HANDBOOK OF CHILD PSYCHOLOGY

HANDBOOK OF CHILD PSYCHOLOGY

FIFTH EDITION

Volume 4: Child Psychology in Practice

Editor-in-Chief

WILLIAM DAMON

Volume Editors

IRVING E. SIGEL and K. ANN RENNINGER

John Wiley & Sons, Inc.

New York • Chichester • Weinheim • Brisbane • Singapore • Toronto

Publisher: Jeffrey W. Brown

Editor: Kelly A. Franklin

Managing Editor: Maureen B. Drexel

Composition
and Management: Publications Development Company of Texas

This text is printed on acid-free paper.

Library of Congress Cataloging-in-Publication Data:

Handbook of child psychology / William Damon, editor. — 5th ed.
p. cm.
Includes bibliographical references and index.
Contents: v. 1. Theoretical models of human development / Richard M. Lerner, volume editor — v. 2. Cognition, perception, and language / Deanna Kuhn and Robert Siegler, volume editors — v. 3. Social, emotional, and personality development / Nancy Eisenberg, volume editor — v. 4. Child psychology in practice / Irving E. Sigel and K. Ann Renninger, volume editors.
ISBN 0-471-07663-5 (v. 4 : cloth : alk. paper). — ISBN 0-471-17893-4 (set : alk. paper)
1. Child psychology. I. Damon, William, 1944–
BF721.H242 1997
155.4—dc21 96-49157

Printed in the United States of America

10 9 8 7 6 5 4 3 2 1

Editorial Advisory Board

Contributors

Marilyn Jager Adams, Ph.D.
Department of Human Development and Psychology
Graduate School of Education
Harvard University
Cambridge, Massachusetts

David J. Bearison, Ph.D.
Program in Psychology, The Graduate School and University Center of the City University of New York, and Mount Sinai Medical Center and School of Medicine
New York, New York

Maggie Bruck, Ph.D.
Department of Psychology
McGill University
Montreal, Canada

Stephen J. Ceci, Ph.D.
Department of Human Development and Family Studies
Cornell University
Ithaca, New York

Dante Cicchetti, Ph.D.
Departments of Psychology, Psychiatry, and Pediatrics
Mount Hope Family Center
University of Rochester
Rochester, New York

Philip A. Cowan, Ph.D.
Department of Psychology
University of California, Berkeley
Berkeley, California

Carolyn Pape Cowan, Ph.D.
Department of Psychology
University of California, Berkeley
Berkeley, California

Robert E. Emery, Ph.D.
Department of Psychology
University of Virginia
Charlottesville, Virginia

Herbert P. Ginsburg, Ph.D.
Department of Human Development
Teachers College
Columbia University
New York, New York

Gail S. Goodman, Ph.D.
Department of Psychology
University of California, Davis
Davis, California

Beth L. Green, Ph.D.
Department of Psychology
Portland State University
Portland, Oregon

Mark T. Greenberg, Ph.D.
Department of Psychology
University of Washington
Seattle, Washington

Patricia M. Greenfield, Ph.D.
Department of Psychology
University of California, Los Angeles
Los Angeles, California

Christina J. Groark, Ph.D.
University Center for Social and Urban Research
Office of Child Development
University of Pittsburgh
Pittsburgh, Pennsylvania

Jeffrey J. Haugaard, Ph.D.
Department of Human Development and Family Studies
Cornell University
Ithaca, New York

Aletha C. Huston, Ph.D.
Department of Human Ecology
University of Texas
Austin, Texas

Alice Klein, Ph.D.
Institute of Human Development
University of California, Berkeley
Berkeley, California

Michael E. Lamb, Ph.D.
Section of Social and Emotional Development
National Institute of Child Health and Human Development
Bethesda, Maryland

Robert B. McCall, Ph.D.
University Center for Social and Urban Research
Office of Child Development
University of Pittsburgh
Pittsburgh, Pennsylvania

Vonnie C. McLoyd, Ph.D.
Center for Human Growth and Development
University of Michigan
Ann Arbor, Michigan

Gil G. Noam, Ed.D., Ph.D.
Medical School and Department of Human Development
and Psychology
Harvard University
Cambridge, Massachusetts
and Hall-Mercer Laboratory of Developmental Psychology
and Developmental Psychopathology
Belmont, Massachusetts

Douglas Powell, Ph.D.
Department of Child Development and Family Studies
Purdue University
West Lafayette, Indiana

Michael Pressley, Ph.D.
Department of Psychology
University of Notre Dame
Notre Dame, Indiana

K. Ann Renninger, Ph.D.
Program in Education
Swarthmore College
Swarthmore, Pennsylvania

Irving E. Sigel, Ph.D.
Education Policy Research Division
Educational Testing Service
Princeton, New Jersey

Prentice Starkey, Ph.D.
School of Education
University of California, Berkeley
Berkeley, California

Sidney Strauss, Ph.D.
School of Education
Tel Aviv University
Tel Aviv, Israel

Mark S. Strauss, Ph.D.
University Center for Social and Urban Research
Office of Child Development
University of Pittsburgh
Pittsburgh, Pennsylvania

Lalita K. Suzuki, M.A.
Department of Psychology
University of California, Los Angeles
Los Angeles, California

Sheree L. Toth, Ph.D.
Department of Psychology
Mt. Hope Family Center
University of Rochester
Rochester, New York

Rebecca Treiman, Ph.D.
Department of Psychology
Wayne State University
Detroit, Michigan

Roger P. Weissberg, Ph.D.
Department of Psychology
The University of Illinois at Chicago
Chicago, Illinois

John C. Wright, Ph.D.
Department of Human Ecology
University of Texas
Austin, Texas

Foreword

PAUL MUSSEN

This fifth edition of the *Handbook of Child Psychology* belongs to an invaluable scholarly tradition: the presentation, at approximately 15-year intervals, of a well-planned, comprehensive, authoritative account of the current state of the field. Successive editions of the *Handbook* (or *Manual,* as it was called in the first three editions) reflect the history of the study of human development over the past half-century.

The first two editions (the second, a moderately revised version of the first) reported the accomplishments of the field in an earlier era during which there were relatively few developmental psychologists. *Description* and *measurement of changes over time* were the principal goals of research and speculation. Very little attention was paid to explanation, theory, systems, or models.

The years immediately following World War II were a watershed for science, a period marked by an immensely powerful surge in interest and activity in all sciences, including psychology. The number of scientifically trained psychologists proliferated, and fields or subdivisions within the discipline became more clearly defined. A more modern form of developmental psychology began to take shape and became a major field that was linked to other areas of psychology and allied disciplines but had its own agendas of research and theory. Continuities with earlier work were evident in new investigations and conceptualizations of standard topics—that is, topics of enduring interest—such as language, intelligence, moral behavior, the nature–nurture controversy, and social influences on development. Not surprisingly, the new investigations surpassed the earlier ones in breadth, depth, and scientific sophistication.

Most significantly, the scope of the field was immeasurably extended to include numerous new topics; innovative, more adequate methods of investigation were devised, and *explanation*—and therefore theories about mechanisms and processes—was emphasized. And, for many reasons, the new generation of developmental psychologists—many of whom were trained in other areas such as social, experimental, and clinical psychology—were generally more productive than their predecessors.

Among the myriad factors that account for the many significant advances in the field are: a basic quest for knowledge, and the self-perpetuating nature of scientific endeavors—investigations that yield interesting, sometimes unexpected, findings prompt new questions (as well as modifications of theories) and, consequently, further research. In addition, and of equal importance, developmental psychologists are generally sensitive to social issues and technological changes that may have significant impacts on children's health and development. These concerns frequently are sources of novel investigations and theories, further expanding the boundaries of the field.

Because developmental psychology had been transformed since the end of World War II, the third (1970) edition of the *Manual,* which I edited, was inevitably vastly different from the first two. In addition to up-to-date chapters on topics of continued interest, it included several chapters on theory, psycholinguistics, aggression, attachment, behavior genetics, and creativity, all of which still stand as central issues.

Like most productive scientific disciplines, developmental psychology continues to progress ceaselessly, in profound and complex ways, and at an ever-increasing rate. In 1983, the fourth edition of the *Handbook* was published. It was twice the size of the third edition, and it encompassed standard topics (usually handled in more refined and penetrating ways) and many new, fruitful areas.

Like the years following World War II, the period since 1980 has been one of unprecedented growth, change, and specialization in developmental psychology. The many theoretical and empirical developments in the discipline generated the need for this new edition. It is virtually impossible to delineate the numerous factors affecting its structure and contents, but some of the most significant influences—only a small sample, hardly an exhaustive list—can be highlighted. For example, compelling evidence of the variety and complexity of the determinants of all parameters of psychological development (and the interactions among them) cast doubt on the explanatory power of major theories that conceptualized development in terms of very few dimensions. In widely accepted current approaches and models, development is viewed as the product of multiple variables operating at multiple levels. This orientation, most explicit in several chapters of Volume 1, is also apparent in many other sections in which person–context interactions are discussed. The multivariate approach also calls attention to the limitations on generalizations from research; conclusions derived from a study with a particular population and under specified conditions may not be valid for other groups or under other circumstances. As a consequence, many chapters in this new edition include in-depth discussions of patterns of development in ethnic minorities and in diverse familial and peer group contexts. Renewed vigorous and innovative research in critical psychological parameters such as temperament, character, and emotion, reflected in several chapters, has also been significantly influenced by the multivariable approach.

As the search for the processes underlying development continues, the need to involve significant advances in other scientific disciplines accelerates. Thus, the present edition has chapters that incorporate information from the cognitive sciences, information processing, neurology, and the cultural psychology of development. Moreover, the boundaries of the field have been substantially broadened and enhanced by recent empirical work and conceptualization about psychological development throughout the life span, as reflected in several chapters.

Fortunately, in recent years, professional practitioners and policy makers have recognized the actual and potential contributions of developmental psychology to the solution of critical social and educational problems—for example, problems of parenting, childrearing in nontraditional families, effective teaching, school drop-out, and violence in television programs. Because of this recognition and the notable advances in applied research, one of the volumes of this edition is devoted exclusively to child psychology in practice.

To assist him in the extraordinarily difficult and complicated task of selecting and organizing the most prominent and exciting areas of contemporary developmental psychology, William Damon, the general editor, chose six volume editors who are recognized leaders in the field and have considerable experience in editing journals and books. Next, outstanding experts were invited to contribute critical, integrated chapters on the theoretical and substantive accomplishments of their area of expertise.

As a consequence of these authors' impeccable scholarship, intuitive and informed insights, dedication, creativity, and painstaking work, the fifth edition of the *Handbook* fully achieves its purpose: the timely presentation of an accurate and comprehensive report of the current state of developmental psychology. Readers who compare these volumes with earlier editions will be impressed with how much our understanding of human development has been enhanced in recent years, how much more solid information is available, and how much deeper and more relevant conceptualizations in the field have become. But this indispensable publication is more than an encyclopedic report, for it is enriched by thoughtful perceptions of key issues and keen insights about where matters stand and what still needs to be done. It is an invaluable aid in mapping out the future directions of this vital and dynamic field. The editors and authors have done the field of developmental psychology a great service. Everyone who is seriously interested in human development is deeply indebted to them.

Preface to The Handbook of Child Psychology, Fifth Edition

WILLIAM DAMON

THE *HANDBOOK'S* BACK PAGES—AND OURS

Developmental questions may be asked about almost any human endeavor—even about the enterprise of asking developmental questions. We may ask: How has the field of developmental study developed? In a field that has been preoccupied by continuity and change, where are the continuities and where are the changes?

Many of the chapters of this fifth edition of the *Handbook of Child Psychology* address our field's growth and progress in connection with the particular topics that they examine, and the three historical chapters (by Cairns, by Overton, and by Valsiner) present a panoramic view of our profession. As general editor of the *Handbook's* fifth edition, I wish to add a further data point: the history of the *Handbook,* which stands as an indicator of the continuities and changes within our field. The *Handbook* has long and notable credentials as a beacon, organizer, and encyclopedia of developmental study. What does its history tell us about where we have been, what we have learned, and where we are going? What does it tell us about what has changed and what has remained the same in the questions that we ask, in the methods that we use, and in the theoretical ideas that we draw on in our quest to understand human development?

It is tempting to begin with a riddle: What fifth edition has six predecessors but just three prior namesakes? Given the context of the riddle, there is not much mystery to the answer, but the reasons for it will tell us something about the *Handbook* and its history.

Leonard Carmichael was President of Tufts University when he guided Wiley's first edition of the *Handbook.* The book (one volume at that time) was called the *Manual of Child Psychology,* in keeping with Carmichael's intention of producing an "advanced scientific manual to bridge the gap between the excellent and varied elementary textbooks in this field and the scientific periodical literature. . . . "[1]

The publication date was 1946, and Carmichael complained that "this book has been a difficult and expensive one to produce, especially under wartime conditions."[2] Nevertheless, the project was worth the effort. The *Manual* quickly became the bible of graduate training and scholarly work in the field, available virtually everywhere that children's development was studied. Eight years later, now head of the Smithsonian Institution as well as editor of the book's second edition, Carmichael wrote, in the preface: "The favorable reception that the first edition received not only in America but all over the world is indicative of the growing importance of the study of the phenomena of the growth and development of the child."[3]

The second edition had a long life; not until 1970 did Wiley bring out a third edition. Carmichael was retired by then, but he still had a keen interest in the book. At his insistence, his own name became part of the title of the third edition: *Carmichael's Manual of Child Psychology.* Paul Mussen took over as editor, and once again the project flourished. Now a two-volume set, the third edition swept across the social sciences, generating widespread interest in developmental psychology and its related disciplines. Rarely had a scholarly compendium become both so dominant in its own field and so familiar in related disciplines. The set became an essential source for graduate students and advanced scholars alike. Publishers referred to *Carmichael's Manual* as the standard against which other scientific handbooks were compared. The fourth edition, published in 1983, was redesignated by John Wiley & Sons as the *Handbook of Child Psychology.* By then, Carmichael had passed away. The set of books, now expanded to four volumes, became widely referred to in the field as "the Mussen handbook."

Words can have the power to reawaken dusty memories. When John Wiley & Sons replaced the title word *Manual* with *Handbook,* an important piece of scholarly history was inadvertently recalled. Wiley's fourth edition had a long-forgotten ancestor that was unknown to most of the new book's readers. The ancestor was called *A Handbook of Child Psychology,* and it preceded Wiley's own first edition by over 15 years. I quote here from two statements by Leonard Carmichael:

> Both as editor of the *Manual* and as the author of a special chapter, the writer is indebted . . . [for] extensive excerpts and the use of other materials previously published in the *Handbook of Child Psychology, Revised Edition.* . . .[4]

> Both the *Handbook of Child Psychology* and the *Handbook of Child Psychology, Revised Edition,* were edited by Dr. Carl Murchison. I wish to express here my profound appreciation for the pioneer work done by Dr. Murchison in producing these handbooks and other advanced books in psychology. The *Manual* owes much in spirit and content to the foresight and editorial skill of Dr. Murchison.[5]

The first quote comes from Carmichael's preface to the 1946 edition, the second from his preface to the 1954 edition. We shall never know why Carmichael waited until the 1954 edition to add the personal tribute to Carl Murchison. Perhaps a careless typist dropped the laudatory passage from a handwritten version of the 1946 preface, and its omission escaped Carmichael's notice. Perhaps eight years of further adult development increased Carmichael's generosity of spirit; or perhaps Murchison or his family complained. In any case, Carmichael from the start directly acknowledged the roots of his *Manual,* if not their author. Those roots are a revealing part of the *Handbook's* story—and of our own "back pages," as intellectual descendants of the early pioneers in the Murchison and Carmichael handbooks.

Carl Murchison was a scholar/impresario who edited *The Psychological Register;* founded and edited key psychological journals; wrote books on social psychology, politics, and the criminal mind; and compiled an assortment of handbooks, psychology texts, autobiographies of renowned psychologists, and even a book on psychic beliefs (Sir Arthur Conan Doyle and Harry Houdini were among the contributors). Murchison's first *Handbook of Child Psychology* was published by a small university press in 1931, when the field itself was still in its childhood. Murchison wrote:

> Experimental psychology has had a much older scientific and academic status [than child psychology], but at the present time it is probable that much less money is being spent for pure research in the field of experimental psychology than is being spent in the field of child psychology. In spite of this obvious fact, many experimental psychologists continue to look upon the field of child psychology as a proper field of research for women and for men whose experimental masculinity is not of the maximum. This attitude of patronage is based almost entirely upon a blissful ignorance of what is going on in the tremendously virile field of child behavior.[6]

Murchison's masculine figures of speech, of course, are from another time; they might supply good material for a social history study of gender stereotyping. That aside, Murchison was prescient in the task that he undertook and the way that he went about it. At the time this passage was written, developmental psychology was known only in Europe and in a few American labs and universities. Nevertheless, Murchison predicted the field's impending ascent: "The time is not far distant, if it is not already here, when nearly all competent psychologists will recognize that one-half of the whole field of psychology is involved in the problem of how the infant becomes an adult psychologically."[7]

For his original 1931 *Handbook,* Murchison looked to Europe and to a handful of American centers (or "field stations") for child research (Iowa, Minnesota, University of California at Berkeley, Columbia, Stanford, Yale, Clark). Murchison's Europeans included a young epistemologist named Jean Piaget, who, in an essay on "Children's Philosophies," quoted from verbal interviews of 60 Genevan children between the ages of 4 and 12 years. Piaget's chapter would provide most American readers with their introduction to his initial research program on children's conceptions of the world. Another European, Charlotte Bühler, wrote a chapter on children's social behavior. In this chapter, which still reads freshly today, Bühler described intricate play and communication patterns among toddlers—patterns that developmental psychology would not rediscover until the late 1970s. Bühler also anticipated the critiques of Piaget that would appear during the sociolinguistics heyday of the 1970s: "Piaget, in his studies on children's talk and reasoning, emphasizes that their talk is much more egocentric than social . . . that children from three to seven years accompany all their manipulations with talk which actually is not so much intercourse as monologue . . . [but] the special relationship of the child to each of the different members of the household is distinctly reflected in the respective conversations."[8] Other Europeans included Anna Freud, who wrote on "The Psychoanalysis of the Child," and Kurt

Lewin, who wrote on "Environmental Forces in Child Behavior and Development."

The Americans whom Murchison chose were equally distinguished. Arnold Gesell wrote a nativistic account of his twin studies—an enterprise that remains familiar to us today—and Louis Terman wrote a comprehensive account of everything known about the "gifted child." Harold Jones described the developmental effects of birth order, Mary Cover Jones wrote about children's emotions, Florence Goodenough wrote about children's drawings, and Dorothea McCarthy wrote about language development. Vernon Jones's chapter on "children's morals" focused on the growth of *character,* a notion that was to become lost to the field during the cognitive-developmental revolution, but has lately reemerged as a primary concern in the study of moral development.

Murchison's vision of child psychology left room for an examination of cultural differences as well. He included a young anthropologist named Margaret Mead, just back from her tours of Samoa and New Guinea. In this early essay, Mead wrote that her motivation in traveling to the South Seas was to discredit the view that Piaget, Levy-Bruhl, and other nascent structuralists had put forth concerning "animism" in young children's thinking. (Interestingly, about one-third of Piaget's chapter in the same volume was dedicated to showing how it takes Genevan children years to outgrow animism.) Mead reported some data that she called "amazing": "In not one of the 32,000 drawings (by young 'primitive' children) was there a single case of personalization of animals, material phenomena, or inanimate objects."[9] Mead parlayed these data into a tough-minded critique of Western psychology's ethnocentrism, making the point that animism and other beliefs are more likely to be culturally induced than intrinsic to early cognitive development. This is hardly an unfamiliar theme in contemporary psychology. Mead also offered a research guide for developmental field workers in strange cultures, complete with methodological and practical advice, such as: translate questions into native linguistic categories; don't do controlled experiments; don't do studies that require knowing ages of subjects, which are usually unknowable; and live next door to the children whom you are studying.

Despite the imposing roster of authors that Murchison had assembled for the 1931 *Handbook of Child Psychology,* his achievement did not satisfy him for long. Barely two years later, Murchison put out a second edition, of which he wrote: "Within a period of slightly more than two years, this first revision bears scarcely any resemblance to the original *Handbook of Child Psychology.* This is due chiefly to the great expansion in the field during the past three years and partly to the improved insight of the editor."[10]

Murchison also saw fit to provide the following warning in his second edition: "There has been no attempt to simplify, condense, or to appeal to the immature mind. This volume is prepared specifically for the scholar, and its form is for his maximum convenience."[11] It is likely that sales of Murchison's first volume did not approach textbook levels. Perhaps he also received negative comments regarding its accessibility. For the record, though, despite Murchison's continued use of masculine phraseology, 10 of the 24 authors in the second edition were women.

Murchison exaggerated when he wrote that his second edition bore little resemblance to the first. Almost half of the chapters were virtually the same, with minor additions and updating. Moreover, some of the authors whose original chapters were dropped were asked to write about new topics. So, for example, Goodenough wrote about mental testing rather than about children's drawings, and Gesell wrote a more general statement of his maturational theory that went well beyond the twin studies.

But Murchison also made some abrupt changes. Anna Freud was dropped, auguring the marginalization of psychoanalysis within academic psychology. Leonard Carmichael made his first appearance, as author of a major chapter (by far, the longest in the book) on prenatal and perinatal growth. Three other physiologically oriented chapters were added as well: one on neonatal motor behavior, one on visual–manual functions during the first two years of life, and one on physiological "appetites" such as hunger, rest, and sex. Combined with the Goodenough and Gesell shifts in focus, these additions gave the 1933 *Handbook* more of a biological thrust, in keeping with Murchison's long-standing desire to display the hard-science backbone of the emerging field.

Leonard Carmichael took his 1946 *Manual* several steps further in the same direction. First, he appropriated five Murchison chapters on biological or experimental topics such as physiological growth, scientific methods, and mental testing. Second, he added three new biologically oriented chapters on animal infancy, on physical growth, and on motor and behavioral maturation (a *tour de force* by Myrtal McGraw that instantly made Gesell's chapter in the same volume obsolete). Third, he commissioned Wayne Dennis to write an adolescence chapter that focused exclusively on physiological changes associated with puberty. Fourth, Carmichael dropped Piaget and Bühler.

But five Murchison chapters on social and cultural influences in development were retained: two chapters on environmental forces on the child (by Kurt Lewin and by

Harold Jones), Dorothea McCarthy's chapter on children's language, Vernon Jones's chapter on children's morality (now entitled "Character Development—An Objective Approach"), and Margaret Mead's chapter on "primitive" children (now enhanced by several spectacular photos of mothers and children from exotic cultures around the world). Carmichael stayed with three other psychologically oriented Murchison topics (emotional development, gifted children, and sex differences), but selected new authors to cover them.

Carmichael's 1954 revision—his second and final edition—was very close in structure and content to the 1946 *Manual.* Carmichael again retained the heart of Murchison's original vision, many of Murchison's original authors and chapter topics, and some of the same material that dated all the way back to the 1931 *Handbook.* Not surprisingly, the chapters that were closest to Carmichael's own interests got the most significant updating. As Murchison had tried to do, Carmichael leaned toward the biological and physiological whenever possible. He clearly favored experimental treatments of psychological processes. Yet Carmichael still kept the social, cultural, and psychological analyses by Lewin, Mead, McCarthy, Terman, Harold Jones, and Vernon Jones, and he even went so far as to add one new chapter on social development by Harold and Gladys Anderson and one new chapter on emotional development by Arthur Jersild.

The Murchison/Carmichael volumes make for fascinating reading, even today. The perennial themes of the field were there from the start: the nature–nurture debate; the generalizations of universalists opposed by the particularizations of contextualists; the alternating emphases on continuities and discontinuities during ontogenesis; and the standard categories of maturation, learning, locomotor activity, perception, cognition, language, emotion, conduct, morality, and culture—all separated for the sake of analysis, yet, as authors throughout each of the volumes acknowledged, all somehow inextricably joined in the dynamic mix of human development.

These things have not changed. Yet much in the early handbooks/manuals is now irrevocably dated. Long lists of children's dietary preferences, sleeping patterns, elimination habits, toys, and somatic types look quaint and pointless through today's lenses. The chapters on children's thought and language were done prior to the great contemporary breakthroughs in neurology and brain/behavior research, and they show it. The chapters on social and emotional development were ignorant of the processes of social influence and self-regulation that soon would be revealed through attribution research and other studies in social psychology. Terms such as *behavior genetics, social cognition, dynamic systems, information processing,* and *developmental psychopathology* were unknown. Even Mead's rendition of the "primitive child" stands as a weak straw in comparison to the wealth of cross-cultural knowledge available today.

Most tellingly, the assortments of odd facts and normative trends were tied together by very little theory throughout the Carmichael chapters. It was as if, in the exhilaration of discovery at the frontiers of a new field, all the facts looked interesting in and of themselves. That, of course, is what makes so much of the material seem odd and arbitrary. It is hard to know what to make of the lists of facts, where to place them, which ones were worth keeping track of and which ones are expendable. Not surprisingly, the bulk of the data presented in the Carmichael manuals seems not only outdated by today's standards but, worse, irrelevant.

By 1970, the importance of theory for understanding human development had become apparent. Looking back on Carmichael's last *Manual,* Paul Mussen wrote: "The 1954 edition of this *Manual* had only one theoretical chapter, and that was concerned with Lewinian theory which, so far as we can see, has not had a significant lasting impact on developmental psychology."[12] The intervening years had seen a turning away from the norm of psychological research once fondly referred to as "dustbowl empiricism."

The Mussen 1970 handbook—or *Carmichael's Manual,* as it was still called—had an entirely new look. The two-volume set carried only one chapter from the earlier books—Carmichael's updated version of his own long chapter on the "Onset and Early Development of Behavior," which had made its appearance under a different title in Murchison's 1933 edition. Otherwise, as Mussen wrote in his preface, "It should be clear from the outset . . . that the present volumes are not, in any sense, a *revision* of the earlier editions; this is a completely new *Manual.*"[13]

And it was. In comparison to Carmichael's last edition 16 years earlier, the scope, variety, and theoretical depth of the Mussen volumes were astonishing. The field had blossomed, and the new *Manual* showcased many of the new bouquets that were being produced. The biological perspective was still strong, grounded by chapters on physical growth (by J. M. Tanner) and physiological development (by Dorothy Eichorn), and by Carmichael's revised chapter (now made more elegant by some excerpts from Greek philosophy and modern poetry). But two other cousins of biology also were represented, in an ethological chapter by Eckhard Hess, and a behavior genetics chapter by Gerald McClearn. These chapters were to define the major directions of biological research in the field for at least the next three decades.

As for theory, Mussen's *Handbook* was thoroughly permeated with it. Much of the theorizing was organized around the approaches that, in 1970, were known as the "three grand systems": (a) Piaget's cognitive-developmentalism, (b) psychoanalysis, and (c) learning theory. Piaget was given the most extensive treatment. He reappeared in the *Manual,* this time authoring a comprehensive (and some say, definitive) statement of his entire theory, which now bore little resemblance to his 1931/1933 sortings of children's intriguing verbal expressions. In addition, chapters by John Flavell, by David Berlyne, by Martin Hoffman, and by William Kessen, Marshall Haith, and Philip Salapatek, all gave major treatments to one or another aspect of Piaget's body of work. Other approaches were represented as well. Herbert and Ann Pick explicated Gibsonian theory in a chapter on sensation and perception, Jonas Langer wrote a chapter on Werner's organismic theory, David McNeill wrote a Chomskian account of language development, and Robert LeVine wrote an early version of what was soon to become "culture theory."

With its increased emphasis on theory, the 1970 *Manual* explored in depth a matter that had been all but neglected in the *Manual's* previous versions: the mechanisms of change that could account for, to use Murchison's old phrase, "the problem of how the infant becomes an adult psychologically." In the process, old questions such as the relative importance of nature *versus* nurture were revisited, but with far more sophisticated conceptual and methodological tools.

Beyond theory building, the 1970 *Manual* addressed an array of new topics and featured new contributors: peer interaction (Willard Hartup), attachment (Eleanor Maccoby and John Masters), aggression (Seymour Feshback), individual differences (Jerome Kagan and Nathan Kogan), and creativity (Michael Wallach). All of these areas of interest are still very much with us at century's end.

If the 1970 *Manual* reflected a blossoming of the field's plantings, the 1983 *Handbook* reflected a field whose ground cover had spread beyond any boundaries that could have been previously anticipated. New growth had sprouted in literally dozens of separate locations. A French garden, with its overarching designs and tidy compartments, had turned into an English garden, a bit unruly but often glorious in its profusion. Mussen's two-volume *Carmichael's Manual* had now become the four-volume Mussen *Handbook,* with a page-count increase that came close to tripling the 1970 edition.

The grand old theories were breaking down. Piaget was still represented by his 1970 piece, but his influence was on the wane throughout the other chapters. Learning theory and psychoanalysis were scarcely mentioned. Yet the early theorizing had left its mark, in vestiges that were apparent in new approaches, and in the evident conceptual sophistication with which authors treated their material. No return to dust-bowl empiricism could be found anywhere in the set. Instead, a variety of classical and innovative ideas were coexisting: ethology, neurobiology, information processing, attribution theory, cultural approaches, communications theory, behavioral genetics, sensory-perception models, psycholinguistics, sociolinguistics, discontinuous stage theories, and continuous memory theories all took their places, with none quite on center stage. Research topics now ranged from children's play to brain lateralization, from children's family life to the influences of school, day care, and disadvantageous risk factors. There also was coverage of the burgeoning attempts to use developmental theory as a basis for clinical and educational interventions. The interventions usually were described at the end of chapters that had discussed the research relevant to the particular intervention efforts, rather than in whole chapters dedicated specifically to issues of practice.

This brings us to the present—the *Handbook's* fifth (but really seventh) edition. I will leave it to future reviewers to provide a summation of what we have done. The volume editors have offered introductory and/or concluding renditions of their own volumes. I will add to their efforts by stating here the overall intent of our design, and by commenting on some directions that our field has taken in the years from 1931 to 1998.

We approached this edition with the same purpose that Murchison, Carmichael, and Mussen before us had shared: "to provide," as Mussen wrote, "a comprehensive and accurate picture of the current state of knowledge—the major systematic thinking and research—in the most important research areas of the psychology of human development."[14] We assumed that the *Handbook* should be aimed "specifically for the scholar," as Murchison declared, and that it should have the character of an "advanced text," as Carmichael defined it. We expected, though, that our audience may be more interdisciplinary than the readerships of previous editions, given the greater tendency of today's scholars to cross back and forth among fields such as psychology, cognitive science, neurobiology, history, linguistics, sociology, anthropology, education, and psychiatry. We also believed that research-oriented practitioners should be included under the rubric of the "scholars" for whom this *Handbook* was intended. To that end, we devoted, for the first time, an entire volume to "child psychology in practice."

Beyond these very general intentions, we have let chapters in the *Handbook's* fifth edition take their own shape. We solicited the chapters from authors who were widely acknowledged to be among the leading experts in their areas of the field; although we know that, given an entirely open-ended selection process and budget, we would have invited a very large number of other leading researchers whom we did not have the space—and thus the privilege—to include. With only two exceptions, every author whom we invited chose to accept the challenge.

Our directive to authors was simple: Convey your area of the field as you see it. From then on, the 112 authors took center stage—with, of course, much constructive feedback from reviewers and volume editors. But no one tried to impose a perspective, a preferred method of inquiry, or domain boundaries on any of the chapters. The authors freely expressed their views on what researchers in their areas attempt to accomplish, why they do so, how they go about it, what intellectual sources they draw on, what progress they have made, and what conclusions they have reached.

The result, in my opinion, is yet more glorious profusion, but perhaps contained a bit by some broad patterns that have emerged across our garden. Powerful theoretical models and approaches—not quite unified theories, such as the three grand systems—have begun once again to organize much of the field's research and practice. There is great variety in these models and approaches, and each is drawing together significant clusters of work. Some have been only recently formulated, and some are combinations or modifications of classic theories that still have staying power.

Among the formidable models and approaches that the reader will find in this *Handbook* are the dynamic system theories, the life-span and life-course approaches, cognitive science and neural models, the behavior genetics approach, person–context interaction theories, action theories, cultural psychology, ecological models, neo-Piagetian and neo-Vygotskian models. Although some of these models and approaches have been in the making for some time, my impression is that they are just now coming into their own, in that researchers now are drawing on them more directly, taking their implied assumptions and hypotheses seriously, using them with specificity and with full control, and exploiting all of their implications for practice. A glance at the contents listings for the *Handbook's* four volumes will reveal the staggering breadth of concerns addressed through use of these models and approaches.

The other pattern that emerges is a self-conscious reflection about the notion of development. The reflection is an earnest one, yet it has a more affirmative tone than similar discussions in recent years. We have just passed through a time when the very credibility of a developmental approach was itself thrown into question. The whole idea of progress and advance, implicit in the notion of development, seemed out of step with ideological principles of diversity and equality.

Some genuine intellectual benefits accrued from that critique: the field has come to better appreciate diverse developmental pathways. But, like many critique positions, it led to excesses that created, for some in the field of developmental study, a kind of crisis of faith. For some, it became questionable even to explore issues that lie at the heart of human development. Learning, growth, achievement, individual continuity and change, common beliefs and standards—all became suspect as subjects of investigation.

Fortunately, as the contents of this *Handbook* attest, such doubts are waning. As was probably inevitable, the field's center of gravity has returned to the study of development. After all, the story of growth during infancy, childhood, and adolescence is a developmental story of multi-faceted learning, of acquisitions of skills and knowledge, of waxing powers of attention and memory, of formations and transformations of character and personality, of increases in understanding of self and others, of advances in emotional and behavioral regulation, of progress in communicating and collaborating with others, and of a host of other achievements that are chronicled in this *Handbook*. Parents and teachers in every part of the world recognize and value such developmental achievements in their children, although they do not always know how to foster them. Neither do we in all cases. But the kinds of scientific understanding that the *Handbook's* authors explicate in their chapters—scientific understanding created by themselves as well as by fellow researchers in the field of developmental study—have brought us all several giant steps toward this goal.

NOTES

1. Carmichael, L. (Ed.). (1946). *Manual of child psychology*. New York: Wiley, p. viii.
2. Carmichael, L. (Ed.). (1946). *Manual of child psychology*. New York: Wiley, p. vi.
3. Carmichael, L. (Ed.). (1954). *Manual of child psychology: Second edition*. New York: Wiley, p. v.

4. Carmichael, L. (Ed.). (1946). *Manual of child psychology.* New York: Wiley, p. vi.
5. Carmichael, L. (Ed.). (1954). *Manual of child psychology: Second edition.* New York: Wiley, p. vii.
6. Murchison, C. (Ed.). (1931). *A handbook of child psychology.* Worcester, MA: Clark University Press, p. ix.
7. Murchison, C. (Ed.). (1931). *A handbook of child psychology.* Worcester, MA: Clark University Press, p. x.
8. Buhler, C. (1931). The social participation of infants and toddlers. In C. Murchison (Ed.), *A handbook of child psychology.* Worcester, MA: Clark University Press, p. 138.
9. Mead, M. (1931). The primitive child. In C. Murchison (Ed.), *A handbook of child psychology.* Worcester, MA: Clark University Press, p. 400.
10. Murchison, C. (Ed.). (1933). *A handbook of child psychology: Second edition (Revised).* Worcester, MA: Clark University Press, p. viii.
11. Murchison, C. (Ed.). (1933). *A handbook of child psychology: Second edition (Revised).* Worcester, MA: Clark University Press, p. viii.
12. Mussen, P. (Ed.). (1970). *Carmichael's manual of child psychology.* New York: Wiley, p. x.
13. Mussen, P. (Ed.). (1970). *Carmichael's manual of child psychology.* New York: Wiley, p. x.
14. Mussen, P. (Ed.). (1983). *Handbook of child psychology.* New York: Wiley, p. vii.

Acknowledgments

The fifth edition of the *Handbook* was truly a team effort. The six volume editors have my deepest gratitude for their countless hours of devoted work. No project editor has ever had a finer group of collaborators. I also thank Kelly Franklin, of John Wiley & Sons, Inc., for her inspired editorial efforts from the time of the project's inception. Without Kelly's persistence and good sense, publication in 1998 would not have been possible.

Many people contributed invaluable advice during one or another phase of the fifth edition's production. They are far too many to mention here, even if I had managed to keep systematic records of all conversations on the project's development. The final product has benefited greatly from the insights and feedback of all those who responded. In particular, I note two giants of the field whose wise counsel and generosity remain prominent in my mind: Paul Mussen and Eleanor Maccoby.

In slightly altered form, my preface was published in *Human Development* (March–April, 1997). I am grateful to Barbara Rogoff for her editorial help in this process, and to Anne Gregory for her help in obtaining background materials. Josef and Marsy Mittlemann's support has been vital in facilitating this and other scholarly activities at the Brown University Center for the Study of Human Development. My assistant, Pat Balsofiore, deserves our unending gratitude for her valiant work in helping to organize this vast endeavor.

William Damon

Preface to Volume 4
Child Psychology in Practice

IRVING E. SIGEL and K. ANN RENNINGER

We enthusiastically accepted the invitation of William Damon and the Advisory Committee of the *Handbook of Child Psychology* to edit this volume dedicated to Child Psychology and Practice, because we believe that behavioral research, whether basic or applied, must be accessible. The present volume should be useful to scholars interested in general developmental principles that may be revealed in contexts of practice; developmental researchers who themselves have sought practical applications of their work; researchers who have considered engaging in practice-oriented work, but who have not yet done so; and researchers interested in broadening the theoretical and empirical bases of their work. This volume should also be of interest to those who interpret research as consultants in such field settings as community clinics, public and independent schools, and government agencies, or as evaluators of intervention programs. Finally, this volume should be useful for faculty and students involved in graduate or professional educational programs in applied developmental science.

At first glance, it might seem a straightforward activity to identify the critical research findings in child psychology and articulate how these findings can be used in the world of practice: in the family, the school, the clinic, and the community. The task, however, is quite complicated, in part because the field of practice is always in the process of being defined, and in part because research relevant to the health and welfare of children is the province of a large number of fields. The situation is further complicated by increasing specialization and the sheer amount of literature in each of these fields.

In a sense, the problems facing researchers and practitioners are similar—how to gain access to the information overload. The researcher needs to streamline such access in order to keep abreast of the field within which he or she works. The practitioner needs current findings in order to consider their implications for his or her practice. The difference between the researcher and the practitioner (a consumer of research), however, is a difference in the nature of their needs.

The researcher studying infant perception, for example, typically focuses on a highly specialized problem and must be accountable for a reasonably discrete literature. In contrast, ideally, the practitioner working with new parents on parenting is familiar with changing understanding about infant perception as well as a wide-range of information about infant development. Thus, the practitioner requires a general, interdisciplinary understanding of topics relevant to infants: issues of normative and atypical development across childhood, pediatrics, and so on.

There has been increasing interest in how to enable practitioners to access information from research so that it can be used in practice (cf., Fischer & Lerner, 1994; Morrison, Lord, & Keating, 1984; Scholnick, Fisher, Brown, & Sigel, 1988). Reviews of the research have been written to provide this information service, but they are often more scholarly than practical. They enable researchers within a topic area to share their work with each other, but these reviews typically are not readily accessible to the community of practitioners. From the perspective of a practitioner, reading such a review may give a feeling that he or she has missed some prior conversation. Terms are not used in exactly the same way, the work of most of the authors cited is unfamiliar, and there is little context for understanding the gist of research concerns in the field.

This volume on *Child Psychology and Practice* stands apart from the other three volumes of the *Handbook* because it specifically addresses practice. The basic sciences reviewed in the other volumes provide the theoretical and empirical base for the topics addressed by the authors in this volume. The discussions begun in the other volumes are extended to address the role of research in practice, which requires a broad and interdisciplinary view of the field, technical knowledge of practice, and an appreciation of the complexity of applying research to practice.

As we began to discuss the scope of child psychology and the possible topics to be covered here, we grappled with the breadth and so-called fragmentation of the field since it was first described in Murcheson's (1931) *Handbook of Child Psychology.* We recognize and appreciate the role of the number of specialties that keep emerging as reflections of the responsiveness of the field to developments both in basic research and in the specific needs of practice. We used as our criteria, however, socially relevant topics that have influenced and continue to influence the lives of children.

We focused on traditional topics of study that continue to be viable areas for further study and have much to contribute to practice. We opted for more conventional topics because of their specific links to social and welfare concerns and because they represent bodies of research that practitioners seek. They share the developing child as a focus, across settings that overlap: the home, the school, the clinic, and the community. Yet we recognize that many of the topics addressed either apply to development across the life span and/or require consideration of the developmental status of the adult others with whom the child is engaged.

Having identified the scope of the chapters to be included, we approached authors who not only have strong research credentials, but also work with and think about applied problems. We asked them to prepare chapters that would be accessible and useful to practitioners as well as to their research-focused colleagues. We considered "use" broadly in terms of action and application to a practical setting, and enhancement of a perspective.

Specifically, we asked authors to include in their chapters the most relevant and up-to-date literature and, where appropriate, to place it in the context of the larger field of which it is a part. We asked that the literature review be defined as those bodies of knowledge most useful to practice, reflecting sources of information available for study and use. We asked the authors to identify the questions of practice at the outset of their reviews, and to use these to frame their reviews of research. We further asked that they consider each of the following questions:

1. What is the accepted knowledge base from which you and your colleagues work in this field?
2. What are some of the major questions being addressed in this field at this time?
3. How has the research base been used in practice?
4. What, in your opinion, are some of the substantive, practical, and political factors that influence the acceptance of such application, either positively or negatively? For example, is the research too discrete, or does it not address current problems of concern (that is, is it ahead of its time), or is it reflecting different objectives—those of the practitioner?
5. What can researchers learn from practitioners? How might they engage in a partnership on the basis of such interactions?
6. What suggestions do you have for future directions to create working relations between research and application—for example, graduate training, internship arrangements, or incorporating researchers into the field organization so that they are integral to practice?

These questions provide a common outline for each of the chapters. The authors made judgments about their mode of communication (choice of language and level of detail) and set the boundaries of the field in conjunction with reviews from both of their editors, and from peers. Reviewers for each chapter were selected on the basis of their expertise as researchers interested in practice, or as practitioners concerned with children's development.

Shepherding this volume to its completion has been a challenge. We have learned that the process of bridging research and practice is very difficult. Even for developmental psychologists steeped in practice, it is difficult to write a review chapter that relies to some extent on inference for the very *Handbook* that in the past has served as a standard of dispassionate, scientific rigor. It is one thing to talk about and consult on the questions of practitioners; it is a very different proposition to commit this knowledge to paper and use it to organize the basis of a review.

We appreciate the help of our many colleagues who have participated in this effort, particularly the chapter authors, who have been patient with us and have accepted our sometimes imperious suggestions in good faith, and even with occasional humor. We also want to give special thanks and recognition to Linda Kozelski at Educational Testing Service, for her organizational skills in keeping this project on target. The reviewers and authors are acknowledged in the forthcoming pages.

REFERENCES

Fisher, C. B., & Lerner, R. M. (1994). *Applied developmental psychology.* New York: McGraw-Hill.

Morrison, F. J., Lord, C., & Keating, D. P. (Eds.). (1984). *Applied developmental psychology* (Vol. 1). Orlando, FL: Academic Press.

Murcheson, C. (Ed.). (1931). *A handbook of child psychology.* Worcester, MA: Clark University Press.

Scholnick, E. K., Fisher, C. B., Brown, A. C., & Sigel, I. E. (1988). Report on applied developmental psychology. *APA Division 7 Newsletter,* pp. 6–10.

Contents

Child-Rearing and Family

Education in School

Mental and Physical Health

Community and Culture

Epilogue

Child-Rearing and Family

CHAPTER 1

Parenting Interventions: A Family Systems Perspective

PHILIP A. COWAN, DOUGLAS POWELL, and CAROLYN PAPE COWAN

Work on this chapter was supported in part by a grant from the National Institute of Mental Health to Philip and Carolyn Cowan (MH-31109).

For decades, books on childbirth and infant care dominated the parenting or family sections of bookstores. More recently, these books have been surrounded by volumes that summarize the stages of child development and offer advice to parents of children from toddlerhood through late adolescence. Newsstands are dotted with magazines devoted to rearing healthy children. Newspapers run daily columns answering questions from anxious parents. Community colleges and places of worship offer courses and lectures on child-rearing strategies. Brightly illustrated brochures advertise costly audiotaped or videotaped "seminars" designed to increase positive communication between parents and their children. Comprehensive programs at the infant, preschool, and elementary school levels provide modules for parents whose children are at risk for serious mental health and behavior problems. For parents at the end of their rope, hotlines and "warm"-lines offer anonymous telephone support to help parents resist the impulse to batter a persistently whiny or crying child. Parents who know they need counseling or psychotherapy for themselves and their emotionally disturbed children face long waiting lists at mental health clinics. Clearly, contemporary parents from families all along the continuum from low risk to serious distress are seeking assistance to become more effective parents. Too many will not find the help they need.

As we will show, interventions designed to help parents rear healthy, secure children come in an array of modalities (print and broadcast media, classes, psychotherapy), settings (homes, schools, religious institutions, health and mental health clinics), and formats (individual parent counseling, family sessions, parenting group meetings). In each of these contexts, programs vary in terms of their goals and target populations. They address a variety of parents, from well-functioning fathers and mothers who wish to enhance their relationships with their children, to families recruited into programs designed to prevent incipient distress from spreading, to families with members already identified as mentally ill and in need of therapeutic assistance and social services.

We begin in the first section with a discussion of some basic concepts. We define what we mean by parenting and by parenting interventions. We distinguish between risk models and causal models of parenting effects on children's development. We introduce a family systems perspective for understanding how parents affect their children's development and adaptation, a view that is consistent with ideas in the newly emerging field of developmental psychopathology (Cicchetti & Cohen, 1995; Rutter & Garmezy, 1983) and provides a strong justification for programs that emphasize prevention and early intervention with parents—before family relationship problems escalate in severity or scope.

In the second section, we present a brief historical survey to highlight the trends and issues in parenting interventions from the mid-nineteenth century to the present day. This survey highlights the fact that parent education and parenting interventions emerge and flourish in particular cultural and political contexts and it shows that support for parenting programs has shifted along with historical changes in these contexts.

A central emphasis of this chapter is the reciprocal relationship between theories of parenting and parenting interventions. In the third section we show that, although they are often implicit, theories about how parents influence children underlie the procedures and practices of all parenting intervention programs. We present a checklist that summarizes nine theoretical perspectives on how parents affect their children's adaptation or distress.

The fourth through sixth sections provide examples of parenting intervention programs that are based on one or more of the nine theoretical perspectives outlined in the checklist. The fourth section describes child-focused intervention programs based on theories that emphasize biological and psychological change mechanisms within the child. In these programs, the parents' task is conceptualized as providing a "good-enough environment" to allow the child's inner developmental processes to unfold. The fifth section describes intervention programs that focus primarily on changing parents' behavior. The sixth section describes programs that combine child- and parent-focused perspectives to improve the quality of parent-child relationships and interrupt the tendency of negative or dysfunctional parent-child relationship patterns to repeat themselves across the generations.

Because almost all theories of parenting have been constructed and tested in studies of mothers and children, it is not surprising to find that most intervention programs have been directed toward mothers. In the seventh section, we present a theoretical perspective that adopts a more contextual, systemic view of parenting—as it occurs in the context of all of the relationships within the family (mother-child, father-child, sibling, marital, three-generational) and between the family and the larger social systems in which families live and develop. In the eighth section, we describe a number of new and promising comprehensive interventions based on this systemic approach.

Throughout the chapter, we consider examples of two apparently different kinds of parenting interventions. One is designed to attract parents who have not identified serious problems in the family or asked for a "cure" for acute distress but who want to learn more about parenting strategies. A second type of parenting intervention is addressed to families in which the psychological difficulty of one or more of the members precipitates a request for treatment. Although it is commonly believed that these represent two very different kinds of intervention approaches involving different principles and qualitatively different skills required of the interveners, our survey of both types of intervention suggests that there may be more similarities than differences.

The ninth section attempts to summarize what we have learned from our survey of the current "state of the art" in parenting interventions. We suggest some new directions for intervention programs and outline some of the issues that might profitably be addressed in intervention research. We conclude in the tenth section with a brief discussion of value and ethical issues inherent in the parenting intervention enterprise, and of social policy issues that are bound to affect the development of parenting interventions over the next decade.

BASIC DEFINITIONS

> Despite the fact that most people become parents and everyone who ever lived has had parents, parenting remains a mystifying subject about which almost everyone has opinions, but about which few people agree. Freud once listed bringing up children as one of the three "impossible professions"—the other two being governing nations and psychoanalysis. (Bornstein, 1995a, p. xxii)

This quote is from the editor's preface to a recent four-volume *Handbook of Parenting* (Bornstein, 1995b). Given that parenting seems mysterious and difficult, it makes sense that over the centuries, many have attempted to provide guidance for parents as they traverse this daunting terrain. We begin our account of parenting interventions with a discussion of three central definitional questions: What do we mean by parenting? What do we mean by parenting intervention? Which models are most appropriate and useful in explaining the impact of parents on their children's adaptation and distress: "causal models" that describe characteristics or behaviors of parents that lead directly to their children's growth or problems, or "risk models" that examine the role of potential buffers and vulnerabilities in accounting for whether specific risks result in negative effects on children's development?

What Is Parenting?

In the 59 chapters included in Bornstein's four-volume *Handbook,* well-known researchers describe different types of parents (mothers, fathers, single parents, adolescent parents, adoptive parents, lesbian and gay parents), who are responsible for the care of different kinds of children (boys and girls of different ages, normally developing children, and those with physical, cognitive, social, and emotional disabilities or difficulties). The authors examine the impact of parents on children, and the impact of biological, psychological, and social forces that affect parents and how they rear their children. But nowhere in these four volumes are we presented with a definition of parenting. Is everything that a parent does "parenting"? Conversely, can anything that a parent does *not* do be thought of as parenting? Our goal here is not to resolve these complex questions, but rather to provide a beginning map of the parenting territory.

Merriam-Webster's Collegiate Dictionary (1994) provides an acceptable starting place. Parenting is defined as "the raising of a child by its parents; the act of caring for someone in the manner of a parent." Bornstein (1995b) takes us a little farther by describing four essential functions of caregiving: (a) nurturant caregiving meets the physical requirements of the child; (b) material caregiving constructs and organizes the child's physical world; (c) social caregiving includes the variety of behaviors parents use in engaging their children in interpersonal exchanges; and (d) didactic caregiving consists of the variety of strategies parents use in stimulating children to engage in and understand the world outside the parent-child dyad.

The central task of parents, then, is not simply to keep their infants alive or to provide appropriate discipline but to create the conditions in which children can develop to their fullest capacity both inside and outside the family. This view provides a broad perspective on parenting. First, Bornstein's description of parenting as a set of functions does not limit the focus of discussion to biological parents; other biological relatives and caretakers who are unrelated to the child may also be centrally engaged in parenting. The assumption that mothers as primary caregivers have the most powerful effects on their children's development is open to question and empirical investigation. Second, Bornstein makes the point that parenting is a relationship that unfolds over time. Third, he emphasizes the responsibilities of parents to socialize children to help them become well-functioning members of the culture in which they live. Fourth, he defines parenting not solely by what parents believe about child rearing or how they behave toward their children—the typical parenting questions addressed by child development researchers—but extends the topic to a consideration of how parents create family environments that foster children's development.

More Than One View: Parenting Style, Parenting Practices, and Parenting Roles

There are almost as many ways of conceptualizing and assessing parent-child relationships as there are researchers and authors. Darling and Steinberg (1993) identified two major types of approaches in their influential review of parenting research. Some investigators think about parenting in global dimensions that are typically called *parenting style*—the emotional climate in which parenting behaviors are expressed. Others look at more microanalytic *parenting practices*—specific socialization behaviors we can observe when parents interact with their children. A third related approach emphasizes the different *parenting roles* of mothers and fathers in their children's lives—as nurturers, disciplinarians, gatekeepers, and so on.

Parenting Style. Diana Baumrind (1972) categorized parents' interactions with their children using a typology based on the configuration of two major stylistic dimensions of parenting: warmth/responsiveness and control. Control refers to discipline but also includes providing structure, setting limits, and communicating expectations for competent, age-appropriate behavior. Baumrind describes parents who are warm and responsive to their children and who provide a structure for their learning, set limits when their behavior threatens to go out of control, and set explicit standards for competent behavior, as *authoritative.* Parents who are warm and responsive but exert little control and make few maturity demands are described as *permissive.* Parents who are controlling in a cold, unresponsive way are described as *authoritarian.* By and large, children and adolescents whose parents have an authoritative parenting style show higher levels of instrumental and social competence than children raised by parents using either of the other two styles (Baumrind, 1991).

An important variant on Baumrind's view of parenting style was proposed by Maccoby and Martin (1983), who noted that a three-category typology, however useful, may not capture the range of behaviors that can be observed as parents work and play with their children. In their comprehensive review, Maccoby and Martin suggested that parenting style be assessed along two separate linear dimensions, responsiveness and demandingness, which they combine to produce four parenting types (authoritative, authoritarian, permissive, and disengaged). Dix (1991) notes that an essential ingredient in parenting styles is the way in which emotions aroused in parents lead them to regulate their children's emotions.

Parenting Practices. Darling and Steinberg (1993) argue that both the Baumrind and Maccoby and Martin approaches describe global dimensions of family context that moderate the impact of specific parenting practices on children's development. For example, parents' active involvement in the child's schooling (a "practice") has a stronger facilitative effect on adolescents' academic achievement for authoritative than for nonauthoritative parents (Steinberg, Lamborn, Dornbush, & Darling, 1992). One might speculate that authoritative parents are more effective during school-related interactions with the child, such as helping the adolescent choose courses, "because their use of explanations, their encouragement of discussion, and their acknowledgment of the adolescent's perspective help the adolescent make more intelligent decisions" (Darling & Steinberg, 1993, p. 493).

Parents' Role as Managers of Children's Experiences. A number of researchers (Ladd & Hart, 1991; Parke & Buriel, Volume 2) have suggested that parents influence their children not only by what they do but also by the role they play in structuring the physical and social environment. In their role as arrangers of child care, activities, lessons, and visits with friends, parents function as "gatekeepers" who restrict or encourage their children's access to the world outside the family. There is some evidence to suggest that when parents expose young children to a wider variety of these experiences, the children show higher levels of social adaptation (e.g., Bryant, 1985).

Based on this very brief summary, we can see how interveners might consider addressing their programs to any of these aspects of the parent-child relationship known to enhance children's development: the overall emotional climate represented by parenting styles, specific parenting practices, and parents' roles as managers of their children's or adolescents' daily lives.

What Constitutes a Parenting Intervention?

Parenting interventions come in a rich variety of contexts and formats and have few common observable features. Consider the following:

- A parent buys and reads a book on well-baby care.
- A Public Health nurse makes weekly home visits in which she teaches a mother how to provide her infant with increased cognitive stimulation.
- A mother and father attend a weekly group in which couples discuss issues of common concern about how to care for their newborns.
- The Employee Assistance Program at a parent's workplace sponsors noontime meetings to discuss parenting issues such as discipline and how to recognize drug problems.
- A parent of an adopted child diagnosed with Attention Deficit Hyperactivity Disorder watches a television program about hyperactive children.
- Both parents attend a support group for parents who have children diagnosed as autistic.
- A mother brings her whole family to six months of weekly therapy sessions because one of the adolescents has developed a severe substance abuse problem.

Each parent participating in these interventions will have different motivations and experiences. We use these as examples of *parenting interventions* because the books, classes, home visitors, doctors, support groups, and therapists are all attempting to effect some change in the parent's understanding or in the quality of transactions between parent and child, with the ultimate goal of optimizing the child's developmental course.

Throughout this chapter we take a broad, systemic perspective on parenting. Parenting includes stable biological and personality characteristics of each parent as they are revealed in interaction with the child; collectively, these qualities shape the environment of the developing child. Consistent with our systemic definition of parenting, we describe a wide array of programs to help parents. We include traditional interventions designed to modify important aspects of mothers' or fathers' behavior toward the child as well as newer interventions that focus on the parents' relationship as a couple or include parenting as one aspect of a comprehensive family-school intervention. We include some examples of interventions for "low-risk" populations, characterized as parent education or preventive intervention, and others designed for "high-risk" populations, often described as parent or family therapy. Our view is that the theoretical assumptions and practices underlying intervention approaches for families from low- and high-risk populations are more similar than different, but the extent of similarity and difference is an important topic for further study.

Causal Models and Risk Models of Parenting

Causal Models

A few intervention programs attempt to recruit participants by focusing on potential benefits for parents themselves, but almost all hope to achieve some positive impact on the children as well. The reasoning here is that if interventions affect parents, and parents affect children, there is reason to hope that the intervention program will ultimately affect children's behavior and adaptation. Until recently, both public and scientific discourse about the impact of parents on children used the language of causality: certain behavior in the parent leads to or causes certain outcomes in the child.

$$\text{A (Parent behavior)} \rightarrow \text{B (Child outcome)}$$

Causal relationships are generally very difficult to establish in science. In this case, we would need to determine that (a) when antecedent A is present, outcome B is present; (b) when antecedent A is absent, outcome B is absent; and (c) that B is not traceable to factors other than A (e.g., factors within the culture rather than within the family). In studies of parent-to-child effects, causality is virtually impossible to determine. Because almost all studies of parents and children are correlational in design, it is not possible to establish whether parents' behaviors are affecting the child, the child's behaviors are affecting the parents, the child's behavior is a product of the parent-child relationship, or the child's behavior is attributable to familial and extrafamilial factors that are separate from parenting.

There is another even more difficult problem with validating causal hypotheses in most of the research on parenting effects. Causal reasoning about parenting proceeds *from* parent *to* child, but the research almost always begins with children's outcomes (e.g., problem vs. nonproblem) and tests for differences between groups in the parents' behavior. This *follow-back* or case control design leads many researchers to make logically flawed inferences about causality; from the finding that B implies A (a particular child outcome is associated with a particular type of parenting behavior), they conclude that A implies or causes B (parents' actions caused the child's behavior).

Why not, then, test causal hypotheses in a *follow-forward* or prospective study that recruits parents with different parenting styles and examines pathways to adaptation or dysfunction? This certainly allows the researcher to establish time sequences from earlier to later, but the inference problems in determining the direction of effects cannot be completely resolved with longitudinal research designs. The fact that a parent's behavior at Time 1 is highly correlated with a child's behavior at Time 2 does not establish parental influence, because the parent's Time 1 behavior may have been influenced by the child's behavior prior to the Time 1 assessment or by other factors in the parent's experience.

Risk Models

Instead of beginning with a specific child behavior as outcome and attempting to determine its cause, we can begin by focusing on a parent behavior thought to function as a *risk factor* with respect to a given outcome and attempt to map the paths of development of children at greater and lesser risk. Risk, a term originally developed by insurers of ships and adopted as a central construct in the theory and practice of Public Health, refers to the probability of a negative outcome in a population, given a specific antecedent factor (Cowan, Cowan, & Schulz, 1996; Garmezy, Masten, & Tellegen, 1984; Rutter, 1987). For example, given a specific parenting practice as a risk factor, what is the probability of the children's being diagnosed as anxious, depressed, or conduct disordered?

The origins of risk analysis are interwoven with the aims of action and intervention. Insurance brokers were not just wondering idly about the odds on a ship's returning from a perilous journey: they wanted to know whether to put up insurance money or to advise their merchant clients not to set sail during the winter months. In the Public Health field, epidemiologists have attempted to identify high-risk environments so that they can be modified or eliminated to improve the physical health of the population. Parent educators and interveners use ideas about risk to target the most likely populations for their services and determine the most effective focus of the intervention. For example, Patterson and Capaldi (1991) have shown that when parents of adolescents are not effective "monitors" (knowing where their children are and setting limits on being away from home) their children are at risk for aggression and delinquency. This evidence suggests that interventions can focus on protecting children from these serious problems by teaching their parents more effective monitoring skills.

Risks do not always produce negative outcomes. Some families in which parents fail to monitor their adolescents have children who are *not* aggressive and delinquent. In the framework of causal analysis, this finding disconfirms the hypothesis that parents' behavior is linked with children's behavior. By contrast, in the framework of risk models, the "exceptions" inform us about fruitful avenues for further investigation because they reveal potential buffers or protective factors that reduce negative outcomes *despite* the presence of risk. For example, parents who are ineffective monitors of their children may enroll them in schools that provide structured programs to encourage prosocial behavior. Grandparents or neighbors who live nearby may be functioning as effective parent surrogates who provide structure and positive encouragement to teens who might otherwise get into trouble with unsupervised peers.

In some cases, risks fail to produce the expected negative effects not because of the presence of protective or buffering mechanisms but because the child is resilient. Some formulations of resilience imply a kind of "inner Teflon" in the child that prevents risks from producing negative effects, whereas others view resilience as the outcome of a process in which risks present challenges that stimulate highly adaptive responses (Garmezy et al., 1984).

In some families, the effects of risk are magnified by vulnerabilities (genetic, temperamental, intrapsychic, experiential). Without one or more of these vulnerabilities, the risks would not be expected to produce such problematic outcomes. Like a sailboat with a patched hull that remains afloat on calm days but sinks in a storm, a child can carry genetic vulnerabilities that result in problems only under conditions of very high stress.

As Rutter (1987) argued a decade ago, risks are not static events. Rather, they set in motion a series of mechanisms that link the risks with a variety of outcomes. A central task of both researchers and creators of intervention programs is to identify these mechanisms. It may not be possible to change a risk or vulnerability factor such as genetic inheritance, but it may be possible to modify some of the consequences of genetic inheritance that have a disruptive impact on parent-child relationships. In other words, locating specific vulnerabilities in the child or the family can help us to focus and hone the target of intervention. Information about protective mechanisms helps to pinpoint forces that can be mobilized to foster well-being in both parents and children. A clearer understanding of naturally occurring resilience can inform interveners about where to look for resources to help individuals and families cope with inevitable but unexpected adversities.

Risk models provide us with a fresh, essentially developmental perspective on childhood adaptation and dysfunction. Ultimately, these models encourage researchers to examine family members' complex developmental journeys into or out of periods of maladaptation, a perspective adopted by the relatively new field of developmental psychopathology (Cicchetti & Cohen, 1995; Rutter & Garmezy, 1983). This field constitutes the foundation of the emerging science and practice of prevention (Coie et al., 1993). From a developmental psychopathology perspective, risks are not inevitably harbingers of doom, but warning signals that parenting intervention programs can interpret as a call to action. We draw repeatedly on the formulations provided by these risk models in our descriptions of how parents affect children's development and how interventions can be designed to help parents function more effectively.

ISSUES IN THE CREATION OF PARENTING INTERVENTIONS: A HISTORICAL PERSPECTIVE

Attempts to influence parents' beliefs and behaviors through the printed word, sermons, lectures, or more intense interventions are as old as human culture. Because parents' child-rearing responsibilities have been viewed as fundamental to societal well-being in every historical period, treatises on the condition and future of the social order typically give considerable attention to parental duties (Brim, 1959). Classics such as Plato's *Republic* and Rousseau's *Emile* offered perspectives on the child and the proper role of parents and provided the philosophical foundation of the nature/nurture debate that continues today.

At the core of parenting interventions across all periods of U.S. history is a view of parents as central agents for the maintenance or improvement of society through the proper socialization of the younger generation. In the tripartite organization of society/parent/child, parents function as the "middlepersons" who provide a connection between societal practices or ideals and children's daily life and learning. Consciously and unconsciously, parents select a set of prescriptions and norms that they attempt to pass on to their children. The conduit works the other way, too. Children's needs influence parents to act as protectors, advocates, and emissaries who reach out for help on behalf of children, and this outreach links the family with institutions in the larger society.

Our historical survey of parenting interventions as they have been evolving over the past two centuries in the United States indicates that the field has been struggling to answer four basic questions: Why are parenting interventions needed? Who are the interventions designed to reach? Who should deliver them? and Who should pay for them? As we shall see, the answers reveal little evidence of linear historical shifts in which later notions build on or replace earlier ones. Rather, most of the issues and dilemmas raised at different times over the past two hundred years continue to be debated in both academic and political discussions of whether and how to provide assistance for contemporary parents. These issues provide a backdrop for understanding the variety of intervention programs that we describe in some detail in the fourth through eighth sections of the chapter.

Why Are Parenting Interventions Needed?

We have found four quite different answers to the questions: Do parents actually need help? and Why can't they manage to rear children on their own?

1. "Parents are central to children's development but they lack natural competence"

In the nineteenth century, focus on the importance of the parental role was heightened by the emerging belief that the early years of childhood constitute a critical, formative period of human development (Aries, 1962). Since that time, parents have been viewed as the chief architects of the family environment; they gain others' respect when their offspring develop well and become the chief targets of blame when their children are in trouble.

Coupled with the assumption that parents are the dominant influence on a young child's life is the idea that parents are ill prepared for fulfilling their child-rearing responsibilities effectively. An official report of the first meeting of the National Congress of Mothers in February 1897 indicates that "as they listened to G. Stanley Hall's keynote address, mothers realized that they lacked those intellectual habits which would enable them to play their parts competently as parents" (National Congress of Parents and Teachers, 1944, p. 144). This view of parental (maternal) incompetence continues to be reinforced by modern theories of child development, most of which convey the message that laypersons need to be trained in appropriate methods of bringing up children (Kessen, 1979). In its extreme form, this message implies that parents are deficient in important ways and need guidance from "experts" about the skills necessary for adequate child rearing.

2. "Traditional parenting practices need revising in light of scientific findings"

A second perspective justifying parenting interventions begins with the premise that child-rearing practices dictated by tradition are far from ideal. In almost every age, some argue that "old-fashioned" traditional ideas about parenting fail to promote optimal levels of child development and may actually retard societal progress (Brim, 1959). The reasoning here is that well-informed, more effective parents will produce healthier, more resourceful children, and that the improvement of the citizenry across the generations will ultimately result in healthier societies governed by better-adjusted decision makers who will make wiser decisions.

3. "Reinstitute traditional practices in light of contemporary family disarray"

A third rationale that justifies interventions for parents heads in a direction opposite to the second—back to the traditions on which the culture was established. Proponents base their argument on a series of demographic shifts. During the past 150 years in the United States, the migration of families from farms to cities has left nuclear families increasingly isolated, distant from their kinfolk, and lacking child-rearing support and advice that used to be available within extended families and communities (Brim, 1959). This isolation has been accompanied by signs that the American family is not in good health. Over the past four decades, families have increasingly been torn apart by marital separation and divorce (Emery, 1988). Adolescent parenthood and single-parent households are on the increase (Burns & Scott, 1994). Gaps between rich and poor continue to widen, with the result that many families are struggling with economic vulnerability and outright poverty (Children's Defense Fund, 1984).

A number of family scholars (cf., Popenoe, 1993) and politicians (e.g., Bennet, 1992) interpret these trends and statistics as evidence that the modern family is in a state of decline approaching catastrophe. The root causes of this decline from this point of view are the abandonment of traditional family values and child-rearing practices. Contemporary social scientific theory and research, rather than providing solutions for today's families, are seen as part of the problem in that social scientists tolerate and support diverse family forms that meet the needs of parents but not of children (Elkind, 1994). From this perspective, parents need help and support to move back to the "traditional" family structure with two biological parents and mothers at home to look after the children.[1] Part of the current conservative agenda in the United States involves an explicit rejection of "modern secular influences" on parenting and a return to the tenets of more fundamental religious principles (Bennet, 1992).

[1] What constitutes a traditional family structure depends on temporal context. In the span of human history, the traditional nuclear family household with mothers at home and fathers working outside the home is quite new (Skolnick, 1991).

4. "Families need support"

Other family scholars (e.g., Skolnick, 1991; Stacey, 1996) and political commentators (e.g., Clinton, 1996) view the disturbingly high level of strain and distress in the lives of mothers, fathers, and children as evidence that family-based policies and interventions are needed to enhance the ability of contemporary parents and children to cope with the diverse challenges they face. From this perspective, parenting interventions constitute only a subset of the possible interventions for contemporary parents in need of help. Some policies and intervention programs are designed to provide material supports for parents or to remove some of the barriers to accessing societal resources (e.g., making it easier for poor families to obtain medical services).

All four of these justifications for parenting interventions have been challenged. The view that parents lack competence is at best an overgeneralization that does injustice to many men and women who seem to grow into the parent role naturally and rear healthy, well-adjusted children despite the considerable challenges they face on their family journeys. The argument that traditional parenting practices are outmoded and in need of revision in light of new scientific information is, in turn, rejected by those who advocate traditional approaches as the solution to the distress of contemporary family life.

The tension between arguments for moving toward or away from tradition is heightened in writings about ethnic and racial differences in American family life. Some argue that acculturation in the form of assimilation to the dominant Euro-American culture may have negative consequences for ethnic families and that a return to cultural "roots" may provide a source of family stability and strength (e.g., Staples & Johnson, 1993). Others argue that ethnic families can meet the challenge of the modern world through the adoption of a bicultural identity that selects from both the old and the new (e.g., Rueschenberg & Buriel, 1995).

Despite the range of explanations for why contemporary families are under strain, most actually agree that families need shoring up. However, there is no consensus about whether parenting interventions or other forms of family support (e.g., medical, financial) ought to be a high priority for public or private funding. There are, then, no universally accepted justifications for supporting wide access to parenting interventions. Our own view is closest to the argument that parents on the brink of the millennium need support for family making, which has become an increasingly complex endeavor. We provide data to support this view in several subsequent sections of this chapter.

Who Delivers Parenting Services?

A Multiplicity of Service Deliverers

In the nineteenth century, parenting "experts" were likely to be mothers who volunteered their services to help other mothers. In the early years of the twentieth century, increases and declines in support for parenting interventions were closely tied to the resourcefulness of volunteer organizations such as the Child Study Association and the Parent-Teacher Association, both founded in the late 1800s. The current debate about whether parents can learn from one another was accepted as a given a century ago.

A variety of professionals became involved in parenting interventions as a by-product of their professional roles. Physicians, of course, have always provided advice for parents of children who are physically or emotionally ill, but their involvement in more general and systematic efforts at parent education has occurred through the popular media (e.g., Dr. Spock, Dr. Brazelton, Dr. Leach). Social workers in settlement houses at the turn of the twentieth century were among the earliest professionals to talk with parents as part of their role in helping to improve the life of the community. Although preschool teachers were not necessarily experts in dealing with parents, by the 1920s it was common for them to encourage classroom observations, to hold group meetings for parents, to offer frequent parent-teacher conferences and home visits, and to provide a consultation service for parents so that they could discuss child-rearing problems on an individual basis with a professional. Elementary school teachers later followed suit with regular parent-teacher conferences. More recently, organized outreach programs, in which state departments of education, schools, and mental health agencies collaborate to help parents work with their children, have offered a specialized source of child-rearing information and advice (Weiss, 1990). Similar services for parents have become a regular offering of religious institutions across many denominations.

The history of mental health services for children reveals increasing involvement of parents in the treatment of their children, although parent education was not originally the primary focus of the therapy. The first child guidance clinic in the United States was opened by Lightner Witmer in 1896 at the University of Pennsylvania. The clinic set a model for the next 60 years, in which a psychiatrist worked with the child in individual treatment, a psychologist, if there was one, provided psychological assessment, and a social worker met with the parent, virtually always the mother. When psychoanalysts who had initially treated adults began to conduct therapy with children (A. Freud, 1965), the role of the parent in the child's treatment was similar to that in the child guidance clinic—as an adjunct to the "real" work of therapy with the child.[2]

Public Health also began to take on parent education functions in the twentieth century, especially as part of health-related programs to serve the urban poor. Most of the early services were provided by visiting nurses, but over time a variety of professionals, paraprofessionals, and nonprofessionals became involved in providing child-rearing advice and instruction along with other consultative services (Powell, 1993; Wasik, 1993).

By the third decade of the twentieth century, an independent profession of parent educators began to emerge. Research on parent education became a focused activity of scholars, primarily at the Child Welfare Research Station at the University of Iowa and through the National Council of Parent Education. During the same period, research on a more clinically oriented child guidance program for parents was spearheaded by Jean Macfarlane (1938) in the context of the Berkeley Longitudinal Studies at the University of California. Professional education programs for parent educators continued to expand in the 1930s through the National Council of Parent Education and especially through colleges and universities. Today, parent education is taught in various academic settings, with primary homes located in departments of family studies, education, and psychology.

Training for Parenting Interveners

The emergence of a profession devoted to educating parents does not mean that parent educators have *replaced* other professionals and nonprofessionals offering help to parents. In fact, as parenting programs have expanded to serve diverse and more troubled populations, there has been an increase in the number of paraprofessionals (without formal degrees but with systematic training) and nonprofessionals (with only limited training) conducting direct interventions for parents. In a survey of home visiting programs, Roberts and Wasik (1990) found that 76% employed at least some paraprofessionals, and 49% offered no in-service training for their home visitors. There are some obvious advantages to recruiting paraprofessional and nonprofessional personnel. Their salaries are much lower, and paraprofessionals are usually recruited from the same community and ethnic group as the client

[2] We will see in the section on parenting theories that newer mental health interventions for children and adolescents give parents a much more central role in the process of therapy.

families they serve. Because they know the territory, they are thought to be better able to translate the program plan to make it more useful and to enlist the trust and participation of parents who might be skeptical of offers of help from "outsiders."

Wasik's (1993) general comments about the effectiveness of paraprofessionals in home visiting programs can be applied to parenting interventions more generally: "very little research exists to answer empirically the question of whether one should employ professional or paraprofessional home visitors, much less from what discipline a professional should be" (p. 144). The issue of staff training for the most effective delivery of parenting interventions has not received the attention it deserves (Cowan & Cowan, 1995), and we return to it in a later section.

Whom Are Parenting Intervention Programs Designed to Reach?

The intended audience for parenting interventions expanded considerably in the last half of the twentieth century; it now includes fathers as well as mothers in economically and ethnically diverse families. In our view, the current state of parenting education and intervention is best understood in the context of social changes in America after World War II, which foreshadowed the political upheaval of the 1960s and the political backlash against some of those changes that emerged in the 1990s. The decade of the 1960s saw the emergence of several major political movements, government programs, and social changes that had profound implications for family life: the women's movement, the civil rights movement, the War on Poverty, and the increasing fragmentation of the nuclear family. Against this backdrop of social change, recent shifts in the focus of parenting interventions become more understandable.

The Women's Movement: Expanding the Focus of Parenting Interventions

During the 1960s, the women's movement emerged from a coalition of forces working toward a more egalitarian role for women both inside and outside the family. Since that time, women's participation in the workforce has increased markedly, with more than half the mothers of children under the age of 3 now working at least 20 hours per week outside the home (Matthews & Rodin, 1989). Mothers with children under 1 year of age constitute the subgroup of mothers with the greatest increase in participation in the labor force (Hayghe, 1986).

As the women's movement challenged mothers to reenter the world of work, and as feminist scholars (e.g., Chodorow, 1989) and clinicians (McGoldrick, Anderson, & Walsh, 1989) urged a shift in spouses' division of family work, a cultural ideological shift promoted a more central role for men in the family and in their children's development. Researchers were slow to acknowledge this shift. Eleven years after the publication of the first version of the present *Handbook of Child Psychology* (Carmichael, 1954), Nash (1965) pointed out that "father" had not been included in the index. In the past decade, a more central role for fathers has begun to emerge, as reflected in the literature on child development (e.g., Parke, 1996), in research on fatherhood (e.g., Bronstein & Cowan, 1988), in popular parenting manuals (e.g., Kuttner, 1991), and in some clinical interventions (e.g., Dadds, Schwartz, & Sanders, 1987). Even though the realities of fathers' direct participation in child rearing fall far short of some contemporary images of egalitarianism (Cowan & Cowan, 1988, 1992; Pleck, 1988), empirical data make it clear that fathers have an enormous impact on their children's development.

Based on a growing understanding that the parent-child relationship is influenced by forces within and outside the family, some parenting intervention programs have shown interest in the family as a whole. Increasingly, interventions target various relationships in the family system (three generations, marital dyad, mother-child dyad, father-child dyad). Some professionals work with the system as a whole in conjoint family meetings in efforts to increase the scope of program effects by addressing the multiple forces that affect parenting behavior and children's development.

One outgrowth of the 1960s has been a new interest in the social context of family life and a renewed faith in the power of social support. In some parenting intervention programs, the content has broadened to include friends and other peers outside the nuclear family system, often in group meetings (e.g., Christensen & Thomas, 1980; Webster-Stratton, 1984). Discussing questions about child rearing with other parents who face similar issues and dilemmas can provide much-needed support—emotional (relief that others are in the same boat), social (emerging friendships), and instrumental (shared child care resources).

Civil Rights, the War on Poverty, and the Extension of Parenting Intervention Programs to Diverse Populations

The U.S. civil rights movement and the War on Poverty emerged from similar political roots. Increasingly activist in nature, the campaign for civil rights in the South spread across the country, bringing increased recognition that racial and economic discrimination go hand in hand. Both movements were fueled in part by passionate convictions that governments, especially the federal government, should be active in improving the quality of family life when it falls below some minimum economic and social standard. Many ambitious efforts were initiated in the 1960s to combat poverty and establish increased civil rights for minority families through parenting programs for economically disadvantaged parents (Chilman, 1973). During this era, most of the model programs of early childhood intervention for low-income populations included a parent education or parent involvement component as a primary or secondary focus (cf., Consortium for Longitudinal Studies, 1983).

The drive toward civil rights and the War on Poverty, then, resulted in broadening the target populations for parenting intervention programs. It was not a new idea to extend parenting programs to high-risk populations defined on the basis of low income and education. What may be new is the proliferation of programs for parents in different ethnic groups, parents designated in specific categories of risk (e.g., teen mothers, single mothers, parents likely to abuse their children), and parents whose children have already been diagnosed with a specific problem or disorder (e.g., aggression, Attention Deficit Hyperactivity Disorder [ADHD], mental retardation, schizophrenia). In general, this extension has occurred by taking over programs initially designed for middle-class parents. Because we are far from knowing enough about the uniqueness or generalizability of patterns across ethnic and economic groups, it is not clear at this time how serious a problem has been created by the "one size fits all" approach to intervention design.

Largely as a function of the increasing diversity and risk status of the families served, there is a growing pattern of offering parenting interventions in connection with other services aimed at parents and/or other family members. This reflects a movement away from providing parenting interventions as stand-alone programs. For example, attempts to strengthen parenting are included in a genre of interventions known as two-generation programs that address the development of children *and* their parents. In addition to a parenting intervention component, two-generation programs include an assessment of child and family needs, high-quality early childhood education and care, preventive health services, case management, and self-sufficiency services leading to employment and a living wage for the parents (Smith & Zaslow, 1995).

Trouble in the American Family and the Ideology of Prevention

As we noted earlier, the ferment of social change that began in the 1960s was accompanied by a rapid and troubling increase in many negative indicators of the quality of American family life. Politically conservative social critics (e.g., Blankenhorn, Bayme, & Elshtain, 1990; Popenoe, 1993) blame the liberal social agenda for *causing* the difficulties now being experienced by the American family. They argue that the increased ease of divorce, the prevalence of single parenthood, and the participation of women in the labor force are responsible for the increasing prevalence of problems in children and adolescents. Others, including the present authors, believe that it is a logical fallacy to infer causation from correlated social changes, and that difficulties experienced by contemporary families stem from the same sources that led to the search for equality embodied in the struggles for civil rights, women's rights, and the rights of the poor.

Regardless of the explanation, there is consensus that many parents of young children are experiencing distress and that their children are at risk for suffering the consequences. Between 7 and 14 million children in the United States under 18 meet the criteria for at least one mental or emotional disorder (National Plan for Research on Child & Adolescent Mental Disorders, 1990). Of the 5- to 5.5-year-olds entering kindergarten, at least 20% have academic and social problems serious enough to warrant intervention (Lambert, 1988), but less than half will receive psychological services (Saxe, Cross, & Silverman, 1988). An additional significant proportion of the young student population is *at risk* for distress by virtue of their parents' psychopathology (Sameroff, Siefer, & Zax, 1982), marital conflict (Cummings & Davies, 1994), or ineffective parenting (Patterson & Capaldi, 1991).

There is convincing evidence that children tend to move along developmental trajectories that follow from their earliest success or failure at school (Alexander & Entwisle, 1988); those in difficulty in the first two elementary school grades are at risk for a variety of serious difficulties as adolescents, including academic underachievement, dropping out of school, and internalizing or externalizing problems with peers (Kellam, Simon, & Ensminger, 1982; Lambert, 1988). What these data make clear is that a substantial proportion of the children in the United States are experiencing major problems in academic and social adaptation, and that many of them can be identified as being at risk when they are quite young.

Prevention and Early Intervention. We have seen that one outgrowth of social changes in the 1960s was increased effort to create parenting interventions that reach high-risk families. Another legacy of the 1960s was a renewal of interest in the concept of preventive intervention. The prevention model is based on the notion of deterring, hindering, or reducing the risk of problems or dysfunctional patterns. Prevention was encouraged by the federal government during the War on Poverty, and its encouragement in medical and academic settings led to the emergence of the fields of community psychiatry (cf., Caplan, 1964) and community psychology (Sarason, 1974). The prevention model contrasts with a treatment model, which attempts to remedy or ameliorate a disorder, a disease, or their consequences (Cowen, 1985).

Although prevention often has the connotation of warding off problems before they occur, another significant aspect of preventive intervention is the enhancement of individual and family life. In summarizing future directions for a national program of prevention research, Coie et al. (1993) remind us that the goals of health promotion and problem prevention are interrelated and advocate "universal interventions to promote health in broad populations and more focused interventions to prevent severe disorders in targeted populations at risk" (p. 1019). The main argument for preventive intervention programs for families is that if we develop competence-promoting interventions for parents early in families' developmental course—before risk factors become stabilized and less amenable to influence—we maximize the chance of reducing the seriousness of later developmental problems and clinical disorders in all family members.

Who Pays? What Happens When Political Values Change?

To examine the impact of political changes on the availability of funding for parenting intervention programs, we return briefly to the beginning of the twentieth century. Since the early 1900s, interventions for bettering family life have been supported by the federal government. The Children's Bureau was established in 1912 and formed the organizational base for the publication of the first edition of *Infant Care* two years later. The Smith-Lever Act of 1914 made provisions for some 2,000 county home demonstration agents as part of the Department of Agriculture's efforts to support child rearing and home management. Four years later, in 1918, the U.S. Public Health Service established parent education programs focused on child health issues (Brim, 1959). Clearly, the U.S. government took a significant role in providing financial support for parenting intervention programs long before the 1960s War on Poverty, and it has continued to do so throughout this century under both Republican and Democratic presidents and majorities in Congress.

Government support for parenting interventions has always been supplemented by organized charities and religious institutions. Between the 1920s and 1940s, the professional education, research, and program development base of parent education was supported financially in large measure by the Laura Spelman Rockefeller Memorial from 1918 to 1928, and by one of its direct successors, the Spelman Fund. Financial support from the Memorial helped establish or expand child study centers at such institutions as Teachers College, and the Universities of California, Iowa, and Minnesota. The Memorial also supported curriculum development and fellowships in parent education at Teachers College and in home economics departments at institutions of higher education nationally, and encouraged the entry into the parent education field of numerous national organizations, including the American Home Economics Association and the National Congress of Parents and Teachers.

Beginning in the 1940s, the federal government's interest in parenting interventions for targeted populations expanded through the mental health movement, stimulated in part by the rapid increase in mental health services made available to veterans returning from the war. The increase was also supported through the National Mental Health Act of 1946, which provided funds to community mental health programs. Monies available for mental health services stimulated the growth of parenting interventions in the 1950s as funding from the Laura Spelman Rockefeller Memorial and Spelman Fund had done in the 1920s and 1930s (Brim, 1959).

The increase in federal, state, and local funding of parenting interventions in the 1960s, 1970s, and 1980s, then, was built upon an already expanding base. Evaluations of parenting interventions increased during that same period, mostly due to the availability of funding for systematic research through the National Institute of Mental Health. Many of the specific programs that we describe later owe at least part of their existence to government funding for both service delivery and research evaluation. There is no doubt, then, that political and social forces have had a profound impact on the shape, size, and direction of parenting intervention programs.

In the 1990s, the social climate is shifting again. We are now in a period of economic "downsizing" and social backlash against an activist role for government. Cutbacks are the order of the day in both private and public sectors of the economy. Beyond issues of available funds lie explicit negative reactions to what some see as the "failed policies" of the 1960s (Bennet, 1992; Gingrich, 1995). "Social programs" are dismissed by some as "government social work." Federal funds are being withdrawn from these programs and transferred to state governments with as yet unknown consequences. Funds to support preventive interventions, never a top priority of governments or service delivery systems, are certain to be more difficult to obtain. In times of scarcity, choices are determined by those with the power to make them. As of this writing, it is impossible to forecast the impact of the current climate on the availability of funding for parenting interventions. We discuss some of the value and policy issues and dilemmas facing decision makers in the last section of this chapter.

Our survey of the historical context of present-day parenting interventions leads us to two seemingly contradictory conclusions. First, in some sense little has changed over the past two centuries with regard to parenting interventions in the United States: the issues about why parenting interventions are needed, who will deliver them, and who will use them have been debated over the decades with no apparent resolution. Second, in some sense a great deal has changed, especially the marked and rapid social changes of the past 50 years. The move toward inclusion of greater heterogeneity in the population of parents targeted for parenting interventions, along with fewer public resources available for social programs, has created a set of unresolved tensions in the parenting intervention field.

A CHECKLIST OF THEORIES ABOUT PARENTING EFFECTS: NINE ALTERNATIVE PERSPECTIVES

We turn now to an exploration of the basic ideas underlying parenting intervention programs. Assume for a moment that you, the reader, are about to become an intervention agent involved in working with parents. You may be a beginning practitioner consulting with parents as part of your professional role (a pediatrician, nurse, teacher, parent educator, or therapist), or you may be considering the creation of a new intervention program. You are faced immediately with variations of the questions we raised in summarizing the history of the parenting intervention field: Why is this parenting intervention needed? Who will deliver your parenting intervention? Who are the targets of the intervention (which families, which family members)?

We assume that you have already justified the need for intervention, at least to your own satisfaction. The next step is to determine what you ought to do as an intervention agent to enhance parenting. This is where your assumptions, hypotheses, and theories about how parents affect children enter the picture. If you assume that parents affect children's development by reinforcing or ignoring specific behaviors, your intervention may provide direct teaching to parents to help them minimize negative and ineffective reinforcement strategies and maximize positive, effective ones. If you assume that parents influence children's adaptation through actions that facilitate or interfere with the unfolding of their inner development, your intervention will have a different content and focus. Your theory about the mechanisms of parental influence, then, shapes the selection of risks that you target and the curriculum and format that you offer. In this section, we present a checklist that outlines nine alternative perspectives on the mechanisms by which parents are thought to influence their children's development. Each serves as a foundation for intervention approaches to be described in subsequent sections of the chapter.

Orienting Assumptions

The parenting effects checklist is based on four orienting assumptions:[3]

1. Theorists differ in their view of whether the primary locus of the forces regulating developmental change and stability is internal to the child (child-focused), external to the child (parent-focused), or a product of the interaction between internal and external forces (parent-child relationship focused).
2. Within internal, external, and interaction perspectives, three general levels of analysis are represented in modern theories of parenting—biological, psychological, and social interactional—each focusing on a different set of mechanisms thought to be central in explaining human development. Although the three types of developmental mechanisms are often considered separately, a biopsychosocial approach is becoming more common in the fields of both child development (e.g., Hetherington & Parke, 1993) and abnormal psychology (e.g., Davison & Neale, 1996).

We arrive at precisely nine items on our theory checklist by considering the fact that according to different points of view, the forces regulating developmental change are located in the child, in the parent, or in the relationship between them; these effects are thought to occur through the operation of one of three types of mechanisms (biological, psychological, social). From the combination of three locations and three mechanisms regulating developmental

[3] This checklist is based on the notion of a 9-cell matrix that organizes alternative theories of normal development, psychopathology, and intervention (P. Cowan, 1988).

stability and change, we derive a matrix containing nine "boxes" (3×3), with each box containing a similar set of theories to explain how parents contribute to their children's adaptation or distress. We do not assume that each theory fits neatly into one and only one box, nor do we believe that it is necessary to choose one among nine approaches as the best or most correct theory of parenting, with others discarded or ignored. We argue instead that each theoretical view has merit as a potential contributor to our understanding of meaningful variations in children's development. A schematic representation of the checklist in the form of a 9-box matrix is presented in Figure 1.1.

3. We assume that each theory of normal development embodies a theory of psychopathology, just as each theory of psychopathology contains a theory of normal development.

4. Every theory of normal and pathological development is associated with an explicit or implicit theory of intervention.

Taking these last two assumptions together, we show that theories of parenting effects tend to come in "boxed sets" that contain comparable models of normal development, psychopathology, and intervention. For example, if the child's ability to resolve Oedipal conflicts in his or her relationships with both parents is seen as setting the pattern for development over the life course (S. Freud, 1938), then intervention programs might help parents focus on avoiding or repairing the consequences of their children's distressing Oedipal struggles during childhood. By contrast, as we shall see, if the parent's pattern of reinforcements is seen as the primary force in shaping children's development, very different intervention strategies will be suggested.[4]

MECHANISMS OF DEVELOPMENT	LOCUS OF DEVELOPMENT: Child	Parent	Parent-child
Biological	Child-focused biological	Parent-focused biological	Interactive biological
Psychological	Child-focused psychological	Parent-focused psychological	Interactive psychological
Social	Child-focused social relationship	Parent-focused social relationship	Interactive social relationship

Figure 1.1 Nine theories of how children change: the parenting effects checklist.

Child-Focused Theories

1. Child-Focused Biological Theories

In this first box we locate biological theories that focus on parents' genetic, constitutional contributions to their child's development (e.g., Gottesman, 1991). Although genes literally come *from* the parents, it is *inside the child* that we see the operation of genetic, biochemical, neurophysiological, and physical systems that regulate the child's normal growth and development. The same kind of biological mechanisms that account for normal development are invoked as determinants of psychological disorders such as schizophrenia, depression, and antisocial personality.

With all of the recent excitement about genetic and neuropsychological theories of development and psychopathology, it has almost been forgotten that Arnold Gesell and his colleagues at Yale University, who held strict biological maturation views of development, were leading lights of child psychology from the 1930s to the early 1950s (Gesell & Ilg, with Learned & Ames, 1943). Their descriptions of the average age at which children pass a number of physical, cognitive, social, and emotional developmental milestones conceptualized development as a maturational unfolding over time. Parents could use information about age norms to assess whether their children's progress was offtrack or "normal," but it was assumed that they could do little to influence the general content and pace of the child's biologically determined developmental trajectory beyond giving them "the gift of time."

Two quite different implications for intervention can be drawn from the child-focused biological approach. First, many theorists, researchers, and health service providers assume that biologically caused disorders or disorders associated with biological risk factors will respond best to biological treatments. To take one example, current practice influenced by the biological determinism view emphasizes the use of psychoactive drugs in the treatment of schizophrenia, depression, anxiety, and ADHD (e.g., Lickey, 1991). The role of the parents in the treatment is primarily to administer and monitor the medication.

[4] Theorists and service providers act as if theories about risks or causes of a disorder *should* determine the intervention strategy. Our view is that etiology and treatment are both logically and empirically independent.

Another inference from theories that focus on *genetic* biological mechanisms is more consistent with deductions drawn from Gesell's maturation theories. If a trait (intelligence, for example) or a disorder (schizophrenia) is inherited, it is inferred that there is little one can do in the way of intervention for parents except to help them cope with the consequences of biological determinism. From this perspective, parenting interventions designed to treat or alleviate the disorder in the child are bound to fail. When we discuss the implications of theory for child-focused intervention programs, we will show that this inference is unwarranted on both logical and empirical grounds.

2. Child-Focused Psychological Theories

In child-focused psychological theories, intrapsychic forces are predominant in affecting children's adaptation. Humanists (Maslow, 1962; Rogers, 1961) assume that inner forces push children and adults toward self-actualization and that parents disrupt this force only through extremes of neglect or inappropriate care. Psychoanalytic theorists (A. Freud, 1965; S. Freud, 1938; Klein, 1932) assume that various forms of psychopathology are not created by parents directly but are set in motion by the child's reaction to threat and deprivation. Although the distal actions of parents in both humanistic and psychoanalytic theories receive most of the blame for childhood psychopathology, the more proximal causes of distress and the locus of the psychopathology reside in the child. Parents are relegated to the role of conscientious gardeners who plant the seed where it will receive adequate nutrients from the soil, provide optimal amounts of water and sunlight, and wait for the internal processes to unfold and reveal what kind of flower has emerged.

Parents' contributions to their children's developmental trajectories from the child-focused psychological perspective are evaluated in terms of whether they provide a "good-enough" environment (Winnicott, 1987) to allow the child to feel safe and to facilitate the unfolding of internal processes. If this environment is not established, the provocation of internal disequilibrium may be too great for the child's intrapsychic system to manage. Parent educators working from this perspective try to help parents to acquire normative developmental information about what children require to feel secure and learn active listening skills so that, armed with this information, they can provide a family environment that is conducive to the child's development. In treating an emotionally disturbed child using a humanistic or psychoanalytic perspective, the therapist provides a safe "holding environment" (Masterson, 1992) in which the child's defenses can relax enough to allow the normal developmental processes to operate effectively on their own. Parents are included as collateral to the main therapy, with the explicit goal of allaying their anxieties so that they can provide a more secure and nurturing environment for the child at home.

3. Child-Focused Social Relationship Theories

The emphasis in child-focused *social* theories of parenting influences remains on the child's internal processes, but highlights the mechanisms by which the child internalizes schemas or "working models" of parent-child *relationships.* Object relations theories (Klein, 1932; Winnicott, 1987) and attachment theories (Ainsworth & Wittig, 1969; Bowlby, 1980; Main, Kaplan, & Cassidy, 1985) share the premise that the most important effect of early experience is what infants and young children learn about intimate relationships from their experiences with their primary caretakers. It is assumed that this early learning is preserved in the form of "templates"—"object relations schemas" (Kernberg, 1985) or "working models" (Bowlby, 1980)—that shape the individual's expectations and reactions in subsequent intimate relationships. For example, if children form a working model based on the premise that they cannot depend on the ones they love to be there for them when they need them, this expectation may color and even override children's later actual experience in adult love relationships.

Although theoretical formulations (Kernberg, 1985), clinical case reports (Scharff & Birtles, 1994), and research studies (Erickson, Korfmacher, & Egeland, 1994) indicate that it is difficult to alter object relations schemas and working models, some long-term psychotherapies with adults claim success in helping clients reconstruct their early representations of familial relationships so that they influence their current perceptions in less maladaptive ways (Kernberg, 1985). Parent education approaches conducted from this point of view focus less on changing parents' working models and more on making their models more conscious so that expectations about what can happen in intimate relationships are modified. It is expected that these alterations will help break intergenerational cycles of unrewarding and maladaptive behavior (cf. Minde & Hesse, 1996).

Parent-Focused Theories

4. Parent-Focused Biological Theories

Parent-focused theories that emphasize biological factors in children's development examine the parents' genetic makeup and their active management of the child's physical biological environment.

Taking Action Based on Family Genetic Histories. In some medical conditions (e.g., sickle cell disease, Tay-Sachs disease, cystic fibrosis) and certain psychological conditions (e.g., retardation attributable to phenylketonuria [PKU]), it is possible to estimate the probable outcomes for the child, given the father's and mother's genetic history and current status (Harper, 1993). At present, there are no technologies available to alter parents' genes and chromosomes in ways that could have predictable, positive effects on the child. Intervention from a parent-focused biological perspective comes in the form of genetic counseling programs designed to help parents who are carriers of some conditions to make decisions about whether to conceive a child or carry a child to term in light of the risks (Pauker & Pauker, 1987).

Parent's Active Management of Specific Physical Environmental Conditions. Internal biological processes unfold within physical/biological environments. Especially when children are young, parents play a central role in managing these environments in ways that have powerful effects on children's physical, intellectual, social, and emotional development. On the positive side, parents' provision of adequate nutrition and an organized, reasonably uncrowded physical environment contribute directly to desirable developmental outcomes (Politt & Gorman, 1984). On the negative side, parents' failure to prevent children's exposure to environmental toxins (lead paint, chemical waste) has direct adverse effects on their health and their physical and cognitive development (Fein, Schwartz, Jacobs, & Jacobson, 1983). In studies of parent effects, the mother's uterus and umbilical cord are often neglected as prebirth environmental sources of biological influence on the child's development. This has been brought to public attention recently as the effects of mothers' drug use have been implicated in their babies' early neurological and emotional development (Lewis & Bendersky, 1995).

5. Parent-Focused Psychological Theories

Theories located in this box are consistent with traditional socialization approaches emphasizing the top-down parent-to-child effects of reinforcement. Children's development and difficulties can be accounted for by the influences of classical conditioning, reinforcement, and observations of what significant others do (Bandura & Walters, 1963; Skinner, 1938; Watson, 1928). In contrast with the parents-as-gardeners metaphor, behavioral theories conceptualize parents as teachers who write on essentially blank slates.

Why do we categorize an approach that rests heavily on the links between observed parent and child behavior as psychological? Although some of the earliest learning theorists attempted to rid themselves of concepts of mind, all of them assumed that an association process inside the person connects the stimulus and response so that old stimuli evoke new behaviors and new stimuli become attached to old response patterns. In parent-focused psychological theories, the psychological perceptions and learning mechanisms within the child behave like videotape machines that record and preserve experiences of parents' reinforcement patterns.

If, as parent-focused psychological theorists assume, children's adaptation is a function of parental treatment, then changing children's behavior in a more desirable direction would be a matter of altering parents' and significant adults' behavior. This theoretical box contains the traditional behavior modification techniques that are employed in programs for families with troubled children and in behavioral parent education programs for nonclinical families (e.g., Patterson & Gullion, 1973).

6. Parent-Focused Social Theories

Parent-focused social theories of children's development attend to the quality of the parent-child *relationship* rather than to the parent's behavior (e.g., Baumrind, 1991). Is the relationship between parent and child warm or cold, structured or chaotic, hierarchical or egalitarian? Whereas parenting research and parenting books have tended to focus on what parents should or should not *do,* the theories in Box 6 assert that the power of parents' influence on normal development and psychopathology lies in the positive or negative qualities of the relationship that they establish with their children. Theories using this approach tend to be based on studies in which parents and children are observed in interaction, at home or in the laboratory. Global or microanalytic coding schemes are used to assess the quality of the parent-child relationship, which is then correlated with certain child outcomes of interest (see A Contextual, Systemic Perspective on Parenting, below).

Theories with an Interactive Focus on Both Parent and Child

7. Parent-Child Interactive Biological Theories

While most theorists endorse some form of interaction between biological and psychosocial factors, the interactive biological box of our checklist is reserved for theories that focus more narrowly on transactions between the child and environmental *biological/physical* factors. In contrast with the hypothesis derived from traditional theories that biological forces operate from within, newer theories describe bidirectional effects, in which biological factors that affect physical development are modified by physical factors such as nutrition (Sigman, 1995). Similarly, adverse conditions (e.g., extreme heat or extreme cold) may have different effects on individuals with different genetic constitutions. Thus, in reciprocal fashion, biological differences in vulnerability or resilience modify the impact of external risk factors. For example, although babies born to mothers addicted to crack cocaine suffer long-term developmental delays as a group, some appear to be endowed with biologically given mechanisms that resist the negative impact of the drug passed from the mother's system through the placenta (Lewis & Bendersky, 1995).

8. Parent-Child Interactive Psychological Theories

In contrast with parent-focused and child-focused psychological theories, interactive psychological theories of child development and psychopathology give *equal* weight to parents' and children's psychological characteristics. In these theories, a match or optimal mismatch between parent and child facilitates the children's growth, whereas a greater than optimal mismatch is a risk factor for developmental delay or psychological distress.

Jean Piaget (e.g., 1967) is a prime example of a psychological interaction theorist. The impact of *any* stimulus on a child is shaped by the structure of his or her logic system, which is determined by his or her developmental stage. All stimuli are assimilated—altered in meaning—by the child's existing cognitive structures. The tendency for human beings to assimilate helps to explain long-term stability in behavior and widespread generalization of problem-solving strategies across situations. But stability and consistency across time and contexts is only half of the story. Because new situations are surprising and present obstacles, they raise problems that past learning proves inadequate to solve. Thus, cognitive structures are continually in the process of modification (accommodation) to respond to these challenges.

Within the Piagetian perspective, the child's growth is stimulated and development proceeds when the actions of parents, teachers, and others present challenges for the child that are slightly above the child's developmental level. Given an optimal degree of match or mismatch between external challenge and internal organization, the child moves through increasingly complex developmental stages in a continual process of equilibration: the balancing of assimilation and accommodation processes (Turiel, 1974). Psychopathology from the Piagetian view (e.g., P. Cowan, 1978; Schmid-Kitsikis, 1973) occurs in two ways: (a) when there is a failure to proceed through the developmental stages, as when an adolescent is still reasoning with concepts based on how things look rather than how they "really are"; or (b) when there is a functional imbalance in the assimilation-accommodation process that leads either to overassimilation (e.g., getting lost in fantasy) or to overaccommodation (e.g., hypersensitivity to changes in stimulation) in response to environmental challenge.

9. Parent-Child Interactive Social Theories: A Limited Family Systems View

Consistent with traditional socialization theories, the parent-focused theoretical view retains a unidirectional view of causal forces as external to the child. By contrast, family systems views of development assume that causality is circular rather than linear (e.g., Steinglass, 1987), so that in any dyad, influence is bidirectional. Thus, mother-infant studies of the past two decades began to focus attention on the idea of mutual regulation systems (e.g., Stern, 1985). The point at which a transaction between parent and child "starts" is largely a matter of arbitrary convenience selected by the researcher. Is the parent who holds the child at arm's length creating a negative reaction in the child or reacting to the child's pulling away when the parent attempts to cuddle? This view asserts that each participant in the transaction is both acting and reacting to the other in a reciprocally regulated relationship *system.*

The concept of a mutual regulation relationship system is quite revolutionary for psychology, which has its roots in the study of individual psyches. As Hinde and Stevenson-Hinde (1988) note, the concept of mutual regulation systems forces us to develop a new language of *relationships.* What happens between a parent and a child is governed not only by the characteristics of each individual but also by the *pattern of transactions* between them. This subtle reformulation is extremely important. It means that it is impossible to make sense of and predict the quality of a relationship between two family members without examining the forces that contribute to and emerge from their transactions. Whether the mother or father responds warmly at any given moment is determined not only by that parent's characteristic warmth and the infant's characteristic responsiveness, but also by the patterns they have created jointly and therefore come to expect in their relationship.

According to social interactive theories of parenting, we cannot locate psychopathology in the parent or the child, but rather in the distressing pattern of interaction between them (Cicchetti & Toth, this volume). Thus, interventions to address specific problems in the child must be directed at changing the pattern of parent-child transactions. We call this a limited family systems view because the focus is limited to the parent-child dyad. As we show below, a full family systems approach examines parenting in the context of all of the relationships within the family—and between the family and the larger culture.

Using the Parenting Effects Checklist

Our nine-box checklist of parenting effects was organized from the multitude of competing theories about how parents influence children's development. Our typology reflects the fact that parents, experts, and researchers endorse a variety of alternative ideas about how children's development is affected by their parents. The box membership of a specific theory or program is not always clear. We believe, for example, that the assumptions of psychoanalytic theorists focus *primarily* on internal psychological mechanisms within the child, but the theory also posits biological and social components and includes external as well as internal forces that affect children's development. In other words, placement in a specific theoretical box is a matter of emphasis and balance among the competing theoretical alternatives.

So far, we have presented each set of theories as mutually exclusive descriptions of how parents contribute to children's development. In many polemic accounts, the impression is left that one approach must be accepted and all others rejected. A more reasonable assumption is that a combination of perspectives will provide a more differentiated and integrated understanding of the complex contributors to children's development. That is, we may learn more about parenting by considering the interaction of effects described in the nine boxes. In general, this view is consistent with a diathesis-stress model (e.g., Mednick et al., 1981): difficulties occur when a stressor (e.g., childhood trauma) occurs in the presence of a vulnerability (e.g., a genetic predisposition for schizophrenia).

The Checklist as a Reminder of Possibilities

We recommend the nine-box checklist of parenting effects theories as a reminder of possibilities to be explored when an intervention agent attempts to provide help for parents. Let us use an example to illustrate. Parents attending a weekly class reveal that their 5-year-old son is somewhat impulsive and aggressive and is having trouble making friends. From a child-focused perspective, the class instructor might be thinking about temperamental sources of impulsivity in the parents' family history, the child's psychological coping style, the child's attachment to the parent, or the recent loss of a major attachment figure. From a parent-focused or external perspective, the instructor might consider toxic conditions in the neighborhood, the parents' control of the child's nutrition, each parent's tendency to model or reinforce aggression, and the quality of each parent's interactions with the child. An interactive perspective would lead to questions about vulnerabilities and buffers available to child and parents that might decrease the mismatch between what the child needs and what the parents can provide. The instructor could cover the checklist of alternatives in class or in written materials to be read by the parents between meetings.

We realize that it is not possible for an individual educator or clinician working with parents to evaluate risks and buffers in all nine theoretical boxes, or to provide nine different kinds of interventions. Like other interveners, parent educators have a limited range of preferred approaches and limitations of money, time, and personnel. Even if training were truly multitheoretical and financial resources were unlimited, there is a limit to the complexity of data that a single intervener or family can process, and a limit to the number of possibilities that can be considered in any assessment or intervention. We also recognize that alternative explanations of parenting effects do not come easily for true believers and that it is possible for theorists, educators, and interveners to be so wedded to their particular paradigm that alternatives are resisted or rejected out of hand.

Nevertheless, we urge parenting interveners to consider a range of theoretical possibilities. Factors in all nine theoretical boxes may be implicated in the explanation of a specific developmental outcome and treatment, but those in some boxes will seem more salient than others for a given family. In the example of the parents with the 5-year-old impulsive child, it is possible to estimate the relative "weights" of risk factors that may be associated with the problematic outcome (difficulties making friends), and to identify those factors that appear to be contributing most directly to the problem. Then, work with parents can focus on modifying the central contributors.

The checklist can also function as a mental reminder for researchers who want to be certain that they have *considered* the relevant possibilities in their investigations of normal development or psychopathology. Here, too, practical limits will preclude the incorporation of variables from all nine boxes within a single research design, but a consideration of the alternatives may expand the range of potential alternatives and make the final selection more systematic.

Having identified nine types of theories and some possible combinations of theories to account for parents' influence on children's development, we turn to their potential application in parenting intervention programs. Almost all of the programs noted in subsequent sections of the chapter have been evaluated, or are in the process of being evaluated, in systematic studies. Not all of these studies have adequate research designs, if we restricted our account to programs with rigorously designed evaluations we would be quite limited in what we could say about the field of parenting interventions. We chose examples to describe programs that are designed for populations at different points along the continuum of risk, ranging from (a) nonclinical populations at low risk for distress, through (b) families with children at risk for later developmental difficulties based on their troubled environments, to (c) families with children already showing signs of cognitive developmental delay, behavior problems, or emotional disturbance.

Space limitations preclude accounts of each parenting intervention program in full detail. We vary our presentation strategy, depending in part on the available written information. In some cases, we provide illustrative examples from a number of similar programs of the same type. In others, we focus on a single complex program because it embodies a range of examples. We describe the curriculum or content focus of each type of intervention and some of the intervention techniques related to parenting. When they are available, we summarize results of systematic program evaluations. Because our accounts of programs are based on reports in the extant literature and not on direct observation, they may reflect the intent or design of the program more than the program as actually implemented. We wish to recognize further that because intervention models evolve over time, as we see in several instances below, our descriptions may vary somewhat from the most current version of some programs.

CHILD-FOCUSED PARENTING INTERVENTIONS: BIOLOGICAL AND PSYCHOLOGICAL APPROACHES

In this section we describe child-focused parenting interventions that emphasize biological and psychological explanations of children's development. Our concern here is not primarily with interventions in which the child participates, but rather interventions designed for parents to enhance or remediate developmental forces within the child.

Child-Focused Parenting Interventions Emphasizing Biological Mechanisms

The assumption that children's paths toward adaptation and psychopathology are regulated primarily by internal biological mechanisms has led to a search for drug treatments for specific categories of pathology. It has also led, we will argue, to the erroneous view that psychosocial interventions for conditions with a predominantly biological etiology are not likely to work.

Drug Treatment: Parents as Administrators of Treatment Regimens for the Child

Theoretical and Empirical Rationale. ADHD occurs in about 5% of the school-age population (Pelham & Hinshaw, 1992). Children with this diagnosis are described as showing developmentally inappropriate levels of inattention, impulsivity, and motoric activity for at least six months. It has long been supposed that biological risk mechanisms of genetic inheritance and neurotransmitter deficits play a central role in the etiology or cause of the disorder (see Barkley, 1990; Whalen, 1989).

Intervention. More than 90% of the children diagnosed with ADHD have been treated with psychostimulant medication, primarily Ritalin and Dexedrine (Safer & Krager, 1988). A review of studies by Hinshaw and McHale (1991) indicates that the administration of stimulant medication increases the child's focus of attention and reduces (a) stealing and property destruction during laboratory tasks, (b) noncompliance and social disruption in the classroom, (c) noncompliance in structured but not free-play interactions with mothers, and (d) negative aggressive behavior with peers.[5] Despite these encouraging results, other convincing findings suggest that psychostimulant medication for children with ADHD is far from a panacea (Hinshaw, 1994). Between one-fifth and one-third of the diagnosed children show either no effects or negative side effects (sleepiness, sadness, agitation). Most important, the benefits of the medication last only a few hours and seem to have no cumulative effects in the absence of psychosocial interventions.

Although psychostimulant drugs are sometimes administered by school personnel with parents' permission, parents are usually in charge of the child's medication regimen. That is, although the focus of change is on the child, intervention with parents is usually a central part of the process. And yet, this part of the treatment has received relatively little systematic attention. It would be important to know what parents are taught about ADHD, about the medication, and about issues of eliciting treatment compliance in taking the medication, but very little has been written about the parenting aspects of what is essentially a

[5] Despite these positive effects, it is also associated with an *increase* in covert deviations such as cheating.

child-focused psychopharmacological intervention. As far as we know, there are no studies that evaluate whether training parents of children with ADHD, specifically around their role as medication monitors, has any effect on either the short-term or long-term effectiveness of psychostimulant drugs.

Do Child-Focused Genetic and Maturational Theories Imply That Parenting Interventions Will Be Ineffective?

Biological theories of mental retardation, schizophrenia, depression, anxiety, antisocial personality, and ADHD implicate genetic transmission (e.g., Plomin, 1994; Rowe, 1986), biochemical imbalances (Davis, Kahn, Ko, & Davidson, 1991), and neurological malfunctions (Andreasen, Swayze, & Flaum, 1990) as major risk factors in delayed development and psychopathology. Genetic theories have also been applied to explanations of less serious behavior problems and personality styles (Plomin, 1994). The "boxed set" assumption in the parenting effects checklist implies that if genetic mechanisms play a primary role in the etiology of the disorder, genetic interventions ought to be featured in treatment. Acceptance of this assumption implies that until we develop interventions that will alter the transmission and functioning of genetic mechanisms that regulate the child's development, the primary goal of interventions for parents of children with genetically transmitted disorders can be palliative only—to help families accept and deal with the child's mental or emotional disorder. From this point of view, prospects for parenting interventions appear to be dim.

This chapter is being written in a period of heated debate over Herrnstein and Murray's *The Bell Curve* (1994), a book that attempts to justify limited government intervention in Head Start and other programs for the economically disadvantaged on the grounds that intelligence is largely an inherited characteristic. There have been many rejoinders to Herrnstein and Murray, most focusing on attempts to refute their conclusion that a substantial amount of the variation in intelligence is inherited (e.g., Sternberg, 1995). We will not debate some of the important issues raised by *The Bell Curve:* the nature of intelligence, how it is measured, or whether current IQ tests are selectively biased against ethnic minority or socioeconomic status groups. Our view is that *regardless* of the merits of the argument about the heritability of intelligence or any other human characteristic, the inference that psychosocial interventions for parents to increase their children's cognitive competence will be futile, is based on two serious flaws in reasoning about biological influences on development.

The first and most obvious reason to consider the utility of parenting interventions for children with low tested IQ is that, *at most,* genetic factors account for half the variation in intelligence.[6] Clearly, then, genetic theories of intelligence do not rule out the possibility that environmental interventions have the potential to affect aspects of intelligence influenced by environmental factors. The same argument can be applied to genetic explanations of schizophrenia and other psychiatric disorders. Evidence from twin studies showing that there is a significant genetic component in the etiology of schizophrenia reveals that about half the genetically identical twin siblings of individuals diagnosed as schizophrenic do *not* receive the same diagnosis. That is, while twin data can be used to provide evidence for genetic theories of schizophrenia and other outcomes, the same data support the hypothesis that family environments make a substantial contribution to the child's development and level of adaptation (Plomin, 1994; Reiss, 1995).

A second flaw in reasoning about genetic influences is centered on one of the basic assumptions in the boxed-set approach: that theories of causality and theories of intervention are inextricably intertwined. Is it *necessarily* the case that biological treatments are optimal for biologically caused disorders? Certainly not. Even if biological factors can be identified as primary causes of a child's troubled behavior, psychosocial factors almost certainly operate to maintain it. Parents who transmit a genetic vulnerability for a specific disorder to their child may react to the child's behavior in ways that maintain or exacerbate the problem. Furthermore, even if we could establish that biological factors are implicated in a given behavior or disorder, we cannot guarantee that biological interventions are fully effective change agents, as we noted in studies of drug treatment of ADHD.

A third challenge to the automatic linking of biological cause and biological intervention is the fact that psychosocial treatments are often highly effective even when biological causes have been suspected or established. Studies by Ramey and his colleagues (Campbell & Ramey, 1994; Ramey & Ramey, 1992) reveal significant gains—from 8 to 20 IQ points—following early home and preschool interventions with children from very poor families. Curiously, Herrnstein and Murray (1994) acknowledge that intellectual performance can be influenced by environmental intervention. They report, for example, that the strongest influence on IQ is adoption of a child by parents with high IQs. Presumably, this effect follows from what

---

[6] Hernstein and Murray (1994) claim that the estimate of heritability should be 60% or higher, but others strongly disagree (e.g., Sternberg, 1995). Our analysis applies even if heritability is 100%.

these parents *do,* but none of their extensive discussions of social policy mention the possibility of home-based interventions for parents.

No one would argue that because height is highly heritable we should forgo nutrition programs to increase children's stature. And yet, this is the kind of argument that Herrnstein and Murray and other biologically oriented theorists are making to minimize the potential utility of psychosocial interventions in children's development. We are not claiming that biological theories of causality and intervention are *unrelated* but that regardless of the assumed causes or risk factors associated with a problematic outcome, a variety of parenting intervention strategies may be effective in addressing the problem. We focus attention here on *The Bell Curve* because of the potentially profound influence of this line of argument on social policy and the provision of intervention programs for parents. We fear that this reasoning could cause unwarranted rejection of interventions proven to be helpful for parents and their children.

Although we argue for separating theories of cause and outcome, we do not discount the importance of biological theories about risks or causal influences on development. First, identifying causes or risk factors is important in determining how to target interventions for parents of children who are already having problems (Coie et al., 1993). Second, it is absolutely necessary to identify primary causes to plan *preventive* interventions. Interventions for parents of drug-exposed babies may be helpful in reducing the child's acting-out behavior, but only the full-scale elimination of drug taking by pregnant women will prevent the occurrence of the disorder (see parent-focused interventions, below).

Child-Focused Parenting Interventions That Emphasize Psychological Mechanisms

Child-focused interventions that emphasize *psychological* sources of stability and change are designed to inform parents about children's development and to help parents understand their children's psychological needs in order to communicate with them in more growth-facilitating ways.

Parenting Groups and Classes

Theoretical Rationale. The child-focused psychological box of the parenting effects checklist is based on the assumption that the development of the child unfolds from within, and that it is the parents' task to provide an environment that is supportive enough to encourage this unfolding. Given the widespread acceptance of programs based on theories in this box, it is not surprising to find that most of the programs using this approach are addressed to "average" parents who seek information about child development, reassurance about their parenting competence, and, possibly, increased social contact with other parents. They may also be experiencing concern about a child who presents problems but has not been identified as in need of mental health services. The use of parenting groups has a rich past (Auerbach, 1968; Brim, 1959) that was bolstered by Kurt Lewin's theoretical and empirical work on individual change through peer group interaction in the 1940s and 1950s (e.g., Lewin, 1947), by the self-help group movement in the 1960s and 1970s (Jacobs & Goodman, 1989), and by the parenting social support literature in the 1980s and 1990s (Gottlieb, 1988).

Curriculum. Child-focused programs certainly have specific ideas that they want to convey to parents, but consistent with their orientation to the child, the interventions are much less structured, didactic, and agenda-oriented than the parent-focused programs we describe below. One of the prototypes, still active today, is the parent study group, developed in Chicago in 1939 by Rudolf Dreikurs (Dreikurs & Stoltz, 1964), based on ideas derived from Alfred Adler (1927), an associate of Freud's in Vienna. The ultimate aim of the group is to help parents understand that children's "misbehavior" results from four reasonable and quite understandable goals: gaining attention, seeking revenge, displaying inadequacy, and, especially, obtaining power. A currently popular program with a similar theoretical foundation, Systematic Training for Effective Parenting (S.T.E.P.), was created by Dinkmeyer and McKay (1976), who were students of Dreikurs.

Adlerian parent study groups typically consist of 8 to 12 members, preferably couples, and meet for approximately two hours weekly for 8 to 12 weeks. The task of the parent is to discover and provide natural and logical consequences for children's behavior, not to learn how to establish reward and punishment discipline techniques. The basic idea is that encouragement of positive behavior in the child will increase his or her motivation to develop self-control and self-sufficiency. The S.T.E.P. program, not wedded to Adlerian parent group formats but exploring similar ideas, focuses primarily on parents' communication strategies, including reflective listening, problem-solving, and "I" messages. This style of communication informs children how parents feel as a result of the children's behavior. The assumption is that if children are not castigated, blamed, and punished, but rather informed about the negative impact of their behavior on their parents, they will be motivated to change what they do.

Another popular version of interventions that focus on the child are Parent Effectiveness Training (P.E.T.) groups developed by Thomas Gordon (1980). His approach, derived from Rogers's (1961) theory and practice of client-centered therapy, is based on a humanistic model of development in which internal forces unfold in the direction of positive growth unless parents interfere with the process. In P.E.T. groups, parents are encouraged to take roles similar to nondirective client-centered therapists (e.g., Axline, 1964), by being genuine, present, and unconditionally accepting. As in the Adlerian and S.T.E.P. groups, the focus is on teaching parents communication skills that include open, honest expression of feelings and resolution of conflicts. The assumption is that this stance on the part of parents will result in an environment that fosters their children's self-esteem in particular and their overall development in general.

A third type of program, MELD (Minnesota Early Learning Design), developed originally for first-time parents, attempts to blend or "meld" social support and information about child and parent development. There is a curriculum guide from which parents select topics as a springboard for discussions; topics range from infant behavior to managing relations with in-laws (Ellwood, 1988).

Intervention Techniques. The leaders of parenting groups within this tradition are generally parents who receive short-term training and ongoing consultation on group facilitation. The MELD program uses a modified self-help group facilitated by volunteer parents whose children are slightly older than those of the participants ("near peers") (Ellwood, 1988). Generally, the leaders are not "experts" who function as problem solvers, but as facilitators of group process. In some programs, such as the Adlerian groups, the leader offers a brief presentation, followed by open discussion and presentation of group exercises that include breaking the larger group into subgroups or dyads and role-playing or discussing common parent-child issues. The most valuable learning is expected to come not so much from information imparted by the group leader as from the active involvement of the parents in the group. In the Adlerian program, for instance, the style of the parent groups is to be a model for family communication and problem solving (Gamson, Hornstein, & Borden, 1989), and the training of leaders is often identical to the format of the parent groups.

Program Effectiveness. Parent groups with a child-focus appeared to enjoy a high level of popularity through the 1970s, and numerous studies of their effectiveness have been conducted. In a study of a peer discussion group involving low-income African American mothers, Slaughter (1983) found positive effects on mothers' attitudes and teaching styles and on children's verbal skill. One observational study of 101 two-hour meetings of long-term discussion groups comprised of low-income and working-class mothers found that discussion of parent and child topics decreased, whereas group attention to contextual factors such as income, family relationships, neighborhood resources, and personal development increased over a 12-month period (Powell & Eisenstadt, 1988).

Unfortunately, the research designs of studies of child-focused parenting groups are the least adequate of any of the types of interventions we describe here. Critical reviews of evaluations of Adlerian study groups and other popular parenting programs such as P.E.T. point to serious methodological weaknesses in a large number of investigations and to mixed results across studies regarding changes in parents' and children's behaviors and attitudes (Todres & Bunston, 1993). It is clear that these programs attract participants and meet many of the parents' needs, but it is not clear whether they provide demonstrable benefits for the participants' children.

Parenting Aspects of Intrapsychically Oriented Child Therapy

Rationale and Curriculum. In humanistically oriented child-centered nondirective therapy (Axline, 1964) and in psychoanalytic therapy for children (Fonagy & Moran, 1990), the therapist attempts to create the "good-enough" environment that the parents have been unable to provide. The medium of exchange between child and therapist is largely the process of symbolic play. In an attempt to repair the damage caused by earlier trauma or ongoing deprivation, the therapist provides a warm and safe "container" or "holding environment" (Masterson, 1992) in which the child's feelings are gently reflected and fears and self-doubts are carefully explored. Eventually, the safety and psychological holding allow the child's defenses to relax and normal developmental coping processes to take over.

Parents are included as collateral to the main therapy, with the explicit goal of allaying their anxieties so that they will be able to provide a more stable, secure environment for the child at home. In our reading of the literature on child therapy, we have been surprised by the fact that the enterprise is so child-focused that work with parents is given only passing reference and not described in detail. We imagine that the messages conveyed to parents, consistent with the orientation of the child therapy, are similar to those we described for the Adlerian and S.T.E.P. interventions for nonclinical families. In contrast with the idea of teaching parents to use specific behavior management skills, it is assumed that parents who feel less anxious and are able to show warmth, encouragement, and understanding will be better able to react intuitively in ways that facilitate their children's development (Elkind, 1994). The assumption of this approach is that the child's disturbing behavior will no longer be necessary if the emotional atmosphere of the family does not inhibit growth.

Program Effectiveness. It is clear from meta-analyses of a large number of child therapy studies that the average child receiving therapy of any kind is better off than about 75% of children with problems who receive no treatment (Weisz, Donenberg, Han, & Weiss, 1995). We are handicapped on two counts in assessing the impact of the parent intervention component in child-focused therapies. First, despite the view held by child clinicians that psychodynamic therapies are effective, only about 1% of all systematic studies of therapy evaluate interventions using this child-focused approach, compared with 72% of the child therapy studies of parent-focused behavioral or cognitive-behavioral therapy (Weisz et al., 1995). The sparse evidence from studies that compare behavioral and psychodynamic treatment of children diagnosed with either internalizing or externalizing disorders suggests that the behavioral approaches are more effective than the psychodynamic, but given the imbalance in systematic research on the two approaches, it is possible that this conclusion is premature. A second obstacle to assessing the impact of work with parents whose children are in therapy is that we are not aware of a single study in this tradition that examines the parenting part of the intervention. That is, neither the relative benefits to the child from the parent's intervention nor the potential benefits to the parents have been systematically assessed (cf., Weisz et al., 1995).

In sum, there are few well-designed studies of child-focused psychologically oriented parenting interventions for relatively well-functioning families, or of humanistic and psychodynamically oriented therapies for children in distress. In most cases, research has not shown that the programs are *in*effective, but inadequate designs prevent true tests of the programs' impact.

PARENT-FOCUSED INTERVENTIONS: BIOLOGICAL AND PSYCHOLOGICAL APPROACHES

In contrast with child-focused interventions, which assume that the locus of developmental influence is in the child, parent-focused interventions are guided by theoretical models of parenting that give weight to external influences on children's development. We begin with programs that emphasize the biological and psychological aspects of parents' influence on their children's development.

Parent-Focused Biological Interventions

Parents cannot change their own or their child's genetic makeup, but they can consider their own genetic history in making decisions about whether to conceive or terminate a pregnancy, and they can take actions to influence the environmental factors that affect the child's physical/biological development.

Genetic Counseling

Theoretical Rationale. Over the past four decades, information about the genetic factors involved in specific conditions has increased, and a technology for prebirth genetic assessment of a fetus has emerged. The relatively new field of genetic counseling helps parents trace their medical histories and genetic status to help them make decisions before attempting to become pregnant or after receiving the results of amniocentesis on a developing fetus (Harper, 1993).

Curriculum. No single theoretical approach dominates genetic counseling programs or defines the process by which genetic counselors talk with men and women who are considering whether to conceive a baby or terminate a pregnancy. Although there are several medical conditions that genetic counselors typically address (sickle cell anemia, Tay-Sachs disease, some forms of retardation), there are relatively few outcomes for which family histories or current genetic status provide highly accurate outcome information. For example, despite substantial evidence that alcoholism and antisocial personality disorders "run in families," not enough is known to offer definitive guidance to men and women who have family members diagnosed with alcohol dependence or antisocial personality disorder and are considering parenthood (Harper, 1993).

Pre-conception genetic counseling and amniocentesis diagnoses represent qualitatively different decision-making situations. Genetic diagnosis through amniocentesis often gives more precise information about probable developmental outcomes for the child than pre-conception assessments of family histories do, but even here the information is based on probabilities, with no way of predicting whether the child will function at the upper or lower end of the intellectual range. The issues parents must face are often moral, ethical, and psychological (Parker & Gettig, 1995). Given a high probability of a child with severe physical or intellectual problems, what are expectant parents to do? Some choose to carry the fetus to term regardless of the circumstances, based on religious convictions, psychological factors ("I can cope"), or the state of their relationship ("We can weather this together"). Other parents choose to terminate the pregnancy, some in spite of religious beliefs, based on their judgment about the quality of life for the child or of their resources to manage what could be a lifelong challenge for them and for their child.

The genetic counselor's role in this decision-making process is similar to that of other family counselors who have a psychoeducational emphasis. The single principle agreed upon in this field is that the counselor's task is not to make recommendations, but to present as much factual information as possible to help parents arrive at the best possible decision for them in light of their beliefs, their resources, and the facts (Burke & Kolker, 1994). Training for genetic counselors is one of the unresolved issues in the field: whether it is appropriate for master's level professionals with specific training in counseling techniques to offer this counseling or whether it should be done by M.D.s or Ph.D.s (Pencarinha, Bell, Edwards, & Best, 1992).

Parents' Role in Regulating Environments That Affect Children's Biological Processes

Federal programs funded by the U.S. Department of Agriculture's Cooperative Extension Service, and state programs funded by agricultural extension programs associated with land-grant universities, offer parent education programs that focus on helping parents provide adequate and nutritious food for children. These programs, often stimulated by a commitment to preventive intervention, include (a) direct services for mothers, with some that include written material, recipes, and videotapes on how to prepare nutritious meals and snacks; and (b) material for pediatricians and health care providers to distribute to mothers. Given that infants in poor families are at risk for inadequate nutrition, and that poor nutrition has unfortunate intellectual, emotional, and social consequences (Lozoff, 1989; Sigman, 1995), programs showing how parents can provide low-cost, healthy nutrition for infants may have long-term positive effects. Unfortunately, systematic long-term evaluations of these programs do not appear to be available in the research literature.

Parent-Focused Psychological and Behavioral Interventions

The general intent of parent-focused psychological interventions is to strengthen parents' contributions to a child's adaptive functioning in cognitive, social, or emotional domains. Here we consider two types of parent-focused psychological interventions, one dealing with the enhancement of children's intellectual competence, another with the control of children's aggression.

Parent-Child Interventions with a Focus on Intellectual Competence

Theoretical and Empirical Rationale. The centrality of reading skills, language, and literacy to children's cognitive development and academic achievement during the early years of school makes it imperative that children enter kindergarten well equipped to learn to read. Correlational data from longitudinal risk studies indicate that children whose parents have read to them and talked more with them during the preschool years tend to have more advanced language skills in both the preschool years and adolescence (Fredman, 1990; Wells & Egan, 1988). These findings stimulated early preventive intervention efforts for low-income families focused on parents' contributions to their children's intellectual skills.

Curriculum. Parent-child language interactions, often around joint book-reading, are a common target of interventions aimed at increasing children's intellectual competence. For example, a "dialogic intervention" was developed as a prevention program by Whitehurst and colleagues (Arnold & Whitehurst, 1994; Whitehurst et al., 1988) at the State University of New York at Stony Brook for low-income African American, Hispanic American, and European American families. The program's attempt to encourage and enhance parents' reading to their children emphasizes (a) evocative techniques to encourage an active child role during reading; (b) parental feedback in the form of expansions, modeling, corrections, and praise; and (c) progressive raising of the adult's standards for the child's performance. The parents receive instruction at their children's preschools. In two assignments, three weeks apart, parents are taught to ask "what" questions, follow the child's answers with additional questions, repeat what the child says as a way of reinforcing correct responses through repetition, and offer praise and encouragement.

Some interventions have a broader focus than parent-child verbal exchanges. In the Mother-Child Home Program developed on Long Island, New York (Levenstein, 1977, 1988), commercially available toys and books are provided by the program to give focus to the verbal interaction curriculum. Home visitors use the materials to illustrate verbal interaction techniques, with illustrations becoming gradually more complex with each successive item. The Home Instruction Program for Preschool Youngsters (HIPPY), developed originally in Israel and now in use throughout the United States (Lombard, 1981), involves activity packets for parents to use with their preschool-age children. The activities focus on language development, sensory and perceptual discrimination, and problem-solving skills.

How Parents Are Taught. As in the Adlerian parent education programs, interveners' methods to teach parents tend to mirror the strategies they recommend to parents for teaching their children. Attention is given to both direct influences (e.g., typical daily parent-child interactions) and indirect influences of the parent on the child (e.g., selection of nursery school). The instructional technique of modeling is so central to the Mother-Child Home Program that home visitors are called "toy demonstrators" (Levenstein, 1977). In addition to modeling, the dialogic reading intervention uses direct instruction to describe techniques to the mother and direct feedback in a situation where the trainer pretends to be a child and the mother practices the technique (Arnold & Whitehurst, 1994). Paraprofessional home visitors in the HIPPY program use role playing exclusively as a strategy for teaching the activity lessons that parents are to use in turn with their child. In the role play, the parent is to take the part of the child and the home visitor is to be the parent; the expectation is that parents will come to better appreciate the child's perspective and experiences (Lombard, 1981).

Just as parents are taught how to reinforce their children's responses, most parent-focused intervention programs try to provide built-in reinforcers for parents. Teachers in the home-based Portage Project for young children prepare prescriptions for parent-child activities that break tasks into smaller, attainable goals as a way to provide parents with "rapid reinforcement since what is learned by the child is a direct result of parental teaching" (Shearer, 1987, p. 274). Making toys from common household items for use in the intervention has been viewed for years as a strategy for bolstering parents' self-esteem and sense of efficacy (Gordon, Guinagh, & Jester, 1977). This activity also provides a concrete way to introduce such concepts as visual and auditory stimulation and eye-hand coordination in an informal presentation while mothers prepare the toys (Walker, Rodriguez, Johnson, & Cortez, 1995).

Program Evaluation. In one evaluation of the Whitehurst, Arnold, Epstein, and Angell (1994) dialogic intervention, preschoolers whose parents read to them at home showed significantly higher posttest expressive vocabulary scores than children whose teachers read to them at school or than children with no additional reading stimulation. More generally, studies of parenting programs aimed at promoting the cognitive and linguistic development of young children in low-income families show mixed results. In studies of interventions established in the 1960s and 1970s, children's IQ increased in the short term but not in the long term (Lambie, Bond, & Weikart, 1974; Slaughter, 1983).

Recent investigations have considered a broader range of child and parent outcomes. Although the results across studies continue to be uneven, they are quite informative. In a review of 15 randomized trials of home visiting programs aimed at promoting the cognitive and linguistic development of young children in low-income families, Olds and Kitzman (1993) found that only six produced significant overall program benefits for children's intellectual functioning. An instructive observation was that five of the six successful programs employed professionals or highly trained staff: nurses, teachers, or psychology graduate students. In total, compared with randomized controls, 71% of the interventions that employed professionals but only 29% of the programs staffed by paraprofessionals produced significant positive outcomes for the children of participants. Olds and Kitzman were careful to point out that employing professional staff did not guarantee program success, nor were intervention failures attributable solely to the lack of professional training. Parenting programs staffed by paraprofessionals tend to have a narrow rather than broad focus, and narrowly focused programs are typically less successful in obtaining positive results.

Parent-Child Interventions with a Focus on Control of Aggression

Theoretical and Empirical Rationale. Here we describe early behavior management programs (Forehand & McMahon, 1981; G. Patterson, 1974; Wahler, 1980) designed to teach parents new techniques for altering their children's behavior. Our prime example comes from the work of G. Patterson (1974) the pioneer in this field, whose work with colleagues Forgatch, Reid, and Dishion at the Oregon Social Learning Center (OSLC) had a seminal influence on the creation of therapy programs for aggressive, antisocial boys and their parents. The Center's focus on children identified as high in aggression stems from a body of research indicating that early-onset aggression, studied primarily in boys, is a predictor of peer rejection and academic problems in elementary and junior high school, and of dropping out of school, delinquency, and conduct disorders in adolescence (Asher & Coie, 1990).

Curriculum. The parents (usually mothers) of aggressive boys are seen individually at the Center or at home and asked to identify specific child behaviors they wish to change. To establish a pretreatment baseline, they are taught to keep careful daily records of the undesirable behaviors. The intervention focuses on teaching parents how to avoid reinforcing negative behaviors by using distraction, ignoring the behavior, or, when it cannot be ignored (e.g., during hitting or tantrums), creating a "time out" for the child alone in his or her room (Patterson & Gullion, 1973). Even more important, parents are encouraged to shift their attention from reacting angrily to their child's antisocial behavior to encouraging and reinforcing prosocial behavior when it occurs. The Patterson program and all subsequent behavioral management programs attempt to provide parents with positive reinforcement techniques as alternatives to physical punishment. Six to ten sessions is the average length of treatment, with the specific length for each family based on their willingness to continue and on how quickly they achieve the agreed-upon goals.

The OSLC approach and other parent training programs use a variety of media, formats, and contexts to get their points across. Direct teaching by professionals is supplemented by audiotaped and videotaped instruction, written exercises, and between-session telephone consultations.

For school-age children (Patterson, Dishion, & Chamberlain, 1993), the focus of the intervention is more on helping parents to provide consistent discipline and to offer symbolic incentives, such as stars or points, which are turned in for privileges or money. Issues addressed in treating families with children in this age group include improving the child's compliant behavior at home, completing school assignments and other aspects of academic performance, and encouraging prosocial behavior with peers at school. With adolescents, a central aspect of the program is monitoring their behavior outside the family—especially with peers—based on the finding that adolescents whose parents fail to monitor their whereabouts tend to show higher levels of antisocial and delinquent behavior (Patterson, 1982). Partly because the problems of adolescents are part of longer-standing patterns, treatment for families with older children typically lasts longer than work with younger children's families (20 to 30 sessions). Children may or may not attend each session with parents. The focus is not so much on what happens in treatment sessions as on "homework" that translates parenting ideas into action. Systematic daily record keeping, home observations by staff, and telephone contacts with parents help both patient and therapist monitor the ongoing progress of treatment.

Outcome Evaluation. According to comparisons of participant families with randomly selected, nontreated controls, early versions of parent training for the treatment of children's aggression were effective (Patterson et al., 1993). One study that contrasted interventions with and without the parent training component (Bank, Marlowe, Reid, Patterson, & Weinrott, 1991) found that behavioral interventions with the child alone did not affect aggressive behavior, but the addition of parent training yielded significant positive effects. Furthermore, families with younger children showed stronger and more positive effects of treatment than families with older children, suggesting that parents' and children's behavior patterns in families of older aggressive children are more intractable, probably because the patterns tend to be longstanding.

The behavioral interventions we have described are directed toward families with children identified as at high risk for problems or already in distress. Virtually identical principles are advocated for families with children *not* identified as at risk or in distress—in books (Patterson & Forgatch, 1989) or in parenting classes offered in community colleges or other parent education centers (Dembo, Sweitzer, & Lauritzen, 1985). Careful recording of baseline frequencies of the specific behaviors to be changed, systematic and consistent reinforcement for prosocial behaviors, and withdrawal of reinforcement or time out for antisocial behaviors are all part of the behaviorist's "tool kit" for parents, regardless of the seriousness of the problem presented by the child.

In sum, evaluation studies of parent-focused interventions show that although programs with a biological emphasis lack systematic evaluation, interventions that help parents to stimulate their children's intellectual competence or to control aggression appear to be quite promising. A clear implication in the literature on parent-focused interventions is that similar principles are applicable for parents in quite different populations ranging in level of risk from low to high. This premise has not been examined systematically.

INTERVENTIONS WITH AN INTERACTIVE FOCUS ON BOTH PARENT AND CHILD

Intervention approaches based on theories that emphasize biological and psychological mechanisms of development attempt to improve the match between characteristics of the child and the environment. In addition to considering general principles of reinforcement or child development, this type of intervention matches the actions of the parent with the specific behaviors or attributes of the child. Theories that emphasize interactive social mechanisms of development have led to a number of unique parenting interventions designed to improve the quality of parent-child relationships.

Biological Interactive Approaches

Temperament and Goodness of Fit

Child-focused intervention programs and advice books often discuss children's temperament; right from birth, some babies are "easy" (calm, predictable, sleep on schedule), some are "difficult" (cry a lot, easily distracted, fearful), and some are "slow to warm up" (initially fearful, they approach if given time; Chess & Thomas, 1987). From the perspective of biological interactive theories, the issue is not the child's temperament per se but the "goodness of fit" between child and parent: how well the parents' personalities, temperaments, and expectations mesh with the child's (Chess & Thomas, 1986). It seems reasonable that a wiry, irritable infant may cause greater disruption for placid, "laid back" parents, and that more reactive parents may find it less stimulating and rewarding to relate to a placid, quiet baby.

The concept of goodness of fit is elusive and difficult to measure (Seifer, 1995). Given the implication from its basic definition that temperament is resistant to modification, what can a parenting intervention do to increase the match between parent and child? Advice to parents (Brazelton, 1969; Chess & Thomas, 1987) or to pediatricians to pass on to parents (Chess & Thomas, 1986) suggested that parents become aware not only of their infant's temperamental style, but also of their own temperament-related reactions. The hope is that when parents are aware of both parts of the equation, they will be able to avoid blaming the infant for the problem or blaming themselves for not responding effectively, and find it easier eventually to adjust their responses to meet the infant's needs.

Psychological Interactive Approaches

The psychological interactive parent-child interventions we consider in this section pay more attention to the specific match between parent and child: a metaphoric goodness of fit model that does not simply refer to biologically based temperament characteristics. We make a small departure from our practice of describing existing theoretically based intervention programs, because not all of the theories in this box of the checklist have led to programs that have been described in the literature. Instead, we include some ideas based on psychological interactive principles that have been or might be helpful to parents.

Piaget's Cognitive Developmental Theory

Writers in the Piagetian tradition have suggested how parenting interventions might operate (P. Cowan, 1978; Schmid-Kitsikis, 1973). The generic principle involves matching the intervention to the child's developmental level and paying attention to the child's tendency to emphasize assimilation or accommodation.

Developmental Level. Parenting interventions that emphasize parent-child communication often have a remarkably a-developmental framework, as if being direct, open, and honest means the same thing to a 2-year-old, a 12-year-old, and a 22-year-old. Piaget's (e.g., 1967) developmental stage theory shows that children move through a sequence of logic systems between birth and late adolescence, with each stage representing a Copernican revolution in terms of understanding the physical, social, and emotional world. To take just one example, we know that 2- to 4-year-olds in the preconceptual stage cannot fully separate their own perspective from that of another. They do not yet use a two-dimensional category system (round, red). Their concept of self or identity does not include the idea that the self endures over time. Sometimes a very angry child says "I hate you" to a parent. The parent may interpret this statement as if the child has a clear notion of "I," a clear conception of a separate other, and an image of an enduring (negative) relationship between the two. But the preconceptual child is probably using words like "hate" to convey the feeling "You're making me mad right now!" Because of the qualitative difference in these two meanings, children often recover their spirits quickly, whereas adults take much longer to get over the hurt. Five minutes after a tantrum, a 3-year-old may return to ask cheerfully, "What's for dinner?" while the still-upset parent is picking himself or herself up from the emotional floor (P. Cowan, 1978). Interventions that take a psychological interactive perspective on development can help parents to assess their children's level of understanding and match their behavior and interpretations more closely to that level.

Functional Style. We described Piaget's theory of normal development earlier, which involves a balance between interpreting the world according to one's present understanding (assimilation) and reorganizing one's present understanding in response to an external challenge (accommodation). Accounts of disturbed children (Schmid-Kitsikis, 1973) suggest that they may have an enduring imbalance between these two functions—in the direction of overassimilation (e.g., reliance on fantasy), overaccommodation (e.g., overreactiveness), or oscillation between the two. A child who is highly assimilative (lost in a fantasy world) may be more likely to engage in therapy with a play or fantasy orientation, but could also benefit from the gradual introduction of behavioral techniques such as limit setting or reinforcement to induce greater accommodation. Contingent reinforcement may help the parent regain some control over the behavior and in the process help the child adapt more effectively to the demands of the external world. By contrast, children who are highly accommodative and react excessively to stimulation might respond well to behavioral strategies at first, but they may also benefit from the gradual introduction of child-focused interventions that emphasize assimilative play and fantasy; here they can learn to impose order on the world rather than to simply react to events imposed on them.

Vygotsky's Scaffolding Construct

Another psychological interactive theory that might lead to promising interventions was created by the Russian psychologist Vygotsky (e.g., 1978). Among the differences between Piagetian and Vygotskian perspectives (Duncan, 1995), Vygotsky's work emphasizes parents' teaching activities rather than children's stage of development. Vygotsky believed that children's learning proceeds most effectively when teachers or parents present materials in the child's "zone of proximal development." This zone is defined in terms of tasks that are difficult for the child to perform independently but have components that can be accomplished with direct support and guidance. The Vygotskian concept of "scaffolding," introduced by Wood and Bruner (Wood, 1980; Wood, Bruner, & Ross, 1976), suggests that adults' teaching is most effective when they intervene at the appropriate level (in the zone of proximal development) *when the child is having difficulty* with a task. Although this point is consistent with Piaget's notions, Vygotsky adds the important idea that to promote a child's intellectual competence, adults must also step back once the child understands the problem and is able to manage the rest of the task successfully alone. This sophisticated second principle does not come naturally to most parents, nor is it usually conveyed in parenting interventions.

Sigel's Distancing Construct

Distancing, another interactive parental teaching strategy related to Piaget's and Vygotsky's theories but different in its particulars, was enunciated by Sigel (1987, 1992) and investigated in collaboration with McGillicuddy-De Lisi (1990). The distancing construct is based on the premise that adults can foster children's cognitive development by helping them get some distance from their immediate experience. For example, although play in itself is valuable for children, they receive added stimulation in a progressive developmental direction when they are encouraged to tell others *about* their play.

In a preschool-based intervention program based on this concept, teachers challenged children to think about problems in the past or future rather than the here and now ("What did you do before? What will you do next time?"); search for alternative actions when the first attempt does not succeed ("What else could you try?"); recognize that every object is made up of more than one property ("It's round *and* it's red"); and become aware of temporal and physical relations among objects, events, and people represented in various media or symbols ("What happened to make the boy in the picture jump into his father's arms?"). Preschool children whose parents were trained in distancing strategies showed higher levels of cognitive development in second grade compared with a no-intervention control group (Sigel, 1987).

Cognitive-Behavioral Treatments

The examples we have given of interactive theory-based interventions have emphasized cognitive development. Interventions based on cognitive-behavioral theories apply an interactive theoretical framework to problems in the emotional-social domain. Cognitive-behavioral theories are interactive in the sense that they conceptualize psychopathology as a product of reinforcement or punishment experiences *and the child's interpretive construction of these experiences.* For example, some children or adults who are prone to depression tend to focus on experiences in which they fail to obtain reinforcement (good grades or approval) and ignore many counterexamples in which they are successful. Children become depressed when they conclude that it is useless to take action on their own behalf, a stance that reinforces feelings of sadness and hopelessness (Seligman, 1991).

Cognitive-behavioral interventions attempt to help children modify their interpretations of their experience (change their internal view) and take action to obtain reinforcement (change their behavior). Increasingly, therapists who work with aggressive, impulsive children, or the parents of these children, train the child in self-monitoring and self-control; the child is taught to talk aloud while performing tasks to analyze the problem, delay impulsive responding, and formulate a plan for a solution. Therapy for depressed children encourages them to question their negative self-descriptions and to take action on their own behalf; here again, parents can help in encouraging an active rather than passive and helpless approach to the world. As depressed children interpret the world differently, they are more likely to take some action; as they act, they are more likely to get results that disconfirm their negative beliefs (Meichenbaum, 1995).

Cognitive-behavioral treatments alleviate both externalizing and internalizing problems in comparison with a randomly assigned no-treatment control condition (Weisz et al., 1995).[7] We know very little about the parent intervention aspects of the treatment. As in our accounts of child-focused psychodynamic therapies, parents usually participate when children are enrolled in cognitive-behavioral therapies, but the role of the parent is neither well described nor systematically evaluated in the literature.

Social Relationship Interventions: Strengthening the Parent-Child Relationship System

The application of social relationship theories to parenting interventions was influenced in part by the work of Sameroff and Chandler (1975), who proposed a *transactional* view of familial risk. The "continuum of caretaking casualty" defines risk factors for children, not in terms of parent or child alone, but in terms of their dynamic interaction. For some vulnerable children, exceptionally skilled and responsive parents can provide buffers that prevent the appearance of problems or reduce the severity of distress or disorder. The transactions between parent and child are also implicated when children we would expect to do well wind up in difficulty as a consequence of maladaptive patterns of caretaking. Theories that emphasize social relationship mechanisms in accounting for developmental change, and the interventions based on them, assume that interaction patterns are bidirectional, created jointly and fairly equally by parent and child. The goal of parenting interventions is to alter the quality of the parent-child relationship, which affects the child's adaptation, which, in circular fashion, affects the quality of the parent-child relationship.

The quality of parent-child relationships can be assessed from an insider view (the perceptions, beliefs, expectations, and feelings of each of the participants) and an outsider view (observations of the behavioral interaction patterns). The difference in perspectives, even though both focus on relationships, leads to different parenting intervention models. First, there are child-focused social relationship interventions based on psychodynamic object relations and attachment theories (insider views). Several programs, described collectively as infant mental health interventions (Zeanah, 1993), were influenced significantly by the early work of Selma Fraiberg (1980) with parents of blind children. While the central ideas about attachment that underlie these interventions emphasize the role of the child's internal working models of parent-child relationships, in practice, these interventions attempt to rework current interaction patterns between parent and child. Second, there are parent-focused social relationship interventions within the behavioral tradition that have moved from a primary emphasis on changing the child to attempts to modify the pattern of transactions between parent and child (e.g., G. Patterson, 1982).

Parent-Child Relationship Programs Focused on Working Models of Attachment

Theoretical and Empirical Rationale. In the box describing child-focused social relationship theories of children's development, the assumption is that object relations schemas or working models formed in our early relationships with primary caregivers serve as filters that color our interpretations of current relationships, particularly when we are threatened by conflict, harm, or loss. Individuals who have internalized negative working models of parent-child relationships or insecure states of mind with reference to attachment with their parents are more likely to have diagnosable disorders themselves (Kohut & Wolf, 1978),[8] and repeat negative relationships from their families of origin in the families they create in adulthood (Main & Goldwyn, 1984). Three relatively new, sophisticated infant mental health parenting interventions attempt to provide ongoing positive relationships with an intervener. It is expected that these caring relationships will help to improve mothers' adjustment, alter their negative working models of early intimate relationships, and ultimately result in more nurturant mother-child relationships.

Curriculum and Intervention Techniques. The programs we describe briefly are Project STEEP (Steps Toward Effective Enjoyable Parenting) at the University of Minnesota (Egeland & Erickson, 1993); the Family Development Service Program at the University of California at Los

---

[7] This optimistic generalization may not apply to children diagnosed with ADHD (Hinshaw & Erhardt, 1991).

[8] This a theoretical assertion and not an empirical finding.

Angeles (Heinicke, 1991); and the Infant-Parent Psychotherapy Program developed by Lieberman and Pawl (1993) at San Francisco General Hospital. These programs are for mothers who are at risk by virtue of low income, of having grown up in a troubled family, or of having an already troubled relationship with a young child. Each program focuses on the relationships among the mothers and their mothers, their children, and the interveners. Staff in the three programs range from paraprofessionals given extensive on-the-job training to mental health professionals with advanced degrees. All programs view the relationship of mother and intervener as a key mechanism in modifying the mothers' expectations and models of attachment relationships.

Steps taken to establish a supportive and empathic relationship with the parent begin with the first contact with the parent. In Project STEEP in Minnesota, for example, the initial contact with a prospective participant is made during pregnancy, before the mother can be judged in any way to be a failure as a parent. If there are missed appointments, the program worker continues to show up for as many visits as have been promised, to demonstrate that the worker will not reject or abandon the mother. Continuity of program staff is a central goal; the person who recruits the mother is the one who works with her throughout the program in both home visit and group sessions, and the van driver assists during the group session (Egeland & Erickson, 1993). Project STEEP uses videotapes of mother and infant in a variety of naturalistic interactions at home (feeding, bathing, during play) to help the mother recognize the role of reciprocity and mutual influence in her relationship with her baby. Mother and intervener watch the tapes together, with the latter using a nonjudgmental approach to enhance the mother's understanding of the baby and her relationship with the baby, to promote perspective taking, and to increase her sensitivity to cues ("What do you think your baby was feeling then?" or "What is your baby telling you here?"). This is intended to help the mother recognize and affirm her knowledge of her particular baby rather than teach her what a typical 3-month-old does (Egeland & Erickson, 1993).

In the Family Development Service Program in Los Angeles, using cognitive-behavioral intervention principles, the intervener attempts to establish with each mother a supportive context for the relationship, and to help her focus her concerns and perceive them in new ways. The intervener and parent jointly observe the child, followed by discussion, provision of information, or modeling of alternative solutions. Three additional aspects of the Family Development Service Program serve to differentiate it from the other infant mental health programs discussed in this section. First, the intervener places a great deal of emphasis on helping mothers work with the child's father (approximately half of them are living with the father, and the other half are in varying degrees of contact). Second, the intervener attempts to reinforce and support mothers for becoming advocates for themselves and their families with people and institutions outside the nuclear family. Third, the intervention provides weekly group meetings for mothers as a way of enhancing their social support (Heinicke, Fineman, Ruth, Recchia, & Guthrie, 1996; Heinicke, Goorsky, et al., 1996). That is, although the contact is with mother and child, the focus of the intervention covers a number of domains of family life.

In the Infant-Parent Psychotherapy Program in San Francisco, the initial session is viewed as a key time to address sensitively a mother's negative expectations about the therapist and/or the program by (a) showing consistent respect for her reluctance to accept an offer of treatment, (b) legitimizing the appropriateness of her emotional responses, and (c) dealing directly with her worries about the therapist. The therapist also directs her attention to coping with life issues in the world outside the family. For some mothers, the provision of concrete instrumental support, such as driving her to an appointment or helping her fill out a form, is a trust-building experience because it demonstrates that the therapist can see things from the parent's point of view. For many parents, this represents "a first encounter with the notion that relationships can be rewarding and helpful rather than burdensome, disappointing, or abusive" (Lieberman & Pawl, 1993, p. 433).

Program Effectiveness. The evaluations of Project STEEP are in their preliminary phase (Quint & Egeland, 1995). In the months after the intervention, mothers had lower depression and anxiety scores, were more competent in managing their daily lives, and showed a greater ability to provide a stimulating and organized home environment for their babies than mothers who did not take part in the intervention. Despite these shifts in mothers' behaviors, there were no intervention effects on mothers' models of adult attachment or on the babies' security of attachment. It may be that this kind of change is not likely to be produced by the paraprofessional interveners in this study, even though they were well trained and supervised. It is also possible that later follow-ups will find shifts in parents' and/or children's security of attachment status.

Preliminary results evaluating the Family Development Service Program in Los Angeles are very encouraging (Heinicke, Fineman, et al., 1996; Heinicke, Goorsky, et al., 1996). Although there were few differences between randomly assigned intervention and control mothers at six months postpartum, there were clear differences after one year of weekly intervention. Mothers working with home visitors perceived more support from their partners and other family members, and were observed to have more positive and responsive relationships with their infants. The infants were more involved in tasks during home observation[9] and more often classified as securely attached at 1 year of age than the infants of mothers in the control group. Furthermore, mothers who participated more consistently in the intervention and were rated as having a more positive working relationship with the intervener, showed more positive outcomes for them and for their children.

Lieberman, Weston, and Pawl's program (1991), like the Los Angeles program, used clinically trained professionals and also found positive effects on the parents, the children, and the quality of their interactions. The intervention mothers had higher scores than controls on empathy and interactiveness with their children, and their toddlers had higher scores than controls on quality of partnership with their mothers. At 24 months of age, toddlers who had earlier shown avoidance, resistance, and anger when their mothers returned after a short absence now showed increased signs of secure attachment after their mothers received one year of intervention. The control toddlers who entered the study with anxious attachments but whose mothers had no intervention showed no improvement over the same period.

In the San Francisco Infant-Parent Program, improvement was most marked when the mother used the sessions with the therapist to work through negative feelings toward important people in her life, especially her parents. The findings from these last two programs lend support to the theoretical assumptions on which these intervention programs are based: mothers who came to view their negative models of attachment relationships in a more understanding light became more interactive and empathic with their toddlers, and, in turn, their children became less angry, avoidant, and resistant toward them after the therapy. These are the kinds of intervention results that provide validation for the theoretical links—and the mechanisms underlying the links—between parents' experience of their own early relationships and their current relationships with their children. In a review of 12 earlier intervention studies, van IJzendoorn, Juffer, and Duyvesteyn (1995) found effects on mothers' behavior but not on their models of attachment. What is especially impressive about both the Family Development Service and Infant-Parent Psychotherapy programs is that the interventions with mothers are having measurable impact on the quality of attachment between them and their young children. Both of these programs used staff who were clinically trained to deal with parent-child issues and to focus on relationships between the mothers and other significant figures in their lives. This intensive graduate-level training may help account for the difference in results between these two programs and Project STEEP.

[9] Some of these ratings were based on those used in the STEEP project.

Parent-Child Relationship Programs Focused on Behavior Management

Despite the proven success of the early parent-focused behavior management programs based on psychological theories that focus on parents as sources of change, researchers became concerned by the fact that the initially positive treatment effects quickly disappeared and a substantial proportion of families failed to improve at all (Miller & Prinz, 1990). Miller and Prinz describe a progression from a "first-generation" intervention approach that emphasized parents' behaviors as reinforcers or punishers of children's undesirable behavior, to a "second-generation" set of interventions that focus on parent-child relationship quality.

Curriculum and Intervention Techniques. Here we describe one example of a second-generation program designed to enhance parent-child relationships, conducted by Carolyn Webster-Stratton (1992) at the University of Washington in Seattle. The centerpiece of Webster-Stratton's intervention is a set of videotapes containing approximately 200 vignettes that show parents and children attempting to resolve family issues with effective or ineffective parenting strategies. Initially tested as a four-session package with parents of 3- to 8-year-old aggressive children (a nonclinical designation), a subsequent, more intensive program (9–10 sessions) was offered as therapy for young children diagnosed as "conduct-disordered."

In the Webster-Stratton approach, didactic presentations by the group leader or therapist are minimized, and open discussion of the videotaped vignettes and how they apply to each parent's relationship with the child are encouraged. Drawing ideas from the behavioral social learning tradition, especially the work of Forehand and King (1977) and Patterson and Forgatch (1989), Webster-Stratton's program sessions teach parents how to set limits, handle misbehavior, and play effectively with their children. We classify this intervention as parent-child relationship-focused because at least half of the intervention sessions are devoted to helping parents communicate with their children authoritatively, in a nurturant, warm, and playful manner, and to respond sensitively to their children's unique characteristics. Recent descriptions of the Oregon Social Learning Center parenting interventions by Patterson and his colleagues (1993) make it clear that they too now focus a great deal of their attention on the parent-child dyad in attempts to interrupt the coercive cycles that lead to escalating negative interactions between parents and children, and to teaching communication and mutual problem-solving strategies to improve the quality of the relationship.

Program Effectiveness. In an impressive set of evaluations, Webster-Stratton (1984) has shown that two-thirds of the aggressive and oppositional children whose parents participated in the group sessions showed greater reductions than controls in negative behavior at one-month and one-year follow-ups. A three-year follow-up compared (a) videotape plus therapist-led discussion groups with (b) individually self-administered videotape sessions and (c) discussion groups without videotape (Webster-Stratton, 1990). While all three treatment conditions led to significant improvement in the short run, only the families in the videotape plus therapist-led discussion group *maintained* their initial gains over a three-year period. The self-administered videotape program for parents resulted in less aggression in participants' children than in waiting list controls, but the impact of the videotape program was stronger when a therapist-consultant was made available to parents who viewed the videotapes by themselves (Webster-Stratton, 1990).

In sum, relationship-oriented parenting interventions derived both from child-focused attachment theories and parent-focused behavioral theories appear to be effective in helping parents cope with children who display severe emotional disturbance and high levels of aggression. It is too early to tell whether attachment and behavioral perspectives on relationships have specific advantages or drawbacks for treating different kinds of child and family problems. It is also too early to tell whether relationship-focused interventions are effective in nonclinical populations, or how their effects compare to child-focused and parent-focused approaches.

A CONTEXTUAL, SYSTEMIC PERSPECTIVE ON PARENTING

In earlier sections we described a sampling of parenting interventions—child-focused, parent-focused, and parent-child relationship-focused—based on different assumptions about the mechanisms by which parents influence their children's development. In this section, we move to what Bronfenbrenner (1974) has described as an "ecological" perspective on parent-child relationships and children's development. One of his central contributions was to stimulate developmental researchers to think about families from a systemic point of view by placing the study of families in the context of the wider society and culture. We begin by showing how the parent-child domain of the family contains a complex set of relationships between two or more parents and often more than one child. We then outline a six-domain model describing the connections among various aspects of family life, and cite studies that are consistent with an ecological view of the mutual influences among relationship domains inside and outside the nuclear family. The implications of this research for parenting intervention seem straightforward. Although it makes sense to offer direct help with parenting to mothers and fathers, interveners who keep the systemic view in mind can choose a number of strategic intervention points to foster positive outcomes in parent-child relationships.

The System inside the Parent-Child Domain

More Than One Parent

Researchers in the 1950s and 1960s focused most attention on the impact of father *absence* through military service, divorce, or death. We now have an accumulation of systematic data to show that fathers who are present, even infrequently, make unique contributions to their children's development (Parke, 1996; Parke & Buriel, Volume 3). Not only do fathers in two-parent families contribute centrally to their children's development, but also stepfathers, adoptive fathers, divorced fathers, single-parent custodial fathers, biological fathers who have never lived with the mothers of their children, and live-in or non-live-in partners of the children's mothers shape children's adaptation (Furstenberg & Harris, 1993).

In addition to the complexity of multiple parent-child relationships that follow divorce and remarriage, more than two parents are often in the picture for children reared by gay or lesbian parents. In gay male couples, one of the fathers is usually the biological parent, who, along with the child, has an ongoing relationship with the child's mother. Some lesbian couples incorporate the insemination donor as a part of the family (C. Patterson, 1995a, 1995b). Regardless of parents' marital status or sexual orientation, then, understanding the effects of parenting necessitates a consideration of *at least* two parent-child relationships (see Figure 1.2).

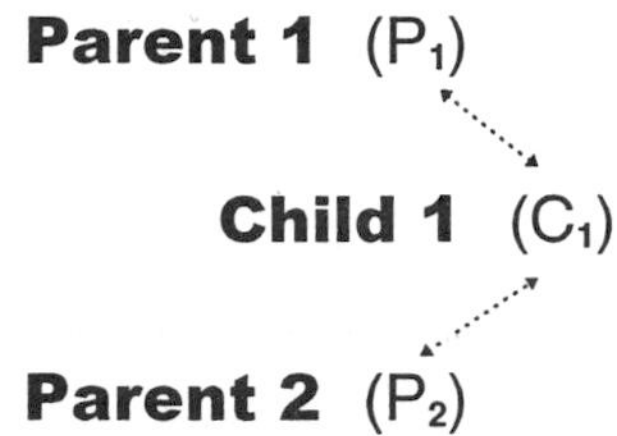

Figure 1.2 Each child has at least two parents.

More Than One Child

Most families have two or more children, so from a family systems framework, there are at least four distinct parent-child relationships to consider (see Figure 1.3). The number expands to six parent-child relationships with three children, eight with four children, and so on. Noting that the "same" parents are *not* the same for each of their children, Dunn (1995), Plomin (1994), and their colleagues (Hetherington, Reiss, & Plomin, 1994) have drawn attention to the importance of understanding the variation in parent-child relationship quality *within* families. Children in the same family may be treated differently because they differ in age, cognitive level, personality characteristics, sex, or personal experiences. We know that it is common for each sibling to believe that "Mom loves you more than me." Family life events, transitions, or traumas (e.g., parents' divorce) may be experienced differently by each child (Wallerstein & Kelly, 1980). Combined with variation in genetic makeup, within-family variation in parental treatment is a potent factor in accounting for why children in the same family are different from one another (Dunn & Plomin, 1990; Hetherington et al., 1994).

Moving beyond the Parent-Child Relationship: A Six-Domain Family Systems Model

In the 1980s, a number of research groups began to apply family systems models developed by family therapists to investigations of family formation and early child development. Each group used similar complex, multidomain schematic diagrams to summarize their theoretical approaches. Belsky's (1984) process model of parenting,

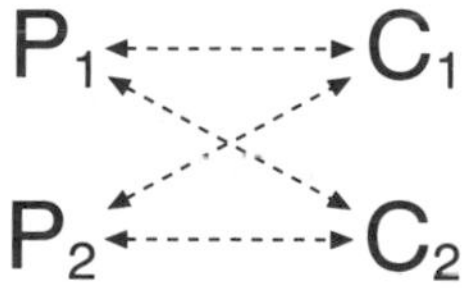

Figure 1.3 Most parents have more than one child.

Parke and Tinsley's (1982) model of the family environment of premature infants, and Cowan and Cowan's (Cowan et al., 1985) five-domain model of couple and family adaptation during the transition to parenthood all suggest that five central aspects of family life combine to shape the course of children's early development. Because these multidomain family models were based on studies of parents and a first child, they did not include information about the relationships between siblings. We propose that to understand variations in the quality of parent-child relationships and their effects on children's development throughout childhood and adolescence, we need information about *six* domains of family functioning:

1. The biological and psychological characteristics of each individual in the family.
2. The quality of relationships in parents' families of origin and in the current relationships among grandparents, parents, and grandchildren.
3. The quality of the relationship between the parents, with special emphasis on their division of roles, communication patterns, and roles as coparents to their children.
4. The quality of relationship between the siblings.
5. The relationships between nuclear family members and key individuals or institutions outside the family (friends, peers, work, child care, school, ethnic group, government) as sources of stress, support, models, values, and beliefs.

All five of these domains affect, and are affected by, the domain we are concentrating on in this chapter:

6. The quality of the relationship between each parent and child.

The six domains of family life form the elements of a structural model of family adaptation. Each domain describes a different level of the family system and its connection with other family domains. The model is presented schematically in Figure 1.4, with circles representing individual family members and arrows representing relationships between people or between domains. The family system lies inside the enclosure, but relates to other key people and institutions in the larger society.[10]

---

[10] To avoid clutter in the figure, we have ignored the fact that grandparents influence grandchildren directly and omitted the arrows.

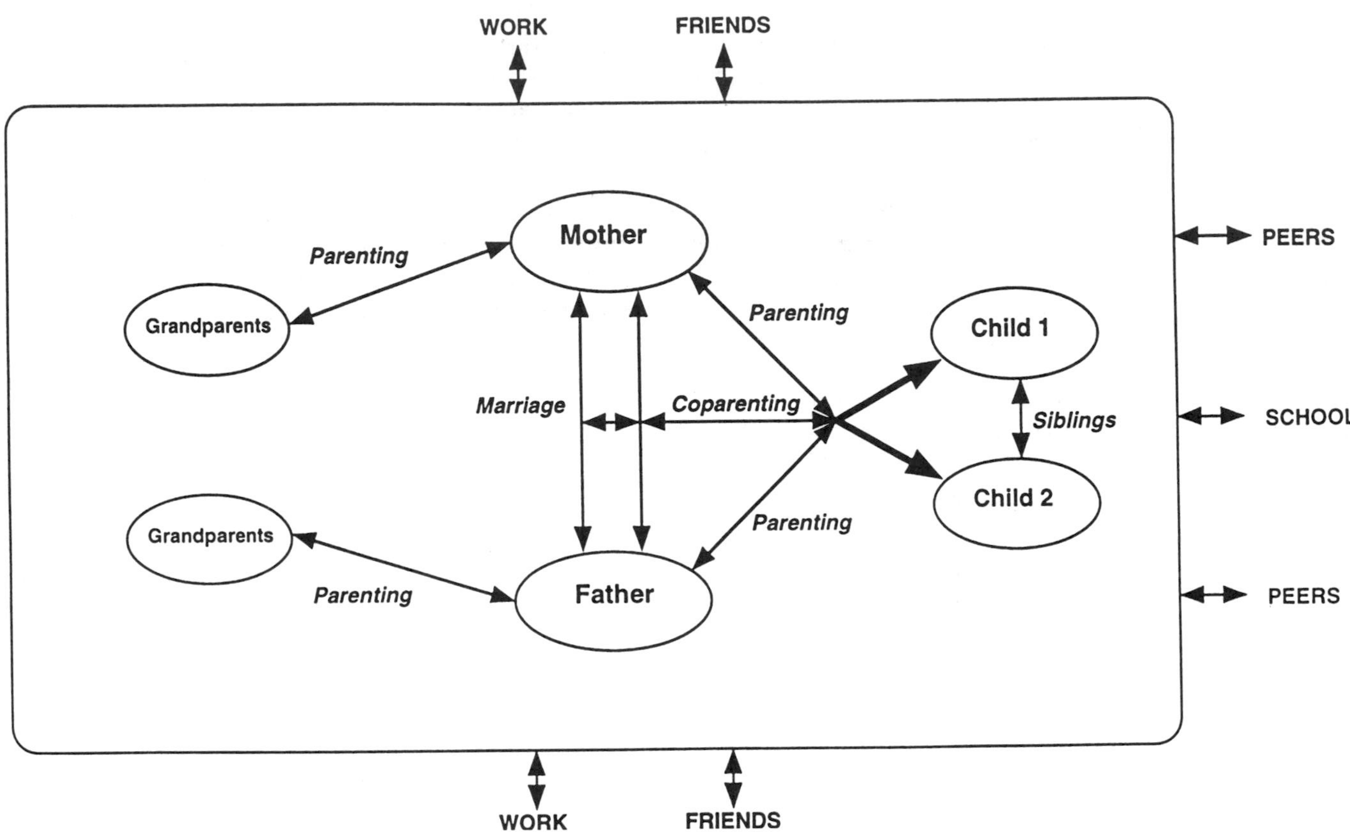

Figure 1.4 A family systems view of parenting.

How the Family System Works

The multidomain family model in Figure 1.4 is consistent with four central assumptions made by family systems theorists (e.g., Broderick, 1993; Steinglass, 1987; Wagner & Reiss, 1995). First, the whole is greater than the sum of its parts. In the present context, this means that the structure or organization of the relationships in the family affects the quality of the relationship between any two family members. For example, both parents' histories of relationships with their parents affect their ability to work together to parent their child. Second, interactions among family members are seen by observers and by family members themselves as patterned, with regularities that permit rules to be inferred ("We cannot express negative feelings in this family"). Third, like cybernetic systems, family systems are self-regulating. The domains of the family are dynamically interconnected in the sense that change in any one aspect of the system can lead to change in other aspects. A major life transition for one family member is likely to have ripple effects throughout the family. Finally, as we noted above, influences within the family system and between the family and social systems in the larger culture are circular rather than linear; it is difficult, if not impossible, to tell where the "first cause" of any behavior lies. This idea is represented by the two-headed arrows linking each domain. The implications of this systemic family view for intervention are quite broad: in thinking about preventing or treating psychological or behavioral difficulties in any member of the family, we might consider directing interventions at one or more of the many transactions within or between these family domains.

How do events and relationships in one domain influence the state of affairs in another? Luster and Okagaki (1993) describe five alternative direct and indirect pathways:

1. Difficulties in a number of domains have a simultaneous additive or cumulative impact (e.g., parents' characteristics, children's characteristics, and contextual factors combine to affect parenting behavior).
2. Negative events or feelings generated in one family domain overflow and contaminate relationships in another domain (e.g., marital conflict spills over into the parent-child relationship).
3. Events in one domain can prevent risks from leading to negative outcomes (e.g., a nurturant marriage can act as a buffer to negative experiences in one parent's family of origin, thus protecting the child from ineffective parenting).
4. Characteristics of the person at Time 1 influence life trajectories in a way that affects parent-child relationships at Time 2. (e.g., irritable, unstable adults may make life choices that affect family environments and parenting style at later points in time).
5. Contexts at Time 1 (e.g., low-income neighborhoods) may influence other life stressors at Time 2 (e.g., qualities of the school environment) that affect the child, and, in turn, affect the child's parents.

Readers following the arrows in Figure 1.4 can identify many other possible pathways in which family domains have cascading effects on each other and on children's development. All of these pathways are avenues by which programs can affect the quality of parent-child relationships. This is what we mean by the family system context of parenting interventions.

Evidence Supporting the Validity of the Six-Domain Model

Although studies designed with a contextual, systemic approach to parenting are relatively new, results reveal consistent links between parent-child relationship quality and the quality of life in other family domains. We will show that this pattern of findings provides important clues for new directions in (a) defining targets of parenting interventions and (b) identifying mechanisms of change that might be built into an intervention curriculum.

Parents' Individual Characteristics and Parenting Patterns

Parents' Stage of Life. Some literature for parents emphasizes the idea that children change over time and that effective parenting requires different strategies as children mature (e.g., Brazelton, 1992). What this literature tends to ignore is that parents are also in a process of development. Parent-infant relationships are complex not only because it is difficult to interpret the meaning of newborns' cries, but also because new mothers and fathers are struggling with the disequilibrating changes of the transition to parenthood (Belsky & Kelly, 1994; Cowan & Cowan, 1992). A child's normative, expectable transition to elementary school may be accompanied by a mother's choice to return to work (Moorehouse, 1993). Parent-adolescent relationships may be strained by the teenagers' struggles with issues of identity, autonomy, and sexuality, and also by their parents' struggles with their own midlife issues of identity and sexuality (Johnson & Irvin, 1983). *Family* development involves the simultaneous unfolding of parents' and children's developmental needs and trajectories (Elder, 1991). Parenting interventions based on this point of view could help parents anticipate the consequences of their own life transitions (job change, retirement, death of a parent) for their relationships with their children.

Parents' Symptoms and Psychopathology. Studies of families who have no diagnosed mental health problems find few systematic links between parents' personality characteristics or subclinical levels of psychiatric symptoms and their children's personality or adaptation (Clarke-Stewart, 1977). Reviewers of this research (e.g., Vondra & Belsky, 1993) suggest that links between parents' personality and child outcomes, if any, are indirect. For example, a study of farm families with adolescent children (Conger et al., 1992) found that mothers' and fathers' symptoms of depression had no direct association with aggressive behavior observed in their children. However, parents who endorsed a greater number of depressive symptoms were more likely to describe an unhappy and conflictful marriage. Parents who were more depressed *and* in discordant marriages were less effective in disciplining their adolescent boys and girls, who had lower scores on a variety of indices of adjustment.

In contrast with the results from nonclinical samples, studies that identify severe psychopathology in either parent (schizophrenia, depression, antisocial personality) show direct increased risks for cognitive, social, and emotional difficulties in the children (Goldstein, 1985; Sameroff et al., 1982). Nevertheless, these studies also indicate that the influence of parents' personality or pathology usually occurs through their impact on parenting behavior and the quality of the parent-child relationship (Zahn-Waxler, Iannotti, Cummings, & Denham, 1990). It is clear, then, that the impact of parents' difficulties in adaptation may be amplified when these difficulties spill over into the parent-child relationship or buffered when this spillover is reduced or eliminated. These findings help to justify *parenting* interventions in both clinical and nonclinical populations.

The Child's Contribution to the Equation. The finding that parenting styles or behaviors are correlated with children's development does not explain how that impact occurs. One possible linking mechanism can be found in biological characteristics of the child. For example, in an extensive review of the literature on the development of conduct disorder, Dodge (1996) cites evidence from a longitudinal study (Bates, Pettit, & Dodge, 1995) showing that infants' biological characteristics in infancy, such as hyperreactivity, attention problems, impulsivity, and difficult temperament, have a small but significant ability to predict externalizing problems 10 years later in seventh grade. However, the predictive power increases when the investigators add information about parenting quality; biological characteristics in the preschool period predict harsh parenting at age 4, which, in turn, accounts for variation in externalizing behavior in seventh grade. A similar pattern of results was reported by Boxer (1996), who found that parents' prebirth attitudes about parenting combined with their postbirth perceptions of their baby's temperament to predict marital quality, parenting style, and the children's externalizing and internalizing problems in kindergarten. In these ways, infants' characteristics contribute to their adjustment as children and to adaptation in a number of family relationships.

Another possible contribution of children to their own developmental progress is the way they construe the world and themselves. Dodge, Pettit, Bates, and Valente (1995) show that the child's social information processing style forms a link in the chain that connects parenting styles with children's behavioral outcomes. Measelle (1993) used an interview "conducted" by puppets (the Berkeley Puppet Interview; Ablow & Measelle, 1993) to assess preschoolers' views of their intellectual competence. Children who described themselves as "very smart" but in fact had low scores on a vocabulary measure—overestimators—were described by their teachers in kindergarten one year later as significantly less task-oriented, less self-regulated, and less academically competent than children who were accurate self-estimators or underestimators. Furthermore, in dyadic interactions in the laboratory, mothers of overestimators were significantly more disengaged (low in warmth and structure), and fathers of overestimators were significantly more permissive (high in warmth but low in structure) than parents of underestimators or children who evaluated themselves more realistically. The findings are consistent with the hypothesis that parenting may alter children's self-perceptions, and that self-perceptions may moderate the impact of parenting style on children's adaptation.

Three-Generational Transmission of Parenting Patterns

An intriguing new body of research on working models of intimate relationships has emerged in which adults are asked about their memories of early relationships with *their* parents using the Adult Attachment Interview (AAI; Main & Goldwyn, in press). Coders analyze both content and formal discourse of the interview to create categories that are thought to represent the quality of adults' working models of their early attachments. The AAI does not claim to provide an accurate assessment of those early primary relationships, but rather a view of the adult's current working models or schemas of their early family relationships. Studies show that parents who describe early relationships with parents dismissively or with low levels of coherence (insecure working models of attachment) are likely to have young children classified as insecurely attached on the basis of laboratory assessments (van IJzendoorn, 1992). Mothers with insecure working models tend to have less effective parenting strategies (van IJzendoorn, 1992), and their preschoolers are more likely to show symptoms of both internalizing and externalizing behavior problems (Crowell, O'Connor, Wollmers, Sprafkin, & Rao, 1991). *Fathers'* working models of early attachment, not examined until very recently, show very similar links with their parenting styles (Cohn, Cowan, Cowan, & Pearson, 1992; Fonagy, Steele, Moran, & Steele, 1993). These results demonstrate what appears to be cross-generational continuity of both adaptive and maladaptive relationships.

Negative intergenerational cycles can be interrupted if an adult with an insecure working model of early attachment chooses a partner with a secure working model. A study by Cohn et al. (1992) takes the pattern of *both* parents' attachment histories into account. When both parents were classified as having secure working models of attachment relationships, the quality of their parenting, observed in separate interactions with their child, was high in warmth and limit setting. When both parents were classified as having insecure working models, their individual parenting styles showed little warmth and limit setting. The unique finding of this study was that when women classified as insecure had spouses classified as secure, the women's parenting quality was as effective as that of mothers classified as securely attached. The quality of the marital interaction for these insecure-secure pairs was more positive and less negative than that of couples in which both husband and wife were classified as insecure (Cohn, Silver, Cowan, Cowan, & Pearson, 1992).[11] It seems that a nurturant marriage can buffer the negative impact of one partner's impoverished early experiences and provide a family environment conducive to effective parenting in the next generation.

This study illustrates our general thesis that a combination of data from multiple family domains (individual, marital, three-generational) does more to explain variations in the quality of parent-child relationships than data from one or two domains alone. It provides additional support for the idea that intergenerational interventions as described above may be effective in altering the climate of the family system.

The Central Role of Marital Quality in Family Adaptation

What we see as the noteworthy contribution of recent studies of parent-child relationships is compelling evidence that parents' marital quality plays a key role in children's development (Engfer, 1988). In Figure 1.4 we can see that two aspects of the couple relationship may have important effects on the child: the intimate relationship between the parents, and the coparenting alliance—the extent to which the parents function as adversaries or cooperative partners in their parenting roles.

Couple Relationships and Children's Development. Ironically, the idea that unresolved marital conflict is detrimental to children's development was first studied systematically in divorcing families. On the average, the negative impact of parents' divorce on the child's academic achievement and social behavior can be seen for at least two years (Emery, 1988; Hetherington, Cox, & Cox, 1982; Wallerstein & Kelly, 1980). The most significant risk factor for children's postdivorce adjustment is the ex-spouses' continuing marital discord (Johnston, Kline, & Tschann, 1989).

Over the past 15 years, interest in the effects of the parents' relationship as a couple extended to studies of intact two-parent families. In a set of well-worked-out analog experiments and observations, Cummings and Davies (1994) showed that children's direct observations of conflict between their parents can be upsetting. The most thoroughly investigated indirect path, however, is the cascade from marital distress (dissatisfaction or conflict) to parent-child relationship quality to children's adaptation (Amato & Keith, 1991; Katz & Gottman, 1994). In an impressive meta-analysis of 68 studies, Erel and Burman (1995) reported a moderate but substantial link between marital atmosphere and parent-child relationship quality (effect size d = .46). Burman and Erel (1993) suggest that marital conflict in intact families may compromise parents' ability to establish supportive parent-child relationships. Consistent with this hypothesis, Wilson and Gottman (1995) summarize research to show that parents in conflictful marriages with escalating negative affect are less able to (a) coach their children to express and regulate negative emotions, (b) regulate their children's behavior, or (c) help their children self-soothe and regulate their own physiological stress response.

Recent effort has been devoted to exploring how the child's perception of marital conflict—the "insider's" view—can contribute to our understanding of the spillover from marital conflict to the child's behavior. Grych and Fincham (1993) demonstrated that the impact of parents' fighting depends in part on whether children are exposed to the conflict and how they interpret it. Ablow (1994) recently used the Berkeley Puppet Interview (Ablow & Measelle, 1993) to assess 5-year-olds' perceptions of their parents' marital conflict. She showed that kindergartners who believed that they were to blame for their parents' conflict were described by their teachers as more depressed; those who reported that their parents fought a lot but did *not* feel they were to blame were described by their teachers as more aggressive. These provocative findings about young children's perceptions suggest that even if we cannot yet identify all of the specific mechanisms of transmission from the parents' marital quality to the children's adjustment, we can be reasonably confident that (a) marital conflict is a risk factor for the development of behavior problems in the children, and (b) there is a risk of spillover from marital distress to the quality of parent-child relationships to distress in the children.

The Coparenting Alliance. Until very recently, researchers have blurred or ignored the distinction between marital functioning and coparenting—how husbands and wives interact while parenting their children (Cowan & McHale, 1997; Gable, Crnic, & Belsky, 1994). It seems surprising that we know so little about coparenting, given that developmentalists (P. Minuchin, 1985; Walsh, 1993) and clinical family theorists (S. Minuchin & Fishman,

[11] In this sample, there were too few couples in which fathers had insecure working models of early relationships and mothers had secure models to examine the impact of this combination on parenting style.

1981) have long stressed the potentially damaging consequences for children's development of a weak alliance between the parents. Systematic research to test this theory has begun to emerge. In the Pennsylvania State Child and Family Project (Gable et al., 1994), observers watched and recorded behavioral and emotional patterns of triadic interaction of mothers, fathers, and their firstborn 15-month-olds, and did home observations six months later. Correlational findings suggested that as stresses in a number of domains of family life increased, parents were less able to ask for and receive assistance from one another and more likely to undermine each other's efforts or openly criticize one another in front of the child. In a recent study of California couples alone and at play with their 8- to 11-month-old infants, McHale (1995) found that marital distress observed in a dyadic problem-solving discussion was associated with hostile-competitive coparenting behavior with sons, and differing levels of parental involvement with daughters.

Kahen (1995) found that when parents of 6-year-olds did not work well together as a team with their child, their coparenting in the triad was a significantly better predictor of the children's externalizing problem behavior than measures of the parents' individual parenting styles in mother-child and father-child dyads. The findings from correlational studies of coparenting support the studies of marital conflict in suggesting that, when possible, parenting interventions should try to include both parents and to improve the quality of relationship between them as a way of reducing the children's risk of developing problematic behavior.

Siblings

It was not until the 1970s that sibling relationships drew the attention of family researchers (Dunn & Kendrick, 1982; Lamb, 1978). One of the unfortunate consequences of this omission was that the role of siblings as caregivers to each other was virtually ignored (Zukow-Goldring, 1995). Negative sibling relationships are more likely when the siblings experience differential treatment by their parents, and differential treatment is exacerbated by marital distress (Bondar, 1995; McHale, Crouter, McGuire, & Updegraff, 1995). Patterson's (e.g., Bank, Patterson, & Reid, 1996) work suggests that some siblings act as "fight trainers," which increases the risk of high levels of aggression in peer relationships outside the family; other siblings function as protectors, in which case the likelihood of peer aggression is reduced despite the parents' marital distress.

Perhaps as a reflection of the fact that there has been little research on sibling relationships until recently, parenting books typically contain one short section or chapter on dealing with sibling relationships (for an important exception, see Dunn, 1995). Parenting intervention programs tend to discuss treatment of children generically, but rarely refer to issues of troubled sibling relationships, unwarranted differential treatment by parents placing one child at a disadvantage, or necessary differential treatment when different children have different characteristics and needs. These are topics that most parenting intervention programs could profitably address.

The Outside-the-Family Context of Parenting

Illustrations of the fact that parents and children affect and are affected by their social environments are drawn from studies of the impact of life stressors, social supports, peer relationships, ethnicity, and poverty on parents and on children's development.

General and Specific Stressors and Supports for Parents. There is ample evidence that work stress, job loss, peer relationship difficulties, and other stressors outside the family disrupt parent-child relationships, thereby interfering with children's optimal development and adjustment (e.g., Cutrona & Troutman, 1986; Patterson & Capaldi, 1991). Conversely, the availability of social support buffers parents from the effects of external stressors that might otherwise put added strain on parent-child relationships (Crockenberg, 1981).

The fact that the proportion of dual-worker parents with young children has increased dramatically in recent decades led to interest in the links between parents' work stress and family adaptation. Although a number of investigators have examined spillover from work to home life using separate samples of men and women (e.g., Repetti, 1987), few have examined the joint impact of fathers' and mothers' work stress when they return to the family at the end of the work day. One exception is a study by Schulz (1994), who asked mothers and fathers of young children to give ratings of stress and negative affect at work and at home on three successive days. His results show that spillover of work stress to the family depended on the parents' evaluation of their marital relationship. For husbands, negative affect at work was likely to spill over to their relationships with their wives and children on their highest stress days if they were *less* maritally satisfied. For wives, negative affect at work tended to spill over on their highest stress days if they were *more* maritally satisfied. Schulz speculates that for wives, a satisfying marital relationship provides a safe environment in which expression of negative emotions feels possible. This study provides another example in which the impact of negative events in one family domain depends in part on the state of the marriage.

Children's Peer Relationships. In the past decade there has been a growing body of evidence that children's peer relationships play a central role in their development (Asher & Coie, 1990; Coie & Dodge, Volume 3). Peer rejection is remarkably stable over time, even when the membership of the peer group changes; rejection by peers appears to precede rather than follow the development of behavior problems (Coie & Krehbiel, 1990; Kupersmidt, Coie, & Dodge, 1990). A number of studies show that the quality of children's peer relationships in both early childhood and adolescence is predictable, in part, from family factors: (a) the parent's role as a direct coach of social behavior; (b) the parent's role as a provider of social opportunities; and (c) the quality of parent-child and sibling relationships (cf., Parke, Burks, Carson, Neville, & Boyum, 1994). Because early peer status appears to be so strongly predictive of externalizing problems in late adolescence, a great deal of interest has developed in interventions that attempt to teach children social skills. These programs appear to have limited success unless they are paired with interventions that alter significant aspects of the child's social context in the family and school (see Comprehensive Multidomain Interventions, below).

The Generality of the Six-Domain Model across Contexts

We have shown that parent-child relationships play out in the context of a complex six-domain family system. The question to be explored in this section is whether the general idea behind the six-domain model can be applied to a variety of different populations defined by poverty status, ethnicity, family structure (two-parent vs. single-parent) and level of risk (high vs. low).

Poverty

The multidomain family model we have described has been supported by studies composed mainly of middle-class, urban families. Would we obtain the same findings in low-income or nonurban populations? In an extensive literature review, McLoyd (1990) summarized studies of the negative impact of poverty on young Black children's development. Low income and other social stressors associated with poverty set in motion a series of processes that disrupt parents' well-being, the tone of their marriage, and the quality of their relationships with their children. This cumulative disruption in many central aspects of family life increases the risk that boys and girls will develop externalizing and internalizing behavior problems at home and at school.

Conger and his colleagues (Conger & Elder, 1994) conducted a comprehensive set of studies of the effects of the 1980s economic recession on Iowa farm families and their adolescent children. The patterns they describe resemble those summarized by McLoyd. Overall, the data support the hypothesis that poverty increases parents' stress levels and disequilibrates the family system by interfering with parents' ability to provide warmth, structure, and control. In other words, poverty operates like other stressors and through similar mechanisms as those described in studies of middle-class families. Our tentative conclusion is that multidomain models like the one in Figure 1.4 appear to be relevant for explaining variations in parenting quality in both low- and high-income families.

Ethnicity

Because poverty and ethnicity are often confounded when minority groups are subject to enduring economic and social discrimination (Coll, Meyer, & Brillon, 1995), it is difficult to make generalizations about differences in family processes among groups of people identified by race or ethnicity. We also recognize that ethnic comparison studies raise political and value controversies. If, as has usually been the case, Caucasian families are taken as the norm or standard (Guthrie, 1976; Jones & Korchin, 1982), there is a danger that differences between any group and the "standard" are likely to be thought of as "deviant" and interpreted in negative terms.

As in our discussion of the effects of poverty, the key question is whether the correlational links between parenting behavior or other aspects of family functioning and children's adaptation hold across cultures and subcultures. At this point, we have research findings supporting both affirmative and negative answers. In a paper entitled "No More Than Skin Deep: Ethnic and Racial Similarity in Developmental Processes," Rowe, Vazsonyi, and Flannery (1994) argue that conclusions about the relations among various family domains can be generalized across ethnic groups. They analyzed data from six large epidemiological studies of African American, Hispanic American, and Caucasian American samples that assessed child and adolescent outcomes such as academic achievement, aggression, and drug use. LISREL structural models of the patterns of covariance among a variety of family factors showed that the same correlational models fit all three ethnic groups. Despite the fact that there were average differences among groups on many measures, the pattern of association among the variables was similar in each data set. From this finding, Rowe et al. concluded that "developmental processes in different ethnic and racial groups were statistically indistinguishable" (p. 407), although they acknowledge that developmental process was *inferred* from the pattern of association among variables, and that few of the studies used direct observational assessments of behavioral outcomes. Despite the fact that these results are consistent with the hypothesis of racial similarity in developmental processes, correlational data are not sufficient to demonstrate that the same causal mechanisms are operating in the different samples. Resolution of this issue is important for the design of parenting interventions. If the same parenting behaviors are not associated with the same outcomes in each group, then interventions developed and evaluated as successful in one ethnic group may not be applicable to another.

An interesting controversy has arisen concerning a set of findings that reveal different patterns of correlation between parenting style and children's development in families from different ethnic backgrounds. Baumrind's (1972, 1991) results, derived from a primarily middle-class Caucasian sample, suggest that in general, authoritative parenting (warmth/responsiveness and control) is associated with positive developmental outcomes, whereas authoritarian parenting (cold, hostile, nonresponsive, and controlling) is associated with negative developmental outcomes in the years from preschool through adolescence. Baumrind noted, however, that in a small subsample of African American families, positive developmental outcomes were associated with harsh but not abusive parenting (1972).

Drawing on an ethnically diverse sample of approximately 10,000 high school students, Steinberg and his colleagues (Steinberg, Darling, & Fletcher, in collaboration with Brown & Dornbush, 1995; Steinberg, Mounts, Lamborn, & Dornbush, 1991) found that parental authoritativeness was more strongly associated with grade-point average (GPA) in Caucasian than in African American or Asian American adolescents. Compared with Caucasian American adolescents, Asian American students rated their parents as more *authoritarian,* yet they had higher GPA scores than all other subgroups. Chao (1994; Chao & Sue, in press) recently addressed the interpretation of "authoritarian" parenting in Asian American families by presenting data showing that (a) the control exerted by Chinese families is directed specifically toward academic work and achievement, and (b) control with regard to academic work is viewed as "training" and as supportive rather than as harsh discipline. This finding reinforces the importance of obtaining children's perceptions and interpretations of their parents' behavior.

We can draw several preliminary conclusions from this line of research. First, while there is reason to expect many similarities in the connections between process and outcome in different ethnic groups, it is important to consider exceptions to the rule. One potential area of difference may be seen in more benign associations between an authoritarian parenting style and children's development in African American and Asian American groups, or in lower-income families. The differences may reflect the fact that parents from different ethnic groups believe in or require different approaches to parenting, depending on their family's situation, and/or the fact that the same approach to parenting means different things in the context of different cultures—from the parents' and/or the children's point of view.

The implications of ethnic group differences for parenting interventions are unclear. Indications that some ethnic groups encourage the expression of emotion whereas others are more concerned with regulation, or that some groups place special emphasis on respect for elders, make it imperative that parent educators and clinicians be sensitive to cultural values and anticipate resistance in some groups, for example, to attempts to encourage children's autonomy or expression of feelings. Paying attention to cultural differences will move us toward different or, at the very least, ethnically sensitive interventions for families of different ethnic backgrounds.

Family Structure

To what extent are theories and findings from two-parent families relevant to single-parent families? Designers of parenting interventions need to know the answer to this question because participants are likely to come from both groups. Between 1960 and 1980, the number of mother-headed families in the United States tripled, with African American and Hispanic children even more likely than Caucasians to be living with single mothers (Furukawa, 1994). Although divorce remained the major source of mother-headed and father-headed families through the 1980s, its proportional contribution declined and that of births outside of marriage increased (Burns & Scott, 1994). There is consensus that a majority of single mothers shoulder the triple burden of being the only parent and sole breadwinner with scarce economic resources (Burns & Scott, 1994).

Given that single parenthood may elevate the level of stresses associated with the rearing of young children, the question most relevant to intervention is whether there are different risks in families with one parent or two, and whether the risks are differentially connected to negative outcomes for parents and children. As we have seen, the list of risk factors for children's adjustment in two-parent families includes parents' economic and psychological stress, their symptomatology, troubled relationships in their families of origin, marital conflict, and ineffective parenting. The list of major risk factors for single-parent families is remarkably similar (Burns & Scott, 1994). In both divorced and never-married single-parent families, negative relationships with members of the family of origin and conflict between ex-spouses or between single mothers and their partners are key factors associated with internalizing or externalizing problems in children. In samples of both divorced and never-married single mothers, effective parenting functions as a buffer, protecting the child from the negative impact of stressors that affect the custodial parent (Chase-Lansdale, Brooks-Gunn, & Zamsky, 1994; Hetherington & Clingempeel, 1992; Pianta, Egeland, & Hyatt, 1986). It is possible that in these families, mother-grandmother relationships play a role much like marital relationships do in two-parent families, although we cannot neglect the potential impact of the mother's relationship with the father of the child or a new partner. Although we could not find a study that explicitly tested interconnections among the six domains in mother-headed families, our working hypothesis is that the multidomain approach presented schematically in Figure 1.4 applies to mother-headed families and may apply to father-headed families as well.

High- versus Low-Risk Status

The studies we have cited in this section have been drawn from research on families at both the low and high ends of the continuum, from no risk to serious psychological distress. Virtually identical path models linking parents' individual adjustment, marital interaction, parenting styles, and children's outcomes have been found in nonclinical samples of California families with 3.5-year olds and Georgia families with preteen children (Miller, Cowan, Cowan, Hetherington, & Clingempeel, 1993), and very similar models were useful in explaining these family factors in Iowa low-income farm families (Conger et al., 1992). Each of these models resembles those presented by researchers at the Oregon Social Learning Center, who studied aggressive children ranging in age from 10 through early adolescence. We do not claim that the pattern of linkage is *identical* across these populations, but rather that (a) regardless of the risk status of the families, there appears to be considerable coherence in both the measures and the explanations of adaptation across family domains, and (b) information from multiple domains in combination provides more accurate predictions of children's developmental outcomes than data from any one domain alone. The finding that similar linkages among family context, parent-child relationships, and children's adaptation occurs in both high-risk and low-risk samples is not surprising when we consider the fact that there is actually a great deal of overlap between the two groups. In high-risk samples, a majority of individuals and families are coping with a great deal of personal adversity, but some are doing well, whereas in low-risk samples, a majority of the individuals and families are adapting well in most areas of life inside and outside the family, but some are experiencing marked distress.

Implications of the Six-Domain Model for Parenting Interventions

We have shown that the parent-child domain is in reality a complex system of dyadic relationships among two or more parents and one or more children. Furthermore, the parent-child domain affects and is affected by the adjustment status of individual family members, the relationships among grandparents, parents, and children, the quality of the parents' marriage, the quality of relationships between siblings, and factors in the culture that have powerful influences on family equilibrium.

The studies we have summarized all attempt to document the connections among two or more of the six family domains. Only recently have family studies attempted to account for variations in children's adjustment using assessments of all six areas of family life. For example, data analyzed using path models that include information about parents' conflict in their families of origin, prebirth marital satisfaction, postpartum life stress, symptoms of depression, marital conflict, and parenting style predicted 51% of the variance in children's academic achievement scores at the end of kindergarten (Cowan, Cowan, Schulz, & Heming, 1994). Although this model accounted for less than 30% of the variance in the children's externalizing and internalizing behavior at school, adding measures of fathers' adult attachment made it possible to explain 69% of the variance in children's externalizing behavior, and adding mothers' attachment scores made it possible to explain 60% of the variance in their internalizing behavior in kindergarten (Cowan, Cohn, Cowan, & Pearson, 1996). These findings, based on relatively small urban family samples (44 families) of young school-age children, are very similar in form to those of Conger and his colleagues (1992) from a much larger sample of rural families with adolescent children.

What is the relevance of these complex multidomain models of family functioning to practitioners? First, supportive evidence from correlational data does not prove that the state of adaptation in each domain is causally linked with specific child outcomes, or that interventions in each family domain will necessarily lead to positive outcomes for children; only systematically evaluated intervention trials can serve that purpose. Nevertheless, research evidence helps to pinpoint potential risks for children's distress and potential buffers of those risks, both of which help us decide where the focus of interventions might lie. The six-domain model opens up a world of possibilities to interveners concerned with the quality of parent-child relationships. Child-focused, parent-focused, and parent-child relationship focused interventions may be effective, but they are not the only possible points of entry for the promotion of more effective parenting. Although positive outcomes are never guaranteed, intervention in any of the six domains of family life *may* have important beneficial consequences for the relationships between parents and children in single-parent, two-parent, and other combinations of blended families.

COMPREHENSIVE MULTIDOMAIN INTERVENTIONS

Comprehensive multidomain interventions began to emerge in the 1980s based on different but related versions of the systemic, contextual models of parenting we have just described. In some interventions for low-income and middle-class parents, interveners work only with parents but also focus their discussion on a number of domains inside and outside the family. Other comprehensive programs intervene in multiple domains of the family system (marital, parenting, whole family). Still others conduct interventions in more than one setting (home, classroom, school playground).

A Multidomain Family-Based Preventive Program for Low-Risk Parents

It has been well established that major life transitions elevate the risk for individual and family dysfunction (P. Cowan, 1991). For example, results of more than 20 studies show that when relatively well-functioning couples become parents for the first time, they experience negative or disturbing changes in individual, three-generational, and outside-the-family domains of family life. These shifts have a negative impact on the marital relationship, and subsequently on the relationships that parents establish with their children (Cowan & Cowan, 1995). The data, then, provide the justification for a preventive intervention for new parents during the transition to parenthood and the early years of child rearing.

Curriculum. In the Becoming a Family Project at the University of California, Berkeley (Cowan & Cowan, 1992), a couples group meeting weekly for 24 weeks was offered to a randomly selected one-third of the expectant couples entering a longitudinal study of the transition to parenthood. Using a combination of structured agendas and open-ended discussions, professionally trained couples serving as group leaders met weekly with each group of four participant couples as they made their transition to first-time parenthood. The babies became part of the groups as soon as they were born.

Agendas were formed collaboratively by participants and leaders. Guided by a five-domain model of family functioning (there were no siblings in these first-child families), leaders raised topics for discussion from each domain. Over time, they helped parents notice links between and among various aspects of their lives: how marital conflict could affect their relationship with the baby; how their own experiences of being parented influenced their ideas, feelings, and practices of parenting *their* children. Staff couples attempted to help participant couples (a) alter the kinds of processes that research has shown are associated with risk and vulnerability, such as resolving marital conflict more effectively, and (b) adopt patterns that are known to buffer risks and optimize resilience, such as taking time to replenish their energy as individuals and as couples and seeking more support from others.

Program Evaluation. When the babies were 6 and 18 months old, the Cowans and their colleagues (Cowan et al., 1985) compared adaptation in new parents with and without the intervention. Results showed positive intervention effects for husbands, for wives, and for the relationship between the partners. Men who had participated in a couples group described themselves as more psychologically involved in their roles as fathers than men with no intervention. Women from the groups maintained their prebaby level of satisfaction with the division of family work, but mothers without an intervention became more unhappy with their role arrangements. Men and women from the groups also reported fewer negative changes in their sexual relationship after giving birth than parents without the intervention. Perhaps the most noteworthy effects of the intervention were on parents' marital satisfaction and stability 18 months into parenthood. In contrast to the declines in marital satisfaction reported in most longitudinal studies of new parents (Belsky & Pensky, 1988), marital satisfaction remained stable between 6 and 18 months postpartum in couples who participated in the group intervention. Whereas the separation and divorce rate of the no-treatment couples was 12.5% when the babies were 18 months old, the marriages of *all* the intervention couples were still intact. These positive effects on the group couples' marriages lasted throughout the first three years of parenthood.

At a three-and-a-half-year follow-up, the intervention effects on parents' individual and marital adaptation began to wane, and two years later, when the children entered elementary school, almost five years after the couples groups ended, marital differences between intervention and no-intervention couples had disappeared. This is a vivid illustration of the fact that preventive intervention effects cannot be expected to last forever without some kind of "booster shot," particularly in the family-making years when so many aspects of life are in flux and require adaptation on the part of both parents.

The Cowans and their colleagues (Cowan & Cowan, in press; Heming, 1997) are currently conducting a second intervention study with a new sample of families, with intervention beginning as the children are about to make the transition to elementary school. In this new intervention, trained clinicians conduct 16-week couples groups for parents that emphasize marital *or* coparenting issues during their first child's transition to elementary school. Preliminary results suggest that a couples group with a coparenting focus has the most positive effects two years after the intervention: the fathers report higher levels of self-esteem, couples argue less in front of their children, and their children show higher levels of academic achievement and fewer behavior problems at the end of first grade according to individually administered achievement tests and teachers' reports. It is not clear at this point whether the maritally focused group intervention was less effective or whether the effects of marital interventions take longer to lead to shifts in the parent-child relationship. The answer to these questions will contribute to the design of future parenting interventions and to theories about family mechanisms in children's adaptation and distress.

Comprehensive Family-Based Interventions for High-Risk Families

Multidomain Interventions for Low-Income Families

Curriculum. Comprehensive programs with parenting components have come about in response to the pressing problems of low-income families, especially parents' employability and prospects for escaping poverty. Illustrative are the two-generation interventions noted earlier, in which the child's development and the parent's job-related skills are targets of change, and parenting education is one component aimed at improving child outcomes (Smith & Zaslow, 1995). There is a tendency for parenting components of comprehensive interventions to be adapted from existing parent education program models, especially those available commercially (St. Pierre & Swartz, 1995).

It is noteworthy that in comprehensive interventions, particularly those with major adult education or job training components, fewer resources are devoted to the parenting component than to other adult services. For example, in the New Chance intervention, a national multisite demonstration program aimed at young mothers on welfare, participants spent an average of 13 hours in parenting education compared to 56 hours of participation in the education component (e.g., G.E.D. instruction) during a four-month period (Quint & Egeland, 1995). The average parent in the federal Even Start Family Literacy Program participated in 7 hours of parenting education compared to 13 hours of adult education a month (St. Pierre & Swartz, 1995). The integration of components of comprehensive interventions, such as the inclusion of parenting information in the adult education service (e.g., reading material about parenting in the adult education class), appears to be highly variable across programs. In Even Start, for example, component integration seems to depend partly on whether one or a number of different agencies are responsible for delivering the individual components.

Some programs for high-risk parents assume that bolstering a mother's interpersonal competence is a prerequisite for improving her child-rearing abilities. The design of an infant intervention program at the University of Washington is based on this two-step assumption—to strengthen the interpersonal competence of mothers at high risk because of poverty and single-parent status by focusing on improving their social skills—and only then providing information on child development and rearing (Booth, Mitchell, Barnard, & Spieker, 1989).

Outcome Studies. A large-scale Parent-Child Development Center (PCDC) program (Dokecki, Hargrove, & Sandler, 1983), evaluated through experimental designs in three sites, had positive effects on children's Stanford-Binet scores at the time of program termination, when children were 36 months of age. These gains were maintained one year after the program ended (Andrews et al., 1982) but not beyond (Bridgeman, Blumenthal, & Andrews, 1981). Program mothers at each of the sites scored significantly higher than control group mothers on various indexes of positive maternal behavior at the end of the program (Andrews et al., 1982). In one of the PCDC sites, a follow-up study found that boys of program group mothers exhibited fewer negative social behaviors than boys of control mothers (Johnson & Breckenridge, 1982). A 10-year follow-up evaluation of the Syracuse University Family Development Research Program, which began with families of early school-age children, found lower incidence and severity of juvenile delinquency, more positive attitudes toward themselves and the environment in program children and their parents (i.e., problem-solving orientation), and higher school performance of program girls, though not boys, in junior high school (Lally, Mangione, & Honig, 1988).

Evaluations of most of the newer, comprehensive, two-generation interventions are underway now. An early analysis of the federal Even Start Family Literacy Program found no effects on parents' expectations for their children's school success, parent-child reading behaviors, home environment quality, or parents' depression and sense of self-efficacy. Curiously, though, the number of hours parents spent in the parenting component was positively correlated with children's expressive language skills (St. Pierre & Swartz, 1995); benefits for the children's academic success may follow in later evaluations.

A program with a multidomain focus at the University of Washington reported by Barnard, Morisset, and Spieker (1993) focused on various aspects of maternal competence, but not specifically on jobs. Compared with low-income mothers in a less intense intervention, mothers visited regularly by nurses with master's-level training not only made more contacts with their home visitors but also showed enhanced social competence in interaction with their children.

Multidomain Marital and Family Interventions for Parents of Children with Diagnosed Problems

Marital Interventions. Webster-Stratton (1990) noted in her own data that aggressive children whose parents suffered individual and marital distress were not affected as positively by her videotape parent intervention as children whose parents were not in distress. In response to this finding, she developed ADVANCE, a new videotape treatment added to the "basic" parenting component to help parents cope with marital distress through improved communication, problem solving, and self-control (1994). Both ADVANCE and the basic program produced similar positive changes in parents and children at short-term follow-up, but ADVANCE produced additional significant improvement in parents' communication, problem-solving skills, and satisfaction with the program. The results appear promising, but without controls and long-term follow-ups, the specific contributions of the focus on parents as individuals and in relationships cannot yet be determined.

Using a similar rationale and intervention strategy, Griest and his colleagues (Griest et al., 1982), and Dadds and his colleagues (Dadds, Sanders, Behrens, & James, 1987) showed that adding a maritally focused segment to regular behavior management training for parents of children with conduct problems resulted in increased positive impact on both family relationships and children's behavior. The effect was especially strong for maritally distressed couples in the treatment program. Since both studies found that initial treatment gains for the parent-training-only condition tended to be lost when parents continued to be high in marital conflict, we have converging evidence that interventions that address the marital relationship appear to strengthen the effectiveness of parent-child relationships and reduce aggressive problem behavior in young children.

Family Interventions. Still other programs for high-risk parents attempt to alter patterns in the whole family system. It became clear to the Oregon Social Learning Center group (Patterson & Forgatch, 1989) that when adolescents are showing seriously aggressive behavior, interventions are needed for many of the family subsystems: the child, the sibling groups, and the family as a whole. Therapists meet conjointly with family members in home or office. It is in this program that the researcher-clinicians discovered that many siblings of aggressive children, although not identified as aggressive themselves, function as "fight trainers" and stimulate aggression in the identified patient (Dishion, Duncan, Eddy, & Fagot, 1994). Patterson et al. (1993) cite a growing number of intervention studies that evaluate the impact of parent training in combination with family systems therapy. Preliminary indications are that enhanced family-oriented treatment has a stronger effect on marital relationships, parent-child relationships, and child outcomes than parenting interventions alone (Brunk, Henngeler, & Whelan, 1987; Wells & Egan, 1988).

Several family-focused intervention and research projects for parents of adult children diagnosed as schizophrenic adopt a psychoeducational approach that combines direct teaching, family communication and problem solving, and behavioral training of parenting skills (Cole, Kane, Zastowny, Grolnick, & Lehman, 1993; Falloon et al., 1985). The parents are taught directly about the nature of schizophrenia and about techniques for parenting their adult child, especially at home after the patient is discharged. Compared with a supportive family intervention with no family problem-solving and communication component, the Cole et al. (1993) intervention reduced the central negative aspects of parental communication (critical and intrusive comments in family problem solving) that are associated with schizophrenic symptomatology, and improved the patients' level of functioning. In general, these programs have advantages over individual treatment for the patient alone because they help to reduce the tendency for patients to be rehospitalized (Falloon et al., 1985).

Finally, multisystemic therapy (MST; Henggeler, Schoenwald, & Pickrel, 1995) represents a strategy midway between the interventions with families we have been describing and the multisetting interventions we describe in the next section. Focused on treatment of inner-city youth, interventions begin by focusing on child and family problems with a goal of establishing effective parenting, but quickly expand the focus to the multiple systems in which family members are embedded (school, community) in an attempt to mobilize these resources in support of the family. A recent summary of studies by Henggeler and his colleagues (Henggeler et al., 1995) demonstrates the success of MST in randomized trials, at first using doctoral-level students in clinical psychology to deliver home-based services, and more recently mounting interventions within community-based mental health and juvenile justice systems.

Comprehensive Interventions in Multiple Settings

Theoretical Rationale. In a comprehensive review of intervention programs designed to prevent conduct disorder, Reid (1993) notes that as children make the transition from preschool to elementary school, they enter expanding domains of risk. Whereas rates of overall aversive behavior for well-adjusted boys drop dramatically during this period, the opposite is true of children referred for conduct problems. These boys respond less competently to the challenges of peer groups, are judged by their teachers to be troublesome in the classroom, and are more likely to experience learning difficulties and school failure. "The challenge for the next generation of prevention trials for CD is to develop programs targeting important subsets of these antecedents across settings" (p. 256). Meeting this challenge requires active intervention with children and parents, not only in the family but also in the classroom and the peer group.

We describe three programs based on the logic of this approach. Although systematic evaluations of these interventions have not yet been completed, we present the programs here because many of the intervention components, including those focused on parenting, have been tested and evaluated as effective in prior studies.

A Universal Intervention for Preventing Conduct Disorder. Reid (1993) describes a study that includes a universal preventive intervention designed for all first-graders in one set of Oregon schools and a control sample of comparable students in no-intervention schools. Interventions are carried out in the home and at school with children all along the range of risk for conduct disorder by virtue of their level of aggressive behavior. In cooperative learning groups, parents, teachers, and children are taught principles of behavior management to be applied at home, in the classroom, and on the playground. To facilitate parent-teacher collaboration, teachers use an answering machine to record short, weekly messages describing current classroom activities to parents. Parents call in for the messages and are encouraged to leave specific messages of their own. A preliminary report of the evaluation study suggests that the intervention produces positive outcomes, but we will have to await further analyses and follow-up (Reid, 1996).

A Targeted Intervention for Preventing Conduct Disorder. Six investigators at four sites have formed a cooperative preventive intervention project named FAST Track (Families and Schools Together) to mount a multidomain, multisetting program based primarily on social learning principles. The aim is to reduce the incidence of conduct disorder in a sample of children at high risk for oppositional defiant disorder and conduct disorder when they first enter school. Consistent with practices in the emerging science of prevention (Coie et al., 1993), these investigators identify children early (in kindergarten) and target their interventions to ameliorate the risk factors known to be associated with conduct disorder. Children are individually tutored on academic skills. Individual and group social skills training helps them change their patterns of thinking about peer relationships and getting along with other children (cf., Crick & Dodge, 1994). Classroom interventions that include teacher consultation and programs for all children in the class facilitate the development of self-control, a positive peer climate, emotional awareness, and interpersonal problem-solving skills.

The parent training component (McMahon, Slough, & the Conduct Problems Prevention Research Group, in press), conducted primarily by a family coordinator in weekly (grade 1) or bimonthly (grade 2) groups of five to seven parents, is modeled on examples we have already described by Forehand and McMahon (1981), Webster-Stratton (1989), and Patterson (1982), and on a program specifically developed to help parents help children with schooling (Burgoyne, Hawkins, & Catalano, 1991). Discussion and group exercises focus on factors found to be associated with children's adaptation: (a) establishing positive family-school relations; (b) increasing parental self-control; (c) developing reasonable and appropriate expectations for children's behavior; and (d) improving parenting skills to increase positive parent-child interaction and decrease acting-out behaviors. In addition to group discussions, parents learn to use a daily school-home notebook to communicate with teachers and to practice in a subsequent parent-child sharing time at school and at home. Home visitors work with parents every other week on personal issues and family skills.

A first public presentation of intervention results reports on data from the children and parents at the end of first grade (Coie, 1996). Compared with comparable children not in the intervention, FAST Track children demonstrate better word-attack skills and social problem-solving skills, greater acceptance of authority in the classroom and seeking help from adults, higher levels of social acceptance by classmates, and less tendency to start fights with peers. Compared with controls, parents in the intervention report less use of physical punishment, more use of appropriate discipline, greater involvement in the child's school, more warmth and involvement with their children, and describe their children as warmer to them. Thus, at this point, the investigators see modest but important gains in children's social cognition, playground behavior, peer-nominated social status, parent-child relationship quality, and academic skills. Promising results concerning intervention effects on the child's externalizing behavior are just beginning to be found (Coie, 1977, personal communication). The investigators will continue the interventions and follow-ups throughout the primary levels into middle school.

A Targeted Intervention for Treating Children with ADHD. Based on the finding that no single-domain treatment for children with ADHD has been shown to have long-term effects, a new multisite, multimodal treatment study of children with ADHD has recently been organized (Richters et al., 1995). A preliminary statement of the central questions addressed by this research and intervention study illustrates the breadth of the approach: "Under what circumstances (co-morbid conditions, age, gender, family background) do which treatment combinations (medication, behavior therapy, parent training, school-based intervention) have what impacts (improvement, stasis, deterioration) on what domains of child functioning (cognitive, academic, behavioral, physical, peer relations, family relations) for how long (short- vs. long-term), to what extent (effect sizes, normal vs. pathological range), and why (processes underlying change)?" (p. 997). Answers to these important questions await completion of the studies.

It is symbolic of the current state of the field that we end this section with a description of ongoing multisetting intervention programs and a set of questions that do not as yet have empirical answers because none of the investigators has completed evaluations of the interventions. Multisetting interventions based on contextual family systems models take a great deal of time to plan and execute; each involves issues of measurement, data reduction, and analysis that are extremely complex and take years to complete.

We should make clear that we do not yet know whether comprehensive interventions, touted as more inclusive, complex, and broadly contextual, are necessarily better or more effective than single-domain parenting interventions. There are as yet no studies comparing child-focused, parent-focused, parent-child, and comprehensive interventions. In part, designers of intervention programs choose to focus on multiple domains in recognition of the emerging body of research and theory that paints a complex systemic picture of individual and family development. We have argued that theories of etiology should not necessarily restrict our intervention strategies. If the system theorists are correct, intervention in any domain has a potential for producing positive effects throughout the system. Only subsequent testing of the effects of the component aspects of comprehensive interventions will increase our understanding of the separate and combined impact of these interventions on different family domains and on specific outcomes for the child.

TOWARD THE FUTURE OF PARENTING INTERVENTIONS

To weave together many of the threads in this chapter, we begin by restating our initial questions about parenting interventions and offer some provisional answers. We then look toward the future of parenting interventions. We consider the interconnections between parenting interventions and parenting theories, and conclude this section with some suggestions for both.

What Have We Learned? Provisional Answers to Some Historical Questions

The Availability of Parenting Interventions

Based on the wide array of intervention programs we have described, we are concerned that the reader will come away with the impression that many programs are available to the general public. Our view is that a range of programs is available, especially for families at the low-risk end of the continuum, but *empirically validated* programs are in short supply. In 1994, there were 34,018,000 U.S. households with children under 18 and more than 60,000,000 biological parents. As we have noted, estimates suggest that at least 20% of their children may be diagnosable with academic, social, or emotional problems at some time during childhood or adolescence (National Plan for Research on Child & Adolescent Mental Disorders, 1990); some estimate as many as 40% (Gillham, Reivich, Jaycox, & Seligman, 1995). A significant proportion of the parents of these children need assistance to find more effective parenting strategies to create more satisfying relationships with their children, but only half of those who need services can be expected to receive them (Saxe, Cross, & Silverman, 1988); many of the existing services for children do not include a parenting intervention component.

Let us be clear that only a few of the programs we have described—sadly, the ones with least evidence about their effectiveness—have been widely disseminated. Many exciting and well-designed programs are funded for systematic trials in a university or clinic setting. They serve a limited number of parents and/or children for a limited time and end when the time-limited funding period ends. Even programs that prove effective in a systematic trial may not have the funding or staffing support to be mounted for a larger number of families in need. Without being able to document precisely the discrepancy between supply and demand, we conclude that parents in millions of U.S. households who have children suffering an array of academic, emotional, and social problems have no access to parenting intervention services that might address their children's developmental difficulties.

What is the situation for families whose children have *not* been identified as having problems? Of course, many mothers and fathers facing the normal stresses and strains of family life will not feel the need of parenting help. But consider the parent of a young toddler whose tantrums are becoming more frequent, or the parents of a school-age child whose nightmares are worrisome and keeping the adults and child from getting enough regular sleep, or the parent of an adolescent who is experimenting with drugs and beginning to show slipping grades and pervasive withdrawal from friends and family? Some parents want guidance to address these troubling problems before they escalate into full-blown behavioral problems or mental health disorders. Even parents who are not worried about serious childhood problems may feel in need of feedback or consultation during the 15, 20, or more years that they are intensively involved in trying to rear healthy children.

Parents in low-risk families can find many opportunities to obtain parenting advice in popular books and magazines or in parenting classes associated with their religious institution or community college. The problem here is that almost none of these resources are backed by evidence of their effectiveness. Although they may have access to parenting interventions, parents in low risk families rarely know how these resources measure up. It seems curious that if parents want to purchase a household product or child's toy, they have access to consumer information and product tests, but if they want to select a parenting intervention, no such information is available.

Who Delivers Parenting Interventions?

Our historical survey of parenting interventions revealed that the field has always included untrained volunteers, paraprofessionals, and professionals who are not trained specifically to conduct parenting interventions. This is still the case. In recent decades, as comprehensive intervention programs have expanded in size and scope to target low-income and minority populations, roles for paraprofessionals have expanded. Although the results of several evaluation studies suggest that professionally trained interveners may be more effective than paraprofessionals or nonprofessionals at producing positive results, this conclusion is far from well established on the basis of empirical research. At this point, because of the dearth of writing about this issue, the question of who can be an effective intervention agent for what kinds of populations of parents is largely unresolved.

Both common sense and research evidence suggest that work with high-risk families with a multitude of problems (cf., Blechman, 1991) requires staff who have comprehensive training. Commenting on the level of training required for parenting interventions, Doherty (1995) presents a useful model describing different levels of family involvement for the intervener in different types of parenting interventions. Level 1 interventions involve brief contact with parents around a child issue (e.g., parent-teacher conferences). Level 2 interventions include educational activities around child development, parenting, and family life issues. Interveners at Level 3 elicit the feelings and experiences of parents or family members and use those personal disclosures as part of an educational process with parents. According to Doherty's model, Level 4 interventions go beyond Level 2 and 3 programs by "including an assessment and a planned effort to help the parent change a troublesome parenting problem, a broader family interaction pattern, or larger systems problem" in families with special needs and multiple stressors (p. 355). Family therapy is a Level 5 intervention, and it is only at this level that Doherty feels it appropriate to move beyond parenting into couple relationship issues, family of origin problems, and mental disorders in individual family members. In his view, extensive professional training for work at this level is a necessity. In our view, the complexity of the contextual model of parent-child relationships that we have presented in this chapter suggests that professional training for work with parents at each of the five levels is highly desirable.

Who Parenting Interventions Are Designed to Reach

Our historical survey noted increasing attempts to broaden the target audience for parenting intervention programs and increasing efforts to reach populations at risk by virtue of low income, minority status, or psychopathology. Given space limitations, we have not described programs designed to reach specific subgroups of parents, including fathers (Hawkins, Christiansen, Sargent, & Hill, 1993; Parke & Beitel, 1986) and divorced mothers (Wolchick et al., 1993). Despite risks for developmental problems in adopted children (Sullivan, Wells, & Bushness, 1995), we could find no intervention programs for adoptive parents that have been systematically evaluated. Some programs *are* available, however, for parents of children with already identified medical or psychological difficulties and disorders: feeding difficulties (Turner, Sanders, & Wall, 1994), asthma (Mesters, Van Nunen, Crebolder, & Meertens, 1995), physical disabilities (Volenski, 1995), head injuries (Singer, Glang, Nixon, & Colley, 1994), Down syndrome (Shapiro & Simonson, 1994), and autism (Bristol, Gallagher, & Holt, 1993). Although each target population has some unique concerns and needs, most of these programs try to help parents help their children with an eclectic mix of the techniques and approaches that we have already described under the general heading of child-focused, parent-focused, or parent-child–focused interventions. For example, the MELD program, a model of parent education and social support based on modified self-help groups, has versions for adolescent mothers, parents who are deaf, parents of children with special needs, Latino parents, and Hmong parents (Ellwood, 1988), although evaluations of each of these programs are not yet available. We suspect that groups for parents experiencing similar life transitions or similar child-focused problems can be powerful in creating a supportive intervention environment. We do not yet know whether parenting interventions with a homogeneous or heterogeneous focus are ultimately more effective.

Future Directions for Parenting Interventions

Prevention

Research evidence that supports the six-domain family systems model of parenting indicates that we have the ability to identify family risk and protective factors associated with children's behavior problems and academic and social competence. Not only are there concurrent correlations between parenting and children's adaptation, but there is considerable predictive power from parenting measured at Time 1 to children's outcomes measured at Time 2. When we add information about parents' experiences in their families of origin, the quality of their intimate relationships, and the balance between life stress and social support, we can do remarkably well in predicting which parents and children will be likely to have problematic outcomes.

Our ability to predict later distress from earlier measures of family adaptation provides the scientific base required by prevention science to shape the direction of preventive interventions. It makes good sense to increase efforts devoted to the creation of prevention programs for parents. Interventions early in the life of a family, or early in the development of family problems, give promise of staving off more serious problems farther along the family developmental trajectory. Unfortunately, financial resources have not been available to mount prevention programs on a wide scale (Snowden, 1982).

Moving beyond Child and Adolescent Aggression

The reader has probably noted that a substantial proportion of the interventions we have described focus on teaching parents about discipline and limit setting to reduce their children's aggression. Several programs have begun to target children's depression and social withdrawal as serious problems that call for substantial prevention efforts (cf., Gillham et al., 1995). However, there are very few interventions devoted specifically to helping parents deal with their children's anxiety, depression, social withdrawal, or other manifestations of internalizing disorders. We believe that it is time to rebalance intervention efforts so that aggressive children do not monopolize all the intervention resources and the problems of quiet, sad children begin to be addressed.

Families with Multiple Risks

Even if they were more widely available, prevention programs would not eliminate the need for parenting interventions for families at serious risk or already in distress. Over the decades, parenting interventions that attempt to reach the burgeoning high-risk populations have developed increasingly complex multidomain intervention strategies. Recent promising interventions for high-risk/high-distress families (see sections above on interactive focus and multidomain interventions) suggest three conclusions about future efforts to work with parents with multiple risks. First, these comprehensive intervention programs require more time and effort than the short-term interventions typically offered to parents; an eight-week series of classes or home visits is not likely to be sufficient for families with multiple problems. Second, because the parent-child relationship is embedded in a network of interconnected domains, interventions that go beyond the enhancement of parenting skills will be required to address some of the life issues parents face: poverty, their feelings of incompetence, and troubled relationships with other people and institutions. Third, given the complexity of the problems experienced in these families and the difficulties involved in altering family dynamics *and* social institutions, the level of training and clinical skills of the interveners on the front lines are of particular importance.

Diverse Populations and Problems

As interventions are developed to provide assistance for diverse populations at many levels of risk, it is critical that attention be paid to whether the parenting models developed on largely middle-class Caucasian populations are appropriate to each new sample. Studies by Rowe et al. (1994) and Steinberg et al. (1995) provide both reassurance and a note of caution: reassurance in that at least some connections between family domains appear to have wide generality; caution in that an unknown number of ideas about effective parenting may require modification for work with members of various ethnic and culturally defined groups.

The once prevalent "one size fits all" notion is being replaced by attempts to match programs more closely to participants' individual, family, and cultural circumstances. Strategies to increase the *accessibility* of a program include: (a) expanded locations (e.g., home visits, waiting rooms of health clinics, shopping malls, neighborhood centers) or ease of contact (e.g., telephone "warm lines"); (b) additional supports to encourage participation (e.g., transportation, child care, food); (c) language familiarity (e.g., attention to local terms and language); and (d) use of local staff (laypersons from the community as frontline program workers). Among these various options, perhaps the greatest level of activity has been the increase in the number of home visiting programs nationally, largely as a means of serving difficult-to-reach populations (Roberts & Wasik, 1990).

Developmental Parenting in a Family Context

Popular parenting books (e.g., Brazelton, 1992; Spock, 1957) make it clear that parenting is a developmental enterprise. Children at each age and stage have characteristic developmental tasks (Gesell et al., 1943), and parents need to learn to respond appropriately to infants, toddlers, and adolescents, because what works and can be understood at one age may not be effective at another. As we have noted, parents too have developmental tasks (Johnson & Irvin, 1983). Although a few commentators have noted that parents are having a difficult time meshing their life trajectories with those of their children (Elkind, 1994), there is very little in the popular literature, and nothing at all in the research literature, about more effective ways to bring the two developmental paths together. Further, while we know that parents of older children need different repertoires than parents of younger children, we know very little about general principles for describing optimal and less optimal shifts in parenting strategies as children mature. Here is another arena that future parenting research and intervention might profitably address.

The Entrepreneurial Context of Parenting Interventions

We have written about the field of parenting interventions as if it is conducted by interveners who are trying to establish a rational balance between estimates of parents' needs and ideas that have been validated by systematic intervention research. This rational calculus has been disrupted by a commercial or entrepreneurial spirit that drives some of the program development and dissemination in the field, particularly in the case of books and packaged audiovisual programs for individuals and parenting groups. Even when programs are not driven by a profit motive, many policy-driven interventions sponsored by cities and states seem to be based on decisions concerning what should be offered, not necessarily on what families need or what has been shown to be effective. These motivations for designing parenting programs stand in sharp contrast to developmental programs that (a) focus on pressing family problems and issues, (b) are based on well-established measures of risk and outcome, and (c) incorporate ideas about change mechanisms as defined by results of systematic research.

Is "Parenting Intervention" a Field?

As we surveyed literatures from many disparate sources in preparing this chapter, we found ourselves struggling with the question of whether this body of knowledge represents a coherent field. Our tentative answer at this point in history is no, or at least not yet. Theorists and interveners have come to the enterprise of addressing the serious problems of contemporary parents and their children from many fields: parent education, religious education, counseling, nursing, public health, sociology, social work, psychology, and psychiatry, to name a few. Theorists and clinicians who discuss parenting in low-risk populations tend not to refer to the literature on interventions for high-risk populations. Parent educators tend not to read the literature published by clinicians who work with troubled parents and children, and vice versa. Family psychologists, social workers, and sociologists interested in parenting are beginning to engage in dialogue, but professionals in those disciplines tend not to read the literature in public health. School-based interventions for parents typically ignore what is known about family interventions, and family-based interventions rarely focus on what happens to children in schools.

Of course, the problem of intellectual isolation or parochialism is not unique to the study of parent-child relationships and parenting interventions. Increased specialization within each field and the proliferation of publication outlets make it quite a challenge to become familiar with these disparate sources, yet increased integration and dialogue seem essential. We can only hope that by the time the next *Handbook* is published, increasing collaboration, convergence, and integration will have brought more coherence to the field of parenting interventions than exists today.

Cross-Fertilization of Theory and Intervention

Reconceptualizing the Distinction between Low Risk and High Risk

In this chapter, most of the parenting programs we described had been subjected to systematic evaluation. One consequence of this choice was that the majority focused on high-risk rather than low-risk populations. Throughout the chapter, we have attempted to compare findings from studies of these two populations and have argued that there are marked similarities in pattern even when the levels of risk and distress are clearly different.

Our survey of family research and parenting interventions has made clear to us that the distinction between high-risk and low-risk families requires redefinition. There are important policy implications that follow from the use of these terms (Cowan & Cowan, 1997). Quite appropriately, policymakers and those who direct service delivery systems have become concerned about addressing the family problems of high-risk families. The inference is that low-risk families do not need services precisely because they are characterized as not at risk.

We believe that we must pay more attention to the distinction between risk—a potential for negative outcomes—and actual distress or disorder. There is mounting evidence (cf., Cowan & Cowan, 1995) that many apparently advantaged parents are at risk for serious social and emotional problems, and that a substantial proportion show signs of serious distress as individuals (depression), as couples (marital distress and dissolution), and as parents (parenting stress, difficulties in managing the problems of their children). The data make clear that when parents suffer from these individual, marital, and parenting problems, their children are more likely to have academic and behavior problems and difficulty relating to their peers. Low risk does not mean "problem-free." Conversely, although research rarely tells this side of the story, many high-risk parents and couples adapt well to both normative and nonnormative life stresses. High risk does not mean "problem-filled."

This discussion brings us back to a question we raised at the beginning of the chapter: Is there an inherent difference between interventions designed for interested parents who want to learn more about parenting, and interventions designed for parents from clinical populations? Our experience with both types of intervention indicates that there is often, though not always, more tension in families who seek treatment rather than education, and these interventions require more specialized clinical skills and more intensive effort over longer periods of time. Although these are important differences, the conceptual underpinnings of intervention as outlined in the parenting effects checklist are very similar in both cases. For example, behavioral principles apply to both normal tantrums and oppositional defiant disorder. The need to understand the inner experience of the child is equally strong in the case of a whiny, anxious child and a child who is destructive and out of control. Ultimately, we need studies that reveal whether parenting interventions have differential effects for families at different points along the continuum of risk and distress.

What the Parenting Effects Checklist Means for Intervention

Our description of nine approaches to explaining parents' influence on children's development was offered as a checklist to assist interveners in identifying the assumptions underlying their program, and to consider whether alternative approaches based on alternative assumptions might be considered. Our intent was not to be prescriptive nor to suggest that all of these approaches must or should be used in every intervention. Although there are nine identifiable theories about how parents contribute to children's development and adaptation, we found it convenient to focus on four major groupings of parenting interventions: child-focused, parent-focused, parent-child focused, and comprehensive. The evidence evaluating the child-focused parenting interventions is sparse, but we have no reason to conclude that any one of these approaches is markedly superior or inferior to any of the others. There is no single "right answer," no "owner's manual" that has universal applicability to parent-child relationships. The checklist may help the creators of intervention programs devote less effort to making generalizations about "what's best" for parents and children, and more to maximizing the fit between programs and the families they serve.

What the Six-Domain Family Systems Model Means for Intervention

The Multidomain Perspective. Our proposal of a multidomain family systems model is consistent with our use of the parenting effects checklist. The comprehensive systems model shows that (a) parent-child relationships exist in a context of relationships, (b) interventions focused directly on parent or child may not always be effective, and (c) multidomain perspectives may be helpful in considering alternative intervention approaches. Our intent is not to mandate family interventions in multiple settings, but rather to help those designing interventions to consider the range of contexts that may be affecting the parent-child relationship.

The Developmental Perspective: An Emphasis on Life Transitions. The six-domain model in Figure 1.4 is like a photograph that freezes a moment in time. In reality, family members are always in the process of development so that the system is always in the process of change. It is no surprise that nonnormative, highly catastrophic and unexpected transitions such as the death of a parent, serious physical or mental illness, and natural disasters elevate the risks for family disruption, distress, and dysfunction (Caplan, 1964). We know now from longitudinal studies that marital dissolution, especially continued conflict between the parents, disrupts the quality of the parent-child relationships and the children's adaptation for an average of two years (Hetherington et al., 1982). What has proved surprising to both researchers and parents is that normative, expectable, positive life transitions such as becoming a family, starting school, or changing jobs can also elevate the risk for individual distress and family conflict over the same period of time.

More than 30 years ago, during the rise of community psychology and community psychiatry, Caplan (1964) suggested that normative transitions were ideal times to provide preventive interventions for families—to work with their current vulnerabilities in the hope of warding off subsequent crisis and psychopathology. Given the assumption of most interaction theories of development that disequilibrium is *necessary* for growth to occur, Caplan's proposal places interveners on the side of helping parents and children to take advantage of the natural growth-inducing properties and challenges of what could otherwise be seen as threatening life changes or crises. It is an idea whose time has come.

The Contribution of Intervention Programs and Evaluations to Parenting Theories

We have focused primarily on how parenting theories can contribute to the development and focus of parenting interventions. Here, we consider briefly what intervention programs and evaluation research have to offer parenting theories. First, we have cited substantial evidence to show that when parents participate in intervention programs, their children's behavior often changes in a positive direction. This result poses no problem for bidirectional interaction theories of parenting: any intervention that alters one participant's behavior in a mutual regulation system ought to result in changes in the other participant's reactions.

Second, recent research on the effects of parenting programs provides support for complex, contextual, systemic theories of parenting effects. The development of multidomain interventions was stimulated in part by the limited success of some single-theory, single-locus interventions. If comprehensive programs are found to have value-added effects, especially in high-risk populations, contextual theories of parenting will have received substantial support.

Third, and perhaps most important for the field of developmental psychopathology, intervention studies go beyond correlational risk studies in informing us about mechanisms of change. The correlational models we have presented imply that marital conflict spills over into parent-child relationships, suggesting that marital relationships are driving the family system. The preliminary results of the Schoolchildren and Their Families Project Intervention (Cowan & Cowan, in press) suggest that, at least in some contexts, coparenting influences marital quality more than the other way around. Only intervention studies can test hypotheses about the direction of effects when one domain of the family system changes.

Future Directions for Parenting Intervention Research

The Need for More Systematic Program Evaluations

A decade ago, a number of reviewers of parenting intervention studies reached the disappointing conclusion (Dembo, Sweitzer & Lauritzen, 1985; Levant, 1988; Powell, 1988) that research results are confusing and fail to demonstrate support for the effectiveness of parenting interventions. These reviewers asserted that to overcome design and measurement flaws in existing studies, intervention studies require a number of things: samples larger than 10 to 15 families; inclusion of fathers as well as mothers; inclusion of no-treatment or alternative treatment controls; random assignment to experimental conditions; and multimeasure, multimethod assessments that include parent self-reports, parents' reports about children, observations of parents' behavior, and independent assessments by both teachers and researchers of outcomes such as children's cognitive and social competence and behavior problems. Based on the newest research, we would add that data from the children's perspective—about themselves, their family relationships, their relationships with peers, and their academic successes and failures—will broaden the scope of our understanding about how best to help children and their parents. Recent reviews of the literature failed to find more than a handful of studies that include more than one or two of these desiderata (for exceptions see Olds, Kitzman, & Cole, 1995; Webster-Stratton, 1992). Even behaviorally oriented interventions that emphasize empirical evaluations often provide surprisingly limited information from small samples of families, with the result that the findings have questionable generalizability (see Patterson et al., 1993).

Evaluation challenges become acute when methods well suited to a research laboratory are transferred to investigations of community-based programs. For these reasons, experimental designs have rarely been used to examine the effects of parenting interventions. Particularly in field studies, random assignment of families to treatment and control group conditions has typically been deemed unworkable on ethical, political, or logistical grounds. Despite these problems, experimental designs have been employed in studies of a few large-scale, long-term parenting interventions (e.g., Andrews et al., 1982; Klaus & Gray, 1968), and treatment-partitioning designs that randomly assign parents to interventions of differing focus or intensity have been recommended increasingly (e.g., Seitz, 1987) as viable alternatives to true experimental design (e.g., Olds, Henderson, Tatelbaum, & Chamberlin, 1986).

A Partial List of Unanswered Research Questions

Is Work with Parents Essential to Affecting Children's Outcomes? A lingering question in all types of parenting intervention programs described here is whether direct work with parents is *essential* to improving children's outcomes. Because the ultimate goal of most parenting interventions focuses on children, the anticipated or actual benefits tend to be weighed in relation to primary or exclusive direct work with the child. Accordingly, parenting interventions are considered an alternative to direct intervention with the child or a value-added component that boosts and/or sustains the results of direct work with the child.

One impediment to answering the value-added question is that changes in the child may trigger changes in the parent, rather than the other way around (Lazar, 1983). In the early childhood intervention field, Bronfenbrenner's (1974) influential conclusion that parent participation and family support were key features of effective programs was derived empirically from several small-scale studies (e.g., Radin, 1972). Few experimental studies have compared the benefits of child- versus parent-focused work, or examined different combinations of parent- and child-focused interventions.

What Is the Role of Parents' and Children's Gender in Parenting Intervention Programs? Many interveners focus on mothers as primary caretakers and ignore essential gender inequalities in the structure and process of family interaction (Chodorow, 1989; Mason, 1988). Feminist family therapists (e.g., McGoldrick et al., 1989; Walters, Carter, Papp, & Silverstein, 1988) have taken the family therapy establishment to task for ignoring these inequalities in the course of family therapy and for forgetting that communication is often qualitatively different in nature and impact from wives to husbands than from husbands to wives (Ball, Cowan, & Cowan, 1995). To direct an intervention to "parents" without recognizing the politics and psychology of gender in family roles is to disregard an issue that may affect the intervention results. The effect of gender issues between husbands and wives on the process and outcome of parenting interventions is an important topic for further investigation.

In child development and family studies, it is frequently the case that differences between mothers and fathers are evaluated, as are differences between boys and girls, but little attention is given to the possibility that the links between risks and outcomes are different for mothers and daughters, mothers and sons, fathers and daughters, and fathers and sons. The existence and extent of gendered parent-child relationships has been hotly debated (e.g., Block, 1984; Maccoby & Jacklin, 1974), but Parke and Tinsley (1987) provide extensive evidence that fathers, especially, tend to treat sons and daughters differently. One possible reason for conflicting viewpoints and findings in research on gender effects in family interaction may be that gender differences in parenting are heightened under some family circumstances and not others. For example, Kerig, Cowan, and Cowan (1993) found that the slight tendency of parents of 3.5-year-old sons to be more positive toward their children than parents of 3.5-year-old daughters was a function of the level of conflict in the marriage. When their marriage had low levels of conflict, parents of sons treated their children similarly to parents of daughters. By contrast, parents in high-conflict marriages treated daughters much more harshly, especially maritally dissatisfied fathers.

Virtually all parenting intervention programs we have read about have been "gender neutral"—intervening with only male or female children, or not making distinctions between them. Reports of parenting intervention programs do not report outcomes separately for girls and boys. The question of whether gender pairing of parent and child makes a difference in these interventions is an empirical one; at this point, we have no answers.

What Are the Mechanisms of Change in Parenting Interventions? In the past few years, a number of researchers studying parent training have realized that the finding of mean differences between intervention and control groups on various child outcome measures does not in itself constitute proof of the intervention's effectiveness. It is necessary to show that interventions targeted to changing parents' behavior actually do so, and that when these behaviors change in the desired direction, children's behavior improves. Such internal analysis of correlation patterns *within* the intervention group will provide information about parenting mechanisms that is necessary to theories of parenting effects. We have a few excellent qualitative descriptions of the processes involved in interventions (e.g., Webster-Stratton & Herbert, 1993), but very little systematic process research, and almost no information about which specific aspects in parenting interventions produce particular outcomes in parents and children.

Research most closely relevant to the process-outcome issue can be found in "module" studies that compare, for example, parenting interventions with parenting plus maritally focused interventions (Dadds, Schwartz, & Sanders, 1987) and conclude that the intervention enhancement produces stronger positive effects. We also need studies of intervener-client interactions and group process interactions that are associated with specific positive and negative outcomes. These investigations will begin to identify the active ingredients of intervention programs that are essential to the planning of new, more effective parenting interventions.

What Is the Most Effective Parenting Intervention for a Specific Family? In their zeal to demonstrate the success of intervention programs, researchers tend to focus on the analysis of mean differences between intervention participants and controls, and to ignore the fact that a substantial number of intervention participants reap no benefits. As we have illustrated with the work of Webster-Stratton (1992) and Patterson (Patterson et al., 1993), some investigators have begun to examine the characteristics of individuals or families who change in positive ways after participating in intervention programs. A careful and systematic delineation in every intervention study of who is likely to benefit most could reveal a more differentiated picture of how to match interventions and prospective participants more effectively. Such matching would result in more cost-effective programs by providing greater benefits for larger numbers of parents.

If it is true that some participants show benefits and others fail to change, is it possible that some parenting interventions may leave some parents and children in more distress than before? To put the question in more blunt terms, can parenting interventions result in harm? We know of no published studies that examine this question. Program evaluators must move beyond analysis of group trends to identify participants who may be at risk for increased distress as a result of participating in an intervention.

How Long Do Intervention Effects Last? We have been struck by a curious phenomenon. The general expectation appears to be that intervention effects will be most visible immediately after the intervention and then will "decay" over time. A number of investigators find, however, that the positive effects of the intervention are stronger over time, sometimes more than a year or two after the intervention ended (Cowan et al., 1995; Markman, Renick, Floyd, & Stanley, 1993; Olds, Kitzman, & Cole, 1995). These "sleeper" effects can be explained by organismic developmental theories such as Piaget's (1967) or Werner's (1948). An intervention may stimulate initial disequilibrations of organized behavior systems, which may result in disorganization in the short run but reorganization at a new structural level in the long run (Langer, 1969). During and shortly after a parenting intervention, parents may be confused and uncertain, which leads them to attempt several new approaches without evaluating them systematically. Over time, as they struggle with new ideas and patterns and become aware of what works and what doesn't, they begin to evolve more effective parenting strategies. There are no guidelines that we are aware of to identify how long this reorganization can be expected to take. Until we have more informative data about this phenomenon, evaluations of programs, whenever possible, should continue over time until the change trajectory has been thoroughly examined.

Just as the concept of crisis has a double meaning of "danger" and "opportunity," so does the fact that there are many as yet unanswered questions in the field of parenting intervention research. On the one hand, we are left with the impression that too much of what is offered in the way of help for parents has not been subject to even the most cursory evaluation. On the other, we are excited about the challenging research opportunities for those who design and evaluate parenting interventions during the next decade.

VALUE ISSUES AND POLICY IMPLICATIONS

Discussions of parenting and the family context of children's adaptation inevitably raise issues of values. In this final section of the chapter we discuss three different but interrelated value issues: the values underlying our descriptions of better and worse intervention outcomes; ethical considerations in conducting parenting intervention research; and the values underlying policy decisions about the allocation of resources to support parenting intervention services.

Value Perspectives in Defining Positive Intervention Outcomes

All interventions impose an authoritative conception of "the good, the desirable, and the healthy" (Sigel, 1983, p. 8), and programs to change or support parents' and children's ideas and behaviors are no exception to this general principle.

Children's Outcomes

Throughout the chapter, we have followed accepted practice of defining "good" outcomes for the child as intellectual competence, some degree of emotional regulation, and "getting along" with peers—a child who is neither too withdrawn nor too aggressive. It should be obvious that while many families would agree on these general outcomes as positive, there is much less agreement on the details. It is good to encourage intellectual competence, but it is not clear within the academic community how intellectual competence should be defined and measured (Sternberg, 1995). There is wide variation within families in defining what is an acceptable level of intellectual competence in the child (are C and B grades tolerated, or will only As be acceptable?). There is even less agreement on what constitutes an optimal level of social engagement and aggression. Should a child who spends hours by himself in solitary play or a child who never fights back when she is pushed be labeled as troubled? The answer depends in part not only on statistical and cultural norms but also on parents' and observers' values about what behavior is desirable. Evaluations of parenting programs necessarily contain adult-determined values about what it is the programs are designed to encourage or discourage.

Effective Parenting

Concepts of goodness in relation to parenting undergo special scrutiny due to a deeply held American view of families as autonomous units that are free to establish their own values and norms of conduct, within broad boundaries. To complicate matters further, the definition of effective parenting is embedded in sets of conflicting cultural values. Varied ideas about parenting based on political outlook, social class, ethnic group membership, and geographic location pervade modern society. Is spanking a child sometimes justified? Is affectionate touching between adolescents and parents advisable? Should children be obedient or autonomous, and at what ages? At what age is a child too old to sleep in a parent's bed? It is possible to develop programs that allow parents to find their own way on each of these issues, but whether programs receive government or private support may depend the funders' views about the values espoused in the intervention.

The move by psychology and other health and mental health disciplines from a primary focus on Caucasian middle-class populations to study and work with families from various ethnic, racial, and sexual minorities has been accompanied by a growing concern about the lack of cultural sensitivity in both research and intervention programs. Early research on diverse populations tended to take an *etic,* comparative approach (Berry, 1969) in which Caucasian middle-class norms were treated as the standard and discrepancies interpreted as deviance and dysfunction (Coll et al., 1995). More recently, there has been advocacy of an *emic* approach, which examines a culture or ethnic group on its own terms, without comparative evaluations. This is difficult to do, especially for researchers who are not members of the group they are studying. We are not advocating the idea that same-race or same-sex observers must be used in gathering and interpreting data from parenting interventions. Same-group membership can lead to blind spots as well as to increased understanding and tolerance. What we are emphasizing here is the idea that the standards defining intervention program success are heavily influenced by the values of those who offer the interventions and conduct the research.

Ethical Considerations in Parenting Interventions

Ethical problems in designing and offering parenting interventions have received sporadic attention from professionals. The most recent focus on ethics in the parenting intervention literature took the form of cautionary responses to the widespread interest in parenting programs of the 1970s. The cautions seemed to reflect a growing concern about the imposition of institutional agendas on families (Lasch, 1977).

Intervener-Client Relationships

Of the myriad ethical issues, the greatest attention appears to have been paid to the implications of the presumed superiority of the interventionist in defining parents' needs, prescribing and providing solutions, and evaluating the efficacy of the intervention. In this model of professional or program roles, the helper is assumed to be more resourceful than the helpee, and the flow of influence is unidirectional, from professional to client (Tyler, Pargament, & Gatz, 1983). Numerous criticisms of this orientation have appeared in the parenting intervention literature. It has been suggested, for instance, that a dominant professional role in parent education programs and child-rearing advice literature can convey a mistrust of the family, undermine parents' sense of confidence, create dependence on external resources, and diminish the authority of the family (Hess, 1980, p. 155). Further, competent parenting is difficult to define in a pluralistic society, and parent education may "melt away sociocultural diversity" by imposing the dominant culture's standards of parenting on others (Laosa, 1983, p. 337). Parents' values may be in conflict with the individually held values of the professional or program staff as well as with the philosophical base of research findings promoted in the intervention (Sigel, 1983), and this problem is intensified when participation in interventions is mandatory, imposed by the juvenile justice system or by family courts as a condition of child custody arrangements.

The Gap between Parenting Interventions and Evaluation Research

As we have pointed out, the correlational design of most empirical investigations of parent-child relations places severe restrictions on justifying particular parenting practices on the basis of research. Even when we find correlations between parent behavior and child outcome, the level of association is generally low and may not be helpful in diagnosis or in designing an appropriate parenting intervention strategy. Ethical problems arise when child-rearing information or advice transcends the limits of the research or clinical base. Interventions that overstate the power of parental or familial influences on the child have been criticized for contributing to parents' unrealistic understanding of their power over the child and for potential negative consequences when parents are unable to fulfill their goals for the child. Parenting interventions have been criticized for elevating parents' contributions to their children's problems or well-being inappropriately, and for not paying attention to nonparental influences on a child's functioning (Schlossman, 1976), including characteristics of the child (Lamb, 1980).

A related ethical concern pertains to the validity of implicit or explicit messages about the effectiveness of a particular parenting intervention. Overzealous communications about a program's effectiveness that are based on weak or limited evidence may prompt parents to develop simplistic expectations about the likelihood or ease with which a situation can be changed. Titles of many popular magazine articles and books on child problems are illustrative of this tendency (e.g., Ten Steps to . . . ; Eight Weeks to . . .). The implicit messages are three-fold: expert knowledge and techniques for dealing with children are available; parents can acquire these skills rapidly; and, if the intervention is not successful, it is the parents' fault (Hess, 1980). A variant of this general problem occurs when an intervention imposes a method (open-ended peer-group discussion) on a population whose cultural traditions emphasize a different means of learning (e.g., lecture by an authority; Powell, Zambrana, & Silva-Palacios, 1990).

Beyond the issue of exaggerated claims for parenting intervention lies the more common and serious ethical issues involved when no claims for validity are asserted because no evidence is available. Dilemmas can be seen at a number of levels. Should a parenting expert offer help to parents who need it even if the recommended course of action has not been validated, or should the expert rely on experience to supplement the rather thin body of parenting program evaluation research? In the absence of definitive information, how much training is necessary for a parenting intervener? Should government or business sponsor parenting interventions or wait until at least pilot programs have demonstrated their effectiveness? All of these questions, like many ethical and political questions in the current debate about the use of societal resources, involve tensions between meeting immediate needs now with available techniques, and meeting needs later with services that may reach a much higher level of effectiveness. These issues raise pragmatic questions of how to allocate resources (see below). Here we are raising the ethical issues involved in offering services without adequate evaluations of the "product."

Implementation

Ethical considerations are involved in the subtle matter of how an intervention is implemented. Does the structure of the intervention accommodate early terminations? Are friendly exit opportunities built into the program, or does early departure carry a stigma? How do staff accommodate a parent's needs in an intervention where the goodness of fit is problematic? What safeguards exist to prevent manipulations of a parent's goals, excessive pressure to alter behavior, and demands for information that the parent may deem to be private (Sigel, 1983)?

Implications for Social Policy

Despite frequent references to "family values" during national, state, and local elections during the 1990s in the United States (Lakoff, 1996), very little in the way of a coherent family policy has been enunciated by governmental bodies controlled by either of the major political parties. To be sure, governments pass laws, make regulations, and create programs that have profound effects on citizens and implications for their quality of family life. For example, some laws and regulations have the effect of defining families (who is considered a legitimate parent), regulating family structure (through marriage, divorce, and adoption laws), and defining family responsibilities (child support laws). Along with laws and regulations in the workplace (e.g., family leave policies), financial and social service programs such as welfare and child care attempt to encourage or discourage a number of family-related decisions.

Nevertheless, compared with most industrialized countries, the United States has devoted little attention to creating policies that are actively supportive of family life quality for parents or children (Kagan & Weissbourd, 1994). Unlike Germany, France, and the Scandinavian countries, the United States has no overall system of paid family leave, no widespread assistance for quality child care, very little support outside the welfare system for single mothers, and no family allowances—programs widely accepted in other industrialized countries but still controversial in the United States. These omissions are not accidental. They stem in part from a philosophy of individualism and self-reliance (Bellah, Madsen, Sullivan, Swidler, & Tipton, 1985), evident in the current increasing pressure to keep government "out" of the business of supporting, and thereby regulating, family life. This attitude is expressed by many lawmakers, politicians, and members of the general public, all of whom are also concerned about the widespread perception that family life quality is declining and that increasing numbers are experiencing financial and psychological distress (Lakoff, 1996).

The Multiplicity of Family Forms

Policy involves making moral and financial choices among competing alternatives. Family policies and programs have been slow to adapt to the reality that "traditional" nuclear families with fathers as breadwinners and mothers as full-time homemakers are in the minority. This reluctance appears to stem, in part, from a fear that support for "alternative" forms of parenting, such as single parenthood or lesbian and gay parenthood, would imply approval of a departure from traditional family forms. The problem here is that when voters and politicians express reluctance to enact laws or allocate resources to provide support for children in *all* families, they effectively deny help to millions of young children who have not been party to the lifestyle decisions of their parents.

Poverty and Families

Effort devoted to parenting interventions, especially for families at high risk by virtue of their economic circumstances, may have the unintended consequence of blaming the victims for their difficulties. It is certainly the case that economic forces, neighborhood circumstances, societal pressures, and discrimination will not be affected by interventions that focus on family relationships and ignore living conditions. It seems to us that policy choices must involve a balanced emphasis on social and economic context factors as well as on raising the level of parenting effectiveness.

Resource Dilemmas

We have noted the discrepancy between the need for support services for children, youth, and families and the services available for families in distress (Saxe et al., 1988; Snowden, 1982). An even smaller proportion of so-called low-risk families have access to formal parenting programs. While the "obvious" conclusion is that more services are needed for families with children, we recognize that this is not an auspicious time to recommend additional services. Nevertheless, the results of longitudinal studies of low- to moderate-risk families, along with data from interventions with parents all along the continuum of risk, suggest that without intervention, the problems and vulnerabilities of new parents will spill over into other relationships in the family. Longitudinal data make it clear that this will place many young children at greater risk for compromised academic, social, and emotional development during their elementary and high school years.

Results from new, systematically evaluated interventions suggest that some of these problems can be addressed and modified in ways that affect the parents' relationships with their children and reduce the liability of children developing academic, emotional, and social problems. When there is no support from government or business for such assistance, parents are virtually on their own to address the competing needs of their children, their marriage, and their family responsibilities. The ideal of the completely self-sufficient family provider, while ideologically attractive to many Americans, is not an attainable goal for large numbers of men and women. Gershenson (1993) notes with sorrow the decline in the quality of human services in the face of demonstrated ability to provide effective interventions. In our view, a serious concern about the preservation of strong family relationships would lead to the allocation of resources for programs to strengthen families all along the risk continuum.

The policy dilemma that we cannot settle here is how to divide limited resources among programs designed to alleviate current distress and interventions designed to prevent or reduce the severity of future distress. To some extent, the issue raises empirical questions to which we do not yet have adequate answers: How effective will the preventive intervention be, and will the costs of prevention *now* result in savings in the future? Our perception is that recent decisions by government and funding agencies have leaned heavily in the direction of treating individuals and families already in difficulty. We propose a reconsideration of the balance to fully explore the longer-term impact on family functioning of preventive programs for parents.

CONCLUSIONS

We see a number of discrepancies between the literature on family research and parenting interventions and discussions of social policy regarding the allocation of resources for families. Two of these discrepancies warrant comment here. First, a growing body of findings from family research indicates that many millions of children are experiencing cognitive, social, and mental health difficulties that compromise their healthy development. Without intervention, many will suffer serious health and mental health consequences as they make their way through adolescence and young adulthood. The results of intervention studies show that some of these difficulties could be reduced or alleviated with the help of programs for their parents and other family members. The dilemma is that research evidence points to the need for more well-designed intervention services for parents at a time when political forces are pushing for reductions in social programs.

Second, there is a discrepancy between the academic formulation of the field of parenting interventions and the level of discourse with which family support issues are discussed. We have attempted to illustrate the complexity of understanding the links between parents' behavior and children's developmental outcomes. Parenting itself must be viewed in the broader context of the family, neighborhood, and societal contexts in which parents and children live their daily lives. Even when interventions are successful, they are not successful for every family, and positive effects are not maintained indefinitely over time. What may work best for specific populations of children and their families is comprehensive interventions that address the particular risks in their family environments. But policymakers are looking for more straightforward, less complex solutions.

Policy discussions of specific issues are often phrased in terms of dichotomous alternatives: "We should/should not support this program." Decisions made on the basis of program cost rarely take into account the financial, emotional, psychological, and societal costs of *not* intervening. We cannot guarantee that government support of parenting programs will inevitably produce the desired results for children, but we urge that discussions of family policy, particularly support for parenting, be more differentiated than they are at present.

We are at a point now that resembles the situation in the 1950s, before space travel began: the technology had become available to explore the moon and solar system; some could imagine the long-term benefits of such a program, but comprehensive programs had not yet been mounted. How do particular problems rise to the top of the public agenda? Glazer (1994) believes that a key element has to do with whether or to what extent there is a clear course of action toward an effective solution for the problem, and that only those issues with clear solutions move forward. We are suggesting that we have the ability to identify families and children who are at risk for serious academic, social, and emotional difficulties, and that with adequate commitments of resources, services could be designed that would begin to address a significant proportion of these family problems. It is clear that many parents need more assistance than is currently available. The question is whether we as a society are willing to devote energy and resources toward the creation of comprehensive programs for families all along the continuum from low risk to high distress.

ACKNOWLEDGMENTS

The authors would like to thank the editors of this volume and a number of additional readers for their helpful and stimulating comments on an earlier draft of this chapter: Ann McGillicuddy-DeLisi, Jennifer Ablow, Jeffrey Measelle, Stephen P. Hinshaw, and Vanessa Kahen Johnson.

REFERENCES

Ablow, J. (1994). *Young children's perceptions and processing of interparental conflict: Predicting behavioral adjustment.* Unpublished master's thesis, University of California, Berkeley.

Ablow, J., & Measelle, J. (1993). *The Berkeley Puppet Interview.* Unpublished instrument, University of California, Berkeley.

Adler, A. (1927). *Understanding human nature.* New York: Greenberg.

Ainsworth, M. D. S., & Wittig, B. A. (1969). Attachment and exploratory behavior of one-year-olds in a strange situation. In B. M. Foss (Ed.), *Determinants of infant behavior* (Vol. 4, pp. 113–136). London: Methuen.

Alexander, K. L., & Entwisle, D. (1988). Achievement in the first 2 years of school: Patterns and processes. *Monographs of the Society for Research in Child Development, 53*(2, Serial No. 218).

Amato, P. R., & Keith, B. (1991). Parental divorce and the well-being of children: A meta-analysis. *Psychological Bulletin, 110,* 26–46.

Andreasen, N. C., Swayze, V. W., & Flaum, M. (1990). Ventricular enlargement in schizophrenia evaluated with computed topographic scanning: Effects of gender, age, and stage of illness. *Archives of General Psychiatry, 47,* 1008–1015.

Andrews, S. R., Blumenthal, J. B., Johnson, D. L., Kahn, A. J., Ferguson, C. J., Lasater, R. M., Malone, P. E., & Wallace, D. B. (1982). The skills of mothering: A study of Parent Child Development Centers. *Monographs of the Society for Research in Child Development, 47*(6, Serial No. 198).

Aries, P. (1962). *Centuries of childhood: A social history of family life.* New York: Random House.

Arnold, D. S., & Whitehurst, G. J. (1994). Accelerating language development through picture book reading: A summary of dialogic reading and its effects. In D. K. Dickinson (Ed.), *Bridges to literacy: Children, families and schools* (pp. 103–128). Cambridge, England: Blackwell.

Asher, S., & Coie, J. D. (Eds.). (1990). *Peer rejection in childhood.* Cambridge, England: Cambridge University Press.

Auerbach, A. A. (1968). *Parents learn through discussion: Principles and practices of parent group education.* New York: Wiley.

Axline, V. (1964). *Dibs: In search of self: Personality development in play therapy.* Boston: Houghton Mifflin.

Ball, F. L. J., Cowan, P. A., & Cowan, C. P. (1995). Who's got the power? Gender differences in partners' perceptions of influence during marital problem-solving discussions. *Family Process, 34,* 303–322.

Bandura, A., & Walters, R. (1963). *Social learning and personality development.* New York: Holt, Rinehart and Winston.

Bank, L., Marlowe, J. H., Reid, J. B., Patterson, G. R., & Weinrott, M. R. (1991). A comparative evaluation of parent-training interventions for families of chronic delinquents. *Journal of Abnormal Child Psychology, 19*(1), 15–33.

Bank, L., Patterson, G. R., & Reid, J. B. (1996). Negative sibling interaction patterns as predictors of later adjustment problems in adolescent and young adult males. In G. H. Brody (Ed.), *Sibling relationships: Their causes and consequences. Advances in applied developmental psychology: Vol. 10.* Norwood NJ: ABLEX.

Barkley, R. A. (1990). *Attention Deficit Hyperactivity Disorder: A handbook for diagnosis and treatment.* New York: Guilford Press.

Barnard, K., Morisset, C., & Spieker, S. (1993). Preventive interventions: Enhancing parent-infant relationships. In C. H. Zeanah (Ed.), *Handbook of infant mental health* (pp. 386–401). New York: Guilford Press.

Bates, J. E., Pettit, G. S., & Dodge, K. A. (1995). Family and child factors in stability and change in children's aggressiveness in elementary school. In J. McCord (Ed.), *Coercion and punishment in long-term perspectives* (pp. 124–138). New York: Cambridge University Press.

Baumrind, D. (1972). An exploratory study of socialization effects on Black children: Some Black-White comparisons. *Child Development, 43,* 262–267.

Baumrind, D. (1991). Effective parenting during the early adolescent transition. In P. A. Cowan & M. E. Hetherington (Eds.), *Family transitions: Advances in family research* (Vol. 2, pp. 111–164). Hillsdale, NJ: Erlbaum.

Bellah, R. N., Madsen, R., Sullivan, W. M., Swidler, A., & Tipton, S. M. (1985). *Habits of the heart: Individualism and commitment in American life.* Berkeley: University of California Press.

Belsky, J. (1984). The determinants of parenting: A process model. *Child Development, 55,* 83–96.

Belsky, J., & Kelly, J. (1994). *Transition to parenthood.* New York: Delacorte Press.

Belsky, J., & Pensky, L. (1988). Marital change across the transition to parenthood. *Marriage and Family Review, 12,* 133–156.

Bennet, W. J. (1992). *The devaluing of America: The fight for our culture and our children.* New York: Simon & Schuster.

Berry, J. W. (1969). On cross-cultural comparability. *International Journal of Psychology, 4,* 119–128.

Blankenhorn, D., Bayme, S., & Elshtain, J. B. (Eds.). (1990). *Rebuilding the nest: A new commitment to the American family.* Milwaukee, WI: Family Service America.

Blechman, E. (1991). Effective communication: Enabling multiproblem families to change. In P. A. Cowan & E. M. Hetherington (Eds.), *Family transitions: Advances in family research* (pp. 3–30). Hillsdale, NJ: Erlbaum.

Block, J. H. (1984). *Sex role identity and ego development.* San Francisco: Jossey-Bass.

Bondar, V. (1995). *Marital discord, differential treatment of siblings, and sibling relationship quality.* Unpublished honor's thesis, University of California, Berkeley.

Booth, C. L., Mitchell, S. K., Barnard, K. E., & Spieker, S. J. (1989). Development of maternal skills in multiproblem families: Effects on the mother-child relationship. *Developmental Psychology, 25,* 403–412.

Bornstein, M. H. (1995a). Introduction to handbook of parenting. In M. Bornstein (Ed.), *Handbook of parenting* (Vol. 1, pp. xxiii-xxiv). Hillsdale, NJ: Erlbaum.

Bornstein, M. H. (1995b). Parenting infants. In M. H. Bornstein (Ed.), *Handbook of parenting* (Vol. 1, pp. 3–39). Hillsdale, NJ: Erlbaum.

Bowlby, J. (1980). *Attachment and loss: Vol. 3. Loss, sadness and depression.* New York: Basic Books.

Boxer, C. C. (1996). *The family context of infant temperament in predicting children's behavioral difficulties in kindergarten.* Unpublished doctoral dissertation, The Wright Institute, Berkeley, CA.

Brazelton, T. B. (1969). *Infants and mothers: Differences in development.* New York: Delacorte Press.

Brazelton, T. B. (1992). *Touchpoints: Your child's emotional and behavioral development.* Reading, MA: Addison-Wesley.

Bridgeman, B., Blumenthal, J., & Andrews, S. (1981). *Parent Child Development Center: Final evaluation report.* Princeton, NJ: Educational Testing Service.

Brim, O. G. (1959). *Education for child rearing.* New York: Russell-Sage Foundation.

Bristol, M. M., Gallagher, J. J., & Holt, K. D. (1993). Maternal depressive symptoms in autism: Response to psychoeducational intervention. *Rehabilitation Psychology, 38,* 3–10.

Broderick, C. B. (1993). *Understanding family processes: Basics of family systems theory.* Newbury Park, CA: Sage.

Bronfenbrenner, U. (1974). *Is early intervention effective? A report on longitudinal evaluations of preschool programs* (Vol. 2). Washington, DC: Department of Health, Education and Welfare, Office of Child Development.

Bronfenbrenner, U. (1979). *The ecology of human development: Experiments by nature and design.* Cambridge, MA: Harvard University Press.

Bronstein, P., & Cowan, C. P. (Eds.). (1988). *Fatherhood today: Men's changing role in the family.* New York: Wiley.

Brunk, M. A., Henggeler, S. W., & Whelan, J. P. (1987). A comparison of multisystemic therapy and parent training in the brief treatment of child abuse and neglect. *Journal of Consulting and Clinical Psychology, 55,* 171–178.

Bryant, B. (1985). The neighborhood walk: Sources of support in middle childhood. *Monographs of the Society for Research in Child Development, 50*(3, Serial No. 210).

Burgoyne, K., Hawkins, D., & Catalano, R. (1991). *How to help your child succeed in school.* Seattle, WA: Developmental Research and Programs.

Burke, B. M., & Kolker, A. (1994). Directiveness in parental genetic counseling. *Women and Health, 22,* 31–53.

Burman, B., & Erel, O. (1993, March). *The linkage between marital quality and the parent-child relationship: A meta-analysis.* Paper presented at the meeting of the Society for Research in Child Development, New Orleans, LA.

Burns, A., & Scott, C. (1994). *Mother-headed families and why they have increased.* Hillsdale, NJ: Erlbaum.

Campbell, F. A., & Ramey, C. T. (1994). Effects of early intervention on intellectual achievement: A follow-up study of children from low-income families. Children and poverty [Special issue]. *Child Development, 65,* 684–698.

Caplan, G. (1964). *Principles of preventive psychiatry.* New York: Basic Books.

Carmichael, L. (1954). *Manual of child psychology* (2nd ed.). New York: Wiley.

Chao, R. K. (1994). Beyond parental control and authoritarian parenting style: Understanding Chinese parenting through the cultural notion of training. *Child Development, 65,* 1111–1119.

Chao, R. K., & Sue, S. (in press). Chinese parental influence and their children's school success: A paradox in the literature on parenting styles. In S. Lau (Ed.), *Youth and child development in Chinese societies.* Hong Kong: Chinese University Press.

Chase-Lansdale, P. L., Brooks-Gunn, J., & Zamsky, E. S. (1994). Young African-American multigenerational families in poverty: Quality of mothering and grandmothering. Children and poverty [Special issue]. *Child Development, 65,* 373–393.

Chess, S., & Thomas, A. (1986). *Temperament in clinical practice.* New York: Guilford Press.

Chess, S., & Thomas, A. (1987). *Know your child: An authoritative guide for today's parents.* New York: Basic Books.

Children's Defense Fund. (1984). *American children in poverty.* Washington, DC: Children's Defense Fund.

Chilman, C. S. (1973). Programs for disadvantaged parents. In B. M. Caldwell & H. N. Ricciuti (Eds.), *Review of child development research* (Vol. 3, pp. 403–465). Chicago: University of Chicago Press.

Chodorow, N. (1989). *Feminism and psychoanalytic theory.* New Haven, CT: Yale University Press.

Christensen, O. C., & Thomas, C. R. (1980). Dreikurs and the search for equality. In M. J. Fine (Ed.), *Handbook on parent education* (pp. 53–74). New York: Academic Press.

Cicchetti, D., & Cohen, D. J. (Eds.). (1995). *Developmental psychopathology: Vol. 1. Theory and methods.* New York: Wiley.

Clarke-Stewart, A. (1977). *Child care in the family.* New York: Academic Press.

Clinton, H. (1996). *It takes a village and other lessons children teach us.* New York: Simon & Schuster.

Cohn, D. A., Cowan, P. A., Cowan, C. P., & Pearson, J. (1992). Mothers' and fathers' working models of childhood attachment relationships, parenting styles, and child behavior. *Development and Psychopathology, 4,* 417–431.

Cohn, D. A., Silver, D. H., Cowan, C. P., Cowan, P. A., & Pearson, J. (1992). Working models of childhood attachment and couple relationships. *Journal of Family Issues, 13,* 432–449.

Coie, J. D. (1996, May). *Effectiveness trials: An initial evaluation of the FAST Track Program.* Paper presented at the Fifth National Conference on Prevention Research, Washington, DC.

Coie, J. D., & Krehbiel, G. (1990). Adapting intervention to the problems of aggressive and disruptive rejected children. In S. R. Asher & J. D. Coie (Eds.), *Peer rejection in childhood* (pp. 309–337). Cambridge, England: Cambridge University Press.

Coie, J. D., Watt, N. F., West, S. G., Hawkins, D., Asarnow, J. R., Markman, H. J., Ramey, S. L., Shure, M. B., & Long, B. (1993). The science of prevention: A conceptual framework and some directions for a national research program. *American Psychologist, 48,* 1013–1022.

Cole, R. E., Kane, C. F., Zastowny, T., Grolnick, W., & Lehman, A. (1993). Expressed emotion, communication, and problem solving in the families of chronic schizophrenic young adults. In R. E. Cole & D. Reiss (Eds.), *How do families cope with chronic illness?* (pp. 141–172). Hillsdale, NJ: Erlbaum.

Coll, C. T. G., Meyer, E. C., & Brillon, L. (1995). Ethnic and minority parenting. In M. H. Bornstein (Ed.), *Handbook of parenting* (Vol. 2, pp. 189–209). Hillsdale, NJ: Erlbaum.

Conduct Problems Prevention Research Group. (1992). A developmental and clinical model for the prevention of conduct disorder: The FAST Track Program. *Development and Psychopathology, 4,* 509–528.

Conger, R. D., Conger, K. J., Elder, G., Lorenz, F., Simmons, R., & Whitbeck, L. (1992). A family process model of economic hardship and adjustment of early adolescent boys. *Child Development, 63,* 526–541.

Conger, R. D., & Elder, G. H., Jr. (Eds.). (1994). *Families in troubled times: Adapting to change in rural America.* New York: Aldine de Gruyter.

Consortium for Longitudinal Studies. (Ed.). (1983). *As the twig is bent: Lasting effects of preschool programs.* Hillsdale, NJ: Erlbaum.

Cowan, C. P., & Cowan, P. A. (1988). Who does what when partners become parents: Implications for men, women, and marriage. *Marriage and Family Review, 13,* 105–132.

Cowan, C. P., & Cowan, P. A. (1992). *When partners become parents: The big life change for couples.* New York: Basic Books.

Cowan, C. P., & Cowan, P. A. (1995). Interventions to ease the transition to parenthood: Why they are needed and what they can do. *Family Relations, 44,* 412–423.

Cowan, C. P., & Cowan, P. A. (1997). New families: Modern couples as new pioneers. In S. Sugarman, M. A. Mason, & A. Skolnick (Eds.), *The evolving American family: New policies for new families.* New York: Oxford University Press.

Cowan, C. P., & Cowan, P. A. (in press). Working with couples during stressful life transitions. In S. Dremen (Ed.), *The family on the threshold of the 21st century: Trends and implications.* Hillsdale, NJ: Erlbaum.

Cowan, C. P., & Heming, G. (1997, April). *A preventive intervention for parents of children entering elementary school.* Poster presented at the meeting of the Society for Research in Child Development, Washington, DC.

Cowan, C. P., Cowan, P. A., Heming, G., Garrett, E., Coysh, W. S., Curtis-Boles, H., & Boles, A. J. (1985). Transitions to parenthood: His, hers, and theirs. *Journal of Family Issues, 6,* 451–481.

Cowan, P. A. (1978). *Piaget: With feeling.* New York: Holt, Rinehart and Winston.

Cowan, P. A. (1988). Developmental psychopathology: A nine-cell map of the territory. In E. Nannis & P. Cowan (Eds.), *Developmental psychopathology and its treatment. New Directions for Child Development* (No. 39, pp. 5–30). San Francisco: Jossey-Bass.

Cowan, P. A. (1991). Individual and family life transitions: A proposal for a new definition. In P. A. Cowan & E. M. Hetherington (Eds.), *Family transitions: Advances in family research* (Vol. 2, pp. 3–30). Hillsdale, NJ: Erlbaum.

Cowan, P. A., Cohn, D. A., Cowan, C. P., & Pearson, J. L. (1996). Parents' attachment histories and children's internalizing and externalizing behavior: Exploring family systems models of linkage. *Journal of Consulting and Clinical Psychology, 64,* 53–63.

Cowan, P. A., Cowan, C. P., & Schulz, M. (1996). Risk and resilience in families. In E. M. Hetherington & E. Blechman (Eds.), *Risk and resilience: Advances in family research* (Vol. 5, pp. 1–38). Hillsdale: NJ. Erlbaum.

Cowan, P. A., Cowan, C. P., Schulz, M., & Heming, G. (1994). Prebirth to preschool family factors predicting children's adaptation to kindergarten. In R. Parke & S. Kellam (Eds.), *Exploring family relationships with other social contexts: Advances in family research* (Vol. 4, pp. 75–114). Hillsdale, NJ: Erlbaum.

Cowan, P. A., & McHale, J. P. (1997). *Family-level dynamics and children's development. New directions.* San Francisco: Jossey-Bass.

Cowen, E. L. (1985). Person-centered approaches to primary prevention in mental health: Situation-focused and competence-enhancement. *American Journal of Community Psychology, 13,* 31–48.

Cox, M. J., Owen, M. T., Lewis, J. M., & Henderson, V. K. (1989). Marriage, adult adjustment, and early parenting. *Child Development, 60,* 1015–1024.

Crick, N. R., & Dodge, K. A. (1994). A review and reformulation of social information-processing mechanisms in children's social adjustment. *Psychological Bulletin, 115,* 74–101.

Crockenberg, S. B. (1981). Infant irritability, mother responsiveness, and social support influences on the security of infant-mother attachment. *Child Development, 52,* 857–865.

Crowell, J., O'Connor, E., Wollmers, G., Sprafkin, J., & Rao, U. (1991). Mothers' conceptualizations of parent-child relationships: Relation to mother-child interaction and child behavior problems. *Development and Psychopathology, 4,* 431–444.

Cummings, E. M., & Davies, P. T. (1994). *Children and marital conflict: The impact of family dispute and resolution.* New York: Guilford Press.

Cutrona, C. E., & Troutman, B. R. (1986). Social support, infant temperament, and parenting self-efficacy: A mediational model of postpartum depression. *Child Development, 57,* 1507–1518.

Dadds, M. R., Sanders, M. R., Behrens, B. C., & James, J. E. (1987). Marital discord and child behavioral problems: A description of family interactions during treatment. *Journal of Clinical Child Psychology, 16,* 192–203.

Dadds, M. R., Schwartz, S., & Sanders, M. R. (1987). Marital discord and treatment outcome in behavioral treatment of child conduct disorders. *Journal of Consulting and Clinical Psychology, 55,* 396–403.

Darling, N., & Steinberg, L. (1993). Parenting style as context: An integrative model. *Psychological Bulletin, 113,* 487–496.

Davis, K. L., Kahn, R. S., Ko, G., & Davidson, M. (1991). Dopamine and schizophrenia: A review and reconceptualization. *American Journal of Psychiatry, 148,* 1474–1486.

Davison, G. C., & Neale, J. M. (1996). *Abnormal psychology* (Rev. 6th ed.). New York: Wiley.

Dembo, M., Sweitzer, M., & Lauritzen, P. (1985). An evaluation of group parent education: Behavioral, PET, and Adlerian programs. *Review of Educational Research, 55,* 155–200.

Dinkmeyer, D., & McKay, G. (1976). *Systematic training for effective parenting (STEP): Parent's handbook.* Circle Pines, MN: American Guidance Service.

Dishion, T. J., Duncan, T. E., Eddy, J. M., & Fagot, B. (1994). The world of parents and peers: Coercive exchanges and children's social relationship systems. *Social Development, 3,* 255–268.

Dix, T. (1991). The affective organization of parenting: Adaptive and maladaptive processes. *Psychological Bulletin, 110,* 3–25.

Dodge, K. A. (1996, May). *Psychosocial perspectives on the development of Conduct Disorder.* Paper presented at the fifth National Conference on Prevention Research, Washington, DC.

Dodge, K. A., Pettit, G. S., Bates, J. E., & Valente, E. (1995). Social information-processing patterns partially mediate the effect of early physical abuse on later conduct problems. *Journal of Abnormal Psychology, 104,* 632–643.

Doherty, W. J. (1995). Boundaries between parent and family education and family therapy: The levels of family involvement model. *Family Relations, 44,* 353–358.

Dokecki, P., Hargrove, E., & Sandler, H. (1983). An overview of the Parent Child Development Center social experiment. In R. Haskins & D. Adams (Eds.), *Parent education and public policy* (pp. 80–111). Norwood, NJ: ABLEX.

Dreikurs, R., & Stoltz, V. (1964). *Children: The challenge.* New York: Meredith Press.

Duncan, R. M. (1995). Piaget and Vygotsky revisited: Dialogue or assimilation. *Developmental Review, 15,* 458–472.

Dunn, J. (1995). *From one child to two.* New York: Fawcett Columbine.

Dunn, J., & Kendrick, C. (1982). Social behavior of young siblings in the family context: Differences between same-sex and different-sex dyads. *Annual Progress in Child Psychiatry and Child Development,* 166–181.

Dunn, J., & Plomin, R. (1990). *Separate lives: Why siblings are so different.* New York: Basic Books.

Egeland, B., & Erickson, M. (1993). Implications of attachment theory for prevention and intervention. In H. Parens &

S. Kramer (Eds.), *Prevention in mental health: Now, tomorrow, ever?* (pp. 23–50). Northvale, NJ: Jason Aronson.

Elder, G. (1991). Family transitions, cycles, and social change. In P. A. Cowan & E. M. Hetherington (Eds.), *Family transitions: Advances in family research* (Vol. 2, pp. 31–58). Hillsdale, NJ: Erlbaum.

Elkind, D. (1994). *Ties that stress: The new family imbalance.* Cambridge, MA: Harvard University Press.

Ellwood, A. (1988). Prove to me MELD makes a difference. In H. B. Weiss & F. H. Jacobs (Eds.), *Evaluating family programs* (pp. 303–313). Hawthorne, NY: Aldine de Gruyter.

Emery, R. E. (1988). *Marriage, divorce, and children's adjustment.* Newbury Park, CA: Sage.

Engfer, A. (1988). The interrelatedness of marriage and the mother-child relationship. In R. A. Hinde & J. Stevenson-Hinde (Eds.), *Relationships within families: Mutual influences* (pp. 104–118). Cambridge, England: Cambridge University Press.

Erel, O., & Burman, B. (1995). Interrelatedness of marital relations and parent-child relations: A meta-analytic review. *Psychological Bulletin, 18,* 108–132.

Erickson, M. F., Korfmacher, J., & Egeland, B. (1994). Attachments past and present: Implications for therapeutic intervention with mother-infant dyads. *Development and Psychology, 4,* 495–507.

Falloon, I. R. H., Boyd, J. L., McGill, C. W., Williamson, M., Razani, J., Moss, H., Gilderman, M., & Simpson, G. M. (1985). Family management in the prevention of morbidity of schizophrenia. *Archives of General Psychiatry, 42,* 887–896.

Fein, G. G., Schwartz, G. G., Jacobs, S. W., & Jacobson, J. L. (1983). Environmental toxins and behavioral development: A new role for psychological research. *American Psychologist, 38,* 1188–1197.

Fonagy, P., & Moran, G. S. (1990). Studies on the efficacy of child psychoanalysis. *Journal of Consulting and Clinical Psychology, 58,* 684–695.

Fonagy, P., Steele, M., Moran, G., & Steele, H. (1993). Measuring the ghost in the nursery: An empirical study of the relation between parents' mental representations of childhood experiences and their infants' security of attachment. *Journal of the American Psychoanalytic Association, 41,* 957–989.

Forehand, R., & King, H. E. (1977). Noncompliant children: Effects of parent training on behavior and attitude change. *Behavior Modification, 1,* 93–108.

Forehand, R., & McMahon, R. J. (1981). *Helping the noncompliant child: A clinician's guide to parent training.* New York: Guilford Press.

Fraiberg, S. (Ed.). (1980). *Clinical studies in infant mental health.* New York: Basic Books.

Freud. A. (1965). *Normality and pathology in childhood.* New York: International Universities Press.

Freud, S. (1938). *The basic writings of Sigmund Freud* (A. A. Brill, Trans.). New York: Modern Library.

Furstenberg, F., Jr., & Harris, K. M. (1993). When fathers matter/why fathers matter: The impact of paternal involvement on the offspring of adolescent mothers. In A. Lawson & D. L. Rhode (Eds.), *The politics of pregnancy: Adolescent sexuality and public policy* (pp. 189–215). New Haven, CT: Yale University Press.

Furukawa, S. (1994). *The diverse living arrangement of children: Summer, 1991* (U.S. Bureau of the Census, Current Population Reports, Series P70, No. 38). Washington DC: U.S. Government Printing Office.

Gable, S., Crnic, K., & Belsky, J. (1994). Coparenting within the family system: Influences on children's development. *Family Relations, 43,* 380–386.

Gamson, B., Hornstein, H., & Borden, B. L. (1989). Adler-Dreikurs parent study group leadership training. In M. J. Fine (Ed.), *Handbook on parent education* (pp. 101–121). New York: Academic Press.

Garmezy, N., Masten, A. S., & Tellegen, A. (1984). The study of stress and competence in children: A building block for developmental psychopathology. *Child Development, 55,* 97–111.

Gershenson, C. (1993). The child well-being conundrum. *Readings, 8*(2), 8–11.

Gesell, A., & Ilg, F. L. (with Learned, J., & Ames, L. B.). (1943). *Infant and child in the culture of today: The guidance of development in home and nursery school.* New York: Harper & Bros.

Gillham, J. E., Reivich, K. J., Jaycox, L. H., & Seligman, M. E. P. (1995). Prevention of depressive symptoms in schoolchildren: Two-year follow-up. *Psychological Science, 6,* 343–351.

Gingrich, N. (1995). *To renew America.* New York: HarperCollins.

Glazer, N. (1994, Spring). How social problems are born. *Public Interest, 115,* 31–44.

Goldstein, M. (1985). Family factors that antedate the onset of schizophrenia and related disorders: The results of a fifteen-year prospective longitudinal study. *Acta Psychiatrica Scandinavia Supplementum, 319,* 7–18.

Gordon, I. J., Guinagh, B., & Jester, R. E. (1977). The Florida Parent Education Infant and Toddler Programs. In M. C. Day & R. K. Parker (Eds.), *The preschool in action: Exploring early childhood programs* (pp. 97–127). Boston: Allyn & Bacon.

Gordon, T. (1980). Parent Effectiveness Training: A preventive program and its effects on families. In M. J. Fine (Ed.), *Handbook on parent education* (pp. 101–121). New York: Academic Press.

Gottesman, I. I. (1991). *Schizophrenia genesis.* New York: Freeman.

Gottlieb, B. H. (Ed.). (1988). *Marshaling social support: Formats, processes, and effects.* Thousand Oaks, CA: Sage.

Griest, D. L., Forehand, R., Rodgers, T., Breiner, J., Furey, W., & Williams, C. (1982). Effects of parent enhancement therapy on the treatment outcome and generalization of a parent training program. *Behaviour Research and Therapy, 20,* 429–436.

Grych, J. F., & Fincham, F. D. (1993). Children's appraisals of marital conflict: Initial investigations of the cognitive-contextual framework. *Child Development, 64,* 215–230.

Guthrie, R. V. (1976). *Even the rat was white: A historical view of psychology.* New York: Harper & Row.

Harper, P. S. (1993). *Practical genetic counseling* (4th ed.). Boston: Butterworth-Heinemann.

Hawkins, A. J., Christiansen, S. L., Sargent, K. P., & Hill, E. J. (1993). Rethinking fathers' involvement in child care: A developmental perspective. Fatherhood [Special issue]. *Journal of Family Issues, 14,* 531–549.

Hayghe, H. (1986, February). Rise in mothers' labor force activity includes those with infant. *Monthly Labor Review,* 43–45.

Heinicke, C. M. (1991). Early family intervention: Focusing on the mother's adaptation-competence and quality of partnership. In D. G. Unger & D. R. Powell (Eds.), *Families as nurturing systems: Support across the life span* (pp. 127–142). Binghamton, NY: Haworth Press.

Heinicke, C. M., Fineman, N., Ruth, G., Recchia, S., & Guthrie, D. (1996). *Relationship-based intervention with at-risk mothers: Outcome in the first year of life.* Unpublished manuscript, University of California, Los Angeles.

Heinicke, C. M., Goorsky, M., Moscov, S., Dudley, K., Gordon, J., Schnieder, C., & Guthrie, D. (1996). *Relationship-based intervention with at-risk mothers: Factors affecting variations in outcome.* Unpublished manuscript, University of California, Los Angeles.

Henggeler, S. W., Schoenwald, S. K., & Pickrel, S. G. (1995). Multisystemic therapy: Bridging the gap between university and community-based treatment. *Journal of Consulting and Clinical Psychology, 63,* 709–717.

Herrnstein, R. J., & Murray, C. (1994). *The bell curve: Intelligence and class structure in American life.* New York: Free Press.

Hess, R. D. (1980). Experts and amateurs: Some unintended consequences of parent education. In M. D. Fantini & Rene Cardenes (Eds.), *Parenting in a multicultural society* (pp. 141–159). New York: Longman.

Hetherington, E. M., & Clingempeel, G. (1992). Coping with marital transitions. *Society for Research in Child Development Monograph, 57*(Nos. 2–3).

Hetherington, E. M., Cox, M. J., & Cox, R. (1982). Effects of divorce on parents and children. In M. E. Lamb (Ed.), *Nontraditional families* (pp. 233–288). Hillsdale, NJ: Erlbaum.

Hetherington, E. M., & Parke, R. D. (1993). *Child psychology: A contemporary viewpoint* (4th ed.). New York: McGraw-Hill.

Hetherington, E. M., Reiss, D., & Plomin, R. (Eds.). (1994). *Separate social worlds of siblings: The impact of nonshared environment on development.* Hillsdale, NJ: Erlbaum.

Hinde, R. A., & Stevenson-Hinde, J. (1988). *Relationships within families: Mutual influences.* Oxford, England: Clarendon Press.

Hinshaw, S. P. (1994). *Attention deficits and hyperactivity in children.* Thousand Oaks, CA: Sage.

Hinshaw, S. P., & Erhardt, D. (1991). Attention-deficit hyperactivity disorder. In P. C. Kendall (Ed.), *Child and adolescent therapy: Cognitive-behavioral procedure.* New York: Guilford Press.

Hinshaw, S. P., & McHale, J. P. (1991). Stimulant medication and the social interactions of hyperactive children: Effects and implications. In D. G. Gilbert & J. J. Connolly (Eds.), *Personality, social skills, and psychopathology: An individual differences approach* (pp. 229–253). New York: Plenum Press.

Jacobs, M. K., & Goodman, G. (1989). Psychology and self-help groups: Predictions on a partnership. *American Psychologist, 44,* 536–545.

Johnson, C. L., & Breckenridge, J. N. (1982). The Houston Parent-Child Development Center and the primary prevention of behavior problems in young children. *American Journal of Community Psychology, 10,* 305–316.

Johnson, C. L., & Irvin, F. S. (1983). Depressive potentials: Interface between adolescence and midlife. In H. L. Morrison (Ed.), *Children of depressed parents* (pp. 115–137). New York: Grune and Stratton.

Johnston, J. R., Kline, M., & Tschann, J. M. (1989). Ongoing postdivorce conflict: Effects on children of joint custody and frequent access. *American Journal of Orthopsychiatry, 59,* 576–592.

Jones, E. E., & Korchin, S. J. (1982). Minority mental health: Perspectives. In E. E. Jones & S. J. Korchin (Eds.), *Minority mental health* (pp. 3–36). New York: Praeger.

Kagan, S. L., & Weissbourd, B. (Eds.). (1994). *Putting families first: America's family support movement and the challenge of change.* San Francisco: Jossey-Bass.

Katz, L. F., & Gottman, J. M. (1994). Patterns of marital interaction and children's emotional development. In R. Parke & S. Kellam (Eds.), *Exploring family relationships with other social contexts: Advances in family research* (Vol. 4, pp. 49–74). Hillsdale, NJ: Erlbaum.

Kellam, S. G., Simon, M. B., & Ensminger, M. E. (1982). Antecedents in first grade of teenage drug use and psychological well-being: A ten-year community-wide prospective study. In D. Ricks & B. Dohrenwend (Eds.), *Origins of psychopathology: Research and public policy* (pp. 17–51). New York: Cambridge University Press.

Kerig, P. K., Cowan, P. A., & Cowan, C. P. (1993). Marital quality and gender differences in parent-child interaction. *Developmental Psychology, 29,* 931–939.

Kernberg, O. F. (1985). *Borderline conditions and pathological narcissism.* Northvale, NJ: Jason Aronson.

Kessen, W. (1979). The American child and other cultural inventions. *American Psychologist, 34,* 815–820.

Klaus, R. A., & Gray, S. W. (1968). The Early Training Project for disadvantaged children. *Monographs of the Society for Research in Child Development, 33*(Serial No. 120).

Klein, M. (1932). *The psychoanalysis of children.* London: International Psychoanalytic Library.

Kohut, H., & Wolf, E. S. (1978). The disorders of the self and their treatment: An outline. *International Journal of Psychoanalysis, 59,* 413–425.

Kupersmidt, J. D., Coie, J. D., & Dodge, K. A. (1990). The role of peer relationships in the development of disorder. In S. Asher & J. D. Coie (Eds.), *Peer rejection in childhood* (pp. 274–305). Cambridge, England: Cambridge University Press.

Kuttner, L. (1991). *Parent and child: Getting through to each other.* New York: Morrow.

Ladd, G. W., & Hart, C. H. (1991). *Parents' management of children's peer relations: Patterns associated with social competence.* Paper presented at the 11th meeting of the International Society for Behavioral Development, Minneapolis, MN.

Lakoff, G. (1996). *Moral politics: What conservatives know that liberals don't.* Chicago: University of Chicago Press.

Lally, J. R., Mangione, P. L., & Honig, A. S. (1988). The Syracuse University Family Development Research Program: Long-range impact of an early intervention with low-income children and their families. In I. E. Sigel (Series Ed.) & D. R. Powell (Vol. Ed.), *Advances in applied developmental psychology: Vol. 3. Parent education as early childhood intervention* (pp. 79–104). Norwood, NJ: ABLEX.

Lamb, M. E. (1978). Interactions between eighteen-month-olds and their preschool-aged siblings. *Child Development, 49,* 51–59.

Lamb, M. E. (1980). What can "research experts" tell parents about effective socialization? In M. D. Fantini & R. Cardenas (Eds.), *Parenting in a multicultural society* (pp. 160–169). New York: Longman.

Lambert, N. (1988). Adolescent outcomes for hyperactive children: Perspectives on general and specific patterns of childhood risk for adolescent educational, social, and mental health problems. *American Psychologist, 43,* 786–799.

Lambie, D. Z., Bond, J. T., & Weikart, D. P. (1974). *Home teaching with mothers and infants. Monographs of the High/Scope Educational Research Foundation, No. 2.* Ypsilanti, MI: High/Scope Press.

Langer, J. (1969). *Theories of development.* New York: Holt, Rinehart and Winston.

Laosa, L. M. (1983). Parent education, cultural pluralism, and public policy: The uncertain connection. In R. Haskins & D. Adams (Eds.), *Parent education and public policy* (pp. 331–345). Norwood, NJ: ABLEX.

Lasch, C. (1977). *Haven in a heartless world.* New York: Basic Books.

Lazar, I. (1983). Discussion and implications of the findings. In Consortium for Longitudinal Studies (Ed.), *As the twig is bent . . . Lasting effects of preschool programs* (pp. 461–466). Hillsdale, NJ: Erlbaum.

Levant, R. F. (1988). Education for fatherhood. In P. Bronstein & C. P. Cowan (Eds.), *Fatherhood today: Men's changing role in the family* (pp. 253–275). New York: Wiley.

Levenstein, P. (1977). The Mother-Child Home Program. In M. C. Day & R. K. Parker (Eds.), *The preschool in action* (pp. 27–49). Boston: Allyn & Bacon.

Levenstein, P. (1988). *Messages from home: The Mother-Child Home Program and the prevention of school disadvantage.* Columbus: Ohio State University Press.

Lewin, K. (1947). Group decision and social change. In T. Newcomb & E. Hartley (Eds.), *Readings in social psychology* (pp. 330–344). New York: Holt, Rinehart and Winston.

Lewis, M., & Bendersky, M. (Eds.). (1995). *Mothers, babies, and cocaine: The role of toxins in development.* Hillsdale, NJ: Erlbaum.

Lickey, M. E. (1991). *Medicine and mental illness: The use of drugs in psychiatry.* New York: Freeman.

Lieberman, A. F., & Pawl, J. H. (1993). Infant-parent psychotherapy. In C. H. Zeanah (Ed.), *Handbook of infant mental health* (pp. 427–442). New York: Guilford Press.

Lieberman, A. F., Weston, D. R., & Pawl, J. H. (1991). Preventive intervention and outcome with anxiously attached dyads. *Child Development, 62,* 199–209.

Lombard, A. (1981). *Success begins at home.* Boston: Lexington Books.

Lozoff, B. (1989). Nutrition and behavior. Children and their development: Knowledge base, research agenda, and social policy application [Special issue]. *American Psychologist, 44,* 98–102.

Luster, T., & Okagaki, L. (1993). Multiple influences in parenting: Ecological and life-course perspectives. In T. Luster &

L. Okagaki (Eds.), *Parenting: An ecological perspective* (pp. 227–250). Hillsdale, NJ: Erlbaum.

Maccoby, E. E., & Jacklin, C. N. (1974). *The psychology of sex differences.* Stanford, CA: Stanford University Press.

Maccoby, E. E., & Martin, J. A. (1983). Socialization in the context of the family: Parent-child interaction. In P. H. Mussen (Series Ed.) & E. M. Hetherington (Vol. Ed.), *Handbook of child psychology: Vol. 4. Socialization, personality and social development* (4th ed., pp. 1–101). New York: Wiley.

Macfarlane, J. W. (1938). Studies in child guidance: I. Methodology of data collection and organization. *Monographs of the Society for Research in Child Development, 3*(6, Serial No. 19).

Main, M., & Goldwyn, R. (1984). Predicting rejection of her infant from mother's representation of her own experience: Implications for the abused-abusing intergenerational cycle. *Child Abuse and Neglect, 8,* 203–217.

Main, M., & Goldwyn, R. (in press). Adult attachment classification system. In M. Main (Ed.), *A typology of human attachment organization: Assessed in discourse, drawings and interviews.* New York: Cambridge University Press.

Main, M., Kaplan, N., & Cassidy, J. (1985). Security in infancy, childhood, and adulthood: A move to the level of representation. In I. Bretherton & E. Waters (Eds.), Growing points of attachment theory and research. *Monographs of the Society for Research in Child Development, 50*(Serial No. 209), 66–106.

Markman, H. J., Renick, M. J., Floyd, F. J., & Stanley, S. M. (1993). Preventing marital distress through communication and conflict management training: A 4- and 5-year follow-up. Special Section: Couples and couple therapy. *Journal of Consulting and Clinical Psychology, 61,* 70–77.

Maslow, A. H. (1962). *Toward a psychology of being.* Princeton, NJ: Van Nostrand.

Mason, M. A. (1988). *The equality trap: Why working women shouldn't be treated like men.* New York: Simon & Schuster.

Masterson, J. F. (1992). The vital therapeutic alliance with borderline and narcissistic patients: A developmental, self and object-relations approach. In J. K. Zeig (Ed.), *The evolution of psychotherapy: The second conference* (pp 171–188). New York: Brunner/Mazel.

Matthews, K. A., & Rodin, J. (1989). Women's changing work roles: Impact on health, family, and public policy. *American Psychologist, 44,* 1389–1393.

McGillicuddy-De Lisi, A. V. (1990). Parental beliefs within the family context: Development of a research program. In I. E. Sigel & G. H. Brody (Eds.), *Methods of family research: Biographies of research projects: Vol. 1. Normal families* (pp. 53–85). Hillsdale, NJ: Erlbaum.

McGoldrick, M., Anderson, C. M., & Walsh, F. (Eds.). (1989). *Women in families: A framework for family therapy.* New York: Norton.

McHale, J. P. (1995). Coparenting and triadic interactions during infancy: The roles of marital distress and child gender. *Developmental Psychology, 31,* 985–996.

McHale, S. M., Crouter, A. C., McGuire, S. A., Updegraff, K. A. (1995). Congruence between mothers' and fathers' differential treatment of siblings: Links with family relations and children's well-being. *Child Development, 66,* 116–128.

McLoyd, V. C. (1990). The impact of economic hardship on Black families and children: Psychological distress, parenting, and socioemotional development. *Child Development, 61,* 311–346.

McMahon, R. J., Slough, N. M., & the Conduct Problems Prevention Research Group. (in press). Family-based intervention in the FAST Track program. In R. D. Peters & R. J. McMahon (Eds.), *Prevention and early intervention: Childhood disorders, substance abuse, and delinquency.* Thousand Oaks, CA: Sage.

Measelle, J. (1993). *Individual differences in the accuracy of preschoolers' perceptions of competence: Linking family process and children's adaptation to kindergarten.* Unpublished master's thesis, University of California, Berkeley.

Mednick, S. A., Parnas, J., & Schulsinger, F. (1987). The Copenhagen high-risk project, 1962–1986. *Schizophrenia Bulletin, 13,* 485–495.

Meichenbaum, D. H. (1995). Cognitive-behavioral therapy in historical perspective. In B. M. Bongar & L. E. Beutler (Eds.), *Comprehensive textbook of psychotherapy: Theory and practice* (Vol. 1, pp. 140–158). New York: Oxford University Press.

Merriam-Webster's Collegiate dictionary. (1993). Springfield, MA: Merriam-Webster.

Mesters, I., Van Nunen, M., Crebolder, H., & Meertens, R. (1995). Education of parents about pediatric asthma: Effects of a protocol on medical consumption. *Patient Education and Counseling, 25,* 131–136.

Miller, G. E., & Prinz, R. J. (1990). Enhancement of social learning family interventions for childhood conduct disorder. *Psychology Bulletin, 108*(2), 291–307.

Miller, N. B., Cowan, P. A., Cowan, C. P., Hetherington, E. M., & Clingempeel, G. (1993). Externalizing in preschoolers and early adolescents: A cross-study replication of a family model. *Developmental Psychology, 29,* 3–18.

Minde, K., & Hesse, E. (1996). The role of the Adult Attachment Interview in parent-infant psychotherapy: A case presentation. *Infant Mental Health Journal, 17*(2), 115–126.

Minuchin, P. (1985). Families and individual development: Provocations from the field of family therapy. Family development [Special issue]. *Child Development, 56,* 289–302.

Minuchin, S., & Fishman, H. C. (1981). *Family therapy techniques.* Cambridge, MA: Harvard University Press.

Moorehouse, M. (1993). Work and family dynamics. In P. A. Cowan, D. Field, D. A. Hansen, A. Skolnick, & G. E. Swanson (Eds.), *Family, self, and society: Toward a new agenda for family research* (pp. 265–286). Hillsdale, NJ: Erlbaum.

Musick, J. S., & Stott, F. (1990). Paraprofessionals, parenting, and child development: Understanding the problems and seeking solutions. In S. J. Meisels & J. P. Shonkoff (Eds.), *Handbook of early childhood intervention* (pp. 651–667). New York: Cambridge University Press.

Nash, J. (1965). The father in contemporary culture and current psychological literature. *Child Development, 36,* 261–298.

National Congress of Parents and Teachers. (1944). *The parent-teacher organization: Its origins and development.* Chicago: Author.

National plan for research on child and adolescent mental disorders. (1990). (DHHS Publication No. ADM 90-1683). Washington, DC: U.S. Government Printing Office.

Olds, D. L., Henderson, C. R., Tatelbaum, R., & Chamberlin, R. (1986). Improving the delivery of prenatal care and outcomes of pregnancy: A randomized trial of nurse home visitation. *Pediatrics, 77,* 16–28.

Olds, D. L., & Kitzman, H. (1993). Review of research on home visiting for pregnant women and parents of young children. *Future of Children, 3,* 53–92.

Olds, D. L., Kitzman, H., & Cole, R. (1995, March). *Influence of prenatal and infancy home visitation on the outcomes of pregnancy and childbearing in the first year of life.* Paper presented at the biennial meetings of the Society for Research in Child Development, Indianapolis, IN.

Parke, R. D. (1996). *Fatherhood* (2nd ed.). Cambridge, MA: Harvard University Press.

Parke, R. D., & Beitel, A. (1986). Hospital-based intervention for fathers. In M. E. Lamb (Ed.), *The father's role: Applied perspectives* (pp. 293–323). New York: Wiley.

Parke, R. D., Burks, V. M., Carson, J. L., Neville, B., & Boyum, L. A. (1994). Family-peer relationships: A tripartite model. In R. Parke & S. Kellam (Eds.), *Exploring family relationships with other social contexts: Advances in family research* (Vol. 4, pp. 115–146). Hillsdale, NJ: Erlbaum.

Parke, R. D., & Tinsley, B. (1982). The early environment of the at-risk infant: Expanding the social context. In D. D. Bricker (Ed.), *Intervention with at-risk and handicapped infants* (pp. 153–177). Baltimore: University Park Press.

Parke, R. D., & Tinsley, B. (1987). Family interaction in infancy. In J. Osofsky (Ed.), *Handbook of infancy* (2nd ed., pp. 579–641). New York: Wiley.

Parker, L., & Gettig, E. (1995). Ethical issues in genetic screening and testing, gene therapy, and scientific conduct. In F. R. Bloom, D. J. Kupfer, B. S. Bunney, R. D. Ciaranello, K. L. Davis, G. F. Koob, H. Y. Meltzer, C. R. Schuster, & R. I. Shader (Eds.), *Psychopharmacology: The fourth generation of progress: An official publication of the American College of Neuropsychopharmacology* (pp. 1875–1881). New York: Raven Press.

Patterson, C. J. (1995a). Lesbian mothers, gay fathers, and their children. In A. R. D'Augelli & C. J. Patterson (Eds.), *Lesbian, gay, and bisexual identities over the lifespan: Psychological perspectives* (pp. 262–290). New York: Oxford University Press.

Patterson, C. J. (1995b). Lesbian and gay parenthood. In M. H. Bornstein (Ed.), *Handbook of parenting* (Vol. 3, pp. 255–276). Hillsdale, NJ: Erlbaum.

Patterson, G. R. (1974). Interventions for boys with conduct problems: Multiple settings, treatments, and criteria. *Journal of Consulting and Clinical Psychology, 42,* 471–481.

Patterson, G. R. (1982). *Coercive family process.* Eugene, OR: Castalia Press.

Patterson, G. R., & Capaldi, D. (1991). Antisocial parents: Unskilled and vulnerable. In P. A. Cowan & M. E. Hetherington (Eds.), *Family transitions. Advances in family research* (Vol. 2, pp. 195–218). Hillsdale, NJ: Erlbaum.

Patterson, G. R., Dishion, T. J., & Chamberlain, P. (1993). Outcomes and methodological issues relating to treatment of antisocial children. In T. R. Giles (Ed.), *Handbook of effective psychotherapy* (pp. 43–88). New York: Plenum Press.

Patterson, G. R., & Forgatch, M. S. (1989). *Parents and adolescents living together: Vol. 1. The basics. Vol. 2. Family problem-solving.* Eugene, OR: Castalia Press.

Patterson, G. R., & Forgatch, M. S. (1990). Initiation and maintenance of process disrupting single-mother families. In G. R. Patterson (Ed.), *Advances in family research: Depression and aggression in family interaction* (pp. 209–246). Hillsdale, NJ: Erlbaum.

Patterson, G. R., & Gullion, E. R. (1973). *Living with children: New methods for parents and teachers* (Rev. ed.). Champaign, IL: Research Press.

Pauker, S. P., & Pauker, S. G. (1987). The amniocentesis decision: Ten years of decision analytic experience. In G. Evers-Kiebooms, J.-J. Cassiman, H. Van Den Berghe, & G. dYdewalle (Eds.), *Genetic risk, risk perception, and decision making: Birth defects, original articles series* (Vol. 23, No. 2). New York: Liss.

Pelham, W. E., & Hinshaw, S. P. (1992). Behavioral intervention for attention deficit hyperactivity disorder. In S. M. Turner, K. S. Calhoun, & H. E. Adams (Eds.), *Handbook of clinical behavior therapy* (2nd ed., pp. 259–283). New York: Wiley.

Pencarinha, D. F., Bell, N. K., Edwards, J. G., & Best, R. G. (1992). Ethical issues in genetic counseling: A comparison of M.S. counselor and medical geneticist perspectives. *Journal of Genetic Counseling, 1,* 19–30.

Piaget, J. (1967). *Six psychological studies* (D. Elkind, Ed.). New York: Random House.

Pianta, R. C., Egeland, B., & Hyatt, A. (1986). Maternal relationship history as an indicator of developmental risk. *American Journal of Orthopsychiatry, 56,* 385–398.

Pleck, J. H. (1988). Fathers and infant care leave. In E. F. Zigler & M. Frank (Eds.), *The parental leave crisis: Toward a national policy* (pp. 177–191). New Haven, CT: Yale University Press.

Plomin, R. (1994). *Genetics and experience: The interplay between nature and nurture.* Thousand Oaks, CA: Sage.

Politt, E., & Gorman, K. S. (1984). Nutritional deficiencies as developmental risk factors. In C. A. Nelson (Ed.), *Threats to optimal development: Integrating biological, psychological, and social risk factors. The Minnesota Symposia in Child Psychology* (Vol. 27, pp. 121–144). Hillsdale, NJ: Erlbaum.

Popenoe, D. (1993). American family decline, 1960–1990. *Journal of Marriage and the Family, 55,* 527–541.

Powell, D. R. (1988). Emerging directions in parent-child early intervention. In I. E. Sigel (Series Ed.) & D. R. Powell (Vol. Ed.), *Advances in applied developmental psychology: Vol. 3. Parent education as early childhood intervention* (pp. 1–22). Norwood, NJ: ABLEX.

Powell, D. R. (1990). Home visiting in the early years: Policy and program design decisions. *Young Children, 45,* 65–73.

Powell, D. R. (1993). Inside home visiting programs: Home Visiting [Special issue]. *Future of Children, 3,* 23–38.

Powell, D. R., & Eisenstadt, J. W. (1988). Informal and formal conversations in parent education groups: An observational study. *Family Relations, 37,* 166–170.

Powell, D. R., & Grantham-McGregory, S. (1989). Home visiting of varying frequency and child development. *Pediatrics, 84,* 157–164.

Powell, D. R., Zambrana, R., & Silva-Palacios, V. (1990). Designing culturally responsive parent programs: A comparison of low-income Mexican and Mexican-American mothers' preferences. *Family Relations, 39,* 298–304.

Pratt, M. W., Kerig, P. K., Cowan, P. A., & Cowan, C. P. (1988). Mothers and fathers teaching three-year-olds: Authoritative parenting and adults' use of the zone of proximal development. *Developmental Psychology, 24,* 832–839.

Quint, J., & Egeland, B. (1995). New Chance: Comprehensive services for disadvantaged families. In I. E. Sigel (Series Ed.) & S. Smith (Vol. Ed.), *Advances in applied developmental psychology: Vol. 9. Two generation programs for families in poverty: A new intervention strategy* (pp. 91–133). Norwood, NJ: ABLEX.

Radin, N. (1972). Three degrees of maternal involvement in a preschool program: Impact on mothers and children. *Child Development, 43,* 1355–1364.

Ramey, C. L., & Ramey, C. T. (1992). Early educational intervention with disadvantaged children: To what effect? *Applied and Preventive Psychology, 1,* 131–140.

Reid, J. (1993). Prevention of conduct disorder before and after school entry: Relating interventions to developmental findings. Toward a developmental perspective on conduct disorder [Special issue]. *Development and Psychopathology, 5,* 243–262.

Reid, J. (1996, May). *Efficacy trials in the prevention of conduct disorder.* Paper presented at the fifth National Conference on Prevention Research, Washington, DC.

Reiss, D. (1995). Genetic influence on family systems. *Journal of Marriage and the Family, 57,* 543–560.

Repetti, R. L. (1987). Linkages between work and family roles. In S. Oskamp (Ed.), *Applied social psychology annual: Vol. 7. Family processes and problems* (pp. 98–127). Beverly Hills, CA: Sage.

Richters, J. E., Arnold, E., Jensen, P. S., Abikoff, H., Conners, C. K., Greenhill, L. L., Hechtman, L., Hinshaw, S. P., Pelham, W. E., & Swanson, J. M. (1995). National Institute of Mental Health collaborative multisite multimodal treatment study of children with Attention-Deficit Hyperactivity Disorder (MTA): I. Background and rationale. *Journal of the American Academy of Child and Adolescent Psychiatry, 34,* 1–10.

Roberts, R. N., & Wasik, B. H. (1990). Home visiting programs for families with children birth to three: Results of a national survey. *Journal of Early Intervention, 14,* 274–284.

Rogers, C. R. (1961). *On becoming a person: A therapist's view of psychotherapy.* Boston: Houghton Mifflin.

Rowe, D. C. (1986). Genetic and environmental components of antisocial behavior: A study of 255 twin pairs. *Child Development, 54,* 473–489.

Rowe, D. C., Vazsonyi, A. T., & Flannery, D. J. (1994). No more than skin deep: Ethnic and racial similarity in developmental process. *Psychological Review, 101,* 396–413.

Rueschenberg, E. J., & Buriel, R. (1995). Mexican American family functioning and acculturation: A family systems perspective. In A. M. Padilla (Ed.), *Hispanic psychology: Critical issues in theory and research* (pp. 15–25). Thousand Oaks, CA: Sage.

Rutter, M. (1987). Psychosocial resilience and protective mechanisms. *American Journal of Orthopsychiatry, 57,* 316–331.

Rutter, M., & Garmezy, N. (1983). Developmental psychopathology. In P. H. Mussen (Series Ed.) & E. M. Hetherington (Vol. Ed.), *Handbook of child psychology: Vol. 4. Socialization, personality, and social development* (pp. 775–911). New York: Wiley.

Safer, D. J., & Krager, J. M. (1988). A survey of medication treatment for hyperactive/inattentive students. *Journal of the American Medical Association, 260,* 2256–2258.

St. Pierre, R. G., & Swartz, J. P. (1995). The Even Start Family Literacy Program. In I. E. Sigel (Series Ed.) & S. Smith (Vol. Ed.), *Advances in applied developmental psychology: Vol. 9. Two generation programs for families in poverty: A new intervention strategy* (pp. 37–66). Norwood, NJ: ABLEX.

Sameroff, A. J., & Chandler, M. J. (1975). Reproductive risk and the continuum of caretaking casualty. In F. D. Horowitz, E. M. Hetherington, S. Scarr-Salapatek, & G. Siegel (Eds.), *Review of child development research* (Vol. 4, pp. 187–244). Chicago: University of Chicago Press.

Sameroff, A. J., Siefer, R., & Zax, M. (1982). Early development of children at risk for emotional disorder. *Monographs of the Society for Research in Child Development, 47*(7, No. 199).

Sarason, S. B. (1974). *The psychological sense of community: Prospects for a community psychology.* San Francisco: Jossey-Bass.

Saxe, L., Cross, T., & Silverman, N. (1988). Children's mental health: The gap between what we know and what we do. *American Psychologist, 43,* 800–807.

Scharff, D. E., & Birtles, E. F. (Eds.). (1994). *From instinct to self: Selected papers of W. R. D. Fairbairn: Vol. 1. Clinical and theoretical papers. Vol. 2. Application and early contributions.* Northvale, NJ: Jason Aronson.

Schlossman, S. (1976). Before Home Start: Notes toward a history of parent education in America, 1897–1929. *Harvard Educational Review, 46,* 436–467.

Schmid-Kitsikis, E. (1973). Piagetian theory and its approach to psychopathology. *American Journal of Mental Deficiency, 77,* 694–705.

Schulz, M. S. (1994). *Coping with negative emotional arousal: The daily spillover of work stress into marital interactions.* Unpublished doctoral dissertation, University of California, Berkeley.

Seifer, R. (1995). Perils and pitfalls of high-risk research. Special Section: Parental depression and distress: Implications for development in infancy, childhood, and adolescence. *Developmental Psychology, 31,* 420–424.

Seitz, V. (1987). Outcome evaluation of family support programs: Research design alternatives to true experiments. In S. L. Kagan, D. R. Powell, B. Weissbourd, & E. F. Zigler (Eds.), *America's family support programs* (pp. 329–361). New Haven, CT: Yale University Press.

Seligman, M. E. P. (1991). *Learned optimism.* New York: Knopf.

Shapiro, J., & Simonson, D. (1994). Educational/support group for Latino families of children with Down syndrome. *Mental Retardation, 32,* 403–415.

Shearer, D. E. (1987). The Portage Project: A home approach to early education of young children with special needs. In J. Roopnarine & J. Johnson (Eds.), *Approach to early childhood education* (pp. 269–282). Columbus, OH: Merrill.

Sigel, I. E. (1983). The ethics of intervention. In I. E. Sigel & L. M. Laosa (Eds.), *Changing families* (pp. 1–21). New York: Plenum Press.

Sigel, I. E. (1987). Educating the young thinker: A distancing model of preschool education. In J. Roopnarine & J. Johnson (Eds.), *Approach to early childhood education* (pp. 237–252). Columbus, OH: Merrill.

Sigel, I. E. (1992). The belief-behavior connection: A resolvable dilemma? In I. E. Sigel, A. V. McGillicuddy-DeLisi, & J. Goodenow (Eds.), *Parental belief systems: The psychological consequences for children* (2nd ed., pp. 433–456). Hillsdale, NJ: Erlbaum.

Sigman, M. (1995). Nutrition and child development: More food for thought. *Current Directions in Psychological Science, 4,* 52–55.

Singer, G. H. S., Glang, A., Nixon, C., & Colley, E. (1994). A comparison of two psychosocial interventions for parents of children with acquired brain injury: An exploratory study. *Journal of Head Trauma Rehabilitation, 9,* 38–49.

Skinner, B. F. (1938). *The behavior of organisms: An experimental analysis.* New York: Appleton-Century.

Skolnick, A. (1991). *Embattled paradise: The American family in an age of uncertainty.* New York: Basic Books.

Slaughter, D. T. (1983). Early intervention and its effects on maternal and child development. *Monographs of the Society for Research in Child Development, 48*(4, Serial No. 202).

Smith, S., & Zaslow, M. (1995). Rationale and policy context for two-generation interventions. In I. E. Sigel (Series Ed.) & S. Smith (Ed.), *Advances in applied developmental psychology: Vol. 9. Two-generation programs for families in poverty: A new intervention strategy* (pp. 1–35). Norwood, NJ: ABLEX.

Snowden, L. R. (Ed.). (1982). *Reaching the underserved: Mental health needs of neglected populations.* Beverly Hills, CA: Sage.

Spock, B. (1957). *Baby and child care.* New York: Pocket Books.

Stacey, J. (1996). *In the name of the family: Rethinking family values in the postmodern age.* Boston: Beacon Press.

Staples, R., & Johnson, L. B. (1993). *Black families at the crossroads: Challenges and prospects.* San Francisco: Jossey-Bass.

Steinberg, L., Darling, N. E., & Fletcher, A. C. (in collaboration with Brown, B. B., & Dornbush, S. M.). (1995). Authoritative parenting and adolescent adjustment: An ecological journey. In P. Moen, G. Elder, Jr., & K. Luscher (Eds.), *Examining lives in context: Perspectives on the ecology of human development* (pp. 423–466). Washington, DC: American Psychological Association.

Steinberg, L., Lamborn, S. D., Dornbush, S. M., & Darling, N. (1992). Impact of parenting practices on adolescent achievement: Authoritative parenting, school involvement, and encouragement to succeed. *Child Development, 63,* 1266–1281.

Steinberg, L., Mounts, N. S., Lamborn, S. D., & Dornbush, S. M. (1991). Authoritative parenting and adolescent adjustment across varied ecological niches. *Journal of Research on Adolescence, 1,* 19–36.

Steinglass, P. (1987). A systems view of family interaction and psychopathology. In T. Jacob (Ed.), *Family interaction and psychopathology: Theories, methods, and findings* (pp. 25–65). New York: Plenum Press.

Stern, D. (1985). *The interpersonal world of the infant: A view from psychoanalysis and developmental psychology.* New York: Basic Books.

Sternberg, R. J. (1995). *In search of the human mind.* Ft. Worth, TX: Harcourt Brace.

Sullivan, P. F., Wells, J. E., & Bushness, J. A. (1995). Adoption as a risk factor for mental disorders. *Acta Psychiatrica Scandinavica, 92,* 119–124.

Todres, R., & Bunston, T. (1993). Parent education program evaluation: A review of the literature. *Canadian Journal of Community Mental Health, 12,* 225 257.

Turiel, E. (1974). Conflict and transition in adolescent moral development. *Child Development, 45,* 14–29.

Turner, K. M. T., Sanders, M. R., & Wall, C. R. (1994). Behavioral parent training versus dietary education in the treatment of children with persistent feeding difficulties. Behavior therapy and schizophrenia: I [Special issue]. *Behavior Change, 11,* 242–258.

Tyler, F. B., Pargament, K. I., & Gatz, M. (1983). The resource collaborator role: A model for interactions involving psychologists. *American Psychologist, 38,* 388–398.

van IJzendoorn, M. H. (1992). Intergenerational transmission of parenting: A review of studies in nonclinical populations. *Developmental Review, 12,* 76–99.

van IJzendoorn, M. H., Juffer, F., & Duyvesteyn, M. G. C. (1995). Breaking the intergenerational cycle of insecure attachment: A review of the effects of attachment-based intervention on maternal sensitivity and infant security. *Journal of Child Psychology and Psychiatry and Allied Disciplines, 36,* 225–248.

Volenski, L. T. (1995). Building school support systems for parents of handicapped children: The parent education and guidance program. *Psychology in the Schools, 32,* 124–129.

Vondra, J., & Belsky, J. (1993). Developmental origins of parenting: Personality and relationship factors. In T. Luster & L. Okagaki (Eds.), *Parenting: An ecological perspective* (pp. 1–33). Hillsdale, NJ: Erlbaum.

Vygotsky, L. S. (1978). *Mind in society: The development of higher psychological processes.* Cambridge, MA: Harvard University Press.

Wagner, B., & Reiss, D. (1995). Family systems and developmental psychopathology: Courtship, marriage, or divorce. In D. Cicchetti & D. J. Cohen (Eds.), *Developmental psychopathology: Vol. 1. Theory and methods* (pp. 696–730). New York: Wiley.

Wahler, R. G. (1980). The insular mother: Her problems in parent-child treatment. *Journal of Applied Behavior Analysis, 13,* 207–219.

Walker, T. B., Rodriguez, G. G., Johnson, D. L., & Cortez, C. P. (1995). Advances in parent-child education programs. In I. E. Sigel (Series Ed.) & S. Smith (Vol. Ed.), *Advances in applied developmental psychology: Vol. 9. Two-generation programs for families in poverty: A new intervention strategy* (pp. 67–90). Norwood, NJ: ABLEX.

Wallerstein, J., & Kelly, J. (1980). *Surviving the breakup.* New York: Basic Books.

Walsh, F. (Ed.). (1993). *Normal family processes* (2nd ed.). New York: Guilford Press.

Walters, M., Carter, B., Papp, P., & Silverstein, O. (1988). *The invisible web: Gender patterns in family relationships.* New York: Guilford Press.

Wasik, B. H. (1993). Staffing issues for home visiting programs. Home Visiting [Special issue]. *The Future of Children, 3,* 140–157.

Wasik, B. H., Ramey, C. T., Bryant, D. M., & Sparling, J. J. (1990). A longitudinal study of two early intervention strategies: Project CARE. *Child Development, 61,* 1682–1696.

Watson, J. B. (1928). *Psychological care of infant and child.* London: Allen & Unwin.

Webster-Stratton, C. (1984). Randomized trial of two parent-training programs for families with conduct-disordered children. *Journal of Consulting and Clinical Psychology, 52*(4), 666–678.

Webster-Stratton, C. (1989). *The parents and children series.* Eugene, OR: Castalia Press.

Webster-Stratton, C. (1990). Enhancing the effectiveness of self-administered videotape parent training for families with conduct-problem children. *Journal of Abnormal Child Psychology, 18,* 479–492.

Webster-Stratton, C. (1992). Individually administered videotape parent training: "Who benefits?" *Cognitive Therapy and Research, 16*(1), 31–35.

Webster-Stratton, C. (1994). Advancing videotape parent training: A comparison study. *Journal of Consulting and Clinical Psychology, 62*(3), 583–593.

Webster-Stratton, C., & Herbert, M. (1993). "What really happens in parent training?" *Behavior Modification, 17*(4), 407–456.

Weiss, H. B. (1990). Beyond parent practices: Building policies and programs to care for ones own and others' children. *Children and Youth Services Review, 12,* 264–284.

Weisz, J. R., Donenberg, G. R., Han, S. S., & Weiss, B. (1995). Bridging the gap between laboratory and clinic in child and adolescent psychotherapy. *Journal of Consulting and Clinical Psychology, 63,* 688–701.

Wells, K. C., & Egan, J. (1988). Social learning and family systems therapy for childhood oppositional disorder: Comparative treatment outcome. *Comprehensive Psychiatry, 29,* 138–145.

Werner, H. (1948). *Comparative psychology of mental development* (Rev. ed.). New York: International Universities Press.

Whalen, C. K. (1989). Attention Deficit Hyperactivity Disorder. In T. H. Ollendick & M. Hersen (Eds.), *Handbook of child psychopathology* (2nd ed., pp. 131–169). New York: Plenum Press.

Whitehurst, G. J., Arnold, D. S., Epstein, J. M., & Angell, A. L. (1994). A picture book reading intervention in day care and home for children from low-income families. *Developmental Psychology, 30,* 679–689.

Whitehurst, G. J., Falco, F., Lonigan, C. J., Fischel, J. E., Valdez-Menchaca, M. C., & Caulfield, M. (1988). Accelerating language development through picture-book reading. *Developmental Psychology, 24,* 552–558.

Wilson, B. J., & Gottman, J. M. (1995). Marital interaction and parenting. In M. H. Bornstein (Ed.), *Handbook of parenting* (Vol. 4, pp. 33–56). Hillsdale, NJ: Erlbaum.

Winnicott, D. W. (1987). *The child, the family, and the outside world.* Reading, MA: Addison-Wesley.

Wolchick, S. A., West, S. G., Westover, D., Sandler, I. N., Martin, A., Lustig, J., Tein, J.-Y., & Fisher, J. (1993). The children of divorce parenting intervention: Outcome evaluation of an empirically based program. *American Journal of Community Psychology, 21,* 293–330.

Wood, D. (1980). Teaching the young child: Some relationships between social interaction, language, and thought. In D. Olson (Ed.), *The social foundations of language and thought* (pp. 280–296). New York: Norton.

Wood, D., Bruner, J., & Ross, G. (1976). The role of tutoring in problem solving. *Journal of Child Psychology and Child Psychiatry, 17,* 89–100.

Zahn-Waxler, C., Iannotti, R. J., Cummings, E. M., & Denham, S. (1990). Antecedents of problem behaviors in children of depressed mothers. *Development and Psychopathology, 2,* 349–366.

Zeanah, C. H. (Ed.). (1993). *Handbook of infant mental health.* New York: Guilford Press.

Zukow-Goldring, P. (1995). Sibling caregiving. In M. H. Bornstein (Ed.), *Handbook of parenting* (Vol. 3, pp. 177–208). Hillsdale, NJ: Erlbaum.

CHAPTER 2

Nonparental Child Care: Context, Quality, Correlates, and Consequences

MICHAEL E. LAMB

This chapter is concerned with variations in the extent to which young children receive care from adults other than their parents and the effects that such care arrangements have on their development. As readers will quickly note, the underlying issues are more complex than they appear, and thus our understanding remains quite limited. In addition, researchers have learned in recent years to be wary of facile generalization across contexts or cultures when studying such issues. It is naïve to ask such questions about the universal consequences of child care experiences as Is day care good or bad for children? or Is center day care better for children than family day care? Instead, researchers must examine children's development in the context of the rich array of experiences to which children around the world are exposed. Nonparental care is and has been experienced to a greater or lesser degree in almost every society. Care of poor quality and care patterns that are inconsistent with the other experiences and needs of children may be harmful, but—contrary to the claims of popularizers like White (1985, 1988, 1995)—the evidence reviewed in this chapter makes clear that children are not inevitably harmed just because they experience nonparental care.

Most of the published research is concerned with the situation in the United States, but I have tried wherever possible to report and evaluate relevant research conducted in other countries. Such studies help place in context and perspective the results of research conducted in the United States, and should foster caution about the universality, generalizability, and interpretability of the research literature. This perspective is especially helpful when evaluating conclusions regarding children's intrinsic or endogenous tendencies and the inevitability of certain causal associations or effects; as do historical perspectives, cross-cultural perspectives often provide a cautionary brake on the widespread tendency of researchers to overstate and overgeneralize their findings. Needless to say, it is especially necessary when attempting to reach inferences regarding practical implications.

Unfortunately, social scientists tend to have a very myopic view of human history, often treating popular or widespread practices as basic species-typical givens without analyzing their origins and history. Because formal schooling has been mandatory in most developed countries for several generations, for example, the potential effects of schooling on child-parent relationships are largely ignored, although concerns are raised about the potential effects of nonparental care on younger children. The fact that formal education (or productive labor away from family members) is a much more recent and culturally restricted innovation than nonparental child care for young children elicits little attention. The transition to school is viewed as normal and normative; enrollment in infant day care, by contrast, is questioned, popularly and professionally.

Of course, preoccupation with the potentially harmful effects of *preschool* care is not accidental; it reflects the belief, partially attributable to psychoanalysis and its incorporation into popular North American belief systems, that early experiences have disproportionately powerful influences on child development. Fortunately, commitment to the early experience hypothesis is not as profound today as it was as little as four decades ago, when psychologists implied that major early experiences had long-lasting effects that were nearly impossible to overcome. Many researchers and theorists have since come to believe that "all periods are critical" and that development is best viewed as a continuing process in which successive experiences modify, modulate, amplify, or ameliorate the effects of earlier experiences on remarkably plastic individuals (Lerner, 1984). This life span view of development undeniably complicates efforts to study longer-term effects on child development—particularly the effects of less salient and significant events—but appears to represent better the determinants and course of human development.

Over the past decade, researchers have also come to recognize the diversity and complexity of child care arrangements and their effects on children. Children grow up in a heterogeneous array of cultural and family circumstances, and many also experience multiple types of nonparental care. The diversity of family circumstances, the disparate array of nonparental care arrangements that exist, and the complex effects of endogenous differences among children all ensure that day care per se is unlikely to have clear, unambiguous, and universal effects, either positive or negative, when other important factors are taken into account (Lamb & Sternberg, 1990; Lamb, Sternberg, Hwang, & Broberg, 1992). Instead, researchers must focus on the nature, extent, quality, and age at onset of care, as well as the way these factors together affect children with different characteristics, from different family backgrounds, and with different educational, developmental, and individual needs. In this endeavor, contemporary researchers will need to focus increasingly on the crucial intersection between familial and nonfamilial child care settings. Similarity in the practices and values manifest in the two contexts may play an important role in facilitating healthy development.

In the first substantive section of this chapter, I attempt to place the contemporary patterns of day care in their broader sociocultural and historical context. Nonparental care is a universal practice with a long history, not a dangerous innovation representing a major deviation from species-typical and species-appropriate patterns of child care. Specific patterns of child care vary cross-culturally, of course, with different nations choosing to emphasize different national goals in their support of different patterns of formal and informal child care. These divergent goals and representations are revealing to the extent that they underscore the need to view any research on the *effects* of day care in the context of the goals, values, and practices of particular cultures at specific points in time.

I next sketch the changing patterns of child care in the contemporary United States, where most of the recent research on the effects of day care has been conducted. Over the past three decades, nonparental care has become a normative pattern for preschoolers in the United States, where formal out-of-home care arrangements are made for children of all races, from all socioeconomic backgrounds, and of all ages, beginning in infancy. Over the same period, major changes have also taken place in the average age of exposure to regular nonparental care and in the relative popularity of different forms of care.

The effects of day care become central in the sections that follow. In the past decade, researchers have emphasized the need to evaluate the quality of care when assessing effects on children, and the parameters of this debate, as well as the popular indices of quality, are introduced in the third section. Increasing awareness that the quality of care may play a crucial role in determining how children are affected by nonparental care has fostered efforts to understand *how* care providers behave and how they should be trained to provide growth-promoting care for children (Bredekamp, 1987a, 1987b).

Unfortunately, "high-quality alternative care" is a construct that is much more difficult to define than one might think. Quality is not a single, readily quantifiable dimension. Some simple and concrete measures can be used to assess structural aspects of the quality of care, including adult–child ratios, levels of care provider training and experience, staff stability, and the adequacy of the physical facilities. These dimensions are most likely to be emphasized by state standards, which set the minimal acceptable standards on a state-by-state rather than federal basis (Phillips & Zigler, 1987). Structural characteristics affect the likelihood of high-quality care, but they do not guarantee it: centers that are characterized by good adult–child ratios and are staffed by well-trained providers may still provide care of poor quality. Extensive training, education, and experience, like generous adult–child ratios, have to be translated into sensitive patterns of interaction, displays of appropriate emotion, and the intuitive understanding of children that make the experiences richly rewarding for children. The ease with which and the extent to which structural factors are translated into quality clearly vary depending upon the culture, the context, and the alternative opportunities available to children, care providers, and parents. Furthermore, even the benefits of high-quality care may be compromised when the demands of the parents' work roles result in excessively long periods of nonparental care. It is thus impossible to write a recipe for high-quality care that is universally applicable. High-quality care needs to be defined with respect to the characteristics and needs of children and families in specific societies and subcultures rather than in terms of universal dimensions. Additionally, the practices and values of the care facility must be consistent with the values of the home.

Debates about the effects of day care on children's development, which become the focus of the fourth and fifth sections, have varied over time in response to a multitude of social, economic, and scientific factors. Initially, research efforts were focused on 3- and 4-year-old children in an attempt to address the implicit question Is day care bad for children? By the early 1980s, the results of several studies, mostly conducted in high-quality day care centers, had fostered a widespread consensus that, contrary to popular fears, nonparental care begun in the third year of life or later need not have adverse effects on psychosocial development (Belsky & Steinberg, 1978; Belsky, Steinberg, & Walker, 1982; Clarke-Stewart & Fein, 1983). This conclusion had to be qualified, however, because most of the studies involved atypically good programs, ignored family day care and in-home sitter arrangements, and paid no attention to group differences in parental values or attitudes prior to enrollment in nonparental care.

These limitations notwithstanding, public concerns about day care changed in the 1980s either because out-of-home care had become a normative and manifestly nonharmful experience for preschoolers, or because the accumulated evidence had become overwhelming. Instead, concern was focused on infants and toddlers—children who began receiving nonparental care before they had time to establish and consolidate attachments to their parents. The controversies surrounding infant day care and its effects thus come to the fore in the fourth section. Following intensive and contentious research, substantial evidence about the immediate effects of infant day care on infant-mother attachment has now been gathered. Focus on infant-mother attachment has also fostered research concerned with the effects of infant day care on other important aspects of development such as compliance with adults, peer relationships, behavior problems, and cognitive/intellectual development. In all literatures other than that concerned with infant-mother attachment, quality of care has emerged as a crucially important issue.

In some respects, debates concerning the risks posed by infant day care parallel controversies a decade or two earlier concerning the effects of nonparental care on preschoolers (discussed in the fifth section). In the 1970s, anxieties about the effects of nonmaternal care on child-mother attachment had predominated, with professionals warning that damaged attachments would in turn lead to maladaptation in other aspects of development. Only in discussions regarding the benefits of compensatory education for impoverished children were these concerns submerged, presumably because the risks were viewed as less serious than the potential gains. Research on nonparental care initiated after infancy has been considerably less intensive than research on infant and toddler day care in the past decade, and thus the section on preschoolers is considerably shorter than the section on infants. In the case of both early- and late-initiated care, however, quality of care appears to be an important consideration.

As noted earlier, public and professional concerns about the effects of nonparental care have been focused on infants, toddlers, and preschool-age children, but increases in the rates and extent of maternal employment have also left many parents searching to arrange supervision and care for their elementary school-age children. What little is known about the differential effects of self-care and various forms of afterschool care is summarized in the sixth section. The chapter ends with an integrative summary and conclusion.

DAY CARE IN CULTURAL CONTEXT

Recent media hyperbole notwithstanding, arrangements regarding nonparental child care do not represent a new set of problems for the world's parents. In fact, decisions and arrangements about children's care and supervision are among the oldest problems faced by human society. The fact that they were not discussed frequently in the past may reflect the failure of the men with political and intellectual power to discuss a "women's issue" as well as the fact that maternal care at home has been the dominant mode of early child care in the groups and times of primary interest to social and political scientists.

Unfortunately, the long history of attempts to make child care arrangements has not reduced the complexity of the issues faced by contemporary parents and policymakers, although it has ensured that a diverse array of solutions or resolutions has been developed. In this section, I sketch some of the arrangements that have developed in various parts of the world. The goal is to provide a framework for analyzing these individual solutions and for making cautious and informed comparisons among them. In the first subsection, child care is placed in the context of species-typical behavior patterns and needs. I then discuss the various purposes that nonparental child care can be designed to serve. In the third subsection, I describe the ideological dimensions along which countries can be arrayed and the resulting dangers of superficial generalization from one country to another. Finally, the implications for policymakers, researchers, and practitioners are summarized. These implications are revisited later in the chapter after the empirical literature has been examined.

Human Ecology

The evolution of Homo sapiens created a species for which decisions about child care arrangements and the division of time and energy among child care, provisioning, and other survival-relevant activities have always been necessary (Lancaster, Rossi, Altmann, & Sherrod, 1987). For biological and anatomical reasons, humans are born at a much earlier stage of individual development than are the young of any other mammalian species (Altmann, 1987). As a result, a larger proportion of development takes place outside of the womb in humans than in any other mammal, and this ensures that the period of dependency, and thus the process of socialization, are greatly extended. As a consequence, parental investment in each child must be extremely high for the child to survive. In addition, humans have long been forced to develop complex and extended alliances and arrangements with others to ensure the survival of both themselves and their offspring. Many theorists believe that pair-bonding represents one adaptation to the basic needs of human parents to cooperate in the provisioning, defense, and rearing of their offspring (Lancaster & Lancaster, 1987): the family emerged as a result. In some environments, multifamily units developed to maximize individual survival in circumstances where, for example, hunting or gathering required cooperative strategies.

Studies of modern hunter-gatherers provide insight into the social organizations that might have developed in circumstances such as these. In many such societies, within-family divisions of responsibility between men and women are paralleled by cooperative hunting strategies among men and cooperative gathering strategies among women. Depending on the task, the season, the children's ages, the availability of alternatives, and the women's condition, children accompany one or the other parent or are left under the supervision of older children or adults. Although the strategies of provisioning, protection, and child care are different in industrialized countries as well as in those societies where pastoral or agricultural traditions have replaced nomadic hunting and gathering, similar choices must always be made. Exclusive maternal care throughout the period of dependency was never an option in what Bowlby (1969) called "the environment of evolutionary adaptedness," and there are no societies today in which it is the typical practice. Indeed, exclusive maternal care through adulthood was seldom an option in any phase of human history; it emerged as a possibility for a small, elite segment of society during one small portion of human history. According to Weisner and Gallimore (1977), infants in 40% of the cultures they sampled were cared for more than half the time by people other than their mothers, and rates are surely higher where toddlers, preschoolers, and young children are concerned. It is thus testimony to the power of recent mythology and ignorance of the dominant human condition throughout history that exclusive maternal care came to be labeled as the "traditional" or "natural" form of human child care, with all deviations from this portrayed as unnatural and potentially dangerous. Braverman (1989) decries this creation of "the myth of motherhood," and Silverstein (1991) has bemoaned the way the historically recent "essentializing" of maternal care has shaped the popular and scholarly approach to conceptualizing and studying various forms of nonmaternal care. Such patterns of care are portrayed as deviant, even though they predominate overwhelmingly in both the developed and developing world. What does differ, however, is the willingness of parents in industrialized countries to leave their children in the care of a succession of unrelated paid care providers, rather than the neighbors or kin who shared in the care of young children in most cultures historically and currently (Werner, 1984).

Individual choices among the available options are determined by economic circumstances, local social demography, history, and cultural ideology. Of these, economic forces—particularly the need for women to work outside the home to support their families—play the major role in determining whether and what types of nonparental care arrangements are made. To complicate matters, however, economic, demographic, ideological, and historical factors often exert inconsistent and contrasting pressures. In most Western European and North American countries, for example, parents began to seek extensive assistance with children before such practices were popularly endorsed. In this fashion, economic circumstances forced families to make nonmaternal care arrangements of which many parents and their peers disapproved. Only later did the ideology change. It is not uncommon both for ideology to be shaped by practice rather than vice versa and for ideology to exert a cautious brake on change rather than being the driving force behind such change.

The central prominence of economic forces can be illustrated with many examples. In agricultural societies, for example, infants are typically left in the care of siblings, relatives, or neighbors while their mothers work in the fields (e.g., Leiderman & Leiderman, 1974; Nerlove, 1974; Weisner & Gallimore, 1977). Economic factors are also important in more developed countries. Mason and Duberstein (1992) have shown that the availability and affordability of child care influences maternal employment in the United States, and this realization motivated the design of family policy in many socialist and communist countries. Sweden's remarkably comprehensive, well-integrated, and carefully planned national family policy was developed because the rapid industrialization of Sweden and the sustained demands for the products of Swedish industry produced a national labor shortage. To increase the number of women who were employed and to increase the willingness of young families to bear and rear future workers, it was necessary to develop a comprehensive system in which women were paid well, early child care could be accomplished without professional or financial sacrifices, and the assured availability of high-quality nonparental child care facilities made it a positive experience to have and rear children (Broberg & Hwang, 1991; Gunnarsson, 1993; Haas, 1992; Hwang & Broberg, 1992; Lamb & Levine, 1983).

The communist countries of Eastern Europe likewise made child care facilities widely available to facilitate the increased participation of women in the paid labor force (Kamerman & Kahn, 1978, 1981). These governments were not motivated by noble ideologies any more than were the brief attempts by the U.S. and Canadian governments to become involved in the financial support and supervision of nonmaternal child care facilities during the Second World War (Griswold, 1993; Tuttle, 1993). The establishment and funding of day care centers in North America during this era was motivated by the need to enable or encourage women to work in war-related industries while potential male workers were away at war. Not surprisingly, therefore, when the men were demobilized, support for the day care centers rapidly disappeared. In place of Rosie the Riveter emerged the myth of the traditional American family, a powerful image that led women out of the paid labor force and into domestic roles and responsibilities.

Similarly, in what is now Israel, small agricultural settlements called kibbutzim were established in the early part of the 20th century by Jewish socialists from Eastern Europe who were determined to establish a new lifestyle by cultivating the land of Israel after centuries of exile (Infield, 1944). The malaria-infested swamplands and rocky desert soils posed severe problems for the idealistic and inexperienced farmers. Because of the poor economic and housing conditions and the need for female labor, it was expedient to have one person, usually a woman, take care of several children rather than have each mother care for her own child. To maximize productivity, the original kibbutznikim decided that children should live in collective dormitories, visiting their parents for several hours every day (Neubauer, 1965). Over the ensuing decades, the emergence of the communal child care system has been attributed to ideological commitment and the role played by economic necessity has been downplayed. Interestingly, most of the kibbutzim have prospered economically and have abandoned many of their socialist and communalistic ideals, including the central "children's houses," though they still provide well-equipped child care facilities (Rosenthal, 1991b). Contemporary lifestyles on the kibbutzim contrast with the values upon which the kibbutz system was founded, leading to frequent inconsistencies between the expressed goals of the child rearing system and its actual implementation.

The tendency to develop post hoc ideological explanations of cultural patterns is pervasive in human societies and tends to obscure the central role of economic circumstances in the development of nonparental care arrangements. Lamb, Sternberg, Hwang, and Broberg (1992) could identify no country in which the basic demand for nonmaternal child care at the societal level was not driven primarily by economic forces, although subgroups (e.g., the British upper class) occasionally sought child care assistance (e.g., nannies) for other reasons.

The Goals and Purposes of Nonparental Child Care

The crucial role of economic forces—in particular, the increasing need for women to seek employment outside the home—forces us to ask whose interests nonparental child care arrangements should or do serve. Because developmental psychologists have studied the effects on children, and opponents of nonparental care often cite adverse effects on children to justify their opposition, one might mistakenly conclude that nonparental care was designed primarily to serve the needs of children. In fact, nonparental care arrangements have typically proliferated because parents need to seek employment and cannot simultaneously care for their children (Lamb, Sternberg, Hwang, & Broberg, 1992). With economic need driving demand and availability, however, nonparental child care has been used in various countries to serve a variety of purposes. Four purposes or goals recur with sufficient regularity to merit attention here: fostering equal employment opportunities, providing acculturation and ideological indoctrination, encouraging economic self-sufficiency, and enriching children's lives.

Fostering Female Employment

As mentioned earlier, child care policies in many countries have been designed at least in part to promote female employment and to equalize the potential employment opportunities of men and women (Cochran, 1993; Lamb, Sternberg, Hwang, & Broberg, 1992). The formerly communist countries of Asia and Eastern Europe, for example, made this a central feature of their family policies (Foteeva, 1993; Kamerman & Kahn, 1978, 1981; Korczak, 1993; Nemenyi, 1993; Zhengao, 1993). Unfortunately, equality of opportunity has never been achieved anywhere despite the costly and extensive investment in child care facilities. Even in countries like Sweden, with a long-established and popular commitment to gender equality, almost all child care providers are women. Ironically, therefore, whether or not it is economically possible for both men and women to be gainfully employed outside the home, most employed women are engaged in female-typed activities—often the same activities they would otherwise perform at home without pay. And in most countries, women do not enjoy equitable pay, whether or not their professions are integrated.

Acculturation of Immigrants

Child care facilities have frequently been used to facilitate acculturation or ideological indoctrination as well. In northern Italy, for example, the number of children in preschools nearly doubled in the 1960s because the educational philosopher Ciari believed that preschools could be used to provide cultural foundations for children from different backgrounds (Corsaro & Emiliani, 1992). In Israel, meanwhile, the speed with which successive waves of Jewish immigrants have risen to positions of economic and political power can be partially attributed to the participation of immigrant children in preschool programs where they learn Hebrew and the norms of Israeli culture (Rosenthal, 1992). The children in turn socialize and teach their parents. In the People's Republic of China, child care was made available in the early 1950s ostensibly to help children learn the importance of hard work and individual sacrifice (Lee, 1992). Universal day care also permitted parents to participate in reeducation programs, sponsored by the new communist government as part of its plan for the reconstruction of China. Finally, Shwalb and his colleagues (1992) point out that preschool education was made widely available to 4- and 5-year-old Japanese children in 1941 in part because the government wanted to use educational institutions to foster nationalism.

Reduction of Welfare Dependency

Child care facilities have also been provided to encourage women to seek job training or paid employment and thus to cease being the beneficiaries of welfare; in the United States, pursuit of this goal has led politicians to propose major revisions of the welfare system in the 1990s. This goal has been promoted with greatest vigor in the United States by politicians who have opposed other governmental involvement in child care. Similar goals have been pursued in Israel by politicians of diverse ideological persuasions.

Enrichment of Children's Lives

Some child care facilities and policies have been developed because policymakers want to enrich the lives of children (Getis & Vinovskis, 1992). The impetus to develop and invest in intervention programs grew in the late 1950s and early 1960s, following the determination by experts that poor children experienced understimulation, overstimulation, or inappropriate stimulation, which in turn led them to perform poorly in school and on achievement tests (Clarke-Stewart, 1977; Fein & Clarke-Stewart, 1973; Hess, 1970). The development in the United States of the Head Start program in 1965 exemplified such a motivation to enrich the lives of children from the poorest and most disadvantaged families (Lamb, Sternberg, & Ketterlinus, 1992; Zigler & Valentine, 1979). Likewise, despite its strong opposition to nonmaternal care, the Catholic Church in Italy came to view preschools as an effective technique for socializing children from impoverished homes whose parents were considered incapable of effective socialization (Corsaro & Emiliani, 1992; New, 1993); only later was preschool deemed acceptable for children in better socioeconomic circumstances. In Great Britain, day care is still considered a service for children at risk because their parents cannot cope (Melhuish & Moss, 1992); popular disapproval of day care is reinforced there by a policy of channeling government funding to day care centers serving disadvantaged, troubled, and disabled children. In Canada, meanwhile, it took the recommendations of a government task force in the mid-1980s to recast day care as a service of potential value to all Canadian families, rather than solely a service for disadvantaged and immigrant children (Goelman, 1992; Pence, 1993).

In most cases, however, concern with enriching the lives of children does not motivate the initial development of nonparental care facilities: it represents an attempt to make the best of existing practice. Parents and their governmental representatives may hope for care of adequate quality, but there is ample evidence that parents often accept care of lower quality, perhaps because they simply have no choice but to make such arrangements (National Academy of Science, 1990). Where parents, groups, and societies have seriously considered the needs and best interests of children, these have often been secondary considerations. Many politicians and social commentators argue further that few societies, whether industrialized or nonindustrialized, have addressed children's needs satisfactorily.

Dimensions of Cross-Cultural Variation

Although the need to supervise children while their parents are employed is widespread, cultures clearly differ with respect to the other goals that nonparental child care is expected to serve. In addition, there are four major philosophical or ideological dimensions along which contemporary societies can be compared. The first is one that has already been broached: the ideology concerning *equality between men and women* and the ways the availability of nonmaternal care programs increases female labor participation and allows women to advance themselves economically and professionally.

Consider next international variations in the extent to which the provision of child care is viewed as a *public responsibility* rather than a *private* or individual *concern.* The United States and the United Kingdom probably represent the extremes among the capitalist societies holding that decisions about child care should be left to individual families, that the cost and quality of care should be set by the competition between the unregulated forces of supply and demand, and that governmental intrusions of all kinds should be resisted on the grounds that they would simply reduce efficiency (Cohen, 1993; Lamb, Sternberg, Hwang, & Broberg, 1992; Scarr, 1992; Spedding, 1993). At the other extreme stand the democratic-socialist countries of Scandinavia and the formerly communist countries of Eastern Europe, in which society as a whole was believed to share responsibility for the care and welfare of all children (Hwang & Broberg, 1992; Kamerman & Kahn, 1978, 1981; Stoltenberg, 1994). The child care systems that evolved in each country necessarily reflected that society's position regarding public and private responsibilities. Contributions to Lamb, Sternberg, Hwang, and Broberg's (1992) volume suggest that the best quality nonparental care is provided or regulated by governmental agencies in the context of comprehensive family policies. By contrast, countries or regions that have failed to develop comprehensive family policies tend to provide care of much poorer average quality.

Third, societies vary with respect to whether child care is viewed as a *social welfare program* or an *early educational program.* Since all industrialized countries and most developing countries regularly assign responsibility for children older than 5 or 6 years of age to educational authorities, many countries have expanded the availability of care settings for young children by emphasizing the educational value of preschool care. Because public education is a widely accepted concept, it has proven relatively easy to direct public finances to the support of preschool settings when this strategy is adopted, as exemplified recently by attempts in the United States to establish "Schools of the 21st Century": full-day all-year educational programs for children ages 3 to 13 (Zigler & Finn-Stevenson, 1996; Zigler & Lang, 1991). By contrast, when nonparental care is viewed as a custodial babysitting service addressing the goals of social welfare, it has proven harder to obtain support for the concept of public responsibility and harder yet to make quality of care a relevant dimension. Thus, the presumed character of nonparental care has major and far-reaching implications for the quality, type, and public support of nonparental care services. In Italy, the United Kingdom, France, and the Netherlands, for example, the portrayal of day care as an educational service ("nursery schools") rather than a welfare service altered perceptions of its value by middle- and upper-class families and thus legitimized its widespread utilization (Clerkx & Van IJzendoorn, 1992; Corsaro & Emiliani, 1992; Lamb, Sternberg, Hwang, & Broberg, 1992; Melhuish & Moss, 1992; Musattii & Mantovani, 1990). Olmsted (1992) notes that, among the developed countries, higher percentages of preschoolers are enrolled in nonparental care settings when there have been educational rather than custodial goals. O'Connor (1995) has chronicled the emergent distinctions at the turn of the century between day nurseries and kindergartens in St. Louis; the latter came to be seen as part of the educational process and flourished, whereas day nurseries experienced the struggle for support that continues to this day. Cahan (1989), too, chronicled the emergence of separate child care and early childhood education pathways in the nineteenth and twentieth centuries.

The last, infrequently considered factor concerns *basic conceptions of childhood and developmental process.* Many inhabitants of the Western industrialized countries are steeped in the Freudian and post-Freudian belief that early experiences are crucially important; they seldom step back and recognize this belief as an ideological statement of faith rather than an empirically proven statement of fact. As a consequence, Western social scientists seldom recognize that this belief in the crucial importance of the early weeks, months, and years of life is not shared by most people on this planet today, and that many societies, particularly in Asia, emphasize the formative effects of experiences occurring after the age of reason (6 or 7 years) rather than before (Lee, 1992; Shwalb & Chen, 1996). In such societies, it is not unreasonable to emphasize custodial aspects of care designed largely to ensure survival until the age of reason begins. Thus, these differing belief systems have major implications for child care practices and the seriousness of concerns about the quality of care.

Analysts of comparative child care practices and policies need to consider these four dimensions (ideologies concerning male and female roles, perceptions of private and public responsibilities, educational and custodial goals, and conceptions of developmental processes) when evaluating the policies and systems of diverse countries because international differences on these dimensions make it difficult, probably inappropriate, and perhaps dangerous to generalize from one country to another and to use any country's social policies as models for adoption by others. Only when we fully understand the social structures and the ideologies that led to the development of a particular child care system are we likely to learn from the experiences of other societies.

To illustrate this point, consider Sweden, whose family policies are widely envied and often cited as exemplary models for the rest of the world. Less frequently noted is the fact that the nation's history, economy, and ideology are about as unique as its family policies. Sweden is a culturally and linguistically homogeneous country of about 8 million people; it experienced relatively little immigration for several centuries. The dominant political ideology—democratic socialism—was so well established that the Social Democratic Party remained in power for all but 3 of the 50 years between 1932 and 1991. The country also has a long and sincere history of commitment to the attainment of gender equality. Historically, Sweden switched with remarkable rapidity from a basically agrarian economy to a highly industrialized country. After remaining neutral and relatively untouched by the two World Wars that ravaged the rest of Europe, Sweden emerged from the Second World War as the only European country with a functioning, undamaged, and modern industrial base capable of providing consumer goods to the rest of the world. As a result, Sweden has since experienced a degree of affluence shared by few other countries. The generous family policies that Swedes enjoy are the product of these factors, which made it relatively easy to develop a comprehensive universal child care system.

Affluence alone was not the key, and it is dangerous to look uncritically toward Sweden (or any other country) as a universal model, just as it is dangerous to generalize research results from one society to another in the face of important differences at the level of measurement, at the level of constructs, and in the meaning of certain behaviors that may limit the relevance and validity of research in other countries. Some universals presumably exist, but the equivalence of the effects and developmental processes should be demonstrated, not assumed. Consider, by way of comparison, that Switzerland and Sweden have comparably affluent standards of living. The Swiss speak four distinct languages, however, and owe allegiance to 23 cantons and three cities with a history of rivalry and independence. A national system like that developed in Sweden does not constitute a useful model for Switzerland. Nor does Sweden provide a good model for a geographically huge and populous country like the United States, characterized by cultural heterogeneity, ideological diversity, economic inequality, and insistent commitments to individualism and capitalism.

In addition, differences in parental and national goals lead to differences in the implementation of programs and in the effects of child care, and the evaluation of those outcomes differs from society to society. Within the United States, for example, some view assertiveness as a desirable goal, whereas others view it as one manifestation of undesirable aggression. Everywhere debate persists over the relative value of individualism and cooperation. Is compliance an index of passive acquiescence or of being well socialized? As long as disagreements persist concerning these values, it becomes impossible to determine whether any given pattern of child care has "positive" or "negative" effects.

Few countries have actually developed integrated child care systems that address all the functions of child care equally well. Even the best-developed and most carefully integrated systems must deal with the contradictory impulses created by pursuit of these different goals; in most countries a patchwork array of solutions has emerged over time, with different and often contradictory policies designed to address each of these needs. At its best, pursuit of the highest possible quality of care forces ideologically liberal governments toward a dilemma. Better quality care almost invariably involves more adults taking care of fewer children, and this becomes expensive. In fact, after concluding that it is cheaper to provide infant care at home than to provide out-of-home care of good quality, successive Swedish governments have gradually extended the duration of paid parental leave permitting parents to stay at home with their children—a generous resolution that may strengthen parent-child relationships at the expense of other worthy goals for both parents and children. Does high-quality nonparental care provide some unique and valuable formative experiences of which children in exclusive parental care will be deprived? What happens to the goals of gender equality and salary equity when families almost invariably conclude that mothers rather than fathers should withdraw from paid work to care for their children? What values are conveyed by the assignment of child care to members of an immigrant lower class (Wrigley, 1995)? How can one satisfy the competing agendas that child care policies must address?

Summary

Clearly, individuals and societies have developed a large number of solutions to age-old needs for child care. The variety and diversity of these solutions illustrate the ways historical, economic, ideological, and demographic realities shape the context in which individuals, families, and societies operate, and constrain the solutions or policies they can develop. Employed parents need to obtain care for their children, and this chapter is concerned largely with the circumstances in which they make these decisions as well as with their effects on child development.

The development of child care policies has become increasingly important to governments around the world. As a result, new policies, plans, and practices are being developed worldwide. But despite the development of family policies and child care facilities, the demand for child care far outstrips the available supply in almost every country. This in turn maintains the pressure on governments, private agencies, and parents to make arrangements that are not optimal.

Interestingly, discussions of the needs for child care have, with few exceptions, portrayed child care as a women's issue, whereas decisions about how and where children will be raised concern both mothers and fathers. Swedish sociologists and policymakers recognized more than three decades ago (e.g., Dahlström, 1962) that major changes in paternal involvement were unlikely unless they were preceded by changes in the underlying expectations about the appropriate roles and responsibilities of men and women and changes in the opportunities available to men and women within the home as well as in the world of paid employment. In this regard, it is conceivable that group care settings may instill greater concern for the community and a commitment to less sexist values. These possibilities have not been explored empirically, but the near exclusive reliance on female care providers makes it unlikely that day care gives children a less sexist view of which adults are most responsible for child care, whether or not mothers are employed.

Decades of research have made clear that one cannot make blanket statements about the superiority of exclusive maternal care, paternal care, or nonparental care (Lamb, 1986; Lamb & Sternberg, 1990). In each case, the quality of care appears crucial; the development of most children is affected by the quality of care received both at home and in out-of-home care facilities and by the extent to which the care is sensitively adjusted so as to be appropriate given children's developmental and individual needs. The implication is that societies need to provide an array of options that allow parents to choose child care arrangements that are most appropriate given their children's ages and individual styles, the family's economic and social circumstances, and the values and attitudes the parents hold.

Furthermore, nonparental child care must be viewed in the context of the whole ecology of socialization, because child care patterns are manifestations of the wider social structure. Development is a complex, multifaceted process, and thus we are only likely to understand it if we look, not simply at patterns of nonparental care, but at these patterns of care in the context of other experiences, ideologies, and practices. Nonparental child care arrangements do not exist in social vacuums and are likely to have relatively small discrete and direct effects on development, though they may be important parts of the web of influences and experiences that shape children's development. Because development is such a multifaceted and complicated process, it is essential to understand the role played by each of those experiences in shaping the course of human development. With that in mind, I next consider evidence concerning the extent to which children, especially in the United States, experience nonparental care in the first few years of their lives.

CHANGING PATTERNS OF NONMATERNAL CARE IN THE UNITED STATES

"Day care" was once viewed as a service used primarily by single mothers and disadvantaged Black families; middle-class families sent their children to "nursery schools" and "child development centers" (Phillips, 1989). Recent statistics illustrate that this view is inaccurate, and that Black and White families have very similar needs for nonparental care. The proportions of employed Black and White mothers of preschoolers were the same by 1995, with a larger proportion of White than of Black mothers of school-age children in the workforce. Likewise, there are few differences in the employment rates of married and single mothers (Hayghe, 1995). Approximately 66% of preschool children and 75% of school-age children had mothers in the workforce by 1995 (Hayghe, 1995). Even higher proportions had employed fathers. And whereas employed mothers in European countries tend to work part time, employed mothers in the United States tend to work full time because there is a dearth of well-paying part-time jobs (Cherlin, 1992).

In popular discourse, a wide variety of nonparental care arrangements are referred to as day care. Day care has become a generic term referring to various types of nonparental care—family day care, care by nonparental relatives, in-home babysitters, nursery schools, and day care centers—for anywhere between 5 and 55 hours per week. The purpose of this section is to summarize available information about the extent of variation in the patterns of care that infants, toddlers, and preschoolers receive, and to quantify recent changes in these patterns.

The Census Bureau's annual reports, *Who's Minding the Kids?,* which use Survey of Income and Program Participation (SIPP) data and data from the National Child Care Survey (NCCS) conducted by Hofferth and her colleagues (Hofferth, 1992b; Hofferth, Brayfield, Deich, & Holcomb, 1991; Willer, Hofferth, Kisker, Divine-Hawkins, Farquhar, & Glantz, 1991), provide the most extensive and up-to-date information about child care patterns drawn from nationally representative samples.

The Census Bureau's child care data have been collected as a supplement to the SIPP since 1984. The most recently published Census data on child care were collected between October 1991 and January 1992, although some unpublished SIPP data from 1993 are included in Table 2.1. Child care data in the SIPP are gathered using samples of about 3,400 households in which mothers are employed either full or part time. These households are randomly drawn from the noninstitutionalized U.S. population, although, because of the selection criteria, the child care arrangements of the 300,000 preschool children who live alone with their fathers, of the 700,000 preschool children whose mothers are studying full time, and of the 9 million children whose mothers are not employed are not included or represented in these data.

When conducting the NCCS, by contrast, Hofferth et al. (1991) contacted a random sample of households located in 100 counties across the United States and identified families with children under 13. Between October 1989 and May 1990, 4,392 parents (mostly mothers) were interviewed over the telephone about their child care arrangements, as well as about a host of demographic characteristics. To complement the Census Bureau data, Hofferth and her colleagues interviewed families with both employed and nonemployed mothers, as well as respondents in father-only households. In a parallel study, A Profile of Child Care Settings (PCS), Hofferth and her colleagues (Kisker, Hofferth, Phillips, & Farquhar, 1991) surveyed child care providers and family day care centers in the same 100 counties during the same study period.

Table 2.1 Primary Child Care Arrangements for Children under 5 (expressed in percentages)

	Employed	Unemployed	All	Full-Time	Part-Time	All Employed
Parent	30	65	46	20	44	29
Father				15	29	20
Mother				5	15	9
Relative (nonparent, in or out of child's home)	18	11	15	24	23	23
In-home (nonrelative)	4	2	3	6	5	5
Family Day Care (out of home, unrelated provider)	19	3	11	21	13	18
Center	26	15	20	28	15	23

Source: First three columns, National Child Care Survey, 1990; second three columns, SIPP, 1991 (Hofferth et al., 1991; U.S. Bureau of the Census, 1993).

In 1991, there were about 19.5 million children under 5 years of age in the United States, and 9.9 million of them lived in families with employed mothers (U.S. Census, 1994). About 63% of these mothers were employed full time. Maternal employment rates rise as preschoolers grow older. According to the 1990 NCCS, 25% of mothers with children under age 1 were employed full time and 15% were employed part time, whereas 39% of mothers with children aged 3 to 4 were employed full time and 19% were employed part time (Willer et al., 1991). The National Institute of Child Health and Human Development (NICHD) Early Child Care Research Network (in press) reported that, in their prospective longitudinal study, the proportion of infants receiving care from someone other than their mothers for 30 hours or more per week in the first year of life was 58%, with 74% receiving 10 hours or more. Nationally, 55% of mothers with children under 1 year of age were employed or looking for work by 1994 (Hayghe, 1995).

Child care arrangements vary considerably depending on the employment status of the mother (see Table 2.1). Mothers working full time were almost twice as likely as those employed part time to use child care centers (28% versus 15%), about 50% more likely to use family day care (21% versus 13%), and less than half as likely to rely on parental child care (20% versus 44%). In families with mothers who were employed part time, fathers were twice as likely to be the primary nonmaternal care provider as they were in families with mothers employed full time (29% versus 15%). The rates of relative care and in-home nonrelative care did not vary depending on whether mothers were employed part or full time, however.

Parental child care was by far the most common care arrangement in families in which mothers were not employed: the NCCS estimates that almost two-thirds of the preschoolers in these families were primarily cared for by their parents (65%) and that nearly three-quarters (73%) of the children under age 3 were primarily cared for by one of their parents. These families were consequently less likely to make any use of nonparental care. Interestingly, however, by ages 3 to 4, there was little difference between families with nonemployed and employed mothers in preschool and kindergarten enrollment rates (50% versus 60% in 1991; U.S. Bureau of the Census, 1993). As would be expected, however, children of nonemployed mothers spent much less time in child care centers than their peers whose mothers were employed: about 80% of children with nonemployed mothers spent less than 20 hours a week, whereas 55% of the children with employed mothers spent 35 or more hours a week at child care facilities.

Examination of Table 2.2 reveals that, between 1977 and 1991, care by relatives and family day care providers became less common, whereas center care became more popular, especially between 1977 and 1985, after which utilization rates stabilized. Between 1970 and 1989, the proportion of 3- and 4-year-olds enrolled in center-based programs nearly doubled from 21% to 39% (Hofferth et al., 1991). The proportion of preschoolers in families with employed mothers (both part and full time) who were primarily cared for by their parents remained fairly constant (around 25%). Between 1988 and 1991, the proportion of preschoolers who were cared for by their fathers while their mothers worked increased by a third (15% to 20%), after remaining at around 14% to 15% between 1977 and 1988. Many families rely on nonoverlapping work schedules to permit exclusive reliance on parental care, although the motivations for preferring such arrangements remain poorly understood (Presser, 1986, 1988, 1992a; Presser & Cain, 1983).

In addition to maternal employment status, a number of demographic characteristics, including family income, marital status, age of the child, and region of residence, seem to be associated with differences in child care arrangements (see Table 2.3). Parents in two-income families whose annual incomes exceed $54,000 are more apt to use center care than those whose combined income is less than $18,000 per annum (34% versus 21%). Conversely, low-income families with employed mothers are more likely than high-income families to rely on parental care (28% versus 20%) and care by relatives (29% versus

Table 2.2 Primary Child Care Arrangements for Children under 5 with Employed Mothers (expressed in percentages)

	1977	1985	1988	1990	1991	1993
Parent (either)	25	24	23	24	29	22
Father	14	16	15	16	20	16
Mother (at work)	11	8	8	8	9	6
Relative (nonparent, in or out of child's home)	31	25	23	23	23	25
In-home (nonrelative)	7	6	5	5	5	5
Family Day Care (out of home, unrelated provider)	22	22	24	20	18	17
Center	13	23	26	27	23	30

Source: Census data (from the SIPP database) (Hofferth et al., 1991; U.S. Bureau of the Census, 1993).

Table 2.3 Primary Child Care Arrangements for Children with Employed Mothers, by Demographic Characteristics of the Family, 1991 (expressed in percentages)

	Parent	(Father)	(Mother)	Relative	In-Home	Family Day Care	Center
Income							
<poverty	37	27	10	28	4	11	19
>poverty	27	19	8	23	6	19	24
<$15,000	48	22	2	8	15		
<$18,000	28	21	7	29	4	16	21
$18–36,000	35	25	10	26	3	16	19
$36–54,000	28	20	8	24	5	19	22
>$54,000	20	12	8	15	9	21	34
Race							
White	30	21	9	21	6	18	23
Black	18	14	4	35	1	17	27
Hispanic	25	19	6	31	9	10	22
Marital Status							
Married, with spouse present	33	23	10	21	6	17	23
All other	11	7	4	36	5	21	25
Region							
Northeast	36	27	9	27	8	12	16
Midwest	33	23	10	20	5	21	20
South	20	15	5	25	2	21	30
West	29	18	11	23	7	15	25
Metropolitan							
Greater Metropolitan	30	21	9	23	6	17	23
Center city	31	24	7	24	7	17	23
Rural	26	18	8	24	4	21	24

Source: SIPP, 1991, except third line, which provides 1990 data from the NCCS. Families with employed *and* unemployed mothers are included in these figures only (Hofferth et al., 1991; U.S. Bureau of the Census, 1993).

15%). When maternal employment status is ignored, however, families with incomes between $15,000 and $25,000 per annum are the most likely to rely on parental care (49%). Presumably, families with higher annual income depend on the earnings of two working parents, and thus have a greater need for nonparental care, whereas families with annual incomes between $15,000 and $25,000 are more likely to be supported by a single wage earner, and also tend not to be eligible for many of the subsidized programs available to low-income families.

In 1991, preschoolers whose mothers were married were at least three times more likely to be cared for by their fathers than were preschoolers whose mothers were not married (23% versus 7%), although the proportion of preschoolers with unmarried mothers who were cared for by their fathers almost tripled between 1988 and 1991. On the other hand, single mothers' children were more likely than married mothers' children to be cared for by their grandparents or other relatives (36% versus 21%).

Child care arrangements also differ across regions of the country, most notably in center care utilization. Preschoolers in the South were the most likely to be enrolled in day care centers, the primary care arrangement for about 30% of them, compared with only 16% and 20% in the Northeast and Midwest, respectively.

According to the PCS (Kisker et al., 1991), about 65% of the centers serving preschoolers were nonprofit organizations, and the remainder were under for-profit auspices. For-profit agencies were much more likely to be in the South (where the largest proportion of preschoolers go to child care centers) and in rural and suburban areas. Most (83%) for-profit centers were independent rather than members of a chain. About 60% of nonprofit centers were operated under the auspices of another organization, primarily religious organizations (23%), Head Start (14%), or public schools (12%).

Age of the child also influences parents' child care choices and decisions (see Table 2.4). According to the PCS (Kisker et al., 1991), over 80% of infants under age 1 with employed mothers were cared for in homes, either their own or another's, whereas only 12% were cared for in child care centers and 8% by their mothers at work. For 1- and 2-year-olds, in-home care arrangements were made for 73%, while the proportion in center care rose to 18%. By contrast, in-home care was received by 56% of 3- to 4-year-old children, and center care by 33%. Table 2.4 also shows that, over the preschool years, care by relatives steadily decreases in importance, but center care becomes increasingly prominent. Over 60% of preschoolers in organized center care were 3 to 4 years old, 31% were 1 to 2 years old, and only 8% were under 1 year old.

Using NCCS data, Hofferth (1994) also looked at the characteristics of families who used Head Start, a comprehensive, federally funded child care program designed to serve the poorest families. To be eligible for Head Start, families must have a child between the ages of 3 and 5 and have incomes below the poverty level or collect Aid to Families with Dependent Children (AFDC); 68% of the families whose children attend Head Start collect AFDC (Brayfield, Deich, & Hofferth, 1990). Given these restrictions, fewer than one-quarter (23%, according to Hofferth, 1994) of eligible children enroll in Head Start programs (see also Chafel, 1992). One reason for the overrepresentation of unemployed families may well be the limited hours of care provided by Head Start programs, which usually provide part-time care that is not sufficient for employed mothers. The availability of places doubtless limits enrollment as well. African American children, children whose mothers did not complete high school, children with two nonworking parents, and children whose mothers attended job training programs are also more likely than their eligible counterparts to participate in Head Start. Single parents, both employed and nonemployed, are less likely to enroll their children in Head Start, perhaps because it is more difficult for them to arrange drop-off and pickup, especially at part-day programs. Interestingly, eligible children who live in communities with higher standards of living are also more likely to enroll, perhaps because such communities make better-organized efforts to obtain and maintain Head Start funding. Although Head Start was designed to serve the poorest families, Hofferth found that within the group of the Head Start–eligible, the degree of poverty did not predict enrollment.

According to Hofferth's (1994) survey, the most common child care arrangement among nonenrolled Head Start–eligible children was parental care (45%); another 17% relied on relatives. A little less than a quarter (23%) of the children received center-based care, only about half of the time in programs offering "comprehensive services." About 56% of these programs were school-based (35% public and 21% private), 26% were church-based, and 18% were programs in community centers. Although these church- and school-based programs sometimes offered many of the same services as Head Start, they were usually not as extensive (Hofferth, 1994).

Summary

Over the past two decades, dramatic increases in the rates of maternal employment and single parenthood have taken place, bringing with them substantial increases in reliance on nonparental care. The majority of infants in the United States are now cared for on a regular basis by someone other than their mothers or fathers, and the same is true of more than two-thirds of the children under 4 years of age. Similar trends are evident in most of the developed countries. In

Table 2.4 Primary Child Care Arrangements for Children under 5 with Employed Mothers (expressed in percentages)

Type of Care	< 1 Year Old	1 to 2 Years Old	3 to 4 Years Old	All Preschoolers
Parent	29	31	26	29
Father	22	21	18	20
Mother	8	10	8	9
Relative (nonparent, in or out of child's home)	31	25	19	23
In-home (nonrelative)	7	5	4	5
Family Day Care (out of home, unrelated provider)	20	20	14	18
Center	11	17	33	23

Source: SIPP (1991) (Hofferth et al., 1991; U.S. Bureau of the Census, 1993).

France, for example, Balleyguier (1988) reported that 30% of French children under 3 were in family day care homes, 15% were in day care centers, and only 40% were cared for exclusively by their parents. In many countries, infants tend to receive care in home-like settings but are moved to center arrangements as they grow older, for either ideological or economic reasons. Only a small proportion of preschoolers are enrolled in formal enrichment programs or model day care or nursery schools, where much of the research—especially the early research—was conducted.

The statistics presented in this brief section illustrate that exposure to nonparental care has become a normative experience for American preschoolers, although the types and extent of nonparental care vary widely, as do the motivations and practices of the parents concerned. One implication for researchers is that there may be differences prior to enrollment in day care between parents who utilize full-time and part-time day care; likewise, children in day care may have different day care histories and trajectories depending on their parents' employment circumstances and schedules. These obviously complicate efforts to discern the effects of day care.

Researchers have been remarkably inattentive to variations in the types of arrangements made by parents. For many years, researchers tended to study children in day care centers, often rather atypical university-affiliated model programs, even though fewer than 15% of the children receiving nonparental care were enrolled in centers in that era (Klein, 1985). Although a far greater proportion were in family day care, such arrangements received little empirical attention. (Ironically, researchers' increased attention to family day care has coincided with an increasing reliance on center care!)

The misplaced focus of researchers has had significant implications: it raised questions about the extent to which one can generalize from available research findings. Family day care, center-based day care, and care provided by relatives and in-home babysitters differ structurally and institutionally and provide different types of experiences for children. Generalization is further imperiled by the tendency of researchers to act as though children were randomly assigned to day care and exclusive parental care groups. This remains an indefensible assumption. By failing to take into account possible differences in the values, practices, and backgrounds of parents who do or do not enroll their children in day care, or in different types of care at different ages, researchers run the risk of attributing group differences to day care when these should be attributed (at least in part) to differences in the values and behavior of the parents and the communities in which they live. Likewise, researchers should (but seldom do) assess the comparability of children and families prior to the assignment to various care arrangements before they interpret later differences in terms of the effects of day care. In addition, of course, none of these types of care should be viewed as homogeneous "treatments," as there are wide variations in the nature and quality of care provided within any group of centers, homes, or babysitters and many, if not most, children experience multiple types of nonmaternal care, serially or contemporaneously. Fortunately, researchers have recently attempted to move beyond main effects studies to studies that take into account family background and child care history. An even larger number have begun to assess the quality of care, and their progress is discussed in the next section.

QUALITY OF CARE

Just as researchers have come to appreciate the diverse array of care arrangements children experience and the possible importance of wide variations in their pre-enrollment characteristics and backgrounds, so too have they come to acknowledge vast differences in the quality of care that children experience both in and outside their homes. As a result, the measurement of quality has improved dramatically in the last decade and this has permitted significant progress in evaluating the effects of variations in the quality of care on children's development.

Process Measures of Quality

Two approaches to the measurement of quality have been pursued: process and structural measures. Conceptually, structural, and process measures differ to the extent that factors indexed by the structural measures potentiate high-quality interaction and care but do not guarantee it, whereas process measures try to quantify the actual care received by children. In practice, however, some of the most popular process measures include indications of environmental features (including those that index safety, for example) as well as indications of interactional quality.

Observational measures of the settings and of the interactions between care providers and children are often described as process measures, and standardized measures developed by Thelma Harms and Richard Clifford have been employed by most researchers in the United States. The Infant/Toddler Environment Rating Scale (ITERS; Harms, Cryer, & Clifford, 1986, 1990) and the Early Childhood Environment Rating Scale (ECERS; Harms &

Clifford, 1980) contain 35 and 37 items, respectively, on which the quality of care is rated by trained observers; from these ratings, scores on seven highly intercorrelated scales can be computed. Scores can also be reduced to two factors—appropriate caregiving and developmentally appropriate activities—although these two tend to be highly intercorrelated as well (Phillips, Voran, Kisker, Howes, & Whitebook, 1994). The Family Day Care Rating Scale (FDCRS; Harms & Clifford, 1989) was developed to provide a 6-factor assessment of the quality of home-based care using 32 items.

In addition to Harms and Clifford's measures, other measures have also been used in major studies. Abbott-Shim and Sibley (1987, 1992) developed the Assessment Profile for Early Childhood Programs (APECP), which contains over 150 items, and Arnett (1989) developed an observational measure of teacher sensitivity that has been used in several large-scale studies. A briefer (26-item) Classroom Practices Inventory (CPI) was developed by Hyson, Hirsh-Pasek, and Rescorla (1990) to tap those aspects of quality subsumed under the National Association for the Education of Young Children's (NAEYC) Guidelines for Developmentally Appropriate Practices (Bredekamp, 1987b). The CPI has not yet been widely used, although Dunn (1993) reported that higher ECERS scores were associated with more developmentally appropriate practices, as assessed using the CPI. Scores on the various process measures are in fact highly correlated with one another, making it possible to use composite measures containing fewer items to measure quality than the complete measures do (Petrogiannis, 1995; Scarr, Eisenberg, & Deater-Deckard, 1994). Items on three of the most widely used process measures are listed in Table 2.5.

The measures just described have proven to be less useful as indices of the quality of care in Western Europe, perhaps because the quality of care available there is less variable and of higher average quality. In Sweden, for example, attempts to use the ECERS scales were abandoned because all the centers sampled achieved near-perfect scores (Wessels, Lamb, Hwang, & Broberg, in press). As the scores did not vary, they were not helpful in efforts to explore the effects of varying quality of care, and thus these researchers were forced to rely on a lesser known spot-sampling technique developed by Belsky and Walker (1980) to assess observable aspects of the quality of care (see Broberg, Hwang, Lamb, & Ketterlinus, 1989; Broberg, Wessels, Lamb, & Hwang, 1997; Hwang, Broberg, & Lamb, 1991; Lamb, Hwang, Bookstein, Broberg, Hult, & Frodi, 1988; Lamb, Hwang, Broberg, & Bookstein, 1988; Wessels et al., in press). Recognizing the need for more systematic and comprehensive measures that could be used internationally, Pierrehumbert and his colleagues (Pierrehumbert, Ramstein, Krucher, El-Najjar, Lamb, & Halfon, 1996) in Switzerland have begun developing measures of quality that could be used in Switzerland, Sweden, and other countries where day care is reported to be of very high quality. Another measure, the Child Care Facility Schedule (CCFS), has been developed for use in countries outside the United States where quality is highly variable (Dragonas, Tsiantis, & Lambidi, 1995). Its predictive and construct validity have yet to be established, however.

Structural Measures of Quality

Instead of process variables, many researchers index quality using a number of structural indices: measures of teacher training and experience, group size, teacher:child ratios, crowding, staff turnover, and the like (e.g., Barnas & Cummings, 1994; Howes & Olenick, 1986). Most of these factors can be and often are regulated, although such factors as stability and continuity obviously cannot be regulated.

Group size and staff–child ratios are popular and easily quantified structural measures. The Panel on Child Care Policy of the National Research Council (1991) recommended group sizes of 6 to 8 for infants, 6 to 12 for 1- to 2-year-olds, 14 to 20 for 3-year-olds, and 16 to 20 for 4- and 5-year-olds, as well as child–staff ratios of 4:1 for infants and 1-year-olds, between 4 and 6:1 for 2-year-olds, between 5 and 10:1 for 3-year-olds, and between 7 and 10:1 for 4- and 5-year-olds. Not surprisingly, standards vary dramatically among states, with about half requiring that licensed care providers obtain child-related training (Phillips, Lande, & Goldberg, 1990; Morgan, Azer, Costley, Genser, Goodman, Lombardi, & McGimsey, 1993). Licensed care providers are, in turn, more likely to offer stimulating environments and nutritious food (Fosburg, Hawkins, Singer, Goodson, Smith, & Brush, 1970; Stallings, 1980).

According to Howes (1983), the adult–child ratio and the extent of teacher training are the best structural indices of high-quality center-based care, whereas group size, the degree of safety, and the appropriateness of care provider behavior best index the quality of family day care. The care providers' salaries provide a valuable indirect measure of the quality of care because salary levels predict the rate of staff turnover reasonably well (Howes, in press). Howes has also introduced an important distinction between the conventional structural measures of quality (group size,

Table 2.5 Items on Three Popular Process Measures of Child Care Quality

ECERS[1]

Personal care routines
1. Greetings/farewells
2. Meal/snack schedule
3. Nap/rest
4. Diapering/toileting
5. Personal grooming

Furnishings and display
6. For routine care
7. For learning activities
8. For relaxation and comfort
9. Room arrangement
10. Child-related display

Language-reasoning experiences
11. Receptive language
12. Expressive language
13. Reasoning/use of concepts
14. Informal language use

Motor activities
15. Perceptual/fine motor
16. Supervision/fine motor
17. Space for gross motor
18. Gross motor equipment
19. Scheduled gross motor activities
20. Supervision

Creative activities
21. Art
22. Music/movement
23. Blocks
24. Sand/water
25. Dramatic play
26. Scheduled/opportunities for interesting activities
27. Supervision

Social development
28. Space to be alone
29. Free play
30. Group activity time
31. Cultural awareness
32. Tone of interaction
33. Provision for exceptional children

Adult needs
34. Adult personal area
35. Opportunities for professional growth
36. Adult meeting area
37. Provisions for parents

Global Rating Scale[2]

Positive relationship
1. Speaks warmly to children
2. Listens when children speak
3. Seems to enjoy children
4. Explains rule violations
5. Encourages new experiences
6. Seems enthusiastic
7. Is attentive to individuals
8. Talks at appropriate level
9. Encourages prosocial behavior
10. Adopts children's level

Punitiveness
11. Seems critical of children
12. Values obedience
13. Speaks with irritation
14. Threatens
15. Punishes without explanation
16. Finds fault
17. Prohibits many activities
18. Unnecessarily harsh

Permissiveness
19. Doesn't control
20. Doesn't reprimand misbehavior
21. Firm when necessary
22. Expects self-control

Detachment
23. Seems distant/detached
24. Spends time in other activities
25. Uninterested in children's activities
26. Not close supervision

APECP[3]

Safety and health
1. Classroom safe
2. Supplies and materials safe
3. Teacher prepared for emergencies
4. Personal hygiene encouraged
5. Teacher responsible for basic health care

Learning environment
6. Physical layout encourages independence
7. Classroom respects individuality
8. Outdoor materials support varied opportunities
9. Teacher active outdoors

Scheduling
10. Scheduling occurs
11. Varied activities on written schedule
12. Teacher organized
13. Varied classroom activities

Curriculum
14. Materials support varied experiences
15. Materials encourage cultural awareness
16. Alternative techniques used
17. Children active in learning
18. Individualization

Interacting
19. Teacher initiates positive interactions
20. Teacher responsive
21. Teacher manages children positively
22. Food served in positive atmosphere
23. Children happy and involved

Individualizing
24. Systematic child assessment
25. Assessments used in planning activities
26. Teacher identifies special needs
27. Teacher cooperative with adults
28. Provisions made for special needs
29. Conferences planned regularly
30. Parental activity encouraged

[1] Early Childhood Environment Rating Scale (Harms & Clifford, 1980). All items are rated on a 7-point scale, anchored by definitions of inadequate (1), minimal (3), good (5), and excellent (7). Similar items, adjusted for age and context, appear on the Family Day Care Rating Scale (Harms & Clifford, 1989) and the Infant/Toddler Environment Rating Scale (Harms, Cryer, & Clifford, 1986, 1990).

[2] Arnett (1989). All rated on 4-point scale, with item scores combined into 4 factor scores.

[3] Assessment Profile for Early Childhood Programs (Abbott-Shim & Sibley, 1987). Each of the 30 topics listed here subsumes several specific items (150 in all), each rated as "present" or "absent" on the basis of observations or reports.

adult–child ratio, care provider training) and more comprehensive and empirically derived measures such as number of care providers present at any given time, staff turnover, number of settings experienced by each child, care provider sensitivity and involvement, and the provision of developmentally appropriate activities. Unfortunately, site- or care-provider-specific measures of quality fail to take account of the substantial frequency of moves by children from one setting to another (NICHD Early Child Care Network, 1995a). From an individual point of view, such instability may be developmentally disruptive.

Relations between Structural and Process Measures of Quality

Because the many structural measures are all believed to indicate conditions conducive to high-quality interactions and experiences, one might expect at least modest relations among them, but this has not always been the case. Scarr et al. (1994) found that scores on various structural measures of quality were poorly correlated with one another and were not correlated with scores on the process measures of quality. In their large multisite study, only teachers' wages predicted the quality of care they provided, as indexed on process measures. Other researchers have reported clearer and stronger associations between scores on structural and process measures of quality: the better the salaries, benefits, and level of training received by care providers, the better the quality of care they provide and the less they are likely to quit their jobs (Berk, 1985; Kontos & Stremmel, 1988; Phillips, Howes, & Whitebook, 1991; Ruopp, Travers, Glantz, & Coelen, 1979). In one recent multisite study, furthermore, the quality of day care—assessed using process measures of quality—was correlated with higher staff–child ratios, better staff training and education, and higher teacher wages (Cost, Quality, and Child Outcomes in Child Care Centers, 1995). In the latter study, as in another study by Phillips, Mekos, Scarr, McCartney, and Abbott-Shim (1995), average levels of quality within the states sampled were related to the stringency of state standards: states with more demanding licensing standards had fewer centers providing care of poor quality. Except in North Carolina, where licensing regulations are quite lax and for-profit centers provided care of significantly lower quality, there was no difference in the quality of care provided by for-profit and not-for-profit centers, in part because nonprofit church-based centers provided care of such poor quality. Nonprofit centers did have higher staff–child ratios, better-educated, better-trained, more experienced staff, and lower rates of staff turnover, however.

Howes, Phillips, and Whitebook (1992) reported that classrooms with appropriate teacher:child ratios were more likely than those with poorer ratios to provide care of better quality and to promote secure child-teacher attachments. Galinsky, Howes, Kontos, and Shinn (1994) and Galinsky, Howes, and Kontos (1995a, 1995b) reported that family day care providers who received training were more likely to behave warmly, attentively, and responsively and receive higher scores on Harms and Cliffords' (1989) FDCRS, perhaps because such training enhances self-esteem and professionalism (Dombro, 1995; Dombro & Modigliani, 1995). In an independent sample of family day care providers, training was in fact the most powerful predictor of the observed quality of care as indexed on the FDCRS (Fischer & Eheart, 1991); it is thus significant that the social service agencies in Israel provide continuous on-site training for family day care providers (Rosenthal, 1990). Bollin (1993) reported that family day care providers were most likely to continue providing care when they had held previous child care jobs and were not trying to combine paid child care work with care of their own young children. The NICHD Early Child Care Research Network (1995d, 1996a) reported that the observed quality of care provider–child interaction was higher when group sizes were smaller and child–adult ratios were lower. Specialized training predicted the quality of interaction in home-based settings, but not in day care settings.

Quality of care provider–child interaction has also been linked to group size in family day care (Kontos, 1994; Stith & Davis, 1984;) and care provider–child ratios in both center and family-based care (Howes, 1983; Howes & Rubenstein, 1985). In an interesting natural experiment, Howes, Smith, and Galinsky (1995) reported that the introduction of stricter standards of training and provider–child ratios led to improvements in the quality of child–care provider interaction and higher scores on the ECERS scale. Ghazvini and Readdick (1994) reported a positive correlation between the quality of center care, as assessed on the ECERS, and the frequency of parent–care provider communication. Petrogiannis (1995), however, reported no relations among the observed quality of care provider–child interaction, ITERS scores, and structural indices of quality in his study of Greek child care centers. In Israel, Rosenthal (1991a) reported little association between the quality of care provider–child interaction and the quality of the education that caregivers provided.

The latter findings notwithstanding, there is substantial evidence that scores on diverse structural and process indices of quality are intercorrelated, with Scarr et al.'s (1994) findings representing the exception rather than the rule. The convergence reported by other researchers underscores the substantial consensus regarding the components and nature of high- (or low-) quality care, despite the rather heterogeneous range of items considered as indices of quality, while identifying some of the difficulties inherent in attempts to regulate the quality of care using easily measured structural indices, particularly when parents' ratings of quality and satisfaction are often uncorrelated with researchers' estimates of quality (see, for example, Clarke-Stewart, Gruber, & Fitzgerald, 1994; Galinsky, 1992; Mason & Duberstein, 1992; Phillips, 1992). Consensus regarding the components of quality also gives additional weight to claims by authors of several major national studies that the average quality of care provided in the settings sampled was barely "adequate," as indexed by the Harms and Clifford inventories (Cost, Quality, and Child Outcomes in Child Care Centers, 1995; Galinsky, Howes, Kontos, & Shinn, 1994; Kontos, Howes, Shinn, & Galinsky, 1994; Whitebook, Howes, & Phillips, 1989). This conclusion is especially alarming when one considers that the centers and care providers providing care of higher quality are likely to be overrepresented in these studies because those providing care of poorest quality might be disproportionately likely to refuse to participate. In this context, it is thus somewhat reassuring to learn that the average quality of care, at least as indexed by provider training and education level, has improved recently although average group sizes and turnover rates have increased (Hofferth, 1992b). In addition, Haskins (1992) and Clarke-Stewart (1992) have questioned the assumption that "adequate" day care quality represents a case for concern, and the results of the NICHD Early Child Care Research Network (1995d) suggested that three-quarters of the infants studied had sensitive care providers.

Correlates of the Quality of Care

In the early 1980s, several researchers noted a disturbing tendency in both Canada and the United States for quality of care and social class to be confounded. Children from economically and socially disadvantaged backgrounds appeared to receive nonparental care of poorer quality than those from more advantaged backgrounds. This led researchers to fear that these children were doubly handicapped, suffering the adverse effects of poor-quality care both at home and in their out-of-home care settings (Anderson, Nagle, Roberts, & Smith, 1981; Clarke-Stewart, Gruber, & Fitzgerald, 1994; Goelman, 1988; Goelman & Pence, 1987a, 1987b; Howes & Stewart, 1987; Kontos & Fiene, 1987). Although the NICHD Early Child Care Research Network (1995c) reported that children receiving better out-of-home care had more optimal home environments as well, most recent large-scale studies have noted a curvilinear rather than linear relationship between social class and the quality of out-of-home care especially with respect to center care (NICHD Early Child Care Research Network, 1997a; Phillips, Voran, Kisker, Howes, & Whitebook, 1994; Voran & Whitebook, 1991; Waite, Leibowitz, & Witsberger, 1991; Whitebook et al., 1989; Zaslow, 1991). Centers serving children from advantaged backgrounds indeed seem to provide care of the highest quality (see also Holloway & Reichhart-Erickson, 1989; Kontos, 1991), but the worst care is apparently provided by centers predominantly serving children from middle-income families rather than the poorest families. Centers serving children from low-income families do not differ from those serving advantaged families on most measures of quality, although the teachers in centers serving poorer children tend to be less sensitive and harsher, perhaps because the children behave more poorly. According to the survey by Phillips and her colleagues (1994), quality varies across an especially wide range in centers serving disadvantaged families. Community-based centers had smaller groups and better teacher–child ratios, although their teachers had obtained less education and were more poorly trained. Interestingly, children from middle-income families are especially likely to attend for-profit centers, where quality is often significantly poorer (Coelen, Glantz, & Calore, 1979; Kagan, 1991; Phillips, Howes, & Whitebook, 1992). In the NICHD Early Child Care Research Network (1997a) study, the quality of center care was lowest for children in families just above the poverty level, and the quality of home care was correlated with the quality of family day care.

Family social status, parental income, and parental education are not the only factors correlated with indices of the quality of care children receive. Bolger and Scarr (1995) reported that authoritarian attitudes toward child rearing were also associated with lower-quality care, and that, at least in the middle-class sample they studied, variation in the state standards for child care quality did not attentuate the powerful relation between family background and child care quality. Phillips, McCartney, and Scarr (1987) reported that parents who valued social skills tended to choose centers with higher quality than those who valued conformity, although Kontos (1991) reported that parents who chose high-quality facilities placed less emphasis on the development of social skills. Children may also end up in centers of lower quality if their parents are too preoccupied with other problems to thoroughly evaluate their child care options (Howes & Olenick, 1986). Psychosocial characteristics of the parents were not consistently associated with indices of quality in the NICHD Early Child Care Study (National Institute of Child Health and Human Development Early Child Care Research Network, 1997a), however.

Much of the literature reviewed below confirms that quality of care is indeed an important consideration: children perform better on many dimensions when they have received care of higher quality. Such findings raise obvious questions: How good is good enough? Is there a linear relationship between quality of care and children's adjustment? Or is there a threshold beyond which improvements in quality no longer have demonstrable effects? The results of the Göteborg Child Care Study suggest a preliminary answer to this question (Broberg et al., 1989; Hwang et al., 1991; Lamb, Hwang, Bookstein, et al., 1988; Lamb, Hwang, Broberg, et al., 1988). In Sweden, nonparental care is government subsidized and strictly regulated to ensure high quality (Broberg & Hwang, 1991; Hwang & Broberg, 1992). Despite limited variations in the quality of care across settings, however, quality of out-of-home care was one of the most important and consistent correlates of children's personality maturity, social skills, and compliance with maternal requests in the Göteborg Child Care Study described below.

Scarr and her colleagues (Scarr, Eisenberg, & Deater-Deckard, 1994; Scarr, McCartney, Abbott-Shim, & Eisenberg, 1995) have not only reported poor intercorrelation among measures of quality, but have also offered the more skeptical opinion that quality of out-of-home care is much less significant than many advocates believe. Their research suggested that socioeconomic and family background variables were much more influential sources of variance than the quality of care, which explained statistically significant but practically trivial portions of the variance in behavioral adjustment. Further research involving diverse samples and measures is obviously necessary to evaluate the merits of this argument, which has substantial implications for both parents and public authorities. At the very least, however, Scarr's argument underscores the importance of viewing the type, quality, and extent of out-of-home care in broader context, thereby recognizing that day care does not replace home care and does not render family processes and family background irrelevant. These factors clearly remain important; the relative importance of different factors (like the quality of out-of-home care) obviously varies depending on the sample studied and the number and type of other factors considered.

Summary

The results of both small- and large-scale studies over the past decade have revealed substantial agreement among experts regarding the components or dimensions of high-quality care, even though parents' assessments of quality and their appraisals of satisfaction seem to be determined very differently than experts' assessments. Researchers have distinguished in their endeavors between process indices of quality, which quantify development-promoting care provider behavior or environments, and structural indices, which identify conditions in which such behavior should be more likely. Empirical evidence confirms that the many objective indices of high-quality care are highly intercorrelated, and that observable aspects of appropriate care provider behavior are more likely to be evident when the structural indices suggest auspicious circumstances for such high-quality care. Research reviewed later in this chapter also supports the assumption that high-quality care promotes adaptive development in a variety of domains.

Unfortunately, the most popular indices of quality have proven less useful when employed in Western and Northern European countries. Their failure has been attributed to measurement insensitivity when levels of quality are very high, but it is also possible, if not likely, that cultural differences in the definition of quality restrict the validity of these measures as well. Exploration and specification of these cultural differences would be extremely informative, not only to students of nonparental care but to those who study cultural practices and beliefs. In addition, repeated reports that the quality of care is correlated with various outcome measures often lead researchers to ignore the small size of the associations, especially in predictive analyses. At least in part, these disappointing findings can be attributed to the rather general way that quality is typically measured. In the next decade, researchers should thus focus their efforts on attempts to identify more precisely the particular aspects of quality that promote or impede development in specific domains and for children with particular characteristics, thereby moving beyond global indices of quality and sharpening our understanding of "quality" and its effects.

INFANT DAY CARE

Effects on Infant-Parent Attachment

Even casual observers acknowledge that infants (and young children) initially respond with distress to enrollment in a new child care setting. This distress diminishes over time, however, to be replaced by smiling, vocalization, and increased interest in peers (Fein, 1995; Fein, Gariboldi, & Boni, 1993; Field, Gewirtz, Cohen, Garcia, Greenberg, & Collins, 1984; Schaffer & Callendar, 1959). Is this behavioral adjustment benign, or does it signal major underlying changes in infants' attachment relationships, as might be inferred by generalization from research on institutionalization (Bowlby, 1951, 1969)? Does day care fundamentally alter the interactions between infants and their parents—especially mothers, as theorists have never worried that the daily separations accompanying paternal employment might be harmful? Attempts to answer these questions have been controversial, to say the least, although it now seems clear that most infant-mother attachments are not adversely affected by regular nonmaternal care.

When observed at home with their 5- to 6-month-old and 1-year-old infants, employed mothers and homemaking mothers interact and behave very similarly (Stith & Davis, 1984; Zaslow, Pedersen, Suwalsky, & Rabinovich, 1989), although infants with homemaking mothers are more sociable and engaged when their fathers are also present. Beginning in 1986, however, a series of reports in the popular media and in the professional literature suggested that early-initiated nonparental care might adversely affect infant-parent attachment and related aspects of psychosocial development (Belsky, 1986, 1988, 1989, 1992, 1994). In many of the relevant studies, the Strange Situation procedure (Ainsworth, Blehar, Waters, & Wall, 1978) was used to assess socioemotional adjustment. This procedure was designed to measure the quality of infant-adult attachment by observing the child's reaction to reunion with the parent following brief separations in an unfamiliar context (Ainsworth, Blehar, Waters, & Wall, 1978; Lamb, Thompson, Gardner, & Charnov, 1985). Following such separations, most infants greet the returning parent warmly, either by approaching, asking to be picked up, or smiling and vocalizing. Infants who behave in this fashion are deemed securely attached. Other infants are deemed insecure because they behave avoidantly (ignoring the adults' bids, failing to greet, and perhaps even withdrawing from their parents) or resistantly (ambivalently mingling bids for contact with angry rejection of contact when that is offered).

Reviewing the results of four studies (Barglow, Vaughn, & Molitor, 1987; Belsky & Rovine, 1988; Chase-Lansdale & Owen, 1987; Jacobson & Wille, 1984) in which the Strange Situation had been used, Belsky (1988) reported that the proportion of insecure (especially insecure-avoidant) attachments was higher (41%) among middle-class children receiving out-of-home care than among children in home care (26%) comparison groups. Belsky (1989) argued that, "on the basis of the findings just reviewed . . . it is clear that when methodologically informed distinctions are made between studies, a strong and highly reliable association exists between extensive nonmaternal care in the first year of life and elevated risk of insecure infant-mother attachment (and insecure infant-father attachment in the case of boys)" (p. 34).

Conceptual Concerns

This conclusion provoked a series of rebuttals, some focused on conceptual and some on empirical and methodological issues. Of the criticisms on conceptual grounds, the tendency to rely primarily upon the Strange Situation to assess the effects of infant day care is most often mentioned. This dependence on one measure is fraught with several problems, particularly when the validity and reliability of this measure of infant-mother attachment have been challenged (Lamb, Thompson, Gardner, & Charnov, 1985). Further questions are raised by the failure to find the expected correspondence between assessments of attachment security in the Strange Situation and on the basis of Q-sort ratings by trained observers of naturalistic interactions at home (Belsky, 1995).

Because the Strange Situation was developed and validated with infants who were cared for primarily by their mothers, there was some question regarding its validity for assessing attachment in infants experiencing day care. Reactions to the Strange Situation are powerfully influenced by social and cultural contexts (Lamb et al., 1985), and thus the Strange Situation may not have the same psychological meaning for infants of employed and unemployed mothers. It is thus inappropriate to speak of insecure attachment in the absence of information concerning the antecedents or consequences of "insecure" or "avoidant" behavior in day care children, among whom "avoidant" behavior may not have the same adverse implications for future behavior as it might for the infants typically studied using this procedure. Associations between Strange Situation behavior and measures of later performance tend to be impressive only when there is stability over time with respect to family circumstances and caretaking arrangements (Goldsmith & Alansky, 1987; Lamb, Thompson, Gardner, & Charnov, 1985; Lamb, Thompson, Gardner, Charnov, & Estes, 1984; Thompson, 1988), and thus the hypothesized relation between insecure-avoidant attachment and subsequent problematic behavior in day care infants needs to be evaluated empirically (Belsky, 1989). There is as yet no evidence that "avoidant" day care infants in fact behave any differently in future years than day care infants who behave "securely" in the Strange Situation. Research involving other longer-term outcome measures than behavior in the Strange Situation is thus needed.

Both Clarke-Stewart (1988, 1989) and Thompson (1988) suggested that infants who had experienced frequent separations from their mothers might find the brief separations in the Strange Situation less stressful than would other children, and might thus appear unfazed and/or more independent. Such infants might be misclassified as avoidant, they worried. In fact, the results of several early studies fail to support the hypothesis that day care experiences make infants or preschoolers less distressed by separations from their mothers (e.g., Hock, 1980; Moskowitz, Schwarz, & Corsini, 1977; Portnoy & Simmons, 1978; Ragozin, 1977; Ricciuti, 1974; Roopnarine & Lamb, 1978; Wynn, 1979). Similar results were reported by Sagi, Lamb, Lewkowicz, Shoham, Dvir, and Estes (1985), who studied the attachments formed by infants in Israeli kibbutzim. In a more narrowly focused study, Belsky and Braungart (1991) reported that 11 avoidant infants who had experienced extensive nonmaternal care were more (rather than less) distressed in the Strange Situation than were 9 avoidant infants with less experience of nonmaternal care. This finding did not, of course, address Clarke-Stewart's hypothesis about the effects of repeated separation on infant behavior because the study only included avoidant infants and did not demonstrate that the Strange Situation has the same validity when used to assess attachment in infants who have had experiences (such as repeated separations) likely to affect behavior in the test situation. In addition, Fox, Sutton, and Newcombe (1993) reported contrasting findings in a similar study.

On the face of it, the results of both studies suggest that the Strange Situation procedure may indeed be viewed differently by infants with and without nonmaternal care histories, although there are no reliable indications of the actual differences. In addition, McGurk, Caplan, Hennessy, and Moss (1993) criticized Belsky and Braungart (1991) for computing summary scores that exaggerated chance group differences, for reporting uninterpretable mean scores, and for excluding comparable information about securely attached infants. Furthermore, investigators in the NICHD Early Child Care Research Network (1996) reported that mean levels of distress were similar across attachment categories regardless of whether the infants had experienced little, none, or a lot of nonmaternal care. These findings clearly failed to support Clarke-Stewart's hypothesis. The same researchers also demonstrated that the Strange Situation classifications of infants in both groups were associated with indices of maternal security in earlier brief observations; these findings supported the external validity of the Strange Situation classifications regardless of the infants' child care histories.

Methodological and Empirical Reactions

Belsky's claims regarding the harmful effects of infant day care on infant-mother attachment also provoked criticisms of his methods as well as efforts to explore the issue further through empirical research. Arguing that Belsky's review was selective, Clarke-Stewart (1988, 1989, 1992) used data from all known studies in which the Strange Situation had been used, regardless of socioeconomic status (Ainslie & Anderson, 1984; Barglow et al., 1987; Beckwith, 1987; Belsky & Rovine, 1988; Benn, 1986; Burchinal & Bryant, 1988; Chase-Lansdale & Owen, 1987; Easterbrooks & Goldberg, 1985; Easterbrooks & Harmon, 1987; Goossens, 1987; Jacobson & Wille, 1984; Lipsitt & LaGasse, 1987; Owen & Cox, 1988; Owen, Easterbrooks, Chase-Lansdale, & Goldberg, 1984; Rodning, 1987; Thompson, Lamb, & Estes, 1982; Vaughn, Gove, & Egeland, 1980). In this rather heterogeneous sample, 36% of the infants in full-time care were classified as insecure, compared with 29% of the infants who received part-time or no nonmaternal care. Acknowledging an elevated "risk" of insecure attachment among infants in day care, Clarke-Stewart emphasized the need to (a) explore a variety of factors other than emotional insecurity that might explain these differences in child behavior and (b) use a wider range of measures in evaluating the adjustment to day care.

Thompson (1988), Phillips, McCartney, Scarr, and Howes (1987b), and Melhuish and Moss (1991b) likewise concluded that it was too early to reach responsible conclusions about the effects of day care on infants' socioemotional development. In an attempt to clarify this controversy, Lamb, Sternberg, and Prodromidis (1992) obtained raw data from several investigators, recoded the data, and reexamined the effects of day care on the security of infant-mother attachment. They excluded samples from outside the United States, those involving preterm infants, and those including overlapping samples, and added data from some recently completed studies. The resulting sample drew data from 13 studies primarily focused on Caucasian infants from middle-class backgrounds (Ainslie, 1987; Barglow et al., 1987; Belsky & Rovine, 1988; Benn, 1986; Chase-Lansdale & Owen, 1987; Howes, Rodning, Galluzo, & Myers, 1988; Jacobson & Wille, 1984; Krentz, 1983; Lipsitt & LaGasse, 1987; Owen & Cox, 1988; Suwalsky, Klein, Zaslow, Rabinovich, & Gist, 1987; Teti & Ablard, 1989; Thompson et al., 1982). Access to raw data allowed Lamb, Sternberg, and Prodromidis to assess the effects of such factors as extent of care and age of enrollment more fully than had been possible in the previous meta-analyses. Their reanalysis showed that infants receiving regular nonmaternal care were more likely to be insecurely attached (37%) than were those cared for exclusively by their mothers (29%).

Lamb, Sternberg, and Prodromidis (1992), like Lamb and Sternberg (1990), remarked on the great variation in operationalization of "the day care experience." As discussed earlier, day care is not a clear-cut, homogeneous treatment but a complex range of experiences influenced by a variety of factors. Belsky (e.g., 1989, 1992) has emphasized the importance of age of enrollment and extent of care in modulating the effects of day care on infant-parent attachment, but there is a great deal of variability in the way *extent of care* is defined, and the evidence regarding age of enrollment is mixed. The term *full-time day care* is used by different researchers to refer to day care experiences ranging from 20 (Barglow, Vaughn, & Molitor, 1987; Lamb, Sternberg, & Prodromidis, 1992), to 30 (Vandell & Corasaniti, 1988), to 35 (Belsky & Rovine, 1988) hours of nonparental care per week. Some researchers distinguish between two groups of children—those in day care and those in home care—and some report only the average amount of day care without specifying the criteria used to assign children to their day care group. Such inconsistencies across studies make it difficult to compare results and may lead reviewers to draw unwarranted conclusions. For example, if babies receiving part-time care are often securely attached to their mothers, then the effects of out-of-home care might be obscured depending on whether these part-timers were ignored, grouped with infants receiving no out-of-home care, or grouped with those receiving full-time care. In Lamb, Sternberg, and Prodromidis's (1992) reanalysis, furthermore, part-timers (those receiving 5 to 20 hours of care per week) resembled the parental-care infants when assessed under 15 months of age but resembled full-timers (those receiving more than 20 hours of care per week) when assessed between 15 and 26 months of age. Perhaps a more fruitful way of approaching this issue in the future would be to view nonparental care as a continuous variable, particularly as most infants in the United States now experience at least some nonmaternal care on a regular basis (NICHD Early Child Care Research Network, 1997a, in press; Suwalsky, Klein, Zaslow, Rabinovich, & Gist, 1987). There is clearly need for further research designed to determine whether quality of nonparental care is an important determinant of impact, and this research will not be productive in the absence of clarity regarding the definition of terms and measurement of the extent of care.

The results of studies not included in Lamb, Sternberg, and Prodromidis's reanalysis reveal no or modest associations between day care and attachment security. Two studies using Q-sort ratings rather than behavior in the Strange Situation to assess attachment security revealed no relationship between infant day care and attachment security (Belsky & Rovine, 1990; Weinraub, Jaeger, & Hoffman, 1988), although Belsky and Rovine (1990) found that use of the maternal Q-sort data in association with Strange Situation data did reveal significant effects. Roggman, Langlois, Hubbs-Tait, and Rieser-Danner (1994) reported no significant relationship between infant day care and security of attachment as assessed in the Strange Situation, while Pierrehumbert (1990) reported that Swiss children were more likely to behave securely in the Strange Situation at 21 months when they attended child care centers (but not family day care homes) instead of remaining in exclusive maternal care. In a multisite study of over 1,000 infants, furthermore, (NICHD Early Child Care Research Network, 1996b) researchers reported no direct link between child care experience and the security of infant-mother attachment at 15 months of age.

Few infants in Lamb, Sternberg, and Prodromidis's (1992) data set entered care between 7 and 12 months of age, but the rates of insecurity were higher among these children than among those who entered care between birth and 6 months of age or remained in the exclusive care of their parents. The analyses also included few children receiving part-time nonparental care, but results suggested that the rates of insecurity tended to be nonsignificantly higher for those in care for more rather than less than 20 hours a week. Because the sample sizes were so small, however, the findings about both the extent of care and the age of enrollment must be viewed cautiously until further research has been conducted. In fact, Weinraub and Jaeger (1990) reported that infants whose mothers returned to work before 8 months of age were less likely to behave securely in the Strange Situation than infants whose mothers returned to work between 8 and 16 months. Stifter, Coulehan, and Fish (1993) reported that infants were no more likely to be rated as insecure in the Strange Situation when their mothers returned to work by 5 months of age than if they remained unemployed at least until their babies were 10 months old. Roggman et al. (1994) found that infants receiving part-time care tended to have more negative outcomes. Field, Masi, Goldstein, Perry, and Parl (1988) observed the reunions between 2- to 5-year-olds in a university-affiliated day care center and their mothers and found no differences between those in full-time care who entered day care before or after reaching 6 months of age; only about 6% of the children in either group were rated insecure, however, which raises questions about the sensitivity of measurement. Furthermore, age of entry was not directly associated with attachment security in the multisite NICHD Study of Early Child Care (NICHD Early Child Care Research Network, 1996b).

Because parents' decisions about enrollment in day care reflect their values, needs, and circumstances, we must assume that family characteristics may directly affect the extent and timing of maternal employment as well as behavior in the Strange Situation (Symons & McLeod, 1994). Burchinal, Bryant, Lee, and Ramey (1992) reported that full-time center care initiated at 7 months of age was not associated with elevated rates of insecure attachment or reductions in the quality of maternal behavior after controlling for differences in the willingness to choose infant day care. Benn (1986) reported that employed mothers who provided sensitive and responsive care when with their sons had securely attached infants, whereas less sensitive employed mothers had insecurely attached infants. Belsky and Rovine (1988) reported that differences in maternal personality within the day care group predicted differences in attachment security. However, Stifter et al. (1993) found that mothers who returned to work early and reported greater levels of separation anxiety were more likely to behave intrusively and to have insecurely attached infants. Weinraub et al. (1988) reported that when mothers were satisfied with their child care arrangements and had frequent social contacts, their infants were more likely to be rated as secure by their mothers. Nonemployed mothers' responses were differently correlated, though the small sample size relative to the large number of measures makes it difficult to evaluate the patterns of correlations.

At present there is little or no evidence that either family- or center-based day care is "better" for infants (Barglow et al., 1987; Clarke-Stewart, 1992a, 1992b; Moore, Snow, & Poteat, 1988). We might expect, however, that any effects of the type of care would vary depending on characteristics of the child, family, and setting. Wide variations in the types of care received (Belsky & Rovine, 1988; Chase-Lansdale & Owen, 1987; Hofferth & Phillips, 1987; Howes, Rodning, Galluzzo, & Myers, 1987) and the fact that some children experience a variety of care settings either sequentially or simultaneously further complicate efforts to evaluate the independent effects of specific types of care.

Although most scholars allude to the importance of high-quality care, quality of care has been assessed comprehensively in relatively few studies concerning the association between infant day care and attachment. The researchers who contributed data for Lamb, Sternberg, and Prodromidis's (1992) reanalysis seldom obtained structural measures of quality and were even less likely to obtain process measures of quality, and thus the effects of quality could not be assessed reliably. Quality of care *was* assessed in the large multisite study initiated by the NICHD (Friedman, 1993; NICHD Early Child Care Research Network, 1994, 1995c, 1995f, 1995g, 1996b, 1997a). The results of this study revealed no main effect for the quality of out-of-home care on the security of infant-mother attachment in the Strange Situation, although rates of insecurity were disproportionately elevated when infants were exposed to such multiple risks as poor-quality (insensitive) care both at home and in nonparental care settings, more extensive care, and less stable care (NICHD Early Child Care Research Network, 1996b).

Unfortunately, most studies employ samples that are too small to reveal effects of the size that appear common, and this has prompted several efforts to combine data from multiple studies into single analyses (Belsky, 1988; Clarke-Stewart, 1988, 1989; Lamb, Sternberg, & Prodromidis, 1992). Selection biases, attributable to the nonrandom assignment to conditions, are also pervasive. Evoking Rosenthal's (1979) "file drawer problem," Roggman et al. (1994) have also bemoaned the tendency of researchers and journal editors to withhold or prevent publication of studies like their own revealing no significant effects of day care enrollment. As a result, they argue, the published literature drawn upon by analysts like Belsky, Clarke-Stewart, and Lamb, Sternberg, and Prodromidis, as well as by other reviewers, is likely to inflate or exaggerate the actual relationship between day care and attachment. (Needless to say, similar biases affect the published literature on all topics covered in this *Handbook,* as well as in other sections of this chapter.) Despite such biases, the empirical evidence reveals that enrollment in infant day care is problematic only when it co-occurs with other indices of risk, including poor-quality care at home and unstable care arrangements. When studies have revealed significant associations between nonparental care and insecure attachment, they may have been attributable to sampling biases, as well as to the unrecognized co-ocurrence of multiple adverse risk conditions. After determining that infant day care per se is not harmful, researchers now need to specify what types of care are potentially harmful and potentially beneficial for specific subgroups of infants and families, and to define with greater precision those aspects of quality likely to be of particular significance in defined circumstances.

Whether day care increases the frequency of insecure attachments, and whether insecure-avoidant attachments predict subsequent psychosocial problems, the observation of Strange Situation behavior at best provides a very narrow assessment of the effects of day care. We need studies, like those reviewed in later sections of this chapter, that sample a broad range of outcomes and follow subjects through time so that the extent and longevity of any effects can be traced. Regardless of their breadth and perseverance, furthermore, the increased "risk" associated with day care is such that the majority of infants receiving out-of-home care have secure attachments to their mothers and fathers. It is obviously important not to exaggerate the potentially negative effects of nonparental care and to view out-of-home care in combination with other social and familial variables that may have important influences on infant-parent attachment. When evaluating risks to public mental health, furthermore, we should place the risks associated with infant day care in a broader context, mindful of the many factors—including maternal and paternal neglect, poverty, family stress, and drug abuse—that separately and together affect the likelihood that infants will behave insecurely, questions about the validity of the Strange Situation notwithstanding.

Because a variety of factors may interact to determine the effects of day care on infant development in general, and infant-mother attachment in particular, it is also important to obtain information about child and family characteristics prior to enrollment in day care. Symons and McLeod (1993, 1994) reported that prenatal assessments of mothers' plans, anxieties about separation, and autonomy distinguished among mothers' later employment decisions. Other researchers have reported, not surprisingly, that mothers' concerns about separation and employment are correlated with their tendencies to seek paid employment (DeMeis, Hock, & McBride, 1986; Hock, 1980; Hock & DeMeis, 1990; Hock, DeMeis, & McBride, 1988; Hock, McBride, & Gnezda, 1989; Hock & Schirtzinger, 1992; McBride & Belsky, 1988). Cohn, Campbell, and Ross (1991) found that when depressed mothers sought employment by the time their children were 6 months old, it had a salutory effect on the security of their infants' behavior in the Strange Situation six months later. There is also some evidence that variables such as birth order (Barglow, Vaughn, & Molitor, 1987), temperament (Belsky, 1988; Melhuish, 1987), level of familial stress (Belsky & Rovine, 1988; Howes, 1987), maternal role satisfaction (Hock, 1980), and the availability of social support may mediate the effects of day care experiences on infant-mother attachment; thus, it is important to identify and measure these factors and take any group differences into account when interpreting the effects of day care. In a recent retrospective study of middle-class 6- to 12-year-olds, furthermore, Burchinal, Ramey, Reid, and Jaccard (1995) reported that African Americans who had been enrolled in out-of-home care in infancy had more negative perceptions of their mothers, whereas Whites who experienced nonparental infant care viewed their mothers more positively.

Relationships with Care Providers

Instead of studying reactions to brief separations, several researchers have asked whether children in day care develop attachment-like relationships with care providers or teachers, and, if so, how these relationships compare with mother-child relationships. The evidence suggests that enrollment in day care allows children to form additional significant relationships but does not lead care providers to displace mothers as the primary objects of attachment. As in the case of infant-parent attachments, the quality or security of infant–care provider attachment is influenced by the care provider's sensitivity and responsiveness.

After observing infants interacting with their mothers and care providers, Farran and Ramey (1977) found that the children showed an overwhelming preference for proximity to and interaction with their mothers, as did the children in a similar study by Ainslie and Anderson (1984). Not surprisingly, children also behave differently in alternative care centers than at home. Meudec and Balleyguier-Boulanger (1991) reported that French 6- to 8-month-olds were more passive and less person-oriented when observed in alternative care facilities with their care providers than when observed at home with their mothers (Balleyguier, Meudec, & Chasseigne, 1991). Subsequent research showed that these patterns were especially evident in full-time day care centers, and that children in family day care showed what the authors described as "a better balance" of attention to people and objects (Balleyguier, Meudec, Comfort, & Fullard 1994).

Such behavioral patterns are likely to vary both over time and in relation to the quality of the relationships children have been able to establish with care providers. Cummings (1980) reported that children revealed a preference for regular over irregular care providers as their parents left the day care, but that in a laboratory they rarely approached care providers, preferring instead to stay close to their mothers; they were often upset when left alone with one of the care providers. They were also more positive in the presence of the regular or stable care providers, however (see also Rubenstein & Howes, 1979). Anderson, Nagle, Roberts, and Smith (1981) reported more contact seeking, distance interaction, and exploration in the presence of highly involved than less involved care providers, whereas all these behaviors were less common in the presence of strangers than of the less involved care providers.

In a later study, Barnas and Cummings (1994) observed interactions between 40 toddlers (average age 21 months) and their care providers. The toddlers consistently sought comfort from the "stable" care providers—those who had provided care to the child longer—when distressed, interacted with them preferentially when not distressed, and were more rapidly soothed by them than by "unstable" providers. These differences did not seem related to the characteristics or skills of the providers; stable and unstable providers were equally likely to be sought by newer children in the groups. Instead, Barnas and Cummings (1994) speculated that the children had been able to form attachments to the care providers who had been regular sources of care. As it is presumably beneficial for children to have access to attachment figures when their primary (parental) attachment figures are absent (Ainslie & Anderson, 1984; Rutter, 1981), these findings underscore the importance of minimizing staff turnover so as to maximize the stability of care. Interestingly, Rubenstein, Pedersen, and Yarrow (1977) and Raikes (1993) both reported that more stable care providers also provided care of better quality. Howes and Hamilton (1993) also reported that when children's primary teachers changed when they were between 12 and 18 months of age, the children subsequently behaved more aggressively (particularly with peers); the same was true of children who experienced more turnover among care providers before age 4. The effect was greatest when the children lost a teacher with whom they had a good relationship. The interpretation of these associations is not obvious; it may simply be that better-motivated care providers are both more sensitive and more likely to keep their jobs.

Infants indeed form attachments to care providers (Krentz, 1983), and the security of infant–care provider attachment is not simply determined by the security of infant-mother attachment (Goosens & van IJzendoorn, 1990; Howes & Hamilton, 1992a, 1992b; Sagi et al., 1985; Seltenheim, Ahnert, Rickert, & Lamb, 1997). As with parents, the security of infant–care provider attachments is associated instead with the sensitivity, involvement, and quality of care provided by the specific care providers (Howes & Hamilton, 1992b; Howes, Phillips, & Whitebook, 1992; Seltenheim et al., 1997). Using Q-sort ratings of many child–care provider relationships to derive profiles, Howes and Smith (1995) were able to discern three profiles—secure, avoidant, and difficult—that very much resembled the patterns of attachment frequently described in studies of infant-parent attachment. Howes and Hamilton (1992b) reported stability over time in the quality of teacher-child attachment, assessed using the Attachment Q-set, when children had the same teachers, whereas relationship quality understandably changed when the teachers themselves changed. After observing 5- to 6-month-old infants with their mothers and their family day care providers, Stith and Davis (1984) reported that the 10 substitute caregivers studied provided considerably less stimulation, affect, and fewer contingent responses than did the mothers when observed in their own homes. This would lead one to expect less secure infant–care provider than infant-mother attachments. Interestingly, Galinsky, Howes, and Kontos (1995a, 1995b) reported that the security of infant–care provider attachment, assessed using a Q-sort rating, improved after the family day care providers participated in a training program that enhanced the quality of care they provided. Improvements in the level of teacher training also led to increases in the proportion of children who behaved securely (Howes, Smith, & Galinsky, 1995). Such findings were especially important in light of evidence that more than half of the infants in family day care were insecurely attached to their care providers (Galinsky, Howes, Kontos, & Shinn, 1994) and underscores for practitioners the value of care provider training. Insecure infant care provider attachments were also common in Seltenheim et al.'s (1997) study of infants in German day-care centers.

Secure infant–care provider relationships promote more advanced types of play (Howes, Matheson, & Hamilton, 1994) and more positive peer relationships (Howes & Hamilton, 1993). Indeed, the nature of the relationship with the primary teacher may be more influential than the number of changes in teachers experienced (Howes & Hamilton, 1993). Not surprisingly, Howes, Rodning, Galluzzo, and Myers (1988) found that the security of infant–mother and infant–care provider attachment, assessed using both the Strange Situation and Q-sorts, both predicted the level of competence exhibited when playing with adults as well as the degree of engagement in play with peers. Security of infant-caregiver interaction apparently does not affect the basic orientation of infants to peers and adults, however (Galluzzo, Matheson, Moore, & Howes, 1988). Oppenheim, Sagi, and Lamb (1988) reported that the security of infant–care provider attachments significantly predicted the personality development of Israeli kindergartners, whereas neither the security of infant-mother nor infant-father attachment was predictively informative. Infants who behaved securely toward care providers in the Strange Situation were later less ego-controlled and more empathic, dominant, purposive, achievement-oriented, and independent than those whose relationships were insecure-resistant four years earlier.

Viewed together, these findings suggest that, even though the quality of nonparental care does not consistently affect the security of infant-mother attachment (see previous section), it does have beneficial consequences for children mediated by the enhanced quality of infant–care provider relationships. The addition of child–care provider relationships to the list of influences on child development and adjustment also reduces the relative significance of child-parent relationships, and this may concern some parents.

Few researchers have studied the adaptation to day care and new care providers longitudinally. Fein, Gariboldi, and Boni (1993) reported that, over the six months immediately following enrollment in day care centers, Italian infants became less distressed, more active, and more expressive of positive emotions. These changes in the infants' demeanour paralleled changes in the behavior of care providers, who shifted from an emphasis on comforting to an emphasis on play. Fein (1995) noted that infants who were object-centered, happy, and socially unengaged after six months of care received less attention from caregivers, however, leading her to suggest that infants manifesting "detachment-like" symptoms might fail to elicit from care providers the type of care they need.

Compliance with Parents and Care Providers

As noted earlier, researchers such as Belsky (1988, 1989) view insecure infant-mother attachment as a likely consequence of early and extensive nonmaternal care and point out that, according to attachment theory, noncompliance is a common consequence of insecure infant-mother attachment (Ainsworth et al., 1978; Arend, Gove, & Sroufe, 1979; Londerville & Main, 1981). This leads to the prediction that early nonmaternal care should foster subsequent noncompliance. Consistent with this hypothesis, the results of several early studies suggested that nonmaternal child care was associated with inappropriate noncompliance with adult demands (Finkelstein, 1982; Rubenstein, Howes, & Boyle, 1981; Schwarz, Strickland, & Krolick, 1974). Indeed, in a large study of kindergartners in Missouri, children at home continuously from infancy were rated by their teachers as more compliant than children who had experienced any of a variety of part- and full-time care arrangements in the first four years of life (Thornburg, Pearl, Crompton, & Ispa, 1990). In a retrospective study of third-graders, furthermore, Vandell and Corasaniti (1990a, 1990b) reported that children who received extensive nonmaternal care beginning in infancy were perceived by both teachers and mothers as less compliant, even after group differences in family and socioeconomic background were taken into account.

Belsky and Eggebeen (1991) subsequently analyzed data drawn from the National Longitudinal Survey of Labor Market Experience of Youth (NLSY); they found that 4- to 6-year-old children were rated by their mothers as less compliant when the mothers had been employed from the first or second years of their children's lives. These differences were still evident after controlling for several family and socioeconomic background variables. Critics of this report noted the failure to recognize the impact of later differences in the families' situations, the uniqueness of the subsample studied, weaknesses in the NLSY measures of adjustment and child care histories, small effect sizes, and the manner in which the statistical analyses were conducted (McCartney & Rosenthal, 1991; Scarr, 1991; Vandell, 1991), further underscoring the difficulties inherent in conducting research using such large complex data sets.

In the first study intensively focused on the association between day care and noncompliance, Howes and Olenick (1986) studied 18-, 24-, 30-, and 36-month-olds at home, in their day care centers, and in a standardized laboratory situation, and reported quite different results. Compliance with adult requests at home and in the laboratory did not vary depending on the quality of out-of-home care or even on whether the children had any regular out-of-home care experiences, although children without day care experience were least likely to regulate their own behavior and emotions in the laboratory. In the laboratory, children from high-quality centers were more compliant and less resistant than children in low-quality centers, perhaps because their parents and care providers were most invested in their compliance. In exploratory regression analyses, quality of center care was the most powerful predictor of compliance, but unfortunately, the different measures of compliance were not stable over situations, making it inappropriate to speak of compliance and noncompliance as traits. It is also unclear how many of these children entered day care in infancy and whether age of enrollment was a significant determinant of variations in compliance. At the very least, these findings cast doubt on the notion that compliance and noncompliance represent traits that are stable across contexts and relationships (with parents and care providers, for example) and further suggest that the association between child care history and noncompliance may be more limited and narrow then it once appeared. Research on children who entered care later (see below) supports this conclusion. Belsky, Woodworth, and Crnic (1996) also demonstrated recently that early and more extensive (over 20 hours per week) nonmaternal care in the first year of life was associated with increases in the likelihood that families would become troubled (i.e., that the parents would have more difficulty controlling and managing their toddlers) in response to stresses posed by poor marital quality, deficient social networks, and adverse parental personality factors. An alternative interpretation might emphasize the fact that unsatisfactory child care arrangements sometimes produce anxiety and personal distress, which impede the quality of parent-child interaction and thereby diminish the security of child-parent attachments and relationships (Mason & Duberstein, 1992; Phillips, 1992; Presser, 1992a). Nevertheless, the association between early experiences of nonparental care and subsequent noncompliance has been reported with sufficient frequency to merit continuing concern and further research.

Relationships with Peers

Initially motivated by the assumption that early and extensive exposure to peers would foster the development of social skills, researchers have more recently sought to discern effects of nonparental care placements on both prosocial and agonistic behavior with peers. In early studies, primarily of infants enrolled in intervention/enrichment programs, researchers reported that infant day care was associated with later aggression toward peers, although the aggression diminished over time (Barton & Schwarz, 1981; Farber & Egeland, 1982; Haskins, 1985; Rubenstein, Howes, & Boyle, 1981; Schwarz, Strickland, & Krolick, 1974). Most of these studies involved unrepresentative high-risk samples, argued Clarke-Stewart (1988, 1989), and more recent studies have yielded mixed results. Hegland and Rix (1990) reported no differences in the aggression and assertiveness of children who had experienced infant day care and those who had remained in the exclusive care of their parents. Similarly, British 6-year-olds who began family or center day care in infancy were no more aggressive or otherwise behaviorally problematic than peers who received care only at home (Melhuish, Hennessy, Martin, & Moss, 1990). Somewhat surprisingly, Thornburg et al. (1990) reported that the least aggressive kindergartners were those who had either been continuously at home or continuously in full-time care. However, teachers reported that children in continuous part- or full-time care and children who remained at home for the first two years had interactions of the poorest quality with their peers. In addition, Vandell and Corasaniti (1990a, 1990b) found that third-graders who had begun extensive nonmaternal care in infancy had poorer peer relationships and were less popular than children who received no nonmaternal care or entered care later. In this study, child care history was a better predictor than family and socioeconomic background.

Unmeasured differences in the quality of care and in children's initial orientation—including differences in temperament—may help account for these inconsistent findings. In an intriguing exploratory study, for example, Volling and Feagans (1995) reported that socially fearful infants developed more positive relations with peers when they received high-quality care, whereas their social relations deteriorated when placed in centers of lower quality. Other studies speak to the beneficial effects of high-quality care, although statistical interactions between quality of care and individual characteristics continue to receive little attention. Care of higher quality was associated with peer interactions of higher quality in a large study of toddlers and preschoolers (Howes, Smith, & Galinsky, 1995). Field, Masi, Goldstein, Perry, and Parl (1988) reported that children enrolled in a high-quality center before 6 months of age were more socially competent and socially active than those who entered later in infancy, although early enrollees were also rated as more assertive and aggressive by their teachers. The longer the children remained in child care, however, the more friends they had as 5- to 7-year-olds and the more popular, mature, and less aggressive they were in their mothers' eyes (Field, 1991). Sixth graders who had attended other high-quality facilities from the first two years of life were rated by their teachers as more assertive and more likely to express their emotions physically than children who had spent less time in the same facilities. Comparing 4-year-olds who entered day care before or after 6 months of age, Field et al. (1988) reported no differences in the quality of peer interaction, whereas children in part-time care were less socially engaged and engaged in less cooperative play than did those in full-time care. Those who had received full-time care were rated as more aggressive and assertive by their teachers, however, regardless of age at enrollment. Unfortunately, family interaction variables were not considered in this study.

The potential benefits of high-quality care were also illustrated by Andersson (1989), who found that 8-year-old Swedish children who entered out-of-home care as infants were rated by their teachers as more persistent, more independent, less anxious, more verbal, and as having made the transition from preschool to school more easily. By age 13, the children who received out-of-home care from infancy were more socially competent in the views of their teachers than children without such experiences (Andersson, 1992), once the effects of family and socioeconomic background were taken into account. Israeli toddlers in family day care settings interacted with their peers most competently and positively when the care providers encouraged frequent group interaction (Rosenthal, 1994). Agonistic interactions were rare, but more common when care providers expected social skills to develop faster than cognitive skills, preferred power-assertive means of control, and when the poorer physical qualities of the out-of-home care settings apparently frustrated children from more advantaged family backgrounds.

The most extensive programmatic research on the associations between early child care and relationships with peers has been conducted by Carollee Howes and her colleagues. Howes (1988) reported that preschoolers were more sociable with their peers when they began day care in infancy. Subsequent research revealed that low-quality care beginning in infancy was associated with poorer relations with peers at kindergarten age (Howes, 1990), whereas early-initiated care of high quality did not have adverse effects. Early enrollment in day care also appeared to increase the impact of teacher behavior and decrease the impact of parental behavior on the children's behavior. In light of the concerns reported earlier that many infants are enrolled in care of poor quality, the results of this longitudinal study raise concerns about the adverse effects on their social skills.

In a later longitudinal study, Howes, Hamilton, and Matheson (1994) followed 48 children who entered full-time day care (either center- or family-based) in the first year of life (the average age at enrollment was 5 months). The first data collection took place one year after enrollment and subsequent data gathering occurred every six months thereafter. The more secure the teacher-child relationships, the more complex, gregarious, and less aggressive was the play observed with peers at age 4, whereas dependence on teachers was associated with social withdrawal and hostile aggressive behavior. These predictive relations parallel other reports that, among preschoolers, children who have secure relations with their teachers and care providers are more socially competent with peers (Howes, Phillips, & Whitebook, 1992; Pianta & Nimetz, 1991; Sroufe, Fox, & Pancake, 1983). They also suggest that the reliable associations between infant day care and later aggressiveness may be mediated via poor relationships with care providers, rather than by the effects of separation on infant-mother attachment.

Behavior Problems

Aggressive behavior is frequently studied along with other behavior problems, and in this research literature there are again troubling reports of misbehavior on the part of children exposed to nonparental care beginning in infancy. Balleyguier (1988) reported that French infants in day care cried more, threw more tantrums, and were more oppositional at home during the second year of life than were those who remained in the exclusive care of their parents. In an analysis of data from the NLSY, Bayder and Brooks-Gunn (1991) reported that White 4-year-olds who began receiving nonmaternal care in the first year were believed by their mothers to have more behavior problems than those who began receiving nonmaternal care later or not at all. Using the same data set but different statistical controls, however, Ketterlinus, Henderson, and Lamb (1992) reported that children who started day care in the first or second years of life and were in day care for at least two years did not have more reported behavior problems than children who experienced no day care. In a retrospective study of 6- to 12-year-olds in middle-class families, Burchinal, Ramey, Reid, and Jaccard (1995) similarly reported that infant day care had no effect on maternal reports of children's externalizing and internalizing behavior problems and multiple raters' reports of positive social characteristics after family and social background factors were taken into account. Boys who received out-of-home care in infancy were rated more positively by observers than other boys were, but a similar effect was not evident for girls. High-quality day care, initiated at 12 months of age for preterm low-birthweight infants participating in an intensive intervention study, was also associated with a decline in the incidence of behavior problems reported by mothers on the Behavior Checklist and Child Behavior Checklist when their children were 26 to 36 months old (Brooks-Gunn, Klebanov, Liaw, & Spiker, 1993; Infant Health and Development Program, 1990). The contrasting results of a large though retrospective study were more sobering. Bates, Marvinney, Kelly, Dodge, Bennett, and Pettit (1994) reported that, on a composite measure of adjustment that included many indices of difficulties with peers, infant day care was associated with less positive adjustment to kindergarten even after the effects of later care arrangements were taken into account.

Egeland and Hiester (1995) reported that, in annual assessments from kindergarten through sixth grade, children from impoverished families who entered day care in infancy did not manifest more externalizing behavior problems than children who did not receive infant day care. However, exploratory analyses suggested that securely attached infants who entered day care in infancy tended to manifest externalizing behavior problems in kindergarten, whereas insecurely attached children who did not experience day care were less withdrawn and more self-competent. Attachment status predicted later adjustment for the children who did not enter day care in infancy but not for those who did, suggesting (as did Oppenheim et al.'s 1988 study of kibbutz-reared Israelis) that early-initiated, continuing nonparental care may reduce the formative salience of parent-child relationships. Unfortunately, interpretation of Egeland and Hiester's results is complicated by the small cell sizes, lack of information about later day care experiences, frequent changes in attachment security between 12 and 18 months, and the fact that, in every case, day care began before the first assessment of attachment security. Rosenthal (1994) found that Israeli toddlers in family day care displayed most distress when they had younger and more stressed mothers, when their co-enrollees tended to be older than they, and when their care providers had age-inappropriate expectations. Such findings suggested that quality of care, rather than the experience of nonparental care per se, is associated with the manifestation of behavior problems. Unfortunately, few of the studies focused on behavior problems have assessed quality of care systematically, and the actual behavior problems at issue are a heterogeneous melange including poor relationships with peers, aggression, and noncompliance. More focused research may be more informative than research on diffuse constructs like "behavior problems."

Effects on Cognitive Competence

By contrast, much of the research associating nonparental care and cognitive development has been extremely focused. Experimental research has documented that out-of-home schooling can have positive and enduring effects on cognitive performance, particularly among children from less stimulating homes, while nonexperimental studies paint a less impressive picture of the benefits.

Ramey and his colleagues (Ramey, 1992; Ramey & Smith, 1977) have continued to study those children who were enrolled as infants in the Abecedarian intervention project in North Carolina. All of the children came from impoverished backgrounds and were of African American ancestry. When they were 3 months old, half of the children were enrolled in a full-time center-based intervention program designed to prepare them for school; this program continued until kindergarten. Upon enrollment in kindergarten, half of the children in each group were given further intervention that continued through the first three years of elementary school. In every assessment between 6 and 54 months, a greater proportion of the children in the intervention group had IQs in the normal range (Martin, Ramey, & Ramey, 1990); at the time of entry into kindergarten, the children in the experimental group had IQ scores 8.5 points higher than those in the comparison group, although the difference narrowed to 5 IQ points by second grade (Ramey & Campbell, 1984, 1987, 1992). At the beginning of kindergarten, the children in the enrichment group also performed better on measures of narrative skills than children in the control group, but these differences were no longer evident by the spring (Feagans & Farran, 1994). Other children in their classrooms performed better on measures of paraphrasing than did children from either the enrichment or comparison group. Children in the intervention group also performed better on tests of conservation at ages 5, 6, and 7 (Campbell & Ramey, 1990).

Significant group differences favoring the children who received early enrichment persisted through seven years of school, although the elementary school supplement had little impact either on the maintenance of preschool intervention effects or on its own account (Campbell & Ramey, 1994, in press). Similar effects were evident on measures of academic achievement and school performance. Grade retention and assessments of special educational needs in the first three years of school were also reduced by the preschool treatment (Burchinal, Campbell, Bryant, Wasik, & Ramey, in press; Hovacek, Ramey, Campbell, Hoffman, & Fletcher, 1987). Wasik, Ramey, Bryant, and Sparling (1990) later showed that the Abecedarian intervention was even more influential when it was supplemented by a home-based family education program in Project CARE. At every assessment through 54 months of age, children receiving both center- and family-focused intervention in Project CARE performed better than those receiving only center-based intervention. According to Ramey, Ramey, Hardin, and Blair (1995), however, intensive home visits by themselves had no effect on the children's performance or on their families, even though home visiting has proven effective in other studies (Seitz, 1990).

Burchinal, Lee, and Ramey (1989) compared the developmental trajectories of Black children from impoverished backgrounds who (a) entered the intensive intervention programs described above at 2 to 3 months of age, (b) were enrolled in community day care at an average of 20 months, or (c) had minimal or no day care experiences. Semiannual assessments between 6 and 54 months using the Bayley MDI, the Stanford-Binet, and the McCarthy scales revealed that the children in the intervention group consistently performed the best, followed by those in community care settings, followed by those who had minimal day care experiences. This suggests that community day care can have beneficial effects on the cognitive performance of children from impoverished unstimulating homes, although the lack of random assignment to the two nonexperimental comparison groups compromises the assessment of causality. The same is true of the New York City Infant Day Care Study (Golden et al., 1978), in which disadvantaged children whose parents chose to enroll them in day care centers had higher IQ scores at 18 and 36 months than children whose parents chose to keep them primarily at home.

Sparling, Lewis, Ramey, Wasik, Bryant, and La Vange (1991) later developed an intensive intervention program modeled after the Abecedarian program for a large-scale randomized control study of low-birthweight premature babies, the Infant Health and Development Program (1990). Mothers and infants in this study were randomly assigned to either program (intervention) or control groups. The program involved weekly home visits for three years after hospital discharge, high-quality educationally oriented day care from 12 to 36 months of age, and parent group meetings on a bimonthly basis. Enrollment in this program led to significant improvements in the IQs of infants at age 36 months (Ramey, Ramey, Hardin, & Blair, 1995). The effects on the heavier babies was greater than on the lighter babies, but was statistically significant in both cases at the time of the three-year follow-up (Ramey, Ramey, Hardin, & Blair, 1995), although by 5 and 8 years of age, significant effects were only evident among those who were heavier at birth (Brooks-Gunn et al., 1994; McCarton et al., 1997). Intervention had substantially more powerful effects on the infants whose mothers had the lowest education and had no effect on the infants whose mothers were college graduates (Ramey, Ramey, Hardin, & Blair, 1995). Additional analyses showed that the magnitude of the effects on IQ varied depending on the extent to which the families participated and took advantage of the services offered to them (Blair, Ramey, & Hardin, 1995; Ramey, Bryant, Wasik, Sparling, Fendt, & La Vange, 1992). This is consistent with other evidence suggesting that more intensive programs have a greater impact on child development than less intensive programs do (Ramey & Ramey, 1992). Furthermore, the results of the Infant Health and Development Program, the Abecedarian Program, and Project CARE all underscore the importance of providing care and stimulation directly to children in out-of-home contexts.

In contrast to the results of intervention programs, the results of nonexperimental studies designed to explore the effects of community day care are quite contradictory and inconsistent. In a retrospective study of third-graders who had received varying amounts of nonmaternal care, Vandell and Corasaniti (1990a, 1990b) reported that extensive care beginning in infancy was associated with poorer scores on standardized cognitive measures, whereas Thornburg, Pearl, Crompton, and Ispa (1990) reported no effects of early day care (full or part time, initiated before or after infancy) on the cognitive achievement scores of a large group of Missouri kindergartners. Likewise, Ackerman-Ross and Khanna (1989) reported no differences in receptive language, expressive language, and IQ between middle-class 3-year-olds who remained home and those who received high-quality day care beginning in infancy. Burchinal et al. (1995) reported no association between infant day care and cognitive performance (PPVT and WISC-R scores) at 6 to 12 years of age in a sample of middle-class White and African American children. In a smaller study of Swiss infants, Pierrehumbert, Ramstein, and Karmaniola (1995) reported that the more nonmaternal care infants experienced, the lower their cognitive test performance at age 2. This effect was not evident, however, when the number of changes in day care arrangements and the quality of the infant-mother relationships were taken into account. The test scores of children who had positive relationships with care providers improved between ages 2 and 5, although by 5 years of age only the socioeconomic status of the family was correlated with cognitive performance (Pierrehumbert, Ramstein, Karmaniola, & Halfon, in press). In Greece, Petrogiannis (1995) found that length of time in day care predicted improved cognitive and language skills among 18-month-olds, although there were no mean differences between children in home-care and center-care settings. Small group sizes and higher quality care amplified the positive effects. Rosenthal (1994) reported that toddlers in family day care played with objects most competently when their care providers encouraged frequent group interaction, and most often interacted positively when the homes were less crowded and when the groups contained children of varying ages. Age, sex, and family background variables were more influential than characteristics of the child care setting, however, and the results of nonexperimental research using data from the NLSY suggest that the effects may differ depending on family social class. Caughy, DiPietro, and Strobino (1994) reported that enrollment in day care before age 1 was associated with better reading recognition scores for 5- and 6-year-old children from impoverished backgrounds and poorer scores for children from more advantaged backgrounds. Center-based care begun in the first three years was also associated with higher math performance scores in children from impoverished backgrounds and lower math scores for children from more stimulating homes. Unfortunately, it is not known how many of these children were enrolled in formal intervention programs. Using subjects drawn from the same data set, Baydar and Brooks-Gunn (1991) reported that day care during the first year was associated with poorer verbal abilities in 3- and 4-year-olds, and Desai, Chase-Lansdale, and Michael (1989) reported that infant day care was associated with poorer cognitive functions during the preschool years by boys from advantaged families.

Quite different results were reported in a long-term longitudinal study conducted in Sweden by Andersson (1989, 1992). Retrospective accounts of the age of enrollment in day care were employed in analyses suggesting that children who entered day care early—probably in the second half of the first year—scored significantly better on standardized measures of cognitive ability and teacher ratings of academic achievement at both 8 and 13 years of age, even after controlling for differences in their family backgrounds. Such results probably reflect the generally high quality of care provided in Swedish day care centers, which most of these children attended (Broberg & Hwang, 1991; Hwang & Broberg, 1992).

Scarr and her colleagues (McCartney, 1984; McCartney, Scarr, Phillips, & Grajek, 1985; McCartney, Scarr, Phillips, Grajek, & Schwarz, 1982) conducted a longitudinal study of 166 Bermudan children in day care centers varying in quality. Scarr and Thompson (1994) reported no differences in cognitive performance at age 2 depending on whether the mothers had been employed at all, part time (less than 20 hours per week), or full time (more than 20 hours per week) during the first year of the infants' lives once differences in family background were taken into account. However, children in high-quality centers scored better on measures of language development and were rated by teachers as more considerate and sociable between 3 to 5 years of age than children in low-quality centers (McCartney et al., 1985; Phillips, McCartney, & Scarr, 1987), although the effects of the quality of care were no longer evident when the children were reassessed at 5, 6, 7, and 8 years, by which times family background and maternal IQ measures were better predictors of academic achievement and teachers' ratings of social competence (Chin-Quee & Scarr, 1994).

The results of other studies suggest that the quality of care can be significant. Rosenthal (1990, 1994) reported that Israeli children in high-quality family day care homes engaged in more cognitively stimulating activities. Likewise, Field (1991) reported that extensive exposure to high-quality infant care was associated with superior academic performances at age 11. In a correlational study of children in four states, furthermore, children had better verbal abilities (receptive language skills) when they received care of high quality (Cost, Quality and Child Outcomes in Child Care Centers, 1995). These effects were evident even after controlling for the effects of social class and other aspects of the family background. Finally, the NICHD Early Child Care Research Network (1997b) reported that quality of care was positively related to measures of cognitive and language development throughout the second and third years, although the effects were very small, albeit significant even after controlling for family background variables.

In general, it seems clear—as it did 20 years ago (Belsky & Steinberg, 1978; Belsky, Walker, & Steinberg, 1982)—that high-quality educationally oriented programs have positive effects on cognitive performance, particularly for children from disadvantaged backgrounds. Unfortunately, few attempts have been made to evaluate the relative effectiveness of different curricula or pedagogical approaches, so we cannot identify the salient aspects of successful programs. Follow-up studies are also uncommon, but all show that significant effects are often attenuated over time unless maintained by continuing care or education of high quality. Care of poorer quality presumably has effects that vary depending on its quality relative to the quality of care and stimulation that children would receive at home. As a result, the performance of some children from well-organized and stimulating families may be affected adversely by out-of-home care experiences. It is also possible that the potential for infection and its detection in group care settings may mediate some of the effects of cognitive stimulation. Feagans, Kipp, and Blood (1994) showed that, when children in day care had chronic ear infections, they were much less likely to pay attention during book reading sessions than children without ear infections. These children were also rated as more distractable and nonattentive by their mothers. Unfortunately, researchers have paid little attention to the role that illness may play in mediating the effects of day care, although children in group care settings are obviously more susceptible to illness and infection than children who are exposed to fewer sources of possible infection.

Summary

Intensive research on the effects of infant day care over the past decade has greatly clarified our understanding of this important issue. It now appears that infant day care in itself does not reliably affect infant-mother attachment. Adverse effects on infant-mother attachment appear to occur only when infant day care co-occurs with other risky conditions, such as insensitive maternal behavior, although it is still not clear whether the insecure behavior of children who have been in day care is predictive of poorer adjustment later in childhood. In addition, although quality of care has proved to be a crucial consideration in research on the association between infant day care and other aspects of development, it appears not to moderate the association between infant care and infant-mother attachment. Researchers have shown that infants do form attachments to other care providers when afforded the opportunity to do so, and that the quality and security of these relationships is determined by the sensitivity and warmth of the care providers' interactions with the child. Relationships with care providers influence the infants' contemporaneous and subsequent behavior with adults as well as peers and thus may compensate for or magnify the effects of infant-mother attachment on subsequent behavior and adjustment.

Whether or not it is mediated through the quality of attachments to care providers, the quality of nonparental child care appears to modulate the effects of infant day care on many aspects of child behavior and adjustment. Thus, children who have experienced nonparental care from infancy tend to be more aggressive and assertive than their peers as well as less compliant with adults, although the associations are weaker, if not nonexistent, when the quality of care is better. Effects on noncompliance with adults must be summarized more cautiously, both because compliance and noncompliance have been studied less extensively and because noncompliance appears to be situation- and relationship-specific, rather than traitlike. High-quality day care from infancy clearly has positive effects on children's intellectual, verbal, and cognitive development, especially when the children would otherwise experience impoverished and relatively unstimulating home environments. Care of unknown quality may have deleterious effects in the intellectual performance of children from more advantaged backgrounds, presumably when such children miss out on the beneficial effects of stimulating and enriching experiences at home.

RESEARCH ON DAY CARE FOR PRESCHOOLERS

As indicated in the section on changing patterns of nonmaternal care, there have been steady increases in the rates of maternal employment over the past 30 years. Initially, mothers of preschoolers sought employment for themselves and day care for their children, and this precipitated popular and professional concerns about effects on the children. As mothers of younger children moved into the paid workforce, the status of infants and toddlers has attracted most popular concern. Research emphases have paralleled these trends: whereas the earlier studies focused on the effects of day care on 3- to 4-year-olds, the focus shifted to infants and toddlers in the mid-1980s. As a result, most of the studies reviewed in this section, where I focus on children entering care in the third through fifth years of life, were conducted before the most recent phase of research on infant care began. In general, greater public acceptance of nonparental care for older preschoolers has paralleled a tendency for researchers to emphasize the potential benefits rather than the risks associated with out-of-home care. Such conclusions are not universal, however, as my review makes clear.

Effects on Mother-Child Relationships

Although Bowlby's (1951) work on maternal deprivation and separation had highlighted the effects of extended separation on infants, the same interpretive framework was initially applied by researchers concerned about the effects of day care on preschoolers that is, 2.5- to 5-year-olds. Buttressed by attachment theory (Ainsworth, 1967, 1969; Bowlby, 1958, 1969), professionals warned that repeated daily separations might harm psychosocial development, and thus the initial research was designed to address the implicit question, Is day care bad for preschoolers? In the first systematic attempt to compare the effects of nonparental and exclusive home care, Caldwell, Wright, Honig, and Tannenbaum (1970) studied two groups of 2.5-year-old children, half attending a high-quality day care facility and half receiving care exclusively at home. Ratings of child-mother and child-other interactions revealed no differences between the day care and home care children.

In a widely cited study, Blehar (1974) then compared 2- and 3-year-old children receiving full-time group day care with children of similar ages cared for exclusively at home. The children were observed with their mothers in the Strange Situation procedure described above and disturbances in the day care children's attachments were discerned. More specifically, the 2-year-olds exhibited "detachment-like behavior" (i.e., avoidance) and the 3-year-olds exhibited "anxious, ambivalent attachment behaviors": day care 3-year-olds explored less, were more distressed by separation, and sought more proximity to and contact with their mothers on reunion than did the other 3-year-olds. Because these findings seemed to confirm that day care had the predicted negative effects and thus contradicted Caldwell et al.'s conclusions, several investigators attempted to replicate Blehar's study. None were successful (e.g., Kagan, Kearsley, & Zelazo, 1978; Moskowitz et al., 1977; Portnoy & Simmons, 1978; Ragozin, 1980), suggesting that the effects Blehar observed may have reflected temporary maladjustment because the children had only recently entered day care (Blanchard & Main, 1979) or were attributable to factors other than enrollment in day care. In addition, the Strange Situation was designed to assess infant-mother attachment, not attachments between 2- to 3-year-olds and their parents. The validity of the assessments in the Strange Situation was thus unknown, and other researchers have suggested different interpretations of "detachment-like behavior." For example, Clarke-Stewart and her colleagues (1994) reported that children in day care were more independent of their mothers in unfamiliar test situations than were children in home care. In their study, independence from mother was correlated with several measures of social competence with unfamiliar adults, and thus did not appear to reflect inadequate or insecure mother-child relationships.

Roopnarine and Lamb (1978) adopted a somewhat different strategy. Three-year-old children were observed in the Strange Situation immediately before they were enrolled in day care and again three months later. When children in this group were compared with others, matched in all respects except for the fact that their parents had no plans to enroll them in day care, these investigators found that the day care children were initially more anxious about and distressed by brief separations than the other children were. After three months of day care, however, these group differences had disappeared. Roopnarine and Lamb (1980) later replicated these findings, again showing that group differences in responses to brief separation were greater in pre-enrollment than postenrollment assessments. The results of these studies underscored the need for pre-enrollment assessments: group differences that are observed in a single posttreatment assessment cannot be interpreted as "effects" of nonparental care, and the absence of group differences in a posttest does not necessarily mean that nonparental care has no effects. Unfortunately, researchers still tend to ignore pre-enrollment characteristics in studies designed to assess the effects of day care on young children.

In more recent studies concerned with child-mother relationships among children in day care, researchers have focused on group differences in compliance, motivated both by earlier observations that infant day care may promote noncompliance and aggression (see section on infant day care) and by Belsky's (1988, 1989) claims that later noncompliance was a likely consequence of insecure attachment relationships.

In 1981, Lamb and his colleagues (Lamb, Hwang, Bookstein, Broberg, Hult, & Frodi, 1988) began a longitudinal study tracing the development of 145 firstborn Swedish children who averaged 16 months of age at the time of recruitment, the Göteborg Child Care Study. At the time, all the children were still being cared for at home by their parents, but all were on the waiting lists for enrollment in day care centers. Because the available supply was inadequate, only 53 of the children were accommodated; a further 33 were enrolled by their parents in family day care settings, while the rest of the children ($n = 54$) remained at home in the care of their parents. All the families in this study thus sought center care arrangements for their children, with the assignment to groups (center care, family day care, home care) determined by availability rather than parental ideology. Subsequent analyses confirmed that the families in the three groups had similar socioeconomic characteristics and comparable attitudes regarding parenting and child care at the time of recruitment, so group differences later observed are unlikely to reflect group selection factors (Wessels, Lamb, & Hwang, 1996). In addition, this study included measures of the quality of care received at home as well as pre-enrollment measures of many family and child characteristics.

In this study, compliance with mothers' requests were assessed in home observations when the children were 28 and 40 months of age (Ketterlinus, Bookstein, Sampson, & Lamb, 1989; Sternberg, Lamb, Hwang, Broberg, Ketterlinus, & Bookstein, 1991). No reliable dimension of compliance was evident at 28 months, but individual differences in noncompliance at 40 months were predicted by the quality of both home and alternative care and by the amount of nonparental care received before age 2. Compliance was highly correlated with the degree of parent-child harmony, suggesting that compliance is best viewed as an aspect of cooperation with the parents rather than as a characteristic of the individual child. Subsequently, Prodromidis, Lamb, Sternberg, Hwang, and Broberg (1995) supplemented the observational measures of mother-child compliance with ratings made by teachers and parents through 80 months of age. Once again, no consistent or reliable dimension was evident at 28 months; indices of compliance with teachers and mothers loaded on the same factor but were not stable over time and were uncorrelated with any aspects of the children's child care histories. Noncompliant children received care of poorer quality at home and were more likely to have controlling parents regardless of their child care experiences.

In a large study of children in Missouri kindergartens, Thornburg, Pearl, Crompton, and Ispa (1990) reported that children who had been at home continuously since infancy were rated by their teachers as more compliant with adults. By contrast, Clarke-Stewart et al. (1994) reported that middle-class 2- to 4-year-old children in day care, especially those in center care, were more friendly toward and more compliant with unfamiliar experimenters than those in the exclusive care of their parents. These children were most socially competent when they experienced intermediate amounts of care on a regular basis (10–30 hours per week) and when the care was of good quality. Observed levels of compliance with parents at home were higher for children in day care, although there was some evidence that the different indices of compliance did not form a single coherent dimension. In addition, family variables and parental behavior had a greater impact on compliance than day care variables did. By contrast, sociability with the mothers was not predicted by day care experiences, although they were predicted by indications that the mothers were more attentive, more responsive, and less controlling, whether or not the children were in day care. Crockenberg and Litman (1991) reported that maternal employment did not adversely affect the quality of maternal behavior at home; indeed, mothers who worked more were more responsive to and provided more guidance to 2-year-olds than nonemployed mothers did. Boys with employed mothers were more defiant of their mothers in the laboratory but not at home.

Taken together, these reports reveal a tendency for early enrollment in day care to be associated with noncompliance and less harmonious child-mother interactions at home. As reviewed in the earlier section, research on the effects of infant day care also suggests that the earlier nonparental care is initiated, the greater the likelihood of noncompliant behavior, particularly when the care is of poorer quality. However, several contradictory findings, and evidence that noncompliance does not constitute a coherent cross-situational trait, imply that the association is context-specific and poorly understood. This signals the need for further efforts to understand the origins, reliability, and implications of these potentially important correlates or effects.

Peer Relationships

Until recently, surprisingly little attention was paid to the effects of day care on peer relationships, even though children in group care settings typically spend more time interacting with peers than do children cared for exclusively by their parents, and research on infants suggests that nonparental care experiences are sometimes associated with elevated levels of aggression.

Somewhat surprisingly, Howes, Matheson, and Hamilton (1994) reported no differences in peer interaction skills between groups of children who entered child care in infancy ($M = 5$ months), early toddlerhood ($M = 19$ months), and late toddlerhood ($M = 33$ months). However, Harper and Huie (1985) found that group care experiences indeed facilitated the development of children's social participation, and Clarke-Stewart, Umeh, Snow, and Pederson (1980) and Clarke-Stewart et al. (1994) reported that children in alternative care settings were more socially competent and more cooperative with unfamiliar peers than were children cared for exclusively at home, even after individual differences in family background were taken into account. In the latter study, interestingly, increased opportunities for interaction with other children were not the causal factor, whereas among children in day care centers, quality of care and amount of attention from care providers were predictively important. Poor-quality care was associated with more negative and aggressive behavior with peers.

The results of two retrospective longitudinal studies were more troubling, although in neither case were data available concerning either pre-enrollment differences in the children's characteristics and experiences or the quality of care received. Bates et al. (1994) created a composite measure of adjustment including many indices of peer relationships: scores based on teacher reports of aggression, sociometric nominations, teacher ratings of popularity, social competence and skills, and observations of peer interaction. These researchers reported that the extent of out-of-home care was significantly associated with maladjustment in kindergarten. In another study, teachers in Missouri rated kindergartners as more aggressive when they had experienced out-of-home care unless they had received full-time care from infancy (Thornburg et al., 1990). Children in part-time care from infancy had the poorest quality relations with their peers.

An earlier report by Vandell and Powers (1983) suggests that quality of care may be an important consideration, and quality was not assessed in the studies by Bates et al. (1994) and Thornburg et al. (1990). Vandell and Powers observed 55 middle-class White 4-year-olds during free play in either poorly equipped, crowded, inadequately staffed centers with large groups of children or centers of higher quality. Quality of interaction with the teachers was correlated with the quality of the center, and children in low-quality centers spent more time unoccupied and in solitary play. Unfortunately, only 20 of the children were restudied four years later (Vandell, Henderson, & Wilson, 1987, 1988), but of these, the children who had been in high-quality centers were more socially competent, happier, and less shy than peers who had received care of poorer quality. Positive relations with the teachers at 4 years were correlated with greater empathy, social competence, and peer acceptance at 8 years.

Although Holloway and Reichhart-Erickson (1988) did not create a composite index of quality, they too reported some modest relationships between markers of quality and the amount of time spent by 4-year-olds in solitary play, but not the quality of free play with other children. In a quasi-experimental study in Florida, however, changes in state regulations led to improvements in both the quality of care and the quality of peer interactions observed among toddlers and preschoolers (Howes, Smith, & Galinsky, 1995). Kontos (1994) reported a positive relationship between the quality of family day care and the frequency of social play with 3- and 4-year-old peers.

The authors of a large multisite study of Cost, Quality, and Child Outcomes in Child Care Centers (1995) in four states (California, North Carolina, Colorado, and Connecticut) also concluded that children enrolled in centers providing care of high quality had superior social skills even after controlling for the effects of social class, ethnicity, and other aspects of family background. Howes, Matheson, and Hamilton (1994), meanwhile, reported that children who had secure relationships with their first teachers were rated as optimally ego-controlled (i.e., neither over- nor undercontrolled), and those who were classified as secure with their teachers at 4 years of age were more gregarious, ego-resilient, popular, and socially adept than children who had insecure relationships with their teachers. As noted earlier, previous research by these investigators suggested that the security of child-teacher relationships was influenced by the sensitivity of the teachers' behaviors. Interestingly, the quality of mother-child relationships was unrelated to children's social competence with peers.

The results of longitudinal research conducted by Lamb and his colleagues (1988a, 1988b) confirmed that the quality of care was influential. In the Göteborg Child Care Study, children were observed interacting with familiar peers at home before any of the children had out-of-home care experiences, as well as one and two years after some of the children entered center or family day care settings. Children in nonparental care settings were also observed interacting with peers in that context. Observational measures of social competence with both peers and unfamiliar adults were quite stable over time (such that the best predictors of social competence were earlier measures of the same construct), as well as by the quality of care received both at home and in the out-of-home care settings (Broberg, Hwang, Lamb, & Ketterlinus, 1989; Lamb et al., 1988; Lamb, Hwang, Broberg, & Bookstein, 1988). Children in the different care groups did not differ significantly when observed interacting with peers at home, although children in family day care engaged in more positive and more competent play with peers than did children in center care when observed in the alternative care facilities (Lamb, Sternberg, Knuth, Hwang, & Broberg, 1994). Prodromidis et al. (1995) showed that individual differences in the aggressiveness (mostly toward peers) of these children were moderately stable over the period from 16 to 80 months, and were best predicted by variations in the quality of home care. They were not related to child care history and were only modestly related to individual differences in noncompliance.

Taken together, the results of several studies thus suggest that simple enrollment in day care during the preschool years does not reliably facilitate or impede the development of positive relationships with peers. Instead, it seems that the quality of nonparental care is important: children receiving care of high quality have superior relationship skills, whereas children receiving care of poor quality have deficient social skills and may behave more aggressively than children without such experiences.

Personality Maturity

The personality maturity of children in day care has not often been studied, although there is some evidence that nonparental care of high quality fosters maturity. In the Göteborg Child Care Study, mothers described the children's personalities at 28 and 40 months of age using Block and Block's (1980) California Child Q-set (CCQ); their ratings were used to generate scores for the children's ego resilience, ego control, and field independence (Lamb et al., 1988a, 1988b; Broberg et al., 1989). Perceived personality maturity was quite stable over time and was best predicted by observational measures of the quality of care received at home and in the alternative care settings. The children viewed as most mature by their mothers were those who had received care of higher quality from the care providers as well as from their parents. There were no differences between children in the home care, family day care, and center care groups on any of the personality measures at either age.

Most (87%) of the children in this study were reassessed immediately prior to enrollment in first grade (80 months of age) and toward the end of the second grade (101 months of age). Once again, personality maturity was assessed using the CCQ, but a different pattern of results was now evident. Children who had been enrolled since toddlerhood in family day care settings appeared less mature than those in the other groups (Wessels, Lamb, Hwang, & Broberg, in press). Over time, ego undercontrol decreased less, while ego resilience and field independence increased less in the children in family day care than in those who remained at home with their parents or received center care. The quality of home and out-of-home care did not moderate or qualify these effects, which were evident in analyses of both the children who had received the same type of care since enrollment as well as among those who later shifted into another group.

No other researchers have explored type of care effects, and most have examined contemporaneous associations rather than longitudinal relations. Hestenes, Kontos, and Bryan (1993) showed that 3- to 5-year-olds were observed to express more positive affect when their day care arrangements were of higher quality. The appropriateness of the adult's behavior, along with the extent to which they manifested high levels of engagement, was especially significant. Positive self-perceptions were also correlated with high-quality care, even after controlling for differences in social class, ethnicity, and family background, in a large-scale study of infants, toddlers, and preschoolers in child care centers (Cost, Quality, and Child Outcomes in Child Care Centers, 1995). Howes, Matheson, and Hamilton (1994) found that children who had secure relationships with their care providers—presumably because these care providers behaved more sensitively and supportively—were more ego-resilient and more appropriately ego-controlled than those who had insecure relationships with their care providers. Reynolds (1994) reported that preschool and elementary school intervention was associated with improved teacher ratings on various indices of mature adjustment to school in the fifth grade.

Although the number of studies is quite small, the available evidence suggests that center care of high quality has positive effects on personality maturity, whereas children receiving care of lower quality tend to be less mature. Further exploration in large samples is called for, however, particularly in light of Wessels et al.'s (in press) findings that the effects of quality diminish over time.

Behavior Problems

Whereas high-quality care appears to foster personality maturity, nonparental care in the preschool years may promote the development of behavior problems. In the retrospective study mentioned earlier, Bates et al. (1994) assessed relations between the extent of nonmaternal care in the first, second to fourth, and fifth year of life and scores on multiple teacher- and mother-reported indices of adjustment after controlling for family background, sex, and other possible correlates. The extent of care in the most recent period was most influential, with children who were currently in day care appearing to be most poorly adjusted. In addition, infant care predicted less positive adjustment in kindergarten even after the effects of later care histories were taken into account. Interestingly, however, greater day care exposure was associated with teacher reports of fewer internalizing symptoms (e.g., somatic complaints, anxiety, depression). Burchinal et al. (1995) likewise found that middle-class 6- to 12-year-old children with preschool experience had higher levels of externalizing problems than did children with no preschool experiences, although there was no comparable association between child care history and internalizing problem behaviors. Interestingly, preschool experience predicted more positive ratings of the social behavior of African American but not of White children in this study.

Possible effects on behavioral problems were also suggested by Borge and Melhuish (1995), who followed all the children in a rural Norwegian community from their fourth birthdays through third grade. Behavior problems were no more common at either 4 or 8 years of age among those who had received nonmaternal care in their first three years. Children who experienced more center care between ages 4 and 7 had significantly fewer behavior problems at ages 7 and 10 years in the views of both mothers and teachers, even though there was little association between the behavior problems reported by mothers and teachers. Teachers, but not parents, reported that children who experienced more day care before 4 years of age behaved more poorly at age 10.

The association between nonparental care and behavioral problems was not evident in several other studies, both small and large scale. Pierrehumbert (1994; Pierrehumbert & Milhaud, 1994) reported that Swiss children who behaved insecurely with their mothers in the Strange Situation at 21 months were rated as more aggressive by their mothers at 5 years of age unless they had experienced more than average nonmaternal care in the first five years, in which case their levels of aggression were not elevated. Furthermore, Scarr, McCartney, Abbott-Shinn, and Eisenberg (1995) reported that length of time in center care had no effect, and the observed quality of care had minimal effects on children's behavioral adjustment and manageability as reported by both parents and teachers. However, family background (social class, parental stress, ethnicity) accounted for substantial portions of the variance in this large multisite study of infants, toddlers, and preschoolers. Meanwhile, Jewsuwan, Luster, and Kostelnik (1993) reported that 3- and 4-year-old children who were rated by their parents as anxious had more difficulty adjusting to preschool, whereas children rated by their parents as sociable had a more positive reaction, especially to their peers.

In sum, the available evidence suggests that nonparental care is associated with increased behavioral problems. These problems tend to involve externalization and likely reflect the same behavioral patterns (aggression, assertiveness) earlier discussed as adverse effects of nonparental care on peer relationships. Unfortunately, quality of care has not been considered in the research on behavior problems, although investigators who have focused more narrowly on peer interactions (see above) conclude that poor quality care is of particular concern.

Cognitive and Intellectual Competence

As in the case of infants, there has been considerable research on the association between nonparental care and intellectual development in preschoolers. Most of the research on the cognitive and intellectual correlates of nonparental child care has been gathered in the course of evaluating intervention programs designed to enhance the school readiness and academic performance of children from disadvantaged family backgrounds (see section on Enrichment Programs for Preschoolers, below). Several researchers have also examined the intellectual, cognitive, and academic performance of children in nonexperimental community programs, however, and the results tend to show that high-quality out-of-home care has positive effects on intellectual development, at least in the short term. Thus, Dunn (1993) reported that the intelligence of 4-year-olds from middle-class families was correlated with the quality of alternative care, even after controlling for family background variables. In a study focused on low-income mothers and their second-graders, Vandell and Ramanan (1992) likewise reported that maternal employment in the first three years was associated with superior academic performance especially when the mothers remained employed for the remainder of the preschool years. The effects of early maternal employment on math achievement remained significant even after controlling for various maternal and socioeconomic background characteristics. And a prospective longitudinal study of children from educationally advantaged backgrounds revealed positive effects of a one-year preschool program on a battery of achievement measures administered in second and third grade (Larsen & Robinson, 1989). The program benefited boys but not girls, however. Less generalized effects were also found in a retrospective study of middle-class 6- to 12-year-olds by Burchinal et al. (1995), who reported beneficial effects of preschool attendance on the PPVT scores of African American but not White children. Meanwhile, Clarke-Stewart et al. (1994; Clarke-Stewart, 1984, 1987) reported that middle-class 2- to 4-year-old children in centers scored better on many measures of cognitive development than children who remained in the exclusive care of their parents, had in-home sitters, or were in family day care, and that the effects were greater in centers of higher quality. The effects of attendance remained significant after the effects of family social class were partialed out. Interestingly, the amount of time spent each week in day care was curvilinearly related to the children's performance; those in care for 10 to 30 hours per week scored better than those receiving either less or more care, although it is unclear whether these differences are attributable to those factors that determine extent of care rather than extent of care per se. Care providers who took an active role in interaction and teaching had more positive effects than those who assumed more passive, custodial roles, and the predictive significance of these familial factors was not reduced by enrollment in nonparental care settings.

Broberg, Hwang, Lamb, and Bookstein (1990) assessed the development of verbal intelligence in the children participating in the Göteborg Child Care Study. Focusing on those children who had continued receiving the same type of care from 16 through 40 months of age, these researchers showed that scores on the Griffiths (1954, 1970) Developmental Scales at 28 and 40 months were predicted by independent observations of the children's sociability with unfamiliar adults as well as by earlier and contemporaneous indices of the quality of care received at home. The quality and type of out-of-home care were not related to the children's verbal abilities.

The children were reassessed several years later when they were nearing the end of the second grade (average age, 101 months). At this stage, the children's performance on standardized measures of cognitive ability (Häggström & Lundberg, 1990; Ljung & Pettersson, 1990; Ljungblad, 1967/1989) was predicted by the number of months the children had spent in center-based care before 3.5 years of age and the quality of care received in these centers (Broberg, Wessels, Lamb, & Hwang, 1997). By contrast, children in family day care performed more poorly than those in the center care and home care groups. The quality of home care was no longer associated with indices of the children's abilities or school performance, and preexisting group differences or differences in family background were not responsible for the effects observed. These results were largely consistent with those of Andersson (1989, 1992), who studied Swedish children who began out-of-home care in infancy (see above), as well as with the results of retrospective studies in Norway (Hartmann, 1991), New Zealand (Smith, Inder, & Ratcliff, 1993) and Britain (Wadsworth, 1986). In these studies enrollment in day care had either positive or no significant effects after the effects of maternal education and family SES had been partialed out. In a further assessment at age 20, furthermore, Hartmann (1995) reported that children who received high-quality center care between 4 and 7 years of age achieved higher levels of educational competence, and also saw themselves as more independent and autonomous, than a matched group of peers who received preschool care exclusively from their parents.

Taken together, the published literature reveals that center-based day care, presumably of high quality, can have positive effects on children's intellectual development, regardless of family background, and does not seem to have negative effects on any groups of children. However, too few researchers have studied family day care to permit confident conclusions about the effects of this form of care.

Enrichment Programs for Preschoolers

Numerous attempts have been made to evaluate the long- and short-term effects of compensatory enrichment programs for children from disadvantaged backgrounds. The amount of attention paid to this topic reflects in large part the tremendously optimistic fanfare that accompanied the rapid nationwide expansion of these programs in the mid-1960s as part of President Johnson's twin crusades, the Great Society and the War on Poverty (Steiner, 1976; Zigler & Muenchow, 1992; Zigler & Valentine, 1979). In this context, the establishment of Head Start in 1965 took center stage and remains a centerpiece of U.S. efforts to enhance the welfare of its poorest children. Because of its tremendous costs and broad constituency, furthermore, efforts to demonstrate its efficacy have been extensive, and the debates have been contentious.

In the late 1950s, social scientists began to marshal evidence suggesting that human abilities were more pliable than the hereditarians had previously acknowledged (e.g., Bloom, 1964; Hunt, 1961). In response to this, a small number of model programs had been developed and evaluated prior to the creation of Head Start; they pointed to the value of compensatory education but primarily sought to contrast the relative efficacy of different curricula and pedagogical approaches (e.g., Bereiter & Engelmann, 1966; Caldwell & Richmond, 1968; Copple, Sigel, & Saunders, 1984; Gray & Klaus, 1965; Stanley, 1973). Before this programmatic research had really expanded to permit the evaluation and fine-tuning of intensive model interventions, political pressures and the availability of funds led to the premature launching of Head Start on a nationwide scale. Originally intended as a summer-long pilot program for children from impoverished backgrounds, Head Start quickly became a year-round program attended by preschoolers in the year or two before they entered the public school system. A half million children were enrolled by the summer of 1965, and in 1992, some 621,000 children attended Head Start programs, mostly for a few hours per day, while some of their mothers attended parent education and skill development classes, often in the same building (Administration for Children, Youth, & Families, 1993). Head Start programs vary greatly, in large part because of an explicit determination to remain attentive to the grassroots clientele whose loyalty has allowed the program to prosper for more than three decades. A common theme has been to emphasize the direct delivery of services to children, and this is viewed as most effective (Ramey & Ramey, 1992; Roberts, Casto, Wasik, & Ramey, 1991; Wasik, Ramey, Bryant, & Sparling, 1990). Parent participation is widely viewed as an important adjunct to successful early intervention programs but varies greatly from program to program (Comer, 1980; Powell, 1982; Powell & Grantham-McGregor, 1989; Seitz, 1990), and potentially valuable home visiting components are part of only a small number of Head Start programs (Roberts & Wasik, 1990, 1994).

Originally intended as a broadly focused compensatory and enrichment program, Head Start's political proponents quickly came to depict it as a program designed (in large part) to improve children's school performance. Evaluations shortly after enrollment could not, of course, track either behavior or achievement at school and so the fateful decision was made to measure IQ, a construct with which psychologists and educators had extensive experience and were able to measure quickly and reliably (Kagan et al., 1969). Unfortunately, this helped foster unrealistic and simplistic views of the problems posed by poverty, and of their susceptibility to intervention (Sigel, 1990).

Despite evidence that short-term increases in IQ could be attributed to enhanced motivation rather than intelligence (Zigler & Butterfield, 1968), initial reports pleased Head Start's political and academic progenitors: the IQ scores of children in Head Start programs increased over the time they were enrolled and the IQ scores of children attending Head Start programs were significantly higher than those of comparable children who did not attend the programs. However, the euphoria quickly faded following publication of the Westinghouse Report in 1969 (Cicirelli, 1969). The results of this large multisite evaluation confirmed that children who had attended Head Start programs indeed had higher IQs, although these advantages quickly faded after the children left the programs and entered the regular public school system. The methodological sophistication of the Westinghouse Report was widely criticized (Campbell & Erlebacher, 1970; Datta, 1976; Lazar, 1981; Smith & Bissell, 1970), but similar findings were reported by other researchers (McKey, Condetti, Granson, Barrett, McConkey, & Plantz, 1985). Together, these reports fueled (a) criticisms that compensatory education was a wrongheaded failure that should be abandoned (Jensen, 1969, 1973; Spitz, 1986); (b) efforts to underscore that the other—nonintellectual—goals of Head Start (such as improved medical, mental health, and dental care) had not been evaluated (Cohen, Solnit, & Wohlford, 1979; Hale, Seitz, & Zigler, 1990; National Head Start Association, 1990; North, 1979; Zigler, Piotrkowski, & Collins, 1994); (c) arguments that practitioners needed to build on the acknowledged short-term contributions of Head Start by complementing them with continuing enrichment following enrollment in public school (Doernberger & Zigler, 1993; Ramey & Ramey, 1992); (d) arguments that interventions would be more effective if children were enrolled at much younger ages (Ramey & Ramey, 1992); and (e) awareness that poverty had multiple facets and impacts, such that amelioration of its effects would require complex, multifaceted, multidisciplinary, and extensive interventions (Sigel, 1990). The recent emergence of Early Head Start for children under 3 years of age represents one belated response to this need, as did the earlier Parent-Child Centers.

Unfortunately, public school enrichment programs (like Program Follow Through) designed to attenuate the IQ decline that typically occurs when children leave Head Start programs (Doernberger & Zigler, 1993; Kennedy, 1993) never achieved strong financial support, and thus implementation has been limited despite a small but persuasive body of evidence showing that programs of this sort can indeed be beneficial. Abelson, Zigler, and DeBlasi (1974) and Seitz, Apfel, Rosenbaum, and Zigler (1983) showed that one cohort of children who went from Head Start to Follow Through programs in New Haven maintained higher scores on measures of IQ, school achievement, and social-emotional development than children who attended traditional school programs through grade 9. A comparable demonstration program involving comprehensive preschool and school-age intervention, complemented by parental involvement during the preschool and early elementary years, was conducted in Chicago, although, as in New Haven, children were not assigned randomly to the two groups. Fuerst and Fuerst (1993) and Reynolds (1992a, 1993, 1994) reported that, after controlling for family background, graduates had better reading and mathematics achievement scores, were significantly more likely to be retained in grade, were less likely to be referred for special education, and were more likely to graduate from high school than children who received traditional schooling. Reynolds (1994) further found that participation in the elementary school component of the program had beneficial effects independent of the preschool component. Participation in the preschool component alone had significant effects through the sixth grade, although there was very little difference between the effects of one- and two-year enrollment periods, suggesting that it might be more effective to expand the number of children served than to extend the length of time each was enrolled (Reynolds, 1995). Maintenance of parental involvement also played an important role in ensuring the long-term continuity of effects on the children's performance (Reynolds, 1992b). Taylor and Machida (1994) likewise reported that parental participation in school activities was associated with learning skills and more strongly associated with classroom behavior after several months in Head Start. As summarized earlier, the results of early intervention programs initiated in infancy indicated that supplementary intervention in the school-age years has weaker effects than it has when associated with preschool intervention. This suggests that intensive intervention that begins early enough in development might have enduring effects, whereas less intensive interventions that begin later in development require supplementation.

The Consortium of Longitudinal Studies (1978, 1983; Darlington, Royce, Snipper, Murray, & Lazar, 1980; Lazar, Darlington, Murray, Royce, & Snipper, 1982) followed participants in 11 early intervention studies using a uniform set of measures. Their analyses confirmed that effects on IQ quickly faded following graduation from the programs, although they were able to identify impressive group differences in other aspects of school performance, including retentions in grade and premature school leaving. Few of these longitudinal studies involve Head Start graduates, in part because assignment to Head Start and comparison groups is not random and in part because there is so much diversity among Head Start programs that consistent effects should perhaps not be expected. Notwithstanding such methodological shortcomings, other reports suggest better school performance on the part of Head Start graduates.

Hebbeler (1985), McKey et al. (1985), and Copple, Cline, and Smith (1987) reported that Head Start graduates were more likely than children from comparable backgrounds who did not attend Head Start to be promoted, perform adequately at school, and have adequate nutrition and health care. Because the quality of Head Start programs is so variable, it is possible that the effects of Head Start would appear greater and more enduring if focus was placed on the good programs and their graduates (Gamble & Zigler, 1989). Consistent with this hypothesis, Bryant, Burchinal, Lau, and Sparling (1994) reported that the quality of Head Start classrooms, assessed using Harms and Clifford's (1980) ECERS scales, was correlated with scores on standardized measures of achievement, school readiness, and intelligence at the end of the Head Start year, regardless of the quality of home care. Most of the classrooms were rated "adequate" in quality; none were deemed "developmentally appropriate." These findings underscore the need for improvements in the overall quality of Head Start (Gamble & Zigler, 1989). Nevertheless, it is surprising how little evidence exists concerning the effects of Head Start, particularly considering the enormous cumulative and annual public costs of the program (Haskins, 1989).

Of the early intervention programs that have managed to follow their graduates over extended periods of time, most attention has been paid to the Perry Preschool Program in Ypsilanti, Michigan, which began in 1962 (Barnett, 1985, 1993; Berrueta-Clement, Schweinhart, Barnett, Epstein, & Weikart, 1984). One hundred and twenty-eight African American children from low-income families were randomly assigned to control and intervention groups. Beginning when they were 3 to 4 years old, children received 2.5 hours of class instructions per day throughout a 30-week school year, 13 for one year and 45 for two years. In addition, mothers and children were visited at home weekly for about 90 minutes. The children and their official records were reevaluated annually through 11 years of age as well as at 14, 15, 19, and 28 years of age using a battery of measures primarily focused on achievement, ability, and school performance (Schweinhart, Barnes, & Weikart, 1993). These data revealed that children in the program had higher achievement scores at ages 9 and 14, were more likely to graduate from high school, were more likely to be employed and not to have been arrested by age 19, earned more and were less likely to have a history of frequent arrests by age 28, and were less likely to go on welfare.

Much of the popular attention paid to this program reflects the decision to estimate in dollar terms the costs and benefits of enrollment in the preschool program (Barnett, 1993). The most widely publicized figures suggest that an average investment of $12,356 per child who participated in the program resulted in benefits through age 28 of $70,876. These benefits reflected the additional costs of completed education and higher wages and the lower costs of incarceration and welfare. Benefits are projected to continue as well, presumably justifying an initial investment per child that was substantially greater than the average cost of typical public preschool programs or Head Start programs.

The results of the Perry Preschool Project underscore the potential value of an extended preschool intervention of high quality, but do not reflect the likely effects of large established programs like Head Start, which serve a somewhat different clientele over a briefer period of time with much less rigorous control over quality (Zigler & Styfco, 1994). Greater attention to quality might improve the average effectiveness of early intervention programs like Head Start. Likewise, extension of the programs by enrolling children at younger ages, providing full-day services, and/or continuing to provide enriching services after enrollment in public school might enhance the effects of preschool on the intellectual performance of children from impoverished backgrounds.

Unfortunately, little effort has been made to specify the influential aspects of intervention programs so that attempts can be made to fine-tune their effectiveness. As in research on day care, which was mired too long in argumentative responses to the question Is day care bad for children?, proponents and critics have focused on determining whether Head Start is effective, instead of determining which aspects of which programs are of particular value to which children from which types of families. It is a shocking testament of our inattention to curricular issues that this chapter can offer only the most general conclusions about the beneficial effects of "high-quality" care rather than empirically supported conclusions about the value of particular programs and approaches.

AFTERSCHOOL CARE

The need for nonparental care does not end when children enter the elementary educational system at around 6 years of age (enrollment ages vary across cultures and communities), particularly as parental employment rates continue to rise in association with children's ages, and have always been higher for parents with school-age than preschool-age children or infants (see section on the changing patterns of nonmaternal care, above). In the United States, an estimated 75% of the mothers with school-age children were employed outside the home by 1995, compared with 40% in 1970 (Hayghe, 1995; Hofferth & Phillips, 1987; U.S. Bureau of Labor Statistics, 1987). The typical school day extends for only six hours, and in most European countries, children are expected to go home for lunch either at the end of or in the middle of the school day. As a result, many parents must make provision for the care and supervision of their children in the periods that they are at work and their children are not at school, although others fail to do so. The U.S. Bureau of the Census (1987) estimated that 7% of the children between 5 and 13 years of age stay at home unsupervised by an adult at least part of the time they are out of school. Contrary to popular belief, furthermore, unsupervised children are not more likely to be found in impoverished, minority communities. Cain and Hofferth (1989) reported that upper-income White families were more likely to leave their children unsupervised after school than were poorer or African American families. Similarly, Vandell and Ramanan (1991), using data from the NLSY, reported that children were more likely to be supervised after school when family income and social support levels were lower, and Steinberg (1986) found self-care most common when mothers worked full time and parents were divorced or separated.

Since the 1970s, great concern has been expressed about the safety and welfare of unsupervised or "latchkey" children (Bronfenbrenner, 1976; Genser & Baden, 1980), whose circumstances fit the legal definition of child neglect in most states. Perhaps because this legal characterization makes parents unwilling to admit the care status of their children, there has been much less research on the psychosocial and behavioral adjustment of young children (i.e., those in the first elementary grades) than on the status of children in middle school, with surprisingly little attention paid to their differing developmental needs. While a case can be made that eighth-graders benefit from learning to be responsible and independent during periods of unsupervised self-care, for example, the same argument should not be made with respect to first-graders living in urban communities.

Much of the concern about latchkey children was prompted by Woods (1972), who studied African American inner-city fifth-graders and found that the latchkey girls scored more poorly on measures of cognitive/academic, social, and personality adjustment than did peers in the care of adults. In particular, unsupervised girls had poorer achievement test scores and poorer relationships with their peers at school. On the basis of open-ended interviews with children in self-care arrangements, furthermore, Long and Long (1983, 1984) also concluded that latchkey children were at risk for a wide variety of social, academic, and emotional problems. Richardson and colleagues (1989) later reported that eighth-graders in the Los Angeles and San Diego metropolitan areas were more likely to abuse illicit substances when they spent more time in self-care.

By contrast, Galambos and Garbarino (1983) reported no differences in achievement, classroom orientation, adjustment to school, and fear between fifth- and seventh-graders who were either adult-supervised or cared for themselves after school in a rural community. Neither did Rodman, Pratto, and Nelson (1985), who studied fourth- and seventh-graders, matched on age, sex, family composition, and socioeconomic status. There were no differences in locus of control, behavioral adjustment, and self-esteem. Sharply criticizing Rodman et al.'s conclusions on the grounds that their measures were poorly chosen and the actual afterschool arrangements were not well defined, Steinberg (1986, 1988) argued that researchers need to distinguish among several groups of children who are all unsupervised by their parents after school: those who stay home alone; those who go to a friend's house, where they may be but typically are not supervised by the friend's parent; those who "hang out" in the mall or some other public place, and so on. These differences may be associated with important differences in the psychosocial status of the children concerned, argued Steinberg, particularly if they lead to differences in exposure to antisocial peer pressure. As predicted, suburban fifth-, sixth-, eighth-, and ninth-graders in fact appeared more susceptible to antisocial peer pressure (as indexed by the children's responses to hypothetical vignettes on a measure developed by Berndt, 1979) when they tended to "hang out" in public places, and those who went to a friend's house were more susceptible than those who stayed home alone (Steinberg, 1986). Children who stayed home alone, in fact, did not differ from those who were under adult supervision. Steinberg also reported group differences in the children's reports of their parents, with the parents of boys in self-care being more permissive than those of boys in adult care of some sort, and the permissiveness of girls' parents being correlated with the degree to which they were unsupervised (adult care, self-care at home, at friend's house, hanging out). Child-reported parental permissiveness was itself associated with the susceptibility to peer pressure, whereas authoritative parental practices (Baumrind, 1967, 1971) were associated with greater resistance to peer pressure.

Comparable results were obtained by Galambos and Maggs (1991) in a longitudinal study of sixth-graders living with both of their parents in suburban Canadian communities. Children who were not at home after school were more involved with peers. Unsupervised girls were more likely to have deviant peers, poor self-images, and be at risk of problem behavior, although the risks were reduced by less permissive and more accepting parental behavior. As earlier reported by Steinberg (1986) and Rodman et al. (1985), children who stayed at home unsupervised did not differ from those who were under adult supervision. And after evaluating data from teachers, parents, school records, standardized tests, peers, and the children themselves, Vandell and Corasaniti (1988) concluded that White suburban middle-class third-graders in self-care after school did not differ from children in the care of their mothers on any dimensions. In fact, the latchkey children appeared to function better at school and in the peer group than peers who went to formal afterschool programs. The mothers' marital status did not moderate any of these differences or nondifferences.

Vandell and Ramanan (1991) later studied third- to fifth-graders whose mothers were participants in the NLSY; the children were thus disproportionately likely to be born to adolescent, poor, minority parents, and only 28 of the 390 children were unsupervised after school, which further limits the strength of the conclusions that can be drawn from the study. Results showed no differences between latchkey and mother- or other-care children in the total number of behavior problems, although those who were unsupervised after school were rated as more headstrong and hyperactive than those in other- (but not mother-) care after school. Children in other-care after school had fewer behavior problems and higher PPVT scores than children cared for by their mothers after school. However, all of these differences disappeared following statistical controls for family income and emotional support, presumably because mother-care was the arrangement most likely to be chosen by the poorer, less emotionally supported families.

In a later study of third-graders in Milwaukee, which again oversampled single-parent, African American, low-income families, Vandell and Posner (in press; Posner & Vandell, 1994) sought to describe the components and effects of formal afterschool programs. Formal care was more likely when mothers were better educated and family incomes were lower; Whites were more likely to leave their children unsupervised, and African Americans were more likely to count on informal afterschool care arrangements. After controlling statistically for these factors, Vandell and Posner found that children attending formal afterschool programs received better grades for math, reading, and conduct than did peers in the mother-care and other-care groups. The former also had better work habits and better peer relations than those in the other-care group. These results are perhaps attributable to the facts that children in the formal settings spent more time in academic and enrichment activities and with both adults and peers, but less time watching television or playing with siblings than children in the other group. Unlike Vandell and Ramanan (1991), Posner and Vandell (1994) found that children in the other-care group performed more poorly than those in mother-care with respect to reading grades, work habits, and behavior problems, perhaps because these arrangements seemed quite inconsistent and variable from day to day. Unfortunately, quality of care has not been studied by researchers other than Vandell and her associates (Rosenthal & Vandell, 1996).

In sum, there is evidence that direct adult supervision may remain an important determinant of children's adjustment at least through midadolescence, although researchers have paid inadequate attention to developmental differences and have failed to study the psychosocial adjustment of the youngest children left unsupervised. In light of demographic data suggesting that some kindergartners are left alone regularly, it is noteworthy that the research literature has focused on children in third grade or higher, with most studies concerned with young adolescents. Third-graders seem to do better academically and behaviorally when they are in formal afterschool programs, although this may not be true of children from more affluent families. From the fifth grade on, children who are regularly at home behave and perform similarly whether or not an adult is present, but the distance from adult supervision explains differences in the outcomes of unsupervised children who do not go home after school. Parental disciplinary practices appear to modulate these differences in predictable ways. Unfortunately, all of these findings are compromised by the absence of longitudinal data and the strong possibility that differences among children (in their preferences to be and act with peers, for example) may precede rather than be consequences of the differing types of supervision.

CONCLUSION

After nearly three decades of intensive research on nonparental child care, considerable progress has been made, although we still have much to learn about the mechanisms by which out-of-home care affects children's development. In large part, our continuing ignorance about developmental processes reflects the extent to which researchers were preoccupied too long with the wrong questions—first asking Is day care bad for children? instead of How does day care affect children's development?—and later remained focused on the effects of day care per se instead of recognizing that day care has myriad incarnations and must always be viewed in the context of other events and experiences in children's lives. We should not be surprised that children's experiences away from their homes are formatively significant, though not in obvious or simple ways. However, simplistic assessments of these experiences and limitations on the opportunities for truly experimental research have impeded progress.

In addition, there is vast (and often poorly specified) variability within and among studies with respect to the actual care arrangements, the amount of care received, the age at which it began, the number and type of changes in the patterns of care, and the ways outcomes were assessed. Even when the same outcomes are assessed, variations in the ages of assessment and enrollment, means of quantification, and the composition and selection of comparison groups often preclude more than tentative conclusions about specific care arrangements. Whether or not one shares Silverstein's (1991) belief that researchers should shift their focus from the possible negative effects of nonparental care to documenting "the negative consequences of *not* providing high quality, affordable child care" (p. 1026), we can only hope that the current wave of research on day care yields clearer and more refined conclusions than those of the past 30 years.

Clumsy investigative strategies notwithstanding, we can actually answer a few of the simpler questions with some confidence. We now know, for example, that day care experiences *need not* have harmful effects on children's development and on their family relationships, although they *can* do so. The relationships enjoyed with parents by the majority of infants and children receiving out-of-home care do not differ systematically from those experienced by the majority of children cared for exclusively at home. Most children in out-of-home facilities remain attached to their parents and still prefer their parents over teachers and care providers. Meaningful relationships are often established with peers and care providers, however, and these can affect children's later social behavior, personality maturity, and cognitive development for good or for ill, depending on the quality and stability of these relationships. Researchers have consistently shown, for example, that early exposure to nonparental care fosters excessive assertiveness, aggression, and noncompliance in some children for reasons that are not yet well understood. Because nonparental care experiences are not reliably associated with insecure infant-mother attachment, the speculation that nonparental care fosters insecure attachment that in turn fosters subsequent misbehavior is not supported. One alternative interpretation—that early out-of-home care simply brings earlier exposure to societal norms of individualism—has not been explored systematically, but there is now evidence that poor relationships with care providers mediate the effects of out-of-home care on children's aggressiveness. Children in high-quality facilities who enjoy good relationships with stable providers are not more aggressive than peers who have experienced care only from their parents.

Assertions that nonparental care does not consistently or inevitably have either positive or adverse effects on children's development must be qualified on a number of grounds. Some of the most important qualifications stem from the fact that, with few exceptions, true experimental studies have not been possible. Because the children and families studied are thus not assigned randomly to nonparental and exclusive parental care groups, preexisting group differences—particularly those that led to the enrollment of some but not other children in nonparental care settings in the first place—may continue to explain at least some of the between-group variance discerned. Statistical controls for some of the known group differences and potentially influential factors reduce but do not completely eliminate the problem, limited as they are to imperfect indices of factors that are operationalized as linear and independent sources of influence. Still, it is comforting to note that researchers are continuing to refine their understanding of the factors that influence parental choices among child care options.

Social class (as manifested in varying levels of parental education and the richness of resources made available to children) is correlated with many indices of child development and thus needs to be considered in research on day care. In addition, although researchers have more recently done a much better job of sampling the range of settings experienced by most children receiving nonparental care, in-home placements and settings providing care of the poorest quality are likely to be overlooked and to refuse participation disproportionately. The most intensive studies still tend to overrepresent middle-class, White North Americans in placements of better-than-average quality, whereas the larger multisite studies and surveys include more diverse and ethnically representative groups. For a variety of reasons, the large multisite studies are least likely to include longitudinal components, however, so sampling limitations are an especially important consideration when longer-term outcomes are at issue.

In general, the quality of care received both at home and in alternative care facilities appears to be important, whereas the specific type of care (exclusive home care, family day care, center day care) appears to be much less significant than was once thought. Poor-quality care may be experienced by many children, according to the authors of many recent surveys, and poor-quality care can have harmful effects on child development. Type of care may also have varying effects depending on the ages at which children enter out-of-home care settings, with the planned curricula of day care centers becoming increasingly advantageous as children get older. Interactions between the type of care and the age of the child must obviously be considered, although claims about the formative importance of the amount of nonparental care and the age of onset have yet to be substantiated empirically. It also appears likely that different children will be affected differently by various day care experiences, although we remain ignorant about most of the factors that modulate these differential effects. Child temperament, parental attitudes and values, preenrollment differences in sociability, curiosity, and cognitive functioning, sex, and birth order may all be influential, but reliable evidence is scanty.

Over time, researchers' focus has clearly shifted from between-group to within-group (correlational) strategies. Many researchers embracing such strategies have attempted to assess the predictive importance of the quality of care, and there is a clear consensus that the quality of care, broadly defined and measured, modulates the effects of nonparental child care on child development. Interestingly, improvements in quality appear to have significant positive effects even at the highest end of the range sampled, suggesting that there is no threshold beyond which quality of care no longer matters. The magnitude of the effect is considerably less clear than its reliability, however, and the fact that researchers must estimate the importance of quality in the context of complex correlational models that also include a range of other potential predictors in studies involving widely varying samples makes it doubtful that we will ever really know how important quality is in an absolute sense. Furthermore, the recent and widespread focus on the quality of care often leads to an unwarranted neglect of the many other factors that affect children's development. Developmentalists now know that all aspects of behavioral development are multiply and redundantly determined, and, as a result, the absolute magnitude of each individual influence is likely to be quite small when all important factors are taken into account simultaneously. It would thus be a mistake to conclude that quality of care is not really important because its coefficients are small; by this logic, almost any factor could be deemed insignificant. A realistic appreciation of how complex developmental processes really are should instead foster a shift from the simplistic search for magic bullets to the patient but tedious evaluation of complex models of development.

Out-of-home care of superior quality is clearly beneficial to children and preferable to care of poor quality; however, parents and regulators need to evaluate the relative costs and benefits of incremental improvements in quality. Researchers, meanwhile, need to shift their attention to more detailed considerations of quality so as to define, more clearly than has been possible with the current generation of crude indices, what features of care providers and out-of-home care settings have the greatest impact on specific aspects of development. Progress in this domain is likely to be slow; researchers are only beginning to specify the effects of individual differences in parental behavior (Lamb, Ketterlinus, & Fracasso, 1992), and it may well be even harder to specify the crucial dimensions and mechanisms associated with day care. Nevertheless, the global indices of quality that have served a first generation of researchers and regulators so well must now yield center stage to a generation of more refined measures and concepts that allow practitioners to determine whether and how specific practices have the desired effects on children's learning and development. Among other things, such studies might explore why the quality of care, as currently measured, has equivalent effects on the social-emotional adjustment of all children, regardless of sociocultural background, whereas the effects on cognitive development often differ for children from differing backgrounds. Such insight should, in turn, permit the development of enriching programs for children from all sociocultural backgrounds.

Although it seldom receives the amount of attention it deserves, there is clear evidence that the quality of children's interactions and relationships with their parents and family members and the quality of care children receive at home continue to be the most important sources of influence on the development of young children, even when they receive substantial amounts of care outside the home. It remains an article of faith that nonparental care is likely to be most beneficial when it complements the quality of family care most successfully, and most likely to be harmful when there are differences in ideology, belief, and behavior. One implication of this would be that, beyond a certain level, different parents will evaluate different characteristics of alternative care providers quite differently, and that in the pursuit of different developmental goals for their children, their subjective evaluations of quality and choices among alternatives may begin to differ. Research findings that more clearly and carefully link specific practices to specific outcomes in defined circumstances would obviously benefit such rational choice, as would efforts to make parents better evaluators than they currently appear to be.

In all, we have learned a great deal about the effects of out-of-home care, and we have, in so doing, learned that these "effects" are a good deal more complex than was once thought. The challenge for the next decade is to determine how different experiences inside and outside the home are associated with specific outcomes for children in defined contexts and cultures. We know that extended exposure to nonparental child care indeed has a variety of effects on children, but when asked about specific patterns of effects or even whether such care is good or bad for children we still have to say *It depends.*

ACKNOWLEDGMENTS

I am grateful to the many colleagues who read earlier drafts of this chapter and helped me to shape the final form—Jay Belsky, Susan Chira, Diane Eyer, Ron Haskins, Carollee Howes, Philip Hwang, Blaise Pierrehumbert, Irving Sigel, and Edward Zigler—as well as to Kimberly Monroe, Lisa Laumann Billings, and Katie Brittin, who helped me to gather material and prepare successive drafts of the manuscript.

REFERENCES

Abbott-Shim, M., & Sibley, A. (1987). *Assessment profile for childhood programs.* Atlanta, GA: Quality Assistance.

Abbott-Shim, M., & Sibley, A. (1992). *Research version of the assessment profile for childhood programs.* Atlanta, GA: Quality Assistance.

Abelson, W. D., Zigler, E. F., & DeBlasi, C. L. (1974). Effects of a four-year Follow Through program on economically disadvantaged children. *Journal of Educational Psychology, 66,* 756–771.

Ackerman-Ross, S., & Khanna, P. (1989). The relationship of high quality day care to middle-class 3-year-olds' language performance. *Early Childhood Research Quarterly, 4,* 97–116.

Administration on Children, Youth and Families. (1993). *Project Head Start: Statistical fact sheet.* Washington, DC: Author.

Ainslie, R. C. (1987, August). *The social ecology of day care infants with secure and insecure maternal attachments.* Paper presented at the meeting of the American Psychological Association, New York.

Ainslie, R. C., & Anderson, C. W. (1984). Daycare children's relationships to their mothers and caregivers: An inquiry into the conditions for the development of attachment. In R. C. Ainslie (Ed.), *The child and the day care setting: Qualitative variations and development* (pp. 98–132). New York: Praeger.

Ainsworth, M. D. S. (1967). *Infancy in Uganda.* Baltimore: Johns Hopkins University Press.

Ainsworth, M. D. S. (1969). Object relations, dependency, and attachment: A theoretical review of the infant-mother relationship. *Child Development, 40,* 969–1025.

Ainsworth, M. D. S., Blehar, M. C., Waters, E., & Wall, S. (1978). *Patterns of attachment.* Hillsdale, NJ: Erlbaum.

Altmann, J. (1987). Life span aspects of reproduction and parental care in anthropoid primates. In J. B. Lancaster, J. Altmann, A. S. Rossi, & L. R. Sherrod (Eds.), *Parenting across the life span: Biosocial perspectives* (pp. 15–29). Hawthorne, NY: Aldine de Gruyter.

Anderson, C. W., Nagle, R. J., Roberts, W. A., & Smith, J. W. (1981). Attachment to substitute caregivers as a function of center quality and caregiver involvement. *Child Development, 52,* 53–61.

Andersson, B.-E. (1989). Effects of public day care: A longitudinal study. *Child Development, 60,* 857–866.

Andersson, B.-E. (1992). Effects of day care on cognitive and socioemotional competence of thirteen-year-old Swedish school children. *Child Development, 63,* 20–36.

Arend, R., Gove, F., & Sroufe, L. A. (1979). Continuity in early adaptation from attachment security in infancy to resiliency and curiosity at age five. *Child Development, 50,* 950–959.

Arnett, J. (1989). Caregivers in day care centers: Does training matter? *Journal of Applied Developmental Psychology, 10,* 541–552.

Balleyguier, G. (1988). What is the best mode of day care for young children: A French study. *Early Child Development and Care, 33,* 41–65.

Balleyguier, G., Meudec, M., & Chasseigne, G. (1991). Modes de garde et temperament chez le jeune enfant [Types of care and temperament in the young child]. *Enfance, 12,* 154–169.

Balleyguier, G., Meudec, M., Comfort, M., & Fullard, W. (1994). *Infant temperament and day care setting: Observations of child behavior with caregiver.* Unpublished manuscript, Université de Tours, Tours, France.

Barglow, P., Vaughn, B. E., & Molitor, N. (1987). Effects of maternal absence due to employment on the quality of infant-mother attachment in a low-risk sample. *Child Development, 53,* 53–61.

Barnas, M. V., & Cummings, E. M. (1994). Caregiver stability and toddlers' attachment-related behavior towards caregivers in day care. *Infant Behavior and Development, 17,* 141–147.

Barnett, W. S. (1985). Benefit-cost analysis of the Perry Preschool programs and its policy implications. *Educational Evaluation and Policy Analysis, 7,* 333–342.

Barnett, W. S. (1993). Benefit-cost analysis. In L. J. Schweinhart, H. V. Barnes, & D. P. Weikart (Eds.), *Significant benefits: The High/Scope Perry Preschool Study through age 27* (pp. 142–173). Ypsilanti, MI: High/Scope Press.

Barton, M., & Schwarz, J. C. (1981, August). *Daycare in the middle class: Effects in elementary schools.* Paper presented at the meeting of the American Psychological Association, Los Angeles.

Bates, J. E., Marvinney, D., Kelly, T., Dodge, K. A., Bennett, D. S., & Pettit, G. S. (1994). Child-care history and kindergarten adjustment. *Developmental Psychology, 30,* 690–700.

Baumrind, D. (1967). Child care practices anteceding three patterns of preschool behavior. *Genetic Psychology Monographs, 75,* 43–88.

Baumrind, D. (1971). Current patterns of parental authority. *Developmental Psychology Monographs, 41*(1, Pt. 2), 1–103.

Baydar, N., & Brooks-Gunn, J. (1991). Effects of maternal employment and child care arrangements on preschoolers' cognitive and behavioral outcomes: Evidence from the children of the National Longitudinal Survey of Youth. *Developmental Psychology, 27,* 932–945.

Beckwith, L. (1987). [Longitudinal study at UCLA of high-risk preterm infants]. Unpublished raw data.

Belsky, J. (1986). Infant day care: A cause for concern? *Zero to Three, 6,* 1–9.

Belsky, J. (1988). The "effects" of infant daycare reconsidered. *Early Childhood Research Quarterly, 3,* 235–272.

Belsky, J. (1989). Infant-parent attachment and day care: In defense of the Strange Situation. In J. Lande, S. Scarr, & N. Gunzenhauser (Eds.), *Caring for children: Challenge to America* (pp. 23–48). Hillsdale, NJ: Erlbaum.

Belsky, J. (1992). Consequences of child care for children's development: A deconstructionist view. In A. Booth (Ed.), *Child care in the 1990s: Trends and consequences* (pp. 83–95). Hillsdale, NJ: Erlbaum.

Belsky, J. (1994, September). *Effects of infant day care: 1986–1994.* Paper presented at the meeting of the British Psychological Society Section on Developmental Psychology, Portsmouth, England.

Belsky, J., & Braungart, J. M. (1991). Are insecure-avoidant infants with extensive day care experience less stressed by and more independent in the Strange Situation? *Child Development, 62,* 567–571.

Belsky, J., & Eggebeen, D. (1991). Early and extensive maternal employment and young children's socioemotional development: Children of the National Longitudinal Survey of Youth. *Journal of Marriage and the Family, 53,* 1083–1098.

Belsky, J., & Rovine, M. J. (1988). Nonmaternal care in the first year of life and the security of infant-parent attachment. *Child Development, 59,* 929–949.

Belsky, J., & Rovine, M. J. (1990). Q-set security and first-year nonmaternal care. *New Directions for Child Development, 49,* 7–22.

Belsky, J., & Steinberg, L. D. (1978). The effects of daycare: A critical review. *Child Development, 49,* 929–949.

Belsky, J., Steinberg, L. D., & Walker, A. (1982). The ecology of daycare. In M. E. Lamb (Ed.), *Nontraditional families* (pp. 71–116). Hillsdale, NJ: Erlbaum.

Belsky, J., & Walker, A. (1980). *Infant-toddler center spot observation system.* Unpublished manuscript, Department of Individual and Family Studies, Pennsylvania State University, University Park.

Belsky, J., Woodworth, S., & Crnic, K. (1996). Trouble in the second year: Three questions about family interaction. *Child Development, 67,* 556–578.

Benn, R. K. (1986). Factors promoting secure attachment relationships between employed mothers and their sons. *Child Development, 55,* 1224–1231.

Bereiter, C., & Engelmann, S. (1966). *Teaching disadvantaged children in the preschool.* Englewood Cliffs, NJ: Prentice-Hall.

Berk, L. E. (1985). Relationship of caregiver education to child-oriented attitudes, job satisfaction, and behavior toward children. *Child Care Quarterly, 14,* 103–129.

Berndt, T. (1979). Developmental changes in conformity to peers and parents. *Developmental Psychology, 15,* 608–616.

Berrueta-Clement, J. R., Schweinhart, L. J., Barnett, W. S., Epstein, A. S., & Weikart, D. P. (1984). *Changed lives: The effects of the Perry Preschool program on youths through age 19.* Ypsilanti, MI: High/Scope Press.

Blair, C., Ramey, C. T., & Hardin, J. M. (1995). Early intervention for low birthweight, premature infants: Participation and intellectual development. *American Journal on Mental Retardation, 99,* 542–554.

Blanchard, M., & Main, M. (1979). Avoidance of the attachment figure and social-emotional adjustment in day-care infants. *Developmental Psychology, 15,* 445–446.

Blehar, M. C. (1974). Anxious attachment and defensive reactions associated with day care. *Child Development, 46,* 801–817.

Block, J. H., & Block, J. (1980). The role of ego-control and ego-resiliency in the organization of behavior. In W. A. Collins (Ed.), *The Minnesota Symposia on Child Psychology* (Vol. 13, pp. 39–101). Hillsdale, NJ: Erlbaum.

Bloom, B. S. (1964). *Stability and change in human characteristics.* New York: Wiley.

Bolger, K. E., & Scarr, S. (1995). Not so far from home: How family characteristics predict child care quality. *Early Development and Parenting, 4,* 103–112.

Bollin, G. G. (1993). An investigation of job stability and job satisfaction among family day care providers. *Early Childhood Research Quarterly, 8,* 207–220.

Borge, A. I. H., & Melhuish, E. C. (1995). A longitudinal study of childhood behavior problems, maternal employment and day care in a rural Norwegian community. *International Journal of Behavioral Development, 18,* 23–42.

Bowlby, J. (1951). *Maternal care and mental health.* Geneva, Switzerland: World Health Organization.

Bowlby, J. (1958). The nature of the child's tie to his mother. *International Journal of Psychoanalysis, 39,* 350–373.

Bowlby, J. (1969). *Attachment and loss: Vol. 1. Attachment.* New York: Basic Books.

Bowman, B. T. (1992). Child development and its implications for day care. In A. Booth (Ed.), *Child care in the 1990s: Trends and consequences* (pp. 95–101). Hillsdale, NJ: Erlbaum.

Braverman, L. B. (1989). Beyond the myth of motherhood. In M. McGoldrick, C. M. Anderson, & F. Walsh (Eds.), *Women and families* (pp. 227–243). New York: Free Press.

Brayfield, A. A., Deich, S. G., & Hofferth, S. L. (1990). *Caring for children in low-income families: A substudy of the National Child Care Survey, 1990.* Washington, DC: Urban Institute Press.

Bredekamp, S. (Ed.). (1987a). *Accreditation criteria and procedures of the National Academy of Early Childhood Programs.* Washington, DC: National Association for the Education of Young Children.

Bredekamp, S. (1987b). *Developmentally appropriate practice in early childhood programs serving children from birth through age 8.* Washington, DC: National Association for the Education of Young Children.

Broberg, A. G., & Hwang, C. P. (1991). The Swedish child care system. In E. C. Melhuish & P. Moss (Eds.), *Day care and the young child: International perspectives* (pp. 75–101). London: Routledge & Kegan Paul.

Broberg, A. G., Hwang, C. P., Lamb, M. E., & Bookstein, F. L. (1990). Factors related to verbal abilities in Swedish preschoolers. *British Journal of Developmental Psychology, 8,* 335–349.

Broberg, A. G., Hwang, C. P., Lamb, M. E., & Ketterlinus, R. D. (1989). Child care effects on socioemotional and intellectual competence in Swedish preschoolers. In J. S. Lande, S. Scarr, & N. Gunzenhauser (Eds.), *Caring for children: Challenge to America* (pp. 49–75). Hillsdale, NJ: Erlbaum.

Broberg, A. G., Wessels, H., Lamb, M. E., & Hwang, C. P. (1997). The effects of day care on the development of cognitive abilities in eight-year-olds: A longitudinal study. *Developmental Psychology, 33,* 62–69.

Bronfenbrenner, U. (1976). Who cares for America's children. In V. C. Vaughn & T. B. Brazelton (Eds.), *The family: Can it be saved?* (pp. 3–32). Cambridge, MA: Harvard University Press.

Brooks-Gunn, J., Klebanov, P. K., Liaw, F., & Spiker, D. (1993). Enhancing the development of low-birthweight, premature infants: Changes in cognition and behavior over the first three years. *Child Development, 64,* 736–753.

Brooks-Gunn, J., McCarton, G. M., Casey, P. H., McCormick, M. C., Bauer, C. R., Bernbaum, J. L., Tyson, J., Swanson, M., Bennett, F. C., Scott, D. T., Tonascia, J., & Meinert, C. L. (1994). Early intervention in low-birth-weight premature infants: Results through age 5 years from the Infant Health and Development Program. *Journal of the American Medical Association, 272,* 1257–1262.

Bryant, D. M., Burchinal, M., Lau, L. B., & Sparling, J. J. (1994). Family and classroom correlates of Head Start children's developmental outcomes. *Early Childhood Research Quarterly, 9,* 289–309.

Burchinal, M. R., & Bryant, D. M. (1988). [Longitudinal study at the Frank Porter Graham Center of a mixed SES sample]. Unpublished raw data.

Burchinal, M. R., Bryant, D. M., Lee, M. W., & Ramey, C. T. (1992). Early day care, infant-mother attachment, and maternal responsiveness in the infant's first year. *Early Childhood Research Quarterly, 7,* 383–396.

Burchinal, M. R., Campbell, F. A., Bryant, D. M., Wasik, B. H., & Ramey, C. T. (in press). Early intervention and mediating processes in intellectual development among low-income African-American children. *Child Development.*

Burchinal, M. R., Lee, M., & Ramey, C. T. (1989). Type of day care and preschool intellectual development in disadvantaged children. *Child Development, 60,* 182–187.

Burchinal, M. R., Ramey, S. L., Reid, M. K., & Jaccard, J. (1995). Early child care experiences and their association with family and child characteristics during middle childhood. *Early Childhood Research Quarterly, 10,* 33–61.

Cahan, E. D. (1989). *Past caring: A history of U.S. preschool care and education for the poor, 1820–1965.* New York: National Center for Children in Poverty.

Cain, V. S., & Hofferth, S. L. (1989). Parental choice of self-care for school-age children. *Journal of Marriage and the Family, 51,* 65–77.

Caldwell, B. M., & Richmond, J. (1968). The Children's Center in Syracuse. In C. P. Chandler, R. S. Lourie, & A. P. Peters (Eds.), *Early child care* (pp. 326–358). New York: Atherton Press.

Caldwell, B. M., Wright, C., Honig, A., & Tannenbaum, J. (1970). Infant day care and attachment. *American Journal of Orthopsychiatry, 69,* 690–697.

Campbell, D. T., & Erlebacher, A. (1970). How regression artifacts in quasi-experimental evaluations can mistakenly make compensatory education look harmful. In J. Hellmuth (Ed.), *Compensatory education: A national debate* (Vol. 3, pp. 185–210). New York: Brunner/Mazel.

Campbell, F. A., Burchinal, M., Wasik, B. H., Bryant, D. M., Sparling, J. J., & Ramey, C. T. (1995). *Early intervention and long term predictors of school concerns in African American children from low-income families.* Unpublished manuscript, University of North Carolina, Chapel Hill.

Campbell, F. A., & Ramey, C. T. (1990). The relationship between Piagetian cognitive development, mental test performance, and academic achievement in high-risk students with and without early educational experience. *Intelligence, 14,* 293–308.

Campbell, F. A., & Ramey, C. T. (1994). Effects of early intervention on intellectual and academic achievement: A follow-up study of children from low-income families. *Child Development, 65,* 684–698.

Campbell, F. A., & Ramey, C. T. (1995). Cognitive and school outcomes for high risk African-American students at middle adolescence: Positive effects of early intervention. *American Education Research Journal, 32,* 743–772.

Caughy, M. O'B., DiPietro, J. A., & Strobino, D. M. (1994). Day care participation as a protective factor in the cognitive development of low-income children. *Child Development, 65,* 457–471.

Chafel, J. A. (1992). Funding Head Start: What are the issues? *American Journal of Orthopsychiatry, 62,* 9–21.

Chase-Lansdale, P. L., & Owen, M. T. (1987). Maternal employment in family context: Effects on infant-mother and infant-father attachments. *Child Development, 58,* 1505–1512.

Cherlin, A. (1992). Infant care and full-time employment. In A. Booth (Ed.), *Child care in the 1990s: Trends and consequences* (pp. 209–215). Hillsdale, NJ: Erlbaum.

Chin-Quee, D. S., & Scarr, S. (1994). Lack of early child care effects on school-age children's social competence and academic achievement. *Early Development and Parenting, 3,* 103–112.

Cicirelli, V. G. (1969). *The impact of Head Start: An evaluation of the effects of Head Start on children's cognitive and effective development.* Washington, DC: Westinghouse Learning Corporation.

Clarke-Stewart, K. A. (1977). *Child care in the family: A review of research and some propositions for policy.* New York: Academic Press.

Clarke-Stewart, K. A. (1984). Day care: A new context for research and development. In M. Perlmutter (Ed.), *The Minnesota Symposium on Child Psychology* (Vol. 17, pp. 61–100). Hillsdale, NJ: Erlbaum.

Clarke-Stewart, K. A. (1987). Predicting child development from child care forms and features: The Chicago Study. In D. A. Phillips (Ed.), *Quality in child care: What does research tell us?* (pp. 21–42). Washington, DC: National Association for the Education of Young Children.

Clarke-Stewart, K. A. (1988). "The effects of infant day care reconsidered" reconsidered: Risks for parents, children, and researchers. *Early Childhood Research Quarterly, 3,* 293–318.

Clarke-Stewart, K. A. (1989). Infant day care: Maligned or malignant? *American Psychologist, 44,* 266–273.

Clarke-Stewart, K. A. (1992a). Consequences of child care for children's development. In A. Booth (Ed.), *Child care in the 1990s: Trends and consequences* (pp. 63–83). Hillsdale, NJ: Erlbaum.

Clarke-Stewart, K. A. (1992b). Consequences of child care—One more time: A rejoinder. In A. Booth (Ed.), *Child care in the 1990s: Trends and consequences* (pp. 116–127). Hillsdale, NJ: Erlbaum.

Clarke-Stewart, K. A., & Fein, G. C. (1983). Early childhood programs. In P. H. Mussen (Series Ed.) & M. M. Haith & J. J. Campos (Vol. Eds.), *Handbook of child psychology: Vol. 2. Infancy and developmental psychobiology* (4th ed., pp. 917–999). New York: Wiley.

Clarke-Stewart, K. A., Gruber, C. P., & Fitzgerald, L. M. (1994). *Children at home and in day care.* Hillsdale, NJ: Erlbaum.

Clarke-Stewart, K. A., Umeh, B. J., Snow, M. E., & Pederson, J. A. (1980). Development and prediction of children's sociability from 1 to 2 ½ years. *Developmental Psychology, 16,* 290–302.

Clerkx, L. E., & Van IJzendoorn, M. H. (1992). Child care in a Dutch context: On the history, current status, and evaluation of nonmaternal child care in the Netherlands. In M. E. Lamb, K. J. Sternberg, C.-P. Hwang, & A. G. Broberg (Eds.), *Child care in context: Cross-cultural perspectives* (pp. 55–79). Hillsdale, NJ: Erlbaum.

Cochran, M. (Ed.). (1993). *International handbook of child care policies and programs.* Westport, CT: Greenwood Press.

Coelen, C., Glantz, F., & Calore, D. (1979). *Day care centers in the U.S.: A national profile, 1976–1977.* Cambridge, MA: Abt Associates.

Cohen, B. (1993). The United Kingdom. In M. Cochran (Ed.), *International handbook of child care policies and programs* (pp. 515–534). Westport, CT: Greenwood Press.

Cohen, D. J., Solnit, A. J., & Wohlford, P. (1979). Mental health services in Head Start. In E. Zigler & J. Valentine (Eds.), *Project Head Start: A legacy of the war on poverty* (pp. 259–282). New York: Free Press.

Cohn, J. F., Campbell, S. B., & Ross, S. (1991). Infant response in the still-face paradigm at 6 months predicts avoidant and secure attachment at 12 months. *Development and Psychopathology, 3,* 367–376.

Comer, J. P. (1980). *School power.* New York: Free Press.

Consortium for Longitudinal Studies. (1978). *Lasting effects after preschool.* Final report to the Administration on Children, Youth, and Families. Washington, DC: U.S. Government Printing Office.

Consortium for Longitudinal Studies. (1983). *As the twig is bent: Lasting effects of preschool programs.* Hillsdale, NJ: Erlbaum.

Copple, G., Cline, M., & Smith, A. (1987). *Paths to the future: Long-term effects of Head Start in the Philadelphia school district.* Washington, DC: U.S. Department of Health and Human Services.

Copple, G., Sigel, I. E., & Saunders, R. (1984). *Educating the young thinker: Classroom strategies for cognitive growth.* Hillsdale, NJ: Erlbaum.

Corsaro, W. A., & Emiliani, F. (1992). Child care, early education, and children's peer culture in Italy. In M. E. Lamb, K. J. Sternberg, C. P. Hwang, & A. G. Broberg (Eds.), *Child care in context: Cross-cultural perspectives* (pp. 81–115). Hillsdale, NJ: Erlbaum.

Cost, Quality, and Child Outcome in Child Care Centers. (1995). Economics Department, University of Colorado at Denver, Denver.

Crockenberg, S., & Litman, C. (1991). Effects of maternal employment on maternal and two-year-old child behavior. *Child Development, 62,* 930–953.

Cummings, M. E. (1980). Caregiver stability and day care. *Developmental Psychology, 16,* 290–302.

Dahlström, E. (Ed.). (1962). *Kvinnors liv och arbete* [Women's lives and work]. Stockholm: Studieförbundet Näringsliv och Samhälle.

Darlington, R. B., Royce, J. M., Snipper, A. S., Murray, H. W., & Lazar, I. (1980). Preschool programs and the later school competence of children from low-income families. *Science, 208,* 202–204.

Datta, L. (1976). The impact of the Westinghouse/Ohio evaluation on the development of Project Head Start. In C. C. Abt (Ed.), *The evaluation of social programs* (pp. 129–181). Beverly Hills, CA: Sage.

DeMeis, D. K., Hock, E., & McBride, S. L. (1986). The balance of employment and motherhood: Longitudinal study of mothers' feelings about separation from their firstborn infants. *Developmental Psychology, 22,* 627–632.

Desai, S., Chase-Lansdale, P. L., & Michael, R. T. (1989). Mother or market? Effects of maternal employment on the intellectual ability of 4-year-old children. *Demography, 26,* 545–561.

Doernberger, C., & Zigler, E. F. (1993). Project Follow Through: Intent and reality. In E. F. Zigler & S. J. Styfco (Eds.), *Head Start and beyond: A national plan for extended childhood intervention* (pp. 43–72). New Haven, CT: Yale University Press.

Dombro, A. L. (1995). *Child care aware: A guide to promoting professional development in family child care.* New York: Families and Work Institute.

Dombro, A. L., & Modigliani, K. (1995). *Family child care providers speak about training, trainees, accreditation, and professionalism: Findings from a survey of family-to-family graduates.* New York: Families and Work Institute.

Dragonas, T., Tsiantis, J., & Lambidi, A. (1995). Assessing quality day care: The Child Care Facility Schedule. *International Journal of Behavioral Development, 18,* 557–568.

Dunn, L. (1993). Proximal and distal features of day care quality and children's development. *Early Childhood Research Quarterly, 8,* 167–192.

Easterbrooks, M. A., & Goldberg, W. A. (1985). Effects of early maternal employment on toddlers, mothers, and fathers. *Developmental Psychology, 21,* 774–783.

Easterbrooks, M. A., & Harmon, R. A. (1987). [Longitudinal study of pre-term and full-term infants from middle class two-parent families]. Unpublished raw data.

Egeland, B., & Hiester, M. (1995). The long-term consequences of infant daycare and mother-infant attachment. *Child Development, 66,* 474–485.

Farber, E. A., & Egeland, B. (1982). Developmental consequences of out-of-home care for infants in a low-income population. In E. Zigler & E. Gordon (Eds.), *Day care* (pp. 102–125). Boston: Auburn House.

Farran, D. C., & Ramey, C. T. (1977). Infant day care and attachment behaviors toward mothers and teachers. *Child Development, 48,* 1112–1116.

Feagans, L. V., & Farran, D. C. (1994). The effects of day care intervention in the preschool years on the narrative skills of poverty children in kindergarten. *International Journal of Behavioral Development, 17,* 503–523.

Feagans, L. V., Kipp, E., & Blood, I. (1994). The effects of otitis media on the attention skills of day-care-attending toddlers. *Developmental Psychology, 30,* 701–708.

Fein, G. G. (1995). Infants in group care: Patterns of despair and detachment. *Early Childhood Research Quarterly, 10,* 261–275.

Fein, G. G., & Clarke-Stewart, K. A. (1973). *Day care in context.* New York: Wiley.

Fein, G. G., Gariboldi, A., & Boni, R. (1993). The adjustment of infants and toddlers to group care: The first 6 months. *Early Childhood Research Quarterly, 8,* 1–14.

Field, T. (1991). Quality infant daycare and grade school behavior and performance. *Child Development, 62,* 863–870.

Field, T., Gewirtz, J. L., Cohen, D., Garcia, R., Greenberg, R., & Collins, K. (1984). Leave-takings and reunions of infants, toddlers, preschoolers, and their parents. *Child Development, 55,* 628–635.

Field, T., Masi, W., Goldstein, D., Perry, S., & Parl, S. (1988). Infant daycare facilitates preschool behavior. *Early Childhood Research Quarterly, 3,* 341–359.

Finkelstein, N. (1982). Aggression: Is it stimulated by day care? *Young Children, 37,* 3–9.

Fischer, J. L., & Eheart, B. K. (1991). Family day care: A theoretical basis for improving quality. *Early Childhood Research Quarterly, 6,* 549–563.

Fosburg, S., Hawkins, P. D., Singer, J. D., Goodson, B. D., Smith, J. M., & Brush, L. R. (1970). *National day care home study.* Cambridge, MA: Abt Associates.

Foteeva, Y. V. (1993). The Commonwealth of Independent States. In M. Cochran (Ed.), *International handbook of child care policies and programs* (pp. 125–142). Westport, CT: Greenwood Press.

Fox, N. A., Sutton, D. B., & Newcombe, N. S. (1993). *Small samples and large conclusions: A reply to Belsky and Braungart.* Unpublished manuscript, Institute for Child Study, University of Maryland.

Friedman, S. L. (1993). *The NICHD Study of Early Child Care: A comprehensive longitudinal study of young children's lives.* (ERIC Clearinghouse on Elementary and Early Child Education, ED 353 087)

Fuerst, J. S., & Fuerst, D. (1993). Chicago experience with an early education program: The special care of the Child-Parent Center program. *Urban Education, 28,* 69–96.

Galambos, N. L., & Garbarino, J. (1983, July/August). Identifying the missing links in the study of latchkey children. *Children Today,* (2/4), 40–41.

Galambos, N. L., & Maggs, J. L. (1991). Out-of-school care of young adolescents and self-reported behavior. *Developmental Psychology, 27,* 644–655.

Galinsky, E. (1992). The impact of child care on parents. In A. Booth (Ed.), *Child care in the 1990s: Trends and consequences* (pp. 159–172). Hillsdale, NJ: Erlbaum.

Galinsky, E., Howes, C., & Kontos, S. (1995a). *The family child care training study.* New York: Families and Work Institute.

Galinsky, E., Howes, C., & Kontos, S. (1995b). *The family child care training study: Highlights of findings.* New York: Families and Work Institute.

Galinsky, E., Howes, C., Kontos, S., & Shinn, M. (1994). *The study of children in family child care and relative care.* New York: Families and Work Institute.

Galluzzo, D. C., Matheson, C. C., Moore, J. A., & Howes, C. (1988). Social orientation to adults and peers in infant child care. *Early Childhood Research Quarterly, 3,* 417–426.

Gamble, T., & Zigler, E. F. (1989). The Head Start Synthesis Project: A critique. *Journal of Applied Developmental Psychology, 10,* 267–274.

Genser, A., & Baden, C. (Eds.). (1980). *School-aged child care: Programs and issues.* Urbana: University of Illinois. (ERIC Clearinghouse)

Getis, V. L., & Vinovskis, M. A. (1992). History of child care in the United States before 1950. In M. E. Lamb, K. J. Sternberg, C. P. Hwang, & A. G. Broberg (Eds.), *Child care in context: Cross-cultural perspectives* (pp. 185–206). Hillsdale, NJ: Erlbaum.

Ghazvini, A. S., & Readdick, C. A. (1994). Parent-caregiver communication and quality of care in diverse child care settings. *Early Childhood Research Quarterly, 9,* 207–222.

Goelman, H. (1988). A study of the relationship between structure and process variables in home and day care settings on children's language development. In A. R. Pence (Ed.), *Ecological research with children and families: From concepts to methodology* (pp. 16–34). New York: Teachers College Press.

Goelman, H. (1992). Day care in Canada. In M. E. Lamb, K. J. Sternberg, C.-P. Hwang, & A. G. Broberg (Eds.), *Child care in context: Cross-cultural perspectives* (pp. 223–263). Hillsdale, NJ: Erlbaum.

Goelman, H., & Pence, A. R. (1987a). Effects of child care, family, and individual characteristics on children's language development: The Victorian Day Care Research Project. In D. A. Phillips (Ed.), *Quality in child care: What does research tell us?* (pp. 89–104). Washington, DC: National Association for the Education of Young Children.

Goelman, H., & Pence, A. R. (1987b). The relationships between family structure and child development in three types of day care. In S. Kontos & D. L. Peters (Eds.), *Advances in applied developmental psychology* (Vol. 2, pp. 129–146). Norwood, NJ: ABLEX.

Golden, M., Rosenbluth, L., Grossi, M., Policare, H., Freeman, H., & Brownlee, E. (1978). *The New York City Infant Day Care Study.* New York: Medical and Health Resource Association of New York City.

Goldsmith, H. H., & Alansky, J. A. (1987). Infant and maternal predictors of attachment: A meta analytic review. *Journal of Consulting and Clinical Psychology, 55,* 805–816.

Goossens, F. A. (1987). Maternal employment and day care: Effects on attachment. In L. W. G. Tavecchio & M. H. van IJzendoorn (Eds.), *Attachment in social networks* (pp. 135–183). New York: Elsevier.

Goossens, F. A., & van IJzendoorn, M. H. (1990). Quality of infants' attachments to professional caregivers: Relation to infant-parent attachment and day-care characteristics. *Child Development, 61,* 832–837.

Gray, S. W., & Klaus, R. A. (1965). An experimental preschool program for culturally deprived children. *Child Development, 36,* 889–898.

Griffiths, R. (1954). *The abilities of babies.* London: University of London Press.

Griffiths, R. (1970). *The abilities of young children.* London: University of London Press.

Griswold, R. (1993). *Fatherhood in America: A history.* New York: Basic Books.

Gunnarsson, L. (1993). Sweden. In M. Cochran (Ed.), *International handbook of child care policies and programs* (pp. 491–514). Westport, CT: Greenwood Press.

Haas, L. (1992). *Equal parenthood and social policy: A study of parental leave in Sweden.* Albany, NY: SUNY Press.

Häggström, S., & Lundberg, I. (1990). *Prov i svenska för den nationella utvärderingen av kunskaper och fördighetor i den svenska skolan* [Tests in Swedish for the national evaluation of knowledge and skills in Swedish schools]. Umeå: Psykologiska Intitutionem, Umeå Universitet.

Hale, B. A., Seitz, V., & Zigler, E. F. (1990). Health services and Head Start: A forgotten formula. *Journal of Applied Developmental Psychology, 11,* 447–458.

Harms, T., & Clifford, R. M. (1980). *The early childhood environment rating scale.* New York: Teachers College Press.

Harms, T., & Clifford, R. M. (1989). *The family day care rating scale.* New York: Teachers College Press.

Harms, T., Cryer, D., & Clifford, R. M. (1986). *Infant/toddler environment rating scale.* Chapel Hill: University of North Carolina.

Harms, T., Cryer, D., & Clifford, R. M. (1990). *Infant/toddler environment rating scale.* New York: Teachers College Press.

Harper, L. B., & Huie, K. S. (1985). The effects of prior group experience, age, and familiarity on the quality and organization of preschoolers' social relationships. *Child Development, 56,* 704–717.

Hartmann, E. (1991). Effects of day care and maternal teaching on child educability. *Scandinavian Journal of Psychology, 32,* 325–335.

Hartmann, E. (1995). *Long-term effects of day care and maternal teaching on educational competence, independence and autonomy in young adulthood.* Unpublished manuscript, University of Oslo, Oslo, Norway.

Haskins, R. (1985). Public school aggression among children with varying day-care experience. *Child Development, 56,* 689–703.

Haskins, R. (1989). Beyond metaphor: The efficacy of early childhood education. *American Psychologist, 44,* 274–282.

Haskins, R. (1992). Is anything more important than day-care quality? In A. Booth (Ed.), *Child care in the 1990s: Trends and consequences* (pp. 101–116). Hillsdale, NJ: Erlbaum.

Hebbeler, K. (1985). An old and a new question on the effects of early education for children from low income families. *Educational Evaluation and Policy Analysis, 7,* 207–216.

Hegland, S. M., & Rix, M. K. (1990). Aggression and assertiveness in kindergarten children differing in day care experiences. *Early Childhood Research Quarterly, 5,* 105–116.

Hess, R. D. (1970). Social class and ethnic influences upon socialization. In P. H. Mussen (Ed.), *Carmichael's manual of child psychology* (3rd ed.) (Vol. 2, pp. 457–557). New York: Wiley.

Hestenes, L. L., Kontos, S., & Bryan, Y. (1993). Children's emotional expression in child care centers varying in quality. *Early Childhood Research Quarterly, 8,* 295–307.

Hock, E. (1980). Working and nonworking mothers and their infants: A comparative study of maternal caregiving characteristics and infants' social behavior. *Merrill-Palmer Quarterly, 46,* 79–101.

Hock, E., & DeMeis, D. K. (1990). Depression in mothers of infants: The role of maternal employment. *Developmental Psychology, 26,* 285–296.

Hock, E., DeMeis, D. K., & McBride, S. (1988). Maternal separation anxiety: Its role in the balance of employment and motherhood in mothers of infants. In A. E. Gottfried & A. W. Gottfried (Eds.), *Maternal employment and children's development: Longitudinal research* (pp. 191–229). New York: Plenum Press.

Hock, E., McBride, S., & Gnezda, T. (1989). Maternal separation anxiety: Mother-infant separation from the maternal perspective. *Child Development, 60,* 793–802.

Hock, E., & Schirtzinger, M. B. (1992). Maternal separation anxiety: Its developmental course and relation to maternal mental health. *Child Development, 63,* 93–102.

Hofferth, S. L. (1992a). Are parents better off than they were a decade ago? A response to Prosser and McGroder. In A. Booth (Ed.), *Child care in the 1990s: Trends and consequences* (pp. 56–63). Hillsdale, NJ: Erlbaum.

Hofferth, S. L. (1992b). The demand for and supply of child care in the 1990s. In A. Booth (Ed.), *Child care in the 1990s: Trends and consequences* (pp. 3–26). Hillsdale, NJ: Erlbaum.

Hofferth, S. L. (1994). Who enrolls in Head Start? A demographic analysis of Head Start–eligible children. *Early Childhood Research Quarterly, 9,* 243–268.

Hofferth, S. L., Brayfield, A., Deich, S., & Holcomb, P. (1991). *National Child Care Survey, 1990.* Washington, DC: Urban Institute.

Hofferth, S. L., & Phillips, D. A. (1987). Child care in the United States, 1970 to 1995. *Journal of Marriage and the Family, 49,* 559–571.

Holloway, S. D., & Reichhart-Erickson, M. (1988). The relationship of day care quality to children's free-play behavior and social problem-solving skills. *Early Childhood Research Quarterly, 3,* 39–54.

Holloway, S. D., & Reichhart-Erickson, M. (1989). Child care quality, family structure, and maternal expectation: Relationship to preschool children's peer relations. *Journal of Applied Developmental Psychology, 10,* 281–298.

Hovacek, H. J., Ramey, C. T., Campbell, F. A., Hoffman, K. P., & Fletcher, R. H. (1987). Predicting school failure and assessing early intervention with high risk children. *Journal of the American Academy of Child and Adolescent Psychiatry, 26,* 758–763.

Howes, C. (1983). Caregiver's behavior in center and family day care. *Journal of Applied Developmental Psychology, 4,* 99–107.

Howes, C. (1987, December). *Child care for infants and toddlers: Research issues and agenda.* Paper presented at the meeting of the National Center for Clinical Infant Programs, Washington, DC.

Howes, C. (1988). The peer interactions of young children. *Monographs of the Society for Research in Child Development, 53*(1), (Serial no. 217).

Howes, C. (1990). Can the age of entry into child care and the quality of child care predict adjustment in kindergarten? *Developmental Psychology, 26,* 292–303.

Howes, C., & Hamilton, C. E. (1992a). Children's relationships with caregivers: Mothers and child care teachers. *Child Development, 63,* 859–866.

Howes, C., & Hamilton, C. E. (1992b). Children's relationships with child care teachers: Stability and concordance with parental attachments. *Child Development, 63,* 867–878.

Howes, C., & Hamilton, C. E. (1993). The changing experience of child care: Changes in teachers and in teacher-child relationships and children's social competence with peers. *Early Childhood Research Quarterly, 8,* 15–32.

Howes, C., Hamilton, C. E., & Matheson, C. C. (1994). Children's relationships with peers: Differential associations with aspects of the teacher-child relationship. *Child Development, 65,* 253–263.

Howes, C., Matheson, C. C., & Hamilton, C. E. (1994). Maternal, teacher, and child care history correlates of children's relationships with peers. *Child Development, 65,* 264–273.

Howes, C., & Olenick, M. (1986). Family and child care influences on toddler compliance. *Child Development, 57,* 202–216.

Howes, C., Phillips, D. A., & Whitebook, M. (1992). Thresholds of quality: Implications for the social development of children in center-based child care. *Child Development, 63,* 447–460.

Howes, C., Rodning, C., Galluzzo, D. C., & Myers, L. (1987). *Attachment and childcare: Relationships with mother and caregiver.* Unpublished manuscript, University of California, Los Angeles.

Howes, C., Rodning, C., Galluzzo, D. C., & Myers, L. (1988). Attachment and childcare: Relationships with mother and caregiver. *Early Childhood Research Quarterly, 3,* 403–416.

Howes, C., & Rubenstein, J. L. (1985). Determinants of toddler's experience in day care: Age of entry at quality of setting. *Child Care Quarterly, 14,* 140–151.

Howes, C., & Smith, E. W. (1995). Children and their child care caregivers: Profiles of relationships. *Social Development, 4,* 44–61.

Howes, C., Smith, E., & Galinsky, E. (1995). *The Florida Child Care Quality Improvement Study.* New York: Families and Work Institute.

Howes, C., & Stewart, P. (1987). Child's play with adults, toys, and peers: An examination of family and child care influences. *Developmental Psychology, 23,* 423–430.

Hunt, J., McV. (1961). *Intelligence and experience.* New York: Ronald Press.

Hwang, C. P., & Broberg, A. G. (1992). The historical and social context of child care in Sweden. In M. E. Lamb, K. J. Sternberg, C. P. Hwang, & A. G. Broberg (Eds.), *Child care in context: Cross-cultural perspectives* (pp. 27–54). Hillsdale, NJ: Erlbaum.

Hwang, C. P., Broberg, A., & Lamb, M. E. (1991). Swedish childcare research. In E. C. Melhuish & P. Moss (Eds.), *Day care for young children* (pp. 75–101). London: Routledge & Kegan Paul.

Hyson, M. C., Hirsh-Pasek, K., & Rescorla, L. (1990). The Classroom Practices Inventory: An observation instrument based on NAEYC's Guidelines for Developmentally Appropriate Practices for 4- and 5-year-old children. *Early Childhood Research Quarterly, 5,* 475–494.

Infant Health and Development Program. (1990). Enhancing the outcomes of low-birth-weight, premature infants: A multisite, randomized trial. *Journal of the American Medical Association, 263,* 3035–3042.

Infield, H. F. (1944). *Cooperative living in Palestine.* New York: Dryden Press.

Jacobson, J. L., & Wille, D. E. (1984). Influence of attachment and separation experience on separation distress at 18 months. *Developmental Psychology, 20,* 477–484.

Jensen, A. R. (1969). How much can we boost IQ and scholastic achievement? *Harvard Educational Review, 39,* 1–123.

Jensen, A. R. (1973). *Educability and group differences.* New York: Harper & Row.

Jewsuwan, R., Luster, T., & Kostelnik, M. (1993). The relation between parents' perceptions of temperament and children's adjustment to preschool. *Early Childhood Research Quarterly, 8,* 33–51.

Kagan, J. S., Hunt, J. M., Crow, J. F., Bereiter, G., Elkand, D., Cronbach, L. J., & Brazziel, W. F. (1969). "How much can we boost IQ and scholastic achievement?": A discussion. *Harvard Educational Review, 39,* 273–356.

Kagan, J. S., Kearsley, R., & Zelazo, P. (1978). *Infancy: Its place in human development.* Cambridge, MA: Harvard University Press.

Kagan, S. L. (1991). Examining profit and non-profit child care in an odyssey of quality and auspices. *Journal of Social Issues, 47,* 87–104.

Kamerman, S. B., & Kahn, A. J. (Eds.). (1978). *Family policy: Government and families in fourteen countries.* New York: Columbia University Press.

Kamerman, S. B., & Kahn, A. J. (1981). *Child care, family benefits, and working parents.* New York: Columbia University Press.

Kennedy, E. M. (1993). The Head Start Transition Project: Head Start goes to elementary school. In E. F. Zigler & S. J. Styfco (Eds.), *Head Start and beyond: A national plan for extended childhood intervention* (pp. 97–109). New Haven, CT: Yale University Press.

Ketterlinus, R. D., Bookstein, F. L., Sampson, P. D., & Lamb, M. E. (1989). Partial least squares analysis in developmental psychopathology. *Development and Psychopathology, 2,* 351–371.

Ketterlinus, R. D., Henderson, S. H., & Lamb, M. E. (1992). Les effets du type de garde de l'emploi maternel et de l'estime de soi sur le comportement des enfants [The effect of type of child care and maternal employment on children's behavioral adjustment and self-esteem]. In B. Pierrehumbert (Ed.), *L'accueil du jeune enfant: Politiques et recherches dans les différents pays* [Child care in infancy: Policy and research issues in different countries] (pp. 150–163). Paris: Les Editions Sociales.

Kisker, E., Hofferth, S., Phillips, D., & Farguhar, E. (1991). *A profile of child care settings: Early education and care in 1990.* Princeton, NJ: Mathematica Policy Research.

Klein, R. (1985). Caregiving arrangements by employed women with children under one year of age. *Developmental Psychology, 21,* 403–406.

Kontos, S. (1991). Child care quality, family background, and children's development. *Early Childhood Research Quarterly, 6,* 249–262.

Kontos, S. (1994). The ecology of family day care. *Early Childhood Research Quarterly, 9,* 87–110.

Kontos, S. (Ed.). (1994). *Annual advances in applied developmental psychology: Continuity and discontinuity of experience in child care* (Vol. 2, pp. 129–146). Norwood, NJ: ABLEX.

Kontos, S., & Fiene, R. (1987). Child care quality, compliance with regulations, and children's development: The Pennsylvania study. In D. A. Phillips (Eds.), *Quality in child care: What does research tell us?* (pp. 57–80). Washington, DC: National Association for the Education of Young Children.

Kontos, S., Howes, C., Shinn, M., & Galinsky, E. (1994). *Quality in family child care and relative care.* New York: Teachers College Press.

Kontos, S., & Stremmel, A. J. (1988). Caregivers' perceptions of working conditions in a child care environment. *Early Childhood Research Quarterly, 3,* 77–90.

Korczak, E. (1993). Poland. In M. Cochran (Ed.), *International handbook of child care policies and programs* (pp. 453–467). Westport, CT: Greenwood Press.

Krentz, M. (1983, April). *Qualitative differences between mother-child and caregiver-child attachments of infants in family day care.* Paper presented at the meeting of the Society for Research in Child Development, Detroit, MI.

Lamb, M. E. (1986). The changing roles of fathers. In M. E. Lamb (Ed.), *The father's role: Applied perspectives* (pp. 3–27). New York: Wiley.

Lamb, M. E., Hwang, C. P., Bookstein, F. L., Broberg, A., Hult, G., & Frodi, M. (1988). Determinants of social competence in Swedish preschoolers. *Developmental Psychology, 24,* 58–70.

Lamb, M. E., Hwang, C. P., Broberg, A., & Bookstein, F. L. (1988). The effects of out-of-home care on the development of social competence in Sweden: A longitudinal study. *Early Childhood Research Quarterly, 3,* 379–402.

Lamb, M. E., Ketterlinus, R. D., & Fracasso, M. P. (1992). Parent-child relationships. In M. H. Bornstein & M. E. Lamb (Eds.), *Developmental psychology: An advanced textbook* (3rd ed., pp. 465–518). Hillsdale, NJ: Erlbaum.

Lamb, M. E., & Levine, J. A. (1983). The Swedish parental insurance policy: An experiment in social engineering. In M. E. Lamb (Ed.), *Fatherhood and family policy* (pp. 39–51). Hillsdale, NJ: Erlbaum.

Lamb, M. E., & Sternberg, K. J. (1990). Do we really know how day care affects children? *Journal of Applied Developmental Psychology, 11,* 351–379.

Lamb, M. E., Sternberg, K. J., Hwang, C. P., & Broberg, A. (Eds.). (1992). *Child care in context: Cross-cultural perspectives.* Hillsdale, NJ: Erlbaum.

Lamb, M. E., Sternberg, K. J., & Ketterlinus, R. D. (1992). Child care in the United States: The modern era. In M. E. Lamb, K. J. Sternberg, C. P. Hwang, & A. G. Broberg (Eds.), *Child care in context: Cross-cultural perspectives* (pp. 207–222). Hillsdale, NJ: Erlbaum.

Lamb, M. E., Sternberg, K. J., Knuth, N., Hwang, C.-P., & Broberg, A. G. (1994). Peer play and nonparental care experiences. In H. Goelman & E. V. Jacobs (Eds.), *Children's play in childcare settings* (pp. 37–52). Albany: State University of New York Press.

Lamb, M. E., Sternberg, K. J., & Prodromidis, M. (1992). Nonmaternal care and the security of infant-mother attachment: A reanalysis of the data. *Infant Behavior and Development, 15,* 71–83.

Lamb, M. E., Thompson, R. A., Gardner, W., & Charnov, E. L. (1985). *Infant-mother attachment.* Hillsdale, NJ: Erlbaum.

Lamb, M. E., Thompson, R. A., Gardner, W., Charnov, E. L., & Estes, D. (1984). Security of infantile attachment as assessed in the "Strange Situation": Its study and biological interpretation. *Behavioral and Brain Sciences, 7,* 127–147.

Lancaster, J. B., & Lancaster, C. S. (1987). The watershed: Change in parental investment and family formation strategies in the course of human evolution. In J. S. Lancaster, J. Altmann, A. Rossi, & L. R. Sherrod (Eds.), *Parenting across the life span: Biosocial perspectives* (pp. 187–205). Hawthorne, NY: Aldine de Gruyter.

Lancaster, J. B., Rossi, A., Altmann, J., & Sherrod, L. R. (Eds.). (1987). *Parenting across the life span: Biosocial perspectives.* Hawthorne, NY: Aldine de Gruyter.

Larsen, J. M., & Robinson, C. C. (1989). Later effects of preschool on low-risk children. *Early Childhood Research Quarterly, 4,* 133–144.

Lazar, I. (1981). Early intervention is effective. *Educational Leadership, 38,* 303–305.

Lazar, I., Darlington, R., Murray, H., Royce, J., & Snipper, A. (1982). Lasting effects of early education: A report from the Consortium for Longitudinal Studies. *Monographs of the Society for Research in Child Development, 47*(Serial no. 195).

Lee, L. C. (1992). Day care in the People's Republic of China. In M. E. Lamb, K. J. Sternberg, C. P. Hwang, & A. G. Broberg (Eds.), *Child care in context: Cross-cultural perspectives* (pp. 355–392). Hillsdale, NJ: Erlbaum.

Leiderman, P. H., & Leiderman, G. F. (1974). Affective and cognitive consequences of polymatric infant care in the East African highlands. In *Minnesota Symposium on Child Psychology* (Vol. 8, pp. 81–110). Minneapolis: University of Minnesota Press.

Lerner, R. M. (1984). *On the nature of human plasticity.* New York: Cambridge University Press.

Lipsitt, L. A., & LaGasse, L. (1987). [Longitudinal study of normal full-term infants]. Unpublished raw data.

Ljung, B.-O., & Pettersson, A. (1990). *Matematiken i nationell utvärdering. Kunskaper och färdigheter i årskurserna 2 och 5. Rapport no. 5, PRIM-gruppen* [National evaluation of mathematics. Knowledge and skills in grades 2 and 5]. Stockholm, Sweden: Högskolan för Lårarutbildning, Stockholms Universitet.

Ljungblad, T. (1989). *Höstproven* [Fall tests of school readiness]. Stockholm: Psykologiforlaget. (Original work published 1967)

Londerville, S., & Main, M. (1981). Security of attachment, compliance, and maternal training methods in the second year. *Developmental Psychology, 17,* 281–299.

Long, T. J., & Long, L. (1983). *The handbook of latchkey children and their parents.* New York: Arbor House.

Long, T. J., & Long, L. (1984). Latchkey children. In L. Katz (Ed.), *Current topics in early childhood education* (Vol. 5, pp. 141–164). Norwood, NJ: ABLEX.

Martin, S. L., Ramey, C. T., & Ramey, S. (1990). The prevention of intellectual impairment in children of impoverished families: Findings of a randomized trial of educational day care. *American Journal of Public Health, 80,* 844–847.

Mason, K. O., & Duberstein, L. (1992). Consequences of child care for parents' well-being. In A. Booth (Ed.), *Child care in the 1990s: Trends and consequences* (pp. 127–159). Hillsdale, NJ: Erlbaum.

Maynard, R., & McGinnis, E. (1992). Policies to enhance access to high-quality child care. In A. Booth (Ed.), *Child care in the 1990s: Trends and consequences* (pp. 189–209). Hillsdale, NJ: Erlbaum.

McBride, S., & Belsky, J. (1988). Characteristics, determinants, and consequences of maternal separation anxiety. *Developmental Psychology, 24,* 407–414.

McCartney, K. (1984). The effect of quality of day care environment upon children's language development. *Developmental Psychology, 20,* 244–260.

McCartney, K., & Rosenthal, S. (1991). Maternal employment should be studied within social ecologies. *Journal of Marriage and the Family, 53,* 1103–1107.

McCartney, K., Scarr, S., Phillips, D., & Grajek, S. (1985). Day care as intervention: Comparisons of varying quality programs. *Journal of Applied Developmental Psychology, 6,* 247–260.

McCartney, K., Scarr, S., Phillips, D., Grajek, S., & Schwarz, J. C. (1982). Environmental differences among day care centers and their effects on children's development. In E. F. Zigler & E. W. Gordon (Eds.), *Day care: Scientific and social policy issues* (pp. 135–156). Boston: Auburn House.

McCartney, K., Scarr, S., Rocheleau, A., Phillips, D., Eisenberg, M., Keefa, N., Rosenthal, S., & Abbott-Shim, M. (in press). Social development in the context of typical center-based child care. *Merrill-Palmer Quarterly.*

McCarton, C. M., Brooks-Gunn, J., Wallace, I. F., Bauer, C. R., Bennett, F. C., Bernbaum, J. L., Broyles, R. S., Casey, P. H., McCormick, M. C., Scott, D. T., Tyson, J., Tonascia, J., & Meinert, C. L. (1997). Results at age 8 years of early intervention for low-birth-weight premature infants. *Journal of the American Medical Association, 277,* 126–132.

McGurk, A., Caplan, M., Hennessy, E., & Moss, P. (1993). Controversy, theory, and social context in contemporary day care research. *Journal of Child Psychology and Psychiatry, 34,* 3–23.

McKey, R. H., Condelli, L., Granson, H., Barrett, B., McConhey, C., & Plantz, M. (1985). *The impact of Head Start on children, family, and communities: Final report of the Head Start Evaluation, Synthesis, and Utilization Project.* Washington, DC: U.S. Government Printing Office.

Melhuish, E. C. (1987). Socio-emotional behaviour at 18 months as a function of daycare experience, gender and temperament. *Infant Mental Health Journal, 8,* 364–373.

Melhuish, E. C., Hennessy, E., Martin, S., & Moss, P. (1990, September). *Social development at six years as a function of type and amount of early child care.* Paper presented to the International Symposium on Child Care in the Early Years, Lausanne, Switzerland.

Melhuish, E. C., & Moss, P. (Eds.). (1991a). *Day care for young children: International perspectives.* London: Routledge & Kegan Paul.

Melhuish, E. C., & Moss, P. (1991b). Introduction. In E. C. Melhuish & P. Moss (Eds.), *Day care for young children: International perspectives* (pp. 1–9). London: Routledge & Kegan Paul.

Melhuish, E. C., & Moss, P. (1992). Day care in the United Kingdom in historical perspective. In M. E. Lamb, K. J. Sternberg, C. P. Hwang, & A. G. Broberg (Eds.), *Child care in context: Cross-cultural perspectives* (pp. 157–183). Hillsdale, NJ: Erlbaum.

Meudec, M., & Balleyguier-Boulanger, G. (1991, August). *Relationship between day care organizations and infant's behavior at home.* Paper presented to the Prague International Conference on Psychological Development and Personality Formative Processes, Prague, Czechoslovakia.

Moore, M. S., Snow, C. W., & Poteat, M. (1988). Effects of variant types of child care experience on the adaptive behavior of kindergarten children. *American Journal of Orthopsychiatry, 58,* 297–303.

Morgan, G., Azer, S. L., Costley, J. B., Genser, A., Goodman, I. F., Lombardi, J., & McGimsey, B. (1993). *Making a career of it: The state of the states report on career development in early care and education.* Boston: Wheelock College Press.

Moskowitz, D. S., Schwarz, J. C., & Corsini, D. A. (1977). Initiating day care at three years of age: Effects on attachment. *Child Development, 48,* 1271–1276.

Musatti, T., & Mantovani, S. (1990, September). *Child care in Italy: Its effects on children's daily life.* Paper presented to the International Symposium on Childcare in the Early Years, Lausanne, Switzerland.

National Academy of Science. (1990). *Who cares for America's children?* Washington, DC: National Academy Press.

National Head Start Association. (1990). *Head Start: The nation's pride, a nation's challenge. Report of the Silver Ribbon Panel.* Alexandria, VA: Author.

National Institute of Child Health and Human Development Early Child Care Research Network. (1994). Child care and child development: The NICHD study of early child care. In S. L. Friedman & H. C. Haywood (Eds.), *Developmental follow-up: Concepts, domains and methods* (pp. 377–396). New York: Academic Press.

National Institute of Child Health and Human Development Early Child Care Research Network. (1995a, April). *The dynamics of child care experiences during the first year of life.* Poster presented to a meeting of the Society for Research in Child Development, Indianapolis.

National Institute of Child Health and Human Development Early Child Care Research Network. (1995b, April). *Family economic status, structure, and maternal employment as predictors of child care quantity and quality.* Poster presented to a meeting of the Society for Research in Child Development, Indianapolis.

National Institute of Child Health and Human Development Early Child Care Research Network. (1995c, April). *Future directions: Testing models of developmental outcome.* Poster presented to a meeting of the Society for Research in Child Development, Indianapolis.

National Institute of Child Health and Human Development Early Child Care Research Network. (1995d, April). *Measuring child care quality in the first year.* Poster presented to a meeting of the Society for Research in Child Development, Indianapolis.

National Institute of Child Health and Human Development Early Child Care Research Network. (1995e, April). *More than economics? Maternal and child prediction of child care choices.* Poster presented to a meeting of the Society for Research in Child Development, Indianapolis.

National Institute of Child Health and Human Development Early Child Care Research Network. (1995f, April). *NICHD Study of Early child care sampling plan and subject recruitment.* Poster presented to a meeting of the Society for Research in Child Development, Indianapolis.

National Institute of Child Health and Human Development Early Child Care Research Network. (1995g, April). *Overview and conceptual model: NICHD study of early child care.* Poster presented to a meeting of the Society for Research in Child Development, Indianapolis.

National Institute of Child Health and Human Development Early Child Care Research Network. (1996a). Characteristics of infant child care: Factors contributing to positive caregiving. *Early Childhood Research Quarterly, 11,* 269–306.

National Institute of Child Health and Human Development Early Child Care Research Network. (1996b). *Infant child care and attachment security: Results of the NICHD study of early child care.* Paper presented to the International Conference on Infant Studies, Providence, RI.

National Institute of Child Health and Human Development Early Child Care Research Network. (1997a). Familial factors associated with the characteristics of nonmaternal care of infants. *Journal of Marriage and the Family, 59,* 389–408.

National Institute of Child Health and Human Development Early Child Care Research Network. (1997b, April). *Mother-child interaction and cognitive outcomes associated with early child care: Results of the NICHD study.* Paper presented to the Society for Research in Child Development, Washington, D.C.

National Institute of Child Health and Human Development Early Child Care Research Network. (in press). Child care in the first year of life. *Merrill-Palmer Quarterly.*

National Research Council. (1991). *Caring for America's children.* Washington, DC: National Academy Press.

Nemenyi, M. (1993). Hungary. In M. Cochran (Ed.), *International handbook of child care policies and programs* (pp. 231–245). Westport, CT: Greenwood Press.

Nerlove, S. B. (1974). Women's workload and infant feeding practices: A relationship with demographic implications. *Ethnology, 13,* 207–214.

Neubauer, P. B. (Ed.). (1965). *Children in collectives: Child-rearing aims and practices in the kibbutz.* Springfield, IL: Thomas.

New, R. (1993). Italy. In M. Cochran (Ed.), *International handbook of child care policies and programs* (pp. 291–311). Westport, CT: Greenwood Press.

North, A. F., Jr. (1979). Health services in Head Start. In E. Zigler & J. Valentine (Eds.), *Project Head Start* (pp. 231–258). New York: Free Press.

O'Connor, S. M. (1995). Mothering in public: The division of organized child care in the kindergarten and day nursery, St. Louis, 1886–1920. *Early Childhood Research Quarterly, 10,* 63–80.

Olmsted, P. P. (1992). A cross-national perspective on the demand for and supply of early childhood services. In A. Booth (Ed.), *Child care in the 1990s: Trends and consequences* (pp. 26–33). Hillsdale, NJ: Erlbaum.

Oppenheim, D., Sagi, A., & Lamb, M. E. (1988). Infant-adult attachments on the kibbutz and their relation to socioemotional development four years later. *Developmental Psychology, 24,* 427–433.

Owen, M. T., & Cox, M. (1988). Maternal employment and the transition to parenthood. In A. E. Gottfried & A. W. Gottfried (Eds.), *Maternal employment and children's development: Longitudinal research* (pp. 85–119). New York: Plenum Press.

Owen, M. T., Easterbrooks, M. A., Chase-Lansdale, P. L., & Goldberg, W. A. (1984). The relation between maternal employment status and the stability of attachments to mother and to father. *Child Development, 55,* 1894–1901.

Pence, A. R. (1993). Canada. In M. Cochran (Ed.), *International handbook of child care policies and programs* (pp. 57–81). Westport, CT: Greenwood Press.

Petrogiannis, K. G. (1995). *Psychological development at 18 months of age as a function of child care experience in Greece.* Unpublished doctoral dissertation, University of Wales, Cardiff.

Phillips, D. A. (1989). Future directions and need for child care in the United States. In J. S. Lande, S. Scarr, & N. Gunzenhauser (Eds.), *Caring for children: Challenge to America* (pp. 257–274). Hillsdale, NJ: Erlbaum.

Phillips, D. A. (1992). Child care and parental well-being: Bringing quality of care into the picture. In A. Booth (Ed.), *Child care in the 1990s: Trends and consequences* (pp. 172–180). Hillsdale, NJ: Erlbaum.

Phillips, D. A., Howes, C., & Whitebook, M. (1991). Child care as an adult work environment. *Journal of Social Issues, 47,* 49–70.

Phillips, D. A., Howes, C., & Whitebook, M. (1992). The social policy context of child care: Effects on quality. *American Journal of Community Psychology, 20,* 25–51.

Phillips, D. A., Lande, J., & Goldberg, M. (1990). The state of child care regulations: A comparative analysis. *Early Childhood Research Quarterly, 5,* 151–179.

Phillips, D. A., McCartney, K., & Scarr, S. (1987). Child-care quality and children's social development. *Developmental Psychology, 23,* 537–543.

Phillips, D. A., McCartney, K., Scarr, S., & Howes, C. (1987). Selective review of infant day care research: A cause for concern? *Zero to Three, 7*(3), 18–21.

Phillips, D. A., Mekos, D., Scarr, S., McCartney, K., & Abbott-Shim, M. (1995). *Paths to quality in child care: Structural and contextual influences on classroom environments.* Unpublished manuscript, Department of Psychology, University of Virginia, Charlottesville.

Phillips, D. A., Voran, M., Kisker, E., Howes, C., & Whitebook, M. (1994). Child care for children in poverty: Opportunity or inequity? *Child Development, 65,* 472–492.

Phillips, D. A., & Zigler, E. F. (1987). The checkered history of federal child care regulation. In E. Z. Rothkopf (Ed.), *Review of research in education* (Vol. 14, pp. 3–41). Washington, DC: America Educational Research Association.

Pianta, P. C., & Nimetz, S. L. (1991). Relationship between children and teachers: Associations with classroom and home behavior. *Journal of Applied Developmental Psychology, 12,* 379–393.

Pierrehumbert, B. (1990, June). *Attachment et séparation dans le jeune age.* Paper presented to a conference on education familiale, image de soi et reconnaissance, University of Toulouse Le Mirail, Toulouse, France.

Pierrehumbert, B. (1994, September). *Socio-emotional continuity through the preschool years and child care experience.* Paper presented to the British Psychological Society, Developmental Section Conference, Portsmouth, England.

Pierrehumbert, B., & Milhaud, K. (1994, June). *Socio-emotional continuity through the preschool years and child care experience.* Paper presented to the International Conference on Infant Studies, Paris.

Pierrehumbert, B., Ramstein, T., & Karmaniola, A. (1995). Bébés à partager [Babies to share]. In M. Robin, I. Casati, & D. Candilis-Huisman (Eds.), *La construction des liens familiaux pendant la première enfance* [The construction of family ties in infancy] (pp. 107–128). Paris: Presses Universitaires de France.

Pierrehumbert, B., Ramstein, T., Karmaniola, A., & Halfon, O. (1996). Child care in the preschool years, behavior problems, and cognitive development. *European Journal of Educational Psychology, 11,* 201–214.

Pierrehumbert, B., Ramstein, T., Krucher, R., El-Najjar, S., Lamb, M. E., & Halfon, O. (1996). L'évaluation du lieu du jeune enfant [Evaluating the life experiences of young children]. *Bulletin of Psychologie, 49,* 565–584.

Portnoy, F. C., & Simmons, C. (1978). Day care and attachment. *Child Development, 49,* 239–242.

Posner, J. K., & Vandell, D. L. (1994). Low-income children's afterschool care: Are there beneficial effects of after-school programs? *Child Development, 63,* 440–456.

Powell, C., & Grantham-McGregor, S. (1989). Home visiting of varying frequency and child development. *Pediatrics, 84,* 157–164.

Powell, D. R. (1982). From child to parent: Changing conceptions of early childhood intervention. *Annals of the American Academy of Political and Social Science, 481,* 135–144.

Presser, H. B. (1986). Shift work among American women and child care. *Journal of Marriage and the Family, 48,* 551–563.

Presser, H. B. (1988). Shift work and child care among young dual-earner American parents. *Journal of Marriage and the Family, 50,* 133–148.

Presser, H. B. (1992a). Child care and parental well-being: A needed focus on gender and trade-offs. In A. Booth (Ed.), *Child care in the 1990s: Trends and consequences* (pp. 180–189). Hillsdale, NJ: Erlbaum.

Presser, H. B. (1992b). Child-care supply and demand: What do we really know? In A. Booth (Ed.), *Child care in the 1990s: Trends and consequences* (pp. 26–32). Hillsdale, NJ: Erlbaum.

Presser, H. B., & Cain, V. (1983). Shift work among dual earner couples with children. *Science, 219,* 876–879.

Prodromidis, M., Lamb, M. E., Sternberg, K. J., Hwang, C. P., & Broberg, A. G. (1995). Aggression and noncompliance among Swedish children in center-based care, family day care, and home care. *International Journal of Behavioral Development, 18,* 43–62.

Prosser, W. R., & McGroder, S. M. (1992). The supply of and demand for childcare: Measurement and analytic issues. In A. Booth (Ed.), *Child care in the 1990s: Trends and consequences* (pp. 42–56). Hillsdale, NJ: Erlbaum.

Ragozin, A. S. (1977, March). *Attachment behavior of day care and home-reared children in a laboratory setting.* Paper presented to a meeting of the Society for Research in Child Development, New Orleans, LA.

Ragozin, A. S. (1980). Attachment behavior of day care children: Naturalistic and laboratory observations. *Child Development, 51,* 409–415.

Raikes, H. (1993). Relationship duration in infant care: Time with a high ability teacher and infant-teacher attachment. *Early Childhood Research Quarterly, 8,* 309–325.

Ramey, C. T. (1992). High-risk children and IQ: Altering intergenerational patterns. *Intelligence, 16,* 239–256.

Ramey, C. T., Bryant, D. M., Wasik, B. H., Sparling, J. J., Fendt, K. H., & LaVange, L. M. (1992). Infant health and development program for low-birth-weight, premature infants: Program elements, family participation, and child intelligence. *Pediatrics, 89,* 454–465.

Ramey, C. T., & Campbell, F. A. (1984). Preventive education for high-risk children: Cognitive consequences of the Carolina Abecedarian Project. *American Journal of Mental Deficiency, 88,* 515–523.

Ramey, C. T., & Campbell, F. A. (1987). The Carolina Abecedarian Project: An educational experiment concerning human malleability. In S. S. Gallagher & C. T. Ramey (Eds.), *The malleability of children* (pp. 127–139). Baltimore: Brooks.

Ramey, C. T., & Campbell, F. A. (1992). Poverty, early childhood education, and academic competence: The Abecedarian experiment. In A. C. Huston (Ed.), *Children in poverty: Child development and public policy* (pp. 190–221). New York: Cambridge University Press.

Ramey, C. T., Ramey, S. L., Hardin, M., & Blair, C. (1995, May). *Family types and developmental risk: Functional differentiations among poverty families.* Paper presented to the fifth annual conference of the Center for Human Development and Developmental Disabilities, New Brunswick, NJ.

Ramey, C. T., & Smith, B. (1977). Assessing the intellectual consequences of early intervention with high risk infants. *American Journal of Mental Deficiency, 81,* 318–324.

Ramey, S. L., & Ramey, C. T. (1992). Early educational intervention with disadvantaged children: To what effect? *Applied and Preventive Psychology, 1,* 131–140.

Reynolds, A. J. (1992a). *Effects of a multi-year child-parent center intervention program on children at risk.* Unpublished manuscript.

Reynolds, A. J. (1992b). Mediated effects of preschool intervention. *Early Education and Development, 3,* 139–164.

Reynolds, A. J. (1993, November). *One year of preschool intervention or two: Does it matter for low-income black children from the inner city?* Paper presented at the meeting of the National Head Start Research Conference, Washington, DC.

Reynolds, A. J. (1994). Effects of a preschool plus follow-on intervention for children at risk. *Developmental Psychology, 30,* 787–804.

Reynolds, A. J. (1995). One year of preschool intervention or two. Does it matter? *Early Childhood Research Quarterly, 10,* 1–31.

Ricciuti, H. N. (1974). Fear and the development of social attachments in the first year of life. In M. Lewis & L. A. Rosenblum (Eds.), *The origins of fear* (pp. 73–106). New York: Wiley.

Richardson, J. L., Dwyer, K., McGuigan, K., Hansen, W. B., Dent, C., Johnson, C. A., Sussman, S. Y., Brannon, B., & Flay, B. (1989). Substance use among eighth grade students who take care of themselves after school. *Pediatrics, 84,* 556–566.

Roberts, R. N., Casto, G., Wasik, B., & Ramey, C. T. (1991). Family support in the home: Programs, policy, and social change. *American Psychologist, 46,* 131–137.

Roberts, R. N., & Wasik, B. H. (1990). Home visiting programs for families with children from birth to three: Results of a national survey. *Journal of Early Intervention, 14,* 274–284.

Roberts, R. N., & Wasik, B. H. (1994). Home visiting options within Head Start: Current positive and future directions. *Early Childhood Research Quarterly, 9,* 311–325.

Rodman, H., Pratto, D., & Nelson, R. (1985). Child care arrangements and children's functioning: A comparison of self-care and adult-care children. *Developmental Psychology, 21,* 413–418.

Rodning, C. (1987). [Longitudinal research on infants in middle class two-parent families]. Unpublished raw data.

Roggman, L. A., Langlois, J. H., Hubbs-Tait, L., & Rieser-Danner, L. A. (1994). Infant daycare, attachment, and the "file drawer problem." *Child Development, 65,* 1429–1443.

Roopnarine, J. L., & Lamb, M. E. (1978). The effects of day care on attachment and exploratory behavior in a Strange Situation. *Merrill-Palmer Quarterly, 24,* 85–95.

Roopnarine, J. L., & Lamb, M. E. (1980). Peer and parent-child interaction before and after enrollment in nursery school. *Journal of Applied Developmental Psychology, 1,* 77–81.

Rosenthal, M. K. (1990). Social policy and its effects on the daily experiences of infants and toddlers in family day care in Israel. *Journal of Applied Developmental Psychology, 11,* 85–103.

Rosenthal, M. K. (1991a). Behaviors and beliefs of caregivers in family day care: The effects of background and work environment. *Early Childhood Research Quarterly, 6,* 263–283.

Rosenthal, M. K. (1991b). Daily experiences of toddlers in three child care settings in Israel. *Child and Youth Care Forum, 20,* 37–58.

Rosenthal, M. K. (1992). Nonparental child care in Israel: A cultural and historical perspective. In M. E. Lamb, K. J. Sternberg, C. P. Hwang, & A. G. Broberg (Eds.), *Child care in context: Cross-cultural perspectives* (pp. 305–330). Hillsdale, NJ: Erlbaum.

Rosenthal, M. K. (1994). *An ecological approach to the study of child care: Family day care in Israel.* Hillsdale, NJ: Erlbaum.

Rosenthal, R. (1979). The "file drawer problem" and tolerance for null results. *Psychological Bulletin, 86,* 638–641.

Rosenthal, R., & Vandell, D. L. (1996). Quality of care at school-aged child-care programs: Regulatable features, observed experiences, child perspectives, and parent perspectives. *Child Development, 67,* 2434–2445.

Rubenstein, J. L., & Howes, C. (1979). Caregiving and infant behavior in day care and homes. *Developmental Psychology, 15,* 1–24.

Rubenstein, J. L., Howes, C., & Boyle, P. (1981). A two-year follow-up of infants in community-based day care. *Journal of Child Psychology and Psychiatry, 8,* 1–11.

Rubenstein, J. L., Pedersen, F. A., & Yarrow, L. J. (1977). What happens when mothers are away: A comparison of mothers and substitute caregivers. *Developmental Psychology, 13,* 529–530.

Ruopp, R., Travers, J., Glantz, F., & Coelen, G. (1979). *Children at the center.* Cambridge, MA: Abt Associates.

Rutter, M. (1981). Social-emotional consequences of day care for preschool children. *American Journal of Orthopsychiatry, 51,* 4–28.

Sagi, A., Lamb, M. E., Lewkowicz, K. S., Shoham, R., Dvir, R., & Estes, D. (1985). Security of infant-mother, -father, and -metapelet attachments among kibbutz-reared Israeli children. In I. Bretherton & E. Waters (Eds.), *Growing points of attachment theory and research. Monographs of the Society for Research in Child Development, 50*(1/2, Serial No. 209), 257–275.

Scarr, S. (1991). On comparing apples and oranges and making inferences about bananas. *Journal of Marriage and the Family, 53,* 1099–1100.

Scarr, S. (1992). Keep our eyes on the prize: Family and child care policy in the United States, as it should be. In A. Booth (Ed.), *Child care in the 1990s: Trends and consequences* (pp. 215–223). Hillsdale, NJ: Erlbaum.

Scarr, S., Eisenberg, M., & Deater-Deckard, R. (1994). Measurement of quality in child care centers. *Early Childhood Research Quarterly, 9,* 131–151.

Scarr, S., McCartney, K., Abbott-Shim, M., & Eisenberg, M. (1995). *Small effects of large quality differences among child care centers on infants', toddlers', and preschool children's social adjustment.* Unpublished manuscript, Department of Psychology, University of Virginia, Charlottesville.

Scarr, S., & Thompson, W. W. (1994). The effects of maternal employment and non-maternal infant care on development at two and four years. *Early Development and Parenting, 3,* 113–123.

Schaffer, H. R., & Callendar, W. M. (1959). Psychologic effects of hospitalization in infancy. *Pediatrics, 24,* 528–539.

Schwarz, J. C., Strickland, R., & Krolick, G. (1974). Infant day care: Behavioral effects at preschool age. *Developmental Psychology, 10,* 502–506.

Schweinhart, L. J., Barnes, H. V., & Weikart, D. P. (Eds.). (1993). *Significant benefits: The High/Scope Perry Preschool Study through age 27.* Ypsilanti, MI: High/Scope Press.

Seitz, V. (1990). Intervention programs for impoverished children: A comparison of educational and family support models. *Annals of Child Development, 7,* 78–103.

Seitz, V., Apfel, N. H., Rosenbaum, L., & Zigler, E. F. (1983). Long-term effects of Project Head Start. In Consortium for Longitudinal Studies (Eds.), *As the twig is bent: Lasting effects of preschool programs* (pp. 299–332). Hillsdale, NJ: Erlbaum.

Seltenheim, K., Ahnert, L., Rickert, H., & Lamb, M. E. (1997, May). *The formation of attachments between infants and care providers in German daycare centers.* Poster presented to the American Psychological Society, Washington, DC.

Shwalb, D. W., & Chen, S. J. (1996). Sacred or selfish? A survey on parental images of Japanese children. *Research and Clinical Center for Child Development Annual Report, 18,* 33–44.

Shwalb, D. W., Shwalb, B. J., Sukemune, S., & Tatsumoto, S. (1992). Japanese nonmaternal child care: Past, present, and future. In M. E. Lamb, K. J. Sternberg, C. P. Hwang, & A. G. Broberg (Eds.), *Child care in context: Cross-cultural perspectives* (pp. 331–353). Hillsdale, NJ: Erlbaum.

Sigel, I. E. (1990). Psychoeducational intervention: Future directions. *Merrill-Palmer Quarterly, 36,* 159–172.

Silverstein, L. B. (1991). Transforming the debate about child care and maternal employment. *American Psychologist, 46,* 1025–1032.

Smith, A. B., Inder, P. M., & Ratcliff, B. (1993). Relationships between early childhood center experience and social behavior at school. *New Zealand Journal of Educational Studies, 28,* 13–28.

Smith, M., & Bissell, J. S. (1970). Report analysis: The impact of Head Start. *Harvard Educational Review, 40,* 51–104.

Sparling, J., Lewis, I., Ramey, C. T., Wasik, B. H., Bryant, D. M., & La Vange, L. M. (1991). Partners: A curriculum to help premature, low birthweight infants get off to a good start. *TECSE, 11,* 36–55.

Spedding, P. (1993). United States of America. In M. Cochran (Ed.), *International handbook of child care policies and programs* (pp. 535–557). Westport, CT: Greenwood Press.

Spitz, H. H. (1986). *The raising of intelligence: A selected history of attempts to raise retarded intelligence.* Hillsdale, NJ: Erlbaum.

Sroufe, L. A., Fox, N., & Pancake, V. (1983). Attachment and dependency in developmental perspective. *Child Development, 54,* 1615–1627.

Stallings, J. A. (1980). An observational study of family day care. In J. C. Colbert (Ed.), *Home day care: A perspective* (pp. 10–22). Chicago: Roosevelt University Press.

Stanley, J. C. (Ed.). (1973). *Compensatory education for children, ages 2 to 8: Recent studies of educational intervention.* Baltimore: Johns Hopkins University Press.

Steinberg, L. (1986). Latchkey children and susceptibility to peer pressure: An ecological analysis. *Developmental Psychology, 22,* 433–439.

Steinberg, L. (1988). Simple solutions to a complex problem: A response to Rodman, Pratto, and Nelson. *Developmental Psychology, 24,* 295–296.

Steiner, G. Y. (1976). *The children's cause.* Washington, DC: Brookings Institution.

Sternberg, K. J., Lamb, M. E., Hwang, C. P., Broberg, A., Ketterlinus, R. D., & Bookstein, F. L. (1991). Does out-of-home care affect compliance in preschoolers? *International Journal of Behavioral Development, 14,* 45–65.

Stifter, C. A., Coulehan, C. M., & Fish, M. (1993). Linking employment to attachment: The mediating effects of maternal separation anxiety and interactive behavior. *Child Development, 64,* 1451–1460.

Stith, S., & Davis, A. (1984). Employed mothers and family day care substitute caregivers. *Child Development, 55,* 1340–1348.

Stoltenberg, J. (1994). Day care centers: Quality and provision. In A. E. Borge, E. Hartmann, & S. Strom (Eds.), *Day care centers: Quality and provision* (pp. 7–11). Oslo, Norway: National Institute of Public Health.

Suwalsky, J. D., Klein, R. P., Zaslow, M. J., Rabinovich, B. A., & Gist, N. F. (1987). Dimensions of naturally occurring mother-infant separations during the first year of life. *Infant Mental Health Journal, 8,* 3–18.

Symons, D. K., & McLeod, P. J. (1993). Maternal employment plans and outcomes after the birth of an infant in a Canadian sample. *Family Relations, 42,* 442–446.

Symons, D. K., & McLeod, P. J. (1994). Maternal, infant, and occupational characteristics that predict postpartum employment patterns. *Infant Behavior and Development, 17,* 71–82.

Taylor, A. R., & Machida, S. (1994). The contribution of parent and peer support to Head Start children's early school adjustment. *Early Childhood Research Quarterly, 9,* 387–405.

Teti, D. M., & Ablard, K. E. (1989). Security of attachment and infant-sibling relationships: A laboratory study. *Child Development, 60,* 1519–1528.

Thompson, R. A. (1988). The effects of infant day care through the prism of attachment theory: A critical appraisal. *Early Childhood Research Quarterly, 3,* 273–282.

Thompson, R. A., Lamb, M. E., & Estes, D. (1982). Stability of infant-mother attachment and its relationship to changing life circumstances in an unselected middle-class sample. *Child Development, 53,* 144–148.

Thornburg, K. R. (1992). Child care policies: Changing to meet the needs. In A. Booth (Ed.), *Child care in the 1990s: Trends and consequences* (pp. 223–235). Hillsdale, NJ: Erlbaum.

Thornburg, K. R., Pearl, P., Crompton, D., & Ispa, J. M. (1990). Development of kindergarten children based on child care arrangements. *Early Childhood Research Quarterly, 5,* 27–42.

Tuttle, W. M., Jr. (1993). *"Daddy's gone to war": The second world war in the lives of America's children.* New York: Oxford University Press.

U.S. Bureau of the Census. (1987). *After school care of school-age children: December 1984* (Current Population Reports, Series P-23, No. 149). Washington, DC: U.S. Government Printing Office.

U.S. Bureau of the Census. (1993). *Who's minding the kids? Child care arrangements, 1990.* Washington, DC: U.S. Government Printing Office.

U.S. Bureau of the Census. (1994). *Statistical abstract of the United States, 1993.* Washington, DC: U.S. Government Printing Office.

U.S. Bureau of Labor Statistics. (1987). *Statistical abstract of the United States* (107th ed.). Washington, DC: U.S. Department of Commerce.

Vandell, D. L. (1991). Belsky and Eggebeen's analysis of the NLSY: Meaningful results or statistical illusions? *Journal of Marriage and the Family, 53,* 1100–1103.

Vandell, D. L., & Corasaniti, M. A. (1988). *Variations in early child care: Do they predict subsequent social and emotional and cognitive differences?* Unpublished manuscript, University of Texas at Dallas, Richardson.

Vandell, D. L., & Corasaniti, M. A. (1990a). Child care and the family: Complex contributors to child development. *New Directions in Child Development, 49,* 23–38.

Vandell, D. L., & Corasaniti, M. A. (1990b). Variations in early child care: Do they predict subsequent social, emotional, and cognitive differences? *Early Childhood Research Quarterly, 5,* 555–572.

Vandell, D. L., Henderson, V. K., & Wilson, K. S. (1987, April). *A follow-up study of children in excellent, moderate, and poor quality day care.* Paper presented at the meeting of the Society for Research in Child Development, Baltimore, MD.

Vandell, D. L., Henderson, V. K., & Wilson, K. G. (1988). A longitudinal study of children with day care experiences of varying quality. *Child Development, 59,* 1286–1292.

Vandell, D. L., & Posner, J. (in press). Conceptualization and measurement of children's after-school environments. In S. L. Friedman & T. D. Wachs (Eds.), *Assessment of the environment across the lifespan.*

Vandell, D. L., & Powers, C. (1983). Day care quality and children's free play activities. *American Journal of Orthopsychiatry, 53,* 493–500.

Vandell, D. L., & Ramanan, J. (1991). Children of the National Longitudinal Survey of Youth: Choices in after-school care and child development. *Developmental Psychology, 27,* 637–643.

Vandell, D. L., & Ramanan, J. (1992). Effects of early and recent maternal employment on children from low-income families. *Child Development, 63,* 938–949.

Vaughn, B. E., Gove, F. L., & Egeland, B. (1980). The relationship between out-of-home care and the quality of infant-mother attachment in an economically disadvantaged population. *Child Development, 51,* 1203–1214.

Volling, B. L., & Feagans, L. V. (1995). Infant day care and children's social competence. *Infant Behavior and Development, 18,* 177–188.

Voran, M. J., & Whitebook, M. (1991, April). *Inequity begins early: The relationship between day care quality and family social class.* Paper presented at the meeting of the Society for Research in Child Development, Seattle, WA.

Wadsworth, M. E. J. (1986). Effects of parenting style and preschool experience on children's verbal attainment: Results of a British longitudinal study. *Early Childhood Research Quarterly, 5,* 55–72.

Waite, L. J., Leibowitz, A., & Witsberger, C. (1991). What parents pay for: Child care characteristics, quality, and costs. *Journal of Social Issues, 47,* 33–48.

Wasik, B. H., Ramey, C. T., Bryant, D. M., & Sparling, J. J. (1990). A longitudinal study of two early intervention strategies: Project CARE. *Child Development, 61,* 1682–1696.

Weinraub, M., & Jaeger, E. (1990). The time of mothers' return to the workplace: Effects on the developing mother-infant relationship. In J. S. Hyde & M. J. Essex (Eds.), *Parental leave and child care: Setting a research and policy agenda* (pp. 307–322). Philadelphia: Temple University Press.

Weinraub, M., Jaeger, E., & Hoffman, L. (1988). Predicting infant outcome in families of employed and nonemployed mothers. *Early Childhood Research Quarterly, 3,* 361–378.

Weisner, T. S., & Gallimore, R. (1977). My brother's keeper: Child and sibling caretaking. *Current Anthropology, 18,* 971–975.

Werner, E. E. (1984). *Child care: Kith, kin, and hired hands.* Baltimore: University Park Press.

Wessels, H., Lamb, M. E., & Hwang, C.-P. (1996). Cause and causality in daycare research: An investigation of group differences in the Göteborg Child Care Study. *European Journal of Educational Psychology, 11,* 231–245.

Wessels, H., Lamb, M. E., Hwang, C.-P., & Broberg, A. G. (in press). Personality development between 1 and 8 years of age in Swedish children with varying child care experiences. *International Journal of Behavorial Development.*

White, B. L. (1985). *The first three years of life.* New York: Simon & Schuster.

White, B. L. (1988). *Educating the infant and toddler.* Lexington, MA: Lexington Books/Heath.

White, B. L. (1995). *The new first three years of life.* New York: Simon & Schuster.

Whitebook, M., Howes, C., & Phillips, D. A. (1989). *Who cares? Child care teachers and the quality of care in America.* Oakland, CA: Child Care Employee Project.

Willer, B., Hofferth, S., Kisker, E., Divine-Hawkins, P., Farquhar, E., & Glantz, F. (1991). *The demand and supply of child care in 1990: Joint findings from the National Child Care Survey 1990 and a profile of child care settings.* Washington, DC: National Association for the Education of Young Children.

Woods, M. B. (1972). The unsupervised child of the working mother. *Developmental Psychology, 6,* 14–25.

Wrigley, J. (1995). *Other people's children.* New York: Basic Books.

Wynn, R. L. (1979, March). *The effect of a playmate on day care and home-reared toddlers in a Strange Situation.* Paper presented to a meeting of the Society for Research in Child Development, San Francisco, CA.

Zaslow, M. J. (1991). Variation in child care quality and its implications for children. *Journal of Social Issues, 47,* 125–138.

Zaslow, M. J., Pedersen, F. A., Suwalsky, J. T. D., & Rabinovich, B. A. (1989). Maternal employment and parent-infant interaction at one year. *Early Childhood Research Quarterly, 4,* 459–478.

Zhengao, W. (1993). China. In M. Cochran (Ed.), *International handbook of child care policies and programs* (pp. 83–106). Westport, CT: Greenwood Press.

Zigler, E. F., & Butterfield, E. C. (1968). Motivational aspects of changes in IQ test performance of culturally deprived nursery school children. *Child Development, 39,* 1–14.

Zigler, E. F., & Finn-Stevenson, M. (1996). The child care crisis: Implications for the growth and development of the nation's children. *Journal of Social Issues, 51,* 215–231.

Zigler, E. F., & Gordon, E. W. (Eds.). (1982). *Daycare: Scientific and social policy issues.* Boston: Auburn House.

Zigler, E. F., & Lang, M. E. (1991). *Child care choices.* New York: Free Press.

Zigler, E. F., & Muenchow, S. (1992). *Head Start: The inside story of America's most successful educational experiment.* New York: Basic Books.

Zigler, E. F., Piotrkowski, C., & Collins, R. (1994). Health services in Head Start. *Annual Review of Public Health, 15,* 511–534.

Zigler, E. F., & Styfco, S. J. (1994). Is the Perry Preschool better than Head Start? Yes and no. *Early Childhood Research Quarterly, 9,* 241–242.

Zigler, E. F., & Valentine, J. (1979). *Project Head Start.* New York: Free Press.

CHAPTER 3

Children in Poverty: Development, Public Policy, and Practice

VONNIE C. McLOYD

Although fundamentally accepting of wide disparities in economic well-being as an inherent consequence of capitalism, Americans are not inured to economic poverty and its attendant problems. The United States has a long history dating back to colonial times of policies, reforms, and interventions ostensibly intended to reduce the incidence and/or ameliorate the human costs of poverty (Demos, 1986; Schlossman, 1976). Because of Americans' strong bias toward individualistic explanations of poverty (Feather, 1974; Haller, Hollinger, & Raubal, 1990), these efforts have primarily focused on changing poor individuals' putative behavior and characteristics, rather than altering structural conditions that create poverty and its social ills. Further, most antipoverty efforts have focused on children directly or indirectly through their parents, based on the notion that poverty results from an intergenerational cycle that can best be broken during the victim's childhood (de Lone, 1979; Halpern, 1988). Several broad, overlapping categories of antipoverty programs currently exist for children and families, among them, early childhood (preschool) education programs (Barnett, 1995), two-generation programs (St. Pierre, Layzer, & Barnes, 1995; S. Smith, 1995), welfare-to-work programs (Brooks-Gunn, 1995), and home visitation programs for pregnant women and young parents (Olds & Kitzman, 1993).

The major goal of this chapter is to illuminate the dynamic relation between programs for poor children and families on the one hand, and theoretical and empirical work in the field of child development on the other. The United States is the focal geographic context within which these issues are discussed, but cross-national data are presented to highlight characteristics distinctive to the United States that shape its antipoverty policies and practices and ultimately affect the economic well-being of its children. Although the centerpiece of this chapter is a discussion of how theoretical and empirical work in the field of child development has influenced policies and programs for poor children, it is important that we underscore two points at the outset to put this discussion in proper perspective. First, it is our belief that when developmental theory and

Portions of this chapter were prepared while the author was on sabbatical at Duke University.

research have played a role in the formulation of poverty-focused policies and programs, most often it has been a supporting, rather than a leading, role. Political and social forces, not developmental theory and research, typically are the prime movers and wellspring of social policies and programs directed toward poor children and families. Research often is not a prerequisite and is virtually never a sufficient basis for the formulation and maintenance of such policies and programs. Examples abound of policies directed toward poor families that persist in the face of strong research evidence that they are not having their desired effect (e.g., Learnfare; Quinn & Magill, 1994). Conversely, in a number of instances, experimental social policies (e.g., negative income tax experiments of the 1960s and early 1970s) shown by research to have salutary effects on poor children's development have been rejected for universal implementation (Neubeck & Roach, 1981; Salkind & Haskins, 1982). Often underlying such divergences between policy decisions and research are ideological and social forces, especially prevailing public sentiments about how the poor should be treated.

In other instances, the formulation of policies that have or will impact massive numbers of poor children bears little imprint from child development research and theory. Two recent, historic pieces of federal legislation, the Family Support Act of 1988 and the Welfare Reform Act of 1996, are cases in point. Forged out of growing hostility toward the poor and the basic income support program for poor families and children (i.e., Aid to Families with Dependent Children), strong beliefs about parental responsibility to children, the emergence of maternal employment as a normative phenomenon, and increased understanding of patterns of welfare use, both laws, like the welfare debate from which they emerged, lack a clear, consistent focus on children's developmental needs and well-being (Chase-Lansdale & Vinovskis, 1995; Greenberg, 1996). The Family Support Act of 1988 seeks to increase economic self-sufficiency among welfare recipients by mandating participation in educational and employment training programs and strengthening enforcement of existing child support provisions. It provides for child care (and health coverage) for 12 months after families exit from public assistance, but neither quality nor availability of child care is guaranteed (Chase-Lansdale & Vinovskis, 1995).

Projected to push 1.1 million children into poverty and make many children who are poor still poorer, the Welfare Reform Act of 1996 mandates large reductions in the food stamp program, decreased assistance to legal immigrants, cuts in benefits to adult welfare recipients who do not find work after two years, and a five-year lifetime limit on assistance in the form of cash aid, work slots, or noncash aid such as vouchers to poor children and families, regardless of whether parents can find employment. Premised on the unrealistic expectation that the natural job creation process will absorb welfare recipients seeking employment, the law does not provide for a public works program. States can and are expected to adopt time limits shorter than five years and, in any case, have no duty to provide such assistance for any period of time, as the law voids the long-standing principle of entitlement for poor children and adults alike (Greenberg, 1996; Super, Parrott, Steinmetz, & Mann, 1996).

Delineation of how theoretical and empirical work has sanctioned policies and practices directed toward poor children and families also must be tempered with an appreciation of the oftentimes subtle but decided shadows that social and political forces cast on scholarly work itself. The manner in which issues are formulated and, therefore, the nature of knowledge generated in the discipline of child development are influenced by sociohistorical context (Riegel, 1972; Wertsch & Youniss, 1987). Scholars in the field of child development, as in any discipline, bring with them predispositions stemming from laws, customs, economic factors, political beliefs, and the prevailing zeitgeist, among other things, that necessarily shape the nature of and conclusions drawn from their research (Youniss, 1990). Their recommendations about courses of action toward children and interventions in the lives of families follow not just from data but from the interests that they bring to their studies as well. For these reasons, woven into our review of scholarly work that undergirds policies and programs directed toward poor families and children is a discussion of how social and political forces have shaped both of these entities. It represents our attempt to take seriously Youniss's (1990) challenge that "An ethically mature development psychology would not deny its debt to social and cultural forces but seek to know them better for itself and the persons it serves" (p. 287).

The chapter is divided into four major sections. We begin with an overview of various operational definitions of poverty, their respective strengths and weaknesses from both a research and policy perspective, and the relation between definitions of poverty and other indicators of economic well-being such as socioeconomic status. This orienting section is followed by a discussion of the demographic correlates of childhood poverty. Attention is devoted to racial and ethnic disparities in children's economic well-being and to factors that have contributed to these disparities and to recent increases in the incidence of childhood poverty. Included in this section is an analysis of the distinctive characteristics of the U.S. public welfare system that result in exceptionally high rates of child poverty, followed by a brief discussion of the prevailing ideology, attitudes, and values that shape these welfare policies.

In the third section, we turn our attention to the core foci of the chapter, namely, linkages among theory, research, and programs that seek to reduce poverty and/or its negative effects. Our analysis is limited primarily to three categories of programs that provide an array of educational and social services to poor infants, preschoolers, and/or their parents, specifically, early childhood education programs, parent education and training programs, and programs that focus on both parent and child and the broader ecology of family life (e.g., two-generation programs). The organizing framework for our discussion is three assumptions on which these categories of programs are premised: (a) that early experience is a critical determinant of the course of development; (b) that parents and the home environment exert primary influence on children's development; and (c) that the broader ecological context of family life impacts parental behavior and, in turn, children's functioning. We review the theoretical and empirical work that prompted and/or sustained these assumptions and provided the intellectual foundation for these antipoverty programs, along with findings from intervention studies designed to demonstrate the efficacy of these programs and the soundness of the policies that spawned them. The chapter concludes with a discussion of the implications of extant research for policy and practice. The ideological bases and limitations of existing antipoverty programs are considered in light of social-structural and macroeconomic forces, and suggestions are offered to guide the practices of those working with poor children and families.

CATEGORIES AND DEFINITIONS OF ECONOMIC DEPRIVATION

Poverty

Sound definitions and corresponding measures of poverty are important for a range of "scientific" and political reasons. They allow comparisons of economic well-being across different groups and across time; identification of individuals, families, and social groups whose most basic needs remain unmet; and assessments of the effects of poverty, policies, and programs on these individuals, families, and social groups (Ruggles, 1990). Definitions of poverty used in psychological and sociological research fall into three broad categories, each of which establishes a poverty standard defined in economic terms. Hagenaars and de Vos (1988) succinctly summarize these three definitions of poverty in the following way: (a) poverty is having less than an objectively defined, absolute minimum required for basic needs (i.e., food, clothing, housing); (b) poverty is having less than others in society (e.g., lacking certain commodities that are common in the society in question or falling below some cutoff expressed as a proportion of the median income for the society); and (c) poverty is feeling you do not have enough to get along. These characterizations have been commonly labeled *absolute, relative,* and *subjective* poverty, respectively.

For our purposes, absolute poverty is the most relevant of the three classes of definitions because it typically is the focal construct in developmental, socialization, intervention, and policy studies that use a precise definition of poverty. The most common measure of absolute poverty in these studies is defined by cash income using the "official" federal poverty index as a marker. Developed in 1965 by Mollie Orshansky, an economist employed by the Social Security Administration, the federal poverty standard was officially adopted by the government in 1969 during its War on Poverty (Haveman, 1987). Cash income was defined as the pretax, posttransfer annual cash income of a family, excluding capital gains or losses. This value was compared with a threshold based on the estimated cost of food multiplied by 3, adjusted to account for economies of scale for larger families and the differing food needs of children under age 18 and of adults under and over 65. The estimated cost of food was based on the minimum income a family needed to purchase food delineated in the U.S. Department of Agriculture's (USDA) "thrifty" diet. The food multiplier of 3 was based on a household budget study conducted in 1955 indicating that food typically absorbed about a third of the posttax income of families over a wide range of incomes. Today, there are well over 100 different poverty lines or thresholds, adjusted annually by the consumer price index so that the purchasing power they represent does not change over time. Thus, they remain close to those calculated with the "thrifty" food plan (Citro & Michael, 1995; Haveman, 1987). Because this index is an absolute dollar amount, not a percent of the median income or a percentile, it is theoretically possible for everyone to be above the poverty threshold.

The official poverty index has several defects and limitations, the most glaring of these being that (a) it is not adjusted to take account of geographic variation in living costs, in-kind transfers such as food stamps, Medicaid, or employed-provider health benefits, or rising real income or improvements in living standards; (b) money paid in income and payroll taxes is counted as part of family income when determining specifically who is below the threshold of poverty (pretax income), but the poverty index is based on net after-tax income; and (c) it does not reflect how far below (or above) the threshold people fall (the poverty gap). These problems notwithstanding, the official poverty index, or some derivative of it, is widely used in both research and policy. For example, an income-to-needs ratio (calculated as household income/official poverty threshold for household) is increasingly popular among developmental researchers as an indicator of the degree of poverty or affluence characterizing a household (e.g., Brooks-Gunn, Klebanov, & Liaw, 1995; Duncan, Brooks-Gunn, & Klebanov, 1994). An income-to-needs ratio of 1.0 indicates that a household's income is equal to the official poverty threshold, and smaller or larger ratios represent more or less severe poverty (or lesser and greater affluence), respectively. Used in this manner, the poverty line becomes a unit of measure rather than a threshold of need (Hauser & Carr, 1995). Others define poverty in terms of eligibility for federal or state subsidies to the poor (e.g., reduced-cost or free lunch) or family income cutoffs corresponding to those used to determine eligibility for subsidies.

As Vaughan (1993) has pointed out, the resilience of the official measure of poverty is hardly due to widespread agreement about its technical merits or even to the difficulty of updating it in accord with the principles used to first construct it. Rather, it appears to be a product of the economic and social ramifications of changes in poverty thresholds. These issues are enmeshed in larger, rancorous political debates over the extent and causes of poverty, the most effective strategies to reduce rates of poverty, and the validity of the unfavorable current ranking of the United States relative to other Western industrialized countries in terms of poverty rates among children (Smeeding & Torrey, 1988). It is inescapable that any definition of poverty has strengths and weaknesses, involves matters of judgment, and, thus, is subject to criticism. Nevertheless, glaring defects in the government's poverty index should be corrected because it determines the size and characteristics of the poverty population and therefore influences public attitudes about the extent to which poverty reduction should lay claim on national resources and the types of antipoverty policies and programs that should be implemented. (For extensive discussions of the strengths and weaknesses of the official poverty index and other measures of poverty, along with proposals for the development and updating over time of a new official poverty index see Citro & Michael, 1995; Dear, 1982; Hagenaars & de Vos, 1988; Hauser & Carr, 1995; Haveman, 1987; Ruggles, 1990; Vaughan, 1993.)

Low Socioeconomic Status and Economic Loss

Another large category of studies pertinent to this review focuses on low socioeconomic status (SES) as an indicator of economic deprivation. The term *socioeconomic status* typically is used to signify an individual's, family's, or group's ranking on a hierarchy according to its access to or control over some combination of valued commodities such as wealth, power, and social status (Mueller & Parcel, 1981). Although some dispute exists among social scientists about how SES should be defined or measured, there is considerable agreement that important components of SES include the occupation of the father and/or mother, family income, education, prestige, power, and a certain style of life (House, 1981).

Poverty is not isomorphic with low SES. Unlike SES, poverty is based on an absolute standard or threshold and does not signify relative position. Its marker, cash income, is only one of several components or dimensions of SES and is clearly related to but distinct from occupational status, educational level, prestige, and power. In addition, poverty status is considerably more volatile than SES. During adulthood, income relative to need is more likely to shift markedly from one year to another than SES indicators such as educational attainment and occupational status. Duncan's (1984) examination of adjacent-year pairs of data from the national longitudinal Panel Study of Income Dynamics for the period 1969–1978 indicated that one-third to one-half of those who were poor in one year were not poor in the next year. One of the important distinctions that has emerged from this work is persistent versus transitory poverty.

These distinctions between poverty and low SES are crucial conceptually and for public policy discussions. Some research indicates, for example, that poverty and income status have effects on children's socioemotional functioning (i.e., externalizing symptoms) independent of SES indicators (e.g., parent education; Duncan et al., 1994), although too few studies simultaneously assess the effects of poverty status and SES to discern any pattern that might exist in the relative contributions of poverty versus various SES indicators. We do not yet know how stability or instability in poverty and income status acts synergistically with more stable indicators of SES to influence children's development (Huston, McLoyd, & García Coll, 1994). Policy analysts regard the poverty-SES distinction as critical, partly on the proposition that it is generally easier to design and implement programs that alter family income (e.g., increasing welfare benefits, tax credits, minimum wage) than programs that modify a range of family characteristics that mark social class (Duncan, Yeung, Brooks-Gunn, & Smith, in press).

Also important to bear in mind is that neither poverty as measured by official criteria nor low SES can be assumed to be identical to, or even particularly good proxies for, material hardship. Mayer and Jencks (1988) found, for example, that income-to-needs ratios explained less than a quarter of the variance in householders' reports of material hardship (e.g., spending less for food than the "thrifty" food budget published by the USDA; unmet medical and dental needs; housing problems). This is because poverty and low SES rarely come "alone." They often represent a conglomerate of conditions and events that amount to a pervasive rather than a bounded stressor. Scarcity of material resources and services frequently is conjoined to a plethora of undesirable events (e.g., eviction, physical illness, criminal assault) and ongoing conditions (e.g., inadequate housing, poor health care, dangerous neighborhoods, poor diets, environmental toxins) that operate concurrently and often precipitate additional crises (Belle, 1984; Pelton, 1989). In short, in the context of limited financial resources, stressors are highly contagious (Harrington, 1962; Makosky, 1982). Traditional measures of poverty and SES, then, may underestimate the direct and indirect effects of material hardship on children's development.

Whereas poverty and low SES are typically conceptualized as ongoing *conditions* inextricably linked to employment-related factors such as unemployment, underemployment, low wages, and unstable work, another set of studies relevant to our concern here focuses on various *events* as precipitants of economic deprivation. This research assesses the impact on parents and children of job loss, job demotion, and income loss as experienced by working- and middle-class individuals who characteristically are employed (e.g., Conger, Ge, Elder, Lorenz, & Simons, 1994; Flanagan & Eccles, 1993; McLoyd, 1989, 1990). Although they tend to be overrepresented among poor families, these experiences of economic loss or decline do not necessarily push families into poverty. We review this work to the extent that it helps fill gaps in the poverty literature and, in general, furthers our understanding of the processes by which economic deprivation might influence children's development.

Throughout this chapter, we attempt to maintain distinctions among various categories of economic deprivation, especially poverty and low SES on the one hand and economic loss on the other. In our discussion of specific findings, the term is used that most closely approximates the indicator of economic deprivation employed by the researchers. In psychological research published prior to the mid-1980s, the terms *low SES* and *poor* tended to be used interchangeably. Recent research is distinguished by more precise definitions of poverty (e.g., income-to-needs ratios), attention to the multiple dimensions of poverty (e.g., chronicity and contexts of poverty, such as neighborhoods and schools), and a diminution of the tendency to treat poverty as a condition identical to low SES. These conceptual and empirical advances are traceable in large measure to Duncan's (1984) research underscoring the volatility and dynamics of poverty and W. Wilson's (1987) seminal analysis of historical changes in the spatial concentration of poverty in inner-city neighborhoods wrought by structural changes in the economy.

The preeminence in research and policy studies of objective states of economic deprivation operationalized in terms of the official poverty index, low SES, and economic loss should not obscure the fact that some of the impact on individuals of economic deprivation and ameliorative policies and practices undoubtedly is subjective. How parents and children perceive and feel about their economic circumstances is driven partly by subjective evaluation of their circumstances in comparison to some reference group. In contexts distinguished by extraordinary affluence and conspicuous consumption, such as the United States, this comparison process can accentuate "feeling poor" among individuals who are poor in an objective sense and engender "feeling poor" among those who are not (Garbarino, 1992). This subjective state can have direct effects on psychological functioning and mediate as well as moderate the influence of objective states of poverty and other forms of economic deprivation (Conger et al., 1994; Garbarino, 1992; McLoyd, Jayaratne, Ceballo, & Borquez, 1994).

TRENDS IN THE INCIDENCE AND NATURE OF CHILDHOOD POVERTY

America's children are faring less well economically than their counterparts two decades ago. Following a period of decline in the rate of official childhood poverty in the United States from 27% in 1959 to 14% in 1969, the rate rose slightly throughout the 1970s and increased sharply between 1979 and 1984 from 17% to 22%. A short-lived decline between 1984 and 1989 was followed by an increase. As of 1993, 22.7% of children under age 18 were officially classified as poor, and 38% of all poor Americans were children (Danziger & Danziger, 1993; Hernandez, 1997). The post-1970 period also witnessed unprecedented growth in income inequality. Between 1973 and 1990, for example, the adjusted mean cash income among the poorest fifth of American families with children fell by 30%, whereas the mean cash income for the richest fifth of American families increased by 13%. Not since the late 1940s has income inequality been as marked as it is today (Danziger & Danziger, 1993).

The sharp rise in childhood poverty during the past two decades stimulated a burgeoning of scholarly interest in poor children and families, manifested most strikingly by the publication of numerous special issues of journals devoted to the topic. The issues around which this surge of scholarship coalesced included the effectiveness of extant antipoverty programs (Barnett, 1995; Olds & Kitzman, 1993; St. Pierre et al., 1995), the processes that mediate and temper the adverse effects of poverty and economic stress on children's development (e.g., Huston, García-Coll, & McLoyd, 1994; Korbin, 1992; McLoyd & Flanagan, 1990; Routh, 1994; Slaughter, 1988a), and the application of current research on poor children and families to welfare policy and practice (Danziger & Danziger, 1995; Slaughter, 1988a). (For a review of recent research studies and their implications for policy and practice, see McLoyd, in press.) This demographic trend and recently established public policies directed toward the poor also gave impetus to several national research and policy-focused meetings on poor children and families, among them, the 1989 Forum on Children and the Family Support Act (Chase-Lansdale & Brooks-Gunn, 1995) and the 1995 Conference on Consequences of Growing up Poor (Duncan & Brooks-Gunn, 1997), both held at the National Academy of Sciences.

Rates of poverty are substantially higher among African American, American Indian, and certain ethnic subgroups of Latino and Asian American children than among non-Latino White children (Gibbs, Huang, et al., 1989). For example, in 1991, Puerto Rican, African American, and Mexican American children under 18 years of age had poverty rates of 57%, 44% and 36%, respectively, compared to a rate of 15% for non-Latino White children (Reddy, 1993; U.S. Bureau of the Census, 1992). In addition, compared to non-Latino White children, African American children are more subject to major drops in family income relative to need and more likely to fall into poverty following events that reduce family income (e.g., family breakups, cutbacks in work hours of household members, disability of household head; Duncan, 1991). Half of the poorest fifth of African American households have absolutely no financial cushion to fall back on in the event of a disruption of current income (i.e., zero net worth; Shinn & Gillespie, 1994).

Immigration patterns, in concert with macroeconomic changes, may strengthen the link between ethnic minority status and poverty. By the 1980s, 85% of all immigrants arriving in the United States were from Latin American and Asian countries (only 10% were from Europe), contributing to an unprecedented increase during the past decade in the proportion of ethnic minorities in the U.S. population (P. Martin & Midgley, 1994; U.S. Bureau of the Census, 1994). Not only are post-1979 immigrants economically and educationally disadvantaged relative to native-born Americans and to immigrants who entered the United States before 1980, they also may be less able than their predecessors to improve their economic status once they gain experience in the U.S. job market, first, because they are entering a U.S. economy that is less robust and opportunity laden than in earlier times and, second, because a significant proportion are subject to racial/ethnic discrimination evoked by their darker skin color (e.g., Dominicans, Haitians, Mexicans; A. Portes & Zhou, 1993; Rumbaut, 1994).

Primarily affecting ethnic minority children, three interrelated changes in the context and nature of poverty itself have accompanied increases in the incidence of childhood poverty during the past two decades. First, poverty appears to have become more difficult to escape (i.e., more chronic and less transitory) since the 1970s (Rodgers & Rodgers, 1993), though whether or not this trend is found in longitudinal data depends on how poverty and chronicity of poverty are measured (Duncan & Rodgers, 1991). Children exposed to chronic poverty are overwhelmingly from ethnic minority backgrounds, whereas poverty as experienced by non-Latino White children is primarily transitory. In an analysis of longitudinal data from the 1968–1982 waves of data from the Panel Study of Income Dynamics, for example, Duncan and Rodgers (1988) found that African American children accounted for the total number of children who were poor all 15 of the years examined and for almost 90% of the children who were poor during at least 10 of the 15 years. Second, environmental stressors associated with poverty have become more pervasive and life-threatening (e.g., homelessness, street violence, illegal drugs, negative role models; Shinn & Gillespie, 1994; Zigler, 1994).

Both of these changes, to some extent, are by-products of a third trend, namely, the growing concentration of poverty in urban areas. Unlike poor Whites, poor African Americans increasingly live in economically depressed, socially isolated inner-city communities where jobs, high-quality public and private services (e.g., child care, schools, parks, community centers, youth organizations), and informal social supports are less accessible (Duncan, 1991; Shinn & Gillespie, 1994; W. Wilson, 1996; Zigler, 1994). Jargowsky's (1994) recent analysis of national data indicated that between 1980 and 1990, the percentage of poor African Americans in metropolitan areas who lived in census tracts with poverty rates of 40% or more increased from 37% to 45%. This trend is not observed among poor Whites, nor do poor Whites live primarily in high-poverty areas. In 1980, 68% of poor non-Latino Whites lived in low-poverty areas (areas with poverty rates below 20%), whereas only 15% of poor African Americans and 20% of poor Latinos lived in such areas. Conversely, 39% of poor African Americans and 32% of poor Latinos in the five largest American cities lived in high-poverty areas (i.e., areas with poverty rates above 20%), compared to 7% of poor non-Latino Whites (W. Wilson, 1987). Increased rates of residence in economically depressed neighborhoods where inadequate housing units are concentrated, in combination with racism in the housing market (Massey, 1994), contribute to substantially higher rates of homelessness and increased likelihood of living in deficient and overcrowded dwellings among poor African Americans and Latinos compared to poor non-Latino Whites (Shinn & Gillespie, 1994).

Taken together, these trends have conspired to render poverty a harsher, more pernicious condition in a broader context distinguished by rising materialism, conspicuous consumption, and an increasingly monetarized economy. These contextual factors have psychological significance in that they can engender higher economic expectations, a heightened sense of being poor, and, in turn, rising anger, depression, and hostility among the poor (Garbarino, 1992). In the next section, we discuss factors that have contributed to the recent deterioration in children's economic well-being and ethnic disparities in rates of childhood poverty. The latter discussion focuses primarily on African Americans because considerably more data are available on this group.

Contributors to Recent Trends and Race Differences in Childhood Poverty

Macroeconomic Changes

The mid-1970s ushered in a period of national deindustrialization, decline in the manufacturing sector relative to the service sector of the economy, and globalization of economic markets. These macroeconomic changes not only contributed to sluggish economic growth in the United States, but precipitated significant loss of work hours and low-skill, high-wage jobs, displacement of workers into much lower-paying trade and service positions, and rates of unemployment that were higher than at any time since the Depression of the 1930 (Horvath, 1987). Among the consequences were reductions in family income and, in turn, increases in childhood poverty. Whereas median family income grew almost continually between 1950 and 1973, it stagnated during the years that followed. Year-to-year changes in median income between 1950 and 1973 were positive 20 times and negative only 4 times, but during the decade that followed, there were as many year-to-year declines as increases in median family income. By 1989, median income for all families was only 8% higher than in 1973 (Danziger & Danziger, 1993).

Economic attrition brought on by sluggish economic growth and structural changes in the economy has been especially acute among African Americans. For example, between 1973 and 1986, African American families headed by persons 24 years old or younger lost 47% of their real income, compared to 18% for Latino families and 19% for White families (William T. Grant Foundation Commission on Work, Family, and Citizenship, 1988). African American families have fared so poorly for several reasons: (a) rates of job displacement in the manufacturing sector are higher and reemployment rates lower in precisely those blue-collar occupations in which African Americans are overrepresented (James, 1985; Simms, 1987); (b) manufacturing employment has increasingly relocated from central cities, where disproportionate numbers of African Americans reside, to outlying areas; (c) central cities have been transformed from centers of production to centers of administration, generating sharp increases in white-collar employment and thus higher educational requirements for employment, but African Americans rely disproportionately upon blue-collar employment and average lower levels of education than Whites; (d) virtually all of the recent growth in entry-level jobs requiring lower levels of education has occurred in the suburbs and nonmetropolitan areas away from high concentrations of poorly educated African Americans (Fusfeld & Bates, 1984; W. Wilson, 1996); and (e) disproportionate numbers of African Americans work in low-wage industries (e.g., retail, service) whose existence is preserved by high rates of unemployment, lack of union contracts, and large numbers of jobs that are not covered by "protective" legislation (e.g., minimum wage; Fusfeld & Bates, 1984).

Increase in Single-Mother Families

Rising rates of childhood poverty during the 1970s were strongly linked to increases in the proportion of families headed by single mothers, especially never-married mothers. However, during the 1980s, declining income of single mothers, rather than increases in the number of such families, was a significant cause of increases in poverty among children (Bane & Ellwood, 1989). Between 1960 and 1987, the percentage of American children living in female-headed families increased from 8% to over 20% (Eggebeen & Lichter, 1991). These families, compared to two-parent families, are at much greater risk of being poor for many reasons, including reduced likelihood of a second wage earner in the household, lower wages for women than men as a result of discriminatory labor market practices, the low educational attainment of many single mothers, and the large percentage of men who provide little if any child support (Bartfeld & Meyer, 1994; Garfinkel, Meyer, & Sandefur, 1992; Klein, 1983; U.S. Bureau of the Census, 1992).

The risk of long spells of childhood poverty among children in mother-only families is even greater if the mother has never married. The problem of inadequate or nonexistent child support from fathers is especially acute among never-married mothers because it is more difficult to identify the noncustodial father and because many of the fathers are poor (Garfinkel et al., 1992). Adding to their economic vulnerability, never-married mothers have lower levels of education and work experience than either married mothers or other single mothers (i.e., divorced, separated; Danziger & Danziger, 1993; Ellwood & Crane, 1990). These comparisons, however, should not obscure the fact that, contrary to popular perception, *within* each marital status category, including the never-married category, the majority of African American mothers, like White mothers, with children under 18 are currently in the labor force (U.S. Bureau of Labor Statistics, 1992).

African American children are at greater risk of experiencing chronic poverty than are White children because they are much more likely to live in families headed by never-married mothers (Eggebeen & Lichter, 1991). Relatively more common among African Americans than Whites and especially likely among offspring of never-married mothers, spells of childhood poverty that begin at birth tend to be especially long (Bane & Ellwood, 1986). African American children's increased risk of chronic poverty also is related to higher proportions of mother-only families resulting from separation and divorce. Following marital dissolution, African American children, compared to White children, spend more time in a single-parent family before making the transition to a two-parent family and are much more likely to remain in a single-parent family for the duration of childhood (Duncan & Rodgers, 1987). Between 1960 and 1990, the proportion of children living in mother-only families increased from 20% to 51% among African Americans and from 6% to 16% among White Americans (Danziger & Danziger, 1993). Among African Americans, this trend primarily reflects the increased prevalence of out-of-wedlock births and a general decline in fertility among married African American women (Center for the Study of Social Policy, 1986; W. Wilson, 1987).

Some analyses suggest that a major contributor to the rise in mother-only families among African Americans is the shrinking pool of marriageable (i.e., employed or earning above-poverty wages) African American men brought on by the deteriorating economic status of African American men. In the most influential and widely cited work on this issue, W. Wilson and Neckerman (1986) showed that among African Americans below age 35, the ratio of employed males per 100 females in the population fell sharply in the 1970s and early 1980s, a pattern that mirrors the decrease in marriage rates among African American families. Wilson and Neckerman's findings have been replicated in other studies based on data from various regions of the country. They also are in keeping with evidence across different demographic groups that entry into marriage is less likely and marital dissolution more likely if the husband is unemployed or poor than if the husband is employed or more affluent (Bishop, 1977; Furstenberg, 1976; William T. Grant Foundation Commission on Work, Family, and Citizenship, 1988). However, for reasons that are unclear, other studies have failed to replicate Wilson and Neckerman's finding (for a review of these studies, see Ellwood & Crane, 1990).

Even if the declining economic fortunes of African American men is a causal factor, racial differences in family structure clearly are not the sole factor responsible for the increased prevalence of poverty among African American children. The expected prevalence of poverty among African American children living in two-parent families throughout childhood is roughly the same as the expected prevalence of poverty among White children who spend their entire childhood living in single-parent families (3.0 years versus 3.2 years; Duncan & Rodgers, 1987). Institutional barriers deriving directly from past and/or present racial discrimination (e.g., housing patterns in relation to the location of jobs, restricted educational and employment opportunities, marginalization into secondary and casual sectors of the labor market) undoubtedly are implicated in this racial disparity (Brewer, 1988; W. Wilson, 1987, 1996).

Reduced Government Benefits

A third contributor to the increase in childhood poverty is reduction in federal expenditures on programs benefiting children. The total number of children receiving AFDC dropped in the early 1980s due to more restrictive eligibility requirements, despite the increase in childhood poverty during this time. In addition, during the past 20 years, welfare benefits have been eroded substantially by inflation (Danziger & Danziger, 1993; Ellwood & Crane, 1990). For example, between 1971 and 1983, the real value of food stamps and AFDC declined by 22% (Ellwood & Summers, cited in Huston, 1991). Consistent with this attrition, since 1975, government cash transfer programs became less effective in reducing poverty. The percentage of pretransfer poor, mother-only families (i.e., those that would have been poor in the absence of government cash transfers) who were lifted out of poverty as a result of government cash transfer programs declined from 20% to 10% between 1975 and 1990 (Danziger & Danziger, 1993). In addition, the real value of the personal exemption on federal income taxes continued to decline during the 1970s and 1980s, while payroll taxes, borne disproportionately by lower-income wage earners, increased significantly during this time (Huston, 1991).

Childhood Poverty in International Perspective

The posttax and posttransfer rates of child poverty in the United States during the mid-1980s were considerably higher than those in six other Western industrialized countries (Canada, Sweden, Germany, Netherlands, France, United Kingdom), and this difference was most pronounced for children living in single-parent families (Smeeding & Torrey, 1988). In Sweden, the country most often cited as a model welfare state, only 5% of all children and 8.6% of children in single-parent families were poor during this time, whereas in the United States, the comparable figures were 17% and 51%, respectively. Even in Canada, a country whose economy and standard of living are similar to the United States', rates of poverty among all children and those in single-parent families (9.6% and 39%, respectively) were notably lower than those in the United States. Equally as striking, rates of child poverty fell in these countries during the 1980s, when those in the United States rose (Danziger & Danziger, 1993; Smeeding, 1992). This was true even in those countries such as Canada and the United Kingdom that, like the United States, experienced an increase in single mothers during the 1970s and 1980s (Evans, 1992).

The United States owes its exceptionally high rates of child poverty to several distinctive characteristics of its public welfare system. At the most basic level, its cash transfer programs are considerably less effective in reducing poverty than those in other Western industrialized countries. During the mid-1980s, for example, fewer than 20% of the pretransfer poor in the United States were removed from poverty by cash transfers, whereas in other Western industrialized countries, this figure ranged from about 50% to 75% (Smeeding, 1992). Many of the latter countries have social insurance (rather than income-tested welfare benefits that are, by definition, restricted to poor children and families) in the form of universal child allowances, universal health care, and free or inexpensive child care. These forms of child support help reduce poverty among children, just as Social Security and Medicare help to reduce poverty among the elderly in the United States (Danziger & Danziger, 1993; Huston, 1991).

A higher percentage of cash transfer programs are income-tested in the United States compared to other Western industrialized countries, and this has two consequences that serve to increase rates of child poverty. First, income-tested programs such as AFDC overtly and intentionally stigmatize, isolate, and pathologize the poor (Bronfenbrenner & Weiss, 1983; Goodban, 1985; Kluegel, 1987; Marshall, 1982), and this appears to discourage significant numbers of people who are eligible from applying. In 1981, for example, 27% of all poor American families with children received no public income support, as compared to only 1% in both Canada and the United Kingdom (Smeeding & Torrey, 1988).

The United States' overreliance on income-tested programs has the additional effect of dampening labor force participation (de Lone, 1979; Edin, 1995; Wong, Garfinkel, & McLanahan, 1993). Welfare benefits, unlike social insurance, are related to economic need and therefore are reduced when beneficiaries increase their income from earnings. Essentially, this constitutes a tax on earned income, which tends to reduce labor force participation and hours of employment. It follows, then, that poor families have lower earnings in countries that rely more on welfare benefits than on social insurance benefits. Indeed, data show that the earnings of poor American families are markedly lower than those of poor families in West Germany, Sweden, and the United Kingdom (Smeeding & Torrey, 1988). In sum, as a consequence of high levels of inequality in families' access to resources and services needed to promote children's development, U.S. social policies appear to exaggerate rather than minimize the impact of family SES and income on children's development (Garbarino, 1992). This may explain why correlations between measures of family income (or SES) and child development outcomes are often higher in the United States than in other Western industrialized countries (Bronfenbrenner, 1986).

Clearly, prevailing value and belief systems are at the root of America's penurious cash transfers to poor children and relatively high percentage of cash transfer programs that are income-tested. As shown by cross-national survey research, Americans, relative to citizens in other Western industrialized countries, have comparatively less positive attitudes toward social welfare (e.g., reduction of income inequality, universal minimum income), stronger preference for individualistic explanations of economic inequality (e.g., attributing poverty to individual deficits such as insufficient motivation), and greater tendency to perceive current social and economic conditions as equitable (Feather, 1974; T. Smith, 1990). In accord with these differences is Americans' tendency to perceive the effects of poverty (e.g., low levels of education) as ones driven largely by choices made by the poor (Halpern, 1991; Harrington, 1962; Pelton, 1989). These historically rooted sentiments reflect and foment among the American public highly disparaging attitudes toward the poor, even among the poor themselves (Williamson, 1974) and even during periods of prolonged macroeconomic downturns (Kluegel, 1987; Tropman, 1977). They converge to shape welfare policies that are predictably isolating, demeaning, and ineffective in removing Americans from poverty.

Issues of race and racism toward African Americans also shape U.S. welfare policies toward the poor (Edsall & Edsall, 1991; Evans, 1992; Quadagno, 1994). One of the several reasons that universal social welfare programs are anathema to U.S. policymakers, for example, is the perception that African Americans, whose receipt of public welfare benefits is disproportionate to their numbers, are prone to welfare abuse and less imbued with "family values" and the Protestant work ethic. Consider Glazer's (1986) explanations of failed efforts during the Nixon and Carter administrations to implement national policies that would temper demeaning and isolating features of public welfare. He observed that:

> [There was] the fear . . . that the reduction in the stigma of welfare by incorporating it into a national system would not reduce the behavior that makes welfare necessary (i.e., withdrawal from the labor force, male irresponsibility toward their children, creation of broken families, and the increase in illegitimacy) but would simply make it more acceptable. . . . The racial angle is that these behaviors . . . are far more marked among the black population. . . . National systems, treating everyone alike, based on insurance and dignity, do not work in the United States as they do in Europe—or they would in Japan—because America has large differences, related to race and ethnicity, in how people behave. . . . Discrimination is not major today. . . . Nevertheless, the group differences in behavior exist, presumably because of the enormous impact of a heritage of severe discrimination. Group differences are barriers to universalism. . . . When a nation is ethnically homogeneous, it is easier to see social benefits as designed for "us"—all of us—rather than for "them," a minority. (pp. 57–58)

Paradoxically, opposition to universal social insurance for children based on such anti–African American sentiments in effect has relegated large numbers of White American children to poverty status. To wit, the poverty rate for White American children alone is higher than those for all children (nonminority and minority combined) in the six other Western industrialized countries enumerated above (Smeeding & Torrey, 1988). Because of its centrality to issues of poverty, policy, and practice, we return repeatedly in this chapter to the issue of race.

BASIC ASSUMPTIONS OF ANTIPOVERTY POLICIES AND PROGRAMS: LINKAGES TO CHILD DEVELOPMENT THEORY AND RESEARCH

Programs that aim to reduce the prevalence of poverty and/or ameliorate the negative effects of poverty on children have informed and been influenced by developmental research, and both have been shaped by common political and social forces. Although a mainstay of these programs is their principal focus on infants and preschoolers, the research that undergirds the programs, and the programs themselves, have grown more complex and sophisticated over time. A historical overview of these programs reveals progressive shifts toward more comprehensive models whose precursors include changing conceptual frameworks and research foci within the field of child development and evidence from evaluation studies of the limitations of previous programs based on more simplistic models.

In this section of the chapter, we consider three major premises that are the bedrock of major antipoverty policies and programs in the United States: (a) that early experience is a critical determinant of the course of development, setting the child on a trajectory toward successful or problematic adaptation; (b) that parents and the home environment exert primary influence on children's development; and (c) that the broader ecological context of family life impacts parental behavior and, in turn, children's functioning. Our primary goal is to illuminate the theoretical and empirical work that gave rise to and/or affirmed these and other guiding assumptions and, thus, helped shape the nature of antipoverty policies and their implementation. Also reviewed are intervention studies that test the efficacy of programs designed to reduce poverty and/or its negative effects. Historical continuities and discontinuities in the nature of policies and programs for the poor are highlighted, with special attention given to antecedents of discontinuities.

Two qualities of research on poor children are reflected in this review. First, basic and intervention research focused on poor children and families are genealogically and conceptually intertwined. Second, issues of race, ethnicity, culture, and racism are prominently and intricately woven throughout the history of research on poor children, because the U.S. racial caste system has ensured a continued confounding of race and poverty. This confound, however, is not sufficient as an explanation for the fact that the overwhelming majority of basic and intervention studies of poor children focuses on African Americans. Poor White children are largely invisible in the annals of child development research, despite constituting the plurality of America's poor children. We speculate about the precursors of this bias and make note of the limitations it poses for the formulation and implementation of national antipoverty policies. More extensive historical accounts of child development research and its relation to practice and social policies directed toward poor children and families can be found elsewhere (Condry, 1983; Fein, 1980; Laosa, 1984; Schlossman, 1976; Washington & Bailey, 1995; Washington & Oyemade, 1987; Weissbourd, 1987; Zigler & Muenchow, 1992; Zigler & Valentine, 1979).

Early Experience as a Critical Determinant of the Course of Development

The notion that experiences during childhood influence poor children's ability to meet the expectations of broader, mainstream society and to acquire skills necessary for successful adulthood was implicit in many early policies and practices directed toward the poor. British colonists, transporting across the Atlantic the attitudes commonplace in England about poverty and its prevention, sought to prevent the development of a pauper class in Boston with the passage of laws mandating parents to provide children with a basic education and marketable skills. Children whose parents did not fulfill these responsibilities, most of whom were indigent, were indentured as servants. The church complemented interventions of the state during the colonial period with efforts to compel parents to rear their children according to religious doctrines and to provide religious instruction to poor children as an antidote to the "temptations of poverty" (Ross, 1979; Schlossman, 1976).

During the mid- to late nineteenth century, the confluence of industrialization, urbanization, and high rates of immigration sowed urban ghettos populated by the poor and culturally different. Most newcomers of this period were individuals from southern and eastern Europe whose customs, language, and, to a lesser extent, child-rearing practices were unlike those of earlier immigrants from England and western Europe. Plagued by disease, crime, delinquency, and a host of social problems linked to economic exploitation, these urban ghettos were perceived as a threat to the stability of American culture. Large numbers of poor, immigrant women entered the workforce with the new wave of immigration preceding World War I, necessitating out-of-home care of their children. Mainstream, more affluent sectors of the society responded with the introduction into these urban ghettos of three distinct types of interventions, namely, settlement houses, religious missions, and kindergartens. Each was envisioned, in part, as a vehicle of poverty reduction and assimilation of lower-class individuals to mainstream middle-class values, attitudes, and behavior (Braun & Edwards, 1972; Ross, 1979; Shonkoff & Meisels, 1990). Each had elements of a personal helping strategy that was paradigmatic during the latter half of the nineteenth century, namely, "friendly visiting," in which well-to-do women associated with private relief agencies and charity organizations made home visits to poor families "to provide a mixture of support, scrutiny, and advice" (Halpern, 1988, p. 285).

Settlement houses were established during the late nineteenth century in urban neighborhoods, deemed an "experimental effort" by their most prominent exponent, Jane Addams. Young, college-educated professionals staffed and lived in the houses "not to uplift the masses, but to be neighbors to the poor and restore communications between various parts of society" (Addams, cited in Weissbourd, 1987, p. 44). They "settled and developed services in the neighborhood" (Weissman, cited in Halpern, 1988, p. 286) and aimed to strengthen neighborhood and family life by advocating for and empowering the poor, decreasing ethnic, racial, and cultural conflicts, and increasing understanding among individuals from diverse backgrounds (Weissbourd, 1987). Rather than duplicate the services of other family agencies, settlement houses gave priority to linking people with existing services and helping people to utilize them. Settlement workers conducted parent education for immigrant families isolated from traditional sources of child-rearing advice and provided practical assistance with child care, housing, and legal problems. Under the auspices of the settlement movement, nurses also made home visits to care for the sick and to give advice about domestic matters such as child care, diet, and hygiene (Halpern, 1988). Their work and the role of the new social work profession in championing the needs of poor children achieved national attention in the first White House Conference on Children in 1909 (Fein, 1980). Many elements of the community work of settlement workers foreshadowed the strategies and goals of today's parent/family support movement (Halpern, 1988), discussed later in the chapter.

Because missions of Protestant crusaders were largely unsuccessful in modifying the behavior of poor urban adults, attention shifted to young children as instruments of social reform. Subsequent religious missions into poor neighborhoods were intended to "improve the living conditions of families through the lessons the children received in cleanliness, morality, and industriousness" (Ross, 1979, p. 24). The focus on young children continued with the establishment of kindergartens in urban ghettos supported by religious and philanthropic organizations (Braun & Edwards, 1972; Ross, 1979). Espousing the pedagogical philosophy of Froebel, who established the first formal kindergarten classes during the early 1800s in Germany, these kindergartens were grounded in traditional religious values and a belief in the importance of learning through supervised play. However, because of the nature of the social and economic conditions that spawned them, urban kindergartens in the United States sought to satisfy educational and social welfare functions simultaneously. Professional personnel spent mornings as teachers of young children and afternoons as social welfare workers, helping unemployed parents find work, securing health care for children and families, and assisting families in acquiring other needed services. As Braun and Edwards (1972) point out, referring to the social welfare functions performed by these employees, "This was the most important contribution of the pioneer kindergartners, as at this period the kindergarten was frequently the only social agency offering a helping hand in the rapidly-increasing slums" (p. 75). This ecologically oriented approach combining educational services to preschoolers and support services to their parents lost ground in the following decades, regaining currency in the 1970s as interventionists turned their attention to improving the social context of parenthood and children's development (Bronfenbrenner, 1975).

Kindergartens for poor children gave way to nursery schools for middle-class children in the 1930s, which in turn served as models for early childhood education programs established in the 1960s to fight poverty. Participation of middle-class families in institutional forms of child care once reserved exclusively for the poor was the result of a confluence of factors operating in the 1930s, including the growing prominence of child development "experts," angst among middle-class parents about their ability to provide a child-rearing environment adequate for positive child development, economic hardship during the Great Depression, pressure on middle-class women to find employment, and the formation of Works Progress Administration day nurseries (Fein, 1980).

Environmentalism as a Cornerstone of Contemporary Antipoverty Programs: The Role of Basic Research

Not until the 1960s was reduction of poverty and its adverse effects formally articulated as federal policy. Initiated by Johnson as a War on Poverty, this policy and its attendant programs for a Great Society were born of a complex configuration of social and political forces operating at the time, including rapid economic growth and the resulting affluence and optimism of Americans, heightened awareness of the high prevalence of poverty in the United States, the struggle for racial equality waged by the civil rights movement, and the emergence of political leaders (i.e., President Johnson, Sargent Shriver) who had notable personal and professional experiences with poor children (Condry, 1983; Laosa, 1984; Steiner, 1976; Zigler & Valentine, 1979). Educationally oriented early childhood intervention was one of the major categories of antipoverty programs that emerged during this period. Emphasis on "compensatory education" was galvanized by several influential analyses calling attention to widespread school failure among poor children even in the early years and to the correlation between poverty and low levels of education in the adult population (Fein, 1980).

Abundant evidence had accrued prior to the 1960s that lower-class children and children from certain ethnic minority groups performed less well than middle-class White children on indicators of academic achievement and cognitive functioning (e.g., Dreger & Miller, 1960; Guthrie, 1976; Shuey, 1958). Performance on IQ tests was elevated to major significance partly because of its significant correlation with school achievement (C. Deutsch, 1973). The relation between SES and performance on IQ tests was documented in samples of both White and African American children (e.g., M. Deutsch & Brown, 1964; Dreger & Miller, 1960; Kennedy, Van de Riet, & White, 1963), though most early studies confounded SES and race. Studies with race X SES factorial designs were few in number, but they consistently found SES to be more highly related than race to IQ and its environmental correlates (C. Deutsch, 1973).

Inspired by small-scale demonstration programs crafted by individual researchers in the early 1960s to study their effects on poor preschool children (e.g., S. Gray, Ramsey, and Klaus's Early Training Project, initiated in 1962), Head Start was established in 1965 as the first national, publicly funded preschool intervention program (Fein, 1980; Zigler & Valentine, 1979). Early childhood intervention was premised on a strong environmentalist perspective that called for reducing poverty by equipping poor children with academically relevant cognitive skills during the early years of life, which in turn was expected to prevent school failure and, ultimately, low employability, poverty, and economic deprivation. In effect, inadequate cognitive skills were seen as a proximal cause and, therefore, locus for the prevention of poverty. This marked a major shift toward environmental, rather than genetic, factors as the prevailing explanation for social class and race differences in academic and cognitive performance (Laosa, 1984; for historical accounts of controversies surrounding these issues, see Dreger & Miller, 1960; Guthrie, 1976). In addition, the optimal time for remediation of these presumed cognitive deficits was thought to be the preschool years. Although attempts at social reforms had historically focused on young children partly because they were perceived to be more malleable than adults, the 1960s marked the transformation of this notion into a "scientific" tenet that undergirded antipoverty policies and programs.

These core assumptions on which Head Start was based derived principally from two authoritative books, Hunt's (1961) *Intelligence and Experience* and Bloom's (1964) *Stability and Change in Human Characteristics* (Condry, 1983; Laosa, 1984; Zigler & Valentine, 1979). To support his claim that environmental factors have measurable effects on intelligence, Hunt assembled an impressive corpus of studies of both animals and humans exposed to environments varying in stimulation, including the famous investigations of institutionalized infants and children conducted by Skeels (e.g., 1966; Skeels & Dye, 1939) and Spitz (e.g., Spitz & Wolf, 1946). This was followed by Bloom's influential treatise popularizing the concept of a "critical period" in human development. Bloom analyzed several major longitudinal and cross-sectional studies and concluded that just as people achieve half of their adult height by 2.5 years of age, they achieve roughly half of their adult intelligence between conception and 4 years of age. He argued that the effect of the environment on intelligence and other human characteristics is greatest during the early and most rapid periods of development of the characteristics. Therefore, contended Bloom, to ameliorate the effects of environmental deprivation, intervention should occur as early in life as possible. Further bolstering the argument for early intervention was subsequent evidence that social class and race differences in children's performance on IQ tests and school achievement became more pronounced with age, a phenomenon termed "progressive retardation" and "cumulative deficit" (Coleman et al., 1966; Deutsch, 1967).

The notion that early childhood is the critical period for the development of skills required for academic success came under attack in later years as it became clear that early intervention did not inoculate children against continuing economic disadvantage. Critics argued that because development is continuous, a series of dovetailed programs appropriate for each major stage of development would have more beneficial effects on poor children's development than intervention limited to the preschool years (Zigler & Berman, 1983). Nonetheless, that current intervention programs for the poor overwhelmingly focus on infants and preschoolers and/or their parents indicates an abiding belief in the singularly potent influence of early experience.

This belief is likely to be invigorated by recent research indicating that the preschool years are a period of elevated vulnerability to the impact of poverty, at least in terms of years of schooling, although differences in the timing of poverty *within* the preschool period appear to have no effects on children's achievement scores (Smith, Brooks-Gunn, & Klebanov, 1997) or classroom placement (Pagani, Boulerice, & Tremblay, 1997). In a study based on data from the Panel Study of Income Dynamics, Duncan, Yeung, Brooks-Gunn, and Smith (in press) found that poverty during the first five years of a child's life was far more detrimental to children's years of completed schooling than poverty during middle childhood and adolescence. The differential impact of income by childhood stage was especially strong for African Americans, compared to Whites. Duncan et al. (in press) lacked data to explain the timing of poverty effect, but speculated that it may reflect the influence of school readiness, and in turn, teachers' affective responses to and expectancies of children, both of which predict later school achievement (Alexander, Entwisle, & Thompson, 1987; Brooks-Gunn, Guo, & Furstenberg, 1993).

Cultural Deprivation as a Corollary Premise. The establishment of preschool intervention was also premised on the assumption that the early experiences of poor children are inadequate as a foundation for academic success and upward economic mobility. Recognition of the etiological significance of environment in children's development stimulated a proliferation of studies documenting SES differences in an ever-widening range of cognitive and social variables presumably related to later academic functioning (e.g., Coleman et al., 1966; C. Deutsch, 1973; M. Deutsch & Brown, 1964; Hess & Shipman, 1965; Kamii & Radin, 1967). Collectively, these efforts served to build a case for preschool intervention by claiming that poor children were suffering deficiencies that forecast academic failure and, therefore, needed remediation (Laosa, 1984).

Implicitly contrasting *cultural* with *genetic* to underscore the environment as a determinant of behavior seen as inferior and undesirable (Condry, 1983), poor children were labeled "culturally deprived" and disparities in their behavior as compared to middle-class children termed "cultural deficits" (e.g., Bernstein, 1961; M. Deutsch & Brown, 1964; Hess & Shipman, 1965). This terminology is a derivative of the "culture of poverty" concept elaborated by Oscar Lewis (1966). Lewis attributed to poor people living in the ghettos of Latin America many of the psychological characteristics and behaviors that were later conceived as precursors of school failure. Researchers and scholars concerned with the psychological impact of environmental disadvantage during the 1960s borrowed generously from Lewis's writings, applying his culture of poverty notion most consistently and forcefully to inner-city African Americans, although the majority of America's poor were White and lived in rural areas (Condry, 1983). Attempting to explain this peculiarity, J. Patterson (1981) noted, referring to poor, inner-city African Americans, "Their comparative visibility, their geographic concentration, and their color made cultural interpretations of poverty more plausible than they might otherwise have been" (p. 120).

Preschool intervention programs established during the 1960s and 1970s, including Head Start and its educational forebearers (e.g., M. Deutsch, Deutsch, Jordan, & Grallo, 1983; S. Gray & Klaus, 1965), bore the stamp of the cultural deficiency model and drew sustenance from empirical studies conducted under this banner (Laosa, 1984; Zigler & Berman, 1983). This is not to suggest that these programs were homogeneous. Indeed, intervention programs of this period varied greatly in terms of their guiding assumptions, curricula, and structure. Some viewed the so-called deficiencies and, hence, needs of poor children as largely superficial, whereas others viewed them as a product of unfamiliarity with school-related objects and activities (Laosa, 1984). Still others regarded them as more fundamental, the most controversial and flagrant example being the Direct Instruction System for Teaching Arithmetic and Reading (DISTAR), in which classroom activities were prescribed by explicit behavior sequences of stimuli, responses, and positive reinforcements. Developed by Bereiter and Engelmann (1966) for poor African American children, the beginning language program of DISTAR for preschoolers was conceived as "one that starts from zero, assuming no prior mastery of English" (p. 138).

The program structures and curricula of intervention programs that developed during this period, then, differed depending on whether the intent was to supplement the experiences that poor children had in their homes and natural milieux, enhance academic preparation, or counteract the effects of poverty by abrogating children's culture and culture-linked behavior. This diversity aside, common to these programs was the assumption that poor children were suffering deficits that needed remediation by professionals during the preschool years (Laosa, 1984).

Cultural Difference as an Alternative Perspective. By the early to mid-1970s, the concept of cultural deprivation and its companion studies and programs were under scathing attack. They were criticized as perniciously ethnocentric on the grounds that they exalted White middle-class norms as the standard of "health," ignored the vast range of intellectual and social competencies possessed by poor children, and blamed poverty on individual characteristics while ignoring social structural contributors to economic deprivation (e.g., Baratz & Baratz, 1970; Ginsburg, 1972; Hall, 1974; Sroufe, 1970; Tulkin, 1972; Weems, 1974).

The most vehement and prodigious criticisms were reserved for the notion that poor, African American children are impoverished in their means of verbal expression and that nonstandard vernacular impedes complex abstract thought. Linguists excoriated researchers' and interventionists' ignorance of the rules of discourse and syntax of "Black English" and expressed outrage that some intervention programs presumed to remediate verbal deficits in normal speakers of this vernacular. Labov (1970) presented evidence that nonstandard Black English has compensating sets of rules that combine in different ways to express the same logical content and to mark the same distinctions as standard English. The verbal behavior of poor, urban African American children, compared to that of White middle-class children, was seen as a case of cultural difference, not cultural deficit. Far from being deprived of verbal stimulation, they argued, poor, urban African American children are bathed in verbal stimulation and participate in a highly verbal culture.

Labov (1970) demonstrated the powerful influence of social context on verbal behavior and criticized the typical assessment of linguistic competence in poor, urban children for eliciting defensive behavior unrevealing of linguistic competence. He essentially dismissed as misguided and invalid studies using the latter methodology, arguing that because the superficial form of the stimulus is controlled in laboratory studies of verbal behavior and the crucial intervening variables of interpretation and motivation are not, "most of the literature on verbal deprivation tells us nothing about the capacities of children . . . the best we can do to understand the verbal capacities of children is to study them within the cultural context in which they were developed" (p. 170).

In a much-cited paper, Cole and Bruner (1971) sharpened the distinction between competence and performance and expanded the critique of cultural deprivation to encompass other indicators of cognitive functioning. They reviewed a diverse body of data and theoretical formulations that controverted the claim that poor, minority children suffer intellectual deficits, concluding that (a) groups typically diagnosed as culturally deprived have the same underlying competence as those members of the dominant culture; (b) differences in performance derive from the situations and contexts in which competence is expressed; and (c) a simple equivalence-of-test procedure is not sufficient to make inferences about the competence of the two groups involved. Turning their attention to practice, Cole and Bruner conjectured that recognition of the integrity of lower-class culture would enhance poor children's academic performance by raising teachers' expectations and positive affectations. They admonished teachers to stop laboring under the erroneous assumption that they must create new intellectual structures in poor children, to eliminate instructional approaches that disparaged their culture and abilities, and to start concentrating on how to get children to transfer skills they already possessed to the task at hand.

This academic discourse, in concert with forces within preschool intervention programs (e.g., parent involvement), played a role in attenuating the pejorative view of the poor that prevailed in preschool intervention programs and shifting priorities to building on the strengths and cultural experiences that poor children brought to the programs (Zigler, 1985; Zigler & Berman, 1983). As we discuss later, criticism of the deficit model eventually tempered the focus on personal behavior as a target of blame. It helped forge a more ecological approach to early childhood intervention, distinguished by a focus on improving the context of child rearing and child development by reducing stressors and increasing social supports (D. Powell, 1988). Nonetheless, the extent to which Head Start and other preschool intervention programs have fully divested themselves of practices rooted in notions of cultural inferiority is still a matter of some debate (see, e.g., Laosa, 1984; Oyemade, 1985; Washington, 1985; Zigler, 1985).

Resilience of Early Intervention as an Antipoverty Policy: The Significance of Evaluation Research

Providing experiences during early life that are presumed to be intellectually stimulating and enriching remains a major cornerstone of antipoverty policies and programs directed toward poor children, although considerable diversity exists in the implementation of this goal (e.g., provision of services directly to parent vs. child, home visitation vs. center-based education). Head Start is the largest and most enduring exemplar of this antipoverty strategy. It stands as the model for other public, large-scale, non-Head Start preschool education programs established under the auspices of Title I (Chapter I) of the Elementary and Second Education Act, which legislated appropriation of federal funds to school districts with large proportions of poor children (e.g., Child-Parent Center Preschool Program, initiated in 1965 and currently operating under the auspices of the Chicago Public Schools; Fuerst & Fuerst, 1993; Reynolds, 1994, 1995). A multifaceted program that has served over 13 million children and their families since 1965, Head Start offers a wide range of services that include early childhood education, health screening and referral, mental health services, nutrition education, family support services, and opportunities for parent involvement (Zigler & Styfco, 1994a). Head Start programs must adhere to national performance standards but are permitted to adapt components, including the preschool education curriculum, to local needs and resources. Consequently, considerable variation exists among Head Start programs (Zigler & Styfco, 1994b).

Currently, Head Start's basic educational component is a center-based preschool program serving children aged 3 to 5, with the majority (64%) being 4 years old (National Center for Education Statistics, 1995). Head Start preschools have an adult:child ratio that ranges from 1:8 to 1:10, and most consist of half-day sessions held daily throughout the nine-month school year (Slaughter, Washington, Oyemade, & Lindsey, 1988). Fewer than 15% are full day and 35% are open fewer than 5 days per week. Most Head Start children are served for only one year (only 20% are served for two years), with no postpreschool services (Hofferth, 1994; Zigler & Styfco, 1994b). In fiscal year 1993, there were 1,370 Head Start grantees (over 36,300 classrooms) serving over 714,000 children and their families. Of these children, 36% were African American, 33% were Anglo, 24% were Latino, 4% were Native American, and 3% were Asian (National Center for Education Statistics, 1995). Federal guidelines require that at least 90% of children enrolled in Head Start programs be from families with incomes below the official poverty line. In 1993, about 95% of the families were officially poor, and 52% received welfare. Most participating families were single-parent families, and 13% of the children were handicapped. As of 1992, Head Start served only about 30% of all eligible 3- to 5-year-old children. It receives 80% of its funding from the federal government, with the remaining 20% coming from other sources, usually local, in the form of funds or services (Hofferth, 1994; National Center for Education Statistics, 1995; Zigler & Styfco, 1994b).

Evaluations of Head Start's Efficacy. Major landmarks in the evaluation of Head Start include the Westinghouse evaluation (Westinghouse Learning Corporation, 1969), a highly controversial undertaking (M. Smith & Bissell, 1970; S. White, 1970), followed by the Head Start Evaluation, Synthesis, and Utilization Project, commonly known as the Synthesis Project (McKey et al., 1985), and the Educational Testing Service (ETS) Head Start Longitudinal Study (Lee, Brooks-Gunn, & Schnur, 1988; Lee, Brooks-Gunn, Schnur, & Liaw, 1990; Schnur, Brooks-Gunn, & Shipman, 1992). Empirical studies of the effects of large-scale preschool education programs similar to Head Start also have been conducted (Fuerst & Fuerst, 1993; Reynolds, 1994, 1995).

Westinghouse Evaluation. The first large-scale evaluation of Head Start, conducted by the Westinghouse Learning Corporation (1969), was based on a sample of first-, second-, and third-grade children who had attended summer or full-year Head Start programs in 1966–1967. These children were compared with a sample of their grade school peers who had not attended Head Start. Assessment of effects was limited to IQ scores and performance on other cognitive measures, despite the fact that Head Start was designed with the much broader goal of improving poor children's overall development (i.e., physical health and nutritional status, social skills, affective functioning, and motivation). This decision would prove imprudent and occasion serious threats to the survival of Head Start (Caldwell, 1974; Zigler & Berman, 1983). Attendance at summer-only programs was found to have no effects. To the further dismay of advocates, only a few immediate cognitive gains (i.e., school readiness, psycholinguistic skills) were found among children who attended Head Start for a full year, and these gains were small and eroded after a few years in school. The overall lack of robust effects led the researchers to conclude that, "although this study indicates that full-year Head Start appears to be a more effective compensatory education program than summer Head Start, its benefits cannot be described as satisfactory" (Westinghouse Learning Corporation, 1969, p. 11).

Response to the evaluation was intense and rancorous. Jensen (1969), in his famously controversial and racist monograph, asserted on the basis of the Westinghouse evaluation that compensatory education had failed and that attempts to boost IQ were misdirected because genetic factors are far more important than environmental factors in determining IQ. Interwoven into his argument was the claim that African Americans are intellectually inferior to Whites. Other scholars delineated the study's many methodological problems thought to invalidate the findings, among them, the posttest-only design, the absence of true treatment and control groups created by random assignment, the noncomparability of the Head Start and non-Head Start children (the latter came from families with higher SES), the small sample of children who attended full-year Head Start programs, the dubious representativeness of the sample and generalizability of the findings (more than half of the 225 selected sites refused to participate in the evaluation), and lack of attention to the quality and type of Head Start program. The study also was criticized for the restricted range of dependent variables examined and especially for the absence of direct measures of academic functioning such as grades or performance on achievement tests (Condry, 1983; Smith & Bissell, 1970; White, 1970).

Among the most immediate and direct effects of the Westinghouse evaluation were a drastic reduction in the number of summer-only programs beginning in 1970, a corresponding drop in the number of children enrolled in Head Start (offset by the increase in the number of children in full-year programs), acceleration of a more experimental approach to early childhood education, and initiation of a broad program of management and programmatic reforms within Head Start (Condry, 1983; Harmon & Hanley, 1979; Richmond, Stipek, & Zigler, 1979). In the long run, the Westinghouse evaluation, along with other negative critiques of Head Start and related programs, bolstered the case of political opponents of the War on Poverty. In 1971, President Nixon vetoed the Equal Opportunities Amendments, and in 1975, President Ford planned to phase out all support for Head Start (Condry & Lazar, 1982). Threats to downsize and eliminate Head Start in the wake of the Westinghouse evaluation and shifts in government priorities away from social action were deflected by parental, community, and congressional support for Head Start, and the forceful advocacy of Zigler, first director of the Office of Child Development, the government entity responsible for administration and oversight of Head Start. Nevertheless, it was clear that research evidence of positive, long-term effects was needed to bolster Head Start's chances of survival.

It was in this political climate that a group of independent researchers, all of whom had initiated preschool intervention projects between 1962 and 1972, formed the Consortium for Longitudinal Studies in 1975 for the expressed purpose of providing a more definitive answer to the question of whether early education programs were effective in preventing school failure among poor children (Condry, 1983). The Consortium's major findings, discussed in a subsequent section of this chapter, yielded impressive evidence of positive effects and, as such, were critically important in buttressing broad-based public and political support of Head Start. Indeed, reports in the popular media of the positive effects of early childhood education interventions often confused small-scale model programs with Head Start programs or implied that positive effects of model programs would be produced by ordinary, large-scale programs (Zigler & Styfco, 1994b). More astute consumers of research were cognizant of the substantive differences between these two categories of programs and understood the need for authoritative research evidence of Head Start's efficacy, in particular. The Head Start Synthesis Project was conducted to help fill this void.

Head Start Synthesis Project. This project included an analysis and synthesis of 210 published and unpublished research reports on the effects of Head Start on children's cognitive, socioemotional, and physical development and the children's families and communities (McKey et al., 1985). Traditional narrative review methods were used to synthesize 134 of the studies. The 76 remaining studies were submitted to a meta-analysis, to which the research and policy community directed most of its attention. Major findings from this meta-analysis are presented below.

PROCEDURES. Not included in the synthesis were (a) studies that assessed the efficacy of only summer Head Start programs or special Head Start demonstration programs; (b) studies of related programs such as Home Start and Follow Through that did not include separate data for participants in basic Head Start programs; (c) studies that compared Head Start children to middle-class children or to children who attended other preschool or day care programs; and (d) studies that provided inadequate information or statistics needed to compute effect sizes.

FINDINGS. Of the 76 studies remaining after these exclusionary criteria were applied, 72 investigated cognitive functioning, including tests of intelligence, school readiness, and school achievement. Seventeen measured socioemotional gains (self-esteem, social behavior, achievement motivation), and 5 assessed impacts on the relation between parent involvement and children's cognitive performance. Most studies in the meta-analysis assessed effects immediately after the Head Start program ended, with very few examining impacts beyond the second year. For example, only eight treatment-control studies investigated impacts on cognitive development three or more years post–Head Start. Studies were characterized by one of two research designs: (a) a pre-post, intragroup longitudinal design comparing the performance of the same group of children before and after their Head Start involvement, or (b) a between-group, treatment–no treatment design comparing the postintervention performance of children who did and those who did not attend Head Start.

McKey et al. (1985) derived an effect size (ES) for each study by dividing the treatment-control (or pre-post) difference by the standard deviation of the control group. Effect sizes were then averaged across studies. They regarded as "educationally meaningful" an effect size of .25 or greater, a convention established on the basis of evidence that differences this size accompany discernible improvement in classroom performance (Cohen & Cohen, 1983). Because of the paucity of longitudinal studies, McKey et al.'s analyses of long-term effects were based on different Head Start sites at each time point. A comparison of results produced by long-term and cross-sectional studies suggested that variation in effect sizes over time were not an artifact of this admittedly crude analytic strategy.

The overall pattern of findings indicated positive short-term effects of Head Start that usually faded during the early grade school years. Consistent with the Westinghouse evaluation (Westinghouse Learning Corporation, 1969), and regardless of study design, children showed immediate gains (i.e., at the end of the Head Start year) in IQ (ES = .59 in treatment-control studies) that disappeared one year after Head Start. Head Start also produced immediate, positive effects on children's reading and mathematics achievement (ES = .31 and .54, respectively; treatment-control studies). These differences were attenuated, but continued to be in the educationally meaningful range (ES = .21 and .20, respectively) one year after Head Start. By the end of the second year, however, treatment and control group children performed at roughly equivalent levels. McKey et al.'s (1985) meta-analysis included too few studies (a total of three) to warrant conclusions about Head Start's effects on rates of grade retention and assignment to special education classes.

To assess effects on socioemotional development, treatment-control and pre-post studies were combined because so few studies focused on this domain (n = 17). Head Start had immediate positive effects on participants' social behavior (ES = .35), achievement motivation (ES = .22), and self-esteem (ES = .17). Gains in social behavior persisted two years after Head Start, dissipating by the end of the third year. On achievement motivation and self-esteem, however, Head Start children dropped below comparison children a year after Head Start, then returned to the level of non–Head Start children during the next two years.

McKey et al. (1985) also attempted to determine if benefits resulting from one year of Head Start attendance depended on certain program, child, or family characteristics. Academically oriented programs that used didactic, direct instruction methods produced greater immediate cognitive gains (a composite of IQ, school readiness, and achievement test scores) than Montessori, cognitive, or traditional (a more informal approach that places greater emphasis on socioemotional development) curricula, but these differences dissipated after one year. In addition, programs operating more hours per day produced greater immediate cognitive gains. Insufficient data precluded assessment of the persistence of these moderating effects of program characteristics. In terms of child and family characteristics, children who were older when they entered Head Start, children with higher IQs prior to entering Head Start, and children who came from higher SES families made greater immediate cognitive gains during the course of the Head Start year. These patterns were not evident, however, when long-term effects were assessed.

CRITIQUE. Like the Westinghouse evaluation, the Synthesis Project was met with skepticism about its validity. Critics pointed out that it was not based on a national representative sample of Head Start sites, and findings concerning moderating effects were based on very few studies, most designed for other purposes (Schweinhart & Weikart, 1986). The project also was criticized for not illuminating the processes by which positive as well as unanticipated effects were produced and the circumstances under which such outcomes were more or less likely (Gamble & Zigler, 1989). However, the most serious threat to the project's validity appeared to be the inclusion of low-quality studies in the meta-analysis, for, as skeptics pointed out, if a significant proportion of investigations are seriously flawed, inferences drawn from the report are highly questionable (Gamble & Zigler, 1989; Schweinhart & Weikart, 1986). Rather than eliminate studies that fell below minimum standards after the exclusionary criteria noted above were applied, McKey et al. (1985) rated the quality of each study on several factors (e.g., statistical vs. convenience sample, size of sample, nature of comparison group, sources and degree of bias in selection, attrition, instruments, etc.) and then determined whether, within the major outcome variables, each dimension of quality was related statistically to the magnitude of the effect size. In general, these analyses indicated that quality of study was unrelated to effect size and that, to the extent that a relation existed, the higher-quality studies tended to show less of an impact of Head Start than the lower-quality studies.

These analyses notwithstanding, several factors make it difficult to discount critics' concerns, the most central one being the apparent noncomparability of treatment and comparison groups in several studies. In their examination of the comparability of groups in studies with data collected one to three or more years after participation in Head Start ended, McKey et al. (1985) found that treatment and control groups ostensibly were comparable in only 6 of the 32 studies. McKey et al. inexplicably concluded that nonequivalence of groups was not a serious problem in the meta-analysis, but critics thought otherwise (Gamble & Zigler, 1989). A subsequent landmark evaluation, the ETS Head Start Longitudinal Study (Schnur et al., 1992), directly addressed the issue of nonequivalence of groups and, in effect, vindicated critics who believed that failure to control for preintervention differences between Head Start and comparison groups posed a significant threat to the validity of the findings generated by the Synthesis Project.

ETS Head Start Longitudinal Study. Long-standing anecdotal evidence exists that local Head Start staff, faced with an inability to offer Head Start to all eligible children because of limited funds, tend to select the most disadvantaged children for participation in Head Start (Haskins, 1989). There also was some hint of this selection bias in earlier research (e.g., Hebbeler, 1989), but strong empirical confirmation of its existence was unavailable until the long-awaited publication of data from the ETS Head Start Longitudinal Study (Lee et al., 1988, 1990; Schnur et al., 1992). The study began with the collection of data in 1969–1970 from children living in three regions of the United States in the spring *prior* to their possible entry into Head Start. It therefore permitted assessment of preexisting differences between children who enrolled in Head Start and children who were eligible (i.e., poor) but either did not enroll in Head Start or enrolled in a non–Head Start preschool. Another important methodological advantage of the ETS study is its inclusion of two comparison groups, one of children with no preschool experience and another of children who attended non–Head Start preschool programs. This makes it possible to determine whether children benefit from any preschool experience or from a particular preschool experience, compared to none at all.

Preintervention data indicated that children who subsequently enrolled in Head Start indeed were more disadvantaged than their impoverished counterparts (Schnur et al., 1992). Children destined for Head Start programs, compared to poor children who attended a non–Head Start preschool or attended no preschool, had mothers with fewer years of schooling, were more likely to live in families in which the father was absent, and lived in more crowded homes, even after controlling for race. Mothers of Head Start attendees had lower expectations for their children's achievement compared to mothers of children who ultimately attended other preschools. Furthermore, prospective Head Start attendees performed less well on measures of cognitive functioning (administered before entry to preschool) than children who ultimately attended other preschool programs, but were similar to children who attended no preschool after controlling for race, site, and family characteristics.

The findings are a strong caution against ignoring the heterogeneity of the poverty population and suggest that "reports of postintervention differences in evaluations of programs like Head Start that lack initial status information, or that use matching techniques, almost certainly have underestimated the efficacy of the preschool intervention experience" (Schnur et al., 1992, p. 416). Trends evident during the decade of the 1970s may have actually increased this selection bias. These include increases in the number of children eligible for Head Start (i.e., increases in rates of child poverty) but a corresponding decrease in the number of children actually served by Head Start, and increases in the geographic concentration of poverty. Thus, appraisal of effects reported in the Synthesis Project, and in subsequent investigations that assess Head Start's efficacy by comparing groups matched after the intervention, should take account of potential selection bias resulting in an underestimation of effects.

Lee et al.'s (1988) assessment of the immediate effects of one year of Head Start attendance among children in the ETS sample indicated significant gains among African Americans, but not Whites, from the point of program entry (controlling for preexisting differences on measures of cognitive functioning and background demographic factors such as maternal education and father presence). Compared to their counterparts enrolled in no preschool or in a non–Head Start preschool, African American Head Start children showed greater improvement in school readiness (ES = .13 and .32, respectively) and ability to control motoric impulsivity (ES = .27 and .32, respectively). They also improved their categorization skills more than children with no preschool experience (ES = .17), but less than children who attended a non–Head Start preschool (ES = –.23). However, even with their relatively larger gains in school readiness and control of motoric impulsivity, Head Start children still scored lower at posttest in absolute terms than the two comparison groups on all of the dependent measures except motor inhibition.

A one-year longitudinal follow-up of the African American children yielded results consistent with the fade-out effect found in previous evaluations (Lee et al., 1990). Controlling for initial group differences in background and cognitive factors, at the end of kindergarten or first grade Head Start enrollees maintained educationally meaningful gains in cognitive and analytic functioning, especially when compared to children without preschool experience. These gains, however, were attenuated compared to those found immediately after the Head Start experience. Unadjusted group differences in outcomes were relatively minor. The findings suggested that poor, African American children are likely to benefit from typical preschool experiences (and not just from Head Start), compared to none at all.

Evaluations of the Efficacy of Model Programs. To the extent that research played a role in the survival of Head Start and other large-scale, publicly funded non–Head Start preschool education programs during the late 1970s and 1980s, major credit goes to research evaluations of small-scale model programs, rather than to efficacy studies of Head Start that existed during this period. This is because the former evaluations had several methodological advantages that made the evidence they yielded more persuasive (Barnett, 1995; Consortium for Longitudinal Studies, 1983; Haskins, 1989; Zigler & Styfco, 1994b). First, several model programs had long follow-ups and relatively low attrition rates, making possible reasonably sound assessments of the efficacy of early childhood intervention through high school and beyond. In contrast, few well-designed studies of the long-term effects of large-scale preschool intervention programs were published during the late 1970s and 1980s (Barnett, 1995), due in large measure to the precipitous decline in funding for research on Head Start's efficacy (Zigler & Styfco, 1994b).

Second, many model programs used random assignment, the preferred method of evaluation of program effects because it increases confidence that estimated effects are due to program differences rather than to preexisting differences between comparison groups (e.g., Andrews et al., 1982; Berrueta-Clement, Schweinhart, Barnett, Epstein, & Weikart, 1984; M. Deutsch et al., 1983; S. Gray et al., 1983). Lack of random assignment to treatment and control groups is a major methodological weakness of all studies of large-scale preschool programs (Barnett, 1995). Enrollment in basic Head Start programs has never been under experimental control for political reasons, including the fact that the program was instituted on a national, full-scale level, rather than as an experimental pilot program. As a consequence, it was and continues to be open theoretically to all poor children (Condry & Lazar, 1982). Similar factors operating on the local level explain why none of the studies of large-scale early education programs similar to Head Start (e.g., Chicago Child-Parent Center) has used random assignment (Barnett, 1995; Reynolds, 1994).

With random assignment precluded as an option, researchers conducting evaluation studies of large-scale preschool programs typically attempt to match treatment and control group children on various familial and demographic characteristics. Strategies include drawing controls from the same neighborhood or elementary school classes attended by enrollees of the program, selecting children from waiting lists comprised of those who are eligible but not enrolled in the program, and using statistical techniques to control for initial differences. Although preferable to having no comparison group, matching of groups is problematic because it is virtually impossible to rule out the possibility that differences observed between groups of children simply reflect differences that were present prior to the intervention rather than differences resulting from the intervention (Barnett, 1995).

These methodological advantages essentially rendered studies based on model programs more rigorous and sound as tests of the effects of early education intervention. Nonetheless, because model programs typically have lower child:staff ratios, smaller group size, and more highly trained staff than large-scale, public programs such as Head Start, scholars cautioned against assuming that the documented effects of model programs would be produced by ordinary, large-scale preschool programs (Haskins, 1989; Woodhead, 1988). At the same time, they have pointed out that studies of large-scale and model programs are best seen as complementary, with both providing unique and important information needed to guide policy formulation and service delivery. Studies of model programs are often weak on generalizability but strong on internal validity, documenting the effects that can accrue from early childhood education programs implemented under relatively ideal circumstances (Haskins, 1989; Schweinhart, Barnes, & Weikart, 1993). Studies of large-scale programs, on the other hand, are often strong on generalizability in that they provide a close approximation of what effects can be expected to be produced by ordinary, universally available preschool programs. However, they tend to be weak on internal validity (e.g., control of selection bias, uniformity of treatment implementation and test administration, confounding of preschool with other program variations experienced by children after the preschool years).

Several small-scale early childhood educational programs for poor children were initiated prior to and subsequent to the establishment of Head Start. As a group, these programs are very diverse, varying in terms of curriculum, ages and number of children served, length of program, and years of operation, among other dimensions (Barnett, 1995). For example, age of entry into these programs ranges from the prenatal and early infancy period (e.g., Garber, 1988; Jester & Guinagh, 1983) to approximately 4 years, with most programs enrolling children between ages 3 and 4 (Beller, 1983; S. Gray et al., 1983; Horacek, Ramey, Campbell, Hoffman, & Fletcher, 1987; Schweinhart & Weikart, 1983). A few are home-based (e.g., Jester & Guinagh, 1983; Levenstein, O'Hara, & Madden, 1983), but the vast majority are center-based with frequent to occasional home visits (e.g., Beller, 1983; Schweinhart & Weikart, 1983). Program length during the preschool period varies from about two years (e.g., Levenstein et al., 1983; Schweinhart & Weikart, 1983) to five years (e.g., Campbell & Ramey, 1994). Preschool curricula are highly diversified and based on a range of child development and pedagogical models (e.g., Bank Street, Montessorian, Piagetian, Bereiter-Englemann), but most are primarily cognitive in orientation. The majority of model programs operated during the 1960s and had run their course by the early 1970s. Most were part of the Consortium on Longitudinal Studies (1983). We describe two model projects here to illustrate some of the features of these programs and the variation within this category of projects. The first one, the Perry Preschool Project (Berrueta-Clement et al., 1984; Schweinhart & Weikart, 1983; Schweinhart et al., 1993), is the most prominent of the model projects and was part of the Consortium. The second project, the Carolina Abecedarian Project, is the most recent vintage of early education model programs and was not part of the Consortium (Campbell & Ramey, 1994, 1995; Horecek et al., 1987).

Conducted in Ypsilanti, Michigan, between 1962 and 1967, the Perry Preschool project (Berrueta-Clement et al., 1984; Schweinhart & Weikart, 1983; Schweinhart et al., 1993) identified potential participants from a census of the families of students attending the Perry Elementary School in Ypsilanti, referrals by neighborhood groups, and door-to-door canvassing. The sample consisted of 123 low SES families (58 randomly assigned to the treatment group and

65 to the control group) whose children had IQ scores between 70 and 85 but showed no evidence of organic handicap. All of the families were African American and about half were mother-headed and receiving welfare. Forty percent of parents were unemployed, and only 21% of mothers and 11% of fathers had completed high school.

Children entered the program at ages 3 and 4. Those in the treatment group attended two-and-a-half-hour center-based classes five mornings a week from October to May, most (78%) for a period of two years. Teacher:child ratio was 1:5–6. The curriculum was guided by Piagetian theory and emphasized children as active learners. Interactions with children were built around a set of active learning experiences (e.g., creative representation, language, social relations, movement). Teachers made a weekly home visit during the afternoon (with both mother and child present) lasting 90 minutes to involve the mother in the educational process, to enable the mother to provide her child with educational support, and to implement aspects of the center's curriculum in the child's home. Supportive social services such as assistance with housing and nutritional services were not provided. Children who participated in the program have been followed through age 27, the longest follow-up of any early childhood education program (Schweinhart et al., 1993).

The Carolina Abecedarian Project operated between 1972 and 1985 in Chapel Hill, North Carolina (Campbell & Ramey, 1994, 1995; Horecek et al., 1987). This center-based program recruited poor families nominated by social welfare departments and prenatal clinics; most were African American (98%) and headed by an unmarried mother (mean age = 20 years with a range from 13 to 44 years; mean IQ = 85) who had not graduated from high school at the time of the child's birth. A total of 55 families were randomly assigned to the experimental group and 54 to the control group. Children entered the program at 4 months of age on average and remained until they entered public kindergarten at age 5. The child care center operated 8 hours a day, 5 days a week, 50 weeks a year. The caregiver:infant ratio was 1:3. Caregiver:child ratios gradually increased to 1:6 as children moved from the nursery into toddler and preschool groupings.

The curriculum for infants emphasized cognitive, language, and perceptual-motor development and social and self-help skills. In the later preschool years, emphasis was placed on language development (pragmatic features rather than syntax) and preliteracy skills. Parents served on the day care center's advisory board and were offered a series of voluntary classes covering such topics as family nutrition, legal matters, behavior management, and toy making. Supportive social services were available to families to help solve problems related to housing, food, and transportation. The most recent follow-up assessed preschool treatment effects on 15-year-olds (Campbell & Ramey, 1995).

Consortium for Longitudinal Studies: Pooled Analysis. Growing threats to downsize and eliminate Head Start due to changing government priorities and the disappointing findings of the Westinghouse evaluation, in addition to the methodological shortcomings of the latter evaluation, prompted the formation of the Consortium for Longitudinal Studies in 1975. Pivotal for purposes of policy was the Consortium's unique ability to evaluate the long-term effects of early educational interventions on direct measures of children's school achievement, such as performance on achievement tests and rates of grade retention, placement in special education, and high school graduation. With support from the Administration for Child, Youth, and Families (the successor to the Office of Child Development), 11 research groups developed a common protocol for the collection of follow-up data from children in their original treatment and control groups (94% of the original samples were African American children), relocated their samples, collected common data, and submitted the data to an independent group for joint analyses (Condry, 1983). The studies of programs in the Consortium essentially represented independent tests of the hypothesis that early education has positive effects on poor children's development. As Condry (1983) noted, the value of such independent replications is that chance findings tend to cancel each other out. Consequently, common findings across projects increase confidence that effects are reliable. Data on IQ and family background variables were collected at Waves 1 and 2 prior to the establishment of the Consortium. Waves 3 (1976) and 4 (1980) involved collection of a common set of information on developmental outcomes across all projects, during which time children in the Consortium samples were 9 to 19 years and 12 to 22 years, respectively (Condry & Lazar, 1982).

The independent group contracted to analyze the data from the Consortium projects followed an elaborate, stringent plan of analysis. Five projects employed random assignment to a program group and a control group and six projects were quasi-experimental in that the treatment and control groups were matched. The results were pooled, with programs with true experimental designs analyzed separately from those with quasi-experimental programs. Within each program site, treatment children were compared with control children to determine if results were consistent across projects. *P* values from each individual project were then pooled. When pooled results were statistically significant, the project with the highest individual *p* value was dropped and the analysis was repeated. If the pooled *p* values of the remaining programs were still statistically significant, the result was considered robust (Royce, Darlington, & Murray, 1983).

ACADEMIC ACHIEVEMENT. Like the Westinghouse evaluation, data from the Consortium projects indicated a diminution of IQ effects over time. Pooled results of 7 of the 11 projects indicated that after three or four years, program effects on IQ remained statistically significant (mean difference = 3 points), but were not robust. More important, children in the programs, compared to those in the control groups, performed better academically. Pooled results indicated program effects on mathematics achievement that were significant and robust at grade 3, significant but not robust at grades 4 and 5, and neither significant nor robust at grade 6 (number of programs on which pooled results for each grade are based differed, ranging from four to six). Program children had significantly higher scores on reading achievement than controls only at grade 3, but results were not robust for any grade (Royce et al., 1983).

SCHOOL PROGRESS. Programs in the Consortium also proved effective in reducing rates of grade retention and/or placement in special education. The Consortium's pooled analysis (Royce et al., 1983) of these outcomes focused on effects through grade 7 (eight projects; Beller, 1983; S. Gray et al., 1983; Jester & Guinagh, 1983; Karnes, Schwedel, & Williams, 1983; Levenstein et al., 1983; Miller & Bizzell, 1983; Palmer, 1983; Schweinhart & Weikart, 1983) and grade 12 (four projects; Beller, 1983; S. Gray et al., 1983; Karnes et al., 1983; Schweinhart & Weikart, 1983). Some 20% of children in the program group versus 32% in the control group had been retained in grade by grade 7, an effect that was both significant and robust. Likewise, fewer children in the program group than in the control group had been retained in grade by the end of high school (32 % vs. 47%). This effect, however, was not significant after background variables were taken into account (Royce et al., 1983). In contrast, pooled effects on special education were significant as well as robust at both grade levels. At grade 7, the average rate of such placement was 14.5% for program children, compared to 34.9% for control children. At grade 12, the comparable figures were 13.4% and 30.8%, respectively. Using IQ test scores, school competence, and high school completion as the dependent variables, pooled analysis yielded no consistent evidence that program effects were conditioned by children's preprogram IQ test scores, sex, family background (two- vs. one-parent family, maternal education), or the curriculum of the preschool (Royce et al., 1983).

HIGH SCHOOL GRADUATION. Four of the programs in the Consortium had follow-ups sufficiently long to permit assessment of rates of high school graduation (Beller, 1983; Gray et al., 1983; Karnes et al., 1983; Schweinhart & Weikart, 1983). In each of them, program participants were more likely to complete high school than were controls, and the pooled result was statistically significant (65% vs. 53% for program and control groups, respectively). The group difference was statistically significant only for the Perry Preschool Program (and only for female participants in the Perry Preschool Program; Schweinhart & Weikart, 1983), but for the remaining three, the magnitude of the program effect was substantial and educationally meaningful. Follow-up data from three Consortium projects with samples between the ages of 19 and 22 indicated no direct effects of preschool education on measures of labor market participation (e.g., employment and unemployment rates, earnings, type of job) within projects or when results were pooled across projects. However, preschool education indirectly and positively affected employment status by increasing school competence (never placed in special classes nor retained in grade), positive attitudes toward achievement, and rates of high school completion.

MEDIATING PROCESSES. Pooled analyses across six Consortium programs indicated that the effect of preschool education on grade retention, rather than being direct, was mediated through increased IQ scores at age 6. However, preschool education affected placement in special education through two pathways, one independent of IQ score and one mediated through increased IQ scores at age 6. These findings led Lazar and his colleagues (Lazar, Darlington, Murray, Royce, & Snipper, 1982) to conclude that "early education apparently affected children beyond teaching them the concepts and skills measured by intelligence tests yet in ways that were related to school performance" (p. 39). Similar direct and mediated effects were found for the composite variable of met versus did not meet school's requirements (never placed in special classes nor retained in grade), though the mediated effect was only marginally significant.

Lazar et al. (1982) identified three components of IQ test scores that preschool education may have enhanced: (a) developed cognitive abilities; (b) motivation, attitudes, and behavior of the child relevant for both successful test taking and successful learning (e.g., attentiveness to adults, task orientation, persistence); and (c) prior experience with the types of questions used in the test (e.g., "coaching"). They were unable to statistically disaggregate these components, but pointed to two findings suggestive of a genuine increase in the first two components. First, the effect of preschool intervention on IQ scores lasted for up to three or four years, considerably longer than would be expected from "coaching" or training children during the intervention to take IQ tests. Second, the Consortium programs increased children's performance on achievement tests, which arguably reflects a combination of developed cognitive abilities, achievement motivation, and attitudes about learning. On the other hand, they acknowledge the possibility that first-grade teachers may have resisted placing program children in special education because of a temporarily inflated IQ score.

Lazar et al. (1982) also hypothesized that positive effects on school progress not mediated by IQ test scores were due to enhancement of several noncognitive variables such as children's self-esteem, classroom behaviors, and attitudes toward teachers, along with mothers' parenting skills, expectations for their children, self-confidence, and ability to work effectively with teachers and other professionals. Data from individual projects in the Consortium were suggestive of some of these processes, but too few projects measured these hypothetical intervening variables to permit rigorous tests of mediation across studies. These researchers also presented compelling analyses that appeared to rule out some competing interpretations of noncognitive pathways, among them, that teachers in public schools may have been more reluctant to place children in special education classes who were known to have attended preschool. If this process operated, they argued, the difference in school progress between program and control groups should have been greatest after grade 1 or 2 and declined thereafter. To the contrary, the difference between the two groups increased as children progressed through the grades and, indeed, did not become statistically significant until grade 7.

The Consortium's findings were pivotal in stoking policymakers' enthusiasm for early childhood intervention and ensuring continued and incremental funding of Head Start. Condry and Lazar (1982) attribute the Consortium's impact on social policy to three factors: (a) positive and robust findings that concerned specific outcomes the interventions were intended to influence (e.g., placement in special education classes, grade retention, high school graduation) and whose importance and validity were easily understood; (b) cost-benefit analyses of one of the Consortium programs, the Perry Preschool Project, demonstrating a significant return on the original investment of public dollars (Weber, Foster, & Weikart, 1978); and (c) rapid, broad dissemination of the findings to policymakers. The Consortium's findings were disseminated in policy circles as early as 1977, but did not appear in academic publications until the 1980s (Consortium for Longitudinal Studies, 1983; Darlington, Royce, Snipper, Murray, & Lazar, 1980; Lazar et al., 1982).

Evaluations of Long-Term Effects of Individual Model Programs. Further buttressing Head Start's favored status was additional evidence of long-term positive effects of model programs released after the Consortium's major reports. Some resulted from additional follow-ups of programs in the Consortium, such as the Perry Preschool Project (Berrueta-Clement et al., 1984). Other highly influential findings were based on programs not in the Consortium, such as the Carolina Abecedarian Project (Campbell & Ramey, 1994, 1995).

ACADEMIC ACHIEVEMENT. The Carolina Abecedarian Project stands out for the longevity and consistency of preschool treatment effects on academic achievement. At the age 8 follow-up, age 12 follow-up, and age 15 follow-up, program children scored significantly higher than controls on numerous measures of academic achievement and cognitive functioning (e.g., reading, mathematics, language, and knowledge subtests of the Woodcock-Johnson achievement test), controlling for maternal IQ. Program-treatment differences at the latter two follow-ups, however, were not as large as those evident at the age 8 follow-up (Campbell & Ramey, 1994, 1995).

LABOR MARKET SUCCESS AND USE OF PUBLIC WELFARE. In contrast to the findings from the Consortium's pooled analyses, Schweinhart et al. (1993) found at the age 27 follow-up that the Perry Preschool Program had a direct and positive effect on program participants' success in the labor market. Self-report data on annual earnings and employment status indicated that program females earned significantly more than their control group counterparts ($14,308 vs. $8,620, respectively, in 1992 dollars) because they were more likely to be employed (80% vs. 55%, respectively) and achieved substantially higher levels of educational attainment. Males in the two groups attained about the same highest year of education and had equivalent employment rates at roughly age 27 (63% vs. 62%, respectively), but program males had a small advantage over control males in annual earnings ($16,397 vs. $16,064, respectively). Schweinhart et al. speculated that the latter difference may be attributable to differences in the quality of education attained by the two groups, including differences in the acquisition of knowledge, skills, and attitudes. In light of the findings from the Consortium's pooled analysis and the absence of other data that corroborate Schweinhart et al.'s findings, it seems reasonable to conclude that preschool education has weak if any direct effects on employment and earnings, especially males.

Data on the effects of preschool intervention on use of public welfare assistance are sparse and conflicting. Gray, Ramsey, and Klaus (cited in Haskins, 1989) reported that at age 21, a slightly *smaller* percentage of program participants was supported by nongovernmental sources (i.e., themselves, their spouse, their parents), compared to individuals in two control groups. This suggests that program participants were not less likely than controls to depend on public welfare. In contrast, the age 27 follow-up of the Perry Preschool sample (Schweinhart et al., 1993) found reductions in the use of public welfare among participants as indicated by public welfare records and self-reports. However, the magnitude of these reductions depended on individuals' sex and the time period in question. Program males were significantly less likely than controls to have received any governmental welfare assistance (e.g., AFDC, food stamps, General Assistance, public housing) during the previous 10 years (52% vs. 77%). However, the two groups did not differ in the number of months on welfare during the previous 10 years or the percentage currently receiving welfare assistance (7% vs. 16%).

A different pattern emerged for females. Compared to control females, program females were less likely to have received welfare assistance during the previous 10 years (85% vs. 68%, respectively) and had been on welfare for fewer months than control females during the previous 10 years, but neither of these differences was statistically significant. Assessments of types of welfare assistance received in the previous 5 years revealed even smaller differences between the two groups. However, at the time of the age 27 interview, program females were significantly less likely than controls to be receiving public welfare assistance (26% vs. 59%; Schweinhart et al., 1993).

ADOLESCENT PARENTHOOD. In addition to school and labor market success, policy analysts have been keenly interested in whether preschool education reduces adolescent parenthood, especially among females. Adolescent mothers are more likely to drop out of high school than teenagers of similar SES background and similar academic aptitude who postpone childbearing. This educational deficit impedes adolescent mothers' ability to secure stable and remunerative employment and increases the likelihood of reliance on public welfare, compared to women who begin childbearing later in life (Furstenberg, Brooks-Gunn, & Chase-Lansdale, 1989). Both Schweinhart et al. (1993) and S. Gray et al. (1983) collected relevant data and neither found significant effects. At the age 19 interview, Perry Preschool participants did not differ noticeably from controls in their rates of adolescent parenthood (44% vs. 58%, respectively, for females; 18% vs. 26%, respectively for males). Likewise, S. Gray et al. found no difference in the percentage of females in the program versus control group who bore children as adolescents.

Although preschool intervention apparently does not inhibit adolescent parenthood, it appears to make a marked difference in terms of whether teenage motherhood proves an obstacle to completion of secondary education. Among adolescent mothers in S. Gray et al.'s (1983) study, those in the preschool intervention group were significantly more likely than controls to complete high school. Similarly, Schweinhart et al. (1993) found that of those females in the Perry Preschool study who became mothers during adolescence (19 years or younger), 73% (8 of 11) of program participants graduated from high school or the equivalent, whereas only 17% (2 of 12) of controls did so. Regardless of preschool experience, the overwhelming majority of adolescent mothers who were neither assigned to special education nor retained in grade graduated from high school or the equivalent (73%), whereas only a minority of adolescent mothers who were assigned to special education or retained in grade did so (14%). It appears, then, that one mechanism by which preschool intervention increases high school graduation among adolescent mothers is through reducing the likelihood of grade retention and placement in special education (Schweinhart et al., 1993).

Congruencies between Policy and Evaluation Findings. It is clear that Head Start is not so potent as to boost enrollees' school readiness and academic competence to the level of poor children who attend non–Head Start preschools, to the level of nonpoor children, or to parity with national norms. However, it is equally clear that Head Start significantly enhances children's school readiness and that the degree of this enhancement has been underestimated due to selection bias. This argues in favor of continuing federal support for preschool education programs for poor children. That Head Start's basic model has remained largely intact over the years is due in some measure to the fact that numerous researchers have looked for, but not found, strong, consistent evidence that program, child, or family characteristics moderate to any significant degree the long-term impact of model or large-scale preschool interventions. Across both Head Start and model programs, program characteristics (e.g., curricular/training model, age of entry) generally do not predict differential effects, nor do certain subgroups of poor children (e.g., those living in single-parent vs. two-parent families) appear to benefit more from preschool attendance than others (McKey et al., 1985; Royce et al., 1983; K. White, 1985/1986).

Duration of intervention is a program characteristic that has evoked considerable interest among policy analysts and interventionists, particularly the question of whether a second year of preschool intervention confers advantages beyond a single year. Advocacy for an additional year of preschool has increased in recent years, on the grounds that it will improve both short-term and long-term effectiveness of interventions (i.e., preventing or attenuating the fading of positive effects) and help counteract the increasingly harsh and corrosive nature of poverty (Chafel, 1992; Lee et al., 1988; Reynolds, 1995; Zigler & Styfco, 1994b).

A few studies of model programs have found higher levels of academic performance during elementary and high school (e.g., school grades, teacher evaluations, lower rates of grade retention) among children who experienced two years (either two years of preschool or one year of preschool and one year of kindergarten) versus one year of intervention prior to first grade, but effects tend to be small or statistically nonsignificant (e.g., Beller, 1983; Levenstein et al., 1983). This pattern also characterizes results from studies of large-scale public programs. For example, two-year participants in the Chicago Child-Parent Center were found by Reynolds (1995) to be more academically competent (e.g., at listening skills, vocabulary, reading readiness, math skills) than one-year participants at the beginning and end of kindergarten. However, during the elementary grades (grades 1–6), differences between the two groups in reading comprehension, mathematics achievement, teacher ratings of social adjustment, and rates of grade retention and special education placement, although consistently favoring the two-year group, were generally not statistically significant or educationally meaningful. Similarly, in an evaluation of the effects of Head Start and Learning to Learn, a cognitive-developmental preschool intervention that emphasized both free-choice play and small-group instruction designed to teach problem-solving strategies, Sprigle and Schaefer (1985) reported no differences in GPA, grade retention, or special education placement during fourth through sixth grade between children who, prior to first grade, participated in the program for two years (preschool and kindergarten) versus one year (kindergarten). Some studies even fail to find immediate positive effects of two years versus one year of preschool on academic readiness (e.g., Gullo & Burton, 1992).

Taken together, studies of model and large-scale programs for poor children, as well as programs serving a more economically diverse sample of children, yield no robust, definitive evidence of benefits bestowed by two years versus one year of preschool at ages 3 and 4 (S. Gray et al., 1983; Gullo & Burton, 1992; Reynolds, 1995; Schweinhart & Weikart, 1988; Sprigle & Schaefer, 1985). Most studies confound duration of intervention exposure and age of entry, but disentangling these factors does not boost the unique effect of two years of intervention as compared to one (Reynolds, 1995). A second year of preschool intervention may reinforce the school readiness skills that children have learned during the first year, but its unique contribution to the acquisition of academic skills is modest at best and decidedly less than that of the first year (Reynolds, 1995).

These findings are consonant with the prevailing practice of providing one rather than two years of Head Start for most children who participate in the program. However, so intuitively appealing is the rationale for a second year of preschool that advocacy for this change seems to prevail despite the absence of strong empirical evidence of beneficial effects. For example, Schweinhart et al. (1993) recommended two years of preschool education beginning when children are 3 years of age, although they concluded that the 13 children who attended the Perry Preschool program for only one school year experienced "essentially the same effects" (p. 234) as the 45 children who attended the program for two school years. Research findings provide a much stronger case for advocating one year of publicly funded preschool intervention for *all* poor children in lieu of two years of such services for a small minority of poor children. At the same time, radical expansion of the scale of service programs can increase the difficulty of delivering high-quality services due to insufficient flexibility in program features and implementation to meet the needs of diverse populations, limited human resources due to insufficient hiring, inadequate training and supervision of staff, and poor quality-control procedures (Schorr, 1989). A recent example of aspects of this problem occurred during the 1980s when expansion of the Head Start program outpaced grantees' ability to provide comprehensive services. This resulted in checkered delivery of health services to Head Start children and inadequate supportive services to families of Head Start children (Kassebaum,

1994). Effective expansion of programs clearly requires planful strategies that minimize these problems. This is a matter of some urgency in the case of Head Start, as it is scheduled for a major expansion by 1998 to serve over 60% of eligible children, compared to the 30% of eligible children currently served (Kassebaum, 1994; Takanishi & DeLeon, 1994).

Paradoxically, although two years of preschool may not be markedly more advantageous than one year of preschool in increasing poor children's cognitive functioning and school achievement, comparisons of treatment effects between and within studies suggest that programs of even longer duration may be optimal (Fuerst & Fuerst, 1993; Madden, Slavin, Karweit, Dolan, & Wasik, 1993; Reynolds, 1995). We turn to this issue next.

Evaluation Findings in Search of Policies

BENEFITS OF LONGER, MORE INTENSE INTERVENTION. Some of the model programs with the largest or most enduring effects on these outcomes have begun educational intervention during the first two years of life and continued at least until children entered kindergarten (Campbell & Ramey, 1995; Garber, 1988; Ramey, Ramey, Gaines, & Blair, 1995; Wasik, Ramey, Bryant, & Sparling, 1990). Additionally, those that are full-day and operate five days per week year-round generally produce larger and more enduring positive effects on children's cognitive and academic functioning than less intensive programs (Campbell & Ramey, 1995; Hauser-Cram, Pierson, Walker, & Tivnan, 1991; Ramey et al., 1995; S. Smith & Zaslow, 1995; Wasik et al., 1990). Such findings argue for increasing the intensity as well as duration of Head Start, in particular, making it a full-day rather than a half-day program, five days per week year-round and implementing a birth-to-3 Head Start (Zigler, 1994).

Other justifications for increasing the intensity and duration of Head Start include child care needs created by welfare reform and the paucity of regulated, high-quality child care. As others have noted, in the wake of the Family Support Act and JOBS program that require welfare recipients to work or receive training, many poor children who could benefit from Head Start will not be able to attend because full-day care is needed. Many, if not most, mothers participating in welfare reform programs are likely to place their children in informal, unregulated child care that, in general, tends to be of lower quality than that provided in Head Start centers (Zigler, 1994).

Rather than extending Head Start downward to children under 3, others have argued for a continuation of intervention services into the primary grades on the grounds that Head Start's positive effects would be less likely to fade. This rationale led to the creation of Follow Through in 1967. Despite original intentions, Follow Through never became a national program, and initial emphasis on comprehensive services has been supplanted with a primary focus on innovative curricula. In the early 1990s, it operated in only 40 schools, and few evaluations of its effectiveness exist (Zigler & Muenchow, 1992). A recent study of poor children who participated in preschool and follow-on interventions suggests that longer education intervention will benefit children academically and that it is of little consequence whether the additional years of intervention occur during preschool or primary school. Reynolds (1994) assessed the effects of center- and school-based follow-on services offered as part of the Child-Parent Center Program (CPC), a large-scale, federally funded program similar to Head Start and Follow Through. A particularly strong feature of the study is its assessment of the independent effects of age of entry and duration of intervention exposure, factors that are confounded in most studies.

Distinctive features of the follow-on (primary grades 1–3) components of the CPC included (a) reduced class size (an average class size of 25 with an adult: child ratio of approximately 1:12, compared to an average class size of 30 in non-follow-on classes); (b) parental involvement activities; (c) a highly individualized, child-centered focus on the acquisition of reading comprehension and writing skills; (d) other educational services (e.g., teacher aide for each class, school-community representative, home visits); and (e) services to meet children's nutritional and health needs. Six intervention groups were formed reflecting differences in the duration and timing of intervention, with the full intervention lasting five to six years (preschool, kindergarten, and grades 1–3). Also included was a non-CPC comparison group that did not participate in the preschool, kindergarten, or primary grade intervention programs but did enroll in a locally developed all-day kindergarten program for children at risk. For this reason, the study's findings may constitute a conservative test of the effects of the CPC program. Intervention groups were not under experimental control (no random assignment).

Findings indicated a four-year threshold effect. At the end of the program (grade 3) and at the two-year follow-up (grade 5), children who had participated in the intervention for four or more years had significantly higher math and reading achievement and a significantly lower rate of grade retention than children with fewer than four years of intervention. At grade 5, follow-on intervention bolstered children's scholastic achievement above the levels observed for participation in only preschool and kindergarten intervention. Although preschool intervention contributed uniquely to the cumulative effect of intervention, it bestowed no particular advantage over primary grade intervention. Children who participated in only the preschool and kindergarten components performed no better than children who participated in only the follow-on component. Findings for grade retention were somewhat less clear-cut, but in general supported the value of both preschool and follow-on intervention. Differential exposure to intervention was unrelated to placement in special education. In sum, this study suggests that intervention has markedly stronger effects if it spans four or more years, irrespective of its timing (preschool vs. primary grades). Further, it underscores the persistent effects of poverty on children's achievement despite educational interventions. The average reading and mathematics achievement scores of the non-retained full intervention group approximated the 30th percentile, one full year below the national mean for fifth-graders.

Other studies have found no positive, unique effect of follow-on intervention, but they may not be especially relevant because of weak methodology or the nature of the intervention. Abelson, Zigler, and DeBlasi (1974) found that third-graders who participated in both Head Start and Follow Through were superior to combined groups of non-Follow Through children on Peabody Picture Vocabulary Test (PPVT) scores, achievement, and curiosity, but Follow Through made no unique contribution to these outcomes when the effects of Head Start were controlled. The negative findings may be due to the small sample and the reduced statistical power to detect differences among groups. Ramey and his colleagues (Campbell & Ramey, 1995; Horacek et al., 1987) also found no significant effects of follow-on services, but this is probably attributable to their modest, parent-mediated nature. Their study assessed the effects of follow-on services as part of a project explicitly designed to compare outcomes in students who experienced preschool versus school-age intervention (public kindergarten through grade 2).

Children were randomly assigned to four educational intervention groups: (a) preschool treatment only (infancy to 5 years); (b) preschool treatment followed by school-age treatment (infancy to 8 years); (c) school-age treatment only (5 years to 8 years); and (d) no preschool or school-age treatment (controls). The Abecedarian Preschool Project described previously constituted the preschool treatment. The school-age treatment was designed to support children's academic development by increasing and enhancing parent involvement in the child's schooling. Families receiving this treatment were assigned a home/school resource teacher (HST) who every other week provided parents with home curriculum activities individually designed for each child to reinforce the reading and mathematics concepts being taught at school. Parents were urged to use these activities for at least 15 minutes each day (the overwhelming majority reported completing the follow-on activities with their children, but there is no way of knowing whether they actually did so). The HST visited the classroom on alternate weeks to acquire information from the classroom teacher about concepts and skills being taught and to consult about the child's adjustment to school. Other duties of the HST included helping families with non-school-related problems (e.g., housing, health, employment) that might compromise their ability to support the children's learning (e.g., referrals to relevant agencies, providing transportation) and advocating for the school within the family and for the child and family within the school.

At the end of the program (age 8), children participating in the preschool intervention followed by the school-age intervention had the lowest rate of retention and the highest level of reading and mathematics achievement. However, the school-age intervention had no independent effect on grade retention or achievement (Horacek et al., 1987). At age 15, seven to ten years after any treatment was provided, the findings were largely consistent with those at age 8. Unlike preschool intervention, school-age intervention made no unique contribution to IQ test scores, mathematics achievement, or grade retention. It had a modest, positive impact on reading achievement only when paired with preschool intervention (Campbell & Ramey, 1995).

The CPC follow-on intervention assessed by Reynolds (1994) may have had a positive effect because it resulted in marked changes in the child's school environment, unlike the home-based follow-on intervention conducted by Ramey and his colleagues (Campbell & Ramey, 1995; Horacek et al., 1987). Alternatively, parents who sought CPC follow-on services may have been different from parents who did not, whereas such selection bias presumably would have been eliminated in Ramey et al.'s project through random assignment. Nonetheless, a number of studies are consistent with Reynolds in reporting positive effects on school progress and achievement of multiple years of education intervention that encompass preschool, kindergarten, and several years of grade school (e.g., Fuerst & Fuerst, 1993; Madden et al., 1993; Meyer, 1984), though they do not clarify the relative contributions of preschool versus follow-on intervention (kindergarten and grade school) to these outcomes. A tentative conclusion that seems warranted from the few existing studies is that direct delivery of educational services to the child and significant changes in the child's learning environment, especially in the school context, are prerequisites for effective follow-on interventions (Barnett, 1995).

ATTENUATED GAINS AMONG AFRICAN AMERICAN BOYS. Sex of the child is a possible exception to the generalization that early educational interventions of the type implemented and assessed in previous studies do not benefit any particular kinds of children more than others (Barnett, 1995). A conspicuous number of higher-quality studies of model programs serving African American children report stronger intervention and follow-on effects on girls' school competence, school progress, and socioemotional functioning than boys', although program by sex interactions have not necessarily been statistically significant. These studies also suggest that sex is a more probable moderator of long-term rather than immediate effects, with sex differences becoming progressively larger over time in some instances (Beller, 1983; S. Gray et al., 1983; Lally, Mangione, & Honig, 1988; Schweinhart et al., 1993; Seitz, Apfel, Rosenbaum, & Zigler, 1983).

Selected examples of these sex differences are presented here. The Perry Preschool Program produced significantly higher levels of schooling and rates of high school graduation and reduced retention rates and number of years in special education among program girls, compared to control group girls. In contrast, none of these treatment-control differences was significant for boys, even though boys either matched or outscored girls on tests of intellectual functioning (but not on tests of school achievement) throughout the elementary school years, regardless of preschool experience (Schweinhart et al., 1993). In essence, boys brought equivalent and, in some instances, superior intellectual abilities to their schooling, but benefited substantially less from schooling than did girls. Lally et al.'s (1988) findings are equally striking in that virtually all of the long-term salutary effects on school achievement and socioemotional functioning were limited to girls. In a similar vein, the impact of S. Gray et al.'s (1983) preschool intervention on GPA, grade retention, personal-social adjustment, and educational and occupational orientation was more pronounced for girls than boys. Differential effects as a function of children's sex also have been found in large-scale early education interventions. The CPC Program in Chicago had much stronger positive effects on the high school graduation rate of females than males, although there were few sex differences among the program group during the course of the intervention (Fuerst & Fuerst, 1993).

Researchers have offered several explanations for these differences, but ascertaining which ones are most credible is difficult because no longitudinal studies exist that track the school, family, and broader social experiences of boys and girls in relation to the preschool experience. Some educational interventions may exert less positive impact on boys than girls because they are less inherently meaningful and responsive to boys than girls (e.g., program curricula, materials, activities, availability of salient or same-sex role models). This explanation is dubious because sex differences in immediate effects typically are not found. Explanations centering around postpreschool factors appear more plausible. A combination of gender and racial stereotypes may condition teachers and school staff to more readily ignore or to respond less positively to improvement in school competence among African American boys. Attention may be directed toward boys' conduct at the expense of their academic competence (Schweinhart et al., 1993). Perhaps poor African American boys, compared to their female counterparts, confront more barriers to academic achievement and/or barriers that are more impervious to preschool intervention. Gender-specific barriers may include an indifferent if not hostile school climate, peer pressure against school achievement, belief that academic competence is not masculine, low expectations of achievement among parents and teachers, and early school failure (Hare & Castenell, 1985; Kunjufu, 1986; Majors & Billson, 1992; Seitz et al., 1983). The conditions and underlying processes that encourage divergence between boys and girls in their long-term response to preschool education are among the most intriguing issues in the vast literature on preschool intervention. Moreover, given the increasingly bleak status of a substantial portion of the African American male population (Gibbs, 1988), few issues are more deserving of systematic study.

Conflicting Findings and Unresolved Issues

RACE AS A MODERATING VARIABLE. Two recent studies of the effects of Head Start, both distinguished by a number of methodological strengths, raise the possibility of race as a determinant of both the short-term and long-term effects of Head Start. As previously discussed, the ETS study found that Head Start produced significant gains in the cognitive functioning and school readiness of African American children, but not White children. Head Start's differential effectiveness for the two groups may reflect lack of statistical power to detect an effect among White children. (Of 414 Head Start enrollees in the study, only 55 were White, whereas 359 were African American.) It also may be due to race differences in cognitive functioning and school readiness at the point of preintervention. In general, children who started out lowest gained the most. African American children were more likely to be big gainers than White children because they were relatively more disadvantaged demographically and scored significantly lower on all four measures in the preintervention year (Lee et al., 1988).

In contrast to the ETS findings, Currie and Thomas's (1995) analysis of data from the National Longitudinal Study of Youth (NLSY) child sample revealed no race differences in the initial gains from Head Start. However, significant race disparities were found in the rate at which gains dissipated. White children retained the benefits of Head Start on the PPVT much longer than did African American children. By age 10, African American children had lost any gains on the PPVT derived from Head Start, whereas 10-year-old White Head Start enrollees retained a gain of 5 percentile points. The rate at which the cognitive benefits of Head Start dissipated among African American children did not depend on maternal IQ, construed by the investigators as a proxy for quality of the home environment. At first glance, one might be inclined to attribute this difference to race disparities in the cultural appropriateness of the PPVT, which may be especially manifest when African American children are no longer in intervention programs devoted to "cultural mainstreaming." However, Currie and Thomas also found race differences in the impact of Head Start on grade retention. Whereas Head Start reduced the probability of grade retention among White children by 47%, compared to their siblings who did not attend preschool, it was unrelated to grade retention among African American children. At least part of the race difference in rate of dissipation may reflect differences in the quality of schools that African American and White children attended once they left Head Start. Curiously, no evidence of a similar race effect in the dissipation of positive effects was found among children who attended non–Head Start preschools.

Currie and Thomas's (1995) provocative findings contrast sharply with other reports of long-term positive effects of large-scale preschool intervention programs on African American children (e.g., Reynolds, 1994). What explains this discrepancy is unclear, but it is notable that unlike most studies of preschool effects, Currie and Thomas used siblings (rather than nonsiblings) of Head Start enrollees who had not attended Head Start as a comparison group and as an explicit strategy to control for family background effects on cognitive outcomes. Their investigation and the ETS study (Lee et al., 1988) raise but do not resolve the question of whether race moderates the immediate and long-term effects of preschool intervention. Studies of model programs do not illuminate this issue because most samples have not included sufficient numbers of White children to permit assessment of race X intervention effects.

MAIN EFFECTS OF PRESCHOOL INTERVENTION ON WHITES AND OTHER ETHNIC GROUPS. The discussion about race as a moderator of preschool effects points up a related gap in the research literature, namely, inadequate study of the impact of preschool education on poor White children and children from other ethnic groups. Studies of preschool effects reveal a preoccupation with African American children (Barnett, 1995). African American children are greatly overrepresented in the population of poor children, but the fact remains that poor White children vastly outnumber poor African American children in an absolute sense. Over the course of Head Start's existence, African American children have comprised from about one-third to two-fifths of its enrollment and Latino children from about one-fifth to one-fourth (National Center for Education Statistics, 1995; Washington & Oyemade, 1987). Historically, a large percentage of the early growth of Head Start centers occurred in poor, African American communities. Taking account of their rates of enrollment, however, African American children are overrepresented in studies of Head Start effects, and White and Latino children are underrepresented. All of the children in studies of the effects of the Chicago CPC program were African American, but this was representative of the population served by the program (Reynolds, 1994, 1995).

More intriguing is the fact that, with the exception of a few studies of preschool programs that targeted Latino children (Andrews et al., 1982; Johnson & Breckenridge, 1982), model programs have focused almost exclusively on African American children. African American children comprised 94% of the original samples of studies of the 11 projects in the Consortium of Longitudinal Studies and the overwhelming majority of participants in most studies of model projects not part of the Consortium (e.g., Campbell & Ramey, 1995). Investigators emphasize pragmatic factors as explanations for their primary focus on African American children. S. Gray and Klaus (1965), for example, noted that racial segregation made it impractical to work with both African American and White children. They based their decision to focus the Early Training Project on African American children on the expectation that these children, for reasons unspecified, would be more responsive to the program than White children.

Other researchers, despite considerable effort, found it difficult to recruit and retain poor White families in what were intended to be racially integrated interventions (Birmingham Parent-Child Development Center [PCDC]; Andrews et al., 1982; Jester & Guinagh, 1983; Lally et al., 1988). In at least one instance, this difficulty ostensibly was linked to White families' discomfort with being part of a "poverty" program (Jester & Guinagh, 1983). The Perry Preschool Project as originally conceived was to focus on a racially diverse group of children, but funding considerations required simplification of the research design. This was achieved by limiting the study to one racial group, African Americans being chosen because of their disproportionately high rates of poverty and school problems (Schweinhart et al., 1993). Other investigators assert that ethnicity was irrelevant as a selection criterion, attributing the exclusive focus on African American children solely to the confounding of ethnicity and poverty status in the local area (e.g., Campbell & Ramey, 1995; Levenstein et al., 1983).

In addition to the pragmatic issues cited by individual investigators, other factors that probably contributed to this strong bias were poor African Americans' geographic concentration and comparative visibility. Another probable contributing factor was the race-related political and social currents reverberating throughout U.S. society during the period when most of these programs were initiated. The 1960s were marked by a wave of protests against long-standing, blatant racial discrimination, various institutional responses to these protests (including increased federal funding for research on African Americans), and the appearance of a multitude of scholarly writings that attributed a "culture of poverty" to African Americans (McLoyd & Randolph, 1985; J. Patterson, 1981). It is inconceivable that these factors exerted no influence on researchers' decisions to target African American children and their families as participants in programs begun during the 1960s.

Whatever its underlying cause, this bias has had at least two unfortunate consequences. First, we know little about the utility of Head Start and preschool education generally to poor White children. Both the Currie and Thomas (1995) study and the ETS evaluation raise cautions against generalizing findings based on African American children to White children. Second, it feeds the stereotype of African Americans as invariably poor and economically dependent, while furthering the tendency of child developmental researchers to ignore poor White children.

Parents and the Home Environment as Determinants of Development

A second major assumption that undergirds antipoverty programs is that parents and the home environment they afford exert major influences on the course of children's development. During the 1960s, rapid growth in research evidence lending support to this assumption, along with other forces, propelled interest in parent education as a form and a major component of early childhood intervention (Clarke-Stewart & Apfel, 1978; D. Powell, 1988). Parent education programs and, to a lesser extent, opportunities for parent involvement in early education interventions were conceived as strategies to alter poor children's outcomes indirectly by increasing parents' knowledge of the principles of child development and, ultimately, modifying parental behavior.

Like interventions that focus directly on children, parent education as an indirect strategy to influence children's development has a long history in America. During the early and late 1800s, surges in the provision and partaking of parent education were precipitated by discovery of corruption and unethical behavior among public officials and the belief that such behavior was evidence that American children were not being raised properly. The periods of moral crises and self-scrutiny that followed spawned wide dissemination of pamphlets, magazines, and sermons on child rearing (Fein, 1980). "Maternal Associations" for mothers interested in child rearing were formed as early as 1820, with the first publication for mothers, *Mother's Magazine,* appearing in 1832 (Wishy, 1972). Interest in parent education waned by 1850, burgeoning again in the 1880s during a period of scandal involving government officials. This time, however, parent education emerged as a movement with recognized national leadership and the imprimatur of "developmental science." Two organizations wielded considerable influence during this period: the Society for the Study of Child Nature, formed in 1888, and the National Congress of Mothers (later known as the Parent-Teacher Association), established in 1897 as the first national organization devoted to parent education and the upgrade of child-care practices. The National Congress was dominated by themes of self-improvement and mutual support and appealed primarily to middle-class mothers raising children in households that were increasingly isolated and nuclear (Fein, 1980). Following the lead of its intellectual patron saint, G. Stanley Hall, the most prominent psychologist of the late nineteenth century, the National Congress sought to popularize knowledge about child development and the science of pedagogy and to translate this knowledge into ameliorative social programs. This mission coexisted with the organization's and Hall's view, common during the Progressive era, that human capacities are determined primarily by hereditary factors and manifested in invariant developmental sequences (Schlossman, 1976).

Poor parents were not excluded altogether from parent education programs during this historical period, but they were exceptional, rather than mainstay, participants. Settlement houses, for example, offered parent education to immigrant families with young children (Halpern, 1988). Members of the National Congress assumed a more paternalistic and condescending stance as "moral and scientific missionaries" to the poor, offering advice to poor mothers about child care and domestic management (Schlossman, 1976, p. 446). They also initiated policies that forecast America's penchant for coercive social policies and intervention programs that stigmatize poor families and reproach them for difficult circumstances. In several cities, for example, local chapters of the National Congress secured passage of laws during the early 1900s requiring that all mothers receiving welfare assistance ("mother's pension") attend parent education classes (Schlossman, 1976).

Modern Parent Education Programs for Poor Mothers

Parent education programs proliferated during the 1950s, but their clientele was almost exclusively middle class (Brim, 1959). Parent education rose to prominence again during the late 1960s and 1970s, but in ways that distinguished it from its predecessors. First, it was now a strategy that principally targeted poor families, on the grounds that enhancing parents' child-rearing skills would, in turn, improve children's ability to effect a successful transition from home to school, to benefit from schooling, and to maximize cognitive gains accrued from preschool education (Chilman, 1973; Clarke-Stewart & Apfel, 1978; D. Powell, 1988). Characterized by a focus on mothers of infants and preschoolers as primary recipients of services, parent education programs marked an evolving direction in early childhood intervention from an almost exclusive focus on children to one that gave major consideration to the roles of parents, the home environment, and parent-child interaction in poor children's development. This trend was strengthened by rising rates of single-parent households, unmarried teenage mothers, divorce, unemployment, and economic instability and increased public awareness of child abuse and neglect, all of which evoked concern that the child-nurturing capacities of American families were in decline (D. Powell, 1988).

Research-Based Antecedents. The reincarnation of parent education during the late 1960s was also different from its predecessors in that it had much deeper foundations in empirical child development research (Clarke-Stewart & Apfel, 1978). Proponents cited popular ideas such as "every child needs—and has a right to have—trained parents" (Bell, 1975, p. 272), but they relied heavily on a diverse set of research findings from child development research to support their cause (Clarke-Stewart & Apfel, 1978; D. Powell, 1988). First, the disappointing effects of Head Start found in the Westinghouse evaluation were interpreted by some advocates as evidence that prevention of cognitive deficits required intervention even before preschool and, relatedly, that the source of cognitive deficits resided somewhere in the home (Clarke-Stewart & Apfel, 1978). Second, a singular and major boost for parent training programs came from Bronfenbrenner's (1975) synthesis of findings from early education interventions, wherein he concluded that the more involved the parents, the greater and more enduring benefits in children such interventions produce. Commenting on the causative factors that underlie parent involvement's moderating influences, Bronfenbrenner noted that during the first three years of life, the parent-child system "is the major source of the forces affecting both the rate and stability of the child's development. . . . It is as if the child himself had no way of internalizing the processes which foster his growth, whereas the parent-child system does possess this capacity" (p. 566). Although Bronfenbrenner's synthesis spoke more directly to the enhanced efficacy of family-centered interventions involving parents and their children, it was viewed as support for the more narrow concept of parent education as well. What was more, data indicated that the positive effects on targeted children of interventions involving parents diffused to younger siblings (e.g., S. Gray & Klaus, 1970), making such programs highly cost-effective.

Third, proponents pointed to interview and laboratory studies documenting the relation of mothers' child-rearing practices, attitudes, and knowledge of child development to children's cognitive abilities. By the early 1970s, a panoply of such research findings was available (for a detailed review of these studies, see Clarke-Stewart & Apfel, 1978). Studies linked countless maternal and home environmental variables to perceptual, cognitive, and intellectual competence in infants and children, including level of maternal stimulation of the child (e.g., playing, talking, elaborating the child's activities), provision of appropriate play materials, opportunities for physical movement and exploration, abstractness of the mother's speech, promptness of the mother's responsiveness to the infant's distress signals, and consistent and firm discipline accompanied by frequent approval (e.g., Ainsworth, 1973; Baumrind, 1967; Becker, 1964; Beckwith, 1971; Clarke-Stewart, 1973; McCall, Appelbaum, & Hogarty, 1973; Schaefer & Emerson, 1964). Investigations also found evidence that maternal attitudes (e.g., love/hostility toward the child) and knowledge about principles of child development predicted both maternal and child behavior (e.g., Baumrind, 1971; Clarke-Stewart, 1973; Tulkin & Cohler, 1973). Yet another stream of findings relevant to child-rearing effects came from laboratory studies, whereby environmental events were controlled and manipulated (with the adult experimenter cast in the role of parent substitute; Clarke-Stewart & Apfel, 1978). These studies demonstrated the impact of social and vocal stimulation (L. Powell, 1974), reinforcement (Stevenson, 1965), punishment, and modeling on infants' and children's behavior (Feshbach & Feshbach, 1972). Also contributing to the credibility of parent training was evidence that parents' behavior could be modified by brief interventions (Clarke-Stewart & Apfel, 1978).

A fourth and critical set of studies on which advocates of parent education relied focused on social class differences in children's home and family environment (Clarke-Stewart & Apfel, 1978). One line of work documented SES differences in child-rearing practices (e.g., teaching strategies, maternal speech patterns, influence techniques) and, on the basis of parent-child correlational data or developmental theory, inferred that these differences accounted for social class variation in children's cognitive and academic functioning (e.g., Bee, Egeren, Streissguth, Nyman, & Leckie, 1969; Bernstein, 1961; Coleman et al., 1966; C. Deutsch, 1973; M. Deutsch & Brown, 1964; Hess & Shipman, 1965; Kamii & Radin, 1967). In a related program of work, poverty, low levels of maternal education, and other indicators of low social status were identified as predictors of both lower IQ in children and less cognitive stimulation in the home environment (Bradley & Caldwell, 1976; Clarke-Stewart & Apfel, 1978; C. Deutsch, 1973).

Some evidence existed that middle-class mothers, compared to lower-class mothers, tended to talk to their infants more when they were in close contact and not involved in other activities, but on the whole, SES differences in maternal as well as infant behavior tended to be negligible during the infancy period (Clarke-Stewart & Apfel, 1978). Research focused on the postinfancy period, however, reported a great number of SES differences, most favoring middle-class mothers and their children. Compared to lower-class mothers, middle-class mothers were found to be more accepting, affectionate, and egalitarian and less commanding, threatening, and punishing in their interactions with the child. They provided more verbal and cognitive stimulation and were more consistent and rewarding, and their children scored higher on tests of intelligence, problem solving, cognitive functioning, and school achievement than did children of lower-class mothers (Clarke-Stewart & Apfel, 1978).

This research continued a long tradition of work on SES as a determinant of child rearing, but its basic thrust, assumptions, and conceptual framework were different than those characterizing research conducted prior to the 1960s and after the mid-1980s. Studies undertaken during the 1940s and 1950s of social class differences in child-rearing patterns were stimulated largely by a desire to explain child and adult personality rather than cognitive and academic functioning. They tended to focus on toilet training, infant feeding, weaning, and responsibility training, and the timing, pacing, and strictness of this training (e.g., Davis, 1941; Davis & Havighurst, 1946; Maccoby, Gibbs, et al., 1954; Sears, Maccoby, & Levin, 1957), with some attention given to the use of reason, praise, deprivation of privileges, and physical punishment as disciplinary techniques (Kohn, 1959; Maccoby, Gibbs, et al., 1954; Sears et al., 1957). Moreover, several of the researchers who conducted these studies were sociologists who emphasized the compatibility of child-rearing practices with certain aspects of the social structure (e.g., characteristics and behavioral requirements of blue-collar versus white collar jobs, Kohn, 1959). In general, they were less given to pejorative and proscriptive judgment about lower-class patterns of child-rearing practices than were their intellectual successors. For example, Davis and Havighurst (1946) asserted that, "whether the middle-class or the lower-class practices are preferable is, of course, largely a matter of private opinion . . . the better childrearing practices can be drawn from both middle and lower-class life and made into a combination which is superior to both of the norms" (p. 708). In contrast, the view of lower-class patterns of child rearing painted by 1960s-era research generally was one of wholesale inadequacy (e.g., Bee et al., 1969; Hess & Shipman, 1965; Kamii & Radin, 1967).

Recent research on parenting and home environmental factors as determinants of cognitive functioning in poor children diverges from 1960s-era research in that it tends to (a) emphasize social structural rather than cultural deficiencies as causal factors in poverty, (b) focus on income poverty rather than social class, and (c) directly assess hypothesized mediational processes. In a recent investigation,

Duncan et al. (1994) found that the quality of children's home environment as measured by the HOME accounted for about one-third of the effect of family income on IQ scores, with the most potent dimension being degree of cognitive stimulation. Other studies conducted recently relate specific dimensions of poverty to home environmental quality. They indicate that the quality of children's home environment, like IQ scores, decreases as families' income-to-need ratios decline and as duration of poverty increases and, further, that improvements in family income have the strongest effects on the quality of children's home environment if children were born poor (versus not born poor) or spent more time in poverty (Dubow & Ippolito, 1994; Garrett, Ng'andu, & Ferron, 1994). These poverty-related effects remain after controlling for the effects of maternal (education, age, and academic ability), household (e.g., number of siblings, adult-to-child ratio), and child characteristics.

The culture of poverty notion that held sway during the 1960s and 1970s led inexorably to interpretations of SES differences that disparaged lower-class patterns of child rearing. These patterns were conceptualized as antecedents of retarded cognitive, linguistic, and socioemotional development and in turn as a major pathway by which poverty is perpetuated from one generation to the next. A natural extension of these arguments was the assertion that poor parents needed training for their child-rearing role more than parents from more affluent backgrounds (Baratz & Baratz, 1970; Laosa, 1984). Although Oscar Lewis's (1966) writings provided an important heuristic, direct inspiration for this line of reasoning came from Basil Bernstein (1961). His analyses and the research investigations they spawned were among the most influential antecedents of parent education programs for the poor. Briefly, Bernstein alleged that in encounters with their children, lower-class parents use a "restricted" code of communication, marked by stereotyped, limited, condensed language and use of descriptive rather than analytic concepts. This communication style, argued Bernstein, is ill suited for the development of higher-level abstract thought, resulting in lower-class children's lesser ability to learn from the environment. In contrast, middle-class parents use an "elaborated" code of communication, distinguished by a high level of differentiation and precision and use of intricate conceptual hierarchies. Consequently, reasoned Bernstein, middle-class children acquire a language that is complex, capable of communicating subtle shades of meaning, and conducive to higher-level learning.

Bernstein's thesis was prominently featured in a symposium entitled "Early Experiential Deprivation and Enrichment and Later Development" presented at the meetings of American Association for the Advancement of Science in 1964. A year later, the symposium was published in *Child Development,* a publication of the Society for Research in Child Development and the premier journal in the field of child development at the time. Two papers reported research based on humans (both focused exclusively on African Americans). One presented a study of the effectiveness of an experimental preschool intervention for poor children (S. Gray & Klaus, 1965), and the other focused on SES differences in maternal teaching strategies and their relation to children's cognitive functioning (Hess & Shipman, 1965). The symposium signaled the impending watershed of psychological and developmental studies on poor and African American children conducted from the late 1960s through the mid-1970s (McLoyd & Randolph, 1985) and heralded the beginning of the heyday of the concept of cultural deprivation.

The foundation on which 1970s-era parent education for poor mothers rested was not nearly as sound as proponents made it out to be. First, much of the research on parental effects on children's development was based on White, middle-class families. Its uncertain generalizability to poor families, and to poor African American families especially, made its use as the basis for recommending policy dubious (Clarke-Stewart & Apfel, 1978). Indeed, a few studies published during the 1970s found the association between children's cognitive functioning and maternal stimulation to be weaker in African American families than in White families. This race disparity may reflect cultural bias in assessment instruments that attenuate correlations among African Americans, but does not appear to be due to mean lower frequency of maternal stimulation in these families (Clarke-Stewart, 1973; Elardo, Bradley, & Caldwell, 1975). Conversely, studies reported that the association between children's cognitive functioning and nonmaternal environmental factors, such as teachers and schools, is stronger in African American families than in White families, raising the possibility that the major pathways through which SES influences children's cognitive functioning differs by race (for a discussion of this issue and a review of relevant studies, see Clarke-Stewart & Apfel, 1978).

Second, serious methodological biases against poor parents, similar to those existing against poor children, limited interpretation of many of the research findings and their applicability to policy. Often, SES was confounded with race and a host of other demographic variables, and poor mothers were assessed with tests normed for middle-class individuals and in settings (e.g., university laboratories) that were likely to elicit nonrepresentative or defensive behavior, all factors that exaggerate SES differences (Clarke-Stewart & Apfel, 1978; McLoyd & Randolph, 1984; Sroufe, 1970). Third, as an intervention that targeted participants principally on the basis of SES status, especially during the early stages of the movement, parent education ignored the considerable hetereogeneity that existed within lower-class parents. Typically, modal behavior of parents, like that of children, is the same at different SES levels, and heterogeneity within social class typically is greater than variation among social classes. Hence, SES is, at best, a crude proxy of presumed differences in parental behavior and home environment (Clarke-Stewart & Apfel, 1978).

As the parent education movement gained momentum, a number of programs with evaluation components began to target specific groups who were thought to be at high risk of parenting difficulties, such as pregnant adolescents, adolescent mothers, and women identified as drug users or potential child abusers (e.g., Field, Widmayer, Stringer, & Ignatoff, 1980; Gutelius, Kirsch, MacDonald, Brooks, & McErlean, 1977; Larson, 1980). In the main, though, the eligibility criterion for most programs was simply low SES. Heightened appreciation in subsequent years of the hetereogeneity within groups of poor individuals prompted basic research studies of parenting practices, home environment, and extrafamilial factors as sources of psychological resilience and academic competence, rather than problematic development, in poor, minority children (Baldwin, Baldwin, & Cole, 1990; Clark, 1983; Jarrett, 1995; Werner & Smith, 1982).

Evaluations of the Efficacy of Parent Education Programs. Most parent education programs initiated during the 1970s emphasized enhancing children's cognitive performance, especially IQ scores, and, more recently, children's literacy skills, although some also aimed to prevent children from developing emotional disorders (Chilman, 1973; Clarke-Stewart & Apfel, 1978; Morley, Dornbusch, & Seer, 1993; Olds & Kitzman, 1993). Diverse strategies have been employed to achieve these goals, as reflected in the vast array of dimensions on which parent education and training programs differ. These dimensions include focus (parent-child dyad vs. parent alone), method of instruction (one-to-one vs. group discussion, toy demonstration and modeling), setting (home vs. center-based), frequency of contact, duration of the program, existence of a predetermined curriculum, and staff credentials (e.g., professional vs. paraprofessionals), among other factors (D. Powell, 1982). Content may include information about various milestones in child development, physical and emotional development, and parenting techniques. Children range in age from young infants to 5-year-olds, though more emphasis is given to the first three years of life. A large number of programs with an evaluation component have focused on African American mothers (e.g., Morley et al., 1993; Olds & Kitzman, 1993).

The vast majority of parent education and training programs do not include an evaluation component. Among those that do, a variety of methodological problems exist that make it difficult to assess their effects and to determine which aspects or kinds of programs are most effective. In their detailed review of these programs, Clarke-Stewart and Apfel (1978) found that most evaluations utilized a pre-post design with no randomly assigned control group. Moreover, the advantages of a true random control group are likely lost in some studies because control and experimental groups live in close proximity and the curriculum may be diffused from program mothers and children to control mothers and children. Other common threats to the validity of evaluations of these programs include repeated testing of children with the same instrument, use of unstandardized and culturally biased measures and measures with unknown psychometric properties, and subject attrition. Few evaluations have included long-term follow-ups or gone beyond demonstrating the overall effectiveness of the program to systematically investigate either processes through which change is effected or factors that moderate overall effectiveness.

Finally, the overwhelming diversity among parent education programs makes it hazardous to compare effects across programs and sites. As we discuss in the next section of the chapter, over the past two decades or so, parent education increasingly was offered as a component of more omnibus intervention programs. In terms of assessment, the thorny problem this creates is sorting out the unique effects of parent education per se from other program components, such as parent support and social services, because these multifaceted programs invariably are not structured to set apart the impact of the parent education component. Some of the largest and best-evaluated interventions are of this nature, such as the Parent-Child Development Centers (Clarke-Stewart & Apfel, 1978; Morley et al., 1993; D. Powell, 1982). On the other hand, some scholars argue that efforts to dissect multifaceted programs into their constituents are misdirected because it is the sum of the parts and the synergistic processes operating among program components that often account for their demonstrated success (Olds & Kitzman, 1990; Schorr, 1989).

Effects on Children. Despite these limitations, existing research supports the general conclusion that well-administered parent education programs produce immediate effects on children's cognitive functioning (for detailed reviews of these studies, see Clarke-Stewart & Apfel, 1978; Halpern, 1990b; Morley et al., 1993). Most programs report moderate IQ gains among program children compared to control children; these gains are usually maintained for one or two years and then gradually fade. In a recent meta-analysis of the effects of 13 programs that offered parent education either alone or in combination with other intervention services to mothers/parents of children under 3 years of age, Morley et al. (1993) found an overall positive though modest effect on children's cognitive development (e.g., performance on Bayley Mental Development Index) that tended to persist for a year or so. Analysis of the effects of parent education alone, unmixed with other interventions, yielded similar findings. Lazar et al. (cited in D. Powell, 1982), synthesizing evidence from several studies of programs in the Consortium for Longitudinal Studies, also concluded that parent education programs are modestly effective in reducing grade retention and placement in remedial classes during elementary school. In general, though, interventions that rely solely on parent-mediated routes to increase children's competencies (e.g., parent education that involves only the parent) produce less positive and enduring effects on children's cognitive development than interventions that provide direct learning experiences to children (Ramey et al., 1995; Wasik et al., 1990).

Considerably less consensus exists about the degree to which the effectiveness of parent education programs on children's development is moderated by program characteristics such as duration, intensity, location, format, focal child's age at inception of the intervention, and curriculum content. It is difficult to assess the independent contribution of these program characteristics because they tend to be confounded within and across programs. Several studies have found no difference in the effects of programs lasting one versus two years, or two versus three years, but when differences are found, they tend to favor longer programs, the latter tending to produce more enduring rather than larger gains (Clarke-Stewart & Apfel, 1978; Morley et al. 1993). There is some suggestive evidence that a more intense program schedule may result in increased benefits, but most studies have confounded intensity with a host of other potentially critical variables. In one of the higher-quality studies of this issue, C. Powell and Grantham-McGregor (1989) varied the frequency with which community health aides provided psychosocial stimulation to infants and toddlers and demonstrated these techniques to their mothers during a two-year period. At the end of the first and second years, children who were visited biweekly had higher intellectual functioning than those who were visited monthly or not at all. Examination of the pattern of scores indicated that the first year of biweekly home visiting increased intellectual functioning, whereas the second year served to maintain this benefit or reinforce the skills that children had learned during the first year—a pattern reminiscent of that found in studies of the effects of two- versus one-year center-based intervention (S. Gray et al., 1983; Gullo & Burton, 1992; Reynolds, 1995; Schweinhart & Weikart, 1988; Sprigle & Schaefer, 1985).

Data do not point to any optimal age during the first five years of the child's life for initiating parent education. Studies that systematically vary by about a year the age of the child at the inception of parent education tend to find no significant age-related difference in immediate effects. Beginning at a younger age may be better in the long run (Clarke-Stewart & Apfel, 1978), though there may be no significant advantage to beginning prior to the child's twelfth month of life (Morley et al., 1993). Some evidence indicates that home-based parent education programs produce more child gains than programs using a group/center-based format (Chilman, 1973). However, other data support the opposite conclusion and evoke questions about whether discrepancies across studies are due to differences in other variables independent of format (e.g., race of group leader, appropriateness of content; D. Powell, 1988; Slaughter, 1983). Discrepancies in findings regarding the relative effectiveness of different formats, along with cultural insensitivity of programs for ethnic minorities, acknowledgment of individual differences in parents, and evidence that exact replication of model programs were not possible because of the need to adapt programs to local circumstances has led to a shift in the parent education field toward matching program content and methods to the needs and characteristics of parents (D. Powell, 1988).

Effects on Maternal Behavior and Attitudes. Data on the effects of parent training programs on maternal behavior and attitudes are less plentiful, but positive changes at the end of programs have been reported. These include use of more complex speech, less authoritarian child-rearing attitudes, and increased confidence in their role as parents. Too few long-term studies have been conducted to know whether these maternal effects persist well beyond the end of the programs. Overall, though, parent education programs have stronger immediate effects on mothers' attitudes and behavior and on the quality of the home environment than on children's cognitive functioning (Clarke-Stewart & Apfel, 1978; Morley et al., 1993). Because evaluation studies have not assessed the relation between changes in maternal and child behavior over time, it remains unclear whether gains in children's cognitive development are indeed caused by increased parental knowledge and changes in parental behavior and attitudes (Clarke-Stewart & Apfel, 1978).

Parent Participation/Involvement in Early Childhood Interventions

During the mid- to late 1970s, emphasis on parent education in a narrow sense began to give way to the broader concepts of parent participation and involvement, whereby professionals, in effect, were to do things "with rather than to parents in early intervention programs" (D. Powell, 1988, p. 11). This realignment of parent-professional relations, seen by some as more rhetorical than substantive, was the product of several forces, including provisions for parent participation in federal legislation establishing programs for the poor, such as the Economic Opportunity Act and its amendments, criticisms of the disparaging view of the parenting behavior of the poor (Cochran & Woolever, 1983; Sroufe, 1970; Tulkin, 1972), and growing concern about professional meddling in private family matters (D. Powell, 1988).

Parent Participation/Involvement as a Source of Empowerment and Institutional Change. The Economic Opportunity Act of 1964 called for "maximum feasible participation" of individuals served by Community Action Programs (CAP), the umbrella entity under which Head Start was implemented and whose philosophy, highly controversial at the time, was that poor citizens should control programs intended to serve them (Califano, 1979). This mandate was a direct result of the consciousness-raising efforts of the civil rights movement. Activists argued that institutionalized racism and structural inequalities in U.S. society created and perpetuated poverty by denying African Americans and other oppressed groups participation in the democratic process and access to economic resources. In the glare of unvarnished evidence of America's fundamental contradictions, some policymakers began to endorse the notion that society needed reforming as much as the poor did (Halpern, 1988).

Parent participation/involvement in federally funded programs for poor children was advocated as a strategy to forge institutional change (e.g., creating a base of political power among the poor to change schools and other social institutions that served them; providing access to employment) as well as individual change (e.g., increasing poor people's sense of control; enhancing parents' confidence in devising and implementing plans in the school setting, with the expectation that these skills would be transferred to the management of home and children; Chilman, 1973; Fein, 1980). More child-centered rationales for parental involvement were also advanced, including parents' responsibility for the welfare of their children, strengthening parents as a political constituency that advocates growth and support of educational programs, and improving parental and family functioning directly and indirectly by increasing awareness of potentially beneficial agencies and services.

Although Head Start was the harbinger of the trend toward parent participation/involvement in early childhood education programs, these issues were subjects of heated debate during its early days. Some members of the original planning committee of Head Start opposed even limited parental involvement in the program, perceiving Head Start parents as deficient in educational and parenting skills and as a primary source of their children's "cultural deficits." Others opposed parent education on the grounds that it assumed parenting deficits and disparaged and threatened African American culture (Zigler & Muenchow, 1992). Parent involvement and parenting education ultimately were incorporated as central components of the Head Start model. By the early 1970s, provisions for parent participation and decision making in Head Start had been clearly enunciated and spanned a wide array of possibilities, among them, participation in the classroom as paid employees, volunteers, or observers; educational activities for parents that they helped to develop; home visits by staff for discussion of ways the parent could contribute to the child's development at home; and leading and serving on committees that made decisions about budgetary matters, curriculum development, health services, program goals, and implementation of program services (Fein, 1980; Parker, Piotrkowski, Horn, & Greene, 1995).

Parent Participation/Involvement as an Enhancer of Preschool Effects. The legitimacy of parent participation/involvement in preschool interventions increased exponentially following Bronfenbrenner's (1975) conclusion, noted previously, that increased parent involvement enhanced the efficacy of early childhood interventions. Advocates pointed to two potential pathways by which this effect is produced. First, it was asserted that helping parents understand and manage their children's developmental needs helps consolidate and maintain the benefits of early education, given parents' uniquely salient and enduring presence in the child's life. Second, involving parents in the planning, implementation, and assessment of programs was thought to enhance programs' sensitivity to the needs of children and, hence, boost positive effects (K. White, Taylor, & Moss, 1992).

In subsequent reviews of research bearing on parental participation/involvement as a moderator of the effects of early childhood intervention, researchers have noted limitations in Bronfenbrenner's analysis (e.g., the sample of programs was small, ages and frequency of home visits were confounded) and concluded that existing research provides no compelling evidence of an enhancing effect of parental participation/involvement (Clarke-Stewart & Apfel, 1978; K. White et al., 1992). Clarke-Stewart and Apfel (1978) identified a number of studies reporting evidence of stronger effects in mother-child programs than programs that focused only on the child. However, they found equally strong evidence that children's cognitive gains were not dependent on their mothers' level of participation/involvement in the program. Moreover, they cited studies in which child-focused programs were more effective than mother-child programs in producing gains in children's test competence and school skills. Clarke-Stewart and Apfel's conclusion of an overall null effect, based on a traditional review of the literature, foreshadowed similar findings from a meta-analysis published several years later (K. White et al., 1992).

K. White et al. (1992) conducted a meta-analysis of over 200 early intervention studies with a treatment versus no-treatment design, comparing those in which treatment was carried out with and without significant parent participation/involvement (i.e., between-study comparison). In these studies, IQ was the most commonly assessed child outcome and teaching children developmental skills in the role of intervener was the most frequent operationalization of parent participation/involvement. Examination of studies with high internal validity suggested that involving parents made little difference in child outcomes. The average effect size was about the same for studies that involved parents and those that did not, and this was true regardless of whether the research was conducted with children who were poor, handicapped, or "at risk," whether the outcome was IQ or some other variable, or whether the programs in question were center-based or home-based.

K. White et al. (1992) identified another corpus of eight early intervention studies of poor children that directly manipulated the degree of parent participation/involvement (within-study comparison). Only one of these studies was published (the other seven were final reports to funding agencies, conference presentations, dissertations, and unpublished papers archived in ERIC documents), and most were rated by K. White et al. as having low internal validity. These studies yielded mixed results, with about half reporting positive effects and the other half reporting no effect or negative effects of parent participation/involvement. The average effect size of the eight studies across all measures of child functioning was .11, with studies of higher methodological quality finding the weakest effects.

In the one published study, Radin (1972) found no immediate effects of maternal participation/involvement on low-income African American and White 4-year-olds participating in a center-based early education program. However, in the follow-up study conducted one year later, children in the two groups with maternal participation/involvement (biweekly home tutorials for children with mothers present during the tutorial sessions, with and without small group meetings for parents) had higher PPVT scores than children in the group without maternal participation/involvement, though no differences were found on the Wechsler Scale of Intelligence. In a third corpus of studies identified by K. White et al. (1992), parent participation/involvement was only one of several variables (e.g., curriculum variation, setting, age of entry) distinguishing two or more intervention groups compared within the same study. They legitimately concluded that these studies provided little valid evidence about the effects of involving parents in intervention programs, so confounded was parent involvement with other program variables.

Taken together, extant investigations yield no consistent evidence that parent participation/involvement enhances the immediate or long-term effects of early intervention on children's development. This may be due to a lack of consensus about the definition of parent participation/involvement. Parent participation/involvement has evolved into a broad and highly diffuse concept whose operationalizations encompass highly disparate activities, including teaching parents specific skills to assist them in becoming more effective socializers of their children, exchanging information between parents and professionals, inviting participation of parents in the planning and implementation of programs, assisting parents in accessing community resources, and providing emotional and social support to family members (K. White et al., 1992). Failure to find an enhancing effect of parent participation/involvement also may be due to insufficient attention to a range of parent behaviors across different settings and populations, inadequate implementation of parent participation/involvement components of intervention programs, and poorly designed research (Reynolds, 1992; K. White et al., 1992).

The most obvious limitation in drawing firm conclusions about the impact of parental participation/involvement, however, is the remarkably small number of studies that have been designed expressly to investigate this issue. A strong, venerable presumption exists that parental involvement in child-directed educational efforts, however defined and measured, is desirable (Fein, 1980; Reynolds,

1992). Perhaps low priority has been given to conducting empirical tests of this assumption because the assumption is so prevalent and held with such certitude. Even if parent participation/involvement does not enhance children's gains from early intervention, this in no way negates its potential importance as a means to achieve other laudable goals (e.g., enhancing poor parents' political power and sense of efficacy).

Although apparently not a robust moderator of effects, it is important to underscore evidence of parent involvement as a mediator of preschool effects. In his longitudinal study of children enrolled in a large-scale preschool intervention program similar to Head Start, Reynolds (1991) found that parental involvement mediated the effect of preschool intervention on reading and mathematics achievement during the first two years of primary school and the effect of children's achievement motivation during kindergarten on academic achievement in first grade.

Ecological Influences on Parenting and Child Development

Intervention strategies that aim to prevent and ameliorate the negative effects of poverty on children's development traditionally have concentrated on providing direct educational experiences to children and modifying the parenting practices and home environment to which poor children are subject, without major regard for contextual, extrafamilial factors impinging on parents and their children. This perspective and its implicit disavowal of the need to change contextual factors and social systems has always had its critics, though they typically have been a minority voice (Chilman, 1973). During the late 1960s and early 1970s, a handful of demonstration models evinced some degree of departure from this traditional approach (Andrews et al., 1982). In addition to parent education and educational experiences for preschoolers, they offered social services to the entire family and attempted to remediate extrafamilial obstacles to optimal parent and child functioning (Halpern, 1988).

It was not until the 1980s, however, that an ecological perspective achieved notable currency in early childhood intervention. At the heart of this evolving direction is increased appreciation of stress, social support, and broader contextual factors as determinants of parenting behavior on the one hand, and as conditioners of parents' and children's ability to profit from an intervention program on the other (Bronfenbrenner, 1975; Chilman, 1973; Halpern, 1984). An overarching goal is improvement of the social and economic contexts of parenting and children's development (D. Powell, 1988). Ecologically sensitive intervention is a highly diverse genre, but a few common denominators distinguish programs in this category. They tend to be expansive in focus (i.e., family-focused, rather than child- or parent-focused) and offer a broad complement of services. Emphasis is given to prevention rather than treatment as a cost-effective approach to human service delivery. In addition, these programs claim espousal of a nondeficit orientation dedicated to building on families' strengths rather than simply remediating their weaknesses, though questions exist about whether this is a substantive change or a public relations maneuver (Laosa, 1984; D. Powell, 1988) .

A multiplicity of strategies is employed to increase supports and reduce stressors at multiple levels of proximity to the parent, child, and entire family (e.g., psychological, sociological, economic; home, neighborhood, workplace). These include direct provision of emotional support to parents and other family members, facilitation of peer support and social networks, assistance of family members in gaining access to and using educational, health, and social services in the community, reinforcement of links between families and both formal and informal sources of support, and mediation between the family and more distal bureaucracies to help families obtain needed services. Considerable variation exists across programs, however, in the degree of emphasis given to each of these services (Bronfenbrenner, 1987; Halpern, 1990b; Kagan & Shelley, 1987; Weiss, 1987; Zigler & Freedman, 1987).

As a form and component of early childhood intervention, parent education also broadened its focus to include ecological factors. By the early 1980s, many parent education programs sought to improve parent functioning via provision of social support to parents, not just dissemination of information about child rearing and the principles of child development. D. Powell (1988) identified two variants of the family/parent support approach that emerged during this period. In the first, the assumption is that parents lack confidence in their child-rearing beliefs and practices. Rather than attempting to modify parental behavior and attitudes in accord with some ideal notion of what a parent should do with children, these programs provide validation and affirmation of the parent's existing child-rearing beliefs and behaviors on the assumption that this alone is sufficient to enhance parental behavior and attitudes. Such programs attempt to replicate some elements of informal support systems traditionally available through networks of friends and family. In the second variant, programs provide social support as a means to increase parents' receptivity to expert information and advice, on the grounds that high levels of stressors and low support inhibit parents' ability to attend to the curriculum content of parent education programs.

The trend toward more ecological approaches to poverty-focused early childhood intervention is part of a broader "family support" movement that surged during the 1980s. Family support programs share the characteristics, emphasis, and perspectives of ecologically sensitive early childhood intervention programs described above, but are distinctive in one major regard. They are committed to universal (rather than means-tested) access to family support services on the grounds that economic and social changes during the past two decades have created widespread support needs that transcend social class and economic boundaries (e.g., increases in cost of living that necessitate two paychecks to maintain a middle-class standard of living; increased geographic mobility that has reduced the availability of extended family members for provision of myriad kinds of support; increase in divorce and single-parent families; Kagan, Powell, Weissbourd, & Zigler, 1987; Weissbourd, 1987). Head Start, especially its demonstration models, laid the foundation for the principles underlying the family support movement (Zigler & Freedman, 1987). Interestingly, just as social and economic pressures during the 1930s led middle-class parents to participate in institutionalized forms of child care once reserved exclusively for the poor (i.e., kindergarten, nursery school; Fein, 1980), similar forces in the 1980s motivated development of programs for economically diverse groups whose tenets rest to a large degree on those established by interventions for impoverished families.

The late 1970s and 1980s also brought a broadening of the developmental outcomes considered in both basic and intervention research. With the burgeoning of intervention programs during the late 1960s and early 1970s, several scholars questioned the preoccupation with cognitive enrichment. They asserted that socioemotional factors contributed as much to school failure as the lack of academic skills and, thus, that studied attention should be extended to socioemotional functioning and the overall development of poor children and their parents (Beller, 1983; Chilman, 1973; Zigler & Berman, 1983). These arguments were buttressed by evidence that children's school achievement was greatly influenced by their expectancy of success, a psychological indicator that derives from an individual's expectations of acquiring specific outcomes as a result of performing certain behaviors and his or her valuation of these outcomes (Coleman et al., 1966; Eccles-Parsons et al., 1983). Evidence also existed that motivational factors influenced children's performance on cognitive tasks (Zigler, Abelson, & Seitz, 1973; Zigler & Butterfield, 1968).

Interest in the impact of early interventions on children's socioemotional functioning exploded during the 1980s, strengthened by rising rates of crime, violence, and antisocial behavior among youth, the growing availability of longitudinal data on preschool intervention effects during late adolescence and early adulthood, when antisocial behavior tends to peak (e.g., Berrueta-Clement et al., 1984; Consortium for Longitudinal Studies, 1983; Johnson, 1988; Schweinhart et al., 1993), and advances in the measurement of socioemotional functioning. Gains in cognitive functioning continue to be regarded as critical indicators of the efficacy of early childhood interventions, but they no longer eclipse focus on socioemotional outcomes (e.g., Brooks-Gunn, 1995; McKey et al., 1985). In the following section, we discuss conceptual and empirical work that triggered and sustained the evolution toward more ecologically oriented approaches in early childhood intervention for poor children and families. We then turn to an appraisal of different categories of interventions whose content reflects some of the hallmarks of this approach.

Precursors of an Ecological Approach to Early Childhood Intervention

A confluence of factors has been credited for the evolving direction of early childhood intervention toward a more ecological approach (Bronfenbrenner, 1987; Halpern, 1990a; D. Powell, 1988), among them (a) prominent model programs developed in the late 1960s that exemplified and documented positive effects of ecologically oriented intervention; (b) Bronfenbrenner's (1975) assertion that ecological intervention and parenting support are essential to effecting positive change in the course of poor children's development and his subsequent elaboration of an ecological model of human development (Bronfenbrenner, 1979, 1986); (c) empirical evidence that family processes, including parenting behavior, and children's development can be undermined by stressful events and conditions, including those that occur in extrafamilial settings (e.g., workplace); (d) empirical evidence that the availability and provision of social support from immediate family members and persons outside the immediate family, such as kin, friends, and neighbors, can enhance psychological functioning and parenting behavior under ordinary and stressful conditions; and (e) persistent criticisms of the deficit model and evidence of its negative effects. We discuss each of these factors, although this is not to suggest that individual interventionists necessarily are cognizant of how these factors have shaped their efforts. Indeed, although the work reviewed below provides strong underpinnings for the policies and practices governing ecologically oriented intervention, its contributions to some of the basic concepts underlying these programs and to some of the programs themselves often have gone unrecognized (Bronfenbrenner, 1987).

Early, Prominent Demonstration Models. Head Start's early experimental program, as well as the Yale Child Welfare Research Programs, all highly visible, help to advance multileveled early childhood interventions by demonstrating how to implement them and documenting their salutary effects on children.

Head Start Experimental Programs. Research findings on SES differences in parenting practices and the relations between parenting practices and child development, discussed previously, were widely disseminated among policymakers during the mid-1960s by a cadre of pediatricians, developmental psychologists, and other social scientists. These dissemination efforts, along with the disappointing findings of the Westinghouse evaluation, according to Halpern (1988), "put the rearing of low-income infants on the public agenda in a historically unprecedented way, complementing the early evaluation findings from Head Start itself" (p. 291). The Office of Economic Opportunity, and later the Office of Child Development and its successor, the Administration for Children, Youth, and Families, responded to the research findings by launching several experimental demonstration projects focused on early parenting in poor families. They included the Parent and Child Centers, followed by the Parent-Child Development Centers, and later, the Child and Family Resource Programs. Carefully conceived, implemented, and evaluated to enhance the probability of replication if they proved effective (all used random assignment), these programs are rightly credited as forerunners of the current family/parent support movement and the source of some of the best evidence about the conditions of effective parent education and support (Halpern, 1988; Zigler & Freedman, 1987). They also reflected the ambivalent impulses of the Office of Economic Opportunity community action programs, evident as well in today's parent-focused programs for the poor. Whereas the programs comported with a nascent ecological perspective on human development arguing for attention to extrafamilial forces that obstruct optimal parenting, they also endorsed traditional child development theory asserting that poor parents should imitate and emulate the child-rearing practices and attitudes associated with middle-class status (Halpern, 1988).

The Parent and Child Centers (PCCs), established in 1967 as the first Head Start experimental programs designed to serve very young children (infants to 3-year-olds) and their families, were multipurpose family centers that provided parent education, health, and social services. Some 33 centers were established, and in 1973, seven of them were provided funds to develop a child advocacy component and to promote services for all children in the community. Whereas center-based Head Start was seen as remedial, the PCCs reached poor children during the earliest years of life and hence, were regarded as preventive. The centers were allowed flexibility in accord with community requirements. For example, the location of programs depended, in part, on whether states permitted center-based care for infants. In Southern states, where center-based care for infants was prohibited, poor children were brought to the homes of middle-class women during the day for educational experiences (Zigler & Freedman, 1987). This initiative was envisioned to become a nationwide program, but its expansion was prevented by shifting political forces and bureaucratic reorganization (Halpern, 1988).

In 1970, three PCCs located in Birmingham (serving African American and White children), Houston (serving Mexican American families), and New Orleans (serving African American families) were selected to become experimental Parent-Child Development Centers (PCDCs). Their general purpose was to define the goals of parent-infant intervention, develop different approaches to meet these goals, and establish appropriate evaluation strategies. The centers adopted different methods of program delivery (in Birmingham, a step system of increasing maternal responsibility for program work, culminating in staff positions; in New Orleans, involvement of paraprofessionals from the community; in Houston, a year of home visits, followed by a year of center programs for both mother and child), but all served families with children from birth to 3 years and were developed and implemented within a common framework that emphasized the role of parents in children's development. Core components in all the centers were (a) a comprehensive curriculum for mothers consisting of information on child development and child-rearing practices, home management, nutrition and health, mothers' personal development, and government and community resources (e.g., community colleges) and how to use them; (b) a simultaneous program for the children of these women (ranging in age from 2 to 12 months at the time of entry into the program); and (c) extensive supportive services for participating families, including transportation, some meals, family health and social services, peer support groups, and a small daily stipend. The programs varied in the amount of weekly participation expected and ended when the child was 36 months of age (Andrews et al., 1982; Halpern, 1988; Zigler & Freedman, 1987).

A description of one of the programs provides a sense of their intensity and scope. Families were recruited into the 24-month Houston program by door-to-door canvassing and randomly assigned to the program group (97 mother-child pairs) and control group (119 mother-child pairs). At entry, more than 90% of the families were intact, and mothers, on average, were 28 years old and had about 7.5 years of formal schooling. Mothers and caregivers entered the program when their children were 1 year old. During the first year, the program was home-based and consisted of about 30 weekly home visits, each lasting about one and a half hours. Home visitors exchanged information with mothers about child development, parenting skills, and the use of the home as a learning environment and gave lessons in a new activity involving a book or toy. Weekend workshops focusing on communication, decision making, problem solving, and family roles were scheduled to include fathers and siblings in the program, as were optional weekly English-language classes. The second year of the program was center-based. Children attended preschool classes organized around a formal curriculum, and mothers attended three-hour sessions four mornings a week for eight months. These sessions alternated between a focus on home management activities and child development/parenting. One instructional strategy involved small-group sessions in which mothers critiqued videotaped classroom interactions between themselves and their children and discussed various issues of child behavior and development evoked by the videotapes (Johnson, 1988; Johnson & Walker, 1987).

Evaluations of short-term effects showed that in all three of the PCDCs, program children scored higher than control children on the Stanford-Binet, although this difference reached statistical significance in only two of the three sites. In general, immediate effects of the PCDC intervention were stronger for mothers than their children. At graduation, program mothers in all three PCDCs showed more positive maternal behavior than controls in videotaped interactions with their children (e.g., giving children praise and emotional support, being affectionate and accepting, encouraging children's verbal communications, participating actively in children's activities, greater use of language to inform rather than restrict and control children). In addition, in the one site where a graduation interview was conducted, mothers who participated in the intervention reported greater use of reasoning, less use of physical punishment, and higher levels of general life satisfaction. The programs suffered a generally high attrition rate, especially among program-group women whose return to work or school made it difficult to continue their involvement in the lengthy and intensive intervention (Andrews et al., 1982).

In a follow-up of children in the Houston PCDC when they were in grades 2 through 5, five to eight years after program completion, positive effects were found on children's academic and socioemotional functioning. Compared to the control group, program children scored significantly better on standardized achievement tests and were reliably more considerate of others, less hostile, restless, impulsive, and obstinate, and less likely to be involved in fights (Johnson, 1988; Johnson & Walker, 1987). However, a more recent and comprehensive follow-up of all three PCDC samples found no residual program effects on a number of child and family variables (Halpern, 1990b). In the context of growing budgetary pressures within the funding agency and the burgeoning need for services among low-income parents, efforts to replicate the centers on a broad scale were abandoned, despite evidence of their short-term efficacy, because of concerns about their costliness and generalizability (Fein, 1980; Halpern, 1988)

The Child and Family Resource Program (CFRP), initiated in 1973 and funded through 1983, had as its core a two-year program of monthly home visits for families with infants from birth to 3 at the beginning of the program. Its distinguishing features were (a) an emphasis on parent support and education (e.g., information on prevention and identification of child abuse, domestic management, use of community services), including helping parents resolve serious family problems (e.g., poor health, substandard housing, alcoholism); (b) facilitation of developmental continuity by providing services before birth and continuing them into elementary school; (c) coordination of comprehensive social services provided directly and via referrals; and (d) an attempt to individualize services through needs assessment and goal setting with each family. Home visits ranged in frequency from monthly to bimonthly, and their focus varied across programs but mostly concerned service brokerage, general family problems, and parents' personal support needs. Referrals for adult education, literacy, and job training were made by case managers on an as-needed basis, but this was not a strong component of the program. Each of the 11 local programs was linked to Head Start centers, where 3- to 5-year-olds in the program attended preschool. Once children began elementary school, staff personnel maintained contact with parents to maximize their involvement in their child's academic progress (Travers, Nauta, & Irwin, cited in St. Pierre et al., 1995; Zigler & Freedman, 1987).

Effects of the program on children were much weaker than those produced by the PCDCs, probably because children received fewer direct services and only uneven attention was given to parent-child interaction. The CFRP had no significant effect on children's Bayley scores or on several other measures of development, health, and behavior. However, the program had significant, positive effects on parenting behavior, feelings of efficacy, and perceived ability to control events. Rate of maternal employment and training, but not household income, also favored program mothers, though this difference was modest (Travers et al., cited in St. Pierre et al., 1995).

Yale Child Welfare Research Program. The Yale Child Welfare Research Program, a family support intervention conducted between 1968 and 1974, was premised on the notion that "chronic stress is a significant impediment to effective family functioning and that poverty both increases the likelihood of such stress and restricts the resources available to families to cope with it" (Seitz, Rosenbaum, & Apfel, 1985, p. 377). The program aimed to enhance children's intellectual and socioemotional development by strengthening the caregiving and problem-solving abilities of their mothers. Eschewing the deficit perspective, the researchers noted that they "did not view severely impoverished families as being different in some psychological way from families with more resources," only in greater need of the services offered by the program (p. 377). Services were received from the point of mothers' pregnancy with their first child to 30 months postpartum and involved home visits, pediatric care, regular developmental assessments of children, and educational day care. Home visitors, who were clinical social workers, psychologists, and nurses, made an average of 28 home visits to help solve some immediate problems facing families (e.g., reducing physical dangers, obtaining more adequate food or housing) and to offer advice regarding educational, marital, and career decisions. They also provided emotional support and a liaison with other service providers in the community.

A pediatrician saw the newborn and mother daily during the postdelivery hospital stay and made house calls if needed. Children received regular well-baby exams as well as periodic developmental examinations. During this time, the examiner discussed maternal concerns about the infant's or toddler's development, and the mother observed the child's abilities as well as the examiner's techniques for handling difficult behavior. All but one of the children attended a high-quality, center-based day care program for periods ranging from 2 to 28 months and averaging 13 months. The staff was highly trained, the caregiver:child ratio never exceeded 1:3, and each child had a primary caregiver. Staff tried to achieve continuity between their child care practices and those of the parents, discussing problems with parents to arrive at mutually agreeable methods of handling them. The primary focus of the center program was on children's emotional and social development (e.g., helping child learn to handle aggression, promoting positive peer interactions). The experimental group consisted of 18 children; a control group of 18 30-month-old children living in the same area as the program children were recruited after the project ended. About 70% of the children in the program and control groups were African American (Seitz et al., 1985).

The program produced immediate gains in children's IQ scores and language skills, and at the age 7 follow-up, experimental children had higher IQ scores, higher school achievement, and better school attendance than control group children (Provence & Naylor, 1983; Trickett, Apfel, Rosenbaum, & Zigler, 1982). At the age 12 follow-up, gains on IQ tests and achievement tests had disappeared. However, program boys, compared to control group boys, had received fewer remedial and special educational services, had better school attendance, were rated significantly less negatively by their teachers, and were more likely to manifest good school adjustment. This follow-up also revealed differences between experimental and control group mothers. In comparison to controls, experimental group mothers had completed significantly more years of education and were more likely to live in a family in which at least one adult was employed on a full-time basis (or the number of jobs held by the adults equaled a full-time job), although the two groups did not differ in education at the birth of their first child. Experimental mothers also were more likely to have initiated consultation with the child's teacher. They did not differ from control group mothers, however, on a number of other self-reported parenting practices (e.g., number of hours of television child watched per day, hours of homework per day, number of household chores child permitted or required to do; Seitz et al., 1983).

Bronfenbrenner's Analyses. In his analysis of the effectiveness of early intervention, Bronfenbrenner (1975) selected for special attention the famous Skeels (1966; Skeels & Dye, 1939) experiment and the extremely invasive and controversial Milwaukee Project (Garber, 1988) to illustrate the potential of ecological interventions to promote cognitive functioning. He noted:

> [The] "enabling act" took the form, in both instances, of a major transformation of the environment for the child

> and the persons principally responsible for his care and development. . . . The essence of the strategy [of ecological intervention] is a primary focus neither on the child nor his parent nor even the dyad or the family as a system. Rather, the aim is to effect changes in the *context* in which the family lives; these changes in turn enable the mother, the parents, and the family as a whole to exercise the functioning necessary for the child's development. . . . The need for ecological intervention arises when the . . . prerequisites [for the family to perform its child-rearing functions] are not met by the environment in which the child and his family live. This is precisely the situation which obtains for many, if not most, disadvantaged families. Under these circumstances no direct form of intervention aimed at enhancing the child's development or his parents' childrearing skills is likely to have much impact. Conversely, once the environmental prerequisites are met, the direct forms of intervention may no longer seem as necessary. (pp. 584–585)

Bronfenbrenner noted further that ecological intervention is rarely carried out because it "almost invariably requires institutional change" (p. 586). He continued his theme concerning the importance of the family's ecology on children's development in a subsequent analysis focusing on basic research. Drawing on a theoretically convergent body of research, Bronfenbrenner (1979, 1986) argued compellingly that children's development is influenced not only by the family system, but by systems well removed from the family's control, among them, parents' workplace, neighborhoods, schools, available health and day care services, and macroeconomic forces that result in stressors such as parental unemployment and job and income loss. He exhorted researchers to take seriously the potency of the family's ecology by undertaking multi-layered, contextual, and more process-oriented analyses of family relations and children's development.

Other analytic advances during this time intensified interest in ecological influences on human development. Ogbu (1981), focusing specifically on poor African American children and families living in urban settings, articulated a cultural-ecological model underscoring the potency of extrafamilial forces on child rearing and child development. His work is an important conceptual anchor in recent research on the links between cultural orientations and development in African American children, the psychological consequences of inconsistencies across social contexts in expectations and definitions of successful developmental outcomes, and the dynamic influences of school and home settings (e.g., Burton, Allison, & Obeidallah, 1995; Jagers & Mock, 1993). More recently, W. Wilson (1987) considered the implications for social norms and children's development of increasingly high concentrations of poor and jobless adults in inner-city neighborhoods. This work has not yet had any discernible, direct influence on intervention programs, but it has precipitated keen interest in and study of the effects of the economic character of neighborhoods on development in poor children and adolescents (e.g., Brooks-Gunn, Duncan, Klebanov, & Sealand, 1993; Chase-Lansdale & Gordon, 1996; Duncan et al., 1994; Jencks & Mayer, 1990).

Research on Relations among Stressors, Parenting, and Adult Psychological Functioning. The 1970s and 1980s brought a rapid growth in research documenting the effects of undesirable life events and chronic conditions on both adult psychological functioning and parenting. A considerable amount of this work focused on economic stressors, prompted in part by the economic downturns of the late 1970s and early 1980s (McLoyd, 1989). However, the most influential work published during this period concerned economic hardship as experienced during the Great Depression of the 1930s. In that research, Elder and his colleagues (Elder, 1974, 1979; Elder, Liker, & Cross, 1984) found that fathers who lost jobs and sustained heavy financial loss became irritable, tense, and explosive, which in turn increased their tendency to be punitive and arbitrary in the discipline of their children. These fathering behaviors were predictive of temper tantrums, irritability, and negativity in young children, especially boys, and of moodiness and hypersensitivity, feelings of inadequacy, and lowered aspirations in adolescent girls. Thus, although the workplace where job and income loss occurred was external to the child's environment, economic loss adversely affected the child's development through the changes it produced in the father's behavior and disposition. Elder et al.'s basic causal pathway linking economic loss to the child through the father's behavior has been replicated in several studies of contemporary families (Conger et al., 1992, 1993; Galambos & Silbereisen, 1987a, 1987b; Lempers, Clark-Lempers, & Simons, 1989). In Lemper et al.'s (1989) study of White working- and middle-class families, for example, economic loss led to higher rates of adolescent delinquency and drug use by increasing inconsistent and punitive discipline by parents.

Further corroboration of the link between economic loss and parenting comes from studies of child abusers and investigations of the relation between the status of an economy (e.g., unemployment rate, inflation rate) and rates of child abuse. These investigations are consistent in showing that child abuse occurs more frequently in families experiencing economic decline (i.e., job and income loss) than in families with stable resources (Garbarino, 1976; Parke & Collmer, 1975). Analyzing data over a 30-month period, Steinberg, Catalano, and Dooley (1981) found that increases in child abuse were preceded by periods of high job loss, confirming the authors' hypothesis that "undesirable economic change leads to increased child maltreatment" (p. 975). Likewise, in a study by Straus, Gelles, and Steinmetz (1980), the rate of child abuse among fathers employed part time was almost twice as high as the rate for fathers employed full time. Paternal unemployment and economic loss can lead to child abuse, in part, by increasing parental frustration and depleting emotional resources as a consequence of financial strain.

Negative life events more generally also were found to predict quality of parenting. Research reported that the occurrence of undesirable life events correlated positively with affectively distant, restrictive, and punitive parenting (Gersten, Langner, Eisenberg, & Simcha-Fagan, 1977). Similarly, mothers who experienced more stressful life events were found to be less nurturant toward their children and, in the case of single mothers, less at ease, less spontaneous, and less responsive to their children's communications (Weinraub & Wolf, 1983). Even ephemeral, relatively minor hassles were found to produce detectable negative changes in maternal behavior. G. Patterson's (1988) observations of mother-child dyads over the course of several days indicated that day-to-day fluctuations in the mother's tendency to initiate and continue an aversive exchange with the child were systematically related to the daily frequency of hassles or crises the mother experienced.

Data linking chronic stressors to the quality of parenting also emerged during this period. Investigators reported that mothers who perceived their neighborhoods as dangerous and crime-infested, compared to those who perceived their neighborhoods as safer, reported more conflict with their children (M. White, Kasl, Zahner, & Will, 1987) and were more likely to use physical punishment as a child management technique (Kriesberg, 1970). One explanation of these findings is that mothers residing in dangerous neighborhoods adopt these parenting strategies more readily to ensure their children's safety and to discourage disobedience of rules because of the potentially grave consequences. From the parents' perspective, achieving these goals may require the use of more severe child management techniques (Dubrow & Garbarino, 1989).

Recent studies extended this line of research by focusing on the relation between adverse events/conditions and another dimension of parenting, namely, the quality of the home environment. Reminiscent of the inverse relation found between children's IQ and number of risk factors (Sameroff, Seifer, Barocas, Zax, & Greenspan, 1987; Whiteman, Brown, & Deutsch, 1967), Brooks-Gunn, Klebanov, and Liaw (1995) found that as the number of risk factors experienced by parents increases (e.g., incidence of stressful life events, parental unemployment), the less stimulating is preschoolers' home environment. Extrapolating from Bee et al.'s (1982) study, in which the relation of family ecology variables (e.g., social support, life change, home learning environment) to children's cognitive functioning was found to be stronger in poor families than more affluent families, it is likely that the impact of these ecology variables on children's home environment increases as economic hardship increases.

Psychological Distress as a Mediator of the Adversity-Parenting Link. Several studies conducted during the late 1970s and 1980s yielded direct as well as indirect evidence that psychological distress mediates the link between negative life events/conditions and harsh, inconsistent parenting. This mediational process was clearly demonstrated in work on economic hardship precipitated by parental job and income loss (Conger et al., 1992, 1993; Elder, 1974, 1979; Lempers et al., 1989) and was thought to operate more generally across a range of stressors. Two types of evidence are relevant to this proposition: (a) research linking adverse events/conditions to adult psychological functioning, and (b) investigations documenting an association between parents' psychological functioning and parenting behavior. Each of these lines of research is discussed below.

A plethora of studies reported strong positive relations between negative life events/conditions and psychological distress in adults as indicated by depression, anxiety, hostility, somatic complaints, eating and sleeping problems, and low self-regard (e.g., Kasl & Cobb, 1979; Kessler & Neighbors, 1986; Liem & Liem, 1978). Parenthetically, several studies conducted during this period found a strong link between negative life events/conditions and psychological distress (including school adjustment problems) in children (Gersten, Langner, Eisenberg, & Orzek, 1974; Pryor-Brown, Powell, & Earls, 1989; Sandler & Block, 1979; Sterling, Cowen, Weissberg, Lotyczewski, & Boike, 1985). Complementing these studies of adults was evidence linking fluctuations in unemployment rates to aggregate-level indices of psychological distress (e.g., admissions to psychiatric hospitals; Dooley & Catalano, 1980; Horwitz, 1984). Research demonstrated cogently that these are true effects and not simply selective factors that lead to job loss or unemployment (Dew, Bromet, & Schulberg, 1987; Kessler, House, & Turner, 1987). Not only is unemployment directly responsible for increasing stress symptoms, but reemployment has health-promoting, restorative effects (Liem, 1983).

Turning to the second line of research, enormous amounts of data were generated during the 1980s about how parents' affective states condition the quality of parent-child interaction (for reviews of this work, see Dix, 1991; Downey & Coyne, 1990; McLoyd, 1990). These data, most from mothers of infants and preschoolers, directly tied negative psychological states in the parent to parental punitiveness, inconsistency, and unresponsiveness. In an observational study of African American and White mothers and children from diverse socioeconomic backgrounds, Conger, McCarty, Yang, Lahey, and Kropp (1984) found that mothers who reported high psychological distress, as compared to mothers reporting lower distress, exhibited fewer positive behaviors (e.g., hugs, praise, supportive statements) and more negative behaviors toward the child (e.g., threats, derogatory statements, slaps). Similarly, investigations indicated that maternal depression and psychological distress are correlated with physical abuse, use of aversive, coercive discipline, and diminished maternal sensitivity and satisfaction with parenting (Crnic & Greenberg, 1987; Daniel, Hampton, & Newberger, 1983; McLoyd & Wilson, 1990; G. Patterson, 1986). Heightened depression and psychosomatic problems appear to explain some of the changes in parenting following divorce, an event promoted by economic hardship. During and following divorce, custodial mothers often become self-involved, uncommunicative, nonsupportive, and inconsistently punitive toward their children (Hetherington, Stanley-Hagan, & Anderson, 1989). Psychological distress also may partly explain the link of perceived neighborhood danger to use of physical punishment and mother-child conflict (M. White et al., 1987). Perceived neighborhood danger and crime, highly correlated with actual crime statistics (Kriesberg, 1970; D. Lewis & Maxfield, 1980), have been found to predict poor mental health among minority women (Kasl & Harburg, 1975; M. White et al., 1987).

The relation between psychological distress and parenting is robust, for it has been found within samples of poor individuals where the range of scores is generally more restricted. Poor parents whose total stress burden is high are reported to be less happy and less involved in the activities of their preschool and adolescent children than poor parents who experience fewer stressors (H. Wilson, 1974). High levels of psychological distress also dispose poor adolescent mothers to custodial and unstimulating contact with their infants (Crockenberg, 1987). Zelkowitz and her colleagues (Longfellow, Zelkowitz, & Saunders, 1982; Zelkowitz, 1982) conducted two highly cited investigations of the relations between psychological distress and child-rearing behaviors in a sample of poor African American and White mothers of 5- to 7-year-olds. Longfellow et al. (1982) found that more highly distressed mothers were less responsive to the child's dependency needs, more hostile and dominating, more likely to yell and hit the child, and less likely to rely on reasoning and loss of privileges in disciplining the child. They also demanded more intensive involvement in household maintenance from their children and placed greater responsibility on them.

Likewise, in Zelkowitz's (1982) investigation, poor mothers who had elevated levels of anxiety and depressive symptomatology were more likely to expect immediate compliance from their children, although they were less consistent in following through on their requests if their children did not comply. They were more likely to see their maternal role as teaching socially appropriate behavior and valued obedience and "good" behavior more highly. The mothers in the sample studied by Zelkowitz (1982) and Longfellow et al. (1982) were not unaware of how negative psychological states affected their parenting behavior. They reported that among the hardest things to do when feeling depressed were being nurturant, patient, and involved with their children. Furthermore, they seemed to be aware that the parenting strategies they were most prone to use when depressed and anxious were, in the main, ineffective and changeworthy. Thus, psychological overload, rather than ignorance of the principles of effective parenting, appeared to underlie differences in mothers' style of interaction with their children.

The studies reviewed up to this point assessed depressive affect and psychological distress on the basis of self-reports on symptom checklists. A number of other investigations conducted during the 1980s assessed parenting behavior among depressed (or manic-depressive) mothers identified on the basis of clinical diagnosis. These mothers exemplify a pattern of parenting marked by unresponsiveness, nonsupportiveness, and hostile coerciveness toward the child. When interacting with their preschool children, depressed mothers are more critical, less positive in affective expression, less responsive to the child's overtures, and less active and spontaneous (Davenport, Zahn-Waxler, Adland, & Mayfield, 1984; Downey & Coyne, 1990; Radke-Yarrow, Richters, & Wilson, 1988). They are more likely to choose conflict-resolution strategies that require little effort, such as dropping initial demands when the child is resistant or enforcing obedience unilaterally rather than negotiating with the child (Kochanska, Kuczynski, Radke-Yarrow, & Walsh, 1987). Other work showed that the more severe the mother's depression, the more likely she is to slap and shout at the child to signal disapproval and the more negative is her perception of the child (Panaccione & Wahler, 1986).

Parallels between Correlates of Poverty and Correlates of Adverse Events/Conditions. By the mid-1980s, the inverse relation between SES (and poverty) and various forms of psychological distress was well established. In addition, enough data existed to conclude that the poor's increased exposure to negative life events and chronic conditions was a major cause underlying this relation (Liem & Liem, 1978; McAdoo, 1986; Neff & Husaini, 1980). Researchers documented that poor and low SES individuals were more likely than economically advantaged counterparts to be confronted with an unremitting succession of negative life events (e.g., eviction, physical illness, criminal assault, catastrophes resulting from substandard housing) in the context of chronically stressful life conditions outside personal control, such as inadequate housing and dangerous neighborhoods. It was also clear from research that psychological impairment was more severe when negative conditions and catastrophic events were not under the control of the individual, a condition more common for the poor (Liem & Liem, 1978). Ongoing stressful conditions associated with poverty and low SES, such as inadequate housing and shortfalls of money, were found to be more debilitating than acute crises and negative events (Belle, 1984; Brown, Bhrolchain, & Harris, 1975; Makosky, 1982). In some studies, after chronic stressors were controlled, the effects of life events on psychological distress were diminished to borderline significance (Dressler, 1985; Gersten et al., 1977; Pearlin, Lieberman, Menaghan, & Mullan, 1981).

If poverty and low SES are markers for a conglomerate of negative life events and chronic stressors and are predictive of higher levels of psychological distress, they should predict child-rearing behaviors and attitudes similar to those linked to specific negative life events, undesirable conditions, and psychological distress, as discussed above. Abundant evidence accumulated over three decades confirms this expectation. These studies found that mothers who are poor or from low SES backgrounds, compared to their economically advantaged counterparts, are more likely to use power-assertive techniques in disciplinary encounters and are generally less supportive of their children. They value obedience more and are less likely to use reasoning and more likely to use physical punishment as a means of disciplining and controlling the child. Lower-class parents also are more likely to issue commands without explanation, less likely to consult the child about his or her wishes, and less likely to reward the child verbally for desirable behavior. In addition, poverty has been associated with diminished expression of affection and less responsiveness to the socioemotional needs explicitly expressed by the child (e.g., Gecas, 1979; Hess, 1970; Kamii & Radin, 1967; Kriesberg, 1970; Langner, Herson, Greene, Jameson, & Goff, 1970; Peterson & Peters, 1985; P. Portes, Dunham, & Williams, 1986; H. Wilson, 1974).

Parallels between poverty and low SES, on the one hand, and specific negative life events, undesirable conditions, and psychological distress, on the other, also were found for child abuse. Poverty, like job and income loss, is a significant predictor of child abuse (e.g., Daniel et al., 1983; Garbarino, 1976). Indeed, it is the single most prevalent characteristic of abusing parents, though it is indisputable that only a small proportion of poor parents are even alleged to abuse their children (Pelton, 1989). Several kinds of data generated during the late 1970s and 1980s contradicted the claim that the relation between poverty and abuse is spurious because of greater public scrutiny of the poor and resulting bias in detection and reporting. First, although greater public awareness and new reporting laws resulted in a significant increase in official reporting in recent years, the socioeconomic pattern of these reports has not changed (Pelton, 1989). Second, child abuse is related to degrees of poverty even within the lower class, which admittedly is more open to public scrutiny; abusing parents tend to be the poorest of the poor (Wolock & Horowitz, 1979). Third, the most severe injuries occur within the poorest families (Pelton, 1989).

In sum, research conducted during the 1970s and 1980s yielded a trove of evidence that poor and low SES individuals are more likely than their economically advantaged counterparts to experience negative life events, undesirable chronic conditions, and psychological distress and that these factors are conducive to less nurturant and more punitive parenting. In addition, the findings of several studies lent support to the hypothesis that child-rearing practices associated with poverty and low SES are partly a function of higher levels of psychological distress brought on by elevated exposure to negative life events and undesirable chronic conditions (McLoyd, 1990). These data, with their clear implications for practice, commanded the attention of the early childhood intervention field. They suggested that, in some cases, stressors and their attendant psychological distress can override knowledge of the principles of child development as a determinant of parenting and that removal or amelioration of acute and chronic stressors can be highly effective as a strategy to improve parenting and, presumably, child functioning. The multidimensionality of poverty and the conglomeration of acute and chronic stressors experienced by the poor accented the poor's need for a broad range of concrete services. These factors also suggested that service delivery should be integrative in approach (e.g., collaboration among individual service providers and clients in developing intervention and evaluation plans; close proximity of service delivery sites) so that it is not yet another source of stress.

Research on Social Support as a Contributor to Positive Psychological and Maternal Functioning. Empirical research on social support as a determinant of adults' psychological well-being, family functioning, and parenting behavior, as well as ecological models of the determinants of parenting (Belsky, 1984; D. Powell, 1979) and family coping patterns (Barbarin, 1983) were powerful stimulants of interventionists' interest in the social context of parenting. Several of the interpersonal-level strategies chosen to promote poor children's development indirectly through the parent (e.g., peer support, strengthening self-help networks, reinforcing links between families and both formal and informal sources of support) are rooted in this rapidly growing literature. They also have been informed by qualitative research that developed methods for professionals to identify and recruit natural helpers in social networks, to collaborate in the matching of needs and resources in neighborhoods, and to link with formal agencies as needed (Watson & Collins, 1982).

The first set of findings from empirical research that proved to be highly significant to the field of early childhood intervention concerned the role of social support as a buffer of the negative effects of stress. Inspired by Caplan's (1974) thesis that social support is a protection against pathology, several studies were published during the late 1970s and thereafter indicating that social support buffered psychological distress among individuals under stress, including unemployed adults (e.g., Gore, 1978; Kasl & Cobb, 1979; Kessler et al., 1987) and mothers on welfare (e.g., Colletta & Lee, 1983; Zur-Szpiro & Longfellow, 1982). A second set of studies documented naturally occurring patterns of informal help seeking (e.g., Cowen, 1982) and poor African Americans' heavy reliance on kinship ties and social networks for primary support and mutual aid (Barbarin, 1983; Stack, 1974; M. Wilson, 1986).

A third set of studies demonstrated the salutary effects of various forms of social support on parents' behavior toward their children (main effect, rather than a buffering effect). Emotional support (i.e., companionship, expressions of affection, availability of a confidant) was found to improve mothers' dispositions and, moreover, to lessen their tendency toward insensitivity and coercive discipline. Both poor and more affluent mothers receiving higher levels of emotional support (i.e., companionship, expressions of affection, availability of a confidant) report being less likely to nag, scold, ridicule, or threaten their children and are observed to interact in a more nurturant, sensitive fashion with their children. They also feel less overwhelmed by their parenting situation, more gratified by the maternal role, and more satisfied with their children (Colletta, 1981; Crnic & Greenberg, 1987; Zur-Szpiro & Longfellow, 1982), factors that may both instigate as well as result from more positive parenting behavior. In Colletta's (1981) study of adolescent mothers, about half of whom were on welfare, emotional support was the strongest predictor of the quality of maternal behavior (other kinds of support included child care, task assistance, and material, financial, and informational support). The relation between emotional support and maternal behavior was strongest when the adolescent's own family was the source of the support, as compared to support from friends or the mother's partner or spouse. Consonant with these findings is evidence that instrumental use of extended family members in the face of child-rearing problems predicts greater parenting skill (e.g., emotional/verbal responsivity, avoidance of restriction and punishment, provision of play materials, encouragement of developmental advance) among poor White adult mothers and poor African American adolescent mothers (Stevens, 1988).

Parenting support in the form of assistance with child care also was found to effect positive changes in parenting behavior. Crockenberg's (1987) observational study of poor adolescent mothers indicated that increases in the number of family members who helped with various household and child care chores predicted increases in maternal sensitivity and accessibility to the baby, as well as promptness in responding to the infant's cries. This is consistent with reports from poor mothers that they are warmer and less rejecting of their preschool children when given an opportunity to break continuous interactions with them for more than two hours (Colletta, 1979) and congruent with evidence that teenage mothers who live with their parents, compared to those who live alone, are less punitive and restrictive in their interactions with their infants (King & Fullard, 1982). Parenting support also increases the mother's ability to give effective directions to the child and her effectiveness in getting the child to conform to rules (Weinraub & Wolf, 1983).

Indirect evidence of the salutary effects of social support emerged from the research literature on child abuse as well.

Studies reported that parents who abused their children, compared to nonabusing parents, were more isolated from formal and informal support networks, less likely to have a relative living nearby, and usually had lived in their neighborhoods for shorter periods of time (Cazenave & Straus, 1979; Daniel et al., 1983; Gelles, 1980; Trickett & Susman, 1988). These findings appeared to suggest that social isolation contributes to child abuse, although it is important to acknowledge that the isolation of abusive families may be partly self-imposed, owing to perceptions of the world as hostile and threatening. In addition, abusive parents may lack interpersonal skills necessary for positive relations, a failing that may discourage other adults from initiating and maintaining social interactions with them, further reinforcing their social isolation (Trickett & Susman, 1988). In any case, research suggested that in addition to indirectly preventing child maltreatment by enhancing parents' psychological functioning, members of parents' social networks directly inhibit child abuse by purposive intervention. Network embeddedness increases detection of child abuse, and a strong sense of obligation fosters direct intervention in the interest of the child (E. Martin & Martin, 1978).

In later years, data were reported supporting the assumption that children accrued benefits from the creation and strengthening of social support systems. For example, researchers found that availability of child care support to the primary caregiver distinguished stress-resilient from stress-affected children (Cowen, Wyman, Work, & Parker, 1990). Similarly, a recent study of rural, two-parent African American families representing a wide income range indicated that adolescents whose mothers received more caregiver support from their spouses had more self-control (e.g., thinking ahead of time about consequences of actions, planning before acting, task persistence), which in turn predicted better academic outcomes and fewer externalizing and internalizing problems (Brody et al., 1994). Increased parenting or emotional support, and more nurturant parenting behavior as a result, may explain why emotional adjustment in poor African American children living in mother-grandmother families is almost as high as that of children living in mother-father families, and significantly higher than that of children living alone with the mother (Kellam, Ensminger, & Turner, 1977). In general, though, the bulk of the evidence suggests that parents' social networks have more indirect than direct effects on the child through their effects on the mother (M. Wilson, 1989).

Although the research literature provides incontrovertible evidence that social support enhances psychological and maternal functioning, it also contains a number of cautionary notes that merit careful attention from those formulating and implementing programs that rely on the creation and strengthening of social support systems for families under stress. First, the protective effects of social support vary by context and circumstance. Support relationships exert a more positive influence on emotional and parental functioning when psychological distress is relatively low (Crockenberg, 1987), during times of major life transitions (Crnic & Greenberg, 1987), and when the source of stress is an event rather than a chronic condition such as persistent poverty or economic hardship (Dressler, 1985). Second, support from individuals who are also major sources of distress reduces the effectiveness of the support (Belle, 1982; Crockenberg, 1987). Likewise, embeddedness in an extended family network, while generally providing psychological and material benefits, is not without costs. These costs include feeling burdened by obligations to the extended family, feeling exploited by those who want more than they need or deserve, disagreement concerning the need for and/or use of aid, and disapproval by extended family members of potential marital partners and child-rearing practices and decisions (Stack, 1974; M. Wilson, 1986). Thus, although parent/family support has been greeted with enthusiasm and high hopes as a balm for the problems of the poor, the research literature sounds some sobering notes that call for, at the very least, guarded optimism.

Persistent Criticisms and Negative Effects of the Deficit Model. Criticism of the deficit model on which early childhood intervention was premised continued relentlessly throughout the 1970s and 1980s, although the nature and practice implications of these criticisms varied (Bronfenbrenner, 1987; Halpern, 1988; Laosa, 1984, 1989; Ogbu, 1981; Oyemade, 1985; Washington, 1985). To the extent that early childhood intervention in general has been torn away from its deficit-based moorings—an issue of some debate still—the variant that was most potent in forging this change argued that "failures" in the social environment, not personal deficiencies, were responsible for the problems of the poor. Its effect was to direct attention to the social ecology of poor families, rather than the individual, as the primary target for transformation (D. Powell, 1988).

This perspective, combined with the notion of empowerment of poor parents (Califano, 1979; Cochran, 1988), is the essence of the compensatory model of helping articulated by Brickman and his colleagues (Brickman et al., 1982). The core tenet of this model is that people are not blamed for their problems, but are held responsible for solving the problems by compelling an unwilling social environment to yield needed resources. People are seen and see themselves as having to compensate, via effort, ingenuity, and collaboration with others, among other strategies, for the hardships and obstacles imposed on them. Likewise, people who help others under the assumptions of this model see themselves as compensating by providing assistance and opportunities that the recipients deserve, but somehow do not have. However, the responsibility for using the help and determining whether the help is successful is seen to lie with the recipients. This ideological perspective is embodied in Jesse Jackson's repeated assertion to urban, economically distressed African Americans that "You are not responsible for being down, but you are responsible for getting up" and that "Both tears and sweat are wet and salty, but they render a different result. Tears will get you sympathy, but sweat will get you change" (Brickman et al., 1982).

An evolving orientation toward transformation of the environment, rather than the individual, was also a product of growing awareness of the ill effects of the deficit or person-blame model. In contrast to the beneficial effects of emotional support from family and friends, several investigations found use of community/neighborhood services to have no enhancing effect on the psychological well-being and parenting behavior of adolescent mothers (Colletta, 1981; Colletta & Lee, 1983; Crockenberg, 1987). In fact, in one study, adolescent mothers were more dissatisfied with professionals than any other group of helpers. Health professionals were often seen as unsympathetic, impatient, disapproving, uninformative, and offering parenting advice that contradicted that of family members or other professionals. In essence, they provided these mothers little, if any, emotional, informational, or instrumental support and hence, had no salutary effect on their mental health or parenting (Crockenberg, 1987). Evidence that attributional biases moderated the impact of economic hardship on adults' psychological functioning also served notice of the dysfunctionality of person-blame attributions. For example, researchers found that men who held themselves responsible for the loss of income or a job (e.g., Buss & Redburn, 1983; Cohn, 1978; Kasl & Cobb, 1979) and poor African American women who blamed themselves for being on welfare (Goodban, 1985) had more psychological and physical health problems than those who did not blame themselves for their economic difficulties. Extrapolating these findings, professional helpers who covertly and overtly heap blame on poor parents for their difficult circumstances essentially compromise their avowed mission because such attributions, reflected in behaviors and attitudes, render the helpers less effective in ameliorating psychological and parenting problems.

Evaluations of Ecologically Oriented Interventions

The research discussed above helped illuminate the ecology of poor families and the multidimensionality of family poverty. As such, it increased understanding of the pathways by which poverty influences children's development and expanded the focal targets of change to include concrete conditions, social circumstances, and other features of the ecology. It also nurtured an appreciation of the heterogeneity of the poverty population and, therefore, a tendency toward developing programs for distinct subgroups within the poverty population. In Schorr's (1989) qualitative evaluation of a broad cross-section of programs for poor children and families, whose services ran the gamut from health, social services, and family support to education, programs judged to be most effective in increasing positive outcomes for poor children were all predicated on an ecological model. Specifically, they typically offered a broad spectrum of coherent, easy-to-use services (recognizing that social and emotional support and help with concrete problems such as food and housing are often prerequisites to a family's ability to make use of other interventions such as parenting education); provided help to parents as adults in order that they could make good use of services for their children; and allowed staff members to exercise discretion, redefine their roles, and cross traditional professional and bureaucratic boundaries to respond to clients' needs. Given these characteristics, Schorr's conclusion that many highly successful interventions are "unstandardized and idiosyncratic" (p. 268) is not surprising.

In the sections that follow, we focus attention on the effects of two categories of ecologically oriented interventions that proliferated during the 1980s and 1990s, namely, home visitation programs and two-generation programs. They are but a small sampling of a multitude of ecologically oriented programs for poor children and families, but are of special interest because of their comparatively strong research designs and because several have been subject to intensive evaluation.

Home Visitation Programs. As noted previously, home visitation programs date back at least to the latter half of the nineteenth century, when well-to-do women associated with private relief agencies and charity organizations made home visits to poor families "to provide a mixture of support, scrutiny, and advice" (Halpern, 1988, p. 285). This helping strategy was revitalized during the late 1970s and 1980s, when several home visitation programs were established to promote positive functioning in poor mothers and children and to prevent several problems associated with poverty. In 1989, the federal government responded to the growing popularity of these programs by authorizing funding of home visitation for pregnant women and infants, by which time a number of state governments had begun supporting maternal and child home visitation programs with Medicaid dollars (Olds & Kitzman, 1990). Home visitation programs are of particular interest because they permit within- and across-study comparisons of the relative effectiveness of programs that are more or less ecological in their approach.

Promotion of Maternal Teaching and Children's Cognitive Development. Several studies exist of randomized trials with poor families that aimed to promote cognitively stimulating mother-child interaction and, in turn, children's cognitive development either through parent education alone (e.g., Levenstein et al., 1983; Scarr & McCartney, 1988) or a combination of parent education and social support (Bernard et al., 1985; Gutelius et al., 1972; Olds, Henderson, Chamberlain, & Tatelbaum, 1986a, 1986b). Both types of home visitation intervention have produced positive effects on maternal parenting and teaching behaviors and on children's cognitive functioning. In general, though, programs that address the broader ecology of the family by providing parent education as well as social support (e.g., help locating needed community resources, establishing a therapeutic alliance between mother and nurse home visitor) produce stronger and more enduring effects on mothers' parenting and teaching behaviors and children's cognitive functioning than programs that provide parent education only, or parent education combined with minimal social support (e.g., referrals without establishment of a therapeutic alliance; Olds & Kitzman, 1993; Schorr, 1989). Across-program comparisons also suggest that home visitation programs that target poor families at particularly high risk of parenting problems (e.g., unmarried adolescent mothers living alone with child, drug-addicted mothers) are generally more effective than those focusing on heterogeneous groups of poor children and families (for a more detailed review of efficacy studies of these programs, see Olds & Kitzman, 1990, 1993).

Prevention of Child Maltreatment. The public institution charged to protect the welfare of dependent, neglected, and abused children is the public child welfare system. In response to criticism that child welfare agencies devote insufficient effort to placement prevention and provide care of questionable quality to children who have been removed from their own homes, the Adoption Assistance and Child Welfare Act was passed in 1980. It mandated that a certain portion of funding of child welfare agencies must be allocated toward services intended to reduce the need for placement of children in foster care, reunify families, and find adoptive families for those children who cannot return home. Family-centered, home-based service programs are among the options available to meet these requirements. These programs focus on the family system, not just the mother, and its social and physical context as the target for change. They typically provide counseling and concrete services such as housekeeping assistance and day care. Unfortunately, very few well-designed studies exist of the effectiveness of this approach versus more traditional approaches to preventing child placement. Existing evaluations tend to be seriously flawed (e.g., lack of comparison or control groups, inadequate descriptions of service activities). Furthermore, almost no research has been done to determine if these programs affect family functioning or to assess the relation between changes in family functioning and placement (Frankel, 1988).

One of the better-quality studies of the effectiveness of different approaches to prevention of child abuse and placement used a design reminiscent of the one employed by Olds et al. (1986a) in their study of intervention effects on preterm delivery and low birthweight. Wolfe, Edwards, Manion, and Koverola (1988) assessed the relative effects of support services alone versus parent education combined with support services on the parenting behavior of mothers who were under supervision from a child protective service agency because public health nurses suspected that a child living in the home was at high risk of maltreatment. In addition to receiving standard agency services (e.g., informal discussion of topics related to health and family, social activities, periodic home visits from caseworkers), mothers in the parent education intervention received didactic instruction and exposure to modeling and rehearsal procedures to increase positive child management skills (e.g., rewarding compliance, using more praise and less criticism, giving concise demands). Results indicated that, in comparison to mothers who received only standard agency services, mothers in the parent education intervention had more positive attitudes and feelings about parenting and reported less depressive symptomatology, though the two groups did not differ on their child-rearing methods as assessed by home observation. One year following treatment, caseworkers rated mothers in the parent intervention group as managing their children significantly better and at lower risk of maltreating the child than mothers in the comparison group.

These findings are in general accord with those from a randomized trial of nurse home visitation of primiparas mothers who were either teenagers, unmarried, or of low SES (Olds et al., 1986b). One group received home visits once every two weeks during pregnancy. For a second group, home visits continued with decreasing frequency until the child was 2 years of age. During these visits, nurses provided mothers with information about infants' development and socioemotional and cognitive needs (e.g., crying behavior and its meaning; infant's need for progressively more complex motor, social, and intellectual experiences), encouraged involvement of relatives and friends in child care and support of the mother, and connected families with community health and human service agencies. Among poor, unmarried teenage mothers, those who were visited by a nurse had fewer instances of verified child abuse and neglect during the first two years of the child's life, reported less conflict with and scolding of their 6-month-old infants, were observed in their homes to restrict and punish their children (10- and 22-month-olds) less frequently, and provided more appropriate play materials, compared to those who received either no services or only free transportation to medical offices for prenatal and well-child care. In addition, during the second year of life, regardless of the families' risk status, babies of nurse-visited women were seen in the emergency room less frequently and were seen by physicians less frequently for accidents and poisoning. However, differences in rates of maltreatment did not persist during the two-year period after the program ended.

Notwithstanding the short-term positive findings from these two studies, randomized trials of programs designed to prevent child maltreatment generally do not demonstrate overall, sustained decreases in maltreatment as evidenced by state Child Protective Services records (Olds & Kitzman, 1990, 1993). Some have found differences that are suggestive of a reduction in maltreatment such as lower rates of severe diaper rash (Hardy & Streett, 1989) or decreased use of medical services associated with child abuse and neglect (e.g., hospitalizations for serious injury; J. Gray, Cutler, Dean, & Kempe, 1979; Hardy & Streett, 1989). In their detailed review of these randomized trials, Olds and Kitzman (1993) detected no clear pattern in findings as a function of program characteristics (e.g., comprehensiveness, intensity), but noted that two of the programs that produced positive effects in a subsample of women or on at least some variables associated with abuse and neglect employed especially well-trained home visitors who remained through the course of the study.

Prevention of Preterm Delivery and Low Birthweight. During the 1980s, rapid growth occurred in home visiting programs to prevent preterm delivery and low birthweight and to improve the health and development of preterm or low-birthweight infants and their parents. Most of these programs focused on poor, unmarried adolescents and young adult women, and many combined health education, parent education, and various forms of instrumental and emotional support (e.g., Olds et al., 1986a; Resnick, Armstrong, & Carter, 1988). The immediate precipitant of these programs was a burgeoning body of research suggesting that poverty adversely affected children's cognitive development partly by impairing their physical health status at birth and restricting their ability to overcome perinatal complications. Numerous studies had found that poor children were overrepresented in premature samples due partly to substandard or total lack of prenatal care and inadequate nutrition. Evidence also existed that poor children were more likely to be exposed prenatally to illegal drugs as well as to legal drugs such as nicotine and alcohol and that such exposure increased perinatal complications such as prematurity, low birthweight, small head circumference, and severe respiratory problems (Randolph & Adams-Taylor, in press). These complications were found to be risk factors for delayed cognitive development, especially in poor children. In particular, research indicated that poor children were less able than affluent children to overcome the problems created by perinatal complications, apparently because they grow up in circumstances marked by fewer social, educational, and material resources (Escalona, 1984; Werner & Smith, 1977).

Olds and Kitzman (1990) contrasted the effects of four home visiting prenatal programs (all randomized trials) on birthweight and length of gestation, three of which adopted a narrow social support model, in contrast to an ecological approach followed in the fourth program. The three programs exemplifying a social support model assumed that high rates of preterm delivery and low birthweight among poor women are caused by high rates of psychosocial stress in the absence of social support. To test this assumption, home visitors in the three programs provided various kinds of social support (e.g., serving as a confidant, providing concrete assistance such as help with transportation and child care, facilitating women's use of community services, helping women with their relationships with family members and friends, involving family members and friends in child care and support of the mother), but actively avoided teaching about health-related behaviors or only provided such information upon request. In contrast, a fourth program followed a broader ecological model, integrating social support with education about health-related behaviors such as smoking, alcohol consumption, nonprescription drug use, and managing the complications of pregnancy. Note that in this across-study comparison, health education, rather than social support, is the distinguishing feature of the approach labeled ecological, as provision of social support to improve the broader context of women's pregnancy is a common denominator of the programs.

Only the ecological program had a discernible positive effect on birthweight and length of gestation, and the effect was concentrated among women who smoked or who were very young (under 17 years) at the time of program entry (Olds et al., 1986a). This pattern of findings suggests that programs are more likely to be effective if they are more comprehensive in their approach and target women with specific risks for preterm delivery or low birthweight (e.g., smoking, alcohol, illicit drug use). However, more corroborating evidence is needed given that the subsample in which effects were identified in the Olds et al. study was quite small and that no similar effects were found in a more recent evaluation of a prenatal, home visiting program that also combined social support with education (Villar et al., 1992). Moreover, Olds et al.'s prenatal home visitation program had no enduring effects on maternal and child functioning (e.g., cognitive performance), despite nurses' attempts to establish a close working relationship with families and their success in improving women's health-related behaviors, the psychosocial conditions of pregnancy, and the health status of babies born to smokers and young adolescents.

Overall, home visiting prenatal programs of varying levels of comprehensiveness generally have not produced significant reductions in preterm delivery or low birthweight or reliable improvement in utilization of routine prenatal services. Even if successful in improving pregnancy outcomes, prenatal home visitation does not appear sufficient to promote long-term maternal and child functioning (Olds & Kitzman, 1993). This pattern of negative findings may be due to insufficient intensity or poor program implementation, but is more likely attributable to failure of most of these programs to concentrate directly on elimination of known behavioral antecedents of poor pregnancy outcomes (e.g., smoking; for a fuller discussion of these issues and a detailed review of the effects of prenatal home visiting programs, see Olds & Kitzman, 1990, 1993).

Two-Generation Programs. The most recent genre of antipoverty programs, labeled two-generation programs, are distinguished by a combination of services for children and a more omnibus parent component that provides parenting education and social support but gives greater emphasis than most of its predecessors to adult education, literacy training, and other job skills training intended to help parents become economically sufficient. Ancillary services such as transportation, meals, and child care are typically provided so that parents can participate in the latter activities. The child-focused component of these programs usually includes educational day care or preschool education, although the intensity of child-focused services of this category of programs varies tremendously (S. Smith, 1995).

Two-generation programs, most of which began in the early 1990s, owe their emergence partly to growing recognition of the limitations of unigeneration programs, whether focused on children or their parents. Among the specific arguments that have laid the groundwork for more omnibus programs are that (a) parenting programs may improve parenting skills, but children cannot wait to accrue the benefits of such programs because some critical aspects of their development occur on their own timetable (St. Pierre et al., 1995); (b) early childhood education programs can confer to children enhanced cognitive and socio-emotional skills, but high-quality parenting can increase the prospects that these skills will translate into school success; and (c) neither child-focused nor parent-focused programs alone provide interventions sufficiently expansive to address the multiplicity of problems and needs that poor families face (e.g., unemployment, limited literacy and job skills) and to significantly improve the economic status of poor families (Larner, Halpern, & Harkavy, 1992; Oyemade, 1985; St. Pierre et al., 1995; Weiss, 1993). These arguments, taken together, have been sufficiently cogent to forge this new category of interventions into the ranks of an already complex array of programs designed to serve poor children and families (St. Pierre et al., 1995; S. Smith, 1995).

Several two-generation programs are part of Head Start, among them the Comprehensive Child Development Program (CCDP) and the Head Start Family Service Centers (FSCs; S. Smith & Zaslow, 1995). One of the earliest two-generation programs, the Child and Family Resource Program (CFRP), described previously, operated as a Head Start demonstration project. This corpus of programs is in keeping with Head Start's long-standing tradition of implementing demonstration projects both within and outside its basic core program to ascertain more effective ways of serving poor children and families (Zigler & Styfco,

1994a). Well-known two-generation program models that are not part of Head Start include Even Start Family Literacy Program (St. Pierre & Swartz, 1995), Avance Parent-Child Education Program (Walker, Rodriguez, Johnson, & Cortez, 1995), and New Chance (Quint & Egeland, 1995).

A description of CCDP is presented here to exemplify the approach that characterizes most two-generation programs. Initiated in 1990, CCDP is a national demonstration program that aims to enhance parents' progress toward economic self-sufficiency by increasing the scope, duration, and intensity of services, while maintaining the services to children provided by Head Start's basic program. It operates in both rural and urban areas and provides integrated, comprehensive, and continuous support services to over 4,440 low-income families with a newborn child for up to five years. Parents and other adult members of the family receive prenatal care, parenting education, health care, adult education, job training, and other supports as needed, such as treatment for mental health problems and substance abuse. Adult literacy education, employment counseling, and job training and placement are typically provided through linkages and referrals to community colleges and other local educational institutions. Job linkages are also made with employers and agencies. CCDP provides relatively low-intensive services to children from birth through age 3, using biweekly home visits for a maximum of 30 minutes. The focus of instruction during these visits is parenting skills. When children reach age 4, they enroll in a Head Start center that provides a year-long, half-day, center-based program (St. Pierre et al., 1995).

In addition to a stronger focus on adult services, several features of CCDP are intended to improve on Head Start's capacity to deliver two-generation services. These include (a) broader eligibility requirements (e.g., a family may remain in the program even if its income rises above the poverty threshold at any time during the program's five-year period); (b) provision of services to all members of a participating family, broadly defined to include any children of the primary caregiver under age 18 in the household and any family member residing in the household having major responsibility for the care of the focal child; (c) provision of services to a parent of the focal child who resides outside the household; and (d) expanded and stronger provisions for ensuring that families can gain access to needed services (Parker et al., 1995).

All six of the two-generation programs cited here have been or are being evaluated via randomized trials (St. Pierre et al., 1995; St. Pierre, Layzer, & Barnes, 1996). The evaluation of the Avance program, however, used random assignment to establish groups at only one of two locations, with a matched group design employed in the second location (Walker et al., 1995). Evaluations of most of these programs have been limited to relatively short-term effects because to date, most families have been followed from the focal child's birth through the fifth year of life only.

Effects on Children. Efficacy studies indicate that two-generation programs have only small or no effects on children's cognitive development, verbal skills, and school readiness. For example, CCDP had a significantly positive effect on the health status of infants, but produced a relatively trivial positive effect (ES = .10) on 2-year-olds' cognitive functioning as measured by the Bayley Scales of Infant Development. Neither Avance nor CFRP had an effect on Bayley scores. Even Start produced a significant gain in children's school readiness skills nine months after entry in the program, but this difference dissipated once children in the control group began school (St. Pierre et al., 1996).

Effects on Mothers. Two-generation programs appear to have stronger short-term effects on parents than on children. Several have produced positive effects on parenting attitudes and behavior. For example, at the end of the first year of participation in the Avance program, program mothers compared to control group mothers had a stronger belief in their ability to determine the nature of their children's educational experiences, provided their children a more educationally stimulating home environment, and interacted in a more positive and stimulating manner with their children during videotaped play sessions (e.g., affect, vocalization, contingent praise, initiation of social interaction with child, time spent teaching child; Walker et al., 1995). Other significant changes in parents' attitudes and behavior resulting from participation in these programs include less authoritarian child-rearing attitudes, more emotional support and nurturance of the child (CCDP, CFRP, New Chance), higher expectations for the child's success, increased time spent with the child (CCDP), and increased presence of reading materials in the home (Even Start; for a more detailed review of these findings, see St. Pierre et al., 1995, 1996). Evaluations generally find relatively high levels of depressive symptomatogy in both program and control group mothers, but no evidence that programs are effective in reducing depressive symptoms or increasing mothers' self-esteem or use of social supports (St. Pierre et al., 1995; Walker et al., 1995).

Of particular significance to any assessment of two-generation programs is whether programs affect parents' educational attainment, employment status, household income, and use of welfare benefits. Longer-term evaluations of these programs are needed to draw firm conclusions about effects on these particular outcomes. At least in the short term, though, effects appear modest at best and tend to be restricted to educational attainment. Evaluations of Even Start, New Chance, and Avance indicated that program mothers, compared to control group mothers, were significantly more likely to attain a GED certificate, but this educational advancement was not accompanied by positive effects on standardized tests of adult literacy. None of the studies that measured annual household income (or average hourly wage among those employed) found positive effects (Even Start, New Chance, CCDP, CFRP, FSC), and only CFRP increased rates of employment. In general, two-generation programs have no immediate effect on use of federal benefits such as AFDC and food stamps (e.g., FSC), or actually increase participants' use of such benefits by heightening participants' awareness of their availability or by rendering more families eligible for them by virtue of increased participation in educational classes (e.g., CCDP, CFRP, New Chance; St. Pierre et al., 1995, 1996; Swartz et al., 1995).

A recent review of studies of the impact on maternal outcomes of a broader, more diverse set of educationally oriented interventions exclusive of recently implemented two-generation programs yielded a more favorable picture, perhaps because several studies followed mothers long enough to capture whatever improvements eventually occurred in mothers' educational and employment outcomes (Benasich, Brooks-Gunn, & Clewell, 1992). All of the programs provided services to poor children for at least six months during the first three years of the child's life and most provided services of some kind to mothers, though the services ranged greatly in scope, nature, and intensity. Of the 11 programs reviewed by Benasich et al. (1992) that assessed maternal education (e.g., years of schooling completed, whether or not mother returned to school) and employment (e.g., employment status, number of hours employed, job classification), all but one (i.e., Berrueta-Clement et al., 1984) found significant differences in favor of the experimental group (5 home-based; 5 center-based; e.g., Andrews et al., 1982; Garber, 1988; Gutelius et al., 1977; Olds et al., 1986a, 1986b; Seitz et al., 1985). Unfortunately, information was unavailable about the long-term poverty status and income-to-need ratios of experimental versus control group families. As is clear from St. Pierre et al.'s (1995) review of two-generation programs, educational advancement at lower levels (e.g., acquisition of GED) does not necessarily translate into higher income. Likewise, employment does not guarantee having income above the poverty line, especially if the job is unstable, has minimum fringe benefits, or pays minimum wage and if the family or household has only one wage earner.

PROGRAMS FOR POOR CHILDREN AND FAMILIES: POLICY AND PRACTICE CONSIDERATIONS

Early Childhood Intervention in Context

Ideological Context

Americans are far more supportive of government action to ensure educational opportunity than other types of social welfare (e.g., universal minimal income and health insurance), and this disparity in preference is much more pronounced among Americans than among citizens in other Western industrialized countries (Haller et al., 1990). It is not surprising, then, that early childhood education, either alone or in combination with other services, is the predominant government-sponsored strategy used in the United States to fight poverty and its negative effects. As a large-scale, publicly funded strategy, it dates back more than 150 years with the establishment of free and universal public education for White American children and the assurance by its proponent, Horace Mann, that this reform would virtually eradicate poverty. It is a natural outgrowth of the United States' tendency to focus on children as instruments of reform (de Lone, 1979).

Between 1989 and 1993, funding for Head Start increased 127% and by 1993 totaled $2.8 billion. Funding is expected to increase to $8 billion by 1998 to permit Head Start to serve a larger proportion of poor children (Kassebaum, 1994; Takanishi & DeLeon, 1994). Head Start's broad-based support derives from several sources, including strong support from Head Start parents and staff, public campaigns by advocacy groups such as the Children's Defense Fund, positive media attention, as well as empirical evidence of early childhood education's effects on children's school readiness and academic achievement (Zigler & Styfco, 1994a, 1994b). Not to be underestimated as a source of its popularity, though, is Head Start's compatibility with Americans' preference for indirect rather than direct approaches (e.g., universal minimal income) to poverty reduction (Datta, 1979; Haskins, 1989; Oyemade, 1985; Zigler, 1985). It is politically palatable because of its avowed promotion of equality of opportunity, rather than equality of condition.

Early childhood interventions touted as antipoverty programs essentially hold out the promise of ending poverty in the next generation, while preserving social harmony and buttressing the Protestant work ethic and beliefs about equal opportunity and unlimited economic and social mobility (de Lone, 1979). Because the ideal of equality of opportunity stands in sharp contrast to the reality of gross economic inequality in the United States, "the mission of childhood in this country has been defined to a considerable extent by the promise of equal opportunity" (de Lone, 1979, p. 34). This promise exerts a powerful grip on the American psyche, for what poor parent dares not hold fast to the dream of rearing offspring who "make it," who do better economically than their parents? Reality, however, is more sobering. The escape hatch is not a large one and, indeed, may be growing smaller if recent research on intergenerational income mobility (Solon, 1992) and the changing prevalence of chronic poverty (Rodgers & Rodgers, 1993) is any indication. Using intergenerational data from the Panel Study of Income Dynamics, Solon (1992) found father-son and mother-son correlations of about .40 or higher in long-run earnings, hourly wages, and family income. Based on this estimate, a son whose father is in the bottom 5% of earners has only a 1-in-20 chance of making it into the top 20% of families, a 1-in-4 chance of rising above the median income of American families, and a 2-in-5 chance of staying poor or near poor. The parent-son correlations for earnings and family income reported by Solon are higher than those typically reported in past studies (most report correlations of .20 or less, and most present data on fathers but not mothers). Correlations for ethnic minorities are likely to be even higher due to racial and ethnic barriers. Solon argues compellingly that previous studies systematically underestimated the correlation between father and son income status (and hence overestimated intergenerational income mobility) as a result of flawed and limited data (e.g., single-year measures of earnings) and unrepresentative, homogeneous samples.

The United States espouses a liberal ideology that minimizes class distinctions and proclaims equal opportunity, yet it has intergenerational mobility rates roughly comparable to those in European countries where class distinctions are exaggerated (de Lone, 1979). This contradiction exists because Americans are less likely to interpret intergenerational mobility as tied to family background and more likely to view it as evidence of the openness of their society than are individuals in, for example, Great Britain, West Germany, Austria, or Italy (T. Smith, 1990). Liberal ideology has tempered class consciousness in the United States, but so has ethnicity, religion, and especially race as sources of identity. The United States' heightened racial and ethnic consciousness is inextricably tied to the lingering effects of its systematic subordination of "castelike" ethnic and racial minorities, including its enslavement and legal segregation of African Americans, conquest and forced displacement of American Indians and Latinos, and the economic exploitation of Asian immigrants (Deparle, 1996; Ogbu, 1978).

Sociostructural and Macroeconomic Context

That many of the causes of poverty and the difficult life conditions confronting poor families are largely impervious to child- and family-level interventions (e.g., historical and contemporary racism in the labor market, lending institutions, housing; poor-quality schools; low wages paid by traditionally "female" jobs; unavailability of affordable, high-quality child care) does not augur well for the success of antipoverty policies whose core strategy involves educating or ministering to the acute needs of poor youngsters in the absence of job creation and the presence of massive numbers of jobs that do not pay their parents a living wage. It is a case of using secondary strategies to deal with primary problems (Halpern, 1988, 1990b).

Rather than effect structural changes to remedy poverty and its social ills, U.S. policymakers have overrelied on a variety of social services and programs that call for ameliorating poverty and its attendant problems largely by changing individuals, not structures. The evolving ecological approach in early childhood intervention, with its emphasis on altering social contexts in ways that enhance family life and children's development, surely represents an advance over more unidimensional, person-centered approaches, but it has not and indeed cannot alone produce significant structural or institutional change in American society. The social and economic conditions that produce developmental risks are as prevalent as ever today, despite an ever increasing proliferation of ecologically sensitive home-based and center-based programs and expansion of our national early childhood education programs for poor children and families. This overreliance on services and programs, many of which were designed to be a last resort rather than the principal resource base for developing children (Garbarino, 1992), reflects either genuine opacity about the limits of what such programs and services can realistically accomplish, or "an unwillingness to acknowledge that many of our most serious problems are a result of chosen social and economic arrangements and a reluctance to use the political process to alter arrangements even when it is acknowledged that they are harmful" (Halpern, 1991, p. 344). Moreover, because the reforms and programs invariably fall markedly short of their promise, insufficient acknowledgment of what they can accomplish bodes well for the cyclical and predictable resurrection of genetic hypotheses proclaiming the intrinsic inferiority of those individuals whom reformers sought to help (de Lone, 1979; see, e.g., Herrnstein & Murray, 1994; Jensen, 1969).

As a genre, early childhood education is no more likely to significantly reduce poverty in America than did universal public education, for it does not directly increase material resources or fundamentally alter most of the environmental conditions that produce problematic developmental outcomes and intergenerational poverty. At best, it only blunts the force of poverty and renders modest improvements in children's environmental circumstances and developmental outcomes. As is clearly documented in research studies reviewed in this chapter, although Head Start and other preschool education programs significantly increase poor children's school readiness, they leave wide gaps between poor children's school competence and that of more economically advantaged children and have only weak, if any, impacts on participants' postschool labor market participation (Royce et al., 1983). Moreover, the positive effects on preschoolers of these interventions, especially large-scale educational programs, are not sustained because of the tangle of environmental risk factors and their multiplicative adverse effects that is the lot of too many poor children in the United States (Rutter, 1979).

This analysis finds support in a recent study by Lee and Loeb (1995) that sought to clarify why the cognitive gains produced by children's participation in Head Start and model programs fade or disappear completely within two to three years after the intervention. Based on a sample of over 15,000 eighth-graders enrolled in 975 middle schools (based on a sample drawn from the National Education Longitudinal Study of 1988), the study points to poor-quality schooling subsequent to preschool intervention as a potential culprit. Compared to students who attended other preschools, former Head Start enrollees were in middle schools that were distinguished by considerably less academic rigor as reported by students, parents, and principals; lower overall quality; lower average student performance on mathematics, science, reading, and social studies achievement tests; and lower SES (i.e., average SES of children attending the school). The middle schools of former Head Start enrollees also were perceived to be more unsafe than those attended by their non–Head Start counterparts. These differences were evident after controlling for family income-to-need ratio, parents' education, and children's race and ethnicity. Similar but less pronounced differences were also found in school quality favoring students who did not attend preschool, as compared to students who formerly attended Head Start. Additional insight could be brought to bear on this issue by tracking changes in children's academic performance from the preschool years through elementary and secondary school in relation to the quality of schooling.

The challenge of producing positive effects potent enough to be of some long-term or even immediate significance in parents' and children's lives, in spite of a multiplicity of ongoing and unremitting environmental stressors, is no less daunting for service programs that are billed, not as instruments of poverty reduction, but as strategies that prevent or ameliorate poverty's negative effects on family life and children's development. As we have seen, randomized trials of home visitation programs, even those that are more comprehensive in nature, have had little overall success in preventing child maltreatment, preterm delivery, and low birthweight. They have proven more effective in promoting positive child-rearing practices and producing gains in children's cognitive functioning, though it is not known whether these effects translate into better long-term outcomes for children (Olds & Kitzman, 1990, 1993).

Recognizing the negative consequences of overoptimism, some of the most ardent supporters of these programs have conceded and even emphasized the limitations of what early childhood intervention programs can accomplish (Oyemade, 1985; Washington, 1985; Zigler & Styfco, 1994a). Zigler and Styfco (1994a), for example, recently lamented that "neither Head Start nor any preschool program can inoculate children against the ravages of poverty. Early intervention simply cannot overpower the effects of poor living conditions, inadequate nutrition and health care, negative role models, and substandard schools" (p. 129). To argue that early childhood education programs or various other forms of social and educational services are insufficient to reduce poverty and its negative effects to a major degree is not to suggest that they be eliminated. Rather, in the spirit of Zigler and Styfco's admonition, it is a call to acknowledge that child- and family-level interventions and service programs can "counter some of the injuries of inequality, but . . . cannot destroy inequality itself" (de Lone, 1979, p. 68). This acknowledgment is essential to relieve these programs of a responsibility they cannot discharge: producing greater equality.

It is too soon to tell whether two-generation programs will be similarly limited in their efficacy, but evaluations of their short-term impacts on children's development, parents' employment status, and household income are not especially impressive (St. Pierre et al., 1995, 1996). In any case, program effects on employment status and wages are likely to be highly dependent on circumstances such as the local economy that are beyond the control of these programs (Swartz et al., 1995). Given trends in the nature and context of poverty, we believe that significant reduction in the incidence of childhood poverty in the United States is ultimately likely to require the creation of government-supported work programs in impoverished communities (W. Wilson, 1996) and child-focused social insurance policies akin to those operating in many European countries (Smeeding & Torrey, 1988).

Several recent studies of the relation between income and children's development are important for their contribution to knowledge and their implications for policy and practice. These studies consistently report that the effects of persistent poverty are both negative and substantial, suggesting that policies that raise the incomes of poor families will enhance children's development, especially their cognitive functioning and educational attainments (Duncan & Brooks-Gunn, 1997; McLoyd, in press). Furthermore, evidence that increases in the incomes of families below or near the poverty line have a greater impact on children's cognitive development and educational attainment than increases in the incomes of middle-class and affluent families (Duncan et al., in press; Smith et al., 1997) bolster the assertion of child advocates that targeting primarily poor families, rather than middle- and upper-income families, for income subsidies and tax relief will have more salutary impacts on children's development generally. Succinctly put, recently documented nonlinear effects of income are consonant with the view that ". . . reducing poverty is associated with improved outcomes for children, whereas increasing affluence is not" (Garbarino, 1992, p. 233).

Barring income increments for all poor families, Duncan et al.'s (in press) research on the differential effects of the timing of poverty may argue for welfare policies that give highest priority to the elimination of deep and persistent poverty during children's early years of life, rather than during middle childhood and adolescence. Evidence that family income is a stronger predictor of IQ and school achievement than are parental education or occupation invites numerous inferences (Duncan et al., 1994), one of which is that programs that raise incomes of poor families directly (e.g., increasing welfare benefits, tax credits, minimum wage) may be comparatively more effective in fostering children's development (in addition to being easier to design and administer) than programs that seek to modify family characteristics that mark low SES and low family income. Resolution of this issue requires careful, cost-benefit analyses in which expenditures on income-transfer programs and service-delivery programs (including preschool education, nutrition, education and job training programs for parents) are compared and "judged by the benefits they produce relative to their costs" (Duncan et al., in press).

Historical Context

Recent trends in childhood poverty raise questions about whether early childhood intervention and service delivery based on models developed during the 1960s and 1970s are even less effective today than in previous times. As we noted at the beginning of this chapter, since the mid-1970s, poverty has become more geographically concentrated and its environmental stressors more pervasive and life-threatening (e.g., homelessness, street violence, illegal drugs; Shinn & Gillespie, 1994; W. Wilson, 1996; Zigler, 1994). It also appears to have become more chronic and less transitory, though the data on this are less conclusive (Duncan & Rodgers, 1991; Rodgers & Rodgers, 1993). Conversely, jobs, public and private services (e.g., parks, community centers, child care), and informal social supports have become less accessible to the poor (W. Wilson, 1996; Zigler, 1994).

These changes in the persistence, context, and environmental correlates of poverty signal more acute needs among the poor. Although Head Start apparently has always served the poorest of the poor (Schnur et al., 1992), the deprivation experienced by that group may well have increased over the years (Slaughter, Lindsey, Nakagawa, & Kuehne, 1989). If the disadvantages resulting from poverty have increased, the injurious effects of poverty may have intensified as well, necessitating modifications in extant programs. This inference is supported by evidence that persistent poverty is more deleterious to children's development and home environments than is transitory poverty and research indicating that neighborhood poverty has adverse effects on children's functioning independent of family-level poverty (Brooks-Gunn et al., 1995; Duncan et al., 1994; Duncan & Brooks-Gunn, 1997). Consequently, programs based on models of intervention, prevention, and service delivery developed prior to the mid-1970s may be less effective in buffering the effects of today's poverty (Takanishi & DeLeon, 1994; Zigler, 1994). Achieving remediation effects equivalent to those produced by interventions implemented in earlier times may require interventions that are more intensive, comprehensive, and integrative. Data directly bearing on this question are not available. Nonetheless, what we do know is that studies of the efficacy of early childhood education that undergird government policy favorable to preschool education for poor children are based on children who participated in those programs during the 1960s and 1970s (Barnett, 1995). This raises crucial questions about the generalizability of the studies' findings and the appropriateness of the programs themselves to the contemporary scene. To some extent, the flexibility accorded Head Start programs, whereby they are permitted to adapt components to local needs and resources, mitigates the latter concern. However, this flexibility does not result in incremental funding if the needs of those to be served increase.

At the very least, the family support services component of Head Start should be shored up (Kassebaum, 1994; Takanishi & DeLeon, 1994) and such a component added to early childhood education programs lacking it. Better integration of services also is needed (Illback, 1994). These recommendations are justified on the basis of the changing nature of poverty and strong evidence of the adverse and cumulative effects on children's cognitive functioning and home learning environment of risk factors such as low social support and stressful life events (Brooks-Gunn et al., 1995; Sameroff et al., 1987). The relation of these risk factors within the family ecology to children's cognitive functioning is consistently stronger in poor families than in affluent families, suggesting that need for these support services may be especially acute and their provision particularly beneficial to children whose parents are poor (Bee et al., 1982).

Working with Poor Children and Families

The effectiveness of programs intended to enhance poor children's intellectual and educational achievement is not only a function of whether the services provided by the programs are sufficiently intensive, comprehensive, content-appropriate, and flexible to meet families' needs. It would be a serious error to ignore the potency of the affective dimension of programs. It is this dimension on which we concentrate here. Schorr (1989) found that staffs of successful programs were not only technically skilled, but were committed to and respectful of the families they served, making it possible for them to establish caring and trusting relationships with service recipients. According families wide latitude to decide what services to utilize and how they wanted to participate and taking account of the families' particular goals for their children were among the ways respect and trust were established and maintained.

The established link between attributional biases and psychological well-being suggests that blaming the poor for their plight will exacerbate their psychological problems, heighten mistrust and apprehension, and undercut the professional's role as facilitator and helper (Belle, 1984; Crockenberg, 1987). Thus, programmatic efforts to ameliorate or prevent negative outcomes in parental functioning, parental psychological well-being, and children's functioning should be unambivalently supportive rather than punitive in nature. Although the family support movement and ecological approaches to intervention essentially endorse this position, effectively actualizing this principle requires recognition of the formidable cognitive challenges it poses to prevailing sentiments.

Americans harbor a profound ambivalence toward and suspicion of poor people, partly because the value and myth of independence and self-sufficiency are so deeply etched in American society as to be virtually sacrosanct. A sense of morality, ethics, and magnanimity moves us to help them, but our steadfast ideological commitment to individual culpability as a primary explanation of poverty compels us to punish them (Halpern, 1991; Pelton, 1989). Racism, cultural ethnocentrism, and ignorance of "non-mainstream" cultural traditions intensify these negative attitudes when the poor in question are ethnic minorities. The typical middle-class service provider or teacher has never experienced the stressors that children and families living in concentrated poverty routinely confront. This lack of common history and experience, combined with the negative view of the poor that prevails in American society, means that persons who work with poor children and families in intervention and prevention programs must confront and work arduously and self-consciously to minimize ambivalence about the character and worth of poor people and to bridge the class- and culture-linked chasms between them and the poor. Otherwise, their effectiveness will be undermined. Visits to clients' neighborhoods and homes, when undertaken as a genuine educational experience, can help interventionists appreciate clients' ongoing struggles to survive and raise their children in the midst of daunting environmental realities (Belle, 1984). Educators and service providers also need to grapple with ethical issues that often arise in intervention programs for poor children and parents (e.g., procedures that restrict the autonomy of participants who are highly vulnerable and in greatest need; activities that usurp the parental role and conflict with the child's family heritage and values; McAdoo, 1990).

Knowing and demonstrating sensitivity to the cultural characteristics and class-linked expressions of the families and children to be served cannot be overemphasized (McAdoo, 1990; Slaughter, 1988b), although it is equally important to recognize the existence of differences within groups of poor and ethnic minority families and individuals. Without this competence, status cues assume exaggerated importance in unfamiliar interpersonal situations, often operating to the detriment of lower-class individuals and hindering the establishment of a trusting and mutually respectful relationship. For example, as early as kindergarten, status cues appear to contribute to negative biases about the intellectual capacity of poor children, which in turn can impede their educational and economic mobility through various classroom dynamics (Gouldner, 1978; Rist, 1970). In a well-designed study of first-grade teachers and students in a socially heterogeneous, urban public school system, Alexander et al. (1987) found that first-grade teachers' own social origins tempered their reactions to the status attributes (i.e., race and SES) of their students and that these reactions had significant implications for children's achievement. High SES teachers (i.e., those who grew up in middle-class homes), compared to low SES teachers (i.e., those who grew up in lower-class homes), held more negative attitudes about the maturity and social competence of poor, African American first-graders and held lower performance expectations for them than for their White peers. African American students in classrooms taught by high SES teachers began first grade with test scores very similar to their White counterparts', but by year's end they had fallen markedly behind. Race differences in grades were especially pronounced. In classrooms taught by low SES teachers, however, pupil race was unrelated to teachers' affective orientations and judgments, and no race differences were found in grades or test performance. Alexander et al. speculate that high SES teachers may be less committed to African American students and think less well of their abilities partly because they are less familiar with poor and minority individuals and their surroundings and culture. This can lead them to misconstrue certain cues (e.g., style of dress, deportment, language usage) as fundamental failings in the child.

It is also the case that negative stereotypes can have untoward effects on the behavior of individuals who are the objects of stereotypes. A case in point is the stereotype of African Americans as intellectually inferior to Whites. In a series of laboratory experiments, Steele and Aronson (1995) found that, controlling for verbal and quantitative scores on the Scholastic Aptitude Test, African American college students at a prestigious private university underperformed in relation to Whites when tests (items taken from the Graduate Record Examination study guides) were presented as diagnostic of intellectual ability, but matched the performance of Whites when the same tests were described as laboratory problem-solving tasks. Even asking students to indicate their race on an information sheet immediately prior to taking the test was sufficient to depress African Americans' performance compared to Whites'; when students were not asked to indicate their race, there were no race differences in performance. If these effects are generalizable to the classroom, we would predict that African Americans would perform less well than Whites of equal ability on tests construed as measures of intellectual ability.

Members of stigmatized groups typically buffer their self-esteem from the prejudice of others through a variety of social and psychological mechanisms. In their extensive literature review, Crocker and Major (1989) presented compelling, convergent evidence of the use of three of these self-protective mechanisms, namely (a) attributing negative feedback to prejudice against members of the stigmatized group, (b) selectively comparing their outcomes with those of members of their own group, and (c) selectively devaluing those attributes on which their group typically fares poorly and valuing those attributes on which their group excels. Although these self-protective mechanisms have positive consequences for self-esteem, each of them may undermine motivation to improve one's individual performance in areas where one's group is disadvantaged. Ultimately, the performance level of the stigmatized group may lag behind that of nonstigmatized groups even when individual capabilities do not warrant these differences. Within the domain of school achievement, these processes can lead to academic "helplessness" and low levels of motivation among poor children and children stigmatized because of their racial and ethnic minority status. Paradoxically, to the degree that they operate, these self-protective strategies advance a trajectory of underachievement set in motion by teachers' prejudiced attitudes and behavior and other stigmatizing experiences in the broader environment. A number of scholars have provided compelling evidence of these dynamics among African American and poor students (Brantlinger, 1991; Fordham, 1988; Fordham & Ogbu, 1986). Treatment of individuals belonging to stigmatized groups in a caring and respectful manner minimizes the need for them to invoke self-protective strategies.

As we indicated at the beginning of this chapter, relatively high rates of immigration among minorities are contributing to the growth in the proportion of racial and ethnic minorities in the U.S. population. Because of the socioeconomic and demographic characteristics of recent immigrants (A. Portes & Zhou, 1993; Rumbaut, 1994), the ethnic diversity of the poverty population will increase, which, in turn, may well intensify the challenges of designing and implementing antipoverty programs for poor children and families that are culturally sensitive (e.g., awareness and respect for socialization values and practices; Halpern, 1992; Williams, 1987). Educational interventions and family support programs that serve African Americans and Latinos have provided valuable lessons about some of the essentials for accomplishing this goal (e.g., Larner et al., 1992; Slaughter, 1988a, 1988b; Walker et al., 1995). However, because newcomers often experience stressors uncommon to or less pronounced among long-time residents (e.g., language barriers, dislocations and separations from support networks, dual struggle to preserve identity and to acculturate, changes in SES status; Rogler, 1994), adaptations in the program content and service delivery may be required to achieve optimal cultural sensitivity and maximum effectiveness in programs serving immigrant parents and their children.

ACKNOWLEDGMENTS

The author expresses appreciation to Sheba Shakir, Jamila Ponton, and Dina Greenberg for their bibliographic and editorial assistance and to the Departments of Psychology at Duke University and the University of Michigan for their support in the preparation of this chapter. Correspondence regarding this chapter should be addressed to the author, who is now at the University of Michigan, Center for Human Growth and Development, 300 N. Ingalls, Ann Arbor, Michigan 48109.

REFERENCES

Abelson, W., Zigler, E., & DeBlasi, C. (1974). Effects of a four-year follow through program on economically disadvantaged children. *Journal of Educational Psychology, 66,* 756–771.

Ainsworth, M. D. (1973). The development of infant-mother attachment. In B. M. Caldwell & H. N. Ricciuti (Eds.), *Review of child development research* (Vol. 3, pp. 1–94). Chicago: University of Chicago Press.

Alexander, K., Entwisle, D., & Thompson, M. (1987). School performance, status relations, and the structure of sentiment: Bringing the teacher back in. *American Sociological Review, 52,* 665–682.

Andrews, S. R., Blumenthal, J. B., Johnson, D. L., Kahn, A. J., Ferguson, C. J., Lasater, T. M., Malone, P. E., & Wallace, D. B. (1982). The skills of mothering: A study of parent child development centers. *Monographs of the Society for Research in Child Development, 47*(6, Serial No. 198).

Baldwin, A. L., Baldwin, C., & Cole, R. E. (1990). Stress resistant families and stress resistant children. In J. Rolf, A. S. Masten, D. Cicchetti, K. Nuechterlein, & S. Weintraub (Eds.), *Risk and protective factors in the development of psychopathology* (pp. 257–280). Cambridge, England: Cambridge University Press.

Bane, M. J., & Ellwood, D. (1986). Slipping into and out of poverty: The dynamics of spells. *Journal of Human Resources, 21,* 1–23.

Bane, M. J., & Ellwood, D. (1989). One fifth of the nation's children: Why are they poor? *Science, 245,* 1047–1053.

Baratz, S., & Baratz, J. (1970). Early childhood intervention: The social science base of institutional racism. *Harvard Educational Review, 40,* 29–50.

Barbarin, O. (1983). Coping with ecological transitions by black families: A psychosocial model. *Journal of Community Psychology, 11,* 308–322.

Barnett, W. S. (1995). Long-term effects of early childhood programs on cognitive and school outcomes. *The Future of Children, 5,* 25–50.

Bartfeld, J., & Meyer, D. (1994). Are there really deadbeat dads? The relationship between ability to pay, enforcement, and compliance in nonmarital child support cases. *Social Service Review, 68,* 219–235.

Baumrind, D. (1967). Child care practices anteceding three patterns of preschool behavior. *Genetic Psychology Monographs, 75,* 43–88.

Baumrind, D. (1971). Current patterns of parental authority. *Developmental Psychology Monograph, 4*(1, Part 2).

Becker, W. C. (1964). Consequences of different kinds of parental discipline. In M. L. Hoffman & L. W. Hoffman (Eds.), *Review of child development research* (Vol. 1, pp. 169–208). New York: Russell-Sage Foundation.

Beckwith, L. (1971). Relationships between attributes of mothers and their infants' IQ scores. *Child Development, 42,* 1083–1097.

Bee, H., Barnard, K., Eyres, S., Gray, C., Hammond, M., Spietz, A., Snyder, C., & Clark, B. (1982). Prediction of IQ and language skill from perinatal status, child performance, family characteristics, and mother-infant interaction. *Child Development, 53,* 1134–1156.

Bee, H., Egeren, L., Streissguth, P., Nyman, B., & Leckie, M. (1969). Social class differences in maternal teaching strategies and speech patterns. *Developmental Psychology, 1,* 726–734.

Bell, T. H. (1975). The child's right to have a trained parent. *Elementary School Guidance and Counseling, 9,* 271–276.

Belle, D. (1982). Social ties and social support. In D. Belle (Ed.), *Lives in stress: Women and depression* (pp. 133–144). Beverly Hills, CA: Sage.

Belle, D. (1984). Inequality and mental health: Low income and minority women. In L. Walker (Ed.), *Women and mental health policy* (pp. 135–150). Beverly Hills, CA: Sage.

Beller, E. (1983). The Philadelphia Study: The impact of preschool on intellectual and socioemotional development. In Consortium for Longitudinal Studies (Ed.), *As the twig is bent: Lasting effects of preschool programs* (pp. 33–69). Hillsdale, NJ: Erlbaum.

Belsky, J. (1984). The determinants of parenting: A process model. *Child Development, 55,* 83–96.

Benasich, A., Brooks-Gunn, J., & Clewell, B. (1992). How do mothers benefit from early intervention programs? *Journal of Applied Developmental Psychology, 13,* 311–362.

Bereiter, C., & Englemann, S. (1966). *Teaching disadvantaged children in the preschool.* Englewood Cliffs, NJ: Prentice-Hall.

Bernard, K. E., Magyary, D., Sumner, G., Booth, C., Mitchell, S., & Spieker, S. (1985). Prevention of parental alterations for women with low social support. *Psychiatry, 51,* 248–253.

Bernstein, B. (1961). Social class and linguistic development: A theory of social learning. In A. Halsey, J. Floud, & C. Anderson (Eds.), *Education, economy, and society* (pp. 288–314). New York: Free Press.

Berrueta-Clement, J., Schweinhart, L., Barnett, W. S., Epstein, A., & Weikart, D. (1984). *Changed lives: The effects of the Perry Preschool Program on youths through age 19. Monographs of the High/Scope Educational Research Foundation* (Vol. 8). Ypsilanti, MI: High/Scope Press.

Bishop, J. (1977). *Jobs, cash transfers, and marital instability: A review of the evidence.* Madison: University of Wisconsin Institute for Research on Poverty.

Bloom, B. S. (1964). *Stability and change in human characteristics.* New York: Wiley.

Bradley, R. H., & Caldwell, B. M. (1976). The relations of infants' home environments to mental test performance at fifty-four months: A follow-up study. *Child Development, 47,* 1172–1174.

Brantlinger, E. (1991). Social class distinctions in adolescents' reports of problems and punishment in school. *Behavioral Disorders, 17,* 36–46.

Braun, S., & Edwards, E. (1972). *History and theory of early childhood education.* Belmont, CA: Wadsworth.

Brewer, R. M. (1988). Black women in poverty: Some comments on female-headed families. *Signs: Journal of Women in Culture and Society, 13,* 331–339.

Brickman, P., Rabinowitz, V., Karuza, J., Coates, D., Cohn, E., & Kidder, L. (1982). Models of helping and coping. *American Psychologist, 37,* 368–384.

Brim, O. (1959). *Education for child rearing.* New York: Russell-Sage Foundation.

Brody, G., Stoneman, Z., Flor, D., McCrary, C., Hastings, L., & Conyers, O. (1994). Financial resources, parent psychological functioning, parent co-caregiving, and early adolescent competence in rural two-parent African-American families. *Child Development, 65,* 590–605.

Bronfenbrenner, U. (1975). Is early intervention effective? In M. Guttentag & E. Struening (Eds.), *Handbook of evaluation research* (Vol. 2, pp. 519–603). Beverly Hills, CA: Sage.

Bronfenbrenner, U. (1979). *The ecology of human development.* Cambridge, MA: Harvard University Press.

Bronfenbrenner, U. (1986). Ecology of the family as a context for human development: Research perspectives. *Developmental Psychology, 22,* 723–742.

Bronfenbrenner, U. (1987). Foreword. Family support: The quiet revolution. In S. Kagan, D. Powell, B. Weissbourd, & E. Zigler (Eds.), *America's family support programs* (pp. xi–xvii). New Haven, CT: Yale University Press.

Bronfenbrenner, U., & Weiss, H. B. (1983). Beyond policies without people. In E. Zigler, S. Kagan, & E. Klugman (Eds.), *Children, families, and government: Perspectives on American social policy* (pp. 393–414). New York: Cambridge University Press.

Brooks-Gunn, J. (1995). Strategies for altering the outcomes of poor children and their families. In P. L. Chase-Lansdale & J. Brooks-Gunn (Eds.), *Escape from poverty: What makes a difference for children?* (pp. 87–117). New York: Cambridge University Press.

Brooks-Gunn, J., Duncan, G., Kelbanov, P., & Sealand, N. (1993). Do neighborhoods influence child and adolescent development? *American Journal of Sociology, 99,* 353–395.

Brooks-Gunn, J., Guo, G., & Furstenberg, F. (1993). Who drops out and who continues beyond high school? A 20-year follow-up of Black urban youth. *Journal of Research on Adolescence, 3,* 271–294.

Brooks-Gunn, J., Klebanov, P., & Liaw, F. (1995). The learning, physical, and emotional environment of the home in the context of poverty: The Infant Health and Development Program. *Children and Youth Services Review, 17,* 231–250.

Brown, G., Bhrolchain, M., & Harris, T. (1975). Social class and psychiatric disturbance among women in an urban population. *Sociology, 9,* 225–254.

Burton, L., Allison, K., & Obeidallah, D. (1995). Social context and adolescence: Perspectives on development among inner-city African-American teens. In L. Crocker & A. Crouter (Eds.), *Pathways through adolescence: Individual development in relation to social context* (pp. 119–138). Hillsdale, NJ: Erlbaum.

Buss, T., & Redburn, F. S. (1983). *Mass unemployment: Plant closings and community mental health.* Beverly Hills, CA: Sage.

Caldwell, B. (1974). A decade of early intervention programs: What we have learned. *American Journal of Orthopsychiatry, 44,* 491–496.

Califano, J. (1979). Head Start, a retrospective view: The founders. In E. Zigler & J. Valentine (Eds.), *Project Head Start: A legacy of the war on poverty* (pp. 43–134). New York: Free Press.

Campbell, F., & Ramey, C. (1994). Effects of early intervention on intellectual and academic achievement: A follow-up study of children from low-income families. *Child Development, 65,* 684–698.

Campbell, F., & Ramey, C. (1995). Cognitive and school outcomes for high-risk African-American students at middle adolescence: Positive effects of early intervention. *American Educational Research Journal, 32,* 743–772.

Caplan, G. (1974). *Support systems and community mental health.* New York: Behavioral.

Cazenave, N., & Straus, M. (1979). Race, class, network embeddedness and family violence: A search for potent support systems. *Journal of Comparative Family Studies, 10,* 281–300.

Center for the Study of Social Policy. (1986). The "flip-side" of black families headed by women: The economic status of black men. In R. Staples (Ed.), *The Black family: Essays and studies* (pp. 232–238). Belmont, CA: Wadsworth.

Chafel, J. A. (1992). Funding Head Start: What are the issues? *American Journal of Orthopsychiatry, 62,* 9–21.

Chase-Lansdale, P. L., & Brooks-Gunn, J. (Eds.). (1995). *Escape from poverty: What makes a difference for children?* New York: Cambridge University Press.

Chase-Lansdale, P. L., & Gordon, R. A. (1996). Economic hardship and the development of five- and six-year-olds: Neighborhood and regional perspectives. *Child Development, 67,* 3338–3367.

Chase-Lansdale, P. L., & Vinovskis, M. (1995). Whose responsibility? An historical analysis of the changing roles of mothers, fathers, and society. In P. L. Chase-Lansdale & J. Brooks-Gunn (Eds.), *Escape from poverty: What makes a difference for children?* (pp. 11–37). New York: Cambridge University Press.

Chilman, C. S. (1973). Programs for disadvantaged parents: Some major trends and related research. In B. M. Caldwell & H. N. Ricciuti (Eds.), *Review of child development research* (Vol. 3, pp. 403–465). Chicago: University of Chicago Press.

Citro, C. F., & Michael, R. T. (Eds.). (1995). *Measuring poverty: A new approach.* Washington, DC: National Academy Press.

Clark, R. (1983). *Family life and school achievement: Why poor black children succeed or fail.* Chicago: University of Chicago Press.

Clarke-Stewart, K. A. (1973). Interactions between mothers and their young children: Characteristics and consequences. *Monographs of the Society for Research in Child Development, 38*(6/7, Serial No. 153).

Clarke-Stewart, K. A., & Apfel, N. (1978). Evaluating parental effects on child development. In L. S. Shulman (Ed.), *Review of research in education* (Vol. 6, pp. 47–119). Itasca, IL: Peacock.

Cochran, M. (1988). Parental empowerment in family matters: Lessons learned from a research program. In I. Sigel (Series Ed.) & D. Powell (Vol. Ed.), *Advances in applied developmental psychology: Vol. 3. Parent education as early childhood intervention: Emerging directions in theory, research, and practice* (pp. 23–50). Norwood, NJ: ABLEX.

Cochran, M., & Woolever, F. (1983). Beyond the deficit model: The empowerment of parents with information and informal supports. In I. Sigel & L. Laosa (Eds.), *Changing families* (pp. 225–245). New York: Plenum Press.

Cohen, J., & Cohen, P. (1983). *Applied multiple regression/correlation analysis for the behavioral sciences.* Hillsdale, NJ: Erlbaum.

Cohn, R. (1978). The effect of employment status change on self-attitudes. *Social Psychology, 41,* 81–93.

Cole, M., & Bruner, J. (1971). Cultural differences and inferences about psychological processes. *American Psychologist, 26,* 867–876.

Coleman, J. S., Campbell, E., Hobson, C., McPartland, J., Mood, A., Weinfeld, F., & York, R. (1966). *Equality of educational opportunity.* Washington, DC: U.S. Government Printing Office.

Colletta, N. (1979). Support systems after divorce: Incidence and impact. *Journal of Marriage and the Family, 41,* 837–846.

Colletta, N. (1981). Social support and the risk of maternal rejection by adolescent mothers. *Journal of Psychology, 109,* 191–197.

Colletta, N., & Lee, D. (1983). The impact of support for black adolescent mothers. *Journal of Family Issues, 4,* 127–143.

Condry, S. (1983). History and background of preschool intervention programs and the Consortium for Longitudinal Studies. In Consortium for Longitudinal Studies (Ed.), *As the twig is bent: Lasting effects of preschool programs* (pp. 1–31). Hillsdale, NJ: Erlbaum.

Condry, S., & Lazar, I. (1982). American values and social policy for children. *Annals of the American Academy of Political and Social Science, 461,* 21–31.

Conger, R. D., Conger, K., Elder, G., Lorenz, F., Simons, R., & Whitbeck, L. (1992). A family process model of economic hardship and adjustment of early adolescent boys. *Child Development, 63,* 526–541.

Conger, R. D., Conger, K., Elder, G., Lorenz, F., Simons, R., & Whitbeck, L. (1993). Family economic stress and adjustment of early adolescent girls. *Developmental Psychology, 29,* 206–219.

Conger, R. D., Ge, X., Elder, G., Lorenz, F., & Simons, R. (1994). Economic stress, coercive family process and developmental problems of adolescents. *Child Development, 65,* 541–561.

Conger, R. D., McCarty, J., Yang, R., Lahey, B., & Kropp, J. (1984). Perception of child, child-rearing values, and emotional distress as mediating links between environmental stressors and observed maternal behavior. *Child Development, 54,* 2234–2247.

Consortium for Longitudinal Studies. (Ed.). (1983). *As the twig is bent: Lasting effects of preschool programs.* Hillsdale, NJ: Erlbaum.

Cowen, E. L. (1982). Help is where you find it: Four informal helping groups. *American Psychologist, 37,* 385–395.

Cowen, E. L., Wyman, P. A., Work, W. C., & Parker, G. R. (1990). The Rochester Child Resilience project: Overview and summary of first year findings. *Development and Psychopathology, 2,* 193–212.

Crnic, K., & Greenberg, M. (1987). Maternal stress, social support, and coping: Influences on early mother-child relationship. In C. Boukydis (Ed.), *Research on support for parents and infants in the postnatal period* (pp. 25–40). Norwood, NJ: ABLEX.

Crockenberg, S. (1987). Support for adolescent mothers during the postnatal period: Theory and research. In C. Boukydis (Ed.), *Research on support for parents and infants in the postnatal period* (pp. 3–24). Norwood, NJ: ABLEX.

Crocker, J., & Major, B. (1989). Social stigma and self-esteem: The self-protective properties of stigma. *Psychological Review, 96,* 608–630.

Currie, J., & Thomas, D. (1995). Does Head Start make a difference? *American Economic Review, 85,* 341–364.

Daniel, J., Hampton, R., & Newberger, E. (1983). Child abuse and accidents in black families: A controlled comparative study. *American Journal of Orthopsychiatry, 53,* 645–653.

Danziger, S., & Danziger, S. (1993). Child poverty and public policy: Toward a comprehensive antipoverty agenda. *Daedalus: America's Childhood, 122,* 57–84.

Danziger, S., & Danziger, S. (Eds.). (1995). Child poverty, public policies and welfare reform [Special issue]. *Children and Youth Services Review, 17*(1/2).

Darlington, R., Royce, J., Snipper, A., Murray, H., & Lazar, I. (1980, April). Preschool programs and later school competence of children from low-income families. *Science, 208,* 202–204.

Datta, L. (1979). Another spring and other hopes: Some findings from national evaluations of Project Head Start. In E. Zigler & J. Valentine (Eds.), *Project Head Start: A legacy of the war on poverty* (pp. 405–432). New York: Free Press.

Davenport, Y. B., Zahn-Waxler, C., Adland, M. L., & Mayfield, A. (1984). Early child rearing practices in families with a manic-depressive parent. *American Journal of Psychiatry, 142,* 230–235.

Davis, A. (1941). American status systems and the socialization of the child. *American Sociological Review, 6,* 345–356.

Davis, A., & Havighurst, R. (1946). Social class and color differences in child-rearing. *American Sociological Review, 11,* 698–710.

Dear, R. B. (1982). No more poverty in America? A critique of Martin Anderson's theory of welfare. *Children and Youth Services Review, 4,* 5–33.

de Lone, R. (1979). *Small futures: Children, inequality, and the limits of liberal reform.* New York: Harcourt Brace Jovanovich.

Demos, J. (1986). *Past, present and personal.* New York: Oxford University Press.

DeParle, J. (1996, March 17). Class is no longer a four-letter word. *New York Times Magazine,* 40–43.

Deutsch, C. (1973). Social class and child development. In B. Caldwell & H. Ricciuti (Eds.), *Review of child development research* (Vol. 3, pp. 233–282). Chicago: University of Chicago Press.

Deutsch, M. (1967). *The disadvantaged child.* New York: Basic Books.

Deutsch, M., & Brown, B. (1964). Social influences in Negro-White intelligence differences. *Journal of Social Issues, 20,* 24–35.

Deutsch, M., Deutsch, C., Jordan, T., & Grallo, R. (1983). The IDS program: An experiment in early and sustained enrichment. In Consortium for Longitudinal Studies (Ed.), *As the twig is bent: Lasting effects of preschool programs* (pp. 377–410). Hillsdale, NJ: Erlbaum.

Dew, M., Bromet, E., & Schulberg, H. (1987). A comparative analysis of two community stressors' long-term mental health effects. *American Journal of Community Psychology, 15,* 167–184.

Dix, T. (1991). The affective organization of parenting: Adaptive and maladaptive processes. *Psychological Bulletin, 110,* 3–25.

Dooley, D., & Catalano, R. (1980). Economic change as a cause of behavioral disorder. *Psychological Bulletin, 87,* 358–390.

Downey, G., & Coyne, J. (1990). Children of depressed parents: An integrative review. *Psychological Bulletin, 108,* 50–76.

Dreger, R., & Miller, K. (1960). Comparative psychological studies of Negroes and whites in the United States. *Psychological Bulletin, 57,* 361–402.

Dressler, W. (1985). Extended family relationships, social support, and mental health in a southern black community. *Journal of Health and Social Behavior, 26,* 39–48.

Dubow, E., & Ippolito, M. F. (1994). Effects of poverty and quality of the home environment on changes in the academic and behavioral adjustment of elementary school-age children. *Journal of Clinical Child Psychology, 23,* 401–412.

Dubrow, N. F., & Garbarino, J. (1989). Living in the war zone: Mothers and young children in a public housing development. *Child Welfare, 68*(1), 3–20.

Duncan, G. (1984). *Years of poverty, years of plenty.* Ann Arbor: University of Michigan Institute for Social Research.

Duncan, G. (1991). The economic environment of childhood. In A. Huston (Ed.), *Children in poverty: Child development and public policy* (pp. 23–50). New York: Cambridge University Press.

Duncan, G., & Brooks-Gunn, J. (Eds.). (1997). *Consequences of growing up poor.* New York: Russell-Sage Foundation.

Duncan, G., Brooks-Gunn, J., & Klebanov, P. (1994). Economic deprivation and early childhood development. *Child Development, 65,* 296–318.

Duncan, G., & Rodgers, W. (1987). Single-parent families: Are their economic problems transitory or persistent? *Family Planning Perspectives, 19,* 171–178.

Duncan, G., & Rodgers, W. (1988). Longitudinal aspects of childhood poverty. *Journal of Marriage and the Family, 50,* 1007–1021.

Duncan, G., & Rodgers, W. (1991). Has children's poverty become more persistent? *American Sociological Review, 56,* 538–550.

Duncan, G., Yeung, W., Brooks-Gunn, J., & Smith, J. (in press). Does childhood poverty affect the life chances of children? *American Sociological Review.*

Eccles-Parsons, J. S., Adler, T. F., Futterman, R., Goff, S. B., Kaczala, C., Meece, J. L., & Midgley, C. (1983). Expectancies, values, and academic behaviors. In J. T. Spence (Ed.), *Achievement and achievement motives* (pp. 75–146). San Francisco: Freeman.

Edin, K. (1995). *The myths of dependence and self-sufficiency: Women, welfare, and low-wage work.* Unpublished manuscript, Center for Urban Policy Research, Rutgers University, New Brunswick, NJ.

Edsall, T., & Edsall, M. (1991, May). When the official subject is presidential politics, taxes, welfare, crime, rights, or values . . . the real subject is race. *Atlantic Monthly, 267,* 53–86.

Eggebeen, D., & Lichter, D. (1991). Race, family structure, and changing poverty among American children. *American Sociological Review, 56,* 801–817.

Elardo, R., Bradley, R., & Caldwell, B. M. (1975). The relation of infants' home environments to mental test performance and to language development at age three. *Child Development, 48,* 595–603.

Elder, G. (1974). *Children of the great depression.* Chicago: University of Chicago Press.

Elder, G. (1979). Historical change in life patterns and personality. In P. Baltes & O. Brim (Eds.), *Life span development and behavior* (Vol. 2, pp. 117–159). New York: Academic Press.

Elder, G., Liker, J., & Cross, C. (1984). Parent-child behavior in the great depression: Life course and intergenerational influences. In P. Baltes & O. Brim (Eds.), *Life-span development and behavior* (Vol. 6, pp. 109–158). Orlando, FL: Academic Press.

Ellwood, D., & Crane, J. (1990). Family change among black Americans: What do we know? *Journal of Economic Perspectives, 4,* 65–84.

Escalona, S. K. (1984). Social and other environmental influences on the cognitive and personality development of low birthweight infants. *American Journal of Mental Deficiency, 88,* 508–512.

Evans, P. (1992). Targeting single mothers for employment: Comparisons from the United States, Britain, and Canada. *Social Service Review, 66,* 378–398.

Feather, N. (1974). Explanations of poverty in Australian and American samples. *Australian Journal of Psychology, 26,* 199–216.

Fein, G. (1980). The informed parent. In S. Kilmer (Ed.), *Advances in early education and day care* (Vol. 1, pp. 155–185). Greenwich, CT: JAI Press.

Feshbach, N., & Feshbach, S. (1972). Children's aggression. In W. W. Hartup (Ed.), *The young child: Reviews of research* (Vol. 2, pp. 284–302). Washington, DC: National Association for the Education of Young Children.

Field, T., Widmayer, S., Stringer, S., & Ignatoff, E. (1980). Teenage, lower-class, black mothers and their preterm infants: An intervention and developmental follow-up. *Child Development, 51,* 426–436.

Flanagan, C., & Eccles, J. (1993). Changes in parents' work status and adolescents' adjustment at school. *Child Development, 64,* 246–257.

Fordham, S. (1988). Racelessness as a factor in black students' school success: Pragmatic strategy or pyrrhic victory. *Harvard Educational Review, 58,* 54–83.

Fordham, S., & Ogbu, J. (1986). Black students' school success: Coping with the "burden of 'acting white.'" *Urban Review, 18,* 176–206.

Frankel, H. (1988). Family centered, home-based services in child protection: A review of the research. *Social Service Review, 62,* 137–157.

Fuerst, J., & Fuerst, D. (1993). Chicago experience with an early childhood program: The special case of the Child Parent Center Program. *Urban Education, 28,* 69–96.

Furstenberg, F. (1976). *Unplanned parenthood: The social consequences of teenage childbearing.* New York: Free Press.

Furstenberg, F., Brooks-Gunn, J., & Chase-Lansdale, L. (1989). Teenaged pregnancy and childbearing. *American Psychologist, 44,* 313–320.

Fusfeld, D., & Bates, T. (1984). *The political economy of the urban ghetto.* Carbondale: Southern Illinois University Press.

Galambos, N., & Silbereisen, R. (1987a). Income change, parental life outlook, and adolescent expectations for job success. *Journal of Marriage and the Family, 49,* 141–149.

Galambos, N., & Silbereisen, R. (1987b). Influences of income change and parental acceptance on adolescent transgression proneness and peer relations. *European Journal of Psychology of Education, 1,* 17–28.

Gamble, T., & Zigler, E. (1989). The Head Start Synthesis Project: A critique. *Journal of Applied Developmental Psychology, 10,* 267–274.

Garbarino, J. (1976). A preliminary study of some ecological correlates of child abuse: The impact of socioeconomic stress on mothers. *Child Development, 47,* 178–185.

Garbarino, J. (1992). The meaning of poverty in the world of children. *American Behavioral Scientist, 35,* 220–237.

Garber, H. L. (1988). *The Milwaukee Project: Prevention of mental retardation in children at risk.* Washington, DC: American Association of Mental Retardation.

Garfinkel, I., Meyer, D. R., & Sandefur, G. (1992). The effects of alternative child support systems on blacks, Hispanics, and non-Hispanic whites. *Social Service Review, 66,* 505–523.

Garrett, P., Ng'andu, N., & Ferron, J. (1994). Poverty experiences of young children and the quality of their home environments. *Child Development, 65,* 331–345.

Gecas, V. (1979). The influence of social class on socialization. In W. Burr, R. Hill, F. Nye, & I. Reiss (Eds.), *Contemporary theories about the family: Research-based theories* (Vol. 1, pp. 365–404). New York: Free Press.

Gelles, R. (1980). Violence in the family: A review of research in the seventies. *Journal of Marriage and the Family, 42,* 143–155.

Gersten, J., Langner, T., Eisenberg, J., & Orzek, L. (1974). Child behavior and life events: Undesirable change or change per se? In B. S. Dohrenwend & B. P. Dohrenwend (Eds.), *Stressful life events: Their nature and effects* (pp. 159–170). New York: Wiley.

Gersten, J., Langner, T., Eisenberg, J., & Simcha-Fagan, O. (1977). An evaluation of the etiological role of stressful life-change events in psychological disorders. *Journal of Health and Social Behavior, 18,* 228–244.

Gibbs, J. (1988). Young black males in America: Endangered, embittered, and embattled. In J. Gibbs (Eds.), *Young, black, and male in America: An endangered species* (pp. 1–36). New York: Auburn House.

Gibbs, J. T., Huang, L., & Associates. (Eds.). (1989). *Children of color: Psychological interventions with minority youth.* San Francisco: Jossey-Bass.

Ginsburg, H. (1972). *The myth of the deprived child: Poor children's intellect and education.* Englewood Cliffs, NJ: Prentice-Hall.

Glazer, N. (1986). Welfare and "welfare" in America. In R. Rose & R. Shiratori (Eds.), *Welfare state: East and west* (pp. 40–63). New York: Oxford University Press.

Goodban, N. (1985). The psychological impact of being on welfare. *Social Service Review, 59,* 403–422.

Gore, S. (1978). The effect of social support in moderating the health consequences of unemployment. *Journal of Health and Social Behavior, 19,* 157–165.

Gouldner, H. (1978). *Teachers' pets, troublemakers, and nobodies: Black children in elementary school.* Westport, CT: Greenwood Press.

Gray, J., Cutler, C., Dean, J., & Kempe, C. (1979). Prediction and prevention of child abuse and neglect. *Journal of Social Issues, 35,* 127–139.

Gray, S., & Klaus, R. (1965). An experimental preschool program for culturally deprived children. *Child Development, 36,* 887–898.

Gray, S., & Klaus, R. (1970). The Early Training Project: A seventh-year report. *Child Development, 41,* 909–924.

Gray, S., Ramsey, B., & Klaus, R. (1983). The Early Training Project: 1962–1980. In Consortium for Longitudinal Studies (Ed.), *As the twig is bent: Lasting effects of preschool programs* (pp. 33–69). Hillsdale, NJ: Erlbaum.

Greenberg, M. (1996). *No duty, no floor: The real meaning of "ending entitlements."* Washington, DC: Center for Law and Social Policy.

Gullo, D., & Burton, C. (1992). Age of entry, preschool experience, and sex as antecedents of academic readiness in kindergarten. *Early Childhood Research Quarterly, 7,* 175–186.

Gutelius, M., Kirsch, A., MacDonald, S., Brooks, M., & McErlean, T. (1977). Controlled study of child health supervision: Behavioral results. *Pediatrics, 60,* 294–304.

Gutelius, M., Kirsch, A., MacDonald, S., Brooks, M., McErlean, T., & Newcomb, C. (1972). Promising results from a cognitive stimulation program in infancy: A preliminary report. *Clinical Pediatrics, 11,* 585–593.

Guthrie, R. (1976). *Even the rat was white: A historical view of psychology.* New York: Harper & Row.

Hagenaars, A., & de Vos, K. (1988). The definition and measurement of poverty. *Journal of Human Resources, 23,* 211–221.

Hall, W. S. (1974). Research in the black community: Child development. In J. Chunn (Ed.), *The survival of black children and youth* (pp. 79–104). Washington, DC: Nuclassics and Science.

Haller, M., Hollinger, F., & Raubal, O. (1990). Leviathan or welfare state? Attitudes toward the role of government in six advanced Western nations. In J. Becker, J. Davis, P. Ester, & P. Mohler (Eds.), *Attitudes to inequality and the role of government* (pp. 33–62). Rijswijk, maart: Sociaal en Cultureel Planbureau.

Halpern, R. (1984). Lack of effects for home-based early intervention? Some possible explanations. *American Journal of Orthopsychiatry, 54,* 33–42.

Halpern, R. (1988). Parent support and education for low-income families: Historical and current perspectives. *Children and Youth Services Review, 10,* 283–303.

Halpern, R. (1990a). Community-based early intervention. In S. Meisels & J. Shonkoff (Eds.), *Handbook of early childhood intervention* (pp. 469–498). New York: Cambridge University Press.

Halpern, R. (1990b). Parent support and education programs. *Children and Youth Services Review, 12,* 285–308.

Halpern, R. (1991). Supportive services for families in poverty: Dilemmas of reform. *Social Service Review, 65,* 343–364.

Halpern, R. (1992). Issues of program design and implementation. In M. Larner, R. Halpern, & O. Harkavy (Eds.), *Fair Start for children: Lessons learned from seven demonstration projects* (pp. 179–197). New Haven, CT: Yale University Press.

Hardy, J. B., & Streett, R. (1989). Family support and parenting education in the home: An effective extension of clinic-based preventive health care services for poor children. *Journal of Pediatrics, 115/116,* 927–931.

Hare, B., & Castenell, L. (1985). No place to run, no place to hide: Comparative status and future prospects of black boys. In M. Spencer, G. Brookins, & W. Allen (Eds.), *Beginnings: The social and affective development of black children.* Hillsdale, NJ: Erlbaum.

Harmon, C., & Hanley, E. (1979). Administrative aspects of the Head Start program. In E. Zigler & J. Valentine (Eds.), *Project Head Start: A legacy of the war on poverty* (pp. 379–396). New York: Free Press.

Harrington, M. (1962). *The other America: Poverty in the United States.* New York: Macmillan.

Haskins, R. (1989). Beyond metaphor: The efficacy of early childhood education. *American Psychologist, 44,* 274–282.

Hauser, R., & Carr, D. (1995). *Measuring poverty and socioeconomic status in studies of health and well-being* (Center for Demographic and Ecology Working Paper No. 94-24). Madison: University of Wisconsin.

Hauser-Cram, P., Pierson, D., Walker, D., & Tivnan, T. (1991). *Early education in the public schools: Lessons from a comprehensive birth-to-kindergarten program.* San Francisco: Jossey-Bass.

Haveman, R. H. (1987). *Poverty policy and poverty research.* Madison: University of Wisconsin Press.

Hebbeler, K. (1985). An old and a new question on the effects of early education for children from low income families. *Educational Evaluation and Policy Analysis, 7,* 207–216.

Hernandez, D. (1997). Poverty trends. In G. Duncan & J. Brooks-Gunn (Eds.), *Consequences of growing up poor* (pp. 18–34). New York: Russell-Sage Foundation.

Herrnstein, R., & Murray, C. (1994). *The bell curve: Intelligence and class structure in American life.* New York: Free Press.

Hess, R. (1970). Social class and ethnic influences upon socialization. In P. Mussen (Ed.), *Carmichael's manual of child psychology* (pp. 457–557). New York: Wiley.

Hess, R., & Shipman, V. (1965). Early experience and the socialization of cognitive modes in children. *Child Development, 36,* 869–886.

Hetherington, E. M., Stanley-Hagan, M., & Anderson, E. (1989). Marital transitions: A child's perspective. *American Psychologist, 44,* 303–312.

Hofferth, S. (1994). Who enrolls in Head Start? A demographic analysis of Head Start–eligible children. *Early Childhood Research Quarterly, 9,* 243–268.

Horacek, H., Ramey, C., Campbell, F., Hoffman, K., & Fletcher, R. (1987). Predicting school failure and assessing early intervention with high-risk children. *American Academy of Child and Adolescent Psychiatry, 26,* 758–763.

Horvath, F. (1987). The pulse of economic change: Displaced workers of 1981–1985. *Monthly Labor Review, 110,* 3–12.

Horwitz, A. (1984). The economy and social pathology. *Annual Review of Sociology, 10,* 95–119.

House, J. (1981). Social structure and personality. In M. Rosenberg & R. Turner (Eds.), *Social psychology: Sociological perspectives* (pp. 525–561). New York: Basic Books.

Hunt, J. M. (1961). *Intelligence and experience.* New York: Ronald Press.

Huston, A. (1991). Children in poverty: Developmental and policy issues. In A. Huston (Ed.), *Children in poverty: Child development and public policy* (pp. 1–22). New York: Cambridge University Press.

Huston, A., García Coll, C., & McLoyd, V. C. (Eds.). (1994). Children and poverty [Special issue]. *Child Development, 65*(2).

Huston, A., McLoyd, V. C., & García Coll, C. (1994). Children and poverty: Issues in contemporary research. *Child Development, 65,* 275–282.

Illback, R. (1994). Poverty and the crisis in children's services: The need for services integration. *Journal of Clinical Child Psychology, 23,* 413–424.

Jagers, R., & Mock, L. (1993). Culture and social outcomes among inner-city African American children: An Afrographic exploration. *Journal of Black Psychology, 19,* 391–405.

James, S. D. (1985). *The impact of cybernation technology on black automobile workers in the U.S.* Ann Arbor, MI: UMI Research Press.

Jargowsky, P. (1994). Ghetto poverty among blacks in the 1980s. *Journal of Policy Analysis and Management, 13,* 288–310.

Jarrett, R. (1995). Growing up poor: The family experiences of socially mobile youth in low-income African American neighborhoods. *Journal of Adolescent Research, 10,* 111–135.

Jencks, C., & Mayer, S. (1990). The social consequences of growing up in a poor neighborhood: A review. In M. McGeary & L. Lynn (Eds.), *Inner city poverty in the United States.* Washington, DC: National Academy Press.

Jensen, A. (1969). How much can we boost IQ and scholastic achievement? *Harvard Educational Review, 39,* 1–123.

Jester, R., & Guinagh, B. (1983). The Gordon Parent Education Infant and Toddler Program. In Consortium for Longitudinal Studies (Ed.), *As the twig is bent: Lasting effects of preschool programs* (pp. 103–132). Hillsdale, NJ: Erlbaum.

Johnson, D. L. (1988). Primary prevention of behavior problems in young children: The Houston Parent-Child Development Center. In R. Price, E. Cowen, R. Lorion, & J. Ramos-McKay (Eds.), *14 ounces of prevention: A casebook for practitioners* (pp. 44–52). Washington, DC: American Psychological Association.

Johnson, D. L., & Breckenridge, J. N. (1982). The Houston Parent-Child Development Center and the primary prevention of behavior problems in young children. *American Journal of Community Psychology, 10,* 305–316.

Johnson, D. L., & Walker, T. (1987). The primary prevention of behavior problems in Mexican-American children. *American Journal of Community Psychology, 15,* 375–385.

Kagan, S., Powell, D., Weissbourd, B., & Zigler, E. (Eds.). (1987). *America's family support programs.* New Haven, CT: Yale University Press.

Kagan, S., & Shelley, A. (1987). The promise and problems of family support programs. In S. Kagan, D. Powell, B. Weissbourd, & E. Zigler (Eds.), *America's family support programs* (pp. 3–18). New Haven, CT: Yale University Press.

Kamii, C., & Radin, N. (1967). Class differences in the socialization practices of Negro mothers. *Journal of Marriage and the Family, 29,* 302–310.

Karnes, M., Shwedel, A., & Williams, M. (1983). A comparison of five approaches for educating young children from low-income homes. In Consortium for Longitudinal Studies (Ed.), *As the twig is bent: Lasting effects of preschool programs* (pp. 133–169). Hillsdale, NJ: Erlbaum.

Kasl, S. V., & Cobb, S. (1979). Some mental health consequences of plant closings and job loss. In L. Ferman & J. Gordus (Eds.), *Mental health and the economy* (pp. 255–300). Kalamazoo, MI: W. E. Upjohn Institute for Employment Research.

Kasl, S. V., & Harburg, E. (1975). Mental health and the urban environment: Some doubts and second thoughts. *Journal of Health and Social Behavior, 16*(3), 268–282.

Kassebaum, N. (1994). Head Start: Only the best for America's children. *American Psychologist, 49,* 123–126.

Kellam, S., Ensminger, M. E., & Turner, R. (1977). Family structure and the mental health of children. *Archives of General Psychiatry, 34,* 1012–1022.

Kennedy, W. A., Van de Riet, V., & White, J. C. (1963). A normative sample of intelligence and achievement of Negro elementary school children in the southeastern United States. *Monographs of the Society for Research in Child Development, 28*(6, Serial No. 90).

Kessler, R., House, J., & Turner, J. (1987). Unemployment and health in a community sample. *Journal of Health and Social Behavior, 28,* 51–59.

Kessler, R., & Neighbors, H. (1986). A new perspective on the relationships among race, social class, and psychological distress. *Journal of Health and Social Behavior, 27,* 107–115.

King, T., & Fullard, W. (1982). Teenage mothers and their infants: New findings on the home environment. *Journal of Adolescence, 5,* 333–346.

Klein, D. (1983). Trends in employment and unemployment in families. *Monthly Labor Review, 106,* 21–25.

Kluegel, J. R. (1987). Macro-economic problems, beliefs about the poor and attitudes toward welfare spending. *Social Problems, 34,* 82–99.

Kochanska, G., Kuczynski, L., Radke-Yarrow, M., & Walsh, J. D. (1987). Resolutions of control episodes between well and affectively ill mothers and their young child. *Journal of Abnormal Child Psychology, 15,* 441–456.

Kohn, M. (1959). Social class and parental values. *American Journal of Sociology, 64,* 337–351.

Korbin, J. (Ed.). (1992). Child poverty in the United States [Special issue]. *American Behavioral Scientist, 35*(3).

Kriesberg, L. (1970). *Mothers in poverty: A study of fatherless families.* Chicago: Aldine.

Kunjufu, J. (1986). *Countering the conspiracy to destroy black boys* (Vol. 2). Chicago: African American Images.

Labov, W. (1970). The logic of non-standard English. In F. Williams (Ed.), *Language and poverty* (pp. 153–189). Chicago: Markham.

Lally, J. R., Mangione, P., & Honig, A. (1988). The Syracuse University Family Development Research Program: Long-range impact on an early intervention with low-income children and their families. In I. Sigel (Series Ed.) & D. Powell (Vol. Ed.), *Advances in applied developmental psychology: Vol. 3. Parent education as early childhood intervention: Emerging directions in theory, research, and practice* (pp. 79–104). Norwood, NJ: ABLEX.

Langner, T., Herson, J., Greene, E., Jameson, J., & Goff, J. (1970). Children of the city: Affluence, poverty, and mental health. In V. Allen (Ed.), *Psychological factors in poverty* (pp. 185–209). Chicago: Markham.

Laosa, L. M. (1984). Social policies toward children of diverse ethnic, racial, and language groups in the United States. In H. W. Stevenson & A. Siegel (Eds.), *Child development research and social policy* (pp. 1–109). Chicago: University of Chicago Press.

Laosa, L. M. (1989). Social competence in childhood: Toward a developmental, socioculturally relativistic paradigm. *Journal of Applied Developmental Psychology, 10,* 447–468.

Larner, M., Halpern, R., & Harkavy, O. (Eds.). (1992). *Fair Start for children: Lessons learned from seven demonstration projects.* New Haven, CT: Yale University Press.

Larson, C. P. (1980). Efficacy of prenatal and postpartum home visits on child health and development. *Pediatrics, 66,* 191–197.

Lazar, I., Darlington, R., Murray, H., Royce, J., & Snipper, A. (1982). Lasting effects of early education: A report from the Consortium for Longitudinal Studies. *Monographs of the Society for Research in Child Development, 47*(2/3, Serial No. 195).

Lee, V., Brooks-Gunn, J., & Schnur, E. (1988). Does Head Start work? A 1-year follow-up comparison of disadvantaged children attending Head Start, no preschool, and other preschool programs. *Developmental Psychology, 24,* 210–222.

Lee, V., Brooks-Gunn, J., Schnur, E., & Liaw, F. (1990). Are Head Start effects sustained? A longitudinal follow-up comparison of disadvantaged children attending Head Start, no preschool, and other preschool programs. *Child Development, 61,* 495–507.

Lee, V., & Loeb, S. (1995). Where do Head Start attendees end up? One reason why preschool effects fade out. *Educational Evaluation and Policy Analysis, 17,* 62–82.

Lempers, J., Clark-Lempers, D., & Simons, R. (1989). Economic hardship, parenting, and distress in adolescence. *Child Development, 60,* 25–49.

Levenstein, P., O'Hara, J., & Madden, J. (1983). The Mother-Child Home Program of the Verbal Interaction Project. In Consortium for Longitudinal Studies (Ed.), *As the twig is bent: Lasting effects of preschool programs* (pp. 237–263). Hillsdale, NJ: Erlbaum.

Lewis, D. A., & Maxfield, M. G. (1980). Fear in the neighborhoods: An investigation of the impact of crime. *Journal of Research in Crime and Delinquency, 17,* 160–189.

Lewis, O. (1966, October). The culture of poverty. *Scientific American, 215,* 19–25.

Liem, R. (1983). *Unemployment: Personal and family effects.* Unpublished manuscript, Boston College, Chestnut Hill, MA.

Liem, R., & Liem, J. (1978). Social class and mental illness reconsidered: The role of economic stress and social support. *Journal of Health and Social Behavior, 19,* 139–156.

Longfellow, C., Zelkowitz, P., & Saunders, E. (1982). The quality of mother-child relationships. In D. Belle (Ed.), *Lives in stress: Women and depression* (pp. 163–176). Beverly Hills, CA: Sage.

Maccoby, E., Gibbs, P., & Staff of the Laboratory of Human Development, Harvard University. (1954). Methods of child-rearing in two social classes. In W. Martin & C. Stendler (Eds.), *Readings in child development* (pp. 380–396). New York: Harcourt Brace.

Madden, N., Slavin, R., Karweit, N., Dolan, L., & Wasik, B. (1993). Success for all: Longitudinal effects of a restructuring program for inner-city elementary schools. *American Educational Research Journal, 30,* 123–148.

Majors, R., & Billson, J. (1992). *Cool pose: The dilemmas of black manhood in America.* New York: Lexington Books.

Makosky, V. P. (1982). Sources of stress: Events or conditions? In D. Belle (Ed.), *Lives in stress: Women and depression* (pp. 35–53). Beverly Hills, CA: Sage.

Marshall, N. (1982). The public welfare system: Regulation and dehumanization. In D. Belle (Ed.), *Lives in stress: Women and depression* (pp. 96–108). Beverly Hills, CA: Sage.

Martin, E. P., & Martin, J. M. (1978). *The black extended family.* Chicago: University of Chicago Press.

Martin, P., & Midgley, E. (1994). Immigration to the United States: Journey to an uncertain destination. *Population Bulletin, 49,* 2–45.

Massey, D. (1994). America's apartheid and the urban underclass. *Social Service Review, 68,* 471–487.

Mayer, S., & Jencks, C. (1988). Poverty and the distribution of material hardship. *Journal of Human Resources, 24,* 88–113.

McAdoo, H. P. (1986). Strategies used by black single mothers against stress. In M. Simms & J. Malveaux (Eds.), *Slipping through the cracks: The status of black women* (pp. 153–166). New Brunswick, NJ: Transaction Books.

McAdoo, H. P. (1990). The ethics of research and intervention with ethnic minority parents and their children. In I. Sigel (Series Ed.) & C. Fisher & W. Tryon (Vol. Eds.), *Advances in applied developmental psychology: Vol. 4. Ethics in applied developmental psychology: Emerging issues in an emerging field* (pp. 273–283). Norwood, NJ: ABLEX.

McCall, R. B., Appelbaum, M. I., & Hogarty, P. S. (1973). Developmental changes in mental performance. *Monographs of the Society for Research in Child Development, 38*(3, Serial No. 150).

McKey, R., Condelli, L., Ganson, H., Barrett, B., McConkey, C., & Plantz, M. (1985). *The impact of Head Start on children, families, and communities* (DHHS Publication No. OHDS 90-31193). Washington, DC: U.S. Government Printing Office.

McLoyd, V. C. (1989). Socialization and development in a changing economy: The effects of paternal job and income loss on children. *American Psychologist, 44,* 293–302.

McLoyd, V. C. (1990). The impact of economic hardship on black families and children: Psychological distress, parenting, and socioemotional development. *Child Development, 61,* 311–346.

McLoyd, V. C. (in press). Poverty, low socioeconomic status, and child development. *American Psychologist.*

McLoyd, V. C., & Flanagan, C. (Eds.). (1990). *New directions for child development: Vol. 46. Economic stress: Effects on family life and child development.* San Francisco: Jossey-Bass.

McLoyd, V. C., Jayaratne, T., Ceballo, R., & Borquez, J. (1994). Unemployment and work interruption among African American single mothers: Effects on parenting and adolescent socioemotional functioning. *Child Development, 65,* 562–589.

McLoyd, V. C., & Randolph, S. M. (1984). The conduct and publication of research on Afro-American children. *Human Development, 27,* 65–75.

McLoyd, V. C., & Randolph, S. M. (1985). Secular trends in the study of Afro-American children: A review of child development 1936–1980. In A. Smuts & J. Hagen (Eds.), *Monographs of the Society for Research in Child Development, 50*(4/5, Serial No. 211), 78–92.

McLoyd, V. C., & Wilson, L. (1990). Maternal behavior, social support, and economic conditions as predictors of psychological distress in children. In V. C. McLoyd & C. Flanagan (Eds.), *New directions for child development: Vol. 46. Economic stress: Effects on family life and child development* (pp. 49–69). San Francisco: Jossey-Bass.

Meyer, L. (1984). Long-term academic effects of the direct instructional Project Follow Thru. *Elementary School Journal, 84,* 380–392.

Miller, L., & Bizzell, R. (1983). The Louisville experiment: A comparison of four programs. In Consortium for Longitudinal Studies (Ed.), *As the twig is bent: Lasting effects of preschool programs* (pp. 171–199). Hillsdale, NJ: Erlbaum.

Morley, J., Dornbusch, S., & Seer, N. (1993). *A meta-analysis of education for parenting of children under three years of age.* Unpublished manuscript, Stanford University, Stanford, CA.

Mueller, C., & Parcel, T. (1981). Measures of socioeconomic status: Alternatives and recommendations. *Child Development, 52,* 13–30.

National Center for Education Statistics. (1995). *Digest of education statistics: 1995.* Washington, DC: U.S. Department of Education.

Neff, J., & Husaini, B. (1980). Race, socioeconomic status, and psychiatric impairment: A research note. *Journal of Community Psychology, 8,* 16–19.

Neubeck, K., & Roach, J. (1981). Income maintenance experiments, politics, and the perpetuation of poverty. *Social Problems, 28,* 308–319.

Ogbu, J. (1978). *Minority education and caste: The American system in cross-cultural perspective.* New York: Academic Press.

Ogbu, J. (1981). Origins of human competence: A cultural-ecological perspective. *Child Development, 52,* 413–429.

Olds, D. L., Henderson, C., Chamberlain, R., & Tatelbaum, R. (1986a). Improving the delivery of prenatal care and outcomes of pregnancy: A randomized trial of nurse home visitation. *Pediatrics, 77,* 16–28.

Olds, D. L., Henderson, C., Chamberlain, R., & Tatelbaum, R. (1986b). Preventing child abuse and neglect: A randomized trial of nurse home visitation. *Pediatrics, 78,* 65–78.

Olds, D., & Kitzman, H. (1990). Can home visitation improve the health of women and children at environmental risk? *Pediatrics, 86,* 108–116.

Olds, D., & Kitzman, H. (1993). Review of research on home visiting for pregnant women and parents of young children. *The Future of Children, 3,* 53–92.

Oyemade, U. J. (1985). The rationale for Head Start as a vehicle for the upward mobility of minority families: A minority perspective. *American Journal of Orthopsychiatry, 55,* 591–602.

Pagani, L., Boulerice, B., & Tremblay, R. (1997). The influence of poverty on children's classroom placement and behavior problems during elementary school: A change model approach. In G. Duncan & J. Brooks-Gunn (Eds.), *Consequences of growing up poor.* New York: Russell-Sage Foundation.

Palmer, F. (1983). The Harlem Study: Effects by type of training, age of training, and social class. In Consortium for Longitudinal Studies (Ed.), *As the twig is bent: Lasting effects of preschool programs* (pp. 201–236). Hillsdale, NJ: Erlbaum.

Panaccione, V., & Wahler, R. (1986). Child behavior, maternal depression, and social coercion as factors in the quality of child care. *Journal of Abnormal Child Psychology, 14,* 273–284.

Parke, R., & Collmer, C. (1975). Child abuse: An interdisciplinary review. In E. M. Hetherington (Ed.), *Review of child development research* (Vol. 5, pp. 509–590). Chicago: University of Chicago Press.

Parker, F., Piotrkowski, C., Horn, W., & Greene, S. (1995). The challenge for Head Start: Realizing its vision as a two-generation program. In I. Sigel (Series Ed.) & S. Smith (Vol. Ed.), *Advances in applied developmental psychology: Vol. 9. Two-*

generation programs for families in poverty: A new intervention strategy (pp. 135–159). Norwood, NJ: ABLEX.

Patterson, G. (1986). Performance models for antisocial boys. *American Psychologist, 41,* 432–444.

Patterson, G. (1988). Stress: A change agent for family process. In N. Garmezy & M. Rutter (Eds.), *Stress, coping and development in children* (pp. 235–264). Baltimore: Johns Hopkins University Press.

Patterson, J. (1981). *America's struggle against poverty 1900–1980.* Cambridge, MA: Harvard University Press.

Pearlin, L., Lieberman, M., Menaghan, E., & Mullan, S. (1981). The stress process. *Journal of Health and Social Behavior, 22,* 337–356.

Pelton, L. H. (1989). *For reasons of poverty: A critical analysis of the public child welfare system in the United System.* New York: Praeger.

Peterson, G., & Peters, D. (1985). The socialization values of low-income Appalachian white and rural black mothers: A comparative study. *Journal of Comparative Family Studies, 16,* 75–91.

Portes, A., & Zhou, M. (1993). The new second generation: Segmented assimilation and its variants. *Annals of the American Academy of Political and Social Science, 530,* 74–96.

Portes, P., Dunham, R., & Williams, S. (1986). Assessing child-rearing style in ecological settings: Its relation to culture, social class, early age intervention and scholastic achievement. *Adolescence, 21,* 723–735.

Powell, C., & Grantham-McGregor, S. (1989). Home visiting of varying frequency and child development. *Pediatrics, 84,* 157–164.

Powell, D. (1979). Family-environment relations and early child-rearing: The role of social networks and neighborhoods. *Journal of Research and Development in Education, 13,* 1–11.

Powell, D. (1982). From child to parent: Changing conceptions of early childhood intervention. *Annals of the American Academy of Political and Social Science, 461,* 135–144.

Powell, D. (1988). Emerging directions in parent-child early intervention. In I. Sigel (Series Ed.) & D. Powell (Vol. Ed.), *Advances in applied developmental psychology: Vol. 3. Parent education as early childhood intervention: Emerging directions in theory, research, and practice* (pp. 1–22). Norwood, NJ: ABLEX.

Powell, L. F. (1974). The effect of extra stimulation and maternal involvement on the development of low-birthweight infants and maternal behavior. *Child Development, 45,* 106–113.

Provence, S., & Naylor, A. (1983). *Working with disadvantaged parents and children: Scientific issues and practice.* New Haven, CT: Yale University Press.

Pryor-Brown, L., Powell, J., & Earls, F. (1989). Stressful life events and psychiatric symptoms in black adolescent females. *Journal of Adolescent Research, 4,* 140–151.

Quadagno, J. (1994). *The color of welfare: How racism undermined the war on poverty.* New York: Oxford University Press.

Quinn, L., & Magill, R. (1994). Politics versus research in social policy. *Social Service Review, 68,* 503–520.

Quint, J., & Egeland, B. (1995). New chance: Comprehensive services for disadvantaged young families. In I. Sigel (Series Ed.) & S. Smith (Vol. Ed.), *Advances in applied developmental psychology: Vol. 9. Two-generation programs for families in poverty: A new intervention strategy* (pp. 91–133). Norwood, NJ: ABLEX.

Radin, N. (1972). Three degrees of maternal involvement in a preschool program: Impact on mothers and children. *Child Development, 43,* 1355–1364.

Radke-Yarrow, M., Richters, J., & Wilson, W. (1988). Child development in a network of relationships. In R. Hinde & J. Stevenson-Hinde (Eds.), *Relationships within families: Mutual influences* (pp. 48–67). New York: Oxford University Press.

Ramey, C., Ramey, S., Gaines, K., & Blair, C. (1995). Two-generation early intervention programs: A child development perspective. In I. Sigel (Series Ed.) & S. Smith (Vol. Ed.), *Advances in applied developmental psychology: Vol. 9. Two-generation programs for families in poverty: A new intervention strategy* (pp. 199–228). Norwood, NJ: ABLEX.

Randolph, S., & Adams-Taylor, S. (in press). The health status of children and adolescents in urban environments. In G. King & W. Davis (Eds.), *The health of black America: Social causes and consequences.* New York: Oxford University Press.

Reddy, M. A. (Ed.). (1993). *Statistical record of Hispanic Americans.* Detroit, MI: Gale Research.

Resnick, M. B., Armstrong, S., & Carter, R. L. (1988). Developmental intervention program for high-risk premature infants: Effects on development and parent-infant interaction. *Developmental and Behavior Pediatrics, 9,* 73–78.

Reynolds, A. (1991). Early schooling of children at risk. *American Educational Research Journal, 28,* 392–422.

Reynolds, A. (1992). Comparing measures of parental involvement and their effects on academic achievement. *Early Childhood Research Quarterly, 7,* 441–462.

Reynolds, A. (1994). Effects of a preschool plus follow-on intervention for children at risk. *Developmental Psychology, 30,* 787–804.

Reynolds, A. (1995). One year of preschool intervention or two: Does it matter? *Early Childhood Research Quarterly, 10,* 1–31.

Richmond, J., Stipek, D., & Zigler, E. (1979). A decade of Head Start. In E. Zigler & J. Valentine (Eds.), *Project Head Start: A legacy of the war on poverty* (pp. 135–152). New York: Free Press.

Riegel, K. (1972). Influence of economic and political ideologies on the development of developmental psychology. *Psychological Bulletin, 78,* 129–141.

Rist, R. (1970). Student social class and teacher expectations: The self-fulfilling prophecy in ghetto education. *Harvard Education Review, 40,* 411–451.

Rodgers, J., & Rodgers, J. L. (1993). Chronic poverty in the United States. *Journal of Human Resources, 28,* 25–54.

Rogler, L. H. (1994). International migrations: A framework for directing research. *American Psychologist, 49,* 701–708.

Ross, C. J. (1979). Early skirmishes with poverty: The historical roots of Head Start. In E. Zigler & J. Valentine (Eds.), *Project Head Start: A legacy of the war on poverty* (pp. 21–42). New York: Free Press.

Routh, D. (Ed.). (1994). Impact of poverty on children, youth, and families [Special issue]. *Journal of Clinical Child Psychology, 23*(4).

Royce, J., Darlington, R., & Murray, H. (1983). Pooled analyses: Findings across studies. In Consortium for Longitudinal Studies (Ed.), *As the twig is bent: Lasting effects of preschool programs* (pp. 411–459). Hillsdale, NJ: Erlbaum.

Ruggles, P. (1990). *Drawing the line: Alternative poverty measures and their implications for public policy.* Washington, DC: Urban Institute Press.

Rumbaut, R. (1994). Origins and destinies: Immigration to the United States since World War II. *Sociological Forum, 9,* 583–621.

Rutter, M. (1979). Protective factors in children's responses to stress and disadvantage. In M. Kent & J. Rolf (Eds.), *Primary prevention of psychopathology* (pp. 49–74). Hanover, NH: University Press of New England.

St. Pierre, R., Layzer, J., & Barnes, H. (1995). Two-generation programs: Design, cost, and short-term effectiveness. *The Future of Children, 5,* 76–93.

St. Pierre, R., Layzer, J., & Barnes, H. (1996). *Regenerating two-generation programs.* Cambridge, MA: Abt Associates.

St. Pierre, R., & Swartz, J. (1995). The Even Start Family Literacy Program. In I. Sigel (Series Ed.) & S. Smith (Vol. Ed.), *Advances in applied developmental psychology: Vol. 9. Two-generation programs for families in poverty: A new intervention strategy* (pp. 37–66). Norwood, NJ: ABLEX.

Salkind, N., & Haskins, R. (1982). Negative income tax: The impact on children from low-income families. *Journal of Family Issues, 3,* 165–180.

Sameroff, A., Seifer, R., Barocas, R., Zax, M., & Greenspan, S. (1987). Intelligence quotient scores of 4-year-old children: Social-environmental risk factors. *Pediatrics, 79,* 343–350.

Sandler, I. N., & Block, M. (1979). Life stress and maladaptation of children. *American Journal of Community Psychology, 7,* 425–440.

Scarr, S., & McCartney, K. (1988). Far from home: An experimental evaluation of the Mother-Child Home Program in Bermuda. *Child Development, 59,* 636–647.

Schaefer, H. R., & Emerson, P. E. (1964). The development of social attachments in infancy. *Monographs of the Society for Research in Child Development, 29*(3, Serial No. 94).

Schlossman, S. L. (1976). Before Home Start: Notes toward a history of parent education in America, 1897–1929. *Harvard Educational Review, 46,* 436–467.

Schnur, E., Brooks-Gunn, J., & Shipman, V. (1992). Who attends programs serving poor children? The case of Head Start attendees and nonattendees. *Journal of Applied Developmental Psychology, 13,* 405–421.

Schorr, L. (1989). *Within our reach: Breaking the cycle of disadvantage.* New York: Doubleday.

Schweinhart, L. J., Barnes, H., & Weikart, D. (1993). *Significant benefits: The High/Scope Perry Preschool study through age 27. Monographs of the High/Scope Educational Research Foundation* (Vol. 10). Ypsilanti, MI: High/Scope Press.

Schweinhart, L. J., & Weikart, D. (1983). The effects of the Perry Preschool Program on youths through age 15: A summary. In Consortium for Longitudinal Studies (Ed.), *As the twig is bent: Lasting effects of preschool programs* (pp. 71–101). Hillsdale, NJ: Erlbaum.

Schweinhart, L. J., & Weikart, D. (1986). What do we know so far? A review of the Head Start Synthesis Project. *Young Children, 41,* 49–55.

Schweinhart, L. J., & Weikart, D. (1988). The High/Scope Perry Preschool Program. In R. Price, E. Cowen, R. Lorion, & J. Ramos-McKay (Eds.), *14 ounces of prevention: A casebook for practitioners* (pp. 53–65). Washington, DC: American Psychological Association.

Sears, R. R., Maccoby, E. E., & Levin, H. (1957). *Patterns of child rearing.* Evanston, IL: Row-Peterson.

Seitz, V., Apfel, N., Rosenbaum, L., & Zigler, E. (1983). Long-term effects of projects Head Start and Follow Through: The New Haven Project. In Consortium for Longitudinal Studies (Ed.), *As the twig is bent: Lasting effects of preschool programs* (pp. 299–332). Hillsdale, NJ: Erlbaum.

Seitz, V., Rosenbaum, L., & Apfel, N. (1985). Effects of family support intervention: A ten-year follow-up. *Child Development, 56,* 376–391.

Shinn, M., & Gillespie, C. (1994). The roles of housing and poverty in the origins of homelessness. *American Behavioral Scientist, 37,* 505–521.

Shonkoff, J., & Meisels, S. (1990). Early childhood intervention: The evolution of a concept. In S. Meisels & J. Shonkoff (Eds.), *Handbook of early childhood intervention* (pp. 3–31). New York: Cambridge University Press.

Shuey, A. (1958). *The testing of Negro intelligence.* Lynchburg, VA: J. P. Bell.

Simms, M. (1987). How loss of manufacturing jobs is affecting blacks. *Focus: The Monthly Newsletter of the Joint Center for Political Studies, 15,* 6–7.

Skeels, H. (1966). Adult status of children from contrasting early life experiences. *Monographs of the Society for Research in Child Development, 31*(Serial No. 105).

Skeels, H., & Dye, H. (1939). A study of the effects of differential stimulation on mentally retarded children. *Proceedings and Addresses of the American Association on Mental Deficiency, 44,* 114–136.

Slaughter, D. (1983). Early intervention and its effects on maternal and child development. *Monographs of the Society for Research in Child Development, 48*(4, Serial No. 202).

Slaughter, D. (Ed.). (1988a). *New directions for child development: Vol. 42. Black children and poverty: A developmental perspective.* San Francisco: Jossey-Bass.

Slaughter, D. (1988b). Programs for racially and ethnically diverse American families: Some critical issues. In H. Weiss & F. Jacobs (Eds.), *Evaluating family programs* (pp. 461–476). New York: Aldine de Gruyter.

Slaughter, D., Lindsey, R., Nakagawa, K., & Kuehne, V. (1989). Who gets involved? Head Start mothers as persons. *Journal of Negro Education, 58,* 16–29.

Slaughter, D., Washington, V., Oyemade, U., & Lindsey, R. (1988). Head Start: A backward and forward look. *Social Policy Report, 3*(2).

Smeeding, T. M. (1992, January/February). Why the U.S. antipoverty system doesn't work very well. *Challenge,* 30–35.

Smeeding, T. M., & Torrey, B. B. (1988, November 11). Poor children in rich countries. *Science, 242,* 873–877.

Smith, J., Brooks-Gunn, J., & Klebanov, P. (1997). Consequences of growing up poor for young children. In G. Duncan & J. Brooks-Gunn (Eds.), *Consequences of growing up poor.* New York: Russell-Sage Foundation.

Smith, M., & Bissell, J. (1970). Report analysis: The impact of Head Start. *Harvard Educational Review, 40,* 51–104.

Smith, S. (Ed). (1995). *Two-generation programs for families in poverty: A new intervention strategy.* Norwood, NJ: ABLEX.

Smith, S., & Zaslow, M. (1995). Rationale and policy context for two-generation interventions. In I. Sigel (Series Ed.) & S. Smith (Vol. Ed.), *Advances in applied developmental psychology: Vol. 9. Two-generation programs for families in poverty: A new intervention strategy* (pp. 1–35). Norwood, NJ: ABLEX.

Smith, T. (1990). Social inequality in cross-national perspective. In J. Becker, J. Davis, P. Ester, & P. Mohler (Eds.), *Attitudes to inequality and the role of government* (pp. 21–31). Rijswijk, maart: Sociaal en Cultureel Planbureau.

Solon, G. (1992). Intergenerational income mobility in the United States. *American Economic Review, 82,* 393–408.

Spitz, R. A., & Wolf, K. (1946). The smiling response: A contribution to the ontogenesis of social relations. *Genetic Psychology Monographs, 34,* 57–125.

Sprigle, J., & Schaefer, L. (1985). Longitudinal evaluation of the effects of two compensatory preschool programs on fourth- through sixth-grade students. *Developmental Psychology, 21,* 702–708.

Sroufe, A. (1970). A methodological and philosophical critique of intervention-oriented research. *Developmental Psychology, 2,* 140–145.

Stack, C. (1974). *All our kin: Strategies for survival in a black community.* New York: Harper & Row.

Steele, C., & Aronson, J. (1995). Stereotype threat and the intellectual test performance of African Americans. *Journal of Personality and Social Psychology, 69,* 797–811.

Steinberg, L., Catalano, R., & Dooley, D. (1981). Economic antecedents of child abuse and neglect. *Child Development, 52,* 975–985.

Steiner, G. (1976). *The children's cause.* Washington, DC: Brookings Institute.

Sterling, S., Cowen, E. L., Weissberg, R. P., Lotyczewski, B. S., & Boike, M. (1985). Recent stressful life events and young children's school adjustment. *American Journal of Community Psychology, 13,* 87–98.

Stevens, J. (1988). Social support, locus of control, and parenting in three low-income groups of mothers: Black teenagers, black adults, and white adults. *Child Development, 59,* 635–642.

Stevenson, H. W. (1965). Social reinforcement of children's behavior. In L. P. Lipsitt & C. C. Spiker (Eds.), *Advances in child development and behavior* (Vol. 2, pp. 97–126). New York: Academic Press.

Straus, M., Gelles, R., & Steinmetz, S. (1980). *Behind closed doors: Violence in the American family.* Garden City, NY: Doubleday.

Super, D., Parrott, S., Steinmetz, S., & Mann, C. (1996). *The new welfare law.* Washington, DC: Center on Budget and Policy Priorities.

Swartz, J., Smith, C., Bernstein, L., Gardine, J., Levin, M., & Stewart, G. (1995). *Evaluation of the Head Start Family*

Service Center Demonstration Projects (Second Interim Report, Wave III Projects). Cambridge, MA: Abt Associates.

Takanishi, R., & DeLeon, P. (1994). A Head Start for the 21st century. *American Psychologist, 49,* 120–122.

Trickett, P., Apfel, N., Rosenbaum, L., & Zigler, E. (1982). A five-year follow-up of participants in the Yale Child Welfare Research Program. In E. Zigler & E. Gordon (Eds.), *Day care: Scientific and social policy issues* (pp. 200–222). Boston: Auburn House.

Trickett, P., & Susman, E. (1988). Parental perceptions of child-rearing practices in physically abusive and nonabusive families. *Developmental Psychology, 24,* 270–276.

Tropman, J. E. (1977, Winter). The image of public welfare: Reality or projection? *Public Welfare, 35,* 17–24.

Tulkin, S. R. (1972). An analysis of the concept of cultural deprivation. *Developmental Psychology, 6,* 326–339.

Tulkin, S. R., & Cohler, B. J. (1973). Child-rearing attitudes and mother-child interaction in the first year of life. *Merrill-Palmer Quarterly, 19,* 95–106.

U.S. Bureau of the Census. (1992). *The Black population in the United States: March 1991* (Current Population Reports, P20-464). Washington, DC: U.S. Government Printing Office.

U.S. Bureau of the Census. (1994). *Statistical abstract of the United States: 1994.* Washington, DC: U.S. Government Printing Office.

U.S. Bureau of Labor Statistics. (1992). *Current population survey: March 1991.* Washington, DC: U.S. Government Printing Office.

Vaughan, D. (1993). Exploring the use of the public's views to set income poverty thresholds and adjust them over time. *Social Security Bulletin, 56,* 22–46.

Villar, J., Farnot, U., Barros, F., Victoria, C., Langer, A., & Belizan, J. (1992). A randomized trial of psychosocial support during high-risk pregnancies. *New England Journal of Medicine, 327,* 1266–1271.

Walker, T., Rodriguez, G., Johnson, D., & Cortez, C. (1995). Advance Parent-Child Education Program. In I. Sigel (Series Ed.) & S. Smith (Vol. Ed.), *Advances in applied developmental psychology: Vol. 9. Two-generation programs for families in poverty: A new intervention strategy* (pp. 67–90). Norwood, NJ: ABLEX.

Washington, V. (1985). Head Start: How appropriate for minority families in the 1980s? *American Journal of Orthopsychiatry, 55,* 577–590.

Washington, V., & Bailey, U. J. (1995). *Project Head Start: Models and strategies for the 21st century.* New York: Garland.

Washington, V., & Oyemade, U. J. (1987). *Project Head Start: Past, present, and future trends in the context of family needs.* New York: Garland.

Wasik, B., Ramey, C., Bryant, D., & Sparling, J. (1990). A longitudinal study of two early intervention strategies: Project CARE. *Child Development, 61,* 1682–1696.

Watson, E., & Collins, A. (1982). Natural helping networks in alleviating family stress. *Annals of the American Academy of Political and Social Science, 461,* 102–112.

Weber, C. U., Foster, P., & Weikart, D. (1978). *An economic analysis of the Ypsilanti Perry Preschool Project. Monographs of the High/Scope Educational Research Foundation* (Vol. 5). Ypsilanti, MI: High/Scope Press.

Weems, L. (1974). Black community research needs: Methods, models and modalities. In L. Gary (Ed.), *Social research and the black community: Selected issues and priorities* (pp. 25–38). Washington, DC: Institute for Urban Affairs and Research, Howard University.

Weinraub, M., & Wolf, B. (1983). Effects of stress and social supports on mother-child interactions in single- and two-parent families. *Child Development, 54,* 1297–1311.

Weiss, H. (1987). Family support and education in early childhood programs. In S. Kagan, D. Powell, B. Weissbourd, & E. Zigler (Eds.), *America's family support programs* (pp. 133–160). New Haven, CT: Yale University Press.

Weiss, H. (1993). Home visits: Necessary but not sufficient. *The Future of Children, 3,* 113–128.

Weissbourd, B. (1987). A brief history of family support programs. In S. Kagan, D. Powell, B. Weissbourd, & E. Zigler (Eds.), *America's family support programs* (pp. 38–56). New Haven, CT: Yale University Press.

Werner, E. E., & Smith, R. S. (1977). *Kauai's children come of age.* Honolulu: University of Hawaii Press.

Werner, E. E., & Smith, R. S. (1982). *Vulnerable but invincible: A study of resilient children.* New York: McGraw-Hill.

Wertsch, J., & Youniss, J. (1987). Contextualizing the investigator: The case of developmental psychology. *Human Development, 30,* 18–31.

Westinghouse Learning Corporation. (1969, June). *The impact of Head Start: An evaluation of the effects of Head Start on children's cognitive and affective development* (Ohio University report to the Office of Economic Opportunity). Washington, DC: Clearinghouse for Federal Scientific and Technical Information.

White, K. R. (1985–1986). Efficacy of early intervention. *Journal of Special Education, 19,* 402–416.

White, K. R., Taylor, M., & Moss, V. (1992). Does research support claims about the benefits of involving parents in early intervention programs? *Review of Educational Research, 62,* 91–125.

White, M., Kasl, S. V., Zahner, G., & Will, J. C. (1987). Perceived crime in the neighborhood and mental health of women and children. *Environment and Behavior, 19,* 588–613.

White, S. H. (1970). The national impact study of Head Start. In J. Hellmuth (Ed.), *Disadvantaged child: Compensatory education: A national debate* (Vol. 3, pp. 163–184). New York: Brunner/Mazel.

Whiteman, M., Brown, B. R., & Deutsch, M. (1967). Some effects of social class and race on children's language and intellectual abilities. In M. Deutsch (Ed.), *The disadvantaged child: Selected papers of Martin Deutsch and Associates* (pp. 319–335). New York: Basic Books.

William T. Grant Foundation Commission on Work, Family, and Citizenship. (1988). *The forgotten half: Pathways to success for America's youth and young families.* Washington, DC: Author.

Williams, K. (1987). Cultural diversity in family support: Black families. In S. Kagan, D. Powell, B. Weissbourd, & E. Zigler (Eds.), *America's family support programs* (pp. 295–307). New Haven, CT: Yale University Press.

Williamson, J. (1974). Beliefs about the motivation of the poor and attitudes toward poverty policy. *Social Problems, 21,* 634–648.

Wilson, H. (1974). Parenting in poverty. *British Journal of Social Work, 4,* 241–254.

Wilson, M. (1986). The black extended family: An analytical consideration. *Developmental Psychology, 22,* 246–258.

Wilson, M. (1989). Child development in the context of the black extended family. *American Psychologist, 44,* 380–383.

Wilson, W. J. (1987). *The truly disadvantaged: The inner city, the underclass, and public policy.* Chicago: University of Chicago Press.

Wilson, W. J. (1996). *When work disappears: The world of the new urban poor.* New York: Knopf.

Wilson, W. J., & Neckerman, K. (1986). Poverty and family structure: The widening gap between evidence and public policy issues. In S. Danziger & D. Weinberg (Eds.), *Fighting poverty: What works and what doesn't* (pp. 232–259). Cambridge, MA: Harvard University Press.

Wishy, B. (1972). *The child and the republic.* Philadelphia: University of Pennsylvania Press.

Wolfe, D. A., Edwards, B., Manion, I., & Koverola, C. (1988). Early intervention for parents at risk of child abuse and neglect: A preliminary investigation. *Journal of Consulting and Clinical Psychology, 56,* 40–47.

Wolock, I., & Horowitz, B. (1979). Child maltreatment and material deprivation among AFDC recipient families. *Social Service Review, 53,* 175–162.

Wong, Y., Garfinkel, I., & McLanahan, S. (1993). Single-mother families in eight countries: Economic status and social policy. *Social Service Review, 67,* 177–197.

Woodhead, M. (1988). When psychology informs public policy: The case of early childhood intervention. *American Psychologist, 43,* 443–454.

Youniss, J. (1990). Cultural forces leading to scientific developmental psychology. In I. Sigel (Series Ed.) & C. Fisher & W. Tryon (Vol. Eds.), *Advances in applied developmental psychology: Vol. 4. Ethics in applied developmental psychology: Emerging issues in an emerging field* (pp. 285–300). Norwood, NJ: ABLEX.

Zelkowitz, P. (1982). Parenting philosophies and practices. In D. Belle (Ed.), *Lives in stress: Women and depression* (pp. 154–162). Beverly Hills, CA: Sage.

Zigler, E. (1985). Assessing Head Start at 20: An invited commentary. *American Journal of Orthopsychiatry, 55,* 603–609.

Zigler, E. (1994). Reshaping early childhood intervention to be a more effective weapon against poverty. *American Journal of Community Psychology, 22,* 37–47.

Zigler, E., Abelson, W., & Seitz, V. (1973). Motivational factors in the performance of economically disadvantaged children on the Peabody Picture Vocabulary Test. *Child Development, 44,* 294–303.

Zigler, E., & Berman, W. (1983). Discerning the future of early childhood intervention. *American Psychologist, 33,* 894–906.

Zigler, E., & Butterfield, W. (1968). Motivational aspects of changes in IQ test performance of culturally deprived nursery school children. *Child Development, 39,* 1–14.

Zigler, E., & Freedman, J. (1987). Head Start: A pioneer of family support. In S. Kagan, D. Powell, B. Weissbourd, & E. Zigler (Eds.), *America's family support programs* (pp. 57–76). New Haven, CT: Yale University Press.

Zigler, E., & Muenchow, S. (1992). *Head Start: The inside story of America's most successful educational experiment.* New York: Basic Books.

Zigler, E., & Styfco, S. (1994a). Head Start: Criticisms in a constructive context. *American Psychologist, 49,* 127–132.

Zigler, E., & Styfco, S. (1994b). Is the Perry Preschool better than Head Start? Yes and no. *Early Childhood Research Quarterly, 9,* 269–287.

Zigler, E., & Valentine, J. (Eds.). (1979). *Project Head Start: A legacy of the war on poverty.* New York: Free Press.

Zur-Szpiro, S., & Longfellow, C. (1982). Fathers' support to mothers and children. In D. Belle (Ed.), *Lives in stress: Women and depression* (pp. 145–153). Beverly Hills, CA: Sage.

Education in School

CHAPTER 4

Developmental Psychology and Instruction: Issues From and For Practice

K. ANN RENNINGER

How students access, process or work through, and finally complete a task is a concern shared by many developmental psychologists and educators.[1] Increasing numbers of developmental psychologists are conducting research on education-related topics (see Bruer's discussion of research in cognitive psychology, 1993; and the edited volume by McGilly, 1994). Others see the implications of their theory and research for practice and are involved at some level in instituting inservices or developing resources for teachers and caretakers (cf. developing community and teacher partnerships: Comer, Haynes, Joyner, & Ben-Avie, 1996; Damon, 1997; Nicolopoulou & Cole, 1993; developing software for anchored instruction: Cognition and Technology Group at Vanderbilt, 1996; establishing school–university collaborations: Baird & Northfield, 1992; facilitating teacher networks: Webb & Romberg, 1994; providing an Internet forum for teacher resources: Renninger, Weimar, & Klotz, 1997; providing training and support for Cognitively Guided Instruction: Fennema, Carpenter, & Peterson, 1989). Yet others have embedded the study of student learning in the ongoing process of classroom practice (cf. Brown & Campione, 1994; Cobb, Yackel, & Wood, 1995).

There are differences in emphasis, however, between researchers trained in developmental psychology and those trained in education, stemming from their differing purposes and goals and reflected in the nature of the issues with which the two groups are concerned. For example, developmental psychologists typically study issues related to how and why children learn, whereas educators are more likely to focus their attention on what and how to teach. Developmental psychologists study learning across a wide variety of contexts largely unrelated to school, whereas educators focus on student learning in school. Developmental psychologists may study an atypicality such as Down Syndrome in order to learn more about typical development; educators primarily read about the populations and subject matter content within which they themselves work. Finally,

[1] Note that in accord with the scope of this volume, even though topics in developmental psychology and instruction are relevant to the life span of the individual, the present chapter focuses primarily on instruction of children and adolescents. Furthermore, this chapter focuses specifically on neurologically intact students, although the general approach to students' needs that is described has relevance to instruction for atypical populations.

although both developmental psychologists and educators study children or adolescents as discrete groups, developmental psychologists refer to their subjects as children or adolescents, while educators call them students and often associate them with grade-level, school-based accomplishments ("second graders do . . . ").[2]

Thus, education-related studies in developmental psychology are often more distal than proximal for educators, meaning that the connections between the research question being addressed and classroom practice are not obvious. Even in cases where researchers specify implications for practice, these often take the form of suggesting that practitioners promote metacognition, for example, rather than specifying how one might actually implement this suggestion in the classroom.

There is almost no developmental research that specifically addresses questions related to classroom practice such as: Is it always bad to give students a task they cannot complete? What do I do with the four kids who just can't keep up with the work? Why don't students learn better when I've given them something interesting to read? How do I get my students to really discuss something? Should students keep the same partners for all of their lab periods? Why aren't my students learning anything when they do small group work? For such questions—the questions of practitioners—the applicability of research findings typically need to be inferred and conclusions treated as working hypotheses.

Recently, researchers in cognitive science, in particular, have been seeking to understand the selection of content for curriculum, including both selection of content that will provide the student with a critical base for subsequent knowledge development, and its sequencing (see Greeno, Collins, & Resnick, 1996 for a review). There also is a need, however, to begin seriously considering what we know about instructional practice: the organization and process of teaching a class of students, an inservice for teachers, and so on (Shulman, 1986).

The content of instruction is the specific topic of other chapters in this *Handbook*. Here, the emphasis is on considering what students need by way of instruction; the knowledge we have about instruction at present; and the resources to which we might turn in order to consider more fully the application or implications of developmental psychology in everyday practice. What might we still need to know, for example, before concluding that lecturing or direct instruction is necessarily bad and small group work needs to occur in all classrooms? While it is a given that instruction never occurs independent of content or subject matter, specific consideration of instruction enables examination of what is and is not understood about the processes through which learning is facilitated. Information about how and why students learn has implications for how students might most effectively be taught.

The chapter has its roots in James' (1899) and Gage's (1978) discussions of learning and the art of teaching, or what has been labeled the problem of theory and practice. It also builds on that of Brown, Bransford, Ferrara, and Campione (1983) in the preceding *Handbook of Child Psychology* (Mussen, 1983). In particular, their description of learning as complex, interactive, and dynamic provides a foundation for the present discussion.

Three working assumptions guide the organization of this chapter:

1. Effective instructional decisions are informed by an articulated and coherent sense of how students learn and develop over time.
2. If more educators (teachers, teacher-educators, administrators, policymakers, parents, etc.) were knowledgeable about developmental theory and research, and had tools to think about classroom decision making that were informed by what is known about how students learn, research in developmental psychology would radically change the mainstream of educational practice.
3. If more researchers were knowledgeable about educational practice—the strengths and needs of teachers and their working knowledge about students—*and* invested time working with educators to consider the implications and directions of their research efforts, research could contribute more directly to educational practice.

This chapter consists of three main sections. The first section overviews the relevance of topics in developmental psychology for instruction. To provide a common set of instructional formats to which the reader can refer throughout the chapter, it opens with two formats for teaching about what makes the Jurassic Period the Jurassic Period: a

[2] It would be even more accurate to describe the continuum of overlap and variation between those trained in developmental psychology or educational psychology and those trained in practice. There are those who have taught and worked with children, those who in their studies have come to be familiar with children of a particular age or grade level, those whose training has consistently involved them in grounding their understanding of theory and research methods in practice, and so on. Differences in background contribute to differences in the lens and language available for describing learning. Here, two endpoints are described by way of establishing the band within which discussions of student learning take place.

lecture format and an interactive format. These are followed by a synthesis of the developmental literature on research and practice that permits consideration of links between instructional formats and conceptions of learning, students' needs, what we know about development, and its implications for the process of instruction.

The second portion of the chapter consists of an overview of issues raised in recent research and reports on large group instruction (lecture and discussion methods), questioning, and classroom grouping. This section is intended to permit consideration of the information or language currently available to educators for thinking about instruction. Following each topic, commentary addresses the way in which the literature reviewed contributes to our thinking about the Jurassic Period case formats and our understanding of students' abilities to access, process or work through, and complete a task. Following this, unanswered questions are identified, particularly those that stem from and might be addressed by research and theory in developmental psychology.

The third section of the chapter further considers the language of instruction as it is reflected in the overview of the literature. It also addresses the tensions between research and practice in general, and developmental psychology and practice more specifically as these are highlighted in this literature. Finally, discussion focuses on current efforts and possibilities for coordinating research and practice.

DEVELOPMENTAL PSYCHOLOGY AND INSTRUCTION

This chapter focuses on the application of developmental psychology to instructional practice, although what might be technically classified as literature from child psychology, cognitive science, developmental education, and educational psychology also form a basis for the discussion.[3] In keeping with the mission of this volume, the specific emphasis of this chapter is the application of developmental psychology to instructional practice.

"Development," or change in how and what students learn, is not simply a matter of identifying differences among students as a function of age or grade level. It refers to transitions or qualitative (stage-related) shifts in students' cognitive, social, and affective functioning (the way in which they problem solve on the playground, in mathematics class, and as they work on choosing words to write a story) and involves an emergent relation between the biological being and psychological self and the physical and social environment. The individual is at the same time both a contributor to and a product of a larger system that includes family, school, and culture (Bronfenbrenner, 1979).

Developmental psychology as it applies to schools appears to have more to do with transitions than qualitative changes, however, since teachers work with students who typically vary in age by no more than two years. The sequences that characterize these transitions and the differences in their organization (Rogoff, 1996) and structure (Kuhn, 1995) can be useful information for teachers. By way of example, an adaptation of Piaget's (1950; see also Sigel, 1986) observations to student learning would suggest that early in students' encounters with a class of objects or events—a subject area or set of concepts to be learned—a characteristic of their thinking is that it is dominated by the connections that can be made to the concepts to be learned. Students more easily make connections to tasks that involve them in making logical extensions based on what they already know, recognizing relations, and working with concepts (applying them to other instances, analyzing their parts, etc.). With experience, students are increasingly able to move between working with concrete and abstract instances, and to understand concepts as they are represented in symbols or abstraction. Just because students can work with symbols or abstraction, this does not obviate their need for opportunities to manipulate or directly experiment with concepts. Students can look as if they understand something when they are still working to understand it, and they can

[3] For purposes of clarity, some definitions of terms related to the topic of developmental psychology and instruction are listed below:

1. *Developmental psychology* describes the study of distinct and shared sequences that characterize human growth.
2. *Applied developmental psychology* refers to the study of developmental psychology in clinical, educational, and policy settings.
3. *Cognitive science* is the study of how the mind works.
4. *Child psychology* is the study of the child's cognitive, social, and affective functioning.
5. *A developmental approach to education* refers to teaching that is responsive to the cognitive and social strengths of the child, and as such involves him or her in optimally challenging tasks.
6. *Developmental education* is a term used by educators to refer to a developmental approach to education; however, in practice it is often misconstrued to be relevant only to the education of slow or atypical learners.
7. *Educational psychology* is the application of principles of psychology to educational issues.

appear to understand material when they are being assisted that they in fact "mostly understand."

As students work with tasks, they are in a position to ask questions (generate hypotheses) that will enable them to further clarify and question what they know. The transitions that occur prior to students' abilities to generate developed and testable hypotheses highlight the benefits of using brainstorms and hypothesis-generation as teaching methods early on in work with students. Students (or the individual student) are always in a process of developing their understanding. There is always more to learn (other ways in which to think about the content, other questions to ask, and so on). Furthermore, learners at different ages are similar in their need to develop a foundation for understanding that begins with their establishing a connection to a concept and learning the skills and information necessary to rerepresent it to themselves as being both abstract and concrete.

It also may be important to underscore the point that acquisition of knowledge about social studies, mathematics, and so forth, is tied to developing cognition. It is not entirely dependent on the structure of the subject matter. Rather, based on what students understand, content-based information can be sequenced and particular methods or formats of instruction employed in order to facilitate their abilities to make connections to it. Such adjustments to instructional practice provide students with the base of skills and knowledge necessary for further developing their understanding. To rely on an external or "adult" model of knowledge to be learned (the structure of a discipline), however, is to ignore the comprehension of the student (Gelman & Brown, 1986; Sigel, 1986). This does not negate the usefulness of mapping students' developing understanding of a subject area or the usefulness of task analysis, but it suggests that instruction for students cannot be optimal if the particular strengths and needs of the students being taught are not taken into consideration.

By definition, then, a developmental approach to instruction involves the simultaneous consideration of the students' characteristics as learners, the nature of the tasks to be learned, methods for adjusting these tasks so that learning can take place, criteria for evaluating what the student still needs to learn (Bransford, 1979; Brown, 1982; Brown et al., 1983; Cronbach & Snow, 1977), and the environment of the learner (Bronfenbrenner, 1979). Furthermore, it involves attention to both the cognitive, social, and affective developmental status of the learner.

Central to such decision making is information about how students learn: how the student perceives information, represents this information to him or herself, and acts upon it (Wozniak, 1985). This information forms the basis for describing implications for practice. At this time what might be called the "working knowledge" of developmental researchers, from a variety of theoretical orientations, includes the following:

1. Each student's knowledge or understanding is individually constructed in relation to the others (i.e., the teacher, other students) and objects (i.e., texts, computer software, classroom rituals, assigned tasks) in the environment;
2. The process of apprehending or perceiving something (i.e., a concept) involves readiness in terms of attentional capacity, short-term memory, prior knowledge or experience, individual interest, and the particular affordances of (or actions suggested by) the task, including how situated within a particular context the learning is;
3. What the individual attends to influences what he or she represents to him- or herself; and
4. What individuals represent to themselves in turn affects the particular action or sets of actions in which they engage or are ready to engage.

This working knowledge provides the basis for thinking about whether and why a student will learn what the teacher is teaching. It does not, however, specifically address actual transitions or change in students' understanding. Information about student learning needs to be linked to real students and their strengths and needs as learners: instruction is a "live" or dynamic and reciprocal relation between a group of students and their teacher. It involves providing opportunities for students to develop their problem-solving abilities and their skills and understanding of specific knowledge (cf. Ammon & Hutcheson, 1989; Baird & Northfield, 1992; Copple, Sigel, & Saunders, 1984; Newman, Griffin, & Cole, 1989; Silver, 1986; Tharp & Gallimore, 1988; Yackel, 1995), as well as their value for themselves as learners based on their current understanding.

Descriptions of effective (Bredekamp, 1993; National Council for the Social Studies, 1994; National Council of Teachers of Mathematics, 1989; see also Brown & Campione's, 1994, discussion of "first principles") and potentially developmentally appropriate practices include:

1. Creating opportunities for student questioning;
2. Providing opportunities for students to practice and begin to own the language of the subject area or domain in which they are working;

3. Appreciating that there is not necessarily one right answer, but that there are different perspectives (dimensions to the problem to be solved, approximations) to the right answer;
4. Emphasizing the *process* of problem solution;
5. Drawing on students' prior experience;
6. Requiring that students reflect on material covered through journals, discussion, written summaries, and so forth;
7. Specifying immediate goals so the student is clear about what is to be accomplished and why;
8. Specifying each student's role in a given task so that he or she knows both what is expected and for what he or she is responsible;
9. Encouraging students' repeated work with skills and discourse-knowledge in different types of contexts;
10. Enabling students to exchange ideas with others in order to gain information or perspective on the work they are undertaking.

It is difficult for many teachers to adjust instructional tasks to accommodate student strengths and needs and then sequence these tasks to enable students to meet the challenges that were once difficult for them. There is no algorithm for what teachers should do. Instead, they need to learn to work with and help students to develop the cognitive strategies that support their abilities to perform the tasks they are assigned (Rosenshine, Meister, & Chapman, 1996).

Take the case of a mathematics teacher who is using one of the newly revised texts that provides problems for students to pursue in small group work. The problems are challenging and require the students to apply what they have been learning in new ways. Neither the teacher nor the students, however, have had much experience with group work. The challenge problems are intended to take a full 40-minute period with all group members fully participating—but short of a description of effective group work behaviors, which the teacher reviewed with the students the first week in class, there is no additional thought on the part of the teacher that she or he needs to teach the students how to do group work. The teacher thinks this information has been covered. Thus, when the group work flounders because some students are not focused and others still come to the teacher with questions, the group work is cut out of the curriculum.

In an alternative scenario, the teacher recognizes that the students need to learn how to work together in groups, and knows that telling them about roles early in the term is no guarantee that they will carry this information through to their own work in small groups. Thus, the teacher might adjust and sequence instruction suggested by the text to meet the strengths and needs of the students. She or he could introduce the students to small group work by having them complete a portion of the work for the problem in the small group and then bring that information back to the larger group for discussion. Following this, the teacher might, over the course of several days, keep involving students in 5- to 10-minute periods of work with a partner that would provide a critical component of the learning for the day. The teacher might also encourage the students to work with a different person each day in order to enable them to practice working with other people. As the teacher moves to involving the students in longer blocks of paired and eventually small group work, she or he can build accountability into the assignment by collecting the problem(s) on which the students have worked at the end of the period of small group work. Finally, following their work in the groups, the teacher can encourage the students to talk about the content of their learning—new insights, connections, and so on—and what has worked for them (and what has not) in the process of working with others. Such information would provide the basis for subsequent planning for that class.

There are no guarantees that using small groups in class is sufficient for students to learn; benefits can accrue from carefully planned use of small groups in teaching, however. (See review of research on small groups by Lou et al., 1996.) In the case of the mathematics classroom described, the process of working together in small groups can give the students practice using the language of mathematics. It also can enable them to gain some perspective on what the possible approaches to problem solution might be. In fact, each member of the group is in a position to discover gaps in both his or her understanding and that of the others in the group (Webb, 1989). This acknowledges the appropriateness of not knowing and coming to know, as part of the process of learning. Furthermore, it provides a context that can lead students to search together for new information, enabling them to expand and solidify the understanding of all group members (Webb, 1989). Finally, the process of working together in groups and then reconvening as part of a larger group discussion of the problem can enable students to know the questions they need to ask or the work they need to take on in order to complete the task as assigned (see discussions in Lindquist, 1989; Yackel, 1995).

There is no algorithm that can provide information about what students will or will not understand. Teachers need to learn from watching and talking with their students about what is still not clear to them (see related discussion in Wood, 1995). They can be assisted by documentation of the types of strategies students might employ in similar situations. This kind of teacher resource is central to projects such as Cognitively Guided Instruction (Fennema et al., 1989) and teaching practice in Japan (Stigler, Fernandez, & Yoshida, 1996). Even when such resources are not available to teachers, however, once teachers are in situations that encourage them to talk with others about the way they work with cognitive strategies—the way they adjust their use of group work, embed strategies into the content of what they are teaching, and are enabled to respond to the developmental strengths and needs of their students—such adjustments in their teaching become a matter of course (Baird & Northfield, 1992; Black & Ammon, 1992; Comer et al., 1996; Wilson, Miller, & Yerkes, 1993).

A significant byproduct of developmental approaches to instruction is that problems with management and teacher-student relationships are significantly reduced and even eliminated when students are able to perform the tasks they have been assigned (Comer, Haynes, & Joyner, 1996; Lindquist, 1989; Palincsar & Klenk, 1991). This makes sense: Students cannot connect to tasks or even figure out what the relevant strategies for a task are if it is so discrepant (so removed from their strengths and needs) that they do not have access to it.

A Case in Two Formats

A case is presented here in two formats: a lecture format and an interactive format,[4] in order to set forth a common set of instructional practices to which the reader can refer throughout the rest of the chapter. The two formats are designed specifically for a second grade class, but they could also be used with preschool, later elementary, middle school, high school, or even college students. Necessary adjustments would include changes in the content to be learned (information, skills, and concepts) and, depending on the students' experience in interactive classrooms, the description of the interactive format (increasing or decreasing its focus on problems, independent learning, using the resources of others to solve problems, etc.).

For the purposes of this portion of the chapter, it is assumed that either the lecture or the interactive format *could* be considered developmentally appropriate practice. Whether this is the case, however, is dependent upon the particular students' prior knowledge, metacognitive awareness, self-concept, as well as the culture of learning (D'Andrade, 1984, 1990) in which they are immersed.[5]

The particular topic of this case—the Jurassic Period—is intended to enable all readers to think about instructional formats and their role in development; the case easily could have been set in a math classroom or a reading class (see the Appendix for a second set of case formats on the topic of U.S. colonization). Both formats are designed to provide an interdisciplinary introduction to the Jurassic Period, in which students address concepts of period, time scale, evolution, decay and fossilization, ecology (the system of the period), and paleontology. Materials for the class include bones and fossils, time lines, the Internet Resource Center,[6] a chart depicting the evolution of dinosaurs, a diagram of a dig, and so on.

An interesting feature of the topic of this case is that there is no prescribed set of information available to us about what students at particular ages know about the Jurassic Period. Whether using a lecture or a more interactive format, a teacher working with these plans will need to attend to what students can talk about and how to use this information to inform subsequent lessons—in fact, such attention is critical to work with even the most well-documented subject matter. Were information available to the teacher about the sequence through which students pass in understanding (and misunderstanding) the Jurassic Period, the teacher would still need to consider what the particular students in his or her class understood and what they needed to figure out in order to understand what distinguishes the Jurassic from any other period.

The information missing from these formats is a description of who the students are as a group and as individuals. Information about students needs to be collected continuously and revised in the process of teaching. This information is omitted here in order to call attention to the role of students in instruction generally, and, more specifically, to focus attention on the instructional format.

---

[4] This case is derived from Stephen Weimar's work with second grade students at The School in Rose Valley during the spring of 1996. A second case example is included in the Appendix. It represents another example of a case in a lecture and an interactive format. Presenting two sets of cases enables the interested reader to consider more fully another example of a lecture and an interactive format and the necessary characteristics of each.

[5] Here, I am referring primarily to the culture of learning that characterizes a school, but clearly the culture of learning for any given student also includes the input of his or her home environment (DiMaggio, 1982; Greenfield & Cocking, 1994) and/or the culture of the specific subject matter (Schoenfeld, 1987).

[6] The Internet Resource Center can be found at: http://forum.swarthmore.edu/~steve/.

Lecture Format

The teacher begins the first class with an explanation that the students will be studying the Jurassic Period. She or he asks them what they know about the time period called the Jurassic Period and writes their ideas on the board. This brainstorming serves as a kind of pretest, and provides a gauge for the teacher to use in thinking about what the students already know and where the explanation needs to start.[7] The teacher then explains that people who study such time periods are called paleontologists or geologists, and gives examples of the kinds of investigations they conduct and what this would mean for studying a particular period such as the Jurassic. The class closes with a review of the information covered. As homework, students are to write a "dino-fact" each day in a dino-journal they will compile during the unit. They can use information from sources found either in the classroom or at home.

During other parts of the school day students:

1. Work on "dinosaur math." They are taught about appropriate units of measure, ratio, the use of perspective and scale, and eventually are asked to compare their findings with what humans of the current "period" (people living today) know;
2. Each student individually writes a chapter book using information that has been gathered about dinosaurs;
3. Participate in an interactive Web-based project developed especially for the class, in which they can ask questions of and receive answers from a current graduate student in geology, "Dr. Dino"; and
4. Explore texts and virtual museums via the Internet Resource Center.

Interactive Format

The teacher begins the first class with a brief overview of the topic to be studied; students will be working to figure out what makes the Jurassic the Jurassic. The teacher then asks the students to brainstorm what they know that they know, what they think they know, and what they want to find out about the Jurassic Period. Large sheets of paper are taped up on the wall and the teacher writes all of the students' ideas under appropriate headings as directed by the students.

Following this, students are led into a discussion of theory and facts: What do they consider to be evidence that they know something? The discussion continues, and the terms *hypothesis* and *theory* are introduced as students consider how to go about moving things from one category to the next. How could we do this? How does one develop confidence in one's decisions? These questions lead in turn to a discussion of where we get our facts: Who does the work necessary to gather facts? How do people do this work? Only after students have offered what they already know does the teacher supplement and summarize the answers given by students to each of these questions.

Summary statements are written on additional big sheets of paper and taped on other sections of the wall so that they will be available to the students for the next several days. These sheets will be reposted later for subsequent discussions that build on this information. The five or six items that remain under "what they want to find out" provide the focus for the students' learning during the unit.

As homework, students are to collect dino-facts for a class dino-challenge that they have elected to set for themselves: They aim to amass 500 dino-facts by the end of the unit. Part of their responsibility in completing this assignment is to note with whom they have conferred in asserting that a fact entered is indeed a fact. This portion of the assignment is also based on their collective decision that for their purposes one other student and an adult need to verify that a fact is a fact.

Student responses to the questions are used to select tasks, establish the level of questioning, and so on, for the first days of the course during which students will be involved in simulations (i.e., a geologic dig), projects (embedding fossils in a terrarium to depict geologic layers), ecosystem modeling (each student is given a slip of paper with a role written on it and must find others to whom he or she would relate), small group brainstorming, fact finding, and discussions of period, evolution, and geologic change.

During other parts of the week students:

1. Work on "dinosaur math." They think of all of the questions they might have about different dinosaurs: how big, how long, how heavy, how much did they eat, how fast did they eat? They work with and help to determine appropriate units of measure, and use of perspective and scale. They will eventually compare their findings with what humans of the current period know, and study ratio.

---

[7] It may already be obvious to the reader, but if not: The purpose of this case description is to emphasize that a lecture format can be developmentally appropriate depending on the strengths and needs of the students and the particular lecture format used. As such, this lecture format intentionally bears only some resemblance to the stereotype of lectures as teacher-directed learning for which students need to be accomplished learners.

2. Each student works on writing a chapter book using information gathered about dinosaurs.
3. Students participate in an interactive Web-based project developed especially for the class in which the students can ask questions of and receive answers from a current graduate student in geology, "Dr. Dino."
4. Students explore texts and virtual museums via the Internet Resource Center.

Linking the Case Formats to Topics in Developmental Psychology

As is reflected in both of these case formats, many different lines of research in developmental psychology can be relevant to instructional practice. Both the lecture and the interactive formats include possibilities for drawing out and allowing for (a) information students already possess about either prehistoric time periods, dinosaurs, paleontology, and so on (knowledge, comprehension, conceptual development, developmental stage, attitudes); (b) the possibility that students have misunderstandings about the nature of history and science generally and prehistoric time periods more specifically (misconception); (c) students' needs to reflect on what they are learning (metacognition, comprehension, conceptual development); (d) the importance of exploring alternative sources of information (strategies, problem solving, concept development, the development of representational competence); and (e) the teacher's need to inform subsequent work in the class using information about what the students already know (zone of proximal development, psychological distance).

In addition, the interactive format also includes *explicit* consideration of (a) potential differences among students in their ability to connect to a topic (affect, interest, temperament, motivation, experience, individual difference, intelligence, knowledge); (b) potential differences among students in both skills and discourse-knowledge (independence, attentional capacity, memory, implicit knowledge, expertise, ability level, strategy use); (c) opportunities to work together as a group (intercultural orientation, gender, social cognition, peers, peer relations, friendship, cooperation); (d) the use of a group to provide assistance and support that enables information to be learned (cognitive change); (e) opportunities to enhance students' self-understanding (self-esteem, self-concept, self-perception, social development); (f) the use of a group to provide different perspectives on a given task (representational competence, strategy use); and (g) the opportunity to make connections between the world outside and the content of school learning (situated learning).

The Format of Instruction and Conceptions of Learning

In addition to reflecting links to topics in developmental psychology, the lecture and interactive formats for instruction may also be understood as reflecting two "ideal," if implicit, conceptions of learning—ideal in the sense that they are exemplars or idealized scripts (Greenfield, 1994), not in the sense that either is necessarily correct (Benjamin, 1949).

Lecture Format

Those subscribing to the lecture format might be said generally to equate learning with acquisition of a hierarchy of materials and skills (Gagne, 1968). It is not necessarily expected, however, that what is learned will become part of the repertoire of the students' knowledge without systematic practice. Nor is it assumed that learning will lead to a qualitative shift in the students' understanding of the information. More typically, in the mind of the practitioner, the content of what is learned in a lecture is discrete and prescribed. The product is known. There is a particular amount of text that needs to be covered, a set number of experiments to run or problems to be done. The teacher is perceived to need to move through content at the pace that has been set by someone beside him- or herself (the grade level administrator, the district). The pace often precludes sequencing the material to meet the strengths and needs of the students, in turn affecting the likelihood that some students will not fully understand the material covered and that others will be bored with what for them is repetition.

From this perspective, culture, gender, interest, motivation, and task orientation are considered to be differing types of intervening variables. It is thought that if students are better prepared, more motivated, or more task-oriented, they will be more effective learners (Pintrich & Schunk, 1995). The emphasis is on self-regulation and the acquisition or mastery of material, not on connections and reconstruction of what had been understood.

Empirical models often fit the conception of learning specified by the lecture method, where the task and the abilities of the students are not necessarily matched. The goal in such data collection is to compare students with respect to their abilities, motivational orientations, learning strategies, and so on. Such studies are designed to ascertain what students can and cannot do, the strategies they employ, and the implicit knowledge they have. While such work contributes to our abilities to map student capacities as a function of age, experience with the task, and so on, they may not map directly onto optimal classroom instruction, even though they are embodied in the way some educators think and teach. The reason for this is that they may show what was accomplished, but do not provide information about on what a particular student is currently working, or the kinds of learning on which he or she is ready to embark (Gardner, 1991; R. Mitchell, 1992; Perrone, 1991). Furthermore, student assignment to groups as a function of performance may not account for the importance of social and emotional well-being for cognitive functioning and the reduction of differences to dichotomies such as strong student/weak student or high achiever/underachiever. Such dichotomies often precondition students' abilities to continue to function effectively in the situation as learners and/or their abilities to develop some revised sense of themselves as learners (Eder, 1981; Harter, 1983).

Interactive Format

Those who subscribe to more interactive methods of teaching consider learning to be an ongoing process of making meaning (acquiring skills, information, and self-knowledge). It is thought to evolve across a wide range of settings and emerges in participation (Rogoff, 1997) or through facilitation by others, text, and/or materials.

Interactive formats for learning often are described as involving students as partners in learning. They ascribe the role of facilitating student learning to the teacher. In the mind of the practitioner, there is no expectation that students can learn any faster than they are ready and able to consolidate what they do know about concepts being covered. Thus, rather than entire bodies of knowledge, selection of content to be learned reflects teacher perceptions of students' needs to begin to develop facility with particular concepts and skills (cf. Griffin, Case, & Siegler, 1994). The expectation here is that provision of tools matched to their development (in other words, tasks that challenge but do not overwhelm them) will enable students to revise or qualitatively change the way in which they have been thinking. Once the student has "learned" something, it can be assumed to be part of his or her repertoire for subsequent learning. From this perspective, practice may include varied opportunities to continue work with a concept; because tasks are sequenced to enable students to build on what they do understand, practice also can be thought about as embedded in the next sets of tasks with which they engage.

Furthermore, based on a host of moderating variables (e.g., culture, gender, interest, motivation, and task orientation), it is expected that students will have a range of useful perspectives on which to draw in considering topics being covered, and that they will take different amounts of time to consolidate information. As a result, tasks for this type of instruction are often somewhat open-ended and include opportunities to engage in multiple types of representation (cf. anchored instruction: Goldman, Pellegrino, & Bransford, 1994; distanced instruction: Copple et al., 1984; principle-based learning: Brown & Campione, 1994; project-based learning: Blumenfeld et al., 1991; thematic-based learning: Gamberg, Kwak, Hutchings, & Altheim, 1988; Katz & Chard, 1989). The tasks can account for what the student and the class are ready to learn and what would be too discrepant a challenge (Vygotsky, 1978), and can involve students in explicit consideration of what they are learning and why they are learning it (Countryman, 1992; Scardamalia, Bereiter, & Lamon, 1994). Such methods typically emphasize students' abilities to access and process the tasks they are assigned; however, they may also overlook the quality of the learning engaged if clear goal structures are not established (see Anderson, Reder, & Simon, 1996). It is possible for interactive classes to constrain learning because they are not matched to students' strengths and needs (see Cobb, 1995). Teachers sometimes use an interactive task more for personal reasons (i.e., they like doing a simulation of a presidential election, or want to use the simulation they have developed on cell mitosis) rather than because it meets appropriate learning goals for students. Furthermore, teachers may overlook the needs of students to process or reflect on such learning, leaving students unaware that they have been working on understanding particular concepts or skills. Thus, even though the interactive format may technically involve the students as "partners" in learning, the partnership needs to be facilitated by a teacher. Adjustment and sequencing of instruction is necessary in order to maximize learning for each group of students.

Comment

On paper, it appears that a singular difference between the lecture and interactive formats of instruction as reflecting conceptions of learning is the perceived relation between the task to be learned and the student. Students exposed to the lecture format may not have the background of skills and discourse-knowledge necessary to engage the lecture and/or the tasks they are assigned, and may therefore not be in a position to learn them in a lecture format. On the other hand, students involved in interactive classrooms are assumed to differ in their preparation for the discussion and so on, and this difference of perspective is thought to contribute to the development of each student's understanding and eventual consolidation of the information to be learned.

In practice, however, most classes do not feature exclusively either a lecture or an interactive format, and one lecture or interactive class is not exactly the same as any other (Good, Grouws, Mason, Slavings, & Cramer, 1990). Some combination of these formats is often employed by teachers in order to pose particular challenges or respond to the specific needs of students.

Similarly, while "the lecture" or "the interactive class" appears to reflect particular assumptions about student learning, it is not a given that these assumptions will be articulated and used to inform practice and research. It is possible for predominantly lecture classes and predominantly interactive classes to meet the strengths and needs of the students being taught.

Mere knowledge that one or the other format is used in a class is no indication of the quality of the connections the student is able to make to the material being learned or the basis this provides for problem posing and problem solving. Ultimately, formats of instruction are probably most accurately thought about as descriptions of potential practice. Whether they will meet the strengths and needs of students in a given class depends on how they are used.

Formats of Instruction and Students' Strengths and Needs

Although both lecture and interactive formats can be used to meet students' strengths and needs, they reflect important differences in the kinds of problems or tasks (complex thinking) they pose for students. On the one hand, the lecture format requires that students actively pose challenges and questions for themselves about the material being covered (by posing "self-questions" or questions they ask themselves; taking notes that paraphrase the lecture; and stretching themselves and their thinking as they listen). On the other hand, the interactive format provides a context in which the student works on developing a knowledge of and an ability to pose questions specific to the subject matter. Ideally, interactive formats provide students with opportunities to develop skills and discourse-knowledge as well as a small enough group of students (i.e., 2 to 4 students) with whom to talk and work through the information to be learned.

Differences among students necessitate differences in the formats that would be considered optimal for them at the beginning of a term (cf. Heath, 1986; Hunt, 1961; Michaels, 1981). There can be vast differences between classrooms of students in terms of prior knowledge, metacognitive awareness, and self-concept, including a sense of possibility, as can readily be seen when juxtaposing students from a housing project being schooled in the inner city and students helping to develop the curriculum they are learning in a progressive private school.

It may be most appropriate to think about effective instruction as embodied in the ability to teach using the plans specified in both the lecture and the interactive formats, depending on the strengths and needs of the students. Such strengths and needs might include the ability to function within a group, to listen, to use information, to set tasks for themselves, and to ask questions. For some students, they might include the ability to sit down, focus on a task, and use words to describe the problem on which they are working.

Thus, instruction, in the sense that it is used here, refers to teaching that enables students to engage new questions, revise current understanding, learn appropriate skills, and recognize that they have the tools necessary for further learning. It involves thinking about the lesson from the perspective of the student and gauging what students do and do not understand (Leinhardt, 1993). It also acknowledges that while students may prefer a particular instructional format and, in fact, perform "best" in that context (Dunn, Giannitti, Murray, Rossi, Geisert, & Quinn, 1990), different instructional formats afford different challenges for students—each of which needs to be considered seriously.

The way in which students have previously been taught may be predictive of what at least initially is considered to be optimal instruction for them regardless of their grade level. This is not to suggest that any group of students should experience either lecturing or interactive teaching continuously: the different formats represent complementary sets of challenges. No group has exhausted its possibilities in terms of the skills or discourse-knowledge it could develop—nor, by definition, will it.

The suggestion that some students are not ready to undertake problem solving as an educational goal, or that such an expectation is a violation of culture (Delpit, 1988), calls attention to the fact that, in some classrooms, students will have no idea what you are talking about if you ask them what they would like to know about the Jurassic Period. Furthermore, there may be a cultural predisposition to experience the interactive format as lacking in seriousness or importance (D'Amato, 1996). Students with this kind of reaction, at first at least, will never follow through on an assignment to confirm that a fact they have proposed is a fact, either because the assignment is not well matched to their questions, or because they are not themselves in a position to assume responsibility for this kind of learning.

This does not mean that these students should never be challenged to set and pose problems for themselves such as those that would be required of them in a more interactive format. It does suggest, however, that a teacher might feel that he or she could best meet the needs of the students in such settings by beginning to teach the class using a plan similar to that specified in the lecture format—especially if this type of teacher-directed instruction is a match for their (and their parents') expectations of school. While this kind of lecture or direct instruction is unlikely to lead students to pose challenges and questions for themselves initially, the format provides them with necessary strategies for task completion, and does not ask them to assume responsibility for which they are not ready (Roehler, Duffy, & Meloth, 1986). In fact, it can provide the students with the self-confidence and necessary strategies to begin posing and finding solutions to questions they have about the materials being taught (Gaskins, Ehri, Cress, O'Hara, & Donnelly, 1997). This approach has a high level of success, especially when the teacher follows through to teach the students explicitly the cognitive strategies in the context of their work on subject matter (Pressley et al., 1990).

Instruction, then, can gradually be adjusted to involve students in a more interactive format. Instructional conversations (Osterman, Christensen, & Coffey, 1985; Williams, 1986), reciprocal teaching or principle-based instruction (Brown & Campione, 1994; Palincsar & Brown, 1984), jigsaws (Aronson, Blaney, Stephen, Sikes, & Snapp, 1978), or even simple "buzz" groups and brainstorms (cf. Cohen, 1988) are all examples of interactive formats that provide a scaffold for students to begin to assume more responsibility for their learning. Through such formats, students develop the necessary capacities for more independent learning such as that posed by interactive formats or lectures.

It is a rule of thumb that within three weeks of gradually adjusted instructional expectations, a shift in instructional practice can be realized (can work well)—even for a large group of students.[8] For change in student learning to occur, however, the process of student learning needs to be understood as a kind of "construction zone" (Newman, Griffin, & Cole, 1989), in which student's (or the group of students') capacities, skills, and self-understanding are in the process of change, and for which students need to develop the necessary strategies with which to work on the tasks they are assigned. This involves teachers in ongoing revisions of their understanding of students' strengths and needs, and involves consideration of how students are thinking about themselves as learners (Harter, 1983; Wittrock, 1986). Furthermore, it necessitates an awareness that the time involved in changed understanding or abilities may well extend beyond the parameters of any one marking period.

Development and the Selection of Instructional Formats

Student Learning: A Synthesis

Developmental theories describe the process of learning as continuous and characterized by sequences or identifiable patterns of action that reflect an increasing ability to work with complexity (cf. across and between domains: Feldman, 1980; in terms of conceptual structures: Case, 1985; intelligence: Piaget, 1950; moral development: Damon, 1988; representation: Karmiloff-Smith, 1992; self-concept [the self-system]: Harter, 1983; skill development: Fischer, 1980; social knowledge: Turiel, 1993; and strategy development: Siegler, 1997). The process of learning is also described as being both dynamic and spirallike (cf. Bruner, 1977; Karmiloff-Smith, 1992; Nelson, 1997; Newman, Griffin, & Cole, 1989; Resnick & Ford, 1981; Sigel & Kelley, 1988; Sternberg, 1985; Voss & Schauble, 1992; Vygotsky, 1978; Werner, 1978). The student receives information, begins to internalize (or processes) it, and uses this understanding to revise his or her present understanding and to seek out new information. Each concept and skill acquired contributes to what might be considered the building blocks of an even richer or more synthetic understanding. This progression or sequence characterizes student learning across both broad categories of and more discrete or microlevel aspects of tasks, ranging from learning to hide a comic book behind the text being used in the class to figuring out how to say what a math problem is asking.

It is important to note, however, that students who have been assigned a particular task can not necessarily be assumed to be working on learning the kinds of things that the teacher (or researcher) intends (Bullinger & Chatillon, 1983; Gelman, 1994; Lave & Wenger, 1991). Furthermore, there seems to be no guarantee that students will always function at the highest level of complexity of which they are capable (Azmitia, 1996; Fischer, 1980), although it does appear that students are likely to engage complex activity in their work with identified objects of interest

[8] Consistent use of the Jigsaw method in teachers' classes over a three-week period was typically found to be enough time to enable students to accommodate to the changed role requirements introduction of this method necessitated (Aronson et al., 1978). In my own work with student teachers, I also have found that 3 weeks is long enough to enable some real change to occur (as long as it is accurately gauged and facilitated). It is also long enough for student teachers to appreciate that the change cannot occur overnight or without support from them.

(identified based on their stored knowledge and stored value for these classes of objects; see Krapp & Fink, 1992; Prenzel, 1992; Renninger 1990; Schiefele, 1990). Interest has been found to influence the way in which students engage and perform on tasks; the demands they understand the tasks to include; the knowledge that a student is in a position to carry to subsequent activity; and the way in which a student works with others especially under conditions that require persistence (see Renninger, 1992, for an overview). Of particular importance is the repeated finding that while students can be identified as having and sharing interests, among students, interest is most likely to vary from one student to the next—as such, each student's interest appears to inform the kind of information to which he or she attends and is largely specific to the individual. This finding provides support for the need to not only recognize but to work with individual variation in learning and its impact on students' abilities to access the tasks they are assigned. As Good, Slavings, Harel, and Emerson (1987) point out, students within the same classroom typically do not all experience instruction in the same way, nor are materials appropriately adjusted to accommodate their learning needs.

Indeed, it appears that there is no one particular sequence of subgoals, strategies, and so on, through which each student will pass in learning to perform a task (Nelson, 1997; Perry, Church, & Goldin-Meadow, 1988; Resnick, 1988; Siegler, 1995; Siegler & Jenkins, 1989). In the process of coming to understand something, students may at first seem to understand it but then appear *not* to understand it before finally having clarity about it (Baird & Northfield, 1992; see also Bidell & Fischer, 1992; Karmiloff-Smith, 1992; Kuhn, Amsel, & O'Loughlin, 1988; Siegler, 1997). Thus, while a range of students' likely responses/actions in working with concepts to be learned and the order of their occurrence can be identified, and students can be expected to move or cycle through these in a similar order (Case, 1996; Fischer & Pipp, 1984), it cannot be expected that students will all go about working with the tasks through which they "acquire" these concepts in exactly the same way. The teacher needs to be able to attend to the connections and questions the students have about the tasks and concepts to be learned.

The processes involved in working with a task or problem—where a problem is some challenge perceived by the student in a task—specifically require the student to first identify what the problem involves. Following this, students need to be able to recognize component parts or features of the problem and invoke and/or learn the requisite skills for its solution, sequence the components of the problem in order to facilitate their work on it, allocate time to the problem and make decisions about the quality of effort necessary for its completion, monitor progress toward obtaining a solution, and work with feedback in order to revisit it, if necessary (see also Mayer, 1984; Perkins, 1992; Polya, 1945; Sternberg, 1985).

The problem solving in which students engage also involves them in developing an understanding of themselves as learners, members of a class, and contributors to the body of known information about the particular topic being covered. As students approach later elementary and middle school, their self-concept affects the attention they give and the choices they make about problems they take on, as well as whether they consider a change in capacity to be likely (Damon & Hart, 1988; Harter, 1983; Helmke, 1994; Krapp, 1997; Markus & Wurf, 1987). The messages students receive from others and the organization of the learning environment contribute to how they come to understand themselves as problem solvers, persons in the world with interesting ideas, collaborators, people entitled to ask questions, and so on (Deci & Ryan, 1985; Fend, 1994; Markus & Nurius, 1986).

As Siegler's (1997) data suggest, student innovation can follow both success and failure. If a student does not also understand this, he or she may impose constraints on what can be learned. Teachers can work to minimize or eliminate such constraints. To do so, however, they need to assume responsibility for the well-being of the student in addition to defining themselves as teachers of a subject area. Deci, Connell, and Ryan (1989) report that as compared to teachers who control student behavior, teachers who support students' abilities and feelings of possibility—their self-determination—positively influence their students' feelings of competence, self-esteem, and intrinsic motivation. Not only is it important that a teacher acknowledge students' feelings and attitudes, but such acknowledgment also provides support for autonomy (Williams & Deci, 1996), encouraging students to initiate activity rather than asking them to conform or behave. In turn, such initiation leads to better integration and internalization of the material to be learned (e.g., Deci, Eghrari, Patrick, & Leone, 1994).

To return to the case formats, then, the decision to use either a lecture method or a more interactive class format for instruction involves not only whether (given a particular format) the student is ready to pose challenges for him- or herself, but also the kind of teacher-student relationship afforded by the particular format (see discussions about the importance of teacher-student relationships in Harter, 1983; Kontos, 1992; Minuchin & Shapiro, 1983; Pianta &

Steinberg, 1992). A traditional lecture will not foster students' feelings of self-determination and autonomy unless the students possess enough knowledge to "stay with it" and have a clear sense that questions can always be posed at its conclusion. Similarly, an interactive class will not necessarily foster students' feelings of self-determination or autonomy unless they understand the goal of the lesson and their role in it (Slavin, 1983).

Students who are having difficulty learning are often stuck at the point of entry, unable to say what the problem or task is (Flavell, 1977), or wondering whether they are in a position to take it on (Fend, 1994). Even when they complete practice problems, write an essay or a lab report, and so on, students are often unclear about what they are learning, why it is important, and that they can, in fact, undertake the challenge it represents (Tobias, 1990). Without such information they can only skim the surface of what could be learned.

At the very least, it appears that such students need instruction that provides them with guidance as they engage the problem solving that they are assigned by helping them to know how to generate questions and summarize the information they are learning (Alvermann, 1981; Hidi & Anderson, 1986; Paris, Cross, & Lipson, 1984; Raphael & Pearson, 1985), and by providing them with opportunities to revisit and consolidate newly learned information by using previously learned information as a basis for introducing new material in a lecture, or by posing it as a basis from which students may do problem solving, undertake a discussion, and so on, in a more interactive class (Kroll & Black, 1989).

Part of being an effective problem solver includes constructing and using strategies that work and getting rid of those that do not (Schoenfeld, 1987). This process involves students in developing an awareness about the way in which they learn and the resources or strategies necessary to establish connections between information to be learned and that which the students already know. This process has been variously labeled *reflective thinking* (Dewey, 1933) or *metacognition* (cf. Flavell, 1977; see also Weinert & Kluwe, 1987). The process of *becoming* an effective problem solver is ongoing. It can be facilitated by instruction that involves students in reflection such as questioning and summarizing, and strategy instruction in which these skills have been embedded into the subject matter to be learned (see Pressley et al., 1990, for elementary level applications; Wood, Woloshyn, & Willoughby, 1995, for secondary level applications). Not surprisingly, students who are considered to be successful are likely to have better understanding of themselves as problem solvers and the problems to be learned. Ellis (in press) points out, however, that those who evidence little awareness about strategies can select appropriate strategies and those who are able to talk about strategies may not. She suggests that available strategies consist not only of those that have been "taught" but also those learned working and watching others solve similar problems. As such, students' choices and awareness of particular strategies reflect information about what their school and/or their individual culture decrees is "appropriate, adaptive, and wise." (p. 5)

In the case of the Jurassic Period lecture format, for example, students are led to reflect on their learning when they review the information covered in the lecture and when they work on writing their chapter book about dinosaurs. In the interactive format, students' reflections are used to frame the sequence of questions in which they engage, their summation of information on the "big paper," their writing of the chapter book on dinosaurs, the process of certifying that a fact is a fact, and so on.

What students attend to and the challenges they represent to themselves in these tasks are linked to the accessibility of the task, the skills and strategies available to engage or process the task, and the likelihood that the task completed will be the task the teacher intended. Thus, the selection of a format for instruction presumably should be informed by whether students can access tasks, the way in which they work with them, and the nature of their work on similar tasks in the past.

Task Access and Student Process as Influences on Performance

As Gardner (1985) has pointed out, there are two ways in which we can describe the developing knowledge base about how students learn. The first specifies the importance of the process involved in how students connect to or access tasks, while the second focuses on what it takes for that engagement to work.

Many kinds of student characteristics have been found to affect the accessibility of tasks (see Karmiloff-Smith, 1992; Prawat, 1989). Among them are the match of the task to the student's ability for that task (cf. Glaser, 1987; Rohrkemper & Bershon, 1984; Stein, Leinhardt, & Bickel, 1989), belief (Pintrich & DeGroot, 1990), cultural independence or interdependence (Greenfield, 1994), gender (Golombok & Fivush, 1994; Hoffmann & Haussler, 1995), individual interest (cf. Krapp & Fink, 1992; Renninger, 1992), learning goals (Diener & Dweck, 1978, 1980), learning related self-concept or self-esteem (Helmke, 1994), misconceptions (Chinn & Brewer, 1993; Perkins & Simmons, 1988), niche (Gauvain, 1995), prior knowledge (cf. Brown, Palincsar, & Purcell, 1986; Palincsar & Brown, 1984), situational interest (Hidi & Baird, 1988; Wade, 1992), social class (Anyon, 1980), task orientation (Nicholls, 1984; Nolan, 1988), temperament (cf. Carey, 1995), understanding of the task assigned (Bullinger & Chatillon, 1983; Gelman, 1994; Lave & Wenger, 1991), and understanding of societal or institutional norms (Perret-Clermont, Perret, & Bell, 1991). The way students access tasks influence how they will be able to process them. Instructional practice can be adjusted to increase the likelihood of task accessibility (cf. adjustment of task interest and task difficulty: Renninger, 1992; instructional methods: Stein et al., 1989; reciprocal teaching: Brown, Palincsar, & Purcell 1986).

The process of working on tasks is further influenced by students' implicit method (Berg, 1994), metacognitive awareness (cf. Schoenfeld, 1985; Palincsar & Brown, 1984), planning ability (cf. Ericsson & Simon, 1980; Gauvain & Rogoff, 1989; Scholnick & Freedman, 1987), and use of strategies (cf. Gaskins, 1994; Pressley, El-Dinary, Marks, Brown, & Stein, 1992; Siegler & Jenkins, 1989). For purposes of application, consideration of students' abilities to process or work through a task can suggest methods for adjusting instructional practice to increase the likelihood of task completion (cf. reciprocal teaching, modeling, and apprenticeship: see Collins, Brown, & Newman, 1989, for an overview; strategy instruction: Gaskins, 1994; Pressley et al., 1992). The ability (skills, strategies, self-confidence, etc.) to work on (or process) a task, places a student in the position of being able to complete the task assigned. It also leads to the increased accessibility of other tasks. If a student is not able to access the task as it is posed, he or she has little chance of learning it. The very range of task access and process variables that have been examined and their direct relation to student performance and subsequent task access provides compelling support for the need to consider seriously the role of individual variation in what students learn. It also suggests that task access is of considerable importance for thinking about the instruction that is employed.

Tasks that afford multiple opportunities for access and reengaging topics (Brown & Campione, 1994; Goldman et al., 1994) provide a wider range of opportunities for student access. Open-ended tasks can be structured in order to provide opportunities for students to learn and strengthen skills, develop subject matter knowledge, and enhance their knowledge about themselves as learners (cf. Brown & Campione, 1994). They also require students to develop their representational competencies, since the organization of such tasks require the student to explore a variety of problem solutions (cf. Copple et al., 1984). They can be structured to enable all students to have a role or function in the task and, as such, permit students to progress through and engage challenges at levels of difficulty matched to their readiness.

In those instances where students are particularly disaffected and/or the tasks assigned to students are more closed and do not involve multiple points of access, information about patterns that emerge from study of individual variation in task access is critical for mapping student functioning. Furthermore, identification of those elements of tasks and/or particular task difficulties or strategies that vary between students would provide critical insights about what is malleable and what might therefore be a good target for intervention or task adjustment.

Study of these variables within student levels and with respect to individualized levels of task difficulty across different subject areas, in particular, should provide useful data about the generalizability of their effects and ways in which they may moderate student learning. This does *not,* however, mean that all tasks or all instruction needs to be individualized for each student (although this is reasonable for purposes of one-on-one work); rather, from such data, the teacher gains information about patterns of variation in development useful for understanding the range of student variation in the given classroom and sequencing strategy instruction. Based on such information, instruction can be and optimally would be individualized for classes of students.

Other subtle but no less important influences on student learning include: (a) the problem finding and problem posing that is modeled for students (Collins, Brown, & Newman, 1989), (b) on what the students are ready to work, and (c) the ability of the teacher to provide supports, or scaffolding, for students that enables them to reconstruct what had been understood in relation to new information. (See Hunt & Minstrell, 1994, for classroom examples and further discussion.)

Comment

Many of the studies on which this synthesis draws are based on children in experimental situations rather than classrooms. These children varied in age, capacities, and the context in which they were studied. Moreover, the children were typically studied in groups, even though they are described in terms of their individual functioning. The findings reported have been corroborated either by studies conducted in different contexts or by the same researchers across several samples of students, so that it seems reasonable to consider them seriously in an effort to describe how students learn.

By now it also should be quite clear that it is no simple issue to consider the implications of how students learn for instructional practice. Research efforts corroborate some of the difficulties that teachers experience in classrooms, namely that students differ much more than we originally might have thought, and that it is not easy to focus students on what we want them to "get" out of the tasks we assign them. Research efforts also suggest that, rather than stopping at observation and more standardized measures, we need to talk with students about what they are thinking as they work on problems, concern ourselves with students as developing selves, and think about the instructional format as a kind of tool and its implementation as a process of responding to students' strengths and needs.

The present synthesis, however, focuses primarily on how students go about "getting" the information they are to learn. It does not tell us much about what a student needs to get when they are learning, nor what this would mean for the way that decisions might be made about instruction when learning is understood to continue beyond the end of the marking period. There are two reasons for this. The first has to do with the importance and relevance of the content of subject matter to the discussion of what students learn. The materials and skills that are covered in a class fall into the category of curriculum, which, as noted earlier, is the topic of other chapters in this *Handbook*. The second reason is linked to the status of research in the field. What students get from their learning is yoked to what are perceived to be prior questions about the processes involved in learning. Thus, research on student learning primarily addresses how students get information. There is little developmental work that addresses what needs to be attained.

In their review of the literature on students' abilities to transfer their knowledge and skills from one situation to another situation, Mayer and Wittrock (1996) suggest that learning (premised on a problem-oriented view of learning) is successful if, upon its completion, the student is in a position to generate or revisit a problem and can use his or her developing base of skills to monitor this effort. It would appear to follow, then, that to the extent that students are not using the specific skills and knowledge that are intended, the process of instruction needs to be adjusted. In practice, as Pressley et al. (1990) note, students appear to be most likely to learn and be able to apply strategies appropriately when strategy instruction is embedded in the content being taught (cf. Palincsar & Brown, 1984; Roehler et al., 1986).

We really do not know the implications of direct instruction for how students understand themselves as learners and what they understand the process of learning or problem solving to be, especially in the long run. Furthermore, we do not know whether there is a discrete set of patterns or strategies that we might expect students to naturally employ on tasks, and whether these are equally effective at a particular age or point in the process of learning something, even if they do not map exactly onto the types of strategies an expert might use in the situation. Rather than providing students with effective strategies, should we, for example, be modeling two or three alternative approaches to any given task? Should the way we work with students around use of strategies vary as a function of variables that have been identified as influencing their access to tasks, that is, age, gender, interest, the culture of schooling, or their inter- or intradependent cultural orientation? What kinds of adjustments in instruction might be suggested with respect to the way in which students go about working on tasks (i.e., their implicit method, planning, etc.)? Can we expect to see transfer if students have identified a problem on which they are working? What kind of range are we talking about when we say a task is appropriately matched to a student's level of problem-solving difficulty—and what does this suggest for classes of students where the level of problem solving often varies as much as two grade levels?

Until more is known about how students actually learn information, it is difficult to talk specifically about what needs to be learned and whether learning has taken place. As Mayer and Wittrock (1996) observe, the findings from study of transfer of learning have been disappointing. In many ways, it appears that information from further study of the process of learning will provide the basis of more successful efforts—but not until this research is conducted.

What we do know about how students learn and the important kinds of questions to ask, however, has implications for practice. It suggests, for example, a shift in the emphasis of classes away from group-based practice ("second graders do") to instruction that addresses the strengths and needs of students in the class. Furthermore, it suggests that instructional formats can be adjusted to meet students' abilities to focus on the task assigned, that it is not the task format itself which necessarily leads to student learning, and that students' feelings about themselves as learners must be an important aspect of instructional planning.

In terms of the selection of instructional formats, we know that there is probably no one instructional format that will meet each student's strengths and needs in a class at all times. In fact, it is likely that one student's strengths will be the needs of the next student, necessitating the use of different combinations of tasks—tasks that will allow one student to further develop strengths while another works on needs, or open-ended tasks that allow students to work on their own particular strengths and needs.

As is suggested by the "best practices" list (cf. Bredekamp, 1993), it further appears that we can talk about practices that optimize the chances of students attending to the tasks we assign or present to them—although it is also important that these practices be employed in a way that is attentive to the individual strengths and needs of the students in the particular class in which they are being used.

Methods such as the lecture and the interactive formats described here appear at least to afford the possibility of students (a) being allowed to define the problems or challenges on which they are working, (b) employing or beginning to practice employing strategies that are modeled/demonstrated for them, (c) revisiting the information being covered in various formats and contexts so that they will have it available as they need it in order to continue working on a task, and (d) understanding that they have learned. From this perspective, like the process of a student working on a task, the process of instruction requires focused attention and reflection. In particular, the selection of instructional format calls for attention to and reflection on the strengths and needs of the particular group of students being taught and how they learn, and it requires information about the formats that might be employed in the classroom and the means to adjust them.[9]

Instruction as a Process

Two general principles emerge from the preceding discussion about development and the selection of formats for instruction:

1. There is often variation in the way students learn what, to an observer, appears to be essentially the same task.
2. There is no one right way to work effectively with students; rather, an accumulating body of research contributes to our understanding of how students learn. Together with information about the strengths and needs of the students to be taught, such research can be used to inform decision making about instruction.

While these principles have been tenets of many educators and psychologists whose writing has focused on how students learn (cf. Dewey, 1938; Montessori, 1917/1965; Pestalozzi, 1855; Polya, 1945), they directly contradict the way most educators and researchers have themselves been taught. They focus on the skills, discourse-knowledge, and self-understanding each student has and still needs to develop rather than on discrete knowledge learned at specific time points according to a previously identified criterion (cf. Mager, 1962).

The work of Skinner (cf. 1968) as spokesperson for Behaviorism, for example, appears to have contributed to a notion shared by many educators that actions and reactions have only linear relations and particular answers,[10] thus suggesting that there is a discrete number of effective ways to work with students and that there is one effective way to learn a task. In fact, Skinner's (1968) research on learning, in particular, his emphasis on baselines of behavior and his discussions of reinforcement and contingency (often reinterpreted) continue to inform educational practice, presumably due to their simplicity, scientific presentation, and the fact that in particular situations they are useful in the classroom. The problem is that his studies do not provide sufficient information with which to begin to consider and respond to the complexity of the processes involved in students' emerging understanding of concepts, skills, and self-knowledge. Information about this complexity is necessary for developing instruction tailored to students' changing strengths and needs.

It may well have been Flavell's (1977) volume on Piaget's research, *Cognitive Development,* and Cole, John-Steiner, Scribner, and Souberman's translation of Vygotsky's (1978) *Mind in Society,* which provided the groundwork necessary to enable psychologists and educators generally to begin

[9] For the purposes of this discussion, content knowledge is an assumed basis of instructional decisions in the classroom. In practice, it is more reasonable to talk about the teacher's developing content knowledge as informing and sometimes constraining decision making about instruction.

[10] Interestingly, most educators do not read Skinner's work in the original, but instead are introduced to his ideas through someone else's syntheses. These are typically focused on ideas presented in the 1968 volume, *The Technology of Teaching,* and do not incorporate further developments of his or other behavioral researchers' studies.

reconsidering how learning might be conceptualized differently and more fully. Certainly, Bruner (1966) and his colleagues' development of the MACOS materials, Cronbach and Snow's (1977) considerations of the relation between aptitude and instructional method, Sarason's (1982) analysis of the problems that arose in the effort to institute New Math, Neisser's (1976) ecological approach to cognition, Bronfenbrenner's (1979) ecological psychology, Jackson's (1968) discussion of the hidden curriculum, Ashton-Warner's (1963) description of literacy development, and Holt's (1964) description of why children fail indicate that across several disciplines, it had become increasingly clear to many that school learning was not at all a discrete process.

The Tetrahedral Model

Jenkins' (1979) scholar's tetrahedron and its elaboration by Brown (1982) and Bransford (1979) provides a much-needed tool for those interested in going beyond the laboratory to address learning in more natural contexts (cf. Brown et al., 1983). The tetrahedral model identifies four components of learning: (a) the characteristics of the learner (skills, knowledge); (b) learning activities (attention, rehearsal); (c) criterial tasks (recognition, recall); and (d) the nature of the materials (modality, physical structure). In specifying the interdependence of these components, the model offers a check on more discrete conceptualizations of learning that earlier stimulus-response models somewhat inadvertently sanctioned.

The tetrahedral model calls attention to points also raised by Cronbach and Snow's (1977) aptitude-treatment-interaction (ATI) and Hunt and Sullivan's (1973) behavior-person-environment (BPE) models. The tetrahedral model, however, has broader applications than either the ATI or BPE model, since it is not limited to matching instruction to student aptitudes or behaviors. Furthermore, rather than focusing on students grouped by type, the tetrahedral model accords a dimension to individually varying student characteristics.

Reminiscent of points raised by James (1890), Baldwin (1906, 1911), and Dewey (1933, 1938) in their discussions of learning, the tetrahedral model also differs from these earlier theories because it posits specific dimensions of learning for which researchers need simultaneously to be accountable. It provides a language for conceptualizing the process of learning as both dynamic and reciprocal, and points to interactions among the components or dimensions that need to be acknowledged. Furthermore, it permits consideration of a range of potential factors and theoretical perspectives on which an educator can draw in making decisions. In fact, the model has provided the theoretical foundation for several current school-based projects designed to investigate the contributions of cognitive science to classroom practice (cf. Bereiter & Scardamalia, 1992; Brown & Campione, 1994; Cognition and Technology Group at Vanderbilt, 1991).

The model does not, however, give us more than a label for the interactions that it so clearly specifies, that is, interactions between the student and the task and among the student, the task, and the criteria for learning, and so on. The model gives us a general sense that adjustment of (or attention to) one component results in other components being affected, but beyond this there was no specification for action. In fact, Jenkins (1979) spoke about researcher selection of vertices for their focus as reflecting "a favorite vertex." . . . "a favorite edge for research" (p. 431).

In order to inform practice, it is critical that one of the vertices under consideration represent the learner (or the community doing the learning). The learner—not the educator, and not the text—consolidates and develops his or her skills and discourse-knowledge (cf. Gelman, 1994; Piaget, 1952). Understanding how text, for example, can be enhanced to increase the likelihood that students will attend to it is only effective if experimental manipulations take into account information about the learner *as learner:* prior knowledge, abilities, individual interests, and so on, in the context of a particular environment (Bronfenbrenner, 1979). Without this information, such research makes too many assumptions about individual students for these data to contribute significantly to classroom practice in useful ways over time (even though it does have a demonstrated effect on learning in the moment, cf. Wade, 1992).

Psychological Distance as a Tool for Instructional Planning

The construct of psychological distance provides an extension and an elaboration of the tetrahedral model for practice. Psychological distance refers to both the distance between what the learner understands and what he or she still needs to understand (intrapsychic understanding, similar to Vygotsky's, 1978, notion of the zone of proximal development), *and* the ways through which others, tasks, and/or the environment facilitate learning by adjusting questions and engagements for the learner (interpsychic understanding) (Sigel, 1970; see discussion, Cocking & Renninger, 1993). These two foci always stand in relation to each other and are central to conceptions of learning and change across a wide range of theoretical models: discrepancy (cf. DeLoache, 1993; Werner, 1978), equilibration (cf. Piaget, 1950; Watson & Fischer, 1993), mediation (cf.

Cobb, 1995; Rogoff, 1990), and social learning (cf. Mischel & Rodriguez, 1993; Shantz, 1993).

In terms of psychological distance, the individual learner (or group of learners) is described as cocreating his or her (their) learning in conjunction with the others (the teacher, other students, etc.) and objects (tasks, texts, etc.) that comprise the environment. It is individuals, in this instance, teachers, who actively and naturally perceive and construct an understanding of their environment (students, text, etc.). The distance or discrepancy lies between what the student understands and what he or she still needs to understand about each of the learning components specified in the tetrahedral model: characteristics of student, task, teacher, and criterion.

Given a question about how to facilitate student understanding of what a paleontologist does, for example, the teacher has in the construct a tool that requires reflection upon the question (issues linked to history, paleontology, the students' present understanding and possible misconceptions) and identification of a plan of action in terms of student strengths and needs. The specifics of such instruction are not fully articulated for the teacher, however—nor can they be if teachers are learning about and responding to the individual strengths and needs of their students in the process of teaching. Rather, the endpoints of psychological distance are specified and their juxtaposition enables the teacher to consider alternative responses. The educator imposes his or her "value" on the construct and, in turn, scaffolds him- or herself into the role of scientist or problem solver. Thus, psychological distance can be said to describe the action or change to be undertaken rather than the locus or potential sources of activity. Change is facilitated through the adjustment of instruction.

Like the tetrahedral model, the construct of psychological distance reflects the complexity of the learning process and the potential of multiple lenses for evaluating learning. It provides a kind of classification scheme that facilitates attention to the patterns that arise in classroom activity, rather than being mired at an individual level (cf. Rogoff, 1997); yet it can be effectively applied to specify change at the level of individual learning as well. Distancing, or the process of using information about psychological distance to inform action, can take the form of questions posed, tasks presented, modeling, and so forth (see Sigel, 1993, for a taxonomy of verbal distancing actions). Its effectiveness is directly related to the way in which it enables the student, educator, researcher, and so on, to rerepresent information (assumptions about what the student understands, how materials have always been sequenced, and so on). This process of rerepresenting information can be instigated by discrepancy (Sigel & Cocking, 1977), can emerge from engaging information that is novel, surprising, complex, uncertain, or curious (Berlyne, 1960). It can also be facilitated through modeling (cf. Rogoff, 1990) and/or mediation such as that provided by small group work (Cobb, 1995) or metacognition (cf. Brown, 1978). During the process of distancing, the teacher concurrently learns about the students and the ways in which materials might be adjusted (questions posed, etc.) to facilitate further student learning either at the individual level or within a group. While the others and the objects that comprise the student's environment affect learning by virtue of their very existence (which explains why some learning goes on in classrooms even though there may not be much attention to students' strengths or needs), they can also serve in more explicit ways to organize or reorganize the relationship of the student to the environment.

Consideration of alternate activity, as afforded by the juxtaposition in the construct of both the distance between what the student (or group of students) knows and still needs to know *and* what might be undertaken to work with him or her on learning it, provides for the likelihood of informed, reflective decision making about instruction. It also increases the likelihood that the tasks in which students engage will be matched to their cognitive and social strengths and, as such, be optimally challenging.

Adjustment of instruction to meet the strengths and needs of students can only occur, however, to the extent that teacher practice is not simply what Berg (1994) has labeled an implicit method. The tool of psychological distance, applied to a problem that the teacher identifies, focuses attention on the teacher's students and ideas about possible actions on their behalf. Just as an open-ended task provides multiple points of access for the student, so psychological distance provides the teacher with a forum for connecting to his or her students' strengths and needs in a given classroom. Applied to the stereotype of the inner-city classroom in which, among other things, assignments are two and three grade levels above that for which the students are ready, psychological distance could focus attention on the students' readiness for: the nature of the tasks (difficulty, interest-value, and so on), the teacher's criteria, and the teacher's actions. Application of the construct involves singling out one component of the learning process at a time and considering it in terms of a particular group of students' (or student's) strengths and needs.

Given a 40-person class of students who are not motivated to learn French, consideration needs to be given to: what the students' sense of themselves as students is, their goals and what they understand about the French they are being taught, what the teacher expects to be mastered and what the students are ready to master, the format of instruction, and so on. If learning is the goal, the dimensions of what currently passes as instructional practice in this classroom clearly need to be reviewed and revised.

In psychological distance, both educators and researchers have a tool for reflecting on their activity—a tool that is dependent on their input. The constructs, including the language, that teachers and researchers have to describe teaching constitutes the set of possibilities, or repertoire, with which they have to work.

In order for us to think further about the possible applications of developmental psychology to practice, it is necessary to consider what knowledge is available to teachers to use as input were they to work with psychological distance as a tool for instructional planning. At a meta-level, such information also provides the researcher (workshop leader, teacher educator, etc.) with information about the "language" teachers may have available.

INSTRUCTION: AN OVERVIEW OF RESEARCH AND REPORTS

In order to consider what we know about the language of instruction and the kind of repertoire the literature provides (or could provide) to the practitioner, an overview of recent work on the topics of large group instruction, questioning, and grouping was undertaken. These topics, or more accurately, these categories of topics, permit reconsideration of what we currently know about how students learn and the links between this information and practice, specifically as these bear on students' access to, processing of, and performance on tasks they are assigned.

A two-part process was involved in selecting literature for each overview. First, using ERIC and PsycINFO with SilverPlatter retrieval software, abstracts of articles addressing the topics (and related headers) were selected and sets of questions or patterns characterizing each of the literatures were identified. These patterns were used to inform the organization of each overview. Finally, articles, reports, and technical documents were obtained, reviewed, and used as resources with particular attention to the inclusion of work that drew on different types of methodologies (case analysis, microanalysis, controlled experiment, etc.). The second part of the literature selection focused on reviews of the topic.

The overviews consist of a synthesis of the issues specific to student learning. Following each synthesis is a summary and a commentary: (a) What does this overview contribute to our thinking about instructional formats depicted in the two Jurassic Period case formats? (b) What does the topic contribute more generally to how we think about student learning and its implications for instruction?, and (c) What might we still want to know about this topic based on developmental theory and research? (In other words, what kind of research might usefully be undertaken?)

Large Group Instruction

Overview of Research and Reports

Despite a sizable literature on discussion, large group instruction[11] is discussed as though it were synonymous with lecturing. In particular, it is described as being both teacher-directed and associated with distant, unindividualized teaching. Articles on large group instruction generally detail ways to minimize the problems of teaching and learning in a classroom with many students and a low teacher-student ratio. Few authors speak about the advantage of large group instruction as a method for learning and teaching. Instead, the advantages typically specified

---

[11] Literature was searched under the following headers: Direct Instruction, Large Group Instruction, Lecture Method, Whole Group Discussion, Discussion-Teaching Technique, Group Discussion, Discussion Groups.

Sample: Research and reports on lecturing focus primarily on undergraduate and graduate student populations; they are reviewed here, however, because teacher lectures or explanation constitutes such a large percentage of classroom instruction in elementary and secondary schools (up to 66% of the time in class, according to Bellack, Kliebard, Hyman, & Smith, 1966). Few considerations of lecturing evaluate either the effects of lecturing on atypical populations, race, ethnicity, or gender as possible factors in learning from lectures.

Research and reports on discussion, on the other hand, focus primarily on elementary and high school populations. Studies of discussion have investigated at-risk students, adult students, and learning disabled students; few studies, however, evaluate the roles of race, ethnicity, or gender as possible factors in learning from discussions.

Content Areas of Focus: Research and reports examining large group instruction and lecturing tend to be conducted in introductory education and biology courses, physiology and home economics courses, and medical school settings. Almost no studies of large group instruction and lecturing have been conducted in foreign language classes. In contrast, studies of discussion span the disciplines, with particular emphasis on literature and reading classes, social studies, and science and foreign language classes.

include such factors as (a) lowered costs, (b) efficient use of faculty time and talent, (c) availability of professional resources, and (d) standardization. Disadvantages include (a) impersonal relationships between teacher and students, (b) limited instruction, (c) management difficulties, (d) inequity in rewards, and (e) lower status for the instructor (Chism, Cano, & Pruitt, 1989). In fact, large group instruction is often described as a problem that has to be "fixed," "dealt with," or "solved."

In contrast to the literature on lectures, large group discussion classes are considered to reflect a shift to student-oriented methods of teaching, permitting students to explore ideas and identify their needs as learners (Conti & Fellenz, 1988). According to Miner (1992), teachers who aim to be effective with large classes look for ways to minimize psychological and physical distance between themselves and their students in order to increase personalization. Solutions to the problem of large classes include peer tutoring, group work, and educator training. Pearson (1990) suggests expanding on what traditional expectations for the large group setting might include. He suggests a need for lecturers to explore opportunities for active participation; development of a supportive climate; provision of rewards for positive behavior; and presentations that include auditory, sensory, and visual input.

The authors of research and reports on lecturing and discussion as methods make clear distinctions between them as different methods of large group instruction. Therefore, overviews of the issues raised in studies and reports on each are undertaken separately.

Lecture Method. Lecturing is the most common form of large group instruction. Cashin (1985) summarizes the instructional goals met by lecturing as including opportunities to (a) share the instructor's interest in the material, (b) present unavailable materials, (c) organize materials in a particular way, (d) cover a lot of information, (e) address numerous students at the same time, (f) model how professionals work through discipline-based problems, (g) exercise control, (h) lessen the threat of direct contact with an authority, and (i) develop skills for listening. Furthermore, a variety of lecture types exist: (a) interactive lectures, which engage student thinking throughout the lesson; (b) mastery lectures, which link new knowledge to familiar concepts and ideas; and (c) traditional lectures, which present information with minimal student activity (Kuzbik, 1992). The predominant focus of research and reports on lecturing, however, is the traditional lecture.

Research and reports on the lecture method appear to focus specifically on (a) comparison of lecturing to other methods of teaching, (b) elements of the lecture that influence student performance, and (c) what instructors need to do in order to be more effective in the classroom.

Comparing Lecturing to Other Methods of Instruction. Studies in which the lecture method is compared to other methods of large group instruction evidence mixed findings. Some studies in which the lecture method is contrasted with student performance in a pretest, posttest design indicate that students taught by the lecture method do less well than those taught using reflective methods (cf. Adyemi, 1992; Grieve, 1992). For example, students in precollege and college algebra lecture classes scored significantly lower on post-tests than did students in a self-paced laboratory format class (Robinson, 1990). Similarly, when DaRosa et al. (1991) compared the effects of lectures and independent study on medical school students' test scores and study time, they concluded that independent study should be given emphasis in the curriculum. Heywood and Heywood (1992) report, however, that high school students did no better in a variety of school subjects when taught with lecture (expository teaching) rather than discovery-based methods. Furthermore, they observed that low-ability students benefited more from the expository lesson, whereas high-ability students benefitted more from the discovery lesson.

The variable of ability appears to influence the impact of lectures on performance; however, the direction of its predicted effect varies. Robinson and Niaz (1991), for example, report that interactive instruction in chemistry is more effective than lectures for low-ability students. Odubunmi and Balogun (1991) also report that high-achieving eighth graders performed no differently in science laboratory or lecture classes, but low achievers in laboratory sections performed better than students in lecture sections, and girls in lectures performed better than boys.

Other variables considered to affect student performance in lectures (or discussion) include student preferences for interactive methods (cf. Heywood & Heywood, 1992), and level of instructor effectiveness (cf. Abeasi & Reigeluth, 1985). Moreover, matching student learning style with instructional method has been demonstrated to be effective, and can make the lecture classroom a successful learning environment for students well suited to it (Katz, 1990). According to Burns (1990), the format a teacher uses, the order of items presented, the presentation style, the timing, the pairing of items, the use of data summaries, and the amount of information presented all influence students' understanding as well as their recall.

Elements of the Lecture that Affect Student Performance. Taking in all of the information conveyed in lecture classes requires well-developed listening and note taking skills. These have been found to pose particular challenges for non-native students (ESL, or English as a Second Language students) who are not as adept at processing English language quickly. Fahmy and Bilton (1990), for example, found that ESL students do not always pick up lecturers' cues signalling key words. In addition, ESL students are not familiar with English abbreviations or shorthand, which makes their note taking difficult and prevents them from taking notes on a lot of information in a short period of time. They conclude that foreign students' listening and note taking skills need to be improved. Another study of non-native-speaking graduate and undergraduate students conducted by Olson and Huckin (1990) provides an analysis of college engineering students' immediate recall summaries following a videotaped lecture. Conclusions from this study also suggest that non-native-speaking students should be taught skills for listening to lectures more strategically.

Findings from a few studies suggest changing the lecture format to improve students' comprehension of information presented. One study, for example, found that two-minute pauses spaced at appropriate points in a videotape lecture were effective for enhancing both learning disabled and nonlearning-disabled students' performance on free-recall and objective test measures, although they did not affect longer-term recall (Ruhl, Hughes, & Gajar, 1990). Other studies suggest that questions embedded in lectures foster greater student involvement with the lecture. Fisher and Jablonski (1985) report, for example, that the type of question posed during a college lecture affects the nature of student participation. Their findings suggest that rhetorical questions allow silent involvement, since they call attention to the perspective being addressed and can provide a summary of the information covered. Discussion questions, on the other hand, demand vocal involvement since they call for an analysis or evaluation of the information presented. Transition questions, in contrast, can call for either silent or vocal responses since they indicate movement to a new topic (i.e., How might we evaluate . . . ?) and can be used to shift the focus of the lecture or to open a discussion.

Another set of reports recommends enhancing lectures through the use of methods that encourage more active student involvement. Bonwell and Eison (1991), for example, suggest a modified lecture format supplemented by visual learning, writing in class, problem solving, computer-based instruction, cooperative learning, debates, drama, role playing, simulations, games, and/or peer teaching.

Williams (1986) describes the "feedback lecture method" as a modification of the traditional lecture method. This approach to lecturing involves ongoing feedback to both the student and the teacher. It includes the following steps: (a) The teacher determines the students' level of knowledge on a given subject by asking questions and giving feedback, (b) the teacher presents the sequential order of the lesson, (c) the teacher presents a list of tasks to be learned and clarifies uncertainties, (d) the teacher presents an overview of material to be covered, (e) the teacher teaches, (f) the students are asked to synthesize and evaluate the newly acquired material in light of their own experiences, (g) the students' comprehension is assessed, (h) written feedback is provided to students for reinforcement, and (i) students evaluate the instructional process and materials.

In another version of a feedback lecture, a study guide is handed out before the lecture, postlecture small group discussions are employed, a lecture outline is provided, and teacher notes are made available. Osterman, Christensen, and Coffey (1985) report that findings from the use of this method indicate that it models effective study skills for students and provides them with opportunities to improve their comprehension, storage, recall, and subsequent application of material.

Yet another suggested adjustment to the lecture method involves asking students to self-question—having students articulate questions prior to the lecture. King (1989a), for example, reports that ninth-grade honors students got the most from a lecture when they posed self-questions during the lecture and discussed answers to their questions following it.

Making expectations for lectures explicit and paying attention to note taking are two more ways in which lectures can be adjusted to enable students to learn efficiently, although there is some dissension among researchers about whether and when students should be encouraged to take notes. Topics addressed in this literature include note taking versus listening, providing notes versus generating notes, note taking efficiency, teaching note taking, and the qualities of a lecture that provide for good note taking (see reviews by Dubois, 1986; Isaacs, 1989).

Anderson and Armbruster's (1986) review of the value of note taking during lectures at college specifies the potential benefits to students of the kind of lecturing that permits deep processing while taking notes, *provided that the tests that follow are consistent with the style of the lecture.* They distinguish among verbatim note taking while listening, selectively noting information, and recording some meaningful reorganization of the lecture. The latter involves a deep level of processing. They further specify that the level of processing will depend on the characteristics of the lecture itself: Speed of presentation and the number of concepts presented also affect the difficulty of processing a lecture and taking notes. Anderson and Armbruster cite the usefulness of collecting and reviewing students' notes early in the term following a lecture. This practice provides feedback about how well the lecture is being understood and which students need to be assisted to develop their note taking skills.

Anderson and Armbruster (1986) recommend that students (a) take complete notes as long as this does not interfere with comprehension; (b) note key ideas and supplement this information later using the text and so on, especially if the lecture is delivered rapidly; (c) use paraphrasing or summaries of the lecture as a method of note taking in order to ensure deep processing; (d) find out about tests given previously and use these as a guide for taking and studying notes; and (e) study notes in a manner that makes it possible to use them in another situation.

Walbaum (1989) further suggests that although there are potential encoding benefits of note taking (attention, assimilation of new information, and meaningful encoding; cf. Peper & Mayer, 1978), it is also likely that some students only experience one or more of these benefits and that they only do so some of the time. She notes, for example, that students are probably not experiencing coding benefits if they struggle to take notes during a rapidly delivered lecture. Furthermore, in note taking, low verbal students who are slow auditory processors may be performing a recording task that keeps them from processing lecture material meaningfully.

Training for Lecturing. The process of effectively attending to lectures can be taught, but it appears that teachers need to learn to structure lectures, acknowledge the context of the information students require to learn, and involve themselves in the development of communication skills.

Chilcoat's (1989) review, for example, emphasizes the importance of structuring lectures to enhance student learning and subsequent achievement. He specifies the importance of (a) providing a preview of information prior to explanation (through overview, set induction, or advanced organizer); (b) organizing information within a step-by-step lesson sequence; (c) assessing student learning when information is being given; (d) signaling transitions; (e) using multiple examples to illustrate information points; (f) stressing important points during explanations; (g) eliminating nonessential information; and (h) frequently summarizing information to be learned.

Murray and Murray (1992) further specify that the systematic preparation of a successful college lecture includes a four-stage process of (a) anticipating student expectations; (b) selecting, preparing, and sequencing the content to be presented; (c) delivering the lecture with attention to speech, demeanor, body language, and timing; and (d) supporting and evaluating the students' learning.

Finally, training for the improvement of lecturing skills is linked by Andrews (1989) to the development of communication and public speaking skills. She suggests the following objectives for helping teachers to be effective lecturers: (a) Gaining and maintaining control of the class; (b) highlighting main ideas; (c) preparing students for forthcoming activities; (d) showing interest and enthusiasm for the subject being taught; (e) providing a role model of good public communication skills; (f) acknowledging and dealing with speech anxiety; (g) anticipating the teaching environment; (h) bringing in other teaching techniques; (i) using visual aids; and (j) seeking feedback on the lecture.

Discussion Method. Studies of discussion as a method for large group instruction reflect a strong commitment to discussion as a means of promoting students' critical thinking skills.[12] A dual assumption appears to inform this work. Namely, learning should be a responsibility shared by teachers and students, and discussions are more effective than lectures because of this. The extent to which teachers and students participate in discussions is understood, however, to depend on the type of discussion in which they are involved. In a cooperative learning situation or a subject mastery discussion, the teacher has been found to serve less as a participant and more as a resource expert and observer. In an issues-oriented discussion, on the other hand, the teacher assumes the role of moderator (Gall & Gall, 1993).

Recent research and reports on discussion appear to be focused specifically on (a) discussion and student learning (justification that students do learn during discussion) and (b) training teachers and students to participate in discussions.

Discussion and Student Learning. Research and reports indicate that teachers can promote students' critical

[12]The literature distinguishes between the characteristics and effects of large and small group discussions. Since another portion of this paper reviews the literature on grouping and the focus of the present overview is large group instruction, small group discussion will not be addressed here.

and creative thinking and stimulate divergent thinking through the use of discussion. Structured discussions in a geography class, for example, have been used to help students (a) learn geographical concepts and critical thinking skills; (b) retain information on a long-term basis; and (c) develop interpersonal skills (Delaney, 1991). Similarly, in the science classroom, discussions can be used to carry out practical work, interpret results, and relate the results to everyday life (Solomon, 1991).

Students' background knowledge and experience have been found both to enhance their participation in discussions and to help them develop as thinkers (Gentile & McMillian, 1992). In their adaptation of Freire's (1970) critical dialogue, Gentile and McMillian report that the use of topics that have direct application to the problems and ethical dilemmas that at-risk students encounter on the streets and in their houses provides them with connections between what they do understand and the subject matter they are expected to master in school. Strategies such as this also enabled Buckelew (1991) to be sensitive to each student's experience when conducting or facilitating discussions in English classes.

Several methods for adjusting the way in which discussions are conducted have also been found to enhance student learning. These include instructional conversations, interactive discussion, and online computer discussions.

Instructional conversations in which content and conversation are combined to promote dialogue are understood to provide students with opportunities to form connections between what they do know and the learning they are undertaking. This serves as a kind of scaffold (or means for making connections) for students and teachers who have not had much experience with discussion-based learning. Instructional conversations are characterized as involving a thematic focus, students' prior knowledge, direct teaching, complex language, few questions with known answers, students' decisions about when to participate, and so on (ED347850, 1992). By way of example, "Questioning the Author" (Beck, 1997) is a technique for involving students in the ideas of a text. They are led through collaborative work to construct an understanding together with others as a response to teacher probes that require rereading for meaning and accuracy. Findings reported by McKeown, Beck, and Sandora (1994) indicate that when students work with Questioning the Author, more than half of the comments from students are directed toward construction of meaning, whereas student comments in baseline classrooms are more or less verbatim repetitions of text.

Dillon (1982a, 1982b, 1994) suggests that students *need* to help direct the flow of discussion in order to construct meaning for themselves (see also Yackel, 1995). In fact, he suggests that teachers might not want to ask questions if they wish to facilitate class discussions. Based on the typical (and expected) practice of teachers to do most of the questioning in discussions, Dillon suggests that at most, teachers should pose one question at the start of a discussion in order to define it. By holding back, so to speak, the teacher provides room for the students to begin to own or shape the conversation based on their understanding. Dillon further suggests that any other comments or questions that the teacher makes should occur only in response to his or her genuine need for clarification.

The premise of interactive discussions is that teachers can work together with students as a group to develop and, where necessary, enable them to reconstruct what they understand about a concept. Similar to the interactive format described for teaching about the Jurassic Period, class members assist each other and work together to both problematize and make sense of discrepant or counterintuitive perspectives (see examples in Alvermann, 1991; Commeyras, 1993; Guzzetti, Snyder, Glass, & Gamas, 1993; Roth, Anderson, & Smith, 1987).

Online computer discussion can be yet another vehicle for student discussion, one that has been shown to generate a large peer audience for student work and enhanced peer performance (cf. Bump, 1990). Other technology-based vehicles for involving students in learning together include the electronic sharing of databases, student communication with identified experts on the topic being studied, and desktop video conferencing in which students work with others who are addressing similar problems (see review chapter by The Cognition and Technology Group at Vanderbilt, 1996).

Studies of the quality of interaction, however, indicate that although the student needs to assume responsibility for learning, the process of the teacher's instruction does affect how this transpires. Ahern, Peck, and Laycock (1992) studied three styles of discourse on line and quality of student participation in a computer-mediated discussion of an introductory college-level education course. They report that the instructor's style of response was the most important factor in determining the amount of student participation and the quality of student responses. A teacher's question posed in response to a student's comment typically led to recitation. Where the teacher reflected on or elaborated on a student's response, spontaneous and rich discussion ensued among students, as well as between teacher and students.

Similarly, Smagorinsky and Fly (1993) report that students' functioning in small group discussions typically reflects the types of behavior modeled by the teacher during teacher-led discussions. Specifically, they suggest that use of small groups for student learning provides a critical support for students' learning to construct meaning for themselves *if* teachers (a) provide opportunities for students to make connections between the material to be learned and the context in which it was written (e.g., relating literature to personal experiences, to current events, or through discussion of how a concept such as *maturity* mapped onto the material read) and (b) identify strategies necessary for critical reading (e.g., establishing the need to ask questions, provide support for points being made, etc.). They conclude that if students experience top-down support for instruction, they are less likely to assume responsibility for their learning than if they are led to participate in interaction that encourages them to elaborate upon what they do and do not understand (see also Cobb, 1995).

Not surprisingly, perhaps, the teacher's goals for a given lesson also have been found to affect the types of discussion that can be held (Alvermann, O'Brien, & Dillon, 1990). In a study of 24 classroom teachers, Alvermann et al. (1990) found that discussion is typically recitation-based when its purpose is review; discussion is recitation-based or a recitation-lecture when the purpose is to define, label, or identify; and finally, discussion is open-ended (the students are encouraged to question the text or discuss the basis of "the facts"), if the purpose is the development of student comprehension. They report that these teachers' definitions of discussion were found to correspond to the few open-ended discussions observed, although the dominant format for discussion among the teachers was lecture/recitation or recitation. Interviews with the teachers revealed that the teachers' concerns about being in control of their classes and covering content meant that, while teachers might like the idea of delving into a topic with their students, they would rarely let this happen.

Training for Discussion. It appears that successful classroom discussions hinge on both teachers' and students' training for their respective roles in a discussion (cf. Coleman, 1992; Mesa-Bains & Shulman, 1991; Thomas, 1992). Learning how to ask reflective questions that promote and enhance discussion must be included in such training (cf. Ciardiello, 1993). Wasserman (1992), for example, describes high school social studies class discussions as "powerful forums" when teachers (a) are purposeful in their teaching, (b) are clear about what students need to understand, (c) apply principles of effective questioning, and (d) are open to further developing their questioning skills.

Marshall, Klages, and Fehlman's (1991) findings with high school students, however, suggest that teachers may have trouble running discussions and may attribute their difficulties to their students rather than to their own lack of skill. Specifically, they report that English teachers in middle-track high school classrooms found it difficult to run student-centered discussions. The teachers attributed their difficulties to student disinterest or inability to participate, whereas the students interviewed from these classes said that they felt that the type of student involved in these classes required the discussion to be teacher-centered. Not surprisingly, perhaps, other findings from this study include the following: (a) Teachers and students were likely to make informative statements when they held the floor, (b) students' remarks were likely to reflect the kinds of questions the teachers asked, and (c) teachers were likely to respond to students by either acknowledging or restating what they had said.

Wood's (1995) description of the "to-ing" and "fro-ing" of a traditional teacher making her way in a reform math classroom provides further evidence of the difficulties involved in changing practice even when there is a high level of support for changed curricular emphasis. The teacher with whom he worked found that she struggled with a desire to intervene in students' discussions when an incorrect solution was being considered, even though she conceptually understood why intervening in the students' efforts would change the nature of what they would learn. Her experiences underscore the importance to teachers of time, practice, changed understanding about students as learners, and support for changed curriculum in order for discussion-based classes to provide forums for classroom-based problem posing and problem solving. (Once this teacher was finished her 3-month commitment to this classroom project, she urged her researcher collaborators to continue it [Cobb et al., 1995]).

As Hauser (1992) points out, teachers may need training before they can teach students how to hold fruitful discussions. In particular, they need to be skilled in effective classroom communication skills in order to enable students to think critically and speak confidently. Hauser's suggestions for fostering discussion in the classroom include: (a) Use of restatements of what the student has said; (b) description of teacher interest, conviction, and so on; (c) request for elaboration; (d) encouragement of questions; and (e) use of wait time (Hauser, 1987; see also Jegede & Olajide, 1995; Wilkerson, Hafler, & Liu, 1991).

Self-evaluation of participant behavior, personal reports of communication apprehension, post-discussion questionnaires, and self-assessments of leadership abilities have all been found to help teachers improve the quality of group discussions (Millar, 1986). Furthermore, several projects point to the importance of providing opportunities for teachers to work with each other on a regular basis around perceived difficulties involved in discussion-based teaching in order for them to begin to understand its possibilities (cf. Northfield, 1992).

Summary of Research and Reports on Large Group Instruction

Research and reports on large group instruction raise a host of considerations about the student learning that occurs in lectures and discussions. In particular, lectures require that students possess well-developed listening and note taking skills. The findings regarding students' abilities to learn from lectures are mixed, however. Some studies suggest that all students benefit from more interactive classes when these are contrasted with lectures. Other studies indicate that high-ability students and girls perform no differently in some lecture and laboratory or discussion-based classes, and low-ability students and boys benefit more from discussion than from lecture classes.

In contrast, research and reports on discussion-based teaching reflect an emphasis on the benefits of discussion for student learning in all subject matter areas rather than on what students need in order to learn from discussions. This literature suggests that discussions provide students with opportunities to build on their background knowledge and experience, rather than needing to have these addressed for them by the teacher. It is argued that in discussions, students develop their abilities to comprehend, since the process of needing to pose an argument, present an opinion, and so on, requires them to both consolidate what is known and to link this with existing knowledge in order to generate an argument.

Discussions of both the lecture method and the discussion method of large group instruction underscore the importance of training teachers in the effective use of these formats, as well as the need for students to develop their skills in learning from lectures and discussions. The instructional conversation or feedback lecture provides a bridge to a more interactive classroom for teachers and students who have not had a lot of experience working with discussion.

Comment

What does this overview contribute to our thinking about instructional formats depicted in the two Jurassic Period case formats? On the one hand, the case formats described for teaching about what makes the Jurassic Period the Jurassic Period offer specific examples of what the teacher might do in a lecture or an interactive class. Both of the case formats meet criteria for effective practice laid out in the overviews of each literature. They reflect the suggestions that teachers should build on student knowledge, include breaks in the lecture/discussion, use post-lecture/discussion work to help students consolidate their understanding of materials covered, have as a product an outline that students generate, or notes that summarize points made during the class.

On the other hand, since the specific strengths and needs of a group of students are not specified, the case formats are simply descriptions of intention. They do not tell us how the instruction will be carried out. (In fact, given the dynamic nature of practice in which teachers are reevaluating and adjusting instruction in response to students, it is useful to recognize that no case could be more than a snapshot of classroom functioning.)

With respect to the lecture format, for example, we do not know anything about how the lectures will be conducted, nor do we know what types of lectures they will be. We do not know, for example, how the original source materials will be used in conjunction with the lecture, to what extent student self-questions will be encouraged, and whether students will be helped to develop the skills necessary for the effective listening and note taking so essential to learning in a lecture class. Furthermore, we do not know anything about the students and what their abilities are—or, for that matter, their familiarity with the skills and language necessary for successfully considering issues of period and paleontology. Thus, it is difficult to assume that a lecture format is generally appropriate for the learner. The lecture assumes a high level of self-regulation and prior knowledge, one not characteristic of most learners, especially younger students (see Schunk & Zimmerman, 1994).

We know a little more with respect to the interactive format. It is clear that a wide range of tasks for student learning is planned, and that the teacher will use information from students' work in these activities (i.e., brainstorming) to inform his or her sense of what they are ready to engage next in terms of their developing skills and discourse-knowledge of history. We really do not know, however, how the interactive tasks proposed will be implemented (i.e., Will all of the contributions to the brainstorm be accepted without comment or ad hoc lecture? Will the teacher be attentive to which students in the class are better able to develop their ideas in a small group, at least at the outset of the term?).

Given that we do not have information about the makeup and abilities of the members of the class, the interactive format appears to be a more optimal starting point for student learning generally. Interactive methods, by definition, encourage and build on students' responses to content, whereas it is not a given that lecturers will be attentive to students' prior knowledge and needs as learners.

What does the topic of large group instruction contribute more generally to how we think about student learning and its implications for instruction? Based on this overview, it appears that student access or connections to material to be covered can be facilitated in a wide variety of ways. It is also clear that such connections may need to be made explicit for students, depending on their abilities.

While there is literature that suggests that lectures can be adjusted to enhance the quality of student comprehension, there is little information that demonstrates the importance of lectures in enhancing student comprehension. In fact, based on the literature overviewed, it appears that if a teacher's goal is for all students to get beyond mere understanding of the material being covered, it is preferable to use discussion-based instruction, that is, discussions that have an open format to which students can readily contribute, not a recitation-type discussion. The literature presented here further suggests that more open-ended discussion is important for enabling students to consider alternative perspectives on a topic and benefits those with less background in a subject area.

Finally, the research and reports on large group instruction seem to reveal mixed findings on the topic of the product (achievement or outcome) of learning. In general, however, students appear to be more likely to consolidate their understanding of new information in discussions than they are in lectures. (This finding may be all the more powerful, given that comparisons of learning in lecture- and discussion-based classes typically employ standardized indices that favor lecture-based instruction.)

What might we still want to know about large group instruction based on developmental theory and research? The literature reviewed here covers students of different ages, in different kinds of educational settings, learning about different kinds of subjects, potentially engaging in different kinds of lectures and discussions, and presented with very different measures of outcome, since these are often specific to the subject matter and the class in which the student is being taught. Furthermore, the type of lecture is never specified in studies of lecturing, and the teacher's particular role in the discussion is almost never specified in studies of discussions.

To some extent, the particular organization of this review exacerbates the problem of drawing conclusions relevant to student learning, since it is organized by issue (i.e., the effects of lectures on student learning), rather than by age, domain, or expertise. Were there a specific consideration of age, domain, or expertise in the literature, however, they would have been acknowledged. Instead, it appears that this literature is rich in a wide range of different and preliminary contributions to an understanding of large group instruction.

Current findings from this literature provide the basis of studies that still need to be conducted. As such, they also provide the basis of informed practice wherein what is known is taken as a basis for experimentation.

Researchers and teachers may wish to experiment with different types of lecture and discussion formats for different organizations of student age, familiarity with material to be taught, and class size (15 students, 35 students, 150 students, etc.). The gross differences in the ages of the sample of students typically studied in lectures (high school and post-secondary school) and discussions (elementary and high school) raise some questions for immediate consideration. It is surprising, for example, that there is no literature on lecturing in elementary schools. Elementary teachers spend a good deal of time giving directions and information to their students, so it seems reasonable that systematic consideration of the impact, optimal organization, and timing of what might be called "short lectures" on student learning could usefully be undertaken.

Furthermore, while the literature reviewed emphasizes the importance of teacher attention to prior knowledge in student learning and the importance of such links to material to be taught, research on student misconceptions in science and mathematics, for example, further suggests that students may well need opportunities to confront and rethink their implicit understandings of different subject areas (cf. Gelman, 1994). Familiarity with dinosaurs or the Jurassic Period, for example, is in no way a guarantee of the accuracy of the students' knowledge or assumptions. In working with students, it is important to explore the base of student knowledge and the ways in which this knowledge may reflect faulty logic (cf. Ginsburg, 1982).

Based on our current understanding of how students learn, it also appears that it is particularly important that students develop the metacognitive tools (including strategies) necessary to identify for themselves the problem under consideration (such as, how the paleontologist confirms findings or knows that a fact is a fact). Students need to recognize how problems relate to their prior understanding, and begin the process of exploring and evaluating approaches for solving problems (cf. Polya, 1945; Scholnick & Freedman, 1987; Sternberg, 1985). This being the case, it would be useful to know whether it would be more effective to use lectures or discussion or some combination of these two methods in order to enable students to identify the problem(s) on which they are to work, consider alternative perspectives, and so on. It would be useful to know whether the same approaches are most effective when the information to be learned is largely novel (i.e., what makes the Jurassic Period a period), rather than being based in some more familiar subject area. It would also be useful to know whether the same approaches are most effective when a student is easily able to generate his or her own questions. Finally, it would be useful to consider within-student variation systematically as a function of student access to tasks.

Although the literature on discussion specifies the importance of more open-ended formats for students to explore ideas, few studies of lectures and discussions specify the type of lecture or discussion being studied, let alone the way in which information from one lecture or discussion to the next is sequenced so that such ideas can be fully explored. Sequenced, open-ended tasks have been found to provide a range of opportunities or entry points for engaging information (cf. Goldman et al., 1994; Kroll & Black, 1993). They enable students both to consolidate what they know and to begin to explore other ways to understand the topic or concepts with which they are working. In fact, they appear to be a useful default format for instruction, especially where student access to a task may be a problem.

Finally, although the nature of the teacher-student relationship is clearly perceived to be important for effective lectures and discussions, the nature of the exchange that takes place in such relationships, the shifts of power that need to occur in order for a student to gradually assume more responsibility for learning, how much of a scaffold needs to be provided, and so on, are largely uncharted information. Based on the data that do exist, it seems reasonable that the teacher-student relationship, at minimum, needs to be recognized as reciprocal by both the teacher and the student. The process of learning to problem solve involves a relationship that is emergent. The two parties adjust their responses in direct relation to each other, even when they are largely unaware that this is the case (Renninger & Winegar, 1985; see also Mehan, Hertweck, Combs, & Flynn, 1982). From this perspective, it is not really tenable to undertake research or practice based on an assumption that either the lecture or the interactive format is teacher-directed or that learning is the sole responsibility of the student(s). As Alvermann et al. (1990) point out, however, instruction and learning are not always understood as involving a joint focus on problem posing and problem solving. The teachers they studied understood themselves to be responsible for student learning.

There is a distinction to be drawn between learning to do what the teacher says and developing a knowledge of problem posing and problem solving (Wood, 1995). From a developmental perspective, students' (and teachers') questions and connections are central to the process of learning. They reflect the differences in strengths and needs that necessitate the adjustment of classroom instruction.

The next section of this review addresses the topic of questioning.

Questioning

Overview of Research and Reports

Recent research and reports on questioning.[13] focus on questioning as a vehicle for promoting student learning, despite Graesser and Person's (1994) observation that they largely reflect idealized goals for classroom learning. It should be acknowledged that even though teachers may ask a lot of questions in their classes, often only about 20% of these require them to make connections between what they know and new information; others are factual or procedural in nature (Gall, 1970; Hare & Pulliam, 1980). The presumed reasons for this include the facts that: (a) curriculum generally is more fact-oriented than thought-oriented, (b) teachers think it is necessary to know facts before progressing to more complex aspects of content and the questions that inform these,[14] and (c) teachers lack skills or resources to articulate higher order questions in the content areas themselves (Gall, 1970).

---

[13] Literature was searched under the following headings: Questioning, Questioning Techniques, Inquiry, Question-Answer Reciprocity, Reciprocal Teaching.

Sample: Research and reports on the topic of questioning include studies focused on students ranging in age from kindergarten through college, with most attention paid to elementary and high school settings. The research examines both typical and atypical populations, including learning disabled, hearing impaired, gifted, low- and high-ability students, English as a Second Language students, and poverty-stricken students. Few studies examine either the average student or differences in questioning as a function of gender or culture.

Content areas of focus: Research and reports that discuss questioning tend to focus on the disciplines of English, mathematics, and social studies; few to no studies address questioning in science or foreign language classrooms.

[14] See Papert (1993) for a discussion of concrete and abstract ways of knowing. Since this issue relates to the content of instruction, it is not discussed further in this chapter.

Furthermore, students almost never ask questions in classes and when they do, the questions are largely of a procedural nature. In fact, between kindergarten and late elementary school, the proportion of procedural questions triples, while the proportion of curiosity questions drops by half (Lindfors, 1991; see also Good et al., 1987). Interviews with students suggest that these behaviors reflect their understanding that *school* asks them to do what is assigned (Lindfors, 1991). As Good et al. (1987) point out, the low-achieving student in particular is eventually silenced by a system where asking questions indicates that "you don't know" (see also Good, 1981; Morine-Dershimer, 1985).

In short, while there are those who do concern themselves with questioning as a reflection of problem solving, this kind of questioning does not reflect common practice in classrooms (van der Meij, 1994; see also Stigler et al., 1996, for cross-cultural considerations). It also should be acknowledged, however, that there are many classrooms in which teachers do employ questioning effectively (cf. in large groups: Ball, 1993; Cobb, Wood, & Yackel, 1993; Hatano & Inagaki, 1991; Lampert, 1986; Lindfors, 1991; in small groups: Copple et al., 1984; Tharp & Gallimore, 1988).

Where the goal of learning is problem posing and problem solving, research and practice addresses students' questions, question generation, and/or what have been called cognitive strategies or procedures for engaging less-structured tasks where the engagement is contingent on the student having generated a question. The types of questions that are considered to promote student learning are those that involve students in seriously considering the information with which they are working. It is presumed that whether students understand information from lectures or interactive classes is contingent on how they have been able to engage that information. Being able to consider discrepancies between material being learned and prior understanding of that information and to use the recognition of a gap between the two to ask a question is an indication of both comprehension and an ability to figure out what still needs to be understood—what is called comprehension monitoring. As Mayer and Wittrock (1996) suggest, the problem solver is one who "manage[s] the way in which prior knowledge is used to solve a new problem" (p. 50).

A problem-solving focus in questioning at the most basic level involves (a) the use of authentic questions (questions for which you do not already have an answer); (b) genuine encouragement of student input; (c) incorporation of previous classroom contributions into questioning; (d) using responses to questions to validate the way in which the students are contributing to the course of the discussion; (e) posing questions that elicit nonroutine generalizations, analyses, or speculations; and (f) encouraging questions that reflect thought (Nystrand & Gamoran, 1988). This approach to questioning reflects the notion that the teacher needs to facilitate students' developing abilities to ask or recognize questions, and that such facilitation requires shifting the power from the teacher as question asker to student as problem solver.

Van der Meij (1994) distinguishes between questions designed to solve problems and questions used to learn how to do something. Citing his own work and that of Siegler (1977) as examples of questioning to solve abstract problems, he points out that older students more often seek to refine their understanding by identifying constraints in the situation than do younger students, and questioning is often more strategic at the outset of a problem since initial questions eliminate more options than do later questions. Research on questioning that involves learning to do something indicates, instead, an interaction between prior knowledge and questioning. Across several task contexts, those with more knowledge have been found to ask more higher order questions—questions that have to do with the organization of the task and its goals (cf. Flammer, Grob, Leuthardt, & Luthi, 1982a, 1982b; Scardamalia & Bereiter, 1992). Van der Meij (1994) further observes that it would be worth examining whether the types of questions at various stages of learning differ in a predictable way—information that has not yet been compiled.

Ciancido and Quirk (1993) report that students as young as those in kindergarten and first grade were quite capable of learning how to respond critically to literature, which suggests that questioning and critical thinking can be taught to younger as well as older students. These findings also indicate that skillful use of questions and guidance by the teacher helps to facilitate critical thinking. Similarly, Feagans (1994) reports that second graders were able to use probes to orally evaluate their own writing and, following modeling by the teacher, were able to write evaluations. The probes appear to have provided a scaffold for students not only to evaluate their own writing, but to enhance and transfer the understanding they developed to other types of writing.

It appears that with instructional support, even very young students can begin to work with questions related to their understanding of concepts and strategy use, although they appear to need instruction to do so. Perry, Vanderstoep, and Yu (1993) found, for example, that Asian teachers asked first graders significantly more addition and subtraction questions that required them to draw on what they knew and to use strategies in order to accomplish these tasks than did U.S. teachers.

The issue of instructional support is critical (cf. Pressley, Johnson, Symons, McGoldrick, & Kurita, 1989). As van der Meij (1993) reports, study of the types of questions fifth- and sixth-grade students ask when reading a text suggests that without instructional support, many students rely on a repertoire of generic questions that can easily be found in the text, rather than generating higher order questions. Similarly, findings from Newman and Schwager (1995) suggest the importance of organizing instruction so that the students understand that the emphasis is on student learning. They found that while sixth graders are generally more likely than third graders to request process-related hints and less likely to simply ask for an answer, when given learning goals, both third and sixth graders were more likely to have adaptive patterns of questioning in their help seeking than were students given performance goals.

Instructional support for questioning can also extend beyond the particulars of the actual questions posed to include instructional formats that involve teachers in working explicitly with students on their abilities to question. Examples of such direct instruction include reciprocal teaching, self-questioning, and elaborative interrogation. Reciprocal teaching (cf. Palincsar & Brown, 1984; see Rosenshine & Meister, 1994 for a review) is frequently cited as an effective method for facilitating student questioning. In reciprocal teaching, the teacher initially models the strategies of question generation, summarizing, clarification, and prediction—strategies that good readers practice spontaneously—and through sequenced instruction gradually encourages the students to assume the role of teacher. Although this kind of structured dialogue was originally developed to work with poor readers (cf. Palincsar & Klenk, 1991), it has been found to benefit the comprehension of all types of students (cf. Frances & Eckart, 1992) in subject areas as varied as reading, math, and science (cf. Brown & Campione, 1994; Brown, Campione, Reeve, Ferrara, & Palincsar, 1991). In fact, Kelly, Moore, and Tuck (1994) report both that gains among grade four students on a reciprocal reading task were maintained at an eight-week follow-up and that the students were able to generalize their understanding across different reading genres.

Instruction in self-questioning is another method for facilitating student questioning. Self-questioning involves students in posing questions during or after lectures or the reading of text. The process of self-questioning provides students with feedback that not only motivates them to examine the topics being covered, but leads them to do so with reflection (see review by Wong, 1985). Encouraging students to use self-questioning has been found to be more effective than other techniques, such as summarizing, presumably because it involves students in considering what they do and do not know about the question posed. As Wong (1985) points out, this process requires them to be actively involved in seeking answers. It also gives them increased responsibility for their learning. Methods that facilitate self-questioning, for example, include assignments to write questions that a particular text does not answer or even raise, formulation of hypotheses and generation of arguments that support and refute them, or deletion of critical information during a lecture or discussion that piques students' need to ask questions (Graesser, 1992). Fenwick and McMillan (1992) further suggest the usefulness of instructors' modeling their own use of self-questions.

Elaborative interrogation is another strategy that involves students in further explaining what they have read by answering "why" questions. In this type of self-generated elaboration, students are explicitly involved in reconstructing their understanding of information they are reading in terms of what they know. Compared to conditions in which students read and studied the same paragraphs, students who took facts from a text and made them into "why" questions had better recall than those who read the text under normal conditions. In fact, even when the students did not answer the why questions, they were still more likely to recall the text than were students who had not generated questions (Pressley et al., 1992).

Pressley et al. (1989), however, caution that when cognitive strategy instruction is only introduced briefly or mentioned to students, there are few gains in their comprehension. When, on the other hand, instruction for self-questioning is part of ongoing instruction, student comprehension is significantly enhanced (cf. Davey & McBride, 1986).

An alternative to the direct teaching of cognitive strategies or self-questions is to provide an environment for students that builds on their questions, within a context that provides the structure necessary to guide them to substantial inquiry. In the Computer Supported Intentional Learning Environments (CSILE) project, for example, the computer is used as a vehicle for communicating among students as they work to answer questions, follow up on questions posed previously, and so on (Bereiter & Scardamalia, 1992). CSILE has been used in a variety of subject matter areas (social studies, literature, mathematics, geography, etc.) and with simple as well as complex assignments.

Students' use of CSILE indicates that they are capable of generating reasoned inquiry and can talk about the strategies that they are using. Scardamalia et al. (1994) report that in grades 1 through 3, students working with CSILE are primarily absorbed in their own work or work with a partner, but can take an interest in what the rest of the class is doing with respect to a project. On the other hand, only one of these teachers reported that a class was able to consider problems of understanding, such as appreciating that claims were claims, rather than immutable facts. By grades 4 through 6, however, students evidence a greater focus on problems of understanding. Scardamalia et al. also note the importance of teacher encouragement in successful collaborative knowledge building at this age. For both grade levels, the success of this project was dependent on having time for reflection and refinement of work, opportunities for public and private displays of work in progress, and access to and exchange of texts, resources, and so on (Scardamalia & Bereiter, 1992; see also project descriptions such as Cobb & Bauersfeld, 1995; Cognition and Technology Group at Vanderbilt, 1991; Brown & Campione, 1994).

Emphasis on questioning that requires student explanation characterizes the environment that Japanese teachers more or less uniformly present for their students (Stevenson & Stigler, 1992). Stigler et al. (1996), for example, report that in the Japanese lessons they studied, the most frequent types of teacher questions were how and why questions (i.e., "How did you find the area of a triangle? or Why is the area here 17?") (p. 166). The next most frequent type of question involved checking the status of explanation with the others in the class—asking if there were any other explanations to be considered.[15] Such questioning stands in contrast to the lessons of teachers from the United States, whose most frequent type of questions ask students to give short-answer responses that name or label the kind of triangle, specify the length of a side, and so on. The second most frequent question asked students for the answer to a specific calculation. Not surprisingly, Japanese students were found to be more likely to talk and explain themselves than were students in the United States.

Interestingly, Japanese teachers have a wealth of information available about the methods students will develop themselves in order to solve problems. As Stigler et al. (1996) point out, the Japanese teacher does not need to generate such responses by him- or herself. The entry-level teacher has a set of resources that specifies the range of possible solution types, in turn, underscoring the importance of explanation for the process of "doing math" and the impossibility of assuming that students' answers might be limited to whether they were able to get the answer. With such resources it is possible to identify a key question on which to focus a lesson and a sense of the kind of explanation with which students new to a concept will be able to work (Kawanaka & Stigler, 1997), something that is not available to most teachers in the United States (with the exception of those working with projects in which the range of possible student responses have been mapped, i.e., Cognitively Guided Instruction [Fennema et al., 1989]).

A further question, however, needs to be asked about what exactly is involved in "training" students to question. It appears that it is only possible to specify what kinds of accomplishments might be set as the goals for learning to question, rather than a specific type or sequence of questions that will be effective in all settings. For example, Au and Jordon (1981) reported that questioning strategies used successfully by teachers of White middle-class students failed with Hawaiian students because these students had different expectations for teacher behavior. As a response, Au and Jordon developed the E-T-R program, which built on students' experience (E), the text (T), and relationships between experience and text (R) (see also Au, 1979, 1981).

Interestingly enough, Tharp (1994) reports that when the E-T-R program developed to improve the reading skills of the Hawaiian students was implemented in Navajo reservation schools, it too needed to be adjusted. In the Hawaiian school, teachers introduced the story by encouraging students to talk about experiences they had had that were similar to those described in the story; following this, the teacher read the text and returned to experience questions to build additional background. Finally, the teacher-guided student processing of the text so that this occurred at various levels of comprehension, leading the students to relate their experiences to new ideas from the texts. In the Navajo setting, because the students objected to being asked questions during the reading of the story, the teachers first needed to ask all of the experiential questions, then read the text with the class, answer questions about the text, and

[15] Stigler et al. (1996) point out, however, that the teaching observed in the Japanese elementary school is quite different than that in the secondary school where the emphasis is on rote memorization. They suggest that the Japanese elementary classrooms are organized to teach students to think. By high school, the inference might be that students are ready to acquire the content on which such skills might be used.

finally relate the texts back to their personal experiences. The skills on which they were working with the Navajo students were the same as those on which the Hawaiian children had worked, but the sequencing of the tasks had to be adjusted.

In their review of question generation, Rosenshine et al. (1996) found it "difficult to derive any prescriptions on how to develop effective procedural prompts" [scaffolds provided for students in cognitive strategies instruction] (p. 198). They were able to determine that the most successful prompts were easy to use and did not demand strong cognitive skills. The three most effective prompts included signal words (i.e., who, what), generic question stems (another example is . . .) or generic questions, and categories of story grammar (i.e., setting, character).

Other elements of instruction that were used (although not all at once) to facilitate student ability to generate questions included providing prompts specific to the strategy being taught, offering models of appropriate responses, anticipating students' difficulties, adjusting the difficulty of the material, providing cue cards, guiding student practice, giving feedback, instructing students in the use of a checklist, and assessing student mastery (Rosenshine et al., 1996).

The notion that there are principles guiding the way in which questioning is undertaken, but that there are not procedures that necessarily have to be implemented in the same way in order to carry out questioning, characterizes Sigel and Kelley's (1988) discussion of questioning strategies (see also discussion of "first principles" in Brown & Campione, 1994). They suggest specifically that working with students to engage a topic involves a spirallike sequence: focus, explore, restructure, (re)focus, and so on.

For example, if students are just about to begin work on a task (focus), Sigel and Kelley suggest using three types of questions: an open-ended question, a question that poses a problem, or a question that introduces some kind of conflict with prior information. They specify what questioning might look like at the point of accessing the problem/task and offer examples of how it might play out, but their scheme is actually predicated on the notion that the teacher needs to determine student readiness for particular questions. The initial task of the teacher is to determine the experiential, cognitive, and emotional status of the learners in relation to the knowledge to be learned or goal to be accomplished. This information represents the psychological distance between the readiness of the students for the task and the goal to be accomplished. The actual distancing in which the teacher engages is determined by the teacher, based on this information. Sigel and Kelley further note that it is not the first question and its answer that provide an indicator of the students' readiness and understanding; rather, it is the students' ability to follow through with a second question that is the critical indicator of engagement or questioning and readiness to move on to a deeper level of understanding.

Where teachers such as those in Japan identify their goals in teaching to work with children on problem posing and problem solving, they can be likened to researchers (Stigler et al., 1996). Kawanaka and Stigler (1997) point out that Japanese teachers' lesson plans are quite detailed and are focused on what students need to be thinking. For each lesson, they have identified at least one question that is intended to focus and further develop the students' thinking. They found, in contrast, that teachers in the United States are more likely to plan what *they* will do in a lesson and to use questions as a check on students' comprehension (Kawanaka & Stigler, 1997).

Without the resources that mapped information about students' difficulties and strategies could provide, many teachers are spontaneous in their questioning, meaning that their questions are poorly phrased and generally do not lead to answers that yield new questions (Gall, 1984). Consistent with findings that suggest the need to facilitate and provide instruction to scaffold students' abilities to question, it appears that simply providing teachers with information about questioning is not sufficient to enable them to change their practice and work with their students on developing questioning skills (Graesser, 1992). Information about cognitive strategies (Duffy, 1993) and/or reform classroom practice (Wood, 1995) does not appear to be a substitute for the opportunity to work with these concepts—being in the position to question them (and others). Peer discussant feedback (Wilen & Campbell, 1992) that builds on teachers' present practice and presents them with links between it and findings from research on reciprocal teaching, and opportunities for collaboration (Palincsar & Klenk, 1991) are methods that have been found to foster teachers' comprehension and awareness of the possibilities for developing their own skills and using questioning in their work with students.

Summary of Research and Reports on Questioning

Questioning forms the basis of research and practice concerned with student learning where learning is understood to involve problem posing and problem solving. It is described as both a reflection of and a contributor to student learning. Research and reports on questioning focus on teacher behaviors that can be used to elicit student questioning. In their classrooms, teachers can ask students for explanations, provide time for students to think about questions, ask open-ended questions, pose problems, have conversations, elaborate on their answers, and so on.

Furthermore, teachers can instruct students in cognitive strategies in order to foster questioning, developing student comprehension, and abilities to monitor their own comprehension, including question posing. Reciprocal teaching, self-questions, use of prompts, class-based problem solving, and distancing strategies are reviewed as methods of working with students on questioning.

Finally, parallels between methods for working with students and teachers to understand the potential of including questioning in classroom instruction are identified.

Comment

What does this overview contribute to our thinking about instructional formats depicted in the two Jurassic Period case formats? Both case formats described for teaching about what makes the Jurassic Period the Jurassic Period open with questions in order to anchor the lesson in the students' knowledge base and as a way for the teacher to figure out what the students do and do not understand about the topic. Using the students' current knowledge and adjusting the level of explanation in light of what they know increases the likelihood that the students will connect to and engage in the material being covered in the lecture. It would also have been possible to specify modeling of self-questioning, instruction in cognitive strategies, or prompts in this lecture format, but given the use of the brainstorm, this was not necessary. The brainstorm was chosen because, in this case, it was the first day of the class, when a brainstorm would provide an opportunity to gather ideas and enable everyone to have a voice.

It is even more clear in the interactive format that students are initially provided with questions to address, and that brainstorming not only triggers their ideas, but provides the basis of their discussion. The students' answers are expected to consolidate what they already know and what their questions may be. This information provides them with the basis for their subsequent efforts to figure out what makes the Jurassic Period the Jurassic Period.

It is apparent that the interactive format provides multiple opportunities for students to address their own and others' questions with peers and/or expert others. Furthermore, the questioning in which the class as a whole is engaged can be expected to range from simple open-ended responses to more focused, text-based considerations. Writing their own chapter books provides a format for students to consolidate their individual understandings of the investigations begun in the classroom in the discussion format. In fact, the organization of the interactive format enables students to turn to the class as a whole or to others in the class for confirmation and elaboration of ideas with which they are working and for strategies for doing the work as these are needed. They also have Ask Dr. Dino, the Web, and classroom materials as resources.

What does the topic of questioning contribute more generally to how we think about student learning and its implications for instruction? Students' access or connections to material can be facilitated by questioning. Questions can be the basis of instruction and can enable students to connect their own questions to the material being covered, and instruction in use of cognitive strategies can provide students with a basis for learning how to make such connections.

The example of the E-T-R reading program and its necessary adjustment further suggests that while the concept being taught through the use of questioning may not change, the actual process of teacher questioning may need to be thought about as always requiring adjustment in response to the strengths and needs of students. Thus, the process of posing a question appears to require that the student be able to identify the problem a task poses (cf. Gall, 1984; Steinberg, 1985), that the student has "focused" on the task and the questions inherent in it, and that the student be ready to "explore," "restructure," and so on (to borrow Sigel & Kelley's, 1988, terminology).

Instructing students in such cognitive strategies as reciprocal teaching and self-questioning provides them with the tools they need to identify the problem under discussion and then begin the process of working through it more closely. Classroom-based problem solving such as that described in the CSILE project accomplishes similar ends. In fact, since the problems come from the students, the struggle to get them to focus on a problem is eliminated. It could also be argued that identifying a problem and generating a problem are two very different tasks, and as such pose different and complementary challenges from which all students can benefit.

What might we still want to know about questioning based on developmental theory and research? The work on questioning focuses on ways in which teachers can build opportunities for students to question—and to learn to question—into their lectures and discussions. The literature reviewed here covers students who range in age, are in different kinds of educational settings, and are learning about different kinds of subjects. Some of them are being presented with different types of experiences to enable them to pose questions; presumably, others are in classrooms where they are not encouraged to ask any questions.

We do not learn much from this literature about students' natural inclinations to question, or whether there is any difference in the effectiveness of cognitive strategy instruction as a function of student age, gender, cultural inter- or independence, interest, school culture, and so on. We also do not learn whether students' questions are "shut down" by particular instructional techniques and what it takes to change such a situation if this is the case.

It appears that students in early elementary school are able to seriously engage questioning and cognitive strategy instruction. We also know that they can contribute to the development of the collective knowledge that characterizes class-based problem solving in CSILE. Interestingly, Scardamalia et al. (1994) report that only one class of students in grades 1 through 3 was able to work on addressing claims as claims rather than as immutable facts. Given that students who worked with the interactive case format on the Jurassic Period described were second graders and were seriously engaged in the verification of facts as facts—problems of understanding—it seems likely that these two classes are not anomalies, but that there may be other developmental considerations in addition to age that could be considered.

One explanation for differences among classes in the level of their work with questioning may have to do with how well matched this kind of problem for understanding is to the curriculum in general (cf. Farnham-Diggory, 1994), the culture of the school (cf. Good et al., 1990), and the personal culture of the students. It seems reasonable to suggest that what may appear to be age-based developmental differences in such settings may actually be mediated by teacher facilitation and work with students to understand what they are doing and why they are doing it, through processing with them the experience of their problem posing.

The importance of instructional support, especially for tasks where the students need to identify (cf. Sternberg, 1985) rather than generate the problem, is clear. What is less clear is the kind of consideration given in cognitive strategy instruction to identifying student difficulties prior to instruction. How is a student's conceptual understanding developed through questioning? Is there a more opportune time to work with and model reciprocal teaching, learning to self-question, and so on, in terms of age, experience with particular instructional formats, or subject area familiarity? Do students learn to question, after much effort, because of the way that they are taught? Is the appropriateness of the questions posed in, say, the eighth grade, dependent on whether a student is led to ask questions, develop ideas and a foundation for understanding, and work with these ideas in earlier schooling? What is the difference in learning if one learns in a sequence that moves from fact to synthesis, rather than learning facts through efforts to synthesize information? What are the implications of developments in our understanding about misconception for thinking about students' (and teachers') questions?

When students do have questions and are encouraged to ask them, there are other questions to be addressed about how to build on students' questions and how to help them become even more resourceful as learners. There are also questions to be asked about the form of questioning that works for students, at what ages, in what kinds of settings, and perhaps with which kinds of conceptions/misconceptions these are most appropriate. Interestingly, descriptions of instructional practice that included questioning in this overview were also descriptions of classroom grouping. In group work, students typically work together anywhere between three minutes to a week or two in order to accomplish the goals of a prescribed task. One benefit of group work is that it enables students to both ask questions of and seek solutions from their peers, in addition to having question asking modeled for them by their peers (Webb, 1989). Another benefit is that it permits students to have different kinds of access to—make different kinds of connections with—the tasks they are assigned.

The overview that follows focuses on grouping in the classroom, including the use of group work.

Grouping

Overview of Research and Reports

In the ERIC database, research and reports on grouping[16] encompass a variety of teaching practices. Although the

---

[16] Literature was searched under the following headers: Grouping for Instructional Purposes, Mixed-Age Groups, Vertical Classroom, Vertical Grouping, Non-Graded Instructional Grouping, Multi-Graded Classes, Heterogeneous Grouping, Homogeneous Grouping, Cross-Age Teaching, Peer Tutoring, Peer Teaching.

Sample: Research and reports on grouping address both the selection of students for particular classes (i.e., ability grouping or tracking) and instruction in which students are grouped for peer learning or teaching and small group instruction. Most of the research on grouping focuses on elementary students, and its predominant focus is gifted students. A few studies have evaluated the effects of grouping on minority students, special education students, students with developmental disabilities, or at-risk students. A few other studies have addressed grouping of secondary students or grouping in day-care programs. Only a few primary foci of these studies and reports are (a) the effects of grouping on students' learning and (b) the training necessary for teachers to use grouping practices in instruction effectively, a competing subtext reflects the strong feelings (pro and con) of these researchers and educators about grouping. For the purposes of this review, this subtext is acknowledged but not taken as a focus.

Grouping, as it is used here, refers to both assignment of students to a class, as well as to the use of flexible grouping within classes. Because the decision to assign students to group work within classes is often informed by what is understood about assignment of students to classes (ability grouping, mixed age grouping, and so on), this overview addresses both assignment of students to classes as well as the use of flexible grouping or what is also simply labeled small group or group work within classes.

Effects of Grouping on Student Learning. Studies of the effects of mixed-age (vertical or nongraded instruction) and ability groupings on student learning have yielded mixed results. In general, the research reveals that mixed-age instruction (classes with students who, in a more traditional setting, would be assigned to different grades) has little effect on student performance when compared to other, more traditional, practices. If there is a difference, it is usually in favor of multi-age classrooms. Jensen and Green (1993) found that children in multi-age groupings performed as well academically as children in single-age groupings (SAGs) and also developed better self-concepts and school attitudes than children in SAGs. Miller's (1990, 1991a, 1991b) reviews affirm such conclusions (see also Pratt, 1986). Furthermore, as Hartup (1996) reports, children and adolescents choose friends who are similar in development, not age. Thus, in multi-age classes, it might be expected that children would more readily find friends, and that such friendship will provide a supportive base from which students can be challenged academically.[17] In fact, in his review, Pratt (1986) suggests that the general picture that emerges from the literature is one of increased competition and aggression within SAGs, and increased harmony in mixed-age classrooms.

Mixed-aged grouping is considered to be particularly beneficial for elementary students, given their varying rates of development (Evangelou, 1989).[18] Katz and Chard (1989) specify that it provides for the development of (a) leadership skills, (b) pro-social behaviors, (c) freedom of involvement and play, (d) self-regulation, (e) social participation, (f) models of more complex behaviors, and (g) adjustment of communication abilities. Mixed-ability grouping also requires that students learn to structure their learning time and to choose strategies appropriate to their needs (Veenman, Lem, & Voeten, 1988). Interestingly, Stright and French (1988) report similar patterns of learning success and leadership behavior among nine-year-old and eleven-year-old students when they were paired with children two years younger than themselves. These findings provide support for the argument that mixed-age peer groups are an important context for learning and the development of leadership skills. At present, however, as DelForge, DelForge, and DelForge (1992) observe, there is no agreed-upon way to group elementary students in mixed-grade or combination classrooms. Variables used to group students include matched levels of academic ability, mixed levels of academic ability, degree of self-discipline, and social maturity.

In contrast to mixed findings regarding particular grouping of students, research on cross-age teaching or tutoring uniformly suggests that this method of grouping students affords both tutors and tutees an opportunity to enlarge their understanding of the topic being taught as well as to improve their social skills and attitudes toward school. Cross-age tutoring is essentially another form of mixed-group work in which, most typically, an older, at-risk, or disadvantaged student tutors a younger student—although students who are tutors do not need to be at risk. Trapani (1988) and Trapani and Gettinger (1989) report that providing fourth- to sixth-grade learning-disabled boys with social skills training and cross-age tutoring resulted in improved achievement and ability to work with others. It appears that tutors benefit from cross-age and peer tutoring

studies have considered either the effects of grouping on average students or the role of gender as a factor in grouping.

Content areas of focus: Studies and reports on grouping tend to be focused on reading, language arts, and mathematics classes. Few studies examine grouping in laboratory or science classes, foreign language classes, or social studies classes.

[17] Azmitia (1996) points out, however, that in adolescence, friends can sustain and repair collaborations, but there is a decline in the incidence of negotiation among friends, suggesting that the synergy that might be expected to be provided by friends to get students through a difficult task is not necessarily energy that will get them to push each other's understanding in a group situation.

[18] How "mixed" the classroom is may adversely affect the benefit, however. Specifically, Sundell (1994) reports that in Swedish schools, differences in students' ages in mixed ability classes are typically three or more years and sometimes as much as six years. Mixed-age classes more typically include students whose age varies by no more than two years.

because in their role as resources for each other, they need to assume responsibility and are put in the position of demonstrating their ability to be the knower. The process of tutoring also requires that they review material, in turn enabling them to further consolidate their understanding of it (Gaustad, 1992).

Based on the findings from cross-age tutoring research, it might be expected that the impact of ability grouping on student learning would be related to the degree to which the curriculum is adjusted to provide resources to students and require them to be responsible for the material they are learning. Not surprisingly, it does appear that the more a grouping arrangement serves to adjust the curriculum to students' abilities, the greater the effect such grouping has on students (Kulik, 1993). Kulik (1992) reports that separate classes for gifted students involving enrichment or accelerated work involve the greatest amount of curricular adjustment and have the greatest effect on student learning.

Findings from study of the consolidation of middle- and upper-track English and social studies classes in a Maine high school indicates, too, that curricular adjustment in heterogeneous classrooms benefits students. Following consolidation, (a) students had high levels of self-esteem, (b) teachers perceived increased self-esteem in the mid-level student, (c) students had a positive perception of the learning environment, (d) staff ability to reorganize the learning environment increased, (e) teachers preferred heterogeneous groups, (f) students' motivation increased, (g) students took responsibility for their learning, (h) students had a positive perception of class activities, (i) teachers diversified and improved their teaching strategies, (j) classes became more student-centered and interactive, and (k) teachers observed a decrease in the gaps between performance and students' identified roles as middle- and upper-level students (Poppish et al., 1990).

It appears that the process of teachers' adjusting or tailoring classes for the students they teach benefits all students, whether they are paired as in cross-age tutoring, placed in homogeneous classrooms as gifted students, or assigned to heterogeneous classes. Such findings provide support for a hypothesis that grouping affects students in direct relation to the extent to which teachers adjust curriculum to meet student abilities. They also suggest that grouping affects students in relation to the particular variables addressed by the study (cf. Hoover, Sayler, & Feldhusen, 1993). For example, when variables such as socialization and psychological effects on students are considered, it appears that gifted students feel less sure about their self-worth when grouped with other high-ability students (Keller, 1991). This finding, however, is mediated by the specific type of classroom placement for the gifted learners (Kulik, 1992), and potentially by how instruction is adjusted to these students' strengths and needs.

Several studies suggest alternatives to ability grouping and tracking of students between classes, and advocate adjusting instruction in the classroom through use of flexible grouping. Flexible grouping refers to grouping of students based on their diverse interests and learning rates. Such grouping can be maintained over time or used for single tasks (cf. Barbour, 1990). Findings from study of the effects of flexible grouping on student learning also are mixed. This, at least to some extent, is presumably due to the range of classroom grouping that is labeled "group work." Good et al. (1990) and Gerleman (1987) distinguish between teachers who teach two or three groups (typically assigned by ability, all of whom receive the same assignment) and classrooms in which a more flexible assignment of students and tasks is used. In the former, students are typically instructed in small groups (organized based on ability) and then do seat work as follow-up to this instruction. In the latter, teachers often make use of the small group time as an opportunity for active, hands-on learning, and follow this format with either (a) whole group instruction that permits follow-up discussion of issues raised in the small groups, links between work engaged previously or that will follow, or (b) group collaboration on projects, worksheets, and so on.

A meta-analysis of the research on flexible grouping did reveal several consistent findings. These include:[19] (a) group work by itself is no guarantee of achievement gains; (b) no one type of grouping is more likely to promote student achievement than another; (c) large classes of students appear to benefit most from flexible grouping; (d) students in math and science classes, in particular, seem to benefit from flexible grouping; (e) grouping is most effective when it is accompanied by modifications of instructional methods and materials to be taught (in other words, the way in which group work is undertaken built on the strengths and needs of the students, including their prior experience with group work, their need for discrete goals and accountability, and so on); (f) 3- to 4-person groups of students are an optimal size for group work; and (g) group work is most effective when students are compatible (Lou et al., 1996).

One of the most common methods of grouping students in the classroom involves pairing them for group work or peer education. Damon (1984), in his review of the literature,

[19] This meta-analysis did not include studies of students paired for group work.

however, suggests distinguishing between the use of peer tutoring and peer collaboration in classrooms based on the intended task. Specifically, his reading of the literature suggests that it is most effective for students to work together as peer tutors when they need to bolster the understanding of *skills* and *information* in which they are receiving more direct instruction, for example, historical facts, word attack skills, multiplication tables, and so on. When students need to be developing their understanding of *concepts* related to classwork, however, he suggests that peer collaboration is more appropriate.

Peer tutoring classically involves same-age peers working together, where one peer teaches the other a skill or strategy. Peer tutoring can be used as whole-class instruction with everyone taking turns in the roles of tutor and tutee (cf. Gartner & Riessman, 1994) as (a) a supplement to instruction (cf. Lundeberg, 1990) and (b) as specific student pairing for learning in classes (cf. Kutnick & Thomas, 1990). On the whole, it appears that as in the results reported on mixed-age and ability groups, peer tutoring also benefits students' academic achievement and social development, enhancing their self-esteem (Gomer, 1992), fostering an exchange of ideas among native and non-native English-speaking ninth graders prior to revision of first drafts (Blake, 1992), and leading to more revisions even among learning-disabled students (MacArthur, Schwartz, & Graham, 1991). Paired tutor-tutee groupings were also found to outperform peers in understanding concepts in chemistry (Kutnick & Thomas, 1990).

Carter and Jones (1993) report, furthermore, that heterogeneous pairing of fifth-grade students in science can be mutually beneficial to low-ability students partnered with high-ability students. They found that (a) low-ability student achievement is greater when students are paired with high-ability partners; (b) low-ability students spoke more and exhibited less distracting behaviors when paired with partners of high-ability; (c) high-ability students spoke more, took more turns speaking, and exhibited more helping behaviors when they were paired with low-ability students rather than with other high-ability students; and (d) ability of partner did not affect achievement of high-ability students. Tudge (1989) reports, however, that while low-ability students paired with high-ability students on a mathematical balance-beam task were more likely to engage the demands of the task in a qualitatively different way than would have been possible if they had been working independently, high-ability students in these pairings regressed in their level of thinking. In another experiment, this regression did not occur when students were provided with feedback about their work (Tudge, 1992). In fact, students working individually on the task also performed better with feedback. These findings are interpreted as evidence that the type and organization of a task (in this case, grouping and provision of feedback) help to determine the benefits of the grouping experience.

Slavin and his colleagues' discussions of effective group work, in particular, underscore the importance of establishing clear group goals and making individuals accountable to the group (see Slavin, 1983). Methods of grouping students for work can range from having pairs of students constitute a group to having sequenced groupings and regroupings of students working together. Two of the more complex and commonly employed versions of such grouping and regrouping are the Jigsaw classroom (Aronson et al., 1978) and the Teams-Games-Tournament (TGT) (Slavin, 1983).[20] Both of these forms of group work can

---

[20] Brief examples of Aronson et al.'s (1978) Jigsaw classroom and Slavin's (1983) Teams-Games-Tournament (TGT) follow, set in the context of the case study at the outset of this chapter.

The Jigsaw classroom was originally developed to facilitate school integration efforts. As such, its structure permits students with varying levels of ability to work together and depend on their work together, while developing content area skills and knowledge. There are two parts to the Jigsaw. In the first, students participate in an information-gathering/demonstration phase. In the second, they are the experts on whatever they did with their group in the first part of the Jigsaw and are responsible for teaching it to the second group of students.

For the first part of a Jigsaw (which can take a half an hour, an hour and a half, or a period a day for a week, depending on the nature of the task), the particular content of the assignments and their accompanying instructions can be tailored to the learning needs of the initial group to which students are assigned. Thus, for example, students in groups of 4 to 5 might receive a reading assignment or a set of tasks about some aspect of a bigger question, such as how to explain change or how to describe a period (for example, as part of the unit on the characteristics of the Jurassic Period). The assignment would or could be tailored to students' reading level or level of comprehension and would not be duplicated in the assignments given to other groups. One group might focus on fossilization, another on a dig and how to convert observations (such as a bone found lying sideways) into explanations, another might write a play about dinosaurs as caregivers, and so on.

If any group in particular needs explicit instruction, they can also receive study questions, sets of instructions, even worksheets that will make them accountable for doing the assignment for each period they work. Once students complete their task for the first part of the Jigsaw, they move to the second part, where they share their work with one person from each of the other groups. A critical feature of the Jigsaw is that students in the

involve students in either cooperative or collaborative group work. Whether the group work is ultimately labeled cooperative or collaborative would depend upon the nature of the task, the goals of the group, and the ability of the group of students to focus on a joint goal.

Slavin's (1983) review of research on cooperative learning indicates that it promotes higher achievement than competitive and individualistic learning structures, promotes healthy ethnic relations, and reduces racial conflict. It is considered to lessen the need for and reduce the use of tracking and separate enrichment programs for the gifted, and to enable students to maximize their own and each other's learning (Slavin, 1983, 1990). Findings reported by Terwel, Herfs, Mertens, and Perrenet (1994) further indicate that students in heterogeneous mathematics classes taught with cooperative learning techniques achieve more than students taught in traditional ability-grouped classrooms.

Webb and Palincsar (1996) point out, however, that there is a distinction to be made between cooperation, where students work together to meet a group goal, and cooperation that evolves into collaboration within the group. Cooperative group work typically involves tasks that serve to build students' base of facts and discrete skills (Slavin, 1987)—although as the footnoted example of the Jigsaw illustrates, cooperative grouping does not have to be limited to work on discrete information. On the other hand, work on classroom-based problem-solving projects (e.g., Bereiter & Scardamalia, 1992; Brown & Campione, 1994; Cobb, Yackel, & Wood, 1995; Cognition and Technology Group at Vanderbilt, in press) might more appropriately be considered instances of collaborative group work where the focus is on understanding that requires discussion and problem solving. Such projects have been designed to capitalize on the reflexive relation between students' verbal exchange and their thinking about concepts that they are learning (Cobb et al., 1995). The process of working together to make sense requires students to clarify the meanings suggested by others and in so doing, they also consolidate their own developing understanding. Thus, collaboration is built into the process of the task.

Central to the effectiveness of this type of group work is its facilitation. The teacher establishes routines for discussion—typically, a problem is posed, students work in small groups to address it, and then the class of students reconvenes as a whole group in order to sort through their understanding and what they still need to know. In Brown and Campione's (1994) Oakland classroom, the routine consisted of students moving with regularity between work groups (computer composition, research, or working with the teacher), reciprocal teaching or jigsaw seminars, and chat groups that included project presentation/discussions as they tackled their current classrooms queries. In both settings, once the routine is understood, it permits the students to focus their attention on the tasks that provide the content of their learning, the process of working together and with the teacher on their questions (Brown & Campione, 1994; Wood, 1995).

As Azmitia (1996) points out in her review of peer interaction across the life span, even young children have been shown to increase their conceptual understanding if engaged in tasks that require coordinating ideas into a general theory or rule, resolving disagreements, and so on (cf. Brownell & Carriger, 1991; Tomasello, Kruger, & Ratner, 1993). Not surprisingly, Azmitia also notes age-related differences in the process of students' work together on the tasks they are assigned. Specifically, (a) elementary students generate fewer and more similar kinds of ideas about what to do on a task than do older students, and (b) preschool and elementary school students are more likely to learn through conflict with another than they are through collaboration (Berkowitz & Gibbs, 1983; Kruger, 1992, 1993). By adolescence, it appears that students are able to build on a partner's ideas and can use conflict (challenges, disagreement, questioning, etc.) as a means to further come to a joint understanding that neither might have developed independently (Forman & McPhail, 1993).

The two areas in which elementary school-aged students' capacities for working together are most likely to evidence change include: (a) The ability to talk about their roles and (b) the ability to focus on a joint or group goal,

---

second part of the Jigsaw do not have access to the materials that students in other groups had for the first part. They must depend on the student who is the expert for learning about that specific part of that task.

In TGT, the teacher first presents the lesson, typically in a lecture format such as that described in the case study. For the purposes of this example, the topic of the lecture will be characteristics of dinosaurs during the Jurassic Period. Following the lecture, teams of 4 to 5 students are organized to represent a cross-section of the class. Students are given two worksheets to fill out—necessitating that they work together—based on information from the lecture. This team study period also prepares them for the tournament. Students from the teams are each assigned to a tournament table where their tournament partners are people who are matched to them in ability. The tournament consists of a rehearsal of information presented in the lecture and on the worksheet used for team study; it often takes the form of a ditto sheet of numbered questions and a stack of cards with numbers.

rather than their own contribution to the project (cf. Azmitia, 1996; Azmitia & Montgomery, 1993). Interestingly, it is these changes that are critical to the success of collaborative learning as a type of flexible grouping, and more recent efforts to create collective communities of learners.

Presumably, the ability to collaborate on a task is also dependent on how open or closed (how accessible) the task is for the particular students, their questions and connections to it, and the way in which the teacher facilitates their meaning-making through it (see Cobb, 1995; Krummheuer, 1995; Wood, 1995; Yackel, 1995).

Training for Group Work. It is not entirely the students who determine the success of peer tutoring (Fantuzzo, Polite, & Grayson, 1990), or, for that matter, any grouping practice. Use of grouping in the classroom is enhanced by teachers' efforts to help students develop responsibility for their own learning and a willingness to help their peers learn. This can be accomplished by: (a) Focusing on student learning, (b) fostering independence and interdependence, (c) emphasizing students' responsibility for their own learning, (d) using cooperative and self-directed student learning tasks, (e) giving clear directions, (f) encouraging self-directed learning strategies, and (g) involving students in peer tutoring (Miller, 1991b; see also Medway, 1991, for similar points regarding effective peer tutoring practice).

Hereford (1993) further specifies the importance of (a) frequently reassessing ability group assignments, (b) varying instructional levels and pace, (c) assigning groups based on demonstrated needs and abilities, (d) grouping students for specific subjects, and (e) using ability groups to teach specific skills (see also Sanacore, 1990).

Teachers, however, are not usually trained to set up, facilitate, or assess multi-age grouping practices, cooperative grouping, peer tutoring, and so on in their classrooms (see Jensen & Green, 1993; Miller, 1991a; Webb & Palincsar, 1996). For group work to function effectively, students cannot simply be assigned to groups, and teachers cannot be assumed to use a book in order to figure out how to plan group work that takes into consideration: (a) the skills to be taught, including those necessary for working together in a group; (b) the topic to be covered; and (c) the needs of the students (Lyman, 1991; Palincsar & Klenk, 1991).

As Webb and Palincsar (1996) point out, in many schools and classrooms, students have had little opportunity to develop the skills needed to work effectively with others. Embedded in cooperative grouping tasks such as the Jigsaw and TGT are specific role and goal prescriptions for each student. The advantage of explicit roles and goals in these tasks is that both teachers and students know what is expected of them during this kind of group work. For similar reasons, perhaps, reciprocal questioning has been found to be more effective for learning than more open group discussions, presumably because students need to learn how to question or be given permission to do so—that is, they need to be given a role—and teachers need to know how to pose the question (Fantuzzo, Riggio, Connelly, & Dimeff, 1989; King, 1989a, 1989b, 1990).

Some projects that have been developed to prepare students (and teachers) for group work have focused on developing norms for group participation and providing students with instruction. Kagan (1992) developed specific tasks to enable students to develop and practice the skills necessary to work with and trust each other in small groups. These include (a) listening, (b) turn taking, (c) helping, (d) resolving differences, (e) appreciating, (f) encouraging, (g) staying on task, and (h) asking for help. Team-building and prosocial development activities have also been used to develop spontaneous prosocial behaviors (Solomon, Watson, Schaps, Battistich, & Solomon, 1990) and change in students' ascribed status expectations for peers (Cohen, Lotan, & Catanzarite, 1990). Other projects have more or less explicitly embedded the process of learning to work together in the process of working on shared tasks. An explicit example is the mathematics learning undertaken in the Teaching Experiment Classroom (Cobb, Wood, & Yackel, 1993). In this type of small group work, the teacher role involves intervening to help the students develop productive relationships (Cobb, 1995; Wood & Yackel, 1990). In this classroom, there was explicit discussion of the importance of persistence, explanation of solutions, listening and making sense, and discussion of solutions when conflict arose (Cobb, 1995). Conflict in particular was found to be an important indicator of students' emerging understanding (Cobb, 1995; Krummheuer, 1995).

Summary of Research and Reports on Grouping

Although the different studies and reports represent a range of foci and grouping types, there is general support for the notion that mixed and flexible grouping can contribute positively to students' academic, social, and emotional development. There is also substantial support for adjusting instruction in relation to the particular groupings of students being taught.

Although the literature is not conclusive about whether there are optimal methods for assigning students to groups, it does appear that paired or smaller groupings of 3 to 4 students are optimal. Flexible grouping does appear to provide opportunities for students to consolidate their understanding of material through discussion and focused work with others. Findings from studies of cross-age tutoring are the most cohesive on this point. This type of grouping appears to ensure clear academic, social, and emotional gains for both tutor and tutee, presumably because the particular roles and goals in this type of grouping are clear. Findings from this literature indicate that even students who may not feel competent in more traditional instructional formats respond positively to being asked to be responsible for what they know, and to having the opportunity to use and build on what they know in their work with one another.

Despite a substantial literature on grouping in classrooms, there appears to be a consensus that students need to learn how to work together in groups and most teachers need both training and support if they are to implement, facilitate, or assess grouping in the classes they teach.

Comment

What does this overview contribute to our thinking about instructional formats depicted in the two Jurassic Period case formats? Although we are not provided with specific information about the students being taught in the case formats described for teaching about what makes the Jurassic Period the Jurassic Period, we know that the range of differences among them is not extreme. By second grade, students with severe learning difficulties typically are no longer mainstreamed (part of the regular classroom). Further, we know that if the lecture format described a classroom of gifted students, these students might learn as effectively and would perhaps cover more content than those in a more interactive class. We also know that it might be particularly important to attend to their feelings about themselves relative to the others in their class *and* as students of the content being covered.

The same gifted students, if taught using the approach described in the interactive format, would probably have a more highly developed conceptual understanding of the material covered, greater comfort with themselves as peer collaborators, and an increased sense of control in relation to their contributions to the classroom knowledge base. They would feel secure in their knowledge and be in a position to generate questions, having worked on learning to do this together with the others in their class.

If the students are average or low-ability students, on the other hand, it might be expected that they would learn less in the lecture format than in the interactive format, since the requirements for listening could present difficulties for them. Taught through an interactive format, however, the students would help to generate the questions on which they would be focused, and would therefore have more ready access to the material to be learned. This in turn would enable them to move on to consolidate their understanding of the topics and skills to be mastered.

In addition to the issues of topic coverage and skill development, however, the interactive format offers all students experience with different types of flexible grouping. Such experience encourages them to individually and collectively develop a coherent narrative about the topic as they work to express their ideas and questions about the material on which they are working. It allows them to work with others who have a similar level of familiarity with the material being introduced, but who bring different sets of experience to their work with it. Finally, the interactive format provides students with a basis for belonging to and being part of a community of learners.

What does the topic of grouping contribute more generally to how we think about student learning and its implications for instruction? Technically, all classrooms are mixed-age classrooms, since students in single-age classes often range in age by as much as two years. In addition, students in all classrooms vary in their levels of experience and competence with the material being taught (cf. Gardner, 1983; Sternberg, 1996), perhaps even more so in tracked or ability-based grouping, since students are typically gifted in particular domains (cf. Feldman, 1980; Meeker, 1976). As Goodlad and Anderson (1963) point out, grouping children on the basis of a single criterion does not produce a homogeneous group. It appears, however, that unless classes are labeled "mixed," or are organized for an interactive format, teachers perceive themselves as working with groups of students who are similar, using methods designed to distinguish between those who complete the assigned tasks and those who have difficulty.

In addition to highlighting student variation for teachers, mixed grouping affords opportunities for student learning not available in homogeneous grouping—not available in classes where instruction is premised on homogeneity. Working in flexible groups, for example, enables students to (a) access prior knowledge because they can pool their understanding in order to complete a task; (b) engage in discussions leading to more sophisticated learning than they could accomplish independently in a relatively short amount of time; (c) share their interest or connection to the materials being covered, which in turn provides a scaffold to the materials for other students; and (d) have peer models for strategies necessary to task completion.

Grouping further influences the process of students' work on tasks because in groups, students (a) engage a range of perspectives on a topic that provides the basis for their emerging understanding of that concept, and (b) are provided with the incremental scaffolding and reworking of concepts (the practice) necessary for conceptual development. Finally, grouping influences the product of student work: Students not only accomplish the assigned tasks, but their frame of reference and strategies for working with and using the concepts they have been studying are enriched—especially if instruction about and reflection on the process of their work occurs.

Students do need to learn how to work in groups, however. Based on the literature presented, there are at least three ways to undertake this process: (a) adjustment of goals and roles in the task while working on subject matter, (b) focus on learning to work in groups as the subject matter, or (c) immersion in classroom-based problem solving. Presumably each of these approaches might be effective, especially if coupled with explicit information about student goals and teacher facilitation of goals, including student reflection (cf. Pressley et al., 1989). The relative merits of teaching a particular group of students through one method or another can only be decided based on information about their strengths and needs when involved in group work and the learning to be accomplished (and what the teacher is in a position to try).

Tasks can be assigned to provide for multiple points of access and differences among students. (See Cohen, 1988 for a useful discussion.) Basic information about how open or closed a task is and its effects on the ways in which students access, process, and are then able to complete the tasks they are assigned appears to be central to understanding how group work (or any other kind of instruction) might be adjusted and sequenced to meet students' strengths and needs.

It is also clear that teachers need to have more knowledge about and support for learning how grouping can be used in the classroom. In addition, they may need to know more about how students learn so as to be able to use grouping in the classroom effectively to meet their students' needs (cf. Rings & Sheets, 1991).

What might we still want to know about grouping based on developmental theory and research? Although much of the work focuses on students in elementary school, the literature reviewed informs the use of grouping with students at the preschool level through high school. Students have been studied across different content areas and schools, as subjects in basic research and as students in whose class grouping of some type was being practiced. We generally do not know anything about their (or their teachers') prior experience with grouping or their particular abilities to handle the content and skills of the grouping in which they are involved. This is complicated because the opportunities for richer learning afforded by group work are conflated with the need to work with students on their learning in small groups. Without information about what experience with group work the students and the teacher being studied have, it is difficult to know where they fit in the continuum of learning to use group work. Furthermore, we have not explicitly addressed the roles of task accessibility and its effect on group process in this literature.

At this time, there is work that suggests that grouping is an effective instructional technique, that during group work, students develop the skills to assume and share responsibility for problem solving, and that with age (or perhaps experience?) students are increasingly able to focus on joint or group goals. Flexible grouping, however, also affords possibilities for the development of misconceptions (cf. Forman & McPhail, 1993; Levin & Druyan, 1993) and the breakdown of students' abilities to work together (Azmitia, 1996). We know very little about the links between open-ended learning experiences, such as those afforded by group work, the development of misconception or faulty information about either content being covered or skills being learned, and the subject matter.

Presumably, there are more and less opportune times to involve students in flexible groups as a function of their understanding of the material to be covered, their readiness to work together, and/or the structure of the task. Are these links different if there is a reward or a demand structure because the teacher has determined the task to be accomplished instead of the student helping to determine the task? At present, information about what works appears dependent on teacher intuition. Can we assume that there are increasingly complex demands represented by open-ended or less structured sets of tasks, and that these can be sequenced in order to facilitate the development of students' abilities to work together in groups (e.g., moving from two-person buzz groups to small groups of three or four for a discrete task, moving back to the large group to reflect on work carried out in groups, and so on)? Or is it the case that if we want students to be problem solvers, it is more advantageous to immerse them in open-ended tasks? Certainly, for many students open-ended tasks are likely to be discrepant relative to their expectations about learning. Possibly because of this, they might just pique their curiosity (cf. Berlyne, 1960). Brown and Campione (1994) and the Cognition and Technology Group at Vanderbilt (Hickey, Moore, & Pellegrino, in press) report high levels of engagement by students who otherwise might be expected to resist alternative formats for learning (cf.

D'Amato, 1996). For students who have not been able to connect to more traditional forms of learning, it is tasks such as these that provide enough in the way of support or scaffolding to enable them to begin taking responsibility for themselves as learners (Slavin, 1990).

There is little research that documents the processes and concepts students and their teachers need to engage in order to learn from and use groups effectively in the classroom, much less the way in which these are mediated by the accessibility of the task for students or students' abilities to process these tasks effectively. Furthermore, what do teachers (and students and parents) need to know or see in order to be willing to do the problem solving involved in learning to work with and adjust grouping tasks in their classrooms? Documentation of change across time in students' abilities to engage particular types of group work in subject areas could be quite useful for teachers who have a hard time imagining their own students ever being able to handle such challenges. As Rosenshine and Meister (1994) comment in their review of the research on reciprocal teaching, one of the limitations of reciprocal teaching is that little attention is given to issues of implementation. (The interested reader is encouraged to look at Marks et al.'s, 1993, efforts to document adaptations of reciprocal teaching in classrooms.) Not only do teachers need clarity about these areas, but researchers, too, need to understand the contextual issues that affect the variables to which they address themselves (see Damon, 1997), since better documentation of implementation facilitates replication and extension of findings.

Information about how students perceive the use of group work in their classes, and how this perception shifts with increased experience in groups, may also be useful for teachers concerned about when and how to incorporate group work into their classes. Furthermore, given that groupings such as Jigsaw and TGT can function to facilitate students' abilities to break through stereotypes and learn to develop the ability to work with others on tasks (cf. Aronson et al., 1978; Slavin, 1983), it would be useful to teachers to know more about the implications of assigning friends—or nonfriends—to work together during subject-area learning, and how task access variables would mediate this.

Studies providing teachers with a clear understanding of the primary task elements to which they might pay attention while planning student work in groups (and as students work in groups) would also be quite useful. These could provide a basis for understanding how to build into instruction periods of reflection about both the topics being addressed and group process. They could also provide a basis for thinking about how to monitor students' efforts in the present in order to adjust and sequence subsequent tasks.

Finally, what does it look like as students learn to take responsibility for their own learning in group work? Do age, level of expertise in subject matter, and different school cultures affect the ways in which they learn to adjust the roles they assume in group work and their ability to engage in joint goal setting? Are students' abilities to assume responsibility for themselves as learners mediated by whether they help to set tasks for themselves or need to meet the demands of a task that is set for them?

ISSUES FROM AND FOR PRACTICE

The Language of Instruction

What does the literature overviewed provide us in the way of answers to the questions from practice posed at the outset of the chapter? (Is it always bad to give students a task they cannot complete? What do I do with the four kids who just can't keep up with the work? Why don't students learn better when I've given them something interesting to read? How do I get my students to discuss something? Should students keep the same partners for all of their lab periods? Why aren't my students learning anything when they do small group work?)

First, the literature suggests that there is not one answer to such educational questions. There are many ways to conduct a lecture or run a discussion, and except for the literature on cross-age tutoring, studies of student achievement in lectures, discussions, questioning, and grouping all reflect mixed findings. Second, the literature suggests that regardless of type (gifted, average, or atypical), all students benefit when instruction is adjusted. Furthermore, students may achieve more and feel better about themselves in some settings than in others; students can learn to work with new instructional formats; they profit from having prior knowledge used as a basis for their learning in any format; they may need to be helped to develop strategies if achievement is a goal; and the way in which the teacher asks questions, engages students in discussion, uses computers, and so on affects the way in which the students do each of these things. Finally, the findings suggest that teachers are likely to need help thinking about how to use lectures, discussions, questioning, and grouping in their classrooms.

More specifically, it seems that teachers may need to recognize that the questions they pose about classroom practice are subjects for further discussion, not discrete answers. Discrete answers overlook the issue of who students are (what they need as learners) and whether they know how to implement the answer. Based on this overview, it also appears that teachers need to identify possible answers to their questions through conversation with others, use of self-questions, or in work with text, and so on.

The literature provides information basic to beginning to answer teachers' questions—here, for example, this includes the information that students benefit from having prior knowledge, reflection (metacognition), and instruction about strategies embedded or built into subject matter on which they are working. The questions posed above, however, belong to the teachers. Teachers know about their context of instruction and their students, and this information is not in the literature. Teachers also are the ones who make decisions about both the academic goals (i.e., learning to summarize, describing what a problem asks in their own words) and the behavioral goals (i.e., staying on task, learning to listen) for the students in their classes. Given that teachers have the information necessary to begin working on or gathering resources for answering the questions they pose, they may need to know that they can answer them. Some teachers (just like some students), may need to recognize first that they have questions about teaching (as opposed to simply having information about what to do). Some teachers (like some students), may need to learn how to locate and develop strategies in order to make use of resources. The literature represents a set of resources, as does further education, some in-service training, and so on. In order for teaching to reflect findings from research in developmental psychology, however, teachers, like their students, may need a way to connect their questions to the possibilities inherent in the developmental literature.

In order for these connections to be developed, it appears to be a necessary condition that teachers contextualize their questions—that they anchor them in their own classrooms, with their own students, within the particular content area they are teaching. This is the basis of "action research" (cf. Oja & Smulyan, 1989), a method of research in which teachers pose questions, that, together with researchers, are then studied in their own classrooms.

From this perspective, teaching can be conceptualized as an ongoing (developmental) process of collecting and developing resources that permit the fine-tuning of content knowledge and skills for working with students (see Lieberman, 1995; Little, 1990). When combined with information from the research literature and reports about others' practice, action research provides a basis for serious consideration of questions from practice.

There is, however, another set of considerations. While at one level of analysis, the literature on instruction largely corroborates points outlined in the synthesis of the developmental work (markers of transition and qualitative changes in understanding, such as the importance of students posing and answering their own questions, the benefits of building on prior knowledge in the organization of tasks, involving students in reflecting on their understanding about their own learning as a means for calling their attention to the problem under consideration and the strategies they are using), it also is more focused on student achievement and the need to train teachers about using tasks than on how students learn. Therefore, terms such as task access, task process, prior knowledge, metacognition, and students are all somewhat differently construed.

Discussion of task access in the literature on instruction is largely focused on the means for getting students to complete tasks, or motivating them to engage in tasks, rather than on individual (or group-based) variability in the way in which they go about working on tasks—identifying the problem under examination (not assuming that because it has been stated or presented that it is therefore understood), considering links between the problem and what they have as information about it, considering resources available for working with the problem, and so on. In fact, it appears that, with the exception of the literature on questioning and classroom-based problem solving, the notion of student access to a task is fused with that of student work on a task. As a result, distinct indices of student processing, such as use of strategies, are more likely to be linked to the demands of the task than to differences among students in their ability to use them, or changes in the way they are used. This means, for example, that the literature on instruction emphasizes the nature of the task, the method of instruction, and the need to embed strategies in the task, rather than focusing on whether students are already employing some strategies, which ones, and perhaps how they understand their use.

Similarly, while the literature on instruction indicates convergence on the importance of metacognition and strategy training as contributors to student learning, this often takes the form of describing the importance of, say, discourse or summaries for student achievement. The role of reflection in bringing the student to the point of being able to identify the problem and learn strategies for working is therefore often subsumed in the focus on achievement. In fact, if achievement is the goal, then assisting students to be able to describe the problems with which they are working and developing their abilities to work with them—including use of discourse and/or strategies for summarizing—may actually mean that students can achieve.

The literature overviewed also attests to the importance of providing opportunities for students to work together on learning. Typically, however, students' connections with other students as motivators or methods for engaging students in tasks are emphasized, rather than the role of the small group in enabling students to consolidate their understanding through working with others who are endeavoring to develop a language of strategy use, representing information in different formats, and the practice involved in reworking materials so that they become their own (task process).

Furthermore, little current attention is being given to the notion of open and closed tasks—tasks that afford multiple opportunities for students to access them, as opposed to tasks that do not. It appears that if open tasks such as those used in classroom-based problem solving (Bereiter & Scardamalia, 1992; Brown & Campione, 1994; Cobb et al., 1995; Cognition and Technology Group at Vanderbilt, in press) heighten task accessibility for students, the difficulty of accessing more closed tasks may well account for the mixed results that characterize student performance on those tasks. In fact, the only literature that does not report mixed results is that on cross-age tutoring. In cross-age tutoring, presumably, the tutor is naturally inclined to adjust the task in the course of working with his or her tutee even if he or she is not reflectively aware of such adjustment.

Students' needs are also described in the literature on instruction in terms of a characteristic of disaffected students, of students in the first year of a subject, and so on, rather than being based in more particularized understandings and misconceptions of an individual or a specific class of students. There is another whole literature in education that specifically focuses on individualization. This literature is typically the province of special educators. As such, it may not be surprising that where individualized needs of students are addressed, these are primarily those of atypical learners or special-needs students. Even the literature on individualization, however, focuses on the needs of students by type, rather than on particular groups of students in particular classrooms.

There is good reason to focus on the level of the task and on types of students rather than the level of the student or students in a particular classroom. Discussion at the level of the task is expedient: the parameters of the task can be specified and the requisite procedures itemized. On the other hand, the literature on instruction does consistently address teachers' needs to be trained to use each of the types of instruction overviewed, suggesting that limiting the discussion of tasks and students to the level of the generic classroom is not sufficient for changed practice.

The generic classroom does not provide information specific to how instruction needs to be adjusted, such as what students already know, what they still need to understand about the skills, discourse-knowledge, and themselves as learners of the subject—and then in relation to this information: what materials to select for the classroom; what tasks to choose and how they might be organized and reorganized for use in a particular classroom setting; selection of questioning; and choice of responses to a range of differences in classroom composition (SES, atypicality, gender, etc.).

Based on the literature overviewed, however, it does not appear that there is any compelling reason for educators to ask questions about these topics or to seek out answers from research. The process of adjusting instruction to meet strengths and needs of particular students is not part of the language with which they or their mentors typically work. In fact, many of the assignments given to education students, such as designing lesson plans or curriculum projects, emphasize the subject matter and tasks employed and de-emphasize the role of the student(s) as influencing how, why, and when particular materials and tasks might be employed.

Developmental Psychology and Practice

It might be useful to consider how the working knowledge of developmental psychologists described at the outset of this chapter maps onto the literature reviewed. This working knowledge has been described as including the following:

1. Each student's knowledge or understanding is individually constructed in relation to the others (i.e., the teacher, other students) and objects (i.e., texts, computer software, classroom rituals, assigned tasks) in the environment;
2. The process of apprehending or perceiving something (i.e., a concept) involves readiness in terms of attentional capacity, short-term memory, prior knowledge or experience, individual interest, and the particular affordances of or actions suggested by, the task including how situated within a particular context the learning is;
3. What the individual attends to influences what he or she represents to him- or herself; and
4. What individuals represent to themselves in turn affects the particular action or sets of actions in which they engage or are ready to engage.

Based on the literature overviewed, it appears that educators are most familiar with the terms raised in (2), for example, student attention, prior knowledge, and interest. Given that the literature is largely focused on achievement of types of students and task access is yoked to the process of working on tasks, it is also understandable why teachers might be inclined to simply think about these as terms to describe why students have difficulty, rather than as a call for action.

It would be ideal if psychological distance or some other construct could help us to clearly identify a student's current level of understanding about a given topic with reference to a next step within a well-understood (by the teacher) set of not necessarily linearly related conceptual attainments, which, in turn, would lead to flexible understanding of a given topic. By definition, however, psychological distance cannot do this for the teacher or the researcher, nor can another construct. What the construct of psychological distance can do is to provide a guide for parameters that need to be considered if the goal is to facilitate change. For change in students' learning, these parameters include assessing what is known and what needs to be known in terms of the possible action or set of actions or distancing necessary to close the gap between them.

Thus, for example, in long-term (i.e., 3 weeks) lesson planning, a teacher working within the parameters set by the construct of psychological distance might identify the topic to be covered and take stock of the students with whom he or she is working in terms of (a) their strengths and needs behaviorally (i.e., listening to other students, focusing on the task assigned, working with others in small groups) and (b) their strengths and needs academically (i.e., ability to explain what the problem posed is asking, comparing and contrasting perspectives, using resources other than the teacher when they have questions). Following this, the teacher would be in a position to target two or three academic and behavioral needs on which to focus, and could chart the sequence of small steps or adjustments necessary to enable the students to learn the topic including its connections to the subject area as a whole, in turn, developing their skills as learners *and* as students of the subject area.[21]

[21] It might be helpful to the reader to know that this is an assignment that I regularly give to student teachers during the fourth week of their practice-teaching experience. It typically provides them with enough of a scaffold to move from being dependent on their cooperating teacher and supervisor to assuming responsibility for the class in consultation with these people. I also have used this task as an opening exercise for workshops with teachers. Similar to a self-question, it grounds subsequent discussion in their situation, strengths, and needs.

The teacher who employs psychological distance as a tool for thinking about changed action imposes his or her understanding of learning on its parameters. It is this teacher who has—or does not have—the content knowledge necessary to make informed decisions about where a student's knowledge falls along the continuum of information that is known. It is also this person who has—or does not have—an understanding of how students learn and the implications of this information for how they might most effectively be taught.

Herein, then, are at least two of the tensions that emerge in considering the implications of developmental psychology for practice. First, the teacher cannot be overlooked in the effort to instruct students. Second, it is neither practical nor developmentally appropriate to overspecify what teachers *should* do in working with students.

The Role of the Teacher

Based on the working knowledge about student development and the overview of the research on instruction, it follows that learning can be enhanced by tasks that are sequenced so that students will further develop their understanding of the content to be learned by being led to re-represent it to themselves. In school, these experiences are typically afforded by texts, other students, and the teacher.

It is usually the teacher who selects texts and juxtaposes them with other resources, and it is the teacher who makes decisions about the tasks used in teaching and the use of grouping within the classroom. Furthermore, it is the teacher who sets the context for and models the use of questioning, reflection, and strategy use. Unfortunately, as a host of authors have pointed out (cf. Cuban, 1984; Gregg, 1995; Sirotnik, 1983), the model that many teachers represent does not map onto working knowledge about how students learn or what is understood about instruction. As Sirotnik (1983) observes, "'The modus operandi' of the typical classroom is still didactics, practice, and little else" (p. 17).

Thus, at the same time that research-driven practice, teacher education, and inservice programs are in place, there is still a gulf between practice and what Brown and Campione (1994) describe as the "first principles of learning": Learning that (a) is active; (b) includes metacognition; (c) acknowledges multiple zones of proximal development; (d) is based in dialogue (shared discourse, negotiated meaning, seeding conversations, legitimizing difference); (e) engenders a community of practice; and (f) addresses content that is contextualized and situated. What Brown and Campione have achieved is the specification of developmentally appropriate endpoints—the basis for what Cohen (1989) has described as "adventurous teaching."

These principles echo findings reported in the literature. They build on students' attention to the task, their need to represent tasks to themselves, and the benefits of a context for learning that facilitates opportunities for active work on reconstructing what has been understood. The complication is that even adventurous teachers can be challenged when they try to figure out how to take these words and work with them in the classroom (Wilson, Miller, & Yerkes, 1993).

As suggested earlier, one reason for this may be that developmental psychologists, even those sincerely committed to educational practice, only appear to speak the same language as educators. The idea of a group of second graders adjusting a task for themselves would be likely to sound like mayhem, particularly if you did not have models with which to work or the support to begin working on restructuring the way in which you have been teaching. It would sound like mayhem if you did not think in terms of individual students, but instead about students in general, and when you thought about students generally you thought about generic types of students, and when you thought about tasks you thought about closed tasks because they were the types of tasks you assigned and understood yourself to be expected to assign.

We need to consider seriously and without judgment what is understood about how students learn and the implications of this understanding for how they should be taught. What does the person who considers classroom-based problem solving to be the equivalent of mayhem understand about it? (How does he or she identify the problem?) This is where a discussion of first principles for practice needs to begin. Given this information, and a sense of the literature or first principles that can be distilled from the literature, it becomes possible to think about how to begin to coordinate educators' and researchers' understanding of possibilities for practice.

Another complication is that there is a history of gifted researchers from leading universities who have described the problems of education largely in terms of curriculum.

> They assumed that students should learn largely on their own as they "discovered" ideas, "did" mathematics, "messed about in science," and the like. But these eminent professors knew as little of schools . . . as they imagined most teachers knew about science. . . . They were particularly ignorant of how classroom teachers might apprehend and use novel materials. As it turned out, few teachers gave students much chance to independently use the new curricula. Hence when teachers used the materials, they did so in ways that made sense to them. Since few knew much of the new science, that meant that their use of the curricula typically was guided both by the inherited knowledge and pedagogy that reformers wanted to circumvent and by teachers' struggles with problems that reformers had never considered, like classroom management and local politics. The curriculum reformers' passion for active learning led them to overestimate the materials' independent power, and their ignorance about schools and teaching led them to underestimate teachers' influence on the use of the materials. (Cohen & Barnes, 1993, p. 215)

Based on present research findings, it is no longer appropriate to assume that students will independently generate the questions and strategies that enable them to learn. Instead, it is recognized that there is a need to focus on students' abilities to connect to curricula and the skills the student needs to develop in order to have access to tasks. Furthermore, teachers need to adjust instruction accordingly, for purposes of management as well as local understanding. This may, of course, involve recognizing that the students are independently generating questions and strategies. It may involve recognizing that students are doing this some of the time and with support might be able to do so more of the time (i.e., How did you make that decision? Will you walk me through your thinking here? I'd like to know what you are doing. How did you think about that? What is the connection between [the topics and skills previously covered, a self-question, etc.] and your efforts here?). Finally, it may necessitate more direct instruction in order to prepare the students to begin assuming responsibility for making their own connections to the topics they are to learn.

Using a task (or a curriculum) exactly as it is described is a first approximation to working with students on learning. If its premises are not understood, it can also be a little like an algorithm. Adjusting instruction involves understanding the intentions of the curriculum design and/or instructional practice, recognizing that questions to be posed may need to be tailored to the class in which they are being used, the length of time used to carry through on a task may need to be adjusted and the task itself broken into smaller units at least initially, the mode of presenting the tasks to the students may need to include alternative and repeated formats given the needs of the students, and so on.

The task that works effectively for one group of students may not work for the next; instruction that was effective at the beginning of the year is not necessarily going to work at the end of the year (Good & Stipek, 1983). The teacher needs to assume responsibility (or be allowed to assume responsibility) for how the tasks in his or her class are adjusted and sequenced. The teacher also needs to feel comfortable about changing his or her mind and experimenting—two qualities that run counter to an expectation that teachers know what they are doing and have the correct answers. As Charney (1997) points out, it is:

> a common misconception that good teachers do *not* have problems . . . the issue is not how to make teaching problem-free, but how to dignify and honor the problem-solving process that is inherent to good teaching. We must pay attention to the questions, the evidence, and the sources that yield our best results and find the time to share with our colleagues the realities of our classroom so we can solve problems together. (p. 1)

Practice should look quite different from one classroom to the next (Brown & Campione, 1994). Encouraging teachers to adjust tasks, however, also means that the researcher needs to sacrifice authority over instructional practice as well as traditional expectations for experimental control.

The Role of Specification

Tasks that enable teachers to use research in practice clearly need to be specified and disseminated. It is critical, however, that they neither be overspecified nor understood as such—the teacher needs to work with his or her students, just as the students need to work with the content about which they are learning. Attempting to teacher-proof tasks (design curricula that works for the students even if the teacher does not understand it) reflects short-sightedness on the part of researchers and has been the downfall of many curriculum efforts (cf. Cohen & Barnes, 1993; Popkewitz, Tabachnick, & Wehlage, 1982; Sarason, 1982).

There is far too much variance in the study of social science to be able to claim that all conditions for learning are equal (Cronbach & Snow, 1977) or, conversely, that an algorithm about instruction will apply to all settings. The dictums of effective research according to Smith (1997), and thus the expectations of effective practice—that findings be generalizable or practice be appropriate for all students, that tasks minimize variability or be executed in particular ways, and that attention be focused on optimal cases or particular indices rather than others—are no longer completely tenable. Instead, as described by the tetrahedral model, the process of learning appears to be most accurately characterized as multidimensional. This lens permits theory building that addresses the "real performances and real intelligences" of students without dismissing data (Smith, 1997; see also Smith & Thelen, 1993). It involves working with patterns of individual variation in learning and study of the organization and transitions of these patterns over time.

Interestingly enough, however, research on individual differences or individual variation has met a relatively quick demise each time it has surfaced in the literature. The major reason for this appears to be the overwhelming numbers of interactions that have been perceived to need documentation when individual differences are studied (cf. Cronbach & Snow, 1977). This perception is logically consistent with two principles that have dominated thinking about learning and instruction—that there is one way to complete tasks, and that there is a discrete set of approaches for working with students.

At present, it is clear that there are multiple approaches to completing tasks and a number of ways of facilitating student learning. Tracking specific interactions is far less useful than identifying patterns of individual variation, except in the case of instances that arise in a particular classroom.

In practice, where there are four or so students in a classroom who are having real difficulty working with a task, and, as a result, are acting out and disturbing others, it makes a significant difference to the functioning of the classroom if the teacher can figure out what these students already understand and what they still need to understand with respect to their understanding of concepts, skill development, and their sense of themselves as learners. In such cases, the focus is specifically directed to the individual or the group of individuals who are having difficulty and their strengths and needs in the particular situation. It should be noted that such adjustments to classroom instruction typically serve to enhance the learning of other students as well as that of the targeted students, since they involve more focused development of skills, and so on. Furthermore, this approach has also proven to be an effective management technique for teachers. Students want to be able to do the tasks assigned in the classroom; however, they need to be able to connect to them in order to do so.

Somewhat similarly, Comer, Haynes, and Joyner (1996) report that as they began collaboration on the School Development Program in the 1970s, they focused the attention of all parties involved on students and their need for interactions that would provide a predictable and caring environment for each of them. They found that once attention was focused on each student's learning, there was no longer any expectation that students would all learn in the same way or that there would be one way to teach them. It appears that focusing on individual students provides a necessary lens for adjusting instruction to meet their strengths and needs.

Commenting on the same program, Gillette and Kranyik (1996) observe that "For an individual teacher and for a school, taking development seriously is a major cultural transformation" (p. 150). They continue to suggest that such work of necessity begins with an appreciation that all students can learn—information that is basic to the working knowledge of developmental psychologists, but which is not typical of most school cultures where the focus is on performance, and where students are given and take on labels like "intelligent," "underachiever," or "creative."

In fact, there has been a recent surge of educator interest in "multiple intelligences" (Gardner, 1983)—that is, recognition that students (and people generally) have a range of strengths and weaknesses, for example, linguistic, personal, logico-deductive, bodily-kinesthetic, and so on. This theory has called educators' attention to issues of difference and the possibility that tasks and assessment practices need to be more broadly defined than they once were (Williams et al., 1996).[22]

For practitioners, attention to patterns of individual variation might be usefully understood as requiring attention to particular individuals (or groups of individuals) in their particular classroom rather than classification of students as types. This focus enables teachers to act in response to specific information on the basis of which they are in a position to effect change.

For the researcher, patterns of individual variation are most usefully described in terms of within-individual functioning rather than particular individuals. At this more general level, the researcher is in a position to provide teachers with basic information about potential sources of within-student difference as this affects task access and process (i.e., boys are more likely to use visualization as a strategy for recall on passages that are about topics of interest than on passages about topics for which they have a noninterest, whereas girls are more likely to use visualization as a strategy for recall on passages that are about topics of noninterest to them than on passages about topics for which they have an interest [Renninger & Stavis, 1995]). The teacher can infer implications from this work for practice. It can provide the basis for experimenting with task adjustment. This type of research also suggests another lens for thinking about, say, student strategy use: information about the particular strategies that are used by students at this age on this kind of task, evidence that there is not one effective strategy for all students, and so on. Such information contributes to the repertoire of knowledge that teachers have about students as learners generally and about strategy use more specifically. It can also contribute to the kind of language they have available for describing student learning—a language, that includes "likelihood," consideration of contextualized information, gender, and so on.

Information from research only specifies *general* patterns, however. The teacher still needs to adjust and sequence instruction for his or her class, and is in a position to do so, in this case, with an enhanced sense of the possibilities for students' use of strategy and aspects of task access. This is no small job. It involves recognizing that not all tasks will be as useful for some students as for others, that there will be a wide range of approaches to tasks even when a task itself is closed, and that there are always other variables to be considered. With continued research efforts to detail the patterns of within-student variation for particular types of problem solving across grade levels and school culture, teachers will have available an increasingly articulated repertoire of information about possibilities for student learning and implications for instruction.

The researchers' findings almost always speak only to the general case. It is the teachers who remain ultimately responsible for working with the particular students assigned to their class(es) that year. The teachers are the ones with information about possibilities in terms of individual (or particular group) functioning and about principles for learning and, as such, are in a position to optimize student learning, including how students feel about themselves as learners of a discipline.

Let us return briefly to the question posed at the beginning of the chapter about whether small group work is necessarily better than lecturing. It should be obvious by now that if the concern involves student learning, this question needs further clarification. For what purposes, for which groups of students, and given this information, how has small group work and lecturing been adjusted for use with the students? What instructional tasks does it precede and follow? Using small group work—or any other instructional task—as a benchmark of effective instruction has its

[22] One complication is that the theory of multiple intelligences has also been subject to assimilation and can be offered as an explanation for difference and lack of progress rather than as an impetus for adjusted or broadened curricula. One explanation for this may be that the concept of multiple intelligences is often overviewed for educators by others rather than read and processed by the educators themselves, meaning that educators are not put in a situation where they need to revise or reconstruct what they already know and consider the notion of multiple intelligences in relation to that.

limitations (see Good et al., 1990; Noddings, 1985, 1989). In order to answer the question, two additional pieces of information are necessary: How and why is the small group work and the lecturing being employed?

Coordinating Research and Practice

Not only do developmental psychologists and educators appear to have somewhat different languages for describing student learning, there are differences in the kinds of questions they pose and the kinds of answers each might expect. Furthermore, developmental psychologists and teachers typically have different concerns—studying and writing about student development versus working with students.

The four types of teacher groups that are seriously engaged in implementing current research on student learning in their practice include:

1. Those in dire straits who have become part of "teacher projects" because their schools have looked to these as a source of support (cf. Comer et al., 1996);
2. Those who are interested in curriculum development and see in the standards of their disciplines methods that could enhance their own teaching, or provide justification for what they have already been trying to use in their classrooms (cf. Wilson et al., 1993);
3. Those in teacher workshops and inservices who are learning how to ask questions, generate summaries, problem solve, and participate in small groups, just as their students might (cf. Baird & Northfield, 1992; Cognition and Technology Group at Vanderbilt, 1991; Palincsar & Klenk, 1991); and
4. Those who in working with a forum such as the World Wide Web or a networked group of teachers find samples of projects and discussions about teaching that, over time, provide enough support for them to see alternate possibilities and ask questions that lead to changed practice (cf. Renninger et al., 1997; Webb & Romberg, 1994).

These teachers have in common a sense that there are alternatives to present practice and real support for engaging in change—not in the form of a half-day inservice or the monthly visit of yet two other people from some project, but months and years of shared time working together, focused on a particular learning environment, and developing a common language and set of purposes for talking and working together. In this kind of coordination of research and practice, there is little emphasis on learning the terminology or facts of research and more emphasis on exploring alternative practices (the implications of the research). There also is little emphasis on demanding that all teachers do the same things on the same timeline. Some teachers have less active or even passive roles initially. They watch the project or effort unfold and elect to join in at some later time (sometimes as much as three years later, according to I. Mitchell, 1992).

Without support for attending to research on student learning, however, teachers may not be inclined to do so—partly because the language of instruction typically used by educators does not describe it as a process of adjusting tasks to meet particular strengths and needs of students. Most preservice (student) teachers do not take courses that address student learning and development for more than one or two class periods. What they are taught, furthermore, is typically filtered through the lens of the instructional literature. Issues of task access, if addressed, are specified in terms of types of students rather than the actual functioning of particular students and the range of patterns that such functioning can depict.

It is also likely that there is a range of misunderstanding about the respective and complementary roles of research on student learning and practice. Typically, teachers also have had little direct experience with research on student learning. They are not clear about the distinctions to be made between general patterns and particular instances in their efforts to apply research—in fact, the notion of research is frightening for many, and they generally do not think about the possibility of seeking implications for practice from research.

Regardless of the particular reason(s), it appears important that both researchers and teachers coordinate what they do know. Our understanding of student learning is currently at a point where findings from disparate foci (i.e., children's language, strategy use in mathematics, etc.) have begun to converge in their descriptions of students' access to and processing of tasks. Similarly, the literatures on instruction that have been overviewed suggest a need for teachers to consider approaches to working with students that are consistent with their prior knowledge, and involve opportunities to question and to work with the material they are presented. Furthermore, studies of performance have not yielded conclusive evidence. In fact, there is some suggestion across the literatures on instruction that tasks of all types are more effective if they are adjusted, and that *teachers need to learn how to do this.*

The coordination of research and practice could begin with a description of what the roles and goals of each include (cf. Slavin, 1983). It also probably needs to build on examinations of what is (Genishi, 1992b; Gillette & Kranyik, 1996; Jervis, 1996) and what is not exemplary. Finally, it needs to consider seriously what has not worked, as well as what has. For example, if one is going to start an afterschool tutoring project focused on homework for students in a housing project, it will be very helpful if previous attempts were recorded, enabling such an effort to build on the efforts of others even if they failed.

Furthermore, it appears likely that rather than thinking about teachers as being resistant to change, it might be more appropriate to appreciate that mandated change based on an understanding of student learning is not something to which teachers are likely to have *access*. Providing teachers with logical explanations about why change is useful is only a partial solution. Teachers really need to know what to *do:* this is how they were previously taught, and this is where coordination of a shared language about student learning and practice needs to begin (cf. Palincsar & Klenk, 1991).

One approach to coordinating research and practice involves collaboration of researchers and practitioners (cf. Bruer, 1993). For students, teachers, and researchers in such projects, it appears that the process of working collaboratively affords the possibility of new understanding—understanding that none could have developed independently (Cognition and Technology Group at Vanderbilt, 1996; Damon, 1997; Wilson et al., 1993). Such collaboration also requires an ongoing discussion about what is and is not working in the collaboration, and why (I. Mitchell, 1992).

Another approach to developing a shared language involves rethinking the way in which we disseminate our findings through both writing and teaching. We need to define terms and be clear about how we are using them. We need to provide examples. We need to accumulate a fund of shared knowledge. If we do not cast the problem being undertaken in language that can be understood, it will not be understood (cf. Genishi, 1992a).

Furthermore, links to practice need to be carefully developed. Our standard practice of including one paragraph at the beginning and/or the end of an article to specify the importance of findings for practice does not help the practitioner think about instruction. This convention requires too much work for anyone who does not speak the language of research and has no experience inferring the implications of research for practice.

Yet another approach to coordinating research and practice involves enabling and expecting teachers to be better prepared to value, seek, and accommodate research findings. Preservice teachers need more than a quick brush with and understanding of student development (Sigel, 1990) in order for it to provide the kind of basis from which they can be problem solvers and, in turn, model problem solving in their classrooms (Renninger, 1996). We need to recognize that our own teaching reflects and communicates our conceptions of how learning works. Using the assigned text as the basis of a lecture suggests something quite different to students than does asking them to pose self-questions at the outset of a lecture, and then at its conclusion, asking them to work on answering these questions with other people sitting nearby.

Finally, coordination of research and practice requires patience. The process of change is not swift if real change is to take place. Coordinating research and practice in developmental psychology and instruction, furthermore, involves a shift in both fields to acknowledge the importance of the learning of each student and teacher. For both researchers and teachers, this shift involves reconstructing working knowledge about what is currently known about how students and teachers learn and the implications of this for how students might be taught. It also means being prepared to acknowledge and revise current working knowledge based on what is learned from practitioners, as well as from subsequent research efforts. In this way, research in developmental psychology will not only come from practice, but it will be understood as essential to practice.

APPENDIX: A SECOND CASE IN TWO FORMATS

This appendix provides the reader with a second case in two formats. The topic, the Colonization of North America, is more mainstream than that of the Jurassic Period; however, like the lecture and interactive formats of that case, both formats described here are examples of instruction that would challenge students, albeit differently. Presenting a second case in two formats is intended to enable the interested reader to consider more fully yet another example of a lecture and an interactive format and the necessary characteristics of each.

Lecture Format

The organization of the course is chronological, starting with the European settlement of North America. Materials for the lecture include references to and overheads of original source materials such as Sewell's Diary, school primers, lists of materials shipped to the early settlers, and so on.

The teacher begins the class with a pretest to find out what the students know. The information from the test is then used in selecting materials for lectures on which the students take notes. The assignment for the first evening involves reading the first chapter in the text and summarizing it in one page. The homework assignment enables students to elaborate upon the information presented in class and requires them to read with enough comprehension to be able to produce a summary of the chapter. Students' summaries allow further consideration of what they have understood to date and what they still do not understand.

Interactive Format

The organization of the course is largely chronological; however, it begins with an introduction to history and the skills of the historian in the present day, then moves back in time to discuss the European settlement of North America. The first class starts with a brief overview of the course content, after which the teacher asks the students to say what they know about the early settlers, and to brainstorm about what history is. The teacher uses the information gleaned during the brainstorm to understand the level and breadth of the students' prior knowledge. This information is then used to inform selection of tasks, level of questioning, and so on for the first days of the course.

Materials for the course include original source materials such as Sewell's Diary, school primers, lists of materials shipped to the early settlers, and so on. Class work consists of short lectures interspersed with a variety of activities that permit students to explore the concepts central to U.S. history and the nature of questions asked by historians. Students keep weekly journals in which they reflect about an historian's questions. The teacher provides questions to help students reflect on such questions in their journals. After several weeks, these questions become increasingly open ended, and support for the students' reflections is no longer necessary.

The teacher starts the class by asking students to work with a person sitting beside them to make lists of all of the kinds of things an historian does. These are shared with the class and written on the board—the teacher decides which of these options to follow based on both the students' facility in generating the list of what they know and the extent of their abilities to listen to each other as different ideas are suggested. Following this, the teacher uses this information to review the students' job for the year: to sharpen their skills as historians as they study U.S. history.

Students then move right into talking about all of the things they know about U.S. history. Standing back from the board, the teacher asks how to organize this information; alternatively, the teacher can ask students to work in groups of three to develop categories for talking about all of the information on the board. Students share information and categories are written on the board. Students are then asked to write in what will be their journal for the class about what an historian does and to list the categories they consider to be the most useful avenues for furthering their understanding of U.S. history.

The assignment for the first evening involves listening to a news broadcast or finding an article in the newspaper that is an example of history in the making, and writing a summary of it to be shared with the class. This assignment provides a foundation for the next class, which focuses on source materials and perspectives, and it begins the process of anchoring the study of U.S. history in the present. It also permits the teacher to learn something about how students follow through on an assignment, their ability to express themselves, and whether they know what a summary is.

ACKNOWLEDGMENTS

I would like to acknowledge the many contributions my students, the teachers with whom I have worked, and my colleagues have made to my thinking about the links (and gaps) between the field of developmental psychology and instructional practice. Research support for this chapter was provided by the Swarthmore College Faculty Research Fund.

I would also like to acknowledge specifically the research assistance of Jane Ehrenfeld, Dana Lehman, Emily Smith, and Cecilia Tomori in the preparation of this chapter and the editorial assistance of Sarah Seastone in compiling it. Finally, I would like to express appreciation to Allen Black, John T. Bruer, Jane Ehrenfeld, Liza Ewen, Andreas Krapp, Wesley Shumar, and Irving E. Sigel for their thoughtful reviews of earlier drafts of this chapter.

REFERENCES

Abeasi, K., & Reigeluth, C. M. (1985). *Group discussion as an effective method of instruction* (IDD&E Working Paper No. 20). (ERIC Document Reproduction Service No. ED 289- 467)

Adyemi, M. B. (1992). The relative effectiveness of the reflective and the lecture approach methods on the achievement of high school social studies students. *Educational Studies, 18*(1), 49–56.

Ahern, T. C., Peck, K., & Laycock, M. (1992). The effects of teacher discourse in computer-mediated discussion. *Journal of Educational Computing Research, 8*(3), 291–309.

Alvermann, D. E. (1981). The compensatory effect of graphic organizers on descriptive text. *Journal of Educational Research, 75,* 44–48.

Alvermann, D. E. (1991). The discussion web: A graphic aid for learning across the curriculum. *The Reading Teacher, 45,* 92–99.

Alvermann, D. E., O'Brien, D. G., & Dillon, D. R. (1990). What teachers do when they say they are having discussions of content area reading assignments: A qualitative analysis. *Reading Research Quarterly, 25*(4), 296–322.

Ammon, P., & Hutcheson, B. P. (1989). Promoting the development of teachers' pedagogical conceptions. *Genetic Epistomologist, 17*(4), 23–30.

Anderson, J. R., Reder, L. M., & Simon, H. A. (1996). *Applications and misapplications of cognitive psychology to mathematics education* [On-line]. Available: http://sands.psy.cmu.edu/personal/ja/misapplied.html

Anderson, T. H., & Armbruster, B. B. (1986). *The value of taking notes during lectures* (Tech. Rep. No. 374). Washington, DC: National Institute of Education. (ERIC Document Reproduction Service No. ED 277 996)

Andrews, P. H. (1989). *Improving lecturing skills: Some insights from speech communication.* Bloomington: Indiana University. (ERIC Document Reproduction Service No. ED 303 839)

Anyon, J. (1980). Social class and the hidden curriculum of work. *Journal of Education, 162,* 67–102.

Aronson, E., Blaney, N., Stephen, C., Sikes, J., & Snapp, M. (1978). *The jigsaw classroom* (p. 56). Beverly Hills, CA: Sage.

Ashton-Warner, S. (1963). *Teacher.* New York: Simon & Schuster.

Au, K. H. (1979). Using the experience-text-relationship method with minority children. *The Reading Teacher, 32*(6), 677–679.

Au, K. H. (1981). The comprehension-oriented reading lesson: Relationships to proximal indices of achievement. *Educational Perspectives, 20,* 13–15.

Au, K. H., & Jordan, C. (1981). Teaching reading to Hawaiian children: Finding a culturally appropriate solution. In H. Trueba, G. P. Guthrie, & K. H. Au (Eds.), *Culture in the bilingual classroom* (pp. 139–152). Rowkey, MA: Newbury House.

Azmitia, M. (1996). Peer interactive minds: Developmental, theoretical, and methodological issues. In P. B. Baltes & U. M. Staudinger (Eds.), *Interactive minds: Life-span perspectives on the social foundations of cognition* (pp. 133–162). New York: Cambridge University Press.

Azmitia, M., & Montgomery, R. (1993). Friendship, transactive dialogues, and the development of scientific reasoning. *Social Development, 2,* 202–221.

Baird, J. R., & Northfield, J. R. (Eds.). (1992). *Learning from the PEEL experience.* Melbourne, Victoria: Monash University Printing Services.

Baldwin, J. M. (1906). *Thought and things: A study of the development and meaning of thought* (Vol. 1). New York: Macmillan.

Baldwin, J. M. (1911). *Thought and things: A study of the development and meaning of thought* (Vol. 3). New York: Macmillan.

Ball, D. L. (1993). With an eye on the mathematical horizon: Dilemmas of teaching elementary school mathematics. *Elementary School Journal, 93*(4), 373–397.

Barbour, N. H. (1990). Flexible grouping: It works! *Childhood Education, 67*(2), 66–67.

Beck, I. L. (1997). *Questioning the author: An approach for enhancing student engagement with text.* Newark, NJ: International Reading Association.

Bellack, A. A., Kliebard, H. M., Hyman, R. T., & Smith, F. L., Jr. (1966). *The language of the classroom teacher.* New York: Teachers College Press.

Benjamin, H. (1949). *The cultivation of idiosyncracy.* Cambridge, MA: Harvard University Press.

Bereiter, C., & Scardamalia, M. (1992). Two models of classroom learning using a communal database. In S. Dijkstra (Ed.), *Instructional models in computer-based learning environments* (pp. 229–241) (NATO-ASI Series F: Computer and Systems Sciences). New York: Springer-Verlag.

Berg, J. (1994). Philosophical remarks on implicit knowledge and educational theory. In D. Tirosh (Ed.), *Implicit and explicit knowledge: An educational approach* (pp. 245–253). Norwood, NJ: ABLEX.

Berkowitz, M. W., & Gibbs, J. C. (1983). The process of moral conflict resolution and moral development. In M. W. Berkowitz (Ed.), *New directions for child development: Peer conflict and psychological growth* (pp. 71–84). San Francisco: Jossey-Bass.

Berlyne, D. E. (1960). *Conflict, arousal, and curiosity.* New York: Grove Press.

Bidell, T. R., & Fischer, K. W. (1992). Cognitive development in educational contexts: Implications of skill theory. In A. Demetriou, M. Shayer, & A. Efklides (Eds.), *The neo-Piagetian theories of cognitive development go to school* (pp. 13–30). London: Routledge & Kegan Paul.

Black, A., & Ammon, P. (1992). A developmental-constructivist approach to teacher education. *Journal of Teacher Education, 43*(5), 323–335.

Blake, B. E. (1992). Talk in non-native and native English speakers' peer writing conferences: What's the difference? *Language Arts, 69*(8), 604–610.

Blumenfeld, P. C., Soloway, E., Marx, R. W., Krajcik, J. S., Guzdial, M., & Palincsar, A. (1991). Motivating project-based learning: Sustaining the doing, supporting the learning. *Educational Psychologist, 26,* 369–398.

Bonwell, C. C., & Eison, J. A. (1991). *Active learning: Creating excitement in the classroom.* (ERIC Document Reproduction Service No. ED 336 049)

Bransford, J. D. (1979). *Human cognition: Learning, understanding, and remembering.* Belmont, CA: Wadsworth.

Bredekamp, S. (1993). *Developmentally appropriate practice in early childhood programs serving children from birth through age eight.* Washington, DC: National Association for the Education of Young Children.

Bronfenbrenner, U. (1979). *The ecology of human development: Experiments by nature and design.* Cambridge, MA: Harvard University Press.

Brown, A. L. (1978). Knowing when, where and how to remember: A problem of metacognition. In R. Glaser (Ed.), *Advances in instructional psychology* (Vol. 1, pp. 77–165). Hillsdale, NJ: Erlbaum.

Brown, A. L. (1982). Learning and development: The problems of compatibility, access, and induction. *Human Development, 25,* 89–115.

Brown, A. L., Bransford, J. D., Ferrara, R. A., & Campione, J. C. (1983). Learning, remembering and understanding. In P. H. Mussen (Ed.), *Handbook of child psychology* (4th ed.) (Vol. 3, pp. 77–166). New York: Wiley.

Brown, A. L., & Campione, J. C. (1994). Guided discovery in a community of learners. In K. McGilly (Ed.), *Classroom lessons: Integrating cognitive theory and classroom practice* (pp. 229–272). Cambridge, MA: MIT Press.

Brown, A. L., Campione, J. C., Reeve, R. A., Ferrara, R. A., & Palinscar, A. S. (1991). Interactive learning and individual understanding: The case of reading and mathematics. In L. T. Landsmann (Ed.), *Culture, schooling, and psychological development* (pp. 136–170). Norwood, NJ: ABLEX.

Brown, A. L., Palincsar, A. S., & Purcell, L. (1986). Poor readers: Teach, don't label. In U. Neisser (Ed.), *The school achievement of minority children* (pp. 105–143). Hillsdale, NJ: Erlbaum.

Brownell, C. A., & Carriger, M. S. (1991). Changes in cooperation and self-other differentiation during the second year. *Child Development, 61,* 1164–1174.

Bruer, J. T. (1993). *Schools for thought.* Cambridge, MA: MIT Press.

Bruner, J. S. (1966). *Toward a theory of instruction.* Cambridge, MA: Harvard University Press.

Bruner, J. S. (1977). *The process of education.* Cambridge, MA: Harvard University Press.

Buckelew, M. (1991, March). *Group discussion strategies for a diverse student population.* Paper presented at the annual meeting of the Conference on College Composition and Communication, Boston. (ERIC Document Reproduction Service No. ED 334 576)

Bullinger, A., & Chatillon, J. F. (1983). Recent theory and research of the Genevan school. In P. H. Mussen (Ed.), *Handbook of child psychology* (4th ed.) (Vol. 3, pp. 231–262). New York: Wiley.

Bump, J. (1990). Radical changes in class discussion using networked computers. *Computers and the Humanities, 24,* 49–65.

Burns, P. A. (1990). The two year college: Designing presentations to help students remember. *Journal of College Science Teaching, 19*(5), 301–305.

Carey, W. B. (1995). *Coping with children's temperament: A guide for professionals.* New York: Basic Books.

Carter, G., & Jones, G. M. (1993). The relationship between ability-paired interactions and the development of fifth graders' concepts of balance. *Journal of Research in Science Teaching, 31*(8), 847–856.

Case, R. (1985). *Intellectual development: Birth to adulthood.* Orlando, FL: Academic Press.

Case, R. (1996). Introduction: Reconceptualizing the nature of children's conceptual structures and their development in middle childhood. In R. Case & Y. Okamoto (Eds.), The role of conceptual structures in the development of children's thought. *Monographs of the Society for Research in Child Development, 61*(1/2, Serial No. 246), 1–27.

Cashin, W. E. (1985). *Improving lectures* (Idea Paper No. 14). (ERIC Document Reproduction Service No. ED 267 721)

Charney, R. S. (1997). *Habits of goodness: Case studies in the social curriculum.* Greenfield, MA: Northeast Foundation for Children.

Chilcoat, G. W. (1989). Instructional behaviors for clearer presentations in the classroom. *Instructional Science, 18*(4), 289–314.

Chinn, C. A., & Brewer, W. F. (1993). The role of anomalous data in knowledge acquisition: A theoretical framework and implication for science instruction. *Review of Educational Research, 63,* 1–49.

Chism, N. V. N., Cano, J., & Pruitt, A. S. (1989). Teaching in a diverse environment: Knowledge and skills needed by TAs. *New Directions for Teaching and Learning, 39,* 23–36.

Ciancido, P. J., & Quirk, B. A. (1993). *Teaching and learning critical aesthetic response to literature: An instructive improvement study in grades K–5* (Elementary Subjects Center Series No. 75). (ERIC Document Reproduction Service No. ED 354 526)

Ciardiello, A. V. (1993). Training students to ask reflective questions. *Clearing House, 66*(5), 312–314.

Cobb, P. (1995). Mathematical learning and small-group interaction: Four case studies. In P. Cobb & H. Bauersfeld (Eds.), *The emergence of mathematical meaning: Interaction in classroom cultures* (pp. 25–129). Mahwah, NJ: Erlbaum.

Cobb, P., & Bauersfeld, H. (Eds.). (1995). *The emergence of mathematical meaning: Interaction in classroom cultures.* Mahwah, NJ: Erlbaum.

Cobb, P., Wood, T., & Yackel, E. (1993). Discourse, mathematical thinking, and classroom practice. In E. Forman, N. Minick, & A. Stone (Eds.), *Contexts for learning: Social cultural dynamics in children's development* (pp. 91–119). Oxford, England: Oxford University Press.

Cobb, P., Yackel, E., & Wood, T. (1995). The teaching experiment classroom. In P. Cobb & H. Bauersfeld (Eds.), *The emergence of mathematical meaning: Interaction in classroom cultures* (pp. 17–24). Mahwah, NJ: Erlbaum.

Cocking, R. R., & Renninger, K. A. (1993). Psychological distance as a unifying theory of development. In R. R. Cocking & K. A. Renninger (Eds.), *The development and meaning of psychological distance* (pp. 3–187). Hillsdale, NJ: Erlbaum.

Cognition and Technology Group at Vanderbilt. (1991). Technology and the design of generative learning environments. *Educational Technology, 31,* 34–40.

Cognition and Technology Group at Vanderbilt. (1996). Looking at technology in context: A framework for understanding technology and educational research. In D. C. Berliner & R. C. Calfee, *Handbook of educational psychology* (pp. 807–840). New York: Simon & Schuster/Macmillan.

Cognition and Technology Group at Vanderbilt. (in press). The Jasper series: A design experiment in complex, mathematical problem solving. In J. Hawkins & A. Collins (Eds.), *Design experiments: Integrating technologies into schools.* New York: Cambridge University Press.

Cohen, D. K. (1989). Practice and policy: Notes on the history of instruction. In D. Warren (Ed.), *American teachers: Histories of a profession at work* (pp. 393–407). New York: Macmillan.

Cohen, D. K., & Barnes, C. A. (1993). Pedagogy and policy. In D. K. Cohen, M. W. McLaughlin, & J. E. Talbert (Eds.), *Teaching for understanding: Challenges for policy and practice* (pp. 207–239). San Francisco: Jossey-Bass.

Cohen, E. G. (1988). *Designing groupwork.* New York: Teachers College Press.

Cohen, E. G., Lotan, R., & Catanzarite, L. (1990). Treating status problems in the cooperative classroom. In S. Sharan (Ed.), *Cooperative learning: Theory and research* (pp. 203–230). New York: Praeger.

Coleman, L. J. (1992). The cognitive map of a master teacher conducting discussions with gifted students. *Exceptionality: A Research Journal, 3*(1), 1–16.

Collins, A., Brown, J. S., & Newman, S. E. (1989). Cognitive apprenticeship: Teaching the crafts of reading, writing, and mathematics. In L. B. Resnick (Ed.), *Knowing, learning, and instruction: Essays in honor of Robert Glaser* (pp. 455–494). Hillsdale, NJ: Erlbaum.

Comer, J. P., Haynes, N. M., & Joyner, E. T. (1996). The school development program. In J. P. Comer, N. M. Haynes, E. T. Joyner, & M. Ben-Avie (Eds.), *Rallying the whole village: The Comer process for reforming education* (pp. 1–26). New York: Teachers College Press.

Comer, J. P., Haynes, N. M., Joyner, E. T., & Ben-Avie, M. (Eds.). (1996). *Rallying the whole village: The Comer process for reforming education.* New York: Teachers College Press.

Commeyras, M. (1993). Promoting critical thinking through dialogical reading lessons. *The Reading Teacher, 46,* 486–493.

Conti, G. J., & Fellenz, R. A. (1988). Stimulating discussions with agree-disagree statements and expanding groups: From theory to practice. *Adult Literacy and Basic Education, 12*(1).

Copple, C., Sigel, I. E., & Saunders, R. (1984). *Educating the young thinker: Classroom strategies for cognitive growth.* Hillsdale, NJ: Erlbaum.

Countryman, J. (1992). *Writing to learn math: Strategies that work, K–12.* Portsmouth: Heinemann.

Cronbach, L. J., & Snow, R. E. (Eds.). (1977). *Aptitudes and instructional methods.* New York: Irvington.

Cuban, L. (1984). *How teachers taught: Consistency and change in the American classroom.* New York: Longman.

D'Amato, J. (1996). Resistance and compliance in minority classrooms. In E. Jacob & C. Jordan (Eds.), *Minority education: Anthropological perspectives* (pp. 181–207). Norwood, NJ: ABLEX.

Damon, W. (1984). Peer education: The untapped potential. *Journal of Applied Developmental Psychology, 5,* 331–343.

Damon, W. (1988). *The moral child.* New York: Free Press.

Damon, W. (1997). Learning and resistance: When developmental theory meets educational practice. In E. Amsel & K. A. Renninger (Eds.), *Change and development: Issues of theory, method, and application* (pp. 287–310). Mahwah, NJ: Erlbaum.

Damon, W., & Hart. D. (1988). *Self-understanding in childhood and adolescence.* Cambridge, MA: Cambridge University Press.

D'Andrade, R. (1984). Cultural meaning systems. In R. Shweder & R. LeVine (Eds.), *Culture theory: Essays on mind, self, and emotion* (pp. 89–119). New York: Cambridge University Press.

D'Andrade, R. (1990). Some propositions about the relations between culture and human cognition. In J. W. Stigler & R. Shweder (Eds.), *Cultural psychology: Essays in compara-*

tive human development (pp. 65–129). New York: Cambridge University Press.

DaRosa, D. A., Kolm, P., Follmer, H. C., Pemberton, L. B., Pearce, W. H., & Leapman, S. (1991). Evaluating the effectiveness of the lecture versus the independent study. *Evaluation and Planning, 14,* 141–146.

Davey, B., & McBride, S. (1986). Effects of question-generation training on reading comprehension. *Journal of Educational Psychology, 78,* 256–262.

Deci, E. L., Connell, J. P., & Ryan, R. M. (1989). Self-determination in a work organization. *Journal of Applied Psychology, 74*(4), 580–590.

Deci, E. L., Eghrari, H., Patrick, B. C., & Leone, D. R. (1994). Facilitating internalization: The self-determination theory perspective. *Journal of Personality, 62,* 119–142.

Deci, E. L., & Ryan, R. M. (1985). *Intrinsic motivation and self-determination in human behavior.* New York: Plenum Press.

Delaney, E. (1991). Applying geography in the classroom through structured discussions. *Journal of Geography, 90*(3), 129–133.

DelForge, C., DelForge, L., & DelForge, C. V. (1992). *Grouping students and helpful suggestions for combination classrooms.* (ERIC Document Reproduction Service No. ED 343 749)

DeLoache, J. S. (1993). Distancing and dual representation. In R. R. Cocking & K. A. Renninger (Eds.), *The development and meaning of psychological distance* (pp. 91–108). Hillsdale, NJ: Erlbaum.

Delpit, L. (1988). The silenced dialogue: Power and pedagogy in educating other people's children. *Harvard Educational Review, 58*(3), 280–298.

Dewey, J. (1933). *How we think.* New York: Heath.

Dewey, J. (1938). *Experience and education.* New York: Collier.

Diener, C. I., & Dweck, C. S. (1978). An analysis of learned helplessness: Continuous changes in performance, strategy, and achievement conditions following failure. *Journal of Personality and Social Psychology, 36,* 451–462.

Diener, C. I., & Dweck, C. S. (1980). An analysis of learned helplessness: II. The processing of success. *Journal of Personality and Social Psychology, 39,* 940–952.

Dillon, J. T. (1982a). The multidisciplinary study of questioning. *Journal of Educational Psychology, 74,* 147–165.

Dillon, J. T. (1982b). Problem finding and solving. *Journal of Creative Behavior, 16,* 97–111.

Dillon, J. T. (1994). *Using discussions in classrooms.* Philadelphia: Open University Press.

DiMaggio, P. (1982). Cultural capital and school success: The impact of status culture participation in the grades of U.S. high school students. *American Sociological Review, 47,* 189–201.

Duffy, G. G. (1993). Teachers' progress toward becoming expert strategy teachers. *The Elementary School Journal, 94*(2), 109–120.

Dunn, R., Giannitti, M. C., Murray, J. B., Rossi, I., Geisert, G., & Quinn, P. (1990). Grouping students for instruction: Effects of learning style on achievement and attitudes. *Journal of Social Psychology, 130,* 485–494.

ED 347 850 ERIC Digest. (1992). *Instructional conversations.* Washington, DC: Office of Educational Research and Improvement.

Eder, D. (1981). Ability grouping as a self-fulfilling prophecy: A micro-analysis of teacher-student interaction. *Sociology of Education, 54,* 151–161.

Ellis, S. (in press). Strategy choice in sociocultural context. *Developmental Review.*

Ericsson, K. A., & Simon, H. A. (1980). Verbal reports as data. *Psychological Review, 87,* 215–251.

Evangelou, D. (1989). *Mixed-age groups in early childhood education.* Washington, DC: Office of Educational Research and Improvement. (ERIC Document Reproduction Service No. ED 308 990)

Fahmy, J. J., & Bilton, L. (1990, April). *Listening and note taking in higher education.* Paper presented at the World Congress of Applied Linguistics, Thessaloniki, Greece.

Fantuzzo, J. W., Polite, K., & Grayson, N. (1990). An evaluation of reciprocal peer tutoring across elementary school settings. *Journal of School Psychology, 28*(4), 309–323.

Fantuzzo, J. W., Riggio, R. E., Connelly, S., & Dimeff, L. A. (1989). Effects of reciprocal peer tutoring on academic achievement and psychological adjustment: A component analysis. *Journal of Educational Psychology, 81,* 173–177.

Farnham-Diggory, S. (1994). Paradigms of knowledge and instruction. *Review of Educational Research, 64*(3), 463–477.

Feagans, H. (1994). Using structured questions to improve writing self-evaluation. *Texas Reading Report, 16*(2), 2, 5–7.

Feldman, D. H. (1980). *Beyond universals in cognitive development.* Norwood, NJ: ABLEX.

Fend, H. (1994). *Die Entdeckung des Selbst und die Verarbeitung der Pubertat.* Bern/Gottigen: Huber.

Fennema, E., Carpenter, T. P., & Peterson, P. L. (1989). Learning mathematics with understanding: Cognitively guided instruction. In J. Brophy (Ed.), *Advances in research in teaching* (pp. 195–221). Greenwich, CT: JAI Press.

Fenwick, J., & McMillan, R. (1992, November). *A question of questions.* Paper presented to the World Conference of the International Council for Distance Education, Bangkok, Thailand.

Fischer, K. W. (1980). A theory of cognitive development: Control and construction of hierarchies of skills. *Psychological Review, 87,* 477–531.

Fischer, K. W., & Pipp, S. L. (1984). Processes of cognitive development: Optimal level and skill acquisition. In R. J. Sternberg (Ed.), *Mechanisms of cognitive development* (pp. 45–80). New York: Freeman.

Fisher, B. F., & Jablonski, C. (1985). *Questions in the lecture.* Bloomington: Indiana University. (ERIC Document Reproduction Service No. Ed 303 840)

Flammer, A., Grob, A., Leuthardt, T., & Luthi, R. (1982a). *Wissen zum Fragen und Fragen nach Wissen* [Knowing to ask and asking to know] (Internal Rep. No. 28). Fribourg: University of Fribourg.

Flammer, A., Grob, A., Leuthardt, T., & Luthi, R. (1982b). *Zur Sicherheit: Frag doch!* [To make sure: Ask!] (Internal Rep. No. 30). Fribourg: University of Fribourg.

Flavell, J. H. (1977). *Cognitive development.* Englewood Cliffs, NJ: Prentice-Hall.

Forman, E. A., & McPhail, J. (1993). Vygotskian perspective in children's collaborative problem solving activity. In E. A. Forman, N. Minick, & C. A. Stone (Eds.), *Contexts for learning: Sociocultural dynamics in children's development* (pp. 213–229). Oxford, England: Oxford University Press.

Frances, S. M., & Eckart, J. A. (1992). *The effects of reciprocal teaching on comprehension.* (ERIC Document Reproduction Service No. ED 350 572)

Freire, P. (1970). *Pedagogy of the oppressed.* New York: Herder and Herder.

Gage, N. (1978). *The scientific basis of the art of teaching.* New York: Teachers College Press.

Gagne, R. (1968). Learning hierarchies. *Educational Psychologist, 6,* 1–9.

Gall, M. D. (1970). The use of questions in teaching. *Review of Educational Research, 40,* 707–721.

Gall, M. D. (1984). Synthesis of research on teachers' questioning. *Educational Leadership,* 43.

Gall, M. D., & Gall, J. P. (1993). Teacher and student roles in different types of classroom discussions. In W. Wilen (Ed.), *Teaching and learning.* Springfield, MA: Charles C. Thomas.

Gamberg, R., Kwak, R., Hutchings, M., & Altheim, J. (1988). *Learning and loving it: Theme studies in the classroom.* Portsmouth, NH: Heinemann.

Gardner, H. (1983). *Frames of mind: The theory of multiple intelligences.* New York: Basic Books.

Gardner, H. (1985). *The mind's new science: A history of the cognitive revolution.* New York: Basic Books.

Gardner, H. (1991). *The unschooled mind: How children think and how schools should teach.* New York: Basic Books.

Gartner, A., & Riessman, F. (1994). Tutoring helps those who give, those who receive. *Educational Leadership, 52*(3), 58–60.

Gaskins, I. W. (1994). Classroom applications of cognitive science: Teaching poor readers how to think, learn, and problem solve. In K. McGilly (Ed.), *Classroom lessons: Integrating cognitive theory and classroom practice* (pp. 129–156). Cambridge, MA: MIT Press.

Gaskins, I. W., Ehri, L. C., Cress, C., O'Hara, C., & Donnelly, K. (1997). Procedures for word learning: Making discoveries about words. *The Reading Teacher, 50*(4), 312–327.

Gaustad, J. (1992). Tutoring for at-risk students. *OSSC Bulletin, 36*(3), 1–74.

Gauvain, M. (1995). Thinking in niches: Sociocultural influences on cognitive development. *Human Development, 38,* 25–45.

Gauvain, M., & Rogoff, B. (1989). Collaborative problem solving and children's planning skills. *Developmental Psychology, 2,* 139–151.

Gelman, R. (1994). Constructivism and supporting environments. In D. Tirosh (Ed.), *Implicit and explicit knowledge: An educational approach* (pp. 55–82). Norwood, NJ: ABLEX.

Gelman, R., & Brown, A. L. (1986). Changing views of cognitive competence in the young. In N. J. Smelser & D. R. Gerstein (Eds.), *Behavior and social science, fifty years of discovery* (pp. 175–207). Washington, DC: National Academy Press.

Genishi, C. (1992a). Looking forward: Toward stories of theory and practice. In C. Genishi (Ed.), *Ways of assessing children and curriculum: Stories of early childhood practice* (pp. 191–207). New York: Teachers College Press.

Genishi, C. (Ed.). (1992b). *Ways of assessing children and curriculum: Stories of early childhood practice.* New York: Teachers College Press.

Gentile, L. M., & McMillian, M. M. (1992). Literacy for students at risk: Developing critical dialogues. *Journal of Reading, 35*(8), 636–641.

Gerleman, S. (1987). An observational study of small-group instruction in fourth-grade mathematics classrooms. *Elementary School Journal, 88*(1), 3–28.

Gillette, J. H., & Kranyik, R. D. (1996). Changing American schools: Insights from the school development program. In J. P. Comer, N. M. Haynes, E. T. Joyner, & M. Ben-Avie (Eds.), *Rallying the whole village: The Comer process for reforming education* (pp. 147–161). New York: Teachers College Press.

Ginsburg, H. (1982). *Children's arithmetic: How they learn it and how you teach it.* Pro-Education.

Glaser, R. (1987). Teaching expert novices. *Educational Researcher, 16,* 5.

Goldman, S. R., Pellegrino, J. W., & Bransford, J. D. (1994). Assessing programs that invite thinking. In E. L. Baker & H. F. O'Neil, Jr. (Eds.), *Technology assessment in education and training* (pp. 199–230). Hillsdale, NJ: Erlbaum.

Golombok, S., & Fivush, R. (1994). *Gender development.* New York: Cambridge University Press.

Gomer, J. R. (1992). *Improving the writing of underachieving ninth graders through peer tutoring.* (ERIC Document Reproduction Service No. ED 348 679)

Good, T. L. (1981). Teacher expectations and student perceptions: A decade of research. *Educational Leadership, 38,* 415–423.

Good, T. L., Grouws, D. A., Mason, D. A., Slavings, R. L., & Cramer, K. (1990). An observational study of small-group mathematics instruction in elementary schools. *American Educational Research Journal, 27*(4), 755–782.

Good, T. L., Slavings, R. L., Harel, K. H., & Emerson, H. (1987, July). Student passivity: A study of question-asking in K–12 classrooms. *Sociology of Education, 60,* 181–199.

Good, T. L., & Stipek, D. J. (1983). Individual differences in the classroom: A psychological perspective. In G. D. Fenstermacher & J. I. Goodlad (Eds.), *Individual differences and the common curriculum: National Society for the Study of Education, Part, 1* (82nd yearbook, pp. 9–44). Chicago: University of Chicago Press.

Goodlad, J. I., & Anderson, R. H. (1963). *The non-graded elementary school.* New York: Teachers College Press.

Graesser, A. C. (1992). *Questioning mechanisms during complex learning* (Reports—Research, 143). Arlington, VA: Office of Naval Research. (Accession Number ED350306)

Graesser, A. C., & Person, N. K. (1994). Question asking during tutoring. *American Educational Research Journal, 31*(1), 104–137.

Greenfield, P. M. (1994). Independence and interdependence as developmental scripts: Implications for theory, research, and practice. In P. M. Greenfield & R. R. Cocking (Eds.), *Cross-cultural roots of minority child development* (pp. 1–40). Hillsdale, NJ: Erlbaum.

Greenfield, P. M., & Cocking, R. R. (Eds.). (1994). *Cross-cultural roots of minority child development.* Hillsdale, NJ: Erlbaum.

Greeno, J. G., Collins, A. M., & Resnick, L. B. (1996). Cognition and learning. In D. C. Berliner & R. C. Calfee (Eds.), *Handbook of educational psychology* (pp. 15–46). New York: Simon & Schuster/Macmillan.

Gregg, J. (1995). The tensions and contradictions of the school mathematics tradition. *Journal of Research in Mathematics Education, 26*(5), 442–466.

Grieve, C. (1992). Knowledge increment assessed for three methodologies of teaching physiology. *Medical Teacher, 14*(1), 27–32.

Griffin, S. A., Case, R., & Siegler, R. S. (1994). Rightstart: Providing the central conceptual prerequisites for first formal learning of arithmetic to students at risk for school failure. In K. McGilly (Ed.), *Classroom lessons: Integrating cognitive theory* (pp. 25–49). Cambridge, MA: MIT Press.

Guzzetti, B. J., Snyder, T. E., Glass, G. V., & Gamas, W. S. (1993). Promoting conceptual change in science: A comparative meta-analysis of instructional interventions from reading education and science education. *Reading Research Quarterly, 28,* 117–155.

Hare, V. C., & Pulliam, C. A. (1980). Teacher questioning: A verification and extension. *Journal of Reading Behavior, 12,* 69–72.

Harter, S. (1983). Developmental perspectives on the self-system. In P. H. Mussen (Ed.), *Handbook of child psychology* (4th ed.) (Vol. 4, pp. 275–385). New York: Wiley.

Hartup, W. W. (1996). The company they keep: Friendships and their developmental significance. *Child Development, 67,* 1–13.

Hatano, G., & Inagaki, K. (1991). Sharing cognition through collective comprehension activity. In L. Resnick, J. Levine, & S. Teasley (Eds.), *Perspectives on socially shared cognition* (pp. 331–346). Washington, DC: American Psychological Association.

Hauser, J. (1987, February). *Stimulating critical thinking and discussion formats: Research and strategies for educators to ponder.* Paper presented at the annual meeting of the Association of Teacher Educators, Houston, TX. (ERIC Document Reproduction Service No. ED 277 704)

Hauser, J. (1992, November). *Dialogic classrooms: Tactics, projects, and attitude conversions.* Paper presented at the annual convention of the National Council of Teachers of English, Louisville, KY. (ERIC Document Reproduction Service No. ED 353 232)

Heath, S. B. (1986). What no bedtime story means: Narrative skills at home and at school. In B. Schieffelin & E. Ochs (Eds.), *Language socialization across cultures* (pp. 97–124). Cambridge, England: Cambridge University Press.

Helmke, A. (1994). Self-concept: Development of. In T. Husen & T. N. Postlethwaite (Eds.), *International encyclopedia of education* (pp. 5390–5394). Oxford, England: Pergamon Press.

Hereford, N. J. (1993). Making sense of ability grouping. *Instructor, 102*(9), 50–52.

Heywood, J., & Heywood, S. (1992). *The training of student-teachers in discovery methods of instruction and learning [and] comparing guided discovery and expository methods: Teaching the water cycle in geography* (Research in teacher education monograph series No. 1/92). (ERIC Document Reproduction Service No. ED 358 034)

Hickey, D. T., Moore, A. L., & Pellegrino, J. W. (in press). Motivational and academic consequences of two innovative elementary mathematics environments. *Educational Psychologist.*

Hidi, S., & Anderson, V. (1986). Producing written summaries: Task demands, cognitive operations, and implications for instruction. *Review of Educational Research, 56,* 473–493.

Hidi, S., & Baird, W. (1988). Strategies for increasing text-based interest and students' recall of expository texts. *Reading Research Quarterly, 23,* 465–483.

Hoffmann, L., & Haussler, P. (1995, April). *Modification of interests by instruction.* Paper presented at the annual meeting of the American Educational Research Association, San Francisco.

Holt, J. (1964). *How children fail.* New York: Delta/Seymour Lawrence.

Hoover, S. M., Sayler, M., & Feldhusen, J. F. (1993). Cluster grouping of gifted students at the elementary level. *Roeper Review, 16*(1), 13–15.

Hunt, D. E., & Sullivan, E. V. (1973). *Between psychology and education.* Hinsdale, IL: Dryden Press.

Hunt, E., & Minstrell, J. (1994). A cognitive approach to the teaching of physics. In K. McGilly (Ed.), *Classroom lessons: Integrating cognitive theory* (pp. 51–74). Boston: MIT Press.

Hunt, J. M. (1961). *Intelligence and experience.* New York: Ronald Press.

Isaacs, G. (1989). Lecture, note taking, learning, and recall. *Medical Teacher, 11*(3/4), 295–302.

Jackson, P. W. (1968). *Life in classrooms.* New York: Holt, Rinehart and Winston.

James, W. (1890). *The principles of psychology.* London: Macmillan.

James, W. (1899). *Talks to teachers on psychology: And to students on some of life's ideals.* London: Longmans, Green.

Jegede, O. J., & Olajide, J. O. (1995). Wait-time, classroom discourse, and the influence of sociocultural factors in science teaching. *Science Education, 79*(3), 233–249.

Jenkins, J. J. (1979). Four points to remember: A tetrahedral model of memory experiments. In L. S. Cermak & F. I. M. Craik (Eds.), *Levels of processing in human memory* (pp. 429–446). Hillsdale, NJ: Erlbaum.

Jensen, M. K., & Green, V. P. (1993). The effects of multi-age grouping on young children and teacher preparation. *Early Child Development and Care, 91,* 25–31.

Jervis, K. (1996). *Eyes on the child: Three portfolio stories.* New York: Teachers College Press.

Kagan, S. (1992). *Cooperative learning.* San Juan Capistrano, CA: Resources for Teachers.

Karmiloff-Smith, A. (1992). *Beyond modularity.* Cambridge, MA: MIT Press.

Katz, L., & Chard, S. C. (1989). *Engaging children's minds: The project approach.* Norwood, NJ: ABLEX.

Katz, N. (1990). Problem solving and time: Functions of learning style and teaching methods. *Occupational Therapy Journal of Research, 10*(4), 221–236.

Kawanaka, T., & Stigler, J. W. (1997, June). *Culture and classroom discourse: Teachers' use of questions in 8th-grade mathematics classrooms in Japan and the United States.* Paper presented at the meetings of the Jean Piaget Society, Santa Monica, CA.

Keller, J. (1991, April). *Self-perception and the grouping of gifted children.* Paper presented at the annual meeting of the American Educational Research Association, Chicago. (ERIC Document Reproduction Service No. ED 334 725)

Kelly, M., Moore, D. W., & Tuck, B. F. (1994). Reciprocal teaching in a regular primary school classroom. *Journal of Educational Research, 88*(1), 53–61.

King, A. (1989a, March). *Effects of a metacognitive strategy on high school students' comprehension of literature.* Paper presented at the annual meeting of the American Educational Research Association, San Francisco.

King, A. (1989b). Effects of self-questioning training on college students' comprehension of lectures. *Contemporary Educational Psychology, 14,* 366–381.

King, A. (1990). Enhancing peer interaction and learning in the classroom through reciprocal questioning. *American Educational Research Journal, 27,* 644–687.

Kontos, S. (1992). The role of continuity and context in children's relationships with nonparental adults. In R. C. Pianta (Ed.), *Beyond the parent: The role of other adults in children's lives* (pp. 109–120). San Francisco: Jossey-Bass.

Krapp, A. (1997). Selbstkonzept und Leistung: Dynamik ihres Zusammenspiels. In F. E. Weinert & A. Helmke (Eds.), *Entwicklung im Grundschulater* (pp. 325–339). Weinheim: Psychologie Verlags Union.

Krapp, A., & Fink, B. (1992). The development and function of interests during the critical transition from home to preschool. In K. A. Renninger, S. Hidi, & A. Krapp (Eds.), *The role of interest in learning and development* (pp. 397–430). Hillsdale, NJ: Erlbaum.

Kroll, L., & Black, A. (1989). Developmental principles and organization of instruction for literacy. *Genetic Epistomologist, 17*(4), 15–22.

Kroll, L., & Black, A. (1993). Developmental theory and teaching methods: A pilot study of a teacher education program. *Elementary School Journal, 93*(4), 417–441.

Kruger, A. C. (1992). The effect of peer and adult-child transactive discussions on moral reasoning. *Merrill-Palmer Quarterly, 38,* 191–211.

Kruger, A. C. (1993). Peer collaboration: Conflict, cooperation, or both? *Social Development, 2,* 165–183.

Krummheuer, G. (1995). The ethnography of argumentation. In P. Cobb & H. Bauersfeld (Eds.), *The emergence of mathematical meaning: Interaction in classroom cultures* (pp. 229–269). Hillsdale, NJ: Erlbaum.

Kuhn, D. (1995). Introduction. *Human Development, 38,* 293–294.

Kuhn, D., Amsel, E., & O'Loughlin, M. (1988). *The development of scientific thinking skills.* New York: Academic Press.

Kulik, J. A. (1992). *An analysis of the research on ability grouping: Historical and contemporary perspectives* (Research-based decision making series). Storrs, CT: National Research Center on the Gifted and Talented. (ERIC Document Reproduction Service No. ED 350 777)

Kulik, J. A. (1993, Spring). An analysis of the research on ability grouping. *National Research Center on the Gifted and Talented Newsletter,* 8–9.

Kutnick, P., & Thomas, M. (1990). Dyadic pairings for the enhancement of cognitive development in the school curriculum: Some preliminary results on science tasks. *British Educational Research Journal, 16*(4), 399–406.

Kuzbik, J. (1992). *Can we talk? Effective learning in the classroom: Instructional strategies series No. 9.* (ERIC Document Reproduction Service No. ED 360 307)

Lampert, M. (1986). Knowing, doing, and teaching multiplication. *Cognition and Instruction, 3*(4), 305–342.

Lave, J., & Wenger, E. (1991). *Situated learning: Legitimate peripheral participation.* New York: Cambridge University Press.

Leinhardt, G. (1993). On teaching. In R. Glaser (Ed.), *Advances in instructional psychology* (Vol. 4). Hillsdale, NJ: Erlbaum.

Levin, I., & Druyan, S. (1993). When sociocognitive transaction among peers fails: The case of misconceptions in science. *Child Development, 63,* 1571–1591.

Lieberman, A. (1995). Restructuring schools: The dynamics of changing practice, structure, and culture. In A. Lieberman (Ed.), *The work of restructuring schools: Building from the ground up* (pp. 1–17). New York: Teachers College Press.

Lindfors, J. (1991). *Children's language and learning* (2nd ed.). Needham Heights, MA: Allyn & Bacon.

Lindquist, M. (1989). Mathematics content and small-group instruction in grades four through six. *Elementary School Journal, 89*(5), 625–632.

Little, J. W. (1990). Conditions of professional development in secondary schools. In M. W. McLaughlin, J. E. Talbert, & N. Bascia (Eds.), *The contexts of teaching in secondary schools* (pp. 187–223). New York: Teachers College Press.

Lou, Y., Abrami, P. C., Spence, J. C., Poulsen, C., Chambers, B., & D'Apollonia, S. (1996). Within-class grouping: A meta-analysis. *Review of Educational Research, 66*(4), 423–458.

Lundeberg, M. A. (1990). Supplemental instruction in chemistry. *Journal of Research in Science Teaching, 27*(2), 145–155.

Lyman, L. (1991). Teaching geography using cooperative learning. *Journal of Geography, 90*(5), 223–226.

MacArthur, C. A., Schwartz, S. S., & Graham, S. (1991). Effects of a reciprocal peer revision strategy in special education classrooms. *Learning Disabilities Research and Practice, 6*(4), 201–210.

Mager, R. F. (1962). *Preparing objectives for programmed instruction.* Palo Alto, CA: Fearon.

Marks, M., Pressley, M., Coley, J. D., Craig, S., Gardner, R., DePinto, T., & Rose, W. (1993). Three teachers' adaptations of reciprocal teaching in comparison to traditional reciprocal teaching. *The Elementary School Journal, 94*(2), 267–283.

Markus, H., & Nurius, P. (1986). Possible selves. *American Psychologist, 4*(9), 954–969.

Markus, H., & Wurf, E. (1987). The dynamic self-concept: A social psychological perspective. *Annual Review of Psychology, 38,* 299–337.

Marshall, J. D., Klages, M. B., & Fehlman, R. (1991). *Discussions of literature in middle-track classrooms* (Report series, 2.17). (ERIC Document Reproduction Service No. ED 337 781)

Mayer, R. E. (1984). Aids to prose construction. *Educational Psychologist, 19,* 30–42.

Mayer, R. E., & Wittrock, M. C. (1996). Problem-solving transfer. In D. C. Berliner & R. C. Calfee (Eds.), *Handbook of educational psychology* (pp. 47–62). New York: Simon & Schuster/Macmillan.

McGilly, K. (Ed.). (1994). *Classroom lessons: Integrating cognitive theory and classroom practice.* Cambridge, MA: MIT Press.

McKeown, M., Beck, I. L., & Sandora, C. (1994, November-December). *Getting inside meaningful classroom discourse.* Paper presented at the annual meeting of the National Reading Conference, San Diego, CA.

Medway, F. J. (1991). A social psychological analysis of peer tutoring. *Journal of Developmental Education, 15*(1), 20–26.

Meeker, M. (1976). The prophecy of giftedness. *Gifted Child Quarterly, 20*(1), 99–104.

Mehan, H., Hertweck, A., Combs, S., & Flynn, P. (1982). Teachers' interpretations of students' behaviors. In L. Wilkinson (Ed.), *Communicating in the classroom* (pp. 297–322). New York: Academic Press.

Mesa-Bains, A., & Shulman, J. H. (1991). *Teaching diverse students: Cases and commentaries. Instructors Guide* (Guides-Classroom-Teacher, 052). Washington, DC: Office of Educational Research and Improvement. (ERIC Document Reproduction Service No. ED 343 889)

Michaels, S. (1981). "Sharing time": Children's narrative styles and differential access to literacy. *Language in Society, 10,* 423–442.

Millar, D. P. (1986). *Introduction to small group discussion.* (ERIC Document Reproduction Service No. ED 278 037)

Miller, B. A. (1990). A review of the quantitative research on multigrade instruction. *Journal of Research in Rural Education, 7*(1), 1–8.

Miller, B. A. (1991a). A review of the qualitative research on multigrade instruction. *Journal of Research in Rural Education, 7*(2), 3–12.

Miller, B. A. (1991b). *Teaching and learning in the multigrade classroom: Student performance and instructional routines.* (ERIC Document Reproduction Service No. ED 335 178)

Miner, R. (1992). Reflections on teaching a large class. *Journal of Management Education, 16*(3), 290–302.

Minuchin, P. P., & Shapiro, E. K. (1983). The school as a context for social development. In P. L. Mussen (Gen. Ed.), *Handbook of child psychology* (4th ed.) (Vol. 2, pp. 197–274). New York: Wiley.

Mischel, W., & Rodriguez, M. L. (1993). Psychological distance in self-imposed delay of gratification. In R. R. Cocking & K. A. Renninger (Eds.), *The development and meaning of psychological distance* (pp. 109–122). Hillsdale, NJ: Erlbaum.

Mitchell, I. (1992). Sustaining support and stimulation: The teacher group, 1986–1989. In J. R. Baird & J. R. Northfield (Eds.), *Learning from the PEEL experience* (pp. 14–36). Melbourne, Australia: Monash University Printing Services.

Mitchell, R. (1992). *Testing for learning: How new approaches to evaluation can improve American schools.* New York: Free Press.

Montessori, M. (1965). *Spontaneous activity in education.* New York: Schocken Books. (Original work published 1917)

Morine-Dershimer, G. (1985). *Talking, listening, and learning in elementary classrooms* (Research on Teaching Monograph Series). New York: Longman.

Murray, J. P., & Murray, J. I. (1992). How do I lecture thee? *College Teaching, 40*(3), 109–113.

Mussen, P. H. (Ed.). (1983). *Handbook of child psychology.* New York: Wiley.

National Council for the Social Studies. (1994). *Curriculum standards for social studies: Expectations of excellence.* Washington, DC: National Council for the Social Studies.

National Council of Teachers of Mathematics. (1989). *Curriculum and evaluation standards for school mathematics.* Reston, VA: National Council of Teachers of Mathematics.

Neisser, U. (1976). *Cognition and reality: Principles and implications of cognitive psychology.* San Francisco: Freeman.

Nelson, K. (1997). Cognitive change as collaborative construction. In E. Amsel & K. A. Renninger (Eds.), *Change and development: Issues of theory, application, and method* (pp. 99–115). Hillsdale, NJ: Erlbaum.

Newman, D., Griffin, P., & Cole, M. (1989). *The construction zone: Working for cognitive change in school.* Cambridge, MA: Cambridge University Press.

Newman, R. S., & Schwager, M. T. (1995). Students' help seeking during problem solving: Effects of grade, goal, and prior achievement. *American Educational Research Journal, 32*(2), 352–376.

Nicholls, J. G. (1984). Achievement motivation: Conceptions of ability—subjective experience, task choice, and performance. *Psychological Review, 91,* 328–346.

Nicolopoulou, A., & Cole, M. (1993). The Fifth Dimension, its play world, and its instructional contexts: The generation and transmission of shared knowledge in the culture of collaborative learning. In N. Minnick & E. Forman (Eds.), *The institutional and social context of mind: New directions in Vygotskian theory and research* (pp. 283–314). New York: Oxford University Press.

Noddings, N. (1985). Small groups as a setting for research on mathematical problem solving. In E. A. Silver (Ed.), *Teaching and learning mathematical problem solving: Multiple research perspectives* (pp. 345–359). Hillsdale, NJ: Erlbaum.

Noddings, N. (1989). Theoretical and practical concerns about small groups in mathematics. *Elementary School Journal, 89*(5), 607–623.

Nolan, S. B. (1988). Reasons for studying: Motivational orientations and study strategies. *Cognition and Instruction, 5,* 269–287.

Northfield, J. R. (1992). Principles for adopting and sustaining an innovation. In J. R. Baird & J. R. Northfield (Eds.), *Learning from the PEEL experience* (pp. 274–282). Melbourne, Australia: Monash University Printing Services.

Nystrand, M., & Gamoran, A. (1988). *A study of instruction as discourse* (Report for the National Center on Effective Secondary Schools). Madison: Wisconsin Center for Educational Research. (ERIC Document Reproduction Service No. ED 328 516)

Nystrand, M., Gamoran, A., & Heck, M. J. (1993). Using small groups for response to and thinking about literature. *English Journal, 82*(1), 14–22.

Odubunmi, O., & Balogun, T. A. (1991). The effect of laboratory and lecture teaching methods on cognitive achievement in integrated science. *Journal of Research in Science Teaching, 28*(3), 213–234.

Oja, S. N., & Smulyan, L. (1989). *Collaborative action research: A developmental approach.* Lewes: Falmer Press.

Olson, L. A., & Huckin, T. N. (1990). Point-driven understanding in engineering lecture comprehension. *English for Specific Purposes, 9*(1), 33–47.

Osterman, D., Christensen, M., & Coffey, B. (1985). *The feedback lecture* (Idea Paper No. 13). (ERIC Document Reproduction Service No. ED 302 562)

Palinscar, A. S., & Brown, A. L. (1984). Reciprocal teaching of comprehension-fostering and comprehension-monitoring activities. *Cognition and Instruction, 1,* 117–175.

Palinscar, A. S., & Klenk, L. J. (1991). Learning dialogues to promote text comprehension. In B. Means & M. S. Knapp (Eds.), *Teaching advanced skills to educationally disadvantaged students. Data Analysis Support Center (DASC) Task, 4. Final Report* (pp. 20–42). Washington, DC: U.S. Department of Education.

Papert, S. (1993). *The children's machine: Rethinking school in the age of the computer.* New York: Basic Books.

Paris, S. C., Cross, D. R., & Lipson, M. Y. (1984). Informed strategies for learning: A program to improve children's reading awareness and comprehension. *Journal of Educational Psychology, 76,* 1239–1252.

Pearson, W. E. (1990). Group learning in the secondary social studies classroom. *OAH Magazine of History, 5*(1), 5–7.

Peper, R. J., & Mayer, R. E. (1978). Note taking as a generative activity. *Journal of Educational Psychology, 70,* 514–522.

Perkins, D. N. (1992). *Smart schools: From training memories to educating minds.* New York: Free Press.

Perkins, D. N., & Simmons, R. (1988). Patterns of misunderstanding: An integrative model for science, math, and programming. *Review of Educational Research, 58,* 303–326.

Perret-Clermont, A. N., Perret, J. F., & Bell, N. (1991). The social construction of meaning and cognitive activity in elementary school children. In J. M. Levine, L. B. Resnick, & S. Teasley (Eds.), *Socially shared cognition* (pp. 41–62). New York: American Psychological Association Press.

Perrone, V. (Ed.). (1991). *Expanding student assessment.* Alexandria, VA: Association for Supervision and Curriculum Development.

Perry, M., Church, R. B., & Goldin-Meadow, S. (1988). Transitional knowledge in the acquisition of concepts. *Cognitive Development, 3,* 359–400.

Perry, M., Vanderstoep, S. W., & Yu, S. L. (1993). Asking questions in first-grade mathematics classes: Potential influences on mathematical thought. *Journal of Educational Psychology, 85*(1), 31–40.

Pestalozzi, J. H. (1855). *Leonard and Gertrude.* Boston: Heath.

Piaget, J. (1950). *The psychology of intelligence.* New York: Harcourt.

Piaget, J. (1952). *The language and thought of the child.* London: Routledge & Kegan Paul.

Pianta, R. C., & Steinberg, M. (1992). Teacher-child relationships and the process of adjusting to school. In R. C. Pianta (Ed.), *Beyond the parent: The role of other adults in children's lives* (pp. 61–80). San Francisco: Jossey-Bass.

Pintrich, P. R., & DeGroot, E. V. (1990). Motivational and self-regulated learning components of classroom academic performance. *Journal of Educational Psychology, 82*(1), 33–40.

Pintrich, P. R., & Schunk, D. H. (1995). *Motivation in education: Theory research, and applications.* Englewood Cliffs, NJ: Prentice-Hall.

Polya, G. (1945). *How to solve it.* Princeton, NJ: Princeton University Press.

Popkewitz, T. S., Tabachnick, B. R., & Wehlage, G. G. (1982). *The myth of educational reform: A study of school responses to a program of change.* Madison: University of Wisconsin Press.

Poppish, S., Trevorrow, J., Ford, J., Hughes, M., LeBlanc, P., Wooten, E., & Fuller, R. (1990). *Assessing student attitudes toward heterogeneous grouping: A pilot study.* (ERIC Document Reproduction Service No. ED 328 397)

Pratt, D. (1986). On the merits of multiage classrooms: Their work life. *Research in Rural Education, 3*(3), 111–116.

Prawat, P. S. (1989). Promoting access to knowledge, strategy, and disposition in students: A research synthesis. *Review of Educational Research, 59,* 1–41.

Prenzel, M. (1992). The selective persistence of interest. In K. A. Renninger, S. Hidi, & A. Krapp (Eds.), *The role of interest in learning and development* (pp. 71–98). Hillsdale, NJ: Erlbaum.

Pressley, M. J., Burkell, J., Cariglia-Bull, T., Lysynchuk, L., McGoldrick, J. A., Schneider, B., Snyder, B. L., Symons, S., & Woloshyn, V. E. (1990). *Cognitive strategy instruction that really improves children's academic performance.* Cambridge, MA: Brookline Books.

Pressley, M. J., El-Dinary, P. B., Marks, M. B., Brown, R., & Stein, S. (1992). Good strategy instruction is motivating and interesting. In K. A. Renninger, S. Hidi, & A. Krapp (Eds.), *The role of interest in learning and development* (pp. 333–358). Hillsdale, NJ: Erlbaum.

Pressley, M. J., Johnson, C. J., Symons, S., McGoldrick, J. A., & Kurita, J. A. (1989). Strategies that improve children's memory and comprehension of text. *Elementary School Journal, 90*(1), 3–32.

Pressley, M. J., Wood, E., Woloshyn, V. E., Martin, V., King, A., & Menke, D. (1992). Encouraging mindful use of prior knowledge: Attempting to construct explanatory answers facilitates learning. *Educational Psychologist, 27,* 91–110.

Raphael, T. E., & Pearson, P. D. (1985). Increasing student awareness of sources of information for answering questions. *American Educational Research Journal, 22,* 217–237.

Renninger, K. A. (1990). Children's play interests, representation, and activity. In R. Fivush & J. Hudson (Eds.), *Knowing and remembering in young children* (Vol. 3, pp. 127–165). New York: Cambridge University Press.

Renninger, K. A. (1992). Individual interest and development: Implications for theory and practice. In K. A. Renninger,

S. Hidi, & A. Krapp (Eds.), *The role of interest in learning and development* (pp. 361–396). Hillsdale, NJ: Erlbaum.

Renninger, K. A. (1996). Learning as the focus of the educational psychology course. *Educational Psychologist, 31*(1), 63–76.

Renninger, K. A., & Stavis, J. (1995, April). *The roles of interest, task difficulty, and gender in the process of students' reconstructive recall of expository text.* Poster presented at the meetings of the Society for Research in Child Development, Indianapolis, IN.

Renninger, K. A., Weimar, S. A., & Klotz, E. A. (1997). Teachers and students investigating and communicating about geometry: The Math Forum. In R. Lehrer & D. Chazen (Eds.), *Designing learning environments for developing understanding of geometry and space.* Mahwah, NJ: Erlbaum.

Renninger, K. A., & Winegar, L. T. (1985). Emergent organization in expert-novice relationships. *Genetic Epistemologist, 14*(1), 14–20.

Resnick, L. B. (1988). Treating mathematics as an ill-structured discipline. In R. I. Charles & E. A. Silver (Eds.), *The teaching and assessing of mathematical problem solving* (pp. 32–60). Hillsdale, NJ: Erlbaum.

Resnick, L. B., & Ford, W. W. (1981). *The psychology of mathematics for instruction.* Hillsdale, NJ: Erlbaum.

Rings, S., & Sheets, R. A. (1991). Students' development and metacognition: Foundations for tutor training. *Journal of Developmental Education, 15*(1), 30–32.

Robinson, P. W. (1990). *A study of the self-paced math lab approach to developmental algebra compared to the traditional lecture method at Brenau: Learning theory and applications.* (ERIC Document Reproduction Service No. ED 328 452)

Robinson, W. R., & Niaz, M. (1991). Performance based on instruction by lecture or by interaction and its relationship to cognitive variables. *International Journal of Science Education, 13*(2), 203–215.

Roehler, L. R., Duffy, G. G., & Meloth, M. S. (1986). What to be direct about in direct instruction in reading: Content only versus process-into-content. In T. E. Raphael (Ed.), *The contents of school-based literacy* (pp. 79–93). New York: Random House.

Rogoff, B. (1990). *Apprenticeship in thinking: Cognitive development in social context.* New York: Oxford University Press.

Rogoff, B. (1996). Developmental transitions in children's participation in sociocultural activities. In A. Sameroff & M. Haith (Eds.), *Reason and responsibility: The passage through childhood* (pp. 273–294). Chicago: University of Chicago Press.

Rogoff, B. (1997). Evaluating development in the process of participation: Theory, methods, and practice building on each other. In E. Amsel & K. A. Renninger (Eds.), *Change and development: Issues of theory, application, and method* (pp. 265–285). Mahwah, NJ: Erlbaum.

Rohrkemper, M. M., & Bershon, B. L. (1984). Elementary school students' reports of the causes and effects of problem difficulty in mathematics. *Elementary School Journal, 85*(1), 127–147.

Rosenshine, B., & Meister, C. (1994). Reciprocal teaching: A review of the research. *Review of Educational Research, 64*(4), 479–530.

Rosenshine, B., Meister, C., & Chapman, S. (1996). Teaching students to generate questions: A review of the intervention studies. *Review of Educational Research, 66*(2), 181–221.

Roth, K. J., Anderson, C. W., & Smith, E. L. (1987). Curriculum materials, teacher talk, and student learning: Case studies in fifth grade science teaching. *Journal of Curriculum Studies, 19,* 527–548.

Ruhl, K. L., Hughes, C. A., & Gajar, A. H. (1990). Efficacy of the pause procedure for enhancing learning disabled and nondisabled college students' long- and short-term recall of facts presented through lecture. *Learning Disabled Quarterly, 13*(1), 55–64.

Sanacore, J. (1990). *Intra-class grouping with a whole language thrust.* (ERIC Document Reproduction Service No. ED 320 114)

Sarason, S. B. (1982). *The culture of school and the problem of change* (2nd ed.). Boston: Allyn & Bacon.

Scardamalia, M., & Bereiter, C. (1992). Text-based and knowledge-based questioning by children. *Cognition and Instruction, 9,* 177–199.

Scardamalia, M., Bereiter, C., & Lamon, M. (1994). The CSILE Project: Trying to bring the classroom into world three. In K. McGilly (Ed.), *Classroom lessons: Integrating cognitive theory and classroom practice* (pp. 201–228). Cambridge, MA: MIT Press.

Schiefele, U. (1990). The influence of topic interest, prior knowledge and cognitive capabilities on text comprehension. In J. M. Pieters, K. Breuer, & P. R. J. Simons (Eds.), *Learning environments* (pp. 323–338). Berlin: Springer-Verlag.

Schoenfeld, A. (1987). What's all the fuss about metacognition? In A. Schoenfeld (Ed.), *Cognitive science and mathematics education* (pp. 189–215). Hillsdale, NJ: Erlbaum.

Scholnick, E. K., & Freedman, S. L. (1987). The planning construct in psychological literature. In S. L. Friedman, E. K. Scholnick, & R. R. Cocking (Eds.), *Blueprints for thinking* (pp. 3–38). New York: Cambridge University Press.

Schunk, D. H., & Zimmerman, B. J. (Eds.). (1994). *Self-regulation of learning and performance: Issues and educational applications.* Hillsdale, NJ: Erlbaum.

Shantz, C. U. (1993). Children's conflicts: Representations and lessons learned. In R. R. Cocking & K. A. Renninger (Eds.), *The development and meaning of psychological distance* (pp. 185–202). Hillsdale, NJ: Erlbaum.

Shulman, L. S. (1986). Those who understand: Knowledge growth in teaching. *Educational Researcher, 15,* 4–14.

Siegler, R. S. (1977). The twenty questions game as a form of problem solving. *Child Development, 48,* 395–403.

Siegler, R. S. (1995). How does change occur: A microgenetic study of number conservation. *Cognitive Psychology, 28,* 225–273.

Siegler, R. S. (1997). Concepts and methods for studying cognitive change. In E. Amsel & K. A. Renninger (Eds.), *Change and development: Issues of theory, method, and application* (pp. 77–98). Mahwah, NJ: Erlbaum.

Siegler, R. S., & Jenkins, E. (1989). *How children discover new strategies.* Hillsdale, NJ: Erlbaum.

Sigel, I. E. (1970). The distancing hypothesis: A causal hypothesis for the acquisition of representational thought. In M. R. Jones (Ed.), *Miami Symposium on the Prediction of Behavior, 1968: Effects of early experience* (pp. 99–118). Coral Gables, FL: University of Miami Press.

Sigel, I. E. (1986). Early social experience and the development of representational competence. In W. Fowler (Ed.), *Early experience and the development of competence.* San Francisco: Jossey-Bass.

Sigel, I. E. (1990). What teachers need to know about human development. In D. D. Dill & Associates (Eds.), *What teachers need to know: The knowledge, skills, and values essential to good teaching* (pp. 76–93). San Francisco: Jossey-Bass.

Sigel, I. E. (1993). The centrality of a distancing model for the development of representational competence. In R. R. Cocking & K. A. Renninger (Eds.), *The development and meaning of psychological distance* (pp. 141–158). Hillsdale, NJ: Erlbaum.

Sigel, I. E., & Cocking, R. R. (1977). Cognition and communication: A dialectic paradigm for development. In M. Lewis & L. A. Rosenblum (Eds.), *The origins of behavior* (Vol. 5, pp. 207–226). New York: Wiley.

Sigel, I. E., & Kelley, T. D. (1988). A cognitive developmental approach to questioning. In J. T. Dillon (Ed.), *Questioning and discussion: A multi-disciplinary study* (pp. 105–134). Norwood, NJ: ABLEX.

Silver, E. A. (1986). Using conceptual and procedural knowledge: A focus on relationships. In J. Hiebert (Ed.), *Conceptual and procedural knowledge: The case of mathematics* (pp. 181–198). Hillsdale, NJ: Erlbaum.

Sirotnik, K. A. (1983). What you see is what you get—Consistency, persistency, and mediocrity in classrooms. *Harvard Educational Review, 53*(1), 16–31.

Skinner, B. F. (1968). *The technology of teaching.* Englewood Cliffs, NJ: Prentice-Hall.

Slavin, R. E. (1983). *Cooperative learning.* New York: Longman.

Slavin, R. E. (1987). Developmental and motivational perspectives on cooperative learning: A reconciliation. *Child Development, 58*(5), 1161–1167.

Slavin, R. E. (1990). Ability grouping, cooperative learning and the gifted. Point-counterpoint—cooperative learning. *Journal for the Education of the Gifted, 14*(3), 3–8.

Smagorinsky, P., & Fly, P. K. (1993). The social environment of the classroom: A Vygotskian perspective on the small group process. *Communication Education, 42*(2), 159–171.

Smith, L. B. (1997). Metaphors and methods: Variability and the study of word learning. In E. Amsel & K. A. Renninger (Eds.), *Change and development: Issues of theory, method, and application* (pp. 153–172). Mahwah, NJ: Erlbaum.

Smith, L. B., & Thelen, E. (Eds.). (1993). *A dynamic systems approach to development.* Cambridge, MA: MIT Press.

Solomon, D., Watson, M., Schaps, E., Battistich, V., & Solomon, J. (1990). Cooperative learning as part of a comprehensive classroom program designed to promote prosocial development. In S. Sharan (Ed.), *Cooperative learning: Theory and research* (pp. 231–260). New York: Praeger.

Solomon, J. (1991). Group discussions in the classroom. *School Science Review, 72*(261), 29–34.

Stein, M. K., Leinhardt, G., & Bickel, W. (1989). Instructional issues for teaching students at risk. In R. E. Slavin, N. L. Karwit, & N. A. Madden (Eds.), *Effective programs for students at risk.* Needham Heights, MA: Allyn & Bacon.

Sternberg, R. J. (1985). *Beyond IQ.* New York: Cambridge University Press.

Sternberg, R. J. (1996). Myths, countermyths, and truths about intelligence. *Educational Researcher, 25*(2), 11–16.

Stevenson, H. W., & Stigler, J. W. (1992). *The learning gap: Why our schools are failing and what we can learn from Japanese and Chinese education.* New York: Summit.

Stigler, J. W., Fernandez, C., & Yoshida, M. (1996). Traditions of school mathematics in Japanese and American elementary classrooms. In P. L. Steffe, P. Nesher, P. Cobb, G. A. Goldin, & B. Greer (Eds.), *Theories of mathematics learning* (pp. 149–175). Mahwah, NJ: Erlbaum.

Stright, A. L., & French, D. C. (1988). Leadership in mixed-age children's groups. *International Journal of Behavioral Development, 11*(4), 507–515.

Sundell, K. (1994). Mixed-age groups in Swedish nursery and compulsory schools. *School Effectiveness and School Improvement, 5*(4), 376–393.

Terwel, J., Herfs, P. G. P., Mertens, E. H. M., & Perrenet, J. (Chr.). (1994). Cooperative learning and adaptive instruction in a mathematics curriculum. *Journal of Curriculum Studies, 26*(2), 217–233.

Tharp, R. G. (1994). Intergroup differences among Native Americans in socialization and child cognition: An ethnographic analysis. In P. M. Greenfield & R. R. Cocking (Eds.), *Cross-cultural roots of minority child development* (pp. 87–106). Hillsdale, NJ: Erlbaum.

Tharp, R. G., & Gallimore, R. (1988). *Rousing minds to life: Teaching, learning, and schooling in social context.* New York: Cambridge University Press.

Thomas, D. A. (1992). Using computer visualization to motivate and support mathematical dialogues. *Journal of Computers in Mathematics and Science Teaching, 11*(3/4), 265–274.

Tobias, S. (1990). *They're not dumb, they're different: Stalking the second tier.* Tucson, AZ: Research Corporation.

Tomasello, M., Kruger, A. C., & Ratner, H. H. (1993). Cultural learning. *Behavioral and Brain Sciences, 16,* 495–552.

Trapani, C. (1988). *Peer tutoring: Integrating academic and social skills remediation in the classrooms.* Paper presented at the annual convention of the Council for Exceptional Children. Washington, DC: National Institute of Handicapped Research. (ERIC Document Reproduction Service No. ED 297 533)

Trapani, C., & Gettinger, M. (1989). Effects of social skills training and cross-age tutoring on academic achievement and social behaviors of boys with learning disabilities. *Journal of Research and Development in Education, 23*(1), 1–9.

Tudge, J. R. H. (1989). When collaboration leads to regression: Some negative consequences of socio-cognitive conflict. *European Journal of Social Psychology, 19,* 123–138.

Tudge, J. R. H. (1992). Vygotsky, the zone of proximal development, and peer collaboration: Implications for classroom practice. In L. C. Moll (Ed.), *Vygotsky and education* (pp. 155–172). New York: Cambridge University Press.

Turiel, E. (1983). *The development of social knowledge: Morality and convention.* Cambridge, England: Cambridge University Press.

van der Meij, H. (1986). *Questioning: A study on the questioning behavior of elementary school children.* Den Haag, The Netherlands: SVO.

van der Meij, H. (1993). What's the title? A case study of questioning in reading. *Journal of Research in Reading, 16*(1), 46–56.

van der Meij, H. (1994). Students questioning: A componential analysis. *Learning and Individual Differences, 6*(2), 137–161.

Veenman, S., Lem, P., & Voeten, M. (1988). Time on task in mixed age classes. *Journal of Classroom Interaction, 23*(2), 14–21.

Voss, J. F., & Schauble, L. (1992). Is interest educationally interesting? An interest-related model of learning. In K. A. Renninger, S. Hidi, & A. Krapp (Eds.), *The role of interest in learning and development* (pp. 101–120). Hillsdale, NJ: Erlbaum.

Vygotsky, L. (1978). *Mind in society.* Boston: Harvard University Press.

Wade, S. (1992). How interest affects learning from text. In K. A. Renninger, S. Hidi, & A. Krapp (Eds.), *The role of interest in learning and development* (pp. 255–278). Hillsdale, NJ: Erlbaum.

Walbaum, S. D. (1989). *Note taking, verbal aptitude, and listening span: Factors involved in learning from lectures.* Paper presented at the annual meeting of the American Educational Research Association, San Francisco.

Wasserman, S. (1992). A case for social studies. *Phi Delta Kappan, 73*(10), 793–801.

Watson, M. W., & Fischer, K. W. (1993). Structural changes in children's understanding of family roles and divorce. In R. R. Cocking & K. A. Renninger (Eds.), *The development and meaning of psychological distance* (pp. 123–140). Hillsdale, NJ: Erlbaum.

Webb, N. L., & Romberg, T. A. (Eds.). (1994). *Reforming mathematics education in America's cities: The Urban Mathematics Collaborative Project.* New York: Teachers College Press.

Webb, N. M. (1989). Peer interaction and learning in small groups. *International Journal of Educational Research, 13,* 21–39.

Webb, N. M., & Palinscar, A. S. (1996). Group processes in the classroom. In D. C. Berliner & R. C. Calfee (Eds.), *Handbook of educational psychology.* New York: Macmillan.

Weinert, F. E., & Kluwe, R. H. (Eds.). (1987). *Metacognition, motivation, and understanding.* Hillsdale, NJ: Erlbaum.

Werner, H. (1978). Process and achievement: A basic problem of education and developmental psychology. In S. S. Barten & M. B. Franklin (Eds.), *Developmental processes: Heinz Werner's selected writings* (Vol. 1, pp. 9–22). New York: International Universities Press.

Wilen, W. W., & Campbell, J. (1992). Using research findings to improve social studies teachers' questions and questioning. *International Journal of Social Education, 7*(1), 61–69.

Wilkerson, L., Hafler, J., & Liu, P. (1991). A case study of student-directed discussion in four problem-based tutorial groups. *Academic Medicine, 66*(9), S79–81.

Williams, B., Supon, V., Rushefski, C., Doby, G., & Clarke, R. (1991, November). *Questions, not answers, stimulate critical thinking.* Paper presented at the annual conference of the National Council of States on Inservice Education, Houston, TX.

Williams, C. R. (1986, October). The feedback lecture method: Teaching the non-traditional adult student. In *Thinking Across*

Disciplines. Proceedings of the Annual Conference of the International Society for Individualized Instruction. Atlanta, GA. (Accession Number ED276440)

Williams, G. C., & Deci, E. L. (1996). Internalization of biopsychosocial values by medical students: A test of self-determination theory. *Journal of Personality and Social Psychology, 70*(4), 767–779.

Williams, W., Blythe, T., White, N., Li, J., Sternberg, R., & Gardner, H. (1996). *Practical intelligences for school.* New York: HarperCollins.

Wilson, S. M., Miller, C., & Yerkes, C. (1993). Deeply rooted change: A tale of learning to teach adventurously. In D. K. Cohen, M. W. McLaughlin, & J. E. Talbert (Eds.), *Teaching for understanding: Challenges for policy and practice* (pp. 84–129). San Francisco: Jossey-Bass.

Wittrock, M. (1986). Students' thought processes. In M. Wittrock (Ed.), *Third handbook of research on teaching* (pp. 297–314). New York: Macmillan.

Wong, B. Y. L. (1985). Self-questioning instructional research: A review. *Review of Educational Research, 55*(2), 227–268.

Wood, E., Woloshyn, V., & Willoughby, T. (Eds.). (1995). *Cognitive strategy instruction for middle and high schools.* Cambridge, MA: Brookline Books.

Wood, T. (1995). An emerging practice of teaching. In P. Cobb & H. Bauersfeld (Eds.), *The emergence of mathematical meaning: Interaction in classroom cultures* (pp. 203–227). Hillsdale, NJ: Erlbaum.

Wood, T., & Yackel, E. (1990). The development of collaborative dialogue within small-group interactions. In L. P. Steffe & T. Wood (Eds.), *Transforming children's mathematical education: International perspectives* (pp. 244–252). Hillsdale, NJ: Erlbaum.

Wozniak, R. H. (1985). Notes toward a co-constructive theory of the emotion/cognition relationship. In D. Bearison & H. Zimiles (Eds.), *Thought and emotion: Developmental issues* (pp. 39–64). Hillsdale, NJ: Erlbaum.

Yackel, E. (1995). Children's talk in inquiry mathematics classrooms. In P. Cobb & H. Bauersfeld (Eds.), *The emergence of mathematical meaning: Interaction in classroom cultures* (pp. 131–162). Hillsdale, NJ: Erlbaum.

CHAPTER 5

Reading, Writing, and Literacy

MARILYN JAGER ADAMS, REBECCA TREIMAN, and MICHAEL PRESSLEY

Some children learn to read and write with remarkable ease. Before school, and without any great effort or pressure on the part of their parents, they pick up books, pencils, and paper, and they are on their way, almost as though by magic (see Bissex, 1980; C. Chomsky, 1971; M. Clarke, 1976; Durkin, 1966; Read 1971; Sulzby, 1985).

For most children, however, learning to read and write is just plain difficult, even given years of formal instruction and enforced practice. Thus, we meet many youngsters who would just as soon not read or write and a number who hate to do so. In watching them read, we see some who balk at every other word. We see others who sound out each word, as in "jirl" for *girl,* regardless of the force of the context. We see some who skip and gloss even to the extent that they forfeit the meaning of the passage. And we see others who, though they seem to read with reasonable fluency and accuracy, leave the text with little notion, much less useful thought, of what it was about. At one point or another, in one way or another, many if not most children labor so arduously in reading and so unproductively in writing that we cannot imagine they are getting anything but frustration from the exercise. These children are at the fulcrum of the literacy debate.

Most often, agree those on both sides of the debate, the problem lies in the students' poor management of the words. Yet their explanations and solutions for this problem are diametrically opposed. In caricature, those on one side of the debate argue that the students' preoccupation with the words reflects a fundamental misunderstanding of the real purposes and mature dynamics of reading. The cure, they suggest, is to design the instructional regimen such that issues of letters, spelling-sound correspondences, and word-recognition accuracy are clearly subordinated to meaning from the start. After all, they argue, if readers would focus their attention on the meaning and message of the text, then the letterwise detail of most words could be glossed through context. Those on the other side of the debate, in contrast, argue that it is the students' inability to recognize the words with adequate ease and speed that prevents them from reading with fluency and comprehension. If this is so, they argue, then giving students the help they need to master the words is necessarily key to the cure.

In its barest essence, this debate will be familiar to all psychologists: Are learning and experience principally built bottom-up, through successive organizations of the physical data available through our senses? Or are learning and effective experience controlled top-down, as available information is selected and structured by our reigning goals, interests, and expectations? For almost any psychologist, this is a good problem at some level of abstraction or granularity.

When perspective is shifted to the classroom, however, this becomes a problem of real practical import. The power and effectiveness of our educational programs pivot on how we conceive its resolution at *every* level of abstraction and granularity as this, in turn, determines the schoolroom issues of what to teach, when, and how. Arguably, the principal motive for universal education is universal literacy. Reviewing a number of studies, the U.S. Office of Technology Assessment (1993) estimated that the literacy competencies of approximately one-quarter of adult Americans—35 to 50 million people—are inadequate for purposes of everyday tasks. The majority of these people have passed through our educational system, but many cannot read beyond the third-grade level. The social and personal impact of this situation cannot be overstated. Virtually every dynamic in which this country has invested itself—democracy, innovation, technology competition, productivity, philanthropy, individual liberties, and self-determination—is predicated on a thoughtful, knowledgeable, self-educating populace.

Yet, even as the social and economic values of literacy are multiplying, so too is the evidence that many American children are not adequately learning to read. Results of the 1992 National Assessment of Educational Progress indicated that, nationwide, the reading performance of 41% of fourth-graders fell beneath the cutoff point for basic level performance: they could not read grade-level narratives and high-interest text well enough to identify obvious themes, locate explicitly given information, summarize, or reflect on character's actions (Mullis, Campbell, & Farstrup, 1993). The dropout and illiteracy statistics are especially marked among youth from language and ethnic minorities. These children will soon constitute the majority of our electorate. As a group, moreover, they are also the children who depend most of all on formal schooling for their literacy education.

THE COGNITIVE REVOLUTION AND THE ASCENDANCE OF THE WHOLE LANGUAGE MOVEMENT

The most recent bout in the so-called Great Debate (Chall, 1967) over literacy instruction began to take shape in the 1960s, at the outset of the cognitive revolution. At the time, both psychology and education were becoming increasingly frustrated with the bottom-up stimulus-response framework that had come to dominate theories of learning. This framework was logical, it was deeply entrenched, and it was mature to the point of nth-order parameters and a burgeoning market in bottom-up teaching designs. But there was also something about it that was somehow incomplete, unsatisfying, inhuman.

At just that moment, there erupted a series of compelling arguments that language, that quintessentially *human* capacity, was special. The physical dimensions of the speech signal were argued to be such that it could not be processed through bottom-up perceptual mechanisms. The complexities and possibilities of syntax were argued to be such that it could not be mastered through any piecewise bottom-up learning regimen. Humans must be endowed with some special, higher-order capacity to respond to structure and meaning in language (Chomsky, 1965; McNeill, 1970).

That the cognitive requirements of oral and written language must overlap at some level may be self-evident. At that time, however, psychologists saw parallels at every level. In Neisser's (1967) words, "Most people . . . can understand what they read without actually identifying many of the individual words. How is this possible?" (pp. 134–135; see also, e.g., Kolers, 1968; F. Smith, 1971, 1973). Having accepted the question, the answer was necessarily sought in the reader's higher-order knowledge and expectations about language and meaning.

Suddenly, reading was an interesting domain of study. For research psychologists, the buzz word was *top-down processing,* and text processing became a major medium for its investigation. Indeed, in the years since then, research on reading is said to have filled more book and journal pages than any other topic in cognitive psychology (Besner & Humphreys, 1991).

Yet, if these speculations were energizing to research psychologists, they were of arresting significance to educators. Specifically, if the separate words and letters of text are functionally irrelevant to the mature reading process, then what is the advantage—and what might be the disadvantages—of making these units so focal in early reading instruction? Were our conventional methods of reading instruction seriously misguided? Could this be why so many young readers bog down on the words? Could it be that the major difference between good and poor readers lay in their ability to divert attention from the letters and words to the meaning of text? Would children learn to read more quickly and productively if, from the start, their attention was directed not to letters and words but to the meaning and message of the texts?

Of course, whether or not skillful readers skip and gloss the letters and words of text while reading, the questions of whether or not young readers can or should do so are separate. Because the interest was intense and the data were sparse, a single research study by Ken Goodman (1965) became highly influential. In designing this study, Goodman reasoned that if the functional cues in meaningful text extend beyond the level of individual words, then growing readers should be more able to read words in context than in isolation. To assess this hypothesis, he constructed word lists from each of a graded sequence of basal stories. His subjects were 100 students in grades 1 through 3. Toward equating the subjective difficulty of the task, each child was tested first on the word lists. When a list was found on which the child missed neither too many nor too few words, she or he was asked to read the story from which that list had been taken. Goodman found that more than half of the words that had been misread or skipped in the lists were read accurately in context, and this was true across all of the children and regardless of grade. Given, as these data suggested, that children find it harder to recognize simple words than to read them in stories, Goodman concluded, "We must abandon our concentration on words in teaching reading and develop a theory of reading and a methodology which puts the focus where it belongs: on language" (p. 134).

Goodman himself became highly active in promoting this very belief and, with remarkable rapidity, it burgeoned into what is now known as the whole language movement. According to the whole language philosophy, reading and writing cannot be nurtured piece by piece; they are holistic acts, learnable and worth learning only as such. Most of all, the whole language philosophy holds that learning is anchored on and motivated by meaning. Further, since meaning and meaningfulness are necessarily defined internally and never by pronouncement, learning can be effective only to the extent that it is cognitively controlled by the learner.

Meanwhile, away from the classroom, research psychologists were also captivated by theories of top-down processing. Working within this framework, they discovered that people's memory and reading times for words were responsive to subtle overlaps in the meanings of words (e.g., Collins & Quillian, 1969; Meyer, Schvaneveldt, & Ruddy, 1975; Tulving & Gold, 1963). Cognitive psychologists showed that readers' ability to comprehend a text at all depends on some larger understanding of what it is about (e.g., Bransford & Johnson, 1973; Dooling & Lachman, 1971). They showed that the particulars remembered from text are strongly influenced by the perspective from which it is read (e.g., Anderson & Pichart, 1978). They showed that readers readily generate inferences to complete and connect the information on the page (e.g., Bransford, Barclay, & Franks, 1972). More generally, research psychologists found broad evidence for the constructive nature of comprehension and memory. Over the same period of time, however, they also found firm evidence that, for skillful adults, reading generally proceeds through relatively thorough processing of the words and letters of text (for reviews, see Adams, 1990; Rayner & Pollatsek, 1989).

Although whole language, its advocates insist, is not a method or program of instruction, it has brought along certain dramatic changes in classroom practices across the grades. These include a general shift from teacher-directed to student-centered classroom dynamics; an emphasis on learning through engagement with quality texts and intrinsically meaningful tasks in place of workbooks and drill; the abandonment of rigid ability grouping in favor of more equitable and flexible support strategies; an early and continuing emphasis on independent writing; and an effort toward integration across the curriculum. For the most part, these changes are long overdue and for the better. On the other hand, whole language advocates have steadfastly, adamantly, and sometimes vitriolically denied the value and rejected the practice of skills instruction, including phonics, and this has been a point of heated contention.

The word *illiterate,* by dictionary definitions, means unable to read or to write. A person who is *literate,* in contrast, is someone who not only can and does read and write but, further, does so in the service of expanding and exploring her or his own thoughts and knowledge and of sharing them with others. In keeping with this, we have divided this chapter into two main sections. The first examines issues involved in learning to read and write, and the second focuses on those involved in learning to use reading and writing in increasingly literate ways. Despite having thus divided the literacy challenge in two, we wish to assert at the outset that the essential cognitive challenge remains the same throughout. Specifically, literacy development at every level pivots on the ability to treat language itself as not merely an instrument, but an *object* of thought, analysis, and reflection.

READING AND WRITING: THE BASICS

The Use of Words by Skillful Readers

The question with which researchers entered this era was *how* skillful readers might exploit context to skip the words. The prior question, *whether* skillful readers might exploit context to skip the words, was presumptively dismissed, ultimately to be appreciated only by force of the data.

In fact, it had long ago been established that, given very brief exposure durations, people could "see" the letters of familiar words more accurately than random strings of letters (Cattell, 1885; Pillsbury, 1897). Surely this was evidence of the higher-order influences in quest. Armed with tachistoscopes, millisecond timers, computers, and the array of new methodologies thereby afforded, research psychologists were remarkably inventive at creating situations in which their subjects' prior knowledge and expectations ought to override the precise letterwise compositions of the words actually displayed. But none of them worked. At least with isolated words, the data stubbornly but ever more strongly indicated that, although somehow letters become more perceptible when they are parts of familiar words, the perception of words was meticulously respectful of the identities of their letters (e.g., Adams, 1979; McClelland & Johnston, 1977; D. Wheeler, 1970).

The pertinence of such word-recognition data to real reading situations became clear only gradually, and largely through the help of computer-mediated eye movement technologies. Physically, after all, it seems that people ought to be able to see more on the page than the word in fixation. Cognitively, however, it seems that they do not. F. Smith's (1971) intuitively appealing hypothesis that fluent reading is propelled by semantic or syntactic preprocessing of peripherally viewed words is counterindicated by the data (see e.g., Inhoff & Briihl, 1991; Rayner & Morris, 1992; Rayner & Pollatsek, 1989). Although readers' eyes do sometimes skip over words, they tend only to skip short function words and rarely to skip more than one at a time. Otherwise, for skillful readers and regardless of the difficulty or predictability of the text, the basic dynamic of connected reading is left to right, line by line, and word by word (Just & Carpenter, 1980). As in the case of isolated words, moreover, the recognition of each fixated word in text entails complete visual processing of its letters as well as early and compulsory translation of its spelling to speech (Pollatsek, Lesch, Morris, & Rayner, 1992; Rayner, Sereno, Lesch, & Pollatsek, 1995).

In the end, it seems that printed words are the basic data on which reading depends. Skillful readers generally *do* fixate most of the words; the information they gain from a text depends tightly on the specific words they have fixated, and their recognition of the words on which they fixate depends integrally on their processing the words' spellings and spelling-speech correspondences. Furthermore, this letter- and wordwise processing does *not* divert attention from meaning and message. Instead, it operates almost automatically, almost autonomously, in support of comprehension. This is possible only because skillful readers possess a remarkably rich, redundant, and flexible system of knowledge about the spellings of words and their links to speech and meaning (Adams, 1990; Rayner & Pollatsek, 1989).

Developmental Data on Word Recognition and Reading

Researchers have not only amassed incontrovertible data for the critical role of spelling and spelling-sound knowledge in skillful reading and word recognition, but have also developed strong explanatory models of how the mind uses this knowledge (e.g., Berent & Perfetti, 1995; Coltheart, Curtis, Atkins, & Haller, 1993; Seidenberg & McClelland, 1989; Van Orden, Pennington, & Stone, 1990). But here is the converse of the issue raised earlier: Even if reading involves thorough processing of spellings and spelling-sound mappings for skillful adults, this may or may not be so for children.

What are the cues to which beginning readers are most sensitive? How do these cues change in nature or balance with reading growth? And how do more and less successful learners differ from one another? Goodman's (1965) report and the surrounding interest accentuated the importance of these questions, and within a few years there appeared in the literature two separate, observational studies of beginners' reading behaviors (Biemiller, 1970; Weber, 1970a, 1970b). Both studies were designed to assess the growth, across the first-grade year, of first-graders' sensitivity to the higher-order cues of context in their daily reading of meaningful, connected text.

Building directly on Goodman's (1965) results, Biemiller's (1970) expectation was that the children's reading errors or miscues would reflect three successively more mature stages in their sensitivity to textual cues: running from nonresponse errors, to orthographically driven errors, to contextually influenced substitutions. On the basis of his recordings of the children's oral reading from October to May, Biemiller did in fact identify these three stages. But their order differed jarringly from his expectations. Specifically, it was only in the first or earliest stage of reading development that context exerted a preemptive influence on word recognition. In this stage, although the children's errors tended to be contextually acceptable (74%), most (81%) seemed graphically unrelated to the print on the page. Further, the longer the children dwelled in this first, context-driven stage of reading, the poorer their progress as measured at the year's end. In the intermediate stage, the children's most common error was no response, as they basically refused to read words they did not know. Finally, Biemiller observed, it was only in the *last* stage, at the *end* of first grade, that the graphemic details of the words began to supersede contextual cues in influencing the children's misreadings.

Weber (1970) obtained a similar pattern of results in a study of two different first-grade classrooms. In keeping with context-based theories of reading, the vast majority (80–94%) of the errors these children made consisted of substituting a word in view with some other. Further, whether the children were in the high, middle, or low reading group, the majority (87–92%) of their substitution errors were grammatically compatible with the preceding context. On the other hand, reported Weber, not only did the better readers make fewer errors per line of running text, but their errors tended to capture *more* of the graphemic detail of the misread word than did those of the poorer readers.

Thus, both Biemiller (1970) and Weber (1970) found ample evidence of young readers' sensitivity to the meaning and flow of their texts. However, the pattern of these errors across development and reading ability was just the opposite of that suggested by Goodman's (1965) study. Among both Biemiller's and Weber's young subjects, reading growth brought with it, not less, but *more* deference to the print on the page.

How could these findings be reconciled? The answer, with hindsight, is methodological. First, Goodman (1965) had collapsed his data by grades regardless of the children's reading ability. Yet, subsequent replications have shown that the context advantage is due mostly to the poor readers, regardless of grade (Allington, 1978; Nicholson, 1991; Nicholson, Bailey, & McArthur, 1991; Nicholson, Lillas, & Rzoska, 1988). Second, the children in Goodman's study were always asked to read the word lists before the stories. When, instead, they are asked to read the stories first, the advantage of context over the word lists is generally diminished; indeed, among better readers, this advantage is generally reversed (Nicholson, 1991; Nicholson et al., 1991; Nicholson et al., 1988).

This basic pattern has been replicated and extended across a variety of research paradigms. From the start, it seems that good readers-to-be are, if anything, more attuned to context than are poor readers-to-be. However, good readers-to-be are also far more sensitive to the spellings of the words and their phonological mappings (Tunmer & Chapman, 1995). This relation continues across years in school such that good readers remain significantly more able to predict upcoming words in context (for reviews, see Perfetti, 1985; Tunmer & Hoover, 1992). Nevertheless, and whether measured by speed or accuracy, the word recognition of good readers is also significantly less dependent on (or susceptible to) context than is that of poor readers (e.g., Allington & Strange, 1977; Juel, 1980; Perfetti & Roth, 1977; West & Stanovich, 1978). Very quickly, and in contrast to poor readers, the ability of good readers to recognize familiar words becomes so fast and sure that supportive context results in little measurable improvement in speed or accuracy of word recognition (for extensive reviews, see Stanovich, 1980, 1986). Alongside, the ability to read unfamiliar words or pseudowords emerges as the singularly most powerful discriminator of overall reading ability (see Perfetti, 1985; Rack, Snowling, & Olson, 1992; Stanovich & Siegel, 1994; Vellutino, 1979).

Overall, the data argue compellingly that letters and words are the basic data of reading (Adams, 1990). This conclusion, in turn, provides a powerful explanation for the findings of numerous studies that poor word-identification skills are strongly coupled with poor reading comprehension in both children (Perfetti, 1985; Rack, Snowling, & Olson, 1992; Stanovich, 1982, 1991b; Vellutino, 1991) and adults (Bruck, 1990; Cunningham, Stanovich, & Wilson, 1990). Moreover, research now affirms that weaknesses in decoding abilities are the most common and debilitating source of reading difficulties (Perfetti, 1985; Shankweiler et al., 1995; Stanovich, 1986; Vellutino, 1991; Vernon, 1971).

Conventional Phonics: A Problematic Solution

The term *phonics* refers to systems of instruction, of which there are literally hundreds (Aukerman, 1971, 1984), that are designed to help children use the correspondences between letters and sounds to learn to read and write. To understand written text, the reader must be able to derive meaning from the strings of printed symbols on the page. Phonics methods are built on the recognition that the basic symbols—the graphemes—of alphabetic languages such as English encode elementary speech sounds. By teaching the relationships between spellings and sounds, phonics methods are intended to assist the learning process by providing young readers and writers with a basis both for remembering the ordered identities of useful letter strings and for deriving the meanings of printed words that, though visually unfamiliar, are in their speaking and listening vocabularies.

Across the centuries, methods to help beginning readers attend to the sequences of letters and their correspondences to speech patterns have been a core element of most approaches to literacy instruction in alphabetic languages (Feitelson, 1988; Mathews, 1966; N. Smith, 1974). Further, whether assessed through large-scale classroom studies, such as the massive U.S. Office of Education first-grade studies (Bond & Dykstra, 1967), or through myriad smaller experimental studies (e.g., see meta-analysis by Pflaum, Walberg, Karegianes, & Rasher, 1980), it has been found with overwhelming consistency that instructional approaches lending explicit attention to phonics result in significantly greater reading growth than those that do not (see also Chall, 1967).

Thus, even in the infancy of the whole language movement, strong data existed to the effect that knowing about spellings and spelling-sound mappings was essential to reading and learning to read. Nevertheless, as the whole language movement grew stronger, so too did its renunciations of phonics instruction. This stance was surely aggravated by the strong anti-phonics rhetoric of Frank Smith (1971, 1973, 1982, 1992). Yet, common sense argues that there had to be some underlying reason for the appeal of Smith's writings. Three can be offered. First, Smith methodically conflated issues of phonics instruction with the urgent social, political, and educational concerns of the whole language movement (see Adams, 1991; Stanovich, 1994). Second, the piecewise, bottom-up nature of conventional phonics instruction was inherently incompatible with the constructivist premises on which the whole language movement was built. Third and, we suspect, most influential, was the frequent plaint that conventional phonics instruction tends to be tedious in progress and iffy in effectiveness; doubtless, many teachers sensed this and were eager for a better approach.

Across this era, the documented advantage of conventional phonics was neither awesomely large nor comfortingly reliable. Even while the studies collectively affirmed that conventional phonics instruction was, on average, a positive component of early reading development, they also demonstrated enormous differences in the outcomes of any program depending on the particular schools, teachers, children, and implementation vagaries involved. In particular, even where phonics was taught, and even where it was taught under the watchful eye of researchers, there remained many children who nonetheless experienced great difficulty in learning to read. Across studies of middle-class schools using conventional programs, it can be estimated that roughly 25% of children fail to catch on by the end of the first grade (Adams, 1990). Clearly, something more than what was conventionally taught was needed to make phonics accessible.

The Wonders of the Alphabet versus the Difficulty of Phonics

Over the centuries and around the world, writing systems that were comprised of large numbers of symbols were naturally the possession of the elite. They were generally passed on only to those few whom it was felt should and, among those, could and would invest the amount of time and study required for their memorization. In view of this, historian David Diringer (1968) describes the invention of the alphabet as "the creation of a 'revolutionary writing,' a script which we can perhaps term 'democratic' (or rather, a 'people's script'), as against the 'theocratic' scripts that preceded it" (p. 161).

The number of symbols in alphabetic systems tends to range between 20 and 35: few enough to be memorized by very nearly anyone and, once memorized, adequate—at least in a perfectly alphabetic system—for purposes of reading and writing any word in the language. Yet, for many children, learning to read an alphabetic script is not easy. It sounds so simple. Why is it that so many have such difficulty?

One possibility is that the difficulty lies in learning the letters. In fact, preschoolers' familiarity with the letters of the alphabet is a strong predictor of their reading success (Bond & Dykstra, 1967; Chall, 1967; Jansky & de Hirsch, 1972; Richek 1977–1978; Silberberg, Iverson, & Silberberg, 1968; Speer & Lamb, 1976), and letter-naming facility continues to correlate with reading success well into the primary grades (Biemiller, 1977–1978; Blachman, 1984; Muter, Hulme, Snowling, & Taylor, 1995). Nowadays, most children from mainstream neighborhoods are found to know most of their letters by first-grade entry (Durrell & Catterson, 1980, cited in Chall, 1983; Mason, 1980; McCormick & Mason, 1986; Nurss, 1979). Importantly, however, there are both children and neighborhoods for which this generality is untrue. For example, Masonheimer (1980, cited in Ehri, 1986) found that although the English-speaking 5-year-olds in her California sample could name most (71%) of the uppercase letters correctly, the Spanish-speaking children could name very few (4%, or roughly one letter).

Letter naming, in short, is very important and warrants earnest assessment and support. On the other hand, both clinical report (e.g., I. Liberman, 1973; Vernon, 1971) and experimental evidence (Doehring, 1976; Jenkins, Bausell, & Jenkins, 1972; Mason, 1980; Ohnmacht, 1969) indicate that, given the opportunity, most children successfully learn their letters as such without too much trouble. Further, for children who know their letter names, but *not* for children who do not (Ehri & Wilce, 1979), neither does learning the sounds of the letters seem a major obstacle (Jenkins et al., 1972; Mason, 1980; Ehri & Wilce, 1979; we discuss the relation of letter-name and letter-sound learning more fully in the section on children's writing).

Rather, reading difficulty asserts itself when, "even when able to sound printed letters and letter groups, they cannot blend these to form whole words" (Vernon, 1971, p. 128; see also Chall, 1967; Critchley & Critchley, 1978). How could this be? The step from having all of the sounds to inducing the word seems so self-evident. It is generally taken for granted by those touting the elegant simplicity of the alphabetic code.

Dyslexia: "Minimal Brain Dysfunction"

Given the seeming ease of the challenge alongside the fact that it nonetheless eludes children who seem normal and intelligent in every other way, a dominant assumption has been that such difficulties reflect some underlying and relatively reading-specific neural aberration. The earliest explanations, for example, attributed the cause of otherwise inexplicable reading problems to a deficiency in those areas of the brain responsible for storing visual images; children with severe difficulties were said to suffer from *congenital word blindness* (Hinshelwood, 1900, 1917; Morgan, 1896). Struck by observations of letter and spelling reversals, Orton (1925, 1937) ascribed the problem to an underlying syndrome he termed *strephosymbolia,* or "twisted symbols." Based on his belief that visual patterns are stored in mirror images in the right and left halves of the brain, Orton theorized that such reversals reflect a delay in establishment of left-hemispheric dominance for language.

Although many of the older theories seem strange or unfounded from a contemporary perspective, all are intended to offer an underlying cause for disturbances in information processing that plausibly could disrupt the word-learning process of young readers. Among the proximal difficulties that such theories were intended to explain are deficiencies in visual-motor coordination, visual matching, visual feature extraction and trace persistence, spatial and directional orientation, figure-ground perception, visual information-processing speed, visual short- or long-term memory, intersensory mappings, cross-modality shifting, intersensory learning, temporal order perception, sequential ordering, and spatial ordering. Vellutino (1979) masterfully critiqued the vast experimental literature on these factors as they separate normal and reading-delayed children. Extending the literature as necessary through work with his own, clean sample of 200 normal and reading-delayed children in grades 2 through 6, he concluded that performance on tasks designed to tap these categories of factors was, at best, weakly or inconsistently associated with specific reading difficulty *unless* the tasks directly or indirectly entailed verbal processing or memory.

Regardless of the research findings, the nonscientific press continues to cite lack of coordination or balance among cerebral functions as the core cause for reading difficulties. Consider, for example, the broadly promulgated hypothesis that there exists some substantial and identifiable group of visually, globally oriented children for whom phonics is, by nature, inferior to visual or meaning-based approaches (see e.g., Carbo, Dunn, & Dunn, 1986). Perhaps because of its fit with the folk psychology on right and left brains, this hypothesis has held remarkably long and strong sway among teachers and reading specialists. For example, a survey of special education teachers in Illinois (Arter & Jenkins, 1977) showed that 95% were familiar with this argument, and, of those familiar with it, 99% believed that modality preferences should be a primary consideration in devising instruction for children with learning difficulties. In addition, nearly all believed this hypothesis to be well supported by research. But it is not.

Instead, and regardless of children's apparent perceptual strengths and styles, successful intervention seems invariably to depend on helping them learn how to sound out words (for reviews, see Arter & Jenkins, 1979; Barr, 1984; Bateman, 1979; Chall, 1967; Cronbach & Snow, 1977; Kampwirth & Bates 1980; Robinson, 1972; Stahl, 1988; Tarver & Dawson, 1988). By all indications, moreover, early intervention is more successful than later intervention (Carter, 1984; Vernon, 1971). No wonder, then, the claim by concerned citizen groups such as the National Right to Read Foundation that early intensive phonics instruction ought to offer a near-universal cure to America's reading ills.

Yet, if the problem were that simple, it surely would have been solved long ago. Again, instruction programs that include a solid, explicit, systematic strand of conventional phonics have been shown to bring along more children than those that do not (Adams, 1990; Aukerman, 1971, 1984; Bond & Dykstra, 1967; Chall, 1967, 1983). But neither are these programs ideal classroom solutions. Regardless of the instruction provided, the accessibility of phonics varies enormously across children: Although some catch on in a wink, others just don't; although the logic and value of phonics is instantly self-evident to some, it stubbornly eludes others. For those children who have already taken off, a bitwise regimen of intensive, systematic phonics is arguably not the most useful way to spend time; for those who have not yet caught on, it is useless. A far better solution would be to understand and address the reasons why phonics is more or less accessible to different children. This is where the most important breakthroughs of the past few years have been.

The Importance of Phonemic Awareness

The Perceptual Nonreality of Phonemes

If the cognitive revolution was triggered by theoretical malaise, it was fueled by a series of compelling arguments that human behavior could not be explained by any piecewise, bottom-up concatenation of simple sensory or motor events (e.g., N. Chomksy, 1965; Hebb, 1949; Lashley, 1951; Neisser, 1967). As relates to research on beginning reading, the most important of these arguments may well have been that, acoustically speaking, phonemes do not exist. This argument was made most forcefully in a classic paper by Alvin Liberman and his colleagues (A. Liberman, Cooper, Shankweiler, & Studdert-Kennedy, 1967).

Meanwhile, being close to these findings through her spouse and involved in reading research herself, Isabelle Liberman was quick to recognize the instructional significance of this claim. Others had mused that the problem for many young readers seemed to lie in developing an awareness of phonemes (e.g., Monroe, 1932; Savin, 1972; Vernon, 1971). In addition, several studies had documented the difficulty of training young children to break words into phonemes (Elkonin, 1973; Rosner & Simon, 1971). But the idea that phonemes were flatly unhearable put a different slant on these reports. Conventional phonics instruction, after all, was firmly predicated on the assumption that there existed some essential and available acoustical invariance within phonemic categories. Yet, if this were not so, then what was a child to make of such standard classroom verbiage as "The sound of the letter *b* is /b/"; "Listen for the sound of the letter *b* in ball, blue, table, and crab"; "What is the first sound of the word *bat?*"; "Name some words that end in the sound of the letter *b*"; and so on.

To assess the reality of this problem more directly, I. Liberman, Shankweiler, Fischer, and Carter (1974) developed a straightforward sound-counting task, logically equivalent to the common classroom question "How many sounds do you hear in the word ______?" Specifically, the task consisted of a set of 42 items, each composed of one to three phonemes. The children were given a wooden stick and asked to tap out the number of phonemes in each item; for example, given the word *mat,* the child was to tap three times, once for each of its phonemes: /m/, /ă/, and /t/. A second, matched group of children was given an analogous task in which they were asked to tap out the number of syllables (one to three) in words. The children were drawn from middle-class preschool, kindergarten, and first-grade classrooms and tested near the end of the school year. For both groups, the test items were preceded by ample training, demonstration, and modeling, and, even within the test trials, feedback was provided for incorrect responses. The children were deemed successful if they correctly tapped out six consecutive items.

Nearly all of the first-graders and roughly half of the kindergartners and preschoolers reached criterion on the syllable-tapping task, and some (50% of the first-graders, 16% of the kindergartners, and 7% of the preschoolers) did so without making a single error. Thus, the basic "play" of the game seemed well within reach for most of the children. Despite that, only 70% of the first-graders, 17% of the kindergartners, and none of the preschool children reached criterion on the phoneme-tapping task. Of those who did, all made errors and most took close to the maximum number of trials (and thus feedback) available. Further, on assessing the reading achievement of the oldest children the following fall, it was found that none of those in the top third of the class had failed the phoneme-tapping test the previous spring. In contrast, of those who had failed the phoneme-tapping task, half were in the lowest third of their class in reading achievement, and none were in the top third. (I. Liberman, Shankweiler, Liberman, Fowler, & Fischer, 1977).

In short, and as suspected, the sort of explicit phonemic awareness measured by the phoneme-counting task seemed strongly related to beginning reading acquisition. More disturbingly, however, the data also suggested that, for many school-age children, this sort of sensitivity to phonemes was neither already established nor easy to acquire. At the same time, the steep increase in segmentation ability across the first-grade year left I. Liberman wondering whether phonemic awareness developed as enabler or consequence of emergent reading and writing. Clearly, with regard to instructional implications, this question is critical. Its answer, with hindsight, seems to be *both.*

The Causal Importance of Phonemic Awareness

In the intervening years, a variety of different tasks has been developed for assessing phonemic awareness. Relevant to issues of construct validity, the common variance of these tasks is generally very substantial (Stahl & Murray, 1994; Stanovich, Cunningham, & Cramer, 1984; Wagner & Torgesen, 1987; Wagner, Torgesen, Laughon, Simmons, & Rashotte, 1993; Yopp, 1988). Collectively, such work yields the conclusion that, even for normal language learners, awareness of phonemes is not a given and is only weakly related to abilities to perceive and discriminate speech sounds (see Backman, 1983; Stanovich, Cunningham, & Cramer, 1984; Yopp, 1988).

Consistent with causal interpretations of phonemic awareness, longitudinal studies have demonstrated over and over that such measures of children's phonemic awareness are powerful predictors of subsequent reading growth, even when competed against, for example, various measures of IQ and nonphonological print/language sophistication (e.g., Bradley & Bryant, 1983; Byrne, Freebody, & Gates, 1992; Catts, 1991a, 1991b; Foorman, Francis, Novy, & Liberman, 1991; Hurford, Schauf, Bunce, Blaich, & Moore, 1994; Jorm, Share, MacLean, & Matthews, 1984; Juel, Griffith, & Gough, 1986; MacLean, Bryant, & Bradley, 1987; Mann, 1984; Mann & Liberman, 1984; Stanovich et al., 1984; Vellutino & Scanlon, 1987; Wagner, Torgesen, & Rashotte, 1994). To give the flavor of this work, and because of its cognitive and pedagogical importance, we describe a sampling of these studies in more detail.

Tunmer and Nesdale (1985) administered the phoneme-tapping task along with a decoding test, a reading comprehension test, and the Peabody Picture Vocabulary Test (to measure verbal IQ) to 68 first-graders from six different classrooms. Based on close statistical analysis of their data, Tunmer and Nesdale concluded that phonemic segmentation skills, as measured by the tapping task, were strongly, directly, and causally related to decoding abilities and that decoding abilities, in turn, were strongly, directly, and causally related to reading comprehension. IQ contributed directly, but weakly, to each of these abilities.

A direct peek at the children's patterns of performance tells the story just as well: all of the students who did well on the decoding test also passed the tapping task; all of those who failed the tapping task also failed the decoding test; an additional number of students passed the tapping task but failed the decoding test. Thus, it seems that phonemic segmentation skills were a necessary precursor to being able to decode, but they were not sufficient. Those who could decode could segment. Those who could not segment could not decode. The third group of children, who could segment but could not decode, were evidently lacking in their mastery of letter-to-sound correspondences (see also Tunmer, Nesdale, & Herriman, 1988).

A similar pattern of results was obtained with children attending a lower-middle-class school in Texas through a longitudinal study conducted by Juel et al. (1986). In place of the tapping test, Juel et al. measured phonemic awareness with a set of six 7-item subtests measuring (a) segmentation (e.g., "Say *no*. What are the two sounds in *no?*"); (b) blending (e.g., "Say /n/, /ī/, /s/. What word is /n/, /ī/, /s/?"); (c) initial phoneme deletion (e.g., "Say *top*. Now say *top* without the /t/."); (d) deletion of last phoneme (e.g., "Say *same*. Now say *same* without the /m/."); (e) substitution of initial phoneme (e.g., "Say *ball*. Instead of /b/, begin a new word with /k/."); (f) substitution of final phoneme (e.g., "Say *park*. Instead of /k/, end a word with /t/.").

Through a hierarchical regression analysis, Juel et al. (1986) found that performance on the phonemic awareness measure at the beginning of first grade predicted 49% of the variance in the children's word recognition or decoding performance at the end of first grade *after* accounting for the contributions of IQ (block design and vocabulary subtests of the Wechsler Intelligence Scale for Children–Revised) and listening comprehension (Iowa test). Further, a comparison of end-of-the-year phonemic awareness and decoding scores revealed the same pattern of results that Tunmer and Nesdale (1985) obtained: no students with average or above-average word-recognition abilities had low phonemic awareness scores, and all students with low phonemic awareness scores had below-average word-recognition abilities.

In extending this study through the children's fourth year of school, Juel (1988) also took periodic measures of their listening comprehension, their generation of ideas in oral storytelling (in response to pictures), and the amount of reading they did outside of school. Although these measures did not distinguish would-be good and poor readers in first grade, all diverged dramatically across the school years. Specifically, for children who were successfully learning to read, performance surged upward on every one of these measures; for children who were not learning to read adequately, performance barely changed at all on any of these measures. Moreover, the likelihood that a child would be a good or poor reader by the end of fourth grade was almost wholly predicted by whether she or he was a good or poor reader at the end of first grade. This, in turn, was strongly predicted by the child's phonemic awareness at the beginning of first grade (Juel, 1988, 1994).

The common variance of the phonemic awareness measures in conjunction with their collective dissociation with indices of IQ, vocabulary, and general language development suggest that the phonemic tasks are tapping some relatively specific factor. At the same time, their predictive strength and the asymmetry of their contingency with word recognition are consistent with the notion that this factor is prerequisite to reading acquisition. Strengthening this view are studies showing that engaging children in activities designed to develop phonemic awareness hastens later reading and writing acquisition (e.g., Ball & Blachman, 1991; Bradley & Bryant, 1983; Byrne & Fielding-Barnsley, 1989, 1991; Castle, Riach, & Nicholson, 1994; Cunningham, 1990; Hatcher, Hulme, & Ellis, 1994; Tangel & Blachman, 1992; Vellutino & Scanlon, 1987; Wallach & Wallach, 1979; Williams, 1979).

The classic study in this category is a training study built on strictly *oral* language activities (no print) that was conducted with Danish preschoolers by Lundberg, Frost, and Petersen (1988). Over the course of the preschool year, these children were engaged in a variety of games and activities involving nursery rhymes, rhymed stories, and rhyme production; segmentation of sentences into separate words and investigations of word length; clapping and dancing to syllabic rhythms and solving puzzles posed by a "troll" who could speak only in a syllable-by-syllable manner; and, finally, segmentation and blending of word-initial and then word-final and word-internal phonemes.

For their control group, Lundberg et al. (1988) went to a district that had historically outscored that of the experimental children in academic measures. At the end of the training year, the performance of the two groups was comparable in both letter knowledge and higher-order language comprehension. However, the experimental children were significantly superior to the controls in their measurable sensitivity to rhymes, syllables, word lengths, and, most of all, phonemes. At the end of first grade—and thus a year after the training program had ended—the children were compared again, this time on measures of word recognition, spelling, mathematics, and a nonverbal IQ test (Ravens' Progressive Matrices). Although (and as expected, given the sampling strategy) the control children slightly outperformed the experimentals on both the math and IQ tests, the experimental children outperformed the controls on both the word-recognition and spelling tests. Retesting at the end of the second grade showed that the experimental children's advantage over the controls by these measures remained as great or even increased. Indeed, although the difference in the experimental and control children's spelling scores was significant in both first and second grade, the difference in word-recognition scores did not reach statistical significance until the second grade.

Phonemic Awareness as a Consequence of Literacy Growth

Such longitudinal data notwithstanding, the prima facie case that phonemic awareness is not cause but consequence of literacy instruction is still simpler: People tend to demonstrate an awareness of phonemes only if they have tried to learn an alphabetic writing system. What, after all, are the alternatives? As discussed earlier, phonemic awareness appears to be relatively independent of general intelligence, general language ability, and perceptual analysis. Could it be a developmentally emergent phenomenon? Evidently not, for a number of studies have shown that adult illiterates essentially lack awareness of phonemes (see Morais, 1991). Is phonemic awareness the product of some gradual tuning or refinement of more general phonological sensitivities? Again, this seems not to be the answer; choosing two illiterate poets especially because of their exceptional sensitivity to phonetic contrasts among syllables, Morais (1991) found that the ability to isolate phonemes was beyond the reach of both. Nor could formal schooling per se be responsible because, as shown by Read, Yun-Fei, Hong-Yin, and Bao-Qing (1986), phonemic awareness generally eludes literate Chinese adults *unless* they have been schooled in an alphabetic writing system.

Although, as demonstrated by Lundberg et al. (1988), phonemic awareness can be trained in the absence of any linkage to print, vanishingly few children have experienced such specialized training. On the other hand, most children, when taught, do learn to read. Given an alphabetic script, the implication is that all such children do acquire phonemic awareness, for reading does not develop without it. Where does this phonemic awareness come from? For most students, it seems to emerge and grow rapidly in the course of their first year of reading instruction (e.g., Bentin, Hammer, & Cahan, 1991; Bowey & Francis, 1991; Cardoso-Martins, 1991; Liberman et al., 1974; Tunmer & Nesdale, 1985).

Logically, anything that is both cause and consequence must also be part and parcel. Thus, the story would be neat and complete—just teach the children to read—except for one thing: with or without reading instruction, gaining phonemic awareness is not easy for many children. This raises two subsidiary questions: Why is phonemic awareness hard? and What, more precisely, is its relation to reading?

The Difficulty of Phonemic Awareness

Historical Patterns

In one way or another, virtually all modern writing systems are parasitic on language. This was not always true. Linguistic mediation of visual communication evolved gradually and uncertainly in both time and levels of abstraction. In the earliest writing systems, referents were represented pictorially, and meaning and messages were represented through complex scenes. Within pictographic genres, conventionalized icons for specific concepts or "words" seem to evolve irrepressibly. Nevertheless, the adoption of logographic systems counts as a relatively rare and distinct communication insight. A key distinction between pictographic and logographic systems is that, in the latter, the icons are arrayed and interpreted sequentially as guided by spoken language constraints (DeFrancis, 1989; Gelb, 1963).

Similarly, although logographies seem inevitably to exploit the use of "sounds-like" symbols for extending their referential power, they evolved into syllabic writing systems only in the rarest of circumstances. More often, syllabic writing systems have become established through cultural borrowing or through their deliberate invention for one language system by somebody—a missionary, king, or emperor—who was literate in some other (DeFrancis, 1989; Gelb, 1963).

The evolution of our present writing system took thousands of years and depended no less on cross-cultural borrowing than on cross-linguistic inappropriateness and adaptation of that which had been borrowed. Due largely to record-keeping exigencies of foreign trade, ancient logographies were displaced by syllabaries. According to one story, at least, the syllabaries gradually degenerated into an alliterative shorthand, which, when adopted by the Greeks, was serendipitously misconceived as an alphabet: the symbols were seen to represent the consonants per se (see Gleitman & Rozin, 1977). Even so, the denotation of vowel phonemes took hundreds more years to settle in (Balmuth, 1982; Mathews, 1966).

The point is that the notion that language can be successively decomposed into words, syllables, and phonemes is not a priori psychologically obvious or compelling. Moreover, the historical ease and order with which cultures have become aware of these levels of abstraction and exploited them as units of writing is mirrored in the developmental ease and order with which children normally do so.

Developmental Patterns: The Attentional Problem

Early reading instruction begins with the assumption that words are individually accessible units of language. The concept of a word and the ability to recognize stand-alone words are taken for granted. Moreover, the word *word* is nearly unavoidable in instructional settings. To make any sense whatsoever out of their classroom activities, children must already understand or quickly catch on to the idea of what a word is.

Yet, evidence concurs that children, like their ancestors, are not naturally prepared either to conceive of spoken language as a string of individual words or to treat words as individual units of meaning (Downing & Oliver, 1973–1974; Ehri, 1975; Holden & MacGinitie, 1972; Huttenlocher, 1964). What children listen for is the full meaning of an utterance, and that comes only after the meanings of the individual words have been combined—automatically and without their attention. More picturesquely, "During this period, the word may be used but not noticed by the child, and frequently it presents things seemingly like a glass, through which the child looks at the surrounding world, not making the word itself the object" (attributed to A. R. Luria by Downing, 1979, p. 27).

Perhaps because of their status as conceptual handles, words attract awareness quite easily, once pointed out. Even in a single sitting, young children can make great progress in segmenting sentences into individual words, although they are extremely resistant to conceding word status to function words and prepositions (Engelmann, 1969; Fox & Routh, 1975). More often, argues Ehri (1976, 1979), the concept of word is evoked through exposure to print. In print, unlike speech, words are physically separated one from the next. As children become aware of the one-by-oneness of words in print, they begin to notice and isolate words in speech. This insight apparently requires no great amount of reading sophistication, for Ehri (1979) has shown that word awareness increases dramatically along with the earliest signs of emerging reading ability. Interestingly, the convention of inserting spaces between printed words popped in and out of practice for hundreds of years, becoming firmly established only with the advent of the printing press.

Like words, neither are syllables spontaneously evident. Unlike words, however, syllables are punctuated physically in the speech stream. Perhaps for that reason, awareness of syllables has also proved relatively easy to establish, both developmentally and historically, once their existence is pointed out. On the other hand, and in contrast with words, the defining characteristic of syllables is strictly phonological. Perhaps this is why the ability to detect syllables in speech or to segment syllables from speech has been shown to predict future reading (Lundberg, Olofsson, & Wall, 1980; Mann & Liberman, 1984), to correlate with the reading progress of beginners (Morais, Bertelson, Cary, & Alegria, 1986; Treiman & Baron, 1983), and to differentiate older disabled or dyslexic readers from normal first-graders (Mann, 1984, 1986; Morais et al., 1986). Syllable awareness tends to precede phonemic awareness both developmentally and historically. Even so, awareness of syllables does not lead readily to awareness of phonemes.

As with words and syllables, the most basic obstacle to phonemic awareness seems to be the normal attentional dynamics of language processing. That is, in normal speaking and listening, the processing of the subunits is essentially automatic, allowing attention to be focused not on the sounds of language, but on the meaning and message that they encode. Even ignoring issues of comprehension, to focus on any individual word, syllable, or phoneme would be too time consuming; we would quickly lose track of the rest of the spoken stream. However, the challenge of developing phonemic awareness clearly involves much more, and is much more difficult, than a mere redirection of attention.

Beyond Attention: The Special Difficulty of Phonemes

All speakers must "know" about phonemes at some level, or they could not produce or understand speech. Indeed, at 1 month of age, infants make phonemic distinctions between elementary speechlike sounds. They not only discriminate between such highly similar sounds as /ba/ and /pa/, but they also lump physically in-between sounds into one category or the other (Eimas, Siqueland, Jusczyk, & Vigorito, 1971). Shortly thereafter, babies begin to practice the phonemes of their language, quickly moving on to the abilities to produce and distinguish them in the rapidly flowing permutations and combinations of continuous speech. Yet, time and use do not serve to reveal the phonemes. As one example, adults can push a button faster when listening for a whole word than when listening for a single phoneme such as /s/, and this is true even when the phoneme is the first sound of the word. Evidently, they can consciously access the phoneme only through the time-consuming and retrospective process of taking apart the syllable that they have already perceived by virtue of its presence (Savin & Bever, 1970; Warren, 1971).

Consistent with such findings, many speech scientists subscribe to the view that phonetic processing is carried out by a precognitive, biologically specialized subsystem that is modular in a strong sense of that word and thus relatively impenetrable to conscious awareness and to non-speech knowledge and processes (see A. Liberman & Mattingly, 1989). If so, however, then it follows that there will "ordinarily [be] nothing in children's experience with speech that will acquaint them with the alphabetic principle—that is nothing to make them [consciously] aware that all words are specified by an internal phonological structure, the shortest elements of which are the phonemes that the letters of the alphabet represent. . . . Saying 'buh a guh' to the child does not necessarily help [her or him to grasp the underlying phonemic structure of the word *bag*] all that much, since 'buh a guh' is the wrong word. At all events, we can now see that the normal processes of speech not only fail to reveal the internal structures of words, but may, indeed, obscure them" (I. Liberman & Liberman, 1990, pp. 60–61).

Significantly, it was the last part of this message—that the sounds of phonemes spoken one at a time bear little resemblance to their sounds in running speech—that registered most clearly in the educational community. In response, many instructional programs were redesigned in the 1970s to discourage both teachers and students from voicing the phonemes in isolation. The purpose, of course, was one of avoiding referential confusion; the effect, however, was an untenable loss of referential clarity (see Adams, 1990). In the absence of the direct alternative, word mediation became the most widespread technique for introducing or discussing the sounds of individual phonemes, for example, "The letter *f* makes the sound you hear at the beginning of *food, father,* and *frost.*"

The uselessness of such instruction for children who do not already have phonemic awareness should be obvious. Where attention was turned to multiple phonemes, as, for example, in blending, the bind was even worse. The following excerpt from a teachers' guide was originally cited in a paper by MacGinitie (1976): "The teacher is instructed to write the word *girls* on the board. The teacher then says, 'You can find out what this word is. With what consonant does it begin? With what consonant does it end? You know the sounds that *g* and *r* and *l* and *s* stand for. I am going to say something and leave out this word at the end. When I stop, think of a word that begins with a sound *g* stands for, ends with the sounds *r* and *l* and *s* stand for and makes sense with what I said' " (p. 372). Thus, just as the very value of phonics instruction was coming under assault by the whole language movement, its endorsed conduct was made essentially unmanageable—and especially for those children who needed it most. No wonder so many teachers turned away.

Auditory versus Motoric Conceptions of the Phoneme

Linguists have long distinguished between phonetics and phonemics. Whereas phonetics is concerned with all perceptible differences among speech sounds, phonemics is concerned with only the functional differences in speech sounds or, roughly, the differences captured by the graphemic conventions of the written language. In contrast to phonetics, speech scientists found they could define phonemes quite neatly and systematically in terms of their place and manner of articulation (e.g., Jones, 1956; Jakobson, Fant, & Halle, 1961). Having done so, they soon discovered further that the perceptual confusability of phonemes generally clustered on these articulatory dimensions (e.g., Miller & Nicely, 1955). Ultimately, the view emerged that these motorically based conceptions of phonemes were not merely descriptively convenient but, indeed, psychologically real. In particular, the view emerged that the phonemes were essentially undiscriminable except as the listener might manage to reconstruct the speech signal in terms of the underlying sequence of articulatory gestures through which it was generated by the speaker (A. Liberman et al., 1967).

From this perspective, the practice of encouraging children to articulate each phoneme at issue would seem to make far more sense than discouraging them from doing so. If, in fact, phonemes are defined by their ideal place and manner of articulation, then how better might one anchor their identities than by asking children to produce and explore them motorically? Indeed, successful phonemic awareness programs commonly engage the children in articulation of the individual phonemes (e.g., Ball & Blachman, 1991; Byrne & Fielding-Barnsley, 1991; Lundberg et al., 1988; Wallach & Wallach, 1979; Williams, 1979). In addition, speech therapists have long pointed to the value of articulatory training in promoting reading (e.g., VanRiper & Butler, 1955). In this vein, whether used remedially or with entering first-graders, the Auditory Discrimination in Depth (ADD) program (Lindamood & Lindamood, 1975), which begins by engaging students in a systematic and reflective exploration of the articulatory features and voicing of the phonemes, has been shown to accelerate reading growth dramatically (see Truch, 1991).

A study by Skjelfjord (1976) provides a closer view of how such articulatory training may hasten children's phonological awareness. The subjects were Norwegian preschoolers, roughly 6 years old. Each lesson focused on one particular phoneme. After the children heard a story containing several instances of the phoneme, they were asked to find out how the sound was produced by trying to "feel it in the mouth." They were then given pictures and asked to find out if the phoneme was present in the illustrated words, again by trying to feel it in the mouth. Finally, the children were asked to try to find out whether the sound was found in the initial, medial, or final position in the word. These exercises lasted 10 to 20 minutes a day, and three phonemes were covered every second week until all 27 of the Norwegian phonemes had been covered. The week before the first lesson and every odd week thereafter were spent individually testing the children, first on their ability to identify either a taught or as yet untaught phoneme in a specified position of several three-phoneme words and then on their ability to identify all three phonemes of a nonword in sequence.

In the pretest, the children's responses tended to be spontaneous and swift, but they evidenced little ability to analyze the words into phonemes. Forty-eight percent of the answers showed no analytic ability, and 15% were syllable-size answers. Meanwhile, although the children did produce a number of phoneme-size responses (37%), these consisted almost exclusively of vowels. Moreover, the vowels and syllable-size units reported in these early test sessions reflected almost total indifference to the position requested.

By the second test session, after only one week of training, the phoneme-size responses rose to 63%, and the nonanalytic responses fell to 22%; by the final session, these percentages were 95 and 1. Moreover, the students were nearly as successful at finding untaught as taught phonemes, suggesting that their performance was based as much on the strategy of feeling the segments as on familiarity with the specific phonemes. In keeping with this, improvements in the children's performance was marked by a shift from the rapid responding of early trials to slow and laborious whispering of the words prior to giving an answer. Alongside, the vowels shifted from the most frequent to the most difficult of the phonemes for the children to report, which Skjelfjord (1976) tentatively attributes to the vowels' lack of articulatory distinctiveness.

Although the children's ability to report the requested position improved markedly alongside their phonemic sensitivity, it remained error-prone. From observations of the children, Skjelfjord (1976) concluded that the reason for this difficulty was that the children were not selectively listening for the sound in the named position. Instead, they determined their responses by slowly uttering the whole word, phoneme by phoneme, and then deciding—retrospectively and sometimes incorrectly—which of the uttered phonemes occurred in the named position. Finally, Skjelfjord observed, in a number of instances the students uttered all of the sounds in the test word correctly, only to report some sound that was similar to but different from any of those just uttered. This, he conjectured, reflected the students' awareness of the phonemes' contextual lability. Rather than report the sound as perceived, they responded with a sound they had previously learned and that they judged could be its prototype.

Skjelfjord's (1976) arguments and observations interlace provocatively with A. Liberman et al.'s (1967) hypothesis that the consonant phonemes are "hearable" only as the listener can reconstruct their underlying articulatory gestures. As such, his work points out a major limitation to such articulatory training even as it underscores its utility. Yes, phonemes are defined by an ideal place and manner of articulation. In reality, however, they become physically blurred and compromised as the speaker rushes from one to the next in a way that sacrifices precision to comfort and efficiency. In consequence, articulatory analysis of functional speech can give back no better than a lumpy distribution of noisy phonemic tokens; nor does it afford any means of insight into the ideal nature of the types they represent or even how many such types there might be. In short, toward awakening the insight that speech consists of series of phoneme-size vocal gestures, activities that engage students in reflective articulation are arguably necessary and clearly valuable. Toward helping the students to identify the phonemes, however, they are not sufficient.

From Awareness of Phonemes to the Alphabetic Insight

Suppose you were working with Skjelfjord's (1976) young students, and you wanted to make it easier for them to enumerate the phonemes. Very likely, the first thing you would try would be some sort of visual mnemonic. One widely used technique (see e.g., Clay, 1979), invented by the Russian psychologist, Elkonin (1973), is to demarcate the separate phonemes with empty squares, asking the children to slide out counters or bingo markers to fill the squares, left to right, for each phoneme they hear (see Figure 5.1). The advantages of the Elkonin procedure over Liberman et al.'s (1974) tapping task are that it visually emphasizes the sequentiality of the sounds even as it results in an inspectable and, thus, discussable record of the effort. Another approach, championed by Lindamood and Lindamood (1975), is to ask the children to represent the string of phonemes with a row of colored blocks. The advantage of using blocks over bingo markers is that the colors of the blocks can be made to correspond to the phonemes they represent. Thus, for example, by letting the blue block correspond to /p/s in *pot, top,* and *pop,* the child is visually induced to consider the underlying similarities and differences of the phonemes as well as their order.

In terms of mnemonics, of course, if the goal is one of phoneme identification, then having a distinct visual symbol for each phoneme ought to be still better. In keeping with this, positive effects on reading have been obtained by pairing the phonemes with distinctive letterlike symbols during training (Fox & Routh, 1984). Yet, the letters of the alphabet also lend themselves well to this purpose and do so with direct downstream value. As demonstrated by Lundberg et al. (1988), training phonemic awareness in the absence of print can significantly hasten later reading and spelling growth. Across studies, however, the gains have been more consistent and robust when phonemic awareness has been trained together with letter-sound correspondences than when it has not (Ball & Blachman, 1991; Bradley & Bryant, 1983; Byrne & Fielding-Barnsley, 1989, 1991; Goldstein, 1976; Treiman & Baron, 1983; Vellutino & Scanlon, 1987; Wallach & Wallach, 1979; Williams, 1979).

Figure 5.1 Elkonin boxes for phoneme segmentation.

One advantage of training the letters and sounds together is surely that the letters serve to anchor the phonemes perceptually. Equally important, however, may be the value of the letter-sound pairings for persuading the children that words must be treated differently from other visual patterns. In particular, young children are inclined to examine words, not as any left-to-right sequence of separately informative symbols, but more holistically in terms of overall visual pattern and special features (see e.g., Byrne, 1992; Masonheimer, Drum, & Ehri, 1984). And no wonder: this, after all, is the right approach for virtually every other visual stimulus in their world or ours, *except* strings of letters and numbers. The suggestion, in short, is that awareness of letters and spellings, on one hand, and of phonemes, on the other, may well promote each other. In support of this, we turn to a series of studies by Byrne and his colleagues (see Byrne, 1992).

As noted by Gough and Hillinger (1980), beginning readers are generally faster to learn lists of dissimilar than similar words. Exploring this effect with preschoolers, Byrne (1992) found that it was the visual similarity more than the phonological similarity of the words that made the difference. Further, the visual similarity or distinctiveness of the words seemed to derive almost entirely from their initial or leftmost letters. To ask whether this initial-letter salience might be a useful step toward inducing the alphabetic principle, Byrne tried training the children to recognize *fat* and *bat* and then tested their ability to choose between initial-*f* and initial-*b* words such as *fun* versus *bun* and *big* versus *fig.* But the children's transfer performance was at chance.

Continuing with the train-transfer paradigm, Byrne set out to ask why children perform so poorly in the transfer task. Is it the logic of the task? Is it that children are disinclined to treat visual patterns analytically, as a string? (No, they figure it out if the separate symbols represent words rather than phonological information.) What if the initial symbol-sound correspondence is restricted to *s*-/s/ versus *m*-/m/? After all, /s/ and /m/ seem especially salient as phonemes go. (Transfer performance was still at chance.) What if the number of items in the training set is expanded so that finer discriminations are required in the training phase? (No matter.) What if the children are first trained to segment the words, as in "s . . . at" (only 8 of 12 mastered this task), then will they catch on? (No.) What if these same children are also taught to discern which of a set of spoken words begin with the same sounds as /sat/ versus /mat/ (only 5 of the 12 eventually managed to do so), *then* would they learn to discriminate the printed words on the basis of the correspondence between their initial letters and sounds? (Again, transfer performance was at chance.)

Be careful not to miss the point here: Byrne's young subjects blithely learned the words that went with the training stimuli in each of these experiments. The problem was that, time and again, doing so neither involved nor provoked any transferable appreciation of the underlying print-speech relationships.

And so, Byrne asked, what if, in addition to segmenting and recognizing initial sounds, these children are also taught that the letter *s* says /s/ and the letter *m* says /m/. At last: not only were the letter-sound pairings easy for the children to learn, but now training on *sat* and *mat* transferred readily to choice discrimination of *sow* versus *mow, set* versus *met,* and so on. However, this was true if and only if the children had also succeeded in the segmentation and first-sound matching tasks: those who had succeeded in both of the speech tasks made no errors on the reading challenge; those who had failed at both tasks performed at chance.

Through further study, Byrne and his colleague, Fielding-Barnsley, have generalized and extended these findings (Byrne & Fielding-Barnsley, 1989, 1991). Learning to segment the initial consonant from a /consonant-vowel-consonant/ word is hard for preschoolers. The ability to segment, in turn, appears necessary but not sufficient for hearing that, for example, /sad/ and /sow/ begin with the "same" sound as /sat/. Finally, provided that the children can hear the initial similarity between such words as /sat/ and /sow/, teaching them that the letter *s* says /s/ and *m* says /m/ leads easily to the ability to discriminate between such printed pairs as *sat-mat,* and *sow-mow.* But there is more: having provided all this support with *s*-/s/ and *m*-/m/, Byrne and Fielding-Barnsley (1991) have further demonstrated that the mere teaching of *f* says /f/ and *b* says /b/ is generally adequate for the children to infer that, for example, of printed *fin* and *bin,* the first says /fin/.

Back to Dyslexia

As evidence accrued for the strength of the relationship between phonemic awareness and reading growth in the general population, the question inevitably arose as to whether phonological difficulties might constitute the elusive core deficit underlying dyslexia. Consistent with this hypothesis, reading-disabled children and adults evidence weak phonological processing across a variety of tasks, including poor short-term memory for phonological information and difficulties in repeating spoken pseudowords (see Brady, 1991), difficulties in naming objects (Wolf, 1991) and retrieving words (see Katz, 1986), and less sharpness in phoneme discrimination (e.g., Lieberman, Meskill, Chatillon, & Schupack, 1985). Inasmuch as such phonological difficulties appear early in childhood, they cannot be dismissed as consequences of reading difficulties.

The concept of specific reading disability or dyslexia was originally invented because of the clinical need to recognize—even without the ability to explain—the occurrence of children with marked reading disability who were otherwise earnest, healthy, well-nurtured, and cognitively advanced. Given the failure, across much research, to identify any other more specific diagnostic index (see Critchley & Critchley, 1978; Vellutino, 1979; Vernon, 1971), the criterion by which dyslexia was identified was broadly formalized, by both clinicians and policymakers, as a discrepancy between a child's reading and her or his IQ or nonverbal achievement that could not be ascribed to environmental factors (see Lyon, 1995). As this criterion was equally applied to the disbursement of special funds and allowances for remedial assistance, dyslexia came to be known as a rich kids' syndrome.

Although a number of people (see especially Siegel, 1989, 1992) have adduced a number of very good reasons for mistrusting and even disavowing the discrepancy definition, it prevailed in part because of the firm belief that reading disability was a discrete syndrome—etiologically distinct and symptomatically distinguishable from garden-variety reading difficulties—and otherwise because of the simple need for *some* screening rule. As it turns out, however, reading ability or disability is normally distributed; it is "not an all-or-none phenomenon but, like hypertension and obesity, occurs in varying degrees of severity" (Shaywitz, Escobar, Shaywitz, Fletcher, & Makuch, 1992, p. 149). Furthermore, and regardless of whether or not it is "specific"—that is, regardless of a child's IQ, socioeconomic status, or achievement in other areas, and despite the coexistence of other behavioral syndromes such as attention deficit disorder—reading disability is robustly associated with poor phonological sensitivity and a marked difficulty in decoding pseudowords (Fletcher et al., 1994; Shankweiler et al., 1995; Stanovich & Siegel, 1994). This fact, in turn, carries two important practical implications with respect to diagnosis and treatment of reading disability.

First, the discrepancy-based definitions of reading disability are educationally counterproductive because they inappropriately exclude children who have linguistic, performance, or emotional difficulties in addition to low reading scores. Second, the discrepancy-based definitions are risky in any case because, by nature of the criteria on which they rest, they do not afford diagnosis of reading disability until well into a child's school career (i.e., a first-grader cannot be a "grade level behind" in reading). Moreover, given the responsiveness of reading and spelling growth to early phonemic intervention together with the persistence of phonological and decoding difficulties among dyslexics diagnosed even a few years later in life (Bruck, 1990, 1992), the pressing question is: To what extent could the prevalence or degree of reading disability be reduced by giving the children proper guidance and assessment early in the acquisition process? (Adams & Bruck, 1993).

From Letters and Sounds to Spellings and Sounds

In summary, research both demonstrates and explains the importance of letter-sound instruction for children. Moreover, concurring with age-old pedagogical conventions, the acquisition of word-initial letter-sound pairs seems universally and necessarily the first real entry into alphabetic learning. Yet, these studies also bound the value of such instruction from both below and above.

On one hand, this research affirms that letter-sound knowledge alone is not sufficient to seed the alphabetic insight, for the ability—logical, perceptual, and mnemonic—to assimilate letter-sound instruction is itself predicated on a basic awareness of phonemes and a relatively comfortable familiarity with the letters of the alphabet (see Adams, 1990; Share, 1995). As discussed above, phonemic awareness is difficult, and it is far more difficult for some children than others. Similarly, the letters of the alphabet are ill designed for any crash course; to the young child, they surely look more like each other than anything else she or he has been asked to learn before. The implication is that movement into reading should be significantly accelerated—and failure significantly mitigated—if children are given ample opportunity to play with the letters and to explore their sounds prior to formal reading instruction, ideally in preschool and kindergarten. Indeed, it is precisely this outcome that is so resoundingly demonstrated by the training studies we have reviewed.

On the other hand, these studies beg the question of how any usefully detailed knowledge of spellings and sounds might grow from this word-initial alphabetic insight. The quick answer is that this does not happen instantly or automatically. The ability to "hear" the phonemic structure of the rest of the word emerges gradually.

Toward gaining a better understanding of this process, Stahl and Murray (1994) analyzed children's performance across a battery of phonemic awareness tasks. At the most primitive level, the children in Stahl and Murray's study were capable only of dividing the (monosyllabic) words into two parts: the initial consonant(s) or *onset,* and the balance of the word or the *rime,* for example, /c-at/, /tr-ick/. The ability to separate the rime into its vowel and its consonant coda came next. The ability to analyze consonant clusters came still later, with isolation of the last consonant of word-final clusters preceding isolation of the leading consonant of word-initial clusters. In other words, the children were inclined to respond to sounds such as /pl/ and /dr/ as though they were each composed of a single vocal gesture. Arguably, the children are correct—except that the spelling conventions of English have recognized that these sounds adequately can, and therewith have decreed that they properly should, be conceived as a concatenation of two separate gestures, /p/-/l/ and /d/-/r/ (see also Share, 1995; Treiman, 1993).

Thus, the chicken-egg relationship between phonemic awareness and letter knowledge continues well beyond the basics. Perhaps for this reason, both continue, independent of one another, to exert a significant influence on word recognition and reading growth well into the primary years (Muter et al., 1995; Wagner et al., 1995).

How can children's learning of word-internal spelling-sound connections best be fostered? Synthetic phonics, or the practice of teaching children to read words by sounding them out, offers itself as one possibility. However, children are very good at learning what a word looks like (at least for the duration of the instructional foray), and they are not very good at paying attention to noninstrumental verbiage. After all, why sound out *cat* if you can already recognize it?

An alternate strategy, urged in a prescient thought-piece by Lewkowicz (1980), is to engage the children in inventive spelling. Because the memory burden of each successive sound is relieved as soon as each is written, spelling affords a work space for phonemic analysis of words that is cognitively easier than aural segmentation tasks (for empirical affirmation, see Stahl & Murray, 1994). Indeed, ample early experience in spelling independently seems not—as once feared—to obstruct but to promote children's ability to learn conventional spellings when taught and, significantly, to learn them in a way that translates readily to improved word recognition and fluency in reading (Uhry & Shepherd, 1993). More generally, because independent spelling is a way of engaging children in thinking actively and reflectively about the sounds of words in relation to their lettered representations, it proves itself a powerful medium for developing (L. Clarke, 1988; Griffith, 1992) and evaluating (Gerber, 1985; Mann, Tobin, & Wilson, 1987; Tangel & Blachman, 1992) their growing phonemic and orthographic awareness. Finally, because the output of independent spelling is a scrutible record of the child's efforts, it is also an invaluable medium for studying the development of the knowledge and understanding on which it depends. In view of these considerations, discussion of early writing and spelling is in order before returning to issues of reading development.

Children's Writing as a Window on the Cognition of Early Literacy

Jamie was a 3½-year-old Scottish child (M. Jones, 1990). Asked by an adult to write a shopping list for a teddy bear who had been knocked down by a car and was not feeling well enough to write it himself, Jamie produced the string of symbols depicted in Figure 5.2. Some of the symbols could be *o*s, but others are not real letters. Nevertheless, they look a good deal like letters. The symbols are arranged in a linear sequence, as are letters in real writing. Jamie, like many children of this age, has already begun to distinguish writing from drawing.

Five-year-old Bobby was told by his mother that he must wear a jacket or sweater when he went outside so that he would be warm enough. Indignant, Bobby got a piece of paper and a pencil and wrote the note depicted in Figure 5.3. Bobby's message, unlike Jamie's, is made up wholly of real letters. "Why should I be warm enough?" it demands. Bobby was in a combined kindergarten/first-grade program that emphasized the usefulness of writing. This was the first time that he had written a complete sentence on his own outside of school without asking an adult for help in spelling words or forming letters. Bobby could read only a few words at the time he produced this message. He wrote in capital letters without leaving spaces between words. His writing would be hard to decipher if one did not know what prompted the message.

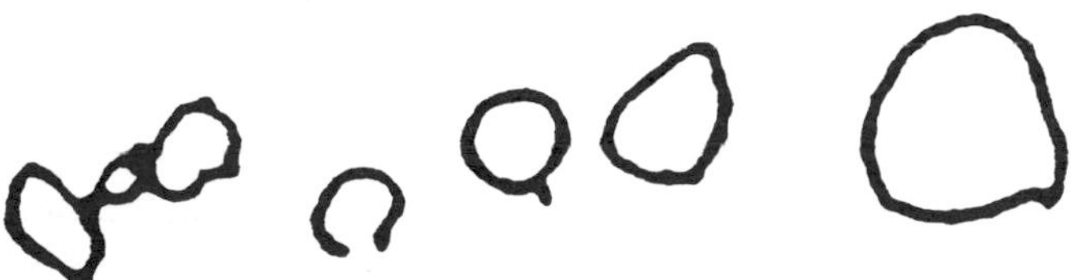

Figure 5.2 Teddy bear's shopping list, by Jamie (age 3½).

Figure 5.3 "Why should I be warm enough?" by Bobby (age 5).

Trevor was in a whole-language first-grade class in a middle-class suburb. He was learning to read and kept a word bank of words that he was able to recognize. Children in this classroom began to keep a daily journal once they had accumulated a number of words in their word banks. Figure 5.4 shows sections from Trevor's earliest journal entries. On October 5 his entry read, "When I go outside I ride my bike and I play on my bike ride." The next day he wrote, "I like to eat pizza and I like to drink pop." Trevor's writing is about the here and now. It is hard to decipher because there are no spaces between words and because there are many misspelled words, such as "pa" for *play* and

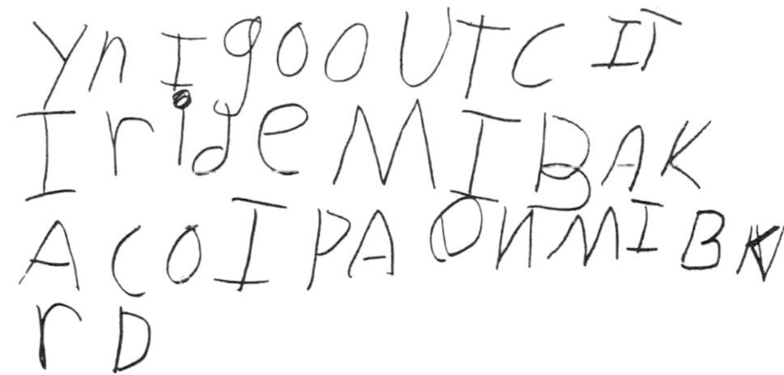

Figure 5.4 October 5: "When I go outside I ride my bike and I play on my bike ride." October 6: "I like to eat pizza and I like to drink pop." by Trevor (first grade).

"grak" for *drink.* As we will see, though, most of Trevor's spelling errors are typical of those of beginning writers. His spellings are not as random or unmotivated as they might first appear to be.

Jillian was a classmate of Trevor's. When she began writing in her journal, her writings were very similar to Trevor's. She improved rapidly, by late March producing the story in Figure 5.5. This story depicts the events of the preceding spring involving the growth of a sunflower. Jillian now puts spaces between words and uses primarily lower-case letters, but she does not include punctuation. Although she makes numerous spelling errors, such as "bigr" for *bigger* and "seds" for *seeds,* her story is nevertheless readable. Jillian's teacher was so pleased with this work that she had it "published," or typed up for Jillian to share with her classmates.

Shayna and Missy were fourth-graders who participated in the longitudinal study, discussed earlier, by Juel and colleagues (Juel, 1994; Juel et al., 1986). They attended a large elementary school in Austin, Texas, that served a lower-class neighborhood. As part of Juel's study, Shayna and Missy were shown colorful pictures of animals in a classroom and were asked to write a story about the picture. Shayna, a poor reader and writer, produced the relatively simple description shown on the left side of Figure 5.6. Missy, a good reader and writer, produced the more elaborate story shown on the right side. Missy's story has a more expressive and varied vocabulary than Shayna's, including some less common words such as *arrangements* and *sandstorm.* Missy shows an awareness of the reader and a playful attitude toward language, telling the researchers that she wrote "very" a large number of times so that the reader would realize how long the trail felt to the hikers. Missy also stated that when writing "they hiked for hours

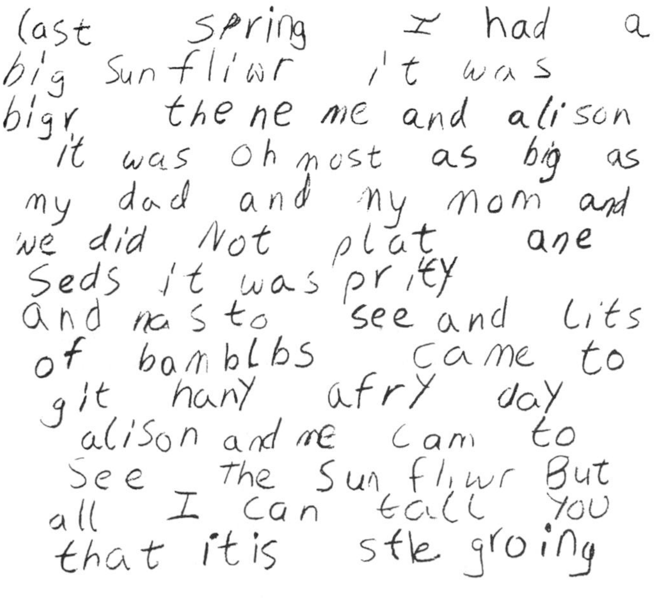

last spring I had a
big Sunfliwr it was
bigr then me and alison
it was ohmost as big as
my dad and my mom and
we did Not plat ane
Seds it was prity
and nas to see and lits
of bamblbs came to
git hany afry day
alison and me cam to
See the Sun fliwr But
all I can tall you
that it is stle groing

Figure 5.5 Sunflower story, by Jillian (first grade).

Shayna's story:

There's is a teacher with Her class. One of the kids is asking her a quastion most of the kids are working, playing and talking and there are. pitcher's on the wall there. is also a door. there is a window and they have desk and they have chairs. And Some are reading book's to.

Missy's story:

The class is going on a fieldtrip tomorrow. They need to do extra work for tomorrow. Lenny mouse does not understand fractions. Larry porcupine is eating some of his lunch. Lisa feild mouse is drawing Mrs. Lee a picture. Laura squirrel is reading a story. Lucky bunny is throwing spitballs. The class is never going to get their work done! Lupie hamster is quietly doing his work. Lea ground squirrel is chattering to Lisa. Tomorrow they are going to have a lot of fun. Finaly they finish all of their work for today. But they have to finish tomorrow's work. But Larry porcupine did not finish his work so he had to stay to do it after shcool if he wanted to go on the field trip. By the time lunch arrived Lucky ate so quickly he had a stomach-ache. He went to the nurses office she said it would be allright for him to go on the field trip tomorrow, unless his tummy-ache got worse. Lenny mouse talked to his frined Lupie hanster. Lisa and Lea ground squirrel talked about the field trip the next day. They went to the library that after noon. Everyone checked out books. The next day everyone was in their swimming suits. They went to the pond had a picnic and went swimming. Then they went hiking up a very, very long trail. They hiked for hours and hours. Then they got lost a sand storm came and covered up the trail. Everyone go very scared. It was finnaly dawn then Lisa ground squirrel found a cave. The calss stayed there overnight thank god they brought their lunches and had that for their dinner The next day Lenny saw a diffrent trail they droped big rocks on their way so the sandstorm could not cover up their trail. They walked fjor twenty five minutes. Then they came to a cabin knocked. then they opened the door then they discoverd it was a summer cabin. They found a map followed it back to their school. Everyone took turns calling their parents. They went home and never went to school again. They played all day had slumer parties every night. Then Lisa and Mrs. Lee made arangments for a party and everyone spent the night at Lisa's house even Mrs. Lee. The End

Figure 5.6 Shayna and Missy's stories (fourth grade).

and hours," she started a new line for the "and hours" to emphasize the length of the hike.

How does a child move from the primitive productions of Jamie and Bobby to the more advanced levels of writing development exemplified by Missy? Why do some children, like Jillian, progress rapidly, whereas other children, like Shayna, progress more slowly? In the following sections, we will address these questions by reviewing research on the development of writing and spelling ability.

The Precursors of Alphabetic Writing

Preschoolers may "write" by making marks with a crayon or pencil even before they know the conventional letters. Their writing, unconventional as it is, is noticeably different from their drawing. For example, Jamie (Figure 5.2) used a linear string of discrete units to write a grocery list—a different configuration than typically found in drawing.

The results of Tolchinsky-Landsmann and Levin (1985) support the idea that children distinguish between writing and drawing from an early age. These investigators worked with middle-class Israeli children aged 3, 4, and 5. The children were asked to both write and draw utterances such as "a house" and "a red flower." By the time the children were 4, adults could easily tell which of the children's productions were meant as writing and which were meant as drawing. The 4-year-olds' writings generally consisted of linearly arranged strings of units separated by blanks. The writings tended to be smaller in size than the drawings. When writing, the 3-year-olds either used characters of unidentifiable origin, mostly undifferentiated into units, or nonletters that bore some resemblance to Hebrew letters. Four-year-olds used a combination of real Hebrew letters, digits, and letters of the Roman alphabet, which these children had probably seen in addition to Hebrew letters. It was not until the age of 5 that children predominantly used real Hebrew letters in their writing. Still, these letters were often not the ones found in the conventional spelling of the utterance. The majority of 5-year-olds wrote in the direction that is standard for Hebrew, from right to left.

Further support for the idea that children differentiate between writing and drawing from an early age comes from Ferreiro and Teberosky's (1982) case studies of Argentinian children. When asked to write words or sentences, some 4- and 5-year-olds produced curved characters linked together by wavy lines that resembled cursive writing. Other children produced separate characters composed of curved and/or straight lines that resembled print, as Jamie (Figure 5.2) did.

Lavine (1977) tested children's ability to differentiate between writing and drawing by asking them to sort cards containing various kinds of graphic displays. The children in this study were American preschoolers aged 3, 4, and 5. Lavine asked the children to put those cards that had writing on them into a play mailbox and those that did not have writing on them into another container. Even the 3-year-olds accurately discriminated writing from pictures. Although some of the 3-year-olds tested by Tolchinsky-Landsmann and Levin (1985) did not differentiate between writing and drawing in their own productions, they may have been able to do so in a task like Lavine's, in which examples of writing and drawing were shown to them. The children tested by Lavine appeared to use linearity as one criterion for writing: they considered linearly arranged displays as writing more often than nonlinear displays. In addition, displays that included a variety of symbols were more likely to be labeled as writing than those in which the same symbol was repeated several times. As long as the units in a display looked similar to letters, the 3- and 4-year-olds accepted them as writing. It was not until age 5 that children showed signs of differentiating Roman letters from similar-looking nonletters.

Lavine's (1977) results, together with those of Tolchinsky-Landsmann and Levin (1985) and Ferreiro and Teberosky (1982), indicate that children begin to grasp the characteristics of writing from an early age. They learn about the superordinate features of writing, such as its linearity and its size, before they learn about the detailed characteristics of its units. This learning reflects the exposure to print that children have in a literate society. Even before they learn to read, children see words on street signs, cereal boxes, and food cans. They see words in books and newspapers. As a result of this exposure, children begin to learn about the salient characteristics of writing from an early age.

Although children as young as 3 or 4 know that writing looks different from drawing, they do not yet understand why. As discussed earlier, the notion that written symbols might represent the sounds of language is relatively abstract. Thus, many young children seem to believe instead that the forms of written words reflect their meanings. Variations in the written forms of objects' names, they believe, correspond to differences in the properties of the objects themselves in much the same way that variations among pictures mirror variations among objects. For example, 4-year-old Gustavo (Ferreiro & Teberosky, 1982) wrote the word *pato* (duck) using a wavy line. The researchers then asked him to write *oso* (bear). They asked the child whether the word for bear would be longer or shorter than the word for duck. Gustavo replied that the word for bear would be bigger. Because bears are bigger than ducks, Gustavo reasoned, the word for bear must be longer than the word for duck.

The results of several studies support the idea that young children consider the meanings of words when they write. Levin and Tolchinsky-Landsmann (1989) asked 5- and 6-year-old Israeli children to write pairs of nouns such as *elephant* and *ant, cucumber* and *tomato,* and *ball* and *rope.* Children sometimes indicated the size of an object by using more marks for a larger object (e.g., elephant) than for a smaller object (e.g., ant). They sometimes indicated the color of an object by choosing a red marker to write *tomato* and a green one to write *cucumber.* Representation of shape was also noted, especially among the 5-year-olds. For example, these children might use one or more round letters to write *ball* and a widely spaced string of letters to write *rope.*

Levin and Korat (1993) followed up these findings by focusing on children's tendency to use many marks for words that denote several objects or large objects and relatively few marks for words that denote few objects or small objects. They asked 5- and 6-year-old Israeli children to write words such as *tree, forest, coop,* and *chicken.* The Hebrew word for tree contains one syllable, whereas the word for forest contains two syllables. For this pair of words, then, the longer-sounding word denotes a group of many objects and the shorter-sounding word denotes a single object. The situation is reversed for *coop* and *chicken:* the Hebrew word that refers to a place housing a collection of chickens is, like the English word *coop,* shorter than the word that refers to a single chicken. Levin and Korat counted the number of characters that children wrote for each word. For pairs like *tree* and *forest,* where longer words denoted more or bigger objects, both 5- and 6-year-olds produced more signs for the longer words. For pairs like *coop* and *chicken,* where longer words denoted fewer objects, 5-year-olds did not produce more signs for the longer words, although 6-year-olds did. Overall, Levin and Korat's results suggest that semantic cues play a role in early spelling but that their role decreases as children grow older.

In a related study of children's use of semantic cues, Lundberg and Torneus (1978) showed Swedish nonreaders two printed words. For example, one word might be *arm* and the other word might be *ambulance.* The researchers asked the children which printed word was *arm.* Children did better if the word denoting the smaller object was written with fewer letters, as in this example, than if the word denoting the larger object was written with fewer letters.

Further evidence for the primacy of meaning in early writing, according to Ferreiro and Teberosky (1982), is that young children expect nouns to be represented in print but do not understand that verbs can also be represented. Support for this suggestion comes from the findings of Tolchinsky-Landsmann and Levin (1987) with Israeli children. These researchers asked 4-, 5-, and 6-year-olds to write words, phrases, and sentences. When a noun was added to a phrase or sentence, the children were apt to write an additional character. They were less likely to add a character when a verb was added. For example, 5-year-old Yafit used one character to write words that corresponded to single objects, such as *wave* and *wheel.* She used a single sign to write *Tali* (a girl's name), two signs to write the phrase *Tali and Eran* (the names of a girl and a boy), and three signs to write the sentence *Tali and Eran are building a tower.* When asked to read what she had written, Yafit divided the spoken sentence into three units: *Tali / and Eran / are building a tower.* She pointed successively to each of the three signs she had written while saying each unit. Thus, the number of units in Yafit's writing corresponded to the number of people or objects referred to. Yafit used a single character to write *a girl, a girl is dancing,* and *a girl is dancing and singing.* Only nouns, she seemed to believe, deserved representation in print.

As children progress, they discover that writing represents the spoken form of language. All of the words in a spoken utterance are symbolized, not just the nouns. This realization may come about as children observe that the number of separate units in a written sentence is typically greater than the number of objects referred to. Moreover, the physical features of a word and of the letters it contains do not necessarily correspond to the physical features of the corresponding object. For example, the written word *Dad* has fewer letters than the written word *Bobby,* even though Dad is bigger and older than Bobby.

Ferreiro and Teberosky (1982) proposed that, mirroring history, children at first conceive the correspondence between writing and speech to be at the level of the syllable. For example, 5-year-old Erik wrote two characters for the bisyllabic words *sapo* and *oso* but three characters for the trisyllabic word *patito.* Similarly, the 5- and 6-year-old Israeli children studied by Levin and Korat (1993), Levin and Tolchinsky-Landsmann (1989), and Tolchinsky-Landsmann and Levin (1987) tended to use more characters to write phonologically longer words than phonologically shorter words. However, inasmuch as phonologically longer words contain more phonemes as well as more syllables than do phonologically shorter words, the results of these studies do not provide unambiguous support for the syllabic hypothesis (see Jones, 1990).

Some children, as observed by Ferreiro and Teberosky (1982), use their own invented letter forms to represent syllables. Other children use real letters but do not do so in a consistent manner: they represent a given syllable with one letter on one occasion and with another letter on a second occasion. Still other children develop stable spellings for certain syllables, often relying on their knowledge of letter names. Regardless of such variations, such research challenges the assumption (Gentry, 1982) that children are stringing letters together in a random manner even where their spellings bear no obvious relationship to the sounds in spoken words.

Bobby (Figure 5.3) appears to understand that writing symbolizes the words of a spoken utterance, the verbs as well as the nouns. For the most part, he seems to relate print and speech at the syllabic level, using letters to represent syllables. Thus, he writes the monosyllabic words *should* and *be* with one letter each: *c* for *should* and *b* for *be.* The use of *b* for *be* reflects the letter's name; the use of *c* for *should* may reflect the similarity between the name of the letter *c,* /sē/, and the first sound in the spoken form of *should,* /sh/. Bobby's spellings of *why* as "ye" and *I* as "ie" reflect a syllabic hypothesis overlaid with the effects of experience. Bobby's older brother had told him that, when a letter says its name, an *e* should be added to the end of the word. Thus, Bobby included an *e* after his *y* spelling of *why* and his *i* spelling of *I.* The syllabic hypothesis also shows through in Bobby's two-letter spelling of *enough.* He uses *n* to symbolize the first syllable of this word and *f* to symbolize the second syllable. Note that Bobby's choices of letters to represent syllables are often influenced by his knowledge of letter names.

Had Bobby not attempted the word *warm,* we might have concluded that he linked writing and speech solely at the level of syllables. However, Bobby's "wom" spelling of *warm* reveals the beginnings of the idea that letters in print reflect the individual phonemes in the spoken forms of words. Bobby seems to have segmented the spoken word *warm* into three units of sound, writing *w* for the initial /w/, *o* for the middle part of the word, and *m* for the final /m/. His failure to represent the /r/ with a separate letter is typical of beginning spellers and is discussed below. Bobby's case forms a bridge between what we have called the precursors of alphabetic writing and the emergence of the alphabetic principle.

The Alphabetic Principle Emerges

When children first begin to relate print and speech, they tend to do so at the level of syllables. However, this syllabic hypothesis turns out to be untenable. Children may begin to realize that the syllabic hypothesis is unsatisfactory when they learn to write or recognize their own name and try to understand why it is spelled as it is (Ferreiro & Teberosky, 1982). At the age of 3½, for example, Bobby knew that his name was spelled as *b, o, b, b, y.* He seemed to understand the function of the *b*s because he could hear the syllable /bē/ in the spoken form of his name. However, he was puzzled about the function of the *o* and *y* in the spelling of his name. After all, there was no /ō/ or /wī/ in the name's spoken form. Having heard his parents and his older brother discuss the silent *k* of *knife* and other orthographic peculiarities of English, Bobby offered a conclusion: the *o* and *y* in his name were silent letters. Solutions such as these, creative as they are, cannot last forever.

As children begin to learn the conventional spellings of words such as *Dad, Mom,* and *stop,* they observe that the number of letters in a word's spelling does not usually match the number of syllables in its spoken form. Their beginning experiences with print force children to go beyond the syllabic hypothesis and to relate print and speech at a more fine-grained level. At age 5, Bobby shows the beginnings of alphabetic writing in his spelling of *warm* (Figure 5.3).

Trevor (Figure 5.4), a year older than Bobby and with more knowledge of reading, shows a stronger grasp of the alphabetic principle. Trevor uses the alphabetic principle more or less consistently instead of only sporadically, as Bobby does. For example, the spoken word *eat* contains two phonemes, /ē/ and /t/. Trevor uses *e* to symbolize the first sound of this word and *t* to symbolize the second. His choice of *e* for /ē/ is surely motivated by the fact that /ē/ is the name of the letter *e.* The spoken word *pop* has three sounds, /p/, /ŏ/, and /p/, and Trevor spells it with three letters: *p* for the two /p/s and *a* for the /ŏ/. Trevor seems to fall back on a syllabic strategy when he writes *like* as "l" on the second line of his October 6 journal entry. On the first line of this entry, though, he writes this same word as "lak," with one letter for each of its three sounds.

Trevor does not always succeed in dividing words into individual phonemes and representing each phoneme with a letter or letter group. For example, he fails to spell the /l/ of *play,* writing "pa." He does not use a separate letter to represent the /ng/ of *drink,* the nasal sound that precedes the final /k/. He also chooses an unconventional letter to spell the initial /d/ of this same word, resulting in the apparently odd—but, as we shall see, developmentally common—spelling "grak" for *drink.* The only spelling of Trevor's that is at all unusual is "aco" for *and,* which he produces on both October 5 and 6. The next day, though, he switches to "ad," again failing to represent the first phoneme of a final cluster.

Jillian (Figure 5.5) makes some of the same kinds of spelling errors as Trevor. For example, she omits the second consonant of the initial /st/ cluster when spelling *still* as "sile." She fails to spell the first consonant of the final cluster when writing "plat" for *plant.* Although Jillian is a better speller than Bobby or Trevor, she too sometimes uses the names of letters as a guide to spelling. For example, she spells the /ē/ of *seeds* with *e,* the letter that has this name, rather than with the conventional *ee.*

Most of the research on children's writing has focused on children whose spellings are similar to Trevor's and Jillian's. These children have grasped the alphabetic nature of English writing but have not fully mastered the system. The pioneering research in this area was carried out by Charles Read (1975). Read studied 32 children from the United States who began to write as preschoolers, generally when they were between about 2½ and 4 years old, and in advance of reading or reading instruction. All in all, Read examined a total of over 2,500 spellings. Read carried out detailed analyses of the children's errors in an attempt to understand the reasons behind them. His results suggested that children approach the task of spelling primarily by trying to symbolize the sounds in words rather than by trying to reproduce memorized strings of letters. However, because the children in Read's study began to write much earlier than average, Gibson and Levin (1975) suggested that Read's results might not generalize to children who learn to write at school.

In answer to this reservation, Treiman (1993) gathered a large collection of first-graders' writings and performed detailed linguistic analyses of their spellings. Treiman's study differed from Read's (1975) in that it examined children who were not precocious or advanced but who were learning to read and write at school. Although school policy dictated that the children be given some instruction in phonics, the children's teacher, who was a strong believer in the whole language approach, put most stress on independent writing. Because the teacher believed that children should figure out the spellings of words on their own, she did not tell the children how to spell a word even if they asked. After children had finished writing, they brought their work to the teacher or teacher's aide and read aloud what they had written. The adult wrote the child's words on the paper, using conventional spelling, and also wrote the date. At the beginning of the school year, some children spent their writing period drawing pictures and writing their names. Other children produced strings of letters that bore no obvious correspondence to the sentences that they read back. As the school year progressed, the children's written productions showed increasing understanding of the alphabetic principle. Their texts grew longer, with print occupying more and more space on their papers and pictures less. Treiman collected a total of 5,617 spellings from the writings of 43 children who were in this same teacher's first-grade class during two successive school years.

Errors in Early Spelling

Naturalistic data such as those analyzed by Read (1975) and Treiman (1993) allow us to see the spellings that are produced by children engaged in meaningful writing. It happens, however, that children do not necessarily choose to spell those words that might best shed light on their operating principles. Further, those words that they do choose to spell differ in a number of ways. To compensate for these sorts of weaknesses, a number of experimental studies have been conducted in which children are asked to spell words—or, to eliminate familiarity factors, nonwords—of particular types. The combination of naturalistic data and experimental data allows stronger conclusions about spelling development than afforded by either type of data alone.

In the following sections, we will discuss four conclusions about early alphabetic spelling that are suggested by the results of the naturalistic and experimental research. To anticipate, the first conclusion is that certain spelling errors accurately reflect aspects of words' sounds that may not be obvious to adults. A second conclusion is that children's omissions of letters also tend to be phonologically based rather than random. Third, children's knowledge of letter names has an important influence on their early spellings. Fourth, in addition to trying to represent the sounds of words, children also try to reproduce the kinds of letter patterns they have seen in print.

Unconventionalized Sensitivity to the Sounds of Words. A child who misspells *plaid* as "plad" has clearly used the alphabetic principle. This child has analyzed the word into individual phonemes—/p/, /l/, and /ă/ and /d/—and has chosen a reasonable letter to symbolize each. The child's only error is in picking *a* rather than *ai* to represent the vowel. The letter *a* is in fact the most typical spelling of /ă/ in English; it is the *ai* in the conventional spelling of *plaid* that is unusual. Misspellings such as "plad" for *plaid* are often called phonetic errors and are generally taken to indicate that a child is successfully using the alphabetic principle.

Read (1975) observed that some of children's errors, although not phonetic in the sense just described, nevertheless accurately represented aspects of words' sounds. For example, the children in his study sometimes spelled /d/ before /r/ as *g* or *j,* as in "gradl" for *dreidel* or "jragin" for *dragon.* This is the same kind of error that Trevor (Figure 5.4) makes when spelling *drink* as "grak." Similarly, the children sometimes symbolized /t/ before /r/ as *ch,* for example spelling *try* as "chrie" or *truck* as "chrac." These errors make sense phonetically. When /d/ occurs before /r/, the contact between the tongue and the top of the mouth is made further back in the mouth than when /d/ occurs before a vowel. Also, the closure is released more slowly than when /d/ precedes a vowel. This gives /d/ before /r/ a degree of frication or turbulence that is similar to (although not as marked as) the frication that occurs in /j/ . Likewise, /t/ becomes similar to /ch/ when it occurs before /r/. Errors such as "gradl" for *dreidel* and "chrie" for *try* are thus reasonable spellings that reflect the sound properties of the words.

The occurrence of such spellings such as "jrad" for *drowned* and "chrap" for *trap* in Treiman's (1993) naturalistic first-grade data confirms that such errors on /d/ and /t/ before /r/ are not confined to precocious spellers. Further, the same kinds of errors have been documented in experimental studies in which kindergartners and first-graders were asked to spell or provide the first letters of words and nonwords with initial /tr/ and /dr/ (Read, 1975; Treiman, 1985c). Such errors cannot be ascribed to any general confusion of *d* with *g* or *j* for they tend not to occur except when /d/ is followed by /r/ (Treiman, 1985c, 1993). Moreover, children who make the errors for /dr/ tend to do the same for /tr/ (Treiman, 1985c). The errors seem to be based on the sound properties of words.

A similar tendency to represent sounds in unconventional but plausible ways is associated with certain consonants—stop consonants—when they occur after /s/. English has two series of stop consonants: the voiceless stops /p/, /t/, and /k/ and the voiced stops /b/, /d/, and /g/. These sounds are called stops because the flow of air is completely obstructed for a short period of time, a small burst of sound being produced when the obstruction is released. At the beginnings of words, voiced and voiceless stops contrast with one another. The vocal cords begin to vibrate sooner for the voiced stops /b/, /d/, and /g/ than for the voiceless stops /p/, /t/, and /k/. Thus, English speakers distinguish *cot*, which begins with the voiceless stop /k/, from *got*, which begins with the voiced stop /g/.

In contrast, voiced and voiceless stops are not distinguishable from one another when they occur after initial /s/. The English writing system assumes that stops are voiceless in this context and so *Scot* is spelled with *c* rather than *g*. In terms of certain phonetic properties, though, the second sound of *Scot* is more similar to /g/ than to /k/ (Klatt, 1975; Lotz, Abramson, Gerstman, Ingemann, & Nemser, 1960; Reeds & Wang, 1961). If one takes a tape recording of *Scot* and erases the portion corresponding to the initial /s/, speakers of English will almost always report hearing *got* rather than *cot*.

Children's tendency to symbolize stops after /s/ with letters that are appropriate for the voiced stops /b/, /d/, and /g/ has been documented (Treiman, 1985d). In this study, kindergartners and first-graders were asked to choose between a spelling representing a voiced stop (e.g., *b*) and a spelling representing a voiceless stop (e.g., *p*) to represent the second consonant of syllables like /spō/. The children selected for this particular study were able to choose *l* over *f* as a spelling for the second consonant of /slē/, demonstrating that they could choose the conventional spelling for the second consonant of a cluster provided its sound was unambiguous. Nevertheless, stop consonants after /s/ were often categorized as voiced, especially by the kindergartners.

A third case in which children spell sounds in an unconventional but plausible manner involves syllabic /r/. In most varieties of American English, a word like *her* does not contain a separate vowel as it is pronounced. Rather, the /r/ takes the place of the vowel and is said to be syllabic. The children in the naturalistic studies of Read (1975) and Treiman (1993) often omitted the vowels in these contexts, producing many errors such as "hr" for *her* and "brutr" for *brother*. Jillian (Figure 5.5) made the same sort of error when she spelled *bigger* as "bigr" and *sunflower* as "sunfliwr."

Indeed, the precocious spellers studied by Read (1975) and the kindergartners studied by Treiman, Berch, Tincoff, and Weatherston (1993) omitted the *es* of words like *her* and *brother* more often than they included them. Moreover, Treiman, Berch, Tincoff et al. found that even the first-graders in their study who were average to above-average readers and who had surely seen common words such as *her, work,* and *mother* omitted the vowel between one-third and two-thirds of the time when spelling syllabic /r/. This problem cannot be explained as an across-the-board failure to include vowels or middle letters in spellings, for children are less likely to omit the vowels of words like *war* (which have a true vowel in the middle) than of words like *her* (which have a syllabic /r/). Nor is the problem peculiar to the letter *r* for, as illustrated by Jillian's spelling of *bumblebees* as "bamblbs," children exhibit a similar tendency to omit vowels from their spellings of syllabic /l/ (Treiman, 1993; Treiman, Berch, Tincoff, et al., 1993).

Rather, the spelling errors seem to reflect the children's perception of the sound properties of the words. Thus, young British children were found to produce errors like "ble" for *blur* and "docke" for *doctor*. In the dialect of these children, *her* is pronounced without a final /r/. American children, in contrast, were more likely to make errors like "blrr" and "dkr" (Treiman, Goswami, Tincoff, & Leevers, 1996).

In short, children's tacit analyses of spoken words do not always match those of adults. This in turn leads to several other relevant observations. First, the division between phonetic and nonphonetic errors that forms the basis of many schemes of classifying spelling errors (e.g., Boder, 1973; Bruck & Waters, 1988; Finucci, Isaacs, Whitehouse, & Childs, 1983; Nelson, 1980) may be misleading when applied to young children. As we have seen, errors such as "gradl," "sgie," and "hr" reflect fine sensitivity to the sounds of spoken words. We would miss this sensitivity if we categorized a misspelling like "gradl" for *dreidel* as phonetically incorrect on the grounds that /d/ is never symbolized as *g* in English. A child who makes a so-called nonphonetic error is not necessarily failing to attend to the sounds of words when spelling.

Second, people have long blamed the irregularity of the English writing system for children's difficulties in learning to write and read and have urged that the writing system be reformed (Venezky, 1980). Yet, spelling reform cannot eliminate all of children's problems during the early stages of learning, not, at least, if spelling-sound regularity is defined from the viewpoint of literate adults. Learning to read and write seems to shape people's conceptions of speech, causing changes in their classification of certain potentially ambiguous sounds (see Derwing, 1992; Fowler, 1991).

Third, these studies indicate that for children mastering the alphabetic principle, spelling is a creative, language-based process rather than a process of rote visual memorization. Children's sound-based errors show that spelling is to a large extent a process of symbolizing the linguistic structure of spoken words.

Omissions of Letters. Bobby, Trevor, and Jillian all produced errors in which they omitted consonant phonemes. For example, Trevor spelled *play* as "pa," omitting the second consonant of the initial cluster, and Bobby spelled *warm* as "wom," deleting the first consonant of the final cluster. In fact, children often omit the internal phonemes of both initial and final consonant clusters. Though the factors that regulate these errors seem to be slightly different, both seem to be rooted in still unconventional analyses of the words' phonemic structure.

In analyzing his collection of preschoolers' writings, Read (1975) noticed that the children frequently failed to symbolize the nasal consonants /m/, /n/, and /ng/ when they occurred as the first phoneme of a final consonant cluster, for example, spelling *and* as "ad" or *stamps* as "staps." These omissions were more common if the following stop consonant was voiceless, as with the clusters /nt/ and /ngk/, than if it was voiced, as with /nd/ (see also Read, 1986; Snowling, 1994). As it happens, there are position effects in spelling such that letters in the middle of a word are more likely to be omitted than letters at the beginning or at the end of a word (Jensen, 1962; Kooi, Schutz, & Baker, 1965; Mendenhall, 1930; Treiman, Berch, & Weatherston, 1993). However, position alone cannot explain why *n* is more susceptible to omission before letters such as *t* and *k,* which stand for voiceless stops, than before letters such as *d,* which stand for voiced stops. Read's (1975) hypothesis was that these errors related to the sound properties of nasals in final clusters and, in particular, to the fact that nasals are very short before final consonants, especially if these consonants are voiceless (MalKcot, 1960).

The first-graders in Treiman's (1993) study made the same kinds of nasal omission errors as Read's (1975) preschoolers, for example, spelling *think* as "theeck" and *stand* as "stad." Importantly, though, the first-graders' omissions of consonants in final clusters were not restricted to nasals. As Marcel (1980) found among older poor spellers, Treiman's first-graders also tended to omit liquids in final clusters, as in "hos" for horse and "od" for *old.* And they omitted obstruents such as /t/ and /s/, as in "las" for *lets* and "foret" for *forest.* (Obstruents include stop consonants such as /t/ and /d/, together with sounds such as /s/ and /z/.) Thus, Treiman's data indicate that children are inclined to omit the interior phonemes of final consonant clusters in general. Indeed, across two-consonant final clusters such as /rs/ and /ld/, the children omitted the first consonant 25% of the time but the final consonant at less than half that rate. With three-consonant final clusters such as /mps/, the first and second consonants of the cluster both had omission rates of 25% or more; again, the final consonant was omitted much less often.

To further examine the breadth of consonant omissions in final clusters, Treiman, Zukowski, and Richmond-Welty (1995) asked first-graders to repeat and then spell nonsense words such as /jink/, /sanch/, and /dulb/ that had various types of final clusters. As observed by Read (1975), nasals were frequently omitted before voiceless obstruents, with omission rates ranging from 57% to 81% across experiments. In addition, nasals before voiced obstruents were omitted at rates between 42% and 51%; liquids that were the first phonemes of final clusters between 40% and 63%; and obstruents as the first elements of final clusters between 13% and 23%. Because the children in this study had been asked to repeat each item before spelling it, the researchers were able to reject the possibility that their failures to spell consonants reflected failures to pronounce them. Rather, their explanation for these errors was that children analyze spoken syllables differently than adults do.

In particular, children seem to treat liquids and nasals as qualities of the vowel that precedes them rather than as phonemes in their own right. Because children consider /r/-ness to be a quality of the vowel rather than a separate unit, they do not use the separate letter *r* in spelling *born,* producing "bon." With *lets,* in contrast, the obstruent /t/ is less likely to be grouped with the vowel and is more likely to be spelled. To corroborate this hypothesis, Treiman et al. (1995) asked the children to pronounce the nonwords sound by sound, putting down one token for each sound. For nonwords such as /morl/, children often used just three tokens and pronounced just three sounds: /m/, /or/, and /l/. These same children performed the phoneme counting task very accurately with syllables that did not contain such blends.

As illustrated by Trevor's spelling of *play* as "pa," young children also tend to omit the internal consonants of word-initial clusters. In Treiman's (1993) study of first-graders' classroom writings, children omitted the second consonants of two-consonant syllable-initial clusters almost 25% of the time. Examples include "sak" for *snake,* "afad" for *afraid,* and "set" for *sweat.* With three-consonant initial clusters, both the second and the third consonants were omitted at rates of 25% or more. In contrast, the first consonants of initial clusters were rarely omitted. Omissions of consonants in initial clusters have also been reported in other studies of young children's writing (Bruck & Treiman, 1990; Miller & Limber, 1985; Treiman, 1991). Moreover, while some children rarely make such errors, a few children do so very frequently (Treiman, 1991). Of note, whereas omissions of consonants in final clusters vary with the phonological makeup of the cluster, no such influences have been detected for initial clusters (Treiman, 1991, 1993). For all types of syllable-initial clusters, the interior phonemes appear more likely to be omitted than the exterior phonemes.

Among normal children, in short, failures to spell consonants in initial clusters do not seem related to failures to pronounce these consonants (Bruck & Treiman, 1990; Treiman, 1991). Nor do they seem to reflect serial position effects, for children are much more likely to omit the *l* of *blows* than the *l* of *along,* even though *l* is the second letter in both words (Treiman, 1985b). Instead, the spelling data suggest that children are disinclined to break the initial clusters, or onsets, of syllables into two separate phonemes, treating them instead as a single spoken unit. In effect, they consider *snow* to contain the initial consonant unit /sn/ followed by the vowel /ō/. This suggestion is consistent with the evidence discussed earlier that the onsets of syllables form cohesive units for both children and adults (Goswami & Bryant, 1990; Stahl & Murray, 1994; Treiman, 1985a, 1989, 1992).

How might children be taught to analyze the internal structure of words? Extra drill on individual letter-sound correspondences is unlikely to eliminate the errors, for children who produce, for example, "pat" and "so" for *pant* and *snow* usually spell /n/ with the appropriate letter when the sound occurs at the beginning of a word. Neither do the necessary insights follow readily from reading experience for, as found by Treiman et al. (1995), first-graders who had learned to read such words as *went* frequently omitted consonants in clusters when spelling similar nonsense words.

Perhaps a faster and more efficient way to get children to revise their analyses of words like *pant* and *snow* is through phonemic awareness activities designed toward that end. For example, children could learn a secret language in which words are said without their first consonants. Thus, *sat* becomes *at* and *Ned* becomes *Ed.* Given a word like *snow,* children's first response is likely to be *oh* (Bruck & Treiman, 1990). Yet, designed and played properly, such a game could lead them to notice that *no* is actually a better answer. If such activities result in improved spelling, it would be yet another demonstration of the value, discussed earlier in this chapter, of helping children to develop phonemic awareness (e.g., Ball & Blachman, 1991; Bradley & Bryant, 1983; Byrne & Fielding-Barnsley, 1989, 1991; Goldstein, 1976; Lundberg et al., 1988; Treiman & Baron, 1983; Vellutino & Scanlon, 1987; Wallach & Wallach, 1979; Williams, 1979).

In general, linguistic factors that influence the perceptual salience of phonemes seem also to influence the ease with which they are represented. Thus, other linguistic variables that have an effect on children's tendency to omit consonant and vowel phonemes include the position of the phoneme in the word, the length of the word, and the stress of the syllable (Stage & Wagner, 1992; Treiman, 1993; Treiman, Berch, & Weatherston, 1993). Moreover, English has more clusters than many other languages of the world, and this may well be a factor in making learning to spell difficult for young English speakers. In future research, it will be useful to examine beginning spelling in other languages that have many consonant clusters. Caravolas and Bruck (1993) have made a start in this direction by studying Czech; their results indicate that Czech children, like English-speaking children, are more likely to omit the interior phonemes of consonant clusters than the exterior phonemes of these clusters.

In any case, the results on phoneme omissions underscore the fact that spelling is a linguistic process, not just a process of rote visual memorization. In turn, a better understanding of how children spell and why they make the errors that they do depends on a better understanding of the phonological structure of the language.

The Role of Letter Names in Beginning Spelling. Middle-class North American children typically learn to sing the alphabet song well before they begin formal schooling. They learn the names of the letters, and they learn what many of the letters look like. Parents, children's television programs, and preschools are just some of the sources from which children acquire this information. In one study (Mason, 1980), almost two-thirds of 4-year-olds were said by their parents to "very often" recite the alphabet without error, and over half of the children could recognize more than 20 letters of the alphabet by name. In another study (Worden & Boettcher, 1990), children could recite or sing 5 or more letters of the alphabet by the age of 4 and were almost perfect by the age of 5. Shown uppercase letters and asked to name them, the 4-year-olds were correct on about 14 of the 26 letters, and the 5-year-olds were correct on about 22. In contrast, the 4-year-olds could provide the sounds for only about 6 letters and 5-year-olds for only 8.

Given that children enter school with a good deal of knowledge about letter names, what role, if any, does this knowledge play in learning to write and read? One might argue that letter-name knowledge cannot directly benefit spelling or reading because written letters symbolize phonemes and not the letters' names. After all, *bat* is pronounced /băt/ rather than /bē/-/ā/-/tē/. However, most English letter names contain the phoneme that is commonly represented by the letter. Thus, a child who does not know or has forgotten how to spell the sound /b/ might search her or his memory for a letter name that contains /b/. Furthermore, this strategy will succeed with most of the phonemes—but not all.

For example, the English phonemes /g/ and /h/ do not occur in the name of any letter. If children use the names of letters to remember or figure out their sounds, they should have more difficulty spelling phonemes such as /g/ and /h/ than phonemes such as /b/, /t/, and /l/. The spellings of Treiman's (1993) first-graders were consistent with this hypothesis, but Treiman, Weatherston, and Berch (1994) have provided firmer evidence.

In the latter study, preschoolers and kindergartners were asked to supply the first letters of syllables like /bŏ/, /lŏ/, and /gŏ/ and, in another condition, the last letters of syllables like /ŏb/, /ŏl/, and /ŏg/. Children were required, not to write, but only to say the first or last letters of the spoken syllables. Again, while the phonemes /b/ and /l/ occur in the names of the letters *b* and *l,* the name of the letter *g* does not contain the phoneme /g/. Correspondingly, Treiman and her colleagues found that children indeed did better on syllables for which letter-name knowledge could help them (e.g., /bŏ/ and /lŏ/ in the supply-the-first-letter task; /ŏb/ and /ŏl/ in the supply-the-last-letter task) than on syllables for which letter-name knowledge was misleading (e.g., /gŏ/ and /ŏg/). Moreover, children did better with letters like *b,* where the phoneme that the letter symbolizes is at the beginning of its name, /bē/, than with letters like *l,* where the phoneme that the letter symbolizes is at the end of its name, /ĕl/. This difference may arise because /b/ is in the salient onset position of the letter name /bē/. As discussed earlier, children gain the ability to segment syllables into their onsets and rimes at an early age (e.g., Bowey & Francis, 1991; Kirtley, Bryant, MacLean, & Bradley, 1989; Treiman, 1985a, 1992). In contrast, the /l/ of /ĕl/ is in a less salient position in the spoken syllable and is more difficult to separate from the vowel.

A few English letter names suggest the wrong spellings for sounds. For example, the /w/ sound occurs at the beginning of the name of the letter *y* but /w/ is never spelled as *y* in English. Instead, /w/ is typically spelled with the letter *w,* which has the unusual name "doubleyou." Thus, Trevor spelled *when* with initial *y* in one of his earliest first-grade journal entries (Figure 5.4), although *w* spellings of /w/ began to emerge soon afterwards. The preschoolers and kindergartners studied by Treiman, Weatherston, and Berch (1994) spelled /w/ as *y* between 17% and 18% of the time. For example, some kindergartners spelled *wet* as "yat" and *work* as "yrk." For the most part, these errors are gone by first grade (Treiman, 1993; Treiman, Weatherston, & Berch, 1994). Nevertheless, early errors like "yrk" for *work* suggest that some children's initial ideas about the sounds that letters make are influenced by their knowledge of the letters' names.

Another way letter-name knowledge can affect early spelling is exemplified by errors such as Trevor's "et" for *eat* and Jillian's "seds" for *seeds.* In these cases, children spell a vowel with the letter that has that name rather than with the conventional spelling. These kinds of spellings are very frequent for vowels (Beers, Beers, & Grant, 1977; Read, 1975; Treiman, 1993). Letter-name spellings of vowels are often correct, as in *he* and *bacon,* and perhaps this is why letter-name spellings of vowels persist longer than letter-name spellings that are never correct, such as *y* for /w/.

Just as children sometimes spell a single vowel phoneme with the letter that has that name, they sometimes spell a sequence of phonemes with the letter that has that name. Examples are "lefit" for *elephant,* "frmmr" for *farmer,* and Jillian's "bamblbs" for *bumblebees* (Figure 5.5). In these cases, first-graders use a single consonant letter to symbolize all of the phonemes in the letter's name. For example, the *l* of "lefit" represents the entire syllable, /ĕl/. Such letter-name spellings with consonants have been noted by a number of researchers (e.g., Chomsky, 1979; Ehri, 1986; Gentry, 1982; Read, 1975; Treiman, 1993, 1994).

According to Gentry (1982), beginning spellers use a letter-name strategy whenever it is possible to do so. When they encounter a phoneme or sequence of phonemes that matches the name of an English letter, they spell it with the corresponding letter. This claim may be too broad, however. First, children may be particularly apt to produce letter-name spellings for vowels. Even for consonants, letter-name spellings appear to be more frequent in some cases than in others. In Treiman's (1993) study of first-graders, children sometimes used the consonant letters *r, l, m,* and *n* to spell their names. Errors such as "bl" for *bell* were more common than errors such as "bl" for *ball.* However, letter-name spellings did not occur at levels significantly above those expected by chance for letters such as *b* and *d.* For example, an error such as "bt" for *beat* was not more common than an error such as "bt" for *boat.*

To verify that letter-name spellings do not occur equally often for all consonants, Treiman (1994) asked children to spell syllables that contained various types of letter-name sequences. In the first experiment, first-graders spelled /vär/, which contains the name of the letter *r,* /vĕl/, which contains the name of the letter *l,* and /pĕm/ and /kĕf/, which contain the names of *m* and *f.* If children use a letter-name spelling strategy whenever it is possible to do so, they should spell these nonwords as "vr," "vl," "pm," and "kf." The first-graders, who were tested in October and November, did make some of these letter-name errors. However, the errors were by far most frequent for nonwords containing the name of *r.* For nonwords like /vär/, 41% of the children's spellings were letter-name errors such as "vr." The letter-name errors occurred less often for *l,* with a rate of 9% errors such as "vl" for /vĕl/. Vowel omissions in spellings of nonwords containing the names of *m, n, f,* and *s* were even less common, occurring between 2% and 4% of the time. Again, the results suggest that some letter-name sequences are more likely to be spelled as units than others.

Treiman's (1994) second experiment was designed to investigate these differences further. In addition to examining letters with vowel + consonant names, the second study also included letters with consonant + vowel names. Children were screened to ensure that they knew the names of the critical letters. The children were asked to spell syllables containing phoneme sequences that matched the names of English letters. The letters considered were *r, l, m, n, f, s, t, p,* and *k.* For example, /gär/ contains the letter name for *r,* or /är/, /zĕf/ contains the letter name for *f,* or /ĕf/, and /tĕb/ contains the letter name for *t,* or /tē/. Kindergartners and first-graders produced most consonant + consonant spellings for syllables containing the name of *r.* Indeed, kindergartners made errors like "gr" for /gär/ 61% of the time, and first-graders did so 50% of the time. Syllables containing the letter name *l* were the next most likely to receive letter-name spellings, with 41% such errors for kindergartners and 19% for first-graders. Letter-name spellings were less common for syllables that contained the names of the letters *m, n, f, s, t, p,* and *k.* Nevertheless, children did produce more letter-name spellings for these syllables than for control syllables that did not contain letter-name sequences.

How can we explain the observed differences among consonant letters in their susceptibility to letter-name spellings? These differences may reflect, in part, the sound properties of the letters' names (Treiman, 1993, 1994). To spell a word such as *far,* children attempt to divide the spoken word into individual sounds or phonemes and to represent each phoneme with a letter. However, the /är/ sequence in this word is difficult to segment. As we argued earlier, children tend to group vowels and following /r/s, treating them as a single unit. Given this fact, and given the strong association that children have between /är/ and *r,* they may spell *far* as "fr." The unusual nature of the name of *r* may further contribute to this error. The vowel phoneme in the name of *r,* /ä/, occurs in no other English letter name. In contrast, the recurrence of vowel phonemes across other consonant letter names may help children to understand that the letters are used to represent the consonant phonemes that distinguish their names. Thus, a child may come to realize that the letter names /bē/, /dē/, /pē/, /tē/, and so on share the vowel /ē/ and that the letters *b, d, p,* and *t* symbolize the consonants that distinguish these letter names. The same may be true for the letter names /ĕl/, /ĕf/, /ĕm/, /ĕn/, and /ĕs/. How much of a contribution the uniqueness of the vowel in /är/ among the letter names of English makes to children's use of *r* letter-name spellings remains to be investigated.

In summary, children who learn the names of letters at an early age, as most North American children do, use this knowledge as a guide to sound-spelling correspondence. The extent to which they do so depends on their experience with print, their phonological analysis abilities, and the sound properties of the letter names themselves. Children's misspellings of words do not reflect simple lapses in the memorization and recall of letter strings. Were this the case, we could not explain why errors like "br" for *bar* are more common than errors like "bd" for *bad.* Instead, children's errors reflect the knowledge that they bring with them to the spelling task. Children's knowledge of letter names and their knowledge of phonology help to explain the high rate of misspelling errors like "br" for *bar.*

The misspellings reviewed in this section again challenge the dependence of productive letter-sound learning on rote, paired-associate memory. Rather, children who know the names of letters and who have enough phonological analysis ability to divide the letter names into smaller units use this knowledge to help them learn sound-spelling correspondences. For English, in which the names of letters are not always good guides to the letters' sounds, this strategy can lead to errors like "yrk" for *work.* Conversely, languages in which letters' names are more reliable guides to sound may offer an advantage compared to English. In comparing children's learning of reading and writing across orthographies, therefore, it may be necessary to take into account the systems of letter names as well as the regularity of sound-spelling correspondence and other factors. Note, too, that children in English-speaking cultures where letter names are less strongly emphasized in early education may not make some of the errors that North American children do.

The Influence of Orthographic Experience on Children's Spellings. As we discussed in the previous section on the precursors of alphabetic writing, children in a literate society have a good deal of experience with print even before they learn to read and write. As a result of this experience, prereaders begin to learn about the salient visual characteristics of print, such as the fact that it consists of strings of units arranged in a linear pattern. With time, children focus more and more on the letters within printed words and on how they are arranged. In this section, we discuss children's developing knowledge of the letter patterns in printed words and the way this knowledge affects their spelling.

The words of English, or of any other language, are not random strings of letters. Instead, the letters are arranged in certain patterns. Some of the patterns reflect the sound patterns of the spoken language. For example, printed words do not begin with *bw* because spoken words do not begin with /bw/; /bwăt/ is not a possible word of English. Printed words generally contain at least one vowel letter because spoken words generally contain at least one vowel sound; /pd/ is not a possible word of English.

Other constraints on the arrangements of letters in printed words are not motivated by sound but instead are purely orthographic. For example, *ck* may occur in the middles and at the ends of English words, as in *packet* and *pack.* This digraph (or two-letter sequence) does not occur at the beginnings of words. The ban against initial *ck* does not reflect a ban against the initial /k/ sound; many words begin with /k/ spelled as *k* or *c.* Rather, the nonoccurrence of initial *ck* is an orthographic feature of English. Other orthographic patterns involve doublets, or two-letter spellings in which the two letters are identical. Certain letters may occur as doublets, such as the double *e* of *peel* and the double *l* of *ill.* Other letters, such as *v* and *i,* rarely double. Doublets typically occur in the middles and at the ends of words, as in *supper* and *inn;* they rarely occur at the beginnings of words. Venezky (1970) has described a number of such orthographic patterns.

Do beginning spellers appreciate these orthographic patterns? The results of several early research studies suggested that they do. Rosinski and Wheeler (1972) presented first-, third-, and fifth-graders (tested in October) with pairs of nonwords such as *tup-nda* and *dink-xogl.* Within each pair, one nonword was orthographically regular and pronounceable and the other was orthographically irregular and unpronounceable. The children were instructed to point to the item in each pair that was more like a real word. The first-graders performed at chance levels, whereas the third- and fifth-graders performed significantly above chance. In a similar study, Niles, Grunder, and Wimmer (1977) used pairs such as *ateditol-ijhbwstt.* First- through sixth-graders (tested near the end of the school year) were able to pick the correct item at better than chance levels, whereas kindergartners performed at the level of chance. However, a problem with these early studies is that orthographic regularity and pronounceability were confounded in the nonword pairs. Thus, the children could have been using one or both of the features as a basis for their decisions.

Treiman (1993) attempted to get around the confounding effects of pronounceability in testing children's knowledge of orthographic constraints. Her orthographic constraints test included 16 pairs of nonwords. Each pair tested a constraint or regularity of the English writing system. One nonword in a pair conformed to the regular pattern, and the other word did not. However, both nonwords were pronounceable. For example, one pair was *ckun* and *nuck.* Children were asked which item looked more like a real word. If children make their judgments on the basis of sound only, both items would be equally likely to be chosen. However, if children consider orthographic acceptability in making their judgments, the item that conforms to the orthographic constraint should be chosen more often. Treiman found that middle-class kindergartners (tested in May), first-graders (tested in March), and second-graders (tested in May) all chose the conforming item significantly more than 50% of the time. The percentages of correct responses were 56% for kindergartners, 62% for first-graders, and 83% for second-graders. The above-chance performance of kindergartners and first-graders supports the idea that knowledge of orthography begins to emerge at an early age.

The tests used by Niles et al. (1977), Rosinski and Wheeler (1972), and Treiman (1993) contained a variety of nonword pairs. Knowledge of no one constraint was explored in detail. Two further studies, however, specifically investigated children's knowledge of double consonants and vowels (Cassar, 1995). Cassar's first study focused on consonants. In English, consonant doublets may occur in the middle or at the end of a word but not at the beginning. In addition, medial doublets normally follow short vowels in words of more than one syllable, as in *latter.* Single consonants normally follow long vowels, as in *later.* Pairs of nonwords were designed to test children's knowledge of these conventions. In pairs testing knowledge of position, one nonword contained an initial doublet and the other nonword contained a final doublet. An example is *nnus* and *nuss.* If children know where consonant doublets may occur, they should judge that *nuss* is more likely to be a word than *nnus.* In pairs examining the phonetic environment for doubling, one nonword contained a medial single consonant, as in *salip,* and the other contained a medial doublet, as in *sallip.* Cassar asked whether participants listening to pronunciations for the nonwords chose *salip* for a pronunciation with /ā/ in the first syllable and *sallip* for a pronunciation with /ă/.

The participants in Cassar's (1995) first study were children in kindergarten, first, second, third, sixth, and ninth grades, as well as college undergraduates. One group at each grade level was assigned to an auditory condition in which they chose which spelling looked best for the word they heard. The other group was assigned to a visual condition in which they viewed pairs of spellings and chose the one they thought looked more like a real word. For the pairs testing knowledge of position (e.g., *nuss* and *nnus*), even kindergartners tested in the first semester of the school year picked the final doublet spellings significantly more often than chance. Not until sixth grade and above did children show clear knowledge of the correspondence between short vowels and spellings with medial doublets. That is, only the older children reliably chose *sallip* for /săl ĭp/ and *salip* for /sālĭp/. These latter results support Henderson's (1985) claim that knowledge about the complex pattern of short vowel plus double consonant in two-syllable words develops later than the first few years of elementary school. However, young children's above-chance performance on the test of knowledge about the positions of consonant doublets suggests that knowledge of simpler orthographic patterns emerges much earlier in the course of spelling acquisition.

Cassar's (1995) second study further investigated children's knowledge of double consonants and also investigated their knowledge of double vowels. As in the first study, an orthographic choice test employed pairs of nonwords. One nonword in each pair contained an acceptable vowel or consonant doublet. The other nonword contained an unacceptable doublet. The doublets occurred in the medial or final positions of the spellings, both of which are acceptable for doublets. Sample pairs are *noss* and *novv* and *geed* and *gaad.* If children know which letters are allowed to double, they should choose *noss* and *geed* as more wordlike than *novv* and *gaad.* Kindergarten, first-, and second-grade children were tested during February. First- and second-graders, but not kindergartners, chose spellings containing allowable doublets over spellings containing unallowable doublets. That is, they judged that *noss* and *geed* were more like real English words than *novv* and *gaad.* By first grade, then, children have some appreciation for which letters may double and which letters may not. Different children served in Cassar's first and second studies and so comparisons between the two studies must be made with caution. However, it appears that knowledge of which particular letters may double, as tested in the second study, may develop later than knowledge of where double letters may occur in words, as tested in the first study.

The results of a study by Pick, Unze, Brownell, Drozdal, and Hopmann (1978) speak to children's developing knowledge of another orthographic constraint, the fact that words are rarely composed of all consonants or all vowels. In this study, children were asked to sort cards with various types of letter strings printed on them into words and nonwords. The youngest children in the study, who were 3 and 4 years old, accepted most of the items as words. Between nursery school and kindergarten, though, there was a significant decline in the acceptability of items like *mptc* and *aiue.* Based on these results, Pick and her colleagues suggested that kindergartners know something about the combinations of letters that occur in words. Even though most kindergartners cannot yet read, they are learning that words are not composed of all consonant letters or of all vowel letters.

If children have some implicit knowledge about the kinds of letter sequences that may occur in English words, as the findings just reviewed suggest, then this knowledge may be reflected in their own spellings. Children should make spelling errors that follow the orthographic patterns of English more often than spelling errors that deviate from these patterns. For example, children may misspell *cake* as "kack," following the pattern that *ck* may occur at the ends of English words. Children should be unlikely to misspell this word as "ckak," for this spelling violates the constraints of English. Looking at the classroom writings of first-graders, Treiman (1993) examined the degree to which the errors honored the orthographic patterns of English. For each pattern that was investigated, the first-graders usually, though not always, followed the pattern. Consider the results for *ck*. The children used this digraph (or two-letter spelling) 38 times when it was not a part of a word's correct spelling. They used the digraph at the beginning of a word only twice. The digraph occurred in the middle of a word 11 times, as in "mrckut" for *market,* and at the end of a word 25 times, as in "bick" for *bike.* Apparently, the children had begun to pick up the restriction against initial *ck.* This restriction, like the other orthographic patterns studied, was not formally taught at school. The children probably discovered the pattern on their own from seeing words such as *sick* and *package* but not words like *ckan.*

As another example, consider digraphs that end in *y,* such as *ay* and *oy,* and digraphs that end in *i,* such as *ai* and *oi.* As Venezky (1970) pointed out, digraphs ending in *y* generally occur before vowels and at the ends of words, as in *mayor* and *boy.* Digraphs ending in *i* usually appear before consonants, as in *maid* and *coin.* Similar alternations occur for digraphs ending in *w,* such as *ow,* and those ending in *u,* such as *ou.* The former usually occur before vowels and at the ends of words, as in *power* and *how;* the latter usually occur before consonants, as in *ouch.* Treiman (1993) examined errors that contained one of the digraphs in question where the digraph did not occur in the word's conventional spelling. Errors were classified as either honoring or violating the orthographic pattern. For example, "seilf" for *self* honors the pattern because it has a digraph ending in *i* before a consonant; "plew" for *play* is also legal because it has a digraph ending in *w* at the end of a word. Errors that violate the orthographic pattern include "ai" for *a,* which has a digraph with final *i* at the end of a word, and "ewt" for *it,* which has a digraph with final *w* before a consonant. Errors that followed the graphemic pattern significantly outnumbered errors that violated it. Moreover, children's adherence to the pattern was significantly greater for *i* and *y* than for *u* and *w.* This difference may arise because the *i/y* alternation has fewer exceptions in conventional English than the *u/w* alternation. For example, the common words *you* and *down* deviate from the typical *u/w* alternation. That children followed the pattern more often in the case of *i* and *y* than in the case of *u* and *w* strengthens the view that exposure to print rather than explicit teaching of rules is the important factor in the learning of orthographic patterns. It is unlikely that an adult would point out a rule to a first-grader but then tell the child that the rule has more exceptions in one case than another.

In Treiman's (1993) study of first-graders' classroom spelling errors, compliance with the orthographic constraints tended to be greater during the second half of first grade than during the first half. Even during the first half of first grade, though, the children showed some knowledge of the patterns. Thus, children begin learning about the letter patterns within printed words from an early age. This learning may even start before children are able to read and spell words on their own. Once children begin to write, their spellings tend to honor the orthographic patterns that they have observed.

In conclusion, children learn about the kinds of letter patterns that occur in words from their experience with print. In their own spellings, they attempt to reproduce the sorts of patterns that they have seen. First-graders' spellings like "bick" for *bike* or "seilf" for *self* show, at a more advanced level, a sensitivity to print similar to Jamie's linearly arranged symbols (Figure 5.2). In both cases, children observe the features of the print around them and attempt to reproduce those features in their own writing. Whereas the 3½-year-old Jamie mimics the superordinate features of print, such as its linear organization, the 6-year-old reproduces more detailed features pertaining to the organization of letters within words.

Toward More Sophisticated Spelling

As children progress, their knowledge of the spelling system grows and deepens and they become better and better spellers. In this section, we will discuss four changes that occur with increasing spelling skill. To anticipate, one change is that children gradually internalize the classifications of sounds that are embodied in the conventional writing system. For example, children see that *her* is classified as having a consonant + vowel + consonant structure, like *war,* rather than a consonant + vowel structure, like *he.* Errors like "hr" for *her* become less common beyond the first grade. Second, children learn the range of spellings that are possible for various sounds. Rather than relying on the names of letters as a guide to spelling, children now spell sounds in conventional ways. Thus, children beyond the first grade may misspell *plaid* as "plad," using *a* rather than *ai* for /ă/, but are unlikely to spell *when* as "yn." Third, children rapidly improve in their understanding of and adherence to orthographic patterns. For example, children in first grade and above rarely produce spellings that begin with double consonants, having seen very few such spellings in English. Finally, children learn that the printed forms of English words reflect the meanings of words as well as their sounds. For example, *health* shares the *heal* of *heal,* even though this sequence is pronounced differently in the two words. Older children and adults gradually come to grips with the way meaning is represented in the English writing system and use the spellings of words as a way of learning more about relationships among them.

Learning to Classify Sounds in Accordance with the Conventional Orthography. As children learn to read, they see how sounds are classified by the conventional writing system. For example, the first sound of *drag* is classified as /d/, *her* is considered to contain a vowel, and *went* is considered to contain /n/. All of these classifications are embodied in the conventional spellings of the words. In each case, though, another choice might have been possible. For example, the first sound of *drag* has characteristics in common with /j/ as well as with /d/. Before they learn to read, some children's choices in ambiguous cases such as these do not always match those of the conventional writing system. For example, some children seem to classify the first sound of *drag* as a type of /j/ rather than as a type of /d/ and to spell it accordingly. As children see that this sound is always spelled with *d,* their classifications change. The change does not happen overnight as a result of learning to read a few *dr* and *tr* words. For example, one first-grader tested by Treiman (1985c) read the word *tray* correctly but spelled /dr/ and /tr/ in a nonstandard manner on every possible occasion. By second grade, though, children make only a few unconventional spellings of /dr/ and /tr/ (Treiman, 1985c). The case of syllabic /r/ provides another example of how experience with conventional print changes children's ideas about sounds. As children progress from kindergarten to first grade to second grade, they are increasingly likely to include a vowel in their spellings of words such as *sir* and *work* (Treiman, Berch, Tincoff, & Weatherston, 1993). By second grade, most children include a vowel in such words. They also use a vowel when spelling similar nonwords, showing that they have learned something beyond the conventional spellings of specific real words.

The suggestion that learning the conventional spellings of words can change the way children think about sounds is supported by the results of Ehri and Wilce (1980, 1986). In the first of these two studies, Ehri and Wilce (1980) had fourth-graders practice reading nonwords. Some of the spellings, such as *zitch,* included letters that suggested the existence of extra sounds. Other spellings, such as *zich,* did not include these extra letters. Although the two words were pronounced alike, the children considered *zitch* to contain more sounds than *zich.* In the second study, working with second-graders, Ehri and Wilce (1986) used real words, such as *notice,* that the children did not yet know how to spell. Half of the children were taught how to spell the words, the other half were not. The children who were taught that *notice* contained a *t* in its spelling generally considered it to contain a /t/ in its pronunciation. The children in the control group were more likely to think that *notice* contained a /d/. This is a reasonable judgment given that the middle sound of *notice,* which is called a *flap,* is voiced like /d/ rather than voiceless like /t/.

Older children's and adults' thinking about sounds is thus colored by their knowledge of spellings. Literate people find it difficult to think about sounds as divorced from letters, as any teacher of phonetics can testify. Orthography, originally learned as a representation of speech, takes on a life of its own. Once learned, it influences our views about language itself.

The Assimilation of Spelling Conventions. When children first start to write, they may know the conventional spellings of only a few words. For example, at the time that Bobby wrote the message in Figure 5.3, he knew how to spell his own name, the names of other family members, and a few common words like *no.* Such children have a very limited stock of knowledge on which to base their spellings of sounds. If the children cannot or do not ask an adult how to spell sounds (like Bobby, who wanted to write the message of Figure 5.3 on his own) or if the adult will not provide such information (like the teacher in the classroom studied by Treiman, 1993), the children must come up with spellings on their own. It is not surprising that such children use their knowledge of letters' names as a guide to the spellings of sounds. For example, Bobby spelled *be* as "b" because the name of the letter *b* matches the word *be.*

As children learn the conventional spellings of more and more words, they acquire a broader base of knowledge from which to induce the spellings of sounds. In addition, many children are taught the letters that are used to spell particular sounds in school. As a result, children come to spell sounds in conventional ways. Unconventional spellings that are influenced by letter names, such as *y* for /w/ and *r* for /är/, become less common (Treiman, 1994; Treiman, Cassar, & Zukowski, 1994).

Those letter-name spellings that occur in the conventional spellings of words seem to persist longer than those that do not. For example, even third- and fourth-graders occasionally misspell *spike* as "spick" or "spic," using *i* to represent its name (Beers et al., 1977). These errors may last longer than errors such as *y* for /w/ because the /ī/ sound is spelled with *i* in real words such as *island* and *china*. To children, *i* seems to be an excellent way to spell the /ī/ sound. It takes time for them to understand that, in some cases, an *e* must be added to the end of the word to "lengthen" the vowel (Henderson, 1985). Children's uncertainty about the function of final *e* shows up, too, in incorrect use of final *e* after "short" vowels, as in Jillian's "thene" for *then* (Figure 5.5).

As children move from using letter names as a basis for symbolizing sounds to using information gained from an increasingly large body of known words, their spellings become more and more conventional. Children still make errors, but these errors involve possible spellings of sounds that are used in the wrong contexts rather than nonstandard spellings. For example, the fourth-grader Missy (Figure 5.6) used *ei* to spell the /ē/ of *field*. This is one spelling of the /ē/ sound, as witnessed by the word *ceiling*. What Missy did not yet know was the context in which *ei* spellings of /ē/ occur. As another example, Missy misspelled *finally* as "finnaly" and as "finaly" in the same story. She knew that *n* and *nn* are possible spellings of /n/, but she did not seem to know that double-letter spellings occur after "short" vowels, whereas single letters occur after "long" vowels. Cassar's (1995) results, described earlier, confirm that knowledge of this pattern does not develop until sometime between third and sixth grade (see also Henderson, 1985).

Children do better on words in which each sound is spelled in the most common manner, or regular words, than on words for which this is not the case. For example, Waters, Bruck, and Malus-Abramovitz (1988) found that spellers in the third, fourth, fifth, and sixth grades performed more accurately on words like *must*, for which there are few or no alternative legal spellings, than on words like *street*, for which there are other possible spellings *(streat, strete)*. In a study by Treiman (1984), third- and fourth-graders did significantly better on regular words such as *glad* than on exception words such as *plaid*, for which there is an obvious alternative spelling *(plad)*.

Spelling becomes more and more correct as children sort out the contexts in which various spellings occur and as they learn the conventional spellings of more and more words. Missy (Figure 5.6) shows evidence of this in her correct spellings of difficult exception words such as *squirrel* and *stomach-ache*. She would have made errors like *squirl* and *stummuck-ake* had she not seen and learned the spellings of these particular words.

As we discussed earlier, even young children know a good deal about the letter patterns that may appear in printed words. For example, the first-graders studied by Treiman (1993) were learning that *ck* is restricted in where it may occur in words. Even in their errors, they were more likely to use *ck* at the ends or in the middles of words than at the beginnings. Orthographic knowledge increases rapidly across the early school years (Cassar, 1995; Niles et al., 1977; Pick et al., 1978; Rosinski & Wheeler, 1972; Treiman, 1993). As children acquire a body of known words, they make generalizations about the kinds of letter sequences that do and do not occur in the language. Their spellings, even when wrong, "look right." Thus, most of Missy's spelling errors in Figure 5.6—"feild," "finaly," "finnaly," "frined," and others—could be real English words. Although these spellings are incorrect, they contain sequences of letters that occur in real words.

Developing Awareness of Morphemes. The English writing system is typically considered to be an alphabet, albeit an irregular one. For words that contain more than one unit of meaning, however, English often deviates systematically from the alphabetic principle. The spelling of a word that contains more than one meaningful unit often reflects meaning rather than sound. For example, one would expect *health* to be spelled *helth* based on the sounds that it contains. The conventional spelling, though, indicates the similarity in meaning between *health* and *heal*. As another example, *jumped* and *hemmed* end with different sounds: /t/ for *jumped* and /d/ for *hemmed*. The final sounds of the two words, although different, both represent the past tense marker. The English writing system chooses to represent the level of meaning by spelling both words with final *ed*.

It takes some time for children to learn about the way meaning is reflected in spelling (Carlisle, 1988; Ehri, 1986; Gentry, 1982; Henderson, 1985; Templeton, 1992; Waters et al., 1988). Indeed, poor adult spellers may never fully master this aspect of English spelling (Fischer, Shankweiler, & Liberman, 1985). The third- through sixth-graders tested by Waters et al. (1988) had difficulty spelling words like *sign*. The correct spelling of this word can be predicted if one relates it to *signal*, which has the same root; the word is unlikely to be spelled correctly otherwise. Missy showed an apparent failure to analyze *finally* into its root *(final)* and suffix *(ly)* when she spelled this word as "finnaly" and "finaly." Had she divided the word into units of meaning, she would presumably have spelled it with double *l.* Sterling (1983) found similar errors among 12-year-olds. For example, one child apparently did not divide *closely* into the stem *close* plus the suffix *ly,* writing the word as "closlay."

Children's spelling errors on words such as *sign* and *finally* may arise, in part, because they do not yet know that *sign* is related to *signal* or that *finally* is related to *final.* A word such as *signal* may not even be in a young child's vocabulary; the word, if present, may not be related to *sign.* In addition, children may not have mastered the often complex rules by which suffixes and prefixes are added to poken words (Carlisle, 1988). For example, the changes that take place between *magic* and *magician* or between *original* and *originality* involve variations in pronunciation and stress.

With simple suffixes and relatively common words, young children show some ability to represent meaning relationships among words in their spelling. Evidence for this claim comes from a study by Treiman, Cassar, and Zukowski (1994). These researchers compared children's spellings of words like *dirty* and words like *attic. Dirty* is related to *dirt,* whereas *attic* is not related to *at.* Both *dirty* and *attic* contain flaps. As discussed previously, children often misspell flaps as *d* because they are voiced. However, if children use the root word *dirt* to aid their spelling of *dirty,* they should be less likely to make *d* errors on *dirty* than on *attic.* This result was found with children as young as kindergarten. Young children did not use their knowledge of the stem as much as they could have, in that they were not as likely to spell *dirty* with a *t* as to spell *dirt* with a *t,* but they did use it to some degree. Thus, young children appear to have some ability to represent meaning relations in spelling if these relations are clear and transparent.

Many of the meaning relations that are reflected in English spelling are more like *magic* and *magician* or *heal* and *health* than like *dirt* and *dirty.* In these cases, learning to spell may deepen and expand the learner's vocabulary and suggest new relations among words (Templeton, 1992). For example, a child may first learn to spell *health* as an unanalyzed unit, an exception to the general pattern that /ĕ/ is spelled with *e.* Having mastered the conventional spelling, the child may then realize that *health* is related to *heal* and that its spelling makes sense on this basis. Thus, learning to read and write may shape people's ideas about how words are related, just as it shapes their thinking about sounds. Orthography, once learned, is not simply a reflection of linguistic knowledge. It plays a powerful role in influencing and shaping our knowledge about language.

From Understanding to Automaticity in Reading

In all, independent writing offers a superlative medium for developing young readers' basic understanding of the sounds and spellings of words. As compellingly documented by the work on phonemic awareness, such understanding is vital for learning to read. But it is not enough. Whereas, by its nature, writing affords reflective consideration and review of spellings, fluent reading requires that words be apprehended at a glance. In particular, skillful reading depends on acquiring deep, automatized, and detailed knowledge of spelling patterns and their mappings to speech: in significant measure, just as this learning is specific to reading, it can only be gained through reading.

Developmental investigations of children's perceptual sensitivity to orthographic patterns show that it accrues in a gradual but systematic fashion (for a review, see Barron, 1981). As discussed earlier, kindergarten and first-grade readers' sensitivity to whether the spellings of the strings they see are regular is limited. Whether reading words, pseudowords, or nonwords, they tend to process them in a simple letter-by-letter manner (Juola, Schadler, Chabot, & McCaughey, 1978; Lefton & Spragins, 1974; McCaughey, Juola, Schadler, & Ward, 1980).

Toward the end of first grade, normal readers begin to show a distinct advantage for pronounceable consonant-vowel-consonant sequences such as *rop* over irregular and unpronounceable nonwords such as *rjp* (Doehring, 1976; Gibson, Osser, & Pick, 1963; Thomas, 1968). Over the course of second grade, normal readers (but not poor readers) additionally become sensitive to the consonant pairs that frequently occur at the beginnings of words, such as *bl* and *pr* (Santa, 1976–1977). Furthermore, even given relatively long (seven-letter) strings, the speed with which normal second-graders can decide whether or not a word is real proves sensitive to the frequency of the spelling patterns. Nonword decisions are slowed by both the likelihood of the individual consonant pairs in the strings (e.g., *shrnld* is slower to be rejected than *hgjcpl*) and the presence or absence of vowels (e.g., *turild* is slower to be rejected than *shrnld*). Moreover—and perhaps most interestingly—the mere presence of one or more vowels is enough to slow their rejection of even an otherwise unlikely string (e.g., *kugafp, vbejic,* and *gsecfp* are slower to be rejected than *dtscfk,* etc.; Henderson & Chard, 1980).

By the time normal readers are in the fourth grade, the presence of a vowel slows their ability to decide that a string is not a word only if it appears in likely surroundings in the string, for example, *clasty* and *grilts* but not *kigafp* and *vbejic* (Henderson & Chard, 1980). By that time, too, normal readers generally exhibit the adult pattern of pseudoword/nonword differences, even for long strings (Gibson et al., 1963; Lefton & Spragins, 1974). In addition, it is during the fourth grade that normal readers begin to perceive syllables more quickly and accurately than single letters (Friedrich, Schadler, & Juola, 1979) and become able, like adults, to vocalize words faster in response to print than to pictures (Marmurek & Rinaldo, 1992).

Complementing such findings with extensive work of her own, Ehri (see 1980, 1992) has offered a "word identity amalgamation theory" to explain this remarkable growth. At the first level, according to her theory, children must acquire a working familiarity with the shapes and sounds of letters. In addition, they must acquire basic phonemic awareness and, in particular, the ability to detect systematic relationships between the sound segments of spoken words and the letters in their spellings. Working from these abilities, the children begin to build orthographic images of the words they read by matching the letters of each to its phonemic segments.

At first, children may proceed by matching just a few—usually the first and sometimes the last—of the individual graphemes of each word to its phonemic segments. As they become more and more familiar with the words and with the grapheme-phoneme relationships, their orthographic images become more and more complete and cohesive, such that, eventually, the full image of a word may be evoked at a glance. As the children's repertoires of printed words grow in number and completeness, they begin to learn about more complex spelling-sound patterns too. And as these complex patterns support more efficient mapping of spellings to sounds, it becomes easier and easier for them to read and remember newly encountered words. Meanwhile, through their reading experience, semantic and syntactic information also becomes "amalgamated" with the orthographic images of the words.

Perfetti (1992) similarly accepts that the process of skillful word recognition necessarily involves interactive connections between letters and words, letters and phonemes, and phonemes and words (where the "letter" and "phoneme" representations almost certainly include multiletter and multiphoneme units). However, he continues, the larger research on word recognition argues that these interactions are independent of, even insulated from, the influence or bias of the reader's prior knowledge and expectations about linguistic flow and meaning. To be sure, such higher-order expectations are an integral part of the reading complex, but their job is to assist interpretation, not recognition. This "encapsulation" or isolation of the word-recognition processes is possible for mature readers only because the mind's response to the graphic representation is fully and redundantly specified by its word, letter, and phoneme knowledge. It is because the word is triggered by the print in a wholly deterministic way that the mind is responsive, and need be responsive, only to the input features.

Thus, in its very structure and explanatory objective, Perfetti's (1992) theory directly rejects the merit and plausibility of meaning-driven notions of word learning. And though stage theories may remain useful as gross descriptions of orthographic growth, they too are dismissed as causal explanations. That is, if the development of children's word-recognition facility proceeds through increases in the number of words that are represented and the precision and redundancy of those representations, then the automaticity and autonomy of their ability to recognize a word must be a function, not of any general characteristic of their developmental level, but of their knowledge and experience with the particular word or spelling in view. On the other hand, Perfetti's theory is richly consistent with both the developmental data that Ehri (1992) sought to explain and with the burgeoning research on mature word recognition. Specifically, the ability to decode quickly and accurately while reading depends integrally and inalterably on familiarity, not just with individual letter-sound correspondences, but with the spelling patterns from which frequent words and syllables are composed (see Adams, 1990).

Arguably, the human memory system is designed to learn quite automatically about such sequential patterns through experience—but *only* to the extent that experience has treated the patterns in that way. Children's tendency, discussed earlier, instead to view words as holistic patterns is therefore a real impediment, such that, from this perspective, phonics instruction per se takes on a very special value: the process of sounding out a new word requires attention to each and every one of its letters, in left to right order.

Even so, it is not just teaching children phonics that makes a difference but persuading them to use it. As a case in point, Juel and Roper-Schneider (1985) studied two groups of children across their first-grade year. Both groups of children received the same program of phonics instruction, complete with teacher scripts and exercises. In addition, as demonstrated by accompanying tests, both groups of children learned the taught phonics, and equally well. Despite that, the first group showed consistent evidence of using their phonic knowledge while reading and, importantly, of extending it beyond what they had been taught such that, by the end of the year, the first group was significantly better at reading new words than their peers. Why? Whereas the texts in the initial books or preprimers of the first group were built around short, decodable words, those of the second group used a text in which vocabulary was biased toward high-interest words instead. (The wordings of the children's books were more or less comparable beyond the preprimer.) Evidently, a strong determinant of whether or how well children will use their phonic knowledge lies in whether or not they find it useful in their earliest efforts after print.

Contrary to such findings, prominent whole language advocates have cautioned against encouraging children to sound out new words as they read (Goodman, 1993; F. Smith, 1973). Doing so, they have claimed, induces children to become "word-callers"—to become so absorbed in the decoding process that they lose track of meaning. In fact, research affirms that, midway through first grade or so, many children tend toward "word calling." As a group, that is, they measurably shift away from contextually appropriate miscues in deference to responses that maintain graphemic similarity to the print on the page (Biemiller, 1970; Juel & Roper-Schneider, 1985; Weber, 1970a, 1970b). Yet, these same studies also demonstrate that as the children's word-recognition skills improve, their sensitivity to context reblossoms.

More generally, research—as opposed to armchair musings—convergingly suggests that, at every age, the inclination to examine rather than gloss the spellings of less familiar words in text is a strong determinant of orthographic facility, which, in turn, is significantly related to overall reading ability (Frith, 1980; Stanovich, West, & Cunningham, 1991). Nor, for normal readers, does it take many such efforts to conquer a new word. Recall that in Nicholson's (1991) replication of Goodman's (1967) classic study, having read the words of a text just once days before, in a decontextualized list, was sufficient to overcome any advantage of context for the good readers, and more so with advancing grade. Indeed, Reitsma (1983) has shown that for normal second-graders, once an unfamiliar word has been decoded and reread just a few times, its recognition remains speeded significantly and quite enduringly. In contrast, he found poor readers to demonstrate relatively little savings across repeated encounters with words (Reitsma, 1989). Working with reading-level matched children in the United States, Ehri and Saltmarsh (1995) have replicated this contrast between good and poor readers in retention of orthographic detail.

One explanation for such findings, considered by Bowers and Wolf (1993) and Stanovich (1992), is that poor readers may suffer a deficit in visual consolidation of the orthographic patterns they encounter. Another (though not necessarily exclusive) explanation, suggested by the theories of Ehri (1980, 1992) and Perfetti (1992), is that the orthographic knowledge of the poor readers in these studies was too poorly articulated or underdeveloped to absorb the spellings of the target words with useful efficiency and cohesion. Still another, slightly different, explanation is that dyslexics may characteristically adopt a reading strategy that relies more on visual than phonological information (Share, 1995); if so, the dyslexic's orthographic knowledge will be suboptimally structured for interword transfer. In support of this hypothesis, Seigel, Share, and Giva (1995; see also Stanovich & Seigel, 1994) have reported that, among children with a range of matching reading levels, normal readers are superior at decoding nonwords, although dyslexics are superior at judging their orthographic typicality.

In any case, and regardless of a child's reading ability, if too many of the words of a text are problematic, both comprehension and reading growth itself are impeded (Adams, 1990). Thus, high error rates are negatively correlated with achievement gains and low error rates are positively correlated with achievement gains (for a review, see Rosenshine & Stevens, 1984). Further, the younger or less able the readers, the stronger are these correlations until, at the extreme—for beginning readers—reading comprehension is strongly predicted by word-recognition abilities but, with that factor discounted, not at all by how far children have been moved through their basal reading books (Juel, 1994).

But, of course, neither can children's abilities grow if their texts contain no new words, which raises the question of how to arrange optimal levels of reading challenge. As rules of thumb, it has been suggested that error rates for instructional texts should not exceed 1 in 5 words for older, better readers (Rosenshine & Stevens, 1984), or 1 in 20 for younger, poorer readers (Clay, 1979; Juel, 1994). After all, younger poorer readers are working harder even on those words that they do read correctly. Alternatively, students can be asked to read the text several times. Not surprisingly, doing so is shown to result in increases in reading fluency and comprehension of the reread text; surprisingly, it is also shown to boost readers' performance on new texts (Samuels, 1979, 1985). Granted that nobody could become a proficient reader by reading and rereading the same paragraph even a million times over, the reread-transfer effect begs special explanation. Its underlying source, as it turns out, depends on the subjective difficulty of the texts: overlap in the content of the practice and transfer texts produces facilitation only for subjectively easy texts; otherwise, the bulk of the reread-transfer effect is due to the readers' increasing facility with the texts' specific wording (Faulkner & Levy, 1994; Rashotte & Torgesen, 1985).

A ready inference from such findings is that, beyond the basics, gains in both the ease and productivity of reading might best be promoted by asking students to read and reread as broadly, deeply, and often as possible. Yet, even here, prominent whole language advocates have taken issue: "Literacy," wrote Frank Smith (1989), "doesn't generate finer feelings or higher values. It doesn't even make anyone smarter" (p. 354).

Such pronouncements notwithstanding, the data broadly support the benefits of reading. In line with the foregoing discussion, amount of reading is strongly related to orthographic growth, as measured by both word recognition and spelling facility (Cunningham & Stanovich, 1990, 1991; Juel, 1994). Amount of reading also predicts growth in reading comprehension across the elementary school years even after controlling for entry-level differences in reading comprehension (Anderson, Wilson, & Fielding, 1988; Cipielewski & Stanovich, 1992). It predicts the quantity and quality (language, vocabulary, and structure) of students' writing (Cunningham & Stanovich, 1991; Juel, 1994; Stotsky, 1984) as well as the ideational richness of their oral storytelling (Juel, 1994). In addition, it predicts receptive vocabulary, verbal fluency, content area achievement, and all manner of declarative knowledge even when other measures of school ability, general intelligence, age, education, and reading comprehension itself are partialed out of the equation (for a review, see Stanovich, 1993).

In short, provided that children *can* read, there is arguably no more powerful lever on their overall cognitive growth than inducing them *to* read. Yet, even in a literate culture, the amount of reading that people do ranges dramatically (Guthrie & Greany, 1991). Among U.S. fifth-graders studied by Anderson et al. (1988), the 90th percentile student reported reading about 200 times more text per year than the 10th percentile student. Anderson et al. also estimated that, altogether, in school and out, the median fifth-grade student encounters approximately 1 million words of text per year, which includes less than five minutes of out-of-school book reading per day (see also Allen, Cipielewski, & Stanovich, 1992). Although setting time aside for reading in school has been shown to make a difference (Rosenshine & Stevens, 1984), classroom time is limited. Thus, activity outside the classroom—where that significantly includes summer reading—contributes very heavily to the huge performance differential in U.S. students' reading abilities (Hayes & Grether, 1983).

Other Influences on Early Literacy Development

What Else besides Phonemic Awareness and Letter Knowledge?

As our collective analyses of reading predictors and precursors have become increasingly refined and disconfounded, nearly all of our more conventional hypotheses about what makes a difference in learning to read have been discounted. Repeatedly and convergingly, the heavy majority of the variance in beginning reading success has been traced to just two factors—familiarity with the letters of the alphabet and phonemic awareness—whereas the measurable contributions of even our most intuitively compelling contenders appear weak, evanescent, and remote.

The issue raised in this section is not whether letter familiarity and phonemic awareness are crucial and powerful factors in beginning reading: inarguably, they are. Yet, there remains the possibility that such analyses inadvertently discount other factors that are also key. After all, within the logic of the statistical procedures undergirding these analyses, the only means of distinguishing the contribution of one factor from any other with which it is correlated is by entering both in the analysis. Thus, the possibility remains that there exist other potent predictors that are poorly measured by or missing from the set of independent variables in the contrast.

Fueling this concern, Clay's (1979) Concepts about Print test has been found to absorb significant variance above and beyond phonemic awareness and letter knowledge when entered into the equations. Examining this test to discover what—not counting letter knowledge, phonemic awareness, and word recognition—it taps, reveals a few very basic probes, for example: Which is the front of the book and which is the back? Which way should one turn the pages? Do the words come from the print (as opposed to the pictures or the page numbers)? In what direction does one follow the print (left-right and top-bottom)? Is the child aware of words and the convention of separating them by spaces in print?

So here is a puzzle: What is the nature of the variance that these items are capturing? To pose the problem in a different way, our tests of letter familiarity, phonemic awareness, and decoding are directly and unsubtly designed to measure those particular and specific abilities. We understand how letter familiarity, phonemic awareness, and decoding are involved in the reading process and that they, per se, are critical. We know that instruction that effectively instills, repairs, or strengthens abilities in any of these areas commensurately effects improvements in reading capabilities, and we know that to be effective, the requirements of such instruction are nontrivial in design or delivery. In contrast, although we could sit any 5-year old down for a few minutes and teach her or him how to tell the front from the back of a storybook and which way to turn the pages, it would very likely make not a whit of difference in her or his reading potential.

The suggestion, in other words, is that page turning and so on are proxies or indirect indices of some set of factors that really do matter. By their nature, moreover, this set of factors seems closely tied to the nature or amount of children's prior experience with books.

Indeed, reading aloud to young children is broadly held to be among the most important of parenting activities (e.g., Bush, 1990; PTA, 1987)—or at least this is true in the public forum. Scouring the research forum on this topic, Scarborough and Dobrich (1994) found that relevant studies were surprisingly few and collectively weak in design. Moreover, the correlations among the various outcome variables of interest and quantity or quality of parent-preschooler reading that could be gleaned from these studies suggested that the effects are quite modest, accounting for no more than 8% of the variance in concurrent or subsequent literacy-related abilities (see also Bus, van IJzendoorn, & Pellegrini, 1995).

Given the research base from which Scarborough and Dobrich (1994) were working, reservations to this conclusion are not inappropriate: more and better research is clearly needed. Regardless of specifics, however, Scarborough and Dobrich offer a blanket caveat that warrants serious consideration: Where the nature of the relation between parent-preschooler reading and any given outcome variable is nonlinear, such studies will necessarily underestimate its impact. "That is, it might matter a great deal whether a preschooler experiences little or no shared reading with a responsive partner, but beyond a certain threshold level, differences in the quantity or quality of this activity may have little bearing" (p. 285). In keeping with this, Stevenson and Fredman (1990) found that the reading, spelling, and IQ scores of a sample of 550 13-year-olds were strongly predicted by the frequency with which their parents reported having read to them as preschoolers. However, they wrote, "There seemed to be a cutoff point whereby children who were read to less than four times a week achieved less well than those read to more regularly" (p. 690).

What is at issue here is not merely the precision, but the very appropriateness of the linear statistical models on which the field so strongly relies: in fact, the data suggest that the frequency of parent-preschooler storybook reading is strikingly bimodal. For example, across a sample of middle-class 2- and 3-year-olds studied by Whitehurst et al. (1988), the average frequency of home book reading was roughly eight sessions per week. Extrapolating from six months to six and one-half years, we point out that this weekly average cumulates to about 2,500 book-sharing sessions prior to school entry. In contrast, in a two-year study of home literacy activities conducted in a neighborhood with historically poor literacy success, Teale (1986) found that only 3 of the 24 preschoolers in the sample had been read to with any appreciable regularity; for the majority, he found no evidence of any storybook reading whatsoever. Feitelson and Goldstein (1986) found similar differences in the home literacy support of Israeli kindergartners from neighborhoods with records of high versus low school achievement: whereas the homes of the kindergartners in the school-oriented neighborhoods had an average of 54 children's books in the home, 61% of those in the other neighborhood had none at all (see also McCormick & Mason, 1986); whereas 96% of the kindergartners in the school-oriented neighborhood were read to daily, 24% of those in the other neighborhood were read to "sometimes" and 61% not at all (see also Heath, 1983); further, even among those in the neighborhood with poor schooling success who did read with their children, none began before their children were 4 or 5 years old. The predictive significance of each of these variables has been independently affirmed by Payne, Whitehurst, and Angell (1994) through a study of the language development of 323 4-year-olds attending Head Start in the United States.

Meanwhile, if ample exposure to stories and books is valuable, so too must be the linguistic, rhetorical, and conceptual exploration that such book-sharing sessions afford. Across parent-child dyads who regularly share storybooks, the sessions are nearly routinized and highly interactive, as the "reading" is sensitively tailored to the child's developing abilities and punctuated with questions and discussions of the words, concepts, and events raised by the text (Ninio & Bruner, 1978; Snow & Ninio, 1986; Sulzby, 1985; P. Wheeler, 1983). But again, data suggest that the instructional range of these interactions is more limited among low-SES parent-child dyads (Ninio, 1980).

Book-Sharing Interventions

The strong cultural variation in both the quantity and quality of home book sharing urges the question of whether the behaviors can be effectively taught. Working from this perspective, Whitehurst and his colleagues (1988) gave a one-hour training session on interactive story reading to parents of 15 children between 2 and 3 years old. Rather than just read to their children, these parents were encouraged to pause every so often and to ask open-ended (as opposed to yes/no) questions such as "What is Eeyore doing?" They were also encouraged to expand on their children's answers, suggest alternative possibilities, and pose progressively more challenging questions. The parents were then asked to tape-record their home reading sessions with their children for one month. Meanwhile, the parents of 15 other children, matched in age and language development to the first group, were also asked to tape-record their home reading sessions. Analyses of the tapes indicated that both groups read equally often, about eight times per week. They also confirmed that the parents who had participated in the training session followed its recommendations. Analyses of the children showed that at the end of the month, those whose parents had been trained were 8.5 months ahead of the others on a test of verbal expression and 6 months ahead on a vocabulary test—substantial differences for people who are only 30 months old.

The parents involved in Whitehurst et al.'s (1988) first study were college-educated volunteers, from intact homes, who had already established solid storybook practices and rapport with their children. As a stronger test of the value of this approach, Valdez-Menchaca and Whitehurst (1992) ventured to reproduce it with 2-year-olds in a public day care center for low-income families in Mexico. The day care center did neither storytelling nor storybook reading with the children, and few of the children had ever been read to at home. For the intervention, a trained graduate student engaged each of the 10 experimental subjects, one-on-one, in 10-minute sessions of interactive storybook reading daily for six weeks. Afterwards, the experimental subjects significantly outgained their matched controls both in vocabulary and on a variety of expressive language measures. The gains, though not as dramatic as in the study involving middle-class parents, were substantial and consistent across measures.

Having thus demonstrated the effectiveness of their interactive reading routines, the group turned their attention to the challenge of training children's regular caretakers to engage in effective book-sharing activities. They began by putting together an instructional videotape (Whitehurst, Arnold, & Lonigan, 1990) and verifying that its use produced solid gains among the children of well-schooled, highly motivated (reporting a preintervention storybook reading rate of 12.8 times per week), middle-class volunteers (Arnold, Lonigan, Whitehurst, & Epstein, 1994). Even so, efforts to extend this experience to parents from low-SES homes have been disappointing: enlistment of parents is difficult, the attrition rates are high, and, even given compliance, the measured effects on children's language growth have been relatively meager (DeBaryshe, Rodarmel, Daly, & Huntley, 1992; Lonigan, 1993; Morisset, 1993; Needlman & Fitzgerald, 1993).

As an alternative strategy, Whitehurst et al. (1994) used their video to train Head Start teachers and parents in interactive or, in their terms, "dialogic" reading. The study involved 15 classrooms, half designated as experimental and half as controls. Because assessment was more extensive, outcomes were clustered into four factors for analysis: language development, writing, print concepts, and linguistic awareness (words, syllables, and phonemes). Postintervention analyses showed no impact on the linguistic awareness factor, alongside a modest but significant advantage for experimental classrooms in writing and print concepts. In contrast, the responsiveness of the language factor depended strongly on the extent that the children's parents did, as promised, read with them at home; exposure in the classroom alone had no measurable effect.

As Whitehurst et al. (1994) review, evidence of such special dependence of language growth on home language and literacy support has been found in other studies, too. The question is why. One immediate hypothesis is that the key controlling variable was the amount or frequency of shared reading, which, after all, should have been doubled for the children who were also read to at home. Another possibility, however, is that the educational power (and perhaps, absent intervention, the very dynamic) of interactive reading pivots, most of all, on the reader's sensitivity to the child's own responsiveness and contributions—and that sensitivity is only afforded in a one-on-one setting. If so, then there is nothing specific that one can teach teachers or parents to do or say that will make the difference. On the other hand, to the extent that parents complied by reading at home, the effects of Whitehurst et al.'s Head Start study were strong. This raises the hopeful possibility that, in modeling the appropriate dynamic for both the parents (as was done through the video-training session) and the children (as was done in the classroom), Whitehurst et al. have discovered a key to setting up novice parent-preschooler dyads for rewarding and self-engendering experience with books.

The importance of optimizing the child's give and take in book-sharing sessions notwithstanding, the focus of these exchanges also makes a difference. Thus, Feitelson, Goldstein, Iraqi, and Share (1993) conducted a kindergarten book-sharing intervention in an Arab town in which, for reasons of the marked difference between written Arabic and the spoken language of the community, virtually no parents read to their preschoolers regardless of social background variables. In response to this situation, the emphasis of the intervention was on developing the children's appreciation of the language of the written register and of story structure. Commensurately, Feitelson et al.'s subjects evidenced strong gains in both linguistic facility with formal Arabic—as evidenced by their listening comprehension and the complexities of their expressive language—and in their tendency to impose canonical story structures and express the causal connections between events in telling stories about picture sequences. Similarly, the Whitehurst et al. (1990) program emphasizes the use of good children's literature as a platform for expanding and refining the child's vocabulary and expressive command of language. Consistent with this, the program has produced gains in both the vocabulary and the complexity of the children's descriptive speech, but not in letter or phonic knowledge. In contrast, in McCormick and Mason's (1986) intervention, which was centered on inducing parents to share preprimer-like books with children, gains were observed in the children's letter, word, and "reading" performance, but not their vocabulary or linguistic sophistication. On the other hand, children's phonological sensitivities are found to be stubbornly indifferent to their book-sharing histories (Cunningham & Stanovich, 1993). Phonemic awareness is not easy or natural; it is rarely induced without special guidance.

Vocabulary and Syntax

The primary purpose of beginners' texts is to support basic reading processes and fluency development. By design, therefore, these texts tend to be simple and familiar in vocabulary, concept, and both inter- and intrasentential structure. No doubt, it is largely for this very reason that, as reviewed above, the majority of the variance in beginning reading success is absorbed by measures of letter knowledge, phonemic awareness, and—through them—word recognition and decoding ability.

In contrast, where the primary purpose of text becomes instead one of conveying new information and ideas, it is convenient to introduce new words and necessary to express novel relations among familiar ones. To understand a text, children must be able to understand both the meanings of the words and the intended interrelations among them. Thus, although measured vocabulary does not carry much weight in predictions of beginning reading success, it becomes a potent correlate of reading achievement in the middle grades and up (Chall, 1983; Stanovich, Cunningham, & Feeman, 1984; Thorndike, 1973).

Research suggests that the single most powerful contributor to vocabulary development is reading itself, yielding about half of the roughly 3,000 new words that adequately performing schoolchildren are expected to learn each year (Nagy, Anderson, & Herman, 1987). Yet, this raises certain educational dilemmas. First, because the likelihood of learning any *given* word from text is very small, the possibility of learning lots of words through reading depends on reading lots of text of the sort that contains some reasonable sampling of new words. In effect, this raises a new literacy barrier for poor readers, who have neither the capacity nor the disposition to keep up, much less catch up. Second, as implied by componential theories of meaning representation, the ease of vocabulary learning should depend on the depth, breadth, and organization of the vocabulary already learned. In keeping with this, data indicate that children with stronger vocabularies in the first place absorb new words more easily than those with weaker vocabularies (Robbins & Ehri, 1994). In all, the question of how better to support vocabulary growth for those who need it most is urgent. Further, if a literate vocabulary is suddenly required at grade 4, then it cannot be good policy to wait until grade 4 to work on its development. A few promising programs have been developed (see e.g., Beck, Perfetti, & McKeown, 1982; O'Rourke, 1974). Overall, however, and despite the rich history of work on the representation and access of word meanings by adults, work on vocabulary development and its underlying dynamics is relatively scant. We will return to this topic in the section on comprehension.

The situation is still vaguer with respect to syntactic development. The importance of syntactic awareness to reading is strongly suggested by differences in the use (Tunmer & Chapman, 1995) as well as the structure (Chafe & Danielewicz, 1987; Halliday, 1987; Perera, 1988) and processing requirements (Adams, 1980; Huggins & Adams, 1980) of written as opposed to oral syntax. Consistent with this, based on a meta-analysis of relevant literature, Bus et al. (1995) concluded that familiarization with the written register is the strongest and most important outcome of reading aloud with preschoolers. The importance of instructionally supporting early syntactic development is further indicated by longitudinal studies of children with language delay. Unless they recover by 5½ years of age, preschoolers with expressive and receptive language delay, whether specific or secondary (which includes environmentally induced delay), are repeatedly shown to be delayed in reading achievement across the primary school years (e.g., Bishop & Adams, 1990; Catts, 1991b; Scarborough & Dobrich, 1990; Whitehurst & Fischel, 1994). In addition, a number of studies have shown performance on syntactically specific tasks to separate good and poor readers (for a review, see Tunmer & Hoover, 1992).

Nevertheless, when measures of syntactic facility are competed against measures of phonological sensitivity, the former have been found to contribute precious little to the reading equation (Gottardo, Stanovich, & Siegel, 1995; Shankweiler et al., 1995; but see Tunmer et al., 1988). Where samples include beginning or disabled readers, one might argue that any effects of syntax are liable to be swamped. Alternatively, one might argue that the apparent nonsignificance of syntax may derive from poorly conceived measures thereof: since the 1960s, when children were declared syntactically competent by age 4 (McNeill, 1970; Slobin, 1971), the development of syntax across the school years has been a flagrantly neglected topic of research. The other possibility, of course, is that maybe syntax really doesn't much matter. Again, however, to understand a text, children must be able to understand both the meanings of the words and the intended interrelations among them; in written text about unfamiliar constructs, syntax is the primary means of conveying such relations.

Revisiting this section at a more molar level of analysis, an inherent difficulty in studying the general impact of parent-preschooler reading is that the domain is composed of so many different books and adults and, across them, so many different aspects of language and literacy that might or might not be explored with any given child. When concern is expanded to the more general issues of good language and literacy support, the complexities only multiply. In the interest of progress, the diffuseness of the domain is important in at least three ways. First, it challenges the informativeness of our outcome measures; for example, should we be surprised that the strongest *common* outcome across the various studies reviewed by Scarborough and Dobrich (1994) was an increase in children's *interest* in literacy-related activities? Should we expect the Peabody Picture Vocabulary Test to yield an appropriate or adequately sensitive metric of consequent linguistic growth? Do we even have a usefully refined measure of syntactic competence? Second, the prospect of bringing all children to full literacy depends on inventing practicably efficient and effective instructional strategies for ensuring that all children have the knowledge and cognitive abilities that literacy development presumes or entails. Third, resolution of these problems as well as the larger progress and productivity of the science of cognitive development will depend on discovering not just what works, but why and how it does so.

Summary

Over the past several decades, the field has established a solid research base on the critical importance of word-recognition abilities and how best to support their development. For the next several decades, the goal must be one of extending this science beyond issues of word recognition. We must turn, with the same tenacity and rigor, and with due respect for their respective social, educational, and linguistic backgrounds, to questions of what can be done to foster language and literacy most fully and effectively for all of our children.

COMPREHENSION AND COMPOSING: HIGHER-LEVEL READING AND WRITING

The ultimate goal of reading education is for students to be able to comprehend text. To this end, there have been many analyses of comprehension and comprehension instruction. Without a doubt, more attention has been given to the development of comprehension through comprehension strategies instruction than through any other approach. Thus, that is the main focus of this section on comprehension, which emphasizes connections between historically prominent work on comprehension and comprehension strategies instruction as it was studied in the 1980s and continues to be studied in the 1990s. Alternatives to strategies instruction are then considered, with the discussion concluding by emphasizing the connections between comprehension research past and present.

The Historical Foundations of Comprehension Strategies Instruction

Most of the scientific work on comprehension instruction was conducted in the past two decades. There was rapid progress during this period largely because of seven related developments in the 1970s. In this subsection, two are reviewed: (a) the need for comprehension instruction became apparent, and (b) serious doubts about traditional study skills instruction arose. In subsequent subsections, five additional factors that stimulated research on comprehension instruction will be considered: (c) a number of theories of meaning representation were introduced, with many suggesting comprehension processes that might be taught; (d) the nature of conscious processing by skilled comprehenders began to be examined through verbal protocol analyses; (e) metacognitive theory was developed; (f) theories about the development of self-regulated cognition emerged as important; and (g) reader response emerged as an important approach to language arts.

The Need

Before there is an intervention, there must be a need for an intervention. One study (Durkin, 1978–1979) more than any other made apparent the need to instruct students how to comprehend text (Hoffman, 1991; Pearson & Fielding, 1991; Shulman, 1986). In a series of studies, Durkin observed classrooms and students in grades 3 and 6, watching for comprehension instruction during reading and social studies. She saw little of it. Instead of teaching students how to comprehend, teachers were assessing comprehension, asking students questions about material they had read. Similarly, the teachers' manuals provided little guidance about how to teach comprehension but much material to aid assessment of reading comprehension (i.e., comprehension questions; Durkin, 1981). Although some argued that Durkin underestimated the amount of comprehension instruction occurring in schools (Heap, 1982; Hodges, 1980), her conclusions stimulated researchers to study comprehension strategies instruction, teachers to teach them, and materials producers to change their basal materials to include much more about how to teach comprehension.

The interest in reading comprehension assessment reflected the concern that reading, in the sense of accurate and fluent decoding, might occur without high levels of comprehension. For example, Wiener and Cromer (1967) proposed that some weak child readers were "difference"-poor readers, who could decode but could not construct meaning capturing the overall messages in text. In addition, prominent developmental psychologists were turning attention to the difficulties young children sometimes experience in identifying main ideas (e.g., Brown & Smiley, 1977) and in drawing straightforward inferences from simple prose (e.g., Paris & Upton, 1976).

In the late 1970s, there was not an adequate response to the need for comprehension instruction. Pearson and Johnson (1978) provided a candid appraisal, flagging that much more needed to be known about teaching comprehension processes to students.

Durkin, Wiener and Cromer, Paris and Upton, Brown and Smiley, and Pearson and Johnson were all influenced in their analyses and thinking by cognitive psychology. Not surprising, most of the research that would occur in reaction to their analyses would be conceived in cognitive psychological terms.

Doubts about Study Skills

Study skills manuals have been published throughout the twentieth century (Forrest-Pressley & Gilles, 1983). Even the earliest included comprehension strategies instruction. Thus, Sandwick (1915) instructed students to reflect before they read a passage, calling to mind what they already knew about the topic. After studying the entire passage, students were advised to return to difficult portions of it. Sandwick urged students to study aloud, drill on information that was important to remember, visualize the content of text, and summarize it. Swain's (1917) study skills manual favored self-questioning and summarizing during reading.

F. Robinson (1946) introduced the SQ3R approach: students using this approach first *survey* (S) the text, then generate *questions* (Q) about the text based on boldface headers, followed by *reading* (first R), *reciting* (second R) of the text, and *reviewing* (third R) it, including attempting to recall the text. Although SQ3R continues even today to be well known in study skills circles (e.g., Nist & Diehl, 1990), it and other study skills approaches have something of a checkered history. First, there is relatively little evaluation of it, with the comparative studies that do exist not of high quality and not particularly supportive of the method: SQ3R does not produce much better learning of a text than simply reading and rereading it (Caverly & Orlando, 1991; Johns & McNamara, 1980). SQ3R is difficult for children to understand. For example, surveying means skimming, a process not well understood by students in the early elementary grades (Forrest-Pressley & Gilles, 1983; Forrest-Pressley & Waller, 1984). Elementary-level students also have difficulties constructing anything but low-level, factual questions unless they are taught how to construct questions stimulating deep reflection on text (e.g., Davey & McBride, 1986). Students who lack background knowledge related to the topic of a reading also can have difficulty with the questioning phase of SQ3R (e.g., Bean, Smith, & Searfoss, 1980). If the headers and subheaders in a text are poorly constructed and mismatched to the important ideas in text, and they often are, using them to generate questions can direct attention away from more important ideas in favor of less important ones (Anderson & Armbruster, 1984). In addition, the method is better matched to tasks requiring recall of text content than to other tasks, for example, ones requiring application of the ideas in the text (Anderson & Armbruster, 1984). In short, many difficulties with SQ3R, the centerpiece of much of study skills, became apparent in the late 1970s and early 1980s.

Two other study skills approaches deserve mention here, because they were precursors of reciprocal teaching, an important cognitive strategies intervention evaluated in the 1980s (Palincsar & Brown, 1984) and taken up later in this chapter. The first, Manzo's (1968) ReQuest procedure, involved students and teacher reading part of a text and then taking turns asking each other questions about it (i.e., engaging in reciprocal questioning). Through generation of questions, the teacher models questioning for the students. The teacher also provides feedback to students about the questions they generate. The second, Stauffer's (1969) Directed Reading-Thinking Activity approach (DRTA) focused on three steps: predicting the content of text (based on title, subheaders, illustrations, etc.), reading, and revising predictions. After reading, revision of predictions is prompted by teacher questions: Were your predictions correct? What do you think now? The teacher also solicits predictions about the content to come: What do you think will happen? That neither ReQuest nor DRTA enjoyed much empirical support became apparent with the publication of Tierney, Readence, and Dishner (1980), which detailed for reading educators the classical study skills approaches and the thin evidentiary bases for many of them. There was a need for something better than traditional study skills.

Theories of Meaning Representation

An important concern of cognitive psychologists is the determination of how meaning is represented in the mind and how mental representations of meaning determine comprehension of complex ideas, such as those represented in text. There was much new theory and debate about representation during the 1970s. The various representational theories stimulated hypotheses about the nature of effective comprehension strategies instruction.

Many experimental studies of children's reading took the following form: One condition in the experiment would involve instruction encouraging a particular type of comprehension processing; a second condition would be a control condition, often one in which readers were left on their own to process text as they naturally would. The assumption was that children's low comprehension relative to adult comprehension was due to incomplete processing of text, so that children were creating incomplete representations of texts. We review here four of the more important representational theories of the 1970s and the types of strategies and instructional experiments they spawned. In each case, the studies produced outcomes that proved replicable as the 1980s proceeded.

Kintsch and van Dijk's Theory

According to Kintsch and van Dijk (1978; van Dijk & Kintsch, 1983), skilled readers parse text into micropropositions, the smallest units of meaning. A microproposition can be conceived as a verb or preposition and semantic roles that are related by the verb or preposition. Thus, a microproposition can contain information about an agent performing an action specified by a verb, as well as information about the object of an action specified by a verb, goals accomplished by the action, the recipient of the action (referred to as a patient in this system), time of the action, and so on. Micropropositions are equivalent to sentences in logic and are represented using a standard format that emphasizes the relationship specified by the verb or preposition. Thus, the proposition UNDER (DOG, HOUSE) specifies a relationship between a dog and a house, that the dog is under a house; TYPES (MICHAEL) conveys that Michael types. All of the micropropositions specified in a text combine to capture the full meaning of the text. Of course, no one remembers every idea specified in a text. What people remember is the gist, which is the main idea of the text, which is encoded as macropropositions, according to Kintsch and van Dijk. Macropropositions are distilled from the micropropositions of the text. Thus, macropropositions for *A Christmas Carol* would include that Scrooge met ghosts who changed his life philosophy.

A number of cognitive theorists assumed that the construction of macropropositions was not as certain with children as with skilled adult readers. Thus, they hypothesized that children's understanding and memory of text would be improved if they were taught to generate summaries as they read. The result was a number of studies in which summarization was taught to students in the elementary grades (mostly in the middle and later grade school years) in various ways (e.g., Doctorow, Wittrock, & Marks, 1978; Taylor, 1982). One of the most prominent of these studies was devised by Brown and Day (1983). They taught students a series of rules to apply as they processed text: (a) delete trivial information; (b) delete redundant information; (c) substitute superordinate terms for lists of items; (d) integrate a series of events into a superordinate action; (e) select a topic sentence from among the sentences in a passage; and (f) invent a topic sentence if one cannot be found. Students' memory and comprehension of text typically improved following their use of summarization strategies.

Paivio's Dual-Coding Theory and Imagery Generation

Paivio (e. g., 1971, 1986; Clark & Paivio, 1991) proposed that knowledge is composed of complex associative networks of verbal and imaginal representations. The verbal system contains wordlike codes for objects and events and abstract ideas, codes that are only arbitrarily related to what they represent (e.g., the word *book* has no physical resemblance to an actual book). The imagery system contains nonverbal representations that retain some resemblance to the perceptions giving rise to them (e.g., an image of a book shares features with the perception of an actual book). Elements in the imagery representational system are linked to elements in the verbal representational system. Thus, there is a connection between most people's image of a book and their verbal representation of a book, with such referential connections permitting construction of mental images given words as stimuli and generation of names when objects are seen in pictures.

A series of images can be linked according to dual-coding theory, for instance, to create a nonverbal representation of the contents of a story. Thus, Levin (e.g., 1973), Pressley (e.g., 1976), and others made the case that children's imagery generation during reading was typically less extensive than it could be, and thus, they proposed that teaching children to construct images when reading a text might increase activation of the imagery system. In general, when children constructed mental images representing the content of texts, their memory (e.g., as tested by literal, short-answer questions) and understanding (e.g., as tested by questions tapping inferences that could be made during reading of the text) improved relative to when same-age students read as usual (see Pressley, 1977).

Story Grammar Theory and Story Grammar Analysis

Stories have a conventional structure: a beginning, including information about the time, setting, and characters in the story; an initiating event setting a goal or leading to a problem; a series of attempts to achieve the goal or overcome the problem; achievement of the goal or resolution of the problem; and character reactions to the resolution. Good readers understand this structure implicitly and use it to understand stories, with their memory of a story reflecting essential story elements (e.g, Mandler, 1984; Stein & Glenn, 1979).

In a study conducted in 1980, Short and Ryan (reported in 1984) hypothesized that not all children understand story grammar, or, if they do, some fail to use their story grammar knowledge to comprehend stories. To test this idea, they taught weak grade 4 readers to ask themselves a series of questions as they read, questions orienting the reader to story grammar elements of stories: (a) Who is the main character? (b) Where and when did the story take place? (c) What did the main characters do? (d) How did the story end? and (e) How did the characters feel? Use of this strategy increased the text recall of the weak readers relative to comparable-ability control readers, who read as they usually read. More impressively, the strategy-instructed students recalled at the level of skilled grade 4 readers.

Schema Theory and Prior Knowledge

Without a doubt, the most prominent representational theory among reading researchers and educators during the late 1970s and early 1980s was schema theory, as reviewed by Anderson and Pearson (1984). A schema integrates a number of concepts that commonly co-occur into an orderly system of procedures and expectations. Events and situations are presumed to have skeleton structures that are more or less constant, although the particular ways the skeleton takes on flesh varies from instance to instance. For example, the schema for a ship christening includes its purpose: to bless the ship. It includes information about where it is done (in dry dock), by whom (a celebrity), and when it occurs (just before launching of a new ship). The christening action is also represented (breaking a bottle of champagne that is suspended from a rope). Once some small part of the ship christening schema is encountered, for example, by the mention of a bottle of champagne breaking on the bow of a ship, the entire schema is activated. Once activated, comprehension and processing of the ship christening text will be affected. Schematic processing is top-down in that activation of the higher-order idea occurs first and constrains thinking about the details of the situation. The activated schema will permit reasonable inferences to be made during reading about details of the event. For example, as the bottle is seen breaking on the bow, the viewer might infer that there was a platform beside the ship with one or more persons on it, one of them a celebrity. It will also affect the allocation of attention to information in the text, for example, to the celebrity, to the name of the ship, and memory of the event.

Schema activation can dramatically affect comprehension, inferences, attention allocation, and memory of what is read (see Anderson & Pearson, 1984, for a review). Thus, schema theory implies that strategic activation of prior knowledge, which is largely schematic, according to this theory, will affect understanding and learning of text. It was for this reason that schema theorists encouraged students to make predictions about text before reading, relate information encountered in text to prior knowledge, and ask themselves questions about the reasons for the relations specified in text, operations that were proved to affect comprehension and memory of text.

Summary

Representational theorists in the late 1970s and early 1980s believed that if children failed to understand and remember text, the fault may be that they were not constructing complete representations. That is, children were failing to generate macropropositions as completely as they could, failing to form images capturing the semantic relations in a story, failing to construct representations that adequately reflected story grammar elements or intermeshed with schematic prior knowledge. The solution was to encourage students to construct fuller representations through instruction. What resulted were strategies for enhancing mental representations of texts, ones that could be applied before, during, and after reading (Levin & Pressley, 1981).

Theory and Research on Comprehension Control

Verbal Protocols of Skilled Reading

An important analytical tool for cognitive psychologists is the verbal protocol analysis, which involves thinking aloud while performing a task. Such protocols have been collected throughout the twentieth century (e.g., Marbe, 1901; McCallister, 1930; Piekarz, 1954; Titchener, 1912a, 1912b).

The prominence of the methodology in reading research increased substantially with the publication of Olshavsky (1976–1977). She studied the reading of 12 good grade 10 readers and 12 weak grade 10 readers. Each silently read a short story. The students were informed that the purpose of the study was to determine how grade 10 students read, not to test an individual participant's reading ability. The students were instructed to read silently until they encountered a red dot and then to "talk about what happened in the story and about what you were doing and thinking as you read it" (p. 663). Red dots were placed after each independent clause.

The verbal protocols were analyzed for cognitive strategies. Three word-level strategies were detected: using contextual cues to infer the meanings of unknown words, attempting to substitute synonyms for unknown words, and simply acknowledging when a word is not understood. Many more strategies aimed at understanding the meanings of sentences and paragraphs were detected. These included rereading segments of text that were not understood, attempting to infer information not explicitly stated in text, relating information in the text to personal prior knowledge, making predictions, and relating information in a just-encountered clause to the theme of the passage emerging during reading.

Five prominent verbal protocol analyses of reading appeared within five years of the Olshavsky report (Christopherson, Schultz, & Waern, 1981; Collins, Brown, & Larkin, 1980; Hare, 1981; Lytle, 1982; Olson, Mack, & Duffy, 1981), with these studies including a wide range of readers and a variety of reading genres. Although the amount of strategy use observed in these studies varied (e.g., they were not as predominant in the protocols of children as in some protocols of high school and college students), and the particular processes varied, strategies were consistently observed in these studies, with strategic processing considered as skillful processing by the protocol analysts.

Emergence of Metacognitive Theory

Metacognition is cognition about cognition, an idea first introduced into the developmental literature by Flavell (1971). Metacognition plays an important regulatory role in cognition. Thus, the long-term knowledge that intentionally creating a summary of something just read increases memory of it is important metacognitive knowledge, conditional knowledge (Paris, Lipson, & Wixson, 1983) about summarization, that can inform a student how to proceed when confronted with text containing main ideas that must be remembered. That is, conditional knowledge increases the likelihood of long-term, appropriate use of strategies (for reviews, see Pressley, Borkowski, & O'Sullivan, 1984, 1985). Other metacognitive knowledge is generated online, via cognitive monitoring. Thus, a reader's awareness that comprehension is not going well is metacognitive knowledge, knowledge that also can inform and motivate subsequent cognitive actions, for example, the decision to reread, read more slowly, or give up on a text.

Both Flavell's (1977) prominent book, *Cognitive Development,* and Flavell and Wellman (1977) offered analyses of how metacognition might regulate cognitive strategies in various tasks. That memory strategies were definitely teachable also became well established during this era, with many different strategies proving teachable (Pressley, Heisel, McCormick, & Nakamura, 1982). However, it also became obvious that long-term use of taught strategies only occurred when memory strategies instruction was metacognitively embellished, as when information about the usefulness of a trained strategy was included in instruction (Borkowski, Levers, & Gruenenfelder, 1976; Cavanaugh & Borkowski, 1979; Kennedy & Miller, 1976; Posnansky, 1978). Metacognitive theory was thriving as a function of the first analyses and tests of it in the realm of children's memory, with metacognitive theory implicating strategies as critical in effective thinking.

At about the same time, Ellen Markman (1977) introduced the idea of comprehension monitoring as an important form of metacognition during text processing, arguing that children were often unaware when they did not understand text. How might awareness of comprehension and miscomprehension improve, according to Markman's analyses? One possibility was through processes that could be thought of as strategic, such as explicitly comparing the ideas in the part of text just read with ideas presented earlier in a reading (Elliott-Faust & Pressley, 1986). Not only could metacognition contribute to strategies regulation, but strategies use could result in important metacognitive understandings. Metacognitive theory provided justification for teaching of strategies to promote self-regulation of reading.

The Development of Internalized Cognitive Competence

More than half a century ago, Vygotsky (translated in 1978) recognized that (a) adults often assist children in thinking about problems they are confronting; (b) these interactions are thinking, thinking involving two heads; (c) although the child cannot work through many problems without assistance, with parental support, there may be fine progress; and (d) long-term participation in such interactions leads to internalization by the child of the types of actions once carried out between the child and the adult: thought processes that were once interpersonal become intrapersonal. Cognitive development proceeds largely because the child is in a world that provides assistance when the child needs it and can benefit from it. When the child can get along alone, the same adults remain in the background. The same adults also encourage the child away from situations and tasks that are well beyond her or his competence.

Critical developmental interactions between adults and children occur with tasks that the child cannot do independently but can do with assistance, tasks that are within the child's *zone of proximal development,* according to Vygotskian theory. A child learns how to perform tasks within her or his zone by interacting with more competent and responsive others who provide hints, prompts, and assistance to the child as needed. The regulative processing that goes on between adult and child during these interactions is eventually internalized by the child; that is, the child ultimately can perform the task without assistance, a development stimulated by the supportive interactions with others before autonomous functioning was possible. Beginning in the late 1970s, Vygotsky's perspective on the zone of proximal development did much to stimulate developmentally oriented researchers and educators to embrace the teaching of cognitive skills not fully developed in children, but ones that could develop with adult support—-such as comprehension strategies.

There were other analyses in this era for explicit adult support of competencies that the child initially can do only with support but can come to control through participation in supportive interactions. Forty years after Vygotsky, Wood, Bruner, and Ross (1976) also observed that adults often assist children, eventually yielding control to the children themselves as they learn how to carry out a task during interactions with adults. Wood et al. (1976) offered the metaphor of a scaffold to describe such teaching. Recall that a scaffold is used when a building is being erected and is gradually removed as the building becomes self-supporting. So it is with the prompts and hints provided by an adult or older child to a younger child.

Meichenbaum (e.g., 1977) also developed an extremely visible position about how adults could interact with children to encourage their acquisition and autonomous use of new cognitive skills, with Meichenbaum's theoretical thinking and research informed by Vygotsky's thinking. Vygotsky (translated in 1962) advanced the idea that *inner speech* is an important mechanism in mature thought. Compared to overt speech, inner speech is abbreviated and fragmentary, with complex meanings captured in a few words or syllables. Vygotsky provided a developmental model of how such speech-for-self develops, a model reflecting his belief that speech-for-self begins as interpersonal, overt speech between adults and children, with the adult role highly directive at first, gradually fading as children increasingly internalize directive speech. By the middle 1970s, there were a number of American analyses suggesting that the development of self-directive speech plays an important role in the development of children's self-regulation (e.g., Kohlberg, Yaeger, & Hjertholm, 1968; Patterson & Mischel, 1976; Wozniak, 1972).

Thus, in the late 1960s and early 1970s, Meichenbaum (Meichenbaum & Goodman, 1969a, 1969b, 1971) hypothesized that children could learn a variety of cognitive skills if they were taught simultaneously to use self-speech to direct their use of these skills. Meichenbaum (1977) offered an entire volume summarizing research consistent with the idea that children could be taught to self-regulate through interactions with adults who initially modeled self-regulative speech and gradually yielded cognitive control to the students themselves.

Meichenbaum's general approach can be illustrated through review of a study by Bommarito and Meichenbaum (reported by Meichenbaum & Asarnow, 1979). They taught comprehension strategies to middle school students who could decode but were experiencing difficulties understanding what they read. Instruction began with an adult modeling self-verbalized regulation of the comprehension strategies of looking for the main idea, attending to the sequence of important events in a story, and attending to how characters in a story feel and why they feel the way they do, as well as some other strategies helpful during reading. The students saw the adult read as they heard the following verbalizations by the adult:

> Well, I've learned three big things to keep in mind before I read a story and while I read it. One is to ask myself what the main idea of the story is. What is the story about? A second is to learn important details of the story as I go along. The order of the main events or their sequence is an especially important detail. A third is to know how the characters feel and why. So, get the main idea. Watch sequences. And learn how the characters feel and why. While I'm reading I should pause now and then. I should think of what I'm doing. And I should listen to what I'm saying to myself. Am I saying the right things? Remember, don't worry about mistakes. Just try again. Keep cool, calm, and relaxed. Be proud of yourself when you succeed. Have a blast. (Meichenbaum & Asarnow, 1979, pp. 17–18)

By the end of six training sessions, the students were self-verbalizing covertly, with control gradually transferred to the students over the course of six sessions. Did the self-verbalization instruction affect reading comprehension? There was greater pretest-to-posttest gain on a standardized comprehension test than for control condition participants.

In summary, there was substantial cognitive developmentally oriented instructional theory in the late 1970s supporting explicit teaching of cognitive strategies, with theoretical triangulation (Mathison, 1988) for the conclusion that adults could advance the cognitive development of children through scaffolded teaching of important cognitive processes.

Reader Response Theory

In 1938, Rosenblatt made a then radical proposal: that the meaning of a text must vary somewhat from reader to reader. Like Vygotsky, Rosenblatt would be discovered anew in 1978, in her case, with the publication of her theoretical masterpiece, *The Reader, the Text, the Poem.* Reader response theory, as defined by the 1978 book, had an enormous impact on the language arts education community. It legitimized the teaching of active and interpretive reading (see Clifford, 1991; Holland, Hungerford, & Ernst, 1993), although reading that respected the text much more than did other prominent literary analyses of the era (e.g., Eco, 1978; Fish, 1980). According to reader response theory, interpretations vary because the meaning of a text involves a transaction between a reader, who has particular perspectives and prior knowledge, and a text, which can affect different readers in different ways (e.g., Beach & Hynds, 1991; Rosenblatt, 1978). What is critical from the perspective of reader response theory is how the reader experiences and reacts to the text. Sometimes readers form impressions of characters in stories, and frequently they relate their personal and cultural experiences to events encountered in text. They may respond to difficult-to-understand text by treating meaning-making as an exercise in problem solving, requiring probing analysis of text and posing of numerous questions as part of attempting to determine what a text might mean. As part of responding to text, readers sometimes explain events in a text to themselves. Often, they form vivid images. In short, language arts theorists and educators viewed the processes that psychologists considered to be comprehension strategies as reader responses. Reader responding was acceptable to the language arts community in the late 1970s and continues to be so. That is, the cognitive psychologists and the language arts specialists had the same idea of prompting child readers to be more active as they read.

Summary

A number of intellectual directions converged in the late 1970s and early 1980s, inspiring prominent research on comprehension strategies instruction in the 1980s. An important factor in this convergence was the federally funded Center for the Study of Reading at the University of Illinois. Durkin's (1978–1979) study establishing the need for comprehension instruction was conducted at the Center. Tierney et al.'s (1980) impressive review of all existing study skills packages pertaining to reading was put together at Illinois, a summary that made obvious the lack of support for most of the study skills approaches. There was substantial interest among Center faculty in the effectiveness of particular comprehension strategies. For example, Brown and Day (1983) were exploring summarization as a strategy. Richard Anderson (e.g., Anderson & Hidde, 1971), the director of the Center, had a long-time interest in mental imagery and its role in learning of connected materials. Schema theory (Rumelhart, 1980) was the driving force at the Center, however, stimulating much interest in validation of prior knowledge activation strategies. Ann Brown and her colleagues (e.g., Brown, 1978) were exploring the implications of metacognitive theory. The Center faculty were definitely aware of the insights about text processing emerging from protocol analyses, providing input and feedback to important studies such as Lytle's (1982) dissertation study of elementary-level students thinking aloud as they read. Brown and her colleagues (see Brown, Bransford, Campione, & Ferrara, 1983) also recognized the importance of and interrelations among Vygotsky's theory, Wood et al.'s (1976) conception of scaffolding, and Meichenbaum's (1977) self-instructional perspective. The professional organization that would provide much impetus for reader response theory was the National Council for Teachers of English, headquartered at the University of Illinois, with its positions well known to anyone at Illinois concerned with the language arts. Thus, the stage was set at the end of the 1970s at Champaign-Urbana for an important advance in comprehension strategies instruction. Annemarie Palincsar and Ann Brown would make that advance, with their work the first stop on our tour of the advances in comprehension strategies instruction that were made in the 1980s.

Comprehension Strategies Instruction

A great deal of progress was made in the 1980s and 1990s in determining whether and how students could be taught to coordinate comprehension strategies. Because the need for such instruction was great and research on comprehension strategies instruction was largely driven by theoretical concerns, such as the ones just reviewed, the research detailed in this section had a wide audience, practitioners as well as researchers and theorists. We cover here the most visible of the contributions, each of which made a great deal of sense given the research that had preceded it.

Reciprocal Teaching

Without a doubt, the most visible report of research on comprehension strategies instruction in the 1980s was Palincsar and Brown's (1984).

Study 1. Twenty-four grade 7 readers who were adequate decoders and poor comprehenders participated in the study, with six assigned to a condition. In one of the conditions, the participants were taught four comprehension strategies—predicting, questioning, seeking clarification when confused, and summarizing—using the reciprocal teaching method, a variant of the reciprocal teaching questioning originally devised by Manzo (1968) as part of ReQuest. In the second condition, participants were taught a different strategy, one for locating information in text in response to postreading questions about the content of a text. Participants in the third, test-only condition, experienced all of the assessments (pretests, posttests, daily assessments) that the participants in the first two groups experienced but received no training in strategy use. The fourth group was a control condition in which the participants received the same pretests and posttests as strategies-instructed students but received no instruction and did not experience daily assessments. Because of space limitations, we take up in detail only the procedures in the reciprocal teaching group and limit discussion to the reciprocal teaching versus control group comparisons.

For the students in the reciprocal teaching group, baseline (pretest) data were collected over a period of four to eight days. One set of pretests involved 400- to 475-word passages, which were read silently by participants, followed by 10 comprehension questions. Also, given a set of summarization rules, like those devised by Brown and Day (1983), students were asked to apply them to two other passages. The students were also asked to generate 10 questions like the ones teachers might generate for each of two 400- to 475-word passages. In addition, students also read some stories line by line. Some of these stories contained semantic anomalies, and the children's task was to indicate when something in the text being read did not make sense. Control condition participants also participated in baseline sessions, experiencing the comprehension, summarization, question-generation, and detecting anomalies measures. There were approximately 20 days of intervention for the students in the reciprocal teaching condition, followed by 5 days of posttesting immediately after the intervention period. Eight weeks later, there were 3 days of long-term follow-up testing.

Each intervention day began with the adult teacher discussing the topic of the day's text, calling for predictions about the content of the passage based on the title, if the passage was completely new, and calling for a review of main points covered thus far for passages that had been begun the previous day. The adult teacher then assigned one of the two students to be the "teacher." Adult teacher and students then read the first paragraph of the day's reading silently, with the student teacher then posing a question about the paragraph, summarizing it, and then either predicting upcoming content or seeking clarification if there was some confusion about the ideas in the paragraph. If the student teacher faltered, the adult teacher scaffolded these activities with prompts (e.g., "What question do you think a teacher might ask?"), instruction (e.g., "Remember, a summary is a shortened version . . ."), and modifying the activity (e.g., "If you're having a hard time thinking of a question, why don't you summarize first?"). Students were praised for their teaching and given feedback about the quality of it (e.g., "You asked that question well"; "A question I would have asked would have been . . ."). Students took turns as the student teacher, with a session lasting about 30 minutes.

Throughout the intervention, the students were explicitly informed that questioning, summarizing, predicting, and seeking clarification were strategies that could help them to understand better and that they should try to use the strategies when they read on their own. The students were also informed that being able to summarize passages and being able to predict the questions on upcoming tests were good ways to assess whether they understood what they had read.

At the end of each day, the reciprocal teaching participants read a 400- to 475-word assessment passage, which was followed by 10 questions about its content. Control participants did not receive these daily assessments.

Both reciprocal teaching and control participants experienced the following assessments during the period corresponding to intervention or as posttests:

- During the study there were two classroom probes, consisting of passages and 10-item tests, like the daily assessment passages, with these placed unobtrusively into ongoing social studies and science instruction.

- Comprehension passages with 10-item tests were administered as posttests as well.
- Summarization, question-generation, and anomaly-detection tasks like the ones administered as pretests were given as posttests.

Reciprocal teaching positively impacted all of these measures. The instruction affected processing as it was intended to do, increasing summarization skills, question-generation competencies, and monitoring, as reflected by detection of semantic anomalies (Markman, 1977). This translated into much better performance on the comprehension assessments in the reciprocal teaching condition than in the control condition.

In addition, there were two other analyses involving the students in the reciprocal teaching condition. Individual students' performances on the daily assessments were plotted. Because the baseline period varied between four and eight days, the point when intervention began varied. Importantly, for all six reciprocal teaching students, daily assessment performance jumped shortly after the onset of the reciprocal teaching intervention. An especially important outcome was obtained on a standardized comprehension measure, important because dramatic effects on standardized comprehension measures would be cited prominently to make a case for reciprocal teaching (e.g., Brown & Campione, 1990a, 1990b). Gates-MacGinitie comprehension measures were available for all reciprocal teaching condition participants, with the test readministered to these students at the conclusion of the study. Four of the six students in the condition showed striking gains on this measure: 15, 17, 20, and 36 months' growth. One of the remaining two students made 2 months' growth, and one had no growth. There were interpretive difficulties with this outcome, however. The comparable data were not available for control participants, so that a variety of alternative interpretations of the outcomes could not be ruled out (e.g., practice effect, maturation). In addition, because the pretest data were collected in a group and the posttest data through individual assessment, it could be that much of the improvement was due to differences in testing conditions on the two occasions.

In short, Study 1 provided plenty of reason for enthusiasm about reciprocal teaching. Nonetheless, with only two students per teacher and an experimenter as a teacher, it was difficult to make a case for the classroom validity of the intervention. In their Study 2, Palincsar and Brown (1984) evaluated the usefulness of reciprocal teaching in a realistic classroom situation.

Study 2. Four small groups of middle school students who could decode adequately but who experienced comprehension problems participated in reciprocal teaching reading groups. With the exception that these groups were taught by the students' own teachers, all four of whom received several days of training and practice with reciprocal teaching, the procedures were similar to the reciprocal teaching condition of Study 1. In general, the pretest-to-posttest improvements obtained in the first study were replicated, although no standardized comprehension data were collected in this study. Similar to Study 1, the daily assessments were plotted for each of the four reading groups. In each case, performance on the daily assessments jumped shortly after the onset of intervention.

Discussion. Reciprocal teaching reflected well the traditions that had stimulated it. It responded directly to the rising concern (e.g., Wiener & Cromer, 1967) over readers who could decode but who had comprehension problems. It was also strongly influenced by study skills, elaborating on Manzo's (1968) reciprocal questioning approach and emphasizing prediction (Stauffer, 1969) and summarization (Brown & Day, 1983) as learning strategies. Summarization effects on awareness were also emphasized in the Palincsar and Brown (1984) report, reflecting the impact of metacognitive theory: if a person cannot summarize after reading, it is a sign of comprehension failure and the need to process the text additionally before reading on. The importance of scaffolding by the teacher was framed in Vygotskian (1962) terms, with reference to Bruner (1960). The importance of self-control as Meichenbaum (1977) had defined it was apparent in Palincsar and Brown, with the study also framed in terms of Meichenbaum and Asarnow's (1979) analysis (see also Brown et al., 1983; Brown & Palincsar, 1982). Dialoguing about text, which is so important, according to reader response theorists (Rosenblatt, 1978), was emphasized as a critical part of learning via reciprocal teaching, with numerous examples of dialogue presented in the Palincsar and Brown article (see also Palincsar, 1986; Palincsar, Brown, & Martin, 1986).

The reciprocal teaching research had a substantial impact on practice. For example, it stimulated publishers of basal readers to include strategies instruction in their teacher guides, with questioning, predicting, seeking clarification, and summarizing the centerpiece strategies for comprehension instruction. Its direct effect on research was to inspire additional study of the method. Rosenshine and Meister (1994) carefully analyzed 16 studies of reciprocal teaching and summarized the effects on reading produced by the intervention. There were consistent, striking effects on cognitive process measures, such as those tapping summarization and self-questioning skills. With respect to standardized comprehension, however, the effects have been less striking, with an average effect size of .3 standard deviations. A further finding of Rosenshine and Meister's (1994) meta-analysis was that reciprocal teaching was more successful when there was more direct teaching of the four comprehension strategies. This outcome is important in light of conclusions we offer later in favor of greater direct explanation as part of strategies instruction.

Paris's Informed Strategies for Learning

Paris and his associates (1984) devised a comprehension strategies instructional package, Informed Strategies for Learning, that could be covered in the course of a single school year. The program included 20 modules, each aimed at developing understanding of the reading process, teaching specific strategies, and/or increasing students' awareness as they read. There were four sets of five 3-lesson modules, with each lesson intended to take about 30 minutes, for approximately 30 hours of instruction in total. The main strategies emphasized in the program were elaboration, inference, integration, activation of prior knowledge, summarization, rereading, self-questioning, checking consistencies, and paraphrasing.

The first two lessons in each module introduced the lesson with a metaphor (e.g., for a lesson introducing comprehension strategies, "A bagful of tricks"), described the processes being emphasized in the lesson, and outlined how to apply the processes during reading. In the third, "bridging" lesson, students practiced the new process with content-area materials, such as science or social studies, from their regular studies. The lessons were supported by workbook materials, passages for practice of the processes being taught, and posters depicting the metaphor for each lesson.

A number of instructional mechanisms were employed in the lessons. Teachers explained and modeled use of the processes being taught. There were teacher-student discussions about the value of the processes taught, revolving around questions such as "When should you use this strategy?"; "When could it be inappropriate?"; "Why is it helpful?"; and "How did you use it?" The discussions covered how, when, and where to use the processes being taught, as well as the ease, benefits, and difficulties associated with each strategy. Instruction was scaffolded in that teacher modeling gradually gave way to student self-direction in the selection of strategies to be used to accomplish lesson tasks, and student independence was increasingly expected for the workbook assignments as lessons proceeded.

Informed Strategies for Learning was evaluated at the grade 3 and grade 5 levels in two studies, one small in scale (4 classrooms per condition; Paris, Cross, & Lipson, 1984; Paris & Jacobs, 1984) and one much larger (46 Informed Strategies for Learning teachers, 25 control teachers; Paris & Oka, 1986). There were several consistent benefits in the two studies: Informed Strategies for Learning improved students' strategic awareness as measured by a 20-item multiple-choice instrument devised by the Paris group (see Jacobs & Paris, 1987). Most of the items on the metacognitive awareness scale tapped processes taught directly in the curriculum, and thus, this measure permitted the conclusion that Informed Strategies for Learning students did in fact learn about cognitive processing as a function of experiencing the curriculum. However, although the effects on the metacognitive scale were significant, they were not large, with only a 1- or 2-item advantage seen on the scale at posttesting.

Students in the Informed Strategies for Learning condition also outperformed controls on a cloze task and an error-detection task. The cloze task required the students to fill in missing words on a test version of a passage just read; the error-detection task involved reading passages containing anomalous information and underlining the parts of the text that did not make sense. Given that Informed Strategies for Learning participants experienced many examples of similar cloze and error-detection items as part of the strategies instruction curriculum, the advantages for them on these tasks were not surprising. Again, however, the effects were never very large.

Informed Strategies for Learning was designed to be much like classic study skills programs in many ways, with the program even published as a boxed kit, much as many study skills programs are available. It taught strategies that had been validated separately in well-designed studies (e.g., summarization), incorporated important insights from metacognitive theory (e.g., to emphasize conditional knowledge as part of strategies instruction, teaching comprehension monitoring), and reflected the Vygotskian/Brunerian/Meichenbaumian approach to scaffolded instruction as a way to increase self-controlled use of strategies. Paris's studies of Informed Strategies for Learning were logical outgrowths of the converging lines of theory and evidence considered important at the end of the 1970s and beginning of the 1980s by cognitive developmentalists interested in reading instruction. Disappointingly, however, Informed Strategies for Learning failed to have any effect on standardized comprehension test performance in either of the two evaluations of the method, which for many traditional reading educators is a benchmark of a successful comprehension instructional intervention. This contrasted with the perception in the mid-1980s that reciprocal teaching did impact performance on standardized tests. It also contrasted with the outcomes of another strategies instruction study that became prominent in the mid-1980s.

Bereiter and Bird

Bereiter and Bird's (1985) approach was first to collect verbal protocols of reading from adults they believed to be good readers to obtain insights about comprehension strategies that should be taught to students. The initial verbal protocol study of mature readers was followed by a training experiment with middle school children.

Study 1. Ten adults, two graduate students and eight middle-class professionals, read 6,500-word passages—an exposition, a narration, a personal opinion essay, a discussion of a controversy, and a procedural description—and talked aloud about their cognitive processing as they read. A variety of comprehension strategies was reported by these readers: restatement or rephrasing of a difficult portion of text, backtracking to seek clarification, demanding relationships (i.e., deciding to watch for causes for effects, reasons, links among topics, particular information that should be in text), formulating a problem and trying to solve it (i.e., by inference, closer examination of text, rejection of information), prediction, imagery, and recall of related information.

Study 2. Eighty average readers in grades 7 and 8 were assigned to one of four experimental conditions: (a) In the modeling plus explanation condition, four of the strategies observed in Study 1—restating, backtracking, demanding relationships, and formulating a problem to solve—were taught by a teacher. The students practiced using the trained strategies and judging appropriate use of the strategies. (b) In the second condition, there was modeling and practice of the strategies. (c) In the third, exercise, condition, the strategies were neither modeled nor explained; the students only did exercises that entailed the processes associated with the strategies rather than learned how to apply the strategies. (d) Controls only experienced the tests administered in the other three conditions. The participants in the first three conditions received six hours of teaching and practice. Think-aloud protocols were collected as participants read passages from one standardized comprehension test, both at the beginning and at the end of the study. A second standardized comprehension test was administered silently at pretest and posttest.

Increased use of trained strategies from pretest to posttest was clearly evidenced only in the verbal protocols of the children of the modeling plus explanation condition. Although there were pretest-to-posttest improvements in all conditions on the silently read standardized comprehension test, the greatest gains were in the modeling plus explanation condition. Specifically, there was a little less than a grade-level improvement in the other three conditions versus a 2.7 grade-equivalent increase in the modeling plus explanation condition.

Although modeling and explanation occurred in reciprocal teaching and Informed Strategies for Learning, these explicit teaching processes were much more prominent in Bereiter and Bird's (1985) modeling plus explanation condition, comprising fully 40% of the intervention. The striking gains on a standardized comprehension test produced by the explanation plus modeling condition provided strong evidence in favor of direct explanation and modeling as an approach to comprehension strategies instruction.

Duffy et al.

Direct explanations in Roehler and Duffy's (1984) model begin with teacher explanations and mental modeling, or showing students how to apply a strategy by thinking aloud (Duffy & Roehler, 1989), and then proceed to student practice. Practice is monitored by the teacher, with additional explanations and modeling provided as needed. Instruction is scaffolded in that explanations and feedback are reduced as students become more and more independent. The information provided to students during practice depends very much on the particular problems the students encounter and the particular ways that their understandings are deficient. Reinstruction and reexplanations as well as follow-up mental modeling are responsive to student needs and usually are an elaboration of student understandings up to that point.

Duffy et al. (1987) produced an extremely well-designed study of the effects of direct explanation strategy instruction on third-graders' reading, with 10 of 20 groups of weak readers assigned randomly to the direct explanation condition and the remaining 10 groups, or controls, receiving their usual instruction. The researchers taught third-grade teachers to explain directly the strategies, skills, and processes that are part of skilled reading at this level, with the study occurring over the course of an entire academic year. The teachers were taught first to explain a strategy, skill, or process and then to mentally model use of it for students. Then came guided student practice, with the students initially carrying out the processing overtly so that the teacher could monitor their use of the new strategy.

Assistance was reduced as students became more proficient. Teachers encouraged transfer of strategies by going over when and where the strategies being learned might be used. Teachers cued use of the new strategies when students encountered situations where the strategies might be applied profitably, regardless of when these occasions arose during the school day. Cuing and prompting were continued until students autonomously applied the strategies they were taught.

By the end of the year, students in the direct explanation condition outperformed control students on standardized measures of reading. Disappointingly, there was only a slight trend toward better performance in the direct explanation compared to the control condition on the comprehension section of the Stanford Achievement Test administered at the end of the year. This lack of a difference, however, occurred in the context of many other clear differences favoring direct explanation, including a standardized measure of reading achievement given the year after the direct explanation intervention had been administered. These results had a profound effect on the reading education community, with direct explanation as Duffy et al. (1987) defined it subsequently used by many educators as a basis for implementing comprehension strategies instruction in their own schools.

Transactional Strategies Instruction

Beginning in 1989, Pressley and his colleagues set out to study school-based, educator-developed strategies instruction that seemed to work, that is, where educators could offer evidence, such as pretest-posttest performance differences, that their instruction was having an impact on students. Their first studies were conducted at Benchmark School in Media, Pennsylvania, a school dedicated to helping elementary-age children overcome reading problems (Gaskins, Anderson, Pressley, Cunicelli, & Satlow, 1993; Pressley, Gaskins, Cunicelli, et al., 1991; Pressley, Gaskins, Wile, Cunicelli, & Sheridan, 1991). A focus of the Benchmark curriculum is comprehension strategies instruction. The Benchmark investigations were followed by studies in two Maryland public school elementary programs dedicated to increasing the use of strategies for reading comprehension (Brown & Coy-Ogan, 1993; El-Dinary, Pressley, & Schuder, 1992; Pressley, El-Dinary, Gaskins, et al., 1992; Pressley, El-Dinary, Stein, Marks, & Brown, 1992; Pressley, Schuder, SAIL Faculty and Administration, Bergman, & El-Dinary, 1992).

A variety of qualitative methods was used in this research, including ethnographies, ethnographic interviews, long-term case studies, and analyses of classroom discourse. Although the three programs in these studies differed in their particulars, a number of conclusions held across them:

- Comprehension strategies instruction was long-term, with teachers offering it in their classroom throughout a school year. The ideal was for it to continue across school years. Teachers recognized that the younger the children, the more that was required for them to understand the individual strategies. Also, the younger the children, the more that was required for them to learn how to coordinate their use of different strategies.
- Teachers explained and modeled effective comprehension strategies. Typically, a few powerful strategies were emphasized, for example, prediction of upcoming information in a text, relating text content to prior knowledge, constructing internal mental images of relations described in text, use of problem-solving strategies such as rereading and analyzing context clues when meaning is unclear, and summarizing.
- The teachers coached students to use strategies as needed, providing hints to students about potential strategic choices they might make. There were many minilessons about when it is appropriate to use particular strategies.
- Both teachers and students modeled use of strategies for one another, thinking aloud as they read.
- Throughout instruction, the usefulness of strategies was emphasized, with students reminded frequently about the comprehension gains that accompany strategy use. Information about when and where various strategies can be applied was discussed often. Teachers consistently modeled flexible use of strategies; students explained to one another how they used strategies in their reading.
- The strategies were used as vehicles for coordinating dialogue about text (see especially Gaskins et al., 1993). In particular, when students related text to their prior knowledge, constructed summaries of text meaning, visualized relations covered in a text, and predicted what might transpire in a story, they engaged in personal interpretation of text, with these personal interpretations varying from child to child and reading group to reading group (Brown & Coy-Ogan, 1993).

Such instruction came to be known as *transactional strategies instruction,* for three reasons relating to alternative theoretical definitions of transaction. First, long-term strategies instruction emphasizes that getting meaning from text involves an active thinker using the text as a starting point for construction of meaning, consistent with transaction as defined in reader response theory (Rosenblatt, 1978). Second, the interpretations of stories that emerge as groups of children apply strategies to stories are different from the interpretations that would occur if children read the stories by themselves; the process is transactional in the sense of the term employed by organizational psychologists interested in communications and problem solving (e.g., Hutchins, 1991). Third, a teacher's and students' reactions and interpretations are codetermined by each other's reactions to and interpretations of stories during group discussions of stories, which are common in this form of instruction; thus, classroom strategies instruction is transactional in a sense identified by developmental psychologists (e. g., Bell, 1968).

In a nutshell, transactional strategies instruction involves direct explanations and teacher modeling of strategies, which is followed by guided practice of strategies. (Thus, it is more similar to Duffy et al.'s 1987 approach than to any other model.) Teacher assistance is provided on an as-needed basis (i.e., strategy instruction is "scaffolded"; Wood et al., 1976). There are lively interpretive discussions of texts, with students exposed to diverse reactions to text.

As they devised instruction, the educators in these settings were aware of the research on comprehension strategies instruction and felt it was relevant to the great need they perceived in their students to learn how to comprehend. These educators felt that short-term instruction would not produce the effects they wanted. Moreover, explanation, modeling, and scaffolded practice had intuitive appeal. Commitments to traditional language arts instruction, with its emphasis on dialogue and interpretation, also affected the development of comprehension strategies instruction in these settings. The result was instruction that looked much like Duffy et al.'s (1987) vision of strategies instruction, even for some schools that had the reciprocal teaching model as their starting point (Marks et al., 1993). The flexibility of direct explanation has a lot of appeal, with educators' elaboration of transactional strategies instruction enjoying increasing support.

In some areas of research, it is possible to produce programs of research consisting of a number of related multifactorial experiments. That is not occurring in the case of transactional strategies instruction, however. The main reason is that a realistic test must occur at least over the course of months, for the model specifies that learning comprehension strategies and how to coordinate their application is a long-term development. We can offer three recent reports of comparative studies of instruction that is transactional as defined by Pressley, El-Dinary, Gaskins, et al. (1992).

Brown, Pressley, Van Meter, and Schuder. Brown et al. (1996) conducted a year-long quasi-experimental investigation of the effects of transactional strategies instruction on second-graders' reading. Five grade 2 classrooms receiving transactional strategies instruction were matched with grade 2 classrooms taught by teachers who were well regarded as language arts teachers but who were not using a strategies instruction approach. In each classroom, a group of readers who were low achieving at the beginning of grade 2 was identified.

In the fall of the year, the strategies instruction condition and control participants in the study did not differ on standardized measures of reading comprehension and word-attack skills. By the spring, there were clear differences on these measures favoring the transactional strategies instruction classrooms. In addition, there were differences favoring the strategies instructed students on strategies use measures as well as interpretive measures. That is, strategies instructed students made more diverse and richer interpretations of what they read than controls.

Collins. Collins (1991) produced improved comprehension in fifth- and sixth-graders by providing a semester (3 days a week) of comprehension strategies lessons. Her students were taught to predict, seek clarification when uncertain, look for patterns and principles in arguments presented in text, analyze decision making that occurs during text processing, solve problems through strategies including backward reasoning and visualization, summarize, adapt ideas in text (including rearranging parts of ideas in text), and negotiate interpretations of texts in groups. Although the strategies instructed students did not differ from controls before the intervention with respect to standardized comprehension performance, treated and control students differed by 3 standard deviations on the posttest, a very large effect for the treatment.

Anderson. Anderson (1992; see also Anderson & Roit, 1993) conducted a three-month experimental investigation of the effects of transactional strategies instruction on reading-disabled students in grades 6 through 11. Students were taught comprehension strategies in small groups, with nine groups of transactional strategies students and seven control groups. Although both strategies instructed and control students made gains on standardized comprehension measures from before to after the study, the gains were greater in the trained group than in the control condition. Anderson (1992) also collected a variety of qualitative data supporting the conclusions that reading for meaning improved in the strategies instructed condition. For example, strategies instruction increased students' willingness to read difficult material and attempt to understand it, collaborate with classmates to discover meanings in text, and react to and elaborate text.

Summary. Comprehension strategies instruction is being disseminated in schools in the 1990s, often consistent with the transactional strategies instruction model. Transactional strategies instruction begins with teacher modeling and explanation of strategies and proceeds to students practicing strategies applications together, using the strategies as part of constructing interpretations of text. This is the way that Duffy et al.'s (1987) research on direct explanation of comprehension strategies is being translated into practice. The transactional strategies instruction approach yields improved results on standardized reading tests, which are still the most broadly used measures of accountability within the U.S. educational system. In addition, transactional strategies instruction seems to produce more interpretive readers, readers better able to discuss their interpretations of text in dialogues that are much more student involved and involving than traditional classroom discussions (cf., Mehan, 1979).

Summary

The strategies instruction of the 1990s is very different from reciprocal teaching, although there is little doubt that the reciprocal teaching research did much to stimulate later research on strategies instruction. Because reciprocal teaching is so familiar to many developmentalists, a principal audience of this volume, we reflect on the transactional strategies instructional approach—which is what comprehension strategies instruction at its best has become—by comparing it with reciprocal teaching, which was the launching conceptualization of comprehension strategies instruction with children.

Both transactional strategies instruction and reciprocal teaching involve teaching of cognitive processes for coming to terms with text. Both include modeling and explanation of strategies. Both include much discussion of what is being read as students practice strategies. Both include teacher scaffolding of instruction: the teacher monitors what is going on and offers supportive instruction as needed. Both cultivate cooperative, supportive relations among students during reading. Both approaches assume that participating in the instructional group and receiving the scaffolded instruction will result in long-term internalization of the cognitive processes being fostered by the group, so that the teacher is progressively less involved as instruction proceeds.

Nonetheless, the differences between reciprocal teaching and direct explanations-based transactional strategies instruction are striking. The most important difference concerns the salience of the teacher. Reciprocal teaching involves quickly reducing the adult teacher's control. The belief is that if students are to internalize decision making with respect to cognitive processes, students need to be the ones controlling the cognitive processes in reading groups. In contrast, the teacher is much more visibly in charge as part of direct explanations, although always with the goal of reducing teacher input; that is, direct explanation teaching is scaffolded, with the teacher cutting back as soon as it is possible to do so.

There is an important consequence of this difference in salience of the teacher in reciprocal teaching and direct explanation, one that, in our view, favors the direct explanation approach. Reciprocal teaching involves a fairly rigid sequence. Each time, after a portion of text is read, the student leader of the moment poses a question for peers; the peers attempt to respond; then the student leader proposes a summary. Only then are the other students in the group invited into the conversation, to seek clarifications by posing questions or make predictions about upcoming text. Those who favor reciprocal teaching correctly argue that these processes are ones that are critical to comprehension of text (e.g., Baker & Brown, 1984). Moreover, they correctly point out that a great deal of flexible discussion of text and issues in text can occur within this framework. The flexibility of discussion certainly is greater during transactional strategies instruction, however, with the direct explanation approach in no way restricting the order of strategies execution or limiting who may participate in group discussion of text. The transactional strategies instructional approach succeeds in stimulating interpretive dialogues in which strategic processes are used flexibly, with consistently high engagement by all group members (see Gaskins et al., 1993).

Transactional strategies instruction, like reciprocal teaching, is a product of a variety of theoretical forces. The specific strategies in transactional strategies instructional programs typically are ones validated in basic research, ones that also are salient in verbal protocols of excellent reading. The metacognitive theoretical emphasis on heightening student awareness is unambiguous in transactional strategies instruction, with many efforts made to increase the understanding of students about the effects of strategies on their reading achievement, to increase their understanding about when, where, and how to apply strategies they are learning. Transactional strategies instructors are determined to teach within their students' zones of proximal development, scaffolding instruction and encouraging students to reflect and then instruct themselves about how to proceed with their reading. Because educators who teach comprehension strategies are committed members of the language arts education communities, interpretation and response are prominent in transactional strategies instruction lessons and dialogues. Although the most directly influential research on transactional strategies instruction was direct explanation as exemplified by Duffy et al. (1987) and others (e.g., Bereiter & Bird, 1985), transactional strategies instruction is the conjunction of many intellectual forces affecting reading instruction at the end of the twentieth century, ones that continue to evolve. This theme will be explored in some detail in the concluding comments to this section on comprehension instruction.

Alternatives to Comprehension Strategies Instruction

In addition to teaching of comprehension strategies, two other general directions have been pursued as a means for increasing student understanding of text. Neither of these, however, have been studied as extensively as comprehension strategies instruction.

Improving Word-Level Processing and Knowledge

As reviewed earlier in this chapter, proficiency in basic decoding processes is associated with later competence in comprehension and overall reading achievement. One question posed by researchers has been whether improving word-level competence translates immediately into comprehension gains. The answer seems to be yes, at least sometimes. For example, improvements in comprehension following decoding instruction have been evident in the most systematic program of research to date assessing instructional improvement of decoding in dyslexic students. This is the work carried on by Lovett and her colleagues at Toronto's Hospital for Sick Children.

Lovett, Ransby, Hardwick, Johns, and Donaldson (1989) succeeded in improving the decoding of dyslexic students ages 9 to 13, with two different training methods proving effective, one involving letter-sound analyses and blending and the other intensive practice in reading and writing. Both of these programs also produced improved performance on a measure of standardized reading comprehension. Lovett, Warren-Chaplin, Ransby, and Borden (1990) also succeeded in improving the decoding of dyslexic students with two different approaches to training, one an exclusive whole word approach and the other varying instruction depending on the nature of the word: a whole word with irregular words, and letter-sound analyses and blending with regular words. The exclusive whole word approach produced improved performance on a standardized measure of comprehension relative to gains in a control condition; the mixed whole word and letter-sound mapping approach produced comprehension gains no better than those occurring in the control condition. An analogous pattern of outcomes was produced by Lovett et al. (1994), who trained dyslexic readers to decode using one of two approaches, either phonological analysis and blending or decoding by analogy (e.g., if child knows *round,* using that knowledge to decode unfamiliar words such as *bound, found, mound,* and *pound*). The former approach increased performance on a standardized comprehension measurement relative to a control condition, although the latter approach failed to do so.

There was no obvious accounting for the different outcome patterns in these studies. The comprehension measures were tangential to the main interest in word-level effects, and thus, there was insufficient measurement to tease out the various effects of word-level processing improvements on comprehension. That improvements in decoding competence might have immediately documentable effects on comprehension is an important hypothesis, with enough preliminary support for it in the studies by Lovett and her colleagues to urge additional study of this problem.

Because the students in the Lovett studies were dyslexic, it is especially important to generate evidence on this problem with respect to the reading of normal readers. That is, when normally achieving children learn to read words using various approaches to decoding instruction, are there immediate improvements in their comprehension? Beyond decoding, does it make much difference in comprehension if students know more about the meanings of words? Given consistent correlations between vocabulary knowledge and reading achievement (see Anderson & Freebody, 1981), there certainly is the possibility of a causal relationship between vocabulary knowledge and comprehension. Without a doubt, the best-known evaluation of this causal hypothesis was Beck et al. (1982; McKeown, Beck, Omanson, & Perfetti, 1983; McKeown, Beck, Omanson, & Pople, 1985). In Beck et al., fourth-graders were taught 104 new vocabulary words over a period of five months, with the students encountering the words often as part of the intervention and using the words in multiple ways as part of instruction. Follow-up measures included pretest-to-posttest gain scores on a standardized comprehension test. Although the effects were not large, at the end of the study, comprehension tended to be better for students receiving the vocabulary intervention compared to those who had not.

In reviewing the relevant studies, some of which produced vocabulary-comprehension associations and some that did not, Beck, McKeown, Sinatra, and Loxterman (1991) concluded that vocabulary interventions affected comprehension positively to the extent that they stimulated students to make deep and extensive connections between vocabulary words and their definitions. They attributed failures to find comprehension effects in some vocabulary intervention studies as reflecting superficial and rote learning of vocabulary-definition linkages. Durso and Coggins (1991) provided an outcome in a true experiment that could be interpreted as consistent with the Beck et al. (1991) interpretation of the between-study differences in outcomes.

So, should students be taught vocabulary explicitly as a means of improving comprehension? There is debate, with some believing there are so many vocabulary words that instruction has no hope of making much of a dent on comprehension (e.g., Nagy & Anderson, 1984). Others argue that the doubters overestimate the number of different words in English that need to be known to read well and that vocabulary instruction is a viable option (e.g., D'Anna, Zechmeister, & Hall, 1991).

An important understanding that has emerged in recent years is that there are Matthew effects in reading, analogous to the Biblical Matthew's conclusion that the rich get richer: all else being equal, good readers will improve faster than weaker readers (Stanovich, 1986). If students can decode, it is easier for them to read. Because it is easier for them to read, they will read more. Yet, as the consequence of doing more reading, good decoders will become still more automatic and skilled in decoding even as they are exposed to more text than poor readers. Moreover, the more skilled the decoding, the greater the learning from any given piece of text. The result, in all, is that not merely reading ability per se but also vocabulary, literary experience, and all manner of book knowledge will increase more rapidly for good decoders than for weaker decoders. As knowledge increases, future reading comprehension is more certain, because comprehension largely depends on prior knowledge, including vocabulary. The research we have just reviewed is consistent with Stanovich's argument that poor decoding constrains comprehension growth. Thus, as educational researchers strive to improve reading comprehension directly, they must not overlook the importance of assessing and supporting word-level abilities. They must recognize the critical importance of lower-order competencies as part of the spiral of experience and growth that enables improvement in higher-order competencies.

Improving the Comprehensibility of Text

Toward increasing the productivity of children's reading, an alternative to increasing children's reading comprehension is that of increasing the comprehensibility of their texts. Psychologists have identified four major approaches for modifying the structure of texts so that their content is easier to comprehend and more memorable (see especially Britton, Woodward, & Binkley, 1993). Developmentally oriented reading educators, however, are not entirely convinced that such modifications should be made to the texts children read.

Signals include the following (Meyer, 1975):

- Use of text conventions that flag the structure of the text (e.g., cause and effect signaled with "because . . ."; sequences with "first . . . second . . . third . . . fourth . . . and so on").
- Advance organizers summarizing a main point before it is developed.
- Summary statements at the end of a section of text.
- A variety of words specifying importance of information, such as "Of less consequence . . ." and "More to the point . . ."

Signaling seems to provide at least slight comprehension advantages to readers (e.g., Lorch, 1989; Meyer, Brandt, & Bluth, 1980). It is especially helpful in making difficult conceptual information comprehensible and useful.

Elaborations and connections can be added to textbooks used by elementary-level students to increase the likelihood that students detect and understand connections among ideas. Often, the students lack prior knowledge assumed by the texts. In addition, many textbook passages are very poorly written if not downright incoherent. Textbook passages can be modified so that essential background information is presented and linkages between ideas in text are made explicit, for example, by adding elaborations and connections to text. Such revision has been shown to produce modest increases in schoolchildren's learning (Beck et al., 1991; McKeown, Beck, Sinatra, & Loxterman, 1992). The benefits of adding connections and elaborations at the high school and college levels have been more striking than the gains at the elementary level (Britton, Van Dusen, & Gülgöz, 1991; Britton, Van Dusen, Gülgöz, & Glynn, 1989; Duffy et al., 1989; Graves & Slater, 1991).

Adjunct questions can be placed before a text, in text, or after text (e.g., Rothkopf, 1966). Both pre- and postquestions enhance memory for material covered by questions (Anderson & Biddle, 1975). Postquestions also improve learning of nonquestioned material, increasing review and reflection of more than just the information that answers the postquestion. Adjunct questioning effects are not large, consistent with the general tendency of most text modifications to produce small effects. In general, adjunct question effects are smaller and less certain with children than with adults (see Pressley & Forrest-Pressley, 1985).

Text accompanied by semantically redundant *illustrations* is more memorable than unillustrated text (Levin, 1982, 1983; Levin & Lesgold, 1978; Levin & Mayer, 1993; Pressley, 1977; Woodward, 1993). Pictures also stimulate inferences that would not occur if text alone were processed (e.g., Guttman, Levin, & Pressley, 1977). The only consistently negative effect of pictures on learning that has been reported is with beginning readers. Pictures can reduce decoding demands for these readers and thus reduce their attention to the words they are reading. If children read words accompanied by their illustrations, their acquisition of the words as sight vocabulary is less likely than if they read them without accompanying illustrations (Samuels, 1970).

Should Text Be Made Easier to Comprehend? Chall, Conard, and Harris-Sharples (1991) concluded that attempting to produce an optimally comprehensible textbook for a given content area at a particular grade level misses the mark. Rather, different textbooks are required for different students, depending on their reading ability. This is consistent with the principle that a little challenge motivates students (e.g., White, 1959), that students will be more motivated if they are reading materials that are not too easy but not too difficult either.

Roller (1990) provided a similar analysis, contending it especially important to have well-structured text when students are processing moderately unfamiliar content. If content is familiar and easy, students will comprehend it regardless of whether the text is well organized. If content is too difficult, students will not understand it even if the text is well organized. When content is moderately familiar (or unfamiliar, depending on how you look at it), organization and clues to text organization make a huge difference (see also Spyridakis & Standal, 1987). Such analyses challenge those who are studying text modification to take developmental and ability differences into account more than they have done in the past.

Summary. Researchers have succeeded in identifying a number of ways to improve comprehension, each of which produces a small amount of improvement in understanding. The case in favor of decoding instruction is overwhelming, as detailed earlier in this chapter. That facility in decoding increases comprehension strengthens the case for decoding instruction. Our reading of the evidence is that there is more support for teaching vocabulary than not. Finally, although we do not endorse one-size-fits-all books for children, making books as easy to understand and remember as possible is reasonable. If the small advantages created by improved presentations in text are complemented by the advantages that can be produced through strategies instruction, as detailed earlier in this section, students might get much more from their texts than they have in the past.

Concluding Comments

There are contemporary parallels to all of the theoretical and pragmatic factors of the late 1970s and early 1980s that motivated the research reviewed in this section. Thus, we expect more research on comprehension, especially expanded teaching of comprehension processes.

Despite the substantial research reviewed here and the dissemination of it, including by a number of elementary curriculum publishers, the need for more comprehension instruction in schools hardly seems to have abated in the 1990s. Accountability for comprehension instruction increased in prominence during the Reagan and Bush years, with the ascent of the National Assessment of Educational Progress (NAEP), the nation's report card, leading the way. With respect to reading, the NAEP test outcomes have changed little since the late 1970s, with U.S. students consistently reported as having comprehension problems. The concern for comprehension instruction has been emphasized with the development of new tests as well, particularly reading performance assessments. Students who manifest the processes stimulated by comprehension strategies instruction receive high scores on these modern assessments (Mitchell, 1992).

There has been increasing recognition in recent years that many high school and college students lack sophisticated comprehension skills (Pressley, El-Dinary, & Brown, 1992), with a concomitant increase in developmental studies and remedial programs. Modern study skills programs have assimilated contemporary strategies instruction (see Flippo & Caverly, 1991), and thus, the symbiotic relationship between the study skills movement and comprehension process instruction continues.

The evidence in favor of individual cognitive strategies continues to accumulate (see Dole, Duffy, Roehler, & Pearson, 1991). Direct explanation approaches to the development of articulated strategies use by students, such as transactional strategies instruction, are now being researched.

The 40-plus extant verbal protocol studies of reading were analyzed by Pressley and Afflerbach (1995). The portrait of sophisticated reading that emerges from this analysis is strongly supportive of comprehension strategies instruction, for excellent readers do much that is strategic as they read. Good readers:

1. Overview before reading.
2. Look for important information in text and pay greater attention to it than other information.
3. Attempt to relate important points in text to one another to understand the text as a whole.
4. Activate and use prior knowledge to interpret text, such as generating hypotheses about text and predicting text content.
5. Reconsider and/or revise hypotheses about the meaning of text based on text content.
6. Reconsider and/or revise prior knowledge based on text content.
7. Relate text content to prior knowledge as part of constructing interpretations of text.
8. Attempt to infer information not explicitly stated in text when the information is critical to comprehension of the text.
9. Attempt to determine the meaning of words not understood or recognized, especially when a word seems critical to meaning construction.
10. Use strategies, such as underlining, repeating, making notes, visualizing, summarizing, paraphrasing, and self-questioning, to remember text.
11. Change reading strategies when comprehension is perceived to not be proceeding smoothly.
12. Evaluate the qualities of text, with these evaluations in part affecting whether text has impact on reader's knowledge, attitudes, behavior, and so on.
13. Reflect on and process text additionally after reading it (reviewing, questioning, summarizing, attempting to interpret, evaluating, considering alternative interpretations, considering how to process the text additionally, accepting one's understanding of a text, rejecting one's understanding of a text).
14. Carry on a responsive conversation with the author.
15. Anticipate or plan for the use of knowledge gained from the reading.

In short, there is much better verbal protocol evidence in the 1990s than was available in the late 1970s for many, many conscious processes as part of excellent, self-regulated reading (e.g., Wyatt et al., 1993).

More complete metacognitive theories of self-regulation have appeared in the past decade than were available in the late 1970s. All of these theories specify that strategies are important in self-regulated thinking, which is portrayed as a product of cognitive processes, metacognitive knowledge and monitoring, conceptual knowledge, and motivational processes and beliefs (e.g., Borkowski, Carr, Rellinger, & Pressley, 1990; Schunk & Zimmerman, 1994).

Transactional strategies instruction is particularly well matched to these contemporary models of self-regulation and the development of self-regulation (Brown et al., 1996), with development through modeling and direct explanation of processes consistent with much modern thinking about the educative development of intellectual autonomy (Deshler & Schumaker, 1988; instruction also meshes well with literary critical theories embraced by contemporary language arts professionals and, in particular, with the reader response approach embraced by those now extending Rosenblatt's (1978) thinking in the elementary and secondary curricula (Beach & Hynds, 1991; Clifford, 1991; Holland et al., 1993; Karolides, 1992).

In summary, there are very strong pragmatic and theoretical reasons for continuing research on comprehension strategies and their development through teaching; such instruction meshes with accountability demands, but also is acceptable to the language arts educator community. The case is strong that transactional strategies instruction stimulates comprehension processing consistent with the processing of excellent readers. Finally, such research and translation into practice will continue largely because there is no obvious competitor approach to meeting what continues to be a very great need. Improving word-level processes has had only slight effect on comprehension in studies to date. Text modifications also have relatively small effects on comprehension.

Contemporary Views on Writing and Writing Instruction

Much has changed in the past two decades with respect to writing instruction in U.S. schools. This is largely due to the efforts of language arts educators to increase the amount of writing occurring in schools, especially expressive writing. For example, Gray (see 1988) began the Bay Area Writing Project in the early 1970s. Bay Area teachers who themselves wrote and taught writing to their students collaborated with other teachers who wanted to increase writing from their students. At the center of this model, which eventually expanded into the National Writing Project, were the beliefs that teachers of writing needed to be writers themselves and that the only way to learn how to teach writing was by becoming a writer. Toward this end, Writing Project teachers organized summer workshops and peer support. With the appearance of a number of visible books urging teachers to teach writing and develop writers in their classrooms (e.g., Atwell, 1987; Calkins, 1986; Graves, 1983), this movement found much support in the professional language arts literature.

The result has been that composing of stories and narratives has become an everyday occurrence in many U.S. elementary classrooms, much more common than such activities were 20 years ago. In contrast, instruction on the formal conventions of writing, such as spelling and grammar, was more common 20 years ago than it is today. As in the case of comprehension, contemporary writing instruction can be understood by considering its historical foundations, for a number of scientific and educational directions in the early 1980s did much to stimulate the development of modern writing strategies instruction.

The Development of Writing Skills

Earlier in this chapter, we discussed how children learn the basics of alphabetic spelling. As important as these skills are, children must go beyond the basics to become skillful writers. Looking back at the stories in Figures 5.3 through 5.6, we see obvious development in such areas as sentence structure, vocabulary, and attention to the reader. What does research have to say about these higher-level aspects of writing?

Learning to spell accurately and automatically is an important part of being a skilled writer. Children who must puzzle over the spelling of each word have little attention left to devote to higher-level aspects of writing. Such children may avoid words that they are unable to spell, limiting their vocabulary and their ability to express themselves. Thus, even though spelling is often considered a low-level skill, it has an important influence on higher-level aspects of writing. The results of Juel (1994) support these claims. As part of her longitudinal study of children in grades 1 through 4, Juel asked judges to rate children's stories (which were elicited in response to a picture) for story development, syntactic maturity, and richness of vocabulary. The raters were specifically instructed to disregard spelling. Two factors were found to account for about 40% of the variation among children in the rated quality of writing. The first of these factors was the children's spelling ability; even though judges were told to ignore spelling when they rated the stories, the good spellers were observed to produce better stories than the poor spellers. The second factor that helped to account for variation in writing ability was the quality of children's story ideas. This was assessed by asking children to tell a story about the same picture they had earlier written about. The oral stories were scored using the same criteria that were used to score the written stories. Children who told better oral stories tended to be better writers. The relative contributions of spelling and story ideas changed across grades. For first-graders, spelling was the dominant influence on the quality of the written stories. By grade 2, the measure of story ideas had become more important, its influence steadily increasing through grade 4. Still, spelling made a significant contribution to writing quality throughout the four years of the study. These results show that, at least in the elementary grades, good spellers tend to be good writers.

Juel (1994) further found that children's ability to tell a good oral story—one determinant of their writing ability—was related to their reading experience. Good readers gained each year on the oral storytelling measure. Poor readers did not improve from grade 1 to grade 4. In fourth grade, as in first grade, the poor readers' oral stories, like their written stories, were often no more than lists of what they had seen in the picture. Children who do not read very much, like the poor readers in Juel's study, have less opportunity to learn about story structure and vocabulary than avid readers do. Their writing is predictably poor.

Although children's ability to tell oral stories is related to their ability to produce written stories, children's written texts are at first less complex and more primitive than their oral productions. O'Donnell, Griffin, and Norris (1967) documented this difference by showing children a silent film. Immediately after seeing the film, children were asked to tell its story to an experimenter and also to write it. The children's written and spoken productions were segmented into T-units, which are the shortest units that can be grammatically punctuated as sentences. Third-graders produced shorter T-units in their writing than in their speech. Moreover, the T-units in writing were less complex, less likely to contain constructions such as embedded clauses. A later study by Loban (1976) reported that, up to about seventh grade, T-units continued to be longer in speech than in writing. These results are consistent with the view that young children's written language is constrained by their oral expression. Because writing makes so many demands on them, young children cannot display their linguistic abilities to the same extent in writing as they do in talking.

At some point during the middle years of schooling, an important shift occurs. Written language now becomes more complex and elaborate than spoken language. O'Donnell et al. (1967) found signs of this shift as early as fifth grade when examining the length of T-units in speech and writing. The shift in T-unit length occurred somewhat later in the study by Loban (1976). In this study, though, differences in elaboration favoring writing were apparent in fifth grade for a random sample of students. These differences appeared in fourth grade for children with high language ability but not until eighth grade for students with low language ability. By late elementary school, then, most children realize that writing is not just talk written down. Children deliberately shape their written productions in a way that they do not normally do in speaking. They learn that certain linguistic forms, vocabulary items, and conventions are used to a greater extent in writing than in talking (Rubin, 1980). It is likely that Missy (Figure 5.6) has already gone through this shift, whereas Shayna (Figure 5.6) has not.

Development is also observed in children's ability to consider the point of view of the reader and the purpose of the writing, for example, whether the goal is to entertain, inform, or persuade. Thus, in a study by Scardamalia, Bereiter, and McDonald that was cited in Bereiter (1980), fourth-graders who were asked to write instructions for playing a novel game did not do a good job of adapting the instructions to the readers. It is not that children of this age are totally egocentric; research on social cognition reveals that they can take another person's point of view into account under some circumstances. Rather, children seem to have difficulty considering the needs of the reader while simultaneously coping with all of the other demands of writing. Missy (Figure 5.6) did apparently consider the reader when she wrote "very" a large number of times so that the reader would realize how long the trail felt to the hikers. Although goal setting and audience consideration improve with age, they remain problems for many student writers at least into the high school years (e.g., Langer, 1986, Ch. 3).

Revision is uncommon in young children's writing, with the first draft often being the final draft (e.g., Bereiter & Scardamalia, 1987; Fitzgerald, 1987). When young children and poor writers do revise, their revisions tend to be superficial. Better writers put more stress on revision (see Fitzgerald, 1992). They attend closely to what they want the reader to get out of the piece and they keep in mind the style that they want to use. In the course of writing, they give more concern to the overall meaning of the text than to the structure of individual sentences or to mechanics. Nevertheless, good revisers do attend to spelling, punctuation, and grammar before they are done.

As children develop, their writing also becomes better organized. For example, Stahl (1977) found that second-graders' compositions on the topic "my house" showed no evidence of attention to selection, arrangement, or balance. The compositions generally just broke off at the end, with no concluding statement. By eighth grade, students presented the content in a coherent arrangement, allocated space in proportion to the importance of the elements, and ended at an appropriate point. Some fifth-graders' stories showed the qualities of the typical second-grade story, whereas other fifth-graders' stories were more like eighth-graders'. Shayna (Figure 5.6) seems to write whatever comes to mind in the way that Stahl observed among second-graders; Missy's writing (Figure 5.6) is more organized.

The writing of young children and of poor writers has been characterized as "knowledge telling." Children add ideas to essays as they come to mind rather than systematically searching their relevant knowledge. Children may fail to notice that what comes to mind may not actually be relevant to the topic at hand (Bereiter & Scardamalia, 1987; Scardamalia & Bereiter, 1986; see also Emig, 1971; Pianko, 1979). As a result, the writing is often less complete than it could or should be. To be sure, Langer (1986) reported improvement in student writing from the elementary to secondary school years. Thus, elementary students tend to write simple stories and expositions that reflect a knowledge-telling strategy, often using packaged expressions such as "Once upon a time" and "They lived happily ever after." These give way to more complex writing, although the book reports and laboratory reports observed in high school are often very uncreative in structure. High school students' longer papers typically begin with a thesis statement, followed by several paragraphs, each of which contains one point related to the thesis, followed by a concluding paragraph. Even still, knowledge telling is not an uncommon strategy among secondary students (Applebee, 1984; Durst, 1984; Marshall, 1984).

Langer and Applebee (1984, 1987; Applebee, 1984) pointed to conventional schooling as a major culprit in shaping students' unreflective knowledge telling. The most frequent writing assignment students experience in school, they argued, is that of writing a short answer as part of an examination, where such answers are not evaluated for style but rather for correctness and completeness of content (Marshall, 1984). What is graded is more often the mechanics than the construction of meaning. Not only do school tests primarily tap content, they often probe items in their order of coverage in the class (Bereiter & Scardamalia, 1987). Even the wording of some test questions (e.g., "what we studied last week") can promote information dumping rather than reflection. Knowledge telling may be further encouraged by asking students to write on topics about which they know already: there is no need to seek out further information and integrate it with what is already known. When reports are assigned in school, a simple listing of pieces of information found in different sources will often earn a high mark. It has also been argued that educator pressure to attend to mechanics such as spelling, capitalization, and punctuation induces students to attend to word-level and sentence-level elements of writing and to ignore whether paragraphs and the essay as a whole make sense (Langer, 1986).

To better understand the thought processes involved in good writing, Flower and Hayes (1980, 1981) collected verbal protocols from college freshmen and college-level composition teachers. The writers were asked to say everything that came to mind as they composed essays on given topics. Analyses of their tape-recorded protocols made clear that expert writers approach writing as a problem-solving challenge, to be solved through three interrelated processes. The first process, planning, includes generating and organizing the content and setting writing goals that place the sought reactions of probable readers in the forefront. The second process, translating the plan into words, results in a rough draft. The third process is revising the draft.

This three-phase conception of writing as planning, translation, and revising was not new (see Rohman, 1965). What was new was how highly interrelated and recursive the three phases were. During drafting, the skilled writer is sensitive to gaps, recognizing when reorganization or more information is needed. Thus, revision begins even during the process of translation, invoking more planning alongside. Layer within layer of planning, translating, and revising cycles were reported by the skilled writers as they wrote.

In contrast, the freshman writers in Flower and Hayes's (1980, 1981) studies were less likely than experts to set goals for their writing. Knowledge telling was observed more frequently, planning was less salient, and revision was much less extensive. Moreover, whereas the novices paid close attention to mechanics throughout their writing, experts did so only at the end, in polishing their piece. Flower and Hayes's work thus documented that even students at an elite university (Carnegie-Mellon) were relatively unskilled in composition and that the weaknesses lay in the process as much as the product. Why might this be?

Contemporary Writing Instruction

Among educators, whole language has been the dominant philosophy on literacy education for the past several decades. The whole language philosophy emphasizes the reading and writing of whole texts while de-emphasizing instruction in basic skills and mechanics per se. Toward bringing the elementary writing curriculum under the whole language umbrella, Graves's (1983) work was particularly influential. At the core of Graves's recommendations was the subordination of basic skills and mechanics to the writing process itself. Students were to be frequently engaged in sustained writing about topics and ideas of their own choosing. During Writer's Workshop, as writing sessions are known in classrooms following the Graves model (see also Atwell, 1987; Calkins, 1986), the optimal teacher-student relationship is collaborative, with the teacher providing assistance and input to students as needed, often as part of conferences concerned with revising a student-produced text.

On the face of it, there is much that is positive about Graves's approach to writing instruction. In contrast to the short-answer syndrome discussed earlier, students in Writing Workshop classrooms are regularly encouraged to write longer pieces and for various purposes. Teacher-student revision conferences create opportunity for the teacher to assess students' spelling, grammar, capitalization, and so on, and to conduct minilessons targeted at their particular needs. In the spirit of Dewey (1913), Graves's approach with its focus on students writing about what they want to anchors instruction on the students' own interests. To reinforce the authenticity of process writing, publication of students' final drafts is encouraged, and this can be motivating, too.

As attractive as Graves's model is—as well as related models, such as the Bay Area and National Writing Projects—it was not particularly well informed about how skilled writers write. In particular, there is more to learning to write than simply writing lots, as revealed by the Flower and Hayes (1980, 1981) analyses. Some educators picked up on the insights produced in the verbal protocol studies, developing instruction that focuses on higher-order dimensions of meaning and message construction. In these approaches, young writers are taught to plan, translate, and revise recursively. Close attention to sentence- and word-level concerns is deferred until the revision stage.

With elementary-level students, the most ambitious exploration of the value of a plan-translate-revise model of writing instruction was carried out by Englert, Raphael, Anderson, Anthony, and Stevens (1991). The instructional program, referred to as Cognitive Strategy Instruction in Writing (CSIW), targeted writing of explanatory and compare-and-contrast essays, and the study involved regular and special education students in the fourth and fifth grades.

CSIW adopted most features of process writing as defined by Writer's Workshop models, including that students chose their own writing topics and that writing instruction occurred in a socially rich milieu in which teacher-student and student-student conferences were frequent. Beyond that, however, students received a great deal of explanation about good and poor explanatory and compare-and-contrast essays. One way this was accomplished was by sharing good and poor examples of writing, with teachers thinking aloud about the example while leading a discussion of its strengths and weaknesses. Reflecting aloud, the teacher asked questions such as "Did the author address what is being explained?" and "Did the author explain where this should take place?" Through think-alouds, teachers also modeled writing of explanatory and compare-and-contrast essays. Thus, to model the planning process, teachers asked themselves a series of questions about what should be in the text they wanted to write. Students watched and heard the teacher mull, "Who am I writing this for? . . . Why am I writing this? . . . What do I know about this? . . . How can I organize all of this?" Similarly, the teacher continued to think aloud while writing and revising the piece together with the class. The similarities with the direct explanation approach to comprehension strategies instruction may be seen to reflect Duffy's (Duffy et al., 1987) impact on his Michigan State colleagues.

Over the school year, as the program proceeded, students took greater and greater control of planning, drafting, and revising. In addition, ongoing supports, such as planning sheets, were provided, for example:

WHO: Who am I writing for?
WHY: Why am I writing this?
WHAT: What do I know? (Brainstorm)
HOW: How can I group my ideas?
How will I organize my ideas? (compare/contrast, problem/solution, explanation, other)

After a year of instruction, CSIW students wrote better than control students who had been engaged in writing without the intensive emphasis on planning, drafting, and revising. The essays produced in the posttraining evaluation were analyzed in a number of ways. Whether scored holistically, with respect to how well the essay as a whole conveyed its intended message, or analytically, with respect to the completeness of the information included in explanation or compare-and-contrast essays, CSIW students did better than controls. This advantage also held when the students were asked to write something other than explanation or compare-and-contrast pieces. The CSIW writers were also more inclined to anticipate potential reader questions and to let readers know when they were offering personal opinions. In general, these positive outcomes were observed both with regular education students and students with mild reading disabilities. (For a review of a number of successes in teaching learning-disabled students to plan, draft, and revise, see Graham & Harris, 1992.)

In similar spirit, several researchers have endeavored to assist the writing of narratives by providing sets of questions such as What happened first? What happened next? What happened last? (Hume, 1983) or Who is the main character? Who else is in the story? When does the story take place? Where does the story take place? What does the main character do or want to do? What do other characters do? What happens when the main character does or tries to do it? What happens with other characters? How does the story end? How does the main character feel? How do other characters feel? (Harris & Graham, 1992). Similarly, in support of expository writing, Graham and Harris (1988) taught learning-disabled students to follow a set of commands: (a) Generate a topic sentence; (b) note reasons; (c) examine the reasons and ask if readers will buy each reason; (d) come up with an ending. Alternatively, toward assisting students' search for topic-relevant information, Bereiter and Scardamalia (1982) explored the value of encouraging use of sentence openers, such as "One reason . . ."; "Even though . . ."; "For example . . ."; and "I think. . . . " In general, such prompting increases at least the amount that students write (Kellogg, 1990) and has often resulted in measurable improvement in writing quality among both regular and learning-disabled students in the later elementary and middle school years (for a review, see Graham and Harris, 1992).

In keeping with the broader interest in comprehension monitoring (Markman, 1981), researchers have shown special interest in the revision process. For example, Beal (1987) determined that children have more difficulty in identifying where a text needs to be revised than in doing the revision itself once the problem is pointed out. Although the ability to detect revisable problems improves across the elementary grades (Beal, 1990), it can also be fostered through instruction. Thus, to help third- and sixth-graders evaluate the need for revisions, Beal, Garrod, and Bonitatibus (1990) taught them to ask a series of questions about their drafts: "Who are the people in the story and what are they like?"; "What is happening in the story?"; "Why are they doing what they did?"; "Where does the story take place?"; and "When does the story take place?" The approach has been shown to improve children's revisions, especially when instruction is rich with examples of problematic narratives. A different tactic, developed by Fitzgerald and Markham (1987), consisted in teaching sixth-grade students to think of revision as a problem-solving task that could be solved through additions to text, deletion of text, substitutions, and rearrangements. Graham and MacArthur (1988) taught students with learning disabilities to pursue revisions through six steps: (a) Read the essay; (b) find a specific sentence that tells something the writer wants in the essay; (c) add two more reasons to the essay to support the point; (d) check each sentence of the essay; (e) make changes; (f) reread and make final changes. All of these studies demonstrate that elementary school students can learn to revise better than they otherwise do.

Summary

Every school day, many U.S. elementary students are writing narrative and exposition. They learn to plan, draft, and revise by doing it. During teacher-student revision conferences, the teachers provide minilessons targeted at aspects of mechanics that seem problematic for the particular student writer. That is, teachers use student drafts to diagnose student instructional needs.

That educational research sometimes makes a difference is dramatically illustrated in the revolution in writing instruction that has occurred in the past decade, with isolated skills- and mechanics-driven teaching of writing largely an approach of the past. This revolution occurred because of converging theoretical analyses and research outcomes, analyses provided by language arts researchers, cognitive scientists, and developmental psychologists. The progress in writing strategies instruction parallels the progress in teaching of comprehension strategies. Scientists from diverse disciplines conducted analyses directly relevant to the development of literacy competencies via instruction, instruction that is necessary because the literacy of young adults is far short of what it could be. Instruction can make an important difference in the development of academic competence.

Research on skilled writing continues. For example, although there is no doubt that skilled writers plan extensively before they write, new analyses (e.g., Kellogg, 1994; Lansman, Smith, & Weber, 1990) suggest that it may not take up the majority of writing time as suggested by earlier analyses based on think-alouds (Hayes & Flower, 1986). How prior knowledge in a domain makes writing easier, although not necessarily better, is becoming better understood. Conversely, how high verbal ability increases the quantity of writing but not necessarily its quality is also becoming better understood (Kellogg, 1993).

Just as research on the writing process improves, so do research programs on writing strategies instruction, such as that by Graham and Harris (1992). This makes sense given that the great need for more effective writing instruction persists, with recent reports on writing from the National Assessment of Educational Progress no more sanguine about student writing than earlier ones. We believe, as do others (e.g., Bruer, 1993) that this is largely because the process writing models that only stimulated more writing are only now being replaced on a large scale by writing instruction consistent with planning-drafting-revising conceptions of writing.

CONCLUSION

In recent years, the field has made reifying progress in understanding the difficulties of learning to read and write as well as ways to ease their progress. Indeed, to the extent that these understandings find realization in the classroom, there is sound reason for expecting the incidence of learning disability in these areas to be reduced dramatically. In particular, the lion's share of the variance in early reading and writing success is absorbed by measures of letter knowledge and phonemic awareness and—through them—word recognition, decoding, and spelling. Succinctly stated, successful entry into print depends first on understanding how our writing system works and then on learning to use it.

Given that children just plain can't read or write unless they can conquer the print, the primacy of these word-level factors probably should not be surprising. On the other hand, if the first goal is to move children comfortably and confidently into reading and writing, it is only because the ultimate goal is to lead them into literacy in the broadest sense of that word. Although the passage from illiteracy depends critically on developing facility with the written word, it remains a long stretch from such basic competencies to true literacy.

Beyond the basics, the firmest prescription from research is that children should read as often, as broadly, and as thoughtfully as possible. In theory, this seems so simple, straightforward, and equitably valid a recommendation. In practice, however, it too is problematic. Given equal opportunity, poor readers cannot possibly read as much in quantity or quality as good readers, nor are they likely to try. Children who do not read well are those who need most to read more, but children who do not read well are very often loathe to read at all.

Issues of uneven access notwithstanding, there are indications that schoolchildren generally are reading more these days. This can only be good news, but even so, what children are reading more of, it seems, are stories and novels; in contrast, what they need most to become good at reading is informational text. Among both children (Mullis et al., 1993) and adults (Guthrie, Schafer, & Hutchinson, 1991) in the United States, the ability to read informational texts remains differentially and disturbingly weak.

We are thus returned to the two issues with which we started. First, why is it so difficult for so many children to learn how to read and write the words? And, second, on what else, besides word facility, does literacy depend—and, in particular, on what else that can be hastened and sharpened through instruction? If we believe we have answered the first of these questions, then it is due time to turn in earnest to the second. We do not know what to do about vocabulary difficulties. We do not know what to ask about syntactic difficulties. Research on strategies instruction has given us better methods for helping students to think actively about reading comprehension difficulties and to write with more clarity and coherence. Clearly, however, our understanding of the underlying nature and optimal development of such higher-order dimensions of literacy is still quite crude.

As one last provocation, then, we leave you with this thought: Strong correlations hold between children's reading and writing abilities (Shanahan & Tierney, 1990; Spivey & King, 1989). As Stotsky (1984) has pointed out, how much and how well students read are firm predictors of the quality of their writing. One wonders: If we had more refined questions and measures, might we find telling reflections of writing on reading as well? Children's early spelling behaviors have served as a powerful database for studying their perceptions, misperceptions, and cognitive command of the phonological and orthographic structures that make beginning reading difficult. Perhaps children's writing will similarly yield an entry into the higher-order linguistic and conceptual difficulties of becoming literate. In any case, and whatever the means, gaining that understanding must be the field's next challenge.

REFERENCES

Adams, M. J. (1979). Models of word recognition. *Cognitive Psychology, 11,* 133–176.

Adams, M. J. (1980). Failures to comprehend and levels of processing in reading. In R. J. Spiro, B. C. Bruce, & W. F. Brewer (Eds.), *Theoretical issues in reading comprehension* (pp. 87–112). Hillsdale, NJ: Erlbaum.

Adams, M. J. (1990). *Beginning to read: Thinking and learning about print.* Cambridge, MA: MIT Press.

Adams, M. J. (1991). Why not phonics and whole language? In W. Ellis (Ed.), *All language and the creation of literacy* (pp. 40–53). Baltimore: Orton Dyslexia Society.

Adams, M. J., & Bruce, B. C. (1982). Background knowledge and reading comprehension. In J. A. Langer & M. T. Smith-Burke (Eds.), *Reader meets author/bridging the gap* (pp. 2–25). Newark, DE: International Reading Association.

Adams, M. J., & Bruck, M. (1993). Word recognition: The interface of educational policies and scientific research. *Reading and Writing: An Interdisciplinary Journal, 5,* 113–139.

Adams, M. J., & Collins, A. M. (1979). A schema-theoretic view of reading. In R. Freedle (Ed.), *New directions in discourse processing* (pp. 1–22). Norwood, NJ: ABLEX.

Adams, M. J., & Huggins, A. W. F. (1985). The growth of children's sight vocabulary: A quick test with educational and theoretical implications. *Reading Research Quarterly, 20,* 262–281.

Allen, L., Cipielewski, J., & Stanovich, K. E. (1992). Multiple indicators of children's reading habits and attitudes: Construct validity and cognitive correlates. *Journal of Educational Psychology, 84,* 489–503.

Allington, R. L. (1978). Effects of contextual constraints upon rate and accuracy. *Perceptual and Motor Skills, 46,* 1318.

Allington, R. L., & Strange, M. (1977). Effects of grapheme substitutions in connected text upon reading behaviors. *Visible Language, 11,* 285–297.

Anderson, R. C., & Biddle, W. B. (1975). On asking people questions about what they are reading. In G. Bower (Ed.), *The psychology of learning and motivation* (Vol. 9). New York: Academic Press.

Anderson, R. C., & Freebody, P. (1981). Vocabulary knowledge. In J. T. Guthrie (Ed.), *Comprehension and teaching: Research reviews* (pp. 77–117). Newark, DE: International Reading Association.

Anderson, R. C., & Hidde, J. L. (1971). Imagery and sentence learning. *Journal of Educational Psychology, 62,* 526–530.

Anderson, R. C., & Pearson, P. D. (1984). A schema-theoretic view of basic processes in reading. In P. D. Pearson (Ed.), *Handbook of reading research* (pp. 255–291). New York: Longman.

Anderson, R. C., & Pichart, J. W. (1978). Recall of previously unrecallable information following a shift in perspective. *Journal of Verbal Learning and Verbal Behavior, 17,* 1–12.

Anderson, R. C., Wilson, P. T., & Fielding, L. G. (1988). Growth in reading and how children spend their time outside school. *Reading Research Quarterly, 23,* 285–303.

Anderson, T. H., & Armbruster, B. B. (1984a). Content area textbooks. In R. C. Anderson, J. Osborne, & R. J. Tierney (Eds.), *Learning to read in American schools* (pp. 193–224). Hillsdale, NJ: Erlbaum.

Anderson, T. H., & Armbruster, B. B. (1984b). Studying. In P. D. Pearson (Ed.), *Handbook of reading research* (pp. 657–679). New York: Longman.

Anderson, V. (1992). A teacher development project in transactional strategy instruction for teachers of severely reading-disabled adolescents. *Teaching and Teacher Education, 8,* 391–403.

Anderson, V., & Roit, M. (1993). Planning and implementing collaborative strategy instruction for delayed readers in grades 6–10. *Elementary School Journal, 94,* 121–137.

Applebee, A. N. (1984). *Contexts for learning to write.* Norwood, NJ: ABLEX.

Arnold, D. S., Lonigan, C. U., Whitehurst, G. U., & Epstein, J. N. (1994). Accelerating language development through picture book reading: Replication and extension to a videotape training format. *Journal of Educational Psychology, 86,* 235–243.

Arter, J. A., & Jenkins, J. R. (1977). Examining the benefits and prevalence of modality considerations in special education. *Journal of Special Education, 11,* 281–298.

Arter, J. A., & Jenkins, J. R. (1979). Differential diagnosis—prescriptive teaching: A critical appraisal. *Review of Educational Research, 49,* 517–555.

Atwell, N. (1987). *In the middle: Reading, writing, and learning from adolescents.* Portsmouth, NH: Heinemann.

Aukerman, R. C. (1971). *Approaches to beginning reading.* New York: Wiley.

Aukerman, R. C. (1984). *Approaches to beginning reading* (2nd ed.). New York: Wiley.

Backman, J. (1983). The role of psycholinguistic skills in reading acquisition: A look at early readers. *Reading Research Quarterly, 18,* 466–479.

Baker, L., & Brown, A. L. (1984). Metacognitive skills and reading. In P. D. Pearson, R. Barr, M. Kamil, & P. Mosenthal (Eds.), *Handbook of reading research* (pp. 353–394). New York: Longman.

Ball, E. W., & Blachman, B. A. (1991). Does phoneme awareness training in kindergarten make a difference in early word recognition and developmental spelling? *Reading Research Quarterly, 26,* 49–66.

Balmuth, M. (1982). *The roots of phonics.* New York: Teachers College Press.

Barr, R. (1984). Beginning reading instruction: From debate to reformation. In P. D. Pearson (Ed.), *Handbook of reading research* (pp. 545–581). New York: Longman.

Barron, R. W. (1981). Development of visual word recognition: A review. In G. E. MacKinnon & T. G. Waller (Eds.), *Reading research: Advances in theory and practice* (Vol. 3, pp. 119–158). New York: Academic Press.

Bateman, B. (1979). Teaching reading to learning disabled and other hard-to-teach children. In L. A. Resnick & P. A. Weaver (Eds.), *Theory and practice of early reading* (Vol. 1, pp. 227–259). Hillsdale, NJ: Erlbaum.

Beach, R. (1976). Self-evaluation strategies of extensive revisers and nonrevisers. *College Composition and Communication, 27,* 160–164.

Beach, R., & Hynds, S. (1991). Research on response to literature. In R. Barr, M. L. Kamil, P. B. Mosenthal, & P. D. Pearson (Eds.), *Handbook of reading research* (Vol. 2, pp. 453–489). New York: Longman.

Beal, C. R. (1987). Repairing the message: Children's monitoring and revision skills. *Child Development, 58,* 401–408.

Beal, C. R. (1990). The development of text evaluation and revision skills. *Child Development, 61,* 247–258.

Beal, C. R., Garrod, A. C., & Bonitatibus, G. J. (1990). Fostering children's revision skills through training in comprehension monitoring. *Journal of Educational Psychology, 82,* 275–280.

Bean, T., Smith, C., & Searfoss, L. (1980). *Study strategies for the content classroom.* Paper presented at the thirteenth annual meeting of the California Reading Association, Newport Beach, CA.

Beck, I. L., McKeown, M. G., Sinatra, G. M., & Loxterman, J. A. (1991). Revising social studies text from a text-processing perspective: Evidence of improved comprehensibility. *Reading Research Quarterly, 26,* 251–276.

Beck, I. L., Perfetti, C. A., & McKeown, M. G. (1982). Effects of long-term vocabulary instruction on lexical access and reading comprehension. *Journal of Educational Psychology, 74,* 506–521.

Beers, J. W., Beers, C. S., & Grant, K. (1977). The logic behind children's spelling. *Elementary School Journal, 77,* 238–242.

Bell, R. Q. (1968). A reinterpretation of the direction of effects in studies of socialization. *Psychological Review, 75,* 81–95.

Bentin, S., Hammer, R., & Cahan, S. (1991). The effects of aging and first year schooling on the development of phonological awareness. *Psychological Science, 2,* 271–274.

Bereiter, C. (1980). Development in writing. In L. W. Gregg & E. R. Steinberg (Eds.), *Cognitive processes in writing* (pp. 73–93). Hillsdale, NJ: Erlbaum.

Bereiter, C., & Bird, M. (1985). Use of thinking aloud in identification and teaching of reading comprehension strategies. *Cognition and Instruction, 2,* 131–156.

Bereiter, C., & Scardamalia, M. (1982). From conversation to composition: The role of instruction in a developmental process. In R. Glaser (Ed.), *Advances in instructional psychology* (Vol. 2, pp. 1–64). Hillsdale, NJ: Erlbaum.

Bereiter, C., & Scardamalia, M. (1987). *The psychology of written communication.* Hillsdale, NJ: Erlbaum.

Berent, I., & Perfetti, C. A. (1995). A Rose is a REEZ: The two-cycles model of phonology assembly in reading English. *Psychological Review, 102,* 146–184.

Besner, D., & Humphreys, G. W. (1991). Introduction. In D. Besner & G. W. Humphreys (Eds.), *Basic processes in reading: Visual word recognition* (pp. 1–9). Hillsdale, NJ: Erlbaum.

Biemiller, A. (1970). The development of the use of graphic and contextual information as children learn to read. *Reading Research Quarterly, 6,* 75–96.

Biemiller, A. (1977–1978). Relationships between oral reading rates for letters, words, and simple text in the development of reading achievement. *Reading Research Quarterly, 13,* 223–253.

Bishop, D. V. M., & Adams, C. (1990). A prospective study of the relationship between specific language impairment, phonological disorders, and reading retardation. *Journal of Child Psychology and Psychiatry, 31,* 1027–1050.

Bissex, G. L. (1980). *GNYS AT WRK: A child learns to write and read.* Cambridge, MA: Harvard University Press.

Blachman, B. A. (1984). Relationship of rapid naming ability and language analysis skills to kindergarten and first-grade reading achievement. *Journal of Educational Psychology, 76,* 610–622.

Boder, E. (1973). Developmental dyslexia: A diagnostic approach based on three atypical reading-spelling patterns. *Developmental Medicine and Child Neurology, 15,* 663–687.

Bond, G. L., & Dykstra, R. (1967). The cooperative research program in first-grade reading instruction. *Reading Research Quarterly, 2,* 5–142.

Borkowski, J. G., Carr, M., Rellinger, E. A., & Pressley, M. (1990). Self-regulated strategy use: Interdependence of metacognition, attributions, and self-esteem. In B. F. Jones (Ed.), *Dimensions of thinking: Review of research* (pp. 53–92). Hillsdale, NJ: Erlbaum.

Borkowski, J. G., Levers, S., & Gruenenfelder, T. M. (1976). Transfer of mediational strategies in children: The role of activity and awareness during strategy acquisition. *Child Development, 47,* 779–786.

Bowers, P. G., & Wolf, M. (1993). Theoretical links among naming speed, precise timing mechanisms and orthographic skill in dyslexia. *Reading and Writing: An Interdisciplinary Journal, 5,* 69–85.

Bowey, J. A., & Francis, J. (1991). Phonological analysis as a function of age and exposure to reading instruction. *Applied Psycholinguistics, 12,* 91–121.

Bradley, L., & Bryant, P. E. (1983). Categorizing sounds and learning to read—a causal connection. *Nature, 301,* 419–421.

Brady, S. A. (1991). The role of working memory in reading disability. In S. Brady & D. Shankweiler (Eds.), *Phonological processes in literacy* (pp. 129–152). Hillsdale, NJ: Erlbaum.

Bransford, J. D., Barclay, J., & Franks, J. (1972). Sentence memory: A constructive versus interpretative approach. *Cognitive Psychology, 3,* 193–209.

Bransford, J. D., & Johnson, M. K. (1973). Considerations of some problems of comprehension. In W. G. Chase (Ed.), *Visual information processing.* New York: Academic Press.

Britton, B. K., Van Dusen, L., & Gülgöz, S. (1991). Reply to "A response to 'Instructional texts rewritten by five expert teams.'" *Journal of Educational Psychology, 83,* 149–152.

Britton, B. K., Van Dusen, L., Gülgöz, S., & Glynn, S. (1989). Instructional texts rewritten by five expert teams: Revisions and retention improvements. *Journal of Educational Psychology, 81,* 226–239.

Britton, B. K., Woodward, A., & Binkley, M. (1993). *Learning from textbooks: Theory and practice.* Hillsdale, NJ: Erlbaum.

Brown, A. L. (1978). Knowing when, where, and how to remember: A problem of metacognition. In R. Glaser (Ed.), *Advances in instructional psychology* (pp. 77–165). Hillsdale, NJ: Erlbaum.

Brown, A. L., Bransford, J. D., Ferrara, R. A., & Campione, J. C. (1983). Learning, remembering, and understanding. In P. H. Mussen (Series Ed.) & J. H. Flavell & E. M. Markman (Vol. Eds.), *Handbook of child psychology: Vol. 3. Cognitive development* (pp. 77–166). New York: Wiley.

Brown, A. L., & Campione, J. C. (1990a). Communities of learning and thinking: A context by any other name. *Contributions to Human Development, 21,* 108–126.

Brown, A. L., & Campione, J. C. (1990b). Interactive learning environments and the teaching of science and mathematics. In M. Gardner, J. G. Greeno, F. Reif, A. H. Schoenfeld, A. DiSessa, & E. Stage (Eds.), *Toward a scientific practice of science education* (pp. 111–139). Hillsdale, NJ: Erlbaum.

Brown, A. L., & Day, J. D. (1983). Macrorules for summarizing texts: The development of expertise. *Journal of Verbal Learning and Verbal Behavior, 22,* 1–14.

Brown, A. L., & Palincsar, A. S. (1982). Inducing strategic learning from texts by means of informed self-control training. *Topics in Learning and Learning Disabilities, 2,* 1017.

Brown, A. L., & Smiley, S. S. (1977). Rating the importance of structural units of prose passages: A problem of metacognitive development. *Child Development, 48,* 1–8.

Brown, R., & Coy-Ogan, L. (1993). The evolution of transactional strategies instruction in one teacher's classroom. *Elementary School Journal, 94,* 221–233.

Brown, R., & Pressley, M. (1994). Self-regulated reading and getting meaning from text: The transactional strategies instruction model and its ongoing evaluation. In D. Schunk & B. Zimmerman (Eds.), *Self-regulation of learning and performance: Issues and educational applications.* Hillsdale, NJ: Erlbaum.

Brown, R., Pressley, M., Van Meter, P., & Schuder, T. (1996). A quasi-experimental validation of transactional strategies instruction with low-achieving second-grade readers. *Journal of Educational Psychology, 88,* 18–47.

Bruck, M. (1990). Word-recognition skills of adults with childhood diagnoses of dyslexia. *Developmental Psychology, 26,* 439–454.

Bruck, M. (1992). Persistence of dyslexics' phonological awareness deficits. *Developmental Psychology, 28,* 874–886.

Bruck, M., & Treiman, R. (1990). Phonological awareness and spelling in normal children and dyslexics: The case of initial consonant clusters. *Journal of Experimental Child Psychology, 50,* 156–178.

Bruck, M., & Waters, G. (1988). An analysis of the spelling errors of children who differ in their reading and spelling skills. *Applied Psycholinguistics, 9,* 77–92.

Bruer, J. T. (1993). *Schools for thought: A science of learning in the classroom.* Cambridge, MA: MIT Press.

Bruner, J. (1960). *The process of education.* Cambridge, MA: Harvard University Press.

Bus, A. G., Van IJzendoorn, M. H., & Pellegrini, A. D. (1995). Joint book reading makes for success in learning to read: A meta-analysis on intergenerational transmission of literacy. *Review of Educational Research, 65,* 1–21.

Bush, B. (1990). Parenting's best kept secret: Reading to your children. *Reader's Digest, 137,* 67–70.

Byrne, B. (1992). Studies in the acquisition procedure for reading: Rationale, hypotheses, and data. In P. B. Gough, L. C. Ehri, & R. Treiman (Eds.), *Reading acquisition* (pp. 1–34). Hillsdale, NJ: Erlbaum.

Byrne, B., & Fielding-Barnsley, R. (1989). Phonemic awareness and letter knowledge in the child's acquisition of the alphabetic principle. *Journal of Educational Psychology, 81,* 313–321.

Byrne, B., & Fielding-Barnsley, R. (1991). Evaluation of a program to teach phonemic awareness to young children. *Journal of Educational Psychology, 83,* 451–455.

Byrne, B., Freebody, P., & Gates, A. (1992). Longitudinal data on the relations of word-reading strategies to comprehension, reading time, and phonemic awareness. *Reading Research Quarterly, 27,* 141–151.

Calkins, L. M. (1986). *The art of teaching writing.* Portsmouth, NH: Heinemann.

Caravolas, M., & Bruck, M. (1993). The effect of oral and written language input on children's phonological awareness: A cross-linguistic study. *Journal of Experimental Child Psychology, 55,* 1–30.

Carbo, M., Dunn, R., & Dunn, K. (1986). *Teaching students to read through their individual learning styles.* Englewood Cliffs, NJ: Prentice-Hall.

Cardoso-Martins, C. (1991). Awareness of phonemes and alphabetic literacy acquisition. *British Journal of Educational Psychology, 61,* 164–173.

Carlisle, J. F. (1988). Knowledge of derivational morphology and spelling ability in fourth, sixth, and eighth graders. *Applied Psycholinguistics, 9,* 247–266.

Carter, L. G. (1984). The sustaining effects study of compensatory and elementary education. *Educational Researcher, 13,* 4–13.

Cassar, M. T. (1995). *Beginning spellers' knowledge about double letters in written English.* Unpublished master's thesis, Wayne State University, Detroit, MI.

Castle, J. M., Riach, J., & Nicholson, T. (1994). Getting off to a better start in reading and spelling: The effects of phonemic awareness instruction within a whole language program. *Journal of Educational Psychology, 86,* 350–359.

Cattell, J. M. (1947). The inertia of the eye and brain. In A. T. Poffenberger (Ed.), *James McKeen Cattell: Man of science.* York, PA: Science Press. (Original work published 1885)

Catts, H. W. (1989). Defining dyslexia as a developmental language disorder. *Annals of Dyslexia, 39,* 50–64.

Catts, H. W. (1991a). Early identification of reading disabilities. *Topics in Language Disorders, 12,* 1–16.

Catts, H. W. (1991b). Early identification of dyslexia: Evidence from a follow-up study of speech-language impaired children. *Annals of Dyslexia, 41,* 58–79.

Cavanaugh, J. C., & Borkowski, J. G. (1979). The metamemory-memory "connection": Effects of strategy training and maintenance. *Journal of General Psychology, 101,* 161–174.

Caverly, D. C., & Orlando, V. P. (1991). Textbook study strategies. In R. F. Flippo & D. C. Caverly (Eds.), *Teaching reading and study strategies at the college level* (pp. 86–165). Newark, DE: International Reading Association.

Chafe, W., & Danielewicz, J. (1987). Properties of spoken and written language. In R. Horowitz & S. J. Samuels (Eds.), *Comprehending oral and written language* (pp. 83–113). Orlando, FL: Academic Press.

Chall, J. S. (1967). *Learning to read: The great debate.* New York: McGraw-Hill.

Chall, J. S. (1983). *Stages of reading development.* New York: McGraw-Hill.

Chall, J. S., Conard, S. S., & Harris-Sharples, S. (1991). *Should textbooks challenge students? The case for easier and harder books.* New York: Teachers College Press.

Chomsky, C. (1971). Write first, read later. *Childhood Education, 41,* 296–299.

Chomsky, C. (1979). Approaching reading through invented spelling. In L. B. Resnick & P. A. Weaver (Eds.), *Theory and practice of early reading* (Vol. 2, pp. 43–65). Hillsdale, NJ: Erlbaum.

Chomsky, N. (1965). *Aspects of a theory of syntax.* Cambridge, MA: MIT Press.

Christopherson, S. L., Schultz, C. B., & Waern, Y. (1981). The effect of two contextual conditions on recall of a reading passage and on thought processes in reading. *Journal of Reading, 24,* 573–578.

Cipielewski, J., & Stanovich, K. E. (1992). Predicting growth in reading ability from children's exposure to print. *Journal of Experimental Child Psychology, 54,* 74–89.

Clark, J. M., & Paivio, A. (1991). Dual coding theory and education. *Educational Psychology Review, 3,* 149–210.

Clarke, L. K. (1988). Invented versus traditional spelling in first graders' writings: Effects on learning to spell and read. *Research in the Teaching of English, 22,* 281–309.

Clarke, M. M. (1976). *Young fluent readers: What can they teach us?* London: Heinemann.

Clay, M. M. (1979). *The early detection of reading difficulties* (3rd ed.). Portsmouth, NH: Heinemann.

Clifford, M. M. (1991). Risk taking: Theoretical, empirical, and educational considerations. *Educational Psychologist, 26,* 263–297.

Collins, A. M., Brown, J. S., & Larkin, K. M. (1980). Inferences in text understanding. In R. J. Spiro, B. C. Bruce, & W. F. Brewer (Eds.), *Theoretical issues in reading comprehension* (pp. 385–407). Hillsdale, NJ: Erlbaum.

Collins, A. M., & Quillian, M. R. (1969). Retrieval time from semantic memory. *Journal of Verbal Learning and Verbal Memory, 8,* 240–248.

Collins, C. (1991). Reading instruction that increases thinking abilities. *Journal of Reading, 34,* 510–516.

Coltheart, M., Curtis, B., Atkins, P., & Haller, M. (1993). Models of reading aloud: Dual-route and parallel-distributed-processing approaches. *Psychological Review, 100,* 589–608.

Cordon, L. A., & Day, J. D. (1996). Strategy use and comprehension on standardized reading tests. *Journal of Educational Psychology, 88,* 288–295.

Critchley, M., & Critchley, E. A. (1978). *Dyslexia defined.* London: Heinemann.

Cronbach, L. S., & Snow, R. E. (1977). *Aptitudes and instructional methods.* New York: Irvington.

Cunningham, A. E. (1990). Explicit versus implicit instruction in phonemic awareness. *Journal of Experimental Child Psychology, 50,* 429–444.

Cunningham, A. E., & Stanovich, K. E. (1990). Assessing print exposure and orthographic processing skill in children: A quick measure of reading experience. *Journal of Educational Psychology, 82,* 733–740.

Cunningham, A. E., & Stanovich, K. E. (1991). Tracking the unique effects of print exposure in children: Associations with vocabulary, general knowledge, and spelling. *Journal of Educational Psychology, 83,* 264–274.

Cunningham, A. E., & Stanovich, K. E. (1993). Children's literacy environments and early word recognition subskills. *Reading and Writing: An Interdisciplinary Journal, 5,* 193–204.

Cunningham, A. E., Stanovich, K. E., & Wilson, M. R. (1990). Cognitive variation in adult students differing in reading ability. In T. Carr & B. A. Levy (Eds.), *Reading and development: Component skills approaches* (pp. 129–159). San Diego, CA: Academic Press.

d'Anna, C. A., Zechmeister, E. B., & Hall, J. W. (1991). Toward a meaningful definition of vocabulary size. *Journal of Reading Behavior, 23,* 109–122.

Davey, B., & McBride, S. (1986). Effects of question-generation training on reading comprehension. *Journal of Educational Psychology, 78,* 256–262.

DeBaryshe, B. C., Rodarmel, S. L., Daly, B. A., & Huntley, L. (1992). *Shared picture book reading in the home: A language enrichment program for Head Start children.* Paper presented at the Conference of Human Development, Atlanta, GA.

DeFrancis, J. (1989). *Visible speech: The diverse oneness of writing systems.* Honolulu: University of Hawaii Press.

Derwing, B. L. (1992). Orthographic aspects of linguistic competence. In P. Downing, S. D. Lima, & M. Noonan (Eds.), *The linguistics of literacy.* Amsterdam, The Netherlands: John Benjamin.

Deshler, D. D., & Schumaker, J. B. (1988). An instructional model for teaching students how to learn. In J. L. Graden, J. E. Zins, & M. J. Curtis (Eds.), *Alternative educational delivery systems: Enhancing instructional options for all students* (pp. 391–411). Washington, DC: National Association of School Psychologists.

Dewey, J. (1913). *Interest and effort in education.* Boston: Riverside.

Diringer, D. (1968). *The alphabet.* London: Hutchinson.

Doctorow, M., Wittrock, M. C., & Marks, C. (1978). Generative processes in reading comprehension. *Journal of Educational Psychology, 70,* 109–118.

Doehring, D. G. (1968). *Patterns of impairment in specific reading disability.* Bloomington: Indiana University Press.

Doehring, D. G. (1976). Acquisition of rapid reading responses. *Monograph of the Society for Research in Child Development, 41.*

Dole, J. A., Duffy, G. G., Roehler, L. R., & Pearson, P. D. (1991). Moving from the old to the new: Research on reading comprehension instruction. *Review of Educational Research, 61,* 239–264.

Dooling, D. J., & Lachman, R. (1971). Effects of comprehension on retention of prose. *Journal of Experimental Psychology, 88,* 216–222.

Downing, J. (1979). *Reading and reasoning.* New York: Springer-Verlag.

Downing, J., & Oliver, P. (1973–1974). The child's conception of "a word." *Reading Research Quarterly, 9,* 568–582.

Duffy, G. G., & Roehler, L. R. (1989). Why strategy instruction is so difficult and what we need to do about it. In C. B. McCormick, G. Miller, & M. Pressley (Eds.), *Cognitive strategy research: From basic research to educational applications* (pp. 133–154). New York: Springer-Verlag.

Duffy, G. G., Roehler, L. R., Sivan, E., Rackliffe, G., Book, C., Meloth, M., Vavrus, L. G., Wesselman, R., Putnam, J., & Bassiri, D. (1987). Effects of explaining the reasoning associated with using reading strategies. *Reading Research Quarterly, 22,* 347–368.

Duffy, T. M., Haugen, D., Higgins, L., McCaffrey, M., Mehlenbacher, B., Burnett, R., Cochran, C., Sloane, S., Wallace, D., Smith, S., & Hill, C. (1989). Models for the design of instructional text. *Reading Research Quarterly, 24,* 434–457.

Durkin, D. (1966). The achievement of pre-school readers: Two longitudinal studies. *Reading Research Quarterly, 1,* 5–36.

Durkin, D. (1978–1979). What classroom observations reveal about reading comprehension instruction. *Reading Research Quarterly, 15,* 481–533.

Durkin, D. (1981). Reading comprehension instruction in five basal reading series. *Reading Research Quarterly, 22,* 347–368.

Durrell, D. D., & Catterson, J. H. (1980). *Manual of directions: Durrell analysis of reading difficulty* (Rev. ed.). New York: Psychological Corporation.

Durso, F. T., & Coggins, K. A. (1991). Organized instruction for the improvement of word knowledge skills. *Journal of Educational Psychology, 83,* 109–112.

Durst, R. K. (1984). The development of analytic writing. In A. N. Applebee (Ed.), *Contexts for learning to write: Studies of secondary school instruction* (pp. 79–102). Norwood, NJ: ABLEX.

Eco, U. (1978). *The open work.* Cambridge, MA: Harvard University Press.

Ehri, L. C. (1975). Word consciousness in readers and prereaders. *Journal of Educational Psychology, 67,* 204–212.

Ehri, L. C. (1976). Word learning in beginning readers and prereaders: Effects of form class and defining contexts. *Journal of Educational Psychology, 67,* 204–212.

Ehri, L. C. (1979). Linguistic insight: Threshold of reading acquisition. In T. G. Waller & G. E. MacKinnon (Eds.), *Reading research: Advances in theory and practice* (Vol. 1, pp. 63–111). New York: Academic Press.

Ehri, L. C. (1980). The development of orthographic images. In U. Frith (Ed.), *Cognitive processes in spelling* (pp. 311–338). London: Academic Press.

Ehri, L. C. (1986). Sources of difficulty in learning to spell and read. In M. L. Wolraich & D. Routh (Eds.), *Advances in developmental and behavioral pediatrics* (Vol. 7, pp. 121–195). Greenwich, CT: JAI Press.

Ehri, L. C. (1992). Reconceptualizing the development of sight word reading and its relationship to recoding. In P. B. Gough, L. C. Ehri, & R. Treiman (Eds.), *Reading acquisition* (pp. 107–143). Hillsdale, NJ: Erlbaum.

Ehri, L. C., & Saltmarsh, J. (1995). Beginning readers outperform older disabled readers in learning to read words by sight. *Reading and Writing: An Interdisciplinary Journal, 7,* 295–326.

Ehri, L. C., & Wilce, L. S. (1979). The mnemonic value of orthography among beginning readers. *Journal of Educational Psychology, 71,* 26–40.

Ehri, L. C., & Wilce, L. S. (1980). The influence of orthography on readers' conceptualization of the phonemic structure of words. *Applied Psycholinguistics, 1,* 371–385.

Ehri, L. C., & Wilce, L. S. (1986). The influence of spellings on speech: Are alveolar flaps /d/ or /t/? In D. B. Yaden & S. Templeton (Eds.), *Metalinguistic awareness and beginning literacy* (pp. 101–114). Portsmouth, NH: Heinemann.

Eimas, P. D., Siqueland, E. R., Jusczyk, P., & Vigorito, J. (1971). Speech perception in infants. *Science, 171,* 303–306.

El-Dinary, P. B., Pressley, M., & Schuder, T. (1992). Becoming a strategies teacher: An observational and interview study of three teachers learning transactional strategies instruction. In C. Kinzer & D. Leu (Eds.), *Forty-first Yearbook of the National Reading Conference* (pp. 453–462). Chicago: National Reading Conference.

Elkonin, D. B. (1973). U.S.S.R. In J. Downing (Ed.), *Comparative reading.* New York: Macmillan.

Elliott-Faust, D. J., & Pressley, M. (1986). Self-controlled training of comparison strategies increase children's comprehension monitoring. *Journal of Educational Psychology, 78,* 27–32.

Emig, J. (1971). *The composition process of twelfth graders.* Urbana, IL: National Council of Teachers of English.

Engelmann, S. (1969). *Preventing failure in the primary grades.* Chicago: Science Research Associates.

Englert, C. S., Raphael, T. E., Anderson, L. M., Anthony, H. M., & Stevens, D. D. (1991). Making strategies and self-talk visible: Writing instruction in regular and special education classrooms. *American Educational Research Journal, 28,* 337–372.

Faulkner, H. J., & Levy, B. A. (1994). How text difficulty and reader skill interact to produce differential reliance on word and content overlap in reading transfer. *Journal of Experimental Child Psychology, 58,* 1–24.

Feitelson, D. (1988). *Facts and fads in beginning reading: A cross-language perspective.* Norwood, NJ: ABLEX.

Feitelson, D., & Goldstein, Z. (1986). Patterns of book ownership and reading to young children in Israeli school-oriented and nonschool-oriented families. *The Reading Teacher, 39,* 924–930.

Feitelson, D., Goldstein, Z., Iraqi, J., & Share, D. L. (1993). Effects of listening to story reading on aspects of literacy acquisition in a diglossia situation. *Reading Research Quarterly, 28,* 70–79.

Ferreiro, E., & Teberosky, A. (1982). *Literacy before schooling.* New York: Heinemann.

Finucci, J. M., Isaacs, S. D., Whitehouse, C. C., & Childs, B. (1983). Classification of spelling errors and their relationship to reading ability, sex, grade placement, and intelligence. *Brain and Language, 20,* 340–355.

Fischer, F. W., Shankweiler, D., & Liberman, I. Y. (1985). Spelling proficiency and sensitivity to word structure. *Journal of Memory and Language, 24,* 423–441.

Fish, S. (1980). *Is there a text in this class?* Cambridge, MA: Harvard University Press.

Fitzgerald, J. (1987). Research on revision in writing. *Review of Educational Research, 57,* 481–506.

Fitzgerald, J. (1992). Variant views about good thinking during composing: Focus on revision. In M. Pressley, K. R. Harris, & J. T. Guthrie (Eds.), *Promoting academic competence and literacy in school* (pp. 337–358). San Diego, CA: Academic Press.

Fitzgerald, J., & Markham, L. (1987). Teaching children about revision in writing. *Cognition and Instruction, 4,* 3–24.

Flavell, J. H. (1971). Stage-related properties of cognitive development. *Cognitive Psychology, 2,* 421–453.

Flavell, J. H. (1977). *Cognitive development.* Englewood Cliffs, NJ: Prentice-Hall.

Flavell, J. H., & Wellman, H. M. (1977). Metamemory. In R. V. Kail & J. W. Hagen (Eds.), *Perspectives on the development of memory and cognition.* Hillsdale, NJ: Erlbaum.

Flavell, J. R., Miller, P., & Miller, S. (1993). *Cognitive development* (3rd ed.). Englewood Cliffs, NJ: Prentice-Hall.

Fletcher, J. M., Shaywitz, S. E., Shankweiler, D. P., Katz, L., Liberman, I. Y., Stuebing, K. K., Francis, D. J., Fowler, A. E., & Shaywitz, B. A. (1994). Cognitive profiles of reading disability: Comparisons of discrepancy and low achievement definitions. *Journal of Educational Psychology, 86,* 6–23.

Flippo, R. F., & Caverly, D. C. (1991). *Teaching reading and study strategies at the college level.* Newark, DE: International Reading Association.

Flower, L. S., & Hayes, J. R. (1980). The dynamics of composing: Making plans and juggling constraints. In L. Gregg & E. Steinberg (Eds.), *Cognitive processes in writing* (pp. 31–50). Hillsdale, NJ: Erlbaum.

Flower, L. S., & Hayes, J. R. (1981). A cognitive process theory of writing. *College Composition and Communication, 32,* 365–387.

Foorman, B. R., Francis, D. J., Novy, D. M., & Liberman, D. (1991). How letter-sound instruction mediates progress in first-grade reading and spelling. *Journal of Educational Psychology, 83,* 456–469.

Forrest-Pressley, D. L., & Gilles, L. A. (1983). Children's flexible use of strategies during reading. In M. Pressley & J. R. Levin (Eds.), *Cognitive strategy research: Educational applications.* New York: Springer-Verlag.

Forrest-Pressley, D. L., & Waller, T. G. (1984). *Cognition, metacognition, and reading.* New York: Springer-Verlag.

Fowler, A. E. (1991). How early phonological development might set the stage for phoneme awareness. In S. A. Brady & D. P. Shankweiler (Eds.), *Phonological processes in literacy: A tribute to Isabelle Y. Liberman* (pp. 97–117). Hillsdale, NJ: Erlbaum.

Fox, B., & Routh, D. K. (1975). Analyzing spoken language into words, syllables, and phonemes: A developmental study. *Journal of Psycholinguistic Research, 4,* 331–342.

Fox, B., & Routh, D. K. (1984). Phonemic analysis and synthesis as word attack skills: Revisited. *Journal of Educational Psychology, 76,* 1059–1064.

Friedrich, F. J., Schadler, M., & Juola, J. F. (1979). Developmental changes in units of processing in reading. *Journal of Experimental Child Psychology, 28,* 344–358.

Frith, U. (1980). Unexpected spelling problems. In U. Frith (Ed.), *Cognitive processes in spelling* (pp. 495–516). New York: Academic Press.

Gaskins, I. W., Anderson, R. C., Pressley, M., Cunicelli, E. A., & Satlow, E. (1993). Six teachers' dialogue during cognitive process instruction. *Elementary School Journal, 93,* 277–304.

Gelb, I. J. (1963). *A study of writing* (2nd ed.). Chicago: University of Chicago Press.

Gentry, J. R. (1982). An analysis of developmental spelling in GNYS AT WRK. *The Reading Teacher, 36,* 192–200.

Gerber, M. M. (1985). Spelling as concept-governed problem solving: Learning disabled and normally achieving students. In B. A. Hutson (Ed.), *Advances in reading/language research* (Vol. 3). Greenwich, CT: JAI Press.

Gibson, E. J., & Levin, J. (1975). *The psychology of reading.* Cambridge, MA: MIT Press.

Gibson, E. J., Osser, H., & Pick, A. D. (1963). A study of the development of grapheme-phoneme correspondences. *Journal of Verbal Learning and Verbal Behavior, 2,* 142–146.

Gleitman, L. R., & Rozin, P. (1977). The structure and acquisition of reading: I. Relations between orthographies and the structure of language. In A. S. Reber & D. L. Scarborough (Eds.), *Toward a psychology of reading* (pp. 1–53). Hillsdale, NJ: Erlbaum.

Goldstein, D. M. (1976). Cognitive-linguistic functioning and learning to read in preschoolers. *Journal of Educational Psychology, 68,* 680–688.

Goodman, K. S. (1965). A linguistic study of cues and miscues in reading. *Elementary English, 42,* 639–643.

Goodman, K. S. (1986). *What's whole in whole language?* Portsmouth, NH: Heinemann.

Goodman, K. S. (1993). *Phonics phacts.* Portsmouth, NH: Heinemann.

Goswami, U., & Bryant, P. (1990). *Phonological skills and learning to read.* Hillsdale, NJ: Erlbaum.

Gottardo, A., Stanovich, K. E., & Siegel, L. S. (in press). The relationships between phonological sensitivity, syntactic processing, and verbal working memory in the reading performance of third-grade children. *Journal of Experimental Child Psychology, 56,* 563–582.

Gough, P. B., & Hillinger, M. L. (1980). Learning to read: An unnatural act. *Bulletin of the Orton Society, 30,* 179–196.

Graham, S., & Harris, K. R. (1988). Instructional recommendations for teaching writing to exceptional children. *Exceptional Children, 54,* 506–512.

Graham, S., & Harris, K. R. (1992). Self-regulated strategy development: Programmatic research in writing. In B. Y. L. Wong (Ed.), *Contemporary intervention research in learning disabilities: An international perspective* (pp. 47–64). New York: Springer-Verlag.

Graham, S., & MacArthur, C. (1988). Improving learning disabled students' skill at revising essays produced on a word processor: Self-instructional strategy training. *Journal of Special Education, 22,* 133–152.

Graves, D. (1983). *Writing: Teachers and children at work.* Portsmouth, NH: Heinemann.

Graves, D. H. (1978). *Balance the basics: Let them write.* New York: Ford Foundation.

Graves, M. F., & Slater, W. H. (1991). A response to "Instructional texts rewritten by five expert teams." *Journal of Educational Psychology, 83,* 147–148.

Gray, J. R. (1988). *National writing project: Model and program design* (National Writing Project). Berkeley: University of California.

Griffith, P. L. (1992). Phonemic awareness helps first graders invent spellings and third graders remember correct spellings. *Journal of Reading Behavior, 23,* 215–234.

Guthrie, J. T., & Greany, V. (1991). Literacy acts. In R. Barr, M. L. Kamil, P. Mosenthal, & P. D. Pearson (Eds.), *Handbook of reading research* (Vol. 2, pp. 68–96). New York: Longman.

Guthrie, J. T., Schafer, W. D., & Hutchinson, S. R. (1991). Relations of document literacy and prose literacy to occupational and societal characteristics of young black and white adults. *Reading Research Quarterly, 26,* 30–48.

Guttman, J., Levin, J. R., & Pressley, M. (1977). Pictures, partial pictures, and children's oral prose learning. *Journal of Educational Psychology, 69,* 473–480.

Halliday, M. A. K. (1987). Spoken and written modes of meaning. In R. Horowitz & S. J. Samuels (Eds.), *Comprehending oral and written language* (pp. 55–82). Orlando, FL: Academic Press.

Hare, V. C. (1981). Readers' problem identification and problem solving strategies for high- and low-knowledge articles. *Journal of Reading Behavior, 13,* 359–365.

Harris, K. R., & Graham, S. (1992). Self-regulated strategy development: A part of the writing process. In M. Pressley, K. R. Harris, & J. T. Guthrie (Eds.), *Promoting academic competence and literacy in school* (pp. 277–309). San Diego, CA: Academic Press.

Hatcher, P., Hulme, C., & Ellis, A. W. (1994). Ameliorating early reading failure by integrating the teaching of reading and phonological skills: The phonological linkage hypothesis. *Child Development, 65,* 41–57.

Hayes, D. P., & Grether, J. (1983). The school year and vacations: When do students learn? *Cornell Journal of Social Relations, 17,* 56–71.

Heap, J. L. (1982). Understanding classroom events: A critique of Durkin, with an alternative. *Journal of Reading Behavior, 14,* 391–411.

Heath, S. B. (1983). *Ways with words.* Cambridge, England: Cambridge University Press.

Hebb, D. O. (1949). *The organization of behavior.* New York: Wiley.

Henderson, E. (1985). *Teaching spelling.* Boston: Houghton Mifflin.

Henderson, L., & Chard, J. (1980). The readers' implicit knowledge of orthographic structure. In U. Frith (Ed.), *Cognitive processes in spelling* (pp. 85–116). New York: Academic Press.

Hidi, S. (1990). Interest and its contribution as a mental resource for learning. *Review of Educational Research, 60,* 549–571.

Hinshelwood, J. (1900). Congenital word-blindness. *Lancet, 1,* 1506–1508.

Hinshelwood, J. (1917). *Congenital word-blindness.* London: Lewis.

Hodges, C. A. (1980). Commentary: Toward a broader definition of comprehension instruction. *Reading Research Quarterly, 15,* 299–306.

Hoffman, J. V. (1991). Teacher and school effects in learning to read. In R. Barr, M. L. Kamil, P. B. Mosenthal, & P. D. Pearson (Eds.), *Handbook of reading research* (Vol. 2, pp. 911–950). New York: Longman.

Holden, M. H., & MacGinitie, W. H. (1972). Children's conceptions of word boundaries in speech and print. *Journal of Educational Psychology, 63,* 551–557.

Holland, K. E., Hungerford, R. A., & Ernst, S. B. (1993). *Journeying: Children responding to literature.* Portsmouth, NH: Heinemann.

Huggins, A. W. F., & Adams, M. J. (1980). Syntactic aspects of reading comprehension. In R. J. Spiro, B. C. Bruce, & W. F. Brewer (Eds.), *Theoretical issues in reading comprehension* (pp. 87–112). Hillsdale, NJ: Erlbaum.

Hurford, D. P., Schauf, J. D., Bunce, L., Blaich, T., & Moore, K. (1994). Early identification of children at risk for reading disabilities. *Journal of Learning Disabilities, 27,* 371–382.

Hutchins, E. (1991). The social organization of distributed cognition. In L. Resnick, J. M. Levine, & S. D. Teasley (Eds.), *Perspectives on socially shared cognition* (pp. 283–307). Washington, DC: American Psychological Association.

Huttenlocher, J. (1964). Children's language: Word-phrase relationship. *Science, 143,* 264–265.

Inhoff, A. W., & Briihl, D. (1991). Semantic processing of unattended text during selective reading: How the eyes see it. *Perception and Psychophysics, 49,* 289–294.

Jacobs, J. E., & Paris, S. G. (1987). Children's metacognition about reading: Issues in definition, measurement, and instruction. *Educational Psychologist, 22,* 255–278.

Jakobson, R., Fant, C. G. M., & Halle, M. (1961). *Preliminaries to speech analysis: The distinctive features and their correlates.* Cambridge, MA: MIT Press.

Jansky, J., & de Hirsch, K. (1972). *Preventing reading failure: Prediction, diagnosis, intervention.* New York: Harper & Row.

Jenkins, J. R., Bausell, R. B., & Jenkins, L. M. (1972). Comparison of letter name and letter sound training as transfer variables. *American Educational Research Journal, 9,* 75–86.

Jensen, A. R. (1962). Spelling errors and the serial-position effect. *Journal of Educational Psychology, 53,* 105–109.

Johns, J. C., & McNamara, L. P. (1980). The SQ3R study technique: A forgotten research target. *Journal of Reading, 23,* 705–708.

Jones, D. (1956). *An outline of English phonetics.* Cambridge, England: Heffner.

Jones, M. (1990). Children's writing. In R. Grieve & M. Hughes (Eds.), *Understanding children: Essays in honor of Margaret Donaldson* (pp. 94–120). Oxford, England: Blackwell.

Jorm, A. F., Share, D. L., MacLean, R., & Matthews, R. (1984). Phonological confusability in short-term memory for sentences as a predictor of reading ability. *British Journal of Psychology, 75,* 393–400.

Juel, C. (1980). Comparison of word identification strategies with varying context, word type, and reader skill. *Reading Research Quarterly, 15,* 358–376.

Juel, C. (1988). Learning to read and write: A longitudinal study of 54 children from first through fourth grades. *Journal of Educational Psychology, 80,* 417–447.

Juel, C. (1994). *Learning to read and write in one elementary school.* New York: Springer-Verlag.

Juel, C., Griffith, P. L., & Gough, P. B. (1986). Acquisition of literacy: A longitudinal study of children in first and second grade. *Journal of Educational Psychology, 78,* 243–255.

Juel, C., & Roper-Schneider, D. (1985). The influence of basal readers on first grade reading. *Reading Research Quarterly, 20,* 134–152.

Juola, J. F., Schadler, M., Chabot, R. J., & McCaughey, M. W. (1978). The development of visual information processing skills related to reading. *Journal of Experimental Child Psychology, 25,* 459–476.

Just, M. A., & Carpenter, P. A. (1980). A theory of reading: From eye fixations to comprehension. *Psychological Review, 87,* 329–354.

Kampwirth, T. J., & Bates, M. (1980). Modality preference and teaching method: A review of the research. *Academic Therapy, 15,* 597–605.

Karolides, N. J. (1992). *Reader response in the classroom: Evoking and interpreting meaning in literature.* New York: Longman.

Katz, R. (1986). Phonological deficiencies in children with reading disability: Evidence from an object-naming task. *Cognition, 22,* 225–257.

Kellogg, R. T. (1990). Effectiveness of prewriting strategies as a function of task demands. *American Journal of Psychology, 103,* 327–342.

Kellogg, R. T. (1993). Observations on the psychology of thinking and writing. *Composition Studies, 21,* 3–41.

Kellogg, R. T. (1994). *The psychology of writing.* New York: Oxford University Press.

Kennedy, B. A., & Miller, D. J. (1976). Persistent use of verbal rehearsal as a function of information about its value. *Child Development, 47,* 566–569.

Kintsch, W., & van Dijk, T. (1978). Toward a model of text comprehension and production. *Psychological Review, 85,* 363–394.

Kirtley, C., Bryant, P., MacLean, M., & Bradley, L. (1989). Rhyme, rime, and the onset of reading. *Journal of Experimental Child Psychology, 48,* 224–245.

Klatt, D. H. (1975). Voice onset time, frication, and aspiration in word-initial consonant clusters. *Journal of Speech and Hearing Research, 18,* 686–706.

Kohlberg, L., Yaeger, J., & Hjertholm, E. (1968). Private speech: Four studies and a review of theories. *Child Development, 39,* 691–736.

Kolers, P. A. (1968). Introduction. In E. B. Huey (Ed.), *The psychology and pedagogy of reading* (pp. xiii-xxxix). Cambridge, MA: MIT Press.

Kooi, B. Y., Schutz, R. E., & Baker, R. L. (1965). Spelling errors and the serial-position effect. *Journal of Educational Psychology, 56,* 334–336.

Langer, J. A. (1986). *Children reading and writing: Structures and strategies.* Norwood, NJ: ABLEX.

Langer, J. A., & Applebee, A. N. (1984). Language, learning, and interaction: A framework for improving the teaching of writing. In A. N. Applebee (Ed.), *Contexts for learning to write: Studies of secondary school instruction* (pp. 169–181). Norwood, NJ: ABLEX.

Langer, J. A., & Applebee, A. N. (1987). *How writing shapes thinking: A study of teaching and learning.* Champaign, IL: National Council of Teachers of English.

Lansman, M., Smith, J. B., & Weber, I. (1990). *Using computer-generated protocols to study writers' planning strategies* (Technical Rep. No. TR90-033). Chapel Hill: University of North Carolina, Department of Computer Science.

Lashley, K. S. (1951). The problem of serial order in behavior. In L. A. Jeffries (Ed.), *Cerebral mechanisms in behavior* (pp. 112–136). New York: Wiley.

Lavine, L. O. (1977). Differentiation of letterlike forms in pre-reading children. *Developmental Psychology, 13,* 89–94.

Lefton, L. A., & Spragins, A. B. (1974). Orthographic structure and reading experience affect the transfer from iconic to short-term memory. *Journal of Experimental Psychology, 103,* 775–781.

Levin, I., & Korat, O. (1993). Sensitivity to phonological, morphological, and semantic cues in early reading and writing in Hebrew. *Merrill-Palmer Quarterly, 39,* 213–232.

Levin, I., & Tolchinsky-Landsmann, L. (1989). Becoming literate: Referential and phonetic strategies in early reading and writing. *International Journal of Behavioural Development, 12,* 369–384.

Levin, J. R. (1973). What have we learned about maximizing what children learn? In J. R. Levin & V. L. Allen (Eds.), *Cognitive learning in childen: Theories and strategies* (pp. 105–134). New York: Academic Press.

Levin, J. R. (1982). Pictures as prose-learning devices. In A. Flammer & W. Kintsch (Eds.), *Discourse processing* (pp. 412–444). Amsterdam, The Netherlands: North-Holland.

Levin, J. R. (1983). Pictorial strategies for school learning: Practical illustrations. In M. Pressley & J. R. Levin (Eds.), *Cognitive strategy research: Educational applications* (pp. 213–237). New York: Springer-Verlag.

Levin, J. R., & Lesgold, A. M. (1978). On pictures in prose. *Educational Communication and Technology, 26,* 233–243.

Levin, J. R., & Mayer, R. E. (1993). Understanding illustrations in text. In B. K. Britton, A. Woodward, & M. Binkley (Eds.), *Learning from textbooks: Theory and practice* (pp. 95–113). Hillsdale, NJ: Erlbaum.

Levin, J. R., & Pressley, M. (1981). Improving children's prose comprehension: Selected strategies that seem to succeed. In C. M. Santa & B. L. Hayes (Eds.), *Children's prose comprehension: Research and practice* (pp. 44–71). Newark, DE: International Reading Association.

Lewkowicz, N. K. (1980). Phonemic awareness training: What to teach and how to teach it. *Journal of Educational Psychology, 72,* 686–700.

Liberman, A. M., Cooper, F., Shankweiler, D., & Studdert-Kennedy, M. (1967). Perception of the speech code. *Psychological Review, 74,* 431–461.

Liberman, A. M., & Mattingly, I. G. (1989). A specialization for speech perception. *Science, 243,* 489–494.

Liberman, I. Y. (1973). Segmentation of the spoken word and reading acquisition. *Bulletin of the Orton Society, 23,* 65–77.

Liberman, I. Y., & Liberman, A. M. (1990). Whole language vs. code emphasis: Underlying assumptions and their implications for reading instruction. *Annals of Dyslexia, 40,* 51–76.

Liberman, I. Y., Shankweiler, D., Fischer, F. W., & Carter, B. (1974). Reading and the awareness of linguistic segments. *Journal of Experimental Child Psychology, 18,* 201–212.

Liberman, I. Y., Shankweiler, D., Liberman, A. M., Fowler, C., & Fischer, F. W. (1977). Phonetic segmentation and recoding in the beginning reader. In A. S. Reber & D. L. Scarborough (Eds.), *Toward a psychology of reading* (pp. 207–225). Hillsdale, NJ: Erlbaum.

Lie, A. (1991). Effects of a training program for stimulating skills in word analysis in first-grade children. *Reading Research Quarterly, 26,* 234–250.

Lieberman, P., Meskill, R. H., Chatillon, M., & Schupack, H. (1985). Phonetic speech perception deficits in dyslexia. *Journal of Speech and Hearing Research, 28,* 480–486.

Lindamood, C. H., & Lindamood, P. C. (1975). *Auditory discrimination in depth.* Boston: Teaching Resources Corporation.

Loban, W. (1976). *Language development: Kindergarten through grade twelve* (NCTE Research Report No. 18). Urbana, IL: National Council of Teachers of English.

Lonigan, C. (1993). Somebody read me a story: Evaluation of a shared reading program in low-income daycare. *Society for Research in Child Development Abstracts, 9,* 219.

Lorch, R. F., Jr. (1989). Text-signaling devices and their effects on reading and memory processes. *Educational Psychology Review, 1,* 209–234.

Lotz, J., Abramson, A. S., Gerstman, L. J., Ingemann, F., & Nemser, W. J. (1960). The perception of English stops by speakers of English, Spanish, Hungarian, and Thai: A tape-cutting experiment. *Language and Speech, 3,* 71–77.

Lovett, M. W., Borden, S. L., DeLuca, T., Lacerenza, L., Benson, N. J., & Blackstone, D. (1994). Treating the core deficits of developmental dyslexia: Evidence of transfer of learning after phonologically- and strategy-based reading training programs. *Developmental Psychology, 30,* 805–822.

Lovett, M. W., Ransby, M. J., Hardwick, N., Johns, M. S., & Donaldson, S. A. (1989). Can dyslexia be treated? Treatment-specific and generalized treatment effects in dyslexic children's response to remediation. *Brain and Language, 37,* 90–121.

Lovett, M. W., Warren-Chaplin, P. M., Ransby, M. J., & Borden, S. L. (1990). Training the word recognition skills of reading disabled children: Treatment and transfer effects. *Journal of Educational Psychology, 82,* 769–780.

Lundberg, I., Frost, J., & Petersen, O. P. (1988). Effects of an extensive program for stimulating phonological awareness in preschool children. *Reading Research Quarterly, 23,* 263–284.

Lundberg, I., Olofsson, A., & Wall, S. (1980). Reading and spelling skills in the first school years predicted from phonemic awareness skills in kindergarten. *Scandinavian Journal of Psychology, 21,* 159–173.

Lundberg, I., & Torneus, M. (1978). Nonreaders' awareness of the basic relationship between spoken and written words. *Journal of Experimental Child Psychology, 25,* 404–412.

Lyon, G. R. (1995). Toward a definition of dyslexia. *Annals of Dyslexia, 45,* 20-45.

Lytle, S. L. (1982). *Exploring comprehension style: A study of twelfth-grade readers' transactions with texts.* Doctoral dissertation, University of Pennsylvania. (University Microfilms No. 82-27292)

MacGinitie, W. (1976). Difficulty with logical operations. *Reading Teacher, 29,* 371–375.

MacLean, M., Bryant, P., & Bradley, L. (1987). Rhymes, nursery rhymes, and reading in early childhood. *Merrill-Palmer Quarterly, 33,* 255–281.

MalKcot, A. (1960). Vowel nasality as a distinctive feature in American English. *Language, 36,* 222–229.

Mandler, J. M. (1984). *Stories, scripts, and scenes: Aspects of schema theory.* Hillsdale, NJ: Erlbaum.

Mann, V. A. (1984). Longitudinal prediction and prevention of early reading difficulty. *Annals of Dyslexia, 34,* 115–136.

Mann, V. A. (1986). Phonological awareness: The role of reading experience. *Cognition, 24,* 65–92.

Mann, V. A., & Liberman, I. Y. (1984). Phonological awareness and verbal short-term memory. *Journal of Learning Disabilities, 17,* 592–598.

Mann, V. A., Tobin, P., & Wilson, R. (1987). Measuring phonological awareness through the invented spellings of kindergartners. *Merrill-Palmer Quarterly, 33,* 365–391.

Manzo, A. V. (1968). *Improving reading comprehension through reciprocal questioning.* Unpublished doctoral dissertation, Syracuse University, Syracuse, NY.

Marbe, K. (1964). Experimentell-psychologische: Untersuchungen uber das Urteil. Leipzig: Engelmann. In J. Mandler & G. Mandler (Eds. & Trans.), *Thinking: From association to gestalt* (pp. 143–148). New York: Wiley. (Original work published 1901)

Marcel, T. (1980). Phonological awareness and phonological representation: Investigation of a specific spelling problem. In U. Frith (Ed.), *Cognitive processes in spelling* (pp. 373–403). London: Academic Press.

Markman, E. M. (1977). Realizing that you don't understand: A preliminary investigation. *Child Development, 46,* 986–992.

Markman, E. M. (1981). Comprehension monitoring. In W. P. Dickson (Ed.), *Children's oral communication skills* (pp. 61–84). New York: Academic Press.

Marks, M., Pressley, M., Coley, J. D., Craig, S., Gardner, R., Rose, W., & DePinto, T. (1993). Teachers' adaptations of reciprocal teaching: Progress toward a classroom-compatible version of reciprocal teaching. *Elementary School Journal, 94,* 267–283.

Marmurek, H. H. C., & Rinaldo, R. (1992). The development of letter and syllable effects in categorization, reading aloud, and picture naming. *Journal of Experimental Child Psychology, 53,* 277–299.

Marshall, J. D. (1984). Schooling and the composing process. In A. N. Applebee (Ed.), *Contexts for learning to write: Studies of secondary school instruction* (pp. 103–119). Norwood, NJ: ABLEX.

Mason, J. M. (1980). When do children begin to read: An exploration of our year old children's letter and word reading competencies. *Reading Research Quarterly, 15,* 203–227.

Masonheimer, P. E. (1982). *Alphabetic identification by Spanish speaking three to five year olds.* Unpublished manuscript, University of California, Santa Barbara.

Masonheimer, P. E., Drum, P. A., & Ehri, L. C. (1984). Does environmental print identification lead children into word reading? *Journal of Reading Behavior, 16,* 257–271.

Mathews, M. M. (1966). *Teaching to read: Historically considered.* Chicago: University of Chicago Press.

Mathison, S. (1988). Why triangulate? *Educational Researcher, 17*(2), 13–17.

McCallister, J. (1930). Reading difficulties in studying content subjects. *Elementary School Journal, 31,* 191–201.

McCaughey, M. W., Juola, J. F., Schadler, M., & Ward, N. J. (1980). Whole-word units are used before orthographic knowledge in perceptual development. *Journal of Experimental Child Psychology, 30,* 411–421.

McClelland, J. L., & Johnston, J. C. (1977). The role of familiar units in perception of words and nonwords. *Perception and Psychophysics, 22,* 249–261.

McCormick, C. E., & Mason, J. M. (1986). Intervention procedures for increasing preschool children's interest in and knowledge about reading. In W. H. Teale & E. Sulzby (Eds.), *Emergent literacy: Writing and reading* (pp. 90–115). Norwood, NJ: ABLEX.

McKeown, M. G., Beck, I. L., Omanson, R. C., & Perfetti, C. A. (1983). The effects of long-term vocabulary instruction on reading comprehension: A replication. *Journal of Reading Behavior, 15,* 3–18.

McKeown, M. G., Beck, I. L., Omanson, R. C., & Pople, M. T. (1985). Some effects of the nature and frequency of vocabulary instruction on the knowledge and use of words. *Reading Research Quarterly, 20,* 522–535.

McKeown, M. G., Beck, I. L., Sinatra, G. M., & Loxterman, J. A. (1992). The contribution of prior knowledge and coherent text to comprehension. *Reading Research Quarterly, 27,* 78–93.

McNeill, D. (1970). The development of language. In P. H. Mussen (Ed.), *Carmichael's manual of child psychology* (pp. 1061–1162). New York: Wiley.

Mehan, H. (1979). *Social organization in the classroom.* Cambridge, MA: Harvard University Press.

Meichenbaum, D. (1977). *Cognitive behavior modification.* New York: Plenum Press.

Meichenbaum, D., & Asarnow, J. (1979). Cognitive-behavioral modification and metacognitive development. In P. C. Kendall & S. D. Hollon (Eds.), *Cognitive-behavioral interventions: Theory, research, and procedures* (pp. 11–35). New York: Academic Press.

Meichenbaum, D., & Goodman, J. (1969a). The developmental control of operant motor responding by verbal operants. *Journal of Experimental Child Psychology, 7,* 553–565.

Meichenbaum, D., & Goodman, J. (1969b). Reflection-impulsivity and verbal control of motor behavior. *Child Development, 40,* 785–797.

Meichenbaum, D., & Goodman, J. (1971). Training impulsive children to talk to themselves: A means of developing self-control. *Journal of Abnormal Psychology, 77,* 115–126.

Mendenhall, J. E. (1930). The characteristics of spelling errors. *Journal of Educational Psychology, 21,* 648–656.

Meyer, B. J. F. (1975). *The organization of prose and its effects on memory.* Amsterdam, The Netherlands: North-Holland.

Meyer, B. J. F., Brandt, D. H., & Bluth, G. J. (1980). Use of top-level structure in text: Key for reading comprehension of ninth-grade students. *Reading Research Quarterly, 16,* 72–103.

Meyer, D. E., Schvaneveldt, R. W., & Ruddy, M. G. (1975). Loci of contextual effects on word recognition. In P. M. A. Rabbitt & S. Dornic (Eds.), *Attention and performance* (Vol. 5). New York: Academic Press.

Miller, G. A., & Nicely, P. E. (1955). An analysis of perceptual confusions among some English consonants. *Journal of the Acoustical Society of America, 27,* 338–352.

Miller, P., & Limber, J. (1985). *The acquisition of consonant clusters: A paradigm problem.* Paper presented at the Boston University Conference on Language Development, Boston, MA.

Miller, S. D., & Yochum, N. (1991). Asking students about the nature of their reading difficulties. *Journal of Reading Behavior, 23,* 465–485.

Mitchell, R. (1992). *Testing for learning: How new approaches to evaluation can improve American schools.* New York: Free Press.

Monroe, M. (1932). *Children who cannot read.* Chicago: University of Chicago Press.

Morais, J. (1991). Constraints on the development of phonemic awareness. In S. Brady & D. P. Shankweiler (Eds.), *Phonological processes in literacy* (pp. 5–27). Hillsdale, NJ: Erlbaum.

Morais, J., Bertelson, P., Cary, L., & Alegria, J. (1986). Literacy training and speech segmentation. *Cognition, 24,* 45–64.

Morgan, W. P. (1896). A case of congenital word-blindness. *British Medical Journal, 11,* 378.

Morisset, C. (1993). SPARK: Seattle's parents are reading to kids. *Society for Research in Child Development Abstracts, 9,* 219.

Mullis, I. V. S., Campbell, J. R., & Farstrup, A. E. (1993). *NAEP 1992 reading report card for the nation and the states.* Princeton, NJ: Educational Testing Service.

Muter, V., Hulme, C., Snowling, M., & Taylor, S. (1995). Segmentation, not rhyming, predicts early progress in learning to read. *Journal of Experimental Child Psychology, 59,* 64–86.

Nagy, W., & Anderson R. (1984). How many words are there in printed school English? *Reading Research Quarterly, 19,* 304–330.

Nagy, W. E., Anderson, R. C., & Herman, P. A. (1987). Learning word meanings from context during normal reading. *American Educational Research Journal, 24,* 237–270.

Needlman, R., & Fitzgerald, K. (1993). Pediatric interventions to promote picture book sharing. *Society for Research in Child Development Abstracts, 9,* 220.

Neisser, U. (1967). *Cognitive psychology,* New York: Appleton-Century-Crofts.

Nelson, H. E. (1980). Analysis of spelling errors in normal and dyslexic children. In U. Frith (Ed.), *Cognitive processes in spelling* (pp. 475–493). London: Academic Press.

Nicholson, T. (1991). Do children read words better in context or in lists? A classic study revisited. *Journal of Educational Psychology, 83,* 444–450.

Nicholson, T., Bailey, J., & MacArthur, J. (1991). Context cues in reading: The gap between research and popular opinion. *Journal of Reading, Writing, and Learning Disabilities, 7,* 33–41.

Nicholson, T., Lillas, C., & Rzoska, A. (1988). Have we been misled by miscues? *The Reading Teacher, 42,* 6–10.

Niles, J. A., Grunder, A., & Wimmer, C. (1977). The effects of grade level and school setting on the development of sensitivity to orthographic structure. In P. D. Pearson & J. Hansen

(Eds.), *Reading: Theory, research, and practice* (pp. 183–186). Clemson, SC: National Reading Conference.

Ninio, A. (1980). Picture book reading in mother-infant dyads belonging to two subgroups in Israel. *Child Development, 51,* 587–590.

Ninio, A., & Bruner, J. (1978). The achievement and antecedents of labeling. *Journal of Child Language, 5,* 1–15.

Nist, S. L., & Diehl, W. (1990). *Developing textbook thinking* (2nd ed.). Lexington, MA: Heath.

Nolte, R. Y., & Singer, H. (1985). Active comprehension: Teaching a process of reading comprehension and its effects on reading achievement. *The Reading Teacher, 39,* 24–31.

Nurss, J. R. (1979). Assessment of readiness. In T. G. Waller & G. E. MacKinnon (Eds.), *Reading research: Advances in theory and practice* (Vol. 1). New York: Academic Press.

O'Donnell, R. C., Griffin, W. J., & Norris, R. C. (1967). *Syntax of kindergarten and elementary school children: A transformational analysis* (NCTE Research Report No. 8). Urbana, IL: National Council of Teachers of English.

Ohnmacht, D. C. (1969). *The effects of letter knowledge on achievement in reading in the first grade.* Paper presented at the meeting of the American Educational Research Association, Los Angeles.

Olshavsky, J. E. (1976–1977). Reading as problem solving: An investigation of strategies. *Reading Research Quarterly, 12,* 654–674.

Olson, G. M., Mack, R. L., & Duffy, S. A. (1981). Cognitive aspects of genre. *Poetics, 10,* 283–315.

O'Rourke, J. P. (1974). *Toward a science of vocabulary development.* The Hague: Mouton.

Orton, S. T. (1925). "Word-blindness" in school children. *Archives of Neurology and Psychiatry, 14,* 581–615.

Orton, S. T. (1937). *Reading, writing, and speech problems in children.* London: Chapman & Hall.

Paivio, A. (1971). *Imagery and verbal processes.* New York: Holt, Rinehart and Winston.

Paivio, A. (1986). *Mental representations: A dual-coding approach.* New York: Oxford University Press.

Palincsar, A. S. (1986). The role of dialogue in providing scaffolded instruction. *Educational Psychologist, 21,* 73–98.

Palincsar, A. S., & Brown, A. L. (1984). Reciprocal teaching of comprehension-fostering and monitoring activities. *Cognition and Instruction, 1,* 117–175.

Palincsar, A. S., Brown, A. L., & Martin, S. M. (1987). Peer interaction in reading comprehension instruction. *Educational Psychologist, 22,* 231–253.

PTA (Parent Teachers Association). (1987). How to encourage a love of reading [Special advertising section]. *Redbook, 169,* 15–21.

Paris, S. G., Cross, D. R., & Lipson, M. Y. (1984). Informed strategies for learning: A program to improve children's reading awareness and comprehension. *Journal of Educational Psychology, 76,* 1239–1252.

Paris, S. G., & Jacobs, J. E. (1984). The benefits of informed instruction for children's reading awareness and comprehension skills. *Child Development, 55,* 2083–2093.

Paris, S. G., Lipson, M. Y., & Wixson, K. K. (1983). Becoming a strategic reader. *Contemporary Educational Psychology, 8,* 293–316.

Paris, S. G., & Oka, E. R. (1986). Children's reading strategies, metacognition, and motivation. *Developmental Review, 6,* 25–56.

Paris, S. G., & Upton, L. R. (1976). Children's memory for inferential relationships in prose. *Child Development, 47,* 660–668.

Patterson, C. J., & Mischel, W. (1976). Effects of temptation-inhibiting and task-facilitating plans on self-control. *Journal of Personality and Social Psychology, 33,* 209–217.

Payne, A. C., Whitehurst, G. J., & Angell, A. L. (1994). The role of home literacy environment in the development of language ability in preschool children from low-income families. *Early Childhood Research Quarterly, 9,* 427–440.

Pearson, P. D., & Fielding, L. (1991). Comprehension instruction. In R. Barr, M. L. Kamil, P. B. Mosenthal, & P. D. Pearson (Eds.), *Handbook of reading research* (Vol. 2, pp. 815–860). New York: Longman.

Pearson, P. D., & Johnson, D. D. (1978). *Teaching reading comprehension.* New York: Holt, Rinehart and Winston.

Perera, K. (1988). Language acquisition and writing. In P. Fletcher & M. Garman (Eds.), *Language acquisition* (pp. 494–518). New York: Cambridge University Press.

Perfetti, C. A. (1985). *Reading ability.* New York: Oxford University Press.

Perfetti, C. A. (1992). The representation problem in reading acquisition. In P. B. Gough, L. C. Ehri, & R. Treiman (Eds.), *Reading acquisition* (pp. 145–174). Hillsdale, NJ: Erlbaum.

Perfetti, C. A., Goldman, S., & Hogaboam, T. (1979). Reading skill and the identification of words in discourse context. *Memory and Cognition, 7,* 273–282.

Perfetti, C. A., & Roth, S. (1977). Some of the interactive processes in reading and their role in reading skill. In A. M. Lesgold & C. A. Perfetti (Eds.), *Interactive processes in reading* (pp. 269–297). Hillsdale, NJ: Erlbaum.

Pflaum, S. W., Walberg, H. J., Karegianes, M. L., & Rasher, S. P. (1980). Reading instruction: A quantitative analysis. *Educational Researcher, 9,* 12–18.

Pianko, S. (1979). A description of the composing processes of college freshmen writers. *Research in the Teaching of English, 13,* 5–22.

Pick, A. D., Unze, M. G., Brownell, C. A., Drozdal, D. G., & Hopmann, M. R. (1978). Young children's knowledge of word structure. *Child Development, 49,* 669–680.

Piekarz, J. (1954). *Individual responses in interpretive responses in reading.* Unpublished doctoral dissertation, University of Chicago.

Pillsbury, W. B. (1897). A study in apperception. *American Journal of Psychology, 8,* 315–393.

Pollatsek, A., Lesch, M., Morris, R. K., & Rayner, K. (1992). Phonological codes are used in integrating information across saccades in word identification and reading. *Journal of Experimental Psychology: Human Perception and Performance, 18,* 148–162.

Posnansky, C. J. (1978). Age- and task-related differences in the use of category-size information for the retrieval of categorized items. *Journal of Experimental Child Psychology, 26,* 373–382.

Pressley, G. M. (1976). Mental imagery helps eight-year-olds remember what they read. *Journal of Educational Psychology, 68,* 355–359.

Pressley, M. (1977). Imagery and children's learning: Putting the picture in developmental perspective. *Review of Educational Research, 47,* 586–622.

Pressley, M., & Afflerbach, P. (1995). *Verbal protocols of reading: The nature of constructively responsive reading.* Hillsdale, NJ: Erlbaum.

Pressley, M., El-Dinary, P. B., & Brown, R. (1992). Skilled and not-so-skilled reading: Good and not-so-good information processing. In M. Pressley, K. R. Harris, & J. T. Guthrie (Eds.), *Promoting academic competence and literacy in school* (pp. 91–127). San Diego, CA: Academic Press.

Pressley, M., El-Dinary, P. B., Gaskins, I., Schuder, T., Bergman, J., Almasi, L., & Brown, R. (1992). Beyond direct explanation: Transactional instruction of reading comprehension strategies. *Elementary School Journal, 92,* 511–554.

Pressley, M., El-Dinary, P. B., Stein, S., Marks, M. B., & Brown, R. (1992). Good strategy instruction is motivating and interesting. In A. Renninger, S. Hidi, & A. Krapp (Eds.), *The role of interest in learning and development* (pp. 333–358). Hillsdale, NJ: Erlbaum.

Pressley, M., & Forrest-Pressley, D. L. (1985). Questions and children's cognitive processing. In A. Graesser & J. Black (Eds.), *Psychology of questions* (pp. 277–296). Hillsdale, NJ: Erlbaum.

Pressley, M., Gaskins, I. W., Cunicelli, E. A., Burdick, N. J., Schaub-Matt, M., Lee, D. S., & Powell, N. (1991). Strategy instruction at Benchmark School: A faculty interview study. *Learning Disability Quarterly, 14,* 19–48.

Pressley, M., Gaskins, I. W., Wile, D., Cunicelli, B., & Sheridan, J. (1991). Teaching literacy strategies across the curriculum: A case study at Benchmark School. In J. Zutell & S. McCormick (Eds.), *Learner factors/teacher factors: Issues in literacy research and instruction. Fortieth yearbook of the National Reading Conference* (pp. 219–228). Chicago: National Reading Conference.

Pressley, M., Harris, K. R., & Marks, M. B. (1992). But good strategy instructors are constructivists!! *Educational Psychology Review, 4,* 1–32.

Pressley, M., Heisel, B. E., McCormick, C. G., & Nakamura, G. V. (1982). Memory strategy instruction with children. In C. J. Brainerd & M. Pressley (Eds.), *Progress in cognitive development research: 2. Verbal processes in children* (pp. 125–159). New York: Springer-Verlag.

Pressley, M., Johnson, C. J., Symons, S., McGoldrick, J. A., & Kurita, J. A. (1989). Strategies that improve memory and comprehension of what is read. *Elementary School Journal, 90,* 3–32.

Pressley, M., & McCormick, C. B. (1995a). *Advanced educational psychology for educators, researchers, and policymakers.* New York: HarperCollins.

Pressley, M., & McCormick, C. B. (1995b). *Cognition, teaching, and assessment.* New York: HarperCollins.

Pressley, M., Schuder, T., SAIL Faculty and Administration, Bergman, J. L., & El-Dinary, P. B. (1992). A researcher-educator collaborative interview study of transactional comprehension strategies instruction. *Journal of Educational Psychology, 84,* 231–246.

Rack, J. P., Snowling, M. J., & Olson, R. K. (1992). The nonword reading deficit in developmental dyslexia: A review. *Reading Research Quarterly, 26,* 28–53.

Rashotte, C. A., & Torgesen, J. K. (1985). Repeated reading and reading fluency in learning disabled children. *Reading Research Quarterly, 20,* 180–202.

Rayner, K., & Morris, R. K. (1992). Information from nonfixated words in reading. *Journal of Experimental Psychology: Human Perception and Performance, 18,* 163–172.

Rayner, K., & Pollatsek, A. (1989). *The psychology of reading.* Hillsdale, NJ: Erlbaum.

Rayner, K., Sereno, S. C., Lesch, M. F., & Pollatsek, A. (1995). Phonological codes are automatically activated during reading. *Psychological Science, 6,* 26–32.

Read, C. (1971). Preschool children's knowledge of English phonology. *Harvard Educational Review, 41,* 1–34.

Read, C. (1975). *Children's categorization of speech sounds in English* (NCTE Research Report No. 17). Urbana, IL: National Council of Teachers of English.

Read, C. (1986). *Children's creative spelling.* London: Routledge & Kegan Paul.

Read, C., Yun-Fei, Z., Hong-Yin, N., & Bao-Qing, D. (1986). The ability to manipulate speech sounds depends on knowing alphabetic writing. *Cognition, 24,* 31–44.

Reeds, J. A., & Wang, W. S.-Y. (1961). The perception of stops after s. *Phonetica, 6,* 78–81.

Reitsma, P. (1983). Printed word learning in beginning readers. *Journal of Experimental Child Psychology, 36,* 321–339.

Reitsma, P. (1989). Orthographic memory and learning to read. In P. G. Aaron & R. M. Joshi (Eds.), *Reading and writing disorders in different orthographic systems* (pp. 51–73). The, Hague, The Netherlands: Kluwer Academic.

Renninger, A., Hidi, S., & Krapp, A. (Eds.). (1992). *The role of interest in learning and development.* Hillsdale, NJ: Erlbaum.

Richck, M. (1977–1978). Readiness skills that predict initial word learning using two different methods of instruction. *Reading Research Quarterly, 13,* 200–222.

Robbins, C., & Ehri, L. C. (1994). Reading storybooks to kindergartners helps them learn new vocabulary words. *Journal of Educational Psychology, 86,* 54–64.

Robinson, F. P. (1946). *Effective study* (2nd ed.). New York: Harper & Row.

Robinson, H. M. (1972). Visual and auditory modalities related to methods for beginning reading. *Reading Research Quarterly, 8,* 7–39.

Roehler, L. R., & Duffy, G. G. (1984). Direct explanation of comprehension processes. In G. G. Duffy, L. R. Roehler, & J. Mason (Eds.), *Comprehension instruction: Perspectives and suggestions* (pp. 265–280). New York: Longman.

Rohman, D. G. (1965). Pre-writing: The stage of discovery in the writing process. *College Composition and Communication, 16,* 106–112.

Roller, C. M. (1990). The interaction of knowledge and structure variables in the processing of expository prose. *Reading Research Quarterly, 25,* 79–89.

Rosenblatt, L. M. (1938). *Literature as exploration.* New York: Modern Language Association.

Rosenblatt, L. M. (1978). *The reader, the text, the poem: The transactional theory of the literary work.* Carbondale: Southern Illinois University Press.

Rosenshine, B., & Meister, C. (1994). Reciprocal teaching: A review of nineteen experimental studies. *Review of Educational Research, 64,* 479–530.

Rosenshine, B., & Stevens, R. (1984). Classroom instruction in reading. In P. D. Pearson, R. Barr, M. L. Kamil, & P. Mosenthal (Eds.), *Handbook of reading research* (pp. 745–799). New York: Longman.

Rosinski, R. R., & Wheeler, K. E. (1972). Children's use of orthographic structure in word discrimination. *Psychonomic Science, 26,* 97–98.

Rosner, J. (1974). Auditory analysis training with prereaders. *The Reading Teacher, 27,* 379–384.

Rosner, J., & Simon, D. P. (1971). The auditory analysis test: An initial report. *Journal of Learning Disabilities, 4,* 384–392.

Rothkopf, E. Z. (1966). Learning from written materials: An exploration of the control of inspection of test-like events. *American Educational Research Journal, 3,* 241–249.

Rubin, A. (1980). A theoretical taxonomy of the differences between oral and written language. In R. J. Spiro, B. C. Bruce, & W. F. Brewer (Eds.), *Theoretical issues in reading comprehension* (pp. 411–438). Hillsdale, NJ: Erlbaum.

Rumelhart, D. E. (1980). Schemata: The building blocks of cognition. In R. J. Spiro, B. C. Bruce, & W. F. Brewer (Eds.), *Theoretical issues in reading comprehension* (pp. 1–34). Hillsdale, NJ: Erlbaum.

Rumelhart, D. E., & Ortony, A. (1978). The representation of knowledge in memory. In R. C. Anderson, R. J. Spiro, & W. E. Montague (Eds.), *Schooling and the representation of knowledge.* Hillsdale, NJ: Erlbaum.

Samuels, S. J. (1970). Effects of pictures on learning to read, comprehension, and attitudes. *Review of Educational Research, 40,* 397–407.

Samuels, S. J. (1979). The method of repeated readings. *The Reading Teacher, 32,* 403–408.

Samuels, S. J. (1985). Automaticity and repeated reading. In J. Osborn, P. T. Wilson, & R. C. Anderson (Eds.), *Reading education: Foundations for a literate America* (pp. 215–230). Lexington, MA: Lexington Books.

Sandwick, R. (1915). *How to study and what to study.* New York: Heath.

Santa, C. M. (1976–1977). Spelling patterns and the development of flexible word recognition strategies. *Reading Research Quarterly, 7,* 125–144.

Savin, H. B. (1972). What the child knows about speech when he starts to learn to read. In J. Kavanaugh & I. Mattingly (Eds.), *Language by eye and by ear* (pp. 319–326). Cambridge, MA: MIT Press.

Savin, H. B., & Bever, T. G. (1970). The nonperceptual reality of the phoneme. *Journal of Verbal Learning and Verbal Behavior, 9,* 295–302.

Scarborough, H. S. (1990). Very early language deficits in dyslexic children. *Child Development, 61,* 1728–1743.

Scarborough, H. S., & Dobrich, W. (1990). Development of children with early language delay. *Journal of Speech and Hearing Disorders, 33,* 70–83.

Scarborough, H. S., & Dobrich, W. (1994). On the efficacy of reading to preschoolers. *Developmental Review, 14,* 245–302.

Scardamalia, M., & Bereiter, C. (1986). Research on written composition. In M. C. Wittrock (Ed.), *Handbook of research on teaching* (3rd ed., pp. 778–803). New York: Macmillan.

Schunk, D., & Zimmerman, B. (1994). *Self-regulation of learning and performance: Issues and educational applications.* Hillsdale, NJ: Erlbaum.

Seidenberg, M. S., & McClelland, J. L. (1989). A distributed, developmental model of visual word recognition. *Psychological Review, 96,* 523–568.

Seigel, L. S., Share, D., & Giva, E. (1995). Evidence for superior orthographic skills in dyslexics. *Psychological Science, 6,* 250–254.

Shanahan, T., & Tierney, R. J. (1990). Reading-writing connections: The relations among three perspectives. In J. Zutell & S. McCormick (Eds.), *Literacy theory and research: Analyses from multiple paradigms* (Thirty-ninth yearbook of the National Reading Conference) (pp. 13–34). Chicago: National Reading Conference.

Shankweiler, D., Crain, S., Katz, L., Fowler, A. E., Liberman, A. M., Brady, S. A., Thornton, R., Lundquist, E., Dreyer, L., Fletcher, J. M., Stuebing, K. K., Shaywitz, S. E., & Shaywitz, B. A. (1995). Cognitive profiles of reading-disabled children: Comparison of language skills in phonology, morphology, and syntax. *Psychological Science, 6,* 149–156.

Share, D. L. (1995). Phonological recoding and self-teaching: Sine qua non of reading acquisition. *Cognition, 55,* 151–218.

Shaughnessy, M. P. (1977). *Errors and expectations: A guide for the teacher of basic writing.* New York: Oxford University Press.

Shaywitz, S. E., Escobar, M. D., Shaywitz, B. A., Fletcher, J. M., & Makuch, R. (1992). Evidence that dyslexia may represent the lower tail of a normal distribution of reading ability. *New England Journal of Medicine, 326,* 145–150.

Short, E. J., & Ryan, E. B. (1984). Metacognitive differences between skilled and less skilled readers: Remediating deficits through story grammar and attribution training. *Journal of Educational Psychology, 76,* 225–235.

Shulman, L. (1986). Paradigms and research programs in the study of teaching: A contemporary perspective. In M. C. Wittrock (Ed.), *Handbook of research on teaching* (3rd ed., pp. 3–36). New York: Macmillan.

Siegel, L. S. (1989). IQ is irrelevant ot the definition of learning disabilities. *Journal of Learning Disabilities, 22,* 469–479.

Siegel, L. W. (1992). An evaluation of the discrepancy definition of dyslexia. *Journal of Learning Disabilities, 25,* 618–629.

Silberberg, N., Iverson, I., & Silberberg, M. (1968). The predictive efficiency of the Gates Reading Readiness Tests. *Elementary School Journal, 68,* 213–218.

Singer, H. (1978). Active comprehension from answering to asking questions. *The Reading Teacher, 31,* 901–908.

Skjelfjord, V. J. (1976). Teaching children to segment spoken words as an aid in learning to read. *Journal of Learning Disabilities, 9,* 297–305.

Slobin, D. I. (1971). *The ontogenesis of grammar: Facts and theories.* New York: Academic Press.

Smith, F. (1971). *Understanding reading.* New York: Holt, Rinehart and Winston.

Smith, F. (1973). *Psycholinguistics and reading.* New York: Holt, Rinehart and Winston.

Smith, F. (1982). *Understanding reading* (3rd ed.). New York: Holt, Rinehart and Winston.

Smith, F. (1989). Overselling literacy. *Phi Delta Kappan, 70,* 353–359.

Smith, F. (1992). Learning to read: The never-ending debate. *Phi Delta Kappan, 74,* 432–441.

Smith, N. B. (1974). *American reading instruction.* Newark, DE: International Reading Association.

Snow, C. E., & Ninio, A. (1986). The contracts of literacy: What children learn from learning to read books. In W. H. Teale & E. Sulzby (Eds.), *Emergent literacy: Writing and reading* (pp. 116–138). Norwood, NJ: ABLEX.

Snowling, M. J. (1994). Towards a model of spelling acquisition: The development of some component skills. In G. D. A. Brown & N. C. Ellis (Eds.), *Handbook of spelling: Theory, process and intervention* (pp. 111–128). Chichester, England: Wiley.

Speer, O. B., & Lamb, G. S. (1976). First grade reading ability and fluency in naming verbal symbols. *The Reading Teacher, 26,* 572–576.

Spivey, N. N., & King, J. R. (1989). Readers as writers composing from sources. *Reading Research Quarterly, 24,* 7–26.

Spyridakis, J. H., & Standal, T. C. (1987). Signals in expository prose: Effects on reading comprehension. *Reading Research Quarterly, 22,* 285–298.

Stage, S. A., & Wagner, R. K. (1992). The development of young children's phonological and orthographic knowledge as revealed by their spellings. *Developmental Psychology, 28,* 287–296.

Stahl, A. (1977). The structure of children's compositions: Developmental and ethnic differences. *Research in the Teaching of English, 11,* 156–163.

Stahl, S. A. (1988). Is there evidence to support matching reading styles and initial reading methods? A reply to Carbo. *Phi Delta Kappan, 70,* 317–322.

Stahl, S. A., & Murray, B. A. (1994). Defining phonological awareness and its relationship to early reading. *Journal of Educational Psychology, 86,* 221–234.

Stanovich, K. E. (1980). Toward an interactive-compensatory model of individual differences in the development of reading fluency. *Reading Research Quarterly, 16,* 32–71.

Stanovich, K. E. (1986). Matthew effects in reading: Some consequences of individual differences in the acquisition of literacy. *Reading Research Quarterly, 21,* 360–406.

Stanovich, K. E. (1992). Speculations of the causes and consequences of individual differences in early reading acquisition. In P. B. Gough, L. C. Ehri, & R. Treiman (Eds.), *Reading acquisition* (pp. 307–342). Hillsdale, NJ: Erlbaum.

Stanovich, K. E. (1993). Does reading make you smarter? Literacy and the development of verbal intelligence. In H. Reese (Ed.), *Advances in child development and behavior* (Vol. 24, pp. 133–180). San Diego, CA: Academic Press.

Stanovich, K. E. (1994). Romance and reality. *The Reading Teacher, 47,* 280–291.

Stanovich, K. E., Cunningham, A. E., & Cramer, B. B. (1984). Assessing phonological awareness in kindergarten children: Issues of task comparability. *Journal of Experimental Child Psychology, 38,* 175–190.

Stanovich, K. E., Cunningham, A. E., & Feeman, D. J. (1984). Intelligence, cognitive skills, and early reading progress. *Reading Research Quarterly, 22,* 8–46.

Stanovich, K. E., & Seigel, L. S. (1994). Phenotypic performance profile of children with reading disabilities: A regression-based test of the phonological-core variable-difference model. *Journal of Educational Psychology, 86,* 24–53.

Stanovich, K. E., West, R. F., & Cunningham, A. E. (1991). Beyond phonological processes: Print exposure and orthographic processing. In S. Brady & D. Shankweiler (Eds.), *Phonological processes in literacy* (pp. 219–235). Hillsdale, NJ: Erlbaum.

Stauffer, R. G. (1969). *Directing reading maturity as a cognitive process.* New York: Harper & Row.

Stein, N. L., & Glenn, C. G. (1979). An analysis of story comprehension in elementary school children. In R. O. Freedle (Ed.), *New directions in discourse processing* (Vol. 2, pp. 53–120). Norwood, NJ: ABLEX.

Sterling, C. M. (1983). Spelling errors in context. *British Journal of Psychology, 74,* 353–364.

Stevenson, J., & Fredman, G. (1990). The social environmental correlates of reading ability. *Journal of Child Psychology and Psychiatry, 31,* 681–698.

Stotsky, S. (1984). Research on reading/writing relationships: A synthesis and suggested directions. In J. Jensen (Ed.), *Composition and comprehending* (pp. 627–742). Urbana, IL: ERIC Clearinghouse on Reading and Communication Skills and National Conference on Research in English.

Sulzby, E. (1985). Children's emergent reading of favorite storybooks: A developmental study. *Reading Research Quarterly, 20,* 458–481.

Swain, G. F. (1917). *How to study.* New York: McGraw-Hill.

Tangel, D. M., & Blachman, B. A. (1992). Effect of phoneme awareness instruction on kindergarten children's invented spellings. *Journal of Reading Behavior, 24,* 233–261.

Tarver, S., & Dawson, M. M. (1988). Modality preference and the teaching of reading. *Journal of Learning Disabilities, 11,* 17–29.

Taylor, B. M. (1982). Text structure and children's comprehension and memory for expository material. *Journal of Educational Psychology, 74,* 323–340.

Teale, W. H. (1986). Home background and young children's literacy development. In W. H. Teale & E. Sulzby (Eds.), *Emergent literacy* (pp. 173–206). Norwood, NJ: ABLEX.

Templeton, S. (1992). Theory, nature, and pedagogy of high-order orthographic development in older students. In S. Templeton & D. R. Bear (Eds.), *Development of orthographic knowledge and the foundations of literacy* (pp. 253–277). Hillsdale, NJ: Erlbaum.

Thomas, H. (1968). Children's tachistoscopic recognition of words and pseudowords varying in pronounceability and consonant vowel sequence. *Journal of Experimental Psychology, 77,* 511–513.

Thorndike, R. L. (1973). Reading as reasoning. *Reading Research Quarterly, 9,* 135–147.

Tierney, R. J., Readence, J. E., & Dishner, E. K. (1980). *Reading strategies and practices: Guide for improving instruction.* Boston: Allyn & Bacon.

Titchener, E. B. (1912a). Prolegomena to a study of introspection. *American Journal of Psychology, 23,* 427–448.

Titchener, E. B. (1912b). The schema of introspection. *American Journal of Psychology, 23,* 485–508.

Tolchinsky-Landsmann, L., & Levin, I. (1985). Writing in preschoolers: An age-related analysis. *Applied Psycholinguistics, 6,* 319–339.

Tolchinsky-Landsmann, L., & Levin, I. (1987). Writing in four- to six-year-olds: Representation of semantic and phonetic similarities and differences. *Journal of Child Language, 14,* 127–144.

Treiman, R. (1984). Individual differences among children in spelling and reading styles. *Journal of Experimental Child Psychology, 37,* 463–477.

Treiman, R. (1985a). Onsets and rimes as units of spoken syllables: Evidence from children. *Journal of Experimental Child Psychology, 39,* 161–181.

Treiman, R. (1985b). Phonemic analysis, spelling, and reading. In T. Carr (Ed.), *New directions for child development: The development of reading skills* (pp. 5–18). San Francisco: Jossey-Bass.

Treiman, R. (1985c). Phonemic awareness and spelling: Children's judgments do not always agree with adults'. *Journal of Experimental Child Psychology, 39,* 182–201.

Treiman, R. (1985d). Spelling of stop consonants after /s/ by children and adults. *Applied Psycholinguistics, 6,* 261–282.

Treiman, R. (1989). The internal structure of the syllable. In G. Carlson & M. Tanenhaus (Eds.), *Linguistic structure in language processing* (pp. 27–52). Dordrecht, The Netherlands: Kluwer.

Treiman, R. (1991). Children's spelling errors on syllable-initial consonant clusters. *Journal of Educational Psychology, 83,* 346–360.

Treiman, R. (1992). The role of intrasyllabic units in learning to read and spell. In P. B. Gough, L. Ehri, & R. Treiman (Eds.), *Reading acquisition* (pp. 65–106). Hillsdale, NJ: Erlbaum.

Treiman, R. (1993). *Beginning to spell: A study of first-grade children.* New York: Oxford University Press.

Treiman, R. (1994). Use of consonant letter names in beginning spelling. *Developmental Psychology, 30,* 567–580.

Treiman, R., & Baron, J. (1983). Phonemic-analysis training helps children benefit from spelling-sound rules. *Memory and Cognition, 18,* 559–567.

Treiman, R., Berch, D., Tincoff, R., & Weatherston, S. (1993). Phonology and spelling: The case of syllabic consonants. *Journal of Experimental Child Psychology, 56,* 267–290.

Treiman, R., Berch, D., & Weatherston, S. (1993). Children's use of phoneme-grapheme correspondences in spelling: Roles of position and stress. *Journal of Educational Psychology, 85,* 1–12.

Treiman, R., Cassar, M., & Zukowski, A. (1994). What types of linguistic information do children use in spelling? The case of flaps. *Child Development, 65,* 1310–1329.

Treiman, R., Goswami, U., Tincoff, R., & Leevers, H. (1995). *Effects of dialect on American and British children's spelling.* Unpublished manuscript. Wayne State University, Detroit.

Treiman, R., Weatherston, S., & Berch, D. (1994). The role of letter names in children's learning of phoneme-grapheme relations. *Applied Psycholinguistics, 15,* 97–122.

Treiman, R., Zukowski, A., & Richmond-Welty, E. D. (1995). What happened to the "n" of sink? Children's spellings of final consonant clusters. *Cognition, 55,* 1–38.

Truch, S. (1991). *The missing parts of whole language.* Calgary, Alberta, Canada: Foothills Educational Materials.

Tulving, E., & Gold, C. (1963). Stimulus information and contextual information as determinants of tachistoscopic recognition of words. *Journal of Experimental Psychology, 66,* 319–327.

Tunmer, W. E., & Chapman, J. W. (1995). Language prediction skill, phonological recoding, and beginning reading. In C. Hulme & R. M. Joshi (Eds.), *Reading and spelling: Development and disorder.* Hillsdale, NJ: Erlbaum.

Tunmer, W. E., Herriman, M. L., & Nesdale, A. R. (1988). Metalinguistic abilities and beginning reading. *Reading Research Quarterly, 23,* 134–158.

Tunmer, W. E., & Hoover, W. (1992). Cognitive and linguistic factors in learning to read. In P. B. Gough, L. C. Ehri, & R. Treiman (Eds.), *Reading acquisition* (pp. 175–214). Hillsdale, NJ: Erlbaum.

Tunmer, W. E., & Nesdale, A. R. (1985). Phonemic segmentation skill and beginning reading. *Journal of Educational Psychology, 77,* 417–427.

Turner, G. Y. (1992). College students' self-awareness of study behaviors. *College Student Journal, 26,* 129–134.

Uhry, J. K., & Shepherd, M. J. (1993). Segmentation/spelling instruction as part of a first-grade reading program: Effects on several measures of reading. *Reading Research Quarterly, 28,* 218–233.

U.S. Office of Technology Assessment. (1993). *Adult literacy and new technologies.* Washington, DC: U.S. Government Printing Office.

Valdez-Menchaca, M. C., & Whitehurst, G. J. (1992). Accelerating language development through picture book reading: A systematic extension to Mexican day care. *Developmental Psychology, 28,* 1106–1114.

van Dijk, T. A., & Kintsch, W. (1983). *Strategies of discourse comprehension.* New York: Academic Press.

Van Orden, G. C., Pennington, B. F., & Stone, G. O. (1990). Word identification in reading and the promise of subsymbolic psycholinguistics. *Psychological Review, 97,* 488–522.

VanRiper, C. G., & Butler, K. G. (1955). *Speech in the elementary classroom.* New York: Harper & Row.

Vellutino, F. R. (1979). *Dyslexia: Theory and research.* Cambridge, MA: MIT Press.

Vellutino, F. R. (1991). Introduction to three studies on reading acquisition: Convergent findings on theoretical foundations of code-oriented versus whole-language approaches to reading instruction. *Journal of Educational Psychology, 83,* 437–443.

Vellutino, F. R., & Scanlon, D. M. (1987). Phonological coding, phonological awareness, and reading ability: Evidence from a longitudinal and experimental study. *Merrill-Palmer Quarterly, 33,* 321–363.

Venezky, R. L. (1970). *The structure of English orthography.* The Hague: Mouton.

Venezky, R. L. (1980). From Webster to Rice to Roosevelt: The formative years for spelling instruction and spelling reform in the U.S.A. In U. Frith (Ed.), *Cognitive processes in spelling* (pp. 9–30). London: Academic Press.

Vernon, M. D. (1971). *Reading and its difficulties.* Cambridge, England: Cambridge University Press.

Vygotsky, L. S. (1962). *Thought and language.* Cambridge, MA: MIT Press.

Vygotsky, L. S. (1978). *Mind in society: The development of higher psychological processes.* Cambridge, MA: Harvard University Press.

Wagner, R. K., & Torgesen, J. K. (1987). The nature of phonological processing and its causal role in the acquisition of reading skills. *Psychological Bulletin, 101,* 192–212.

Wagner, R. K., Torgesen, J. K., Laughon, P., Simmons, K., & Rashotte, C. A. (1993). Development of young readers' phonological processing abilities. *Journal of Educational Psychology, 85,* 83–103.

Wagner, R. K., Torgesen, J. K., & Rashotte, C. A. (1994). Development of reading-related phonological processing abilities: New evidence of bidirectional causality from a latent variable longitudinal study. *Developmental Psychology, 30,* 73–87.

Wallach, M. A., & Wallach, L. (1979). Helping disadvantaged children learn to read by teaching them phoneme identification skills. In L. A. Resnick & P. A. Weaver (Eds.), *Theory and practice of early reading* (Vol. 3, pp. 227–259). Hillsdale, NJ: Erlbaum.

Warren, R. M. (1971). Identification times for phonemic components of graded complexity and for spelling of speech. *Perception and Psychophysics, 9,* 345–349.

Waters, G. S., Bruck, M., & Malus-Abramovitz, M. (1988). The role of linguistic and visual information in spelling: A developmental study. *Journal of Experimental Child Psychology, 45,* 400–421.

Weber, R. M. (1970a). A linguistic analysis of first-grade reading errors. *Reading Research Quarterly, 5,* 427–451.

Weber, R. M. (1970b). First-graders' use of grammatical context in reading. In H. Levin & J. P. Williams (Eds.), *Basic studies on reading* (pp. 147–163). New York: Basic Books.

Wells, G. (1985). Preschool literacy-related activities and success in school. In D. Olson, N. Torrance, & A. Hildyard (Eds.), *Literacy, language, and learning: The nature and consequences of reading and writing* (pp. 229–255). New York: Cambridge University Press.

West, R. F., & Stanovich, K. E. (1978). Automatic contextual facilitation in readers of three ages. *Child Development, 49,* 717–727.

Wheeler, D. D. (1970). Processes in word recognition. *Cognitive Psychology, 1,* 59–85.

Wheeler, P. (1983). Context-related age characteristics in mothers' speech: Joint book reading. *Journal of Child Language, 10,* 259–263.

White, R. W. (1959). Motivation reconsidered: The concept of competence. *Psychological Review, 66,* 297–333.

Whitehurst, G. J., Arnold, D. S., & Lonigan, C. J. (1990). *Dialogic reading: The hear-say method—A video workshop.* Stony Brook, NY: Acorn Films.

Whitehurst, G. J., Epstein, J. N., Angell, A. L., Payne, A. C., Crone, D. A., & Fischel, J. E. (1994). Outcomes of an emergent literacy intervention in Head Start. *Journal of Educational Psychology, 86,* 542–555.

Whitehurst, G. J., Falco, F., Lonigan, C. J., Fischal, J. E., DeBaryshe, B. D., Valdez-Manchaca, M. C., & Caulfield, M. (1988). Accelerating language development through picture book reading. *Developmental Psychology, 24,* 552–559.

Whitehurst, G. J., & Fischel, J. E. (1994). Practitioner review: Early developmental language delay: What, if anything, should the clinician do about it? *Journal of Child Psychology and Psychiatry, 35,* 613–648.

Wiener, M., & Cromer, W. (1967). Reading and reading difficulty: A conceptual analysis. *Harvard Educational Review, 37,* 620–643.

Williams, J. P. (1979). The ABD's of reading: A program for the learning disabled. In L. A. Resnick & P. A. Weaver (Eds.), *Theory and practice of early reading* (Vol. 3, pp. 227–259). Hillsdale, NJ: Erlbaum.

Wolf, M. (1991). Naming speed and reading: The contribution of the cognitive neurosciences. *Reading Research Quarterly, 26,* 123–141.

Wood, S. S., Bruner, J. S., & Ross, G. (1976). The role of tutoring in problem solving. *Journal of Child Psychology and Psychiatry, 17,* 89–100.

Woodward, A. (1993). Do illustrations serve an instructional purpose in U.S. textbooks? In B. K. Britton, A. Woodward, & M. Binkley (Eds.), *Learning from textbooks: Theory and practice* (pp. 115–134). Hillsdale, NJ: Erlbaum.

Worden, P. E., & Boettcher, W. (1990). Young children's acquisition of alphabet knowledge. *Journal of Reading Behavior, 22,* 277–295.

Wozniak, R. (1972). Verbal regulation of motor behavior: Soviet research and non-Soviet replications. *Human Development, 15,* 13–57.

Wyatt, D., Pressley, M., El-Dinary, P. B., Stein, S., Evans, P., & Brown, R. (1993). Reading behaviors of domain experts processing professional articles that are important to them: The critical role of worth and credibility monitoring. *Learning and Individual Differences, 5,* 49–72.

Yopp, H. K. (1988). The validity and reliability of phonemic awareness tests. *Reading Research Quarterly, 23,* 159–177.

CHAPTER 6

Cognitive Development and Science Education: Toward a Middle Level Model

SIDNEY STRAUSS

The issues related to how cognitive developmental psychology and science education can inform each other are extraordinarily rich and complex (see the edited volume by Gabel, 1994).

A middle level model of science education is proposed here as a means of capturing both this richness and complexity. At the middle level, cognitive developmental psychologists and science educators could come together to find common ground and parlance. Some have already conjoined at this nexus, and the result has been a fast-moving and exciting area of research and development. This chapter documents where the nexus is and the kind of work that has been and could be done there.

This middle level model should be viewed as heuristic. It frames a way to think about where and how science education and cognitive developmental psychology can and do meet. It is an organizing notion, and it lacks precision to measure deep, middle, and surface levels of cognition.

The middle level model focuses on the deceptive ordinariness of science education. Throughout the Western world, science teaching has much in common—hence, a feeling of ordinariness. But the knowledge we are developing about cognitive aspects of science education reveals that science teaching is anything but ordinary. An extraordinary complexity imbues the elements of science education—theory building, research, and practice—and enormous efforts are being made to understand and influence their significance and interrelationship.

The key topics of the chapter are:

1. Aspects of cognitive developmental psychology that have potential to be informed by and to inform science education.

2. The parts of science education that could be informed by and could inform cognitive developmental psychology.
3. The nature of the relations that could exist between the domains of cognitive developmental psychology and science education.

There is, at present, very little overlap between these two domains; the reasons for this gap are explored. The middle level developmental model shows how the domains can be connected. The nature of teachers' cognition about science and about the classroom instruction of children is then reviewed in detail. Curricula for children's study of science and for teacher education in the subject are presented, with emphasis on how the curricula might look if cognitive developmental issues were taken into account.

OVERLAPS BETWEEN COGNITIVE DEVELOPMENTAL PSYCHOLOGY AND SCIENCE EDUCATION

It would not be unreasonable to assume that considerable overlap exists between cognitive developmental psychology and science education. Cognitive developmental psychologists attempt to describe: the epistemological foundations of knowledge and its representations in individuals; the psychological principles of how that knowledge is organized mentally and how it is operated on; the biological constraints on the types of knowledge that can be constructed; the societal influences on cognition and ontogenesis; the developmental principles about how knowledge becomes reorganized; and the developmental sequences that originate from those principles of developmental reorganization.

Science educators are interested in understanding the approaches and methods that influence effective teaching and lead to cognitive change in individuals. The relations among the learner, the classroom environment (including the curriculum), and the teacher are among the variables included in science education theory, research, and practice. If we restrict the discussion of science education to the cognitive aspects, there should be considerable overlap between the two domains. Instead, there are tensions. Cognitive developmental psychologists rarely involve themselves in topics that are of interest to science educators. There is often little resemblance between what is being tested about cognitive development and what happens cognitively in the classroom where children are being taught science. Similarly, curriculum developers, when designing science curricula, often do not take into account the cognitive development of the children who must learn the prescribed subjects. I suggest the following five reasons for this lack of overlap:

1. The content of research chosen by cognitive developmental psychologists and science educators is often very different. Developmentalists often avoid studying the growth of children's understanding of the science concepts that are taught in school, whereas that is exactly what science educators study and teach.
2. Developmental psychologists and science educators map out sequences of development differently. Although strongly emphasized in Piaget's psychogenetic theory of development, more contemporary models of cognitive development also include sequential development. Examples include Case's (1985, 1992; Case & McKeough, 1990) neo-Piagetian model, Fischer's (1980) skill theory, Halford's (1982) information processing/structuralist model, and Karmiloff-Smith's (1985, 1992, 1994) phase model.

   Most science educators do not concern themselves with mapping out developmental sequences, although there are some who believe that without a clear understanding of the developmental landmarks of children's normative, commonsense understanding of school-taught concepts, the sequence and timing of instruction for these concepts cannot be determined (Driver & Oldham, 1985; Fischbein, 1975; Shayer & Adey, 1981).

   There is no inconsistency, in principle, between cognitive developmental psychology and science education; however, developmental psychologists often look for developmental sequences, and science educators often do not.
3. Cognitive developmental psychologists often focus on universal laws of human cognition and its development among all humans, without taking into account any special environmental conditions (Feldman, 1994). These forms of cognition and their developmental courses are so deep that they are virtually unchangeable except, perhaps, by genetic engineering.

   Science educators are interested in a level of cognitive development that is changeable—the level where learning occurs. This is a middle level cognition; it occupies a space between the deep cognitive structures that developmental psychologists look for and the surface knowledge states that are tied to specific tasks but have little generality or transferability. This middle level cognition gets carried out in special environments such as school classrooms.
4. The two groups study different units of psychological entities. Cognitive developmental psychologists

generally conduct their research with individuals. They study ontogenesis. Some researchers may study interactions between two or sometimes three children, but the effects of these interactions are studied at the level of the individual.

In contrast, science educators often look at the classroom as their psychological unit, although data about individuals are relevant and are often sought. The shifting realities of classroom learning—with all the competing agendas of youngsters, teachers, and the classroom situation—lead to a situated learning description of that orchestrated complex.

Recently, cognitive developmental psychologists (Brown, Campione, Reeve, Ferrara, & Palincsar, 1991; Pea, 1993) with an interest in science education have begun to take the "communities of learners" approach to cognitive development. They exemplify those who work within cognitive developmental psychology traditions to solve science education problems. Increasing use of this framework for organizing theory construction and research in cognitive developmental psychology is anticipated.

5. Cognitive developmental psychologists and science educators come from very different academic backgrounds and research traditions. The former usually get their doctorate degrees from psychology departments, where the course emphasis is on cognitive development. Their science background is sometimes not very strong. The latter often have a master's or doctorate degree in one of the sciences, and their background in cognitive development is sometimes weak. It is rare to find individuals with both a strong developmental and science background, which suggests that collaboration between the two fields is in order.

These five explanations for the large gap between the fields of cognitive developmental psychology and science education (the part that is based on developmental and learning issues) illustrate the differing interests and concerns of the two domains. Despite these differences and the tensions that result from them, the claim herein is that the two fields can overlap and enrich one another.

A Developmental View of Science Education, and a Science Education View of Development

Cognitive developmental psychology and science education can maintain their own integrity while sharing an intersecting area where something new emerges. This emergent area is a middle level cognitive developmental psychology of science education.

Compared to their traditional nonoverlapping status, both cognitive developmental psychology and science education would look different in this area. First, school-learned science concepts, processes, and so on, could be included as part of the content that describes cognition and its development.

Second, in addition to searching for deep cognitive organizations and their development, cognitive developmental psychologists would look for middle level mental organizations and how they change.

Third, given the interventionist view allowed by middle level mental organizations, cognitive developmental psychologists would have to search for ways to describe the nature of the artificial, designed-for-intervention environment. This could, in turn, lead to a cognitive developmental psychology that attempts to find ways to modify cognitive structures via planned tutoring environments.

Science education would have a different look in the intersecting area in two principal ways. First, it would be concerned with mapping out developmental sequences which, in the middle level model, are important in assessing the developmental landmarks for the science content that is taught in the schools. As pointed out earlier, this mapping activity has been missing in most science education work.

Second, science educators would also be searching for middle level cognitive organizations and mechanisms that govern children's development.

Research in traditional science education often careens between searching for deep cognitive organizations and developmental mechanisms, and searching for ways to bring individuals' specific performances under experimental control, in the hope of transferring this control to the classroom. The former is too general and the latter is too specific to be of concern to science educators. Middle level cognitive organizations offer a place where change can occur through intervention, and when it does, its effects are general.

To recap, there are reasons for the gap between cognitive developmental psychology and science education, but these differences need not deter us from seeking a middle level developmental model of science education that takes something from the traditions of both. Cognitive developmental psychology would be informed by science education issues, and science educators would bring developmental theory more integrally into their educational decisions. The resulting intersection would allow an emergent cognitive developmental psychology committed to changing developing cognitive organizations via instructional intervention to achieve a higher level of children's understandings of science concepts and processes.

I now turn to how the middle level developmental model of science education can make this happen.

A MIDDLE LEVEL COGNITIVE DEVELOPMENTAL MODEL OF SCIENCE EDUCATION

This section is devoted to a brief outline of some characteristics of the middle level model and the basic positions that serve as the underpinnings of this location.

Characteristics of the Middle Level Model

The middle level cognitive developmental model of science education refers to (a) the nature of the psychological entity that occupies that ground and (b) its location on the continuum on which developmental theory and science education practice serve as the poles.

The Middle Level Psychological Entity

The choice of the psychological entity one chooses to investigate and to teach is determined, in part, by one's professional identity. Traditional cognitive developmental psychologists often choose to investigate the development of concepts located at a level of mental organization that is so general and deep, and so tied to phylogenetic selection that it is virtually unchangeable. Development is viewed as occurring naturally and spontaneously in the world of natural objects, language, and so on. Were we able to change those mental organizations, we could bring off profound cognitive change. But schooling cannot budge this level of mental organization.

The other pole of the continuum is occupied by entities that are at the surface level, where the cognitive organizations are close to a description of children's behaviors. Siegler's (1981) rule assessment procedure provides us with a good case in point. He described children's rules for solving tasks such as the balance scale. The children first took into account the weights on both sides of the scale, the distance of the weights from the center, and ways to combine these two variables. For solving the shadows task, the children were asked to predict the size of a shadow on a screen. The variables tested were the size of the object being projected onto the screen and the distance of the object from the light source.

Although both the balance scale and the shadows tasks tap children's understanding of proportions, Siegler (1981) made no claims about the generality of the rules thought to underlie task solution. In fact, he claimed that the rules used to solve the balance scale task were somewhat different from those used to solve the shadows task. In other words, the claim was that the rules were closely tied to the tasks and the children's solutions to those tasks.

Cognitive entities at this level may be amenable to change through intervention, including schooling, but if such change were actually pulled off, we would have changed the cognitive entities (rules, in Siegler's case) that children had tied to specific tasks. In other words, such a change would have no generality, which is not what one wants in school learning.

Middle level psychological entities occupy a space between the levels of deep and surface mental organizations. They are close enough to the surface to be changeable through schooling, and when they do change, some generality results from that change. As an example, consider children's understanding of thermal phenomena (Wiser, 1988; Wiser & Carey, 1983). Children's and adults' intuitive thermal models seem to be fairly general and coherent. They include thermal equilibrium, heat as an intensive quantity, and a model of expansion due to heating. For cognitive developmental psychologists and science educators working at the middle level, this mild generality and coherence are a source of both hope and difficulty. By being somewhat general and coherent, the change should lead to moderately general cognitive restructuring; however, the same moderate generality and coherence make the change difficult to bring off.

The Middle Level between Cognitive Developmental Psychology Theory and Science Education Practice

The second continuum onto which the middle level model is placed has theory and practice at its poles. There are no precise benchmarks for deciding the distance between these poles on the continuum, but the position here is that theory is, by and large, decontextualized whereas practice is mostly situation-specific. The middle level, occupying a space between these two poles, is analogous to the role engineering has in relation to science and to the solution of specific engineering problems.

These distinctions are fraught with philosophical problems, but space considerations do not allow me to enter the fray. Suffice it to say that this criterion is intended to position investigators so that they do not get bogged down in the description of the actual teaching of specific content as it gets played out in a particular classroom at a particular moment with a particular teacher and particular pupils. Nor does it encourage investigators to attempt to describe the general characteristics of universal cognitive change, which may be a helpful backdrop for science education but is unable to guide it. What the middle level *does* allow is a description of the principles of a science education that is informed by general cognitive developmental theory and by specific educational practice in the form of teaching and curriculum development (in the broadest sense of those terms). By being in contact with the macro and micro levels, it is informed by them and informs them in return.

The middle level, as I describe it, is also eclectic. It is not bound to any one theory of cognition and development. Schooling is too diverse and school learning is too contextual for any one theory to be the sole guide for fostering learning in science classes. In keeping with this dictum, I offer, in other sections of this chapter, examples of descriptions of transition mechanisms and curriculum materials. Some are inspired by the structuralist approach, others are based on the sociohistorical perspective, and still others are more compatible with information processing approaches.

Underpinnings of the Middle Level Model

Six basic positions serve as the underpinnings of this model: (a) research content, (b) misconceptions, (c) multiple representations, (d) semiotic technologies, (e) normative development, and (f) models of cognitive transition. Each is presented briefly in an attempt to describe how connections can be made between cognitive developmental psychology and science education, connections that can be less tentative than those in the current literature.

Research Content

The content of our research, in the framework of the middle level cognitive developmental model of science education, should be school-taught subject matter. Two criteria for the teacher in a school and the researcher in a lab are: (a) the content must have significance for a domain of science (e.g., the concepts of heat and temperature in physics, photosynthesis in biology, matter in chemistry) and/or (b) the content must have generality across science domains (e.g., the concept of the arithmetic mean, the understanding of graph productions, the nature of argumentation for a position of theory).

A relevant example of cognitive developmental psychology and science education content could be children's developing understanding of the epistemology of scientific experimentation, including the relations among theory, research methods, the nature of data and their roles in theory development, and more.

An example of developmental and science education work that would *not* be relevant is research on, say, developmental aspects of how children learn word lists of nonsense words. Research of this sort might be of interest to developmental psychology if it is suitably embedded in developmental theory and if the research is done to elaborate some aspects of the theory under test. But such research would not be within the confines of the middle level developmental model of science education because its content is not school-based science content.

The principal reason for requiring that school-taught content be within the purview of the middle level model is to connect cognitive developmental theory and research with aspects of science education. General developmental principles covering many aspects of human cognitive development are not focused enough to help us understand what children's developing notions will be. In other words, for us to have an understanding of, say, how children's concepts of light develop, we must investigate just that. If we do not investigate children's developing concepts of light, we will not have a clue from the general theories of cognitive development as to how that concept develops.

I have been approached many times by curriculum developers for the sciences and by science teachers who ask: "What do X-year-old children know about Y? Can I teach those children Y?" Unfortunately, they consider my usual reply generally inadequate: "I do not know what X-year-old children know about Y, but I can look it up in the literature. And if there is nothing in the literature about it, I know a way of finding out. I do not know what we can teach these children, but if we can determine what they know and then figure out where we want them to change to, I know of ways we can try to help them make that change."

To readers who believe they can provide a better answer than mine, I suggest that, in advance of your actual research and before you read the research literature on the topic, you attempt to determine the nature of children's developing conceptions of light, based on general theories of cognitive development. Also, try to describe how you can arrange teaching situations where progressive cognitive change is likely to occur. Answers to these questions are hard to come by.

In short, domain-general theories of cognitive development cannot tell us what to expect in terms of children's understanding of specific science concepts, nor can they tell us what the developmental trajectory of those specific concepts will be. What we have are methods to determine (a) the nature of children's understanding of science concepts and the scientific enterprise, and (b) the developmental courses of this understanding. In the middle level developmental model of science education, we must make these determinations on a concept-by-concept basis.

Misconceptions

The content that should interest us is the science content for which children and/or adults do *not* have a correct understanding. This is a pragmatic position. Children study science for only a few hours each week, so we must limit our teaching to those concepts and processes that are not going to be understood correctly by children without some supplementary teaching. In other words, if research shows that children have an incorrect understanding of a particular scientific concept or enterprise and that misconception or misunderstanding remains stable or is replaced by another that is also incorrect, we have a candidate for research and development that fits the second criterion of the middle level developmental model.

The concept of light fits this second position. Research has shown that young children, adolescents, and adults have various misconceptions about light (Andersson & Karrvqvist, 1981). This concept, then, is a candidate for research and development because, apparently, without school-based intervention, children and adults have persistent misconceptions.

An example of a concept that does *not* fit this second position is the concept of conservation, an academic bread-and-butter concept that has attracted considerable research energy. In fact, there may not be a more researched concept than the various kinds of conservation first noted by Piaget. Why does this concept *not* fit the second criterion? Because it is understood correctly by virtually all children by the age of 9 or 10 years. And, following the reasoning inspired by the second criterion, if children will correctly understand a concept without having been taught it, why bother to teach it?

The fallout from the second position states that, given the limited time we have to teach science concepts in schools, we ought to focus on concepts, processes, skills, modes of argumentation, and so on, that require instruction.

Multiple Representations

Children and adults have multiple representations about the world (see, e.g., Bamberger, 1982; Lave, 1988; Pea, 1993; Reif & Larkin, 1991).

Vygotsky's (1978, 1987) distinction between everyday/spontaneous and scientific/cultural knowledge is useful here. Spontaneous knowledge is described as unconscious, nonreflective, nonsystematic, originating in children's direct and personal experiences with the world, developing in an inductive and data-driven manner, and not in need of formal instruction in order to be constructed mentally. In contrast, scientific/cultural knowledge is described as conscious, reflective, systematic, originating in social mediation, developing in a deductive, theory-driven manner, and in need of instruction in order to be constructed mentally.

Reif and Larkin (1991) have elaborated some of the distinctions between these two kinds of knowledge. They also introduced the notion of school science knowledge, which is different from the knowledge of science as practiced and developed in universities and laboratories, and from everyday science knowledge. Reif and Larkin proposed a number of distinctions between everyday and scientific domains of knowledge, including the goals of the two domains and the kinds of cognition that pervade both. Their comparison suggests that teachers and curriculum developers should be aware of and should address the differences between these kinds of knowledge. In other words, children's everyday understanding about science content may be very different from the school science concepts they are taught in science classes. And both may be very different from the science concepts held by practicing scientists.

Curriculum developers and teachers, when deciding on and teaching science curricula, should take into account: (a) students' multiple representations of science concepts, which are constructed spontaneously about the subject matter being taught, (b) scientists' representation and understanding of science content; (c) the representation of knowledge of science as it is presented in the classroom via the curriculum and teaching, and (d) the differences among the three.

If all these elements are not taken into account, science teaching in classrooms will fail in bringing about the desired change in students' representations of the world of science. Their spontaneous mental representations will be unable to approximate the representations held by scientists.

Semiotic Technologies

In semiotics, different mental representations are clothed in symbolic and notational systems. These semiotic systems are cultural technologies—spoken and written language, mathematics, and graphs. They have been invented for many purposes. One of them is the amplification of knowledge gained through either a natural, spontaneous track or a cultural, scientific track (e.g., being able to predict scientific phenomena using mathematical representations of laws of physics). Another purpose of these semiotic technologies is to "freeze" our constantly changing world (e.g., written language captures and holds spoken language, which disappears the moment it is spoken; graphs capture the nature of relations among variables, relations that often elude our sensory system).

These semiotic systems are part of our cultural knowledge, and they have their own developmental trajectories. The idea of cultural technologies and their developmental trajectories can be illustrated by analyzing children's developing understanding of the concept of temperature, which will be dealt with in various sections of this chapter.

Children have direct experience playing with and feeling water and its temperature. Their experience with the temperature of water is sensory. When they use natural language to describe the temperature they feel sensorially, they call the temperature of the water "hot," "cold," "tepid," and so on. This is a semiotic technology that describes in nominal terms—what Carnap (1966) called classification—what is felt sensorially.

Children can also use comparative terms, such as "more," "less," and "same," in their natural language (Carnap, 1966). Their intellectual competence and their use of these terms allow them to make transitive inferences about comparative temperatures. For example, with these comparative terms, children can argue that if substance A is hotter than substance B and if substance B is hotter than substance C, then substance A is hotter than substance C. This inference is impossible if they have only nominal or classification terms. Children do not have a full-blown, mature understanding of these comparative terms from the moment they appear in their lexicon. Children's understanding and use of these terms follow a developmental course. They do not have a full understanding of the transitive relation from the inception of these lexical items, as has been shown in countless studies.

With the aid of a thermometer (a material tool), one can measure temperature and ascertain, for example, that the temperature of a body of water is, say, 10°C, or 50°F. The temperature, as described by this semiotic system, is scalar. It allows precision that is unavailable via other semiotic systems. Children's understanding of scalars (a semiotic technology) follows a developmental course, which is described in another section of this chapter. In other words, children's grasp of this aspect of the numerical semiotic system has a developmental trajectory, too.

To recap, children describe temperature they feel sensorially with different semiotic systems. They use natural language to describe the water's temperature, sometimes in a classificatory manner (hot, cold, tepid), sometimes comparatively (hotter, colder, same temperature), and sometimes numerically (10°C). All three are descriptions of the temperature of a body of water that is felt sensorially. The semiotic technologies that are the media of description are different from each other. Each has its own constraints and power, and each develops differently.

To better understand children's developing science concepts, we must be aware of the type of semiotic system in which the concepts are clothed. We should also be aware of the developmental courses of children's grasp of those semiotic technologies. (I will have more to say about this in later sections of this chapter.)

Normative Development

The developmental model must inform and be informed by work on normative development—how children spontaneously understand science content taught in school. Without a clear understanding of the developmental landmarks of children's spontaneous, commonsense understanding of concepts taught in schools, we will not be in a position to insightfully determine the sequence and timing of instruction for these concepts. (This idea is illustrated in the section on curriculum development.)

Models of Cognitive Transitions

One needs models of cognitive transitions (learning and development) to describe how children move from an initial understanding of a concept to a deeper understanding of the same concept. Without models of how learning and development take place, we will be hard-pressed to decide how to foster progressive cognitive transitions, which is one of the goals of science education.

Notice that several aspects are embedded in this position. First, the kinds of transitions that interest us here occur as a consequence of instruction. We are less interested in the developmental transitions that occur spontaneously and are not in need of special, manufactured environments such as schools and museums. We are more interested in learning that occurs in school settings, which were established so that children could go beyond their commonsense understanding of the world and of science.

Second, work in this area should concern cognitive transitions that occur when attempting to teach school science content. How teachers teach science concepts and how curriculum developers present science ideas to children belie an underlying notion of (a) children's initial knowledge states, (b) the final knowledge states they want children to achieve as a consequence of having been taught and having worked with the curriculum materials, and (c) an implicit understanding of how children move from the initial to the final state.

The sixth position of the middle level developmental model addresses this understanding of cognitive transitions. Transition mechanisms, as conceived by both curriculum developers and teachers, are generally implicit. In various sections of this chapter, an argument is made for the need to make explicit these implicit understandings of cognitive transitions. Cognitive developmental psychologists and science educators must make these models of cognitive transitions a central area of research and theory-building. The models will serve the interests of academicians in this area, science educators who engage in curriculum development and teaching, and teachers who teach science in classrooms.

These six positions of the middle level developmental model of science education have been presented in an attempt to reconcile some deep differences among the domains of developmental psychology, academic science education, and science education practice. The area created where these three domains intersect—that is, the area created by the middle level model—allows work to be done because each domain informs and is informed by the others.

Even though there is an emergent area in the middle level, life goes on as normal for those who remain out of that intersect. People from all three domains continue to do their traditional work. Classical developmental psychologists search for deeper levels of mental organization than the one needed to do educational work; for example, they seek a logic of meanings to describe deep mental structures. Traditional science educators continue to work in areas that are not necessarily developmental; for example, they study the roles of subject matter in curriculum development. And teachers practice their profession in ways that are not clearly motivated by developmental considerations—for example, their roles as classroom managers in laboratory classes.

In addition, there are still some commonalities among those who work in the intersect and those who do not.

This point can be elaborated by showing that the same studies can be conducted by those who do and do not work in the middle level, but whose research can be done for different purposes.

Training studies are a good illustration. For reasons of theory construction in cognitive developmental psychology, it is of importance to know whether progressive cognitive change can be induced via training that attempts to run a version of the model that represents mechanisms of cognitive change. These are not change studies, to see whether we can induce change for the sake of inducing change. Rather, these are studies whose purposes are to test our ideas about mechanisms of cognitive development. These studies also help us to understand the developmental trajectory of children's science concepts.

These same training studies, by serving as *developmental tools,* can enable us to gain valuable insights into pragmatic areas of education. We can see whether children's understanding of the content we choose to study follows a developmental course and, if so, what that course is.

These studies can also be *diagnostic tools.* If we map out the developmental trajectory of children's understanding of science concepts, we can determine whether children at initially identical or similar levels in the developmental trajectory move to the same or different points along that trajectory as a consequence of instruction. This is Vygotsky's (1978) famous *zone of proximal development* (ZPD). Notice that although the ZPD helps us conceptualize how learning can proceed, it is an empty vessel. We cannot know from the notion of the ZPD what any learning sequence will be. Developmental research allows us to fill the vessel so that we will know, in general terms, what trajectory to expect.

As an example, Strauss and Stavy (1982) found that, for the intensive quantity aspect of temperature [pouring same-temperature water from two containers into a third (empty) container and asking children what the temperature of the mixed water is], there was a U-shaped behavioral growth curve. Young children solved the task correctly, older children solved the same task incorrectly, and still older children solved it correctly. Strauss and Stavy (1982) described this curve as indicating progressive cognitive advance. Instruction in the ZPD, if informed by these research findings and the theory construction that interpreted the findings, could be very helpful for teachers when they attempt to move children along the ZPD. They would know, for example, that a drop in children's performance signifies cognitive advance.

We can also determine the nature of the difficulties children encounter in understanding the science concepts or processes presented in that instruction. Diagnosing these difficulties can help us to understand what appears to stand in the way of children's correct representations of the problems at hand, and this, in turn, could guide us in curriculum construction and teaching.

These intervention studies can serve as *mapping tools* for teachers. As just shown, we can suggest, through careful analysis, effective instructional techniques for bringing about progressive cognitive advance. If, as a consequence of our research, teachers have an understanding of children's developmental course progress, they might be in a better position to help children negotiate that course. The developmental course we find in our training studies could be used as a map, allowing teachers to see where different children are heading and how far they have traveled in their personal trajectory.

The training studies can also be used as *instructional tools* for teachers. Teacher education often involves helping teachers become sensitive to the transactions between them and their pupils during teaching. Were we to have data from training studies about children's developing understanding about certain science concepts, and were teachers, both future and present, to work out the complexity of the teaching task with the guidance of those who have developmental backgrounds, these teachers could become more aware of the complexities involved in teaching those science concepts.

These same training studies can be a *curriculum development tool.* How this happens is spelled out in a later section on curriculum development. I simply note here that all of the above tools could be useful for the curriculum developer.

In short, training studies in the domain of cognitive development, which are conducted for the purpose of describing mechanisms of cognitive advance by those working outside the middle level, can be used by people working within the confines of the middle level model of science education as developmental, diagnostic, instructional, and curriculum development tools. Other examples of how cognitive development work could be exploited for science education purposes could be worked out. The same research can be conducted by cognitive developmentalists and science educators for the same or different purposes.

Now that the broadest outlines of this middle level cognitive developmental model of science education have been proposed, where learning and development are at its core, let us look at how theories of cognitive development can be expressed in science education theory, research, and practice.

HOW COGNITIVE DEVELOPMENT AND SCIENCE EDUCATION THEORY AND RESEARCH CAN CONJOIN

Along with the learning and development part of cognitive developmental psychology, the educational part of science education deals with cognitive transitions. There are many explanations of what these transitions are and how they are accomplished (Kuhn, 1995; Strauss, 1993a, 1993c). In part, these explanations are related to how one describes something that is thought to be changing. Descriptions might include the nature of children's initial cognitive states, their final states, and the transition mechanisms that allow children to go from the initial to the final state. All three are theory-bound, of course.

In keeping with the middle level model of science education, the psychological entities that give rise to the initial-state understandings described here are middle level. They are neither deep psychological entities, such as Piaget's mental structures, nor surface psychological entities, such as Siegler's rules. And in keeping with the eclectic nature of the middle level model, the descriptions of the initial states and transition mechanisms will come from several theories of cognition and its development.

Initial State

The initial state of children's cognition, as presented here, has been tested in three main areas in science education: (a) misconceptions, preconceptions, and alternatives for science concepts, (b) everyday versus scientific knowledge, and (c) understanding of the scientific enterprise: research, models, discoveries, and the nature of the inferences one can make from data to theory and vice versa. Other areas have been tested, but space constraints do not allow their inclusion here.

Misconceptions, Preconceptions, and Alternative Frameworks

In the past 15 years or so, there has been a burgeoning of research on children's misconceptions, preconceptions, and alternative frameworks. This area has grown into a virtual cottage industry, and the literature is now filled with accounts of research findings on how individuals misconstrue science concepts. The idea is to test children's (or university students') conceptions of school-science subject matter, to determine the nature of their understanding of these conceptions, and to compare them to conventional conceptions of experts in science. Generally (and not surprisingly), children's concepts are different from those of experts—the reason for the "mis" in the term "misconceptions."

Where does this research come from? Why would investigators turn their energies to determining the nature of children's preconceptions and misconceptions? One reason is that science educators became unenamored with Piaget's account of children's cognitive achievements. In his view of cognitive developmental psychology, science concepts were seen as structural products of interactions between the logico-mathematical structures that children constructed and the environment.

As much as this satisfied cognitive developmental psychologists in the era when Piaget was the central figure in that field, it was not a satisfying position for science educators. In the Piagetian scheme, there is no room for children's understanding of science concepts that *are taught in schools.* When a cognitive developmental psychologist of the Piagetian brand attempts to describe the nature of children's science concepts, the tasks presented to children and the analysis of children's understanding of those tasks are in terms of the structure of logical reasoning posited to give rise to children's concepts.

In Piaget's theory, one addresses children's science concepts as structural products or forms of reasoning about science content. The psychological entities thought to underlie these science concepts are mental structures, and the contents of these structures are logico-mathematical operations. Children's developing science concepts are treated less in terms of their science content and more in terms of how they allow us to infer children's forms of logical reasoning.

Because of dissatisfaction with this stance, science educators attempted to test children's understanding of science concepts where those concepts were the stuff of their knowledge organization. This stance removed logico-mathematical structures from children's minds and replaced them with science concepts, which were part of the children's knowledge organization.

I do not review all the research literature in the area of misconceptions because the number of references is far beyond the scope of this chapter. For a comprehensive compilation of studies and their findings in various areas of the sciences, see Pfundt and Duit (1988). However, I would like to note that the literature in the various areas of children's preconceptions and misconceptions has been impressive. International studies seem to show that children from many European countries and from North America, at similar ages, have similar misconceptions about various science domains.

Along with the impressive uniformity of misconceptions found among children come two problems. First, there is a relative dearth of theory that informs the search for these misconceptions. By and large, science education researchers (a) list the microdomains, to use Karmiloff-Smith's (1992, 1994) terminology, of science concepts that are taught in school, and (b) test how children conceptualize them. In short, the search for children's conceptions, which generally turn out to be misconceptions when compared to experts' conceptions, do not seem to be guided by issues of theory. Instead, the research has a pragmatic ring to it: Let's see what children know about what we want to teach them.

This is fine as far as it goes, but this approach to misconceptions research is not theory-free. The methods that researchers use to study children's (mis)conceptions belie an implicit understanding of the cognitive entity they are looking for. Even if the theory is not stated explicitly, it is there between the lines.

A second problem with the misconceptions research in science education is noted by Smith, diSessa, and Roschelle (1993), who argue that children are largely seen as holding flawed concepts (i.e., nonexpert views) of the domain under test and being quite resistant to intervention. This overemphasis on resistance to instruction unduly emphasizes the differences between expert and novice knowledge and deemphasizes how experts became experts; they, too, were once novices.

The bald fact is that some people *do* become experts in the sciences. They overcome their science misconceptions, most likely through school learning. Smith et al. (1993) argue that we would be better off changing our stance about misconceptions; rather than noting a resistance to change, we should attempt to change it. The attempts to intervene for the purpose of helping children overcome their misconceptions are briefly reviewed in the section on transition mechanisms.

A third problem with the misconceptions research is that it tells us what children's concepts are not: They are not the concepts held by scientists. This is a negative understanding of children's science concepts. A more positive view would allow us to see what these misconceptions tell us about what children *do* understand. Children hold these misconceptions for good reasons. The question to ask, then, is not how these children incorrectly understand some science concepts, but what those misunderstandings reveal about the nature and structure of children's minds.

Children's misconceptions are not random. Similar misconceptions are found among children in many other countries. My assumption is that they exist for good reasons and that they may be adaptive understandings for other situations and occasions. One goal of the search for middle level cognitive entities, then, is to find out the nature of these adaptive understandings. As demonstrated in the curriculum section, later in this chapter, one can sometimes use adaptive understandings for instructional purposes, as Hunt and Minstrell (1994) have done.

Everyday versus Scientific Knowledge

The dichotomy between everyday/spontaneous and scientific/social knowledge is central to Vygotsky's (1978, 1987) sociohistorical theory and to neo-Vygotskian theory (Brown & Campione, 1994; Pea, 1993). This epistemological distinction carries implications for a number of deep psychological issues, four of which I present here.

1. The sources of these two kinds of knowledge are different. Everyday concepts are the product of one's direct experiences with one's physical, social, biological, musical, or other environment. In contrast, social knowledge is mediated through social interactions between individuals or through individuals' cultural interactions.
2. Consciousness plays different roles in the existence and development of the two kinds of knowledge. Everyday concepts are not conscious; we are not aware we hold

them. Cognitive developmental psychologists attempt to describe their nature, their organization, and the mechanisms that underlie their change. Scientific concepts are conscious. Not only do we talk about them, but we discuss their ontological status, the ways we can prove their existence, how we can test them through experimentation, and how we can infer them from research data.

3. The developmental courses involved are thought to be different. Everyday concepts develop bottom up, are inductive in nature, and are data-driven. Scientific concepts develop top down, are essentially deductive in nature, and are theory-driven.
4. The semiotic technologies of cognition are different between these kinds of knowledge, noted in the previous section on the middle level developmental model of science education.

To illustrate some of these distinctions, work has focused on the development of children's concepts of heat and temperature (Strauss, 1981, 1987; Strauss & Stavy, 1982). We can describe heat as an extensive physical quantity, and temperature as an intensive physical quantity. Intensive physical quantities remain unchanged despite changes in their amount or extent. Examples are: temperature, sweetness, viscosity, pressure, and hardness. A task to measure children's understanding of intensive physical quantity for temperature is conducted as follows: Two containers of equal-temperature water are poured into a third (empty) container. Although the water's extensive physical quantity (amount) has changed, its intensive physical quantity (temperature) has not.

If we present this task qualitatively, telling the children that the water in the two containers is equally cold, we have presented the intensive physical quantity with natural language. Using another language (a semiotic system) to describe the identical task, we represent the intensive physical quantity task numerically. We can measure the water's temperature with a thermometer. Let's say that the temperature we record is 10°C. The temperature of the mixed water, poured from the two containers, will be 10°C, too.

Note that the qualitative and the numerical tasks are identical in terms of the physics of the problem. We used the same water and we performed the same transformations; nothing is different in the two tasks from the point of view of the physical laws that underlie them.

Sociohistorical proponents would argue, however, that the tasks *are* different in fundamental ways. The former task is closer to the everyday knowledge side of the continuum. Children, when playing with water, inevitably add different- and same-temperature water. They heat the mixture, cool it off, and so on. Their everyday experiences with temperature become abstracted into everyday concepts. This is not the case for the numerical task, which is closer to the scientific or cultural side of the same continuum. In the numerical task, children use a cultural tool, the thermometer, which has a developmental history. It records the water's temperature and indicates it by a single number. Numbers are also a cultural invention.

Note also that identical *physics* tasks, in terms of the laws of physics that underlie them, can be different *psychological* tasks when they are presented in different languages: natural; qualitative versus cultural; or numerical. The epistemological distinction that Vygotsky created (between common sense and cultural knowledge) has psychological reality. In a series of studies by Strauss and Stavy (1982), children, across a wide age span, were given tasks of the kind described above and were asked what the temperature of the mixed water in the container would be if the water in the original containers was cold (the qualitative task) or was 10°C (the numerical task).

The results from the two tasks had different developmental trajectories. The qualitative task, which tapped children's everyday knowledge about temperature, showed a U-shaped behavioral growth curve. Young children (ages 4 to 5 years) solved the task correctly; older children (ages 6 to 8 years) solved the same task incorrectly; and still older children (ages 9 years or more) solved the task correctly. The numerical task, which tapped children's scientific/social knowledge about temperature, was solved by very few children until approximately age 9 years, and then the percentage of children who solved the task correctly increased with age.

The above results indicate the psychological reality of the epistemological distinction Vygotsky made between everyday and scientific knowledge. Children solve identical physics task differently when the tasks are presented in two versions: one that taps everyday knowledge and one that taps scientific knowledge.

Understanding the Scientific Enterprise

Let us now look at some developmental research that informs us of children's developing understanding of aspects of the scientific enterprise, especially: (a) the goals of science; (b) the nature of scientific knowledge, theory, and evidence; and (c) the purposes and uses of science models.

Children's Understandings of Scientific Goals. Reif and Larkin (1991) have discussed the nature of scientific goals, as well as the means employed to attain those goals. Science is a knowledge domain about which scientists have certain beliefs. Children almost surely have different beliefs about science as a knowledge domain. And what is presented in schools as the knowledge domain of science is not necessarily what scientists believe about their domain. Is it any wonder that children encounter difficulties learning those aspects of science?

Reif and Larkin (1991) lay out a 2×2 taxonomy of kinds of domain knowledge and domain cognition that are understood and worked out in everyday and scientific ways. The four categories (and the subcategories within these categories) are found in Table 6.1. This taxonomy, which compares everyday and scientific knowledge, is a remarkably rich and useful way for middle level model science education people and cognitive developmental psychologists to view their domains of theory. It can serve as a map of what could be understood in terms of theory and what could be tested empirically.

Table 6.1 A Taxonomy of Representations of Scientific Knowledge

	Everyday Domain	Scientific Knowledge
Domain Goals		
Main Goals		
Central goal	Leading a good life	Optimal prediction and explanation
Subgoal	Adequate prediction and explanation	
Requirements	Adequate generality, parsimony, precision, consistence	Maximal generality, parsimony, precision, consistency
Working Goals		
Understanding	Few inferences Various acceptable premises	Many inferences Well-specified premises
Assessing validity	Moderate importance Various acceptable premises Plausible inference rules	Central importance Observation-based premises Well-specified inference rules
Domain Cognition		
Knowledge Structure		
Concept specification	Implicit and scheme-based	Explicit and rule-based
Knowledge organization	Locally coherent Associative organization	Globally coherent Local organization
Methods		
Problem solving	Short inferences based on rich compiled knowledge	Long inferences based on parsimonious knowledge
Types of methods	Nonformal	Complementary formal and nonformal
Quality Concerns		
Quality control	Nonformal	Strict and explicit
Efficiency	Naturally efficient everyday tasks	Designed for efficiency in complex tasks

Children's Understanding of Scientific Knowledge, Theory, and Evidence. One of the hallmarks of scientific work is theory building, which, when aided by empirical research, involves relations among theory, hypotheses that flow from theory, and evidence that confirms or refutes hypotheses. An aspect of cognitive developmental and science education research that has received some attention is the ways children conceptualize scientific knowledge and the purposes and nature of research. Four research programs have emerged in this area: (a) Piagetian research, (b) research on hypothesis generation and the evaluation of evidence, (c) understanding scientific knowledge and research, and (d) developing search strategies in a scientific problem space.

Piagetian Research. Research on a part of this area was reported in Inhelder and Piaget's (1958) account of what constitutes formal operational reasoning. Their main claim was that only formal operations children are able to isolate variables, manipulate them systematically and fully, test their effects on the problem under consideration, and then draw conclusions about the variables' effects. These children can construct a hypothetical list of variables and their combinations to test, and they can then go about empirically testing that list and eventually drawing proper conclusions, given what the data showed. Children at lower stages, when solving tasks that required the above reasoning, isolated some of the variables, manipulated several yet drew conclusions about only one of them, and, in general, were not able to come up with an exhaustive list of variables that was generated hypothetically.

The Piagetian claim was that there are qualitative differences in the ways children at different stages conceptualize problems when they are asked to solve tasks of the type intended to measure children's hypotheticodeductive reasoning. The mental structures children construct give rise to the solutions they produce when they are presented with such tasks. Piaget argued that the radical differences between younger and older children (and adults) in their solutions to scientific reasoning tasks are a consequence of their qualitatively different mental structures.

The bottom line here is that, before the formal operations stage, as defined by Piaget, children do not have the mental structure needed to conduct research. Unlike the plentiful investigations into children's intuitive and concrete operations stages, research and theory constructions about formal operations reasoning are rather scarce. This was the case for the proponents and the opponents of Piaget's psychogenetic approach. By default, then, Piaget's was the generally accepted idea among many cognitive developmental psychologists regarding children's developing conceptions of the myriad aspects of reasoning needed to conduct scientific experimentation. On the other hand, among science education researchers, there was considerable research on formal operational reasoning, which was within the Piagetian tradition.

All of this changed, at least among cognitive developmental psychologists, when Kuhn, Amsel, and O'Laughlin's (1988) research program was first published. I now turn to their work.

Research on Hypothesis Generation and the Evaluation of Evidence. Kuhn et al.'s (1988) work looked at children's developing abilities to understand scientific reasoning that includes (a) producing hypotheses about some part of our world, based on theory considerations, and (b) using evidence to change these theories. Their work concentrated on children's developing abilities to evaluate evidence. They presented rather simple tasks that tested children's understanding of what variable produces an effect—for example, the effect of tennis racket size on the speed of a serve. They concluded that children and some adults cannot differentiate among theories, hypotheses of cause and effect, and the evidence needed to confirm or refute these hypotheses, and that they seem to have difficulty distinguishing between the goal of understanding a phenomenon and making it occur.

This research area is growing rapidly now that there is a non-Piagetian way of thinking about the development of scientific reasoning in children. And because the theory part has loosened up, different methodologies to test that reasoning have been developed. The area is still in controversy, however, as various theorists and investigators disagree about the import of Piaget's and Kuhn's work.

One line of disagreement centers on Kuhn's et al.'s claims. For example, Sodian (1995) and Sodian, Zaitchik, and Carey (1991) showed that young elementary school children *do* distinguish between testing a belief and producing a desirable effect. They understand that indirect evidence can be generated to verify whether a test result or a belief is true or false. And older elementary school children understand that testing causal beliefs includes comparing critical conditions.

These research findings contradict those of Kuhn et al. (1988). Without getting into the reasons for these differences, we see here that research on hypothesis generation and the evaluation of evidence is rapidly growing, which points to potentially important work both for cognitive developmental psychology and for science education. For cognitive developmental psychologists, the area of children's developing abilities to mentally navigate among theory, knowledge, and evidence is important because it involves children's developing epistemology of a knowledge domain: science. For science educators and teachers, it contributes to decisions about curriculum development and teaching at different grade levels—decisions that are based on research about children's developing conceptions of the epistemology of science.

1. *Understanding scientific knowledge and research.* Susan Carey and her coworkers (Carey, Evans, Honda, Jay, & Unger, 1989; Carey & Smith, 1993) have been conducting research on children's understanding of scientific knowledge and its relations to research. Carey et al. (1989) showed that middle school and high school children's understanding of experimentation as an activity for generating ideas and testing theories is organized at three levels. At the first level of understanding, children believe that an activity is done for its own sake. A scientist tries to learn whether "it" works; however, "it" is ambiguous. Scientists aim to discover facts, get answers about the world, and invent things. At this level, children believe that knowledge is a copy of the part of the world that is encountered by the knower. Wellman (1990) has found similar ideas regarding different tasks among 3- and 4-year-olds.

At the second level, children distinguish between experiments and ideas. Children believe that an experiment is conducted to test an idea and to determine whether the idea is right. But, at this level, an idea is equated with a guess on the part of the scientist. Children at this level do not understand that an idea is a prediction derived from a theory, and if there is a revision of the original idea, it must include both the data described by the previous idea and the new data.

At the third level, children differentiate between experiments and the ideas they are intended to test. They understand that experiments are performed to test or to explore consequences of theories, and they appreciate the goal of science to develop continually deeper explanations of scientific domains.

2. *Developmental search strategies in a science problem space.* The third position of research in this area adopts a science-as-problem-solving view. Dunbar and Klahr (1989) sought to understand developing search strategies in a science problem space. Their work aimed at discovering both the strategies used by children and adults in a scientific reasoning task, and their knowledge representation of the task at hand. In this way, they attempted to test processes and knowledge in concert, rather than in isolation.

Here is an example of the ways they tested. Children and adults were given a computer-controlled vehicle that could move when given commands. The subjects were first trained in how to program the vehicle to move. They were then asked to discover how a "repeat" command works. The ways they searched for solutions to the problem were part of the experimental data collected by Dunbar and Klahr (1989).

Their findings about developmental differences between children and adults in solving science problems of the above sort were dependent on the level of analysis used to describe the observed behaviors. At a very general level, both children and adults could understand the nature of the task (how to get the device to behave so as to learn how it works) and could arrive at a summary statement about the device's workings in a general manner. At this very general level, there were no differences between children and adults.

However, there were differences in success rate. The adults had a 95% success rate, whereas the children's success rate was only 10%. Dunbar and Klahr offered two explanations for these differences: (a) Children have less demanding criteria for evaluating hypotheses than adults do. This leads to the children's being able to accept hypotheses in the face of incomplete evidence and inconsistency. (b) Metacognitive skills are lacking in children and are present adults.

This area of research has been summarized, and the different approaches to it—and the controversies that surround it—have been noted. Although there is no general agreement about this area, identical research can be conducted by both cognitive developmental psychologists, who have a science education orientation, and science educators, who have a developmental bent. This is one of the features of the middle level developmental model of science education. Both groups could use it to find out what children's developing ideas are about scientific theory, hypothesis testing, the nature of evidence, and inferences that can be drawn from experiments.

Research in this domain could be interesting for cognitive developmental psychologists because, through the model, we could better understand how children conceptualize a significant aspect of domain knowledge. There is potential here for cognitive development theory-building.

Research in this area could also be of importance and interest to science educators and teachers because were we to find that children's belief systems differ from those of scientists and from the school presentation of the roles of experimentation (Reif & Larkin, 1991), we would then be in a position to (a) understand the nature of the difficulties children have in understanding those aspects of the scientific enterprise, and (b) consider ways to rectify the situation through instruction.

Children's Developing Understanding of Scientific Models. Scientists use models to summarize an idea or theory, explain how something works, predict the consequences of an application or solution, and so on. Models are ubiquitous in scientists' knapsacks of technological ideas, and models can be powerful tools for scientific researchers. It is virtually impossible to think of a science domain that has not produced attendant models.

Models can be presented in various media. They can be mathematical equations, sketches of atoms, life-size plastic mannequins of the human body with "organs" that can be removed and replaced, computer simulations of gas transfer in the leaves of plants, and more.

Models can be found in most schools and are used extensively. As technological devices, their purpose is to give children a better understanding of a phenomenon under study. They are science teachers' aids for instruction.

Among curriculum materials, textbooks present models of various kinds, and computer programs with graphics often have models of science phenomena.

Despite models' ubiquity in scientific enterprises and in teaching about those enterprises, very little research has investigated the cognitive aspects of how students understand: what purposes models serve, who creates them and decides the ways in which they are to be constructed, the conditions under which they can and should be revised, the different ways the same thing can be represented by different models, and what models actually represent.

Recent work has begun to shed light on these details (see Grosslight, Unger, Jay, & Smith, 1991; Smith, Snir, & Grosslight, 1992). Children and experts (scientists) were asked to speak about what models are used for, what designers have to think about when making the models, how scientists use models, and so on. A picture of a house, a map of a subway system, a schematic diagram of the ground-to-clouds water cycle, a toy plane, and similar objects, were presented, and children were asked whether these objects could be called models and why.

Scientists had different and deeper knowledge about models than did 13- and 18-year-old children, but the experts' and children's understanding of models had some overlapping features. Grosslight et al. (1991) found three general levels of how children understand the relationships of models to reality, and the roles that ideas play in constructing models.

At the first level of understanding, children think that models are toys or simple copies of actual objects or actions. The developing psychological entities that create the levels of understanding are at the second or middle level. This level of understanding is characterized by children's believing that the model does not need to match the real-world object exactly. Changes can be made in the model, and it can still be a model of a piece of reality. Children also realize that an explicit purpose mediates the way models are constructed. In other words, the modeler's ideas begin to play a role here. But students at this level attend more to the reality being modeled than to the ideas portrayed via the model. And tests of the model are seen as tests of the workability of the model itself, and not the workability of the ideas underlying the model.

The third level of understanding has two principal features: (a) models are constructed so as to develop and test ideas (and they do not serve as a copy of reality itself) and (b) the modeler is an active constructor of the model and may change the language the model is embedded in so that the model best suits the modeler's purposes.

For cognitive developmental psychologists, this area of study is potentially interesting because it gets at the intersect of children's understanding of representations of realities; the forms and technologies used to embody those realities; and the ways that understanding of the representations and of their technological forms can interact with children's developing cognition.

For science educators, it is important to gain an understanding of children's developing conceptions of models in the manner just suggested. The teachers can then engage children's developing notions of this topic more successfully in their instruction. Similarly, based on research findings, curriculum developers can organize curriculum materials for the purposes of capitalizing on what is known of children's understanding about the above, and advancing their understanding to a higher level. As things stand now, many teachers use models to teach aspects of science concepts, and curriculum developers construct curricula that incorporate models without a clear understanding of children's developing conceptions about what models are.

I now turn to transition mechanisms that allow children to move from their initial state of understanding of the topic of interest to their next higher level of understanding.

Transition Mechanisms

Transitions are at the heart of cognitive developmental psychology because they capture the dynamics of cognitive change. And they should be no less at the heart of science education because a central goal of science education is to help move cognitive change from less advanced to more advanced cognitive states.

In this section, I describe how cognitive developmental theory about transition mechanisms has influenced attempts to foster children's understanding of aspects of science. This is one of the places where cognitive development and science education overlap in the middle level model. It is therefore one of the places where cognitive developmental psychology has implications for science education.

Misconceptions, Preconceptions, and Alternative Frameworks

Considerable research has shown that children's everyday, commonsense science preconceptions, some of which may be misconceptions, are remarkably resistant to intervention. Because of this resistance, various researchers have attempted to find ways to enlist, circumvent, and overcome the preconceptions. By and large, there have been few attempts to remove them or to activate what Bamberger (1982) calls the wipeout theory, mostly for the pragmatic reason that researchers have found removal to be virtually impossible.

As already noted, Smith et al. (1993) suggested that work on misconceptions places undue emphasis on children's resistance to intervention. In that spirit, two ways of bringing off cognitive change of science misconceptions are presented: (a) analogy construction and (b) conceptual change models of science concepts.

Analogy Construction and Learning by Analogy. Reasoning by analogy has been viewed by different theories as being central to human cognition. It imbues learning and is important in scientific discovery and creativity.

Goswami (1992) pointed out that structuralist, information processing, and knowledge-based theories use analogies as ways to describe learning. Each has its own ways of characterizing reasoning by analogy, the developmental constraints on this reasoning, and the educational implications for this reasoning. I briefly discuss the structuralist and knowledge-based theories.

Structuralist theory, or the structuralist account, declares that analogy reasoning is similar to proportional reasoning. The reasoning A:B::C:D sets up a relation between A and B, a relation between C and D, and a relation of the two relations (A:B and C:D) to each other. This was thought by Inhelder and Piaget (1958) to be similar to proportional reasoning where, for example, on the balance scale task, a child evaluates the weight and distance relation on one side (A/B) and on the other side (A′/B′) and then relates these relations when deciding whether the scale balances or one side tips down.

As for the developmental constraints in this account of reasoning by analogy, only children who have constructed the formal operations structure are capable of reasoning by analogy. Children who are at lower structural levels and who understand the content involved in the analogies are incapable of reasoning by analogy because their mental structure cannot produce the second-order reasoning required to solve analogy problems.

The educational implications are rather restricting here. If children cannot successfully engage in reasoning by analogy before the formal operations structure is constructed (at approximately ages 11 to 12 years), there is no point in giving them these problems to solve. We must wait for children to construct the formal operations structure before we can introduce analogy problems.

Knowledge-based theory has a different read on reasoning by analogy. Adherents to this approach (Gentner, 1989; Goswami, 1992) claim that reasoning by analogy is dependent, first and foremost, on one's conceptual knowledge of the content under discussion. If the content is represented conceptually and the relations in the analogy have been worked out, reasoning by analogy should ensue. If the relations in the analogy have not been fully worked out in the child's knowledge structure, that factor could prevent reasoning by analogy. In that circumstance, the individual cannot recognize the similarity between the two sides of the analogy.

By this account, there are no developmental constraints on reasoning by analogy. If a child's conceptual knowledge has the relations in the analogy embedded in it, then reasoning by analogy should be unencumbered. Goswami (1992), who advocates a strong version of the knowledge-based explanation of reasoning by analogy, reviewed research literature on infants' and toddlers' ability to apply the relational similarity constraint and concluded that it is used by both age groups. Goswami's review supports the claim that there may be no developmental constraints on reasoning by analogy.

To elaborate slightly on the knowledge-based theory, note that its devotees separate children's (and adults') problem knowledge representation from their solution procedure for the problem. When students solve science problems incorrectly, there are two major reasons for their difficulties: (a) they may have an adequate representation for the problem at hand, but their solution procedure may be inadequate for a solution, or (b) they may have adequate solution procedures but their problem representation may be askew.

Although the constructs of problem representations and solution procedures may be attractive and compelling, Novick and Hmelo (1994) argue that the line separating them is quite fragile. They investigated the construction of problem representations that are presented symbolically, for example, through spatial diagrams such as networks, hierarchies, matrices, and so on (cf. Larkin & Simon, 1987). In particular, they attempted to invoke representational transfer from the target problem to a similar problem (sometimes called a base domain) that had underlying structures similar to the target domain. In short, Novick and Hmelo used analogies to study the transfer of symbolic representations across problems.

The educational implications of the knowledge-based theory are promising (Duit, 1991; Treagust, Harrison, & Venville, 1996). Before dealing with that topic, however, a further elaboration of analogy construction is necessary.

Analogy construction involves knowledge about a base domain, a target domain, and rules for mapping from the former to the latter. Some recent theoretical (Gentner, 1983; Goswami, 1992) and empirical (Novick & Hmelo, 1994; Reed, 1987) work has led to ways of describing how rules get mapped from the base to the target domain.

The work here distinguishes between objects in the two domains and the relations among objects within each of the domains. A structure-mapping analogy preserves the relations among objects but not the attributes of those objects. An example frequently used to illustrate these ideas is the analogy between an atom and the solar system. The objects of the two domains are: electrons and a nucleus in the case of atoms, and planets and the sun in the case of the solar system. The relations between the objects in the domain are that electrons revolve around the nucleus of the atom, and planets revolve around the sun. The mapping from the base domain to the target domain is on the *revolving* rather than on the properties of the domains' objects. Electrons and planets differ in their properties, as do nuclei and the sun.

Analogy construction has generally used school-learned knowledge in both the source and target domains. The example of teaching the representation of the solar system through analogy with atoms is paradigmatic; both the atom and the solar system are school-learned knowledge. A notable exception is the work conducted by Clement, Brown, and Zietsman (1989), who used children's everyday knowledge as anchors and who slowly built intermediate analogies until they finally arrived at the scientific concept they wanted the children to learn.

With the exception of Clement et al. (1989), it is not clear why investigators believe that helping children construct, in nature, analogies between knowledge representations that are school-learned should help overcome the obstacles raised by everyday, spontaneous representations of science misconceptions. Instead, one could imagine building analogies from everyday knowledge representations (in the base domain) to school-learned knowledge representations (in the target domain), something that has not been consciously done to date. For a brief description of such a research attempt by Strauss and Salinger (1988), see the section on curriculum development in this chapter.

Researchers and theoreticians in cognitive development and science education, who work in the area of analogy construction for the learning of science concepts, can push forward the edges of our knowledge about how transitions occur between knowledge representations held by students from the base to the target domains. Results from such research could help in theory construction about the learning mechanisms involved.

Research and theory construction of this sort has an implication for science education in classrooms. Teachers constantly make analogies between domains as part of their normal instruction. Some analogies may be helpful, but only for some children. Were teachers more aware of the nature of their students' knowledge representations about the two domains they want to connect through analogy, they might be more judicious in their use of analogies. They might also consider the kinds of analogies that might more effectively foster in their students the kinds of knowledge they want to communicate. The same can be said for curriculum developers. For example, Thiele and Treagust (1996) found that chemistry textbooks were replete with problems when analogies were used to explain phenomena in chemistry.

Conceptual Change Models

Perhaps more than any other theoretical body of work, conceptual change is inspired by the philosophy and history of science. The area of conceptual change has proponents both in science education and in cognitive developmental psychology. Posner, Strike, Hewson, and Gertzog (1982), Strike and Posner (1985), Chi (1992, 1993) and Chi, Slotta, and deLeeuw (1994) attempted to connect such work to science education. Carey (1985) developed the naïve theories framework as an alternative to prevailing cognitive developmental theories, such as Piaget's.

In one of the shifts that led to conceptual change models, cognition was viewed in a light other than the one suggested by Piaget. Piaget (1970) looked at children's cognition in terms of the logical structures thought to underlie children's behaviors on tasks designed to reveal those structures. The content of those mental structures included operations and their relations. The content of children's science concepts was a product of the interactions between the children's mental structures and the environment.

The shift brought about by Posner et al. (1982) and Carey (1985) identified the nature of the content of children's concepts per se. A search ensued for a description of children's knowledge organizations (not logical mental structures) in which the content was science beliefs (not mental operations). Posner et al. and Carey argued that a way to describe these knowledge organizations was in terms of theories. In other words, the philosophy of science about theories of science could be used to describe students' organization of knowledge. They claimed that students have naïve theories about the world of science.

Their next step was to claim that students' naïve theories change in ways that are similar to the ways theories change in the sciences. Both research groups pointed out that there are significant differences between how a field changes and how individuals change. Yet both noted some similarities, which will now be discussed.

According to Posner et al. (1982) and Strike and Posner (1985), some basic tenets of conceptual change have conceptual conflict at their core. Hewson and Hewson (1984) took a similar stance. All of them proposed these tenets for conceptual change: (a) scientists and students must be dissatisfied with existing concepts; (b) there must be a minimal understanding of the new concepts; (c) the new concepts must have some initial plausibility; and (d) the new concepts should suggest new areas of inquiry.

There is some similarity between these tenets and Piaget's notions of qualitative cognitive change. Piaget (1970) wrote about the two faces of cognition: (a) the face that looks outward or the adaptational face that seeks accord between mental structures and the environment, and (b) the face that looks inward or the organizational face that seeks accord with itself. Mental structures maintain equilibrium between themselves and the environment (adaptational equilibrium) and within themselves (organizational equilibrium). This equilibrium balances assimilation, a coherence mechanism that allows for meaning-making, and accommodation, a mechanism that allows mental structures to deal with the changing nuances of the environment.

Disequilibrium is, in Piaget's scheme of things, the major explanation of cognitive development. Disequilibrium can be adaptational or organizational. When there is a conflict between the mental structure and the environment, or when a conflict exists between structures, conditions are set for cognitive change. Disequilibrium does not always lead to cognitive change, however.

Despite the similarity among Hewson and Hewson's conceptual conflict model of cognitive change, Posner et al.'s (1982) and Strike and Posner's (1985) conceptual change view of learning, Piaget's disequilibrium model of cognitive change, and the fascination of cognitive developmental psychologists and science educators with the place of conflict in cognitive development, work in the area has virtually stopped among cognitive developmentalists and has come under attack by some science educators (Chi, 1992, 1993; Chi, Slotta, & deLeeuw, 1994; J. Smith et al., 1993).

Decline in interest in Piaget's theory is one reason for the change of the cognitive conflict model in cognitive developmental psychology. Although central and compelling approximately 20 years ago, it is virtually absent in contemporary work. Science educators also relate this decline to a belief that cognitive conflict is not adequate as a mechanism for change (Chi, Slotta, & deLeeuw, 1994; Smith et al., 1993). Among the reasons offered are: (a) conflict between differing understandings does not explain why the more correct understanding wins out over the misconception; (b) misconceptions have been argued to be resistant to change and schooling, so it is unclear why conflict, which purports to show an alternative to children's understandings, should be more successful in bringing about cognitive change; and (c) choosing among understandings requires a judgment about which understanding is more reasonable. Conflict does not include this rational choice. In addition, decision making of this sort has been found to be developmental (Kuhn & Phelps, 1982).

Chi (1992, 1993; Chi et al., 1994) offers another interpretation of the notion of conceptual change and suggests ways to overcome children's science misconceptions. In an attempt to explain why some misconceptions are so difficult to change, Chi begins with the premise that there are ontological categories (matter, processes, and mental states), and within each are hierarchies (trees) so that, for example, matter can be subdivided into natural kinds and artifacts. A schematic representation of these trees is given in Figure 6.1. The categories within a given tree are different ontologically from those within other trees.

Chi's premise (1992, 1993; Chi et al., 1994) pertains to epistemological assumptions about the nature of entities in

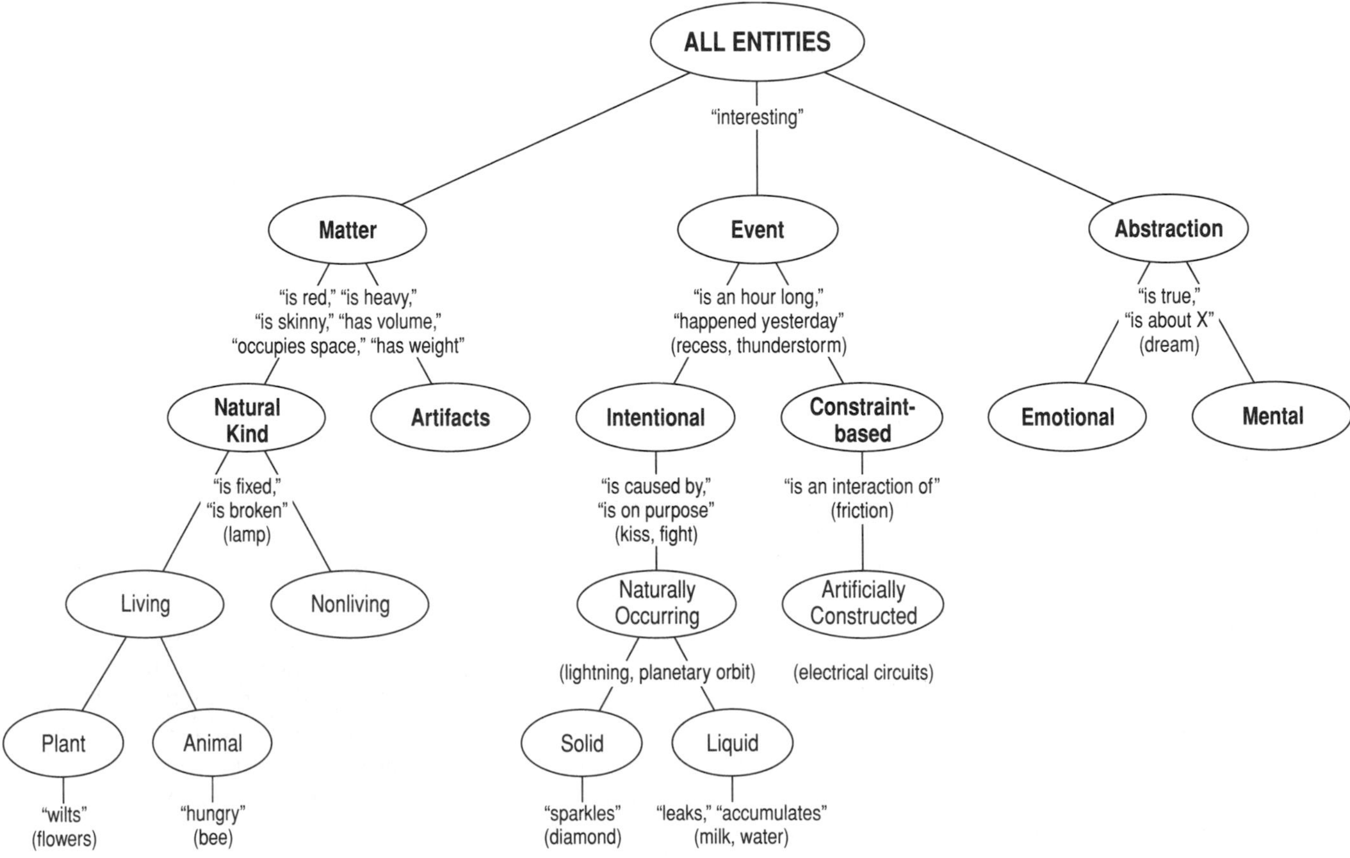

Figure 6.1 A schematic representation of ontological categories.

the world. She also makes metaphysical and psychological assumptions about the same trees. Her claim about science misconceptions is that children and adults often assign concepts to the wrong ontological tree. For example, children believe that heat (a constraint-based process) is a kind of matter. They also believe that animals grow (a biological phenomenon) because they want to (part of mental states). When there is a mismatch between the categorical representation that children bring to a learning situation and the ontological category of which the concept being learned is a part, the prediction is that we will be in the presence of a science misconception.

For children to overcome their misconception and learn a science concept in the way scientists understand it, they must make a radical conceptual change requiring a shift across trees. They must learn how to categorize the misconception under a different tree.

In short, this classification system allows a way to predict which science concepts will be misconceptions that are resistant to conventional instruction and which will be less resistant to such instruction. What the system does not tell us is the nature of transitional mechanisms: how one goes from conceptualizing a concept under one tree to conceptualizing it under another tree. Analysis shows that learning processes—analogy construction, discrimination, generalization, and so on—cannot transform a concept from one tree to another. The search for learning via radical conceptual change must therefore be taken elsewhere.

Chi (1992) describes a three-step learning process by which children and adults reassign a concept under a different tree. First, the new ontological category's properties must be learned via acquisition processes. Students must be told that the concepts they put in one category belong in another category that has different properties. Learning these properties is the focus of the first step.

In the second step, students learn the meaning of individual concepts within this ontological category. Traditional instruction techniques are used; their purposes are to bring about discrimination, generalization, and so on. But in Chi's (1992) scheme of things, this is done within the framework of the new ontological category.

The third step involves a reassignment of the concept to the new ontological category. Three possible sets of processes can lead to this reassignment. The first process is replacement: Students abandon the original meaning they attributed to the concept and essentially replace it with the new meaning. The second process is addition: The new meaning is added to the first, and both exist side-by-side in the students' representations. One or the other gets called up, depending on the context of the task. The third process is similar to the first: Students replace the assignment of the concept in question under the new ontological category rather than under the former one. But in this third process, the concept in the new category is called up automatically, without requiring conscious effort. The new category is more coherent and robust than the former one.

The final class of transition mechanisms revolves around students' consciousness of the ways they understand the science concepts before the concepts are being taught.

Metacognition

One of the insights gained from Vygotsky's sociohistorical approach is the importance of consciousness or self-awareness in learning. Neo-Vygotskian work has come to emphasize this metacognitive part of human cognition.

Understanding and control over that understanding are the characteristics of metacognition. In metacognition, children (and adults) are aware of themselves as thinkers. They think about their thinking, monitor it, and eventually control it. This is one of the characteristics of efficient learning, and it should be a goal of science education (Brown, 1975, 1978).

One part of this argument is that a condition for learning is the achievement of an insight into one's own understanding of the content being taught before being presented with alternative content. In other words, if pupils do not know what they think about the content that is about to be taught, they will be less likely to incorporate the taught material into their existing knowledge. Under those conditions, there will be less understanding on the part of the children.

Having pupils become aware, during the learning process, of their own thinking about their conceptual models and understanding of science has been the subject of some recent work. Two promising undertakings on self-explanations and conceptual models for solving science problems have been reported. Another exciting and ambitious undertaking in metacognition as it relates to science education is that of Brown and Campione (1994). I do not review their work here, but it is an excellent example of how metacognition can be used to help foster children's understanding of science.

Self-Explanation. Self-explanation involves generating explanations to oneself. It is a form of self instruction. As students read a science text or solve a science problem, self-explanations allow them to learn and better understand examples or sequences of actions that are not well explained in the text.

Although proponents of self-explanations research do not frame their work in literature on metacognition, I believe a case can be made for that approach. Let us take the example of students explaining to themselves, say, the principle of photosynthesis or a law of Newtonian mechanics, which they are attempting to understand from an example in a textbook. As they self-explain, they become aware of what they know, what they do not know, and what they need to learn if they are to have a more correct understanding of the topic. In short, these children are monitoring their knowledge and are strategically attempting to overcome what they view as problematic in their understanding. When this is done in a deliberate manner, students are testing their knowledge and understanding against a statement of a principle. This testing makes them more conscious of the principle than when they read examples without trying to resort to self-explanation.

Chi and her colleagues tested the roles of self-explanation in learning physics problems (Chi, Bassok, Lewis, Reimann, & Glaser, 1989; Chi, deLeeuw, Chiu, & LaVancher, 1994; Chi & VanLehn, 1991). Chi et al. (1989) examined how college students study and use examples from a physics text. Through analysis, examples from physics texts were found to be almost always underdetermined; they required the reader to fill in knowledge and inferences. There have been few attempts to measure students' representations when they read worked-out solutions of problems, which are commonly found in science texts.

Chi et al.'s (1989) main purpose was to study the relations between text encoding, as tested by the completeness of the representation of the knowledge students acquire when they read from a physics text, and problem solving. The text included examples of worked-out solutions for a physics problem involving Newtonian particle dynamics.

The investigators wanted to determine whether difficulties in problem solving could be attributed to less-than-complete representations of knowledge on the part of students when they attempted to encode examples from the physics text. They also tested the roles of individual differences in text encoding and subsequent problem solving.

Text encoding was measured by having students describe and explain what they were thinking. A classification system was worked out that included explanations, monitoring statements (e.g., "I'm getting lost here"), and a category called "others," which included students' paraphrases, mathematical elaborations, and metastrategies.

The researchers found good and poor text encoders; some had more and others had less complete representations of the problem and its solutions. Good encoders, when attempting to understand the examples, solved close and far transfer tasks at a higher level than poor encoders. In other words, Chi et al. (1989) found that varying levels of knowledge representation, gained from encoding examples from a science text, influence students' problem solving on similar and different tasks.

This study showed that there are differences in self-explanation among students. Good problem solvers generate many more self-explanations than poor problem solvers. Because self-explanation is considered a way for students to infer additional pieces of information that are not in the text but are part of the problem solution, Chi et al. (1989) concluded that self-explanation mediates self-instruction.

Chi and VanLehn (1991), who analyzed further the nature of the self-explanations the students produced, found four categories of knowledge: (a) systems, (b) technical procedures, (c) principles, and (d) concepts. Within these categories, there were 110 distinct pieces of constituent knowledge. Good problem solvers produced significantly more constituent knowledge pieces when self-explaining than did poor problem solvers.

The implications of Chi's studies for science education practice are clear. If we were to enhance students' self-explanation strategies, the students' problem solving might improve. This possibility was studied by Chi, deLeeuw, Chiu, and LaVancher (1994) during an attempt to teach self-explanation skills to 14-year-olds. The text's topic was the circulatory system.

This study differed from others in several ways: the age group was younger (elementary school versus college students); the domain was different (biology versus physics); the text had a self-explaining approach versus one that had worked-out examples; attention was paid to the students' understanding of concepts versus learning a problem-solving procedural skill; and students' self-explanations were prompted versus recording their spontaneous generation.

The study found that self-explanation fosters learning and understanding of a text that presents new knowledge. This was the result for children who received promptings for self-explanation and for others in a control group who did not get these prompts. The result was the same for high and low explainers.

One implication garnered from Chi's studies pertains to theories of learning: Students can generate new knowledge that is not in the text. This new knowledge comes from self-explanations that suggest to the students where they have gaps in their knowledge or where their knowledge might be inadequate. In other words, their knowledge generation is constructive in nature.

A second implication is that children can change their misconceptions via self-explanation. This was found in the research on Newtonian mechanics among college students and in the research on the circulatory system among elementary school children. When explaining how this could be so, Chi, deLeeuw, Chiu, et al. (1994) argued that self-explanation allows students to go beyond their instantiating existing knowledge and its direct encoding. It allows new information to become integrated with prior knowledge and, in the process, new knowledge is created.

A third implication is that self-explanation is domain-general. It is a cognitive mechanism that describes how learners gain deeper understandings of science concepts presented in texts. It is not a mechanism specific to, say, Newtonian physics.

An implication of these findings for science education is that children learn science concepts with relatively deep understanding when they are prompted to self-explain. This suggests that curriculum materials can be constructed in ways that foster self-explanation. And science teachers might use these ideas by setting up classroom situations that encourage children to attempt to self-explain science texts.

Conceptual Models. Research by Smith, Snir, and Grosslight (1992) was aimed at fostering the differentiation of the concepts of weight, size, and density. The differentiation of relatively global functions and structures has been described by Werner (1937, 1957) as a basic component of development, as elaborated in his orthogenetic theory. Smith, Carey, and Wiser (1985) discussed extensively the roles of differentiation in ontogenesis and in historical development. The differentiation of weight, size, amount, and density was the focus of their discussion of the concept of differentiation in cognitive developmental theory.

The method used by Smith et al. (1992) to help foster the differentiation of global, syncretic mental models was to first have children produce, on paper (via computer programs), their own model of size, amount, weight, and density. The idea was to make the children aware of the model they held about these concepts. Once they explicated their own model of these concepts and their relations, they were in a position to evaluate it against other models of the same concepts and their relation to models that physicists have developed. A key point is that the students were in a position to use their personal model as a tool when they became aware of which model they held.

Metacognition, it should be emphasized, is a precondition for some kinds of learning. Helping students become aware of their conceptual system does not guarantee that they will be able to change it. Metacognition simply sets the stage for some kinds of learning to take place. There must also be strategic and active control over one's own cognitive processing. (This theme is picked up in a discussion of curricula for teacher education, in the section on curriculum development.)

The previous sections of this chapter focused on children's developing science concepts and the transition mechanisms that are thought to underlie moves from initial to next states. The focus now shifts to teachers' concepts of science and their understandings of how to teach science to children.

TEACHERS' COGNITION ABOUT SCIENCE AND CHILDREN'S MINDS, LEARNING, AND INSTRUCTION

This section deals with various aspects of theory and research on teachers' cognition and classroom science instruction.

Teachers' Cognition

This topic is divided into discussions of teachers' understanding of the science they teach, teachers' mental models about children's minds and how children learn science, and teachers' subject matter knowledge and their mental models about how children learn that subject matter.

Teachers' Understanding of Science

Several aspects of understanding science are relevant for cognitive developmentalists, science educators, and science teaching practitioners: (a) understanding science concepts (subject matter knowledge) and (b) understanding the epistemology of science, which includes understanding scientific goals, scientific models, and relations between scientific theory and evidence. There has been minimal research in these areas as they pertain to teachers. As a consequence, the present section is more a map of what could be done than a summary of what has been done. Only teachers' understanding of scientific concepts is presented here; however, the same reasoning and conclusions apply to teachers' understanding of the epistemology of science.

Considerable research and theory development have been done in the area of how children understand (and misunderstand) science concepts, but similar research about teachers has been scant. In fact, one of the first calls for such research was made only a bit more than a decade ago (Munby, 1984).

Why are theory building and research in the area of teachers' subject matter knowledge of interest? The first reason is the varying amounts and kinds of science education that teachers receive and the uneven levels of their understanding of the science concepts they study.

Despite the scant research on science teachers' concepts, the many studies of college and university science majors' understanding of science concepts leave little doubt that misconceptions abound in many subdomains of the sciences (e.g., for the concept of force, see Caramazza, McCloskey, & Green, 1981; Clement, 1982; diSessa, 1982, 1983; Driver, Guesne, & Tiberghien, 1985; Helm & Novak, 1983; McDermott, 1984; Trowbridge & McDermott, 1980, 1981; Viennot, 1979; B. Y. White, 1983).

Should we expect the teachers of science in elementary schools and high schools to be different from these college students? Not when many college and university nonscience majors, who are to become elementary school teachers, have taken relatively few courses in the sciences. If science majors have misconceptions about science, we can reasonably expect that college and university nonscience majors who are preparing to teach science would have misconceptions as well.

A taxonomy of those misconceptions might reveal some that are deeply rooted and resist change even after instruction (e.g., university graduate students in the sciences) versus others that are less robust and change in response to varying amounts and kinds of instruction. This taxonomy could lead to speculation about the reasons these concepts have different levels of resistance to instruction. How do science concepts, human cognition, and the roles of instruction in fostering science concepts intersect in our future science teachers?

A second reason for the importance of theory building and research in the area of teachers' understanding of science concepts is connected to teachers' knowledge of the science curriculum. In particular, how does teachers' subject matter knowledge match their knowledge of pedagogical methods? Can the teachers communicate their knowledge about science concepts, methods, and principles so that pupils will learn them? The conventional wisdom of the literature in this area is that teachers with more and better organized subject matter knowledge will teach differently (and better) than teachers who have less knowledge and whose knowledge is less well-organized. However, that projection may not be valid.

Teachers' Mental Models about Children's Minds and Science Teaching

Teaching at children's level of understanding, and fostering learning are among teachers' major responsibilities. This is an aspect of a general area that has been dubbed *pedagogical content knowledge* by Shulman (1986). Nobody has seen a child's mind, nor does anyone truly know what learning is and what conditions are necessary to bring it about. All of these elements are controversial. Yet, teachers are charged with the task of bringing about learning in their pupils. Teachers take on this task with an intuitive description (what I will call a mental model) of what children's minds are like, how learning takes place in children's minds, and their own roles, as teachers, in fostering that learning.

Research in cognition and education has shown repeatedly that mental models organize how students learn what is taught in a domain, and these models are quite resistant to change via instruction (see, e.g., Clement, 1982; diSessa, 1982; McCloskey, 1983; McCloskey & Kargon, 1988). If we see that teachers have certain mental models about children's minds and the learning of science, and we are going to teach about learning and conceptions of the mind in our teacher education courses, we would then know what in teachers' thinking has to be addressed.

Teacher education courses may be able to influence teachers' mental models. And in so doing, they might influence the ways future teachers reach their pupils' minds so that learning can take place.

A brief review may achieve three main purposes: (a) to gain a deeper understanding of teachers' implicit mental models, which guide their actual teaching; (b) to enable teachers to be more reflective about the implications of their mental models of children's minds and children's learning; and (c) to help teachers construct additional ways of conceptualizing children's minds and learning and, therefore, additional ways of teaching.

The area of teacher cognition or teacher thinking is relatively new. Shulman's (1986) ground-breaking work established a new way of understanding it. Clark and Peterson (1986) classified research on teachers' thinking into three categories: (a) preactive and postactive planning, (b) interactive thinking, and (c) teachers' theories and beliefs. Teachers' theories and beliefs are discussed here.

Shulman (1986) and Wilson, Shulman, and Richert (1987) created a taxonomy of teachers' theories, beliefs, and knowledge. Schulman's term, pedagogical content knowledge, includes teachers' knowledge about pupils' minds and learning; pupils' preconceptions about subject matter; the concepts and skills that are particularly difficult for children to learn (and what makes them difficult); ways to simplify difficult concepts and skills, and more.

Pedagogical content knowledge relies on the psychological entities that imbue this discussion: mental models.

Gentner and Stevens (1983) and Johnson-Laird (1983) proposed that mental models are powerful organizers of people's understanding of aspects of their world. I argue further that these mental models are middle level cognitive entities and, as such, are relevant to the middle level cognitive developmental model of science education.

Norman (1983) claimed that a major purpose of a mental model is to enable a user of that model to predict the operation of the domain under study. In the domain under scrutiny here, the users are teachers and future teachers and the domain is children's minds and learning. Norman argued that mental models have three important functional factors, which are summarized here in terms of children's minds and learning: (a) teachers' mental models reflect their beliefs about children's minds and learning; (b) there is a correspondence between the parameters and states of the mental model and the aspects and states of children's minds and learning; and (c) the mental model has predictive power in that it allows teachers to understand and anticipate the nature of children's minds and how learning takes place in them.

Mental models are implicit. They are hidden, internal, and inaccessible by direct observation. They are inferred from what is observable, external, and explicit. Implicit mental models organize explicit behaviors, and through these behaviors, we come to describe the mental models.

Teachers have two kinds of implicit mental models: (a) espoused and (b) in-action. This distinction, made by Argyris and Schon (1974) and Schon (1983, 1987), identifies important differences between what teachers know when they speak about their profession (their espoused model) and what they know when they practice it (their in-action model).

We infer implicit *espoused* mental models of children's minds and learning from what teachers say about how they teach. If we were to ask teachers what they think children's minds and learning are, they would recite what they remember about Piaget and Vygotsky from their university courses. Instead, we ask them *how they teach* difficult material and infer their implicit mental models of learning from what they say. This inference is reasonable because teachers' purpose is to have learning take place in children's minds.

As an example, in discussions with teachers about how they teach difficult subject matter, they might say that because complex material is difficult for children, breaking up the complex materials into parts makes the material easier to learn. From this explicit statement, we infer a maxim of the teacher's implicit mental model: Smaller pieces of knowledge can get into children's minds more easily than larger pieces of knowledge. This is implicit (it was not what the teacher said), but what we inferred had organized that statement. Teachers' implicit espoused mental models underlie their explicit statements.

Implicit *in-action* mental models held by teachers about children's minds and learning are inferred from teachers' actual teaching. The external, explicit teaching reveals teachers' mental models of minds and learning. We infer from their teaching what those models might be. For example, a teacher who asks children, at the beginning of a lesson, "Do you remember what we did in the last lesson in science?" is getting the children to find the place in their memory where the knowledge from the last science lesson is stored and to recall that knowledge. In teachers' implicit in-action mental models of children's minds and learning, prior knowledge exists in children's minds; it can be located and "pulled out" from memory. We infer these implicit beliefs from what the teacher did as a tiny part of the teaching.

Teachers' Subject Matter Knowledge and Their Mental Models about Children's Learning

Claims have been made that teachers' subject matter knowledge has great importance for their teaching (e.g., Grossman, 1991; Grossman & Stodolsky, 1994; Stodolsky, 1988). A part of these claims is problematic. The view presented here is that teachers' mental models of children's minds and learning have priority over their science subject matter knowledge. Because this view flies in the face of others' findings, it requires justification.

The argument is as follows. Teachers' purpose when they teach subject matter to children is to have learning take place. Teachers' mental models of children's minds and learning guide their teaching. Whether teachers have a large or a small amount of science subject matter knowledge, or whether their knowledge of science concepts is deep or shallow, teachers will teach in the same ways, and these ways belie their mental models of children's learning.

For example, as shown above, one aspect of teachers' mental model of children's minds and learning suggests that complex science material, which is difficult to learn, should be broken up into component parts so that it will be easier to learn. This aspect guides the teaching. The subject matter will be broken up, regardless of whether teachers have considerable or little subject matter knowledge about the concepts in question, or whether that subject matter knowledge is organized deeply or superficially. This suggests that pedagogical content knowledge overrides and has precedence over subject matter knowledge when it comes to *how* teachers teach. How teachers teach reflects their mental model of children's minds and learning.

Concurrently, however, *what* teachers teach is influenced by teachers' subject matter knowledge about science. Let us take two teachers as an example. One has considerable knowledge, deeply organized, and the other has less knowledge, superficially organized. What will happen when these teachers realize that the science material is too complex for the children? Both teachers will break up the material into component parts, reflecting both teachers' mental models of children's learning. But the places where they will break up the material will be different, depending on the teachers' knowledge organization. In other words, the two teachers will carve the science subject matter at its joints, but the joints will be different, given the teachers' subject matter knowledge.

Teachers' mental models of children's minds and learning also have precedence over the ages of the children they teach. In the above example, the breaking up of material so that it will be easier to learn will be done by teachers who teach children at different ages.

Research Findings about Teachers' Espoused and In-Action Mental Models

Having presented very general ideas about implicit espoused and in-action mental models, I now give the findings from studies conducted under my direction at Tel Aviv University (Mevorach & Strauss, 1996; Strauss, 1993b; Strauss & Shilony, 1994).

Teachers' Espoused Mental Models

Regarding teachers' implicit espoused mental models, we interviewed novice and experienced high school teachers who teach the sciences and the humanities (Strauss, 1993a; Strauss & Shilony, 1994). Using a semistructured clinical interview format, we posed the same initial question to each teacher and then followed up each answer with other questions. Teachers' statements were classified and organized. Their organization constituted our description of teachers' espoused mental model of children's minds and learning. As the initial question, we asked each teacher how he or she teaches material that is difficult for children to learn. Because teachers' purpose is to have learning take place, we could infer their mental model of children's minds and learning from their statements.

The mental model we found among the teachers bears a family resemblance to the information-processing models of the 1960s, such as that of Atkinson and Shiffrin (1968). Briefly, the mental model of children's minds and learning shows an engineering vision on the part of the teachers. The basic premise of the model is that knowledge is possessed by the teacher, and it is external to children's minds. When one takes that position, two engineering problems follow: (a) How does one get the external information inside the child's mind? and (b) Once it gets there, how can one move it along to the place where it gets stored or, in other words, gets learned?

For learning to occur, the content must first enter the children's minds, which teachers conceive as openings of a certain size that allow information to enter. Their notion of the "opening size" recalls the notion of working memory capacity. Teachers believe that good pedagogy involves serving up knowledge in chunk sizes that can "get through" the openings. For example, teachers said that what makes some subject matter difficult is that it is too complex and, as a result, it may not be able to get "in" when it reaches the mind. Teachers see their task as reducing this complexity by breaking the material into component parts so that it will be able to enter the mind's opening. However, even if the material were of the right complexity, it may never enter the mind if the child's affective states are not primed to receive the content. Conceived of metaphorically, the entrances to children's minds have "flaps" that are open when children are attentive. If children are uninterested or unmotivated, the flaps go down and the material cannot enter the mind.

Teachers believe that the content that gets through must somehow connect with already existing knowledge by means of analogies, associations, familiar examples, and so on. This corresponds to an elaborative processing model. Accordingly, teachers believe they should facilitate making a connection between new and old knowledge. If there is no existing knowledge to get connected to, the new knowledge can get driven into memory through repetition, rehearsal, and practice until this new knowledge becomes part of the knowledge that is already learned. How does the new knowledge affect the prior knowledge? Teachers believe that there are changes in the amount and organization of prior knowledge. The prior knowledge gets broadened and generalized, and it rises to higher levels of abstraction than were present in the previous knowledge.

These are some of the solutions to the two engineering problems that result from teachers' mental models of the structure of children's minds: how learning takes place in those minds, and how instruction fosters that learning.

Figure 6.2 illustrates the mental model. Teachers hold 11 general categories of knowledge about children's minds, learning, and instruction. Each category has a

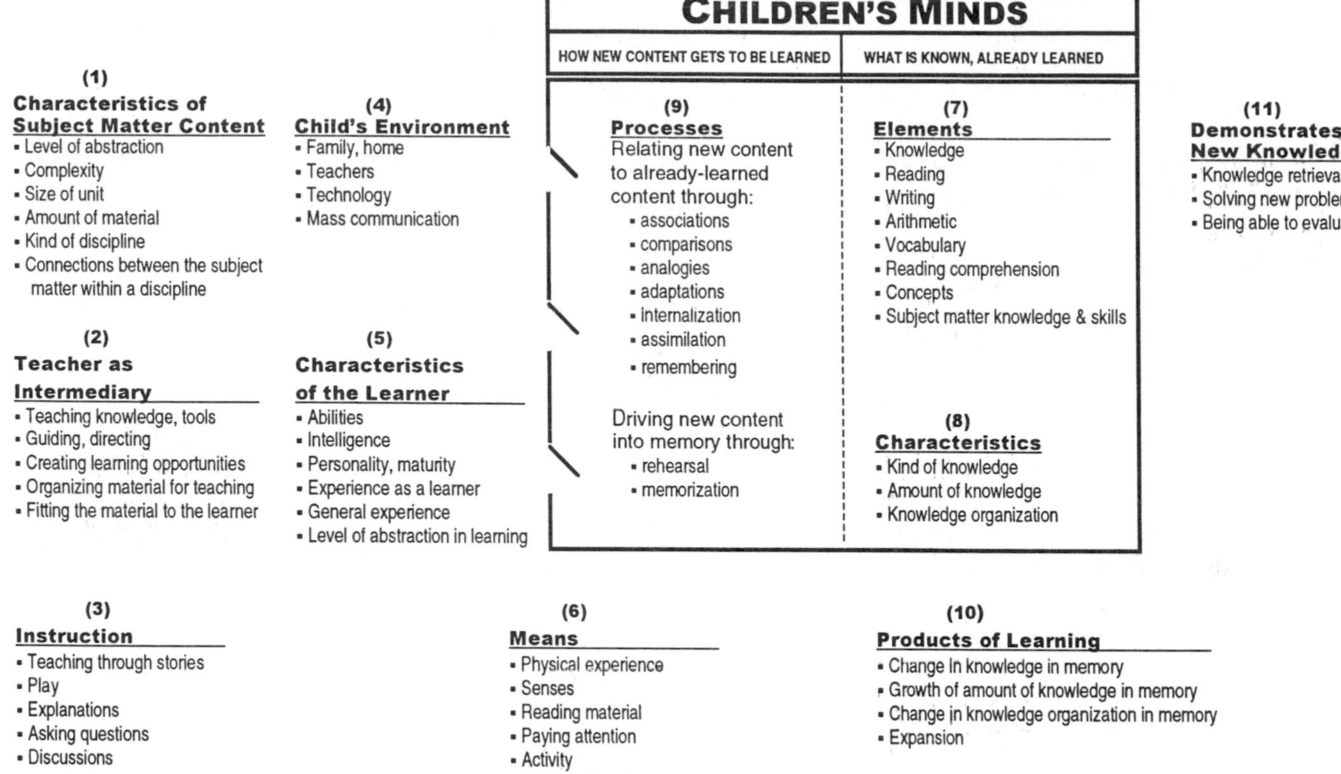

Figure 6.2 Teachers' espoused mental model of children's minds and learning.

The child's mind is the box. Through instruction, teachers attempt to get material into the mind, and moved along in the mind in such a way that it stays there for a long time—which is another way of saying that it gets learned.

On the left side of Figure 6.2 are categories that are not part of learning as such, but which do influence it. These five categories include: (1) Characteristics of the Material to be taught (e.g., that it is complex); (2) the Teacher as Intermediary between the material and the learner (e.g., the teacher breaks a problem into parts for the children); (3) aspects of Instruction (e.g., asking questions); (4) aspects of the Child's Environment (e.g, mass communication); and (5) Characteristics of the Learner (e.g., abilities and intelligence).

We move next from the categories that are not learning as such to the sixth (6) category, which involved *how* the material enters the child's mind. That category has been labeled "Means," because its components are the means by which material external to the mind enters the mind. The Means gets a the seam between the external world and the mind. The openings have "flaps" next to them, allowing material to enter when they are up, or preventing material from entering if they are down. As mentioned above, these flaps are regulated by the affective system; i.e., if the child is interested and motivated or not.

The mind itself has five categories: (7) Already-Learned Knowledge that exists in the mind (concepts, skills, and so forth which have already been learned); (8) Characteristics of Already-Learned Knowledge—such as amount of knowledge; (9) mental Processes which allow new material which just entered the mind to become part of the already-learned knowledge (that is, to become learned). An example of a Process would be analogies between new and old knowledge. The next category, Products (10), deals with what happens to the old knowledge when new knowledge gets learned (e.g., it gets expanded). We labeled this Products because they are products of learning. And there is a category of the mind that involves the ways the learner (11) Demonstrates Uses of New Knowledge; e.g., the learner solves problems that are similar to those just learned.

number of components, only some of which appear in the figure. The caption accompanying Figure 6.2 describes the model.

Interestingly, none of the teachers was taught that model in any university or teacher training courses. What they were taught is *not* held as a mental model, and the mental models they *do* hold were not taught. I believe this research tapped teachers' implicit espoused mental models, which are similar to the preconceptions mentioned above. And I believe that our findings, like those of Clement, diSessa,

McCloskey, and others, show that teachers' mental models are resistant to instruction.

Teachers' In-Action Mental Models

To determine the existence and nature of mental models, we (Mevorach, 1994; Strauss, 1993b; Strauss & Mevorach, 1996) videotaped classroom episodes to record teachers' teaching. The videotapes provided observable, explicit teaching behaviors from which we inferred teachers' implicit mental models of children's minds and learning. Twenty-four first-grade teachers (8 student, 8 novice, and 8 experienced teachers) taught the same arithmetic lesson, using the same curriculum unit. The teachers taught addition using Cuisenair rods, and the lessons lasted between 20 and 30 minutes.

We devised a two-tier category system that allowed us to classify teachers' instructional behaviors and to infer the mental models they hold about children's minds and learning.

The first tier classified teachers' explicit teaching behaviors. We found that they were organized into units that bear a resemblance to those described by both Flanders (1970) and Cazden (1988). The first tier has four units: (a) behaviors, (b) episodes, (c) events, and (d) lessons. The teachers' and pupils' *behaviors* can be as simple as asking a question. Each behavior at this level is meaningless. We described 11,000 behaviors among all the teachers and all the lessons.

An *episode* is a combination of several behaviors on the part of the teacher and pupils, for example, the teacher asks a question, a pupil answers the question, and the teacher remarks about the answer. We categorized 12 kinds of episodes.

An *event* includes several episodes, for example, teacher asks–pupil answers–teacher responds. The aim of the episode may be to define the subject being presented. Behaviors from the first unit gain meaning in the events. We categorized 12 kinds of events.

A *lesson* is comprised of a number of events and has a particular purpose, for example, introducing the subject matter: addition.

The second tier is inferential and is based on the teachers' behaviors we observed in the first tier. *The units of the second tier, which comprise teachers' mental models,* are interrelated and are related to the teachers' teaching behaviors. The units are:

1. *Cognitive goals* teachers want their pupils to achieve (e.g., connecting the new material being taught to what the pupils already know).
2. *Cognitive processes* teachers identify as leading to these cognitive goals (e.g., retrieval of already learned material from memory).
3. *Assumptions* about how teaching in a particular way leads to these processes, which, in turn, lead to the cognitive goals (e.g., mentioning a prior lesson leads to the retrieval of already learned material from memory, which allows new material to be connected to it).
4. *The mother of all assumptions* (metaassumptions) about learning and teaching (e.g., knowledge is stored, knowledge can be retrieved). (The reader can surmise when we came up with the name of the fourth unit.)

Table 6.2, an excerpt from a lesson, illustrates how we infer these units from teachers' teaching. The table shows 23 behaviors on the part of the teacher and children. Space considerations do not allow analysis of each behavior and all of the units from the two tiers. But, to give a flavor of the enterprise, I present a partial analysis, beginning with the *first tier's* behaviors. In behavior (1), the teacher verbally presents material, thus beginning the task. Behavior (2) is a question through which the teacher attempts to define the domain of the exercise. Behaviors (3) and (4) are children's answers to the teacher's question. Behavior (5) is the teacher's response to the children's answers, acknowledging that the answers were correct.

Strauss and Mevorach's (1996) coding system has many kinds of behaviors; for example, teachers ask seven kinds of questions, each with a different pedagogical purpose, showing different aspects of their in-action mental models of children's minds and learning. Although it was indicated that the teacher asks a question, it was not noted which of the seven kinds of questions was asked.

As mentioned, events are a series of interactions at the level of teachers' and children's behaviors. Generally, the teacher asks a question, a child answers, and the teacher evaluates the answer. In the above interactions, we noted and classified four events.

A key unit in the first tier consists of episodes (Table 6.2), which are comprised of a number of events. The first episode, comprised of the first and second events, is labeled "Using Already Learned Knowledge." The second episode, "Broadening Children's Arithmetic Operations," is comprised of the third and fourth events. Here the teacher attempts to move the children beyond the already learned knowledge. They are to find one rod that is the same length as the two rods that are placed side-by-side.

In the second tier, the *cognitive goal* of the first episode was to guide the children to mentally use arithmetic

Table 6.2 A Teaching Segment in Terms of Units from the First Tier of Teachers' In-Action Mental Model

In the classroom, the teacher is seated with five first-grade youngsters. The other children are doing an assignment. A box of Cuisenair rods is close to the teacher. The children have already been introduced to Cuisenair rods in a prior lesson. In what follows, each number that appears in parentheses is the number of a behavior. The following occurred in the classroom:

EVENT 1: USING ALREADY LEARNED KNOWLEDGE

EPISODE 1: Demonstration. The teacher holds up two Cuisenair rods, one whose length is 4 units and one whose length is 2 units.

T(eacher): (1) "I want to present something to you that I am going to build. Tell me what you see." (The teacher puts the two rods together end-to-end.) (2) "What did I do?"
C(hild): (3) "It's adding, adding."
C: (4) "Adding."
C: (5) "Adding."
T: (6) "It's an adding problem, right?"
C: (7) "Yes."
T: (8) "An adding problem."

EPISODE 2: Recall.

T: (9) "Can someone tell me what kind of problem this is?"
C: (10) "We're learning."
T: (11) "We're learning, but which numbers? Which numbers?" (12) "Pay attention to the adding problem."
C: (13) "4 and 2."
T: (14) "Very good. 4 and 2. Right."

EVENT 2: BROADENING CHILDREN'S ARITHMETIC OPERATIONS

EPISODE 3: Recall.

T: (15) "Now, what I'd like to ask, let's see who can pull the right rods out of the box [the rods are of different lengths], but listen to the instructions. Don't build the exercise yet. Here, for this adding exercise, I have two rods, right?"
C: (16) "Yes."
T: (17) "An adding exercise that's made up of [pause]?"
C: (18) "Two rods."
T: (19) "Two rods."

EPISODE 4: Extension of Children's Arithmetic Operations.

T: (20) "I'd like you to find one rod, but the exact same length as these two rods." (21) "Do you understand what I mean?"
C: (22) "Yes."
T: (23) "Those who understand should do the exercise. Those who don't should wait, should think."

operations. This teacher believes that the children's *process* for allowing this cognitive goal to be achieved is identification of the appropriate arithmetic operations that are stored as already learned knowledge. This teacher's *assumptions* about the cognitive processes are: using rods as concrete material and demonstrating the results of putting two small rods together causes children to identify the appropriate already learned arithmetic operations that are stored in their minds.

The claim made here is that teachers' in-action mental models of children's minds and learning guide their teaching practice. That is, the mental model found in the second tier of our analysis gives rise to the various teaching behaviors found in the first tier. This claim is based on analyses within each tier and between the two tiers. In this sense, the in-action mental model we found fits Johnson-Laird's (1983) and Norman's (1983) definition of mental models as a set of connected cognitive elements that represent the external world. We found clear connections within and between the two tiers. And the second tier, which comprises teachers' mental models, represents the world of the child's mind and learning.

Teachers stand outside of children's minds and teach in ways that reflect their implicit in-action mental models of the nature of a child's mind and how learning takes place in it. This teaching, as captured by the units of the first tier, is the external, explicit manifestation of the implicit mental model, which is captured by the second tier's units. In other words, the mental model gives rise to the teaching behaviors. It organizes the ways teachers teach. This mental model, then, is a psychological entity of significance in teachers' teaching practice. Along with teachers' espoused mental model, it will serve as an object of intervention.

This has been a very brief description of teachers' implicit espoused and in-action mental models of children's minds and learning, as culled from our research. Our findings show that teachers have remarkably rich, deep, and powerful implicit espoused and in-action mental models of children's minds and learning. Because these middle level psychological entities have significant implications for how teachers teach, they are the mental entities that must be addressed in teachers' preservice and in-service education.

Teachers may hold these mental models before they become students in teacher education courses, but we know that these models are not taught in these courses. It is possible that mental models not engaged in teacher education courses remain unchanged. Or, through the mental models, preservice teachers may understand the material they are learning about children's minds and learning. In either case, it appears that these deep and powerful mental models are somewhat resistant to change. The challenge before us is to see whether there is a way for these mental models to be elaborated, embellished, and extended.

In sum, teachers' cognition is of importance for science education research and for the construction of teacher education courses. This leads us to the final section in this chapter that deals with how we can construct science curricula for children and for teachers, given the perspective of the middle level developmental model of science education.

COGNITIVE DEVELOPMENTAL PSYCHOLOGY AND CURRICULUM DEVELOPMENT IN THE SCIENCES

This section suggests how curriculum development might look when we take the view of the middle level developmental model of science education. Ideas are presented about what a curriculum is and what steps are needed for curriculum construction, where each step has cognitive developmental underpinnings. Illustrations show how curriculum materials can be constructed, for children and teachers, based on ideas of how cognitive entities change.

What Is a Curriculum?

A curriculum has two significant parts: an external part and an intentional part that belies the meanings of the external part. The external, literal curriculum is the content and form of the book or booklets, or the computer programs, children learn from in school settings. Reading assignments and laboratory work are facets of the external curriculum, as are the actual science problems children are asked to solve and the informal aspects of science education, such as field trips and trips to museums.

Using this as their sole definition, some speak of *the* curriculum. However, this definition leaves us at a somewhat vacuous level of examining the textbook's or computer program's content relative to the subject matter, as understood by experts in the field.

In my view, the curriculum is more appropriately described as a system derived from the intentions and meanings of the authors of the external curriculum, even if the authors did not have these intentions and meanings consciously in mind when writing it. The messages between the lines count here.

Curriculum authors have subject matter knowledge in mind when they write about the subject matter and its organization. They have something in mind about how children learn and develop, too. For example, if a curriculum has several examples of how problems are solved, and then presents problems to be solved by the pupil, the curriculum authors believe children learn by example and practice. They have in mind something about how teachers understand the subject matter and how they might teach it to their pupils. The kinds of topics curriculum developers have in mind cover a wide range. The subject matter knowledge part is perhaps most explicit for the curriculum authors, whereas the knowledge they have about how children learn and how teachers might understand the material and teach it to their youngsters is likely to be implicit.

Phases in Curriculum Construction

The middle level developmental model of science education suggests several phases in curriculum construction, all centered around children's developing science concepts and their developing understandings of the scientific process. There are four major phases in curriculum development, and each requires considerable information:

1. Getting normative data about developmental trajectories.
2. Training to induce progressive cognitive change for understanding difficult science concepts, processes, and so on.
3. Translating the findings of the first and second phases into a curriculum unit.
4. Assessing or evaluating the curriculum's effectiveness.

Normative Data. The first step in curriculum construction is to assess the normative development of children's understanding of the content and processes of interest. The goal of the search is to understand the nature and the developmental trajectories of children's concepts and processes. This search requires a deep analysis of the structure of the concepts and processes of interest, as well as deep analyses of children's evolving understanding of concepts and processes.

Expertise in the domain of science at hand is necessary here. Developmental psychologists who do not have that expertise can bring a subject matter expert into the research and development team. Similarly, scientists who do not have developmental expertise can have a developmentalist join the research and development team. There is a need for science teachers who teach at the grade levels toward which the curriculum is aimed. The normative research envisioned by adherents of the middle level cognitive developmental model requires expertise in: science subject matter content, the developmental courses children traverse when constructing understandings of that content, and ways to engagingly teach the subject matter. Teams with this expertise have been formed on the Jasper Project (The Cognition and Technology Group at Vanderbilt, 1994).

Tasks that are built to measure children's understanding of the content, when wide-ranging and not narrowly restricted to a limited portion of the concepts under test, often allow deep probes of children's understanding of the content and are more attuned to curriculum construction, which is rarely very circumscribed. Tasks that are built to gain normative developmental data also can be used to assess the effects of the curriculum materials on children's learning.

Having gained a deep understanding of children's normative science concepts and their normative developmental trajectories, we are in a position to evaluate which concepts are difficult for children. Those concepts are candidates for the next phase of curriculum building: *training studies* to help children overcome their difficulties.

Training Studies. The purpose of a training studies phase is to test the models used for mechanisms of developmental transitions. This topic is of clear importance to developmental psychologists and to curriculum developers because those mechanisms are an aspect of the intentional part of the curriculum. Those who build curriculum materials for the sciences have in mind how learning takes place in children. The curriculum's activities are built in a sequence that fosters learning on the part of the children who study from that curriculum.

We are not lacking models that describe mechanisms of cognitive change. An early section of this chapter noted some of them. Were curriculum developers more aware of these models and more willing to incorporate them into curriculum materials, we would be witness to curricula that are better informed by contemporary cognitive developmental psychology's theory-building and research data.

Translation into a Curriculum Unit. A curriculum has two main parts: (a) the material with which children work and (b) a teacher's guide.

Any translation from theory and research to actual curriculum materials is neither straightforward nor obvious. It is one thing to have tested children's developing normative trajectories of understanding science concepts and processes, and the results of principled interventions based on theories of mechanisms of cognitive advance. It is quite another matter altogether to produce a curriculum unit that embodies those ideas.

Studies conducted to gain normative data and to foster children's progressive cognitive advance based on theories of cognitive change mechanisms are generally conducted with individual children. The curriculum is written with a classroom in mind. The curriculum is intended to produce, for a classroom or groups of children, the success found when individual children participated in studies during the first and second phases. Normative, aggregated data obtained in studies with individual children represent children's understanding of the science content we study.

In my experience, a good way to go about implementing the curriculum is to try it out in several regular classrooms, with one of the curriculum builders teaching the unit and with the classroom teacher and others from the research and development team observing. Pilot teaching is often done in a large number of classrooms; however, teaching the curriculum unit in a small number of classes allows the curriculum writing team to observe, in depth, what happens when the curriculum is implemented. If there are problems with the implementation in the classroom, there is then a basis, in both theory and research findings, to understand the curriculum's inadequacies and to enlist principled ways to revise it.

After the classroom activities have been worked out and revised to reflect the results in several classrooms, the curriculum unit is ready for a trial run in a large number of schools. For this enlarged testing, a teacher's guide must be prepared.

No matter how well constructed the curriculum unit may be, it is critical that teachers who will be teaching the unit know as much as possible about: (a) the nature of the science subject matter that is being taught in the curriculum, (b) children's understanding of that subject matter, as tapped in the first phase of curriculum development, (c) the models of children's learning that inform the curriculum unit, and (d) some findings that show the characteristic ways children dealt with and understood the subject matter when they were being taught in the training phase of curriculum development. This information should help teachers identify children's gropings toward a more complete understanding of the subject matter, and should be a source of reassurance that the children are moving along in characteristic ways, often (but not always) in a progressive manner. Because teachers often do not read teachers' guides, in-service courses on the above four aspects of the curriculum can be helpful.

Curriculum Assessment. In this last phase of curriculum development, pre- and postdesign studies, with a control group, can be used to determine whether the curriculum contributes to children's understanding of the curriculum's subject matter. The tests used in the pretest and posttest are those developed in the first phase of curriculum development to test children's normative understanding and developmental trajectories.

These are idealized general guidelines for constructing curriculum materials for the sciences. They are idealized because they do not necessarily occur in that order. Some curriculum developers begin constructing curricula without a very informed idea about children's developing notions of what the curriculum is intended to teach, and as curriculum development proceeds, the curriculum authors learn about those developments and their trajectories.

The ideas above were implemented in the construction of three topical units: (a) the arithmetic average, (b) the concepts of heat and temperature, and (c) weight–density differentiation. They are described below for illustrative purposes. Other curricula based on a learning communities approach to cognitive development are then presented.

Curriculum Materials for the Arithmetic Average Based on Analogy as a Learning Mechanism

The arithmetic average is a concept that fits the criteria of material that could be included in research and development using the middle level developmental model of science education. For example, evidence from research studies showing that university students have conceptual difficulties with the weighted average (Mevarech, 1983; Pollatsek, Lima, & Well, 1981) meets the criterion that adults have misconceptions about the content under scrutiny. The arithmetic average is simply ubiquitous. Whenever there are numerical descriptions of objects, events, and processes, the arithmetic average can be found lurking around. The extraordinary range of content across domains to which it is applied fulfills one of the criteria for inclusion in the middle level developmental model.

Children's Normative Understandings of the Arithmetic Average

Strauss and Bichler (1988), in a study of children's developing concepts of *properties* of the average, showed that, quite unlike the procedural side of calculating the arithmetic average, the development of children's understanding of the average is neither straightforward nor simple.

Among the properties tested were: the sum of the deviations around the arithmetic mean is zero; the average is located between the extreme values; the average is influenced by values other than the average; the average does not necessarily equal one of the values that was summed; the average can be a fraction that has no counterpart in reality; and the average is representative of the values that were averaged.

Data for the first property (the sum of the deviations around the arithmetic mean is zero) are presented here. To test this property, Strauss and Bichler (1988) devised several tasks that could be part of children's everyday experiences. One was as follows:

> Children in a class brought picture playing cards to school. They put all of their cards into a pile and then passed them out to every child so that each one got the same number of cards. When they did that, it turned out that each child got four cards. Afterward, the children got back all of the original cards they had brought to school. The teacher then divided the class into two groups: those who had more than four cards and those who had fewer than four cards. The children who had more than four cards gave their extras to the teacher. The teacher then passed out the extras to the other children in the group, so that each child in the group would have four cards. When she did this, did she have any cards left? Did she have too few to pass out? Why do you think so?

The basic idea here is that the number of cards that were extras (above the average) equaled the number of cards missing among the group who had fewer than four cards (below the average), and the teacher had none left (zero) when she finished passing out the extras (adding those above the average to those below the average).

Strauss and Bichler found that 10% of the 8-, 10-, and 12-year-olds and 30% of the 14-year-olds tested produced correct judgments for tasks that measured this property of the arithmetic average. Few children justified their correct judgments with the idea that, when passing out the cards, the surplus should equal the deficit. Justifications for the incorrect judgments were often of the following nature: "I do not have enough data. Were I to know how many children and/or cards there were, I could tell you if the teacher was left with any extras, but since I don't have the exact number, I can't tell you."

This kind of reply shows how children think about an important property of the arithmetic average, when that property is presented qualitatively. We can reasonably assume that were children presented this property numerically, they would have even greater difficulty in understanding it. And even if they were taught how to calculate the property, it is unlikely that they would understand its significance because their qualitative understanding of the same property is problematic.

This example only hints at the normative data we collected on children's understanding of a number of properties of the arithmetic average. As shown, children have difficulty grasping an aspect of the arithmetic average. Attempts were made to help children overcome their natural conceptual difficulties. Analogy lessons created to teach this property were one of these attempts.

Training via Analogies

As discussed previously, the use of analogy as a method for inducing progressive cognitive change rests on several assumptions: (a) analogies serve as a tool for generating new knowledge and are a source of understanding of domains yet unknown; (b) knowledge can be mapped from the base to the target domain, where the base domain knowledge that is faulty may be a powerful source of resistance to understanding a domain in instructional situations; and (c) analogies can be used as an instructional tool to help children (and adults) restructure their understanding of a domain.

As mentioned before, research on analogies, for the most part, has studied differences in school-learned knowledge. In the research described here, we attempted to help children construct analogies between different kinds of knowledge: spontaneous, commonsense knowledge, and school-learned knowledge.

Strauss and Salinger (1988), in testing children's understanding of a property of the arithmetic average (the sum of the deviations from the mean equals zero), did so via three tasks: building a sand castle, cards, and numerical tasks. For the *sand castle* task, we asked children what they do when they build a sand castle at the beach. Most began with leveling the area where the castle was to be built. They were then asked what it meant to "level sand," and either spontaneously or through a short discussion they came to the understanding that it entails filling the areas that were below the level with the sand that was above it, so that, when the filling was done, there was no sand above or below the level. The *cards* task was identical to the one just described, using cards as the medium. The *numerical* task involved presenting children with numbers: 1,1,2,3,5,5,5,7, and 7. The children were to work out the average (36/9 = 4), separate those numbers that were above the average from those numbers that were below the average, calculate the difference between each number and the average, and then add all those differences.

The three tasks have similarities and differences. Their content is different: the sand castle task's content is physical (sand) and is, essentially, continuous; the cards task's content is physical and discrete; and the numerical task's content is numerical and continuous. The kinds of knowledge tapped by each task are also different. In the sand castle and cards tasks, we tapped children's everyday, commonsense qualitative knowledge; in the numerical task, we tapped children's school-learned knowledge that was numerical in nature. Along with these differences, there is a significant similarity: The relations between the parts is isomorphic in all three tasks. Despite their different physical content and knowledge, there is a mean, there are values above and below the mean, and when the values that deviate from the mean are added, the sum is zero.

The study included a pre- and postdesign with analogy training for the experimental group and no training for a control group. Two age groups were tested: 8- and 11-year-olds. The training part of the study had children talking about their understanding of what happened in the three kinds of tasks, where we began with their correct understanding of the sand castle task and used that as the base domain knowledge structure to help the children construct a correct understanding of one target domain in the cards task. And we used their correct understanding of the sand castle task and their newly correct understanding of the cards task as base domain knowledge to help them draw analogies between this knowledge and the new target domain: the numerical task.

For the 8- and 11-year-olds, respectively, 23% and 10% of the control group and 75% and 60% of the experimental group changed from incorrect to correct understanding of the numerical task. Overall, the training was helpful for children who understood, during the training, that the sand castle and cards tasks were analogous. Most of the children could successfully construct the correct representation of the numerical task after training, even though they had had an incorrect understanding of the task prior to training. Of the children who solved the numerical task incorrectly after training, most did not understand the analogy between the sand castle and the cards tasks during training. These children focused on the content differences (continuous sand and discrete cards), which tended to obscure the underlying structural analogies. In other words, what did not map as expected or desired in the analogy can occupy center stage in some children's understanding and can render the structural analogies difficult to grasp.

Curriculum Development and Implementation

Based on the above findings, we constructed worksheets for the purpose of teaching the property of the arithmetic average—that the sum of the deviations equals zero. The activities pages were designed to build on the analogies between children's spontaneous understanding of the qualitative sand castle and cards tasks and their numerical, school-based knowledge of the same principle. The pages were constructed so that the children could be asked to work together to discuss the problems posed. This allowed children at different levels to interact.

The worksheets were put into two classrooms to evaluate their effectiveness for bringing about the planned-for conceptual change. One was a stronger class than the other. Although the classes had 37 and 38 children, respectively, only 31 were given the pre- and posttests because of absences, special events in the school, and so on. The worksheets were presented to children in two mathematics lessons separated by two days. Each lesson lasted approximately 45 minutes. All the children were interviewed on the pre- and posttests, and the posttest was administered one week after the children finished the worksheets. The pre- and posttests included the sand castle, cards, and numerical tasks, as well as several other qualitative tasks that were designed for this evaluation.

The effects of the curriculum that was tested in the classrooms were that there were significant pre- postdifferences on all the tasks for both the stronger and the weaker classes. In the stronger and weaker classes, respectively, 52% and 37% of the children solved correctly the posttest numerical task when it was presented with odd numbers, and 65% and 43% solved the posttest numerical task correctly when it was presented with even numbers. These figures are encouraging, but far from ideal.

Curriculum Materials for the Concepts of Heat and Temperature Based on Cognitive Conflict as a Learning Mechanism

Research has shown that the differentiation between the concepts of heat and temperature is difficult for both children and adults to grasp (Linn, Songer, & Eylon, 1996; Strauss & Stavy, 1982). One way of characterizing the difference between temperature and heat is that the former is an intensive physical quantity and the latter is an extensive physical quantity (Carnap, 1966). An intensive physical quantity remains unchanged despite changes in its amount or extensive physical quantity. The class of intensive physical quantities is central for the field of physics and includes, among other examples, sugar water concentrations, viscosity, hardness, density, and pressure. The fact that children and adults have difficulty differentiating these two concepts, and the centrality of the concepts for physics make them candidates for research and development with respect to the middle level cognitive developmental model of science education.

The four phases of curriculum development for teaching children the concepts of heat and temperature are presented below.

Children's Normative Development of Heat and Temperature

Considerable research has been conducted on children's developing concepts of heat and temperature (Arnold & Millar, 1996; Erickson, 1979, 1980; Linn & Songer, 1991). In one task given to children, they were told that two cups had cold water at the same temperature. When the contents were poured into a third, empty cup, the children were asked what the water's temperature was. As noted above, we found U-shaped behavioral growth for these tasks (Strauss, 1982). These drops in behavior were seen as signs of progressive cognitive advance.

This task can also be presented numerically. For example, we can use a thermometer to measure the water's temperature in the two containers. Let's say the water recorded in each cup is 10°C. As in the qualitative task, the water is then poured into a third, empty cup, and the children are asked what the temperature of the water is in that cup. When questions of this sort are asked, the overwhelming majority of children through age 13 years answer that the mixed water's temperature is 20°C. Children add the numbers as if the addition models the joining of extensive physical quantities.

The same child could produce a correct judgment on the qualitative version of the task (cold + cold = ?) and an incorrect judgment on the numerical version of the identical task (10°C + 10°C = ?). Children's representations of this task are different when the task is presented in a qualitative, everyday form and a numerical, school-based form. In other words, some children produce conflicting judgments when the same task is given in two versions.

Training via Cognitive Conflict

The conflict noted above is between judgments produced by an individual child. This type of conflict, sometimes termed *organizational disequilibrium conflict,* has been shown to be effective in inducing cognitive change (Snyder & Feldman, 1977; Strauss & Ilan, 1975; Strauss & Rimalt, 1974).

Another kind of conflict, termed *adaptational disequilibrium conflict,* takes place between a child's cognitive structure and environmental information. To use the earlier example, children can measure the temperature of the water in the mixed-water cup. When they do so, they find out that the water is 10°C, and not 20°C, as they had thought. The child's mental representation of the task's solution is contradicted by the environmental information (the thermometer's reading). To indicate what can happen when such an adaptational disequilibrium conflict occurs, virtually all children who had this conflict thought their thermometer was "stuck" at 10°C, even when they made several measures with different thermometers.

In organizational disequilibrium conflict, children produce contradicting judgments. The children's contradictory judgments here, in Vygotskian terms, are between spontaneous everyday concepts and cultural school-based concepts.

Children from ages 7 to 11 years were confronted with organizational conflicts between their judgments on the qualitative and numerical tasks. Before asking them to address their contradictory judgments or to share their thoughts about them, we tried to establish with the children that the two tasks (qualitative and numerical) were identical. Many of the children found it difficult to understand that the same task was being asked in different ways. This, too, supports the epistemological distinction drawn by Vygotsky (1978, 1987) between spontaneous and cultural knowledge.

After discussion, the children understood that the tasks were the same: They both began with cold water in two cups, the water was poured from the two cups into a third one, and so on. We found three age-related responses to the conflict. The youngest children (the 7-year-olds and some 8-year-olds) did not recognize that a conflict existed. They argued that cold water when mixed with cold water remains cold water, and that the same water, when heated to be 10°C and then mixed, becomes water at 20°C. Or, as many of the children stated, "It's different when you have numbers."

The second type of response to the conflict was found among somewhat older children (8- and 9-year-olds). Their response was to change their correct qualitative judgment to an incorrect one, by arguing that cold water when mixed with cold water becomes colder. These children gave up their correct understanding of the qualitative task, even though it was confirmed by the environment and had been held by them for a number of years. And they did so when the numbers contradicted their commonsense understanding of temperature. There is a drop in performance here; one representational system carries with it a set of rules (additivity of numbers) that overrides another representational system whose symbol system is different. In our example, the experience-based commonsense representation of temperature is overridden by a numerical-based representational system.

The third response to this contradiction was found among the oldest children (many 10-year-olds), who changed their incorrect numerical judgments to correct ones (10°C + 10°C = 10°C). Space limitations do not allow a full discussion of why this conflict resolution occurs, but children who argue that 10°C + 10°C = 10°C have had a minor intellectual revolution because, in school, it is almost always true that 10 + 10 = 20. These same children tell us that two containers of 10 liters of water, when poured into a larger empty container, will yield 20 liters. In other words, these children now know that there are times when one should add numbers and times when one should not add them, and that these times are dependent on the physical reality being modeled by the arithmetic problem. If the physical reality is extensive and additive, as in the case of the liters of water, one adds the numbers. If, on the other hand, the physical reality is intensive and nonadditive, one does not add the numbers. In other words, these children have come to differentiate intensive from extensive physical quantities and the ways we describe them numerically. The claim here is that this understanding was accomplished by inducing organizational disequilibrium conflict among the older children.

The intervention studies just described suggest three points. First, they indicate that conflicting representational systems are the source of progressive cognitive development, and the mechanism of cognitive development brings conflicting representational systems into contact with each other. Second, qualitative tasks are understood correctly before numerical tasks. This gives us information about the sequence of materials within a curriculum unit on heat and temperature. Third, most children in the oldest age group, (10 to 11 years) resolved the organizational conflict situation in a way that led to a correct understanding of the qualitative and numerical versions of the same task. This gives us important information about the timing of the curriculum unit. We would want to introduce it to 10- and 11-year-olds and not to younger children.

Given the findings on how to conduct our studies—(a) gather normative data about the development of children's understandings of intensive and extensive physical quantities when they are clothed in different symbol systems, and (b) induce progressive cognitive development as a test of a model of mechanisms that underlie developmental transitions—we are in a position to attempt to develop a curriculum unit that exploits our knowledge about children's developing representations of heat and temperature.

Curriculum Development and Implementation

The work described here was done by a curriculum development team (including Ruth Stavy, Varda Bar, and Baruch Berkowitz) working on the development of a curriculum unit on "Temperature" for the Tel-Aviv University Elementary School Science Project (MATAL). MATAL's science units were used in approximately 60% of Israel's elementary schools.

A typical Israeli elementary school class has 35 to 40 children, so any unit that is constructed must take into account the fact that a teacher will have little opportunity to pose conflicting judgment problems to children on an individual basis. The conflicting situations must be provoked in the unit's activities in order to lead the children to confront their contradictions and to discuss their ideas with other children in the class.

Here is an example of how this was accomplished. A work page was constructed in such a way that the qualitative scale could be aligned with the numerical scale on the following page. This allowed children to compare their qualitative and numerical judgments about same-temperature water.

The children were first requested to judge the temperature that results from mixing equal amounts of hot and cold water, and then to do the same for water that was hot and measured to be 90°C and water that was cold and measured to be 10°C. In both cases, they marked their judgment on a scale prepared for the purpose of engaging their qualitative and numerical representations. Next, the children were asked whether the two tasks were the same. This query was included to help the children overcome a problem we found in our research: Many children did not recognize that, except for the language used to describe them, the two tasks were identical. They were then asked to fold one page onto the second page and to determine whether there were differences in their answers to the numerical and the qualitative tasks. This question was posed to make the children aware of their conflict. The children were then asked to choose which of the answers was correct—yet another way to make the conflict obvious to them.

This sequence was an attempt to indicate how research findings from the normative and transition mechanisms research can inform aspects of curriculum design. The example given was one of several that attempted to induce cognitive conflict between the children's commonsense, qualitative representations of the problem and their cultural, numerical representation of the same problem.

As shown above, even research and theory-based curricula must be tested to determine whether what was developed and implemented in schools brings about the kinds of changes intended in the curriculum. This brings us to the fourth phase of curriculum development: evaluation.

Curriculum Evaluation

The purpose of curriculum evaluation is to determine whether the curriculum fosters cognitive advance when it is introduced into a regular classroom under regular school conditions.

Such an evaluation was conducted by Stavy and Berkowitz (1980) to test the results of the curriculum unit on temperature. Two classrooms of 35 children, all 10 years old, participated in the study. They were given pretest items that included mixing equal and unequal amounts of water at the same and different temperatures. The pretest established a baseline for placing the children in one of three groups: (a) those who were administered the curriculum unit on temperature, which was based on the ideas presented above; (b) those who were given conflict training on an individual basis (i.e., the experimenter gave the conflict conditions to individual children); and (c) those who were in a control group. All of the children were administered two posttests: one immediately after the training and another a month after the first posttest.

Three results were of interest. First, the children were equivalent on their pretest representations of the qualitative and numerical versions of intensive physical quantities tasks, and tasks that measured the results of mixing water that had different temperatures. Second, both the individual instruction group and the curriculum unit group significantly improved their numerical representations from incorrect to correct for both the intensiveness tasks and the more difficult tepidness tasks (90°C + 10°C) from the pretest to both posttests. Third, the control group did not improve significantly from the pretest to the two posttests.

In short, the findings were: The curriculum unit, when implemented in regular classrooms, was effective in bringing off progressive cognitive change in children's numerical representations of intensiveness tasks and the more difficult tasks that tap their understandings of intermediate temperatures.

Curriculum Materials for Weight–Amount–Density Differentiation Based on Conceptual Models as a Learning Mechanism

The differentiation among weight, amount, and density is an important component in understanding physics and chemistry. And, as will be shown, the centrality of these concepts and the fact that children and adults have difficulties differentiating among them create a candidate for the middle level developmental model of science education.

The curriculum materials that are briefly presented below were designed to help children differentiate among weight, amount, and density by using their cognitive models as a point of discussion for changing them. The curriculum has a deep connection to research on the normative development of children's understanding of the density–weight differentiation and their understanding of models. The curriculum development here, by and large, followed the four phases suggested by the middle level developmental model of science education. The training part and the curriculum construction and implementation parts were combined, rather than kept separate.

Children's Normative Development of Weight–Density Differentiation

The differentiation among weight, amount, and density is exceptionally difficult for children (Inhelder & Piaget,

1958; Rowell & Dawson, 1977a, 1977b; Smith et al., 1985; Strauss, Globerson, & Mintz, 1983). Most cognitive development research has focused on how children conceptualize density, and the findings were that children's and adolescents' understanding of density ranges from weight, density, and amount being quite undifferentiated to a partial differentiation between the concept of density and its components.

In addition to the components listed above, there can be an atomistic conception of nature. For example, Strauss et al. (1983) presented children with the following task. Two full cups of water, each with the same amount of water at the same temperature, were provided. The children were asked whether the same amount of water was in the two cups and whether the cups had the same weight. The children answered these questions correctly. The water in one cup was then heated and it rose into a tube that was attached to a stopper that plugged up the cup. The children were then asked whether the water was the same amount and the same weight in each cup.

Some children argued that the same amount of water was present and that it must weigh the same because no water had been added. These children showed no differentiation between amount and weight. Other children showed an initial differentiation. They argued that the amounts were different because the water expanded in one of the cups, but the weights were the same because no water had been added.

The children were then asked: If we were to take an amount of water from the heated water and the same amount of water from the unheated water, would they weigh the same or not? The correct answer is that the heated water would weigh less because it contains fewer water molecules. Few children gave full differentiation as the (correct) answer. Most thought that when there is the same amount of the same material, it should weigh the same.

Training via Modeling, Curriculum Development, and Implementation

With this experience as a cognitive developmental backdrop, Smith, Snir, and Grosslight (1987, 1992) attempted to teach children the concept of density via children's conceptual models. In addition to basing the curriculum materials on developmental research about children's developing differentiation of notions of size, amount, and density, Smith et al. (1987, 1992) based their curriculum on findings from research that tapped children's developing concepts of models and their uses (Grosslight et al., 1991). Children's conceptual models were simulated on a computer, with dots representing molecules. The total number of dots and the dots per varying sizes of units were the objects of discussion.

The children produced their models of size, amount, and density via drawings on paper and via computer programs. Discussions were held about the nature of the models they constructed as representations, the relations between the different kinds of models they constructed, and so on. The children also tested their models by experimenting with real objects. One of the tests was whether objects float or sink. The children, through discussion, were asked to understand that tests of real objects' floating or sinking were tests of their models of what should float and what should sink. These discussions were informed by the research findings on children's developing notions of models (Grosslight et al., 1991).

In the curriculum, the children were asked to test their undifferentiated models of sinking and floating where absolute weight was the variable the children used as a model for sinking and floating. This model was tested, for example, by trying to "making a raft sink,"—attempting to make an object sink by making it bigger and heavier—or making a sinking object float by removing some of its material. The curriculum activities were informed by the research literature on children's developing understanding of the weight–density differentiation.

Three attempts to construct curriculum materials were presented. Their common denominator was the attempt to connect curriculum development in the sciences to cognitive developmental models about: (a) children's developing normative understanding of the content under investigation and (b) models of how the psychological entities that organize those normative understandings change. In presenting these three curriculum materials and the ways they were constructed, there was endorsement of the ways the curriculum developers went about connecting cognitive developmental work and curriculum construction.

Community of Learners' Approaches to Curriculum Development in the Sciences

There is a view of curriculum development and implementation that is complementary to the one just presented. This complementary view, based on a community of learners approach, is inspired by neo-Vygotskian theory development (Pea, 1993; Wertsch, 1991). It expands the idea of curriculum to include other learners (in the classroom and the school), community resources, and distance learning—for example, through the Internet.

One part of the theory informs these science curriculum programs: the basic idea that knowledge is distributed across individuals and institutions, and that this knowledge base is one from which communities of learners can draw. This view also suggests that different people have different areas and kinds of expertise, which are used by various members of the community.

A view of cognition as being distributed in a community of learners has been developed in sociology and the cognitive sciences (e.g., Lave, 1988; Lave & Wenger, 1991). And a theory of learning that includes this view includes ideas about expertise, knowledge, how expertise is achieved, how knowledge is distributed, ways that individuals gain access to the distributed knowledge, relations between individuals and the community, and more.

Scientists interested in research and development in science education have begun to use the community of learners view of cognition and learning. Two such curricula have been developed by the Cognition and Technology Group at Vanderbilt (1994) and the Guided Discovery work done by Brown and Campione (1994).

Both groups of researchers have used the neo-Vygotskian theory about distributed cognition, and the notions of learning that follow from that theory, to inform what they teach and, perhaps more important, how they organize classrooms for learning to take place. In this sense, their work is similar to the work described in the three curriculum units described above. The curriculum developers use their ideas of cognition and learning as bases for deciding how to arrange classroom situations where such learning takes place.

Cognition and Technology Group at Vanderbilt

Those working on the project of the Cognition and Technology Group at Vanderbilt (1994, 1995) arrange classrooms with technology that allows for Internet contact with others outside the classroom and the school. Children are asked to solve complex, real-world problems that require many steps for their solution. An example problem is: A person has to get home down the river, and it is uncertain whether he can make it home with his boat. The problem requires children to consider the distance that must be traveled, the amount of fuel available, the speed at which the boat travels, and so on.

The curriculum designers obtained normative data about pupils and teachers by analyzing their representations of the problem and its solution. The curriculum designers then established a baseline understanding of others' problem solving, in order to be able to assess whether the curriculum influenced this understanding. Among those who had difficulty solving these problems were 13-year-old children and college students.

Classroom activities that reflect the community of learners approach are as follows. Projects, not lessons, are the focus of classroom activities. The projects are built in such a way that project team members use each other's expertise in a collaborative manner. For a full account of this work, see Cognition and Technology Group at Vanderbilt (1994) and Barron et al. (1995).

Guided Discovery

Brown and Campione (1994) used notions of (a) "reciprocal teaching" they had developed in previous work on helping children overcome reading problems (Brown & Palincsar, 1982, 1989) and (b) a modified version of the jigsaw method of cooperative learning (described below; see also Aronson, 1978) to develop curriculum materials for the sciences.

Curriculum themes are assigned to children. As is true for the Cognition and Technology Group at Vanderbilt, the problems are complex and deal with real world problems. An example is changing populations. The theme is divided into subtopics (e.g., extinct, endangered, artificial, assisted, and urbanized populations).

After the children in a group decide which subtopic they want to work on, learning about it is their responsibility. Groups of children working on the same topic form research groups so as to study and learn about the various subtopics. Sources of knowledge for that learning are varied. They may include books; other pupils in the class, the school, or other schools; experts; and the teacher.

The children then prepare materials that can be used to teach the other children in their theme group. The theme group reconvenes at appropriate times, and the children hold reciprocal teaching seminars about the subtopic for which they are responsible. Each child in the theme group teaches his or her part of the theme, with all the pieces fitting together in jigsaw fashion. Although all children are responsible for teaching their area of newfound expertise, they are also responsible for all the theme's material.

These curricula were constructed so that they could be implemented in classrooms in a way that would enhance children's learning of science concepts or processes that have proven to be very difficult for children and adults to understand. Along with these materials for the children, curricula often have teacher guides. Generally, these guides present material about the subject matter, as viewed by scientists, and give some helpful hints—for example, how to organize the classroom for the various activities. Teachers' guides generally do not include material about children's difficulties in grasping the material at hand, nor is there mention of what the curriculum developers believe are the ways that children learn, even though these ways are embedded in the design of the curriculum.

Even if there were some discussion, in the teachers' guide, about the curriculum developers' conceptions of children's learning, which underlie the curriculum activities, there is no guarantee that teachers would hold a similar view of children's learning. In fact, as noted above, recent research (Mevorach & Strauss, 1996; Strauss, 1993b; Strauss, 1996; Strauss & Shilony, 1994) shows that teachers have mental models of children's learning that almost surely do *not* jibe with those of curriculum developers, at least those curriculum developers who have asked themselves how they believe children learn and how their curriculum units can be developed in accordance with those beliefs.

We now turn to curriculum development for teachers.

CURRICULA FOR TEACHERS

A fundamental educational problem is addressed here: There is a gap in our knowledge of teachers' cognition and a related fundamental weakness in current approaches to the education of science teachers. I address this general problem by proposing a way to think about teacher education, a way that is founded in theory and research in the cognitive sciences and in cognitive developmental psychology.

In the earlier section on teachers' cognition, it was claimed that teachers have middle level mental models of children's minds and learning. That subject of that learning could be science. Teachers' mental models are consistent with a nonconstructivist version of information processing (Atkinson & Shiffrin, 1968). On the assumption that we would be interested in teachers' having a more constructivist notion of children's learning, we should find ways to help teachers construct such a notion. This assumption has its detractors (Anderson, Reder, & Simon, 1996) because teacher education has not been a great success in this respect. The search, then, should be for a teacher education curriculum that encourages modifying teachers' mental models so that they could embrace a more constructivist notion of children's learning. A curriculum of this kind would have several phases, as described in the next section.

A Way to Think about How Teachers' Mental Models and Teaching Can Change

The science teacher education curriculum is based, in part, on a Vygotskian model of how teachers' concepts of children's minds and learning can be elaborated and restructured (Anderson et al., 1995; Vygotsky, 1978, 1987; Wertsch & Tulviste, 1992).

In education of the Vygotskian type, one attempts to make explicit those mental entities that are implicit. This is necessary because the teaching of cultural knowledge, which is sometimes nonintuitive, is not likely to be accepted by pre- and in-service teachers if they are unaware that they hold a model of the subject under discussion. If we do not make the attempt to be explicit, the alternatives we present to our students will not be seen as alternatives because the students will not know that they have a (commonsense) mental model for which the cultural model is an alternative. This may account for my findings that teachers have espoused and in-action mental models that are different from what they have been taught (Strauss, 1993b). *One purpose of the first part of the teacher education curriculum is to make explicit teachers' implicit espoused and in-action mental models.*

In the sociohistorical perspective, there can be an important merging of these two kinds of knowledge; a connection can be made that enriches commonsense knowledge by giving it cultural underpinnings, and enriches cultural knowledge by grounding it in personal experience. This connection can be made when the formerly implicit mental models have been made explicit, when teachers can talk about their mental models. *Another purpose of the curriculum, then, is to help teachers connect their espoused and in-action mental models.*

Both steps—making implicit mental models explicit and connecting them—are necessary for bringing about more enriched and elaborated classroom teaching. But these aspects of our proposed intervention are not sufficient to achieve one of the aims of the curriculum: elaborating and restructuring teachers' mental models and, as a consequence, their teaching.

One goal of the curriculum is to have teachers understand that there is an alternative conception of children's minds and learning—an alternative to the information processing of the implicit mental models they hold. That alternative is constructivist in nature. The child's mind is seen as actively constructing the environment, and children's mental organizations are central to how they gain an understanding of their world. By having that understanding, in addition to their capacity for information processing, teachers will have a broader perspective about children's learning and might then be able to apply more flexibility to teaching situations.

The knowledge that, as a teacher, one has a mental model of this kind or that, or has connected the different salient mental models, or understands that there are alternative conceptions of children's minds and learning—these traits, as necessary as they are for teacher education, cannot by themselves lead to the change we are looking for. Teachers need to know how to teach with their newly explicit and elaborated mental models of children's minds and learning.

In an analogy to psychoanalysis, having insights into one's psychodynamics does not inexorably lead to behavioral change; one needs to learn how to behave differently in light of these insights. *Another purpose of the curriculum is to create conditions in which teachers will learn how to teach differently,* based on their explicit and connected mental models and their understanding of an alternative, constructivist understanding of children's learning.

There has been a not-so-quiet change in research in the area of theories of mind among those who study child development. Among the attempts to determine the nature of children's changing conceptions of the mind, some have studied the earliest occurrences of signs that children understand that the mind exists. These researchers note when words such as *think, want,* and *am happy,* which refer to the mental states of belief, desire, and emotion, occur in children's lexicon, indicating their awareness of the mind (Bartsch & Wellman, 1995). For an interesting review of some of the literature in this area, see Astington & Pelletier (in press).

Why is this area important for science education? I believe that some of what happens in classroom teaching and learning involves the connecting of teachers' and children's mental models of science learning. The classroom is the arena where teachers' and children's mental models of children's learning meet.

The content being taught is science content. But the ways the classroom teaching of science is organized belie teachers' mental models of children's learning science. For example, a teacher who reminds children about what they learned in the previous science lesson believes that knowledge is stored and can be accessed. This is evidence of a teacher's mental models of children's minds and learning. A teacher might also attempt to connect the new material to the already learned material by asking a series of leading questions. This, too, is a part of teachers' mental models of children's minds and learning.

Children have mental models of their own minds and learning. Research shows that, at a remarkably young age, children already have a concept of their mind and how it works. And that concept undergoes developmental changes (Astington & Pelletier, in press).

Research into children's developing concepts of their own minds and the minds of others is an area of significance. Were we to have a good description of (a) children's developing mental models of the mind and learning and (b) teachers' mental models of children's minds and learning, we would be in a position to conduct research on what happens when the two meet in classroom instruction. The bottom line here is: More research is needed in the areas of children's and teachers' mental models of the mind and learning.

On the assumption that the nature of both teachers' and children's minds will yield to experimentation and, as a consequence, we will have good descriptions of those mental models, we can look forward to research in the area of their juncture in the classroom. For example, we would be able to follow the nature of assumptions teachers and children have about learning, and the ensuing interactions between teachers and children as the teachers attempt to explain science concepts and the children attempt to grapple with them, where both the instruction and the grappling are directed by mental models of learning.

Here is yet another example of how cognitive developmental psychologists could conduct research in an area that is, in my view, a gold mine for theory construction in an important and growing research area, and that has significant implications for science education theory and educational practice. Similarly, if science education researchers can join efforts in this area, their read would have different purposes. Both groups could conduct the same research, but for different reasons. Or, the two groups could exploit the area for theory building in cognitive developmental psychology and science education and for science education practice. This is one of the hallmarks of the middle level developmental model of science education.

SUMMARY

A middle level developmental model of science education has been proposed here. It has a number of theoretical underpinnings that allow us to circumscribe what we look at in the intersect that emerges when we connect developmental psychology and science education. The emergent area changes both traditional cognitive developmental psychology and science education, and these changes can be to the betterment of both domains. The emergent middle level of cognitive development and science education informs both areas so that each is enriched by the other.

Among the aims of this emergent area is the improvement of our science education to a point where decisions about curriculum development, teaching, and teacher education are better informed about cognitive development. Cognitive developmental psychology would become richer and deeper by virtue of wrestling with issues of science education. What would be the results in cognitive developmental psychology? An opening of the domain to the wider and profoundly challenging area of how children come to learn science concepts that, if not taught, will remain misconceptions. This challenge of wedding science to children's betterment is a worthy goal. It also leads to a deeper cognitive developmental psychology and science education.

ACKNOWLEDGMENTS

Thanks go to the editors of this volume and the two reviewers whose comments were extremely helpful and added to this chapter's clarity of exposition and conceptual framework. Thanks are also extended to the members of the Unit of Human Development and Education at Tel Aviv University, whose comments over the years have helped shape my thoughts.

REFERENCES

Anderson, J. R., Reder, L. M., & Simon, H. A. (1996). *Applications and misapplications of cognitive psychology to mathematics education.* Unpublished manuscript, Carnegie Mellon University, Pittsburgh.

Anderson, L. M., Blumenfeld, P., Pintrich, P. R., Clark, C. M., Marx, R. W., & Peterson, P. (1995). Educational psychology for teachers: Reforming our courses, rethinking our roles. *Educational Psychologist, 30,* 143–157.

Andersson, B., & Karrvqvist, K. (1981). *Light and its properties.* Institutionen for Praktisk Pedagogik, Gotesborg University.

Argyris, C., & Schon, D. (1974). *Theory in practice: Increasing professional effectiveness.* San Francisco: Jossey-Bass.

Arnold, M., & Millar, R. (1996). Learning the scientific 'story': A case study in the teaching and learning of elementary thermodynamics. *Science Education, 80,* 249–281.

Aronson, E. (1978). *The jigsaw classroom.* Beverly Hills, CA: Sage.

Astington, J. W., & Pelletier, J. (1996). The language of the mind: Its role in learning and teaching. In D. R. Olson & N. Torrance (Eds.), *Handbook of education and human development: New models of learning, teaching, and schooling* (pp. 593–619). Oxford, England: Blackwell.

Atkinson, R. C., & Shiffrin, R. M. (1968). Human memory: A proposed system and its control mechanisms. In K. W. Spence & J. Spence (Eds.), *The psychology of learning and motivation: Advances in research and theory* (Vol. 2, pp. 89–195). New York: Academic Press.

Bamberger, J. (1982). Revisiting children's drawings of simple rhythms: A function for reflection-in-action. In S. Strauss (Ed.), *U-shaped behavioral growth* (pp. 191–226). New York: Academic Press.

Barron, B., Vye, N., Zech, L., Schwartz, D., Bransford, J., Goldman, S., Pelligrino, J., Morris, J., Garrison, S., & Kantor, R. (1995). Creating contexts for community-based problems-solving: The Jasper challenge problem series. In C. N. Hedley, P. Antonacci, & M. Rabinowitz (Eds.), *Thinking and literacy: The mind at work* (pp. 47–71). Hillsdale, NJ: Erlbaum.

Bartsch, K., & Wellman, H. M. (1995). *Children talk about the mind.* New York: Oxford University Press.

Brown, A. L. (1975). The development of memory: Knowing, knowing about knowing, and knowing how to know. In H. W. Reese (Ed.), *Advances in child development and behavior* (pp. 103–152). New York: Academic Press.

Brown, A. L. (1978). Knowing when, where, and how to remember: A problem of metacognition. In R. Glaser (Ed.), *Advances in instructional psychology* (pp. 77–165). Hillsdale, NJ: Erlbaum.

Brown, A. L., & Campione, J. C. (1994). Guided discovery in a community of learners. In K. McGilly (Ed.), *Classroom lessons: Integrating cognitive theory and classroom practice* (pp. 229–270). Cambridge, MA: MIT Press.

Brown, A. L., Campione, J. C., Reeve, R. L., Ferrara, R. A., & Palincsar, A. S. (1991). Interactive learning and individual understanding: The case of reading and mathematics. In S. Strauss (Series Ed.) & L. Tolchinsky-Landsmann (Vol. Ed.), *Human development: Vol. 4. Culture, schooling, and psychological development* (pp. 136–170). Norwood, NJ: ABLEX.

Brown, A. L., & Palincsar, A. S. (1982). Inducing strategic learning from texts by means of informed, self-control training. *Topics in Learning and Learning Disabilities, 2,* 1–17.

Brown, A. L., & Palincsar, A. S. (1989). Guided, cooperative learning and individual knowledge acquisition. In L. B. Resnick (Ed.), *Knowing, learning, and instruction: Essays in honor of Robert Glaser* (pp. 393–451). Hillsdale, NJ: Erlbaum.

Bruner, J. (1996). *The culture of education.* Cambridge, MA: Harvard University Press.

Caramazza, A., McCloskey, M., & Green, B. (1981). Naive beliefs in "sophisticated" subjects: Misconceptions about trajectories of objects. *Cognition, 9,* 117–123.

Carey, S. (1985). *Conceptual development in childhood.* Cambridge, MA: MIT Press.

Carey, S., Evans, R., Honda, M., Jay, E., & Unger, C. (1989). "An experiment is when you try to see it and see if it works": A study of grade 7 students' understanding of the construction of scientific knowledge. *International Journal of Science Education, 11,* 514–529.

Carey, S., & Smith, C. (1993). On understanding the nature of scientific knowledge. *Educational Psychologist, 28,* 235–251.

Carnap, R. (1966). *Philosophical foundations of physics.* New York: Basic Books.

Case, R. (1985). *Intellectual development: Birth to childhood.* New York: Academic Press.

Case, R. (1992). *The mind's staircase: Exploring the conceptual underpinnings of children's thought and knowledge.* Hillsdale, NJ: Erlbaum.

Case, R., & McKeough, A. (1990). Schooling and the development of central conceptual structures in the development of scientific and social thought. In C. A. Hauert (Ed.), *Advances in psychology: Developmental psychology* (pp. 225–246). Amsterdam, The Netherlands: Elsevier.

Cazden, C. B. (1988). *Classroom discourse.* Portsmouth, NH: Heinemann Educational Books.

Chi, M. T. H. (1992). Conceptual change within and across ontological categories: Examples from learning and discovery in science. In R. Giere (Ed.), *Cognitive models of science: Minnesota studies in the philosophy of science* (pp. 129–186). Minneapolis: University of Minnesota Press.

Chi, M. T. H. (1993). Barriers to conceptual change in learning science concepts: A theoretical conjecture. *Proceedings of the Fifteenth Annual Cognitive Science Society Conference* (pp. 312–317). Hillsdale, NJ: Erlbaum.

Chi, M. T. H., Bassok, M., Lewis, M. W., Reimann, P., & Glaser, R. (1989). Self-explanation: How students study and use examples in learning to solve problems. *Cognitive Science, 13,* 145–182.

Chi, M. T. H., de Leeuw, N., Chiu, M.-H., & LaVancher, C. (1994). Eliciting self-explanations improves understanding. *Cognitive Science, 18,* 439–477.

Chi, M. T. H., Slotta, J. D., & de Leeuw, N. (1994). From things to processes: A theory of conceptual change for learning science concepts. *Learning and Instruction, 4,* 27–43.

Chi, M. T. H., & VanLehn, K. A. (1991). The content of physics self-explanation. *Journal of the Learning Sciences, 1,* 69–105.

Clark, C., & Peterson, P. L. (1986). Teachers' thought processes. In M. C. Wittrock (Ed.), *Handbook of research on teaching* (3rd ed., pp. 255–296). New York: Macmillan.

Clement, J. (1982). Students' preconceptions in introductory mechanics. *American Journal of Physics, 50,* 66–71.

Clement, J., Brown, D., & Zietsman, A. (1989). Not all preconceptions are misconceptions: Finding "anchoring conceptions" for grounding instruction on students' intuitions. *International Journal of Science Education, 11,* 554–565.

Cognition and Technology Group at Vanderbilt. (1994). From visual word problems to learning communities: Changing conceptions of cognitive research. In K. McGilly (Ed.), *Classroom lessons: Integrating cognitive theory and classroom practice* (pp. 157–200). Cambridge, MA: MIT Press.

diSessa, A. A. (1982). Unlearning Aristotelian physics: A study of knowledge-based learning. *Cognitive Science, 6,* 37–75.

diSessa, A. A. (1983). Phenomenology and the evolution of intuition. In D. Gentner & A. Stevens (Eds.), *Mental models* (pp. 15–33). Hillsdale, NJ: Erlbaum.

Driver, R., Guesne, E., & Tiberghien, A. (Eds.). (1985). *Children's ideas about the physical world.* London: Open University Press.

Driver, R., & Oldham, V. (1985, August). *A constructivist approach to curriculum development in science.* Paper presented at the symposium Personal Construction of Meaning in Educational Settings, Sheffield, England.

Duit, R. (1991). On the role of analogies and metaphors in learning science. *Science Education, 75,* 649–672.

Dunbar, K., & Klahr, D. (1989). Developmental differences in scientific discovery processes. In D. Klahr & K. Kotovsky (Eds.), *Complex information processing: The impact of Herbert A. Simon* (pp. 109–143). Hillsdale, NJ: Erlbaum.

Erickson, G. L. (1979). Children's conceptions of heat and temperature. *Science Education, 63,* 221–230.

Erickson, G. L. (1980). Children's viewpoint of heat: A second look. *Science Education, 64,* 323–336.

Feldman, D. H. (1994). *Beyond universals in cognitive development* (2nd ed.). Norwood, NJ: ABLEX.

Fischbein, E. (1975). *The sources of probabilistic thinking in children.* Dordrecht, The Netherlands: Reidel.

Fischer, K. W. (1980). A theory of cognitive development: The control and construction of hierarchical skills. *Psychological Review, 87,* 477–531.

Flanders, N. A. (1970). *Analyzing teacher behavior.* Reading, MA: Addison-Wesley.

Gabel, D. L. (Ed.). (1994). *Handbook of research on science teaching and learning.* New York: Macmillan.

Gentner, D. (1983). Structure-mapping: A theoretical framework for analogy. *Cognitive Science, 7,* 155–170.

Gentner, D. (1989). The mechanisms of analogical learning. In S. Vosniadov & A. Ortony (Eds.), *Similarity and analogical reasoning* (pp. 199–241). Cambridge, England: Cambridge University Press.

Gentner, D., & Stevens, A. L. (Eds.). (1983). *Mental models.* Hillsdale, NJ: Erlbaum.

Goswami, U. (1992). *Analogical reasoning in children.* Hillsdale, NJ: Erlbaum.

Grosslight, L., Unger, C., Jay, E., & Smith, C. (1991). Understanding models and their use in science: Conceptions of middle and high school students and experts. *Journal of Research in Science Teaching, 28,* 799–822.

Grossman, P. L. (1991). What are we talking about anyhow? Subject matter knowledge of secondary English teachers. In J. Brophy (Ed.), *Advances in research on teaching* (pp. 245–264). Greenwich, CT: JAI Press.

Grossman, P. L., & Stodolsky, S. S. (1994). Considerations of content and the circumstances of secondary school teaching. In L. Darling-Hammond (Ed.), *Review of Research in Education, 20,* 179–221.

Halford, G. S. (1982). *The development of thought.* Hillsdale, NJ: Erlbaum.

Helm, H., & Novak, J. D. (Eds.). (1983). *Proceedings of the international seminar on misconceptions in science and mathematics.* Ithaca, NY: Cornell University Press.

Hewson, P. W., & Hewson, M. A. G. (1984). The role of conceptual conflict in conceptual change and the design of science instruction. *Instructional Science, 13,* 1–13.

Hunt, E., & Minstrell, J. (1994). A cognitive approach to the teaching of physics. In K. McGilly (Ed.), *Classroom lessons: Integrating cognitive theory and classroom practice* (pp. 51–74). Cambridge, MA: MIT Press.

Inhelder, B., & Piaget, J. (1958). *The growth of logical thinking from childhood to adolescence.* New York: Basic Books.

Johnson-Laird, P. N. (1983). *Mental models: Towards a cognitive science of language, inference, and consciousness.* Cambridge, MA: Harvard University Press.

Karmiloff-Smith, A. (1985). Language and cognitive processes from a developmental perspective. *Language and Cognitive Processes, 1,* 61–85.

Karmiloff-Smith, A. (1986). From metaprocess to conscious access: Evidence from children's metalinguistic and repair data. *Cognition, 23,* 95–147.

Karmiloff-Smith, A. (1992). *Beyond modularity: A developmental perspective on cognitive science.* Cambridge, MA: MIT Press.

Karmiloff-Smith, A. (1994). Precis of *Beyond Modularity:* A developmental perspective on cognitive science. *Behavioral and Brain Sciences, 17,* 693–707.

Kuhn, D. (Ed.). (1995). Development and learning: Reconceptualizing the intersection [Special issue]. *Human Development, 38.*

Kuhn, D., Amsel, E., & O'Laughlin, M. (1988). *The development of scientific thinking skills.* Orlando, FL: Academic Press.

Kuhn, D., & Phelps, E. (1982). The development of problem-solving strategies. In H. Reese (Ed.), *Advances in child development and behavior* (Vol. 17, pp. 1–44). New York: Academic Press.

Larkin, J. H., & Simon, H. A. (1987). Why a diagram is (sometimes) worth ten thousand words. *Cognitive Science, 11,* 65–99.

Lave, J. (1988). *Cognition in practice.* Boston: Cambridge University Press.

Lave, J., & Wenger, E. (1991). *Situated learning: Legitimate peripheral participation.* New York: Cambridge University Press.

Linn, M. C., & Songer, N. B. (1991). Teaching thermodynamics to middle school students: What are the appropriate cognitive demands? *Journal of Research in Science Teaching, 28,* 885–918.

Linn, M. C., Songer, N. B., & Eylon, B. (1996). Shifts and convergences in science learning and instruction. In D. Berliner & R. Calfee (Eds.), *Handbook of educational psychology* (pp. 438–490). New York: Macmillan.

McCloskey, M. (1983). Naive theories of motion. In D. Gentner & A. L. Stevens (Eds.), *Mental models* (pp. 299–324). Hillsdale, NJ: Erlbaum.

McCloskey, M., & Kargon, R. (1988). The meaning and use of historical models in the study of intuitive physics. In S. Strauss (Ed.), *Ontogeny, phylogeny, and historical development* (pp. 49–67). Norwood, NJ: ABLEX.

McDermott, L. C. (1984). Research on conceptual understandings in mechanics. *Physics Today, 37,* 24–32.

Mevarech, Z. R. (1983). A deep structure model of students' statistical misconceptions. *Educational Studies in Mathematics, 3,* 415–428.

Mevorach, M. (1994). *First grade student, novice, and experienced teachers' in-action mental models of children's minds and learning when they are taught an arithmetics lesson.* Unpublished doctoral dissertation, Tel Aviv University, Tel Aviv, Israel.

Mevorach, M., & Strauss, S. (1996). *Teachers' in-action mental models of children's minds and learning.* Unpublished manuscript.

Munby, H. (1984). A qualitative approach to the study of a teacher's beliefs. *Journal of Research in Science Teaching, 21,* 27–38.

Norman, D. A. (1983). Some observations on mental models. In D. Gentner & A. L. Stevens (Eds.), *Mental models* (pp. 7–14). Hillsdale, NJ: Erlbaum.

Novick, L. R., & Hmelo, C. E. (1994). Transferring symbolic representations across non-isomorphic problems. *Journal of Experimental Psychology: Learning, Memory, and Cognition, 20,* 1296–1321.

Pea, R. D. (1993). Learning scientific concepts through material and social activities: Conversational analysis meets conceptual change. *Educational Psychologist, 28,* 265–277.

Pfundt, H., & Duit, R. (1988). *Bibliography: Students' alternative frameworks and science education* (2nd ed.). Kiel: Institute for Science Education.

Piaget, J. (1970). Piaget's theory. In P. H. Mussen (Ed.), *Carmichael's manual of child psychology* (3rd ed.) (Vol. 1, pp. 703–732). New York: Wiley.

Pollatsek, A., Lima, S., & Well, D. (1981). Computation or concept: Students' understanding of the mean. *Educational Studies in Mathematics, 12,* 191–204.

Posner, G. J., Strike, K. A., Hewson, P. W., & Gertzog, W. A. (1982). Accommodation of a scientific conception: Toward a theory of conceptual change. *Science Education, 66,* 211–227.

Reed, S. K. (1987). A structure-mapping model for word problems. *Journal of Experimental Psychology: Learning, Memory, and Cognition, 13,* 124–139.

Reif, F., & Larkin, J. H. (1991). Cognition in scientific and everyday domains: Comparison and learning implications. *Journal of Research in Science Teaching, 28,* 733–760.

Rowell, J. A., & Dawson, C. J. (1977a). Teaching about floating and sinking: An attempt to link cognitive psychology with classroom practice. *Science Education, 61,* 243–251.

Rowell, J. A., & Dawson, C. J. (1977b). Teaching about floating and sinking: Further studies towards closing the gap between cognitive psychology and classroom practice. *Science Education, 61,* 527–540.

Schon, D. A. (1983). *The reflective practitioner: How professionals think in action.* London: Temple Smith.

Schon, D. A. (1987). *Educating the reflective practitioner.* New York: Basic Books.

Shayer, M., & Adey, P. (1981). *Towards a science of science teaching.* London: Heinemann Educational Books.

Shulman, L. S. (1986). Those who understand: Knowledge growth in teaching. *Educational Researcher, 15,* 4–14.

Siegler, R. S. (1981). Developmental sequences within and between concepts. *Monographs of the Society for Research in Child Development, 46*(2, Serial No. 189).

Smith, C., Carey, S., & Wiser, M. (1985). On differentiation: A case study of the development of the concepts of size, weight, and density. *Cognition, 21,* 177–237.

Smith, C., Snir, J., & Grosslight, L. (1987). *Teaching for conceptual change using a computer-based modeling approach: The case of weight/density differentiation* (Tech. Rep. 87-11). Cambridge, MA: Harvard Graduate School of Education, Educational Technology Center.

Smith, C., Snir, J., & Grosslight, L. (1992). Using conceptual models to facilitate conceptual change: The case of weight-density differentiation. *Cognition and Instruction, 9,* 221–283.

Smith, J. P., diSessa, A. A., & Roschelle, J. (1993). Misconceptions reconceived: A constructivist analysis of knowledge in transition. *Journal of the Learning Sciences, 3,* 115–163.

Snyder, S., & Feldman, D. H. (1977). Internal and external influences on cognitive developmental changes. *Child Development, 48,* 937–943.

Sodian, B. (1995, April). *Children's and lay adults' understanding of the relation between theories and evidence.* Paper presented at the annual meeting of the American Educational Research Association, San Francisco, CA.

Sodian, B., Zaitchik, D., & Carey, S. (1991). Young children's differentiation of hypothetical beliefs from evidence. *Child Development, 62,* 753–766.

Stavy, R., & Berkowitz, B. (1980). Cognitive conflicts as a basis for teaching quantitative aspects of the concept of temperature. *Science Education, 64,* 679–692.

Stodolsky, S. S. (1988). *The subject matters: Classroom activity in math and social studies.* Chicago: University of Chicago Press.

Strauss, S. (1981). Cognitive development in school and out. *Cognition, 10,* 295–300.

Strauss, S. (Ed.). (1982). *U-shaped behavioral growth.* New York: Academic Press.

Strauss, S. (1987). Educational-developmental psychology and school learning. In L. Liben (Ed.), *Development and learning: Conflict or congruence?* (pp. 133–158). Hillsdale, NJ: Erlbaum.

Strauss, S. (1993a). Theories of learning and development for academics and educators. *Educational Psychologist, 28,* 191–203.

Strauss, S. (1993b). Teachers' pedagogical content knowledge about children's minds and learning: Implications for teacher education. *Educational Psychologist, 28,* 279–290.

Strauss, S. (Ed.). (1993c). Learning and development [Special issue]. *Human Development, 28.*

Strauss, S. (1996). Confessions of a born-again constructivist. *Educational Psychologist, 31,* 15–21.

Strauss, S., & Bichler, E. (1988). The development of children's concepts of the arithmetic average. *Journal of Research in Mathematics Education, 19,* 64–80.

Strauss, S., Globerson, T., & Mintz, R. (1983). The influence of training for the atomistic schema on the development of the density concept among gifted and nongifted children. *Journal of Applied Developmental Psychology, 4,* 125–147.

Strauss, S., & Ilan, J. (1975). Length conservation and the speed concept: Organization disequilibrium training between concepts. *Journal of Educational Psychology, 67,* 470–477.

Strauss, S., & Mevorach, M. (1996). *Teachers' in-action mental models of children's minds and learning.* Unpublished manuscript, Tel Aviv University, Tel Aviv, Israel.

Strauss, S., & Rimalt, I. (1974). Effects of organizational disequilibrium training on structural elaboration. *Developmental Psychology, 10,* 526–533.

Strauss, S., & Salinger, A. (1988). *Instructing via analogies for the understanding of a property of the arithmetic average: A case study from a developmental model of instruction.* Unpublished manuscript, Tel Aviv University, Tel Aviv, Israel.

Strauss, S., & Shilony, T. (1994). Teachers' mental models of children's minds and learning. In L. Hirschfeld & S. A. Gelman (Eds.), *Mapping the mind: Cognition and culture* (pp. 455–473). New York: Cambridge University Press.

Strauss, S., & Stavy, R. (1982). U-shaped behavioral growth: Implications for developmental theories. In W. W. Hartup (Ed.), *Review of developmental research* (pp. 547–599). Chicago: University of Chicago Press.

Strike, K. A., & Posner, G. J. (1985). A conceptual change view of learning and understanding. In L. H. T. West & A. L. Pines (Eds.), *Cognitive structure and conceptual change* (pp. 211–231). Orlando, FL: Academic Press.

Thiele, R. B., & Treagust, D. F. (1996). Analogies in chemistry textbooks. *International Journal of Science Education, 17,* 783–795.

Treagust, D. F., Harrison, A. G., & Venville, G. J. (1996). Using an analogical teaching approach to engender conceptual change. *International Journal of Science Education, 18,* 213–229.

Trowbridge, D. E., & McDermott, L. C. (1980). Investigation of student understanding of the concept of velocity in one dimension. *American Journal of Physics, 48,* 1020–1028.

Trowbridge, D. E., & McDermott, L. C. (1981). Investigation of students understanding of acceleration in one dimension. *American Journal of Physics, 49,* 242–253.

Viennot, L. (1979). Spontaneous reasoning in elementary mechanics. *European Journal of Science Education, 1,* 205–221.

Vygotsky, L. S. (1978). In M. Cole, V. John-Steiner, S. Scribner, & E. Souberman (Eds.), *Mind in society: The development of higher psychological processes.* New York: Plenum Press.

Vygotsky, L. S. (1987). In R. W. Rieber, & A. S. Carton (Eds.), *The collected works of L. S. Vygotsky: Vol. 1. Problems of general psychology.* New York: Plenum Press.

Wellman, H. M. (1990). *The child's theory of mind.* Cambridge, MA: Bradford Books/MIT Press.

Werner, H. (1937). Process and achievement. *Harvard Educational Review, 7,* 353–368.

Werner, H. (1948). *Comparative psychology of mental development.* New York: Universities Press.

Werner, H. (1957). The concept of development from an organismic-developmental point of view. In D. Harris (Ed.), *The concept of development* (pp. 125–148). Minneapolis: University of Minnesota Press.

Wertsch, J. V. (1991). *Voices of the mind: A sociocultural approach to mediated action.* Cambridge, MA: Harvard University Press.

Wertsch, J. V., & Tulviste, P. (1992). L. S. Vygotsky and contemporary developmental psychology. *Developmental Psychology, 28,* 1–10.

White, B. Y. (1983). Sources of difficulty in understanding Newtonian mechanics. *Cognitive Science, 7,* 41–65.

Wilson, S. M., Shulman, L. S., & Richert, A. E. (1987). "150 different ways" of knowing: Representations of knowledge in teaching. In J. Calderhead (Ed.), *Exploring teachers' thinking* (pp. 104–124). London: Cassell.

Wiser, M. (1988). The differentiation of heat and temperature: History of science and novice-expert shift. In S. Strauss (Ed.), *Ontogeny, phylogeny, and historical development* (pp. 28–48). Norwood, NJ: ABLEX.

Wiser, M., & Carey, S. (1983). When heat and temperature were one. In D. Gentner & A. Stevens (Eds.), *Mental models* (pp. 267–297). Hillsdale, NJ: Erlbaum.

CHAPTER 7

The Development of Children's Mathematical Thinking: Connecting Research with Practice

HERBERT P. GINSBURG, ALICE KLEIN, and PRENTICE STARKEY

This chapter presents an account of how research on the development of mathematical thinking has been applied to the practice of mathematics education. The chapter first offers a brief history of the field and then gives a summary of key aspects of contemporary research. Next, the chapter turns to a discussion of three applications: (a) mathematics textbooks, (b) teacher development, and (c) techniques of assessment. The chapter ends with a discussion of the ways in which research gets translated into practice; a reflection on both the power and the limitations of contemporary research for purposes of application; and a proposal concerning the vital role that psychological research should play in the education of teachers, which is arguably one of the key problems—if not the *central* problem—of American education.

The long and distinguished history of research on mathematical thinking has included the work of notable figures from a variety of disciplines: the philosopher John Dewey (McLellan & Dewey, 1895), the educational psychologist E. L. Thorndike (1922), the mathematician Jacques Hadamard (1945), and, of course, the developmental psychologist (genetic epistemologist) Jean Piaget (1952), whose constructivist theory set the stage for contemporary work. During the past 30 years or so, research in this area has proliferated and prospered to the point where it is a recognizable and popular subfield of the area of cognitive development. Now, researchers specialize in "doing number" or "studying math," and publish their work both in mainstream journals such as *Child Development* and *Developmental Psychology* and in journals dedicated to work in this area (for example, *Journal for Research in Mathematics Education* and *The Journal of Mathematical Behavior*).

The result is an impressive and fascinating body of knowledge that covers a wide variety of topics, including infants' perception of numerosity, the nature and development of counting, preschoolers' informal understanding of addition, the mental arithmetic of children in schooled and unschooled cultures, gender differences in mathematical abilities, the early use of mathematical symbols, the nature and origins of systematic errors (or "bugs") in calculational routines, and the understanding of formal mathematical concepts. This work provides a rich understanding of

Financial support was provided by The Spencer Foundation, Grant B-1074.

the ways in which children construct an informal knowledge of mathematics in the everyday environment and then attempt to make sense of the formal mathematics taught in school.

Research on the development of mathematical thinking is of interest not only to developmental psychologists but also to scholars from many disciplines: philosophers (Is early mathematical knowledge innate?), anthropologists (How do cultures differ in their understanding of quantity?), educational psychologists (How do children process the mathematics taught in school?), and mathematics educators (How should we teach mathematics?). The research can also be relevant for teachers and parents who wish to foster children's learning of what is all too often (at least in the United States) a difficult and anxiety-laden topic.

The section on research involves an account and an evaluation of major findings deriving from this varied, interesting, and often successful field. Our review is not comprehensive and all-inclusive. We make no attempt to cover all facets of the diverse research on mathematical thinking; indeed, it would be impossible to do so in a chapter of this length (for recent general reviews, see Baroody, 1987a; Geary, 1994; Ginsburg, 1989; Grouws, 1992; Nunes & Bryant, 1996). Rather, our account is selective, in three senses. First, in accordance with the purpose of this volume of the *Handbook,* we have chosen to review only those aspects of the basic research that we believe are relevant for applications to mathematics education in the broadest sense. Second, we focus on a limited age range—children from birth through roughly the end of elementary school—paying scant attention (because of limitations of space) to the important years beyond. Third, we focus primarily on major findings, methods, and ideas relating to children's acquisition of number, and we slight or neglect such interesting topics as children's knowledge of probability and statistics, or of geometry. We chose to focus on number because that topic has received the most extensive attention in the research literature, and because it is most directly relevant to the perceived needs of elementary educators. Nevertheless, in one important sense, the chapter is catholic rather than selective: we cull these findings, methods, and ideas from wherever we can find them. Mathematics education and educational psychology often have as much to contribute to the enterprise of understanding mathematical thinking as does what might officially be called developmental psychology; boundaries among these fields are shifting and evanescent.

An entire section of the chapter deals with the challenges of *applications.* We live in a society in which mathematical knowledge is commonly portrayed as vitally important for economic success, and indeed for everyday functioning. Yet, in recent years, both politicians and citizens have expressed increasing concern, even anxiety, about the adequacy of the U.S. system of mathematics education. International comparisons have portrayed U.S. children's mathematics achievement test performance as inferior to that of children and youth from many countries (Stevenson & Stigler, 1992). American textbooks cover less challenging material than do those in other countries (Stigler, Fuson, Ham, & Kim, 1986). American elementary school teachers are poorly prepared in their subject matter and display astounding ignorance of key mathematical concepts they are supposed to teach (Simon, 1993). Although American children are relatively successful in reading, they do not seem to learn mathematics very well. Less well publicized and understood is the fact that within the United States, the low levels of performance are strongly associated with race and class. African Americans and Hispanics generally perform at a lower level than do Whites, and, as a group, lower socioeconomic status children do not perform as well as their more affluent peers (Natriello, McDill, & Pallas, 1990). Schools in inner-city and rural school districts are often in such a state of disrepair and so poorly funded that conditions resemble those of Third World countries (Berliner, 1993). Perhaps there is a new crisis in American education; perhaps the situation is no worse than it ever has been. In any event, a good deal needs fixing.

Over the years, research on the development of mathematical thinking has been applied in diverse ways to improve mathematics education. The research has influenced the creation of television shows such as *Sesame Street* (Lesser, 1974), innovative mathematics curricula and materials for children and teachers, computer software, procedures for testing and assessment, and mathematics textbooks. Our review is highly selective; we examine three key areas of application.

We chose *textbook development* as our first topic because textbooks are central to formal education in the United States and indeed in most countries around the world. Textbooks influence the lives of literally millions of children every day of the school year. For good or evil, children in schools usually learn mathematics from textbooks. Hence, understanding how research influences and fails to influence textbook development is of considerable practical importance. But the route from research to textbook creation is indirect and complex. To understand it, we must examine how public policies concerning mathematics education have been influenced through the *Curriculum and Evaluation Standards* of the National Council of Teachers of Mathematics (1989); how the policies are implemented through the State adoption criteria (California Department of Education, 1992); and how the textbooks are finally produced by the moguls and editors of the publishing industry. Textbook development is influenced by a great many factors other than psychological research, not the least of which are economic and political forces.

A second application involves teacher development, specifically the *Cognitively Guided Instruction* (CGI) program for teaching elementary mathematics (Carpenter & Fennema, 1992), which we chose to examine for several reasons. First, it deals in an interesting way with what we believe to be one of the major problems of mathematics education: the training of teachers. CGI is one of the few systematic efforts aimed at supporting the professional development of teachers. Second, CGI is an extensive and thorough application, not merely a clever but circumscribed development. And third, this application is relatively "pure" in the sense that the researchers have almost fully controlled its development. (This stands in stark contrast to the decidedly "impure" example of textbook development.) But purity has its disadvantages; applications like these tend to have limited impact on the number of children affected.

The last application we examine is *assessment,* which is central to mathematics education. One of the main functions of assessment is (or should be) to provide the teacher with information concerning what children have learned, so as to improve instruction. Dissatisfied with standardized testing, educators cry out for alternative methods for assessing mathematical knowledge and for gaining insight into the processes of mathematical thinking. Researchers can contribute to the desired reform-minded assessment practices. Indeed, assessment is one of the most direct and powerful applications that can result from psychological research, which at its heart is perforce concerned with issues of sensitive and valid measurement of cognitive and other processes. Psychologists have made and can make even greater contributions to helping educators improve *their* brand of research into children's mathematical thinking.

We examine these applications—textbooks, CGI, and assessment—from several points of view. First, we inquire into the process of application itself. How does research get translated into practice? What are the forces that facilitate applications and what are the forces that hinder their implementation? This is a sociology of science and practice, a story of how research knowledge gets disseminated, used, and applied. We argue that the classic notion of "application"—a scientist has a good idea, applies it to a real problem, achieves a solution of the problem, disseminates the solution to eager recipients, and receives heartfelt thanks from all concerned—is hopelessly naïve. Unfortunately for cloistered academics, the world does not work in that way. The process of application is complex; many factors intervene between the psychologist's investigation and the outcome.

Second, we examine the contributions of research. What types of research knowledge do we and others find it useful to apply? What aspects of the research are most informative, relevant, and productive for various practitioners? This is a story about the goodness and relevance of the research—*for practitioners.* But again, the story is not simple. Like beauty, goodness and relevance are in the eye of the beholder. In the case of mathematics education, the beholders are the teachers, the textbook developers, the testers, the administrators, and the parents. The question then becomes: What do these practitioners find useful in the research? Their ideas of goodness and relevance do not necessarily coincide with the researcher's. Furthermore, experience with applications shows that questions of utility cannot be separated from those of value: what is seen as useful depends in part on what is valued. Because this is true, applications of research knowledge get caught up in swirls of controversy in American political life, particularly in clashes between fundamentalists and progressives.

Third, we ask about the ways in which the available research is deficient in speaking to the educational challenge. How does the research fail to meet real educational needs? This is the story of the limits of current research and researchers. The existence of such limits should not be surprising. After all, research on the development of mathematical thinking does not have as its chief aim the improvement of mathematics education, and researchers are typically not trained to engage in applications. But, to be effective, to take the next step, we need to understand our limitations.

Fourth, we ask what we can do to improve our contributions to the world of applications. How can psychologists get more productively involved in producing useful applications? What unanticipated problems need to be addressed? What are fruitful areas for application in the future? What can involvement in applications teach researchers about the limitations of their research? What kinds of new research, theory, and researchers are needed? We argue that successful application requires research that is sensitive to the ecology in which mathematical thinking develops; that application requires "translation" for teachers in particular; and that application requires researchers to engage in attempts to understand and influence the larger forces that shape education in the real world. If we can accomplish some small part of this, then the next edition of this *Handbook* will contain a chapter on the development of mathematical thinking that can report even greater accomplishments than this one.

HISTORY

Mathematics education and psychology are both about 100 years old (Kilpatrick, 1992) and have been intertwined throughout their history. The chief aim of mathematics educators is, of course, to teach mathematics effectively. But in attempting to do this, they have found it necessary to draw on psychology or to invent their own. From the earliest days of the field, mathematics educators have made psychological assumptions and observations about children's learning, about the nature of mathematical knowledge, and about methods for teaching mathematics.

Thus, in 1842, Colburn wrote: "The idea of number is first acquired by observing sensible objects. Having observed that this quality is common to all things with which we are acquainted, we obtain an abstract idea of number. We first make calculations about sensible objects; and we soon discover the same calculations will apply to things very dissimilar; and finally that they can be made without reference to any particular thing. Hence from particulars we establish general principles, which serve as the basis of our reasonings, and enable us to proceed, step by step, from the most simple to the most complex operations" (p. 4). Colburn was, in effect, proposing a realist theory of perceptual learning in which ideas of number are induced from concrete experience and gradually extended to increasingly abstract problems. Many educators today continue to hold similar views.

Possessing this propensity to analyze the learning process and the psychology of the child (how could they avoid it?), mathematics educators were naturally attracted to the contributions of psychologists. From the end of the 19th century, mathematics education has viewed psychology as a kind of foundation discipline. This is not to say that the relations between the two fields have been uniformly harmonious. Many mathematics educators have felt a certain ambivalence about our field, partly because they see some psychologists as understanding little about mathematics and failing to appreciate what aspects of the discipline are important to teach. Thus: "To be sure, the psychologists have shown us how to teach better some things which would better go untaught, but they have also . . . discovered many useful facts and laws about how children learn most easily . . . " (Reeve, 1929, p. 148).

Psychologists' contributions to mathematics education have reflected the complexity of a field that involves the teaching of different kinds of mathematics to individuals from preschool through the college years. Psychologists have focused on several different aspects of mathematics learning, including the mathematical knowledge children possess on arrival at school, the child's processes of thinking, the nature of mathematical knowledge acquired in school, the processes of learning, effective techniques for instruction, the assessment of the child's achievement and knowledge, and individual and group differences. This array of topics is the province of no single branch of psychology. Developmental psychologists have a stronger interest in some of these topics than in others, and the same can be said about educational psychologists, cognitive psychologists, and others. But although researchers may find it possible to isolate aspects of the child's functioning, they are inseparable in the real world of schools. Consequently, psychologists interested in mathematics learning often find themselves crossing disciplinary boundaries in an effort to understand and solve problems of mathematics education. As a result, it is often difficult to classify work in this area as pure developmental psychology, educational psychology, cognitive psychology, or some other discipline.

Whatever their approach, psychologists have been attracted to the topic of mathematics learning for several reasons. Some—but not all—wish to contribute to mathematics education; others see mathematics as an important and convenient *vehicle* for studying complex human learning. The vehicle can be observed to make many noteworthy trips: Mathematical knowledge is a basic aspect of everyday cognition and it is also a key subject to learn in school; it ranges from the concrete to the abstract; it involves both practical measurement and the most intellectually advanced theory; it is valued for its "cumulative, hierarchical structure . . . and the range of complexity and difficulty in the learning tasks it can provide" (Kilpatrick, 1992, p. 5).

So the study of number or of mathematical thinking more generally has been an attractive topic for some of the most distinguished psychological theorists and researchers. One of the earliest contributors to the field was the philosopher John Dewey, who may be said to have originated the "constructivist school" of thought in this area.

Dewey's work[1] boldly proclaimed several themes that resonate today among many researchers. One is the use of psychology as a foundational science for education: "Knowing the nature and origin of number and numerical properties as psychological facts, the teacher knows how the mind works in the construction of number, and is prepared to help the child to think number. . . . [R]ational method in arithmetic must be based on the psychology of number" (McLellan & Dewey, 1895, p. 22). Education must be built on psychological knowledge.

---

[1] The work was indeed written by McLellan and Dewey, but Dewey seems to have been responsible for the more theoretical portions, particularly as they involve psychology.

A second theme is constructivism. Although Dewey offered no psychological data other than his informal observations of children and uncommon good sense, he stressed the constructed nature of number and of knowledge generally. "Number is not a property of the objects which can be realized through the mere use of the senses, or impressed upon the mind by so-called external energies or attributes" (p. 24). "Number . . . is not a bare property of facts, but is a certain way of interpreting and arranging them—a certain method of constructing them" (pp. 21–22). For Dewey, as for Piaget, number was not an empirical discovery, but a construction of the mind reflecting on actions related to objects.[2] Dewey proposed this view one year before Piaget was born.

A third theme is context. Dewey stressed the development of mathematical thinking within the context of everyday experience and motivation. In the natural world, number arises from need: We develop number because we need to measure, and we need to measure because we want more of this than that, or we want to make two quantities equivalent in value. This kind of "ecological" approach is only now receiving wide currency.

Unfortunately, Dewey did not pursue the psychology of mathematical thinking beyond his first foray into the area, so that many of his ideas were not explored in depth. Yet three remarkable persons from the University of Chicago—Charles H. Judd; his student, Guy T. Buswell; and their student, William A. Brownell—did work that was, in some respects, consistent with Dewey's approach.[3] Like Dewey, Judd stressed the foundational importance of a psychology of mathematical thinking. His goal was to help teachers "to understand the nature and complexity of arithmetic ideas . . . [This] will operate to modify the somewhat blind procedures which now characterize the teaching of arithmetic . . . " (Judd, 1927, p. 6). Through his many empirical investigations of the "fundamentals of arithmetic," Judd attempted to show that mathematics learning is a meaningful activity involving organized structures of thought. "[T]he mind generalizes experiences and organizes its operations into certain systematic schemes" (p. 78). He cited gestalt psychology to the effect that: "there are no elements in consciousness . . . number experiences are gradually matured through organization into higher and more general types of thinking" (p. 110).

At the same time, Judd departed from the "discovery-oriented" approach usually associated with Dewey and other progressive educators. Judd's preference was to "give explicit instruction in the meaning of the process of addition and thus hasten the arrival of the pupil at an understanding of the general idea" (p. 113). Instruction was necessary, he felt, because: "The expectation that little children are going to show a spontaneous interest in number such as they show in good things to eat . . . is certain to meet with disappointment" (p. 108). Although the disappointment may have been premature, these sentiments led to an instructional psychology of the type championed by Ausubel (1968).

Judd was among the first to promote research methods other than standardized tests. Indeed, he felt that standard testing has a negative effect on the research enterprise: "Very little has been done . . . by way of direct investigations of the mental processes involved in the development of number ideas. . . . The reason . . . is to be found in part in the preoccupation of students of education in tests . . . " (p. 17). "[T]he test method does not contribute greatly to the detailed analysis of mental processes. Tests are excellent devices for comparative studies of the survey type. They were formulated especially for that purpose. They can also be advantageously used in locating the difficulties and deficiencies of pupils. Where analyses of the processes of thinking are to be made, tests prove to be inadequate" (p. 98).[4]

Buswell and John (1926) explored alternative methods for examining mathematical thinking, particularly young children's strategies for arithmetic computation. Their goal was to gain insight into the cognitive processes underlying children's mistakes in the ordinary calculations of addition, subtraction, multiplication, and division. Their

---

[2] This position led in turn to an approach to mathematics teaching in which Dewey warned against the thoughtless use of what we would today call *manipulatives:* "[S]o far as [teaching] emphasizes the objects to the neglect of the mental activity which uses them, it . . . makes number meaningless; it subordinates thought to things" (McLellan & Dewey, 1895, p. 60). Messing around with objects has an educational use only when the activity produces abstract thought.

[3] Unlike Dewey, however, "Judd thought that University professors should formulate laws of learning that teachers would then implement, whereas Dewey saw educational research as an ongoing collaborative process in which both professors and teachers collaborated" (Ellen Lagemann, personal communication, October 22, 1995). The two also differed in other respects, for example, the importance of instruction as opposed to discovery (Lagemann, 1989).

[4] Judd (1927) even suggested the possibility that "the person who knows the rules thoroughly but has little comprehension of processes makes better scores on tests than does the individual who has a more fundamental form of knowledge" (p. 112). This is an interesting and by no means implausible hypothesis, at least when tests consist entirely of boring calculational items.

method—in the 1920s!—was the "think aloud" procedure, and they used it with great success to identify for the first time virtually all of what are known today as "bugs" and "slips" (J. Brown & VanLehn, 1982; VanLehn, 1990). Lacking the terminology of computer science, Buswell and John spoke of "habits," which included "bugs" (systematic strategies leading to error, as in 28 + 14 = 312), "slips" (errors of execution, as in forgetting to write down a number in a complex computation), and even "invented strategies" (for example, counting on the fingers to get a number fact). The evidence suggests that these habits have not changed a great deal over the past 70 years.

Buswell and John's work formed the basis for a test, the goal of which was *not* to determine relative success in computation but to describe the student's underlying strategies. In this sense of emphasizing process and downplaying product, the Buswell and John test was, so far as we know, the first truly cognitive measuring device in mathematics education. And the authors went one step further; in an innovative procedure, they developed "teacher workshops" based on discussion of the test results. The tests were used as a vehicle for teacher analysis of their students' cognitive processes.

Brownell (1935) elaborated on Judd's approach to meaningful learning. Number "is the creation of the observer; it is a concept or an idea which the observer imposes on the objective data" (p. 20). "The 'meaning' theory conceives of arithmetic as a closely knit system of understandable ideas, principles, and processes. According to this theory, the test of learning is not mere mechanical facility in 'figuring.' The true test is an intelligent grasp upon number relations and the ability to deal with arithmetical situations with proper comprehension of their mathematical as well as their practical significance" (p. 19).

Like Judd and Buswell, Brownell was skeptical of the utility of standard tests and championed the use of methods designed to uncover children's thinking. In particular, Brownell advocated the use of interview methods in both research and instruction. The teacher "will insist on an interpretation and upon a defense of his solution. She will make the question, 'Why did you do that?' her commonest one in the arithmetic period. Exposed repeatedly to this searching question, the child will come soon to appreciate arithmetic as a mode of precise thinking . . . " (p. 29).

These aspects of the work of Dewey, Judd, Buswell, and Brownell (despite important differences among them) seem remarkably in tune with recent developments in psychological research. Unfortunately, their approach was overshadowed by the connectionist theory of Edward L. Thorndike at Teachers College, Columbia University. "Edward L. Thorndike won and John Dewey lost" (Lagemann, 1989, p. 185) in virtually all aspects of educational theory and practice.

Consider three features of Thorndike's extensive work on children's arithmetic: connectionist (or associationist) theory, drill, and testing. First is the proposal that learning proceeded in an upward direction from the formation of elementary connections (stimulus–response bonds) to the development of abstraction and reason (Thorndike, 1922). The child must first establish basic connections (between such stimuli as 2 + 3 and such responses as 5) with great reliability. Later, the connections will "grow together into an orderly, rational system of thinking" (p. 74). "The newer pedagogy [that is, Thorndike's!] is careful to help [the pupil] build up these connections or bonds ahead of or along with the general truth or principle, so that he can understand it better" (p. 74). As is well known, from about the 1930s until the 1960s (the onset of the "cognitive revolution"), this kind of elementaristic, behaviorist approach held sway in psychology.

Second, Thorndike's connectionism led to an emphasis on drill, as opposed to meaningful learning. "The constituent bonds involved in the fundamental operations with numbers need to be much stronger than they now are" (1922, p. 102). And the way to strengthen them was through systematic drill. "For bonds of ordinary difficulty [number facts like 11–3] in the case of the median or average pupil, we may estimate twenty practices in the week of first learning, supported by thirty, and maintained by fifty practices well spread over the later periods" (pp. 133–134). The practical impact of Thorndike's work cannot be overlooked. It led to, or justified the prior existence of, a less than exciting educational experience for many (millions?) of children—a deadening drill in number facts, or what some mathematics educators refer to as "drill and kill."

Thorndike's third legacy is standardized testing. According to his famous dictum: "If any given knowledge or skill or power or idea exists, it exists in some amount" (1922, p. 27) and therefore can be measured with standard tests. Under Thorndike's influence, standardized testing became the norm for both educational research and practice. Many tests of calculational skill and memory for number facts were created; after all, it is possible to measure their *amount.* And as these tests proliferated, they came to dominate the curriculum: Many teachers teach to the tests. But as subsequent theory has shown, measuring the *amount* of knowledge ignores what is more important from the point of view of cognitive theory and educational practice—the *nature* of the knowledge. It does not seem unfair to maintain that Thorndike is responsible both for the triviality of a good deal of educational and psychological research and for the pernicious effects of standard testing on the mathematics curriculum. After all, Thorndike won and Dewey lost.

The general result of the Thorndike victory was that the work of Dewey, Judd, Buswell, and Brownell remained obscure; indeed, most modern researchers are probably unfamiliar with their theories and research. Later, the cognitive revolution snatched away Thorndike's victory. The most influential figure in that revolution, at least for developmental psychologists, was Jean Piaget, who influenced the field in at least four ways: (a) his theory of number, (b) his constructivist approach, (c) his theory of equilibration, and (d) his clinical interview methodology.

Piaget (1952) presented a detailed analysis of the basic concepts of number, portrayed in terms of the synthesis of classes and relations. In the foreword to his book (written with the often unacknowledged but important collaboration of Alina Szeminska), Piaget boldly proposed: "Our hypothesis is that the construction of number goes hand in hand with the development of logic, and that a pre-numerical period corresponds to the pre-logical level. . . . [L]ogical and arithmetical operations therefore constitute a single system that is psychologically natural, the second resulting from generalization and fusion of the first" (p. viii). For Piaget, the acquisition of basic concepts of number can be explained as resulting from qualitative changes in the underlying structures of thought (preoperational thinking being supplanted by the concrete operations, and these, in turn, by the formal operations). Thus, the child's ability to conserve the equivalence relations between two sets—the numerical equivalence existing between one line of n objects and another line of n objects is conserved over visible transformations in physical arrangement—is the result of developmental changes in the underlying structures of thought. At first, the preoperational child focuses on the mere appearance of the objects and hence fails to conserve the equivalence relation; later, with development, the child coordinates classes and relations to arrive at a synthesis that enables the conservation of numerical equivalence.

A corollary, which did not receive a prominent place in accounts of Piaget's work, was that culturally transmitted mathematical knowledge such as counting or paper-and-pencil arithmetic does not play a major role in the development of the fundamental structures of children's mathematical thinking. Indeed, the Piagetian study of basic concepts of number did not require any examination of culturally transmitted mathematical knowledge. "[T]here is no connection between the acquired ability to count and the actual operations of which the child is capable" (1952, p. 61).

Piaget's theory of number became enormously popular among both psychologists and educators. It was commonplace to perform replications of research on the conservation problem, often with number. Indeed, the Piagetian paradigm became so popular that, through the 1970s, most research on children's mathematical thinking (and cognitive development generally) addressed Piagetian themes (e.g., Markman, 1979; Rosskopf, 1975; Rosskopf, Steffe, & Taback, 1971; Wohlwill, 1960). The conservation phenomenon is easily replicated; following Piaget's method, anyone can observe the failure to conserve. In fact, the conservation experiment is probably the most frequently replicated result in psychology. At the same time, some researchers, questioning Piaget's interpretation of the young child's failure to conserve, argued that Piaget's tasks were insensitive to numerical concepts that develop early in life (for an example of this debate, see Beilin, 1968; Mehler & Bever, 1967).

Psychologists and educators took several lessons from Piaget's discussion of the thought processes underlying the child's concept of number. One was that children's thought is dramatically different from adults'. Children will say that a line of five saucers is more numerous than a line of five teacups, even though the teacups had previously been sitting in the saucers, and even though the child had accurately counted both sets. A second lesson, at least for some, was that mathematics education should be tied to the Piagetian conception of the child's cognitive development. Shulman, a prominent educational psychologist, wrote that Piaget's "characterization of the number-related concepts understood by children at different ages . . . has influenced our grasp of what children at different stages can be expected to learn meaningfully. . . . To determine whether a child is ready to learn a particular concept or principle, one analyzes the structure of that to be taught and compares it with what is already known about the cognitive structure of the child at that age" (1970, p. 42). This approach stresses *limits* on the child's learning: If the appropriate cognitive stage has not been attained, the child will not be ready to learn certain subject matter. And a third lesson was that number is a fascinating subject to study, both for its own sake and because it was seen as a domain through which general principles of the child's cognitive functioning and development could be discerned.

But Piaget's contribution was not limited to his theory of the particular cognitive operations underlying the child's concept of number. Indeed, his general constructivist approach ultimately proved more enduring and influential.

Piaget proposed that number, like other major cognitive acquisitions, is constructed—it is not innate and it is not "picked up" from stimulation (Gibson, 1969), or otherwise imposed by experience. Number is an idea that children have to "invent" on their own. "Real comprehension of a notion or theory implies the reinvention of this theory by the subject" (Piaget, 1977, p. 731). Children cannot discover number or have the idea of number imposed on or imparted to them; they must construct it. Today, the notion of constructivism is among the most popular concepts in mathematics education, but constructivism is not necessarily tied to the particular theory of number development that Piaget proposed. One can adopt constructivism as a general theoretical stance, without accepting, for example, Piaget's theory of the concrete operations. In fact, late in his life, Piaget himself downplayed his theoretical account of the structures of thought in terms of concrete operations and the like (Ginsburg & Opper, 1988).

Piaget's third contribution was his theory of equilibration. Leaving out, for now, the rather complex details, Piaget's general point was that the child's learning often involves the manipulation of objects, and is always active, self-regulated, and particularly sensitive to disequilibrium between the current cognitive state and the immediate demands of the environment. As Shulman (1970) interpreted it: "Piaget's emphasis upon action as a prerequisite to the internalization of cognitive operations has stimulated the focus upon direct manipulation of mathematically relevant materials in the early grades. His description of cognitive development occurring through auto-regulation has reinforced tendencies to emphasize pupil-initiated, problem-solving activities as a major vehicle of mathematics instruction" (p. 42).

Piaget's fourth contribution was the clinical interview method. Piaget proposed: "In dealing with these new problems, appropriate methods must be used. We shall still keep our original procedure of free conversation with the child, conversation . . . governed by the questions put, but . . . compelled to follow the direction indicated by the child's spontaneous answers. Our investigation of sensorimotor intelligence has, however, shown us the necessity for actual manipulation of objects" (1952, p. vii). The use of objects was designed both to concretize the mathematical problem for the child and to allow the child to externalize thought through the manipulation of objects. And the clinical interview method was considered to combine the advantages of observation, experimentation, and testing (Piaget, 1976).

When Piaget's work became prominent, North American psychologists in particular felt that his method was preliminary, sloppy, and in need of standardization (Pinard & Laurendeau, 1964). They failed to realize that the clinical interview method was created on principled grounds: its lack of standardization was deliberate, intended to overcome some of the serious limitations of standard tests. Piaget's method was not "unscientific"; rather, it was based on a distinctive theoretical approach (Ginsburg, 1997). In recent years, as understanding of Piaget's work has deepened, the tide has changed and interview methods of one kind or another are considered respectable methods of research (e.g., A. Brown & Campione, 1994; Gelman, 1980; Siegler & Crowley, 1991).

As one of the first to recognize the magnitude of Piaget's contribution to the study of cognitive development, Jerome Bruner played an important role in legitimating Piaget's theory in the eyes of American psychologists and in interesting them in research concerning education. Further, Bruner conducted an influential study of mathematical thinking in an instructional context. The method was "close in spirit to that of Piaget and of ethologists like Tinbergen" (Bruner, 1966, p. 54). It focused not on children's right and wrong answers but on the processes of learning and teaching. Mathematics was seen as an especially important topic and vehicle for research, because it can lead to "a simplified set of propositions about teaching and learning" (p. 39). The resulting formulation held that mathematics learning involves a progression in forms of representation, from enactive, to iconic, and then to symbolic. More importantly, Bruner urged that instruction take into account "the nature of the knower and of the knowledge getting process. . . . We teach a subject not to produce little living libraries on that subject, but rather to get a student to think mathematically for himself . . . to take part in the process of knowledge getting. Knowing is a process, not a product" (p. 72). This account owes much to Piaget in its emphasis on observational method and the processes of thinking (in Piaget's famous phrase, "To understand is to invent"). At the same time, Bruner did not base his theory on the Piaget thought structures per se. He did not couch his account of process only in terms of the concrete or formal operations. With his catholic frame of mind, Bruner introduced various concepts (like *strategy*) from information processing and other cognitive theories (e.g., Bartlett, 1932).

Bruner's contributions were many. His work not only popularized many of Piaget's notions, but also had the salutary effect of opening up the field of inquiry to other cognitive ideas and theories. Bruner's point of view made it acceptable not only to replicate Piaget but encouraged the undertaking of independent cognitive investigations into the development of mathematical thinking (we might say that he allowed researchers to "go beyond the Piagetian given"). Bruner's work also spurred the creation of a cognitive brand of instructional theory, and, not unimportantly, this leader of the cognitive revolution persuaded cognitive psychologists that the study of education was a scientifically respectable activity.

If Piaget stimulated modern interest in the development of mathematical thinking, and if Bruner helped to broaden psychologists' approach to this area of research, the ideas of another major theorist—Lev Semenovich Vygotsky—have recently come to exert great influence on contemporary researchers. Although Vygotsky himself did not conduct investigations of mathematical thinking per se, he recognized the importance of doing so, and he contributed several major theoretical ideas to the study of cognitive development in general.

In contrast to Piaget, Vygotsky stressed the contribution of social factors to intellectual development. For Vygotsky, "social interactions were a critical vehicle whereby natural processes in cognitive development were redirected by social and historical influences" (Saxe, 1991, p. 10). The social environment, and instruction in particular, exerts a nurturing influence on development, prodding the child to create increasingly complex and systematic cognitive constructions.

Vygotsky's elaboration of this notion in regard to schooling is of particular interest. In his view, children enter school with "spontaneous concepts" (according to Russian-speaking informants, a better translation is probably "everyday concepts" or "common life knowledge") developed in the ordinary environment. In the case of mathematics, Vygotsky (1978) proposed that "children's learning begins long before they enter school . . . children begin to study arithmetic in school, but long beforehand they have had some experience with quantity—they have had to deal with operations of division, addition, subtraction, and the determination of size. Consequently, children have their own preschool arithmetic, which only myopic psychologists could ignore" (p. 84).

Moreover, these spontaneous concepts have a special character. "Spontaneous concepts . . . are strong in what concerns the situational, empirical, and practical" (Vygotsky, 1986, p. 194). When children enter school, they encounter "scientific concepts" (a better translation is probably "systematic concepts"), including the formal system of mathematics. Scientific concepts are organized, systematic, and abstract. They impose new demands on the child's cognition and thus provoke development. "[T]he rudiments of systematization first enter the child's mind by way of his contact with scientific concepts" (p. 172).

Further, the relation between spontaneous and scientific is complex. "[T]he development of the child's spontaneous concepts proceeds upward, and the development of his scientific concepts downward. . . . The inception of a spontaneous concept can usually be traced to a face-to-face meeting with a concrete situation, while a scientific concept involves from the first a 'mediated' attitude toward its object. . . . In working its slow way upward, an everyday concept clears a path for the scientific concept and its downward development . . . [giving it] body and vitality. Scientific concepts, in turn, supply structures for the upward development of the child's spontaneous concepts towards consciousness and deliberate use" (pp. 193–194).

Vygotsky's theory has recently been received with great enthusiasm because it suggests a research agenda involving several novel components. One is the investigation of ways in which the social environment contributes to cognitive development generally and to the development of mathematical thinking in particular. Except for early speculations (Piaget, 1962) about the effects of peer interaction on cognitive development, Piaget himself neglected issues of social experience (Ginsburg, 1981) that are of obvious importance for the educational enterprise. A second is the investigation of the development of academic knowledge in the context of the school. From Vygotsky's point of view, changes in the structure of academic knowledge are as important to understand as changes in the spontaneous concepts studied by Piaget: Academic knowledge promotes systematic and organized thinking. And a third part of the research agenda is the examination of the interaction between the social-historical and the individual—the manner in which the individual's intuitions give energy to the social wisdom, which in turn helps to organize the personal. This powerful conceptualization of the process of education deserves serious consideration.

This brings us then to the "modern period" of research on mathematical thinking, which we date from the early 1960s (roughly the beginning of the cognitive revolution) and which the next section reviews in detail. Contemporary research may be said to focus on three major topics: (a) early mathematical competence, (b) academic knowledge, and (c) sociocultural influence. The focus on early competence may be said to have originated in the pioneering investigations of P. Bryant (1974), Gelman and Gallistel (1978), and Mehler and Bever (1967). Gelman and Gallistel's theory and extensive data on the early development of counting and related concepts were especially influential because they were interpreted as demonstrations—contrary to Piaget's view—both that counting plays a major role in the early development of number and that preschool children exhibit a surprising cognitive competence (Gelman, 1979). In Gelman and Gallistel's view, preschool children's counting, even at age 3 years, is not merely a rote, verbal activity (as Piaget had proposed) but rather is based on important mathematical principles. Given these findings, researchers were spurred to conduct extensive investigations of early counting and to undertake a search for other aspects of mathematical competence in early childhood and even in infancy, as we shall see in the next section.

The study of academic knowledge is another concern of the current era. Instead of focusing on the kinds of basic but nonacademic knowledge investigated by Piaget, researchers have undertaken an examination of the mathematical knowledge children acquire in the school setting. The focus is not on achievement as conventionally defined by grades or standard tests, but on the child's knowing—the child's strategies and conceptual understanding. To some extent, this emphasis derives from Piaget's general focus on the processes rather than the products of thought. But we can also trace this approach to the work of Robert Davis, a prominent mathematics educator who undertook some of the first empirical investigations of children's mathematical knowledge (Cochran, Barson, & Davis, 1970; Davis & Greenstein, 1964), and who influenced other early work in this area (Ginsburg, 1971).

A third trend in research is a consideration of the sociocultural context of children's early mathematical development. Much of this work can be traced to an early study of African mathematics (Gay & Cole, 1967), and to other research of Michael Cole and his colleagues (Cole & Scribner, 1974). This body of work introduced others both to the exciting possibilities of cross-cultural research (Saxe & Posner, 1983) and to the importance of Vygotsky's sociocultural perspective (Lave, 1988). As we shall see in the next section, this work eventually led to investigations both in foreign cultures (Nunes, Schliemann, & Carraher, 1993) and within the United States (Saxe, Guberman, & Gearhart, 1987).

For the past 30 years or so, research on the development of mathematical thinking has proliferated, and there has been a large increase in the number of published studies in this area. Until 1960, there were fewer than 50 research studies a year in the area, broadly conceived. The average from 1892 to 1960 was approximately 25 or less. By 1970, somewhere between 300 and 400 papers were being published each year (Kilpatrick, 1992). Another sign of the popularity of this research area is the proliferation of organizations and meetings. Research on mathematical thinking is commonly presented at meetings of the Society for Research in Child Development, the American Psychological Association, and the American Educational Research Association. And interest in this area of research is of course not limited to the United States. The International Group for the Psychology of Mathematics Education, which held its first meeting in Utrecht in 1977, is a vibrant international organization that has stimulated research in many countries around the world.

Why has this area of research become so popular? Among the reasons are the distinguished intellectual ancestors whose work we have described. Also, much of the research has been successful and of obvious interest for both psychology and education. But another important influence must be mentioned: money. During this period of time, the U.S. federal government has provided substantial funding for research in this area, particularly through the National Science Foundation and the Department of Education.

This brief historical review leads to several conclusions. First, for many years, psychological research and theory—from Dewey's and Thorndike's work to Piaget's and Bruner's—have played a major role in mathematics education. Psychology has indeed served as a foundation discipline for mathematics education. Second, psychological ideas have been used not so much to produce practical methods for the teaching of mathematics (although Thorndike's theory led to the development of procedures for drill) as to interpret phenomena of mathematics education. Psychologists' ways of looking at the world influence how educators conceptualize the teaching and learning of mathematics. Third, psychologists have hardly been of one mind concerning their theories of mathematical thinking. Witness, for example, the contrast between Thorndike's theory of elementary bonds and Brownell's meaning theory, or between Piaget's emphasis on the individual and Vygotsky's on the social community. Fourth, some of the disagreement is only apparent, resulting from the fact that various psychologists focus on different aspects of the process of mathematics education. Developmentalists have tended to focus on the child's informal knowledge, whereas educational psychologists tend to concern themselves with classroom instruction. And finally, in its first 70 or 80 years, psychology's contribution to mathematics education has been both distinguished and influential.

We consider next the major findings of the contemporary era of research.

RESEARCH

Our review of the research literature is divided into four major sections. The first spans infancy and toddlerhood, and focuses on mathematical abilities that are innately endowed or develop very early in life, without substantial sociocultural influence. The second section reviews the preschool years, focusing on informal knowledge, particularly the acquisition of counting and related knowledge influenced by culture. The third section covers middle to late childhood. The primary focus is the formal mathematics knowledge acquired in elementary school classrooms. The final section considers the influence of sociocultural context on mathematical thinking.

We conclude the review of research with a capsule summary in the form of basic principles of mathematics learning.

Origins of Informal Mathematical Knowledge

When does numerical knowledge first develop in the young child? Does it depend on the availability of the language of counting and on culture more generally, or is it innate like many perceptual abilities? To answer questions like these, investigators have studied the development of number-related skills in preverbal infants. Babies possess some basic numerical abilities that can be used with small sets of objects. They have the ability to determine exactly how many objects are contained in small sets, to determine which of two sets is more numerous, and to engage in a simple kind of arithmetic reasoning.

Enumeration

Young, preverbal infants possess an ability to enumerate small sets of objects, that is, to empirically determine and then represent the precise number of objects in a set. Starkey and Cooper (1980) presented 4- to 5-month-old infants with displays of two-dimensional objects (dots) using a habituation–dishabituation of looking paradigm. (This involves repeated presentation of the same stimulus until attention to it decreases, and then presentation of a new stimulus. If the latter results in renewed attention, one may conclude that it has been discriminated from the former.) Infants were habituated to displays containing a repeated number of objects (e.g., 3) and then were presented with a test display containing a new number of objects (e.g., 2). Infants dishabituated (i.e., their looking times increased) when set numerosity changed from 2 to 3 objects or from 3 to 2, but not when it changed from 4 to 6 or from 6 to 4. Antell and Keating (1983) conducted a closely related study with much younger infants—neonates in a hospital nursery. These infants dishabituated when numerosity changed from 2 to 3 or the reverse. Thus, from the earliest point in life, well before language or social agents could instill mathematical knowledge from the culture, infants possess an ability to enumerate small objects.

How robust is this early enumerative ability? It has been found that infants can enumerate small sets regardless of whether the objects are similar or dissimilar (Strauss & Curtis, 1981), static or moving (van Loosbroek & Smitsman, 1990), or presented sequentially or simultaneously (Canfield & Haith, in press). Indeed, babies can even match the number of objects they see with the number of sounds they hear (Starkey, Spelke, & Gelman, 1983, 1990). Thus, well before children begin to count, babies possess a primitive ability to enumerate small sets. Numerical competence is present from the beginning of life.

Number Relations

Other evidence indicates that, from 12 and 18 months of age, infants can determine which of two small sets is more numerous. In one study (Cooper, 1984), infants were repeatedly presented with a pattern involving two sets of 1 to 4 objects, presented sequentially. In the "more-than" pattern, infants were shown two sets presented in order of ascending numerosity: a 1-object set followed by a 2-object set; a 2-object set followed by a 3-object set; and so forth. After habituating to the more-than pattern, infants were presented with exemplars of a novel pattern such as "equal to" (same numbers of objects) or "less than" (descending numerosity; e.g., a 3-object set followed by a 2-object set). The youngest infants in the study, those 6 to 8 months old, habituated slowly and appeared to fail to discriminate the various types of numerical patterns. Those 10 to 12 months old discriminated shifts from equal-to to more-than and less-than patterns and the reverse, but not from more-than to less-than patterns. Apparently, babies at this age can see numbers of objects as same or different, but cannot distinguish between more than and less than. But this difficulty is overcome by age 12 to 14 months, when babies can also discriminate shifts from more than to less than and the reverse. Thus, from an early point in life, children detect simple numerical patterns involving sameness and more-than and less-than patterns.

Arithmetic Reasoning

Simple arithmetic reasoning is another aspect of numerical cognition that begins to develop early in life. Arithmetic reasoning involves more than enumerating a set of objects or comparing two sets. This type of reasoning is used to determine the numerical effects of transformations on sets. Sophian and Adams (1987) investigated young children's (ages 14, 18, 24, and 28 months old) understanding of the directional effects of addition and subtraction. First, children were shown two sets, with one object in each. Then these sets were hidden by a screen, and, in full view of the children, one object was either added to or subtracted from one set. Under these conditions, when the children knew the size of the original sets and could see only the act of addition or subtraction but not the results, 24- and 28-month-olds reached for the more numerous set, but 14- and 18-month-olds chose the set that had been transformed, regardless of the nature of the transformation. So, at least by 24 months, children know that adding makes more and subtracting yields less. What the study did not reveal was whether toddlers were computing the precise sums or remainders produced by these transformations.

Starkey (1992) developed a "searchbox" task to study young children's ability to compute precise sums and remainders. In one experiment, children from 18 months to 2 years were presented with a set of from 1 to 5 identical objects (balls), which they then placed one-by-one into an opaque container, the searchbox. The experimenter then either visibly added one object by placing it into the searchbox, or subtracted one object by reaching into the searchbox and removing it. Thus, the child might have placed a set of 3 objects in the searchbox and then the experimenter might have added 1 more, to make a total of 4. The children's task was to remove all objects—in this example, 4—from the searchbox after the transformation had been performed. A hole in the top of the searchbox was covered by elastic material that allowed reaching in without revealing the balls inside. The searchbox had a false floor and trap door that were operated by a remote switch. With this hidden mechanism, it was possible to operate the searchbox in such a way that only one object was actually in the main chamber of the searchbox while children were searching inside it (so that they could not discover by touch that more objects needed to be removed). The measure of interest was the number of times children reached into the searchbox to remove an object from the set. This indicated how many objects they thought should be inside the searchbox after the addition or subtraction transformation had been performed. It was found that even the youngest children could compute the exact sums or remainders for small-numerosity problems. The 18-month-olds solved addition and subtraction problems when the largest set size (i.e., the sum or minuend numerosity) did not exceed 2 (1 + 1 and 2–1). The 24-month-olds solved some (typically subtraction) problems in which the largest set was 3 objects, and 30-month-olds were successful with both types of problems when the largest set was 3 or fewer. At none of the age levels did children compute sums or remainders when a set of 4 or more objects was involved, and verbal counting was rarely observed. Thus, even in late infancy, children can compute exact sums and remainders for very small sets, and they do this without overt counting.

One study (Wynn, 1992) reported that considerably younger infants can engage in simple arithmetic reasoning. Infants first saw an object disappear behind a screen. Next, they saw another object being placed behind the screen. The screen was then removed and either the correct number of objects (2) or an incorrect number (1) was displayed. Infants tended to look longer at the incorrect number than at the correct number, as if a numerical expectation had been violated when only 1 object was present. A comparable subtraction problem was presented in the same general way. Infants looked longer at the incorrect number of objects (2) than at the correct number (1).

In summary, mathematical cognition originates in early infancy and undergoes developmental change during infancy and toddlerhood. These early mathematical competencies include the enumeration of small numerosities, an ability to relate sets numerically, knowledge of the directional effects of addition and subtraction, and an ability to compute the exact sum or remainder produced by an addition or subtraction transformation. Infants' earliest mathematical competence does not depend on language or cultural transmission. It is as natural for humans to think mathematically as it is to use language or tools, for "humans are born with a fundamental sense of quantity" (Geary, 1994, p. 1).

Informal Mathematical Thinking during the Preschool Years

If biology provides the foundation for number, the child erects its structure from quantitative opportunities provided by the material and social environments. The human mind always develops in an environment that is both physical and social, and the quantitative environment is so pervasive that we are often oblivious to it. From early in development, children encounter small discrete objects that can be manipulated, touched, and counted. Indeed, in manipulating objects, infants and young children can create many examples of addition and other numerical problems (Langer, 1986).

The physical environment of quantity appears to offer rich stimulation across widely diverse cultures. In what culture, however impoverished, does the child lack things to count? In what culture cannot one add to what there is? Children also encounter a social environment affording important notions of quantity. Culture makes available vital tools: the number words and the processes of counting. These social environments vary considerably from culture to culture, but almost all known cultures traditionally offer a number-word system, often highly elaborate, with a base system such as base 10 and extending to rather large numbers (Dantzig, 1954). Given the opportunities afforded by these rich environments, children's almost inevitable response is the construction of elementary forms of mathematical knowledge. After all, children are endowed with an innate mathematical competence of the type described above (in Piaget's terms, "specific heredity") and also with a biological propensity to learn, to construct, and to make sense of the environment (Piaget's "general heredity").

There is general consensus among researchers that preschool children construct a set of informal mathematical concepts prior to formal schooling in arithmetic (e.g., Carpenter, Moser, & Romberg, 1982; Resnick, 1989). Underlying this view is a critical distinction between *informal* and *formal* mathematical knowledge. Informal knowledge is grounded in problem-solving situations with concrete objects, and children construct it through their interactions with the physical and social world. In contrast, formal knowledge entails the manipulation of a system of written symbols, and children typically acquire this type of mathematical knowledge in school. Although the rate of development of some informal knowledge is subject to sociocultural influence, the basic components of informal mathematical knowledge are universal across diverse cultural and social class groups (Ginsburg, Choi, Lopez, Netley, & Chi, 1997; Klein & Starkey, 1988). Child development researchers and educators have come to recognize that children's developing informal knowledge of mathematics is a necessary foundation for formal mathematical knowledge. In this section, we emphasize the development of informal mathematical knowledge that parents and educators can reasonably expect children to have when they enter elementary school.

The preschool period marks the point in development when culturally specific numerical knowledge such as the English number-word system begins to play a prominent role in children's mathematical thinking. Children acquire this knowledge through processes of mathematical enculturation, beginning with the acquisition of number words and counting, the first mathematical tool that cultures provide. Around age 2 years, many children begin to acquire the enumerative process of counting. As we have seen, children do not approach this acquisition as a tabula rasa mathematically, but rather with considerable mathematical knowledge already in place. We argue that the acquisition of counting is essentially a constructive process whereby prior mathematical knowledge becomes integrated with and enhanced by this culturally transmitted intellectual tool. By age 4 years, children integrate counting with their arithmetic knowledge, and in doing so, they invent counting strategies to compute the effects of addition and subtraction operations on sets of objects (e.g., Ginsburg, 1989; Groen & Resnick, 1977). Thus, counting proves to be a powerful intellectual tool that children use in the construction of informal mathematical knowledge. Not until they receive formal mathematics instruction in school does a potentially more powerful type of tool becomes available to them—a written number system such as the Hindu-Arabic system.

Subitizing and Counting

Culture first enters children's mathematical thinking when they acquire the conventional number names for small numbers: one, two, three, and so on. These names appear to be used initially to label the cardinal value of small sets of objects. Children begin to assign number names to sets of things quite early in life. The first number word children use is typically "two," and this word sometimes appears before children are 2 years of age and hence before they have begun to count (Wagner & Walters, 1982). Within a year after the first number word appears, children use "one" and "three" in the presence of small sets. (For a review of acquisition of number words, see Fuson, 1988.) "Four" is not acquired until children have begun to count.

How do children determine that a set should be characterized by a certain number? By age 3 years, children can enumerate sets by subitizing them or by counting. "Subitizing" (which derives from the Latin verb *subitare,* to arrive suddenly) is a rapid enumerative procedure used with small sets (for adults, typically sets of 1 to 4 or 5 objects). To demonstrate, have a friend place a small number of pennies beneath a cover and then briefly remove the cover. Try to determine exactly how many pennies are in the set without counting, "One, two," and so on. If the set is small enough, you will know how many pennies are in the set without having to count.

Children subitize small sets from an early point in life, and the subitizing range—the range of set sizes that can be accurately subitized—changes with development (Cooper, 1984; Starkey & Cooper, 1995a). Toddlers who have not yet begun to count verbally have a subitizing range of 1 to 3. This range is identical to the accurate enumeration range of infants (Starkey & Cooper, 1995a, 1995b). Over the preschool years, the subitizing range expands from 1 to 4 at age 3 years to 1 to 5 in some children at age 4 or 5 years.

A second enumerative procedure is counting: the assigning of number words, in sequence, to the individual members of a set, with the final number denoting cardinal value. Thus, the child points to an object and pairs it with the number "one," points to the next object and pairs it with the number "two," and concludes that there are "two" altogether (the cardinal value).

Counting seems so easy to adults that they forget what a major cognitive achievement it represents for the very young and how long it takes them to learn it. Only months after the first conventional number words are acquired, children begin the protracted process of acquiring the number words and learning to count.

The first major account of this process was presented in *The Child's Understanding of Number* (Gelman & Gallistel, 1978), which proposed that counting is a fundamental, conceptually based process in children's mathematical development. In this view, at no point in development is children's counting a rote (nonconceptual) activity; instead, counting is guided by a central set of innate how-to-count principles: (a) the one-one principle asserts that it is necessary to assign one and only one distinct tag (e.g., an English number name) to individual objects in a set as they are counted; (b) the stable order principle asserts that it is necessary to arrange in a stable (repeatable) order the tags assigned to individual objects being counted (e.g., the ordered English number names, one, two, three, and so on); (c) the cardinal principle asserts that the final tag used in counting a set represents the number of objects contained in the set. Together, these principles form the child's counting scheme, the conceptual structure of counting.

The Gelman and Gallistel theory is quite remarkable in proposing that the child's earliest mathematical activity—the apparently trivial counting of small sets of objects—is based on important mathematical principles of one-to-one correspondence, order, and cardinality. This represents a sharp break with the tradition of Piaget, which held that counting is a peripheral activity and that key mathematical ideas emerge only later in development, with the elaboration of general intellectual structures. And the theory certainly contradicts Thorndike's view of counting as a collection of meaningless connections.

It is now widely accepted that preschool children's counting is conceptually grounded. This does not guarantee, however, that the counting will be error-free. Gelman and Gallistel (1978) found that 3-year-olds, when counting sets of 2 to 5 objects, made errors involving double counting or omission of an object about 33% of the time. For 5-year-olds, the errors occurred 19% of the time. Several factors lead young children to err when they count: the arrangement of objects, the number of items, and whether the items can be touched or moved (Greeno, Riley, & Gelman, 1984). The easiest type of set for young children to count is a numerically small, linear arrangement of distinct, touchable items. As features of the set depart from this prototype, counting becomes more difficult.

The failure of a child's counting behavior to be constrained by a given counting principle does not necessarily imply that the child does not possess the principle. A general rule in life is that worthy principles are easier to espouse than to implement. The procedural demands of counting—for example, remembering exactly which objects were counted and which were not—cause the child to lose sight of the principle. To test this possibility, Gelman and Meck (1983) used an error-detection task (adapted from Saxe, 1979) in which a puppet held by the experimenter counted, either correctly or not, while a preschool child watched. The child's task was to judge whether the puppet's counting was "OK or not OK." By making the puppet responsible for the act of counting, certain procedural demands were reduced. For example, during the count, it was the puppet's responsibility to keep track of which objects in the set had already been counted and which had not, and of which number name was used most recently to tag an object during the count. Gelman and Meck found that preschool children readily judged correct counts as correct, and detected the errors in counts that violated any of the how-to-count principles. Thus, the error-detection task adds support to Gelman and Gallistel's argument that counting by preschool children is conceptually based.

Briars and Siegler (1984) also used an error-detection task with 3- to 5-year-old children. In addition to presenting children with correct and principle-violating counts, they presented counts that were unconventional but did not violate a counting principle. For example, when presented with a linear array of objects that alternated in color (black-white-black-white, and so on), the puppet did not count in the usual left-to-right manner, but instead first counted all objects that were one color and then doubled back and counted the objects that were the other color. Briars and Siegler replicated Gelman and Meck's findings: The 4- and 5-year-olds judged correct-conventional counts as correct, and they detected principle-violating errors in incorrect counts. Several children, however, sometimes judged the correct-unconventional counts to be incorrect. This finding suggests that the counting of preschool children is constrained by mathematically unnecessary conventions. A developmental task for children, then, is to more fully differentiate the essential from the conventional (but nonessential) features of counting.

Not only is preschool children's developing counting ability more constrained than was originally thought, but there is also considerable evidence that the counting of beginning (i.e., 2- to 3-year-old) counters is less grounded conceptually (see discussions by Baroody, 1992; P. Bryant, 1995; Frydman, in press; Siegler, 1991; Starkey & Cooper, 1995a). Most research has focused on the cardinality principle. When 2- or 3-year-olds first begin to exhibit counting behaviors, they do not relate counting to the cardinal value of a set (e.g., Frye, Braisby, Love, Maroudas, & Nicholls, 1989; Fuson, 1988, 1992; Sophian & Adams, 1987; Wynn, 1990). When asked to count a set of 4 objects, young children may correctly count, "One, two, three, four," but then fail to report that the set has a cardinal value of 4. When the experimenter then asks, "How many things are there?" young children often count the set again instead of stating the final number name used in the count (e.g., Fuson, 1988; Gelman & Gallistel, 1978; Schaeffer, Eggleston, & Scott, 1974). Several researchers take this reaction as evidence that young children do not initially understand the cardinality function served by the final number name in the count.

To summarize, the development of counting has been a very active research area, and remarkable progress has been made in describing the course of its development. Counting is a cultural tool that children begin to acquire at 2 to 3 years of age, often before entry into preschool. This tool is not simply internalized, however; rather, it builds on prior mathematical knowledge. This process takes some time, as indicated by the finding that children do not appear to know initially that counting can be used to determine the cardinal value of a set. Over time, counting becomes fully grounded conceptually in the child's developing mathematical cognition.

Informal Addition and Subtraction

The development of informal mathematical knowledge in the preschool years encompasses more than subitizing and counting. Arithmetic knowledge also develops during these years. The knowledge that develops, albeit incomplete, constitutes a foundation for the subsequent development of a formal arithmetic system.

Research has shown that very young children can compute the effects of addition and subtraction on small sets without counting, before they develop counting methods to perform calculations on larger sets. Earlier, we described studies that used a searchbox methodology to present simple addition and subtraction problems to 1.5- and 2-year-olds (Starkey, 1992). Groups of 3- and 4-year-olds were also included to determine whether preschool children, unlike infants and toddlers, spontaneously use counting strategies to solve addition and subtraction problems. The results showed that, when given simple addition and subtraction problems, children searched a correct number of times and then stopped searching. Children erred on the larger-set problems, either by searching exhaustively until no further balls were found or by searching an incorrect, fixed number of times. Children rarely exhibited a counting strategy, did not use fingers as mnemonic aids, and generally solved the problems in silence. One explanation posits that the solutions were obtained through a subitizing process that is successful with very small numbers. The 3- and 4-year-olds were able to solve arithmetic problems involving somewhat larger sets than those solved correctly by the younger children, perhaps because of the expansion of the subitizing range that occurs during the preschool years.

Other studies confirm that across a variety of task contexts 3-year-olds solve small-numerosity addition and subtraction problems without using overt, counting-based strategies. Siegler and Robinson (1982) and Starkey and Gelman (1982) found that 3-year-olds usually did not spontaneously use counting to solve addition problems. Even when they had been instructed to count an initial set, 3-year-olds rarely went on to use counting to compute the effects of addition or subtraction on the set. These findings lend further support to the view stated earlier: Counting in toddlers and young preschoolers has not yet developed to the point of being a procedure children use to determine the cardinal value of sets.

At about age 4 years, children begin to use counting spontaneously in solving arithmetic problems. They do so under a variety of conditions: when a visible set of concrete objects undergoes an addition or subtraction transformation (Groen & Resnick, 1977), when an initially visible set that has been enumerated is then screened and transformed as in the searchbox studies (Starkey & Gelman, 1982), and when the set and transformation are never displayed but are described verbally in a word problem (Siegler & Robinson, 1982). Children's initial counting strategies are closely tied to the structure of the problem as it is presented, and they include mathematically irrelevant properties such as the order in which addends are presented. Later in their development, children invent counting strategies that are less directly tied to mathematically irrelevant properties of the problem (e.g., Baroody, in press). For example, children begin to count on from the cardinal value of the initial addend instead of recounting the entire set after it has undergone addition; later, they rearrange the order of addends so they can count on from the larger of the two addends.

Young children typically use a mix of strategies in solving addition and subtraction problems. The observations of Siegler and Robinson (1982) are typical. Children from 3 to 5 years of age were presented with simple word problems in which single sets of imaginary objects were described as undergoing an addition transformation. The experimenter described the type and number of objects comprising the initial set, and the type and magnitude of the transformation. Children were told, "I want you to imagine that you have a pile of oranges. You have *m* oranges, and I'm going to give you *n* to add to your pile. How many do you have altogether?" It was found that 3-year-olds consistently solved only the numerically small problems. The 4- and 5-year-old children were able to solve problems involving larger sets, and they used a variety of strategies. By our calculation, they used overt strategies on 38% of the problems and one or more covert strategies on 62% of the problems, including most small-set problems.

The overt strategies included *finger counting* (holding up fingers as substitutes for the imaginary objects and then counting them), *verbal counting* (counting but without using fingers or other physical props), and *fingers* (holding up fingers but not overtly counting them). It is not clear how children are actually solving problems when they use the fingers strategy: perhaps they subitize or covertly count their fingers, or perhaps, as Siegler and his colleagues have suggested, the fingers remind the children of the number facts to be retrieved from long-term storage. Whether a covert enumerative procedure or a number-fact retrieval accompanies the use of fingers, it is clear that preschool children possess diverse methods for solving simple concrete addition problems.

Research has documented that children develop and use the same general mix of strategies to solve simple subtraction problems (Siegler, 1987; Starkey & Gelman, 1982). Children's informal subtraction knowledge has been studied less than their informal addition knowledge, but the general patterns of development of the two appear to be the same. In both cases, covert strategies appear first in development and are initially used by children to solve problems involving small sets. Counting strategies develop later and are used with larger sets. Over time, counting strategies become more efficient and reflect increasing mathematical sophistication. It is as yet unclear whether addition problem solving has developmental priority over subtraction. For example, it is not known whether children first invent finger-counting to solve informal addition problems and, only later, adapt finger counting to solve informal subtraction problems.

In summary, during the preschool years, children develop and use several strategies for computing the effects of addition and subtraction transformations on single sets of objects. The earliest type of strategy is limited to representations of small, concrete sets and utilizes subitizing, either to calculate sums or remainders, or perhaps (as some have argued) to store and retrieve number facts. Next, within about a year from when counting has developed into a scheme with a cardinal underpinning, 4-year-old children invent counting-based strategies for solving addition and subtraction problems. Children can compute the effects of simple transformations on objects in an observed, screened, or imagined set. As we will describe in more detail in the review of mathematical thinking in the elementary school years, these strategies continue to develop in the lower grades of elementary school.

Ideas of Addition and Subtraction

Reasoning about the effects of addition and subtraction on sets of objects (as opposed to *computing* particular sums or remainders) also develops during early childhood. Researchers have examined children's knowledge of arithmetic operations apart from the ability to compute. Converging evidence from several studies indicates that preschool children understand the directional effects of addition and subtraction operations (addition to a set produces more, and subtraction produces less). To illustrate one type of task, Klein (1984) presented preschoolers with two linear arrays of eight objects, displayed in spatial one-to-one correspondence, so that it was easy for them to determine without counting that the sets were equal in number. After children had inspected the initial arrays (without counting) and judged them to be equal, both arrays were screened from view. Then two objects were added to or subtracted from one of the initial arrays. The developmental question is when children know that adding objects to one of the sets makes it have more.

Four-year-old children are highly successful in solving this type of problem (Brush, 1978; Klein, 1984), and related research has found this ability to be present even in 2- and 3-year-olds (Cooper, 1984). Thus, young children's understanding of adding and subtracting is consistent with their ability to perform arithmetic computations. It stands to reason that preschoolers have to know the direction in which to perform an arithmetic computation in order to use counting strategies, such as counting on, to solve addition and subtraction problems.

Other research has demonstrated that young children's arithmetic reasoning is limited and develops over a protracted period of time. Some nonequivalence problems are particularly difficult for 4- and 5-year-olds to solve (Blevins-Knabe, Cooper, Mace, Starkey, & Leitner, 1987; Brush, 1978; Klein, 1984). For example, suppose that children are presented with initial sets that are unequal—they contain 10 and 7 objects, respectively—and then 2 objects are added to the smaller set. To solve this problem, children have to integrate information concerning the addition transformation with information about the inequality between the two sets (i.e., 2 objects were added to the smaller set, making it more numerous than it was originally, but it still had fewer objects than the untransformed set of 10).

The errors that preschoolers make on these problems reflect a qualitative change in their ability to reason arithmetically about the numerical relation between two sets (Klein, 1984). Younger preschoolers exhibit directional errors: they consider only the direction of the arithmetic transformation without any regard to the initial inequality between the sets. Thus, if something is added to a set, that set is judged to be the larger. In contrast, older preschoolers make integration errors. They attempt to integrate the arithmetic transformation with the initial inequality, but they do this only in an imprecise way, failing to quantify the initial difference between the sets and to balance the transformation against the initial inequality. They judge that the outcome is an equal number of objects in the two sets. In general, children are not successful on this type of two-set problem until 6 or 7 years of age.

In brief, preschoolers have the ability not only to compute, but also to understand something about the operations of addition and subtraction. They realize that adding makes more and subtracting yields less, at least when two initially equal sets are involved, but they have difficulty with more complex problems involving initial inequalities.

Informal Division

Several studies have examined the developmental origins of children's knowledge of division. Klein and Langer (1991) presented concrete division problems to 2- and 3-year-old children. The children were asked to give a set of objects (e.g., slices of bread, cookies)—the "source set"—to two toy dogs. "Put the bread on your dogs' plates." In a *simultaneous* condition, the entire source set was presented at the beginning of a division problem. In a *sequential* condition, the source set was presented object-by-object from a dispenser apparatus. The division problems were varied on several dimensions, in order to determine whether the numerosity of the source set (4 or 8) or its class composition (one or two equal or unequal classes) affected children's ability to divide the source set into two equal sets.

The results showed that children shift from predominantly one-set constructions (giving one dog all the objects) at 24 months to predominantly two-set constructions (giving each dog at least one object) at 30 months. Children divided the source set into two equal sets (i.e., sharing the objects equally between the two toy dogs) on a majority of problems at 36 months in the simultaneous condition and at 42 months in the sequential condition. More small sets were divided equally than large sets.

Children used two principal types of strategy. The *consecutive* strategy involved distributing objects in turn, first to one quotient set and then to the other. The *overlapping* strategy involved shifting back and forth between two sets in distributing the objects. In some (but not all) cases, one-to-one correspondence was used in the overlapping strategy (e.g., one for Dog A and one for Dog B, etc.). Both strategies appeared at 30 months of age when children were beginning to construct two sets. The overlapping strategy was used more on large-numerosity problems and eventually emerged as the more general-purpose approach.

Other research on informal division has revealed some extensions and limitations of this early mathematical knowledge (Frydman & Bryant, 1988; Miller, 1984). Four- and 5-year-olds can use divisors of 2, 3, or even 4, and can successfully divide large numerosity sets (12 and 24). Also, use of one-to-one correspondence is greater at this age level than in younger children. Children experience difficulty when presented with sets that do not divide evenly and thus have a remainder.

Carpenter, Ansell, Franke, Fennema, and Weisbeck (1993) presented kindergarten children, throughout a school year, with division problems that were accompanied by concrete objects that could be manipulated. By the end of the year, the children were able to solve both partitive division problems (e.g., John gave each doggie the same number of cookies) and measurement division problems (e.g., Mary had 8 guppies. She put 2 into each jar. How many jars did she have?). Thus, children can deal with simple division problems at a much younger age than is usually expected.

In brief, even at the preschool level, children demonstrate considerable informal knowledge of division as sharing.

Conclusion

Our review has shown that, despite evident limitations, children's informal mathematics is more fully developed and powerful than many have realized. Mathematics educators in particular need to be cognizant of the ways in which preschool children count, add, subtract, and divide, and of the kinds of mathematical understanding they possess when they enter school. Indeed, there is widespread consensus that children's informal mathematics can serve as a useful foundation for much early mathematics education (Baroody, 1987a; Nunes, 1993; Resnick, 1989). How can we successfully teach young children unless we are aware of the knowledge into which they assimilate formal instruction?

Mathematical Thinking during the Elementary School Years

We have seen that counting serves as a surprisingly effective basis for young children's arithmetic. Yet, counting has obvious limits for computation and is particularly cumbersome to use for multiplication and division. Children can enrich their knowledge and technique by learning the arithmetic taught in school. This arithmetic is *codified:* it is written, it is arranged systematically, and it has explicit rules and procedures. Codified arithmetic allows the user to deal with imaginary mathematical objects, to remember the calculations he or she has done, and to communicate the results to others. Just as counting can be viewed as an intellectual tool that extends the infant's mathematical knowledge, so written notation systems and formal algorithms can extend the young child's ability to represent and compute. Children cannot by themselves reinvent the conventional symbols and methods of arithmetic. Codified arithmetic needs to be taught through a process of *formal* instruction—that is, through organized teaching in the classroom or in tutorial sessions. Written arithmetic is a cultural legacy; it represents the accumulated wisdom of the race, put in written form so as to be available to all, and it is obviously far superior to children's informal arithmetic.

We now discuss how children, already possessing an informal mathematics, enter a new and specially designed environment, the artificial culture of the school, where they encounter the world of academic mathematics. The course of learning formal mathematics is often far from smooth. Indeed, we are faced with a great paradox: codified mathematics is enormously powerful, but few children easily understand it or find it useful.

We review major aspects of psychological research on children's learning of school mathematics: the evolution of counting strategies; number facts; invented strategies; bugs; word problems; and understanding. Our review is selective in two ways. We focus on material that is *relevant* for mathematics education and that offers *general principles* for understanding children's mathematics learning. The relevance criterion means that we do not cover research that is more germane to psychologists' theorizing (for example, about the specific processes by which number facts might be represented in memory) than to children's learning of school mathematics. The relevance criterion also means that we cover material concerning invented strategies, bugs, understanding, and the like, because these concepts are important for anyone engaged in the teaching of mathematics. The criterion of general principle means that we do not cover in detail the development of all mathematical concepts that have been investigated. Thus, instead of presenting a comprehensive account of the development of division, fractions, decimals, geometric ideas, and other content areas learned in school, we review general ideas such as the nature of invented strategies, because they seem relevant for understanding any specific content area in mathematics. (The interested reader will find reviews of the learning of specific content areas in Grouws, 1992; and Lesh & Landau, 1989.)

The Evolution of Counting Strategies

Recall from our review of mathematical thinking in the preschool years that young children possess a variety of strategies for solving simple arithmetic problems. To add or subtract visible, hidden, or imagined objects, young children tend to use counting-based strategies of one kind or another. Most children have and use several of these strategies but rely primarily on just a few.

Children continue to use these types of strategies to solve simple addition and subtraction problems into the lower grades of elementary school (Ashcraft, 1990; Carpenter et al., 1982; Siegler, 1987). Furthermore, these counting-based strategies become more efficient over time (Baroody, 1987b). Reliance on the inefficient *counting-all* (or *sum*) strategy, in which an entire set is recounted after an addition transformation, is replaced by the more efficient strategy of *counting-on-from-first number* (or *first*) strategy, in which children count up from the initial addend the exact number of times corresponding to the numerosity of the second addend. Children's switch from a counting-all to a counting-on strategy has been found to occur around age 6 to 7 years (Grade 1).

Children next develop a more efficient counting-based addition strategy, the *counting-on-from-larger number (min)* strategy. When presented with two numbers to add, children count up from the larger one. Acquisition of this strategy appears to depend on implicit knowledge of additive composition. Turner and Bryant (in press) found that children who could count-on-from-larger had knowledge of additive composition—an empirical generalization that the same sum is achieved when two sets are combined in different orders. To summarize, in the first 2 to 3 grades, children progress from a *counting-all* strategy to *counting-on-from-first number* and then to *counting-on-from-larger number.*

When children have counting-based strategies in place, the stage is set for several developments in their arithmetical cognition, particularly the acquisition of number facts, and the development of invented strategies for solving and giving meaning to paper-and-pencil arithmetic problems.

Number Facts

For a considerable amount of time, children use the various strategies described above when they *compute* the answers to small arithmetic problems like $5 + 7$. But eventually, as they acquire experience with problems like these, and as they are subjected to frequent drill, children store small number facts in long-term memory. Children increasingly come to rely on retrieval to answer simple arithmetic problems, and, over the several years of elementary school, retrieval becomes more rapid and increasingly automatic (Ashcraft, 1990, 1992).

Some number facts are harder to learn than others. Difficulty of number-fact learning is related to size: larger number-fact problems are often harder to master than smaller ones. This effect is evident at least as early as kindergarten and indeed across the life span (Geary & Wiley, 1991; Hamann & Ashcraft, 1985). One reason for this result is that textbooks present more examples of smaller facts than of larger ones (Ashcraft & Christy, 1995).

Children do not simply retrieve all of their number facts from long-term memory. There are at least two senses in which children construct number facts. First, children use known facts to *derive* unknown facts (e.g., $6 + 6 = 12$, so $6 + 8$ is 2 more than 12, and hence must be 14) (Carpenter & Moser, 1982). Use of such *derived facts* is extremely widespread, appearing even in unschooled individuals (Ginsburg, Posner, & Russell, 1981b), and indeed is often encouraged by teachers and textbooks.

Second, some classes of facts can be generated by children through the use of a general rule. Thus, the relative difficulty of these number facts is determined more by semantic factors than by problem size (Baroody, 1994). As one set of examples, consider the facts involving doubles ($5 + 5$, 8×8, and so on). These are learned easily (Parkman & Groen, 1971), not only because mathematics textbooks provide children with a good deal of practice with doubles (Siegler, 1988), and doubles are psychologically salient, but also because simple rules govern doubles (e.g., all sums of the addition doubles are even numbers and are part of the skip-count sequence produced when counting by twos). The $5 \times n$ and $10 \times n$ combinations are also governed by simple rules (e.g., to multiply n by 10, add a 0 to the end of n). Because of an awareness of these rules and prior practice in skip counting (e.g., by 5s), children master these combinations quickly without learning them fact-by-fact (Baroody, 1995). Other examples of number facts that children can generate through rule use are the sums involving an addend of 0 and the products involving a multiplier of 1 (Baroody, 1993). If the child understands that adding 0 or multiplying by 1 "makes no difference," then it is not necessary to memorize each individual combination involving the addition of 0 or the multiplication by 1. Similarly, if the child understands and applies the principle of commutativity—order of adding or multiplying does not affect the result—then the answer to the problem $3 + 4$ can be deduced from the already known number fact, $4 + 3 = 7$. Indeed, knowledge of commutativity reduces by about half the amount of addition and multiplication facts that need to be learned.

In brief, children memorize number facts over the course of elementary schooling. They also engage in reasoning strategies—simple constructive activities of deriving new number facts from those already available, and generating answers by using general rules instead of retrieval from long-term memory. Thus, children do not use a single strategy (recall); they use a mix of strategies.

Invented Strategies

To help children deal with number problems too large to remember, we teach them the standard methods of calculation. Indeed, much elementary school mathematics education is devoted to teaching the written methods for addition, subtraction, multiplication, and division with whole numbers. These *algorithms,* developed and codified over the course of centuries, produce correct results. When used properly, the algorithms always work.

But children do not always do arithmetic as it is taught. Often, they assimilate the written arithmetic taught in school into what they already know. The results are various constructed forms of knowledge, including what are sometimes called "invented strategies." Invented strategies make use of existing procedures, such as counting, and available information, such as known number facts. For example, Peter, a 13-year-old, was given the following problem (Ginsburg, 1971):

> **I:** Suppose you have 48 divided by 6. Go ahead. Do it any way you want.
>
> **P:** [He wrote a 7 in the quotient's place.] Wait . . . 8.
>
> **I:** How do you know that's right?
>
> **P:** Cause 6 times 6 is 36 and add 7 more to it and that's going to make 42 and another 8 more would be 48.

Peter's strategy seems to have been the following. First, he converted the division problem ($48 \div 6$) into one involving multiplication ($6 \times ? = 48$), but he could not remember that $6 \times 8 = 48$, which would have given him the answer. Consequently, he had to use a combination of methods. He began by drawing on what he already knew, namely that $6 \times 6 = 36$. Then he acknowledged an equivalence between multiplication and repeated addition. He added 6 to 36, which told him how much is 6×7. As he described this, he mistakenly said, "Add 7 to 36." But this seemed to mean: If you add 6 to 36, you get the same result as when you multiply 6×7. Then Peter added 6 to 42, which told him how much is 6×8 and gave him the missing multiplier, 8. Again he described his computations incorrectly ("another 8 more would be 48"); but, again, verbal mistakes only obscure his understanding of the relation between multiplication and addition.

Peter transformed a division problem to multiplication; used a multiplication fact he remembered; and went on to use addition to solve a multiplication problem. At the same time, he could not accurately describe what he was doing!

Some children develop genuinely interesting invented procedures. One of the most remarkable of these was developed by Kye, an 8-year-old (Cochran et al., 1970). Kye's teacher had written on the board:

$$\begin{array}{r} 64 \\ -28 \\ \hline \end{array}$$

and was explaining that "You can't take 8 from 4, so you have to regroup the 64 as. . . . "

At this point, Kye interrupted, saying, "Oh, yes you can. Four minus 8 is negative 4." He wrote:

$$\begin{array}{r} 64 \\ -28 \\ \hline -4 \end{array}$$

"And 40 and negative 4 give you 36. . . . The answer is 36." He wrote:

$$\begin{array}{r} 64 \\ -28 \\ \hline -4 \\ 40 \\ \hline 36 \end{array}$$

In brief, Kye subtracted 8 from 4, getting negative 4. He subtracted 20 from 60, getting 40; and then he added negative 4 to the 40, getting 36, which is the correct answer. Kye's invented method is in fact a perfectly adequate algorithm for subtraction.

Other common invented strategies exploit properties of the base 10 system, making it easy to solve problems like 236 + 127. A simple approach (Ginsburg et al., 1981b; Kamii, 1985) is to break the problem up into convenient parts like (200 + 100) + (30 + 20) + (6 + 4 + 3), which can be solved by rules involving simple number combinations. Thus, 200 + 100 is 300 (because it is obvious that 2 + 1 = 3); 30 + 20 is 50 (by the same type of rule) which gives 250 so far; and 6 + 4 is 10 (an easy-to-remember number combination), giving 260 so far; and then there are 3 left for a total of 263.

Notice that decomposing problems in this way exploits the base 10 structure of the numbers. Rearrangements like these involve grouping numbers by 100s, 10s, and so on. This is also the idea that underlies the conventional algorithm. Written addition starts with units, then goes to 10s, etc. The main difference between the two methods is that the mental procedure goes from large numbers to small ones (left to right) whereas the algorithm goes from small to large (right to left).

In brief, children often use several types of invented procedures. Usually, they begin by using counting methods of one kind or another, such as counting on from the larger number, to solve addition problems. Then they develop more elaborate and efficient procedures for the purposes of calculation. For example, they may combine counting with remembered addition facts to get a sum. Or they may rearrange numbers into convenient combinations for the purposes of mental calculation. Sometimes they convert difficult problems into simpler ones, as when they solve a multiplication problem by adding. Occasionally, they even create genuinely novel approaches.

Errors

Children's invented strategies do not always result in correct solutions. Some strategies are systematically flawed, and therefore produce consistent errors under certain conditions. Such errors suggest that mathematical knowledge is constructed gradually. Errors are a natural part of the knowledge construction process. Systematic errors are sometimes called "bugs" (by analogy with flawed software).

In doing subtraction, many children use the following common bug, "Subtract the smaller from the larger." Asked to do

$$\begin{array}{r} 21 \\ -5 \\ \hline \end{array}$$

Bob came up with the answer 24. He had subtracted 1 from 5 to get 4 and then simply brought down the 2 (or subtracted 0 from it) (Ginsburg, 1989, p. 166).

A less common bug involves adding individual digits. Sherry, a third grader, was asked to add 52 + 123 + 4. She got 17, an apparently absurd answer—so absurd that it must have been the result of an unthinking guess. But Sherry's explanation was: "First I added 5 and 2 and then I added 1 and 4 and the 2 and 3." In other words, Sherry simply added the individual digits without regard to place value (Ginsburg, 1989, p. 166).

Bugs have been investigated from the early part of the 20th century (Buswell & John, 1926) until the present

(J. Brown & VanLehn, 1982; VanLehn, 1986, 1990). The message seems to be consistent: children's errors in arithmetic can result not simply from guesses or slips, but from systematic strategies that lead to predictable errors. These strategies, serving as windows into mathematical thinking, indicate incomplete learning by the child. Furthermore, bugs may be thought of as resulting from the child's attempt to make sense out of what is taught, perhaps in a confusing manner. If a teacher, parent, or peer proclaims, without adequate explanation, "Always subtract the smaller from the larger," is it any wonder that the child constructs a strategy—a bug—that does just that?

Word Problems

Word problems involve the verbal description of some quantitative event in the "real world," and the student's task is to use mathematics to answer some question about the event. Thus, "Luis had 5 marbles. His brother gave him 4 more marbles. How many marbles did Luis have altogether?" A common rationale for word problems is that they purport to provide real-world contexts, which presumably motivate children and make it easier for them to apply their mathematical skills.

In any event, word problems, even if they are what we might call "secondhand applications," are common in textbooks, and researchers have investigated how children go about solving them. Later, in discussing Cognitively Guided Instruction (CGI), we present an account of children's approach to common addition and subtraction word problems. For now, we review a few general propositions about word problems.

Word problems that have the same formal mathematical features on the surface require different cognitive resources (Riley, Greeno, & Heller, 1983). For example, consider the following two problems, both of which may be considered to involve subtraction. "Six apples were in the bag and then 4 were given away. How many apples were left in the bag?" By contrast, consider: "Six apples were in the bag. Four were red and the rest were green. How many were green?" Note that both problems may be solved by subtracting 4 from 6. Yet the semantics of each problem are quite different. The first involves separation, a kind of literal "take away," in which a portion of the whole is removed and the task is to discover what remains. The second is more complex, involving part–whole relations. Here, the task is to use information on the whole set (6 apples) and a known subset (4 red apples) to obtain the number of the unknown subset. In the first case, the child has a whole and takes away from it; in the second, the child must keep in mind set and subsets, whole and parts, and consider the relations among them to obtain a solution. Despite the fact that the formal solution method for the two problems is identical (and trivial, involving the mere subtraction of 4 from 6, a task that even a 5-year-old can typically perform), their deep structures differ radically. The first involves removing a part from a whole; the second requires considering relations among the whole and its parts.

The semantic structure of word problems, not the surface structure, is a major determinant of children's difficulties in solving them. Even preschoolers can solve simple "change problems" in which something is added onto an existing set ("Pretend that you have 1 orange. Then I give you 2 more oranges. How many do you have altogether?") (Siegler & Robinson, 1982). First graders typically begin to solve problems involving part–whole relations, reminiscent of the notion of "class-inclusion," that Piaget argued was attained at the beginning of the period of concrete operations, around age 6 or 7 years. And progress in dealing with different types of deep structures is made throughout elementary school (Morales, Shute, & Pellegrino, 1985; Riley & Greeno, 1988; Stern, 1993).

For educators, this research offers two basic lessons. One is that it is important to consider the underlying mathematical and logical structures of commonly used word problems. Despite requiring the *same calculation,* word problems may involve radically *different concepts.* The second lesson is that the difficulty of these concepts may be related to the developmental level of the child. Educators need to be aware of both the underlying mathematics and cognition.

Another major determinant of children's ability to solve word problems is their nonmathematical content. The "real-life," relatively concrete character of word problems is intended to arouse interest and to help children situate the problems in an everyday context. A possible criticism, of course, is that common word problems are not very intriguing (who cares how many marbles Luis gets?) and are themselves rather abstract (it is one thing to see and touch Luis's marbles and quite another merely to read about them). Renninger and Stavis (1995) found that fifth and sixth graders were more successful in solving structurally difficult word problems with content that was interesting to them (e.g., soccer or music-television programs) than similar problems with uninteresting content.

In summary, research on word problems has shown that the semantic structure of problems influences how children try to solve them and the age at which they are successful. Problems that primarily consist of adding to or subtracting from an existing set can be solved early in elementary school, and even before. Other addition and subtraction problems, especially those involving the relations between two sets, are not solved until later in elementary school. Finally, the likelihood that children will solve a word problem is influenced by the degree of interest they find in the content.

Understanding

From almost any cognitive point of view, understanding involves far more than accurate computation or correct verbal statements or high levels of achievement. Current views tend to conceptualize understanding as a web of connections among different aspects of mathematical knowledge (Ginsburg et al., 1992; Greeno, 1977; Mack, 1990; Pirie, 1988; Van den Brink, 1989).

According to this approach, the child tries to make sense of the formal mathematics presented in school by assimilating it into or linking it with various aspects of existing knowledge. Understanding seems to involve interpreting a given aspect of formal mathematics in terms of various informal notions and procedures, intermediary schemas and metaphors, and various other formal notions and procedures.

Consider a very simple example. Suppose that the child encounters a school activity or lesson presenting the idea that $2 + 3 = 5$. The child can deal with this situation in several different ways. On the one hand, the child can simply attempt to memorize the number combination, without any connection to anything else. Whether the child succeeds or fails in this attempt is of little interest from the point of view of understanding; in either event, the performance involves simple rote memorization. On the other hand, the child may attempt to link the simple number combination with other aspects of mathematical knowledge. The child may connect the combination with already available counting procedures, realizing that if a set of 2 elements is combined with a set of 3 and the total is counted, 5 will be the result. Associated with this informal procedure may be informal knowledge to the effect that when 2 sets are combined, the result is larger than either set.

The child may also connect the number combination $2 + 3$ with various formal ideas or procedures. Thus, the child may link the combination with operations on the number line: if you move forward 3 spaces from the number 2, you end up on the number 5. This in turn may be linked with formal principles such as commutativity, so that the child realizes that moving 3 spaces from the number 2 gives the same result as moving 2 spaces from the number 3.

The child may also link the number combination to an "intermediary schema" or manipulative such as unifix cubes. Thus, the child may realize that the numeral 2 corresponds to two cubes, that the numeral 3 corresponds to three cubes, that the + refers to combining the cubes, and that the numeral 5 corresponds to the result obtained. The child may also realize that the 2 cubes are just like 2 fingers, and that combining 2 and 3 cubes gives the same result as combining 2 and 3 fingers. In this respect, the cubes and fingers serve as a bridge between informal knowledge (counting, addition concepts) and the written symbols, concepts, and procedures of formal mathematics (the numerals 2 and 3, the symbol +, the concept of commutativity). The bridge allows the formal mathematics to be assimilated into the informal knowledge.

In brief, this approach asserts that understanding involves relationships among different areas of knowledge; it is much more (and more complicated) than correct response, words, or calculation. The notion of understanding as connected knowledge resonates with educators' intuition that measuring "real understanding" requires more sensitive methods of assessment than standard tests, and that whatever achievement tests measure, it is usually not real understanding.

The Development of Mathematical Thinking in Context

Mathematical thinking was one of the first areas to be investigated by cross-cultural researchers because it is used in such a broad range of human endeavors and from such an early point in life. Much of the pioneering work was formulated and conducted within Piagetian or Vygotskian theoretical frameworks (Saxe & Posner, 1983). The Piagetian work (Dasen, 1977) focused on structural universals in the development of mathematical cognition. Researchers in this tradition showed that both schooled and unschooled children seemed to display the development of number concepts as described by Piaget, at least up to the period of formal operations. Although the rate of development varied among cultures, what was important for the Piagetians was the universal sequence of development (Piaget, 1972).

In general, Piagetian studies did not seek to discover cultural variables that influence the form of mathematical knowledge or the rate of development of universal types of mathematical abilities. Yet the importance of such cultural variables is evident: merchant economies have led some societies to invent elaborate number-word systems (Saxe, 1991; Schmandt-Besserat, 1992); agrarian and mercantile societies vary considerably in regard to the mathematical knowledge required of their members (Ginsburg, 1982).

Studies in the Vygotskian tradition (Gay & Cole, 1967; Lave, 1988; Scribner, 1986) have made the unique contribution of focusing attention on culturally distinct forms of mathematical knowledge. Specifically, research within this framework involves an analysis of the variety of representational systems, strategies, and other aspects of mathematical thinking individuals use to solve mathematical problems that arise in some customary activity. The research typically examines the influence of cultural variables such as economic specialization, schooling, and number-word systems on the development of mathematical thinking. Originally, much of the Vygotskian work focused on the mathematical thinking used by adults in their work, and failed to shed light on the development of mathematical thinking.

During the past decade or so, research on the sociocultural context of children's mathematical thinking (and cognitive development generally) has rapidly expanded. Theoretical approaches have evolved, and researchers have chosen to investigate many interesting phenomena. Here, we focus on three sets of issues. One concerns the development of mathematical thinking within the context of a practice such as street vending. The issue is the nature and power of mathematical thinking developed in a "real-life" context. A second set of issues concerns the early development of mathematical thinking in children of poverty. The question is whether the materially deprived context of poverty adversely affects mathematical development. The third set of issues concerns the role of culturally based number-word systems in the early development of mathematical thinking. The question is whether special characteristics of East Asian languages facilitate mathematical thinking.

The Context of Practice

Two programs of research (Nunes et al., 1993; Saxe, 1991) have successfully blended a neo-Piagetian structural developmental approach and a Vygotskian contextual approach to study the development of mathematical thinking in children in urban Brazil. Saxe's study is representative and will be discussed in some detail. The research focused on children at three age levels (5 to 7, 8 to 11, and 12 to 15 years), with little or even no formal education (mean years of schooling, 1.6), who engaged in the practice of candy selling on the street. As they engage in their practice, mathematical problems arise, and as they find ways to solve these problems, cognitive growth can ensue. Various comparison groups were used, including nonselling children who received formal education.

Candy selling is a complex economic activity involving four distinct phases: (a) purchasing candy wholesale from clerks, (b) preparing to sell, which sometimes involves assistance from other sellers, (c) selling to customers, and (d) preparing to purchase candy wholesale, which may involve assistance from other sellers. Mathematical goals arise during the different phases of candy selling. In the selling-to-customers phase, for example, the goals include the identification of currency units, the use of arithmetic operations with currency, and the making of ratio comparisons when customers offer to buy a greater quantity at a lower per-unit price. Saxe investigated the development of knowledge and use of the currency system ("form–function relations") by presenting sellers and nonsellers with problems that might arise within practice.

For example, one set of problems was presented to determine whether—and, if so, how—children could add or subtract currency (for example, 17 bills totaling 17,300 units). The results are complex, and here we focus on a developmental comparison within the group of sellers. Many of the younger children (primarily 5- to 7-year-olds) had difficulty in doing addition and subtraction, and instead interpreted the task as involving currency identification; they simply identified the nominal value of each bill. Other young children interpreted the task in terms of counting: they determined the number of bills. With increasing age, children learned to add by using a grouping strategy to form convenient subsets. Thus, without paper and pencil, an 11-year-old ordered the 12 bills from largest to smallest, in groupings of 1,000 units, as far as possible. He began with a 10,000-unit bill. Then he added three 1,000-unit bills; then five 200-unit bills; then three pairs of 500-unit bills; and, finally the remaining 200- and 100-unit bills, to reach a correct total of 17,300 (Saxe, 1991, pp. 81–82). So, with development, essentially unschooled children create "invented strategies" to deal with the addition of relatively large numbers.

Saxe also presented children with problems in which they were asked to make price adjustments for inflation. For example, in one problem, children were told that the initial wholesale price of a box of candy was 4,000 units, and they were asked to propose a retail price for that box. Then they were told that, after inflation, the wholesale price would be 7,000 units for the same box of candy. What then should the retail price be, adjusting for inflation? Nonsellers had more difficulty with this problem than did sellers. For example, one nonselling 10-year-old said that if the wholesale price were 4,000 units, he would sell the box for 5,000 units at retail, a markup of 1,000 units. Suppose then that inflation raised the price of the box to 7,000 units. What should the retail price be? He proposed 8,000 units, the same *absolute* amount of markup, but proportionally *less* profit. By contrast, a 12-year-old seller said that the retail price for the 4,000-unit box should be 8,000 units, and that, if inflation raises the wholesale price to 7,000 units, then the retail price should be 14,000 units. Why? Because "it's half-half. I take 7,000 of the 14,000 for the purchase, and 7,000 for me" (Saxe, 1991, p. 96). In this case, the child, who had only a second-grade education, seemed to think in terms of a 1:1 ratio of cost to profit. In general, sellers, despite their meager education, tended to engage in proportional reasoning to a greater extent than more highly educated nonsellers.

Saxe also investigated the transfer of mathematical knowledge from one ecological context to another. The focus was on knowledge transfers from the practice of candy selling to school mathematics, and from school to practice. It was found that school experience sometimes helped and sometimes did not help children solve practice-related problems. School mathematics helped children decode the numerals written on currency to indicate the denomination of the bill. In school, children also learned arithmetic algorithms that were used to add and subtract currency. But no aspect of school mathematics helped children solve ratio problems.

Knowledge transfer also flowed from the practice of candy selling to school mathematics, particularly the regrouping knowledge that sellers used to form convenient values of currency (e.g., groups of 500 units). Sellers in second or third grade (age 11 to 12 years) used regrouping in school mathematics much more often than a comparison group of nonsellers at the same grade and age levels. Thus, transfer of mathematical knowledge can occur in both directions, from practice to school and the reverse.

In brief, children who are relatively uneducated nevertheless develop useful invented strategies for dealing with everyday mathematical problems. They can profit from some material learned in school, but important aspects of their learning do not depend on schooling. They even transfer some of what they learn in their practice to the task of learning mathematics in school.

Poor and Minority Children

One of the most striking facts about American education is the existence of pervasive social-class and ethnic differences in achievement. In the United States, poor children, as a group, generally perform less adequately in school than do more affluent children (National Research Council, 1989; Natriello et al., 1990; Oakes, 1990). The failure is even more severe in the case of African Americans and Hispanics who are poorer than Whites and hence are at especially high risk for school failure (McLloyd, 1990). African American and Hispanic children perform especially poorly in school mathematics and science (Natriello et al., 1990; Oakes, 1990).

Why do poor children, and especially African Americans and Hispanics, do so badly in school? One possibility is that their informal mathematical knowledge has not yet developed to the extent necessary for them to be ready to learn the school mathematics curriculum. According to this view, poor and minority preschool children do not receive sufficient environmental support to construct a broad foundation of informal mathematical knowledge. Their informal mathematical knowledge is *developmentally immature.* Another possibility is that these children suffer from a real *deficiency* in informal mathematical knowledge (a version of the "cognitive deficit" hypothesis). The *lack* of informal mathematical knowledge subsequently hinders their success in school mathematics.

The hypotheses of developmental delay or deficiency do not of course rule out other explanations of poor children's substandard performance in school. One obvious explanation is that schooling for poor children is often inadequate (Kozol, 1991). Another theory points to a discontinuity between poor children's abilities and the culture of the middle-class-dominated school (Moll, Amanti, Neff, & Gonzalez, 1992; Ogbu, 1982).

Several studies provide evidence concerning the development of informal mathematics in poor children. Kirk, Hunt, and Volkmar (1975) examined several aspects of enumeration (e.g., producing sets of a given number; counting a set of blocks) in African American and White children, some lower socioeconomic status (SES) and others middle-class nursery school children, probably all White, in a small town. The results showed that lower-SES children, both African American and White, performed at a significantly lower level than middle-class children. One limitation of this study is the narrow set of tasks that were included: all could be solved through enumeration, and none required arithmetic reasoning. Another problem with this study is that the testing procedures appear to have been somewhat rigid and therefore may not have been maximally effective in eliciting children's competence.

Subsequent studies have included a broader set of mathematical tasks. Ginsburg and Russell (1981) presented 4- and 5-year-old, African American and Caucasian, lower-class and middle-class children with several informal mathematical tasks. The findings showed very few differences associated with ethnicity (holding SES constant), but several differences were associated with SES. Middle-class children were correct more often than the lower-class children on rote counting, cardinality, number conservation, and numerical equivalence tasks but not on other tasks such as enumeration and addition operations. The statistically significant social class differences generally favored the middle class, but they were usually not large.

Saxe et al. (1987) presented 2- and 4-year-old, Caucasian, working-class and middle-class children with a range of numerical tasks, including some that were drawn from Ginsburg and Russell's study. Middle-class children were correct more often than working-class children on a number reproduction task (similar to the type of task presented by Kirk et al.), and on cardinality, addition and subtraction, and complex counting. No social class differences were found on other tasks (e.g., reciting the counting words, reading numerals, comparison of the magnitudes of number words, or counting accuracy).

Hughes (1986) employed a searchbox task (described earlier) in which preschool children stated the cardinal value of a sum or remainder set that was screened from view. The youngest children were 3-year-olds and came from either working-class or middle-class families. Significantly fewer one-set arithmetic problems were solved by 3-year-old working-class children than by middle-class children. Hughes also reported differences in concrete addition between middle- and working-class British children at 4 and 5 years of age, with working-class children performing about a year behind their middle-class peers. Thus, SES differences in informal mathematical development appear as early as 3 years of age.

A limitation of these studies is the inclusion of working-class children in the low-SES samples. To examine the effects of poverty on early mathematical development, it is important for research of this type to make finer distinctions within the low-SES group. "Underclass" (extremely impoverished) and working-poor families seem to differ from working-class families in important ways that might conceivably affect children's mathematical development. Research studies should not confound these groups.

Starkey and Klein (1992) included only 4-year-old children from families who were below the federally established poverty line (as indicated by their qualification for Aid to Families with Dependent Children) in their ethnically mixed, low-SES sample. These children and a comparison group of middle-class 4-year-olds were presented with a broad set of numerical tasks including: standard counting, counting-error detection, number reproduction, verbal one- and two-set addition and subtraction, modified number conservation, and numerical comparison. On every task, the middle-class children's solutions were more advanced developmentally than the economically disadvantaged children's solutions. Differences were most pronounced on two-set addition and mathematical reasoning tasks. Thus, children's early mathematical development does not flourish in severely impoverished circumstances. Ginsburg et al. (1997) obtained similar results with respect to the effects of extreme poverty on mathematical thinking.

Jordan, Huttenlocher, and Levine (1994) studied arithmetic problem solving in impoverished (Head Start) and middle-class 3- and 4-year-olds. Children were presented with addition and subtraction tasks that required either a nonverbal answer (the children could simply show the sum or remainder with objects, or select an answer from among four choices provided by the experimenter) or a verbal statement of the answer. A counting task in which children were asked to count sets of 1 to 4 objects was also administered. Middle-class children performed equally well on verbal and nonverbal arithmetic tasks. In contrast, impoverished children performed less well on verbal than on nonverbal tasks. Social class comparisons revealed more correct solutions to verbal problems by middle-class children than by impoverished children. Jordan et al. found that impoverished children's counting was poor, especially that of the 3-year-olds. Some knew few or no number names and answered verbal arithmetic problems by holding up fingers instead of producing number names. Middle-class children's performance was better on the verbal tasks, due, at least in part, to a richer knowledge of number names.

Jordan, Huttenlocher, and Levine (1992) also presented verbal and nonverbal addition and subtraction problems to impoverished and middle-class kindergarten children. The kindergarten findings were consistent with the preschool findings. No effect of social class was evident on the nonverbal tasks, but middle-class children were correct more often than impoverished children on all types of verbal tasks.

Taken together, these findings make it possible to characterize in broad strokes the nature of impoverished children's early mathematical development. The research shows that poor and minority children do possess basic, informal mathematical abilities. Thus, the empirical findings put to rest the "cognitive deficit" hypothesis. Nevertheless, many of these abilities, especially in the very poor, develop at a slower rate than in middle-class children. The immaturity of their mathematical development makes it difficult for many extremely impoverished children to learn formal mathematics upon entrance to school. Thus, these findings support the view that many economically disadvantaged children enter school less than fully prepared to learn formal mathematics.

Researchers have recently begun to examine the home and school environments of poor children. Consider the availability of mathematical supports in the home. In a recent study of the home environments of 4-year-old Head Start children, Klein and Starkey (1995) found that low-income parents provided a very narrow base of support for mathematical development. Parents generally fostered traditional numeracy skills such as numeral or shape recognition, but rarely provided activities that foster informal arithmetic or geometric reasoning. Similar findings were obtained by Saxe et al. (1987), who reported that their sample of working-class children engaged in significantly fewer and less complex number activities in their homes than did middle-class children.

An examination of preschool classrooms serving impoverished children also revealed a paucity of developmentally appropriate supports for mathematical development (Bryant, Burchinal, Lau, & Sparling, 1994). Moreover, in a survey of public preschool teachers in North Carolina, it was found that many teachers did not know how to support children's developing numerical abilities (Farran, Silveri, & Culp, 1991). The limited availability of mathematical supports in the preschool classroom is particularly problematic given impoverished mothers' views on preparing their children for school (Holloway, Rambaud, Fuller, & Eggers-Pierola, 1995): low-income mothers tend to believe that the preschool teacher is responsible for providing instruction in math.

In brief, the research shows that poor children possess the basic components of informal mathematical knowledge, but many of these components develop more slowly in poor children than in middle-class children. On the one hand, the results do not contradict the claim that basic components of informal mathematics are universal across cultures and social classes (Klein & Starkey, 1988; Saxe & Posner, 1983). On the other hand, these results have important implications for understanding impoverished children's underachievement in school mathematics. The lag in their informal mathematical development makes them less ready to learn the school mathematics curriculum. Thus, the developmental seeds of underachievement may be sown before improverished children enter school.

At the same time, one should not ignore the equally important role of the schools in producing poor children's school failure. American mathematics education suffers from so many deficiencies—for example, teachers' limited knowledge of the mathematics that they are supposed to teach (Post, Harel, Behr, & Lesh, 1991)—and the education of poor children is so inadequate (Kozol, 1991), that it would be imprudent to assert that the sole cause of failure is the children's immature intellectual ability upon entrance to school.

Number-Word Systems and Early Mathematical Development

Anthropologists have documented that most number systems around the world utilize bases of 5, 10, or 20 (Menninger, 1969; Zaslavsky, 1973), presumably deriving from the digits of the body—5 fingers, 10 fingers, 20 fingers and toes. The base-10 system, which has become the world standard, uses the ten written Arabic numerals (0, 1, 2, . . . , 9) alone or in combination, and the place-value convention allows the value of these numerals to be dependent on their place in a sequence of numerals designed to represent one number. Thus, the numeral *1* can stand for one unit (as in the number 1), ten units (as in 10), one hundred units (as in 100), etc. Each place in a number is ten times the size of the numeral to its right. The Arabic numerals, together with the place-value convention, make it possible to represent any natural or counting number with combinations of only ten numerals. This written notation system for representing numbers is an intellectual tool that supports the development of more extensive mathematical knowledge, such as the standard algorithms for performing arithmetic computations.

To use the written notation system, children must know that the Arabic numerals are used to represent numbers, and that place-value and base-10 conventions organize the system. The conventional base of the number system is first introduced through the system of number names children use in counting. In some languages, including Asian languages such as Chinese, Japanese, and Korean, the base structure is clearly coded in number names, and number names are highly regular. For example, in these languages, counting proceeds from the equivalents of "one, two . . . ten" (which are completely arbitrary and must be memorized in all languages using a base-10 system) to the rule-based "ten-one, ten-two . . . ten-nine, two-ten, two-ten-one, two-ten-two . . . . three-ten . . . . nine-ten-nine." The system is perfectly regular; the number names are stated in the same order as the numerals are written, as in "ten-four" for 14. In European languages such as English, French, German, Italian, Spanish, and Swedish, the system of number words is less regular than is the Asian counting system. Thus, in English, at least some of the number words between 11 and 19 have a number-name order that is the reverse of the numeral order, as in "fourteen," instead of "ten-four" for 14. Given these differences, researchers have argued that the Asian number-word system should facilitate the development of children's mathematical thinking (Fuson & Kwon, 1992b; Miura, 1989), particularly counting, informal arithmetic problem solving, multidigit addition and subtraction, and the use of currency based on decade systems.

To test the hypothesis that the development of counting should be facilitated by the regular Asian number-word system, Miller and Stigler (1987) investigated 4- to 6-year-old Taiwanese and American children's ability to recite the number names. American children encountered more difficulty than did Taiwanese children, particularly in reciting numbers in the teens, which are irregular in English, but not in Chinese.

Fuson and Kwon (1992b) examined Korean second- and third-grade children's understanding of written, multidigit addition and subtraction problems that were vertically displayed. The children exhibited knowledge of place-value names ("ten" and "hundred") and considerable facility at solving multidigit addition and subtraction problems larger than those they had been taught in school (i.e., 3-digit problems instead of 2-digit problems). Both the place-value knowledge and the problem-solving proficiency of the Korean children were more developmentally advanced than typically exhibited by American children. The same type of result has been obtained with Japanese children (Miura, 1989; Miura, Okamoto, Kim, Steere, & Fayol, 1993). Fuson and Kwon point out that, in addition to the number-word system, other cultural tools that use a decade system (the abacus and the metric system) may help children become proficient in dealing with base structure.

If the Asian number-word system (and perhaps other cultural tools) facilitates children's understanding of base-10, then Asian children may be more facile at converting money back and forth from single-unit denominations (e.g., pence or one-pound notes) to ten-unit denominations (e.g., ten-pence coins and ten-pound notes). Lines, Nunes, and Bryant (in press) gave British and Taiwanese children a shopping task in which they were to use money in single denominations (ones or tens) or in mixed denominations (ones and tens). The groups of children performed at similar levels when using a single denomination, but the British children encountered more difficulty than did the Taiwanese children when using mixed denominations of ones and tens. Apparently, the British children had a less developed understanding of the currency's decade structure than did the Taiwanese children.

In brief, the extremely regular Asian number system seems to provide its users with an advantage in the area of counting, understanding the base-10 system, and even using decade-based currencies. It is unlikely, however, that the number system alone can explain the well-documented superiority in mathematics achievement shown by Chinese, Japanese, and Korean children (Stevenson, Lee, & Stigler, 1986). No doubt many factors associated with Asian culture and schooling contribute to their superior achievement (Stevenson & Stigler, 1992).

Summary: The Essential Principles of Mathematics Learning Revealed

The beauty of the research literature is in the eye of the beholder. It can teach different lessons to different people. Consider now some general principles designed to be of interest not to the researchers themselves but to educators concerned with using the research.

1. *Even babies possess an informal mathematics.* Babies are born with some fundamental notions of quantity. They can see that there is more here than there, or that this has the same amount as that. They realize that adding makes more, and subtracting makes less. Although crude, and effective only with very small numbers of objects, their judgments seem to be genuinely quantitative. Much of this occurs before the onset of language and extensive cultural transmission. Like crawling or perceiving, the fundamentals of mathematical cognition have a strong basis in human biological endowment.

2. *Young children's counting is guided by abstract principles.* The social environment provides young children in virtually all cultures with a rich counting system, which can serve as a basic tool for mathematical thinking. Children are active in making good use of this environment. They learn the counting words. But more importantly, from the outset, children's counting employs mathematical principles of one-to-one correspondence, order, and cardinality. To a large extent, early counting is an abstract, principled activity.

3. *Young children use counting as a practical instrument of calculation.* Before entering school, children spontaneously develop operational definitions of addition and subtraction. Addition is combining sets and then counting the elements to get a sum; subtraction is taking away a subset from a larger set and then counting the elements to get a remainder. Over the course of the preschool years, children refine these strategies, making them more efficient, and extending their use from concrete objects to imaginary ones.

4. *Young children reason about addition and subtraction.* For young children, addition and subtraction are not simple mechanical routines or mindless algorithms. These operations make sense. Adding is interpreted in terms of increments, and subtracting is seen in terms of decrements. Young children's reasoning about these operations suffers from some basic limitations, but reflects the beginnings of what could be a sound understanding of basic mathematical ideas.

5. *The acquisition of informal mathematics is a constructive process guided by biology, physical environment, and culture.* Biology provides an elementary framework for appreciating number—for perceiving differences in quantity and even the effects of quantitative transformations. The physical environment is replete with quantitative phenomena and events; they are so pervasive that they often go unnoticed. The social world provides children in all cultures with a basic tool for mathematical thinking—the system of counting words. Before entrance to school, children exploit the opportunities offered by the physical and social environments: They construct an informal mathematics. Children count and reason about number in their own principled ways, which do not simply copy or mimic adult mathematics.

6. *Informal mathematics can serve as a useful foundation for formal instruction in mathematics.* Despite evident limitations, the child's informal mathematics is more fully developed and powerful than is often realized. Mathematics educators need to appreciate young children's informal mathematics upon entrance to school—their versions of counting, adding and subtracting, and understanding. Indeed, this informal mathematics can serve as a useful foundation on which much early mathematics education can be built.

7. *Informal mathematics is extremely widespread, if not universal, across cultures.* Children in many different cultures and social circumstances possess the fundamentals of informal mathematics. Even when provided with little or no education, children in some cultures nevertheless invent useful strategies for dealing with everyday mathematical problems—for example, those involving calculation of money. Poor children possess basic, informal mathematical abilities. Yet, many of these abilities, especially in the very poor, develop at a slower rate than in children from more economically advantaged groups.

8. *Children assimilate school mathematics into their informal knowledge.* Schooling offers children a formal mathematics different from and more powerful than their own informal system. Formal mathematics is *codified:* written, arranged systematically, with explicit rules and procedures. Its written notation systems and formal algorithms—cultural legacies developed over many years—can extend the young child's mathematical power. Children do not simply absorb formal mathematics as such. They do memorize and mimic some elements of what is taught. But more importantly, they assimilate formal mathematics into their own informal knowledge, and in the process construct their own procedures and understanding.

9. *Children learn number facts both by counting and memorization.* Children solve some small arithmetic problems (like 3 + 2)—the "number facts"—by a process of retrieval from memory. But they also solve some problems like these by means of counting and other informal calculational procedures, or by an inventive process in which already known facts are used to *derive* unknown facts. Even the most trivial mathematical knowledge—learning the number facts—is in part a constructive process. Encouraging such constructions provides children with sensible "back-up strategies" that can be used if memory fails.

10. *Children develop invented strategies for calculation.* Although standard *algorithms,* developed and codified over the course of centuries, are guaranteed to achieve correct results, children do not always use them. Instead, they employ a variety of "invented strategies" involving counting, or counting combined with remembered addition facts, or the rearrangement of numbers into convenient combinations, or the converting of difficult problems into simpler ones. These methods are usually based on sound, if implicit, principles. Occasionally, children even create genuinely novel approaches.

11. *Children sometimes construct consistently incorrect strategies.* Given complex and sometimes incoherent input, children's invented strategies do not always result in correct solutions. Some constructed strategies, today sometimes called "bugs" (and called "bad habits" in an earlier era), are systematically flawed and therefore produce consistent errors under certain conditions.

12. *The underlying structure of word problems influences children's method of solution and their success.* Word problems are intended to provide real-world contexts that presumably motivate children and make it easier for them to apply their mathematical skills. But word problems may differ in important ways that affect children's learning. Despite requiring the same calculation on the surface, word problems may involve radically different concepts at a deeper level. And this underlying structure influences children's strategies of solution and their success. Moreover, word problems differ in the degree of interest they generate, and this too affects accuracy.

13. *Understanding is connecting.* Understanding is not simply correct calculation or correct verbal statements, or high levels of achievement or "mastery." It is a complex web of connections among different aspects of mathematical knowledge. Children try to make sense of the formal mathematics presented in school by assimilating it into or linking it with various aspects of existing knowledge. Understanding involves relationships among different areas of knowledge; it is connected knowledge.

14. *Culture shapes the learning of mathematics.* One example is provided by Asian number systems, which provide some advantages for learning mathematics. Languages like Chinese, Japanese, and Korean are extremely regular and transparently constructed on the base-10 system. Indeed, the system is so regular and conceptually clear that it provides its users with an advantage in learning to count, in understanding the base-10 system, and in using decade-based currencies. Another example is provided by research on everyday practice. In the course of everyday activities like commerce, individuals develop effective methods for dealing with and thinking about quantitative issues.

We consider next how knowledge derived from research has and has not affected basic applications.

APPLICATIONS

Research yields a distinctive form of knowledge derived from observations made under special and often artificial conditions. Research is designed to answer specific questions stemming from the researcher's curiosity, from serendipitous findings, from the community of researchers, and from government or foundation requests for proposals, among other sources. The researcher studies children's "counting on" or "bugs" because other researchers study those issues, because support is available for studying them, and/or because they are intriguing topics. To succeed, research usually has to maintain a narrow focus. It needs to hone in on one type of bug, or on counting back from numbers of a certain magnitude, or on a particular aspect of the process of construction. It is no criticism to say that the knowledge produced by such research is of necessity distinctive and narrow; that is the reality. It is also no criticism to say that research knowledge may not necessarily meet the needs of practitioners—the teachers who are responsible for children's learning, the producers of textbooks, the designers of assessment procedures. These people may not need to know as much about the fine details of counting back, or bugs, or construction as researchers (think they) need to know. Indeed, the practitioners may (think they) need to know about some things that are not of particular interest to researchers.

The question now is: How do the special forms of knowledge provided by research get "applied" to practice, and how and why does some of it fail to get applied? Has the research in fact made useful contributions to practice? What are the processes of application? What are the forces that block application? To begin to answer some of these questions, we consider some of the ways in which insights from research on mathematical thinking have been applied to the practical problems of:

1. Textbook development—including the story of how educational policy is created and implemented, and how textbooks are produced by the publishing industry, partly in response to economic and political forces.
2. Professional development—helping teachers to understand children's thinking and the principles of "constructivist" mathematics education.
3. Assessment—providing teachers with both standardized and alternative forms of assessment designed to obtain information concerning children's learning and knowledge, for the purpose of improving instruction.

We argue that research has indeed made useful contributions to these areas, but the processes of application are not simple and direct, and the fruits of research are as likely to be general ideas as specific materials and practices.

Textbooks

Curriculum materials are the devices and activities teachers use to help children learn mathematics. Curriculum materials—the "stuff" that children use in their everyday classroom learning—are usually textbooks, but can also be "manipulatives" such as base-10 blocks, or computer software, or exploratory activities designed by teachers. Although many innovative curriculum materials have been developed over the years—see, for example, the wonderful Madison Project materials (Davis, 1967, 1980)—we focus on textbooks because they are used extensively and they are the norm in the real world of education. They are the most common tool of the practitioner. We attempt to determine how research knowledge has affected the development of these conventional curriculum materials. Have the applications in fact been useful, and how can they be improved?

Textbooks are the primary method of mathematics instruction—and instruction in all other academic fields, with the possible exception of music—around the world. Across the United States, some $240 million was spent on mathematics textbooks, at all grade levels, in 1994.[5] We learn mathematics, history, and psychology from textbooks. Indeed, even constructivists who tend to sneer at the use of textbooks use them to present constructivist arguments. Piaget himself wrote textbooks (and gave formal lectures too).

Most mathematics textbooks sell far more copies, and earn more money, than most novels; textbook publishing is a very lucrative business. In 1994, total textbook sales in the United States were approximately $942 million.[6] Partly because of these economics, textbook writing and publishing is an intricate process. A mathematics textbook is typically not

---

[5] Figures provided by the Association of American Publishers. According to this group, sale of mathematics textbooks accounts for about 25% of the total, second only to reading textbooks, which account for about 35% of the total.

[6] Figures provided by the Association of American Publishers.

written by an "author," and it undergoes an elaborate process of development. In this section, we describe how the process unfolds through the development of "curriculum standards" proposed by a national organization of mathematics teachers; the dissemination of these standards through journals and other means; the imposition of curriculum "frameworks" by some states; the contribution of editors, publishing executives, and writers; the nature of the textbooks themselves; and, finally, teachers' use of the textbooks in the classrooms. We attempt to determine how research knowledge affects all stages of this process. Our account is based partly on an examination of the available literature, partly on interviews with participants, and partly on our own experience with the process.[7]

Curriculum Standards

To understand the textbooks of the 1990s, we must begin with an account of the political atmosphere in the United States in the 1980s. The American economy was in some difficulty, particularly in comparison with the Japanese, and the United States seemed to be losing its preeminence in world economic affairs. As the standard of living declined, American politicians expressed a need to reestablish dominance in the world economy. The economic crisis called forth a national self-examination, and the main target was the educational system.[8] Distinguished committees, formed to examine the state of American education, issued reports such as *A Nation at Risk: The Imperative for Educational Reform* (National Commission on Excellence in Education, 1983), the title of which conveys a message that failure to reform the educational system places the republic at peril. Many stressed the need for reform of mathematics education in particular. The argument was that economic success requires a highly educated workforce who possess mathematical abilities adequate to an increasingly technological workplace and society.[9]

This line of argument was naturally seized on by the mathematics educators' professional organization, the National Council of Teachers of Mathematics (NCTM)—a very large and influential group, with some 123,000 members[10]—which proclaimed that "new methods of production demand a technologically competent work force" (National Council of Teachers of Mathematics, 1989, p. 3). Partly in response to this perceived need, the NCTM initiated a planning process, in the late 1980s, to "create a set of standards to guide the revision of the school mathematics curriculum and its associated evaluation . . . " (p. 1). The NCTM *Standards* would guide practice and thinking about mathematics education "(1) to ensure quality, (2) to indicate goals, and (3) to promote change" (p. 2).

The NCTM *Standards* were influenced not only by economic considerations but by research deriving from developmental and educational psychology. The way in which this occurred is partly a story about the diffusion of knowledge by influential "gatekeepers." The *Standards* were prepared by committees presumably chosen to represent constituencies within the NCTM. The committees were composed of various individuals, including classroom teachers, mathematicians, mathematics educators, and "educational researchers." The Chair of the effort was Thomas A. Romberg, a mathematics educator who was quite familiar with research on mathematical thinking. Indeed, in the late 1970s, Romberg was one of the organizers of a conference at Wingspread, Wisconsin, which brought together, from around the world, researchers who shared an interest in mathematical thinking (Carpenter et al., 1982).[11] The Chair of the NCTM Commission was thoroughly conversant with the research literature.[12]

---

[7] Ginsburg has been involved in consulting and writing for Silver Burdett Ginn, a major publisher of mathematics textbooks for grades Kindergarten through 9.

[8] In a personal communication, Ellen Lagemann points out that throughout American history, "when there is a general social/political/economic problem that people do not know how to handle, they look to schools and generally blame them." This she calls the "displacement function of educational policy."

[9] This may or not be true. It is possible to argue that American industry's failures are more likely the results of management's errors than workers' lack of technical skill (Bracey, 1993). The apparent resurgence of the American economy since the 1980s is seldom attributed to an improvement in the educational system. Also, the more sophisticated the technology, the less users need to understand what is below its friendly surface—for example, computers that can understand speech eliminate users' need to learn programming.

[10] This figure was provided by the NCTM Media Relations Department. In 1995, the registration count for the national meetings in Boston was 20,844.

[11] The present writers attended that conference, as did many others whose work has been cited in earlier sections of this chapter: J. S. Brown, Carpenter, Case, Fuson, Gelman, Hatano, Resnick, and Vergnaud, among others.

[12] Romberg also helped to found the *Journal for Research in Mathematics Education,* which began with 3,000 subscribers in 1970, and by 1995 enjoyed a circulation of 11,000 (Johnson, Romberg, & Scandura, 1994).

The *Curriculum and Evaluation Standards,* published in 1989, were followed by the *Professional Standards for Teaching Mathematics* (National Council of Teachers of Mathematics, 1991), and, most recently, by the *Assessment Standards for School Mathematics* (National Council of Teachers of Mathematics, 1995). These various reports have been extremely influential in the field of mathematics education, and indeed have come to serve as models for reform efforts in various academic disciplines.

The stated goals of the *Standards* (National Council of Teachers of Mathematics, 1989) are to help students learn to value mathematics, to be confident in their abilities, to become problem solvers, to communicate mathematically, and to reason mathematically (p. 5). These goals, of course, do not depend on psychological research. But the *Standards* go on to say:

> Research findings from psychology indicate that learning does not occur by passive absorption alone. . . . Instead, in many situations individuals approach a new task with prior knowledge, assimilate new information, and construct their own meanings. For example, before young children are taught addition and subtraction, they can already solve most addition and subtraction problems using such routines as "counting on" and "counting back." . . . This constructive, active view of the learning process must be reflected in the way much of mathematics is taught. (p. 10)

The *Standards* assert that children begin school with the belief that "learning mathematics is a sense-making experience" (p. 15). "When most children enter school, they can use objects and counting to solve many kinds of problems" (p. 41). "Young children are active individuals who construct, modify, and integrate ideas by interacting with the physical world, materials, and other children. . . . [Teachers] need to listen carefully to children and to guide the development of their ideas" (p. 17). "Young children understand the underlying structure of many numerical problems and use counting to solve them. It is important to tie these conceptual ideas to more abstract procedures such as adding and subtracting" (p. 32).

We offer several comments about the *Standards* and the role of psychological research in shaping them. First, they are intentionally quite general. The *Standards* were intended to serve as a kind of "slogan system" (Apple, 1992) that, in effect, gives marching orders to the organization and sets the tone for organizing future work. The *Standards* are not intended to present a compendium of research findings; rather, they state some general ways of looking at mathematics learning.

Second, although they take the form of slogans, the *Standards* have clearly been influenced by psychological research. As we have seen, the *Standards* sometimes are couched in specific language: "Research findings from psychology indicate that . . . " (p. 10). And even when specific attribution to research is lacking, some of the ideas in the *Standards* clearly derive from research studies, as in: "When most children enter school, they can use objects and counting to solve many kinds of problems" (p. 41). The influence of research on mathematics education is not new; as we have seen, researchers from Thorndike (1922) to Bruner (1966) have influenced mathematics education. But the current influence is strong and important.

Third, the current research contribution to mathematics education is of two types, one partly old and the other relatively new. The old part uses a form of the "constructivist" approach to explain how children learn and how they should be taught. The view that mathematics is a "sense-making activity" in which children "construct their own meanings" (National Council of Teachers of Mathematics, 1989, p. 10) is not very different from the early theories of progressive educators such as John Dewey (McLellan & Dewey, 1895) and even earlier figures such as Pestalozzi (Kilpatrick, 1992). The current versions of constructivism are more substantially supported by evidence and are buttressed by more sophisticated theorizing. Indeed, some form of constructivism is now an orthodox position of psychology. Nevertheless, constructivism is not new for progressive mathematics educators; it is a familiar point of view that serves to legitimate what at least some mathematics educators already believe, or already know (or think they know) from their experiments in the classroom.

The new contribution from psychological research (as highlighted earlier in this chapter) is a body of empirical data and theory concerning both the nature of mathematical knowledge and the methods for assessing this knowledge. It describes children's early informal mathematics, including their addition concepts and strategies, and their rules for and beliefs about counting. The research also provides empirical data and theory concerning children's later knowledge of the formal mathematics taught in school—the development of "invented strategies," bugs, the nature of understanding, and the like. Much of this was not known by earlier generations of psychologists, at least in the kind of rich detail that is now available.

Dissemination

The NCTM *Standards* were not an isolated event. In 1989, a good year for such reports, the National Research Council (NRC) also published a report calling for mathematics reform, *Everybody Counts: A Report to the Nation on the Future of Mathematics Education* (Mathematical Sciences Education Board, 1989). That this document advocated positions similar to those of the NCTM *Standards* should come as little surprise because of the overlap in authorship. The ubiquitous Professor Romberg and other NCTM officials—all of whom championed the *Standards*—contributed to the NRC report as well. A fairly tight network of "players" is involved in mathematics education reform, and their ideas tend to get sanctioned by official governmental and professional groups and by money-granting foundations. This legitimating process is not unimportant in the dissemination of scientific ideas.

The NCTM followed through on its reform efforts by publicizing the *Standards* through its professional journals, *Teaching Children Mathematics* (formerly *The Arithmetic Teacher*), which in 1995 was distributed to some 19,961 subscribers (elementary level teachers, principals, etc.), and the *Mathematics Teacher,* aimed at mathematics educators of older students. The *Standards* are frequently mentioned (with reverence) in these journals, and, occasionally, the NCTM solicits papers on aspects of the *Standards,* as in the February 1995 "focus" issue of *Teaching Children Mathematics,* which dealt with the topic of communication.

In that issue, the first paper, by a teacher of a "blended first-, second-, and third-grade classroom" (Buschman, 1995) begins with a reference to the NCTM *Standards* position that "the process by which a student arrives at the answer to a problem becomes as important as the answer itself. Answers alone often fail to reveal the nature of a student's thinking, the strategies used in the problem-solving process, or the level of understanding. . . . Teachers must help students make their thinking visible to others by encouraging them to talk and write about the process they use to solve problems." (p. 324). He then describes methods he has developed for accomplishing these goals.

The second paper, by professors of elementary education (Cramer & Karnowski, 1995), deals with the issue of how informal mathematical language can be used to help children understand mathematics. Relying on psychological research (Lesh, 1979), the authors propose that: "Understanding in mathematics can be defined as the ability to represent a mathematical idea in multiple ways and to make connections among different representations. Students' informal mathematical language mediates the translations among different representations . . . " (p. 333). The paper then goes on to describe "teaching scenarios" designed to implement these ideas.

Similar ideas appear in other issues of the journal not specifically dedicated to *Standards* themes. Thus, in the April 1995 issue of *Teaching Children Mathematics,* every article citing references quotes either the *Standards* or a piece of developmental research (Kamii, 1982; Stigler & Perry, 1990). It is no exaggeration to say that the NCTM has done a masterful job in disseminating its point of view.

But has its audience assimilated the message? Yes and no. Leaders in the schools, such as curriculum supervisors, are certainly familiar with and often supportive of the *Standards,* and they have some familiarity with the research on which the *Standards* are (in part) based. And these are precisely the people who have a large say in the selection of textbooks. Other dedicated professionals, such as professors of mathematics education, some of whom may be textbook writers, also are knowledgeable about the *Standards* and related research. Yet, observation suggests that many other educators remain unaware of or uninterested in the *Standards.* Principals often have little to do with the substance of curriculum; and many elementary teachers are not comfortable with (and indeed avoid) the teaching of mathematics. Also, there are 1,361,775 (exactly!) elementary teachers in the United States (Office of Educational Research and Improvement, 1994), and only 19,961 subscribers to *Teaching Children Mathematics,* so that the message is probably reaching only a small segment of the potential audience.

And even if aware of the existence of the *Standards,* some educators' understanding of them may be primitive. At a PTA meeting, a parent asked what the school was doing about the NCTM *Standards.* "Without hesitation, the principal said, 'Yes, we know about the *Standards* and we did them last fall'" (Reys, 1992, p. 3).

The Encouragement of Research

The NCTM has also served as a publication outlet for research and has disseminated research. Its *Journal for Research in Mathematics Education* publishes basic research on children's mathematical thinking, as well as more applied studies. *Teaching Children Mathematics* has a regular section on *Research into Practice,* which offers brief accounts of research studies judged to be relevant for educational practice. Such dissemination is influential because it is conducted by members of the mathematics education community who can convey their message in ways that are directly relevant to practitioners.

State Adoption Criteria

Findings and ideas deriving from research also filter down to textbooks through a very influential process of State adoption criteria. In the United States, some States (including large ones like California, Florida, and Texas) require publishers to receive official approval before their textbooks may be offered for sale. Thus, a State will announce that in May 1997, for example, publishers are invited to submit for approval new textbooks to be bought by local school districts beginning in 1998. (Other States, called "open States" by the publishers, allow local districts to buy any textbooks they choose.) The States publish both adoption criteria describing the types of textbooks desired, and legal rules and regulations designed to monitor the processes of submission and approval. The adoption criteria, sometimes called "frameworks," are usually written by committees designated by a State Board of Education, which also appoints committees entrusted with the responsibility for evaluating publishers' submissions. The committees that promulgate the frameworks and evaluate the textbooks are often composed of teachers, curriculum supervisors, administrators, professors of education, and State education officials.

The adoption process is very important for publishers; they cannot even attempt to sell in an adoption State unless they "make the list." And the potential market is quite large. In California, for example, some $104 million was allocated for the purchase of instructional materials in all subject matter areas for the school year 1995–1996, and at least 70% of these funds were required to be spent on State-approved textbooks.[13] At the same time, receiving State approval does not guarantee sales. As we shall see, the features of textbooks that permit publishers to "make the list" are not necessarily those that appeal to buyers.

In preparing adoption criteria, many States—including Florida and New Jersey (Bolduc, n.d.; New Jersey Mathematics Coalition, 1993), to cite two large and prominent examples—rely heavily on the NCTM *Standards* (and thus are indirectly influenced by ideas derived from the research literature). But California has produced what is in some ways the most "radical" set of adoption criteria (California Department of Education, 1992), and in doing so has generated considerable and instructive controversy about mathematics education.

The committee that designed the "California Framework" was composed of a variety of educators, some of whom are quite familiar with the NCTM *Standards* and serve on NCTM committees, and at least one of whom (Alan Schoenfeld) is a prominent researcher. This is another example of the kind of networking that exists in the mathematics education community.

Some aspects of the California Framework are explicitly psychological. For example, it quotes research (Resnick, 1987) on the nature of higher-order thinking: "Higher-order thinking involves *self-regulation* of the thinking process" (California Department of Education, 1992, p. 21). The Framework also presents a section on the learning of mathematics that makes heavy use of both constructivist ideas (the partly "old" theoretical approach that has underpinned progressive education for many years) and research on the nature of children's mathematical knowledge (the "new" contribution of contemporary researchers). Thus, "children actively create their own understanding of the world. In fact, by the time they come to school, they have already developed a rich body of knowledge about the worlds around them, including well-developed, informal systems of mathematics" (p. 33).

The Framework is also heavily influenced by Piaget's theory of egocentrism as a general cognitive characteristic of primary-level children (grades K through 2), who, it is claimed, "have a hard time holding more than one idea in their mind at a time. . . . Have shorter attention spans. . . . Are more egocentric. . . . Often work on a task in parallel alongside other children . . . " (p. 73).

Drawing on its interpretation of constructivism, the California Framework requires what some in the State have seen as a radical approach to the creation of textbooks. The Framework decrees that, to be adopted by schools in California, curriculum materials must stress meaningful learning, the construction of knowledge, independent thinking, and extended investigations and explorations; and the Framework requires publishers to downplay rote learning, memorization, and the passive absorption of knowledge.

Thus, the Framework contrasts "traditional" and "desired" practices as follows. In traditional practice, "Procedures are given major focus. Emphasis is placed on learning the steps to perform an algorithm and on providing enough practice so that the procedure becomes automatic . . . " (p. 199). By contrast, the desired practice requires students to "develop a range of computational procedures, with greater emphasis on number sense than on algorithms. They invent and use a number of different computational procedures. . . . Students are expected to decide the most efficient means of calculating an answer for a given situation; that is . . . with the mind only or with . . . paper and pencil or a calculator" (p. 199).

The California Framework uses ideas from research (for example, the notion of invented strategies, cited above) to set the requirements for textbook development and adoption.

The Publishing Industry

It should come as no surprise that, in developing textbooks, publishers are influenced not only by research findings but also by the financial "bottom line." Most large publishers

[13] Figures provided by the California State Department of Education.

(often, subsidiaries of even larger conglomerates) exist to make money; contributing to the improvement of mathematics education is a means to an end, not their primary concern. These businesses will not publish research-based textbooks if doing so results in economic losses or only very small profits. Other, usually smaller publishers are more ideologically driven; their goal is more likely to be the promotion of particular approaches to mathematics education. At least at the outset, in their days of idealism, before tasting economic success, these smaller publishers do not exist only to make money; but they must make money to exist. The largest and most influential publishers (about seven large publishers are said to control over half of the U. S. sales[14]) do not take this approach to the publication of mathematics text books.

Given the need to produce a product that will sell, publishers are strongly influenced by State adoption criteria. The marketing and editorial staff—those individuals directly employed by the publishing company—keep track of the State deadlines (and, in fact, keep charts listing them over a 5- or 10-year period) and study the State curriculum frameworks with great interest. Indeed, in deciding on the purchase of a textbook series, local districts often ask publishers to demonstrate the extent to which the books meet the adoption criteria. The editorial staff must stay current on the essential features of State mandates and figure out how they can be fulfilled. Publishers pay particular attention, of course, to the desires of large-population States where sales are potentially lucrative and serious economic consequences would result from failing to make the list. Because a large proportion of a company's sales can be generated in a State like California, if that State desires a "constructivist" textbook, the publishers will tend to comply.[15] In this sense, then, economic necessity drives publishers in the direction of being responsive to the research literature.

Publishers are also influenced, although less directly, by the NCTM *Standards.* Editorial staff members study the *Standards* for several purposes, the first of which is to guide textbook development. They seek to develop a product that achieves the NCTM goals of promoting construction of mathematical ideas, problem solving, and all the rest. (As we shall see below, other considerations act to *prevent* the publishers from implementing the *Standards.*) Publishers know that the States and local districts are strongly influenced by the *Standards,* which now represent the orthodoxy in mathematics education. Demonstrating a fit between the publishers' textbooks and the *Standards* is important for sales. Indeed, publishers cite the *Standards* in their advertising and cover blurbs. A typical self-endorsement states that a book is: "A not-so-standard way of meeting the math standards. . . . Learning math—and meeting the NCTM math standards—can be more fun and interesting with ______ (for grades 3–4)." Publishers' enthusiasm for the *Standards* resembles politicians' espousal of religion. At the very least, one must *say* one believes in it. No mainstream publisher would deliberately announce rejection of the *Standards.*

The *Standards* are also a guide for damage control. If a manuscript or a published text does not in fact meet the criteria set by the *Standards,* it must be made to *appear* to meet them. This can sometimes be done via minor revisions, such as rewording the headings on pages (for example, change *drill* to *problem solving,* or *lesson* to *exploration).* Even the sales staff need to learn about the *Standards* so that they can point to those features of the text that satisfy them and downplay other features that do not.

The editorial staff are also influenced by the NCTM journals, particularly *Teaching Children Mathematics,* which contains many reports of psychological research. The editorial staff are often former teachers and other individuals with a sincere interest in helping children learn. Although they know that various factors will prevent them from making textbooks as "constructivist" as they might like, the editors nevertheless attempt to become knowledgeable about the research and to use it in developing texts. Staff members not only read the journals but attend professional meetings, especially those of the National Council of Teachers of Mathematics (no math editor has yet been sighted or cited at the SRCD or APA meetings). Publishers occasionally invite guest lecturers and consultants to inform them of the latest research developments.[16]

---

[14] This is an estimate provided by a knowledgeable mole in the publishing industry.

[15] The publishers also attend to needs and desires of the "open States"—those that merely recommend, but do not *mandate* selection of textbooks conforming to their Curriculum Framework. In open States like New York, local districts often base purchasing decisions, at least in part, on the criteria proposed by the (nonmandatory) Framework.

[16] One mathematics educator with knowledge of publishers partly agrees and disagrees with our account. In a personal e-mail communication of November 22, 1994, Frank Lester, former editor of the *Journal for Research in Mathematics Education* maintains that: "The matter of whether, how, and to what extent commercial textbook publishers are influenced by research is a particularly thorny issue. My experience has been that publishers are influenced by research but only indirectly. When a body

Textbook development is also influenced by the authors' knowledge of the research, which may sometimes be their own. Publishers employ various authors to work with the editorial staff—authors who are knowledgeable in the mathematics of various grade levels, in the cultural aspects of mathematics, and even in psychological research. (Publishers also make a point of contracting with authors who represent particular parts of the country—not surprisingly, they may favor residents of States that adopt large quantities of textbooks.) Most authors are professors of mathematics education; some are teachers; some are connected with committees of the NCTM; and some are identified with psychological research. In the textbook publishing environment, authors do not actually write books in the same sense that novelists write them or psychologists write chapters like this. The writing of mathematics textbooks, at least those directed at grades K through 8, is a group process, and the publisher's editorial and marketing staff may make as many decisions about the content as do the "authors."[17] Nevertheless, the authors often introduce psychological considerations into the process of textbook development.

Although these factors—the NCTM *Standards* and publications, the State adoption criteria, the economics of publishing, and the editorial staff's and writers' knowledge—lead to the production of textbooks based, at least to some degree, on the psychological research literature, and indeed have resulted in some general improvement of mathematics textbooks, other forces, such as the anticipated demands of teachers, political controversies, and the nature of the printed page, conspire to push publishers in other directions.

of research built up over time (say 10 years or so) indicates something particular about children's learning of math, textbook publishers learn about this only through professional meetings, agitation from teachers on textbook selection committees, and so forth. The emphasis on thinking strategies for learning basic arithmetic facts today is a result not of publishers' looking at the research so much as their being forced by popular demand to include more of this in texts. An unfortunate side effect of this is that these publishers never actually read any research and, as a result, come up with a mongrelized interpretation of what the research says." Our own view is that the editorial staff do sometimes read reports of research, and of course sometimes create a "mongrelized interpretation" (or perhaps "construction") of it, although that could be said about many psychologists, too.

[17] Indeed, it is said that, in some publishing houses, the editorial staff are largely responsible for the writing, and the "authors" provide general consulting and their names. Some introductory psychology textbook writing is said to take this form too.

Anticipated Demands of Teachers

In planning textbook development, publishers realize that even if they meet the State adoption criteria and make the list, they still have to sell to the local districts, which have the power to choose among the books on the approved list. In planning the books, the publisher has to meet the demands of both the State adoption criteria and the local district selectors, some of whom may be teachers, or curriculum supervisors, or school administrators, or parent representatives. The publishers must be as sensitive to grass-roots sentiment as they are to the *Standards* and to State adoption criteria. The demands and preferences of the local districts may be assessed through such organized techniques as focus groups, interviews, and questionnaires; often, local sentiment is inferred from informal conversations with teachers and administrators, or intuited based on general experience.

Thus, publishers come to believe that some substantial proportion of teachers—a proportion that may vary by State and region of the country—may not want "constructivist" textbooks. Some teachers do not approve of the kind of thinking that motivates the NCTM *Standards;* some teachers, believing in drill and practice and in the general proposition that children ought to do what they are told, want to teach in traditional ways; and some teachers, not liking mathematics, not knowing it very well, or not wanting to teach it, try to get through the whole process as quickly and with as little effort as possible.

Other teachers, publishers believe, do not object in principle to the thinking behind the *Standards,* but are concerned primarily with accomplishing all the things they are supposed to do each day with an increasingly diverse student population and with few resources. These teachers are not interested in textbooks that require them to do more than they already do in a very busy class. Thus, they are interested in getting through the lesson, not in finding out how children think or in encouraging children's invention of interesting computational procedures. They prefer traditional textbooks that supply specific activities and familiar routines to occupy the day.

Sad to say, publishers are probably correct in their assessment of the preferences of many teachers. Research indicates that many elementary teachers are poorly prepared to teach mathematics (Weiss, 1990), do not know it very well (Post et al., 1991; Simon, 1993), hold traditional views about teaching it (Battista, 1994; Civil, 1993; Thompson, 1992), and favor "whole class instruction with seat work and recitations" (Stodolsky, 1988, p. 74). If this is the case, then publishers must attempt to "water down" those aspects of textbooks which the NCTM and at least some of the State Education Departments most wish to promote.

Political Controversies

Not only does mathematics education arouse anxiety in children, parents, and (to a greater extent than is often acknowledged) teachers; it also elicits strong negative feelings in community groups and politicians. Indeed, it provokes a degree of political controversy that is both surprising and informative with respect to American intellectual life and ideology. The State of California presents an interesting case study in this regard.

California, a large and complex State, is home to many immigrants and to diverse ethnic and racial groups. It is also home to varied and extreme political organizations, from conservative elements in Orange County to radicals in the northern region. In this volatile political climate, controversy about mathematics education has flourished. After the California Framework for evaluating textbooks (California Department of Education, 1992) was introduced, some individuals and community groups objected with great outrage to its recommendations. One newspaper columnist wrote:

> If the proposed framework is approved, California's third graders could be taught that even math is relative. [The program] would teach children that there are different "strategies" for solving simple equations. Instead of memorizing $5 + 4 = 9$, the program would tell children to find creative ways to find the answer, such as: "I think of $5 + 5$, because I know that $5 + 5 = 10$. And $5 + 4$ is 1 less, so it's 9." . . . Maureen DiMarco, Governor Wilson's point person on education and candidate for state schools superintendent, dismisses new-new math as "fuzzy crap." (Saunders, 1994a, p. A20)

This article is not unique: others like it have appeared in the press.[18] The controversy has been widespread, and the State has appointed a commission to review the California Framework. Saunders's piece reveals some important cultural attitudes and assumptions, and it suggests why mathematics has been drawn into what, gratefully following Ms. DiMarco's pungent lead, we might call the "slimy crap" of politics.

The newspaper columnist is horrified that California's innocent children could be *taught* (not that they might themselves *learn*) that "even math is relative." This scenario proposes that mathematics is but one weapon in the arsenal of those relativists who wish to undermine traditional values and certainties. Children would be discouraged from *memorizing* what their elders tell them is true, and would actually be taught to use *strategies* and even to be *creative!* In this point of view, mathematics has become a surrogate for modernism, and the NCTM *Standards* are a blueprint for teaching children disrespect for the established order. Anti-intellectualism and fundamentalism are enduring features of American political life.

The columnist's evidence for the evils that the modernist conspiracy has wrought is precisely those features of children's thinking that others (like the authors of the NCTM *Standards*) find so fascinating, worthy of encouragement, and indeed captivating. Saunders is outraged when children do not need to memorize $5 + 4 = 9$, and instead construct an invented strategy to obtain the solution ("I think of $5 + 5$, because I know that $5 + 5 = 10$. And $5 + 4$ is 1 less, so it's 9."). But others believe that this kind of constructed knowledge is the essence of mathematical thinking and that memorization (Piaget's "memory in the narrow sense") is a trivial activity that educators should discourage. The dispute does not revolve around evidence or theory; presumably, Saunders would not dispute the research showing that children in fact develop invented strategies. The issue is not science, but values. The fundamentalists do not believe that education should promote creative or critical thinking.

Indeed, the fundamentalists feel that modern education threatens the very fabric of traditional life. In another piece, titled "Math Agnostics Breed Math Illiterates,"

---

[18] Here is another example: "If you are the parent of a student in a California public elementary or middle school, prepare to feel out of touch come next fall when your child sits down to do math homework. . . . When adding . . . is required, it might not matter if a student uses a calculator. And if your child says there is no right answer, he or she is probably telling the truth. Sound disorienting? Discouraging? Don't feel too bad, because in all likelihood, your son or daughter's teacher will be confounded as well" (Colvin, 1995, pp. A1, A16). The article goes on to say: "In Palo Alto, parents objected to a state-sponsored program to promote the 'thinking' curriculum in middle schools. Parents' fears that children were being steered away from math fundamentals led to angry confrontations with teachers . . . " (p. A17). Later in the article, Ms. DiMarco was quoted as saying: "I'm truly alarmed that some radicals have taken ahold (sic) of the curriculum, and are convinced that basic skills are not important, when everybody knows that solid basic skills are the foundation on which you work to get to those higher order skills" (p. A17).

Saunders (1994b) writes: "[E]ducrats won't let math be math. They want to twist math into a multicultural, quality-time-with-the-parents, journal-keeping, do-your-own-thing and make-the-teacher-stand-back activity. They are math agnostics about to breed math illiterates" (p. A25). It is no accident that Saunders uses the imagery of religion—true believers versus agnostics—in portraying a dispute over mathematics education.

So, even mathematics—that cold, rational, neutral, nerdy subject matter—can become embroiled in political dispute, at least when hot issues of values are introduced. Alfred Binet did not believe that politicians would bother themselves with educational issues: "What is taught to children at school! As though legislators could become interested in that! . . . We cannot readily imagine a secretary of state busying himself with a question of this kind" (Binet & Simon, 1916, p. 262). But he was wrong. He did not anticipate that, in California, even State officials like Maureen DiMarco are clearly taken with the finer points of mathematics education.

The Printed Page

Any medium of communication is limited by its very nature. The printed page can show pictures of things to explore, but the things on the page cannot be explored except by vision. The printed page can picture "manipulatives," but the manipulatives on the page cannot be moved and joined to one another, except in imagination. The static page cannot vividly portray transformations over time—for example, the actions of adding, or taking away. There are limits to what books can do to engage young children in the construction of mathematics.[19]

Publishers are well aware of these constraints, and they know that it is easier to produce "drill and kill" textbooks—pages crowded with numerical problems—than it is to develop textbooks that promote exploration, open-ended problem solving, and the like. From a publisher's point of view, the printed page resists implementation of the kind of mathematics education suggested indirectly by some research (for example, building on children's informal knowledge).

The Publishers' Dilemma

Consider the very difficult dilemma faced by publishers. On the one hand, several forces promote applying research ideas and findings to the development of children's mathematics textbooks: The NCTM *Standards* for curriculum have been influenced by research findings. The *Standards* have in turn been disseminated widely through the NCTM's journals. The *Standards* and the research have helped to shape State criteria for the adoption of textbooks. To sell textbooks, publishers must be responsive to the details of the State criteria in particular and to the *Standards* as a kind of article of faith. Editorial staff of publishing houses read the research literature and attend professional meetings. Authors do the same, and some conduct research themselves.

But opposing forces militate against the application of research. Teachers may not want nontraditional textbooks. Fundamentalists believe that children should accept the traditional wisdom (and values) and should not attempt to construct their own approaches to understanding mathematics. And the printed page is not an ideal medium for encouraging an exploratory, manipulative approach.

These countervailing forces give rise to the publishers' dilemma. By investing in textbooks that attempt to meet State criteria, publishers risk producing a "constructivist" product that some teachers and some political groups may not accept. The NCTM *Standards* and State adoption criteria, which attempt to incorporate research findings, push publishers in one direction; but certain grass-roots constituencies—some teachers and political groups—may band together to push them in another. In some cases, State policy conflicts with market forces. What are publishers to do?

The result is a complex series of compromises. Given the goal of maximizing sales (and profits), publishers naturally wish to have their textbook cake and eat it too. To some extent, publishers try to satisfy all sides in the controversy. Although important differences among them should not be minimized, publishers tend to produce the following mélange of material, all within one textbook or teachers' manual at any given grade level.

Traditional Pages. Every textbook contains traditional pages involving drill, routine memorization of facts, instruction in following directions, and the like. For example, Figure 7.1 illustrates a page in a first grade book

---

[19] At the same time, we would point out that *any* medium is perforce limited. Manipulatives can promote activity that is too concrete. Many children learn to work with sticks or blocks and learn nothing from this about mathematics. For Piaget (1970), the use of manipulatives was only a temporary means toward the end of mental activity: "Although the child's activity at certain levels necessarily entails the manipulation of objects, . . . at other levels the most authentic research activity may take place in the spheres of reflection, of the most advanced abstraction, and of verbal manipulation . . . " (p. 68).

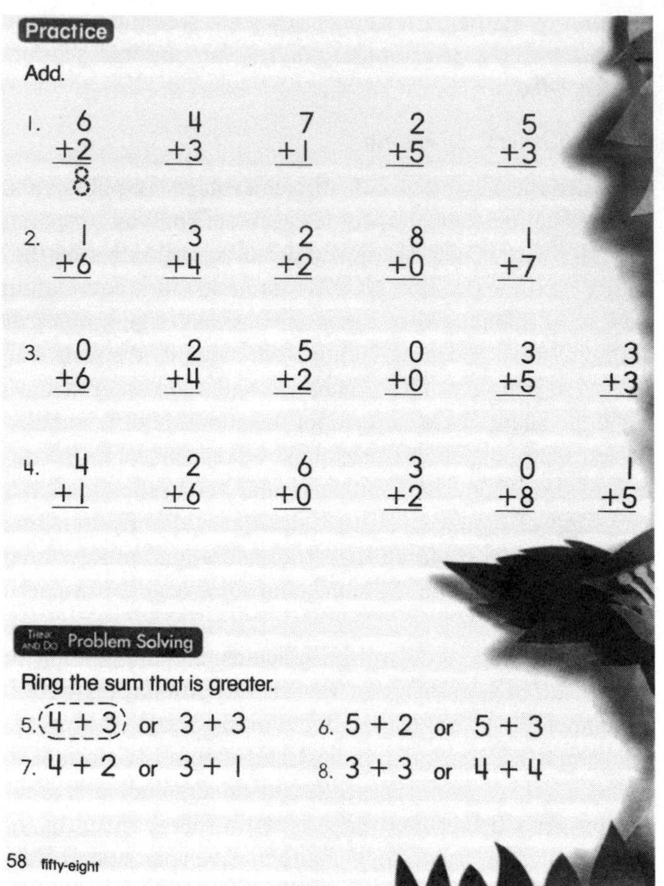

Practice

Add.

1. 6 +2 8 | 4 +3 | 7 +1 | 2 +5 | 5 +3

2. 1 +6 | 3 +4 | 2 +2 | 8 +0 | 1 +7

3. 0 +6 | 2 +4 | 5 +2 | 0 +0 | 3 +5 | 3 +3

4. 4 +1 | 2 +6 | 6 +0 | 3 +2 | 0 +8 | 1 +5

Think and Do Problem Solving

Ring the sum that is greater.

5. (4 + 3) or 3 + 3 6. 5 + 2 or 5 + 3

7. 4 + 2 or 3 + 1 8. 3 + 3 or 4 + 4

58 fifty-eight

Figure 7.1 First-grade textbook page. From Silver Burdett Ginn. (1995). *Mathematics: Exploring Your World. Grade 1.* Morristown, NJ: Author. Copyright © 1995 by Silver Burdett Ginn. Reprinted with permission.

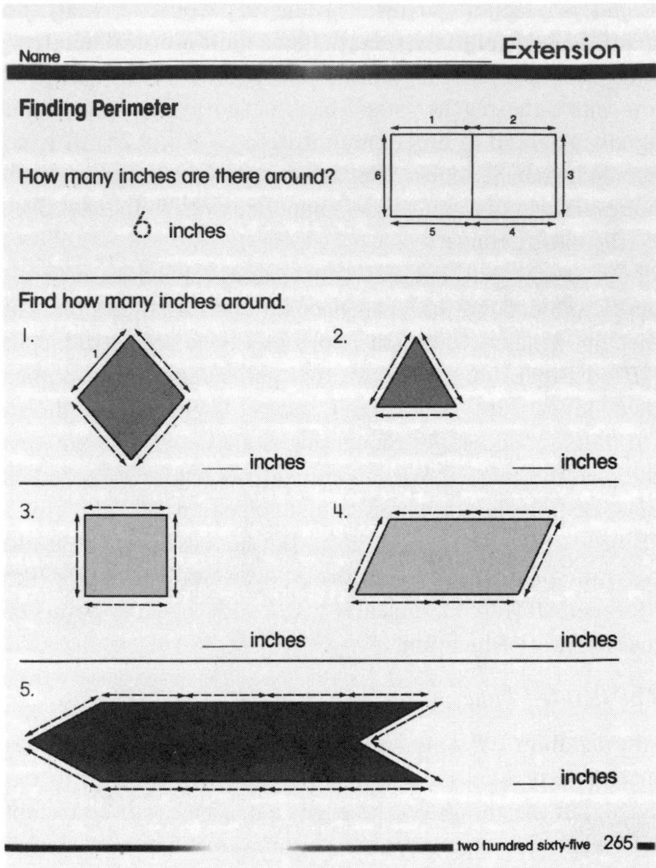

Name ________ Extension

Finding Perimeter

How many inches are there around?

6 inches

Find how many inches around.

1. ___ inches 2. ___ inches

3. ___ inches 4. ___ inches

5. ___ inches

two hundred sixty-five 265

Figure 7.2 First-grade textbook page. From Silver Burdett Ginn. (1995). *Mathematics: Exploring Your World. Grade 1.* Morristown, NJ: Author. Copyright © 1995 by Silver Burdett Ginn. Reprinted with permission.

(Silver Burdett Ginn, 1995b, p. 58),[20] which provides straightforward drill on the addition facts and on the "greater than" relation. Figure 7.2 illustrates another page in the same book (p. 265), which first shows students how to find the perimeter of a rectangle, and then directs students to solve similar problems. The emphasis is entirely instructional and directive.[21]

Artful Dodge Pages. Publishers can be clever at giving the appearance of meeting the State adoption criteria while still offering traditional pages. For example, it is easy to devise constructivist-sounding titles of books, or headings for pages offering drill. Thus, in Figure 7.1, the lower part of the page is labeled "Problem Solving," an act that surely required more imagination from the publisher than the page does from the student.

Research Influenced Pages. Some aspects of textbooks and teachers' manuals have been thoroughly changed—and,

[20] Ginsburg was one of the "authors" of this series but had nothing to do with the writing or planning of any of the textbook pages referred to in this chapter.

[21] Even a constructivist might argue that such an approach is not a bad idea, at least when used in moderation for certain specific purposes. In this view, there are some relatively uninteresting aspects of mathematics that one must learn more or less by rote, partly because it is difficult to summon the enthusiasm necessary to construct sensible approaches to dealing with them. In this vein, Piaget (1970) commended the use of Skinnerian teaching machines for learning certain dull material: "[It] is possible that the use of teaching machines will save time that would have been needlessly wasted by more traditional methods and therefore augment the number of hours available for active work" (pp. 78–79).

in our view, improved—by research findings. We have no evidence as to the proportion of such pages in textbooks, but we can assert that they do exist and they represent one way in which our field's research has been "applied."

Consider first some introductory material in a teachers' manual. Manuals of this type, given to teachers along with the textbooks, are intended to provide guidance in the use of the textbooks. One manual (Hope & Small, 1993) for teachers at the third grade level, in an introductory section called "The Approach to Learning," begins with a quote from the NCTM *Standards,* and then states that this textbook "views the learner as an active participant in the learning process. As the children interact with objects and materials, with people, with ideas and thoughts, they explore, experiment, discover, gain information, and construct knowledge" (p. 17). Later, in describing work on addition, the authors say: "When children connect the symbols 3 + 4 = 7 with the action of combining 3 objects and 4 objects, we have some confidence that they understand at least one aspect of addition" (p. 26). To support their ideas, the writers go on to cite studies from the research literature (indeed, several done by members of the CGI group, whose work will be discussed below).[22]

Recent textbooks also reflect the influence of the research literature. A relevant textbook page is shown in Figure 7.3 (Silver Burdett Ginn, 1995c, p. 5). The page takes an active approach to learning; the exercise is designated an "Activity," the goal of which is "Investigating Order." The lesson begins with pictures of a child who is using her fingers to conduct a mathematical investigation. In the first picture, her hands are straight in front of her, and she has paper rings on four fingers of her right hand and three fingers of her left hand. In the second picture, her hands are crossed, so that the positions of the units of three ringed fingers and four ringed fingers are switched.[23] The intention is to show the child (and the teacher) that one can learn about number by performing "experiments" on physical objects, that even fingers are an acceptable tool for conducting such investigations and for promoting mathematical thinking, that learning mathematics involves discovering (reinventing?) principles as well as (or even instead of) memorizing number facts or calculational routines, and that the learning process involves the active engagement of

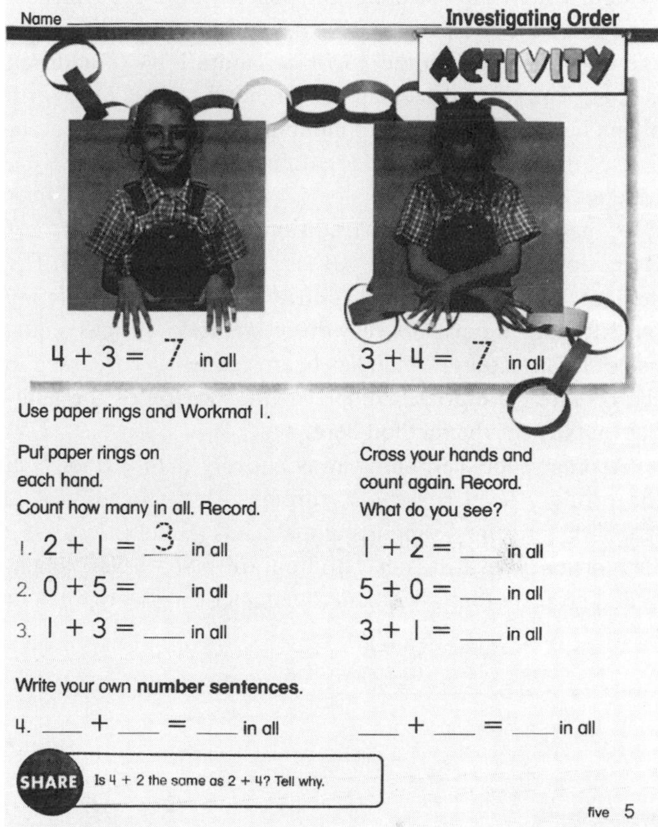

Figure 7.3 Second-grade textbook page. From Silver Burdett Ginn. (1995). *Mathematics: Exploring Your World. Grade 2.* Morristown, NJ: Author. Copyright © 1995 by Silver Burdett Ginn. Reprinted with permission.

[22] By contrast, consider introductory material from a somewhat older text, also at the third grade level (Strayer & Upton, 1934): "This series of books aims to give the child the ability to compute easily and accurately . . . these books incorporate the most valuable findings of modern experimentation . . . including the results of important researches conducted by the authors themselves [an appraisal generously provided by the authors themselves] . . . these texts require the pupil to take only one new step at a time and supply him with enough exercises to assure mastery of that step before proceeding to the next one. . . . All the abstract exercises have been scientifically constructed so as to provide drill. . . . The pupil thereby acquires that automatic mastery of the basic combinations which is so essential to rapid and accurate computation" (pp. iii–iv). It is interesting to note that the authors prided themselves on using research to guide textbook construction, and that the innovation of the day was to make the problems "practical," in the sense of relating to everyday life situations like buying merchandise in stores. But all the problems are written and the book is filled with pages of numerical computations.

[23] This example also illustrates the inherent limitations of the page: it cannot show the child in the act of crossing her hands; a video would be required for that. Ultimately, multimedia "texts" may provide a partial solution, although they too cannot provide the child with actual objects to manipulate.

the learner. At the bottom of the page, children are encouraged to derive their own problems, and even to think about and communicate to others *why* commutativity of addition is true. The overall message is intended to be: Work with objects to construct ideas of number, devise your own problems, think about what you are doing, and express what you have learned.

A page from a more traditional textbook (Harcourt Brace Jovanovich, 1992, p. 101) is shown in Figure 7.4. The student is invited to solve addition problems by counting on. Although the page is very directive, it does focus on the use of this strategy, which has been frequently discussed in the research literature. Simple memorization of the number facts is not the method here.

Another publisher, doing away entirely with textbooks at the primary level (grades K through 2), publishes only a teachers' guide and supporting materials (Scholastic, 1995). In a primary-level lesson, children are given a very open-ended problem that asks them to conduct an investigation of

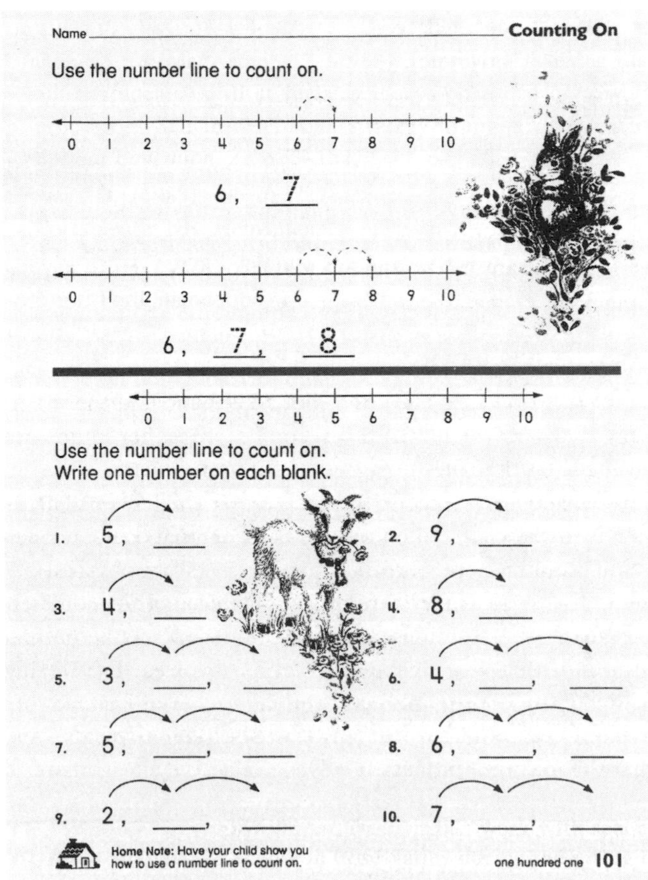

Figure 7.4 First-grade textbook page. From Harcourt Brace Jovanovich, I.. (1995). *Mathematics Plus: Grade 1.* Orlando, FL: Author. Copyright © 1995 by Harcourt Brace Jovanovich. Reprinted with permission.

how many offspring various animals produce over a period of years. The teachers' guide states: "Have children share their strategies. Talk about the operations children used to figure out how many offspring their animals would have over 10 years. Some children may create a chart showing all 10 years and then add the numbers. Others may figure out how many offspring there would be in 2 years and use repeated addition to add the same number 5 times" (p. 34). Note that the manual informs teachers that children invent their own procedures, and indeed encourages an open discussion of the various methods. The manual fails, however, to guide teachers in how to work with the various strategies. What should the teacher do? Encourage the strategies? Use them in some way? The clear message is that children construct their approach to solving problems, and this creativity should be encouraged.

In another teachers' manual, the first grade lesson on "joining and separating" begins with the advice: "Children use their own strategies for finding the addition and subtraction facts. Children discuss and share these strategies throughout the unit, helping others validate and extend their own thinking" (Addison-Wesley, 1995b, p. 185). The unit begins by asking children to make up and act out stories involving joining and separating. The page in the children's textbook (Addison-Wesley, 1995a, p. 44) is basically an empty space in which children are asked: "Record one of your stories. Use pictures, words, or numbers to help you." After this, children are encouraged to use a manipulative to help them solve the problem posed by the story. The teacher is advised: "Watch to see how children model the joining and separating situations" (Addison-Wesley, 1995b, p. 197). The goal is to encourage use of strategies invented by the children.

Teachers' Use of Textbooks. The fruits of research have indeed been "applied" to textbooks, the most prevalent medium of mathematics instruction around the world. But how are these textbooks used by teachers in classrooms? Little is known about implementation at the elementary level.[24] But consider the extent to which the

[24] Research examining high school math department chairs' written reports (concerning course outlines, syllabi, textbooks, plans, and classroom practice) shows that reforms advocated by the NCTM *Standards* are making gradual inroads, although progress is slow and limited. "Elements [of reform] embodied in new materials, such as calculators and textbooks, were more changed than elements of practice that require extensive learning by teachers and substantial commitments of time by teachers" (Garet & Mills, 1995, p. 386). It is surely easier to change textbooks than teachers' classroom practices.

research-oriented textbook pages make demands on teachers. These pages do not offer a cookbook for teaching; they are not "teacher-proof." Just the opposite is true: the constructivist approach depends on the intelligence of the teacher, who must construct an understanding of the child's learning in order to foster it. To use these pages, teachers must think in a flexible manner, responding to the needs and unique constructions of individual children. Textbook pages are merely a resource; they can set direction but cannot guarantee what teachers will do.

Consider how much a teacher must know in order to use, in the way it was intended, the page shown in Figure 7.3. The teacher needs to understand that:

1. Because they possess an informal mathematics, children already understand something about addition before arriving in school.
2. Children think of early addition as combining and counting sets.
3. Even if encouraged, use of the fingers for counting does not necessarily persist into adulthood.
4. Even at a tender age, children can "discover," "induce," or "construct" abstract mathematical principles.
5. Children have minds of their own and are capable of learning on their own.
6. The empirical activity of counting can be a precursor of and provide a basis for understanding.
7. Children may overgeneralize principles learned from concrete activity (thus, children may construct the incorrect belief that subtraction is commutative too—an indication that their thinking is not necessarily too concrete but can in fact err on the side of excessive abstraction).
8. Children should think about why they get the answers they do.
9. Children's "incorrect" verbalizations may in fact express mathematical ideas very accurately.

This list represents a minimum level of the knowledge and sophistication required for teachers to work effectively with this material. Unfortunately, many teachers are unable to meet the challenges offered by research-influenced pages like the one shown in Figure 7.3, and can easily use them in a traditional, rigid manner. If so inclined, a teacher could begin with a little lecture on commutativity, largely ignoring the paper rings on the fingers of the girl pictured, and simply telling the children that the order of adding makes no difference: If you add 4 + 3 to get 7, the result is the same when you calculate 3 + 4. Then the teacher could direct the children to do the problems at the bottom of the page, without paper rings, whereupon the children could quickly figure out that the answer in the second column is always supposed to be the same as the answer in the first. After this has been completed, the teacher could tell the children to write in the blank spaces and solve 3+ 2 and 2 + 3. Finally, the teacher could teach the children to *say* that 4 + 2 is the same as 2 + 4 because "order makes no difference."

Good intentions can be subverted. Innovative material can be used badly. Everything depends on the training and skill of the teacher. The implications of these facts for psychology and for mathematics education are enormous.

Conclusions. The application of research knowledge to textbook development affects millions of students. The next section considers what it teaches us about: the process of applying research to practice; the contributions of research; the deficiencies of research; and the prospects for improving our contributions to mathematics education.

Reflections on the Path from Research to Textbook Use

Examination of the application of research to textbook development reveals a most complex and interesting process that ultimately has implications both for the training of researchers and for educational policy.

Characteristics of the Research. The contemporary research that has influenced mathematics education has several characteristics. First, the results of the research are consistent. Researchers easily agree on the general idea that, before entering school, children possess some kind of informal mathematics, and counting is a key element of it. This is not a subtle result; virtually anyone interviewing a small child can replicate the main findings.

Second, the findings are relatively easy to communicate to educators. The main points can be demonstrated vividly and with immediacy. It is easy to make appealing videotapes that demonstrate to teachers how small children use invented strategies or employ complex forms of understanding.

Third, the research findings are interesting and relevant for mathematics educators. Most educators (and parents) are fascinated and charmed by children's informal mathematics, invented strategies, and bugs. These phenomena immediately capture attention and suggest ways of thinking about the teaching and learning of mathematics. Some of the details that become obsessions to researchers (such as how many different ways of adding by counting may be observed) are probably of little interest to educators (and to many psychologists too). But the main ideas are clearly important.

Fourth, research on mathematical thinking has had high prestige within the psychological community. Perhaps one reason is that the very word mathematical sounds impressive. In our math-phobic society, anyone who is studying *mathematics* must be doing something very difficult, scientific, and prestigious (even if that person is examining how children use their fingers to solve problems of the magnitude of 2 + 2). More importantly, an extremely prominent group of researchers has worked on issues of mathematical thinking—Gelman, Greeno, Saxe, and Siegler, to mention only a few (and offend many more)—and their work has, in turn, attracted others.

Fifth, very early on, the research took on an interdisciplinary character, involving educational psychologists, cross-cultural psychologists, and mathematics educators, as well as developmental psychologists. As mentioned earlier, one of the first conferences in this area, held at the Wingspread Center, involved participants from several of these disciplines and from several countries (Carpenter et al., 1982). Robert Davis, one of the most prominent mathematics educators in the United States, founded the *Journal of Children's Mathematical Behavior,* which was one of the first outlets for research in the area, and was influential in propagating a psychological point of view within the mathematics education community. The International Group for the Psychology of Mathematics Education was founded in Germany in the early 1970s and to this day involves many researchers from around the world who combine an interest in psychological research and mathematics education. The multidisciplinary nature of the research made it easier to disseminate through different journals to various disciplines, including mathematics education.

Influential Receivers of Research. Research may not have much influence if the only people who read it are other researchers. But the research in question was read and sanctioned by an elite and very constructive group of gatekeepers within the mathematics education community. Robert Davis was one of these, as was Thomas Romberg, who played an important role in championing the research within the NCTM in particular. The gatekeepers had a legitimating role, ensuring that the research would affect a much wider audience than if left only to the efforts of the researchers.

Dissemination through Official Documents. One activity of the gatekeepers is to produce various official documents. The gatekeepers influence professional organizations like the NCTM to produce the equivalents of biblical tracts (the various *Standards* documents) which, to some degree, incorporate, disseminate, and sanction the research. Similarly, they influence the National Research Council to produce publications like *Everybody Counts* (Mathematical Sciences Education Board, 1989), which also draws on and disseminates the research. These kinds of official documents and blessings carry considerable weight in influencing policy.

Other Forms of Dissemination. Much primary research gets read by only a relatively small number of subscribers to professional journals. But ideas related to the research in question have been disseminated widely through the NCTM journals, in writings and speeches of the gatekeepers and of the researchers themselves. In the process of dissemination, the research results can be distorted to some degree, and it is not always certain that the recipients of the message assimilate it in the form intended. Nevertheless, the general findings of the research have been communicated to mathematics educators, teachers, administrators, public officials, newspaper writers (e.g., Goleman, 1992), and textbook editors.[25]

Quasi-Legal Effects. Via the various forms of dissemination, the research has contributed to one of the most important influences on publishers: the State criteria for textbook adoption. As we have seen, States like California draw on the research to construct their regulations for textbook selection. Publishers cannot ignore these legally binding mandates, at least some of which have stressed what they consider to be a constructivist approach.

Exogenous Forces. Research knowledge is not the only influence on textbook production. Because of the need to make a profit, publishers are sensitive to the "grass roots"—the demands of teachers, parents, and political groups. The reluctance of some teachers to use anything other than a highly traditional, structured approach is in turn influenced by working conditions. If required to teach class after class, all day, without time off for preparation and with little assistance, they cannot easily do the work

[25] For example, in a paper in *Mathematics Teaching in the Middle School,* Lambdin, Kloosterman, and Johnson (1994) describe for teachers the work of Carraher and colleagues (e.g., Carraher, Carraher, & Schliemann, 1985) on the calculational abilities of street children in Brazil and advise: "Although such research does not tell us what to do in the classroom, it does raise important questions for instruction. What do we, as teachers, really know about the mathematical skills and concepts that our students bring with them to school from other contexts? How can we build our instruction on this prior knowledge?" (p. 39).

required to teach a new and innovative curriculum in a sensitive manner. (By contrast, Japanese teachers are given adequate preparation time and seem to use it to devise coherent lessons [Stevenson & Stigler, 1992]. These teachers also enjoy the benefits of good pay and respect.) Fundamentalism and anti-intellectualism are potent forces in American life, and mathematics education does not escape their attention.

Summary. The research on mathematical thinking seems to have had an impact because it is consistent, easy to communicate to educators, relevant, interesting, conducted by prominent researchers, and multidisciplinary. It has been sanctioned by influential gatekeepers within the mathematics education community and then incorporated into official and prestigious reports at the national and State levels. The research, sometimes in derivative forms, has been disseminated to practitioners through journals, conference presentations, and the popular press. The research has influenced State criteria for textbook adoption—and, therefore, the publishers who must respond to them. At the same time, other forces mitigate against applying the lessons of research. For one thing, it is hard to implement on a static page an active approach to learning. More importantly, teachers, parents, and political groups often oppose the kind of active mathematics learning suggested by the research. It is opposed by some teachers because of their own poor knowledge of and training in mathematics and mathematics education, and by some parents and political groups because of their fundamentalist values. The research has not been applied to textbook production in a straightforward way; nevertheless, it has achieved some important successes in influencing the development of textbooks.

The Contributions of Research to Textbook Development

Mathematics educators have found value in two aspects of the research. One is a general theoretical approach—the ideas of constructivism, of children's possession of an informal mathematics, of children's assimilating what is taught into what they already know. These are general ideas that to some extent merely confirm and validate the previously existing views of progressive educators. But the theory does more than that: It helps these educators to deepen their vision, to understand more clearly what they had only intuited in a vague way. And, the theory provides radically new insights to those educators who had not already acquired these intuitions.

A second contribution lies in some of the particulars of the research—the specific ways in which children use counting to add, or the various bugs that they employ, or the ways in which they invent strategies for doing column addition. As illustrated above, these particulars have helped to shape lessons in textbooks (as well as various activity-oriented approaches). This second contribution is, by its nature, more limited than the first, and that is as it should be. There is a danger in basing mathematics education too narrowly on the findings of psychologists. Children do add by counting, as psychologists have documented. But to limit the curriculum to adding by counting would be a mistake (analogous to limiting the curriculum to the Piagetian stages, as in Kamii & DeVries, 1976). Children are capable of many activities of which psychologists are unaware and have not studied. Indeed, it sometimes occurs that clever mathematics educators invent activities on which children display unsuspected abilities—or at least abilities unsuspected by psychologists. For example, in the Mason mathematics program (Miss Mason's School, 1976), preschoolers seem to employ and understand something like negative numbers. What psychological theory would have predicted that?

The Available Research Is Deficient in Contributing to Textbook Development

The research does not provide much guidance on how children learn from books. It does not help us to understand how first graders interpret pictures of addition and subtraction; it does not provide much information on how second graders read mathematical symbols. This should come as no surprise. These issues have not been the focus of most of the research, which, in an attempt to obtain an accurate and rounded assessment of mathematical competence, has focused on children's abilities in informal settings or on their mental activities. So, we have been provided with useful information about how children think and learn, but not about how they think and learn from textbooks.

Fruitful Areas for Application in the Future

From the point of view of the textbook developer, design issues are crucial. How should one create a page so that it promotes mathematics learning in the kindergarten child or first grader? How should pages differ for younger and older children? We need a kind of developmental-instructional psychology of the textbook page.

We have seen that textbook adoption gets entangled in politics. This is at least partially desirable. The public at large should have an interest in and should play a role in deciding what children learn in school and how they are taught. One danger in this situation, however, is that, for the most part, the public has very little sound knowledge about mathematics education and, specifically, about how children learn and think about mathematics. Indeed, most parents, like most teachers, probably have decidedly unsound ideas about mathematics education because of the ways they themselves were taught. If this is the case, it is incumbent on psychologists to publicize their work—that is, to make its content and its implications for education understandable to the public. As we have seen, influential gatekeepers have played this role for the mathematics education community. But the attempt has seldom been made to disseminate psychological research on mathematics learning to the public at large so as to inform a debate (as in the case of California) that sometimes gets more wrapped up in ideology than simple facts about children's learning.

One largely unanticipated outcome of the NCTM reforms has been increased pressure on teachers (Apple, 1992). A constructivist approach is the antithesis of the teacher-proof approach. Even the constructivist-oriented textbook (not to mention the activity approach, which eschews textbooks) makes heavy intellectual demands on teachers. As we have seen, to implement a constructivist approach, teachers need, among other things, to understand individual children's thinking and to have a grasp of the important features of its development. Consequently, a major area for future research and application is teacher development in the broadest sense. We need to understand more about how teachers develop understanding of both mathematics and students' learning of mathematics, and more effective methods for educating those teachers must be developed. The goal is to avoid the common situation where "a teacher could use the materials and alter some teaching behaviors without coming to grips with the conceptions or beliefs underlying the innovation the textbook is designed to promote" (Fullan, 1982, p. 30). Some models for this process already exist. The Cognitively Guided Instruction project, to which we turn next, devotes major effort to problems of teacher development.

Teacher Development

We have identified teacher education as the Achilles heel for those interested in textbook development. Implementation of any program—a textbook or an innovative set of manipulatives and activities—must "be mediated through the hearts and minds of teachers" (Knapp & Peterson, 1995, p. 41). We chose to examine Cognitively Guided Instruction (CGI) because its attempt to touch those hearts and minds provides important lessons concerning teacher education. Further, CGI has several important characteristics: It utilizes research knowledge in a thoughtful, creative, and thorough manner; it is not an isolated, one-shot experiment. CGI attempts to evaluate outcomes, for both teachers and students, over a period of several years. And finally, CGI is a relatively "pure" case: that is, its development has been fully under the control of researchers. This provides a contrast with the decidedly impure process of textbook development.

Attempts to improve the teaching of early mathematics might proceed in any one of several different directions. One might be called *expository*—teachers are helped, first, to understand what mathematics children ought to learn, and, second, to present it as logically and simply as possible. In this view, the mathematics is the starting point, and the rest is a matter of careful and effective exposition. This method has been the most common approach to teaching by mathematics educators at the higher grade levels (and to textbook writing by authors).

Another method is helping teachers to use what is *available,* whether relatively traditional, or relatively innovative: a curriculum, textbook, set of materials or manipulatives, games, piece of software, and the like. "Math methods" courses typically teach prospective teachers to use various manipulatives and materials. Many school districts run workshops of this type, at least on a superficial basis. Typically, teachers are required to attend only one or two such workshops during the course of a school year, so the effects cannot be very profound. Unfortunately, even when an entirely new curriculum is introduced to a district, teachers are often given little or no training in its use. Publishers cannot afford to provide extensive training in the use of their texts; and, with their budgets cut, school districts cannot afford to provide the necessary training either. Publishers do provide manuals ("teachers' editions") offering some information on how the texts should be used, but these are often of poor quality (although they do typically supply the right answers) and, by common report, they are seldom read. Some dedicated teachers attend extensive summer and intraterm workshops in the use of innovative materials, offered, for example, by the University of Chicago School Mathematics Project, or by Marilyn Burns and other creative mathematics educators. Probably, the attendees are teachers who are already doing reasonably well in their mathematics teaching.

These first two methods have important roles: (a) teachers should understand mathematics and be able to present material clearly, and (b) it is important for teachers to know how to use the curriculum materials available to them. But both suffer from the limitation that they do not take into consideration the psychology of the child. Consequently, we focus on a third method, which involves helping teachers use general principles derived from the psychology of mathematical thinking as their guide to instruction. Here, the dominating force is *psychological theory* about children's knowledge and learning, not mathematical content or curriculum materials. This approach has two key features: (a) identification of useful psychological principles and (b) a method for helping teachers to use them. The approach is seldom employed, but we focus on it because it exploits a valuable contribution of psychological research.

We use CGI as our extended example of this third approach. The founders of the project, Thomas P. Carpenter, Elizabeth Fennema, and Penelope L. Peterson, are researchers deeply involved in issues of mathematical learning. Their strategy was to provide teachers with an approach to instruction based on principles supported by research. We now consider several aspects of CGI: its psychology, the educational implications drawn from the psychology, the work with teachers, and the evaluation.

Psychological Assumptions

The general psychological rationale for CGI is: "Initially young children have quite different conceptions of addition, subtraction, multiplication and division than adults do; but this does not mean that their conceptions are wrong or misguided. In fact, their conceptions make a great deal of sense, and they provide a basis for learning basic mathematical concepts and skills with understanding" (Carpenter, Fennema, & Franke, 1994, p. 1). To flesh out this view, CGI draws heavily on a detailed psychological analysis of arithmetic problems and children's strategies for solving them. Solidly grounded in research evidence, the analysis describes the types of problems children encounter, the strategies children use to solve them, and some general principles of learning and cognition.

The first proposition is that arithmetic problems vary in important ways that are related to children's attempts to deal with them. In the case of addition and subtraction (CGI offers similar analyses for multiplication and division), four basic classes of problems have been identified: *Join, Separate, Part-Part-Whole,* and *Compare. Join* problems involve adding new elements to an existing set ("Three flies were in the ointment, and then 2 more flies landed in the ointment. How many flies were in the ointment then?"). *Separate* problems involve taking away elements from a set ("Seven pigs were in the pen and then 3 went for a stroll. How many pigs were left in the pen?"). In both cases, action is a key part of the problem. By contrast, *Part-Part-Whole* problems involve a relationship between two subsets and their larger set ("Eight cows were in the barn. Five were brown and the rest were spotted. How many were spotted?"). *Compare* problems require comparisons between two disjoint (nonoverlapping) sets ("There were 9 canoes on the lake and 3 rowboats. How many more canoes than rowboats are there?"). Note that *Join* and *Separate* problems seem, at least in terms of surface structure, to involve addition and subtraction, respectively, whereas *Part-Part-Whole* and *Compare* problems seem to have more to do with relationships (in the former, set–subset; and in the latter, set–set).

Each of these different classes of problems *(Join, Separate, Part-Part-Whole,* and *Compare)* can be further analyzed in terms of which quantity is unknown. For example, in the *Join* problems, one may distinguish among Result Unknown ("Begin with 3 things, add 2 more. How many are in the total?"), Change Unknown ("Begin with 3 things, add some, get 5 as the sum. How many were added?"), or Start Unknown ("Begin with some things, add 2 more, get 5 as the sum. How many did you start with?"). These can be described in simple number sentences as follows: Result Unknown: $3 + 2 = \ $. Change Unknown: $3 + \ = 5$. Start Unknown: $\ + 2 = 5$. Similar analyses are offered for *Separate, Part-Part-Whole,* and *Compare* problems.

To this point, the analysis has focused on classes of problems. The different types of problems, with different types within each class, offer distinct challenges to children attempting to solve them. Thus, *Join* problems seem to require different solution processes than do *Compare* problems, and *Join* (Result Unknown) problems present different obstacles than do *Join* (Start Unknown). The next issue is the methods children use to deal with the problems. CGI proposes that "the problem types are generally reflected in children's solution processes which tend to reflect the action or relationships described in a problem" (Carpenter et al., 1994, p. 14). So, if the essence of a problem seems to be joining, then the child is likely to engage in some kind of joining activity to solve it. At the same time, the structure of the problem should not be confused with the method of the solution. For example, although a problem may be conceptualized as *Join* (e.g., a Change Unknown problem: "Harry has 3 hippos. How many more hippos does he need to have 7 altogether?"), the child may choose to solve it by subtracting (7, take away 3).

Solutions are said to follow a developmental sequence. Children begin by using objects or fingers to model the actions or relationships portrayed in each problem, and they then invent mental counting strategies, which are finally replaced by memory for the number facts. The modeling strategy may be thought of as "enactive" (Bruner, 1966). The child places himself or herself in a hypothetical situation and solves the problem by enacting or mimicing the activity. Figure 7.5, describes six Direct Modeling Strategies. In the first problem, the child responds to a *Join* (Result Unknown) problem ("Ellen had 3 tomatoes. . . . ") by employing a *Joining All* strategy, which essentially involves representing the 3 tomatoes with 3 objects or fingers, "picking" 5 more tomatoes (again represented by fingers or objects), and then literally combining or joining the surrogate tomatoes to get the sum. The underlying structures of some problems are easier to capture in action than others, and that is one reason why a *Join* (Results Unknown) problem is easier to solve than a *Join* (Start Unknown) problem.

Strategy	Description
Joining All Ellen had 3 tomatoes. She picked 5 more tomatoes. How many tomatoes does Ellen have now?	Using objects or fingers, a set of 3 objects and a set of 5 objects are constructed. The sets are joined and the union of the two sets is counted.
Separating From There were 8 seals playing. Three seals swam away. How many seals were still playing?	Using objects or fingers, a set of 8 objects is constructed. 3 objects are removed. The answer is the number of remaining objects.
Separating To There were 8 people on the bus. Some people got off. Now there are 3 people on the bus. How many people got off the bus?	A set of 8 objects is counted out. Objects are removed from it until the number of objects remaining is equal to 3. The answer is the number of objects removed.
Joining To Chuck had 3 peanuts. Clara gave him some more peanuts. Now Chuck has 8 peanuts. How many peanuts did Clara give him?	A set of 3 objects is constructed. Objects are added to this set until there is a total of 8 objects. The answer is found by counting the number of objects added.
Matching Megan has 3 stickers. Randy has 8 stickers. How many more stickers does Randy have than Megan?	A set of 3 objects and a set of 8 objects are matched one-to-one until one set is used up. The answer is the number of objects remaining in the unmatched set.
Trial and Error Deborah had some books. She went to the library and got 3 more books. Now she has 8 books altogether. How many books did she have to start with?	A set of objects is constructed. A set of 3 objects is added to or removed, and the resulting set is counted. If the final count is 8, then the number of elements in the initial set is the answer. If it is not 8, a different initial set is tried.

Figure 7.5 Six modeling strategies.

In the latter ("Deborah had some books. . . . "), the child is reduced to Trial and Error, the last option in Figure 7.5.

The strategies then go underground and are converted into mental activities involving counting. In the case of *Join* (Result Unknown) problems, children typically employ the familiar *Counting-All* ("Three and 2 is 1, 2, 3, 4, 5") and then *Counting-On-from-Larger* ("Three and 2 is 3, 4, 5") strategies. As understanding of part–whole relationships and of reversibility develops (Piaget, 1952; Resnick, 1989), children become more flexible and more skilled in the use of these strategies than one might suspect. For example, even kindergarten children can use effective strategies for the solution of multiplication problems (Carpenter et al., 1993), which suggests that much of our early curriculum could be more challenging than it is now.

The next step in the developmental sequence is for the child to learn and use "number facts" to solve the problems. Because a good deal of confusion surrounds the notion of number facts, and because the teaching of number facts is a heated issue in mathematics education, we offer a few words of clarification, which seem consistent with the CGI approach.

First, number facts refer to the relatively small number combinations (for addition, usually from $1 + 0$ to $9 + 9$). What is accepted as "small" is entirely arbitrary and has nothing to do with mathematics. Among persons with very large memory capacity, $43 + 22$ might be considered a small number combination. Second, number facts are not really facts; they are truths or logical necessities (in Piaget's terms) about numbers: $3 + 2$ must be 5. Or, one can think of them as generalizations about the empirical activity of adding (Judd, 1927). Combining 3 objects and 2 objects always yields 5 objects, regardless of what the objects are. Third, in common parlance, "knowing" or "using the number facts" means memorizing the facts and then recalling them to solve problems, without calculating or otherwise thinking.

Fourth, and perhaps most importantly, the teaching of number facts is a contentious and heated issue in American education. One approach owes much to connectionist theory (Thorndike, 1922) and, as we have seen in the case of the California controversies over textbook adoption, owes perhaps even more to fundamentalism in American political life. This approach is to teach students to memorize the number facts so that they can be recalled speedily and used *without any thought.* In this view, when students encounter a problem like $8 + 7$, they should not have to think, but should immediately "know"—or, it would be more accurate to say, *recall*—that $8 + 7 = 15$. In this view, figuring out the answer by using a calculator (or, God forbid, the fingers) is to be avoided. It is no exaggeration to say that some consider calculating under these circumstances to be tantamount to cheating. Knowing the number facts in the sense of recall is claimed to have some advantages. It allows one to engage in effective estimation and calculation of large numbers, and to devote attention to more interesting issues.

The traditional approach leads to drill, often involving flash cards or glitzy computer programs (which amount to the same thing) in which students are taught to memorize the facts and to recall them quickly, without thought. In many schools, drill-memorization occupies a central and quite large place in the mathematics curriculum, so that a good part of the first several grades is devoted to learning the number facts in this way.[26] Under these conditions, many children have little choice but to learn to memorize the number facts as taught. From the Thorndike point of view, this is success.

But consider several possible negative outcomes. One is that, if memory fails, children lack backup strategies (Siegler, 1988) to help solve the number combination problems. A second is that the pressure of memorization may produce anxiety in some children (although others find security in mindless activity). A third result is perhaps most important: Memorizing number facts is not doing mathematics. It is a dull, trivial activity that is a poor model for mathematical thinking. Drill in the number facts probably teaches children the unintended lesson that *mathematics is a subject in which one must get right answers quickly without thinking.*

Against this background, consider the CGI analysis of the learning of number facts. The basic theory is that number facts can be learned over a period of time in a meaningful way, with memorization playing only a minor role. Over time, children spontaneously memorize some number facts, especially simple doubles like 3 + 3, both in school and out. Why? Partly because they get bored calculating sums all the time. It is dull to figure out the sums repeatedly; after a while, it is more efficient to memorize them. Perhaps another reason is that children want to show how smart they are. What self-respecting 6-year-old does not know 2 + 2? In any event, some number facts are committed to memory. Then, again without instruction, children use these memorized facts to derive others. Thus, 6 + 7 is 13 "because I know that 6 + 6 is 12 and then one more is 13." Reasoning of this type is interesting: "Derived number solutions are based on understanding relations between numbers. . . . In many CGI classes, most children use Derived Facts before they have learned all the number facts at a recall level" (Carpenter et al., 1994, pp. 22–23). Children also use counting procedures in a very rapid way to solve small combinations problems, thus giving the appearance of recall when in fact calculation has been used. The CGI group is not alone in this account of number fact development (Baroody & Ginsburg, 1982; Ginsburg, 1989).

In brief, the developmental sequence is something like this. To deal with problems of joining, separating, and the like, children first model the actions and then develop mental solution procedures. And as all this is going on, children spontaneously memorize some number facts, without instruction; derive other number facts in a principled way; and may calculate still others very quickly (so that they appear to have been recalled). At the end of this process, children have achieved the desirable goal of memorizing many number facts. More importantly, if memory fails, they can get the answers in other ways, sometimes calculating or reasoning so fast that they appear to be drawing on memory. Also, they have *not* learned that *mathematics is that subject in which one must get right answers quickly without thinking.*

Educational Implications

This view of the developmental sequence leads to an emphasis on modeling as a general problem-solving strategy; on meaning and the understanding of relations rather than drill; and on the encouragement of invented strategies.

According to CGI, young children attempt to solve problems by modeling, or acting out, the action or relationships perceived in the problems. "The conception of problem solving as modeling could provide a unifying framework for thinking about problem solving in the primary grades" (Carpenter et al., 1993, p. 427). Students could benefit from attempting to act out solutions to many problems they do not understand in the course of learning school mathematics. Modeling is a method for sense making. Unfortunately, as students progress through the educational system, they seem to abandon this sensible approach in favor of a "mechanical application" of symbols, formulas, algorithms, and the like. The CGI view may be seen as "romantic," a story of lost innocence, of children abandoning their sense-making approach as they make their way

[26] One of Ginsburg's students, Marjorie-Hélène L. Déjean, reports that one commonly used textbook for first graders is divided into 13 chapters, 6 of which deal with addition and subtraction facts: addition facts through 7, addition facts through 10, subtraction facts through 7, subtraction facts through 10, addition and subtraction facts through 12, and addition and subtraction facts through 18. At the end of the book, there are 26 pages of extra practice, 13 of which cover addition and subtraction. One chapter provides 283 practice problems in addition facts with sums less than or equal to 7; another has 380 addition problems with sums less than or equal to 10.

through the mindless exercises of schooling. There is much to recommend this perspective (Ginsburg, 1996).

CGI adopts a distinctive perspective toward the learning of number facts—a topic of central importance to many teachers, parents, and administrators. The basic idea is not to let the learning of number facts—in the sense of memorizing them for recall—assume such a central place in mathematics education. Instead, the CGI view stresses building on children's "intuitive modeling skills" in order to promote "meaning making." Children should be encouraged to develop their modeling of problems and of the internalization of strategies, both of which help children to make sense of the number facts. Then, children should be helped to develop an understanding of the relations underlying the number combinations—patterns like commutativity, the "number families" ($3 + 4 = 7$ and $7–4 = 3$, and the like). In the course of this learning, children will spontaneously memorize some number facts, will learn to derive others, and will learn patterns that eliminate the need to memorize other number facts. Drill on number facts occupies a very minor role, if any, in this system.

Another example of the CGI approach involves invented strategies. Much early mathematics instruction involves learning algorithms, like the one for adding a column: "regrouping" (or what used to be called "carrying"), as in adding $24 + 37$. Before children learn the algorithm, they already understand something about adding as joining, and they are already capable of mental addition. In general, when presented with a problem of this type, children use the following type of strategy: "20 and 30 is 50, 4 and 7 is 11, 50 and 10 is 60, and 1 more is 61." Strategies like these are quite "natural." They appear even among unschooled individuals faced with the need to add (Petitto & Ginsburg, 1982). By contrast, the approach underlying the standard algorithm is "7 and 4 is 11, 20 and 30 is 50, the 10 (from the 11) makes it 60, and then 1 more is 61."

The standard algorithm has been created and agreed on (at least within certain cultures) as the convention because it is more efficient than the mental procedure (starting with the units allows one to cumulate all of the carried-over 10s and then to add all of the 10s at once). But, as CGI points out, this algorithm, and others like it, are not "transparent" with respect to why they work (this is particularly true of long division, which almost no one understands). Hence, learning it becomes a matter of rote memory and is very dull.

What to do? The CGI answer is to allow children to "invent" their own algorithms, as in the example above. Typically, an understanding of the base-10 system is implied: children intuitively break up the numbers into 10s and 1s. They add the 10s first, then the 1s, and then the 10s again if necessary. In a sense, the standard algorithm is simply a variant of the invented procedure (which, after all, must have come first in historical time). Another way of putting it is that children's invented procedure already contains the knowledge that the algorithm obscures. Therefore, CGI, along with others (Kamii, 1985; Madell, 1985), advocates allowing children to invent their own algorithms, which are meaningful, grounded as they are in the base-10 conceptual structure, and can lead to the development of estimation techniques (like rounding) and general number sense. Some authors go a step further, proposing that invented strategies can be used as the basis for explicit discussion of the base-10 logic behind the standard algorithm (Ginsburg, 1989).

Teacher Workshops and Support

Given this psychological theory and the educational principles that derive from it, CGI could have developed in several different directions. One direction might have been curriculum development. For example, in the CGI view, children derive number facts from an understanding of basic mathematical principles. Thus, understanding that addition is commutative, the child knows that if $6 + 3$ is 9, then $3 + 6$ must be 9 too, thus reducing by about half the number combinations that need to be learned. This approach might lead to the development of number facts curricula based on the learning of principles, not rote memory. Some authors have in fact done this (Thornton, 1979; Trivett, 1980).

But CGI has taken another approach: the education of teachers. It is assumed that teaching is based to a significant extent on teachers' knowledge (theories, beliefs) concerning students' cognition and learning (Carpenter, Fennema, & Franke, 1996). Consequently, helping teachers to develop a deeper understanding of students' knowledge and its development is a key to reforming mathematics education. Moreover, this understanding should be personally relevant to the teachers themselves. The overall goal is to "help teachers construct models of student thinking at a level of detail that is meaningful to teachers and useful to them in understanding their own students' thinking and making instructional decisions." (p. 14).

The CGI approach to doing this has several interesting characteristics. CGI begins by focusing teachers' attention on a relatively narrow domain—how children develop various strategies (especially modeling, counting, and invented procedures) for dealing with the types of *Join*, *Separate*, and other problems described above. Although this hardly covers everything that is important about children's mathematical thinking, it is a good starting point.[27] Further, it is assumed that what teachers learn from this experience—the conceptual frameworks they create—can deepen their understanding of children's mathematical thinking in general, as well as of mathematics itself, the mathematics curriculum, and general principles of teaching (Carpenter et al., 1996). The idea is that, in the process of learning about a particular strategy, such as counting on, teachers may come to realize that children develop interesting procedures on their own, and teachers may better appreciate—or appreciate *for the first time*—what addition is all about, how the curriculum needs to deal with it, and how it may be taught in an effective manner.

This seems like a tall order, but the argument is plausible. For example, seeing that a child adds mentally (as in the previous example of 24 + 37 is "20 and 30 is 50, 4 and 7 is 11, 50 and 10 is 60, and 1 more is 61") may force teachers to confront some basic issues previously ignored: Does the child know something interesting without having been taught? Is this common? What else might the child know? Is the child in fact doing something that is mathematically sensible? What principles is the child using, and how do they relate to the principles in the textbook about the base-10 system? Is the child doing anything very different from what the book teaches? If not, why does the child have so much trouble with what is in the book and yet appear so facile in the use of mental addition? How can addition be taught in a more effective way? What is good teaching? Teachers will and should develop different answers to these questions. But the experience of attempting to understand a child's learning may provide, to teachers who themselves have feared mathematics, or learned it poorly, or never *thought* about it very much, fundamental insights into children, mathematics, and teaching.

A second key feature of the CGI approach is shared with other programs (Schifter & Fosnot, 1993; Wood, Cobb, & Yackel, 1991): a constructivist approach to teacher education. The basic idea is that teachers should experience the same kind of learning we would like them to provide for their students. The teachers should be helped to construct, in their own terms, their own approach to mathematics education. This is done not through formal presentations, but through in-service activities, including interactions with students, which help teachers elaborate on their informal knowledge of students' thinking and learning.

The in-service program is carefully designed to promote certain kinds of constructions by the teachers (just as a good mathematics curriculum is designed to have students discover or construct certain kinds of ideas rather than others). In the CGI program, several implicit but nevertheless basic themes "permeated the teacher development program: (a) children can learn important mathematical ideas when they have opportunities to engage in solving a variety of problems; (b) individuals and groups of children will solve problems in a variety of ways; (c) children should have many opportunities to talk or write about how they solved problems; (d) teachers should elicit children's thinking; and (e) teachers should consider what children know and understand when they make decisions about mathematics instruction" (Fennema et al., 1996, p. 9).

The CGI teacher development program has two major components: workshops and classroom support. The workshops, attended by groups of teachers, most of whom are volunteers and some of whom were volunteered by administrators,[28] took place over several years,[29] and involved "many videotapes of individual children solving word problems which were carefully selected to illustrate critical aspects of children's thinking" (Fennema et al., in press, p. 9). Teachers engaged in discussion of the tapes, attempting to interpret children's behavior and what it means. (Anyone who has observed such videotapes knows that the images they present are very striking and arouse deep interest and involvement on the part of teachers, and lively discussion among them.) After the discussion, teachers were given written materials that described the official CGI analyses of the various episodes. Teachers were encouraged to test the validity of their own and the CGI interpretations against their own classes' behavior. Teachers returned to the classroom to give their students certain problems and to ascertain their methods of solution. In the next workshop, teachers returned to discuss their findings,

---

[27] We have been informed that, over the years, CGI has extended its focus beyond addition and subtraction, and, as of 1995, has included work on fractions and geometry. We look forward to publications describing CGI work in these areas.

[28] According to a personal communication from Tom Carpenter (August 10, 1995): "In theory all the teachers are volunteers, but in the recent study we used entire schools as the unit, so a number of teachers got volunteered either by the principal or through pressure from other teachers. Even in the initial study, many of the teachers were pressured into participating by administrators. In fact one district required all teachers to participate. The short answer is it is a bit of a mix."

[29] In the late spring of the first year, teachers attended a two-and-a-half-day workshop. The next year, there was a two-day workshop before school started and then fourteen three-hour workshops during the year. In the third and fourth years, there were few workshops, some of which were used for reflection.

revise their interpretations, and, in this manner, gradually construct new frameworks for understanding children's thinking and learning.

In the course of these workshops, teachers raised questions about what and how to teach. The CGI response was not to offer a specific curriculum, nor to urge the teachers to abandon the textbook in favor of some particular manipulatives or activities, but to help the teachers develop deeper knowledge of the children. "[W]e emphasized that the important criteria for making decisions about what and how to teach were children's understandings . . . we emphasized that they were professionals who should decide how their emerging knowledge of children's thinking should and could be used in their classrooms" (Fennema et al., 1996, p. 11).

The second component was classroom support, provided by CGI staff members and mentor teachers. They attended workshops, visited classrooms, discussed issues with teachers, and, in general, tried to help them in efforts to base instruction on their own analyses of children's thinking. During the first full year of the project, classroom visits took place about once a week; during the second full year, about once every two weeks; and in the last year, only occasionally.

Evaluation

The CGI team has made a careful (and rare) effort to evaluate what it has accomplished by examining teacher beliefs, teacher classroom practices, and student achievement. The evaluation work is still in progress, and the results are extensive; here, we report only a few illustrative findings. One study reports on 21 female teachers of grades 1, 2, and 3, who taught in schools in or near Madison, Wisconsin, a Midwestern, nonurban area. One of the schools was rural and had a 99% White population; another school was similar; and the third had 70% White children, of whom 26% were benefiting from a lunch subsidy program and were presumably not affluent. Data include transcriptions of classroom observations, interviews, scores on a scale of teacher beliefs, field notes of informal interactions, and student scores on tests of concepts, problem solving, and computational skill.

The results showed that, by the end of the three-year period of exposure to CGI, teachers' instruction had changed to include "increased emphasis on problem solving, more communication by the children about their problem-solving strategies, and clear evidence that the teacher was more apt to be attending to her own students' thinking when she made instructional decisions" (Fennema et al., in press, p. 19). Although there was a good deal of individual variation, teachers' beliefs about children became more cognitively guided over time, as illustrated, for example, by acceptance of the idea that children can develop strategies without direct instruction, and that the teachers' "role was to find out what children knew, and . . . that what children knew should be a major influence on all instructional decisions" (p. 32). Another study (Knapp & Peterson, 1995) showed that four years after being exposed to one year of CGI experience, 19 of 20 teachers continued to use elements of CGI in their classroom teaching, although only half reported using CGI as the "main basis" for their classroom work in mathematics. About a quarter of the teachers (6 of 20) were enthusiastic about CGI at the outset but, after several years, used the approach only occasionally.

Further, in all classrooms, children's performance on concepts and problem-solving tests improved with the introduction of CGI. Despite the CGI focus on strategy, invented algorithms, and the like, and despite the CGI de-emphasis on drill, students' computational skill did not decline. Students in CGI classes "did better than students in control classes" on measures of problem solving and number fact knowledge (Knapp & Peterson, 1995, p. 42). Also, there was a small positive relationship between teachers' change toward a CGI instructional approach and students' achievement: a correlation of .32 between teachers' CGI-type beliefs and students' problem solving (Peterson, Fennema, Carpenter, & Loef, 1989). Informal observations suggest that CGI children were "different" in that they showed an unusual degree of enthusiasm about mathematics and enjoyed talking about their thinking.

CGI is to be commended for its serious attention to evaluation. At the same time, we may point to weaknesses in some of the evaluation studies. To date, the CGI studies tend to employ measures of student outcome that have a fairly traditional focus on overt performance more than on underlying strategies, concepts, and the like.[30] Also, at least one of the evaluation studies (Fennema et al., in press) lacks a control group (a comparison with teachers and children not receiving CGI). In general, the quantitative data provide a limited (although useful) view of the accomplishments of CGI. By contrast, the qualitative data—particularly interviews with teachers (Fennema, Carpenter, Franke, & Carey, 1993; Knapp & Peterson, 1995)—provide a more detailed and convincing portrait of the rich learning experienced by CGI teachers.

Conclusions

Consider several basic questions about CGI—the same questions concerning application and research that we

[30] CGI researchers have also employed some relatively qualitative interview measures that have not yet been published.

raised earlier, in connection with textbook development—which lead us to some general reflections concerning the development of teacher training programs.

What Does CGI Teach Us about the Process of Application? CGI is a relatively small-scale and "pure" application. The route from research to application is fairly direct and simple. Basically, committed researchers obtained the funds to implement their approach, and then did it in a relatively small number of schools. This is child's play in comparison with the way research is brought to bear on the development of textbooks. The big question for CGI is: What happens next? Is there a way that CGI can be applied in the larger arena of American schools?

What Aspects of the Basic Research Were Most Useful for CGI? The project uses both general constructivist principles (children develop their own strategies, attempt to make sense, and so on) and a very specific analysis of certain aspects of mathematical knowledge—for example, the typology of problems (*Join,* etc.) and the strategies used to solve them, and base-10 and place-value concepts. In a way, this is an odd combination. The constructivism might at first seem to clash with the highly detailed analysis of children's knowledge. Must children encounter *only* these problems and develop *only* these strategies of solution? Yet, CGI's rationale for combining the two makes sense: The specific examples of coping with *Separate* problems, base-10 issues, and the like provide the evidentiary basis for teachers to develop more general frameworks for understanding the development of mathematical thinking. In the absence of such examples, constructivism becomes simply a slogan—and a politically correct one, at that. Another way of looking at it is to say that use of constructivist principles—a focus on how children construct meanings—helps teachers to teach *children* and to promote *mathematical thinking,* and, in a sense, enables both teachers and children to go beyond the specific mathematics that happens to be involved.

For CGI, the metaphor of modeling as problem solving is basic. The child acts out a joining problem to solve it. This notion is useful, and similar ideas have been advocated by others (Papert, 1980). But attention will have to be devoted to the issue of how far one can push the idea of modeling in mathematics education.

Constructivist theory was useful in guiding CGI's approach to teacher education. Most in-service education involves lecturing to teachers who do not listen to the lectures. CGI takes seriously the notion that, like their students, teachers need to experience situations designed to help them construct their own personal understandings. Teachers need to reinvent constructivism just as children need to reinvent mathematics.

How Are the Available Research and Theory Deficient in Speaking to the Educational Problems CGI Wishes to Solve? One possible criticism of CGI is that the project's focus on joining and separating, part–whole relations, and comparison during the early years of schooling is overly narrow. In two senses, this criticism is probably not valid. First, CGI has already broadened its research base to include topics such as base-10 concepts and multiplication (Carpenter et al., 1994). Second, the whole point of focusing on specific material is to use it as a stepping-off point for teachers to develop more general frameworks for dealing with children's thinking and learning. The project's reliance on a relatively narrow range of research is not necessarily the liability it may appear to be.

Despite these arguments, there seems to be a real danger in the CGI approach. The amount of detail provided teachers about the classes of problems and the solution processes—through written materials and lectures as well as the videotapes—might serve to bias teachers' frameworks more than the CGI philosophy intends. By the time one figures out the intricacies of all the problem types and strategies, one's mind is a bit numb, and it may be hard to set aside this elaborate theory in an effort to move in new conceptual directions. Despite its constructivism, does the CGI immersion of teachers in the details of Joining and Separating promote a view of mathematics as calculation, and slight the roles of open-ended and playful inquiry? The flavor of CGI is strongly calculational, even within its sense-making context, and calculation is not all that mathematical thinking is about.

CGI's assertion of the value of building on children's informal mathematics needs to be tempered. Young children believe: "Numbers are what you get when you count things and combine or take apart [other numbers]" (Gelman, 1994, p. 70). Yet, much of mathematics involves dealing with numbers of a different sort, like the rationals or imaginary numbers, which do not involve simple counting, and which are notoriously difficult for children to learn (Behr, Lesh, Post, & Silver, 1983). Consequently, "further learning often requires that one transcend the principles that guided early learning. . . . [C]ontinued adherence to these principles could yield misinterpretations" (Gelman, 1994, p. 70). Perhaps this clash between what the child brings to the task of learning and the nature of the rational numbers explains children's pervasive difficulty with fractions. Some aspects of children's informal knowledge, like their heavy reliance on counting, may not be a very good foundation on which to build school instruction in topics like fractions and in fact may need to be overcome. The constructivist mind can produce bugs and misconceptions, as well as clever invented strategies and informal concepts.

How Can CGI Be Improved? The project might profit from more input from mathematicians. Mathematicians interested in education (many are not) sometimes feel that psychologists understand little about mathematics and teach aspects of it that are less than scintillating. They may be right. Perhaps more contact with mathematicians would serve to broaden the rather narrow focus of CGI.

CGI proposes to provide teachers with general principles to guide mathematics education, not to give them specific activities. The general approach is to help teachers to think, not to tell them what to do. It is certainly important to help teachers to think, and it is also true that simply telling teachers what to do—providing very specific activities—does not work if teachers do not understand what they are doing. But expecting teachers essentially to create their own curriculum on the basis of the general principles may be unrealistic and unfair. Teachers *are* professionals, but some do not have enough time to create activities; others do not have a good enough knowledge of mathematics to do it; others are simply not very creative; and almost all are overworked. There is something entirely realistic in teachers' saying, "Tell me what to do today." Perhaps teachers need more help in creating curriculum than the general CGI principles, or other psychological insights, can give them (Ginsburg, 1996).

The most impressive contributions of CGI may be that it takes seriously the problem of teacher education and it attempts to incorporate psychological research and principles into that process. This stance takes an enormous amount of thought and effort, but it is only the first step. Next, CGI needs to face the issue of further dissemination. How does a pure application step out into the real world? How does a labor-intensive program like CGI get implemented for thousands of needy teachers, and what happens to it when it encounters the multitude of inner-city schools that have a desperate need for educational reform at all levels?[31]

General Reflections on Teacher Education Programs. The essence of CGI's approach is to help teachers develop their own ways of thinking about children's mathematics. Our criticisms were that perhaps some of the specifics of CGI may get in the way of this goal and perhaps teachers need more than such ways of thinking. Despite these possible difficulties, we wish to emphasize the novelty and importance of the CGI approach. In a way, it is an implementation of two venerable ideas. One was Dewey's dictum that "rational method in arithmetic must be based on the psychology of number" (McLellan & Dewey, 1895, p. 22). CGI relies heavily on general ideas about constructivism and specific ideas about adding, base 10, and the like. Other efforts at teacher education might rely on different principles, such as those of Vygotsky (Tharp & Gallimore, 1991). Whatever psychology is employed, the goal is to enable teachers to use psychological principles to guide their work. If teachers are to perform as genuine *professionals,* they must be able to rely on principled ideas to inform their action.

A second venerable principle stems from William James, who maintained that teachers must create, out of scientific psychology, their own personal and psychological theories, which could guide their teaching in the concrete world of the classroom. "Psychology is a science, and teaching is an art; and sciences never generate arts directly out of themselves. An intermediary inventive mind must make the application, by using its originality" (James, 1958, pp. 23–24). CGI takes the radical step of placing confidence in the teacher's "intermediary inventive mind." In our view, such an approach is essential to a constructivist approach to education. Teachers need to create personal theories to understand and influence individual children's sometimes idiosyncratic constructions of mathematics. Whether CGI is the best method to nurture the intermediary inventive minds may be debated. But the goal of empowering teachers to think about their students' mathematical thinking needs to be taken seriously by all those concerned with teacher education.

Assessment

The final application we consider is assessment—how theories and methods from developmental psychology have been used to develop novel approaches to measuring children's performance and knowledge. These techniques range from standard tests to clinical interviews to methods for examining knowledge in the zone of proximal development (ZPD).

The Demand

In the 1980s and 1990s, there were many calls for new approaches to the assessment of mathematics achievement.

[31] We are informed that CGI is already involved in activities in several American cities and intends to get involved in national dissemination of its approach, so that data concerning these thorny questions will eventually be available.

The NCTM, which played a major role in this process, issued a *Standards* document devoted exclusively to the topic of assessment (National Council of Teachers of Mathematics, 1995). The general argument was that the kind of reforms NCTM envisions in mathematics education—among them, to encourage student thinking and understanding, to introduce complex mathematics in meaningful ways, to encourage mathematics achievement in minority groups—cannot be accomplished without major improvements in assessment. "[T]raditional assessment practices . . . are inconsistent with these new views of mathematics and how learning progresses" (p. 3).

Why is traditional assessment inadequate? The criticisms are familiar and plausible to anyone who has ever taken standard achievement tests in school. The tests tend to emphasize computation, often not demanding a great deal of thought. Because teachers teach to the tests, the curriculum ends up placing heavy emphasis on computation. Under these conditions, students are not encouraged to grapple with the concepts and ideas of mathematics; instead, they attempt to learn whatever is needed to get them through the tests—usually, procedures of one kind or another. Further, the traditional tests tend to underestimate the abilities of students, and "have been used unintentionally as filters that deny underrepresented groups access to the further study of mathematics" (p. 1). Partly because they tend to be given at the end of the year, and partly because their essence is basically to rank students along a common scale, achievement tests fail to provide information of practical value to students and teachers in the classroom. Test data do not help teachers to teach, nor students to learn. In view of these deficiencies, new views of and approaches to testing are sorely needed.

The *Standards* propose several reforms. First, assessments should focus on understanding, on thinking, and on problem solving, not on the mechanical aspects of mathematics. According to the California Framework (which, as we have seen, is modeled on the *Standards*), "We must be interested in what students are really thinking and understanding. Students may be able to answer correctly but still have fundamental misunderstandings. It is through the probing of students' thinking that we get the information we need to provide appropriate learning experiences" (California Department of Education, 1992, p. 52). Second, assessment should provide information useful for teaching, as the preceding quotation indicates. Third, assessment should employ information from multiple sources, not just tests, and especially not achievement tests given at the end of the school year (preventing the current teacher from using the results). "Observing, listening, and questioning are the most common methods for gathering evidence of learning during instruction" (National Council of Teachers of Mathematics, 1995, p. 46). And finally, assessment is to be done in the classroom, by teachers: "Teachers are the persons who are in the best position to judge the development of students' progress and, hence, must be considered the primary assessors of students" (p. 1). As with CGI, there is "a shift toward relying on the professional judgment of teachers" (p. 2).

In brief, according to the *Standards,* assessment is a responsibility of teachers, who should gather information from several sources in order to gain practical insights into students' thinking—specifically, insights that will contribute to the process of instruction.

Nature and Components of Assessment

In our view (Ginsburg, 1986a), assessment is research in miniature—research designed to achieve an understanding of an individual case. Assessment is not fundamentally different in method from what is ordinarily considered to be research. Both use, or aspire to use, reliable and valid techniques of data gathering to arrive at new psychological theory. We use *theory* in the broad sense—models, understanding, insights, hypotheses, ideas about people. The main distinction between research and assessment is in the degree of generalization intended. Research is meaningless unless it can be generalized beyond the initial source of data; by contrast, the aim of assessment is to comprehend the individual case—the original source of data—not to generalize beyond it. But both research and assessment use data to generate new theory, whether of the individual as such, or of people or phenomena in general. In this usage, classroom assessment involves teachers' obtaining evidence to create practical theories about the psychological functioning and learning of their students.

If assessment and research are similar in the ways described, then research has many lessons to offer for the improvement of assessment. Research into children's mathematical thinking has employed various investigative techniques other than standard tests. Examples include Piaget's clinical interview method and Vygotsky's notion of the zone of proximal development (ZPD). These innovative methods of research stem from developments in theory. As Vygotsky (1978) put it: "Any fundamentally new approach to a scientific problem inevitably leads to new methods of investigation and analysis" (p. 58). The new methods of investigation and analysis may be among the most important contributions of cognitive researchers. They have much to offer with respect to practical problems of assessment in mathematics education.

We consider the methodological "applications" of researchers under the following rubric. Assessment may be considered to focus on four aspects of functioning: (a) performance ("Can José add two-digit numbers?"), (b) traits ("Does he have good 'calculation skill'?"), (c) processes ("What are the strategies used for adding?"), and (d) learning potential ("Can he learn to add?"). Each of these may be measured, with varying success, by different techniques: standard testing, observation, think aloud, clinical interview, and "testing the limits."

Performance. The assessment of performance at first seems very simple. The teacher wants to investigate whether a child can do a certain type of work, such as adding fractions with unlike denominators, or rounding decimal values. The assessment question may center solely on the individual or may involve a comparison of the individual with an appropriate group. In the first case, the issue is whether Fatimah can or cannot add the fractions, regardless of what anyone else is doing. This is a question of "criterion-referenced" testing. In the second case, by contrast, the issue is normative—how Fatimah's performance compares with that of her peers.

For the most part, performance is measured in one of two ways. The first is through classroom tests, constructed by teachers, which are composed of problems representative of the domain of interest and which examine students' simple success or failure. Another method is the standardized achievement test, which uses similar problems (although often in multiple-choice format) and usually involves national or at least State norms. Such standardized tests are one part of Thorndike's legacy (or his curse, depending on how you evaluate them).

In one sense, classroom tests and standardized achievement tests do not need a great deal of improvement. Teachers know what aspects of students' performance they want to measure, and, generally, they are capable of devising test problems in the area of interest. Similarly, achievement tests are reasonably effective at measuring routine aspects of mathematical performance, particularly involving calculations. After all, the question is simply whether the child can solve certain problems or knows certain number facts, and/or whether the child does this better or worse than the other children in the class. The issue is not whether the classroom or achievement test accurately measures the child's potential or provides insight into thought processes.

Tests of performance can yield useful information. We want to know whether a child has mastered certain specific areas of knowledge, such as simple number facts. And we almost always want to know whether the child's performance is roughly at the level of peers', or is severely deficient, or precocious.[32] Judicious interpretation is essential. Low scores should not necessarily be interpreted as measures of ability, potential, or mathematical aptitude; indeed, they may only point to poor teaching.

At the same time, we should recognize that performance tests, no matter how reliable and valid, may produce unintended negative consequences. For one thing, what they measure (reliably and validly) may have less than earth-shattering importance from a mathematical point of view. This would be of no great significance were it not for the fact that what tests measure unfortunately often drives the curriculum. "Short, closed, stereotyped examination questions are bound to encourage imitative rehearsal and practice on similar tasks in the classroom" (Bell, Burkhardt, & Swan, 1992, p. 119). If the curriculum is to offer challenging mathematics, then assessment tasks themselves should "represent learning activities of high educational value" (p. 121). Stated another way: It is hardly worthwhile to expend effort on measuring performance on tasks that are not worth teaching in depth.

Several efforts to improve both classroom and achievement tests have been initiated by mathematics educators. For example, the British Shell Centre Group (Bell et al., 1992) has developed an extensive system of achievement testing that has been explicitly designed to include material of practical relevance, require complex and comprehensive problem-solving skills, permit a wide range of responses, and require an extended period of problem-solving skills. Tasks of a similar nature have been developed and are widely used in The Netherlands (de Lange, 1993). Performance tests like these are said to have "curriculum validity" in that spending time on them benefits student learning; indeed, it would be educationally useful for them to drive instruction. Others have proposed a similar approach (Frederiksen & Collins, 1989).

This kind of approach has affected everyday classroom testing as well. Publishers have developed materials stress-

[32] One of us has suggested another use for performance tests. Even "a dumb test can be exploited as a useful assessment technique, provided children are encouraged to reflect on and reveal the solution processes employed" (Ginsburg et al., 1992, p. 286). Thus, after giving a standard performance test, the teacher can explore with students how they solved the problems in question. This exercise usually reveals a wealth of interesting cognitive activities and mathematical ideas, and may teach students that they in fact solve even uninteresting problems in interesting ways that contain a good deal of implicit mathematical knowledge. (It can also reveal that some students are clueless.)

ing "authentic assessment" for use in the classroom (Silver Burdett Ginn, 1995a), and these emphasize relatively open-ended problems requiring complex processes of solution.

In essence, the new types of tests attempt to change the criteria for both the "good" problem and the "correct" response. They get away from the traditional focus on calculational problems with short responses, and open up the playing field to more complex and interesting tasks and richer responses. Still, they yield information on whether and to what extent the student "gets it," but what the student now has to get in order to be successful on these tests is very different from what was required before. (The tests also yield some information about strategies of solution, as discussed below.)

For the most part, these reforms have been influenced only in a very general (but still important) way by psychological research on the development of mathematical thinking. The "constructivist" (of whatever variety) theoretical approach leads to the valuing of responses that are very different from those encouraged by traditional achievement tests. In the new theoretical atmosphere, simple correct responses (for example, to number fact problems) are considered "mechanical," "merely rote," and hardly worth measuring—at least if one is concerned with genuine understanding and complex problem solving. If this is so, then the fact that scores on traditional achievement tests correlate with one another and with grades is not particularly impressive. What is considered to be the main evidence for the concurrent and predictive validity of achievement tests only confirms their banality. In brief, the newer theories lead one to focus on complex content and methods of solution, to downplay the importance of the traditional achievement tests in measuring significant learning, and to realize that those tests do not have a monopoly on scientific respectability. To this not inconsiderable extent, then, current research and theory have influenced the creation of tests of performance.

Traits or General Psychological Characteristics. Psychologists and educators often find it useful to conceptualize others' minds in terms of various "traits"—general psychological characteristics, such as "ability"—which are thought to have a certain explanatory power. Thus, we say that a child is creative or inquisitive or rigid in thinking. Psychological concepts at this level do not offer the specificity of cognitive process explanations (for example, a child got the answer 5 because he or she counted on 2 more from 3), and may even appear to be similar to performance measures. (Thus, in practice, how different is the trait of rigidity from repeated performances of rigid behavior, or high math achievement from high math proficiency?) Trait notions have the advantage of generality and convergence with everyday, commonsense notions. Several psychological theories posit traits like these (Sternberg, 1985), and certainly their use is common in the everyday discourse of teachers and educators.

In the area of mathematical thinking, several traditional diagnostic tests—chief among them, the KeyMath Diagnostic Arithmetic Test (Connelly, Nachtman, & Pritchett, 1976)—have attempted to provide measures of general mathematical ability or more specific "traits" such as computational ability or conceptual skill (see Baroody, 1987a, for a critical review). Such tests provide normative information; from them, one might learn that a particular child ranks at the 20th percentile in computational skill and at the 43rd percentile in conceptual ability. Tests like these, usually administered and interpreted by school psychologists, are valuable to the extent that (a) they provide the educator with information illuminating important psychological characteristics of children and (b) they lead to effective educational activities. For the teacher, learning that a child is proficient in calculational ability but not computational skill may be of some use in attempting to understand the child's learning and in designating broad areas of strength or weakness that deserve closer attention.

Recent research and theory have influenced the development of at least one normative test, the Test of Early Mathematics Ability (TEMA) (Ginsburg & Baroody, 1983, 1990), which provides trait information (and, as we shall see, information concerning process as well). Nationally normed, the TEMA focuses on various aspects of informal and formal knowledge in children from preschool through approximately third grade. The test items were selected from data-gathering procedures used in cognitive developmental research on mathematical thinking, particularly the work of Ginsburg and colleagues (Baroody & Ginsburg, 1982; Ginsburg, Posner, & Russell, 1981a; Ginsburg et al., 1981b; Ginsburg & Russell, 1981; Houlihan & Ginsburg, 1981). The general procedure was to modify relevant tasks from these studies so that they could be easily administered to individual children by school psychologists and classroom teachers. Some tasks involve concrete objects, others require written materials, and still others are entirely mental, involving no materials at all.

The test provides information at several different levels. The tester can use national norms to obtain an overall ranking of the child relative to peers in terms of a general "Math Quotient" (analogous to an IQ score); can compare the child's performance in Informal Mathematics Ability and Formal Mathematics Ability; and can examine the child's performance in various subareas of formal and informal mathematical thinking (e.g., concepts of relative magnitude, number facts, and counting).

How useful is this information? TEMA scores correlate reasonably well with those of other relevant tests,[33] but, more importantly, teachers report that TEMA results are useful in pointing to children's unexpected proficiency in the "trait" of Informal Mathematics Ability. Most often, tests like the TEMA are given to children experiencing difficulty in school mathematics, and the teacher already knows about existing deficiencies, particularly in written calculation. Therefore, the Formal Mathematics Ability score may not be particularly valuable because, like an achievement test score, it simply confirms what the teacher already knows. But what the teacher may not realize is that the child who cannot do some aspect of written arithmetic nevertheless may display informal skills in related areas of mental calculation, just like the children in various research studies (Nunes et al., 1993). In this way, the TEMA may help school psychologists and teachers to think differently about their students' mental functioning with respect to mathematics.[34]

Tests are based, at least implicitly, on theories of mind. To the extent that tests are derived from useful research and theory, they may help educators to conceptualize students' mathematical thinking. In other words, the contribution of theory-based tests like the TEMA may not be so much to predict relative success under current conditions (achievement tests already do that quite accurately) as to help educators think differently about children's learning. Indeed, tests have the potential to do this on a very wide scale because they affect the lives of a great many children. According to the publisher's estimate, by the end of 1995, the TEMA had been given to some 400,000 children, and the KeyMath had probably been administered to many more.

Process. There is widespread agreement that psychological tests, particularly those designed for use in education, need to focus on more than overt performance, achievement, and general psychological traits. Information about these matters may be useful, but tests must also provide insight into the workings of children's minds—the concepts, understandings, and strategies responsible for a child's mathematical behavior. Research and theory have made their most important contributions to the development of assessment procedures like these. We now consider three approaches to the measurement of the underlying process—standardized tests, probes, and clinical interviews—and conclude this section with a discussion of learning potential and the Brown–Campione approach to assessment.

Standardized Tests. The most traditional approach to measuring the processes of mathematical thinking involves standard tests. Several authors have proposed that new kinds of tests be developed to assess underlying cognitive processes (Glaser, 1981; Royer, Cisero, & Carlo, 1993), particularly in the area of mathematical thinking (Lesh & Lamon, 1992). Instead of measuring mathematics achievement or calculational ability, such tests would assess children's strategies and concepts.

The essence of most of these tests is the method of *standardized administration,* which demands that the tester exert control sufficient to ensure that the administration of test items is virtually identical for all subjects. The basic argument is: "If the scores obtained by different persons are to be comparable, testing conditions must obviously be the same for all. . . . Such a requirement is only a special application of the need for controlled conditions in all scientific observations" (Anastasi, 1988, p. 25). All subjects must receive the same test stimuli in the same manner. To do otherwise, the argument goes, would be to render the data uninterpretable. If subjects were to receive different test stimuli, then the tester could not confidently attribute subsequent variations in performance to individual differences or to variations in the way the test was administered.

Few standardized tests have been developed to measure processes of mathematical thinking. The TEMA (Ginsburg & Baroody, 1983, 1990) allows the examiner to make some inferences about underlying process, although the test was designed mainly to provide information concerning "trait" scores of Informal and Formal Mathematics Ability. Thus, one item, which is intended mainly to contribute to an assessment of the child's Formal Mathematics Ability, presents the child with a column addition problem and is scored "correct" if the child uses the standard algorithm. But the tester could use the item as an opportunity to observe whether the child employs another procedure, like an invented procedure or a bug.

Similarly, the achievement tests developed in Britain (Bell et al., 1992) and The Netherlands (de Lange, 1993)

[33] For example, the TEMA correlates significantly with the Diagnostic Achievement Battery Math Calculation subtests at the 6- and 8-year-old levels, with *r*s of .40 and .59, respectively, and with the Slossen Intelligence test, the *r* being a highly significant .66.

[34] Some children perform poorly on informal mathematical tasks. In these cases, the test may helps the teacher see the need for remedying difficulties with informal mathematics before launching into formal mathematics.

were intended to provide insight into complex problem-solving procedures and "higher order thinking skills" (de Lange, 1993, p. 274). For example, in one problem, children are presented with a graph that "describes what happens when three athletes . . . enter a 400-meter hurdles race. Imagine that you are the race commentator. Describe what is happening as carefully as you can. You do not need to measure anything accurately" (Bell et al., 1992, p. 132). Children need to employ more interesting and complex thought processes on open-ended tasks like these than they do on most standard tests, and, presumably, children's responses to the test items mirror those thought processes in some way.

With respect to this approach to testing, the key question then refers to the kind of system the test employs to score and otherwise interpret the rich responses it elicits. The authors' general approach is to score primarily to measure achievement, rather than to obtain detailed information about cognitive processes. Figure 7.6 presents the authors "suggested marking scheme" for six students who have solved the problem (students A–F), as well as a sample script from student C (Simon). The scoring system assigns points for reading correctly certain features of the graph (for example, that runner C stopped at a certain point) and also involves an evaluation of the general quality of the student's written explanation. All of this may be very valuable for achievement testing, but it does not exploit as fully as possible the information concerning mathematical thinking available in students' responses: the test authors fail to provide systematic ways of conceptualizing and assessing the thought processes in question. Indeed, doing this would be a rather large task. Because children's responses to the open-ended questions are so rich, a rather elaborate coding system—perhaps too elaborate for the needs of most teachers—would be required.

The Diagnostic Test of Arithmetic Strategies (DTAS) (Ginsburg & Mathews, 1984) is distinctive in that it was designed entirely on the basis of available research to provide explicit information concerning strategies underlying children's calculation. For the present discussion, the most interesting parts of the test involve the measurement of *Strategy* and of *Mental Calculation* (for each of the standard arithmetic operations—addition, subtraction, multiplication, and division). The DTAS allows the examiner to determine whether the child employs (accurately or not) the standard algorithms to solve arithmetic problems in the areas of addition, subtraction, multiplication, and division, or instead uses various invented algorithms or bugs. The test is not normed; the goal is simply to identify the use of various strategies, not to rank the child against peers.

		Script					
		A	B	C	D	E	F
1 mark for each of these	At start, C takes lead		1	1		1	1
	After a while, C stops	1	1	1	1	1	
	Near end, B overtakes A		1	1	1	1	
	B Wins		1	1	1	1	
2 marks for 4 of these, or 1 mark for 2 of these	A and B Pass C		✓	✓			
	C starts running again		✓		✓	✓	
	C runs at slower pace					✓	
	A slows down *or* B speeds up	✓	✓	✓	✓	✓	
	A is second *or* C is last		✓	✓	✓	✓	
Quality of commentary		0	2	1	2	0	1
TOTAL		1	8	6	7	3	4

Example 8. Sample scripts.

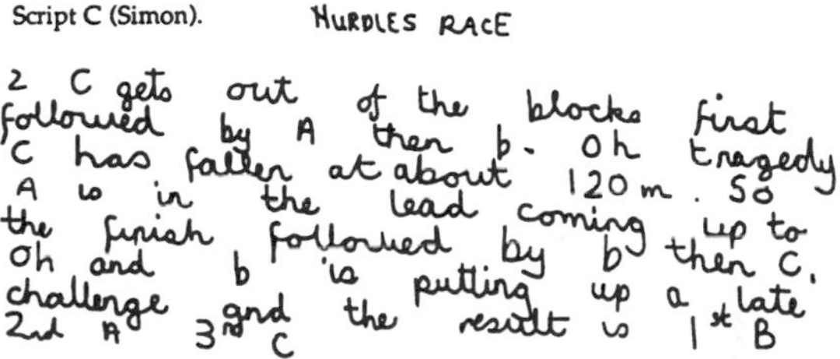

Figure 7.6 Marking scheme. From "Balanced assessment of mathematical performance," by A. Bell, H. Burkhardt, & M. Swan, 1992. In R. Lesh & S. J. Lamon (Eds.), *Assessment of authentic performance in school mathematics* (pp. 119–144). Washington, DC: American Association for the Advancement of Science Press. Copyright © 1992 by the American Association for the Advancement of Science Press. Reprinted with permission.

The section on mental calculation presents the child with four problems (in the case of addition, the problems are given verbally: 14 and 13; 35 and 20; 42 and 17; and 29 and 12) as follows: "Now I want you to do some adding problems in your head. Do them any way you want. Tell me out loud how you are doing the problem in your head" (p. 12). Thus, the presentation of problems is standardized, although the examiner relies not only on the child's spoken answer but also on a "thinking aloud" method to obtain information about methods of solution. The scoring system requires the tester to identify the child's response as falling into any of the following categories, the first two of which derive from research findings on mental addition:

- Counting (from the larger number, fingers, tallies).
- Simplification: converting to simpler form (as in 14 and 13 is 10 and 10, and then 4 and 3).
- Imaginary column addition.
- Other.
- No response, or a guess.

The section on written calculation draws on both old (Buswell & John, 1926) and new research on "habits" and "bugs" underlying children's calculation (Brown & Burton, 1978). It presents children with carefully selected problems designed to reveal specific bugs. Thus, the two addition problems,

$$\begin{array}{r} 32 \\ \underline{+7} \end{array} \quad \text{and} \quad \begin{array}{r} 21 \\ \underline{+6} \end{array}$$

can be done correctly by using the standard algorithm, but the bug "addition like multiplication" will yield distinctive incorrect answers: 109 and 87, respectively. The test employs standard problems designed to identify the most common and important bugs: addition like multiplication; zero makes zero (as in 26 + 20 = 40); no carry, all digits on the bottom (as in 28 + 14 = 312), and so on. This test then can provide the school psychologist or teacher with a very precise account of the thought processes underlying the child's calculations, both correct and incorrect, formal and informal.

Although useful in measuring clearly defined cognitive processes, standard tests of this type suffer from several limitations. One difficulty involves validity. It may not be clear that the intended bug is really being measured, because observed responses can often be generated by a number of bugs. For example, if a child does 26 + 20 = 40, one reasonable explanation is that the child used the "zero makes zero" bug. Thus, the child added 6 + 0 = 0 because of the belief that zero added to something makes zero, and then added 2 + 2 = 4, to get the answer 40. But there are other possibilities as well. For example, the child could have been using a multiplication bug, multiplying by units. Operating with this bug, the child begins by multiplying units by units (6 × 0 = 0) and then 10s by 10s (2 × 2 = 4) and also gets the answer 40. Because both bugs generate the same answer—that is, both are sufficient but not necessary explanations—the interpretation of the child's response is ambiguous and the answer itself is not an infallible guide to the underlying bug.

Another difficulty arises when the child employs a bug that the test is not designed to measure. Research shows that there are literally hundreds of distinguishable bugs (Brown & Burton, 1978), so that it is impossible for a standardized test, which necessarily must be administered in about 30 minutes, to measure many, let alone all of them. Hence, on a test of this type, answers generated by bugs that were not intended to be measured must remain uninterpretable. (In this situation, a computer-driven test might prove more effective.)

In brief, standard tests of this type suffer from two basic limitations: (a) a strategy different from the one postulated can produce the observed behavior (the postulated strategy is *sufficient,* not necessary), and (b) an unanticipated strategy may go unidentified (or merely be categorized as "other").

Probes. If standard tests provide inconclusive information concerning underlying process, one solution is the "organized probe"—a highly structured and limited form of clinical interviewing (Ginsburg, 1990), which was developed to be used in parallel with the TEMA but is also of some general interest. The intent was that after the TEMA had been given in standard fashion, many examiners would find it useful to probe further into the thought processes that produced the observed performance, particularly in the case of errors. Most examiners, however, have not had training or experience in assessing students' thinking. Consequently, an attempt was made to provide examiners with a structured and comfortable procedure for probing the strategies and concepts underlying students' responses to the TEMA. These probes provide a useful introduction to the more difficult (and, it will be argued, more rewarding) activity of clinical interviewing.

The probes for each of the 65 items of the TEMA first attempt to establish whether the student has understood the basic question. Often, students produce an incorrect response because they have misinterpreted a minor feature of the question. The probes attempt to distinguish this situation from one in which students do not understand the question because they fail to comprehend the relevant concept.

For example, one of the TEMA items attempts to deal with addition of multiples of 10s by asking: "Here are some questions about adding money. We'll pretend that you have some money and I give you some more. If you start with nine dollars and I give you one ten-dollar bill, what do you end up with?" The wording, of course, was intended to be clear in the first place, but some children misunderstand the question, perhaps from confusion about the phrase, "What do you end up with?" Consequently, the probes make available an alternative wording: "If you have nine dollars and I give you one ten-dollar bill, how much do you have altogether?" In response to this, some children suddenly see the light and exclaim, "Oh, is that what you meant!"

Next, the probes attempt to determine the strategies and processes used by the student to solve the problem. For example, in the case of concrete addition, the basic TEMA question is: "Joey has two pennies. He gets one more penny. How many does he have altogether? If you want, you can use your fingers to help you find your answer." (As the questions are asked, the examiner shows the child the numbers of pennies involved.) Under conditions of standard test administration, the examiner may or may not learn from the child's overt behavior what problem-solving process was employed. In an effort to clarify this matter, the probes then attempt to determine whether the student used such procedures as counting on the fingers, mental counting, or memorized number facts. Three types of maneuvers are suggested. The first is: "It's OK to use your fingers. Put your hands on the table and show me how you do this. Tell me out loud what you are doing." This encourages externalization of the strategy in behavior and thinking aloud. In response, some children, who had previously thought that it was improper or even cheating to use the fingers, breathe a sigh of relief and show the examiner their finger-counting procedure or tell about it. A second question is: "How did you know the answer was ______?" In this case, some children say, "I know that 3 and 2 is 5 because I just knew the answer. I learned it." If the answer was given quickly, the child's explanation may be a good indication of the use of memorized facts. A third question is: "Why does 6 pennies and 2 make ______ altogether?" In response to this question, some children say, "It had to be 8 because I know that 6 and 1 is 7 and then 1 more must be 8." Here, the use of a reasoning strategy is evident. Probes appear to be a very useful procedure in educational testing and seem to merit careful evaluation.

Clinical Interviews. The essence of standardized administration is the constraint that the interviewer test all children in as constant and unvarying a manner as possible. Under conditions of standard administration, the tester is not allowed to rephrase the question if the child does not seem to understand it, and the tester is certainly not allowed to pose different questions to different children.

In the course of his work with IQ tests, Piaget concluded that standardized testing—despite its laudable goal of avoiding bias in testing—often provides little insight into children's thinking (Piaget, 1976). The main weakness of standardized testing, according to Piaget, is its very essence (and, in a sense, its strength): the requirement that all children be treated in the same manner. If this is done, the examiner cannot effectively deal with misunderstanding of questions and cannot probe for methods of solution. For example, if a child who speaks a dialect fails to understand a key word, the examiner cannot reword the question, in dialect, to tap the child's understanding. Or, if the hypothesis is that a response is produced by a particular strategy, then the examiner is constrained from devising new questions to identify it. Although effective in ranking children's performance, standardized testing is often inadequate for the purpose of uncovering their thinking.

To overcome these weaknesses inherent in standard testing, Piaget developed the "clinical interview" method, which we believe is the most informative—and difficult—technique available for the purpose of assessing mathematical thinking. The clinical interview is not a sloppy form of pilot work that needs to be standardized. It is a principled method that, for some purposes, is superior to standardized administration. Indeed, in our view, it is one of Piaget's most important contributions (Ginsburg, 1997a) to psychology.

The goal of the clinical interview is to identify the child's underlying processes of thought. The essence of the clinical interview is its flexible, responsive, and open-ended nature. Although at the outset the interviewer has available several tasks likely to be appropriate for the topic at hand, initial questions are intentionally quite general, allowing the child's response to influence the direction and content of the interview. The interviewer employs nonspecific questions such as "How did you do it?" or "What did you say to yourself?" or "How would you explain it to a friend?" so as to encourage rich verbalization and to avoid biasing response. The clinical interview is a distinctive form of discourse in which the interviewer asks the child to reflect on and articulate thinking processes. As the interview evolves, tasks and questions are determined in part by the child's responses. Tasks are varied and modified, becoming more specific in order to focus on particular aspects of thinking, and more difficult in order to test the limits of understanding. In the clinical interview, the examiner's behavior is to some degree contingent on the child's; in the standard test, the child's behavior is always contingent on the examiner's questions.

The interview is a highly theoretical activity in which the interviewer constantly makes and tests hypotheses about the child's thinking. The interview combines several methods: observation, test, experimentation, and "think aloud." The interviewer (a) observes the child's behavior and listens to the child's verbalizations; (b) presents "test items"—problems of various sorts, often involving concrete objects; (c) experiments with different questions or tasks (for example, comparing the effects of large and small numbers, as one varies conditions in an experiment) to test hypotheses; and (d) asks the child to think aloud, to verbalize thought processes as explicitly as possible.

An interview is time-consuming and demanding; it requires 20 to 60 minutes of concentrated effort. A good interviewer is theorist, methodologist, and clinician all rolled into one. He or she must have command of relevant mathematical content; must be familiar with typical mathematical thinking—that is, with normative behavior—at the child's level; must be able to generate, on the spot, useful hypotheses concerning the child's thinking; must have the ability to devise methods for testing these hypotheses, again "online"; and must be sensitive to the nuances of the child's affect and motivation so as to establish rapport and motivate the child.

Educators have long had an interest in something like clinical interviewing as a method for investigating individual children's thinking. Recall Judd's (1927) view that "Where analyses of the processes of thinking are to be made, tests prove to be inadequate" (p. 98). Similarly, in a more recent historical period: "We know that children do not think uniformly, in the same way, when dealing with a given quantitative situation. . . . Instruction in arithmetic cannot be most effective unless the teacher is first aware of the levels of thinking employed by the children in her class . . . and then differentiates her instruction appropriately" (Weaver, 1955, p. 40). Citing the work of Buswell, described briefly in our review of the field's history, Weaver then stressed use of the interview, "in which children individually 'think out loud' as they respond to specific quantitative situations, which have been designed carefully for a specific purpose" (p. 41). In such interviews, the teacher may "interject pertinent questions . . . if she felt them to be necessary or helpful at any time" (p. 41).

As mentioned above, the NCTM has been advocating the use of "authentic" assessment in classrooms, including the conduct of "informal" interviews.[35] Many would agree that the interview method is powerful. But can it be used effectively by ordinary teachers? Or, more precisely, can teachers who put the effort into learning the method make practical use of it in the hurly-burly of the everyday classroom? Several different approaches to interviewing in the classroom have been developed.

The NCTM journals frequently describe interview methods for teachers and give examples of their use. For example, Peck, Jencks, and Connell (1989) described how students might be interviewed every five to six weeks at the beginning of a new topic of study. Another study reported research involving administration of 10- to 15-minute interviews by a mathematics specialist, who was then able to uncover difficulties hidden by correct responses on tests, and to provide diagnostic information helpful to the teacher and the students' parents (Dionne & Fitzback-Labrecque, 1989).

Recently, a major textbook publisher has made available a series of booklets describing clinical interview activities designed to be used in connection with its texts (Silver Burdett Ginn, 1995a).[36] Thus, in connection with a first grade lesson on the use of manipulatives to represent place value, teachers are presented with questions to investigate students' understanding of what has been taught. For example, "How many tens are in your number? How many ones? How do you know?" (p. 22).

Others have described how interview activities can be integrated into, and indeed can transform, classroom instruction (Ginsburg, Jacobs, & Lopez, 1993; Moon & Schulman, 1995). For example, one second grade teacher (described in Ginsburg et al., 1993) frequently used the following procedure. She began by writing a simple computational problem, such as $9 + 7 = \_\_\_$, on a large piece of paper displayed in front of the class. She asked the students to solve the problem in their own way and to write down the answer. After this had been done, the teacher spent a good part of the "math lesson" using interview techniques to explore student strategies. Among the strategies were:

- "I took 2 away from the 9 and that was 7. 7 + 7 = 14. I add 2 more and I got 16."
- "First I took the 7 and then I put up 9 fingers and I counted up 7 8 9 10 11 12 13 14 15 16."
- "I knew 10 + 7 = 17, but 9 is 1 less than 10, so 1 less than that = 16."

She asked all of the students in the room to explain their method of solution. Sometimes, she encouraged them to describe it in writing. In the course of exercises like these,

[35] Educators seem to have a distaste for the word "clinical," presumably because it suggests to them a focus on pathology. Piaget used it because the interview method was based partly on what he had learned in a psychiatric setting; but Piaget was not interested in pathologies of thought. In any event, educators substitute for "clinical" words like "flexible" or "informal."

[36] Ginsburg advised the publisher on this project.

students provided interesting information concerning the different strategies they employed. And, over time, students' ability to articulate the strategies improved.

With the assistance of the investigators, the teacher developed a simple scheme for coding the observed strategies. The scheme included simple descriptions of procedures commonly observed in the research literature: recall of number facts; concrete counting involving fingers or other easily available objects; mental counting procedures, like counting on; and various "derived strategies," such as: "6 and 4 is 10 because I know that 4 and 4 is 8 and the answer is only 2 more than that." It was relatively easy for the teacher to record students' use of these strategies on a simple checklist, which provided a convenient record.

Note that the clinical interview was not used simply as a technique. Rather, its use transformed the entire atmosphere of the classroom. In essence, the teacher's focus was not on mathematics as a fixed body of knowledge, but on the students' mathematical thinking. She had conveyed to her students that the use of different strategies was not only acceptable but desirable and interesting, and she used interview techniques to help the students to describe and thus become aware of those strategies. The clinical interview was both assessment and teaching method, and the subject matter of the curriculum was not mathematics, but students' thinking about mathematics.

Learning Potential. One essential aspect of assessment, at least as far as teachers are concerned, is information concerning children's ability to profit from instruction. The teacher is interested in both what the child knows or has mastered at any given point in time, and the extent to which the child is capable of learning new material. The goal is to understand children's learning potential and gain insight into the kind of instructional or educational experiences that will be most effective in helping children to learn.

In recent years, the concepts of two major theorists, Vygotsky and Feuerstein, have legitimated and stimulated efforts to develop techniques to assess children's learning potential. At the core of Vygotsky's theory, which is now so well known that it requires only minimal description here, is the concept of the zone of proximal development (ZPD), defined as the "distance between the actual developmental level, as determined by independent problem solving, and the level of potential development, as determined through problem-solving under adult guidance, or in collaboration with more capable peers" (Vygotsky, 1978, p. 86). The basic idea is that standardized achievement tests, intelligence tests, and the like typically provide some understanding of the child's current level of functioning—what the child is capable of at the present time. But this information is not sufficient; indeed, it may be misleading. Imagine, Vygotsky says, that standard intelligence tests have determined the mental age of two children to be 8 years. Imagine further that an adult provides some assistance—hints, suggestions, leading questions, and even the beginnings of a solution—to each of the children. Under these conditions, one child solves problems at a 12-year level, but the other remains fixed at the measured mental age of 8 years. Surely these children are very different one from the other; and surely this information concerning the difference in their learning potential is of great relevance for their teachers.

Feuerstein (1979), much of whose work centered around the assessment of disadvantaged children's mental abilities, proposed a system of "dynamic assessment," in which the examiner engages in assisted instruction as a method for measuring the child's learning potential.

It is interesting to note that both of these theorists were engaged in attempting to solve the problem that motivated Alfred Binet's initial work on intelligence testing, which was a response to the French Minister of Public Instruction's desire that "no child suspected of retardation should be eliminated from the ordinary school and admitted into a special class, without first being subjected to [an] . . . examination from which it could be certified that because of the state of his intelligence, he was unable to profit . . . from the instruction given in ordinary schools" (Binet & Simon, 1916, p. 9). For Binet, as for Vygotsky and Feuerstein, the goal was to measure not static intelligence but the ability to learn.

To date, the assessment of learning potential is more applauded than implemented. School psychologists and educators generally continue to assess the child's current level rather than the potential level. Indeed, diagnoses of learning disabilities are made all the time without any direct consideration of learning potential. Nevertheless, we can report on some interesting work on the development of techniques designed to assess learning potential in mathematics.

The Brown–Campione Approach. Brown, Campione, Webber, and McGilly (1992) approach the assessment of mathematics learning potential with two fundamental goals. "Our idea was to assess the facility with which students learn from others and the flexibility with which they could use what they had learned" (p. 154). To achieve these goals, assessment must involve several steps. First, the examiner needs to obtain a baseline measure of the child's current understanding of the subject matter. This is the pretest or assessment of the child's "actual developmental level" (in Vygotsky's terms). The examiner then provides the child with a series of hints, suggestions, and the like, until the child can solve the problem (or, presumably, until nothing works). "The amount of help each student needs is taken as the estimate of her learning efficiency *within that domain* and *at that particular point in time*" (p. 155). After that, the child is given a series of transfer problems, involving near, far, or very far transfer. "Transfer performance is taken as an index of the extent to which the students *understand* the procedures they had been taught" (p. 155). In this paradigm, assessment has two foci: (a) the child's ability to profit from adult assistance, and (b) the child's ability to use what has been learned in an independent and flexible way to deal with new problems.

Consider how this approach was implemented by the Brown–Campione research team in the case of young children's mathematics. First, the baseline was established using a standard measure of kindergarten children's mathematical knowledge (similar to the TEMA) in the areas of basic principles of counting (e.g., one-to-one correspondence), oral counting, and the counting of objects.

Then the 5-year-olds were asked to learn to solve addition and subtraction word problems, such as: "Cookie Monster starts out with 3 cookies in his cookie jar, and I'm putting 2 more in the jar. Now how many cookies are there in the cookie jar?" (Ferrara, 1987, p. 165). If the child was not immediately successful, the examiner provided each child with a very carefully designed series of "gradually more explicit hints" (p. 164) until the child solved the problem.

The hints ranged from "simple memory prompts through concrete aids to leading the child through the steps of a particular strategy for solving the problem" (p. 164). Indeed, the hints are based on an interesting conceptual system. At first, the examiner begins with "simple negative feedback," informing the child that the answer was incorrect, and that the child ought to try again. Then the examiner provides "working memory refreshers," which simply repeat key aspects of the problem situation to help the child who had forgotten basic terms of the problem. The third type of hint involves "numerals as memory aids." The child is asked to write down numerals representing key aspects of the problem. Fourth is a "transfer hint," in which the child is asked to approach the current problem in the same way an earlier, relevant problem was attacked. Fifth are "strategy hints," which suggest specific methods for solving the problem (e.g., counting). Sixth is the "complete demonstration and rationale," in which the examiner demonstrates and explains a particular strategy. A seventh type of hint involves "strategic orientation," in which the examiner provides information concerning the conditions under which the child should use a particular strategy. The last set of hints is "abandon ineffective strategy," involving an explicit instruction to stop using an ineffective strategy and to substitute a better one.

After this, each child is presented with a series of increasingly novel transfer problems—ranging from simple 2-digit problems of the sort given in the original problem to 3-digit problems $(4 + 2 + 3)$ and to missing addend problems $(4 + ? = 9)$—in order to assess the degree to which independent, flexible learning has been achieved. Finally, a posttest of mathematical knowledge is administered to determine how much the children have learned during the course of the assessment (with hints) procedure.

How successful is the assessment of learning potential? One way of answering this question is provided by examining the degree to which learning potential scores (the fewer the number of hints required and the greater the degree of transfer, the higher the learning potential) predict gains in knowledge from pretest to posttest. The results showed that the higher the learning potential, the more likely it was that the children would learn from the assessment experience. And learning potential scores were better predictors of learning than were measures of the children's initial knowledge or IQ. Stating the matter in Vygotsky's terms, knowing a child's zone of proximal development was more informative with respect to understanding the child's learning than was knowing the child's actual level of development.

This work is important for several reasons: (a) it is one of the few attempts to measure potential for learning mathematics in a rigorous way; (b) the system of graduated hints provides an operational definition of Vygotsky's rather vague notions of adult help; and (c) the system links assessment to the instructional process.

Probes. As in the case of flexible interviewing, the assessment of learning potential can be enormously informative but very difficult to conduct. To reduce the difficulty, especially for novice assessors, Ginsburg (1990) has developed a series of organized probes to assess learning potential. The approach is very similar to the sequence of hints developed by Ferrara (1987). The issue is whether the student can learn the type of material covered in the TEMA (Ginsburg & Baroody, 1990) with a minimum of hints or whether more substantial teaching is required. In the first case, it is clear that the student is close to "understanding"; in the second case, the student is not.

For example, one TEMA item (p. 22) assesses the child's understanding of the "mental number line" by posing such questions as: "Which is just a little different from 7—1 or 9?" The learning potential probes are of two types. First, the examiner provides a hint: "Try to do it by counting. See if that will help." If this minimal amount of help is successful, clearly the child's potential for learning about this concept is substantial; indeed, the concept may be considered to have been on the tip of the "mental tongue." If the hint is not successful, the examiner goes on to offer "teaching," a much more directive approach: "You can tell how close they are by counting. First, you count from 7 to 9, like this, '8, 9.' That's two counts. Then you count from 1 to 7: '2, 3, 4, 5, 6, 7.' That's six counts, so 1 is far away from 7, and 9 is close." If the child succeeds with this kind of help, there is again some potential for learning. If the child does not, learning potential—for this task, at this time—may be severely limited.

In brief, the theories of Vygotsky and Feuerstein have pointed the way to attempts at the assessment of potential for mathematics learning. The initial work is promising, but much more needs to be done in this area, especially in linking these assessments to suggestions for improved instruction.

Conclusions

The work on assessment may be evaluated as follows.

1. *What does the assessment work teach us about the process of application*? The review of assessment shows us that research exerts its effects in both indirect and direct ways. The indirect effect is that psychological research has influenced the climate surrounding assessment in the schools. Thus, the NCTM Assessment Standards document (National Council of Teachers of Mathematics, 1995) draws on psychological concepts and research to argue for alternative approaches to assessment. The direct effects are fairly straightforward. Several psychologists have devised particular tests (Ginsburg & Baroody, 1990) or assessment procedures (Campione, Brown, Ferrara, & Bryant, 1984), sometimes in connection with their attempts to develop innovations in educational practice (as in the Brown–Campione *Fostering a Community of Learners* project). Others have contributed directly to publishers' efforts to provide teachers with alternative methods of assessment (Silver Burdett Ginn, 1995a).

2. *What aspects of the basic research were most useful for developing new assessment procedures?* The research on the development of mathematical thinking has made several different kinds of contributions. As mentioned above, one is to help in creating a climate in which traditional forms of testing are recognized as inadequate and in which a need for alternatives is widely accepted. If children's thinking is complex, involving the construction of knowledge, then education requires more than tests that focus only on overt behavior and achievement. In effect, the research has contributed to changing the assumptions about what tests should attempt to measure and hence the goals of testing.

As a second contribution, the research suggests particular forms of mathematical knowledge that assessment techniques should examine. Thus, the research has informed tests that focus on bugs or derived strategies, informal and formal knowledge, strategies and learning potential.

A third contribution of the research is to offer new techniques of assessment—in particular, alternatives to standardized testing. The field offers nontraditional research techniques like the clinical interview method and the examination of learning potential. Many educators, believing in the necessity for "authentic assessment," have begun to explore methods like these.

3. *How is the available research and theory deficient in speaking to the need for new forms of assessment?* On one level, the research does not speak to some of the issues that concern teachers in their everyday interactions with children—questions of motivation, cognitive style, and the like. Teachers want to understand children's feelings about and attitudes toward mathematics, as well as their styles of thinking and learning. But these topics are not prominent in the mathematics learning research literature. The research focuses mainly on children's thinking; teachers do not have the luxury of considering mathematical learning in isolation from the motives, feelings, attitudes, and personalities that shape it.

On another level, the important methods of assessment suggested by psychological research do not always find their way into the classroom. (In a sense, this situation is reminiscent of the scenario involving achievement tests.) Tests of traits (e.g., the KeyMath or the TEMA), tests of process (e.g., the DTAS), and techniques like the probes are usually administered by school psychologists, and the results may or may not reach classroom teachers in a form that is useful to them. Clinical interviewing is difficult to conduct, and few teachers seem to attempt it. The various methods' considerable potential for influencing classroom practice has gone largely unrealized. Considerable work remains to be done in translating the methods for use by teachers, in training teachers to use them, and in evaluating the resulting efforts.

4. *How can we improve our contribution to problems of assessment*? The new climate places educators in a difficult situation. They have been encouraged to employ alternative or "authentic" forms of assessment. They have been urged to abandon standard tests in favor of observational methods, portfolios, or clinical interviews. But educators are then left in the lurch, in at least two different ways.

First, teachers receive very little assistance in learning how to do observations, conduct interviews, or evaluate portfolios. One of the biggest challenges presented by the alternative methods is understanding *what to assess.* Assessment is a highly conceptual activity. It is research in miniature. It requires gathering evidence to make inferences about underlying cognitive processes.[37] But making those inferences depends on having an educationally relevant, practical theory of mathematical thinking. One cannot properly interpret the observations, or evaluate the portfolio, or conduct and profit from the clinical interview unless one has a good idea of what children's mathematical thinking is all about. A practical theory of the individual child's thinking is necessary both for asking a good interview question and for evaluating a student's response. It is not enough for the NCTM to advocate alternative assessment, or for psychologists to make available methods like the clinical interview. Alternative assessment will not be successful unless educators get help in understanding children's mathematical thinking.

Enhancement of the development of alternative forms of assessment could be one of psychologists' most important contributions to education. But both psychologists and educators must recognize that assessment is, at bottom, a conceptual activity in which teachers need considerable education. Psychologists should find ways to contribute to that educational process.

A second way in which teachers are left in the lurch is that, for the most part, they continue to be judged by their students' success on standardized tests. While the NCTM and leaders in mathematics education call for authentic assessment—or at least a dual system involving both standard tests and authentic assessment—the day-to-day reality in most school districts is that unless students perform well on conventional achievement tests, all hell breaks loose. So, although teachers are encouraged to learn new forms of assessment, the ultimate rewards and sanctions revolve around achievement tests. Authentic assessment is the slogan, but high scores are the bottom line. When high stakes are involved, such as evaluation of programs, or rate of college admissions—standard tests are the measures that really count.

[37] Or, as the NCTM puts it, assessment "is defined as *the process of gathering evidence about a student's knowledge of, ability to use, and disposition toward, mathematics and of making inferences from that evidence for a variety of purposes*" (National Council of Teachers of Mathematics, 1995, p. 3).

What can researchers do about this? Probably not a great deal except to engage in another kind of educational effort: helping the public to understand learning and education generally, and particularly to appreciate the need in mathematics education for an emphasis on thinking and understanding.

GENERAL CONCLUSIONS

This chapter has been about applications—about connecting research with practice. What can we conclude about the kinds of contributions psychological research has made and can make to the improvement of mathematics education?

Ideas and Methods

Researchers have contributed useful general ideas to mathematics education, and their power should not be underestimated. They include notions of constructivism, informal knowledge, invented strategies, bugs, innate mathematical ideas, cultural adaptation, learning in the context of everyday life, and understanding as a web of ideas. The clearer, simpler, and more compelling these ideas are, the more likely that they will appeal to those who would put them into practice.

Psychological ideas have been used by the mathematics education community in several ways. First, they serve as a framework for educational reform, providing a general "philosophy" and powerful slogans that serve as "economizers of thought," "demolishers of illusions," and "energizers of practice" (Sierpinska et al., 1993). The development of the NCTM *Standards* and of the State guidelines for textbook adoption shows how general ideas serve to influence ideology and opinion in the mathematics education community—or to reinforce existing ideology and opinion—and thus shape the climate of mathematics education. Second, they have helped teachers to gain a fresh and deeper understanding of children's learning. Teachers following the NCTM *Standards,* using CGI, reading the journals that report on research, and using the newer textbooks must think differently about children and expect different things of them. Third, they have provided a new approach to the development of textbook pages, at least some of which have indeed been affected by ideas stemming from research. Fourth, they have drawn a rationale and a general blueprint for teacher education, as the example of CGI attests. One major conclusion is, therefore, that general *ideas* matter; they have helped to change mathematics education.

Specific ideas matter, too. The research has resulted in specific knowledge concerning the development of counting-based addition strategies, the ways in which particular languages facilitate the understanding of base-10 ideas, the nature of bugs in subtraction, the particular strategies that children invent. This specific knowledge allows the teacher to understand why one child gets a wrong answer (she used the "subtract smaller from larger" bug), or how another child solves a problem mentally that he cannot do correctly on paper (when he added, he used the invented strategy of chunking numbers into convenient elements that he could deal with). The specific knowledge allows States to mandate that children should not only learn the standard algorithms, but should be encouraged to develop alternative procedures for addition. The specific knowledge enables textbook writers to create lessons on finger counting or on how a variety of methods, not only memorization, can be used to solve number fact problems. The specific knowledge points test developers in new directions; now, they not only attempt to measure general achievement, but they can focus on whether the child employs a particular bug or invented strategy. The research thus puts flesh on the bones of the general philosophy.

One of the most important contributions of research is methodology. Making clear the inadequacies of standard testing, Piaget's and Vygotsky's theories provide a fresh perspective on the nature and goals of assessment. To quote Vygotsky (1978) again: "Any fundamentally new approach to a scientific problem inevitably leads to new methods of investigation and analysis" (p. 58). But the theories not only fan the fires of dissatisfaction with standard testing; they offer specific alternatives. Thus, Piaget's theory leads to the clinical interview method and Vygotsky's to the measurement of the zone of proximal development. These methods can have an enormous impact on mathematics education, because they can be used every day by ordinary teachers in ordinary classrooms.

Research into Practice

How does research get translated into practice? Researchers should not be so naïve as to think that their good ideas—at least in their own eyes—lead easily to enthusiastic applications. We have seen that, in the case of a high-stakes application—textbooks, the sales of which involve millions of dollars—the process is by no means simple. At least two sets of forces determine the ways in which research knowledge gets applied (if it does get applied) into educational policy, State mandates, and the actual development of textbooks. On the one hand are gatekeepers who disseminate the research, legitimize it in the eyes of the educational community, and use it to create educational policy; State officials who draw on the research to propagate quasi-legal guidelines that influence the purchase of textbooks; and writers and editors who base their work at least partly on knowledge of the research literature. On the other hand are forces that tend to dilute or negate application of the research. Among them are publishers driven by a market economy; teachers who, for one reason or another, are not prepared to implement a constructivist approach; and fundamentalist political opinion.

Note that, in this process, the researchers provided the original ideas but, in a sense, have generally not been responsible for the applications stemming from the new perspectives they have suggested. In a way, these applications are too important to be left to researchers, who tend to be naïve when it comes to the daily challenges of mathematics education in the schools. Researchers generally are not competent to devise general guidelines for mathematics education or to write an exciting textbook page. These practical applications are better accomplished by mathematics educators, curriculum developers, teachers, and textbook writers—all of whom know how to exploit the psychological ideas more effectively than most researchers do.

In short, the application of research to textbook development is a complex affair in which many forces—social, political, and scientific—play important roles. In this process, researchers have provided some of the ideas, but the applications have often been accomplished by others.

The other examples we examined—teacher training and test development—tell a somewhat different story about the applications of research. For both CGI and the development of various tests and assessment procedures, researchers played a direct and independent role in the creation of the "product." Several researchers were responsible for the CGI model for teacher training; others created the various tests and assessment procedures described. In these cases, the more classical notion of application has some merit—researchers felt they had some good ideas that could be applied to a practical problem, and they went ahead and devised the application.

But that is only the beginning of the story. Once the application is created, it lives only in the researcher's vita unless it is implemented in the real world. And that is where the complexity begins. The implementation of CGI will undoubtedly be more complex than its creation. School districts have to decide to commit to the CGI philosophy, to buy into the project, to spend money on it, to allocate teacher time to it. Parents will need to decide whether CGI, as interpreted by local teachers, is their cup of tea—and, as we have seen, the fundamentalists disapprove of certain beverages. Similarly, the use of flexible assessment procedures will depend on testing policy in a school district. If the State mandates the use of standard tests as the ultimate criterion, there is little incentive to engage in alternative forms of assessment. If parents want clear and objective criteria by which to judge their schools and to propel their children into college, there is again little incentive to invest considerable time, energy, and money in programs designed to enable teachers to employ the more difficult and subjective forms of assessment.

In brief, the process of application is complex. Ideas derive from research matter, but they are only one competitor in the marketplace of ideas, values, and special interests. The application of these ideas usually involves many participants, not always acting in concert, and not always holding dear the findings of research.

Limitations of Research

Although research on the development of mathematical thinking has certainly produced important insights, it also suffers from limitations, at least so far as applications to mathematics education are concerned. These limitations may be of little interest to many researchers who quite legitimately judge the success of their work by the criterion of whether it helps to answer the questions that motivated it. But mathematics educators just as legitimately are concerned with a different set of issues, to which the current psychological research provides only limited answers. From the point of view of mathematics education, then, and not the point of view of the psychological investigator, how has the research fallen short? What kind of research could psychologists do to make a greater contribution?

Psychological research, particularly with younger children, has tended to focus on simple aspects of number, on addition and subtraction, on number facts. This is all well and good, but the focus is limited; it reflects a narrow view of the scope and content of mathematics. From the point of view of mathematics education, the memorization of number facts is of little significance. Engagement in problem solving, in critical thinking, in the exploration of mathematical ideas, in the creation of conjectures, in the identification of patterns—these are central to mathematics, not some minor (but essential) calculations. One shortcoming—even a danger—of the psychological research is that its focus too narrowly limits, and even trivializes, what should be thought of as mathematical. Perhaps psychological researchers fall into this trap because their understanding of mathematics is often limited.

Psychological research has also tended to slight the "ecology" in which mathematical thinking occurs. The research often fails to examine in any depth the environments—the textbooks, teachers, classroom conditions, and social context—in which children learn mathematics. The research focuses single-mindedly on the minds of individual children. This is a particular pitfall when the subjects of the research are children whose performance is substandard—children with "learning disabilities," or poor children. In these cases, the psychological researcher's tendency to focus on single minds often results in blaming the victim—attributing failure primarily to deficiencies in the mind of the child, and ignoring the causative role of all the obvious factors, such as inadequate instruction (Ginsburg, 1997b).

The research also slights the richness and complexity of motivation underlying the child's school learning. Academic success and failure result from more than invented strategies and bugs. Children learn or fail to learn school mathematics for many reasons—self-concept, identification, motivation, peer relations, interactions with the teacher, and racial identity (Fordham & Ogbu, 1986; Ginsburg & Asmussen, 1988), to mention only some. These are issues of which many cognitive developmental researchers are blissfully unaware. But, in the real world of schools, they are crucial.

Most developmental research does not deal with development. Drawing on cross-sectional samples, it deals with states of knowledge at different points of time and typically fails to examine transitions from one point to the next. Similarly, research focuses more on mathematical knowledge than on mathematical learning. It provides little insight into the acquisition of knowledge, particularly the processes of exploration, of "messing around" (Hawkins, 1974). To do so would take us far beyond the comfortable examination of simple strategies of arithmetic.

Finally, in focusing on what is taken to be the typical child—that is, the modal White, middle-class mind—the research tends to ignore the increasing diversity of student backgrounds in the United States (Secada, 1991). We know very little about the learning experiences of poor children and children from disadvantaged minorities.

As a result of all of these limitations, we must be cautious in "applying" our research to the complex context of mathematics education in the schools, particularly in the United States.

Needed Applications

What kinds of applications can make a contribution to mathematics education in the 21st century? Many can be useful: improved mathematics textbooks, manipulatives, multimedia materials, television programming, tests and assessment devices. But, in our view, the most essential and most needed application is to teacher education. Indeed, teacher education is one of the most fundamental problems in mathematics education and, indeed, in education generally.

The constructivist approach to mathematics education championed by the NCTM places especially heavy demands on teachers. "The teaching that reformers seem to envision would require vast changes in what most teachers know and believe" (Cohen & Barnes, 1993, p. 246). "Teachers who take this path must work harder, concentrate more. . . . They must also have unusual knowledge and skills. They require, for instance, a deep understanding of the material. . . . They must be able to comprehend students' thinking, their interpretations of problems, their mistakes . . . they must have the capacity to probe thoughtfully and tactfully. These and other capacities would not be needed if teachers relied on texts and worksheets" (Cohen, 1988, p. 75).

But, as we have seen, American teachers often have a poor grasp of mathematics and teach it poorly—in good measure, because they themselves have been taught it poorly from elementary school through the college and graduate levels. Teachers do not have a sophisticated understanding of children's minds or of the methods needed to reveal them—probably because teachers have been exposed to psychology courses that are largely irrelevant to understanding real children in real classrooms.

If teachers are indeed so poorly prepared in mathematics, pedagogy, and psychology, they cannot take advantage of exciting curricula and materials, or sensitive approaches to assessment. Failing to see what manipulatives can accomplish, teachers merely let children play with blocks without connecting the activity to mathematics. Unable to understand children's thinking, teachers simply collect portfolios without knowing how to interpret them.

As Reeve (1929) put it many years ago: "While the greater part of this report concerns itself with the content of courses in mathematics . . . the National Committee must emphasize strongly that *even more fundamental* is the problem of the teacher—his [sic] qualifications and training, his personality, skill and enthusiasm. . . . *Good teachers have in the past succeeded . . . in achieving highly satisfactory results with the traditional material; poor teachers will not succeed even with the newer and better material*" (p. 185).

If all this is true, then a fundamental problem for mathematics education is not the creation of more effective curricula or assessment methods, but the education of teachers.

How can psychologists contribute to this effort? Perhaps the most important contribution we can make is to find ways to help teachers understand children's minds and mathematics learning. The CGI project has already made an important contribution to this effort. But a good deal more needs to be done to help teachers use psychological ideas in their daily practice. We need to learn more about how teachers ordinarily think about children's learning of mathematics. What are their "naïve theories" of the mathematical mind? We need to learn more about the kind and level of psychological ideas that are most useful for the "intermediary inventive mind" (James, 1958, p. 24) which is at the heart of educational practice. After all, we must be aware that the kind of psychological ideas teachers need may be different from those required by researchers. Finally, we need to learn how to teach better ourselves. How can we be more effective in "transmitting," or helping teachers to construct, a meaningful psychology?

Training Researchers (and Ourselves)

What lessons does this chapter offer for the training of researchers interested in applications of psychology to mathematics education?

To apply research, the psychologist cannot be isolated in the "laboratory." It is certainly a disservice to lead students to believe that the world revolves around, or even cares much about, their research. Unless students are helped to become aware of the place of their research in the larger ecology of education, and of the complex forces influencing practice, their approach will be egocentric and ineffective. Our students need to learn about the lives of students and teachers in ordinary schools, and to understand the conditions under which teachers work and children study. Our students need to understand the political forces shaping education, the machinations of the textbook industry, the concerns of parents. Our students need to listen to teachers, to hear their questions, to understand their skepticism about outsiders helping them, and to benefit from their ideas.

Our students also need to learn that interesting research questions can arise from practice. Often, mathematics educators develop interesting curricula without the benefit of psychological research. Indeed, these curricula may be said to have been developed *despite* the psychological research. An example is Miss Mason's Math, which teaches negative numbers to preschoolers, with apparent success (Miss Mason's School, 1976). Psychological research would never have predicted that this could be done, and probably would be interpreted to say that it cannot be done. How can "preoperational" children understand negative numbers? But Miss Mason's Math seems to lead them to do it. If so, then researchers are faced with interesting questions, and indeed need to reexamine their views of preschoolers' intellectual competence.

Another example is provided by the Madison Project's demonstration that fourth and fifth grade inner-city elementary school children can do interesting work with functions (Davis, 1967). At the time this work was done, psychological theories (Jensen, 1969) pictured these children as cognitively deficient and incapable of such abstract thinking. Again, the practice was in advance of the psychology and provided it with interesting questions for research.

The lesson is this: Practice does not always (or even frequently) derive from applications of psychological research. Instead, practice may suggest psychological questions of deep interest to researchers.

To teach our students these things, we need to learn (and practice) them ourselves, which is often harder than conveying them to others. In any event, the education of researchers interested in application must be a good deal broader than it typically is now.

Finally, we need to think more about the role of values in our work. Those of us who appreciate constructivism in education hold certain values that are not necessarily shared in all sectors of the educational community. Indeed, as we have seen in the case of the California textbook controversy, there is a serious value conflict between constructivists and fundamentalists. Constructivists espouse values that others do not hold. Further, "The instructional practices that reformers wish to eliminate contain views of knowledge, teaching and learning to which many parents, teachers, and students have deep loyalties" (Cohen, 1988, p. 48). What are we to do if a teacher holds a traditional orientation toward instruction? Should we try to change that orientation or help the teacher use psychological ideas to implement it more effectively?

Research and Public Responsibility

The potential contributions of psychological research need to be kept in perspective. American education is afflicted by many serious problems involving funding, demands on and support of teachers, communication between parents and teachers, standards for those entering the teaching profession, student discipline, teacher unions, school bureaucracies, schools of education, an uninformed and often math phobic general populace, and a general neglect of children in our society.[38] Without improvements in these contexts in which education is embedded, what we learn from psychological research will have only minor effects on improving children's learning of mathematics. Our small attempts at improving children's learning need to be integrated within a larger movement for educational reform.

[38] These remarks were prompted by some of Art Baroody's comments on a draft of this paper.

ACKNOWLEDGMENTS

The authors wish to acknowledge the valuable assistance of several reviewers and colleagues who took the time to provide thoughtful comments on the manuscript: Arthur Baroody, Thomas Carpenter, Ellen Lagemann, Jean Liccione, Ann Renninger, Geoffrey Saxe, and Irving Sigel. This chapter was initiated while Ginsburg was a Fellow at the Center for Advanced Study in Behavioral Sciences. Klein and Starkey were primarily responsible for writing the section titled "Research" and Ginsburg for the rest.

REFERENCES

Addison-Wesley. (1995a). *Quest 2000: Exploring mathematics (pupil edition).* Menlo Park, CA: Author.

Addison-Wesley. (1995b). *Quest 2000: Exploring mathematics (teachers' edition).* Menlo Park, CA: Author.

Anastasi, A. (1988). *Psychological testing* (6th ed.). New York: Macmillan.

Antell, S., & Keating, D. (1983). Perception of numerical invariance in neonates. *Child Development, 54,* 695–701.

Apple, M. W. (1992). Do the Standards go far enough? Power, policy, and practice and mathematics education. *Journal for Research in Mathematics Education, 23*(5), 412–431.

Ashcraft, M. H. (1990). Strategic processing in children's mental arithmetic: A review and proposal. In D. F. Bjorklund (Ed.), *Children's strategies: Contemporary views of cognitive development* (pp. 185–212). Hillsdale, NJ: Erlbaum.

Ashcraft, M. H. (1992). Cognitive arithmetic: A review of data and theory. *Cognition, 44,* 75–106.

Ashcraft, M. H., & Christy, K. S. (1995). The frequency of arithmetic facts in elementary texts: Addition and multiplication in grades 1–6. *Journal for Research in Mathematics Education, 26,* 396–421.

Ausubel, D. P. (1968). *Educational psychology: A cognitive view.* New York: Holt, Rinehart and Winston.

Baroody, A. J. (1987a). *Children's mathematical thinking.* New York: Teachers College Press.

Baroody, A. J. (1987b). The development of counting strategies for single-digit addition. *Journal for Research in Mathematics Education, 18,* 141–157.

Baroody, A. J. (1992). The development of preschoolers' counting skills and principles. In J. Bideaud, C. Meljac, & J. P. Fischer (Eds.), *Pathways to number* (pp. 99–126). Hillsdale, NJ: Erlbaum.

Baroody, A. J. (1993). Early mental multiplication performance and the role of relational knowledge in mastering combinations involving two. *Learning and Individual Differences, 4,* 215–235.

Baroody, A. J. (1994). An evaluation of evidence supporting fact-retrieval models. *Learning and Individual Differences, 6,* 1–36.

Baroody, A. J. (1995). Mastery of basic number combinations: Internalization of relationships or facts? *Journal for Research in Mathematics Education, 16,* 83–98.

Baroody, A. J. (in press). Self-invented addition strategies by children classified as mentally handicapped. *American Journal on Mental Retardation.*

Baroody, A. J., & Ginsburg, H. P. (1982). Generating number combinations: Rote process or problem solving? *Problem Solving, 4,* 3–4.

Bartlett, F. C. (1932). *Remembering.* Cambridge, England: Cambridge University Press.

Battista, M. T. (1994). Teacher beliefs and the reform movement in mathematics education. *Phi Delta Kappan,* 462–470.

Behr, M. J., Lesh, R., Post, T. R., & Silver, E. A. (1983). Rational-number concepts. In R. Lesh & M. Landau (Eds.), *Acquisition of mathematics concepts and processes* (pp. 91–126). New York: Academic Press.

Beilin, H. (1968). Cognitive capacities of young children: A replication. *Science, 162,* 920–921.

Bell, A., Burkhardt, H., & Swan, M. (1992). Balanced assessment of mathematical performance. In R. Lesh & S. J. Lamon (Eds.), *Assessment of authentic performance in school mathematics* (pp. 119–144). Washington, DC: American Association for the Advancement of Science Press.

Berliner, D. C. (1993). Mythology and the American system of Education. *Phi Delta Kappan, 75,* 632–640.

Binet, A., & Simon, T. (1916). *The development of intelligence in children.* Baltimore: Williams & Wilkins.

Blevins-Knabe, B., Cooper, R. G., Mace, P. G., Starkey, P., & Leitner, E. (1987). Preschoolers sometimes know less than we think: The use of quantifiers to solve addition and subtraction tasks. *Bulletin of the Psychometric Society, 25,* 31–34.

Bolduc, R. (n.d.). *Florida model curriculum project: Mathematics grades K–5.* Tallahassee: Florida Department of Education.

Bracey, G. W. (1993). The third Bracey Report on the condition of public education. *Phi Delta Kappan, 75,* 104–117.

Briars, D. J., & Siegler, R. (1984). A featural analysis of preschoolers' counting knowledge. *Developmental Psychology, 20,* 607–618.

Brown, A. L., & Campione, J. C. (1994). Guided discovery in a community of learners. In K. McGilly (Ed.), *Classroom lessons: Integrating cognitive theory and classroom practice* (pp. 229–270). Cambridge, MA: MIT Press/Bradford Books.

Brown, A. L., Campione, J. C., Webber, L. S., & McGilly, K. (1992). Interactive learning environments: A new look at assessment and instruction. In B. R. Gifford & M. C. O'Connor (Eds.), *Changing assessments: Alternative views of aptitude, achievement, and instruction* (pp. 121–211). Boston: Kluwer.

Brown, J. S., & Burton, R. B. (1978). Diagnostic models for procedural bugs in basic mathematical skills. *Cognitive Science, 2,* 155–192.

Brown, J. S., & VanLehn, K. (1982). Towards a generative theory of "bugs." In T. P. Carpenter, J. M. Moser, & T. A. Romberg (Eds.), *Addition and subtraction: A cognitive perspective* (pp. 117–135). Hillsdale, NJ: Erlbaum.

Brownell, W. A. (1935). Psychological considerations in the learning and teaching of arithmetic. In W. D. Reeve (Ed.), *The teaching of arithmetic* (10th Yearbook of the National Council of Teachers of Mathematics) (pp. 1–31). New York: Columbia University, Teachers College, Bureau of Publications.

Bruner, J. S. (1966). *Toward a theory of instruction.* Cambridge, MA: Belknap Press of Harvard University Press.

Brush, L. R. (1978). Preschool children's knowledge of addition and subtraction. *Journal for Research in Mathematics Education, 9,* 44–54.

Bryant, D. M., Burchinal, M., Lau, L. B., & Sparling, J. J. (1994). Family and classroom correlates of Head Start children's developmental outcomes. *Early Childhood Research Quarterly, 9,* 289–309.

Bryant, P. (1974). *Perception and understanding in young children.* New York: Basic Books.

Bryant, P. E. (1995). Children and arithmetic. *Journal of Child Psychology and Psychiatry, 36,* 3–32.

Buschman, L. (1995). Communicating in the language of mathematics. *Journal for Research in Mathematics Education, 1*(6), 324–329.

Buswell, G. T., & John, L. (1926). *Diagnostic studies in arithmetic* (Supplementary Educational Monographs No. 30). Chicago: University of Chicago.

California Department of Education. (1992). *Mathematics framework for California public schools: Kindergarten through grade twelve.* Sacramento, CA: Author.

Campione, J. C., Brown, A. L., Ferrara, R. A., & Bryant, N. R. (1984). The zone of proximal development: Implications for individual differences and learning. In B. Rogoff & J. V.

Wertsch (Eds.), *Children's learning in the zone of proximal development. New directions for child development* (pp. 77–91). San Francisco: Jossey-Bass.

Canfield, R. L., & Haith, M. M. (in press). Number-based expectation and sequential enumeration by 5-month-old infants. *Developmental Psychology.*

Carpenter, T. P., Ansell, E., Franke, M. L., Fennema, E., & Weisbeck, L. (1993). Models of problem-solving: A study of kindergarten children's problem-solving processes. *Journal for Research in Mathematics Education, 24*(5), 427–440.

Carpenter, T. P., & Fennema, E. (1992). Cognitively guided instruction: Building on the knowledge of students and teachers. *International Journal of Educational Research, 17*(5), 457–470.

Carpenter, T. P., Fennema, E., & Franke, M. L. (1994). *Children's thinking about whole numbers.* Wisconsin Center for Education Research, Madison, WI.

Carpenter, T. P., Fennema, E., & Franke, M. L. (1996). Cognitively guided instruction: A knowledge base for reform in primary mathematics instruction. *Elementary School Journal, 97*(1), 3–20.

Carpenter, T. P., & Moser, J. M. (1982). The development of addition and subtraction problem-solving skills. In T. P. Carpenter, J. M. Moser, & T. A. Romberg (Eds.), *Addition and subtraction: A cognitive perspective* (pp. 9–24). Hillsdale, NJ: Erlbaum.

Carpenter, T. P., Moser, J. M., & Romberg, T. A. (Eds.). (1982). *Addition and subtraction: A cognitive perspective.* Hillsdale, NJ: Erlbaum.

Carraher, T. N., Carraher, D. W., & Schliemann, A. S. (1985). Mathematics in streets and schools. *British Journal of Developmental Psychology, 3,* 21–29.

Civil, M. (1993). Prospective elementary teachers' thinking about teaching mathematics. *Journal of Mathematical Behavior, 12*(1), 79–109.

Cochran, B. S., Barson, A., & Davis, R. B. (1970). Child-created mathematics. *Arithmetic Teacher, 17,* 211–215.

Cohen, D. K. (1988). Teaching practice: Plus que ça change . . . . In P. W. Jackson (Ed.), *Contributing to educational change: Perspectives on research and practice* (pp. 27–84). Berkeley, CA: McCutchan.

Cohen, D. K., & Barnes, C. A. (1993). Pedagogy and policy. In D. K. Cohen, M. W. McLaughlin, & J. E. Talbert (Eds.), *Teaching for understanding: Challenges for policy and practice* (pp. 207–239). San Francisco: Jossey-Bass.

Colburn, W. (1842). *Intellectual arithmetic upon the inductive method of instruction.* Boston: Hilliard, Gray.

Cole, M., & Scribner, S. (1974). *Culture and thought.* New York: Wiley.

Colvin, R. L. (1995, March 12). New math plan: A plus for pupils? *Los Angeles Times,* pp. A1, A16, A17.

Connelly, A. J., Nachtman, W., & Pritchett, E. M. (1976). *Keymath diagnostic arithmetic test.* Circle Pines, MN: American Guidance Service.

Cooper, R. G. (1984). Early number development: Discovering number space with addition and subtraction. In C. Sophian (Ed.), *The origins of cognitive skill* (pp. 157–192). Hillsdale, NJ: Erlbaum.

Cramer, K., & Karnowski, L. (1995). The importance of informal language in representing mathematical ideas. *Journal for Research in Mathematics Education, 1*(6), 332–335.

Dantzig, T. (1954). *Number: The language of science* (4th ed.). New York: Macmillan.

Dasen, P. (1977). *Piagetian psychology: Cross-cultural contributions.* New York: Gardner Press.

Davis, R. B. (1967). *Explorations in mathematics: A text for teachers.* Palo Alto, CA: Addison-Wesley.

Davis, R. B. (1980). *Discovery in mathematics: A text for teachers.* New Rochelle, NY: Cuisenaire Company of America.

Davis, R. B., & Greenstein, R. (1964). Jennifer. *Mathematical Teachers Journal, 19,* 94–105.

de Lange, J. (1993). Real tasks and real assessment. In R. B. Davis & C. S. Maher (Eds.), *Schools, mathematics, and the world of reality* (pp. 263–287). Boston: Allyn & Bacon.

Dionne, J. J., & Fitzback-Labrecque, M. (1989). The use of "mini-interviews" by "orthopédagogues": Three case studies. In C. A. Maher, G. A. Goldin, & R. B. Davis (Eds.), *Proceedings of the eleventh annual meeting* (pp. 315–321). New Brunswick, NJ: Psychology of Mathematics Education.

Farran, D. C., Silveri, B., & Culp, A. (1991). Public preschools and the disadvantaged. In L. Rescorla, M. C. Hyson, & K. Hirsh-Pasek (Eds.), *Academic instruction in early childhood: Challenge or pressure?* (pp. 65–73). San Francisco: Jossey-Bass.

Fennema, E., Carpenter, T. P., Franke, M. L., & Carey, D. A. (1993). Learning to use children's mathematics thinking: A case study. In R. B. Davis & C. A. Maher (Eds.), *Schools, mathematics, and the world of reality* (pp. 93–117). Boston, MA: Allyn & Bacon.

Fennema, E., Carpenter, T. P., Franke, M. L., Levi, L., Jacobs, V. R., & Empson, S. B. (1996). A longitudinal study of learning to use children's thinking in mathematics instruction. *Journal for Research in Mathematics Education, 27,* 403–434.

Ferrara, R. A. (1987). *Learning mathematics in the zone of proximal development: The importance of flexible use of knowledge.* Doctoral dissertation, University of Illinois at Urbana, Champaign.

Feuerstein, R. (1979). *The dynamic assessment of retarded performers: The learning potential device, theory, instruments, and techniques.* Baltimore: University Park Press.

Fordham, S., & Ogbu, J. U. (1986). Black students' school success: Coping with the burden of "acting White." *Urban Review, 18,* 178–206.

Frederiksen, J. R., & Collins, A. (1989). A systems approach to educational testing. *Educational Researcher, 18*(9), 27–32.

Frydman, O. (in press). The concept of number and the acquisition of counting concepts: The "when," the "how," and the "what" of it. *Cahiers de Psychologie Cognitive.*

Frydman, O., & Bryant, P. E. (1988). Sharing and the understanding of number equivalence by young children. *Cognitive Development, 3,* 323–339.

Frye, D., Braisby, N., Love, J., Maroudas, C., & Nicholls, J. (1989). Young children's understanding of counting and cardinality. *Child Development, 60,* 1158–1171.

Fullan, M. (1982). *The meaning of educational change.* New York: Teachers College Press.

Fuson, K. C. (1988). *Children's counting and concepts of number.* New York: Springer-Verlag.

Fuson, K. C. (1992). Relationships between counting and cardinality from age 2 to age 8. In J. Bideaud, C. Meljac, & J. P. Fischer (Eds.), *Pathways to number* (pp. 127–149). Hillsdale, NJ: Erlbaum.

Fuson, K. C., & Kwon, Y. (1992a). Effects on children's addition and subtraction of the system of number words and other cultural tools. In J. Bideaud, C. Meljac, & J.-P. Fischer (Eds.), *Pathways to number: Children's developing numerical abilities* (pp. 283–306). Hillsdale, NJ: Erlbaum.

Fuson, K. C., & Kwon, Y. (1992b). Korean children's understanding of multidigit addition and subtraction. *Child Development, 63,* 491–506.

Garet, M. S., & Mills, V. L. (1995). Changes in teaching practices: The effects of the *Curriculum and Evaluation Standards. Mathematics Teacher, 88*(5), 380–389.

Gay, J., & Cole, M. (1967). *The new mathematics and an old culture.* New York: Holt, Rinehart and Winston.

Geary, D. (1994). *Children's mathematical development: Research and practical applications.* Washington, DC: American Psychological Association.

Geary, D., & Wiley, J. G. (1991). Cognitive addition: Strategy choice and speed-of-processing differences in young and elderly adults. *Psychology and Aging, 6,* 474–483.

Gelman, R. (1979). Preschool thought. *American Psychologist, 34,* 900–905.

Gelman, R. (1980). What young children know about numbers. *Educational Psychologist, 15,* 54–68.

Gelman, R. (1994). Constructivism and supporting environments. In D. Tirosh (Ed.), *Implicit and explicit knowledge: An educational approach* (pp. 55–82). Norwood, NJ: ABLEX.

Gelman, R., & Gallistel, C. R. (1978). *The child's understanding of number.* Cambridge, MA: Harvard University Press.

Gelman, R., & Meck, E. (1983). Preschoolers' counting: Principles before skill. *Cognition, 13,* 343–359.

Gibson, E. J. (1969). *Principles of perceptual learning and development.* New York: Appleton-Century-Crofts.

Ginsburg, H. P. (1971). The case of Peter. *Journal of Children's Mathematical Behavior, 1,* 60–71.

Ginsburg, H. P. (1981). Piaget and education: The contributions and limits of genetic epistemology. In I. E. Sigel, D. M. Brodzinsky, & R. M. Golinkoff (Eds.), *New directions in Piagetian theory and practice* (pp. 315–330). Hillsdale, NJ: Erlbaum.

Ginsburg, H. P. (1982). The development of addition in contexts of culture, social class, and race. In T. P. Carpenter, J. M. Moser, & T. A. Romberg (Eds.), *Addition and subtraction: A cognitive perspective* (pp. 191–210). Hillsdale, NJ: Erlbaum.

Ginsburg, H. P. (1986a). Academic diagnosis: Contributions from developmental psychology. In J. Valsiner (Ed.), *Individual subject and scientific psychology* (pp. 235–260). New York: Plenum Press.

Ginsburg, H. P. (1986b). The myth of the deprived child: New thoughts on poor children. In U. Neisser (Ed.), *The school achievement of minority children: New perspectives* (pp. 169–189). Hillsdale, NJ: Erlbaum.

Ginsburg, H. P. (1989). *Children's arithmetic: How they learn it and how you teach it* (2nd ed.). Austin, TX: Pro-Ed.

Ginsburg, H. P. (1990). *Assessment probes and instructional activities: The test of early mathematics ability* (2nd ed.). Austin, TX: Pro-Ed.

Ginsburg, H. P. (1996a). Taming the math monster. In G. Brannigan (Ed.), *The enlightened educator* (pp. 3–25). New York: McGraw-Hill.

Ginsburg, H. P. (1996b). Toby's math. In R. J. Sternberg & T. Ben-Zeev (Eds.), *The nature of mathematical thinking* (pp. 175–202). Hillsdale, NJ: Erlbaum.

Ginsburg, H. P. (1997a). *Entering the child's mind: The cognitive clinical interview in psychological research and practice.* New York: Cambridge University Press.

Ginsburg, H. P. (1997b). Mathematics learning disabilities: A view from developmental psychology. *Journal of Learning Disabilities, 30,* 20–33.

Ginsburg, H. P., & Asmussen, K. (1988). Hot mathematics: Children's mathematics. *New Directions for Child Development, 41,* 89–111.

Ginsburg, H. P., & Baroody, A. J. (1983). *The test of early mathematics ability* (1st ed.). Austin, TX: Pro-Ed.

Ginsburg, H. P., & Baroody, A. J. (1990). *The test of early mathematics ability* (2nd ed.). Austin, TX: Pro-Ed.

Ginsburg, H. P., Choi, Y. E., Lopez, L. S., Netley, R., & Chi, C.-Y. (1997). Happy birthday to you: The early mathematical thinking of Asian, South American, and U.S. children. In T. Nunes & P. Bryant (Eds.), *Learning and teaching mathematics: An international perspective* (pp. 1–45). East Sussex, England: Erlbaum/Taylor & Francis.

Ginsburg, H. P., Jacobs, S. F., & Lopez, L. S. (1993). Assessing mathematical thinking and learning potential. In R. B. Davis & C. S. Maher (Eds.), *Schools, mathematics, and the world of reality* (pp. 237–262). Boston: Allyn & Bacon.

Ginsburg, H. P., Jacobs, S. F., & Lopez, L. S. (in press). *Flexible interviewing in the classroom: Learning what children know about math.* Boston: Allyn & Bacon.

Ginsburg, H. P., Lopez, L. S., Mukhopadhyay, S., Yamamoto, T., Willis, M., & Kelly, M. S. (1992). Assessing understandings of arithmetic. In R. Lesh & S. J. Lamon (Eds.), *Assessment of authentic performance in school mathematics* (pp. 265–289). Washington, DC: American Association for the Advancement of Science Press.

Ginsburg, H. P., & Mathews, S. C. (1984). *Diagnostic test of arithmetic strategies.* Austin, TX: Pro-Ed.

Ginsburg, H. P., & Opper, S. (1988). *Piaget's theory of intellectual development* (3rd ed.). Englewood Cliffs, NJ: Prentice-Hall.

Ginsburg, H. P., Posner, J. K., & Russell, R. L. (1981a). The development of knowledge concerning written arithmetic: A cross-cultural study. *International Journal of Psychology, 16,* 13–34.

Ginsburg, H. P., Posner, J. K., & Russell, R. L. (1981b). The development of mental addition as a function of schooling and culture. *Journal of Cross-Cultural Psychology, 12,* 163–178.

Ginsburg, H. P., & Russell, R. L. (1981). Social class and racial influences on early mathematical thinking. *Monographs of the Society for Research in Child Development, 46*(6, Serial No. 193).

Glaser, R. (1981). The future of testing: A research agenda for cognitive psychology and psychometrics. *American Psychologist, 36,* 923–936.

Goleman, D. (1992, August 27). Study finds babies at 5 months grasp simple mathematics. *New York Times,* p. A1.

Greeno, J. G. (1977). Process of understanding in problem solving. In N. J. Castellan, D. B. Pisoni, & G. R. Potts (Eds.), *Cognitive theory* (pp. 43–83). Hillsdale, NJ: Erlbaum.

Greeno, J. G., Riley, M. S., & Gelman, R. (1984). Conceptual competence and children's counting. *Cognitive Psychology, 16,* 94–143.

Groen, G., & Resnick, L. B. (1977). Can preschool children invent addition algorithms? *Journal of Educational Psychology, 69,* 645–652.

Grouws, D. A. (Ed.). (1992). *Handbook of research on mathematics teaching and learning: A project of the National Council of Teachers of Mathematics.* New York: Macmillan.

Hadamard, J. (1945). *The psychology of invention in the mathematical field.* New York: Dover.

Hamann, M. S., & Ashcraft, M. H. (1985). Simple and complex mental addition across development. *Journal of Experimental Child Psychology, 40,* 49–72.

Harcourt Brace Jovanovich, I. (1992). *Mathematics plus: Grade 1.* Orlando, FL: Author.

Hawkins, D. (1974). *The informed vision.* New York: Agathon Press.

Holloway, S. D., Rambaud, M. F., Fuller, B., & Eggers-Pierola, C. (1995). *What is "appropriate practice" in home and in child care? Low income mothers' views on preparing their children for school.* Presented at the biennial meeting of the Society for Research in Child Development, Indianapolis, IN.

Hope, J., & Small, M. (1993). *Interactions 3: Program information.* Toronto, Canada: Ginn.

Houlihan, D. M., & Ginsburg, H. P. (1981). The addition methods of first- and second-grade children. *Journal for Research in Mathematics Education, 12,* 95–106.

Hughes, M. (1986). *Children and number: Difficulties in learning mathematics.* New York: Basil Blackwell.

James, W. (1958). *Talks to teachers on psychology: And to students on some of life's ideals.* New York: Norton.

Jensen, A. R. (1969). How much can we boost IQ and scholastic achievement? *Harvard Educational Review, 39,* 1–123.

Johnson, D. C., Romberg, T. A., & Scandura, J. M. (1994). The origins of the *JRME:* A retrospective account. *Journal for Research in Mathematics Education, 25*(6), 560–582.

Jordan, N. C., Huttenlocher, J., & Levine, S. C. (1992). Differential calculation abilities in young children from middle- and low-income families. *Developmental Psychology, 28,* 644–653.

Jordan, N. C., Huttenlocher, J., & Levine, S. C. (1994). Assessing early arithmetic abilities: Effects of verbal and nonverbal response types on the calculation performance of middle- and low-income children. *Learning and Individual Differences, 6,* 413–432.

Judd, C. H. (1927). *Psychological analysis of the fundamentals of arithmetic* (Supplementary Educational Monographs No. 32). Chicago: University of Chicago.

Kamii, C. (1982). *Number in preschool and kindergarten.* Washington, DC: National Association for the Education of Young Children.

Kamii, C. (1985). *Young children reinvent arithmetic.* New York: Teachers College Press.

Kamii, C., & DeVries, R. (1976). *Piaget, children, and number.* Washington, DC: National Association for the Education of Young Children.

Kilpatrick, J. (1992). A history of research in mathematics education. In D. A. Grouws (Ed.), *Handbook of research in mathematics teaching and learning* (pp. 3–38). New York: Macmillan.

Kirk, G. E., Hunt, J. M., & Volkmar, F. (1975). Social class and preschool language skill: V. Cognitive and semantic mastery of number. *Genetic Psychology Monographs, 93,* 131–153.

Klein, A. (1984). The early development of arithmetic reasoning: Numerative activities and logical operations. *Dissertation Abstracts International, 45,* 375B–376B.

Klein, A., & Langer, J. (1991). *The early development of division: Social sharing or numerical distribution.* Presented at the meeting of the Jean Piaget Society, Philadelphia, PA.

Klein, A., & Starkey, P. (1988). Universals in the development of early arithmetic cognition. In G. Saxe & M. Gearhart (Eds.), *Children's mathematics* (pp. 5–26). San Francisco: Jossey-Bass.

Klein, A., & Starkey, P. (1995). *Preparing for the transition to school mathematics: The Head Start Family Math project.* Presented at the meeting of the Society for Research in Child Development, Indianapolis, IN.

Knapp, N. F., & Peterson, P. L. (1995). Teachers' interpretations of "CGI" after four years: Meanings and practices. *Journal for Research in Mathematics Education, 26*(1), 40–65.

Kozol, J. (1991). *Savage inequalities: Children in America's schools.* New York: Crown.

Lagemann, E. C. (1989). The plural worlds of educational research. *History of Education Quarterly, 29,* 185–214.

Lambdin, D. V., Kloosterman, P., & Johnson, M. (1994). Connecting research to teaching. *Mathematics Teaching in the Middle School, 1*(1), 38–43.

Langer, J. (1986). *The origins of logic: One to two years.* Orlando, FL: Academic Press.

Lave, J. (1988). *Cognition in practice: Mind, mathematics, and culture in everyday life.* Cambridge, England: Cambridge University Press.

Lesh, R. (1979). Mathematical learning disabilities: Considerations for identification, diagnosis, and remediation. In R. Lesh, D. Mierkiewicz, & M. G. Kantowski (Eds.), *Applied mathematical problem solving.* Columbus, OH: ERIC/SMEAC.

Lesh, R., & Lamon, S. J. (Eds.). (1992). *Assessment of authentic performance in school mathematics.* Washington, DC: AAAS Press.

Lesh, R., & Landau, M. (Eds.). (1989). *Acquisition of mathematics concepts and processes.* New York: Academic Press.

Lesser, G. S. (1974). *Children and television: Lessons from Sesame Street.* New York: Random House.

Lines, S., Nunes, T., & Bryant, P. E. (in press). *Number naming systems in English and Chinese: Linguistic effects on number understanding and basic mathematical skill.*

Mack, N. K. (1990). Learning fractions with understanding. *Journal for Research in Mathematics Education, 21,* 16–32.

Madell, R. (1985). Children's natural processes. *Arithmetic Teacher, 32,* 20–22.

Markman, E. M. (1979). Classes and collections: Conceptual organization and numerical abilities. *Cognitive Psychology, 11,* 394–411.

Mathematical Sciences Education Board. (1989). *Everybody counts: A report to the nation on the future of mathematics education.* Washington, DC: National Academy Press.

McLellan, J. A., & Dewey, J. (1895). *The psychology of number and its applications to methods of teaching arithmetic.* New York: Appleton.

McLloyd, V. (1990). The impact of economic hardship on Black families and children: Psychological distress, parenting, and socioemotional development. *Child Development, 61,* 311–346.

Mehler, J., & Bever, T. (1967). Cognitive capacity of very young children. *Science, 158,* 141–142.

Menninger, K. (1969). *Number words and number symbols: A cultural history of numbers.* Cambridge, MA: MIT Press.

Miller, K. F. (1984). The child as measurer of all things: Measurement procedures and the development of quantitative concepts. In C. Sophian (Ed.), *Origins of cognitive skills* (pp. 193–228). Hillsdale, NJ: Erlbaum.

Miller, K. F., & Stigler, J. W. (1987). Counting in Chinese: Cultural variation in a basic cognitive skill. *Cognitive Development, 2,* 279–305.

Miss Mason's School. (1976). *Mason math.* Princeton, NJ: Author.

Miura, I. T. (1989). Comparisons of U.S. and Japanese first graders' cognitive representations of number and understanding of place value. *Journal of Educational Psychology, 81,* 109–113.

Miura, I. T., Okamoto, Y., Kim, C. C., Steere, M., & Fayol, M. (1993). First graders' cognitive representation of number and understanding of place value: Cross-national comparisons—France, Japan, Korea, Sweden, and the United States. *Journal of Educational Psychology, 85,* 24–30.

Moll, L. C., Amanti, C., Neff, D., & Gonzalez, N. (1992). Funds of knowledge for teaching: Using a qualitative approach to connect homes and classrooms. *Theory into Practice, 31,* 132–141.

Moon, J., & Schulman, L. (1995). *Finding the connections: Linking assessment, instruction, and curriculum in elementary mathematics.* Portsmouth, NH: Heinemann.

Morales, R. V., Shute, V. J., & Pellegrino, J. W. (1985). Developmental differences in understanding and solving simple mathematics word problems. *Cognition and Instruction, 2,* 41–57.

National Commission on Excellence in Education. (1983). *A nation at risk: The imperative for educational reform.* Washington, DC: U.S. Government Printing Office.

National Council of Teachers of Mathematics. (1989). *Curriculum and evaluation standards for school mathematics.* Reston, VA: Author.

National Council of Teachers of Mathematics. (1991). *Professional standards for teaching mathematics.* Reston, VA: Author.

National Council of Teachers of Mathematics. (1995). *Assessment standards for school mathematics.* Reston, VA: Author.

National Research Council. (1989). *Everybody counts: A report to the nation on the future of mathematics education.* Reston, VA: National Council of Teachers of Mathematics.

Natriello, G., McDill, E. L., & Pallas, A. M. (1990). *Schooling disadvantaged children: Racing against catastrophe.* New York: Teachers College Press.

New Jersey Mathematics Coalition. (1993). *New Jersey mathematics curriculum standards (draft copy).* New Brunswick, NJ: Author.

Nunes, T. (1993). Learning mathematics: Perspectives from everyday life. In R. B. Davis & C. A. Maher (Eds.), *Schools, mathematics, and the world of reality* (pp. 61–78). Boston: Allyn & Bacon.

Nunes, T., & Bryant, P. E. (1996). *Children doing mathematics.* Oxford, England: Basil Blackwell.

Nunes, T., Schliemann, A. D., & Carraher, D. W. (1993). *Street mathematics and school mathematics.* Cambridge, England: Cambridge University Press.

Oakes, J. (1990). *Multiplying inequalities: The effects of race, social class, and tracking on opportunities to learn mathematics and science.* Santa Monica, CA: Rand.

Office of Educational Research and Improvement. (1994). *Digest of educational statistics* (30th ed.). Washington, DC: U.S. Department of Education.

Ogbu, J. U. (1982, Winter). Cultural discontinuities and schooling. *Anthropology and Education Quarterly, 13*(4), 290–307.

Papert, S. (1980). *Mindstorms: Children, computers, and powerful ideas.* New York: Basic Books.

Parkman, J. M., & Groen, G. J. (1971). Temporal aspects of simple addition and comparison. *Journal of Experimental Psychology, 89,* 335–342.

Peck, D. M., Jencks, S. M., & Connell, M. L. (1989). Improving instruction through brief interviews. *Arithmetic Teacher, 37,* 15–17.

Peterson, P. L., Fennema, E., Carpenter, T. P., & Loef, M. (1989). Teachers' pedagogical content beliefs in mathematics. *Cognition and Instruction, 6,* 1–40.

Petitto, A. L., & Ginsburg, H. P. (1982). Mental arithmetic in Africa and America: Strategies, principles, and explanations. *International Journal of Psychology, 17,* 81–102.

Piaget, J. (1952). *The child's conception of number* (C. Gattegno & F. M. Hodgson, Trans.). London: Routledge & Kegan Paul.

Piaget, J. (1962). *The moral judgment of the child* (M. Gabain, Trans.). New York: Collier Books.

Piaget, J. (1970). *The science of education and the psychology of the child* (D. Coleman, Trans.). New York: Orion Press.

Piaget, J. (1972). Intellectual evolution from adolescence to adulthood. *Human Development, 15,* 1–12.

Piaget, J. (1976). *The child's conception of the world* (J. A. Tomlinson, Trans.). Totowa, NJ: Littlefield, Adams.

Piaget, J. (1977). Comments on mathematical education. In H. E. Gruber & J. J. Voneche (Eds.), *The essential Piaget* (pp. 726–732). New York: Basic Books.

Pinard, A., & Laurendeau, M. (1964). A scale of mental development based on the theory of Piaget: Description of a project. *Journal of Research in Science Teaching, 2,* 253–260.

Pirie, S. E. B. (1988). Understanding: Instrumental, relational, intuitive, constructed, formalized . . . How can we know? *For the Learning of Mathematics, 8*(3), 2–6.

Post, T. R., Harel, G., Behr, M. J., & Lesh, R. (1991). Intermediate teachers' knowledge of rational number concepts. In E. Fennema, T. P. Carpenter, & S. J. Lamon (Eds.), *Integrating research on teaching and learning mathematics* (pp. 177–198). Albany: State University of New York Press.

Reeve, W. D. (1929). United States: Significant changes and trends in the teaching of mathematics throughout the world since 1910. In W. D. Reeve (Ed.), *Fourth yearbook of the national council of teachers of mathematics.* New York: Teachers College.

Renninger, K. A., & Stavis, J. (1995). *The roles of interest, task difficulty, and gender in the process of students' work with mathematical word problems.* Presented at the meeting of the Society for Research in Child Development, Indianapolis, IN.

Resnick, L. B. (1987). *Education and learning to think.* Washington, DC: National Academy Press.

Resnick, L. B. (1989). Developing mathematical knowledge. *American Psychologist, 44,* 162–169.

Reys, R. E. (1992). The *Standards?* We did them last fall. *Arithmetic Teacher.*

Riley, M. S., & Greeno, J. G. (1988). Developmental analysis of understanding language about quantities and of solving problems. *Cognition and Instruction, 5,* 49–101.

Riley, M. S., Greeno, J. G., & Heller, J. I. (1983). Development of children's problem-solving ability in arithmetic. In H. P. Ginsburg (Ed.), *The development of mathematical thinking* (pp. 153–196). New York: Academic Press.

Rosskopf, M. F. (Ed.). (1975). *Children's mathematical concepts: Six Piagetian studies in mathematics education.* New York: Teachers College Press.

Rosskopf, M. F., Steffe, L. P., & Taback, S. (1971). *Piagetian cognitive development research and mathematics education.* Washington, DC: National Council of Teachers of Mathematics.

Royer, J. M., Cisero, C. A., & Carlo, M. S. (1993). Techniques and procedures for assessing cognitive skills. *Review of Educational Research, 63*(2), 201–243.

Saunders, D. (1994a, September 26). Duck, it's the New-New Math. *San Francisco Chronicle,* p. A20.

Saunders, D. (1994b, October 21). Math agnostics breed math illiterates. *San Francisco Chronicle,* p. A25.

Saxe, G. B. (1979). Developmental relations between notational counting and number conservation. *Child Development, 50,* 180–187.

Saxe, G. B. (1991). *Culture and cognitive development: Studies in mathematical understanding.* Hillsdale, NJ: Erlbaum.

Saxe, G. B., Guberman, S. R., & Gearhart, M. (1987). Social processes in early number development. *Monographs of the Society for Research in Child Development, 52*(2, Serial No. 216).

Saxe, G. B., & Posner, J. (1983). The development of numerical cognition: Cross-cultural perspectives. In H. P. Ginsburg (Ed.), *The development of mathematical thinking* (pp. 291–317). New York: Academic Press.

Schaeffer, B., Eggleston, V. H., & Scott, L. H. (1974). Number development in young children. *Cognitive Psychology, 6,* 357–379.

Schifter, D., & Fosnot, C. T. (1993). *Reconstructing mathematics instruction.* New York: Teachers College Press.

Schmandt-Besserat, D. (1992). *Before writing.* Austin: University of Texas Press.

Scholastic, I. (1995). *Math place: Numbers in the wild.* New York: Author.

Scribner, S. (1986). Thinking in action: Some characteristics of practical thought. In R. Sternberg & R. K. Wagner (Eds.), *Practical intelligence: Nature and origins of competence in the everyday world* (pp. 13–60). Cambridge, MA: Harvard University Press.

Secada, W. (1991). Diversity, equity, and cognitivist research. In E. Fennema, T. P. Carpenter, & S. J. Lamon (Eds.), *Integrating research on teaching and learning mathematics.* Albany: State University of New York Press.

Shulman, L. S. (1970). Psychology and mathematics education. In E. G. Begle (Ed.), *Mathematics education* (69th Yearbook of the National Society for the Study of Education, Pt. 1) (pp. 23–71). Chicago: University of Chicago Press.

Siegler, R. S. (1987). Strategy choices in subtraction. In J. A. Sloboda & D. Rogers (Eds.), *Cognitive processes in mathematics* (pp. 81–106). Oxford, England: Clarendon Press.

Siegler, R. S. (1988). Individual differences in strategy choices: Good students, not-so-good students, and perfectionists. *Child Development, 59,* 833–851.

Siegler, R. S. (1991). In young children's counting, procedures precede principles. *Educational Psychology Review, 3,* 127–135.

Siegler, R. S., & Crowley, K. (1991). The microgenetic method: A direct means for studying cognitive development. *American Psychologist, 46*(6), 606–620.

Siegler, R. S., & Robinson, M. (1982). The development of numerical understandings. In H. W. Reese & L. P. Lipsitt (Eds.), *Advances in child development and behavior.* New York: Academic Press.

Sierpinska, A., Kilpatrick, J., Balacheff, N., Howson, A. G., Sfard, A., & Steinbring, H. (1993). What is research in mathematics education, and what are its results? *Journal for Research in Mathematics Education, 24*(3), 274–278.

Silver Burdett Ginn. (1995a). *Authentic assessment: Grades K through 8.* Morristown, NJ: Author.

Silver Burdett Ginn. (1995b). *Mathematics: Exploring your world. Grade 1.* Morristown, NJ: Author.

Silver Burdett Ginn. (1995c). *Mathematics: Exploring your world. Grade 2.* Morristown, NJ: Author.

Simon, M. A. (1993). Prospective elementary teachers' knowledge of division. *Journal for Research in Mathematics Education, 24*(3), 233–254.

Sophian, C., & Adams, N. (1987). Infants' understanding of numerical transformations. *British Journal of Developmental Psychology, 5,* 257–264.

Starkey, P. (1992). The early development of numerical reasoning. *Cognition, 43,* 93–126.

Starkey, P., & Cooper, R. G. (1980). Perception of numbers by human infants. *Science, 210,* 1033–1035.

Starkey, P., & Cooper, R. G. (1995a). The development of subitizing in young children. *British Journal of Developmental Psychology, 13,* 399–420.

Starkey, P., & Cooper, R. G. (1995b). *The enumeration range of human infants.* Manuscript submitted for publication.

Starkey, P., & Gelman, R. (1982). The development of addition and subtraction abilities prior to formal schooling in arithmetic. In T. P. Carpenter, J. M. Moser, & T. A. Romberg (Eds.), *Addition and subtraction: A cognitive perspective* (pp. 99–116). Hillsdale, NJ: Erlbaum.

Starkey, P., & Klein, A. (1992). Economic and cultural influences on early mathematical development. In F. L. Parker, R. Robinson, S. Sombrano, C. Piotrowski, J. Hagen, S. Randolph, & A. Baker (Eds.), *New directions in child and family research: Shaping Head Start in the 90s* (pp. 440–443). New York: National Council of Jewish Women.

Starkey, P., Spelke, E. S., & Gelman, R. (1983). Detection of intermodal numerical correspondences by human infants. *Science, 222,* 179–181.

Starkey, P., Spelke, E. S., & Gelman, R. (1990). Numerical abstraction by human infants. *Cognition, 36,* 97–128.

Stern, E. (1993). What makes certain arithmetic word problems involving comparison of sets so difficult for children? *Journal of Educational Psychology, 85,* 7–23.

Sternberg, R. J. (1985). *Beyond IQ: A triarchic theory of human intelligence.* Cambridge, England: Cambridge University Press.

Stevenson, H., Lee, S. S., & Stigler, J. (1986). The mathematics achievement of Chinese, Japanese, and American children. *Science, 56,* 693–699.

Stevenson, H. W., & Stigler, J. W. (1992). *The learning gap: Why our schools are failing and what we can learn from Japanese and Chinese education.* New York: Summit.

Stigler, J. W., Fuson, K. C., Ham, M., & Kim, M. S. (1986). An analysis of addition and subtraction word problems in American and Soviet elementary mathematics textbooks. *Cognition and Instruction, 3,* 153–171.

Stigler, J. W., & Perry, M. (1990). Mathematics learning in Japanese, Chinese, and American classrooms. In J. W. Stigler, R. A. Shweder, & G. Herdt (Eds.), *Cultural psychology: Essays on comparative human development* (pp. 328–353). New York: Cambridge University Press.

Stodolsky, S. S. (1988). *The subject matters: Classroom activity in math and social studies.* Chicago: University of Chicago Press.

Strauss, M. S., & Curtis, L. E. (1981). Infant perception of number. *Child Development, 52,* 1146–1152.

Strayer, G. D., & Upton, C. B. (1934). *Stayer-Upton practical arithmetics: Book 3.* New York: American Book.

Tharp, R. G., & Gallimore, R. (1991). *Rousing minds to life: Teaching, learning, and schooling in social context.* New York: Cambridge University Press.

Thompson, A. G. (1992). Teachers' beliefs and conceptions: A synthesis of the research. In D. A. Grouws (Ed.), *Handbook of research in mathematics teaching and learning* (pp. 127–146). New York: Macmillan.

Thorndike, E. L. (1922). *The psychology of arithmetic.* New York: Macmillan.

Thornton, C. (1979). Basic fact mastery: Guides to success for the LD child. *Focus on Learning Problems in Mathematics, 1*(1), 34–42.

Trivett, J. (1980). The multiplication table: To be memorized or mastered? *For the Learning of Mathematics, 1*(1), 21–25.

Turner, M., & Bryant, P. E. (in press). *Do children understand what they are doing when they add?*

Van den Brink, J. (1989). Transference of objects. *For the Learning of Mathematics, 9*(3), 12–16.

VanLehn, K. (1986). Arithmetic procedures are induced from examples. In J. Hiebert (Ed.), *Conceptual and procedural knowledge: The case of mathematics* (pp. 133–180). Hillsdale, NJ: Erlbaum.

VanLehn, K. (1990). *Mindbugs: The origins of procedural misconceptions.* Cambridge, MA: MIT Press.

van Loosbroek, E., & Smitsman, A. W. (1990). Visual perception of numerosity in infancy. *Developmental Psychology, 26,* 916–922.

Vygotsky, L. S. (1978). *Mind in society: The development of higher psychological processes.* Cambridge, MA: Harvard University Press.

Vygotsky, L. S. (1986). *Thought and language* (A. Kozulin, Trans.). Cambridge, MA: MIT Press.

Wagner, S. H., & Walters, J. (1982). A longitudinal analysis of early number concepts: From numbers to number. In G. E. Forman (Ed.), *Action and thought: From sensorimotor schemes to symbolic operations* (pp. 137–161). New York: Academic Press.

Weaver, J. F. (1955). Big dividends from little interviews. *Arithmetic Teacher, 2,* 40–47.

Weiss, I. R. (1990). Mathematics teachers in the United States. *International Journal of Educational Research, 14*(2), 139–155.

Wohlwill, J. F. (1960). A study of the development of number by scalogram analysis. *Journal of Genetic Psychology, 97,* 345–377.

Wood, T., Cobb, P., & Yackel, E. (1991). Change in teaching mathematics: A case study. *American Educational Research Journal, 28,* 586–616.

Wynn, K. (1990). Children's understanding of counting. *Cognition, 36,* 155–192.

Wynn, K. (1992). Addition and subtraction by human infants. *Nature, 358,* 749–750.

Zaslavsky, C. (1973). *Africa counts: Number and pattern in African culture.* Boston: Prindle, Weber & Schmidt.

Mental and Physical Health

CHAPTER 8

Perspectives on Research and Practice in Developmental Psychopathology

DANTE CICCHETTI and SHEREE L. TOTH

Considerable progress has occurred in our understanding of the origins, course, sequelae, treatment, and prevention of mental disorders (Institute of Medicine [IOM], 1985, 1989, 1994; National Advisory Mental Health Council, 1993). Despite these gains, mental illness continues to challenge millions of individuals as well as to place major stress on the service delivery system and on the research community that strive to better understand psychopathology and thereby contribute to improved treatment and prevention efforts (Hoagwood, Jensen, Petti, & Burns, 1996; Howard et al., 1996; IOM, 1985, 1994). In 1990, the cost of mental illness in the United States was estimated at 147 billion dollars. This figure does not include the approximately 164 billion dollars expended for the treatment of drug and alcohol abuse. Monetary numbers alone, however, fail to capture the costs associated with the suffering experienced by those confronted with a mental disorder. Many of the treatment

Our work on this project was supported, in part, by grants from the William T. Grant Foundation, the National Center on Child Abuse and Neglect, the National Institute of Mental Health, and the Spunk Fund, Inc.

advances that have benefited individuals with mental disorders can be attributed to improvements in our knowledge of epidemiology, diagnosis, and the matching of treatment to diagnosis that have occurred over the past several decades.

With respect to the child and adolescent segment of the population, a great deal is known about the types of disorders that affect children. However, although progress is being made in our understanding of the course of disorder over time, many questions remain unanswered (Sroufe, 1997). Considerably less is known about the causes of mental illness or the factors that contribute to vulnerability rather than resistance to disease (IOM, 1989). Moreover, although our understanding of childhood mental disorders has profited from knowledge derived from the study of adult psychopathology, childhood psychopathology is a unique field that requires utilization of a developmental perspective if it is to be fully understood (IOM, 1989).

In response to requests from the United States Senate and House of Representatives, and as a result of growing concern that too little was being done to treat or prevent mental disorders in children, the National Institute of Mental Health issued its National Plan for Research on Child and Adolescent Mental Disorders (NIMH, 1990). The 5-year plan articulated three primary goals: (a) to develop and sustain a critical mass of basic and clinically oriented researchers to study mental disorders of childhood and adolescence; (b) to stimulate basic and clinical research; and (c) to form a consortium of NIMH program staff to implement the national plan (NIMH, 1990).

A "report card" was issued to assess progress made in the implementation of the national plan. Gains were noted in the areas of services and prevention research. Investments in research training and career development, however, were considered to be only modest. Of significant concern was the conclusion that NIMH had not yet taken sufficient steps to educate the public about the nature and impact of child and adolescent mental disorders (Leckman et al., 1995).

In recognition of its importance, the IOM (1994) highlighted developmental psychopathology as one of four core sciences considered to be necessary for expanding the frontiers of prevention and intervention efforts. In this chapter, a developmental psychopathology perspective is applied toward the elucidation of the etiology, course, consequences, prevention, and treatment of mental disorders of childhood and adolescence. Although developmental psychopathologists are invested in understanding high-risk conditions and mental disorders across the life span (Cicchetti & Cohen, 1995b), in this chapter we limit ourselves to a consideration of child and adolescent disorders and their treatment because this volume focuses on research and practice as they pertain to children and adolescents. However, when applicable, we discuss long-term follow-up studies and disorders beyond the adolescent years. The literatures related to child maltreatment and depression, the areas that we use to illustrate our approach to developmental psychopathology, are extensive. Therefore, we have limited our discussion of relevant research findings to those studies that meet adequate methodological standards and that incorporate developmental considerations into their design.

To begin, a description of the field of developmental psychopathology is provided, along with its definitional parameters and tenets. The ways in which a developmental approach to psychopathology can contribute to reducing the schisms that have prevented the productive interface between researchers and practitioners are then explored, followed by a discussion of how developmental theorizing and research can enhance the design and implementation of prevention and treatment efforts for high-risk conditions and mental disorders of children and adolescents. The importance of theory in organizing and conducting research and treatment is emphasized and the organizational framework on development is presented as one such approach for conceptualizing risk, disorder, and resilience. A developmental epidemiological framework is utilized to improve our understanding of the identification of the incidence and prevalence of risk conditions and mental disorders, and the implications of such a framework for illustrating the mutually enriching interplay between developmental theory and epidemiologically based preventive interventions are examined. Research on illustrative risk conditions and disorders of childhood and adolescence is then reviewed, and the practice implications emanating from this work are discussed. Throughout our review of this research the ways in which principles derived from an organizational perspective on normal development elucidate various aspects of maladaptation and disorder are explicated. Conversely, illustrations are provided on how the study of these atypical populations can inform our existing theories of normal development. In our penultimate sections, we focus on a discussion of ethical issues and training needs that accompany service provision and research on high-risk conditions and mental disorders of childhood and adolescence. We conclude the chapter with an integrative summary statement and a view toward the future for research and practice in the field of developmental psychopathology.

DEFINITIONAL PARAMETERS OF DEVELOPMENTAL PSYCHOPATHOLOGY

It has been only within the past two decades that the field of developmental psychopathology has emerged as a new interdisciplinary science (Cicchetti, 1984, 1993; Rutter & Garmezy, 1983). Despite its relatively recent crystallization as a coherent framework for examining and conceptualizing the links between the study of psychopathology and the study of development, developmental psychopathology owes its ascendance and coalescence to many historically based endeavors within a variety of areas and disciplines (Cicchetti, 1990). Prior to the emergence of developmental psychopathology as an integrative perspective with its own integrity, the efforts of those working in these areas had been separate and distinct. Some of the lack of integration stemmed from long-standing tensions between the philosophical traditions underlying clinical practice and academic training and between experimental versus applied research (see Cahan & White, 1992; Cicchetti, 1984, 1993; Santostefano, 1978, 1991; Santostefano & Baker, 1972).

Throughout its matriculation as an increasingly mature scientific discipline, an ongoing goal of developmental psychopathology has been to become a science that not only bridges fields of study and aids in the discovery of important new truths about the processes underlying adaptation and maladaptation across the life span, but also to provide the best means of preventing and ameliorating maladaptive and pathological outcomes (Cicchetti, 1989; Cicchetti & Toth, 1992b; Sroufe & Rutter, 1984). Moreover, the field of developmental psychopathology has continuously sought to reduce the dualisms that exist between empirical research and the clinical study and treatment of childhood and adult high-risk conditions and disorders, between the behavioral and biological sciences, and between basic and applied research.

Although some advances have been made in breaking down the barriers that exist between basic and applied research and between practitioners and researchers, a great deal of work remains to be completed before true progress is achieved (cf., Beutler, Williams, Wakefield, & Entwistle, 1995; Cicchetti & Toth, 1991, 1993; Peterson, 1995; Stricker & Trierweiler, 1995). As Neal Miller (1995) noted, it is critical that "all of the different specialties—ranging from the basic to the applied and from the biological to the social and cultural—are needed to advance our common goal of better understanding human behavior" (p. 910). Furthermore, Miller (1995) stated, "Clinical observations can direct the attention of laboratory workers to significant new problems" and "laboratory experiments can refine and correct clinical observations" (p. 901). Even though Miller was discussing the importance of basic and applied research, and a multidomain and interdisciplinary perspective for the field of neuroscience, his recommendations echo the basic principles and philosophical beliefs of developmental psychopathologists (cf., Cicchetti, 1993; Cicchetti & Toth, 1991; Santostefano, 1978; Santostefano & Baker, 1972).

A further examination of the ways in which the investigation of psychopathology and development have been intertwined historically reveals that many of the most influential theoreticians and researchers in embryology, molecular genetics, the neurosciences, philosophy, psychoanalysis, psychiatry, and clinical, developmental, and experimental psychology have reasoned that we can learn more about the normal functioning of organisms or individuals by studying their pathological condition, and, likewise, more about their pathology by examining their normal condition (see Cicchetti, 1990; B. Kaplan, 1967; and Overton & Horowitz, 1991, for an in-depth explication). A number of the integrative thinkers from these diverse scientific fields conceived psychopathology as a magnifying mirror in which normal biological, psychological, and social processes could better be observed (Cicchetti & Cohen, 1995b). Because these systematizers conceptualized psychopathology as a distortion or exaggeration of the normal condition, the study of pathological phenomena was thought to throw into sharper relief one's understanding of normal processes (cf., Weiss, 1961; Werner, 1948).

A basic theme in the writings of these early thinkers is that because all psychopathology can be conceived as a distortion, disturbance, or degeneration of normal functioning, it follows that, if one wishes to comprehend psychopathology more fully, then one must understand the normal functioning with which psychopathology is compared. Not only is knowledge of normal biological, psychological, and social processes exceedingly useful for assessing, diagnosing, understanding, treating, and preventing psychopathology, but also the deviations from and distortions of normal development that characterize pathological processes indicate in exciting ways how normal development may be better investigated and understood. The essence and the uniqueness of a developmental psychopathology approach lie in its focus on both normal and abnormal, adaptive and maladaptive, developmental processes (Cicchetti, 1984, 1990, 1993; Rutter, 1986; Rutter & Garmezy, 1983; Sroufe, 1990; Sroufe & Rutter, 1984).

In the foreword to an edited volume on child psychiatry that had been dedicated in his honor, Jean Piaget (1975) wrote that he looked ahead "with great expectation to the emergence of developmental psychopathology as a new discipline" (p. ix). Rather than focusing on distinguishing different clinical entities or on psychological assessments of family conflict and their impact on individual functioning, Piaget urged that researchers in developmental psychopathology should aim to form an integrative "science of ontogenetic development" (Piaget, 1975, p. vii), a goal that involved the construction of "a common language" that would enable psychological disorder to be conceptualized in terms of the "ensemble of elements involved" (i.e., the organization and integration of the biological and psychological systems in their extant contexts).

Sroufe and Rutter (1984) originally defined developmental psychopathology as ". . . *the study of the origins and course of individual patterns of behavioral maladaptation,* whatever the age of onset, whatever the causes, whatever the transformations in behavioral manifestation, and however complex the course of the developmental pattern may be" (p. 18; italics theirs). More recently, authors of the Institute of Medicine (1989) report stated that the developmental psychopathology perspective should take into account ". . . the emerging behavioral repertoire, cognitive and language functions, social and emotional processes, and changes occurring in anatomical structures and physiological processes of the brain" (p. 14). Although some definitional divergence exists, it is generally agreed that developmental psychopathologists should investigate functioning through the assessment of ontogenetic, genetic, biochemical, biological, physiological, societal, cultural, environmental, family, cognitive, social-cognitive, linguistic, representational, and socioemotional influences on behavior. Theory and research conducted within the discipline of developmental psychopathology seek to unify, within a life-span framework, the many contributions to the study of high-risk and disordered individuals emanating from multiple fields of inquiry, including psychiatry, psychology, cognitive science, the neurosciences, genetics, physiology, cultural anthropology, sociology, epidemiology, statistics, and psychometrics (Achenbach, 1990; Cicchetti, 1990). It is our conviction that the principles of developmental psychopathology provide a much needed conceptual scaffolding for the facilitation of this multidisciplinary integration, as well as for fostering an increased synergy between research and practice.

From the perspective of developmental psychopathology, it is critical to engage in a comprehensive evaluation of these biological, psychological, and social factors and to ascertain how these multiple levels of analysis may influence individual differences, the continuity of adaptive or maladaptive behavioral patterns, and the pathways by which the same developmental outcomes may be achieved (Cicchetti & Rogosch, 1996a; Cicchetti & Schneider-Rosen, 1986; Pennington & Welsh, 1995; Robins & Rutter, 1990; Sroufe, 1989, 1997). In practice, this entails a comprehension of and an appreciation for the developmental transformations and reorganizations that occur over time, an analysis of the risk and protective factors and mechanisms operating in the individual and his or her environment throughout ontogenesis, the investigation of how emergent functions, competencies, and developmental tasks modify the expression of a disorder or lead to new symptoms and difficulties, and the recognition that a particular stress or underlying mechanism may result in different biological and psychological difficulties, depending on when in the developmental period the stress occurs (Cicchetti & Aber, 1986; Cicchetti & Lynch, 1993; IOM, 1989, 1994; Rutter, 1988, 1990, 1995). Moreover, various problems will constitute different meanings for an individual depending on cultural considerations. The interpretation of the experience, in turn, will affect the adaptation or maladaptation that ensues.

Consequently, the field of developmental psychopathology transcends traditional disciplinary boundaries and provides fertile ground for moving beyond descriptive facts to a process level understanding of normal and abnormal developmental trajectories. Rather than competing with existing theories and facts, the developmental psychopathology perspective provides a broad, integrative framework within which the contributions of separate disciplines can be fully realized in the broader context of understanding individual development and functioning. Research conducted within a developmental psychopathology framework may challenge assumptions about what constitutes health or pathology and may redefine the manner in which the mental health community operationalizes, assesses, classifies, communicates about, and treats the adjustment problems and functioning impairments of infants, children, adolescents, and adults (Richters & Cicchetti, 1993b; Sameroff & Emde, 1989; Zeanah, 1993, 1996; Zero-To-Three Task Force on Diagnostic Classification in Infancy, 1994). Thus, its own potential contribution lies in the heuristic power it holds for translating facts into knowledge, understanding, and practical application.

A focus on the boundary between normal and abnormal development also is central to a developmental psychopathology analysis (Cicchetti, 1984, 1990, 1993, 1996b; Rutter, 1986; Rutter & Garmezy, 1983; Sroufe, 1990). Such a perspective emphasizes not only how knowledge from the study of normal development can inform the study of high-risk conditions and psychopathology, but also how the investigation of risk and pathology can enhance our comprehension of normal development. Even before a psychopathological disorder emerges, certain pathways signify adaptational failures in normal development that probabilistically forebode subsequent pathology (Cicchetti & Rogosch, 1996a; Sroufe, 1989). Similarly, information obtained from studying pathology can enhance the comprehension of normal development.

Despite the importance of such studies, investigations of the determinants of human behavior are greatly hampered by the ethical impossibility of conducting experiments that will compromise the integrity of biological and psychological ontogenetic processes. Therefore, we believe that we must direct our attention toward "experiments of nature" to elucidate our understanding of developmental processes and mechanisms. These so-called natural experiments "are especially important for the purpose of dissociating possible mechanisms that offer competing explanations" (Rutter, 1994, p. 935). Moreover, the examination of individuals with high-risk conditions and mental disorders can provide a natural entree into the study of system organization, disorganization, and reorganization that is otherwise not possible due to constraints associated with human participants. Because there are limits to experimental manipulations that can be invoked with humans, utilization of individuals who are experiencing difficulties frequently is the only way to examine developmental processes in their full complexity.

Often, the investigation of a system in its smoothly operating normal or healthy state does not afford the opportunity to comprehend the interrelations among its component subsystems. Noam Chomsky (1968) reflected on this state of affairs when he asserted: "One difficulty in the psychological sciences lies in the familiarity of the phenomena with which they deal. . . . One is inclined to take them for granted as necessary or somehow 'natural'" (p. 21). Furthermore, Chomsky (1968) lamented, "We also lose sight of the need for explanation when phenomena are too familiar and 'obvious.' We tend too easily to assume that explanations must be transparent and close to the surface" (p. 22).

Because pathological conditions such as brain damage, mental disorder, and growing up in a malignant environment enable scientists to isolate the components of the integrated system, their investigation sheds light on the normal structure of the system, and prevents us from falling prey to the problems identified by Chomsky. Consequently, examinations of developmental extremes and imperfections must be conducted. The anthropologist Stephen Gould (1980) has articulated the central role that the discovery of anomalies can play in elucidating the history of evolution. Gould noted that whereas "good fits" between organisms and their ecological niches generate so great an array of interpretations as to be uninformative, the identification of anomalies greatly decreases the number of explanations possible. As Gould (1986) stated: "We must look for imperfections and oddities because any perfection in organic design or ecology obliterates the paths of history and might have been created as we find it" (p. 63).

We agree with Michael Scriven's view (cited in A. Kaplan, 1964) that one can learn more from studying disarray than by disregarding it. If we choose simply to ignore or bypass the study of these atypical phenomena, then the eventual result is likely to be the construction of theories that are contradicted by the revelation of critical facts in risk and psychopathology (cf., Lenneberg, 1967). Similar to genetic research on pathological embryos and to neurobiological and genetic linkage studies on psychopathology, investigations of the ecological, biological, and psychological factors that cause development to go awry can help to inform our understanding of more normative ontogenetic processes. When extrapolating from nontypical populations with the goal of informing developmental theory, it is critical to investigate a range of high-risk and mentally disordered individuals. The study of a single pathological or risk process may result in spurious conclusions if generalizations are made based solely on that condition or disorder. However, if a given biological or behavioral pattern is viewed in the light of an entire spectrum of disordered modifications, then it may be possible to attain significant insight into the processes of development not generally achieved through sole reliance on studies of relatively nondisordered populations (cf., Lenneberg, 1967).

Developmental psychopathologists are as interested in individuals at high risk for the development of pathology who do not manifest it over time, as they are in individuals who develop an actual disorder (Sroufe & Rutter, 1984). Relatedly, developmental psychopathologists also are committed to understanding pathways to competent adaptation despite exposure to conditions of adversity (Cicchetti & Garmezy, 1993; Masten, Best, & Garmezy, 1990; Rutter, 1990; Skuse, 1984). In addition, developmental psychopathologists emphasize the need to understand the functioning of individuals who, after having diverged onto deviant developmental pathways, resume more positive functioning and achieve adequate adaptation (Cicchetti & Richters, 1993).

Because of the interrelations between the investigation of normal and abnormal ontogenesis, developmental psychopathologists must be aware of normal pathways of development within a given cultural context, uncover deviations from these pathways, articulate the developmental transformations that occur as individuals progress through these deviant ontogenetic courses, and identify the processes and mechanisms that may divert an individual from a particular pathway and onto a more or less adaptive course (Sroufe, 1989). According to Zigler and Glick (1986), a central tenet of developmental psychopathology is that persons may move between pathological and nonpathological forms of functioning.

The central focus of developmental psychopathology involves the elucidation of developmental processes and how they function as indicated and elaborated by the examination of extremes in developmental outcome. In addition to studying extremes in the distribution (i.e., individuals with disorders), developmental psychopathologists also direct attention toward variations in the continuum between the mean and the extremes. These variations may represent individuals who are currently not divergent enough to be considered disordered, but who may progress to further extremes as development continues. Such individuals may be vulnerable to developing future disordered outcomes, or, viewed within Wakefield's (1992, 1997) concept of harmful dysfunction, developmental deviations may, for some individuals, reflect either the earliest signs of an emerging dysfunction or an already existing dysfunction that is partially compensated for by other processes within or outside the individual. Therefore, tracking the developmental course of these individuals is likely to broaden the complexity of understanding ontogenetic processes.

Additionally, developmental psychopathology underscores that, even in the midst of pathology, patients may display adaptive coping mechanisms. Only through the consideration of both adaptive and maladaptive processes does it become possible to delimit the presence, nature, and boundaries of the underlying psychopathology. Furthermore, developmental psychopathology is a perspective that is especially applicable to the investigation of transitional turning points in development across the life span. With respect to the emergence of psychopathology, all periods of life are consequential in that the developmental process may undergo a pernicious turn toward mental disorder at any phase. Developmental psychopathologists acknowledge that disorders may appear at any point in the life span (for examples, see Breslin & Weinberger, 1990; Moffitt, 1993; Rogers & Kegan, 1991; Rutter, 1996; Zigler & Glick, 1986) and advocate the examination of the course of disorders once manifest, including their phases and sequelae (Post, Weiss, & Leverich, 1994; Post et al., 1996; Zigler & Glick, 1986).

Not only is the emergence of psychopathology possible at any developmental stage, but also operating at higher stages of development may usher in more serious forms of psychopathology than evident in individuals functioning at less advanced stages (Noam, Chandler, & Lalonde, 1995; Rogers & Kegan, 1991). According to Fischer (1980), development proceeds through successively more complex levels of control systems, thereby bringing about not only more sophisticated cognition, language, representation, and emotion, but also the possibility of more complex psychopathology (Fischer & Ayoub, 1994). Thus, psychopathology becomes increasingly complex throughout developmental time. Although such complexity may initiate the emergence of more advanced skills that subsequently enhance adaptive functioning in a particular environment, these very abilities may create more complicated forms of difficulty. For example, physically abused children may learn to avoid eye contact with their parents to minimize future abuse; however, if friends, teachers, and other nonparental adults are interacted with in a similar fashion, then it is unlikely that these children's perpetuation of avoidance will result in competent relations with teachers or peers (Cicchetti, Lynch, Shonk, & Manly, 1992).

In another illustration of the assertion that achievement of a high developmental level of self-functioning does not grant immunity to psychopathology, even in its most serious manifestations, Borst and her colleagues demonstrated that different forms and expressions of psychopathology are manifest at different levels of ego development. In an important study, Borst, Noam, and Bartok (1991) posed the question: Can individuals who function at higher levels of a developmental sequence end up more disturbed or symptomatic than individuals operating at earlier developmental positions? Interestingly, contrary to what one would expect from Piaget's (1971) or Kohlberg's (1984) assertions that more advanced stages of cognitive and moral development should be associated with more adaptive functioning, Borst and associates found that, in fact, increased ego development did not protect hospitalized adolescents from committing suicide. Adolescents who were characterized by higher levels of ego development revealed more internalizing and less action-oriented problems than did adolescents operating at less developmentally complex levels of ego functioning. The higher levels of ego development and internalizing symptomatology apparently eventuated in elevated depression and self-blame, and these in turn brought about an increase in suicidal behavior. In contrast, adolescents who were functioning at less developmentally complex levels of ego development manifested greater externalizing behavior, such as blaming others for their own problems, or engaging in acting-out behaviors.

An important conclusion that can be drawn from these illustrations is that any given pathway will eventuate in an array of outcomes rather than in a single linear endpoint. A major reason for the variations in outcome associated with a particular pathway is the concept of differentiation in development (Werner, 1957). Thus, children diagnosed with conduct disorder may, as adults, develop antisocial personality, alcoholism, depression, or schizophrenia, or manifest normal functioning (Richters & Cicchetti, 1993b; Robins, 1966). A critical task for future research will be to ascertain if, and when, the developmental pathways for maladaptive patterns and mental disorders become strongly canalized and, theoretically, more difficult to deflect from a negative course.

Diversity in process and outcome are hallmarks of the developmental psychopathology perspective. With the acquisition of more knowledge about diversity in development, it has become increasingly recognized that the same rules of normal development do not necessarily exist for, or apply to, all children and families (e.g., Baldwin, Baldwin, & Cole, 1990). In this regard, the principles of equifinality and multifinality, derived from general systems theory, are relevant (von Bertalanffy, 1968; Cicchetti & Rogosch, 1996b). Equifinality refers to the observation that a diversity of paths may lead to the same outcome (Sroufe, 1989). Accordingly, the breakdown, as well as the maintenance, of a system's function can occur in many ways, especially when taking into account environment-organism interactions and transactions. As such, instead of a singular primary pathway, a variety of developmental progressions may eventuate in a given disorder. In contrast, multifinality suggests that single pathways can lead to multiple outcomes. Thus, a particular adverse event should not necessarily be seen as contributing to the same psychopathological or nonpsychopathological outcome in every individual. The pathology or health of a system must be identified in terms of how adequately its essential functions are maintained. Consequently, any one component may function differently depending on the organization of the system in which it operates.

In the absence of this sophisticated understanding of the range of diversity in normal development, developmental psychopathologists would have been severely hampered in their attempts to elucidate the pathways to adaptation and maladaptation in high-risk and disordered individuals from varying backgrounds. Using conduct disorder as an example, it is expected that there are multiple contributors to conduct-disordered outcomes in any individual, that the contributors vary among individuals who have the disorder, that there is heterogeneity among conduct-disordered children in the features of their disturbance, and that there are numerous pathways to any particular manifestation of conduct-disordered behavior (Goldsmith & Gottesman, 1994; Richters & Cicchetti, 1993b). Achenbach (1993) argued cogently for the existence of two different yet overlapping syndromes of antisocial behavior, one with and one without significant levels of overt aggression. Even among those with similar patterns of aggressive behavior, there may be multiple, alternative causal pathways influencing aggression. Relatedly, Sroufe (1989) found multiple pathways to attention-deficit/hyperactivity disorder (ADHD), one predominantly biological, the other largely attributable to insensitive caregiving. Likewise, Richters and Cicchetti (1993b) proposed that there were diverse etiological pathways to conduct disorder. In a further illustration of equifinality, Gjerde (1995) provided evidence that there may be different developmental trajectories to depression for young adult females and males. In a longitudinal study, Gjerde found that the reliable prospective correlates of depressive symptoms of young adults originated earlier in boys than in girls. Moreover, Gjerde discovered that there were different behavioral indicators of depression in boys and girls.

Similarly, Neumann, Grimes, Walker, and Baum (1995) offer support that there are different developmental pathways to schizophrenia. The behavior problems that are antecedents to schizophrenia were found to vary in their developmental course, with some behavior problems revealing an insidious but consistent escalation across childhood, and other behavior problems manifesting more precipitous increases in adolescence. Finally, a third subgroup was identified that displayed more pronounced behavior problems that increased with age and that exhibited more neuromotor anomalies (cf., Walker, 1994).

With regard to multifinality, it would be very informative to examine the functioning characteristics of individuals formerly diagnosed with a depressive disorder who have returned to a nondisordered condition. Congruent with the concept of multifinality, it may be possible to identify core characteristics of functioning that remain stable but that no longer give rise to depression because of compensatory factors within the individual or the environment (Cicchetti & Aber, 1986). Conceivably, such research might reveal that certain functioning characteristics that were once causally relevant to developing a depressive disorder in an earlier environment have become positively adaptive in a new environment. They not only may not detract from, but also actually may facilitate, adaptive and successful functioning. It also may be erroneous to assume that normalized behavior necessarily reflects improvements in processes that were once causal to the development of depression. Thus, a developmental psychopathology perspective encourages us to remain open to the possibility that many of the characteristics we typically view as functioning deficits in fact may be neutral. That is, they may translate into deficits or assets depending on other characteristics of the individual or the environment.

Because adaptation at any point is the product of extant circumstances and conditions as well as prior experiences and adaptations (Carlson, Jacobvitz, & Sroufe, 1995; Cicchetti & Tucker, 1994; Sroufe, Egeland, & Kreutzer, 1990), maladaptation and mental disorder may best be comprehended in terms of current potentiating and compensatory factors within the context of prior developmental experiences that have been hierarchically integrated into the individual's present organization of biological and behavioral systems. When psychopathology is conceptualized in this manner, it becomes crucial to identify the specific developmental arrests or failures and the unsuccessfully resolved developmental tasks implicated in an episode of mental illness, the environmental stressors involved, and the biological and psychological circumstances that may have interfered with the resolution of the developmental issues. Furthermore, it is essential to characterize each mental disorder in terms of its specific form of nonintegration, or its own integration of pathological structures, to distinguish it from other forms of mental disorder, each of which leaves its own fingerprint of incompetence by leading to peculiar patterns of maladaptation.

This developmental conceptualization of psychopathology acknowledges human development and functioning in its full complexity and subtlety. In contrast to the often dichotomous world of mental disorder/nondisorder in clinical psychology and psychiatry, a developmental perspective recognizes that normality often fades into abnormality, adaptive and maladaptive may take on differing definitions depending on whether one's time referent is immediate circumstance or long-term development, and that processes within the individual can be characterized as having shades or degrees of psychopathology.

Now that we have discussed the major principles of developmental psychopathology, the ways in which it differs from related fields of inquiry such as developmental and clinical psychology and psychiatry begin to emerge. If taken in isolation, then many components of a developmental psychopathology perspective are equally applicable to other disciplines. However, the incorporation and integration of previously discrete concepts serve to set developmental psychopathology apart as a unique approach. Moreover, a developmental perspective can augment our understanding of psychopathology in ways that a nondevelopmental approach may overlook. In the absence of a developmental conceptualization, one may focus on symptomatic continuity and fail to attend to age-specific manifestations of psychopathology (Cicchetti & Schneider-Rosen, 1986; A. Freud, 1965; Sroufe & Rutter, 1984). In addition, whereas a purely nondevelopmental psychopathology tradition might, for example, focus on between-group differences and view group similarities as reflective of a lack of statistically significant differences on the dependent variables in question, developmental psychopathologists, in contrast, believe that the investigation of between-group similarities can provide clues concerning the mechanisms by which multiple pathways can eventuate in the same outcome. Perhaps most importantly, developmental psychopathologists strive to reduce the schisms that so often separate scientific research from the applications of knowledge to disadvantaged, high-risk, or clinical populations (Cicchetti, 1984; Santostefano, 1978).

BRIDGING THE SCHISM BETWEEN RESEARCH AND PRACTICE

Although the scholarly relevance of the work described in this chapter is apparent, the application of such knowledge to the very populations from which it has been derived all too often does not occur. Despite the mutual value that can result from dialogue between those whose primary interest is in the treatment of child and adolescent psychopathology and those who focus on conducting research on psychopathology, far too little communication occurs between these two camps. Regardless of area of expertise, there is substantial agreement among mental health professionals regarding the gap between the clinician's office and the research laboratory, with many practitioners questioning the value of research to their daily practices (cf., Weisz, Donenberg, Han, & Weiss, 1995). Similarly, many psychopathology researchers feel that the practice arena has little relevance to the conduct of scientific investigations. Despite the complex and somewhat adversarial relationship that exists between the science and practice of clinical psychology, a survey of 325 psychologists found that practitioners value research and believe that their practices can be augmented by the incorporation of scientific findings into the applied arena (Beutler et al., 1995). In fact, the authors of this survey conclude that clinicians value and attend to scientific findings more than scientists respect the input of clinicians. Unless a two-way network of communication can be forged, it is highly unlikely that more productive interchanges will occur between scientists and practitioners. Of immediate concern in the rapidly changing climate of health care is the fear that the gap between clinicians and researchers may widen rather than diminish (Carlson, 1995). As researchers are forced to devote more and more time to grant-writing in a quest for ever-shrinking research dollars, they will have even less time to grapple with the realities of patient care. Similarly, issues related to reimbursable services are likely to restrict the number of clinically oriented academics available to serve on editorial boards and grant review study sections, thereby reducing the influx of clinical concerns into the research arena even further (Carlson, 1995).

The dangers associated with a lack of communication between researchers and practitioners are articulated by Weisz and his colleagues (Weisz et al., 1995) in their examination of differences between psychotherapy outcome studies conducted in laboratory versus clinical settings. Weisz and his colleagues conclude that the therapy provided in most research-based outcome studies differs from therapy typically provided in clinic settings and that the "clinic" therapy shows markedly poorer outcomes. These authors propose "bridging" research to improve the flow of information from academic to applied settings. They advocate: (a) the conduct of more outcome research in clinical settings; (b) the articulation of those aspects of "research" outcome studies that account for positive outcome; and (c) the exportation of laboratory-tested therapies to service delivery sites, and the subsequent evaluation of their efficacy (Weisz et al., 1995).

We believe that the discipline of developmental psychopathology holds great promise for reducing the gap between research and practice. Because research conducted within a developmental psychopathology framework frequently utilizes clinical populations and contexts, practical information and clinical insights derived from applied settings must be incorporated into research designs. In addition to benefiting from such knowledge, researchers also are in an excellent position to share findings that can be incorporated into the clinical arena, thereby improving services to the population being studied.

Although the bridging of research and practice is a laudable goal, it would be naïve to assume that such a nexus can occur easily, or that significant obstacles do not need to be overcome before a more mutually enriching dialogue can occur. First and foremost, our training programs must be committed to an integrative approach to research and practice. Unless this occurs, there will be too few clinicians trained in the provision of empirically proven methods of intervention, and too few researchers committed to evaluating treatment outcome. Similarly, scientists must strive to overcome isolation among themselves based on areas of subspecialization (Beutler et al., 1995). Rather than maintaining scientific compartmentalization because of one's theoretical perspective, communication among scholars conducting clinically meaningful research could facilitate the dissemination of results to practitioners.

To reduce the chasm between research and practice, service funders must be committed to providing resources for clinic-based practitioners to continue to acquire new knowledge if intervention in applied settings is to benefit from growing research knowledge. Similarly, funding must be made available to support the evaluation of clinic services. Despite the increased rhetoric on the importance of "evaluating" clinical services that has accompanied cost consciousness and health care reform efforts, most clinics lack the expertise or personnel to conduct evaluation studies. Moreover, third-party funders similarly lack the knowledge required to recognize that financial resources are required to evaluate service delivery effectively. Thus, practitioners are being placed in a potentially impossible position; they are being asked to provide data to support the efficacy of their treatments without being allocated any resources to conduct such evaluations. This situation is likely to result in frustration among clinicians and in a widening of the very gap that needs to be reduced. Equally disconcerting is the likelihood of the conduct of methodologically unsound "evaluations" that, in actuality, answer nothing despite alleging to do so. To avoid such scenarios, efforts must be made not only to educate service providers regarding results of research and evaluation methodology, but also to convey information on the need for research support to those who control the allocation of service dollars.

Because findings suggest that practitioners are more open to integrating scientific knowledge into the practice arena than scientists are to acknowledging the importance of clinically derived information, much of the onus for bridging the science-practice gap falls to academicians (Beutler et al., 1995). Whereas practice will most likely survive with or without scientific input (although calls to document efficacy of services provided may increase the importance of research to the practice arena), clinical science may be placed in a precarious position if research findings do not find their way into the practice arena. Researchers must strive to make their research findings relevant and accessible to those faced with providing treatment or implementing social policy.

There is much to be gained from an increase in communication between those in academic and applied settings, and much to be lost from a failure to negotiate this interface more effectively. Perhaps of most concern, it is the children in need of mental health services who will ultimately lose if we fail to reduce the research-service schism. In the next section, we discuss aspects of development that have implications for the practice arena.

IMPLICATIONS FOR PRACTICE

General Developmental Considerations

Despite the logical links that exist between developmental theory and research and the provision of interventions to children and adolescents, too few connections have been forged between these realms (Cicchetti & Toth, 1992b; Cicchetti, Toth, & Bush, 1988; Kellam & Rebok, 1992; Noam, 1992; Shirk, 1988a; Shirk & Russell, 1996; Shonkoff & Meisels, 1990). Just as adult criteria for the diagnosis of mental disorders have been assumed to be equally applicable to childhood psychopathology, so, too, have principles derived from adult therapy been applied, often indiscriminately, to children and adolescents. This "developmental continuity myth" of psychotherapy (Shirk, 1988a), which suggests that symptomatology manifests itself similarly regardless of age and therefore does not require therapeutic techniques that are sensitive to developmental change, is likely to impede efforts to provide more theoretically guided, developmentally appropriate services to children and adolescents. Moreover, decision making regarding what constitutes an action that is in a child's best interest cannot be made adequately unless the child's developmental level and accompanying capacity to understand certain events is considered (cf., Shirk & Russell, 1996). Productive dialogue between basic researchers and those invested in providing developmentally guided prevention and intervention has increased over the past decade. Much of this progress can be attributed to the findings from programs of developmentally informed research that will be presented in the next section of this chapter. In general, a developmental psychopathology approach to service provision requires consideration of a number of areas.

To begin, the hierarchical nature of development possesses important implications for prevention and intervention efforts. Because all stage-salient issues are life-span issues, ongoing differentiation, integration, and organization occur. Of special note for purposes of intervention, each point of reorganization and the resultant disequilibrium may make the individual more amenable to change. In view of the disequilibrium generated during periods of transition, targeting prevention and intervention efforts at times of transition might be especially effective in bringing about change (Cicchetti & Toth, 1992b). Moreover, at times it may be useful to generate a state of disequilibrium to afford the opportunity for an intervention that could achieve a higher level of organization (Futterweit & Ruff, 1993). Naturally occurring events that result in disequilibration of the individual also may provide especially timely opportunities to initiate intervention. Although a therapist may be reluctant to confront a patient during times of stress and instead decide to provide a more supportive function, such a stance could result in the loss of a prime period for providing a more growth-promoting intervention.

A hierarchical model of development also suggests that interventions may be optimally effective if targeted at emergent skills rather than at those already consolidated. The possibility of the existence of "sensitive periods" for intervention needs to be considered: Interventions might be more effectively targeted when a pathology-inducing insult occurs, or during a time at which a deviant process is initiated. By developing more focused and circumscribed approaches, intervention effectiveness could increase and the need for more prolonged treatment might decrease. The knowledge of early developmental deviations and their link with subsequent psychopathology also could be used to prevent the emergence of full-blown psychopathology, thereby decreasing both time and money expended in the treatment of more entrenched and often severe clinical conditions (Carnegie Task Force on Meeting the Needs of Young Children, 1994; Hamburg, 1992; IOM, 1989, 1994). Such a conceptualization suggests that the developmental timing of interventions or preventive efforts may be as or more important than the actual content of the intervention. Relatedly, the magnitude of the effect of a given intervention may be maximized or minimized depending on the timing of an event. Once an intervention has ended, a developmental perspective also suggests that the provision of "booster" interventions during developmental transitions holds promise for sustaining positive outcomes (Cicchetti & Toth, 1992b).

In addition to considerations associated with periods of developmental transition and the timing of intervention in relation to the resultant disequilibration, aspects of the developmental course of illness also possess implications for intervention. The previously discussed concepts of equifinality and multifinality should alert all clinicians to the importance of utilizing multiple strategies of treatment, predicated on issues such as individuals' stage in the life cycle, their current functioning and developmental organization across psychological and biological domains, and any characteristics specific to the group of individuals being treated. Likewise, interventions must be directed at a range of developmental domains (e.g., cognition, language, emotion, biology, etc.), rather than focusing on a single area of functioning. Moreover, because multiple risk factors, both intra- and extraorganismic, drawn from psychological, biological, and environmental forces, characterize the pathways to maladaptive and disordered outcomes, interventions must address the broader causal matrix or be destined to produce ineffective and short-lived results. Additionally, as the presence of many risk factors at multiple levels of the ecology and the individual are associated with more chronic, enduring, and maladaptive outcomes than those characterized by fewer and more circumscribed risk factors, interventions with more serious pathological conditions (e.g., manic depressive illness; schizophrenia) must incorporate a longitudinal perspective and employ a series of interventions over time in an effort to reduce risk factors to a manageable level.

In his discussion of affective disorders, Post (1992) suggests that different types of intervention may be more or less effective as a function of stages in the development and course of the illness. In presenting findings about behavioral sensitization and electrophysiological kindling in recurrent mood disorders, Post posits that psychodynamic therapies may be more effective for an initial depressive episode, whereas recurrent episodes might be more responsive to behavioral and cognitive techniques of therapy. Moreover, Post argues that because most psychotherapeutic techniques require the reworking of cortical control using the limbic and cortically based representational memory systems, depressed patients with hypoactive cortical systems may not be amenable to dynamic therapies. Rather, Post advocates the use of behavioral and cognitive techniques in combination with pharmacological or electrophysiological approaches that can enhance cortical mechanisms. Finally, Post maintains that different drug therapies are differentially effective during various stages of disease evolution. Post's work is especially compelling because he addresses developmental aspects of the progression and course of mental illness as they relate to prevention and intervention (Post et al., 1994, 1996). Additionally, Post strives to convey the relevance of psychophysiological substrates of illness for psychotherapeutic forms of intervention.

Ontogenesis is an integrated, multiply determined process, which has implications for prevention and intervention efforts. Considerations such as when and why a disorder occurs, how long it persists, and the identification of the precursors to disordered functioning all require a developmental approach to ensure that prevention and intervention strategies are appropriately timed and guided (Kellam & Rebok, 1992). Additionally, targeting prevention efforts at key areas prior to the emergence of full-blown psychopathology requires an in-depth understanding of adaptive components of development so that their emergence can be facilitated and, subsequently, serve as compensatory factors or protective mechanisms. Developmental psychopathologists may advocate a focus on subclinical indicators, such as how stage-salient issues are resolved, as they strive to prevent and treat risk conditions and mental disorders.

It is critical that prevention and intervention efforts recognize that a given factor may affect various individuals very differently. This variable effect may be the result of the developmental period during which a stressor occurs, prior quality of adaptation, or it may be due to the specific vulnerabilities or compensators available for access by the child. Although always difficult, the effects of parental death during childhood and its link to subsequent depression may be affected by whether the child is in a period of developmental transition, the quality of adaptation prior to the loss, as well as by the availability of other external supports to assist in coping. An assessment of internal resources available to the child, as well as any genetic propensity toward an affective disorder also would be of considerable importance in identifying how best to help the child cope adaptively.

Because development is viewed as a naturally unfolding process that emerges from the child and his or her characteristics, in combination with the caregiving environment, issues related to whether or not to intervene also require careful evaluation. This may be especially relevant for prevention efforts, where intervention is provided prior to the crystallization of a mental disorder. Although it is often assumed that prevention can do no harm, this premise is not necessarily true (cf., Rutter, 1981). The importance of fully understanding development so as not to intervene unnecessarily or in an iatrogenic manner is proffered by Thomas (1979), who argues that intervention for one component of a complex system contains a significant risk of resulting in unanticipated negative consequences for other parts of the system. A similar position that is relevant to the practice arena is discussed by Howitt (1992), who examines how a desire to protect children from abuse can actually lead to harm if intervention into families is misguided. Although seemingly a quite negative perspective, these positions underscore the risks of initiating intervention without fully considering its potential impact on the developing system. Such issues assume special relevance in cases of child maltreatment, where decisions regarding the adequacy of parenting and possible placement of children in foster care occur routinely. Especially disconcerting is the lack of incorporation of any data on developmental processes into this decision-making process. Decision making related to the development and provision of prevention and intervention services that is not theory-informed and data-driven is all too frequently the norm. Developmental differences among children and the implications of these varied capabilities for intervention need to be considered. Therefore, we highlight aspects of development with special relevance to the provision of child therapy (Shirk, 1988a; Weisz, 1997). This discussion also is pertinent to our subsequent examination of interventions that target stage-salient issues of development.

Causal Reasoning

An agreed-on goal of psychotherapy is to help a child construct a new understanding of internal or external issues through the use of interpretations. Such techniques are effective only if the child is able to understand the interpretive process used by the therapist. The causal structure of an interpretation can be viewed as varying along several dimensions that influence outcomes. These dimensions are the internal versus external, past versus present, and conscious versus unconscious (Shirk, 1988b). With respect to internal versus external attributions (e.g., the degree to which a child believes he or she is responsible for an outcome versus the belief that outcome is the result of forces beyond his or her control), evidence suggests that children's understanding of the causes of behavior become more psychological and less situational with increasing age (Shirk, 1988b). Thus, expecting a preschool or kindergarten-age child to understand events as related to internal, nonobservable sources is likely to be ineffective unless the therapist is able to concretize the cause for the child. Although an adolescent may easily follow subtle interpretations, therapeutic style must be modified in accord with the child's cognitive reasoning capabilities.

The temporal dimension associated with interpretations also assumes different significance depending on developmental level (Shirk & Russell, 1996). In general, prior to middle childhood, children have difficulty linking past events with current emotions or behavior. Therefore, the child's ability to relate the past to the present must be considered during the course of therapy. With young children, a focus on current concomitants of affect or behavior is likely to be the most fruitful approach (Shirk, 1988b).

A final area to consider in child therapies that use interpretation to foster change relates to the conscious-unconscious dimension. Generally, unconscious explanations of behavior are difficult for children to comprehend. Thus, if two available explanations of behavior are feasible, one conscious and therefore observable and one unconscious, prior to adolescence most children will reject the unconscious explanation in favor of the more overtly evident cause (Shirk, 1988b). Such behavior, easily confused with "resistance" or "denial" is more likely to be a result of cognitive developmental constraints.

Emotion Understanding

In an examination of research on emotion understanding, Nannis (1988) summarizes investigations in a number of areas, including knowledge of feelings, ability to experience multiple feelings, control of emotion, and attributions of the causality of emotions. Overall, research suggests that as children mature, their understanding of emotion becomes increasingly complex, with a shift from reliance on external to more internally based explanations. With respect to multiple feelings, young children cannot articulate the experience of two feelings simultaneously (Harris, 1989; Harter, 1977, 1983). Additionally, children were found to be able to understand multiple emotions based on sequential experiences before they grasped multiple feelings based on simultaneous occurrences. Generally, the relation between cognitive development and emotion understanding has been supported (Harris, 1989; Nannis, 1988), with younger children's understanding of emotion tending to be more bound by contextual cues. The implications of such developmental trajectories for purposes of intervention must be considered to avoid confusion for the child and frustration for the therapist that will result if the therapist does not recognize the child's developmental constraints with the processing of emotional content.

Self-Understanding

Several researchers have hypothesized that there are developmental shifts in self-understanding, beginning with a focus on more physical external attributes and progressing to more internal, psychological constructs (Damon & Hart, 1982, 1988; Harter, 1983; Rosenberg, 1986). Rosenberg (1979) links developmental differences with various forms of psychotherapy, suggesting that the young child acts like a behaviorist, the older child functions like a trait theorist, and the adolescent assumes a psychoanalytic stance. This formulation possesses some interesting implications for therapy, as it could be inferred that children would be most receptive to interventions that are consistent with their self-conceptions. Structural changes in the self are thought to accompany these more content-related alterations, with the self being described in more abstract terms in older children (Harter, 1988). Advances in the accuracy of children's self-assessments also typically occur with increasing age, with middle childhood ushering in an ability to incorporate the opinions of significant others (Harter, 1988). Developmental constraints in a child's ability to recognize the cognitive perspective of others on activities, events, and oneself may impose limits on the outcome of interventions that require children to see situations from the perspective of others (Weisz, 1997). In evaluating the psychotherapeutic implications of research findings on self-understanding, Harter (1988) argues that prior to adolescence children do not possess the introspective capacities needed to experience intrapsychic conflict and therefore lack the related desire to change. Harter suggests that interventions for children need to be somewhat didactic and that they need to target factors that *determine* self-esteem, rather than self-esteem itself. Inadequate understanding of the development of the self on the part of the therapist may limit the facilitation of positive change.

Language Ability

Developmental variations in children's capacities to encode and decode language also need to be considered in the provision of child therapy (Weisz, 1997). Limitations in encoding skills can restrict a child's ability to share inner thoughts and feelings, thereby impeding the provision of an intervention matched to the child's inner state. Decoding constraints on a child's ability to understand comments made by a therapist also will limit how helpful the intended intervention is. Finally, developmental differences in children's abilities to use inner speech to guide behavior are likely to result in differences in children's responsiveness to therapies that use language to facilitate self-control (Weisz, 1997).

Conceptions of Social Relationships

Children's understanding of social relationships represents a final area to consider regarding developmental transformations for intervention strategies. This understanding is important because, in addition to the frequency of aggressive and withdrawn peer problems during childhood and the resultant need for intervention, the psychotherapeutic arena is based on a type of social relationship between the child and the therapist. Therefore, knowledge of the child's capacity to understand and benefit from social interactions is critical to implementing a successful intervention plan.

Bierman (1988) summarizes research on children's social conceptions and social reasoning abilities that demonstrates developmental progressions in the acquisition of information about others, about the behaviors and attitudes associated with social roles, and about the changes in the ability to reason regarding the role of multiple informational cues. As development proceeds, children become increasingly able to construct models that enable them to guide their own social behavior, as well as to predict the social behavior of others. Because certain kinds of abstract reasoning do not emerge until the advent of formal operations in adolescence, social skills programs that require children to generate hypothetical situations, think of various ways of responding, envision how others might react to their responses, and imagine alternative outcomes that can occur, may be beyond the reasoning abilities of young children (Weisz, 1997). These changing abilities can be assessed and factored into the design of interventions that are most likely to be effective in improving a child's social relationships or in allowing a child to benefit from historical and current social interactions, including those of a psychotherapeutic nature.

In the following section, we describe a theoretical perspective that holds considerable promise for informing our efforts to prevent and treat the mental disorders of childhood and adolescence.

THE IMPORTANCE OF THEORY: ILLUSTRATIONS FROM THE ORGANIZATIONAL PERSPECTIVE ON DEVELOPMENT

Although the field of developmental psychopathology is not characterized by the acceptance of any unitary theoretical approach, the organizational perspective on development (Cicchetti, 1993; Cicchetti & Schneider-Rosen, 1986; Cicchetti & Sroufe, 1978; Cicchetti & Toth, 1995; Cicchetti & Tucker, 1994; Sroufe, 1996; Sroufe & Waters, 1976) offers a powerful theoretical framework for conceptualizing the intricacies of the life-span perspective on risk and psychopathology, as well as on normal ontogenesis. Drawing on the concepts of Werner's (1948; Werner & Kaplan, 1963) organismic-developmental theory, adherents of the organizational perspective conceptualize development as consisting of a series of structural reorganizations within and between the biological and behavioral systems of the individual that proceed by means of differentiation and hierarchical integration (i.e., Werner's "orthogenetic principle"). The relationship between the relatively immature and the relatively mature is the relationship between a state of globality and lack of articulation and a state of greater differentiation, articulation, coordination, complexity, and consolidation, effectively organized into hierarchical systems and subsystems (von Bertalanffy, 1968). The concept of organization can be conceptualized as the tendency of systems to extend themselves while maintaining their overall integrity (Mayr, 1982; Piaget, 1971).

A distinction can thus be drawn between chronological age and developmental age, where the latter is determined by the individual's state of articulation and hierarchical integration (Wohlwill, 1973). An important consequence of the orthogenetic principle for the investigation of psychopathology is that, because development must be viewed in terms of integration and qualitative reorganization rather than mere accretion or expansion, one should not necessarily expect phenotypic isomorphism (i.e., homotypic continuity) across developmental levels.

At each junction of reorganization in development, the concept of hierarchic motility specifies that prior developmental structures are incorporated into later ones by means of hierarchic integration. In this way, early experience and its effects on the individual are carried forward within the individual's organization of biological and behavioral systems rather than through having reorganizations override previous organizations. As a result, hierarchic motility suggests that previous areas of vulnerability or strength within the organizational structure may remain present (i.e., accessible) although not prominent in the current organizational structure. Nevertheless, the presence of prior structures in times of stress, crisis, novelty or creativity may exert an influence on the outcome. Thus, a behavioral or symptomatic presentation of a depressed or hypomanic individual may appear discrepant with recently evidenced adaptation, but in effect indicates the activation of prior maladaptive structures that were retained in the organizational structure through hierarchical integration.

Werner (1957) conjectured that all problem-solving behavior involves first a regression via hierarchic motility to a relatively immature level of functioning in the relevant domain, and the renewed differentiation and integration, which takes the problem into account. Environmental stressors or crises, for example, may fruitfully be conceptualized as "problems" requiring "solutions" by the child. Our expectation is that children who possess a great deal of hierarchic motility would, in general, be better able to cope with crises or stressors by utilizing a strategy that initially may appear to be immature and regressive, but that later may be seen to be effective. Moreover, we would expect that, with development and increased experience, the child becomes more competent at negotiating minor regressions in response to stress so that integrity of functioning may be more readily maintained with a concomitant reduction in the overt manifestation of disorganization or anxiety. Pathology in turn may result or partly be caused by a lack of motility or else an inability to redifferentiate after regression in response to crises or stressors.

Each epoch of development poses new challenges to which the individual must adapt. At each juncture, successful adaptation or competence is signified by an adaptive integration within and among the biological and behavioral systems, as the person masters current developmental challenges. Because earlier structures of the individual's organization are incorporated into later structures in the successive process of hierarchical integration, early competence tends to promote later competence. An individual who has adaptively met the developmental challenges of the particular stage will be better equipped to meet successive new challenges in development. This is not to suggest that early adaptation ensures successful later adaptation, because major changes or stresses in the internal and external environment may tax subsequent adaptational capacities. However, early competence provides a more optimal organization of biological and behavioral systems, thus offering, in a probabilistic manner, the greatest likelihood that adaptive resources are available to encounter and cope with new developmental demands.

In contrast, incompetence in development is generated by difficulties or maladaptive efforts to resolve the challenges of a developmental period. Inadequate resolution of these challenges may result in a developmental lag or delay in one of the biobehavioral systems such as the emotional system. As a result, less than adequate integration within that system will occur, and that poor within-system integration will compromise adaptive integration among biological and behavioral systems as hierarchical integration proceeds. Thus, incompetence in development may be viewed as a lack of integration within and among the biological and behavioral systems as the individual adapts to the challenges of his or her period of ontogenesis, as an integration of pathological structures, and/or as the development of a behavioral pattern that is rigid and leads to future maladaptation (cf., B. Kaplan, 1966).

Of particular importance are advances and lags in one biological or behavioral system with respect to the others, because the presence of capacities of one of these systems may be a necessary condition for the development or exercise of capacities of another system. Lags in these systems may then result in compensatory development that, in some instances, may leave the child vulnerable to psychopathology. Over time, difficulty in the organization of one biological or behavioral system may tend to promote difficulty in the way in which other systems are organized as hierarchical integration between the separate systems occurs. The organization of the individual may then appear to consist of an integration of poorly integrated component systems. As the converse of the effects of early competence, early incompetence will tend to promote later incompetence because the individual arrives at successive developmental stages with less than optimal resources available for responding to the challenges of that period. Again, however, this progression is not inevitable but probabilistic. Changes in the internal and external environment may lead to improvements in the ability to grapple with developmental challenges, resulting in a redirection in the developmental course.

Organizational theorists emphasize the active role that individuals play in their own development. Moreover, they acknowledge the dialectic that exists between the canalization of ontogenetic processes and the belief that there is continued opportunity for change (i.e., developmental plasticity) throughout life (Ciaranello et al., 1995). Although more distal historical factors are critical to examine in an organismic perspective, individual choice and self-organization play important roles in determining the course of development. Moreover, plasticity (change) can be brought about either by psychological or biological self-organization (Cicchetti & Tucker, 1994). We conjecture that it may be during transitional turning points or sensitive periods of development that the ontogenetic process is most susceptible, positively or negatively, to the individual's self-organizational strivings. The importance of individual choice to the organizational perspective implies that individuals are neither unaffected by their earlier experiences nor immutably controlled by them. Change in developmental course is always possible as a result of new experiences and reorganizations and the individual's active self-organizing strivings for adaptation.

Across the developmental course, the evolving capacities of individuals and their active choices allow for new aspects of experience, both internal (i.e., biological) and external, to be coordinated in increasingly complex ways. At each developmental transition, individuals are confronted with specific developmental tasks central to that era (Sroufe, 1979; Waters & Sroufe, 1983). From infancy through adulthood, new developmental tasks arise during sensitive periods that are of primary importance during their particular stage of ascendance. However, despite subsequent developmental issues gaining greater salience at later points in the ontogenetic cycle, each developmental task remains an issue of life-span significance. Through differentiation and hierarchic integration, the quality of the resolution of each stage-salient issue is coordinated with the prior organization of biological and behavioral systems, and reorganization occurs, moving individuals forward in development. The quality of the resolution of each stage-salient issue primes the way subsequent developmental issues are likely to be negotiated. It is through their active role in the ontogenetic process that individuals begin to proceed down different developmental pathways.

Given the importance of a life-span view of developmental processes and an interest in delineating how prior development influences future development, a major issue in developmental psychopathology involves how continuity in the quality of adaptation across developmental time is determined. Sroufe (1979; see also Caspi & Moffitt, 1995) has articulated the concept of coherence in the organization of behaviors in successive developmental periods as a means of identifying continuity in adaptation despite changing behavioral presentations of the developing individual. Crucial to this concept is a recognition that the same behaviors in different developmental periods may represent quite different levels of adaptation. Behaviors indicating competence within a developmental period may indicate incompetence when evidenced within subsequent developmental periods. Normative behaviors early in development may indicate maladaptation when exhibited later in development. Thus, the manifestation of competence in different developmental periods is rarely indicated by isomorphism in behavioral presentation. Homotypic continuity is likely to be an unusual occurrence, particularly early in development when the ontogenetic process is quite rapid (Kagan, 1971).

Additionally, because the same function in an organized biobehavioral system can be fulfilled by two dissimilar behaviors, whereas the same kind of behavior may serve two different functions in different contexts (Werner & Kaplan, 1963), and given that the same behavior also may play different roles in different biobehavioral systems (Cicchetti & Serafica, 1981), it is especially important to distinguish between similarities and differences in *molar* and *molecular* symptomatology during different developmental periods. Because of the reorganization of biological and behavioral systems that takes place at each new level of development, one cannot expect to see, for any symptom, isomorphism at the molecular level, even if there is isomorphism at the molar level. For example, the child whose depressive episode spans the transition from preoperational to concrete-operational thought may display excessive and inappropriate guilt, a loss of self-esteem, and a decrease in activity throughout the episode. Consequently, at a molar level, the depressive symptoms at the later period will be isomorphic to those of the earlier period. Nonetheless, the particular manifestation of the guilt feelings, loss of self-esteem, and psychomotor retardation may change and develop during the transition, when the child's biological and behavioral systems undergo a rather radical development. In this way, there may be noteworthy differences at the molecular level.

A Transactional Approach to Investigating the Nature of the Relation between Normality and Pathology

Until this point, much of our theoretical discussion has focused on the organization of biological and behavioral systems occurring within the developing individual. Our emphasis shifts now to examining the means by which individual differences in developmental outcomes are conceptualized. Proponents of a transactional model recognize the importance of transacting genetic, constitutional, neurobiological, biochemical, psychological, and sociological factors in the determination of behavior, and state that these factors change through their dynamic transaction, thus providing the framework for a developmental perspective on how internal and external sources of influence are coordinated to shape the organizational structure of individuals along alternate pathways over the course of ontogenesis (Cicchetti & Rizley, 1981; Cicchetti & Schneider-Rosen, 1986; Sameroff & Chandler, 1975). Adherence to a transactional model thus decries reductionism; in particular, it denies that a pathological process can be viewed as an emerging characteristic of some biological, psychological, or environmental process *alone,* except perhaps in the most extreme cases. Rather, various factors operate together through a hierarchy of dispositions. A genetic diathesis may constitute a disposition to biochemical anomalies only given the action of some psychological mechanism; these biochemical anomalies in turn may constitute a disposition to the development of psychological anomalies only given a particular pattern of socialization (cf., Cicchetti & Aber, 1986). Thus, whereas some factors act as *permissive* causes by constituting dispositions, others act as *efficient* causes by realizing these dispositions (Carnap, 1936; Pap, 1958; Sellars, 1958). In addition, it need not be the case that, as in the traditional diathesis-stress model (cf., Gottesman & Shields, 1972), only genetic or biological factors act as permissive causes, whereas psychological or environmental factors function only as efficient causes. Long-standing patterns of social interaction in a child's social environment may constitute a permissive cause for depression (Cummings & Cicchetti, 1990) or for altering the organization, structure, or functioning of the brain in children and adults exposed to chronic trauma such as childhood physical and sexual abuse (Cicchetti, 1993, 1996b, in press) and in adults with combat-related posttraumatic stress disorder (PTSD) (Bremner et al., 1995), whereas transient biological or biochemical changes during development may be efficient causes of depression (Cicchetti & Schneider-Rosen, 1986). Furthermore, not only may the particular risk mechanisms vary in significance over time, as well as in their importance in the operation of alternative permissive or efficient causes but also, with development, the organization of the biological and behavioral systems, and the integration between these systems, may introduce protective mechanisms that moderate against maladaptation and disorder.

The transactional model specifies that the interrelations between the organization of biological and behavioral systems and the environment are in a progressive exchange of mutual influence. Not only is the individual influenced by environmental inputs resulting in transformation and reorganization, but also the environment is influenced by and responds to characteristics of the individual. At successive points in development, the organizational structure of both the individual and the environment are in a state of bidirectional influence. Early temperamental differences in children are transformed into a range of attachment organizations in response to variations in responding from caregivers (Belsky & Rovine, 1987; Goldsmith & Alansky, 1987). Subsequently, there also are likely to be alterations within caregivers as they respond to new variations in behavioral presentations of the child. Both qualities of the child and of the environment are being mutually influenced as each evolves. These transactions of bidirectional influence will generate variations in the quality of the organization of their different biological and behavioral systems. At subsequent points in development, variations in the organization of the child (i.e., competent vs. incompetent) will alter how the child can respond to new experiences, positive or negative, and the pathways toward adaptation or maladaptation that unfold.

Risk Factors and the Development of Psychopathology

Numerous reasons can be invoked to explain the heterogeneity in outcome found in individuals exposed to adversity (Cicchetti & Aber, 1986; Kopp, 1994), including when in development the individual is first exposed to the risk, variations in the duration and intensity of exposure to the risk (Garmezy & Masten, 1994; Rende & Plomin, 1990; Richters & Weintraub, 1990), and a multiplicative synergism that often occurs among combinations of risk factors (Rutter, 1979, 1987; Sameroff, Seifer, Barocas, Zax, & Greenspan, 1987). Moreover, it has been revealed that even children from the same family are differently affected by their experiences with adverse circumstances. These so-called "nonshared environment" effects, revealed through behavior genetic designs, are critical both for elucidating the operation of environmental forces and for specifying which aspects of the environment exert the most profound impact on developmental outcome for different individuals (DiLalla & Gottesman, 1995; Plomin & Daniels, 1987; Reiss, Plomin, & Hetherington, 1991; Rutter et al., 1997). The investigation of risk factors as they relate to the development of maladaptation and psychopathology has been an active area of inquiry in recent decades (Haggerty, Sherrod, Garmezy, & Rutter, 1994; Luthar, Burack, Cicchetti, & Weisz, 1997; Rolf, Masten, Cicchetti, Nuechterlein, & Weintraub, 1990). Many of the internal and external processes implicated in the causes and consequences of maladaptive and disordered outcomes tend not to occur in isolation (Rutter, 1979; Sameroff et al., 1987; Walker, Downey, & Nightingale, 1989). This co-occurrence of risk factors often renders difficult the critical task of disentangling mediating and moderating influences on outcome. In some instances, suspected causal processes genuinely may be the products of other converging systems and only spuriously related to the risk or disordered condition being studied. In other instances, a process may indeed influence a risk condition or a mental disorder, but the nature and extent of its causal effect may be masked or clouded by the influences of other interacting systems (Rutter, 1994). One strategy for disentangling causal influences among multiple interacting systems is to identify and investigate the functioning of individuals who possess specific functioning deficits and not others (Richters & Cicchetti, 1993b). Multiple processes studied individually in this way may yield significant insights into the individual roles they play in normal adaptation, and into how those roles might change and require reconceptualization within a broader matrix of functioning deficits.

In concert with our developmental formulation, it is likely that a multitude of rather general factors across the broad domains of biology, psychology, and sociology are at least indirectly related to the etiology, course, and sequelae of risk conditions and mental disorders. A comprehensive articulation of the vulnerability and protective processes or mechanisms that have promoted or inhibited the development of competent adaptation over the course of ontogenesis may be more important than specific predictors of the immediate or proximal onset of a psychopathological disorder (Sroufe, 1989; Sroufe & Rutter, 1984). Vocisano, Klein, Keefe, Dienst, and Kincaid (1996) examined the developmental course of a group of patients with major depressive disorder who not only had been continuously symptomatic for prolonged time periods, but also were so impaired in their adaptive functioning that they required years of ongoing care in psychiatric facilities or by family members. These investigators found that birth-related problems, physical disorders in infancy, and poor premorbid functioning in childhood and adolescence played a major role in the deteriorated adaptive functioning in the adult depressed inpatients (Vocisano et al., 1996).

An examination of factors that may contribute to adaptive or maladaptive functioning is necessary to better understand diversity in functioning. Vulnerability factors are typically regarded as enduring or long-standing life circumstances or conditions that promote maladaptation (Cicchetti & Rizley, 1981; Zubin & Spring, 1977). Major domains of influence on the child, including those external (e.g., intrafamilial, social-environmental) and internal (e.g., genetic, biological, temperamental, psychological) to the individual, may serve as sources of vulnerability if they detract from the achievement of successful adaptation and competence. Throughout ontogenesis, these vulnerability factors transact with the evolving organization of the biological and behavioral systems of the individual child to reduce the attainment of competence and may promote a pathological organization across the biological and psychological domains of development. For example, children with more difficult temperaments who lived in high-conflict families developed more internalizing and externalizing behavior problems than did children residing in similar families but who had easy temperaments (Tschann, Kaiser, Chesney, Alkon, & Boyce, 1996; see also Carey, 1990).

In contrast, there also are enduring protective factors that promote competent adaptation in the child. These features are likely to enhance rather than hinder development. Protective factors may operate in a compensatory manner, counterbalancing the effects of known risk factors. Alternatively, protective factors may operate as mechanisms or moderators, interactively influencing outcomes more potently under conditions of high risk while providing minimal influence under conditions of low risk; the protective mechanism moderates or reduces the strength of the effect of high levels of risk (Rutter, 1990).

In addition to these enduring competence-detracting and competence-promoting factors, transient influences also exist that, though temporary in duration, may have a critical negative (i.e., "challenging") or positive (i.e., "buffering") impact (Cicchetti & Aber, 1986), depending on the timing of such events or on transitions in circumstances and the pertinent developmental issues that the child is confronting at the time. Moreover, the potency of risk and protective factors in influencing development will vary as a result of the developmental period during which they occur (Bell, 1986); a specific factor may be more influential in one developmental period as compared with another. Furthermore, the same factor may function differently depending on the context in which it occurs. Thus, it is important to evaluate the effect of risk and protective processes based both on the developmental and social-environmental context in which they occur.

For any individual child, the enduring and transient features encountered, both vulnerability and challenger and protective and buffering, respectively, will vary and exist within a dynamic balance. A greater likelihood for the development of incompetence and a pathological organization will occur for those children for whom vulnerability factors and challengers outweigh protective and buffering influences. Psychopathological disorders have the potential to emerge in those individuals for whom a pathological organization has evolved transactionally through development and whose coping capacities and protective resources are no longer effective in counteracting long-standing vulnerability and current stressors or acute risk factors.

For example, depressive disorders have the potential to emerge in those individuals for whom a depressotypic organization of biological and behavioral systems had evolved transactionally through development and whose coping capacities and protective resources are no longer effective in counteracting long-standing vulnerabilities and current stressors or acute risk factors. Moreover, the action of these factors can differ. Some are mechanism-specific, whereas others operate in a general fashion. A factor is mechanism-specific if it potentiates or compensates by playing a role in a proposed mechanism of a given disorder or high-risk condition, whereas its action is general if it can potentiate or compensate in a variety of ways in varied circumstances. Additionally, causal inferences become greatly strengthened when the effects of risk factors are specific rather than global and undifferentiated (Rutter, 1994).

Rutter (1990) has cautioned that risk potentiators (vulnerability and challenger factors) and risk compensators (protective and buffering factors) are not variables causing pathological outcomes per se, but rather that they are indicators of more complex processes and mechanisms that impact on individual adaptation. Specification of the process or mechanism involved is therefore essential. In our conceptualization, these factors are expected to operate primarily through the significance they have in promoting or detracting from the development of competence at progressive stages of development and the consequent likelihood of an emerging pathological organization. For example, parental death per se does not cause depressive disorder, but in some children it may contribute to a sequence of negative transformations in the biological and behavioral systems over the course of development. These changes, in turn, may result in the emergence of a prototypic depressive organization and a strong potential for depressive outcomes (Brown, Harris, & Bifulco, 1986). As the preceding discussion intimates, the concept of risk connotes uncertainty, either about whether or when a problem will eventuate, or about the aftermath once a hazard has transpired. Moreover, risk factors differ from correlates in that the former must temporally precede hazardous events and increase the likelihood of the occurrence of the events beyond the base rates found in the general population (Meehl & Rosen, 1955), whereas correlates take place contemporaneously with hazardous events.

Investigations that concentrate on the antecedent characteristics of particular maladaptive outcomes customarily uncover a multifarious number of risk factors. Research has revealed that the accumulation of multiple risk factors may be more critical in determining outcomes than the specific combination of co-occurring risks (Garmezy & Masten, 1994). Moreover, similar outcomes may be produced by diverse combinations of risk factors (i.e., equifinality) (Garmezy & Masten, 1994). In addition, the same risk factors may be predictive of different developmental outcomes (i.e., multifinality), raising the specter of doubt about the causal specificity of these risks (Cicchetti & Aber, 1986; Rutter, 1994). Furthermore, the effects of interacting risk factors are often magnified such that their overall effect on the developmental process is more harmful than risk factors occurring in isolation.

Several other important points must be made before we address the empirical literature on risk and resilience. The same characteristic is capable of serving as an enduring vulnerability or a transient challenger risk factor for a particular outcome, while functioning as an enduring protective factor or a transient buffer for another outcome (Stouthamer-Loeber et al., 1993). Likewise, a given characteristic may serve as a potentiator (i.e., vulnerability factor or challenger) of a disorder and/or of a negative developmental outcome for one individual and as a compensator (i.e., protective or buffering factor—see Cicchetti & Rizley, 1981) against the occurrence of these events for another individual. Furthermore, whereas a characteristic may function as a compensator at one point during development, it also may serve as a potentiator at another developmental period. Finally, certain risk factors also may exert more salient impacts on individuals than other risk factors. For example, sexually abused children whose maltreatment is perpetrated by their caregiver would most certainly be more adversely affected than those whose maltreatment resulted from abuse at the hands of a stranger (Kendall-Tackett, Williams, & Finkelhor, 1993; Toth & Cicchetti, 1996b).

In addition to studies that have sought to examine the potentiating or compensatory effects of a single risk factor, studies also have sought to assess the role of cumulative risks. In an important series of papers, Rutter and colleagues (1979, 1985; Rutter & Quinton, 1987) demonstrated the enhanced power of multiple risk indices for predicting later psychiatric disorder. Six variables, each reflective of chronic family adversity, were identified:

1. Severe marital discord.
2. Low socioeconomic status.

3. Overcrowding or large family size.
4. Parental criminality.
5. Maternal psychiatric illness.
6. Placement of a child in the family out of the home.

In the sample of 10-year-old children that Rutter (1979) investigated, psychiatric risk in the offspring increased from 2% in children with zero or one risk index, to 6% in children with two or three risk indices, to 21% in children with four or more risk indices.

Along similar lines, Kolvin and his colleagues (Kolvin, Miller, Scott, Gratznis, & Fleeting, 1988) utilized indicators that paralleled those employed by Rutter (1979) to investigate how these cumulative risk factors influenced the development of criminality. Although the presence of a single risk was associated with a 29% rate of later criminality, two indicators augmented the criminality rate to 69%. In addition, the investigation of Kolvin and his colleagues (1988) attested to the dynamic nature of cumulative risk. When the number of indicators of disadvantage increased, children's subsequent rate of criminality increased. In contrast, as deprivation decreased, the children's subsequent criminality rates declined.

Biederman and his colleagues (1995) utilized Rutter's 6 chronic family adversity variables to examine whether there was any relationship between these indicators of adversity and the diagnosis of ADHD and ADHD-related psychopathology (i.e., depression, anxiety, and conduct disorder) and ADHD-associated impairments (e.g., cognitive impairments, learning disabilities, and psychosocial dysfunction). These investigators studied 140 ADHD and 120 normal control children who were all Caucasian males between the ages of 6 and 17 years. Consistent with the findings of the prior studies that employed Rutter's indices of family adversity, Biederman et al. (1995) found that the odds ratio for the diagnosis of ADHD increased as a function of the number of family adversity indicators experienced by the child. Moreover, higher scores on the family adversity index predicted ADHD-related psychopathology and its associated cognitive, psychiatric, and psychosocial impairments.

In a longitudinal examination of this sample, 128 of the 140 children with ADHD and 109 of the 120 normal controls were reassessed 4 years later by Biederman and his colleagues (1996). Of the children with ADHD, 85% continued to manifest the disorder, whereas 15% of the disorders were found to be remitted. Included among the predictors of persistent ADHD were the genetic familiarity of the disorder, comorbidity with conduct, mood, and anxiety disorders, and the family adversity indicators noted in the initial investigation (Biederman et al., 1995).

In a related vein, Williams and colleagues (1990) examined the relation between a cumulative disadvantage score and childhood behavioral problems in a group of 11-year-old children. The cumulative risk index comprised factors that included single parenthood, low socioeconomic status, number of residence and school changes, marital separation, young motherhood, maternal mental illness symptoms, and seeking guidance for a problematic marriage. Williams, Anderson, McGee, and Silva (1990) divided their sample into five groups, each of which was characterized by increasing levels of risk. Once again, as the number of indices of disadvantage increased, so, too, did the percentage of children manifesting problem behavior. For example, only 7% of the children from families where there were fewer than two risk indices developed behavior problems, whereas for those who experienced eight or more disadvantages, the behavior problem rate was 40%.

In the Rochester Longitudinal Study (RLS), Sameroff and his colleagues (1987) created a cumulative risk index that chronicled the total number of risks for each family. These risk factors, similar to those utilized in the aforementioned investigations, were related to children's socioemotional functioning and intelligence at age 4. On an intelligence test, children who had no environmental risks scored more than 30 IQ points higher than children who had 8 or 9 risk factors. Thus, on average, each individual risk decreased children's IQ scores by approximately 4 points. With respect to socioemotional competence, nearly two standard deviations in functioning separated the lowest and highest groups of children.

To date, very few investigations have examined continuities of environmental adversity over time. Duncan and Brooks-Gunn (1994) discovered that the best predictor of functioning during early childhood was the number of prior years that the family had lived in poverty and not the current economic circumstances of the family. Likewise Bolger, Patterson, Thompson, and Kupersmidt (1995) demonstrated that, for both African American and Caucasian children, enduring economic hardship was associated with a wide range of indicators of psychological adjustment. Specifically, children whose families had experienced persistent poverty were more likely to have difficulties forming effective peer relations, to manifest conduct disturbances at school, and to report low self-esteem than were children whose families were not characterized by economic hardship. Additionally, the psychosocial adjustment of children from families where there was intermittent poverty fell between the other two groups.

In a prospective longitudinal follow-up of the 4-year-olds who were participants in the RLS, Sameroff, Seifer, Baldwin, and Baldwin (1993) examined the longitudinal continuity of the cumulative risk index when the children were between 4 and 13 years of age. Notably, few major shifts occurred in the number of risk factors that existed in families across the 9-year interval since the last child assessment. Other than maternal education, where the number of mothers without a high school education or its equivalent decreased by approximately 10%, Sameroff and colleagues (1993) found remarkable consistency of disadvantage in the environments of the children in their sample. Moreover, intelligence at age 4 was highly positively correlated with intelligence at age 13 ($r = .72$). Because there was such high stability in the amount of environmental risk experienced by these families over time, Sameroff and colleagues (1993) could not ascertain whether the effects of early adversity or contemporary risk had the greatest impact on later intellectual competence (cf., Sroufe et al., 1990).

As another illustration of the predictive synergy found in multiple risk indices, Sameroff et al., (1993) discovered that, at age 4 years, 22% of the children with 4 or more risk factors had IQs lower than 85, whereas none of the children with a 0 or 1 risk factor had an IQ lower than 85. Equally striking, whereas 59% of the children with 1 or fewer risk factors had an IQ above 115, only 4% of the children with 4 or more risk indicators had an IQ above 115. When the children were reassessed at age 13 and the same cumulative risk factor group cutoffs employed at age 4 were utilized, the percentage of children in the 4 or greater risk factor group with IQs below 85 increased from 22% to 46%. These data provide strong confirmation that high-risk environments operate in a synergistic fashion that places children experiencing these multiple disadvantages in a downward spiral of increasingly incompetent functioning.

A final example of the predictive power of multiple risk factors is provided by the work of Richters and Martinez (1993). In a cross-sectional sample of 72 children attending their first years of elementary school in a violent neighborhood, Richters and Martinez (1993) found that the odds of early adaptational failure among children from stable, safe homes were approximately 6%; these odds were augmented by over 300% for children living in homes rated as either unstable or unsafe, and by greater than 1,500% for children residing in homes rated as both unstable and unsafe. Strikingly, 100% of the children who were directly experiencing instability and danger in the families were classified as adaptational failures, defined as children who were performing poorly or failing in school and who were rated by their parents as suffering from behavior problems that were clinically significant. Because the transition into the early grade school years is a developmentally significant life turning point (cf., Meyer, 1957), the unsuccessful adaptation of the children from the riskiest environments is especially troubling.

Resilience

Understanding how children overcome significant stressors and go on to function adaptively is an area that holds considerable promise for informing both developmental theory and prevention and intervention efforts. Resilience has been operationalized as the individual's capacity for adapting successfully and functioning competently despite experiencing chronic stress or adversity, or following exposure to prolonged or severe trauma (Masten et al., 1990; Rutter, 1990). The roots of work on resilience can be traced back to prior research in diverse areas, including investigations of schizophrenia, poverty, and response to trauma.

The empirical literature on schizophrenia can be viewed as one founding base in providing exemplars of resilience in the presence of serious psychopathology. Schizophrenics who were characterized by a less severe course of illness usually had shown a premorbid history of competence in work, social relations, marital status, and capacity to fulfill responsibility. The adaptive early histories, manifest signs of premorbid competence, and differentiated symptom patterns displayed by these atypical schizophrenics eventuated in the creation of a dichotomy between the more common "chronic" long-term pattern of schizophrenia and the briefer and more adaptive life history pattern designed as the "reactive" type of schizophrenia (Garmezy, 1970). This reactive pattern also was frequently associated with recovery.

Resilience also was evident in other situations associated with exposure to chronic stress. Poverty inevitably provides a plenitude of stressors (Huston, Garcia-Coll, & McLoyd, 1994), yet the literature reveals the patterning of positive behaviors in many children exposed to economic and social deprivation. Examples include Pavenstedt's (1965) comparison of the adaptations of children reared in upper-lower and very low-lower social environments; Elder's (1974) *Children of the Great Depression;* Festinger's (1983) *No One Ever Asked Us,* detailing the outcomes in adulthood of young children reared in foster homes and institutional settings; Long and Vaillant's (1984) follow-up study of Glueck and Glueck's (1950) investigations of delinquency during the 1940s; Schorr and Schorr's (1988) *Within Our Reach: Breaking the Cycle of Disadvantage;* the Kandel et al. (1988) study of a Danish cohort that demonstrated the avoidance of potential delinquency among children with severely criminal fathers, and Jerrold Ladd's (1994) *Out of the Madness,* a stunning and compelling autobiographical account of an African American's triumph over the poverty and racism that defeats so many.

Finally, historical instances of adaptive functioning in individuals exposed to trauma have contributed to the foundation on which theories and investigations of resilience have been built. These events include children exposed to the "cauldron of turmoil" in Northern Ireland (Harbison, 1983) who have remained resilient and adaptable, and have coped surprisingly well with Northern Ireland's "troubles"; children of the Holocaust grown to adulthood (Epstein, 1979; Moskovitz, 1983); and the "malleability" of poor and minority children (Clark, 1983; Comer, 1980; Gallagher & Ramey, 1987; Monroe & Goldman, 1988; Neisser, 1986). Children exposed to disasters provide a supplemental portrait of the presence of "malleability" for some, but not for all youngsters (Masten et al., 1990; Terr, 1991).

The work of Adolf Meyer (1957) likewise played a prominent role in the upsurge of interest displayed toward uncovering the determinants of resilient functioning. Emphasizing the need to investigate how individuals adapted to key developmental turning points throughout the life course, Meyer's writings underscored the important role that one's ability to deal with challenge plays in determining the ultimate outcome. Relatedly, Lois Murphy's investigations of vulnerability, coping, and mastery emphasized the active role that the individual plays in the adaptive process (Murphy, 1962; Murphy & Moriarty, 1976). In keeping with our viewpoint, both Meyer and Murphy believed that the individual's active self-organization exerted a critical role in determining whether an adaptive or a maladaptive pathway would be traversed (cf., Cicchetti & Tucker, 1994).

The more contemporaneous roots of resilience can be traced to the seminal work of Norman Garmezy and his colleagues (Garmezy, 1971; Garmezy & Streitman, 1974). Garmezy's writings were among the earliest examples of efforts to emphasize the importance of examining protective factors in at-risk populations and they laid the groundwork for the present-day work in the area of resilience. Current efforts to understand the mechanisms and processes leading to resilient outcome have been facilitated by investigators conducting work within the arena of developmental psychopathology (Cicchetti & Garmezy, 1993; Rutter, 1987). As the developmental perspective has assumed a more prominent role in psychopathology research, there has been a growing interest in the study of resilience. By uncovering the mechanisms and processes that lead to competent adaptation despite the presence of adversity, our understanding of both normal development and psychopathology is enhanced. Within this context, it is important that resilient functioning not be viewed as a static or trait-like condition, but as being in dynamic transaction with intra- and extra-organismic forces (Cicchetti & Schneider-Rosen, 1986).

The incorporation of an organizational developmental perspective into work in the area of resilience also underscores the need to examine functioning across multiple domains of development. Whereas a child may appear to be adapting positively within the school arena if outcome measures focus solely on cognitive abilities, the same child may manifest impaired social relationships. Unless multiple domains of development are assessed, only a partial picture of adaptation can be formulated. This is especially problematic if significant maladaptation subsequently emerges because it would appear to be an unexplained divergence when, in reality, the earlier portrayal of adaptive functioning was incorrect. As the work of Luthar and her colleagues with inner-city adolescents highlights (e.g., Luthar, 1991; Luthar, Doernberger, & Zigler, 1993), resilience is not an all-or-none construct. Adolescents from disadvantaged backgrounds who manifest resilient functioning in some areas are often at risk for experiencing difficulties in other realms of functioning (Luthar, 1991; Luthar et al., 1993). Of particular interest, Luthar's work documents that children functioning well despite experiencing high levels of stress are likely to express their distress in the form of internalizing symptoms. Thus, resilient children are not herculean in their resistance to stress. Rather, they are capable of maintaining competent functioning despite an interfering emotionality. This conceptualization is important in its emphasis on the dialectic that exists between successful adaptation and the struggles associated with this process (cf., Jamison, 1993). By recognizing that even "resilient" children require support and may be vulnerable throughout their lives, we will be helping to ensure the provision of adequate and necessary services for these children. In fact, the very availability of support may be a critical component in the continued expression of resilience. Furthermore, the field of resilience also offers great promise as an avenue for facilitating the development of prevention and intervention strategies. Through the examination of the proximal and distal processes and mechanisms that contribute to positive adaptation in situations that more typically eventuate in maladaptation, researchers and clinicians will be better prepared to devise ways of promoting positive outcomes in high-risk populations.

Likewise, from an organizational perspective, the necessity of examining children's functioning across multiple settings becomes paramount. Thus, some children may fare poorly in the school arena, yet function adaptively in more "real-world" contexts. Luthar and McMahon (in press) found that inner-city youth whose peer reputations were aggressive nonetheless were popular with their peers. Thus, in addition to the more typical pathway to peer popularity (e.g., prosocial behaviors, academic success), Luthar and McMahon (in press) identified a less typical pathway characterized by disruptive and aggressive behaviors and poor academic functioning. These results are strikingly different from those reported in a large number of studies utilizing other samples of children that have consistently indicated strong links between aggressive and disruptive behaviors and rejection by peers (Newcomb, Bukowski, & Pattee, 1993), and they underscore the diversity of pathways to adaptive outcome.

Consistent with the developmental-contextual approach advocated by organizational developmental theorists, Luthar and McMahon (in press) explained this alternate pathway with respect to sociocultural factors (cf., Cicchetti & Toth, in press; Weisz, 1989). Luthar and McMahon hypothesized that within the crime-, violence-, and poverty-laden, disenfranchised communities that these youth reside, aggressive behaviors not only may be normative, but also, in some contexts, are adaptive. As Richters and Cicchetti (1993b) theorized, behaviors that are viewed as deviant by the mainstream may be associated with prestige and high status among particular sociocultural groups (see also Coie & Jacobs, 1993).

Furthermore, psychopathologists who adhere to an organizational view of the developmental process advocate the importance of incorporating age- and culturally-appropriate assessments of biological, psychological, and psychosocial factors on the same individuals in their striving to uncover the roots of resilient adaptation (Garcia-Coll et al., 1996; Richters & Cicchetti, 1993b). Along these lines, Staudinger, Marsiske, and Baltes (1995) present a life-span developmental perspective on resilience and reserve capacity in their studies of elderly persons in Germany. Staudinger and her colleagues demonstrate through their empirical work that, in later adulthood, reserve capacity (i.e., an individual's current maximum performance potential) increasingly becomes allocated to resilience-related processes (i.e., maintenance of adult functioning and recovery from dysfunction) rather than to growth. Believing that plasticity and growth can occur throughout the life span, Staudinger et al. (1995) argue that the elderly retain the potential for selective growth. Moreover, these investigators illustrate how various interventions (e.g., with elderly persons suffering from depression or dementia) can enhance reserve capacity and promote successful aging through the protective mechanisms of selection (e.g., domains of expertise), optimization (e.g., training, self-efficacy), and compensation (e.g., alternate pathways).

Finally, the ability to function resiliently in the presence of biological, psychological, environmental, and sociocultural disadvantage may be achieved through the use of developmental pathways that are less typical than those negotiated in usual circumstances. Thus, an important question for researchers to address is whether the employment of alternative pathways to attaining competence renders individuals more vulnerable to manifesting delays or deviations in development. Although only prospective longitudinal investigations can fully address this issue, it is critical to ascertain whether these individuals are more prone to developing maladaptation or psychopathology in later life. Given the nonstatic nature of the construct, we do not expect children identified as resilient to be immune to declines in functioning at each future assessment period (cf., Egeland, Carlson, & Sroufe, 1993). In addition to attaining competence in the face of acute and chronic adversity (Garmezy & Masten, 1994; Garmezy & Rutter, 1985), it is as important to discover the processes underlying recovery of function as it is to discern the mechanisms that contribute either to ongoing resilient adaptation or to a decline from such functioning.

An array of factors have been identified by researchers that enhance the functioning of both high-risk and low-risk groups of individuals. Included among these protective factors are easy temperament, level of autonomic arousal, positive coping skills, the ability to garner support from peers and elders in the community, the ability to maintain some psychological distance from the family, active participation in a church community, attendance at colleges, a supportive friend or marital partner, the presence of family religious beliefs, and the presence of affectional ties that encourage the development of trust, autonomy, and initiative (Cicchetti & Garmezy, 1993; Masten et al., 1990; Raine, Venables & Williams, 1995; Werner & Smith, 1992). Because the aforementioned positive predictors of good outcome regardless of risk status have been discovered at various points in the life course, in a number of studies, and with several different high-risk and pathological populations (Cicchetti & Garmezy, 1993; Werner, 1995), we consider them to be an impressive documentation of their compensatory nature.

Although most of the research in the field of resilience has uncovered protective factors that enhance the functioning of both the high-risk and low-risk groups, several groups of investigators have begun to discover protective mechanisms that augment the adaptation only of the high-risk group. Included among these protective mechanisms for various high-risk groups are intelligence (Garmezy, Masten, & Tellegen, 1984; Luthar & Zigler, 1992), easy temperament (Maziade et al., 1990; Tschann et al., 1996), positive future expectations (Rutter, 1979; Werner & Smith, 1982; Wyman, Cowen, Work, & Kerley, 1993), humor (Masten, 1986), maternal social competence (Conrad & Hammen, 1993), positive friendships (Conrad & Hammen, 1993), close secure relations with nonparental adults (Beardslee & Podorefsky, 1988), and effective planning (or "planful competence") that helps to set off positive feedback that promotes virtuous chains of circumstances (Quinton & Rutter, 1988). Importantly, because individual differences in resilience are not fixed qualities residing within the person, once the mechanisms underlying particular protective factors are discovered, it should be possible to design interventions to promote their development in high-risk individuals or groups. However, these protective mechanisms may not function in a similar fashion across all high-risk individuals or groups and a protective mechanism may not operate identically across all developmental periods.

Rutter (1990), in keeping with the beliefs of Adolf Meyer and congruent with one of the major theoretical propositions of the organizational perspective, viewed key life turning points as times (e.g., sensitive periods—see Cicchetti & Tucker, 1994) when protective mechanisms could help individuals redirect themselves from a risk trajectory onto a more adaptive developmental pathway (Cicchetti & Toth, 1992b). Again, the ability of individuals to deal effectively with life changes and to handle stressful or adverse circumstances adaptively plays a critical role in determining developmental outcome. We concur with Rutter (1990) that resilience is not a static trait that exists in the "psychological chemistry of the moment" (p. 210). It is a dynamic construct and both biological and psychological processes of self-organization exert a vital role in how individuals fare when they are exposed to adverse circumstances.

Now that an overarching theoretical framework for conceptualizing risk, disorder, and resilience in childhood and adolescence has been presented, we turn our attention toward epidemiological considerations that possess relevance for research and practice.

DEVELOPMENTAL EPIDEMIOLOGY

As noted earlier, efforts to apply an epidemiological perspective to disorders of childhood and adolescence were initiated in the late 19th century, with the goal of classifying and caring for children with severe disabilities (Costello & Angold, 1995). To address increased concern about the role of social factors in mental illness (Earls, 1979), by the mid-20th century epidemiologists had shifted their focus to examining the borderline between normality and abnormality. In the past two decades, a renewed interest in the prevalence of psychiatric disorders has occurred (Costello & Angold, 1995). Despite these shifts in emphasis, the basic focus of epidemiology has continued to be an investment in the identification of causal links between risk factors and disorders, with the goal of predicting and preventing illness (Costello & Angold, 1995).

After culling a range of epidemiological studies, the report of the Institute of Medicine (IOM, 1989) conservatively estimated that 12% of U.S. children under the age of 18 suffer from a mental disorder. However, this report recognized that in populations who are exposed to extreme psychosocial adversity the rate of mental illness may exceed 20% (see Knitzer, 1982). In reviewing major prevalence studies of the past 25 years that have yielded information pertinent to developmental epidemiology, Costello and Angold (1995) report the overall prevalence of child psychopathology to be in the region of 20%. This incidence rate derives from surveys including Wave 2 of the Isle of Wight study (Graham & Rutter, 1973), the Dunedin study (McGee et al., 1990), and the New York Study (Velez, Johnson, & Cohen, 1989). Moreover, Achenbach and Howell (1993) compared problems and competencies as reported by parents and teachers for a random sample of 7- to 16-year-olds assessed by parents in 1976 and by teachers for a 1981 to 1982 sample. These investigators found that problem scores were higher and competence scores were lower in 1989 than they were in earlier assessments. Additionally, when evaluating clinically significant symptomatology, more untreated children were viewed as in need of intervention in the 1989 than in the 1976 sample. In view of these estimates of prevalence, it is especially disconcerting that the rate of treatment in mental health settings is close to only 1% (Costello & Angold, 1995). The prevalence of psychiatric problems in young children seen in primary care settings and the tendency for pediatricians to underidentify such problems suggest the importance of collaborative work between pediatricians and mental health professionals if mental illness in children is to be more accurately identified and treated (Lavigne et al., 1996; Resnick & Kruczek, 1996).

To gain an understanding of the contributions of epidemiology to our knowledge of child and adolescent psychopathology, a brief look at relevant history is useful.

The first wide-scale epidemiological investigation of child disorders was undertaken in the mid-1950s by Lapouse and Monk (1958, 1964). This study was important in documenting the high rate of emotional and behavioral problems in 6- to 12-year-old children. It also demonstrated a lessening of problems with increasing age and highlighted the discrepancy between maternal and child reports of symptomatology. However, it was limited in scope because psychiatric diagnoses were not assigned to the children (Rutter, 1989a).

The first large-scale epidemiological study to incorporate a more explicit psychiatric focus was conducted on the Isle of Wight during the mid-1960s. Rutter (1989a) summarizes a number of important findings that emerged from the Isle of Wight studies, many of which continue to be relevant to our understanding of the developmental epidemiology of childhood disorders. Issues related to comorbidity of disorders, low agreement between parent and teacher reports of child behavior, and varied illness course as a function of age of onset were elucidated by the Isle of Wight studies. Although much was learned, some omissions also were apparent. Perhaps most significantly, younger children were not included in the Isle of Wight studies, thereby limiting the attainment of a portrayal of disorders at various developmental periods.

A number of other epidemiological studies, however, did provide information on younger children (Earls, 1980a, 1980b; Minde & Minde, 1977; Richman, Stevenson, & Graham, 1982; Wolkind, 1985). Most notably, the London study found that three fifths of disorders present at age 3 persisted over a 5-year period (Richman et al., 1982), thereby casting doubt on the previously held assumption that disorders in preschool children were transient and therefore did not warrant intervention. Of equal importance for purposes of intervention was the finding that improvements in family functioning did not necessarily translate into disease remission in children for whom psychosocial stressors were considered to be contributory to the emergence of psychopathology. According to Rutter (1989a), this negative finding suggests a number of possibilities with relevance for intervention. It could be that greater environmental change is required to promote remission, or that once a disorder is present, factors intrinsic to the child result in self-perpetuation of the disorder. An alternate, though not exclusionary, explanation might be that factors leading to the onset of a disorder are different from those affecting its course. Issues related to the course of disorders over time emphasize the importance of adopting a developmental perspective in epidemiological investigations.

Until recently, epidemiology did not incorporate the importance of development into its methodology (cf., Kellam, Brown, Rubin, & Ensminger, 1983). According to Costello and Angold (1995):

> Developmental epidemiology is about continuity and change in psychopathology; *describing* how disorders develop, *explaining* the observed patterns in terms of what is known about both human development and the development of disease, *predicting* the distribution of disorders in the population, and using this knowledge for *controlling* the development of disorders. (p. 50)

The ramifications of the omission of a developmental perspective for understanding the prevalence and course of childhood disorder need to be considered in arriving at a developmental epidemiology (Costello & Angold, 1995; Kellam & Rebok, 1992). The use of scaled-down adult nomenclature regarding etiology, course, and outcome poses significant problems for the epidemiologist interested in explaining disease distribution in the community. Unless the concept of varied rates of development is taken into account, differing prevalence rates for a given disorder over time and across genders cannot be explained.

By attending to development as "goal-directed change toward developmentally appropriate 'normal' behavior" (Costello & Angold, 1995, p. 46), developmental epidemiologists can study patterns of pathology, and link the study of normal development with the emergence of disease. Such an approach holds great promise for improving the effectiveness of our approaches to prevention and intervention for childhood psychopathology. In this regard, issues of continuity and discontinuity of disorder are especially important considerations.

Although historically many disorders of childhood were viewed as transient and therefore of little concern, evidence has increasingly called this assumption into question (IOM, 1989). Within global patterns of psychopathology, an increasing consensus is emerging regarding continuity of disorder (Cicchetti & Toth, 1991; Costello & Angold, 1995). This continuity has been most consistently demonstrated with respect to externalizing disorders in children age 6 and older (Loeber, 1982; Robins, 1966, 1979; Rutter & Giller, 1983). McGee, Freehan, Williams, and Anderson (1992) found that externalizing disorders in 11-year-old boys were predictive of externalizing disorders at age 15. For girls, similar predictive power was attained for internalizing disorders. In a 5-year longitudinal investigation, Costello, Stouthamer-Loeber, and DeRosier (1993) found that for both boys and girls internalizing disorders in childhood predicted internalizing disorders in adolescence and externalizing disorders in childhood predicted externalizing disorders in adolescence. Cohen, Cohen, and Brook (1993) calculated the probability of adolescents who had the same diagnosis 2.5 years earlier receiving a specific diagnosis relative to nondiagnosed adolescents. For attention deficit disorder, conduct disorder, oppositional disorder, overanxious disorder, and alcohol abuse, the odds ratios were significantly above chance. Moreover, for all disorders except alcohol abuse, greater severity at initial assessment resulted in greater odds ratios 2.5 years later. In a study of a community sample conducted in Canada, the strongest predictor of conduct disorder was a diagnosis of conduct disorder 4 years earlier (Offord et al., 1992). Thirty-four percent of children diagnosed with hyperactivity and 25% of children diagnosed with anxiety or depression had received the same diagnosis 4 years earlier (Offord et al., 1992).

To illustrate the development of psychopathology in a sample of children that included those younger than age 6, Achenbach and his colleagues (Achenbach, Howell, McConaughy, & Stanger, 1995a) traced the 6-year predictive paths to outcome via parent, teacher, and self-reports in 4- through 12-year-old children. Aggressive behavior was found to be the most predictable syndrome for both boys and girls. Delinquent behavior was less predictable, leading the investigators to conclude that it may emerge from a range of developmental precursors. Attention problems were stable over time, but this syndrome was associated with more diverse difficulties among girls, whereas the anxious/depressed syndrome was associated with more diverse difficulties among boys (Achenbach et al., 1995a). In their nationally representative sample, Achenbach and his colleagues (Achenbach, Howell, McConaughy, & Stranger, 1995b) also were able to identify specific predictive paths for each sign of disturbance for both sexes over a 6-year period. This national study lends considerable support to the concept of continuity of disorder over time.

Continuity of disorder also has been demonstrated in samples containing exclusively very young children. Pianta and Caldwell (1990) assessed a normative sample of children at their entry into kindergarten and followed them through first grade. Substantial stability in externalizing symptomatology was evidenced for both boys and girls over the 2-year period, with concurrent learning problems found to be associated with higher than expected continuity of dysfunction. In a similar study of internalizing disorders, only low to moderate continuity was found (Pianta & Castaldi, 1989).

Considerable stability of behavior problems also has been obtained in preschool children. In an examination of the stability of behavior problems in 2- to 5-year-olds, continuity for externalizing symptomatology was obtained over a 3-year period, whereas internalizing scores were stable only between ages 4 and 5 (Rose, Rose, & Feldman, 1989). Overall, studies have found high stability of behavior problems in preschoolers over a 1- to 2-year period (Campbell, Breaux, Ewing, & Szumowski, 1986; Egeland, Kalkoske, Gottesman, & Erickson, 1990).

Longer-term follow-up studies similarly have revealed relatively high stability from the preschool period to elementary school age (Campbell & Ewing, 1990; Egeland et al., 1990; Richman et al., 1982). Moreover, in her recent review of behavior problems in preschool children, Campbell (1995) reports that despite variations in sample, definitional issues, and geographic site of studies, children identified as hard-to-manage at age 3 or 4 have a high probability of continuing to evidence difficulties throughout the elementary school years and into adolescence. Additionally, although only a few studies have examined infant precursors of later behavior problems, there is some indication that maternal ratings of infant difficultness predict later ratings of behavior problems, especially with respect to externalizing symptomatology in boys (Bates & Bayles, 1988; Bates, Maslin, & Frankel, 1985). However, a possible interaction between infant characteristics and the quality of parenting, as well as parental biases and expectations, cannot be excluded from exerting a role in these estimates of stability.

In general, then, studies have consistently revealed continuity over time with respect to the presence of behavioral disorders of childhood. Importantly, this continuity has been found to exist even when problems have been identified during infancy. Because studies have rarely looked specifically at internalizing disorders in children below the age of 6, much of our knowledge on continuity during the early years of life relates to externalizing disorders. During the school-age years and adolescence, however, continuity for internalizing symptomatology also has been found. In moving beyond continuity across childhood and adolescence, investigators also have been interested in continuity between childhood disorders and psychopathology in adulthood (Rutter, 1989b).

The Epidemiological Catchment Area (ECA) studies provide a window into links between childhood onset disorders and their relevance for functioning in adulthood (Robins & Regier, 1991). These surveys of over 20,000 individuals age 18 or older in the United States revealed that the median age of onset for manic-depressive illness, phobias, and drug abuse or dependence was in the teen years. Although these findings are affected by limitations associated with retrospective recall, taken in conjunction with the prospective evidence on continuity from childhood to adolescence, they bode poorly for the outcome of individuals afflicted with childhood mental illness.

In a follow-up of 6- to 12-year-old boys initially diagnosed with hyperkinetic reaction of childhood, Gittelman, Manuzza, Shenker, and Bonaguro (1985) found that 31% of the sample met criteria for hyperactivity at ages 16 to 23. Continuity for hyperactivity also was reported for an 8-year follow-up, with 72% of boys initially diagnosed as hyperactive continuing to meet criteria at ages 12 to 20 (Barkley, Fischer, Edelbrock, & Smallosh, 1990). Kandel and Davies (1986) reported moderately high stability for depressive symptomatology over a 9-year period for adolescents initially assessed at 15 to 16 years of age. In an investigation of the 4-year course of behavioral and emotional problems from adolescence into young adulthood in a general population sample, Ferdinand, Verhulst, and Wiznitzer (1995) found that almost 40% of adolescents initially classified as deviant continued to be so 4 years later. This continuity occurred for both internalizing and externalizing disorders. Achenbach and his colleagues also found strong predictive relations from adolescent to adult syndromes in their sample of 13- to 16- and 16- to 19-year-olds who were subsequently assessed at 19 to 22 years of age (Achenbach et al., 1995b). Increasing information also has been obtained on continuity within specific disorders (see, e.g., Rutter, 1995). However, unlike the earlier literature that generally focused on a search for direct continuities of the same disorder, there has been an increasing recognition of the implications of heterotypic continuity (Rutter, 1995). The role of heterotypic continuity of disorder, in conjunction with realities associated with substantial comorbidity between disorders presumed to be separate, may well result in higher estimates of continuity of disorder than has been obtained to date. The problems of childhood and adolescence must not be ignored if efforts to reduce the emotional and monetary costs associated with mental illness are to be successful.

Our prior discussions of the definitional and theoretical parameters of developmental psychopathology and epidemiology can be used to guide the efforts of researchers and practitioners who are invested in better understanding and ameliorating disorders of childhood and adolescence. With this as a base, we next turn our attention toward stage-salient issues of development for three illustrative conditions: child maltreatment, offspring of depressed parents, and child and adolescent depression. The implications of this research for practitioners are discussed following the presentation of research findings on each issue.

ILLUSTRATIVE RISK CONDITIONS AND DISORDERS OF CHILDHOOD AND ADOLESCENCE

Our understanding of a number of high-risk conditions and mental disorders, including alcoholism and drug abuse (Cicchetti, 1996a; Tarter & Vanyukov, 1994; Zucker, Fitzgerald, & Moses, 1995), autism (Bailey, Phillips, & Rutter, 1996; Baron-Cohen, 1995; Baron-Cohen, Tager-Flusberg, & Cohen, 1993; Courchesne, Townsend, & Chase, 1995), childhood depression (Cicchetti & Schneider-Rosen, 1986), schizophrenia (Benes, Turtle, Khan, & Farol, 1994; Bloom, 1993; Cannon et al., 1994; Gooding & Iacono, 1995; Mednick, Cannon, Barr, & La Fosse, 1991; Mednick, Cannon, Barr, & Lyon, 1991; Weinberger, 1987), mental retardation (Cicchetti & Beeghly, 1990; Cicchetti & Pogge-Hesse, 1982; Hodapp & Zigler, 1995; Zigler, 1969), child maltreatment (Cicchetti & Carlson, 1989; Cicchetti & Toth, 1993), anxiety disorders (Manassis & Bradley, 1994), conduct disorder (Cicchetti & Richters, 1993; Moffitt, 1993; Richters & Cicchetti, 1993a, 1993b), and attention-deficit/hyperactivity disorder (Castellanos et al., 1994; Hinshaw, 1987; Sroufe, 1989; Taylor, 1995) has been enhanced by knowledge of normal psychological and biological developmental processes (see Cicchetti & Cohen, 1995a, for other examples). We focus on child maltreatment, the offspring of depressed parents, and childhood depression as interesting exemplars of how theory and research in the area of normal development can help to elucidate the etiology, course, sequelae, and treatment of high-risk conditions and disorders of childhood and adolescence. Moreover, we use these conditions to illustrate how the study of risk and psychopathology can reciprocally inform normal developmental theory. Our discussion of these topics is guided by an adherence to an organizational perspective on development because we believe that sound theory is critical for organizing and guiding research and treatment efforts in this field.

CHILD MALTREATMENT

Child maltreatment represents a severe dysfunction in parenting, as well as a substantial disturbance in parent-child relationships, that may result in serious child maladaptation and aberrant development. Although other risk conditions posing threats to optimal child development (e.g., parental psychopathology, parental substance abuse, poverty, marital discord) also may entail compromised parental functioning, child maltreatment, by definition, involves grossly inadequate and destructive patterns of parenting (Cicchetti & Barnett, 1991b). In fact, child maltreatment may represent the greatest failure of the caregiving environment to provide opportunities for normal development.

In terms of an "average expectable environment" (Hartmann, 1958; Winnicott, 1958), maltreating parents are at best an aberration of the supportive, nurturant adults that are expected by the individual in the evolutionary context of species-typical development (Scarr, 1993). Moreover, numerous studies indicate that maltreating families characteristically provide fewer supports and opportunities for mastery outside the family than are expected from an environment that is "good enough" (Scarr, 1992; Winnicott, 1958). Knowledge of normative parental functioning assists in forming a context in which to understand the deviations inherent in child maltreatment; conversely, the investigation of maltreatment in parenting also informs the study of normative parenting by illuminating the effects on parent, child, and family when adaptive parenting is not present.

According to the developmental psychopathology perspective, a recognition of the developmental and contextual aspects of maltreatment is a requisite for understanding its causes and consequences. A caregiver must be able to adapt to the changing needs of a child. Failure to do so could constitute an act of maltreatment, depending on the developmental level of the child. Thus, whereas close monitoring and physical proximity are expected with a newborn, a similar parenting style with an adolescent would be inappropriate and, taken to extremes, emotionally abusive. The actual consequences of child maltreatment also manifest themselves differently according to a number of factors, including the perpetrator and the child's developmental level. Accordingly, methods of documenting psychological harm will need to vary with the child's age for accurate assessment of possible sequelae. In addition to child-relevant considerations, alterations in the parent, the family, and the broader extrafamilial environment need to be considered in any definition of maltreatment (see Barnett, Manly, & Cicchetti, 1993).

Definitional Considerations in Maltreatment

Because extensive research information is required if it is to be useful in making policy decisions, researchers must be able to communicate their findings and compare their results across laboratories and across samples. Standardizing and unifying definitions of child maltreatment reflect fundamental steps toward improving research and hence the knowledge base about abuse and neglect. Systematized definitions also represent an essential aspect of ensuring consistent and adequate services to children in need.

The problems in constructing effective operational definitions include a lack of social consensus about what forms of parenting are unacceptable or dangerous; uncertainty about whether to define maltreatment based on adult behavior, child outcome, or some combination of the two; controversy over whether criteria of harm or endangerment should be included in definitions of maltreatment; and disagreements about whether similar definitions should be used for scientific, legal, and clinical purposes.

The last issue in particular has proved to be a continuing source of disagreement because scientists, lawmakers, and clinicians all use separate definitions of maltreatment to best suit their particular needs. In legal settings, for example, definitions focusing on the demonstrable harm done to the child may be useful in prosecuting cases (Juvenile Justice Standards Project, 1977). However, a number of investigators have argued that for research purposes definitions of maltreatment that focus on the specific acts that endanger children may be more appropriate (Barnett et al., 1993; Cicchetti & Barnett, 1991b). This allows researchers to concentrate on identifiable behaviors that make up part of the child's caretaking environment rather than the uncertain consequences of those parental actions, such as some form of harm that may or may not be demonstrable. The challenge for researchers, though, is to develop precise operational definitions that minimize relying on professional opinion. This lack of consensus about what constitutes maltreatment makes clear communication and collaboration among the respective fields difficult.

In general, four categories of child maltreatment are usually distinguished from each other:

1. *Physical Abuse.* The infliction of bodily injury on a child by other than accidental means.
2. *Sexual Abuse.* Sexual contact or attempted sexual contact between a caregiver or other responsible adult and a child for purposes of the caregiver's gratification or financial benefit.
3. *Neglect.* The failure to provide minimum care and the lack of appropriate supervision.
4. *Emotional Maltreatment.* Persistent and extreme thwarting of a child's basic emotional needs (Aber & Zigler, 1981; Giovannoni & Becerra, 1979).

Each of these subtypes of maltreatment represents a clear deviation from the average expectable environment. However, even an issue as seemingly straightforward as identifying maltreatment subtypes can become unclear. It would be a mistake to think that maltreatment always occurs in discrete subtypes. There is a high degree of comorbidity among maltreatment subtypes, indicating that many maltreated children experience more than one form of maltreatment (Cicchetti & Barnett, 1991b; Cicchetti & Rizley, 1981). In many instances, it may be theoretically or clinically necessary to focus on the major subtype of maltreatment in a particular case; however, the actual experience of many children is much more complicated, and this presents significant challenges for both researchers and clinicians. For more detailed operational definitions of subtypes of maltreatment, the reader is referred to Barnett et al. (1993).

Moving toward a uniform agreement on what constitutes maltreatment and instituting a standardized means of recording the pertinent information regarding identified maltreatment are essential steps for the future. Despite some important groundbreaking work in this direction, much research remains to be conducted. The challenge is to adopt a consistent method of systematizing maltreatment that is feasible and that satisfies the needs of individuals addressing various related issues.

An Ecological-Transactional Model of Maltreatment

Cicchetti and Lynch (1993) have proposed an ecological-transactional model that can be used to examine the way in which serious disturbances in caregiving environments, such as child maltreatment, impact individual development and adaptation. Cicchetti and Lynch (1993) explain how forces from each level of the environment as well as characteristics of the individual parent and child exert reciprocal influences on each other and shape the course of child development. Thus, the multileveled ecology of child maltreatment can be seen as demonstrating broad-based environmental failure and as indicating a deviation from the average expectable environment. In combination with characteristics of the individual parent and child, these environmental disturbances shape the probabilistic course of maltreated children's development.

According to Cicchetti and Lynch (1993), potentiating and compensatory risk factors associated with maltreatment are present at each level of the ecology. Risk factors within a given level of the model can influence outcomes and processes in surrounding levels of the environment. These constantly occurring transactions determine the amount of biological and psychological risk that the individual faces. At higher, more distal levels of the ecology, such as the macrosystem and the exosystem (cf., Bronfenbrenner & Ceci, 1994), potentiating factors increase the potential of conditions that support maltreatment, whereas compensatory factors decrease the potential of such conditions (Coulton, Korbin, Su, & Chow, 1995; Osofsky, 1995; Thompson, 1995). Risk factors within the microsystem also contribute to the presence or absence of maltreatment and to the adaptiveness of family functioning. Characteristics of the microsystem exert the most direct effects on children's development because it is the level of the ecology most proximal to the child.

The manner in which children handle the challenges presented to them by family, community, and societal dysfunction is seen in their own ontogenic (i.e., individual) development. It is the particular pathway that individual development takes that results in ultimate adaptation or maladaptation. An increased presence at all ecological levels of the enduring vulnerability factors and transient challengers associated with different forms of violence and maltreatment represents a deviation from the average expectable environment, making the successful resolution of stage-salient developmental issues problematic for children (Cicchetti, 1989). The result is a greater likelihood of negative developmental outcomes and psychopathology (Cicchetti & Toth, 1995). Conversely, such an ecological-transactional approach provides a powerful theoretical perspective for conceptualizing resilient outcomes in some children. The presence of enduring protective factors and transient buffers at any level of the ecology may approximate some conditions of an average expectable environment and, in accord with an organizational perspective on development, may help to explain why some children display successful adaptation in the face of maltreatment and other disturbances in the caretaking environment. In applying such a model to predictions about individual adaptation, it will ultimately be critical to know the child's level of adaptation prior to the occurrence of maltreatment, as this will play a significant role in how the child responds to subsequent stressful experiences (Carlson et al., 1995; Cicchetti & Tucker, 1994; Sroufe et al., 1990).

We use the Cicchetti and Lynch (1993) ecological-transactional model as a heuristic for organizing and synthesizing the literature on the consequences of child maltreatment for biological and psychological development. We limit our focus here to one ecological system, the microsystem, and its impact on individual ontogenetic development. Elaborate treatments of the role that the macrosystem and exosystem play in the etiology, course, and sequelae of child maltreatment may be found in the writings of Belsky (1980, 1993) and Cicchetti (Cicchetti & Lynch, 1993; Cicchetti & Rizley, 1981).

Following Belsky's (1980) usage, the microsystem represents the family environment. This is the immediate context in which child maltreatment takes place. In addition, the microsystem incorporates many other related components such as family dynamics and parenting styles, and the developmental histories and psychological resources of the maltreating parents. However, Bronfenbrenner (1977) does not limit the microsystem to the family. According to him, it includes any environmental setting (e.g., home, school, workplace) that contains the developing person.

With this expanded conceptualization of the microsystem, any form of maltreatment directly experienced or witnessed by children, whether it be physical and/or sexual abuse, physical neglect, emotional maltreatment, or some act of domestic violence, is considered to occur within the microsystem. This point has theoretical significance because it places all actual experiences of maltreatment in an ecological level that is proximal to children's ontogenetic development, suggesting that any experience of maltreatment or exposure to domestic violence should have direct effects on children (Margolin, 1995). Research on posttraumatic stress experienced by children is relevant in this regard. Several studies have documented that children exhibit posttraumatic symptoms over prolonged periods in response to being victimized by severe acts of personal violence (Pynoos, Steinberg, & Wraith, 1995; Terr, 1991; Udwin, 1993).

In the case of child maltreatment, the microsystem in which children develop is characterized by stressful, chaotic, and uncontrollable events (Cicchetti & Howes, 1991; Howes & Cicchetti, 1993). The most obvious feature of this ecological level is the maltreatment experience itself. The type, severity, and chronicity of maltreatment are potent characteristics of the maltreating microsystem (Cicchetti & Barnett, 1991b). Furthermore, there is mounting evidence for the independent and interactive effects these factors exert on children's development (Manly, Cicchetti, & Barnett, 1994).

Other related features of the microsystem with regard to maltreatment are important as well. Parents' prior developmental histories may be the first contributors to evolving family microsystems (Belsky & Vondra, 1989). In addition, the personal resources—psychological and biological—of maltreating parents also shape the microsystem. A number of studies indicate that maltreating parents are lacking in impulse control, especially when stressed and aroused (Brunquell, Crichton, & Egeland, 1981). Moreover, maltreating parents respond to stressful situations with greater arousal than do nonmaltreating parents. Frodi and Lamb (1980) have demonstrated that abusive mothers report more aversion to infant cries than nonabusers, and that they are more physiologically aroused. Likewise, Wolfe, Fairbank, Kelly, and Bradlyn (1983) found that abusive mothers display greater emotional arousal (i.e., increased skin conductance and respiration) to stressful stimuli than do nonabusive mothers, and that abusive mothers *remain* more aroused during both stressful and nonstressful stimuli. Furthermore, parental substance abuse has been linked with increased violence toward children (Wolfner & Gelles, 1993). Finally, higher rates of parental psychopathology, including depression, anxiety disorder, alcoholism, substance abuse, and antisocial personality disorder, appear to be associated with maltreatment (Dinwiddie & Bucholz, 1993; Egami, Ford, Greenfield, & Crum, 1996; Murphy et al., 1991). The interaction of parental psychopathology with the experience of maltreatment poses serious threats to normal child development (Walker, Downey, & Bergman, 1989).

Aspects of Maltreating Parenting

Disruptions in all aspects of family relationships are often present in the families of maltreated children. Maltreating parents interact with their children and display more negative affect toward them than do comparison parents (Burgess & Conger, 1978). In addition, anger and conflict are pervasive features of maltreating families (Trickett & Susman, 1988), although interpersonal conflict may be more characteristic of abusive parents and social isolation may be more indicative of neglecting families (Crittenden, 1985). Overall, husbands and wives in maltreating families are less warm and supportive, less satisfied in their conjugal relationships, and more aggressive and violent than spousal partners in nonabusive families (Howes & Cicchetti; 1993; Rosenbaum & O'Leary, 1981; Rosenberg, 1987; Straus, Gelles, & Steinmetz, 1980). In general, family interactions in maltreating families tend to be unsupportive and the family system is characterized by chaos and instability (Cicchetti & Howes, 1991).

Because parenting comprises a matrix of behaviors, cognitions, and emotions within a family through which parents function to provide care, socialization of the child, and a fundamental relationship experience, we next focus on specific aspects of the organization of parenting that may contribute to child maltreatment.

Processes of Attachment Organization in Maltreating Parents

Attachment theory and research have been used increasingly as an organizing framework for understanding not only the deleterious effects of maltreatment on children (Cicchetti & Toth, 1995; Cicchetti, Toth, & Lynch, 1995;

Crittenden & Ainsworth, 1989), but also as a system for conceptualizing adult relational capacities, intimate partner relationships, family dynamics, and parenting quality in regard to child maltreatment (Cicchetti & Howes, 1991; Crittenden, Partridge, & Claussen, 1991; Howes & Cicchetti, 1993; Main & Goldwyn, 1984). Attachment theory (Bowlby, 1969/1982) delineates how cognition, emotion, and behavior are integrated and influence ongoing and future relationships with others and the understanding of the self. In the early years, as infants seek to balance needs for internal security and connectedness in the context of the relationship with the primary caregiver, secure and insecure or anxious patterns of attachment behavior have been consistently identified and linked to variations in caregiver responsivity and sensitivity (Ainsworth, Blehar, Waters, & Wall, 1978; Isabella, 1993). The secure pattern (B) is associated with caregiver sensitivity and responsivity, whereas the avoidant pattern (A) has been linked to caregiver rejection and intrusiveness and the ambivalent pattern (C) to caregiver inconsistency. Moreover, highly insecure and disorganized patterns of attachment have been identified in maltreated infants and toddlers (Carlson, Cicchetti, Barnett, & Braunwald, 1989; Lyons-Ruth, Repacholi, McLeod, & Silva, 1991). Frightened and/or frightening parental behaviors are hypothesized to be the causal mechanisms underlying disorganized attachments (Main & Hesse, 1990).

The need for attachment relationships and their negotiation is a lifelong quest, and secure and insecure patterns of attachment organization also have been delineated for 3- to 4-year-olds, older children, adolescents, and adults (George, Kaplan, & Main, 1985; Kobak & Sceery, 1988; Lynch & Cicchetti, 1991; Main & Cassidy, 1988; Main, Kaplan, & Cassidy, 1985; Ward & Carlson, 1995). As development proceeds onward from infancy, behavioral patterns signifying the quality of the attachment relationship are carried forward in the form of internalized mental representations. Internal representational models of the attachment relationship, incorporating aspects of both the self and the attachment figure, are constructed along with the affects associated with experiences in the attachment relationship (Sroufe & Fleeson, 1986). Qualitatively different internal representational models are formed in accord with variations in the security of the relationship with the attachment figure. Increasingly, internal representational models are used to process information about relational experiences and to guide interpersonal encounters that maximize internal security. In accord with different relationship histories, the internal representational models are thought to act as guides for interpersonal behavior, thereby processing relational information differently and selectively attending to and interpreting experience in ways that are likely to be consistent with the model. As a result of this selective processing, interpersonal behavior increasingly is organized and directed in accord with the expectations of the individual's model. Although internal representational models are not impervious to revision based on new and qualitatively different experience that is inconsistent with the model, selective processing tends to validate the internal representations, and continuity is preserved unless sustained and marked changes in relational experience occur.

Internal representational models are likely to have a strong influence on parents' relationships with their own children and the character of concomitant parenting behavior. For parents who were themselves maltreated in childhood, internal representational models derived from those experiences potentially may contribute to relationship disturbances with their children, thereby increasing the risk for maltreatment. For individuals who have had abusive or neglectful experiences of being parented in childhood, the insecure patterns of adult attachment patterns are likely to predominate. Furthermore, these insecure patterns of attachment organization are prevalent in maltreating parents (Crittenden & Ainsworth, 1989).

Not only is parental behavior guided by the internal representational models, but these models also have a powerful influence on the selection of and relational quality between spouses or parenting partners (Crittenden et al., 1991). In examining a sample of maltreating mothers and their spouses or partners, Crittenden and her colleagues found rates of dismissing or preoccupied-engaged adult attachment organizations in both the females and males in excess of 90%. The melding of insecure attachment organizations in the spousal subsystem in maltreating families poses further risks for the quality of parenting these parents are likely to implement, based on dysfunctional relational patterns that are extended across relationships to interactions with children. These patterns in couples are likely to result in considerable disharmony and frequent conflicts. A pattern of coerciveness and victim-victimizer relational interactions is frequent in maltreating families (Howes & Cicchetti, 1993). Spousal violence and abuse also are common. These conflictual partner relationships are likely to detract from attention paid to the children's needs as well as increase the volatility of the emotional climate in the family, thereby intensifying the risk for violence being extended to the children. These findings underscore the importance of providing interventions directed at ameliorating dysfunctions inherent in the marital system.

Although in some maltreating families, marital or partner relationships are enduring, it is more likely that partner relationships are unstable. Howes and Cicchetti (1993) state that either partners go through frequent and erratic separations and reunions, or mothers may have a series of idealized relationships that quickly deteriorate and are terminated impulsively (Howes & Cicchetti, 1993). These authors note a customary peripheral role of men in maltreating families. These patterns of couple instability are likely to relate to the inability of the individuals to integrate their experiences of the relationship and the associated aspects into their internal representational models. This inability increases the likelihood of repetition of these problems (Crittenden & Ainsworth, 1989), and perpetuates the chaotic, disorganized character of family life in which parenting is conducted.

Thus, attachment theory has been instructive in organizing aspects of the parent's cognitive and affective experience in regard to parenting as well as other relationships in the parent's life that influence parental functioning. Notably, insecure internal representational models of maltreating parents, derived from past relationship experiences, promote continuity in relationship disturbances being extended to the parent-child relationship. Effective parenting is jeopardized as insecure representational models of maltreating parents, in conjunction with their negative expectations about relationships, contribute to distortions in the way they perceive and respond to their children. As a result, the potential for maltreatment is heightened. From this organizational viewpoint on attachment, further aspects of parenting by maltreating parents are now explored, with special attention directed toward cognitive, behavioral, and affective features of parenting.

Cognitions and Behavior in Maltreating Parents

In maltreating families, often the goals parents have for their children may center around their own personal needs as well as solutions to short-term rather than long-term child outcomes (Grusec & Walters, 1991). Parent-focused goals, such as gaining affection or emotional gratification from the child, acquiring economic assistance, and improving the parent's self-esteem through child success, lead to parenting practices tailored to the attainment of these goals rather than to optimizing the development of competence in the child. Short-term solutions to crises rather than a long-term focus on furthering adaptive functioning in the child (e.g., eliminating the child's noxious crying rather than focusing on the growth of self-esteem) similarly lead to parenting practices that do not further optimal socialization. The emotional communications of the authoritarian or neglecting parenting styles concomitant with these parental goals will likely detract from parents being effective in achieving their goals and contribute to child resistance, further diminishing parental effectiveness. Even these inappropriate goals are likely to be frustrated in their realization, contributing to coercive or abusive episodes or parental withdrawal and neglect.

Along with a growing realization that global parental attitudes do not correspond substantially to parental behavior, there has been an increased interest in parental cognitions and beliefs, as they may influence parent-child interaction (Sigel & Kim, 1996). Social cognitions are used as guides to interpret situations when those situations are ambiguous and do not provide clear cues to understanding events. The attributions parents make about specific child behaviors have been suggested to influence the disciplinary approaches parents use (Dix & Grusec, 1985). Attributions of intentionality and responsibility for child misdeeds or inappropriate behavior are likely to decrease parental attempts to reason with children and increase disciplinary tactics. Abusive parents also have been shown to be more likely to attribute malevolent intentions to their children (Bauer & Twentyman, 1985). When parents are prone to make attributions of spitefulness or intentionality, they also may become more vigilant to perceiving confirmatory evidence from minor variations in the child's behavior, resulting in greater intrusiveness and negative reactivity to the child's behavior. Abusive parents also have been shown to respond to variations in child misdeeds with the same highly punitive response rather than modifying their approach in accord with the degree of transgression (Trickett & Kuczynski, 1986). The attributions of seriousness may not correspond to the character of the child's behavior. Maltreating parents are also more likely to react with increased hostility if they attribute the cause of child inappropriate behavior to stable, internal, and global features of the child instead of to unstable, external, and specific situational aspects. Maltreating parents have been shown to make dispositional attributions for negative child behavior and situational attributions for positive child behavior (Bauer & Twentyman, 1985). This pattern of attributions is similar to that found in the cognitive distortions posited by the learned helplessness theory of depression (Abramson, Seligman, & Teasdale, 1978), and suggests that maltreating parents may regard themselves as helpless in regulating child misbehavior and overreact as a consequence of their attributions.

Parents' attributions of power and efficacy in parenting also may affect their parenting behavior. Persons who perceive limited control in stressful situations are more likely to respond with emotion-focused than with problem-focused coping (Lazarus, 1981), and for highly stressed parents with limited resources, emotional responses to parenting dilemmas may be more common, contributing to maltreatment. Bugental, Blue, and Cruzcosa (1989) have shown that mothers with low perceived control in parenting situations are more likely to use abusive and coercive discipline. These parents take little responsibility for child-care successes, and either blame themselves or their children for caregiving difficulties (Bugental, Mantyla, & Lewis, 1989). Parents with low perceived power and control in parenting are also likely to have a lower threshold for what they consider to be difficult child behavior and are quicker to react negatively. Vasta (1982) showed that abusive parents are more easily aroused by aversive child behavior. Thus, parental attributions made by maltreating parents may increase the likelihood that child behavior will be misperceived and punitive measures will be more likely.

Emotion Processes in Maltreating Parents

Dix (1991) synthesized theory and research on how emotion processes are coordinated with parental cognitions and behaviors, thereby contributing to adaptive and maladaptive patterns of parental functioning. Examples of the importance of emotion in parenting and maltreatment are suggested by the fact that high levels of intense negative emotion, particularly anger, are pervasive in the parenting of abusing mothers (Lahey, Conger, Atkensen, & Treiber, 1984), whereas restrictions in emotion may be operating in neglecting families, and inconsistent or situationally inappropriate emotions may play a role in parenting disturbance. Dix (1991) proposes a model of affective processes in parenting that has substantial relevance for child maltreatment. In the model, the components of emotion activation, emotion engagement, and emotion regulation are specified.

In emotion activation, goals or concerns of parents contribute to how parent-child interaction is evaluated, with differences in appraisal contributing to variations in the emotions activated in parents. Differences in child behavior and stresses from other areas of the parent's life also contribute to the appraisals made and the emotions that are activated. When parent concerns are incompatible with child concerns and mutually satisfying behaviors and outcomes are not achieved, parents experience more negative and less positive emotion. Negative emotion is more likely when parents select forceful and coercive strategies to reduce incompatibility between parent and child concerns. Because child concerns are not promoted, cooperation between parent and child is restricted, and child resistance and noncompliance are heightened.

Abusive mothers often have unrealistic expectations for mature behavior in their children (Azar, Robinson, Hekimian, & Twentyman, 1984), and they are more likely to experience negative emotion because their expectations frequently cannot be met. They also have a greater self-focus than child-focus (Crittenden, 1981) and have less empathy for their children (Feshbach, 1989). Negative emotion is generated as a result of frequent frustration in gaining child cooperation because of the lack of attention to child concerns and capabilities. This negative emotion accompanying failures in meeting their self-concerns often contributes to perceptions of failure or lack of competence in the parenting role. Anger and dysphoria are communicated to the children, further limiting parental efficacy (Bugental et al., 1989). Negative affect may be perpetuated if maltreating parents make stable, general, and uncontrollable attributions for difficulties in actualizing the parenting goals (Abramson et al., 1978), and if they make negative, intentional, and dispositional attributions for children's failure to conform to parental wishes (Bauer & Twentyman, 1985). Further, as maltreated children develop a wide range of behavioral and emotional incompetencies and disturbances, they become more difficult interactional partners, contributing to a cyclical perpetuation of conflict and negative affect in parent-child relationships (Cicchetti, 1989). The stresses of low socioeconomic status, violent neighborhoods, and poverty experienced by many maltreating parents also contribute to the generation of considerable distress and negative affect. Thus, numerous aspects of parenting and parent-child relationships, as well as social contextual stresses, activate substantial negative affect in maltreating parents, and this excess of negative affect may fuel inappropriate parenting practices and maltreatment.

Through their effects on parental motivation, cognition, communication patterns, and behavior, activated emotions engage and organize processes affecting parenting (Dix, 1991). Chronically high levels of activated negative emotion are likely to contribute to disturbances in parenting and maltreatment through poor impulse control, cognitive distortions, and reduced sensitivity. High negative emotion in parents increases tendencies to focus on immediate reduction in the negative affect. This need to reduce high negative affect results in an emphasis on short-term, parent-centered goals over long-term, child-centered developmental goals. The exertion of power tactics in parenting to gain immediate control (Maccoby & Martin, 1983) and impulsive power assertion fueled by negative emotion may contribute to maltreatment. Maltreating parents have been shown to have reduced empathic responsiveness to their children (Feshbach, 1989), also contributing to self-focused goals, particularly when negative affect is activated. Similarly, hypersensitivity in maltreating parents to child aversive stimuli (Frodi & Lamb, 1980) may also increase the likelihood of impulsive responses to reduce the parents' negatively aroused affect. High negative emotion can disrupt parental reasoning and can contribute to more reflexive emotional responding from maltreating parents in efforts to gain control (Vasta, 1982). Negative expectations, perceptions, and evaluations of children also are more likely when negative affect is aroused in parents. Dix (1991) proposed that high negative emotion contributes to parental cognitive distortions, disrupts parental problem solving, and interferes with appropriate monitoring and attention. Each of these processes may reduce parental effectiveness and increase the potential for maltreatment. High negative emotion in parents is also expressed to children directly, increasing the likelihood of eliciting reciprocal negative emotion in children and contributing to negative, coercive interchanges (Patterson, 1982). The prominent emotional instability of maltreating parents (Pianta, Egeland, & Erickson, 1989) also may create considerable ambiguity or confusion for children in understanding parent expression of emotion, promoting poor cooperation and coordination in parent-child interactions, and increasing maltreatment potential (Bugental et al., 1989).

Finally, attempts by parents to regulate their emotions are important for understanding parenting effectiveness (Dix, 1991). Vasta (1982) suggested the disrupted ability of maltreating parents to anticipate the dire consequences of their behavior for their children, and this limitation may contribute to deficits in their regulation of the expression of negative emotion and concomitant punitive parenting behavior. Nonmaltreating parents may use cognitive and affective strategies to control or inhibit their expression of negative emotion (Dix, 1991), whereas lack of control over negative emotion in maltreating parents is a prominent characteristic (Feshbach, 1989; Vasta, 1982).

A multiplicity of cognitive, affective, and behavioral processes conspire to reduce effective parenting in maltreating parents, contributing to restrictions in these parents' abilities to promote their children's welfare and heightening the likelihood of escalating relational problems and potential maltreatment. Maltreating parents frequently function in a social contextual matrix that challenges rather than supports their parenting efforts. Their own developmental experiences and consequent internal representational models that guide their relationships with their children and others impede their interpersonal relationship capacities and abilities to parent competently.

In terms of the average expectable environment, the microsystem associated with maltreatment represents substantial environmental failure in providing the necessary conditions for normal ontogenesis. In general, at the level of the microsystem, maltreating parents do little to foster the successful adaptation of their children on the major tasks of individual development. All these negative potentiating inputs from the maltreating microsystem may be internalized and carried forward by maltreated children in the form of relatively enduring vulnerability factors as they proceed through the tasks of development. Sroufe and Fleeson (1988) contend that whole relationships (including complex family relationships) are internalized and perpetuated by the individual. As a result, the individual's internalized relationship history can influence his or her attitudes, affects, and cognitions, thus organizing the self and shaping individual development.

Ontogenic Development

We next examine how growing up in a maltreating environment that deviates from the average expectable conditions affects children's individual development. Much progress has occurred in our understanding of the sequelae of child maltreatment since Kempe, Silverman, Steele, Droegemueller, and Silver's (1962) seminal paper on the "battered child syndrome." Our review is organized around ascertaining how maltreated children resolve the central developmental tasks of infancy and childhood. Because little is known about the adolescent outcomes of children who have been maltreated in infancy or childhood or about maltreated adolescents, we focus on the early years of life. However, because each issue is operative throughout the life course, we begin with each task's period of ascendance as a salient issue and track what is known about it as it unfolds to become coordinated and integrated with later emerging developmental tasks. For each stage-salient issue, practice implications that can be derived from the research presented are discussed.

Homeostatic and Physiological Regulation

Research Findings. One of the first tasks of development is the maintenance of physiological or homeostatic regulation (Emde, Gaensbauer, & Harmon, 1976; Sroufe, 1979). The goal of a homeostatic system is to maintain a set point of functioning or homeostatic equilibrium. Departure from this point introduces tension into the system, which serves as the motivation for biological and behavioral systems that subsequently act to dissipate tension and return the system once more to a state of homeostasis (Bischof, 1975). During the first months of life, tension is defined in terms of changes in the infant's arousal level and the physiological discomfort caused by these experiences. When the infant is overly aroused or physically uncomfortable, homeostatic tension is generated. At later stages of development, however, with the onset of representational skills and the formation of a core sense of self, threats to psychological coherence and consistency create tension as well.

To a large extent, maturation and development of physiological regulation may be guided by the infant's experiences with his or her caregiver during dyadic interaction (Sander, 1962). Caregivers play a critical role in the development of this homeostasis as they help the infant to establish basic cycles and rhythms of balance between inner need states and external stimuli (Hofer, 1987). By directly aiding infants in the maintenance of physiological homeostasis in the early weeks and months of life, caregivers may influence the development and organization of neurological systems (Black & Greenough, 1986). Such influences on the part of the caregiver during a period of rapid neurological growth and maturation may have long-term effects on the organization and development of the infant's brain. In fact, the existence of an open homeostatic system at this time in development suggests that interactions with the environment may be necessary for the brain to mature fully. Consequently, the development of some neurological systems may be "experience expectant"; that is, for complete differentiation and development to occur, certain types of external input by caregivers are essential, and, usually, readily available (Greenough, Black, & Wallace, 1987). By providing stable routines and responding appropriately to their infants' needs, caregivers help infants to modulate physiological tension and support their development of physiological regulation (Derryberry & Rothbart, 1984; Field, 1989).

The level of maternal sensitivity and responsivity needed to support this kind of homeostatic regulation is a specific weakness of maltreating parents. As a result, signs of physiological dysregulation are evident in maltreated infants and children (Lewis, 1992). Van der Kolk (1987) and Perry, Pollard, Blakley, Baker, and Vigilante (1995) report evidence suggesting that childhood maltreatment may enhance children's long-term hyperarousal and decrease their ability to modulate strong affect states. Additionally, van der Kolk (1987) hypothesizes that abused children may require much greater external stimulation to affect the endogenous opioid system for soothing than is the case for children whose good quality early caregiving enables them to more easily access the biological concomitants of comfort.

Practice Implications. Because caretakers are integral to the facilitation of homeostatic regulation, intervention therefore necessarily needs to target the caregiver or the parent-child dyad. Although there is a paucity of empirical data on homeostatic regulation in maltreated infants, largely because when maltreatment is identified in the early months of life it is generally so severe that infant injury and removal from the home are common, the overall maladaptations in the caregiver-child relationship suggest that homeostatic and physiological regulation should be an important target for preventive interventions.

Because full-blown psychopathology is not common during infancy, efforts to facilitate successful resolution of the developmental task of physiological and homeostatic regulation are amenable to an educational approach. Parents can be provided with information on the importance of interactions with and appropriately sensitive responsivity to their infants at this young age. Our work with maltreating parents has elucidated the extensive misinformation that exists regarding infant needs and appropriate parenting. Many parents believe that crying infants should be ignored to avoid "spoiling" them. In case of infant developmental disabilities and temperamental differences, an educative intervention also can be useful in helping parents respond most appropriately to their infants.

In addition to educational services, intervention also can be provided directly for maltreating parents. Techniques designed to induce more positive moods and to facilitate relaxation in mothers could result in increased maternal sensitivity to infant signaling systems. Finally, the provision of massage therapy to mothers and infants could alleviate stress in mothers (Field, Morrow, Valdeon, & Larson, 1992), while reducing problematic infant behavior such as colic and sleep dysregulation, thereby increasing the probability of positive interactions occurring between infant and caregiver.

As it has been suggested that maltreatment may dampen the endogenous opiod system, an assessment of optimal levels of stimulation in the caregiving system is important to help maltreating parents interact with their infants more appropriately. For example, a therapist or intervenor might need to observe mother-infant interactions directly to determine whether the infant is being over- or understimulated by the caregiver. Although much of the work in the area of homeostatic regulation and maltreatment is in its early stages, the incorporation of measures of physiological regulation into the assessment of intervention efficacy could provide insights into the malleability or plasticity of these early neurobiological structures and functions.

In view of our earlier discussion of periods of transition and the accompanying disequilibration, the failure to facilitate the acquisition of homeostatic and physiological regulation could result in significant difficulties for the developing infant. Moreover, these infant problems, in turn, could lead to the introjection of stress into the caregiving relationship, thereby resulting in a lack of resolution of this early developmental issue and initiating a trajectory of maladaptation. The earlier one can intervene into these regulatory problems, the greater the likelihood that the intensity and severity of the maltreated child's response to trauma can be ameliorated (Cicchetti & Tucker, 1994; Perry et al., 1995). Such early intervention should lessen the probability that maltreated children will develop sensitized neural systems that eventuate in long-term hyperarousal, dissociative symptoms, or both (Perry et al., 1995).

Affect Regulation and Differentiation

Research Findings. Affect regulation, defined as the intra- and extraorganismic factors by which affect arousal is redirected, controlled, modulated, and modified to enable an individual to function adaptively in emotionally arousing situations, has increasingly come to be viewed as a primary developmental task with wide-ranging implications for children's development (Cicchetti, Ganiban, & Barnett, 1991; Thompson, 1990a). Because the infant remains heavily in need of the caregiver for external scaffolding and support, the quality of care and interactions with the caregiver contribute to "experience dependent" individual differences in patterns of affect differentiation, expression, and regulation that emerge (Greenough et al., 1987; Schore, 1996). As early affect-regulatory processes emerge within the context of the caregiver-child relationship, disruptions in the development of affect regulation are likely in children who have experienced maltreatment (cf., Lewis, 1992). Thus, in accord with a developmental psychopathology perspective, adequate affect regulation would serve as a foundation for the development of secure attachment relationships, an autonomous and positive self, and effective relations with peers, whereas early affect-regulatory failures would place a child at risk for future insecure attachment relationships, self-system deficits, and peer difficulties, including later adult relationship difficulties (Howes & Cicchetti, 1993).

The roots of affect-regulation deficits have been noted in maltreated infants. Gaensbauer, Mrazek, and Harmon (1980) observed four patterns of affect differentiation in infants who had been maltreated: developmentally and affectively retarded, depressed, ambivalent and affectively labile, and angry. These investigators believed that the pattern displayed was dependent on an interaction between the caregiving experienced and the infant's biological predisposition. In a case study design, different types of maltreatment were related to the development of various affective patterns (Gaensbauer & Hiatt, 1984). Infants who were physically abused were found to demonstrate high levels of negative affects such as fear, anger, and sadness, and a paucity of positive affect, whereas an emotionally neglected infant presented as affectively blunted, evidencing little negative or positive affect.

Similar results with respect to affect dysregulation were obtained in a longitudinal investigation, where maltreated toddlers were found to be more angry, frustrated, and noncompliant during an experimental task than were nonmaltreated comparison children (Erickson, Egeland, & Pianta, 1989). During the preschool years, these children also were rated as more hyperactive, distractible, lacking in self-control, and evidencing a high level of negative affect. In kindergarten, the maltreated children were viewed as more inattentive, aggressive, and overactive by their teachers.

Corroboration for the belief that maltreated children are at risk for a developmental progression from affect-regulatory problems to behavioral dysregulation has been obtained in a number of cross-sectional investigations. Maltreated preschool (Alessandri, 1991; Haskett & Kistner, 1991) and grade-school children (Kaufman & Cicchetti, 1989; Shields, Cicchetti, & Ryan, 1994) have been found to exhibit a range of dysregulated behaviors that are frequently characterized by disruptive and aggressive actions. Maltreated toddlers also have been shown to react to peer distress with poorly regulated and situationally inappropriate affect and behavior, including anger, fear, and aggression, as opposed to the more normatively expected response of empathy and concern (Main & George, 1985; Troy & Sroufe, 1987).

Youngsters who have been physically abused manifest the later vestiges of early affect-regulatory problems in the coping patterns they evidence when exposed to interadult anger. Physically abused preschool boys who witnessed an angry simulated live laboratory interaction directed at their mothers by an adult female evinced greater aggressiveness and more coping responses aimed at alleviating the distress of their mothers than did nonabused boys (Cummings, Hennessy, Rabideau, & Cicchetti, 1994). Rather than habituating to others' hostility as a result of their history of exposure to familial violence, these abused children appeared more aroused and angered by it and more motivated to intervene. Moreover, because level of arousal is related to one's subsequent propensity for aggressive behavior, hypervigilance and arousal in response to aggressive stimuli among abused children could contribute to the development of aggressive patterns, particularly if conflict in the home is chronic (cf., Lewis, 1992).

In a related study, Hennessy, Rabideau, Cicchetti, and Cummings (1994) presented physically abused school-age children with videotaped segments of adults in angry and friendly interactions and asked children questions about their responses after each episode. Abused children reported greater distress than nonabused children in response to various forms of interadult anger, particularly in response to anger that was unresolved between adults. Moreover, the physically abused children reported greater fear in response to different forms of angry adult behavior. Similar to the findings reported by Cummings et al. (1994), these findings support a sensitization model whereby repeated exposure to anger and familial violence leads to greater emotional reactivity. Likewise, the distress responses to different forms of interadult anger exhibited by the abused children in this study may provide an early indication of the potential for developing internalizing problems in children exposed to high levels of familial violence.

These patterns of affective interactions and expectations exert an impact on how maltreated children's affect regulation continues to differentiate with development. The internal, experiential components of affect become divorced from the outward expressions of affect, allowing for the adoption of specific affect-regulatory strategies consistent with the qualities of the child's environment. Camras, Sachs-Alter, and Ribordy (1996) found that maltreated children, in explaining the story characters' emotional reactions to a situation, often distorted the story by adding extraneous material that seemed to be particularly related to their own maltreatment experience. Moreover, Camras and colleagues (1996) reported that some maltreated youngsters also were less capable of using information about the past experience of a story character to accurately comprehend the protagonist's current emotional reactions to a situation or to resolve apparent discrepancies that existed between facial and situational emotional cues. Thus, affect-regulation difficulties may also play a role in the disorganization found in maltreated children's attachment relationships.

Finally, we see some of the coping skills that maltreated children acquire in the cognitive control functioning that they use for affect regulation. Rieder and Cicchetti (1989) found that maltreated children were more hypervigilant to aggressive stimuli and recalled a greater number of distracting aggressive stimuli than did nonmaltreated children. Maltreated children also assimilated aggressive stimuli more readily, even though this may result in less cognitive efficiency and impaired task performance. Hypervigilance and ready assimilation of aggressive stimuli may develop originally as an adaptive coping strategy in the maltreating environment, alerting the child to signs of imminent danger and keeping affects from rising so high that they would incapacitate the child. This strategy also may help the child to identify specific elements of the current situation that will facilitate the determination of the most adaptive response. However, this response pattern becomes less adaptive when the child is faced with nonthreatening situations, and it may even undermine the child's ability to function adaptively under normal circumstances (Rogosch, Cicchetti, & Aber, 1995).

Although most of the research on the sequelae of child maltreatment has been focused on the behavioral level, there is increasing interest in the physiological correlates of maltreatment. Physiological adjustments to chronic stress, particularly when they occur early in development, may play a role in the behavioral and emotional sequelae of maltreatment. Physiological and behavioral responses to maltreatment are expected to be interrelated and to lead children to make choices and respond to experiences in ways that support pathological development (Cicchetti & Tucker, 1994).

Even though we possess limited empirical knowledge about the neurobiology of children who have grown up in a maltreating environment, information is accumulating on the functioning of the hypothalamic-pituitary-adrenocortical (HPA) system in maltreated children. Activity of the HPA system also may be related to the emergence of emotional pathology among individuals who have experienced childhood maltreatment. There have been relatively few studies in children of HPA activity in response to chronic adverse life events.

Research conducted in Romanian orphanages suggests that maternal deprivation contributes to marked HPA system dysregulation in the infants; extremely elevated cortisol concentrations were found in the infants residing in the orphanages (Carlson et al., in press). Although interest in the neuroendocrine correlates of maltreatment has increased, there are relatively few studies comparing neuroendocrine activity in maltreated and nonmaltreated children. Many of those that exist have focused predominantly on sexually abused girls and have been conducted in a clinical laboratory.

Thus, Putnam, Trickett, Helmers, Dorn, and Everett (1991) found higher morning and lower afternoon cortisol values for sexually abused girls, yielding a more marked diurnal decrease in cortisol compared with controls. In another study whose findings are consistent with a dampening of reactivity, DeBellis and colleagues (1994) found that sexually abused girls displayed attenuated adrenocorticotropic hormone (ACTH) responses to corticotropin releasing hormone (CRH). DeBellis and associates (1994) suggest that the attenuated ACTH response to CRH may reflect homeostatic neuroregulatory adjustments in the HPA system that might maintain cortisol concentrations within normal bounds.

Several neuroendocrine studies of more heterogeneous groups of maltreated children have been conducted in complex social settings, a context that does not allow the same level of experimental control as does assessment in a clinical laboratory. In an investigation conducted in a camp setting, Kaufman (1991) found that depressed, maltreated children were likely to show suppressed midmorning cortisol levels and a rise from morning to afternoon, indicating marked dysregulation of the diurnal pattern of cortisol secretion. However, because Kaufman (1991) did not include a comparison group of nonmaltreated children, she could not determine whether maltreatment, independent of depression, affected diurnal cortisol activity.

To address these limitations, Hart, Gunnar, and Cicchetti (1996) investigated the effects of maltreatment on physiological and affective functioning in a group of maltreated and nonmaltreated children attending a summer day-camp setting. Hart and colleagues (1996) found that maltreated children had slightly elevated afternoon cortisol concentrations, whereas their morning concentrations did not differ significantly from those of nonmaltreated children. Neither clinical levels of depression, nor internalizing nor externalizing problems were predictive of these elevated afternoon values. Depression among maltreated children was, however, associated with altered activity of the HPA system. Depressed maltreated children displayed lower morning cortisol concentrations compared with nondepressed maltreated children and were more likely to show a rise rather than the expected decrease in cortisol from morning to afternoon. These data replicated the earlier findings of Kaufman (1991). In addition, there was no evidence that depressed, nonmaltreated children exhibited this change in diurnal cortisol activity.

Additionally, Hart, Gunnar, and Cicchetti (1995) examined the salivary cortisol concentrations and social behavior (via observations and teacher reports) of maltreated and nonmaltreated children. The maltreated youngsters were studied while they attended a therapeutic preschool for abused and neglected children and the nonmaltreated children were studied while they were enrolled in a preschool that served economically disadvantaged families. Each child's cortisol values over a number of days were used to compute measures of basal activity (median cortisol) and reactivity (ratio of quartile ranges). A child with a reactive HPA system would be expected to have a larger positive than negative quartile range.

Hart and colleagues (1995) discovered that median cortisol was not significantly correlated with social behavior measures. Moreover, these investigators found that cortisol reactivity was positively correlated with social competence and negatively correlated with shy/internalizing behavior. Furthermore, maltreated children exhibited less cortisol reactivity than did comparison children. Maltreated children also scored lower in social competence and higher in shy/internalizing and acting-out/externalizing behaviors. In additional analyses, maltreated children failed to show elevations in cortisol on days of high versus low social conflict in the classroom. Social competence was also found to correlate positively with cortisol levels on high-conflict days. Taken in tandem, the results suggest a reduction in cortisol reactivity in maltreated children related to the impairment in social competence frequently noted among these children.

Practice Implications. The infant's ability to elicit caregiver responsivity, as well as caregiver sensitivity to infant cues, is critical to the successful resolution of affect regulation and differentiation. In view of the difficulties that maltreating parents experience in tolerating negative child affect, and the affect-regulatory deficits evidenced by maltreating caregivers, this issue is subject to significant disruption. Preventive interventions designed to educate caregivers and/or target the caregiver-infant dyad again emerge as potentially useful strategies for this issue of development.

Because maltreated infants display negative affects such as fear, sadness, and anger at an earlier age than do nonmaltreated infants (Izard et al., 1995; Sroufe, 1996), it is conceivable that the experience of maltreatment facilitates the premature development of the negative affect pathways in the brain (Cicchetti, in press). Assessments of brain structure, functioning, and organization of maltreating parents and maltreated infants prior to and after the completion of intervention will provide important insights into the contributions of genetics and experience on neurobiological development, as well as an entree into the malleability of these maladaptive patterns of neural wiring. For example, recording the resting EEGs of maltreated infants and their parents to ascertain whether hemispheric asymmetries of negative affect exist and to discern whether they are modifiable through intervention, as well as the utilization of a variety of brain-imaging techniques to investigate whether brain structures and functions that were, in whole or part, altered by the experience of maltreatment are amenable or refractory to intervention, all could be useful techniques. The demonstration that maltreatment experiences can modify neurobiological ontogenesis and subsequent evidence that these maladaptive changes can be improved through intervention will be an important illustration of the transactional relation that exists between brain development and social experience (cf., Cicchetti & Tucker, 1994; Eisenberg, 1995).

Likewise, investigations that address whether intervention can modify the altered neuroendocrine reactivity of maltreated children should be conducted. As Yehuda, Giller, Southwick, Lowy, and Mason (1991) have noted, the glucocorticoid response to aversive stimulation may help to normalize the increased activity of limbic midbrain structures in response to events that stimulate strong negative emotions. Long-term dampening of the HPA system response to stressors, thus, may play a role in maltreated children's maladaptive emotion regulatory capacities, reduced ability to engage in active avoidance in stressful circumstances, and increased likelihood of passive avoidancelike behaviors.

Conduct problems frequently emerge in maltreated children, in part because of early difficulties with affect regulation originating in the caregiving context; thus, intervention must be directed toward ameliorating these difficulties in later childhood. To prevent behavior problems and deficits in emotional regulation and social-cognition associated with externalizing disorders, Greenberg, Kusche, and Speltz (1991) propose that parents provide a warm, supportive presence, facilitate child recognition and mediation of affective states, and involve children in interactions that support planning and anticipation of future events.

An approach that incorporates these goals in the treatment of preschool conduct problems has been described by Speltz (1990), who modified a behavioral parent-training model to incorporate aspects of attachment theory. Although retaining components of operant parenting skills such as praise and limit-setting, consideration is given to the encouragement of negotiation and joint planning between parent and child, the discussion of parental affects and the facilitation of child identification of internal states, and a focus on parent and child attributions for behaviors.

In view of the problems noted in the affective-cognitive balance of maltreated children, intervention also needs to be directed toward this area. Cognitive Control Therapy (Santostefano, 1985) can be used to help work toward the integration of cognition, inner experience, and the external environment, thereby addressing possible peer difficulties associated with either an overly inner or outer directed style. The overarching goal of therapy is the facilitation of a reality-based view of the world, rather than reliance on preconceived and potentially invalid assessments of the environment.

Finally, in view of the affect regulatory problems noted in traumatized adolescents and adults, treatment also needs to be directed toward this issue with older populations. For example, van der Kolk and colleagues (1996) concluded that there are a spectrum of symptomatic responses to childhood and adult trauma, including PTSD, dissociation, somatization, and affect dysregulation. Moreover, van der Kolk et al. point out that persons who have been traumatized may suffer from combinations of the aforementioned adaptations to trauma over the course of development. Van der Kolk et al. advocate a multimodal treatment approach with traumatized adolescents and adults. Depending on the symptom cluster presented by the patient, these include (a) work on desensitizing the traumatic memory, with the goal of habituating the afflicted individual to the stimuli that precipitate the reexperiencing of traumatic events; (b) work on helping these individuals improve their emotion recognition and discrimination abilities, including their own internal states and the discrimination of past from present experiences; (c) work on enhancing these individuals' capacity to integrate social cues in the context of current realities; and (d) work on the cognitive integration and self-regulation of experience.

The Development of Attachment Relationships

Research Findings. Although maltreated children form attachments, the main issue here concerns the quality of their attachments and their internal representational models of attachment figures, the self, and the self in relation to others. Children form such representational models based on their relationship history with their primary caregiver (Bowlby, 1969/1982). Through these models, children's affects, cognitions, and expectations about future interactions are organized and carried forward into subsequent relationships (Sroufe & Fleeson, 1986).

Several studies have shown that the attachments maltreated children form with their caregivers are more likely to be insecure than those of nonmaltreated children (Crittenden, 1988; Egeland & Sroufe, 1981; Schneider-Rosen, Braunwald, Carlson, & Cicchetti, 1985). In a contribution to normal developmental theory and research made through observations of maltreated children, a number of investigators have observed patterns of attachment behavior that do not fit smoothly into the original Ainsworth et al. (1978) classification system (e.g., Egeland & Sroufe, 1981). Unlike infants with more typical patterns of attachment, maltreated infants often lack organized strategies for dealing with separations from and reunions with their caregiver.

Main and Solomon (1990) describe this pattern of attachment as "disorganized/disoriented" ("Type D"). In addition, these infants display other bizarre symptoms in the presence of their caregiver such as interrupted movements and expressions, dazing, freezing and stilling behaviors, and apprehension.

Within a revised attachment classification scheme that includes these atypical patterns of attachment, maltreated infants and toddlers demonstrate a preponderance of insecure and atypical attachments (Carlson et al., 1989; Crittenden, 1988; Lyons-Ruth, Connell, Zoll, & Stahl, 1987). The findings on the prevalence and stability of insecure and atypical attachments in maltreated children point to the extreme risk these children face in achieving adaptive outcomes in other domains of interpersonal relationships. Internal representational models of these insecure and often atypical attachments, with their complementary models of self and other, may generalize to new relationships, leading to negative expectations of how others will behave and how successful the self will be in relation to others. It is believed that the insecurity and disorganization found in many maltreated children's attachments are the result of the inconsistent care and the fear that are common elements of being maltreated (Carlson et al., 1989). If maltreated children's representational models reflect insecurity and fear, and if these models are generalized to new relationships with negative expectations that lead to the same type of approach/avoidance conflicts that are seen in their attachment relationships, then the result may be maladaptive patterns of relating with their new partners. Furthermore, in some samples, as high as 82% of maltreated infants exhibit disorganized attachments (Carlson et al., 1989; Crittenden, 1988; Lyons-Ruth et al., 1991). This is in comparison with only 20% of demographically matched nonmaltreated infants having disorganized attachments. Moreover, maltreated children demonstrate substantial stability of insecure attachment, whereas securely attached maltreated children generally become insecurely attached (Cicchetti & Barnett, 1991a; Schneider-Rosen et al., 1985). In contrast, for nonmaltreated children, secure attachments are highly stable, whereas insecure attachments are more likely to change (Lamb, Thompson, Gardner, & Charnov, 1985).

As children grow older, the likelihood that they will have an atypical pattern of attachment seems to decrease. In an investigation of the attachments of maltreated preschool children of different ages (Cicchetti & Barnett, 1991a), 30-month-old children who had been maltreated were significantly more likely to have atypical patterns of attachment than were nonmaltreated children. However, although approximately one third of the 36- and 48-month-old maltreated children were classified as having an atypical attachment classification, this was not significantly greater than the proportion of nonmaltreated children who had atypical attachment patterns. Along these lines, Lynch and Cicchetti (1991) found that maltreated school children between the ages of 7 and 13 were more likely to have nonoptimal (i.e., insecure) patterns of relatedness with their mothers and that approximately 30% of the maltreated children described "confused" patterns of relatedness with their mothers, an atypical nonoptimal pattern in which children report not feeling close to their mothers despite feeling warm and secure with them. This finding suggests that distortions in maltreated children's relationships with and mental representations of their caregivers may persist at least through the preadolescent years, although at lower rates than found in infancy.

The life-span significance of maltreatment experiences on attachment organization also has been demonstrated. Research has found that mothers who were maltreated during childhood and who possessed dismissing or preoccupied-engaged adult attachment organizations were likely to provide maladaptive parenting to their own children (Main & Goldwyn, 1984), whereas the perpetuation of maltreatment was unlikely in women who had processed their negative childhood histories (Egeland, Jacobvitz, & Sroufe, 1988; Hunter & Kihlstrom, 1979). Moreover, in a retrospective study, Alexander (1992, 1993) found that only 14% of women who reported childhood histories of sexual abuse described themselves as securely attached, whereas 13%, 16%, and 57% rated themselves as preoccupied-engaged, dismissing, and fearful/disorganized, respectively. The absence of secure attachment also was predictive of the avoidance of memories of abuse, as well as hypothesized to be associated with several personality disorders (Alexander, 1992, 1993).

Dismissing attachment organizations were thought to predispose an adult survivor of sexual abuse toward a denial-based coping strategy, avoidance of memories of the sexual abuse, and debilitation in expressing emotion and forming intimate relationships with others. Preoccupied-engaged attachment organizations render an adult survivor of sexual abuse to being overly concerned about love relationships and as having a tendency to overidealize romantic partners and adopt negative representations of the self. Alexander (1992) believed that the adult with a preoccupied-engaged attachment organization also was more likely to develop symptoms of anxiety and depression, and to be at increased risk for borderline personality disorder. Lastly, fearful/disorganized adult attachment organizations were thought to eventuate in a confused or dissociative style of coping and a high risk for the development of

PTSD symptoms, borderline personality disorder, and multiple personality disorder. In addition to the linkages of insecure attachment organizations to relationship difficulties and self-pathologies in women with histories of sexual abuse, the insecure attachment organizations may contribute to intergenerational vulnerabilities for subsequent victimization.

These results demonstrate that maltreatment and its relationship to attachment extend beyond infancy and early childhood. The representational models that emerge from the maltreating caregiving matrix influence the individual's conceptualization of self, as well as responses to potential relationship partners. Because maltreated children have been found to evidence a preponderance of insecure attachment relationships, they are at risk for developing emotional disorders in childhood and adulthood, as well as for continuing the maladaptive relationship patterns of their childhoods. This potentially bleak scenario underscores the critical need for providing theoretically grounded interventions geared toward the prevention of maltreatment, as well as the treatment of those individuals who have been damaged by their traumatic childhood experiences.

Practice Implications. A considerable amount of research has documented the presence of attachment dysfunctions in maltreated children. Because even infants and young children may develop attachment disorders (Chisholm, Carter, Ames, & Morison, 1995; Provence & Lipton, 1962; Richters & Volkmar, 1994; Zeanah, 1996) and because attachment-related deficits may contribute to a range of psychopathology and be experienced across the life course, this issue warrants serious intervention. Moreover, due to the hierarchical nature of development, the effects of maladaptation on earlier issues may be manifested more overtly in attachment difficulties.

Many therapeutic interventions have been developed to address attachment-related dysfunctions. Because of the salience of the attachment relationship during the 12- to 18-month age period, it is not surprising that the bulk of attachment-driven approaches to intervention have targeted the early mother-child relationship. Perhaps one of the most widely used interventions for attachment problems during infancy had its origins in the work of Selma Fraiberg (Fraiberg, Adelson, & Shapiro, 1975). Subsequently, infant-parent psychotherapy has focused on the possible contributions of both parent and child to attachment dysfunction (Lieberman & Pawl, 1988). Through an elaboration of the role that parental attachment representations exert on the caregiving context, infant-parent psychotherapy seeks to ameliorate disorders of attachment. This technique also can be modified for use with toddlers (Lieberman, 1993). In an evaluation of the effectiveness of infant-parent therapy with low-SES immigrant mothers, Lieberman, Weston, and Pawl (1991) found that a 12-month program of intervention was effective in enhancing maternal empathy and mother-child interaction, increasing the goal-corrected partnership between mother and child, and decreasing child avoidance, resistance, and anger.

Another intervention directed toward parent-child attachment targeted a population similar to that of the Lieberman et al. (1991) sample. Mothers at risk for parenting difficulties due to the presence of a number of stressors, including poverty, limited education, social isolation, and stressful life circumstances, received a variety of services, including home visitation and parenting informational and support groups. The goal of the intervention was the modification of the insecure attachment relationship between mother and infant. Services were initiated during the mother's second trimester of pregnancy and continued through the child's first birthday (Egeland & Erickson, 1990; Erickson, Korfmacher, & Egeland, 1992).

Although governed by the belief that the alteration of both parent and child working models of relationships was necessary to improve the maladaptive attachment, the multiservice nature of the program made it difficult to attribute therapeutic change to attachment-specific factors. However, the influence of attachment theory can be seen throughout the structure of the intervention, beginning with the efforts to address maternal representations of the unborn child, a factor shown to be a powerful predictor of the quality of postbirth attachment relationships (Fonagy, Steele, & Steele, 1991). Erickson and her colleagues also describe a number of important attachment-driven therapeutic principles, including providing consistency to the mother, the identification and affirmation of strengths in mother and baby, maternal empowerment, communication directed at the alteration of internal working models, and elucidation of interactional patterns between the mother and the intervenor with the goal of linking these styles with the maternal relationship history (Erickson et al., 1992). Preliminary data on the effectiveness of this program suggest that the intervention improved maternal understanding of infant needs, resulting in more appropriate home environments and in a decrease in maternal emotional problems (Erickson et al., 1992). Although no differences in security of attachment were found at the conclusion of the intervention, follow-up assessments revealed a trend for intervention dyads to move toward a more secure relationship during the infant's second year.

Another intervention designed to promote positive parent-child relationships in impoverished families with caregiving difficulties was initiated when infants were less than 9 months old (Lyons-Ruth, 1992). Not surprisingly and in accord with attachment theory predictions, Lyons-Ruth (1992) found that mothers who had experienced more stable childhood environments provided more attentive, involved care to their infants than did mothers from less cohesive homes. Hostile-intrusive maternal behavior also was related to a history characterized by family conflict, severe punishment, lack of warmth, maternal psychopathology, and poor peer relationships. Intervention consisted of weekly home visitation designed to promote adequate parenting and to address the family's social service needs. Although varied interventions were provided, Lyons-Ruth conceptualizes and attributes the success of the intervention to its attachment focus. Improvements in mother-child interaction were noted when infants reached 12 months of age, with insecure-disorganized attachment being twice as high in infants of depressed mothers who did not receive intervention.

In addition to attachment-based interventions for the infancy and toddler periods, the provision of intervention during the preschool and later childhood years is important. Although such approaches have not been evaluated, individual psychotherapy that is informed by attachment theory is an important model of intervention. By providing the child with a therapeutic relationship that challenges existing negative representational models of relationships, it may be possible to prevent the coalescence of a representational model through which all potential relationship partners will be viewed negatively. The concomitant provision of intervention to caregivers with the goal of "opening" their representational models of relationships also is indicated.

Experiences of maltreatment and resultant attachment dysfunction have been implicated in a number of mental disorders. Consequently, we consider the development of a secure attachment to be a central issue requiring concerted intervention across the life course. The developmental hierarchy and the associated consolidation of earlier issues into subsequent ones also highlight the role of attachment in successfully resolving the subsequent salient developmental issues of self, peer relationships, and school adaptation.

The Development of the Self-System

Research Findings. During the second half of the second year of life, children experience an increased sense of themselves as autonomous. Before this age, processes of emotion regulation are primarily sensorimotor in origin. As a sense of self emerges, however, an increase in representational capacities arises (Sroufe, 1990; Stern, 1985). Consequently, children become able to use symbolic capacities such as play and language to convey their needs and feelings. This developmental transition also marks a shift in the burden of self-regulation from the caregiver to the child. However, caregiver availability and responsivity continue to remain necessary to the facilitation of this developmental task. During this period, children are able to rely on representations of caregivers to alleviate their distress during separations (Cicchetti, Ganiban, & Barnett, 1991). Thus, the representational models of self and others that had their origins in the early caregiving relationship exert a significant impact on the continued development of the self-system.

An examination of visual self-recognition, an early index of self-awareness in maltreated toddlers, revealed no differences between maltreated and nonmaltreated youngsters (Schneider-Rosen & Cicchetti, 1984, 1991). However, differences were detected with regard to affective responsivity. Maltreated toddlers were more likely than comparison children to display either neutral or negative affect on seeing their rouge-marked images in a mirror, possibly indicating an early precursor to a generalized low sense of self-worth. In contrast, nonmaltreated toddlers were more likely to evince positive affective reactions.

In another investigation of the self-system, Beeghly and Cicchetti (1994) examined the internal-state language of maltreated and nonmaltreated toddlers during interactions with their mothers in a number of different contexts. The ability to talk about the feelings, emotions, and other internal states of self and other is an age-appropriate development of late toddlerhood hypothesized to reflect toddlers' emergent self-other understanding and to be fundamental to the regulation of social interaction. The emergence of this ability may be viewed as part of a larger developmental transformation during toddlerhood characterized not only by general lexical advances such as the ability to talk in sentences, but also by developments that reflect toddlers' emerging self-other differentiation, including an increase in self-descriptive utterances, shifting personal pronouns, a growing empathic concern for others, the emergence of the ability to tease and deceive, the "social" emotions such as guilt and shame, and active agency during symbolic play (Beeghly & Cicchetti, 1994; Bretherton & Beeghly, 1982). Beeghly and Cicchetti (1994) found that whereas children did not differ on receptive vocabulary, significant group differences on productive and internal-state language variables emerged. Maltreated toddlers used proportionately fewer internal-state words, showed less differentiation in their attributional focus, and were more context-bound in their use of internal-state language than their nonmaltreated peers.

The tendency for maltreated toddlers to use fewer internal-state words may stem from parental disapproval of the expression of affect or of a certain class of affects. We suggest that the use of negative emotion terms, references to the self, and the self's desires has provoked responses in the mother that generate anxiety in the child that necessitate regulation and control. Thus, maltreated children, in an attempt to control their anxiety, may modify their language (and perhaps even their thinking) to prevent the anxiety engendered by certain aspects of language and discourse in general.

Alessandri and Lewis (1996) examined the self-conscious emotion expressions of shame and pride in maltreated children. These self-conscious emotions evolve, in part, from the child's burgeoning cognitive abilities between the second and third year of life. Included among the self-conscious emotions are embarrassment, pride, shame, and guilt. In particular, the ability to mentally represent standards for comparison, objective self-awareness and self-evaluation, and the capacity to reflect on and attribute outcomes to personal competence, appear to be the prerequisite cognitive capabilities for the development of shame and pride (Kagan, 1981; Lewis, 1992).

Alessandri and Lewis (1996) found that maltreated girls displayed more shame and less pride than nonmaltreated girls. On the other hand, maltreated boys exhibited less shame and pride than nonmaltreated boys. Notably, the finding that maltreated girls manifested less pride and more shame in the achievementlike situations used to evoke these self-conscious emotions suggests that these girls are at high risk for developing dysfunctions or disorders of the self and for adapting poorly to school (cf., Cicchetti, 1989). In contrast, maltreated boys displayed a reduction of the self-conscious emotions of shame and pride, developed attributional strategies that attributed their difficulties to characteristics of others, and employed acting-out behaviors to cope with their interpersonal difficulties.

Findings revealing the presence of negative representations of the self in maltreated children also have been mounting. Support for this view derives primarily from research on maltreated children that has revealed lower self-esteem (Browne & Finkelhor, 1986; Egeland, Sroufe, & Erickson, 1983; Kaufman & Cicchetti, 1989), and poorer social functioning (Rogosch & Cicchetti, 1994) when compared with nonmaltreated children. Evidence of exaggerated and overinflated as well as impaired perceptions of competence (Vondra, Barnett, & Cicchetti, 1989, 1990) and denial of authentic needs and feelings have contributed to the belief that maltreated children are prone to develop a "false self." According to this conceptualization, maltreated children often act compulsively compliant with their caregivers and display insincere positive affect (Crittenden & DiLalla, 1988).

Guided by Fischer's (1980) skills theory of development, Calverley, Fischer, and Ayoub (1994) investigated the perceptions and representations that sexually abused adolescents had of themselves and their worlds. Calverley and her colleagues found that the sexually abused adolescents attributed significantly more negative self-perceptions to their core selves, and displayed greater "polarized affective splitting" (e.g., described the self as "happy," "sad," "lonely," and "good" in the absence of any obvious conflict) than did nonsexually abused adolescent females. Despite their differences in self-representation, the sexually abused adolescents revealed no delays in their level of self-development, and, in fact, operated on the same level or better than their nonsexually abused counterparts. Consistent with the viewpoint of developmental psychopathologists, the experience of trauma did not necessarily result in developmental delay. Instead, it eventuated in an alternative and unique path of adaptation to their extreme experiences and not to a developmental fixation or regression to an earlier developmental level (Cicchetti & Schneider-Rosen, 1986). In the words of Calverley and colleagues (1994), rather than "not growing up, sexually abused girls grow up differently" (p. 209). Consequently, traumatic experiences such as sexual abuse may be transformed throughout the course of ontogenesis, leading to the development of progressively more complex forms of affective splitting. Furthermore, it is conceivable that through this alternative ontogenetic pathway arising from sexual abuse, these adolescent females may subsequently develop psychopathology (e.g., dissociative disorders—Putnam, 1995).

Practice Implications. The "self-system" deficits evident in maltreated children highlight the importance of considering this issue in the development and provision of prevention and intervention services. Moreover, in view of the developmental progression in self-understanding previously discussed, the child's ability to benefit from intervention directed toward the self-system must be assessed. For younger children, intervention is likely to be most effective if the child is encouraged to be actively involved in experiences that are focused on the development of mastery. Determining an area of interest for a child (e.g., sports, music) and encouraging the child to foster skill development, while simultaneously praising effort and goal achievement is a technique that could be used by therapists, teachers, or parents. Because a child who has experienced maltreatment is likely to have internalized a negative self-view and to be wary of taking any risks for fear of failure, considerable encouragement is necessary for a positive impact on the child's passivity and helplessness. School-age children also are excellent candidates for the provision of cognitive behavioral methods of intervention (cf., Beck, 1979). The provision of early intervention in such situations may be effective in preventing the emergence and subsequent consolidation of child maladaptive self-representations.

Cognitive therapeutic approaches geared toward the articulation and remediation of destructive belief systems involving self-blame also are likely to be helpful (Alessandri & Lewis, 1996). Because childhood beliefs may become entrenched due to modeling and reinforcement occurring at an impressionable age, negative beliefs need to be challenged repeatedly for a child to feel empowered (Alessandri & Lewis, 1996).

As children mature, both increased opportunities and greater difficulties can be identified in working with negative self-system processes. Children's growing cognitive sophistication results in increased capacities to benefit from interventions that seek to understand the more distal roots of negative self-representation. With maturation, however, the magnitude and duration of self-system deficits also are likely to become more firmly entrenched. Thus, because preventive approaches may be less effective, more sustained psychotherapeutic strategies are indicated. Although our discussion of interventions for negative self-system development has focused on efforts geared toward the individual, the increasing importance of peer relations in later childhood and the potential for adaptive peer interactions to impact positively on self-related issues also emerges as an area for remediation. Peer-mediated therapies are addressed following the discussion of research on peer relationships.

Peer Relationships

Research Findings. In their review of this literature, Mueller and Silverman (1989) identified two main themes that summarize the knowledge base on peer relations in maltreated children. One set of findings indicates that maltreated children, especially physically abused children, tend to show heightened levels of physical and verbal aggression in their interactions with peers (George & Main, 1979). The exploiter-exploited relationships that maltreated children engage in with their parents often take other forms, such as when a physically abused child becomes hostile toward a peer partner (Troy & Sroufe, 1987). It is more alarming that some maltreated children have been observed to respond with anger and aggression both to friendly overtures from their peers (Howes & Eldredge, 1985) and to signs of distress in other children. In some instances, comforting and attacking behaviors were intermingled (Klimes-Dougan & Kistner, 1990; Main & George, 1985).

The second set of findings that Mueller and Silverman (1989) described is that there is a high degree of withdrawal from and avoidance of peer interactions in maltreated children, compared with nonmaltreated children (both toddlers and school-age children). Hoffman-Plotkin and Twentyman (1984) found that neglected children tended to be more generally withdrawn from social interaction with peers. This social withdrawal may be an active strategy of avoidance on the part of maltreated children and not merely a passive orientation toward peer interaction. In combination with the heightened aggressiveness found in some maltreated children, their social withdrawal may lead to increasing isolation and peer rejection (Rogosch & Cicchetti, 1994; Salzinger, Feldman, Hammer, & Rosario, 1993).

Rogosch and Cicchetti (1994) identified a subgroup of maltreated and nonmaltreated children who are perceived by their peers as demonstrating a combination of aggressive and withdrawn behavior. In particular, maltreated children who are viewed by their peers as relatively high on both aggression and withdrawal evidence substantially lower social effectiveness than is the case for nonmaltreated comparison youngsters. An attachment theory perspective may be useful to account for the effects of maltreatment among the children who exhibit the mixed aggressive and withdrawn presentation. Given the high prevalence of blending of aggression and withdrawal in maltreated infants and toddlers and the patterns of disorganization and disorientation in those attachments (Carlson et al., 1989), it is interesting to speculate on the mixing of aggression and withdrawal found among maltreated children. The presence of intense frightening experiences in the maltreating parent-child relationship may contribute to these intermingled patterns in that fearful and frightening behavior by caregivers has been associated with disorganized attachment behaviors (Main & Hesse, 1990). This co-occurrence of aggression and withdrawal may reflect representations carried forward from the attachment relationship into new social encounters, resulting in disturbances in social adaptation (cf., McCrone, Egeland, Kalkoske, & Carlson, 1994). The aggressive-withdrawn strategy may be used protectively to diminish the anticipated negative aspects of interpersonal relations; aggression may be employed to terminate perceived interpersonal threats, whereas isolation may be used to avoid threats.

By revealing indications of a predisposition to both "fight" and "flight" responses in maltreated children's interactions with their peers, these findings lend support to the claim that maltreated children internalize both sides of their relationship with their caregiver (Troy & Sroufe, 1987). As a result, maltreated children's representational models may include elements of being both a victim and a victimizer. Overall, heightened aggressiveness, avoidance of social interaction, and aberrant responses to friendly overtures and signs of distress leave maltreated children unprepared to develop effective relationships with their peers. On the contrary, contact with peers seems to elicit stressful reactions from maltreated children and further decreases the likelihood of successful interaction.

Howes and Espinosa (1985) found that maltreated children seem to have the most difficulty with unfamiliar peers. When placed in a new peer group, maltreated children demonstrated less social competence than nonmaltreated children. They exhibited fewer positive emotions, directed less behavior toward peers, initiated fewer interactions, and engaged in less complex play. This lack of social competence demonstrated with novel peers obviously would make it difficult for maltreated children to establish new peer relationships and friendships. However, Haskett and Kistner (1991) found that peer difficulties in a group of physically abused 3- to 6-year-old children continued to be evidenced even when they had been in a day-care peer group for at least 1 year. In this study, abused children initiated fewer positive interactions with peers and exhibited a higher proportion of negative behavior than nonabused comparison children. Peers also viewed maltreated children as less well liked and they were less likely to reciprocate the initiations of abused children.

In an investigation of the peer relations of maltreated and nonmaltreated children in the school setting, Salzinger et al. (1993) found that peers viewed maltreated children as evidencing more antisocial behaviors (i.e., aggressiveness, meanness, and disruptiveness), and fewer prosocial behaviors such as leadership and sharing. These peer-perceived differences were related to higher proportions of rejected sociometric status and lower proportions of popular status for the maltreated compared with the nonmaltreated children (cf., Rogosch & Cicchetti, 1994). Kaufman and Cicchetti (1989) similarly found evidence of peer difficulties among maltreated school-age children in a summer camp setting. Maltreated children were rated as lower in self-esteem and prosocial behavior and higher in withdrawal than nonmaltreated children. Peers rated children with multiple forms of maltreatment as higher in disruptive behavior. Moreover, Rogosch and Cicchetti (1994) obtained teacher and peer assessments of the social functioning of maltreated and comparison children. Maltreated children were rated as lower in social competence and higher in externalizing problems by both teachers and peers.

Furthermore, concurrent difficulties in emotion regulation among maltreated children have been shown to mediate the relations between maltreatment and lower levels of social competence exhibited when they are engaged in peer interactions (Shields et al., 1994). Finally, in a prospective longitudinal investigation, Rogosch and his colleagues (1995) found that negative affect understanding mediated both the relation of maltreatment on later dysregulated behavior in the peer setting and the effect of physical abuse on later rejection by peers.

In a related vein, Parker and Herrera (1996) conducted lengthy observations of preadolescent and young adolescent physically abused children with their closest friends and compared these relationships to friendships that did not contain abused members. In keeping with the predictions of attachment theory, the children who were physically abused by their parents experienced problems developing and maintaining close personal relationships. Physically abused children and their friends displayed less intimacy in their interactions than nonabused children and their friends. Friendships that consisted of physically abused children were more conflictual than friendships containing no abused members. Interestingly, these difficulties were most apparent during interactions that taxed the emotion regulation skills of the abused children, such as while playing competitive games. Finally, important gender differences were detected. Abused boys and their friends displayed more negative affect during game playing than dyads of nonabused companions. In contrast, abused girls and their friends exhibited less positive affect than dyads of nonabused companions.

Practice Implications. When developing interventions for children who are experiencing peer problems, the diversity of these difficulties must be considered. Moreover, because the peer arena can provide children with a natural context within which to develop positive relationships, the child has the opportunity to acquire relationship partners that may be discrepant with his or her previously formed negative representational models of relationships. Because research has shown maltreated children to be at risk for peer difficulties, the peer arena is a potentially productive forum within which to intervene.

The use of peers in promoting improved interactions can be beneficial. Peer-mediated strategies were developed largely in response to dissatisfaction with earlier intervention techniques. Peer therapy involves using a more well-adjusted child to effect changes in a child with dysfunctional social skills (Fantuzzo & Holland, 1992). Because experiences with age-mates fulfill many important needs, the use of peers in cases where children experience difficulties with social interaction can be very helpful. Peer interactions can provide opportunities for learning to control aggression, improving perspective-taking abilities, and engaging in intimate relations, to name only a few areas (Hartup, 1983, 1996; Parker, Rubin, Price, & Herrera, 1995).

A potentially rich area for interventions in the area of social development of maltreated children pertains to improving the interactions of withdrawn children. Because socially withdrawn children are deficient in expressing their opinions, gaining cooperation, and attracting the attention of peers (Kohn & Rosman, 1972; Rubin & Lollis, 1988), interventions designed to improve skills in this area are indicated.

Peer-pair counseling (Selman, Schultz, & Yeates, 1991) is a technique that can be applied toward helping children to avoid a cycle of relational dysfunction. In this approach, children meet in pairs with an adult trainer. The overall goal of the intervention is to help children learn more mature strategies for interpersonal problem negotiation and to enable them to practice the new strategies in a supportive context. Because maltreated children frequently are rejected by their peers (Rogosch & Cicchetti, 1994; Salzinger et al., 1993) and tend to misread ambiguous peer behavior as having hostile intent (Dodge, Pettit, & Bates, 1990), therapeutically structured experience with a peer can help alter the course of maltreated children away from a cumulative experience of negative social interactions.

Peer pairing has been used with school-age children from low-income neighborhoods characterized by high rates of violence and substance abuse (Selman et al., 1992). Children who participate in this program are referred by teachers due to their aggressive behavior or social withdrawal, and pairing combines children with opposing styles. Although not specifically identified as maltreated, it is likely that some of the children who participated in the intervention came from violent homes. The effectiveness of this intervention for vulnerable youth is noteworthy, and it has potential for being applied to children who have experienced familial violence.

A similar approach to facilitating positive peer relations in withdrawn, maltreated preschool children has been developed by Fantuzzo (Fantuzzo & Holland, 1992). In an evaluation of the resilient peer treatment (RPT), the effects of using a higher functioning peer or a familiar adult as the agent of treatment were assessed. Results indicated that children receiving peer-mediated intervention evidenced increases in positive social behaviors (Fantuzzo et al., 1988). Interestingly, children in the adult mediated treatment group exhibited a decrease in positive social behavior.

These studies support the efficacy of using peers to help improve the social functioning of less competent peers. This technique is especially applicable to classroom settings where consultation by a mental health professional can be provided to help teachers implement peer-guided social interaction paradigms. Because resources in schools for children with special needs are limited, utilization of a naturally occurring resource such as peers can be especially helpful in providing a cost-effective and convenient modality to many children.

In addition to peer-mediated therapeutic interventions for fostering more positive interaction in withdrawn children, research suggests the provision of interventions designed to help maltreated children more accurately read the cues and intent of peers, and to respond accordingly. Toward this end, therapists might consider the use of role plays to help maltreated children learn more adaptive styles of interaction. Group therapy with older children and adolescents also might provide a forum through which age-mates can challenge and help to modify the distorted processing that can adversely affect the peer relationships of maltreated children.

Finally, the potential for improved peer interactions to exert a positive impact on the self-organization of children who have been maltreated cannot be underestimated. By becoming active participants in relationships that challenge negative views of self in relation to others, maltreated children may begin to value themselves and learn that the representational models formed in the early caregiving relationship are open to modification.

Adaptation to School

Research Findings. As with the salient developmental issues discussed previously, the child's experience in the home provides an important foundation on which the transition to the school setting is built. The children most likely to fail in school are those whose families are less able to prepare them for a rewarding educational experience (Cicchetti, Toth, & Hennessy, 1993). It is not surprising that children who have been maltreated are at extremely high risk for school failure. Thus, a potentially positive experience that could serve to reverse an earlier trajectory of maladaptation more often confirms the maltreated child's negative history and maladaptive relationship patterns.

In their prospective study on the antecedents and consequences of child maltreatment, Erickson, Egeland, and Pianta (1989) asked teachers to rate social adaptation and response to demands accompanying school entry in a group of maltreated children. Among the physically abused children studied, Erickson and her colleagues found that aggressive, noncompliant, acting-out behavior was very common. In addition, teachers reported that the maltreated children functioned more poorly on cognitive tasks and in the classroom. Quite strikingly, the conduct of these physically abused children in the school setting was so problematic that approximately half of them were referred either for special intervention services or were retained by the end of their first year of school.

Erickson et al. (1989) also found that the neglected children in their sample displayed the most severe and variable problems in school. These children performed more poorly on cognitive assessments than the physically and sexually abused youngsters. In the classroom, neglected children were described as anxious, inattentive, unable to understand their school work, lacking initiative, and heavily reliant on the teacher for help, approval, and encouragement. In social situations, they manifested both aggressive and withdrawn behavior and were not well liked by their peers. These neglected children were uncooperative with adults (i.e., teachers) and were insensitive and unempathic with their peers. Moreover, they rarely expressed positive affect or a sense of humor. By the end of their first year in school, 65% of the neglected children already had been referred for special intervention or were retained. A possible interpretation for the extremely poor functioning of the neglected children is that they have experienced a chronic and pervasive history of deprivation across all domains of development—cognitive, socioemotional, and linguistic.

Sexually abused children also exhibited various problems adapting to the school environment. Their performance in school suffered because of their marked anxiety, inattentiveness, and inability to comprehend classroom expectations. These children also were not popular with their peers and were predominantly withdrawn or aggressive in social interactions. Most notably, Erickson and her colleagues (1989) highlighted the excessive dependency that sexually abused children displayed toward their teachers. Specifically, these youngsters' interactions with teachers were characterized by a strong need for approval and physical closeness in combination with a high incidence of seeking assistance in the classroom. The passive, dependent nature of these sexually abused children is congruent with the victim roles that they have experienced in their homes.

Difficulties in the school functioning of maltreated youngsters also were revealed in a large-scale, well-controlled investigation conducted by Eckenrode, Laird, and Doris (1993). These investigators compared the academic outcomes of 420 maltreated youngsters (neglected, physically abused, sexually abused) in nonspecialized kindergarten through Grade 12 placements with a demographically matched group of nonmaltreated children. Maltreated children scored significantly lower than the nonmaltreated children on math and reading standardized test scores. Among the maltreated group and consistent with the result of Erickson et al. (1989), Eckenrode and his colleagues found that the neglected children performed most poorly on this standardized index of academic ability. Interestingly, the test scores of sexually abused children were not significantly different from that of controls.

With respect to other measures of school functioning, maltreated children received poorer grades than nonmaltreated comparison children. Similar to the results obtained from the standard test score performance measure, neglected children received the lowest grades, whereas the grades of sexually abused children were not significantly different from those of the comparison group. As a group, maltreated children were 2.5 times more likely to repeat a grade than were comparison children. Within the maltreated sample, the neglected and physically abused youngsters were those who were most likely to be retained in a grade.

Maltreatment also was associated with difficulties in the arena of social adjustment in the school setting (Eckenrode et al., 1993). In particular, maltreated children were more likely to be referred to the principal, with physically abused youngsters receiving the highest number of referrals. In contrast, sexually abused children were no more likely to visit the principal than were the nonmaltreated youngsters. Furthermore, in junior and senior high school, maltreated children were significantly more likely than nonmaltreated children to be suspended from school. An examination of maltreatment subtype differences revealed that physically abused children received the most suspensions; neglected and sexually abused children were similar to nonmaltreated youngsters.

The combination of controlling environments and high performance demands found in maltreating homes has been linked to an extrinsic motivational orientation toward task performance (Lepper, 1981) and has been viewed as exerting a negative influence on classroom functioning (Harter, 1981). In fact, Aber and Allen (1987) found that maltreated children evidenced less independent mastery motivation and a more extrinsically oriented approach than comparison children. Thus, it appears that maltreated children have motivational orientations that may contribute to deficits in their school achievement.

In a related vein, school adaptation may be affected by secure readiness to learn. Aber and Allen (1987) proposed that important aspects of children being able to adjust to the school environment are the intrinsic desire to deal competently with one's environment and successful relations with unknown adults that are characterized by neither dependency nor wariness. Aber and Allen (1987) investigated whether maltreated preschool and early-school-age children subordinated their desire to learn to the need to establish secure relationships with novel adults. Consistent with findings obtained with other socially deprived youngsters, Aber and Allen found that maltreated children scored lower than nonmaltreated children on a factor measuring secure readiness to learn in the company of unknown adults. The secure readiness to learn factor was composed of high effectance motivation and low dependency.

Like the construct of attachment security, secure readiness to learn appears to reflect a balance between establishing secure relationships with adults and feeling free to explore the environment in ways that will promote cognitive competence. In both the earlier years and the school-age years, maltreatment interferes with the balance between the motivation to form secure relationships with adults and the motivation to explore the world in competence-promoting ways. In fact, many of the problems that maltreated children manifest in school appear to be traceable to a central problem—an overconcern with security issues due to an expectation of unresponsivity and rejection from adults. The preoccupation with security-promoting issues is a mediating factor that links a history of maltreatment with difficulties in school adaptation.

Toth and Cicchetti (1996b) also examined the role of relationship patterns in contributing to school adaptation in a sample of maltreated and demographically comparable nonmaltreated children. Toth and Cicchetti found that the security that a child experienced in relation to his or her mother, in interaction with maltreatment status, significantly affected adaptation in school. Nonmaltreated children who reported secure patterns of relatedness to their mothers exhibited less externalizing symptomatology, more ego-resilience, and fewer school record risk factors (e.g., attendance problems, poor achievement test performance, suspensions, failure in 50% of courses, grade retention) than did maltreated children who reported insecure patterns of relatedness. Additionally, nonmaltreated children with secure patterns of relatedness to their mothers exhibited more positive adaptation in school than did nonmaltreated children who reported insecure patterns of relatedness. For maltreated children, the positive effects of secure relatedness on school functioning were evident only in school record risk data, suggesting that a positive relationship with a maltreating parent may actually exert a negative impact on some aspects of school adaptation.

Commensurate with the difficulties experienced on earlier stage-salient issues, children who have experienced maltreatment exhibit significant difficulties with the negotiation of all aspects of the school environment. Because school personnel may be unaware of the precipitants of the difficulties manifested by maltreated children, these children may fail to receive the school services that could be most effective in setting them on a more adaptive course.

Practice Implications. In recent years, the educational system in our society has been subjected to scrutiny due to perceived failures and shortcomings of its existing structure (Tharinger et al., 1996). Currently, the schools are unable to meet the mental health service needs of our most vulnerable youth (Knitzer, 1993). Because of the significance of school functioning for cognitive as well as for socioemotional development, interventions designed to ameliorate difficulties in the school setting are indicated. Moreover, because child advocates are increasingly calling for a system that would integrate schooling, child care, and family education and support (Zigler, 1989), the school setting is in an excellent position to serve a critical support and preventive function within communities (Carlson, Tharinger, Bricklin, DeMers, & Paavola, 1996; Paavola et al., 1996).

School-based interventions are especially critical for children who have been maltreated, as individuals in the school setting may be the child's only out-of-home, and potentially positive, contact. Therefore, a number of intervention strategies might be implemented. Because maltreated children manifest behavioral difficulties in the classroom setting, teachers often feel they must focus on controlling child behavior. This, in turn, may result in the overcontrolling teaching styles that have been found to undermine an intrinsic motivational orientation in school (Deci, 1975). Rather than undoing the reliance on extrinsic reinforcement that has been linked with maltreatment, teachers may inadvertently foster the maintenance of an externally based orientation. In turn, such teaching styles may result in additional failure experiences for the maltreated child, which are likely to increase anxiety and further undermine self-esteem.

On the basis of theories of a hierarchical emergence of motives (Harter, 1978; Maslow, 1954), one would not expect maltreated children to be motivated to achieve and to do well in school. Considering the home environments of these children, one would predict that their physical needs, issues of safety, and need for love and acceptance are almost certainly more salient. Guided by this perspective, teachers and mental health professionals can gain insight into why maltreated children spend more energy on acting out and limit testing in the classroom than on mastery and achievement. By developing an understanding of the behavioral problems of maltreated children, therapists also can consult with classroom teachers around the development of management strategies that will not further undermine the attainment of an intrinsic orientation to school performance.

As discussed earlier, studies have revealed that the representational models of maltreated youngsters are likely to affect the establishment of new relationships adversely; therefore, another area on which to focus intervention efforts is the provision of positive adult relationship models for maltreated children. Because such impairments in relations with novel adults may affect children's ability to negotiate entry into nursery school, kindergarten, and elementary school (cf., Aber & Allen, 1987; Sroufe, 1983), interventions designed to facilitate interactions with and trust toward new adults are especially important. Involvement in individual therapy and the provision of positive adult "friends" (e.g., Big Brother/Sister programs) can be useful in this regard. By providing maltreated children with multiple positive adults with whom they can practice relationship experiences, these youngsters may learn to challenge historical representations of relationships and to more realistically respond to relationship partners as they negotiate the tasks of the school years.

Because research has shown the importance of the family in fostering school success for children (Toth & Cicchetti, 1996b), it behooves schools to reach out to families and to strive to integrate parents into their child's school experience. Moreover, because children who do not have positive relationships with caregivers are likely to be viewed as difficult in the classroom because of behavior problems, it is important that teachers continue to try to reach these youngsters.

Finally, the school setting may provide an excellent opportunity to educate parents regarding normal developmental progressions, as well as to the variability inherent in normal development. An educational approach can sensitize parents to likely points of child vulnerability during the developmental process and suggest ways of facilitating positive child adaptation. By understanding the process of development, parents may be better able to interact with their children in growth-promoting ways.

When considering the implementation of parenting programs, the bidirectional parent-child influence cannot be overemphasized. Parental responses are mediated by child characteristics, including gender, developmental level, and temperament. Therefore, when exploring interventions for specific conditions of childhood, it is necessary to consider the role of the child's strengths and weaknesses in conjunction with the parent's characteristics. In this regard, issues related to the risk and protective factor models discussed earlier are especially applicable. When child characteristics complement parental styles, positive interactions are more likely to occur (Belsky & Vondra, 1989). Sensitizing parents to principles of child rearing, as well as to how the developmental progression of their child can interact with their own developmental characteristics and needs, can facilitate the emergence of competence during childhood.

If the potential preventive value afforded by schools is to be realized fully, then researchers must become increasingly invested in devising and conducting investigations that have relevance for promoting mental health within the school setting. Just as importantly, concerted efforts must be made to disseminate these findings to school personnel and to those educating future teachers (Cicchetti, Rogosch, Lynch, & Holt, 1993). It is critical that schools become an integral component of a mental health system designed to meet the needs of vulnerable children and families more adequately. Because schools represent a community resource that does not suffer from the stigma so often associated with seeking mental health support, the involvement of schools in prevention and intervention could increase the number of children and adolescents who receive services.

The Emergence of Behavior Problems and Psychopathology

As opposed to the usual response to an average expectable environment, the ecological conditions associated with maltreatment set in motion a probabilistic path of ontogenesis for maltreated children characterized by an increased likelihood of failure on many of the stage-salient issues of development. These failures may be isolated to particular domains of functioning, or they may occur in combination with failures in other domains. As research has shown, maltreated children are likely to exhibit atypical physiological regulation, difficulties in affect differentiation and regulation, dysfunctional attachment relationships, anomalies in self-system processes, perturbations in representational development, problematic peer relationships, and trouble adapting successfully to school. These repeated developmental disruptions create a profile of relatively enduring vulnerability factors that places maltreated children at high risk for future maladaptation (Cicchetti & Lynch, 1993). Although not all maltreated children who have trouble resolving stage-salient issues will develop psychopathology, let alone the same form of pathology, later disturbances in functioning are likely to occur. In fact, maltreated children have evidenced elevated levels of disturbance across a wide range of areas.

Physical abuse has been linked with higher levels of child depressive symptomatology, dysthymia, and depression (Kaufman, 1991; Kazdin, Moser, Colbus, & Bell, 1985; Sternberg et al., 1993; Toth, Manly, & Cicchetti, 1992) and to conduct disorder and delinquency (Lewis, Mallouh, & Webb, 1989). In comparing 5- to 10-year-old maltreated and nonmaltreated children on child and parent semistructured interviews assessing clinical disturbances, Famularo, Kinscherff, and Fenton (1992) found significantly higher rates of diagnoses for attention-deficit/hyperactivity disorder, oppositional disorder, and PTSD among maltreated children. In addition, child interviews revealed increased rates of anxiety and personality disorder, whereas parent interviews identified higher rates of mood and conduct disorders in maltreated children. Although generalizations from existing data must be made cautiously because of the sample composition and the presence of co-occurring risk factors, in general, maltreatment, especially physical and sexual abuse, is related to a number of psychiatric complaints in childhood and adulthood, including panic disorders, anxiety disorders, depression, substance abuse, eating disorders, somatic complaints, dissociation and hysterical symptoms, sexual dysfunction, and borderline personality disorder (Browne & Finkelhor, 1986; Green, 1993; Malinowsky-Rummell & Hansen, 1993; Stein et al., 1996; Wolfe & Jaffe, 1991). Moreover, adults who have been maltreated as children manifest increased violence toward other adults, dating partners, and marital partners (Feldman & Downey, 1994; Malinowsky-Rummell & Hansen, 1993). The experience of maltreatment in childhood increases the risk of arrest as a juvenile by 53%, as an adult by 38%, and for a violent crime by 38% (Widom, 1989). Thus, across childhood and into adulthood, maltreatment poses increased risk for a wide range of disturbances in functioning and varied forms of psychopathology.

The inherent severity of some forms of abuse may create especially high risk for psychopathology. Sexual abuse, in particular, presents a major source of chronic trauma for many children. Viewing the effects of sexual abuse from a model of chronic trauma, a number of interrelated areas of development are likely to be impaired including the development of self-esteem and self-concepts; beliefs about personal power, control, and self-efficacy; the development of cognitive and social competencies; and emotional and behavioral self-regulation (Putnam & Trickett, 1993). Such widespread impairment is highlighted in investigations of the links between sexual abuse and both PTSD and the dissociative states related to multiple personality disorder.

Child sexual abuse has been shown to produce both immediate and long-term PTSD symptoms in some individuals. McLeer, Callaghen, Henry, and Wallen (1994) found that sexually abused children are far more likely than a well-matched group of nonmaltreated disadvantaged children to develop PTSD. In general, sexually abused children display a variety of PTSD symptoms, and at higher rates than children experiencing other forms of abuse (Kendall-Tackett et al., 1993). Specific aspects of the abuse such as penetration, duration and frequency of the abuse, the use of force, and the perpetrator's relationship to the child, all affect the degree of PTSD symptomatology.

Dissociation is a complex psychophysiological process manifested by a disruption in the normally integrative processes of memory, identity, and consciousness (American Psychiatric Association, 1994). Dissociation is conceptualized as occurring along a continuum ranging from the normal minor dissociations of everyday life, such as daydreaming, to the pathological manifestations seen in the profound disruptions to self and memory that may occur in multiple personality disorder (Fischer & Ayoub, 1994; Putnam & Trickett, 1993). In general, the experience of sexual abuse appears to render victims especially vulnerable to disturbances related to body and self. Higher rates of dissociation and affective splitting are seen in sexually abused children than in other comparison groups (Calverley et al., 1994). These disturbances in self-functioning may be especially apparent in problems with self-definition and integration, and in problems with self-regulatory processes (Cole & Putnam, 1992). Once again, characteristics of the abuse such as age of onset, as well as the presence of family psychopathology, appear to be related to the development of dissociative symptoms.

As knowledge on the sequelae of child maltreatment has burgeoned, investigators have become increasingly interested in examining the links between maltreatment and psychopathology. Although researchers have documented the negative effects of child maltreatment, including the emergence of both internalizing and externalizing disorders, less work has been conducted on the mechanisms that may be contributing to manifestations of disorder in children who have been maltreated.

The aforementioned findings of increased depressive symptomatology in maltreated children, taken in conjunction with studies documenting insecure attachment relationships among maltreated children, suggest that insecure attachment relationships and the resulting negative representational models of the self and of the self in relation to others may be a central mechanism contributing to the emergence of disturbances in children who have been maltreated (Toth et al., 1992). In fact, investigators are directing increased attention toward elucidating the effect of various types of maltreatment experience on the etiology of self-disorders.

Considerable effort has been directed toward examining the effects of sexual abuse on self-pathology. With respect to long-term effects of childhood sexual abuse, a number of adult psychiatric outcomes have been identified, including borderline personality disorder, eating disorders, multiple personality disorder, somatization disorder, and substance abuse (Putnam & Trickett, 1993). With respect to the acute impact of childhood sexual abuse, research is less clear, with as many as half of sexually abused children seeming to be asymptomatic on initial evaluation (Kendall-Tackett et al., 1993). Of children evidencing problems, common symptoms include sexualized behavior, posttraumatic stress disorder, fears, depression, low self-esteem, and behavior problems, to name only a few.

Toth and Cicchetti (1996a) applied an attachment theory based framework to examine the possible mechanisms contributing to increased depressive symptomatology in sexually abused, physically abused, and neglected children and in demographically comparable nonmaltreated children. These investigators found that maltreated children with confused patterns of relatedness with mother reported more depressive symptomatology than maltreated children with optimal/adequate relatedness to mother. Especially noteworthy was the discovery that sexually abused children who had confused patterns of relatedness with their mother reported extremely elevated levels of depressive symptomatology that were consistent with depression considered to be of clinical significance. These findings contrasted markedly with the nonclinical level of depressive symptomatology endorsed by sexually abused children who reported optimal/adequate relatedness to mother. The results of this investigation are a step toward elucidating the possible mechanisms that may account for the heterogeneity in functioning among samples of maltreated children. Because developmental psychopathologists must grapple with the heterogeneity of outcome *among* maltreated children, efforts to identify moderating and mediating factors that may be contributing to diverse outcome are critical.

Resilient Outcomes

The notion that an average expectable environment is necessary for species-typical development suggests that competent outcomes in maltreated children are highly improbable because of wide-ranging disturbances in the maltreatment ecology. However, although there is documented risk for maladaptation associated with maltreatment, the absence of an average expectable environment does not condemn maltreated children to negative developmental outcomes later in life. Despite the relatively low probability of adaptive outcomes for maltreated children (compared with nonmaltreated children), individuals' self-righting tendencies (Waddington, 1942, 1957), in combination with any additional intraorganismic as well as extraorganismic protective mechanisms and compensatory or protective factors, may result in some maltreated children achieving developmental competence.

In an investigation of resilience in school-age children, maltreated children as a group displayed lower overall competence across multiple areas of adaptation than did nonmaltreated children (Cicchetti et al., 1993). However, whereas more maltreated children than nonmaltreated children exhibited low levels of competence, an equal proportion of maltreated and nonmaltreated children demonstrated moderate to high levels of competence. Ego-resilience, ego-overcontrol, and positive self-esteem each accounted for significant amounts of variance in the adaptive functioning of maltreated children. In contrast, only ego-resilience and positive self-esteem contributed unique variance to accounting for adaptation in nonmaltreated children. This finding of a differential contribution of ego-overcontrol for the two groups in predicting adaptive or resilient functioning suggests that ego-overcontrol may serve a protective function for maltreated children. A reserved, controlled approach to the environment may help these children to be more attuned to adapting to the adverse conditions of their home environments, and may protect them from being targets of continued maltreatment incidents (Cicchetti et al., 1993; Crittenden & DiLalla, 1988; Werner & Smith, 1992). Pulling back from conflict in the family, detaching from high-intensity affect in the family, and being compliant with the wishes of one's caregiver all can help one to escape abuse and/or to achieve competent adaptation.

Contributions of the Study of Child Maltreatment to Normal Development: Illustration from the Study of the Relation between Caregiving Casualty and Neurobiological Development

Adverse life circumstances, exemplified by the experience of child maltreatment, are thought to affect both physiological and psychological processes. Because maltreated children experience the extremes of caregiving casualty, they provide one of the clearest opportunities for scientists to discover the myriad ways in which psychological stressors and adverse experiences can affect biological systems. Comparisons between maltreated and nonmaltreated children can elucidate the understanding of the caregiving processes that contribute to the development of regulated neurobiological systems. As Torsten Wiesel (1994) articulated: "Genes controlling embryonic development shape the structure of the infant brain; the infant's experience in the world then fine-tunes the pattern of neural connections underlying the brain's function. Such fine-tuning . . . must surely continue through adulthood" (p. 1647).

Early stresses, either physiological or emotional, may condition or sensitize young neural networks to produce cascading effects through later development, possibly constraining the child's flexibility to adapt to new challenging situations with new strategies rather than with old conceptual and behavioral prototypes. There has been remarkable evidence that early psychological trauma may result not only in emotional sensitization (Cummings et al., 1994; Hennessy et al., 1994; van der Kolk, 1987), but also in pathological sensitization of neurophysiological reactivity (Cicchetti & Tucker, 1994; Perry et al., 1995). Pollak, Cicchetti, Klorman, and Brumaghim (1997) elicited event-related potentials (ERPs) from maltreated and nonmaltreated school-age children. Children were presented with photographs depicting posed facial expressions of anger, happiness, and neutrality. In each of two conditions, children were instructed to attend and respond to the angry or the happy face by pressing a button held in their preferred hand. Pollak et al., (1997) discovered that nonmaltreated children evinced comparable ERPs in both conditions. In contrast, maltreated children displayed lower ERP amplitudes to happy, as compared with angry, stimuli. These findings are indicative of increased neurophysiological activity in maltreated children to angry affect and suggest increased psychological salience of negative affect, and possibly anger, for children with histories of maltreatment. Moreover, these results can be interpreted as suggesting that anger activated more affective representations for maltreated children than did happiness. Indeed, such patterns of activation or arousal would be adaptive for coping with environments marked by stress and threat. However, diminished responsiveness to positive affect combined with biases toward negative affect would certainly create difficulties for the children when interacting with others in nonmaltreating contexts (cf., Dodge et al., 1990; Rieder & Cicchetti, 1989; Rogosch et al., 1995).

Relatedly, Shearer, Peters, Quaytman, and Ogden (1990) found that the medical disorders of adult females with a history of sexual trauma included a high percentage of complex seizure disorder. These seizures were not present in a sample of women who had only been physically abused, suggesting that the EEG abnormalities may not have been attributable to the neurological consequences of head injury. Shearer and colleagues (1990) hypothesized that the repetitive childhood traumas experienced by these sexually abused women might have kindled limbic system alterations that eventually manifested in later life as a seizure disorder in combination with an enduring PTSD.

Particularly in a temperamentally sensitive brain (Bates & Wachs, 1994), psychological insults such as child maltreatment may create emotional sensitizations that ripple through the developmental process with effects that are neuropsychological more than neurophysiological, but that nonetheless compound themselves into relatively enduring forms of maladaptation or psychopathology. The processes through which this occurs may be complex enough that, as the dynamics of the brain's maturation unfold, it may be impossible to predict the eventual outcome that is set in place by each psychological insult. In these instances, the best predictions ultimately may be made on the basis of the more proximal mechanisms, the homeostatic, feedback-regulated mechanisms of self-organization, through which the child spontaneously strives for consistency and order in a chaotic self-and-world matrix. The self in this context is not just an abstract psychological entity. It may represent the configuration of adaptive homeostatic mechanisms that strive to achieve organizational coherence within the massively distributed, dynamically differentiating neural networks of the human cortex.

We have only begun to examine the self-organizing capacities of the brain, and many domains remain to be discovered as we become increasingly integrative in our theories and research programs on the ways in which biological and psychological systems transact, differentiate, integrate, and reorganize, thereby exerting their reciprocal influences on normal and pathological ontogenesis. The integration of cognitive neuroscience and developmental psychology within a developmental psychopathology perspective, despite being a formidable task, has the potential to add more precision to the classic organismic theories, as well as to address old questions in new ways. Investigations of other high-risk groups of children who experience varying degrees of negative or inconsistent caregiving not only will offer insight into the specificity of these neurological system dysregulations in response to maltreatment and its associated stressors, but also will contribute increasing precision to our knowledge of which aspects of caregiving experiences are critical for normal neurobiological and psychological development.

DEPRESSIVE DISORDERS IN CHILDHOOD AND ADOLESCENCE

Although the mood disorders of children and adolescents have been investigated for a shorter period than their adult counterparts, in recent decades there has been a proliferation of research activity in the area of childhood and adolescent depression. In contrast to earlier beliefs that questioned whether depressive illness could occur prior to puberty (e.g., Lefkowitz & Burton, 1978; Rie, 1966), contemporary research emphases have shifted from a prior focus on debating which criteria should be used to diagnose childhood mood disorders, to more sophisticated examinations of the epidemiology, causes, course, sequelae, and treatment responses of mood-disordered children, as well as of children who have one or more relatives with a mood disorder (Cicchetti & Schneider-Rosen, 1984, 1986; Cicchetti & Toth, 1992a; Downey & Coyne, 1990; Kovacs, 1989; Puig-Antich, 1986).

Current diagnostic classification systems (e.g., APA, 1994) define mood disorders as including all disorders that have a disturbance in mood as the predominant feature. Mood disorders are divided into the Depressive Disorders and the Bipolar Disorders (i.e., Manic-Depressive Illness; cf., Goodwin & Jamison, 1990). Depressive Disorders are characterized by at least 2 weeks of depressed mood or loss of interest in usual activities, accompanied by at least four additional symptoms, such as weight loss, insomnia or hypersomnia, psychomotor agitation or retardation, fatigue, feelings of worthlessness, diminished ability to concentrate, and recurrent thoughts of death. Dysthymic Disorders, a type of depression, also are characterized by depressed mood; however, the depression must be generally present for at least 2 years. Bipolar Disorders are characterized by disturbances in mood involving both depressive and manic episodes. In the *DSM-IV* (APA, 1994), some efforts have been made to recognize that symptoms of these disorders may be manifested differently in children and adolescents. For example, a Major Depressive Episode in children and adolescents may involve irritability rather than sadness. Moreover, certain symptoms such as somatic complaints, irritability, and social withdrawal are especially common in children, whereas psychomotor retardation, hypersomnia, and delusions are less common prior to puberty. The focus in this section is on Depressive Disorders because the majority of research on mood disorders and development has been conducted with either the offspring of depressed mothers or on depressed children.

Epidemiology

The IOM (1989) reported the prevalence of depression to be approximately 2% in prepubertal children. Moreover, Weissman and her colleagues (1987) have discovered that prepubescent and adolescent children of clinically depressed parents had a greater prevalence of major depressive disorder than did children of parents without a psychiatric disorder.

Investigations indicate that the prevalence of depression in adolescence increases substantially, with between 5% and 10% of adolescents manifesting a major depressive disorder at any point in time (Fleming & Offord, 1990; Lewinsohn, Hops, Roberts, Seeley, & Andrews, 1993). A recently conducted epidemiological investigation of 1,507 adolescents in a randomly selected community sample revealed that the mean age of onset of first depressive episode was approximately 15 years (Lewinsohn, Clarke, Seeley, & Rohde, 1994). Early onset of depressive disorder in this adolescent community sample was associated with being female and having thoughts about committing suicide.

Additionally, Warner, Weissman, Fendrich, Wickramaratne, and Moreau (1992) examined the 2-year course, first onset, recurrence, and recovery from major depression in a sample of 174 children with a parent who had a major depressive disorder. At 2 years, the incidence rate of major depression in these children was 8.5%. Moreover, 16.1% of the children also had experienced a recurrent episode. Congruent with the conclusion of Kovacs (1989), one of the best predictors of recurrent depression in these children was a prior comorbid diagnosis of dysthymic disorder. Within a 2-year period, the majority of these children had recovered (87%), with the mean time to recovery being 54 weeks. Children who experienced their first affective disorder at or before the age of 13, and those who had been exposed to multiple parental depressions, displayed protracted courses of recovery. In particular, children whose first episode occurred prior to age 13 took an average of 74 weeks to recover, while those who had experienced two or more bouts of parental depression needed nearly 79 weeks to recover on average.

As part of a seminal prospective longitudinal investigation of the development of major depressive disorder in childhood, Kovacs and her colleagues (Kovacs, Feinberg, Crouse-Novak, Paulauskas, & Finkelstein, 1984; Kovacs, Feinberg, Crouse-Novak, Paulauskas, Pollock, & Finkelstein, 1984) examined the duration of the first illness, the course of recovery from this initial episode onset, and the time to recurrence of a subsequent major depressive bout in a school-age, clinically referred sample. The investigators discovered that dysthymia had an earlier age of onset than did major depressive disorder. Moreover, dysthymia persisted for approximately 3 years, whereas depressive disorders took nearly 8 months to remit. When these depressed children recovered, they continued to be examined until they developed a recurrent episode of major depression. Forty percent of the children developed a subsequent depression and none of these youngsters had a recovery period of more than 2 years before they experienced their first remission. Those children who had an underlying dysthymic disorder had an elevated risk for experiencing recurrent or periodic depressive disorder.

In a more protracted prospective longitudinal investigation of this sample, Kovacs, Akiskal, Gatsonis, and Parrone (1994) compared the course of functioning in a group of 60 children whose first mood disorder was dysthymic disorder, and a group whose first affective illness was major depressive disorder. Kovacs and her colleagues (1994) found that children with first-onset dysthymic disorder had an earlier age of onset, similar symptoms of affect dysregulation, lower rates of anhedonia and vasovegetative symptoms, and a greater overall risk for developing any subsequent mood disorder than was the case for the youngsters whose first affective disorder was major depressive illness. Kovacs et al., (1994) found that 76% of dysthymic children developed a first-episode major depressive disorder and that 69% combined dysthymia and depression (i.e., manifested "double depression"). Moreover, 40% of the dysthymic youngsters had comorbid anxiety disorders, while 31% of dysthymic children had comorbid conduct disorder. Furthermore, 13% of the dysthymics subsequently "switched" to bipolar disorder diagnoses. After the first episode, the course and subsequent rates of recurrent mood disorders of the dysthymic children were similar to that exhibited by the children whose first affective disorder was major depression.

Sanford and colleagues (1995) followed up a group of 67 adolescents with major depression over a 1-year period. The depressed adolescents were drawn from consecutive referrals to psychiatric clinics in a defined geographic catchment area. Adolescents and their parents were administered clinical interviews and questionnaires at both inception and at 1-year follow-up. Over the course of the 1-year time period, major depression remitted in nearly two thirds of the adolescents. A number of characteristics were found to distinguish between those adolescents whose depression persisted and those whose depression remitted. Persisters were characterized at inception as older, more likely to have comorbid anxiety disorders or to use substances, to have less involvement with their fathers, and to be less responsive to their mother's discipline compared with remitters.

In an investigation of the episode duration and the time to recurrence of major depressive disorder in an adolescent community sample, Lewinsohn and his colleagues (1994) discovered that the average episode length was 26 weeks and the median length was 8 weeks. Those adolescents who took longer to recover were characterized by an earlier age of first episode onset, the presence of suicidal ideation, and the seeking of treatment for the mood disorder. Five percent of the recovered adolescents relapsed within 6 months, 12% developed a recurrent depressive episode within a year, and nearly one third became subsequently depressed within 4 years.

Rohde, Lewinsohn, and Seeley (1994) conducted a 1-year follow-up of the adolescents from the Lewinsohn et al., (1994) community sample. Of the 45 adolescents who had experienced and recovered from their first onset of major depression, a number of psychosocial scars (i.e., characteristics that were present after but not prior to the depression episode) were found. Compared with a group of never-depressed adolescent control subjects who also were assessed on an array of psychosocial variables both prior and subsequent to the depression episode, the depressed adolescents had a number of psychological sequelae, including increased stressful major life events, excessive reliance on others, internalizing problems, and subsyndromal depression symptoms.

Harrington, Fudge, Rutter, Pickles, and Hill (1990, 1991) examined the adult outcomes of childhood and adolescent depression. Using the clinical data summaries of children who attended the Maudsley Hospital in London, Harrington and his colleagues identified a cohort of 80 children and adolescents who were depressed and a demographically matched control group of nondepressed psychiatric patients. Over 80% of these children and adolescents were studied at approximately 18 years from their original contact at the Maudsley. The depressed and nondepressed psychiatric controls, assessed "blindly" to their status, did not differ with respect to the number of nondepressive adult psychiatric disorders. However, the depressed group demonstrated an enhanced risk for affective disorder in adulthood, suggesting that substantial specificity exists in the continuity of mood disorders between childhood and adulthood (Harrington et al., 1990).

In a subsequent reanalysis of this sample, Harrington and his coworkers (1991) discovered that depressed children who are comorbid for conduct disorder had a poorer short-term outcome and engaged in significantly more criminal activity in adulthood than did the depressed children who were without conduct problems. Furthermore, depressed children with conduct disorder displayed very similar patterns of maladaptation in adulthood to conduct-disordered children without depression. Finally, although findings did not quite reach statistical significance, Harrington et al. (1991) uncovered suggestive evidence that depressed children with conduct problems were less likely to develop depression in adulthood than were depressed children without conduct problems.

Rao and her colleagues (1995) examined the longitudinal course and adult consequences of a group of adolescents with major depression and a control group of adolescents who had participated in a cross-sectional EEG sleep and neuroendocrine study. Adolescents were interviewed approximately 7 years after the depression initially had been diagnosed. The depressed adolescent group manifested high recurrence rates of major depression during the interval since the first assessment period: Of these depressed adolescents, 69% experienced recurrent depression episodes; moreover, 19% had elevated rates of new-onset disorders (cf., Strober, Lampert, Schmidt, & Morrell, 1993). Following an initial diagnosis of major depression, 23% of the adolescents had no additional depressive episodes subsequent to that assessment. In contrast, 21% of the controls experienced new onset depression during the follow-up period.

Parenting and the Child-Rearing Context

A number of difficulties in children with depressed caregivers have been linked to dysfunctional parenting. Compared with nondepressed caregivers, parents with depression have been described as more inconsistent, lax, and ineffective in their child management and discipline (Zahn-Waxler, Iannotti, Cummings, & Denham, 1990) and as less engaged and involved in interaction with their children (DeMulder, Tarullo, Klimes-Dougan, Free, & Radke-Yarrow, 1995). In contrast, depressed caregivers also have been found to use more forceful control strategies (Fendrich, Warner, & Weissman, 1990). Moreover, the behavior of depressed mothers in interaction with their children has been shown to be related to the mothers' personality disorder, a type of mental illness often found to co-occur with maternal depression (Cicchetti, Toth, & Rogosch, 1997; DeMulder et al., 1995). Interestingly, DeMulder and colleagues (1995) discovered that paranoid, schizoid, and schizotypal personality disorders predominated among their sample of mothers with unipolar depression; these categories are particularly indicative of interpersonal impairments, an area that commonly reveals dysfunction in depressed persons.

Overall, it appears that depressed caregivers try to avoid conflict with their children by accommodating to their child's demands and tolerating noncompliance. However, when these caregivers try to set limits on child demands, they also are less likely to reach a compromise with their children (Kochanska, Kuczynski, Radke-Yarrow, & Welsh, 1987). Because relations have been reported between inconsistent, controlling, and lax parenting and externalizing child behavior problems (Loeber & Dishion, 1984), this style of parenting may contribute to the externalizing symptomatology reported in offspring of depressed caregivers. Increased inhibition to unfamiliar situations also has been noted in toddlers with depressed mothers, especially for mothers with the most severe illnesses (Kochanska, 1991). This inhibition has been attributed to less involvement and less sensitivity in response to child wariness by depressed caregivers, in combination with infrequent encouragement of child exploration and frequent angry criticism of the child (Kochanska, 1991).

The self-critical styles of depressed caregivers also appear to be transmitted to their offspring. One such mode of transmission relates to the speech used by depressed parents. Murray, Kempton, Woolgar, and Hooper (1993) found that the speech used by depressed women to their infants expressed more negative affect, was less focused on infant experience, and evidenced less acknowledgment of infant agency. Even in adolescence, increased irritability has been observed in the verbal interchanges between affectively ill mothers and their adolescents (Tarullo, DeMulder, Martinez, & Radke-Yarrow, 1994). The emotion socialization that is conveyed by depressed caregivers also may be especially important to consider for child development. In describing the emotions depicted by photographs of infants, Zahn-Waxler and Wagner (1993) reported that depressed mothers tended to view infants as more tearful and less joyous than did well mothers. Depressed mothers also were either more or less likely to identify sorrow in infants, a finding that suggests that depressed mothers may either deny the existence of sadness in their own infants, or overattribute its presence (Zahn-Waxler & Wagner, 1993). Depressed mothers also have been shown to make more negative attributions about their children during mother-child interactions than well mothers (Radke-Yarrow, Belmont, Nottelmann, & Bottomly, 1990). Depressed caregivers also have been shown to use more anxiety-and-guilt-inducing methods of discipline in combination with voiced disappointment in their children (Susman, Trickett, Iannotti, Hollenbeck, & Zahn-Waxler, 1985). The criticality of depressed caregivers also has been found to manifest itself through shouting and slapping (Panaccione & Wahler, 1986) and in its more extreme forms may result in hostile, coercive parenting.

In addition to the previously discussed dysfunctional parenting that characterizes the depressed caregiver, research concerning the marital relationship and the role of the nondisordered parent needs to be considered. It may be the context accompanying depression and not the illness itself that contributes to poor parenting and child maladaptation. Depressed persons tend to reside in adverse circumstances that may precede, co-occur with, and persist beyond their depression (Downey & Coyne, 1990). Chronic interpersonal difficulties commonly occur, particularly in close relationships (Coyne, 1976), and depressed women have a high rate of marital conflict (Weissman & Paykel, 1974). Moreover, research findings suggest that the interpersonal difficulties of depressed persons are more serious during a depressive episode (Weissman & Paykel, 1974) and that persons experiencing an active depression exert a markedly greater impact on their spouse's adjustment than recovered depressed persons (Coyne et al., 1987). Moreover, because of the tendency for assortative mating in depressed persons (Merikangas & Spiker, 1982) and for depression in one spouse to arouse stress in the marital partner (Coyne, 1976), children with a depressed parent are at high risk for poor parenting from both caregivers. Thus, it is unlikely that the nondepressed spouse can compensate adequately for the poor quality caregiving of depressed persons.

In an especially relevant study, Keller et al. (1986) investigated the effect of severity and chronicity of parental depression and marital discord on child psychopathology and adaptive functioning in a large group of children of unipolar depressed parents. Both severity of parental illness and marital distress were associated with poor adaptive functioning on current and lifetime *DSM-III* diagnoses (Keller et al., 1986). Likewise, Emery, Weintraub, and Neale (1982) found that marital discord was a stronger predictor of child competence in the offspring of depressives than in the offspring of schizophrenics or in controls. The role of the marital relationship and of the nondisordered spouse are important for understanding the sources of influences on the caregiving environment.

Rutter and Quinton (1984) have identified three possible mechanisms through which marital discord may contribute to child outcomes in children with a depressed caregiver. They discuss (a) marital discord as predating the emergence of a psychiatric disorder; (b) psychiatric disorder as causing impaired marital relationships; and (c) a process by which marital discord and psychiatric disorder are caused by prior conditions. Because research has shown that children are affected not only by their interactions with others, but also by what they observe, exposure to negative parental interactions may constitute a major risk (Cummings & Davies, 1994). After reviewing the literature on parental depression and child outcome, Downey and Coyne (1990) concluded that marital discord provides an alternative explanation for the adjustment problems evidenced by the offspring of depressives.

The difficulties experienced by children with a depressed caregiver also may be exacerbated by factors external to the nuclear family. Because depression frequently accompanies other adverse circumstances such as poverty, limited knowledge of child development, and stressful life events, disruptions in parenting are especially likely to occur. Similarly, these stressors may exacerbate parental depression, resulting in a negative cycle of depression, adverse circumstances, and maladaptive parenting. Over time, child behavior problems may emerge and enter into the negative cycle.

The isolated lifestyles of depressed persons also may result in increased adversity for their children, who may be prevented from developing an extrafamilial support network (Cummings & Davies, 1994). To further compound the lack of extrafamilial supports, Zahn-Waxler and her colleagues have found that the few individuals outside the family that the child may have access to are themselves frequently mentally ill or emotionally disturbed (Zahn-Waxler, Iannotti, Cummings, & Denham, 1990).

Thus, findings suggest that the parenting provided by depressed caregivers, as well as the caregiving context within which they raise their children, may conspire to place these children at substantial risk for developmental failure and emotional difficulties (Downey & Coyne, 1990). However, whereas a depressive illness may be immodifiable during its emergence and course, this is not the case for parenting and associated aspects of the caregiving context. Therefore, although parenting difficulties and a negative caregiving context may be present in conjunction with parental depression, it is also possible that even in the midst of parental depression positive parenting and related family circumstances may serve to buffer the adverse consequences of parental depression.

Ontogenic Development

In the next section, we present what is known about the unfolding of a number of stage-salient issues in individuals who either have, or are at increased risk for, the development of a depressive disorder. Rather than discussing all stage-salient issues, we focus on those that have generated the most research relevant to the etiology of the depressive disorders. We provide illustrative data on how offspring of depressed parents resolve each of these stage-salient issues, and on how depressed children and adolescents fare on these tasks. Where empirical evidence exists, we document how these individuals negotiate each of these issues as they go beyond their period of ascendancy to become coordinated and integrated with subsequent tasks. Practice implications of the research presented for each stage-salient issue also are discussed.

The development of a depressive disorder, as well as the age of its onset, is influenced not only by the emergence of salient issues or tasks that must be confronted throughout the life course, but also by timed biological events that create challenges and provide new opportunities as they figure prominently in every developmental phase (for an elaboration, see Dahl, 1996; Dahl & Ryan, 1996). For example, the family members of patients with depressive disorder manifest an elevated risk for developing a depressive illness (McGuffin & Katz, 1993). Furthermore, the empirical literature reveals that, in general, the greater the percentage of genes shared with the affected individual, the greater the probability that the relative will be similarly affected (Tsuang & Faraone, 1990). In addition, there is an increased rate of affective disorder in the biological relatives and not in the adopted relatives of the adoptees (for a review, see Tsuang & Faraone, 1990). Moreover, twin studies of affective disorder have consistently found the concordance rates for monozygotic twins to be substantially higher than in dizygotic twins (Kendler, Neale, Kessler, Heath, & Eaves, 1992; McGuffin & Katz, 1993). These genetic factors, or lack thereof, though not all expressed at the earliest moments of life, contribute sources of vulnerability as well as resilience to the probabilistic unfolding of depressive illness.

Molecular geneticists have discovered that gene action, like psychological growth, persists throughout the life span and is not only a phenomenon of the early period of existence (Goldsmith, Gottesman, & Lemery, 1997; Watson, Hopkins, Roberts, Steitz, & Weiner, 1987). Consequently, both genetic factors and psychological experiences can bring about developmental change across the life course. Furthermore, just as is true for psychologically mediated effects, consequences that are genetically mediated may be modified, both by subsequent experience and through later mechanisms of gene action (Goldsmith & Gottesman, 1994). Although the effects of some genes may be enduring, others may be transient. During different developmental periods, genes may be activated or deactivated, and diverse factors that regulate gene activity are likely to vary developmentally. Thus, whereas genes may create particular physical structures early in ontogenesis (e.g., receptors for particular neurotransmitters in a specific tissue-type), and the functioning of these structures subsequently may play a role in the unfolding of a particular normal or pathological behavioral disposition (e.g., withdrawal, negative affectivity, passivity), it nonetheless is possible for gene action to occur at any point in the life course that either could modify these structures or cause a physiological process to unfold that affects particular individual behavioral dispositions (Goldsmith & Gottesman, 1994).

Homeostatic and Physiological Regulation

Research Findings. Information pertaining to the homeostatic regulation of infants of parents with an affective disorder stems from a number of sources. As early as the neonatal period, infant offspring of depressed parents have been shown to have more difficult temperaments as indexed by greater difficulty in self-quieting, irritability, less social responsiveness, lower activity levels, and more negative affect (Sameroff, Seifer, & Zax, 1982).

In an important experiment, Cohn and Tronick (1983) investigated the face-to-face interaction of nondepressed mothers with their 3-month-old infants. In one of the counterbalanced experimental conditions, mothers were requested to simulate depressive affect during interaction with the baby. During periods of simulated depression, infants evidenced wariness, protest, and gaze aversion. Cohn and Tronick (1983) concluded that even simulated depression could result in negative infant affectivity, subsequently impairing the infant's capacity to engage in effective self-regulation. These findings revealed that the flexibility in rhythms evidenced during sequences of normal interaction were significantly impaired during phases of simulated depression. Additionally, Field (1984) compared dyadic interactions between a sample of mothers suffering from postpartum depression and a sample of normal mothers simulating depression. A difference in coping strategy emerged, with infants in the postpartum group showing resigned, passive, and mimicking behavior, whereas infants in the simulated depression group were active in their protests (Field, 1984).

Field and her colleagues (1988) found that 3- to 6-month-old infants of depressed mothers are more stressed (e.g., have elevated heart rate, lower vagal tone) during infant-mother interactions than are infants of nondepressed mothers. Moreover, the lower incidence of interest in the facial expressions of infants who have depressed mothers and who have mothers with very low scores on a self-report inventory of depression (considered to reflect denial of depression) may be due to the fact that these mothers display a diminished facial repertoire when compared with well mothers.

Field et al. also (1988) examined the face-to-face interactions of 3- to 6-month-old infants of depressed and nondepressed mothers. Not surprisingly, depressed mothers and their babies displayed less positive behavior during their interaction than did well dyads. However, with the exception that they showed more head and gaze aversion with their mothers, the infants of depressed mothers exhibited the same depressed style of interacting with a stranger as they did with their mother.

Field, Pickens, Fox, Nawrocki, and Gonzalez (1995) investigated the vagal tone of 3- and 6-month-old infants of depressed and nondepressed mothers. Although vagal tone of the infants did not reveal between-group differences at 3 months, lower vagal tone was found in the 6-month-old infants of depressed mothers. Thus, the increase in vagal tone that occurred for the infants of nondepressed mothers between 3 and 6 months of age was not present in the infants of depressed mothers, suggesting a less mature autonomic development in infants exposed to maternal depression. Furthermore, correlational analyses revealed that higher vagal tone at 6 months of age was related to more optimal infant neurological status and increased infant vocalization. The lower vagal tone in the offspring of depressed mothers is consistent with the aforementioned results obtained during infant-mother and infant-stranger interactions (Field et al., 1988). Moreover, infants with lower vagal tone are typically less emotionally expressive and less reactive and have higher cortisol levels, both characteristic of depressed individuals at later ages.

Field and her colleagues (Field, Healy, Goldstein, & Guthertz, 1990; Field, Healy, & LeBlanc, 1989) have conducted several studies of behavior-state matching and synchrony in depressed and nondepressed mother-infant dyads. Field et al. (1990) studied 48 depressed and nondepressed mother-infant dyads when the babies were 3 months of age. These investigators discovered that the depressed mothers and their babies matched negative behavior states more frequently and positive behavior states less frequently than did the nondepressed dyads.

In another study, Field et al. (1989) found that African American depressed mothers and their 3-month-old infants not only shared negative behavior states more often and positive behavior states less frequently than nondepressed dyads, but also revealed less synchrony between mother-infant behavior states than nondepressed dyads (i.e., that the depressed mothers were less behaviorally *attuned* to their babies). Moreover, Field et al. (1989) discovered that nondepressed mothers and their babies likewise revealed a greater match between maternal heart rate and infant behavior (i.e., the nondepressed mothers also were more physiologically attuned to their babies than were the depressed mothers).

In a longitudinal investigation, Campbell, Cohn, and Meyers (1995) studied the interactions of postpartum depressed and nondepressed mothers with their infants when the babies were 2, 4, and 6 months of age. These investigators found that women whose depression persisted through the entire 6 months were less positive with their infants and that their infants were less positive during face-to-face interaction with their mothers. These longitudinal data underscore the importance of distinguishing between more enduring and transient mood disorders in determining the impact of depression on mother-infant interaction and infant development.

Practice Implications. In view of the findings on the tendency for depressed mothers to attend to negative affective states in their infants and the greater likelihood that nondepressed mothers will be physiologically attuned to their babies, an approach that helps depressed women recognize the possible effects of their depression on their infants is indicated. Similar to the educative approach discussed in relation to parents of maltreated children, depressed parents can be helped to recognize the importance of attending to the positive affective cues of their infants. The technique of videotaping face-to-face interactions could increase parental awareness of their differential responsivity to infant affective states.

The passivity observed in the infants of depressed women, regardless of the origins of the passivity, also could extinguish maternal efforts to initiate interactions and respond to infant cues. Because depressed mothers are likely to perceive themselves as ineffective and are prone to feelings of helplessness, a paucity of reinforcement from their infants will promote a tendency not to engage with the infant. Moreover, when infant signals are ignored, the resulting lack of effectance in relation to the environment will increase infant passivity. The resulting negative transactional pattern between parent and infant will be detrimental to both members of the dyad and could promote a more sustained learned helplessness in both parent and child. Interventions designed to ameliorate these negative transactions by modifying parental behavior and helping the mother to recognize increases in infant responsivity are indicated. Once a more reinforcing pattern can be initiated, ongoing intervention may not be required.

In addition to dyadically focused interventions, interventions designed to address the symptoms of parental depression as quickly as possible also could reduce the more enduring effects of parental depression on infant development and regulation. The early provision of antidepressant medication, in conjunction with psychotherapy, might be indicated to alleviate acute depression, thereby minimizing the effects on the developing infant (Persons, Thase, & Crits-Christoph, 1996).

Affect Regulation and Differentiation

Research Findings. Pickens and Field (1993) examined the facial expressions of 84 three-month-old infants of mothers classified as depressed, nondepressed, or low scoring on the Beck Depression Inventory (BDI; Beck, 1967).

They found that infants of depressed mothers displayed sadness and anger expressions significantly more often, and interest expressions less often, than babies with well mothers. Interestingly, infants whose mothers scored low on the BDI also exhibited higher incidences of sadness and anger, paralleling the emotion expression of the infants of depressed mothers. Although the higher frequency of sadness expressions is not surprising, the greater rate of anger expressions suggest that infants of depressed mothers may be more upset during interactions with their mothers.

Empirical evidence of affect regulatory difficulties beyond the early months of life can be seen throughout the toddler and childhood periods in children with depressed caregivers. Gaensbauer, Harmon, Cytryn, and McKnew (1984) found dysregulation of emotion in infants and toddlers of parents with an affective disorder. When compared with control children, youngsters of parents with a unipolar and/or bipolar disorder exhibited more fear in situations where one would normally experience less fear (e.g., during free play and during reunion with mother after a brief separation at 12 months) and displayed less fear in situations where more would be expected (e.g., during a brief maternal separation at 15 months). These investigators interpreted these findings as indicating that the children of mood-disordered parents appear to prolong the experience and expression of affect (e.g., a slow recovery time from a disruptive emotion). In their research, this general tendency was inferred from the children apparently carrying affect into a subsequent episode when its expression was most relevant to coping with the prior episode.

Zahn-Waxler, Iannotti, Cummings, and Denham (1990) found that toddlers of depressed mothers were more likely to manifest dysregulated out-of-control aggressive behavior than toddlers of nondepressed mothers. Moreover, the maladaptive aggression displayed by the toddlers of depressed mothers predicted externalizing behaviors in these youngsters at age 5 (mother report) and age 6 (child self-report). However, toddlers of depressed mothers who exerted modulated control, provided structure and organization during mother-toddler play, and could take the child's viewpoint exhibited fewer externalizing behavior problems than toddlers of depressed mothers who did not employ these proactive child-rearing methods.

Practice Implications. The regulatory difficulties evidenced by the offspring of depressed caregivers during infancy and early childhood possess important implications for continued development. Unless these youngsters become able to modulate their behaviors more effectively, they will be at high risk for the development of mood disorders and externalizing disorders such as conduct disorder, as well as for personality disorders that are characterized by impulsivity and affective lability (e.g., borderline personality disorder).

In view of the very early tendency for offspring of depressed caregivers to exhibit more negative affective states, efforts either to modify parental behaviors to preclude the socialization of negative infant affect or to provide the infant with alternate opportunities for positive affective interchange should be considered. If a mother is severely depressed, perhaps a more active role of the father in engaging positively with the infant can be promoted. Additionally, enrollment in day care might be an appropriate intervention to consider to expand the baby's sphere of social interactions until parental symptomatology can be addressed.

The affect regulatory difficulties experienced by children with depressed caregivers also underscore the importance of addressing this issue. The provision of cognitive control therapy discussed earlier might be appropriately invoked with these children. Difficulties associated with the generalization of disruptive emotions also suggest the need to help parents and teachers understand why a child may be perseverating on a negative affective state and introjecting it into an arena that no longer seems to be related to the initial stimulus situation. Rather than becoming frustrated at the child, thereby increasing the likelihood that a negative situation will continue and escalate, caregivers need to understand that the child requires additional help to regain affective regulation. Support around helping the child resolve the feelings aroused by an altercation before moving on to the next event is critical.

The Development of Attachment Relationships

Research Findings. Throughout his writings on separation and loss, Bowlby (1969/1982, 1973, 1980) argued that, when faced with separation from their primary caregiver, children experience anxiety. In cases of prolonged or sustained loss, an intense mourning process, with its socioemotional, cognitive, representational and biological components, ensues and, if continued beyond the normally expected period of grieving, is viewed as a reflection of an unresolved loss. Without the presence of a secure internal working model of the primary caregiver, Bowlby believed that any loss would be experienced as paramount. Conversely, the development of a secure internal working model of the major attachment figure was thought to serve as a buffer for minimizing the extent and duration of devastation experienced in the face of loss.

In terms of the development of internal working models, the psychological unavailability of parents for long periods can be viewed as a powerful influence on shaping expectations that attachment figures are unavailable and the self is unlovable. The implicit communication to the child is that he or she is unworthy of love, that is, worthless and rejected, and that the parent is "lost" to the child. The recurrent loss of the parent as a function of the decreased emotional availability that may accompany major depressive episodes may be equivalent in impact on the child's self-concept to the effects of recurrent major separations. This loss also can be seen as parallel to the perceptions of loss that precipitate depressive patterns (Beck, 1967). Early experiences of loss may be particularly powerful because they mold fundamental biological, cognitive, socioemotional, and representational response patterns (Akiskal & McKinney, 1973; Cicchetti & Tucker, 1994). The psychological unavailability of parents, the development of insecure attachments and working models of attachment figures and of the self in relation to others in children, children's developing precursors of depression, and clinical depression thus may be conceptualized as interrelated processes (cf., Blatt & Homann, 1992).

Children of depressed parents are particularly likely to be faced with the psychological unavailability of parents for long periods, especially during, but not necessarily restricted to, episodes of depression. Such children are exposed to sad and dysphoric affect, helplessness and hopelessness, irritability and confusion, and in manic-depressive illness to these episodes sometimes alternating with periods of euphoria and grandiosity. Thus, there are compelling reasons for considering psychological unavailability of the parent to be a risk factor for the development of insecure attachment in children of depressed parents.

Several studies have examined the quality of attachment relationships in the offspring of parents with a mood disorder. Gaensbauer and his colleagues (1984) found no differences in the percentage of 12-month-old infants securely attached to affectively ill and healthy parents; however, by 18 months there was a dramatic decrease in the percentage of securely attached infants of parents with an affective disorder, but not for the infants of the healthy parents. These results parallel short-term longitudinal findings reported by Egeland and Sroufe (1981). As part of a larger prospective study of children at developmental risk due to poverty, they assessed infant security of attachment at 12 months and again at 18 months for a subsample of infants whose maltreating mothers were "psychologically unavailable" (but not physically abusive) to their infants and for a subsample of comparison infants whose mothers were at risk for maltreating their infants because of psychosocial disadvantage but who had not maltreated their children to date. For the subsample of infants of psychologically unavailable mothers who were not physically abused, the number of securely attached infants fell from 57% at 12 months to 0% at 18 months; whereas there was a slight rise in secure attachments among the control infants from 12 to 18 months.

Although the psychologically unavailable mothers in the Egeland and Sroufe (1981) study were not formally diagnosed as clinically depressed, the descriptions of their interactions with their infants and toddlers resemble both clinical and research descriptions of the effects of depression on adult social interaction in general, and parental caretaking behavior in particular (Downey & Coyne, 1990). Perhaps psychological unavailability is one of the common features shared by some maltreating parents and by most depressed parents that affects the security of the attachment relationship between parent and infant.

Radke-Yarrow, Cummings, Kuczynski, and Chapman (1985) compared patterns of attachment in children of mothers with major unipolar and bipolar depression, minor depression, and no affective disorder. When these investigators examined the patterns of attachment in their four groups, they found a higher proportion of insecure attachments in children of parents with major unipolar and bipolar depressive illness than in children from the other two groups. Interestingly, in families in which the mothers were depressed, the presence of depression in the father did not exacerbate the likelihood that an insecure attachment would develop between the mother and child. However, if depressed mothers did not have a husband within the household, then the risk of an insecure mother-child attachment relationship was increased.

In a prospective longitudinal follow-up investigation of this sample, Radke-Yarrow and colleagues (1995) assessed the links between quality of attachment rated during the toddler or preschool years and psychosocial development during the early school-age years. Radke-Yarrow and her colleagues examined the influence of attachment and stressor conditions (e.g., maternal mood disorder, abusive relationships, marital discord) in combination as they relate to later problematic and adaptive child outcomes. These investigators found that, under some circumstances, secure attachment may not be protective for all children, and insecure attachment may confer some advantages. Some children who had developed a secure attachment relationship with a severely ill mother with unipolar illness exhibited problems that were of clinical concern by the early school years, whereas the development of an insecure attachment relationship with a mother with bipolar illness was associated with the absence of problematic anxiety during the early school years. The children of bipolar mothers who did not develop anxiety problems at age 6 were typically uninhibited temperamentally and often took refuge in autonomous activities. Continued longitudinal data are necessary on these children to distinguish between adaptive and maladaptive insecure attachments. Additionally, it will be important to ascertain how these children of bipolar parents fare on other developmental issues at different points in the life span.

Teti, Gelfand, Messinger, and Isabella (1995) also investigated the relations between maternal depression and attachment security among a group of 61 infants and preschoolers who had a depressed mother, and 43 infants and preschoolers who had nondepressed mothers. Teti and his colleagues found that 80% of infant-depressed mother and 87% of preschool-depressed mother attachments were insecure. In contrast to studies that solicited their mothers via advertisements and then screened for the presence of depression, Teti and colleagues recruited mothers who were in therapy because their depressions were sufficiently severe to disrupt their lives. These differences in sampling likely explain the increased rates of insecurity found in the offspring of depressed mothers in the Teti et al. (1995) investigation and underscore that, in the investigation of the relation between early attachment organization and maternal depression, the severity and chronicity of the mother's mental illness are critical dimensions. In addition to the high percentages of insecurity, Teti et al. (1995) discovered that 40% of infants of depressed mothers and 29% of preschoolers of depressed mothers had disorganized or atypical patterns of attachment.

In a follow up to an intervention study in infancy, 4- and 6-year-old children with depressed mothers were rated by their preschool teachers. The most powerful predictor of deviant levels of hostile behavior toward peers was disorganized-disoriented attachment status. Looking backward from the teacher assessment to earlier assessments, it was found that 71% of hostile preschoolers were classified as having a disorganized attachment at their 18-month Strange Situation assessment. In contrast, only 12% of children manifesting deviant hostile behavior were securely attached during infancy. It is likely that for some infants, disorganized attachment may prove to be a potential precursor of later maladaptation, long before actual childhood disorders develop and become manifest.

In the most recent longitudinal follow-up assessment of the Lyons-Ruth et al. (1987; Lyons-Ruth, Connell, Grunebaum, & Botein, 1990) sample, Easterbrooks, Davidson, and Chazan (1993) assessed these children's attachment to mothers at age 7 in an hour-long separation-reunion procedure in the laboratory. In addition, the mothers and teachers of these children provided reports of the children's behavior problems using the Child Behavior Checklist (CBCL; Achenbach & Edelbrock, 1981). The Main and Cassidy (1988) separation-reunion codings revealed that 45% of the sample were insecurely attached to their caregivers (19%, A; 12%, C; 14%, D). Quality of attachment also was related to children's reported behavior problems. Both mothers and teachers rated children who were securely attached as manifesting fewer internalizing and externalizing symptoms and as evidencing fewer total behavior problems than children who were classified as insecurely attached.

In a further exploration of the behavior problems data, classifications were made as to whether the children's behavior problem scores fell into the "clinical range" using the standard Achenbach and Edelbrock (1981) cutoff scores. The results of these analyses revealed that maternal reports placed 42% of the children in the clinical range, while teachers' ratings resulted in a 24% placement above the clinical cutoff. Examinations of the relationship between attachment status and the presence of behavior problems in the clinical range revealed that securely attached children were significantly less likely to be placed in the clinical range by either mother or teacher CBCL ratings. Finally, 45% of the children with a secure attachment relationship to their mother received scores above the clinical cutoff from either their mothers or teachers, compared with 83% of those with insecure attachment relationships (88% of A's; 60% of C's; and 100% of the D groups).

Armsden, McCauley, Greenberg, Burke, and Mitchell (1990) examined the security of parent attachment in several groups of young adolescents, including clinically depressed, nondepressed psychiatric controls, and nonpsychiatric controls. Depressed adolescents reported significantly less secure attachments to their parent than either of the control groups. Moreover, consistent with the predictions of cognitive models of depression (e.g., Abramson et al., 1978; Beck, 1967), associations were found among attachment security to parents, attributional style, and presence of a depressive disorder. These findings provide support for the belief that insecure attachment and concomitant negative representational models of self and other promote the development of negative cognitive schemata, which contribute to the development of a depressive disorder and problems in interpersonal relations.

Kobak, Sudler, and Gamble (1991) examined the relations between adolescents' quality of attachment on the Adult Attachment Interview (AAI) (George, Kaplan, & Main, 1985) and their self-reported depressive symptoms. The AAI's were scored using the Q-set developed by Kobak. Adolescents who were characterized by insecure attachment strategies had elevated levels of depressive symptomatology, both concurrently and 10 to 11 months prior to receiving the AAI. In contrast, teenagers' who had secure strategies had significantly lower levels of depressed symptomatology. Thus, an adolescent's ability to generate coherent discourse abut him- or herself in relation to attachment figures appeared to act as a protective factor against depressive symptoms. The findings reported by Kobak and his colleagues (1991) dovetail nicely with an earlier study by Kobak and Sceery (1988) that found an association between adolescent secure attachment strategies and positive outcomes during the transition to college. Furthermore, the reported association between insecure attachment strategies and depressive symptoms provides evidence that attachment continues to be an important developmental task in adolescence.

A wealth of data have accumulated from research conducted with groups of infants, toddlers, preschoolers, school-age children, and adolescents who have depressed caregivers. Additionally, studies examining links between attachment organization and the development of depression in nonrisk and high-risk samples, as well as in individuals with dysthymia and major depression have begun to emerge. To date, however, direct evidence of a relationship between early insecure attachment and later clinical depression has not been obtained. Insecure attachment can only be regarded as a risk factor for deviant outcomes, including depression, within the context of a complex developmental model (Cummings & Cicchetti, 1990). It is important to remember that there are diverse parental mechanisms through which depression might be linked with insecure attachment and risk for depression. These include maternal attributions toward the child, child-rearing practices associated with the socialization of affect, and facial expressions and body posture as aspects of the caregiver's emotion language (Cicchetti & Schneider-Rosen, 1986; Cohn, Matias, Tronick, Connell, & Lyons-Ruth, 1986). Identification of the links between parental depression and insecure attachment is only an initial step toward delimiting the bases for such relations. If depression in parents is linked with insecure attachment, it may be attributable to the effect that depression has in influencing aspects of parent-child interaction, as well as to its role in determining broader aspects of the child-rearing environment. An important aspect of this caregiving environment is likely to be the psychological unavailability of the parent during periods of depression.

Early insecure attachment relationships may lead children to be more vulnerable to depression by causing them to have very low internalized felt security. When faced with stress, such children are likely to have few resources for coping and may easily be prone to developing lower self-esteem, intensified feelings of insecurity, and sad affect. In addition, the cognitions that the insecurely attached individual develops in the context of attachment relationships may contribute to the emergence of thought processes and affect that are associated with depression. As noted by Cummings and Cicchetti (1990), the cognitions that center around loss and the unacceptability of the self are likely to resemble patterns of cognitive processes that have been linked with depression in adults (Beck, 1967).

Other mechanisms whereby maternal depression may bring about insecure attachment may be neurobiological in nature. It is conceivable that each developmental reorganization throughout ontogenesis is a "sensitive period" during which timed biological and psychological developments either render an organism vulnerable to psychopathology or present the individual with the opportunity to develop new strengths that buffer or protect it against pathological outcomes (Cicchetti, 1993; Cicchetti & Tucker, 1994).

Thus, one can hypothesize that parental depression and its concomitant biological, interpersonal, affective, and cognitive difficulties that render parenting problematic may either delay or impair the development of brain mechanisms that are the biological substrates of interpersonal attachments, and/or facilitate the development of genetically vulnerable neuronal circuits to the loss of reinforcement (cf., Akiskal & McKinney, 1973). Because human depression is associated with the withdrawal of contact from significant persons and the dissolution of attachment relationships (Akiskal & McKinney, 1975; Gentile, Cicchetti, Rogosch, & O'Brien, 1992; Lewinsohn, 1974), children of depressed caregivers may develop a biological reward system that is especially susceptible to abandonment, unavailability, disappointment, and loss. Akin to Akiskal and McKinney's (1973) conceptualization, it is conceivable that, although reversible, the punishment system of the brain (e.g., the periventricular system) could assume an imbalanced dominance over the reward system (e.g., the medial forebrain bundle). Moreover, these genetically and psychologically induced neurobiological anomalies may form the basis of a neurobiology of representational models that sets the tone for depressed individuals' views of themselves as hopeless and helpless with respect to their fate (Abramson, Metalsky, & Alloy, 1989), the dysregulation of the serotonergic, dopaminergic, noradrenergic, and cholinergic neurotransmitter systems (Antelman & Caggiula, 1977; Siever & Davis, 1985), neuronal excitability and hyperarousal, and ineffective coping (Akiskal & McKinney, 1975).

Regardless of the processes and mechanisms that contribute to the evolution of an insecure attachment relationship, the presence of such an attachment organization has been linked with the seriousness of psychopathology in adulthood, as well as with responsivity to psychotherapeutic intervention. Dozier (1990) administered the Adult Attachment Interview (George et al., 1985) to 40 adults with serious psychopathological disorders. Adults who were rated as more secure were more likely to have affective disorders than thought disorders. Additionally, greater security was associated with more treatment compliance, whereas stronger avoidant tendencies were accompanied by increased rejection of therapists, less self-disclosure, and poorer treatment utilization (Dozier, 1990). These findings suggest that attachment history exerts a role not only in the emergence of psychopathology, but also in the potential effectiveness of intervention.

Practice Implications. Many of the attachment-based interventions described for maltreating parents are equally applicable to dyads in which parental depression is present.

In view of the role of insecure attachment relationships in depression, efforts to facilitate the development of secure attachment relationships and positive internal working models of the self and of the self in relation to others are necessary. Because there is a high likelihood that a depressed caregiver is struggling with a history of negative representational models, therapies directed at improving parental representational models of relationships are a potentially useful approach to employ (Guidano & Liotti, 1983). The provision of individual therapy and the minimization of environmental stress is required to address this goal. Because parental sensitivity to child needs is likely to be possible only after their own negative relationship histories have been reworked (Egeland et al., 1988), the timely provision of therapy to parents may prevent extensive damage to their children's emerging self-systems.

The Development of the Self-System

Research Findings. Evidence on the effects of parental depression on the self-system of young children emerges from a number of investigations. Radke-Yarrow et al. (1990) studied mothers with unipolar ($N = 13$) and bipolar ($N = 4$) disorder, as well as a group of control mothers with no psychiatric disorder, interacting with their 2½-year-old toddlers. Although this investigation revealed that mood-disordered mothers were similar to nonmood-disordered mothers in the quantity and content of their attributions, mood-disordered mothers conveyed significantly more negatively toned affect in their attributions. This occurred most often with negative attributions about child emotions. These findings are significant, because, as we discuss later, depressed children have been shown to selectively process negative self-referent words as opposed to positive self-referent words.

Additionally, mood-disordered mother-child dyads evidence higher correspondence of affect tone of attributions and of self-reference than nonmood-disordered dyads (e.g., mother says "I hate myself," child says "I'm bad"). Radke-Yarrow et al. (1990) interpreted these results as suggesting a heightened vulnerability to maternal attributions in the offspring of mood-disordered mothers. The potential for increases in negative self-attributions for these children and the impact of this vulnerability for the development of a later mood disorder are strikingly evident in these findings. Moreover, these results emphasize the importance of mother-child discourse for the development of children's emerging sense of self.

Kochanska (1991) studied patterns of inhibition to the unfamiliar in toddlers of nondepressed, unipolar, and bipolar mothers. Toddlers of recently symptomatic mothers with unipolar depression were the most inhibited (cf., Kagan, 1994). Toddlers of well mothers and of mothers with bipolar illness did not manifest inhibition to a new environment or to a stranger. Kochanska proffered two possible interpretations of these findings. First, she stated that it was conceivable that the inhibition observed in toddlers of depressed mothers may be part of a more general response to living in a highly stressed environment brought on by the mother's depression. Alternatively, Kochanska theorized that the depressed mothers may have reacted anxiously to the experimental context and communicated their tension to the child.

In a study of communication patterns among mothers and older children, Tarullo et al. (1994) examined the interactions of unipolar, bipolar, and well mothers with their preadolescent and adolescent children. Preadolescent children of well mothers were rated as more happy/comfortable than were children of mood-disordered mothers. Mothers and their children were rated as more irritable/critical with each other when the child had a psychiatric illness. Whenever mothers met diagnostic criteria for a major depressive episode within the preceding month, their interactions with their adolescent daughters were rated as more critical.

For the child who develops an insecure representational model of the self and others based on experiences in the attachment relationship, we observe what may be regarded as the germinal signs of a depressionlike organization, with interpersonal, emotional, cognitive, linguistic, representational, and biological components. By extending this analysis to later points in development, we can examine how affective components of the self that are relevant to the mood disorder (e.g., self-esteem), are intertwined with growing cognitive and representational components of the self (e.g., self-understanding, self-cognitions, self-schemata). Such a developmental perspective may then provide insights into comprehending how cognitive distortions, learned helplessness, hopelessness, and other responses to one's own mood disorder, may have evolved throughout ontogenesis.

Dodge (1993) formulated a theoretical model of the etiology of depression by integrating his research on social information processing and various knowledge structures into a developmental framework. Dodge hypothesized that experiences in early life and biologically based limits on memory and neural functioning interact to yield constantly evolving knowledge structures that consist of schema for experiences in the past, expectations about future occurrences, and affectively charged vulnerabilities. He speculated that when an individual encounters particular stimuli, these knowledge structures organize the manner in which information is processed. Dodge conjectured that either early life experiences of interpersonal loss and instability or excessive pressure to achieve at an unrealistic level, both of which are increasingly likely if one has grown up with a mood-disordered parent, may lead children to develop in memory both negative self-schema and low self-esteem. As such, when children encounter loss, abandonment, or failure, the negative self-schema held in memory cause these children to direct heightened attention to the negative aspects of these stressful events and to attribute their occurrence to internal, stable, and global characteristics of the self. The children, in turn, then readily retrieve depressive memories and present in a depressed fashion. Because of the depressogenic processing patterns that are utilized and the negative self-schemata that are formed, it becomes increasingly likely that such children will develop chronic dysthymia or depression.

Quiggle, Garber, Panak, and Dodge (1992) examined the social information processing patterns of depressed, aggressive, depressed and aggressive, and normal children. The children, between 9 and 12 years of age, reported on their depressive symptomatology and were administered intention cue detection vignettes to detect potential attributional biases in their information processing. In addition, their classmates rated their peer relationship skills, and teacher ratings were used to index levels of child aggression.

The aggressive children displayed hostile attributional biases and stated that they could readily commit aggressive acts. Although depressed children likewise revealed hostile attributional biases, they attributed these negative situations to internal, stable, and global causes. Moreover, the depressed children stated that they would not be likely to employ assertive responses and believed that engaging in such aggressive acts would be more likely to eventuate in negative outcomes. The comorbid aggressive and depressed children manifested the cognitive patterns of both the aggressive and the depressed children, comorbid children performed like aggressive children, and for those variables related to depression, they mirrored the responses of depressed children. Although the results of this study cannot address the origins of these biased patterns of social-information processing, they are consistent with a number of developmental cognitive formulations (e.g., Cummings & Cicchetti, 1990; Dodge, 1993; Rose & Abramson, 1992).

In a related study, Lauer and colleagues (1994) investigated the effects of clinical depression on memory and metamemory performances in 9- to 12-year-old children. Memory *impairment* was found only in the most severely depressed children; in addition, all depressed children, regardless of their level of severity, exhibited performance *deficits* on the metamemory battery. Depressed children also were more likely to overestimate their memory abilities. The authors suggest two interesting hypotheses to account for their findings. They speculate that the overestimation of memory ability attributions exhibited by depressed children may be their attempt to compensate for feelings of inferiority or inadequacy brought about by their overly critical thought processes. Alternatively, depressed children could set themselves up to fail by setting unrealistic standards for themselves, thereby confirming their negative self-cognitions. Of special relevance, these distortions or overestimations may cause depressed children's information processing to be impaired, resulting in poor judgment in selecting how to respond appropriately to ambiguous or negative situations.

Zahn-Waxler, Kochanska, Krupnick, and McKnew (1990) investigated patterns of guilt in 5- to 9-year-old children of depressed and nondepressed mothers. The younger children of depressed mothers in this sample displayed patterns of overarousal to projective stimuli depicting hypothetical situations of distress and interpersonal conflict. These youngsters exhibited high levels of involvement and responsibility in their responses to the hypothetical problems of others. In contrast, the older children (i.e., the 9-year-olds) of depressed mothers did not reveal explicit guilt themes to these projective stimuli. Rather than assuming that these older children of depressed mothers were not experiencing guilt, Zahn-Waxler, Kochanska, and their colleagues (1990) hypothesized that these children were engaged in an inner struggle against experiencing it.

Overall, patterns of guilt in children of depressed mothers of all ages did not cohere with assessments of their other areas of adaptation such as empathy. The differing patterns of organization for children of depressed and well mothers may reflect different developmental pathways or trajectories for these groups of children. In keeping with the organizational perspective on development, the investigators speculated that the intense involvement and arousal in the problems of others from an early point in development may alter how children of depressed mothers resolve the salient tasks of attachment and self-other differentiation. In addition, having a needy, depressed mother may make it difficult for the child to become integrated into the peer group. Being deprived of these crucial peer group experiences, thought to be central for developing morality and social competence, could conceivably affect the ability of these children to experience guilt and responsibility in relationships in an adaptive fashion (Zahn-Waxler & Kochanska, 1990).

The narrative themes of the children of depressed mothers to the hypothetical situations contained distortions that reflect defensiveness against experiencing guilt feelings. Zahn-Waxler, Kochanska, and their colleagues (1990) discovered several types of distortions. For some, the narrative response conveyed a striking sensitivity to others' problems, a quality that could eventuate in either problematic or constructive later outcomes (see also Hay, 1994). Beardslee and Podorefsky (1988) hypothesized that one pathway to resilience in adolescent children of parents with an affective disorder is developing advanced levels of role-taking, interpersonal maturity, and empathy. Conceivably, as noted by Zahn-Waxler, Kochanska, Krupnick, and McKnew (1990), children who develop empathic over-involvement with their parents' problems may also need to develop the ability to protect themselves by distancing from the burden of parental depression. A potential risk of adopting such a stance is that as their feelings of guilt and responsibility persist without resolution, these children may develop an affective disorder later in life.

In an important study, Nolen-Hoeksema, Girgus, and Seligman (1992) conducted a 5-year prospective longitudinal investigation examining the interrelationships among children's depressed symptoms, negative life events, explanatory style, and helplessness behaviors in school and achievement contexts. The children were enrolled in the study when they were in the third grade and were assessed on the noted constructs at 6-month intervals. Nolen-Hoeksema and her colleagues (1992) found that in early childhood negative events, and not explanatory style, predicted later depressive symptoms. In later childhood, however, a pessimistic explanatory style (cf., Peterson & Seligman, 1984) surfaced as a predictor of depressive symptoms, either alone or in combination with negative events. During episodes of depression, children's explanatory styles not only worsened, but also remained pessimistic even when the depression remitted. Thus, a pessimistic explanatory style increased the risk for future depressive episodes. Moreover, depressed children exhibited consistent helplessness in both interpersonal and achievement contexts.

A number of the major psychological theories of adult depression have focused on the cognitive processing and functioning of depressed persons. Beck's (1967) theory placed emphasis on the "cognitive triad" of faulty information processing, distorted cognitions, and negative self-schemas of depressed individuals. Beck (1967) hypothesized that individuals who are depressed possess negative self-schemas, processes believed to be a stable characteristic of the way depressed individuals process information even during nondepressed periods.

Longitudinal work on the development of self-schemas would help to illuminate the role that they play in the development and sequelae of depression. Our position, although speculative, is that early loss, inadequate maternal care, an insecure attachment relationship, poor quality representational models of the self and the self in relation to others, an impoverished environment, parental mood disorder, and/or a temperamental predisposition to heightened awareness or social unease may lead to the formation of depressogenic schemas, which make an individual vulnerable to depression. Through time, these cognitive structures may then be elaborated and organized by experiences congruent with them (Rose & Abramson, 1992). Although the basic cognitive distortions may remain relatively stable, new information can be systematically integrated and organized into them. These structures can then be activated either by general or specific stress, or by prolonged negative affect.

Numerous studies have demonstrated that children exhibit enhanced recall of personal adjectives considered to be self-descriptive. Depressed and nondepressed children also show differential facilitated memory for negative and positive adjectives, respectively (Hammen, 1992). For example, Zupan, Hammen, and Jaenicke (1987) found that children between the ages of 8 and 16 years of age who had current or prior histories of depression demonstrated greater recall of negative self-descriptive adjectives. Interestingly, the number of previous depressions was not predictive of the degree of negativity of the children's self-schemas over and above that predicted by their current mood. Zupan and his colleagues (1987) viewed their findings as congruent with a developmental model of self-schemas in which prior negative experiences may enhance the accessibility of negative thoughts once the self-schema are activated.

In an impressive culling together of normal developmental theory to address the cause of adolescent suicide, Chandler (1994) argues that the identity formation demands associated with the transition to adolescence can strip away the sense of identity necessary for maintaining an investment in the future. In the absence of a sense of self-continuity, Chandler believes that suicide may result. In efforts to test this hypothesis, Chandler (1994) classified hospitalized adolescents into those at "low" or "high" risk for suicide. Remarkably, more than 80% of the high-risk adolescents failed to find any means of justifying their own or other's self-continuity in the face of change. Only 8% of the low-risk adolescents, and none of the nonpatient controls, evidenced this inability.

Practice Implications. Research has consistently demonstrated clear links between perturbations in the self-system and depression. Although causal relationships cannot be documented, the hierarchical model of development we propose suggests that self-system difficulties may emanate from the parent-child relationship and, in turn, contribute to a vulnerability to depression across the life course. Increased credibility for this conceptualization can be garnered from clinical work with depressed individuals. The origins of the pervasive negative self-views, passivity, and hopelessness that permeate the presentation of many depressed persons can be traced back to insults to the self experienced during childhood. Although therapists may opt to modify current self-views through techniques involving cognitive restructuring and may obtain success, it is rare for the underpinnings of a depressive style to originate from current experiences. Rather, self-conceptualizations and the resulting processing of information about the self and the world generally develop out of the caregiving history that has been experienced. Although departures from a negative history certainly are possible, those individuals who present with depression are often struggling with a historically based negative self-view.

In view of the prevalence of self-disorders among those suffering from various forms of psychopathology, interventions designed to modify these maladaptations are critical. When considering the needs of infants and toddlers who have a depressed caregiver, prevention and early intervention are indicated. Addressing parent-child interaction and modifying the environment as necessary emerge as strategies of intervention.

Because symbolic representation is a skill that affects the development of the self-system, dyadic interventions for parent and toddler that strive to modify parental communication should be considered. In cases where a depressed parent has contributed to or is instrumental in sustaining child negative self-views, it may be necessary to broaden the experience base of young children so that the parent is not the sole channel of attributional statements. In a related vein, sensitizing depressed caregivers to the impact that their own self-statements may have on their child also holds promise as an intervention strategy that may prevent the emergence and coalescence of negative child self-views.

The extensive data on negative self-schema in offspring of depressed caregivers and in depressed children suggests that cognitive behavior therapy is an important intervention strategy to utilize. By directly targeting negative self-views and reframing them more positively, the pervasive negative expectations of the future observed in these children and the effect of these expectations in perpetuating negative life experiences may be prevented.

Data that suggest both memory impairment and an overestimation of memory abilities in depressed children also raise interesting implications for intervention. It may be important to facilitate the development of realistic appraisals of ability in depressed children so as to avoid failure experiences. By possessing inflated expectations of competence, children at risk for depression are ensuring a course replete with failure and resulting feelings of helplessness. To avoid this trajectory, the unrealistic expectations must be challenged and the child helped to develop kinder attitudes toward the self.

Research on guilt and empathy in children at risk for developing a depressive disorder also suggest areas that may require intervention. Although advanced perspective-taking abilities and empathy may be viewed as positive attributes, there is a perilously fine line between adaptive and maladaptive functioning in this arena. Being reared by a depressed caregiver may well result in increased child sensitivity. However, if the child comes to believe that his or her value depends on successfully alleviating the pain of others, then a tendency to meet the needs of others to the exclusion of one's own needs may result. In the absence of intervention, the perpetuation of this interactional pattern into future relationships can eventuate in significant self-deficits. Therapies designed to elucidate the child's feelings of responsibility for parental well-being and to identify any beginning tendencies to apply this stance to other relationships may be helpful in preventing a life-long pattern of self-sacrifice and resultant feelings of inadequacy.

Contributions of the Study of Depression to Normal Development: Illustration from the Investigation of Hemispheric Activation Asymmetries

Many psychophysiological investigations suggest that there may be individuals who are vulnerable to depression, as evidenced by long-term hemispheric activation asymmetries (Davidson, 1991). A plausible explanation is that the hypoactivation of the left hemisphere and the overactivation of the right hemisphere may have a genetic basis. On the other hand, it also is conceivable that particular experiences can affect the developing brain structures and prime them for chronic activation asymmetry (see, e.g., Tucker, 1981). Because hemispheric asymmetries may be mediated by both genetic factors and socialization, the offspring of depressed parents may be especially at risk for developing a negative affect bias. Work by Dawson and her colleagues is beginning to shed important light on this topic.

Dawson, Grofer Klinger, Panagiotides, Hill, and Spieker (1992) investigated frontal lobe activation and affective behavior in a group of infants whose mothers had elevated depressed symptomatology and in a group of babies whose mothers did not display increased depressive symptomatology. The researchers recorded EEG frontal and parietal activity in both groups of infants.

The EEGs of these babies, 14 months old on average, were recorded during resting and several emotion-eliciting conditions. Compared with infants of nonsymptomatic mothers, the babies whose mothers exhibited elevated depressed symptomatology displayed reduced left frontal brain activation during baseline and playful interactions with their mothers. Moreover, infants of mothers with elevated depressed symptoms did not display the typical pattern of greater right frontal activation shown by the infants of nonsymptomatic mothers during a condition that elicits distress (i.e., maternal separation).

Additionally, the infants of symptomatic mothers manifested less distress during the maternal separation condition than did the infants of nonsymptomatic mothers. The two groups of infants also did not differ in their behavior during the playful condition with mother. Finally, the infants of symptomatic mothers did not differ in their patterns of parietal lobe brain activity, suggesting that the differences obtained in brain activation were specific to the frontal lobe region.

In a further examination of this same sample, Dawson, Grofer Klinger, Panagiotides, Spieker, and Frey (1992) investigated the relation between quality of infant-mother attachment and frontal and parietal brain activation patterns in response to the positive- and negative-emotion-eliciting conditions described in their initial paper. Both during baseline and the free-play interaction with their mothers, securely attached infants of symptomatic mothers displayed left frontal hypoactivation asymmetries compared with securely attached babies of nonsymptomatic mothers. Additionally, during the maternal separation condition, infants of symptomatic mothers, independent of their attachment classification, exhibited reduced right frontal activation patterns and lower levels of behavioral upset. Dawson and her colleagues (1992) interpret these findings as evidence that both the emotional wellness of the mother and the quality of her attachment relationship with her infant can exert influence on infant frontal lobe brain activation and on emotional behavior.

Hemispheric asymmetries also have been found in even younger infants. Jones and colleagues (1997) found that 1-month-old offspring of depressed mothers exhibited greater relative right frontal EEG asymmetry than did infants of nondepressed mothers. Similarly, Field, Fox, Pickens, and Nawrocki (1995) found evidence of right frontal EEG asymmetry in both depressed mothers and their 3- to 6-month-old infants.

Results of studies such as these (e.g., Dawson, Grofer Klinger, Panagiotides, Hill, & Spieker, 1992; Dawson, Grofer Klinger, Panagiotides, Spieker, & Frey, 1992; Field et al., 1995; Jones et al., 1997) parallel those of Davidson and his associates (e.g., Davidson, 1991), who discovered that depressed adults exhibited left frontal activation asymmetries during resting EEGs. Thus, the EEGs of infants with symptomatic mothers may be interpreted either as reflective of a lower threshold for experiencing negative affect or of a higher threshold for the experience of positive emotions. Consequently, the infants with symptomatic mothers appear to have an enhanced tendency toward developing negative emotionality (cf., Watson & Clark, 1984).

The securely attached offspring of the depressed mothers in the Dawson, Grofer Klinger, Panagiotides, Spieker, and Frey (1992) study displayed the reduced left frontal activation, whereas the insecurely attached infants of depressed mothers did not differ from the infants of the nondepressed mothers. Although preliminary, these results suggest that the negative effects of maternal depression on infant brain activation is not mediated exclusively through an insecure attachment relationship. In fact, the development of an insecure relationship with a symptomatic mother may protect the infant from developing some of the negative sequelae associated with her condition. Finally, when the effects of maternal depressive symptoms and attachment security on parietal EEG were investigated, no statistically significant findings occurred, suggesting that the obtained group differences in attachment security and elevated maternal depressed symptomatology were specific to the frontal lobe area. These data also are consistent with those reported in the adult depression literature (see, e.g., Davidson, 1991).

The findings of investigators who have examined hemispheric asymmetries in infants with depressed mothers are intriguing. In his important book *Neural Darwinism,* Edelman (1987) describes the great variability that is found in patterns of synaptic connection and states that some of this heterogeneity takes place as a result of differential experiences during sensitive periods for synaptogenesis. Consistent with Edelman's (1987) thesis, and our prior discussion of how caretaking casualty can affect brain structure, organization, and functioning in maltreated children, the findings of Dawson and her colleagues further buttress the thesis that a mother's emotional condition (and implicitly her interactions with her baby) can impact developing patterns of synaptogenesis in the early years of life (see, e.g., Cicchetti & Tucker, 1994). Moreover, baseline and treatment follow-up assessments of the nature of hemispheric activation asymmetries in the offspring of depressed persons should be incorporated into future evaluations of the efficacy of developmentally informed interventions employed with mood-disordered individuals. Such examinations will reveal whether maladaptive neurobiological structures, functions, and organization are modifiable or are refractory to intervention.

DEVELOPMENTAL CONSIDERATIONS IN ETHICAL PRACTICE

Now that the importance of research in child and adolescent developmental psychopathology for informing practice efforts has been articulated, we consider it to be equally necessary to address ethical considerations that accompany the conduct of such work. Although considerable attention has been directed toward ethics in adult psychiatry, much less effort has focused on ethical issues in research and practice with children and adolescents (Fassler, 1992). This omission has been even more striking for developmental considerations or special circumstances posed by high-risk and mentally disordered children. To be effective in efforts to understand and address the mental health needs of children and adolescents, developmentalists must grapple with thorny ethical dilemmas. A successful regimen of prevention and treatment for child and adolescent mental disorders requires a comprehensive understanding of biological as well as psychosocial contributors to psychopathology (Arnold et al., 1995). Therefore, ethics related to both of these areas must be considered.

Research Ethics

Because of children's special vulnerability, society has established legal and ethical protection for their research participation. A number of federal agencies and professional organizations possess codes aimed at providing guidelines and standards for research with adults and minors (e.g., *Protection of Human Subjects,* Department of Health and Human Services, 1983; *Ethical Principles of Psychologists and Code of Conduct,* American Psychological Association, 1992; *Ethical Standards of the American Educational Research Association,* 1992; and *Ethical Standards for Research with Children,* Society for Research in Child Development, 1993).

A cornerstone of decision making in research with children and adolescents involves an assessment of potential risks and benefits. In 1983, the Department of Health and Human Services (DHHS) adopted regulations involving research with children (DHHS, 1983). These standards established levels of research risk, with "minimal risk" being defined as the risk of harm not greater than that "ordinarily encountered in daily life or during the performance of routine physical or psychological examinations or tests" (DHHS, 1983, 45 CFR 46.102[g]). Studies involving minimal risk could be approved by the DHHS contingent on the permission of parents or guardians for child participation, and child assent. Under these conditions, no requirements of predictable benefits to the child, guardians, or society were necessary. For research involving more than minimal risk, approval could be given if an intervention from which the child was likely to benefit was provided or if a monitoring procedure that was likely to contribute to the child's well-being was involved; under these conditions, the Institutional Review Board (IRB) also needs to conclude that risk can be justified by benefits to the child and that the risk-benefit ratio is no less favorable to the child than that of any alternative procedures that are available. Although these stringent criteria suggest that greater than minimal risk research cannot be approved unless the child benefits *directly,* approval still can be given if an IRB finds that the risk is a "minor increase" over minimal risk, that the research involves situations that are consistent with those commonly experienced during daily pursuits, and that the research is likely to result in "generalizable knowledge" that is of "vital importance" for understanding the child's disorder or condition (DHHS, 1983, 45 CFR 46.406). It is important to recognize that this conceptualization includes the broader benefits to society as well as child-specific benefits (Thompson, 1992).

Additionally, the DHHS (1983) is able, under certain conditions, to approve research that does not satisfy "minimal risk" or "minor increase" provisions if the research provides an opportunity for understanding, preventing, or alleviating a "serious problem affecting the health or welfare of children" (p. 16). Although technically the regulations apply only to federally supported projects, federal requirements for IRBs and their review of all institutional research bring all research under the purview of these standards.

In conducting risk-benefit analyses, four broad ethical principles typically are relied on (NCPHS, 1979). Thompson (1992) summarizes the implications of these principles. The first principle, *respect for persons,* subsumes the concept of autonomy. It manifests itself with respect to procedures for obtaining informed consent, protection of privacy, confidentiality, freedom to withdraw from research participation, limits of deception in research, and utilization of debriefing procedures. *Nonmaleficence,* the second principle, mandates that researchers minimize the risks of harm to research participants. This principle, in combination with the third principle of *beneficence,* or the responsibility to remove harm and provide benefits to participants, comprise the undergirdings of risk-benefit analyses. The fourth ethical principle used to evaluate research is that of *justice.* Justice mandates an obligation to treat equally those in similar circumstances and to treat those who differ in relevant ways differently. This requires impartiality and fairness in the treatment of research participants. Although laudable, the breadth of these principles and the ambiguity of regulatory language suggests that they are not able to address the ethical gray areas so often encountered in the design and evaluation of research investigations. These guidelines are even more ineffectual in offering solutions to developmentalists who strive to apply the scientific method to understanding and improving the status of mentally disordered or high-risk youth (Fisher & Rosendahl, 1990). If ethical research on child and adolescent disorders is to proceed, and is, in fact, in the best interest of the child, then several issues need to be considered (cf., Fisher, 1993).

Informed Consent

In addressing informed consent and the role of parental permission, it is important to factor in the nature of the research question being asked. In investigations of child development and parental mental illness or child abuse, consent of the parent might not adequately attend to child well-being. In such cases, child assent in conjunction with IRB approval is important. Additionally, if the investigator believes that a child is adversely affected as a result of research participation, then a decision to discontinue the experimental procedure should occur, even if the parent minimizes the significance of the child's distress.

Agreement to participate in a research project also may be motivated by a parent's desire to seek professional help. In this regard, parents of children who are the most vulnerable or parents who themselves are experiencing significant difficulties might be likely to consent to research in hopes of obtaining assistance. If assistance is not to be forthcoming, then this must be made very clear to parents. Additionally, if a possibility of assistance is available but its provision is a function of random assignment, then it is critical that parents fully understand that they may not receive the help that they seek. Moreover, although the methodology of an intervention investigation may be adversely affected by parents obtaining intervention elsewhere, researchers must apprise parents of their right to secure services outside the research investigation.

It is equally important that investigators consider the impact of incentives on parental decisions to allow their children to participate in research investigations. Where parents are impoverished, investigators must consider the possibility of coercion on gaining an agreement to participate. Again, it is the responsibility of the investigator to ensure that child interests are not obscured by parents' needs to obtain financial benefit.

Parameters of informed consent also may be altered by the circumstances that surround children. Often, developmental research assumes that children reside within a secure setting where children and parents share loving relationships (Gaylin & Macklin, 1982; Levine, 1986). However, when conducting research with children who are living in adverse situations that are replete with child abuse and/or parental mental illness, reliance on parents or guardians for informed consent poses significant problems. Again, in such cases, investigator ethics become critical.

Confidentiality

Issues related to confidentiality assume special importance in investigations with mentally ill parents or high-risk and mentally disordered children and adolescents. Procedures that identify previously undetected developmental lags or permutations pose special challenges for confidentiality. What is ethically appropriate—maintaining confidentiality or ensuring that appropriate services are made available? Ideally, researchers should confront issues such as these prior to the conduct of research. A proactive approach enables a balance between confidentiality and the well-being of the child. Therefore, consent forms should articulate procedures if a mental illness or disability is discovered during research.

In accord with principles of the Society for Research in Child Development *Ethical Standards for Research with Children:*

> When, in the course of research, information comes to the investigators' attention that may jeopardize the child's well-being, the investigator has a responsibility to discuss the information with the parents or guardians and with those expert in the field in order that they may arrange the necessary assistance. (SRCD, 1993, p. 338)

Although some investigators maintain that limitations in the accuracy of developmental research assessments preclude them from sharing results with parents, one must consider whether providing or withholding information is to the benefit of the child.

Decisions on whether and how to intervene when concerns arise as a result of research participation are particularly difficult in cases where informing a parent of a child's problem may jeopardize the welfare of the child rather than result in assistance. For example, if an investigator determines that a child is suffering from an emotional disorder such as depression, but the child reports that he or she is fearful of a parent being informed of their problems, then taking action may be more harmful than helpful. Anticipating cases such as this suggests that informed consent also should state that school personnel may be informed if concern over child well-being arises.

The detection of child maltreatment also poses significant challenges for the researcher, especially in studies of high-risk or maltreating populations. Ethically, many states would consider the researcher to be responsible for reporting suspected maltreatment to authorities, but decisions to do so might result in sample attrition, thereby affecting the integrity of the research and its potential benefit to society. Concern for the child must take precedence; however, in view of limitations in the resources available to authorities to deal with increasing cases of abuse, action often is limited only to cases that are deemed to be the most severe. Consequently, reports of questionable instances of maltreatment could jeopardize the research, adversely affect the child due to parental anger, and ultimately lead to little or no positive outcome. Overall, it is critical that the best interest of the child be considered fully before any action is taken by investigators. While seemingly well motivated and overtly in accord with ethical and legal standards, failure to consider fully the ramifications of a given action may prove to be detrimental to the child. Fully understanding the parameters of state and federal regulations and then evaluating their applicability to a given situation, considering the developmental status of the child participant, and assessing the probable outcome of acting or failing to do so are likely to result in the conduct of the most ethically grounded research.

Thompson (1992) discusses characteristics of children that pose unique challenges to addressing ethical concerns. To begin, the limited cognitive competencies and experiences of children limit their ability to make well-informed decisions regarding research participation. The minimal social power of children also makes them vulnerable to coercion, even if indirectly. Finally, their ambiguous legal rights and the role of parents and guardians in the consent process may not always result in decisions being made in the best interest of the child. Possible divergences between child and parent interest become especially important when dealing with high-risk populations, where parental mental illness or economic circumstances may inhibit parental ability to be an appropriate advocate for or protector of their child (Fisher, 1993). Moreover, considerations of "minimal risk" may vary markedly when the gauge of normally encountered risks of daily life is applied to children residing within very different circumstances. For example, the "normal risk" experienced by a child living in an impoverished, high crime urban area differs dramatically from the "risk" environment common to a child from a wealthy family who attends a private school. If the minimal risk guideline were to be applied based on the former child's typical experiences, then it would be difficult to maintain that the guideline had been appropriately invoked. In addition, although the principle of justice calls for equal treatment of all research participants, this hypothetical example of two very different children also highlights challenges likely to be encountered in the implementation of the justice principle. Moreover, as Thompson (1992) emphasizes, the heterogeneity of children and the nuances of vulnerabilities that change with development possess important obligations for researchers. On the surface, the DHHS regulations appear to be sensitive to the vulnerabilities of children, but a rigid adherence to the underlying tenets may result in guidelines that fail to address adequately the changing needs of children and adolescents.

Thompson (1992) proposes a developmental formulation that addresses how changing cognitive skills, experiential backgrounds, and social power modify the pattern of age-related vulnerabilities warranting consideration in an evaluation of the ethics of research. In so doing, he draws on the developmental research literature. To summarize, Thompson proposes that the following premises be considered in evaluating research ethics to ensure their applicability to children and adolescents.

- Younger children are at greater risk for behavioral and socioemotional distress in response to stressful experiences.
- Threats to a child's self-concept are likely to increase as the child's understanding of the self develops.
- With increasing age, the effects of social comparison information become more significant.
- The ability to make inferences regarding others' motives, attitudes, and feelings increases with age.
- Once self-conscious emotions such as shame, guilt, embarrassment, and pride emerge, young children may be more vulnerable to their arousal due to a more limited understanding of these emotional reactions.
- Young children are more vulnerable to coercive manipulations than older children.
- Concerns about privacy increase with age.
- Older children are more likely to be sensitive to cultural and socioeconomic biases in research.

Overall, such an analysis suggests that, as discussed earlier, vulnerabilities vary with age; a linear analysis that views young children as most vulnerable and in need of protection fails to consider the complexity of development. Moreover, although an improvement over more simplistic models, even a more sophisticated consideration of development must attend to individual differences among children (Fisher, 1993; Thompson, 1990b).

The issue of individual differences assumes paramount importance in the conduct of research with special needs populations. Thus, in the area of childhood and adolescent psychopathology, all children can be assumed to be more vulnerable to the potential risks of research. This baseline risk becomes exacerbated in situations involving incapacitated or absent caregivers, where adequate protection of the child may not be present; child incarceration or hospitalization, where institutional interests may take precedence over individual child well-being; and severe family psychosocial deprivation, where any incentive to participate may adversely affect parental judgment. In situations such as these, impartial individuals who are not invested in the conduct of a given program of research are in the best position to evaluate ethical dilemmas.

Although the bulk of ethical decision making seems to fall on the side of "protecting" children from *participating* in research, equally powerful arguments can be made regarding the dangers of *excluding* children from research participation. Klin and Cohen (1994) state that responsible clinical concern for the welfare of patients might be viewed as imposing an ethical mandate to conduct, or minimally to support research. Although all individuals vested in the well-being of children as a vulnerable population believe that research should be approached with appropriate care and caution, this position may result in an extremist view that *all* research is abhorrent, and, subsequently, interfere with the acquisition of knowledge necessary to address child needs (Kopelman, 1989). Failure to conduct research on disorders of childhood with children as participants may force clinicians to extrapolate their findings on adults to children (Arnold et al., 1995). Because a developmental approach to psychopathology recognizes that such generalizations may be inappropriate, reluctance to enroll children as research participants is antithetical to a developmental psychopathology framework. In fact, failure to conduct research with children can lead to ethical dilemmas. For example, a significant problem surfaces in the practice arena regarding whether to deprive children of a potentially effective treatment or to utilize an intervention where efficacy has not been demonstrated. Additionally, reliance on adult research might fail to elucidate the effectiveness of a treatment for children, thereby deeming it "ineffective" and removing it as a treatment option for children (Arnold et al., 1995). Finally, although the use of animal models may provide potential solutions to some areas of treatment, reliance on animal studies may have more limited value with children than with adults. For example, although children have been found to metabolize drugs more rapidly than adults, some studies have found that adult animals metabolize drugs faster than young animals (Arnold et al., 1995). Thus, determining how to apply animal findings to children can prove to be especially challenging. Overall, in an examination of ethical issues associated with biological psychiatric research with children and adolescents, Arnold and colleagues (1995) concluded:

> The consequences of not conducting research in children and adolescents might include the perpetuation or introduction of harmful practices, failure to discover etiology of illness, and failure to develop new treatments for psychiatric disorders of childhood and adolescence. (p. 93)

Although this statement focuses on biological research, this view is consistent as well with our position on research that examines psychosocial development. Although critics of research with children and adolescents consider extreme protectiveness to be beneficial, in fact, reluctance to conduct research on child populations will limit the availability of sound information on which to base clinical decisions. In attempting to apply research knowledge to practical settings, a number of issues must be addressed (Sigel, 1990). The ethical use of research findings is especially challenging, in that there are more guidelines pertaining to the conduct of research than there are to the integration of research data into the practice arena. Although the individual who conducts research has some responsibility for its ultimate use, the aegis for appropriate utilization falls on the individuals who are attempting to translate research findings into practical pursuits (Sigel, 1990). Thus, while perhaps seemingly disparate, ethical decision making with respect to research possesses significant implications for the practice arena when one seeks to incorporate research into clinical practice. The synergy that can occur among scientific advances, ethical standards, and clinical practice is elucidated by Hoagwood, Jensen, and Fischer (1996) in their book *Ethical Issues in Mental Health Research with Children and Adolescents.*

Practice Ethics

In the area of practice ethics, the professional codes of psychologists, psychiatrists, or other relevant disciplines are most heavily relied on. Informed consent, confidentiality, and client-therapist relationships are among the issues that have received the most attention.

The provision of clinical services to children differs markedly from work with adults, in terms of both developmental and ethical issues that are encountered. Similar to informed consent issues present in research, children generally are not considered to be capable of providing consent for treatment. Therefore, their parents or guardians are the individuals who enter into a service contract. Additionally, most commonly it is the parent who feels that the child needs treatment, and not the child who is seeking treatment. These issues all pose potentially complex ethical issues for the therapist, especially when the role of development is considered.

Historically, children have been considered to be the property of their parents, and as such parents have been held to possess a "right of control" over their children (Koocher & Keith-Spiegel, 1990). In fact, only in the 1960s were children considered to be due protection under the Bill of Rights. However, in the area of ethics and child mental health, parents typically continue to exercise control over their children. For our purposes, the ability of children to make informed decisions about their lives and to understand the implications of such decision making permeates many areas of ethics. Therefore, a solid understanding of developmental transformations that occur and their impact on the decision-making process are important to consider.

The assessment of child competence is a critical component of ethical decision making with children considered to be in need of treatment due to the presence of psychopathology. To determine whether or not a child is competent, four key elements of competence must be evaluated: (a) the child's ability to understand information that is provided regarding the possible consequences of a decision; (b) the child's ability to express a decision; (c) the way in which the decision is made; and (d) the nature of the resulting decision (Leikin, 1983; Weithorn & Campbell, 1982). To move through such a decision-making process, developmentally relevant issues such as cognitive competence, assertiveness and autonomy, rational reasoning, understanding of future consequences, and judgments in the absence of complete information all must occur (Koocher & Keith-Spiegel, 1990). It is therefore the responsibility of the therapist to possess enough knowledge about the developmental progression of these capacities to determine when and if a child is likely to be competent to make decisions regarding him- or herself. Determinations regarding child competence are especially critical when a therapist questions whether or not a parent or guardian is acting in the best interest of the child.

Similar to limitations discussed with parental decision making about their child's participation in research, parents who are struggling with their own issues may be incapable of acting on behalf of their child with regard to seeking treatment. This situation becomes even more complicated, as a decision not to provide treatment may also have negative ramifications for a child. Moreover, if the parent is the primary reporter of child difficulties, and the therapist has no other sources of information regarding child functioning, then decisions on whether the provision of treatment is in the best interest of the child become even more difficult. A related but different ethical issue arises when a child seeks treatment without the knowledge of his or her parent or guardian. In cases such as this, the child may report being fearful of possible consequences if his or her parent learns that the child has sought help. Typically, legal standards suggest that only if a minor has been declared "emancipated" may treatment be offered without parental consent. However, if the therapist believes that a younger child is capable of providing consent for treatment and will be in jeopardy if the parent is notified, then very thorny ethical determinations arise. Similarly, therapists often must grapple with how to address parental decisions to stop treatment if the therapist and the child feel continued therapy is necessary. No simple answers are available to questions such as these, but seeking to factor information on child capabilities into the legal process with relation to consent for treatment and issues related to child emancipation could be helpful.

The issue of confidentiality also can be extremely difficult to resolve when conducting child therapy. From the perspective of the legal system, prior to the age of 18 parents possess the legal ability to make all privacy-related decisions for their children. Basically, from a legal standpoint, confidentiality in child therapy applies only if the parent grants permission for this. From a developmental perspective, however, very different issues are present. For example, can a child who is functioning at the preoperational stage of cognitive development truly believe that any adult, therapist or otherwise, can withhold information from an "omniscient" parent? If the child cannot understand the concept of confidentiality, then it may be meaningless to the therapeutic process. This issue may be confounded when the child knows that the therapist and parent have regular communications. In these cases, it may be unfathomable to the child that "secrets" are not being shared.

Even when a therapist seeks to clarify issues of confidentiality with parent and child, situations may arise when confidentiality no longer is possible. If the therapist is concerned about the welfare of the child, then confidentiality must be broken. Although optimally the therapist should discuss this possibility with the child initially, young children are unlikely to understand the issues involved with the maintenance or dismissal of confidentiality. Even if they cognitively have the capacity to understand when the issue is initially broached, it is most unlikely that children will remember the caveats associated with confidentiality if a situation arises when something shared during therapy must be revealed. When issues related to confidentiality arise during therapy, the child's cognitive capacities must be considered when determining how best to help the child understand the therapist's decision-making process.

Thus, as this discussion suggests, being knowledgeable about developmental constraints on child understanding is an important aspect of ethical decision making with respect to the treatment of children and adolescents. Although legal guidelines and ethical standards do not always mesh and may appear to be at cross-purposes at times, attention to the child's capacity to function in his or her own best interest can be extremely helpful in determining how to proceed in a given situation.

PERSPECTIVES ON TRAINING

When reflecting on what is known about the epidemiology, causes, course, and sequelae of child and adolescent mental disorders, the urgency of providing training that will foster the development of professionals who are prepared to meet the challenges of addressing disorders of childhood and adolescence becomes apparent. Given the preponderance and diversity of mental disorders across the life span, a critical mass of competently trained researchers and practitioners must be available if progress is to occur in the understanding and treatment of mental disorders. With respect to individuals trained to conduct developmentally informed research on mental illness, the availability of competent professionals is not keeping pace with demand (Cicchetti & Toth, 1991; Haviland, Pincus, & Dial, 1987; IOM, 1989; Pion, 1988). Moreover, training that incorporates a developmental focus into the preparation of child clinicians also is lacking.

In a survey of PhDs in clinical psychology conducted by the American Psychological Association (APA), Pion (1988) reported that half of doctoral recipients who responded to the survey spent none of their time engaged in research, 85% spent from zero to 20% of their time conducting research, and only 4% spent over 50% of their time carrying out scientific investigations. A similar scenario is apparent in psychiatry, where fewer than 5% of all medical students choose to specialize in psychiatry, and only 20% to 30% of those who do so want to enter the field of child psychiatry (Weissman & Bashook, 1986). Moreover, of those planning to specialize in psychiatry, only one third of graduating medical students professed an intent to engage in any research (Haviland et al., 1987). The majority (76.9%) of those with an interest in research wanted to be only "somewhat involved" or "involved in a limited way." Even more severe shortages exist for professionals trained to conduct research on psychopathology from a developmental perspective. Moreover, although it may be assumed that programs in clinical child psychology provide students with a solid grounding in developmental theory and its relevance for the provision of intervention services, we maintain that severe shortages of developmentally knowledgeable professionals also exist in the practice arena.

In accord with a developmental psychopathology perspective, it is critical that specialists be trained in methods of developmentally guided research that explore the interfaces among biological, psychological, and social aspects of functioning in conditions of psychopathology (Cicchetti & Toth, 1991). Similarly, individuals invested in focusing on the provision of treatment must learn to apply research knowledge to intervention strategies and to utilize knowledge derived from service provision to inform research programs on treatment efficacy. Although historically such a reciprocal approach was the goal of the majority of clinical psychology training programs, current trends in training and bifurcation between practitioners and researchers threaten to jeopardize mutually enhancing interchanges between research and practice. In view of increased scrutiny by policy analysts of intervention effectiveness and related decision making regarding reimbursable services, such a departure from an integrated approach to research and treatment of mental disorders may result in dire consequences. Before moving to a discussion of aspects of training that are important to the attainment of a developmentally informed approach, a review of historically relevant training in clinical psychology is informative.

Historical Perspectives on Training in Clinical Psychology

Academicians and clinicians have struggled with how best to meet the needs of students who have basic and applied research, as well as clinical interests. In particular, a great deal has been written about the education of clinical psychologists (e.g., Cattell, 1954; Korchin, 1983; McFall, 1991, 1996; Meehl, 1964, 1971, 1972, 1973; Raimy, 1950; Shaffer, 1947; Shakow, 1938, 1939, 1942).

Over half a century ago, David Shakow (1938, 1939, 1942) argued that diagnosis, research, and therapy should be the major responsibilities of clinical psychologists. Shakow also discussed the importance of a clinical internship and further argued that research opportunities should be an integral part of the internship (Shakow, 1942, 1946). Shakow supported the scientist-practitioner model that dominated much of the training of clinical psychologists for over two thirds of the discipline's 100-year history (Peterson, 1991).

However, subsequent to Shakow's articulation of his position on training, clinical psychology periodically has been depicted as a profession in search of an identity (e.g., Blank & David, 1963; Garfield & Kurtz, 1976; Kahn & Santostefano, 1962; Meehl, 1954, 1957, 1964, 1972, 1987; Peterson, 1976a, 1976b; Routh, 1994; and Tryon, 1963). In fact, several landmark conferences have been held in which the training of clinical psychologists has been debated and the goals of training have been formulated (Korman, 1976; Matarazzo, 1983; Peterson, 1985; Raimy, 1950; Strickland, 1988). Training in clinical psychology also was discussed at length during two national conferences, one in Miami (Roe, Gustad, Moore, Ross, & Skodak, 1959), and one in Salt Lake City (Bickman, 1987). Training issues related more specifically to clinical child psychology also were addressed during a 1985 conference at Hilton Head (Tuma, 1985).

The first major conference on training in clinical psychology occurred during August 1949 in Boulder, Colorado (Raimy, 1950). Societal factors related to the large number of World War II veterans in need of mental health services and the paucity of clinical psychologists able to address these needs served as the impetus for the conference. In accord with Shakow's position, the scientist-practitioner model of training was recommended. Subsequent conferences held at Stanford University in 1955 (Strother, 1956) and in Chicago in 1965 (Hoch, Ross, & Winder, 1966) reaffirmed a commitment to an integration of science and practice in the training of clinical psychologists. However, the Chicago conference also acknowledged the need for diversification in training and raised the possibility of implementing more practitioner-oriented training programs.

This possibility was first explored in 1964 when the APA formed an ad hoc committee on the Scientific and Professional Aims of Psychology. This committee, commonly referred to as the Clark Committee, proposed a two-track, practice-research (PsyD-PhD) system of training (APA, 1967). Despite the stature of the committee members, including Jerome Bruner, Paul Meehl, Carl Rogers, and Kenneth Spence, the ideas proposed by the Clark Committee fell largely on deaf ears. In the ensuing years, however, and in response to the need for clinically oriented psychologists, practitioner-oriented schools were established. The resultant diversity in clinical psychology was recognized and substantiated at a second conference on graduate education in Salt Lake City (Altman, 1987; Spence, 1987), where discipline unity and diversity were acknowledged as the critical issues facing psychology.

A consideration of important components of clinical training raises the role of developmental theory in education. Over 50 years ago, Robert Woodworth, an early leader in the field of clinical psychology, stated, "Increasing knowledge of child development will be one of the chief contributions of the science to the resources of clinical psychology" (1937, p. 4). Moreover, although issues specific to clinical child psychology were addressed at the Hilton Head conference, training in clinical child psychology has most often been viewed as an "add on" to an adult curriculum (Serafica & Wenar, in press). Consequently, providing clinical child psychology programs that are sufficiently grounded in developmental theory has been a rarity. This situation has been exacerbated by the APA's failure to recognize clinical child psychology as an independent specialty (Serafica & Wenar, in press). Thus, training in clinical child psychology has been plagued not only by the identity questions that have permeated the history of clinical psychology more generally, but also by issues unique to acquiring competence in child-related pursuits. When the goal of incorporating a truly developmental perspective into such training is added, it is not surprising that few exemplars exist. Although a more in-depth discussion of curricular considerations in the provision of such a model can be found in Cicchetti and Toth (1991) with respect to developmental psychopathology and in Serafica and Wenar (in press) with regard to applied developmental psychology, the following précis highlights issues important to a developmental psychopathology model of training.

Training in Developmental Psychopathology

Consistent with the objectives of unity, diversity, quality control, and responsivity to societal needs that emerged from the second conference on training at Salt Lake City, some modifications in traditional methods of training clinical psychologists are needed. We believe that a developmental psychopathology approach to training will be a necessary addition to attaining the goals articulated at the Utah conference. Moreover, a renewed commitment to fostering research in clinical programs is integral to furthering the development of clinical psychology. Although the application of a developmental psychopathology approach to training is an outgrowth of the Boulder model, we feel that the problems of the Boulder model can be attributed, at least in part, to the lack of an overarching conceptual framework to unify training. Thus, although similar in some respects to the Boulder model, a developmental psychopathology approach to training differs in important ways.

First and foremost, the utilization of the developmental approach as a unifying framework serves to add a critical dimension to clinical training programs. Typically, conventional scientist-practitioner programs have contained an adult focus, and various theoretical orientations may be incorporated into the program structure. Perhaps worse, a total absence of theory also may occur. Training in developmental psychopathology departs from this approach and, as a "macroparadigm" (Achenbach, 1990), provides a cohesive way of conceptualizing and organizing a wide array of phenomena. The life-span perspective advocated by developmental psychopathologists also departs from the more traditional "split" between training in adult versus child psychopathology. Rather, development is viewed as continuing from infancy through old age and, as such, the psychologist trained in this model must be knowledgeable regarding the entire range of development. Although certainly decisions to specialize in a certain age period may occur, that period must be conceptualized within the broader frame of development. This may serve to combat the status of child clinical training as secondary to adult training. For developmental psychopathology, both children and adults are given equal importance and the life-span view is considered to be integral to gaining competence, regardless of area of specialization.

In view of the paucity of researchers trained to address problems of clinical import, we also propose that training in developmental psychopathology emphasize the acquisition of research skills. Toward this end, we advocate the involvement of faculty from diverse scientific disciplines, all unified by a developmental perspective. From the inception of training, the development of scientific skills with regard to the conduct of research with clinical populations, as well as those at risk for the development of psychopathology, will be stressed. Although a developmental psychopathology approach to training emphasizes the importance of acquiring research skills, clinical training will not be neglected. Rather, such a perspective would urge students to carve out an area of research that is also of interest to them clinically. As such, the conduct of research and their clinical training could prove to be reciprocally informative and could serve as a model for subsequent professional endeavors.

As developmentalists, we believe that varied pathways to acquiring expertise as developmental psychopathologists are possible. Here, we focus on aspects of training at the graduate level. Because of issues related to credentialing, we advocate the inclusion of developmental psychopathology programs into departments offering doctoral degrees in clinical psychology. Ideally, such programs would be housed within a university that is sufficiently large to offer students exposure to a range of courses within psychology. Open access to departments outside psychology, such as biology and physiology, also is critical if students are to obtain sufficient breadth of knowledge. As a function of the developmental focus that must permeate all coursework, such a program also would require a strong department of developmental psychology and open relations between clinical and developmental psychology.

Beginning in the student's second year, we consider a placement in a clinical facility where therapy is provided to be an integral component of training in developmental psychopathology. Because, unlike applied developmental programs, developmental psychopathology is invested in grappling with and treating severe psychopathology, we believe learning to intervene with clinical populations is important to the student's growth and development. Additionally, because developmental psychopathologists are equally invested in understanding the relation between normality and abnormality, exposure to nondisordered and high-risk populations also is necessary. Regardless of subsequent decisions to focus on research or service provision, we strongly advocate for a strong combination of research and clinical training. Such an integration of research and clinical endeavors also is recommended during the internship year, as pure clinical placements may disrupt research pursuits and further convey that subsequent integrations of research and clinical pursuits are infeasible. Moreover, it is equally important that interns be exposed to role models who are successfully integrating clinical and research activities. If necessary, a 2-year internship might be optimal to achieve this integration. Thus, a program in developmental psychopathology would advocate the integration of research expertise with clinical skills. Within such a dual focus, students might be able to emphasize one area over the other as their future goals become more clear. However, under no circumstances do we believe that either aspect of training should be omitted. Therefore, we next address some more specific training issues with relevance to research and practice.

Training in Ethnic and Cultural Diversity

For more than two decades, nearly every conference on the education and training of professional psychologists has addressed the issue of cultural and ethnic diversity and has emphasized the importance of preparing all psychologists to function in a multicultural, multiracial, multiethnic society (cf., APA, 1987; Belar & Perry, 1991; Jones, 1985; Korman, 1974; Stricker et al., 1990). Nevertheless, because the majority of psychologists continue to be Caucasians who have been trained by predominantly Caucasian faculty members, ethnic issues have been largely ignored or included in training programs as an afterthought (Meyers, Echemendia, & Trimble, 1991). The failure to integrate racial/ethnic diversity and cultural pluralism into departments of psychology has resulted in a paucity of culturally sensitive research and theory (Highlen, 1994; Ivey, 1993; Yutrazenka, 1995). In fact, the majority of our knowledge of developmental psychopathology has been generated from research conducted in Western cultures (Spencer, in press; Weisz, Weiss, Alicke, & Klotz, 1997). Although useful, such research may fail to elucidate the diverse paths development may follow, the different factors that may contribute to dysfunction, or the varied definitions of abnormality that may be derived from different cultures (Weisz et al., 1997). Reliance on a monocultural database also might result in a blurring of the distinction between phenomena that are culture-specific and those that are culture-general (Draguns, 1982; Jackson, 1993; Ogbu, 1985). Thus, both researchers and practitioners need to be well grounded in issues of racial and ethnic diversity.

Ecological and cultural considerations have rarely been included in normative developmental theorizing or in designs of empirical research (Spencer & Dupree, 1996). These egregious omissions have threatened to result in a monocultural science, where theories and data are based on, and therefore relevant to, only the nonminority sectors of society. This is extremely disparate from the view held by developmental psychopathologists who consider cross-cultural perspectives and ethnic/racial diversity as an integral component of the discipline. Spencer and Dupree (1996) argues that consideration of how membership in a "favored" or "disfavored" group may impact on functioning can provide an opportunity for improved construction of developmental theories. Because members of minority groups grow up in milieus that differ dramatically from those most typically encountered by members of nonminority groups, the mechanisms that contribute to adaptive versus maladaptive outcome are likely to differ as well. Failure to address the unique contributions that research with non-Caucasian youth can make to theory development is a disservice, not only to children and families of color, but also to the field of psychology and mental health more generally (Cicchetti & Toth, in press).

Similarly, little work has been directed toward efforts to understand and apply culturally sensitive modes of intervention (Cicchetti & Toth, 1995). To be effective, interventions must incorporate knowledge of family cultural values (Toth & Cicchetti, 1993). Therefore, therapists must be trained in issues related to cultural diversity to be able to determine what is or is not normative for a given subculture. Moreover, an understanding of culturally specific value systems must be present if therapists are to be effective in developing and providing effective interventions.

Numerous models for incorporating ethnic and cultural diversity into training curricula have been developed over the past two decades (cf., Bluestone, Stokes, & Kuba, 1996; Yutrzenka, 1995). Our challenge is even more complex as it must reflect a developmental understanding of these differences. How then might training in developmental psychopathology proceed to ensure adequate knowledge of racial and ethnic diversity? To begin, programs must be committed to recruiting and retaining faculty of color. Toward this end, utilization of multicultural developmental models might be helpful (cf., Highlen, 1994). If multicultural individuals are not present on the core faculty, then, minimally, efforts must be made to have adjunct faculty available to provide culturally informed material. In a similar vein, recruitment of a culturally diverse student body is a necessary step. Additionally, faculty must be committed to incorporating research on minority populations into standard curricular coursework. When such research is unavailable for a given area, this needs to be addressed and the implications of the omission examined. With respect to research and clinical placements, students must acquire experience with minority populations. Students minimally should develop a research proposal to address cultural gaps in more mainstream theory and research. Ideally, at least some portion of clinical supervision should be provided by a culturally diverse supervisor.

Professional Training and Therapy Outcome

In considering aspects of training with special relevance to the practice arena, the link between training and psychotherapy outcome surfaces as an important issue. Despite the critical need to address psychotherapy outcome and elucidate variables that contribute to effectiveness, research to date has been limited and that which does exist has not been unequivocally supportive regarding the importance of professional training (typically defined as graduate training or postgraduate experience in a mental health discipline) to outcome (Beutler & Kendall, 1995). Reviews of research have, at times, concluded that there is little correlation between professional training and clinical efficacy (Beutler, Machado, & Neufeldt, 1994). However, because many studies of professional training and outcome have utilized oversimplified research designs, clear conclusions cannot be made about the relation between therapist training and therapy effectiveness. Failure to attend to differences in level of expertise and type of training as they relate to various treatment modalities or to address specific effects that might be attributable to different interventions and diverse disorders can result in inaccurate conclusions regarding the failure of therapist training and experience to contribute to positive therapy outcome (Beutler & Kendall, 1995). To date, the majority of information on the relation between therapist training and effectiveness has been garnered from more general therapy outcome studies.

In their classic meta-analysis of psychotherapy outcome studies, Smith and Glass (1977) found an overall effect size of -.01 between therapist experience and treatment outcome. The authors excuse this small effect size by questioning the reliability, or lack thereof, in their estimates of therapist experience. With respect to child therapy, Weisz et al. (1987) found a significant interaction between client age and therapist training. Professionals were found to be equally effective with all age groups of children, whereas graduate students and paraprofessionals were deemed to be more effective with younger clients. Differences based on training also emerged with respect to child presenting problem. Professionals were more effective in treating overcontrolled problems, whereas level of training was not related to effectiveness in treating problems of undercontrol (Weisz et al., 1987). Overall, recent reviews suggest that professional training enhances clinical effectiveness, especially if type of training, practice setting, and patient population are considered (Beutler & Kendall, 1995; Stein & Lambert, 1995).

It is much more difficult to look specifically at training in developmental psychopathology and to evaluate its role in treatment outcome. A glimmer of the importance of developmental considerations emerges from the Weisz et al. (1987) meta-analysis, where training seems to play a role in differential therapy effectiveness with older children. However, the paucity of clinical training programs grounded in developmental theory and their relatively recent ascendance precludes the availability of data linking training with effectiveness as a therapist. Despite this gap, it is possible to reflect on those components of training in developmental psychopathology that could be important in contributing to effectiveness as a child therapist. Issues related both to the meaning of child communication as a function of development and to the child's ability to process therapist communication exert a major influence on the child's utilization of and ability to benefit from psychotherapy (Shirk, 1988a; Shirk & Russell, 1996).

In conceptualizing child communications during therapy, it is critical to consider developmental differences in their understanding and subsequent communication of events. If a therapist is not familiar with developmentally changing conceptions of, for example, self-understanding (Damon & Hart, 1988; Harter, 1988), reconciliations of discrepant information with respect to person perception (Bierman, 1988), or attributions of causality (Shirk, 1988b), erroneous conclusions can be made about child play or verbal communication. Similarly, children's ability to extract meaningful content from therapist communication is constrained by their cognitive development. Shirk (1988b) discusses how therapist verbalizations that seek to link behavior or emotion to distal causes may exceed the school-age child's level of causal reasoning. In such instances, the therapeutic intervention is likely to be ineffective.

Although child psychotherapy outcome research typically has not considered developmental level of the child (Barrett, Hampe, & Miller, 1978; Shirk, 1988a; Shirk & Russell, 1996), conceptual links between cognitive development and therapeutic outcome have been made (Shirk, 1988a). A number of theorists consider cognitive-developmental level to act as a moderator of treatment effectiveness (cf., Harter, 1988; Kegan, 1982; Leahy, 1988; Shirk, 1988b; Shirk & Russell, 1996). Cognitive-developmental growth also has been conceptualized as a goal of intervention (Noam, 1992; Schorin & Hart, 1988) or as a way of promoting therapeutic growth across domains of development (Bierman, 1988; Schorin & Hart, 1988). Regardless of one's conceptual focus, sufficient knowledge of development and its role in the therapeutic process is likely to be a critical contributor to outcome in child therapy (cf., Shirk & Russell, 1996). It is encumbent on child clinical programs to incorporate a developmental psychopathology focus into their training strategies.

Training in Community Consultation and Policy Implementation

In addition to functioning in more traditional clinical and research settings, developmental psychopathologists also are in the position to contribute to real-world decision making. Research on issues such as the effects of day care on child development, children's memory and its relation to court testimony, and the attachment relationship and the impact of removal from parents all have benefited, or can profit from an influx of developmental knowledge into decision making. Because the nature of development must be considered to best determine appropriate interventions or actions for a given child, the training of a developmental psychopathologist can be invaluable to fostering subsequent roles in the social policy arena. However, unless individuals are knowledgeable about how to communicate effectively, information may fail to reach those responsible for policy formulation (Cicchetti & Toth, 1993). Therefore, we advocate training programs to provide students with research and clinical opportunities that interface with the social policy arena, and that thereby teach students how to communicate their findings effectively. Venturing into the policy arena carries with it a heavy social responsibility and an accompanying responsibility to consider the ramifications of the provision of information. Thus, training in the ethical dissemination of data is critical.

Training in Ethics

A final area of training, and one that all too often is neglected, pertains to ethics. As evident in our discussion of ethical issues, knowledge of child development is intimately related to determinations of how best to proceed when ethical dilemmas are encountered. Because cognitive and moral judgment mature over time, a continuum of child reasoning capability is present and must be considered when evaluating what is or is not in a child's best interest. An understanding of cognitive development must be factored into decisions such as whether a child can provide consent to participate in research or to refuse clinical treatment. We, therefore, strongly advocate that a course addressing ethical decision making from a developmental perspective be provided in developmental psychopathology training programs. Case vignettes and active student discussion would be important components of such a course (Sondheimer & Martucci, 1992).

Moreover, encouraging students to think about the ethics involved with disseminating research findings, and how best to make clear the developmental considerations that may limit findings for certain subgroups of children should be grappled with. For example, a great deal of research on child memory and its role in abuse cases has recently been used in court cases involving sexual abuse (Ceci & Bruck, 1993). Of concern, however, is that the majority of this work has been conducted with "normal" children who have not been exposed to trauma. One cannot assume that memory operates similarly in a child who has experienced trauma as it does in a normal child. In fact, some research has revealed processing differences between maltreated and nonmaltreated children (cf., Dodge et al., 1990; Rieder & Cicchetti, 1989; Rogosch et al., 1995). Moreover, traumatic experiences may affect brain structure, organization, and functioning, thereby resulting in very different perceptions and abilities as a result of history (Bremner et al., 1995; Cicchetti & Tucker, 1994; Perry et al., 1995; van der Kolk, 1987). Similarly, significant ethical responsibilities are associated with disseminating findings on the effects of parental depression on child development. Unless the *group* nature of data and their lack of applicability to individuals is stressed, depressed parents may be unnecessarily alarmed about the possible adverse effects of their depression on their children. Moreover, because studies often fail to assess the full range of factors that can buffer or exacerbate possible negative effects (e.g., supportive vs. absent spouse), the conveyance of partial explanations regarding parental depression and child outcome may be misleading to parents. Ethics training in developmental psychopathology must help students consider the implications of these issues.

INTEGRATIVE SUMMARY AND FUTURE DIRECTIONS

We have used a developmental psychopathology framework to organize theory and research on risk conditions and mental disorders of childhood and adolescence. The value of a developmental psychopathology perspective and of research conducted within this tradition for informing prevention and intervention efforts also has been addressed. Moreover, the role embodied by a developmental psychopathology approach for reducing the schisms between normality and abnormality, biology and psychology, and research and practice, and the value of increased integration among these areas for improving our understanding of risk conditions and mental disorders and of prevention and treatment efforts has been emphasized throughout the chapter. To realize its potential as an integrative perspective that can generate knowledge of relevance to child and adolescent psychopathology, we believe that the field of developmental psychopathology must continue to evolve. Toward this end, we articulate our perspectives on future challenges and necessary accomplishments for the field.

The field of developmental psychopathology must become increasingly interdisciplinary in nature. Because adequate assessments must be made of multiple domains of development, expertise in a broad range of assessment strategies and methodologies is required. The developmental considerations raised in this chapter make clear that progress toward a process-level understanding of high-risk conditions and psychopathology will require research designs that allow for the simultaneous consideration of multiple domains of variables within and outside the individual. For some questions, reference to variables measured in other domains is essential to clarify the role(s) of variables of interest. In other cases, variables from other domains are necessary to consider as competing explanations for hypothesized etiologic pathways. We believe that the most pressing and important research questions are those that can be answered only in the broader context of theoretically informed variables within and outside the individual, particularly as those variables change and influence one another over developmental time. Moreover, the organizational perspective, with its emphasis on understanding the differentiation, integration, and organization of biological and psychological development, and its focus on studying the whole person in context, will play an important role in framing the questions as we seek to explore the relations among environmental, psychological, and biological factors in the etiology, course, sequelae, and treatment of various high-risk conditions and mental disorders. Furthermore, the organizational framework possesses the integrative power to guide research on the interface between normality and pathology. The meaning of any one attribute, process, or psychopathological condition needs to be considered in light of the complex matrix of individual characteristics, experiences, and social-contextual influences involved, the timing of events and experiences, and the developmental history of the individual.

To help realize the exciting potential of the developmental psychopathology approach, future investigations must strive to attain enhanced fidelity between the elegance and complexity of our theoretical models and the measurement and data-analytic strategies employed in our studies (Richters, 1997). Likewise, because major variability exists within and across all psychological and biological domains, it is crucial to investigate the processes that underlie the individual differences. This attention to diversity in origins, processes, and outcomes in understanding developmental pathways does not suggest that prediction is futile as a result of the many potential individual patterns of adaptation (Sroufe, 1989). There are constraints on how much diversity is possible, and not all outcomes are equally likely (Cicchetti & Tucker, 1994; Sroufe et al., 1990). The existence of equifinality and multifinality in development requires that researchers increasingly should strive to demonstrate the multiplicity of processes and outcomes that may be articulated at the individual, person-oriented level as opposed to the prevailing variable-oriented strategies that dominate the field (cf., Bergman & Magnusson, 1997). Future endeavors must conceptualize and design research at the outset with these differential pathway concepts as a foundation (Cicchetti & Rogosch, 1996a). Doing so will help investigators in achieving the unique goals of developmental psychopathology—to explain the development of individual patterns of adaptation and maladaptation.

There also is a need for unbroken dialogue between developmental psychopathologists and developmentalists of all persuasions to prevent a premature compartmentalization of the issues that we must confront. Throughout history, a number of developmentalists have called for cross-fertilization of developmental psychology with other areas of psychology and with other disciplines (Cicchetti, 1990; Gottesman, 1974; Hinde, 1992). Moreover, recent national conferences on graduate training in applied developmental science have advocated an integration of perspectives from pertinent biological, social, and behavioral sciences (Fisher et al., 1993). Discussions of training in developmental psychopathology similarly have called for a broad-based, multi- and interdisciplinary approach (Cicchetti & Toth, 1991). Additionally, there is growing consensus on the importance of incorporating diversity in graduate training programs, including calls for cultural pluralism and racial/ethnic diversity. Much of the momentum of developmental psychopathology has stemmed from an openness to preexisting knowledge in combination with a willingness to question established theory, thereby continuing to promote growth. Furthermore, the integration of methods and concepts derived from areas of endeavor that are too often isolated from each other has resulted in knowledge gains that might have been missed in the absence of cross-disciplinary dialogue.

When considering the interface and mutually informing potential of research and practice, a number of recommendations for the future surface. Our knowledge of the hierarchical nature of development underscores the importance of providing *preventive* services as early as possible after a maladaptive or pathological process has been identified. Such an approach may help to avoid the emergence of more serious maladaptation. To provide a needed continuum of mental health care for children, Hoagwood and Koretz (1996) advocate the criticality of incorporating theoretically grounded preventive services into the service delivery system. Relatedly, rather than focusing exclusively on the *prevention* of *psychopathology,* increased attention must be directed toward the *promotion* of *wellness* (Cowen, 1994). Such a perspective can be most effective if it builds on knowledge of normal development to foster adaptive functioning. Lessons derived from resilience research also can inform preventive efforts.

Developmental considerations must be factored into the design and implementation of both prevention and intervention services. Similarly, evaluations of service efficacy must be increasingly conducted in actual clinical settings and such evaluations must be guided by developmental theory to assess adequately the impact of the intervention. Just as the concomitants of a risk or pathological process may vary as a result of the developmental period during which the event occurred, so too, may the effectiveness of therapy depend on the sensitivity of the approach to developmental considerations. The provision of therapy without attention to either the developmental impact of events or the child's capacity to utilize therapy is likely to be ineffective. It is critical that any effort to evaluate therapeutic outcome take issues related to the developmental appropriateness of intervention into account. Moreover, because research is increasingly demonstrating varied consequences of disorders at different periods of ontogenesis, the design and targeting of intervention toward the psychological and biological sequelae associated with specific developmental issues is a promising avenue to pursue.

When providing prevention and intervention services to high-risk populations or those with complex clinical problems, continuity of services assumes importance. Because such clients may manifest difficulties over time as a function of developmental transitions, the availability of accessible services, even if full-blown psychopathology has not surfaced, is indicated. Similarly, use of an ecological model wherein intervention is delivered within the child's natural environment (e.g., home, school) becomes important to service effectiveness (Olds & Henderson, 1989; Santos, Henggeler, Burns, Arana, & Meisler, 1995; Shonkoff & Meisels, 1990; Zigler, 1989). Program comprehensiveness, integration, and responsivity to the needs of the population all are important and require a departure from status quo systems of delivery of mental health services.

In a related vein, increased integration among mental health, special education, and social welfare systems must occur. Historically, the provision of services to children with mental disorders has been hampered by splintering among the assumption of responsibility for various areas of functioning. Because childhood psychopathology cuts across discrete areas typically associated with each system, an integrated program of intervention has not been developed. Therefore, rather than coalescing in the best interests of children, intervention efforts often work at cross-purposes. This lack of coordination is exacerbated by separate funding streams and difficulties associated with accessing services across areas. Parallel to approaches that treat various domains of development as separate entities (e.g., cognitive and emotional development), service systems tend to focus on discrete needs. To achieve a truly integrated approach to service delivery for disorders of childhood, sweeping change in the structure of the mental health, educational, and child welfare systems is needed.

A critical area in fostering improvements for the delivery of mental health services to children and adolescents is improved dissemination of research findings on childhood psychopathology and treatment outcome. Currently, the flow of information from the academic research arena into the policy forum is a trickle at best. Although a great deal of research in the area of childhood psychopathology possesses policy implications, far too little actually reaches the desks or chambers of those in positions to implement change. This failure is not a unidirectional occurrence, as researchers and formulators of policy are equally responsible for communication failure. Researchers too often conceive their questions without giving sufficient thought to the real-world issues with which child advocates are grappling. Once concluded, the results from many potentially informative investigations are buried in scientific, nonaccessible journals. Researchers must become increasingly skilled and interested in framing and disseminating their findings so that they can be incorporated into the policy arena. Similarly, efforts must be increased by child advocates to seek out information that may not be readily available to them. Simply stated, both researchers and child advocates must become increasingly invested in striving to learn from each other. The role of universities in this process cannot be minimized, as we believe that the philosophical orientation and value systems espoused by academic institutions can either promote or impede such community-academic interchanges.

Finally, social scientists who are invested in contributing to children's well-being must become more vocal and active advocates in the social policy arena. An interesting example of the reluctance of social scientists to enter the policy arena is the paucity of input that has occurred in relation to the United Nations Convention on the Rights of the Child (United Nations, 1989), and subsequent discussions about U.S. ratification of the treaty. Even in the absence of treaty ratification, the Convention poses important challenges for social scientists (Limber & Flekkoy, 1995). First, the Convention's emphasis on the best interest of the child and the child's sense of dignity requires scientists and practitioners to reevaluate how they interact with children in therapeutic, research, and educational settings. Second, the Convention challenges social scientists to use their expertise in helping to monitor compliance with the provisions of the treaty. The incorporation of knowledge derived from developmentally informed investigations is especially relevant in this regard. Third, social scientists may play important roles in helping children understand and express the rights granted to them under the Convention, and in providing input on how to teach children about their rights. The Convention on the Rights of the Child represents a significant human rights treaty that promises to improve the conditions affecting children worldwide (Limber & Flekkoy, 1995). Although ratification of the treaty within the United States faces strong political opposition, it is imperative that developmentalists recognize the unique contributions they can make to discussions about ratification.

As the field of developmental psychopathology ushers in its next era of scientific and clinical challenges, opportunities for fascinating collaborations on pressing theoretical, empirical, and social issues should abound as a consequence of enhanced sensitivity to the urgent sociopolitical issues of our time. We have not yet succeeded in educating society about the importance of research in the area of mental health. It is imperative that we become more effective at conveying the benefits that can be derived from developmentally informed research conducted with high-risk and mentally disordered populations.

We cannot lose sight of the importance of linking research with high-quality patient care. Because one of the goals of a developmental psychopathology perspective involves minimizing the schisms that typically occur between clinical practice and academic pursuits, we believe that researchers in this field should have exposure to a range of normal, high-risk, and psychopathological populations. This does not mean that all developmental psychopathologists must engage in the provision of therapy; however, it is essential for them to have firsthand experience with atypical populations (Cicchetti, 1993; IOM, 1989). Similarly, therapists need to be informed consumers of research in the area of psychopathology and developmental theory to meet the needs of patients most effectively.

In a relatively brief period, developmental psychopathologists have contributed significantly to our understanding of risk, disorder, and adaptation across the life course. Numerous challenges lie ahead, and we must have the courage to continue to critically examine the implicit as well as the explicit conceptual and scientific assumptions that exist in the fields of development and psychopathology to sustain our momentum and to foster new advances (Cicchetti & Richters, 1997). We believe that the continuation and elaboration of the mutually enriching interchanges that have occurred within and across disciplines interested in normal and abnormal development will enhance not only the science of developmental psychopathology, but also the benefits to be derived for society as a whole.

ACKNOWLEDGMENTS

This chapter is dedicated to the memory of Dr. Roland D. Ciaranello. His loss to his family, friends, and the field is great, but his work and spirit live on.

REFERENCES

Aber, J. L., & Allen, J. P. (1987). The effects of maltreatment on young children's socio-emotional development: An attachment theory perspective. *Developmental Psychology, 23,* 406–414.

Aber, J. L., & Zigler, E. (1981). Developmental considerations in defining child maltreatment. *New Directions for Child Development, 11,* 1–29.

Abramson, L. Y., Metalsky, G. I., & Alloy, L. B. (1989). The hopelessness theory of depression: Does the research test the theory? In L. Y. Abramson (Ed.), *Social cognition and clinical psychology: A synthesis* (pp. 33–65). New York: Guilford Press.

Abramson, L. Y., Seligman, M. E. P., & Teasdale, J. D., (1978). Learned helplessness in humans: Critique and reformulation. *Journal of Abnormal Psychology, 87,* 49–74.

Achenbach, T. M. (1990). What is "developmental" about developmental psychopathology? In J. Rolf, A. Masten, D. Cicchetti, K. Nuechterlein, & S. Weintraub (Eds.), *Risk and protective factors in the development of psychopathology* (pp. 29–48). New York: Cambridge University Press.

Achenbach, T. M. (1993). Taxonomy and comorbidity of conduct problems: Evidence from empirically based offenders. *Development and Psychopathology, 5,* 51–64.

Achenbach, T. M., & Edelbrock, C. S. (1981). Behavioral problems and competencies reported by parents of normal and disturbed children aged four through sixteen. *Monographs of the Society for Research in Child Development, 46*(188).

Achenbach, T. M., & Howell, C. T. (1993). Are America's children's problems getting worse? A 13-year comparison. *Journal of the American Academy of Child and Adolescent Psychiatry, 32,* 1145–1154.

Achenbach, T. M., Howell, C. T., McConaughy, S. H., & Stanger, C. (1995a). Six-year predictors of problems in a national sample of children and youth: II. Signs of disturbance. *Journal of the American Academy of Child and Adolescent Psychiatry, 34,* 488–669.

Achenbach, T. M., Howell, C. T., McConaughy, S. H., & Stanger, C. (1995b). Six-year predictors of problems in a national sample of children and youth: III. Transitions to young adult syndromes. *Journal of the American Academy of Child and Adolescent Psychiatry, 34,* 658–669.

Ainsworth, M. D. S., Blehar, M. C., Waters, E., & Wall, S. (1978). *Patterns of attachment: A psychological study of the Strange Situation.* Hillsdale, NJ: Erlbaum.

Akiskal, H. S., & McKinney, W. T. (1973). Depressive disorders: Toward a unified hypothesis. *Science, 162,* 20–29.

Akiskal, H. S., & McKinney, W. T. (1975). Overview of recent research in depression: Integration of ten conceptual models into a comprehensive clinical frame. *Archives of General Psychiatry, 32,* 285–305.

Alessandri, S. M. (1991). Play and social behaviors in maltreated preschoolers. *Development and Psychopathology, 3,* 191–206.

Alessandri, S. M., & Lewis, M. (1996). Development of the self-conscious emotions in maltreated children. In M. Lewis & M. Sullivan (Eds.), *Emotional development in atypical children* (pp. 185–201). Hillsdale, NJ: Erlbaum.

Alexander, P. C. (1992). Applications of attachment theory to the study of sexual abuse. *Journal of Consulting and Clinical Psychology, 60,* 185–195.

Alexander, P. C. (1993). The differential effects of abuse characteristics and attachment in the prediction of long term effects of sexual abuse. *Journal of Interpersonal Violence, 8,* 346–362.

Altman, I. (1987). Centripetal and centrifugal trends in psychology. *American Psychologist, 42,* 1058–1069.

American Psychiatric Association. (1994). *Diagnostic and statistical manual of mental disorders* (4th ed.). Washington, DC: Author.

American Psychological Association. (1987). Resolution approved by the National Conference on Graduate Education in Psychology. *American Psychologist, 12,* 1070–1084.

American Psychological Association. (1992). Ethical principles of psychologists and code of conduct. *American Psychologist, 47,* 1597–1611.

American Psychological Association, Committee on the Scientific and Professional Aims of Psychology. (1967). The scientific and professional aims of psychology. *American Psychologist, 22,* 49–76.

Antelman, S., & Caggiula, A. (1977). Norepinephrine-dopamine interactions and behavior. *Science, 195,* 646–651.

Armsden, G., McCauley, E., Greenberg, M., Burke, P., & Mitchell, J. (1990). Parent and peer attachment in early adolescent depression. *Journal of Abnormal Child Psychology, 18,* 683–697.

Arnold, L. E., Stoff, D. M., Cook, E., Cohen, D. J., Kruesi, M., Wright, C., Hattab, J., Graham, P., Zametkin, A., Castellanos, F. X., McMahon, W., & Leckman, J. F. (1995). Ethical issues in biological psychiatric research with children and adolescents. *Journal of the American Academy of Child and Adolescent Psychiatry, 34,* 929–939.

Azar, S. T., Robinson, D. R., Hekimian, E., & Twentyman, C. T. (1984). Unrealistic expectations and problem-solving ability in maltreating and comparison mothers. *Journal of Consulting and Clinical Psychology, 52,* 687–691.

Bailey, A., Phillips, W., & Rutter, M. (1996). Autism: Towards an integration of clinical, genetic, neuropsychological, and neurobiological perspectives. *Journal of Child Psychology and Psychiatry, 37,* 89–126.

Baldwin, A. F., Baldwin, C., & Cole, R. E. (1990). Stress-resistant families and stress-resistant children. In J. Rolf, A. S. Masten, D. Cicchetti, K. H. Nuechterlein, & S. Weintraub (Eds.), *Risk and protective factors in the development of psychopathology* (pp. 257–280). New York: Cambridge University Press.

Barkley, R. A., Fischer, M., Edelbrock, C. C., & Smallosh, L. (1990). The adolescent outcome of hyperactive children diagnosed by research criteria: I. An 8-year prospective follow-up study. *Journal of the American Academy of Child and Adolescent Psychiatry, 29,* 546–557.

Barnett, D., Manly, J. T., & Cicchetti, D. (1993). Defining child maltreatment: The interface between policy and research. In

D. Cicchetti & S. L. Toth (Eds.), *Child abuse, child development, and social policy* (pp. 7–73). Norwood, NJ: ABLEX.

Baron-Cohen, S. (1995). *Mindblindness.* Cambridge, MA: MIT Press.

Baron-Cohen, S., Tager-Flusberg, H., & Cohen, D. J. (Eds.). (1993). *Understanding other minds: Perspectives from autism.* New York: Oxford University Press.

Barrett, C. L., Hampe, I. E., & Miller, M. C. (1978). Research on child psychotherapy. In S. L. Garfield & A. E. Bergin (Eds.), *Handbook of psychotherapy and behavior change: An empirical analysis* (2nd ed., pp. 411–435). New York: Wiley.

Bates, J. E., & Bayles, K. (1988). Attachment and the development of behavior problems. In J. Belsky & T. Nezworski (Eds.), *Clinical implications of attachment* (pp. 253–297). Hillsdale, NJ: Erlbaum.

Bates, J. E., Maslin, C., & Frankel, K. (1985). Attachment security, mother-child interaction, and temperament as predictors of behavior problem ratings at age three years. In I. Bretherton & E. Waters (Eds.), Growing points in attachment theory. *Monographs of the Society for Research in Child Development, 50,* 167–193.

Bates, J. E., & Wachs, T. (Eds.). (1994). *Temperament: Individual differences at the interface of biology and behavior.* Washington, DC: American Psychological Association.

Bauer, W. D., & Twentyman, C. T. (1985). Abusing, neglectful, and comparison mothers' responses to child-related and non-child-related stressors. *Journal of Consulting and Clinical Psychology, 53,* 335–343.

Beardslee, W., & Podorefsky, M. (1988). Resilient adolescents whose parents have serious affective and other psychiatric disorders. Importance of self-understanding and relationships. *American Journal of Psychiatry, 145,* 63–69.

Beck, A. T. (1967). *Depression: Causes and treatment.* Philadelphia: University of Pennsylvania Press.

Beck, A. T. (1979). *Cognitive therapy and the emotional disorders.* New York & Searborough, Ontario: Times Mirror.

Beeghly, M., & Cicchetti, D. (1994). Child maltreatment, attachment and the self system: Emergence of an internal state lexicon in toddlers at high social risk. *Development and Psychopathology, 6,* 5–30.

Belar, C. D., & Perry, N. W. (Eds.). (1991). *Proceedings of the national conference on scientist-practitioner education and training for the professional practice of psychology.* Sarasota, FL: Professional Resource Exchange.

Bell, R. Q. (1986). Age-specific manifestations in changing psychosocial risk. In D. C. Farran & J. D. McKinney (Eds.), *The concept of risk in intellectual and psychosocial development.* New York: Academic Press.

Belsky, J. (1980). Child maltreatment: An ecological integration. *American Psychologist, 35,* 320–335.

Belsky, J. (1993). Etiology of child maltreatment: A developmental-ecological analysis. *Psychological Bulletin, 114,* 413–433.

Belsky, J., & Rovine, M. (1987). Temperament and attachment security in the strange situation: An empirical rapprochement. *Child Development, 58,* 787–795.

Belsky, J., & Vondra, J. (1989). Lessons from child abuse: The determinants of parenting. In D. Cicchetti & V. Carlson (Eds.), *Child maltreatment: Theory and research on the causes and consequences of child abuse and neglect* (pp. 153–202). New York: Cambridge University Press.

Benes, F., Turtle, M., Khan, Y., & Farol, P. (1994). Myelination of a key relay zone in the hippcampal formation occurs in the human brain during childhood, adolescence, and adulthood. *Archives of General Psychiatry, 51,* 477–484.

Bergman, L. R., & Magnusson, D. (1997). A person-oriented approach in research on developmental psychopathology. *Development and Psychopathology, 9,* 291–319.

von Bertalanffy, L. (1968). *General systems theory.* New York: Braziller.

Beutler, L., & Kendall, P. (1995). Introduction to the special section: The case for training in the provision of psychological therapy. *Journal of Consulting and Clinical Psychology, 63,* 179–181.

Beutler, L., Machado, P., & Neufeld, S. (1994). Therapist variables. In S. Garfield & A. Bergin (Eds.), *Handbook of psychotherapy and behavior change* (4th ed., pp. 259–269). New York: Wiley.

Beutler, L., Williams, R., Wakefield, P., & Entwistle, S. (1995). Bridging scientist and practitioner perspectives in clinical psychology. *American Psychologist, 50,* 984–994.

Bickman, L. (1987). Graduate education in psychology. *American Psychologist, 42,* 1041–1047.

Biederman, J., Faraone, S., Milberger, S., Curtis, S., Chen, L., Marrs, A., Ouellette, C., Moore, P., & Spencer, T. (1996). Predictors of persistence and remission of ADHD into adolescence: Results of a four-year prospective follow-up study. *Journal of the American Academy of Child and Adolescent Psychiatry, 35,* 343–351.

Biederman, J., Milberger, S., Faraone, S., Kiely, K., Guite, J., Mick, E., Ablon, S., Warburton, R., & Reed, E. (1995). Family-environment risk factors for attention-deficit hyperactivity disorder. *Archives of General Psychiatry, 52,* 464–470.

Bierman, K. L. (1988). The clinical implications of children's concepts of social relationships. In S. Shirk (Ed.), *Cognitive development and child psychotherapy* (pp. 247–272). New York: Plenum Press.

Bischof, N. (1975). A systems approach toward the functional connections of attachment and fear. *Child Development, 46,* 801–817.

Black, J., & Greenough, W. (1986). Induction of pattern in neural structure by experience: Implications for cognitive development. In M. Lamb, A. Brown, & B. Rogoff (Eds.), *Advances in developmental psychology* (Vol. 4, pp. 1–44). Hillsdale, NJ: Erlbaum.

Blank, L., & David, H. P. (1963). The crisis in clinical psychology training. *American Psychologist, 18,* 216–219.

Blatt, S. (1995). The destructiveness of perfectionism: Implications for the treatment of depression. *American Psychologist, 50,* 1003–1020.

Blatt, S., & Homann, E. (1992). Parent-child interaction in the etiology of dependent and self-critical depression. *Clinical Psychology Review, 12,* 47–91.

Bloom, F. (1993). Advancing a neurodevelopmental origin for schizophrenia. *Archives of General Psychiatry, 50,* 224–227.

Bluestone, H., Stokes, A., & Kuba, S. (1996). Toward an integrated program design: Evaluating the status of diversity training in a graduate school curriculum. *Professional Psychology: Research and Practice, 27,* 394–400.

Bolger, K., Patterson, C., Thompson, W., & Kupersmidt, J. (1995). Psychosocial adjustment among children experiencing persistent and intermittent family economic hardship. *Child Development, 66,* 1107–1129.

Borst, S. R., Noam, G. G., & Bartok, J. (1991). Adolescent suicidality: A clinical-developmental approach. *Journal of the American Academy of Child and Adolescent Psychiatry, 30,* 796–803.

Bowlby, J. (1951). *Maternal care and mental health* (WHO Monograph No. 2). Geneva: World Health Organization.

Bowlby, J. (1973). *Attachment and loss: Vol. 2. Separation.* New York: Basic Books.

Bowlby, J. (1980). *Attachment and loss: Loss, sadness, and depression.* New York: Basic Books.

Bowlby, J. (1982). *Attachment and loss* (Vol. 1). New York: Basic Books. (Original work published 1969)

Bremner, J. D., Randall, P., Scott, M., Bronen, R., Seibyl, J., Southwick, S., Delaney, R., McCarthy, G., Charney, D., & Innis, R. (1995). MRI-based measurement of hippocampal volume in patients with combat-related post traumatic stress disorder. *American Journal of Psychiatry, 152,* 973–981.

Breslin, N. A., & Weinberger, D. R. (1990). Schizophrenia and the normal development of the prefrontal cortex. *Development and Psychopathology, 2,* 409–424.

Bretherton, I., & Beeghly, M. (1982). Talking about internal states: The acquisition of an explicit theory of mind. *Developmental Psychology, 18,* 906–921.

Bronfenbrenner, U. (1977). Toward an experimental ecology of human development. *American Psychologist, 32,* 513–531.

Bronfenbrenner, U. (1979). *The ecology of human development: Experiments by nature and design.* Cambridge, MA: Harvard University Press.

Bronfenbrenner, U., & Ceci, S. (1994). Nature–nurture reconceptualization in developmental perspective: A bioecological model. *Psychological Review, 101,* 568–586.

Brown, G. W., Harris, T. O., & Bifulco, A. (1986). Long-term effects of early loss of parent. In M. Rutter, C. E. Izard, & P. B. Read (Eds.), *Depression in young people* (pp. 251–296). New York: Guilford Press.

Browne, A., & Finkelhor, D. (1986). Impact of child sexual abuse: A review of the literature. *Psychological Bulletin, 99,* 66–77.

Brunquell, D., Crichton, L., & Egeland, B. (1981). Maternal personality and attitude in disturbances of child-rearing. *American Journal of Orthopsychiatry, 51,* 680–691.

Bugental, D. B., Blue, J., & Cruzcosa, M. (1989). Perceived control over caregiving outcomes: Implications for child abuse. *Developmental Psychology, 25,* 532–539.

Bugental, D. B., Mantyla, S. M., & Lewis, J. (1989). Parental attributions as moderators of affective communication to children at risk for physical abuse. In D. Cicchetti & V. Carlson (Eds.), *Child maltreatment: Theory and research on the causes and consequences of child abuse and neglect* (pp. 254–279). New York: Cambridge University Press.

Burgess, R. L., & Conger, R. D. (1978). Family interaction in abusive, neglectful, and normal families. *Child Development, 49,* 1163–1173.

Cahan, E., & White, S. (1992). Proposals for a second psychology. *American Psychologist, 47,* 224–235.

Calverley, R., Fischer, K., & Ayoub, C. (1994). Complex splitting of self-representations in sexually abused adolescent girls. *Development and Psychopathology, 6,* 195–213.

Campbell, S. B. (1995). Behavior problems in preschool children: A review of recent research. *Journal of Child Psychology and Psychiatry, 36,* 113–149.

Campbell, S. B., Breaux, A. M., Ewing, L. J., & Szumowski, E. K. (1986). Correlates and predictors of hyperactivity and aggression: A longitudinal study of parent-referred problem preschoolers. *Journal of Abnormal Child Psychology, 14,* 217–234.

Campbell, S. B., Cohn, J., & Meyers, T. (1995). Depression in first-time mothers: Mother-infant interaction and depression chronicity. *Developmental Psychology, 31,* 349–357.

Campbell, S. B., & Ewing, L. J. (1990). Hard-to-manage preschoolers: Adjustment at age nine and predictors of continuing symptoms. *Journal of Child Psychology and Psychiatry, 31,* 871–889.

Camras, L., Sachs-Alter, E., & Ribordy, S. (1996). Emotion understanding in maltreated children: Recognition of facial expressions and integration with other emotion cues. In M. Lewis & M. Sullivan (Eds.), *Emotional development in atypical children* (pp. 203–225). Hillsdale, NJ: Erlbaum.

Cannon, T., Mednick, S., Parnas, J., Schulsinger, F., Praestholm, J., & Vestergaard, A. (1994). Developmental brain abnormalities in the offspring of schizophrenic mothers: II. Structural brain characteristics of schizophrenia and schizotypal personality disorder. *Archives of General Psychiatry, 51,* 955–962.

Carey, W. B. (1990). Temperament risk factors in children: A conference report. *Journal of Developmental and Behavioral Pediatrics, 11,* 28–34.

Carlson, C., Tharinger, D., Bricklin, P., DeMers, S., & Paavola, J. (1996). Health care reform and psychological practice in schools. *Professional Psychology: Research and Practice, 27,* 14–23.

Carlson, E. A., Jacobvitz, D., & Sroufe, L. A. (1995). A developmental investigation of inattentiveness and hyperactivity. *Child Development, 66,* 37–54.

Carlson, G. (1995). The report card: Progress report or final grade? *Archives of General Psychiatry, 52,* 724–726.

Carlson, M., Dragomir, C., Earls, F., Farrell, M., Macovei, O., Nystrom, P., & Sparling, J. (in press). Effects of social deprivation on cortisol regulation in institutionalized Romanian infants. *Society of Neuroscience Abstracts.*

Carlson, V., Cicchetti, D., Barnett, D., & Braunwald, K. (1989). Disorganized/disoriented attachment relationships in maltreated infants. *Developmental Psychology, 25,* 525–531.

Carnap, R. (1936). Testability and meaning. *Philosophy of Science, 3,* 420–471.

Carnegie Task Force on Meeting the Needs of Young Children. (1994). *Starting points: Meeting the needs of our youngest children.* New York: Carnegie Corporation.

Caspi, A., & Moffitt, T. E. (1995). The continuity of maladaptive behavior: From description to understanding in the study of antisocial behavior. In D. Cicchetti & D. Cohen (Eds.), *Developmental psychopathology: Vol. 2. Risk, disorder, and adaptation* (pp. 472–511). New York: Wiley.

Castellanos, F. X., Giedd, J., Eckburgh, P., Marsh, W., Vaituzis, A. C., Kaysen, D., Hamburger, S., & Rapoport, J. (1994). Quantitative morphology of the caudate nucleus in attention deficit hyperactivity disorder. *American Journal of Psychiatry, 151,* 1791–1796.

Cattell, R. (1954). The meaning of clinical psychology. In L. A. Pennington & I. A. Berg (Eds.), *An introduction to clinical psychology* (pp. 3–25). New York: Ronald.

Ceci, S. J., & Bruck, M. (1993). Suggestibility of the child witness: A historical review and synthesis. *Psychological Bulletin, 113,* 403–439.

Chandler, M. (1994). Adolescent suicide and the loss of personal continuity. In D. Cicchetti & S. L. Toth (Eds.), *Rochester Symposium on Developmental Psychopathology: Vol. 5. Disorders and dysfunctions of the self* (pp. 371–390). Rochester, NY: University of Rochester Press.

Chisholm, K., Carter, M., Ames, E., & Morison, S. (1995). Attachment security and indiscriminately friendly behavior in children adopted from Romanian orphanages. *Development and Psychopathology, 7,* 283–294.

Chomsky, N. (1968). *Language and mind.* New York: Harcourt Brace Jovanovich.

Ciaranello, R., Aimi, J., Dean, R., Morilak, D., Porteus, M., & Cicchetti, D. (1995). Fundamentals of molecular neurobiology. In D. Cicchetti & D. Cohen (Eds.), *Developmental psychopathology: Vol. 1. Theory and methods* (pp. 109–160). New York: Wiley.

Cicchetti, D. (1984). The emergence of developmental psychopathology. *Child Development, 55,* 1–7.

Cicchetti, D. (1989). How research on child maltreatment has informed the study of child development: Perspectives from developmental psychopathology. In D. Cicchetti & V. Carlson (Eds.), *Child maltreatment: Theory and research on the causes and consequences of child abuse and neglect* (pp. 377–431). New York: Cambridge University Press.

Cicchetti, D. (1990). An historical perspective on the discipline of developmental psychopathology. In J. Rolf, A. Masten, D. Cicchetti, K. Nuechterlein, & S. Weintraub (Eds.), *Risk and protective factors in the development of psychopathology* (pp. 2–28). New York: Cambridge University Press.

Cicchetti, D. (1993). Developmental psychopathology: Reactions, reflections, projections. *Developmental Review, 13,* 471–502.

Cicchetti, D. (1996a, August). *A developmental psychopathology perspective on drug abuse.* Invited address, American Psychological Association, Toronto, Ontario.

Cicchetti, D. (1996b). Child maltreatment: Implications for developmental theory. *Human Development, 39,* 1–17.

Cicchetti, D. (in press). *Emotion, early experience, and brain: Illustration from the developmental psychopathology of child maltreatment. Advancing research on developmental plasticity: The interaction of behavioral sciences and neuroscience.* Rockville, MD: National Institute of Mental Health.

Cicchetti, D., & Aber, J. L. (1986). Early precursors to later depression: An organizational perspective. In L. Lipsitt & C. Rovee-Collier (Eds.), *Advances in infancy* (Vol. 4, pp. 81–137). Norwood, NJ: ABLEX.

Cicchetti, D., & Barnett, D. (1991a). Attachment organization in preschool aged maltreated children. *Development and Psychopathology, 3,* 397–411.

Cicchetti, D., & Barnett, D. (1991b). Toward the development of a scientific nosology of child maltreatment. In D. Cicchetti & W. Grove (Eds.), *Thinking clearly about psychology: Essays in honor of Paul E. Meehl* (pp. 346–377). Minneapolis: University of Minnesota Press.

Cicchetti, D., & Beeghly, M. (Eds.). (1990). *Children with Down syndrome: A developmental perspective.* New York: Cambridge University Press.

Cicchetti, D., & Carlson, V. (Eds.). (1989). *Child maltreatment: Theory and research on the causes and consequences of child abuse and neglect.* New York: Cambridge University Press.

Cicchetti, D., & Cohen, D. (Eds.). (1995a). *Developmental psychopathology: Vol. 1. Theory and methods. Vol. 2. Risk, disorder, and adaptation.* New York: Wiley.

Cicchetti, D., & Cohen, D. (1995b). Perspectives on developmental psychopathology. In D. Cicchetti & D. Cohen (Eds.), *Developmental psychopathology: Vol. 1. Theory and method* (pp. 3–20). New York: Wiley.

Cicchetti, D., Ganiban, J., & Barnett, D. (1991). Contributions from the Study of high risk populations to understanding the development of emotion regulation. In K. Dodge & J. Garber (Eds.), *The development of emotion regulation* (pp. 15–48). New York: Cambridge University Press.

Cicchetti, D., & Garmezy, N. (Eds.). (1993). Milestones in the development of resilience [Special issue]. *Development and Psychopathology, 5*(4), 497–774.

Cicchetti, D., & Howes, P. (1991). Developmental psychopathology in the context of the family: Illustrations from the study of child maltreatment. *Canadian Journal of Behavioural Science, 23,* 257–281.

Cicchetti, D., & Lynch, M. (1993). Toward an ecological/transactional model of community violence and child maltreatment: Consequences for children's development. *Psychiatry, 56,* 96–118.

Cicchetti, D., Lynch, M., Shonk, S., & Manly, J. (1992). An organizational perspective on peer relations in maltreated children. In R. D. Parke & G. W. Ladd (Eds.), *Family-peer relationships: Modes of linkage* (pp. 345–383). Hillsdale, NJ: Erlbaum.

Cicchetti, D., & Pogge-Hesse, P. (1982). Possible contributions of the study of organically retarded persons to developmental theory. In E. Zigler & D. Balla (Eds.), *Mental retardation: The developmental-difference controversy* (pp. 277–318). Hillsdale, NJ: Erlbaum.

Cicchetti, D., & Richters, J. (1993). Developmental considerations in the investigation of conduct disorder. *Development and Psychopathology, 5,* 331–344.

Cicchetti, D., & Richters, J. (Eds.). (1997). The conceptual and scientific underpinnings of research in developmental psychopathology [Special issue]. *Development and Psychopathology, 9*(2), 189–471.

Cicchetti, D., & Rizley, R. (1981). Developmental perspectives on the etiology, intergenerational transmission, and sequelae of child maltreatment. *New Directions for Child Development, 11,* 31–55.

Cicchetti, D., & Rogosch, F. (Eds.). (1996a). Developmental pathways [Special issue]. *Development and Psychopathology, 8*(4), 597–896.

Cicchetti, D., & Rogosch, F. (1996b). Equifinality and multifinality in developmental psychopathology. *Development and Psychopathology, 8,* 597–600.

Cicchetti, D., Rogosch, F., Lynch, M., & Holt, K. (1993). Resilience in maltreated children: Processes leading to adaptive outcome. *Development and Psychopathology, 5,* 629–647.

Cicchetti, D., & Schneider-Rosen, K. (1986). An organizational approach to childhood depression. In M. Rutter, C. Izard, & P. Read (Eds.), *Depression in young people, clinical and developmental perspectives* (pp. 71–134). New York: Guilford Press.

Cicchetti, D., & Serafica, F. (1981). The interplay among behavioral systems: Illustrations from the study of attachment, affiliation and manners in young Down syndrome children. *Developmental Psychology, 17,* 36–49.

Cicchetti, D., & Sroufe, L. A. (1978). An organizational view of affect: Illustration from the study of Down's syndrome infants. In M. Lewis & L. Rosenblum (Eds.), *The development of affect* (pp. 309–350). New York: Plenum Press.

Cicchetti, D., & Toth, S. L. (1991). The making of a developmental psychopathologist. In J. Cantor, C. Spiker, & L. Lipsitt (Eds.), *Child behavior and development: Training for university* (pp. 34–72). Norwood, NJ: ABLEX.

Cicchetti, D., & Toth, S. L. (1992a). *Introduction. Rochester Symposium on Developmental Psychopathology: Vol. 4. Developmental perspectives on depression.* Rochester, NY: University of Rochester Press.

Cicchetti, D., & Toth, S. L. (1992b). The role of developmental theory in prevention and intervention. *Development and Psychopathology, 4,* 489–494.

Cicchetti, D., & Toth, S. L. (Eds.). (1993). *Child abuse, child development, and social policy.* Norwood, NJ: ABLEX.

Cicchetti, D., & Toth, S. L. (1995). Child maltreatment and attachment organization: Implications for intervention. In S. Goldberg, R. Muir, & J. Kerr (Eds.), *Attachment theory: Social, developmental, and clinical perspectives* (pp. 279–308). Hillsdale, NJ: Analytic Press.

Cicchetti, D., & Toth, S. L. (in press). Child maltreatment in African American families: Risk and resilience. In J. Fray & J. King (Eds.), *Psychosocial and physiological dimensions of Black child development.* Hillsdale, NJ: Erlbaum.

Cicchetti, D., Toth, S. L., & Bush, M. (1988). Developmental psychopathology and incompetence in childhood: Suggestions for intervention. In B. Lahey & A. Kazdin (Eds.), *Advances in clinical child psychology* (Vol. 11, pp. 1–71). New York: Plenum Press.

Cicchetti, D., Toth, S. L., & Hennessy, K. (1993). Child maltreatment and school adaptation: Problems and promises. In

D. Cicchetti & S. L. Toth (Eds.), *Child abuse, child development, and social policy* (pp. 301–330). Norwood, NJ: ABLEX.

Cicchetti, D., Toth, S. L., & Lynch, M. (1995). Bowlby's dream comes full circle: The application of attachment theory to risk and psychopathology. In T. Ollendick & R. Prinz (Eds.), *Advances in clinical child psychology* (Vol. 17, pp. 1–75). New York: Plenum Press.

Cicchetti, D., & Tucker, D. (1994). Development and self-regulatory structures of the mind. *Development and Psychopathology, 6,* 533–549.

Clark, R. M. (1983). *Family life and school achievement: Why poor Black children succeed or fail.* Chicago: University of Chicago Press.

Cohen, P., Cohen, J., & Brook, J. (1993). An epidemiological study of disorders in late childhood and adolescence: 2. Persistence of disorders. *Journal of Child Psychology and Psychiatry, 34,* 869–877.

Cohn, J., Matias, R., Tronick, E., Connell, D., & Lyons-Ruth, K. (1986). Face-to-face interactions of depressed mothers and their infants. *New Directions for Child Development, 34,* 31–45.

Cohn, J., & Tronick, E. (1983). Three-month-old infants' reaction to simulated maternal depression. *Child Development, 54,* 185–193.

Coie, J. D., & Jacobs, M. R. (1993). The role of social context in the prevention of conduct disorder. *Development and Psychopathology, 5,* 263–275.

Cole, P., & Putnam, F. (1992). Effect of incest on self and social functioning: A developmental psychopathology perspective. *Journal of Clinical and Consulting Psychology, 60,* 174–184.

Comer, J. P. (1980). *School power.* New York: Free Press.

Conrad, M., & Hammen, C. (1989). Role of maternal depression in perceptions of child maladjustment. *Journal of Consulting, and Clinical Psychology, 57,* 663–667.

Conrad, M., & Hammen, C. (1993). Protective and resource factors in high- and low-risk children: A comparison of children with unipolar, bipolar, medically ill, and normal mothers. *Development and Psychopathology, 5,* 593–607.

Costello, E. J., & Angold, A. (1995). Developmental epidemiology. In D. Cicchetti & D. Cohen (Eds.), *Developmental psychopathology: Vol. 1. Theory and method* (pp. 23–56). New York: Wiley.

Costello, E. J., Stouthamer-Loeber, M., & DeRosier, M. (1993, February). *Continuity and change in psychopathology from childhood to adolescence.* Paper presented at the annual meeting of the Society for Research in Child and Adolescent Psychopathology, Santa Fe, NM.

Coulton, C., Korbin, J., Su, M., & Chow, J. (1995). Community level factors and child maltreatment rates. *Child Development, 66,* 1262–1276.

Courchesne, E., Townsend, J., & Chase, C. (1995). Neurodevelopmental principles guide research on developmental psychopathologies. In D. Cicchetti & D. Cohen (Eds.), *Developmental psychopathology: Vol. 1. Theory and methods* (pp. 195–226). New York: Wiley.

Cowen, E. L. (1994). The enhancement of psychological wellness. *American Journal of Community Psychology, 22,* 149–179.

Coyne, J. C. (1976). Toward an interactional description of depression. *Psychiatry, 39,* 28–40.

Coyne, J. C., Kessler, R., Tal, M., Turnball, J., Worthman, C., & Greden, J. (1987). Living with a depressed person: Burden and psychological distress. *Journal of Consulting and Clinical Psychology, 55,* 347–352.

Crittenden, P. M. (1981). Abusing, neglecting, problematic, and adequate dyads: Differentiating by patterns of interaction. *Merrill-Palmer Quarterly, 27,* 201–218.

Crittenden, P. M. (1985). Maltreated infants: Vulnerability and resilience. *Journal of Child Psychology and Psychiatry and Allied Disciplines, 26,* 85–96.

Crittenden, P. M. (1988). Relationships at risk. In J. Belsky & T. Nezworski (Eds.), *Clinical implications of attachment theory* (pp. 136–174). Hillsdale, NJ: Erlbaum.

Crittenden, P. M., & Ainsworth, M. D. S. (1989). Attachment and child abuse. In D. Cicchetti & V. Carlson (Eds.), *Child maltreatment: Theory and research on the causes and consequences of child abuse and neglect* (pp. 432–463). New York: Cambridge University Press.

Crittenden, P. M., & DiLalla, D. (1988). Compulsive compliance: The development of an inhibitory coping strategy in infancy. *Journal of Abnormal Child Psychology, 16,* 585–599.

Crittenden, P. M., Partridge, M. F., & Claussen, A. H. (1991). Family patterns of relationship in normative and dysfunctional families. *Development and Psychopathology, 3,* 491–512.

Cummings, E. M., & Cicchetti, D. (1990). Attachment, depression, and the transmission of depression. In M. T. Greenberg, D. Cicchetti, & E. M. Cummings (Eds.), *Attachment during the preschool years* (pp. 339–372). Chicago: University of Chicago Press.

Cummings, E. M., & Davies, P. T. (1994). Maternal depression and child development. *Journal of Child Psychology and Psychiatry and Allied Disciplines, 35,* 73–112.

Cummings, E. M., Hennessy, K., Rabideau, G., & Cicchetti, D. (1994). Responses of physically abused boys to interadult anger involving their mothers. *Development and Psychopathology, 6,* 31–42.

Dahl, R. (1996). The regulation of sleep and arousal: Development and psychopathology. *Development and Psychopathology, 7,* 3–27.

Dahl, R., & Ryan, N. (1996). The psychobiology of adolescent depression. In D. Cicchetti & S. L. Toth (Eds.), *Rochester Sympo-*

sium on Developmental Psychopathology: Vol. 7. Adolescence: Opportunities and challenges (pp. 197–232). Rochester, NY: University of Rochester Press.

Damon, W., & Hart, D. (1982). The development of self-understanding from infancy through adolescence. *Child Development, 53,* 841–864.

Damon, W., & Hart, D. (1988). *Self-understanding in childhood and adolescence.* New York: Cambridge University Press.

Davidson, R. (1991). Cerebral asymmetry and affective disorders: A developmental perspective. In D. Cicchetti & S. L. Toth (Eds.), *Rochester Symposium on Developmental Psychopathology: Vol. 2. Internalizing and externalizing expressions of dysfunction* (pp. 123–154). Hillsdale, NJ: Erlbaum.

Dawson, G., Grofer Klinger, L., Panagiotides, H., Hill, D., & Spieker, S. (1992). Frontal lobe activity and affective behavior of infants of mothers with depressive symptoms. *Child Development, 63,* 725–737.

Dawson, G., Grofer Klinger, L., Panagiotides, H., Spieker, S., & Frey, K. (1992). Infants of mothers with depressive symptoms: Electroencephalographic and behavioral findings related to attachment status. *Development and Psychopathology, 4,* 67–80.

DeBellis, M. D., Chrousos, G. P., Dorn, L. D., Burks, L., Helmers, K., Kling, M. A., Trickett, P., & Putnam, F. W. (1994). Adrenal axis dysregulation in sexually abused girls. *Journal of Clinical Endocrinology and Metabolism, 78,* 249–255.

Deci, E. L. (1975). *Intrinsic motivation.* New York: Plenum Press.

DeMulder, E., Tarullo, L., Klimes-Dougan, B., Free, K., & Radke-Yarrow, M. (1995). Personality disorders of affectively ill mothers: Links to maternal behavior. *Journal of Personality Disorders, 9,* 199–212.

Department of Health and Human Services. (1983, March 8). *Protection of human subjects* (45 C.F.R. 46). Washington, DC: Department of Health and Human Services.

Derryberry, D., & Rothbart, M. (1984). Emotion, attention, and temperament. In C. E. Izard, J. Kagan, & R. Zajonc (Eds.), *Emotions, cognition, and behavior* (pp. 132–166). New York: Cambridge University Press.

DiLalla, D., & Gottesman, I. (1995). Normal personality characteristics in identical twins discordant for schizophrenia. *Journal of Abnormal Psychology, 104,* 490–499.

Dinwiddie, S., & Buchholz, K. (1993). Psychiatric diagnoses of self-reported child abuses. *Child Abuse and Neglect, 17,* 465–476.

Dix, T. (1991). The affective organization of parenting: Adaptive and maladaptive processes. *Psychological Bulletin, 110,* 3–25.

Dix, T., & Grusec, J. E. (1985). Parent attribution processes in the socialization of children. In I. E. Sigel (Ed.), *Parental belief systems* (pp. 201–234). Hillsdale, NJ: Erlbaum.

Dodge, K. A. (1993). Social-cognitive mechanisms in the development of conduct disorder and depression. *Annual Review of Psychology, 44,* 559–584.

Dodge, K. A., Pettit, G. S., & Bates, J. E. (1990). Mechanisms in the cycle of violence. *Science, 250,* 1678–1683.

Downey, G., & Coyne, J. C. (1990). Children of depressed parents: An integrative review. *Psychological Bulletin, 108,* 50–76.

Dozier, M. (1990). Attachment organization and treatment use for adults with serious psychopathological disorders. *Development and Psychopathology, 2,* 47–60.

Draguns, J. G. (1982). Methodology in cross-cultural psychology. In I. Alissa (Ed.), *Culture and psychopathology* (pp. 33–70). Baltimore: University Park Press.

Duncan, G. J., & Brooks-Gunn, J. (1994). Economic deprivation and early childhood development. *Child Development, 99,* 353–395.

Earls, F. (1979). Epidemiology and child psychiatry: Historical and conceptual development. *Comprehensive Psychiatry, 20,* 256–269.

Earls, F. (1980a). Epidemiological child psychiatry: An American perspective. In E. F. Purcell (Ed.), *Psychopathology of children and youth: A cross-cultural perspective.* New York: Macy Foundation.

Earls, F. (1980b). Prevalence of behavior problems in 3-year-old children: A cross-national replication. *Archives of General Psychiatry, 37,* 1153–1157.

Easterbrooks, M. A., Davidson, C., & Chazan, R. (1993). Psychosocial risk, attachment, and behavior problems among school-aged children. *Development and Psychopathology, 5,* 389–402.

Eckenrode, J., Laird, M., & Doris, J. (1993). School performance and disciplinary problems among abused and neglected children. *Developmental Psychology, 29,* 53–62.

Edelman, G. (1987). *Neural Darwinism.* New York: Basic Books.

Egami, Y., Ford, D., Greenfield, S., & Crum, R. (1996). Psychiatric profile and sociodemographic characteristics of adults who report physically abusing or neglecting children. *American Journal of Psychiatry, 153,* 921–928.

Egeland, B., Carlson, E., & Sroufe, L. A. (1993). Resilience as process. *Development and Psychopathology, 5,* 517–528.

Egeland, B., & Erickson, M. F. (1990). Rising above the past: Strategies for helping new mothers break the cycle of abuse and neglect. *Zero to Three, 11,* 29–35.

Egeland, B., Jacobvitz, D., & Sroufe, L. A. (1988). Breaking the cycle of abuse. *New Directions for Child Development, 11,* 77–92.

Egeland, B., Kalkoske, M., Gottesman, N., & Erickson, M. F. (1990). Preschool behavior problems: Stability and factors accounting for change. *Journal of Child Psychology and Psychiatry, 31,* 891–909.

Egeland, B., & Sroufe, L. A. (1981). Developmental sequelae of maltreatment in infancy. *New Directions for Child Development, 11,* 77–92.

Egeland, B., Sroufe, L. A., & Erickson, M. F. (1983). Developmental consequence of different patterns of maltreatment. *Child Abuse and Neglect, 7,* 459–469.

Eisenberg, L. (1995). The social construction of the human brain. *American Journal of Psychiatry, 152,* 1563–1575.

Elder, G. (1974). *Children of the Great Depression.* Chicago: University of Chicago Press.

Emde, R. N., Gaensbauer, T., & Harmon, R. (1976). *Emotional expression in infancy: A biobehavioral study.* New York: International Universities Press.

Emery, R., Weintraub, S., & Neale, J. (1982). Effects of marital discord on the school behavior of children of schizophrenic, affective disordered, and normal parents. *Journal of Abnormal Child Psychology, 16,* 215–225.

Epstein, H. (1979). *Children of the Holocaust.* New York: Penguin Books.

Erickson, M., Egeland, B., & Pianta, R. (1989). The effects of maltreatment on the development of young children. In D. Cicchetti & V. Carlson (Eds.), *Child maltreatment: Theory and research on the causes and consequences of child abuse and neglect* (pp. 647–684). New York: Cambridge University Press.

Erickson, M. F., Korfmacher, J., & Egeland, B. (1992). Attachments past and present: Implications for therapeutic intervention with mother-infancy dyads. *Development and Psychopathology, 4,* 495–507.

Famularo, R., Kinscherff, R., & Fenton, T. (1992). Psychiatric diagnoses of maltreated children: Preliminary findings. *Journal of the American Academy of Child and Adolescent Psychiatry, 31,* 863–867.

Fantuzzo, J. W., & Holland, A. (1992). Resilient peer training: Systematic investigation of a treatment to improve the social effectiveness of child victims of maltreatment. In A. W. Burgess (Ed.), *Child trauma: I. Issues and research.* New York: Garland.

Fantuzzo, J. W., Jurecic, L., Stovall, A., Hightower, D. A., Goins, C., & Schachtel, D. (1988). Effects of adult and peer initiations on the social behavior of withdrawn, maltreated preschool children. *Journal of Consulting and Clinical Psychology, 56,* 34–39.

Fassler, D. (1992). Ethical issues in child and adolescent psychiatry. *Journal of the American Academy of Child and Adolescent Psychiatry, 31,* 392.

Feldman, S., & Downey, G. (1994). Rejection sensitivity as a mediator of the impact of childhood exposure to family violence on adult attachment behavior. *Development and Psychopathology, 6,* 231–247.

Fendrich, M., Warner, V., & Weissman, M. M. (1990). Family risk factors, parental depression, and psychopathology in offspring. *Developmental Psychology, 26,* 40–50.

Ferdinand, R. F., Verhulst, F. C., & Wiznitzer, M. (1995). Continuity and change of self-reported problem behaviors from adolescence into young adulthood. *Journal of the American Academy of Child and Adolescence Psychiatry, 34,* 680–690.

Feshbach, N. D. (1989). The construct of empathy and the phenomenon of physical maltreatment of children. In D. Cicchetti & V. Carlson (Eds.), *Child maltreatment: Theory and research on the causes and consequences of child abuse and neglect* (pp. 349–373). New York: Cambridge University Press.

Festinger, T. (1983). *No one ever asked us.* New York: Columbia University Press.

Field, T. M. (1984). Early interactions between infants and their post-partum depressed mothers. *Infant Behavior and Development, 7,* 517–522.

Field, T. M. (1989). Maternal depression effects on infant interaction and attachment behavior. In D. Cicchetti (Ed.), *Rochester Symposium on Developmental Psychopathology: Vol. 1. The emergence of a discipline* (pp. 139–163). Hillsdale, NJ: Erlbaum.

Field, T. M., Fox, N., Pickens, J., & Nawrocki, T. (1995). Relative right frontal EEG activation in 3- to 6-month old infants of "depressed" mothers. *Developmental Psychology, 31,* 358–363.

Field, T. M., Healy, B., Goldstein, S., & Guthertz, M. (1990). Behavior-state matching and synchrony in mother-infant interactions of nondepressed versus depressed dyads. *Developmental Psychology, 26,* 7–14.

Field, T. M., Healy, B., Goldstein, S., Perry, S., Bendell, D., Schanberg, S., Zimmerman, E., & Kuhn, C. (1988). Infants of depressed mothers show "depressed" behavior even with nondepressed adults. *Child Development, 59,* 1569–1579.

Field, T. M., Healy, B., & LeBlanc, W. (1989). Sharing and synchrony of behavior states and heart rate in nondepressed versus depressed mother-infant interactions. *Infant Behavior and Development, 12,* 357–376.

Field, T. M., Morrow, C. J., Valdeon, C., & Larson, S. (1992). Massage reduces anxiety in child and adolescent psychiatric patients. *Journal of the American Academy of Child and Adolescent Psychiatry, 31,* 125–131.

Field, T. M., Pickens, J., Fox, N., Nawrocki, T., & Gonzalez, J. (1995). Vagal tone in infants of depressed mothers. *Development and Psychopathology, 7,* 227–231.

Fischer, K. W. (1980). A theory of cognitive development: Control and construction of hierarchies of skills. *Psychological Review, 87,* 477–531.

Fischer, K. W., & Ayoub, C. (1994). Affective splitting and dissociation in normal and maltreated children: Developmental pathways for self in relationships. In D. Cicchetti & S. Toth (Eds.), *Rochester Symposium on Developmental Psychopathology: Vol. 5. Disorders and dysfunctions of the self* (pp. 149–222). Rochester, NY: University of Rochester Press.

Fisher, C. B. (1993). *Integrating science and ethics in research with high-risk children and youth.* Social policy report, Vol. 2. Ann Arbor, MI: Society for Research in Child Development.

Fisher, C. B., Murray, J., Dill, J., Hagen, J., Hogan, M., Lerner, R., Rebok, G., Sigel, I., Sostek, A., Smyer, M., Spencer, M., & Wilcox, B. (1993). The national conference on graduate education in the applications of developmental science. *Journal of Applied Developmental Psychology, 14,* 1–10.

Fisher, C. B., & Rosendahl, S. A. (1990). Psychological risk and remedies of research participation. In C. B. Fisher & W. W. Tryon (Eds.), *Ethics in applied developmental psychology: Emerging issues in an emerging field* (pp. 43–60). Norwood, NJ: ABLEX.

Fleming, J., & Offord, D. (1990). Epidemiology of childhood depressive disorders: A critical review. *Journal of the American Academy of Child and Adolescent Psychiatry, 29,* 571–580.

Fonagy, P., Steele, H., & Steele, M. (1991). Maternal representations of attachment during pregnancy predict the organization of infant-mother attachment at one year of age. *Child Development, 62,* 891–905.

Fraiberg, S., Adelson, E., & Shapiro, V. (1975). Ghosts in the nursery: A psychoanalytic approach to impaired infant-mother relationships. *Journal of the American Academy of Child Psychiatry, 14,* 387–421.

Freud, A. (1965). *Normality and pathology in childhood: Assessments of development.* New York: International Universities Press.

Freud, S. (1955a). An outline of psycho-analysis. In J. Strachey (Ed.), *The standard edition of the complete works of Sigmund Freud* (Vol. 23). London: Hogart. (Original work published 1940)

Freud, S. (1955b). Fetishism. In J. Strachey (Ed.), *The standard edition of the complete works of Sigmund Freud* (Vol. 21). London: Hogarth. (Original work published 1927)

Frodi, A., & Lamb, M. (1980). Child abusers' responses to infant smiles and cries. *Child Development, 51,* 238–241.

Futterweit, L. R., & Ruff, H. A. (1993). Principles of development: Implications for early intervention. *Journal of Applied Developmental Psychology, 14,* 153–173.

Gaensbauer, T. J., Harmon, R. J., Cytryn, L., & McKnew, D. (1984). Social and affective development in infants with a manic-depressive parent. *American Journal of Psychiatry, 141,* 223–229.

Gaensbauer, T. J., & Hiatt, S. (1984). Facial communication of emotion in early infancy. In N. A. Fox & R. J. Davidson (Eds.), *The psychobiology of affective development* (pp. 207–230). Hillsdale, NJ: Erlbaum.

Gaensbauer, T. J., Mrazek, D., & Harmon, R. (1980). Affective behavior patterns in abused and/or neglected infants. In N. Frude (Ed.), *The understanding and prevention of child abuse: Psychological approaches* (pp. 120–135). London: Concord Press.

Gallagher, J. J., & Ramey, C. T. (1987). *The malleability of children.* Baltimore: Brooks.

Garcia Coll, C., Lamberty, G., Jenkins, R., McAdoo, H. P., Crnic, K., Waskik, B. H., & Vasquez Garcia, H. (1996). An integrative model for the study of developmental competencies in minority children. *Child Development, 67,* 1891–1914.

Garfield, S. L., & Kurtz, R. (1976). Clinical psychologists in the 1970s. *American Psychologist, 31,* 1–9.

Garmezy, N. (1970). Process and reactive schizophrenia: Some conceptions and issues. *Schizophrenia Bulletin, 2,* 30–74.

Garmezy, N. (1971). Vulnerability research and the issue of primary prevention. *American Journal of Orthopsychiatry, 41,* 101–116.

Garmezy, N., & Masten, A. S. (1994). Chronic adversities. In M. Rutter, E. Taylor, & L. Hersov (Eds.), *Child and adolescent psychiatry: Modern approaches* (3rd ed., pp. 191–208). London: Blackwell.

Garmezy, N., Masten, A. S., & Tellegen, A. (1984). The study of stress and competence in children: A building block for developmental psychopathology. *Child Development, 55,* 97–111.

Garmezy, N., & Rutter, M. (1985). Acute reactions to stress. In M. Rutter & L. Hersov (Eds.), *Child psychiatry: Modern approaches* (2nd ed., pp. 152–176). Oxford, England: Blackwell.

Garmezy, N., & Streitman, S. (1974). Children at risk: The search for the antecedents of schizophrenia. *Schizophrenia Bulletin, 8,* 14–90.

Gaylin, W., & Macklin, R. (1982). *Who speaks for the child: The problems of proxy consent.* New York: Plenum Press.

Gentile, J., Cicchetti, D., Rogosch, F., & O'Brien, R. (1992). Functional deficits in the self and depression in widows. *Development and Psychopathology, 4,* 323–339.

George, C., Kaplan, N., & Main, M. (1985). *Adult Attachment Interview.* Unpublished manuscript, University of California, Berkeley.

George, C., & Main, M. (1979). Social interactions of young abused children: Approach, avoidance, and aggression. *Child Development, 50,* 306–318.

Giovannoni, J., & Becerra, R. (1979). *Defining child abuse.* New York: Free Press.

Gittelman, R., Manuzza, S., Shenker, R., & Bonaguro, N. (1985). Hyperactive boys almost grown up: I. Psychiatric status. *Archives of General Psychiatry, 42,* 937–947.

Gjerde, P. (1995). Alternate pathways to chronic depressive symptoms in young adults: Gender differences in developmental trajectories. *Child Development, 66,* 1277–1300.

Glueck, S., & Glueck, E. (1950). *Unraveling juvenile delinquency.* Cambridge, MA: Harvard University Press.

Goldsmith, H. H., & Alansky, J. A. (1987). Maternal and infant temperamental predictors of attachment: A meta-analytic review. *Journal of Consulting and Clinical Psychology, 55,* 805–816.

Goldsmith, H. H., & Gottesman, I. (1994). Developmental psychopathology of antisocial behavior: Inserting genes into its ontogenesis and epigenesis. In C. Nelson (Ed.), *Threats to optimal development: The Minnesota Symposia on Child Psychology* (pp. 69–104). Hillsdale, NJ: Erlbaum.

Goldsmith, H. H., Gottesman, I., & Lemery, K. (1997). Epigenetic approaches to developmental psychopathology. *Development and Psychopathology, 9,* 365–387.

Gooding, D. C., & Iacono, W. G. (1995). Schizophrenia through the lens of a developmental psychopathology perspective. In D. Cicchetti & D. Cohen (Eds.), *Developmental psychopathology: Vol. 2. Risk, disorder, and adaptation* (pp. 535–580). New York: Wiley.

Goodwin, F., & Jamison, K. (1990). *Manic-depressive illness.* New York: Oxford University Press.

Gottesman, I. (1974). Developmental genetics and ontogenetic psychology: Overdue detente and propositions from a matchmaker. In A. Pick (Ed.), *Minnesota Symposium on Child Psychology* (pp. 55–80). Minneapolis: University of Minnesota Press.

Gottesman, I., & Shields, J. (1972). *Schizophrenia and genetics: A twin study vantage point.* New York: Academic Press.

Gould, S. (1980). *The Panda's thumb.* New York: Norton.

Gould, S. (1986). Evolution and the triumph of homology, or why history matters. *American Scientist, 74,* 60–69.

Graham, P., & Rutter, M. (1973). Psychiatric disorders in the young adolescent: A follow-up study. *Proceedings of the Royal Society of Medicine, 66,* 1226–1229.

Green, A. (1993). Child sexual abuse: Immediate and long-term effects and intervention. *Journal of the American Academy of Child and Adolescent Psychiatry, 35,* 890–902.

Greenberg, M. T., Kusche, C. A., & Speltz, M. (1991). Emotional regulation, self-control, and psychopathology: The role of relationships in early childhood. In D. Cicchetti & S. Toth (Eds.), *Rochester Symposium on Developmental Psychopathology: Vol. 2. Internalizing and externalizing expressions of dysfunction* (pp. 21–55). Hillsdale, NJ: Erlbaum.

Greenough, W., Black, J., & Wallace, C. (1987). Experience and brain development. *Child Development, 58,* 539–559.

Grusec, J., & Walters, G. (1991). Psychological abuse and child-rearing belief systems. In R. H. Starr & D. A. Wolfe (Eds.), *The effects of child abuse and neglect: Issues and research* (pp. 100–128). New York: Guilford Press.

Guidano, V. F., & Liotti, G. (Eds.). (1983). *Cognitive processes and emotional disorders: A structural approach to psychotherapy.* New York: Guilford Press.

Haggerty, R., Sherrod, L., Garmezy, N., & Rutter, M. (Eds.). (1994). *Stress, risk, and resilience in children and adolescents.* New York: Cambridge University Press.

Hamburg, D. (1992). *Today's children.* New York: Random House.

Hammen, C. (1992). The family-environmental context of depression: A perspective on children's risk (pp. 251–281). In D. Cicchetti & S. L. Toth (Eds.), *Rochester Symposium on Developmental Psychopathology: Vol. 4. Developmental perspectives on depression* (pp. 252–281). Rochester, NY: University of Rochester Press.

Harbison, J. (Ed.). (1983). *Children of the troubles.* Belfast, Ireland: Stranmillas College.

Harrington, R., Fudge, H., Rutter, M., Pickles, A., & Hill, J. (1990). Adult outcomes of childhood and adolescent depression: I. Psychiatric status. *Archives of General Psychiatry, 47,* 465–473.

Harrington, R., Fudge, H., Rutter, M., Pickles, A., & Hill, J. (1991). Adult outcomes of childhood and adolescent depression: II. Risk for antisocial disorders. *Journal of the American Academy of Child and Adolescent Psychiatry, 30,* 434–439.

Harris, P. (1989). *Children and emotion.* New York: Blackwell.

Hart, J., Gunnar, M., & Cicchetti, D. (1995). Salivary cortisol in maltreated children: Evidence of relations between neuroendocrine activity and social competence. *Development and Psychopathology, 7,* 11–26.

Hart, J., Gunnar, M., & Cicchetti, D. (1996). Altered neuroendocrine activity in maltreated children related to depression. *Development and Psychopathology, 8,* 201–214.

Harter, S. (1977). A cognitive-developmental approach to children's expression of conflicting feelings and a technique to facilitate such expression in play therapy. *Journal of Consulting and Clinical Psychology, 45,* 417–432.

Harter, S. (1978). Effectance motivation reconsidered: Toward a developmental model. *Human Development, 21,* 34–64.

Harter, S. (1981). A model of intrinsic mastery motivation in children: Individual differences and developmental change. In A. Collins (Ed.), *Minnesota Symposia on Child Psychology* (Vol. 14, pp. 215–255). Hillsdale, NJ: Erlbaum.

Harter, S. (1983). Developmental perspectives on the self system. In E. M. Hetherington (Ed.), *Handbook of child psychology* (pp. 275–385). New York: Wiley.

Harter, S. (1988). Developmental and dynamic changes in the nature of the self-concept: Implications for child psychotherapy.

In S. Shirk (Ed.), *Cognitive development and child psychotherapy* (pp. 119–160). New York: Plenum Press.

Hartmann, H. (1958). *Ego psychology and the problem of adaptation.* New York: International Universities Press.

Hartup, W. (1983). Peer relations. In P. Mussen (Ed.), *Handbook of child psychology* (pp. 103–196). New York: Wiley.

Hartup, W. (1996). The company they keep: Friendships and their developmental significance. *Child Development, 67,* 1–13.

Haskett, M. E., & Kistner, J. A. (1991). Social interactions and peer perceptions of young physically abused children. *Child Development, 62,* 979–990.

Haviland, M., Pincus, H., & Dial, T. (1987). Career research involvement, and research fellowship plans of potential psychiatrists. *Archives of General Psychiatry, 44,* 493–496.

Hay, D. (1994). Prosocial development. *Journal of Child Psychology and Psychiatry, 35,* 29–71.

Hennessy, K., Rabideau, G., Cicchetti, D., & Cummings, E. M. (1994). Responses of physically abused children to different forms of interadult anger. *Child Development, 65,* 815–828.

Highlen, P. (1994). Racial/ethnic diversity in doctoral programs of psychology: Challenges for the twenty-first century. *Applied and Preventive Psychology, 3,* 91–108.

Hinde, R. (1992). Developmental psychology in the context of other behavioral sciences. *Developmental Psychology, 28,* 1018–1029.

Hinshaw, S. (1987). On the distinction between attentional deficits/hyperactivity and conduct problems/aggression in child psychopathology. *Psychological Bulletin, 101,* 443–463.

Hoagwood, K., Jensen, P., & Fisher, C. B. (Eds.). (1996). *Ethical issues in mental health research with children and adolescents.* Mahwah, NJ: Erlbaum.

Hoagwood, K., Jensen, P., Petti, T., & Burns, B. (1996). Outcomes of mental health care for children and adolescents: I. A comprehensive conceptual model. *Journal of the American Academy of Child and Adolescent Psychiatry, 35,* 1055–1063.

Hoagwood, K., & Koretz, D. (1996). Embedding prevention services within systems of care: Strengthening the nexus for children. *Applied and Preventive Psychology, 5,* 225–234.

Hoch, E. L., Ross, A. O., & Winder, C. L. (Eds.). (1966). *Professional preparation of clinical psychologists.* Washington, DC: American Psychological Association.

Hodapp, R. M., & Zigler, E. (1995). Past, present, and future issues in the developmental approach to mental retardation and developmental disabilities. In D. Cicchetti & D. Cohen (Eds.), *Developmental psychopathology: Vol. 2. Risk, disorder, and adaptation* (pp. 299–331). New York: Wiley.

Hofer, M. A. (1987). Early social relationships: A psychobiologist's view. *Child Development, 58,* 633–647.

Hoffman-Plotkin, D., & Twentyman, C. T. (1984). A multimodal assessment of behavioral and cognitive deficits in abused and neglected preschoolers. *Child Development, 55,* 794–802.

Howard, K., Cornille, T., Lyons, J., Vessey, J., Lueger, R., & Saunders, S. (1996). Patterns of mental health service utilization. *Archives of General Psychiatry, 53,* 696–705.

Howes, C., & Eldredge, R. (1985). Responses of abused, neglected, and non-maltreated children to the behaviors of their peers. *Journal of Applied Developmental Psychology, 6,* 261–270.

Howes, C., & Espinosa, M. P. (1985). The consequences of child abuse for the formation of relationships with peers. *International Journal of Child Abuse and Neglect, 9,* 397–404.

Howes, P., & Cicchetti, D. (1993). A family/relational perspective on maltreating families: Parallel processes across systems and social policy implications. In D. Cicchetti & S. L. Toth (Eds.), *Child abuse, child development and social policy* (pp. 249–300). Norwood, NJ: ABLEX.

Howitt, D. (1992). *Child abuse errors: When good intentions go wrong.* New Brunswick, NJ: Rutgers University Press.

Hunter, R. S., & Kihlstrom, N. (1979). Breaking the cycle in abusive families. *American Journal of Psychiatry, 136,* 1320–1322.

Huston, A. C., Garcia-Coll, C. T., & McLoyd, V. C. (Eds.). (1994). Special issue on children and poverty. *Child Development, 65*(2), 275–718.

Inhelder, B. (1968). *The diagnosis of reasoning in the mentally retarded.* New York: Day. (Original work published 1943)

Institute of Medicine. (1985). Research on mental illness and addictive disorders: Progress and prospects. *American Journal of Psychiatry, 142*(Suppl.), 1–41.

Institute of Medicine. (1989). *Research on children and adolescents with mental, behavioral, and developmental disorders.* Washington, DC: National Academy Press.

Institute of Medicine. (1994). *Reducing risks for mental disorders: Frontiers for preventive intervention research.* Washington, DC: National Academy Press.

Isabella, R. A. (1993). Origins of attachment: Maternal interactive behavior across the first year. *Child Development, 64,* 605–621.

Ivey, A. E. (1993). On the need for reconstruction of our present practice of counseling and psychotherapy. *Counseling Psychologist, 21,* 225–228.

Izard, C., Fantauzzo, C., Castel, J., Haynes, O. M., Rayias, M., & Putnam, P. (1995). The ontogeny and significance of infants' facial expressions in the first 9 months of life. *Developmental Psychology, 31,* 997–1013.

Jackson, J. F. (1993). Multiple caregiving among African-Americans and infant attachment: The need for an emic approach. *Human Development, 36,* 87–102.

Jamison, K. (1993). *Touched with fire: Manic-depressive illness and the artistic temperament.* New York: Free Press.

Jones, J. M. (1985). The socio-political context of clinical training in psychology: The ethnic minority case. *Psychotherapy, 22,* 453–456.

Jones, N., Field, T., Fox, N., Lundy, B., & Devalos, M. (1997). EEG activation in one-month-old infants of depressed mothers. *Development and Psychopathology, 9,* 491–505.

Juvenile Justice Standards Project. (1977). *Standards relating to child abuse and neglect.* Cambridge, MA: Ballenger.

Kagan, J. (1971). *Change and continuity in infancy.* New York: Wiley.

Kagan, J. (1981). *The second year: The emergence of self-awareness.* Cambridge, MA: Harvard University Press.

Kagan, J. (1994). *Galen's prophecy: Temperament in human nature.* New York: Basic Books.

Kahn, M. W., & Santostefano, S. (1962). The case of clinical psychology: A search for identity. *American Psychologist, 17,* 185–190.

Kandel, D., & Davies, M. (1986). Adult sequelae of adolescent depressive symptoms. *Archives of General Psychiatry, 43,* 255–262.

Kandel, E., Mednick, S., Kirkegaard-Sorensen, L., Hutchings, B., Knop, J., Rosenberg, R., & Schulsinger, F. (1988). IQ as a protective factor for subjects at a high risk for antisocial behavior. *Journal of Consulting and Clinical Psychology, 56,* 224–226.

Kaplan, A. (1964). *The conduct of inquiry.* San Francisco: Chandler.

Kaplan, B. (1966). The study of language in psychiatry: The comparative developmental approach and its application to symbolization and language in psychopathology. In S. Arieti (Ed.), *American handbook of psychiatry* (pp. 659–688). New York: Basic Books.

Kaplan, B. (1967). Meditations on genesis. *Human Development, 10,* 65–87.

Kaufman, J. (1991). Depressive disorders in maltreated children. *Journal of the American Academy of Child and Adolescent Psychiatry, 30,* 257–265.

Kaufman, J., & Cicchetti, D. (1989). The effects of maltreatment on school-aged children's socioemotional development: Assessments in a day camp setting. *Developmental Psychology, 25,* 516–524.

Kazdin, A. E., Moser, J., Colbus, D., & Bell, R. (1985). Depressive symptoms among physically abused and psychiatrically disturbed children. *Journal of Abnormal Psychology, 94,* 298–307.

Kegan, R. (1982). *The evolving self.* Cambridge, MA: Harvard University Press.

Kellam, S., Brown, C., Rubin, B., & Ensminger, M. (1983). Paths leading to teenage psychiatric symptoms and substance use: Developmental epidemiological studies in Woodlawn. In S. Guze, F. Earls, & J. Barrett (Eds.), *Childhood psychopathology and development* (pp. 17–51). New York: Raven Press.

Kellam, S., & Rebok, G. (1992). Building developmental and etiological theory through epidemiologically based preventive intervention trials. In J. McCord & R. Tremblay (Eds.), *Preventing antisocial behavior: Interventions from birth through adolescence* (pp. 162–195). New York: Guilford Press.

Keller, M., Beardslee, W., Dorer, D., Lavori, P, Samuelson, H., & Klerman, G. (1986). Impact of severity and chronicity of parental affective illness on adaptive functioning and psychopathology in children. *Archives of General Psychiatry, 43,* 930–937.

Kempe, C. H., Silverman, F. N., Steele, B. B., Droegemueller, W., & Silver, H. K. (1962). The battered child syndrome. *Journal of the American Medical Association, 181,* 17–24.

Kendall-Tackett, K. A., Williams, L. M., & Finklehor, D. (1993). The impact of sexual abuse on children: A review and synthesis of recent empirical studies. *Psychological Bulletin, 113,* 164–180.

Kendler, K., Neale, M., Kessler, R., Heath, A., & Eaves, L. (1992). A population-based twin study of major depression in women: The impact of varying definitions of illness. *Archives of General Psychiatry, 49,* 257–266.

Klimes-Dougan, B., & Kistner, J. (1990). Physically abused preschoolers' responses to peer distress. *Developmental Psychology, 26,* 599–602.

Klin, A., & Cohen, D. J. (1994). The immortality of not knowing: The ethical imperative to conduct research in child and adolescent psychiatry. In J. Hattab (Ed.), *Ethics in child psychiatry.* Jerusalem: Gelfen.

Knitzer, J. (1982). *Unclaimed children: The failure of public responsibility to children and adolescents in need of mental health services.* Washington, DC: Children's Defense Fund.

Knitzer, J. (1993). Children's mental health policy: Challenging the future. *Journal of Educational and Behavioral Disorders, 1,* 8–16.

Kobak, R., & Sceery, A. (1988). Attachment in adolescence: Working models, affect regulation and perceptions of self and others. *Child Development, 59,* 135–146.

Kobak, R., Sudler, N., & Gamble, W. (1991). Attachment and depressive symptoms during adolescence: A developmental pathways analysis. *Development and Psychopathology, 3,* 461–474.

Kochanska, G. (1991). Patterns of inhibition to the unfamiliar in children of normal and affectively ill mothers. *Child Development, 62,* 250–263.

Kochanska, G., Kuczynski, L., Radke-Yarrow, M., & Welsh, J. D. (1987). Resolution of control episodes between well and affectively ill mothers and their young child. *Journal of Abnormal Child Psychology, 15,* 441–456.

Kohlberg, L. (1984). *Essays on moral development: Vol. 2. The psychology of moral development.* San Francisco: Harper & Row.

Kohlberg, L., LaCrosse, J., & Ricks, D. (1972). The predictability of adult mental health from childhood behavior. In B. Wolman (Ed.), *Manual of child psychopathology* (pp. 1217–1284). New York: McGraw-Hill.

Kohn, M., & Rosman, B. (1972). Relationship of preschool social-emotional functioning to later intellectual achievement. *Developmental Psychology, 6,* 445–452.

Kolvin, L., Miller, F., Scott, D., Gatznis, S., & Fleeting, M. (1988). *Adversity and destiny: Explorations in the transmission of deprivation. Newcastle Thousand Families Study.* Gower: Aldershot.

Koocher, G. P., & Keith-Spiegel, P. C. (1990). *Children, ethics, and the law.* Lincoln: University of Nebraska Press.

Kopelman, L. M. (1989). Children as research subjects. In L. M. Kopelman & J. L. Moskop (Eds.), *Children and health care: Moral and social issues* (pp. 73–87). Boston: Kluwer Academic.

Kopp, C. (1994). Trends and directions in studies of developmental risk. In C. Nelson (Ed.), *Threats to optimal development: The Minnesota Symposium on Child Psychology* (pp. 1–33). Hillsdale, NJ: Erlbaum.

Korchin, S. (1983). The history of clinical psychology: Some personal views. In M. Hersen, A. Kazdin, & A. Bellack (Eds.), *The clinical psychology handbook* (pp. 5–19). New York: Pergamon Press.

Korman, M. (1976). *Levels and patterns of professional training in psychology.* Washington, DC: American Psychological Association.

Kovacs, M. (1989). Affective disorders in children and adolescents. *American Psychologist, 44,* 268–269.

Kovacs, M., Akiskal, H., Gatsonis, C., & Parrone, P. (1994). Childhood-onset dysthymic disorder: Clinical features and prospective naturalistic outcome. *Archives of General Psychiatry, 51,* 365–374.

Kovacs, M., Feinberg, T. L., Crouse-Novak, M. A., Paulauskas, S. L., & Finkelstein, R. (1984). Depressive disorders in childhood: I. A longitudinal prospective study of characteristics and recovery. *Archives of General Psychiatry, 41,* 229–237.

Kovacs, M., Feinberg, T. L., Crouse-Novak, M. A., Paulauskas, S. L., Pollock, M., & Finkelstein, R. (1984). Depressive disorders in childhood: II. A longitudinal study of the risk for a subsequent major depression. *Archives of General Psychiatry, 46,* 643–649.

Ladd, J. (1994). *Out of the madness: From the projects to a life of hope.* New York: Warner Books.

Lahey, B. B., Conger, R. D., Atkenson, B. M., & Treiber, F. A. (1984). Parenting behavior and emotional status of physically abusive mothers. *Journal of Consulting and Clinical Psychology, 52,* 1062–1071.

Lamb, M., Thompson, R., Gardner, W., & Charnov, E. (1985). *Infant-mother attachment.* Hillsdale, NJ: Erlbaum.

Lapouse, R. L., & Monk, M. A. (1958). An epidemiological study of behavior characteristics in children. *American Journal of Public Health, 48,* 1134–1144.

Lapouse, R. L., & Monk, M. A. (1964). Behavior deviations in a representative sample of children: Variation by sex, age, race, social class and family size. *American Journal of Orthopsychiatry, 34,* 436–446.

Lauer, R., Giordani, B., Boivin, M., Halle, N., Glasgow, B., Alessi, N., & Berent, S. (1994). Effects of depression on memory performance and metamemory in children. *Journal of the American Academy of Child and Adolescent Psychiatry, 33,* 679–685.

Lavigne, J., Gibbons, R., Christoffel, K., Arend, R., Rosenbaum, D., Binns, H., Dawson, N., Sobel, H., & Isaacs, C. (1996). Prevalence rates and correlates of psychiatric disorders among preschool children. *Journal of the American Academy of Child and Adolescent Psychiatry, 35,* 204–214.

Lazarus, R. S. (1981). The stress and coping paradigm. In C. Eisendorfer, D. Cohen, A. Kleinman, & P. Maxim (Eds.), *Models for clinical psychopathology.* New York: Spectrum.

Leahy, R. (1988). Cognitive therapy of childhood depression: Developmental considerations. In S. Shirk (Ed.), *Cognitive development and child psychotherapy* (pp. 187–206). New York: Plenum Press.

Leckman, J., Elliott, G., Bromet, E., Campbell, M., Cicchetti, D., Cohen, D., Conger, J., Coyle, J., Earls, F., Feldman, R., Green, M., Hamburg, B., Kazdin, A., Offord, D., Purpura, D., Solnit, A., & Solomon, F. (1995). Report card on the national plan for research on child and adolescent disorders: The midway point. *Archives of General Psychiatry, 52,* 715–723.

Lefkowitz, M. M., & Burton, N. (1978). Childhood depression: A critique of the concept. *Psychological Bulletin, 135,* 716–726.

Leikin, S. L. (1983). Minors' assent or dissent to medical treatment. *Journal of Pediatrics, 102,* 169–176.

Lenneberg, E. (1967). *Biological foundations of language.* New York: Wiley.

Lepper, M. R. (1981). Intrinsic and extrinsic motivation in children: Detrimental effects of superfluous social controls. In W. A. Collins (Ed.), *Minnesota Symposia on Child Psychology* (Vol. 14, pp. 155–214). Hillsdale, NJ: Erlbaum.

Lerner, R., & Kauffmann, M. (1985). The concept of development in contextualism. *Developmental Review, 5,* 309–333.

Levine, R. J. (1986). *Ethics and regulation of clinical research* (pp. 170–172). Baltimore: Urban and Schwartzenberg.

Lewinsohn, P. M. (1974). A behavioral approach to depression. In R. J. Freidman & M. M. Katz (Eds.), *The psychology of depression: Contemporary theory and research.* Washington, DC: Winston.

Lewinsohn, P. M., Clarke, G., Seeley, J., & Rohde, P. (1994). Major depression in community adolescents: Age at onset, episode duration, and time to recurrence. *Journal of the American Academy of Child and Adolescent Psychiatry, 33,* 809–818.

Lewinsohn, P. M., Hops, H., Roberts, R., Seeley, J., & Andrews, J. (1993). Adolescent psychopathology: I. Prevalence and incidence of depression and other *DSM-III-R* disorders in high school students. *Journal of Abnormal Psychology, 102,* 133–144.

Lewis, D. O. (1992). From abuse to violence: Psychological consequences of maltreatment. *Journal of the American Academy of Child and Adolescent Psychiatry, 31,* 282–391.

Lewis, D. O., Mallouh, C., & Webb, V. (1989). Child abuse, delinquency, and violent criminality. In D. Cicchetti & V. Carlson (Eds.), *Child maltreatment: Theory and research on the causes and consequences of child abuse and neglect* (pp. 707–721). New York: Cambridge University Press.

Lewis, M. (1992). *The exposed self.* New York: Free Press.

Lieberman, A. F. (1993). *The emotional life of the toddler.* New York: Free Press.

Lieberman, A. F., & Pawl, J. H. (1988). Clinical applications of attachment theory. In J. Belsky & T. Nezworski (Eds.), *Clinical implications of attachment* (pp. 327–351). Hillsdale, NJ: Erlbaum.

Lieberman, A. F., Weston, D., & Pawl, J. H. (1991). Preventive intervention and outcome with anxiously attached dyads. *Child Development, 62,* 199–209.

Limber, S. P., & Flekkoy, M. G. (1995). *The U.N. convention on the rights of the child: Its relevance for social scientists.* Social Policy Report, Vol. 9. Ann Arbor, MI: Society for Research in Child Development.

Loeber, R. (1982). The stability of antisocial and delinquent child behavior: A review. *Child Development, 53,* 1431–1446.

Loeber, R., & Dishion, T. J. (1984). Boys who fight at home and school: Family conditions influencing cross-setting consistency. *Journal of Consulting and Clinical Psychology, 52,* 759–768.

Long, J. V. F., & Vaillant, G. E. (1984). Natural history of male psychological health: XI. Escape from the underclass. *American Journal of Psychiatry, 141,* 341–346.

Luthar, S. (1991). Vulnerability and resilience: A study of high-risk adolescents. *Child Development, 62*(3), 600–616.

Luthar, S., Burack, J., Cicchetti, D., & Weisz, J. (1997). *Developmental Psychopathology: Perspectives in adjustment risk and disorder.* New York: Cambridge University Press.

Luthar, S., Doernberger, C. H., & Zigler, E. (1993). Resilience is not a undimensional construct: Insights from a prospective study on inner-city adolescents. *Development and Psychopathology, 5,* 703–717.

Luthar, S., & McMahon, T. (in press). *Peer reputation among adolescents: Use of the Revised Class Play with inner-city teens.* Manuscript submitted for publication.

Luthar, S., & Zigler, E. (1992). Intelligence and social competence among high-risk adolescents. *Development and Psychopathology, 4,* 287–299.

Lynch, M., & Cicchetti, D. (1991). Patterns of relatedness in maltreated and nonmaltreated children: Connections among multiple representational models. *Development and Psychopathology, 3,* 207–226.

Lyons-Ruth, K. (1992). Maternal depressive symptoms, disorganized infant-mother attachment relationships and hostile-aggressive behavior in the preschool classroom: A prospective longitudinal view from infancy to age five. In D. Cicchetti & S. L. Toth (Eds.), *Rochester Symposium on Developmental Psychopathology: Vol. 4. Developmental perspectives on depression* (pp. 131–171). Rochester, NY: University of Rochester Press.

Lyons-Ruth, K., Connell, D., Grunebaum, H., & Botein, S. (1990). Infants at social-risk: Maternal depression and family support services as mediators of infant development and security of attachment. *Child Development, 59,* 1569–1579.

Lyons-Ruth, K., Connell, D., Zoll, D., & Stahl, J. (1987). Infants at social risk: Relationships among infant maltreatment, maternal behavior, and infant attachment behavior. *Developmental Psychology, 23,* 223–232.

Lyons-Ruth, K., Repacholi, B., McLeod, S., & Silva, E. (1991). Disorganized attachment behavior in infancy: Short-term stability, maternal and infant correlates, and risk-related subtypes. *Development and Psychopathology, 3,* 377–396.

Maccoby, E. E., & Martin, J. A. (1983). Socialization in the context of the family: Parent-child interaction. In P. H. Mussen (Ed.), *Handbook of child psychology: Vol. 4. Socialization, personality, and social development* (pp. 1–102). New York: Wiley.

Main, M., & Cassidy, J. (1988). Categories of response to reunion with a parent at age 6: Predictable from infant attachment classifications and stable over a 1-month period. *Developmental Psychology, 24,* 415–426.

Main, M., & George, C. (1985). Response of abused and disadvantaged toddlers to distress in agemates: A study in the day care setting. *Developmental Psychology, 21,* 407–412.

Main, M., & Goldwyn, R. (1984). Predicting rejecting of her infant from mother's representation of her own experience:

Implications for the abused-abusing intergenerational cycle. *Child Abuse and Neglect, 8,* 203–217.

Main, M., & Hesse, E. (1990). Parents' unresolved traumatic experiences are related to infant disorganized attachment status: Is frightened and/or frightening parent behavior the linking mechanism? In M. Greenberg, D. Cicchetti, & E. M. Cummings (Eds.), *Attachment during the preschool years* (pp. 161–182). Chicago: University of Chicago Press.

Main, M., Kaplan, N., & Cassidy, J. C. (1985). Security in infancy, childhood and adulthood: A move to the level of representation. In I. Bretherton & E. Waters (Eds.), Growing points of attachment theory and research. *Monographs of the Society for Research in Child Development, 50*(1/2, Serial No. 209), 66–104.

Main, M., & Solomon, J. (1990). Procedures for identifying infants as disorganized/disoriented during the Ainsworth Strange Situation. In M. Greenberg, D. Cicchetti, & E. M. Cummings (Eds.), *Attachment during the preschool years* (pp. 121–160). Chicago: University of Chicago Press.

Malinowsky-Rummell, R., & Hansen, D. (1993). Long-term consequences of childhood physical abuse. *Psychological Bulletin, 114,* 68–79.

Manassis, K., & Bradley, S. (1994). The development of childhood anxiety disorders: Toward an integrated model. *Journal of Applied Developmental Psychology, 15,* 345–366.

Manly, J. T., Cicchetti, D., & Barnett, D. (1994). The impact of maltreatment on child outcome: An exploration of dimensions within maltreatment. *Development and Psychopathology, 6,* 121–143.

Marans, S., & Cohen, D. J. (1991). Child psychoanalytic theories of development. In M. Lewis (Ed.), *Child and adolescent psychiatry: A comprehensive textbook* (pp. 613–621). Baltimore: Williams & Wilkins.

Margolin, G. (1995, January). *The effects of domestic violence on children.* Paper presented at the conference on Violence against Children in the Family and the Community, Los Angeles, CA.

Maslow, A. H. (1954). *Motivation on personality.* New York: Harper.

Masten, A. S. (1986). Humor and competence in school-aged children. *Child Development, 57,* 461–473.

Masten, A. S., Best, K., & Garmezy, N. (1990). Resilience and development: Contributions from the study of children who overcome adversity. *Development and Psychopathology, 2,* 425–444.

Matarazzo, J. D. (1983). Education and training in health psychology: Boulder or bolder? *Health Psychology, 2*(1), 73–113.

Mayr, E. (1982). *The growth of biological thought.* Cambridge, MA: Harvard University Press.

Maziade, M., Caron, C., Cote, R., Merette, C., Bernier, H., Laplante, B., Boutin, P., & Thivierge, J. (1990). Psychiatric status of adolescents who had extreme temperaments at age 7. *American Journal of Psychiatry, 147,* 1531–1536.

McCrone, E., Egeland, B., Kalkoske, M., & Carlson, E. (1994). Relations between early maltreatment and mental representations of relationships assessed with projective storytelling in middle childhood. *Development and Psychopathology, 6,* 99–120.

McFall, R. (1991). Manifesto for a science of clinical psychology. *Clinical Psychologist, 44,* 75–88.

McFall, R. (1996). Making psychology incorruptible. *Applied and Preventive Psychology, 5,* 9–15.

McGee, R., Freehan, M., Williams, S., & Anderson, J. C. (1992). *DSM-III* disorders from 11 to age 15 years. *Journal of the American Academy of Child and Adolescent Psychiatry, 31,* 50–59.

McGee, R., Freehan, M., Williams, S., Partridge, F., Silva, P. A., & Kelly, J. (1990). *DSM-III* disorders in a large sample of adolescents. *Journal of the American Academy of Child and Adolescent Psychiatry, 29,* 611–614.

McGuffin, P., & Katz, R. (1993). Genes, adversity, and depression. In R. Plomin & G. McLearn (Eds.), *Nature, nurture, and psychology* (pp. 217–230). Washington, DC: American Psychological Association.

McLeer, S. V., Callaghen, M., Henry, D., & Wallen, J. (1994). Psychiatric disorders in sexually abused children. *Journal of the American Academy of Child and Adolescent Psychiatry, 33,* 313–319.

Mednick, S., Cannon, T., Barr, C., & LaFosse, J. (Eds.). (1991). *Developmental neuropathology of schizophrenia.* New York: Plenum Press.

Mednick, S., Cannon, T., Barr, C., & Lyon, M. (Eds.). (1991). *Fetal neural development and adult schizophrenia.* New York: Cambridge University Press.

Meehl, P. E. (1954). *Clinical versus statistical prediction: A theoretical analysis and a review of the evidence.* Minneapolis: University of Minnesota Press.

Meehl, P. E. (1957). When shall we use our heads instead of the formula? *Journal of Consulting Psychology, 4,* 268–273.

Meehl, P. E. (1962). Schizotaxia, schizotypy, schizophrenia. *American Psychologist, 17,* 827–838.

Meehl, P. E. (1964, October). *Let's quit kidding ourselves about the training of clinical psychologists.* Paper presented at the conference on Professional Education in Clinical Psychology sponsored by the Graduate School of the University of Minnesota, Stillwater.

Meehl, P. E. (1971). A scientific, scholarly, nonresearch doctorate for clinical practitioners: Arguments pro and con. In R. R. Holt (Ed.), *New horizons for psychotherapy: Autonomy as a profession.* New York: International Universities Press.

Meehl, P. E. (1972). Second-order relevance. *American Psychology, 27,* 932–940.

Meehl, P. E. (1973). Why I do not attend case conferences. In P. E. Meehl (Ed.), *Psychodiagnosis: Selected papers* (pp. 225–302). Minneapolis: University of Minnesota Press.

Meehl, P. E. (1987). Theory and practice: Reflections of an academic clinician. In E. F. Bourg, R. J. Bent, J. E. Callan, N. F. Jones, J. McHolland, & G. Stricker (Eds.), *Standards and evaluation in the education and training of professional psychologists* (pp. 7–23). Norman, OK: Transcript Press.

Meehl, P. E., & Rosen, A. (1955). Antecedent probability and the efficiency of psychometric signs, patterns, or cutting scores. *Psychological Bulletin, 52,* 194–216.

Merikangas, K., & Spiker, D. (1982). Assortative mating among inpatients with primary affective disorder. *Psychological Medicine, 12,* 753–764.

Meyer, A. (1957). *Psychopathology: A science of man.* Springfield, IL: Thomas.

Meyers, H. F., Echemendia, R. J., & Trimble, J. E. (1991). The need for training ethnic minority psychologists. In H. F. Myers, P. Wohlford, L. P. Guzman, & R. J. Echemendia (Eds.), *Ethnic minority perspectives on clinical training and services in psychology* (pp. 1–12). Washington, DC: American Psychological Association.

Miller, N. E. (1995). Clinical-experimental interactions in the development of neuroscience: A primer for nonspecialists and lessons for young scientists. *American Psychologist, 50,* 901–911.

Minde, K., & Minde, R. (1977). Behavioral screening of preschool children: A new approach to mental health? In P. J. Graham (Ed.), *Epidemiological approaches in child psychiatry.* London: Academic Press.

Moffitt, T. E. (1993). "Life-course-persistent and adolescent-limited" antisocial behavior: A developmental taxonomy. *Psychological Review, 100,* 674–701.

Monroe, S., & Goldman, P. (1988). *Brothers.* New York: Morrow.

Moskovitz, S. (1983). *Love despite hate.* New York: Schocken Books.

Mueller, E., & Silverman, N. (1989). Peer relations in maltreated children. In D. Cicchetti & V. Carlson (Eds.), *Child maltreatment: Theory and research on the causes and consequences of child abuse and neglect* (pp. 529–578). New York: Cambridge University Press.

Murphy, J., Jellinek, M., Quinn, D., Smith, G., Poitrast, F., & Goshko, M. (1991). Substance abuse and serious child mistreatment: Prevalence, risk, and outcome in a court sample. *Child Abuse and Neglect, 15,* 197–211.

Murphy, L. B. (1962). *The widening world of childhood.* New York: Basic Books.

Murphy, L. B., & Moriarity, A. (1976). *Vulnerability, coping, and growth: From infancy to adolescence.* New Haven, CT: Yale University Press.

Murray, L., Kempton, C., Woolgar, M., & Hooper, R. (1993). Depressed mothers' speech to their infants and its relation to infant gender and cognitive development. *Journal of Child Psychology and Psychiatry, 34,* 1083–1101.

Nannis, E. D. (1988). A cognitive-developmental view of emotional understanding and its implications of child psychotherapy. In S. Shirk (Ed.), *Cognitive development and child psychotherapy* (pp. 91–115). New York: Plenum Press.

National Advisory Mental Health Council. (1993). Health care reform for Americans with severe mental illnesses. *American Psychologist, 50,* 1447–1465.

National Commission for the Protection of Human Subjects of Biomedical and Behavioral Research (NCPHS). (1979). *The Belmont Report: Ethical principles and guidelines for the protection of human subjects of research.* Washington, DC: U.S. Government Printing Office.

National Institute of Mental Health. (1990). *National plan for research on child and adolescent mental disorders: A report requested by the US Congress submitted by the national advisory mental health council* (Publication No. 90-1683). Rockville, MD: U.S. Department of Health and Human Services, Alcohol, Drug Abuse, and Mental Health Administration.

Neisser, U. (1986). *The school achievement of minority children: New perspectives.* Hillsdale, NJ: Erlbaum.

Neumann, C., Grimes, K., Walker, E., & Baum, K. (1995). Developmental pathways to schizophrenia: Behavioral subtypes. *Journal of Abnormal Psychology, 104,* 558–566.

Newcomb, A. F., Bukowski, W. M., & Pattee, L. (1993). Children's peer relations: A meta-analytic review of popular, rejected, neglected, controversial, and average sociometric status. *Psychological Bulletin, 113,* 99–128.

Noam, G. (1992). Development as the aim of clinical intervention. *Development and Psychopathology, 4,* 679–696.

Noam, G., Chandler, M., & Lalonde, C. E. (1995). Clinical-developmental psychology: Constructivism and social cognition in the study of psychological dysfunctions. In D. Cicchetti & D. Cohen (Eds.), *Developmental psychopathology: Vol. 1. Theory and method* (pp. 424–464). New York: Wiley.

Nolen-Hoeksema, S., Girgus, J., & Seligman, M. (1992). Predictors and consequences of childhood depressive symptoms: A 5-year longitudinal study. *Journal of Abnormal Psychology, 101,* 405–422.

Nowakowski, R. S. (1987). Basic concepts of CNS development. *Child Development, 58,* 568–595.

Offord, D. R., Boyle, M. H., Racine, Y. A., Fleming, J. E., Cudman, D. T., Blum, H. M., Byrne, C., Links, P. S., Lipman, E. L., Macmillin, H. L., Grant, N. I. R., Sanford, M. N., Szatmari, P., Thomas, H., & Woodward, C. A. (1992). Outcome, prognosis, and risks in a longitudinal follow-up study. *Journal of American Academy of Child and Adolescent Psychiatry, 31,* 916–923.

Ogbu, J. U. (1985). A cultural ecology of competence among inner-city Blacks. In M. B. Spencer, G. K. Brookins, & W. R. Allen (Eds.), *Beginnings: Social and affective development of Black children* (pp. 45–66). Hillsdale, NJ: Erlbaum.

Olds, D., & Henderson, C. (1989). The prevention of maltreatment. In D. Cicchetti & V. Carlson (Eds.), *Child maltreatment: Theory and research on the causes and consequences of child abuse and neglect* (pp. 722–763). New York: Cambridge University Press.

Osofsky, J. (1995). The effects of exposure to violence on young children. *American Psychologist, 50,* 782–788.

Overton, W., & Horowitz, H. (1991). Developmental psychopathology: Integration and differentiations. In D. Cicchetti & S. L. Toth (Eds.), *Rochester Symposium on Developmental Psychopathology: Vol. 3. Models and integrations* (pp. 1–42). Rochester, NY: University of Rochester Press.

Paavola, J., Carey, K., Cobb, C., Illback, R., Joseph, H., Routh, D., & Torruella, A. (1996). Interdisciplinary school practice: Implications of the service integration movement for psychologists. *Professional Psychology: Research and Practice, 27,* 34–40.

Panaccione, V. F., & Wahler, R. G. (1986). Child behavior, maternal depression, and social coercion as factors in the quality of child care. *Journal of Abnormal Child Psychology, 14,* 263–278.

Pap, A. (1958). Disposition concepts and extension logic. In H. Feigl, M. Scriven, & G. Maxwell (Eds.), *Minnesota studies in the philosophy of science* (Vol. 2, pp. 196–224). Minneapolis: University of Minnesota Press.

Parker, J. G., & Herrera, C. (1996). Interpersonal processes in friendship: A comparison of maltreated and nonmaltreated children's experiences. *Developmental Psychology, 32,* 1025–1038.

Parker, J. G., Rubin, K. H., Price, J. M., & DeRosier, M. E. (1995). Peer relationships, child development, and adjustment: A developmental psychopathology perspective. In D. Cicchetti & D. Cohen (Eds.), *Developmental psychopathology: Vol. 2. Risk, disorder, and adaptation* (pp. 96–161). New York: Wiley.

Patterson, G. R. (1982). *A social learning approach: Vol. 3. Coercive family process.* Eugene, OR: Castalia Press.

Pavenstadt, E. (1965). A comparison of the childrearing environment of upper-lower and very low class families. *American Journal of Orthopsychiatry, 35,* 89 98.

Pennington, B. F., & Welsh, M. (1995). Neuropsychology and developmental psychopathology. In D. Cicchetti & D. Cohen (Eds.), *Developmental psychopathology: Vol. 1. Theory and methods* (pp. 254–290). New York: Wiley.

Perry, B., Pollard, R., Blakley, T., Baker, W., & Vigilante, D. (1995). Childhood trauma, the neurobiology of adaptation, and "use-dependent" development of the brain: How "states" become "traits." *Infant Mental Health Journal, 16,* 271–291.

Persons, J., Thase, M., & Crits-Christoph, P. (1996). The role of psychotherapy in the treatment of depression: Review of two practice guidelines. *Archives of General Psychiatry, 53,* 283–290.

Peterson, C., & Seligman, M. (1984). Causal explanations as a risk factor for depression: Theory and evidence. *Psychological Review, 91,* 347–374.

Peterson, D. R. (1966). Professional program in an academic psychology department. In E. L. Hoch, A. O. Ross, & C. L. Winder (Eds.), *Professional preparation of clinical psychologists.* Washington, DC: American Psychological Association.

Peterson, D. R. (1976a). Is psychology a profession? *American Psychologist, 31,* 572–581.

Peterson, D. R. (1976b). Need for the Doctor of Psychology degree in professional psychology. *American Psychologist, 40,* 441–451.

Peterson, D. R. (1985). Twenty years of practitioner training in psychology. *American Psychologist, 40,* 441–451.

Peterson, D. R. (1991). Connection and disconnection of research and practice in the education of professional psychologists. *American Psychologist, 46,* 422–429.

Peterson, D. R. (1995). The reflective educator. *American Psychologist, 50,* 975–983.

Piaget, J. (1952). *The origins of intelligence in children.* New York: International Universities Press.

Piaget, J. (1971). *Biology and knowledge.* Chicago: University of Chicago Press.

Piaget, J. (1975). Foreword. In E. J. Anthony (Ed.), *Explorations in child psychiatry* (pp. vii-ix). New York: Plenum Press.

Pianta, R., & Caldwell, C. B. (1990). Stability of externalizing symptoms from kindergarten to first grade and factors related to instability. *Development and Psychopathology, 2,* 247–258.

Pianta, R., & Castaldi, J. (1989). Stability of internalizing symptoms from kindergarten to first grade and factors related to instability. *Development and Psychopathology, 1,* 305–316.

Pianta, R., Egeland, B., & Erickson, M. (1989). The antecedents of child maltreatment: Results of the Mother-Child Interaction Research Project. In D. Cicchetti & V. Carlson (Eds.), *Child maltreatment: Theory and research on the causes and consequences of child abuse and neglect* (pp. 203–253). New York: Cambridge University Press.

Pickens, J., & Field, T. (1993). Facial expressivity in infants of depressed mothers. *Developmental Psychology, 29,* 986–988.

Pion, G. (1988). *Clinical and development psychology: A preliminary overview of human resources.* Unpublished manuscript, American Psychological Association.

Plomin, R., & Daniels, D. (1987). Why are children in the same family so different from each other? *Behavioral and Brain Sciences, 10,* 1–16.

Pollak, S., Cicchetti, D., Klorman, R., & Brumaghim, J. (1997). Cognitive brain event-related potentials and emotion processing in maltreated children. *Child Development, 68,* 773–787.

Post, R. (1992). Transduction of psychosocial stress into the neurobiology of recurrent affective disorder. *American Journal of Psychiatry, 149,* 999–1010.

Post, R., Weiss, S., & Leverich, G. (1994). Recurrent affective disorder: Roots in developmental neurobiology and illness progression based on changes in gene expression. *Development and Psychopathology, 6,* 781–814.

Post, R., Weiss, S., Leverich, G., George, M., Frye, M., & Ketter, T. (1996). Developmental neurobiology of cyclic affective illness: Implications for early therapeutic interventions. *Development and Psychopathology, 8,* 273–305.

Provence, S., & Lipton, R. (1962). *Infants reared in institutions.* New York: International Universities Press.

Puig-Antich, J. (1986). Psychobiological markers: Effects of age and puberty. In M. Rutter, C. Izard, & P. Read (Eds.), *Depression in young people* (pp. 341–382). New York: Guilford Press.

Putnam, F. W. (1995). Development of dissociative disorders. In D. Cicchetti & D. Cohen (Eds.), *Developmental psychopathology: Vol. 2. Risk, disorder, and adaptation* (pp. 581–608). New York: Wiley.

Putnam, F. W., & Trickett, P. K. (1993). Child sexual abuse: A model of chronic trauma. *Psychiatry, 56,* 82–95.

Putnam, F. W., Trickett, P. K., Helmers, K., Dorn, L., & Everett, B. (1991). Cortisol abnormalities in sexually abused girls. *Proceedings of the 144th Annual Meeting of the American Psychiatric Association, 107.*

Pynoos, R. S., Steinberg, A. M., & Wraith, R. (1995). A developmental model of childhood traumatic stress. In D. Cicchetti & D. Cohen (Eds.), *Developmental psychopathology: Vol. 2. Risk, disorder, and adaptation* (pp. 72–95). New York: Wiley.

Quiggle, N., Garber, J., Panak, W., & Dodge, K. (1992). Social information processing in aggressive and depressed children. *Child Development, 63,* 1305–1320.

Quinton, D., & Rutter, M. (1988). *Parenting breakdown: The making and breaking of intergenerational links.* Brookfield, VT: Avebury.

Radke-Yarrow, M., Belmont, B., Nottelmann, E., & Bottomly, L. (1990). Young children's self-conceptions: Origins in the natural discourse of depressed and normal mothers and their children. In D. Cicchetti & M. Beeghly (Eds.), *The self in transition* (pp. 345–361). Chicago: University of Chicago Press.

Radke-Yarrow, M., Cummings, E. M., Kuczynski, L., & Chapman, M. (1985). Patterns of attachment in two- and three-year-olds in normal families and families with parental depression. *Child Development, 56,* 884–893.

Radke-Yarrow, M., McCann, K., DeMulder, E., Belmont, B., Martinez, P., & Richardson, D. (1995). The role of attachment in the context of other relationships. *Development and Psychopathology, 7,* 247–265.

Raimy, V. (Ed.). (1950). *Training in clinical psychology.* Englewood Cliffs, NJ: Prentice-Hall.

Raine, A., Venables, P., & Williams, M. (1995). High autonomic arousal and electrodermal orienting at age 15 years as protective factors against criminal behavior at age 29 years. *American Journal of Psychiatry, 152,* 1595–1600.

Rao, U., Ryan, N., Birmaher, B., Dahl, R., Williamson, D., Kaufman, J., Rao, R., & Nelson, B. (1995). Unipolar depression in adolescents: Clinical outcome in adulthood. *Journal of the American Academy of Child and Adolescent Psychiatry, 34,* 566–578.

Reiss, D., Plomin, R., & Hetherington, E. M. (1991). Genetics and psychiatry: An unheralded window on the environment. *American Journal of Psychiatry, 148,* 283–291.

Rende, R., & Plomin, R. (1990). Quantitative genetics and developmental psychopathology: Contributions to understanding normal development. *Development and Psychopathology, 2*(4), 393–408.

Resnick, R., & Kruczek, T. (1996). Pediatric consultation: New concepts in training. *Professional Psychology: Research and Practice, 27,* 194–197.

Richman, N., Stevenson, J., & Graham, P. J. (1982). *Preschool to school: A behavioral study.* London: Academic Press.

Richters, J. E. (1997). The Hubble hypothesis and the developmentalist's dilemma. *Development and Psychopathology, 9,* 193–229.

Richters, J. E., & Cicchetti, D. (Eds.). (1993a). Toward a developmental perspective on conduct disorder [Special issue]. *Development and Psychopathology, 5*(1/2), 1–344.

Richters, J. E., & Cicchetti, D. (1993b). Mark Twain meets *DSM-III-R:* Conduct disorder, development, and the concept of harmful dysfunction. *Development and Psychopathology, 5,* 5–29.

Richters, J. E., & Martinez, P. E. (1993). Violent communities, family choices, and children's chances: An algorithm for improving the odds. *Development and Psychopathology, 5,* 609–627.

Richters, J. E., & Weintraub, S. (1990). Beyond diathesis: Toward an understanding of high-risk environments. In J. Rolf,

A. S. Masten, D. Cicchetti, K. G. Nuechterlein, & S. Weintraub (Eds.), *Risk and protective factors in the development of psychopathology* (pp. 67–96). New York: Cambridge University Press.

Richters, M. M., & Volkmar, F. (1994). Reactive attachment disorder: Case reports. *Journal of the American Academy of Child and Adolescent Psychiatry, 33,* 328–332.

Rie, H. E. (1966). Depression in childhood: A survey of some pertinent contributions. *Journal of the American Academy of Child Psychiatry, 5,* 653–685.

Rieder, C., & Cicchetti, D. (1989). Organizational perspective on cognitive control functioning and cognitive-affective balance in maltreated children. *Developmental Psychology, 25,* 382–393.

Robins, L. N. (1966). *Deviant children grown up.* Baltimore: Williams & Wilkins.

Robins, L. N. (1979). Follow-up studies. In H. Quay & J. Werry (Eds.), *Psychopathology disorders of childhood* (pp. 483–514). New York: Wiley.

Robins, L. N., & Regier, D. A. (Eds.). (1991). *Psychiatric disorders in America.* New York: Free Press.

Robins, L. N., & Rutter, M. (Eds.). (1990). *Straight and devious pathways from childhood to adulthood.* New York: Cambridge University Press.

Roe, A., Gustad, J. W., Moore, B. V., Ross, S., & Skodak, M. (Eds.). (1959). *Graduate education in psychology.* Washington, DC: American Psychological Association.

Rogers, S. L., & Kegan, R. (1991). Mental growth and mental health as distinct concepts in the study of developmental psychopathology: Theory, research, and clinical implications. In D. Keating & H. Rosen (Eds.), *Constructivist perspectives on developmental psychopathology and atypical development* (pp. 103–147). Hillsdale, NJ: Erlbaum.

Rogosch, F., & Cicchetti, D. (1994). Illustrating the interface of family and peer relations through the study of child maltreatment. *Social Development, 3,* 291–308.

Rogosch, F., Cicchetti, D., & Aber, J. L. (1995). The role of child maltreatment in early deviations in cognitive and affective processing abilities and later peer relationship problems. *Development and Psychopathology, 7,* 591–609.

Rohde, P., Lewinsohn, P., & Seeley, J. (1994). Are adolescents changed by an episode of major depression? *Journal of the American Academy of Child and Adolescent Psychiatry, 33,* 1289–1298.

Rolf, J., Masten, A., Cicchetti, D., Nuechterlein, K., & Weintraub, S. (Eds.). (1990). *Risk and protective factors in the development of psychopathology.* New York: Cambridge University Press.

Rose, D., & Abramson, L. (1992). Developmental predictions of depressive cognitive style: Research and theory. In D. Cicchetti & S. L. Toth (Eds.), *Rochester Symposium on Developmental Psychopathology: Vol. 4. Developmental perspective on depression* (pp. 323–349). Rochester, NY: University of Rochester Press.

Rose, S. L., Rose, S. A., & Feldman, J. F. (1989). Stability of behavior problems in very young children. *Development and Psychopathology, 1,* 5–20.

Rosenbaum, A., & O'Leary, D. (1981). Marital violence: Characteristics of abusive couples. *Journal of Consulting and Clinical Psychology, 49,* 63–71.

Rosenberg, M. S. (1979). *Conceiving the self.* New York: Basic.

Rosenberg, M. S. (1986). Self-concept from middle childhood through adolescence. In J. Suls & A. G., Greenwald (Eds.), *Psychological perspectives on the self.* Hillsdale, NJ: Erlbaum.

Rosenberg, M. S. (1987). New directions for research on the psychological maltreatment of children. *American Psychologist, 42,* 166–171.

Routh, D. (1994). *Clinical psychology since 1917: Science, practice, and organization.* New York: Plenum Press.

Rubin, K. H., & Lollis, S. P. (1988). Beyond attachment: Possible origins and consequences of social withdrawal in childhood. In J. Belsky & T. Nezworski (Eds.), *Clinical implications of attachment* (pp. 219–252). Hillsdale, NJ: Erlbaum.

Rutter, M. (1979). Protective factors in children's responses to stress and disadvantage. In M. W. Kent & J. E. Rolf (Eds.), *Primary prevention in psychopathology: Social competence in children* (Vol. 8, pp. 49–74). Hanover, NH: University of New England Press.

Rutter, M. (1981). Stress, coping, and development: Some issues and some questions. *Journal of Child Psychology and Psychiatry, 22,* 324–356.

Rutter, M. (1985). Resilience in the face of adversity: Protective factors and resistance to psychiatric disorder. *British Journal of Psychiatry, 128,* 493–509.

Rutter, M. (1986). Child psychiatry: Looking 30 years ahead. *Journal of Child Psychology and Psychiatry, 27,* 803–840.

Rutter, M. (1987). Parental mental disorder as a psychiatric risk factor. In R. Hales & A. Frances (Eds.), *American psychiatric association annual review* (Vol. 6, pp. 647–663). Washington, DC: American Psychiatric Press.

Rutter, M. (1988). Epidemiological approaches to developmental psychopathology. *Archives of General Psychiatry, 45,* 486–495.

Rutter, M. (1989a). Isle of Wight revisited: Twenty-five years of child psychiatric epidemiology. *Journal of the American Academy of Child and Adolescent Psychiatry, 28,* 633–653.

Rutter, M. (1989b). Pathways from childhood to adult life. *Journal of Child Psychology and Psychiatry, 30,* 23–51.

Rutter, M. (1990). Psychosocial resilience and protective mechanisms. In J. Rolf, A. S. Masten, D. Cicchetti, K. H. Nuechterlein, & S. Weintraub (Eds.), *Risk and protective factors in the development of psychopathology* (pp. 181–214). New York: Cambridge University Press.

Rutter, M. (1994). Beyond longitudinal data: Causes, consequences, and continuity. *Journal of Consulting and Clinical Psychology, 62,* 928–940.

Rutter, M. (1995). Relationships between mental disorders in childhood and adulthood. *Acta Psychiatrica Scandinavica, 91,* 73–85.

Rutter, M. (1996). Transitions and turning points in developmental psychopathology: As applied to the age span between childhood and mid-adulthood. *International Journal of Behavioral Development, 19,* 603–626.

Rutter, M., Dunn, J., Plomin, R., Simonoff, E., Pickles, A., Maughan, B., Ormel, H., Meyer, J., & Eaves, L. (1997). Integrating nature and nurture: Implications of person-environment correlations and interactions for developmental psychopathology. *Development and Psychopathology, 9,* 335–364.

Rutter, M., & Garmezy, N. (1983). Developmental psychopathology. In E. M. Hetherington (Ed.), *Socialization, personality and social development* (pp. 775–911). New York: Wiley.

Rutter, M., & Giller, H. (1983). *Juvenile delinquency.* New York: Guilford Press.

Rutter, M., & Quinton, D. (1984). Parental psychiatric disorder: Effects on children. *Psychological Medicine, 14,* 853–880.

Rutter, M., & Quinton, D. (1987). Parental mental illness as a risk factor for psychiatric disorders in childhood. In D. Magnusson & A. Ohman (Eds.), *Psychopathology: An interactional perspective* (pp. 199–219). Orlando, FL: Academic Press.

Salzinger, S., Feldman, R. S., Hammer, M., & Rosario, M. (1993). The effects of physical abuse on children's social relationships. *Child Development, 64,* 169–187.

Sameroff, A. J. (1983). Developmental systems: Contexts and evolution. In P. Mussen (Ed.), *Handbook of child psychology* (Vol. 1, pp. 237–294). New York: Wiley.

Sameroff, A. J., & Chandler, M. J. (1975). Reproductive risk and the continuum of caretaking casualty. In F. D. Horowitz (Ed.), *Review of child development research* (Vol. 4, pp. 187–244). Chicago: University of Chicago Press.

Sameroff, A. J., & Emde, R. (Eds.). (1989). *Relationship disturbances in early childhood: A developmental approach.* New York: Basic Books.

Sameroff, A. J., Seifer, R., Baldwin, A., & Baldwin, C. (1993). Stability of intelligence from preschool to adolescence: The influence of social and family risk factors. *Child Development, 64,* 80–97.

Sameroff, A. J., Seifer, R., Barocas, R., Zax, M., & Greenspan, S. (1987). Intelligence quotient scores of 4 year children: Social-environmental risk factors. *Pediatrics, 79,* 343–350.

Sameroff, A. J., Seifer, R., & Zax, M. (1982). *Early development of children at risk for emotional disorder. Monographs of the Society for Research in Child Development* (Vol. 47). Chicago: University of Chicago Press.

Sander, L. (1962). Issues in early mother-child interaction. *Journal of the American Academy of Child Psychiatry, 1,* 141–166.

Sanford, M., Szatmari, P., Spinner, M., Munroe-Blum, H., Jamieson, E., Walsh, C., & Jones, D. (1995). Predicting the one-year course of adolescent major depression. *Journal of the American Academy of Child and Adolescent Psychiatry, 34,* 1618–1628.

Santos, A. B., Henggeler, S. W., Burns, B. J., Arana, G. W., & Meisler, N. (1995). Research on field-based services: Models for reform in the delivery of mental health care to populations with complex clinical problems. *American Journal of Psychiatry, 152,* 1111–1123.

Santostefano, S. (1978). *A bio-developmental approach to clinical child psychology.* New York: Wiley.

Santostefano, S. (1985). *Cognitive control therapy with children and adolescents.* Elmsford, NY: Pergamon Press.

Santostefano, S. (1991). Coordinating outer space with inner self: Reflections on developmental psychopathology. In D. Keating & H. Rosen (Eds.), *Constructivist perspectives on developmental psychopathology and atypical development* (pp. 11–40). Hillsdale, NJ: Erlbaum.

Santostefano, S., & Baker, A. H. (1972). The contribution of developmental psychology. In B. Wolman (Ed.), *Manual of child psychopathology* (pp. 1113–1153). New York: McGraw-Hill.

Scarr, S. (1992). Developmental theories for the 1990s: Development and individual differences. *Child Development, 63,* 1–19.

Scarr, S. (1993). Biological and cultural diversity: The legacy of Darwin for development. *Child Development, 64,* 1333–1353.

Schneider-Rosen, K., Braunwald, K., Carlson, V., & Cicchetti, D. (1985). Current perspectives in attachment theory: Illustration from the study of maltreated infants. In I. Bretherton & E. Waters (Eds.), Growing points in attachment theory and research. *Monographs of the Society for Research in Child Development, 50*(Serial No. 209), 194–210.

Schneider-Rosen, K., & Cicchetti, D. (1984). the relationship between affect and cognition in maltreated infants: Quality of attachment and the development of visual self-recognition. *Child Development, 55,* 648–658.

Schneider-Rosen, K., & Cicchetti, D. (1991). Early self-knowledge and emotional development: Visual self-recognition and affective reactions to mirror self-image in maltreated and non-maltreated toddlers. *Developmental Psychology, 27,* 481–488.

Schore, A. N. (1996). The experience-dependent maturation of a regulatory system in the orbital prefrontal cortex and the origin of developmental psychopathology. *Development and Psychopathology, 8,* 59–87.

Schorin, M. Z., & Hart, D. (1988). Psychotherapeutic implications of the development of self-understanding. In S. Shirk (Ed.), *Cognitive development and child psychotherapy* (pp. 161–186). New York: Plenum Press.

Schorr, L., & Schorr, D. (1988). *Within our reach: Breaking the cycle of disadvantage.* New York: Anchor Press.

Sellars, W. S. (1958). Counterfactuals, dispositions, and the casual modalities. In H. Feigl, M. Scriven, & G. Maxwell (Eds.), *Minnesota studies in the philosophy of science* (Vol. 2, pp. 225–308). Minneapolis: University of Minnesota Press.

Selman, R. L., Schultz, L. H., Nakkula, M., Barr, D., Watts, C., & Richmond, J. B. (1992). Friendship and fighting: A developmental approach to the study of risk and prevention of violence. *Development and Psychopathology, 4,* 529–558.

Selman, R. L., Schultz, L. H., & Yeates, K. O. (1991). Interpersonal understanding and action: A development and psychopathology perspective on research and prevention. In D. Cicchetti & S. L. Toth (Eds.), *Rochester Symposium on Developmental Psychopathology: Vol. 3. Models and integrations* (pp. 289–329). Rochester, NY: University of Rochester Press.

Serafica, F. C., & Wenar, C. (in press). Integrating applied developmental science and clinical child psychology. In C. B. Fisher, J. P. Murray, & I. E. Sigel (Eds.), *Applied developmental science: Graduate training for diverse disciplines and educational settings.* Norwood, NJ: ABLEX.

Shaffer, L. F. (Ed.). (1947). Fifty years of clinical psychology [Special issue]. *Journal of Consulting Psychology, 11,* 1–54.

Shakow, D. (1938). An internship year for psychologists with special reference to psychiatric hospitals. *Journal of Consulting Psychology, 2,* 73–76.

Shakow, D. (1939). The functions of the psychologist in the state hospital. *Psychology, 6,* 277–288.

Shakow, D. (1942). Training of the clinical psychologist. *Journal of Consulting Psychology, 10,* 191–200.

Shakow, D. (1946). The Worcester internship program. *Journal of Consulting Psychology, 10,* 191–200.

Shearer, S., Peters, C., Quaytman, M., & Ogden, R. (1990). Frequency and correlates of childhood sexual and physical abuse histories on adult female borderline inpatients. *American Journal of Psychiatry, 147,* 214–216.

Shields, A. M., Cicchetti, D., & Ryan, R. (1994). The development of emotional and behavioral self regulation and social competence among maltreated school-age children. *Development and Psychopathology, 6,* 57–75.

Shirk, S. (Ed.). (1988a). *Cognitive development and child psychotherapy.* New York: Plenum Press.

Shirk, S. (1988b). Causal reasoning and children's comprehension of therapeutic interpretations. In S. Shirk (Ed.), *Cognitive development and child psychotherapy* (pp. 53–89). New York: Plenum Press.

Shirk, S., & Russell, R. (1996). *Change processes in child psychotherapy: Revitalizing treatment and research.* New York: Guilford Press.

Shonkoff, J., & Meisels, S. (1990). Early childhood intervention: The evolution of a concept. In S. Meisels & J. Shonkoff (Eds.), *Handbook of early intervention* (pp. 3–31). New York: Cambridge University Press.

Siegel, A., & White, S. H. (1982). The child study movement: Early growth and the development of the symbolized child. *Advances in Child Development and Behavior, 17,* 233–285.

Siever, L., & Davis, K. (1985). Overview: Toward a dysregulation hypothesis of depression. *American Journal of Psychiatry, 142,* 1017–1031.

Sigel, I. E. (1990). Ethical concerns for the use of research findings in applied settings. In C. B. Fisher & W. W. Tryon (Eds.), *Advances in applied developmental psychology: Vol. 4. Ethics in applied developmental psychology: Emerging issues in an emerging field* (pp. 133–142). Norwood, NJ: ABLEX.

Sigel, I. E., & Kim, M.-I. (1996). The answer depends on the question: A conceptual and methodological analysis of a parent belief-behavior interview regarding children's learning. In S. Harkness & C. M. Super (Eds.), *Parents' cultural belief systems: Their origins, expressions, and consequences* (pp. 83–120). New York: Guilford Press.

Skuse, D. (1984). Extreme deprivation in early childhood: II. Theoretical issues and a comparative review. *Journal of Child Psychology and Psychiatry, 25,* 543–572.

Smith, M. L., & Glass, G. V. (1977). Meta-analysis of psychotherapy outcome studies. *American Psychologist, 32,* 752–760.

Society for Research in Child Development. (1993). Ethical standards for research with children. In *Directory of members* (pp. 337–339). Ann Arbor, MI: Author.

Sondheimer, A., & Martucci, C. (1992). An approach to teaching ethics in child and adolescent psychiatry. *Journal of the American Academy of Child and Adolescent Psychiatry, 31,* 415–422.

Speltz, M. L. (1990). Contributions of attachment theory to the treatment of preschool conduct disorders. In M. T. Greenberg, D. Cicchetti, & E. M. Cummings (Eds.), *Attachment during the preschool years* (pp. 399–426). Chicago: University of Chicago Press.

Spemann, H. (1938). *Embryonic development and induction.* New Haven, CT: Yale University Press.

Spence, J. T. (1987). Centrifugal versus centripetal tendencies in psychology: Will the center hold? *American Psychologist, 42,* 1052–1054.

Spencer, M. B., & Dupree, D. (1996). African American youth's eco-cultural challenges and psychosocial opportunities: An alternative analysis of problem behavior outcomes. In D. Cicchetti & S. Toth (Eds.), *Adolescence: Opportunities and challenges. Rochester Symposium on Development Psychopathology* (Vol. 7, pp. 259–282). Rochester, NY: University of Rochester Press.

Sroufe, L. A. (1979). The coherence of individual development: Early care, attachment, and subsequent developmental issues. *American Psychologist, 34,* 834–841.

Sroufe, L. A. (1983). Infant-caregiver attachment and patterns of adaptation in preschool: The roots of maladaptation and competence. In M. Perlmutter (Ed.), *Minnesota Symposium in Child Psychology* (pp. 41–83). Hillsdale, NJ: Erlbaum.

Sroufe, L. A. (1989). Pathways to adaptation and maladaptation: Psychopathology as developmental deviation. In D. Cicchetti (Ed.), *Rochester Symposium on Developmental Psychopathology: Vol. 1. The emergence of a discipline* (pp. 13–40). Hillsdale, NJ: Erlbaum.

Sroufe, L. A. (1990). An organizational perspective on the self. In D. Cicchetti & M. Beeghly (Eds.), *The self in transition: Infancy to childhood* (pp. 281–307). Chicago: University of Chicago Press.

Sroufe, L. A. (1996). *Emotional development: The organization of emotional life in the early years.* New York: Cambridge University Press.

Sroufe, L. A. (1997). Psychopathology as an outcome of development. *Development and Psychopathology, 9,* 251–268.

Sroufe, L. A., Egeland, B., & Kreutzer, T. (1990). The fate of early experience following developmental change: Longitudinal approaches to individual adaptation in childhood. *Child Development, 61,* 1363–1373.

Sroufe, L. A., & Fleeson, J. (1986). Attachment and the construction of relationships. In W. Hartup & Z. Rubin (Eds.), *Relationships and development* (pp. 51–72). Hillsdale, NJ: Erlbaum.

Sroufe, L. A., & Fleeson, J. (1988). The coherence of family relationships. In R. A. Hinde & J. Stevenson-Hinde (Eds.), *Relationships within families* (pp. 27–47). Oxford, England: Clarendon.

Sroufe, L. A., & Rutter, M. (1984). The domain of developmental psychopathology. *Child Development, 55,* 17–29.

Sroufe, L. A., & Waters, E. (1976). The ontogenesis of smiling and laughter: A perspective on the organization of development in infancy. *Psychological Review, 83,* 173–189.

Staudinger, U. M., Marsiske, M., & Baltes, P. B. (1995). Resilience and reserve capacity in later adulthood: Potentials and limits of development across the life span. In D. Cicchetti & D. Cohen (Eds.), *Developmental psychopathology: Vol. 2. Risk, disorder, and adaptation* (pp. 801–847). New York: Wiley.

Stein, D., & Lambert, M. (1995). Graduate training in psychotherapy: Are therapy outcomes enhanced? *Journal of Consulting and Clinical Psychology, 63,* 182–196.

Stein, M., Walker, J., Anderson, G., Hazen, A., Ross, C., Eldridge, G., & Forde, D. (1996). Childhood physical and sexual abuse in patients with anxiety disorders and in a community sample. *American Journal of Psychiatry, 153,* 275–277.

Stern, D. (1985). *The interpersonal world of the infant.* New York: Basic Books.

Sternberg, K. J., Lamb, M. E., Greenbaum, C., Cicchetti, D., Dawud, S., Cortes, R. M., Krispin, O., & Lorey, F. (1993). Effects of domestic violence on children's behavior problems and depression. *Developmental Psychology, 29,* 44–52.

Stouthamer-Loeber, M., Loeber, R., Farrington, D., Zhang, Q., van Kammen, W., & Maguin, E. (1993). The double edge of protective and risk factors for delinquency: Interrelations and developmental patterns. *Development and Psychopathology, 5,* 683–701.

Straus, M. A., Gelles, R. J., & Steinmetz, S. (1980). *Behind closed doors: Violence in American families.* Garden City, NJ: Anchor Press/Doubleday.

Stricker, G., Davis-Russell, E., Bourge, E., Duran, E., Hammond, W. R., McHolland, J., Polite, K., & Vaughn, B. E. (Eds.). (1990). *Toward ethnic diversification in psychology education and training.* Washington, DC: American Psychological Association.

Stricker, G., & Trierweiler, S. (1995). The local clinical scientist: A bridge between science and practice. *American Psychologist, 50,* 995–1003.

Strickland, B. R. (1988). Clinical psychology comes of age. *American Psychologist, 43,* 104–107.

Strober, M., Lampert, C., Schmidt, S., & Morrell, W. (1993). The course of major depressive disorder in adolescents: I. Recovery and risk of manic switching in a follow-up of psychotic and nonpsychotic subtypes. *Journal of the American Academy of Child and Adolescent Psychiatry, 32,* 34–42.

Strother, C. R. (1956). *Psychology and mental health.* Washington, DC: American Psychological Association.

Susman, E. J., Trickett, P. K., Iannotti, R. J., Hollenbeck, B. E., & Zahn-Waxler, C. (1985). Childrearing patterns in depressed, abusive, and normal mothers. *American Journal of Orthopsychiatry, 55,* 237–251.

Tarter, R., & Vanyukov, M. (1994). Alcoholism: A developmental disorder. *Journal of Consulting and Clinical Psychology, 62,* 1096–1107.

Tarullo, L., DeMulder, E., Martinez, P., & Radke-Yarrow, M. (1994). Dialogues with preadolescents and adolescents: Mother-child interaction patterns in affectively ill and well dyads. *Journal of Abnormal Psychology, 22,* 33–51.

Taylor, E. (1995). Dysfunctions of attention. In D. Cicchetti & D. J. Cohen (Eds.), *Developmental psychopathology: Vol. 2. Risk, disorder, and adaptation* (pp. 243–273). New York: Wiley.

Terr, L. C. (1991). Childhood traumas: An outline and overview. *American Journal of Psychiatry, 148,* 10–20.

Teti, D., Gelfand, D., Messinger, D., & Isabella, R. (1995). Maternal depression and the quality of early attachment: An examination of infants, preschoolers, and their mothers. *Developmental Psychology, 31,* 364–376.

Tharinger, D., Lambert, N., Bricklin, P., Feshbach, N., Johnson, N., Oakland, T., Paster, V., & Sanchez, W. (1996). Education reform: Challenges for psychology and psychologists. *Professional Psychology: Research and Practice, 27,* 24–33.

Thomas, L. (1979). *The medusa and the snail: More notes of a biology watcher.* New York: Viking Press.

Thompson, R. A. (1990a). Emotions and self-regulation. In R. Thompson (Ed.), *Nebraska Symposium on Motivation: Vol. 36. Socioemotional development* (pp. 367–467). Lincoln: University of Nebraska Press.

Thompson, R. A. (1990b). Vulnerability in research: A developmental perspective on research risk. *Child Development, 61,* 1–16.

Thompson, R. A. (1992). Developmental changes in research risk and benefit: A changing calculus of concerns. In B. Stanley & J. E. Sieber (Eds.), *Social research on children and adolescents: Ethical issues* (pp. 31–64). Newbury Park, CA: Sage.

Thompson, R. A. (1995). *Preventing child maltreatment through social support: A critical analysis.* Thousand Oaks, CA: Sage.

Toth, S. L., & Cicchetti, D. (1993). Child maltreatment: Where do we go from here in our treatment of victims? In D. Cicchetti & S. L. Toth (Eds.), *Child abuse, child development, and social policy* (pp. 399–438). Norwood, NJ: ABLEX.

Toth, S. L., & Cicchetti, D. (1996a). Patterns of relatedness, depressive symptomatology, and perceived competence in maltreated children. *Journal of Consulting and Clinical Psychology, 64,* 32–41.

Toth, S. L., & Cicchetti, D. (1996b). The impact of relatedness with mother on school functioning in maltreated youngsters. *Journal of School Psychology, 34,* 247–266.

Toth, S. L., Manly, J. T., & Cicchetti, D. (1992). Child maltreatment and vulnerability to depression. *Development and Psychopathology, 4,* 97–112.

Trickett, P. K., & Kuczynski, L. (1986). Children's misbehaviors and parental discipline strategies in abusive and nonabusive families. *Developmental Psychology, 22,* 115–123.

Trickett, P. K., & Susman, E. J. (1988). Parental perceptions of childrearing practices in physically abusive and nonabusive families. *Developmental Psychology, 24,* 270–276.

Troy, M., & Sroufe, L. A. (1987). Victimization among preschoolers: The role of attachment relationship history. *Journal of the American Academy of Child and Adolescent Psychiatry, 26,* 166–172.

Tryon, R. C. (1963). Psychology in flux: The academic-professional bipolarity. *American Psychologist, 18,* 134–143.

Tschann, J., Kaiser, P., Chesney, M., Alkon, A., & Boyce, W. T. (1996). Resilience and vulnerability among preschool children: Family functioning, temperament, and behavior problems. *Journal of the American Academy of Child and Adolescent Psychiatry, 35,* 184–192.

Tsuang, M., & Faraone, S. (1990). *The genetics of mood disorders.* Baltimore: Johns Hopkins University Press.

Tucker, D. (1981). Lateral brain function, emotion and conceptualization. *Psychological Bulletin, 89,* 19–46.

Tuma, J. H. (Ed.). (1985). *Proceedings: Conference on training clinical child psychologists.* Washington, DC: Section on Clinical Child Psychology.

Udwin, O. (1993). Annotation: Children's reactions to traumatic events. *Journal of Child Psychology and Psychiatry, 34,* 115–127.

United Nations. (1989). *Adoption of a convention on the rights of the child* (U.N. Document No. A/44/736). New York: Author.

Valsiner, J. (Ed.). (1987). *Culture and the development of children's action.* New York: Wiley.

van der Kolk, B. (1987). The compulsion to repeat the trauma: Re-enactment, revictimization, and masochism. *Psychiatric Clinics of North America, 12,* 389–411.

van der Kolk, B., Pelcovitz, D., Roth, S., Mandel, F., McFarlane, A., & Herman, J. (1996). Dissociation, somatization, and affect dysregulation: The complexity of adaptation to trauma. *Archives of General Psychiatry, 153,* 83–93.

Vasta, R. (1982). Physical child abuse: A dual-component analysis. *Developmental Review, 2,* 125–149.

Velez, C. N., Johnson, J., & Cohen, P. (1989). A longitudinal analysis of selected risk factors of childhood psychopathology. *Journal of the American Academy of Child and Adolescent Psychiatry, 28,* 861–864.

Vocisano, C., Klein, D., Keefe, R., Dienst, E., & Kincaid, M. (1996). Demographics, family history, premorbid functioning, developmental characteristics, and course of patients with deteriorated affective disorder. *American Journal of Psychiatry, 153,* 248–255.

Von Baer, K. E. (1837). *Uber Entwicklungsgeschichte der Thiere.* Konigsberg: Gerbruder Borntrager. (Original work published 1828)

Vondra, J., Barnett, D., & Cicchetti, D. (1989). Perceived and actual competence among maltreated and comparison school children. *Development and Psychopathology, 1,* 237–255.

Vondra, J., Barnett, D., & Cicchetti, D. (1990). Self-concept, motivation, and competence among preschoolers from maltreating and comparison families. *Child Abuse and Neglect, 14,* 525–540.

Vygotsky, L. S. (1978). *Mind in society: The development of higher psychological processes.* Cambridge, MA: Harvard University Press.

Waddington, C. H. (1942). Canalization of development and the inheritance of acquired characters. *Nature, 150,* 563–564.

Waddington, C. H. (1957). *The strategy of genes.* London: Allen & Unwin.

Wakefield, J. C. (1992). Disorder as harmful dysfunction: A conceptual critique of *DSM-III-R*'s definition of mental disorder. *Psychological Review, 99,* 232–247.

Wakefield, J. C. (1997). When is development disordered? Developmental psychopathology and the harmful dysfunction analysis of mental disorder. *Development and Psychopathology, 9,* 269–290.

Walker, E. (1994). The developmentally moderated expression of the neuropathology underlying schizophrenia. *Schizophrenia Bulletin, 20,* 453–480.

Walker, E., Downey, G., & Bergman, A. (1989). The effects of parental psychopathology and maltreatment on child behavior: A test of the diathesis-stress model. *Child Development, 60,* 15–24.

Walker, E., Downey, G., & Nightingale, N. (1989). The nonorthogonal nature of risk factors: Considerations for investigations of children at risk for psychopathology. *Journal of Primary Prevention, 9,* 143–163.

Ward, M. J., & Carlson, E. A. (1995). Associations among adult attachment representations, maternal sensitivity, and infant-mother attachment in a sample of adolescent mothers. *Child Development, 66,* 69–79.

Warner, V., Weissman, M., Fendrich, M., Wickramaratne, P., & Moreau, D. (1992). The course of major depression in the offspring of depressed parents: Incidence, recurrence, and recovery. *Archives of General Psychiatry, 49,* 795–801.

Waters, E., & Sroufe, L. A. (1983). Competence as a developmental construct. *Developmental Review, 3,* 79–97.

Watson, D., & Clark, L. (1984). Negative affectivity: The disposition to experience aversive emotional states. *Psychological Bulletin, 96,* 465–490.

Watson, J., Hopkins, N., Roberts, J., Steitz, J., & Weiner, A. (1987). *Molecular biology of the gene: Vol. 1. General principles: Vol. 2. Specialized aspects.* Menlo Park, CA: Benjamin/Cummings.

Weinberger, D. R. (1987). Implications of normal brain development for the pathogenesis of schizophrenia. *Archives of General Psychiatry, 44,* 660–669.

Weiss, P. (1961). Deformities as cues to understanding development of form. *Perspectives in Biology and Medicine, 4,* 133–151.

Weissman, M. M., Gammon, G., John, K., Merikangas, K., Warner, V., Prusoff, B., & Sholomskas, D. (1987). Children of depressed parents. *Archives of General Psychiatry, 44,* 847–853.

Weissman, M. M., & Paykel, E. (1974). *The depressed woman: A study of social relationships.* Chicago: University of Chicago Press.

Weissman, S. H., & Bashook, P. G. (1986). A view of the prospective child psychiatrist. *American Journal of Psychiatry, 143,* 722–727.

Weisz, J. R. (1989). Culture and the development of child psychopathology. In D. Cicchetti (Ed.), *Rochester Symposium on Development Psychopathology: Vol. 1. The emergence of a discipline* (pp. 89–117). Hillsdale, NJ: Erlbaum.

Weisz, J. R. (1997). Effects of interventions for child and adolescent psychological dysfunction: Relevance of context, developmental factors, and individual differences. In S. S. Luthar, J. Burack, D. Cicchetti, & J. R. Weisz (Eds.), *Developmental psychopathology: Perspectives on adjustment, risk, and disorder* (pp. 3–22). New York: Cambridge University Press.

Weisz, J. R., Donenberg, G. R., Han, S. S., & Weiss, B. (1995). Bridging the gap between laboratory and clinic in child and adolescent psychotherapy. *Journal of Consulting and Clinical Psychology, 63,* 688–701.

Weisz, J. R., McCarty, C., Eastman, K., Chaiyasit, W., & Suwanlert, S. (1997). Developmental psychopathology and culture: Ten lessons from Thailand. In S. Luthar, J. Burack, D. Cicchetti, & J. Weisz (Eds.), *Developmental psychopathology: Perspectives on adjustment, risk, and disorder* (pp. 568–592). New York: Cambridge University Press.

Weisz, J. R., Weiss, J., Alicke, B., & Klotz, M. L. (1987). Effectiveness of psychotherapy with children and adolescents: A meta-analysis for clinicians. *Journal of Consulting and Clinical Psychology, 55,* 542–549.

Weithorn, L., & Campbell, S. (1982). The competency of children and adolescents to make informed decisions. *Child Development, 53,* 1589–1598.

Werner, E. (1995). Resilience in development. *Current Directions in Psychological Science, 4,* 81–84.

Werner, E., & Smith, R. (1992). *Overcoming the odds: High-risk children from birth to adulthood.* Ithaca, NY: Cornell University Press.

Werner, H. (1948). *Comparative psychology of mental development.* New York: International Universities Press.

Werner, H. (1957). The concept of development from a comparative and organismic point of view. In D. Harris (Ed.), *The concept of development: An issue in the study of human behavior* (pp. 125–148). Minneapolis: University of Minnesota Press.

Werner, H., & Kaplan, B. (1963). *Symbol formation: An organismic-developmental approach to language and the expression of thought.* New York: Wiley.

Widom, C. (1989). The cycle of violence. *Science, 244,* 160–166.

Wiesel, T. (1994). Genetics and behavior. *Science, 264,* 1647.

Williams, S., Anderson, J., McGee, R., & Silva, P. A. (1990). Risk factors for behavioral and emotional disorders in preadolescent children. *Journal of the American Academy of Child and Adolescent Psychiatry, 29,* 413–419.

Winnicott, D. W. (1958). *Through pediatrics to psycho-analysis: Collected papers.* New York: Basic Books.

Wohlwill, J. F. (1973). *The study of behavioral development.* New York: Academic Press.

Wolfe, D. A., Fairbank, J. A., Kelly, J. A., & Bradlyn, A. S. (1983). Child abusive parents' physiological responses to stressful and non-stressful behavior in children. *Behavioral Assessment, 5,* 363–371.

Wolfe, D. A., & Jaffe, P. (1991). Child abuse and family violence as determinants of child psychopathology. *Canadian Journal of Behavioural Science, 23,* 282–299.

Wolfner, G. D., & Gelles, R. J. (1993). A profile of violence toward children: A national study. *Child Abuse and Neglect, 17,* 197–212.

Wolkind, S. (1985). The first years: Preschool children and their families in the inner city. In J. E. Stevenson (Ed.), *Recent research in developmental psychopathology.* Oxford, England: Pergamon Press.

Woodworth, R. S. (1937). The future of clinical psychology. *Journal of Consulting Psychology, 1,* 4–5.

Wyman, P. A., Cowen, E. L., Work, W. C., & Kerley, J. H. (1993). The role of children's future expectations in self-esteem functioning and adjustment to life stress: A prospective study of urban at-risk children. *Development and Psychopathology, 5,* 649–661.

Yehuda, R., Giller, E. L., Southwick, S. M., Lowy, M. T., & Mason, J. W. (1991). Hypothalamic-pituitary adrenal dysfunction in posttraumatic stress disorder. *Biological Psychiatry, 30,* 1031–1048.

Yutrazenka, B. A. (1995). Making a case for training in ethnic and cultural diversity in increasing treatment efficacy. *Journal of Consulting and Clinical Psychology, 63,* 197–206.

Zahn-Waxler, C., Iannotti, R., Cummings, E. M., & Denham, S. (1990). Antecedents of problem behaviors in children of depressed mothers. *Development and Psychopathology, 2,* 271–291.

Zahn-Waxler, C., & Kochanska, G. (1990). The origins of guilt. In R. Thompson (Ed.), *Nebraska Symposium on Motivation: Vol. 36. Socioemotional development* (pp. 183–258). Lincoln: University of Nebraska Press.

Zahn-Waxler, C., Kochanska, G., Krupnick, J., & McKnew, D. (1990). Patterns of guilt in children of depressed and well mothers. *Developmental Psychology, 26,* 51–59.

Zahn-Waxler, C., & Wagner, E. (1993). Caregivers' interpretations of infant emotions: A comparison of depressed and well mothers. In R. Emde, J. Osofsky, & P. Butterfield (Eds.), *Clinical infant reports: The I feel pictures* (pp. 175–184). Madison, CT: International Universities Press.

Zeanah, C. (Ed.). (1993). *Handbook of infant mental health.* New York: Guilford Press.

Zeanah, C. (1996). Beyond insecurity: A reconceptualization of attachment disorders of infancy. *Journal of Consulting and Clinical Psychology, 64,* 42–52.

Zero-to-Three Task Force on Diagnostic Classification in Infancy. (1994). *Diagnostic classification of mental health and developmental disorders of infancy and early childhood.* Arlington, VA: National Center for Clinical Infant Programs.

Zigler, E. (1963). Meta-theoretical issues in developmental psychology. In H. Marx (Ed.), *Theories in contemporary psychology.* New York: Macmillan.

Zigler, E. (1969). Developmental versus defect theories of mental retardation and the problem of motivation. *American Journal of Mental Deficiency, 73,* 536–556.

Zigler, E. (1971). The retarded child as a whole person. In H. E. Adams & W. K. Boardmen (Eds.), *Advances in experimental clinical psychology* (Vol. 1, pp. 47–121). New York: Pergamon Press.

Zigler, E. (1989). Addressing the nation's child care crisis: The school of the twenty-first century. *American Journal of Orthopsychiatry, 59,* 484–491.

Zigler, E., & Glick, M. (1986). *A developmental approach to adult psychopathology.* New York: Wiley.

Zubin, J., & Spring, B. (1977). Vulnerability: A new view of schizophrenia. *Journal of Abnormal Psychology, 56,* 103–126.

Zucker, R. A., Fitzgerald, H. E., & Moses, H. D. (1995). Emergence of alcohol problems and the several alcoholism: A developmental perspective on etiologic theory and life course trajectory. In D. Cicchetti & D. Cohen (Eds.), *Developmental psychopathology: Vol. 2. Risk, disorder, and adaptation* (pp. 677–711). New York: Wiley.

Zupan, B. A., Hammen, C., & Jaenicke, C. (1987). The effects of current mood and prior depressive history on self-schematic processing in children. *Journal of Experimental Child Psychology, 43,* 149–158.

CHAPTER 9

Clinical-Developmental Psychology: Toward Developmentally Differentiated Interventions

GIL G. NOAM

Enormous strides have been made in the understanding of human development since Freud first turned to the stages of childhood to shed light on adult psychopathology. In the domain of the emotions, a clearer conception has evolved of how human beings adapt to their environment and how efforts at adaptation can go awry. In the cognitive realm, progress has been made in understanding how intellectual capacities grow and mature. Where the spheres of emotion and cognition meet, considerable clarity has emerged into the development of the self, of morality, and of how people make meaning in their lives.

But despite the insights that have been gained over the course of the century, more work needs to be done to apply this newfound knowledge to the practice of clinical intervention and prevention. This chapter is intended to address that need. It will examine how the new wealth of developmental knowledge, based on theory and research, can best inform the clinician's work. It will allow the therapist and intervention specialist to make use of the significant advances in those domains of developmental psychology that have not traditionally been incorporated into clinical practice, advances in such areas as the study of cognitive growth and the development of self complexity. It will explore how an understanding of these and other dimensions of development can give the therapist a fuller picture of the origins of a disorder. Beyond this, it will provide a guide for choosing the therapeutic techniques that best treat a disorder as it is understood in the context of development. Finally, it will offer the intervention specialist ways to make use of a patient's strengths in the service of recovery.

Background

It is Freud who is most often credited with introducing a developmental perspective into the understanding of normality, psychopathology, and psychotherapy (e.g., S. Freud, 1958, 1989). The founder of psychoanalysis believed such disorders as hysteria, obsessions, and even the psychoses resulted from fixations in one or another of childhood's psychosexual stages. Research psychologists, philosophers, and social scientists have subjected this idea to their scrutiny, and many have found aspects of it wanting. Seeing the shortcomings of the Freudian paradigm, generations of psychologists and psychoanalysts have refined it in both theory and practice. Yet, despite some limitations, the psychoanalytic perspective with its focus on conflict and fixation remains a model for mental health professionals who seek to use theories of normal development to inform their understanding of abnormality.

In the decades since Freud, British child psychoanalysts, including Anna Freud, Melanie Klein, and Donald Winnicott revolutionized the psychoanalytic notion of development. Winnicott (1965), as well as Klein (1932) and A. Freud (1950), began to turn the focus toward the effects of the social environment. The result was the formulation of the concept of internalized object relations. The theory was developed that in the first years of life representations of caregivers and of the emerging self are internalized by the child, and that these internalized "objects" greatly affect the child's developmental path. Although the ideas coming from these analysts were based mostly on observations of patients in treatment (e.g., Adler, 1986) their insights were equally applicable to nonclinical cases. Their work, therefore, greatly influenced developmental psychologists who were seeking to understand the conflicts, risks, and challenges that normal children and adolescents face (see Noam, Higgins, & Goethals, 1982).

In the tradition of using the consulting room as a base of understanding, Erikson and Sullivan also produced innovative and influential theories. Erikson (1950, 1968) charted adolescent and adult stages of life from the identity formation phase of adolescence through the generativity of the middle years and on to the wisdom of old age. Sullivan (1953) transformed the psychologist's understanding of close relationships (Noam & Fischer, 1996) by identifying and examining the conflicting fears of isolation and engulfment, and by recognizing that this conflict is a central theme in all development.

It is now widely accepted that theories of normal development that are built solely on clinical observations are problematic (e.g., Offer & Schonert-Reichl, 1992). First is the question of applicability that arises when generalizations are made from a sample not randomly chosen. Second is the assumption that the difference between the issues faced in pathological and normal development is one of intensity, rather than kind. For example, the adolescents that populated the western Massachusetts sanitarium in which Erikson worked were upper middle class, and as such they may have had the liberty to struggle with the sorts of questions about identity that would not arise in a group of their less wealthy peers.

While clinicians from Klein to Sullivan were drawing on their experience in the consulting room to construct their theories, Bowlby (1969), also a psychoanalyst, was turning to ethological research and observations of children in natural settings to build a theory of infant attachment. Later, Ainsworth (1982) used systematic studies to test Bowlby's hypotheses. Bowlby and Ainsworth's work on the relationship between an infant's attachment to mother and the child's subsequent mental health remains highly influential. It continues to inform a generation of longitudinal researchers who, in turn, are affecting not only the field of developmental psychology, but the child-rearing practices of our times.

Along with the expansion of the mental health professions at mid-century, the academic discipline of developmental psychology grew rapidly. During this period, which lasted well into the 1980s, the focus of the discipline was on normal development. Cognitive and emotional changes over the life span were examined, as were evolutions in the nature of the self, of moral understanding, and of social relationships. Applied developmental psychology, with its special emphasis on education grew as a specialty (Renninger, 1992; Sigel, 1990).

Coming at this point in the history of developmental psychology, the field of developmental psychopathology faced an important challenge. That challenge was—and continues to be—to integrate the clinician's insights, with the researcher's empirical findings, and the academic psychologist's observations of normal growth. To meet this need, developmental psychopathologists began systematically to apply the researcher's techniques to those questions that are central to the understanding of dysfunction and disorder, questions about the need for attachment and the fear of intimacy (e.g., Cicchetti, 1984; Sroufe & Rutter, 1984), and about long-term course of risk and resiliency (e.g., Hauser et al., 1987; Hauser, Powers, & Noam, 1991; Vaillant, 1977; E. Werner, 1990).[1] In this way, the clinician and the student of development began to enhance one another's work; together these specialists have advanced the field of developmental psychopathology.

Within that field, research in attachment and in risk and resiliency have been highly influential. But significant as these contributions have been, the work in these areas is open to an important criticism. Research in attachment and risk does not fully embrace the notion that the representations that children internalize—of important others, of the self, of the world—are the product of their own interpretation of experiences. I believe that a full understanding of development cannot ignore the significance of interpretation. This is why I have, since the 1980s, taken a constructivist approach to developmental psychopathology (e.g., Noam, 1985, 1988a, 1990, 1992). This approach focuses on how people interpret the events and relationships in their life and how those interpretations change, in a relatively predictable fashion, over the course of the life span. It recognizes that the same events are interpreted differently by different people, as well as by the same person at different points in that person's life. To use the language of the constructivists, this research looks at how people make meaning in their lives. For the intervention specialist, it is important to understand how meaning making grows and develops in the normal course of life. It is only when equipped with such an understanding that the clinician can distinguish between normal and pathological behavior. Not until the typical course of development of the self is fully understood can one best know how to intervene when behavior is pathological.

A constructivist approach to the field of developmental psychopathology promises to provide new principles for therapeutic interventions. The foundation of research on which the field stands affords the clinician a larger repertory of treatments from which to choose, making it possible to tailor intervention to take account of all facets of the patient. With the academic study of human development integrated into the field of developmental psychopathology, clinicians who take advantage of the field's advances will be better able to use the patient's strengths to enhance recovery. These two elements, the tailoring of interventions to the patient and the engagement of the patient's strengths to assist recovery, are the hallmarks of a developmentally differentiated treatment approach.

The clinician[2] who uses a developmentally differentiated model must ask how the patient is organized developmentally. Answers will include an understanding of how the patient perceives herself, her relationship to the world, her problems, and what is motivating her to change. Psychiatric hospitals, schools, pediatric facilities, and private clinicians now use a diagnostic procedure that relies on symptomatology and syndrome classifications (e.g., *DSM-IV,* symptom checklists). Although symptom identification is essential for targeting treatments, intervention could be much improved if the client's developmental profile were also identified and systematically recorded (e.g., Noam & Houlihan, 1990), a perspective also put forward by psychoanalytic ego psychologists (e.g., A. Freud, 1950).

The therapeutic techniques from which today's clinician is required to choose are a balkanized group, each stemming from its own theoretical tradition. Whereas the therapist's own theoretical orientation was once the principal guide for deciding on a course of treatment, this is no longer always the case when pragmatic solutions are sought. The health-care environment in which therapists now function places enormous value on short-term and outpatient interventions. Even when long-term insight-oriented therapy could be useful, brief treatments are often applied. The cheapest and fastest interventions are winning the day, even though they are not always the most humane or the most likely to achieve the desired results.

In proposing that clinical work be developmentally informed, I am encouraging clinicians to step outside the confines of their particular theoretical orientation. My approach is not an atheoretical one; rather, it is an effort to move beyond the dogma that has limited the clinicians' freedom for too long. Although traditional therapeutic approaches have led to useful treatments for certain disorders,

[1] At the close of the century, a major trend in psychology is emerging that, I believe, will enhance the field of developmental psychopathology. The study of neuroscience is leading to a wealth of new findings about how genetics, brain chemistry, brain structure, and mental illness are connected. Discoveries about how the brain develops and functions are being made at an unprecedented pace. This new knowledge, no less than the findings from clinical psychologists and academics and researchers studying development, should be incorporated into the new differentiated treatment.

[2] To simplify the writing style, I will use at different points, "he" or "she" for the therapist as well as the client. I will also use interchangeably the terms *client* and *patient.*

their success has only been partial, and their attempts to explain why their techniques sometimes fail have been mostly disappointing.

In this chapter, I first briefly review the eclectic movement in therapy. This is followed by a discussion of the evolving trend toward tailored, differentiated interventions, in which I demonstrate how an understanding of development across the life span can be used to plan a more effective treatment strategy.

In the section that follows, I set forth the general principles of clinical-developmental psychology. I then describe in detail the five developmental levels of what I call *self complexity.* In later sections, I introduce typical vulnerabilities at each developmental level, and offer examples of differential treatments using actual cases. An empirical section that follows reviews research using constructivist and developmental measures to address issues of psychopathology and clinical intervention. In the Conclusion, I explore the implications of this line of work for research and clinical training.

The chapter grows out of a conviction that the time has come to build a new relationship among psychologists who study psychopathology and those who study normal development. Boundaries between normal and abnormal behavior are less clear now than in the past (see Noam, 1996; Noam, Chandler, & LaLonde, 1995). Although environments that put children at risk for developing psychopathologies are everywhere, it has been found that exposure to risks does not necessarily lead to lifelong maladaptation (e.g., Garmezy, 1983). Longitudinal studies provide many examples of children and adolescents exhibiting behavior and emotional problems, even severe psychopathology, that they outgrow later in life (Kohlberg, LaCrosse, & Ricks, 1972; Noam, 1996; Rutter & Garmezy, 1983; E. Werner, 1990).

This chapter is written for a wide audience. It is meant to speak not only to clinicians from all theoretical schools, but to the growing number of developmental psychologists interested in the study of risk and prevention. It is also directed to those prevention and intervention specialists who have left the private consulting room to practice interventions in schools, pediatric wards, and workplaces. Finally, it is designed to appeal to the many developmental psychologists who are not engaged in clinical work but draw on those ideas of central interest to the intervention specialist in developing the hypotheses they test.

Any attempt to speak to such a diverse audience carries its own difficulties. Each discipline has its particular interests, methods, and theories. In the space allotted here, I cannot translate all my ideas into the language of each field. I have tried, therefore, to write with sufficient clarity to make my ideas comprehensible to a reader with a general knowledge of human development, risk, and psychopathology. In the end, I rely on the reader's willingness to step outside the parameters of her own discipline and embrace new ideas.

THE SHIFT TO ECLECTIC AND DIFFERENTIAL TREATMENTS

More than 20 years ago, a movement began in the field of psychotherapy in which some clinicians set aside their adherence to one or another of the theoretical orientations that divided them and applied only those techniques that were best suited to the particular problems presented. Partisans of this eclectic style of intervention drew on psychotherapy outcome research to find the most effective treatments. What began as a small movement is now quite common in the field: In a 1988 survey of psychotherapists, 68% of those interviewed reported that they practice eclectic therapy (Jensen & Bergin, 1988). Garfield (1980), a leading advocate of this movement, summarizes the philosophy behind the practice this way: "One approach," he writes, "cannot be all things to all men and women" (p. 150).

In the words of Frances, Clarkin, and Perry (1984), eclectic therapists believe, "In most instances, psychiatric treatment cannot be directed simply at the disorder; it must be tailored for the person and circumstances, and also for the multiple interacting factors that influence how the patient is reacting to pathological processes and stressors" (p. xxii). Therefore, a clinician using an eclectic style would draw on the techniques of psychodynamic, client-centered, cognitive, and behavioral therapy, depending on the symptoms presented and the personality of the patient.

However, the first step in devising eclectic treatments was to determine whether psychotherapy is effective at all. Recently, the work of Weisz and Tramontana has focused on this question with regard to adolescents and children. This research has offered some of the more persuasive arguments in favor of the effectiveness of therapy.

In a meta-analysis of the literature on psychotherapy with children and adolescents since 1970, Weisz, Weiss, Han, Granger, and Morton (1995) found that the average youngster was better adjusted after treatment than about four-fifths of those who had not received treatment. Focusing on adolescents only, Tramontana (1980) found a positive outcome in 75% of treated patients, compared with spontaneous improvement in 40% of untreated patients.

Although these outcome studies, as well as many others focusing on adults, show that therapy produces positive outcomes, most research with subjects of all ages reveals that effects are essentially the same regardless of the type of therapy used. For example, research by Smith, Glass, and Miller (1980) suggests that outcome does not depend on type of therapy (whether behavioral, psychodynamic, or client-centered), therapeutic environment (whether group or individual therapy), years of experience the therapist has had, or whether long- or short-term therapy is used. These findings, both that therapy is effective, and that the differences between therapy schools are negligible in terms of outcome, represent the state of our knowledge.

Some exceptions, however, emerge from the literature. Rather than finding that techniques are interchangeable in their effectiveness, some studies have found that the directive methods of the behavioral and cognitive approaches are somewhat more effective than others types of interventions (Smith et al., 1980; Wittmann & Matt, 1986). Also for children and adolescents Weisz, Weiss, Alicke, and Klotz's (1987) excellent meta-analysis showed that behavior treatments had a small but significant advantage over other treatments.

Yet questions about why this is the case remain. In 1984, Frances et al. pointed out that the reason cognitive and behavior therapies appear to have better outcomes than do other types of treatment is that the goal of treatment in directive therapy is to master specific tasks so results are easily observed and noted. Since the patient's problems are more narrowly defined and results more easily measured, treatment appears more effective.

In the same article, Frances noted that few studies have suggested that any single style of therapy is the best one for treating all conditions. Indeed, some studies have shown that it is not the theory behind the intervention, but the type and quality of nonspecific variables, such as the therapist's empathy, reassurance, and support, that account for favorable results. Such variables are believed to be an outgrowth of the therapist's personal style of interacting, not of her theoretical bias. Miller, Taylor, and West (1980) discovered a high correlation (.82) between therapist empathy and success rate. They reported that "it was therapist empathy rather than treatment type that best predicted outcome." This finding is also supported by research showing that therapists who belong to the same theoretical schools can have very different treatment results (Luborsky, McLellan, Woody, O'Brien, & Auerbach, 1985).

Giles (1983) argues:

> The debate about which treatments are generally more effective for all disorders should be replaced by a series of smaller-scale discussions about the specific effects of specific treatments on specific types of clients. To this end, we have suggested the need for continued disorder or problem-focused treatment outcome research, coupled with more intensive investigation of client and therapist individual differences and in-therapy process aimed at identifying how and when change occurs, in order to improve treatments. (p. 85)

Weisz et al. (1987) pursued a strategy by analyzing, for example, effects of treatment depending on age (therapy more effective for children than for adolescents) and level of experience. They also explored differences in outcome by symptom patterns (over controlled vs. under controlled).

Giles' implicit criticism of psychotherapy outcome research is in line with my own regarding the assumptions that are made and questions asked to determine psychotherapeutic technique and outcome. Because outcome studies are most often designed to compare the effectiveness of different types of therapy, those therapists whose work is evaluated are perceived as belonging to only one psychotherapy school. The client, too, is placed in a single category, usually a diagnostic one. These broad labels placed on both therapist and client obscure important processes. Does the therapist, regardless of his orientation, speak a language that is comprehensible to the client? Are the therapist's interventions accessible to the client? Is the therapist's conception of change understandable to the client? What developmental capacities does the client have for insight, for self-observation, and for behavioral change? How alienated is the client from others? How capable of trust is she? What are the strengths and limitations of her cognitive development? Of her ego development? Of her social development? Of her moral development? These are the questions that therapy outcome research should begin to ask.

Most psychological and psychiatric problems involve a number of general reaction patterns, risks, and behavioral manifestations: Why should there be only one treatment of choice? Not all treatments are equally successful for all people and all conditions. For example, where there is a history of abuse, issues of safety and trust become important. Where there is delinquency, work on fairness of rules and negotiation of conflict is needed. Treatment of depression needs to address self-defeating thoughts and behaviors. It is important to address these issues, but whether this is done in a behavioral, client-centered, or psychoanalytic atmosphere does not matter.

Clients at different levels of development can benefit from their treatments in different ways and are in need of different interventions. A young child, for example, can profit greatly from a behavioral program of specific reinforcements, but will not do well with talking methods and insight-oriented treatments. A sophisticated adult can also benefit from behavior modification, especially for specific problem behaviors, but will be more likely to respond to insight into the self.

We have today sufficient developmental knowledge to begin to match treatments to the organizational level of clients, including such relevant domains as self complexity, interpersonal communication strategies, ability to take the perspectives of others, and understanding of the causes of symptoms. It is quite possible that if we take these developmental accomplishments and limitations into consideration we will find that our treatment has differential effects.

How should therapists apply a developmental understanding to create appropriate treatment strategies? Psychotherapists of all schools have long relied on detailed evaluations of the patient's condition, but in an earlier era such diagnoses did not lead clinicians to adapt their techniques very specifically to the complaint. Eclectic therapists, like conventional ones, also begin with a detailed evaluation, but they use their assessments as the bases for selecting treatment. Garfield (1980, p. 145) discussed the need for a detailed assessment of the patient's problems this way: "Since theoretically here the therapist is committed or willing to use a larger array of procedures than is typically the case of a psychotherapist who follows only one particular approach, he or she must have some basis for deciding what procedures will be used in each case."

Omer (1993), in an example of how eclectic therapy can work, points out the advantages of combining the symptom-oriented techniques of behavioral interventions with the person-oriented styles of psychodynamic and experiential therapy. Such a combination allows the clinician to focus at once on the patient's symptoms, personality issues, and life goals.

It is rare today to find a psychology, psychiatry, or social work training institution that is guided by a single model of treatment. Rather, curricula have become quite eclectic, so much so that many programs have abandoned a philosophical base for understanding the nature of development, personality, and psychopathology. Without the guidance of a theoretical base, clinicians now emerging from graduate programs are in danger of becoming technicians who are qualified only to apply techniques to disorders. We have entered a postideological age in therapy, and we greatly need new ways for organizing the myriad views of therapeutic technique, risk, and recovery.

Even among those clinicians who are trying to use the principles of eclectic treatment to create a more carefully tailored, differential therapy, often diagnosis provides the basis for deciding which technique to employ. Because therapeutic techniques are only loosely connected with diagnostic labels, such a system is riddled with problems. For example, conduct disorder, the diagnosis given to delinquent, aggressive, and oppositional adolescents, can lead a differential therapist to any number of courses of action. Whether, or in what combination, inpatient hospitalization, behavior modification, placement in a residential program, supportive therapy, or psychopharmacology is indicated is unclear from the diagnosis alone. Although more detailed divisions are now being made in the existing diagnostic categories, a thicker manual filled with more specific diagnoses will not supply all the information that the developmentally differentiated therapist needs. Those needs can only be satisfied by supplementing the current diagnostic procedures with an in-depth understanding of other important dimensions of the patient.

An additional consideration is that most therapists and intervention specialists do not modify their treatment style to incorporate research findings about therapy outcome. Generally other factors determine the choice of treatment, such as the intervention specialist's training, the dictates of the institution in which the work is performed, and the therapist's personality and style of interacting with others. Also, some treatments have proved valuable despite "thin" research findings for such treatments. One example is play therapy. Therapists of all different theoretical persuasions use play therapy with children. It is hard to imagine that these clinicians would refrain from using this style of treatment even if evidence of the effectiveness of play therapy were not established.

Although few studies have explored the effectiveness of play therapy, the outcome of psychoanalytic treatments has been the subject of much scrutiny. However, many analytically oriented therapists object to this research, believing that it is invalid. In their view, the research methods that are used in these studies do not probe the depth of the analytic experience. These therapists often judge the success of their techniques by the results they see in their patients. No number of empirical studies will sway these clinicians to abandon intervention methods that they have found to work.

Each patient is affected by a number of processes, such as his relationships with family members and friends and his participation in school and his community. In addition, complex developmental processes, and neurochemical and organic influences, are also at work (e.g., Coyle, 1995). These are some of the variables that must be understood by, and incorporated into the treatment strategy of the developmental clinician. In addition, clinical and developmental psychology would do well to explore the "self-righting" tendencies that contribute to natural recovery processes. Clearly, researchers and practitioners find a great deal of continuities in disorders, problems, and symptoms. But there is equal if not more evidence for the self-righting possibilities throughout the life span. Our own longitudinal research (e.g., Noam, Maraganore, Stevens, & Sheinberg, 1997) focuses on these capacities in the transition from adolescence to adulthood. Once more fully understood, these processes can be more directly supported in tailoring differential treatments as outlined in this chapter.

Toward Developmentally Differentiated Treatments

Of the many theoretical approaches to mental health practice, only psychoanalysis has fully embraced a developmental perspective. But it was this embrace, ironically, that led to the more general trend away from a developmental approach in psychiatry. Psychoanalytic theory was the guide that informed the writing of the second edition of the American Psychiatric Association's *Diagnostic and Statistical Manual* (American Psychiatric Association, 1968). Efforts were made to create a more empirically based diagnostic system, and the result was a series of manuals (*DSM-III* in 1980, *DSM-III-R* in 1987, and *DSM-IV* in 1994) that abandoned developmental interpretations in favor of a classification of disorders by symptoms (American Psychiatric Association, 1980, 1987, 1994).

Meanwhile, the success that behavioral psychology was able to claim in treating pervasive developmental delays, phobias, and depression further threatened to make a developmental approach to treatment obsolete. Behavior theory was declaring that cumbersome ideas about the structure of the personality, the nature of development, and the meaning of conflict were not necessary for treatment. The introduction of cognitive theories to behavior therapy has since led many therapists who are inclined to a behavioral approach to acknowledge the role that thoughts, emotions, and attachment play in treatment.[3]

Whether knowingly or intuitively, every clinician enters the patient's developmental space (Noam, 1985). The therapist who has accomplished this might seek to help the patient live successfully at his current level of development or she might work with the patient to achieve new developmental milestones (Erikson, 1950; Neugarten, 1964). A therapist might also use her understanding of where the patient is developmentally by tailoring her style to the patient's cognitive capacities (Ivey, 1986). To take an extreme example, insight-oriented therapy is not a suitable technique for young children because they cannot make sense of interpretations that identify hidden motivations and unconscious processes. Therefore, the clinician who works with children uses therapies that include play and other outlets for the expression of fantasies and feelings.

In doing clinical work with children and adults, progress is only possible in an environment of therapeutic empathy. As previously noted, outcome studies by Miller et al. show that therapist empathy, not treatment type, was the best predictor of results (Miller et al., 1980). But empathy means experiencing the world of the patient on more than an affective level. It means experiencing the meanings that the patient makes of his environment, himself, and his relationships. To empathize, then, is to enter the patient's world both cognitively and affectively (e.g., Wolf, 1988). This can only be accomplished through a developmental understanding of the patient. It is this grasp of a patient's developmental space that makes the clinical enterprise, even as it is practiced now, a developmentally engaged one.

But the considerable knowledge we have amassed about development allows us to do more. In the clinical setting, we can use our understanding that development is not a single process, but rather one that occurs at a different pace in each of the domains of the personality. The development of cognition, emotion, and the self are not fully synchronized; nor are the evolutions of one's resiliency to stress and one's relationships with others. The picture is complicated by the interrelationship of many of these separate domains because the processes of growth in one area can affect the course taken in another. The additional fact that development takes different paths in different cultures makes it extremely difficult to offer meaningful generalizations about patterns of normal growth. The difficulties in using a developmental frame as a guide for treatment now become clear.

In the next section, I focus on the emergence of the self, especially the self in relationships, from the perspective of cognitive development. Using this social-cognitive lens affords a clearer vision of the myriad maladaptive paths that can be taken in development.

---

[3] Therapists can, in fact, generate such information from the TAT stories. I believe that they should do so as a matter of course. To glean such information from the TAT involves following up the child's answers with special "why questions." Developmental assessments can also be made using the Washington University Sentence Completion Test. My associates and I use this test in our lab not only to determine a child's level of ego development, but also to discover the salient developmental themes in the child's life. We also use our own semistructured interview to assess self complexity in different relationship domains.

GENERAL PRINCIPLES OF CLINICAL-DEVELOPMENTAL PSYCHOLOGY

To create a system for applying differential treatment, the researcher must first decide which basic theory of development will be used. Possible conceptual frameworks include attachment theory, Eriksonian psychosocial stages, a longitudinal epidemiological perspective, and a simple focus on chronological age. The orientation I use in this chapter is the constructivist one. From the constructivist point of view, development is understood to be the product of interactions between the various domains of the self and the environment. From this perspective, the meaning that one constructs of the self and others is believed to change dramatically throughout the life span; symptoms and psychological conditions are viewed to be related to these changes (Dobert, Habermas, & Nunner-Winkler, 1987). This constructivist perspective holds special promise for clinicians and prevention/intervention practitioners for the following reasons:

1. Mental health practitioners of most traditions are interested not only in the "reality" of a situation, but also in the meaning the situation holds for the person. Every clinician knows that similar events have different effects on different people (e.g., Beardslee, 1989). Events that reinforce one child's perspective that the world is untrustworthy lead another child to strengthen ties with supportive adults.
2. Personal meanings are not only idiosyncratic internal constructs that one builds from the material of life experiences, but also follow a more general developmental course. Nine-year-olds tend to see the world far more in terms of rules and make far more social comparisons than do preschoolers, who are more involved in the moment-to-moment excitement of their magical worlds. Thus the same significant event (e.g., not being able to perform a task) will have very different effects on children of different ages. In the 9-year-old, it can be integrated into a meaning system of "others can do it better, I am not as good." The preschooler will not have developed this comparative approach and will be far less likely to encode this experience in this way.
3. Although many clinicians do not have time to pursue systematic research, they are often interested in research findings. Constructivists not only share a level of depth with intervention specialists, but also apply research tools (e.g., interviews, observations, and tests) to measure change and development over time. Clinicians work with clients over time as well; they function as applied developmentalists. These professionals, the researcher and clinician, are natural partners in a dialogue about development.

A number of theorists, researchers, and practitioners have used the expression "clinical developmental psychology" to refer to the clinical application of the constructivist-developmental focus (Basseches, 1989; Noam, 1988a; Selman & Yando, 1980). Others have applied the term to the type of clinical psychology that evolved out of Heinz Werner's work (e.g., 1957). For a review of research that has come from this theory, which demonstrates similarities in functioning between psychopathological adults and normal children, see Bibace and Walsh (1981) and Demick (1996). In this chapter, as in earlier publications (Noam, 1988a, 1988b, 1988c; Noam et al., 1995), clinical developmental psychology will specifically mean the clinical application of the constructivist view of development. But "constructivist" does not refer to an exclusively Piagetian point of view. Instead it refers to a broader notion of the centrality of meaning and interpretation that human beings construct to create their realities.

It will be helpful to describe the general principles of clinical-developmental psychology to better situate the discussions of differential treatment within a conceptual framework. I will then introduce a model of self complexity as understood from a constructivist perspective.

Development of Representations of Self and Other

Clinical-developmental psychology has its foundations in an interactionist perspective that views interpersonal relationships and their internalizations as the essential dimension of human development (e.g., Baldwin, 1902; Cooley, 1902; Mead, 1934). The traditional cognitive theorists (e.g., Piaget, 1926) took the interactionist idea and applied it to cognition, giving the concept of relationship an abstract interpretation (e.g., an epistemic, logical subject relating to a generalized other). Although people use the abstract categories of logic to understand themselves and others, relationships are fundamentally meaningful and embedded (e.g., Gilligan, 1982). This is why the clinical-developmental focus represented here is focused on the growth of the self in relationships and draws on essential relational theory approaches (e.g., Gilligan, 1996; Sullivan, 1953).

Evidence has accumulated that significant relationships with parents, teachers, siblings, and friends are actively constructed and interpreted by the self, and that the result is an internal representation (e.g., Noam et al., 1995). The concept that relationships and experiences with important others become represented internally is common to a number of theories of psychology. These theories include classical psychoanalysis and the branches of the modern analytic schools, such as self psychology, object relations theory, and attachment theory. They also include the developmental theories built on the ideas of Vygotsky, Piaget, Mead, and Baldwin.

Although psychoanalysts, attachment theorists, and clinical-developmental psychologists all share the view that the weaving of relationships creates the inner fabric of the self (e.g., Bretherton, 1996; Cicchetti, 1991), the clinical-developmental psychologist examines the typical transformations of relationships over the course of the life span (Noam & Fischer, 1996).

There is evidence from a number of cross-sectional and longitudinal studies for the clinical-developmental view that internal representations of the self and others change over time (e.g., Broughton, 1978; Edelstein, 1990). This view owes much to Piaget and Kohlberg, whose early work on the moral judgment of the child (Kohlberg, 1969; Piaget, 1932) revealed that children's constructions of social rules and relationships change as they grow. Piaget and Kohlberg's ideas have now been refined; new cognitive perspectives on the child's relationship to his social world and to important others exist in the literature (e.g., Damon, 1977; Keller, 1984; Noam, Powers, Kilkenny, & Beedy, 1990; Selman, 1980).

All these models and studies view development as a complex branching out of the child's representations of the self and others. At the earliest stage, a young child perceives relationships in terms of physical attributes. Later, psychological characteristics, such as the ways that thoughts and feelings are shared, dominate the view of relationships. With increased age and maturity, a tolerance of the multifaceted and contradictory nature of relationships comes to the fore. At each step of the way, the representations of how one defines who one is, and what one sees as the most salient features in a relationship, changes. Although clinical-developmental psychology is built on an understanding of the typical cognitive development of the representations of self and relationships, the focus on clinical phenomena has led to significant theoretical extensions:

- There is greater awareness that representations of significant relationships can be quite resistant to change, despite their potential for transformation (e.g., adults tend to represent their parents as still relatively powerful figures, at times viewing them from the perspective of a child; Bretherton, 1996). Although the inner representational life is conservative in nature, most people are capable of changing their perspectives on significant relationships and are able to do what attachment theorists call "updating the working model."
- It is no longer necessary to choose between a psychoanalytic perspective that concentrates on the power of earlier and more primitive representations of relationships and a developmental point of view that focuses on a continued, lifelong, stepwise progression of representations of self and relationships (e.g., Snow, 1991). Clinical-developmental psychology recognizes the fluctuations between progress and regress in development, the resistance to changing one's early representations, and the evolution and progression that can nonetheless take place.
- Clinical-developmental psychology recognizes that children, adolescents, and adults do not possess a single representation of all important relationships, but multiple ones. These different representations present a challenge to the theorist, clinician, and researcher seeking to understand the individual's internal world. They contrast with a focus on overall capacities (e.g., maturity), overall deficiencies (e.g., delay), and the simple dichotomies of normalcy and pathology. For example, an adolescent girl who has had positive mothering experiences will likely develop positive and mature representations of her mother and other maternal figures. That same girl might have had a brother who sexually abused her. In such an event, she would probably develop a representation of her brother that causes her not only to be fearful of him, but afraid of intimacy with any man. It is important to understand the distinction between the internal representations of the girl's mother and brother. Clinical-developmental psychology is a theoretical lens through which we can explore these different facets of the internal world.

The decades of careful work in tracing typical sequences of how the self and relationships develop (e.g., Damon & Hart, 1988; Erikson, 1968; Flavell, 1977; Kegan, 1982; Kohlberg, 1984) has provided the clinical-developmental psychologist with powerful tools. These tools are quite useful, even though the assumption these theorists make that development progresses in a straightforward, stepwise fashion is not shared by the clinical-developmental psychologist. Nor is it what the research with clinical populations supports (e.g., Noam et al., 1995). But the fact that clinicians are beginning to be emancipated from the overemphasis on early childhood fixations as the main source of human suffering is a major step forward.

Normative Development

To understand the developmental dimensions inherent in psychopathology, it is essential to understand what typically occurs in "normal development." How else can we know which challenges arise naturally in life and which represent the beginnings of serious deviation and maladaptation? Anxieties in early childhood are common (e.g., fears of separation, monsters, darkness) and are not necessarily a cause for clinical concern. But severe separation anxiety in middle childhood and adolescence is not typical, and such anxiety often requires clinical attention.

Although theory and clinical observation can clarify what is developmentally normal and what is not, it is only through empirical studies with community samples that these distinctions can be properly made. Such studies can also help determine the prevalence of anxiety, aggression, depression, suicidality, and so on in the child and adolescent population. How do they vary by socio-economic class, geographic location, ethnic group, and gender? And how do these problems change over time? Answers to some of these questions have already come from large-scale longitudinal epidemiological studies (for a review, see Costello & Angold, 1995).

These findings supply the tools to apply, in a meaningful way, the concepts of delay and aberrant pathways that have proved to be so useful to studies of mental retardation, delinquency, and psychosis. We can, for example, trace a delinquent's moral development, allowing us to see that it is delayed compared with that of his nondelinquent peers (e.g., Gibbs, Arnold, Ahlborn, & Chessman, 1984). Such findings provide a developmental focus; they allow us to see that it is not only behavior that distinguishes delinquents from nondelinquents, but also level of sociomoral maturity. More importantly, once we understand the moral delay, we can begin to focus interventions on supporting the process of maturation of the cognitive system that guides moral development. Typically, the delinquent adolescent experiences the world as unsafe and unfair, and thus rationalizes his delinquent actions as revenge and justified responses to unfairness. The clinical-developmental psychologist is interested in helping this adolescent by:

- Taking the delinquent's ways of making meaning seriously instead of only viewing them as psychopathic intellectualizations (which they can be as well).
- Focusing on the adolescent's internal representations, and by doing so offering the patient enough empathy and support to allow him to change his way of seeing the world.
- Applying knowledge about the typical course of development, in this case in the sociomoral domain.
- Guiding the adolescent in the process of development by finding, or creating, developmentally supportive environments, such as prosocial peer groups.
- Remaining committed to the idea that treatment not only means symptom reduction but developmental change.

Clinical-developmental psychology is not just an application of the study of normal development to the realm of psychological dysfunction. It is also a reformulation of a number of traditionally held assumptions of normative theory (e.g., Cicchetti, 1996; Noam, 1996; Noam & Cicchetti, 1996). Key among these reformulations is the view that symptoms may be expressed differently depending on the individual's level of development (e.g., Noam, 1988a, 1988b, 1988c). Typically, in early phases of development, impulsive, action-oriented symptoms are more frequent, whereas later in development, internalizing symptoms such as depression arise with greater frequency (above and beyond the gender findings, with boys tending more toward externalizing and girls toward internalizing disorders and symptoms). Therefore, the idea that higher stages of development are necessarily more adaptive, as is suggested by many developmental theories, requires serious reconsideration. The clinical-developmental psychologist does not view development as progressing simply from egocentric, unsocialized, and impulsive stages to those defined by the ability to see the world from other people's perspectives. Developmental theories have assumed this view for too long. But we now know that the same developmental course that leads to increased self-knowledge in some people leads to alienation, self-deception, and self-destructive behavior in others (e.g., Noam et al., 1995). Reaching formal operations, for example, can throw the adolescent into a dangerous identity crisis, providing so many potential selves that no choice seems possible (e.g., Perry, 1970). Chandler (1973) referred to this cognitive crisis of adolescence as the "epistemological loneliness of formal operations" (p. 381).

Beyond Age Chronology

The clinical-developmental approach is far less focused on chronological age than are most research approaches to development and psychopathology. It has become quite common to label a model or study an example of research in "developmental psychopathology" if age is introduced as an important variable. But chronological age is a very crude indicator of the underlying processes of biological maturation, cognitive capacity, peer and family relations, and self-understanding. Age, of course, plays a role in development in most of these domains, but there is frequently a significant variation in maturity in each of these areas within a single age group.

Age trends also exist in some forms of psychopathology. Suicide rates rise dramatically in adolescence, as do other disorders such as depression and conduct problems. Schizophrenia typically begins in late adolescence or young adulthood. Age, therefore, can serve as a simple way to organize an understanding of many underlying pathogenic processes. However, the simplicity of this approach is deceptive (see Rutter, 1989; Wohlwill, 1973). In psychopathological development, as in normal development, chronological age is by no means a guarantor that basic cognitive and social-cognitive processes have occurred. Despite textbook claims to the contrary, many adolescents and adults never achieve formal-operational thought (i.e., tables in a typical psychology textbook list adolescence next to formal operations as if all adolescents are in that cognitive stage). Although many adolescents have achieved a formal operational level of thinking, others continue to function at the level of concrete operations and, indeed, may remain at this level for the rest of their lives (e.g., Noam et al., 1990).

Consequently, if we use chronological age as the principal developmental marker, then the important variations that occur in every group of normally developing individuals will receive insufficient attention. Reinecke (1993) quoted Steinberg and Hill's 1978 work in which they found that parents tend to judge their sons' intellectual capacities on the basis of their physical growth, which can more directly be related to age than to cognitive maturity. Reinecke (1993) suggests that therapists also can easily misunderstand an adolescent's needs if they view him as having completed his age-appropriate physical maturation, and that "it would be prudent to view adolescents' social, physical, emotional, and cognitive development as domains in need of individual assessment (p. 389)." For the clinical-developmental psychologist, this suggests that chronological age needs to be supplemented with a domain-specific understanding of the person's capacities in different areas of development (Harter, 1994; Henderson, 1989).

For that reason, clinical-developmental psychologists study cognitive, social, and emotional development in relation to symptoms, syndromes, or types of maladaptations without a singular reference to chronological age. Ironically, chronological age becomes more important from such a perspective than it would if it were used as a simple developmental marker because any focus on mental representation and the construction of meaning has to ask whether developmental capacities have "fallen behind" or are accelerated.

In addition, one has to assume that different cognitive and social cognitive capacities will have a different function at different ages, even when those capacities have the same formal structure. Many people reach a third-person perspective-taking position in early adolescence and continue to see themselves and the world from that perspective throughout life. It is unlikely, however, that the basic ways in which a woman of 70 perceives herself and others, and interprets present, past, and future events, will be the same as that of a 15-year-old girl. In other publications, I have drawn a distinction between stage and phase, defining the former as a developmental progression of capacities and skills that is independent of age and the latter as a socially constructed timetable (e.g., graduation from high school, retirement) that is measured in terms of age.

This distinction recognizes the need to use chronological age as a marker; it is especially useful as a shorthand for many clinicians. Even in deciding which treatment to use, age plays a role (e.g., whether or not play therapy is called for depends on the age of the child). But, although capacities are often measured in terms of chronological age, the more sophisticated measurements of development available today call on us to subsume the idea of chronological age into an understanding of progressive adaptation and skill acquisition. In so doing, our research finds significant links between development and psychopathology in adolescents, where chronological age plays only a minor role. I elaborate on this point later when I show that it is the level of social-cognitive functioning, not age per se, that is often associated with specific disorders.

Lifelong Development and Recovery

A premise of clinical-developmental psychology is that how a person relates to himself and others can change in fundamental ways over time. There is much evidence now that internal representations are transformed over the course of a lifetime (e.g., Commons, Richards, & Armon, 1984; Kegan, 1982). Although there are undoubtedly many examples of fixated patterns of object relations, it is perhaps more typical that individuals regularly create new relationships and restructure old ones. These transformed relationships are not only the result of new interactions with these important figures, but also of changes in a person's ways of making meaning about the self and others (see also Bowlby, 1969).

Significant developmental changes can, and regularly do, occur long after childhood and adolescence. The lifelong process of development has been eloquently described by Erikson (1950), Vaillant (1977), and Levinson (1990), among others. For most of these authors, development is marked by the achievement of normative life tasks, the evolution of the self, and the maturing of relationships. Cognitive-developmental researchers are less interested in life tasks; instead, they choose to focus on the pattern of thought known as "postformal operations." In this cognitive stage, the logical thinking that is characteristic of the formal operations stage is less rigid. In its place, a new, process-oriented way of thinking emerges that is more tolerant of contradiction, ambiguity, and exceptions to rules (e.g., Commons et al., 1984; Edelstein & Noam, 1982).

But despite a great progress in understanding the achievement of salient life tasks, meaning making, and cognition, little progress has been made in applying this understanding to psychological treatment and recovery. Indeed, little is known even now about typical problems and psychological dysfunctions that arise with development throughout life (e.g., Baltes & Schaie, 1973). Critical to the clinical-developmental psychologist is the understanding that at each point in life, fundamental shifts in cognitive, emotional, social, and interpersonal development are possible, and that these shifts follow a certain logic and organization. For example, an adult who strongly identifies with work, authority, and control, can become disappointed when others do not live up to his expectations. The inclination to disappointment, perfectionism, and excessive control might be long-standing, stemming from compulsive character traits formed in childhood. But they might also stem from the way the man, as an adult, defines his basic categories of self, world, and relationships. Perhaps the issues most central to him are responsibility, predictability, and accountability. These issues and their salience can change over time into a greater acceptance of human frailty and the limitations of control and predictability. As complex ways of understanding and experiencing change, past rigidities are also revisited. Every new chapter in one's life rewrites the earlier chapters. Understanding the ways that people can transform their representational world allows the developmental therapist to help the patient revisit old relationships, overcome old vulnerabilities, work through past traumas, and help prevent new ones from occurring.

Table 9.1 summarizes the key points of this section. It compares the tenets of clinical-developmental theory with those of traditional psychoanalytic and cognitive-behavior theory by identifying how each of these traditions understand symptoms, relationships, development, and recovery. Although the table is necessarily oversimplified, the goal is to differentiate clinical-developmental psychology from these two therapeutic traditions and to simultaneously show existing overlap. But although the table introduces distinctions between the three paradigms, we are witnessing a convergence of cognitive, relational, and developmental principles. The use of narrative in psychoanalysis (e.g., Schafer, 1976, 1983; Spence, 1982) focuses on the patient's construction of his past from the perspective of the present day. Some cognitive-behavior therapists have turned to a relational perspective and have discovered the regularities in cognitive development (Guidano & Liotti, 1983) that are so essential to the academic developmental psychologist. But despite these interesting ways in which the different clinical paradigms incorporate each other's knowledge base, overall the fields continue to evolve on separate tracks.

DEVELOPMENT OF SELF COMPLEXITY

The principles that have been described all point to increasingly complex forms in the ways a person perceives herself, her relationships, and the world. Over time, people tend to become better able to label emotions, infer motivations, and perceive the internal reality of others. They typically progress from a developmental world in which they make physical distinctions to one in which they make psychological distinctions. In the process, they often become better able to observe themselves more objectively and regulate their behaviors (e.g., delay immediate gratification). Useful differentiations have been overshadowed in the cognitive-developmental literature by a rigid notion of psychological stages. In an effort to formalize the stage theory of development, something of a caricature of developmental progress became established, in which an understanding that was useful for measurement and research design did not correspond to the ways that people actually develop over time. Writing about research and classifying treatment options leads to the same quandary encountered by the stage theorists: It is easier to write about developmental stages than about developmental process. In the interest of communicating my ideas, I use the concept of developmental level, but readers should look at these references to levels as they would to a frozen frame in an evolving film.

To recapitulate, through continuous exchange between the organism and the environment, the person and the culture, the individual and relationships, one is challenged to establish increasingly complex views about the self and others. As these meaning systems about the self evolve with cognitive development, they affect more than thought.

Table 9.1 Differences between Three Therapy Schools

	Cognitive-Behavioral Approach	Clinical-Developmental Approach	Traditional Psychoanalytic Approach
Symptoms	Cognitive attributions lead to self-defeating behaviors. These cognitions are usually global, undifferentiated, primitive, and immature. Underlying meanings of symptoms or cognitions not viewed as important.	New symptoms emerge and are often connected to the most complex forms of meaning and understandings of self and relationships. Earlier problems can develop into more complex ones. Symptoms are related to meanings, but meanings are often conscious and related to present developmental complexity.	Symptoms are related to developmental fixations, arrests, or early self or ego deficiencies. Symptoms have meanings that can be understood.
Relationships	Therapist-patient relationships not an essential part of treatment, although there is a beginning recognition of how important the therapeutic relationships really are.	Strong focus on relationships as causes for problems and context to overcome symptoms. Past vulnerabilities and significant attachments always seen in conjunction with continued relationship development. Thus therapist-patient relationship an essential focus of treatment.	Special focus on archaic relationships which emerge in the transference. Present relationship viewed through lens of "therapeutic alliance"; transference and countertransference the essential aspects of therapeutic process.
Development	In a general way, behavior and cognition develop and change at any point in life, but a formal developmental conception is missing.	Development produces formative points in life not only during the early years but at any time in the life span.	Although very important life span-developmental contributions in theory (e.g., Erikson, Vaillant), the main focus in treatment is the return to early developmental eras and their unresolved conflict (e.g., oedipal, preoedipal).
Recovery	Unlearning of undermining behaviors; directive and playful overcoming of symptoms. No explicit direct link between normative development and recovery.	Recovery tied to the person's potential to develop new meanings, self-understandings, and relationships. Therapeutic relationship does not only return to the past but creates a momentum to evolve natural tendencies to develop and recover.	Return to past, unconscious feelings and thoughts, and working through of the transference and past trauma to free the patient. Connection between development and recovery conceptualized as a developmental process but focus is on early (preoedipal, oedipal) development.

At each new stage, affects, meanings, and motivations that are typical of that developmental position emerge. From a clinical perspective, each position brings out new strengths and opportunities to rework past vulnerabilities. However, each new set of meanings can also lead to new challenges and problems. It is also possible for old dysfunctions to become more complex.

Through social interactions, the self continually evolves, and greater self complexity can result. Past publications have discussed the development of self complexity in some detail (e.g., Noam, 1988c; Noam et al., 1990). I will briefly summarize it here. The self is always a self-in-relationship; it emerges out of early attachment relationships and continues to develop within relationships throughout the life span. The self is a constructed meaning system that is both updated and modified constantly and yet prefers to hold onto old ways of interpreting experience. It evolves through internalizations of relationships throughout life. The shape these internalizations take depends on the complexity and maturity of development. The internalizations of interaction patterns with others are the building blocks of both positive and negative adaptations.

Self complexity refers to the developmental pathway of these components, namely understandings and experiences of close relationships and biographical meanings of the self. It builds on an underlying logic of what I call *self perspective.* This expression has its roots in Baldwin (1902), Mead (1934), and other role-taking theorists. Especially helpful has been Selman's (1980) operationalization of these concepts through developmental studies on the evolution of perspective-taking in childhood and adolescence. However, Selman, as well as others who have employed a role-taking or social perspective approach (e.g., Chandler, 1973; Flavell, 1977), have not taken the step of developing an explicit theory of self-in-relationships. An understanding of self complexity attempts to address this need. The concept of self complexity parallels other social cognitive and constructivist-developmental ideas, including Loevinger's (1976) model of ego development, Damon and Hart's (1988) theory of self understanding, Broughton's (1978) definitions of self and mind, and Kegan's (1982) subject-object development. But as mentioned earlier, the nature of the levels differs significantly in that I posit continuous multiple-level functioning, not a simple stagewise progression. Figure 9.1 shows the dynamic and recursive model of the self.

Multiple-Level Functioning

I have labeled a source of fluctuations of meaning making at different levels of complexity "encapsulations." Encapsulations are old meaning systems that are guided by the cognitive and affective logic that governed at the time the encapsulation occurred. Prone to significant distortions, internalized early events and important others become tied to powerful meanings and strong emotions. People remain loyal to them even when they are not adaptive and cause pain and conflict. Without necessarily knowing this consciously, the feeling of loss caused by detaching from an encapsulation is experienced as more painful than the anticipated gains are liberating.

The assertion that individuals can develop only in some areas, and therefore function at different developmental levels at the same time, is consistent with findings of neo-Piagetian researchers (e.g., Fischer, 1980; Fischer & Ayoub, 1994). Most explanations of development asynchrony state that the limited generalization of transformation is due to a lack of opportunity to try new skills. Social

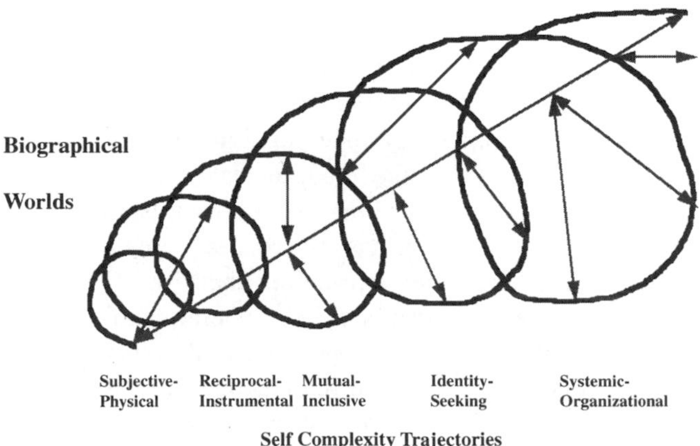

Figure 9.1 Developmental-transformation model: biography and self complexity.

and cognitive development do not occur as context-independent unfoldings of innate abilities. Instead, the abilities evolve in the active exchange of person and opportunities in the environment. The self has to be stimulated and challenged, contradictions need to be experienced, and support needs to be offered to find new and more complex solutions. These are the reasons opportunities can be available in some areas of a person's life but not in others. For example, a thoughtful, artistic youngster loves to paint and pursues the visual medium in museums and books, but mathematics frightens this adolescent, who is also suffering from a mild learning disability. Exposure to numbers led to a "closing off" early in his school career. Adequate supports were not introduced because the learning problems had not been detected. The result was an anxious turning away from the world of numbers and formulas. Not only is this youngster lagging behind his classmates, but essential capacities of logic are not being developed. Yet in the artistic realm, this boy explores, invents, and is developing skills and expertise.

From the perspective of the self, I am suggesting an additional interpersonal interpretation for the discrepancies: Internal relationships can keep a person from experimenting with new situations and responses. This is why, for example, impulse control and the delay of gratification do not necessarily reach mature levels even when an understanding of interpersonal relationships has matured.

The model of encapsulations does not correspond with traditional psychoanalytic fixation theory. Even when aspects of the self do not join the overall thrust of development, it is essential to understand the continued developmental path of the self and to view what is left behind always in relation to the more complex self positions. Furthermore, fixations refer to early experiences, and encapsulations can occur at any developmental level in life.

Depending on the developmental level in which the encapsulations occurred, they can be physical in nature (based on magical thinking, focused on the body-self and images of bodily survival during physical separations), (e.g., Fish-Murray, 1993) concrete action oriented (based on a view of the self as an agent that acts on the world or needs to manipulate the world to have needs gratified), or psychological (a state where needs are expressed in symbolic form around identifications with others).

Developmental Positions of Self Complexity

Having established that a great deal of fluctuation exists in development and that the developmental positions are usually not fully integrated and synthesized, we need to describe the developmental positions of self complexity as they give shape to new symptomatology and represent opportunities for specific interventions. For this reason, each developmental position is labeled and described in terms of strengths and weaknesses. Brief descriptions are elaborated on in tables and case examples presented later in this chapter.

Most people fluctuate in the perspectives they take; they do not exist in a single level of self complexity. Every person is a complex dynamic of past experiences and unevolved meanings and beliefs that coexist with more complex forms of knowing the self, others, and the world at large. The developmental levels of self complexity are important, though, for two main reasons: (a) to find the most complex form that allows for a sense of a "cutting edge," a new developmental possibility of transforming the self; and (b) earlier, encapsulated aspects of the self can be revisited with the tools of the most complex forms of self-observation. The less evolved forms of self complexity still exert power over the self and can be better understood if we know how they are structured. This is similar to the psychoanalyst's ability to distinguish between early "dyadic, pre-oedipal material" centered around fear of abandonment and fear of losing body integrity and a "triadic, oedipal psychology" which is more differentiated, competitive, and ambivalent. For these reasons, a detailed assessment of a person involves an analysis of all levels of self complexity in the life of that person.

The first self complexity position is what I call the *subjective-physical position.* This level permits the child little consideration of the other's interests and desires as different from those of the self. There is an emerging awareness of the distinction between physical and psychological characteristics in people, but actions are primarily evaluated in terms of physical consequences. Impulsive responses are typical and feelings are expressed in action language. Strengths are found in the emerging ability to distinguish between fantasy and reality, to pursue wishes and desires by translating them into directed action, to display a will, and to demonstrate an independent curiosity. These strengths are in part based on the achievement of object constancy (e.g., Mahler, Pine, & Bergman, 1975), the conviction that the other continues to exist even when separated from the self.

In the *reciprocal-instrumental self complexity position,* self interests can be identified as separate from the goals and intents of others. Conflicting interests between self and other can be resolved through instrumental exchange, often understood in instrumental ways. An acknowledgment of the power of the other can lead to a compromise. The person can step out of the concrete bounds of the self, thus allowing for a view of reciprocity in relationships. The perspective one has of oneself and others also changes. A distinction is made between the "public self" and the "inner hidden self." This allows for the possibility of deception. For example, a person may be afraid but not show fear, thus appearing "cool." In addition, the self imposes strong boundaries at this stage.

Conflict at this point usually does not lead to submission or impulsive action, but to self-protective assertion of control. When faced with powerful or guilt-inducing authorities, a return to fearful submission can occur. Nonetheless, there is typically a stronger capacity to resist authority, either directly or through deception. The positive outcome is an ability to control feelings, to concentrate on tasks, to be a team player, and to understand rules. The limitation of the reciprocal-instrumental position is the view that relationships are not built on trust, but rather guided by an interest in power. This often leads to opportunism, exploitation, and manipulation.

With the *mutual-inclusive self-complexity position,* a person understands others in relationships, and this understanding is coordinated through a generalized perspective. The person experiences different points of view according to the "Golden Rule" of seeing reality through the eyes of another person. This perspective creates the context for an increase in altruistic actions. Attitudes and values are seen as persisting over time, often leading to stereotypes like "I am that kind of person who . . . " These "self-traits," in addition to the new internal perspective, lead to more complex self-observational capacities. The limitations of this form of self complexity, however, are an overidentification with the views of the other and the potential for overly conformist social behavior: What do others think? What is normal? It is crucial for the self to be liked at all times and appreciated to maintain self-esteem. Typical feelings of low self-esteem and a proneness to experience depression and anxiety are linked to a sense of abandonment and feeling "lost in the world."

The *identity-seeking self-complexity position* is marked by a strong tension between defining the self through the eyes of others and the attempt to create a more unified sense of self and identity out of the various identifications that marked childhood and are powerful in adolescence. The person experiences the limits of being a different kind of person in each relationship and tries to create strong cross-contextual coherence. In the process of developing a stronger sense of destiny and differentiation, issues of choice become paramount. The person is often in great conflict over the wish to avoid the loss of approval from others while at the same time becoming increasingly concerned with issues of authenticity and autonomy. While these issues exist throughout life, the complex nature with which they are addressed and the central importance given to them is specific to the identity-seeking self-complexity position.

The *systemic-organizational self-complexity position* makes possible the distinction between the societal point of view and the interpersonal one. Multiple mutual perspectives can be integrated into a broader view. When the self takes a systemic perspective on relationships, the communication between people is seen as existing on a number of levels simultaneously. Individual relations are interpreted in terms of their place within a larger system of consciously defined roles and rules. System-maintenance of the self becomes the hallmark of this stage. The person views the self as having control over its own destiny. This is also the point, however, at which the person realizes the existence of parts of the self not easily managed by the system's control, conscious or unconscious. The societal perspective also brings out strong motivations of achievement, duty, and competition. The limitations of the systemic self-complexity perspective are the attempt to overcontrol the self and others, to reflect on social relations excessively in terms of power, role, and status, and to take so many perspectives on the self and other that obsessive-compulsive indecision can result.

A Case Example: Rachel

I want to bring these developmental distinctions to life by describing an adolescent girl called Rachel. Her clinical and developmental profile illustrates how self complexity adds a significant dimension to the traditional psychoanalytic-developmental view. Rachel also teaches us about the multiplicity of complexity levels coexisting within one person.

Rachel is a 13-year-old girl who was admitted to a psychiatric hospital's child and adolescent unit because of a serious depression. For about a year, she exhibited strong mood swings, attempted suicide, and isolated herself from her family. In addition to the depressive symptoms, she was also quite impulsive and aggressive. Her parents reported that she lied, stole, was truant, and experimented a great deal with drugs and alcohol. The aggression was limited to the family (she had threatened her mother and brother with a knife), but many of her other behaviors were more pronounced within a delinquent peer group. Although Rachel reported that she never felt close to her parents and was viewed by them as an "unhappy child," she was able to function quite well before adolescence.

On hospitalization, Rachel was perceived by the treatment staff as "developmentally extremely delayed and cognitively quite limited." Although she was seen as intelligent, the staff complained that she showed little insight into her problems. Her depression, along with her impulsivity, made her a serious suicide risk in the eyes of her therapist. The diagnosis, based on a structured research interview, the Diagnostic Interview Schedule for Children (Costello, Edelbrock, Dulcan, Kalas, & Klarie, 1984) was conduct disorder and major depression. On the Symptom Checklist (Achenbach & Edelbrock, 1978), she scored high on both the internalizing scale (which includes symptoms such as perfectionism, sadness, and anxiety) and on the externalizing scale (which includes symptoms like destroying property, truancy, and aggressive behavior).

A standard psychological test battery, which included a Rorschach, Thematic Apperception Test, and Wechsler Intelligence Scale for Children (WISC), provided a detailed portrait of her internal world. The psychologist wrote: "When tasks are relatively unstructured or when elaborated social reasoning is involved, personal concerns intrude and performance worsens. There is a marked reluctance to involve the self with others and mistrust of others is so profound that virtually no sharing of personal information occurs. There is even an avoidance of the examination of personal feelings and reactions when alone. Although Rachel can present herself as social and related, her real disconnectedness from others cannot be overemphasized." A senior consultant known for his thoughtful clinical assessments viewed her as "infantile," suspected that she had suffered a "developmental arrest at the age of six," and was concerned about her "absence of abstract thinking," as was evident in her concreteness, denial, and a lack of introspection.

But whereas our diagnostic and symptom instruments were similar to those of the psychological tester and clinical team, the results of our developmental interviews and tests were different. On Loevinger's Washington University Sentence Completion Test (for a description, see Loevinger, 1976), Rachel scored higher than the great majority of her hospitalized agemates. She demonstrated a great deal of complex thought, empathy, and an ability to view herself through the perspective of others. Rachel wrote, for example, "A good mother . . . is listening to your child, giving advice, and trusting them to make the right decision. And knowing how to let go." She also wrote, "What gets me into trouble . . . is my attitude that I want to be a troublemaker." These sentences demonstrate an understanding that the parent-child relationship is built on trust, communication, and parental support of the child's autonomy. She also recognizes that she is responsible for the trouble she makes. In writing that she wants to be a troublemaker, she sees herself as an agent of action. Because it is important to distinguish the words chosen to complete a sentence stem from their underlying meanings, I use a semistructured interview focusing on the self in relationships with parents, peers, romantic friends, and so on, to assess self complexity in various relationship domains (Noam et al., 1990). This interview revealed in Rachel an interesting split between a mutual-inclusive complexity level and many responses, especially in her relationship with her family, that were at earlier developmental levels, particularly the reciprocal-instrumental level.

Our recognition of Rachel's mature developmental capacities has important implications for understanding who she is and what problems she faces. Rachel has the developmental capacities that are typical of the position of mutual-inclusive self complexity. For example, she demonstrates a concern for others even when she does not receive a direct benefit in return. The last sentence quoted from the Loevinger test reveals an ability to take some perspective on her acting-out behavior; she states that she chooses to create trouble and that it is her attitude (rather than other people or outside events) that gets her into trouble. Her statement about her mother demonstrates a complex view of self and relationships (the notion of listening, trust, letting go at the appropriate time, and so on).

How are we then to understand the discrepancy in view between the skillful staff who perceived this adolescent to be extremely immature and the developmental testing results that showed her to have relatively mature developmental competencies? We are faced with a paradoxical situation: The treatment staff's insistence on Rachel's primitive functioning fails to recognize her more mature social-developmental abilities, whereas the developmental account fails to capture her immature cognitive and affective processes. Rachel is not unusual in that she displays variations in modes of thought, and experiences and expressions of feeling. Only when we relate the mature parts of the self to the immature parts can we capture the full strength of a clinical-developmental perspective that can enlighten our work, not just with Rachel, but with children and adolescents in general.

The profile from the sentence completion test is significant. It shows a great deal of variation in response complexity (responses range from very low to a very high). But the test is scored in such a way as to give a single, overall stage score, ignoring important variations. This strategy of scoring is quite typical in the cognitive and social-cognitive traditions and should give way to a multilevel assessment that takes account of the different developmental capacities coexisting simultaneously.

Rachel describes a world in which people she cared about are unreliable and hurtful. She has constantly felt rejected, from early childhood onward. This corresponds with her parents' report that she was an unwanted child. Rachel's core themes, including a pervasive feeling of rejection, are based on the experience that the important people in her life were untrustworthy. As a consequence, Rachel has become self-protective and vindictive; it is this that accounts for her aggressiveness when faced with close relationships that might lead to disappointment.

But as mentioned earlier, Rachel reached a mutual-inclusive organization. Her self-esteem rests on group affiliations, and her need for affirmation is at its most intense in intimate relationships. Her distrust of others and her isolation reveal that aspects of her personality remain in the earlier reciprocal-instrumental stage, but they create more internal conflict than would be expected of someone at that stage. Rachel's motivation for closeness and intimate sharing is quite pronounced. In fact, a need for trust in relationships is one of the hallmarks of this stage, and the feeling of being unable to trust becomes especially painful. Her aggression can be understood as a response to her unfulfilled need for closeness. Rachel chose a delinquent group of peers not for concrete rewards in the way of stolen goods, but to protest against her parents and to find a setting where she could feel accepted.

This example demonstrates the need for clinicians to really understand the process of development, to develop a language for the continued evolution of self and relationships, and to view symptoms and behavior as part of meaningful expressions of the self.

SOCIAL-COGNITIVE DEVELOPMENT AND THERAPY

In this section, I review constructivist-developmental contributions to child and adolescent therapy. Among the scholars and clinicians who have bridged the gap between cognitive developmental psychology and clinical practice are Ivey, Ivey, and Simek-Morgan (1993), Guidano and Liotti (1983), Noam (1988a, 1988b, 1988c), Rosen (1985), Rosen and Kuehlwein (1996), Selman and Schultz (1990), and Shirk (1988). Although each of these theorists offers a view of developmental therapy that is unique, in this section I will outline the common themes, which help establish differential intervention strategies.

These themes include the constructivist view, which focuses on the ways therapist and patient develop meaning and how symptoms are related to underlying beliefs and theories about the self. Developmentalists make a distinction between what a patient is capable of and what he does in therapy. Instead of assuming that a patient is resisting if he does not gain insight when presented with an interpretation, research now suggests that not everyone has the necessary tools to be "insightful" (Harter, 1988; Shirk, 1988). In addition, some constructivist theorists stress the importance of multiple-level functioning; they do not apply a stage model of development. As discussed earlier, one purpose of clinical-developmental psychology is to access and integrate earlier ways of knowing and experiencing as development progresses.

In *Cognitive Development and Child Psychotherapy,* Shirk (1988) edited an important volume of nine essays exploring cognitive, self, and interpersonal aspects of child therapy from a constructivist perspective. One concept shared in these works is that "child psychotherapy is a developmental context in which children's cognitive abilities are applied to interpersonal and intrapsychic content over time" (p. 2).

Shirk stresses that the therapist needs to assess the child's developmental level accurately and communicate to the child on his level, otherwise the child is unlikely to benefit from the interaction (e.g., the child will either ignore the communication or interpret it though the perspective of his developmental level and thereby distort its content). This point provides a rationale for a developmental approach to child and adolescent psychotherapy.

According to Shirk, Noam (1986a, 1986b), and Selman (1980), an especially difficult concept for children is unconscious motivation. The paradox of unconscious motivations (things are done for a reason, and yet not done on purpose) is beyond the child's understanding. Shirk offers an example of a troubled schoolchild who was placed in foster care. The child began to act out against a substitute teacher in school. In a discussion with the school principal, the child attributed his disruptive behavior to the fact that the teacher gave too much work. The child's therapist, however, suspected that the amount of work was only one reason for the child's intense reaction. He believed that the behavior was also a result of an "unconscious transference reaction . . . [in which] feelings intended for the 'substitute' parent have been transferred to the substitute teacher" (p. 80). When the therapist presented him with this interpretation, the child dismissed it, calling it "stupid," and continued to blame the teacher. Shirk argues that this response should be understood in its whole complexity, not merely as "resistance." It is likely that the child's cognitive level rendered him incapable of recognizing his psychological processes.

In a similar fashion, Nannis (1988) argues that children's conceptions of emotions are related to their cognitive level. Therefore, a child's denial of conflictual feelings is not necessarily a manifestation of pathology, rather it may be an indication that the child does not possess the cognitive capacities to behave otherwise. Child therapists, therefore, should be especially careful in their assessment. Rather than follow their intuitions regarding the child's understanding of feelings, they must examine what the child is capable of. A child who is highly verbal is often perceived as having achieved relatively high level of reasoning, which can give the therapist "a false sense of progress." Later in therapy, when the child demonstrates thinking at a cognitive level appropriate to her age, the therapist might be tempted to interpret the behavior as "regression." Nannis describes this unfortunate misunderstanding well when she writes, "It is more likely that the child had never truly functioned at a higher level. Rather, the child sounded as if he or she had. It is part of the therapist's responsibility to assess how information is internalized and processed, not just how it is verbalized" (p. 112).

Harter (1988) makes a similar point regarding an adequate evaluation of competence. She believes that the degree of similarity between the child's developmental level and the therapist's communication will determine whether or not the insight offered by the therapist will facilitate change. She points out that the therapist's interest in self-reflection, thoughts, and emotions often stand in contrast to children's interest in concrete activities in the outside world. As a result, overly "psychological" interventions that require introspection and self-reflection on the part of the child are likely to fail since they do not match the child's interests. Thus, for school-age children, action-oriented techniques, such as direct modeling, are likely to be more effective than are insight-oriented ones.

Bierman (1988) argues that preschoolers and young school-age children are unable to integrate inconsistent information about people. For example, if they learn that a movie star committed a crime, most young children will deny that the star can still be a star. Similarly, a child's abrupt change in feeling toward a friend or a significant other may be a normal reaction for the child's level of cognitive development.

Multiple Functioning

Clinicians tend to recognize that their patients often function at multiple levels simultaneously (e.g., Van der Kolk, 1996). Clients often come to treatment because they are troubled or less mature in one area, but they can be quite mature and possess good coping styles in other areas. This experience of multiple functioning and domain specificity has made some clinicians skeptical about the usefulness of developmental perspectives based on stage theories. A number of developmental theorists have begun to address this concern (see, e.g., Noam & Fischer, 1996).

As reported earlier (Noam, 1988a, 1988b, 1988c), advances in social cognition might not reduce symptoms, but rather shift them to a higher developmental level (e.g., the same underlying conflict will be expressed in a higher level symptom). In fact, in many cases greater complexity in self-conception can lead to more sophisticated ways of self-deception and alienation. It is essential not to view symptoms and psychopathology as necessarily primitive and developmentally immature (Noam & Borst, 1995). Also important is the idea that social-cognitive development is not uniform across all aspects of personality, but rather that there are encapsulations of old meaning systems. These old meaning systems, usually in the area of emotional and interpersonal functioning, are governed by a lower cognitive level and resist integration to the higher-level system. Encapsulations can be understood in terms of internalizations. The emphasis in child therapy on advancing development is not helpful to the child if it neglects encapsulated areas. Instead, the therapist should attend to the interrelation between the different developmental levels by engaging in careful analysis of (a) the broader gestalt of the client's core themes in their relationships, (b) encapsulations, and (c) the patient's most mature developmental capacities.

In support of Noam, Leahy (1988) believes that an individual's maladaptive notions regarding herself and her relationships might be the product of the developmental stage in which those notions were formed (as are encapsulations). These early self-schemas often do not change despite cognitive development in other areas. Furthermore, Leahy suggests that progress in social-cognitive development may have negative results. The ability to take a third-person perspective can lead to excess self-reflection which, in turn, may result in self-reproach. Similarly, more complex moral development can produce excessive guilt feelings. These new capacities may make the person more vulnerable to "self-critical depression" (p. 196). Thus, higher stages are not necessarily better; they can bring new vulnerabilities as well as positive changes.

Russell and van den Broek (1988) hold that children's difficulties with therapeutic tasks are not a result of their general cognitive level, but of excessive demands in a specific domain, such as attention or memory. They suggest that therapists complement less-developed aspects of children's cognitive functions to counterbalance demands that are beyond their cognitive abilities. Russell and van den Broek view child psychotherapy as "a process of collaborative problem solving in which the therapist's cognitive abilities support the child's active attempts at problem mastery" (p. 325).

From a moral perspective, Blakeney and Blakeney (1990) introduced a typology of conduct problems. They created three categories of moral misbehavior in a population of severely emotionally disturbed girls in residential treatment at the Berkeley Academy in California. The first category is that of the "rebel." This group of girls usually defied authority and claimed that they did not know how to do their work (in making these claims, they managed to denigrate others). They frequently skipped school, abused drugs and alcohol, stole from others, and sold drugs. The girls tended to justify their behavior as the "practical solution to the problem of unfair distribution" (p. 101).

The second category of moral misbehavior is that of the "martyr." Girls in this category tended to run away from home or school. They often engaged in self-injurious behaviors such as drug and alcohol abuse, self-mutilation with knives or razor blades, and sex with strangers. Their behavior vacillated from temper tantrums to inviting protective attention. They often described "feelings" as the motivation for their behavior, particularly of sadness, abandonment, and rage.

The third category is that of the "professional orphan." These girls frequently exhibited extreme behaviors, both alone and in public, such as hiding in closets, setting fires, masturbating in public, and disrupting their class. They often justified their behavior by claiming that they were "just playing."

Blakeney and Blakeney's perspective is that "by understanding the relationship between the pattern of moral misbehavior and the structure of moral thought and feeling in the social context, we are able to understand the function of the child's misbehavior" (p. 102). Only when the clinician understands the function served by the deviant behavior in maintaining the child's psychic equilibrium can a child be treated by bringing latent moral capacities to awareness and trying to construct new ways of feeling, thinking, and interacting with others. Blakeney and Blakeney argue that an assessment of type of moral misbehavior and the meaning that a particular behavior holds for the child is essential for deciding on a treatment strategy. Such treatment, they say, should be focused on reconstructing the child's underlying moral beliefs rather than on reconstructing the child's actual behavior.

This work on the need of the therapist to understand the developmental capacities of the child and adolescent, and for the developmentalist to evolve theories and research methods that account for multiple functioning, is very promising. It helps create research-based knowledge for the intervention specialist that shares in the depth the clinician seeks when thinking about self and relationships.

DIFFERENTIAL TREATMENTS IN CLINICAL-DEVELOPMENTAL PERSPECTIVE: DIFFERENTIATION OF VULNERABILITIES AND SYMPTOMS

Clinical observations and research (to be described in greater detail in the next section) have led me to discover the regular occurrence of problems and vulnerabilites at particular levels of self complexity. Many clinicians use psychiatric diagnoses to differentiate among symptoms and determine a course of treatment. Therapists and researchers have begun to identify risk factors to help them understand the client's problems and vulnerabilities (e.g., Rutter, 1990). These useful approaches do not compete with the developmental perspective that I propose. But they do neglect the relationship between typical development and the symptoms and vulnerabilities that the client exhibits. In response to this need, this chapter relates self complexity levels to symptoms and vulnerabilities. But in doing so, I do not claim that development is the cause of the vulnerabilities. The causes can be many, including biological predisposition or environmental stresses, but the capacities and limits at any point in development shape how the vulnerability is expressed.

Table 9.2 provides descriptions of vulnerabilities and symptomatology typical of each of the five complexity positions. These positions, which are found in adolescents and adults as well as children, are not meant to convey that earlier problems never reappear in later development, nor that problems cannot occur earlier than the time when they are most commonly observed. The table serves as a rough map for locating vulnerabilities and symptomatology within a developmental framework; it is a guide that incorporates an understanding of the development of cognition, of meaning making, and of self complexity. The table combines theory, empirical findings, and clinical observations, and should be considered heuristically. Under each of the developmental positions is a description of the vulnerabilities that can occur in self identity and interpersonal relationships. Typically occurring symptoms are also described.

The reader may wish to refer back to this table to better understand the case examples and applications of developmentally differentiated treatments as I present them.

Developmentally Differentiated Interventions

From developmental and psychoanalytic treatments, client-centered therapy, and other modalities (e.g., expressive, group, and family interventions) it is possible to extract general ideas about the nature of change in therapy. Three factors seem to be most often at work in producing change:

1. The establishment of a strong bond to the therapist, indeed a bond so strong that the client's hopes and desires are placed in the relationship with the therapist.
2. The feeling and expression of strong emotions on the part of the client (which the safety of the therapeutic relationship allows the patient to experience).
3. And the therapist's fostering of the client's cognitive development by exploring the meanings that the client's behaviors and feelings hold for him.

These cognitive, affective, and relational elements are some of the ingredients that make recovery possible in therapy. But these elements still need to be understood in modern developmental terms. The understanding of development put forth by psychoanalysis is being updated inside and outside the field; it was first promulgated long before we knew all that we now know about development. The conception of disorders as originating in preoedipal, oedipal, or postoedipal periods is insufficient. We now know that cognitive and emotional processes undergo changes throughout the life span. Thus when we speak of observing capacities and insight, we have to ask about the organizing principles of the present-day self. What vulnerabilities can we expect? What tools are available in development with which we can ally ourselves to foster recovery?

The differences in the basic cognitive, emotional, and relational organization of the child and adolescent require that we create alternative therapeutic strategies. Focusing on the needs that adolescents themselves have to use *their* tools in the service of recovery might help teach us how to treat a patient differentially. No battle between therapy schools will resolve this problem because the needs that children and adolescents have for developmentally appropriate treatment have not been satisfied by any one treatment modality. Only with a developmental understanding of vulnerabilities and capacities can we formulate a truly differential therapy.

Table 9.2 Typical Vulnerabilities at Five Levels of Self Complexity

Self-Complexity Levels				
Subjective-Physical	Reciprocal-Instrumental	Mutual-Inclusive	Identity-Seeking	Systemic-Organizational
Vulnerabilities in Self-Identity				
• Concrete definitions of self (I am small, strong, etc.). • Little ability to synthesize different parts of self (i.e., tolerance of ambivalence). • Differentiation of self occurs in physical terms (closed doors, not being present).	• "Anti-identity" created in distinction of what others expect. • "Lone Ranger" ideology. • Others are out for themselves, "I have to do it myself." • No question of "Who am I?"; instead, "What do I want?"	• Very fragile and conformist psychological identity as the self is overly dependent on the approval of others. • Acknowledgment that self requires ability to separate and individuate, but a sense of handicap for not being able to do so. • Terror about asking, "Who am I?"; posed in terms of "Who am I in the eyes of others?"	• Insisting on self agency, yet very fragile about boundaries, great fears about needs for autonomy. • Strong ambivalence about emerging anger and other differentiating emotions. • Fluctuations between having a clear direction in focus and trying to appease important others, even when the direction is not experienced as "right."	• Self is often overly cognitive and rational, suppression of feelings. • Overly rigid superego, sense of duty. • Living too much in the self, schizoid. • Believing too much that self can control destiny.
Vulnerabilities in Interpersonal Relationships				
• Needs to be in constant physical touch to confirm existence of relationship. • Lack of sense of survival without others. • Submissive interpersonal stance (others own me). • Relationships are viewed not in psychological terms but based on appearances and simple distinctions of "good" and "bad."	• Relationships are seen in terms of different partners who pursue their own interests. • Prone to instrumental and exploitative relations. • On guard; nonrevealing; lack of trust. • Often part of a peer group, gang, etc., instead of individual relationships. • Sexuality as a way to have needs met, often promiscuous. • Taking on too little of others; world based on belief that they will be hurt and taken advantage of.	• Great need for closeness, but in contrast to subjective-physical position, taking the form of psychological sharing, talking, etc. • Taking on too much of others' wishes and desires, but also demanding too much to be taken care of. • Sense of not deserving love and affection from others. • No right to differentiate. • Great fear of expressing anger in relationships.	• Confusion about needing others to define who the self is, but others' definitions are inevitably contradictory.	• Outrage at weaknesses of others. • Fearful of too much "dependence." • Need for internal life, difficulty with too many demands for intimacy from others. • Perfectionist demands toward self and others. • Prone to isolation.
Typical Symptomatology				
• Especially prone to psychotic episodes under stress. Takes the form of separation = death; images of explosions. • Prone to depression, but incomprehensible to the subject. • If hyperactive or suffering from attention-deficit disorder, especially impulsive, very few compensating strategies available to control behavior. • Problems of controlling bodily functions (e.g., encopresis). • Violent acts committed without considering consequences. • Anxiety about monsters, ghosts, darkness.	• Antisocial activity and conduct problems; planned deception to affirm self. • Violence as revenge. • Proneness to drug and alcohol experimentation. • Usually few disorganized psychotic episodes; if any psychosis, often suspiciousness. • Little acknowledged or experienced depression. • Danger of harming self through lifestyle (accidents, etc.).	• Suicidal gestures to attain attention from loved ones and suicide danger because of sense of abandonment. • Frequent regression to earlier functioning with the goal of avoiding separation. • Feelings of depersonalization and anxiety; separation-related phobias (e.g., agoraphobia). • Feeling "lost in the world"; sense of loneliness. • Social anxieties.	• Fragile self needing to take too much control. • Overly harsh differentiations, extreme limit setting. • Chronic anger as a new definer of self. • Chronic fluctuation between giving up, holding on. • Feeling overly responsible for everything. • Seemingly unsolvable dilemma between—How do I please others? How am I authentic with myself? • Simultaneous behavioral inhibition and action-orientation.	• Indecision, too many choices, and need for ideal solutions. • Rage reactions. • Overly intellectualized. • Obsessive-compulsive symptoms. • Cutoffness, schizoid. • Existential depression. • Perfectionism. • Nihilism as a philosophy of life. • Delusional symptomatology including paranoia.

Tables 9.3 through 9.8 describe self complexity positions in terms of the clinical issues that clients in these positions frequently present. The tables presented after each case example are organized around categories that most intervention specialists, working within their own clinical tradition, are concerned with. *Treatment Focus* refers to the overall aims and structure of the interventions. *Setting* addresses the fact that treatment does not take place only in the one-on-one therapeutic environment, but in a world that includes institutions and other personal relationships. The *Support* category deals with what the person will experience as helpful in creating a foundation for the difficult work of psychological change. *Insight* deals with the fact that at any developmental point the person is able to gain personal knowledge that can aid the process of recovery. Finally, *Typical Therapeutic binds* are being introduced recognizing that every type of treatment has its own pitfalls, and that those can either lead to failure or to the successful resolution of a previously unresolved problem. Table 9.8, at the end of this section, is a composite of the previous tables facilitating comparison across developmental levels.

Because the telegraphic language of these tables could lead to misunderstanding, examples of clinical cases are provided, each of which represents a different level of self complexity. It is important to remember several issues here. I intend the self complexity positions to represent continuous processes, not stages. Therefore, it is with some trepidation that I refer to "levels." The language I use seems to resemble that of stages too closely. It does not capture the idea that I mean to present: that development is a dynamic process in which the different aspects of the self progress, remain static, or regress separately. In these tables, the limitations of language only allow me to approximate my meaning. The words I use present a still picture of stagelike progression, but what I intend to convey is the idea that development is a dynamic interchange between each domain of the self and the environment, and that this interchange is constantly evolving. It follows, then, that I do not intend that clinicians simply tailor their treatment techniques to the patient's developmental "level." To do this would be to misapply my model. The levels of self complexity and their related vulnerabilities and strengths presented in the table are summaries of the most complex dimension of the self and interpersonal organization. As mentioned earlier, in normal development some aspects of the self are less evolved than others, and those less developed aspects represent segments of the self that are most affected by the conflicts the person has encountered. It is these areas that I refer to when I speak of encapsulations (e.g., Noam 1986a, 1986b). It should be clear that different treatment techniques must be combined to reach a patient at all her developmental levels. However, when treatment methods are combined, it is the most advanced level of self complexity that should define what the most prominent technique should be. The reason for this is that the technique that matches the client's most mature level is likely to engage her reflective capacities in the service of developing her less mature dimensions.

Subjective-Physical Self Complexity

Sometimes we cause anxiety in our patients by offering an interpretation that exceeds their capacity to observe themselves in a complex manner. In the preceding section, I made reference to several developmental psychologists who cautioned clinicians against this. I am reminded of a young adolescent who functioned at the subjective-physical position and repeatedly ran away from the residential treatment center in which he lived because he wanted to be united with his parents. The rules of the unit made clear to the boy that he would not get "privileges" to go home on the weekend if he left during the week. At a meeting called to discuss the boy's behavior, the staff considered the possibility that the boy was running away not only to be close to his parents, but also to assure that he would not be able to stay with his chaotic family for an entire weekend. This discussion was reported to the adolescent by a well-meaning staff member. The result was that the boy felt utterly misunderstood by the treatment staff. How could he convey not wanting to go home by the very act of going home, he wondered? What the staff member who spoke to the boy assumed was that the adolescent would be able to understand that manifest behaviors can cover up or serve unconscious motivations. This understanding, which marks a turning point in development when it does come, had not yet taken place in this adolescent. The cognitive prerequisites for this discovery usually begin to emerge in the self complexity position that follows the level that the boy was in. In deciding to talk to the boy, the staff member was guided by the idea that adolescents are, in general, capable of the distinctions between behavior and unconscious motivation. Many adolescents are, in fact, capable of this, but not those whose most evolved developmental system has not exceeded the subjective-physical position.

Mismatches between an adolescent's capacities and a clinician's perception of those capacities can be damaging to the treatment process. As this vignette shows, a patient can be left feeling distressed and can lose faith in the clinician's ability to understand and help. Although such a

Table 9.3 Clinical-Developmental Interventions with Adolescents: Subjective-Physical Self-Complexity Level

Treatment Focus

- Interventions that focus on cognitive and emotional disorganization, impulsivity, attention problems, lack of control over bodily functions.
- Focus on the constant need for physical presence of authority figures.
- Supportive and behavioral treatments in a structured environment; interventions to change environment (e.g., classroom, family structure).

Setting

- Usually structured environment (e.g., classroom) needed to contain serious impulsivity, depression, and potential for short psychotic episodes.
- Setting must provide strong limits and rules that foster the learning of consequences of self's actions; incentives must be provided to apply and internalize structure.
- Predictable staff, teachers, or clinicians must be readily available.

Support

- Strong boundaries and limits with goal of internalizing external rules. Support with often enmeshed and/or abandoning family system or disorganized school environment.

Insight

- Work with emerging ability to review behaviors, feelings, and thoughts.
- Begin to recognize that multiple feelings can coexist about the same person or situation.
- Learn that strategies being used are self-destructive.

Typical Therapeutic Binds

- Attempt by therapist, counselor, and teacher to interpret behavior in terms of symbolic meanings when they are only understood in concrete and behavioral terms.
- Feeding into split between "good family"—"bad peer world," "good therapist"—"bad parents" (or vice versa) often leads to a breakdown of the work.

break in empathic understanding can usually be repaired, a chronic misunderstanding often leads to a premature termination of treatment.

The treatment focus for children and adolescents at the subjective-physical position will differ depending on the type and severity of the disorder, family constellation, gender, and cultural background. But an astonishing number of developmental issues cut across these differences. For all adolescents at the subjective-physical position, clinical efforts should involve creating conditions that will encourage the development of self regulation and the management of impulses and overwhelming affects in the client. Adolescents at this level often have a history of impulse disorders and school-related problems. These problems make the hurdles of middle childhood and adolescence difficult; the demands of school, families, and peers can be too much for these children. Difficulty in following rules, curtailing impulses, and concentrating on a task makes getting through even the first grade hard. As children burdened with these problems grow older, they encounter more and more trouble from the demands of their environment. Their impulsivity often becomes increasingly dangerous to themselves and others, and the fear that they can engender in peers and adults often leaves them isolated.

These children and adolescents tend to engage in splitting; the people in their lives are all good or all bad. They have not yet discovered that both positive and negative traits can exist in the same person. The concept of ambiguity is foreign to them. This makes them especially vulnerable because they often see themselves as "bad." It is important for the clinician to help the adolescent discover that good and bad elements can coexist in the family and peer world. Since many of these children and adolescents come from abusive and disorganized backgrounds, the support they receive in helping them overcome this splitting is often greeted with suspicion. A child who is challenged to change in this way often interprets this effort as a threat designed to rob him of his protective defenses. One possible consequence of splitting is a tendency to run away from the "bad" environment. In combination with a lack of inhibition and impulse control, a tendency toward projection can make some of these adolescents (and adults) quite dangerous. Treatment should begin early because many of these adolescents are on a path that will take them into the hands of the criminal justice system.

Treatment should take place in an atmosphere of containment, which generally means a residential treatment center or structured environment. The environment should have clear and strong rules, both so that the client feels safe and so he can internalize this structure. Management skills that the self slowly develops under such conditions are necessary for learning to control impulses, delay gratification, and focus on and attend to tasks.

Strong relationships with adults need to be formed; however, they should be as activity-based as possible. A traditional therapist-client relationship remains a mystery to these children and adolescents. Such a relationship is not advisable. Instead, "talking while doing" is more effective. This method should be coupled with the fostering of an attachment to a readily available member of the treatment staff. Clinicians must understand that the adolescents always feel that the thoughts that pass through their minds are accessible to everyone. Clinicians must assist them in creating concrete boundaries. The adolescents tend to learn a great deal of positive and negative boundary skills from those delinquents in the same residential environment who function at the reciprocal-instrumental position (e.g., keeping secrets, manipulating, delaying short-term gains for longer-term gains, etc.).

Although these separate treatment objectives are important, what is most important is that the clinician's work have the following overarching goal: to create a concrete and external structure, supported by a behavioral system of rewards and consequences, which are direct, immediate, and clearly understandable. The role of such an environment is to help the client internalize a predictable system of rules that helps organize his universe so that a more independent person emerges. Such a person will feel safer and will be better able to make friends and gain the respect of his peers, teachers, and coaches. Good treatment methods include concrete help in developing friendship skills, especially pair therapy and group methods that involve other children with whom these skills can be practiced.

Treatment may also have to include behavioral techniques to help the client control body functions (e.g., enuresis and encopresis). It is also essential to recognize how disorganized the internal world of these children and adolescents can be; many come from chaotic families. The level of aggressive preoccupations, as well as of self-destructive thoughts and actions, needs to be a constant concern for the clinician. Any method using play therapy with children or talking techniques with adolescents has to find ways of imposing a structure on the child's cognitive distortions. Methods can include cognitive control therapy that helps build an inner shield against the massive aggressive intrusion that these patients can encounter. For the purpose of overcoming difficult experiences and engaging the family (in an effort to create a healthier holding environment for the child), family therapy can be extremely useful. Again, it will be essential to keep the interventions concrete and understandable, to demonstrate psychological events in concrete ways and to engage the parents in parenting training. These efforts are geared toward protecting the child and family from chaos.

Reciprocal-Instrumental Self Complexity

At this developmental level of self complexity, many treatments can be applied, but they all need to be activity-focused and supportive. When treating children, the therapist should not expect a strong capacity for insight and self reflection and should feel comfortable pursuing play therapy, going out of the office and playing ball, or involving the child in joint projects, such as stories, tape recordings, or drawing (e.g., Bricker & Cripe, 1992; VanderVen, in press). These activities build trust; they invite the child into a safe place and make use of those styles of expression that are most suited to the child. The goal is to encourage the child to express, symbolically or directly, his frustrations and other feelings, including his hopes and joys. The material he offers is bound to suggest that he struggles with issues of control and a need for more freedom and understanding from parents, teachers, and other authority figures who are preoccupied with their own needs. The question of whether the therapist is just as needy as these other authority figures is inevitable. Using play and activities to help develop more room for expressing the self and to evolve more self-esteem by gaining better control over the world represents powerful help in the life of these children.

Often group therapy can help those children who are too isolated or so ashamed of themselves that they are shy with their peers. Useful for children who have difficulty making friends are treatments that help them with skills in developing and maintaining close peer relationships. Social rejection by peers is especially hurtful at this age; so are the beginnings of a secretive attitude that can cause distrust in friends or lead to the establishment of a delinquent subculture. Early intervention is essential. Our present strategies for child intervention, which combine multiple treatments in schools, the home, and the peer world, have great potential.

Establishing treatments for adolescents who function at the reciprocal-instrumental self complexity level is far

Table 9.4 Clinical-Developmental Interventions with Adolescents: Reciprocal-Instrumental Self-Complexity Level

Treatment Focus

- Treatment focus on issues of fairness and support for behavior that takes other people into consideration.
- Central role for peer learning, as struggles with authority figures are typical (e.g., AA, group interventions, community meetings).
- Concrete activities with adult role models who work on skills and abilities, and fun tasks (e.g., coaches, mentors, Outward Bound coordinators).

Setting

- Containment needed for a long period of time, especially when antisocial tendencies are strong.
- Despite seeming disinterest in individual therapy, one-to-one relationships are important to create trust, but need to entail mutually satisfying activities (e.g., eating, sports, walks).
- Support to get needs met in a nondelinquent way.

Support

- Support in experience of unfairness that results in having to confront externalizing stance ("others are at fault").
- Experience of nurturing relationship is critical (many patients have experienced trauma and neglect), but special attention must be given so that supportive stance will not be exploited.
- Address the child's manipulative behavior, but always in context of supportive environment.

Insight

- Emerging recognition that world can be influenced in productive ways and that rejections by others do not have to be addressed in terms of revenge and hostility.
- Close relationships provide a possibility to begin to view the world through a sense of mutuality and community.

Typical Therapeutic Binds

- Person confuses the therapist's "being on my side" with jointly breaking the rules (e.g., smoking in office before age).
- Fear of consequences can lead to a style of nondisclosure.
- Difficulty in talking about problems emerging in the relationship and past hurts because a biographical and transference focus has not yet developed.

more difficult. First, these adolescents are viewed by society as delayed and often have many problems adjusting to the demands placed on them. Adding to these problems is that play therapy is not appropriate at this level because it seems infantalizing to them. Many intervention specialists take account of the well-developed verbal capacities of these adolescents in devising a treatment strategy and expect them to talk about their problems. But talking therapies generally do not work, nor do treatments that require a great deal of self-reflection and insight. The therapist who tries such an approach is usually greeted with contempt and hostility and can expect communication to break down.

And yet, it is these adolescent girls and boys who are especially at risk for developing problems at school, dropping out, using drugs and alcohol, behaving aggressively, and running away from home. They need a great deal of support and mentoring, in the forms of individual therapy and group interventions, to learn how to negotiate life and how to develop goals that do not "get them into trouble." If adults are conducting the intervention, it is important they orient the work toward joint goals, giving the adolescent a great deal of room to decide what should happen. It is also important that the therapist not get caught up in questions like "what kind of therapy am I pursuing," but instead that she remain flexible, leaving the office when it is appropriate to play, eat, or walk. It is not by chance that coaches and youth workers are successful with these adolescents; they are often perceived as nonthreatening and available when the adolescent needs them.

It is also essential to create contexts of peer learning and therapy for these adolescents. These environments can help these adolescents learn how to overcome their difficulties in empathizing with others. So used are they to authorities being abusive and selfish, that working with a new authority figure can be extremely difficult. When conflicts arise (e.g., lying, aggression, problems in school and in the home), the adolescent views the therapist as another untrustworthy adult, and the treatment alliance breaks down.

Working through these problems with the kind of sympathetic adult who also sets limits can be useful, but it is harder for the adolescent to go through the same process with peers. Groups inspire loyalty, and even when this loyalty is shaken, group members often demand conformity from those who dare to defy the group's norms of behavior. This combination of developing group intimacy and confronting problem behavior has the power to help the adolescent overcome an overreliance on self-protection and move toward a more mature developmental understanding of the self and the world.

The following vignettes describe two adolescents, a boy and a girl, in greater detail. Richard, 16 years old, was referred to a residential setting by a juvenile court. Before deciding his case, the court asked for a recommendation from the treatment staff. The parents had originally asked the court to intervene because they could not control Richard's acting-out behavior at home. He was frequently truant from school, ran away from home on several occasions, abused drugs and alcohol, and had threatened his parents a number of times. One disagreement with the father had led to a dangerous, physical fight.

Richard was the second of two sons born to a wealthy lawyer and a teacher. As the boy himself described it, he had a long history of problems. He felt his parents did not understand him, behaved disrespectfully toward him, were excessively controlling, and tried to enforce inappropriate rules. He described his father (the lawyer) as a weak man and his mother (the teacher) as cold, manipulative, and aggressive. He remembered with pride his physical fight with his father. Richard's most serious troubles began when his brother was diagnosed with an incurable (but not life-threatening) illness and when his grandmother died. Richard, 11 at the time of both events, became depressed; he scratched his wrist and cut himself repeatedly with a knife. Over the course of the next two years he became harder to manage and frequently exploded at his parents, who were frightened at the intensity of his anger. Richard's behavior vacillated between aggressive and self-destructive acts.

During the course of hospitalization, Richard wanted to return home on his parents' terms, if they would retract the court petition. To the treatment staff, the proposal seemed like a way to negotiate his way out of the hospital, rather than a genuine change of direction. Richard refused to talk about himself and his parents in detail, so most of the staff's information came from observation in family therapy, which he had begun to attend with some interest. Indeed, he encountered much distance from both his parents, who showed only superficial concern for him. Richard felt close only to the family dog. He became very sad when he described his relationship with his dog, whom he missed greatly. "She is the only one who really is happy when I come home." He often shared his room with her and took her on long walks.

Richard had many friends and found it easy to make new ones. But they found pleasure mainly in the shared distribution and consumption of drugs and alcohol: "We go out, have fun, and get high." He liked to talk about one friend who was different from the rest: "He is someone who is really there when you need him, and I am there for him." The friend left the area and Richard missed him. Because his mother disapproved of this friend, however, Richard could only make occasional secret phone calls to him. Although he did well academically, Richard never liked school very much and began to stay away frequently. He rarely cooperated with the teachers, got into power struggles, and did not develop any goals for the future.

Richard's preoccupation with his own self-interest and his manipulation of the staff (by setting different people up against each other) earned him the title "staff-splitter." Richard was too self-contained. He gave the staff an unsettling feeling that he had sense of a master plan behind his actions. He became part of the adolescent patient group that planned activities which caused problems for the more vulnerable and dependent patients.

With regard to treatment, Richard could see no purpose in psychotherapy meetings and came only because it was required. As a result, he tried to find ways to avoid coming while not losing "privileges." For example, he would become ill just before our therapy hour, but recover soon thereafter. The initial period of therapy, however, was quite positive. During that time, he described in great detail (with much focus on concrete actions) what he most liked to do and why he hated the hospital, his parents, and all other authorities. Although he could not understand what talking would do to help him, he began to see the therapist as an ally against other authorities. He did not consider the meetings therapeutic because he did not feel that he should be in the hospital in the first place. His definition of his problem was that he was getting in trouble with the law and his parents, and it was their inflexibility that led to this "punishment." Richard frequently said that he would plan an escape if there was nothing in the hospitalization that he wanted. However, he wanted the staff to protect him from the judges. Given the choice between a psychiatric institution and a detention center for juvenile delinquents, he preferred the hospital. As he saw it, the meetings with staff were negotiations of deals in which the clinicians were to help him out of his legal problems. The brief work ended with a court decision to transfer him to a residential school, where he remained for more than a year and succeeded in mastering a number of his problems.

From the start, Richard was functioning at a more advanced level of self complexity than those children and adolescents at the subjective-physical position described earlier. The child and adolescent applying this developmental perspective (which often emerges around the age of 6 or 7) can usually control immediate impulses and plan his behavior (although there may be many impulsive breakthroughs, as occurred in Richard's case). Associated with this increased control over concrete physical needs is a capacity to mentally leave the self and view thoughts and actions from an outside perspective. This capacity to self-reflect provides individuals with a more constant sense of themselves over time than is possible in the subjective-physical orientation. Nevertheless, this kind of patient is unable to integrate his needs with those of others, resulting in a self-protective or nonmutual stance. It is only in the transition to the next developmental position that the self can fully take the perspective of the other in relationships.

Richard expressed his frustration at his parents' inability to understand him as rage ("I am going to kill them"). His fear of abandonment was expressed in his belief that people did not care. He interpreted his parents' appeal to the court as a renewed sign of uncaring. Only in the relationships with his brother and his friend was he able to express the wish to be close and be taken care of. But here his experience was that they, too, would become ill or leave him. In Richard's case, as is common at the reciprocal-instrumental self complexity position, fear of engulfment was a prominent theme, as was seen in his need to distance himself, to be isolated and removed, and distrust any adult. Specifically, he feared that adults would take over, and he would be forced to submit to their will. He was not aware that this fear could also contain an element of wish. He struggled for independence from the family, but in ways that would recreate his childhood experiences of running away and being brought home. On many occasions, beginning at age 4, Richard ran away from home and was brought back by the police. His parents were unable to provide the safety net he needed. He increasingly experienced them as distant and overly involved in their careers and their marital relationship. Members of the treatment staff began to observe in their own relationships with Richard the kind of painful formality and distance that seemed to mark the boy's relationship with his parents. It was as if they were talking to him over the telephone a continent away.

Therapy with adolescents at the reciprocal-instrumental level of self complexity often breaks down during the initial contact. The relationship is defined by the patient as wanting the therapist to "help out." If such a construction does not fit all the time and is replaced by limit setting and exploration, power struggles—the hallmark of the acting-out adolescent—soon follow. The patient begins to feel victimized, which reinforces his conviction that no one can be trusted. If the patient has a choice, he or she terminates the therapy; if the therapist has a choice, he stops performing the service. Usually the relationship ends when the adolescent storms out of a therapy session. The outwardly calmer, yet equally angry, therapist labels the patient as "primitive." If a total breakdown of the therapy does not occur, it is often because the adolescent and therapist force themselves to continue, and a new compromise is found. The therapist and patient are seen walking together to the cafeteria or interacting at sports events or other activities; ideally they share in an activity which is of interest to both. A relationship is built around the mutual satisfaction of needs. This helps trust to emerge slowly.

At this point in the therapy, the therapist builds a relationship around helping the patient pursue goals more adaptively. Actively developing trust is for the patient at this developmental level as crucial as boundary establishment is for the patient at the physical level. Early feelings of abandonment by important family members lead to a profound belief that the world is unsafe and that one cannot rely on anybody. Coming close means getting hurt. The developmental thrust to the next developmental level, with its opening of boundaries and strong group identification, is experienced in part as a regression. Evoked for the patient are memories of a time when the self was little protected, often abandoned, and within the cycle of running away and being brought home. Meanwhile, the patient follows an "oath": Never to allow the self to be hurt again, never to care that much again. This early attitude contributes to a developmental delay. The repetitive theme is to avoid closeness while feeling abandoned and victimized. The resultant self-protective attitude stands in the way of those experiences that support a move to the mutual-inclusive level of self complexity. As mentioned, often group environments and group therapy provide the patient with peer experiences that support change by sidestepping biographical recapitulations with adult authority figures. In place of the latter, the patient experiences shared values and emotional ties with his peers, and a tentative intimacy is established.

As Richard moved beyond his self-protective stance, he was able to overcome his cycle of disappointment, resentment, and running away. In the process, he was able to open up to friends, but not without becoming more depressed. Richard's transition led to more symptoms, making it appear that he was getting worse. Such a view is misleading. As the self opens, all earlier intimate relationships, along with their great disappointments, become the focus of treatment. Experiences of loneliness, emptiness, and sadness come to the fore and lead, at first, to more acting out. But ultimately, this hard sequence is the road to recovery. The move to the next developmental position makes the reworking of the past possible, and the reworking of the past creates the opportunity for real change.

The work with Melissa represents another example of work with an adolescent at this level of self complexity. In the course of the work, she underwent an important developmental transformation.

Melissa was 15 when she was hospitalized at a major psychiatric institution. A thin, attractive, and frail-looking girl, she was angry at her parents, the staff, and the therapists at the hospital. She had "gotten into trouble with her family" and constantly fought with her mother, who favored Melissa's younger sister. All the bad events in the family were blamed on Melissa, who began to feel that nothing she did made any difference, "so why try?" Her mother responded to her demands for attention by stating that Melissa should be more grown up and help. The mother wanted assistance from her older daughter, not additional demands.

Melissa did well in her early years of school, although she became a loner, withdrawing from her peers and teachers. She became independent and took great pride in being able to do things alone, to do better than the other students, and to speak only when she had something to say. She was rarely seen in the school yard playing with others, but usually stayed by herself, thinking, and watching. She became fascinated with nature and began identifying and cataloguing birds, trees, and flowers. Her knowledge in these areas impressed her teachers and she developed the idea that one day she would become a great scientist with her own laboratory. Melissa made some friends, but these relationships were rather distant. She looked forward to her books at home and would retreat into her room. She does not remember feeling depressed, but she began to trust only herself. Her father, whom she valued, began to work longer hours; her mother focused more and more attention on her younger child.

Although she found ways of coping with her family problems in middle childhood, the situation became intolerable after she reached puberty. She was still not interested in a peer group and close friends. A family move left her and the whole family isolated; she began to fight with her mother over any issue. Her mother could not make her do anything and any request led to a hostile response. Her father retreated even further, and her mother became increasingly involved with Melissa's sister. Melissa was not able to maintain a sphere of success in school; she began to be truant and to associate with the more delinquent children in her class. But she also felt herself to be an outsider there and usually went into stores by herself to steal. She lost interest in pursuing plans for college and a career. She even stopped reading books. When her mother began to confront her about her schoolwork, Melissa began to fight with her, throwing things at her (on two occasions, Melissa threw knives) and storming out of the house. She became a "Youth Services Case" when she wandered the streets alone one night and her mother called the police to search for her. At about this time, she was caught stealing and found in possession of marijuana. The court recommended a psychiatric evaluation and possible residential treatment.

Melissa's early experiences, including frustration and isolation, led to a detached stance. The rejecting mother, who favored the sister, and the absent father contributed to a self-reliance and distrust in the availability of important others. The view that "I have to do it alone," "I have to look after myself because no one else will do it," generalized to school life. Melissa avoided playing with classmates and became interested in nature. While other children were experiencing the excitement of group play, Melissa was keeping a distance. She began to talk to herself. She stayed away from teachers and sought to find solutions to problems by herself. Melissa's early experiences suggest that her place in the web of complex family interaction supported the development of her tendency to be distant from others. In middle childhood, this style still was directed in productive age-appropriate activities: an interest in nature. The concrete reciprocal-instrumental level of self complexity supported the orderly division of self and world, of facts and feelings. It can be hypothesized that the strong separations at home led to a strengthening of the boundary style during middle childhood, a time when boundaries are strengthened in most children. In Melissa's case, the process of boundary establishment took extreme forms and was not balanced by supportive relationships. When she had reached adolescence and continued to function at the reciprocal-instrumental level of self complexity, she began to get into trouble. Phasic demands of adolescence, as described earlier in this chapter, create a tension for adolescents at this level of self complexity because the reworking of the relationship with parents and the creation of new intimacy with peers demand more complex self-understanding and conflict resolution, usually achieved at the mutual-inclusive position of self complexity. For Melissa, the switch from studiousness in middle childhood at the reciprocal-instrumental level of self complexity to adolescent rebellion at the same developmental position was radical, even though there was no change of underlying developmental organization.

Melissa began treatment at the hospital with a young therapist whose approach was formal and who wanted to discuss her thinking about herself and her family. He was conducting what one could call insight-oriented therapy geared toward a more advanced level of self-observation and self-reflection. It is not surprising that she rejected this option and felt victimized and again misunderstood. The psychoanalytic transference interpretation of the therapist, that she was repeating with him what she had experienced with her family, was greeted with a mixture of laughter, contempt, and disbelief. The therapeutic relationship broke down.

When I began seeing her, I could build on her earlier therapy experience and was aware of her concrete and externalizing stance. I did not view it mainly as defensive, but as reflecting a momentary developmental ceiling. I had to answer her constant question, "What do I get out of this?" Her manipulativeness and distancing maneuvers emerged, but so did a desire to be closer to people. While she was arguing with me and other staff members about authority issues, she was also building important peer relations, took in a cat, and, after another few months, began a very intensive friendship with a girl of similar background. She described the excitement of having someone with whom to share secrets and whom she could trust, but she did not want to provide details about the friendship.

Melissa's first therapist had pushed for too much intimacy and self-reflection; the adolescent's history of disappointments and her boundary style in connection with her reciprocal-instrumental stage position did not permit successful application of his therapy model. More supportive approval that respected both her limited self-observation and boundaries proved successful because it avoided unnecessary power struggles. Her movement into the peer group and the establishment of an intense friendship in which she began sharing some of her disappointments in her family all reflect a move into the mutual-inclusive self position. This move took almost 10 months and was accompanied by many setbacks, such as her running away when angry or when she felt victimized.

In the next phase of treatment, Melissa began to make use of me in a very different way. She thought more about her past, about future aspirations, and about the pain of being part of a rejecting family, but also about her own participation in the painful struggles with her family. She became an engaged student and put a great deal of thought into planning a career—marine biology—with fantasies of travel to remote areas for scientific explorations. Her friendship with Joanne had become less intense because Melissa felt that Joanne had become too "clingy" and not interested in living her own life. Melissa had, by now, moved to a residential school and was preparing for college.

"Delay" as a Productive Force in Development. This discussion of the two earliest developmental self-complexity positions ends with a caution: The reader should not evaluate and treat children or especially adolescents as if they are only in need of maturation. There is an inherently protective, even productive element in "delaying" development. Traditionally, in both clinical and developmental psychology, and across different theoretical frames, psychopathology and symptoms were usually traced to some kind of delay or fixation. This impressive body of literature by now includes not only clinical reports but substantial empirical research. Most of these studies show a firm association between immature cognition and social cognition and externalizing, aggressive, and impulsive behaviors (e.g., Noam et al., 1984). Two assumptions underlie the discussions of these findings: Being aggressive and externalizing is unproductive and thus "bad," and functioning below age norms requires intervention.

But what if we were to try to understand delay in development, not only as a deficiency, but as a productive attempt to regulate complicated life experiences? Or as an attempt to temporarily ward off threatening knowledge that proceeding to a more complex developmental position might bring a greater amount of psychological vulnerability that the individual is not yet capable of dealing with? At the least, it is essential to understand the complex mechanisms implicit in so-called delayed psychological positions. The field of developmental psychopathology can provide insight into these questions because most clinical and research efforts focus on subjects who function on more delayed levels.

In many of the interviews from our longitudinal study, the adolescents who were evaluated by our research methods as lagging behind, actually talked of their developmental worlds in a far more positive and rational way than we had expected. We began to wonder whether we were not missing an entire level of experience of these youngsters and whether they could point us to a new direction of understanding the logic and purpose of delay. Again using Loevinger's scheme as an example, we need to ask: What if the first measurable ego stage called "impulsive" were defined by the capacities to express strong wishes, to assert the self, and to learn to draw crucial boundaries between self and others? That "impulsive child" is, after all, learning how to gain control over the environment and to negotiate powerful caretakers, and is exploring ways to handle the most powerful childhood anxiety: the fear of separation and loss of parents. But instead, the descriptions in the literature on Loevinger's scheme and in others are mostly negative, depicting a child suffering from conceptual simplemindedness, dependent, and authority bound.

An example that shifts us from ego development to a symptom often associated with delay can be useful here: a lying child. Most parents become quite anxious when their child is not telling the truth and see before them already the delinquent adolescent and the antisocial adult. The research simultaneously supports and disproves such fears. Lying is a typical childhood behavior engaged in by the majority of children at some time and is of no concern whatsoever for any long-term consequences. Yet, lying can be part of a larger syndrome of conduct problems with a high rate of continuity and with more severe consequences the earlier it begins.

One useful approach to any psychological behavior and symptom is to avoid stereotyping and dichotomizing and instead to try to understand what developmental capacities are involved in such behaviors and what issues the child might be working out. In the case of lying in children, we can identify the implicit developmental abilities that go into the behavior and often represent important testing grounds for developmental accomplishments. These include experimentation with the boundary between private and public self, differentiation from parents, the understanding that nonshared knowledge is power, and goal-directed behavior. Such a perspective does not free the child from responsibility, nor the adult from taking a stance against such behavior, but it does represent a different perspective of understanding and even appreciating the child's capacity for the anticipatory behavior involved in secrecy and deception.

Mutual-Inclusive Self Complexity

We will now turn to the nondelayed adolescents who employ the *mutual-inclusive self complexity,* a perspective that usually does not emerge before early adolescence. At this position, talking therapy has a real potential for making the adolescent feel understood and supported. Sharing one's

Table 9.5 Clinical-Developmental Interventions with Adolescents: Mutual-Inclusive Self-Complexity Level

Treatment Focus

- Interpersonal therapy with focus on depression and low self-esteem emerging in closer relationships.
- Special emphasis on one-on-one relationship.
- Sharing of experiences to overcome loneliness in groups as well as in individual treatment.

Setting

- Individual treatment (often in conjunction with family treatment) to help express internalized feelings and, when necessary, short residential treatments (long, regressive hospitalizations to be avoided), but suicidality can make safe environment necessary.
- Support groups offer opportunities for "identification first, individualism later."

Support

- Strong commitment in every aspect of person's experiences (e.g., clothes, sports, peer group).
- Encouragement of assertiveness needed.
- Support of the expression of anger and frustration.
- Help with tendency to have negative feelings "go underground" and to attend to the needs of others while neglecting oneself.

Insight

- Beginning reflection of what is occurring in the relationship as a pattern (e.g., "Every time I am silent, I feel ashamed").
- Understanding regression and low self-esteem as a result of not being "master of own destiny."
- Exploring the problems of expression of anger and the tendency to turn against the self.

Typical Therapeutic Binds

- Silences in the treatment (or other relationship) and feeling rejected by therapist require very taxing proofs of acceptance (e.g., midnight phone calls).
- Expressed dependency of patient creates anxiety in therapist.
- Danger of fluctuation of therapist between demand for too much insight and self-observation on part of patient and underestimating the patients' capacity to observe relationship patterns and feeling states.

inner life with adults and peers and framing it in psychological terms becomes a powerful motivation toward intimacy and recovery. We have seen the typical vulnerabilities and symptoms that we encounter at this position. Now the therapist is even more prone to overestimating the capacities for insight because all the developmental capacities appear to be in place. But when we listen carefully to what these adolescents have to teach us, we still do not encounter an Eriksonian identity crisis. The adolescent can certainly experience a great deal of crisis, but does not take a perspective on his identifications to transform them into a new identity. Instead, identifications are sought after and lived, the self is mutual, at home with these idealized friends and adults. Group conformity is at its height, and so is the constant fear of losing the "relationship base," of abandonment by parents, teachers, and friends. It is this fear of losing those who define the self, and of not fitting in, that is a core feature of this adolescent.

The ability of these youngsters to frame experiences in psychological terms, to describe feeling states and interactions with important others, encourages most therapists to explore patterns and motivations, autonomous self-observation, and critical judgment about self and relationships. These explorations usually lead to surprisingly superficial descriptions that frustrate both therapist and client. Surprised by this "lack of self," the therapist may interpret this state as an early, and primitive manifestation of a separation-individuation problem. The client, consequently, feels incompetent, sensing that he is not living up to expectations. Feeling inadequate leads to feeling hopeless, and the client is thereby silenced. The silence in turn makes the therapist and client often feel quite uncomfortable, increasing the potential for low self-esteem and depression.

No therapeutic model clearly fits this adolescent, which is surprising because so many adolescents who enter therapy function at this level. One reason might be that we did not know about this developmental gestalt before the emergence of research on social cognition. Existing therapy methods that use supportive strategies run the risk of underchallenging the patient. The relationship can easily become stale as the adolescent waits for some challenge or some guidance in framing the problems in new ways.

Insight-oriented therapy, on the other hand, requires an observation of systematic patterns of the self that is not available to adolescents at this developmental position. Questioning existing conventions, creating new ones, and following a set of goals experienced as self-chosen require a differentiation between the part of the self steeped in prescribed pathways and conventions and the part that is reflecting, doubting, and questioning. The therapist can be sure that she has an ally in the patient who can cognitively contain, at least under supportive conditions, both sides of the self. For that reason more traditional psychodynamic therapy can be applied, which becomes even more viable as the person grows into full adulthood.

Between these two therapy forms—supportive and insight-oriented—we need to establish new developmentally guided methods. The adolescent at the *mutual-inclusive position* is apt to observe one set of processes with great care: the fluctuations in the relationship, the feelings of inclusion and protection, the sense of abandonment and despair. These adolescents respond vigilantly to the wishes and desires of others and lack anger and self-assertion. Help is needed to deal with these strengths and vulnerabilities. Therapy is not and will not be viewed as a manifestation of inner conflicts and life themes. But therapist and client can focus on the pattern of their and other relationships. They can wonder together about the lack of anger when the self has been violated and share, almost as friends, the victories and disappointments of the adolescent.

I remember one adolescent with whom I worked who always asked me about my opinions, what I considered normal and pathological, and what I would do in a given situation. At the time, I pursued a position of not answering these questions and noticed the girl becoming more and more disappointed and removed. I explained the reasons but to no avail. She wanted to end therapy. Out of desperation, I began to answer more and more questions, and our relationship became unstuck. I felt powerful and effective, and she felt pleased and acknowledged. Only, I noticed that we did not move forward and that many of my answers cemented her insecurities. As a supervisor, I see many young clinicians fall into this same trap.

Since then, I have learned to find a different path. I turn the questions into a *joint* exploration. I try not to over- or underchallenge the patient. The adolescent's insecurities are often related to a long history of insecure attachments and should not be repeated in the therapy. A strategy has to be found that locates the power of finding solutions neither in the patient nor in the therapist, but in *their relationship*. It is not that you have to find *your* answers, which pulls for the identity-seeking position not yet reached, nor is it that I will answer for you, which supports the nonassertive and dependent attitude that the therapy tries to address. Instead, *we* will find solutions, that are, at least in part, located in our relationship. At every developmental position, a focus on the relationship is essential; however, at each point the relationship capacities, meanings, and methods will be fundamentally different.

Identity-Seeking Self Complexity

A new observational capacity emerges when the self begins to view itself as trying to create an internal set of standards and a more chosen sense of identity. Many middle and late adolescents, and even adults, are dealing with issues relevant to this developmental world. Typically, at this transitional position, adolescents struggle in a new way with wanting to conform and desiring to "fit in." They continue to identify strongly with parents and peers, trying to emulate them as much as possible. But simultaneously, and with increasing urgency, they question who they are and what goals they hold beyond the expectations of others. Preoccupied with questions about their origins and their futures, they explore what was given and what is chosen. In contrast to later developmental worlds when identity and relationships are more firmly established, at the identity-seeking self-complexity level the tension between these two aspects of the self are often enormous.

These adolescents want to break out from many of the demands placed on them throughout childhood, even as they persist in trying to conform. They want to be good members of their families, but because they are also deeply concerned about the truthfulness of conventions and their emerging selves, they cannot accept hypocrisy and implicit requests for submission to the rules under which they are placed. An additional difficulty for the identity-seeking adolescent arises because loss often increases identification. While these themes are common in adolescence, the conflict has a specific frame in the identity-seeking developmental level. The emerging capacities for self awareness, coupled with the strengthening of the formal operational cognitive system facilitates the view of the self as consisting of multiple parts and possibilities. Multiplicity of possibilities emphasizes the power these adolescents have in deciding their own paths; but it also is a source of great anxiety. Confronted with so many possibilities, the adolescent often loses clear direction and the epistemological certainty of the "right way" and the "true self." Relativism as Perry (1970) has shown, represents a great liberation as well as threat to the self because it can only be resolved through active commitments. Commitments, however, require some sense of direction, which is most tenuous in the process of seeking identity. Frequently just as new freedoms emerge in establishing more individualized life styles and a set of personal commitments, the loss of identification with parents and peers makes the people and rules

Table 9.6 Clinical-Developmental Interventions with Adolescents: Identity-Seeking Self-Complexity Level

Treatment Focus

- Insight-oriented therapy supporting the emerging capacities to "choose" a self from among many different possibilities.

Setting

- Individual treatment often effective as the therapist can become an ally in reviewing the past relationships and be a sounding board in creating life goals and plans.
- Including the context (friends, family, etc.) can be useful, but focus has to be not only on being part of relationships but also on the need for differentiation.

Support

- Person needs to be supported through the inevitable confusions of wanting to be close to others and be like them while trying to come to terms with being different and standing up for a life project that might not be in line with others' expectations.

Insight

- Taking a perspective on the dilemma of needing approval from significant others while listening to an inner direction.
- Coming to terms with the fact that pursuing one's identity can mean making unpopular decisions and being excluded.
- Focus on potential for being overly differentiated and becoming "ideologically pure" but isolated.

Typical Therapeutic Binds

- Difficulty in handling conflicts that arise from experimenting with identity (e.g., risk-taking to prove that one is different from family, searching out experiences of self through drugs, ideological struggles with authorities, etc.).
- Leaving important relationships for the sake of "finding oneself," including the therapeutic relationship, without adequately thinking through the consequences of isolation and lack of support.

from which the adolescent tries to differentiate seem exceedingly powerful and important.

In terms of intervention, the therapist can now be involved in what is traditionally referred to as *insight-oriented therapy.* A part of the self can actually do the observing, an activity implied by insight-oriented treatments. A productive split between an acting and experiencing self, and one that can begin to make connections, understand motivations, and bring some organization to the multitude of conscious and unconscious experiences, now becomes possible. Often individual therapy is the most important form of intervention, and should be focused both on creating a close bond between therapist and client, and on carrying a goal of reviewing strengths and difficulties in important relationships. The therapist frequently becomes the sounding board in the exploration of creating life goals and plans. Most in-depth psychoanalytic treatments require at least this level of self-reflection in order for transference to be interpretable and for a productive "split in the self" to occur.

The therapist should not underestimate the fragility of this newly emerging identity-seeking self, or the struggle against the powerful relationships which continue to define who the person is to be. Sometimes the client has to separate as he or she becomes increasingly involved in the treatment. These separations serve to protect the person from "losing the self." Fortunately, the client is usually able to observe these needs, but the more fragile the self, the more need there will be to act on these "separation desires." Differentiation from these overpowering internal and interpersonal realities provides the essential developmental drive.

A portion of Michelle's story illustrates some of these points. Very early in the treatment with this 19-year-old woman who was struggling with issues typical for this developmental position, I was just beginning to get ready to do in-depth work while she felt the work was almost done. She had wanted alleviation of some symptoms (anxiety, concentration problems, conflict with her parents); as she felt better, and was afraid she was going to lose her sense of self by engaging in a strong relationship with me. One day she brought a bouquet of flowers to say good-bye. She informed me she was going to work for a college and travel throughout the country while searching for the direction her life would take. She stated she might come back but she was not sure. She just knew she needed to leave for the time being. Against the objection of the clinic at the time, I kept the "file" open and told her I would do so. I wanted to convey to her that the separation did not mean that I was not going to be available, and more, that I saw her leaving as part of our therapy relationship. Michelle was gone for many months, and all the while the clinic worried about being liable for her. She wrote a number of postcards describing her experience and how important the travel and work were for her. After six months I received a phone call from Arizona saying that she was returning and she wanted to set up a time with me. This was the beginning of an intense phase of work in my office. The months of separation were, however, an important part of her identity-seeking developmental phase.

This short vignette can teach us the important lessons. One, it is very easy to misunderstand the enormous need of the person to protect the self from merging and from a sense of weakness in intimate relationships as borderline disorders. Of course, many people with a history of fragile sense of self are especially prone to a "loss of self" at this developmental position, but the typical need to distance and differentiate in order to gain enough of a "transitional space" to explore identity is not a sign of disorder but one of development. Two, we need to develop far more flexible therapeutic arrangements which allow for active separations, breaks, and returns. Maybe this will also help us get beyond the dichotomous debate between long-term and short-term treatment since for some patients long-term treatment consists of a number of developmentally focused short-term interventions. Three, it is essential for therapists working with patients at this developmental level to understand how threatening therapy can be and how easily therapy can become part of the problem and not the solution. The patient will not let the therapist know how much space he or she needs in order to explore an emerging sense of self and how difficult it is still to express the increasingly available feelings such as anger and hurtful honesty which have been taboo for most people at the mutual inclusive developmental position.

Systemic-Organizational Self Complexity

At the systemic organizational self complexity level, which does not appear until well into adolescence or later, a whole set of new treatments becomes possible. The person is now very interested in the many sides of the self. There is a strong reliance on one's "identity" and on loyalty to one's own beliefs. Many adolescents at this developmental level become "parentified," thereby taking on too many adult responsibilities prematurely. Others become despairing as they isolate themselves and become preoccupied with their inner lives. In vulnerable populations in which support is missing, the move into this developmental world can bring with it great risks of alienation, depression, and suicidality. The person at this developmental level experiences problems mostly as inner conflicts and resists the yearning for others, viewing it as weakness. Engagement in any helping

Table 9.7 Clinical-Developmental Interventions with Adolescents: Systemic-Organizational Self-Complexity Level

Treatment Focus

- Strong focus on expression of emotions and relaxation of the rigid moral and self-reliant position; push toward more self-empathy and balancing needs in life—less workaholism, less competitiveness.

Setting

- Individual therapy often essential as the person needs help in reflecting on his or her life. But because it is important that the client does not remove self from the world, groups are also effective.

Support

- The person feels easily out of control and angry at different parts of self for not falling in line.
- Support for more self-acceptance and less self-criticism.

Insight

- Insight is quite typical, but often intellectualized. Person needs help in understanding how removed he or she can get, how achievement focus can constrict the self.
- New ways of integrating feelings have to be found. Special focus also on anger at the self as well as suicide potential.

Typical Therapeutic Binds

- Therapist is seen as not understanding because of a sense of being too nice. The focus on one's biography lets many old vulnerabilities and issues emerge that become hard to work on. Being cut off from one's feelings makes it hard to discuss and deal with the need for closeness.
- Insights can easily fuel self-criticism.

relationship or therapy is viewed in very negative terms. Because of the suspicious feelings about needing help, supportive treatments are usually not helpful, nor is any intervention seen as helping that is too oriented toward action: doing things, playing ball, and so on.

Instead, the systemic organization's self complexity is best served by an insight-oriented approach that engages the significant observational capacities of the client. Psychoanalytic treatment, with its special emphasis on past experiences, can be useful since the patient frames the self in a historical perspective and is often interested in the interplay between what is conscious and what is unconscious, fascinated by symbols, and intrigued by the causes of behavior. The client-centered approaches can also be helpful because they counterbalance the adolescent's significant propensity toward intellectualization and cognitive control. Gaining broader access to the emotional world, which is so important to the client-centered therapist, can be extremely helpful in supporting mental health. Since the self is preoccupied with issues of control (and yet, full control always eludes those who are preoccupied with it), some people do not want help in making the system more flexible and open to emotions. Instead, they want help in making the self more efficient, managerial, and controlling. These people can benefit from cognitive-behavior therapy and behavioral management techniques. But in general, if there is any possibility of using the crisis that leads up to the intervention to challenge the totalitarian issues around control, it has the potential to alter the adolescent's life well into adulthood. Group therapy can be quite effective, but groups should not be formed based only on the group members' shared age of adolescence and "adolescent issues." It is important to create group contexts that recognize significant intellectual curiosity and sophistication, or the adolescent may end up feeling bored and isolated in the peer group.

The following example involves a 17-year-old, whom I shall call John.

John, a senior in high school, came to therapy because of depression, which included feelings of meaninglessness, despair, dysphoria, anger toward his parents and teachers, and failure. He had always been at the top of his class and was accepted to one of the best colleges in the country, a goal his father had not attained. John soon became an average student. He was apathetic before exams. "Nothing I do will ever be of importance; I lost my chance; my time is running out."

John often feels angry at himself for not living up to his own expectations of his performance in creative writing, analytic thinking, and flexible exploration. He resents the absurdity of life but draws some satisfaction from absurdist literature and surrealistic art. John feels he is a failure in the eyes of the world and in his own judgment. He feels alone in a world of perceived possibilities. He wishes for a close relationship with a woman, but his few and fleeting attempts have led to a strong sense of despair: As he put it, "I can't let myself come close." He described several efforts to get close to women, but these relationships collapsed in the confused and intolerant expectations the women and John had of each other. John says he no longer feels honest because he is unable to live according to his ideals.

It may be possible to see John's struggle in terms of his unsuccessful (or too successful) competition with his father, or as a result of the lack of empathic understanding in his childhood, or as the expression of an adolescent identity crisis. Yet, notwithstanding these features of John's experience, I view his dysphoria as shaped by an underlying level of self complexity. He has a pervasive sense of falling short of his own (unreachable) goals and has a conviction that his negative self-evaluation is justified. John is concerned with his standards. He cannot "reach out" and lives in a self-imposed isolation. Such attitudes are commonly described in this stage. When locked-out feelings appear to intrude, John experiences them as perverse, weak, sinful, shameful (threats to personal control or psychological self-government). He describes guilt in terms of self-evaluation, the shame and humiliation of publicly failing his own standard. The language of self, relations, and emotions is bound to the tensions between intimacy and isolation and between psychological autonomy and the inability to share psychological power.

In this system, it is self-regulations, rather than mutuality, that is ultimate, and other selves are viewed in terms of their nourishment of, or threat to, the good order and enhancement of the autonomous organization. As John begins to transcend this stage of development, he may experience himself as isolated rather than autonomous, or, alternatively, as dangerously and wrongfully out of control.

John appears to experience emotions that are made up of the motion of transition. Although he continues to structure his experience mainly along the lines described earlier, his feelings of loneliness and self-criticism for not getting close to another person point beyond the systemic-organizational level of self complexity. It is this desire for intimate relationships and wish to bring a sense of identity into more synchrony that often leads him to step out of this overdifferentiated world and to make use of insight-oriented therapy. The move brings into the foreground the tension between self-attack for not performing well alone and feelings of self-loss for exploring the opening of the rigid boundaries between self and other.

John's case brings to an end the discussion of developmentally differentiated treatments.

Table 9.8 (see pp. 620–621) summarizes the differential treatment approach at five developmental positions. Again, it is important to remember that individuals function at multiple levels and that treatment methods have to be tailored accordingly. The developmental cutting edge must be engaged as much as the areas of lag, vulnerability, and encapsulations.

EMPIRICAL EVIDENCE FOR A RELATIONSHIP BETWEEN DEVELOPMENT AND PSYCHOLOGICAL SYMPTOMS AND DISORDERS

Having examined the implications of applying a developmental perspective to the practice of therapy and other forms of intervention, in this final section I review the empirical evidence for the relationship between children and adolescents' level of development and their symptoms or disorders. Since clinical-developmental psychology represents a new three-way relationship among theory, research, and practice, a review of empirical research in this area is especially important. It is essential that the theories that guide the practitioner are scrutinized and empirically validated, and it is equally important that the applied-developmental researcher focus her energies on exploring those questions that are critical to the clinician's work.

The clinical-developmental psychologist begins with the premise that a person's understanding of relationships, her development of self, and the meaning she makes of life, are connected to the problems, symptoms, and disorders she suffers from. Even if these factors are not the causes of her dysfunction, the ways in which she constructs her reality affects how she experiences her problems. To identify the link between the way people perceive, understand, construct, and interpret, and the symptoms they display is one goal that therapists coming from most schools of clinical practice set for themselves. Even behaviorists, who are coming out of a tradition that had rejected any notion of the "black box" of the mind, are now practicing cognitive-behavior therapy in increasing numbers, and are fascinated by the relationship between behavior and thought (e.g., Guidano & Liotti, 1983; Leahy, 1988). Psychoanalysts and dynamic psychotherapists have always been interested in fantasy, play, and symbolic expression in relationship to psychopathology. For both of these traditions, and for the hundreds of child and adolescent therapies that exist today,

Table 9.8 Clinical-Developmental Interventions with Adolescents

Self-Complexity Levels				
Subjective-Physical	Reciprocal-Instrumental	Mutual-Inclusive	Identity-Seeking	Systemic-Organizational
Treatment Focus				
• Interventions that focus on cognitive and emotional disorganization, impulsivity, attention problems, lack of control over bodily functions. • Focus on the constant need for physical presence of authority figures. • Supportive and behavioral treatments in a structured environment; interventions to change environment (e.g., classroom, family structure).	• Treatment focus on issues of fairness and support for behavior that takes other people into consideration. • Central role for peer learning, as struggles with authority figures are typical (e.g., AA, group interventions, community meetings). • Concrete activities with adult role models who work on skills and abilities, and fun tasks (e.g., coaches, mentors, Outward Bound coordinators).	• Interpersonal therapy with focus on depression and low self-esteem emerging in closer relationships. • Special emphasis on one-on-one relationship. • Sharing of experiences to overcome loneliness in groups as well as in individual treatment.	• Insight-oriented therapy supporting the emerging capacities to "choose" a self from among many different possibilities.	• Strong focus on expression of emotions and relaxation of the rigid moral and self-reliant position; push toward more self-empathy and balancing needs in life—less workaholism, less competitiveness.
Setting				
• Usually structured environment (e.g., classroom) needed to contain serious impulsivity, depression, and potential for short psychotic episodes. • Setting must provide strong limits and rules that foster the learning of consequences of self's actions; incentives must be provided to apply and internalize structure. • Predictable staff, teachers, or clinicians must be readily available.	• Containment needed for a long period of time, especially when antisocial tendencies are strong. • Despite seeming disinterest in individual therapy, one-to-one relationships are important to create trust, but need to entail mutually satisfying activities (e.g., eating, sports, walks). • Support to get needs met in a nondelinquent way.	• Individual treatment (often in conjunction with family treatment) to help express internalized feelings and, when necessary, short residential treatments (long, regressive hospitalizations to be avoided), but suicidality can make safe environment necessary. • Support groups offer opportunities for "identification first, individualism later."	• Individual treatment often effective as the therapist can become an ally in reviewing the past relationships and be a sounding board in creating life goals and plans. • Including the context (friends, family, etc.) can be useful, but focus has to be not only on inclusion but also on the need for differentiation.	• Individual therapy often essential as the person needs help in reflecting on his or her life. But because it is important that the client does not remove self from the world, groups are also effective.
Support				
• Strong boundaries and limits with goal of internalizing external rules. Support with often enmeshed and/or abandoning family system or disorganized school environment.	• Support in experience of unfairness that results in having to confront externalizing stance ("others are at fault"). • Experience of nurturing relationship is critical (many patients have experienced trauma and neglect), but special attention must be given so that supportive stance will not be exploited. • Address the child's manipulative behavior, but always in context of supportive environment.	• Strong commitment in every aspect of person's experiences (e.g., clothes, sports, peer group). • Encouragement of assertiveness needed. • Support of the expression of anger and frustration. • Help with tendency to have negative feelings "go underground" and to attend to the needs of others while neglecting oneself.	• Person needs to be supported through the inevitable confusions of wanting to be close to others and be like them while trying to come to terms with being different and standing up for a life project that might not be in line with others' expectations.	• The person feels easily out of control and angry at different parts of self for not falling in line. • Support for more self-acceptance and less self-criticism.

Table 9.8 ***(Continued)***

Subjective-Physical	Reciprocal-Instrumental	Mutual-Inclusive	Identity-Seeking	Systemic-Organizational
Insight				
• Work with emerging ability to review behaviors, feelings, and thoughts. • Begin to recognize that multiple feelings can coexist about the same person or situation. • Learn that strategies being used are self-destructive.	• Emerging recognition that world can be influenced in productive ways and that rejections by others do not have to be addressed in terms of revenge and hostility. • Close relationships provide a possibility to begin to view the world through a sense of mutuality and community.	• Beginning reflection of what is occurring in the relationship as a pattern (e.g., "Every time I am silent, I feel ashamed"). • Understanding regression and low self-esteem as a result of not being "master of own destiny." • Exploring the problems of expression of anger and the tendency to turn against the self.	• Taking a perspective on the dilemma of needing approval from significant others while listening to an inner direction. • Coming to terms with the fact that pursuing one's identity can mean making unpopular decisions and being excluded. • Focus on potential for being overly differentiated and becoming "ideologically pure" but isolated.	• Insight is quite typical, but often intellectualized. Person needs help in understanding how removed he or she can get, how achievement focus can constrict the self. • New ways of integrating feelings have to be found. Special focus also on anger at the self as well as suicide potential.
Typical Therapeutic Binds				
• Attempt by therapist, counselor, and teacher to interpret behavior in terms of symbolic meanings when they are only understood in concrete and behavioral terms. • Feeding into split between "good family"—"bad peer world," "good therapist"—"bad parents" (or vice versa) often leads to a breakdown of the work.	• Person confuses the therapist's "being on my side" with jointly breaking the rules (e.g., smoking in office before age). • Fear of consequences can lead to a style of nondisclosure. • Difficulty in talking about problems emerging in the relationship and past hurts because a biographical and transference focus has not yet developed.	• Silences in the treatment (or other relationship) and feeling rejected by therapist require very taxing proofs of acceptance (e.g., midnight phone calls). • Expressed dependency of patient creates anxiety in therapist. • Danger of fluctuation of therapist between demand for too much insight and self-observation on part of patient and underestimating the patients' capacity to observe relationship patterns and feeling states.	• Difficulty in handling conflicts that arise from experimenting with identity (e.g., risk-taking to prove that one is different from family, searching out experiences of self through drugs, ideological struggles with authorities, etc.). • Leaving important relationships for the sake of "finding oneself," including the therapeutic relationship, without adequately thinking through the consequences of isolation and lack of support.	• Therapist is seen as not understanding because of a sense of being too nice. The focus on one's biography lets many old vulnerabilities and issues emerge that become hard to work on. Being cut off from one's feelings makes it hard to discuss and deal with the need for closeness. • Insights can easily fuel self-criticism.

empirically based findings that reveal the relationships between symptoms and developmental capacities would be welcome. If we could establish a developmentally focused understanding of symptoms and other psychological dysfunctions, we would be one step closer to refining our treatment methods. If symptomatology is connected to development, then it is likely that recovery is as well. Investigators must first try to construct typical symptom profiles associated with levels of self complexity; only then will it be possible to turn to the topic of treatment and psychological recovery.

To pursue these questions, we turn to developmental psychopathology, the study of dysfunction from a developmental point of view. Once again, the perspective through which I view this is a constructive-developmental one. In adopting this perspective, my focus is on the processes of the active meaning maker, whose interpretations about self and relationships develop in systematic and predictable ways. From within the literature on meaning making, I only make use of one measurement tradition: Loevinger's model of ego development. Loevinger's model and method, the Sentence Completion Test (Loevinger & Wessler, 1970), have been used in many studies of "normal" populations and increasingly to explore variations in development (Hauser et al., 1991; Loevinger, 1968). The Harvard Laboratory of Developmental Psychology and Developmental Psychopathology uses the test with clinical populations; the results allow us to piece together a very useful picture of developmental symptomatology (Noam, in press).

The ego, as Loevinger describes it, is the master around which personality is constructed. Her theory posits that each person has a customary orientation to self and to the world, and that there are stages and transitions along which these "frames of reference" may be grouped. Those in Loevinger's earliest stage of ego development are impulsive and are dependent on, or exploitative of, others. The three stages that share these characteristics are called "preconformist." Those in the next higher, or "conformist," stages are particularly concerned with interpersonal acceptance and often express their views in clichés and stereotypes. Those who have reached the "postconfomist" stages of ego development generally cope with inner conflict through a high degree of self-awareness. They typically show more cognitive complexity and have interpersonal styles that emphasize mutuality and respect for individual differences. These later stages tend to appear only during late adolescence or adulthood.

Ego Development, Psychiatric Symptoms, and Mental Health: A Line of Research

My laboratory uses psychological structures of meaning (as does Loevinger), rather than age, as markers for development and developmental psychopathology. A number of intriguing findings have resulted from this approach.

All the research to be cited, except where otherwise stated, was conducted with an inpatient sample of adolescents admitted for care at a psychiatric hospital affiliated with the Harvard Medical School. Because data for this sample are constantly being updated, different sample sizes in different studies reflect particular data sets available at the time of analysis. The adolescent group consists of patients aged 11 to 16 years. The patients are primarily Caucasian and come from social classes 1 to 5 (Hollingshead, 1957). Patients presented a variety of symptoms for which a full range of treatment services were available (e.g., individual therapy, group therapy, medication). In all the studies, subjects with Wechsler Full-Scale IQ levels below 85 have been eliminated from analyses.

Approximately 80% of the adolescents were found to be functioning at developmentally delayed, preconformist levels of ego functioning. However, these adolescents should not be considered to be members of a single group because each of the three preconformist stages of ego development carries its own distinct meaning system, interpersonal style, and level of moral understanding. This finding argues against a perception of adolescence as a unitary stage. Rather, it argues in favor of the idea, introduced in an earlier publication, of "adolescent worlds" (Noam et al., 1990). In that publication, we introduced a developmental model that accounts for differential conceptualizations of relationships with parents, peers, friends, and role models. Such a model suggests that disorders and symptoms can be subdivided from a developmental point of view.

Taken as a whole, this clinical sample, as well as others from the lab, exhibited a delay in ego development (Browning, 1986). Yet, some adolescents within the samples did not show a delay. The range of ego functioning within the sample allows exploration of how symptomatology differs at different levels of maturity.

Is There a Relationship between Early Stages of Ego Development and Externalizing Symptomatology?

In a study of 140 male and female adolescent inpatients (Noam et al., 1984, associations between levels of ego development and types of maladaptive behavior were studied. We asked whether externalizing behaviors (e.g., aggression, delinquency) were significantly associated with immature ego development. The answer was important both for exploring the relationship between social cognition and behavior and for understanding the distinction between internalizing and externalizing symptoms in developmental terms (Achenbach, 1982; Phillips & Zigler, 1964).

Using the Child Behavior Checklist (Achenbach & Edelbrock, 1987), it was found that both internalizing and externalizing symptoms were significantly and negatively related to increases in ego development. When controlling for the effects of age, gender, and socioeconomic status, level of ego development made a significant contribution to the variance in externalizing scores, but not in internalizing scores.

This result was consistent with findings of other researchers that suggest a correlation between the lower stages of ego development and externalizing symptoms. Powitzky (1976), for example, found that relatively low levels of ego development were prevalent. among less socialized young offenders (bank robbers, drug offenders). Frank and Quinlan (1976) also found differences in ego development when comparing delinquent and nondelinquent teenage girls from the inner city. In addition, Browning (1986) reported that whereas adolescent inpatients at lower stages of ego development frequently demonstrate externalizing symptoms, no correlation between internalizing symptoms and higher stages of ego development was found.

This led to further research in which we refined our measurement of symptoms and diagnoses. The resulting study (Noam et al., 1984) found that adolescents functioning at lower levels of ego development reported significantly more symptoms of all kinds than those functioning at a higher stage. Using this finding, it was hypothesized that differences might begin to emerge in the symptoms and diagnoses exhibited by adolescents at different stages of ego development. In another study of 320 adolescent psychiatric admissions (141 males and 179 females) Noam, Kilburn, and Ammen-Elkins (1989) found robust correlations between both externalizing behaviors and lower ego levels, and internalizing symptoms and higher levels of ego development. The study used a self-report measure (Youth

Self Report) to determine levels of externalizing and internalizing behaviors.

The relationship between symptomatology and level of ego functioning was further explored in a sample of 140 adolescents, 74 males and 66 females (Noam & Houlihan, 1990). Arranging diagnostic categories in order of severity, from relative adjustment to psychosis, a consistent pattern emerged. With the exception of the affective disorders, as severity of diagnosis increased, so did the number of subjects at preconformist levels of ego development.

Is There a Relationship between Ego Development, Symptoms, and Defenses?

Emerging from this research were patterns of symptoms and syndromes that covaried with levels of ego development. The correlation between externalizing symptoms and preconformist levels of ego development was fairly robust. So, too, was the correlation between symptom severity and lower ego levels. These findings led us to ask whether level of ego functioning sheds light on the mechanisms that link cognitive maturity to symptom expression. With that goal in mind, my associates and I undertook studies examining the relationship between defenses and ego level.

We found that there was indeed a correlation between type of defense and level of ego development. Similar results have been found in several studies that use the Defense Mechanism Inventory (DMI: Ihilevich & Gleser, 1986) and Loevinger's measure in nonclinical populations. In a normative study of adolescents, Levit (1989) reported that turning against others (TAO; i.e., responding to conflict by attacking an external source) was inversely related to ego development. Labouvie-Vief, Hakim-Larson, and Hobart (1987), in a study of nonclinical subjects aged 10 to 77 years, found that turning against others (TAO) and projection (PRO; i.e., attribution of negative characteristics as justification for aggression) were associated with lower ego development. Turning against self (TAS; i.e., responding to conflict by directing aggression inward), reversal (REV; i.e., responding neutrally or positively to frustration), and principalization (PRN; i.e., coping with conflict by separating affect from the source of conflict through, for example, rationalization or isolation of affect, were positively linked to ego development. Not all studies of defenses and ego development have found similar relationships, though (e.g., Vaillant & McCullough, 1987).

In a later study (Recklitis & Noam, 1990) of 291 adolescent inpatients (122 males and 169 females), we examined the relationship between aggressive behavior, defenses, and ego development. Using incidents of restraints of the hospitalized adolescents and staff reports of aggressive behavior as criteria, the link between externalizing behaviors (assaults) and lower ego levels was clearly demonstrated. A pattern linking externalizing behaviors to the defenses that fit under the broader categories of TAO, PRO, and REV was also demonstrated. Turning against others and projection were negatively and significantly associated with higher ego development, whereas the more ideational and internalizing defenses of principalization, turning against self and reversal, were positively correlated (also significantly) with higher ego development. Dividing subjects into assaultive and nonassaultive groups revealed significant differences, in the expected direction, between levels of ego functioning in the two groups. The defense in which the difference between these groups was most pronounced was PRN (coping with conflict through intellectualization, rationalization, and isolation of affect). This suggests that the more psychosocially mature adolescents (i.e., those at conformist stages) were able to adopt a more cognitive approach to conflict resolution and use that approach as an inhibitor against impulsive action. Further work is needed to ascertain whether the relationship between ego development and symptoms is mediated by a third set of variables, such as defenses. Our findings show that such an association does exist, but that it is the relationship between ego development and symptoms that is most distinct.

Is There a Relationship between Higher Ego Development and Internalizing Symptoms?

In a study of 277 inpatient adolescents, 124 males and 153 females (Noam, Paget, Valiant, Borst, & Bartok, 1994), we grouped diagnoses into categories of conduct disorders, affective disorders, and a mix of the two. It turned out that conduct and mixed conduct/affective disorders were more prevalent among adolescents in the preconformist stage. Affective disorders, on the other hand, were more commonly associated with females and those at the conformist level of ego development. One important finding was that more advanced ego development was related to an increase in incidents of "pure depression" (compared with incidents of "comorbidity between aggression and depression").

In research on suicidality, we also found a link between higher stages of ego development and increased rates of suicide (Borst, Noam, & Bartok, 1991; Borst & Noam, 1993). Retrospective studies of adolescents who committed suicide have found that 95% were suffering from a *DSM-III-R* disorder (Shafii, Carrigan, Whittinghill, & Derrick, 1985). Depression has often been linked to suicide attempts in adolescence (Pfeffer, Newcorn, Kaplan, Mizruchi, & Plutchik, 1989; Robbins & Alessi, 1985), but research has also identified a significant proportion of suicidal adolescents who were not depressed, but rather sought treatment for conduct disorders and antisocial behavior (Apter, Bleich, Plutchik, Mendelsohn, & Tyano, 1988). Comorbidity of psychiatric disorder has been found to increase the risk of suicide (Brent, Perper, Goldstein, & Kolko, 1988; Kreitman, 1986). In a psychological autopsy of adolescents who killed themselves, Shafii, Steltz-Lenarsky, Derrick, Beckner and Whittinghill (1988) found that comorbidity, usually depression, substance abuse, and conduct disorder or another disorder, was present in 81% of victims. It has been suggested that the mix of conduct and affective disorders may be a potent one leading to suicidality.

The complex nature of suicidality suggests the need for a more complex model than the simple link that has been made between developmental level and suicidal behaviors. Borst et al. (1991) investigated the relationship between ego development, age, gender, and diagnosis, on the one hand, and serious suicidal ideation and attempts, on the other, among 219 inpatient adolescents, 96 males and 123 females. In addition to the established risk factors of gender and diagnosis (e.g., males tend to be more aggressive and females more depressed), it was found in a cross-sectional study that with increasing ego development adolescents became more prone to suicidal ideation and behaviors. Although suicidality was prevalent among the preconformist adolescents, it usually coexisted with externalizing problems and disorders. The depressed, unaggressive (toward others) adolescent was typically at the conformist level. We concluded that higher levels of ego development could be a risk factor in a vulnerable population, leading to an increase in depression and suicidality. More longitudinal work building on these findings is presently under way.

Can We Use Ego Development to Subdivide Symptoms and Disorders?

Although suicidal behavior was not an exclusive phenomenon of the conformist stage, we found a higher proportion of suicide attempters in that group. Although these adolescents were in the conformist level, most of those studied had lower levels of ego development. This finding is consistent with earlier reports of developmental delays among adolescents hospitalized with psychiatric disorders (Noam et al., 1984). Hence, although 62% of conformist inpatients were found to have attempted suicide, of all the adolescents studied who attempted suicide, the majority (79%) were at preconformist stages of ego development. These findings led us to propose two distinct profiles of suicidal adolescents—defiant and self-blaming. Defiant suicidal adolescents are explicitly angry, impulsive, concrete, and often view suicide as form of revenge. Self-blaming adolescents are more depressed, inclined to see themselves from a sociocentric perspective, and view suicide as a response to the loss and abandonment they feel they have suffered.

The use of distinct profiles of suicidality to shed light on the relationship between ego level, defenses, and psychiatric symptoms was explored further in Noam and Borst (1994). A sample of 139 inpatient psychiatric females, aged 13 to 16, were divided into four groups based on dimensions of suicidality (suicidal/non-suicidal) and stage of ego development (preconformist/ conformist). Preconformist attempters were characterized by comorbidity of symptoms, both high internalizing and externalizing behaviors (i.e., depressive and aggressive behaviors) and externalizing defenses (i.e., projection, reversal). The conformist attempter showed primarily internalizing symptoms, (i.e., depression) and scored highest on internalizing defenses (i.e., principalization).

Do We Find a Decrease of Symptomatology with Ego Development?

This same pattern was revealed in research conducted with adult psychiatric patients. Noam and Dill (1991) examined symptom severity and ego development in a sample of 86 adult outpatients (34 males and 52 females aged 19 to 71 with a median age of 30). Subjects ranged from social class 1 to 5, with approximately 10% of subjects divided evenly between the highest and lowest categories and 36% in the middle category. Correlations between advanced levels of ego development and symptom severity were uniformly negative across all but two symptom scales (obsessive-compulsive disorder and interpersonal sensitivity). These results indicate that symptomatology generally decreases as ego level increases or that severe psychopathology interferes with ongoing development. Another possible interpretation of this finding is that as the ego develops, internalized symptomatologies and pathologies arise. To study the relationship between reduction of symptoms and ego development, we followed these subjects longitudinally.

A second longitudinal study further examined the relationship between defenses and symptomatology, this time among a small sample of adolescents, 21 males and 16 females, who were evaluated at admission to a psychiatric hospital and reevaluated 9 months later. Two "ego pathways" were identified in this study: that of the progressors and that of the nonprogressors. Progressors were subjects who advanced at least one-half stage in ego development during the 9-month period between evaluations. Nonprogressors were subjects who regressed or remained at the same ego level during this period (Noam & Dill, 1991). Although both groups showed significant reductions of symptoms in the 9 months, that of ego progressors was greater. Furthermore, while style of defense remained virtually unchanged in the 9 months for nonprogressors, progressors demonstrated a decrease in the use of projection and reversal.

Summary

This section provides evidence that the development of social-cognitive capacities as measured by the Washington University Sentence Completion Test is related to symptoms, diagnoses, and defensive styles. To offer such evidence is also to show that the meaning that people give to their relationships and to the events in their lives finds expression in their actions and symptoms. But this relationship is not a simple one. In vulnerable populations, the earlier levels of ego development can lead to externalizing, aggressive, and impulsive symptoms. As social cognition matures, these symptoms decrease. But the maturation of ego development, or social cognition, does not guarantee that all symptoms abate. Rather, with this maturation can come an increase in internalizing symptoms, such as depression and suicidality.

This kind of research should now focus on intervention and prevention. What sorts of interventions help a child and adolescent at a particular level of self complexity and ego maturity? What is perceived by the client as the most empathic and useful kind of intervention. Which interventions are too simplistic for the client? Which are too complex? What makes for the best match between client's needs and therapist's strategies? We are now in a position to conduct such research by making use of the model presented in this chapter. In so doing, we should take account of the therapist's own level of self complexity, thereby acknowledging that she, too, is a developing human being, not just an "agent of change."

This research should focus not only on global developmental features, such as the ego or the self, but also on more narrow facets of development. It should use a minimalist, rather than maximalist, approach to the self (Noam, 1990), and in so doing should focus (e.g., perspective taking). And yet, other domains also need to be studied as they relate to specific disorders; for example, the capacity for distinguishing between reality and fantasy in those suffering from psychosis, the moral development of delinquents, the development of shame and guilt in victims of depressions, and the development of self-esteem in those suffering from a narcissistic disorder. By focusing on the specific areas of vulnerability and relating them to particular developmental lines, we can hope to learn how to treat patients differentially. Such a differential treatment would be based both on a domain-specific understanding of development and on an understanding of the various disorders; the differential therapist will focus treatment on that point where development and disorder intersect in the patient.

For the time being, better assessment methods should be created to allow the clinician to begin tailoring interventions to the client's developmental level. Typically, a test battery that assesses symptoms and diagnosis is now used. Sometimes neuropsychological, intelligence, and projective tests, such as the Rorshach and the TAT, are also given. But none of these tests gives the clinician a sense of what developmental tools the client uses to understand himself and his social world. In addition, the clinician cannot derive sufficient information from these test results to determine the client's strengths.

Yet, it is not the particular measure used, but the clincian's understanding of the developmental world of the child that is important. A good understanding of the client's developmental space, and a constant reassessment of "where the client is," are essential elements for a productive treatment.

CONCLUSION AND OUTLOOK

A strong tradition, psychoanalysis, has been established in this century for bringing an understanding of development to bear on clinical work. But despite the many creative theories that have emerged from this union, we are just starting to tailor our treatments in a life span, developmentally differentiated fashion. We are now in a position to extend significantly the application of our knowledge of development to the clinical arena. Our understanding of human cognition, emotional development, psychosocial adaptation, and biological maturation has evolved dramatically. Furthermore, more researchers who study development are working in that area where typical and "atypical" development intersect (e.g., Cicchetti, 1996; Noam, 1996; Noam & Cicchetti, 1996; Rutter, 1990; Sroufe, 1979). In addition, clinicians of all persuasions have become more willing, in the interest of practicality, to step over traditional disciplinary boundaries. For example, psychoanalysists have expanded on ideas about empathy (e.g., Kohut, 1978) that had previously been a strong focus in other psychological traditions such as client-centered psychotherapy. Behavioral psychologists are now discovering the power of relationships, attachments, and development. Family therapists are recognizing that there is an individual meaning maker within the family system.

Although this trend is encouraging, a deeper understanding of how to match intervention strategies to the specific needs of patients is still called for. Refinements of traditional diagnostic categories will help. But it is just as important for the intervention specialist to have an understanding of the role of development in treatment. Interventions for at-risk populations that are designed to engage a person's capacity to overcome adversity and develop buffers to deal with new disappointments and stressors are equally vital. Innovations in training, research, and modes of application are required in order to realize these goals in the coming years.

Implications for Therapy

There is a trend toward a more pragmatic approach to mental health practice. Breaking down some of the traditional boundaries between schools of therapy is a welcome change. Among clinicians and those specializing in intervention and prevention there is also a greater need to evaluate the outcomes of the interventions they use. Thus, what began early in the century as a theoretically unified approach has evolved into a multitude of treatment methods, theories, and perspectives. Psychoanalysis and psychodynamic theory share the stage now with many other useful and effective strategies that support growth and reduce symptoms.

We live in an age of experimentation and change in various therapy traditions. Some of these changes have been caused by social trends, such as the reduction in the availability of mental health services. In the United States, hospitalizations are brief now and interventions are often provided through community-based services, such as mental health centers, schools, and after-school programs. Short-term and group therapies are on the rise.

How does one choose the right treatment in this environment? What are the best ways to develop an intervention strategy? With the expansion of our knowledge about human growth in many domains, one would expect an understanding of development to be critical to making decisions about treatments and interventions. One might also expect that the new emphases on the psychology of risk and on developmental psychopathology would underline the importance of basing a treatment strategy on an understanding of development. But the fact remains that most treatments are decided on on the basis of symptoms and disorders. Although there is some wisdom in such an approach, most disorders are not homogeneous and may call for a variety of treatments (e.g., as discussed earlier, there is not one right treatment for an adolescent diagnosed as having a conduct disorder). We need to move away from developing treatment methods for "the" suicidal child, intervention strategies for "the" user of drugs, and programs for "the" violent adolescent, as if all people who suffer from these problems fit the diagnostic prototype. Often, these problems do not exist in isolation; indeed, the recent attention on "comorbidity" and "dual diagnoses" is a recognition of this fact. Those who live in high-risk environments often suffer from a multitude of stressors and symptoms (e.g., Noam, 1996). It is imperative in these situations to recognize the utility of intervention strategies that focus on the person's understanding of self, relationships, symptoms, and life context.

This kind of developmental approach can help us understand why some treatments work and others do not. It can also help the practitioner select among the available interventions. A greater focus on treatment outcome research has developed over the years. Now, it is important to apply an understanding of capacities at different developmental levels to the results of this research; such an application will lend new insight to therapy outcome research.

Implications for Short-Term Treatment

Any developmental approach has to come to terms with two contradictory realities. Results of prevention and intervention projects with aggressive, delinquent, and depressed adolescents suggest that strategies should be multimodal, incorporating the services of various of institutions and personnel and providing intervention over a sustained period of time. But reforms in the health insurance industry in the United States and increasingly in other countries have brought pressure on mental health professionals to provide mostly short-term interventions. And yet, mental health professionals do not have the clinical equivalent of medicine's antibiotics; there are no quick fixes for most psychological complaints.

Far more research is needed before we will be in a position to properly distinguish those who require long-term treatment intervention from those who need only short-term support or therapy. Psychotherapy outcome research has shown that treatment that lasts as little as a few sessions can nonetheless be useful. Nevertheless, few professionals would want to place a violent gang member in short-term treatment with the goal of getting him to give up this lifestyle. On the other hand, a circumscribed phobia can be treated with a limited number of sessions and does not require a biographical reconstruction of the onset and evolution of the anxiety (N. Miller, 1991).

Can a developmental approach to treatment differentiation be useful for determining the best short-term treatment and intervention strategies? Although the answer to this question is not yet known, it is possible to make some generalizations from clinical experience. First, from a developmental point of view, clinical intervention works because the client is a developmental being and a set of developmental forces exist with which the clinician can ally him or herself. Most development occurs over long periods of time and requires a great deal of support, empathy, and challenge. To do short-term interventions, a therapist must have a mental map of the patient's cognitive, emotional, and social development, and must make use of those existing strengths in the person's repertoire to combat the symptoms. The goal in short-term therapy is often to help the patient become developmentally unstuck so that he can continue to grow on his own. This often means that the therapist will seek out for the patient those contexts in the external environment that encourage growth, rather than fostering a dependency on the clinician as the source of the change.

Second, short-term treatment from a developmental point of view requires a very different approach toward termination. Instead of viewing the treatment as having a beginning, middle, and clearly defined end, the therapist must look beyond the parameters of the treatment period to consider what supports can be put in place so that symptoms do not recur. Thus, differential treatment involves clarifying not only what the individual needs in the treatment itself, but also what he will need at later points in development.

A patient who enters short-term therapy early in adolescence with complaints of depression and isolation at home and school, can, in a year or two, be suffering less from these complaints and more from an uncertain identity, an ideological isolation, and rejection of herself. None of these issues can be resolved in short-term treatment, but they can be clarified. Decisions can be made about how to pursue answers for these questions in self-enhancing, rather than self-destructive, ways. Most people have experienced the power of an encounter with a compassionate mentor who quickly grasps the meaning of the other person's conflict in brief, intense, discussions. Often such a profound mirroring experience is remembered for a long time. Based on it, much work can be done in all areas of life. Short-term treatments can have the same effect. This is especially likely if the same therapist is available for the client at different points in development, as is a pediatrician or family doctor. The patient-therapist relationship in such a case is long-term, although the encounters are short. No treatment approach is more in need of a clear developmental understanding than the short-term modality. The goal of such treatment is often to jump-start developmental processes that support recovery. But without a developmental map, it is difficult, indeed, to focus on these processes.

Implications for Training

Typically, training in development for practitioners of mental health services consists of an introduction to psychoanalytic developmental thinking. This theory has served as a guide for generations of child and adult therapists. The psychoanalytic theories of Erik Erikson, John Bowlby, Margaret Mahler, Peter Blos, Anna Freud, and Donald Winnicott have been part of the curricula for students of developmental psychology. Developmental knowledge, however, has broadened and is now, methodologically speaking, exceedingly sophisticated. Every conceivable developmental question is researched carefully. Taken together, this work has catapulted developmental thinking into a full-blown science. But despite the enormous progress that has been made, most mental health professionals do not receive sufficient training to participate in this evolving developmental discourse. Only recently, have the curricula in some individual child psychology and child psychiatry training programs been reformed. Clinical psychology and social work programs are also beginning to change their curricula, and some have made sufficient progress to develop bridges between their clinical and developmental programs. In most universities, however, the boundaries between these programs are rigidly maintained.

Where clinical and developmental theorists, researchers, and clinicians have come together, they are usually still in the early stages of collaboration. Their efforts need to be nurtured; it is important to develop infrastructures to support applied developmental thinking. One such infrastructure might consist of training supervisors who bring these concepts to life around typical clinical dilemmas. In addition, developmental psychologists should also be encouraged to receive postgraduate clinical training without being stigmatized for entering clinical psychology through the "back door." Their lifelong goal might not be the treatment of patients, but their training and experience will better enable them to collaborate with clinical researchers.

Without a basic knowledge of developmental principles, it is impossible to make substantive progress in the area of differential treatment. We are better able to understand the underlying developmental principles that influence the ways risks and symptoms are formed and maintained over time. It is also within our reach to understand how symptoms, problems, and pathologies become transformed by a patient into more complex forms, and how shifts to better adaptation occur. These developmental issues require a developmental focus. The plethora of existing longitudinal studies provides a great deal of the relevant data. What is less established is the systematic dissemination of developmental thought in mental health training programs. Developmental psychology and developmental psychopathology need to become "basic sciences" for the mental health field (e.g., Rolf, Masten, Cicchetti, Nuechterlein, & Weintraub, 1990). A focus on differential treatment from a developmental point of view is a useful way of organizing the immense literature, allowing clinical trainees to incorporate the ideas and use them in their daily work.

Implications for Research

Studies should be conducted to generate knowledge about differential treatment from a developmental point of view. One fruitful approach would be to interview clients in greater detail than has been done to date about which intervention strategies, in their opinions, worked for them. By relating their answers to their developmental capacities and problem areas, it would be possible to refine our treatment methods.

Additional research could use videotapes of therapist-client interactions. Again, by focusing on the developmental world of the client, it would be possible to distinguish those interventions that seem to work from those that do not. This method could also be used to determine the developmental orientation of the therapist to facilitate a matching of client and therapist. A number of studies have shown the importance of matching client and therapist, but we know very little about the connection between this relationship and the client's and the therapist's development.

A third kind of research that needs to be done is longitudinal studies of patients in therapy and after they leave treatment. Are the people who improve through treatment also the ones who are more likely to mature in terms of their self-observational skills and interpersonal understanding? A longitudinal approach would also examine treatment recidivism. Are the clients who are relieved of their symptoms but did not mature developmentally more inclined to return to treatment than those who matured? Or are processes at work that have more to do with the type of psychopathology and symptomatology than with development?

Subjects that are studied in all the research areas that have been described must be compared to control groups of children, adolescents, and adults who are at risk but do not receive treatment or intervention. Even now, many of these studies are under way, some within our own developmental psychology lab at Harvard. Some of them have already been conducted in one form or another, but the research has used a single developmental framework, such as self or ego development. It is important to explore different domains of development and to find further links between specific symptoms and impaired areas of development. This includes, for example, the issue of the development of perfectionism and body image in anorexic patients, of dissociation in traumatized patients, and of moral judgment and moral action in delinquency.

Implications for Program Development for At-Risk Children and Adolescents

We know that prevention and intervention programs with at-risk children and adolescents require a number of features, including a multimodal approach, changes in context such as schools that include experiential learning, student participation, and peer learning (Dryfoos, 1990; Noam, Winner, Molad, & Rhein, 1996). We also know that programs have to be in place for a sustained period of time and that "quick fixes" are not possible. Supporting at-risk adolescents also requires the building of individual relationships. Most of these programs are generic: They focus on a general type of at-risk child and adolescent, or on a general problem such as early pregnancy, alcoholism, or drug use. However, young people do not usually fit so neatly into a single risk category. An adolescent who has a drug addiction might also be delinquent, live in a dysfunctional family, and have academic problems in school (e.g., Masten, 1989). In such a case, focusing on a single risk factor is insufficient.

Furthermore, an understanding of the meaning of risk is needed because the building of protective mechanisms involves not only changing the client's environmental context and peer culture, but also teaching him to internalize inhibitions and consider alternative strategies of behavior (e.g., Dodge, 1980). When it comes to understanding how to encourage these internalizations and the cognitive processes that protect the child and adolescent from risk, it becomes essential to build interventions and prevention methods around a careful developmental understanding. Many interesting projects are underway with children and adolescents in various community and school settings (e.g., Nakkula, Ayoub, Noam, & Selman, 1996; Noam et al., 1996).

These endeavors will produce a great deal of new knowledge that promises to unite the efforts of prevention, intervention, clinical knowledge, education, research, and clinical practice. But in bringing these facets of psychology together, it will be important not to superimpose, but rather to integrate, developmental principles with the various domains of the mental health field. Just as developmental psychologists have a great deal to learn from clinicians, prevention practitioners, and researchers, clinical scholars/scientists can benefit enormously from the new ideas that are emerging from developmental psychopathology. Mental health professionals, clinical and developmental researchers, and education reformers are at the threshold of an exciting era in which our knowledge of development will yield far better intervention and prevention strategies. This chapter represents an attempt to generate more momentum in this direction.

ACKNOWLEDGMENTS

A number of people have been generous with time and advice. I am grateful to Claudia Cooper and Alison Carper for her excellent editorial skills and her dedication throughout the work on this project. Karen Hoffman provided me with excellent comments as did the editors of this volume, Irving Sigel and Ann Renninger. My colleagues at the Clinical-Developmental Institute participated in discussions that sharpened my thinking. Comments by Ann Fleck Henderson, Laura Rogers, and Michael Basseches were especially helpful. Pam Woronoff and Amy Briggs were very helpful in reviewing some of the literature used in this chapter. Francie Fries provided expert assistance in manuscript preparation.

REFERENCES

Achenbach, T. M. (1982). *Developmental psychopathology* (2nd ed.). New York: Wiley.

Achenbach, T. M., & Edelbrock, C. (1978). The classification of child psychopathology: A review and analysis of empirical efforts. *Psychological Bulletin, 85,* 1275–1301.

Achenbach, T. M., & Edelbrock, C. (1987). *Manual for the youth self report and profile.* Burlington: Department of Psychiatry, University of Vermont.

Adler, G. (1986). Psychotherapy of the narcissistic personality disorder patient: Two contrasting approaches. *American Journal of Psychiatry, 143*(4), 430–436.

Ainsworth, M. (1982). Attachment: Retrospect and prospect. In C. Parkes & J. Stevenson-Hinde (Eds.), *The place of attachment in human behavior.* London: Tavistock.

American Psychiatric Association. (1968). *Diagnostic and statistical manual of mental disorders.* Washington, DC: Author.

American Psychiatric Association. (1980). *Diagnostic and statistic manual* (3rd ed.). Washington, DC: Author.

American Psychiatric Association. (1987). *Diagnostic and statistical manual of mental disorders* (3rd ed., Rev.). Washington, DC: Author.

American Psychiatric Association. (1994). *Diagnostic and statistical manual of mental disorders* (4th ed.). Washington, DC: Author.

Apter, A., Bleich, A., Plutchik, R., Mendelsohn, S., & Tyano, S. (1988). Suicidal behavior, depression, and conduct disorder in hospitalized adolescents. *Journal of the American Academy of Child and Adolescent Psychiatry, 27,* 696–699.

Baldwin, J. M. (1902). *Social and ethical interpretations in mental development.* New York: Macmillan.

Baltes, P. B., & Schaie, K. W. (1973). On life-span developmental research paradigms: Retrospects and prospects. In P. B. Baltes & K. W. Schaie (Eds.), *Life-span developmental psychology: Personality and socialization* (pp. 366–395). New York: American.

Basseches, M. (1989). Towards a constructive-developmental understanding of the dialectics of individuality and rationality. In D. A. Kramer & M. Bopp (Eds.), *Transformation in clinical and developmental psychology.* New York: Springer-Verlag.

Beardslee, W. R. (1989). The role of self-understanding in resilient individuals: The development of a perspective. *American Journal of Orthopsychiatry, 59*(2), 266–278.

Bibace, R., & Walsh, M. E. (1981). *Children's conceptions of health, illness, and body functions.* San Francisco: Jossey-Bass.

Bierman, K. L. (1988). The clinical implications of children's conceptions of social relationships. In S. R. Shirk (Ed.), *Cognitive development and child psychotherapy* (pp. 247–272). New York: Plenum Press.

Blakeney, C., & Blakeney, R. (1990). Reforming moral misbehavior. *Journal of Moral Education, 19,* 101–113.

Borst, S. R., & Noam, G. G. (1993). Developmental psychopathology in suicidal and non-suicidal adolescent girls. *Journal of the American Academy of Child and Adolescent Psychiatry, 32,* 501–508.

Borst, S. R., Noam, G. G., & Bartok, J. A. (1991). Adolescent suicidality: A clinical-developmental approach. *Journal of the American Academy of Child and Adolescent Psychiatry, 30,* 796–803.

Bowlby, J. (1969). *Attachment and loss: Vol. 1. Attachment.* New York: Basic Books.

Brent, D. A., Perper, J. A., Goldstein, C. E., & Kolko, D. J. (1988). Risk factors for adolescent suicide: A comparison of adolescent suicide victims with suicidal inpatients. *Archives of General Psychiatry, 45,* 581–588.

Bretherton, I. (1996). Internal working models of attachment relationships as related to coping. In G. G. Noam & K. W.

Fischer (Eds.), *Development and vulnerabilities in close relationships* (pp. 3–27). Mahwah, NJ: Erlbaum.

Bricker, D., & Cripe, J. (1992). *An activity-based approach to early intervention.* Baltimore: Brookes.

Broughton, J. (1978). *The development of concepts of self, mind, reality, and knowledge. New directions in child development: Social cognition.* San Francisco: Jossey-Bass.

Browning, D. L. (1986). Psychiatric ward behavior and length of stay in adolescent and young adult inpatients: A developmental approach to prediction. *Journal of Consulting and Clinical Psychology, 54,* 227–230.

Chandler, M. J. (1973). Egocentrism and anti-social behavior: The assessment and training of social perspective taking skills. *Developmental Psychology, 9,* 326–332.

Cicchetti, D. (1984). *Developmental psychopathology.* Chicago: University of Chicago Press.

Cicchetti, D. (1991). Fractures in the crystal: Developmental psychopathology and the emergence of self. *Developmental Review, 11,* 271–287.

Cicchetti, D. (1996). Child maltreatment: Implications for developmental theory and research. *Human Development, 39,* 18–39.

Commons, M. L., Richards, F. A., & Armon, C. (1984). *Beyond formal operations: Late adolescent and adult cognitive development.* New York: Praeger.

Cooley, C. H. (1902). *Human nature and the social order.* New York: Scribners.

Costello, A., Edelbrock, C., Dulcan, M., Kalas, R., & Klarie, S. (1984). *Development and testing of the NIMH diagnostic interview schedule for children on a clinical population: Final report* (Contract RFP-DB-81-0027). Center for Epidemiologic Studies, National Institute for Mental Health, Washington, DC.

Costello, E. J., & Angold, A. (1995). Developmental epidemiology. In D. Cicchetti & D. J. Cohen (Eds.), *Developmental psychopathology* (Vol. 1). New York: Wiley.

Coyle, J. T. (1995). The neuroscience perspective and the changing role of the psychiatrist. *Academic Psychiatry, 19*(4), 202–212.

Damon, W. (1977). *The social world of the child.* San Francisco: Jossey-Bass.

Damon, W., & Hart, D. (1988). *Self-understanding in childhood and adolescence.* New York: Cambridge University Press.

Demick, J. (1996). Life transitions as a paradigm for the study of adult development. In M. L. Common, J. Demick, & C. Goldberg (Eds.), *Clinical approaches to adult development.* Norwood, NJ: ABLEX.

Dobert, R., Habermas, J., & Nunner-Winkler, G. (1987). The development of the self. In J. M. Broughton (Ed.), *Critical theories of psychological development: PATH in psychology* (pp. 275–301). New York: Plenum Press. (Original work published 1977)

Dodge, K. (1980). Social cognition and children's aggressive behavior. *Child Development, 51,* 162–170.

Dryfoos, J. G. (1990). *Adolescents at risk: Prevalence and prevention.* New York: Oxford University Press.

Dryfoos, J. G. (1994). *Full-service schools: A revolution in health and social services for children, youth, and families.* San Francisco: Jossey-Bass.

Edelstein, W. (1990). Child development and social structure: A longitudinal study of individual differences. In P. B. Baltes, D. L. Featherman, & R. M. Lerner (Eds.), *Life-span development and behavior* (pp. 151–185). Hillsdale, NJ: Erlbaum.

Edelstein, W., & Noam, G. G. (1982). Regulatory structures of the self and "postformal" stages in adulthood. *Human Development, 25,* 407–422.

Erikson, E. (1950). Growth and crisis of the healthy personality. *Psychological Issues, 1,* 50–100.

Erikson, E. (1968). *Identity, youth, and crisis.* New York: Norton.

Fischer, K. W. (1980). A theory of cognitive development: The control and construction of hierarchies of skills. *Psychological Review, 87,* 477–531.

Fischer, K. W., & Ayoub, C. (1994). Affective splitting and dissociation in normal and maltreated children: Developmental pathways for self in relationships. In D. Cicchetti & S. Toth (Eds.), *Rochester Symposium on Developmental Psychopathology: Disorders and dysfunctions of the self* (Vol. 5, pp. 149–222). New York: University of Rochester Press.

Fish-Murray, C. C. (1993). Childhood trauma and subsequent suicidal behavior. In A. A. Leenaars, A. L. Berman, P. Cantor, R. E. Litman, & R. W. Maris (Eds.), *Suicidology: Essays in honor of Edwin S. Shneidman* (pp. 73–92). Northvale, NJ: Jason Aronson.

Flavell, J. H. (1977). *Cognitive development.* Englewood Cliffs, NJ: Prentice-Hall.

Frances, A., Clarkin, J., & Perry, S. (1984). *Differential therapeutics in psychiatry: The art and science of treatment selection.* New York: Brunner/Mazel.

Frank, S., & Quinlan, D. (1976). Ego development and adjustment patterns in adolescence. *Journal of Abnormal Psychology, 85,* 505–510.

Freud, A. (1950). *The ego and mechanisms of defense.* New York: International Universities Press.

Freud, S. (1958). *On creativity and the unconscious.* New York: Harper.

Freud, S. (1989). *Introductory lectures on psychoanalysis.* New York: Norton.

Gardner, H. (1993). *Creating minds.* New York: Basic Books.

Garfield, S. (1980). *Psychotherapy: An eclectic approach.* New York: Wiley.

Garmezy, N. (1983). Stressors of childhood. In N. Garmezy & M. Rutter (Eds.), *Stress, coping, and development in children.* New York: McGraw-Hill.

Gibbs, J. C., Arnold, K. D., Ahlborn, H. H., & Chessman, F. L. (1984). Facilitation of socio-moral reasoning in delinquents. *Journal of Consulting and Clinical Psychology, 52,* 37–45.

Giles, T. R. (1983). Probable superiority of behavioral intervention: I. Traditional comparative outcome. *Journal of Behavior Therapy and Experimental Psychiatry, 14,* 29–32.

Gilligan, C. (1982). *In a different voice.* Cambridge, MA: Harvard University Press.

Gilligan, C. (1996). The centrality of relationship in human development: A puzzle, some evidence, and a theory. In G. G. Noam & K. W. Fischer (Eds.), *Development and vulnerabilities in close relationships* (pp. 237–261). Mahwah, NJ: Erlbaum.

Guidano, V. F., & Liotti, G. (1983). *Cognitive processes and emotional disorders: A structural approach to psychotherapy.* New York: Guilford Press.

Habermas, T. (1989). Entfremdungserleben und Fahigkeit zur Perspektivenubernahme [Depersonalization and the development of perspective-taking]. *Zeitschrift fur Kinder- und Jugendpsychiatrie, 17*(1), 31–36.

Harter, S. (1988). Development and dynamic changes in the nature of the self-concept: Implications for child psychotherapy. In S. R. Shirk (Ed.), *Cognitive development and child psychotherapy* (pp. 119–160). New York: Plenum Press.

Harter, S. (1994). Psychosocial risk factors contributing to adolescent suicidal ideation. In G. G. Noam & S. Borst (Eds.), *Children, youth, and suicide: Developmental perspectives. New Directions for Child Development* (Vol.64, pp. 71–91). San Francisco: Jossey-Bass.

Hauser, S., Houlihan, J., Powers, S., Jacobson, A., Noam, G., Weiss, B., & Follansbee, D. (1987). Interaction sequences in families of psychiatrically hospitalized and other adolescents. *Psychiatry, 50,* 308–319.

Hauser, S., Powers, S., & Noam, G. (1991). *Adolescents and their families: Paths of development.* New York: Free Press.

Henderson, A. F. (1989). Learning, knowing, and the self: A constructive developmental view. In K. Field, B. J. Cohler, & G. Wool (Eds.), *Learning and education: Psychoanalytic perspectives.* Madison, CT: International Universities Press.

Hollingshead, A. B. (1957). *Two factor index of social position.* Unpublished report, New Haven, CT.

Ihilevich, D., & Gleser, G. C. (1986). *Defense mechanisms.* Owosso, MI: DMI Associates.

Ivey, A. E. (1986). *Developmental therapy.* San Francisco: Jossey-Bass.

Ivey, A. E., Ivey, M. B., & Simek-Morgan, L. (Eds.). (1993). *Counseling and psychotherapy.* Boston: Allyn & Bacon.

Jensen, J. P., & Bergin, A. E. (1988). Mental health values of professional therapists: A national interdisciplinary survey. *Professional Psychology Research and Practice, 19,* 290–297.

Kegan, R. (1982). *The evolving self.* Cambridge, MA: Harvard University Press.

Keller, M. (1984). An action-theoretical reconstruction of the development of social-cognitive competence. *Human Development, 27*(3/4), 211–220.

Klein, M. (1932). *The psychoanalysis of children.* London: Hogarth Press.

Kohlberg, L. (1969). Stage and sequence: The cognitive-developmental approach to socialization. In D. Gloslin (Ed.), *Handbook of socialization, theory and research* (pp. 347–480). New York: Rand McNally.

Kohlberg, L. (1984). *Essays on moral development: Vol. 2. The psychology of moral development.* San Francisco: Harper & Row.

Kohlberg, L., LaCrosse, J., & Ricks, D. (1972). The predictability of adult mental health from childhood behavior. In B. Wolman (Ed.), *Manual of child psychopathology.* New York: McGraw-Hill.

Kohut, H. (1978). Selected problems of self psychological theory. In J. Lichtenberg & S. Kaplan (Eds.), *Reflections on self psychology.* Hillsdale, NJ: Erlbaum.

Kreitman, N. (1986). The clinical assessment and management of the suicidal patient. In A. Roy (Ed.), *Suicide* (pp. 181–195). Baltimore: Williams & Wilkins.

Labouvie-Vief, G., Hakim-Larson, J., & Hobart, C. J. (1987). Age, ego, and the life-span development of coping and defense processes. *Psychology and Aging, 2*(3), 286–293.

Leahy, R. L. (1988). Cognitive therapy of childhood depression: Developmental considerations. In S. R. Shirk (Ed.), *Cognitive development and child psychotherapy* (pp. 187–206). New York: Plenum Press.

Levinson, D. J. (1990). A theory of life structure development in adulthood. In C. N. Alexander & E. J. Langer (Eds.), *Higher stages of human development: Perspectives on adult growth.* New York: Oxford University Press.

Levit, D. B. (1989). *A developmental study of ego defenses in adolescence.* Unpublished doctoral dissertation, Boston University, Boston.

Loevinger, J. (1968). The relation of adjustment to ego development. In S. S. Sales (Ed.), *The definition and measurement of mental health* (pp. 161–180). Washington, DC: U.S. Government Printing Office.

Loevinger, J. (1976). *Ego development.* San Francisco: Jossey-Bass.

Loevinger, J., & Wessler, R. (1970). *Measuring ego development: I. Construction and use of sentence completion test.* San Francisco: Jossey-Bass.

Luborsky, L., McLellan, A. T., Woody, G. E., O'Brien, C. P., & Auerbach, A. (1985). Therapist success and its determinants. *Archives of General Psychiatry, 42,* 602–611.

Mahler, M. S., Pine, F., & Bergman, A. (1975). *Psychological birth of the human infant.* New York: Basic Books.

Masten, A. (1989). Resilience in development: Implications of the study of successful adaptation for developmental psychopathology. In D. Cicchetti (Ed.), *Rochester Symposium on Developmental Psychopathology: Vol. 1. The emergence of a discipline* (pp. 261–294). Hillsdale, NJ: Erlbaum.

Mead, G. H. (1934). *Mind, self, and society.* Chicago: University of Chicago Press.

Miller, N. (1991). Emergent treatment concepts and techniques. *Annual Review of Addictions Research and Treatment, 1,* 1–14.

Miller, W. R., Taylor, C. A., & West, J. C. (1980). Focus versus broad-spectrum behavior therapy for problem drinkers. *Journal of Consulting and Clinical Psychology, 48,* 590–601.

Nakkula, M., Ayoub, C., Noam, G. G., & Selman, R. (1996). Risk and prevention: An interdisciplinary master's program in child and adolescent development. *Journal of Child and Youth Care, 11,* 8–31.

Nannis, E. D. (1988). A cognitive-developmental view of emotional understanding and its implications for child psychotherapy. In S. R. Shirk (Ed.), *Cognitive development and child psychotherapy* (pp. 91–118). New York: Plenum Press.

Neugarten, B. L. (1964). *Personality in middle and late life.* New York: Atherton Press.

Noam, G. G. (1985). Stage, phase, and style: The developmental dynamics of the self. In M. Berkowitz & F. Oser (Eds.), *Moral education: Theory and application* (pp. 232–246). Hillside, NJ: Erlbaum.

Noam, G. G. (1986a). Borderline personality disorders and the theory of biography and transformation (Part 1). *McLean Hospital Journal, 11,* 19–43.

Noam, G. G. (1986b). The theory of biography and transformation and the borderline personality disorders: A developmental typology. *McLean Hospital Journal, 11,* 79–105.

Noam, G. G. (1988a). A constructivist approach to developmental psychology. In E. Nannis & P. Cowan (Eds.), *Developmental psychopathology and its treatment* (pp. 91–122). San Francisco: Jossey-Bass.

Noam, G. G. (1988b). The self, adult development and the theory of biography and transformation. In D. R. Lapsky & P. F. Clark (Eds.), *Self, ego and identity-integrative approaches.* New York: Springer-Verlag.

Noam, G. G. (1988c). Self-complexity and self-integration: Theory and therapy in clinical-developmental psychology. *Journal of Moral Education, 17,* 230–245.

Noam, G. G. (1990). Beyond Freud and Piaget: Biographical worlds-interpersonal self. In T. E. Wren (Ed.), *The moral domain* (pp. 360–399). Cambridge, MA: MIT Press.

Noam, G. G. (1992). Development as the aim of clinical intervention. *Development and Psychopathology, 4,* 679–696.

Noam, G. G. (1996). High-risk youth: Transforming our understanding of human development. *Human Development, 39,* 1–17.

Noam, G. G. (in press). Solving the "ego development–mental health riddle." In M. Westenberg, A. Blasi, & L. Cohen (Eds.), *Ego development.* Mahwah, NJ: Erlbaum.

Noam, G. G., & Borst, S. (1994). Developing meaning, losing meaning. In G. G. Noam & S. Borst (Eds.), *Children, youth, and suicide: Developmental perspectives. New directions for child development* (Vol. 64). San Francisco: Jossey-Bass.

Noam, G. G., Chandler, M., & LaLonde, C. (1995). Clinical-developmental psychology: Constructivism and social cognition in the study of psychological dysfunctions. In D. Cicchetti & D. J. Cohen (Eds.), *Developmental psychopathology: Vol. 1. Theory and methods.* New York: Wiley.

Noam, G. G., & Cicchetti, D. (1996). Reply. *Human Development, 39,* 49–56.

Noam, G. G., & Dill, D. L. (1991). Adult development and symptomatology. *Psychiatry, 54,* 208–216.

Noam, G. G., & Fischer, K. W. (1996). *Development and vulnerabilities in close relationships.* Hillsdale, NJ: Erlbaum.

Noam, G. G., Hauser, S., Santostefano, S., Garrison, W., Jacobson, A., Powers, S., & Mead, M. (1984). Ego development and psychopathology: A study of hospitalized adolescents. *Child Development, 55,* 184–194.

Noam, G. G., Higgins, G., & Goethals, G. (1982). Psychoanalysis as a development psychology. In R. Wolman (Ed.), *Handbook of developmental psychology.* New York: Prentice-Hall.

Noam, G. G., & Houlihan, J. (1990). Developmental dimensions of *DSM-III* diagnoses in adolescent psychiatric patients. *American Journal of Orthopsychiatry, 60*(3), 371–378.

Noam, G. G., Kilburn, D., & Ammen-Elkins, G. (1989). *Adolescent development and psychiatric symptomatology.* Unpublished Report, McLean Hospital, Belmont, MA.

Noam, G. G., Maraganore, A., Stevens, D., & Sheinberg, N. (1997, June). *Trajectories of the development of resiliency: Cognitive and relational processes.* Paper presented at the annual meeting of the Jean Piaget Society, Los Angeles.

Noam, G. G., Paget, K., Valiant, G., Borst, S., & Bartok, J. (1994). Conduct and affective disorders in developmental perspective: A systematic study of adolescent developmental psychopathology. *Development and Psychopathology, 6,* 519–532.

Noam, G. G., Powers, S., Kilkenny, R., & Beedy, J. (1990). The interpersonal self in life-span developmental perspective. In P. B. Balts, D. L. Featherman, & R. M. Lerner (Eds.), *Life-span development and behavior* (Vol. 10). Hillsdale, NJ: Erlbaum.

Noam, G. G., Winner, K., Molad, B., & Rhein, A. (1996). The Harvard RALLY Program and the prevention practitioner. *Journal of Child and Youth Care Work, 11,* 32–47.

Offer, D., & Schonert-Reichl, K. (1992). Debunking the myths of adolescence: Findings from recent research. *Journal of the American Academy of Child Adolescent Psychiatry, 3,* 1006–1014.

Omer, H. (1993). The integrative focus: Coordinating symptom- and person-oriented perspectives in therapy. *American Journal of Psychotherapy, 47,* 283–295.

Perry, W. S. (1970). *Forms of intellectual and ethical development in the college years.* New York: Holt, Rinehart.

Pfeffer, C. R., Newcorn, J., Kaplan, G., Mizruchi, M. S., & Plutchik, R. (1989). Subtypes of suicidal and assaultive behaviors in adolescent psychiatric patients: A research note. *Journal of Child Psychology and Psychiatry and Allied Disciplines, 30,* 151–163.

Phillips, L., & Zigler, E. (1964). Role orientation, the action-thought dimension, and outcome in psychiatric disorder. *Journal of Abnormal and Social Psychology, 68,* 381–389.

Piaget, J. (1926). *The language and thought of the child.* New York: Harcourt.

Piaget, J. (1932). *The moral judgement of the child.* New York: Harcourt.

Powitzky, R. (1976). *Ego levels and types of federal offenses.* Unpublished doctoral dissertation, University of Texas Health Sciences Center, Dallas.

Recklitis, C. J., & Noam, G. G. (1990, August,). *Aggression in adolescent psychopathology: Developmental and personality dimensions.* Paper presented at the Psychological Association meeting, Boston.

Reinecke, M. A. (1993). Outpatient treatment of mild psychopathology. In P. H. Tolan & B. J. Cohler (Eds.), *Handbook of clinical research and practice with adolescents.* New York: Wiley.

Renninger, K. A. (1992). Individual interest and development: Implications for theory and practice. In K. A. Renninger, S. Hidi, & A. Krapp (Eds.), *The role of interest in learning and development.* Hillsdale, NJ: Erlbaum.

Robbins, D. R., & Alessi, N. E. (1985). Depressive symptoms and suicidal behavior in adolescents. *American Journal of Psychiatry, 142,* 588–592.

Rogers, L. (1987). *Developmental psychopathology: Studies in adolescent and adult experiences of psychological dysfunction.* Unpublished doctoral dissertation, Harvard Graduate School of Education, Cambridge, MA.

Rogers, L., & Kegan, R. (1991). Mental health and mental development. In D. P. Keating & H. Rosen (Eds.), *Constructivist perspectives on developmental psychopathology and atypical development.* Hillsdale, NJ: Erlbaum.

Rolf, J., Masten, A., Cicchetti, D., Nuechterlein, K., & Weintraub, S. (Eds.). (1990). *Risk and protective factors in the development of psychopathology.* New York: Cambridge University Press.

Rosen, H. (1985). *Piagetian dimensions of clinical relevance.* New York: Columbia University Press.

Rosen, H., & Kuehlwein, K. T. (Eds.). (1996). *Constructing realities: Meaning-making perspectives for psychotherapists* (pp. 3–51). San Francisco: Jossey-Bass.

Russell, R. L., & van den Broek, P. (1988). A cognitive-developmental account of storytelling in child psychotherapy. In S. R. Shirk (Ed.), *Cognitive development and child psychotherapy* (pp. 19–52). New York: Plenum Press.

Rutter, M. (1989). Age as an ambiguous variable in developmental research: Some epidemiological considerations from developmental psychopathology. *International Journal of Behavioral Development, 12,* 1–34.

Rutter, M. (1990). Psychosocial resilience and protective mechanisms. In J. Rolf, A. Masten, D. Cicchetti, K. Nuechterlein, & S. Weintraub (Eds.), *Risk and protective factors in the development of psychopathology* (pp. 181–214). New York: Cambridge University Press.

Rutter, M., & Garmezy, N. (1983). Developmental psychopathology. In E. M. Hetherington (Ed.), *Mussen's handbook of child psychology: Socialization, personality, and social development* (pp. 775–911). New York: Wiley.

Schafer, R. (1976). *A new language for psychoanalysis.* New Haven, CT: Yale University Press.

Schafer, R. (1983). *The analytic attitude.* New York: Basic Books.

Selman, R. L. (1980). *The growth of interpersonal understanding: Developmental and clinical analyses.* New York: Academic Press.

Selman, R. L., & Schultz, L. H. (1990). *Making a friend in youth: Developmental theory and pair therapy.* Chicago: University of Chicago Press.

Selman, R. L., & Yando, R. (Eds.). (1980). *Clinical-developmental psychology* (Vol. 7). San Francisco: Jossey-Bass.

Shafii, M., Carrigan, S., Whittinghill, J. R., & Derrick, A. (1985). Psychological autopsy of completed suicide in children and adolescents. *American Journal of Psychiatry, 142,* 1061–1064.

Shafii, M., Steltz-Lenarsky, J., Derrick, A. M., Beckner, C., & Whittinghill, J. R. (1988). Comorbidity of mental disorders in the post-mortem diagnosis of completed suicide in children and adolescents. *Journal of Affective Disorders, 15,* 227–233.

Shirk, S. R. (1988). *Cognitive development and child psychotherapy.* New York: Plenum Press.

Sigel, I. E. (1990). Psychoeducational intervention: Future directions. *Merrill-Palmer Quarterly, 36*(1), 159–172.

Smith, M. L., Glass, G. V., & Miller, T. I. (1980). *The benefits of psychotherapy.* Baltimore: Johns Hopkins University Press.

Snow, C. E. (1991). Building memories: The ontogeny of autobiography. In D. Cicchetti & M. Beeghls (Eds.), *The self in transition: Infancy to childhood* (pp. 213–242). Chicago: University of Chicago Press.

Speicher, B., & Noam, G. G. (in press). Clinical-developmental psychology. In J. Day, R. Mosher, & D. Youngman (Eds.), *Human development across the lifespan: Education and psychological application.* New York: Praeger.

Spence, D. (1982). *Narrative truth and historical truth.* New York: Norton.

Sroufe, L. A. (1979). The coherence of individual development: Early care, attachment and subsequent developmental issues. *American Psychologist, 34,* 834–841.

Sroufe, L. A., & Rutter, M. (1984). The domain of developmental psychopathology. *Child Development, 55,* 17–29.

Sullivan, H. S. (1953). *The interpersonal theory of psychiatry.* New York: Norton.

Vaillant, G. E. (1977). *Adaptation to life.* Boston: Little, Brown.

Vaillant, G. E., & McCullough, L. (1987). The Washington University Sentence Completion Test compared with other measures of adult ego development. *American Journal of Psychiatry, 144,* 1189–1194.

Van der Kolk, B. A. (1996). A general approach to treatment of posttraumatic stress disorder. In B. A. Van der Kolk, A. C. McFarlane, & L. Weisaeth (Eds.), *Traumatic stress: The effects of overwhelming experience on mind, body, and society* (pp. 417–440). New York: Guilford Press.

VanderVen, K. (in press). Activity programming: Its developmental and therapeutic role in group care. In F. Ainsworth & L. Fulcher (Eds.), *Group care practice with children.* London: Tavistock.

Weisz, J. R., Weiss, B., Alicke, M. D., & Klotz, M. L. (1987). Effectiveness of psychotherapy with children and adolescents: A meta-analysis for clinicians. *Journal of Consulting and Clinical Psychology, 55,* 542–549.

Weisz, J. R., Weiss, B., Han, S., Granger, D., & Morton, T. (1995). Effects of psychotherapy with children and adolescents revisited: A meta-analysis of treatment outcome studies. *Psychological Bulletin, 117*(3), 450–468.

Werner, E. (1990). Protective factors and individual resilience. In S. Meisels & J. Shonkoff (Eds.), *Handbook of early childhood intervention.* Cambridge, MA: Harvard University Press.

Werner, H. (1957). The concept of development from a comparative and organismic point of view. In D. Harris (Ed.), *The concept of development.* Minneapolis: University of Minnesota Press.

Winnicott, D. W. (1965). *The maturational processes and the facilitating environment.* New York: International Universities Press.

Wittmann, W., & Matt, G. E. (1986). Meta-Analyse ab Integration von Forschungsergebnissen am Beispiel deutschsprachiger Arbeiten zur Effektivitaet von Psychotherapy. *Psychologische Rundschau, 37,* 20–40.

Wohlwill, J. F. (1973). The concept of human development: S or R? *Human Development, 16,* 90–107.

Wolf, E. S. (1988). *Treating the self: Elements of clinical self psychology.* New York: Guilford Press.

CHAPTER 10

Pediatric Psychology and Children's Medical Problems

DAVID J. BEARISON

DISCIPLINARY CONCERNS AND PROFESSIONAL DEVELOPMENT

The Advent of Pediatric Psychology

Because pediatric psychology is a young discipline (25 years, according to Wallander, 1995) and is still emergent, it is appropriate to begin this chapter with some consideration of how it has evolved and how pediatric psychologists have contributed to our understanding of the impact of medical conditions that affect children and their families. An adequate definition of the field is provided on the masthead of the *Journal of Pediatric Psychology* (Roberts, La Greca, & Harper, 1988): "Pediatric psychology is an interdisciplinary field addressing physical, cognitive, social, and emotional functioning and development as they relate to health and illness in children, adolescents, and families." Its areas of inquiry include the "psychosocial and developmental factors contributing to the etiology, course, treatment, and outcome of pediatric conditions; assessment and treatment of behavioral and emotional concomitants of disease, illness, and developmental disorders; the role of psychology in health-care settings; behavioral aspects of pediatric medicine; the promotion of health and health-related behaviors; the prevention of illness and injury among children and youth; and issues related to the training of pediatric psychologists." This way of conceptualizing pediatric psychology tacitly assumes that all human experience has psychosocial as well as biological correlates that are interactive and are potentially modifiable (Porges, Matthews, & Pauls, 1992).

The disciplinary boundaries of pediatric psychology incorporate and build on other divisions of psychology—

This chapter was prepared in connection with research activities supported by the National Institute of Child Health and Human Development (Grant No. HD27229) and while the author was Visiting Professor of Pediatrics, The Mount Sinai Medical Center and School of Medicine, New York, NY.

educational psychology, clinical psychology, social and personality psychology, developmental psychology, rehabilitation psychology, community psychology, environmental psychology, and child psychology—as well as such allied disciplines as pediatric medicine, nursing, child life, social work, child psychiatry, medical ethics, family medicine, public health, occupational therapy, and physical therapy. To a varying extent, all of these disciplines and subdisciplines are concerned with psychosocial issues among pediatric patients and their families. Pediatric psychology, therefore, must cross disciplinary boundaries to situate common grounds of practice and inquiry. This need to accommodate a range of interdisciplinary interests has led to a variety of labels to designate the practice of pediatric psychology: behavioral pediatrics, pediatric behavioral medicine, child health psychology, developmental pediatrics, clinical behavioral pediatrics, clinical developmental psychology, and family health psychology (Gross & Drabman, 1990). Research in pediatric psychology is published in both psychological and medical journals. Most notable among the former are the *Journal of Pediatric Psychology, Health Psychology,* and the *Journal of Applied Developmental Psychology,* and, among the latter, *Pediatrics,* the *Journal of Pediatrics,* the *Journal of Behavioral Medicine,* and the *Journal of Pediatric Hematology/Oncology.*

Clinical and Developmental Approaches

The annals of pediatric psychology reflect complementary but also conflicting interests of clinical and developmental psychologists. Pediatric psychology initially was conceptualized as a subspecialty of clinical psychology (Brantley, Stabler, & Whitt, 1981; Tuma, 1975; Tuma & Grabert, 1983) and reflected either behavioristic or psychodynamic orientations common among clinical psychologists. These involved either the clinical application of behavioral techniques such as reinforcement, modeling, progressive relaxation, systematic desensitization, and biofeedback (Sulzer-Azaroff & Mayer, 1977), or the application of psychoanalytic models of assessment and intervention aimed at enhancing ways of coping with stress (A. Freud, 1952). The clinical psychology approach, in general, and the psychoanalytic approach, in particular, were adapted largely from psychiatry and fostered a psychopathic orientation to children's medical problems, along with a conception of children who have medical problems as being at risk for symptoms of psychopathology. It relied on psychometric procedures derived primarily from measures used to assess psychopathology among physically well children. These measures included various kinds of coping, anxiety, and depression scales that generally were insensitive to detecting the kinds of adjustment problems that occur within the range of normal psychosocial functioning (Mooney, 1984; Perrin, Stein, & Drotar, 1991).

Today, pediatric psychologists increasingly recognize the value of normative-based models derived from a developmental perspective (Maddox, Roberts, Sledden, & Wright, 1986; Rowland, 1990), and, accordingly, pediatric psychology constitutes a significant domain of applied developmental psychology. Unlike a psychopathological approach, a developmental approach to children's medical problems is concerned less with boundaries between health and illness, or normality vs. pathology, than with the extent of adaptation along a variety of change dimensions (Werner, 1948). Developmental psychology does not reflect a particular content area as much as a method of behavioral analysis that seeks explanations in terms of dimensions of change—including, but not limited to, temporal, ontogenetic, historical, and cultural dimensions. It is particularly sensitive to the ways in which cognitive and linguistic development mediates and transforms behavior. Instead of interpreting behavioral responses to illness in terms of psychopathology, a developmental approach considers developmentally adaptive changes in response to stressful and abnormal conditions that are ontogenetically, socially, historically, culturally, and biologically constrained (Bibace & Walsh, 1979; Futterman & Hoffman, 1970; Schulman & Kupst, 1979). This approach has led to new assessment techniques that focus on children's medical problems. These techniques replace methods adapted from cases of pathology and instead use samples chosen from among classes of normal (i.e., emotionally adjusted) children who have particular medical problems (Kupst, 1994; Rolland, 1984). Such assessments and comparisons recognize the inherent limitations caused by particular medical conditions (e.g., limited mobility, compromised sensory modes and neurologic functions), how these limitations might impact on children's social and cognitive competencies, and the potential ways of compensating for them.

Psychological inquiries about children's medical problems, however, involve more than simply accommodating psychosocial models of development to the needs of a special population. They also require an understanding of and appreciation for the biomedical aspects of disease symptomatologies and etiologies, in order to account for how manifestly similar behavioral phenomena can have different meanings when they are embedded in different biomedical contexts, and, conversely, how biological conditions do not uniformly determine people's reactions (Susman et al., 1981). A developmental orientation in pediatric psychology recognizes the reciprocal and transformative relations between psychosocial development and biomedical development and, therefore, requires collaboration with pediatricians and appreciation for certain medical aspects of the conditions that need behavioral intervention (Bray & Rogers, 1995; Dym & Berman, 1986). Such mastery often involves the following kinds of issues: (a) the nature and etiology of the condition in terms of biomedical systems [e.g., congenital, infectious, neoplastic (i.e., new growth), metabolic, traumatic, and iatrogenic], (b) how the condition medically and behaviorally presents itself in the patient (i.e., symptomatology), (c) the conditional range of prognoses (including late effects and quality-of-life variables), and (d) treatment and related management issues.

Differences between clinical and developmental approaches to issues in pediatric psychology also are reflected in the traditional modes of training psychologists for the delivery of services in health care settings. Clinical psychologists, trained to intervene in cases of psychopathology, have found their venue in medical centers' psychiatric departments; they fulfill a liaison role, assisting pediatricians when patients' problems of adjustment and coping exceed the limits of ordinary pediatric practice. Developmental psychologists, who have a different frame of reference, fulfill a different role in pediatric practice. Trained to study the vicissitudes of normative modes of adjustment across developmental domains, they have found their institutional venue in pediatric rather than psychiatric departments, and they are concerned primarily with emotionally adjusted children who have medical problems. Their expertise concerning psychosocial aspects of normal child development is more in keeping with the kinds of issues that pediatricians ordinarily deal with in their daily practice.

According to Richmond (1967), a pediatrician, child development is a "basic science for pediatrics," and pediatrics has a stronger functional alliance with child development than with clinical child psychology or psychiatry. The latter are concerned with psychopathic conditions and with theories derived largely from retrospective accounts of patients in psychotherapeutic treatments. Pediatricians' practice is concerned less with children who are emotionally disturbed than with emotionally adjusted children who have medical problems. Thus, their frame of reference is the developing child, including "the dynamic development of individual differences in behavior patterns, the observation of child rearing practices and their consequences, the emergence of curiosity, learning patterns, coping behavior, and personality, and the capacities of children and families to master adversity. Such observations are available to pediatricians in their daily work" (p. 653). According to Richmond, the teaching of child psychiatry (and, by implication, child clinical psychology) "fell on the relatively deaf ears of pediatric trainees, with the frustration level high on both sides—as it inevitably must when there are inappropriate expectations by each" (p. 653). The compelling nature of this contention led the American Academy of Pediatrics to supplant its Section on Mental Health with a Section on Developmental and Behavioral Pediatrics.

In a very practical sense, the need for pediatric medicine to disengage pediatric psychology from some of the assumptions borrowed from psychopathological models of clinical psychology and psychiatry can be seen in current efforts by the American Academy of Pediatrics to replace the *Diagnostic and Statistical Manual of Mental Disorders,* fourth edition (DSM-IV; American Psychiatric Association, 1994) with new standards of diagnostic and treatment taxonomies in pediatric practice: the *Diagnostic and Statistical Manual for Primary Care: Child and Adolescent Version.* There is increasing recognition among both pediatricians and pediatric psychologists that the existing diagnostic nomenclatures of DSM-IV are inadequate for clinical practice because they essentially are based on a model of psychopathological functions aimed at identifying children needing a limited range of psychiatric interventions (medication and/or psychotherapy). Hence, the DSM-IV does not allow ways of classifying a broad range of behavioral problems that are within the normal range of adaptation to stress but that, because of their association with chronic and acute illnesses and treatment conditions, require behavioral interventions (e.g., secondary depression as a normal reaction to limited functions that are disease-related). According to Mulhern, Fairclough, Smith, and Douglas (1992), these diagnostic contingencies present a dilemma for the pediatrician and pediatric psychologist seeking guidelines to discriminate between physically ill children who have psychiatric symptoms secondary to their medical conditions, and children whose symptoms are primary expressions of emotional disturbance. For example, among many hospitalized patients, and particularly among oncology patients, "chemotherapy and radiation therapy may induce nausea and vomiting resulting in anorexia and weight loss. Steroid therapy often results in weight gain. Apathy and diminished interest in the environment may be secondary to prolonged fever and neutropenia (low blood counts) or to the effects of antiemetic therapies with sedative properties. Disturbances of sleep–wake cycles are associated with sedation as well as routine inpatient nursing procedures at night. Problems with concentration and decision making may be a direct result of chemotherapies with known acute central nervous system toxicities" (p. 315).

The DSM-IV also fails to recognize a range of behavioral issues that are specific to disease management; among them might be noncompliance with treatment procedures and high-risk behaviors related to specific diseases (e.g., unrestricted dietary intake by a diabetic). Also, there is inadequate recognition of (a) the social and environmental issues specific to disease and chronic illness and (b) the different culturally specific modes of expressing illness-related behavioral problems.

Theory and Practice

Ideally, research in pediatric psychology should be a "two-way street" on which, in one lane, theory and findings from established areas of psychology are moving toward better understanding of health and illness, while, in the other lane, findings from research in pediatric psychology are arriving to enrich basic theory in the behavioral and social sciences. Examples of the first lane's content might be the need to evaluate the psychological toxicity of a new treatment regimen so that the efficacy/toxicity ratio can be compared to the clinical standard; or efforts to improve cure rates by enhancing medication compliance. Examples of the second lane could include opportunities to study clinical populations in order to address theoretical concerns about basic behavioral principles, such as how developmental processes relate to children's capacities to comprehend and respond adaptively to stressful experiences.

Clinical populations represent, for the investigator, naturally occurring conditions and treatment events. They can be used to systematically test basic theories and behavioral processes that, for various reasons (including ethical and practical constraints), cannot otherwise be achieved by standardized manipulations of experimental conditions. For example, children might have a voiding cystourethrogram (VCUG) procedure, a stressful invasive procedure that requires an adult to have physical contact with the children's genitalia for the purpose of fluoroscopically examining the urinary system in an effort to correct frequent urinary tract infections. Such a medical procedure replicates, in part, the conditions for understanding factors that influence children's memories (accurate and inaccurate) of such traumatic childhood events as childhood sexual abuse (Goodman, Quas, Batterman-Faunce, Riddlesberger, & Kuhn, 1994; Merritt, Ornstein, & Spicker, 1994). Using the medically induced conditions of this procedure to study normative development is responsive to a pressing need to know how children are able to recall and adapt to abusive sexual encounters with adults (Benedek & Schetky, 1987a, 1987b; Ceci & Bruck, 1995). The VCUG procedure does not mimic the sexual abuse of children but it involves activities that, in some critical ways, are similar to a sexual assault, such as genital contact, painful physical penetration committed against the children's will, and, for most children, personal embarrassment. It thereby affords the investigator a naturally occurring event that cannot be experimentally replicated, together with a means of systematically varying experimental factors (e.g., age differences, opportunities for parental communication about the event, and children's emotional reactions to the event) that could not be systematically studied under naturally occurring conditions of sexual abuse nor experimentally induced in a randomized factorial design. Another way in which a naturally occurring condition in pediatrics might inform basic sciences in psychology concerns the site variability of malignant tumors across different ages, which can index the natural development of highly specific kinds of psychoneurological functions. Our understanding of other basic issues—developmental relationships between affect and cognition, causal attribution, decision making, relations between state and trait anxieties, situation-based modes of coping, and factors affecting the development of self-esteem and self-construal—also benefit from studying the naturally occurring conditions occasioned by children's medical problems. The unsettling presence of medical problems in children allows us to pose questions about basic developmental processes that might not otherwise even come to mind.

Despite the potential of practice informing theory and theory informing practice, early studies in pediatric psychology were primarily concerned with applying existing psychological knowledge to pediatric problems arising, for the most part, from how chronic and life-threatening illness affected children and their families. Such inquiries were pursued by psychologists who, as participants in the pressures of pediatric practice in major medical centers, were responsive to the need to find practical solutions to problems that *pediatricians* found meaningful and clinically relevant (Drotar, 1991). Accordingly, most of the research done by psychologists in pediatric practice has been necessarily dependent on and a reaction to new medical developments and has been motivated less by psychological theory than by the compelling daily needs of pediatric practice (Mulhern & Bearison, 1994).

Recently, some investigators have begun to use psychological theories to define their empirical questions and to sample patients experiencing a range of medically relevant variables, in search of common behavioral patterns that generalize across disease and treatment categories. For example, styles of coping with medical trauma may depend more on child, family, and community resources than on specific kinds of diseases and their prescribed treatments. The two research approaches are capable of coming together, but strong collaborative relationships between physicians and behavioral scientists are required (see Drotar, 1993, 1995, for a discussion of the dimensions of such collaborative activities). An example might be the design of intervention studies in which psychological theories are used to specify the parameters of controlled medical interventions. Thus, although theory typically is thought to lead practice among psychologists in academic settings, those in pediatric practice settings often had to let practice lead psychological theory and, as a consequence, most of their studies have been descriptive and atheoretical. They sought to verify the incidence of psychological phenomena associated with illness and to identify factors that place children and/or their families at risk for adverse psychological outcomes. Reliance on theory-driven hypotheses to explain relationships between illness and behavior, or the use of theories to justify clinical interventions that might alter such relationships, was to come later. There remains today a notable lack of theory-driven research in pediatric psychology (Harper, 1991). About 60% of all studies published in the *Journal of Pediatric Psychology* are atheoretical and are clearly of an applied rather than a basic kind (Roberts, 1992).

Despite intermittent clarion calls for more theory-driven research in pediatric psychology (e.g., Harper, 1991), it must be acknowledged that the relative lack of such research doesn't necessarily reflect the limits of experimental paradigms in pediatric psychology as much as the limits of psychological theories to reflect the situated, local, and unusual conditions faced by children (and their families) who have chronic medical problems (Bibace & Walsh, 1982). Practice in pediatric psychology challenges some of our theoretical assumptions about children's development and adjustment and generates productive tensions that can advance our theoretical efforts and inform our basic research.

Areas of Research in Pediatric Psychology

Prevention Research

Research in pediatric psychology can be categorized as being of three kinds: (a) prevention research, (b) intervention research, and (c) research on relationships between psychological factors and medical conditions. Despite the avowed focus on prevention as an area of primary interest in pediatric psychology and the need for interventions to promote health and prevent accidents among children, very little prevention research has been done (Kaufman, Holden, & Walker, 1989; Roberts, 1994; Walker, 1988). According to Roberts (1992), less than 4% of the published studies in pediatric psychology are directed toward prevention. Research in this area has focused primarily on educational and behavioral programs to teach children prevention of injury and accidents (particularly in motor vehicle collisions but also from drowning, falls, fires, poisoning, and unintentional shootings from playing with firearms), to improve nutrition and dietary decisions, to increase exercise activities, and to avoid substance abuse (e.g., drugs, alcohol, and cigarettes). Other areas of prevention research have focused on avoidance of child abuse (Wolf, 1993), AIDS/HIV infection (Brooks-Gunn, Boyer, & Hein, 1988; Whitt, 1995), and adolescent pregnancies (Brooks-Gunn, 1992), as well as the co-occurrence of a range of pernicious health-related behaviors such as early sexual intercourse (before 14 or 15 years of age), smoking, drinking, and the use of illegal substances (Ensminger, 1987; Furstenberg, Brooks-Gunn, & Morgan, 1987; Irwin & Millstein, 1991).

Despite the small proportion of studies that address prevention in pediatric psychology, there is compelling evidence for greater effort in this area. For example, each year in the United States, approximately 1 million children sustain burn injuries (Dimick, 1979) and there are 2.4 million cases of reported child abuse (1,200 to 5,000 children die as a result of abuse; see Willis, Holden, & Rosenberg, 1992, for a comprehensive overview of the extent of this problem). Accidents and unintentional injuries comprise the leading cause of death among children ages 1 to 14 years (Califano, 1979; Jones, McDonald, & Shinske, 1990; see Finney et al., 1993, for further consideration of the role of pediatric psychology and injury control). Adolescent violence (Eron, Gentry, & Schlegal, 1994), suicide (Berman & Jobes, 1991), and drug trafficking (Stanton, 1994) have become national problems that impact all aspects of our society. Aside from concerns about the welfare of children, there are clear and compelling relationships between causes of death across the life span and habitual styles of behaving that are established early in childhood (e.g., amount of exercise, smoking, diet, and ways of coping with stress), all of which offer further reasons for promoting child prevention research.

Intervention Research

Psychological interventions to improve medical conditions would seem to be the central concern of pediatric practice and, consequently, the primary research activity of psychologists working in pediatric settings (Glasgow & Anderson, 1995). The bottom line in consultative relationships between psychologists and pediatricians is for psychologists to prescribe some kind of effective intervention to ameliorate psychosocial problems occasioned by medical conditions and treatment protocols. For example, pediatricians are less interested in learning what proportion of their patients are likely to be noncompliant with treatment, or even which categories of patients are more likely than others to be noncompliant, than they are in learning practical and effective behavioral interventions to ensure that their patients follow the treatment regimens they prescribe. However, intervention research constitutes only 9% of published studies (Roberts, 1992), and its proportion had not risen in a recent five-year period (Rae, 1995). Most intervention studies focus on stress management, coping skills, and treatment adherence. Because intervention studies are labor-intensive and require extended periods of time within a longitudinal design to obtain sufficient data, they are not common. Yet they provide the most direct means of reducing the stress and adversities of chronic illness in children. They also provide a means of experimentally testing causal explanations among psychological and pediatric variables.

Correlational Research

Intervention studies rely on identifying psychological correlates of children's medical problems in order to improve our ability to predict what concurrent and delayed developmental consequences may occur. If we are able to ascertain in advance the likelihood of certain kinds of psychological problems among certain kinds of children with certain kinds of illnesses at certain times in the course of their treatment and survivorship, then pediatric psychologists will be able to intervene at optimal times to prevent serious psychological consequences and thus ensure that children achieve their developmental potential within the restraints imposed by illness conditions.

Accordingly, most of the research in pediatric psychology consists of studies of relationships among a variety of psychologic and pediatric variables (75%, according to Roberts, 1992). Studies of this kind encompass a broad range of pediatric diseases and medical conditions; the principal disease is cancer, followed by cystic fibrosis, diabetes, pediatric AIDS, asthma, and preterm and low-birth-weight infants. The principal psychological variables include: (a) children's adjustments to (and coping with) chronic illness, (b) siblings' and families' adjustment to chronic illness, (c) treatment compliance, (d) neuropsychological effects of treatments, (e) psychological consequences (including late effects) of treatments, (f) quality of life, (g) children's concepts, knowledge, beliefs, and understanding of diseases and medical treatments, and (h) pain and procedural stress management in children.

Table 10.1 is a comprehensive list of medical conditions and related procedures that have been studied in pediatric psychology. It was derived from literature searches in pediatric psychology from Medline and Psychlit databases covering the past ten years. These medical conditions and procedures affect approximately 9% to 14% of children and youth in the United States (Cadman, Boyle, Szatmari, & Offord, 1987; Gortmaker, Walker, Weitzman, & Sobol, 1990; Hobbs & Perrin, 1985; Willis, Culbertson, & Mertens, 1984). Of these, 1% to 2% have severe chronic medical conditions (Gortmaker & Sappenfield, 1984).

Focus and Organization of the Chapter

The present chapter inevitably reflects the limits of current knowledge, given the early stages of much of the research in pediatric psychology. While the chapter is addressed, in part, to the needs of practitioners, it is not a practical guide to the psychosocial care of children with medical problems. It is an attempt to provide a fair and adequate, yet selective topical review of the literature in pediatric psychology and to critically review it relative to unresolved issues. In place of an encyclopedic compendium, the present chapter reflects the perspectives of the author on several broadly conceived domains of research within the field of pediatric psychology: compliance; adjustment and coping; procedural stress and pain management; late effects of illness and treatment; death and dying; and knowledge, understanding, and communication about illness. The chapter provides some new insights into complex areas of pediatric care and encourages new approaches to many unresolved issues that continue to vex practical concerns and that reflect some basic difficulties in doing research about psychological issues in pediatrics.

Pediatric Oncology as a Paradigmatic Case

It is beyond the scope of a single chapter to consider the range of research that has come to constitute the field of pediatric psychology or even that part of the field dealing with children's medical problems. Even in such a new and emergent field as pediatric psychology, the information explosion has rendered such an approach obsolete (see Gross & Drabman, 1990; Lavigne & Burns, 1981; Roberts & McNeal, 1995; Russo & Varni, 1982; Tuma, 1982; Wright, Schaefer, & Solomons, 1979, for general reviews). Therefore, in the present chapter, the kinds of research that pediatric psychologists do; the problems they address; the theories that guide their research; their methods and findings; and the implications for the practice of pediatrics—all are discussed in a broad yet paradigmatic context that often is concerned with psychosocial issues among children who have cancer, and their families. Despite the personal tragedy that a diagnosis of cancer brings, pediatric cancer allows the study of a comprehensive range of psychosocial factors in chronic illness

TABLE 10.1 Primary Medical Conditions and Procedures Studied in Pediatric Psychology

Diseases	
Cystic fibrosis	Renal disorders
Cancer (including bone marrow transplantation)	High blood pressure
Diabetes	Seizure disorders
Pediatric AIDS and HIV infection	Phenylketonuria (and neurological function)
Asthma	Neurofibromatosis
Cerebral palsy	Scoliosis
Epilepsy	Osteogenesis imperfecta
Head injuries/brain injuries	Inflammatory bowel disease (ulcerative colitis & Crohn's disease)
Sickle cell disease	Deafness
Hypothyroidism	Blindness
Hemophilia	Cardiac disorders
Significantly short stature	Dwarfism
Headaches and migraines	Myelomeningocele
Craniofacial deformities	Hypospadias
Rheumatic diseases (including arthritis)	Precocious puberty
Spina bifida	Cleft lip and palate
Hydrocephalus	Recurrent abdominal pain*
Turner's syndrome & Klinefelter's syndrome	Failure to thrive*
Tourette's syndrome	
Procedures	
Intensive care other than neonatal	Pain perception and management
Plastic surgery	Liver or other solid organ transplantation
Terminal care and bereavement	Bone marrow transplantation
Newborn circumcision	Neonatal intensive care
Amputation	
Developmental and Behavioral Issues	
Prenatal exposure to toxic substances (e.g., effects of fetal alcohol syndrome, cocaine, marijuana, cigarettes, etc.)	Child abuse (effects)
Preterm and low-birth-weight infants (effects)	Autism
Obesity/eating disorders (anorexia nervosa; bulimia)	Mental retardation
Attention deficit disorder	Adolescent pregnancies
Childhood stuttering	Enuresis
Psychosomatic disorders in childhood (e.g., nonorganic hearing loss, elective mutism, habit cough, and psychosocial dwarfism)	Encopresis
Lead exposure in children	Constipation
Surgeries (effects)	Sleep disorders
Children conceived by IVF (effects)	Learning disabilities
Emotional disorders/psychopathologies	Language delays
	Substance abuse
Trauma	
Burn injuries	Injuries and accidents

* Disease or developmental and behavioral.

because it encompasses more medical and psychological components than any other pediatric disease (Mulhern & Bearison, 1994). For example, because it potentially affects nearly every major organ system—cardiac, pulmonary, endocrine, visual, and orthopedic—psychologists can study the psychological effects of amputation, sensory deficits, brain damage, and developmental delays; because it involves periods of acute illness that occur in the context of prolonged chronic disease, psychologists can study mechanisms of coping and adaptation, school absence, quality of life, and family and community relationships over time; because its treatment is invasive, involving painful medical procedures and self-regulated routines (including self-medication), psychologists can study pain management and treatment compliance; because its causes are unknown and treatments often rely on experimental protocols, psychologists can study patient control issues, causal attributions of health and illness, informed consent and barriers to consent, and physician–patient relationships; because it can be curable, psychologists can study adjustment among long-term survivors; and because it is potentially fatal, psychologists can study terminal and hospice care and family adjustment to grief and mourning. These characteristics make pediatric cancer a useful model for studying the psychosocial effects of children's medical problems and the ways that psychological findings contribute to the practice of pediatric medicine. (See Bearison & Mulhern, 1994, for a comprehensive review of psychological research in pediatric oncology.)

Growth of the Profession

It is worthwhile to explore how pediatric psychology has evolved in collaboration with pediatric oncology over the past decade because it serves, in many ways, as a paradigmatic model that portends the growth of pediatric psychology within other branches of medicine besides psychiatry. There is today a highly disproportionate number of psychological studies in pediatric oncology, given the number of children affected by cancer compared with the number suffering from other diseases (Roberts, 1992). Yet, prior to the advent of modern cancer treatment, children's deaths from cancer were rapid and painful and, consequently, there were few opportunities for psychologists to work in this area. Also, opportunities were limited because of a professional attitude of concealment (even the word "cancer" was not used in discussing the diagnosis with children) rather than the present "open approach" about the effects of cancer (Bearison, 1991a; Koocher, 1994). The role of psychologists then was limited to assisting physicians in the palliative care of children, and behavioral research was limited to a few studies of families' coping, anticipatory grieving, and mourning. The changes in prognoses occasioned by improvements in medical treatment changed professional attitudes (at least in this country) about sharing information with patients and their families, and promulgated awareness of the psychosocial aspects of having cancer. For example, in 1961, 90% of American physicians responded in a survey that they preferred not telling cancer patients their diagnosis; 16 years later, 97% preferred openly discussing the diagnosis (Novack et al., 1979).

As the treatment of pediatric cancers advanced, the course of treatment became biologically more aggressive, more stressful, and, in individual cases, more uncertain. For children who cannot be cured, advances prolong their survival with active disease and complicate their dying process. For children who are cured, there are long-term uncertainties about having undergone medical regimens whose adverse late effects are yet to be fully understood. Also, the families and friends of children who have cancer are profoundly affected by the experience. Consequently, rapid and dramatic medical advances occasioned a dual need for pediatric psychologists to enter the field: (a) to improve the quality of life for children who have cancer, and their families, and (b) to collaborate with pediatric oncologists toward further advancing medical regimens that reflect biological as well as behavioral aspects. Psychologists began to enter pediatric oncology at an astonishing rate, first as practitioners and then, increasingly, as applied and then basic researchers. Once psychologists were in place in pediatric divisions, new opportunities quickly arose for them to collaborate with pediatric oncologists in the design and implementation of studies concerned with experimental treatment protocols, quality of life, cancer control, and long-term effects, and also to study other related diseases, such as sickle cell disease and AIDS.

Working with pediatricians to formulate methods of assessing neuropsychological functioning among pediatric cancer patients receiving chemotherapy and radiation treatment constituted the initial core commitment of psychologists in pediatric oncology divisions. Early findings had begun to show significant deficits in cognitive functioning among children receiving central nervous system (CNS) radiation, a treatment condition for children with brain tumors and leukemia, the most common kinds of pediatric cancer. Psychologists initially responded to a compelling need to design measures and formulate procedures commensurate with treatment protocols in order to monitor both immediate and delayed effects of chemotherapy and radiation on children's cognitive functioning. As more protocols began to incorporate psychological measures, the need for pediatric oncology divisions in medical centers to employ pediatric psychologists grew. Today, nearly 60% of pediatric oncology divisions employ psychologists.

Increasing opportunities to bring pediatric psychologists into hospital settings in the context of pediatric practice dramatically expanded the role of psychological studies in pediatric oncology and led to the increasing involvement of pediatricians in psychological research. From the initial studies of neuropsychological effects of treatment, psychologists have sought means to improve the quality of life for children who have cancer and to work with pediatricians to advance medical regimens that reflect the behavioral as well as the biological aspects of pediatric oncology. They have sought to promote healthier ways by which society can deal with children who have cancer, and their families. They have developed and provided interventions that help children and their families cope with the fears, uncertainties, anger, frustration, and realities of having cancer—the pain of treatment, the medical side effects, and the need for treatment compliance. They have advocated and suggested means of more open communication and informed consent from children about treatments and their effects. They have considered the consequences of long-term survival, and they have helped families mourn the loss of children who have failed to survive.

This paradigmatic model of the advent of the scientist/practitioner in pediatric psychology rests on establishing a place for psychologists in the clinical milieu of hospital practice to work alongside of and in collaboration with physicians and other members of medical treatment teams. With such collaborations come opportunities for pediatric psychologists to balance patient service with continuing scientific research and, thereby, to gain credibility among physicians in the conduct of meaningful and clinically relevant research. An added benefit is that clinical populations become more accessible to psychologists working outside medical settings. This has been the course (although to a lesser extent) of the growth of pediatric psychology in other subspecialties and of health psychology in other branches of medicine. It clearly has been facilitated in the past decade by an expanding "medical marketplace" that today unfortunately is threatened by more fiscally competitive medical environments (Drotar, 1991).

COMPLIANCE

Successful and cost-effective medical treatment of children depends not only on adequate prescribed treatment, but also on patients' compliance with treatment. Therefore, pediatricians and pediatric psychologists need to consider issues of compliance along with ways of promoting it as a responsibility shared between the patients and their parents to ensure that therapeutic outcomes will be based on the biological responsiveness of the disease (Festa, Tamaroff, Chasalow, & Lanzkowsky, 1992; Johnson, 1993). However, studies of psychosocial issues in medication compliance and treatment adherence have not been able to clearly and causally account for the disturbingly high incidence of noncompliance nor to predict which patients are at risk for noncompliance (Bearison, 1994).

Studies typically have found an overall rate of compliance of about 50% for self-administration (i.e., administration by parent, in the case of young children) of pediatric medication (Litt & Cuskey, 1980). This rate has not varied for at least the past 20 years (Dunbar, 1983; Dunbar, Dunning, & Dwyer, 1993) and is comparable to the rate found among adults (Haynes, Taylor, & Sackett, 1979). Because studies of compliance include only those patients who consent to participate and because there are multiple problems in adequately assessing compliance, these rates for compliance may be grossly overestimated (Epstein & Cluss, 1982; La Greca, 1988a). Although it might be expected that patients with more severe or life-threatening illnesses would be at lower risk for noncompliance, there is no consistent evidence to support this conclusion. Contrary to common wisdom, studies have found that disease severity, or severity of symptoms, generally has not correlated with compliance rates (Haynes, 1979). High rates of medication noncompliance are common even in life-threatening conditions (Korsch, Fine, & Negrete, 1978; Smith, Rosen, Trueworthy, & Lowman, 1979). Furthermore, the various adverse side effects of medication do not typically appear to have an important effect on medication compliance, although they affect the likelihood of patients' keeping their clinic appointments (Richardson, Marks, & Levine, 1988; Richardson, Shelton, Krailo, & Levine, 1990) and other prescribed behavioral procedures (La Greca, 1988a). Compliance has been found to be associated with children's immediate sense of the negative consequences of noncompliance but not with awareness of its long-term consequences (La Greca & Hanna, 1983). The chronicity of a disease consistently has been found to be associated with poorer rates of compliance; compliance decreases with the length of treatment (Litt & Cuskey, 1980; Shope, 1981). Such variables as the age and gender of the pediatric patient, the frequency or severity of symptoms, and the educational level and socioeconomic status of the parents have not generally distinguished compliers from noncompliers (Haynes et al., 1979; Litt & Cuskey, 1980; Tamaroff, Festa, Adesman, & Walco, 1992; Tebbi et al., 1986). Even patients' declared intent to comply with therapeutic regimens generally has not been predictive of their compliance (Giardi, DePisa, & Cianfriglia, 1992). The failure to find relationships between compliance rates and the severity of different disease states, medication side effects, common patient demographics, or avowed intentions, contradicts the common knowledge that we often use to make predictions about people's behavior (Mellins, Evans, Zimmerman, & Clark, 1992). These findings not only substantiate the complexity of compliance as a behavioral phenomenon in pediatrics, they also pose a formidable challenge to clinicians seeking ways to intervene in children's (and parents') behavior to enhance their compliance systematically and reliably.

Measures and Incidence of Noncompliance

Measures

Investigators have used several different kinds of behaviors to measure noncompliance: refusal, to varying extent, of a procedure or treatment; failure to keep appointments; delays (usually defined as a lapse of more than three months) or "lagtime" between the appearance of symptoms and seeking medical consultation; and failure to reliably self-administer prescribed amounts of oral medication at the specified times. These different kinds of compliance measures have been correlated in some studies (Dolgin, Katz, Doctores, & Siegel, 1986) but not in others (Inui, Carter, Pecorato, Pearlman, & Dohan, 1980; Taylor, Lichtman, & Wood, 1984). Many studies relied on informant ratings or self-reports to measure compliance. However, ratings of compliance completed by different informants (e.g., parents, physicians, nurses, and patients) were not highly correlated (La Greca, 1990a). Patient and parent reports tended to overestimate levels of compliance (Epstein & Cluss, 1982; La Greca, 1988a). Also, there was poor correlation between attending physicians and pediatric nurse practitioners on ratings of compliance among pediatric oncology patients (Manne, Jacobsen, Gorfinkle, Gerstein, & Redd, 1993), and physicians have not been able to predict better than chance which of their patients will not comply (Charney et al., 1967). In some cases, the lack of concordance between parent and child informants was indicative of conflicts about children's responsibility for managing their care (e.g., Allen, Tennen, McGrade, Affleck, & Ratzan, 1983; Johnson, Silverstein, Rosenbloom, Carter, & Cunningham, 1986, for children with diabetes).

Compliance typically is reported in terms of the proportion of patients who either are or are not compliant. However, there is not a common marker or threshold among investigators to indicate noncompliance. For example, is a patient who takes 90% of the prescribed medication compliant, or 80%, or any amount sufficient to achieve the therapeutic goal? In studies in which medication compliance is measured according to drug assays, there is not adequate means to compensate for individual variations in drug absorption rates. The lack of standardized operational definitions to measure compliance limits the ability to make generalizations across studies, even when similar measures are being used.

Medication Compliance

Typically, a variety of behavioral procedures, aside from self-medication, are prescribed for children who have chronic illness. These might include mouth care to prevent oral sores, hygienic care of a child's catheter, hydration during chemotherapy, and monitoring of treatment reactions and such side effects as fever and pain for children who have cancer; glucose testing, dietary restrictions, daily urine or blood tests, adjusted insulin injection, and exercise for children who have diabetes; dietary supplements, chest percussion several times a day, and pulmonary treatments for children who have cystic fibrosis. Although several studies examined compliance in terms of some of these kinds of prescribed procedures, most focused on adherence to medication regimens because it is the most reliable and efficacious marker of noncompliance and it reflects its most direct and pernicious effects. Indirect methods used to measure compliance with self-administration of oral medications in pediatrics included patients' and/or parents' self-reports, physicians' estimates, pill counts, prescription renewals, the occurrence of predictable side effects, and indexes of therapeutic outcomes. These kinds of indirect methods, however, tended to overestimate rates of compliance (Evans & Spelman, 1983; Mazur, 1981; Ruth, Caron, & Bartholomew, 1970; Wilson & Endres, 1986). For example, children younger than 10 years of age were not reliable reporters of their own compliance (Johnson, 1993); physician estimates have been found to be one of the least accurate methods (Brody, 1980; Roth & Casen, 1978); a wish to appear compliant often motivated patients to dump their medications (Mellins et al., 1992); and our knowledge of what levels of medication absorption were necessary for particular therapeutic outcomes or contributed to particular side effects is generally limited and highly variable across individuals. A more valid and *direct* method of measuring medication compliance is to use biological assays that assess levels of drugs in urine, serum, or saliva.

Incidence

Pediatric oncology can serve as a paradigmatic case for most issues in compliance research. Although it was assumed at one time that the severity of cancer and its life-threatening condition would ensure compliance among pediatric oncology patients, there is today sufficient evidence that medication compliance cannot be assumed for any patient at any time during treatment. Adolescents who have cancer are significantly more likely than younger patients to be noncompliant. In the most frequently referenced study of medication noncompliance among pediatric cancer patients, Smith et al., (1979) found that 59% of adolescents with leukemia were noncompliant based on random urine levels of oral prednisone. The rate of noncompliance among children younger than 13 years was

33%. These findings have been replicated by Lansky, Smith, Cairns, and Cairns (1983), Dolgin et al. (1986), Tebbi et al. (1986), and Festa et al. (1992).

Although it often is assumed that compliance is better among children than adolescents because of parental administration of oral medication for children, children have been found to have considerable autonomy in self-administering medication. For example, 20% of third-grade children and 45% of seventh-grade children reported taking medication without adult participation, and parents reported that they believed most children were able to take medication on their own by 12 years of age (Iannotti & Bush, 1993). For many adolescents with chronic illnesses, compliance issues are exacerbated because of problems that often arise in the parent–child relationship around issues regarding the transfer of responsibilities for self-care at a time when they normally are assuming greater autonomy and independence, as well as ambiguous and evasive patterns of communicating illness-related issues between parents and adolescents (Anderson & Coyne, 1993; Mulhern, Crisco, & Camitta, 1981; Spinetta & Maloney, 1978). Noncompliance among adolescents also may reflect their denial of illness and its consequences (Tamaroff et al., 1992; Zeltzer, 1980). Despite the differences in compliance rates between children and adolescents, noncompliance even among young children is high enough to consider it a significant risk factor in the clinical management of all patients.

Among pediatric cancer patients, medication noncompliance (with oral prednisone) has been found to occur during initial induction of therapy and in late remission (Klopovich & Trueworthy, 1985). Compliance generally has been found to decline during therapy (Dolgin et al., 1986; Haynes, 1979; Tebbi et al., 1986). For example, using validated self-reports, Tebbi et al. (1986) found a decline from 81% compliance at 2 weeks from diagnosis to 61% compliance at 20 weeks. A study of adult oncology patients found that self-administration of one medication (e.g., prednisone) correlated significantly with self-administration of another medication (e.g., allopurinol), suggesting that medications routinely are either taken or not taken as a group (Richardson et al., 1990). The complexity of a medication regimen also was associated with compliance. While both the frequency of the dose and the number of different drugs prescribed were positively correlated with noncompliance, multiple drugs had a greater negative effect on compliance than multiple dosages. Compliance was found to be significantly impaired when the number of prescriptions reached three or more daily, or the dosage frequency was four or more times daily (Blackwell, 1973). Consistency in complying with different medications did not necessarily hold for multiple nonmedication components of treatment adherence. For example, among children with diabetes, adherence to behaviors other than medication compliance (e.g., blood glucose testing, dietary restrictions, injection, and exercise) was not highly correlated, suggesting that there are different determinants of compliance to different aspects of a regimen (Glasgow, 1991; Glasgow, McCaul, & Schafer, 1987; Hanson, DeGuire, Schinkel, & Henggeler, 1992; Johnson, 1992, 1993; La Greca, 1988b).

Experimental and Therapeutic Outcomes

High rates of medication noncompliance can potentially confound medical studies of experimental treatment protocols (Feinstein, 1979; Goldsmith, 1979). They could explain, in part, why children with the same kinds of diagnoses and the same drug regimens show such wide variations in responses (e.g., induction rates and remission lengths for experimental cancer protocols; Smith et al., 1979). Differential compliance rates between children and adolescents with leukemia might contribute, in part, to poorer outcomes for adolescents compared with younger children (Lansky, List, & Ritter-Sterr, 1989; Sather, 1986). Also, difficulties in replicating treatment effects across institutions using the same protocols might be attributed to differential patterns of patient compliance (Smith et al., 1979). Differential rates of compliance occurring in different arms of an experimental treatment protocol also could bias findings (Bonadonna & Valaquessa, 1981) and could limit our understanding of what level of compliance is necessary for achieving therapeutic outcomes. Consequently, studies of experimental protocols that involve self-medication need to consider the effects of compliance on the efficacy of the treatment being tested.

Although compliance would be expected to have a causal influence on therapeutic response rates, a few studies, including a study of prophylactic antibiotic therapy to prevent infection from chemotherapy-induced granulocytopenia in patients with cancer (Pizzo et al., 1983), found that treatment outcome was independent of whether patients were administered the actual drugs or placebos. Patients with less than total compliance showed no significant decrease in infection incidence, and patients with excellent compliance had a significant decrease regardless of whether they had been randomly selected to receive drugs or placebos. Such a finding implies that patient compliance can function as a surrogate marker for other factors that might relate to treatment outcomes.

Causal Relationship

The logical test for the effect of compliance on treatment efficacy calls for a 2-by-2 factorial design in which patients are randomly assigned to drug or placebo conditions and retrospectively assigned to compliant or noncompliant groups. Statistical analyses of the results from such a study would provide a test of the efficacy of the experimental drug as a main effect on treatment outcome, compliance as a main effect on treatment outcome, and the interaction between the drug and compliance on outcome (Epstein, 1984). However, with serious medical conditions, it is inappropriate to use placebo-controlled trials. Instead, new drugs typically are compared with conventional standards of known efficacy. However, the Pizzo et al. (1983) finding suggests that medication compliance reflects a broader range of behaviors and attitudes (e.g., hygiene, diet, etc.) that can potentially influence outcomes in ways that are not yet understood.

Although compliance with prescribed medication regimens is not typically measured in clinical trials, there is evidence of a causal link between compliance and prognosis in cancer studies. Richardson et al. (1990) found a causal relationship between self-administered medication compliance with allopurinol and survival rates among adult cancer patients. Allopurinol is a supportive drug in cancer treatment and, although it would not be expected to directly influence survival rates, it served as a marker for the self-administration of other medications that would have direct effects. Trueworthy (1982) found a causal relationship between noncompliance with self-administered prednisone in children with cancer and the occurrence of relapses. Among 17 children with acute lymphoblastic leukemia, 12 had urine assays consistent with taking prednisone and had no relapses. Among the 5 patients who did not have urine values consistent with taking prednisone, 4 relapsed. The relationship between compliance and relapses was independent of the initial prognostic conditions of the patients (Klopovich & Trueworthy, 1985). Another study of prednisone adherence among adolescents (Festa et al., 1992) found that 5 of 11 noncompliers had relapses, compared with 1 of 10 compliers. Although further studies using larger samples of patients are warranted, these findings underscore the critical consequences of medication noncompliance and establish noncompliance as a significant risk factor.

Psychosocial Factors Associated with Noncompliance

Despite the high incidence of medication noncompliance in pediatrics, studies to date have not been able to explain why patients are noncompliant nor have they been able to reliably predict which patients are at risk for noncompliance. There does not appear to be a reliable pattern of demographic variables that predicts compliance. For example, noncompliance has *not* been found to be associated with a patient's age, gender, ethnicity, or socioeconomic status (SES) among adult cancer patients (Richardson et al., 1988) and among adolescent cancer patients (Tamaroff et al., 1992; Tebbi et al., 1986). Although some studies have found families' lower SES predicted failure to keep appointments (Manne, Jacobsen, et al., 1993), this variable was not associated with indicators of medication compliance (Tebbi et al., 1986). Such treatment variables as the presence of medical complications and the number of infections among children and adolescents with leukemia have not been related to compliance levels (Tebbi et al., 1986). Although parental marital status was not correlated with compliance among adolescent cancer patients, one study found that patients who had fewer siblings were more compliant (Tebbi et al., 1986). The effects of drug toxicity, such as hair loss, nausea, loss of appetite, fever, weakness, pain, and bleeding also have not been correlated with compliance levels in pediatric oncology (Richardson et al., 1988; Richardson et al., 1990; Tebbi et al., 1986).

Knowledge and Compliance

Patients' knowledge of their illness, medication instructions, and medication effects would seem to be an obvious prerequisite for compliance; consequently, this has been a common variable in compliance studies. However, findings regarding a relationship between compliance and patients' knowledge of their disease, in general, and their medication, in particular, have been equivocal in both correlation and intervention studies among adolescents and adults with a variety of chronic diseases. For example, studies of pediatric patients with renal transplants (Beck et al., 1980), juvenile diabetes (Etzwiler & Robb, 1972), asthma (Tettersell, 1992), and hematologic malignancies (Richardson et al., 1987), and of adults with diabetes (Graber, Christman, Alonga, & Davidson, 1977) found that intervention programs that increased patients' medication knowledge did not increase their medication compliance. Richardson et al. (1987) concluded that "knowledge did not affect any aspect of compliance" (p. 184); Graber et al. (1977) concluded that "correlations of test scores (knowledge) with the patients' compliance . . . has shown no consistent trends" (p. 62); and Beck et al. (1980) stated, "There was no association between compliance and the patient's initial, final, or improvement in medication knowledge" (p. 1096).

Among adolescent cancer patients, Tamaroff et al. (1992) found no differences between compliers' and noncompliers' knowledge of their illness and their understanding of treatment. Tebbi et al. (1986) found that adolescent cancer patients' knowledge of their illness and belief in the effectiveness of their medication were not correlated with compliance nor were compliant adolescents any more likely than noncompliant ones to actively seek information about their condition and treatment from their physician or anyone else. They did find, however, that compliers reported being better informed than noncompliers about instructions concerning how to self-administer their medications. However, an association between reported knowledge of medication instructions and compliance is just as likely to be a consequence of compliance as a cause for compliance.

In general, attempts to enhance adolescents' understanding of disease processes have not yielded greater adherence to treatment regimens (Cromer & Tarnowski, 1989). In the few cases in which interventions that were aimed specifically at improving patients' medication knowledge have been shown to enhance compliance, the effects were not long lasting (Litt & Cuskey, 1980). Haynes (1976) conducted a "methodologic analysis" of 185 compliance studies and found that "the problem of noncompliance is rarely one of lack of knowledge" (p. 81). Shope (1981), in an extensive review of studies of pediatric medication compliance, concluded that "knowledge about the disease being treated has rarely had any relationship to compliance behavior" (p. 19). Despite repeated failures to find a causal or even a correlational association between medication compliance and patients' knowledge of their illness, treatment, and medical instructions, most intervention programs designed to enhance medication compliance continue to focus on educational efforts. Although the failure to find associations between compliance and patient education should not belie the importance of carefully explaining treatment regimens to children, even very young children, in an age-appropriate manner, it should be obvious from present findings that something more is going on.

Coping and Compliance

Children's emotional demeanor, personality traits, modes of coping with stress, and sense of control of the clinical outcome of their illness, together with family styles of coping and support, all influence how children understand and make sense of their medical condition. These kinds of psychosocial variables would be expected to have an impact on adherence to medical procedures. Instead of considering compliance as a function of whether children and their parents know what to do and understand the need to do it, it might be more worthwhile to consider compliance as part of the broader issues of how patients and families cope with and adjust to chronic illnesses. Thus, issues of compliance in pediatrics can be reconceptualized from being a focal problem in patient management to being an integral aspect of the psychological changes that patients and their families undergo when faced with chronic illnesses.

In support of such an approach, variables dealing with aspects of psychosocial adjustment have been found to be consistently associated with levels of compliance in studies of chronically ill adults and adolescents. Studies have found that noncompliant patients had significantly greater adjustment problems than compliant patients, although it was not clear whether these were preexisting or reactive. For example, scores on anxiety (Kleigher & Dirks, 1979), depression, and locus of control measures (Blackwell, 1973; Duke & Cohen, 1975; Kirscht, 1972) were associated with compliance among adults with chronic illness. Richardson et al. (1987) found that, among adult cancer patients, perceived satisfaction with their overall medical care, but not their knowledge, was correlated with compliance for appointment keeping. They further found that patients' levels of depression about their medical problems were inversely related to their perceived satisfaction and thus served to mediate overall compliance rates. Increasing levels of depression correlated with poorer compliance rates for prednisone self-administration. Among adolescent patients, Korsch et al. (1978) found that noncompliance with immunosuppressive therapy following renal transplants was associated with poor self-esteem and socialization as well as psychological problems prior to the onset of illness. In a study of adolescents with juvenile rheumatoid arthritis, noncompliers had significantly poorer self-esteem and felt that they had less autonomy than did compliers (Litt, Cuskey, & Rosenberg, 1982). Self-esteem, along with parents' reports of children's social functioning, also was found to correlate with compliance among children and adolescents with diabetes (Jacobson et al., 1987).

In one of the few studies that systematically considered personality traits of both parents and their children, it was found that compliance with oral prednisone was related more to the parents' personality [as measured by the Minnesota Multiphasic Personality Inventory (MMPI)] than to their children's (Lansky et al., 1983). Although rates of compliance were comparable for boys and girls, psychological traits associated with compliance were different for boys and girls as well as for their mothers and fathers. Among parents, several personality traits that typically are considered maladaptive were found to correlate with compliance among their children according to a gender of parents/gender of child interaction. Among compliant boys, mothers were compulsive, anxious, and high in self-control, whereas fathers were hostile and aggressive. Mothers of compliant girls, on the other hand, were calm instead of anxious, but their fathers tended to avoid facing problems. These findings were thought to reflect different compliance expectations that parents have for their sons compared with their daughters, despite the absence of gender effects in the children's compliance rates; they expected their sons to be more vulnerable and in need of supervision, and their daughters to be more responsible. Among the few studies of psychosocial adjustment and medication compliance among pediatric cancer patients, Jamison, Lewis, and Burish (1986a) found that overall treatment compliance, based on nurses' ratings, including but not limited to medication compliance, was inversely correlated with adolescents' poor self-image and external locus of control. Generally, when adolescents with cancer were compared with healthy peers, they had significantly lower internal and higher external locus-of-control scores about health-related issues. Such findings were interpreted as reflecting their increased vulnerability to feeling helpless and losing control, which in turn, was thought to contribute to their noncompliance (Jamison, Lewis, & Burish, 1986b; Kellerman, Zeltzer, Ellenberg, Dash, & Rigler, 1980). Shope (1981) found that parents of patients who felt that they had some control over their child's health (internal locus of control) were better compliers. Others, however, have not found a relationship between locus of control and compliance (Tamaroff et al., 1992; Tebbi et al., 1986).

The construct of locus of control has received considerable attention in studies of adjusting to illness and would be thought to have obvious implications in compliance issues. Locus of control supposedly reflects the degree to which individuals perceive that they are responsible for and have the ability to control factors affecting their lives. It generally has been reported that individuals who have an internal locus of control adjust better to illness than those who have an external locus of control, the latter reflecting a sense of being unable to control health-related events (Marks, Richardson, Graham, & Levine, 1986; Simonds, Goldstein, Kilo, & Hoette, 1987). Because compliance issues might be one of the few treatment domains where patients and their families feel that they can assert some control, relationships between locus of control and medication compliance seem worth considering in terms of interventions to enhance children's and their families' sense of control of treatment regimens.

Until we have better means of predicting which children from which families will have compliance problems, we should assume that all patients are at risk for medication noncompliance. Consequently, there is a need to actively monitor compliance, throughout treatment, in the context of patients' perceptions and beliefs about their illness, their satisfaction with the medical care they are receiving, and how they see themselves in broader social contexts involving the community, school, family, and other patients they come to know in the hospital. In a recent editorial about compliance among asthmatics, Mellins et al. (1992) addressed the problem in the following way: "The narrow definition of compliance as 'getting them to take the medicine' has to be broadened with concepts of open communication about both the patient's and the physician's concerns and objectives, shared responsibility and mutual agreement on the medical regimen. A shift is needed in the way physicians prescribe and counsel patients, away from an exclusive focus on the clinician's goals (i.e., to use particular medicines in a predetermined schedule) to one that also includes the patient's goals and concerns (e.g., fitting in with school or work schedules or not disrupting daily life patterns)" (p. 1376). Such an approach gives families a greater sense of control for managing medical problems, even in cases when medical demands reduce the actual control that they are able to exercise to more of an illusory status. Psychological studies have long established that people's sense of control of a situation in medical practice, rather than their practice of control, is a critical factor in their adjustment to that situation (Bowers, 1968; Langer, Janis, & Wolfer, 1974; Lefcourt, 1973). Compliance, therefore, might be considered one of the few domains of treatment where children and families can exert some direct control, even as they sense an abandonment of control in other domains of treatment management.

COPING AND ADJUSTMENT

Theoretical Approaches

No area of interest in pediatric psychology has received more study than that of coping and adjustment among chronically ill children and their families. Between 1928 and 1959, there were 44 articles on this topic; between 1960 and 1969, 81 articles; and since 1970, 600 articles (Lavigne & Faier-Routman, 1992). Since the 1960s, there have been over 200 articles on pediatric oncology alone (Kupst, 1994).

Research on children's coping has relied extensively on models of coping in adults, and it has encompassed several different psychological perspectives that have varying relevance to studies of coping in pediatric psychology. Among clinical psychologists, coping has been used to refer to stable personality traits. Experimental psychologists have studied coping in terms of escape and avoidance learning among animals. From a biological perspective, coping has been viewed in terms of cortical stimulation of the hypothalamus region and the pituitary–adrenocortical system. Coping research also has had a long and productive legacy in social-personality psychology (Kugelmann, 1992), and it is this perspective that appears most relevant to recent studies of coping in pediatric psychology. From this perspective, coping typically has been defined as "constantly changing cognitive and behavioral efforts to manage specific external and/or internal demands that are appraised as taxing or exceeding the resources of the person" (Lazarus & Folkman, 1984, p. 141). Yet, according to Folkman (1992), "Despite the steady increase in coping research, we still know remarkably little about the extent to which coping accounts for individual differences in response to stress and the mechanisms through which coping mitigates the harmful physical and psychological effects of stress" (p. 32). Pediatric psychologists who seek to apply basic findings about stress and coping to particular conditions occasioned by chronic illnesses are limited by the lack of a comprehensive theoretical model of coping. Lazarus and Folkman's (1984) process model of coping, although useful as a heuristic, too often has been reified and treated as the phenomenon of interest (Ouellette, 1994). Coping is then reduced to whatever a given coping scale measures. As will be seen, this often has led to some rather strange findings.

In addition to the lack of a comprehensive theoretical model of adult coping, investigators in pediatric psychology often are stymied by a failure to consider the developmental features of children's cognitive and social competencies and how they affect their coping strategies. The extent to which children are able to garner resources for coping with potentially stressful situations is dependent on their developing competencies in such areas as self-esteem, achievement motivation, social perception, perceptual motor skills, attention, linguistic ability, motivation, problem-solving skills, and fantasy and symbolic play (Anderson & Messick, 1974). Thus, for example, older children are less likely to report using primary control strategies (e.g., attempting to directly modify a stressful situation) and more likely to use secondary control strategies [e.g., attempting to modify their own subjective psychological states (Band & Weisz, 1988)]. Even coping among very competent children is unlikely to resemble adults' ways of coping, and individual differences among children of the same age preclude finding a simple relationship between age and coping. Most studies of how children cope with medical stressors have focused on middle childhood (8 to 12 years old) and have not tested for age-related trends (Peterson, Harbeck, Chaney, Farmer, & Muir-Thomas, 1990). Other variables of interest that have not been systematically studied involve children's gender role expectations along with culturally conventionalized ascriptions of modes of coping that vary with both gender and age (Altshuler & Ruble, 1989).

One reason why findings of children's coping with medical problems have not advanced relative to adults' coping is that children's varying developmental levels have complicated and made difficult any investigations relying on traditional methodologies adapted from adult studies, such as using paper-and-pencil type self-report scales. Also, the inconsistencies in how coping is defined at different periods of child development are exacerbated by a general lack of functional criteria of coping. That is, coping often is defined a priori rather than in terms of specific behavioral observations of how people react to stress in specific situations. Another problem of studying coping in children concerns the occasion of its assessment. Most studies examine children's coping in anticipation of a stressful procedure, such as impending hospitalization or elective surgery, but measures of anticipatory stress and coping do not necessarily correlate with measures of how children behave during stressful procedures (i.e., stimulus encounters). Only recently have investigators begun to examine procedural (rather than anticipatory) coping with illness-specific invasive procedures.

Health Belief Models and Locus of Control

Few psychologists would dispute that how people understand and represent events is a primary determinant of how they respond to them. In the field of health psychology, Leventhal, Meyer, and Nerenz (1980; see also Leventhal, Nerenz, & Steele, 1984) have presented compelling evidence of the strength of patients' mental representations of health threats (illness schemas) in determining how patients cope. Increasingly, investigators are trying to understand issues of coping in terms of patients' and families' beliefs about locus of control and how such beliefs might serve as mediators between experience and patients' ways of adapting to it. Studies of the consequences of having a sense of control over one's life have long been a major topic in social psychology, and an increasing proportion of these studies are health-related (Peterson, 1980). Perceived control is "the *belief* that one can determine one's own internal states and behavior, influence one's environment, and/or bring about desired outcomes" (Wallston, Wallston, Smith, & Dobbins, 1987, p. 5). The perception of control has been shown to be more important than veridical control.

Because early studies found that it was not easy to manipulate perceived control in health care settings, perceived control was conceptualized as a trait-like dimension. However, according to Bandura (1977), there is little empirical justification to consider perceived control as a personality-like trait that remains stable over time and situations. Instead, it appears to vary across time and situations. This is particularly relevant to health issues. For example, individuals might believe that although they had little control over getting a disease such as cancer, they can control their response to the disease (Wallston et al., 1987). Several studies found that those who had an internal sense of control regarding the **cause** of their cancer (but not the course of their treatment) had poorer levels of adjustment compared to those who had an external sense of the cause of their cancer (Bearison, Sadow, Granowetter, & Winkel, 1993; Watson, Greer, Pruyn, & Van den Borne, 1990). These findings regarding the causal attribution of an illness like cancer are particularly important because of the unknown etiologies of almost all kinds of childhood cancers.

Early studies of perceived control in health contexts conceived of it as a unidimensional construct that varied from high internal sense of control to high external sense of control. Generally, it was assumed that the more internal one was, the better off one was. According to Wallston (Wallston et al., 1987), hundreds of studies were done comparing those with an internal to those with an external locus of control and "almost always, the 'internals' came out on top" (p. 8; see also Strickland, 1978; and Wallston & Wallston, 1978, for a general review of this early work). Since then, however, the construct has been reconceptualized both theoretically and psychometrically as constituting three orthogonal dimensions operationally defined by the Multidimensional Health Locus of Control Scales (Wallston, Wallston, & DeVellis, 1978): (a) internal, or the extent to which one perceives one's health status as being influenced by one's own actions; (b) powerful other, or the extent to which one perceives one's health status as being influenced or controlled by powerful other people; and (c) external, or the extent to which one perceives one's health status as being controlled by fate or luck.

In a study of the distress of children (4 to 18 years old) during a venipuncture, it was found that their perceived source of control in anticipation of the procedure contributed to their cooperativeness during the procedure. Children who had a perception of control in terms of who they perceived as being responsible for helping them cope with the procedure (themselves, their parents, or a mutual effort) were able to cope better with the procedure and had less anticipatory procedural distress than children who believed that no one could help them cope (Carpenter, 1992). Neither age nor gender was related to their perceived source of control.

Family Systems Theory

A promising impetus for applying theoretically relevant constructs to assess and intervene in children's coping with chronic illness is provided by recent attempts to apply a family systems and social-ecological model of adaptation. In such an approach, the individual coping resources of chronically ill children are seen in the broader context of their families' structure and ways of functioning, along with the medical, psychosocial, and educational resources available to them (Kazak, 1989, 1994). Understanding pediatric medical problems in regard to family systems theory leads the investigator to pose different kinds of basic questions and to reframe problems about stress and coping that require different modes of analysis. The family, rather than the individual, is conceived as the unit of analysis. For example, a family systems approach might predict that a child who came from a family that, prior to the stress of a child's illness, had a high number of adjustment problems and was less cohesive and less adaptable (i.e., more rigid) in dealing with external stressors would be at great risk, independent of the individual child's contributions, medical condition, and experiences. According to a family systems perspective, children develop in interaction with different subsystems that can be conceptualized as a set of concentric rings transversing social–ecological space from the centered individual to the family and to the community. These represent multidirectional and overlapping microsystems, mesosystems, and exosystems, respectively (Bronfenbrenner, 1979; Kazak, Segal-Andrews, & Johnson, 1995).

Family systems theory is based on an adaptation of general systems theory that sees systems and subsystems as being composed of interrelated and mutually reciprocal parts that maintain a dynamic state of balance or homeostasis such that a change in one part is associated with changes in all the other parts (von Bertalanffy, 1968). Consideration of childhood illnesses, according to family systems theory, therefore, necessitates attention to interrelationships among additional sets of variables, along with those traditionally identified in studies of stress and coping. The added variables include: the psychological distress of the child's parents, individually and in terms of their marital relationship (Cummings, 1976; Sabbeth & Leventhal, 1984), and the child's siblings (Carpenter & LeVant, 1994; Horwitz & Kazak, 1990; Madan-Swain, Sexson, Brown, & Ragab, 1993); parenting responsibilities (Kazak & Marvin, 1984); peer relationships (La Greca, 1992); the family's social support network (Kazak & Meadows, 1989; Kazak, Reber, & Carter, 1988; Krahn, 1993); and the family's ongoing interactions with medical, educational, and social service systems (Chesler & Barbarin, 1984, 1987; Cole & Reiss, 1993; Kazak, 1987).

The structural complexity of families as dynamic interacting systems, along with the cultural and ethnic diversities that characterize interpersonal interactions both within and between families, makes research on stress and coping considerably more difficult than more traditional individual approaches and obfuscates reliance on psychometric norms. For example, the ways that African American and Hispanic families cope with medical stress, and how it affects relationships among child-patient, family, and medical systems, are areas of research that remain relatively unexplored (Kazak & Nachman, 1991) and hampered by dubious assumptions about the nature of cultural homogeneity (Reid, 1994). Studies of families' coping with pediatric diseases that occur predominantly among particular ethnic groups need to consider comparative conditions that make sense relative to the cultural values, conventions, and practices of the targeted ethnic group. Studies of African American families' strategies for coping with the pain associated with sickle cell disease is one example (e.g., Armstrong, Lemanek, Pegelow, Gonzalez, & Martinez, 1993; Gil, Williams, Thompson, & Kinney, 1991). From a family systems approach, it would be inappropriate to make general comparisons of familial coping strategies across disease conditions without considering the incidence of disease along ethnic and cultural variables (e.g., comparing how families cope with a child who has an asthmatic crisis to how families cope with a child who has a sickle cell crisis).

Coping studies also need greater recognition of how families develop in reciprocal relationships, given the condition of each of their members. For example, the impact on a family when an infant has a chronic medical problem is different from the experience of having an adolescent with the same problem. Other factors must be explored: Is this a first child, an only child, or one of several (sick or well) children? If the family is intact, has the child come early or late in the parents' marriage? Is the parenting couple married or divorced/remarried, or is there a single parent? These developmentally relevant family variables reciprocally affect the experience of chronic illness for children and their families or extended families.

Coping with Illness

Children who have chronic diseases or who are injured often experience extended hospitalization, separation from their families and friends, and frequent painful medical procedures. Consequently, their ability to cope may be severely compromised, and the extent of their adherence to treatment may become a disruptive issue for the family and treatment teams. Therefore, care must be taken to help children achieve developmentally appropriate ways of coping. This requires assessing basic developmental parameters in order to identify how the nature of a given illness or injury—its cause, treatment, and adverse effects—might disrupt the process of normal development and family interaction. The ultimate utility of stress and coping studies in pediatric practice is to predict future health behavior and status so as to identify which patients and families might be at risk for adjustment problems. Interventions can then be implemented prior to the onset of problems.

Multimodal Factors

A major limitation to studying adjustment to most kinds of chronic illnesses is the confluence of multimodal factors that bear on the experience. For example, in cases of cancer, it is almost impossible to systematically unconfound, in a neat factorial design, the effects due to the experience of cancer per se; aversive treatments, including chemotherapy and central nervous system radiation; the duration and prognostic course of the illness; premorbid stressors and modes of adapting; disruption of children's accustomed and expected daily routines (including school) and social relations; cultural attitudes toward cancer patients; how children understand and make sense of the uncertainties associated with having cancer (including the threat of dying); the financial burdens placed on the family; the chronic condition of cancer survivorship; and the inevitable interaction among these inherent and exogenous factors (Bearison & Pacifici, 1984).

Few consequences of any note in pediatric psychology are singly or uniquely determined; almost all are multiply determined in complex mediational relationships. For example, although many children with spina bifida, cerebral palsy, and hydrocephalus have been found to have serious adjustment problems, their disability parameters, ambulatory status, or extent of physical disability—if taken alone—were not predictive of their psychological adjustment (Fletcher et al., 1995; Wallander, Varni, Babani, Banis, DeHaan, & Wilcox, 1989; Wallander, Varni, Babani, Banis, & Wilcox, 1988). Such findings suggest that the disrupting effects of even such salient quality-of-life and lifestyle variables are mediated by a range of other, subtler variables (Wallander et al., 1989).

Cayler, Lynn, and Stein (1973) provided a dramatic illustration of how an exogenous variable associated with a serious illness in children can be confounded with the process of adjusting to the illness. A group of children (7 to 10 years old) who had been misdiagnosed as having cardiac disease (their condition 3 to 10 years later was discovered to be an "innocent" heart murmur) was compared to a sample of healthy children. Among the children with cardiac "nondisease," some had their activities restricted by physicians, but others had no restrictions imposed on them. The WISC scores for the medically restricted children were significantly lower than the scores for the nonrestricted misdiagnosed children and the healthy children ($M = 97$ vs. 111 and 114, respectively), although there were no known neurological differences among the three groups. Thus, it was concluded that the restrictions imposed on the children's activities affected their adjustment, rather than any inherent conditions of illness.

Methods of Study

Studies of coping and adaptation employ several methods. A global index of coping or adaptation typically is based on standardized scales and compares pediatric medical samples to "normal" samples. In studies of this kind, measures of coping and adaptation are based on mean scale scores that do not typically consider variations in the expression of symptoms, either between subjects or within subjects at different times. Another method seeks interaction effects that mediate relationships between specific medical conditions and specific aspects of psychosocial functioning. The method is based on comparisons both within and between groups. Studies of the latter kind can inform the design of appropriate kinds of interventions, which can then constitute a third kind of study that provides a causal test of the effects of the mediational variables. These methods, while far from frequent in the literature, are most evident in studies of children who have cancer.

Case studies and anecdotal evidence also document the kinds of adjustment problems that children encounter. These kinds of studies are valuable in documenting the psychosocial effects of new interventions and medical regimens (e.g., see Patenaude, Szymanski, & Rappeport, 1979, and Patenaude & Rappeport, 1982, regarding the psychological impact of bone marrow transplantations; and Fritz, Rubinstein, & Lewiston, 1987, regarding psychological factors in fatal childhood asthma). Studies like these are important because they capture the multimodal complexity of behavioral phenomena in the context of clinical practice. Therefore, they can address the assessment and intervention issues that directly challenge practitioners. Case histories can contribute to the formulation and design of empirical studies by helping investigators to identify relationships among ecologically validated variables. On the other hand, they can augment findings from empirical studies by providing clinical depth and relevance in interpreting findings from purely quantitative databased statistical analyses (Yin, 1993). The reporting of case studies has been a central mode of scientific discourse in medical literature, but it is considerably less common in developmental and pediatric psychology literature and reflects an unfortunate distancing between empirical research and clinical practice in pediatric psychology (Drotar, La Greca, Lemanek, & Kazak, 1995).

Having a child with a chronic medical problem is a significant stressor for the family as well as the child, but there is considerable controversy as to the extent that children (and families) with chronic medical problems are at increased risk for adjustment problems. Some investigators have found increased rates of behavioral and emotional problems among children with chronic medical problems; others have not. As will be seen, much of this controversy rests on judgments regarding the adequacy of the measures used to assess different aspects of coping and adjustment in samples of children with different medical problems (Bennett, 1994). Some of these measures have been designed to assess adjustment (and psychopathology) in physically healthy children; other have been developed specifically for use in assessing the adjustment of children with medical problems. Table 10.2 catalogs measures that commonly have been used in studies of children with medical problems. The measures are listed according to the specific attributes they are intended to measure, the type of scale they employ, and their primary references. Each of the listed measures has been used in more than a single study and has been shown to have certain adequate psychometric properties (e.g., item consistency and reliability, though not necessarily ecological or concurrent validity). Together, they reflect the range of variables, both general and disease-specific, used to index coping and adjustment in pediatric psychology.

There also is controversy about whether rates of psychological adjustment change over the course of a child's illness and about the extent to which such findings are dependent on the kinds of measures and empirical designs that have been used. Thompson, Gustafson, George, and Spock (1995) studied the adjustment of children (7 to 17 years old) with cystic fibrosis at the time of initial evaluation and then 12 months later, and Thompson et al. (1994) studied children with sickle cell disease at initial evaluation and 10 months later. They found that, for both illness conditions, the rates of adjustment remained relatively constant over time, although there was less stability in the particular type of behavioral problems that marked individual children's adjustment. Breslau and Marshall (1985) conducted a five-year follow-up of the adjustment of children with cystic fibrosis, cerebral palsy, or spina bifida, and

TABLE 10.2 Adjustment and Coping Measures Used in Pediatric Psychology Studies

Measure	Attributes	Type of Scale	Primary References
Children's Depression Inventory	Depression	27-item, 3-pt. self-report	Kovacs, 1992; Kovacs & Beck, 1977
Beck Depression Inventory	Depression	21-item, 4-pt. self-report	Beck, Ward, & Mendelson, 1961
Revised Children's Manifest Anxiety Scale	Anxiety	37-item, 2-pt. (yes/no) self-report	Reynolds & Richmond, 1978
Attributional Style Questionnaire	Attribution	48-item forced choice	Seligman et al., 1984
Child Behavior Checklist	Behavioral adjustment	138-item, 3-pt. parent report & 113-item self-report & teacher report	Achenbach, 1978; Achenbach & Edelbrock, 1983
Matching Familiar Figures Test	Impulsivity	12-item, 6–8-pt. visual match to sample items	Kagan, 1966
Conners' Parent Rating Scale/Revised	Hyperactivity	48-item, 3-pt. parent report	Goyette, Conners, & Ulrich, 1978
Eyberg Child Behavior Inventory	Conduct disorders	36-item, 7-pt. parent report	Robinson, Eyberg, & Ross, 1980
Revised Fear Survey Schedule for Children	Fears	80-item, 3-pt. self-report	Ollendick, 1983
Medical Fear Questionnaire	Fears	12-item, 3pt. self-report	Broome, 1986
Hospital Fears Rating Scale	Fears	25-item, 5-pt. visual analogue scale	Melamed & Sigel, 1975; Melamed, Dearborn, & Hermecz, 1983
Coping Strategies Inventory	Coping	72-item, 5-pt. report	Tobin, Hjoloryd, Reynolds, & Wigal, 1989
Vincland Social Maturity Scale	Adaptiveness	117-item, 2-pt. (yes/no) parental questionnaire	Doll, 1953
Parenting Stress Index	Parental stress	101-item, 5-pt. parent report	Abidin, 1983
Children's Embedded Figures Test	Impulsivity	Visual discrimination items	Karp & Konstadt, 1971
Nowicki–Strickland Locus of Control Scale for Children	Perceived control	40-item, 2-pt. (yes/no) self-report	Nowicki & Strickland, 1973
Multidimensional Health Locus of Control Scales	Perceived control	18-item, 6-pt. self-report (3 subscales)	Wallston, Wallston, & DeVillis, 1978; Parcel & Meyer, 1978
Piers–Harris Self-Concept Scale	Self-concept	80-item, 2-pt. (yes/no) self-report	Piers, 1977
Visible Physical Impairment Rating Scale	Physical impairments	4-item, 4-pt. professional report	Koocher & O'Malley, 1981
Functional Disability Inventory	Functioning due to illness	15-item, 5-pt. self-report	Walker & Greene, 1991
State-Trait Anxiety Inventory for Children	Anxiety	20-item, 3-pt. self-report	Spielberger, 1973
State-Trait Anxiety Inventory	Anxiety	40-item, 4-pt. self-report	Spielberger, 1983
Children's Depression Inventory	Depression	27-item, 3-pt. self-report	Kovacs, 1980/1981
Post-Traumatic Stress Disorder Reaction Index	Traumatic stress	20-item, 4-pt. self-report	Frederick, 1985
Strategies for Coping with Illness Parents' Scale	Coping	109-item, 4 pt. parent report	Erickson, 1990
Self-Perception Profile for Children	Self-concept	45-item, 4-pt. self-report	Harter, 1985

(Continued)

TABLE 10.2 *(Continued)*

Measure	Attributes	Type of Scale	Primary References
Medical Compliance Incomplete Stories Test	Compliance	5-item, 3-pt. story completion task/child & parent versions	Koocher, Czajkowski, & Fitzpatrick, 1987
KIDCOPE	Coping	13-item, 4-pt. self-report	Spirito, Stark, & Williams, 1988
Family Environment Scale	Family adjustment	90-item, 2-pt. (true–false) self-report	Moos, 1974
Family Environment Scale, 2nd ed.	Family adjustment	90-item, 4-pt. report	Moos & Moos, 1986
Coping Strategies Inventory	Coping	72-item, 5-pt. self-report	Tobin et al., 1989
Lansky Play Performance Scale for Children	Quality of life	100-item, 2-pt. (yes/no) parent questionnaire	Lansky, List, Lansky, Ritter-Sterr, & Miller, 1987
Parenting Dimensions Inventory	Parenting style	26-item, 6-pt. parent report	Slater & Power, 1987
Temperament Assessment Battery for Children	Temperament	48-item, 7-pt. parents' self-report	Martin, 1987
Observational Scale of Behavioral Distress	Distress	8 observational codes	Elliott, Jay, & Woody, 1987
Perception of Procedures Questionnaire	Parents' perception of children's medical stress	21-item, 7-pt. self-report	Kazak et al., 1995
Quality of Life—Bone Marrow Transplant (QOL—BMT)	QOL for BMT survivors	30-item, 100-pt. visual analogue questionnaire	Grant et al., 1992
Dyadic Pre-stressor Interaction Scale	Anticipatory stress	10 observational codes of parent and child behaviors	Bush, Melamed, Sheras, & Greenbaum, 1986
Children's Global Rating Scale (CGRS)	Pain and fear	Single item, 5-pt. self-report	Carpenter, 1990
Infant Pain Behavior Rating Scale	Pain expression	13-pt. observational coding scale	Craig, McMahon, Morison, & Zaskow, 1984
Faces Pain Scale	Pain intensity	Single item, 7-pt. self-report	Bieri, Reeve, Champion, Addicoa, & Ziegler, 1990
Procedure Behavior Rating Scale	Behavioral distress	13-item observational coding scale	Katz, Kellerman, & Siegel, 1980; Jacobsen et al., 1990
Child–Adult Medical Procedure Interaction Scale (CAMPIS)	Behavioral distress & coping	35-item observational coding scale for child and parent interaction	Blount, Sturges, & Powers, 1990
Children's Behavioral Style Scale	Coping style: Monitoring/Blunting	4 scenarios with 6 free choices, self- & parent reports	Phipps, Fairclough, & Mulhern, 1995
Rosenberg Self-Esteem Scale	Perceived self-competence	10-item, 4-pt. self-report	Rosenberg, 1979
Multidimensional Measure of Children's Perceptions of Control (Medical Procedures)	Perceived control	22-item, 4-pt. self-report	Carpenter, 1992
Behavioral Checklist	Behavioral distress	21-item, 2-pt. observer report	Katz, Kellerman, & Siegel, 1980
Children's Global Rating Scale	Anticipatory distress	Single item, 5-pt. self-report	Carpenter, 1990
Miami Quality of Life Questionnaire	Functional adaptation	55-item, 5-pt. questionnaire (parent and child forms)	Armstrong, Tolendano, Lackman, & Miloslavich, 1991
Rand Child Health Status Scale	Health status	Variable no. of items, parent report	Eisen, Ware, Donald, & Brook, 1979
Pediatric Oncology Quality of Life Scale	Physical and emotional functions	21-item, 7-pt. parent report	Goodwin, Boggs, & Graham-Pole, 1994

TABLE 10.2 *(Continued)*

Measure	Attributes	Type of Scale	Primary References
Ways of Coping Inventory	Coping	68-item, 2-pt. (yes/no) checklist	Folkman & Lazarus, 1988
Coping/Health Inventory for Parents	Coping	45-item, 4-pt. parent report	McCubbin, McCubbin, Nevin, & Cauble, 1981
Social Support Rating Scale	Social support	5- & 7-pt. scales	Cauce, Felner, & Primavera, 1982
Family Adaptability and Cohesion Evaluation Scales-III (FACES-III)	Family cohesion & adaptability	40-item, 7-pt. self-report	Olson, Portner, & Bell, 1982
Offer Self-Image Questionnaire for Adolescents (OSIQ)	Adolescent self-concept	130-item, 6-pt. scales (12 subscales)	Offer, 1969
Health Resources Inventory	Self & social competence	54-item, 5-pt. teacher report	Gesten, 1976
Personal Adjustment and Role Skills Scale (PARS III)	Psychosocial adjustment	28-item, 4-pt. scale	Ellsworth, 1978
Neonatal Facial Coding System (NFCS)	Infants' responses to pain	7-item, 2-pt. (present/absent) behavioral observation scale	Craig, Hadjistavropoulos, Grunau, & Whitfield, 1994
Behavioral Upset in Medical Patients—Revised (BUMP-R)	Emotional distress	56-item, 4-pt. parent report	Rodriguez & Boggs, 1994
Minnesota Preschool Affect Rating Scales (MN-PARS)	Emotional & social adjustment	12-item, 7-pt. observational scale	Shapiro, McPhee, & Abbott, 1994
Pediatric Anger Expression Scale—3rd ed. (PAES-III)	Anger	15-item, 3-pt. self-report	Hagglund et al., 1994
Child Behavioral Style Scale (CBSS)	Monitoring vs. blunting coping styles	4 scenarios, each with 6 endorse/don't endorse responses; self- & parent report versions	Miller, Sherman, Roussi, Caputo, & Krus, in press
Children's Health Care Attitudes Questionnaire (CHCAQ)	Health care attitudes	24-item, 5-pt. scale	Bush & Holmbeck, 1987
Illness Causality Scale (ICS)	Illness concepts	7-item, 6-pt. scale	Sayer, Willett, & Perrin, 1993
Coping Strategies Questionnaire (CSG)	Illness-related coping	78-item, 7-pt. self-report (with 13 subscales)	Rosensteil & Keefe, 1983; Gil, Abrams, Phillips, & Keefe, 1989
Child Attitude Toward Illness Scale (CATIS)	Attitudes about having a chronic illness	13-item, 5-pt. self-report	Austin & Huberty, 1993
Social Distance Questionnaire	Attitudes toward the handicapped	12-item, 6-pt. attitude scale	Westervelt, Brantley, & Ware, 1983

children with multiple physical disabilities, and found little change in mean scores on their screening inventory except for improvement among children with cystic fibrosis.

Despite these findings of relative stability in the use of some general coping strategies among some children, it is more likely that specific coping strategies vary intraindividually across different illness-related stressors and between illness-related and non-illness-related situations. Such findings would require using differentiated measures that mark specific kinds of coping strategies instead of mean scale scores. In these types of studies, basic coping strategies—distraction, blaming others, and emotional regulation—have not been found to be stable over time or invariant across situations (Spirito, Stark, Gil, & Tyc, 1995). Also, findings of this kind can be ascertained only by using situation-specific intraindividual longitudinal methods that mark occasion-based events for study instead of the passage of standardized time. To illustrate, a study of how children adjust to the persistent rigors of bone marrow transplantation might target the administration of measures to: when the child is first apprised of the procedure, when a donor has been identified, when the child is admitted to the protected germ-free environment, when he or she is given the transplant infusion, when engraftment begins, and when symptoms of graft versus host disease (GVHD) appear. Each of these events is emotionally, if not medically, stressful, but they occur sequentially at different time intervals in any single regimen. For example, the lapsed time from admission to transplantation can span 1 to 10 days, depending on the effects of high-dose chemotherapy (with or without total body irradiation), and the time between transplant and engraftment can last from 2 to 4 weeks (see Phipps, 1994, for a discussion of the psychological stressors involved in bone marrow transplantation). Longitudinal studies that use standardized times for assessment (e.g., at 2, 6, 8, or 12 weeks postadmission) would fail to capture changes in coping as a function of the variety of specific medical stressors. Situation-specific intraindividual longitudinal studies of children's coping with medical stressors, however, have not been done, aside from those focusing on single short-term procedures, such as a venipuncture.

When studying developmental change, the concepts of intraindividual and interindividual change have critical methodological consequences. Group data reflect attributes of the referent group but not of any individual within the group, and they have limited value for conveying information about the developmental change of a specific individual (Wohlwill, 1973). This is a particularly critical consideration for those seeking to reference empirical findings in order to justify clinical interventions that affect behavioral change in individuals, because the source of individual differences in a given trait cannot be taken as evidence for the source of group differences in the same trait. When psychosocial interventions are based on the needs of an individual patient rather than the condition of some reference group, both interindividual and intraindividual methods of studying behavioral change are necessary. When aggregated group means is the only method used to detect behavioral change in pediatric psychology, the plasticity of individual behavior remains undetected and contributes to the "error" of within-group variance (Herson & Barlow, 1976; Russo, 1986). Therefore, we must be careful in how we use empirical findings from aggregated data to prescribe individual interventions. We must consider such findings relative to the range and relevance of the kinds of variables that have been measured and entered into data analyses.

The complexity and covariation of individual clinical problems in psychosocial interventions in medical treatment often yield confounding variables that preclude aggregating data across subjects for factorial and longitudinal analyses. Particularly when the sample size is limited, the use of single-subject designs using time series analyses should be considered. There are now statistical procedures to correct for potential problems of serial dependency across multiple measures (i.e., autocorrelation, r_k) in single-subject studies (Bloom, Fischer, & Orme, 1995; Wampold & Worsham, 1986). Furthermore, meta-analysis techniques can be used as an adjunct to single-subject designs to aggregate findings from individual subjects and evaluate their generality (White, Rusch, Kazdin, & Hartmann, 1989).

According to some researchers, children with more severe illnesses do not generally appear to be at greater risk for adjustment problems (Bennett, 1992; Nelms, 1989), nor are there differences among children according to the severity of a given disease (see Sharpe, Brown, Thompson, & Eckman, 1994; Thompson, Gil, Burbach, Keith, & Kinney, 1993, for sickle cell syndrome; Kovacs et al., 1990, for diabetes; MacLean, Perrin, Gortmaker, & Pierre, 1992, for asthma; Thompson, Gustafson, Hamlett, & Spock, 1992, for cystic fibrosis). However, according to others, disease severity and duration are positively correlated with adjustment problems, such as those found for children with juvenile rheumatoid arthritis (Daniels, Moss, Billings, & Miller, 1987). Often, children's adjustment problems have been attributed to the physical and/or sensory limitations imposed by the illness, problems with adhering to medical regimens, high rates of school absences, reduced opportunities for social support and peer relations, and an increased sense of helplessness, loss of control, and dependency.

Among hospitalized children, depression and suicidal ideation are the most common reasons for psychiatric consultation (Olson et al., 1988; Rait, Jacobsen, Lederberg, & Holland, 1988). Kashani, Barbero, and Bolander (1981) found that 7% of hospitalized pediatric patients were clinically depressed (DSM-III criteria; American Psychiatric Association, 1987) compared with a 1.9% prevalence rate among the general population of children (Kashani & Simmonds, 1979). Rates of depression sometimes have been found to be even higher among children who have cancer. For example, Tebbi, Bromberg, and Mallon (1988) reported 17% of adolescents with cancer were depressed, and most psychiatric consultations in pediatric oncology were requested because of adjustment disorders with depressed mood (31%), major depression (12%), or dysthymic disorder (3%) (DSM-III criteria; American Psychiatric Association, 1987; Rait et al., 1988).

Pharmacologic Effects

Although it is not unusual for children who have serious and chronic medical problems, particularly those who have cancer, to exhibit, at times, various symptoms of depression (e.g., lethargy, poor attention and concentration, low self-esteem, irritability, and somnolence), the iatrogenic (i.e., treatment-induced) effects of the various medication regimens also must be considered as contributing factors. For example, commonly used chemotherapeutic agents given to children who have acute lymphoblastic leukemia include methotrexate, L-asparaginase, and steroid therapy, each of which, alone or in combination, can produce immediate and delayed psychiatric symptomatology. Although difficult to test in a controlled factorial design (protocols typically include combinations of therapeutic agents, and the use of placebos would be inappropriate), the iatrogenic effects of many of the medications used to treat these children produce symptoms associated with dysthymia and depression (Madan-Swain & Brown, 1991).

Measures

Our understanding of children's adjustment to chronic illness rests on the adequacy and psychometric properties of a variety of measures used to assess adjustment. Measures used to assess coping and adjustment in pediatric psychology pose particular challenges to both clinicians and investigators. Few measures to date have been developed specifically for use with pediatric populations who have specific illness-related impairments. Consequently, most studies have adapted measures from those that were validated among physically healthy children who had a psychometrically adequate range of behavioral symptoms of psychopathology. It is questionable whether such measures can be sufficiently sensitive to detect adjustment problems in chronically ill children and/or their families, or can generalize from physically healthy children to those with medical problems (Mulhern et al., 1992). For example, the presence of somatic symptoms (e.g., fatigue or poor appetite) in many adjustment scales can inflate chronically ill children's scores for adjustment problems, and the symptoms of certain illnesses and treatment effects can mimic those attributable to a depressive syndrome and thereby lead to both false-positive and false-negative diagnoses (Mulhern et al., 1992).

The most commonly used psychometric to assess children's adjustment to illness in terms of behavioral symptoms is the Child Behavior Checklist (Achenbach, 1978; Achenbach & Edelbrock, 1983). It consists of three instruments: (a) a parent rating form (CBCL), (b) a teacher rating form (TRF)—both are suitable for children 4 to 16 years old—and (c) a self-report form (YSR) suitable for children 11 to 18 years old. Each of these forms has been standardized separately from factor analyses of different gender and age groupings. Each resulting subscale is based on two kinds of standardization samples, one of children referred for mental health treatment and the other of children not referred. Given these standardization samples, the instruments are not necessarily appropriate for children with chronic illness. Nevertheless, they have become what Perrin, Stein, and Drotar (1991) described as the "gold standard" for assessing psychological functions in pediatric psychology. These researchers have disclosed several causes for concern when using these and other similar rating scales for pediatric populations. As many as 10 of the items in the different forms of the CBCL refer to physical symptoms that might accompany or be exacerbated by chronic illnesses and, consequently, bias scores. Such items include: "feels dizzy," "lacks energy," has "speech problems," and has "headaches." Another commonly used measure of adjustment, the Children's Depression Inventory (Kovacs & Beck, 1977), contains items on appetite, sleep, fatigue, and decreased school attendance—behaviors that may be symptomatic of depression but may also be associated with particular medical conditions and treatment effects. A more serious concern is that these scales were developed for the purpose of identifying instances of psychopathology in children. Therefore, they are not sensitive to instances of subtle or mild behavioral problems that, although within the range of normal functioning, are of particular concern to pediatricians and pediatric psychologists dealing with chronic illness in children. Nor do these scales tap a sufficiently comprehensive range of social competencies to capture the potential impact of a chronic condition on children's peer relations and social adaptation (La Greca, 1990b). Because the CBCL scales are normed independently for rater (i.e., parent, teacher, and self), gender, and age groups, they preclude unbiased comparisons across these conditions that many investigators fail to appreciate when reporting comparative findings.

There also is evidence that parents' ratings of their children's functioning on behavioral checklists are significantly influenced by the parents' level of distress and marital adjustment, independent of their children's functional status. For example, Sanger, MacLean, and Van-Slyke (1992) collected data from parents of 110 children (ages 2 to 12 years) who were referred to a pediatric clinic for a variety of behavioral problems. They found that ratings of the mothers' psychological distress, marital adjustment, and negative life events accounted for a significant amount of the variance in maternal child behavior ratings over and above that accounted for by fathers' ratings of the same behaviors.

Meta-analytic Reviews

Lavigne and Faier-Routman (1992) conducted a meta-analytic review of psychological adjustment among children who had a wide variety of physical disorders and chronic illnesses, including asthma, blindness, burns, cardiac disorders, cancer, cerebral palsy, cystic fibrosis, deafness, diabetes, neurologic disorders, and renal disorders. Comparing effect sizes across 87 studies, they found that target children, compared to controls, had higher levels of adjustment problems. Specifically, the target children had more internalizing-type symptoms (e.g., anxiety, depression, and social withdrawal) than externalizing-type symptoms (e.g., hyperactivity, conduct disorder, and aggression), and experienced lower levels of self-esteem. In almost all cases, measures were based on a limited range of rating scales and questionnaires, the most common being the Child Behavior Checklist (CBCL; Achenbach & Edelbrock, 1983), the Piers-Harris Self Concept Scale (Piers, 1977), and the Children's Depression Inventory (Kovacs & Beck, 1977). Where ratings were made independently by parents and teachers, it was found that, although there were no effect sizes between internalizing and externalizing symptoms among children as rated by their parents, teachers were more likely than parents to rate children for internalizing symptoms and less likely to rate them for externalizing symptoms. Silverman and Eisen (1992) also concluded, in their review of the literature, that parents have more difficulty in reliably reporting their children's internalizing compared to their externalizing symptoms. Also of note was that effect sizes generally were smaller in studies that used a control group recruited for that particular study and, thereby, matched with the experimental group along some meaningful standard (e.g., age, gender, SES, type of illness, limits of disability, etc.) compared to studies that relied on instrument-based normative samples.

Lavigne and Faier-Routman (1992) also compared effect sizes across different kinds of medical disorders. Those disorders presenting a "very large" effect size (i.e., .75 or more) were inflammatory bowel disease, seizure disorders, burns, and deafness; those presenting a "large" effect size (i.e., between .50 and .74) were cerebral palsy, cardiac disorders, blindness, and diabetes; those presenting a "moderate" effect size (i.e., between .25 and .49) were cystic fibrosis, cancer, asthma, juvenile rheumatoid arthritis, and orthopedic disorders.

A meta-analysis by Bennett (1994) focused solely on depression, one of the several internalizing symptoms identified by Lavigne and Faier-Routman (1992) as having been associated with chronic illness. Sixty studies of depressive symptoms among children and adolescents with chronic medical problems (most notably, asthma, cancer, cystic fibrosis, diabetes, inflammatory bowel disease, recurrent abdominal pain, and sickle cell disease) were reviewed. Bennett found that ratings of depressive symptoms among these children were approximately one-fourth of a standard deviation above the mean for control groups.

Most studies reported no consistent gender, age, or duration-of-illness effects (with the exception of Worchel et al., 1988, and Kovacs et al., 1990, who found a positive relation between duration of illness and self-reports of depression for children with cancer; and Daniels et al., 1987, for children with rheumatic disease). However, there were positive associations between the severity of restrictions due to illness and children's depressive symptoms (e.g., Mulhern et al., 1992, and Greenberg, Kazak, & Meadows, 1989, for children with cancer; and Gizyunski & Shapiro, 1990, for comparisons between children with asthma and cancer). In several studies, parents' ratings of the extent of their children's depressive symptoms were greater than the children's self-reports (e.g., Worchel et al., 1988, for children who have cancer). Worchel et al. (1988) also found that the children's ratings of depressive symptoms (from the Child Depression Inventory, Kovacs & Beck, 1977) were lower than those obtained from healthy controls. Canning, Canning, and Boyce (1992) also found lower levels of self-reported depression among adolescents with cancer compared to healthy controls. Mulhern et al. (1992) found "unexpectedly low correlations" among nurses', parents', and children's self-reports of depressive symptomatology, despite significant positive correlations of estimates of the children's somatic symptomatology among the three groups of raters.

Self-Reports

It generally is surprising to find that chronically ill children have acknowledged *fewer* or similar depressive symptoms on self-report measures than healthy controls and psychometric norms (e.g., Canning et al., 1992; Kaplan, Busner, Weinhold, & Lennon, 1987; Phipps & Srivastava, in press; Tebbi et al., 1988; Worchel, 1989; Worchel et al., 1988; Worchel, Rae, Olson, & Crowley, 1992, for children with cancer; Noll, Bukowski, Davies, Koontz, & Kulkarni, 1993, for late effects among children with cancer; Kovacs, Brent, Steinberg, Paulauskas, & Reid, 1986, for children with diabetes; Mayes, Handford, Kowalski, & Schaefer, 1988, for children with hemophilia; Lemanek, Moore, Gresham, Williamson, & Kelly, 1986, for children with sickle cell disease; and Landry, Robinson, Copeland, & Garner, 1993, for children with spina bifida). For example, Phipps and Srivastava (in press) compared the scores of children who had cancer with a control group of healthy children (7 to 16 years old) on the Children's Depression Inventory (Kovacs, 1992) and found that, although the scores of the control group were fairly typical, the cancer group had mean scores "well below expected values" (p. 13). They also had lower scores on the State-Trait Anxiety Inventory for Children (STAIC; Spielberger, 1973). A series of studies of depression among adolescent cancer patients using the Beck Depression Inventory (Beck, Ward, & Mendelson, 1961; eliminating 8 of the 21 items that refer to physical symptoms) found that depression among adolescent cancer patients was no greater than might be expected among a group of physically healthy cohorts. Kaplan, Hong, and Weinhold (1984), for example, found that 78% of their subjects were not depressed (Beck scores between 0 and 9), 13% were mildly depressed (scores between 10 and 15), 7% were moderately depressed (scores between 16 and 23), and no subjects were severely depressed. Similarly, Tebbi et al. (1988) found 83% of their sample of adolescents with cancer were not depressed, and Plumb and Holland (1977) found that their sample subjects were not more depressed than physically healthy next-of-kin. Susman, Dorn, and Fletcher (1987) found that children newly diagnosed as having cancer did not score significantly different from healthy children on measures of state and trait anxiety. Such seemingly counterintuitive findings have led some investigators to question "why so few adolescent cancer patients appear depressed" and "whether their expression of depressive symptomatology is somehow masked" (Tebbi et al., 1988, p. 188; see also Kellerman, 1980; Worchel et al., 1988).

Although many studies using self-report measures of adjustment for children who have cancer or who are long-term survivors of pediatric cancer have reported adequate levels of psychosocial functioning, studies using other kinds of measures have not. For example, Koocher and O'Malley (1981), using clinical interviews and behavioral ratings by clinicians, found that 23% of their sample was moderately to severely psychologically impaired. Fritz and Williams (1988) found that although cancer survivors reported normal self-concept scores on a standardized self-report measure, more than half of them, in interviews, expressed serious concerns about the potential for relapses and about their physical appearance, and showed evidence of somatization and hypochondriasis. Kashani and Hakami (1982), using interviews, reported that 17% of their sample of children with cancer met the DSM-III (American Psychiatric Association, 1987) criteria for a major depressive episode.

Correspondence between Child and Parent Reports

The generally poor correspondence between children's self-reports and parents' reports of their children's depression and anxiety raises questions about the validity of these methods. Among a nonclinical sample of children, across age (8 to 16 years) and gender, parent–child correspondence was low when using either parents' perceptions of their children's anxiety or their predictions of how their children would self-rate their own anxiety (Revised Children's Manifest Anxiety Scale, Reynolds & Richmond, 1978; State-Trait Anxiety Inventory for Children, Spielberger, 1973). Correspondence between mothers' and fathers' ratings was moderately high (Engle, Rodrique, & Geffken, 1994). Achenbach, McConaughy, and Howell (1987) found an average parent–child correlation of .25 in their meta-analysis of the cross-informant correspondence literature. Wachtel, Rodrique, Geffken, Graham-Pole, and Turner (1994) found correlations for parent–child agreement on anxiety ratings of children awaiting invasive medical procedures ranging from .01 to .30 on measures of state and trait anxiety. Studies typically have found that parents tended to report more child problems and higher levels of problem severity than did their children (Angold et al., 1987; Kazdin, Colbus, & Rodgers, 1986).

Several investigators have begun to suspect that self-reports of children who have serious chronic illnesses, particularly cancer, are biased toward minimizing affective distress. For example, Worchel (1989) reported that children with cancer typically used denial in response to being directly questioned about their emotional state. According to Phipps and Srivastava (in press), "If self-report is accepted as a valid estimate of affective functioning in this population, then one must assume the presence of some uniquely adaptive coping behaviors in children with cancer, or alternatively, that there are aspects of the cancer experience that promote exceptional mental health in children" (p. 2).

Repressor Adaptation

Canning et al. (1992) have considered "repressor adaptation" as a way of explaining the infrequent incidence of depressive symptoms in children who have cancer and other chronic diseases. Unlike denial, repressor adaptation "is associated with self-deception, not just deception of others" (p. 1120). Based on Weinberger, Schwartz, and Davidson's (1979) work with adults, repressors are those who score below the mean in self-reported anxiety scales but exhibit high levels of defensiveness as evidenced by above-the-median scores on a social desirability scale (i.e., score low on trait anxiety and high on defensiveness or social desirability). Canning et al. (1992) sampled 31 adolescents with cancer (12 to 18 years old) and found that, overall, they scored significantly lower on depression than a physically healthy comparison group (based on the Children's Depression Inventory, Kovacs, 1992) but, according to the above criteria, a significantly higher proportion of adolescents with cancer, when compared to the control group, were identified as repressors (52% vs. 30%). Furthermore, Canning et al. found that repressor status accounted for a significant portion of the variance in depression scores beyond that explained by the illness group. This finding was replicated by Phipps and Srivastava (in press) using much larger samples of experimental and control subjects (107 pediatric cancer patients 7 to 16 years old, and a comparison group of 442 healthy children). Children with cancer scored significantly lower on measures of depression and trait anxiety and higher on measures of defensiveness. Subjects identified as repressors in both groups reported the lowest levels of depression, and the oncology group had a significantly greater proportion of repressors (45% vs. 27%). Fritz, Spirito, and Young (1994) found that children identified as repressors also scored low on a measure of expressive anger.

Consistent with findings from adults (Weinberger, 1990), adolescent repressors were thought to avoid awareness of their anxiety by deceiving themselves as well as others. They appeared well adjusted on traditional self-report measures by relying on a style of adaptation that obscured their symptoms of distress but that often began to deteriorate with increasing difficulties and medical complications that interfered with effective coping (Canning et al., 1992). For example, compared to high anxious or true low anxious individuals, repressors were found to show greater psychophysiological reactivity to stressors, despite having the lowest self-reports of anxiety (Weinberger et al., 1979).

Defensive Denial

The potential for subjects to use defensive denial in self-report kinds of measures of coping, along with the willingness of investigators to accept such self-report data at face value, has been discussed, at least in regard to adults, in terms of "the illusion of mental health." It is a particularly potent argument in regard to coping with chronic illness. Shedler, Mayman, and Manis (1993) have been able to demonstrate that defensive deniers present themselves on standardized self-report scales in an illusory manner by administering a self-report measure (e.g., the Beck Depression Inventory; Beck et al., 1961) to a sample of adult subjects who also were evaluated by clinical judges. When self-report and clinical judgment converged in indicating health, subjects were classified as being "genuinely healthy"; when self-report measures indicated health but clinical judgment indicated distress, subjects were classified as having "illusory mental health" (based on defensive denial of distress); when both data sources indicated distress, subjects were classified as "manifestly distressed." Subjects were then exposed to a series of psychological stressors in a laboratory, and changes in their heart rate and blood pressure were monitored in order to ascertain physiological reactivity to stressful situations. In several studies, they found that subjects with illusory mental health showed higher levels of physiological reactivity to stress than either genuinely healthy or manifestly distressed subjects. Consequently, they concluded that self-report kinds of coping scales assess different things in different people and that, among those classified as having illusory mental health, these scales "were not assessing mental health . . . but instead were assessing defensive denial" (Shedler et al., 1993, p. 1127).

Approach–Avoidance Styles

Another kind of coping style that has been studied and is different from repressor adaptation or defensive denial is the tendency to either approach or avoid threat-relevant information under stress (such as in vigilant-avoidant or monitor-blunter coping styles). *Theoretically,* approach–avoidance, as a style of coping, is thought to differ from denial or repression (a defensive process) in that the former is a conscious effortful act whereas the latter is thought to occur outside of conscious awareness (Lazarus & Folkman, 1984). Phipps, Fairclough, and Mulhern (1995), using the Children's Behavioral Style Scale (Miller, Sherman, Roussi, Caputo, & Krus, 1995), found a significantly greater endorsement of avoidant or blunting kinds of coping behaviors among children with cancer than among a sample of healthy controls. Children (6 to 15 years old) were given a set of hypothetical scenarios (e.g., "Imagine you are in school and the teacher tells you the principal wants to see you at recess") and were then asked to either endorse or denounce responses indicative of either monitoring (e.g., "Think about what the principal might do to you") or blunting (e.g., "Think about other things to get your mind off the principal"). Children with cancer endorsed significantly more blunting items (but not monitoring items) than did children in the control group. Also, blunting scores declined with age in the control group, but they increased with age in the group of children who had cancer. Their scores also increased with the time elapsed since their diagnosis, suggesting that blunting was a mode of coping that developed, in part, in response to adjusting to a life-threatening illness. Smith, Ackerson, Blotcky, and Berkow (1990), however, found, over time, an increase in information-seeking behaviors and a decrease in avoidance behaviors among children with cancer who were undergoing invasive procedures.

These collective findings should caution us about reports of coping and adjustment among chronically ill children that are based solely on standardized self-report or trait-based scales of depression, despite their ubiquitous use. To illustrate just how popular self-report measures have become in psychological studies, the *Social Sciences Citation Index* listed 2,000 studies from 1989 to 1993 referencing the Beck Depression Inventory (Beck et al., 1961) alone (Shedler, Mayman, & Manis, 1994). Patterson (1990), in a review of studies published in the 1980s on families and health, reported that 80% of the studies relied on data that were either self-reports or family (usually, parents') reports. Such studies raise questions regarding the validity of findings that suggest that children who are chronically ill are not depressed and do not exhibit adjustment problems. Often, they mistakenly lead investigators (e.g., Brantley et al., 1981) to conclude that children who have chronic illness, and their families, are able to easily adjust on their own to the myriad stressors of illness.

Such findings reveal the need for methodologically sound studies of the validity of self-report and parent-report measures of health-related behaviors. Consideration needs to be given to factors that incline respondents to certain demand characteristics—self-attributions having to do with social desirability factors, and tendencies to want to either please or displease caregivers who elicit responses from them. Issues of self-and-other denial reflect basic and fundamental concerns about adjustment to illness and recovery in sociocultural contexts that both reward and punish the ill and the recovered. Rather than treating these kinds of measures as providing an unbiased index of self-construal, coping, or adjustment in pediatric studies, they ought to be the focus of independent analysis and concurrent validity.

There is a growing need for devising methods other than (or ancillary to) self-report scales to assess children's adjustment to and ability to cope with medical stress. For example, studies using projective measures, such as responses to pictures (Waechter, 1971) and spontaneous drawings (Bach, 1974), reported that, compared to other chronically ill children, children who had cancer were more likely to express themes of dying, bodily mutilation, loneliness, and separation. A now classic study by Spinetta, Rigler, and Karon (1973) is notable in demonstrating the use of a projective technique to assess young children's (6 to 10 years old) adjustment to illness and hospitalization in terms of their sense of "interpersonal distance" (see Duke & Nowicki, 1972, for a discussion of this construct). Children with leukemia were matched with children with other chronic illnesses on a series of demographic variables as well as the seriousness and amount of medical intervention and the number of times hospitalized. The measure of interpersonal distance consisted of having the children arrange scaled hospital-room furniture, and dolls representing various members of the hospital staff, and family members, in a three-dimensional model of their hospital room. A doll placed in the hospital bed represented the child-patient. Simple quantification of the children's sense of "personal space" was obtained by computing the distance between the various doll placements and the doll in the bed. Children with leukemia placed the dolls significantly farther away from the patient doll than did the other chronically ill children, and, although the distance of placement increased with both groups after subsequent hospital admissions, leukemic children increased the distance significantly more than did the other chronically ill children. These findings were interpreted to reflect the sense of growing isolation felt by children as they approach issues of death and dying.

Other promising measures come from efforts to devise systematic behavioral coding systems to index aspects of social interaction that can be adapted to health care settings. Among these are the Procedure Behavior Rating Scale (PBRS; Katz, Kellerman, & Sigel, 1980) to assess procedural pain in children, and the Child–Adult Medical Procedure Interaction Scale (CAMPIS; Blount, Sturges, & Powers, 1990), as adapted by Manne, Bakeman, et al., (1992) and Manne, Bakeman, Jacobsen, and Redd (1993) in their studies of children's reactions to invasive procedures. (See Bakeman & Quera, 1995, for a fuller discussion of how behavioral interactions can be coded and sequentially analyzed.) Using codes to differentiate facial musculature as a situated index of emotional adjustment offers another promising approach (Izard, 1979, 1986). How children attribute meaning to and make sense of a series of hypothetical dilemmas or scenarios (e.g., Miller et al., in press) is still another alternative way of assessing coping and adjustment in children with chronic illness. Compared to self-report questionnaires, these projective measures, clinical interviews, and behavioral coding are labor- and time-intensive, but, at this stage of data gathering in pediatric psychology, they hold greater promise of capturing situated dimensional features of adaptive functioning that are directly relevant to children's medical problems.

Coping with Procedural Stress

Studies of children's coping with procedural stress generally are of two kinds (see Rudolph, Dennig, & Weisz, 1995, for a general review of children's coping with procedural stress). One group of studies is concerned with how children react to general pediatric procedures such as having a physical examination or anticipating hospitalization and/or elective surgery. Another group is concerned with children's experiences of acute, painful, and invasive medical procedures. Among children who have cancer, for example, bone marrow aspirations were perceived as being the most painful and distressing procedure, followed by lumbar punctures and then by venipunctures (Jay, Ozolins, Elliott, & Caldwell, 1983). Studies of children's reactions to these kinds of procedures typically segment them into anticipatory, encounter, and recovery phases. Some studies, using across-subject analyses, have found that children vary in the acute distress they exhibit across these phases (Blount et al., 1989; Jay, Elliott, Katz, & Siegel, 1987), although children typically display more distress and cry more during the encounter phase (Katz et al., 1980). Within-subject analyses have found that children's distress and styles of coping generally remain stable across the procedure, suggesting that children have characteristic ways of responding to medical procedures (Manne, Bakeman, et al., 1992). For example, children who engaged in more adaptive coping (i.e., distraction and deep breathing) during the anticipatory phase continued to cope adaptively and children who were distressed or cried during the anticipatory phase continued during the subsequent phases of the procedure.

Children's procedural distress did not consistently decrease over time in treatment (Kellerman, Zeltzer, Ellenberg, & Dash, 1983); in many cases, it increased or remained constant with the number of procedures experienced (Katz et al., 1980; Manne, Bakeman, et al., 1993). Furthermore, children's (and their families') memories of procedural distress often remained upsetting and recurrent years after having been off treatment (Kazak et al., 1992).

Active to Avoidant Strategies

Studies of how children naturally cope with more general kinds of predictable medical stressors typically have sampled children hospitalized for elective surgery (e.g., tonsillectomy, myringotomy [puncture of the tympanic membrane for removal of fluid], plastic surgery, hernia repair, circumcision, strabismus repair, and exploratory surgery). It is clear from these studies that coping is not a unidimensional variable. Different studies have looked at different facets of coping to define styles of coping and/or individual differences, such as active versus passive, internal versus external, attenders versus distractors, or problem- versus emotion-focused coping. With increasing age and cognitive maturity, children have available to them a broader array of coping strategies to control pain and anxiety, moving from relatively primitive behavioral kinds of strategies to more cognitively oriented strategies (Gedaly-Duff, 1991). For example, young children have more difficulty than older children using cognitive distraction as a coping strategy (Altshuler & Ruble, 1989; Band & Weisz, 1988).

Gender differences in how children cope with procedural stress have not been found as consistently as have age differences. Some investigators (e.g., Katz et al., 1980) have reported that girls were more likely to cry, cling, and request emotional support, and boys were more likely to engage in stalling behaviors; others (e.g., Jacobsen et al., 1990; Jay et al., 1983; Jay et al., 1987) have not found significant differences in types of distress as a function of gender.

According to Peterson (1989), in a review of studies of children's coping during hospitalization for elective surgery, the variety of natural coping styles studied, the theoretical orientations discussed, and the measures used can be captured by a singular dimension of coping ranging from "passive or avoidant to information seeking or actively approaching the medical procedure" (p. 382). Despite the diversity of methods of conceptualizing and the ways of measuring children's coping—for example, play observations (Burstein & Meichenbaum, 1979), procedural observations (Hubert, Jay, Saltoun, & Hayes, 1988), self-report questionnaires (LaMontagne, 1987), Rorschach interpretations (Knight et al., 1979), palmar sweat index (Melamed, 1982), interviews (Peterson & Toler, 1986), and urine cortisol levels (Knight et al., 1979)—findings suggested that children who scored at the active end of the scale were better able to cope with stress and were better adjusted during hospitalization and medical procedures than children at the passive end. The following kinds of reactions represented passive components of coping: "the tendency to avoid or deny stress by selecting toys that are not relevant to one's current medical encounter, by reacting to ambiguous Rorschach and interview stimuli with denial, by advocating remaining quiet and not disturbing the physician with questions, and by looking away during preparation for a medical event . . ." (Peterson, 1989, pp. 383–384). In general, avoidance strategies involved a shifting of attention away from an unpleasant experience (distraction) or attempting to block out awareness of it (escape or denial). Active strategies, on the other hand, reflected "a willingness to encounter information, as in playing with medically relevant toys, watching the preparation narration intently, or advocating question asking" (p. 384).

Given the generally positive findings associated with active styles of coping, it would seem that interventions that actively engage children to seek out information, either directly or through such indirect means as role playing about hospitalization and medical procedures, should facilitate their adjustment. However, it is not clear whether children who actively sought information benefited from the information gained or whether it reflected a personality-like trait indicative of adaptive coping. That is, because almost all of the studies on this topic were correlational, it was not possible to discern whether inducing information seeking in children will have beneficial effects; it could only be noted that children who spontaneously seek information are less distressed. Thus, it is questionable whether exposing children and sensitizing them to information about medical procedures would be helpful for those children who have characteristic defensive styles of repression and denial. Perhaps, to help these children cope, a better approach would be to distract them, which is more in keeping with their style of repressing information.

Knowledge of Coping Strategies and Coping Behaviors

Because many interventions designed to teach children more adaptive ways of coping use cognitive developmental or information-processing approaches, questions about the relationship between children's knowledge of coping strategies and their actual coping behavior are important. In practice, children often are asked in advance of a procedure how well they believe they will be able to cope with it and what was most effective in helping them cope with previous procedures (Zeltzer, 1994). Experimentally, measures of what children know about coping strategies often are derived from hypothetical scenarios. However, there is little evidence of a relationship between children's knowledge of the coping strategies available to a hypothetical child in a hypothetically stressful medical situation and their own observed behavior in medically stressful situations. Altshuler, Genevro, Ruble, and Bornstein (1995), for example, found no associations between children's awareness of either approach or avoidance coping strategies and their self-reports of approach or avoidance behavior while hospitalized for elective surgery; the coping behavior that children most often self-reported was behavioral distraction. Also, children's reports of their own coping behaviors were not related to observers' reports of their approach and avoidance behaviors. The authors concluded that there is "little evidence that children in stressful situations did what they said they knew, or (even) that they did what they said they did" (p. 73). Peterson and Toler (1986), however, found that children's reported knowledge of information seeking as a means of coping correlated with their information-seeking behavior.

Parent–Child Relations

Because parents and medical staff help children regulate their emotions and behavior, it is important to study the role that they play in children's ways of coping with medical stress. Studies have indicated that parents and staff have considerable influence on children's coping behavior prior to, during, and after stressful medical procedures. There currently is conflicting evidence about whether the presence of a parent during pediatric medical procedures helps or hinders children's coping and adjustment (Gross, Stein, Levin, Dale, & Wojnilower, 1983; Shaw & Routh, 1982). Despite children's wishes to have a parent present, several studies of children's responses to brief medical procedures, such as a venipuncture, have found that the behavior of children of varying ages was more stressful when a parent (typically, mother) was present (Gonzalez et al., 1989, for children 13 months old to 7 years, 9 months old; Gross et al., 1983, for 4- to 6-year-old and 7- to 10-year-old children; Shaw & Routh, 1982, for 18-month-old and 5-year-old children). When parents and children were separated, the children's distress usually increased immediately after but did not continue into the enactment phase of the medical procedure. There also is some evidence that, in times of stress, parents' anxiety has a disorganizing effect on their ability to help their children cope (Duffy, 1972; Jay et al., 1983; Kaplan, Smith, Grobstein, & Flischman, 1973).

The utility of these findings, however, must be interpreted in light of children's frequently expressed desire to have a parent present with them during stressful medical procedures. For example, 99% of 720 children (aged 9 to 12 years) who were interviewed expressed that the "thing that helped most" during painful medical procedures was having a parent present (Ross & Ross, 1984). Therefore, it probably is best to ask children whether they want a parent (and which parent) to be present during medical procedures and to work with parents to help them help their children to cope better. Often, parents' anxiety and distress result from their lack of knowledge about how to help their children cope, and they are responsive to efforts to inform them. However, parents whose distress is emotionally overwhelming may need to be referred for professional help to deal with issues of their children's illness and treatment.

Because it is not always clear what kinds of specific parenting behaviors enhance children's responses to specific medical stressors, nor how children's reactions affect their parents' behavior, observational studies of parent–child interactions during procedural distress are important. The effects that parents have on children's coping with medical stressors are best studied in the dyadic context of parent–child interactions and should not simply be left to independent measures or self-reports of parent and child reactions. For example, self-reported maternal state anxiety (State-Trait Anxiety Inventory; Spielberger, 1983) and self-reported hospital fears (Hospital Fears Rating Scale; Melamed & Siegel, 1975) were not related to observations of how mothers and children interacted in a medical setting (Bush, Melamed, Sheras, & Greenbaum, 1986). Dahlquist, Power, Cox, and Fernbach (1994), found that parents' reported anxiety was only significantly related to observed distress among older children (8 to 17 years old), and then only during the enactment phase (of a bone marrow aspiration). They also found that parents of younger children (2 to 7 years old) were more agitated during the procedure than parents of the older age group.

However, significant relationships were found between behavioral observations of mother–child (4 to 10 years old) interactions and children's ability to tolerate stressful medical experiences (Bush et al., 1986). Not surprisingly, less concordance was found between mother–child patterns of interacting among older children (8 years and above) compared to younger children (less than 5 years, 9 months)—a finding that is consistent with older children's greater capacity for emotional self-regulation and control (Maccoby, 1980). Maternal use of distractions (e.g., engaging the child in conversation and play unrelated to the medical situation) and low rates of ignoring, for example, were associated with lower rates of child distress and increased prosocial behaviors. Children's active exploration of the situation was more likely to occur when their mothers provided them with information and was less likely when the mothers gave only verbal reassurance. Both maternal reassurance (e.g., telling a child not to worry, that the procedure will not be so bad, expressing empathy, etc.) and overt maternal agitation (e.g., crying, pacing, verbally expressing anger, dismay, fear, etc.) were associated with maladaptive kinds of child responses (Blount et al., 1989; Bush et al., 1986; Dahlquist et al., 1994). Blount, Landolf-Fritsche, Powers, and Sturges (1991) and Blount et al. (1989) also found that adults' reassurances were not helpful and were associated with children's distress during invasive procedures. Adults' nonprocedural talk (i.e., distraction), however, was associated with children's adaptive coping. Bush and Cockrell (1987) also found that maternal agitation and reassurance were associated with increased child distress and that they were inversely correlated with maternal use of distraction.

Although it seems counterintuitive that maternal reassurance, while seeming to be empathic and oriented to children's emotional reactions, would not be helpful, parents' attempts to reassure their children may be more reflective of their attempts to deal with their own distress rather than with their children's. Such reassurances ("Everything will be all right," "It won't hurt," etc.) might have the effect of denying children's legitimate and reasonable fears.

The effects of distraction in reducing distress have been well documented (Jay, 1988; McCaul & Malott, 1984). Blount et al. (1991) found that parents of children (5 to 13 years old) who showed relatively little procedural distress, and who were coping well, distracted their children and coached them in deep breathing. In a sequential analytic study of parent–child interactions during a venipuncture procedure with children (3 to 9 years old) who were being treated for cancer, Manne, Bakeman, et al. (1992) found that the only parent behavior that reduced the children's distress was distraction. All other kinds of parental behaviors, including praise and directives to engage in coping, had a negative impact on children's coping. Of particular interest was the finding that parents' attempts to explain the medical procedure to their children during preparation were associated with more distress during enactment, and that parents then increased their use of explanations in an attempt (albeit a poor one) to soothe children who were already upset. Thus, while parents' attempts to explain medical procedures to their children may be intended to reduce children's stress and help them cope, it was not found to be a particularly effective strategy compared to distraction. Jacobsen et al. (1990) found that parents' explanations about a medical procedure to distressed children early in the preparatory phase seemed to reduce the children's distress, whereas the same explanations, when given to children who were not overly distressed, seemed to increase their distress. Parents' explanations to distressed children during the enactment phase may have exacerbated the children's distress; however, children who spontaneously sought information about the procedure and asked questions were less anxious and more cooperative than children who avoided information (Manne, Bakeman, et al., 1993; Peterson & Toler, 1986). Giving the child some sense of control over an aspect of the procedure during the preparatory phase (e.g., "Which hand do you want me to look at first?" or "Do you want a board to rest your arm on?") has been found to sometimes be an effective means of reducing stress during the enactment phase of the procedure.

Because findings of parent–child interactions during invasive medical procedures were based on correlations of naturalistic observations, they precluded a causal explanation of how parents can facilitate children's coping with procedural stress. To test a causal relationship, Gonzalez, Routh, and Armstrong (1993a) experimentally manipulated mothers' verbal reactions during intramuscular injections administered to their children (3 to 7 years old) by instructing mothers how to use either nonprocedural talk (distraction) or reassurance. They found that children in the maternal distraction condition exhibited significantly less distress than those in the reassurance or control condition.

These findings highlight the complexity of relationships between parent–child interactions in the coping process and how they are mediated by both individual and phase-specific situational variables. In general, it appears that information seeking, as a coping strategy, works best in preparing for and anticipating medical procedures, and distraction is best during the procedural enactment.

Interventions

Limitations on staff time and issues of cost-effective use of staff resources often preclude preventive interventions and, although all children could benefit from some kind of intervention during invasive medical procedures, guidelines need to be developed to identify those children who are at higher risk than others for developing pain-related distress. Gillman and Mullins (1991) reviewed how pediatric psychologists who are consulted for pain management can incorporate a multidisciplinary team approach involving the child, parents, medical staff, and psychologists (see also Drotar, 1995; McGrath, 1990; Tarnowski & Brown, 1995; Zeltzer, 1994).

The most widely used psychological intervention to prepare children to cope with the anticipation of a painful medical procedure involves providing them with information about what they can expect the procedure to be like, including information of both a sensory (i.e., what it may feel like) and a procedural (i.e., what will be done to them) kind (Zeltzer, Jay, & Fisher, 1989). The rationale for this kind of preparation is that unexpected stress is more anxiety-provoking than predictable stress, but, for some children who have an avoidant anticipatory coping style and a distractor encounter style, this kind of intervention may not be helpful and may even arouse their anxiety. Other kinds of interventions involve desensitization, positive self-statements, positive reinforcement, distraction techniques (e.g., Kelley, Jarvie, Middlebrook, McNeer, & Drabman, 1984), modeling and rehearsal (e.g., Melamed & Siegel, 1975), relaxation and deep breathing (e.g., Blount et al., 1989), guided imagery (e.g., Jay, Elliott, Ozolins, Olson, & Pruitt, 1985), hypnosis (e.g., Zeltzer & LeBaron, 1982), and stress inoculation (e.g., Turk, 1978). In addition, family- and school-based interventions have been used with some success (Kazak, 1994; Kazak & Nachman, 1991). Often, interventions consist of treatment packages employing several of the above components (e.g., filmed modeling, breathing exercises, imagery/distraction, an incentive, behavioral rehearsal, and coaching; Jay et al., 1985; Jay & Elliott, 1990). According to Varni, Blount, Waldron, and Smith (1995), although comparative studies do not generally support the superiority of cognitive–behavioral kinds of interventions over hypnosis, there is, for a variety of reasons (not least of which is the mystique associated with being hypnotized), a shift toward greater reliance on cognitive–behavioral kinds of interventions. Studies of the effectiveness of these various kinds of interventions generally have found that children gain at least partial control over their distress, although it is still not clear why some children seem to benefit more from certain kinds of interventions than other children do, and how such interventions interact with children's spontaneous modes of coping (see Ellis & Spanos, 1994; Gillman & Mullins, 1991; McGrath, 1990; Tarnowski & Brown, 1995; Zeltzer, 1994 for reviews of these studies).

Parental Interventions

The clinical implications of findings regarding parent–child interactions in coping are that children benefit from parents who are able to distract them from the immediacy of the putative threat and to coach them during the enactment phase of the medical procedure. For parents of children who have cancer, invasive procedures are among the most traumatic aspects of treatment, and parents' procedure-related distress has not been found to diminish with the length of time their children are in treatment, despite their satisfaction with their children's quality of medical care (Kazak et al., 1995; Manne et al., 1990). Surveys have found that parents of children who have cancer want to become more involved in their children's care during difficult medical procedures, and that, although mothers typically report having more involvement, fathers, perhaps because of their lesser involvement, report wanting even greater involvement than mothers (Kazak et al., 1995). Several studies have shown that both parents and children benefit (in terms of less anxiety and more adaptive coping) from preventive preparation programs that involve parents in several kinds of medically stressful situations, including surgery, venipunctures, bone marrow aspirations, lumbar punctures, treatments for burn injuries, catheterization, and dental examinations (e.g., Blount et al.,1992; Blount, Powers, Cotter, Swan, & Free, 1994; Campbell, Clark, & Kirkpatrick, 1986; Elliott & Olson, 1983; Fowler-Kerry & Lander, 1987; Jay et al., 1987; Jay & Elliott, 1990;

Melamed & Siegel, 1975; Peterson & Shigetomi, 1981; Siegel & Peterson, 1980). For example, parents and children who together viewed a preparatory film (preferably narrated by a child rather than an adult) were less anxious about a hospitalization experience than control participants (Pinto & Hollandsworth, 1984).

Parents can be trained to serve as coaches to help their children cope with medical procedures during the enactment phase (e.g., Manne et al., 1990; Manne, Bakeman, Jacobsen, Gorfinkle, & Redd, 1994; Meng & Zastowny, 1982; Peterson & Shigetomi, 1981). These training programs typically have included combinations of relaxation (e.g., deep breathing), attentional distraction, and preparation (e.g., information about what to expect). Behavioral interventions for infants undergoing aversive medical procedures have included rocking, soothing talk, stroking, nonnutritive sucking, and swaddling (Berman, Duncan, & Zeltzer, 1992). The ultimate aims of psychological interventions are to enhance children's own coping abilities and to increase their sense of self-efficacy and mastery. Children who are unable to benefit from interventions designed to divert their attention away from the aversive aspects of a medical procedure may require pharmacological interventions, including conscious sedation (Zeltzer et al., 1989).

Match–Mismatch Interventions

An increasing interest in studying individual differences in children's ways of experiencing and coping with pain may aid in promoting individualized methods of intervention. Toward this end, researchers are beginning to test whether the different ways that pain is experienced is a critical variable in selecting a particular intervention strategy. Using a "cold pressor procedure" (i.e., prolonged arm immersion in cold water) to assess children's pain tolerance, Fanurik, Zeltzer, Roberts, and Blount (1993) classified children as either "attenders," those who primarily direct their focus of attention toward the pain (i.e., cold pressor-induced sensations), or "distractors," those who divert their attention away from the pain. As expected, distractors had the highest levels of pain tolerance. Children were then taught coping strategies that were either matched or mismatched to their experiential style. Matching the intervention to the children, however, worked only for children who were distractors, not attenders. Distractors who were taught self-hypnosis (a matched intervention) increased their tolerance for pain, and those who were taught sensory monitoring techniques (a mismatched intervention) decreased their tolerance.

Smith, Ackerson, and Blotcky (1989) paired one of two single-component behavioral interventions (distraction or sensory information) with one of two coping styles (repressors or sensitizers) to create either a match (repression–distraction, sensitization–information) or a mismatch (repression–information, sensitization–distraction) between interventions and coping styles among children (6 to 18 years old) who had cancer and were undergoing invasive medical procedures. Contrary to expectation, they found that children who were taught to use an intervention that was consistent with their coping style (i.e., repressors using distraction, and sensitizers provided with information) self-reported more pain during the procedures than those taught to use an inconsistent intervention (i.e., repressors provided with information, and sensitizers using distraction). They also found that children who were provided with information about the procedures (independent of coping style) had higher anticipatory anxiety (i.e., higher heart rates). Children's choice of coping was found to be related to their time in treatment (Smith et al., 1989; Smith et al., 1990); that is, compared to sensitizers, repressors had cancer for a shorter period of time and had experienced fewer procedures, suggesting that as children had time to adapt to the conditions of having cancer and became more familiar with medical procedures, they were better able to deal with learning about procedures.

Pediatric Pain

Pharmacologic Pain Management

A controversial issue in clinical practice is the role of pharmacological versus psychological interventions to help children cope with pain. Today, an impressive array of both kinds of interventions is available for controlling pediatric pain, and they need not be seen as being mutually exclusive. Multicomponent approaches, combining pharmacological with behavioral and cognitive techniques, seem to have the most success with children. Because pain is a highly subjective experience for children as well as adults, it is difficult to assess; therefore, physicians often must rely on behavioral observations together with their knowledge of the specific pathophysiologic processes involved (Walco & Dampier, 1990). Although most studies of children's experience of pain have concerned behavioral responses to a given noxious stimulus (usually, an invasive medical procedure), children with chronic illnesses also experience pain in situations other than invasive medical procedures: postoperative pain; conditions such as sickle cell disease or juvenile rheumatoid arthritis, for which there is a biological etiology for pain; and conditions in which pain occurs unpredictably and recurrently and has an unpredictable duration and intensity (see Armstrong, Pegelow, Gonzalez, & Martinez, 1992, regarding sickle cell disease; Bush & Harkins, 1991, for a general discussion of issues of pain in children; Ilowite, Walco, & Pochaczevsky, 1992, regarding juvenile rheumatoid arthritis). Often, it is impossible to separate the experience of pain from the anxiety and fear that children associate with a medical procedure or an illness crisis. Consequently, behavioral studies are needed to assist physicians in the pharmacologic management of pain (see Zeltzer et al., 1989, for general guidelines regarding pharmacologic management of procedural pain).

Pharmacologic management of pain has become a prominant issue corroborated by studies in pediatric psychology. There is mounting evidence that painful procedures have not been managed appropriately at many pediatric oncology centers (Zeltzer et al., 1990) and that, in general, pain has been undertreated in children (Schechter, 1989; Schechter, Allen, & Hansen, 1986). For example, Beyer, DeGood, Ashley, and Russell (1983) compared the postoperative prescription and administration of analgesics following cardiac surgery and found that children received only 30% of all analgesics prescribed for them, and they received significantly fewer potent analgesics than adults.

According to Walco, Cassidy, and Schechter (1994), possible reasons for the undertreatment of pain in children include "incorrect assumptions about pain and its management, individual and social attitudes toward pain, the complexity of assessing pain in children, and inadequate research and training" (p. 541). Also, beliefs that children's nervous systems are immature and that, therefore, they do not experience the same pain intensity as do adults; that children are at greater risk for addiction and respiratory depression from narcotic analgesics; and that children cannot be relied on to communicate their pain have contributed to the undertreatment of pain in children. However, according to McGrath (1991) each of these beliefs has been refuted by empirical findings. For example, children have been found to experience pain to the same degree as adults (Eland & Anderson, 1977). Studies of factors that influence professional decisions about administering analgesic pain medication to children have become a consequential area of pediatric psychology.

Recent findings support long-standing clinical speculation that factors other than the assessment of pain influence medication decisions in pediatric practice. For example, Armstrong et al. (1992) found that, regardless of their perception of pain intensity following an initial administration of morphine to children with sickle cell disease, and independent of their beliefs and attitudes about pain, nurses (but not pediatric residents) recommended fewer narcotic analgesics for children who had been hospitalized more often for pain. Ross, Bush, and Crummette (1991) studied children who had undergone surgical procedures and found that nurses, in spite of their perception of pain intensity, recommended fewer analgesics as the elapsed time after the children returned from surgery lengthened. One explanation offered for these findings was suspicion that patients were malingering or achieving secondary gains when initial efforts to alleviate their pain were unsuccessful (Armstrong et al., 1992). Because nurses (pediatric as well as general-care nurses) believed that children felt less pain than did adults, despite an equivalent clinical assessment of pain for children and adults, they administered fewer doses to children than to adults in comparable postoperative situations (Gonzalez, Routh, & Armstrong, 1993b). Similar findings were reported for nurses in pediatric burn units (Perry & Heidrich, 1982).

The opportunity now available for children to administer their own doses of opiates through patient-controlled analgesia (PCA) delivery systems offers new ways of studying the psychological aspects of pain management, particularly in regard to comparisons between patients' feelings of helplessness about the pain experience versus their sense of self-efficacy (see Zeltzer, 1994, for a description of how PCA delivery systems operate). For example, early studies using the PCA systems have found that patient-administered analgesia resulted in lower cumulative analgesia dosages than nurse-administered analgesia (Rodgers, Webb, Stergios, & Newman, 1988) and that even adolescents titrated a balance between comfort and opiate side effects (Tyler, 1990).

Assessment of Pediatric Pain

Pediatric pain is a complex interplay of biological, cognitive-developmental, situational, and affective factors (see Zeltzer, 1994, for a discussion of how these factors interact). Pediatric psychologists often are called on to treat a child's anticipatory distress after he or she has learned that a medical procedure is painful. There is growing evidence that such distress is not only emotional but can result in adverse physiological consequences as well (Zeltzer, 1994). Once children have had one or more painful experiences with invasive medical procedures, their memory of the experience contributes to the development of anxiety reactions in anticipation of future procedures, and they, in turn, contribute to the overall aversiveness of the pain experience (Zeltzer et al., 1989). Other kinds of pain in children are related to disease symptomatologies, and children's ability to adequately express the extent of their pain is crucial to the management of their treatment. In some cases, such as with children who have sickle cell disease, the children's expression of pain is the only factor in decisions regarding the need for and length of hospitalization. Thus, helping children to express their pain experience in a reliable and standard way is important for pediatricians. It also is important in giving children some sense of control and empowerment of their illness and related medical decisions.

Assessing pain in children is a challenging task because methodological and developmental issues complicate the procedure. Assessing the extent and intensity of children's pain involves both asking them and observing their behavior, because pain symptoms are compounded by individual, situational, and contextual differences in children's verbal and nonverbal expressions of pain (LeBaron & Zeltzer, 1984). Therefore, children's overt pain responses do not always provide an adequate measure of their pain. For example, a quiet and withdrawn child might be afraid to express his or her pain, for a variety of reasons, and an irritable or disruptive child may resort to acting-out behaviors as a way of either coping with severe pain or simply expressing exacerbated fear or anger. Older children and adolescents tend to exhibit more controlled expressions of pain (e.g., flinching and muscle tension) than do younger children, so that assessments based on gross observations might erroneously assume that adolescents have less pain than younger children (Zeltzer, 1994).

Methods of assessing children's pain can be psychological or physiological (McGrath, 1990), although physiological methods are infrequent (Tarnowski & Brown, 1995) compared with self-reports and observer ratings. Despite a common practice of having adults judge the pain status of children, pain is such a subjective experience that "self-report should be relied upon . . . for assessing pain" (Manne, Jacobsen, & Redd, 1992; p. 45). However, there are methodological problems regarding children's self-reports of pain assessment (see Dahlquist, 1990, for a review of such studies). According to some, young children lack the cognitive and linguistic abilities to self-evaluate and adequately respond to commonly used measurement techniques (Spirito & Stark, 1987; Venham & Gaulin-Kremer, 1979). The use of Likert-type pain-rating scales for assessing children's perception of pain has been found to present particular problems of concurrent validity and reliability for young children (see Andraski, Burke, Attanasio, & Rosenblum, 1985, regarding headaches; Hilgard & LeBaron, 1982, regarding bone marrow aspirations). Therefore, the use of visual analogue scales (VAS; e.g., a range from happy to sad faces) is probably preferable. Byer and Wells (1989) found that children younger than 7 years provided more reliable ratings with a vertical rather than a horizontal visual analogue scale. Although, for the most part, VAS and numerical scales are recommended, even these kinds of scales are said by some to be useful only for children older than 7 years (McGrath, Cunningham, Goodman, & Unruh, 1986). Zeltzer et al. (1988), however, found that supplementing the VAS with brief vignettes describing a child experiencing the target stressor assisted children as young as 5 years to better understand the pain-related health concepts being assessed. Pain scales also have been suspect because, among older children, they often have been found to correlate highly with age and there is no reason to expect that the nociceptive experience of pain should vary by age (Jay, 1988).

There is an important caveat concerning the use of visual analogue scales with all children, even adolescents. Asking children and adolescents simply to rate their pain from 1 to 10 (or to select a representative face from among several faces pictured as ranging from sad to happy) distorts the intended purpose of the scale. Instead, they need to be carefully and reliably taught how to anchor their ratings to situated instances of their perceived pain so that a reliable standard of relativity is established for each respondent and within respondents, when one occurrence is compared with another.

Carpenter (1990) found predictive and convergent validity among 4- to 8-year-old children (independent of age) for a visual analogue-type self-report technique based on five horizontal lines varying in their waiver. Five lines (a flat line followed by four progressively wavier lines) depicted the amplitude of pain experienced during an invasive medical procedure. Also, body outline figures have been used to help children experiencing musculoskeletal pain (e.g., with juvenile rheumatoid arthritis) to report the location and intensity of their pain (Savedra & Tesler, 1989).

When data from different raters (e.g., self, parents, nurses, and physicians) are inconsistent, questions arise whether ratings from certain sources are biased and inaccurate compared with other sources. An alternative approach is to consider that each informant is responsive to and targets a different aspect of children's pain, and, consequently, it would be useful to systematically determine the different variables that influence each informant's ratings. Manne, Jacobsen, and Redd (1992) obtained four different measures of pain (behavioral codes, self-report, parent rating, and nurse rating) for children 3 to 10 years old undergoing venipuncture during cancer therapy. They found that different demographic and medical variables were associated with each method of pain assessment. For example, younger children self-reported more pain, although it was not clear what aspects of the pain experience their self-reports were capturing. More difficult venous access was related to greater ratings of pain made by nurses and parents but not by children, suggesting that children's self-reports were not directly proportional to the intensity of the noxious stimulus; instead, they may have reflected their fear and distress associated with the situation rather than the experienced pain per se. Overt distress accounted for significant variance in nurses' ratings but not in parents' ratings, which suggested that parents were strongly influenced by their expectations of how much pain their children would experience and their own anxiety about the procedure. Even among adult patients, correlations between self-reports and nurses' ratings were not high (e.g.,$r = .38$ according to Teske, Dart, & Cleeland, 1983). On the other hand, several studies found high correlations among children's, parents', and physicians' ratings using a visual analogue scale (Ilowite et al., 1992; Ross, Lavigne, Hayford, Dyer, & Pachman, 1989; Vandvik & Eckblad, 1990).

Children's ability to self-report pain also can be dependent on the nature of the pain they are asked to reference. For example, chronic musculoskeletal pain in juvenile rheumatoid arthritis is notably different from the kind of pain experienced in an invasive medical procedure such as a venipuncture. Overall, studies have found that disease activity was not highly correlated with reported levels of pain among children with juvenile rheumatoid arthritis and that psychological variables (e.g., children's and mothers' distress) had a substantial influence on children's perceived pain (Kvien, Hoyeraal, & Sandstad, 1982; Ross et al., 1993).

LATE EFFECTS

Of all chronic childhood diseases, cancer is among the most life-threatening and individually uncertain, and it involves some of the most invasive kinds of treatments. Because of dramatically improved prognoses in the past two decades, pediatric psychologists increasingly have been addressing psychosocial issues of cancer survival and its late effects. In 1960, for example, only 1% of acute leukemia patients (the most common kind of pediatric cancer) survived to 5 years postdiagnosis. Today, the overall cure rate for leukemia (5-year survival) is 70% (60% for all pediatric cancers), and this rate continues to improve. Of all children who reach age 20 today, 1 in 1,000 is a survivor of pediatric cancer (see Granowetter, 1994, for a concise medical overview of pediatric oncology, prepared for psychologists). Late effects are defined as occurring after the successful completion of medical therapy and usually 2 or more years from the time of diagnosis. Studies of late effects generally are concerned with (a) the sequelae of treatments used to cure pediatric cancer and (b) the quality of life (e.g., emotional, social, and vocational adjustment) among survivors of pediatric cancer.

Treatment-related sequelae include the effects of cranial irradiation and/or chemotherapy on intellectual development and academic achievement, growth, fertility, and the potential for other medical problems, not the least of which is the potential of a second malignancy; survivors of pediatric cancers are at 10 to 20 times greater risk for a second malignancy compared with the risk for a first malignancy in the general population (Meadows, 1991). The potential for infertility among survivors of pediatric cancers is a particularly profound issue, and many survivors' parents have reported that they have not discussed this issue with their children. In part, the reluctance to talk about infertility reflects the uncertainty and discomfort of discussing the cancer experience in general as well as discomfort with this particular topic (Kazak, 1994). Also, there is a need for parents and members of the treatment teams to understand better how to talk with adolescent males, when appropriate, about opportunities and procedures for sperm banking. Disease-specific treatment effects for different kinds of pediatric malignancies can result in growth deficiencies, problems with sexual maturation, hypothyroidism, scoliosis (i.e., spinal curvature), dental and facial abnormalities, cardiac disease, pulmonary problems, liver damage, urinary tract problems, and cataracts (Meadows & Silber, 1985). The enduring effects of surgery include limb amputation and the sequelae of limb-sparing surgery. For new treatment regimens that are being introduced, the long-term sequelae are not yet known.

Neuropsychological Sequelae

Although treatment advances, such as intrathecal chemotherapy and preventive cranial irradiation for leukemia, indisputably are responsible for increasing survival rates, they also have contributed to cognitive impairments in many survivors of pediatric cancer, particularly in areas associated with short-term memory, attention and concentration, psychomotor speed and motor skills, and performance (i.e., nonverbal) deficits (Mulhern, Fairclough, & Ochs, 1991). These effects, in turn, have been associated with both subtle and dramatic problems in academic achievement and the incidence of various types of learning disabilities (Brown et al., 1992; Sawyer, Toogood, Rice, Haskell, & Baghurst, 1989).

Most findings of neuropsychological deficits associated with treatment sequelae involved children who had been treated for acute lymphoblastic leukemia. The most commonly used psychological index of neurotoxicity has been the IQ score or the pattern of IQ subtest scores. Studies have found significantly lower IQ scores among irradiated compared with nonirradiated survivors (Copeland et al., 1985: 91.2 vs. 105.6; Moss, Nannis, & Poplack, 1981: 98.6 vs. 102.8; Rowland, Glidewell, & Sibley, 1984: 91.6 vs. 106.2; Schlieper, Esseltine, & Tarshis, 1989: 95.1 vs. 102.1). Several studies have found, for reasons not yet understood, that girls were more likely than boys to suffer deleterious effects. The effects, as they relate to children's age at the time they received CNS treatments, remain equivocal; some studies, but not others, have found increased risk of lowered IQ among children treated at younger ages (Fletcher & Copeland, 1988). Some recent longitudinal studies have found variable latency periods before neurological deficits associated with CNS prophylaxis became manifest and chronic, if not progressive (Rubenstein, Varni, & Katz, 1990). However, longitudinal findings of neuropsychological effects can often be confounded by using different IQ measures as children become older (e.g., WPPSI, WISC-R, and WAIS-R) or the use of subsequent editions of the same IQ measures. Mulhern et al. (1991) illustrated the effects of such a confound by either making or not making statistical adjustments for changes in versions of IQ tests. They found that, without adjustments, they replicated the magnitude of decline found by Rubenstein, Varni, and Katz (1990), but the decline in IQ was not significant when they made the statistical adjustments. Another potential confound in this area of research concerns the failure to control across studies for elapsed time between the initiation of CNS treatment and the follow-up assessment.

Another area of neuropsychological studies concerns factors that place children at risk following treatment for pediatric brain tumors; this population comprises 20% of all pediatric cancer patients (Carpentieri & Mulhern, 1993; Carpentieri, Mulhern, Douglas, Hanna, & Fairclough, 1993). Research is still needed to tease out the specific pattern of associations among (a) the effects of medication and irradiation dosage and chronicity compared to, or in addition to, other modes of treatment; (b) patients' age at treatment; (c) patients' age at manifestation of late effects; (d) emotional impact on achievement factors; (e) school absences during treatment; (f) the sensitivity of parents and school personnel to the potential for difficulties, and their willingness to intervene; and (g) the site of the tumor itself (see Mulhern, 1994; Mulhern & Ochs, 1994; Ris & Noll, 1994, for comprehensive reviews of the neuropsychological impact of pediatric cancer). There is a conspicuous lack of studies in response to a growing need for neuropsychological interventions to test whether neuropsychological deficits incurred by treatment can be remediated (Mulhern, 1994). Butler and Namerow (1988) discuss a controversial type of cognitive rehabilitation program intended to improve attentional skills and cognitive abilities among children who have been treated for cancer; others (e.g., Carney & Gerring, 1990) have discussed cognitive remediation for children with traumatic brain injuries.

Sickle Cell Disease and HIV Infection

Studies also have been done on the neuropsychologic functioning of children with sickle cell disease (Fowler, Johnson, & Atkinson, 1985; Fowler et al., 1988) and HIV-infected children (e.g., Whitt et al., 1993, regarding seropositive children who have hemophilia; Epstein et al., 1986; Brouwers, Belman, & Epstein, 1991, regarding perinatally infected children).

An increasing number of recent studies have found that children with sickle cell disease, compared with siblings or healthy subjects, are at risk for developing global and/or specific neuropsychological impairments involving visual-motor integration, attention and concentration, arithmetic, memory, and reading (Brown, Buchanan, et al., 1993; Fowler et al., 1988; Swift et al., 1989; Wasserman, Wilimas, Fairclough, Mulhern, & Wang, 1991; see Brown, Armstrong, & Eckman, 1993, for a review of findings). For example, despite no differences in their IQ scores, children with sickle cell disease scored significantly lower than nondisease siblings on a reading decoding achievement test and a sustained-attention task associated with frontal-lobe functioning (Brown, Armstrong, & Eckman, 1993; see also Wasserman et al., 1991). Because substantial development of the frontal lobe occurs between 6 and 8 years of age (Becker, Isaac, & Hynd, 1987), early educational interventions may diminish the extent of neurological deficits for children with sickle cell disease. Furthermore, Brown, Armstrong, and Eckman (1993) found that the hemoglobin levels were predictive of intellectual functioning, fine-motor skills, and overall academic achievement. Because hemoglobin is correlated with the amount of oxygen delivery to the brain, these findings suggest that therapy aimed at increasing hemoglobin levels (e.g., transfusion or bone marrow transplantation, a procedure already in place in many institutions for selected high-risk patients; see Kodish et al., 1991) may prevent further cognitive impairment.

Children who experienced sickle cell-related strokes had significantly lower IQ scores than matched nonstroke children with sickle cell disease (Harriman, Griffith,

Hurtig, & Keehn, 1991). A recent study of 194 children with sickle cell disease found that children with a clinical history of strokes (cerebrovascular accidents, CVA) were at greatest risk for neuropsychological abnormalities, including impairment in global cognitive functions, specific areas of language and verbal abilities, visual-motor and visual-spatial processing and performance, sequential memory, and academic achievement (Armstrong et al., 1996). Children who showed evidence on MRI of "silent cerebral infarcts" (i.e., strokes without apparent clinical evidence) generally had better performance than children with CVA, but had significantly impaired performance on measures of arithmetic, vocabulary, and visual-motor speed and coordination compared to children with no MRI abnormality (Armstrong et al., 1996). These findings further document the need for a battery of neuropsychological screening tests for children with sickle cell disease. Early detection of cognitive impairments that can adversely affect school performance will allow focused educational plans to be instituted early for these children.

Studies of the cognitive development of children with perinatally acquired HIV infection are difficult because these children tend to come from families that have fewer economic resources, minimal education, a single parent, and more than one family member infected (Crocker, Cohen, & Kastner, 1992). Many of these children are in foster care or live with relatives or unrelated caretakers (Hopkins, 1989). Thus, it is difficult to separate socioeconomic status and maternal factors from clinical status. Future studies of cognitive effects, therefore, will have to include measures of cerebral atrophy or other physiological evidence of a cerebral insult (Armstrong, Seidel, & Swales, 1993). Findings of cognitive impairment have included decreased intellectual functioning, specific learning problems, mental retardation at multiple levels, visual-spatial and visual-motor deficits, decreased alertness, short-term memory deficits, and expressive and receptive language delays. Areas of the brain commonly affected by HIV often have been linked to functional deficits associated with other diseases, such as those found in children treated with cranial radiation for leukemia. Much less is known about the extent of cognitive impairment associated with asymptomatic HIV infection in children (see Armstrong, Seidel, & Swales, 1993, for a review of findings of neuropsychological effects of pediatric HIV infection).

Psychosocial Sequelae

The range of psychosocial sequelae occasioned by having survived pediatric cancer has yet to receive adequate study. There is a need to define a normative range of the patterns of emergence that survivors experience as they endeavor to integrate the history of their illness into their present lives (Kazak, 1994; Patenaude, 1995b). A now classic study of the psychosocial impact of disease-related sequelae is Koocher and O'Malley's (1981) study of 177 cancer survivors (mean age = 18.04 years with a mean of 12.44 years since initial diagnosis). They found "a high rate of adjustment problems with 59% showing at least mild psychiatric symptomology" (p. 608) and 23%, moderate to severe symptomatology. "What appeared most striking in these interviews [with cancer survivors] was the universal use of denial as a coping mechanism for such an overwhelming bodily insult" (p. 615). For some, the use of denial was relatively ego syntonic and helped them adjust to the conditions of chronic survivorship; for others, it contributed to their adjustment problems.

Other studies comparing the adjustment of survivors of pediatric cancer with survivors of other chronic but not life-threatening illnesses, or with healthy controls, have found a significantly higher incidence of emotional stress and adjustment problems among those who had cancer (Schuler et al., 1981; Spinetta & Maloney, 1975; Zeltzer et al., 1995). Other studies have not found such effects (e.g., Fritz, Williams, & Amylon, 1988; Kazak & Meadows, 1989; Spirito et al., 1990). Survivors who were younger at diagnosis (Zeltzer et al., 1995) and who had a relapse (Fritz & Williams, 1988) had a higher range of emotional sequelae (including anxiety and depression).

Many survivors of pediatric cancer must learn to cope with physical and/or cognitive late effects long after they have been pronounced "cured" and are symptom-free. Potential effects include subsequent short stature; weight gain; scoliosis; subtle, or sometimes dramatic, body disfigurements; cardiac problems due to anthracycline toxicity; Sjogren's syndrome, causing blocked tear ducts, following bone marrow transplantation; and premature menopause in women who had bone marrow transplantation or intensive chemotherapy or radiation. Often, it is distressing for those who survive leukemias or brain tumors (and their families) to recall a time when they were able to achieve and accomplish more. For some parents, the sense of elation that came with knowing that their child had been cured of cancer is displaced by a deep and enduring sense of disappointment because they never got back the same child that they had brought to treatment.

Several studies have found that survivors of pediatric cancer were less likely to marry, or married at a later age (Gogan, Koocher, Fine, Foster, & O'Malley, 1979; Green, Zevon, & Hall, 1991; Hays et al., 1992). Other studies have found that a significant number of survivors of pediatric cancer were at risk for interpersonal problems; for example, survivors were less sociably competent than their peers (Olson, Boyle, & White, 1987; Spirito et al., 1990) or they were seen by their peers as being left out, shy, socially isolated, and withdrawn (Noll, Bukowski, Rogosch, LeRoy, & Kulkarni, 1990). Many adolescents who survived cancer were found to be avoidant, guarded, or cautious in sexual relationships and most were uncomfortable talking about the experience of having had cancer. The issue of infertility was particularly difficult for survivors to acknowledge (Fritz & Williams, 1988), and half of them claimed that they did not even know whether they were infertile (Wasserman, Thompson, Wilimas, & Fairclough, 1987).

All survivors are anxious, to varying extents, about the risk of cancer recurring, the potential risk that their children will acquire cancer, or other risks to their children because of their having been treated for cancer. As we are beginning to understand the genetic predispositions to cancer, a small but significant number of survivors also will have cause to worry about the cancer risk to their children because of predisposing mutations, and will have to consider whether they want to have predisposition genetic testing for themselves and/or their children (Patenaude, 1995a; a subsequent section of this chapter discusses genetic testing of children).

Other studies have found that survivors of pediatric cancer face psychosocial barriers to employment and to medical, disability, and life insurance (Baker et al., 1993; Bloom, Knorr, & Evans, 1985; Cairns, Clark, Black, & Lansky, 1979; Mellette & Franco, 1987; Mostow, Byrne, Connelly, & Mulvihill, 1991). For example, Koocher and O'Malley (1981) found that 40% of pediatric cancer survivors 18 years old and older reported that they had experienced some discrimination in employment and insurance coverage because of their history of cancer.

Several investigators (Nir, 1985; Pot-Mees, 1989) have interpreted surviving pediatric cancer as a form of posttraumatic stress that is consistent with the general symptoms of that disorder: (a) persistent reexperiencing of the traumatic events, (b) persistent avoidance of circumstances that are reminders of the traumatic events, and (c) increased arousal and hypervigilance (DSM-IV; American Psychiatric Association, 1994). Based on self-report measures of survivors 7 to 19 years old who were off treatment for at least 2 years, and their parents, Stuber, Christakis, Houskamp, and Kazak (1996) found that 12.5% of the survivors, 39.7% of their mothers, and 33.3% of their fathers reported symptoms that were consistent with a *severe* level of posttraumatic stress, including "feeling afraid or upset when they think about cancer . . . ; feeling 'alone inside' . . . re-experiencing of disturbing scenes . . . intrusive thoughts of cancer . . ." (p. 257). The occurrence of these symptoms was independent of the length of time since treatment, supporting the chronicity of late effects found by others. The dramatically higher rate of prevalence among parents, compared with their surviving children, confirms the familial effects of having and surviving pediatric cancer.

Although such findings suggest a need for long-term psychosocial interventions for survivors of pediatric malignancies, such interventions need to acknowledge individual response styles and be responsive to individual needs and variability in the experience of having had cancer. For example, even survivors who seem well adjusted rely on different coping styles. "Some well-adjusted survivors had embraced their cancer and had become experts and advocates; others had encapsulated the illness and acknowledged it as little as possible. . . . A concrete, nonphilosophical approach served some survivors well, while others ascribed a larger purpose or meaning to the illness. Maximal use of hospital resources was adaptive for some; avoidance of all but the most essential services was the preference for others" (Fritz et al., 1988, p. 560). Fritz et al. also found that illness-related variables surprisingly were *not* predictive of psychosocial adjustment for survivors. For example, "The length, difficulty, error, or uncertainty in the diagnostic process; the child's prognosis; the severity of the treatment protocol; and the complications encountered during the active stages of the illness were not significant determinants of psychosocial outcome" (p. 560). Peer support and opportunities for open communication, however, did predict more positive outcomes.

Bone Marrow Transplantation

In the past decade, the use of bone marrow transplantation (BMT) has become standard therapy for some of the most high-risk leukemias and the preferred option after leukemic relapse (Sullivan, 1989). A variety of genetic and/or metabolic diseases, for example thalassemia, are also treated with BMT. The psychosocial effects of BMT are notable not only because of the particularly aggressive and invasive nature of its regimen, but also because of the need for patients to be hospitalized in germ-free isolation, often in a laminar air-flow room, for a period of from 1 to 3 months. The rapid development and utilization of BMT have left a lag between medical advances and the psychological and neuropsychological impact and sequelae of the procedure. The multiple and intense psychological stressors associated with BMT are just beginning to be understood (see Phipps, 1994, for a comprehensive review of this area).

Late Effects for Parents

From family systems theory, we would expect that the psychosocial sequelae of children who survived cancer also would be evident among the parents (and siblings) of these children. After treatment ends, most parents, like their children, are anxious about the uncertainty of the recurrence of cancer in their children (Peck, 1979). Other lasting concerns about their children, as reported by parents, are: school performance, social relations, employment opportunities, and marriage prospects (Greenberg & Meadows, 1991; Koocher & O'Malley, 1981). Several studies comparing parents of cancer survivors with parents of healthy children found no differences in levels of reported parental distress or anxiety (Greenberg et al., 1989; Kazak & Meadows, 1989; Nixon Speechley & Noh, 1992). However, a recent study of 133 parents of 70 children who had survived and had been off treatment for cancer for periods ranging from 6 months to 7 years, 9 months, found significant psychosocial effects among parents of survivors (Van Dongen-Melman et al., 1995). The study reported that "most parents (mothers and fathers) of childhood cancer survivors continue to be uncertain about the well-being of their children and report lonely feelings but at the same time these concerns are not accompanied by high levels of distress as measured by anxiety, depression, disease-related fear, sleep disturbances, or psychological and physical distress" (p. 852). These concerns persisted over time and were independent of the lapse of time since treatment. Some factors associated with increased risk for late effects among parents were low socioeconomic status, having no stated religious affiliation, and having another member of the family with chronic disease besides the child who survived cancer. Surprisingly, variables such as the child's prognosis, relapse, length of time in treatment, intensity of treatment, or irradiation were not related to the occurrence of late effects among parents, although parents of children with medical late effects such as organ damage, sterility, and learning problems reported a greater sense of loss of control and negative feelings. Van Dongen-Melman et al. concluded that uncertainty about the survival status of their children and their children's psychosocial functioning were the "main problems for parents of cancer survivors" (p. 584). This suggests that (a) parents need continuing medical information long after their child's treatment has ended, (b) given the lingering uncertainties about late effects, they might need more information than what is available, and (c) their quest for information marks their struggle to adjust to the loss of the illusion of normalcy in their family—an after effect of having had a child who survived the trauma of cancer.

Kupst et al. (1995) studied maternal coping with pediatric leukemia 10 years after treatment and found—contrary to Van Dongen-Melman et al. (1995)—that the level of mothers' coping improved significantly from diagnosis to 6 years posttreatment and then declined between 6 and 10 years posttreatment. Kupst et al. did not account for this posttreatment decline after 6 years, but they found that a significant predictor of mothers' adjustment after treatment was their child's level of coping and adjustment. Maternal coping also was positively associated with SES.

More research is clearly warranted before we can reach general conclusions regarding the psychosocial status of survivors of pediatric cancer (and their families); until then, it remains a controversial area. One interpretation is that most survivors do not have significant psychological problems, but there is a "troubling subset" of survivors for whom the problems are significant (Kazak, 1994). Estimates of this subset range from 25% to 33% (Kupst et al., 1995). Another interpretation is that "long-term survivors of childhood cancer have a much higher incidence of both internalizing (anxiety, worries, and withdrawal) and externalizing (aggressiveness and poor impulse control) behavior problems than healthy children. . . . In addition, they report many more somatic complaints" (Armstrong, 1992, pp. 206–207). Further research is needed to determine the risk and resistance factors that predispose children and parents to developing problems in coping and adaptation. Research in this area will have to consider (a) the choice of relevant comparison groups (e.g., sibling controls); (b) the use of more discrete age and disease categories than have so far been considered; (c) variations in lag time used to operationally define survival, (d) the use and availability of family and sociocultural support systems; and (e) measures used to assess adjustment that are considerably more differentiated along a number of dimensions specific to the illness experience.

The kind of measures that investigators choose to assess adjustment is at the heart of much of the controversy about how to interpret findings on late effects. For example, in studies where adjustment is measured according to employment, marital status, school attendance, or engagement in risky activities, it is important to recognize that such measures are surrogate markers for other, more immediate psychological factors that affect survivors' adjustment and that need to be more directly assessed. Also, reliance solely on self-report measures of coping and adjustment in regard to late effects often can mask problems because survivors and their families will want to present themselves to medical staff (as well as to themselves) as capable and well functioning—an element of their sense of gratitude for having been cured. As previously noted, the use of self-report measures designed to differentiate between psychopathology and normality can mask the presence of late effects because these measures are insensitive to identifying essential and specific aspects of the illness experience and its effects (Van Dongen-Melman et al., 1995). Studies of late effects also must consider sampling confounds due to mortality rates as a function of lapsed time from diagnosis to posttreatment effects. For example, in the 10-year follow-up study reported by Kupst et al. (1995), 35 of 64 of the original sample were alive after 10 years. Nevertheless, it was not reported how the late survivors and their families differed on earlier adjustment and coping measures from those who had died.

Findings regarding late effects and quality of life among survivors of pediatric cancer have important implications for those who survive other kinds of chronic medical conditions, and further research is needed in these other areas. For example, there is a growing need for findings of late effects among children who have survived organ transplants.

DYING CHILDREN AND THEIR FAMILIES

Care of Dying Children

Issues about how to care for terminally ill children (and their families) are increasingly important concerns for pediatric psychologists. Often, in their positions in university teaching hospitals, pediatric psychologists are expected to advise medical residents on how and when to inform pediatric patients and their families about the loss of hope of recovery and the process of dying, and how to distinguish between adequate and inadequate modes of coping for the dying patient and anticipatory grief and mourning for the family. The process of dying refers to the terminal or end stage of an illness, when it is beyond cure and there is progressive clinical deterioration. Uncertainty about how to delineate a terminal phase and the lack of specific criteria to establish when a child is dying or is terminally ill complicate research in this area.

To create an alternative to the once common practice of admitting terminally ill children to hospitals to die, studies of home (Hutter, Farrell, & Meltzer, 1991) and pediatric hospice (Corr & Corr, 1983) care programs are furthering consideration of these venues for children who have terminal conditions. However, there still is very little research concerning the death of children and how the dying process is experienced by children, parents, siblings, and health professionals (see Armstrong-Dailey & Goltzer, 1993; Krulik, Holaday, & Martinson, 1987; Martinson & Papadatou, 1994, for reviews of studies of dying children and the bereaved). Early studies in this area were predominantly anecdotal and case-oriented. Researchers were primarily concerned with the clinical implications of children's awareness of the seriousness of their medical condition and their impending death (e.g., Kubler-Ross, 1983). Most of the early studies were hampered by investigators' reluctance to gather information directly from children who were dying; instead, they relied on reports from parents and staff. Also, early studies lacked control or comparison groups (e.g., Morrissey, 1963; Natterson & Knudson, 1960).

Another area of inquiry concerned ways of communicating with dying children, their parents, and health professionals (Karon & Vernick, 1968; Solnit & Green, 1963). Many early studies concluded that fatally ill children under 10 years of age did not understand the implication of their pending death and, consistent with the now-obsolete practice of not informing children of their diagnosis of cancer, they could be "protected" by not being told about their grave condition (see Speece & Brent, 1984, for a comprehensive review of studies of children's understanding of death). Waechter (1987), using projective measures that were more sensitive to the limitations young children have in verbally expressing ambiguous concerns about death and dying—concerns that they often were admonished not to think about or articulate—found that children with cancer were overly concerned about their future, and themes about death and dying were a part of their projective stories. Early studies by Waechter (1971) and Spinetta (1974; see also Spinetta, Rigler, & Karon, 1974) found that fatally ill children had a much higher anxiety level in general and had greater concern about their bodily integrity, hospital procedures, and medical staff, regardless of whether they spoke openly about death and dying, or whether their lives were immediately threatened. These findings were particularly striking because adults caring for these children tended not to speak to them about death and maintained that the children were not aware of the fatal nature of their illness. Children's feelings about their terminal illness often were intensified when they learned about the death of another patient with whom they had been close (Bluebond-Langner, 1978).

According to Martinson and Papadatou (1994), these studies were "a major impetus for advocating a more open approach with children, for encouraging them to express their concerns, and for having their questions answered honestly" (p. 200). Other studies subsequently have confirmed these findings about feeling anxious, isolated, and frightened, along with the consequent clinical implications of being more direct and open when communicating with dying children and their families (Bearison, 1991a; Bluebond-Langner, 1978; Koocher, 1974; Reilly, Hasazi, & Bond, 1983; Spinetta et al., 1974; Spinetta & Deasy-Spinetta, 1981).

Because cultural attitudes and religious beliefs influence the ways that children understand death and dying (McIntire, Angle, & Struempler, 1972; Spinetta, 1984), they need to be acknowledged when creating conditions that are appropriate for talking to children about dying. For some children who have a fatal illness, and perhaps for all of them at certain times, it is preferable to "talk" about death and dying nonverbally, using dramatic and symbolic play, art, music, puppetry, and dance (Schmitt & Guzzino, 1985). When talking about death with children who are dying, it is best to be specific and literal and to avoid euphemistic expressions about death. The goal of communicating with children who are dying is to meet their particular needs at times that are relevant for them, rather than to educate them or ensure that they have a mature understanding of death. It is important to empower children as much as possible regarding the circumstances surrounding their death. This includes recognizing when they need to be alone as well as when they want to share their feelings with others (Adams & Deveau, 1984; Faulkner, 1993; Spinetta & Deasy-Spinetta, 1981).

Abundant evidence suggests that hospitals are ill prepared to handle the psychosocial issues of the dying. There is a need for formal palliative care training of hospital staff in order to alter the ideology of avoidance and denial that characterizes much of the care of the dying (Callahan, 1993; Hafferty & Franks, 1994). Many physicians consider a death a basic failure of medicine. They also have difficulties with countertransference issues regarding patients and their own fear of death. Pediatric psychologists can assume a central role in the training of pediatric staff to better understand their own and their patients' (and families') concerns about death and dying, and can suggest ways to provide palliative care.

Parents and Siblings of Dying Children

Studies of how parents react to their awareness of their child's impending death have questioned the nature and value of anticipatory grief on how parents are able to adjust to the death of their child. Some studies have found that anticipatory grieving can have a beneficial effect on parents' postdeath experience (e.g., Friedman, Chodoff, Mason, & Hamburg, 1963; Futterman, Hoffman, & Sabshin, 1972). Others have found anticipatory grieving unrelated to bereavement outcomes (e.g., Spinetta, Swarner, & Sheposh, 1981). Factors that influenced the effect included the duration and circumstances of anticipatory grieving, and how various forms of grieving were expressed and experienced within the family and cultural contexts during the terminal period. The intensity of their grief reactions at the time of their child's death did not necessarily index their need for support, although parents who had had the opportunity to grieve during the terminal period usually exhibited less intense reactions compared with parents whose child died suddenly (Miles, 1985).

Another area of study concerns patterns of adjustment among families grieving the loss of a child due to terminal illness. Researchers have found that there is no optimal pattern or duration associated with long-term adjustment (McClowry, Davies, May, Kulenkamp, & Martinson, 1987; Miles, 1985; Moore, Gilliss, & Martinson, 1988; Spinetta et al., 1981). Factors associated with families' adaptive coping were structured on their having had good communication with their children during the course of the illness (Spinetta et al., 1981). Studies have found that the duration of the illness and the severity of physical symptoms were not related to parents' postdeath adjustment (Martinson, Davies, & McClowry, 1987; Moore et al., 1988).

Several studies of surviving children's reactions and their adjustment to the loss of a sibling due to illness have indicated that the loss is a major stressor for them and often places them at risk for serious adjustment problems (Balk, 1983; Binger et al., 1969; Davies, 1990; Hogan & Greenfield, 1991; Lansky, Cairns, Hussanein, Wehr, & Lowman, 1978). However, not enough is understood about the specific factors that place siblings at risk and the factors that, in time, reduce their risk.

KNOWLEDGE AND ATTITUDES ABOUT ILLNESS

Developmental psychology's notable history in the study of cognitive functions is distinguished by theoretical advances and experimental ingenuity. In the past decade, several shifts in the ways in which many developmental psychologists (e.g., Bearison, 1991b; Bearison & Zimiles, 1986; Bruner, 1990; Cole, 1988; Damon, 1991; Rogoff, 1990; Selman, 1981; Wertsch, 1991) conceptualized the domain of children's cognitive development have brought this field of inquiry in line with key issues that are pertinent to pediatric psychology. Especially notable were: a shift from universal structural accounts to greater appreciation for the situational specificity of cognition and the sociohistorical and cultural contexts of knowing; a shift from formal reflective kinds of knowing to practical knowledge and its deployment in everyday situations; and greater awareness of narrative as well as paradigmatic genres of knowing and representing what is known. Today, there is greater appreciation that children's experiences in particular domains often result in striking developmental changes, even when only minor changes might occur in basic cognitive processes.

Thus, children's concepts, beliefs, and memories about illness are relevant to both basic and applied concerns in developmental psychology; they inform us about basic cognitive developmental processes, and they help us to understand practical issues regarding children's adjustment to chronic medical problems. Improved understanding about how children conceptualize health and illness also contributes to more effective means of promoting the prevention and treatment of pediatric illnesses, improving patient care and self-management, and communicating with children about the biologic nature of their medical problems and symptoms as well as their comprehension, beliefs, expectations, and assumptions about having a chronic illness (Potter & Roberts, 1984). A better understanding of how children conceptualize illness enhances efforts to involve children in their own health and treatment decisions and to consider their informed consent for treatment. The need for improving how we discuss illness issues with children and their families is illustrated by findings that, for example, half of the parents of children who had cancer (12 of 23) reported, three months after learning the diagnosis, that not only had they taken in little or none of the information communicated to them—some of which was still confusing or conflicting—but their children understood little of what was taking place (Eden, Black, MacKinlay, & Emery, 1994).

Physician–Patient Communication

In this country, children under 5 years of age have an average of 6.7 physician contacts per year, and children 5 to 17 years have 3.3 contacts (National Center for Health Statistics, 1986). Consequently, pediatricians provide almost the entire range of psychosocial interventions by addressing emotional, developmental, and behavioral problems of children and adolescents—problems that typically are not psychopathic in nature but still warrant various levels of psychosocial intervention. Although pediatricians are the single largest referral source for children's psychological services, it has been shown that a significant proportion of children who are seen by pediatricians do not receive appropriate diagnosis, treatment, or referral in this area (Costello et al., 1988; Lavigne et al., 1991).

For most adults, including nurses and physicians, young children often appear to have weird or irrational ideas about illness and bodily functions, and adolescents often appear to be concerned with factors that are irrelevant or contradictory to health-related concerns (e.g., their body image). There is a rich depository of vignettes in pediatric psychology describing children's "weird," sometimes "cute," or irrational ideas. However, a greater appreciation by caregivers for the logic behind children's weird, cute, or seemingly irrational ideas about illness will enable children to talk about their symptoms, fears, anger, and frustrations in ways that establish a basis for maintaining a mutual and unambiguous dialogue with adults who care for them. For example, when talking with a 5-year-old child about impending surgery and hospitalization or trying to explain to a child the efficacy of medications or medical procedures, it is developmentally appropriate to focus on external observable events because children at this age lack cognitive competencies for abstract logical reasoning that would allow them to understand medical procedures in anatomical and physiological terms (Bibace & Walsh, 1981). From a cognitive-developmental perspective, it is not simply a matter of using simpler vocabulary or translating medical terms to metaphors familiar to young children, but of recognizing and honoring qualitatively different forms of knowing at different developmental levels. Physicians (or parents) who just simplify or "down-speak" complex medical procedures and physiologic processes often confuse children, raise unspoken fears about the uncertainties of their condition, and inhibit them from seeking information and advice in their struggle to make sense of their experience of being sick (Bearison, 1991a).

Studies suggest that health professionals have limited understanding of children's ways of reasoning about illness. In a survey of practicing pediatricians, 79% judged their formal training in child development to be inadequate (Dworkin, Shonkoff, Leviton, & Levine, 1979) and only 30% reported feeling highly competent in assessing children's normal development (American Academy of Pediatrics Task Force, 1978). These statistics have important clinical implications, given that about half of the questions that pediatric residents typically ask mothers during well-child examinations concern child development issues (Wissow, Roter, & Wilson, 1994). Pediatricians have been found to generally overestimate the conceptual sophistication with which younger children understand illness and to underestimate older children's understanding (Perrin & Perrin, 1983). This might account for the reluctance of many physicians, including pediatricians, to directly engage children in discussions about the nature, prognosis, and self-management of their medical conditions (Pantell, Steward, Dias, Wells, & Ross, 1982).

Pantell et al. (1982) conducted one of the few studies that have directly addressed how physicians communicate with children. The interactions of physicians, parents, and child patients (4 to 14 years old) in 115 routine pediatric office visits to 49 family practitioners were studied, with attention to how children were included in the visit. Although a considerable amount of the total communication (45.5%) was between the physicians and the children, the physicians used different patterns when communicating with the parents and with the children. More information about the presenting problem was elicited by the physicians from the children, but the parents received 4.4 times as much information about the nature, prognosis, and management of the problem (28.2% vs. 6.4%). Also, physicians conveyed more medical information to boys compared to girls (6.5% vs. 4.0%) independent of education, SES, and race. Physicians maintained control of the interaction by initiating most of the verbal units, but their distribution was disproportionate between children and their parents; they initiated 8.3 times as many statements as did children, compared to 1.8 times as many as did parents. This finding might reflect a general lack of responsiveness on the part of children when visiting a family physician, and this, in turn, would have influenced the ways in which physicians communicated with them. Korsch, Gozzi, and Francis (1968) also found that few pediatric interactions were child-directed and only .8% of child-directed statements were health-oriented rather than social. Whitt (1982) sampled 500 pediatricians treating patients with chronic illnesses (e.g., diabetes, cystic fibrosis, epilepsy, and asthma) and found that only 15.9% of them ever met alone with children between the ages of 8 and 11 years to explain their illness directly to them.

There is convincing evidence that how pediatricians pose questions, at least to mothers of their patients, affects the kind of issues that mothers are likely to bring to the pediatricians' attention. For example, mothers often claimed that they were reluctant to discuss with pediatricians their children's behavioral or emotional symptoms even when they constituted their single greatest concern about their children's health (Good, Good, & Cleary, 1987). In another study of pediatricians' communication with 800 parents of child patients, 25% of the parents reported that they would have liked to have felt comfortable about asking their pediatrician more questions than they typically did (Korsch et al., 1968).

According to Novack, Volk, Drossman, and Lipkin (1993), "the remarkable scientific advances in medicine have not changed the fact that physicians' core clinical skills are interpersonal" (p. 2101), and there is accumulating evidence that the communication process cannot be separated from the physician's overall quality of care. In the past 20 years, studies of physician–patient patterns of communicating have addressed a variety of topics, such as power and dominance within the interaction (Henley, 1977), who is more likely to interrupt whom (West, 1984), nonverbal and extraverbal modes of communicating in the interaction (Hall, Harrigan, & Rosenthal, 1995; Harrigan, 1985; Street & Buller, 1988), reciprocity in the expression of emotions such as anger and anxiety (Hall, Roter, & Rand, 1981), the match or mismatch between physicians and patients according to such variables as gender and ethnicity (Hall, Irish, Roter, Ehrlich, & Miller, 1994), the interactional synchrony between patients and physicians (Engestrom, 1993), and how patients' physical appearance affected the communication (i.e., how attractive, well dressed, or neat patients were perceived to be by physicians; Hadjistavropoulos, Ross, & von Baeyer, 1990; Hooper, Comstock, Goodwin, & Goodwin, 1982; Knapp & Hall, 1992). The overall quality of communication during the medical encounter, including physicians' skills in communicating and in assessing patients' comprehension of the information provided, has been found to be related to several outcome variables: patients' satisfaction with their care; patients' sense of empathy, interest, and concern on the part of physicians; patients' compliance with treatment regimens; patients' ability to adjust to and cope with the exigencies of their medical conditions; the elicitation by physicians of illness-specific information; patients' proclivities to ask more questions in an effort to seek more information about their medical condition from their physicians; physicians' satisfaction with their patients and with their sense of their own quality of care; physicians' ability to assess psychosocial stressors that would likely compromise their patients' quality of care; and judgments of the clinical competence of medical residents by their professors (Beckman & Frankel, 1984; Hall et al., 1995; Korsch, Freemon, & Negrete, 1971; Korsch, Negrete, Mercer, & Freemon, 1971; Roter & Hall, 1987; Street & Wiemann, 1987). The most provocative studies of physician–patient communication explicitly considered the possibility that patients influenced physicians as much as physicians influenced patients. These studies incorporated methods to empirically assess the mutual reciprocity between physicians and patients in the interaction (e.g., Engestrom, 1993).

Given the scope and clinical value of these findings, there is a clear need for more studies of how pediatricians and children communicate with each other. Such studies might address how pediatricians' styles of interacting give form to children's understanding of the nature of their medical condition, and their willingness to share with others their thoughts and feelings about being sick. Also of interest would be how pediatricians communicate prognoses and treatment decisions to children at different phases of the treatment for a long-term chronic condition, and how pediatricians' styles of communicating vary as a function of children's (and their families') adjustment and biological responses to their medical condition and treatment.

Knowledge of Health and Illness

Children's concepts of treatment and illness causality progress through a sequence of developmental stages, from global and phenomenological concepts characteristic of preoperational thinking to increasingly more sophisticated kinds of concepts characteristic of formal operational modes of thinking (Bibace & Walsh, 1979, 1980, 1981). Aside from studies of children's global conceptions of illness, studies have addressed children's knowledge of other health-related phenomena: their conceptions of sexuality and birth (Bernstein & Cowan, 1981; Goldman & Goldman, 1982), psychological disorders (Dollinger, Thelen, & Walsh, 1980), smoking (Meltzer, Bibace, & Walsh, 1984), death (Childers & Wimmer, 1971; Koocher, 1973, 1981; Reilly et al., 1983), medical procedures (Steward & Steward, 1981), biological functions (Cary, 1985; Crider, 1981; Gellert, 1962; Nagy, 1953), and menstruation and contraception (Morrison, 1985).

Early studies of how children conceptualized illness generally were based on psychoanalytic approaches that construed children's responses in terms of oedipal conflicts. These approaches fostered interpretations that children understood illness as a kind of punishment, and, when sick, they tended to blame themselves (Brewster, 1982; Brodie, 1974; Kister & Patterson, 1980). Guilt and self-blame also were considered common kinds of attribution among adult cancer patients at a time when the etiology of most adult cancers was still unknown (Abrams & Finesinger, 1953; Bard & Dyk, 1956). Such findings regarding children, however, might have been a function of how the data were obtained. For example, although 71% of kindergarten and first-grade children thought that misbehavior somehow caused illness (Gratz & Pilivian, 1984), they rarely selected punishment as a cause for illness when presented with other options in a multiple-choice-type format (Hergenrather & Rabinowitz, 1991). Also, although children who have cancer typically are told that the cause of their illness is not known, about half of them (and almost three/fourths of their parents) were found to have constructed their own, seemingly irrational causal attributions which, while not necessarily involving punishment or self-blame, correlated, in some cases, with their ability to cope with their illness (Bearison et al., 1993). Thus, although children's sense of illness as punishment might characterize the feelings of some (mostly younger) children for some kinds of illnesses (those with uncertain or ambiguous etiologies) in particular situations, it doesn't capture the breadth and depth of their understanding (Kister & Patterson, 1980).

Bibace and Walsh (1979, 1980, 1981) conducted one of the first theoretically conceived, and now classic, systematic studies of the development of children's understanding of illness, its cause, and its cure. Their findings advanced previous findings that explained children's knowledge of illness according to simple age differences by providing a cognitive developmental framework with which to make sense of children's conceptions of illness and which has become a benchmark for most of the subsequent research in this area (Burbach & Peterson, 1986). They conceptualized the problem relative to a qualitatively different and invariant sequence of stages marking the development of children's logical reasoning about causality and their ability to differentiate between self and other (Laurendeau & Pinard, 1962; Piaget, 1952; Werner, 1948).

On the basis of a series of guided clinical interviews regarding children's notions about several common illnesses (e.g., a cold, a heart attack, measles, headache, and pain), Bibace and Walsh (1981) distinguished six types of formal explanations that corresponded to the three major periods of children's cognitive development: prelogical, concrete logical, and formal or abstract logical. They found that the six types of explanations were sequenced according to children's developmental status between the ages of 4 and 11 years, and that children made sense of the experience of being ill (themselves or others) by assimilating the experience to cognitive schemes that reflected the ontogenetic evolution of knowledge. These six types of explanations, along with representative examples, are presented in Table 10.3. Contagion-type explanations were given by 54% of 4-year-old children but not by older children. Their sense of contagion, however, was more reflective of their understanding about human activity (e.g., "when someone gets near you") than their knowledge about infection transmission (Hergenrather & Rabinowitz, 1991). Contamination-type explanations were given by 38% of 4-year-old

TABLE 10.3 Stages of Children's Conceptions of Illness (from Bibace & Walsh, 1980, 1981)

Stage	Description	Example
1. Phenomenism	Illness is understood as an external concrete phenomenon that is spatially and temporally remote from the conditions of illness.	You catch a cold "from the sun," or "from God; God does it in the sky."
2. Contagion	Illness is caused by people or objects that are proximate to, but not touching, the child.	People get colds when "someone else gets near them."
3. Contamination	Illness is caused by people, objects, or actions that are external to the child, and it is transmitted by physical contact or harmful action.	You get a cold when "you're outside without a hat."
4. Internalization	Illness is understood as a process of internalization (e.g., swallowing or inhaling).	People get colds breathing in "bacteria . . . and it goes to the nose."
5. Physiologic	Illness is understood as the malfunctioning of an internal physiologic organ or process and is explained as a step-by-step sequence of events.	People get colds "from viruses. . . . Other people have the virus, and it gets into your blood stream and it causes a cold."
6. Psychophysiologic	Illness is understood physiologically, but the child also can consider the influence of psychological factors (i.e., thoughts and feelings).	You get a heart attack "when your heart stops working right . . . pumping too slow or too fast . . . [and] it can come from being all nerve-racked . . . the tension can affect your heart."

children, 63% of 7-year-old children, and 4% of 11-year-old children; internalization-type explanations by 4% of 4-year-old children, 29% of 7-year-old children, and 54% of 11-year-old children; and physiological-type explanations by 8% of 7-year-old children and 34% of 11-year-old children. No 4-year-old children gave physiological or psychophysiological-type explanations, and the latter were given only by 8% of 11-year-old children. These findings have been replicated by Potter and Roberts (1984), Susman et al. (1987), and Young, McMurray, Rothbery, and Emery (1987).

Methodologically, it is notable that, according to Bibace and Walsh (1981), these qualitatively differentiated levels of reasoning about illness were not typically apparent in children's initial responses to interview questions but, consistent with Piaget's (1930) "clinical method" of eliciting children's explanations of causal relations, they required nondirective probing. Therefore, paper-and-pencil type questionnaires and rating scales, despite their ease of administration, will not uncover children's basic levels of reasoning about illness.

Consistent with these findings, others have found that, as children develop, their conceptions of illness become more complex; more related to internal body cues; more differentiated according to specific kinds of illnesses, symptoms, and causes; more abstract and principled; more dependent on process/cause kinds of relationships; and more multidetermined. As children develop, they understand illness as being less vulnerable to chance occurrences, and they gain a greater perception of control over illness as well as greater reliance on internal (compared to external) cues (Beales, Lennox-Holt, Keen, & Mellor, 1983; Campbell, 1975; Carandang, Folkins, Hines, & Steward, 1979; Hergenrather & Rabinowitz, 1991; Kister & Patterson, 1980; Neuhauser, Amsterdam, Hines, & Steward, 1978; Perrin & Gerrity, 1981; Perrin & Perrin, 1983; Potter & Roberts, 1984; Redpath & Rogers, 1984; Susman et al., 1987).

Empirical tests of relationships between children's cognitive development and their illness concepts entail more than simply mapping responses as a function of age (Burbach & Peterson, 1986). They require a measure of children's level of cognitive development, which seemingly is independent of their domain-specific knowledge of health and illness, in order to assess developmental status apart from chronological age (Wohlwill, 1973). Consequently, many studies have relied on one or more Piagetian-type tasks of causal and logical reasoning to provide (relatively) domain-"independent" or metaconceptual measures of cognitive development. Among studies of children's concepts of illness, these tasks have included the pendulum problem (Susman et al., 1987), the movement-of-clouds conundrum (Perrin & Gerrity, 1981; Sayer, Willett, & Perrin, 1993; Simeonsson, Buckley, & Monson, 1979), the conservation of quantities (Brewster, 1982; Koocher, 1981; Neuhauser et al., 1978; Perrin & Gerrity, 1981; Sayer et al., 1993; Simeonsson et al., 1979), and social role-taking problems (Simeonsson et al., 1979). According to how children responded to these kinds of problems, they were assigned a level of logical reasoning (e.g., prelogical, concrete logical, or abstract logical), which was compared to their level of reasoning about a domain-specific target of inquiry (e.g., illness, medical procedures, treatment regimens, etc.). For example, Perrin and Gerrity (1981) found that, despite considerable variation in children's (5 to 13 years old) levels of understanding of different aspects of illness (e.g., causality, hospitalization, illness prevention, etc.), their illness-related knowledge overall correlated highly ($r = .81$) with their seemingly basic concepts about physical causality. They had most difficulty understanding how to prevent illness; ideas about how people get better and how medication works were more easily understood at a younger age.

Children's levels of knowing about illness issues, however, consistently lagged somewhat behind their more basic knowledge; no child received a higher score for illness causality than for physical causality. Similar to Bibace and Walsh (1980, 1981), Perrin and Gerrity (1981; see also Perrin & Perrin, 1983) concluded that there is a stage-sequential pattern to the development of children's illness concepts, and this pattern is consistent with children's basic levels of cognitive development.

Health Status

Children's health status would be expected to have an effect on how they conceptualize illness in terms of comparisons between healthy and ill children and between ill children with different kinds of medical problems. Among children who are seriously ill, questions about illness concepts are not hypothetical or reflective but are drawn from their subjective experiences of a series of intrusive and often painful medical conditions to which they must continually adjust and about which they actively struggle to make sense. Thus, children who have chronic medical problems would be expected to have different ideas about illness than healthy children. However, studies that compared illness knowledge among samples of healthy and ill children in order to assess the impact of illness and/or hospitalization on children's illness concepts have provided equivocal and sometimes conflicting findings (e.g., Brewster, 1982; Myers-Vando, Steward, Folkins, & Hines, 1979; Perrin, Sayer, & Willett, 1991; Redpath & Rogers, 1984; Sayer et al., 1993; Shagena, Sandler, & Perrin, 1988; Susman et al., 1987; Williams, 1978). Redpath and Rogers (1984), for example, found that second graders, but not preschoolers, who had had prior hospitalizations had more advanced understanding of illness concepts than children with no notable medical history. Sayer et al. (1993) found that healthy children, compared to children with a variety of chronic illnesses (diabetes, asthma, seizure disorders, and orthopedic conditions), had better understanding of illness concepts. Myers-Vando et al. (1979) found no differences according to children's health status, but Williams (1978) found that hospitalized children had a better understanding of illness causality. Armstrong, Lemanek, et al. (1993) found no differences in knowledge of sickle cell disease between children (or their parents) who had mild and severe disease-related lifestyle disruptions.

Despite empirical findings comparing healthy and ill children's broad rather than specific knowledge of illness concepts, there is ample clinical evidence that children who are seriously ill actively struggle to make sense of their medical conditions, and, by so doing, they often display a seemingly precocious discernment of complex medical procedures and medication effects (Bearison, 1991a; Bluebond-Langner, 1978).

Symptom Perception

Several kinds of chronic illnesses (e.g., asthma, diabetes, and cancer) entail considerable self-management that depends, in part, on children's ability to accurately perceive their symptoms. For example, the ability to perceive pulmonary changes in the early stages of bronchial asthma allows patients to make appropriate changes in their activity level, to alter their surrounding environment, or to initiate pharmacotherapy. Yet, there is considerable variability in the accuracy of symptom perception for children with moderate to severe asthma. One study (Fritz, Klein, & Overholser, 1990) found that, among children 7 to 15 years old, one-fifth had "quite accurate" perceptions but more than one-third had "extremely inaccurate" perceptions of their symptoms. Correlations between subjective perception of symptoms and objective measures of pulmonary functions for a given child ranged from 0.86 to −0.16 (Fritz et al., 1990). The children's perceptual accuracy was not related to age, gender, and duration or severity of asthma. Another study found that only 46% of children with asthma were able to recognize their acute attacks (Ashkanazi, Amir, Volovitz, & Varsano, 1993). The ability to discriminate asthma severity and perception of respiratory functions, however, was not much better among adult patients (Kendrick, Higgs, Whitfield, & Laszlo, 1993).

Children's ability to recognize and understand the clinical implications of their symptoms depends on several psychological factors, including their cognitive abilities, modes of coping, self-efficacy, and baseline anxiety levels (Fritz, Yeung, & Taitel, 1994). In many cases, it also depends on their visceral autonomic perception, and there is considerable evidence that even healthy adults and adolescents have difficulty assessing such autonomic systems as blood pressure, heart rate, gastric motility, skin temperature, and galvanic skin response (Pennebaker, 1987). Subjective/objective correlation of symptom perception based on blood glucose among adult diabetics was only 0.66 (Cox, Gonder, Pohl, & Pennebaker, 1983). Interventions to enhance symptom perception among children with chronic medical problems has been largely unstudied.

Informing Children

Children who are seriously ill and/or are hospitalized often struggle to learn about and make sense of their medical condition and treatment regimens, in spite of being falsely reassured by adults that there is nothing for them to worry about. For example, regardless of what, how, and when they are told, even very young children who have cancer are able to gather enough incidental cues from parents, hospital peers who have cancer, and medical staff to realize that their condition is serious enough to be life-threatening. Often, without being directly informed by adults, they are able to grasp the biomedical implications of sequentially more toxic forms of chemotherapy and the prognostic consequences of relapses following progressively briefer periods of remission (Bearison, 1991a; Bluebond-Langner, 1978; Chesler & Barbarin, 1987).

Studies have found that children who are told about their having cancer early in their treatment are better able to cope than children who indirectly learn about their diagnosis later (Slavin, O'Malley, Koocher, & Foster, 1982); therefore, there is no defensible reason for withholding a diagnosis of cancer from children, as was once common practice (Holland, Geary, Marchini, & Tross, 1987; Novack et al., 1979). Indeed, there is today a more open attitude about informing all children, not just those who have cancer, about the nature of their medical condition, the diagnosis, prognosis, and treatment procedures, and, when appropriate, the painful and uncertain consequences of treatment. Such open communication has been associated with better psychosocial adjustment (Slavin et al., 1982; Spinetta & Maloney, 1978). Further study is warranted, however, about how to inform children in developmentally appropriate ways, and about the value of using various kinds of materials and media (e.g., films, video games, toys, puppets, books, pamphlets, and interactive computer programs) to supplement direct face-to-face communication. These media allow children more control in seeking information about their medical problems, and they give them a greater sense of mastery and empowerment in regard to their medical care (see Bearison, 1991a, for a discussion about informing children of cancer).

A notable exception to the growing practice of full disclosure to children about their illness involves children with HIV infection. Studies have found that most parents of children (4 to 7 years old) who have HIV do not want their children to know about their illness (Hardy, Armstrong, Routh, Albrecht, & Davis, 1994; Mellins & Ehrhardt, 1993). Staff members' collusion with parents in withholding information from children about their illness and treatment breeds a situation that can compromise the kinds of relationships that parents expect the medical staff to have with their children. Consequently, a pivotal question in clinical practice today is whether to discuss the nature and treatment of HIV infection and AIDS symptoms with these children, despite parents' negative admonitions. This issue involves ethical considerations regarding children's rights to understand the purpose and nature of medical procedures that are performed on them.

Children's Script Knowledge

One approach to studying children's understanding of their medical problems and treatment follows from substantial findings regarding children's script knowledge. According to many cognitive developmental psychologists (e.g., Mandler, 1983; Nelson, 1986), children's knowledge of recurring social events is cognitively organized in the form of scripts—schematic representations of generalized and temporal sequences of socially contexted activities leading to the attainment of particular goals (Schank & Ableson, 1977). Scripts reflect the comprehension, representation, recall, and behavior of individuals in familiar social contexts, and they determine, in part, how individuals interact with one another (Nelson, 1986). Because children as young as 3 years spontaneously organize their knowledge of familiar events in the form of scripts (Nelson, 1981), this method is particularly useful in assessing very young children's procedural understanding of events (i.e., episodic knowledge). The kinds of recurrent medical procedures that children with chronic illness experience lend themselves to scripted forms of organization and representation. They typically involve a recurring pattern of activities involving children and medical personnel that are temporally sequenced. Script knowledge is obtained by asking children, "What happens when . . ." types of questions. These questions are directed to children's comprehension of their direct experiences rather than to their conceptual knowledge. Because these kinds of questions tap children's conceptual knowledge as it is deployed or enacted in their experience, they are more likely to elicit a fuller and more differentiated account of what children know about events than when simply asking them decontexted questions about hypothetical conditions. In the context of eliciting children's comprehension of illness, script knowledge questions are probably a more veridical kind of measure than the kinds used to compare the knowledge of illness between healthy and ill children (and they might account for the equivocal findings from the studies previously discussed). Because these kinds of questions are experientially based, they can't be used to compare knowledge as a simple function of "health status."

Bearison and Pacifici (1989) compared children's script knowledge of their visits to outpatient clinics for chemotherapy ("What happens when you come to the clinic?") with their script knowledge of other common recurrent events in their lives, such as going to a restaurant or a birthday party. The scripts of older children contained more procedure-related events presented with greater consistency across time, across topics, and between subjects than those from younger children (4 to 6 years old vs. 7 to 17 years old), but even the youngest children had scripts that were temporally sequenced, general in form, and relatively accurate. The event-sequence errors made by the youngest group of children primarily involved events such as bone marrow aspirations and chemotherapy procedures—the most aversive and complex aspects of the clinic visit. By age 7 years, children's scripts were well established; the recall and organization of knowledge about cancer treatment among 7- to 9-year-old children did not differ significantly from those of older children and adolescents (10 to 17 years), suggesting that, by this age, most children can comprehend simple yet authentic explanations of complex medical procedures. There were no differences relative to time in treatment, gender, and prognostic condition (suggesting that the children's knowledge of having cancer was established early in treatment). Even children as young as 4 years had the cognitive competencies to mentally represent complex medical procedures in terms of the sequence of events that they experienced, if not in terms of their comprehension of the physiological correlates of the events.

Another group of studies, similar in form to studies of children's script knowledge, has focused on children's episodic memory of pediatric examinations. In these studies, young children (usually, between 3 and 7 years old) were interviewed at variable delay intervals (e.g., immediate, then 1, 3, or 6 weeks) about their recall of routine well-child pediatric examinations. Calculations were based on each of 21 features of the examination (e.g., heart check, urine sample, etc.). Initially, they were spontaneously recalled in response to open-ended questions, and then they were recalled with successively more specific probes. Clubb, Nida, Merritt, and Ornstein (1993) and Baker-Ward, Gordon, Ornstein, Larus, and Clubb (1993) found considerable variability in children's recall of the components of the physical examination. For example, a finger prick to obtain a blood sample was recalled by almost all 5-year-old children initially (.93) and after 6 weeks (.67), but the pediatrician's check of their wrist was not well remembered at any time. Younger children (3 years old) consistently provided less information in response to open-ended questions than did older children, and they relied more on specific probes. Retention over time varied directly with age; there was little forgetting among 7-year-old children but a considerable amount of forgetting among 3-year-old children. However, even at the 6-week interval, 5-year-old children had minimal errors of intrusion to questions about routine features of the examination that were not part of a given child's checkup.

Other studies tested the effects of different kinds of enhancement procedures on children's recall. For example, providing 3-year-old children with a doll at the time of recall (to demonstrate the enactment of the procedure) did not improve their recall (Gordon et al., 1993). In a subsequent study, 3- and 5-year-old children were provided with medical instruments that had been used (and some that had not been used) during their medical examination (e.g., eye chart, urine analysis cup, stethoscope, etc.), and recall was assessed by verbal and/or behavioral enactments of events. Children were able to spontaneously recall more detailed information about the examination in the enactment condition compared to the verbal-only condition, and the rate of improvement was more dramatic among 3-year-old than among 5-year-old children (Follmer & Gordon, 1994). However, children in the enactment condition also showed a substantial increase in the recall of procedures that were not included in the actual examination (i.e., spurious information). Using a memory recognition protocol (i.e., questions describing an event that required a yes or no response) with 3- and 6-year-old children, it was found that the 3-year-old children did not perform much better than chance and, compared to the 6-year-old children, they had a considerable number of affirmative responses to events that didn't take place in their examination (probably due to a tendency for response set biases). Thus, contrary to other kinds of memory studies with preschool children (e.g., Brown & Scott, 1971), these various methods designed to enhance children's recall of medical examinations (i.e., dolls, enactment protocols, and recognition protocols) did not enhance recall among the 3-year-old children.

Procedural Stress and Recall

Merritt et al. (1994) tested children's (3 to 7 years old) recall of a voiding cystourethrogram (VCUG) procedure. More novel, aversive, and stressful than a routine physical examination, a VCUG includes cleansing the genital area, inserting a catheter into the urethra, filling the bladder with contrast fluid to allow fluoroscopic filming, and then voiding the fluid. Children were able to recall 88% of the components of the VCUG procedure immediately after the procedure and evidenced higher levels of spontaneous recall than did 5-year-old children in the previous studies of recall of routine physical examinations (65% vs. 42%). They demonstrated little forgetting over a 6-week interval, and their recall, unlike in the previous findings, was not subject to suggestibility; they correctly denied 95% of misleading questions. Behavioral codings and salivary cortisol assays confirmed that the children were very distressed by the VCUG procedure. The extent of their behavioral stress, but not their salivary cortisol levels, was negatively correlated with their immediate and delayed recall (–.56 and –.58, respectively), suggesting that how the children interpreted the stress of the procedures that they experienced, more than their physiognomic reaction to stress, affected how they cognitively processed (i.e., encoded, stored, and retrieved) the experience. Children's recall also was correlated with measures of their temperament. Although it is difficult to speculate about the recall performance of children in particularly stressful and invasive medical procedures (compared to recall of a routine medical examination) on the basis of a single study of a single procedure, Ornstein, Shapiro, Clubb, Follmer, and Baker-Ward (1996) suggested that the intensively personal nature of the VCUG might have led to the children's heightened attention to each of its features, and thereby accounted for their "excellent" recall, even though they could not have thoroughly understood the features. Ornstein et al. (1996) also suggested that the greater internal structure due to the highly embedded connection of features "linked together by a set of temporally invariant causal enablements" in the VCUG procedure, compared to the seemingly unrelated components of a routine medical examination, might have accounted for the excellent recall performance.

Goodman et al. (1994) also tested children's (3 to 10 years old) recall of a VCUG procedure at approximately 12 days following the procedure. They found that 3- and 4-year-old children, compared to the older children, had poorer free recall and made more errors of commission and omission in response to both specific and misleading questions. They also measured mothers' emotional support and communication to children about the event, and the children's own emotional reactions—all of which were associated with the accuracy of the children's recall. For example, mothers who, following the procedure, talked sympathetically to their children about it, or physically comforted them, had children who recalled more correct information.

AIDS and HIV Infection

Most children with AIDS (76%) were born to mothers infected with the HIV virus (i.e., vertical transmission from mother to child prenatally or perinatally); an additional group of children (mostly those with hemophilia) acquired AIDS through past practices of transfusing blood (Parks & Scott, 1987). Although there are only about 1% of documented cases of AIDS among adolescents (accrual of 14,127 cases among persons 13 to 24 years old by September 1993; Centers for Disease Control, 1993), the long incubation period of the HIV virus implies that many adults diagnosed in their 20s were infected when they were adolescents, as a result of either unprotected sexual activities or intravenous drug abuse (Brooks-Gunn, Boyer, & Hein, 1988). Advocacy for HIV/AIDS education for children as young as 6 years of age (APA Task Force on Pediatric AIDS, 1989; Centers for Disease Control, 1988) has raised questions regarding not only adolescents' but also young children's understanding of the mechanisms of viral transmission in relation to risk behavior. Also, how can such disease-specific knowledge be integrated with children's developing conceptions of illness in general? In addition to instruction directed toward reducing high-risk behaviors, such as unprotected sexual activities and intravenous drug abuse, giving children accurate, developmentally appropriate information about AIDS is necessary to promote their social acceptance of others who have AIDS and to help children who have AIDS adjust to the exigencies of treatment and care. However, finding appropriate ways of talking about AIDS with children in order to achieve these aims is not just a matter of matching illness concepts with their levels of cognitive development. It also involves prudent consideration of affective, attitudinal, and motivational factors in light of children's sense of personal vulnerability, their behavioral intentions, and their competence to negotiate social situations (Whitt, 1995). There remains today a compelling need for AIDS education and what we can learn in this domain will generalize to better ways of promoting children's health in other domains.

Adapting methodologies that they had used in their previous studies of the development of children's understanding of common illnesses, Walsh and Bibace (1991) interviewed children (5 to 13 years old) about the definition, cause, treatment, and prevention of AIDs ("Have you ever heard of AIDS?" "What is AIDS?" "How do people get AIDS?" "What do doctors do for people with AIDS?" and "What can people do so they won't get AIDS?"). Their findings confirmed that the way in which children think about AIDS conforms to the ways in which they think about illness in general. Younger children (in the prelogical period of cognitive development) understood AIDS as being related to any event, person, or object with which AIDS had been associated in any way (i.e., mere proximity). For example, one child identified AIDS as a "terrible sickness you die from" and, because his grandmother had recently died from a "terrible sickness," he concluded that "AIDS is when your grandmother dies" (p. 278). Children at the concrete logical period understood AIDS as a mechanism that invaded the body according to a unilateral and temporal or spatial sequence of events that resulted in internal body symptoms, although such symptoms were understood in a vague and diffuse way (e.g., "'Your blood gets all filled up with it.' ['Filled up with what?'] 'with AIDS'" [p. 279]). At the abstract or formal logical period, AIDS was understood in terms of the malfunction of internal organs or biological processes as a result of interaction of multiple causes and/or effects. Other studies have since confirmed that children's understanding of AIDS follows the same developmental progression as does their understanding of other illnesses (De Loye, Henggeler, & Daniels, 1993; Osborne, Kistner, & Helgemo, 1993).

A recent study of over 1,000 children in the third through sixth grades found that their basic knowledge about the three primary routes of HIV transmission was "strikingly high" (Wells et al., 1995). For example, over 98% of the sample knew that HIV can be transmitted by having sex with a person with HIV; 97%, by sharing a contaminated needle; and 93%, by an HIV mother transmitting it to her unborn baby. However, children in the sample were not nearly as knowledgeable about the mechanisms of HIV transmission, and they had many serious misconceptions about activities associated with transmission. For example, 56% of the third graders thought that sharing a cup with someone who is HIV-positive can transmit the virus, or that drinking too much alcohol (39%), or smoking marijuana (50%) or cigarettes (31%) can transmit the virus. Although there were no differences as a function of gender, there were significant grade, race/ethnicity, and SES effects.

These findings indicate that very young children will not comprehend the cause of AIDS if it is explained in terms of the mechanisms of viral transmission, but they can understand a causal association between external contiguous events (e.g., ". . . dirty needles that people might use to take drugs can give you AIDS"). Although even very young children might associate sexual activity with AIDS (e.g., "You get AIDS from sex"), their understanding of sexual activity and of AIDS is highly limited and concrete (e.g., external body contact), and, therefore, they do not grasp the process of transmittal that associates sexual activity with AIDS. Even among adolescents (14 to 16 years old) the mechanism of AIDS transmittal was found to be confusing (Eiser, Eiser, & Lang, 1990). By the time children are at the concrete logical level of reasoning, they are able to adopt an internalized view of AIDS, but not until they are at the abstract level of logical reasoning are they able to begin to appreciate an agent or mechanism as somehow causing internalized malfunctions. At the highest level of abstract logical reasoning, they are able to understand malfunctions in terms of biological organs and systems (e.g., immune deficiency). These stages of reasoning about AIDS present formidable challenges that have not been consistently fulfilled by those who devise school curricula on AIDS education (National AIDS Information Clearinghouse, 1989).

Knowledge and Attitudes

Because of the continuing charge to find ways to modify people's behavior in regard to AIDS-related activities, and to promote more caring and humane attitudes toward people who have AIDS, issues regarding the relationship between knowledge and attitudes have become important in pediatric AIDS research. Findings regarding children's knowledge of AIDS and their attitudes toward people who have AIDS have, so far, been equivocal. Despite a negative correlation, among adults, between their knowledge of AIDS and their tendency to stigmatize people who have AIDS (Temoshok, Sweet, & Zich, 1987), the correlation between children's knowledge and attitudes about AIDS generally has been low or not significant in some studies (Brown & Fritz, 1988; Fassler, McQueen, Duncan, & Copeland, 1990; Kegeles, Adler, & Irwin, 1988), but not in other studies (e.g., McElreath & Roberts, 1992; Osborne et al., 1993). McElreath and Roberts (1992), for example, found that the more accurate children's knowledge was about AIDS, the more likely the children would express positive or tolerant attitudes about people with AIDS (independent of their scores on the information subtest of the WISC-R).

General findings about relationships between parental belief systems and children's attitudes (e.g., Goodnow & Collins, 1991; Sigel, 1985) have encouraged several investigators to study relationships between children's and their parents' knowledge and attitudes about AIDS. According to McElreath and Roberts (1992), children's (9 to 13 years old) knowledge of AIDS was not correlated with their parents' knowledge but was moderately correlated with their parents' attitudes about people who have AIDS. Osborne, Kistner, and Helgemo (1995) detected a moderate association between children's and parents' attitudes about a hypothetical child with AIDS, independent of parents' and children's knowledge of AIDS. De Loye et al. (1993) also found that children's (7 to 13 years old) knowledge about AIDS was not associated with their mothers' knowledge about AIDS.

Perhaps more interesting than these correlative findings are the simple findings that only 29% of children identified their parents as sources of AIDS information, and 62% mentioned television (McElreath & Roberts, 1992; see Henggeler, Melton, & Rodrique, 1992 for a discussion of the impact of television as a primary source of children's information about AIDS). Although, compared to the influence of television and peers, parents probably are not the primary socializers of children's knowledge and attitudes about AIDS, certain patterns of familial dynamics seem to influence children's awareness about AIDS. For example, Sigelman, Derenowski, Mullaney, and Siders (1993) and Sigelman, Mukai, Woods, and Alfeld (1995) studied the frequency and content of parent–child (6 to 18 years old) communication about AIDS-related topics. They found that although the frequency of parent–child communication about AIDS was not associated with children's general knowledge or attitudes (i.e., willingness to interact) about AIDS, parents' knowledge about six common transmission myths involving AIDS predicted their children's knowledge about these transmission myths, but only among families in which parent–child communication about AIDS was relatively frequent.

Adolescents who reported having known someone with AIDS were more tolerant of the prospect of interacting with a person with AIDS, but such familiarity was not associated with their perceptions of being personally vulnerable to acquiring AIDS (Zimet et al., 1991). Because studies have found that children's attitudes toward disabled peers (e.g., children who use wheelchairs, are obese, are learning-disabled, or have behavior disorders) are, in part, a function of their ascription of personal responsibility to those who have the disability (Sigelman & Begley, 1987), Santilli and Roberts (1993) used a set of vignettes about a hypothesized peer in order to systematically vary the effects of being labeled as a person with AIDS (vs. someone with cystic fibrosis or someone with no label) and the extent of attributed responsibility for having the illness as a function of children's (9 to 14 years) knowledge about AIDS. They found that, regardless of the extent of the target's attributed responsibility for having acquired AIDS and subjects' knowledge of AIDS, the label of AIDS had a negative impact on subjects' attitudes toward the hypothetical peer. However, when subjects were given specific information that the peer was not responsible for his or her illness (i.e., statements that the ill peer did nothing wrong and could not have prevented his or her illness), their attitudes were more positive than when given no information about personal responsibility. Consistent with others' findings, subjects' knowledge about AIDS was not correlated with their attitudes about the hypothetical peer who had AIDS. However, their knowledge was inversely related to their sense of personal vulnerability about acquiring AIDS.

High-Risk Adolescents

Studies of adolescents have found that those who were delinquent, abused, neglected, had run away from home, or were in detention facilities were at higher risk for HIV infection than other adolescents (DiClemente, 1991; Nader, Wexler, Patterson, McKusick, & Coates, 1989; Rotheram-Borus, Becker, & Kaplan, 1991). Male adolescents were more likely than female adolescents to report having engaged in high-risk behaviors related to AIDS, and African American adolescents were less likely than non-African American adolescents to have reported using condoms consistently (DiClemente, 1991). Also, older compared to younger adolescents who engaged in sexual activities were more likely to have been consistent users of condoms (DiClemente, 1991). Among adolescents in residential care settings (due to delinquency, abuse, and neglect), knowledge of AIDS was not associated with either their attitudes about preventing AIDS or their self-reports of having engaged in activities that placed them at risk for AIDS (Slonim-Nevo, Auslander, & Ozawa, 1995). Further evidence suggests that, among this group of adolescents, their quality-of-life aspirations predicted their risk-related behavior.

Sampling Biases

Because AIDS is a sensitive topic of inquiry for many children and adults, findings from studies about AIDS are qualified by participant biases in recruitment (including needing parental consent to allow children to participate). Most studies did not report rates of consent among their sample subjects, nor did they consistently report demographic differences between their sampled and consenting subjects, although the prevalence of AIDS cases varies according to certain demographic variables. According to Osborne et al. (1995), the *highest* reported participation rate among all studies of parents' knowledge and/or attitudes about AIDS was 55%. Hardy et al. (1994) compared demographic variables between children (4 to 7 years old) who had AIDS and children who had cancer. The children were recruited from the same medical center and had consented to participate in their study. Compared to participants who had cancer, children who had AIDS came from families with lower SES, were more likely to be African American than caucasian, came from single-parent or foster homes, and, based on parent reports, were less likely to be aware of their diagnosis. Also, the geographic area from which participants are sampled can bias comparisons across studies because the prevalence of AIDS cases in a community can be expected to affect the likelihood of participants' knowing someone with AIDS, their practical knowledge about AIDS, and their sense of feeling vulnerable to acquiring AIDS. There is a higher incidence of AIDS in urban areas (Centers for Disease Control, 1989; Timmerman, McDonough, & Harmeson, 1991). Almost all psychological studies of AIDS (except Santilli & Roberts, 1993) failed to report whether their samples came from geographic areas in which there was a low or high prevalence of AIDS cases.

Even among those who choose to participate or allow their children to participate, findings are further subject to cohort effects occasioned by changes from year to year about public awareness of AIDS as a national health problem. Public awareness of AIDS (including knowledge and attitudes) has consistently changed, reflecting changes in media coverage since the virus was first disclosed in 1981.

GENETIC TESTING OF CHILDREN: A NEW DIRECTION FOR PEDIATRIC PSYCHOLOGY

The past two decades have witnessed remarkable growth in pediatric psychology. Addressing an increasing range of children's medical problems, the discipline clearly has come into its own as a field of basic and applied inquiry. As the discipline has shifted from a psychopathological to a more developmental orientation, it also has come more in line with common concerns of pediatric practice. Therefore, although one might assume many stances when considering new directions for pediatric psychology, it is particularly germane to consider opportunities arising from new and often unprecedented advances in pediatric practice—the kind of unprecedented advances that occurred in the subspecialty of pediatric oncology and led pediatric psychologists to innovative and sustaining opportunities that encompassed more than strictly medical concerns. Current research in the field of clinical genetics carries similar potential for psychological study in pediatrics. The next step in the growing discovery of disease-related genes is DNA-based tests that will provide presymptomatic diagnoses of certain genetic-based disorders and will discern predispositions to a range of genetically influenced disorders.

There presently are several scenarios in which the genetic testing of children is being considered. In the first scenario, genetic testing will offer immediate medical benefits for a child through either prevention or early treatment (e.g., removing the colon in cases of familial polyposis coli to prevent cancer, or implementing diet and medication regimens to reduce cholesterol levels in cases of familial hypercholesterolemia) or will avoid unnecessary and invasive diagnostic evaluations (e.g., a child with FAP gene negative may be spared annual colonoscopies). In the next scenario is genetic carrier testing, which offers no health benefits for the child but would be useful in making reproductive decisions in the future (e.g., testing for autosomal or X-linked recessive disorders such as cystic fibrosis, hemophilia, or fragile X syndrome), or presymptomatic testing to prepare the child for adult-onset disorders (e.g., Huntington disease). A third scenario involves testing children in order to allow their parents to use prenatal diagnosis in pregnancy planning and abortion (Wertz, Fanos, & Reilly, 1994).

At present, there are no widely accepted standards for considering the psychosocial implications of these scenarios. Considerable discrepancies exist between clinical geneticists and pediatricians regarding even such basic questions as whether children ought to be tested. In a recent survey (Working Party of the Clinical Genetics Society, 1994), 79% of pediatricians, compared to only 40% of clinical geneticists believed that it is the right of each family to decide whether its children should be tested. Most pediatricians thought that testing children for carriers of recessive conditions (i.e., gene carrier status) would result in more responsible attitudes toward reproduction as adults. Most geneticists did not agree. Presently, no data exist to support either view. There also were differences in attitudes about the rights of parents to independently arrange for the genetic testing of their children.

In a recent survey of parents of pediatric oncology patients (Patenaude, 1995c, 1995d), 92% indicated that they would want to have their children tested if it might reduce the likelihood of their having cancer (i.e., it would produce some medical benefit), but 43% also indicated that they would favor testing for their children "just to know," even if there was no present method of reducing risk. Regarding the test findings, 66% indicated that they would inform their children, and 95% said they would if the children were 18 years or older. But 32% indicated that they would not want their children's pediatricians informed because of confidentiality and the need to "protect" their children's medical records. They cited possible discrimination in the workplace and the risk of not being able to obtain insurance. Findings from this survey raise additional questions about how consumers view the psychosocial implications of genetic testing for children. For example, when similar surveys in regard to genetic testing for Huntington disease, a condition for which no treatment is yet available, were conducted among family members at 50% risk (and prior to when the genetic test was available), 57% to 84% of respondents indicated that they would consent (Evers-Kiebooms, Swerts, Cassiman, & Van den Berghe, 1989; Kessler, Field, Worth, & Mosbarger, 1987; Mastromauro, Myers, & Berkman, 1987). However, now that genetic linkage testing for Huntington disease is available, only 12% to 45% of at-risk populations have requested it (Craufurd, Dodge, Kerzin-Storrar, & Harris, 1989). Such discrepant findings document the extent of overestimation of the utilization of predictive testing for Huntington disease in the first decade of its availability and should caution us about heretofore unrecognized factors influencing the utilization of predictive testing for other medical problems, such as cancer (Patenaude, in press).

Informing even adults about the meaning of predictive test results for a disease-related gene is difficult because of the abstract nature of the information, the multifactorial causes of most diseases, and the variable degree of penetrance of most genes. Issues about who should decide whether children should be informed of test results, and at what age, raise legal questions regarding the rights of children versus the rights of their parents in matters of assent, consent, and the age of competence and "emancipated minor" status regarding medical decisions (Leiken, 1982). Giving to parents test results that are relevant to their children's health care but that the parents dare not share with their children's pediatricians threatens the quality of care that children may receive.

Another way in which the psychosocial sequelae of genetic testing would have implications for medical management might be that children found to have a predisposing disease mutation might try to reduce anxiety, as they develop, by explicitly avoiding disease-related procedures such as screening and medical examinations, while those found not to have a predisposing gene might become less vigilant and develop a false sense of reassurance against other than genetic determinants. There already is sufficient behavioral evidence among adults who have been advised of medical risks due to high cholesterol counts, or workers with asbestos-related mesothelioma, to question whether early disclosure offers greater psychological benefit and preventive health practices than its concealment (Lerman, Rimer, & Engstrom, 1991). Also, if disclosure of test results to children were delayed, could it be assumed that all parents would be able to convey full and accurate information to their children years after a test was performed and, if not, then who should be designated as the archival source and messenger of such information? There is, as yet, no relevant case law in these and other related matters (Wertz et al., 1994).

Genetic testing is still an emergent area of medical research in which human values bear on medical technologies, and questions of what can be done in clinical practice need to be tempered by what ought to be done in consideration of the psychological and social impact on children and their families. The psychological questions raised by the promise of genetic testing not only transcend health-related concerns, but are shot through with social, cultural, historical, economic, political, and prejudicial interests and ideologies. They stretch our ethical and legal principles in ways that have not yet been realized and will have considerable effects on the social fabric of our society. Relevant research in pediatric psychology appears to be a necessary next step in formulating evidence-based policies regarding the psychological and social consequences of genetic testing of children. Despite the continuing advance, if not the onslaught, of molecular genetic technologies, the availability of the genetic services that they portend awaits such policies.

Until the psychosocial effects of genetic testing of children are further documented, the U.K. Clinical Genetics Society (Working Party of the Clinical Genetics Society, 1994) has concluded, as have most pediatricians, that predictive genetic testing of children is appropriate only if disease onset regularly occurs in childhood or if there is an effective therapeutic intervention (e.g., diet, medication, or surveillance for complications). It is best avoided among untreatable late-onset disorders such as Huntington disease, prion protein, Alzheimer dementias, and other neurodegenerative disorders. In regard to genetic carrier testing, the Society concluded that, until there is sufficient research to ascertain the psychosocial consequences, it should be deferred until children are developmentally competent to fully comprehend not only the full implications of genetic testing, including the emotional and social consequences, but also issues of diminished confidentiality if third parties such as employers and insurers coerce their consent for access to test results.

Genetic testing challenges pediatric psychologists to extend and adapt previous findings and to devise new methods of study, in collaboration with pediatricians, to bear on an innovative, yet controversial, domain of clinical practice. Some of these research questions are:

- If children come from families in which someone has an inherited disorder that places the children at potential risk for genetic predisposition, will testing help them to develop adaptive coping strategies and health-promoting behaviors, when the finding is positive, or will knowing prospectively that they are at highly increased risk of developing a serious and chronic condition such as cancer exceed their limits of adequate coping?

- Who should make decisions about which children should be genetically tested and when, and should standards be uniformly adopted for everyone?
- What is the optimal age when children should be informed that they are at genetic risk for a serious disorder, in terms of their ability to develop adaptive coping strategies and health-promoting behaviors?
- How might family relationships change due to genetic testing? Although parents may think that they have their children's best interests at heart, will they alter their expectations, distribution of resources, attention, investment, and overall regard for their children relative to their gene-positive and gene-negative status? Will they be less likely to assume a "When you grow up . . ." or "When you have children of your own . . ." kind of attitude toward their gene-positive children?
- As parents and children come to comprehend the path of heritability of a disease in the family, will it exacerbate feelings of guilt among parents and children found not to have the deleterious gene, or depression among those children who do have it?
- Will the adoption of children who have genetic risk be hampered if testing is done prior to adoption? Who has the right of consent if the testing of an adopted child is carried out for the benefit of a biological family member?
- How can risk information be communicated and responses be monitored in order to best deal with reactions of denial, low self-esteem, anxiety, guilt, and feelings of being stigmatized (particularly with regard to marriage and procreation)?
- How can informed consent be ensured and polices be devised to resolve potential conflicts between autonomy and protection of genetic privacy, when many of the outcomes, benefits, and risks of testing remain unknown?
- What are the psychosocial sequelae of labeling children as being at-risk, and what factors will influence who is likely (or unlikely) to alter his or her behavior in health-relevant ways?
- Must genetic testing remain voluntary on an individual basis at all costs, or are there certain conditions in which genetic testing should be mandated for the protection of the public welfare?

Genetic predictive and carrier testing programs hold the promise of enhanced prevention and cure of chronic medical problems, and there already is consensus that, in some situations, children should be included in these programs. In such early- and late-onset diseases as diabetes, cystic fibrosis, obesity, neurological degenerative diseases, heart disease, and cancer, the genetic testing of children is likely to become widespread. Genetic testing for sickle-cell disease and thalassemia already is commonly done; some testing is underway for FAP and Rb, and some is planned for p53 (Patenaude, 1995a).

Genetic testing raises hopes for prevention and protection from environmental and lifestyle exposures, early detection, and, eventually, medication–prevention programs that will reduce morbidity and mortality. For children from high-risk families who are found not to carry a deleterious gene, there is a freedom from anxiety. However, genetic testing also presents considerable ethical and psychological questions. A recent editorial in the *Journal of Medical Genetics* cited the need for research to document the psychological effects of genetic testing in children as the "necessary first step to achieving consensus" (Marteau, 1994, p. 743). This proposal poses bold, provocative, and challenging domains of study and empirical inquiry for pediatric psychologists, and it bodes well for how the discipline can advance in collaboration with medical research.

AFTERWORD

When considering the range of studies in pediatric psychology, one is understandably left questioning the value and relevance of such research to the clinical practice of the profession. Does the corpus of research reviewed, discussed, and sometimes criticized here guide the practitioner in practical ways in the kinds of activities that pediatric psychologists pursue? Are they responsive to the kinds of questions that pediatricians ask about psychosocial issues in their practice? In many critical respects, I think research in pediatric psychology is remarkably responsive to practice—often, because the kinds of issues studied have arisen from practical concerns. Pediatricians turn to pediatric psychologists to find out what kinds of psychosocial interventions work, and sometimes even *why* they work. They have never asked me what kinds of theoretical considerations led to what kinds of hypotheses that substantiated a given way to intervene. To put it bluntly, for those of us in the press of pediatric practice, when our intervention works, we're heroes and we're an integral part of the pediatric team; when it doesn't, well . . . we're just psychologists.

Some common problems about which pediatricians often elicit advice from pediatric psychologists are:

- How can we tell when a child or adolescent is experiencing pain or when he or she is malingering or using the expression of pain for secondary gain?
- How can we reliably elicit sensitive information from an adolescent regarding substance abuse and sexual activity when such information is crucial to pursuing a differential diagnosis?
- How can we inform a child and his or her parents that treatment is no longer effective, and assist them in considering alternative therapies (including experimental treatments) or the option of palliative care?
- What can we say to a parent (or adolescent) to ensure medication compliance when noncompliance can be fatal?
- How can we establish rapport with a child who refuses to communicate or discuss his or her medical condition with the staff?
- How can we deal with parents who refuse to allow their child to know his or her positive HIV status and the reasons for treatment and hospitalization?
- Will altering the administration of CNS radiation in a high-risk leukemic patient (e.g., administering less rads per dose but a greater number of doses) reduce his or her risk for cognitive deficits, and, if so, how long after receiving radiation will the effects be manifest?

In some domains of practice, we have been more responsive than others. On the negative side, for example, we continue to document the alarming incidence of medication noncompliance but have not been successful in finding ways to ameliorate it. We have not adequately addressed the need for preventive studies in pediatric medicine. On the more positive side, many of the kinds of interventions that have been studied to help children endure the pain of invasive medical procedures or a prolonged confinement in medical centers are being widely used and have made the hospital experience more tolerable for children and their families. Some of the demonstrated late effects of CNS treatment for children with cancer have resulted in altered yet equally efficacious treatment regimens, but we still need to better understand the nature of cognitive as well as psychosocial late effects so that we can more adequately monitor children's development. A new era of openness in informing and communicating with children about their illness and treatment has dramatically changed the reciprocal roles of patients and pediatricians, and this is nowhere more dramatic than in the most unfortunate cases when medicine fails and children begin the process of dying. The development of palliative care consultation services in the pediatric departments of many medical centers is extending the concept of medical education to more fully encompass the entire range of patient care. Studies in pediatric psychology contribute to how we communicate with dying children and their families, and how we teach residents to do so.

The kinds of methodological concerns that need to be advanced in studies in pediatric psychology are not very different from those in other areas of psychology, particularly those that have applied contexts associated with them. We need more sensitive and situated measures that reflect the particular concerns of the children and families with whom we work, rather than adapting generalized trait-based self-report paper-and-pencil kinds of questionnaires; we need more intervention studies to replace simple correlational kinds of studies; and we need to study change effects longitudinally rather than cross-sectionally. To achieve these research aims, we need to train pediatric psychologists to be sensitive clinicians as well as developmental researchers who both understand and appreciate the scientist/practitioner model of training.

Finally, it is unreasonable to expect that scientific findings from pediatric psychology, or any other scientific discipline, will adequately resolve practitioners' questions. Scientific findings are based on data aggregated from samples of participants who are known for study only in terms of a few variables that are systematically varied in order to test outcomes and effects. All other ways in which study participants vary from one another are left to error variance. The challenge of practice, however, always involves a novel case; a certain patient or family in a certain situation at a certain time. Meeting the challenge requires clinical experience, judgment, local or idiographic knowledge, ethical considerations, and close and enduring collaborations with others in the context of practice. Scientific findings serve the challenge but never in a calculated or deterministic way because practice is not simply applying science. This is as it ought to be because, otherwise, the accumulation of scientific findings, along with technological advancements in storing, organizing, and disseminating them, would convert the quality of clinical practice to increasingly technological parameters such that the telos would become a computerized formula steering the practitioner along each step, from diagnosis to cure. Such a model of development is no more appropriate for medicine than it is for pediatric psychology.

ACKNOWLEDGMENTS

Preparation of this chapter was assisted by Linda Granowetter, M.D., who provided medical consultation; Andrea

Sadow, who provided bibliographic assistance; and colleagues, reviewers, and editors.

REFERENCES

Abidin, R. R. (1983). *Parenting stress index.* Charlottesville, VA: Pediatric Psychology Press.

Abrams, R. D., & Finesinger, J. E. (1953). Guilt reactions in patients with cancer. *Cancer, 6,* 474–482.

Achenbach, T. M. (1978). The child behavior profile: 1. Boys aged 6–11. *Journal of Consulting and Clinical Psychology, 46,* 478–488.

Achenbach, T. M., & Edelbrock, C. (1983). *Manual for the Child Behavior Checklist.* Burlington: University of Vermont.

Achenbach, T. M., McConaughy, S. H., & Howell, C. T. (1987). Child/adolescent behavioral and emotional problems: Implications of cross-informant correlations for situational specificity. *Psychological Bulletin, 101,* 213–232.

Adams, D. W., & Deveau, E. J. (1987). When a brother or sister is dying of cancer: The vulnerability of the adolescent sibling. *Death Studies, 11,* 279–295.

Allen, D. A., Tennen, H., McGrade, B. J., Affleck, G., & Ratzan, S. (1983). Parent and child perceptions of the management of juvenile diabetes. *Journal of Pediatric Psychology, 8* 129–141.

Altshuler, J. L., Genevro, J. L., Ruble, D. N., & Bornstein, M. H. (1995). Children's knowledge and use of coping strategies during hospitalization for elective surgery. *Journal of Applied Developmental Psychology, 16,* 53–76.

Altshuler, J. L., & Ruble, D. N. (1989). Developmental changes in children's awareness of strategies for coping with uncontrollable stress. *Child Development, 60,* 1337–1349.

American Academy of Pediatrics Task Force. (1978). *The future of pediatric education.* Evanston, IL: American Academy of Pediatrics.

American Psychiatric Association. (1987). *Diagnostic and statistical manual of mental disorders* (3rd ed.). Washington, DC: Author.

American Psychiatric Association. (1994). *Diagnostic and statistical manual of mental disorders,* (4th ed.). Washington, DC: Author.

Anderson, B. J., & Coyne, J. C. (1993). Family context and compliance behavior in chronically ill children. In N. A. Krasnegor, L. Epstein, S. B. Johnson, & S. Yaffe (Eds.), *Developmental aspects of health compliance behavior* (pp. 77–89). Hillsdale, NJ: Erlbaum.

Anderson, S., & Messick, S. (1974). Social competency in young children. *Developmental Psychology, 10,* 282–293.

Andraski, F., Burke, E. J., Attanasio, V., & Rosenblum, E. L. (1985). Child, parent, and physician reports of child's headache pain: Relationships prior to and following treatment. *Headache, 25,* 421–425.

Angold, A., Weissman, M. M., John, K., Merikangas, K. R., Prusoff, B. A., Wickramaratne, P., Gammon, G. D., & Warner, V. (1987). Parent and child reports of depressive symptoms in children at low and high risk of depression. *Journal of Child Psychology and Psychiatry, 28,* 901–915.

APA Task Force on Pediatric AIDS. (1989). Pediatric AIDS and human immunodeficiency virus infections: Psychological issues. *American Psychologist, 44,* 258–264.

Armstrong, F. D. (1992). Psychosocial intervention in pediatric cancer: A strategy for prevention of long-term problems. In T. Field, P. McCabe, & N. Schneiderman (Eds.), *Stress and coping in infancy & childhood* (pp. 197–218). Hillsdale, NJ: Erlbaum.

Armstrong, F. D., Lemanek, K. L., Pegelow, C. H., Gonzalez, J. C., & Martinez, A. (1993). Impact of lifestyle disruption on parent and child coping, knowledge, and parental discipline in children with sickle cell anemia. *Children's Health Care, 22,* 189–203.

Armstrong, F. D., Pegelow, C. H., Gonzalez, J. C., & Martinez, A. (1992). Impact of children's sickle cell history on nurse and physician ratings of pain and medication decisions. *Journal of Pediatric Psychology, 17,* 651–664.

Armstrong, F. D., Seidel, J. F., & Swales, T. P. (1993). Pediatric HIV infection: A neuropsychological and educational challenge. *Journal of Learning Disabilities, 26,* 92–103.

Armstrong, F. D., Thompson, R. J., Wang, W., Zimmerman, R., Pegelow, C. H., Miller, S., Moser, F., Bello, J., Hurtig, A., & Vass, K. (1996). Cognitive functioning and brain MRI in children with SCD. *Pediatrics, 97,* 864–870.

Armstrong, F. D., Tolendano, I. S., Lackman, L., & Miloslavich, K. (1991, April). *Quality of life issues in acute lymphocytic leukemia.* Paper presented at the meeting of the Pediatric Oncology Group, St. Louis, MO.

Armstrong-Dailey, A., & Goltzer, S. Z. (1993). *Hospice care for children.* New York: Oxford University Press.

Ashkanazi, S., Amir, J., Volovitz, B., & Varsano, I. (1993). Why do asthmatic children need referral to an emergency room? *Pediatric Allergy Immunology, 4,* 93–96.

Austin, J. K., & Huberty, T. J. (1993). Development of the Child Attitude Toward Illness scale. *Journal of Pediatric Psychology, 18,* 467–480.

Bach, S. R. (1974). Spontaneous pictures of leukemic children as an expression of the total personality, mind and body. *Acta Paedopsychiatry, 41,* 86–104.

Bakeman, R., & Quera, V. (1995). *Analyzing interaction: Sequential analysis with SDD and GSEQ.* Cambridge, England: Cambridge University Press.

Baker, L. H., Jones, J., Stovall, A., Zeltzer, L. K., Heiney, S. P., Sensenbrenner, L., Tebbi, C. K., Spoerl, E. J., & Zook, D.

(1993). American Cancer Society workshop on adolescents and young adults with cancer. *Cancer, 71,* 2410–2425.

Baker-Ward, L., Gordon, B. N., Ornstein, P. A., Larus, D. M., & Clubb, P. A. (1993). Young children's long-term retention of a pediatric examination. *Child Development, 64,* 1519–1533.

Balk, D. (1983). Effects of sibling death on teenagers. *Journal of Public Health, 53,* 14–18.

Band, E. B., & Weisz, J. R. (1988). How to feel better when it feels bad: Children's perspectives on coping with everyday stress. *Developmental Psychology, 24,* 247–253.

Bandura, A. (1977). Self-efficacy: Toward a unifying theory of behavioral change. *Psychological Review, 84,* 191–215.

Bard, M., & Dyk, R. D. (1956). The psychodynamic significance of beliefs regarding the cause of serious illness. *Psychoanalytic Review, 43,* 146–162.

Beales, J. G., Lennox-Holt, P., Keen, J., & Mellor, V. (1983). Children with juvenile chronic arthritis: Their beliefs about their illness and therapy. *Annals of Rheumatic Diseases, 42,* 481–486.

Bearison, D. J. (1991a). *"They never want to tell you"—Children talk about cancer.* Cambridge, MA: Harvard University Press.

Bearison, D. J. (1991b). Interactional contexts of cognitive development: Piagetian approaches to sociogenesis. In L. T. Landsmann (Ed.), *Culture, schooling and psychological development.* Norwood, NJ: ABLEX.

Bearison, D. J. (1994). Medication compliance in pediatric oncology. In D. J. Bearison & R. K. Mulhern (Eds.), *Pediatric psychooncology: Psychological perspectives on children with cancer.* New York: Oxford University Press.

Bearison, D. J., & Mulhern, R. K. (Eds.). (1994). *Pediatric psychooncology: Psychological perspectives on children with cancer.* New York: Oxford University Press.

Bearison, D. J., & Pacifici, C. (1984). Psychological studies of children who have cancer. *Journal of Applied Developmental Psychology, 5,* 263–280.

Bearison, D. J., & Pacifici, C. (1989). Children's event knowledge of cancer treatment. *Journal of Applied Developmental Psychology, 10,* 469–486.

Bearison, D. J., Sadow, A. J., Granowetter, L., & Winkel, G. (1993). Patients' and parents' causal attributions for childhood cancer. *Journal of Psychosocial Oncology, 11,* 47–61.

Bearison, D. J., & Zimiles, H. (Eds.). (1986). *Thought and emotion: Developmental perspectives.* Hillsdale, NJ: Erlbaum.

Beck, A. T., Ward, C. H., & Mendelson, M. (1961). An inventory for measuring depression. *Archives of General Psychiatry, 4,* 561–571.

Beck, D. E., Fennel, R. S., Yost, R. L., Robinson, J. D., Geary, M. B., & Richards, G. A. (1980). Evaluation of an education program on compliance with medication regimens in pediatric patients with renal transplants. *Journal of Pediatrics, 96,* 1094–1097.

Becker, M G., Isaac, W., & Hynd, G. W. (1987). Neuropsychological development of nonverbal behaviors attributed to "frontal lobe" functioning. *Developmental Neuropsychology, 3,* 275–298.

Beckman, H. B., & Frankel, R. M. (1984). The effect of physician behavior on the collection of data. *Annals of Internal Medicine, 101,* 692–696.

Benedek, E. P., & Schetky, D. H. (1987a). Problems in validating allegations of sexual abuse: Part 1. Factors affecting perception and recall of events. *Journal of the American Academy of Child and Adolescent Psychiatry, 26,* 912–915.

Benedek, E. P., & Schetky, D. H. (1987b). Problems in validating allegations of sexual abuse: Part 2. Clinical evaluation. *Journal of the American Academy of Child and Adolescent Psychiatry, 26,* 916–921.

Bennett, D. S. (1992). Adolescent health—a time for action. *Journal of Adolescent Health, 13,* 340.

Bennett, D. S. (1994). Depression among children with chronic medical problems: A meta-analysis. *Journal of Pediatric Psychology, 19,* 149–169.

Berman, A. L., & Jobes, D. A. (1991). *Adolescent suicide: Assessment and intervention.* Washington, DC: American Psychological Association.

Berman, D., Duncan, A. M., & Zeltzer, L. K. (1992). The evaluation and management of pain in the infant and young child with cancer. *British Journal of Cancer, 66,* S84–S89.

Bernstein, A. C., & Cowan, P. A. (1981). Children's concepts of birth and sexuality. In R. Bibace & M. E. Walsh (Eds.), Children's conceptions of health, illness, and bodily functions [Special issue]. *New Directions for Child Development, 14,* 9–30.

Beyer, J. E., DeGood, D. E., Ashley, L. C., & Russell, G. A. (1983). Patterns of postoperative analgesic use with adults and children following cardiac surgery. *Pain, 17,* 71–81.

Bibace, R., & Walsh, M. E. (1979). Developmental stages in children's conceptions of illness. In G. C. Stone, F. Cohen, & N. E. Adler (Eds.), *Health psychology* (pp. 285–301). San Francisco: Jossey-Bass.

Bibace, R., & Walsh, M. E. (1980). Development of children's concepts of illness. *Pediatrics, 66,* 912–917.

Bibace, R., & Walsh, M. E. (1981). Children's conceptions of illness. In R. Bibace & M. E. Walsh (Eds.), *New directions for child development: Children's conceptions of health, illness, and bodily functions* (pp. 31–48). San Francisco: Jossey-Bass.

Bibace, R., & Walsh, M. E. (1982). Conflict of roles: On the difficulties of being both scientist and practitioner in one life. *Professional Psychology, 13,* 389–396.

Bieri, D., Reeve, R., Champion, G., Addicoa, L., & Ziegler, J. (1990). The Faces Pain Scale for the self-assessment of the severity of pain experienced by children: Development, initial validation and preliminary investigation for ratio scale properties. *Pain, 41,* 139–150.

Binger, C. M., Ablin, A. R., Feuerstein, R. C., Kushner, J. H., Zoger, S., & Mikkelsen, C. (1969). Childhood leukemia: Emotional impact on patient and family. *New England Journal of Medicine, 303,* 414–418.

Blackwell, B. (1973). Patient compliance. *New England Journal of Medicine, 289,* 249–252.

Bloom, M., Fischer, J., & Orme, J. G. (1995). *Evaluating practice: Guidelines for the accountable professional* (2nd ed.). Boston: Allyn & Bacon.

Bloom, B., Knorr, R., & Evans, E. (1985). The epidemiology of disease expenses: The costs of caring for children with cancer. *Journal of the American Medical Association, 253,* 2393–2397.

Blount, R. L., Bachanas, P. J., Powers, S. W., Cotter, M. C., Franklin, A., Chaplin, W., Mayfield, J., Henderson, M., & Blount, S. D. (1992). Training children to cope and parents to coach them during routine immunizations: Effects on child, parent and staff behaviors. *Behavior Therapy, 23,* 689–705.

Blount, R. L., Corbin, S. M., Sturges, J. W., Wolfe, V. V., Prater, J. M., & James, L. D. (1989). The relationship between adults' behavior and child coping and distress during BMA/LP procedures: A sequential analysis. *Behavior Therapy, 20,* 585–601.

Blount, R. L., Landolf-Fritsche, B., Powers, S. W., & Sturges, J. W. (1991). Differences between high and low coping children and between parent and staff behaviors during painful medical procedures. *Journal of Pediatric Psychology, 16,* 795–809.

Blount, R. L., Powers, S. W., Cotter, M. W., Swan, S., & Free, K. (1994). Making the system work: Training pediatric oncology patients to cope and their parents to coach them during BMA/LP procedures. *Behavior Modification, 18,* 6–31.

Blount, R. L., Sturges, J. W., & Powers, S. W. (1990). Analysis of child and adult behavioral variations by phase of medical procedure. *Behavior Therapy, 21,* 33–48.

Bluebond-Langner, M. (1978). *The private worlds of dying children.* Princeton, NJ: Princeton University Press.

Bonadonna, G., & Valaquessa, P. (1981). Dose-response effect of adjuvant chemotherapy in breast cancer. *New England Journal of Medicine, 43,* 169.

Bowers, K. (1968). Pain, anxiety and perceived control. *Journal of Consulting and Clinical Psychology, 32,* 596–602.

Brantley, H. T., Stabler, B., & Whitt, J. K. (1981). Program considerations in comprehensive care of chronically ill children. *Journal of Pediatric Psychology, 6,* 229–237.

Bray, J. H., & Rogers, J. C. (1995). Linking psychologists and family physicians for collaborative practice. *Professional Psychology: Research and Practice, 26,* 132–138.

Breslau, N., & Marshall, I. A. (1985). Psychological disturbance in children with physical disabilities: Continuity and change in a 5-year follow-up. *Journal of Abnormal Psychology, 13,* 199–216.

Brewster, A. (1982). Chronically ill hospitalized children's concepts of their illness. *Pediatrics, 69,* 355–362.

Brodie, B. (1974). Views of healthy children toward illness. *American Journal of Public Health, 64,* 1156.

Brody, D. S. (1980). Physician recognition of behavioral, psychological and social aspects of medical care. *Archives of Internal Medicine, 140,* 1286–1289.

Bronfenbrenner, J. (1979). *The ecology of human development.* Cambridge, MA: Harvard University Press.

Brooks-Gunn, J. (1992). Why do adolescents have difficulty adhering to health regimes? In N. A. Krasnegor (Ed.), *Developmental aspects of health and compliance behavior.* Hillsdale, NJ: Erlbaum.

Brooks-Gunn, J., Boyer, C., & Hein, K. (1988). Preventing HIV infection and AIDS in children and adolescents: Behavioral research and intervention strategies [Special issue]. *American Psychologist: Psychology and AIDS, 43,* 958–964.

Broome, M. E. (1986). The relationship between children's fears and behavior during a painful event. *Children's Health Care, 14,* 142–145.

Brouwers, P., Belman, A. L., & Epstein, L. G. (1991). Central nervous system involvement: Manifestations and evaluation. In P. A. Pizzo & C. M. Wilfert (Eds.), *Pediatric AIDS: The challenge of HIV infection in infants, children, and adolescents* (pp. 318–355). Baltimore: Williams & Wilkens.

Brown, A. L., & Scott, M. S. (1971). Recognition memory for pictures in preschool children. *Journal of Experimental Child Psychology, 11,* 401–412.

Brown, L. K., & Fritz, G. K. (1988). Children's knowledge and attitudes about AIDS. *Journal of the American Academy of Child and Adolescent Psychiatry, 27,* 504–508.

Brown, R. T., Armstrong, F. D., & Eckman, J. R. (1993). Neurocognitive aspects of pediatric sickle cell disease. *Journal of Learning Disabilities, 26,* 33–45.

Brown, R. T., Buchanan, I., Doepke, K., Eckman, J. R., Baldwin, K., Goonan, B., & Schoenherr, S. (1993). Cognitive and academic functioning in children with sickle cell disease. *Journal of Clinical Child Psychology, 22,* 207–218.

Brown, R. T., Madan-Swain, A., Pais, R., Lambert, R. G., Sexson, S., & Ragab, A. (1992). Chemotherapy for acute lymphocytic leukemia: Cognitive and academic sequelae. *Journal of Pediatrics, 121,* 885–889.

Bruner, J. (1990). *Acts of meaning.* Cambridge, MA: Harvard University Press.

Burbach, D. J., & Peterson, L. (1986). Children's concepts of physical illness: A review and critique of the cognitive-developmental literature. *Health Psychology, 5,* 307–325.

Burstein, S., & Meichenbaum, D. (1979). The work of worrying in children undergoing surgery. *Journal of Abnormal Child Psychology, 7,* 121–132.

Bush, J. P., & Cockrell, C. S. (1987). Maternal factors predicting parenting behaviors in the pediatric clinic. *Journal of Pediatric Psychology, 12,* 505–518.

Bush, J. P., & Harkins, S. W. (Eds.). (1991). *Children in pain: Clinical and research issues from a developmental perspective.* New York: Springer-Verlag.

Bush, J. P., & Holmbeck, G. N. (1987). Children's attitudes about health care: Initial development of a questionnaire. *Journal of Pediatric Psychology, 12,* 429–433.

Bush, J. P., Melamed, B. G., Sheras, P. L., & Greenbaum, P. E. (1986). Mother–child patterns of coping with anticipatory medical stress. *Health Psychology, 5,* 137–157.

Butler, R. W., & Namerow, N. S. (1988). Cognitive retraining in brain-injury rehabilitation: A critical review. *Journal of Neurological Rehabilitation, 2,* 97–101.

Byer, J., & Wells, N. (1989). Assessment of pain in children. *Pediatric Clinics of North America, 36,* 837–854.

Cadman, D., Boyle, M., Szatmari, P., & Offord, D. R. (1987). Chronic illness, disability and mental and social well-being: Findings of the Ontario Child Health Study. *Pediatrics, 79,* 805–813.

Cairns, N., Clark, G., Black, J., & Lansky, S. (1979). Childhood cancer: Nonmedical costs of the illness. *Cancer, 43,* 403–408.

Califano, J. A. (1979). *The surgeon general's report on health promotion and disease prevention.* Washington, DC: U.S. Government Printing Office.

Callahan, D. (1993). *The troubled dream of life: Living with mortality.* New York: Simon & Schuster.

Campbell, J. D. (1975). Illness is a point of view: The development of children's concepts of illness. *Child Development, 46,* 92–100.

Campbell, L., Clark, M., & Kirkpatrick, S. E. (1986). Stress management training for parents and their children undergoing cardiac catheterization. *American Journal of Orthopsychiatry, 56,* 234–243.

Canning, E. H., Canning, R. D., & Boyce, W. T. (1992). Depressive symptoms and adaptive style in children with cancer. *Journal of the American Academy of Child and Adolescent Psychiatry, 31,* 1120–1124.

Carandang, M., Folkins, C., Hines, P., & Steward, M. (1979). The role of cognitive level and sibling illness. *American Journal of Orthopsychiatry, 49,* 474–481.

Carney, J., & Gerring, J. (1990). Return to school following severe closed head injury: A critical phase in pediatric rehabilitation. *Pediatrician, 17,* 222–229.

Carpenter, P. J. (1990). New method for measuring young children's self-report of fear and pain. *Journal of Pain and Symptom Management, 5,* 233–240.

Carpenter, P. J. (1992). Perceived control as a predictor of distress in children undergoing invasive medical procedures. *Journal of Pediatric Psychology, 17,* 757–773.

Carpenter, P. J., & LeVant, C. S. (1994). Sibling adaptation to the family crisis of childhood cancer. In D. J. Bearison & R. K. Mulhern (Eds.), *Pediatric psychooncology: Psychological perspectives on children with cancer* (pp. 122–142). New York: Oxford University Press.

Carpentieri, S. C., & Mulhern, R. K. (1993). Patterns of memory dysfunction among children surviving temporal lobe tumors. *Archives of Clinical Neuropsychology, 8,* 345–357.

Carpentieri, S. C., Mulhern, R. K., Douglas, S., Hanna, S., & Fairclough, D. L. (1993). Behavioral resiliency among children surviving brain tumors: A longitudinal study. *Journal of Clinical Child Psychology, 22,* 236–246.

Cary, S. (1985). *Conceptual change in childhood.* Cambridge, MA: MIT Press.

Cauce, A., Felner, R., & Primavera, J. (1982). Social support in high-risk adolescents: Structural components and adaptive impact. *American Journal of Community Psychology, 10,* 417–428.

Cayler, G., Lynn, D., & Stein, E. (1973). Effects of cardiac "non-disease" on intellectual and perceptual motor development. *British Heart Journal, 35,* 543–547.

Ceci, S. J., & Bruck, M. (1995). *Jeopardy in the courtroom.* Washington, DC: American Psychological Association.

Centers for Disease Control. (1988). Guidelines for effective school health education to prevent the spread of AIDS. *Health Education, 19,* 6–13.

Centers for Disease Control. (1989). HIV epidemic and AIDS: Trends in knowledge—United States, 1987 and 1988. *Morbidity and Mortality Weekly Report, 38,* 353–363.

Centers for Disease Control. (1993, October). HIV/AIDS surveillance report, third quarter edition (pp. 1–19).

Charney, E., Bynum, R., Eldredge, D., Frank, D., MacWhinney, J. B., McNabb, N., Scheiner, A., Sumpter, E. A., & Iker, H. (1967). How well do patients take oral penicillin? A collaborative study in private practice. *Pediatrics, 40,* 188–195.

Chesler, M., & Barbarin, O. (1984). Relating to the medical staff: How parents of children with cancer see the issues. *Health and Social Work, 9,* 59–65.

Chesler, M., & Barbarin, O. (1987). *Childhood cancer and the family: Meeting the challenge of stress and support.* New York: Brunner/Mazel.

Childers, P., & Wimmer, M. (1971). The concept of death in early childhood. *Child Development, 42,* 1299–1307.

Clubb, P. A., Nida, R. E., Merritt, K., & Ornstein, P. A. (1993). Visiting the doctor: Children's knowledge and memory. *Cognitive Development, 8,* 361–372.

Cole, M. (1988). Cross-cultural research in the socio-historical tradition. *Human Development, 31,* 137–157.

Cole, R. E., & Reiss, D. (Eds.). (1993). *How do families cope with chronic illness?* Hillsdale, NJ: Erlbaum.

Copeland, D. R., Fletcher, J. M., Pfefferbaum-Levine, F., Jaffe, N., Ried, H., & Maor, M. (1985). Neuropsychological sequelae of childhood cancer in long-term survivors. *Pediatrics, 75,* 745–753.

Corr, C. A., & Corr, D. M. (Eds.). (1983). *Hospice care principles and practice.* New York: Springer.

Costello, E. J., Edelbrock, C., Costello, A., Dulcan, M., Burns, G., & Brent, D. (1988). Psychopathology in pediatric primary care: The new hidden morbidity. *Pediatrics, 82,* 415–424.

Cox, D. J., Gonder, F. L., Pohl, S., & Pennebaker, J. W. (1983). Reliability of symptom–blood glucose relationships among insulin-dependent diabetics. *Psychosomatic Medicine, 45,* 357–360.

Craig, K. D., Hadjistavropoulos, H. D., Grunau, R. V., & Whitfield, M. F. (1994). A comparison of two measures of facial activity during pain in the newborn child. *Journal of Pediatric Psychology, 19,* 305–318.

Craig, K. D., McMahon, R., Morison, J., & Zaskow, C. (1984). Developmental changes in infant pain expression during immunization injections. *Social Science Medicine, 19,* 1331–1337.

Craufurd, D., Dodge, A., Kerzin-Storrar, L., & Harris, R. (1989). Uptake of presymptomatic testing for Huntington's disease. *Lancet, 2,* 603–605.

Crider, C. (1981). Children's conceptions of the body interior. In R. Bibace & M. E. Walsh (Eds.), *Children's conceptions of health, illness and bodily functions* (pp. 49–66). San Francisco: Jossey-Bass.

Crocker, A. C., Cohen, H. J., & Kastner, T. A. (Eds.). (1992). *HIV infection and developmental disabilities: A resource for service providers.* Baltimore: Brooks.

Cromer, B. A., & Tarnowski, K. J. (1989). Noncompliance in adolescents: A review. *Journal of Developmental Behavioral Pediatrics, 10,* 207–215.

Cummings, S. (1976). The impact of the child's deficiency on the father: A study of fathers of mentally retarded and chronically ill children. *American Journal of Orthopsychiatry, 46,* 246–255.

Dahlquist, L. M. (1990). Obtaining child reports in health care settings. In A. La Greca (Ed.), *Through the eyes of the child: Obtaining self-reports from children and adolescents* (pp. 395–439). Boston: Allyn & Bacon.

Dahlquist, L. M., Power, T. G., Cox, C. N., & Fernbach, D. J. (1994). Parenting and child distress during cancer procedures: A multidimensional assessment. *Children's Health Care, 23,* 149–166.

Damon, W. (1991). Problems of direction in socially shared cognition. In L. B. Resnick, J. M. Levine, & S. D. Teasley (Eds.), *Perspectives on socially shared cognition* (pp. 384–397). Washington, DC: American Psychological Association.

Daniels, D., Moos, R. H., Billings, A. G., & Miller, J. J. (1987). Psychosocial risk and resistance factors among children with chronic illness, healthy siblings, and health controls. *Journal of Abnormal Child Psychology, 15,* 295–308.

Davies, B. (1990). Long-term follow-up of bereaved siblings. In J. Morgan (Ed.), *The dying and bereaved teenager.* Philadelphia: Charles Press.

De Loye, G. J., Henggeler, S. W., & Daniels, C. M. (1993). Developmental and family correlates of children's knowledge and attitudes regarding AIDS. *Journal of Pediatric Psychology, 18,* 200–219.

DiClemente, R. J. (1991). Predictors of HIV-preventive sexual behavior in a high-risk adolescent population: The influence of perceived norms and sexual communication on incarcerated adolescents' consistent use of condoms. *Journal of Adolescent Health, 12,* 385–390.

Dimick, A. R. (1979). *Practical approaches to burn management.* Deerfield, IL: Flint Laboratories.

Dolgin, M. J., Katz, E. R., Doctores, S. R., & Siegel, S. E. (1986). Caregivers' perceptions of medical compliance in adolescents with cancer. *Journal of Adolescent Health Care, 7,* 22–27.

Doll, E. A. (1953). *The measurement of social competence: A manual for the Vineland Social Maturity Scale.* Circle Pines, MN: American Guidance Service.

Dollinger, S. J., Thelen, M. H., & Walsh, M. L. (1980). Children's concepts of psychological problems. *Journal of Clinical Child Psychology, 9,* 191–194.

Drotar, D. (1991). Coming of age: Critical challenges to the future development of pediatric psychology. *Journal of Pediatric Psychology, 16,* 1–12.

Drotar, D. (1993). Influences on collaborative activities among psychologists and pediatricians: Implications for practice, training, and research. *Journal of Pediatric Psychology, 18,* 159–172.

Drotar, D. (1995). *Consulting with pediatricians: Psychological perspectives.* New York: Plenum Press.

Drotar, D., La Greca, A. M., Lemanek, K., & Kazak, A. (1995). Case reports in pediatric psychology: Uses and guidelines for authors and reviewers. *Journal of Pediatric Psychology, 20,* 549–565.

Duffy, J. C. (1972). Emotional reactions of children to hospitalization. *Minnesota Medicine, 55,* 1168–1170.

Duke, M. P., & Cohen, B. (1975). Locus of control as an indicator of patient cooperation. *Journal of the American College of Dentistry, 42,* 174–178.

Duke, M. P., & Nowicki, S. A. (1972). A new measure and social-learning model for interpersonal distance. *Journal of Experimental Research in Personality, 6,* 119–132.

Dunbar, J. (1983). Compliance in pediatric populations: A review. In P. J. McGrath & P. Fireston (Eds.), *Pediatric and adolescent medicine: Issues in treatment.* New York: Springer.

Dunbar, J., Dunning, E. J., & Dwyer, K. (1993). The development of compliance research in pediatric and adolescent populations: Two decades of research. In N. Krasnegor, S. Johnson, I. Epstein, & S. Jaffe (Eds.), *Developmental aspects of health compliance behavior.* Hillsdale, NJ: Erlbaum.

Dworkin, P. H., Shonkoff, J., Leviton, A., & Levine, M. D. (1979). Training in developmental pediatrics: How practitioners perceive the gap. *American Journal of Diseases of Childhood, 133,* 709–712.

Dym, B., & Berman, S. (1986). The primary health care team: Family physician and family therapist in joint practice. *Family Systems Medicine, 4,* 9–21.

Eden, O. B., Black, I., MacKinlay, G. A., & Emery, A. E. (1994). Communication with parents of children with cancer. *Palliative Medicine, 8,* 105–114.

Eisen, E., Ware, J. E., Donald, C. A., & Brook, R. H. (1979). Measuring components of children's health status. *Medical Care, 27,* 254–268.

Eiser, C., Eiser, J. R., & Lang, J. (1990). How adolescents compare AIDS with other diseases: Implications for prevention. *Journal of Pediatric Psychology, 15,* 97–103.

Eland, J. M., & Anderson, J. E. (1977). The experience of pain in children. In A. K. Jacox (Ed.), *Pain: A source book for nurses and other health professionals* (pp. 453–471). New York: Little, Brown.

Elliott, C. H., Jay, S. M., & Woody, P. (1987). An observation scale for measuring children's distress during medical procedures. *Journal of Pediatric Psychology, 12,* 543–551.

Elliott, C. H., & Olson, R. (1983). The management of children's behavioral distress in response to painful medical treatments for burn injury. *Behavior Research and Therapy, 21,* 675–683.

Ellis, J. A., & Spanos, N. P. (1994). Cognitive-behavioral interventions for children's distress during bone marrow aspirations and lumbar punctures: A critical review. *Journal of Pain and Symptom Management, 9,* 96–108.

Ellsworth, R. B. (1978). *Personal Adjustment and Role Skills Scale.* Palo Alto, CA: Consulting Psychologists Press.

Engestrom, Y. (1993). Developmental studies of work as a testbench of activity theory: The case of primary care medical practice. In S. Chaiklin & J. Lave (Eds.), *Understanding practice: Perspectives on activity and context* (pp. 64–103). Cambridge, England: Cambridge University Press.

Engle, N. A., Rodrique, J. R., & Geffken, G. R. (1994). Parent–child agreement on ratings of anxiety in children. *Psychological Reports, 75,* 1251–1260.

Ensminger, M. E. (1987). Adolescent sexual behavior as it relates to other transition behaviors in youth. In S. L. Hofferth & C. D. Hayes (Eds.), *Risking the future: Adolescent sexuality, pregnancy, and child bearing* (Vol. II, pp. 36–55). Washington, DC: National Academy Press.

Epstein, L. H. (1984). The direct effects of compliance on health outcome. *Health Psychology, 3,* 385–393.

Epstein, L. G., Sharer, L., Oleske, J., Connor, E. M., Goudsmit, J., Bagdon, L., Robert-Guroff, M., & Koenigsberger, M. R. (1986). Neurologic manifestations of human immunodeficiency virus infection in children. *Pediatrics, 78,* 678–687.

Epstein, L. M., & Cluss, P. A. (1982). A behavioral medicine perspective to long-term medical regimens. *Journal of Consulting and Clinical Psychology, 50,* 950–971.

Erickson, C. J. (1990). *Strategies for coping with illness: Parents' Scale.* Unpublished manuscript, Columbia-Presbyterian Medical Center, New York.

Eron, D. L., Gentry, J., & Schlegal, P. (Eds.). (1994). *Reason to hope: A psychosocial perspective on violence and youth.* Washington, DC: American Psychological Association.

Etzwiler, D. D., & Robb, J. R. (1972). Evaluation of programmed education among juvenile diabetics and their families. *Diabetes, 21,* 967–971.

Evans, L., & Spelman, M. (1983). The problem of noncompliance with drug therapy. *Drugs, 25,* 63–76.

Evers-Kiebooms, G., Swerts, A., Cassiman, J. J., & Van den Berghe, H. (1989). The motivation of at-risk individuals and their partner in deciding for or against predictive testing for Huntington disease. *Clinical Genetics, 35,* 29–40.

Fanurik, D., Zeltzer, L. K., Roberts, M. C., & Blount, R. L. (1993). The relationship between children's coping styles and psychological interventions for cold pressor pain. *Pain, 53,* 213–222.

Fassler, D., McQueen, K., Duncan, P., & Copeland, L. (1990). Children's perceptions of AIDS. *Journal of American Academy of Child and Adolescent Psychiatry, 29,* 459–462.

Faulkner, K. W. (1993). Children's understanding of death. In A. Armstrong-Dailey & S. Z. Goltzer (Eds.), *Hospice care for children* (pp. 9–21). New York: Oxford University Press.

Feinstein, A. R. (1979). Compliance bias and the interpretation of therapeutic trials. In R. B. Haynes, D. W. Taylor, & D. L. Sackett (Eds.), *Compliance in health care.* Baltimore: Johns Hopkins University Press.

Festa, R., Tamaroff, M. H., Chasalow, F., & Lanzkowsky, P. (1992). Therapeutic adherence to oral medication regimens by adolescents with cancer: Laboratory assessment. *Journal of Pediatrics, 120,* 807–811.

Finney, J. W., Christophersen, E. R., Friman, P. C., Kalnins, I. V., Maddux, J. E., Peterson, L., Roberts, M. C., & Wolraich, M. (1993). Society of Pediatric Psychology Task Force Report: Pediatric psychology and injury control. *Journal of Pediatric Psychology, 18,* 499–526.

Fletcher, J. M., Brookshire, F. L., Landry, S. H., Bohan, T. P., Davidson, K. C., Francis, D. J., Thompson, N. M., & Miner, M. E. (1995). Behavioral adjustment of children with hydrocephalus: Relationships with etiology, neurological, and family status. *Journal of Pediatric Psychology, 20,* 109–125.

Fletcher, J. M., & Copeland, D. R. (1988). Neurobehavioral effects of central nervous system prophylactic treatment of cancer in children. *Journal of Clinical and Experimental Neuropsychology, 4,* 495–538.

Folkman, S. (1992). Making the case for coping. In B. N. Carpenter (Ed.), *Personal coping: Theory, research and application.* Westport, CT: Praeger/Greenwood.

Folkman, S., & Lazarus, R. S. (1988). *Ways of Coping questionnaire.* Palo Alto, CA: Consulting Psychological Press.

Follmer, A., & Gordon, B. N. (1994, April). *Does enactment facilitate children's recall of a pediatric examination?* Paper delivered at the biennial meetings of the Conference on Human Development, Pittsburgh, PA.

Fowler, M. G., Johnson, M. P., & Atkinson, S. S. (1985). School achievement and absence in children with chronic health conditions. *Journal of Pediatrics, 106,* 683–786.

Fowler, M. G., Whitt, J. K., Lallinger, R. R., Nash, K. B., Atkinson, S. S., Wells, R. J., & McMillan, C. (1988). Neuropsychologic and academic functioning of children with sickle cell anemia. *Journal of Developmental and Behavioral Pediatrics, 9,* 213–220.

Fowler-Kerry, S., & Lander, J. (1987). Management of injection pain in children. *Pain, 30,* 169–175.

Frederick, C. J. (1985). Selected foci in the spectrum of post-traumatic stress disorders. In J. Laube & S. A. Murphy (Eds.), *Perspective on disaster recovery* (pp. 110–130). East Norwalk, CT: Appleton-Century Crofts.

Freud, A. (1952). The role of bodily illness in the mental life of children. *Psychoanalytic Study of the Child, 7,* 69–81.

Friedman, S. B., Chodoff, P., Mason, J. W., & Hamburg, D. A. (1963). Behavioral observations of parents anticipating the death of a child. *Pediatrics, 32,* 610–625.

Fritz, G. K., Klein, R. B., & Overholser, J. C. (1990). Accuracy of symptom perception in childhood asthma. *Journal of Developmental and Behavioral Pediatrics, 11,* 69–72.

Fritz, G. K., Rubinstein, S., & Lewiston, N. J. (1987). Psychological factors in fatal childhood asthma. *American Journal of Orthopsychiatry, 57,* 253–257.

Fritz, G. K., Spirito, A., & Young, A. (1994). Utility of the repressive defense style construct in childhood. *Journal of Clinical Child Psychology, 23,* 306–313.

Fritz, G. K., & Williams, J. (1988). Issues of adolescent development for survivors of childhood cancer. *Journal of the American Academy of Child and Adolescent Psychiatry, 27,* 712–715.

Fritz, G. K., Williams, J. R., & Amylon, M. (1988). After treatment ends: Psychosocial sequelae in pediatric cancer survivors. *American Journal of Orthopsychiatry, 58,* 552–561.

Fritz, G. K., Yeung, A., & Taitel, M. S. (1994). Symptom perception and self-management in childhood asthma. *Current Opinion in Pediatrics, 6,* 423–427.

Furstenberg, F. F., Brooks-Gunn, J., & Morgan, S. P. (1987). *Adolescent mothers in later life.* New York: Cambridge University Press.

Futterman, E. H., & Hoffman, I. (1970). Transient school phobia in a leukemia child. *Journal of the American Academy of Child Psychiatry, 9,* 477–494.

Futterman, E. H., Hoffman, I., & Sabshin, M. (1972). Parental anticipatory mourning. In B. Schoenberg, A. C. Carr, D. Peretz, & C. Kutscher (Eds.), *Psychosocial aspects of terminal care* (pp. 243–272). New York: Columbia University Press.

Gedaly-Duff, V. (1991). Developmental issues: Preschool and school age children. In J. Bush & S. Harkins (Eds.), *Children in pain: Clinical and research issues from a developmental perspective* (pp. 195–230). New York: Elsevier.

Gellert, E. (1962). Children's conceptions of the content and functions of the human body. *Genetic Psychology Monographs, 65,* 293–405.

Gesten, E. L. (1976). A health resources inventory: The development of a measure of the personal and social competence of primary grade children. *Journal of Consulting and Clinical Psychology, 44,* 775–786.

Giardi, P., DePisa, E., & Cianfriglia, F. (1992). Compliance with treatment for head and neck cancer: The influence of psychologic and psychopathologic variables: A longitudinal study. *European Journal of Psychiatry, 6,* 40–50.

Gil, K. M., Abrams, M. R., Phillips, G., & Keefe, F. J. (1989). Sickle cell disease pain: Relation of coping strategies to adjustment. *Journal of Consulting and Clinical Psychology, 57,* 725–731.

Gil, K. M., Williams, D. A., Thompson, R. J. J., & Kinney, T. R. (1991). Sickle cell disease in children and adolescents: The relation of child and parent pain-coping strategies to adjustment. *Journal of Pediatric Psychology, 16,* 643–663.

Gillman, J. B., & Mullins, L. L. (1991). Pediatric pain management: Professional and pragmatic issues. In J. P. Bush & S. W. Harkins (Eds.), *Children in pain: Clinical and research issues from a developmental perspective* (pp. 117–148). New York: Springer-Verlag.

Gizyunski, M., & Shapiro, V. B. (1990). Depression and childhood illness. *Child and Adolescent Social Work, 7,* 179–197.

Glasgow, R. E. (1991). Compliance in diabetes regimens: Conceptualizations, complexity, and determinants. In J. A. Cramer & B. Spilker (Eds.), *Patient compliance in medical practice and clinical trials.* New York: Raven Press.

Glasgow, R. E., & Anderson, B. J. (1995). Future directions for research on pediatric chronic disease management: Lessons from diabetes. *Journal of Pediatric Psychology, 20,* 389–402.

Glasgow, R. E., McCaul, D. K., & Schafer, L. C. (1987). Self-care behaviors and glycemic control in type 1 diabetes. *Journal of Chronic Diseases, 40,* 399–412.

Gogan, J. L., Koocher, G. P., Fine, W. E., Foster, D. J., & O'Malley, J. E. (1979). Pediatric cancer survival and marriage: Issues affecting adult adjustment. *American Journal of Orthopsychiatry, 49,* 423–430.

Goldman, R. J., & Goldman, J. D. (1982). How children perceive the origins of babies and the role of mothers and fathers in procreation: A cross-national study. *Child Development, 53,* 491–504.

Goldsmith, C. H. (1979). The effect of compliance distributions on therapeutic trials. In B. Haynes, D. W. Taylor, & D. L.

Sackett (Eds.), *Compliance in health care.* Baltimore: Johns Hopkins University Press.

Gonzalez, J. C., Routh, D. K., & Armstrong, F. D. (1993a). Effects of maternal distraction versus reassurance on children's reactions to injections. *Journal of Pediatric Psychology, 18,* 593–604.

Gonzalez, J. C., Routh, D. K., & Armstrong, F. D. (1993b). Differential medication of child versus adult postoperative patients: The effect of nurses' assumptions. *Children's Health Care, 22,* 47–59.

Gonzalez, J. C., Routh, D. K., Saab, P. G., Armstrong, F. D., Shifman, L., Guerra, E., & Fawcett, N. (1989). Effects of parent presence on children's reactions to injections: Behavioral, physiological, and subjective aspects. *Journal of Pediatric Psychology, 14,* 449–462.

Good, M., Good, B., & Cleary, P. (1987). Do patient attitudes influence physician recognition of psychosocial problems in primary care? *Journal of Family Practice, 25,* 53–59.

Goodman, G. S., Quas, J. A., Batterman-Faunce, J. M., Riddlesberger, M. M., & Kuhn, J. (1994). Predictors of accurate and inaccurate memories of traumatic events experienced in childhood. *Consciousness and Cognition, 3,* 269–294.

Goodnow, J., & Collins, A. (1991). *Ideas according to parents.* Hillsdale, NJ: Erlbaum.

Goodwin, D. A., Boggs, S. R., & Graham-Pole, J. (1994). Development and validation of the Pediatric Oncology Quality of Life Scale. *Psychological Assessment, 6,* 321–328.

Gordon, B. N., Ornstein, P. A., Nida, R. E., Follmer, A., Crenshaw, M. C., & Albert, G. (1993). Does the use of dolls facilitate children's memory of visits to the doctor? *Applied Cognitive Psychology, 7,* 459–474.

Gortmaker, S. L., & Sappenfield, W. (1984). Chronic disorders: Prevalence and impact. *Pediatric Clinics of North America, 31,* 3–18.

Gortmaker, S. L., Walker, D. K., Weitzman, M., & Sobel, A. M. (1990). Chronic conditions, socioeconomic risks, and behavioral problems in children and adolescents. *Pediatrics, 85,* 267–276.

Goyette, C. K., Conners, C. K., & Ulrich, R. F. (1978). Normative data on revised Conners Parent and Teacher Rating Scales. *Journal of Abnormal Child Psychology, 46,* 221–236.

Graber, A., Christman, B., Alonga, M., & Davidson, J. K. (1977). Evaluation of diabetes patient education program. *Diabetes, 26,* 61–64.

Granowetter, L. (1994). Pediatric oncology: A medical overview. In D. J. Bearison & R. K. Mulhern (Eds.), *Pediatric psychooncology: Psychological perspectives on children with cancer* (pp. 9–34). New York: Oxford University Press.

Grant, M., Ferrell, B., Schmidt, G. M., Fonbuena, P., Niland, J. C., & Forman, S. J. (1992). Measurement of quality of life in bone marrow transplantation survivors. *Quality of Life Research, 1,* 375–384.

Gratz, R., & Pilivian, J. (1984). What makes kids sick: Children's beliefs about the causative actors of illness. *Children's Health Care, 12,* 156–162.

Green, D. M., Zevon, M. A., & Hall, B. (1991). Achievement of life goals by adult survivors of modern treatment for childhood cancer. *Cancer, 67,* 206–213.

Greenberg, H. S., Kazak, A. E., & Meadows, A. T. (1989). Psychological functioning in 8- to 16-year-old cancer survivors and their parents. *Journal of Pediatrics, 114,* 488–493.

Greenberg, H. S., & Meadows, A. T. (1991). Psychosocial impact of cancer survival on school-age children and their parents. *Journal of Psychosocial Oncology, 9,* 43–56.

Gross, A. M., & Drabman, R. S. (1990). Clinical behavioral pediatrics: An introduction. In A. M. Gross & R. S. Drabman (Eds.), *Handbook of clinical behavioral pediatrics.* New York: Plenum Press.

Gross, A. M., Stein, R. M., Levin, R. G., Dale, J., & Wojnilower, D. A. (1983). The effect of mother–child separation on the behavior of children experiencing a diagnostic medical procedure. *Journal of Consulting and Clinical Psychology, 51,* 783–785.

Hadjistavropoulos, H. D., Ross, M. A., & von Baeyer, C. L. (1990). Are physicians' ratings of pain affected by patients' physical attractiveness? *Social Science and Medicine, 31,* 69–72.

Hafferty, F. W., & Franks, R. (1994). The hidden curriculum, ethics teaching, and the structure of medical education. *Academic Medicine, 69,* 861–871.

Hagglund, K. J., Clay, D. L., Frank, R. G., Beck, N. C., Kashani, J. H., Hewett, J., Johnson, J., Goldstein, D. E., & Cassidy, J. T. (1994). Assessing anger expression in children and adolescents. *Journal of Pediatric Psychology, 19,* 291–304.

Hall, J. A., Harrigan, J. A., & Rosenthal, R. (1995). Nonverbal behavior in clinician–patient interaction. *Applied and Preventive Psychology, 4,* 21–37.

Hall, J. A., Irish, J. T., Roter, D. L. E., Erlich, C. M., & Miller, L. H. (1994). Gender in medical encounters: An analysis of physician and patient communication in a primary care setting. *Health Psychology, 13,* 384–392.

Hall, J. A., Roter, D. L., & Rand, C. S. (1981). Communication of affect between patient and physician. *Journal of Health and Social Behavior, 22,* 18–30.

Hanson, C. L., DeGuire, M. J., Schinkel, A. M., & Henggeler, S. W. (1992). Comparing social learning and family systems correlates of adaptation in youths with IDDM. *Journal of Pediatric Psychology, 17,* 555–572.

Hardy, M. S., Armstrong, F. D., Routh, D. K., Albrecht, J., & Davis, J. (1994). Coping and communication among parents and children with human immunodeficiency virus and cancer. *Developmental and Behavioral Pediatrics, 15,* S49–S53.

Harper, D. C. (1991). Paradigms for investigating rehabilitation and adaptation to childhood disability and chronic illness. *Journal of Pediatric Psychology, 16,* 533–542.

Harrigan, J. A. (1985). Self-touching as an indicator of underlying affect and language processes. *Social Science and Medicine, 20,* 1161–1168.

Harriman, L. M., Griffith, E. R., Hurtig, A. L., & Keehn, M. T. (1991). Functional outcomes of children with sickle-cell disease affected by stroke. *Archives of Physical Medicine Rehabilitation, 72,* 498–502.

Harter, S. (1985). *The self-perception profile for children: Revision of the perceived competence scale for children. Manual.* Denver, CO: University of Denver.

Haynes, R. B. (1976). Strategies for improving compliance: A methodological analysis and review. In D. L. Sackett & R. B. Haynes (Eds.), *Compliance with therapeutic regimens.* Baltimore: Johns Hopkins University Press.

Haynes, R. B. (1979). Determinants of compliance: The disease and the mechanics of treatment. In R. B. Haynes, D. W. Taylor, & D. L. Sackett (Eds.), *Compliance in health care.* Baltimore: Johns Hopkins University Press.

Haynes, R. B., Taylor, D. W., & Sackett, D. L. (1979). *Compliance in health care.* Baltimore: Johns Hopkins University Press.

Hays, D. M., Landsverk, J., Sallan, W. E., Hewett, K. D., Patenaude, A. F., Schoonover, D., Zilber, S. L., Ruccione, K., & Siegel, S. E. (1992). Educational, occupational, and insurance status of childhood cancer survivors in the fourth and fifth decades of life. *Journal of Clinical Oncology, 10,* 1397–1406.

Henggeler, S. W., Melton, G. B., & Rodrique, J. (1992). *Pediatric and adolescent AIDS: Research findings from the social sciences.* Newbury Park, CA: Sage.

Henley, N. M. (1977). *Body politics: Power, sex, and nonverbal communication.* Englewood Cliffs, NJ: Prentice-Hall.

Hergenrather, J. R., & Rabinowitz, M. (1991). Age-related differences in the organization of children's knowledge of illness. *Developmental Psychology, 27,* 952–959.

Herson, M., & Barlow, D. H. (1976). *Single-case experimental design: Strategies for studying behavior change.* New York: Pergamon Press.

Hilgard, J. R., & LeBaron, S. (1982). Relief of anxiety and pain in children and adolescents with cancer: Quantitative measures and clinical observations. *International Journal of Clinical and Experimental Hypnosis, 4,* 417–422.

Hobbs, N., & Perrin, J. M. (Eds.). (1985). *Issues in the care of children with chronic illness.* San Francisco: Jossey-Bass.

Hogan, N. S., & Greenfied, D. B. (1991). Adolescent sibling bereavement symptomatology in a large community sample. *Journal of Adolescent Research, 6,* 97–112.

Holland, J. C., Geary, N., Marchini, A., & Tross, S. (1987). An international survey of physician attitudes and practice in regard to revealing the diagnosis of cancer. *Cancer Investigation, 5,* 151–154.

Hooper, E. M., Comstock, M. S., Goodwin, J. M., & Goodwin, J. S. (1982). Patient characteristics that influence physician behavior. *Medical Care, 20,* 630–638.

Hopkins, K. M. (1989). Emerging patterns of services and case finding for children with HIV infection. *Mental Retardation, 27,* 219–222.

Horwitz, W., & Kazak, A. (1990). Family adaptation to childhood cancer: Sibling and family systems variables. *Journal of Clinical and Child Psychology, 19,* 221–228.

Hubert, N. C., Jay, S. M., Saltoun, M., & Hayes, M. (1988). Approach/avoidance and distress in children undergoing preparation for painful medical procedures. *Journal of Clinical Child Psychology, 17,* 194–202.

Hutter, J. J., Farrell, F. Z., & Meltzer, P. S. (1991). Care of the child dying from cancer: Home vs. hospital. In D. Papadatou & C. Papadatos (Eds.), *Children and death* (pp. 197–208). Washington, DC: Hemisphere.

Iannotti, R. J., & Bush, P. J. (1993). Toward a developmental theory of compliance. In N. A. Krasnegor, L. H. Epstein, S. B. Johnson, & S. J. Yaffe (Eds.), *Developmental aspects of health compliance behavior* (pp. 59–76). Hillsdale, NJ: Erlbaum.

Ilowite, N. T., Walco, G. A., & Pochaczevsky, R. (1992). Assessment of pain in patients with juvenile rheumatoid arthritis: Relation between pain intensity and degree of joint inflammation. *Annals of Rheumatic Diseases, 51,* 343–346.

Inui, T. S., Carter, W. B., Pecorato, R. E., Pearlman, R. A., & Dohan, J. J. (1980). Variation in patient compliance with common long-term drugs. *Medical Care, 18,* 986–993.

Irwin, C. E., & Millstein, S. G. (1991). Risk-taking behaviors during adolescence. In R. M. Lerner, A. C. Petersen, & J. Brooks-Gunn (Eds.), *Encyclopedia of adolescence* (pp. 935–943). New York: Garland Press.

Izard, C. E. (1979). *The maximally discriminative facial movement coding system (max).* Newark: University of Delaware Instructional Resources Center.

Izard, C. E. (1986). Approaches to developmental research on emotion-cognition relationships. In D. J. Bearison & H. Zimiles (Eds.). *Thought and emotion: Developmental perspectives.* Hillsdale, NJ: Erlbaum.

Jacobsen, P. B., Manne, S., Gorfinkle, K., Schorr, O., Rapkin, B., & Redd, W. (1990). Analysis of child and parent behavior during painful medical procedures. *Health Psychology, 9,* 559–576.

Jacobson, A. M., Hauser, S. T., Wolfsdorf, J. I., Houlihan, J., Millery, J. E., Herskowitz, R. D., Wertlief, D., & Watt, E. (1987). Psychologic predictors of compliance in children with recent onset of diabetes mellitus. *Journal of Pediatrics, 110,* 805–811.

Jamison, R. N., Lewis, S., & Burish, T. G. (1986a). Cooperation with treatment in adolescent cancer patients. *Journal of Adolescent Health Care, 7,* 162–167.

Jamison, R. N., Lewis, S., & Burish, T. G. (1986b). Psychological impact of cancer on adolescents: Self-image, locus of control, perception of illness, and knowledge of cancer. *Journal of Chronic Diseases, 39,* 609–617.

Jay, S. M. (1988). Invasive medical procedures: Psychological intervention and assessment. In K. D. Routh (Ed.), *Handbook of pediatric psychology* (pp. 401–423). New York: Guilford Press.

Jay, S. M., & Elliott, C. H. (1990). A stress inoculation program for parents whose children are undergoing painful medical procedures. *Journal of Consulting and Clinical Psychology, 58,* 799–804.

Jay, S. M., Elliott, C. H., Katz, E., & Siegel, S. E. (1987). Cognitive-behavioral and pharmacologic interventions for children's distress during painful medical procedures. *Journal of Consulting and Clinical Psychology, 55,* 860–865.

Jay, S. M., Elliott, C. H., Ozolins, M., Olson, R. A., & Pruitt, S. D. (1985). Behavioral management of children's distress during painful medical procedures. *Behavior Research and Therapy, 23,* 513–520.

Jay, S. M., Ozolins, M., Elliott, C., & Caldwell, S. (1983). Assessment of children's distress during painful medical procedures. *Journal of Health Psychology, 2,* 133–147.

Johnson, S. B. (1992). Methodological issues in diabetes research: Measuring adherence. *Diabetes Care, 15,* 1658–1667.

Johnson, S. B. (1993). Chronic disease of childhood: Assessing compliance with complex medical regimens. In N. A. Krasnegor, L. H. Epstein, S. B. Johnson, & S. J. Yaffe (Eds.), *Developmental aspects of health compliance behavior* (pp. 157–184). Hillsdale, NJ: Erlbaum.

Johnson, S. B., Silverstein, J., Rosenbloom, A., Carter, R., & Cunningham, W. (1986). Assessing daily management in childhood diabetes. *Health Psychology, 5,* 545–564.

Jones, R. T., McDonald, D., & Shinske, F. (1990). Accident prevention: Overview and reconceptualization. In A. M. Gross & R. S. Drabman (Eds.), *Handbook of clinical and behavioral pediatrics* (pp. 383–402). New York: Plenum Press.

Kagan, J. (1966). Reflection-impulsivity: The generality and dynamics of conceptual tempo. *Journal of Abnormal Psychology, 71,* 17–24.

Kaplan, D. M., Smith, A., Grobstein, R., & Flischman, S. E. (1973). Family mediation of stress. *Social Work, 18,* 60–69.

Kaplan, S. L., Busner, J., Weinhold, C., & Lennon, P. (1987). Depressive symptoms in children and adolescents with cancer: A longitudinal study. *Journal of the American Academy of Child and Adolescent Psychiatry, 26,* 782–787.

Kaplan, S. L., Hong, G. K., & Weinhold, C. (1984). Epidemiology of depressive symptomatology in adolescents. *Journal of the American Academy of Child Psychiatry, 23,* 91–98.

Karon, M., & Vernick, J. (1968). Approaches to emotional support of fatally ill children. *Clinical Pediatrics, 7,* 274–280.

Karp, S. A., & Konstadt, N. (1971). *Children's Embedded Figures Test.* Palo Alto, CA: Consulting Psychologists Press.

Kashani, J. H., Barbero, G. J., & Bolander, F. D. (1981). Depression in hospitalized pediatric patients. *Journal of the American Academy of Child Psychiatry, 20,* 123–134.

Kashani, J. H., & Hakami, N. (1982). Depression in children and adolescents with malignancy. *Canadian Journal of Psychiatry, 27,* 474–477.

Kashani, J. H., & Simmonds, J. F. (1979). Incidence of depression in children. *American Journal of Psychiatry, 20,* 1203–1205.

Katz, E. R., Kellerman, J., & Siegel, S. E. (1980). Behavioral distress in children with cancer undergoing medical procedures: Developmental considerations. *Journal of Consulting and Clinical Psychology, 48,* 356–365.

Kaufman, K. L., Holden, E. W., & Walker, C. E. (1989). Future directions in pediatric and clinical psychology. *Professional Psychology, 20,* 148–152.

Kazak, A. E. (1987). Professional helpers and families with disabled children: A social network perspective. *Marriage and Family Review, 11,* 177–191.

Kazak, A. E. (1989). Families of chronically ill children: A systems and social-ecological model of adaptation and challenge. *Journal of Consulting and Clinical Psychology, 57,* 25–30.

Kazak, A. E. (1994). Implications for survival: Pediatric oncology patients and their families. In D. J. Bearison & R. K. Mulhern (Eds.), *Pediatric psychooncology: Psychological perspectives on children with cancer* (pp. 171–192). New York: Oxford University Press.

Kazak, A. E., Boyer, B. A., Brophy, P., Johnson, K., Scher, C. D., Covelman, K., & Scott, S. (1995). Parental perceptions of procedure-related distress and family adaptation in childhood leukemia. *Children's Health Care, 24,* 143–158.

Kazak, A. E., & Marvin, R. (1984). Differences, difficulties and adaptation: Stress and social networks in families with a handicapped child. *Family Relations, 33,* 67–77.

Kazak, A. E., & Meadows, A. (1989). Families of young adolescents who have survived cancer: Social-emotional adjustment, adaptability, and social support. *Journal of Pediatric Psychology, 14,* 175–191.

Kazak, A. E., & Nachman, G. S. (1991). Family research on childhood chronic illness: Pediatric oncology as an example. *Journal of Family Psychology, 4,* 462–483.

Kazak, A. E., Reber, M., & Carter, A. (1988). Structural and qualitative aspects of social networks in families with young chronically ill children. *Journal of Pediatric Psychology, 13,* 171–182.

Kazak, A. E., Segal-Andrews, A. M., & Johnson, K. (1995). Pediatric psychology research and practice: A family/systems approach. In M. C. Roberts (Ed.), *Handbook of pediatric psychology* (2nd ed.). New York: Guilford Press.

Kazak, A. E., Stuber, M., Torchinsky, M., Houskamp, B., Christakis, D., & Kasiraj, J. (1992, August). *Post-traumatic stress in childhood cancer survivors and their parents.* Poster presented at the annual meeting of the American Psychological Association, Washington, DC.

Kazdin, A. E., Colbus, D., & Rodgers, A. (1986). Assessment of depression and diagnosis of depressive disorder among psychiatrically disturbed children. *Journal of Abnormal Child Psychology, 14,* 499–515.

Kegeles, S., Adler, N., & Irwin, D. (1988). Sexually active adolescents and condoms: Changes over the year in knowledge, attitudes and use. *American Journal of Public Health, 78,* 460–461.

Kellerman, J. (1980). *Psychological aspects of childhood cancer.* Springfield, IL: Thomas.

Kellerman, J., Zeltzer, L., Ellenberg, L., & Dash, J. (1983). Adolescents with cancer: Hypnosis for the reduction of the acute pain and anxiety associated with medical procedures. *Journal of Adolescent Health Care, 4,* 85–90.

Kellerman, J., Zeltzer, L., Ellenberg, L., Dash, J., & Rigler, D. (1980). Psychological effects of illness in adolescence: Anxiety, self-esteem and perception of control. *Journal of Pediatrics, 97,* 126–131.

Kelley, M. L., Jarvic, G. J., Middlebrook, J. L., McNeer, M. F., & Drabman, R. S. (1984). Decreasing burned children's pain behavior: Impacting the trauma of hydrotherapy. *Journal of Applied Behavioral Analysis, 17,* 147–158.

Kendrick, A. H., Higgs, C. M., Whitfield, M. J., & Laszlo, G. (1993). Accuracy of perception of severity of asthma: Patient treated in general practice. *British Medical Journal, 307,* 422–424.

Kessler, S., Field, T., Worth, L., & Mosbarger, H. (1987). Attitudes of persons at risk for Huntington disease toward predictive testing. *American Journal of Medical Genetics, 26,* 259–270.

Kirscht, J. P. (1972). Perceptions of control and health beliefs. *Canadian Journal of Behavioral Sciences, 4,* 225–237.

Kister, M. C., & Patterson, C. J. (1980). Children's conceptions of the causes of illness: Understanding of contagion and use of immanent justice. *Child Development, 51,* 839–846.

Kleigher, J. H., & Dirks, J. F. (1979). Medication compliance in chronic asthmatic patients. *Journal of Asthma Research, 16,* 225–237.

Klopovich, P. M., & Trueworthy, R. C. (1985). Adherence to chemotherapy regimens among children with cancer. *Topics in Clinical Nursing, 7,* 19–25.

Knapp, M. L., & Hall, J. A. (1992). *Nonverbal communication in human interaction* (3rd ed.). Ft. Worth: Holt, Rinehart and Winston.

Knight, R. B., Atkins, A., Eagle, C. J., Evans, N., Finkelstein, J. W., Fukushima, D., Katz, J., & Weiner, H. (1979). Psychological stress, ego defenses, and cortisol production in children hospitalized for elective surgery. *Psychosomatic Medicine, 41,* 40–49.

Kodish, E., Lantos, J., Stocking, C., Singer, P. A., Siegler, M., & Johnson, F. L. (1991). Bone marrow transplantation for sickle cell disease: A study of parents' decisions. *New England Journal of Medicine, 325,* 1349–1353.

Koocher, G. P. (1973). Children, death, and cognitive development. *Developmental Psychology, 9,* 369–375.

Koocher, G. P. (1974). Taking with children about death. *American Journal of Orthopsychiatry, 44,* 404–411.

Koocher, G. P. (1981). Children's conceptions of death. In R. Bibace & M. E. Walsh (Eds.), *Children's conceptions of health, illness, and bodily functions* (pp. 85–100). San Francisco: Jossey-Bass.

Koocher, G. P. (1994). Foreword. In D. J. Bearison & R. K. Mulhern (Eds.), *Pediatric psychooncology: Psychological perspectives on children with cancer* (pp. ix–x). New York: Oxford University Press.

Koocher, G. P., Czajkowski, D. R., & Fitzpatrick, J. R. (1987). *Manual for the Medical Compliance Incomplete Stories Test (MCIST).* Boston: Children's Hospital Medical Center.

Koocher, G. P., & O'Malley, J. E. (1981). *The Damocles syndrome: Psychological consequences of surviving childhood cancer.* New York: McGraw-Hill.

Korsch, B. M., Fine, R. N., & Negrete, V. F. (1978). Noncompliance in adolescents with renal transplants. *Pediatrics, 61,* 872–876.

Korsch, B. M., Freemon, B., & Negrete, V. F. (1971). Practical implications of doctor–patient interaction analysis for pediatric practice. *American Journal of Diseases of Childhood, 121,* 110–114.

Korsch, B. M., Gozzi, E. K., & Francis, V. (1968). Gaps in doctor–patient communication: Interaction and patient satisfaction. *Pediatrics, 42,* 855–871.

Korsch, B. M., Negrete, V. F., Mercer, A. S., & Freemon, B. (1971). How comprehensive are well-child visits? *American Journal of Diseases of Childhood, 122,* 483–488.

Kovacs, M. (1980/1981). Rating scales to assess depression in school-aged children. *Acta Paedopsychiatrica, 46,* 303–315.

Kovacs, M. (1992). *Children's Depressive Inventory (CDI) manual.* North Tonawanda, NY: Multi-Health Systems.

Kovacs, M., & Beck, A. T. (1977). An empirical-clinical approach toward a definition of childhood depression. In J. G. Schulterbrandt & A. Raskin (Eds.), *Depression in childhood: Diagnosis, treatment and conceptual models* (pp. 1–25). New York: Raven Press.

Kovacs, M., Brent, D., Steinberg, T. F., Poulauskas, S., & Reid, J. (1986). Children's self-reports of psychologic adjustment and coping strategies during first year insulin-dependent diabetes mellitus. *Diabetes Care, 9,* 472–479.

Kovacs, M., Iyengar, S., Goldston, D., Stewart, J., Obrosky, D., & Marsch, A. (1990). Psychological functioning of children with insulin-dependent diabetes mellitus: A longitudinal study. *Journal of Pediatric Psychology, 15,* 619–632.

Krahn, G. (1993). Conceptualizing social support in families of children with special health care needs. *Family Processes, 32,* 235–248.

Krulik, T., Holaday, B., & Martinson, I. M. (Eds.). (1987). *The child and family facing life-threatening illness.* Philadelphia: Lippincott.

Kubler-Ross, E. (1983). *On children and death.* New York: Macmillan.

Kugelmann, R. (1992). *Stress: The nature and history of engineered grief.* Westport, CT: Praeger/Greenwood.

Kupst, M. J. (1994). Coping with pediatric cancer: Theoretical and research perspectives. In D. J. Bearison & R. K. Mulhern (Eds.). *Pediatric psychooncology: Psychological perspectives on children with cancer* (pp. 35–60). New York: Oxford University Press.

Kupst, M. J., Natta, M. B., Richardson, C. C., Schulman, J. L., Lavigne, J. V., & Das, L. (1995). Family coping with pediatric leukemia: Ten years after treatment. *Journal of Pediatric Psychology, 20,* 601–617.

Kvien, T. K., Hoyeraal, H. M., & Sandstad, B. (1982). Assessment methods of disease activity in juvenile rheumatoid arthritis evaluated in a prednisone/placebo double-blind study. *Journal of Rheumatology, 9,* 696–702.

La Greca, A. M. (1988a). Adherence to prescribed medical regimens. In D. K. Routh (Ed.), *Handbook of pediatric psychology* (pp. 299–320). New York: Guilford Press.

La Greca, A. M. (1988b). Children with diabetes and their families: Coping and disease management. In T. M. Field, P. M. McCabe, & N. Schneiderman (Eds.), *Stress and coping across development* (pp. 139–159). Hillsdale, NJ: Erlbaum.

La Greca, A. M. (1990a). Issues in adherence with pediatric regimens. *Journal of Pediatric Psychology, 15,* 423–436.

La Greca, A. M. (1990b). Social consequences of pediatric conditions: A fertile area for future investigation and intervention? *Journal of Pediatric Psychology, 15,* 285–307.

La Greca, A. M. (1992). Peer influences in pediatric chronic illness: An update. *Journal of Pediatric Psychology, 17,* 775–784.

La Greca, A. M., & Hanna, N. C. (1983). Health beliefs of children and their mothers: Implications for treatment. *Diabetes, 32*(Suppl. 1), 66.

LaMontagne, L. L. (1987). Children's preoperative coping: Replication and extension. *Nursing Research, 36,* 163–167.

Landry, S. H., Robinson, S. S., Copeland, D., & Garner, P. W. (1993). Goal-directed behavior and perception of self-competence in children with spinal bifida. *Journal of Pediatric Psychology, 18,* 389–396.

Langer, E. J., Janis, I., & Wolfer, J. (1974). Effects of a cognitive coping devise and preparatory information on psychological stress in surgical patients. *Journal of Experimental Social Psychology, 11,* 155–163.

Lansky, S. B., Cairns, N. U., Hussanein, R., Wehr, B., & Lowman, J. (1978). Childhood cancer: Parental discord and divorce. *Pediatrics, 62,* 184–188.

Lansky, S. B., List, M. A., Lansky, L. L., Ritter-Sterr, C., & Miller, D. R. (1987). The measurement of performance in childhood cancer patients. *Cancer, 60,* 1651–1656.

Lansky, S. B., List, M. A., & Ritter-Sterr, C. (1989). Psychiatric and psychological support of the child and adolescent with cancer. In P. A. Pizzo & D. G. Poplack (Eds.), *Principles and practice of pediatric oncology.* Philadelphia: Lippincott.

Lansky, S. B., Smith, S. D., Cairns, N. U., & Cairns, G. F. (1983). Psychological correlates of compliance. *American Journal of Pediatric Hematology/Oncology, 5,* 87–92.

Laurendeau, M., & Pinard, A. (1962). *Causal thinking in the child.* New York: International Universities Press.

Lavigne, J. V., & Burns, W. J. (1981). *Pediatric psychology: An introduction to pediatricians and psychologists.* New York: Grune & Stratton.

Lavigne, J. V., Christoffel, K. K., Binns, H. J., Rosenbaum, D., Arend, R., & Smith, K. (1991, September). *Psychopathology among preschoolers in pediatric primary care: Prevalence and pediatric recognition.* Presented at the 5th Annual NIMH International Research Conference on the Classification, Recognition, and Treatment of Mental Disorders in General Medical Settings, Bethesda, MD.

Lavigne, J. V., & Faier-Routman, J. (1992). Psychological adjustment to pediatric physical disorders: A meta-analytic review. *Journal of Pediatric Psychology, 17,* 133–157.

Lazarus, R. S., & Folkman, S. (1984). *Stress, appraisal, and coping.* New York: Springer.

LeBaron, S., & Zeltzer, L. (1984). Assessment of acute pain and anxiety in children and adolescents by self-reports, observer reports, and a behavior checklist. *Journal of Consulting and Clinical Psychology, 55,* 729–738.

Lefcourt, H. (1973). The function of the illusions of control and freedom. *American Psychologist, 28,* 417–425.

Leiken, S. (1982). Minor's assent or dissent in medical treatment. In President's Commission for the Study of Ethical Problems in Medicine and Biomedical and Behavioral Research (Ed.), *Making health care decisions* (pp. 175–191). Washington, DC: U.S. Government Printing Office.

Lemanek, K. L., Moore, S. L., Gresham, F. M., Williamson, D. A., & Kelly, M. L. (1986). Psychosocial adjustment of children with sickle cell anemia. *Journal of Pediatric Psychology, 11,* 397–410.

Lerman, C., Rimer, B. K., & Engstrom, P. E. (1991). Cancer risk notification: Psychosocial and ethical implications. *Journal of Clinical Oncology, 9,* 1275–1282.

Leventhal, H., Meyer, D., & Nerenz, D. (1980). The common sense representation of illness danger. In S. Rachman (Ed.),

Contributions to medical psychology (pp. 7–30). New York: Pergamon Press.

Leventhal, H., Nerenz, D., & Steele, D. J. (1984). Illness representations and coping with health threats. In A. Baum, S. E. Taylor, & J. E. Singer (Eds.), *Handbook of psychology and health* (pp. 219–252). Hillsdale, NJ: Erlbaum.

Lipson, M. (1994). Disclosure of diagnosis to children with human immunodeficiency virus or acquired immunodeficiency syndrome. *Journal of Developmental Behavioral Pediatrics, 15,* 61–65.

Litt, I. F., & Cuskey, W. R. (1980). Compliance with medical regimens during adolescence. *Pediatric Clinics of North America, 27,* 15–17.

Litt, I. F., Cuskey, W. R., & Rosenberg, A. (1982). Role of self-esteem and autonomy in determining medical compliance among adolescents with juvenile rheumatoid arthritis. *Pediatrics, 69,* 15–17.

Maccoby, E. E. (1980). *Social development: Psychological growth and the parent–child relationship.* New York: Harcourt Brace.

MacLean, W. E., Perrin, J. M., Gortmaker, S., & Pierre, C. B. (1992). Psychological adjustment of children with asthma: Effects of illness severity and recent stressful life events. *Journal of Pediatric Psychology, 17,* 159–171.

Madan-Swain, A., & Brown, R. T. (1991). Cognitive and psychosocial sequelae for children with acute lymphocytic leukemia and their families. *Clinical Psychology Review, 11,* 267–294.

Madan-Swain, A., Sexson, S. B., Brown, R. T., & Ragab, A. (1993). Family adaptation and coping among siblings of cancer patients, their brothers and sisters, and nonclinical controls. *The American Journal of Family Therapy, 21,* 60–70.

Maddox, J. E., Roberts, M. C., Sledden, E. A., & Wright, L. (1986). Developmental issues in child health psychology. *American Psychologist, 41,* 25–34.

Mandler, J. (1983). Representation. In J. H. Flavell & E. M. Markman (Eds.), *Handbook of child psychology* (Vol. 3, pp. 420–494). New York: Wiley.

Manne, S. L., Bakeman, R., Jacobsen, P. B., Gorfinkle, K., Bernstein, D., & Redd, W. H. (1992). Adult–child interaction during invasive medical procedures. *Health Psychology, 11,* 241–249.

Manne, S. L., Bakeman, R., Jacobsen, P. B., Gorfinkle, K., & Redd, W. H. (1994). An analysis of a behavioral intervention for children undergoing venipuncture. *Health Psychology, 13,* 556–566.

Manne, S. L., Bakeman, R., Jacobsen, P. B., & Redd, W. H. (1993). Children's coping during invasive medical procedures. *Behavior Therapy, 24,* 143–158.

Manne, S. L., Jacobsen, P. B., Gorfinkle, K., Gerstein, F., & Redd, W. H. (1993). Treatment adherence difficulties among children with cancer: The role of parenting style. *Journal of Pediatric Psychology, 18,* 47–62.

Manne, S. L., Jacobsen, P. B., & Redd, W. H. (1992). Assessment of acute pediatric pain: Do child self-report, parent ratings, and nurse ratings measure the same phenomenon? *Pain, 48,* 45–52.

Manne, S. L., Redd, W. H., Jacobsen, P. B., Gorfinkle, K., Schorr, O., & Rapkin, B. (1990). Behavioral intervention to reduce child and parent distress during venipuncture. *Journal of Consulting and Clinical Psychology, 58,* 565–572.

Marks, G., Richardson, J. L., Graham, J. W., & Levine, A. (1986). Role of health locus of control beliefs and expectations of treatment efficacy in adjustment to cancer. *Journal of Personality and Social Psychology, 51,* 443–450.

Marteau, T. M. (1994). Editorial: The genetic testing of children. *Journal of Medical Genetics, 31,* 743.

Martin, R. P. (1987). *Temperament assessment battery for children.* Brandon, VT: Clinical Psychology.

Martinson, I. M., Davies, E. B., & McClowry, S. G. (1987). The long-term effects of sibling death on self-concept. *Journal of Pediatric Nursing, 2,* 227–235.

Martinson, I. M., & Papadatou, D. (1994). Care of the dying child and the bereaved. In D. J. Bearison & R. K. Mulhern (Eds.), *Pediatric psychooncology: Psychological perspectives on children with cancer* (pp. 193–214). New York: Oxford University Press.

Mastromauro, C., Myers, R. H., & Berkman, B. (1987). Attitudes toward presymptomatic testing in Huntington disease. *American Journal of Medical Genetics, 26,* 271–282.

Mayes, S. D., Handford, H. A., Kowalski, C., & Schaefer, J. H. (1988). Parent attitudes and child personality traits in hemophilia: A six-year longitudinal study. *International Journal of Psychiatry and Medicine, 18,* 339–355.

Mazur, F. T. (1981). Adherence to health care regimens. In L. Pradley & C. Prokop (Eds.), *Medical psychology: Contributions to behavioral medicine.* New York: Academic Press.

McCaul, K. D., & Malott, J. M. (1984). Distraction and coping with pain. *Psychological Bulletin, 95,* 516–533.

McClowry, S. G., Davies, E. B., May, K., Kulenkamp, E. J., & Martinson, I. M. (1987). The empty space phenomenon: The process of grief in the bereaved family. *Death Studies, 11,* 361–374.

McCubbin, H. I., McCubbin, M. A., Nevin, R. S., & Cauble, E. (1981). *Coping–health inventory for parents.* St. Paul: University of Minnesota Family Social Services.

McElreath, L. H., & Roberts, M. C. (1992). Perceptions of acquired immune deficiency syndrome by children and their parents. *Journal of Pediatric Psychology, 17,* 477–490.

McGrath, P. A. (1990). *Pain in children.* New York: Guilford Press.

McGrath, P. J. (1991). Intervention and management. In J. Bush & S. W. Harkins (Eds.), *Children in pain: Clinical and research issues from a developmental perspective* (pp. 83–115). New York: Springer-Verlag.

McGrath, P. J., Cunningham, S. J., Goodman, J. T., & Unruh, A. (1986). The clinical measurement of pain in children: A review. *Clinical Journal of Pain, 1,* 221–227.

McIntire, M. S., Angle, C. R., & Struempler, L. J. (1972). The concept of death in midwestern children and youth. *American Journal of Diseases of Children, 123,* 527–532.

Meadows, A. (1991). Follow-up and care of childhood cancer survivors. *Hospital Practice, 26,* 91–100.

Meadows, A., & Silber, J. (1985). Delayed consequences of therapy for childhood cancer. *Cancer Journal for Clinicians, 35,* 271–286.

Melamed, B. G. (1982). Reduction of medical fears: An information processing analysis. In Boulougouris (Ed.), *Learning theory approaches to psychiatry* (pp. 205–218). New York: Wiley.

Melamed, B. G., Dearborn, M., & Hermecz, D. A. (1983). Necessary considerations for surgery preparation: Age and previous experience. *Psychosomatic Medicine, 45,* 517–525.

Melamed, B. G., & Siegel, L. J. (1975). Reduction of anxiety in children facing hospitalization and surgery by use of filmed modeling. *Journal of Consulting and Clinical Psychology, 43,* 511–521.

Mellette, S., & Franco, P. (1987). Psychosocial barriers to employment of the cancer survivor. *Journal of Psychosocial Oncology, 5,* 97–115.

Mellins, C. A., & Ehrhardt, A. A. (1993, April). *Families affected by pediatric AIDS: Sources of stress and coping.* Paper presented at the Fourth Florida Conference on Child Health Psychology, Gainsville, FL.

Mellins, R. B., Evans, D., Zimmerman, B., & Clark, N. M. (1992). Patient compliance: Are we wasting our time and don't know it? *American Review of Respiratory Diseases, 146,* 1376–1377.

Meltzer, J., Bibace, R., & Walsh, M. E. (1984). Children's concepts of smoking. *Journal of Pediatric Psychology, 9,* 41–56.

Meng, A., & Zastowny, T. (1982). Preparation for hospitalization: A stress inoculation training program for parents and children. *Maternal–Child Nursing Journal, 11,* 87–94.

Merritt, K. A., Ornstein, P. A., & Spicker, B. (1994). Children's memory for a salient medical procedure: Implications for testimony. *Pediatrics, 94,* 17–23.

Miles, M. (1985). Emotional symptoms and physical health in bereaved parents. *Nursing Research, 34,* 76–81.

Miller, S. M., Sherman, H. D., Roussi, P., Caputo, G. C., & Krus, L. (1995). Patterns of children's coping with an aversive dental treatment. *Health Psychology, 14,* 236–246.

Mooney, K. L. (1984). The Child Behavior Checklist. In D. J. Keyser & R. C. Sweetland (Eds.), *Test critiques* (pp. 181–182). Kansas City, MO: Westport.

Moore, I. M., Gilliss, C. L., & Martinson, I. M. (1988). Psychosomatic manifestations of bereavement in parents two years after the death of a child with cancer. *Nursing Research, 37,* 104–107.

Moos, R. H. (1974). *Family Environment Scale manual.* Palo Alto, CA: Consulting Psychologists Press.

Moos, R. H., & Moos, B. S. (1986). *Family Environment Scale manual* (2nd ed.). Palo Alto, CA: Consulting Psychologists Press.

Morrison, D. M. (1985). Adolescent contraceptive behavior: A review. *Psychological Bulletin, 98,* 538–568.

Morrissey, J. R. (1963). Children's adaptations to fatal illness. *Social Work, 8,* 81–88.

Moss, H. A., Nannis, E. D., & Poplack, D. G. (1981). The effects of prophylactic treatment of the central nervous system on the intellectual functioning of children with acute lymphocytic leukemia. *American Journal of Medicine, 71,* 47–52.

Mostow, E. N., Byrne, J., Connelly, R. R., & Mulvihill, J. J. (1991). Quality of life in long-term survivors of CNS tumors of childhood and adolescence. *Journal of Clinical Oncology, 9,* 592–599.

Mulhern, R. K. (1994). Neuropsychological late effects. In D. J. Bearison & R. K. Mulhern (Eds.), *Pediatric psychooncology: Psychological perspectives on children with cancer* (pp. 99–121). New York: Oxford University Press.

Mulhern, R. K., & Bearison, D. J. (1994). Future directions in pediatric psychooncology. In D. J. Bearison & R. K. Mulhern (Eds.), *Pediatric psychooncology: Psychological perspectives on children with cancer* (pp. 215–222). New York: Oxford University Press.

Mulhern, R. K., Crisco, J. J., & Camitta, B. M. (1981). Patterns of communication among pediatric patients with leukemia, parents, and physicians: Prognostic disagreements and misunderstandings. *Journal of Pediatrics, 99,* 480–483.

Mulhern, R. K., Fairclough, D., & Ochs, J. (1991). A prospective comparison of neuropsychologic performance of children surviving leukemia who receive 18 Gy, 24 Gy or no cranial irradiation. *Journal of Clinical Oncology, 9,* 1348–1356.

Mulhern, R. K., Fairclough, D. L., Smith, B., & Douglas, S. M. (1992). Maternal depression, assessment methods, and physical symptoms effect estimates od depressive symptomatology among children with cancer. *Journal of Pediatric Psychology, 17,* 313–326.

Mulhern, R. K., & Ochs, J. (1994). Caring for adolescent cancer survivors: Surveillance and intervention for delayed sequelae of malignancy and its treatment. *Adolescent Medicine: State of the Art Reviews, 5,* 259–269.

Myers-Vando, R., Steward, M., Folkins, C., & Hines, P. (1979). The effects of congenital heart disease on cognitive development, illness causality concepts, and vulnerability. *American Journal of Orthopsychiatry, 49,* 617–625.

Nader, P. R., Wexler, D. B., Patterson, T. L., McKusick, L., & Coates, T. (1989). Comparison of beliefs about AIDS among urban, suburban, incarcerated and gay adolescents. *Journal of Adolescent Health Care, 10,* 413–418.

Nagy, M. H. (1953). Children's conceptions of some bodily functions. *Journal of Genetic Psychology, 83,* 199–216.

National AIDS Information Clearinghouse. (1989). *Educational materials database.* Rockville, MD: Department of Health and Human Services.

National Center for Health Statistics. (1986). *Current estimates from the National Health Interview Survey: United States, 1985* (DHHS Publication No. PHS86-1588). Washington, DC: U.S. Government Printing Office.

Natterson, J. M., & Knudson, A. G., Jr. (1960). Observations concerning fear of death in fatally ill children and their mothers. *Psychosomatic Medicine, 22,* 456–465.

Nelms, B. C. (1989). Emotional behaviors in chronically ill children. *Journal of Abnormal Child Psychology, 17,* 657–688.

Nelson, K. (1981). Social cognition in script framework. In J. H. Flavell & L. Ross (Eds.), *The development of social cognition in childhood.* New York: Cambridge University Press.

Nelson, K. (1986). *Event knowledge: A functional approach to cognitive development.* Hillsdale, NJ: Erlbaum.

Neuhauser, D., Amsterdam, B., Hines, P., & Steward, M. (1978). Children's concepts of healing: Cognitive development and locus of control factors. *American Journal of Orthopsychiatry, 48,* 335–341.

Nir, Y. (1985). Post-traumatic stress disorder in children with cancer. In S. Eth & R. Pynoss (Eds.), *Post-traumatic stress disorder in children.* Washington, DC: American Psychiatric Press.

Nixon Speechley, K., & Noh, S. (1992). Surviving childhood cancer, social support, and parents' psychological adjustment. *Journal of Pediatric Psychology, 17,* 15–31.

Noll, R. B., Bukowski, W. M., Davies, W. H., Koontz, K., & Kulkarni, R. (1993). Adjustment in the peer system of adolescents with cancer: A two-year study. *Journal of Pediatric Psychology, 18,* 351–364.

Noll, R. B., Bukowski, W. M., Rogosch, F. A., LeRoy, S., & Kulkarni, R. (1990). Social interactions between children with cancer and their peers: Teacher ratings. *Journal of Pediatric Psychology, 15,* 43–56.

Novack, D. H., Plumer, R., Smith, R. L., Ochitill, H., Morrow, G. R., & Bennett, J. M. (1979). Changes in physicians' attitudes toward telling the cancer patient. *Journal of the American Medical Association, 241,* 897–900.

Novack, D. H., Volk, G., Drossman, D. A., & Lipkin, M., Jr. (1993). Medical interviewing and interpersonal skills teaching in U.S. medical schools. *Journal of the American Medical Association, 269,* 2101–2105.

Nowicki, S., & Strickland, B. R. (1973). A locus of control scale for children. *Journal of Consulting and Clinical Psychology, 40,* 148–154.

Offer, D. (1969). *The psychological world of the teenager.* New York: Basic Books.

Ollendick, T. H. (1983). Reliability and validity of the revised Fear Survey Schedule for Children (FSSC-R). *Behavior Research and Therapy, 21,* 685–692.

Olson, A. L., Boyle, W. E., & White, M. E. (1987). Functional health status of children cured of cancer. *American Journal of Diseases of Children, 141,* 372.

Olson, D. H., Portner, J., & Bell, R. (1982). Family adaptability and cohesion evaluation scales. In D. Olson (Ed.), *Family inventories: Inventories used in a national survey of families across the family life cycle.* St. Paul: University of Minnesota, Department of Family Social Science.

Olson, R. A., Holden, E. W., Friedman, A., Faust, J., Kenning, M., & Mason, P. J. (1988). Psychological consultation in children's hospital: An evaluation of services. *Journal of Pediatric Psychology, 13,* 479–492.

Ornstein, P. A., Shapiro, L. R., Clubb, P. A., Follmer, A., & Baker-Ward, L. (1996). The influence of prior knowledge on children's memory for salient medical experiences. In N. Stein, P. A. Ornstein, C. J. Brainerd, & B. Tversky (Eds.), *Memory for everyday and emotional events.* Hillsdale, NJ: Erlbaum.

Osborne, M. L., Kistner, J. A., & Helgemo, B. (1993). Developmental progression in children's knowledge of AIDS: Implications for education and attitudinal change. *Journal of Pediatric Psychology, 18,* 177–192.

Osborne, M. L., Kistner, J. A., & Helgemo, B. (1995). Parental knowledge and attitudes toward children with AIDS: Influences on educational policies and children's attitudes. *Journal of Pediatric Psychology, 20,* 79–90.

Ouellette, S. C. (1994). Different views of stress and coping research. *Contemporary Psychology, 39,* 873–874.

Pantell, R. H., Steward, T. J., Dias, J. K., Wells, P., & Ross, A. W. (1982). Physician communication with children and parents. *Pediatrics, 70,* 396–402.

Parcel, G. S., & Meyer, M. P. (1978). Development of an instrument to measure children's health locus of control. *Health Education Monographs, 6,* 149–159.

Parks, W., & Scott, G. (1987). An overview of pediatric AIDS: Approaches to diagnosis and outcome assessment. In S. Broder (Ed.), *Modern concepts and therapeutic challenges* (pp. 245–262). New York: Marcel Dekker.

Patenaude, A. F. (1995a, September). *Psychosocial and ethical issues in predictive testing of children for cancer susceptibility genes.* Paper presented at the 25th meeting of the International Society of Paediatric Oncology, Paris, France.

Patenaude, A. F. (1995b, September). *Cure of the child with cancer.* Paper presented at the 25th meeting of the International Society of Paediatric Oncology, Paris, France.

Patenaude, A. F. (1995c, April). *Attitudes toward predictive testing among mothers of pediatric oncology patients.* Paper presented at the meetings of the Pediatric Oncology Group, St. Petersburg Beach, FL.

Patenaude, A. F. (1995c, September). *Ethical and psychological issues in predisposition testing for cancer genes.* Paper presented at the 25th meeting of the International Society of Paediatric Oncology, Paris, France.

Patenaude, A. F. (in press). Psychosocial impact of familial cancers. In D. Malkin (Ed.), *Inherited tumors.* London: Springer.

Patenaude, A. F., & Rappeport, J. M. (1982). Surviving bone marrow transplantation: The patient in the other bed. *Annals of Internal Medicine, 97,* 915–918.

Patenaude, A. F., Szymanski, L., & Rappeport, J. (1979). Psychological costs of bone marrow transplantation in children. *American Journal of Orthopsychiatry, 49,* 409–422.

Patterson, J. (1990). Family and health research in the 1980's: A family scientist's perspective. *Family Systems Medicine, 8,* 421–434.

Peck, B. (1979). Effects of childhood cancer on longer-term survivors and their families. *British Medical Journal, 1,* 1327–1329.

Pennebaker, J. W. (1987). Physical symptoms and sensations: Psychological causes and correlates. In J. T. Cacippo & R. E. Petty (Eds.), *Social psychophysiology* (pp. 543–564). New York: Guilford Press.

Perrin, E. C., & Gerrity, P. S. (1981). There's a demon in your belly: Children's understanding of illness. *Pediatrics, 67,* 841–849.

Perrin, E. C., & Perrin, J. M. (1983). Clinicians' assessments of children's understanding of illness. *American Journal of Diseases of Children, 137,* 874–878.

Perrin, E. C., Sayer, A. G., & Willett, J. B. (1991). Sticks and stone may break my bones: Reasoning about illness causality and bodily functioning in healthy children and children who have a chronic illness. *Pediatrics, 88,* 608–619.

Perrin, E. C., Stein, R. E. K., & Drotar, D. (1991). Cautions in using the Child Behavior Checklist: Observations based on research about children with a chronic illness. *Journal of Pediatric Psychology, 16,* 411–421.

Perry, S., & Heidrich, G. (1982). Management of pain during debridement: A survey of U.S. burn units. *Pain, 25,* 171–186.

Peterson, C. (1980, October). *A sense of control over one's life: A review of recent literature.* Paper presented at the Social Science Research Council's meeting on "The Self and Personal Control over the Life Span," New York.

Peterson, L. H. (1989). Special series: Coping with medical illness and medical procedures. *Journal of Consulting and Clinical Psychology, 57,* 331–332.

Peterson, L., Harbeck, C., Chaney, J., Farmer, J., & Thomas, A. M. (1990). Children's coping with medical procedures: A conceptual overview and integration. *Behavioral Assessment, 12,* 197–212.

Peterson, L. H., & Shigetomi, C. (1981). The use of coping techniques to minimize anxiety in hospitalized children. *Behavior Therapy, 12,* 1–14.

Peterson, L. H., & Toler, S. M. (1986). An information-seeking disposition in child surgery patients. *Health Psychology, 5,* 343–358.

Phipps, S. (1994). Bone marrow transplantation. In D. J. Bearison & R. K. Mulhern (Eds.), *Pediatric psychooncology: Psychological perspectives on children with cancer* (pp. 143–170). New York: Oxford University Press.

Phipps, S., Fairclough, D., & Mulhern, R. K. (1995). Avoidant coping in children with cancer. *Journal of Pediatric Psychology, 20,* 217–232.

Phipps, S., & Srivastava, D. K. (in press). Repressive adaptation in children with cancer. *Health Psychology.*

Piaget, J. (1930). *The child's conception of physical causality.* London: Kegan Paul.

Piaget, J. (1952). *The origins of intelligence in children.* New York: International Universities Press.

Piers, E. V. (1977). *The Piers–Harris Children's Self-Concept Scale.* Los Angeles: Western Psychological Services.

Pinto, R. P., & Hollandsworth, J. G., Jr. (1984, May). *Preparing parents of pediatric surgical patients using a videotape model.* Paper presented at the meeting of the Society of Behavioral Medicine, Philadelphia.

Pizzo, P. A., Robichaud, K. J., Edwards, B. K., Schumaker, C., Kramer, B. S., & Johnson, S. (1983). Oral antibiotic prophylaxis in patients with cancer: A double-blind randomized placebo-controlled trial. *Journal of Pediatrics, 102,* 125–133.

Plumb, M. M., & Holland, J. (1977). Comparative studies of psychological function in patients with advanced cancer: 1. Self-reported depressive symptoms. *Psychosomatic Medicine, 39,* 264–276.

Porges, S. W., Matthews, K. A., & Pauls, D. L. (1992). The biobehavioral interface in behavioral pediatrics. *Pediatrics, 90,* 789–797.

Pot-Mees, C. (1989). *The psychosocial effects of bone marrow transplantation in children.* Delft, The Netherlands: Eubron Delft.

Potter, P. C., & Roberts, M. C. (1984). Children's perceptions of chronic illness: The roles of disease, symptoms, cognitive development, and information. *Journal of Pediatric Psychology, 9,* 13–27.

Rae, W. A. (1995). The president's message. *Newsletter of the Society of Pediatric Psychology, 19*(3), 1.

Rait, D. S., Jacobsen, P. B., Lederberg, M. S., & Holland, J. C. (1988). Characteristics of psychiatric consultations in a pediatric cancer center. *American Journal of Psychiatry, 145,* 363–364.

Redpath, C. C., & Rogers, C. S. (1984). Healthy young children's concepts of hospitals, medical personnel, operations and illness. *Journal of Pediatric Psychology, 4,* 29–39.

Reid, P. (1994). The real problem in the study of culture. *American Psychologist, 49,* 524–525.

Reilly, T. P., Hasazi, J. E., & Bond, L. A. (1983). Children's conceptions of death and personal mortality. *Journal of Pediatric Psychology, 8,* 21–31.

Reynolds, C. R., & Richmond, B. O. (1978). What I think and feel: A revised measure of children's manifest anxiety. *Journal of Abnormal Child Psychology, 6,* 271–280.

Richardson, J. L., Marks, G., Johnson, C., Graham, J. W., Chan, K. K., Sesler, J. N., Kisbaugh, C., Barranday, Y., & Levine, A. M. (1987). Path model of multidimensional compliance with cancer therapy. *Health Psychology, 6,* 183–207.

Richardson, J. L., Marks, G., & Levine, A. M. (1988). The influence of symptoms of disease and side effects of treatment on compliance with cancer therapy. *Journal of Clinical Oncology, 6,* 1746–1752.

Richardson, J. L., Shelton, D. R., Krailo, M., & Levine, A. M. (1990). The effect of compliance with treatment on survival among patients with hematologic malignancies. *Journal of Clinical Oncology, 8,* 356–364.

Richmond, J. B. (1967). Child development: A basic science for pediatrics. *Pediatrics, 39,* 649–658.

Ris, M. D., & Noll, R. B. (1994). Long-term neurobehavioral outcome in pediatric brain-tumor patients: Review and methodological critique. *Journal of Clinical and Experimental Neuropsychology, 16,* 21–42.

Roberts, M. C. (1992). Vale dictum: An editor's view of the field of pediatric psychology and its journal. *Journal of Pediatric Psychology, 17,* 785–805.

Roberts, M. C. (1994). Prevention/promotion in America: Still spitting on the sidewalk. *Journal of Pediatric Psychology, 19,* 267–281.

Roberts, M. C., La Greca, A. M., & Harper, D. C. (1988). Journal of Pediatric Psychology: Another stage of development. *Journal of Pediatric Psychology, 13,* 1–5.

Roberts, M. C., & McNeal, R. E. (1995). Historical and conceptual foundations of pediatric psychology. In M. C. Roberts (Ed.), *Handbook of pediatric psychology* (2nd ed.). New York: Guilford Press.

Robinson, E. A., Eyberg, S. M., & Ross, A. W. (1980). The standardization of an inventory of child conduct problem behaviors. *Journal of Clinical Child Psychology, 9,* 22–29.

Rodgers, B. M., Webb, C. J., Stergios, D., & Newman, B. M. (1988). Patient-controlled analgesia in pediatric surgery. *Journal of Pediatric Surgery, 23,* 259–262.

Rodriguez, C. M., & Boggs, S. R. (1994). Behavioral upset in medical patients—Revised: Evaluation of a parent report measure of distress for pediatric populations. *Journal of Pediatric Psychology, 19,* 319–324.

Rogoff, B. (1990). *Apprenticeship in thinking.* New York: Oxford University Press.

Rolland, J. (1984). Toward a psychosocial topology of chronic and life-threatening illness. *Family Systems Medicine, 2,* 245–262.

Rosenberg, M. (1979). *Conceiving the self.* New York: Basic Books.

Rosensteil, A. K., & Keefe, F. J. (1983). The use of coping strategies in low back pain patients: Relationship to patient characteristics and current adjustment. *Pain, 17,* 33–40.

Ross, C. K., Lavigne, J. V., Hayford, J. R., Berry, S. L., Sinacore, J. M., & Pachman, L. M. (1993). Psychological factors affecting reported pain in juvenile rheumatoid arthritis. *Journal of Pediatric Psychology, 18,* 561–573.

Ross, C. K., Lavigne, J. V., Hayford, J. R., Dyer, A. R., & Pachman, L. M. (1989). Validity of reported pain as a measure of clinical state in juvenile rheumatoid arthritis. *Annals of Rheumatoid Disorders, 48,* 817–819.

Ross, D. M., & Ross, S. A. (1984). The importance of type of question, psychological climate and subject set in interviewing children about pain. *Pain, 19,* 71–79.

Ross, R. S., Bush, J. P., & Crummette, B. D. (1991). Factors affecting nurses' decisions to administer PRN analgesic medication to children after surgery: An analog investigation. *Journal of Pediatric Psychology, 16,* 151–167.

Roter, D. L., & Hall, J. A. (1987). Physicians' interviewing styles and medical information obtained from patients. *Journal of General Internal Medicine, 2,* 325–329.

Roth, H., & Casen, H. D. (1978). Accuracy of doctors' estimates and patients' statements of adherence in a drug regimen. *Clinical Pharmacological Therapy, 23,* 361–370.

Rotheram-Borus, M. J., Becker, C. K., & Kaplan, M. (1991). AIDS knowledge and beliefs, and sexual behavior of sexually delinquent and non-delinquent (runaway) adolescents. *Journal of Adolescence, 14,* 229–244.

Rowland, J. H. (1990). Developmental stage and adaptation: Child and adolescent model. In J. E. Holland & J. H. Rowland (Eds.), *Handbook of psychooncology: Psychological care of the patient with cancer* (pp. 519–543). New York: Oxford University Press.

Rowland, J. H., Glidewell, O. J., & Sibley, R. F. (1984). Effects of different forms of central nervous system prophylaxis on neuropsychological function in childhood leukemia. *Journal of Clinical Oncology, 2,* 1327–1335.

Rubenstein, C. L., Varni, J. W., & Katz, E. R. (1990). Cognitive functioning in long-term survivors of childhood leukemia: A prospective analysis. *Developmental and Behavioral Pediatrics, 11,* 301–305.

Rudolph, K. D., Dennig, M. D., & Weisz, J. R. (1995). Determinants and consequences of children's coping in the medical setting: Conceptualization, review, and critique. *Psychological Bulletin, 118,* 328–357.

Russo, D. C. (1986). Chronicity and normalcy as the psychological basis for research and treatment in chronic disease in children. In N. Krasnegor, J. Arasteh, & M. Cataldo (Eds.), *Child health behavior: A behavioral pediatrics approach.* New York: Wiley.

Russo, D. C., & Varni, J. W. (1982). *Behavioral pediatrics.* New York: Plenum Press.

Ruth, H. P., Caron, H. S., & Bartholomew, P. H. (1970). Measuring intake of prescribed medication: A bottle count and a tracer technique compared. *Clinical Pharmacology Therapy, 11,* 228–237.

Sabbeth, B., & Leventhal, J. (1984). Marital adjustment to chronic childhood illness. *Pediatrics, 73,* 762–768.

Sanger, M. S., MacLean, W. E., Jr., & Van-Slyke, D. A. (1992). Relation between maternal characteristics and child behavior ratings: Implications for interpreting behavior checklists. *Clinical Pediatrics, 31,* 461–466.

Santilli, L. E., & Roberts, M. C. (1993). Children's perceptions of ill peers as a function of illness conceptualization and attributions of responsibility: AIDS as a paradigm. *Journal of Pediatric Psychology, 18,* 193–207.

Sather, H. N. (1986). Age at diagnosis of childhood acute lymphoblastic leukemia. *Medical and Pediatric Oncology, 14,* 166–172.

Savedra, M. C., & Tesler, M. D. (1989). Assessing children's and adolescents' pain. *Pediatrician, 16,* 24–29.

Sawyer, M., Toogood, I., Rice, M., Haskell, C., & Baghurst, P. (1989). School performance and psychological adjustment of children treated for leukemia. *American Journal of Pediatric Hematology/Oncology, 11,* 146–152.

Sayer, A. G., Willett, J. B., & Perrin, E. C. (1993). Measuring understanding of illness causality in healthy children and in children with chronic illness: A construct validation. *Journal of Applied Developmental Psychology, 14,* 11–36.

Schank, R. C., & Abelson, R. R. (1977). *Scripts, plans, goals, and understanding.* Hillsdale, NJ: Erlbaum.

Schechter, N. L. (1989). The undertreatment of pain in children: An overview. *Pediatric Clinics of North America, 36,* 781–794.

Schechter, N. L., Allen, D. A., & Hansen, K. (1986). Status of pediatric pain control: A comparison of hospital analgesic usage in children and adults. *Pediatrics, 77,* 11–15.

Schlieper, A. E., Esseltine, D. W., & Tarshis, M. A. (1989). Cognitive function in long-term survivors of childhood acute lymphoblastic leukemia. *Pediatric Hematology and Oncology, 6,* 1–9.

Schmitt, B. B., & Guzzino, M. H. (1985). Expressive therapy with children in crisis: A new avenue of communication. In C. A. Corr & D. M. Corr (Eds.), *Hospice approaches to pediatric care* (pp. 155–177). New York: Springer.

Schuler, D., Polcz, A., Revesz, T., Koos, R., Bakos, M., & Gal, N. (1981). Psychological late effects of leukemia in children and their prevention. *Medical and Pediatric Oncology, 9,* 191–194.

Schulman, J. L., & Kupst, M. J. (1979). *The emotional impact of childhood cancer on the patient. Proceedings of the American Cancer Society: National Conference on the Care of the Child with Cancer* (pp. 144–149). New York: American Cancer Society.

Seligman, M. E. P., Peterson, C., Kaslow, N. J., Tannenbaum, R. L., Alloy, L. B., & Abramson, L. Y. (1984). Explanatory style and depressive symptoms among school children. *Journal of Abnormal Psychology, 93,* 235–238.

Selman, R. L. (1981). The development of interpersonal competence: The role of understanding in conduct. *Developmental Review, 1,* 401–422.

Shagena, M., Sandler, H., & Perrin, E. C. (1988). Concepts of illness and perception of control in healthy children and in children with chronic illness. *Journal of Developmental and Behavioral Pediatrics, 9,* 252–256.

Shapiro, E. G., McPhee, J. T., & Abbott, A. A. (1994). Minnesota Preschool Affect Rating Scales: Development, reliability and validity. *Journal of Pediatric Psychology, 19,* 325–345.

Sharpe, J. N., Brown, R. T., Thompson, N. J., & Eckman, J. (1994). Predictors of coping with pain in mothers and their children with sickle cell syndrome. *Journal of the American Academy of Child and Adolescent Psychiatry, 33,* 1246–1255.

Shaw, E. G., & Routh, D. K. (1982). Effects of mothers' presence on children's reactions to aversive procedures. *Journal of Pediatric Psychology, 7,* 33–42.

Shedler, J., Mayman, M., & Manis, M. (1993). The illusion of mental health. *American Psychologist, 48,* 113–117.

Shedler, J., Mayman, M., & Manis, M. (1994). More illusions. *American Psychologist, 49,* 974–976.

Shope, J. T. (1981). Medication compliance. *Pediatric Clinics of North America, 28,* 5–21.

Siegel, L., & Peterson, L. (1980). Stress reduction in young dental patients through coping skills and sensory information. *Journal of Consulting and Clinical Psychology, 48,* 785–787.

Sigel, I. E. (Ed.). (1985). *Parental belief systems: The psychological consequences for children.* Hillsdale, NJ: Erlbaum.

Sigelman, C. K., & Begley, N. L. (1987). The early development of reactions to peers with controllable and uncontrollable problems. *Journal of Pediatric Psychology, 12,* 99–115.

Sigelman, C. K., Derenowski, E. B., Mullaney, H. A., & Siders, A. T. (1993). Parents' contributions to knowledge and attitudes regarding AIDS. *Journal of Pediatric Psychology, 18,* 221–235.

Sigelman, C. K., Mukai, T., Woods, T., & Alfeld, C. (1995). Parents' contributions to children's knowledge and attitudes regarding AIDS: Another look. *Journal of Pediatric Psychology, 20,* 61–77.

Silverman, W. K., & Eisen, A. R. (1992). Age differences in the reliability of parent and child reports of child anxious symptomatology using a structured interview. *Journal of the American Academy of Child and Adolescent Psychiatry, 31,* 117–124.

Simeonsson, R. J., Buckley, L., & Monson, L. (1979). Conceptions of illness causality in hospitalized children. *Journal of Pediatric Psychology, 4,* 173–180.

Simonds, J. F., Goldstein, D., Kilo, C., & Hoette, S. (1987). The role of health beliefs in the regimen adherence and metabolic control of adolescents and adults with diabetes mellitus. *Journal of Consulting and Clinical Psychology, 55,* 139–144.

Slater, M., & Power, T. (1987). Multidimensional assessment of parenting in single-parent families. In J. P. Vincent (Ed.), *Advances in family intervention* (pp. 197–228). Greenwich, CT: JAI Press.

Slavin, L., O'Malley, J., Koocher, G., & Foster, D. (1982). Communication of the cancer diagnosis to pediatric patients: Impact on long-term adjustment. *American Journal of Psychiatry, 139,* 179–183.

Slonim-Nevo, V., Auslander, W. F., & Ozawa, M. N. (1995). Educational options and AIDS-related behaviors among troubled adolescents. *Journal of Pediatric Psychology, 20,* 41–60.

Smith, K. E., Ackerson, J. D., & Blotcky, A. D. (1989). Reducing distress during invasive medical procedures: Relating behavioral interventions to preferred coping style in pediatric cancer patients. *Journal of Pediatric Psychology, 14,* 405–419.

Smith, K. E., Ackerson, J. P., Blotcky, A. D., & Berkow, R. (1990). Preferred coping styles of pediatric cancer patients during invasive medical procedures. *Journal of Psychosocial Oncology, 8,* 59–70.

Smith, S. D., Rosen, D., Trueworthy, R. C., & Lowman, J. T. (1979). A reliable method for evaluating drug compliance in children with cancer. *Cancer, 43,* 169–173.

Solnit, A. J., & Green, M. (1963). The pediatric management of the dying child: 2. The child's reaction to the fear of dying. In A. Solnit & S. Provence (Eds.), *Modern perspectives in child development.* New York: International Universities Press.

Speece, M. W., & Brent, S. B. (1984). Children's understanding of death: A review of three components of a death concept. *Child Development, 55,* 1671–1686.

Spielberger, C. D. (1973). *Manual for the State-Trait Anxiety Inventory for Children.* Palo Alto, CA: Consulting Psychologists Press.

Spielberger, C. D. (1983). *Manual for the State-Trait Anxiety Inventory.* Palo Alto, CA: Consulting Psychologists Press.

Spinetta, J. J. (1974). The dying child's awareness of death: A review. *Psychological Bulletin, 81,* 256–260.

Spinetta, J. J. (1984). Measurement of family function, communication, and cultural effects. *Cancer, 53,* 2330–2338.

Spinetta, J. J., & Deasy-Spinetta, P. (1981). Talking with children who have a life-threatening illness. In J. J. Spinetta & P. Deasy-Spinetta (Eds.), *Living with childhood cancer* (pp. 234–253). St. Louis, MO: Mosby.

Spinetta, J. J., & Maloney, L. J. (1975). Death anxiety in the outpatient leukemic child. *Pediatrics, 56,* 1034–1037.

Spinetta, J. J., & Maloney, L. J. (1978). The child with cancer: Patterns of communication and denial. *Journal of Consulting and Clinical Psychology, 46,* 1540–1541.

Spinetta, J. J., Rigler, D., & Karon, M. (1973). Anxiety and the dying child. *Pediatrics, 56,* 841–845.

Spinetta, J. J., Rigler, D., & Karon, M. (1974). Personal space as a measure of a dying child's sense of isolation. *Journal of Consulting and Clinical Psychology, 42,* 751–756.

Spinetta, J. J., Swarner, J. A., & Sheposh, J. P. (1981). Effective parental coping following the death of a child from cancer. *Journal of Pediatric Psychology, 6,* 251–263.

Spirito, A., & Stark, J. S. (1987). Childhood pain: Assessment and significance of self-report. *Behavioral Medicine Abstracts, 8,* 1–4.

Spirito, A., Stark, L. J., Cobiella, C., Drigan, R., Androkites, A., & Hewett, K. (1990). Social adjustment of children successfully treated for cancer. *Journal of Pediatric Psychology, 15,* 359–371.

Spirito, A., Stark, L. J., Gil, K. M., & Tyc, V. L. (1995). Coping with everyday and disease-related stressors by chronically ill children and adolescents. *Journal of the American Academy of Child and Adolescent Psychiatry, 34,* 283–290.

Spirito, A., Stark, L. J., & Williams, C. (1988). Development of a brief coping checklist for use with pediatric populations. *Pediatric Psychology, 13,* 555–574.

Stanton, B. (1994). Adolescent drug trafficking. *Pediatrics, 93*(Suppl.), 1039–1084.

Steward, M. S., & Steward, D. S. (1981). Children's conceptions of medical procedures. In R. Bibace & M. E. Walsh (Eds.), *Children's conceptions of health, illness, and bodily functions* (pp. 67–84). San Francisco: Jossey-Bass.

Street, R. L., Jr., & Buller, D. B. (1988). Patients' characteristics affecting physician-patient nonverbal communication. *Human Communication Research, 15,* 60–90.

Street, R. L., & Wiemann, J. M. (1987). Patients' satisfaction with physicians' interpersonal involvement, expressiveness and dominance. *Communication Yearbook, 10,* 591–612.

Strickland, B. R. (1978). Internal–external expectancies and health-related behaviors. *Journal of Consulting and Clinical Psychology, 46,* 1192–1211.

Stuber, M. L., Christakis, D. A., Houskamp, B., & Kazak, A. E. (1996). Post trauma symptoms in childhood leukemia survivors and their parents. *Psychosomatics, 37,* 254–261.

Sullivan, K. (1989). Current status of bone marrow transplantation. *Transplantation Proceedings, 21,* 41–50.

Sulzer-Azaroff, B., & Mayer, G. R. (1977). *Applying behavioral-analysis procedures with children and youth.* New York: Holt, Rinehart and Winston.

Susman, E. J., Dorn, L. D., & Fletcher, J. C. (1987). Reasoning about illness in ill and healthy children and adolescents: Cognitive and emotional developmental aspects. *Journal of Developmental and Behavioral Pediatrics, 8,* 266–273.

Susman, E. J., Hollenbeck, A. R., Nannis, E. D., Strope, B. E., Hersh, S. P., Levine, A. S., & Pizzo, P. A. (1981). A prospective naturalistic study of the impact of an intensive medical treatment on the social behavior of child and adolescent cancer patients. *Journal of Applied Developmental Psychology, 2,* 29–47.

Swift, A. V., Cohen, M. J., Hynd, G. W., Wisenbaker, J. M., McKie, K. M., Makari, G., & McKie, V. (1989). Neuropsychologic impairment in children with sickle cell anemia. *Pediatrics, 84,* 1077–1085.

Tamaroff, M. H., Festa, R. S., Adesman, A. R., & Walco, G. A. (1992). Therapeutic adherence to oral medication regimens by adolescents with cancer: 2. Clinical and psychologic correlates. *Journal of Pediatrics, 120,* 812–817.

Tarnowski, K. J., & Brown, R. T. (1995). Pediatric pain. In R. T. Ammerman & M. Hersen (Eds.), *Handbook of child behavior therapy in the psychiatric setting* (pp. 453–476). New York: Wiley.

Taylor, S. E., Lichtman, R. R., & Wood, J. V. (1984). Compliance with chemotherapy among breast cancer patients. *Health Psychology, 3,* 553–562.

Tebbi, C. K., Bromberg, C., & Mallon, J. C. (1988). Self-reported depression in adolescent cancer patients. *American Journal of Pediatric Hematology/Oncology, 10,* 185–190.

Tebbi, C. K., Cummings, K. M., Zevon, M. A., Smith. L., Richards, M., & Mallon, J. (1986). Compliance of pediatric and adolescent cancer patients. *Cancer, 58,* 1179–1184.

Temoshok, L., Sweet, D., & Zich, C. (1987). A three-city comparison of the public's knowledge and attitudes about AIDS. *Psychology and Health, 1,* 43–60.

Teske, K., Dart, R. L., & Cleeland, L. S. (1983). Relationships between nurses' observations and patients' self-reports of pain. *Pain, 16,* 289–296.

Tettersel, M. J. (1992). Patients' knowledge in relation to compliance with drug therapy. *Journal of Advanced Nursing, 18,* 103–113.

Thompson, R. J., Jr., Gil, K. M., Burbach, D. A., Keith, B. R., & Kinney, T. R. (1993). Psychological adjustment of mothers of children and adolescents with sickle cell disease: The role of stress, coping methods, and family functioning. *Journal of Pediatric Psychology, 18,* 549–559.

Thompson, R. J., Jr., Gil, K. M., Keith, B. R., Gustafson, K. E., George, L. K., & Kinney, T. R. (1994). Psychological adjustment of children with sickle cell disease: Stability and change over a 10-month period. *Journal of Consulting and Clinical Psychology, 62,* 856–860.

Thompson, R. J., Jr., Gustafson, K. E., George, L. K., & Spock, A. (1995). Change over a 12-month period in the psychological adjustment of children and adolescents with cystic fibrosis. *Journal of Pediatric Psychology, 19,* 189–204.

Thompson, R. J., Jr., Gustafson, K. E., Hamlett, K. W., & Spock, A. (1992). Psychological adjustment of children with cystic fibrosis: The role of child cognitive processes and maternal adjustment. *Journal of Pediatric Psychology, 17,* 741–755.

Timmerman, T., McDonough, S., & Harmeson, P. (1991). AIDS awareness in North Dakota—A knowledge and attitude study of the general population. *Public Health Reports, 106,* 120–123.

Tobin, D. L., Hjoloryd, K. A., Reynolds, R. V., & Wigal, J. K. (1989). The hierarchical factor structure of the Coping Strategies Inventory. *Cognitive Therapy Research, 13,* 343–361.

Trueworthy, R. C. (1982, April). *A new prognostic factor for childhood acute lymphoblastic leukemia: Drug absorption and compliance.* Proceedings of the 4th annual Pediatric Hematology/Oncology Symposium, University of Kansas Medical Center, Kansas City.

Tuma, J. M. (1975). *Pediatric* psychologist . . . ? Do you mean clinical *child* psychologist? *Journal of Clinical Child Psychology, 4,* 9–12.

Tuma, J. (1982). *Handbook for the practice of pediatric psychology.* New York: Wiley.

Tuma, J. M., & Grabert, J. (1983). Internship and postdoctoral training in pediatric and clinical child psychology: A survey. *Journal of Pediatric Psychology, 8,* 245–260.

Turk, D. C. (1978). Cognitive behavioral techniques in the management of pain. In J. P. Foreyt & D. P. Rathjen (Eds.), *Cognitive behavior therapy* (pp. 199–232). New York: Plenum Press.

Tyler, D. C. (1990). Patient-controlled analgesia in adolescents. *Journal of Adolescent Health Care, 11,* 154–158.

Van Dongen-Melman, J. E., Pruyn, J., De Groot, A., Koot, H. M., Hahlen, K., & Verhulst, F. C. (1995). Late psychosocial consequences for parents of children who survived cancer. *Journal of Pediatric Psychology, 20,* 567–586.

Vandvik, I. H., & Eckblad, G. (1990). Relation between pain, disease severity and psychosocial function in patients with juvenile chronic arthritis. *Scandinavian Journal of Rheumatology, 19,* 295–302.

Varni, J. W., Blount, R. L., Waldron, S. A., & Smith, A. J. (1995). Management of pain and distress. In M. C. Roberts (Ed.), *Handbook of pediatric psychology* (2nd ed.). New York: Guilford Press.

Venham, L. L., & Gaulin-Kremer, E. (1979). A self-report measure of situational anxiety for young children. *Pediatric Dentistry, 1,* 91–96.

von Bertalanffy, L. (1968). *General systems theory: Foundations, development, applications.* New York: Braziller.

Wachtel, J., Rodriquc, J. R., Geffken, G. R., Graham-Pole, J., & Turner, C. (1994). Children awaiting invasive medical procedures: Do children and their mothers agree on child's level of anxiety? *Journal of Pediatric Psychology, 19,* 723–735.

Waechter, E. H. (1971). Children's awareness of fatal illness. *American Journal of Nursing, 71,* 1168–1172.

Waechter, E. H. (1987). Children's reactions to fatal illness. In T. Krulik, B. Holaday, & I. M. Martinson (Eds.), *The child and family facing life-threatening illness* (pp. 108–119). Philadelphia: Lippincott.

Walco, G. A., Cassidy, R. C., & Schechter, N. L. (1994). Pain, hurt, and harm: The ethics of pain control in infants and children. *New England Journal of Medicine, 331,* 541–544.

Walco, G. A., & Dampier, C. D. (1990). Pain in children and adolescents with sickle cell disease: A descriptive study. *Journal of Pediatric Psychology, 15,* 643–658.

Walker, C. E. (1988). The future of pediatric psychology. *Journal of Pediatric Psychology, 13,* 465–477.

Walker, L. S., & Greene, J. W. (1991). The functional disability inventory: Measuring a neglected dimension of child health status. *Journal of Pediatric Psychology, 16,* 39–58.

Wallander, J. L. (1995). Pediatric psychology coming of age. *Contemporary Psychology, 40,* 1083.

Wallander, J. L., Varni, J. W., Babani, L., Banis, H. T., DeHaan, C. B., & Wilcox, K. T. (1989). Disability parameters, chronic strain and adaptation of physically handicapped children and their mothers. *Journal of Pediatric Psychology, 14,* 23–42.

Wallander, J. L., Varni, J. W., Babani, L., Banis, H. T., & Wilcox, K. T. (1988). Children with chronic physical disorders: Maternal reports of their adjustment. *Journal of Pediatric Psychology, 13,* 197–212.

Wallander, J. L., Varni, J. W., Babani, L., Banis, H. T., & Wilcox, K. T. (1989). Family resources as resistance factors for psychological maladjustment in chronically ill and handicapped children. *Journal of Pediatric Psychology, 14,* 157–173.

Wallston, B. S., & Wallston, K. A. (1978). Locus of control and health: A review of the literature. *Health Education Monographs, 6,* 107–117.

Wallston, K. A., Wallston, B. S., & DeVellis, R. (1978). Development of the Multidimensional Health Locus of Control (MHLC) scales. *Health Education Monographs, 6,* 160–170.

Wallston, K. A., Wallston, B. S., Smith, S., & Dobbins, C. J. (1987). Perceived control and health. *Current Psychological Research and Reviews, 6,* 5–25.

Walsh, M. E., & Bibace, R. (1991). Children's conceptions of AIDS: A developmental analysis. *Journal of Pediatric Psychology, 16,* 273–285.

Wampold, B. E., & Worsham, N. L. (1986). Randomization tests for multiple-baseline designs. *Behavioral Assessment, 8,* 135–143.

Wasserman, A. L., Thompson, E. I., Wilimas, J. A., & Fairclough, D. L. (1987). The psychological status of survivors of childhood/adolescent Hodgkins disease. *American Journal of Diseases of Childhood, 141,* 626–631.

Wasserman, A. L., Wilimas, J. A., Fairclough, D. L., Mulhern, R. K., & Wang, W. (1991). Subtle neuropsychological deficits in children with sickle cell disease. *American Journal of Pediatric Hematology/Oncology, 13,* 14–20.

Watson, M., Greer, S., Pruyn, J., & Van den Borne. (1990). Locus of control and adjustment to cancer. *Psychological Reports, 66,* 39–48.

Weinberger, D. A. (1990). The construct validity of the repressive coping style. In J. L. Singer (Ed.), *Repression and dissociation: Implications for personality theory, psychopathology, and health.* Chicago: University of Chicago Press.

Weinberger, D. A., Schwartz, G. E., & Davidson, R. J. (1979). Low-anxious, high-anxious, and repressive coping styles: Psychometric patterns and behavioral and physiological responses to stress. *Journal of Abnormal Psychology, 88,* 369–380.

Wells, E. A., Hoppe, M. J., Simpson, E. E., Gillmore, M. R., Morrison, D. M., & Wilsdon, A. (1995). Misconceptions about AIDS among children who can identify the major routes of HIV transmission. *Journal of Pediatric Psychology, 20,* 671–686.

Werner, H. (1948). *Comparative psychology of mental development.* New York: International Universities Press.

Wertsch, J. V. (1991). *Voices of the mind.* Cambridge, MA: Harvard University Press.

Wertz, D. C., Fanos, J. H., & Reilly, P. R. (1994). Genetic testing for children and adolescents: Who decides? *Journal of the American Medical Association, 272,* 875–881.

West, C. (1984). When the doctor is a "lady": Power, status and gender in physician–patient encounters. *Symbolic Interaction, 7,* 87–106.

Westervelt, V. D., Brantley, J., & Ware, W. (1983). Changing children's attitudes toward physically handicapped peers: Effects of a film and teacher-led discussion. *Journal of Pediatric Psychology, 8,* 327–343.

White, D. M., Rusch, F. R., Kazdin, A. E., & Hartmann, D. P. (1989). Applications of meta-analysis in individual-subject research. *Behavioral Assessment, 11,* 281–296.

Whitt, J. K. (1982). Children's understanding of illness: Developmental considerations and pediatric intervention. In M. Wolraich & D. Routh (Eds.). *Advances in developmental and behavioral pediatrics* (Vol. 3, pp. 163–201). Greenwich, CT: JAI Press.

Whitt, J. K. (1995). Current research on children's and adolescents' HIV/AIDS-related knowledge, attitudes, and behavior. *Journal of Pediatric Psychology, 20,* 693–696.

Whitt, J. K., Hooper, S. R., Tennison, M. B., Robertson, W. T., Gold, S. H., Burchinal, M., Wells, R., McMillan, C., Whaley, R. A., Combest, J., & Hall, C. D. (1993). Neuropsychologic functioning of human immunodeficiency virus-infected children with hemophilia. *Journal of Pediatrics, 122,* 52–59.

Williams, P. (1978). Children's concepts of illness and internal body parts. *Maternal–Child Nursing Journal, 1,* 115–123.

Willis, D. J., Culbertson, J. L., & Mertens, R. A. (1984). Considerations in physical and health-related disorders. In S. J. Weaver (Ed.), *Testing children: A reference guide for effective clinical and psychoeducational assessments* (pp. 185–196). Austin, TX: Pro-Ed.

Willis, D. J., Holden, W., & Rosenberg, M. (1992). Child maltreatment prevention: Introduction and historical overview. In D. J. Willis, E. W. Holden, & M. Rosenberg (Eds.), *Prevention of child maltreatment: Developmental and ecological perspectives* (pp. 1–14). New York: Wiley.

Wilson, D. P., & Endres, R. K. (1986). Compliance with blood glucose monitoring in children with type 1 diabetes mellitus. *Journal of Pediatrics, 108,* 1022–1024.

Wissow, L. S., Roter, D. L., & Wilson, M. E. (1994). Pediatrician interview style and mother's disclosure of psychological issues. *Pediatrics, 93,* 289–295.

Wohlwill, J. F. (1973). *The study of behavioral development.* New York: Academic Press.

Wolf, D. A. (1993). Child abuse intervention research: Implications for policy. In D. Cicchetti & S. L. Toth (Eds.), *Child abuse, child development, and social policy* (pp. 369–398). Norwood, NJ: ABLEX.

Worchel, F. F. (1989). Denial of depression: Adaptive coping in pediatric patients? *Newsletter of the Society of Pediatric Psychology, 13,* 8–11.

Worchel, F. F., Nolan, B. F., Wilson, V. L., Purser, J. S., Copeland, D. R., & Pfefferbaum, B. (1988). Assessment of depression in children with cancer. *Journal of Pediatric Psychology, 13,* 101–112.

Worchel, F. F., Rae, W. A., Olson, T. K., & Crowley, S. L. (1992). Selective responsiveness of chronically ill children to assessment of depression. *Journal of Personality Assessment, 59,* 605–615.

Working Party of the Clinical Genetics Society. (1994). The genetic testing of children. *Journal of Medical Genetics, 31,* 785–797.

Wright, L., Schaefer, A., & Solomons, G. (1979). *Encyclopedia of pediatric psychology.* Baltimore: University Park Press.

Yin, R. K. (1993). *Applications of case study research.* Newbury Park, CA: Sage.

Young, M. K., McMurray, M. B., Rothbery, S. A., & Emery, L. (1987). Use of the health and illness questionnaire with chronically ill and handicapped children. *Children's Health Care, 16,* 97–104.

Zeltzer, L. K. (1980). The adolescent with cancer. In J. Kellerman (Ed.), *Psychological aspects of childhood cancer.* Springfield, IL: Thomas.

Zeltzer, L. K. (1994). Pain and symptom management. In D. J. Bearison & R. K. Mulhern (Eds.), *Pediatric psychooncology: Psychological perspectives on children with cancer* (pp. 61–83). New York: Oxford University Press.

Zeltzer, L. K., Altman, A., Cohen, D., DeBaron, S., Munuksela, E. L., & Schechter, N. L. (1990). Report of the subcommittee on the management of pain associated with procedures in children with cancer. Report of the Consensus Conference on the Management of Pain in Childhood Cancer. *Pediatrics, 86*(Suppl.), 826–831.

Zeltzer, L. K., Hamilton, R., Weiss, J., Byrne, J., Mills, J., Meadows, A., & Robinson, L. (1995). Emotional outcome in adult survivors of childhood leukemia. *Proceedings of the American Society of Clinical Oncology, 14,* 504.

Zeltzer, L. K., Jay, S. M., & Fisher, D. M. (1989). The management of pain associated with pediatric procedures. *Pediatric Clinics of North America, 36,* 1–24.

Zeltzer, L. K., & LeBaron, S. (1982). Hypnosis and nonhypnotic techniques for reduction of pain and anxiety during painful procedures in children and adolescents with cancer. *Journal of Pediatrics, 101,* 1032–1035.

Zeltzer, L. K., LeBaron, S., Richie, D. M., Reed, D., Schoolfield, J., & Prihoda, T. J. (1988). Can children understand and use a rating scale to quantify somatic symptoms? Assessment of nausea and vomiting as a model. *Journal of Consulting and Clinical Psychology, 56,* 567–572.

Zimet, G. D., Hillier, S. A., Anglin, T. M., Ellick, E. M., Krowchuk, D., & Williams, P. (1991). Knowing someone with AIDS: The impact on adolescents. *Journal of Pediatric Psychology, 16,* 287–294.

CHAPTER 11

Children's Testimony: Applied and Basic Issues

STEPHEN J. CECI and MAGGIE BRUCK

Children have enormous strengths in recollecting their past. Even very young preschool children are capable of providing highly detailed and accurate accounts of prior interactions, *provided that the adults who have access to them do not do anything to usurp their memories.* In this chapter, we focus on the deleterious consequences of exposing preschoolers to a host of suggestive procedures. This focus is not meant to deny the many real strengths of young children, but rather to illustrate what can happen if interviewers mislead young children.

Since the turn of the century, social scientists have examined the topic of children's suggestibility (see Ceci &

Bruck, 1995, for a historical review). Although a few studies were carried out in the United States from 1900 until the middle of the 1980s, it is only in the past few years that this topic has attained an important status within the fields of developmental and cognitive psychology. Over the past 5 or so years, social scientists from a number of different disciplines have mounted studies in this field. This flurry of important work has been mainly spurred by an applied issue—children's ability to give reliable legal testimony. As will be shown, the methodologies as well as the primary issues of many studies address applied concerns rather than theoretical ones. And yet, the results of these studies have expanded, and at times challenged, some important theoretical concepts.

The practical issues are motivated by the increasing number of children who are entering the legal system to offer testimony in a broad range of cases. Although there are no estimates of the number of children, we have conservatively estimated (Ceci & Bruck, 1993a) that in the United States, 100,000 children annually testify in criminal and civil cases (custody disputes, domestic violence, product liability, termination of parental rights, etc.). If we add to these cases of courtroom testimony, those cases in which children provide legally relevant statements (e.g., through depositions, interviews with legal personnel) but never actually testify in open court (cases that occur "in the shadow of the law," Mnookin, 1985), then the number of youngsters involved in legal proceedings quickly approaches astronomical levels.

In view of the large numbers of children giving statements of legal importance—both in and out of the courtroom—we might ask what researchers have discovered about children's testimony, and what we still do not know. In this chapter, we review the research on the reliability of children's reports and on the suggestibility of children. In doing so, we primarily focus on the most current research that examines the contextual factors that influence the accuracy of children's statements. After laying out the parameters of children's suggestibility, we consider the cognitive and social factors that may underlie or account for the accuracy of their reports. Although we primarily focus on the research carried out in the past 10 years, our description is prefaced with a summary of the research carried out on this topic in the first 80 years of this century. We believe it is important to understand the historical, theoretical, and ideological roots of the current research.

No discussion of this topic is complete without putting the research into legal perspective. We do this throughout the chapter instead of in the final section as might be customary in other venues, because we believe that an integrated approach to discussing the research allows for assessment of its practical relevance along the way rather than making the reader wait until the end to be disabused of studies that fall short on methodological, ecological, or legal grounds. So we begin this chapter by presenting summaries of two recent criminal cases that involved child witnesses.

Finally, no enterprise in which case studies serve as windows into scientific understanding is complete without some discussion of the nature of this enterprise and, specifically, the traditional distinctions between "applied" and "basic" research and research training. We conclude this chapter with a section that suggests that this distinction is more illusory than real, and that there are few principled differences between these two forms of research other than the number of days that elapse before the findings from research become relevant to solving a practical problem, the term *basic* being used to denote research that has longer intervals.

CHILDREN AS WITNESSES: TWO CASE DESCRIPTIONS

The Little Rascals Day Care Case

Bob and Betsy Kelly owned and operated the Little Rascals Day Care Center in Edenton, North Carolina. Betsy was primarily responsible for the day-to-day running of the Little Rascals, and Bob, a licensed plumbing contractor and golf pro, helped out as needed. Set in an idyllic hamlet in northeastern North Carolina, by all appearances the Little Rascals was the premier nursery school for middle-class and upper-middle-class parents to send their preschoolers. All this changed in the winter of 1989 when a parent of one of the children enrolled at the Little Rascals alleged that Bob Kelly had sexually abused her son. This allegation was investigated by Brenda Toppin, an officer with the Edenton Police Department, and by the Department of Social Services. On the basis of their interviews with several children enrolled at the Little Rascals, they concluded that the allegation was valid.

In February 1989, three additional children made allegations. Soon a wave of panic gripped this small town, as parents became more uneasy about whether their own children had also been abused. The police supplied parents with a list of recommended therapists and advised parents to have their children evaluated for abuse.

Although few children made disclosures when repeatedly questioned by their parents and police officers about suspected abuse, eventually these children would make allegations after many sessions of therapy. Some of these children took up to 10 months of therapeutic intervention before they began to make allegations.

Eventually, 90 children would make allegations involving physical and sexual abuse; and 85% of these were evaluated and treated by three therapists. Most of the alleged events were claimed to have occurred between September 1988 and December 1988—3 to 6 months earlier. Although the initial allegations had involved only Bob Kelly, soon they expanded to include dozens of people in the town. Eventually seven adults were arrested and charged with sexual abuse. These included Betsy Kelly, Dawn Wilson, and two other young women who worked at the day-care center, Scott Privott (the owner of the local video store who claimed to have never set foot in the Little Rascals Day Care center), and a worker at a Head Start Center, which was located several miles from the Little Rascals.

The charges against these defendants involved rape, sodomy, and fellatio. Children told of having to perform sexual acts on other children, of having their pictures taken while performing such acts, of having assorted objects, such as pins and markers, placed into vaginal or anal openings. There were allegations involving "ritualistic" abuse: Betsy and Bob burned a cat with a candle; they murdered babies. Some children claimed to have been tied up, to have been hung upside down from trees, to have been set on fire, and to have been given drugs that made them feel sick and drowsy. Finally, even more improbable claims were made, such as being thrown overboard into a school of circling sharks.

One of the more surprising aspects of this case, and others like it, was the fact that none of the parents of the Little Rascals children had observed anything that caused them to suspect that their children were being abused or tortured during the period of the alleged abuses; there were no reports of unusual incidents from their children. Nor did the parents detect anything unusual when, without notice, they dropped in early to pick up their children from the day care. It was only after allegations began to grow that parents also began to remember events or behaviors that were consistent with their child being abused.

The first of the seven trials, Bob Kelly's, began in August 1991 (*State v. Robert Fulton Kelly, Jr.,* 1991–1992). Twelve children and their parents were among the many witnesses who testified about incidents that allegedly occurred three years earlier. These children's memories appear to have been refreshed by their therapy sessions, through meetings with the prosecution, by repeated discussions with their parents about the events, and through attending "court school" to prepare them for their testimony in court. The parents' memories were refreshed through their diaries, and through meetings that were conducted by the district attorney's office.

The jury returned "guilty" verdicts on 99 of 100 charges against Bob Kelly, and he was sentenced to serve 12 consecutive life sentences. One year later, Dawn Wilson *(State v. Kathryn Dawn Wilson,* 1992–1993) was convicted of five counts of abusing four children and was sentenced to life imprisonment. In December 1993, Betsy Kelly who had already spent two years in prison awaiting trial, pleaded no contest. After serving one year of a 7-year prison sentence, she was released on parole. In June 1994, Scott Privott pleaded no contest to 37 charges involving 16 children. After having served 3½ years in jail before posting bond in June 1993, Privott was placed on probation for 5 years. In short, the first four cases represented a clean sweep for the prosecution. However, on May 2, 1995, the Court of Appeals of North Carolina unanimously reversed the convictions of Bob Kelly and Dawn Wilson. On May 23, 1997, after eight years of investigation and prosecution, the prosecutors dropped all charges against three of the defendants, and announced their decision not to retry the cases of Dawn Wilson and Bob Kelly. We refer to this case as *Little Rascals.*

The Wee Care Nursery Case

On August 2, 1988, Margaret Kelly Michaels, a 26-year-old nursery school teacher, was convicted of sexually abusing children at the Wee Care Nursery School in Maplewood, New Jersey (*State v. Michaels,* 1988). Michaels was said to have licked peanut butter off children's genitals, played the piano while nude, made children drink her urine and eat her feces, and raped and assaulted these children with knives, forks, spoons, and Lego blocks. She was accused of performing these acts during regular school hours over a period of 7 months. During this time, none of the alleged acts were noticed by staff or reported by children to their parents. Nor did any of the parents notice any signs of strange behavior or genital soreness in their children, or smell urine or feces on them when they collected the children from school at the end of the day.

The first suspicion that Michaels abused her charges occurred four days after she had left the Wee Care Nursery School to accept a better paying position elsewhere. At that time, a 4-year-old former student was having his temperature taken rectally at his pediatrician's office when he said to the nurse, "That's what my teacher does to me at school." When asked to explain, he replied, "Her takes my temperature." That afternoon, the child's mother notified the state's child protective agency.

Two days later, the child was brought to the prosecutor's office where he inserted his finger into the rectum of an anatomical doll, and told the assistant prosecutor that two other boys also had their temperature taken. When questioned, neither of these other boys seemed to know anything about this claim, but one of them indicated that Michaels had touched his penis. The first child's mother then told a parent member of the school board of her son's disclosures to the pediatrician and assistant prosecutor. This father questioned his son about Kelly Michaels touching him inappropriately, remarking that "he was his best friend and that he could tell him anything." The child disclosed that Kelly had touched his penis with a spoon.

The Wee Care Nursery School sent out a letter to all parents, informing them of an investigation of a former employee "regarding serious allegations made by a child" and invited a social worker who codirected a sexual assault unit at a nearby hospital to make a presentation to the parents. She explained that sexual abuse of children is very common, with one out of three children being victims of an "inappropriate sexual experience" by the time he or she is 18 years old. She encouraged parents to examine their children for genital soreness, nightmares, bed-wetting, masturbation, or any noticeable changes in behavior, and to have them examined by pediatricians for injury.

Over the next two months, a number of professionals interviewed the children and their families to determine the extent to which the abuse occurred. As was true in the *Little Rascals* case, children began to disclose only after they had been interviewed on several occasions by the state's investigators or by their therapists.

The trial began 2½ years after the first allegation was made. On the basis of the testimony provided by 19 child witnesses, Kelly Michaels was convicted of 115 counts of sexual abuse against 20 3- to 5-year-old children. Sentenced to serve 47 years in prison, Michaels was released on bail after serving 5 years as a result of the Appeals Court of New Jersey reversing her conviction. The court ruled that if the prosecution decided to retry the case, they must first hold a pretrial taint hearing and show that despite suggestive and coercive interviewing techniques, the statements and testimony of the child witnesses are sufficiently reliable to admit them as witnesses at trial. In December 1994, the prosecution dropped all charges against Michaels. We refer to this case as *Michaels*.

Throughout this chapter, we will return to these two cases. Against the backdrop of the scientific data that we will present, we examine some of the investigative methods used in these cases and analyze the factors that may have influenced the accuracy of children's testimony. Before doing this, it is important to acknowledge that these cases are not typical of those that bring children into the legal arena. Nevertheless, we selected them for several reasons. First, the single most important context for children who testify in *criminal* trials is that of sexual abuse. We estimated elsewhere that upward of 13,000 children testify each year in sexual abuse cases in the United States (Ceci & Bruck, 1993a), and many thousands more give depositions and unsworn statements to law enforcement officials and social workers. If we add to these the large number of civil and family court cases that also include allegations of sexual impropriety involving a child, then the absolute numbers swell considerably. These figures reflect the prevalence of this problem in North America and other industrialized countries; in the United States alone; estimates of the annual rate of abused children range from 130,000 to 300,000, and the latest national incidence data (U.S. Dept. of Health and Human Services, 1996) indicate that in 1994 there were 1,011,628 reports of children who were determined to have been victims of abuse and/or neglect, based on a total number of reports that exceeded 2.9 million. Approximately 14% of the reported cases involved sexual abuse and 26% involved other forms of physical abuse (see Ceci & Bruck, 1995, for detailed discussion of incidence and prevalence statistics).

Second, our cases include preschoolers because the latest national figures estimate that 47% of victims of maltreatment are preschoolers (U.S. Dept. of Health and Human Services, 1996). Additionally, a substantial proportion of sexually abused children fall into this age range (18% to 30%) and it appears that a disproportionate number of preschoolers end up as witnesses in sexual abuse cases. In Gray's (1993) analysis of child witnesses in sexual abuse cases, although only 18% of abuse victims were 5 years old or younger, 41% of all the cases that ended up in trial involved children of this age. Although day-care center cases may represent only a small proportion of sexual abuse complaints, in absolute numbers they involve a very large number of children (e.g., in the *McMartin* case, 369 children made disclosures of sexual abuse [Sauer, 1993]).

We also focus on the sexual abuse in day-care settings because these present the greatest challenge to the application of social science research in the courtroom. Intuitively, it seems more relevant to draw a parallel between experimental studies of children's memories of unusual and surprising events (e.g., witnessing an argument) that are staged in laboratory settings and the ability of a child witness to accurately recall the details of a witnessed theft or accident. But how do these studies assist in understanding children's allegations of sexual abuse? How can researchers design scientific studies that would help in the assessment of the accuracy of children's allegations of sexual abuse? Throughout these pages, we show how this challenge has been met by social scientists, and describe when developmental science can and cannot assist in understanding real-world problems. Finally, we selected these cases because they highlight the negative dimensions of children's reporting; we did this to explore the bases of this phenomenon that is not well understood by experts and non-experts alike. Thus, these cases involve allegations of ritualistic abuse, which according to Finkelhor, Williams, and Burns (1988), is a common allegation made in such daycare cases. However, there has never been any physical evidence either from these cases or from larger studies to substantiate claims of ritualistic abuse (e.g., Goodman, Qin, Bottoms, & Shaver, 1994; LaFontaine, 1994). Furthermore, although most reports involving childhood sexual abuse are reliable, there are still a significant proportion of reports that are eventually judged to be unfounded (e.g., Jones & McGraw, 1987, report a figure of 23%). Thus the problems raised by the case histories may not represent the most common characteristics of cases involving children, but the problems or profiles of these cases are common enough that they are worthy of study.

All the arguments we make for and against children's testimony in sexual abuse cases apply equally to nonsexual abuse contexts. Although the unique aspects of sexual victimization can result in differences in children's demeanor and behavior, the underlying mechanisms governing their reports are the same even if couched in terms of issues other than sexual abuse. So, our focus on sexual abuse cases serves as a window into the more general issues regarding children's testimonial accuracy in contexts such as acrimonious custody disputes, physical abuse, domestic violence, or eyewitness accounts in criminal proceedings.

DEFINING SUGGESTIBILITY

These two cases highlight different aspects of the reliability of children's reports that have been the focus of research. The first aspect involves the accuracy of recalling events over long periods of time. In both cases, the children sometimes described events that allegedly occurred several years before they gave their testimony. Hundreds of studies have examined the degree to which children are able to accurately encode, store, and retrieve different types of information (for reviews, see Kail, 1989; Schneider & Pressley, 1989). Most of these studies, however, have examined short-term recollections of objects (as opposed to actions), and of peripheral (as opposed to central) events. More importantly, much of the literature, until recently, has not examined very young children's memories of emotional or stressful events. We will return to these issues later in the chapter.

The second aspect of children's reliability highlighted in the case studies concerns their "suggestibility," and it is this aspect that is the focus of the present chapter. Traditionally, suggestibility has been defined as "the extent to which individuals come to accept and subsequently incorporate postevent information into their memory recollections" (Gudjonsson, 1986, p. 195; see also Powers, Andriks, & Loftus, 1979). This definition contains several important implications. In particular, it implies: (a) Suggestibility is an unconscious process (i.e., information is unwittingly incorporated into memory), (b) suggestibility results from information that was supplied after an event as opposed to before it (hence, the term "postevent"), and (c) suggestibility is a memory-based, as opposed to a social, phenomenon. This final point means that suggestions are thought to influence reports through incorporation into the memory system, not through some social pressure to lie or to otherwise conform to expectations.

As we will be shown, early studies of children's suggestibility adhered to this definition. In these early studies, children experienced some event, then they were exposed to some misleading information, which was often embedded in an interviewer's question. For example, children might meet a beardless man in a schoolyard, and the interviewer would later ask, "What color was his beard?" If children reported a color of the beard, then this response reflected their suggestibility.

This traditional conceptualization and demonstration of suggestibility, however, is too restrictive to aid our understanding of the two case studies and the thousands of others like them. Therefore, elsewhere we have broadened the definition of suggestibility to encompass what is usually connoted by its lay usage (Ceci & Bruck,1993b). Hence, we proposed that children's suggestibility refer to the degree to which their encoding, storage, retrieval, and reporting of events can be influenced by a range of internal and external factors. This broader view implies that it is possible to accept information and yet be fully conscious of its divergence from the originally perceived event, as in the case of acquiescence to social demands, lying, or efforts to please loved ones. This broadened definition of suggestibility does not necessarily involve the alteration of the underlying memory; a child may still remember what actually occurred but choose not to report it for motivational reasons. This broader definition also implies that suggestibility can result from the provision of information either before *or* after an event. Finally, our broader definition implies that suggestibility can result from social as well as cognitive factors.

Thus, this broader conceptualization of children's suggestibility accords with both the legal and everyday uses of the term, to connote how easily a child can be influenced by subtle suggestions, expectations, stereotypes, and leading questions that can unconsciously alter memories, as well as by explicit bribes, threats, and other forms of social inducement that can lead to the conscious alteration of reports without affecting the underlying memory. Using this broadened definition of suggestibility, we can now examine how much children's testimonies reflect their incorporation of information provided before or after the event, whether the effect of the suggestions on their testimony is memory based or socially based, and whether children consciously or unconsciously process suggestions.

In this chapter, we examine several issues related to this broadened conceptualization of suggestibility. The first concerns the scope of children's suggestibility; here we explore the parameters of the phenomenon, asking under what circumstances and conditions it might occur. The second issue concerns age differences in suggestibility. Our review of the literature examines the degree to which younger children are more suggestible than older children and the degree to which all children are more suggestible than adults. Third, we examine some social and cognitive mechanisms that may account for developmental and individual differences in suggestibility. Before turning to these issues, it is important to emphasize that we do not mean to imply that adults are not suggestible, or that their memories are always reliable, or that their testimonies are highly accurate. These statements are clearly false. There is a sizable literature both on the suggestibility (e.g., Lindsay, 1990; Loftus, 1992, 1993) and unreliability of adults' memory for highly salient and important events (Neisser, 1982; Ross, 1989). In this chapter, we examine factors that may influence witnesses of all ages, but that we believe may exert a disproportionate influence on the youngest children.

CHILD WITNESSES: A HISTORICAL OVERVIEW OF LEGAL PRACTICES AND RESEARCH FINDINGS

Children in the Courtroom

The appearance of child witnesses in the courtroom is not a phenomenon unique to the final decades of the 20th century. Their presence has been documented for many centuries. The middle years of the 17th century saw massive involvement of children in the criminal justice systems of Europe and America. The context was usually, though not always, witch trials, and the children were called on to provide evidence of celestial apparitions, corporal transmogrifications, and actual bodily evidence that they were the objects of bewitchment (e.g., by falling into spasms on the mention of a witch's name). So believable were the children's statements and bodily responses that thousands of defendants were sent to the gallows on the word of a child. In Sweden, a great witch panic occurred between 1668 and 1676, and hundreds of children were interviewed by village priests about the presumed sorcery of neighbors (Sjoberg, 1994). As a result of the children's statements, 16 adults in one community were burned at the stake, and 27 adults, in another community, were beheaded.

Europe experienced its own witch trials several decades before those in the United States, the most notorious of which were the witch trials in Salem Village and Salem Farms, Massachusetts. During the final decade of the 17th century, a group of children known as the "circle girls" gave false testimony in the witchcraft trials of over 20 Salem residents. The girls claimed to have seen the defendants flying on broomsticks, to have witnessed celestial apparitions in the form of speaking animals, and to have observed the defendants instructing insects to fly into their mouths and deposit bent nails and pins in their stomachs (which they subsequently vomited during their testimony). On the basis of their testimony, 20 defendants were convicted and put to death, and a dozen more were spared execution because they threw themselves on the mercy of the court, and admitted their participation in witchcraft. In the aftermath of the executions, some of the child witnesses publicly recanted their testimonies.

Although some researchers have dismissed the witch trials as irrelevant to modern concerns over the credibility of child witnesses (e.g., Goodman, 1984; Myers, 1995), Ceci, Toglia, and Ross (1990) have argued that the children were subjected to an array of social and cultural forces that are also present in some recent legal cases, though in reduced form. Salem, at the time leading up to the witch trials, was emotionally charged, with accounts of witchcraft commonplace. Nearly everyone in 17th-century Salem believed in the power of witches. Thus, the court's willingness to accept the children's testimony about observing flying broomsticks and celestial apparitions was understandable in terms of their shared beliefs. Also, because of the widespread belief in witchcraft, people exercised particular care to avoid any display of behaviors that resembled those of witches. Therefore, the motivations of some of the child witnesses, whose own behaviors were viewed by some with suspicion, is understandable; their testimony may have been a means of diverting attention from themselves.

Parents and other powerful adults actively encouraged and shaped their children's "recollections" by encouraging them to elaborate on their statements. These adults asked leading questions and provided positive attention for answers congruent with the charge of witchcraft. As will be seen, the issue of the feasibility of using these techniques for eliciting testimony from young children has spurred a great deal of debate and subsequent research.

In the 19th and 20th centuries, there are many examples of children serving as witnesses in European courtrooms (e.g., Whipple, 1911, 1912, 1913). These children provided eyewitness testimony for varied crimes including sexual assault. In contrast, during this same time period children rarely served as witnesses in the United States and other English-speaking countries.

The quantity and quality of research on children's reliability and suggestibility appears to be related to the structure of the legal system at that time, the legal system's view of the reliability of the child witness, and the contribution of social science research. Three factors might explain why until recently, there was little if any social science research on the reliability of children's testimony in North America and other English-speaking countries, whereas such research flourished in Europe at the beginning of the century, especially in Germany and in France.

First, in America the Salem witch trials had lasting legal repercussions on the credibility of child witnesses. For 300 years following those trials, the predominant legal attitude in the United States was one of skepticism when considering the testimony of child witnesses. Children's reliability was sometimes put on a par with that of mental defectives and drug addicts (see Ceci & Bruck, 1995, for examples).

Due to ungenerous views of prominent jurists, children were only rarely permitted into the courts of English-speaking nations to provide uncorroborated testimony; thus, research on children's suggestibility was largely irrelevant in America, Australia, Canada, and Great Britain. On the other hand, children's testimony was allowed in some European courtrooms. And, some of the early European research was designed to directly address issues regarding children's testimony in the courtroom.

A second factor that accounts for the research hiatus in North America reflects the difference between adjudication procedures English-speaking versus other countries. An inquisitorial system of justice prevails in many European countries in which the judge is responsible for calling and questioning witnesses. Because there are often no juries, the European judge is more likely to call on expert witnesses to testify about the competence of witnesses. In the early part of the 20th century, these expert witnesses were often psychologists who carried out experiments to examine the validity of the children's testimony. In contrast, in an adversarial system, such as the one used in the United States, Australia, Canada, and Britain, the use of opposing attorneys and cross-examination as well as a jury are considered sufficient to evaluate witness credibility.

Finally, little research was carried out in North America on forensic issues, such as children's suggestibility because of the attitudes of the court concerning social science research. The proper interrelationship between social science and the law, particularly in reference to the development of rules governing the trial process, is a complex area of argument that continues to this day (Faigman, 1989; Giannelli, 1980; Haney, 1980). Thus, although European courts were, at least on occasion, eager consumers of the earliest psychological research on children's suggestibility, studies of both child and adult witnesses were rejected by the American legal profession (Loh, 1981). The earliest American jurists believed that psychology had little positive to offer the courts that was not already intuitively obvious, a view that could still be seen well into the early 1960s.

It is against this backdrop that research was carried out in the first 80 years of this century on the suggestibility of children. We only provide some highlights of this research to apprise the reader of the issues and methodologies that concerned social scientists. The interested reader is referred to our comprehensive and detailed treatments of this topic (Ceci & Bruck, 1993b, 1995).

Examples of Suggestibility Research: 1900–1980

Four European pioneers—Binet, Varendonck, Stern, and Lippmann—had the most profound influence on subsequent psychological research.

Alfred Binet

Binet, a French developmental psychologist, is best known as the father of the IQ test. Although he is less known for his work in the field of children's suggestibility, his data continue to stand up well in the modern forum. He argued that suggestibility reflected the operation of two types of factor.

The first factor, called *autosuggestion,* develops within the individual and is not the result of another's influence. Binet (1900) believed that autosuggestions paralyzed a child's critical thought processes; Binet attempted to construct experimental situations in which suggestions came from the subject himself. In one task, five lines of increasing length were presented to children and these were followed by a series of "target" lines that were the same length as the longest (final) line of the series. Children were shown each line and asked to reproduce it on paper. Children tended to be swayed by the expectation of ever-increasing lines; that is, their reproductions of the target line were systematically too long because they inferred that it was longer than the line that had preceded it.

Binet questioned the children after the study to determine why they had drawn the target lines so long, and found that many knew that the lines they had drawn were incorrect; they were able to redraw them more accurately on demand. Binet claimed that this ability showed that following the experiment, children could escape the influence of the autosuggestion and regain control of themselves.

Binet realized, however, that suggestibility, even in this very simple situation, could not be attributed to a single factor, leading him to postulate a second set of factors that were external to the child and reflected mental obedience to another person. In one test of external forces, Binet examined the effects of the examiner's language on children's responses. Children studied five objects for 10 seconds. Some children were told to write down everything they saw, whereas others were asked questions about the objects. For example, one of the objects was a button glued onto a poster board. Some children were asked simple direct questions about the button (e.g., "How is the button attached to the board?"); others were asked either mildly leading questions (e.g., "Wasn't the button attached by a thread?") or highly misleading and suggestive questions (e.g., "What was the color of the thread that attached the button to the board?"). There were several major findings of this study. First, free recall ("write down everything you saw") resulted in the most accurate statements, whereas highly misleading questions resulted in the least accurate statements. This was the first demonstration of a pattern of results that was to be often replicated throughout the rest of this century. Second, the children's answers to the questions were characterized by an exactness and confidence, regardless of their accuracy level. Third, when the children were later asked if they had made any mistakes, unlike Binet's previous studies, they did not correct their inaccurate responses to misleading questions. Binet concluded that children's erroneous responses reflected gaps in their memories, which they attempted to fill to please the experimenter. However, once an erroneous response was given, Binet surmised that it became incorporated into their memory.

Another element of external influences in suggestibility concerns the child's willingness to imitate the group response. Binet showed a group of three children the same objects described in the previous study. They were then asked a series of misleading questions. The children were told to call out the answer to each question as quickly as possible. Much to his surprise, Binet found that children who responded second and third were most likely to give the same answer as the first respondent, even if the answer was inaccurate. Thus, Binet concluded that the group is more suggestible than the individual.

J. Varendonck

Varendonck, a Belgian psychologist, conducted several interesting studies on young children's testimony. These studies were primarily motivated by a trial involving allegations by several children that a young girl named Cecile was murdered by a local man. Varendonck, who was an expert witness in this trial, provided the following details (Varendonck, 1911). Two of Cecile's friends, who had played with her on the day of her murder, were awakened that night by Cecile's mother, inquiring after her whereabouts. One of the children, Louise, replied that after leaving Cecile, she had returned home, had dinner, and gone to bed. Still later that night, Louise led the police to the spot where the children had played, not far from where Cecile's body was found. She was the fourth murder victim in a small town within a period of a month. After much suggestive questioning, Louise stated that a tall dark man with a dark moustache had coaxed Cecile to follow him. The next day, the two children were questioned again, and during this interrogation they altered their original testimony. After further questioning, which involved suggestions of the names of potential murderers, one of the children said the name of the man was "Jan." One month later, an anonymous letter was received by the police accusing one of the town members of the murder. On further questioning by powerful authority figures, Louise provided additional details about the murder.

The prosecution's case at the trial centered on the testimony of the two children. Based on the details of the case, Varendonck was convinced of the defendant's innocence. He quickly conducted a series of studies with the specific intent of demonstrating the unreliability of children's testimony.

In one study, 7-year-old children were asked about the color of a teacher's beard. Sixteen of 18 children provided a response, whereas only 2 said they did not know. The teacher in question did not have a beard (Varendonck, 1911). In another demonstration, a teacher from an adjoining classroom came into Varendonck's classroom and, without removing his hat, talked in an agitated fashion for approximately 5 minutes. (Keeping one's hat on when entering a room was uncommon because it was a sign of rudeness in that day's society.) After this teacher had left the classroom, the children were then asked in which hand that teacher had held his hat. Only 3 of the 27 students claimed that the hat was not in his hand. Varendonck claimed that the types of questions that he used in these studies were similar to those used with one of the child witnesses.

On the basis of his demonstrations, Varendonck concluded that the two children's statements to the police were false, the result of suggestions provided by influential adults. He carefully documented how the children changed their testimonies between the first and second interrogations, and how other social factors (e.g., repeated questioning by powerful adult figures) conspired to produce their testimony. Varendonck concluded that children could not observe accurately, and that their suggestibility was inexhaustible. He maintained that children would believe anything that adults wanted them to.

William Stern

Stern (1910), a German psychologist, developed two types of testimony experiment that still are in use today. In the first paradigm, subjects were shown a picture and asked to study it for a short period of time. Immediately after its presentation, they were asked to recall what they had seen in the picture. They were then asked a series of questions, some of which requested information that was in the picture, whereas others were misleading—they requested information about nonexistent objects. In one developmental study that included children between the ages of 7 and 18 years old, free recall produced the fewest errors, whereas misleading questions produced the most errors (Stern, 1910). Although younger children were the most suggestible, Stern found that even the 18-year-olds occasionally were misled by the suggestible questions.

Stern's second paradigm is called the "reality" experiment. This grew out of his desire to mimic situations that were closer to real life. In these real-life experiments, naive subjects observed staged incidents. In a typical experiment, an argument occurred during a seminar between two students, one of whom drew a revolver. The other students in the class were then questioned about the scenario. Although Stern did not report any developmental data, this paradigm is described here because it was adapted by many future researchers to study the reliability of adult and child witnesses' memory of events (e.g., Loftus, 1979; Marin, Holmes, Guth, & Kovac, 1979).

Stern made the following observations, which continue to be important issues of study. He warned about repeatedly questioning subjects about the same event and claimed that a subject's original verbal answers are better remembered than the actual events themselves. Stern also talked about the "force" that questions may have in determining answers. He claimed that many children answer questions because they view them as imperatives. Stern strongly stated that in many cases the questioner, by virtue of the questions asked, is responsible for the unreliable testimony of witnesses. This also has become a current line of research in this field.

O. Lipmann

The work of Lipmann, a German psychologist, is of interest because many of his hypotheses are the focus of modern research. Lipmann (1911) hypothesized that attentional factors in the encoding of the stimuli in addition to social factors could account for the finding that children's reports were less reliable than those of adults. He argued that children pay attention to different attributes of stimuli than do adults; children do not have fewer memories than adults, but different kinds of memories. He stated that when children were questioned by adults, who have great authority over them, about events that are neither essential nor salient to the child, then the child will attempt to compliantly revise his or her memory, making the report consistent with the question. Thus, rather than simply answering "I do not know," the child accepts any material that comes to mind to fill in these gaps whether it is imaginary or real. Eventually, everything that is imagined becomes real because the child fails to differentiate fantasy from reality. Modern researchers would return to the issue of the young child's ability to separate the sources of their information, including whether it was imagined or perceived (for a review, see Johnson, Hashtroudi, & Lindsay, 1993). And modern researchers would also return to the idea that children have different perceptions (or scripts) of the world than adults and that these can also affect their memories (Hudson & Nelson, 1986).

There are three important elements of the early European work on children's suggestibility that deserve mention. The first was an attempt to draw explicit parallels between the experimental contexts and the proceedings in a court of law. All the European researchers during this early period were interested in applications of children's memory research to the legal system. The second noteworthy feature of this early research was its attempt to provide multifactorial explanations, involving cognitive factors (related to children's encoding, storage, and retrieval of events) as well as social factors (related to children's compliance with authority figures or with group pressures). Finally, this early work foreshadowed a large number of findings that were to appear in the modern literature, such as the idea that repeated questioning is detrimental, that questions are interpreted as "imperatives" by young children, requiring answers even if none is available, that free recall produces fewer errors than yes/no questioning, that a witness's confidence is often unrelated to accuracy, that fantasy-reality distinctions are problematic for very young children, and that even adults are suggestible to some degree.

Research in English-Speaking Countries: 1920–1978

Following the spate of European research around the turn of the century, only 16 studies were conducted during the next 60 years in the United States, Canada, and England. Most of these were carried out in the 1920s and the 1930s and, for the most part, are marked by their unoriginality and failure to go beyond the work of their European predecessors. A major focus of these studies was to examine the relationships of age, intelligence, and gender to suggestibility, or to examine the correlations among different suggestibility measures, most of which were adaptations of tasks devised by Binet, Varendonck, and Stern. Children's suggestibility usually was assessed by asking them to write answers to written questions in a testlike atmosphere. Otis (1924) devised a test to measure children's ability to rely on their own judgments. For some items, children were shown three words with a circle under each. Two of the circles contained the word directly above them, the third circle was empty. Children were told to write a word in the third circle. If they wrote the word directly above it, this was counted as a suggestible response. Other questions assessed the influence of external forces. For example, children were shown a picture with a slight resemblance to a horse and were asked "This figure looks like a race horse. Do you not think so?"

A reading of the literature during this period suggests that a consensus was building that children were especially prone to suggestive influences. Furthermore, the data produced during this era indicated that there was a negative correlation between suggestibility and IQ, with those possessing lower IQs being less able to resist suggestion. Because many of these suggestibility measures were paper-and-pencil tests, however, the correlations may reflect that the younger or less able students had more difficulty dealing with written materials, or with keeping their attention focused during long written tasks, rather than with suggestibility of the experimental manipulations.

In contrast to the earlier European studies, the subsequent studies conducted by North American researchers were not couched in legally relevant terms. For reasons stated earlier, there was never any mention of the applicability of these findings to children's courtroom testimony. One is also struck by the simplicity of the methodology. Because all the studies involved giving groups of children paper-and-pencil tests, there was no opportunity to directly observe the questioner's influence on the child, nor how children would react when questioned individually. And, as would be forcefully argued throughout the rest of the century, the results of these types of demonstrations of suggestibility may have little relevance for actual court cases in which children testify.

Entering the Modern Era: 1979–1980s

At the end of the 1970s, there was a small resurgence of studies on children's suggestibility. These studies exhibited a paradigmatic shift in several ways. First, in contrast to the older studies, subjects now viewed a film, or participated in a staged incident, and this was followed by the provision of some misleading information. The effects of the misleading information were assessed in an interview that took place hours, days, weeks, or months later. Thus, for the first time some developmental studies began to provide a glimpse of the long-term effects of providing misinformation. Using this approach, the handful of studies produced at the beginning of the 1980s showed an inconsistent pattern of results not found in earlier work. Sometimes children were found to be more suggestible than adults (e.g., Cohen & Harnick, 1980), whereas in other studies no age differences were noted (e.g., Marin et al., 1979). Due to pressures from the judicial system, social scientists began to attack this area with a renewed vigor and with different and more satisfactory scientific methods. Inconsistent results were less common than inconsistent interpretations of results. But with additional studies, a unified interpretation of the data began to emerge.

THE MODERN ERA: CHANGES IN LEGAL VIEWS AND RESEARCH TRENDS

In the 1980s, there was a resurgence of interest among developmental researchers in the reliability of children's reports. For the most part, the increased number of studies, and the exploration of new areas in child development were more motivated by social and judicial concerns than by theoretical ones. We identify three interrelated factors that account for this dramatic upsurge in the empirical work.

First, beginning in the middle of the 1970s, there was a broadening of admissibility of expert psychological testimony related to the eyewitness accuracy of adults (Loftus, 1986). Thus, social science research, after a long period of being ignored or rejected by judicial policymakers, has come to be viewed, at least on occasion, as relevant to the legal system. Second, in part fueled by the sociopolitical zeitgeist of the late 1960s, social scientists attempted to apply their scientific training to socially relevant issues, particularly those concerning children's rights and the protection of minors.

The third and undoubtedly the biggest stimulus for the explosion of research on children's suggestibility was a result of the changes in the court system regarding the treatment of child witnesses (e.g., McGough, 1994). As a result of society's reaction to the dramatic increases in child abuse, and particularly to the ineffective prosecution of child abuse cases, the legal systems in many English-speaking countries were forced to change some of their rules concerning the admissibility and treatment of child witnesses. During the 1980s, all but a few jurisdictions dropped their corroboration requirement for children in sexual abuse cases, a crime that by its nature lacks corroboration. Many states in the United States, modeling their procedures after the *Federal Rules of Evidence,* began to allow children to testify regardless of the nature of the crime, permitting the jury to determine how much weight to give to the child's testimony. In Canada, with the adoption of Bill C-15, the court could now convict on the basis of a child's unsworn testimony. In England, children over 3 years of age were admitted as witnesses in the courtroom, and could provide unsworn corroborated testimony in sexual abuse cases.

As more and more children have been admitted as witnesses in the courtroom, legal procedures have been modified. For example, some courts have instituted shield laws that permit a child witness to testify either behind a one-way screen or over closed-circuit television, to occlude the child's view of the defendant but not the defendant's view of the child (e.g., *Coy v. Iowa,* 1988; *Maryland v. Craig,* 1990). Hearsay exceptions are also allowed whereby therapists, pediatricians, and others are permitted under certain circumstances to describe what children have said to them. And, most recently, there has been experimentation with mandated videotaping of interviews (Child Victim Witness Investigative Pilot Projects, 1994). These measures serve to assist child witnesses who otherwise might be "psychologically unavailable" to testify in open court (McGough, 1994; Montoya, 1992, 1993).

Interestingly, the modifications in the judicial system regarding the treatment of child witnesses was brought about by social pressures and by the presumption that courtroom modifications will increase testimonial accuracy (*Harvard Law Review* Notes, 1985; Montoya, 1992) rather than by a consideration of the social science data. As a result, jurists and social scientists continue to raise fundamental questions about whether these changes actually facilitate the accuracy of children's testimony, or result in more reliable judgments of a case by fact finders (Montoya, 1992, 1993).[1]

Because of this uncertainty, social scientists and health care professionals frequently have been called to court to testify about the reliability of statements made by child witnesses. It is fair to say that until recently even well-read professionals would have had to base their testimony on speculation. A major problem in the interpretation of the literature was that until the 1980s most studies of children's suggestibility focused on school-age children and adolescents; not a single study during the first 80 years of this century included preschoolers. This void made it difficult if not impossible to evaluate the testimonies of preschool witnesses who were increasingly becoming participants in the legal system. This void has begun to be filled; in the past decade, many studies of children's suggestibility have included preschoolers.

But the predominant problem that the expert faced in interpreting the existing literature was that it was difficult to make any generalizations from the scientific literature to the courtroom because the studies of children's suggestibility bore so little resemblance to the situations that brought children to court. For example, although the consistent finding in this older literature was that younger

---

[1] Few scientific data addressing these issues are yet available, however, although some data on the costs and benefits of courtroom innovations on children's courtroom behavior have been gathered (Batterman-Faunce & Goodman, 1993; Flin, 1993). What is needed is evidence showing that children who experience an emotional, painful, and/or embarrassing bodily event (e.g., a genital catheterization) can provide more accurate descriptions of the event when they are asked to do so behind a one-way screen or in a videotaped interview than when they have to provide such testimony before an open forum. And conversely, it is important to show that when children have been coached or suggestively interviewed that their descriptions of the alleged event are equally deceiving in both the open forum and videotaped procedures. To date, no satisfactory evidence exists. In light of claims that many of the new courtroom modifications challenge the constitutional rights of defendants to confront their accusers (*Coy v. Iowa,* 1988; *Maryland v. Craig,* 1990), it is important to determine whether such modifications do, in fact, facilitate the accuracy of children's testimony (Montoya, 1993).

children are more suggestible than older children or than adults, this conclusion was based on examinations of the influence of one or two misleading questions or suggestions on children's memories of details about neutral events (e.g., stories, slides, movies, or objects). As a result, some researchers have questioned the usefulness of these results in the evaluation of the testimony of a child who makes allegations of sexual abuse or of other potentially distressing events. Perhaps no generalization can be made from the research context to this real-world context of abuse, a point stated by some in the research community itself:

> Most research on children as eyewitnesses has relied on situations that are very different from the personal involvement and trauma of sexual abuse. Researchers have used brief stories, films, videotapes, or slides to simulate a witnessed event. A few have used actual staged events, but these events—for example . . . a man tending plants—are also qualitatively different from incidents of child abuse. The children are typically bystanders to the events, there is no bodily contact between the child and adult, and it is seldom even known whether the events hold much interest for the children. Of even more importance . . . , the questions the children are asked often focus on peripheral details of the incident like what the confederate was wearing, rather than on the main actions that occurred, or more to the point, whether sexual actions were committed. (Goodman & Clarke-Stewart, 1991, pp. 92–93)

In the next sections, where we summarize the most recent research in this area, we discuss two paradigms for addressing these criticisms. The first line of study asks, "Are children so suggestible that they will make inaccurate statements about very important or salient events, especially those involving their own body?" The second line of research is based on the architecture of interviews between children and adults, and examines the effects of various interviewing practices on the accuracy of young children's reports.

ASKING CHILDREN QUESTIONS ABOUT SALIENT EVENTS, ACTIONS, AND THEIR BODIES

Modern researchers face the challenge of developing paradigms that allow for the study of children's reports when they are participants rather than bystanders, where there is bodily contact between the child and the adult, and where the events hold some interest for the child. In developing these new methodologies, researchers have also realized the importance of questioning children about the main actions that occurred during these events rather than only about peripheral details such as the color of the researcher's beard. The ultimate challenge has been to ask questions in an ethically permissible manner about whether or not "sexual" actions occurred during these events.

Some investigators have conducted studies in which children are brought into a university laboratory to participate in some interesting event with a confederate. At some later point, these children are questioned about what happened during the event. Typically, children are first asked open-ended questions; they are asked to tell as much as they can remember about what happened when they came to the laboratory. Then they are asked more direct questions that may require yes-no answers, or one-word answers (e.g., "Did the man show you a picture?") Some of these questions are misleading (e.g., "The man showed you the picture, didn't he?" or "What color was the frame around the picture?" when in fact no picture had been shown). There is an additional feature of these studies. The interviewer asks children a number of questions termed "abuse-related." These are questions which if answered in the affirmative could lead to suspicions of child abuse: for example, "Did the man take off your clothes?" would be classified as a direct abuse question, or "He took off your clothes, didn't he?" would be classified as a misleading abuse question.

As an example of this approach, Rudy and Goodman (1991) examined whether there were differences in the accuracy of children's reports when they were participants in an event as opposed to merely being bystanders. Pairs of 4-year-old and 7-year-old children were left in a trailer with an unfamiliar adult. One child played a game with the adult that involved being dressed in a clown's costume and being lifted and photographed (i.e., the child was a participant), while the other child was encouraged to carefully observe this interchange (i.e., the child was a bystander). Approximately 10 days later, children were questioned about the events. They were first asked some open-ended questions and then 58 specific questions about the event. As described earlier, these questions were either classified as direct or misleading; and some were classified as abuse-related. Surprisingly, there were few differences between participants' and bystanders' responses. As might be expected, the older children were more accurate than the younger children. Older children's responses were more accurate than those of the younger children for all types of questions except misleading abuse questions; for these latter questions there were no age differences in accuracy. A more detailed analysis of the incorrect answers to the misleading abuse questions revealed only one false report of abuse; a 4-year-old bystander falsely claimed that he and the participant had been spanked. Thus, Rudy and Goodman demonstrated that 4-year-olds are more suggestible than 7-year-olds; however, the important finding of this study is that there were no age differences in suggestibility when misleading abuse questions were examined separately. This finding has commonly been used to support the position, that although there may be age differences in suggestibility, and although children in general may be misled, that these conclusions do not apply to suggestions concerning sexual abuse.

A second study by Saywitz, Goodman, Nicholas, and Moan (1991) takes this paradigm one step further. Here, they examined 5- and 7-year-old girls' reports of an earlier visit to their pediatrician. During their pediatric visit, half of each age group had a scoliosis exam and half had a genital exam. Children were tested between 1 and 4 weeks following their exam. As in the previous study, children were asked misleading and direct questions that were abuse- or nonabuse-related. The older children's answers to the misleading nonabuse questions and to the direct abuse questions were more accurate than those of the younger children. However, there was essentially no age differences for the misleading abuse questions (e.g., "How many times did the doctor kiss you?"), with few children at either age giving incorrect responses. The 7-year-old children never made a false report of abuse, and this occurred only three times (out of a possible 215 opportunities) for the 5-year-olds. Again, this result suggests that children cannot be easily misled into making false statements about sexual abuse.

Saywitz and her colleagues stress the importance of specific patterns of results in this study. They conclude that when children's inaccurate reports are examined, they involve mainly omission errors (i.e., failure to report actual experiences) rather than commission errors (i.e., inclusion of false events). Most children in the genital examination condition did not disclose genital contact, unless specifically asked "Did the doctor touch you here?" In the scoliosis condition, when children were asked this question, the incidence of false reports (commission errors) was only 1%:

> Obtaining accurate testimony about sexual abuse from young children is a complex task. Part of the complexity rests in the fact that there are dangers as well as benefits in the use of leading questions with children. The benefits appear in the finding in the studies by Goodman and associates that leading questions were often necessary to elicit information from children about actual events they had experienced (genital touching) . . . The children in the studies by Goodman and associates were generally accurate in reporting specific and personal things that had happened to them. If these results can be generalized to investigations of abuse, they suggest that normal children are unlikely to make up details of sexual acts when nothing abusive happened. They suggest that children will not easily yield to an interviewer's suggestion that something sexual occurred when in fact it did not, especially if non-intimidating interviewers ask questions children can comprehend. (Goodman & Clarke-Stewart, 1991, pp. 102–103)

In general, we agree with the summary of that "children will not easily yield to an interviewer's suggestion that something sexual occurred when in fact it did not. . . ." though, we feel that these authors have overestimated the degree to which "children will not easily yield." Their claim is based on children's responses to misleading abuse questions. In the trailer study, children's correct answers to the misleading abuse questions ranged from 88% to 94%. In the genital-scoliosis study, the rates were even higher, ranging from 96% to 99%. However, when children were asked nonmisleading questions about potentially abusive events (e.g., "Did the man kiss you?"), accuracy rates were not as high: the accuracy rates in the trailer study ranged from 82% to 90%; in the genital-scoliosis study, the accuracy rates were even lower, ranging from 77% to 87% accuracy. It is not clear why children responded more accurately to the misleading than to the direct questions. Perhaps the content of the misleading questions made them more difficult to accept; or, perhaps there were some subtle verbal or nonverbal cues in the phrasing of the questions that alerted children that the misleading questions were in fact misleading. For these reasons, it may be more instructive to focus on the children's responses to the direct nonleading questions; these results suggest that some children are not uniformly accurate in their responses to questions about abuse, a conclusion supported by other studies as well.

Three studies by Ornstein and his colleagues provide additional information on the accuracy of children's recall of events involving bodily touching (see Ornstein, Shapiro, Clubb, Follmer, & Baker-Ward, 1997, for a summary). These studies, which focus on children's recall of their visits to a pediatrician, assess the rate at which memories fade over different periods of delay and the degree to which children include nonoccurring events as part of their reports of their visits.

In these three studies, the children ranged from 3 to 7 years. Following their yearly medical examination, most children were immediately interviewed and then reinterviewed at varying time intervals, ranging from 1 to 12 weeks. In each interview, the children were first asked open-ended questions ("Can you tell me what happened when you went to the doctor?") and then they were asked more specific yes-no questions (e.g., "Did he look in your nose?"). Children were also asked "strange" questions about events that never happen at a doctor's office (e.g., "Did the Doctor cut your hair?") or about silly actions that if responded to affirmatively might be interpreted as sexual (e.g., "Did the Nurse lick your knee?"). The common elements of all these questions is that they involve actions on the child's body.

There are several important findings of these three studies. First, there were significant age-differences in children's immediate and delayed recall, with the 3-year old children performing the poorest on all types of questions. The 3-year-olds were particularly noteworthy for the lack of information that they provided to the open-ended questions, thus forcing the interviewer to ask a large number of specific yes-no questions to obtain a full report about the visit. Second, as the delay intervals increased, there was notable forgetting among the youngest children who were increasingly inaccurate when questioned following delays of 1, 3, 6, and 12 weeks. Seven-year-olds did not show impairment until a delay of between 6 to 12 weeks after the medical examination. A third important finding is that the accuracy of children's answers to the strange and silly questions also varied as a function of age and delay interval. As before, younger children, gave more inaccurate responses to these questions than older children, and in some cases these scores became more inaccurate at various delays. In one study (Gordon, Ornstein, Clubb, Nida, & Baker-Ward, 1991), the 3-year-old children's responses to these "silly" questions (e.g., "Did the nurse lick your knee?") was at chance levels of accuracy when questioned 12 weeks after their examination. Older children's responses to silly questions remained highly consistent across delays and studies (error rates averaging about 10% for silly questions). Older children's relatively stable performance may reflect their well-formed notions (or in technical terms "scripts") of probable and improbable events that occur during a pediatric visit, leading them to automatically reject the latter without even checking their memories for these events.

Results of the Saywitz, Goodman, and Ornstein studies reflect how accurately children report salient events that may include bodily contact when they are asked to give reports immediately following the events or up to a 3-month delay. The children were fairly, but not entirely accurate about a number of salient events that involved bodily touching. Furthermore, their accuracy increased as a function of age (with preschoolers being most inaccurate) and as a function of the delay between the interview and the actual event. Ornstein's data indicate that when accuracy drops off, it is not merely the case that children forget and therefore make errors of omission, but they also make errors of commission. Children, especially the younger children, reported events that never happened and these reported nonevents included not only acts that could conceivably occur in a doctor's office, but also acts that would not occur in the doctor's office and that have sexual connotations, at least to some adults.

Both Ornstein and Goodman have commented on the behaviors of children when they are asked misleading or silly questions. In defense of the position that children cannot be easily led to make false allegations about "sexual" events, they note that children often laugh at some of the experimenter's questions, refusing to take them seriously. Similar responses have also been noted in some of the nationally visible cases. For example in the *Michaels* case, one of the parents claimed that her preschool child had said, "Kelly puts a penis on her nose and she looked like a penis head. It was funny" (child giggles) (see Ceci & Bruck, 1995, for additional descriptions).

The Ornstein and Goodman data reflect how accurately children respond to direct questions, and to misleading questions, which mainly require yes-no answers. The misleading questions in these studies were embedded in an unemotional, neutral interview that contained a host of other questions, so that the interview was not tilted toward having the child respond in only one way. These are the types of questions that one might ask children who provide no information to more general open-ended questions. As we will argue, these are the optimal conditions under which children should be interviewed, and when testimony is obtained in this way, then we can have the most faith in the accuracy of children's statements.

Having said this, the Goodman and Ornstein studies are not informative about the accuracy of children's statements when the latter are obtained by more aggressive interview methods such as those sometimes used with child witnesses. The children in these research studies were not repeatedly interviewed about alleged abusive events, the identical question was not repeated within interviews, nor were there threats or inducements to have the subjects reply in a certain way. The interviewers in these studies were supportive and neutral; in contrast, in many cases, children are questioned by anxious parents, by therapists, and by legal officials. Consequently, child witnesses may be more likely to comply with the suggestions of their interviewers than in analogous experimental situations, where interviewers are generally less important or less imposing to the child subjects.

The studies we have reviewed do not shed light on how a web of motives, threats, and inducements (which might act independently as subtle forms of suggestion, and interact with more explicit forms of suggestion) might tilt the odds one way or another in terms of the accuracy of a child's report. Thus although many of the experimental studies we have reviewed up to this point, may be immensely important in revealing the underlying mechanisms of suggestibility and of children's memory, they may underestimate the potency of suggestive techniques in actual cases. Because important elements are missing from these studies, it makes it difficult to generalize to many forensic situations. This concern has motivated another group of modern researchers to look more closely at the structure of conversations and interviews between children and adults and to examine the effects of various interviewing practices on the accuracy of children's reports.

ARCHITECTURE OF ADULTS' INTERVIEWS WITH CHILDREN

Because the testimony of child witnesses is elicited in interviews, it is crucial to understand the architecture of interviews between children and adults to evaluate the source as well as the reliability of child witnesses' statements. In this section, we discuss some characteristics of interviews that take place between adults and children. Although interviews may be highly structured, they need not be. An interview, at minimum, is a verbal interaction between at least two people in which one of the participants (the interviewer) has the goal of obtaining specific information from one of the participants (the interviewee). As such, interviews are a particular type of conversation that can be carried out by a wide variety of professionals and nonprofessionals, such as child protection workers, police officers, mental health professionals, attorneys, parents, or teachers.

Obtaining accurate information concerning forensically important events in interviews with children is not a straightforward process; it can be impeded by three factors. The first concerns the general linguistic problem of obtaining detailed information from children who are unaccustomed to providing elaborate verbal narratives about their experiences. The second concerns the cognitive problem that arises when children are asked to recall events that happened long before the interview occurred; as a result the child may have problems remembering the information. Finally, reporting information about stressful, embarrassing, or painful events may be very difficult, especially for the young child.

Adults' Everyday Conversations with Children

Obtaining detailed and accurate accounts from children about events that may have happened weeks, months, or even years ago can be a difficult task. Adults encounter this difficulty whether they ask children about everyday neutral events, special pleasant events, or stressful events in which the child was a participant or a victim. When parents ask their young children about what happened at school or at their friend's birthday party, they typically receive answers such as "nothing" or "we played." These noninformative responses to open-ended questions are very common among young children (Pillemer & White, 1989). To obtain more detailed information, adults must structure the conversation and guide the child into providing responses. Analyses of adult-child conversations reveal the following strategies that adults use to obtain information from children.

On the most general level, the adult asks many questions that serve as probes or prompts to assist the child in reporting the appropriate information (see Fivush, 1993, for a review). Adults attempt to structure the interaction around their knowledge (or their script) of the topic. So, when adults question a child about a birthday party, they may begin with a general question: "What happened at John's party?" but after receiving no information, they may ask specific and often leading questions that reflect their knowledge or script of what generally happens at birthday parties (e.g., "What games did you play?" "What did you do after the gifts were opened?"). When adults do not receive a satisfactory answer, they may repeat the questioning. To ensure that the interaction continues, adults may reward children for their responses, making comments like "Wow, that is really funny," or "That is so interesting, and what happened next?" When children go off topic and make unrelated remarks, adults frequently try to pull them back into the topic, by ignoring the unrelated comments, or promising to talk about them at a later time. This often has the intended effect of extinguishing the child's production of extraneous remarks and focusing on the topic at hand. Of course, when adults do not have full knowledge of the actual events or a script for those events, they may have difficulty interpreting a child's statements and come to make inaccurate assessments of the actual event.

One might also argue that when adults have to structure conversations with plenty of questions and prompts, the child merely answers in ways that are consistent with the beliefs of the adult questioner or that the child's answers simply mirror the information that is contained in the adult's questions. Although some investigators of everyday conversations dispute this interpretation (e.g., Fivush, Hamond, Harsch, Singer, & Wolf, 1991), arguing that children incorporate very little of adults' questions into their subsequent recall, there is also other evidence to suggest that children's responses to adults' questions may sometimes reflect what the child thinks the adult wants to hear, rather than what the child actually thinks. This research emphasizes that although children may not provide abundant information during their conversations with adults, they generally are cooperative and compliant participants in verbal interactions. Children supply their questioner with the type of information they think is being requested (e.g., Ervin-Tripp, 1978; Read & Cherry, 1978). This pattern reflects children's desire to comply with a respected authority figure. As a result, when questioned by adults, children sometimes attempt to make their answers consistent with what they see as the desire of the questioner rather than consistent with their knowledge of the event. Also, from an early age, children perceive their adult conversational partners as cooperative, truthful, and not deceptive (Garvey, 1984; Nelson & Gruendel, 1979; Romaine, 1984). Thus, children place more faith in the credibility of adults' statements than in those of their peers (e.g., Ackerman, 1983; Sonnenschein & Whitehurst, 1980).

Another reflection of children's attempts to be cooperative partners in interactions with adults is their attempt to provide answers to adults' questions even when the questions are bizarre. When asked nonsensical questions such as "Is milk bigger than water?" or "Is red heavier than yellow?" most 5- and 7-year-olds will reply "yes" or "no"; they only rarely respond, "I don't know" (Hughes & Grieve, 1980). These data suggest that children perceive adults as cooperative conversational partners who ask honest and logical questions that must have real answers.

Another finding that reflects children's attempts to be cooperative conversational partners is that when children are asked the same question more than once, they often change their answers. They appear to interpret the repeated question as "I must not have given the correct response the first time, therefore to comply and be a good conversational partner, I must try to provide new information" (e.g., Gelman, Meck, & Merkin, 1986; Rose & Blank, 1974; Siegal, Waters, & Dinwiddy, 1988).

Adults' Conversations with Children about Forensically Relevant Events

Some of the elements that characterize adult-child conversations about daily events or about neutral laboratory tasks also characterize adult-child conversations about topics with potential legal implications. But sometimes because of the urgency or seriousness of forensic interviews, the intensity of such interviews increases greatly. This may pose a serious reliability risk when coupled with some special techniques used by professional interviewers.

A major dimension along which they can be characterized is that of "interviewer bias." Interviewer bias characterizes those interviewers who hold a priori beliefs about the occurrence of certain events and, as a result, mold the interview to elicit statements from the interviewee consistent with these prior beliefs. One of the hallmarks of interviewer bias is the single-minded attempt to gather only confirmatory evidence and to avoid all avenues that may produce negative or inconsistent evidence. Thus, while gathering evidence to support a hypothesis, an interviewer may fail to gather any evidence that could potentially disconfirm the hypothesis. The interviewer does not challenge the child who provides abuse-consistent evidence by saying things like "You're kidding me, aren't you?" or "Did that really happen?" The interviewer does not ask questions that might provide alternate explanations for the allegations (e.g., "Did your mommy and daddy tell you that this happened, or did you see it happen?"). And the interviewer does not ask the child about events that are inconsistent with his hypothesis (e.g., "Who else beside your teacher touched your private parts? Did your mommy touch them, too?"). When children provide inconsistent or bizarre evidence, it is either ignored, or else interpreted within the framework of the interviewer's initial hypothesis. Interviewer bias can be found wherever an interviewer thinks he knows the answers before the child divulges them.

Interviewer bias influences the entire architecture of interviews, and it is revealed through many highly suggestive component features. For example, to obtain confirmation of their suspicions, interviewers may not ask children open-ended questions, but quickly resort to a barrage of specific questions, many of which are repeated, and many of which are leading. When interviewers do not obtain information that is consistent with their suspicions, they may repeatedly interview children until they do obtain such information. Thus, children are often interviewed over a prolonged period of time and are reinterviewed on many occasions about the same set of events. In our sample case studies, many of the children were officially interviewed at least six or more times by police, social workers, and attorneys before coming to trial. No one knows how many unofficial interviews were conducted by parents, neighbors, and therapists.

"Stereotype inducement" is another strategy commonly used in these interviews with children—one reflecting the bias of the interviewer. Here the interviewer gives the child information about some characteristic of the suspected perpetrator. For example, children may be told that a person who is suspected of some crime "is bad" or "does bad things."

Interviewer bias is also reflected in the atmosphere of the interview. Sometimes, interviewers provide much encouragement during the interview to put the children at ease and to provide a highly supportive environment. Such encouraging statements, however, quickly lose their impartial tone, when a biased interviewer *selectively* reinforces children's responses by positively acknowledging statements (e.g., through the use of vigorous head nodding, smiling, and statements such as "Wow, that's great!") that are consistent with the interviewer's beliefs or hypotheses, or by ignoring other statements that do not support the interviewer's beliefs. Some interviewers who feel an urgency and responsibility to obtain the desired disclosure may even use threats and bribes. To obtain full compliance, interviewers often try to engage children by co-opting their cooperation. An interviewer may tell a child that he is a helper in an important legal investigation, and sometimes may add that the child's friends have helped or already told, and that he should also tell.

Other characteristics or techniques are specific to interviews between professionals and children. One of these involves the use of anatomically detailed dolls in investigations of sexual abuse. Children may be given these dolls and asked to reenact the alleged or suspected sexual molestation. It is thought that these props facilitate reports of sexual abuse for children with limited language skills, for children who feel shame and embarrassment, and for children with poor memories of the abusive incident.

Another professional technique involves "guided imagery" or "memory work." Interviewers sometimes ask children to first try to remember or pretend if a certain event occurred and then to create a mental picture of the event and think about its details.

Because our description of the architecture of interviews is based on our review of hundreds of transcripts that have been made available to us by judges, attorneys, parents, law enforcement agencies, medical, and mental health professionals, it should be accepted with the following caveat. The materials we have reviewed may not be representative of many of the interviews carried out with children in forensic or therapeutic situations. Interviews come to our attention because they contain components that might be considered to be suggestive in one way or another, and that have the potential to lead the child astray. So when we say "typical" of interviews, we really mean "typical of the interviews that we have been sent." Undoubtedly, there exist many interviews that do not contain these problems. Having said this, some recent studies reveal the pervasiveness of some interviewers' styles. Warren and her colleagues (McGough & Warren, 1994) have analyzed the child sexual abuse investigative interviews conducted by Child Protective Services professionals in the State of Tennessee. These interviewers spent little if any time asking children open-ended questions; 90% of all questions were highly specific requiring one-word answers (see Lamb et al., in press, for similar results for trained Israeli "youth" investigators).

Professionals use these techniques and defend these practices, particularly in investigations of sexual abuse, on a number of related grounds. First, they cite their own experiences as well as a clinical literature that documents the difficulty of extracting reports from sexually abused children. These youngsters feel shame, guilt, embarrassment, or terror about disclosing the details of their abuse. It is common for them to delay when making disclosures, and often when they finally do disclose, a significant proportion recant. Many professional interviewers argue for the necessity of using a variety of tools which, although potentially suggestive, are crucial for digging out reports of sexual abuse, particularly when the child has allegedly been threatened not to tell of the abuse.

When criticized for the use of biased interview techniques that reflect the search for evidence that is consistent with suspicions of sexual abuse and that avoid the search for evidence that is inconsistent with such suspicions, some professionals defend their practices on the basis of the patterns of disclosures commonly found in sexually abused children. They cite several studies suggesting that it is common for children to first deny sexual abuse, then to disclose sexual abuse, and then, because of fear or guilt, to recant their allegations. Because of this pattern, these professionals claim it is important to fully support children's reports of sexual abuse when they occur because any challenge to their reports may drive the children back into denial.

A few studies, however, support the view that a sizable proportion of sexually abused children go through a series of stages in disclosure. Sorenson and Snow (1991) examined 116 cases from a sample of 630 children who had received therapy for sexual abuse. For the majority of the children, the disclosures were accidental, and at some point 75% of the children had denied that abuse had occurred. Even after making a disclosure, 22% of the children recanted their previous disclosures. Another study by Gonzalez, Waterman, Kelly, McCord, and Oliveri (1993) is also cited as evidence that a substantial proportion of sexually abused children recant. In their study of 63 children in therapy for sexual and ritualistic abuse in day care, 27% of the children recanted.

A number of methodological features mar the interpretation of these data. Of primary concern is the possibility that the children in these studies were in fact not sexually abused, but that their disclosures were the result of the interviewing and therapeutic process. This is particularly salient in the Gonzalez et al. study, which examined the disclosure patterns of the McMartin Preschool child witnesses. Certainly, based on research presented earlier in this chapter, the finding that these children made disclosures involving ritualistic abuse is one that ought to have been greeted with greater skepticism than was apparent.

Other studies provide a different perspective on the process of disclosure. Jones and McGraw (1987) found only a 4% recantation rate among 576 sexual abuse cases seen at a child protection agency, and in the most recent study of the patterns of disclosure among sexually abused children, Bradley and Wood (1996) found that among 249 validated cases, 5% of the children denied the abuse and only 3% recanted their earlier reports of abuse. Some percentage of youngsters do appear to disclose their abuse reluctantly, and a smaller percentage recant their disclosures, but the overwhelming majority of children appear to maintain their claims, never denying them to officials. This is an instance where the results of methodologically inferior studies have spawned the lore that children's denials must be pursued to unearth the truth. Even if such pursuit worked to dislodge their disclosures, one needs to consider that the very same tactics could foster false disclosures: Children could recant previous accurate denials.

There are also some data to address the issue of children's reactions to explicit threats made by their perpetrators. These data do not support the common assumption that children's denials or recantations reflect fear of retribution. In a study by Sauzier (1989), the likelihood of disclosure was unrelated to threats of the offender. When the offender used aggressive methods to gain the child's compliance to keep the secret, children were equally likely to tell about the abuse immediately following the event or to never disclose the abuse. Gray (1993) reported that although 33% of a sample of sexually abused children were threatened by the perpetrator not to tell, nevertheless two-thirds of these children still disclosed.

Professional interviewers also support the use of their suggestive techniques on the basis of some of the research on children's suggestibility and memory. One interpretation of this literature is that although it may be possible to influence children to fabricate reports of unimportant details, they cannot be influenced to "lie" about sexual abuse. Some professionals go even further, stating that children are quite unlikely to lie about sexual abuse (Faller, 1984, 1996; Melton, 1985; Veitch & Gentile, 1992). Furthermore, analyses of children's reports of actual events reveal that although they often fail to recall a number of details, what they do recall is highly accurate. According to some studies, when children make mistakes it is because they omit details, not because they add or fabricate details (Ceci & Bruck, 1993a). This research has assured professionals that when children do report sexual abuse, there is no need to question their accuracy, no matter how suggestive the interviewing procedures.

Finally, some interview techniques are defended on the grounds that they are necessary to revive children's memories of events that occurred in the distant past. In many investigations, the alleged events were said to have occurred not days or weeks ago, but months or years ago. Sometimes 5-year-old children are asked about events that allegedly occurred when they were 2 or 3 years old. Several of the techniques are thought to help them organize and cue their recall of forgotten events.

The use of these interviewing techniques is well intentioned. Interviewers use them because they are concerned about the welfare of the child and want to be assured of their future protection; they use them to make children feel comfortable in the interview and to try to extract details of potentially dangerous situations. These techniques are not consciously used to deceive children nor with the aim of producing inaccurate reports that are consistent with the interviewers' beliefs. No interviewer sets out to deliberately elicit a false report; no interviewer sets out with the intention of tainting a child's memory.[2]

Although the road to disclosures may be paved with good intentions, the contents of its structures are now being challenged on empirical grounds. The next part of this chapter examines how different components of biased interviews influence the accuracy of children's statements.

[2] We do not include in this assertion the small percentage of documented cases in which adults purposely coached their children to give false statements (e.g., Terr, 1994).

The research literature that we will describe indicates that when interviews with young children contain suggestive features or strategies, the accuracy of their reports can be compromised, sometimes significantly. This literature cannot be dismissed on the grounds that the events being recalled are neutral or uninteresting and, as a result, are of little relevance to forensic situations. Rather, much of this literature is forensically important: Some studies concern salient events involving the child's own body—events that are painful or embarrassing. These studies challenge the conventional wisdom that when children are inaccurate in their reporting about such events, it is because they fail to report some events (i.e., "errors of omission") and not because they fabricate events out of whole cloth ("errors of commission"). This newer research indicates that under certain conditions, children also make commission errors about nonexperienced events involving their own bodies. Some of these newer studies also demonstrate the far-reaching influences of the use of some suggestive interviewing techniques on the credibility of children's reports. In these newer studies, children do not simply parrot statements made by the interviewer, but rather construct highly elaborate, coherent, and believable autobiographical narratives that happen to be highly inaccurate. Although we do not want to convey that this is an inevitable consequence of the use of suggestive techniques (it is not), it occurs in research studies often enough to engender concern about its possible occurrence in actual field situations.

INTERVIEWER BIASES

Is there any evidence that interviewer biases can, in fact, influence a child's or adult's behavior in a significant manner? The answer is "yes." The topic of interviewer bias, or experimenter bias, has been researched throughout the century.

One of the earliest studies was reported by Rice (1929). He examined 12 experienced interviewers from various social service agencies in New York City who were assigned to interview approximately 2,000 homeless men to ascertain the causes of their destitution. Rice was struck by how some of the interviewers' beliefs influenced the contents of the reports they obtained from the homeless men. The most obvious example of this came in the case of two interviewers who differed in their social orientations, one being known by coworkers as a "socialist," the other as an ardent "prohibitionist." Rice found that the socialist was nearly three times more likely to report that the men's destitution was due to industrial causes beyond their control (e.g., layoffs, plant closings, seasonal labor), whereas the prohibitionist was nearly three times more likely to report that the basis of their destitution was alcohol or drug abuse. Not only were the findings of these two interviewers consistent with their pet hypotheses about the causes of societal dissolution, but the homeless men themselves seem to have incorporated the interviewers' biases into their own explanations of their homelessness. Rice viewed this as an example of interviewer bias acting as a suggestive form of questioning. In fact, although this analysis was conducted 65 years ago, his conclusion is thoroughly modern in terms of its explanatory construct of suggestibility due to interviewer bias.

Since Rice's study, there have been hundreds of other demonstrations of the influences of interviewer biases. One reason that this topic has received so much attention is its implications for conducting both therapy and reliable scientific studies. Thus, numerous studies have examined whether in behavioral experiments, the interviewer or experimenter might influence the subjects' performance in such a way that their behaviors would be consistent with the hypotheses of the study (see Rosenthal, 1995; Rosenthal & Rubin, 1978, for reviews). The results of a number of studies indicate that when experimenters or interviewers are aware of the hypothesis of a study, they unconsciously alter the way they test subjects, resulting in performance consistent with the hypothesis of the study. Often the biases are observed in subtle ways, such as a slight nuance, a smile, a nod of the head, the tone of voice, or the phrasing of a question. Although this line of work highlights the importance of interpersonal expectancy effects, the results do not directly indicate whether interviewers with specific biases or beliefs can influence children's responses to an interviewer's questions. The next question is, "To what extent will children eventually make statements consistent with a biased interviewer's beliefs?" We describe three recent studies that have examined this issue.

Simon Says

Preschoolers played a game similar to "Simon Says" (Ceci, Leichtman, & White, in press). One month later, they were interviewed by a trained social worker. Before the interview, the interviewer was given a written report containing two types of information about the play episode: accurate information and erroneous information. For example, if the event involved one child touching her own stomach and then touching another child's nose, the interviewer correctly would be told that the child touched her own stomach but incorrectly told that she touched the other child's toe. The interviewer was not told that some the information in the report was inaccurate. She was merely told these actions might have occurred during the play episode. She was asked to conduct an interview to determine what each child could recall about the original play episode.

The information provided on the one-page report influenced the interviewer's hypothesis (or beliefs) about what had transpired and powerfully influenced the dynamics of the interview; the interviewer eventually shaped some of the children's reports to be consistent with her hypothesis, even when it was inaccurate. When the interviewer was accurately informed, the children correctly recalled 93% of all events. However, when she was misinformed, 34% of the 3- to 4-year-olds and 18% of the 5- to 6-year-olds corroborated one or more events that the interviewer falsely believed had occurred, even though they had not. Interestingly, the children seemed to become more credible as their interviews unfolded. Many children initially stated details of the false events inconsistently or reluctantly, but as the interviewer persisted in asking leading questions that were consistent with her false hypothesis, a significant number of these children abandoned their contradictions and hesitancy, and endorsed the interviewer's erroneous hypothesis.

During these interviews, the social worker kept notes about the children's reports. Two months later, these notes were given to another interviewer, who reinterviewed the children about the original play episode. It seems that the social worker's notes influenced the beliefs and the hypotheses of the second interviewer, who not only got the children to continue to assent to erroneous statements that were consistent with her hypotheses (e.g., some falsely claimed that their knees were licked and that marbles were inserted in their ears), but the children did so with increasing confidence. If we had continued to reinterview the children in this study, each time passing along the notes of the prior interviewer to a new interviewer, there is no telling how far astray the children might have gone.

A Class Visit

Similar findings were reported from Australia by Pettit, Fegan, and Howie (1990). These investigators examined how interviewers' beliefs about a certain event affect their style of questioning children and the accuracy of children's subsequent reports. Two actors, posing as park rangers, visited the classes of preschool children to ask them to help a bird find a nest for her eggs. During the presentation, one of the rangers accidently knocked over a cake perched on top of a piano. When the cake fell and shattered on the floor, there was an abrupt silence and a halt to all activities. Two weeks later, all children were questioned about the event.

Interviewers' beliefs about the event were manipulated in the following manner. Some interviewers were provided with full accurate knowledge of the event, whereas others were given inaccurate information (i.e., false beliefs). Finally, some interviewers were given no information about the event.

The interviewers were told to question each child until they found out what happened, and they were also asked to avoid the use of leading questions. Despite the warning to avoid leading questions, 30% of all interviewers' questions were leading, and half of these were misleading. Interviewers with inaccurate knowledge (false beliefs) asked four to five times as many misleading questions as the other interviewers. Overall, children agreed with 41% of the misleading questions, and those interviewed by the misled interviewers gave the most inaccurate information. Thus, when an interviewer's belief was contrary to what the child actually experienced, the interview was characterized by an overabundance of misleading questions that, in turn, resulted in children providing highly inaccurate information.

Chester the Molester/Chester the Cleaner

Clarke-Stewart, Thompson, and Lepore (1989, also see Goodman & Clarke-Stewart, 1991) conducted a study in which 5- and 6-year-olds viewed a staged event that could be construed as either abusive or innocent. Some children interacted with a confederate named "Chester" as he cleaned some dolls and other toys in a playroom. Other children interacted with Chester as he handled the dolls roughly and in a mildly abusive manner. Chester's dialogue reinforced the idea that he was either cleaning (e.g., "This doll is dirty, I had better clean it"), or playing with the doll in a rough, suggestive manner (e.g., "I like to play with dolls. I like to spray them in the face with water").

The children were questioned about this event several times on the same day, by different interviewers who differed in their interpretations of the event. The interviewer was either (a) "accusatory" in tone (suggesting that the janitor had been inappropriately playing with the toys instead of working), (b) "exculpatory" in tone (suggesting that the janitor was just cleaning the toys and not playing), or (c) "neutral" and nonsuggestive in tone. In the first two types of interviews, the questions changed from mildly to strongly suggestive as the interview progressed.

Following the first interview, all children were asked to tell in their own words what they had witnessed. They were then asked some factual questions (e.g., "Did the janitor wipe the doll's face?"), and some interpretive questions regarding the janitor's activities (e.g., "Was the janitor doing his job or was he just being bad?"). Then, each child was interrogated by a second interviewer who either reinforced or contradicted the first interviewer's tone. Finally, children were asked by their parents to recount what the janitor had done.

When questioned by a neutral interviewer, or by an interviewer whose interpretation was consistent with the activity viewed by the child, children's accounts were both factually correct, and consistent with the janitor's script. However, when the interviewer contradicted the activity viewed by the child, those children's stories quickly conformed to the suggestions or beliefs of the interviewer. By the end of the first interview, 75% of these children's remarks were consistent with the interviewer's point of view, and 90% answered the interpretive questions in agreement with her point of view, as opposed to what actually happened.

Children changed their stories from the first to second interviews only if the two interviewers differed in their interpretation of the events. Thus, when the second interviewer contradicted the first interviewer, the majority of children then fit their stories to the suggestions of the second interviewer. If the interviewer's interpretation was consistent across two interviews, but inconsistent with what the child had observed, the suggestions planted in the first session were mentioned by the children in the second session. Moreover, when questioned by their parents, the children's answers were consistent with the interviewers' biases. Finally, although the effects of the interviewers' interpretations were most observable in children's responses to the interpretive questions about what the janitor had done, 20% of the children also made errors on the factual questions in the direction suggested by the biased interpretation, even though no suggestions had been given regarding these particular details.

Summary

These three studies provide important evidence that interviewers' biases and beliefs about an event can influence the conduct of their interviews and influence the accuracy of the children's testimony. The data highlight both the benefits and dangers of having only one hypothesis about an event. When the hypothesis is correct, it results in very high levels of accurate recall by young children, but when the hypothesis is incorrect, it can lead to high levels of inaccurate recall.

It might be argued that criteria for conducting unbiased interviews are too rigid for interviewers involved in child abuse cases. These professionals must act quickly to protect the child from further abuse. The requirement that they test a number of relevant alternate hypotheses is unreasonable under these constraints. Furthermore, the requirement that these interviewers not be biased by previous information concerning the allegations may be detrimental to the protection of the child; unless workers have all the background information, they may fail to detect important or relevant information told by the child.

Although we are sympathetic to these constraints, we believe that the risks associated with confirmatory bias are too great to be swayed by these arguments. Although it may not be possible to "blind" interviewers from all case-related information that could lead to the formation of expectancies, they should be told only as much as necessary, and allowed to form and test their own hypotheses based on their investigations. In well-worked fields of scholarship, if scientists do not attempt to disconfirm their hypothesis, others can be counted on to do the job for them—sometimes with embarrassing candor and detail. In clinical and forensic interviews, it is not always the case that others will test alternative hypotheses if front-line professionals fail to do so. Interviewers need training in how to entertain two or more competing hypotheses simultaneously, without conveying disbelief or skepticism to the child. This is not as difficult as it may sound, and competent interviewers probably already do this without being aware they are doing so.

Confirmatory Bias: Examples from Cases

We believe that the evolution of many of the mass allegation day-care cases, as well as some other cases involving sexual abuse, stem from the phenomenon of interviewer bias. Sometimes these initial biases unfold in therapy sessions, in which the therapist pursues a single hypothesis about the basis of the child's difficulties (for review of the evidence that therapists rarely test alternatives and fall prey to illusory correlations and confirmatory biases, see Alloy & Tabachnik, 1984; Brehm & Smith, 1986; Kayne & Alloy, 1988). Following sustained periods of therapy, some children make disclosures that are then pursued in multiple interviews by law enforcement and child protection personnel. At other times, interviewer bias is rooted in the investigative process by officers of the court who initially interview children. And, finally, some allegations grow out of interviews conducted by parents who are convinced that abuse took place and who relentlessly pursue a single hunch in conversations with their children.

Examples of interviewers' biases, blind pursuit of a single hypothesis, and failure to test alternate, equally believable, explanations of the children's behavior characterize many aspects of the *Little Rascals* case. It appears that many of the investigators in the Little Rascals case were poised to find allegations of sexual abuse. The seeds of this case may have been sown in the spring of 1988, months before the first allegations of child sexual abuse had been made. At a three-day conference in the Outer Banks town of Kill Devil Hills, law-enforcement and social-service workers convened to learn about the dangers of child molesters operating day-care facilities. The seminar was cosponsored by a counseling group and assisted by a social worker who would become one of the most active therapists for the child victims in this case. The featured speaker was Ann Burgess, editor of a book *Child Pornography and Sex Rings* (1984). Also attending this conference were H. P. Williams, who would coprosecute the case, and Brenda Toppin, the Edenton police officer who was the first to interview most of the children in the case and to advise the parents of their abuse.

The first allegation was made by Karl B, whose mother was a friend of Brenda Toppin. Mrs. B voiced concern over her son's nightmares and bed-wetting, and his reticence to go to day care. Toppin urged her friend to question her son about what was going on. During this time, in response to his mother's questions, Karl told his mother that he had being playing a "doctor" game with a child across the street. Mrs. B again called the police department, asking how to question her child about these concerns. After a few days of further questioning, Karl claimed that Mr. Bob played doctor with other children, but not with Karl. According to the available evidence, it seems that this doctor game incident with the child across the street was never mentioned during the investigation. Karl was only questioned about the doctor games that Mr. Bob played. The failure to probe the child about playing doctor with his friend across the street reflects the interviewers' bias that there was abuse in the day care, hence, their predisposition to neglect any evidence that the allegations could be explained by other hypotheses.

A few weeks after making his first allegation, Karl B was interviewed by a psychiatric nurse who provided therapy to many children in the case. After a 15-minute interview, she made the diagnosis that he was suffering from posttraumatic stress disorder (PTSD) as a result of sexual abuse in the day-care center. There is no indication from the therapist's notes that she considered the fact that Karl had played doctor with a friend across the street, that his mother and father were away from home for major portions of the day due to their careers, or that prior interrogations might be the basis of his PTSD. She did not note that the family was considering a move. And finally she did not consider that there was much sibling rivalry, involving aggression with his younger brother. Furthermore, there was no attempt on the part of this therapist to elicit details of the alleged abuse. Given the history of this child, several hypotheses that could have been raised concerning his nightmares and reticence to go to school were never seriously entertained. Sexual abuse at the day care might be very low on the list of a skilled child therapist's hypotheses in trying to understand the symptoms of this child. Nevertheless, the therapist and Toppin both concluded that sexual abuse had occurred.

The *Little Rascals* case is characterized by the numerous allegations involving ritualistic abuse that may have arisen as a result of interviewer bias. It does not seem that the children made any spontaneous allegations concerning ritualistic abuse, but rather such allegations unfolded in response to a therapist's probes, which were based on the premise that when sexual abuse takes place in the day care it is sometimes associated with ritualistic abuse. For example, one therapist showed her child clients pictures of satanic symbols (according to one mother, these were sometimes left in the waiting room), in an effort to uncover evidence of devil worship. Although some children claimed to have seen these before, these symbols are easily confusable with other objects that most children could encounter (e.g., Halloween masks).

Examples of interviewers' biases, blind pursuit of a single hypothesis, and failure to test alternate, equally believable, explanations of the children's behavior appear rife in the interviews conducted in the *Michaels* case. These biases are apparent when interviewers' persistently maintained one line of inquiry even when children consistently denied that the hypothesized events occurred. Interviewer biases are also revealed by a failure to follow up on some of the children's inconsistent or bizarre statements when doing so might undermine the interviewer's primary hypothesis.

The following dialogue between the interviewer (Q) and Child A (A) during an early investigatory interview is illustrative of an interviewer's failure to seriously consider any evidence that was contrary to her or his primary beliefs:

Q: Do you think that Kelly was not good when she was hurting you all?

A: Wasn't hurting me. I like her.

Q: I can't hear you, you got to look at me when you talk to me. Now when Kelly was bothering kids in the music room . . .

A: I got socks off . . .

Q: Did she make anybody else take their clothes off in the music room?

A: No.

Q: Yes?

A: No . . .

Q: Did Kelly ever make you kiss her on the butt?

A: No.

Q: Did Kelly ever say—I'll tell you want. When did Kelly say these words? Piss, shit, sugar?

A: Piss, shit sugar?

Q: Yeah, when did she say that, what did you have to do in order for her to say that?

A: I didn't say that.

Q: I know, she said it, but what did you have to do?

The interviewers had developed the belief that Kelly had abused the children with various utensils and also that part of the abuse involved smearing peanut butter on their bodies. In this next example, the investigator pursues these hypotheses with a child who was given an anatomically correct doll and some utensils.

Q: Okay, I really need your help on this. Did you have to do anything to her with this stuff?

A: Okay. Where's the big knife at. Show me where's the big knife at.

Q: Pretend this is the big knife because we don't have a big knife.

A: This is a big one.

Q: Okay, what did you have to do with that? What did you have to . . .

A: No . . . take the peanut—put the peanut butter . . .

Q: You put what's that, what did you put there?

A: I put jelly right here.

Q: Jelly?

A: And I put jelly on her mouth and on the eyes.

Q: You put jelly on her eyes and her vagina and her mouth?

A: On her back, on her socks . . .

Q: And did you have to put anything else down there?

A: Right there, right here and right here and here.

Q: You put peanut butter all over? And where else did you put the peanut butter?

A: And jelly.

Q: And jelly?

A: And we squeezed orange on her.

Q: And you had to squeeze an orange on her?

A: Put orange juice on her.

Q: And did anybody—how did everybody take it off? How did she make you take it off?

A: No. Lick her all up, eat her all up and lick her all up.

Q: You had to lick her all up?

A: And eat her all up.

Q: Yeah? What did it taste like?

A: Yucky.

Q: So she made you eat the peanut butter and jelly and the orange juice off of the vagina too?

A: Yeah.

Q: Was that scary or funny?

A: Funny, funny and scary.

It is clear from these examples that when children's responses contained discrepant, inconsistent, incomprehensible, or no information, the investigators only considered these responses to be consistent with the fact that abuse had taken place or else they chose to ignore these statements. One is struck by the inconsistencies and the bizarre statements made by the children in response to the interviewers' questions. Most adults interacting with children in these situations would try to figure out just what the child was thinking about or why the child might be so confused to make such statements. Yet this did not happen. The children were not reined in (e.g., instructed to only describe things that really happened), nor were they asked commonsense questions such as: "Did this happen to you or are you just pretending that it happened to you?" or "Did you see this happen or did someone tell you that it happened?" Children were rarely challenged about their statements ("This really didn't happen, did it?"). Competent investigative interviewers would have at least asked themselves how it was possible for all these alleged acts, some of which were very painful, to occur without the other day-care workers' or parents' knowledge. The hypothesis that these alleged acts were the products of suggestive interviewing techniques or of children's imagination seems not to have been seriously considered.

Our statements concerning the preconceived biases of the *Michaels* interviewers are not based on conjecture, but on these interviewers' stated beliefs. For example, Dr. Susan Esquilin, a child therapist who presided over two heavily attended parent meetings when allegations were first made, conducted five group therapy sessions with the *Michaels* children and eventually assessed or treated 13 of the 20 child witnesses. She stated that her goal was to induce the children to discuss sexual abuse. In the first group therapy session, she told the children that they were assembled together because of some of the things that had happened at Wee Care with Michaels. Based on courtroom testimony, it seems that at least three children made allegations after their contacts with Esquilin.

Lou Fonolleras, an investigator from the Division of Youth and Family Services, conducted many of the 80 interviews with the *Michaels* children and 19 interviews with their parents, between May 22 and July 8, 1985. At trial, Fonolleras described his interviewing techniques as follows, "The interview process is in essence the beginning of the healing process." To rationalize his use of persistent questions with the children, he stated, "because it is my professional and ethical responsibility to alleviate whatever anxiety has arisen as a result of what happened to them." As described in the next section, one of Fonolleras' major interview techniques was to tell the children about other children's allegations. He thought that this technique was appropriate for "children who needed some reassurance . . . (that) they were not alone." It was only after their interviews with Fonolleras that most of the children (at least 13) began making allegations to their parents; before the Fonolleras interviews, the children had not reported any abusive episodes to their parents.

Eileen Treacy, an expert for the prosecution, also interviewed most of these children several times between November 1986 and February 1987. At trial, she testified on her interviewing techniques, "So you open the interview in an effort to disempower Kelly of these super powers that she allegedly has or that the kids thought she had and also to let the children know that telling about these things was okay and they would be safe." This statement reflects Treacy's view of the case and her role in it. It appears that she saw little if any need for investigatory procedures because these children were clearly abused.

Finally, we do not limit our consideration of interviews to those held between children with legal and therapeutic professionals, but also extend these to conversations between parents and their children. Although we do not have any recordings or descriptions of the structures of these conversations, parents were soon instilled with the belief that abuse had taken place. Two weeks after the first allegation in the *Michaels* case, Peg Foster, a sex abuse consultant, told the parents at a school meeting that three children had been abused and urged them to discover whether their own children had been abused. These parents, as well as parents in many of the other day-care cases, received phone calls from other parents who related the newest disclosures made by some of the children; a parent might be told that their child was named in the most recent disclosure and to question the child about this event. At least some of the parents aggressively questioned their children through all parts of the investigation, right up to the trial itself.

Maybe, some parents of the child witnesses did raise alternative hypotheses, but these were suppressed by the dominant claim that Kelly had abused the children. For example one mother recounted at trial that her child made the following statement:

> Kelly puts a penis in my nose and she looked like a penis head. It was funny (child giggles).

This mother went on to relate how different the child's affect was during this disclosure than during a previous allegation about the child's own father. This child had told her mother and then her baby-sitter that her father had pinched her "thighs" and legs. And when she told of these alleged behaviors by her father, she cried. Nevertheless, the mother had enough confidence in her child's allegations about Kelly to allow her to testify at trial.

If the type of interviewing that we described in this chapter is widespread, then it raises some real concerns. We have already shown and will show again in greater detail, that researchers are beginning to understand that even milder versions of such interview techniques can increase the risk of eliciting false reports, especially if they are conducted repeatedly and over long delay intervals..

THE EFFECTS OF REPEATED QUESTIONING

Repeated Questions across Interviews

When children are witnesses to or victims of a crime they must tell and retell their story many times, to many different people. Although some authorities estimate that the average child witness may be questioned 12 times during the course of an investigation (Whitcomb, 1992), this figure may actually be an underestimate if one considers the number of times that parents, friends, and/or mental health professionals may question these children. There are different purposes for reinterviewing children. The first is purely administrative: Given the legal structure of our society, a witness may have to tell his story to a number of different parties in a legal dispute. A second reason is to provide the witness with ample opportunity to reveal all details of the alleged event: Perhaps additional details and more complete reports will emerge on second or third telling; perhaps certain interviewing techniques will facilitate this process by providing an emotionally and cognitively supportive climate that allows the unblocking of memories or that conveys to the victim a sense that it is safe to tell the story. Finally, as new case-related information becomes known, it may become necessary to reinterview the witness about newly emerging issues that were unanticipated at the time of the earlier interview. For any or all these reasons, it becomes necessary to reinterview a witness.

What theoretical or empirical support is there that repeated interviewing does, in fact, improve the accuracy of reports? Based on a large tradition of memory research, it has been argued that repeated interviewing is itself a form of rehearsal that prevents memories from decaying over a period of time. According to this argument, it is important for the witness to repeatedly recall the details of the event so that they will not be forgotten. The literature also indicates that the formation of a memory (i.e., consolidation) is facilitated when the first recall takes place soon after the target event. Finally, a number of laboratory studies indicate that when given multiple opportunities to recall previously memorized materials, subjects often remember additional details during each session.

When the studies are taken outside the memory laboratories and into more naturalistic settings (where subjects recall a series of events or an episode), some of these findings are replicated. When asked for free recall, both children and adults remember new items with additional interviews, thereby providing additional information for their original descriptions (see Fivush, 1993; Poole & White, 1995; Warren & Lane, 1995, for reviews). So, repeated interviewing of a child is associated with beneficial effects.

For several different reasons, however, repeated interviewing is also associated with baleful effects. First, as interviews are repeated, so is the length of time between the original event and the interview; this allows for weakening of the original memory trace, and as a result of this weakening, more intrusions are able to infiltrate the memory system. In fact, although as mentioned earlier, when asked for free recall, both children and adults remember more with additional interviews, it is also true that their reports become more inaccurate over time (i.e., they recall both more accurate and more inaccurate details over time). Data by Poole and White (1993) suggest that this decline in accuracy over a long delay may be most apparent in children. These researchers retested children and adults 2 years after their initial observation and recall of a staged event. Children (who at the time of follow-up testing were between the ages of 6 and 10 years) provided many more inaccurate details in response to open-ended questions, compared with adults. The children's responses to direct yes-no questions were at chance when interviewed again 2 years following the event. Finally, 21% of the children confused which actors performed certain actions 2 years earlier; such errors were never made by adult subjects.

Thus far in our discussion of the beneficial effects of repeated interviews, we have assumed that each repeated interview is neutral (nonsuggestive) in tone: that witnesses are only required to tell in their own words everything that happened. But this is not the tone of many forensic interviews with children. In these interviews, there are many examples of misleading information at each interview. This raises the possibility that repeated interviews that contain misleading information may ultimately result in impaired and inaccurate recall of events.

We have conducted one study that highlights the deleterious effects of repeating misinformation across interviews on young children's reports (Bruck, Ceci, Francouer, & Barr, 1995a); these effects are particularly pernicious because not only can the repeated misinformation become directly incorporated into the children's subsequent reports (they use the interviewers' words in their inaccurate statements), but it can also lead to fabrications or inaccuracies which, although not directly mirroring the content of the misleading information or questions, are inferences based on the misinformation.

In our study, children visited their pediatrician when they were 5 years old. During that visit, a male pediatrician gave each child a physical examination, an oral polio vaccine, and an inoculation. During that same visit, a female research assistant talked to the child about a poster on the wall, read the child a story, and gave the child some treats.

Approximately one year later, the children were reinterviewed four times over a period of one month. During the first three interviews, some children were falsely reminded that the male pediatrician showed them the poster, gave them treats, and read them a story, and that the female research assistant gave them the inoculation and the oral vaccine. Other children were given no misinformation about the actors of these events. During the final interview, when asked to recall what happened during the original medical visit, children who were not given any misleading information were highly accurate in their final reports. They correctly recalled which events were performed by the male pediatrician and by the female research assistant. In contrast, the misled children were very inaccurate; not only did they incorporate the misleading suggestions into their reports, with more than half the children falling sway to these suggestions (e.g., claiming that the female assistant inoculated them rather than the male pediatrician), but 38% of these children also included nonsuggested but inaccurate events in their reports. They falsely reported that the female research assistant had checked their ears and nose. These statements are inferences that are consistent with the erroneous suggestion that the research assistant had administered the shot, therefore she must have been the doctor, and therefore she carried out procedures commonly performed by doctors. None of the control children made such inaccurate inferences. Thus, young children use suggestions in highly productive ways to reconstruct and at times distort reality (see Clarke-Stewart et al., 1989; Leichtman & Ceci, 1995, for similar results).

Multiple suggestive interviews may have deleterious effects on reporting not only because of their quantity but also because with each additional suggestive interview the delay between the original event and the child's report of it increases. Sometimes these two variables are inseparable and it raises the following question: Is the effect of misinformation less deleterious if it is provided in an interview that occurs soon after an event compared with an interview that occurs long after an event? Perhaps when events are fresh, it is harder to be swayed by suggestions than when the memories for the event have faded. A number of studies with adults and children confirm this pattern (Belli, Windschitl, McCarthy, & Winfrey, 1992; Loftus, Miller, & Burns, 1978; Zaragoza & Lane, 1994).

The pediatrician study just described also illustrates the differential impacts of providing misinformation immediately after an event compared with many months later. In the first phase of this study, we examined the effect of giving different types of feedback to 5-year-old children immediately following their inoculation. Children were given pain-affirming feedback (emphasizing that the shot hurt), pain-denying feedback (emphasizing that the shot did not hurt), or neutral feedback (the shot is over). One week later, when we interviewed these children about their visit, they did not differ in their reports concerning how much the shot hurt or how much they cried.

We found that the children could not be easily influenced to make inaccurate reports concerning significant and stressful procedures involving their own bodies—when their memory for the inoculation was still relatively fresh. The pattern of results changed dramatically when we provided the same children similar feedback during multiple interviews, one year after the inoculation. Thus, during the three visits when the children were given no information or misinformation about the pediatrician and the research assistant, we also provided children with feedback about how much they had cried in the pediatrician's office one year previously. During three separate visits, they were either given additional pain-denying or neutral feedback. At the fourth and final interview, children who were given pain-denying feedback reported that they cried less and that the shot hurt less than did children given neutral feedback. These results indicate that children's reports about stressful events involving their own bodies can be influenced by suggestive interviewing procedures provided on multiple occasions long after the event takes place.

Other researchers have examined the effects of sequencing suggestive and neutral interviews, asking whether early neutral interviews protect against the potential detrimental effects of later suggestive ones. Warren and Lane (1995) found that neutral interviews that occur immediately after an event protect adults from the effects of future suggestive interviews. Under the same conditions, children were also protected, although to a lesser extent. Furthermore, these researchers also found that children who were subjected to two suggestive interviews reported many more suggested details in their free recall reports than did children subjected to only a single suggestive interview.

Taken together, these results suggest that the highest ratio of accurate-to-inaccurate testimony is obtained in the first interview. As the delay between the event and the interview increases and/or as the number of misleading interviews increase, the chance for serious misreporting also appears to increase. So, if an initial interview is neutral, it seems to have the effect of reinforcing the memory, perhaps by providing a rehearsal. As a consequence, subsequent interviews that are suggestive result in less alteration than might be the case if the initial interview is either suggestive or absent.

In turning to our case histories for examples of the potential effects of repeated interviews, we face a real barrier in this exercise. This is because there are no electronic records of any of the initial interviews with the children. Thus, we cannot ascertain the degree to which the allegations that emerged in later taped investigatory interviews were consistent with the first reports made by these children versus the degree to which they reflected the earlier implantation of suggestions. We also do not have verbatim records of the conversations that the children had with their parents; it is possible that some of the allegations that occurred in these later investigatory interviews reflected suggestions incorporated from earlier conversations with parents who were urged by other parents and professionals to look for signs of abuse in their children. But it is clear from the existing records that most of the children in the *Michaels* and *Little Rascals* cases denied abuse when first interviewed. And in both cases, some parents admitted to repeatedly and often relentlessly questioning their children until they finally gave sway and admitted to abuse. The testimony of one of the mothers illustrates how some of these children may have been questioned at home, prior to any of the investigative interviews, and how allegations of sexual abuse may emerge when young children are repeatedly questioned by their parents.

Mom: First time I questioned him, we were laying on my bed and I was just, you know, "Do you like Mr. Bob," "Do you like Ms. Betsy," um, "Has

Mr. Bob ever done anything bad to you," "Has Mr. Bob ever spanked you." And as we were talking I got more specific with him; I asked him "Had Mr. Bob ever touched his privates,"—I didn't feel like he really knew what his privates were called that, and so I asked him, "Has Mr. Bob ever touched your pee-bug," "Has Mr. Bob ever touched your hiney?" "Has he ever put his finger in your hiney." I was using very specific questioning . . . He thought it was funny. He was laughing at me when we were just talking in general . . . He was so young. He wasn't even three years old then . . .

Dick was being questioned a lot from that first time on (i.e., the end of January), quite often. And then that last week then it was probably a few hours every day thing. And on that Friday (the end of April), I got a response out of him. . . . Um, he told me that Mr. Bob had put his penis in his mouth and peed on him.

Attorney: Now, are those things that he just came up with on his own?

Mom: No, sir, he did not . . . he had been hearing it at least once a week since I first started questioning him and then that last week he was hearing it every day.

Attorney: Now, up to this point in your questioning of Dick you said that you had been fairly specific in your statements to him about asking him whether or not Bob did this or whether or not Bob did that; did you name specific acts to him?

Mom: Yes, sir. "Did Bob put his finger in your hiney," things like that, yes, sir, I did.

Attorney: And did some of the time you get no answer to those questions?

Mom: It was "no" the majority of the time, . . . most of the time he didn't know what I was talking about.

In the *Michaels* case, the children's allegations continued to unfold after the investigatory interviews, some of them not emerging until 2 years later. This is unsurprising, as the children were interviewed many times after the initial investigatory interviews. They were interviewed prior to their appearance before the grand jury; they were questioned by therapists and they were questioned by members of the prosecutors' office leading up to trial. Perhaps some of the most suggestive interviews in the *Michaels* case were conducted by Eileen Treacy, a state-appointed expert, who interviewed most of the child witnesses on at least two occasions before the trial.

As stated earlier, repeated suggestive interviews may have their most profound effect after a long delay between the alleged events and the interviews. Treacy's interviews occurred two years after the alleged events. The following give a flavor of the interactions of some of these interviews:

Treacy: Let me ask you this; did she touch boys, did she touch girls, did she touch dogs?

Child: She touched boys and girls.

Treacy: Did she touch them with telephones? Did she touch them with spoons? What kinda spoons?

Child: Teaspoons.

Treacy: I see and did the kids want Kelly to do that peanut butter stuff?

Child: I didn't even think that there was a peanut butter.

Treacy: Well what about licking the peanut butter?

Child: There wasn't anything about peanut butter.

Treacy: Some of the kids told me that things happened with knives. Do you remember anything like that?

Child: No.

(Although the child professed no knowledge of utensil abuse, at trial she testified to numerous abuse allegations.)

Treacy: Well what about that cat game?

Child: Cat game?

Treacy: Where everybody went like this, "Meow, Meow."

Child: I don't think that I was there that day.

(Although the child professed no knowledge of the cat game, at trial she described a cat game in which all the children were naked and licking each other.)

A consideration of the research findings suggests that if the children had not been abused, then this magnitude of repeated suggestive interviewing could have the effect of planting and cementing false reports. Based on our own work with children of this age, we are fairly confident that if we were to interview a random sample of day-care children, and employ the same suggestive technique used by the interviewers of the child witnesses in our sample cases, we could bring a subset of them to assent to abuse-related themes. Most of the children would not assent immediately. But gradually some allegations would probably emerge as suggestions were repeated.

Repeated Questions within Interviews

The previous section documents some of the potential hazards of multiple suggestions across interviews on children's reports. A related concern is the degree to which repeating a question within an interview can taint a child's report (see Ceci & Bruck, 1993b; Poole & White, 1995; Warren & Lane, 1995, for reviews). When interviewing children, adults frequently repeat a question because the child's first response may not provide enough information. In forensic interviews, questions may be repeated to check the consistency of a child's report. Sometimes, interviewers' repetition of questions signals their biases: They seem to keep asking a child the same question, until they receive the answer they are expecting.

A number of studies, from different domains, demonstrate that when young children are asked the same question more than once within an interview, they change their answer. In some studies, it is the youngest children who are most likely to change their answers. We provide some brief descriptions of these studies.

Poole and White (1991) examined the effects of repeated questioning within and across sessions (and thus this study also speaks to some of the issues raised in the previous section). Adults, as well as 4-, 6-, and 8-year-olds witnessed an ambiguous event. Half of the subjects were interviewed immediately after the event as well as one week later. The remaining subjects were interviewed only once—one week after the event. Within each session, all questions were asked three times. Repeated open-ended questions (e.g., "What did the man look like?") both within and across sessions had little effect, positive or negative, on children's or adults' responses. When yes-no questions were repeated (e.g., "Did the man hurt Melanie?"), however, 4-year-olds were most likely to change their responses, both within and across sessions. Also, when children were asked a specific question about a detail for which they had no information (i.e., "What did the man do for a living?"), many answered with sheer speculations. Furthermore, both children and adults used fewer qualifiers with repeated questions (they omitted phrases such as "it might have been") and consequently sounded more confident about their statements. These findings illustrate the danger of repeatedly asking specific questions: Children will often cooperate by guessing but after several repetitions, their uncertainty is no longer apparent.

Thus, the major finding of this study is that repeated questioning may affect very young children's responses to specific questions. Whereas repeating open-ended questions may merely signal a request for additional information, repeating specific questions that have a limited pool of responses (yes-no) may signal to young children that their first response was unacceptable to the interviewer. This finding is important because young children tend to give limited responses to open-ended questions and therefore interviewers often resort to specific questions to elicit additional information. To confirm a child's answer, interviewers frequently repeat the question.

Although Poole and White did not use leading questions, their repeated use of yes-no questions can be viewed as a subtle form of suggestion. As noted, simply repeating a yes-no question could suggest to children that the interviewer is unsatisfied with their initial answer. But other studies directly address what happens when leading questions are repeated within an interview.

Cassel and Bjorklund (1995) questioned children and adults about a videotaped event they had viewed one week earlier. The subjects were asked leading questions. If they did not fall sway to the lead, then they were asked a more suggestive follow-up question. Kindergarten children were most affected by this manipulation. As expected, compared with adults and older children, they were most inaccurate in answering the first misleading question; but also when the second more suggestive question was asked, they were more likely than older subjects to change their answers and to incorporate the suggested answer into their second responses.

These findings demonstrate that younger children are more prone to change their answers when asked the same question within a session. They are sensitive to the question repetition and seem to reason that the interviewer is requesting additional or new information: "The first answer I gave must be wrong, that is why they are asking me the question again. Therefore, I should change my answer." At other times, children may change their answer to please the adult who is questioning them; they appear to reason that the "adult must not have liked the first answer I gave so I will try another answer."

Some have argued that children's answers may change because the interviewer's previous suggestions become incorporated into their memories. For example, children are given a list of items to study and later their memory for these items is tested by asking them to respond "yes" to previously studied items and "no" to items that were not on the study list. This procedure increases the rate of false positives on a later test; that is, the children say that the "no" items from the memory test were on the original study list (Brainerd & Reyna, 1996). Furthermore, there is some evidence that these false recognition responses are as stable, and sometimes more stable than true responses (Brainerd, Reyna, & Brandes, 1995). This last explanation may have more power when applied to repeating misinformation across interviews (when there is some time allowed for the misinformation to be incorporated into memory) than when the repetition occurs within an interview.

There are numerous examples of the risks of question repetition in the actual cases. Perhaps the most dramatic can be seen in the *Little Rascals* children who frequently changed their answers on the witness stand, on being reasked a question by the prosecutor. For example, one child was asked:

Prosecutor: Did you have to lay on top of Bridget?

Bobby: Yes.

Prosecutor: And when you were laying on top of Bridget, where was your private.

Bobby: I forgot.

Prosecutor: Do you remember telling Miss Judy that you had to put your private next to her private? Did you have to do that, Bobby?

Bobby: No Sir.

Prosecutor: What did you say?

Bobby: No Sir.

Prosecutor: Did you say No or Yes?

Bobby: Yes Sir.

A similar example is seen in the *Michaels* case at the Grand Jury hearing:

Prosecutor: Did she touch you with a spoon?

Child: No.

Prosecutor: No? Okay. Did you like it when she touched you with the spoon?

Child: No.

Prosecutor: No? Why not?

Child: I don't know.

Prosecutor: You don't know?

Child: No.

Prosecutor: What did you say to Kelly when she touched you?

Child: I don't like that.

To summarize, repeated interviews and repeating questions within interviews may decrease the accuracy of children's reports and increase their risk for taint when these are conducted by biased interviewers. These techniques allow an avenue for the introjection of misinformation which if repeated enough times may become incorporated by children. As well, these techniques may signal to children the bias of the interview so that eventually children learn how to answer the questions to provide the information that they think the interviewer wishes to hear.

STEREOTYPE INDUCTION: A SUGGESTIVE INTERVIEWING TECHNIQUE

Suggestions do not necessarily have to be in the form of an explicit (mis)leading question such as, "Show me how she touched your bottom" to take their toll on preschoolers' testimonial accuracy. A powerful yet subtle suggestive interviewing technique involves the induction of stereotypes. In the present context, we use the phrase "stereotype induction" to refer to an interviewer's attempt to transmit to a child a negative characterization of an individual or an event, whether it be true or false. Telling a child that the suspect "does bad things" or "tries to scare children" is an example of stereotype induction. (Stereotypes can also be positive, but the negative ones are of most concern in the context of children's testimony.)

The use of stereotype induction in interviews is one of the more blatant reflections of the interviewer's bias; the interviewer is telling the child how powerful adult authority figures as well as their peers characterize the defendant. Interviewers often justify their use of such techniques on the grounds that they provide a hospitable and supportive environment for the child to tell about the abuse. Notwithstanding the assumption that a stereotype induction makes a child feel better about disclosing details, a review of the scientific literature indicates that stereotype induction can have a powerful negative effect on the accuracy of children's subsequent reports. Some naive children may eventually begin to incorporate the interviewers' stereotypes into their own report.

Several of these studies were reviewed earlier. For example, children's reports of what the janitor "Chester" was doing in their classroom depended on the interviewer's stereotype of Chester. When interviewers induced a positive stereotype (e.g., Chester was depicted as doing a good job cleaning the classroom), many children came to report the event in that manner, regardless of what Chester had actually done. Similarly, when the interviewer induced a negative stereotype (Chester was fooling around), many children came to report the event according to this view regardless of Chester's actual behavior (Clarke-Stewart et al., 1989). The following two studies provide further evidence for the powerful effects of stereotype induction on children's reports.

In the first study (Lepore & Sesco, 1994), children ranging in age from 4 to 6 years old played some games with a man called "Dale." Dale played with some of the toys in a researcher's testing room and he also asked the child to help him take off his sweater. Later, an interviewer asked the child to tell her everything that happened when Dale was in the room. For half the children, the interviewer maintained a neutral stance whenever they recalled an action. For the remaining children, the interviewer reinterpreted each of the child's responses in an incriminating way by stating, "He wasn't supposed to do or say that. That was bad. What else did he do?" Thus, in this incriminating condition, a negative stereotype was induced: "Dale does bad things." At the conclusion of these incriminating procedures, the children were asked three highly suggestive, misleading questions ("Didn't he take off some of your clothes, too?" "Other kids have told me that he kissed them, didn't he do that to you?" and "He touched you and he wasn't supposed to do that, was he?") All children were then asked a series of direct yes-no questions about what had happened with Dale.

Children in the incriminating condition gave many more inaccurate responses to the direct yes-no questions than did children in the neutral condition; this was largely because these children made errors on items related to "bad" actions that had been suggested to them by the interviewer. Interestingly, one-third of the children in the incriminating condition embellished their incorrect responses to these questions, and the embellished responses were always in the direction of the incriminating suggestions. The question that elicited the most frequent embellishments was: "Did Dale ever touch other kids at the school?" Embellishments to this question included information about who Dale touched (e.g., "He touched Jason, he touched Tori, and he touched Molly"), where he touched them (e.g., "He touched them on their legs"), how he touched them (e.g., ". . . and some he kissed . . . on the lips"), and how he took their clothes off ("Yes, my shoes and my socks and my pants. But not my shirt"). When they were reinterviewed one week later, children in the incriminating stereotype condition continued to answer the yes-no questions inaccurately and they continued to embellish their answers.

Finally, the incriminating condition had a powerful effect on children's interpretations of Dale's character and actions. In comparison with children in the neutral interview condition, children in the incriminating interview condition were more likely to spontaneously make negative statements about Dale (e.g., "The guy came in and did some bad things") and to agree that Dale intended to be bad, mean, fool around, and not do his job.

The second study (Leichtman & Ceci, 1995) also demonstrates the powerful effects of a stereotype induction when it is paired with repeated suggestive questioning. A stranger named "Sam Stone" visited preschoolers (aged 3 to 6 years) in their classroom for 2 minutes in their day-care center. Following Sam Stone's visit, the children were asked for details about the visit on four different occasions over a 10-week period. During these four occasions, the interviewer refrained from using suggestive questions. She simply encouraged children to describe Sam Stone's visit in as much detail as possible. One month following the fourth interview, the children were interviewed a fifth time, by a new interviewer who asked about two "non-events" that involved Sam doing something to a teddy bear and a book. In reality, Sam Stone never touched either one. When asked in the fifth interview: "Did Sam Stone do anything to a book or a teddy bear?" most children rightfully replied "No." Only 10% of the youngest (3- to 4-year-old) children's answers contained claims that Sam Stone did anything to a book or teddy bear. When asked if they actually saw him do anything to the book or teddy bear, as opposed to "thinking they saw him do something," or "hearing he did something," now only 5% of their answers contained claims that anything occurred. Finally, when these 5% were gently challenged ("You didn't really see him do anything to the book/the teddy bear, did you?") only 2.5% still insisted on the reality of the fictional event. None of the older (5- to 6-year-old) children claimed to have seen Sam Stone do either of the fictional events. These children's responses can be regarded as a baseline against which to measure the effects of stereotype induction paired with repeated questioning.

A second group of preschoolers were presented with a stereotype of Sam Stone before he ever visited their school. Each week, beginning a month prior to Sam Stone's visit, these children were told a new Sam Stone story, in which he was depicted as very clumsy.

The day after Sam Stone's visit, the children were shown a ripped book (the same one that they were reading when Sam Stone came to visit) and a soiled teddy bear (that had not been in the room during Sam Stone's visit). They were asked if they knew how the book had been ripped and the teddy bear soiled. Very few children claimed to have seen Sam Stone do these things, but one fourth of them said that *perhaps* he had done it—a statement that is reasonable, given the stereotype-induction they received prior to his visit.

Following Sam Stone's visit, these children were given four suggestive interviews over a 10-week period. Each suggestive interview contained two erroneous suggestions, one having to do with ripping a book and the other with soiling a teddy bear (e.g., "Remember that time Sam Stone visited your classroom and spilled chocolate on that white teddy bear? Did he do it on purpose or was it an accident?" and "When Sam Stone ripped that book, was he being silly or was he angry?").

One month later, when a new interviewer probed about these events ("Did anything happen to a book?" "Did anything happen to a teddy bear?"), 72% of the youngest preschoolers claimed that Sam Stone did one or both misdeeds, a figure that dropped to 44% when asked if they actually *saw* him do these things. Importantly, 21% continued to insist that they saw him do these things, even when gently challenged. The older preschoolers, though more accurate, still included some children (11%) who insisted they saw him do the misdeeds.

What was most surprising about these reports was the number of false perceptual details as well as nonverbal gestures with which the children embellished their stories of these nonevents. Children used their hands to show how Sam had purportedly thrown the Teddy Bear up in the air; some children reported sighting Sam in the playground, or on his way to the store to buy chocolate ice cream, or in the bathroom soaking the teddy bear in water before smearing it with a crayon. Some children claimed there was more than one Sam Stone. And one child provided every parent's favorite false detail; this child claimed that Sam had come to his house to trash his room.

Critics of the Sam Stone study wonder about its forensic relevance. They argue that the two-minute visit of Sam to their classroom is not a significant event. We agree, but go one step further: There really was *no* event. Some of the children came to tell elaborate stories about an event that never happened. We think it important to make the following distinction: Children's reports can be unreliable because they confuse, omit, or blend details when recounting an actual event. But they can also be unreliable because they fabricate an entire episode or sequence of events within a larger episode. The latter most clearly occurred in the Sam Stone study. This is an important point for it demonstrates that children's inaccurate reports or allegations do not always reflect a confusion between the events or details of an experience, but may at times reflect the creation of an entire experience in which the child did not participate.

We have reviewed three studies that focus on the effects of stereotype induction. These studies vary in their procedures and yet the results are quite consistent, with all showing negative effects of pairing stereotype induction with suggestive questioning. These effects are apparent regardless of whether the child is interviewed one time (as was true in the Dale study) or over the period of several months (as was true in the Sam Stone study). The negative effects are apparent whether or not the stereotype induction took place before an event or after an event.

According to some commentators, the allegations of sexual abuse in the *Little Rascals* case may reflect a much earlier induction of a stereotype that "Mr. Bob does bad things." The following facts have been well documented. In the fall of 1988, several months before the first allegation of sexual abuse, a 4-year-old attending *Little Rascals* told his mother that he had been slapped by Bob Kelly. On hearing this, the mother recalled "My life crumbled. Life would never be the same." She went to Bob and Betsy Kelly demanding an apology. Betsy would not apologize, and according to one of the parents, "(She) had a crying fit." The mother went back to the day care for a second time looking for an apology, which she did not receive. She removed her child from the day care and her husband told Betsy that they were going to start talking about the slapping to others. And they did seem to do this. The first allegation of sexual abuse was reported by another mother soon after she had been told about the slapping incident. The stereotype-induction interpretation of this allegation was that parents had been asking their children whether Mr. Bob had spanked them just as he had spanked one child. It is possible that the children had developed a stereotype that Mr. Bob did bad things and that this stereotype was sufficient to allow the allegations to emerge with additional prompts.

We do not know how many children had been questioned by their parents about being slapped at the day care, but it is interesting that when children were first interviewed by authorities, some of them reported hitting in the day care, although few reported that the hitting happened to them. Other children who were initially silent often began their disclosures with incidents of hitting or of spanking. Only after many interviews, did the allegations become sexual in nature.

The *Michaels* interviews are also rife with examples of stereotype induction. Investigators told the children that Kelly was in jail because she had done bad things. They also promoted the children's fear of Kelly by asking leading questions about whether Kelly had threatened them or their families if they were to tell on her. It is interesting that, despite these statements, many of the children did not completely incorporate the suggested stereotypes of Kelly as seen in the next example.

In one of the few examples we have of two transcribed interviews for the same child, the first of the transcribed interviews (which was not the first interview) reveals that the child was repeatedly asked about bad things that Kelly did. She denied that Kelly did anything bad to her. In the next (transcribed) interview, the following exchange takes place:

Q: Was Kelly a good girl or a bad girl?
Child: She was a bad girl.
Q: She was a bad girl. Were there any other teachers who were bad?
Child: No.
Q: Kelly was the only bad girl? What did Kelly do that made her a bad girl?
Child: She readed.
Q: She what?
Child: She readed and she came to me and I said no, no, no.
Q: Did she hurt you?
Child: I hurted her.
Q: How did you hurt her?
Child: Because I didn't want to write and she write and I said no, no, no, no and I hit her.

OTHER SUGGESTIVE INTERVIEWING TECHNIQUES

In this section, we describe some additional components of suggestive interviewing techniques. Although we have divided these into distinct categories, in reality, these components often blur into one another. Often examples taken from the case studies entail more than one component. Nevertheless, for clarity we have attempted to keep these distinctions separate when possible.

Emotional Tone of the Interview

Interviewers of children place particular importance on building rapport with young clients so they feel relaxed and unthreatened. To achieve this goal, they may spend time talking or playing with the child before beginning the actual interview or test; during this time an interviewer may ask the child to talk about school or family. Ideally, interviewers attempt to provide a supportive atmosphere by paying attention, acting positively toward the child, and taking seriously the child's answers.

Few would criticize such techniques whether they be used with children or adults. Goodman and her colleagues (Goodman, Bottoms, Schwartz-Kenney, & Rudy, 1991) demonstrated some of the benefits of these techniques on young children's recall of a stressful event. In this study 4- and 7-year-old children were questioned about a previous visit to a medical clinic where they had received an inoculation. Half the children were interviewed in a supportive environment: At the beginning of the interview they were given cookies and juice. The interviewer was warm and friendly; she smiled a lot and gave the child considerable but random praise (i.e., praise not contingent on their pattern of answering) such as "You're doing a great job" or "You've got a great memory." The other children were not treated as warmly. They were not given juice or cookies and the interviewer was more distant, occasionally responding "Okay" or "all right." Children in the supportive condition made fewer incorrect statements when asked to tell in their own words what had happened during their inoculation visit. In addition, supportive interviews diminished children's inaccurate answers to misleading questions in some of the conditions. The authors suggest that providing children with a warm interviewing environment increases their resistance to suggestion because it decreases their feelings of intimidation, allowing them to counter the interviewer's false suggestions.

Few would disagree with the recommendations that forensic interviewers create a supportive environment for the child. A problem arises, however, if interviewers presume they are establishing a supportive relationship when in reality they are setting a very different emotional tone through the use of implicit or explicit threats, bribes, and rewards. In forensic contexts to obtain information from child witnesses, interviewers sometimes make some of the following statements, "It isn't good to let people touch you," or "Don't be afraid to tell." They make these statements to help children disclose facts that they may be too frightened or embarrassed to relate.

But these "supportive statements" may create reliability risks because in some contexts they may be ambiguous. That is, these statements may in fact create an accusatory tone (which reflects the interviewer's bias) and a context that promotes false disclosures. In some studies, when some of these so-called supportive statements are used, children become more likely to fabricate reports of past events even in cases when they have no memory of any event occurring, as will be seen. In some cases, these fabrications are sexual in nature.

In one study that was conducted four years after children had played with an unfamiliar research assistant for five minutes, Goodman and her colleagues asked these same children to recall the original experience, and then asked them a series of questions, including abuse-related suggestive questions about the event (Goodman, Wilson, Hazan, & Reed, 1989; also described in Goodman &

Clarke-Stewart, 1991). At this time, the researchers created what they described as "an atmosphere of accusation," by telling the children that they were to be questioned about an important event and by saying such things as, "Are you afraid to tell? You'll feel better once you've told." Although few children had any memory for the original event from 4 years earlier, they were not always very accurate when answering questions that suggested abuse. Of the 15 children, 5 agreed with the interviewer's erroneously suggestive question that they had been hugged or kissed by the research assistant, 2 of the 15 agreed that they had had their picture taken in the bathroom, and 1 child agreed that she had been given a bath. The important conclusion of this study is that children may begin to give incorrect information to misleading questions about events for which they have no memory, if the interviewer creates an atmosphere (emotional tone) of accusation. These forms of emotional atmospherics are conceptually similar to the negative stereotype inductions discussed earlier.

The Effects of Peer Pressure or Interaction on Children's Report

The effects of letting children know that their friends have "already told" is a much less investigated area in the field of children's testimonial research. Certainly, the common wisdom is that a child will go along with a peer group; but will a child provide an inaccurate response just so he or she can be one of the crowd? The results of three studies suggest that the answer is "yes."

First, Binet (1900) found that children will change their answers to be consistent with those of their peer group even when it is clear that the answer is inaccurate. Although Binet based his conclusions about children's suggestibility on their answers to perceptual stimuli ("which line is longer"), there is some indication that the same result would be observed in another domain. Second, in the Pettit et al. (1990) study in which park rangers visited preschoolers' classrooms, seven children were absent from their classrooms when the target event (the cake falling off the piano) occurred. Yet, when questioned 2 weeks later, six of these children indicated that they had been present. One presumes that these six children gave false reports so that they would feel like they were part of the same group as their friends who did participate. Importantly, this study shows how the peer group's actual experiences in an event can lead nonparticipants to fabricate reports of the event.

Finally, Pynoos and Nader (1989) studied people's recollections of a sniper attack. On February 24, 1984, from a second-story window across the street, a sniper shot repeated rounds of ammunition at children on an elementary school playground. Scores of children were pinned under gunfire, many were injured, and one child and a passerby were killed. Roughly 10% of the student body, 113 children, were interviewed 6 to 16 weeks later. Each child was asked to freely recall the experience and then to respond to specific questions. Some of those children who were interviewed were not at the school during the shooting, including those already on the way home or on vacation. Yet, even the nonwitnesses had "memories":

> One girl initially said that she was at the school gate nearest the sniper when the shooting began. In truth she was not only out of the line of fire, she was half a block away. A boy who had been away on vacation said that he had been on his way to the school, had seen someone lying on the ground, had heard the shots, and then turned back. In actuality, a police barricade prevented anyone from approaching the block around the school. (p. 238)

One assumes that children heard about the event from their peers who were present during the sniper attack and they incorporated these reports into their own memories.

The *Michaels* investigators tried to get the children to disclose by telling them what other children allegedly reported. Sometimes the investigators told the children that they could help their friends by telling about abuse:

> All the other friends I talked to told me everything that happened. 29C told me. 32C told me, 14C told me . . . And now it's your turn to tell. You don't want to be left out, do you?
>
> Boy, I'd hate having to tell your friends that you didn't want to help them" (said in response to a child who did not disclose).

Children in both cases were also interviewed together, presumably as a way of getting one or both children to disclose. And other examples suggest that the children did talk to each other about the allegations, or parents told their children about other children's allegations. The two following examples are taken from the *Michaels'* interviews.

Int: Do you know what (Kelly) did?

Child: She wasn't supposed to touch somebody's body. If you want to touch somebody, touch your own.

Int: How do you know about her touching private parts? Is that something you saw or heard?

Child: 21C told me.

Int: . . . when you and the other kids were upstairs in the music room, was she wearing clothes then?

Child: I saw clothes on, but the other kids didn't.

Int: Oh, how do you know that?

Child: Because my mommy told me that.

One might argue that there is some scientific evidence to support the practice of using peers to elicit disclosures from children who have something to disclose. In a study by Moston and Engleberg (1992), 7- and 10-year-olds witnessed a staged classroom incident and were later asked to recall its details. As is customary in such studies, younger children recalled less information about the incident and were more susceptible to suggestive questioning than the 10-year-olds. However, when these 7-year-olds were allowed to discuss the incident with a friend who accompanied them to the interview, age differences were significantly reduced. The presence of a friend at the interview created a favorable emotional environment that resulted in more accurate and less suggestible reports for the youngest children. But these data are relevant only if the children do have something to disclose. Otherwise, such practices may taint the reports of children.

The Effects of Being Interviewed by Adults with High Status

Young children are sensitive to the status and power of their interviewers and as a result are especially likely to comply with the implicit and explicit agenda of such interviewers. To some extent, the child's recognition of this power differential may be one of the most important causes of their increased suggestibility. Children are more likely to believe adults than other children, they are more willing to go along with the wishes of adults. Children are less open to suggestive influences when the suggestions are planted by their peers than when they are planted by adults (Ceci, Ross, & Toglia, 1987).

But children may also be sensitive to status and power differentials among adults. This is a particularly important issue for the testimony of child witnesses who are interviewed by police officers, judges, and medical personnel. A study by Tobey and Goodman (1992) suggests that interviews by high-status adults who tell children of their status may have negative effects on the accuracy of children's reports. In their study, 4-year-olds played a game with a research assistant who was called a "babysitter." Eleven days later, the children returned to the laboratory. Half of the children met a police officer who said:

> I am very concerned that something bad might have happened the last time that you were here. I think that the babysitter you saw here last time might have done some bad things and I am trying to find out what happened the last time you were here when you played with the babysitter. We need your help. My partner is going to come in now and ask you some questions about what happened.

The control children never met the police officer. When the children were later asked to tell everything they could remember, the children in the police condition gave fewer accurate statements and more inaccurate statements than children in the control group. Two of the 13 children in the police condition seemed to be decisively misled by the suggestion that the babysitter had done something bad. One girl said to her mother, "I think the babysitter had a gun and was going to kill me." Later, in her free recall, the same child said, "That man he might try to do something bad to me . . . really bad, yes siree." The second child inaccurately reported his ideas of what something bad might be, by saying, "I fell down, I got lost, I got hurt on my legs, and I cut my ears."

The *Michaels'* children were interviewed by law enforcement agents or by social workers who made reference to their connection to law enforcement agents. The children were explicitly made aware of the status of their interviewers by such comments as:

> I'm a policeman, if you were a bad girl, I would punish you wouldn't I? Police can punish bad people.
>
> After we finish here, depending on how much you guys help me today, I'm going to introduce you to one of the men who arrested Kelly and put her in jail. . . . Remind me before you leave today, I want to introduce you to the policeman who arrested her. So that he can show you his handcuffs, his badge, and he can tell you how hard it is to break out of jail.

A similar example was taken from one of the only surviving taped interviews of a *Little Rascals* child witness.

Prosecutor: Do you know who put him [Mr. Bob] in jail?

Child: The police.

Prosecutor: Right. Did you know that the police work for me? That I tell the police what to do?

Child: Yeah.

Prosecutor: So Mr. Kevin and Ms. Brenda came to me and asked if we should put Mr. Bob in jail and I said let's put Mr. Bob in jail. Why is he in jail, Jed? Do you know?

THE EFFECTS OF USING VISUALIZATION PROCEDURES

In previous sections, we described how suggestive interviewing techniques can influence children's reports, and how these techniques may account for some of the allegations made in some actual cases. But there are other more subtle techniques that therapists and other interviewers sometimes use that could seed the growth of false reports. In this section, we focus on two related mechanisms. The first is termed *reality monitoring* and it refers to one's ability to distinguish reality from fantasy or to distinguish memories of actual events from memories of imagined events. The second concept is termed *source monitoring:* This refers to the ability to keep track of the sources of actual events.

Reality Monitoring

Over the past 100 years, researchers have held markedly different views on young children's ability to differentiate fantasy from reality. According to the early pioneers, such as Freud, young children's wish-fulfilling fantasies tainted the accuracy of their reports. Piaget, supported this view by claiming that young children cannot distinguish something that actually happened from a dream about the same event. He noted that the child's "mind is full of these 'ludistic' (fantasy) tendencies up to the age of seven or eight, which means before that age it is very difficult for him to distinguish the truth" (1926, p. 34).

In the 1970s, this view of young children began to change. Researchers demonstrated that even 3-year-olds could correctly classify real and pretend figures, and that they have a firm understanding of the distinction between imagined and real entities (Flavell, Flavell, & Green, 1987; Morison & Gardner, 1978; Taylor & Howell, 1973). Thus, the predominant view shifted to "children do not confuse fantasy with reality."

Some current research moderates this extreme position. It appears that although children may be able to differentiate the real from the imagined, these distinctions are sometimes fragile especially if children are asked to imagine events and then to report whether or not the imagined events actually happened. Under these circumstances, young children have a tendency to report that what they were asked to imagine was real (e.g., Foley, Harris, & Hermann, 1994; Harris, Brown, Marriott, Whittall, & Harmer, 1991; Parker, 1995).

A host of therapeutic procedures and interviewing techniques are suggestive precisely because they induce fantasies. Asking children to visualize a scene and focus on some aspect of it and then to make up some encounter that may not have taken place is one example. One widely heralded technique, the *cognitive interview,* asks children to visualize how a scene might appear from the perspective of a person or an object that is situated elsewhere in the room, thus encouraging children to use their imagination. Children are encouraged to abandon reality when therapists delve into symbols or dreams or when they ask children to create a journal account of what *could* happen. Also, self-empowerment training, sometimes using ordinary or anatomical dolls as props, is another technique used by therapists with their child clients. These techniques create the risk that fantasies will eventually come to be believed by the child, particularly if the interviewer does not provide a context for reality testing.

An example from the *Little Rascals* case illustrates how therapeutic techniques that encourage children to fantasize may also produce fear in these same children. One of the child witnesses (Claudia) told her therapist that Mr. Bob put hot sauce on her eyes and her tongue. When the therapist asked Claudia when this happened, she replied that she was in outer space where she was taken by Ms. Betsy and Mr. Bob in a hot air balloon. When the therapist asked what happened in outer space, Claudia answered, "Mr. Bob killed the babies in outer space." The therapist continued: "How do you know that Mr. Bob killed the babies in outer space?" and Claudia replied "Because I saw them." Finally, when the therapist tried to probe further, Claudia said, "I'm too scared."

Source Monitoring

This concept is closely related to reality monitoring. It involves identifying the origins of our memories to elucidate them or to validate them. It might entail remembering in what place or at what time an event occurred; it also might entail identifying the speaker of an utterance and keeping track of who did or said what. Adults monitor the sources of memories continuously and often unconsciously. Whereas *reality monitoring* refers to remembering whether an event was imagined or real, *source monitoring* refers to keeping track of the origins of sources that *did* occur. The concepts of reality and source monitoring are sometimes indistinguishable when we try to remember whether something actually happened to us or merely whether someone told us that something happened to us.

Source monitoring confusions can be the basis of suggestibility effects, at least in some situations. If one cannot remember that the source of a false detail provided by an interviewer, one could come to believe that it was actually experienced rather than suggested. Thus, misleading suggestions may at times become incorporated into memory.

Developmental psychologists have begun to examine source monitoring in children. A few studies have shown that young children are more prone than adults to making source confusion errors (e.g., Lindsay, Gonzales, & Eso, 1995). In these studies, children experience an event (e.g., they might see a short film), then later are reminded of details about the event, some of which did not occur. Later, still when asked to recall the details of the original event, subjects often cannot monitor the source of the information; they report that some of the nonoccurring details provided after the event actually happened during the event; they report that they remember hearing or seeing the nonoccurring event. This effect happens at all ages, but younger children seem to make disproportionately more of these errors.

It also appears that when subjects are warned before their final recall not to believe anything that was said to them after the event because it was not true, they nevertheless continue to make source errors. That they do not relinquish such misinformation and insist that it was part of the original event suggests that they have blended the origins of input into their memories. This type of error is most prominent for preschoolers (Lindsay et al., 1995).

Poole and Lindsay (1995) demonstrated how source monitoring errors may occur through subtle interventions, such as parents' reading a book to their child. In this study, preschoolers played with "Mr. Science" for 16 minutes in a university laboratory. During this time, the children participated in four demonstrations (e.g., lifting cans with pulleys). Four months later, the children's parents were mailed a storybook that was specially constructed for each child. It contained a biographical description of their child's visit to Mr. Science. However, not all the information was accurate; although the story described two experiments that the child had seen, it also described two that the child had not seen. Furthermore, each story finished with the following fabricated account of what had happened when it was time to leave the laboratory: "Mr. Science wiped (child's name) hands and face with a wet-wipe. The cloth got close to (child's name) mouth and tasted really yuckie." The parents read the story to their children three times.

These young children were very susceptible to source monitoring errors. When later interviewed by the experimenters, the children reported that they had participated in demonstrations that, in actuality, had only been mentioned in the stories read to them by their parents. When asked whether Mr. Science put anything "yuckie" in their mouths, more than half of the children inaccurately replied "yes," and many of these children elaborated their "yes" answers. Moreover, inaccurate reports of having something "yuckie" put in their mouths increased on repeated questioning. When asked, "Did Mr. Science put something yuckie in your mouth or did your Mom just read you this in a story?" 71% of the children said that it really happened. The children made these claims even though they had been previously warned that some of the things in the story had not happened and they had been trained to say "no" to nonexperienced events.

We have conducted a series of studies to examine whether asking preschoolers to think repeatedly about some event, creating mental images each time they did so, would result in subsequent source misattributions that lead to false memories (Ceci, Crotteau-Huffman, Smith, & Loftus, 1994; Ceci, Loftus, Leichtman, & Bruck, 1994). The events that children were asked to think about were actual events that they experienced in their distant past (e.g., an accident that required stitches) and fictitious events that they never experienced (e.g., getting their hand caught in a mousetrap).

Each week for 10 consecutive weeks, preschool children were individually interviewed by a trained adult. The adult showed the child a set of cards, each containing a different event. The child picked a card and then the interviewer would read it to the child, ask the child to think about it before replying, and ask if the event had ever happened to him or her. For example, when the child selected the card that read: "Got finger caught in a mousetrap and had to go to the hospital to get the trap off," the interviewer would ask: "Think real hard, and tell me if this ever happened to you. Do you remember going to the hospital with a mousetrap on your finger?" Each week, the interviewer simply asked the child to think real hard about each actual and fictitious event, with prompts to visualize each scene (I want you to think about who was with you. What were they wearing? How did you feel?).

After 10 weeks of thinking about both real and fictitious events, the children were interviewed by a new adult who asked them specific and open-ended questions about the true and false events: "Tell me if this ever happened to you: Did you ever get your finger caught in a mousetrap and have to go to the hospital to get the trap off?" . . . "Can you tell me more?" . . . "What happened next?").

Some children who were asked to repeatedly think about fictitious events produced highly detailed, internally coherent, narratives that were, at times, convincing to naive adults. In our first study (Ceci, Loftus, et al., 1994), 58% of the preschool children produced false narratives to at least one of the fictitious events, with a quarter of the children producing false narratives to the majority of the fictitious events. What is so surprising to many who have watched videotapes of these children is the elaborateness of their narratives by the final week. These narratives are frequently embellished, with internally coherent accounts of the context and emotions associated with the accident.

Consider Bill, a 4-year-old, reporting his experience with a mousetrap. At the first session, Bill correctly claimed to have no memory of ever having his hand caught in a mousetrap, and stated that he has never been to a hospital before. By the 10th session, however, an elaborate story has evolved:

> My brother Colin was trying to get Blowtorch (an action figure) from me, and I wouldn't let him take it from me, so he pushed me into the woodpile where the mousetrap was. And then my finger got caught in it. And then we went to the hospital, and my mommy, daddy, and Colin (older brother) drove me there, to the hospital in our van, because it was far away. And the doctor put a bandage on this finger (indicating).

As can be seen, Bill did not simply give yes-no answers after he had been repeatedly asked to think about a fictitious experience during the previous 9 weeks; rather, he provided a richly detailed, plausible account. In fact, Bill went on to "explain" how his father was in the basement collecting firewood at the time of the accident, and he initially went into the basement to request his father to prepare his lunch. It is not only that Bill's story (and those of other children in this study) is so detailed, but it is also very believable to adults who do not know the procedures of the experiment. We think that these children are so believable because at least some of them have come to believe these false stories themselves. This hypothesis was tested in the next study.

Here (Ceci, Crotteau-Huffman, et al., 1994), we repeated the procedures of the mousetrap study with several modifications. First, we now used explicit memory induction procedures, telling the children that the fictitious events actually happened; then we encouraged children to create mental images about the fictional events. The children were asked about four real events and four false events for 11 consecutive weeks. They were given the following instructions:

> I am going to read some things that happened to you when you were little, and I want you to think real hard about each one of them. Try to make a picture of it in your head. What do you think you would have been wearing when it happened? Who would have been with you? How do you think you would have felt? We made this list up by talking to your mother to get her to tell us about some things that happened to you when you were younger. So, after you make a picture of it in your head, and think real hard about each thing for a minute, I want you to tell me if you can remember it or not, okay? Don't worry if you cannot remember it though.

As in the previous study, with each session children increasingly assented to false events. For the 12th week interview, a new interviewer tried to discredit the previous interviewer by telling the children that the previous interviewer had told the children many things had happened to them when they really hadn't happened. This new interviewer then asked the child which of the events had really happened. Our logic was that if children were just being acquiescent in the previous interviews then they might now correctly deny that the false events had occurred, even though they had previously claimed to have remembered them. On the other hand, if the children had come to truly believe that they experienced the false events, then they should continue to maintain that they had occurred even when told the previous interviewer was wrong. The latter is essentially what happened; although a small number of children now told the new interviewer that the false events had never really occurred, most of the children who had assented to false beliefs in previous interviews, continued to hold onto their false statements. And, as is true in many of our other studies, young preschoolers were more prone to these kinds of persistent and false statements than older preschoolers.

One hypothesis to account for the children's difficulty is that there is a confusion between multiple inputs into the memory system. The memory system contains information encoded from actual experience but it also contains information encoded from imaginary events. The same neural architecture subserves both functions, thus producing a functional equivalence in the brain. Very young children have particular difficulty separating these sources of familiarity, often mistaking the familiarity of imagined events for real ones.

Thus, preschoolers appear to be vulnerable to source misattributions when they are repeatedly encouraged to think about or visualize events that never occurred. Many of them appear to think that they actually experienced events that they had only imagined. This finding would seem to have relevance for the testimony of a child who has been in therapy for a long time, engaging in similar imagery inductions and "memory work" techniques. Since repeatedly creating mental images is a pale version of what can transpire in therapy when techniques may be employed that encourage the creation of competing images, our studies provide a fairly conservative test of the hypothesis that repeatedly thinking about a fictional event can lead to false beliefs about their reality.

In our case studies, many of the children were in counseling for months or even years prior to testifying. Records of these therapy sessions, where they exist, document repeated imagery inductions, enjoinders to think hard, and repeated encouragement to enact events with props (e.g., dressing a doll as a witch to represent the defendant). Some therapists asked the children to do "homework" or journal writing. These children were encouraged to go home and try to think "very hard" about some of the things that were difficult to talk about. Some therapists played games with the children. One therapist assumed the role of the perpetrator and encouraged the child to assume the role of a policeman. In one session, this therapist touched the genital area of a doll, so that the child could arrest her; the therapist then insisted that she didn't do anything, and had the child respond to this remark. This same therapist played another game with another child. According to her trial testimony, the therapist asked him if she should play the "pee game." The child assented and then instructed her to have the dolls (representing the children) pee in the pot and then put it in their mouths. The therapist stated that she did this several times until the child "arrested" her. Several months later, she suggested that they switch roles. Now the child played the "pee game" and the therapist arrested him. According to the therapist, the child was willing to have the dolls pee in the pot and then to have the dolls drink from the pot, but he became very anxious after he was arrested. A few months later, the child told his therapist that there had been a game involving a pee pot, that Kelly would pee in the pot and had the children pee in it too.

There is another element present in many of the day-care cases, which could also lead to reality monitoring and source monitoring errors. This involves parents' reading books with abuse themes to their children. When children did not disclose, some therapists gave parents one or more of these books to read to their children. These books typically depict situations in which a fantasy character has a "bad" secret that he is afraid to tell. But once he discloses his bad secret, he feels better.

We are concerned about this book-reading technique on several grounds. First, the results of the Poole and Lindsay (1995) study indicate that when suggestions are couched in books that parents read to their children some children may eventually come to believe that the suggested information actually happened to them. But there is an imperfect correlation between the conditions of this study and conditions under which parents read these books to children suspected of having been abused. In the latter situation, the books were intentionally given to the parents so that they could talk to their children about the themes of the book and to encourage the children to think about whether these same things had happened to themselves. Children were asked whether they knew any bad people, whether they had any secrets, and sometimes whether they had been abused. And sometimes children did not disclose after their parents had read them these books. We do not think that reading the books alone prompted these disclosures, as the children were also visiting their therapists and being questioned by parents and police, all during the same time period. Perhaps these books served as a catalyst to promote disclosures seeded by these other sources.

Certainly, the cataloguing of techniques that may promote monitoring errors is a sensitive issue, as it raises in some people's minds the possibility that children who are repeatedly exposed to such techniques cannot be believed. Such a conclusion is premature until it can be demonstrated that children are this susceptible to source misattributions about sexual events. And even if they are vulnerable to suggestions about sexual events, this does not mean that their claims are inevitably false, but only that they could be. For example, if therapists simply ask young children to think about certain events which may be beyond the experience and comprehension of children that age, and if the child does come to produce a coherent logical story, then perhaps the child is in fact faithfully reporting a memory.

But the risk of using these techniques could be minimized if therapists gently challenged children to make sure that they understand the need to tell the truth, and repeatedly urged them to check their own memories while engaging in visualization techniques. The worry is that these safeguards are not always attended to. Asking a child repeatedly to think about the time when he was scared or uncomfortable or to think about whether he was abused is often used in concert with an array of other suggestive techniques which may provide the details or the script for the child's emerging false memories. So although most 3-year-olds do not have sufficient knowledge to describe oral-genital contact when they are merely asked to repeatedly think about if someone touched them in a funny way, if this request is accompanied by a host of leading questions such as those used in the investigatory interviews that we have reviewed, then visually guided imagery may have a profound influence on the accuracy of the children's recall.

THE EFFECTS OF BEING INTERVIEWED WITH ANATOMICALLY DETAILED DOLLS AND OTHER PROPS

Diagnosing sexual abuse in children is a complicated and difficult process. Often there are no witnesses or medical evidence to confirm or disconfirm a child's claim or a parent's suspicion. To further complicate matters, there is no syndrome or constellation of behaviors, such as depression, anxiety, or nightmares, that is diagnostic of all or even most cases of sexual abuse (Kendall-Tackett, Williams, & Finkelhor, 1993). Because of these diagnostic difficulties, professionals have developed a number of assessment tools, such as anatomically detailed dolls. Child therapists, police, child protection workers, and attorneys frequently employ these dolls in the assessment and treatment of child sexual abuse.

One rationale for the use of anatomical dolls is that they allow children to manipulate objects reminiscent of a critical event, thereby cuing recall and overcoming language and memory problems. A second rationale for the use of these dolls is that they are thought to overcome motivational problems of embarrassment and shyness. Children may feel more comfortable enacting an abusive event using the dolls than verbally recounting it. The dolls have also been used as projective tests. Some professionals claim that if a child actively avoids these dolls, shows distress if they are undressed, or shows unusual preoccupation with their genitalia, this is consistent with the hypothesis that the child has been abused.

Despite the widespread use of anatomically detailed dolls in therapeutic and forensic settings (the rate of doll use in some jurisdictions may be as high as 90%—Boat & Everson, 1988; Conte, Sorenson, Fogarty, & Rosa, 1991), some researchers and professionals have expressed skepticism about their usefulness as diagnostic tools. Two concerns are frequently raised. The first is that the dolls are suggestive; by their very nature, it is claimed that they may encourage the child to engage in sexual play even if the child has not been sexually abused (e.g., Terr, 1988). A child may insert a finger into a doll's genitalia simply because of its novelty or simply because it is there.

A related criticism of the dolls is that they should not be used to make judgments about children's past abuse because the existing data demonstrate that the dolls do not meet the traditional standards of a reliable assessment instrument (e.g., Berry & Skinner, 1993; Wolfner, Faust, & Dawes, 1993).

Because of these concerns, the use of anatomically detailed dolls to provide legal evidence has been banned in a few jurisdictions until scientific data can be produced to attest to their validity. Furthermore, the American Psychological Association's Council of Representatives formally adopted the following statement on the use of anatomically detailed dolls in forensic evaluations:

> Anatomically detailed dolls are widely used in conducting assessments in cases of alleged child sexual abuse. In general, such dolls may be useful in helping children to communicate when their language skills or emotional concerns preclude direct verbal responses. These dolls may also be useful communication props to help older children who may have difficulty expressing themselves verbally on sexual topics. . . . These dolls are available from a variety of vendors and are readily sold to anyone who wishes to purchase them. The design, detail, and nature of the dolls vary considerably across manufacturers. Neither the dolls, nor their use, are standardized or accompanied by normative data. There are currently no uniform standards for conducting interviews with the dolls. . . . We urge continued research in quest of more and better data regarding the stimulus properties of such dolls and normative behavior of abused and nonabused children. (Statement issued by the APA Counsel of Representatives, February 8, 1991, p. 1)

At present, at least 20 studies address three issues related to the use of anatomically detailed dolls: (a) Do abused children interact with the dolls differently than nonabused children? (b) How do normal children interact with the dolls? (c) How accurately do children use dolls to report events? The results of these studies are now summarized (see Berry & Skinner, 1993; Ceci & Bruck, 1993b, 1995; Koocher et al., 1995; Wolfner et al., 1993, for detailed reviews of these studies).

Comparisons of Abused and Nonabused Children's Play with Anatomically Detailed Dolls

At least seven studies have compared abused and nonabused children's free play with anatomically detailed dolls. The results of these studies are inconsistent. Some provide support for the diagnostic utility of anatomical dolls (August & Forman, 1989; Jampole & Weber, 1987; White, Strom, Santili, & Halpin, 1986). Children with known or suspected histories of abuse played with the dolls differently than children with no histories of abuse: compared with nonabused children, these target children were more likely to engage in sexual activity with the dolls, to make more reference to the dolls' private parts, and to show more avoidance of the dolls and generally to demonstrate more "suspicious" behaviors in their doll play. However, although doll play statistically discriminated the two groups in these studies, it was not a perfect indicator of abuse status; children's interactions with the dolls resulted in nontrivially high rates of misclassification in at least some of the studies.

In contrast, the results of other studies indicate that there are no reliable differences in the doll play of children referred for sexual abuse and nonabused children. In two studies, both groups of children showed low and equal rates of sexually explicit behaviors with the dolls (Cohn, 1991; Kenyon-Jump, Burnette, & Robertson, 1991). In two other studies, highly trained professionals could not accurately differentiate abused from nonabused children on the basis of a doll-centered assessment conducted by an experienced child psychiatrist (Realmuto, Jensen, & Wescoe, 1990; Realmuto & Westcoe, 1990). In another study, abused and nonabused preschoolers both showed the same high levels of sexual and aggressive behavior with the dolls (McIver, Wakefield, & Underwager, 1989).

Factors that may account for the inconsistent results include the failure to control for delays between the disclosure of abuse and the experimental interview, the length of the interview sessions, the use of different procedures for eliciting doll play, the failure to "blind" the interviewer or raters to the status of the child (i.e., abuse-referred vs. control group). A more pervasive problem with this group of studies is that the children "suspected" of abuse were compared with children "not suspected" of having been abused. The failure to validate group membership may result in an underestimate of the diagnostic utility of the dolls. On the other hand, the failure to equate abuse-referred and nonabused subjects in terms of their prior conversations or interviews about sexual activities may result in an overestimate of the utility of the diagnostic dolls. Particularly, the possible encouragement of the abused children in preexperimental interviews to discuss sexual themes and/or to explore the dolls' genitalia, may make them more prone than nonabused (noninterviewed children) to play with the dolls in an explicit fashion during the subsequent experimental interview. Thus, the failure to control for differential exposure to the dolls rather than prior abuse history may be the cause of differences in doll use between abused and nonabused children.

Normative Studies of Nonabused Children's Play with Anatomically Detailed Dolls

This line of study represents an attempt to provide more details on how children who are not suspected of abuse engage in free play with anatomical dolls. One general finding is that nonabused children demonstrate few if any explicit sexual activities when playing with the dolls (e.g., Gabriel, 1985; Glaser & Collins, 1989; Herbert, Grams, & Goranson, 1987, Sivan, Schor, Koeppl, & Noble, 1988). However, there are many children who show reticence or avoidance of the dolls (Glaser & Collins, 1989) or, at the other extreme, overt interest in the genitalia of anatomically detailed dolls (Gabriel, 1985; Herbert et al., 1987). In the most ambitious of these studies, Everson and Boat (1990) observed over 200 preschool children play with the dolls in several different conditions. Although none of the 2-year-olds showed suggestive or clear intercourse positioning, between 3% and 18% of the older children did demonstrate such behaviors.

The results of these normative studies suggest that both avoidance of the dolls and preoccupation with the dolls' genitalia is fairly common among nonabused samples; thus, these behaviors cannot be considered diagnostic of sexual abuse. These results also indicate that nonabused children show very low rates of sexually explicit behavior when playing with anatomically detailed dolls for the first time.

The Influence of Dolls on the Accuracy of Children's Reports

A significant shortcoming of the previously mentioned studies is that the children were not asked to use the dolls to depict a previously experienced event. This would seem to be the central issue in evaluating the usefulness of dolls in interviews. If children can accurately depict previous actions and events with the dolls and if this information is more accurate than that given through verbal reports or other means of prompting, then such evidence would support the diagnostic utility of anatomically detailed dolls as an assessment tool. Several studies have attempted to address this issue.

Goodman and Aman (1990) questioned 3- and 5-year-old children, one week after they had played games with a male experimenter. Children were asked to provide general information about their recollection of the event, and they were also asked straightforward as well as misleading questions, some of which related to sexual abuse. Children answered these questions in one of four interview conditions: (a) anatomical dolls, (b) regular dolls (with no anatomical details), (c) regular dolls that the child could see but not touch, and (d) no dolls.

The accuracy of children's reports was similar across all conditions, with 5-year-olds consistently providing more detailed and accurate reports than 3-year-olds. Although the anatomical dolls did not promote inaccurate reports of sexual events, it is important to note that the dolls did not facilitate accurate reports of the original event, suggesting that their mnemonic value may be limited. Furthermore, the fact the 3-year-olds did not show any benefit from the use of the dolls suggests that one of the premises for the use of the dolls may be faulty. One would expect that given their more limited verbal competence, the 3-year-olds would have benefited from the dolls to a greater extent than the older children. But this was not the case.

A study by Gordon and her colleagues (1993) raises further doubts about the usefulness of dolls to obtain accurate reports from young children. Children, aged 3 and 5 years, were asked to report (either verbally or by manipulating normal dolls) the details of a previous visit to their pediatrician. Although the dolls provided some assistance to the older children in their recall, the provision of the dolls resulted in lower recall for the 3-year-olds, in certain instances.

Because one of the purported benefits of the dolls is to provide children with a tool that will allow them to overcome their shyness and embarrassment concerning sexual matters, perhaps anatomically detailed dolls primarily enhance the accuracy of children's reports of embarrassing events of a sexual nature. The earlier study we described by Saywitz and her colleagues (1991) attempted to address this issue by asking 5- and 7-year-old girls to recall the details of a recent doctor's visit. During this visit, half of the children had received a genital examination, and the other half had received a scoliosis examination. One to four weeks later, when asked for a verbal report of their examination, 78% of the children who had received a genital examination failed to disclose vaginal touching and 89% failed to disclose anal touching. When given the opportunity to provide the same information with the dolls ("show me with the dolls what happened") 83% of the children who had received a genital examination failed to disclose genital touching and 89% failed to disclose anal touching. However, when the experimenter pointed to either the genitalia or buttocks of the doll and asked a direct question, "Did the doctor touch you here?" now only 14% failed to report genital touching and 31% failed to report anal touching (i.e., errors of omission).

Children who received the scoliosis examination (i.e., with no genital touching) never made false reports of genital touching (i.e., errors of commission) in either the verbal free recall or the doll enactment conditions. However, when the experimenter pointed to the genital or anal region of the doll and asked, "Did the doctor touch you here?" 2.86% of the children falsely affirmed vaginal touch and 5.56% falsely affirmed anal touch. These results indicate that regardless of interviewing technique, children rarely if ever make false reports about genital touching unless they are asked direct questions with the dolls. The genital examination results, however, indicate that the dolls do not assist the children to divulge potentially embarrassing material, unless the interviewer uses highly directive questioning. It is possible that the same results could have been obtained without the use of the dolls but merely through the use of a direct verbal question, "Did the doctor touch your genitals?" But this question was not asked by these researchers.

The results of these three experiments are discrepant with the notion that dolls enhance the recall of the youngest children, but they are consistent with findings by DeLoache that children younger than 3 years of age have great difficulty appreciating symbolic relationships in which an object stands for something other than itself (see 1990, for a review). In DeLoache's work, children watch an experimenter hide an object in a room and then they are asked to find its counterpart in a small-scale model of the room. Generally, children younger than 28 to 36 months do not successfully retrieve the object. Deloache argues that this reflects their poor understanding of the symbolic nature of the scale model. Thus, perhaps young children might also have difficulty using a doll to enact real-life events because to be successful they must treat the doll as a symbol of themselves. The task is even more difficult in doll-centered interviews, because the dolls are not exact replicas of the real object (the child) in the way that a scale model is an exact replica of a large room.

A study by DeLoache and Marzolf (1995) reveals how difficult it is for young children to accurately use dolls as symbolic objects. These experimenters used dolls to interview 2.5-, 3-, and 4-year-old children about a play session they had just experienced in which a male experimenter played "Simon Says" and placed stickers on different parts of the children's clothed bodies. The dolls did not help the children report their experiences. The younger children, in particular, often spontaneously responded with correct verbal reports or they correctly showed on their own bodies how they had been touched and then after being reminded that they were to demonstrate on the dolls, sometimes proceeded to make an inaccurate demonstration. When asked to place stickers on the doll in the same places that stickers had been placed on their own bodies, many children did not seem to realize that they were supposed to treat the doll as a representation of themselves. Further, several children rejected the suggestion that they "pretend that this doll is you." This last finding is important since a reluctance to play with dolls in forensic or therapeutic interview sessions is sometimes taken as a possible indicant of abuse (Mason, 1991). Generally, these results indicate that very young children may not have the cognitive sophistication to use a doll to represent their own experiences. Hence, the use of dolls with this age group may actually impede or distort accurate communication rather than facilitate and clarify it.

We have completed a study that shares some similarities to the studies already described in this section but also goes beyond them in several ways. In our study (Bruck, Ceci, Francoeur, & Renick, 1995b), 3-year-old children visited their doctor for a routine medical examination. Half of these children received a genital examination where the pediatrician gently touched their buttocks and genitals. The other half of the children were not touched in these areas. Immediately after the examination, an experimenter pointed to the genitalia or buttocks of an anatomically detailed doll and asked the child, "Did the Doctor touch you here?" Only 47% of the children who received the genital exam correctly answered "Yes," a figure approximating that obtained by others for errors of omission (i.e., saying "No" when something really did happen). On the other hand, 50% of the children who did *not* receive a genital exam incorrectly answered "Yes" to this question (i.e., 50% of these children falsely reported touching or made "errors of commission"). When the children were simply asked to "show on the doll" how the doctor had touched their buttocks or genitalia, accuracy did not improve. Now only 25% of the children who had received genital examinations correctly showed how the pediatrician had touched their genitals and buttocks. Accuracy decreased in part because a significant number of female subjects inserted their fingers into the anal or genital cavities of the dolls—something that the pediatrician never did. When the children who did not receive a genital examination were asked to show on the doll how the doctor had touched their genitals and buttocks, only 50% of the children correctly showed no touching; 50% of the children who did not receive genital examinations falsely showed either genital or anal touching when given the dolls.

Our findings indicate that a substantial proportion of 3-year-old children are inaccurate when reporting how and where they were touched, even when the touching occurred 5 minutes prior to the interview. Children who were not touched demonstrated on the dolls that they were touched and children who *were* touched either refused to admit touching, or at the other extreme they showed penetration when none had occurred. The use of the dolls increases this type of inaccurate reporting in 3-year-old children. We have recently obtained similar results for 4-year-old children (Bruck, Ceci, & Hembrooke, in press).

The interview procedures in our study also elicited a number of other behaviors that adults might interpret as sexual. When the children were given a stethoscope and asked to show what the doctor did with it, some children incorrectly showed on their own bodies that he had used the instrument to examine their genitals. The children were also shown a spoon and asked whether the doctor had used it (he had not). A number of the children were inaccurate, stating that he had given them medicine with it. When the children were asked, "How might he use this spoon?" a small but significant number of them (18%) inserted the spoon into the genital or anal openings or hit the doll's genitals with it.

We believe that these "sexualized" behaviors do not reflect 3-year-olds' sexual knowledge or experiences but two other factors. First, the questions and props used in an interview (asking children to name body parts, including genitals, showing children anatomically detailed dolls and asking children to manipulate these dolls) may lead 3-year-olds to think that it is not only permissible but expected for them to respond to the interviewers' questions using these same terms. Second, perhaps children insert fingers or objects into the dolls' openings for the same reasons they would insert a finger into the hole of a doughnut; it is there, it is something to manipulate, it "affords" this activity. It is also possible, however, that the children's actions do have a sexual basis. One might argue that the presentation of anatomical dolls elicits sexual fantasies by allowing children to engage in their natural exploration of sexual themes which from an adult perspective could be regarded as prurient.

The results of our studies are particularly startling because they show that 3-year-old and 4-year-old children are not particularly accurate in giving details of body touches for an event that happened 5 minutes prior to an interview. Furthermore, many of these children made verbal or nonverbal reports of genital touching or digital penetration even though none occurred. The use of the dolls increased this inaccuracy mainly due to false reporting of genital touching or digital penetration. These findings stand in stark contrast to those obtained by Saywitz et al. (1991), who found that not a single 5-year-old exhibited errors of commission. The major explanatory factor appears to be differences in the ages of the children tested. Unlike the 5-year-olds in the Saywitz et al. study, 3- and 4-year-old children may be highly inaccurate when using the dolls to report bodily touches; their inaccuracy when demonstrating on the dolls may merely reflect their poor accuracy in reporting body touches.

But, as already noted, it is precisely the younger children for whom the dolls are claimed to be needed to lessen embarrassment and surmount their linguistic limitations. By the time children are 5 years old (the age of the children in the Saywitz et al. study), there appears to be little advantage to doll use, as their verbal skills are sufficient to express their experiences.

But the dangers that are inherent in using "dolls" in interviews with young children may also extend to the general use of props that have been thought to be useful in eliciting reports from young children (e.g., Price & Goodman, 1990; Ratner, Smith, & Padgett, 1990). Thus if children experience an event and then are asked to recall it, providing them with props at the time of recall enhances recall if the props were actually present in the initial event, but when foils are introduced at recall, then props are associated with higher rates of errors in the children's recalls (Gee & Pipe, 1995). This effect has been reported for both 6-year-olds and for 9-year-olds. It seems that error rates increase whether or not the props are symbolic and less physically similar to originally experienced cues (Salmon, Bidrose, & Pipe, 1995) or whether they are life-size replicas of actual and potential objects that were present during a critical event (Steward, Steward, Farquhar, et al., 1996).

This is an evolving area of research for which there may be no simple conclusions. It is possible that the effects of props or dolls on children's memory or recall may vary as a function of the child's age and as a function of how the props are actually used in interviews. For example, when children are simply presented with the dolls and asked to show "what happened," errors may occur only for young children. However, similar effects might be obtained with older children if during therapy they are repeatedly asked to imagine or to pretend with the dolls or with props that might have been present during a target event. As discussed in the previous section, the integration of these two interviewing techniques may promote source monitoring errors in children across a wide age range.

Although the data, taken together, do not present persuasive evidence for the value of dolls in forensic and therapeutic settings, small pockets of data appear to provide some support for the validity of doll-centered interviews. The results of the studies that examined the doll play of abused versus nonabused children provide the most support for the use of dolls in forensic and therapeutic interviews. However, we feel that these studies are not very relevant to the issue of the diagnostic utility of anatomically detailed dolls because the interviewing procedures bear little relationship to the procedures used in actual interviews with children suspected of sexual abuse. In the latter situation, children are rarely observed for over an hour in a free-play situation, nor are these children merely asked to undress a doll and name its body parts. Rather, children are asked direct, leading, and misleading questions about abuse with the dolls and are often asked to reenact alleged abusive experiences. Often when children do not respond to the interviewer's questions, they are repeated or rephrased.

As one example of the dubious generalizability of the studies in question, consider the following example from the *Little Rascals* case. Mrs. F is the mother of one of the suspected abuse victims, and her testimony concerns the police officer's first interview with her son Fred. She eavesdropped on the doll-centered interview from an adjacent room, and testified as to what she heard through the wall:

Mrs. F: She (the female officer) asked Fred what he liked to play with. He went and got some of his He-Man guys, and he said that those were what he wanted to play with. After a few minutes of the playing back and forth she said she had dolls with her. And he said, no, he preferred playing with his. And she said, you know, she had some she wanted him to see . . . at some point the dolls came out. I remember clearly her saying, "You do realize the difference between little boys and little girls, and little boys have a penis and little girls have an opening here."

She asked him about pretending and did he know how to pretend, and he said "yes." . . . She asked him to pretend that this doll was Mr. Bob and this (other) doll was him. I remember him at one point saying, "I don't want to be the girl doll." He kept getting his toys back out. I don't think he was very attentive. He didn't like playing with her toys. . . . At some point, and I'm not sure how, because it was difficult sometimes to hear her . . . she demonstrated something, I'm surmising because she said, "Have you ever seen anyone do this?" and "Have you ever seen this?" Um, at one point he said, "That's gross." I'm not sure what he saw, but that was his reply.

Attorney: Had your son ever been exposed to that type of anatomical doll prior to this occasion?

Mrs. F: No, but after she left he understood intercourse. He asked me why anybody would want to do that which I think was inappropriate for someone that age. He thought it was pretty disgusting, and thanks to their interview at that young age he was well versed in what it was.

A number of the procedures used in this interview are absent in the experimental studies described in the first part of this chapter. First, the child was asked to pretend that the dolls represented the defendant and himself. Asking the child to engage in pretense play may override the understanding that he should be telling the truth since he was given permission to pretend. Next, this child was given instruction on the sexual parts of the doll. Finally, it seemed that the interviewer manipulated the dolls into sexually explicit positions. In this one case, it does not appear that these suggestive techniques were associated with the child making allegations of sexual abuse. In fact, this child appeared to react negatively to the whole interview. However, it is still possible that a nonabused child who was interviewed in this manner might be easily coaxed into pretense play that mimics the sexual demonstrations of the interviewer, especially if he were to be interviewed a second time. In other words, maybe little Fred will react differently the second time he is interviewed with the dolls, not because they are valid diagnostic tools, but rather because he has become bored with doing the ordinary things with them and begins to explore their cavities the second time.

We are concerned about the potential negative effects of multiple prior interviews with dolls on children's reports. Although there are no empirical data to address these concerns, on the basis of the previous literature that documents the effects of repeated suggestive interviews on children's reports, one would also predict that there should be effects of repeated interviews with dolls, especially when there is a suggestive component. One case study of a normal nonabused child also leads us to predict that perhaps repeated nonsuggestive interviews with dolls will result in tainted reports. We now describe this pilot study (Bruck et al., 1995b).

A 3½-year-old nonabused girl was examined by a pediatrician. She was not given a genital examination. Immediately after the examination, when interviewed by the experimenter, she correctly said that the doctor had not touched her genitals or buttocks. Furthermore, when shown an anatomically detailed doll and told to show how the doctor had touched her genitals and buttocks, she correctly stated that he had not touched her. Three days later, the same child was given an anatomically detailed doll and asked to show all the things that the doctor had done in her previous visit. This time, she inserted a stick into the vagina of the doll and said that this had happened at the doctor's office. However, upon further questioning, she said that the doctor did not do this. Three days later, the child was asked to use the anatomically detailed doll and to show her father everything that had happened at the examination. This time, she hammered a stick into the doll's vagina and then inserted a toy earscope into the doll's anus. When asked if this really happened, she said "Yes it did." When her father and the experimenter both tried to debrief her with such statements as, "Your doctor doesn't do those things to little girls. You were just fooling. We know he didn't do those things," the 3½-year-old tenaciously clung to her claims that she had just demonstrated on the doll.

Thus, repeated exposure to the doll, with minimal suggestions, resulted in highly sexualized play for this 3½-year-old subject. Although this pilot observation calls for more systematic research on the influence of repeated exposure to anatomically detailed dolls in interviews with sexual themes, the dramatic and startling results of this one subject shows the potential suggestiveness of anatomical dolls with nonabused 3-year-olds and it vividly negates extremist claims that the dolls cannot lead to such behaviors.

There are further examples of how the conditions in which children are interviewed in research studies diverge from those conditions present in actual forensic interviews. In the *Michaels* case, anatomically detailed dolls were shown to the children before they said anything about abuse in 20 of the 39 interviews. In 17 of these interviews, silverware was given to the children and they were asked questions such as:

Interviewer: Did Kelly ever do anything to you with a knife that hurt you or bad things to you with a knife?

Child: No.

Interviewer: Did she ever do bad things or hurt you with a spoon?

Child: No.

Interviewer: Did she ever do bad things or hurt you with a knife?

Child: No.

Interviewer: Okay. What about a wooden spoon?

Child: No.

Four children were asked to speculate about how silverware could have been used. The following are examples:

Interviewer: Why don't you show me how you think a little girl can be hurt by the fork?

and:

Interviewer: Why don't you show me what Kelly did with the big wooden spoon.

Often the children resisted these suggestions, but sometimes after much repetition, a child would respond by poking the silverware into the doll's genitalia or buttocks. The information from these interviews contributed to the interviewers' conclusions that the children had been abused and that the abuse involved the use of utensils.

In our own study of 3-year-olds' reports of their medical checkups, we found a small proportion of children who quickly inserted the spoon into one of the openings or hit the doll's genitals with it. Apparently we were more successful than the interviewers in the *Michaels* case as the latter rarely if ever got children to make a sexualized report when first asked how one might use a spoon!

Other examples of practices used with the children in doll-centered interviews involved having the interviewer name the dolls after the defendant and then berating them (the symbolic dolls) for alleged abuses against the children; assuming the role of fantasy characters in doll play; and creating a persistent atmosphere of accusation. Perhaps one of the most salient features of some of these interviews is that the dolls provide the interviewers with opportunities to ask persistent questions involving sexual themes that go beyond the knowledge and experience of the child interviewees, as shown in the following segment from the *Michaels* case.

> **Interviewer:** Did Kelly and Brenda [another teacher] do anything to each other? . . . What did Kelly and Brenda do to each other? . . . Did they kiss? . . . Huh? Nobody can hear us. What did Kelly and Brenda do to each other? What? They kissed? Is that what you're showing me? I can't hear you. They kissed?

We have presented a number of examples of how clinical practices diverge from experimental presentations of anatomically detailed dolls. We did this for two reasons. First, as we have argued earlier, this disjunction between research and practice makes it difficult if not impossible to draw any generalizations based on children's doll play in highly sanitized experimental settings to how abused or nonabused children might interact with dolls in actual forensic and therapeutic situations. As seen, the latter settings are often imbued with fantasy play, accusatory atmospherics, and persistent discussions of sexual themes.

Second, practitioners frequently seem to be unaware of the available research results and, as a result, misinterpret children's doll play. In a recent survey of what professionals consider normal behavior with anatomical dolls, only 16% of mental health and law professionals felt that avoidance of the dolls was normal, and 80% rated digital penetration as abnormal (Kendall-Tackett, 1991). However, the existing data consistently indicate that these types of behaviors are common among nonabused children.

Based on the available literature that we have briefly reviewed, researchers have reached different conclusions about the feasibility of using anatomically detailed dolls in sexual abuse interviews with very young children. At one pole is the opinion that the current research indicates that the dolls are not suggestive (e.g., Everson & Boat, 1994) or that maybe they are only suggestive with preschoolers but that more research is required (e.g., Koocher et al., 1995) or that the dolls may be a valuable tool when used by experienced clinicians (e.g., APA, 1991; Koocher et al., 1995).

A second position reflects our own view (see Berry & Skinner, 1993; Wolfner et al., 1993, for similar conclusions). Simply put, no available scientific evidence supports the clinical or forensic diagnosis of abuse made primarily on the basis of a very young child's interaction with anatomical dolls. In part, this position is based on the grounds that in assessment, tools should only be used if they provide reliable additional information. There is no evidence that the dolls do this; in fact, in some cases, the dolls seem to impede children's reporting, and may even lead to false judgments about the status of abused and nonabused children.

Certainly, it could be argued that the appropriate research has not yet been done, and therefore our position is premature. As empiricists, we accept the possibility that future research may, in principle, provide support for the use of dolls. But, in practice, it is not clear that research can ever be carried out that will generalize to clinical forensic contexts, because for ethical reasons nonabused children cannot be subjected to the practices seen in the case studies (i.e., naming the dolls after the defendant, assuming the role of fantasy characters in doll play, creating a persistent atmosphere of accusation, interviewing the child more than one time, demonstrating suggestive acts with the dolls, encouraging children to discuss sexual themes while in the presence of the dolls).

Further, we do not find the argument persuasive that anatomical dolls are important tools when used by competent clinicians. How are we to define "competent"? How many courses should the clinician take to become experienced in sexual abuse training? What are the qualifications of the trainer of such courses to become certified?

In conclusion, we feel at this point that there has been sufficient concern raised in the literature, and enough evidence of potential misuse, without sufficiently counterbalanced evidence to the contrary, to urge that dolls not be used diagnostically, at least not with very young children. Some skilled professionals will decry the loss of a valuable tool, without which many children will go undiagnosed and be forced to continue living in an abusive situation. On the other hand, there are sufficient data that demonstrate this tool has the potential for serious misuse, including misdiagnosis, which could result in removing nonabused children from their homes, the implantation of false memories in therapy, and the imprisonment of innocent adults. Both conditions are horrific, and our goal should be to find techniques that minimize both consequences, not to support a technique that guards against one type of error at the expense of increasing the other.

SUMMARY TO DATE AND AGE DIFFERENCES

Throughout this chapter, we have discussed studies of children's suggestibility without stating any definitive conclusions about age differences. Here, we attempt to summarize these findings.

First, and foremost, contrary to the claims made by some (e.g., Melton, 1992), there do appear to be significant age differences in suggestibility, with preschool-age children disproportionately more vulnerable to suggestion than either school-age children or adults. This conclusion follows from a synopsis of our previous literature review (Ceci & Bruck, 1993b, see Appendix B) where we reported that in approximately 88% of the studies (14 out of 16) that involved comparisons of preschoolers with older children or adults, preschool children were the most suggestible group. Since that publication, new studies on children's suggestibility are being published on a regular basis; these newer data continue the trend that we reported in 1993, with approximately four out of five studies demonstrating significant age differences.

Although most researchers would agree with our conclusions regarding age differences in suggestibility, there is still some controversy regarding the boundary conditions for younger children's greater suggestibility. Some argue that suggestibility is diminished or even nonexistent when the act in question concerns a significant action, or when the child is a participant (as opposed to a bystander), or when the report is a free narrative (e.g., Fivush, 1993; Goodman, Rudy, Bottoms, & Aman, 1990). The strongest claim of this position is that children are not suggestible about personally experienced central actions, especially those that involve their own bodies.

Although it is probably true that children are less prone to suggestions about actions to their own bodies than to neutral, nonbodily, acts, the literature does not support the strong view that bodily acts are impervious to distortion. There are numerous demonstrations of how suggestive interviewing procedures can lead children to make inaccurate reports about events involving their own bodies; and at times these reports have been tinged with sexual connotations. As noted earlier, young children have made false claims about "silly events" that involved body contact (e.g., Did the nurse lick your knee? Did she blow in your ear?), and these false claims persisted in repeated interviewing over a 3-month period (Ornstein, Gordon, & Larus, 1992). Young children falsely reported that a man put something yuckie in their mouths (Poole & Lindsay, 1995). Three-year-olds falsely alleged that their pediatrician had inserted a finger or a stick into their genitals (Bruck, Ceci, Francoeur, & Renick, 1995). Preschoolers falsely alleged that some man touched their friends, kissed their friends on the lips, and removed some of the children's clothes (Lepore & Sesco, 1994).

There are other examples that we have not discussed that are provided by research by Goodman and her colleagues. In one study, they reported that 3-year-olds gave false answers 32% of the time to questions such as "Did he touch your private parts?" whereas 5-year-olds gave false answers 24% of the time (Goodman et al., 1991). In response to questions such as "How many times did he spank you?" 3-year-olds gave false answers 24% of the time, whereas 5-year-olds gave false answers only 3% of the time (Goodman & Aman, 1990). In another study, when 3- and 4-year-olds were interviewed about events surrounding an inoculation, there was an error rate of 23% on questions such as "How many times did she kiss you?" or "She touched your bottom didn't she?" (Goodman et al., 1990). That is, many of these children replied "yes" even though these events did not occur. Taken together, one can safely conclude that, compared with older children, young children, and specifically preschoolers, are at a greater risk for suggestion about many topics, including those containing sexual themes.

Notwithstanding this conclusion, it is clear that children—even preschoolers—are capable of accurately recalling much that is forensically relevant. In many of our own studies, children in the control group conditions recalled events flawlessly. This indicates that the absence of suggestive techniques allows even very young preschoolers to provide highly accurate reports, although they may be sparse in the number of details. Numerous other studies highlight the strengths of young children's memories (e.g., see Fivush, 1993; Goodman, Batterman-Faunce, & Kenney, 1992, for a review). What characterizes many such studies is the neutral tone of the interviewer, the limited use of misleading questions (for the most part, if suggestions are used, they are limited to a single occasion) and the absence of the induction of any motive or stereotype for the child to make a false report. When such conditions are present, it is a common (although not universal) finding that children are much more immune to suggestive influences, particularly about sexual details.

An important implication of the studies that focus on the strength of children's reports is that although children are generally accurate when they are interviewed by a neutral experimenter who asks few leading questions, and when they are not given any motivation to produce distorted reports, occasionally a few children give bizarre or sexualized answers to leading questions. In the Saywitz et al. study of children's reports of their medical examinations, one child, who never had a genital exam, falsely reported that the pediatrician had touched her buttocks and on further questioning claimed that it tickled and that the doctor used a long stick. In a study of children's recalls of their visit to a laboratory (Rudy & Goodman, 1991), one young child claimed that he had seen bones and blood in the research trailer (see Goodman et al., 1992, for additional examples). Thus, young children occasionally make spontaneous, strange, and unfounded allegations. However, as Goodman and her colleagues point out, many of these allegations can be understood by sensibly questioning the child and parents further. Often these allegations reflect the child's source confusions or anxieties.

One can only imagine what might happen if the rare spontaneous allegations that occurred during experimental interviews were followed up in the same aggressive manner as in some of the case studies. Perhaps participating researchers would have ended up being falsely accused of heinous acts. Conversely, one can imagine that if in the *Michaels* case the child's initial allegation that "Kelly took my temperature" was investigated in the prudent manner used by Goodman et al. in trying to understand their subjects' bizarre statements, perhaps there would have been no charges.

A second important implication of studies that emphasize the strength of children's memories is that they highlight the conditions under which children should be interviewed if one wishes to obtain reliable reports. Again, when children are interviewed by unbiased, neutral interviewers, when the number of interviews as well as the number of leading questions are kept to a minimum, and when there is the absence of threats, bribes, and peer pressure, then children's reports are at considerably less risk for taint.

Although we have concluded that preschool children (those 6 years and younger) are most at risk for suggestibility, this does not imply that children older than 6 years of age are immune to the effects of suggestive interviews. In some of the studies that we have reviewed, significant suggestibility effects were obtained for older children. In some studies, 8-year-old, 9-year-old, and even 10-year-old children were significantly more suggestible than adults (Ackil & Zaragoza, 1995; Warren & Lane, 1995). Although it could be claimed that these studies have less relevance for the courtroom, because children's memories of staged or videotaped events were tested (i.e., observed bystander events), similar findings have been found when children are suggestively interviewed about events in which they themselves participated. We were successful in influencing 7-year-old children's reports of their visit to their pediatrician one year previously (Bruck, Ceci, Francoeur, & Barr, 1995). Also, when asked to recall the details of an event that occurred 4 years previously, children between the ages of 7 and 10 were influenced by the atmosphere of accusation created by the experiments and came to inaccurately report events even though they had no conscious memory of the original experience (Goodman et al., 1989). Finally, even 8-year-olds will report that something "yuckie" was placed in their mouths if these nonevents are incorporated into stories that their parents tell them (Poole & Lindsay, in press).

There are a number of studies where suggestive influences are negligible in older children; and many studies in which children demonstrate near perfect accuracy in their recall of events. In the Sam Stone study, for example, few of the 6-year old children made false reports. The high levels of accuracy observed in some of these studies may reflect two factors. First, when preschoolers are included in the same study as older children, the task is usually designed to be suitable for the preschool children. As a result, the task often may be too easy for older subjects. It is difficult to create experimental situations that have the same meaning, interest, and difficulty for all age groups. A second factor is that older children may easily see through the deception in tasks such as Sam Stone, and thus resist suggestion. This does not necessarily mean, however, that older children are impervious to suggestive interviewing procedures. There are a number of well-known cases in which older children did succumb to interviewers' suggestions, after initially denying any knowledge of abuse (e.g., Jordan, Minnesota, Kern County). It seems that in some cases, children were engaged in highly pressurized interviews after they had been removed from their families or their homes. Children were told that they could help their (imprisoned) parents after they had been removed from their families or their homes. If similar methods were used in our experimental studies, we are of the opinion that we would obtain substantial suggestibility effects in children of all ages. However, this level of deception and coercion would be ethically unacceptable to employ in research.

MECHANISMS

The research in the 1990s has resulted in great advancements in our understanding of the phenomena of children's suggestibility. Researchers have mapped out conditions under which children's reports and memories can be influenced. The research is now turning to a consideration of the psychological variables that may account for individual differences in suggestibility. In this section, we will provide a brief overview of some of the proposed factors that underlie suggestibility in children and adults but that may be particularly important in accounting for the observed age differences discussed in this chapter.

Memory

Some researchers posit that age differences in suggestibility can be directly linked to age differences in memory. Specifically, children's greater susceptibility to suggestion is viewed as a direct outgrowth of their relatively weaker ability to accurately encode, store, retrieve, and monitor different types of information.

This position is based on a fairly large literature that indicates that memory skills do improve with age (e.g., see reviews by Kail, 1989; Schneider & Pressley, 1989) and that younger children tend to lose information from storage more rapidly than older children. It is also based on a theoretical position that, in general, suggestibility is related to the strength of one's memory. According to this hypothesis, if information about an event is weakly encoded or if it becomes degraded or lost in storage (which is more likely to be the case with very young children), then it will be easier to implant a false suggestion than if the memory was strongly encoded and well preserved in storage. For example, if the child does not have a clear memory of an event that occurred several years previously at day care, it may be easier to suggest that "bad things" happened to that child than to another child who has a strong memory of the event.

Some researchers have provided support for the proposal that there is a link between suggestibility and memory strength in children (Pezdek & Roe, 1995; Warren, Hulse-Trotter, & Tubbs, 1991); but others have argued that there is no consistent relationship between a memory's strength and children's susceptibility to suggestion (Howe, 1991; Zaragoza, 1991).

Intuitively, it makes a great deal of sense to link suggestibility-proneness to the strength of memory. Try suggesting to someone that his birthday is different from what he has been repeatedly told it is. No amount of false suggestions will overwrite the original memory because it is simply too strong, due to years of repetition and reinforcement. On the other hand, it is relatively easy to suggest to him that a friend's birthday is different from what he was once told. We anticipate that in the coming years there will be increasing evidence for the principle that the weaker the memory, the greater its proneness to being altered or interfered with as a result of erroneous suggestions.

Knowledge

To a large extent, the ability to encode, store, and retrieve information is directly dependent on the types of knowledge that one possesses. But the amount and structure of one's knowledge about the world can also indirectly influence one's susceptibility to suggestion. Because children have a weaker knowledge base, this may at times account for their greater susceptibility to suggestion. We provide a number of examples of how this mechanism could potentially operate.

Semantic Knowledge

Children differ from adults in the number of facts they have stored in their memories, in their understanding of the structure of events, and in their expectancies about the way the world works. Occasionally, children may have knowledge advantages in certain areas (e.g., when they possess greater knowledge about cartoon characters than adults). But, generally, knowledge increases as a function of age.

The amount and structure of knowledge can lead to different inferences about witnessed events. Usually, increased knowledge facilitates accurate recall (though not invariably). For example, children's memory for events that transpired during a doctor's visit is related to their knowledge of the types of activities that usually occur in a doctor's office (Ornstein et al., in press), and children's memory for chess positions is highly related to their knowledge of chess (Chi, 1978). Another example of this principle is provided by a study of preschool children's recall of a fire drill at their day care (Pillemer, Picariello, & Pruett, 1994). Very young preschoolers, but not older ones erroneously recollected some of the events because of their lack of understanding of the causal structure of the event. For example, younger children recollected that they left the building and then heard the fire drill. This error was not made by older children, presumably because they understood the procedures of a fire drill.

The relationship of semantic knowledge and memory has important implications for understanding age-related differences in suggestibility. Because of their relatively impoverished knowledge base for many types of events and experiences, it may be easier to implant suggestions in children than in adults. This may occur when the suggestion is bizarre or incongruent with the adult's knowledge of the world, but is meaningless to the child because of her sparse knowledge of the topic. This may be particularly important in investigations of sexual abuse, where young children have fairly limited sexual knowledge, allowing the incorporation of false suggestions that would be rejected by older children because of their implausibility. For example, a mother of one of the *Michaels* children gave the following testimony:

> **Mother:** He said that sometimes that he stuck a saw or a sword up Kelly's butt and sometimes a knife. . . . She was very polite. She said, "Thank you."

Scripted Knowledge

Temporally organized, habitual, agent-actor-action routines are referred to as "scripts." For example, a script for going to dinner at a restaurant includes the expectation that the headwaiter first takes a party to its table, then a menu is used to make a selection, followed by eating the entrée that was ordered, followed by dessert, then the bill is paid. Scripts lead to the automatic generation of expectations, and when these expectations run counter to what actually occurred, the result can be that scripts lead to an erroneous reconstruction of the actual events.

Although scripts develop with age, even very young children possess scripts for familiar events, and these influence the way they reconstruct past events by filling in gaps that did not occur (Flannagan & Hess, 1991; Hudson & Nelson, 1986). Scripts can be potent reminders for activities, but they also can lead to erroneous filling in of missing or expected activities.

The relationship between age, scripted knowledge, and recall is quite complex. Once children of different ages have acquired a script, preschoolers' recall may in fact be more vulnerable to the negative effects of script-based knowledge than elementary school-age children (Hudson & Nelson, 1986). Some work suggests that preschoolers' vulnerability to scripted information reflects their difficulty distinguishing special events from scripted events (Farrar & Goodman, 1992). It seems that with age, children become better able to tag unexpected events and to note that they are special; younger children are more likely to incorporate one-time special events into their scripts.

These studies may provide a basis for the observed age-related differences in suggestibility. Younger children may, in part, be more suggestible than older children because they are overly dependent on scripted knowledge and incorporate discrepant or novel events (such as a false suggestions) into their script of the event rather than keeping them tagged as a separate events.

However, there are some situations in which one might expect scripted knowledge to have more negative consequences on the recall of older children and adults than on younger children. When younger children's scripted knowledge is insufficient or poorer than that of older children, the latter might be expected to make more false inferences about events that were not witnessed but that are part of their scripts. For example, when subjects were erroneously told that the film they were viewing depicted cheaters, sixth graders and college students tended to report more cheating than did third graders when the cheating was based on innocent acts such as one student asking another for the time. Because younger children's scripts for cheating did not contain the scenario of asking for the time as a pretext for cheating, their limited "cheating" script made them less prone than older children to the erroneous suggestion (Lindberg, 1991).

Thus, scripted knowledge can exert a potent influence on the susceptibility to suggestion. If an erroneous suggestion is highly congruent with one's script of an event, then it should be easier to implant in memory than if it is highly inconsistent with one's script. Because young children's recall at times appears to be more script-driven than older children's and adults', it may be easier to implant script-congruent suggestions in their reports than when recall is less script-driven. As was seen, however, if younger children do not have a script for an event (e.g., a method of cheating), it may be easier to implant suggestions (that are congruent with the script) in older children who do have this knowledge. This is one of those developmentally reverse trajectories where an absence of knowledge actually facilitates younger children's recall.

Although some researchers emphasize the theoretical importance of knowledge in accounting for suggestibility effects, this literature should be interpreted with some caution. The reason for this is that if children are persistently interviewed, they may actually acquire facts or scripts about the alleged event, even if they had no previous knowledge of this information prior to the interviews. And with the acquisition of knowledge from the interviewing process, children may begin to provide more credible and detailed reports, which happen to be inaccurate.

Language

Because most examples of suggestibility in this chapter involve the influence of misleading verbal information on a child's verbal report, it seems reasonable to assume that linguistic comprehension and production skills might influence the child's suggestibility-proneness (for a full discussion of these issues, see Brennan & Brennan, 1988; Snyder, Nathanson, & Saywitz, 1993; Walker & Warren, in press). When young children are asked to describe events or are asked questions about specific events, their reports may be inaccurate because they fail to understand the question—regardless of whether it is suggestive or not. Similarly, an adult interviewer may incorrectly interpret a child's verbal report as a result of the child's limited linguistic production skills. Children's answers to questions that they have incorrectly understood, in addition to adults' misunderstanding of their limited productions, may be incorporated into future interrogations, further increasing the likelihood of tainted reports. In one study (Goodman & Aman, 1990), some 3-year-old children inaccurately reported that a male experimenter had touched their "private parts." In response to the question "Did he touch your private parts?" they answered "yes" even though the experimenter had not. On further examination, the experimenters noted that the children simply did not know the meaning of the phrase "private parts." As Goodman and her colleagues note, if this term had been used inappropriately in an actual case, a misleading conclusion, eventually leading to a potential false allegation could have occurred (Goodman et al., 1992).

Source Monitoring: Distinguishing Reality from Fantasy

We devote little space to this topic here, as we have reviewed the literature in some detail earlier in this chapter. To remind the reader, it has been proposed that children's increased suggestibility may be directly related to their relative difficulty in differentiating fantasy from reality, and at a more general level in differentiating actual events from imagined events.

Social Factors

Up to now, our discussion of the potential factors that may account for children's suggestibility has focused on cognitive factors. But since the turn of the century, researchers have also emphasized the importance of social factors in accounting for suggestibility effects in adults, but particularly in children.

In experimental situations, some have argued that suggestibility effects arise out of social pressures: the subject accepts the misleading information to please the experimenter or because the experimenter is trusted. At other times, the pressures may be more subtle, and suggestibility may reflect gap-filling strategies (e.g., McCloskey & Zaragoza, 1985): Subjects accept the misleading information because they have no memory for the original event. Instead of telling the interviewer that they can't remember or don't know—something that children may do less than adults—they revise or fill in memory gaps to please the interviewer.

Based on what we know about the social development of children, social factors should play a large role in the creation of suggestible reports. First, adults (who are the interviewers) have high status in the eyes of young children. Children see adults as omniscient and truthful; rarely do they question adult's statements or actions. On most occasions, children try to comply with the adult norms or what they perceive to be the adult's wishes.

This compliant behavior puts the child at risk for suggestion. A child may be willing to accept the suggestions of an interviewer, no matter how bizarre or incongruent the suggestions, merely because the child trusts the interviewer and wants to please him. Although children may be compliant, it is sometimes with much confusion. Impressions that we derived from listening to some of the existing electronic recordings of children in the case studies, and in similar cases not described in this chapter, provide a missing dimension undetectable in the written transcripts: There are long pauses in these interviews, children's answers do not come spontaneously, and there is often hesitation and a feeling of confusion as they come to assent to the interviewer's questions. Thus, in contrast to children who have been repeatedly exposed to erroneous suggestions over long periods of time and who, as a result, come to harbor false beliefs that result in spontaneous answers, compliant children's disclosures frequently seem halting and confused.

More constraints exist in child-adult interactions than in adult-adult interactions. When adults engage children in interviews, the interaction usually ends when the adult wants it to end. Children rarely are allowed to end such interactions by saying, "I am not talking about this any more" or "Stop this, you are bothering me" (or "I want my attorney present"). When children are part of an investigative interview, regardless of the coerciveness or unpleasantness of the interview, they are required to continue until the adult decides to terminate. In comparison with adult witnesses, it would be impermissible for children to say, "Stop questioning me, I already told you that I can't remember." Or, "I already told you that nothing happened." These techniques, which are available to adults, have the impact of warding off potential suggestive and coercive questioning methods.

Lying and Truth-Telling

For the first time in this chapter, we directly address the issue of whether some of the child witnesses' reports were "lies." That is, did the children consciously and deliberately distort the truth with the deliberate goal of deceiving their interviewers? It seems that, for the most part, the children in the case studies and in our empirical studies did not set out to intentionally deceive their interviewers. Although some may have been aware that their answers were not truthful, we argue that they did this to be compliant rather than to be deceitful. Also, based on the data reviewed earlier, it seems that few of the false reports of abuse can be categorized as deliberate and malicious attempts to distort the truth, and of those few that are categorized as blatant lies, most were initiated by adults and not by the child (Jones & McGraw, 1987). The line between false statements that occur because of lying and those that occur because of suggestive practices can at times become blurred. In this section, we present a summary of the literature in the area of children's lies because it may be relevant to age differences in false reporting when it is thought that the false report is a deliberate lie (for full details, see Ceci & Bruck, 1993b; Ceci, Leichtman, & Putnick, 1992; McGough, 1994).

Historically, it was felt that young children were incapable of lying because this act required a level of cognitive sophistication beyond the capability of the young child (e.g., Piaget, 1926). Since the time of Piaget, much progress has been made in understanding the development and definitional features of lying (Flanagan, 1992). With advances in our understanding of young children's cognitive sophistication, there is now evidence that even very young children sometimes do lie, with full appreciation of the differing perspectives of their listeners.

We now focus on studies of preschoolers' deception, ignoring whether behaviors are more appropriately construed as "sabotage," "deceit," "tricking," "politeness," or "tact." Further, we avoid delving into distinctions that have occupied some scholars, such as lying versus telling a lie, and minimal lies versus deception (Ceci, Leichtman, Putnick, & Nightingale, 1993). Recent research has sought to examine the specific conditions that may foster lying. Five motivations to lie or tell the truth have been studied: (a) avoiding punishment, (b) sustaining a game, (c) keeping a promise (e.g., to protect a loved one), (d) achieving personal gains (e.g., rewards, being accepted in a group), and (e) avoiding embarrassment. Existing data show that not all motivations produce comparable levels of lying and truth-telling.

Avoiding Punishment

Children will lie about events when the operative motives are sufficiently salient. Mothers report that the most frequent motivation for their 4-year-olds to lie is to avoid punishment (Stouthamer-Loeber, 1987). Michael Lewis and his colleagues have one experiment that vividly demonstrates young children's willingness to lie to avoid punishment. They found that 88% of 3-year-olds who were instructed not to peek at a toy, proceeded to peek. When asked if they had peeked, only 38% admitted to it, prompting the investigators to conclude, "Thus, we have some evidence . . . that deception strategies are adopted at early ages" (Lewis, Stranger, & Sullivan, 1989, p. 442).

Sustaining a Game

Some children can be induced to tell a lie in the context of a game. For example, an adult experimenter pretended to find a watch left behind by the teacher (Ceci, DeSimone, Putnick, Lee, & Toglia, 1990). After showing the child the watch, the child was told they were going to play a game of hiding it from the teacher. The child was told the game was a secret and was instructed not talk to anybody about it. Later, the returning teacher asked the child who had taken her watch. Only 10% of the preschoolers lied to sustain this game (see also Tate & Warren-Leubecker, 1990). However, when the motivational salience of the experimental procedure was increased by having a well-known adult coach the child to tell a lie about playing with a toy, then 35% of 2- to 8-year-olds lied to sustain a secret game (Tate, Warren, & Hess, 1992). It appears that the degree to which children will lie to sustain a game is context-dependent, and that the use of stronger coaching will result in higher rates of deception.

Keeping Promises

There is consistent evidence that children as young as 3 years of age will omit important information about transgressions and accidents if adults ask them to do so (see Pipe & Goodman, 1991, for a review). In one study, an adult spilled ink on a pair of gloves the child was wearing, and told the child that she (the adult) would "get into trouble" if anyone found out. Subsequently, 42% of the 5-year-olds claimed not to know who spilled the ink, and 25% maintained ignorance on repeated questioning 10 days and 2 months later (Wilson & Pipe, 1989). Some of the children in the Clarke-Stewart et al. (1989) study were told by Chester that he would lose his job if his boss learned that he had played with the dolls. Sixty-nine percent of these children kept the secret when they were interviewed by a neutral interviewer. However, they all eventually revealed the secret when asked suggestive questions.

If children will lie to protect a stranger, they should do so even more readily to protect a loved one. Results of one study support this hypothesis (Bottoms, Goodman, Schwartz-Kenney, Sachsenmaier, & Thomas, 1990). When mothers of 3- and 5-year-olds broke a Barbie doll, only 1 of the 49 children mentioned this to an interviewer who asked what happened. Further, when asked specific questions about the event, 5-year-olds did not tell the secret, even when asked leading questions.

Achieving Personal Gain

Sometimes children will lie to gain a material reward. Material and psychological rewards do not need to be of a large magnitude to be effective. Children as young as 3 years will engage in sabotage behaviors to gain some reward (e.g., covering up a treasure that is in jeopardy of being discovered by a puppet), but they will not engage in verbal deceit for another year (Leekam,1992). In one study, over 50% of nursery school subjects lied to obtain a gumball as a prize by falsely claiming that they had won a game while the interviewer was out of the room (Ceci et al., 1993). Control children who had played the game, but who were not offered any prizes for misreporting, accurately reported that they had not won the game; so memory failure can be ruled as an explanation of the former children's erroneous claims.

Avoiding Embarrassment

Not all behavior is regulated by external outcomes, rewards, and fears of reprisals. In the context of lies, the most relevant internal regulators are guilt, shame, and pride. Although children prior to the age of 7 (Bussey, 1992; Leekam, 1992) appear to be inferior to older children at inferring some of these self-regulatory states (e.g., appreciating that a sense of pride results from telling the truth), even 4-year-olds distinguish between statements meant to minimize the embarrassment of another ("I like your new hairdo") and those meant to cause distress (Bussey, 1992).

In an effort to study lying to avoid personal embarrassment, Ceci et al. (1993) instructed two parents to kiss their 3-year-olds while bathing them the evening before being interviewed. During an interview in which their parents were absent, the children were told that it was naughty to let someone kiss them when they didn't have any clothes on. They were then asked "No one ever kissed you when you didn't have any clothes on, did they? . . . No one kissed you last night when you were in the bathtub, did they?" These instructions provided a motivation to make "errors of omission" or withhold information about an event portrayed as taboo, to avoid the embarrassment of having done something naughty. Immediately following the child's reply, he or she was told, "But it is okay to be kissed by your mommy or daddy because they know you." (Later, the children were asked by their parents whether they had been kissed while being bathed.)

In a different condition, two children who had not been kissed during their baths were told at the start of the interview that parents who loved their children often kissed them and hugged them while they were in the tub, and asked: "Your mommy kissed you when she bathed you last night, didn't she?" Later, their parents also asked this question. The purpose of this condition was to provide a motivation to make "errors of commission" (claims that something happened even though it did not) to avoid embarrassment.

Initially, both children who were told that it was naughty to allow an adult to kiss them while being bathed replied that they had not been kissed. Later, when a parent interviewed them alone, and asked if they had been kissed while being bathed, they affirmed that they had, offering specific and accurate details (e.g., "Yes, I think mommy kissed me three times in the tub last night"). Interestingly, the children quickly added a codicil, that was nearly a verbatim restatement of the interviewer's assurance: "But it's okay, because I know her." One of the two children who had not been kissed during the evening bath reported that she had been, but reversed her report when interviewed by a parent alone. The results of this case study indicate that occasionally children will consciously distort the truth about events that were allegedly perpetrated to their bodies. Both errors of omission and errors of commission were produced by the strong motives used by these researchers.

Although the results of this study are limited because of the small sample size, they demonstrate an important principle that needs to be considered when evaluating the results of laboratory studies and the statements of child witnesses. It seems to us that researchers who have claimed that children cannot be coached to distort their testimony about bodily events have tilted the odds toward finding truthfulness among preschoolers by implicitly employing motives that favor a truthful outcome (e.g., Goodman et al., 1990). That is, there were no motives for the children in these earlier studies to make false disclosures. It might even be claimed that in such studies there were implicit motives to correctly report what happened because to do otherwise (e.g., to claim to have been sexually abused) would bring embarrassment. In other words, if children were to distort what they had witnessed, and claim to have been sexually touched when they were not, this could be expected to result in embarrassment, thus tilting the motivational structure toward truthful reporting. Contrast this approach with one in which a child is induced to make errors of commission to avoid embarrassment (e.g., "He kissed you because he loves you, didn't he?") or to an approach in which a child is asked to make errors of omission to avoid embarrassment (e.g.,"No one ever touched you there, did they?").

In our sample cases, expert witnesses have argued that the children would not lie because children lie "to get out of trouble not to get into trouble." Putting aside the lack of empirical evidence for this claim, these experts have an egocentric perspective of what "out of trouble" refers to. If the child is told that all his friends have already told, that it is a good thing to tell, that he will get rewards for telling and if the child is interviewed until he produces an incriminating statement, one could interpret any resultant disclosure as an attempt to "stay out of trouble."

The most recent research on lying has attempted to approximate real-life crime contexts by weaving affect and motive into studies of recollection, and by using highly familiar contexts such as observing loved ones break toys or being kissed while in the bathtub. Young children will consciously distort their reports of what they witnessed, and they will do so more in response to some motives (e.g., fear of reprisal and avoidance of embarrassment) than to others (to sustain a game, gain rewards). Generally, these studies demonstrate that, like adults, children are sensitive to the demand characteristics of a situation, and therefore succumb to a wide range of motives to lie or withhold information.

However, the literature is limited; most studies of lying have not examined age-related differences because it is difficult to come up with a lie context that has comparable meaning for the younger and older subjects. The safest conclusion that can be reached at this point in time is that subjects of all ages will lie when the motives are right. Children may be no different than adults in this regard. Thus, the argument that children are incapable of "lying" should be discounted as should the insinuation that they are hopeless liars.

The Interaction of Cognitive and Social Mechanisms

Some researchers have attempted to determine the relative importance of social versus cognitive factors in accounting for suggestibility effects. The results of these studies are inconsistent, and the issue as to the ascendance of one factor over the other remains unresolved. As argued in previous work, it seems that for now we can conclude that although social factors (e.g., desire to please powerful authority figures) are quite important, they do not appear to fully account for all suggestibility effects. Cognitive factors (i.e., memory impairment and source monitoring errors) appear to play important roles in explaining some suggestibility effects in children. These conclusions, however, are based almost exclusively on studies in which children are usually interviewed about an event only one time. Therefore they tell us little about the time-course of suggestibility effects or how reports become increasingly distorted over repeated interviews.

Furthermore, a focus on whether cognitive *or* social factors are more important obscures the possibility that both factors interact in producing suggestion. It is possible that the degree to which social factors play a role has a cognitive basis. When memory traces are weak (or when there is no memory at all for the original event), children may be more compliant and willing to accept suggestions because there is no competing memory trace to challenge the suggestion. On the other hand, when the traces are strong, the child (or adult) is less likely to incorporate misleading suggestions into memory.

In addition to cognitive factors underpinning the effectiveness of social factors, it is also possible for social factors to underpin the effectiveness of cognitive mechanisms in producing suggestibility, (e.g., a child may attend more to suggestions from an authority figure (a social factor), thus ensuring greater encoding (a cognitive factor). But this is a hypothesis in need of data.

Finally, it is possible that a child's report may initially be the result of some social factor, but over time the report may become a part of the child's actual memory. In the Sam Stone study, preschool children were given stereotypical knowledge about a clumsy character (Leichtman & Ceci, 1995). Children later used this knowledge to reconstruct what Sam Stone *might* have done, telling the interviewer "Maybe Sam did it," or "It could have been Sam." On repeated postevent questioning, however, these children often became more and more convinced that the clumsy events had actually occurred, as opposed to *might* have occurred. In the legal arena, in response to strongly suggestive—even pressurized—interviews, children may initially realize that they are providing the interviewer with an erroneous account to please him (a social factor), but after repeated retellings to different interviewers, the erroneous account may become so deeply embedded as to be indistinguishable from an actual memory (a cognitive factor). We know from past research that often such children are highly resistant to being debriefed; they argue with the researchers and their parents when told that their reports are incorrect, the result of suggestions.

Although cognitive as well as social factors may play a role in suggestibility effects, the important question, for which we have no empirical data, is whether there are age-related differences in the interaction of these factors. Do younger children differ from older children and adults in terms of how quickly false reports, which may have been initially motivated by social factors, come to be believed (i.e., a cognitive factor)? Much more research is needed to gain a complete understanding of the boundary conditions (e.g., the role of stress level, centrality of event). For now, we must content ourselves with the knowledge that young children are disproportionately more susceptible to suggestive interviews than older children, leaving aside the basic research question "Why."

Anticipating Future Research

In the foregoing section, we have presented an overview of the hypotheses that are being presented to account for suggestibility effects. To date, there is no generally accepted theoretical model of the mechanisms underlying suggestibility. However, we expect that this is the area that will generate the most research in the next decade. By virtue of the phenomenon itself, the ensuing models by necessity will be complex and multidimensional, involving not only a host of cognitive factors (trace strength, mnemonic representation, strategy use) and social factors (interviewer status, stereotypes), but also biological factors (gender, physiological reactivity). Moreover, we anticipate that the most active area of research in the coming decade will entail an examination of so-called individual differences, such as variations among children's personalities (e.g., compliance, field independence, mother's coping style, self-esteem), task factors (e.g., whether the test is retrieval-intensive, number of exposures), and even demographic factors (e.g., we have reported elsewhere large social class differences in suggestibility—see Ceci, Loftus, Leichtman, & Bruck, 1994, for details). We anticipate that eventually researchers will chart both direct and indirect pathways that link individual differences in all classes of cognitive, social, personality and biological factors.

Finally, it is worth repeating a caveat made at the beginning of this chapter. At that time, we noted that children have tremendous strengths in recollecting their pasts, *provided that the adults who have access to them do not do anything to usurp their memories.* Anyone who has even passing experience with preschoolers appreciates this point; they can recall past events with high degrees of accuracy and vividness of detail. In this chapter, we have focused on the baleful consequences of exposing preschoolers to a host of suggestive procedures.

THE DISTINCTION BETWEEN APPLIED VERSUS BASIC RESEARCH

At the outset, we tried to show how the research on children's suggestibility has been driven by practical concerns, at least since the 1980s. It was our contention that the research before that time was not only scarce but quite uninformative about the general issues at hand. Social scientists in the 1980s began to change their focus as a result of the needs of society in general and of the courts in particular. As one example, we felt that it was important to loosen and expand traditional definitions of suggestibility (see earlier pages of this chapter) so that we could examine a wider range of behavior than previously had been the scope of the field of children's suggestibility. As another example, researchers began to broaden the contexts or the experimental settings in which they observed children's reports of various types of events, including bodily touching.

Because of the applied characteristics of this modern work, we were asked to contribute this chapter to the volume on applied developmental research in the *Handbook*. And we now ask whether the research that we have reviewed is truly "applied" and more generally what is the distinction between applied and basic research? We frame these questions, because it seems that there are never-ending trends of preference in the history of psychological inquiry whereby at times basic research occupies the highest pinnacle, whereas at other times, applied research gains the ascendency. And thus we wonder how the research described in this chapter will be viewed toward the end of the present century. To adumbrate our argument in this section, we will suggest that the "basic versus applied" distinction is ill-wrought because (a) there is no principled basis for classifying research along these lines, (b) one type of research is not superior to the other in terms of quality, and (c) neither type of research has proprietary claims to being seminal, more generative, or even more general.

First, is the research described in this chapter basic or applied? Much of the research that we have been describing here would be classified as applied, no doubt due to the nature of the question asked and the proximity of any obtained findings to application in courtrooms. The issues we raised in the *Prologamena* were motivated by actual court cases and the research in the recent past was in part an attempt to abstract and test general principles that arose from these cases. The research represented somewhat of a paradigmatic shift: As social scientists became acutely aware of the shortcomings of the existing memory development research in terms of understanding children's reports and everyday memories, new methodologies, terminologies, and theoretical constructs were developed.

But this is not to say that the work was conducted in a theoretical vacuum, nor was all the basic research ignored. The social scientists who have participated in this field have all had their apprenticeships—if not primary careers—working in the vineyards of memory, developmental, cognitive, or social research. Occasionally, there are strong markers of our history in the "basic-research" camp which has systematically guided some of the research on the reliability of young children's reports. DeLoache's (1990) discovery of an abrupt stagelike shift in symbolic representational thinking between 28 and 36 months of age, led to a number of important studies on young children's interactions with anatomically detailed dolls. But the DeLoache study is one of only a few such examples; for the most part, there were no hints in the basic research camp to guide us in generating hypotheses that were useful to courts.

In fact, the research that we reviewed in this chapter contradicts some common assumptions about the value and necessary preconditions of applied research. It is commonly believed that applied research depends on good basic research for its underpinnings, that basic research establishes contextual invariances that can subsequently be exploited by applied researchers. We can all cite a favorite example of basic research being recruited to serve some applied interest that was unknown at the time the basic research was originally conducted. For example, the scientist who discovered how to splice genes never imagined the applications that would be made of this basic discovery a decade later.

What is seldom recognized, however, is that basic research sometimes benefits from good applied research, too. Sometimes applied researchers' solution of a problem has spurred basic researchers to conduct studies to better understand the principles underlying the solution. For example, bridges and cathedrals stood long before physicists understood why. In a similar vein, we believe that the results of the developmental research that we have discussed in this chapter has and will continue to force changes and reconceptualizations to basic theories of memory and of development.

This then raises the issue of whether some of the work we have discussed is truly applied or whether it could fall more easily into the "basic" camp. There is no principled basis for distinguishing between these two research styles. The only statement that can be made categorically is that they differ in the number of days that it takes before the practical consequences of the research become evident. So-called basic research is carried out in the absence of the knowledge about how the findings will serve some practical solution, and as a result it takes longer before its practical relevance becomes known, unlike so-called applied research, which is carried out in the context of practical solutions. But even these guidelines cause some confusion. Much of the biochemistry research carried out to better understand the AIDS virus is hard to classify as basic or applied because although the practical solution of HIV is what animates such work, the undeniable generality or "basicness" of this research may inform the solution to distant problems that cannot yet even be formulated.

An example from developmental research, indeed, one from our own lab, further highlights the difficulty of distinguishing between basic versus applied research on principled grounds. We have asked whether the structure of knowledge in long-term memory influences the suggestibility of the young child. According to one hypothesis, false suggestions will be effective to the extent that they are congruent with the manner in which a child's knowledge base is structured. For example, if children of varying ages are asked to sort common objects (milk, alligator, tree, cow, eggs, sandwich, soda, deer, cheese, etc.) and their categorizations are subjected to multidimensional scaling, it will be discovered that very young children lack the *dairy* and *predacity* dimensions that characterize older children's sorts. For them, cheese, milk, eggs, and cow will not be clustered in the same semantic space as seen in older children's representations. Instead, very young children cluster milk closer to fluids like soda than to cheese. Hence, if one exposes subjects to a story about a thief who steals cheese, older children ought to be more open to the erroneous suggestion that the thief stole milk whereas younger children, because they lack this cognate dairy dimension, may be more resistant to this false suggestion. This would be one of the rare occasions when younger children would be *less* suggestible than older children.

Based on the preceding description, one can ask whether this research is applied or basic, or both. On the one hand, it is conceptually driven and the design was spawned by theoretical considerations having to do with developmental differences in the way knowledge is represented; it can be seen as a case in which a hypothesis was generated from basic developmental theory. On the other hand, this work was undertaken for avowedly practical reasons—to predict error types among witnesses of varying ages.

We repeat our earlier assertion: There does not appear to be any principled basis along which much of the work described in this chapter can be classified as basic or applied. A more accurate classification may be that *some* applied research is not theoretical or that it is not useful to scientific questions beyond the one that is the focus of the work at hand. But *some* basic research can be criticized on these grounds as well. As already noted, the developmental research that we summarized is probably better distinguished on the basis of the lag between when a finding becomes known and the time it takes before it becomes important for some practical solution. We will leave the reader to decide how the research described in the present chapter meets these different definitions.

ACKNOWLEDGMENTS

Some of the ideas and phrasing in this chapter were taken from two of our major publications: Ceci, S. J., & Bruck, M. (1993b). "The Suggestibility of the Child Witness: A Historical Review and Synthesis." *Psychological Bulletin, 113,* 403–439, and Ceci, S. J., & Bruck, M. (1995). *Jeopardy in the Courtroom: A Scientific Analysis of Children's Testimony.* Washington, DC: American Psychological Association.

REFERENCES

Ackerman, B. (1983). Speaker bias in children's evaluation of the external consistency of statements. *Journal of Experimental Child Psychology, 35,* 111–127.

Ackil, J. K., & Zaragoza, M. S. (1995). Developmental differences in eyewitness suggestibility and memory for source. *Journal of Experimental Child Psychology, 60,* 57–83.

Alloy, L. B., & Tabachnik, N. (1984). Assessment of covariation by humans and animals: The joint influence of prior expectations and current situational information. *Psychological Review, 91,* 112–149.

American Psychological Association Counsel of Representatives. (1991). *Statement on the use of anatomically detailed dolls in forensic evaluations.* Washington, DC: Author.

August, R. L., & Forman, B. D. (1989). A comparison of sexually abused and nonsexually abused children's behavioral responses to anatomically correct dolls. *Child Psychiatry and Human Development, 20,* 39–47.

Batterman-Faunce, J. M., & Goodman, G. S. (Eds.). (1993). *Effects of context on the accuracy and suggestibility of the child witness.* New York: Guilford Press.

Belli, R. F., Windschitl, P., McCarthy, T., & Winfrey, S. (1992). Detecting memory impairment with a modified test procedure: Manipulating retention interval with centrally presented event items. *Journal of Experimental Psychology: Learning, Memory, and Cognition, 18,* 356–367.

Berry, K., & Skinner, L. G. (1993). Anatomically detailed dolls and the evaluations of child sexual abuse allegations: Psychometric considerations. *Law and Human Behavior, 17,* 399–422.

Binet, A. (1900). *La Suggestibilité.* Paris: Schleicher Freres.

Boat, B., & Everson, M. (1988). The use of anatomical dolls among professionals in sexual abuse evaluations. *Child Abuse and Neglect, 12,* 171–186.

Bottoms, B., Goodman, G., Schwartz-Kenney, B., Sachsenmaier, T., & Thomas, S. (1990, March). *Keeping secrets: Implications for children's testimony.* Paper presented at the biennial meeting of the American Psychology and Law Society, Williamsburg, VA.

Bradley, A., & Wood, J. (1996). How do children tell? The disclosure process in child sexual abuse. *Child Abuse and Neglect, 20,* 881–891.

Brainerd, C., & Reyna, V. (1996). Mere memory testing creates false memories in children. *Developmental Psychology, 32,* 467–478.

Brainerd, C., Reyna, V., & Brandes, E. (1995). Are children's false memories more persistent than their true memories? *Psychological Science, 4,* 141–148.

Brehm, S. S., & Smith, T. W. (1986). Social psychological approaches to psychotherapy and behavior change. In S. L. Garfield & A. Bergin (Eds.), *Handbook of psychotherapy and behavior change* (3rd ed., pp. 69–116). New York: Wiley.

Brennan, M., & Brennan, R. (1988). *Strange language.* Wagga Wagga, New South Wales, Australia: Riverina Muury Institute of Higher Education.

Bruck, M., Ceci, S. J., Francoeur, E., & Barr, R. J. (1995). "I hardly cried when I got my shot!": Influencing children's reports about a visit to their pediatrician. *Child Development, 66,* 193–208.

Bruck, M., Ceci, S. J., Francoeur, E., & Renick, A. (1995). Anatomically detailed dolls do not facilitate preschoolers' reports of a pediatric examination involving genital touching. *Journal of Experimental Psychology: Applied, 1,* 95–109.

Bruck, M., Ceci, S. J., & Hembrooke, H. (in press). Children's reports of pleasant and unpleasant events. In D. Read & S. Lindsay (Eds.), *Recollections of trauma: Scientific research and clinical practice.* New York: Plenum Press.

Burgess, A. H. (Ed.). (1984). *Child pornography and sex rings.* Lexington, MA: Lexington Books.

Bussey, K. (1992). Children's lying and truthfulness: Implications for children's testimony. In S. J. Ceci, M. Leichtman, & M. Putnick (Eds.), *Cognitive and social factors in preschoolers' deception* (pp. 89–110). Hillsdale, NJ: Erlbaum.

Cassel, W. S., & Bjorklund, D. F. (1995). Developmental patterns of eyewitness memory, forgetting, and suggestibility: An ecologically based short-term longitudinal study. *Law and Human Behavior, 19,* 507–532.

Ceci, S. J., & Bruck, M. (1993a). Children's recollections: Translating research into policy. *SRCD Social Policy Reports, 7*(3).

Ceci, S. J., & Bruck, M. (1993b). The suggestibility of the child witness: A historical review and synthesis. *Psychological Bulletin, 113,* 403–439.

Ceci, S. J., & Bruck, M. (1995). *Jeopardy in the courtroom: A scientific analysis of children's testimony.* Washington, DC: American Psychological Association.

Ceci, S. J., Crotteau-Huffman, M., Smith, E., & Loftus, E. W. (1994). Repeatedly thinning about non-events. *Consciousness and Cognition, 3,* 388–407.

Ceci, S. J., DeSimone, M., Putnick, M., Lee, J. M., & Toglia, M. (1990, March). *Motives to lie.* Paper presented at the biennial meeting of the American Psychology and Law Society, Williamsburg, VA.

Ceci, S. J., Leichtman, M., & Putnick, M. (1992). *Cognitive and social factors in early deception.* Hillsdale, NJ: Erlbaum.

Ceci, S. J., Leichtman, M., Putnick, M., & Nightingale, N. (1993). Age differences in suggestibility. In D. Cicchetti & S. Toth (Eds.), *Child abuse, child development, and social policy* (pp. 117–137). Norwood, NJ: ABLEX.

Ceci, S. J., Leichtman, M., & White, T. (in press). Interviewing preschoolers: Remembrance of things planted. In D. P. Peters (Ed.), *The child witness in context: Cognitive, social, and legal perspectives.* Holland: Kluwer.

Ceci, S. J., Loftus, E. W., Leichtman, M., & Bruck, M. (1994). The role of source misattributions in the creation of false beliefs among preschoolers. *International Journal of Clinical and Experimental Hypnosis, 62,* 304–320.

Ceci, S. J., Ross, D., & Toglia, M. (1987). Age differences in suggestibility: Psycholegal implications. *Journal of Experimental Psychology: General, 117,* 38–49.

Ceci, S. J., Toglia, M., & Ross, D. (1990). The suggestibility of preschoolers' recollections: Historical perspectives on current problems. In R. Fivush & J. Hudson (Eds.), *Knowing and remembering in young children* (pp. 285–300). New York: Cambridge University Press.

Chi, M. (1978). Knowledge structures and memory development. In R. S. Siegler (Ed.), *Children's thinking: What develops?* (pp. 73–96). Hillsdale, NJ: Erlbaum.

Child Victim Witness Investigative Pilot Projects. (1994, July). Research and evaluation. Final reports from the California Attorney General's Office, Sacremento, CA.

Clarke-Stewart, A., Thompson, W., & Lepore, S. (1989, May). *Manipulating children's interpretations through interrogation.* Paper presented at the biennial meeting of the Society for Research on Child Development, Kansas City, MO.

Cohen, R. L., & Harnick, M. A. (1980). The susceptibility of child witnesses to suggestion. *Law and Human Behavior, 4,* 201–210.

Cohn, D. S. (1991). Anatomical doll play of preschoolers referred for sexual abuse and those not referred. *Child Abuse and Neglect, 15,* 455–466.

Conte, J. R., Sorenson, E., Fogarty, L., & Rosa, J. D. (1991). Evaluating children's reports of sexual abuse: Results from a survey of professionals. *American Journal of Orthopsychiatry, 78,* 428–437.

Coy v. Iowa., 108 S. Ct. 2798 (1988).

DeLoache, J. S. (1990). Young children's understanding of models. In R. Fivush & J. Hudson (Eds.), *Knowing and remembering in young children. Emory Symposia in Cognition* (pp. 94–126). New York: Cambridge University Press.

DeLoache, J. S., & Marzolf, D. P. (1995). The use of dolls to interview young children: Issues of symbolic representation. *Journal of Experimental Child Psychology, 60,* 155–173.

Ervin-Tripp, S. (1978). Wait for me, Roller-Skate. In S. Ervin-Tripp & C. Mitchell-Kernan (Eds.), *Child discourse* (pp. 165–188). San Diego, CA: Academic Press.

Everson, M., & Boat, B. (1990). Sexualized doll play among young children: Implications for the use of anatomical dolls in sexual abuse evaluations. *Journal of the American Academy of Child and Adolescent Psychiatry, 29,* 736–742.

Everson, M., & Boat, B. (1994). Putting the anatomical doll controversy in perspective: An examination of the major uses and criticisms of the dolls in child sexual abuse evaluations. *Child Abuse and Neglect, 18,* 13–129.

Faigman, D. L. (1989). Notes: The battered woman syndrome and self-defense: A legal and empirical dissent. In S. L. Johann & F. Osanka (Eds.), *Representing battered women who kill* (pp. 333–362). Springfield, MA: Thomas.

Faller, K. (1984). "Is the child victim of sexual abuse telling the truth?" *Child Abuse and Neglect, 8*(4), 473–481.

Faller, K. (1996). Interviewing children who may have been abused: A historical perspective and overview of controversies. *Child Maltreatment, 1,* 83–95.

Farrar, M. J., & Goodman, G. S. (1992). Developmental changes in event memory. *Child Development, 63,* 173–187.

Finkelhor, D., Williams, L. M., & Burns, N. (1988). *Nursery crimes: Sexual abuse in day care.* Newbury Park, CA: Sage.

Fivush, R. (1993). Developmental perspectives on autobiographical recall. In G. S. Goodman & B. Bottoms (Eds.), *Child victims and child witnesses: Understanding and improving testimony* (pp. 1–24). New York: Guilford Press.

Fivush, R., Hammond, N. R., Harsch, N., Singer, N., & Wolf, A. (1991). Content and consistency in young children's autobiographical recall. *Discourse Processes, 14,* 373–388.

Flanagan, O. (1992). Other minds, obligations, and honesty. In S. J. Ceci, M. Leichtman, & M. Putnick (Eds.), *Cognitive and social factors in early deception* (pp. 11–126). Hillsdale, NJ: Erlbaum.

Flannagan, D., & Hess, T. (1991, April). *Developmental differences in children's abilities to utilize scripts in promoting their recall for scenes.* Paper presented at the biennial meeting of the Society for Research in Child Development, Seattle, WA.

Flavell, J., Flavell, E., & Green, F. L. (1987). Young children's knowledge about the apparent-real and pretend-real distinctions. *Developmental Psychology, 23,* 816–822.

Flin, R. (1993). Hearing and testing children's evidence. In G. S. Goodman & B. L. Bottoms (Eds.), *Child victims, child witnesses: Understanding and improving testimony* (pp. 279–300). New York: Guilford Press.

Foley, M. A., Harris, J., & Hermann, S. (1994). Developmental comparisons of the ability to discriminate between memories for symbolic play enactment. *Developmental Psychology, 30,* 206–217.

Gabriel, R. M. (1985). Anatomically correct dolls in the diagnosis of sexual abuse of children. *The Journal of the Melanie Klein Society, 3,* 45–50.

Garvey, C. (1984). *Children's talk.* Cambridge, MA: Harvard University Press.

Gee, S., & Pipe, M. E. (1995). Helping children to remember: The influence of object cues on children's accounts of a real event. *Developmental Psychology, 31,* 746–758.

Gelman, R., Meck, E., & Merkin, S. (1986). Young children's numerical competence. *Cognitive Development, 1,* 1–29.

Giannelli, P. C. (1980). *The admissibility of novel scientific evidence:* Frye v. United.

Glaser, D., & Collins, C. (1989). The response of young, nonsexually abused children to anatomically correct dolls. *Journal of Child Psychology and Psychiatry, 30,* 547–560.

Gonzalez, L., Waterman, J., Kelly, R., McCord, J., & Oliveri. (1993). Children's patterns of disclosures and recantations of sexual and ritualistic abuse allegations in psychotherapy. *Child Abuse and Neglect, 17,* 281–289.

Goodman, G. (1984). Children's testimony in historical perspective. *Journal of Social Issues, 40,* 9–31.

Goodman, G., & Aman, C. (1990). Children's use of anatomically detailed dolls to recount an event. *Child Development, 61,* 1859–1871.

Goodman, G. S., Batterman-Faunce, J. M., & Kenney, R. (1992). Optimizing children's testimony: Research and social policy issues concerning allegations of child sexual abuse. In D. Cicchetti & S. Toth (Eds.), *Child abuse, child development, and social policy.* Norwood, NJ: ABLEX.

Goodman, G. S., Bottoms, B. L., Schwartz-Kenney, B., & Rudy, L. (1991). Children's testimony about a stressful event: Improving children's reports. *Journal of Narrative and Life History, 1,* 69–99.

Goodman, G. S., & Clarke-Stewart, A. (1991). Suggestibility in children's testimony: Implications for child sexual abuse investigations. In J. L. Doris (Ed.), *The suggestibility of children's recollections* (pp. 92–105). Washington, DC: American Psychological Association.

Goodman, G. S., Qin, J., Bottoms, B., & Shaver, P. (1994). *Characteristics of allegations of ritualistic child abuse.* Final report to the National Center on Child Abuse and Neglect.

Goodman, G. S., Rudy, L., Bottoms, B., & Aman, C. (1990). Children's concerns and memory: Issues of ecological validity in the study of children's eyewitness testimony. In R. Fivush & J. Hudson (Eds.), *Knowing and remembering in young children* (pp. 249–284). New York: Cambridge University Press.

Goodman, G. S., Wilson, M. E., Hazan, C., & Reed, R. S. (1989). *Children's testimony nearly four years after an event.* Paper presented at the annual meeting of the Eastern Psychological Association, Boston, MA.

Gordon, B., Ornstein, P. A., Clubb, P. A., Nida, R. E., & Baker-Ward, L. E. (1991, October). *Visiting the pediatrician: Long term retention and forgetting.* Paper presented at the annual meeting of the Psychonomic Society, San Francisco, CA.

Gordon, B., Ornstein, P. A., Nida, R., Follmer, A., Creshaw, C., & Albert, G. (1993). Does the use of dolls facilitate children's memory of visits to the doctor? *Applied Cognitive Psychology, 7,* 459–474.

Gray, E. (1993). *Unequal justice: The prosecution of child sexual abuse.* New York: Macmillan.

Gudjonsson, G. (1986). The relationship between interrogative suggestibility and acquiescence: Empirical findings and theoretical implications. *Personality and Individual Differences, 7,* 195–199.

Haney, C. (1980). Psychology and legal change: On the limits of a factual jurisprudence. *Law and Human Behavior, 4,* 147–199.

Harris, P., Brown, E., Marriott, C., Whittall, S., & Harmer, S. (1991). Monsters, ghosts and witches: Testing the limits of the fantasy-reality distinction in young children. *British Journal of Developmental Psychology, 9,* 105–123.

Harvard Law Review Notes. (1985). The testimony of child sex abuse victims in sex abuse prosecutions: Two legislative innovations. *Harvard Law Review, 98,* 806–827.

Herbert, C. P., Grams, G. D., & Goranson, S. E. (1987). *The use of anatomically detailed dolls in an investigative interview: A preliminary study of non-abused children.* Unpublished manuscript, Department of Family Practice, University of British Columbia, Vancouver, BC.

Howe, M. L. (1991). Misleading children's story recall: Reminiscence of the facts. *Developmental Psychology, 27,* 746–762.

Hudson, J., & Nelson, K. (1986). Repeated encounters of a similar kind: Effects of familiarity on children's autobiographic memory. *Cognitive Development, 1,* 253–271.

Hughes, M., & Grieve, R. (1980). On asking children bizarre questions. *First Language, 1,* 149–160.

Jampole, L., & Weber, M. K. (1987). An assessment of the behavior of sexually abused and nonsexually abused children with anatomically correct dolls. *Child Abuse and Neglect, 11,* 187–192.

Johnson, M. K., Hashtroudi, S., & Lindsay, D. S. (1993). Source monitoring. *Psychological Bulletin, 144,* 3–28.

Jones, D., & McGraw, J. M. (1987). Reliable and fictitious accounts of sexual abuse in children. *Journal of Interpersonal Violence, 2,* 27–45.

Kail, R. V. (1989). *The development of memory in children* (2nd ed.). New York: Freeman.

Kayne, N. T., & Alloy, L. B. (1988). Clinician and patient as aberrant actuaries: Expectation-based distortions in assessment of covariation. In L. Y. Abramson (Ed.), *Social cognition and clinical psychology: A synthesis.* New York: Guilford Press.

Kendall-Tackett, K. A. (1991, April). *Professionals' standards of "normal" behavior with anatomical dolls and factors that influence these standards.* Paper presented at the meeting of the Society for Research in Child Development, Seattle, WA.

Kendall-Tackett, K. A., Williams, L. M., & Finkelhor, D. (1993). Impact of sexual abuse on children: A review and synthesis of recent empirical studies. *Psychological Bulletin, 113,* 164–180.

Kenyon-Jump, R., Burnette, M., & Robertson, M. (1991). Comparison of behaviors of suspected sexually abused and nonsexually abused preschool children using anatomical dolls. *Journal of Psychopathology and Behavioral Assessment, 13,* 225–240.

Koocher, G. P., Goodman, G. S., White, S., Friedrich, W. N., Sivan, A. B., & Reynolds, C. R. (1995). Psychological science and the use of anatomically detailed dolls in child sexual abuse assessments. *Psychological Bulletin.*

LaFontaine, J. S. (1994). *The extent and nature of organized and ritual abuse: Research findings.* London: HMSO.

Lamb. M. E., Hershkowitz, I., Sternberg, K. J., Esplin, P. W., Hovav, M., Manor, T., & Yudilevitch, L. (in press). Effects of investigative utterance types on Israeli children's responses. *International Journal of Behavioral Development.*

Leekam, S. (1992). Believing and deceiving: Steps to becoming a good liar. In S. J. Ceci, M. DeSimone, & M. Putnick (Eds.), *Social and cognitive factors in preschool deception* (pp. 47–62). Hillsdale, NJ: Erlbaum.

Leichtman, M. D., & Ceci, S. J. (1995). The effects of stereotypes and suggestions on preschoolers' reports. *Developmental Psychology, 31,* 568–578.

Lepore, S. J., & Sesco, B. (1994). Distorting children's reports and interpretations of events through suggestion. *Applied Psychology, 79,* 108–120.

Lewis, M., Stranger, C., & Sullivan, M. (1989). Deception in three-year-olds. *Developmental Psychology, 25,* 439–443.

Lindberg, M. (1991). A taxonomy of suggestibility and eyewitness memory: Age, memory process, and focus of analysis. In J. L. Doris (Ed.), *The suggestibility of children's recollections* (pp. 47–55). Washington, DC: American Psychological Association.

Lindsay, D. S. (1990). Misleading suggestions can impair eyewitnesses' ability to remember event details. *Journal of Experimental Child Psychology, 52,* 297–318.

Lindsay. D. S., Gonzales, V., & Eso, K. (1995). Aware and unaware uses of memories of postevent suggestions. In M. S. Zaragoza, J. R. Graham, C. N. Gordon, R. Hirschman, & Y. Ben-Porath (Eds.), *Memory and testimony in the child witness* (pp. 86–108). Newbury Park, CA: Sage.

Lipmann, O. (1911). Pedagogical psychology of report. *Journal of Educational Psychology, 2,* 253–260.

Loftus, E. F. (1979). *Eyewitness testimony.* Cambridge, MA: Harvard University Press.

Loftus, E. F. (1986). Ten years in the life of an expert witness. *Law and Human Behavior, 10,* 241–263.

Loftus, E. F. (1992). When a lie becomes memory's truth: Memory distortion after exposure to misinformation. *Current Directions in Psychological Science, 4,* 121–123.

Loftus, E. F. (1993). The reality of repressed memories. *American Psychologist, 48,* 518–537.

Loftus, E. F., Miller, D. G., & Burns, H. J. (1978). Semantic integration of verbal information into a visual memory. *Journal of Experimental Psychology: Human Learning and Memory, 4,* 19–31.

Loh, W. D. (1981). Psychological research: Past and present. *Michigan Law Review, 79,* 659–707.

Marin, B. V., Holmes, D. L., Guth, M., & Kovac, P. (1979). The potential of children as eyewitnesses. *Law and Human Behavior, 3,* 295–304.

Maryland v. Craig, 110 S. Ct. 3157 (1990).

Mason, M. A. (1991). A judicial dilemma: Expert witness testimony in child sex abuse cases. *Journal of Psychiatry and Law,* 185–219.

McCloskey, M., & Zaragoza, M. (1985). Misleading postevent information and memory for events: Arguments and evidence against the memory impairment hypothesis. *Journal of Experimental Psychology: General, 114,* 1–16.

McGough, L. (1994). *Fragile voices: The child witness in American courts.* New Haven, CT: Yale University Press.

McGough, L. S., & Warren, A. R. (1994). The all-important investigative interview. *Juvenile and Family Court Journal, 45,* 13–29.

McIver, W., Wakefield, H., & Underwager, R. (1989). Behavior of abused and non-abused children in interviews with anatomically correct dolls. *Issues in Child Abuse Accusations, 1,* 39–48.

Melton, G. B. (1985). Sexually abused children and the legal system: Some policy recommendations. *American Journal of Family Therapy, 13,* 61–67.

Melton, G. B. (1992). Children as partners for justice: Next steps for developmentalist. *Monographs of the Society for Research in Child Development, 57*(Serial No. 229), 153–159.

Mnookin, R. H. (1985). *In the interest of children.* New York: Freeman.

Montoya, J. (1992). On truth and shielding in child abuse trials. *Hastings Law Journal, 43,* 1259–1319.

Montoya, J. (1993). *When fragile voices intersect with a fragile process: Pretrial interrogation of child witnesses.* Unpublished monograph, University of San Diego School of Law.

Morison, P., & Gardner, H. (1978). Dragons and dinosaurs: The child's capacity to differentiate fantasy from reality. *Child Development, 49,* 642–648.

Moston, S., & Engelberg, T. (1992). The effects of social support on children's eyewitness testimony. *Applied Cognitive Psychology, 6,* 61–75.

Myers, J. E. B. (1994). The literature of the backlash. In J. E. B. Myers (Ed.), *The backlash: Child protection under fire.* Thousand Oaks, CA: Sage.

Myers, J. E. B. (1995). The era of skepticism regarding children's credibility. *Psychology, Public Policy and the Law, 1,* 387–398.

Neisser, U. (1982). *Memory observed: Remembering in natural contexts.* San Francisco: Freeman.

Nelson, K., & Gruendel, J. (1979). At morning it's lunchtime: A scriptal view of children's dialogues. *Discourse Processes, 2,* 73–94.

Ornstein, P., Gordon, B. N., & Larus, D. (1992). Children's memory for a personally experienced event: Implications for testimony. *Applied Cognitive Psychology, 6,* 49–60.

Ornstein, P. A., Shapiro, L. R., Clubb, P. A., Follmer, A. & Baker-Ward, L. (1997). The influence of prior knowledge on children's memory for salient medical experiences. In N. Stein, P. A. Ornstein, B. Tversky, & C. J. Brainerd (Eds.), *Memory for everyday and emotional events* (pp. 83–112). Hillsdale, NJ: Erlbaum.

Otis, M. (1924). A study of suggestibility in children. *Archives of Psychology, 11,* 5–108.

Parker, J. (1995). Age differences in source monitoring of performed and imagined actions on immediate and delayed tests. *Journal of Experimental Child Psychology, 60,* 84–101.

Pettit, F., Fegan, M., & Howie, P. (1990, September). *Interviewer effects on children's testimony.* Paper presented at the International Congress on Child Abuse and Neglect, Hamburg, Germany.

Pezdek, K., & Roe, C. (1995). The effect of memory trace strength on suggestibility. *Journal of Experimental Child Psychology, 60,* 116–128.

Piaget, J. (1926). *The language and thought of the child.* London: Routledge & Kegan Paul.

Pillemer, D. B., Picariello, M. L., & Pruett, J. C. (1994). Very long-term memories of a salient event. *Applied Cognitive Psychology, 8,* 95–106.

Pillemer, D. B., & White, S. H. (1989). Childhood events recalled by children and adults. In H. W. Reese (Ed.), *Advances in child development and behavior* (Vol. 21, pp. 297–340). San Diego, CA: Academic Press.

Pipe, & Goodman, G. S. (1991). Elements of secrecy: Implications for children's testimony. *Behavioral Sciences and the Law, 9,* 33–41.

Poole, D. A., & Lindsay, D. S. (1995). Interviewing preschoolers: Effects of nonsuggestive techniques, parental coaching and leading questions on reports of nonexperienced events. *Journal of Experimental Child Psychology, 60,* 129–154.

Poole, D. A., & Lindsay, D. S. (in press). Effects of parents suggestions, interviewing techniques, and age on young children's event reports. In D. Read & S. Lindsay (Eds.), *Recollections of trauma: Scientific research and clinical practice.* New York: Plenum Press.

Poole, D., & White, L. (1991). Effects of question repetition on the eyewitness testimony of children and adults. *Developmental Psychology, 27,* 975–986.

Poole, D., & White, L. (1993). Two years later: Effects of question repetition and retention interval on the eyewitness testimony of children and adults. *Developmental Psychology, 29,* 844–853.

Poole, D., & White, L. (1995). Tell me again and again: Stability and change in the repeated testimonies of children and adults. In M. S. Zaragoza, J. R. Graham, C. N. Gordon, R. Hirschman, & Y. Ben-Porath (Eds.), *Memory and testimony in the child witness* (pp. 24–43). Newbury Park, CA: Sage.

Powers, P., Andriks, J. L., & Loftus, E. F. (1979). Eyewitness accounts of females and males. *Journal of Applied Psychology, 64,* 339–347.

Price, D., & Goodman, G. (1990). Visiting the wizard: Children's memory for a recurring event. *Child Development, 61,* 664–680.

Pynoos, R. S., & Nader, K. (1989). Children's memory and proximity to violence. *Journal of the American Academy of Child and Adolescent Psychiatry, 28,* 236–241.

Ratner, H., Smith, B., & Padgett, R. (1990). Children's organization of events and event memories. In R. Fivush & J. Hudson (Eds.), *Knowing and remembering in young children.*

Emory Symposia in Cognition (pp. 65–93). New York: Cambridge University Press.

Read, B., & Cherry, L. (1978). Preschool children's productions of directive forms. *Discourse Processes, 1,* 233–245.

Realmuto, G., Jensen, J., & Wescoe, S. (1990). Specificity and sensitivity of sexually anatomically correct dolls in substantiating abuse: A pilot study. *Journal of the American Academy of Child and Adolescent Psychiatry, 29,* 743–746.

Realmuto, G., & Wescoe, S. (1992). Agreement among professionals about a child's sexual abuse status: Interviews with sexually anatomically correct dolls as indicators of abuse. *Child Abuse and Neglect, 16,* 719–725.

Rice, S. A. (1929). Interviewer bias as a contagion. *American Journal of Sociology, 35,* 421–423.

Romaine, S. (1984). *The language of children and adolescents.* Cambridge, MA: Basil Blackwell.

Rose, S., & Blank, M. (1974). The potency of context in children's cognition: An illustration through conservation. *Child Development, 45,* 499–502.

Rosenthal, R. (1995). Critiquing Pygmalion: A 25-year perspective. *Current Directions, 4,* 171–172.

Rosenthal, R., & Rubin, D. B. (1978). Interpersonal expectancy effects. *Behavioral and Brain Sciences, 3,* 377–386.

Ross, M. (1989). Relation of implicit theories to the construction of personal histories. *Psychological Review, 96,* 341–357.

Rudy, L., & Goodman, G. S. (1991). Effects of participation on children's reports: Implications for children's testimony. *Developmental Psychology, 27,* 527–538.

Salmon, K., Bidrose, S., & Pipe, M. E. (1995). Providing props to facilitate children's events reports: A comparison of toys and real items. *Journal of Experimental Psychology, 60,* 174–194.

Sauer, M. (1993, August 29). Decade of accusations. *San Diego Union Tribune,* pp. D1–D3.

Sauzier, M. (1989). Disclosure of child sexual abuse: For better or for worse. *Treatment of Victims of Sexual Abuse, 12,* 455–469.

Saywitz, K., Goodman, G., Nicholas, G., & Moan, S. (1991). Children's memory of a physical examination involving genital touch: Implications for reports of child sexual abuse. *Journal of Consulting and Clinical Psychology, 5,* 682–691.

Schneider, W., & Pressley, M. (1989). *Memory development between 2 and 20.* New York: Springer-Verlag.

Siegal, M., Waters, L., & Dinwiddy, L. (1988). Misleading children: Causal attributions for inconsistency under repeated questioning. *Journal of Experimental Child Psychology, 45,* 438–456.

Sivan, A. B., Schor, D. P., Koeppl, G. K., & Noble, L. D. (1988). Interaction of normal children with anatomical dolls. *Child Abuse and Neglect, 12,* 295–304.

Sjoberg, R., (1994). *Child testimonies during an outbreak of witch hysteria—Sweden 1670–1671.* Unpublished manuscript: University of Stockholm, Sweden.

Skinner, L. J., & Berry, K. K. (1993). Anatomically detailed dolls and the evaluation of child sexual abuse allegations. *Law and Human Behavior, 17,* 399–421.

Small, W. S. (1896). Suggestibility of children. *Pediatric Seminar, 13,* 176–220.

Snyder, L. S., Nathanson, R., & Saywitz, K. (1993). Children in court: The role of discourse processing and production. *Topics in Language Disorders, 13,* 39–58.

Sonnenschein, S., & Whitehurst, G. (1980). The development of communication: When a bad model makes a good teacher. *Journal of Experimental Child Psychology, 3,* 371–390.

Sorensen, T., & Snow, B. (1991). How children tell: The process of disclosure of child sexual abuse. *Child Welfare, 70,* 3–15.

State v. Robert Fulton Kelly Jr., Superior Criminal Court, Pitt County, North Carolina, #91-CRS-4250–4363 (1991–1992).

State v. Kathryn Dawn Wilson, Superior Criminal Court, Perquimans County, North Carolina, 92-CRS-4296–4306; 92-CRS-4309–4312 (1992–1993).

State v. Michaels, Superior Court, Essex County, New Jersey (1988).

Stern, W. (1910). Abstracts of lectures on the psychology of testimony and on the study of individuality. *American Journal of Psychology, 21,* 270–282.

Steward, M., Steward, D., Farquhar, L., Myers, J. E. B., Reinhart, M., Welker, J., Joye, N., Driskill, J., & Morgan, J. (1996). Interviewing young children about body touching and handling. *Monographs of the Society for Research in Child Development, 61,* 1–186.

Stouthamer-Loeber, M. (1987). *Mothers' perceptions of children's lying and its relationship to behavior problems.* Paper presented at the biennial meeting of the Society for Research in Child Development, Baltimore, MD.

Tate, C., Warren, A., & Hess, T. (1992). Adults' liability for children's "lie-ability": Can adults coach children to lie successfully? In S. J. Ceci, M. D. Leichtman, & M. E. Putnick (Eds.), *Cognitive and social factors in early deceptions* (pp. 69–87). New York: Macmillan.

Tate, C. S., & Warren-Leubecker, A. R. (1990, March). Can young children lie convincingly if coached by adults? In S. J. Ceci (Chair), *Do children lie? Narrowing the uncertainties.* Symposium conducted at the biennial meeting of the American Psychology and Law Society, Williamsburg, VA.

Taylor, W., & Howell, R. (1973). The ability of 3-, 4-, and 5-year-olds to distinguish fantasy from reality. *Journal of Genetic Psychology, 122,* 315–318.

Terr, L. (1988). Anatomically correct dolls: Should they be used as a basis for expert testimony? *Journal of the American Academy of Child and Adolescent Psychiatry, 27,* 254–257.

Terr, L. (1994) *Unchained memories.* New York: Basic Books.

Tobey, A., & Goodman, G. S. (1992). Children's eyewitness memory: Effects of participation and forensic context. *Child Abuse and Neglect, 16,* 779–796.

U.S. Department of Health and Human Services. (1996). *Child maltreatment 1994: Reports from the States to the National Center on Child Abuse and Neglect.* Washington, DC: U.S. Government Printing Office.

Varendonck, J. (1911). Les temoignages d'enfants dans un proces retentissant. *Archives de Psycholgie, 11,* 129–171.

Veitch, V., & Gentile, C. (1992), Psychological assessment of sexually abused children. In W. O'Donohue & J. Geer (Eds.), *The sexual abuse of children: Clinical issues* (Vol. 2, pp. 143–187). Hillsdale, NJ: Erlbaum.

Walker, A. G., & Warren, A. R. (in press). The language of the child abuse interview: Asking the questions, understanding the answers. In T. Ney (Ed.), *Allegations in child sexual abuse, assessment and case management.* New York: Brunner/Mazel.

Warren, A., Hulse-Trotter, K., & Tubbs, E. (1991). Inducing resistance to suggestibility in children. *Law and Human Behavior, 15,* 273–285.

Warren, A. R., & Lane, P. (1995). The effects of timing and type of questioning on eyewitness accuracy and suggestibility. In M. S. Zaragoza, J. R. Graham, C. N. Gordon, R. Hirschman, & Y. Ben-Porath (Eds.), *Memory and testimony in the child witness* (pp. 44–60). Newbury Park, CA: Sage.

Whipple, G. M. (1911). The psychology of testimony. *Psychological Bulletin, 8,* 307–309.

Whipple, G. M. (1912). Psychology of testimony and report. *Psychological Bulletin, 9,* 264–269.

Whipple, G. M. (1913). Psychology of testimony and report. *Psychological Bulletin, 10,* 264–268.

Whitcomb, D. (1992). *When the child is a victim* (2nd ed.). Washington, DC: National Institute of Justice.

White, S., Strom, G., Santili, G., & Halpin, B. M. (1986). Interviewing young sexual abuse victims with anatomically correct dolls. *Child Abuse and Neglect, 10,* 519–530.

Wilson, J. C., & Pipe, M. E. (1989). The effects of cues on young children's recall of real events. *New Zealand Journal of Psychology, 18,* 65–70.

Wolfner, G., Faust, D., & Dawes, R. (1993). The use of anatomical dolls in sexual abuse evaluations: The state of the science. *Applied and Preventative Psychology, 2,* 1–11.

Zaragoza, M. (1991). Preschool children's susceptibility to memory impairment. In J. L. Doris (Ed.), *The suggestibility of children's recollections.* Washington, DC: American Psychological Association.

Zaragoza, M. S., & Lane, S. (1994). Source misattributions and the suggestibility of eyewitness memory. *Journal of Experimental Psychology: Learning, Memory and Cognition, 20,* 934–945.

CHAPTER 12

Developmental Psychology and Law: Divorce, Child Maltreatment, Foster Care, and Adoption

GAIL S. GOODMAN, ROBERT E. EMERY, and JEFFREY J. HAUGAARD

Lawyers and psychologists do not always share a common view of human nature. Nevertheless, there has often been a fruitful, yet challenging, working relationship between members of the two disciplines when it comes to forensic issues concerning children. In fact, there are few other areas of law where the courts rely as heavily on social science data as they do for decisions about children's welfare.

Applied developmental research is most useful to the courts when researchers understand legal concepts and questions, and use them to help guide their research. Many of these concepts and questions are not obvious to those who lack legal training. As a result, the legal system challenges developmentalists to expand their knowledge by approaching research from a new and sometimes foreign perspective. The results can lead to fresh insights for both the legal system and scientists. The legal system also provides developmentalists with an arena in which to examine crucial theoretical issues, providing a valuable realm for testing developmental theory. Many intriguing theoretical issues, such as the effects of traumatic abuse on autobiographical memory development and the emotional sequelae of parent-child separation, can be profitably addressed within a legal context. Thus, research that links developmental psychology and law provides the dual opportunity to advance scientific knowledge and improve children's lives.

For the purposes of writing the present chapter, we selected four topic areas in which forensic questions guide research and in which developmental research and theory guide the law. The four topics are divorce, child maltreatment, foster care, and adoption. We first provide a legal framework for considering these topics and develop several themes that will recur throughout the chapter. Then research related to each topic is reviewed. We close with a discussion of the interface between developmental psychology and law in addressing social-policy concerns that profoundly affect children's welfare.

THEMES IN DEVELOPMENTAL PSYCHOLOGY AND LAW

A number of themes that are central to discussions of developmental psychology and law appear throughout the chapter. The most important recurring themes concern: (a) balancing the interests of child, family, and state; (b) integrating psychology and law's distinct paradigms; and (c) determining the proper role of developmental research in social-policy debates.

Balancing the Interests of Child, Family, and State

The law concerning children provides a framework for distributing decisional power among three interest groups: children, parents, and the state (Mnooken, 1978). The balance of power among these three interest groups is perpetually in flux. Although ultimate authority for decisions regarding children rests primarily with parents and the state, legal decisions affect the balance that emerges within the tripartite structure.

Parents have traditionally possessed substantial freedom in rearing their children, an issue often framed as one of family autonomy. In relation to topics discussed in the present chapter, parents' family autonomy rights include having legal custody (guardianship) of their children, unless such rights have been terminated or limited by court action, as may occur in divorce, abuse foster care, and adoption cases. Parents also possess the right to determine their children's living pattern, religion, education, health care, and discipline. The latter right is particularly relevant to child abuse cases. Parents' rights derive in part from their biological relation to their children. The law assumes that birth parents are particularly motivated to care for their offspring. As a result, in many legal decisions, such as contested adoption cases, the legal system gives clear priority to birth parents. However, in exchange for these rights, parents also face many responsibilities for their children, including the provision of financial support, physical care, and emotional care. At times, the courts have to decide what is suitable parenting given families' responsibilities to children, an issue that arises in legal decisions regarding divorce, child maltreatment, foster care, and adoption.

The state also maintains a number of rights and responsibilities over children's welfare. For example, the state has various regulatory rights (e.g., the state's right to govern children's welfare through compulsory school attendance laws, child labor laws, and standards of care for children in foster placement). Moreover, when parents do not meet their responsibilities to their children, the state can intrude into family life to act on behalf of children under the ancient Roman doctrine of *parens patriae* (literally, "parent of the country"). Parens patriae is the legal principle that serves as the basis for the court to use its power to ensure children's adequate treatment. The "best interest rule" is often applied, by which the court tries to implement actions that are in children's best interest. However, when the state is compelled to intervene into family life, it typically prefers the alternative that intrudes least, so that such rights as family autonomy are maintained as much as possible. As will be seen later in this chapter, other rights may at times take precedence over children's best interests.

The state could not adequately raise the country's children on its own. It is in the state's interest to keep families together. In the past, this interest was reflected in laws that made divorce difficult to obtain, in policies requiring social services to reunite families in child abuse cases, and in legal guarantees of parental rights in adoption and foster care situations. The state continually struggles with these issues and in recent years has moved in the direction of allowing families to disperse more easily following parental divorce. However, this more liberal trend has not necessarily carried over to other areas of family law.

How children's own independent interests fit into this picture is not always clear. Children (typically defined in the American legal system as any person under the age of 18 years) have traditionally possessed "object" but not "subject" rights. Object rights include the right to nurturance and freedom from harm. In contrast, subject rights (e.g., the right to vote, to live independently, to travel, to make medical decisions) are gradually bestowed on children in proportion to their perceived competence. For instance, for older but not necessarily for younger children, there is often a legal expectation or requirement that they have a voice in custody decisions. Children must give their consent to be adopted after a certain age in some states (e.g., 14 years in New York). The legal system typically presumes that parents will ensure that children's object rights are satisfied (e.g., that children will not be maltreated) and that eventually (at age of majority) full subject rights will be bestowed.

Over the years, children have gained greater subject rights in some areas. Before 1967, children were considered "nonpersons" under the law; that is, they possessed no constitutional rights. Then, in the landmark *In re Gault* (1967) decision, the U.S. Supreme Court stated that "neither the 14th Amendment nor the Bill of Rights is for adults alone" (p. 28). Nevertheless, children's subject rights are still quite limited. As Melton (1992) remarked, children are in effect "half-persons" under the law—sometimes they have constitutional rights (e.g., when their liberty is at stake, as in delinquency proceedings), but much of the time they do not. For example, children still do not have the legal standing to bring action to the courts, as reflected in Florida's denial of any legal standing to Gregory M., a 12-year-old who tried to file a petition to terminate his birth parents' rights, freeing him for adoption. Despite the matter's significance to Gregory M., as a child he was still a nonperson when it came to independent access to the courts.

In each section of this chapter, the law's attempts to balance the interests of child, family, and state are addressed. At the interface of developmental psychology and law, the issue of balance underlies many complex legal and social policy questions such as the following ones: When should government have the right to intrude into family life to dictate such matters as parenting practices or custody? What actions are in a child's best interest? What constitutes suitable parenting? At what point should children have the right to decide for themselves?

Paradigms in Conflict

Another theme that recurs throughout this chapter is the dissimilarity between the paradigms of law and psychology. Important differences exist in the styles and methods of reasoning, proof, and justification in psychology and law (Haney, 1980). Yet the interaction of psychology and law requires the bringing together of these paradigms. One important difference between the two disciplines is in their overriding goals. Despite the court's truth-seeking mission, the main goal of the law is justice, whereas the main goal of science is truth (Thibaut & Walker, 1975). Thus, to take hypothetical examples from two of our four topics of interest, if scientists showed that maltreated children are so traumatized by hostile cross-examination in court that they cannot provide complete testimony, the courts might still insist on such procedures to ensure a fair trial for the accused. Or, if scientists showed that psychological harm results from separating a child from loving foster parents to whom the child has become deeply attached, the courts might still give custody to a birth parent because the court's view of justice requires that birth parents have rights to their children. Thus, even if psychologists could redesign the legal system to be based on scientific fact, such "factual jurisprudence" would be objectionable to the law if the new system was not also fair.

Moreover, law and science employ different methods and accept different forms of test and proof. Developmental psychologists use the scientific method and statistical analysis in an attempt to ensure objective, replicable results from which logical, if not causal, inferences can be drawn. The law is more likely to employ the adversary system, in which bias and lack of objectivity on the part of each side in a legal contest are assumed and in which cross-examination is viewed as an important test of the truth. From the carefully structured presentation of information from two opposing sides, truth (or at least justice) is expected to emerge.

Another important difference is that the focus of the law is idiographic, or concerned with individual cases; whereas the focus of psychology is typically nomothetic, or concerned with group trends and general principles. In deciding a specific legal case, it is not enough for the courts to know the average effects (e.g., of divorce, foster care, or maltreatment). Instead the courts more often want to know the effects on the specific child in the specific case at hand.

Finally, from a psychologist's perspective, the law often uses terms that may seem imprecise to scientists. For example, although the courts are often guided by the "best interest rule" in regard to children's welfare, the law provides only very general definitions of "best interest." What is a child's best interest in a divorce proceeding, in a proceeding to determine if the child should be removed from an abusive home and placed in foster care, or in a court battle over adoption? Lack of precise definitions permits discretion in legal decision making, but it can perplex and frustrate researchers.

Social Policy, Legal Change, and Developmental Research

A final underlying theme of the present chapter is that developmental research can have an influence on social policy, as well as individual legal cases and courtroom procedures. Social policy for children is determined in several ways, legislation being one. Developmentalists may be asked to testify before legislative bodies or legislative staff to influence the formation or passage of laws concerning children. However, given our pluralistic society and emphasis on individual freedom, legislators are hesitant to intrude into family life (e.g., by setting laws that determine who should obtain custody in divorce proceedings, defining child abuse in a way that might offend a religious group, or determining laws that govern transracial adoption). Moreover, even when the legislature tries to regulate family life, the courts may find the laws unconstitutional. As a result, policies are often decided on a case-by-case basis in court, especially in this era of pluralism in American society.

As discussed more later, developmentalists may serve as expert witnesses in courts of law to educate judges and juries about research findings or about an evaluation of a specific child or family. Developmentalists can contribute to writing amicus (friend-of-the-court) briefs to state or federal courts, including the U.S. Supreme Court. Social policy toward children is influenced by developmentalists in such interactions. Media attention to research can also influence societal opinions and legal decision making. These roles cause scientists to have special responsibilities. Developmentalists must assess whether enough is known to form a scientifically valid opinion; whether caveats, qualifications, and opposing ideas should be mentioned; and whether sufficient ecological validity ensures adequate generalizability of the research to the issue at hand. Answering these questions may raise ethical issues, often because the political process does not tolerate scientific caution and may press for certainty and unequivocal positions.

A final issue relevant to social policy is too often overlooked: Policy decisions affect many children, not just a single child in a single case. Although policy, unlike court cases, is nomothetic, one must consider the consequences of alternative policies for children who may be in very different circumstances. A policy that may benefit some children may hurt others. To date, science cannot provide complete prediction of the outcome of social-policy decisions on the range of children typically affected. Even if it could, the values placed on the outcomes may be matters of serious societal debate (Mnookin, 1985).

Haney (1980) distinguishes three ways in which psychology can affect social policy: psychology in the law (i.e., when the legal system uses psychological knowledge for specific cases), psychology and law (i.e., use of psychological research to examine the legal system's assumptions), and psychology of law (i.e., law as a determinant of social behavior). Much of the research discussed in this chapter falls in the category of "psychology and law." The research we review is relevant to whether social policy and legal assumptions regarding children's abilities and needs are justified. Throughout the chapter, we draw social policy implications of the research base. At the end of the chapter, we expand on Haney's distinctions in relation to our discussion of children and the law.

Some Restrictions

Several restrictions on the scope of this chapter, and on the resulting themes addressed, should be mentioned. First, the scope prohibits discussion of assessment strategies for individual cases and of international perspectives on child forensic issues. Individual forensic assessments require extensive information gathering from all relevant sources. Such assessments are often controversial, in part because of the application of nomothetic principles in an idiographic context. Many books and articles on child, adult, and family assessment and evaluations for the court are available to the interested reader (e.g., Melton, Petrila, Poythress, & Slobogin, 1987; Stahl, 1994). Instead of focusing on assessment strategies, we provide an overview of legal and social science knowledge which, in combination with information about individual cases, may serve as a foundation for both sound assessment and social-policy decisions.

Second, although international perspectives on child forensic issues are of considerable interest, space limitations preclude discussion of children and the law in various countries. Moreover, surprisingly little has been written about psychological research that directly addresses cross-national legal policy for children (but see Bottoms & Goodman, 1996). Greater attention needs to be given to this topic: Social policy in one country can be informed by policies adapted elsewhere, leading to potential benefits for children everywhere.

CHILDREN AND THE COURTS

The American legal system is complex, and psychologists interested in forensic issues must become familiar with its structure. In this chapter, we will be primarily concerned with forensic issues that arise in three types of courts: criminal, juvenile, and family/divorce courts. Children may become the subject of legal action and/or be called on to serve as witnesses in any of these courts. In some circumstances, children may be involved in two or more court systems simultaneously (e.g., for child abuse, a criminal court case involving charges against the alleged perpetrator and a juvenile court case concerning removal of the child from home). Because somewhat different forensic and psychological issues can arise in each type of court, it is important to understand the mandate of each court system.

Criminal Court

Criminal courts and criminal law deal with crimes against the public order; that is, violations considered so serious as to require formal punishment of the offender. Criminal courts are part of the criminal justice system, which also includes law enforcement and corrections. In the United States, criminal justice is guided by the adversary system, which derives from "trial by ordeal" in medieval times. In the past, two sides in a dispute might be represented by two soldiers who physically battled; it was assumed that God would ensure that the right side won. The adversary system is the formalization of such battles within a set of legal guidelines. It is assumed that both sides are zealous advocates who battle under the watchful eye of a trier of fact (jury or judge), who must render a verdict as to the winner. In many other countries, the inquisitorial system of justice is preferred. In inquisitorial systems, judges do more information gathering and questioning of witnesses than in the adversary system, and there is less focus on cross examination by two opposing camps (Myers, 1996; Spencer & Flin, 1993). Despite a number of advantages to the adversary system (e.g., it is viewed as particularly fair to defendants; Thibaut & Walker, 1975), it is a system that may be insensitive, if not harmful, to children forced to step into the legal battleground (Spencer & Flin, 1993).

In most Americans' minds, trial courts serve as the prototype of legal proceedings. However, before a trial commences, a number of pretrial interviews, depositions, and hearings may take place. After a verdict is rendered, the decision may be appealed to higher courts. If a constitutional issue is involved, the U.S. Supreme Court may choose to hear the case, and its decision will determine the "law of the land." Forensic issues concerning children can arise at any point along the delicate and dangerous path from legal investigation to pretrial hearing to trial to appeal and finally to incarceration or freedom.

Children below the age of 18 years typically are not prosecuted in criminal courts, although for some serious crimes such as murder, teenagers can be prosecuted as adults (Ewing, 1990). However, laws to further facilitate criminal-court prosecution of teenagers are currently being enacted in a number of states. Children can, in any case, be subpoenaed to serve as witnesses. Even when a child is the victim of a crime, the child (like adult witnesses) does not traditionally have legal representation in criminal court. However, when the child is the victim, prosecutors often attempt to consider the child's welfare. Some courts appoint a guardian ad litem, often an attorney or certified lay volunteer, who advocates for the child (e.g., informs the court of the child's ability to understand legal proceedings) but cannot introduce evidence or question witnesses in court (Bross, 1984; Haralambie, 1993).

Juvenile and Family Courts

Until the late 1800s, children 7 years of age or older who allegedly broke the law were tried in adult criminal courts, and children 14 years and older were sentenced to penalties provided to adult offenders. Reformers who objected to such harsh treatment of children established the first juvenile courts in 1899, one in Illinois and another in Colorado. By 1917, only three states lacked such courts. Juvenile courts were originally conceived to handle delinquency cases but quickly evolved to deal with dependent and neglected children as well. In contrast to the criminal court's focus on punishment and due process, the juvenile court's focus is on rehabilitation, protection, and individualized treatment. Technically, juvenile courts are civil rather than criminal courts: Civil law governs relations between individuals and defines their legal rights. Most civil matters are regulated by state, not federal law.

Although the exact jurisdiction (legal authority to hear and decide a case) of the juvenile court varies from state to state, in general the juvenile court maintains jurisdiction for children up to 17 years of age in the following types of cases: child maltreatment, adoption, termination of the legal parent-child relationship, appointment of a guardian, delinquency, children in need of supervision, and determination of the legal custody of a child (Costin, 1991). Juvenile courts typically do not have jurisdiction over the custody of children involved in divorce actions, and in some states adoption can be granted without the juvenile court's attention.

In states that have family court systems, some of the juvenile court responsibilities have been combined with those of divorce courts to unify services to families and children. Family courts often have jurisdiction over children alleged to be dependent, neglected, or in need of supervision; delinquent children; couples seeking a divorce, especially when child custody must be decided; financial support, visitation, and paternity; and adoption. Civil, not criminal, law guides family court.

A brief review of the American legal system, as provided here, can merely outline its general structure. Complexities become more apparent as we delve into children's specific interactions with the legal system.

THE ROLES OF PSYCHOLOGICAL EXPERTS IN THE COURTS

What roles do psychologists typically play in court proceedings? Next we discuss several common roles and some of the ethical issues they pose (for further information, see Melton et al., 1987).

Types of Roles

Most witness testimony is restricted to information "known to the senses" (i.e., based on perception). In contrast, there is a well-established tradition for expert witnesses to testify about their professional opinions. This tradition has contributed to developmentalists, especially those with clinical training, playing several roles in legal proceedings concerning children.

Experts can serve as evaluators who examine one or more of the parties in question. Some experts who serve as evaluators make specific recommendations on the "ultimate issues" before the court. (The ultimate issue in a case refers to the main charge or decision to be made in the legal proceeding, for example, whether a child was sexually abused, whether a specific parent should be given custody, whether parental rights should be terminated.) Other experts serving as evaluators take the more conservative route of providing the court with information relevant to the ultimate issue but without drawing conclusions or formulating recommendations. Instead, the trier of fact is left to interpret how the information provided by the expert connects with the ultimate issue.

Psychologists (especially academics) also serve as theoretical experts. In this capacity, the role of the expert is mainly an educative one. Testimony is offered about current psychological theory and research on topics related to the questions before the court. Typically, the expert provides nomothetic information, that is, information about normative group data. Such testimony is routinely sought for many reasons (e.g., to counter the misrepresentation of psychological theory and research offered by other professionals, to offer the court different perspectives to consider in reaching a decision regarding the ultimate issue). Such testimony is not as controversial as ultimate-issue testimony, although different interpretations of the scientific or clinical literature can lead to dispute.

Psychologists also serve a theoretical and educative role when they adopt a "friend of the court" position and submit, with the help of attorneys, an amicus brief on the psychological foundation of the various legal positions the court is considering. The American Psychological Association has taken on this role in several important cases, including ones concerning the right of adolescents to seek abortion without parental consent and of traumatized child-abuse victims to be sheltered from face-to-face confrontation in criminal court (e.g., Goodman, Levine, Melton, & Ogden, 1991). Given the adversary system, it is quite possible for different psychologists to write amicus briefs for opposing sides.

In addition, psychologists can serve as mediators whose goal is to help the parties in a dispute reach a decision regarding the issues before the court and avoid the necessity of a costly and acrimonious trial. This role is especially likely in divorce cases when child custody is at issue, although mediation can also take place in other types of legal proceedings.

Expert Testimony

The courts have a surprisingly low standard for what constitutes expertise. Basically, anyone whose knowledge or experience goes beyond that of the common lay juror can in principle be deemed an expert. Moreover, the courts require only that the admission of expert opinion leads marginally to a better understanding of the evidence in a case (Melton, 1994).

Expert testimony may be provided in several kinds of legal proceedings, such as criminal prosecutions, juvenile court proceedings, child custody litigation, termination of parental rights, civil suits, and sentencing hearings (e.g., see Myers et al., 1989). In juvenile and family courts, more leeway is given to experts than in criminal cases. When the best interests of the child rather than criminal responsibility are at issue, courts are more receptive to expert opinion (Berliner, in press).

In most states, the Federal Rules of Evidence (FRE) frame the admissibility of expert evidence, especially in criminal proceedings. For example, FRE 702 permits admission of a qualified expert's opinion if based on specialized knowledge that will assist the trier of fact. However, in addition to the FRE, a recent U.S. Supreme Court decision in *Daubert v. Merrell Dow Pharmaceuticals* (1993) is leading to the adoption of new standards. The *Daubert* decision emphasizes the reliability of expert information (e.g., is the knowledge reasonably relied on in the field of science? Are the methods falsifiable?), the relevance of the information (e.g., are the findings generalizable to the situation at hand?), and legal sufficiency (e.g., is the testimony more probative than prejudicial?). Research relevant to the *Daubert* decision is beginning and may aid the courts in deciding whether or not to retain the new standards.

As can be inferred, the types of legal proceedings in which experts testify are diverse and the psycholegal questions posed can be quite complex, requiring experts to understand both the legal issues involved and the relevant research base.

Ethical Issues and Expert Testimony

Although psychologists play a number of different roles in legal proceedings, psychologists' interactions with the legal system are not above controversy. Ethical concerns surrounding expert testimony include lack of scientifically accepted theories and methods, lack of impartial testimony, inadequacy of procedures for selecting experts, prejudicial impact of expert testimony, distortion of the limits of expertise, and battles of the experts. Professional ethics place a higher standard on psychologists than does the law (APA, 1994; Golding, 1991). For these reasons and others, psychologists face numerous ethical decisions when asked to serve as experts.

One of the most frequently discussed ethical issues concerns expert testimony about ultimate issues. Should an expert take a position and make a specific recommendation regarding the crucial issues in a case? Many psychological commentators argue that psychologists should not testify as to the ultimate legal issue (Melton & Limber, 1989, but see Myers et al., 1989). Ultimate issues are traditionally matters that are up to the trier of fact to determine. Moreover, it is unclear that psychological findings are strong enough to make ultimate issue predictions, placing experts who testify to ultimate issues in ethically awkward positions. However, some courts have permitted this kind of expert testimony, especially when the opinion is linked to a specific child.

Another ethical issue concerns "dual role" relationships. A not uncommon type of dual role relationship occurs when a clinician who is treating a child is then asked to conduct a forensic examination of the child. As a clinician, the psychologist may view him- or herself as an advocate for the child's mental health; as a forensic interviewer, the psychologist must be as objective as possible. A role conflict and biased expert opinion can result. Generally, it is recommended that psychologists avoid such conflicts of interest. They can be largely avoided by taking on one role only.

Ethical concerns have also been raised about the misuse of psychological tests in the court and the misrepresentation of psychological knowledge. In the past, some experts have testified that children's play with anatomically detailed dolls constitutes a test of whether or not the child was sexually abused or that the MMPI can accurately determine whether a defendant is a child abuser. Partly as a result of the ignoring of standards set for psychological tests, some courts have ruled against introduction of certain types of information in cases concerning children's welfare (e.g., in California, information about sexual abuse gained from children's play with anatomically detailed dolls; see *in re Amber B,* 1987).

Expert testimony can be lucrative. Concerns are rightly voiced about experts becoming "hired guns," whose opinions are influenced by the party paying the bill. Even when an expert is not being paid (directly or indirectly), bias can result from an expert's oversympathisizing with a cause or a party in a case.

The ethical issues that constrain psychologists may be very different from the ethical issues that guide attorneys, an example of paradigms in conflict. Attorneys are trained to believe that the accused deserves the best defense possible, even if the defendant is guilty. The attorney may try to seek a psychologist who will serve that goal, even if biased expert testimony could result. A psychologist may have to decide whether to testify in a case on behalf of the defense even if the defendant is most likely guilty. Should a psychologist testify on behalf of someone who might be a murderer or child abuser? If one takes the position that the expert's job is to communicate what is known based on the extant scientific and clinical literature and that it is then up to the trier of fact (not the expert) to use that information to determine guilt, some professionals argue that testifying for either side of a case can be justified as long as biased testimony is not given. Certainly, a psychologist's personal moral values may influence how she or he feels about serving as an expert under such circumstances.

Several proposals have emerged for alternative approaches to introduction of expert testimony, but each has its pitfalls. Appointment of "neutral" experts by the courts, as occurs in Europe's inquisitorial legal systems, has been proposed as a way to eliminate hired-gun testimony (Myers et al., 1989). However, it is unclear how courts would determine an expert's neutrality. Moreover, fears have been expressed that jurors will overbelieve court-appointed experts, who would carry an implicit endorsement by the courts. However, overbelief in a court-appointed expert may be less of a problem than jurors not processing information as well when it is presented by a neutral expert rather than by opposing experts (Brekke, Enko, Clavet, & Seelau, 1991; Goodman-Delahunty, 1997).

Another creative proposal involves the establishment of an "amicus institute," through which psychologists and others would provide expertise to the courts in amicus briefs and expert testimony. One of many problems with such proposals is the possible bias in selection of professionals associated with such institutes. Most experimental psychologists who testify and consult in criminal cases do so for the defense (Kassin, Ellsworth, & Smith, 1989). Depending on the scientific atmosphere, the neutrality of such institutes and the slant of the research base can be seriously questioned. Especially on topics for which there is still considerable debate, the courts need to hear opposing views. Such is the nature of our legal system.

ORGANIZATION OF THE CHAPTER

We now turn to a review of the developmental and legal literatures relevant to each area of concern. We begin with custody issues raised by parental separation or divorce because, of the topics discussed here, divorce affects the most children. Next, child maltreatment is addressed. This topic is covered in some detail because the forensic issues are particularly complex, involving both juvenile and criminal court. A discussion of foster care and adoption follows the section on child maltreatment because these procedures may result from interventions for child abuse as well as from other sources of family disruption or loss. Regardless of topic, our concern is with the ways in which developmental knowledge is or can be applied to the legal arena. In each section, we will review relevant literature, point out areas of controversy, and draw implications for policy and practice. In each, we will be concerned with the balance of child, family, and state rights, paying particular attention to children's best interests.

Although certain general themes underlie this chapter, some issues that arise in each section are necessarily unique (e.g., joint custody in divorce cases, investigation and criminal court involvement in child maltreatment cases, and kinship placements in foster care cases). Scientific methodologies used to explore specific issues vary as well, although most of the topics impose important limits on the scientific approaches that may be employed. Researchers cannot, for example, randomly assign children to divorced versus nondivorced groups or to maltreated versus nonmaltreated groups, which means that variables are often confounded. For some topics, random assignment and control conditions are possible (e.g., when studying nonabused children's suggestibility), but then ecological validity may have to be sacrificed.

CHILD CUSTODY FOLLOWING SEPARATION AND DIVORCE

Divorce rates escalated dramatically from the late 1960s through the early 1980s, and they have remained at a stable but high level into the 1990s. Current projections indicate that approximately half of all children born to married parents will experience their parents' divorce before the children reach the age of 18 (Cherlin, 1992). Most divorcing parents negotiate a settlement out of court either on their own or with the aid of attorneys and/or a mediator (Maccoby & Mnookin, 1992). Still, the increase in divorce rates has multiplied the number of cases seen in family courts for pre- or postdivorce litigation, and changes in divorce law have greatly complicated both informal negotiations and formal litigation for this unprecedented number of disputing families.

Developmental, child clinical, and family psychologists have played and continue to play central roles in legal issues related to divorce. Much of the involvement of psychologists stems from societal concerns about the mental health of children from divorced families. Therefore, developmental research or expert opinion regarding the emotional well-being of children has often been used by policymakers, judges, and lawyers to help them fashion or apply the laws governing divorce. Psychologists have used research to help (a) shape new legal standards for divorce and custody settlements by consulting with legislative, judicial, and administrative branches of government; (b) promote alternative methods for resolving divorce disputes in courtrooms and in broader jurisdictions; and (c) provide expert opinion either formally in court or informally in consultation with attorneys, sometimes by directing the assessment of individual children and families and in other cases by offering more general information about psychological research.

In the present overview, we only briefly address the last issue, expert testimony, especially individual custody evaluations, even though this is one of the more common roles for psychologists to play in divorce disputes. Our decision to cover custody evaluations in a limited way reflects the very small amount of research actually conducted on custody evaluations and the limited applicability of more basic research on divorce to the custody evaluation context. Developmental research typically deals with groups, not individuals, and the relevance of normative evidence can always be questioned when it is applied idiographically in evaluating individual children or families. In fact, one can question whether psychologists should be involved in performing custody evaluations, given the uncertain application of scientific knowledge and some of the potentially adverse consequences of custody trials for children and families (Emery & Rogers, 1990). Individual cases also receive only passing attention here, because specific judicial determinations set weak precedents in the divorce area. Divorce statutes give judges wide discretion in evaluating each case on its individual merits, thus case law often is of limited relevance to subsequent divorce disputes. In contrast, legal policies and procedures are designed to apply to divorcing families as a group; thus group research on children and divorce is directly relevant to the primary focus of our discussion.

Our overview of developmental research and legal issues in divorce begins with an examination of the *substantive law* regulating divorce; that is, laws pertaining to the content of divorce disputes. We consider past and present rules related to the grounds for divorce and the appropriate settlement of financial and child-rearing disputes. Next, we highlight the implications of both basic and applied developmental research for substantive divorce law. We survey findings on the psychological consequences of divorce for children, key predictors of risk and resilience, and applied developmental issues such as the adjustment of children living in joint versus sole custody. Following this discussion, we consider *procedural law* in the divorce area (i.e., methods used to resolve divorce disputes). Much of this analysis focuses on how traditional legal procedures can increase family conflict in divorce, apparently to the detriment of children. As an alternative to traditional legal procedures, we highlight divorce mediation, a new, more cooperative method for resolving divorce disputes. Finally, we conclude the section by raising a few controversies related to children, divorce, and the law.

The Substantive Law in Divorce: Legal Terminology

When a couple with children ends their marriage, they must negotiate how they will share and divide their family's financial and child-rearing resources and functions. American family law addresses three substantive area of the couple's financial relationship—property division, spousal support, and child support—and two child-rearing commitments—custody and visitation. Family law is controlled by the individual states, not the federal government, and legal standards and terminology can differ substantially between them. Nevertheless, almost all state laws address these five central issues (Freed & Walker, 1986).

Property division involves (a) defining which items of a couple's belongings are individual assets (e.g., an inheritance) or joint assets (e.g., a family home), and (b) deciding how to allocate joint assets between the partners. *Spousal support* is the transfer of money from the partner with higher income to the partner with lower income for the purposes of that partner's support for a fixed or indefinite period of time. *Child support* is money transferred from one parent to the other for the purposes of supporting a minor child or children. In research and in practice, psychologists have paid relatively little attention to these financial aspects of divorce, except for some passing consideration of the highly visible contemporary issue of child support. This neglect is unfortunate, because some evidence indicates that postdivorce living standards are related to children's subsequent psychological well-being. In any case, data demonstrate that children's income relative to needs declines substantially as a result of divorce. In fact, many children move into poverty as a result of divorce, an outcome that obviously is of great concern to psychologists as well as others. It also is clear that child support alone cannot maintain children's standard of living at predivorce levels. Finally, other financial aspects of divorce settlements should be of interest to psychologists. For example, some elements of property division can create major changes for children, such as selling the family home.

In contrast to their inattention to financial matters, developmental and child clinical psychologists (along with other social scientists) have focused considerable empirical and clinical attention on the legal issues of custody and visitation. *Custody* incorporates a general designation both of primary parental authority and of primary residence. *Visitation* refers to the time children spend with the noncustodial parent. The terms custody and visitation are often ill-defined in legislation and used vaguely in legal practice. For example, it has been common for judges to make a determination such as "sole custody to the mother and liberal rights of visitation to the father," but this ruling is unclear with respect to parents' day-to-day sharing of time and parental authority. Similarly, it often is unclear what parental rights are lost or retained by a noncustodial parent, although losing custody does not imply losing *all* parental rights. (All parental rights are *terminated* only in very unusual circumstances, e.g., following prolonged and severe abuse or neglect.) Some parents also view the terms custody and visitation as pejorative. For example, the idea of "visiting" one's own children may seem to diminish the parent-child relationship.

Because of these problems, more specific and palatable terms have been coined in recent years. In this chapter, we frequently use alternative terms that have been adopted in some legislation and increasingly are used in practice by legal professionals. In particular, we use the term *legal custody* to refer to a parent's legal responsibility for a child's upbringing and his or her authority to make major decisions about a child's upbringing; for example, religious training or a choice of schools. *Physical custody* refers to the child's actual residential arrangements.

Although they are an improvement, the terms legal and physical custody can be ambiguous with respect to their specific legal implications or their application in an individual case. In fact, many professionals urge and help parents to write separation agreements that contain many more specific details to avoid the apprehension and conflict created by ambiguity. Such details may include very specific times for when children will reside with each parent (including holidays and vacations), precise times and methods for making changes between residences, lists of the child-rearing decisions that parents will share (e.g., choice of schools), details about how parents will communicate informally to coordinate parenting across two households, and formal procedures for resolving more serious conflicts as they arise (Emery, 1994). In fact, some state laws now require parents to address such topics by drafting detailed *parenting plans* as a part of their divorce agreement (Ellis, 1990; Freed & Walker, 1991).

Historical Overview

Divorce law has evolved considerably over time, and today's legal changes are a part of these broad, historical trends. Two key historical developments are (a) the regulation and the deregulation of marriage and divorce, and (b) changes in custody standards, particularly over the past century. European practices are the focus of this overview, because American law is rooted in English traditions. Still, different countries and cultures vary considerably in terms of their past and present legal regulations, and in terms of their accepted social practices, regarding marriage, childbearing, and divorce.

The Regulation of Marriage and Divorce

European marriage once involved only a private contract between two family groups, but marriage came under civil control and divorce was outlawed during the Middle Ages, largely due to the influence of the Roman Catholic Church (Eekelaar, 1991). The Catholic Church prohibited (and still prohibits) divorce, and the civil control of divorce remained strict even after the Reformation. Civil and some religious control over marriage and divorce were thus transported to the American Colonies from the time they were founded (Halem, 1981). The law in most colonies, and eventually in the states, held that divorce could be granted only if an offense occurred; that is, if there was a finding of "fault." Typically, adultery, desertion, and extreme cruelty were the only acceptable grounds for divorce, and the law often made it more difficult for a husband than a wife to be found at fault (Eekelaar, 1991; Grossberg, 1985).

The regulation of divorce in the United States became less strict throughout the first half of the 20th century, as the judiciary used increasingly broad interpretations of existing fault grounds (Plateris, 1974). The passage of "no-fault" divorce laws in all 50 states in the 1970s and 1980s dramatically altered legal regulations as well as judicial practices. The option of fault divorce has been retained in some states, but no-fault divorces are far more common even when fault is an option. A no-fault divorce is granted when both spouses request it, and/or when the spouses have lived apart for a fixed period of time—generally 6 months or a year (Freed & Walker, 1991). In a broad sense, no-fault laws mean that divorce has been largely deregulated. Contemporary divorce in the United States is essentially a private matter, except when a couple disputes the terms of a settlement and brings this dispute to the attention of a court. In terms of the themes raised at the beginning of the chapter, in the area of divorce, the family has gained increased autonomy from the state.

Although we focus on divorce in this chapter, marriage also has been deregulated across history and especially in recent social practices. As indicated, European marriages were once arranged by family groups, not the marriage partners, and marriages are still arranged by parents in many cultures today (e.g., India). Romantic marriage and the nuclear family replaced this traditional practice in the West, probably as a result of changes in family roles brought about by industrialization (Grossberg, 1985; Halem, 1981). Recent demographic trends indicate further changes in social practices, as a substantial and increasing number of people in the United States and Western Europe are cohabiting and/or bearing children outside marriage (Cherlin, 1992). In the United States, the *majority* of African American children are now born outside marriage, and cohabitation and nonmarital childbirth are increasing rapidly among Whites (Cherlin, 1992; Hernandez, 1993). One pattern that demographers have detected only recently is a rise in the number of cohabiting partners who marry sometime *after* a child is born (Bumpass & Raley, 1993).

The decline in marriage creates major challenges for family law, because many legal assumptions about a couple's obligations to each other and their children flow out of the marriage contract. Contemporary changes in cohabitation and childbearing have caused debates to flare about such topics as whether support obligations are incurred in cohabiting relationships ("palimony"), whether a mother should identify the father of their child at birth, and whether priority in child custody belongs to a child's birth or "social" parents (e.g., stepparent, adoptive parent, or partner of a gay parent). Clear legal policies have yet to be developed with respect to most of these issues. (The issues have been complicated further by innovations in medical technology such as in vitro fertilization and genetic testing for paternity.) The abandonment of clear, but sometimes objectionable, principles in favor of vaguer guidelines is an overriding theme of family law in the United States in the past two decades. The following overview of changes in child custody rules over Western history provides an example of this trend from specific to much more general rules governing divorce and divorce settlements.

Past and Present Custody Standards

For most of Western history, fathers had the legal authority to retain custody of their children following divorce. *Chattel rules* in common law gave men control over their property—their children—from Roman times through the Middle Ages (Derdeyn, 1976). Men's control over their families had diminished considerably but was still generally acknowledged in custody law into the 19th century. However, a new custody standard, the *tender years presumption,* began to emerge during this time, perhaps as a result of the specialized family roles created by industrialization (Grossberg, 1985). The standard asserted that children of "tender years" were best cared for by their mothers. From the late 1800s through the middle of the 20th century, the age range viewed as encompassing children's tender years expanded gradually from infancy upward to include adolescence. By the 1960s, the presumption of father custody based on men's property rights had been completely replaced by a presumption of mother custody based on the tender years doctrine (Weiss, 1979). The only exceptions to the preference for maternal custody occurred when mothers were found to be at fault for the divorce or if they were deemed "unfit." Questions of fitness could be based on severe maternal impairments such as schizophrenia, but they often turned on questions of conventional morality, particularly sexual practices (Weitzman, 1985).

Societal changes in women's roles and questions of sex discrimination caused the tender years presumption to be removed from formal legislation in the 1970s and 1980s. The standard that took its place was the *best interests test,* the doctrine that determinations of child custody should be based solely on children's future best interests. The best interests test actually developed in the early part of the 20th century as an outgrowth of the parens patriae role of juvenile courts (Grossberg, 1985). For most of the century, however, mother custody was assumed to be in children's best interests, as asserted by the tender years presumption.

The "Best Interests" Test and Some of its Problems. As currently defined, the best interests test is a vague principle. For example, 44 states (Freed & Foster, 1991) have adopted the guidelines outlined in the Uniform Marriage and Divorce Act [9(a) U.L.A. 91 (1976)], but this act offers only the following broad rules for determining a child's best interests: (a) The wishes of the child's parents as to custody; (b) the wishes of the child as to custody; (c) the interaction and interrelationship of the child with the parents, the siblings, and any person who may significantly affect the child's best interest; (d) the child's adjustment to home, school, and community; (e) the mental and physical health of all individuals involved.

The vagueness of the best interests standard in contemporary law is a product of objections that have been raised about the prejudicial nature of more determinative principles (e.g., sex discrimination). Although more general guidelines are able to accommodate diversity in a pluralistic society, problems arise from indeterminate legal principles. Law professor Robert Mnookin (1975) foresaw many of the difficulties when he argued that the indeterminant nature of the best interests test (a) encourages litigation by making the outcomes of custody contests uncertain; (b) increases acrimony between warring parents, as almost any derogatory evidence may be deemed relevant to a custody hearing; (c) opens the door for bias in the exercise of judicial discretion; and (d) limits appellate review because of vague judicial guidelines.

In addition to creating these important, practical dilemmas, there are even more basic problems with the best interests test. First, there is little evidence that even highly skilled experts can predict the future development of children based on a choice between one or another parent in an individual case, another reason for our limited discussion of custody evaluations in this chapter (Emery & Rogers, 1990). Second, even if reliable prediction were possible, the potential debates about what alternative futures are "best" would involve difficult value judgments (Mnookin, 1975). Is it better for a child to live with a strict parent who will encourage achievement but offer less nurturance, or with a warm parent who will be loving but more lax?

Because of these problems, legal scholars and developmentalists have searched for new standards that might offer more clarity in determining custody following divorce. Joint custody is the alternative that has received the most attention recently, although we consider some other new proposals for custody standards toward the end of this section.

Joint Custody

All the custody standards discussed to this point assume that one parent must be awarded custody following divorce, or more accurately, that one parent must lose custody, since both parents share custody in marriage. *Joint custody* is an alternative proposal that allows both parents to retain custody following divorce. Consistent with distinctions in terminology discussed earlier, many commentators and some state laws distinguish between joint *legal* custody (shared parental rights and responsibilities) and joint *physical* custody (approximately equal time in each parent's home).

Considerable academic and legal debate has focused on joint custody, and statutes in at least 41 states address the issue (Folberg, 1991). Disparities between different states in their statutory and/or case law reflect the many opposing contemporary views about joint custody. A few states discourage joint custody or allow it only under certain circumstances (e.g., when parents agree to the arrangement); other states encourage joint custody, and a few states allow judges to award joint custody even when parents object to it; most state statutes simply define joint custody and allow it as an option (Folberg, 1991). As we discuss shortly, the findings of developmental research on joint custody are not sufficiently clear or powerful to cause the option to be either widely embraced or abandoned.

Consequences of Divorce for Children

Research on the consequences of divorce for children is of considerable importance to contemporary legal policies and their application in the courtroom. Research on the average or typical consequences of divorce is pertinent to questions about the extent to which marriage and divorce should be regulated, because society has an interest in promoting the well-being of children. Research on the extent to which postdivorce family relationships serve as risk or protective factors is relevant to the law in determining preferred custody arrangements, financial settlements, and procedural matters in divorce. Finally, some social science research has been conducted with the explicit intention of informing divorce law and social policy; for example, by comparing children reared in joint versus sole physical custody. Thus, in this section we note both normative patterns and individual differences in reviewing research related to (a) the adjustment of children from divorced families; (b) interparental conflict, ineffective parenting, and economic hardship as predictors of risk; and (c) research relating children's emotional well-being to mother versus father custody, contact with the nonresidential parent, joint physical custody, and joint legal custody. Because so much developmental, child clinical, and demographic research has been conducted on these topics, our review relies primarily on summaries of the literature rather than on the details of original reports.

The Adjustment of Children from Divorced Families

Concern about the psychological consequences of divorce for children has been at the center of past and ongoing debates concerning whether social policies should make it easier or more difficult for parents to divorce. The concern is embodied in the frequently asked question: "Should parents stay together for the children's sake?"

Many developmental studies have been conducted on children's experience of divorce. A strong conclusion from this body of research is that divorce is not an event, but a *process* that unfolds over a long period of time (Hetherington, Cox, & Cox, 1982; Wallerstein & Kelly, 1980). All investigators agree that, although a separation or divorce sometimes is a relief, the 2-, 3-, or 4-year process of transition is emotionally wrenching for children and parents. Among the key sources of distress are conflicts in the family prior to a separation and following divorce that are trying not only for parents but also for children who are exposed to or caught up in their parents' disputes (Cummings & Davies, 1994; Emery, 1982; Grych & Fincham, 1990). Family life also is disrupted substantially by the physical separation, and children's sense of security is undermined further by subsequent changes in parent-child relationships, including dramatically reduced contact with one parent and, typically, less adequate parenting on the part of both parents (Fauber, Forehand, Thomas, & Wierson, 1990; Hetherington et al., 1982; Wallerstein & Kelly, 1980). Finally, the increased costs associated with living in two households create financial worries and many practical adjustments for all family members. Some of the practical consequences of financial hardship may include changes in residence, increases in parents' work hours, and increased time in child care (Duncan & Hoffman, 1985).

Evidence indicates that the psychological functioning of most children and parents improves as time passes and the family adjusts to divorce (Hetherington, 1989, 1993). Still, a large body of developmental research has examined the lasting psychological problems that might be found among children from divorced families. These investigations have found a range of difficulties including anxiety, depression, low self-esteem, and troubles relating to members of the opposite sex, although externalizing behavior problems are found most consistently (Amato & Keith, 1991; Emery, 1982, 1988). Far fewer studies have searched for psychological *strengths* among children from divorced families (Barber & Eccles, 1992). Most reviews of the empirical literature conclude, however, that although significantly more problems are found among children from divorced than married families, the difference is modest in magnitude

(Atkeson, Forehand, & Rickard, 1982; Chase-Lansdale & Hetherington, 1990; Emery, 1982, 1988; Furstenberg & Cherlin, 1991; Seltzer, 1994a). A meta-analysis of 92 studies of divorce found that, when all studies were combined across all measures of outcome, an average effect size of only .14 standard deviation units distinguished the psychological adjustment of children from divorced and married families (Amato & Keith, 1991).

Despite the rather consistent conclusions of qualitative and quantitative reviews, social scientists continue to disagree about the extent of psychological problems found among children from divorced families. Disagreements are especially prominent in discussions of the legal and policy implications of empirical research, as interpretations sometimes appear to reflect contrasting political agendas (Amato, 1993, and commentaries; Popenoe, 1993, and commentaries). However, disagreements also appear to be related to different research methods: Case studies tend to conclude that children of divorce have the most emotional problems; developmental research on select samples tends to find an intermediate range of difficulties; and demographic studies tend to uncover the fewest problems. As an illustration of this pattern, based on a series of extensive case studies of divorced families, Judith Wallerstein and Sandra Blakeslee (1989) concluded, "Almost half of the children entered adulthood as worried, underachieving, self-deprecating, and sometimes angry young men and women" (pp. 298–299). Mavis Hetherington (1989) concluded from one of her empirical, multimethod, longitudinal studies, "Children in the long run may be survivors, losers, or winners of their parents' divorce or remarriage" (p. 13). Sociologists Paul Allison and Frank Furstenberg (1989) concluded from their demographic study of a national sample, "The proportion of variation in the outcome measures that could be attributed to marital dissolution was generally quite small, never amounting to more that 3%" (p. 546). These illustrations are anecdotal; however, an empirical meta-analysis demonstrated that smaller effect sizes are found when studies were rated as higher in methodological quality (Amato & Keith, 1991).

It can be argued that conclusions about the consequences of divorce for children should not be based solely on studies deemed to be of the highest methodological quality (Emery & Coiro, in press; Emery & Forehand, 1994). Rather, cases histories, observational studies, and population surveys each may reveal different, perhaps unique, information about the psychological consequences of divorce for children. The contrasting results and interpretations can be captured by the term *resilience,* although this construct is defined with care and caution. The resilience interpretation incorporates several findings from research on children and divorce:

1. Children encounter a wide range of emotional, relationship, and economic stressors before and after divorce, as documented by all research traditions.
2. Although divorce is a risk factor, only a small minority of children experience notable psychological problems as a result of divorce, a finding documented in research on national samples.
3. Considerable individual differences in children's outcomes are attributable to how families manage the process of divorce, as has been demonstrated by multimethod developmental research.
4. As suggested by case studies, even successful coping with divorce often leaves children with painful memories, strained relationships, and persistent regrets that are not easily measured using more objective measures.

The resilience perspective indicates that most children successfully cope with divorce, but coping often extracts an emotional cost (Emery & Coiro, in press; Emery & Forehand, 1994).

Prospective Research on Children and Divorce. Recent findings underscore another caution in interpreting research comparing children from divorced and married families that is relevant to legal issues in divorce. A handful of prospective studies have found that many of the psychological problems evidenced by children from divorced families are present *before* their parents separate (Block, Block, & Gjerde, 1986; Cherlin et al., 1991; Doherty & Needle, 1991; Elliott & Richards, 1991). In these studies, many of the differences between children from married and divorced families were greatly diminished when differences in children's preseparation behavior were taken into account. These findings are consistent with the hypothesis that pathogenic family interaction begins before divorce, as well as with the alternative possibility that a common factor (e.g., parents' antisocial behavior; see McGue & Lykken, 1992) influences both selection into divorce and child maladjustment (Emery, Kitzmann, & Aaron, 1995). In either case, the prospective research demonstrates that many of the problems found among children from divorced families cannot be consequences of divorce, since the putative consequences precede divorce.

Should Parents Stay Together for the Children's Sake? What are the implications of the complicated body of research on children for the legal regulation of divorce? Certainly, there is no evidence of extensive mental health problems among children from divorced families, and, in fact, findings in the opposite direction are stronger. Most children cope successfully with divorce. In fact, it has been suggested that children may be harmed by overstatements about the mental health problems they can expect as a result of parental divorce. In contrast to psychological research, the popular media conveys persistently negative images about the emotional consequences of divorce for children (Forehand, 1992).

At the same time that we accept the weight of research evidence, we find it impossible to be sanguine about the consequences of divorce for children, particularly when viewed from a societal rather than an individual perspective. Before we embrace a policy of easy divorce, perhaps even of divorce "for the children's sake" to escape dysfunctional family interaction, we believe it is essential to raise and carefully consider three basic cautions. First, aggregate data mask important individual differences in outcome. Many of the same studies that found modest average differences in children's adjustment also consistently documented that children from divorced families are two to three times as likely to be referred for mental health treatment or to score beyond a clinical cutpoint on measures of child outcome (Hetherington, 1993; McLanahan & Sandefur, 1994; Zill, Morrison, & Coiro, 1993). It is important to know that most children cope successfully with divorce, but policymakers are legitimately concerned about a factor that doubles the risk of psychological treatment for children—especially when half of today's children are expected to encounter that risk.

Second, we again emphasize the costs of coping. Children are resilient in coping with divorce, but other evidence indicates that children are often resilient in the face of poverty or even when confronted with the horrors of the Holocaust (Garmezy, 1994). In these examples, we do not interpret children's successful coping as an indication that such terrible experiences are somehow acceptable. Divorce is a disruptive, unhappy, and unwanted life event for children. Resilience is not the same as invulnerability, and we need to be attuned to children's struggles in coping with divorce, particularly given the limited sensitivity of traditional empirical measures.

Third and most basically, we raise a caution about operationalizing children's "best interests" only in terms of their individual mental health. As reviewed in more detail in the following section, divorce causes many children to lose contact with their fathers, to develop troubled relationships with both of their parents, and to experience considerable economic hardship. Increased poverty and troubled relationships with parents are "bad" outcomes in their own right, whatever their psychological consequences for children. Thus, our major conclusion about policy and the regulation of divorce is this: It is time to shift the debate from its narrow focus on children's mental health to a much broader view of children's global emotional, social, and economic well-being.

Key Risk Factors for Children: Psychological Problems

Considerable developmental research has been conducted on individual differences in children's adjustment to divorce. Research on individual-level risk factors, such as children's age, gender, and temperament, has been of considerable interest to developmentalists. Debates continue to rage about whether divorce is more difficult for boys or girls, or for preschoolers, school-age children, adolescents, or young adults (Emery, 1988; Hetherington & Clingempeel, 1992; Wallerstein & Blakeslee, 1989; Zaslow, 1988, 1989). Most evidence on children's individual characteristics is only indirectly relevant to the law, however, because the individual-level characteristics are either fixed, difficult to change, or do not translate into acceptable social policy.

Ecological models of child development have encouraged researchers to examine risk and protective factors from broader social and community perspectives. Evidence indicates that children are buffered from some of the fallout of divorce when they have positive relationships with others, such as a supportive ethnic community, involved teachers, caring extended family members, or good sibling relationships (Emery & Forehand, 1994; Jenkins & Smith, 1990). As with individual-level factors, however, the law can influence social and community support only to a limited extent; thus, the implications for law and policy are limited for predictors of risk at this level of analysis.

Of much greater policy interest is research evidence on the traditional focus of the law: family factors that predict children's adjustment to divorce. In the following section, we review studies of the three most important and consistent family risk factors: interparental conflict, the quality of the child's relationship with the parent who has physical custody, and family finances. Later, we consider research on other aspects of family relationships of direct relevance to divorce law: mother versus father custody, frequency of contact with the nonresidential parent, joint physical custody, and joint legal custody.

Interparental Conflict and Divorce Policy. A large body of research on children's postdivorce adjustment indicates that high levels of conflict between parents in marriage and following divorce are associated with more psychological difficulties among children. Increasingly refined analogue and field studies point particularly to the risks associated with conflict that is prolonged, is openly angry or violent, focuses on or involves the child, and remains unresolved (for reviews, see Amato & Keith, 1991; Cummings & Davies, 1994; Emery, 1982, 1988; Erel & Burman, 1995; Grych & Fincham, 1990; Long & Forehand, 1987). Moreover, analogue evidence strongly implies that at least some of the relation is causal (Cummings & Davies, 1994; Emery, Fincham, & Cummings, 1992). Studies dating to the 1950s and 1960s, as well as more recent research, have indicated that conflict predicts children's maladjustment in married and divorced families, and that children fare better psychologically in a happy one-parent home than a conflict-ridden two-parent family (e.g., Forehand, McCombs, Long, Brody, & Fauber, 1988; Hetherington et al., 1982; McCord, McCord, & Thurber, 1962). Commentators have frequently referred to this evidence as contradicting the conventional wisdom to "stay together for the children's sake," suggesting that divorce can provide relief from a troubled family life for children as well as adults.

Cautions should be raised, however, in attempting to extrapolate from research on conflict as a risk factor to policies justifying divorce as an escape from conflict. First, conflict may not end, but increase and focus more on the children following divorce (Buchanan, Maccoby, & Dornbusch, 1991; Emery, Matthews, & Wyer, 1991). Second, consistent with the relief hypothesis, some recent, prospective evidence indicates that children adjust better following a divorce if their parents had high-conflict marriages. However, children fare *worse* after divorce if their unhappily married parents had low-conflict relationships (Amato, Loomis, & Booth, 1995). Third, even if a divorce allows parents and children to escape from conflict, there is no doubt that staying together benefits children in other ways, such as contributing to their economic well-being.

Parenting Difficulties and Divorce Policy. Extensive longitudinal research conducted by Mavis Hetherington (1989, 1991, 1993; Hetherington & Clingempeel, 1992; Hetherington et al., 1982), along with numerous additional studies (e.g., Capaldi & Patterson, 1991; Fauber et al., 1990; Forehand, Thomas, Wierson, Brody, & Fauber, 1990), have demonstrated that divorced mothers with physical custody have less adequate parenting skills than their married counterparts. Documented parenting difficulties include less affection, more problems with communication, less effective problem solving, less monitoring of children's activities, and greater inconsistencies in parent-child relationships. Problems also are found in the relationship between children and their residential or nonresidential fathers (e.g., Peterson & Zill, 1986; Zill et al., 1993), although fathering after divorce has been studied far less frequently than mothering.

Less adequate parenting is a risk factor associated with increased psychological problems among children from divorced families (Hetherington, 1989). Some evidence indicates, moreover, that parenting problems account for some of the relation between interparental conflict and children's behavior problems (Fauber et al., 1990). Prospective research indicates that some parenting difficulties are present before divorce, perhaps as a result of marital conflict prior to separation (Block et al., 1986; Shaw, Emery, & Tuer, 1993). There is no doubt, however, that loss of support and added demands associated with single parenting can contribute to emotional difficulties found among children.

Concerns about the parenting of divorced parents have influenced law and policy in at least two important ways. First, evidence on parenting abilities and children's psychological adjustment undoubtedly is used in custody evaluations designed to pick the better parent, a practice that we have already questioned and return to later in this chapter. A second effect of parenting research on policy is the development of education classes for divorced parents. The number of parent education classes offered in legal settings has grown rapidly in recent years, and attendance is encouraged or even made mandatory in some localities (but attendance is not mandatory according to any state law as of this time). The broad goals of these brief classes are to sensitize parents to their children's perspective on divorce, offer education about effective methods of postdivorce parenting (often including alternative physical custody arrangements), and encourage a degree of cooperation between divorcing parents.

Parenting classes have well-intentioned goals, and developmentalists can be heartened because much of the content of the programs is based on the literature cited in this chapter. However, empirical support is tenuous at best for the assertions made by some educational programs (e.g., the superiority of joint physical custody). In addition, the only current evidence of the effectiveness of the education programs is a handful of evaluation research studies that have found a high level of parent satisfaction with the programs (Devlin, Brown, Beebe, & Parulis, 1992; Kramer & Waho, 1993) but uncertain outcomes in terms of actually changing parents' behavior. There is a need to conduct randomized trials examining whether these brief and increasingly popular interventions actually do increase parents' knowledge about their children's perspective on divorce, alter parent-child relationships, improve coparenting, and ultimately facilitate children's adjustment to divorce.

Family Finances and Divorce Policy. Divorce inevitably creates financial strain, because it is cheaper to live in one than in two households. Straightforward analyses of living expenses indicate that, depending on their predivorce standard of living, families need 10% to 25% more income after divorce to maintain their same, predivorce lifestyle (Espenshade, 1979). Prospective, empirical research has demonstrated, moreover, that the economic hardship caused by divorce is experienced disproportionately by children living with single mothers. According to a careful analysis of a national sample, the income relative to needs of mothers and their children fell to 91% of its predivorce level in the year following divorce (Duncan & Hoffman, 1985). Moreover, whereas the income relative to needs of married families (and divorced fathers) rose 30% over the next 5 years, the low income of divorced women remained stable and below predivorce levels—unless they remarried, in which case it rose 25% (Duncan & Hoffman, 1985).

An early and influential review of the literature suggested that much, perhaps all, of children's psychological problems following divorce could be attributed to economic hardship (Herzog & Sudia, 1973). Several developmental researchers have since examined whether family income or other economic measures are associated with children's adjustment to divorce, but economic disadvantage typically accounts for only a small proportion of the variance in children's emotional well-being (Amato & Keith, 1991). Economic variables typically have not been assessed with great care by psychologists, however, and some research indicates the importance of a family's economic measures to certain child outcomes. In a study that used data from several different national surveys, McLanahan and Sandefur (1994) found that income disparities accounted for half of the increased risk for dropping out of school when comparing children from divorced and married families.

The law is greatly concerned with the financial aspects of divorce, as indicated in provisions regarding property, spousal support, and child support. Of these three areas, research has focused primarily on child support. The low dollar amount of support awards and the poor compliance of "deadbeat dads" paying child support as ordered has been well documented in the academic literature (Seltzer, 1994a), as well as in the popular media. According to 1989 census data, about two-thirds of divorced mothers had child support awards, about three-quarters of mothers who had awards received partial or complete support payments, and the average annual amount of support paid was $3,155 among those who received any support (Seltzer, 1994a).

Two additional empirical findings about child support have received far less popular attention, but they are important for policy. First, some evidence indicates that financial support from fathers is more important to children's psychological well-being than other, equal amounts of economic aid. This finding implies that increased paternal involvement with children is an important part of benefits produced by child support payments (Seltzer, 1994a). Second, despite the considerable focus on child support, income transfers do not and cannot restore single mothers and their children to predivorce income levels. Empirical evidence indicates that the combination of spousal and child support makes up only about 10% of the income of divorced women and their children on average (Duncan & Hoffman, 1985). This added income is important, and many mothers receive a far greater proportion of their income from child support and spousal support. Still, economies of scale, as well as disparities in men's and women's employment and earnings, mean that far more than the added cost of rearing children would have to be transferred from fathers to mothers with physical custody to maintain predivorce living standards for them and their children. There simply is no solution to the economic hardships that divorce (and nonmarital childbirth) cause for children and mothers other than extensive family allowances provided by the government, such as those found in some European countries (Furstenberg & Cherlin, 1991). At this time, such programs seem politically unrealistic for the United States.

Although economic problems are less powerful than parenting or conflict in accounting for children's psychological well-being after divorce, we reiterate two points: (a) postdivorce family economic status makes a substantial contribution to some central outcomes for children, particularly educational attainments (McClanahan & Sandefur, 1994) and (b) economic stability is important for children in its own right. As many as 25% of children move into poverty as a result of divorce (Nichols-Caseboth, 1986), and this outcome would seem to be of great concern to parents and policymakers. Policy debates and the developmental literature repeatedly emphasize the psychological problems of children of divorce. If this focus causes us to ignore the economic consequences of divorce, however, our approach may prove to be somewhat inaccurate, perhaps iatrogenic, and certainly myopic. The economic consequences of divorce are legitimate concerns in weighing the best interests of children, particularly from the perspective of the legal regulation of divorce and of parents' financial obligations to their children.

Research on Alternative Legal and Physical Custody Arrangements

In addition to the more basic research on divorce, a number of investigators have studied children's adjustment in alternative postdivorce legal and physical custody arrangements, often with the intention of informing policy. Four key areas of applied research are considered in this section: mother versus father custody, contact with nonresidential parents, joint physical custody, and joint legal custody.

Mother versus Father Custody. Whether children should be placed in the custody of their mother or father is often intensely debated in individual custody battles; it is a question that holds broader interest both for developmental theory and for social policy. The importance of fathers to children's social and emotional development has long been overlooked in developmental research, and to a lesser degree, the topic continues to be neglected (Parke, 1996; Phares & Compass, 1993). Research on divorce is no exception to the general dearth of research on fathers, although there are at least a handful of investigations. Warshak (1986) reviewed seven studies comparing children in mother and father custody homes and concluded that no study found differences in children's well-being attributable to the custody type per se. Several of the studies, however, found better adjustment when children were living in the custody of their same-sex parent (Gregory, 1965; Santrock & Warshak, 1979). A similar sex-of-parent by sex-of-child interaction has been reported in at least two additional studies not included in the review (Camara & Resnick, 1989; Peterson & Zill, 1986).

Implications for Policy and Practice. If boys fare better with their fathers after divorce, and girls with their mothers, such a finding would seem to have obvious implications for legal decision making. In fact, our anecdotal experience indicates that at least a few judges and custody evaluators have used data to justify same-sex custody placements in more than a few divorce disputes. To our knowledge, however, no formal policies indicating a custody preference for placing children with the same-sex parent have been adopted. For several reasons, we view the absence of policy based on the gender of child by gender of parent interaction with relief, just as we view the application of this evidence with concern. First, selection factors must be carefully considered in interpreting the results of these studies. Experience suggests that divorced fathers often are awarded custody of their sons when they are exceptionally good parents, but fathers are more likely to get custody of their daughters when the mother is particularly troubled. The interaction between gender of parent and gender of child would be obtained as a result of such a pattern of selection. Second, a recent investigation of a large national sample failed to find the expected interaction for any of 35 different outcome measures, thus raising serious doubts about the findings from past research on small, select samples (Downey & Powell, 1993). Third, there is a strong tendency in the law to keep sibling groups together, and at least some research indicates that sibling support is important to children's adjustment to divorce (Cowen, Pedro-Carroll, & Alpert-Gillis, 1990; Kempton, Armistead, Wierson, & Forehand, 1991). Gender-based custody determinations obviously would lead to splitting siblings in many families, a cost that would have to be carefully weighed against any benefit of gender matching. As such, we conclude that research on mother versus father custody fails to indicate that there should be an automatic preference for either parent based on gender, and the support is weak at best for a preference for placing children with their same-gender parent.

Contact with Nonresidential Parents. No relation, or only a weak one, has been found between father contact and children's adjustment in several studies that have used survey data from large national samples (Amato & Rezac, 1994; Baydar & Brooks-Gunn, 1991; Furstenberg, Morgan, & Allison, 1987; Peterson & Zill, 1986). In contrast, a number of studies of small or select samples report that children are better adjusted when they have more frequent contact with their nonresidential fathers, provided that a number of conditions hold. Moderating factors include the mental health of the nonresidential parent, whether the nonresidential parent-child relationship is positive, and the degree of conflict between parents (e.g., Camara & Resnick, 1989; Hetherington et al., 1982; Wallerstein & Kelly, 1980). Other evidence indicates that positive benefits are evident only when contact is consistent, especially when contact is frequent (Healy, Malley, & Stewart, 1990). Yet another study reported the provocative finding that frequency of nonresidential mother-child contact, but not nonresidential father-child contact, is related to more positive child adjustment (Zill, 1988).

Inconsistencies across studies are likely due in part to the number of variables that moderate the effects of contact between children and their nonresidential parents.

Under differing circumstances, more frequent contact may have positive, negative, or neutral effects on children's well-being. The number of moderating factors makes it difficult to draw firm conclusions from available evidence, but one inference is clear: Increased contact per se is not strongly related to measures of children's adjustment.

Two important caveats apply to this conclusion. First, we again raise a caution about interpreting null results. Evidence indicates that children value their relationships with their nonresidential fathers even when contact is infrequent (Maccoby, Buchanan, Mnookin, & Dornbusch, 1993). Commonly used measures may be inadequate in assessing more subtle emotions that children feel toward their absent fathers, such as feelings of anger or rejection, yearning or love. It also is possible that the consequences of infrequent contact may only surface during certain developmental periods. For example, children may be particularly likely to feel the loss of contact during their late adolescence when identity concerns cause them to reflect on the meaning of their troubled family relationships for their developing sense of self.

A second caveat is that father contact is quite infrequent on average in studies of national samples, a finding of great importance in its own right. Based on data from a recent survey of a national sample, for example, Seltzer (1991) found that, among fathers separated for 2 years or less, 12.8% had seen their children only once a year or less, while 42.7% saw them once a week or more. She also found that contact declines rapidly over time, particularly following the remarriage or relocation of one or both parents. Among fathers separated for 11 years or more, 50.4% had seen their children only once a year or less, while only 12.0% saw them once a week or more (Seltzer, 1991). In terms of children's well-being, it is possible that the positive effects of father contact may not be evident when contact is so infrequent. For example, the "high contact" group in the widely cited Furstenberg et al. (1987) study included fathers who saw their children as infrequently as 25 days per year. Advocates of joint physical custody assert that much more frequent contact is needed to benefit children, an issue we consider shortly.

Implications for Policy and Practice. The extent to which contact between children and each of their divorced parents should be promoted forms a central debate in legislative and case law, touching on issues ranging from laws for or against joint physical custody to cases where a parent with physical custody wants to relocate over the objections of the nonresidential parent. It is difficult to draw policy implications from the generally weak relation found between contact with the nonresidential parent and children's psychological adjustment. Both psychologists and legal professionals are reluctant to conclude that contact does not matter to children after divorce. Moreover, a positive relation has been found between the frequency of father contact and compliance with child support payments (Seltzer, 1994a). Still, more frequent contact with the nonresidential parent is a relatively *less* important predictor of children's psychological health than the quality of the residential parent-child relationship or the degree of interparental conflict. We therefore conclude that the law should encourage more contact between children and their nonresidential parents, but contact should be given relatively less weight than these other two factors. For example, children may benefit from less frequent contact when conflict is intense because of being exposed to less conflict under this arrangement.

Joint Physical Custody. A number of investigators have compared children living in joint versus sole physical custody families. Some investigators have found that joint physical custody is a better arrangement for children (Folberg, 1991; Maccoby et al., 1993), but others conclude that the arrangement can damage children, particularly when parental conflict is high (Johnston, Kline, & Tschann, 1989). Overall, it appears that joint physical custody is associated with somewhat more frequent nonresidential parent-child contact, increased parental cooperation, and somewhat better functioning among children. Differences between joint and sole custody families typically are small in magnitude, however, and selection factors suggest an important caution in interpreting existing research: Parents who chose joint physical custody differ from other parents (see Emery, 1988). As with research on father contact, the safest conclusion is that benefits of joint physical custody are relatively small and influenced by a number of moderating variables, particularly the degree of parental conflict (Maccoby et al., 1993). On the whole, evidence indicates that children fare somewhat better under joint than sole physical custody arrangements when parents can manage the degree of ongoing cooperation required by the arrangement.

Implications for Policy and Practice. The implications for policy are similar for joint physical custody and father contact. In general, the option should be encouraged but given less weight than decreasing conflict and supporting the central relationship between children and their residential parent. This conclusion indicates that joint physical custody is an unwise compromise for judges who must make a determination between parents who are disputing custody, because the legal dispute typically is an indication of the parents' inability to cooperate (Scott & Derdeyn, 1984). Still, only a small minority of divorcing parents actually have a court hearing, and these typically are the most contentious couples. Thus, whereas joint physical custody is unwise under circumstances of intense legal conflict, a dilemma for policymakers is that one angry parent can undermine another's good intentions of promoting positive relationships between children and both parents. To address this paradox, a number of states have adopted "friendly parent" rules, preferences for awarding sole custody to the more cooperative parent in contested cases (Folberg, 1991), but there is no research on whether such provisions succeed in promoting cooperation. Studies of this topic are needed.

Joint Legal Custody, Father Contact, and the Payment of Child Support. The concept of joint physical custody has received considerable popular attention, but it is an infrequent arrangement. The *highest* estimates indicate that 15% to 20% of parents elect joint physical custody in the states of California and Washington (Ellis, 1991; Maccoby & Mnookin, 1992). Far fewer parents have joint physical custody in other states—7% in a New Hampshire study (Racusin, Albertini, Wishik, Schnurr, & Mayberry, 1989) and 2% a study of Wisconsin families (Seltzer, 1991).

Joint *legal* custody is a far more common postdivorce parenting arrangement. In fact, joint legal custody is becoming normative in many states. In the same studies previously cited, nearly 80% of California families had joint legal custody (Maccoby & Mnookin, 1992), as did 69% of the Washington state families (Ellis, 1990), 65% in New Hampshire (Racusin, Albertini, Wishik, Schnurr, & Mayberry, 1989), and 20% in Wisconsin (Seltzer, 1990).

As noted earlier, the legal implications of joint legal custody are often vague. However, clinicians who work with divorcing parents point to the symbolic importance of joint legal custody as a means of acknowledging the parental role and maintaining a connection with children (Emery, 1994). Such symbolism may matter to parents' subsequent behavior; for example, fathers with joint legal custody maintain more contact with their children over time (Seltzer, 1994b; Wolchik, Braver, & Sandler, 1985). Evidence also indicates that, although joint legal custody may not affect the size of child support awards, it is related to the stability with which child support is paid over time (Pearson & Thoennes, 1988; Seltzer, 1994b).

Because of obvious ethical concerns, no randomized trials have been conducted on joint legal custody, so these findings may reflect selection influences instead of consequences of legal custody. Several investigators have found that parents with joint custody are more educated and have higher incomes than parents with sole custody (e.g., Donnelly & Finkelhor, 1993). Parents with joint legal custody also often are assumed to be more cooperative than other divorced parents. One study, however, found that background characteristics, including prospective measures of the quality of the partners' relationship during marriage, did *not* explain the positive effects of joint legal custody on postdivorce parenting (Seltzer, 1994b).

Implications for Policy and Practice. It can be argued that the policy implications of evidence on joint legal custody do not require the cautions and caveats raised about other issues, because joint legal custody carries few negative implications for divorced families or for the public (Emery, 1988). The precise meaning of joint legal custody could be defined more clearly in the law or in individual separation agreements, but the symbolic value of the arrangement appears to produce modest benefits for little or no cost. Contrary to some psychological arguments insisting that one parent must be given sole parental authority following divorce (Goldstein, Freud, & Solnit, 1973), we conclude, as a rule subject to exceptions, both parents should retain legal custody on divorce.

Legal Procedures and Children's Adjustment to Divorce

To this point, our overview of legal issues in divorce and custody has focused on the substance of the law, but legal procedures have also been an area for reform and a topic for developmental research. As mentioned earlier, the American legal system's method of dispute resolution, the basic foundation for legal procedures, is the adversary system. The philosophy of the adversary system is embodied in traditional legal procedures for resolving divorce disputes. Each parent is represented by a separate attorney who has the ethical responsibility to vigorously represent his or her client's individual interests. The children may also have their own representation, *guardians ad litem,* lawyer or nonlawyer advocates who represent children's interests in a custody dispute.

Lawyers may advise their clients against pursuing custody, counsel them to act cooperatively in coparenting their children, or offer other advice. Still, the lawyer's principal role is to act on the client's wishes, not to question his or her motivations. In one study, for example, only 19% of attorneys reported that they attempted to discourage their clients from seeking custody, even when they thought their client was not the better parent or when they believed their client was vindictive (Weitzman & Dixon, 1979). Guardians ad litem, in contrast, frequently adopt a less adversarial role. In pursuing the children's interests, guardians often act as mediators and encourage a cooperative settlement (Landsman & Minow, 1978).

As noted, most divorcing parents reach a custody agreement outside court. In a study of a large California sample, only 1.5% of custody cases were decided by a judge (Maccoby & Mnookin, 1992). Still, attorneys seek settlements that are to their clients' advantage, and they must be prepared to go to court if they cannot negotiate a settlement. In preparing for a hearing, each attorney develops evidence that favors her or his side and is damaging to the other side. Because of the indeterminant best interests standard, the historical influence of fault in determining custody, and interpretations of parental fitness in moral terms, "evidence" may include virtually any negative information on the opposing side, including the other parent's past or present sexual activities, religious practices, or lifestyle choices (Catania, 1992; Mnookin, 1975). Friends and relatives may be asked to testify for one parent and against the other, and mental health professionals may be hired as witnesses by one or both sides.

Divorce Mediation

Adversary procedures in custody disputes have been argued to be unnecessarily intrusive and divisive for parents, harmful to children, and expensive for both individual families and the state (Emery & Wyer, 1987). Numerous attempts have been made to change the very method of resolving divorce disputes by replacing adversary procedures with more cooperative ones. Divorce mediation is the most prominent of several new methods, and it has rapidly replaced and/or altered adversary practices in resolving divorce disputes throughout the country, particularly in relation to child custody (Emery, 1994).

Mediation is based on the assumption that cooperative negotiation can produce added benefits or so-called win-win outcomes (Axelrod, 1984). Divorced parents are not expected to be friends, but they are encouraged to develop a degree of cooperation in their ongoing, coparenting relationship (Emery, 1994). Philosophically, mediation assumes that divorced parents should be the experts who decide what is in their own children's best interests.

A number of studies have been conducted on divorce mediation, a practice that has grown rapidly in popularity during the 1980s and 1990s. Evidence indicates that mediation greatly reduces the need for custody hearings, somewhat reduces relitigation, increases compliance with court orders, and increases parents' satisfaction with the legal system (Emery, 1994; Kelly, 1990; Pearson & Thoennes, 1984). In contrast to these practical benefits, short-term follow-up research generally has not found clear psychological benefits of mediation for parents' mental health, children's mental health, or family relationships (Kelly, Gigy, & Hausman, 1988; Kitzmann & Emery, 1994; Pearson & Thoennes, 1984). However, some evidence indicates that fathers who mediate maintain more of their commitments to their children in terms of both physical contact and child support payments, and a pilot study suggests that this increased involvement is maintained over the course of 9 years (Dillon & Emery, 1996).

Implications for Policy and Practice. The policy implications of this research are clear, as is indicated by the rapid spread of mediation programs throughout the country. For example, the 11 states of Arizona, California, Delaware, Florida, Kentucky, Maine, Nevada, North Carolina, Oregon, Utah, and Wisconsin have all adopted legislation *mandating* the mediation of custody disputes in at least some of their jurisdictions (Hendricks, 1993–1994). There are continuing controversies about mediation such as whether it should be voluntary or mandatory, what types of legal and physical custody arrangements mediators should or should not advocate, and when mediation should be terminated or not attempted in the first place (Emery, 1994). Still, developmental evidence clearly supports the goal of reducing conflict and increasing cooperation between parents after divorce, and evidence indicates that mediation helps parents to take a step in this direction.

Current Controversies

Divorce law in recent years has evolved rapidly in response to changing demographics, social practices, and developmental evidence. Policies and individual cases have been the focus of considerable controversy, for example, a recent high-profile case in which a mother's employment contributed to an award of custody to the father. In this chapter, we have not focused on such cases, case law, or expert testimony for two basic reasons. First, as was just outlined briefly, an argument can be made that the adversarial resolution of divorce disputes is harmful to children. We believe, therefore, that legal and psychological professionals should direct the bulk of their efforts toward developing alternatives to adversary procedures and, to the extent it is politically feasible, supporting more determinative standards for resolving custody and other divorce disputes.

Second, as noted earlier we have not addressed case law, because precedent rarely is established through individual cases in the divorce arena. Judges are given broad discretion in deciding individual cases, and discretionary judgments are difficult to challenge (Mnookin, 1975). However, judicial decisions can be successfully challenged when opinions are based on general rather than individualized criteria such as explicitly awarding custody based on gender, race, sexual preference, or employment. Although, such generalizable judgments are precisely the sort that might set a precedent, this rarely happens because the statutory law requires individualized judicial decisions.

New Custody Standards?

A prominent example of a more determinative custody rule is the *primary caretaker parent standard* that has been discussed frequently in recent years. The rule states that the parent who was the primary caretaker of the children during the marriage is the preferred custodian after divorce. The rule is argued to be fair to parents who have assumed the child-rearing role in marriage. It also should remove the need for the extensive exercise of judicial discretion, and alleviate the problems that flow from indeterminant rules (Fineman, 1988). There is no doubt that the primary caretaker parent standard has the advantage of clarity, but some critics argue that it is little more than a return to the tender years presumption. Another criticism is that the primary caretaker standard perpetuates the traditional concepts of custody and visitation. In theory, a parent who was responsible for 51% of child-rearing during marriage would be the primary caretaker, and therefore entitled to sole custody following divorce (Scott, 1992).

A new custody standard that combines elements of joint custody and primary caretaker parent rules has been proposed by law professor Elizabeth Scott (1992). The *approximation rule* argues that postdivorce parenting arrangements should, as far as possible, approximate what existed during the marriage. A parent who took care of the children most of the time during marriage would continue to do so after divorce; two parents who were very involved in child-rearing during marriage would continue to share time and parental authority after divorce. Like the primary caretaker parent provision, the approximation rule looks backward in time to determine the future, but like joint custody, the rule envisions a range of possible postdivorce parenting arrangements. At face value, the proposal also seems fair to the divorcing partners and consistent for children, as it envisions both parents continuing with a similar level of involvement with the children. The approximation rule has not been implemented anywhere as a custody rule, but the new proposal strongly suggests the need for more research. Topics for research include such issues as the extent to which postdivorce parenting arrangements approximate predivorce arrangements under current custody laws, and the extent to which parenting involvement normally changes over the course of child development (e.g., when children transition into school or into adolescence).

Custody Evaluations by Mental Health Professionals

As noted, mental health professionals increasingly have become involved in custody disputes by conducting evaluations of children and one or both parents. Professionals who conduct custody evaluations have the task of determining what family factors are most important to the children's emotional well-being. As noted, however, there is little evidence that mental health professionals can reliably and validly predict how alternative family environments will affect the mental health of children in the individual case. This is especially true when there is not a major difference in the child rearing provided by two parents, precisely the circumstance in which custody is most likely to be disputed (Emery & Rogers, 1990). Moreover, we believe that the question of what arrangements are best for children is one that is better answered by parents, and if not parents, by policy, instead of by custody evaluators.

Further reasons for concern are raised by a look at some of the practices of psychologists who conduct custody evaluations. The tests that have been found to be administered most commonly in custody evaluations are the MMPI (71% of cases), the Rorschach (42%), the TAT (38%), the WAIS (29%), the Bender-Gestalt (12%), and projective drawings (6%) (Keilin & Bloom, 1986). Although the MMPI and WAIS can be helpful in evaluating the mental health of each parent, it seems dubious—even frightening—to contemplate the possible influences of projective test responses on custody determinations (Dawes, 1994). As an alternative, few instruments have been developed that purport to measure which parent is the preferred custodian (Ackerman, 1995). However, objective evaluation of these instruments finds them to be sorely lacking in terms of their psychometric properties (Otto & Butcher, 1995).

Despite the questionable reliability and validity of custody evaluations, the recommendations made by mental health professionals appear to have a strong influence on judicial dispositions. The influence may be so strong that evaluators often serve as *de facto* arbiters in custody cases. We view this as an unacceptable circumstance and offer two alternatives. First, evaluators can explicitly refrain from making a custody recommendation, and limit their testimony to their observations as a mental health professional. The role of decision making belongs to the judge in custody and other legal cases, not to the mental health expert (Monahan, 1980), and evaluators can refrain from making recommendations despite frequent judicial pressure to do so. Second, mental health professionals can explicitly assume the role of arbiter, as parents can stipulate that they will accept the mental health professionals' recommendation. This second possibility puts considerable responsibility into the hands of mental health professionals, but it offers a relatively less adversarial method of dispute resolution to parents who cannot decide custody on their own.

At present, perhaps what is needed most is more research on custody evaluations. Opportunities include descriptive research on the evaluations themselves, including the methods used, the content of reports, the recommendations made, and factors used to justify recommendations. More ambitious research would focus on the reliability and validity of custody evaluations, such as the extent of disagreement between impartial experts, the correspondence between recommendations and judicial determinations, parents' views on the evaluation process, and rates of relitigation.

Children's Custody Preferences

Children themselves may become involved in adversary custody proceedings, if they are asked to state a custody preference to an evaluator or testify to their preferences in court. There is some intuitive appeal in having children present testimony in proceedings about their future best interests, and psychological evidence has pointed to some benefits of having control over decisions in one's life that could be extrapolated to the custody context (Melton & Lind, 1982). The benefits of control are not ubiquitous, however, as research on learned helplessness has demonstrated. Attributions of internal control over positive events are related to better mental health, but attributions of internal control for negative events are associated with more mental health problems (Peterson & Seligman, 1983). Choosing between one's parents is likely to be a negative event for many children, thus one could argue that eliciting children's custody preferences can in some instances harm rather than help them.

Children's custody preferences should be considered carefully, and those who have a clear preference should have at least one staunch ally in their family—that parent. When children's preferences are not clear, however, asking them to make a choice would seem to be exactly the wrong approach. If being caught in the middle of their parents' conflict is a major source of their distress (Buchanan, Maccoby, & Dornbusch, 1991), then soliciting children's preference, when their preference is not evident, is hardly a solution to their dilemma.

Implications for Policy and Practice. Expert opinion is undoubtedly used in numerous custody evaluations designed to pick the "better" parent according to the general principles of the best interests test, although few studies have been conducted on expert testimony in divorce custody cases. Custody evaluators certainly are wise to inform themselves of the findings of developmental research, as this recommendation is included in the American Psychological Association's guidelines for custody evaluations (APA, 1994). However, many questions can and should be raised about custody evaluations. As noted earlier, there is little evidence that normative data on parenting can be applied validly to the individual case. And even if evaluations were psychometrically adequate, determinations about what outcomes are "best" necessarily involve value judgments. Another general concern is that the adversary model of picking between parents increases conflict between parents in a way that may be detrimental to children. To this list, we add the cautions that most existing, objective measures of parenting are dimensional scales that were developed for research purposes. The meaning of research on quantitative differences cannot be readily extrapolated to the categorical outcome of which parent is the preferred custodian in a particular case. There has been essentially no adequate research on reliability or validity of custody evaluations themselves, a circumstance that should invite the interest of behavioral scientists—and suggest to practitioners that they conduct custody evaluations with considerable caution or not at all.

Concluding Comments on Custody and Divorce

Several themes have emerged in this overview of the complex interface between developmental research and law and policy concerning children and divorce. One such theme is the increasing autonomy of parents from the state. Adults are essentially free to make decisions about whether to marry or divorce and to order their own affairs following marital dissolution. Parents have also gained increased authority over making decisions regarding their children following divorce, as a means of supporting parenting and avoiding placing children in the middle of their parents' disputes. A second theme is the relevance of normative developmental research for law and policy. Despite the complexity and diversity of the family's experience of divorce, developmental researchers have provided some consistent evidence on children's well-being. The relevance of this research is obvious in the numerous cases in which scientific evidence has contributed to the reshaping of family law. A third theme of the overview, however, is that application of developmental research is far more tenuous in the individual case. A fourth theme is the importance of procedural as well as substantive law to children's and families' experience of divorce, and the role of social scientists in helping to reshape legal procedures. A fifth theme concerns the future: Especially when considering implications for policy, developmental research must be circumspect about the limited nature of our measures. In the future, we hope investigators will pay more attention to measuring both psychological strengths and some of the more subtle psychological struggles that can accompany divorce. Most importantly, we urge a multidisciplinary perspective. We must recognize that economic and social outcomes are important in their own right irrespective of their relations with particular psychological measures. The outcomes of divorce are complicated, and only a suitably broad perspective can encompass them all at once.

CHILD MALTREATMENT

Child maltreatment has existed since the beginning of recorded history and continues to be a perplexing social problem in modern times. Despite its long past, child maltreatment as an area of scientific inquiry is relatively new, although the literature on the topic has quickly become vast (e.g., Cicchetti & Carlson, 1989; Garbarino, Guttman, & Seeley, 1986; Haugaard & Repucci, 1988; Kolko, 1996).

Psychologists play an increasingly influential role in legal issues related to child maltreatment. Psychologists have helped shape state and federal law regarding child abuse by testifying before legislative bodies. Psychologists often serve as experts in child maltreatment cases. When they do so, they typically function as child clinicians who have evaluated a child or family for legal or mental health purposes; as forensic interviewers who, to aid the police, have questioned a child to gather evidence; or as theoretical expert witnesses who discuss relevant research findings (e.g., children's eyewitness memory, psychological sequelae of abuse). Psychologists have also influenced court decisions about child maltreatment through submission of amicus briefs.

Here, we concentrate on forensic issues that arise in child maltreatment cases. We review research relevant to historical issues, definitions of child maltreatment, prevalence rates, emotional effects of child abuse, disclosure of abuse, forensic interviewing, and child abuse victims in juvenile and criminal court. Many of the topics covered in this section are controversial: Although most people agree that child maltreatment contributes importantly to society's ills (e.g., crime, mental illness, substance abuse), many disagree about how to handle child maltreatment cases within the legal system. Thus, discussions of controversial areas are distributed throughout this section.

Several themes from the section on divorce reemerge here. For example, how to balance the rights of parents, child, and the state is an issue in many child maltreatment decisions. These interests often conflict, as when parents compete with state welfare agencies regarding removing a child from the home or when the state prosecutes a parent for child abuse.

Children's competence at different developmental levels is also a theme of this section. Whether children have the capacity to accurately recount abuse experiences in forensic investigations or in court is similar in certain ways to the issue of whether children in divorce cases should be consulted regarding custody. Also, the issue of children's adjustment to maltreatment has parallels to the issue of children's adjustment to divorce.

Historical Overview

Physical Abuse

Current legal and psychological efforts to prevent, understand, and treat child abuse can be viewed within the context of an evolution toward more humane treatment of children. It can also be viewed within the context of a shift away from parental rights to greater rights for children and the state. In ancient times, parents (particularly fathers) had the legal right to sell children into slavery, maim or kill children if they were disobedient, or abandon their children as infants (DeMause, 1975). Some contend that the *average* child of past centuries would be considered a victim of child maltreatment today, given the severity of punishment typically inflicted in past eras by parents, teachers, and clergy (DeMause, 1975). Children were primarily treated as property under the law. Laws focused more on nonparental than parental assault, or on children who were orphaned or delinquent (Levine & Levine, 1992).

Modern efforts to prevent child maltreatment at first concentrated on physical abuse, which could be illustrated by dramatic cases. The classic example involved a child named Mary Ellen (Lazoritz, 1990). Born in 1864, Mary Ellen was raised from age 2 by adoptive parents in the tenements of New York City. At 9, when Mary Ellen's situation was discovered, she was living in virtual servitude, rarely permitted to go outside, and regularly beaten. A social worker who tried to intervene was informed that if a child were beaten in public, the police could act, but not if such acts occurred in the home by legal guardians, unless the child came forward and complained. The social worker appealed to the head of the Society for the Prevention of Cruelty to Animals (SPCA), who took up Mary Ellen's cause. SPCA lawyers argued in court that, as members of the animal kingdom, children should be afforded protection (laws were in place to protect animals, not children). Mary Ellen testified about the abuse she suffered. The SPCA attorneys were successful in having Mary Ellen removed from the home, and shortly thereafter, in 1875, the New York Society for the Prevention of Cruelty to Children (SPCC) was born.

Private charities such as the SPCC then spread throughout the country and began to receive public funds. The societies had virtual police powers and the authority to bring complaints regarding children to court, and to remove children from their homes. The authority given to the SPCCs represented an important shift in state's rights versus parental rights. Gradually, every state developed a child protective services (CPS) division responsible for handling child maltreatment cases.

Sexual Abuse

There is also reason to believe that child sexual abuse was much more common in the past than it is today. According to ancient Talmudic law, female children of 3 years and 1 day could be married if intercourse had taken place (Rush, 1980). Boy brothels flourished in ancient Greece and Rome. Even when sex with "free children" was illegal, sex with slave children was often permitted (DeMause, 1975). Societal prohibitions against sexual relations with children increased over the centuries, but sexual abuse continued privately.

A landmark event in the history of societal responses to child sexual abuse occurred when, in 1896, Freud rediscovered the problem and linked it to symptoms of hysteria. In *The Aetiology of Hysteria,* Freud described his "seduction theory," claiming that at the origin of every case of hysteria was a childhood sexual trauma. In a much debated reversal of that view (Herman, 1981; Masson, 1984; Rush, 1980), Freud later proclaimed that his patients' reports of sexual abuse were fantasies; his revised theory based on children's sexual wishes helped solidify this new view. For years after Freud abandoned the seduction theory, a silence fell over the mental health and legal communities regarding child sexual abuse, reinforced by the Freudian view that children frequently fantasize or lie about sexual abuse. Even the presence of venereal disease was questioned as proof of sexual contact (Lawson & Chaffin, 1992). As Levine and Levine (1992) point out, "Given the awareness of sexual abuse going back to the earliest days of child protection, it is remarkable that child sexual abuse as a social problem disappeared as a cause for concern, not to reemerge until the late 1970s and 1980s" (p. 214).

Mandatory Reporting

Ever since the inception of the child welfare system, any citizen could report suspected child abuse to child protection authorities (Kalichman, 1993). However, C. Henry Kempe is often credited with the establishment of mandatory reporting laws. Kempe's paper on the battered child syndrome showed that some children's injuries would be highly unlikely or even impossible as the result of accidents (Kempe, Silverman, Steele, Droegemueller, & Silver, 1962). In part because of Kempe's efforts, mandatory reporting laws were established nationwide by about 1966 and were then bolstered federally by the Child Abuse Prevention and Treatment Act (CAPTA, 1974). Mandatory reporting laws differ from state to state but generally require professionals who work with children (e.g., doctors, teachers, clinical psychologists) to report suspicions of child abuse. If a mandated reporter notifies authorities in good faith, he or she is immune from criminal or civil liability. However, if a mandated reporter fails to report, legal action can be taken (see Kalichman, 1993).

Once mandatory reporting laws were in force, the task of investigating abuse became highly demanding. Over the past two decades, reports of child maltreatment to child protective service agencies skyrocketed; nationally, there was a 331% increase from 1976 to 1993. It is widely believed that mandatory reporting of suspected child abuse and heightened public awareness account in large part for this increase, as opposed to increases in the rates of maltreatment itself.

Most mandatory reporting laws at first targeted physical abuse. However, as attention to physical maltreatment rose, attention to child sexual abuse was also kindled, in part by survey findings indicating its surprisingly high prevalence (Finkelhor, 1979; Russell, 1983). Mandatory reporting laws were soon amended to cover suspicions of sexual abuse. By the late 1970s and early 1980s, concerns about child sexual victimization peaked, and sensational preschool and custody cases involving charges of sexual abuse received attention. As a result of some of these cases, concern about actual abuse began to give way to concern about false reports (Myers, 1994). Nevertheless, as most professionals agree, actual child abuse is still a much more serious and pervasive problem than false reports (e.g., Lindsay, 1995).

Recent Policy and Practice: Investigation of Child Maltreatment

The state's CPS is often the sole public agency for receiving and investigating reports of maltreatment of children within familial, foster care, and day-care settings. If a CPS investigation begins and a child is found to be in imminent danger, he or she may be immediately removed from the home. If other services (e.g., substance abuse counseling, homemaker services) are deemed sufficient, they will be offered to the family. If the child has been removed or if services to ensure the child's safety are refused, the case will be referred to juvenile court. Juvenile court does not have the authority to punish abusive parents, but it can maintain custody of the child, place the child in foster care, and terminate parental rights. One would hope that families and children facing this serious situation would receive counseling or other constructive interventions. However, lack of CPS staff and insufficient state funds result in hundreds of thousands of families not receiving even basic services to ameliorate the negative effects of maltreatment (McCurdy & Daro, 1994). The cases are mainly monitored or closed, with minimal services provided (U.S. Advisory Board, 1995). Social service agencies have been so overwhelmed by the task of investigating reports of abuse that few resources are left to provide services. For that reason, some now argue that mandatory reporting laws should be revoked.

Assaults on children can also be reported to the police. If intrafamilial abuse is severe or if extrafamilial abuse has occurred, a perpetrator may be criminally prosecuted. Penal codes in each state describe laws covering child abuse. The district attorney's office will determine whether there is sufficient evidence for a case to go forward. At times, the same child abuse case is handled simultaneously by the juvenile and criminal courts.

Authorities who investigate child abuse are often in a position of being "damned if they do and damned if they don't." Children who are left in abusive homes have a 40% to 70% chance of being reinjured and as much as a 5% chance of being killed (Ferleger, Glenwick, Gaines, & Green, 1988; Jellinek et al., 1992; Schmitt & Krugman, 1992). Leaving a child in an abusive home is thus a serious decision. However, if a child is removed without sufficient cause, the psychological damage to the child and parents can be severe.

Definitions and Legal Terminology

Child maltreatment is such an emotional topic that even its definition is controversial. Defining child abuse and neglect is not simply an academic matter: Definitions affect social service and legal investigations and court action, as well as determinations of prevalence rates and research on the causes and consequences of child maltreatment. From a broad perspective, cultures differ in what constitutes child maltreatment (e.g., clitorectomies of girls, conducted with primitive tools and no anesthesia, are not considered abusive in some countries, whereas even spanking is illegal in Sweden). Even within a society, various social forces and belief systems lead groups to different views of acceptable and abusive behavior (e.g., religious groups opposed to modern medicine may contest the state's right to provide a child with medical care; in a number of states, there are exceptions to child abuse laws for religious practices; Bottoms, Shaver, Goodman, & Qin, 1995). Professionals from different academic traditions (e.g., medicine, sociology, psychology) also tend to define child maltreatment differently (e.g., from a psychological perspective, some propose that an act be considered abusive if it is associated with psychological injury; McGee & Wolfe, 1991).

Different definitions are justified for different purposes, but professionals who handle child abuse cases are typically required to use legal definitions. A central goal for the legal system is to have definitions that establish clear guidelines for justifying social service or court intervention. Legal definitions tend to focus on serious harm to a child or strong potential for injury. But do professionals agree on what constitutes child maltreatment? Giovannoni and Becerra (1979) examined the views of professionals (e.g., attorneys, police, social workers) and members of ethnic groups (e.g., White, African American, and Hispanic) on what constitutes child abuse. These researchers found considerable similarity in judgments of relative severity of different forms of child maltreatment, although some groups rated certain acts of abuse as more serious than did other groups. More recent studies show that there can be substantial agreement among professionals in the criteria they weigh in deciding whether abuse is indicated (e.g., Conte, Sorenson, Fogarty, & Rosa, 1991), although their decisions do not always agree for specific cases (e.g., Realmuto & Wescoe, 1992).

From a psycholegal perspective, child maltreatment generally falls into one of two categories: intentional acts of commission (e.g., physical abuse) or omission (e.g., physical neglect) (Garbarino & Gilliam, 1980). *Physical abuse* is often operationalized as nonaccidental acts of commission by an adult that leave signs of physical harm, such as bruises, on the child. Physical abuse can vary from overzealous spanking or hitting of a child to acts that break bones and even acts that lead to death. *Physical neglect* is often defined as "failure to provide by those legally responsible for the care of the child, the proper or necessary support, education as required by law, or medical, surgical, or any other care necessary for his/her well-being" (NCCAN, 1978). Defining neglect is complicated by lack of knowledge about the indispensable, minimally adequate kinds of care children require (Gaudin, 1993). Acts of neglect include inadequate supervision, abandonment, refusal of needed medical care, and permitted drug abuse and truancy. Nonorganic "failure to thrive" (when an infant is acutely malnourished but responds with improved weight gain in the hospital) is also often classified as a form of neglect. It can be difficult to separate physical neglect from poverty, and a correlation exists between maltreatment and poverty. Currently, over 20% of all children in the United States live below the poverty line, and the rate is much higher for children in several minority groups (nearly 50% of African American children grow up in poverty—Huston, 1991). Nevertheless, the majority of families living in poverty take adequate care of their children (Barnett, Manly, & Cicchetti, 1993). Physical neglect is indicated when parents have or can obtain sufficient resources or services to provide their children with basic necessities but fail to do so. Parental drug addiction is a contributor to neglect of children (NCPCA, 1995).

Child sexual abuse can be broadly defined as "interactions between a child and adult for sexual stimulation." However, legal definitions become much more specific. The legal definition in California includes rape, incest, sodomy, oral copulation, penetration of a genital or anal opening by a foreign object, lewd and lascivious acts against a child under 14 years of age (e.g., any sexual touching or intercourse even if it is consensual if the child is under 14 yrs), and child molestation including exhibitionism. Child sexual abuse is sometimes distinguished from sexual exploitation of a child (e.g., depicting minors in obscene acts, promoting or aiding a minor in prostitution). Although there is general agreement about whether some acts constitute child sexual abuse (e.g., incest involving intercourse), there is less agreement about other acts (e.g., a parent's frequent inspection of a prepubescent child's genitals) (Haugaard & Repucci, 1988).

Emotional scars are often more enduring and damaging than physical scars. *Psychological maltreatment,* an overarching link between all forms of child maltreatment (Brassard, German, & Hart, 1987; Garbarino et al., 1986), has been especially difficult to define. However, psychological maltreatment of children and youth can be defined as acts of omission or commission that damage immediately or ultimately the behavioral, cognitive, affective, or physical functioning of the child. Examples of psychological maltreatment include acts of rejecting, terrorizing, isolating, exploiting, and missocializing. Although many people could probably agree on what constitutes extreme forms of emotional maltreatment (e.g., raising a daughter strapped to a potty in a closet for most of her childhood), other child-rearing practices are open to debate (e.g., repeatedly calling children "stupid").

Although generally agreed-on broad definitions of child maltreatment exist, these definitions do not recognize developmental considerations (e.g., an act may be abusive for a younger but not for an older child). In applying the definitions, many factors must be considered (intent, consequences, type of act, age of child, circumstances). All of these can vary independently, making it difficult if not impossible to specify a precise definition in practice. General definitions allow laws to be applied judiciously to individual cases, but they leave room for unequal application.

Prevalence of Child Maltreatment

How common is child maltreatment? Has it increased over the years, or is society simply more aware of it these days? Prevalence of divorce, foster care, and adoption are relatively easy to document, at least in principle, because they are usually public; in contrast, child abuse is shrouded in secrecy. Estimates of the prevalence of child maltreatment depend on whom you ask and how you ask (Haugaard & Emery, 1989). Many adults whose treatment as children meet criteria for abuse do not label themselves as abuse victims, so simply asking "Were you abused as a child?" is insufficient.

Reports to Child Protective Service Agencies

Reports to CPS provide one estimate of the prevalence of child maltreatment. Nationally, reports to CPS agencies in 1996 involved 3.1 million children (NCPCA, 1997). However, on average, only about 31% of these cases were "substantiated" (i.e., CPS determined that abuse had occurred), resulting in nearly 1 million children substantiated as victims of child abuse and neglect, a 3% decrease compared with 1995 (see also NCCAN, 1997). Thus, 14 out of every 1,000 U.S. children were substantiated victims of child maltreatment in 1996.

NCCAN (1997) notes that most official reports to CPS come from professionals, particularly teachers. Persons within the family account for about 18% of the reports. As a result of these reports, regardless of who made them, about 1.6 million investigations of alleged maltreatment took place in 1995. Intentionally false reports accounted for only 4% of the unsubstantiated dispositions, although relatively few states provided data on false reports (and those often failed to explain how such determinations were made). Based on reports of just 21 states, NCPCA (1997) found that over 64,000 children were removed from their homes and placed in alternative care during 1996. This constitutes a significant number of children, but it represents only 2% to 6% of the children reported for child maltreatment. For substantiated cases, court action is initiated for 17% of the children (NCPCA, 1995).

Types of Abuse. Although child murder and child sexual abuse often gain media attention, about half (52%) of all reports to CPS are for neglect. Physical abuse is involved in 24% of reported cases, with only about 13% of the victims involved in sexual abuse cases. Emotional maltreatment is reported for 5% of the children, and medical neglect for only 3%. Other forms of maltreatment, including abandonment, threats to a child, and congenital drug addiction, constitute 15% of the cases (NCCAN, 1997). There is a recent trend for a larger number of neglect cases and fewer sexual abuse cases to enter the system (NCPCA, 1997). We can speculate that the trend for neglect reflects increased poverty, and the trend for sexual abuse to reflect increased skepticism about children's allegations. In any case, these statistics mask the fact that many children are believed to suffer multiple forms of maltreatment (Rosenberg & Rossman, in press).

Over 1,000 children were killed in the United States in 1996 as a result of child abuse—about 3 children per day (NCCAN, 1997). Of these children, 41% had previous or ongoing contact with CPS (NCPCA, 1997). Sadly, CPS lacks adequate risk assessment instruments to prevent such deaths.

Victims. According to NCCAN (1997), 52% of victims of child maltreatment in 1995 were 7 years old or younger. Young children are particularly likely to be killed as a result of child abuse. Of the child victims killed in 1995, 77% were under 3 years, and almost half were under the age of 1. In general, the number of reports of child maltreatment to CPS decrease somewhat as children get older. Reports of sexual abuse involve female victims twice as often as male victims. But males are more likely to be reported victims of physical abuse before adolescence, at which point males are less likely than females to be victims, perhaps because of males' greater strength. In 55% of reported cases, the children were White, in 27% African American, in 10% Hispanic, in 2% American Indian, and in 3%, ethnicity was unreported.

Survey Studies

Because abuse often goes unreported to agencies, random sample survey studies are relied on to provide more sensitive estimates of the prevalence of child maltreatment.

Physical Abuse. Based on parental self-report, survey studies indicate that approximately 700,000 children in the United States were subjected to very severe violent behavior in 1985, a decrease relative to the 1.5 million figure reported in 1975 (Gelles & Straus, 1979, 1987). The highest rates of abusive violence occurred in families with: low incomes (e.g., below the poverty line); four or more children; male children; children aged 3 to 6 years; and drug or alcohol problems (Wolfner & Gelles, 1993). Further decreases in physical violence against children were reported based on a 1992 national survey (Straus & Kantor, 1995). Although the lower rates reported for 1992 are encouraging, they may represent an underestimation because parents were hesitant to report abusive acts. When 10- to 16-year-olds themselves are interviewed, approximately 7.5% report at least one lifetime incident of physical assault by a family member. Nonfamily assaults (22%) were more frequent than family assaults (Finkelhor & Dziuba-Leatherman, 1994).

Interview studies often include the following acts in the severe or abusive violence category: kicked, bit, or hit the child with a fist; hit or tried to hit with an object; beat up; burned or scalded; threatened with a gun or knife; and used a gun or knife. Corporal punishment is not counted as child maltreatment, although adverse emotional effects of such actions have been documented (e.g., Fergusson & Lynskey, 1997; see Straus, 1995, for a review). The vast majority of Americans have been hit by their parents during childhood, thus experiencing officially nonabusive levels of violence (Graziano & Namaste, 1990).

Sexual Abuse. Estimates of the prevalence of sexual abuse vary depending on how sexual abuse is defined. When such acts as exhibitionism are included, prevalence estimates are considerably higher than when such acts are not included. Moreover, retrospective studies, which are common, suffer from a number of problems, such as reliance on respondents' memory, definitions of abuse, and willingness to disclose personal information. Moreover, there may be cohort effects reflecting societal changes in the prevalence of sexual abuse, so that retrospective studies could misrepresent current prevalence.

Using somewhat different definitions of abuse, community surveys of adult women have shown that 38% (Russell, 1983) to 54% (Wyatt, 1985) of women experienced at least one episode of sexual abuse before 18 years of age. Twelve percent experienced abuse before the age of 12 years, and 31% experienced some form of extrafamilial child sexual exploitation (Russell, 1983). Surveys of college students find that 19.2% of the women and 8.6% of the men indicate some form child sexual molestation (Finkelhor, 1979). Williams (1994a) argues that forgotten abuse may lead to underestimates when prevalence rates are based on retrospective self-reports. However, when children (10- to 16-year-olds) were interviewed, the lifetime rate of attempted or completed sexual victimization was 10.5% (Finkelhor & Dziuba-Leatherman, 1994), considerably lower than that indicated in retrospective studies. It is possible that difficulty in obtaining intimate disclosures from teenagers affected these results. Alternatively, perhaps sexual victimization has declined or earlier retrospective reports were inflated.

Survey studies have also examined the prevalence of abuse claims in custody disputes. Studies repeatedly show that sexual abuse allegations are far from commonplace in custody proceedings (e.g., they occur in only 2% of the cases in which custody or visitation is contested and in only 0.8% of the cases overall; McIntosh & Prinz, 1993). Allegations of other sorts (spousal or alcohol abuse) are more common (Sorenson et al., 1995). In contrast, case-study estimates of false reports in custody cases range from about 6% to 55% (Benedek & Schetky, 1985; Faller, 1991; Jones & McGraw, 1987) and indicate that most allegations judged to be false are reported by parents, not children. However, given difficulties of determining whether a case is false, these estimates are suspect.

Implications for Policy and Practice. Several studies suggest that rates of *reported* physical and sexual violence against children may be declining. Whether the actual rate is lower is unknown. Rates are higher than society should tolerate, in any case. And the rates do not even include community violence or witnessing domestic violence, which may also be considered forms of child maltreatment (especially if a definition of "acts resulting in psychological injury" is employed). Although neglect is the most common type of maltreatment reported to agencies, survey studies of representative samples of the general population have not included neglect as a category. The amount of research attention given to physical and sexual abuse may be disproportionately high. Social policy should aim to prevent child abuse so that its prevalence is as low as possible, using a variety of interventions. Education, parenting classes, home services, early prediction, and crisis intervention have all been suggested (Cohn & Birch, 1988).

Adjustment of Child Maltreatment Victims

Although it is difficult to establish specific effects of child abuse a common thread runs through research findings on the effects of child maltreatment. Children who are physically abused tend, on average, to show heightened aggression; children who are sexually abused tend to show heightened sexualized behavior; children who are neglected tend to be socially withdrawn. Regardless of maltreatment type, low self-worth is commonly reported, along with feelings of depression and self-blame. However, there is a broad range of emotional and behavioral reactions, and no one behavior is always associated with a particular kind of maltreatment. Moreover, nonabused children can sometimes exhibit these tendencies as well.

Identifying the effects of child maltreatment is complicated by the frequent presence of multiple confounding factors. Children may suffer more than one type of maltreatment, making it difficult to tease apart the effects of one independent of the other. Children in abusive homes may also suffer the effects of poverty, parental substance abuse, the witnessing of domestic or community violence, and parental emotional disturbance. Children from such homes may be more likely to run away, be placed in foster care, or become involved in legal battles, all of which may affect the long-term outcome. Nevertheless, even when such possibly confounding factors are controlled, adverse effects of abuse are often found. The specific mechanisms underlying these effects are under debate.

Physical Abuse

Several comprehensive reviews of the short- and long-term effects of physical abuse on children are available (Kolko, 1992, 1996; Malinosky-Rummell & Hansen, 1993; Pianta, Egeland, & Erikson, 1989). Perhaps the most common finding is that physically abused children are more aggressive than nonabused controls, and than neglected children as well (Hoffman-Plotkin & Twentyman, 1984; Kinard, 1980). Moreover, children who experience repeated abuse tend to be more aggressive than children who experience less frequent maltreatment (Kinard, 1982). Increased aggression is already apparent in physically maltreated toddlers (George & Main, 1979). These findings support the view that children tend to model or incorporate the aggressive behavior inflicted on them.

Low self-esteem and self-blame are other common sequelae of physical abuse (Martin & Beezley, 1977). As Herzberger and Tennen (1986) point out, several commonly observed emotional consequences of abuse (e.g., docility, withdrawal, depression, apathy, wariness) could derive from feelings of low self-esteem. Moreover, abused children tend to believe they deserved the treatment they received (Amsterdam, Brill, Bell, & Edwards, 1979; Kempe & Kempe, 1978). On average, maltreated children also have lower social competence, difficulty recognizing others' emotions, and less empathy for others (e.g., Camras, Ribordy, Hill, & Martino, 1988; Howes & Eldredge, 1985; Youngblade & Belsky, 1990).

Underlying many of these responses may be biased interpretations of social events. Dodge, Bates, and Pettit (1990) examined the effects of physical violence on children's social information processing. The experience early in life of physical harm at the hands of an adult was associated in 5-year-olds with perceptions of hostile intent. Such children were more aggressive themselves, as indicated by teacher report and playground observations. These findings were not explained by other possibly confounding variables (e.g., SES or temperament). In fact, children who experienced physical harm early in life and did not evidence hostility-biased information processing were more depressed but not more aggressive.

These processing biases may reflect effects of maltreatment on internal working models. Early maltreatment is likely to affect the development of children's models of attachment relations, which are hypothetical mental summaries of interpersonal experiences with caregivers (Bowlby, 1980). In Ainsworth's Strange Situation, a history of child maltreatment is associated in infancy with insecure parent-child attachment relations (Carlson, Cicchetti, Barnett, & Braunwalk, 1989; Cicchetti & Barnett, 1991), including avoidance, resistance, and disorganization. Later behavioral and emotional disorganization, lack of self-esteem, and neediness of abused children can also be linked to attachment patterns (Lynch & Cicchetti, 1991; Youngblade & Belsky, 1990).

The effects of child maltreatment are not short-lived. In a review of the long-term consequences of childhood physical abuse, Malinosky-Rummell and Hansen (1993) concluded that a strong relation exists between physical abuse and later nonfamilial and familial violence. The relation between physical abuse and later violence is especially strong for males (Maxfield & Widom, 1996). For females, child physical abuse is associated with internalizing problems in adolescence and adulthood, such as depression, suicidal and self-injurious behaviors, somatization, dissociation, anxiety, and psychosis (Malinosky-Rummell & Hansen, 1993). These tendencies could be predicted from social information-processing biases evident by the age of 5 years in children harmed early in life (Dodge et al., 1990).

Physical abuse not only takes an emotional toll on children; it is also associated with decrements in cognitive abilities, although significant effects are not always found. Even when SES is statistically controlled, deficits have been noted in IQ scores, language ability, and school performance (e.g., Coster, Beeghly, Gersten, & Cicchetti, 1989; Eckenrode, Laird, & Doris, 1993; Friedrich, Einbender, & Luecke, 1983; Hoffman-Plotkin & Twentyman, 1984). Possible reasons for poorer cognitive performance in abuse samples include deficits in initiation of tasks, physical injury (e.g., brain damage), lack of cognitive stimulation by parents, lack of appropriate scaffolding due to parents' unrealistic expectations, and social emotional sequelae that interfere with learning (Aber & Allen, 1987; Kolko, 1992).

However, children who experience inconsistent child rearing but were not technically abused are also characterized by some of these same tendencies (e.g., "acting out" behavior; Glueck & Glueck, 1968). Such similarity may in part be a function of how maltreatment is defined. "Maltreatment" is not a discrete category, but rather represents a culturally influenced cutoff point on a continuum of child-rearing practices. A certain child-rearing practice may not meet the legal standard for abuse but still have a negative effect on emotional and cognitive development. Certain deleterious parental practices (such as unfair, inconsistent, harsh discipline) do not necessarily qualify as gross abuse or neglect, but nonetheless are associated with long-lasting adverse emotional responses (e.g., alcohol and depressive disorders; Holmes & Robins, 1987). Developmental models of the effects of physical abuse should help clarify where the cutoff points fall on the child-rearing continuum (Cicchetti, 1990).

Sexual Abuse

It is also difficult to pinpoint causal relations in the study of the effects of child sexual abuse. Many of the same potentially confounding factors that influence studies of physical abuse complicate inference in studies of child sexual abuse. However, additional methodological issues confound research on the effects of child sexual abuse. Many studies compare symptomatology in "nonabused" groups (i.e., children with no known history of sexual abuse) and "abused" groups (i.e., children with an alleged history of sexual abuse), in an attempt to determine symptoms specifically associated with abuse. However, because it is difficult to determine whether sexual abuse actually took place, some misclassification may occur. Most of the time, misclassification leads to a conservative estimate of group differences, but in some cases it can result in potentially misleading findings.

Sexual abuse places children at risk for a number of emotional and behavioral problems. In a comprehensive review, Kendall-Tackett, Williams, and Finkelhor (1993) concluded that although two-thirds of child sexual abuse victims evidence abuse-related symptoms, the exact symptoms are quite varied and do not fit into a consistent symptom-profile pattern or syndrome (see also Berliner & Elliott, 1996). The most common symptom in childhood is inappropriate sexual behavior (such as sexualized acting out and frequent masturbation). Although sexually abused versus nonsexually abused children engage in more sexualized behavior (Friedrich et al., 1992), most sexual abuse victims do not engage in sexualized behavior (Friedrich, 1993). Other frequent symptoms associated with sexual abuse include post-traumatic stress disorder (PTSD), poor self esteem, and fears. One-third of sexually abused children do not evidence any symptoms as a result of their abuse. However, when developmental level is considered, Kendall-Tackett et al. surmised that some evidence for symptom profiles emerged. Severity of abuse, duration and frequency, degree of threat, perpetrator-child relationship, and lack of maternal support contribute to level of symptomatology. Surprisingly, few gender differences are consistently observed. Kendall-Tackett et al. also report that symptoms subsided within 2 years following disclosure of abuse for a large proportion of children. For about 10% to 24% of the child victims, symptoms increased over time or a delayed response occurred. For adults, long-term effects of child sexual abuse include sexual dysfunction, self-destructive behaviors, depression, low self-esteem, substance abuse, revictimization, dissociative tendencies, and feelings of isolation, anxiety, and stigmatization (e.g., Beitchman et al., 1992; DiTomasso & Routh, 1993; Friedrich, 1988; Putnam, 1991). Several models have been proposed to explain the wide variety of emotional responses of child sexual abuse victims (e.g., Briere, 1992; Finkelhor & Browne, 1985). To date, these models lack adequate test.

Neglect and Psychological Maltreatment

Although there is less research on the effects of neglect, neglected children have been found to be socially withdrawn and aggressive, to suffer IQ deficits, and to be at risk for delinquency (Hoffman-Plotkin & Twentyman, 1984; Maxfield & Widom, 1996; for reviews, see Erickson & Egeland, 1996; Gaudin, 1993). In infancy and toddlerhood, neglected children fail to develop secure attachments with their neglecting caregiver (Crittenden & Ainsworth, 1989). Neglected preschool children manifest lower self-esteem and poorer control over their impulses than nonmaltreated children (Egeland, 1988). Parental rejection, often a component of neglect, is also associated with feelings of lack of self-worth and anger (Rohner & Rohner, 1980). Crittenden's (1988; Crittenden & Ainsworth, 1989) studies of neglectful families indicate that the mother's inattention leads to the child developing passivity and withdrawing behavior, or random, undisciplined activity.

Similarly, psychological maltreatment is associated with withdrawal, low self-esteem, delinquency, and reduced emotional responsiveness, but also with aggression, inability to become independent or to trust others, and underachievement (Egeland, Sroufe, & Erikson, 1983; Herrenkohl & Herrenkohl, 1981; Main & George, 1985; see Brassard et al., 1987, for a review). However, additional forms of abuse may co-occur with emotional abuse, making causal inference difficult.

Moderator Variables

It is crucial for scientists to investigate moderator variables associated with resilience in the face of child maltreatment. Malinosky-Rummell and Hansen (1993) discuss four kinds of moderator variables: (a) maltreatment characteristics (variables associated with the abuse itself), (b) individual factors (variables pertaining to the abused individual), (c) family factors (variables pertaining to the family), and (d) environmental factors (variables outside the child and family). It has been difficult for researchers to distinguish among these influences, although some researchers report success. Higher IQ and stability of the child's living environment have been identified as modifying the negative effects of maltreatment (e.g., Eckenrode, Rowe, Laird, & Brathwaite, 1995). One of the most compelling factors contributing to resilience is the emotional support of an important adult in the child's life (Garmezy, 1983). Multiple out-of-home placements, multiple life stressors, and parental depression contribute to more negative effects (Gaudin, 1993). Developmental level also moderates the symptoms manifested by abused children (Berliner & Elliott, 1996).

In summary, child maltreatment is associated with both short- and long-term adverse effects on children. As a general simplification, the type of abuse experienced places children at risk of developing problems that mimic the maltreatment—physical abuse is associated with aggression, sexual abuse with sexualized behavior, and neglect with social withdrawal. A number of theories, from social learning theory, to genetic predispositions, to attachment theory, can be used to explain these effects. However, many child victims are nonsymptomatic, and as discussed next, most become nonabusive adults.

Cycles of Abuse

Do maltreated children grow up to abuse their own offspring? Research indicates a relation between early maltreatment and later abusive, sexualized, or aggressive behavior, both in general (Maxfield & Widom, 1996; but see DiLalla & Gottesman, 1991) and specifically toward children (e.g., Ney, 1988). The relation is complex, however. Prospective studies indicate that most children who have suffered maltreatment do not become maltreating parents, although a certain percentage of adults abused as children go on to abuse their own offspring. It is estimated that approximately 30% of physically abused or neglected individuals abuse their own children (Kaufman & Zigler, 1987; Widom, 1989).

Why do some abuse victims become nonabusive caregivers, whereas others become perpetrators themselves? Abused mothers who do not become abusers tend to have higher IQs, greater emotional stability, and less depression and anxiety than abusing mothers (Egeland, 1988; Zimrin, 1986). Also associated with breaking the cycle of abuse is having a supportive partner, benefiting from therapy, and experiencing fewer stressful life events (Egeland, Jacobvitz, & Sroufe, 1988; Hunter & Kilstrom, 1979). Literature on resilient children suggests that one predictor of a more positive outcome is having at least one caretaker in childhood who is emotionally supportive (Garmezy, 1983).

Thus, a relation exists between child maltreatment (especially physical abuse and neglect) and later violent behavior. However, the lack of straightforward relation motivates further research to determine whether violence in childhood is a necessary or sufficient precursor to violent behavior later on (Kolko, 1992).

Implications for Policy and Practice. Child maltreatment is associated with lasting negative effects on children's emotional and cognitive development. Most social service interventions target parents (who, for example, receive substance-abuse counseling or other psychological treatment) rather than children. Children are also in need of services. Research on the cycle of abuse indicates that a supportive relationship (e.g., with a therapist, with a romantic partner) may be an important form of intervention. Although many children who are abused grow up to live successful lives and do not reabuse their own children, successful coping with abuse (like successful coping with divorce) often leaves children with painful memories, strained relationships, and long-term sadness. Again, as for divorce, coping may still extract a lasting emotional cost.

Disclosure of Abuse

Because most forms of child maltreatment are private and occur in the home, society may have no way to know about it unless children disclose.

Disclosure Rates and Factors Affecting Disclosure

Studies confirm that it can be difficult for children to disclose abuse, especially in formal settings and when parental support is lacking. Fear of parental reaction and punishment, self-blame, and family taboos often inhibit children from disclosing (Finkelhor, 1979; Herman, 1981; Sas & Cunningham, 1995). Other people's reactions to disclosure can have a significant effect on children's emotional well-being. Children who experience negative reactions from significant others later evince increased levels of psychopathology (Sas & Cunningham, 1995; Waller & Ruddock, 1993). Moreover, a substantial number of children experience family disruptions after disclosure, which may reinforce fears of abandonment. In one study, child sexual abuse victims who were removed from home displayed higher levels of emotional distress and aggression than children who stayed in their homes (Sauzier, 1989). Although removal from a maltreating home is not always associated with negative effects on emotional well-being (Wald, Carlsmith, & Leiderman, 1988; Widom, 1991), disclosure may still be associated with children's worst fear (i.e., being separated from their family and friends).

The extent of nondisclosure to authorities can be gleaned from interviews with children and retrospective reports by adults. In a survey of 10- to 16-year-olds, Finkelhor and Dziuba-Leatherman (1994) found that, although two-thirds of children's victimization experiences were reported to someone, only a fourth were reported to authorities and only 6% to police. Ironically, in this day of heightened attention to false reports, sexual assaults were rarely reported to authorities, as was true decades earlier (Russell, 1983). A substantial percentage (e.g., 34%) of adults who retrospectively report child sexual abuse indicate that they failed to disclose to *anyone* during childhood (Wyatt, 1985). Both children and adults are much more likely to report abuse histories if simply asked (e.g., Lanktree, Briere, & Zaidi, 1991).

Children disclose for a number of reasons. Understandably, they disclose to stop the abuse, express anger at the abuser, react to the realization that the acts were "bad," protect a sibling, or respond to a child abuse prevention program. Children are more likely to disclose quickly if they were not emotionally close to the abuser, if they did not experience preabuse "grooming" by the perpetrator, and if they were young at initial abuse (Sas & Cunningham, 1995). Especially in cases of sexual abuse, children are most likely to disclose to their mothers (Berliner & Conte, 1995; Finkelhor, 1984). Parents' reactions vary from support and surprise to disbelief and punishment of children for "lying" (reactions especially likely if the mother is intimately involved with the perpetrator) or even attempts to kill the perpetrator (Berliner & Conte, 1995; Everson, Hunter, Runyan, Edelsohn, & Coulter, 1989; Williams, 1994a).

When authorities are contacted, a child may be required to disclose again. Maternal support and child age appear to be key determinants. Lawson and Chaffin (1992) explored predictors of disclosure in 28 children with sexually transmitted diseases (STD). Only 43% made a verbal disclosure of abuse at the initial interview. Sixty-three percent disclosed if they had a supportive mother, compared with only 17% if the mother was unsupportive. Although generalization of the findings may be affected by a small and nonrepresentative sample, this study indicates that maternal support is a crucial factor in children's willingness to disclose abuse. Regarding age effects, Keary and Fitzpatrick (1994) found that, in nonleading forensic interviews, children under 5 years of age were least likely to disclose abuse during formal investigations regardless of whether the children had told someone before. The researchers argued that, with young children, inclusion of some leading questions may be necessary to facilitate disclosure in formal contexts, a point of controversy to which we will return.

After children disclose, they sometimes "recant" (i.e., say that abuse did not occur). If independent corroboration is lacking, it can then be difficult to know whether the disclosure or the recantation represents the truth. Recantation rates hover around 4% to 6% (Bradley & Wood, 1996; Jones & McGraw, 1987), although in some studies they are as high as 27% (e.g., Sorenson & Snow, 1991). Recantation is believed to be especially likely in intrafamilial cases (Summit, 1983).

In summary, children are often loath to disclose abuse. Even children with physical signs of abuse may fail to disclose, and for young children disclosure at home does not necessarily predict disclosure in a formal interview setting. In some cases, disclosure is associated with adverse consequences for children (e.g., lack of maternal support). These conclusions follow mainly from studies of child sexual abuse. Less is known about children's disclosure of physical abuse, neglect, or emotional maltreatment.

Secrecy

Perpetrators' requests for secrecy can be an important deterrent to children's disclosure of abuse. Psychological forces that can silence children include loyalty conflicts, obedience to adult authority, threats, and bribery. In general, such forces interact with cognitive development to determine whether a secret is maintained. Children under about 3 to 4 years generally lack understanding of the concept of secrecy and the self-control needed to keep secrets (Bottoms, Goodman, Schwartz-Kenney, Sachsenmaier, & Thomas, 1990; Bussey, Lee, & Grimbeek, 1993; Pipe & Goodman, 1991). Even for young children, however, threats result in particularly low rates of disclosure of a stranger's transgression, and the presence of the perpetrator in the room while the child is interviewed has an additional "chilling" effect on disclosure (Bussey et al., 1993). And even when the perpetrator is absent, children may withhold information, especially if they are questioned by strangers, feel they consented to keep a secret, are concerned that something bad will happen, or believe the transgressor would get angry (Peters, 1990).

Children are even more readily silenced when the transgressor is a loved one. When 5- to 6-year-olds were asked by their mothers to keep a parental transgression secret, even leading questions failed to pry the information from them (Bottoms et al., 1990). In contrast, leading questions resulted in many 5- to 6-year-olds revealing a stranger's transgression (Clark-Stewart, Thompson, & Lepore, 1989). Thus, although many children by the age of about 5 years will withhold information to protect a loved one or a stranger, they may be particularly unwilling to reveal information that would implicate their parents.

Although the ecological validity of "secret studies" is limited, several factors appear to influence children's disclosure of secret acts. Developmental level is one factor. Older (5- to 6-year-old) rather than younger (3- to 4-year-old) children are more likely to keep secret information that would implicate a transgressor. Threats and promises may be particularly effective silencers. Even use of leading questions may not pry information about parental transgressions from children.

Implications for Policy and Practice. Disclosure of abuse is important for intervention. In cases of physical abuse or neglect, visible evidence (e.g., bruises or lack of clothing) can verify a child's disclosure. Intervention in sexual abuse cases depends more on children revealing what occurred. Because many children hesitate to disclose, parents may understandably try to question children if abuse is suspected. And given the importance of emotional support at time of disclosure to children's mental health, parents are wise to be supportive. However, concerns about parental elicitation of false reports places parents in a difficult bind concerning whether or not to question their children. When a parent is the abuser, a child may be especially likely to fear disclosure. For purposes of social policy, risks of continued abuse must be weighed against chances of false reports when considering policies that affect disclosure. Also at issue when a child discloses is the availability of helpful responses (e.g., therapy may be unavailable, removal of the child may be traumatic, family reunification may return children to dangerous circumstances).

Memories of Abuse and Abuse Victims' Memories

Once a child has disclosed abuse, or suspicions of abuse arise for other reasons, the child may be interviewed about his or her memories of abuse. Does maltreatment affect children's memory abilities in general or eyewitness or autobiographical memory abilities specifically? How accurately can children report memories of traumatic or abusive events?

Memory in Child Maltreatment Victims

Because child maltreatment is associated with adverse emotional reactions and delays in cognitive and language abilities, a history of maltreatment might also influence memory. Although abused children perform more poorly than nonabused children on standardized tests of short-term memory and verbal skills (Friedrich et al., 1983), little is known about abused children's eyewitness or autobiographical memory abilities. In three studies, few differences were found when comparing sexually abused to nonabused children's memory and suggestibility for a neutral social interaction (Goodman, Rudy, Port, England, Bottoms, & Renouf, 1989) or comparing children who had suffered different types of maltreatment in regard to their memory for an anogenital exam (Eisen, Goodman, & Qin, 1995; Qin et al., 1997). Interestingly, in the latter study, children's PTSD symptoms correlated with stress during the exam but not memory after it, whereas children's dissociative tendencies were predictive of children's memory. In addition, clinicians' ratings of maltreated children's adaptive functioning had some predictive value as well.

It is possible that children who have suffered abuse will find different information salient than children who have not suffered abuse; and salience may affect what is remembered and reported. When children involved in sex abuse evaluations, including anogenital exams performed to collect medical evidence, are divided into those with substantiated sexual abuse and those without substantiation, the former children are especially likely to report that the medical exam included anogenital contact (Katz, Schonfeld, Carter, Leventhal, & Cicchetti, 1995). Thus, abusive experiences may affect children's attention and information processing, which in turn affect memory. These findings are consistent with Dodge et al.'s results concerning biases in maltreated children's social information processing. An important topic for future study concerns possible effects of dissociation and PTSD on memory and possible biases in abused children's information processing that may affect memory. Also of interest is how adults who experienced abuse as children report relevant autobiographical events from childhood. Studies of clinic samples of adults (which are likely to contain a substantial percentage of abuse victims) indicate that such individuals report their past histories with considerable accuracy (Brewin, Andrews, & Gotlib, 1993). However, some have proposed that false memories of abuse may arise in part from distortions of actual abuse experiences (Ganaway, 1989), but there are no direct tests of that notion.

Trauma and Memory

Typically, child abuse constitutes a traumatic experience. What are the effects of trauma on children's memory? The psychological lore used to be that stress had a debilitating effect on memory (e.g., Loftus, 1979), but research findings are mixed.

Much recent work with adults supports the view that core features of highly emotional events are often retained in memory with particular durability, although peripheral details may or may not be as strongly retained (Christianson, 1992; Heuer & Reisberg, 1992; Yuille & Cutshall, 1986). Findings from several studies of children's memory for stressful events (e.g., medical procedures, hurricane disasters) are consistent with that view (Goodman, Hirschman, Hepps, & Rudy, 1991; Parker, Bahrick, Lundy, Fivush, & Levitt, 1995; Steward & Steward, 1989, 1996; Warren-Leubecker & Stratwood, 1992), although memories of traumatic events still fade with time (Howe, Courage, & Peterson, 1994; Quas et al., in press). On the other hand, a number of researchers report that greater stress is associated with decrements in children's memory or increases in suggestibility (Baker-Ward, Burgwyn,

Ornstein, & Gordon, 1995; Merritt, Ornstein, & Spicker, 1994). In some of these studies, children's memory for information not integral to the stressor was tested (Bugental, Blue, Cortez, Fleck, & Rodriquez, 1992; Peters, 1991), which may in part account for the results. In others, detrimental effects are restricted to the amount of information provided in free recall, which may reflect unwillingness to talk. Finally, some researchers have reported no or inconsistent relations between stress and memory in children, including children with documented abuse (e.g., Eisen et al., 1995; Howe et al., 1994; Vandermaas, Hess, & Baker-Ward, 1993). Simple counts of the number of studies showing negative, positive, or no effects of stress on memory (e.g., see Ceci & Bruck, 1993) can be misleading, however, because they do not take into account factors that may affect stress and memory relations (e.g., peripheral information was tested).

The mixed results imply that stressful events may be associated with particularly strong memories, but also memories that are in certain ways inaccurate. In a series of clinical studies (Pynoos & Eth, 1984; Pynoos & Nader, 1988; Terr, 1991) concerning children's memories for such horrifying events as homicides of loved ones, kidnappings, and sniper attacks on schools, mostly accuracies but also some important inaccuracies were noted. A mixture of accuracies and inaccuracies might be especially likely in young children's reports of traumatic events if young children have more difficulty than older children and adults keeping event memories separate (Farrar & Goodman, 1990), in which case young children might intrude other traumatic events into their memory reports. Howe et al. (1994) documented a number of such intrusions in young children's memories of traumatic medical procedures.

Inconsistencies across studies may be resolved, in part, by considering individual differences in children's encoding, memory, and subsequent "processing" of stressful experiences, such as abuse, resulting in certain children remembering stressful events more accurately than others. Important individual differences related to children's processing and memory for stressful events have been found in physiological reactivity, attachment, and temperament (Goodman, Quas, Batterman-Faunce, Riddlesberger, & Kuhn, in press; Ornstein, Baker-Ward, Gordon, & Merritt, 1993; Stein & Boyce, 1995). These differences may reflect general tendencies to appraise and interpret situations in certain ways (e.g., as threatening or challenging; Tomaka & Blascovich, 1994). Depending on children's appraisal or interpretation of an event (which may in part be developmentally determined), the specific, discrete emotion (e.g., anger, fear) or emotional blend (e.g., fear and anger) aroused may differ. Specific emotions may direct attention to different features of a situation (e.g., features relevant to escape vs. fighting back), resulting in divergence, on the one hand, in the information encoded and consolidated and, on the other hand, in the information or processing that may be disrupted. After the event, its emotional interpretation may also influence the information that is rehearsed or retained and may be importantly influenced by children's coping strategies and parental reaction (Goodman, Quas, Batterman-Faunce, Riddlesberger, & Kuhn, 1994). Children who do not initially find sexual abuse traumatic but later understand the implications of the acts may show different memory patterns than children who initially realized the act's implications. Children who evidence signs of PTSD (e.g., nightmares) may have intrusive memories that may or may not remain accurate over time (Terr, 1988). One might expect differences in memory between children whose parents told them "just forget about it" or even that "it was your own fault" and children whose parents helped them understand what occurred. Interestingly, findings of individual differences raise the possibility that, in former studies, relations between distress and children's memory may be not causally related but explained by a third variable (e.g., physiological reactivity).

Currently, there is also considerable debate about whether traumatic memories require special memory mechanisms (e.g., repression or dissociation). Some contend that special memory processes need not be postulated to account for memories of trauma (Hembrooke & Ceci, 1995; Howe et al., 1994). Others propose that traumatic events are processed in a substantially different manner than ordinary events (Alpert, 1995; Whitfield, 1995) and that traumatic stress is qualitatively different from ordinary stress (van der Kolk & Fisler, 1995). According to the latter view, when children are confronted with the overwhelming stress of abuse or other traumas, they employ the defense mechanism of dissociation (Janet, 1919/1925). This mode of cognitive avoidance results in the compartmentalization of the traumatic memory. Children's fear of facing the overwhelming emotional memory keeps them from adequately processing the event in a narrative form. Instead, the memory consists largely of sensory perceptions and affective states (Nemiah, 1995; van der Kolk & van der Hart, 1989). Although dissociation has been identified as a key defense mechanism employed by abused children (Briere, 1992; Putnam, 1985), it is unclear that dissociation results in memory deficits. Adequate tests of these ideas will be important before they can be generally accepted by the scientific community.

As can be seen, findings from studies of children's memories of traumatic events are mixed. Simplistic questions about positive or negative effects of stress on memory should be replaced with theory-guided approaches that emphasize developmental and individual differences in appraisals and interpretations of events, effects of discrete emotions on memory, and influences of children's coping with trauma.

Repressed Memory of Abusive and Traumatic Events: A Current Controversy

Can memories of an abusive event, such as sexual abuse, be inaccessible for years, only to vividly re-emerge later? Few issues have engendered such heated debate as that over "repressed" memory of childhood abuse (Alpert et al., 1996; Pezdek & Banks, 1996). In the current debate, there are at least three separable issues: Are abusive events ever forgotten or rendered inaccessible to memory? If so, can such memories be retrieved? Can there be false memories of abusive childhood experiences?

Forgetting Abusive Events. From a developmental perspective, it would not be surprising for some memories of sexual abuse to be forgotten. Sexual abuse comes in many forms, from fondling that may not be viewed as traumatic or memorable when it occurred to violent rape. Memory processes that develop throughout childhood (e.g., rehearsal, retrieval strategies, knowledge base, source monitoring, and narrative skills) may affect retention of personal events (Cowan, in press: Nelson, 1993), even of an abusive nature. The well-established phenomenon of infantile amnesia suggests that if a traumatic event were experienced in the first two years of life, it would not be explicitly remembered in adulthood (Usher & Neisser, 1993). Even in childhood, such memories become unretrievable, at least on interviewer demand (Quas et al., in press). In a study of documented childhood traumas, including child abuse, Terr (1988) found that older children's explicit memory for traumatic events was quickly lost when children were under about 2.5 to 3 years at the time of the incident. Very early trauma led, in Terr's clinical judgment, to personality change (e.g., a child becoming generally fearful) or behavioral memories (e.g., reenactment in play) that incorporated elements of the trauma.

As opposed to cognitive-development processes, Freud (1915) contended that psychic forces can keep traumatic memories out of consciousness and Janet (1919/1925), as discussed earlier, proposed that dissociation may keep traumatic memories compartmentalized. More recently, Terr (1991) hypothesized that memories of repeated traumas become repressed because, sensing that another assault is to begin, children mount defensive processes (denial, dissociation). In contrast, for one-time traumas, children are emotionally unprepared and cannot mount defenses; the event is thus retained with clarity. So far, empirical support for these proposals remains scant. The only studies to date to examine children's memory for a documented, repeated trauma (up to 6 incidents) found no memory decrement (Goodman et al., 1994; Quas et al., in press).

Some evidence for lost memories of abuse is enticing but scientifically fragile, being based on self-report, without substantiation of the abuse. Surveys of adults with alleged histories of child sexual abuse reveal that substantial percentages of respondents (e.g., nearly 60%) indicate that at some point in childhood they had experienced periods of partial to total amnesia for the abuse (Briere & Conte, 1993; Loftus, Polonsky, & Fullilove, 1994). However, these studies did not ensure that respondents indicated lost memories as opposed to lack of thinking about easily recoverable memories.

A more compelling methodology was used by Williams (1994a). She interviewed women who, as children, had been treated at a hospital emergency room for evaluation of sexual abuse. Twenty years after the assaults, approximately 38% of the women evidenced no memory for the earlier emergency room visit or the sexual assault that brought them there. The rates of nonreport remained high even when children abused as infants were removed from the sample. In fact, an even higher percentage of women who did not remember were abused between 4–6 years of age (62%) than between 0–3 years of age (55%)(see also Widom & Morris, 1993). But it is still unclear whether the women forgot the target incident or simply failed to report it; whether memory loss was due to repression or more ordinary cognitive processes; and whether accurate memories could ever be reinstated (Lindsay & Read, 1994; Loftus, Garry, & Feldman, 1994; Williams, 1994b). However, taken as a whole, such studies indicate that memory for childhood abuse can be lost from adults' and children's autobiographical recollections.

Recovery of Abuse Memories. Scientific evidence is less strong for *recovery* of lost memory of childhood trauma. Perhaps the strongest evidence for recovery of traumatic memories comes from studies of recovery from amnesia for traumatic incidents (Christianson & Nilsson, 1989; Cohen, 1995), but in such cases, the amnesia is typically relatively brief. Hypermnesia and memory cuing effects indicate that with repeated recall attempts, new formerly unretrievable information can become accessible, but most such studies have not concerned traumatic events (e.g., Erdeyli, 1985). Dalenberg (1995) reported relatively high levels of verification of recovered memories of child sexual abuse in adult clients, and Corwin and Olafson (1997) provide a provocative case example. Again, given what is known about memory development and memory retrieval, recovery of lost memory seems possible, whether or not lifting of repression is the mechanism responsible.

Falsification of Abuse Memories. False memories of child sexual abuse or other early traumas are also possible. Some authorities doubt that lost memory for entire traumatic events, especially repeated ones, can occur and point instead to suggestive questioning of suggestible individuals, particularly in the therapeutic context, as the basis for repressed-memory reports (Lindsay & Read, 1994: Loftus, 1993; Ofshe & Waters, 1994). One might well doubt the validity of adults' memories of abuse experienced in the first year of life. Some adults seem to use lax criteria to determine whether a thought is a valid memory of an early experience. When pressured or encouraged, about one-third of college students report memories from the first year of life, and a small proportion report memories from the first *week* of life (Malinoski et al., 1995). It is unlikely that such reports represent valid autobiographical memories.

What about false memories for events dating back not to early infancy but to childhood? Loftus and Pickrell (1995) established that approximately 25% of adults could be led to produce full or partial false reports of being lost as children in a shopping mall, if told that their parents had said the event occurred. Pezdek (1995) replicated Loftus and Pickrell's findings for the shopping mall scenario, but found no false memories for an event that more closely resembles sexual abuse—a childhood enema. Pezdek's results indicate that it may not be as easy to create false memories of child sexual abuse as early studies had suggested. Moreover, when false memories are obtained, the susceptible individuals often seem to connect the false information to an actually experienced event in childhood (Hyman, Husband, & Billings, 1995). Regarding memories of abuse, this conclusion implies that at least some "false memory" may have a basis in reality (e.g., a true memory with false details). Susceptibility to false memory may also be related to dissociative tendencies (Hyman & Billings, 1995; but see Leavitt, 1997), which are high for adolescents (often included in false memory studies) and actual child sexual abuse victims. However, studies of false memory have included as errors reports that subjects themselves indicate are not true memories (e.g., "I don't think it's a real memory"). Thus, the amount of false memory indicated may depend on criteria used to score memory as well as on the type of information suggested. Still, some adults report false memories of bizarre, sexually violent satanic rituals that appear to be religion-, therapy- or hypnosis-influenced fabrications (Bottoms, Shaver, & Goodman, 1996; Poole, Lindsay, Memon, & Bull, 1995).

Laboratory studies of false memory that deal with word lists and prototype errors are primarily of theoretical interest, but processes identified in such research may contribute to the formation of false memories of child abuse (e.g., having a schema of a parent as abusive and then basing memory judgments on extrapolations from that schema; generating a vivid image through hypnosis that is then confused with a real memory—Johnson & Raye, 1981; Roediger & McDermott, 1995; but see Freyd & Gleaves, 1996). Some argue that anyone can be induced to form a false memory, even of dramatic events such as satanic ritual abuse, given a specific belief system (e.g., that child-abusing satanic cults probably exist) and a sufficiently suggestive context with an authoritative person (e.g., a therapist—Spanos, 1994). It seems more likely that in addition to a relevant belief system and suggestive context, important individual differences influence proneness to false-memory formation. For instance, depressed adults show greater suggestibility than nondepressed adults (Ellis, 1995); depression is a frequent consequence of abuse and a common reason for entering therapy.

Thus, evidence indicates that abusive events can become inaccessible to memory. However, false memories of abuse can also exist. At present, there is often no known way to distinguish true from false reports of childhood traumas.

Implications for Policy and Practice. Memories of traumatic events may last a lifetime, although not necessarily in pristine form. As Terr (1994) points out, one can have true memories of traumatic events with false details, false memories with true details, and so forth. It would be a serious injustice to deny abuse victims the reality of their experiences; it is also an injustice to foster false memories of abuse, as has sometimes been done by professionals working in clinical and forensic contexts.

Children's Memories of Abuse in Forensic Interviewing Contexts: A Current Controversy

Questions about how to conduct a forensic interview with children have sparked considerable debate in recent years, especially when the interviews concern sexual abuse. How should children be interviewed to ensure accurate reports? How easily are children's memories regarding abusive events contaminated by interviewer bias? Many professionals would probably agree on what constitutes highly coercive, overly suggestive interviewing of children and that such interviewing is to be avoided, but there are grey areas around which debate more understandably revolves.

The debate is relevant to the balance of child, family, and state interests. The state has an interest in protecting children from abuse, which necessitates questioning children to determine if abuse has occurred. But the state also has an interest in protecting innocent adults from false charges and in protecting children and families from unnecessary state intervention. In intrafamilial abuse cases, children and families have an interest in remaining together, but such interests may be abrogated by children's rights to be free from harm. In extrafamilial abuse cases, children and families have an interest in protection from perpetrators. Balancing all such considerations leads to a delicate risk-benefit ratio concerning more or less directive forensic interviewing of children; that is, the risks of children not disclosing abuse and thus lacking protection must be balanced with the risks of eliciting a false report of abuse.

Before the mid-1980s, only a small handful of modern studies of children's eyewitness memory had been published (Goodman, 1984), and none were specifically oriented toward forensic interviews about abuse. Calls for ecologically valid research relevant to child maltreatment helped stimulate relevant research. Now a wealth of germane articles and books are available (e.g., Bottoms & Goodman, 1996; Ceci & Bruck, 1995; Dent & Flin, 1992; McGough, 1994; Spencer & Flin, 1993; Zaragoza, Graham, Hall, Hirschman, & Ben-Porath, 1994). However, because other chapters in this *Handbook* deal with memory development and children's eyewitness memory, our discussion is limited to studies of most relevance to child abuse investigations, particularly investigations of child sexual abuse.

Most psychological research on forensic interviewing of children focuses on issues that arise in sexual abuse cases because these cases rely so heavily on children's statements rather than corroborative evidence. Such evidence (e.g., bruises on the child's body) is expected if physical abuse occurred; in contrast, most child sexual abuse involves acts such as fondling or oral sex, which leave no physical signs. Moreover, reporting delays are often too long for physical evidence to remain, even if it were initially present. And physical evidence still needs to be linked to a specific person. Because sexual abuse is typically a secret act, other adults are unlikely to bear witness to the abuse. Thus, child sex abuse cases often involve weighing a child's word against an adult's word. How the child's allegation was elicited becomes of central concern.

A Continuum of Accuracy

A continuum exists at each point in development along which a child's or adult's report of events such as abuse can be moved toward either greater or lesser accuracy. Developmental level places important constraints on children's abilities to recount abusive events and to resist false suggestion, but accuracy is not solely a function of developmental level or age. Children's memory and suggestibility depend on complex interactions of age (or developmental level), personality, task, and context, including socioemotional and motivational factors. Extreme positions, such as that children are always highly suggestible and unreliable as witnesses, or that children cannot lie about sexual abuse, are not justifiable.

Experimental research on forensic interviewing of children demonstrates that children's reports can be distorted (Ceci & Bruck, Ch. 11, this Volume; Poole & Lindsay, 1995). In contrast, there is also evidence that children's ability to report the central details of salient events is often quite adequate (Goodman, Hirschman, et al., 1991; Howe et al., 1994; Ornstein et al., 1993; Saywitz, Goodman, Nicholas, & Moan, 1991). To complicate matters further, some children are more suggestible than others, and some children may be more likely than others to lie or deceive when interviewed. A set of seemingly discrepant findings has resulted leading to confusion in the courts. An additional complication for the courts in interpreting discrepant research findings stems from researchers' use of different methodologies that move performance toward the accurate or inaccurate ends of the continuum and result in findings that are difficult to compare. Nevertheless, there are many consistent general trends across studies (Eisen et al., in press).

Typically, it is found that even young children can provide valuable forensic information under certain conditions, but that under other conditions, false reports can be elicited. On average, 3- to 4-year-olds provide less complete information and are more prone to error than older children, as expected based on cognitive developmental theory (e.g., Piagetian theory). Error rates fall more gradually thereafter and do not drop to zero even in adulthood. There is also wide consensus that individual differences occur at every age in eyewitness accuracy. Because numerous cognitive, social, and emotional factors affect performance, the interaction of these in a forensic interview influences where on the accuracy continuum a disclosure or denial of abuse falls.

Forensic Interviews

Forensic interviews differ from many other types of interviews, such as those performed for therapeutic purposes (i.e., clinical interviews). Forensic interviews typically must be conducted in a short period of time, are not for the client's own benefit, result in addressing traumatic memories faster than would normally occur in a therapeutic context, and involve matters about which there may be motivation to lie (Melton, 1994). Moreover, for many children, an abuse investigation takes place at a very stressful and confusing time. When children are involved in such investigations, they are often removed from their homes, subjected to repeated interviews, and asked questions about who has hurt or touched them in a sexualized manner. Thus, the abuse investigation provides a unique context for questioning children that is difficult for scientists to study in an internally and externally valid way.

When conducting a forensic interview, it is recommended that interviewers maintain a neutral stance, explore alternate explanations or hypotheses, and videotape or otherwise objectively record the interview (e.g., APSAC, 1994; Raskin & Esplin, 1991; White & Quinn, 1988). Most guidelines regarding forensic interviews about abuse recommend first building rapport with children and then using open-ended, free-recall questions as much as possible, and certainly initially. Use of specific rather than open-ended queries regarding possible abuse raises the specter of leading the witness.

What Is a Leading Question? Some argue that leading questions may be necessary to facilitate disclosure of abuse by children in forensic interviews; others are concerned that leading questions may result in false reports by nonabused children. Because different commentators often mean different things by the term "leading," it is important to understand what constitutes a leading question from a legal perspective. Questions that introduce or imply information not already offered by a witness are typically considered leading. The problem is that almost any question can be leading to some extent. If a child were asked "What happened?" (an open-ended question) and then "What else happened?" the latter question can technically be defined as leading because it implies that something else occurred. A question that includes specific reference to a person and an act (e.g., "Does daddy ever touch your pee-pee?") would be a clear case of a leading question (see *Idaho v. Wright,* 1989). Leading questions take many forms, from strongly leading to minimally leading. Because so many questions qualify as leading and because interviewers are so often attacked for using any leading questions, interviewing children about abuse becomes a difficult task. From research, we know more about what constitutes overly leading questioning than what constitutes sufficiently probing techniques concerning sexual experiences. Nevertheless, once leading questioning is employed, an interviewer runs the risk of legal challenge.

What Constitutes Coercive Interviewing? "Coercive" interviewing techniques have been used in some abuse investigations (e.g., *State v. Michaels,* 1994). Many would agree that when interviewers pressure children (e.g., "You can't go home until you tell me about the time he kissed you") or badger children with repeated questions about abuse while refusing to take "no" for an answer, such techniques are coercive (Ceci, Bruck & Rosenthal, 1995; White & Quinn, 1988). Less clear-cut examples exist, however, which some would term coercive and others would not (e.g., offering a child cookies and juice). How often such techniques are actually employed in forensic interviews is currently being studied (e.g., Lamb et al., 1996; Warren et al., 1995); how often they result in false reports of abuse is unknown. Coercive interviewing can be abusive in itself.

Continuum of Forensic Questioning. It is useful to think of a continuum of forensic questioning from completely open-ended to overly suggestive and coercive. Myers (1992), differentiates between open-ended, focused (e.g., orienting a child to a topic), leading (including specific), and coercive questions, recognizing that the distinction between focused and leading questions is not always clear. Although some argue that leading questions should never be employed, the debate more reasonably centers on when specific questioning becomes too leading.

What constitutes overly leading questioning of children is an increasingly important legal issue. Concerns about false reports of abuse stemming from highly suggestive interviewing recently led the New Jersey courts to impose "taint hearings." If, based on such hearings, the judge determines that interviews were too suggestive and the child's testimony tainted, the child is not permitted to testify, and the case will likely be closed. Because the most frequent defense challenge of child victims in sex assault cases concerns memory and suggestibility (Quas, DeCicco, Bulkley, & Goodman, 1996), taint hearings may be requested in many cases (Myers, 1995). Thus, what constitutes an overly leading interview has important legal implications.

Videotaping. Over the years, there have been debates about whether all forensic interviews with children should be videotaped. There are several advantages to videotaping. It permits fact finders to see how children were interviewed, assess whether or not the interview was overly leading, and observe children's emotional and nonverbal behavior. Moreover, defendants may be more likely to confess when shown a vivid and convincing disclosure of abuse captured on videotape (Davies, Wilson, Mitchell, & Milsom, 1995). Others argue that it is unrealistic to expect all interviews and disclosures to be videotaped (e.g., if the child discloses at home or adds detail while leaving the police station), that videotaping may result in violations of confidentiality (e.g., videotapes of victims being shown on TV or at conferences), and that older children may be inhibited from discussing abuse while being videotaped. Although the debate is not settled, the courts are increasingly leaning toward the view that forensic interviews with children should be videotaped if possible (*Idaho v. Wright*, 1989).

Questioning Children about Abuse

Open-Ended Questions. Research confirms that open-ended questions often result in limited but largely accurate reports from children, assuming the children are not intentionally lying or have not been manipulated into providing false information. There are also indications that in free recall, children tend to recount central or salient information more than peripheral information (Cassel, Roebers, & Bjorklund, 1995), although a child might not know what is central regarding abuse or may have reasons (e.g., concerns about getting into trouble) for failing to reveal such information.

Open-ended questioning of young children may result in information that is too limited for forensic or legal decision making. It also does not guarantee accuracy. One problem arises when the event a child accesses from memory is different from the one of interest to the interviewer. Specific guidance from an interviewer may be necessary to ensure that the child and interviewer are talking about the same event. A subset of children may provide fantasy responses or recall events that are particularly salient to them in response to open-ended questions (see Goodman, Batterman-Faunce, & Kenney, 1993). In an accusatory atmosphere in which children are told that a person may have done something bad, some young preschoolers have been shown in free recall or spontaneous comments to make false statements reflective of their fears (e.g., Tobey & Goodman, 1992).

Specific Questions. Because of children's difficulty with free recall, forensic interviewers in abuse investigations mainly ask specific rather than open-ended questions (Lamb et al., 1996). The amount of relevant information obtained is increased when children are asked specifically about information of interest (e.g., "Did you go into the bedroom?") and when children's memory is triggered by cues (e.g., Gee & Pipe, 1995; Hammond & Fivush, 1991; Ornstein, Gordon, & Larus, 1992). A liability of more detailed questioning and cuing is that inaccuracies tend to increase along with items of correct information (Dietze & Thompson, 1993; Gee & Pipe, 1995), although studies do not typically differentiate between inaccuracies about minor details versus significant actions.

The relative costs and benefits of asking children specific questions about abuse are still largely unexplored by researchers. When not asked directly about genital touch, however, the rate of omission may be high, as indicated by the findings of Saywitz et al. (1991). Five- and 7-year-old children omitted that they had experienced vaginal and anal touch during a doctor examination over 60% of the time *unless* they were asked directly about it; children not touched genitally during the examination produced an 8% false report rate when asked a leading question in connection with an anatomical doll. Thus, 5- to 7-year-olds were not as prone to false reports of abuse as they were to withholding information about genital touch, although some children were more vulnerable than others to error. A similar pattern of findings for 3- to 7-year-olds who were participants in actual abuse investigations was recently reported by Katz et al. (1995).

Errors of omission are not the only errors children produce. Developmental differences in commission errors to abuse-related specific questions have been documented, with children 4 years and younger particularly prone to false responses to abuse-related specific questions (Goodman & Aman, 1991; Goodman, Bottoms, Schwartz-Kenney, & Rudy, 1991). Moreover, error rates increase even for older children when confusing or difficult language is employed (Carter, Bottoms, & Levine, 1996) and under other circumstances as well (e.g., long delays, highly accusatory context; Goodman, Wilson, Hazan, & Reed, 1989; Lepore & Sesco, 1994). Nevertheless, some specific questioning that in a legal sense qualifies as leading may be necessary when interviewing children in abuse cases. At some point, however, specific questioning becomes overly suggestive, increasing the risk of false report beyond legally acceptable levels.

Suggestibility, Consistency, and False Denial about Abuse

There has been considerable concern about false reports of child abuse, particularly sexual abuse, obtained through highly suggestive questioning. Sensational preschool cases, such as the McMartin case in Manhattan Beach, California, and the Kelly Michaels case in Essex County, New Jersey, in which children reported horrific abuse in response to suggestive questions, ignited concerns about children's suggestibility. Most of the interviewing in these sensational preschool cases occurred in the early 1980s, when very little was known about children's eyewitness capabilities. Moreover, the sensational preschool cases that are currently influencing social policy (Ceci, Leichtman, & Bruck, 1995) appear to be "outliers." Data provided by Finkelhor, Williams, and Burns (1988) indicate that, in 1985 (during the height of the preschool case investigations), preschool cases constituted only a tiny portion (1%) of all abuse investigations. Nevertheless, studies demonstrate that, under certain circumstances, children's testimony relevant to abuse can be misled, especially for a subset of preschoolers.

Methodological and Generalizability Issues. Although demonstrations of children's suggestibility are of considerable interest, most are of limited applicability to abuse investigations. First, most studies of this genre have not focused on abusive acts or the categories of children who typically become involved in abuse investigations. Second, most studies involve children observing one-time brief events (often on videotape) that have little personal significance for them. Third, a number of studies include techniques that are unlikely to be used in actual investigations (e.g., Leichtman & Ceci, 1995; Lepore & Sesco, 1994). Fourth, methodological considerations at times make interpretation difficult (e.g., when children who answer a single question inaccurately are grouped with those who answer many questions incorrectly; when errors of commission and omission are combined, despite different legal implications of each error type). As scientists, we are obligated to examine methodology carefully, especially in a field with such important legal implications.

Factors Affecting Resistance and Susceptibility to Suggestion. Suggestibility varies considerably across individuals and situations even within a specific age group (see Bjorklund, Ch. 2, this Volume; Ceci & Bruck, Ch. 11, this Volume; Myers, Saywitz, & Goodman, 1996). Nevertheless, a number of factors may make abusive events particularly resistant to distortion through suggestion. A strong memory for what actually occurred bolsters resistance to suggestion (Loftus, 1979). Abuse is often repeated, and repetition leads to stronger memories, which in certain ways are less subject to memory distortion (Lindsay, 1995; Pezdek & Roe, 1994). Salient, central actions are often stronger in memory than peripheral details, and abusive acts are salient and central. Abusive acts, such as being hit or penetrated, are personally significant and of special interest to children because they relate to children's fears and survival. Interest value (Renninger, 1990) and survival value (Bohannon & Symons, 1993) affect memory strength. Many abusive acts are also fairly unusual (e.g., most adults do not touch children's genitals), and uniqueness facilitates long-term memory (Howe et al., 1994). Active participation in an event can strengthen memory as well, and at times lessens suggestibility (Baker-Ward, Hess, & Flannagan, 1990; Muruchver, Pipe, Gordon, Owens, & Fivush, 1996; Rudy & Goodman, 1991; Tobey & Goodman, 1992). Children who are abused are participants in the abusive event. It has also been proposed that suggestions are more readily accepted when they are plausible, schema-consistent, and non-discrepant from actual experience (Pezdek & Roe, 1994, 1997). For nonabused children, abuse may be less plausible than many other kinds of acts. However, what is viewed as plausible to children may change with development, such that young children may find bizarre information plausible. Thus, especially for young children, suggestibility effects may be obtained even for bizarre information (Ornstein et al., 1993).

Motivational factors (e.g., feeling that it would be embarrassing to agree to an abuse suggestion, believing that one would gain attention and approval for a false report of abuse) are also likely to affect children's suggestibility, although few direct tests of this possibility have been conducted. Abuse-related false suggestions imply socially taboo acts (e.g., being naked in front of a stranger), which may help motivate children to resist agreeing to such implications (Goodman, Rudy, Bottoms, & Aman, 1990). Freedom from intimidation can add to young children's resistance to suggestion about abuse-related events, whereas intimidation may motivate false affirmation of interviewer suggestions. Because young children tend to be easily intimidated, a supportive context may be especially important in bolstering their resistance to suggestive misinformation about abuse (Goodman, Bottoms, et al., 1991).

Developmental level is also an important determinant of resistance to suggestion. Even in a one-time laboratory interview, young children (e.g., 3-year-olds) appear to conform to false suggestions relating to abuse more often than older children (e.g., Goodman & Aman, 1991). Some young children do not seem to realize the impropriety of nudity or genital touch, and thus are not as taken aback by false suggestions about such actions as are older children. Even by 4 or 5 years, many nonabused children show signs of surprise or embarrassment when asked whether a stranger removed their clothes or touched their bottom (Ornstein et al., 1993; Rudy & Goodman, 1991). Moreover, younger children's information-processing limitations (Case, 1985) and difficulties coordinating dual representational systems (Fischer, 1980) may contribute to greater suggestibility through errors in source monitoring and lack of separation of semantic and episodic memory. However, as indicated below, a number of additional factors relevant to abuse investigations can heighten even older children's suggestibility. In sum, suggestibility can be affected by cognitive developmental factors, memory strength, the type of information suggested, and motivation to conform, as well as other factors.

In any case, a child's falsely affirming misinformation does not necessarily mean that memory change occurred, but may simply reflect the child complying with social demands implicit in an interview (Cassel et al., 1995; Lindsay, Gonzales, & Esso, 1995). This is an important issue because courts are concerned that if children's actual memory has been altered through interview questions, cross-examination will be less effective in uncovering the truth (*State v. Michaels,* 1994). It is possible in some cases, however, that both memory change and social compliance influence children's reports (Gee & Pipe, 1995; Lindsay et al., 1995).

The following are several issues of particular relevance to children's suggestibility in abuse investigations (see also Ceci & Bruck, Ch. 11, this Volume).

Parental Influence. When children spontaneously disclose abuse, parents may question them, sometimes repeatedly. In such cases, however, the child's initial disclosure is unprompted, raising less concern about false reports. More controversial is when a parent suspects abuse and questions the child. In a recent study, it was found that in only 10% of the cases was the disclosure elicited by parental questioning (Berliner & Conte, 1995). Because parents are not trained to conduct forensic interviews (e.g., avoiding misleading questions, documenting interviews) and may be highly emotional if they suspect abuse, concerns have been raised about parental influence. Such concerns are especially great when reports of abuse coincide with custody disputes.

Some fear that children may be particularly suggestible when interviewed by their parents. Children may, for example, be motivated to please loved ones and view their parents as authority figures. Young children in particular may confuse what they have been repeatedly told by their parents with the reality of what occurred, but even then children are less likely to incorporate false information about salient body touch (e.g., having their mouth wiped) than about other types of information tested (Poole & Lindsay, 1995). In contrast, there is also reason to expect that children's comfort, familiarity, and trust in their parents might lead to more accurate parent-interview reports. Research evidence on this topic is mixed (Goodman, Sharma, Thomas, & Considine, 1995; Ricci, Beal, & Dekle, 1995). In the only study to include false suggestions of abuse, children were more resistant to such suggestions when questioned by their mothers than by strangers (Goodman et al., 1995).

A related concern is that if a parent has a preconceived bias about what the child experienced, the child will easily be misled by the parent and simply report what the parent told the child to say. There has been surprisingly little research testing this contention for parents or stranger interviewers (Ceci et al., 1995; Dent, 1982), although one study found that while noncoercive interviews by biased compared to unbiased strangers resulted in greater inaccuracies on the part of 4-year-olds, interviews by biased compared to unbiased mothers did not (Goodman et al., 1995).

Although parental influence on suggestibility regarding abuse is of interest, equal attention should be placed on children's false denials of abuse based on parental pressure or desire to protect a loved one. The few relevant studies indicate that children will falsely deny events or even accuse an innocent person to protect their parents (Bottoms et al., 1990; Ceci, Leichtman, Putnick, & Nightingale, 1993; Honts, Devitt, Tye, Peters, & Vondergeest, 1995), facts that child-abuse professionals have known for years (Summit, 1983).

Repeated Questioning. An important forensic issue in abuse cases is the effect of repeated questioning on children. If suspicions of abuse are reported to authorities and the case is substantiated, it is likely that children will be repeatedly interviewed, especially if criminal prosecution is pursued. In such cases, children may be interviewed by parents or other familiar adults, police, social service professionals, attorneys, investigators, mental health professionals, and judges. In one study, the mean number of child interviews by authorities in abuse prosecutions was five (Goodman et al., 1992).

Children are typically interviewed multiple times by professionals because they have already disclosed abuse, although multiple interviews of nondisclosing children take place at times (Bybee & Mowbray, 1993). Concerns about the elicitation of false reports through repeated suggestive interviewing therefore seem to arise more legitimately when children have failed to disclose abuse and there is no corroborative evidence or when children's disclosures become more and more bizarre over time (e.g., new, unlikely perpetrators are identified and the acts described are incredible), as opposed to when children have disclosed spontaneously or during early interviews. It should be kept in mind, however, that there are also risks to conducting a single interview; specifically, the risk of not gaining important information due to children's initial fearfulness, guardedness, or retrieval deficits. Recent research suggests that children at times fail to disclose embarrassing personal information unless repeatedly interviewed with leading questions (Bruck, Ceci, & Hembrooke, in press).

Deleterious effects of repeated misleading questioning on children's memory reports can occur, especially when the repetitions occur within an accusatory context (e.g., Clarke-Stewart, Thompson, & Lepore, 1989; Leichtman & Ceci, 1995; Lepore & Sesco, 1994; Poole & Lindsay, 1995). Most studies have included repeated suggestive questioning across interviews about nonabusive acts and demonstrate adverse effects on a subset of 3- to 4-year-olds. However, simply asking children over and over if an event occurred does not lead to an increase in false reports, on average (Ceci, Huffman, Smith, & Loftus, 1994; Shyamalan, Lamb, & Sheldrick, 1995). Children tend to be inconsistent over trials, sometimes affirming false events and sometimes not. Lower SES and higher scores on imaginativeness scales are associated with more false affirmations. Interestingly, in contrast to false reports (i.e., commission errors), a more robust adverse effect of repeated interviews may be false denial of true events (Shyamalan et al., 1995), a finding relevant to children's recantations of actual abuse.

When the force of repeated suggestions is increased through multiple misleading techniques (e.g., asking misleading questions and instructing children that their parents said that the false events had actually occurred), an increase in false affirmation over trials can occur (Ceci, Loftus, Leichtman, & Bruck, 1994). Importantly, the increase is primarily for neutral and positive events. False affirmation of negative events also appears to increase but less so. However, the generalizability of such findings, when based on few questions—sometimes involving words that young children may not know or events questionably categorized as positive or negative—needs to be established. The main increase in error associated with repeated interviewing often occurs during the first few trials for a subset of children (Ceci et al., 1994), meaning that it is less likely for a child to begin to falsely affirm false events on later trials. Some children, however, may be prone to greater and greater false elaboration with repeated questioning. Future researchers should identify individual-difference predictors of children who produce false elaborations.

There is a difference between simply asking a child if an event occurred and asserting that an event took place through misinformation. If young children are interviewed repeatedly with strongly leading questions containing misinformation, false suggestions may intrude into their reports. Nevertheless, it takes considerable work in research studies to obtain false reports, even for nonabusive acts about which children may be more susceptible to misinformation effects. After weeks of false suggestions, one study found that although many 3- to 4-year-olds initially erred, 79% of them were accurate in the end when gently challenged about their false answers (Leichtman & Ceci, 1995). Moreover, after a 2-year delay, most false reports suggested through misinformation disappeared (Huffman, Crossman, & Ceci, 1996).

One commonality across the studies of repeated interviewing is that, through repeated suggestions, a stronger memory representation may emerge for the false information than for events the child may have experienced. To the extent that preschool children have greater difficulty than older children and adults in source monitoring, separation of semantic and episodic memory, and reasoning about conflicting mental representations (e.g., Welch-Ross, Diecidue, & Miller, 1997), they may be more prone to mistake repeated false suggestions for true memories. If children's memory for an actual event is strong and the questions concern central information, such confusion may be less likely (e.g., Bjorklund et al., 1997).

In any case, despite possible adverse effects of repeated misleading questioning, there is also good evidence that repeated questioning can bolster accurate memory and decrease forgetting (e.g., through rehearsal and memory reinstatement) (Brainerd & Ornstein, 1991; Warren & Lane, 1995). If an event is not rehearsed in memory, then the memory may remain relatively unorganized and fragmentary, becoming increasingly difficult to retrieve over time. This may be especially relevant to cases of abuse if children choose not to think or talk about the event. However, once a coherently organized memory has been established, recall seems to be quite robust and stable (Fivush & Schwarzmueller, 1995). Repeated questioning can help establish a coherently organized, robust memory. Hypermnesia (reminiscence) effects can result in new information being remembered and disclosed with repeated interviewing (Erdelyi & Becker, 1974; Howe, 1991). When children were repeatedly interviewed about a stressful event (i.e., receiving inoculations) across a one-month period, their performance was superior to a group of children who were interviewed only once after a one-month delay (Goodman et al., 1992). In that study, repeated false suggestions related to abuse did not result in more error.

Because children who have disclosed abuse are typically interviewed repeatedly and such repetition can deter memory loss, problems with repeated questioning may be less a matter of memory accuracy than of emotional sequelae (Flin, 1991). It may be emotionally counterindicated for a child to be forced to recall abusive events over and over again to different professionals. For children in actual sexual abuse cases, repeated interviewing was associated with children's more negative feelings about their legal experiences (Tedesco & Schnell, 1987). Many jurisdictions are attempting to limit repeated interviewing by establishing Multidisciplinary Interview Centers (MDICs) (e.g., Myers et al., 1994), where interviews are videotaped to decrease the number of questioning sessions.

Children's Consistency within an Interview. An important forensic issue related to the effects of repeated questioning is consistency in children's reports of abuse. Inconsistency can be a form of suggestibility to the extent that it results from social influence.

In abuse investigations, children have been known to disclose abuse and then recant within the same interview session. Such inconsistencies are troublesome to fact finders, who understandably may not know which statement is true. Consistent testimony is more likely to be believed by jurors than inconsistent testimony (Leippe, Manion, & Romanczyk, 1993). Due to suggestibility effects, young children can be inconsistent in their memory reports when asked the same question repeatedly in an interview (Cassel et al., 1995; Moston, 1987; Poole & White, 1991). Sometimes, the inconsistency reflects a shift from a correct answer to saying "don't know"; at other times, a shift in a yes-no response. Under certain conditions, even 10-year-olds can be prompted to produce inconsistencies. For example, when told they did poorly on an initial memory test, 10-year-olds tended to change their answers to suggestive questions about a story (Warren, Tulse-Trotter, & Tubbs, 1991).

Most studies of children's consistency within an interview do not involve salient body touch, which is of particular interest in abuse investigations. Are children inconsistent in their reports of touch? Quas, Denton, Goodman, and Myers (1996) found that truthful children were less consistent in their reports of being touched than were children coached to lie. These counterintuitive results have important forensic implications: The consistency of a coached child's memory report could be mistaken as an indicator of accurate memory, whereas the inconsistency of a truthful child's report could be mistaken as an indicator of inaccurate memory, when just the opposite may be true.

For repeated interviewing and the consistency of children's reports, "the risk of increased suggestibility lies not so much in repetition as in what message the repetition sends the child" (Myers et al., 1995, p. 923). In a subset of children, repeated interviewing may result in denial of true events or in inaccurate elaborations of false events. Inconsistency is common in young children's memory reports, even when high accuracy is maintained (Fivush, 1993). That is, children do not always mention the same information from one interview to another, or even within the same interview when asked the same question twice. Although consistency of report tends to increase with age, a highly consistent report does not necessarily imply an accurate report. At times, children may have a harder time being consistent about the truth than about a lie.

Long Delays. Some children do not disclose abuse for many years. Even when children disclose quickly, it may be weeks, months, or years before they are interviewed or a trial date set. Thus, effects of delay on children's memory and suggestibility is an important forensic consideration.

It is well known that children's and adults' memories fade with time (e.g., Ornstein et al., 1993; Pipe & Wilson, 1994). If anything, it appears that children's memory fades more quickly than adults' memory (Brainerd, Reyna, Howe, & Kingma, 1990; Flin, Boon, Knox, & Bull, 1992). An increase in memory error can be expected over time, especially if misleading questions are employed. Still, it is surprising how well children can remember some events over long periods of time, if proper cues are provided or postevent reinstatement occurs; if children were not too young when the event took place; and/or if the event had high personal significance (e.g., Fivush & Hammond, 1989; Howe, Courage, & Bryant-Brown, 1993; Terr, 1988). Even after 6 years, many children evidenced memory for special or stressful experiences (e.g., Quas et al., in press), especially when asked specific questions or questioned repeatedly about it over the years, which may keep memory alive (Hudson & Fivush, 1987). Age at the time of a significant life event may be more important than delay in predicting long-term retention (Pillemer, Picariello, & Pruett, 1994; Pipe et al., in press). Thus, even when the events were highly traumatic or abusive, many children show spot or full memories of the experiences after a several-year delay, as long as they were more than about 2.5 to 3 years of age at the time of the trauma (Terr, 1988).

One way to increase suggestibility effects in children is to exploit weak or no memory for an event from the distant past (Bruck, Ceci, Francoeur, & Barr, 1995; Goodman et al., 1995). As is true for adults' memory, as children's memory fades, children may become more subject to suggestion and their reports may become more subject to misinterpretation. In a study intended to mimic suggestive abuse investigations after long delays, children experienced a leading, accusatory forensic interview 4 years after a brief interaction with a man. Although none of the children made outcries of abuse, their responses might have led to false suspicions of abuse (Goodman, Wilson, et al., 1989).

Ideally, all children in abuse investigations would be interviewed immediately, and would provide complete and accurate reports. Reality does not match that ideal. Videotaping of forensic interviews with children may help alleviate some of the problems associated with long delays (McGough, 1994), but given children's frequent delays in disclosure and the legal system's need to ensure fair trials, delays are inevitable.

Implications for Policy and Practice. Most of the studies of suggestibility reviewed here reveal how not to interview nonabused children rather than showing how to interview children who have actually experienced abuse. Because forensic interviewers often do not know whether a child has been abused, they must be mindful of the risks of suggestive interviewing (e.g., false reports; destroying an abused child's credibility). There are developmental trends in children's susceptibility to suggestion; as could be predicted from developmental theory, young preschoolers are particularly susceptible to misinformation. Even for many young children, it takes a fair amount of interviewer manipulation to produce a false report that goes beyond a simple affirmation error. Other children cave in to false suggestions quickly. In any case, most suggestibility studies do not concern suggestions of abuse. Children may be more resistant to false suggestions of abuse than to the types of suggestions often studied. Content matters. Nevertheless, it is likely that some children can be led to make false claims of abuse when a combination of forces (long delays, parental or authority influence, accusatory context, misleading questioning) combine to create an overly suggestive forensic interview. Specialized interviewers are needed who have graduate-level training in memory, cognitive, emotional, and language development, child abuse and trauma, as well as children's eyewitness memory and suggestibility.

Anatomically Detailed (AD) Dolls

Few techniques for interviewing children in abuse investigations have been as controversial as AD dolls (see Koocher et al., 1995, for a review). Within the forensic context, AD dolls were designed to help children recount acts of abuse that might be difficult to articulate because of embarrassment, inhibition, or lack of sophisticated verbal or memory skills (Morgan, 1995). Although AD dolls are frequently used in forensic interviews (Conte et al., 1991), opponents of AD dolls express concern that the dolls may encourage false reports (e.g., Ceci & Bruck, 1993; Gardner, 1991).

Do AD Dolls Encourage Genital Exploration? A number of studies have investigated whether nonabused children demonstrate sexual acts when presented with AD dolls. Across studies, there is surprisingly little support for the idea that exposure to AD dolls in and of itself induces sexually naive, nonabused children to fantasize about sex or to produce sexually explicit enactments, although there are some developmental, ethnic, and SES differences (Everson & Boat, 1990) Everson and Boat claim that AD dolls "provide sexually knowledgeable children with at least implicit permission and perhaps encouragement to reveal their knowledge of sexuality in play" (p. 741). The main forensic question then becomes how children who reveal sexual knowledge gained that information (e.g., from viewing pornography, discussions with older children, or actual abuse). Explicit sexual positioning of AD dolls (e.g., penile insertion into genital openings), especially with spontaneous disclosure that the acts happened to the child, is uncommon among nonreferred, presumably nonabused young children, while insertion of fingers into AD dolls' orifices is routine among nonabused children (Everson & Boat, 1990; Glaser & Collins, 1989).

Another important line of research concerns whether abused and nonabused children react differently to AD dolls. In several studies (e.g., Jampole & Weber, 1987; White, Halprin, Strom, & Santilli, 1988), significant differences emerged between children with a history of sexual abuse and children with no known history of abuse (e.g., children in the former group displayed more sexualized behavior with the dolls). Findings are mixed across studies, however. Allen, Jones, and Nash's (1989) research suggests that degree of family disturbance, in addition to child psychopathology, may influence children's interactions with AD dolls, eliminating differences between abused and nonabused children. For forensic purposes, many child sexual abuse victims do not display sexualized behavior with AD dolls whereas some nonabused children display such behavior (August & Forman, 1989; Jampole & Weber, 1987; White, Strom, Santilli, & Halprin, 1986).

Do AD Dolls Help Children Report Genital Contact? A crucial question about AD dolls is whether children can use them to reenact real abusive experiences or whether the dolls lead to false reports. There are developmental differences in children's ability to employ props, including dolls, as symbolic representational aids for demonstrating autobiographical or script-based experience (Deloache, 1995; Pipe, Gee, & Wilson, 1993). As would be predicted from developmental theory (e.g., Case, 1991; Fischer, 1980), very young children (e.g., 2-year-olds) have difficulty mentally coordinating dual aspects of symbols (e.g., realizing that a doll both stands for something else and is a concrete entity in itself; Deloache & Marzolf, 1995). Several factors (e.g., similarity of symbol to the referent) affect whether or not, and when, children can coordinate such dual aspects.

Although many 3-year-olds can use dolls as symbols, children often provide as much information verbally without dolls as they do with dolls, and dolls increase error rates for young preschoolers (Deloache, 1995; Gordon et al., 1993). Dolls and props may at other times help older children report more information. These findings, obtained for regular (nonAD) dolls, appear to generalize to AD dolls as well (Goodman & Aman, 1991). When children's use of AD dolls in actual abuse investigations is studied, older children are more likely than younger children to disclose abuse using AD dolls (Levy, Markovic, Lainowski, Ahart, & Torres, 1995). This result is consistent with the experimental literature indicating older children's greater ability to recount events using props.

Despite age differences in the effectiveness of props and dolls to elicit accurate and complete memory reports, there may still be a unique advantage for children 3 years of age and older in use of AD dolls. Several studies indicate that these dolls help children demonstrate or acknowledge personally experienced incidents of genital contact (Goodman et al., in press; Katz et al., 1995; Saywitz et al., 1991). With highly leading questions, however, interviewers may be able to obtain false reports of abuse, especially in young children (e.g., 2- to 3-year-olds), whose performance under such questioning conditions may be basically at chance whether AD dolls or their own bodies are used to recount an event (Bruck, Ceci, Francoeur, & Renick, 1995). Some young children may falsely indicate genital touch when none has occurred; other children who have experienced genital touch may omit it or indicate a greater extent of genital contact than actually took place. However, most research on this topic has neglected to include between-subject no-doll conditions. Thus it is unknown whether children would have made the same number of errors if no AD dolls had been employed.

Uses of AD Dolls and Assessments of Abuse. It is clear that AD dolls should not be considered a "test" to "diagnose" sexual abuse (Skinner & Berry, 1993). Boat and Everson (1993; Everson & Boat, 1994) describe the following uses of AD dolls: as a comforter (e.g., to create a relaxed atmosphere); ice breaker (e.g., to focus a child on sexual issues); an anatomical model (e.g., to obtain a child's name for body parts); a demonstration aid (e.g., to help a child show and tell what happened); a memory stimulus (e.g., to trigger the child's memory of sexual acts); and a diagnostic tool (e.g., to differentiate abused from nonabused children based on AD doll interactions). The latter two uses are particularly controversial. When Boat and Everson (1996) examined videotapes of actual CPS interviews, they found that anatomical model and demonstration aid were the most common AD dolls uses, whereas the most common concerning practice was introduction of the AD dolls as a demonstration aid before sufficiently encouraging the child's verbal account. Practices that might be considered the most questionable, such as placing the AD dolls in sexual positions or overinterpreting the child's AD doll behavior, were very rarely observed.

Professionals do not always agree on the disclosure-related acts children demonstrate during forensic interviews, although there may be near-perfect agreement on certain acts, such as children's AD-doll demonstrations of oral-genital sex (Levy et al., 1995). Recent guidelines should help guard against some of the past excesses in AD-doll use (APSAC, 1995).

Children's Drawings. Although scientific research on anatomical dolls is far from extensive, even less research exists on children's use of drawings to recount abusive events or to aid in abuse disclosures. In forensic interviews with children, drawings may be used in several ways: to relieve anxiety and build rapport (e.g., by giving children paper and markers to draw whatever they want while being questioned); to show children pictures as memory cues (e.g., recognition memory); to have children draw as a means of recounting an event (e.g., asking children to draw what happened); or to have children point to a specific picture or part of a picture as a means of conveying information (e.g., showing children an anatomical figure drawing and asking them to point to where they were touched). Relevant research findings are mixed. Several studies suggest that for children 5 years and older, drawings aid in recall of traumatic and nontraumatic information without increasing error rates (e.g., Butler, Gross, & Hayne, 1995; Drucker, Greco-Vigorito, Moor-Russell, & Avaltroni, 1997). However, in one study involving repeated interviews, 25% of 5-year-olds falsely indicated inappropriate touch when shown diagrams of body parts and asked to indicate where they had been touched (Rawls, in press). In terms of practice, it is likely that interviewer skill (e.g., refraining from overinterpreting children's drawings and from being excessively leading) is an important factor in whether or not drawings are useful interview aids, a principle that also applies to interviews with AD dolls. In terms of research, it is likely that mixed results reflect, in part, differences in methodology and scoring, as well as researchers' emphasis on true versus false reports.

Implications for Policy and Practice. Conclusions must be tentative because studies of AD dolls have generally not included repeated interviewing, an accusatory context, or multiple exposures to AD dolls, and very few studies have included highly suggestive interviewing. In a comprehensive review, Koocher et al. (1995) concluded that AD dolls can at times provide "a useful communication tool," but the following caveats were also mentioned: (a) AD dolls are not a psychological test with predictive (or postdictive) validity per se, so use of AD dolls does not constitute a standardized psychological test for sexual abuse; (b) definitive conclusions about whether or not a child has experienced sexual abuse should not be made on the basis of spontaneous or guided "doll play" alone (although sexualized or posttraumatic play may be relevant to conclusions about possible victimization); (c) special caution is warranted when evaluating memory reports of children aged 4 and under, especially when repeated misleading questions have been employed; (d) recognition of normative differences between children of various cultural and SES groups is important for use of AD dolls in forensic evaluations. It should be added that there can be individual differences at any age level in the accuracy of eyewitness memory when AD dolls are employed. Similar caveats apply to use of drawings in forensic interviews.

Identification (ID) of Perpetrators

Relatively little research investigates children's ability to identify perpetrators of abusive acts, although this is a crucial legal issue. Virtually all studies concern ID of strangers viewed briefly during nonstressful events or in films (see Davies, 1993, for a review). Although abuse by strangers tends to be particularly dangerous (e.g., sex abuse involving kidnapping or murder), most abuse is perpetrated by adults familiar to the child (Finkelhor, 1984). Because performance on standard face-recognition tasks is not systematically related to children's ability to recognize people in real-life encounters (Soppe, 1986), the generalizability of many studies in relation to abuse cases is questionable.

Regarding briefly seen strangers, children's photo ID abilities are close to adult levels by about 6 years of age when "target-present" lineups are presented (e.g., Goodman, Bottoms, Schwartz-Kenney, & Rudy, 1991; Parker, Haverfield, & Baker-Thomas, 1986). However, false ID rates regarding briefly seen strangers are high even for older children when "target-absent" lineups are used. That is, children often identify an innocent person when the target person is omitted from the lineup (King & Yuille, 1987; Parker & Ryan, 1993). Children have a strong tendency to guess on target-absent lineup tasks, even when instructed not to do so (Beal, Schmitt, & Dekle, 1995). These patterns hold also for identification of strangers who have performed stressful actions on children's bodies (Goodman, Bottoms, et al., 1991; Oates & Shrimpton, 1991). There has been a modicum of success in training children 5 years and above to make fewer false IDs to target-absent lineups (Goodman, Bottoms, et al., 1991; but see Parker & Ryan, 1993).

An interesting possibility in several experiments is that errors in answers to questions may have resulted from confusions about people's identities. In studies of medical procedures, there can be confusions concerning who was the doctor, the nurse, and the experimenter (e.g., Bruck et al., 1995). Greater attention should be paid to how such confusions affect children's memory performance. Also important are children's ability to identify familiar adults, such as those commonly accused of child abuse (e.g., neighbors, teachers, uncles), and children's confusion about who was present or absent during stressful events (e.g., whether their sibling or a classmate was present). Children's face ID accuracy is far superior for recognition of familiar classmates than for recognition of unknown children (Diamond & Carey, 1977). It is therefore possible that children would make fewer false IDs in lineups of familiar people. But developmental differences can still be expected. Although most 3-year-olds can accurately identify their father in a photo lineup, when they are asked repeated leading questions (e.g., "Is this your daddy?" while pointing to a picture of another "daddy"), some 3-year-olds finally concede (Lewis, Wilkins, Baker, & Woobey, 1995). In an abuse investigation, if a child accurately recounted abuse but identified the wrong person, a serious miscarriage of justice could occur.

Special Interviewing Techniques and Assessments

One approach to ensuring adequate interviewing of children about abuse is to develop special techniques or guidelines for such interviews. A number of such techniques and guidelines have been proposed (APSAC, 1995; Boat & Everson, 1986; Bull, 1995; Geiselman, Saywitz, & Bornstein, 1993; Yuille, Hunter, Joffe, & Zaparniuk, 1993). A "funnel" approach in which open-ended questions are followed by more specific questioning is typically suggested. Studies have not generally pitted special interviewing strategies against each other to determine which ones result in the most useful and valid forensic information.

The "cognitive interview," developed originally by Geiselman and Fischer (Geiselman, Fischer, MacKinnon,

& Holland, 1985) and extended for use with children by Geiselman et al. (1993), shows some promise for older children. It involves instructions such as asking the child to mentally reinstate the context of the event, recount the event forward and backward, and report even unimportant details. This interview has not been validated on preschool children or children who are known to have experienced a traumatic or sexual event. Moreover, recent studies indicate that it may at times be associated with increased errors (e.g., Douglas, 1997; Memon et al., 1995). Success with older children from training programs that teach them to recall forensically relevant categories of information and not to agree automatically with suggestive questions is quite promising (Saywitz & Synder, 1993). But at present, there is no "gold standard" forensic interview, and different interview techniques and approaches may be needed for different situations (e.g., a child has a sexually transmitted disease or is pregnant but will not disclose ever having had intercourse; abuse is suspected based only on accusations by another preschool child in a day-care case).

Assessing True versus False Reports

Development of scientifically valid techniques for determining whether a child's report of abuse is true or false would solve a number of pressing problems. There is as yet no generally accepted, scientifically valid way to determine whether an abuse report is true or false. Although researchers using intuitively based German systems called Statement Validity Analysis (SVA) and Criteria-Based Content Analysis (CBCA) (Undeutsch, 1982) have reported some promising results in discriminating true and false reports by older children of nonabusive events (Honts et al., 1995), there is no scientifically adequate test of SVA or CBCA with abused populations, preschool children, or truthful children who have strong motivation to conceal the truth (see Wells & Loftus, 1991). Moreover, reliability of CBCA coding tends to fall below acceptable levels when corrected for guessing (Anson, Golding, & Gully, 1993). To the extent that children's true and false reports may converge in terms of detail and inconsistencies across interviews (Bruck et al., in press), systems such as CBCL and SVA may fail. Similarly, Gardner (1987) proposed a "test" to distinguish true and false reports of abuse in custody disputes, but it has no documented scientific validity. Nevertheless, attempts are often made to enter analyses based on these systems into court in abuse cases.

Although scientifically based lie-detection techniques for assessing the accuracy of children's reports are lacking, one would hope that the experience of professionals who investigate abuse allegations would advance their ability to distinguish abused from nonabused children's behavior and reports. Mental health professionals cannot always tell accurate from inaccurate reports when children describe nonabusive acts (e.g., Goodman, 1990; Leichtman & Ceci, 1995) and do not always agree on their judgments of whether abuse is indicated (Horner, Guyer, & Kalter, 1993). Nevertheless, CPS workers are significantly more likely than adults without relevant experience to accurately judge cases as unfounded when nonabused children are interviewed as if they were in an abuse investigation, or when abused versus nonabused children interact with their parents (Deitrich-MacLean & Walden, 1988; Goodman, 1990). Interestingly, a certain percentage of professionals with a personal history of abuse may be particularly prone to overinterpret children's ambiguous reports as possibly indicating abuse (Batterman-Faunce & Goodman, 1996; Howe, Herzberger, & Tennen, 1988).

Implications for Policy and Practice. Developmental research can contribute to optimal techniques for interviewing children. Given the range of children involved in abuse cases and the range of their experiences, however, flexibility in interviewing is needed. Although consensus on broad principles of interviewing can be reached (Lamb, 1993), it will be some time before generally agreed-on methods are developed to conduct forensic interviews with children and to determine whether a report of abuse is true or false.

Child Maltreatment Victims in the Juvenile and Criminal Court Systems

Child Maltreatment Victims and Juvenile Court

As CPS became more burdened with abuse investigations, the juvenile courts have become increasingly responsible for handling child maltreatment cases. Cases referred for juvenile court action are typically the most serious intrafamilial ones. Although CPS and the courts try to keep families together, give parents repeated chances to demonstrate adequate care for their children, and try to reunite families, when serious danger to children is feared, a "care and protection" or dependency order may be issued. The juvenile court judge will then determine whether involuntary removal from parental custody or termination of parental rights is warranted. Because foster care placement and termination of parental rights are discussed in depth later in this chapter, only a few issues particularly relevant to child maltreatment are discussed here.

It is estimated that 10% to 24% of all child maltreatment cases result in legal dependency filings (Otto & Melton, 1990; Tjaden & Thoennes, 1992). Because constitutional rights are more relaxed in juvenile court than in criminal court, and the burden of proof is less stringent, judges can use considerable discretion in decisions regarding children. Still, parents retain a number of constitutional rights in dependency proceedings (e.g., right to counsel, right to notification of the hearing). A guardian ad litem is usually assigned to assess the child's circumstances and advise the court (Goldman et al., 1993).

Of all forms of child maltreatment, neglect is the most common reason for dependency orders. In Boston, for instance, the typical child involved in a dependency proceeding is young (e.g., 4 years old), very poor, and being raised by a single parent who is emotionally disturbed or abusing substances. About 30% of the children are returned to their homes following a dependency hearing, but in most cases removal from the home is ordered. Court-ordered removal is especially likely if the parent refuses to comply with recommendations (e.g., to obtain substance-abuse counseling). In Boston, the mean length of time from filing of an official report of mistreatment to the child's final placement (e.g., adoption) is almost 5 years (Jellinek et al., 1992). Jellinek et al. report that nearly half of the children in their sample were still in temporary placements 3.5 years after the filing of the dependency petition and 21% were still in "temporary" placement 7.5 years later (Jellinek, Little, Benedict, Murphy, & Pagano, 1995). Research from other jurisdictions indicates somewhat, though not much, better rates than those reported for Boston.

Children's Experiences in Juvenile Court. Juvenile court proceedings are often closed to the public and to researchers. In many jurisdictions, children rarely testify in juvenile court hearings regarding maltreatment. Instead, professionals are likely to be permitted to repeat children's out-of-court statements, although some children may also talk to the judge in chambers. In other jurisdictions, children are more likely to make a court appearance. In a study of the emotional sequelae of testifying in juvenile court, Runyan, Everson, Edelsohn, Hunter, and Coulter (1988) reported that children who testified as victims in juvenile court showed short-term improvement in behavioral symptoms. However, the level of emotional disturbance shown by children who testified was initially high; at a 5-month follow-up, their disturbance was about the same as that of a group of nontestifiers. Thus the "beneficial" effect may simply reflect regression to the mean. Still, one could conclude that the testifiers were not harmed by taking the stand in juvenile court.

There has been considerable concern that the court process is more harmful to abused children than leaving them in their homes (Wald, 1982). Others argue that removing children from abusive or neglectful homes is the only way to protect seriously maltreated children from further harm (Garbarino, 1982). The long time frame for resolution of such cases does not conform to children's needs for a stable "psychological parent" (Goldstein et al., 1973), and the system does a disservice to children who spend years in "temporary" placements.

Child Maltreatment Victims and Criminal Court

Many more child maltreatment cases are handled by the juvenile courts than by the criminal courts, but charges of child sexual abuse are particularly likely to be referred for criminal court action (American Association for Protecting Children, 1988). Unless there is an especially brutal assault, physical abuse is difficult to differentiate from overzealous discipline and is unlikely to reach the criminal courts. Fatal child abuse cases are prosecuted, but they occur relatively infrequently.

Considerable variability exists across jurisdictions in the number of child abuse cases accepted for prosecution (e.g., range = 1 to 800 cases per year) (Smith, Goretsky-Elstein, Trost, & Bulkley, 1994). Variability is also great concerning the number of children who testify (Goodman et al., 1992; Gray, 1993; Sas, 1991). When "corroboration laws" were common in the United States (i.e., laws requiring physical evidence, a confession, or an independent eyewitness) for child sex abuse cases, relatively few children testified (Rogers, 1982). Since the 1970s, courts in many states and countries dropped corroboration laws, opening courtroom doors, so to speak, to children's testimony. The chance of conviction in trials for child sexual abuse has been found to be about 50–50 in several jurisdictions studied when plea bargains are not considered (e.g., Davies et al., 1995; Goodman et al., 1992; but see Gray, 1993). Such statistics depend considerably on prosecutors' policies concerning the amount of evidence required to go to trial. In most cases, the defendant pleads guilty and a plea bargain is arranged. Only about 10% of cases go to trial (Gray, 1993; Myers, 1993). Prosecutors sometimes accept a plea bargain in part to protect the child from having to testify. Still, many children give depositions, testify at preliminary hearings, or become involved in other kinds of formal legal proceedings, and some children do take the stand at trial.

The decision to prosecute a child maltreatment case is complicated for attorneys. Prosecutors must determine whether there is sufficient evidence and the benefits to the child and society outweigh the costs. The child's age is one factor in this decision. Sexual abuse cases are least likely to go to trial if they involve preschool children as opposed to children in the 9- to 12-year age range (Cross, DeVos, & Whitcomb, 1994; Gray, 1993). Prosecuted cases involving preschool children are more likely to involve intra- than extrafamilial abuse (Gray, 1993). In addition, severity of the abuse, use of force, presence of corroborative evidence, the child having fewer internalizing problems (e.g., depression), and maternal support (e.g., believing the child's disclosure) predict whether a case is prosecuted (Cross et al., 1994). Nonparent adults and stepparents are more likely than biological parents to face criminal prosecution (Tjaden & Thoennes, 1992). Cases are also somewhat more likely to be prosecuted if the child disclosed to friends or acquaintances rather than family members or professionals, and if the police rather than social services conducted the first interview (Cross et al., 1994). Thus, despite (or perhaps because of) concerns about false reports of abuse from preschoolers who disclose to parents or therapists, such cases are less likely to be prosecuted than other kinds of child sexual abuse cases. As a result, scientific studies that show heightened suggestibility in preschool children are relevant to a small percentage of cases accepted for prosecution. Recent societal and legal trends (e.g., concerns about false reports) may change these statistics. Such trends may also affect judges' determinations of a child's competence to testify.

Competence Examinations. The courts make an important distinction between "competence" and "credibility." Competence refers to the general capabilities that any witness must possess to be permitted to testify, which is for the judge to decide. Credibility refers to truthfulness and persuasiveness in the particular case at hand, and that is up to the trier of fact (typically the jury). Until the 1980s, it was common for the courts, by state law, to specify a presumption that children under the age of about 12 years (10 years in some states, up to 14 years in others) were incompetent to testify. Such presumptions could be overcome through a hearing in which competence was demonstrated. When competence laws are in place, a child typically must attend a pretrial hearing in which she or he is questioned about such matters as: (a) the child's ability to differentiate the truth from a lie, and knowledge of what happens if a child tells a lie; (b) the obligation to speak the truth in court; (c) the child's capacity to form an accurate impression of the event when it occurred; (d) the independence of the child's memory; and (e) ability to communicate (Goodman, 1984; Haugaard, Reppucci, Laird, & Nauful, 1991; Myers, 1992). The judge then makes a determination as to whether the child is a competent witness. Interestingly, competence is determined at the time of the competence hearing, not in relation to age at the time of the event. Thus, a child could be 2 years old when abused but 10 years old at trial, and still be found competent.

The more recent trend, as reflected in the Federal Rules of Evidence (601), is to presume children to be competent witnesses unless it can be proven otherwise. In the 1980s, several states passed laws eliminating the incompetence presumption for children in sexual assault cases (Haugaard et al., 1991). However, presumptions in favor of children can also be overturned, again through a hearing. Competence questions tend not to predict children's eyewitness performance (Goodman, Hirschman, et al., 1991; Pipe & Wilson, 1994), but accuracy of testimony is more a matter of credibility than competence anyway.

Children's understanding of the concepts of truth and lie is relevant to competence examinations (e.g., Burton & Strichartz, 1992; Bussey, 1992; Piaget, 1932). Although there are developmental differences in children's understanding of truth-lie concepts, most 4- to 6-year-olds know that a child who makes an intentionally inaccurate statement, either at the request of an adult or to protect a friend, is telling a lie, although a small percentage are confused about such judgments (Haugaard et al., 1991). In addition, many 4- to 10-year-olds know that corroborating an inaccurate statement by one's mother is a lie (Haugaard, 1993). Delays in maltreated children's language skills may affect their ability to answer competence questions. Moreover, abused children's fears of getting in trouble (e.g., severe punishment) may make them particularly hesitant to answer questions about lying (Saywitz & Lyon, 1995).

Relevant developmental research may be helpful to judges who often make difficult competency decisions in abuse cases. Most judges and attorneys have little training in questioning children. As Walker (1993) points out, "When the competency of a witness is an issue in a court case, two of the tests that must be met are the capacity to understand the questions propounded and the ability to make intelligent answers. There is no reciprocal test that a *questioner* must meet, however, that measures his or her competency to ask intelligent, easily understood, and unambiguous questions" (p. 59).

Children's Legal Knowledge. What do children know about the legal system? One would expect developmental differences in the understanding of a system so elaborate and obscure. Limitations in children's understanding of court procedures, personnel, and language may encroach on their ability to act as competent witnesses and may affect their emotional reactions to legal experience.

Children's knowledge of the legal system increases with age, but even older children lack an accurate understanding of important legal concepts and terms (Saywitz, Jaenicke, & Camparo, 1990; Warren-Leubecker, Tate, Hinton, & Ozbek, 1989). Surprisingly, child abuse victims with legal experience display *less* knowledge about courts than nonabused children with no experience (e.g., Melton & Berliner, 1992). This may reflect differences in the children's intelligence or educational achievement, or the extent of parental explanation.

What do children think it will be like to serve as a witness in court? To interview questions about serving as a witness, most children respond negatively. Children express fears of facing the defendant, not being believed, testifying without their mother present, talking to the judge and jury, being sent to jail, not being able to understand or answer questions, not knowing what to do, and being discredited by defense attorneys (Berliner & Conte, 1995; Davies et al., 1995; Flin, Stevenson, & Davies, 1989). Older female children are particularly likely to express negativity about having to testify (Goodman et al., 1992). Programs to allay abused children's fears and prepare them for court are just beginning to be evaluated (Sas, 1991); such programs may make testifying less frightening for children.

Children's Courtroom Experiences and Jurors' Assessments of Child Witnesses

Children's Experiences in Criminal Court. How are child abuse victims treated in criminal courts? Children's experiences in criminal court proceedings have been documented most fully for child sexual abuse prosecutions. Many have compared the child sex victims' experiences in criminal court with those of adult rape victims, who feel put on trial themselves. Indeed, there are some similarities in children's experiences to those of sexual assault victims generally, in terms of both court experiences and jurors' reactions to them. And although a number of innovative methods have been proposed to make testifying less stressful for children, prosecutors are often afraid to implement them for a number of reasons, including the risk that a guilty verdict will be overturned on appeal. In fact, a child abuse conviction in Massachusetts was recently overturned because the child victim/witnesses who testified sat at an angle, facing the jury rather than the defendant. This was deemed to violate the defendant's 6th Amendment rights to face-to-face confrontation (*The Boston Globe,* 1997).

Legal formalities are often loosened during pretrial hearings in criminal cases, but at trial defendants' constitutional rights have a strong effect on children's experiences. At trial, children may be treated like adults, depending on attorneys' strategies. One important difference, however, is that children can be asked leading questions during both direct and cross examination. (Normally, leading questions can be asked only during cross-examination, but the courts have long realized the necessity of asking children leading questions. Without them, children may simply clam up.)

In abuse cases, the child victim is typically called as a witness by the prosecution and cross-examined by the defense attorney. The prosecutor's job is to obtain a description of the assault and an identification of the accused. The defense's job is to discredit the child victim/witness. It is therefore not surprising that in child abuse prosecutions, defense attorneys conduct more hostile, age-inappropriate questioning of children than do prosecutors and ask more about peripheral details (Davies et al., 1995; Goodman et al., 1992). Tactics for discrediting children, such as methods for causing children to contradict themselves, appear suggestible, or be too intimidated to testify, may be used (Myers, 1987). Questions may be asked in "legalese" (e.g., double negatives, highly complex sentence structure) that children cannot understand (Brennan & Brennan, 1988; Walker, 1993) and can result in greater suggestibility and error (Carter et al., 1996). Teenagers are more likely to receive harsh questioning than younger children (Whitcomb et al., 1991). In general, the tables turn in the approach toward children when the defense calls the child as a witness and the prosecutor conducts cross-examination.

Children's caregivers may be prohibited from being in the courtroom when the children testify. Many courts now permit a support person (e.g., a victim advocate) to accompany the child; research indicates that social support promotes more accurate testimony in children (Carter et al., 1996; Moston & Engelberg, 1992). Fear of the defendant is related to children having difficulty answering prosecutors' questions. The experience on the stand is typically not long, about 20 minutes on average, although some children are questioned for days or weeks (Goodman et al., 1992).

When children emerge from the courtroom, they often indicate relief that the event is over. They generally feel that the most negative part was facing the accused. Although testifying can be a grueling experience for an abused child, some children precluded from taking the stand regret not having their day in court, especially if the defendant is found "not guilty" (Goodman et al., 1992). Children involved in prosecutions often indicate that although participation in the criminal justice system is anxiety-provoking, they would rather participate than be excluded (Berliner & Conte, 1995).

Jurors' Assessments of Child Witnesses. When children testify at trial in abuse cases, jurors face the difficult task of judging their credibility. Several general trends in jurors' reactions to children's testimony have been identified, mainly through mock trial research. First, although jurors are typically more biased against children than adults with respect to memory abilities and resistance to suggestion (Goodman, Golding, Helgeson, Haith, & Michelli, 1987; Leippe et al., 1993), in abuse cases certain attributions can lead to children's enhanced credibility. In particular, young children are viewed as not having the knowledge base or cognitive ability to make up a believable, false story of sexual abuse (Bottoms & Goodman, 1994; Isquith, Levine, & Schneider, 1993). Second, compared with females, males on average view children as more suggestible, more responsible for sexual abuse, and more likely to make a false report (e.g., Bottoms, 1993; Isquith et al., 1993). Underlying these gender differences, however, are attitudes regarding empathy toward child victims, sexuality in general, and children's cognitive abilities and motivations, so females who hold negative attitudes on these dimensions may be less prone to believe children than males who hold more positive attitudes (Bottoms, 1993).

A third robust finding is that mock jurors typically have difficulty in distinguishing accurate from inaccurate, as well as truthful from dishonest, child testimony (e.g., Goodman et al., 1989; Leippe et al., 1993; Orcutt, 1995; Wells & Turtle, 1987). Some studies indicate that, if anything, jurors are somewhat more likely to believe children who are inaccurate or lie than children who are accurate and honest (Myers et al., 1995), in part because jurors mistake confident and consistent child testimony for accurate testimony, even when it is not.

Emotional Effects of Criminal Justice System Involvement. It has been suggested that involvement in criminal prosecutions exacerbates the trauma caused by child abuse itself. In the short-term, involvement as victim/witnesses in the criminal justice system is associated with the prolonging of emotional distress for a subset of children (e.g., Goodman et al., 1992; Runyan et al., 1988; Whitcomb et al., 1991). Children who testify repeatedly, who lack maternal support, whose cases lack corroborative evidence, and who are more fearful of the defendant may be at particular risk. Harshness of courtroom treatment is also associated with ill effects, especially in older children (Whitcomb et al., 1991).

Legal experts argue that short-term negative effects of testifying are not only common for many witnesses, but are unavoidable given our legal system (*Coy v. Iowa,* 1990). Few studies exist on the long-term effects on child abuse victims of their legal experiences, and such studies typically suffer from methodological problems that muddy conclusions (e.g., lack of statistical control over correlated variables, low participation rates). However, long-term studies indicate that children who have testified rate the legal process as less helpful than those who have not; some children are still upset about their court involvement years later; testifying more than once is associated with negative long-term outcomes; number of interviews endured is negatively correlated with perceived helpfulness; females and incest victims are more conflicted than males and nonincest victims about the helpfulness of their legal experiences; better adjustment is associated with a guilty adjudication for the defendant and maternal support of the child (Sas, 1993; Tedesco & Schnell, 1987; Whitcomb et al., 1991). Moreover, important differences exist in children's lives after prosecution for those involved in intra- versus extrafamilial cases (e.g., children in intrafamilial cases are more likely to experience a permanent change in family composition) and for girl versus boy victims (e.g., defendants receive lighter sentences when the victim is a girl) (Sas, 1993). Although most studies have not examined long delays (e.g., 10 years), possibly missing changes in perceptions as children emerge into adulthood, the overall impression one gets from the literature is that (a) maternal support is an important predictor of outcomes for children; (b) courtroom testimony and numerous precourt interviews of children can, though need not, contribute to adverse effects on mental health and feelings that the legal process is not helpful; and (c) children involved in intrafamilial cases (typically females who suffered more prolonged abuse) may be most at risk for adverse effects of criminal court involvement.

Courtroom Techniques to Reduce Children's Trauma: Children's Testimony and Jurors' Reactions

Closed-Circuit Television (CCTV). Sixth Amendment rights to confrontation traditionally require all witnesses to testify face-to-face with the defendant and submit to cross-examination. Child testimony via CCTV represents an innovative technique aimed to reduce face-to-face confrontation with the accused. The U.S. Supreme Court ruled in *Maryland v. Craig* (1990) that if, in a sexual abuse prosecution, the child victim/witness would be so traumatized that she or he could not reasonably communicate in open court, the judge could permit the child to testify via CCTV. Nevertheless, child testimony via CCTV has been ruled to be in violation of certain state constitutions (e.g., Pennsylvania). Moreover, most prosecutors prefer to present a live witness: A live witness is thought to have greater influence on the jury, increasing the emotional impact compared with a televised witness (Davies & Noon, 1991).

Experimental and field research confirms prosecutors' fears: CCTV reduces the impact of testimony on jurors and leads to more negative perceptions of child witnesses (Davies & Noon, 1991; Tobey et al., 1995). CCTV does not appear to interfere with jurors' assessments of children's accuracy or truthfulness: Mock jurors' are no better at detecting lying in children who testify live rather than via CCTV (Orcutt, 1995). In the end, jurors' guilt judgments and verdicts are unaffected by open versus CCTV testimony (Murray, 1995; Ross et al., 1994; Swim, Borgida, & McCoy, 1993; Tobey et al., 1995). Some children prefer facing the accused, and thus children should be permitted to choose whether or not to testify via CCTV (Cashmore, 1992).

Although frightened children may profit emotionally from testifying via CCTV, and the legal system may profit in obtaining more complete child testimony, the loss of impact and negative impressions of children's testimony limits its use. Thus, even though CCTV is becoming commonplace in several countries, it seems less and less likely that CCTV will be widely implemented for child abuse victims in the United States.

Hearsay Exceptions and Videotaped Testimony. Although CCTV provides some shelter from courtroom battles, children must still submit to direct and cross-examination by attorneys. Several other approaches to children's evidence further limit children's court appearances. One approach is for an adult to testify in place of the child. If a witness repeats a child's out-of-court statements about abuse (e.g., the child's disclosure to parents or police), such testimony is hearsay. In the United States, hearsay is generally inadmissable in criminal court, but a number of special exceptions to the hearsay rule apply to child abuse cases. Statements made to a physician or nurse (sometimes to mental health professionals) for the purpose of diagnosis can be restated in court. The law assumes that patients want to obtain proper medical treatment and will thus be truthful to medical staff. However, if the child is too young to understand this relation, the judge may bar such hearsay. Statements made by a child while still "under the emotional force of the event" can also be repeated in court under "excited utterance" or *res geste* exceptions. Other important hearsay exceptions are the Child Abuse or Residual Hearsay Exceptions. For these exceptions, hearsay can be admitted at trial if the judge decides the information is sufficiently reliable. The judge evaluates the "immediately surrounding circumstances" under which the child's statement was made, including whether suggestive questioning was employed (*Idaho v. Wright,* 1989).

Similarly, if a videotaped interview is admitted in court in place of a child's testimony, the videotaped interview is hearsay because it contains out-of-court statements. A more likely scenario in the United States is for a child to testify live as a witness and then for the videotaped interview to be used to show possible contradictions in the child's statements. In England, new laws permit videotaped forensic interviews to be introduced in place of a child's direct examination at trial. For purposes of cross-examination, the child testifies at trial via CCTV. In such trials, children appeared less nervous and the questioning was more supportive and age-appropriate in videotaped interviews than when the children were questioned by the attorneys via CCTV. Trial verdicts were unaffected by whether testimony was presented via videotape plus CCTV or CCTV only. Most children preferred to provide testimony via videotape or CCTV as opposed to having to face the accused and testify in open court (Davies et al., 1995).

In the United States, mock-jury research must suffice to examine effects of videotaped interviews as hearsay. Myers et al. (1995) found little difference in mock jurors' reactions to live child testimony, videotaped forensic interviews, or forensic-interviewer hearsay testimony although hearsay testimony was valued somewhat less by the jurors (but see Golding, Sanchez, & Sego, 1997). The accurracy of hearsay witnesses in recounting children's statements has been questioned (Warren et al., 1997), but for the courts, this is simply another instance of necessary reliance on eyewitness memory.

Implications for Policy and Practice. Prosecutors report that jurors' belief in children's testimony is increased by seeing an upset child on the stand (Limber & Etheridge, 1989). Protective measures such as CCTV, hearsay witnesses, and videotaped testimony may adversely affect the credibility and impact of child testimony, but shelter the child from a stressful experience. How to balance the interests of children, defendants, and the state in such cases remains a challenge for social policymakers.

Expert Testimony about Abuse

Many issues are addressed by expert witnesses in maltreatment cases. Expert testimony has been given in criminal prosecutions on the accuracy of children's memory of abuse, children's recantation of abuse or delay in reporting, behaviors commonly observed in abused children, and "profile evidence" concerning persons who perpetrate abuse; in juvenile court hearings on information relevant to termination of parental rights; in child custody litigation on why allegations of abuse may arise when parents divorce; in civil suits on the psychological damage caused by child abuse; and in sentencing hearings in capital murder cases on how a defendant's own abuse as a child led him or her to violence. In criminal cases, testimony regarding evaluation of a specific child is often solicited by prosecutors, whereas the defense increasingly argues for admission of expert testimony on children's suggestibility and convicted defendants' history of abuse (Berliner, in press).

Regarding testimony in court, experts are not permitted to testify as to the credibility of a particular witness (e.g., *State v. Milbradt,* 1988). Opinions that a child has been abused have been criticized as being thinly disguised opinions of credibility. Many psychological commentators argue that psychologists should not testify as to the "ultimate legal issue"; that is, whether or not, in the expert's opinion, a child suffered maltreatment (Melton & Limber, 1989; but see Myers et al., 1989). The major objection concerns sexual abuse, specifically, when expert testimony is designed to assist in determining whether child sexual abuse took place; in contrast, testimony on the "battered child syndrome" is permitted in physical abuse cases (Berliner, in press). In sexual abuse cases, physical evidence of abuse is usually lacking thus requiring an expert to rely on interviews with victims or defendants in regard to the ultimate issue, whereas in physical abuse cases, physical evidence (e.g., bruises, broken bones) typically exists.

Fischer (1995) has recently argued that given the range of behaviors associated with child abuse, and given that many of these behaviors result from other experiences as well (e.g., divorce), psychologists should not testify in court that certain behaviors are necessarily indicative of abuse. As mentioned earlier, Kendall-Tackett et al. (1993) concluded that no one symptom is found in even the majority of sexually abused children. Although certain sexual behaviors are rare in nonabused children, such behavior can occur (Friedrich et al., 1992). Moreover, "profile evidence" concerning an abused child (i.e., that the child's behavior—sexualized play, bedwetting, nightmares—fits a profile consistent with the child having experienced child abuse) can be misleading, according to Melton (1994), who shows how lack of consideration of base rates can lead to inaccurate prediction (e.g., false positive errors) concerning victimization. In a review of appellate court decisions, Mason (1991) found many contradictions in expert testimony given by clinicians on behalf of prosecutors concerning symptoms of maltreatment and a lack of careful scrutiny by the courts of the scientific basis of clinicians' testimony. However, testimony by experimental and clinical psychologists for the defense has also been criticized for bias or exceeding scientifically verifiable bounds (e.g., Lyon, 1995). As is typical in the adversary system, excesses can be found on both sides.

What are the effects on fact finders of expert testimony in child abuse cases? Existing research suggests that mock jurors' knowledge is improved by provision of expert testimony, but that expert testimony is unlikely to affect the verdict, although it is more likely to do so if it concerns the specific case instead of general principles (Crowley, O'Callaghan, & Ball, 1994; Gabora, Spanos, & Joab, 1993; Kovera & Borgida, 1996). In some actual trials involving allegations of child abuse, however, anecdotal evidence attests to the powerful influence of convincing expert witnesses.

Implications for Policy and Practice. Expert witnesses have substantial ethical responsibilities. Because knowledge regarding abuse is imperfect, experts should be prepared to acknowledge the limits of the research and clinical literatures.

Concluding Comments on Child Maltreatment

Although most professionals acknowledge that child maltreatment is an all-too-prevalent problem that contributes substantially to societal ills and individual pain, there is still disagreement about how to prevent child maltreatment, the causes and effects of child maltreatment, and the best ways to intervene. Despite the controversies, child maltreatment represents an area that requires particular balance. Many actions taken by the state in child maltreatment cases aimed at benefiting children may also cause children and families harm (e.g., removal of children from home, prosecution of a child's parent in criminal court). Also, what may help actual abuse victims can be damaging for nonabused children when abuse is suspected (e.g., repeated interviews to obtain a disclosure of abuse). Because scientific knowledge about child maltreatment is imperfect, risk-benefit ratios of state intervention versus lack of intervention must be carefully considered.

Controversies are particularly heated with respect to child sexual abuse. The biggest current controversy revolves around children's and adults' suggestibility for traumatic childhood abuse. For developmental psychologists, there are many theoretical issues of substantial importance within this debate. How does the development of source-monitoring abilities affect suggestibility about traumatic events? How do children come to discriminate reality from fantasy (Foley, Harris, & Hermann, 1994)? Are highly traumatic events, especially of a sexual nature, encoded and retained differently from nontraumatic events as some have claimed? How does PTSD affect children's memory? From an applied perspective, an open question of substantial importance concerns how to balance the need, on the one hand, to obtain accurate memories of abuse from maltreated children and, on the other hand, to avoid false allegations from nonabused children. Developmentalists could make a particularly positive contribution to the legal system by developing techniques to optimize the accuracy and completeness of children's testimony in regard to abusive events.

This review provides a sense of many of the controversial areas, but there are more. For example, how can society prevent child maltreatment? Are sexual abuse prevention programs helpful or detrimental to children? Should mandatory reporting laws be revoked? Is child maltreatment best handled through therapeutic intervention or criminal court action? Should corporal punishment be illegal? Should children be permitted to decide whether to return to abusing parents? There is a need for high-quality developmental research to answer such questions.

Research is also needed on the developmental trajectories that result from child abuse, including neglect and emotional maltreatment. An adequate developmental model of the effects of abuse is missing, though important strides are being made (e.g., Cicchetti & Toth, Ch. 8, this Volume). Although preventing maltreatment should remain the ultimate goal, understanding the effects of child abuse is important for intervention. It is quite possible that child maltreatment will never be eradicated. Thus, to guide intervention, the legal and social service systems need to appreciate the psychological effects of maltreatment on children even while prevention efforts are underway.

If developmentalists can devise realistic, scientifically based means to help CPS and the courts in their work, collaboration between developmental psychology and the legal system would be strengthened. In this way, researchers can contribute to science, justice, and the welfare of children.

FOSTER CARE AND ADOPTION

Over a half million children and their families are involved in the legal system each year through foster care and adoption (Barth, Courtney, Berrick, & Albert, 1994). Most such children have been abused, neglected, or abandoned by their parents. Projections based on children whose parents have HIV or AIDS suggest that soon, for the first time in several decades, a significant number of orphans may also be placed in foster care each year (Taylor-Brown, 1991). Most children who enter the foster care system will return to their birth homes. The parental rights of some children in foster care will be terminated, making these children available for adoption. Other children will remain in foster care, without being freed for adoption, until emancipation (i.e., the court's decision that the child is sufficiently mature and capable to be considered an adult for most purposes). This section describes the experiences of children and parents who are involved in the foster care and adoption systems. It is divided into three parts: the first examines issues in foster care, the second explores the process of terminating parental rights, and the third examines issues related to adoption.

Psychologists and other mental health professionals can become involved with the foster care and adoption systems in two general ways: (a) through the evaluation of individual children and parents as a way of helping a court or an agency determine the best placement for a child, and (b) through efforts to influence state or federal foster care and adoption policy. To be effective in either role, a mental health professional must have a firm understanding of both the law and the social science research pertaining to an individual case or a policy initiative. Knowledge of the law is important because the law dictates which types of information are pertinent to a case at a given point. For example, an assessment of the best interests of a child is of minimal importance during a hearing to terminate parental rights, but is of primary importance in a hearing to determine custody of a child whose parents' rights have been terminated. Similarly, knowledge of relevant social science research is important. For example, research about transracial adoption and about the concept of the "psychological parent" may guide policy decisions about racial matching of children and adoptive parents, and may guide individual decisions about whether to place a child with his or her long-time foster parents of a different race or a new set of parents of the child's same race.

The social science research concerning many of the issues presented here is rudimentary. Several of the issues recently emerged. In addition, there are several methodological and legal barriers to completing empirically sound research on many foster care and adoption issues. Children cannot be randomly assigned to various foster care and/or adoptive homes to examine the mutual influences of the children and the homes on each other. This complicates comparisons of different foster care and adoption arrangements. For example, children available for transracial adoption in this country are likely to be those for whom a same-race adoptive family could not be found, complicating the comparison between those in same-race and transracial placements. In addition, foster and adoptive families have many different characteristics, and it is often difficult for a researcher to find enough families meeting specific characteristics (e.g., single-parent adoptive homes) to study them. This either requires that information be gathered from a heterogeneous sample, with the subsequent concern about its representativeness for any particular subset of the sample, or that limited information be gathered from a geographically diverse sample. As a result, there are few issues in the foster care and adoption areas about which there is sufficient social science evidence on which to draw firm conclusions. Although the social science research may provide some guidelines, it is important that it not be given more weight than it deserves in many areas.

Several themes seen in the previous sections will be found in this section, although often with a different twist. For example, the balance of the rights of parents, child, and the state is an issue in almost all foster-care or adoption decisions. The issue often is more complicated in adoption and foster care because several sets of parents may be involved, each with their own interests. These interests often conflict, as when foster parents compete with state welfare agencies regarding returning a child to his or her birthparents, or when a birth father sues to have his child's adoption nullified and the child returned to him. The state, which has interests in both maintaining birth families and maintaining the process of adoption for children who need new families, often finds itself having to make decisions that will harm one of these two interests.

The theme of the competency of children at different developmental levels also cuts across all three sections. Whether children have the capacities to participate in decisions about their own foster care or adoption is an important issue, and is similar in many ways to whether children should be consulted regarding custody after parental divorce or whether they have the capacity to give an accurate recounting of an incident in which they were sexually abused. As discussed later in this section, whether children at certain ages have the capacity to bring a matter before the court independently or must use a *guardian ad litem* is currently an important issue for the courts. Finally, the issue of ongoing contact between birth parents and their children in foster or adoptive homes has some parallels to the issue of joint custody. Are there consequences to a child's development if he or she is involved with more than one set of parents when these parents may have different beliefs and expectations for the child?

Each of the three parts of this section begins with a general discussion of historical, legal, and research issues. Several issues that are currently controversial or problematic are then discussed. Some important controversies are not included, either because they are of minimal importance to psychologists (e.g., strategies for recruiting minority foster parents) or because there is little or no social science research pertaining to them (e.g., under what circumstances siblings should or should not be placed in the same adoptive home).

Foster Care

Most societies provide some means of caring for children whose parents are unable or unwilling to care for them. The goals of this care, and the ways in which it occurs (e.g., within family or institutional settings) can be important indications of how a society views its children and their upbringing. Care for abused, neglected, or abandoned children has a long history in America. It is interesting to note some of the similarities between current and previous practices as well as the periodic recurrence of various issues and controversies.

Historical Overview

Laws pertaining to dependent children in colonial America were based on the Elizabethan Poor Law of 1601 (Trattner, 1979; for extended review, see Cox & Cox, 1985). The short life span of adults and the prevalence of disease meant that a substantial number of children in each community needed some type of care. Care was provided mainly through indentured servitude, in which children were legally bound to another adult as an apprentice or other worker until the age of 18 or 24 (Bremner, 1970). Even infants and small children could be legally bound in this way. Some communities used *vendue,* or the procedure of obtaining publicly funded care for a child by auctioning the child to the person willing to provide the care for the least amount of money. The social importance of work and discipline was reflected in officials' abilities to remove children from parents who allowed them to grow up in "idleness or ignorance" and place them in a setting where they could learn the value of hard work (Bremner, 1970).

In the early 1800s, as there was less need for the labor of small children, children were often not apprenticed out until middle childhood. The needs of small children were met in large cities through almshouses—which housed destitute, physically ill, and mentally ill adults as well as children. Conditions in most almshouses were deplorable. For example, of the 1,527 children received at New York City's

Foundling Hospital in 1868, all but 80 had died within a year (Geiser, 1973). In reaction to the almshouses, many religious and other charitable groups began sponsoring asylums for orphans, abandoned children, and children with destitute parents. There was general opposition to providing support or relief directly to parents because of the belief that it would promote laziness and dependence on the part of the parents (Bremner, 1970). Consequently, children had to be taken from their parents to receive any aid, and society relied on large institutions to care for needy children. Furthermore, parents had no legal rights to their children once the children had been removed from them (Rothman, 1971). Increases in orphaned and abandoned children brought on by the Civil War expanded the need for custodial institutions for children.

Charles Loring Brace was one of the first people to advocate placing dependent and needy children in foster homes rather than institutions. He encouraged the placement of children from New York City with families on western farms. Technically, the children were not indentured, and the children or the parents could end the relationship at any time. It is unclear, however, whether children could easily have left problematic placements. Brace's ideas were not generally accepted, and there was considerable opposition from Catholic and Jewish groups who were concerned about Catholic and Jewish children being placed in primarily Protestant western families (Bremner, 1970). In addition, several scandals developed when the exploitation of some of the children was reported and it became clear that there was little or no follow-up with the children to ensure that they were not being mistreated (Hollinger, 1991).

The settlement house movement of the late 1800s promoted the importance of prevention and of maintaining dependent children in their families whenever possible. Many private charities developed settlement houses in tenement areas with workers who provided education, support, and aid directly to parents and other adults. The importance of prevention was reinforced by the White House Conference on Children in 1909 which focused on supporting families. The federal Children's Bureau was established as well as the private Child Welfare League of America. The focus on families also reinvigorated Brace's message of caring for dependent children in foster families rather than institutions, and increasing numbers of children were placed in foster families that were supported financially by local government and private funds (Cox & Cox, 1985).

The Social Security Act of 1935 established several programs for dependent children. However, there was little federal financing for foster care until 1961, when the federal government began providing some foster care funds for children who qualified for the federal Aid to Families with Dependent Children (AFDC). Most of the funds were earmarked for out-of-home placements for children, rather than for preventive services for families, which may have had an important influence on the number of children in foster care (Cox & Cox, 1985).

Recent Policy and Practice

The Adoption Assistance and Child Welfare Act (AACWA)—federal legislation passed in 1980—has had an important influence on current foster care practice. The law focused in two areas: mandating the primary importance of services to families to avoid removal of children into foster care, and codifying the concept of *permanency planning,* which required that child welfare agencies form prompt and specific plans for children in foster care either to return them to their birth homes or to provide them with adoptive placements. The law also has had a significant influence on preventive services to families that were at risk for having their children removed into foster care. The Children's Bureau, other state and federal agencies, and private foundations have encouraged the development of intensive interventions with families to help them overcome short-term problems and develop effective parenting skills for the long term. Although these programs are often shown to be successful at reducing out-of-home placement for some children, their overall effect on the foster care system is unclear.

The AACWA also has influenced the length of time children stay in foster care. Between 1977 and 1987, the median length of stay in foster care was reduced by 46%. In addition, in 1987 half of children in foster care were in care longer than 2.4 years and by 1989 (the last year in which such data were gathered) half of the children were in care longer than 1.4 years (Barth et al., 1994).

Based on the requirements of the AACWA, the process of placing a child in foster care is as follows (for additional discussion, see Cahn & Johnson, 1993): If a child welfare agency has determined that it would be unsafe for a child to remain in his or her home, the child can be removed and placed in foster care. Removal decisions must be reviewed by a judge, with the child's birth parents having the right of legal representation. In some jurisdictions, an attorney or other person is appointed to represent the interests of the child. Once the child is in placement, the child welfare agency must develop a case plan that includes *reasonable efforts* to rehabilitate the family so that the child can return home. The AACWA requires that the plan be reviewed every 6 months. A decision about permanent placement for the child must be made by 18 months after placement. If a parent develops the ability to parent adequately, then the child is returned home. If conditions that led to the removal of the child do not improve, the child welfare agency can pursue termination of the parents' rights to the child. Termination proceedings are adversarial and result in a judge weighing the efforts that the agency has made to provide services to the parent, the parent's improvement in areas that had been identified as problematic, and the parents' general capacities to provide adequate parenting. The judge may either send the child home, continue the case if some, but not enough, progress has been made by the parent, or terminate the parent's rights. If termination of parental rights is approved, the parents can appeal the decision, a process that can often take between 2 and 5 years.

There are several impediments to the smooth running of this process. Of primary difficulty is that the courts have never provided clear guidelines about what constitutes reasonable efforts on the part of child welfare agencies to rehabilitate a parent (Cahn & Johnson, 1993). Some judges require that welfare agencies offer extensive services to parents and go to great lengths to facilitate the parents' involvement in the services before they will consider terminating parents' rights. Consequently, welfare agencies may be hesitant to bring cases to court in which the parents have shown any participation in treatment, and this can increase the time that children remain in foster care. This also can result in parents being offered a hodgepodge of services, some of which may not be appropriate.

The irreversibility of terminating parental rights makes many judges reluctant to grant terminations (Sommer, 1994). As a result, lawyers for departments of social services may hesitate to bring final termination procedures to court except in the most obvious cases of parental unfitness (Cahn & Johnson, 1993). The result can be many children in foster care who are unable to return home because of their parents' continuing problems and unable to be adopted because the problems are not sufficiently severe to provide the level of certainty needed for termination to occur. This delay increases the amount of time that a child spends in a foster home and may reduce the child's ability to be adopted at all, because older children are more difficult than younger children to place in adoptive homes (Barth & Berry, 1988).

Trends in Foster-Care Placements. Over the past few decades, the foster care system has been described as being in crisis. The crisis has deepened recently due to an increase in the number of children needing foster placement, a reduction in the number of family foster homes, and the inability of the child welfare and legal systems to move children through the foster care system quickly and into permanent placements in their birth families or in adoptive homes.

The number of children in foster care in the 1970s was about 500,000, a number that declined to about 250,000 in the early 1980s primarily due to federal and state mandates regarding the length of time that children could remain in foster placements (e.g., National Commission on Child Welfare and Family Preservation, 1990). Barth et al. (1994) disagreed with this assessment, suggesting that the 500,000 figure was too high because it was based on an unrepresentative sample of 315 welfare agencies. They suggested that federal and state mandates resulted in only small declines in the foster care population. Data to reconcile this disagreement are not available. The number of children in foster care began to increase in the mid-1980s. From 1982 to 1992 there was a 69% increase in children in foster care, and by 1993 460,000 children were in out-of-home care. This number is expected to rise to over 500,000 by the end of the 1990s (Pasztor & Wynne, 1995).

The increase in children needing foster placements can be traced to dramatic increases in several circumstances resulting in out-of-home placements for children: substantiated reports of child abuse and neglect (National Center on Child Abuse and Neglect, 1995), pregnant and parenting women with significant substance abuse problems (Barth et al., 1994), and family homelessness (Children's Defense Fund, 1987). The greatest growth in children entering care over the past decade has occurred with infants and very young children (Barth et al., 1994). At the same time, the number of family foster homes decreased from about 145,000 in 1984 to 100,000 in 1990. Although it is unclear why the number of homes has decreased, possible reasons include the higher level of problems currently found in foster children and the lower level of agency support due to increased workloads for caseworkers (for reviews, see Chou, 1993; NCFFC, 1991).

As noted previously, the AACWA Act has reduced the average duration of foster placements. Reliable measures of duration remain elusive, however, as procedures that are most commonly used in this research can result in systematic under- or overestimations (for fuller discussions, see Barth et al., 1994). For example, average length of stay is overestimated if it is calculated at a given point in time, because children who have exited the system quickly are less likely to be included at any one time than are children who have remained in the system for a long time. The use of a longitudinal design eliminates this problem, but presents the problem of how to handle children who remain in foster care at the end of the study. If these children are dropped from the analysis, or if their length of stay is simply calculated as being the time from their entry until the end of the study, then an underestimation of average length of stay will occur.

Using a longitudinal design, Benedict and White (1991) found that 30% of a group of 689 children who entered care in Maryland in the early 1980s left care within 1 month, that 50% left care within 6 months, and that 25% were in care for more than 2 years. The median length of care was 6 months. Having developmental delays or school problems, or being placed with relatives, was associated with increased lengths of stay. Similarly, Barth et al. (1994) found that, among children placed since 1988 in California, 10% went home within 2 weeks, 20% within 2 months, 40% within 1 year, and only 50% within 2.5 years. Thus, these data suggest that many children in care are reunited with their birth families relatively quickly, but a substantial number of children remain in care for a long time. Barth et al. (1994) found that reunifications peaked during months of mandated administrative reviews, suggesting that the reviews do have an effect in reuniting children with their families. However, despite laws requiring permanency plans by 18 months after placement, many children languish in foster care.

Children's Adjustment to Foster Care

Determining children's adjustment to short- or long-term foster-care placement is difficult. Foster children are different from most children in many ways other than being in foster care. Most obvious is that they have had experiences within their families that resulted in foster placement—most typically long-standing physical neglect and long-standing or severe abuse. In addition, they often come from low-income homes, have had little stability in their school and peer relationships, and may be vulnerable to many physical and mental disorders because of their prenatal and postnatal environments and/or genetic influences. This makes it difficult to assemble a suitable group of children with which to compare the adjustment of foster children.

Some researchers have assessed the impact of foster care on children without using comparison groups of non-foster children. They have interviewed the children and/or families and have assessed their responses according to the researchers' expectations of how well-adjusted or poorly adjusted people would respond. These studies have typically concluded that most children have fared well in foster care (for review, see Maluccio & Fein, 1985). However, the lack of behavioral assessments and reports from people other than the children or their foster parents reduce the likelihood that these studies were able to assess the adjustment of the foster children accurately.

Other researchers have followed foster children during their placement, assuming that improvements in behavior or academic functioning would indicate that the children were benefiting from foster care. Fanshel and Shinn (1978) followed 624 children entering foster care in New York City in 1966 for 5 years. They employed IQ and personality testing for the children, questionnaires completed by their caseworker and schoolteachers, and interviews with their foster parents. Children in foster care showed a moderate increase in IQ during their first 2 years in care, with no further increase after that. Compared with children who returned to their birth homes, long-term foster children showed greater increases in IQ. Teachers' reports indicated that school achievement increased over the 5 years for children remaining in foster care. There was general behavior improvement over the course of 5 years. Palmer (1979) reviewed the case records of 200 children who had been in foster care for at least 5 years and found that most showed behavioral improvement as indicated by their caseworker notes. However, the median grade completed for the sample was the ninth grade, even though their mean IQ was 94.

Finally, researchers have used comparison groups of children who have been abused or neglected yet not removed into foster care, or children who come from other problematic backgrounds. Runyan and Gould (1985) compared the arrest records of children who had been maltreated and placed in foster care with a group of maltreated children who had been left in their birth homes. The foster children had been in care for an average of 8 years, with an average of 2.6 placements. There was no difference in the number of arrests for children in the two groups. However, the foster children were arrested more frequently for criminal assault than were the comparison children. Leitenberg, Burchard, Healy, and Fuller (1981) compared four groups of maltreated children (those left in their birth homes and those placed in foster care, a residential school, or a group home) on police contact and school attendance. Children ages 11–13 and 14–16 who were in foster care had significantly fewer police contacts than those in group homes or remaining in their birth families and the children in foster care had better school attendance than those in group homes or in their birth homes. There were no differences for children ages 8–10.

Although there are problems with each of the approaches taken by researchers examining adjustment in foster children, most of the evidence suggests that most children are not harmed by foster placement and some of them improve in foster care. This research, however, was conducted several years ago. It is unclear whether today's foster children, who have been described as being more damaged than children entering care 20 to 30 years ago (e.g., Chou, 1993), would respond as favorably to foster-care placement.

Current Controversies in Foster Care

Abuse and Neglect in Foster Homes. Reports of abuse in foster care have raised concerns about the risk of ongoing abuse and neglect to children placed in foster care (Rosenthal, Motz, Edmonson, & Groze, 1991). Some empirical research addresses this issue. Bolton, Laner, and Gai (1981) found reports of abuse or neglect for 7% of children while in foster care in a county in Arizona, and compared this with other research showing a 2% rate of reported abuse and neglect for the county's general population. Benedict, Zuravin, Brandt, and Abbey (1994) examined reports and substantiated cases of abuse and neglect in Baltimore over 4 years. Foster homes were more likely to be reported for both physical abuse and sexual abuse than were other families in the community. However, different substantiation rates were found. Only 9% of the foster-care cases of physical abuse were substantiated, compared with 37% for the general community. Approximately 50% of sexual abuse cases were substantiated for both groups. This resulted in children in foster care being 1.8 times more likely to be physically abused and 3.9 times more likely to be sexually abused than children in other homes in the community. Foster parents were the perpetrators in 80% of the cases of physical abuse and 40% of the cases of sexual abuse. Foster siblings and others were implicated in the remainder of the cases.

Runyan and Gould (1985) compared the substantiated reabuse rate for abused children who were left in their birth homes and the rate of those who were removed to foster care in six counties in North Carolina. Twenty-five percent of the children remaining in their homes were reabused; 11% of those in foster care were reabused. However, half of the subsequent abuse to foster children occurred at the hands of their birth parents during home visits. If just the abuse by foster parents is considered, children remaining in their birth homes were 4.8 times more likely to be reabused than were children placed in foster care.

Efforts to identify characteristics of foster homes that are associated with increased likelihood of abuse and neglect have met with limited success. Zuravin, Benedict, and Somerfield (1993) found that foster homes with a younger mother, poorer health in the foster parents, or low income were more likely to be abusive, as were homes in which the foster children slept together in the same room or in the same room as the parents. Kinship foster homes were less likely to be abusive than nonkinship homes. However, their model predicted only 7% of the 62 abusive families in their sample accurately, indicating that additional factors are important for predicting abuse in foster homes.

These few studies suggest that foster children are at greater risk for abuse and neglect than are children throughout a community, but at less risk than children who have been abused and left in their birth home. A significant amount of the abuse of foster children is not perpetrated by foster parents. Part of the difference between abuse in foster children and those in the general community may be due to reporting. Foster children are visited periodically by their social workers, whose job requires that they inquire about the child's safety. If all families were put under the same scrutiny, the prevalence of abuse and neglect throughout the community might more closely resemble that found in foster homes. It also may be that the different abuse rates accurately reflect differences between foster homes and homes throughout the community. Some abused children's behavior may precipitate reabuse (Sugarman, 1994), and other abused children may perpetrate abuse on their foster siblings as learned behavior (Haugaard & Feerick, 1996). In addition, some foster parents may respond to their foster children's misbehavior with high levels of aggression or may take advantage of some children's fragile emotional state to satisfy their own aggressive or sexual impulses.

Implications for Policy and Practice. Children who enter foster care are not always protected from reabuse, although the research suggests that they are protected more in foster care than if they are left in an abusive home. Little is known about foster-family or foster-parent characteristics that are associated with higher risk of abuse to foster children, but some research suggests that children in families where there is less parental monitoring of the foster children may be at a greater risk. Future research must focus on identifying characteristics of foster families associated with increased and decreased risk for abuse of their foster children.

Kinship Foster Care. Kinship foster care refers to foster care provided by a child's relative. There has been a long history of extended family members caring for children when their parents were unable or unwilling to care for them. Until the late 1970s, however, states generally considered foster care only as care provided by nonrelatives. A relative providing care for a child might qualify for some form of Aid to Families with Dependent Children (AFDC), but could not qualify as a foster parent. In 1979, the Supreme Court ruled that states could not prohibit foster care subsidies to relatives, as long as they met foster-care licensing standards (*Miller v. Youakim,* 1979). The Court stated that the intent of foster care legislation was to provide the best available care for dependent children, and that providing different levels of funding for dependent children based on their placement went against this intent.

The number of kinship foster care homes rose dramatically during the 1980s and 1990s. In 1990, approximately half of all foster children in New York were in homes with kin (Meyer & Link, 1990). In California, the number of children in foster homes with nonrelatives rose from about 22,000 to 25,000 from 1984 to 1993, while the number of children in kinship foster care rose from about 5,000 to about 30,000 (Berrick & Barth, 1994).

The increase in kinship foster care has been driven by several factors, including the increase in children needing placement and the decrease in the number of family foster care homes. In addition, the emphasis on family preservation has encouraged the search for caregivers within dependent children's extended family (Berrick & Barth, 1994). Finally, finding a foster home for a child is often easier among the child's relatives than among strangers, as there are likely to be people who would be willing to provide care to a relative but unwilling to care for an unfamiliar child.

Gleeson and Craig (1994) found a range of policies regarding kinship foster care across 32 states in the United States. Many of the states encouraged the placement of children in kinship foster care homes. Twenty-one states gave first priority to kinship foster homes when a child needed placement. Seventeen states had exemptions to foster care licensing standards for relatives, or had separate standards for kinship homes. Some states allowed a child to remain in a kinship home that did not meet foster care licensing standards, but did not provide foster care board payments to those homes.

Advocates of kinship foster care argue that its principal advantage is that it is less stressful for a child than being placed with a nonrelative. In addition, kinship foster care is seen as promoting the maintenance of family bonds. No research exists to bolster the claim about stress to the child. Evidence regarding birth-parent visitation was provided by Berrick, Barth, and Needell (1994), who compared the experiences of 246 kinship and 354 nonrelative foster care families in California. Fifty-six percent of the children in kinship care and 32% of the children in nonrelative foster care saw their birth parents at least once a month; 19% of children in kinship care and only 3% of children in nonrelative foster care saw their birth parents four or more times a month. A study of 990 adolescents in out-of-home care in Los Angeles found that 49% in kinship care and 37% in nonrelative care had remained in their initial foster placement, suggesting somewhat greater stability of placement in kinship care (Iglehart, 1994). Dubowitz, Feigelman, and Zuravin (1993) found that 76% of the 524 children in kinship care in Baltimore had remained in their initial placement.

There are several concerns about kinship foster care. Kinship foster homes have been found to receive fewer services through their departments of social services (Beerick et al., 1994), and children in kinship foster care are visited by their social workers less frequently than those in nonrelative care (Beerick et al., 1994; Iglehart, 1994). Furthermore, children in kinship care remained in their foster placement longer than those in nonrelative care, and there was less movement toward adoption for children in kinship care (Beerick et al., 1994; Thornton, 1991). However, this research did not address the consequences to the children of these differences. For example, the value to a child or family of one or two extra visits a year by a social worker is unclear. Similarly, if the child feels that placement in kinship care is permanent, then movement toward adoption may not be needed to provide a child with a sense of permanence.

Concern also has been raised about placing a child with a kinship provider who might have influenced negatively the development of the child's abusive or neglectful parent. This is likely to be a problem in some cases but not in others. Meyer and Link (1990) found that in many kinship foster care placements the abusive parent was the only member of the extended family with significant problems.

The significant difference in state payments to kinship foster homes and homes receiving AFDC poses the potential problem of encouraging parents to place their children into a kinship foster home as a way to increase overall family income (especially if the child is spending considerable time living with the relative already). This is a complex issue. The substantial increase in children in foster care since kinship foster care has been encouraged might be seen as supporting the economic-incentive argument. It is not clear whether this correlation points to the influence of kinship care on foster care increases, or whether both kinship foster care and the number of children in the foster care system have increased because of the increased effort to locate and help abused and neglected children. Gleeson and Craig (1994) suggested that the solution to this problem is to raise AFDC support to equal foster care support.

Implications for Policy and Practice. There is no research addressing which children do best in kinship foster homes and which do best in nonrelative foster homes. There is no research suggesting that kinship foster care is more problematic and there is some research suggesting that it may have advantages over nonrelative foster care (e.g., stability of placement, ongoing contact with birth parent). The research does suggest that children in kinship foster care may get less attention from their social workers, but it is unclear that this is problematic for the child. Assessing the safety of the child who might be placed in kinship foster care is essential. The extent to which the foster parents could regulate or prohibit contact with the birth parents is a critical issue, and one that may not be of importance in nonrelative foster care if the birth parents do not know the location of the children. Evaluating the stability of the kinship foster parents is important, given the possibility that the kinship foster parent might have had a negative influence on the development of the child's birth parent. No specific guidelines for this type of assessment appear in the literature, aside from an examination of the frequency of significant problems in the extended family.

Conclusions

As is true for other societies, policies in the United States for caring for needy children reflect many beliefs and priorities, some of which may be in competition. For example, recent changes in federal law have permitted states to keep the money saved by reducing the number of out-of-home foster placements and apply it to preventive efforts to keep families together. This suggests a shift in attitudes about the worthiness of troubled families and their ability to raise their children if provided some help. At the same time, however, federal policy changes have been suggested that could reduce or eliminate financial support to teenage mothers and women who have additional children while receiving AFCD. Such policies could swell the foster-care rolls if these mothers become unable to pay for their children's basic needs. These policies appear to parallel those in colonial times that precluded support to some parents because of the negative consequences to society that the support was believed to encourage. In addition, discussion of the financial benefits of shifting child-care responsibilities from foster families to orphanages and other institutions has resurrected debates that were common when Charles Loring Brace first suggested that foster families were superior to institutions.

The goals of the foster care and the child welfare systems have been to provide for the appropriate upbringing of children whose parents are unavailable or unable to raise them while minimizing the number of children who need to be served by the systems. Huge increases in the number of children in foster care have raised concerns about the competence of the child welfare system to carry out these tasks. Calls to fix the child welfare system are often heard, although it is not clear whether the system is broken or merely overwhelmed by societal distress over which it has no control.

There are many ways in which developmental research can be applied to the issues faced by the foster care system. Little is known about which children may benefit the most from out-of-home placement. It may be that certain experiences at one age are not as troubling as the same experiences at another age, and knowledge of this type might assist foster care professionals in making placement decisions. Similarly, developmentally based research on factors predicting good matches in child and foster-home characteristics would be helpful. For example, are kinship foster homes especially advantageous to children of a certain age or children who have had certain troubling experiences? Finally, little is known about the consequences to a child's development of being in short- or long-term foster care. Basic research on the specific consequences of foster placement would provide important information to mental-health professionals who work with these children.

Termination of Parental Rights

As noted previously, parental rights over the upbringing of children are seen as fundamental in our society. Consequently, the termination of parental rights is considered to be nearly as significant as taking away an individual's freedom through incarceration. At a certain point, however, agents of the state may believe that a child's right to a healthy upbringing can only be obtained if the child is separated permanently from his or her parents. In these cases, the state may seek to terminate a parent's legal rights to his or her child.

The rights that a birth parent has over a child can be terminated either voluntarily or involuntarily. The adoption of infants often involves voluntary termination of birth parents' rights. Although some voluntary terminations may include provisions allowing one or both birth parents to have some ongoing contact with the child (as discussed in the following section on open adoptions), other voluntary terminations result in the birth parents having no further contact with their child (Grotevant, McRoy, Elde, & Fravel, 1994). Voluntary termination of parental rights can also occur with older children who have been in foster care. In some cases, the child's caseworkers will determine that termination of parental rights is the correct course to take with a case, and will be able to convince the birth parents that they should voluntarily terminate their rights as a way of serving the best interests of the child (Haralambie, 1993).

Involuntary terminations typically involve situations in which a child has been abandoned or removed from his or her home by a social service agency and the agency has determined that it would be improper ever to return the child to the birth parents. Involuntary terminations require court proceedings during which the rights and needs of the birth parents, children, and the state are weighed. Although some involuntary terminations may allow for contact between the child and birth parent, or sharing of information about the child with the birth parent, they typically result in the birth parent losing all contact with the child (Cahn & Johnson, 1993). Psychologists and other mental-health professionals may become involved in termination cases at several points: assessing the fitness of birth parents or foster parents or aiding in the determination of the best placement for the child.

Voluntary Terminations

Voluntary terminations must be given freely (Carrieri, 1991). The majority of states do not allow the birth mother to relinquish rights to her infant until after the birth of the child, and the other states allow for revocation of consent given before the child's birth for a time shortly after the birth. This is based on the belief that the mother will not be able fully to understand relinquishment until after giving birth (Selman, 1994).

Birth fathers, including unwed fathers, have rights similar to those of birth mothers (*In re Raquel Marie X.,* 1990). Although the issue of an unwed father's ability to veto adoption and claim custody of a child whom the mother has placed for adoption remains controversial, custody claims of fathers generally take precedence over those of strangers barring a finding of the father's unfitness (for discussion, see Shanley, 1995). Efforts must be made to locate a father who is not aware of the birth of his child and efforts also must be made to identify the father if the mother is unwilling or unable to identify him (e.g., *In re Doe,* 1994). However, a father who knows of the existence of his child and who has made no effort to participate in the life of the child may be considered to have abandoned or neglected the child, thus permitting termination of his rights (Haralambie, 1993; *Lehr v. Robertson,* 1983).

Involuntary Terminations and Parental Rights versus Best Interests of the Child

There is a strong legal tradition supporting the fundamental right to custody and control of children by their birth parents (e.g., *Meyer v. Nebraska,* 1923; *Santosky v. Kramer,* 1982) (for review, see Korn, 1994). In addition, there is the recognition that "few forms of state action are both so severe and so irreversible" as termination of parental rights (*Santosky v. Kramer,* 1982, p. 759). Consequently significant safeguards are provided for parents in termination proceedings. Although not required by the Supreme Court, 46 states require that birth parents be supplied with a lawyer if they cannot afford one during termination procedures, and 46 states require that a *guardian ad litem* be appointed to represent the best interests of the child (Cressler, 1993–1994).

The birth parents must be found to be unfit before their rights can be terminated (*Quilloin v. Walcott,* 1978), and the state must prove that the statutory grounds for termination have been met by "clear and convincing evidence" (*Santosky v. Kramer,* 1982). The issue of whether or not it would be in a child's best interest to remain with his or her birth parents or to live in another home is not an issue at this stage of the legal proceedings—the sole issue is whether or not the state can show that there are legal grounds for terminating the parents' rights. "If best interests of the child were a sufficient qualification to determine child custody, anyone with superior income, intelligence, education, etc., might challenge and deprive the parents of their right to their own children" (*In re Doe,* 1994, pp. 182–183).

Recent, well-publicized cases have demonstrated clearly that the best interests of a child are considered only after a finding of parental unfitness or relinquishment in adoption cases (*In re Adoption of B.G.S.,* 1992; *In re Doe,* 1994). Both cases involved birth fathers who became aware of the existence of their child only after the child had been relinquished for adoption by the birth mother. Both fathers sued for return of their child soon after this discovery. Although the legal battles took several years to complete, resulting in the children becoming attached to their adoptive parents, state supreme courts and the U.S. Supreme Court were clear in their decision that the children needed to be returned to their birth fathers because the fathers had never been found unfit or relinquished their rights (for discussion see Appell & Boyer, 1995).

Current Controversies in Termination of Parental Rights

The Concept of Psychological Parents and Termination Decisions. The concept of the psychological parent, as described by Goldstein et al. (1973), has had a significant influence on many family court proceedings. A psychological parent is "one who, on a continuing, day-to-day basis, through interaction, companionship, interplay, and mutuality, fulfills the child's psychological needs" (Goldstein et al., 1973, p. 98). The essential premise of the theory is that a child's developmental needs require an ongoing relationship with a psychological parent and that a young child does not have the capacity to form relationships with more than one psychological parent or pair of psychological parents.

In foster-care cases, Goldstein et al. suggest that allowing ongoing contact between a birth parent and child will allow the birth parent to maintain the role as psychological parent. However, if sufficient contact is not maintained, the birth parent loses status as a psychological parent. If the foster parent begins to care and value the child the way a birth parent or adoptive parent might, then the foster parent becomes a "common-law" adoptive parent who serves as the child's psychological parent. Once this occurs, it is the foster parent, not the birth parent, who is of primary importance to the child, and it is the bond between the child and the foster parent that should be maintained to promote the child's development.

Although the theory argues strongly against the removal of a child from his or her birth parents except in dire situations, its primary use in the law has been to argue against the return to the birth parents of a child who has been placed in foster care. This is likely because cases contesting a child's initial removal from birth parents are far less likely to reach the appellate level (and thus be published and have an influence on other cases) than are cases contesting the termination of parental rights to a child who is in foster care.

Nitti (1994) traced the use of the theory in New Jersey courts, where it followed a pattern similar to that in other state courts. Prior to release of the theory, courts terminated parental rights only when it appeared impossible for the child to return to birth parents. Within a few years of publication of the theory, courts were terminating parental rights based solely on information asserting that foster parents had become the psychological parents of a child: "an order permanently terminating the biological parent-child relationship can be validly issued despite the absence of present or past parental unfitness" (*In re J.R.*, 1980, p. 67). However, by 1986, the New Jersey Supreme Court ruled that unfitness of a birth parent is an essential component of parental rights termination—requiring a retreat from reliance on the concept of psychological parenting when terminating parental rights (*New Jersey Division of Youth & Family Services v. A.W.*, 1986). Current law states that the attachment to his or her foster parents may be considered in a parental rights termination case, but may not be dispositive (Nitti, 1994).

Whether the psychological parent theory is accurate, and the extent to which it is useful in making decisions about terminating parents' rights, continues to be debated. Several reviewers have commented that an important source of information for the development of the theory came from observations of children who had been separated from their parents because of adverse conditions; consequently, the observed developmental problems exhibited by many of the children could not be traced specifically to separation but might also have been due to the circumstances that caused the separation (e.g., war, death, child abuse) (Eagle, 1994; Waters & Noyes, 1984). Furthermore, a lack of any attachment to an adult, rather than separation from an adult figure, may have been the primary influence on the development of problems (Rutter, 1972). Other research used to support the theory involved retrospective interviews with adolescents and adults with various problems and showed that many of them had experienced childhood loss and separation. However, failure to include nontroubled subjects in these studies did not rule out that loss and separation might also be experienced by many people who do not show subsequent problems (Waters & Noyes, 1984). Thus, the research foundation for the theory is not solid.

Other research refutes some of the basic concepts of the theory. Studies of adopted children, including children adopted after initially living with their birth parents, show that most of them make a good adjustment and feel comfortable in their adoptive homes (e.g., Barth & Beery, 1988; Bohman & Sigvardsson, 1980; Tizzard, 1991). Many adoptees who search for their birth parents in adolescence or adulthood also show a strong attachment to their adoptive homes, suggesting that bonds to their birth parents and adoptive parents coexist (Campbell, Silverman, & Patti, 1991; Trisiliotis, 1973). Abused and neglected children often have strong attachments to their parents, and there is no indication that the strength of these attachments is lessened over time for some children placed in foster care (Crittenden & Ainsworth, 1990). Finally, cross-cultural research has shown that children in a variety of cultures form healthy relationships with more than one set of parental figures (Stack, 1984).

Implications for Policy and Practice. Although the concept of the psychological parent has strong heuristic value, it appears to contradict a significant amount of research in the foster care and adoption areas. In many ways, it appears more applicable when considering the initial removal of a child from his or her birthparents (for which, as noted above, it is used infrequently) than it does when considering the return to birth parents of a child who has spent time in foster care. It does appear that children can integrate more than one psychological parent into their lives.

Although children may find it difficult to separate from foster parents to return to their birth home or move to an adoptive home, long-term benefits of such a move may overshadow the short-term anguish that they can feel.

Children's Abilities to Initiate Termination of Parental Rights Proceedings. In 1992, 12-year-old Gregory Kingsley filed a petition to terminate his birth parents' rights, thereby freeing him for adoption by the family that was then his foster family. He filed the petition after being in and out of foster care for many years and after the state department of social services decided, against Gregory's wishes, to pursue his return to his birth parents. Although a guardian ad litem had been appointed for Gregory two years previously, the guardian had never met with him (Russ, 1993). The initial issue to be decided was whether Gregory, as a minor, had standing to bring a termination petition to court. The trial judge ruled that Gregory did have standing, and based the ruling on the fact that he was a "natural person" under the Florida Constitution, and therefore had the right to pursue happiness and the right of access to the courts of the state. The rights of Gregory's birth parents were terminated at trial. An appellate court overruled the trial court, stating that Gregory did not have standing to initiate court proceedings and citing Florida Civil Procedure statutes stating that "unemancipated minors do not have the legal capacity to initiate legal proceedings in their own names" (*Kingsley v. Kingsley*, 1993, p. 782). However, the appellate court let stand the ruling that Gregory had been abandoned by his mother, thus affirming the termination of her rights.

Children do have standing to bring termination proceedings in a few states (Haralambie, 1993), and the debate about children's standing to initiate termination proceedings may continue to be raised in the courts. Legal arguments include that children should be afforded the same rights as adults to use the courts directly, through a lawyer who vigorously represents the child's point of view. Currently, most children can only gain access to the courts through *guardians ad litem* or "best friends." Although the roles of guardians ad litem continue to evolve, their basic function is to represent what the guardian perceives to be the child's best interest. The legal assumption is that children, like others considered incompetent (e.g., those with severe mental or developmental disabilities), do not have the capacity to consider both the short- and long-term implications of possible legal courses of action, and thus, need the intermediary of a guardian. Opponents of this view propose that children, perhaps as young as 7 years, do have the necessary capacities to appropriately direct a lawyer to represent their views (e.g., Russ, 1993; Sommer, 1994).

There is very little psychological research on this topic. Several studies have been done of children's and adolescents' decision making (Grisso, 1981; Weithorn & Campbell, 1982), but these have not focused on custody-related issues. In one study, Garrison (1991) examined the rationality of 9- to 14-year-olds' reasoning about two hypothetical custody decisions. The rationality of their responses was evaluated based on assessments made by family court judges. The reasoning of the 14-year-olds was similar to that of a comparison group of adults. Although the reasoning of the 9- and 10-year-olds was less rational than that of the adults, it did not differ from the reasoning of the 14-year-olds. Garrison suggested that the results supported the belief that school-age children could make rational decisions about custody issues.

Implications for Policy and Practice. As noted earlier, children do have some of the same legal rights as adults, but not all of them. Currently, most children do not have standing to bring issues to court. Social science has a role in the debate about whether children should have such standing, through the assessment of the capacities of children to make sound decisions regarding the families in which they reside. If children can make adultlike decisions in this regard, then the argument that their views should have direct access to the courts is strengthened; to the extent that they are incapable of making sound decisions, the argument that they need an intermediary to determine and represent their best interests is strengthened. In cases such as *Gregory K.* it may seem reasonable to argue that children should have access to the courts to extricate themselves from abusive or neglectful families. What if, however, a child had a strong desire to return to an abusive family? Would it be appropriate for a lawyer to work strenuously to have the child returned to abusive parents based solely on the child's preference to do so?

Conclusions

The importance of parental rights is reflected in the legal procedural safeguards that are provided to parents who are voluntarily relinquishing their rights to a child or who are having their rights challenged by the state. Recent court decisions have affirmed that, in our society, genetic ties to a child continue to override emotional ties. It has been argued that parental rights are given too much weight, particularly when children languish in temporary foster-care homes as their fate is deliberated by the courts, and procedures to facilitate the termination of some parents' rights have been proposed. Although these procedures have been used in some areas, the courts in general are reluctant to terminate parental rights any more quickly than they currently do.

Developmental researchers could explore several issues associated with termination of parental rights. As just discussed, the ability of children to bring suit in court independently could be influenced by research documenting children's ability to engage in the emotional and cognitive tasks that the legal system expects of someone who brings such a suit. Information about the resiliency of children's attachments to various adults can inform the next round of the debate about the existence, and relative importance, of a psychological parent figure in children's lives. Developmentally based research about the extent to which longer stays in foster care can impede a child's ability to reattach to birth parents or to attach to adoptive parents may provide some impetus for mandating that permanency decisions be made by a certain point in a child's foster-care stay.

Adoption

Adoption serves the needs of children by providing them with permanent families when their birth parents choose not to, or are unable to, retain custody of them. It also serves the needs of adults who are unable to have birth children or who wish to increase their family without giving birth to additional children. The adoptive relationship has been commonly referred to as the *adoption triangle* (e.g., Sorosky, Baran, & Pannor, 1978), consisting of the birth parent, child, and adoptive parent. However, a four-sided figure would be a more apt description of the relationship, because the state has important interests in the institution of adoption as well as in the functioning of adopted children and their families (one could choose a square or rectangle to represent this, but the rhombus provides a better representation through its infinite number of shapes). The needs of the four partners in each adoptive relationship can differ, and in some cases they may conflict. Adoption policy, and individual court decisions, have sought to balance these interests, but this balance has not been achieved.

About 60% of legal adoptions are by relatives—mostly stepparents, but also grandparents and other relatives. These adoptions will not be discussed in this section. The number of infants adopted by strangers in the United States each year has been estimated at 30,000 to 40,000 (Hollinger, 1991), although the actual number is unknown because there is no national repository of adoption data. The number of adoptions of children older than infants has increased dramatically in the past two decades. Approximately 14,000 older and special-needs children are adopted in the United States each year, and an additional 14,000 older or special-needs children each year are freed for and awaiting adoption (Barth & Beery, 1988; National Committee for Adoption, 1989).

The adoption of most older and special-needs children takes place through public agencies. Infant adoptions most commonly occur through private agencies or private agreements between birth mothers and adoptive parents that are facilitated by lawyers or other professionals (Hollinger, 1991).

Historical Overview

Adoption had no place in English common law, although it played an important part in earlier societies, in particular Roman society (see Presser, 1971, for a detailed analysis). Presser attributes this to the strong tradition in English common law of inheritance through blood lines and the potential problem that adopted children could create for this system. In addition, formal adoption was not needed for the care of dependent children as these children were typically placed in apprenticeship roles (a form of informal adoption) in the same way as were nondependent children. As a result of the lack of adoption in English common law, no formal adoption laws were included in early American law. The placement of orphans was dealt with through the will of the child's parents or by the local government placing the child in an apprenticeship or other form of work. Children whose parents could not care for them were placed in almshouses, where they received rudimentary instruction in reading and arithmetic before being placed in a work setting. Some families took in children without parents, but this was done informally.

The first comprehensive adoption law in the United States was passed in 1851 in Massachusetts (Presser, 1971). Most other states passed adoption laws soon after this. Many of these laws did not require judicial approval, and the extent to which the birth parents had to voluntarily consent to the adoption varied. Some states, for example, did not require birth-parent consent if the child had been neglected or if the parents were "morally depraved." Confidentiality was not required and the statute did not prohibit access to the court record (Hollinger, 1991).

As is also true now, statutes differed between states and were interpreted differently by various courts. Adoptions were overturned in some cases in which procedures were not followed strictly (e.g., *Vandermis v. Gilbert,* 1899), and in other cases the courts cited the best interests of the adopted child when overlooking lapses in procedure (*Van Dyne v. Vreeland,* 1857). Some early statutes distinguished between adopted and "natural" children. Adopted children were not considered siblings to the parents' birth children (*Barnhizel v. Ferrell,* 1874) and adopted children had inheritance tax burdens that did not pertain to birth children (*Commonwealth of Pennsylvania v. Nancrede,* 1859). In addition, laws remained unclear about the "exclusivity" of the adoption relationship. Until the 1930s, some state laws were unclear about whether birth parents would be required to support a child financially if the adoptive parents became destitute (Hollinger, 1991). Provisions that allowed the adoptive parents to return the child to an institution continued as a part of adoption law until the 1950s (Hollinger, 1991): "When the opportunity of parental affection and maintenance is extended to a child it is to be expected that respect, obedience and proper filial conduct will be returned by the child, and when that fails, the statute provides that the adoption may be abrogated" (*In re Anonymous,* 1936, p. 827).

Laws requiring confidentiality in adoption proceedings began in the early 1900s. These laws were designed to shield the adopted child from public scrutiny and continued to allow access to the adoption records by all parties to the adoption. Laws requiring the complete sealing of adoption records were enacted in the 1920s and 1930s at the urging of several professional organizations. It was generally believed that sealed records would facilitate a complete break for adopted children from their birth parents, and that this break would be beneficial to the birth parents, adopted child, and adoptive family (Hollinger, 1991). As discussed in an upcoming section, this belief has recently been challenged.

Older children, particularly boys, were in more demand until the 1940s because of their ability to contribute their work to the family. Infants became more popular in the late 1940s. The number of infants available for adoption declined considerably in the 1970s because of the development of more effective contraception, the availability of abortion, and greater tendencies on the part of single mothers to maintain custody of their children (Hollinger, 1991).

Children's Adjustment to Adoption

A fairly common theme in the clinical and research adoption literature is that adoption as an infant or a child increases a person's risk for the development of problematic behaviors or emotional problems. Several explanations for this increased risk have been proposed, including biological vulnerability from birth parents' genes or prenatal and postnatal environments, emotional turmoil caused by bewilderment over one's biological roots, and changes in a child's conceptualization of the adoption process (Brodzinsky, 1987). The data supporting this assumption remain equivocal, however. The research in this area can be divided into two general categories: (a) studies examining the proportion of adopted children and adults in inpatient and outpatient mental-health settings, and (b) studies of the psychological adjustment of nonclinical groups of adopted and nonadopted children and adolescents.

Percentage of Clinical Samples. The strongest evidence for the risk associated with adoption comes from research that has examined whether the percentage of adopted children in inpatient and outpatient mental health settings is greater than their prevalence in the general population. Although the prevalence of adoptees in the general population is unknown, it is generally assumed to be 1%–2%.

Several researchers have examined inpatient samples. Typically, the case records of all patients for several years are examined and the number of those who were adopted is noted. All of these studies have reported a relatively large percentage of adopted children and adolescents in inpatient settings, including 5.5% (Borgatta & Fanshel, 1965), 10.8% (Piersma, 1987), 11.7% (Dickson, Heffron, & Parker, 1990), and 21.2% (Senior & Himadi, 1985). Research with outpatient samples have also reported relatively large percentages, although these are less than those found in research with inpatient samples. Percentages in outpatient samples have included 2.4% (J. Goodman, Silberstein, & Mandell, 1963), 3.6% (Goldberg & Wolkind, 1992), and 7.5% (Kotsoupoulos et al., 1988).

The primary limitation to this line of research is that all adopted children are considered together. Children who were abused and neglected for 6 years prior to adoption, for example, are considered together with newborns adopted from a mother who provided a good prenatal environment. Therefore, it is impossible to understand the extent to which this research is applicable to any of the major subgroups within the adopted population. As a result, researchers must be cautious about using this research to argue that all adopted children are at greater risk.

Psychological Adjustment in Nonclinical Samples. Research using nonclinical samples allows for an assessment of children who represent a broad range of functioning, rather than only those in need of mental health treatment. These studies show mixed results, with some finding differences in psychological adjustment between adopted and nonadopted children, some finding no differences, and some longitudinal studies finding differences at some ages and not others.

In an ongoing study of a cohort of 1,265 children born in Christchurch, New Zealand in mid-1977, Fergusson, Lynskey, and Horwood (1995) assessed internalizing and externalizing behaviors in 16-year-olds who had been either raised by two birth parents, were born to single women and then adopted as newborns into two-parent families, or were born to single women and remained with their birth mothers. Results showed no differences between the adopted adolescents and adolescents in two-parent families for any of the internalizing disorders: mood disorders, anxiety disorders, low self-esteem, or suicidal behaviors. Children raised in single-mother families were significantly lower than the other two groups on self-esteem but similar in the other areas. Several differences in externalizing behaviors between the three groups emerged, with the pattern consistently being that adolescents from single-mother families showed more problems than adopted adolescents, and the adopted adolescents showed more problems than the adolescents in two-parent birth families. These differences occurred for conduct/oppositional disorders, attention deficit-hyperactivity disorders, self-reported offending, daily cigarette smoking, and cannabis use.

Lipman, Offord, Racine, and Boyle (1992) used data from the Ontario Child Health Study (OCHS), which included a stratified random sample of 1,869 families. Of the 3,294 4- to 16-year-old children examined, 104 had been adopted (the time of the adoptive placement was not stated). Controlling for child and family characteristics such as child age, family income, and number of children in the family, no independent influence was found of adoptive status on psychiatric disorder or substance abuse for the children as a whole or when the boys and girls were considered separately.

Brodzinsky, Schechter, Graff, and Singer (1984) and Brodzinsky, Radice, Huffman, and Merkler (1987) studied 130 6- to 11-year-old adopted children and a comparison group of 130 nonadopted children matched by age, sex, race, and SES, using parental reports on the Child Behavior Checklist (CBCL). Adopted girls received higher behavior problem ratings than nonadopted girls on both the internalizing and externalizing scales of the CBCL. Adopted girls also were higher than nonadopted girls on depression, social withdrawal, hyperactivity, delinquency, aggression, and cruelty. Adopted boys were rated higher on the externalizing scale than were nonadopted boys, and no significant differences appeared on the internalizing scale. The adopted boys were higher than the nonadopted boys on scales labeled uncommunicative, hyperactivity, aggression, and delinquency. In addition, 36% of the adopted group were in the clinically significant range on at least one of the nine behavioral subscales, 18% were in the clinically significant range on two subscales, and 12% were in the clinically significant range on three subscales. This was in comparison to 14%, 5%, and 3% of the nonadopted children, respectively.

Several longitudinal studies have been conducted with data obtained from cohorts of children born during particular time periods. The cohort of children born in England, Wales, and Scotland in a single week of March 1958 has been studied several times. At age 7 years, 180 of the adopted children were compared with two other subgroups of the cohort: legitimately born and illegitimately born children who had remained with their birth parent or birth parents (labeled by the authors as the *legitimate* and *illegitimate* groups, respectively) (Seglow, Pringle, & Wedge, 1972). Results from teachers' ratings on the Bristol Social Adjustment Guides showed no overall differences between adopted children and legitimate children. Illegitimate children were significantly less well adjusted than both adopted and legitimate children. When broken down by sex, however, they found that the adopted boys were more likely to be maladjusted than the legitimate boys and that there were no significant differences between the adopted and legitimate girls. At age 11, after controlling for social class, family size, and sex of child, the adopted group was significantly less well adjusted than the legitimate group and was similar to the illegitimate group (Lambert & Streather, 1980). This pattern held for both boys and girls. At age 16, illegitimate adolescents were significantly less well adjusted than legitimate adolescents, with adopted adolescents falling in between and not significantly different from either of the other two groups (Maughan & Pickles, 1990). Maughan and Pickles (1990) employed the Malaise Inventory, which tapped affective disturbance, and gathered data on relationships and employment at the age-23 assessment. At age 23, among males there were no differences between the three groups on a scale of affective disturbance. Among females, the illegitimate group was significantly higher on this scale than either the adopted or legitimate group, with no differences between the adopted and legitimate group.

St. Claire and Osborn (1987) reported on a cohort of children from Great Britain born during one week in April 1970. The children were assessed at 5 and 10 years of age. Ninety-six children had been adopted, mostly in infancy. On several cognitive measures, the adopted children were .2–.3 standard deviations better than the comparison children. Based on mothers' ratings of the children's behavior, the adopted children had slightly fewer antisocial and neurotic behavioral problems than the comparison groups. Scores on four standardized achievement tests at age 10 showed that the adopted children were just slightly better than the comparison group on each of them. Behaviors at age 10 were rated by both mothers and teachers. Teachers rated the adopted children as more antisocial than the comparison children, while the mothers' ratings showed no differences on antisocial behavior between the adopted and comparison children. The teachers' ratings of inattentive behaviors showed no difference between the adopted and comparison children, whereas the mothers of adopted children rated them as more inattentive than did the mothers of the comparison children.

Finally, Bohman (1971) studied 492 children who had been registered for eventual adoption by their birth mothers in Sweden during 2 years in the 1950s. Of these children, 163 were eventually adopted, 205 were raised by their birth mothers, and 124 lived in foster care. Almost all the adopted children spent some time in an institutional infants' home prior to their adoptive placement. At age 11, the social adjustment of these children was assessed by their teachers, and was compared with a group of children selected at random from the classrooms of each of the target children. The adopted boys showed significantly poorer global social adjustment than did the comparison boys. There were no differences in social adjustment between adopted girls and nonadopted girls. At age 15, school grades were collected and teachers were asked to rate several behaviors without knowing the identity of the target children. The adopted boys had lower grades than the comparison boys in two school subjects and similar grades in five subjects; the adopted girls had significantly lower grades than the comparison girls in one subject. The adopted boys were not significantly different from the comparison boys on any of the behaviors that were assessed (tension, withdrawal, aggressiveness, psychomotor activity, ability to concentrate, contact with peers, social maturity, intelligence, and school motivation). The adopted girls were only significantly higher than the comparison girls in their level of tension.

As a group, these studies paint a mixed picture. Where differences exist, they seem to center on children around the age of puberty—few differences exist when younger children or adolescents are examined. Although some studies did find statistically significant differences between groups, the meaningfulness of these differences is not clear. Comparing the adopted children in the studies by Brodzinsky with the norming sample for the CBCL showed few differences between the adopted children and the nonclinical norming sample, and much more problematic behavior in the clinical norming sample than among the adopted children. Similarly, Fergusson et al. (1995) noted, "While it is the case that systematic differences were found . . . these differences were often not large and the child's placement at birth was only a relatively weak predictor of subsequent life history and adolescent adjustment" (p. 613).

Adoption Disruption

The study of families adopting older children has focused on factors associated with adoption disruption (the adoptive family relinquishing the child prior to or after adoption finalization). Disruption has increased over the past few decades, as more older and special-needs children have been adopted (Barth & Beery, 1988; Bass, 1975). Partridge, Hornby, and McDonald (1986) found an 8.6% disruption rate, over a 2.5 year period, for a group of school-age children from six counties in the Northeast. Barth and Beery (1988) found a 16% disruption rate among new special-needs adoptive placements over a 5-year period. Festinger (1990) found a disruption rate of 13% for special-needs adoptions over 3 years, with most of the disruptions taking place in the first year.

Several studies have examined factors associated with disruption. Adoptions of older children are more likely to disrupt, even when only school-age children are considered (e.g., Festinger, 1986; Rosenthal, Schmidt, & Conner, 1988). The presence of a physical disability in the child has not been associated with disruption; however, emotional disturbance has been associated with disruption in many studies (e.g., Barth & Beery, 1988; Partridge et al., 1986). Adoptions of boys may be more likely to disrupt (K. Nelson, 1985; Rosenthal et al., 1988). This may be associated with the tendency of emotionally disturbed boys to act out, and the tendency of adoptions of acting-out children to disrupt more often (e.g., Barth & Beery, 1988). Rosenthal et al. (1988) found an age-by-gender interaction, with the adoption of boys under the age of 10 more likely to disrupt than the adoptions of girls of that age, and the adoption of teenage girls more likely to disrupt than those of teenage boys.

A longer time of the child waiting for adoption has been associated with disruption in some studies (Boneh, 1979; Partridge et al., 1986) but not in others (Festinger, 1986; Zwimpfer, 1983). Prior removal from a foster home because of inadequate parenting by the foster parents also has been associated with increased disruption (Boneh, 1979). A higher number of previous placements has consistently predicted later disruption (e.g., Festinger, 1986; Partridge et al., 1986).

Investigations of family or parent characteristics have focused on parents' income, education, race, age, and marital status. They have yielded conflicting results (for review, see Festinger, 1990). The conflicts are difficult to reconcile, since the studies often employed different methods. A possible explanation is that differing criteria may have been used for matching children with families in the areas where the studies took place, and that these studies were actually measuring these different criteria. For example, acting-out children may be placed with upper-middle-class families more often in some areas and with working-class families more often in others, yielding different conclusions regarding family income and disruption.

The influence of parental beliefs has been investigated only sporadically (e.g., Doelling & Johnson, 1990), even though certain parental beliefs might make it more difficult for a child to assimilate into an adoptive family. A parental belief that has received some examination is the extent to which the adoptive family acknowledges or rejects their differences from other families. According to Kirk (1988), adoptive families that rejected their differences from nonadoptive families were less able to cope successfully with several family problems than those that acknowledged their differences. Brodzinsky (1987) proposed that when adoptive families insisted on using their differences from nonadoptive families as the reason for their problems, they also had a more difficult time adjusting to their status as an adoptive family, and Kaye (1990) provided empirical support for Brodzinsky's model.

Adoptive families in which the parents had higher levels of social support were less likely to experience significant problems (Barth & Beery, 1988; Feigelman & Silverman, 1977; Reid, Kagan, Kaminsky, & Helmer, 1987). The extent to which sources of social support are influenced by an adoption has not been studied. Almost no empirical work has appeared in the literature regarding the influence of preexisting marital and family relationships on the adoptive placement, and of the adoptive placement on the ongoing marital and family relationships.

Current Controversies in Adoption

Open Adoptions. Openness in adoptions refers to contact between birth parents and the adoptive family. Contact can come in several ways, including exchange of information (either directly or through intermediaries), exchange of letters, and personal contact. When contact occurs, some is solely between adopted children and birth parents (typically in the children's adolescence or adulthood), some is solely between birth parents and adoptive parents, and some involves both sets of parents and adopted children.

Adoptions in the United States through the early 1900s generally had some degree of openness to them. As noted earlier, most states' adoption procedures became secret by the 1940s (Kuhns, 1994). A child's original birth certificate was sealed in a court record, and a new birth certificate was produced with the adoptive parents' names. These procedures were designed to (a) reduce the chance that the child would be considered a second-class citizen, especially if the child was illegitimate, (b) allow the birth mother to bring her involvement with the child to closure, and (c) promote the development of the adoptive family by precluding any potentially disruptive involvement with the birth family.

Pressure from adoptees and birth parents has resulted in a greater amount of openness in adoption over the past two decades. The areas of openness fall into two general categories: unsealing of adoption records so that birth parents and adoptees can make contact, and incorporating various levels of openness into adoption agreements for infants and older children.

Unsealing Adoption Records. Efforts to unseal adoption records have been initiated by birth mothers interested in contacting their children and adults who were adopted as children and who are interested in contacting birth parents or siblings. Early efforts to unseal adoption records involved court challenges to sealed records statutes. Legal arguments against sealed records have included that the constitutional guarantee of family privacy extends to an adopted person being able to identify his or her birth parents, that the First Amendment provides the right to receive birth-parent information since the information is necessary for adoptees' development and thus their ability to fully participate in social and governmental decision making, and that sealed records violate the equal protection clause of the Fourteen Amendment since nonadopted individuals have access to their original birth certificates (e.g., *ALMA Society v. Mellon,* 1979; *Mills v. Atlantic City Dept of Vital Statistics,* 1977). None of the legal challenges have been successful. Courts have consistently ruled that the rights of the adopted adults bringing the legal actions were outweighed by the rights of privacy of the birth parents and the need of the state to maintain a viable system for placing adopted children (the assumption being that openness in adoption would reduce the potential pool of adoptive parents) (for review, see Kuhns, 1994).

Subsequent efforts to unseal records then focused on changing state laws that require sealed records. Most states responded by allowing adoptees access to information in their adoption file that did not identify their birth parents (for review, see Hollinger, 1991). Some state statutes were changed to allow for the unsealing of adoption records if "good cause" could be shown by the adoptee. Good cause typically involved obtaining needed medical information or relieving significant distress due to lack of knowledge of one's birth family (e.g., *ALMA Society v. Mellon,* 1979; *In re Assalone,* 1986). However, curiosity or concern about one's birth parents has not been considered good cause (e.g., *Golan v. Louise Wise Services,* 1987). Some states have developed mutual consent registries. If an adoptee and his or her birth parent both register independently, then identifying information is released. Taking these registries one step further, several states have instituted search and consent procedures. These procedures result in state personnel actively searching for birth parents to secure their permission to release identifying information to their child (for a review of Hawaii's procedure, see Lum, 1993). Alaska and Kansas currently allow adult adoptees free access to their birth certificates.

Opponents of policies allowing adoptees access to sealed birth certificates argue that the policies will infringe on the privacy of birth parents, harm the institution of adoption by making potential adoptive parents afraid of unwanted intrusion into their family lives, and potentially harm adoptees by providing emotionally damaging information about their birth parents or through refusals of their birth parents to see them (for reviews, see Ames, 1992; Demick & Wapner, 1988).

Very limited data are available regarding the consequences of opening sealed adoption records. Weidell (1980) examined 332 requests for birth-parent information during the first year of a search and consent procedure in Minnesota. Two hundred and eight birth mothers and 35 birth fathers were located. Of these, 37% of the birth mothers and 49% of the birth fathers permitted identifying information to be released to the adoptee (those who did not respond were presumed to deny permission for release of information). Forty-five percent of the birth mothers and 46% of the birth fathers indicated their desire to have some personal contact with the adoptee. Overall, 25% of the adoptees who requested their original birth certificate received it, 80% of those who requested a genetic history received it, and 30% of those who asked for personal contact were contacted. Weidell provided no information about the outcomes to the adoptees or their families of receiving this information or contact. Lum (1993) interviewed family court personnel involved in searching for birth parents following the enactment of a search and consent procedure in Hawaii. Based on their impressions, the court personnel reported that only a few birth parents had refused permission for identifying information to be released, and that a majority of them were pleased to be contacted and hoped that they could arrange a meeting with their birth child. No information about the impact on the adoptees or their families was presented.

Establishing Open Adoption Agreements. The second general issue related to adoption openness is the extent to which adoptions should include provisions for sharing of information about the adopted child between birth families and adoptive families as well as whether there should be visitation between the two families. In some cases, birth parents may make contact contingent on their relinquishment of their child. This happens most often in cases of infant adoption, but may also be part of an agreement between a child welfare agency and a parent during a voluntary relinquishment of an older child.

Individual birth parents and adoptive parents can reach any sort of formal or informal agreement that is mutually satisfactory. The courts have become involved in cases in which disputes about an agreement develop. These typically involve situations where adoptive parents want to restrict or eliminate contact with the birth parents or the child's other birth relatives. The courts have followed two general paths in resolving these cases. Some states have been guided by the principle of the best interest of the child. Courts have permitted the enforcement of visitation agreements based on this principle in some cases (e.g., *People ex rel. Sibley v. Sheppard,* 1981), and visitation has been prohibited in other cases where the court felt that it was not in the child's best interest (e.g., *In re Department of Public Welfare,* 1981). Other states have been guided by the principle that once an adoption is final, the adoptive parents have control over visitation and the birth parents have no standing to pursue contact. In these states, visitation over the objection of the adoptive parents has not been approved (e.g., *Colorado ex rel M.M.,* 1986; *Hill v. Moorman,* 1988; for additional cases, see Cook, 1991–1992.)

Most research on openness in adoptions has involved small and unrepresentative samples. Generally, these studies found that both birth parents and adoptive parents were pleased with the openness in their relationships and felt that continued association would be beneficial to their children (e.g., Belbas, 1987; McRoy, Grotevant, & White, 1988). A few larger studies are beginning to appear in the literature. Berry (1993) studied 1,307 adoptions that took place in California in 1988 and 1989. Of these, 719 involved some postadoption contact. Contact was most likely in adoptions of infants and children who were not maltreated by their birth parents. Berry characterized the adoptive parents as being "cautiously comfortable" with postplacement contact. Contacts that were planned in advance were viewed more positively than were those that occurred by surprise. When contact occurred prior to placement, postplacement contact was seen more positively. In addition, postplacement contact was viewed more negatively in cases involving maltreatment of the child by the birth parent. Many adoptive parents expressed uncertainty about the effect of openness on their child's development.

Grotevant, McRoy, Elde, and Fravel (1994) studied 190 families that had adopted an infant 4 to 12 years prior to their research. Adoptions occurred through private agencies that had a range of policies about openness. Their sample included 59 families that had ongoing direct contact with the birth mother. Interestingly, almost two-thirds of these families had started out with mediated contact (indirect contact through the adoption agency) or with no contact. The direct contact evolved because of the trust and mutual respect that developed between the adoptive parents and the birth parents. Adoptive parents were generally satisfied with the amount of contact, and almost all of those who were unsatisfied wanted more contact with the birth parents. Significantly fewer adoptive parents with direct contact had fears that the birth mother would try to reclaim the child than did parents without direct contact. Similarly, parents with direct contact had a greater sense of permanence with their adopted child, and had a greater sense of full entitlement to their child, than did other adoptive parents. Grotevant et al. warned that their research does not suggest that higher levels of openness should be mandated at the outset of the adoption—openness evolved over the course of the adoption for most families. Further, they noted that the value of openness to the birth parents and the adopted children was not assessed.

Implications for Policy and Practice. Although there is only a small amount of research on openness in adoption, existing evidence suggests that openness is a positive experience and may actually increase the adoptive parents' sense of permanence with their children in adoptive families, at least those willing to have contact with birth parents. The research to date does not address whether or not openness should be mandated or encouraged across all adoptions. Policies about openness vary widely among adoption agencies, and adoptive parents who are opposed to openness are unlikely to adopt through an agency that expects it. Parents willing to have an open adoption find contact with the birth parents to be positive; however, it is not known how parents opposed to openness would respond to contact with birth parents. Finally, there is little information about the effects of openness on the adopted children or on the relationships within the adoptive family. Research in this area needs to be done before reaching conclusions about adoption openness. Furthermore, the research needs to have a developmental perspective, because it is reasonable to expect that contact with birth parents may result in very different responses from infants, school-age children, and adolescents.

Transracial Adoption. Transracial adoption has been a contentious issue in the 1980s and 1990s. Views on the topic range from the extremes (e.g., children should never be placed with families outside their race; racial matching is not beneficial to adopted children or families) to a more intermediate position of considering racial matching as preferable but not essential. Mental health professionals may be called on to assess whether the best interests of a child would be to be adopted by a family outside his or her race, to be placed with a family within his or her race, or to remain in a foster placement awaiting a within-race adoptive family. Although value judgments may determine this decision for some people, some research is available to inform these assessment decisions.

Transracial adoptions were rare before the 1950s, and several states had laws prohibiting them (Mini, 1994). Their rareness was due to laws placing strict barriers between the races and to the belief of many adoption agencies that matching children and their adoptive parents in as many ways as possible would facilitate the child's development (Bartholet, 1993). In the mid-1960s, increases in transracial adoptions were influenced by the courts striking down laws prohibiting transracial adoptions (e.g., *In re Gomez,* 1967). In addition, transracial adoption became part of the movement toward social integration of the races (Glynn, 1993). Approximately 2,500 transracial adoptions took place in 1971. Transracial adoption came under sharp criticism by the National Association of Black Social Workers in 1972, which declared that it should be completely prohibited. (Other groups have not had as strong a reaction. The NAACP has stated: "If black families are not available for placement of black children, transracial adoption ought to be pursued as a viable and preferred alternative to keeping such children in foster homes" (Hooks, 1992).) Following this criticism, the numbers of transracial adoptions declined considerably and the policy of many adoption agencies was not to complete transracial adoptions, basically returning the situation to what it was prior to the 1960s.

In the 1970s, some White parents sued to adopt Black children who had been in their homes as foster children, bringing transracial adoptions before the courts again. Although the Supreme Court has never ruled on the use of race in adoption decisions, lower courts have ruled that race cannot be the determining factor in an adoption or be given excessive weight in the decision (e.g., *Compos v. McKeithen,* 1972) and that a trial judge cannot defer to a decision made by an agency that used race as a determining factor in an adoption (*In re Moorehead,* 1991). However, the courts have consistently held that consideration of race is a permissible component of an adoption decision. *Drummond v. Fulton County Department of Family and Children's Services* (1977) initially reasoned that the consideration of race was permissible since it did not further a discriminatory end. Following *Regents of University of California v. Bakke* (1978), in which the Supreme Court held that intentional use of race for any reason required strict constitutional scrutiny, a state court ruled that consideration of race in adoption did pass strict scrutiny in that it furthered the compelling state interest of meeting the best interest of the adopted child and did so in a narrow, prescribed way (*In re R.M.G,* 1982). Because trial judges are given latitude in adoption decisions, however, the extent to which race is considered continues to vary from case to case (for review, see Mini, 1994).

Social Science Research on Transracial Adoptions. Several studies have examined the racial identity of minority group children adopted by White families. A problem with this line of research, however, is that racial identity has not been operationalized in a consistent way. For example, McRoy, Zurcher, Lauderdale, and Anderson (1982) and Andujo (1988) used the Twenty Statements Test to assess racial identity. The Twenty Statements Test has the child respond 20 times to the question "Who am I?" McRoy et al. found that 30 Black children adopted by White families referred to their race more frequently than 30 Black children adopted by Black families, and interpreted this as meaning that the transracially adopted children had more conflict about their racial identity. Andujo, on the other hand, found that 30 Mexican American children adopted by White families referred to themselves as Mexican American *less* frequently than 30 Mexican American children adopted by Mexican American families, and interpreted this as indicating that the transethnically adopted children had a poorer general acceptance of their ethnicity.

Some research has examined transracially adopted children's acceptance of their race or ethnicity. Shireman and Johnson (1985) gave the Clark Doll Test (in which children attribute various qualities to either a White or a Black doll) to Black children adopted by either White or Black families. At age 4, the transracially adopted children showed a higher preference for the Black dolls than the children adopted by Black families. By age 8, there were no differences in the preferences between the children adopted by White or Black families. This suggested that the transracially adopted children had as good a view of their race as did the within-race adopted children. However, Andujo (1988) administered a test designed to assess a positive sense of Mexican American identity and found that the children adopted by White families scored significantly lower than children adopted by Mexican American families.

The general self-esteem of transracially adopted children has been explored also. McRoy et al. (1982) found similar levels of self-esteem in Black children (average age of 13) adopted by Black and White families as measured by the Tennessee Self-Concept Scale. Using the same test, Andujo (1988) found similar self-esteem levels with her two groups of adopted Mexican American children (average age of 14). Simon, Altstein, and Melli (1994) found no differences in self-esteem between Black children adopted by White families, the White birth children in the same adoptive families, or a separate group of White children adopted by White families, 12 years after their adoption. Bagley (1993) found no difference on several measures of self-esteem between Black children adopted by White families and White children adopted by White families 12 years after their adoption. In addition, Bagley (1993) found no differences between the two groups of adoptees on several scales of psychological adjustment and educational achievement.

Several studies have included interviews with parents and children to assess the quality of the child's adjustment. Fanshel found that 75% of the adoptive parents of a group of transculturally adopted American Indian children felt that the adoption was successful 21 months after the adoption, and Grow and Shapiro (1974) found that 77% of transracial adoptions of Black children were successful based on parents' and teachers' assessments. From interviews with 58 transracially adoptive families, Feigelman and Silverman (1983) found that, soon after the adoption, 45% of the parents reported that their child had a problem-free adjustment to the adoption and that an addition 50% described their child as mostly well adjusted. At a 6-year follow-up, 77% of the transracial adoptees were described as being mostly well adjusted or having problem-free adjustments, a percentage that was similar to the 78% reported by a comparison group of White children adopted by White families.

White adoptive families that live in integrated neighborhoods, send their transracially adopted child to an integrated school, and continue to help the child learn about his or her cultural heritage, are more likely to have a child with greater pride in Black culture and a greater willingness to identify themselves as Black (Feigelman & Silverman, 1983; McRoy et al., 1982). However, no association has been found between the family's integration with the Black community and the child's overall adjustment (Bagley, 1993; Feigelman & Silverman, 1983) or between the child's sense of racial identity and general self-esteem (McRoy et al., 1982).

Implications for Policy and Practice. Several issues are involved in the controversy about transracial adoption. Some involve the influence of transracial adoptions on individual children and families. Others involve implications of transracial adoptions for cultural and racial groups. Social science research has focused on the influence of transracial adoptions on individuals and families, and has consistently found no overall negative influence on either the adopted children or their families. Most child welfare agencies have policies that promote the adoption of a child by a family within his or her racial or ethnic group. There is reason to believe, other important family characteristics being roughly equal, that a family of the child's race or ethnicity will provide a better environment for the child's full social and emotional development. On the other side, however, there is nothing in the research literature that suggests that it would not be in a child's best interest to join a permanent home outside his or her race or ethnicity rather than remain in foster care or some other temporary placement.

Additional research is needed in this area. Measures to assess characteristics such as racial identity in children must be validated. Longitudinal studies that follow transracially adopted children into adulthood have the potential to provide important information about their overall development.

Adoptions by Single Parents. There are no national statistics on the number of children placed for adoption with single adults. Shireman (1995) reported that 12% of all placements made through Oregon's Children's Services Division in 1991 were to single parents, up from 5% in 1989. Current estimates are that as many as 25% of special-needs children are currently adopted by single parents (Shireman, 1995).

No laws prohibit adoptions by single parents. State appellate courts have overturned trial court rulings prohibiting adoptions by single parents when no other party was seeking to adopt the child (e.g., *In re Alison VV.,* 1995). However, other courts have ruled that single-parent families are less desirable placements than dual-parent families and have awarded custody to the dual-parent families even if the child had lived with the single parent as a foster child (e.g., *In re L.B.T.,* 1982).

Adoptions by single parents have traditionally been viewed by child welfare agencies as appropriate only for children who are hard to place in dual-parent homes (Dougherty, 1978), and single parents have reported more resistance from child welfare agencies to their becoming adoptive parents than couples report (Feigelman & Silverman, 1983). Consequently, single parents have often adopted children for whom no placement in a dual-parent family could be found. These hard-to-place children are generally older, are from an ethnic minority, and/or have emotional or physical disabilities (Feigelman & Silverman, 1983; Groze & Rosenthal, 1991). Thus, the families that are seen by child welfare agencies as having the fewest resources are generally required to adopt a child who has the greatest needs.

Social Science Research with Single-Parent Adoptive Families. Single-parent adoptive families are different in fundamental ways from other single-parent families. Although an increasing number of single adult women are having birth children, the great majority of single-parent families are the result of divorce or separation, or of adolescents having children out of wedlock. Although single-parent adoptive families face many of the issues faced by all single-parent families (Shireman, 1995), many of the potentially troubling aspects of divorced families or families headed by adolescents are not experienced in adoptive families. Consequently, generalizing from research with other forms of single-parent families to adoptive families is likely to be misleading.

Dougherty (1978) found that among 88 single adoptive mothers, 52% had a graduate degree, the average age at the time of adoption was 35, and about 75% had never been married. In a study of adoptive parents in three midwestern states, Groze and Rosenthal (1991) found that single adoptive mothers were about 6 years older than the mothers in adoptive couples and that most single mothers and a substantial minority of single fathers were Black, whereas most dual-parent adoptive parents were White, and that single-parent adoptive families had lower incomes than dual-parent adoptive families. Feigelman and Silverman (1983) had 58 single parents among their nationwide survey of adoptive families. The single parents tended to be more highly educated than the couples and tended to have higher status jobs, although their family income was less primarily due to having only one wage earner in the family. Fourteen percent of the single parents were members of minority groups, whereas only 2% of the adoptive couples were. The single women were older than their counterparts in the couples, and the men in both groups were about the same age.

Groze and Rosenthal (1991) compared single- and dual-parent families that had adopted a special-needs child at least 6 months prior to the study. The single parents reported fewer behavioral problems on the Child Behavior

Checklist than did the couples. There was no difference between the two groups in parental reports about the children's school behavior or enjoyment of school. Feigelman and Silverman (1983) surveyed single- and dual-parent families 6 years after an adoptive placement. They found no significant differences between the single- and dual-parent families in parents' ratings of children's overall adjustment, the frequency of emotional problems, or levels of hyperactivity. Further, they found that the levels of role distress and conflict about adopting a child were similar among the single parents and couples. Shireman and Johnson (1985) followed several groups of mainly minority children adopted as infants from an agency in Chicago. Their results showed similar development among children adopted by single- and dual-parent families. Through self-report measures and interviews with 15 of the original 31 families when their child was age 15, Shireman (1988) concluded that identity formation, gender identity, and level of emotional and behavioral problems were similar for the children adopted by single parents and couples.

Implications for Policy and Practice. Current research shows that the behavioral and emotional development of both special-needs children and infants who are adopted by single parents is similar to that of children adopted by couples. Thus, there is no evidence that children are more likely to experience problems in their development if they are adopted by a single parent. Because single adoptive parents are more likely to have adopted hard-to-place children, it could be argued that the lack of differences between children adopted by single parents and by couples suggests that single parents provide a better environment for the amelioration of the problems that many special-needs children have (Shireman, 1995). Encouraging the placement of children in single-parent adoptive home seems appropriate, given the number of children awaiting adoption, especially in the minority community.

Continued research with single-parent adoptive families is needed before firm conclusions about their functioning can be drawn. The research to date primarily involves parents' reports of their children's behavior and overall adjustment. There may be a tendency on the part of many adoptive parents to minimize the problems experienced by their children, and this may result in similar levels of problems reported by single- and dual-parent adoptive families. Longitudinal studies with larger sample sizes are particularly needed so that any differences in the process by which the adoptive families are formed can be assessed, and so that information can be gathered about whether certain types of children fare better in single-parent families and other types of children fare better in dual-parent adoptive families.

Adoption by Gay or Lesbian Couples or Individuals. Adoptions by gay or lesbian adults have increased over the past decade, but remain controversial. These adoptions occur in two ways. The new partner of a gay or lesbian divorced birth parent may want to adopt the birth parent's child in the same way that a stepparent could adopt a child. In some cases, these adoptions have been successful (e.g., *In re Tammy,* 1993; *In re Evan,* 1992), with the courts noting that the adoptions were in the child's best interest and met statutory requirements. In other cases they have not been allowed based on statutory requirements. For example, a Wisconsin appellate court ruled that the best interests of the child were to be considered only after the statutory requirements for an adoption were met and disallowed an adoption by a lesbian couple (*In re Angel Lace M.,* 1994).

Cases in which gay or lesbian couples or individuals attempt to adopt a nonrelative child center on whether it is in a particular child's best interest to be adopted by them. Although Florida and New Hampshire prohibit adoptions by gay or lesbian couples, adoptions of nonrelatives by gay or lesbian couples have occurred in several other states. However, courts have raised concerns about children raised by gay or lesbian couples. These include that the children will be at increased risk for psychological problems, development of a homosexual sexual orientation, social stigmatization by peers, and isolation from adults (for reviews, see Falk, 1989; Patterson, 1992). An appellate court in Florida reasoned that most adopted children grow up to be heterosexual and reversed an adoption by a gay couple because "it is in the best interests of a child if his or her parents can personally relate to the child's (issues with heterosexual relationships) and assist the child in the difficult transition to heterosexual adulthood" (*State of Florida v. Cox,* 1993, p. 1220).

Social Science Research on Children Raised by Gay or Lesbian Adults. There is no published research examining the development of children adopted by gay or lesbian couples. There is, however, an emerging literature on birth children raised by their gay or lesbian parents. Overall, there is no evidence that children raised by gay or lesbian parents develop abnormally. Limitations of the research, however, make firm conclusions about the development of children raised by gay or lesbian couples difficult. The samples for most studies were gathered through support groups or through word-of-mouth referrals. It is unclear whether these samples are representative of the gay or lesbian parent population. Although the characteristics of volunteer families are a concern in all research, word-of-mouth recruitment does not allow for an estimation of the percentage of possible participants who volunteered to be included. This exacerbates concerns about not knowing who has participated and who has not. In addition, many of the issues that are of concern to researchers in this area (e.g., the gender-role development of children) are not well defined and there are often few or no valid measures for them in children. Many studies have used toy, activity, or peer preferences as a measure of gender development, and it is not clear that these preferences have a meaningful relationship to the child's gender development.

Several studies have examined school-age children's gender identity and gender-role behavior. The samples typically included children from heterosexual relationships who had spent some time living with their fathers but who were now living with their lesbian mothers. Most of the mothers were living without a partner. These studies found no overall differences in preferences between children living with lesbian and heterosexual mothers on toy preferences (Green, 1986; Hoeffer, 1981; Kirkpatrick, Smith, & Roy, 1981), the sex of the figure drawn during a Human Figure Drawing test (Kirkpatrick et al., 1981), favorite television programs (Green, 1986), friendship preferences (Golombok, Spencer, & Rutter, 1983; Green, 1986; Kirkpatrick et al., 1981), and scales measuring general masculine and feminine interests (Golombok et al., 1983).

Several researchers have interviewed adolescents and adults who were raised by lesbian mothers. Part of the interviews included questions about the participant's sexual orientation. Golombok et al. (1983) found that 1 of 9 adolescents in lesbian-headed households and 0 of 11 children in single, heterosexual parent-headed households had a primarily homosexual orientation. Alternately, Huggins (1989) found that 0 of 18 adolescents being raised by lesbian mothers and 1 of 18 adolescents being raised by a heterosexual mother had a gay or lesbian sexual orientation. One study of adult daughters of lesbian and heterosexual mothers showed that approximately 16% were lesbian, and that there was no significant difference in the percentage of lesbian children between the two groups (Gottman, 1990).

Golombok et al. (1983) found that children of divorced lesbian mothers had more contact with their fathers than did children of divorced heterosexual mothers; 12 of 37 children living in lesbian-headed households had contact with their father at least weekly, whereas only 3 of 38 children in heterosexual-headed households had weekly contact. Kirkpatrick et al. (1981) found that lesbian mothers were more concerned that their children have contact with supportive male adults than were heterosexual single mothers.

Several researchers have administered projective or objective tests of personality or psychological adjustment to children of lesbian mothers. Kirkpatrick et al. (1981) found no differences in the overall ratings of emotional disturbance between children of lesbian- and heterosexual-headed households, as assessed by a psychiatrist evaluating a child development history. Similarly, no differences were found on the Holtzman Inkblot Test and the Wechsler Intelligence Scale for Children. Golombok et al. (1983) found no differences in behavioral rating scales completed by mothers and by teachers for children from lesbian- and heterosexual-headed households. Green et al. (1986) found no differences between children in the two groups on IQ. Finally, Gottman's (1990) study of adult daughters of lesbian and heterosexual mothers showed no differences on personality adjustment as measured by the California Psychological Inventory.

Implications for Policy and Practice. The results of social science research raise no concerns about the development of children raised in lesbian-headed households. Although each of the studies has specific methodological shortcomings, the results from all of them point in the same direction, increasing one's confidence that conclusions drawn by the studies are valid. Several adoptions by gay men or lesbians have been of children in the foster care system who had a relatively small chance of being placed in another permanent adoptive home (e.g., *In re Adoption of Charles B.*, 1990). There is no social science evidence suggesting that these children would have been better off remaining in foster care. Additional research using samples gathered in a way that is more representative of families headed by gay or lesbian parents is needed to increase our knowledge about the development of children raised in them.

Conclusions

The past decade has seen significant changes in adoption law, policy, and practice. The characteristics of children waiting for adoption have changed, and the types of couples and individuals who would like to adopt a child have increased in number and diversity. The suitability of this field for developmental research is apparent by the controversy that surrounds decisions about who should and should not be allowed to adopt children (or certain groups of children) and by the assumptions that many in the legal and policy areas make about which families and which children are suitable for inclusion in the adoption process. Research could play an important role in decisions about whether single parents, gay or lesbian parents, or parents of a different race from a child, would make suitable parents. To be the most effective, this research should have a developmental focus, as the age of a child, and/or developmental needs of a parent, may influence the suitability of adoption. Further, developmentally based research on the impact of open adoptions on children, adoptive families, and birth families could inform the ongoing process of policy change in this area.

Concluding Comments on Foster Care and Adoption

As the forces in our society that shape the functioning of single parents, couples, and families continue to change, policy and practice in the area of foster care and adoption also will continue to change. Changes in the forces that influence which children need out-of-home placement (e.g., increases in parental death due to AIDS) will require changes in all areas of foster care, including the recruitment and retention of foster families, support services for foster children and foster families, and placement decisions. In addition, changes in the financing of foster care may require that more children remain in their birth homes as fewer dollars for foster care are available. These same forces may influence which children are available for adoption, the number of individuals or families willing to adopt children, and the willingness of the legal system to place children in families that might once have been considered inappropriate for adoptive placement.

Despite the strong presence of developmental research in the understanding of families, and the influence of these families on the development of the children and adults within them, only a small number of psychologists are working on the many developmentally relevant issues in adoption and foster care. Although these areas have long been the focus of social work researchers, the perspective provided by psychology would enhance our understanding of many foster care and adoption issues. The research methodology common to developmental studies would provide new ways of examining family, couple, and individual development of those involved with foster care and adoption. An increased focus on adoption and foster care by developmental psychologists would provide a stronger research foundation for the many legal, policy, and practice decisions that influence the lives of thousands of foster and adopted children and their families each day.

INTERFACE OF DEVELOPMENTAL PSYCHOLOGY AND LAW

We began this chapter by introducing several themes relevant to the interface of developmental psychology and law. We return to those themes now.

Balancing the Interests of Child, Family, and State

Changes in the balance of child, family, and state interests over the past few decades have been influenced by many factors. One of these influences has been increases in knowledge of child development. Over the decades, the courts have vacillated on how to balance parents' and children's rights in divorce cases and have looked to psychological research for answers. Research indicating that joint custody is beneficial to children helped persuade the courts to became more lenient toward such arrangements. The growing belief that decisions regarding custody in divorce cases are not best handled within an adversary system, as well as the difficulty of choosing between two parents who may both have their children's best interests at heart has motivated the courts to experiment with mediation. Mediation bows, or at least leans, toward the principle of family autonomy, which the courts want to respect when possible.

Child maltreatment represents an area in which the courts have decided that children's rights and those of the state may outweigh those of parents. Normally parents have the right to discipline their children and determine their living patterns and conditions, but when abusive levels of treatment are reached, the balance shifts. Children's object rights to freedom from harm and to adequate care become paramount. Also, the state's interests in protecting dependent citizens and ensuring healthy future generations are viewed as central. In child maltreatment cases, these interests may outweigh the rights of birth parents to custody of their children.

When children are removed from the home, placed in foster care, and eventually adopted, parents' rights may be completely transferred from birth parent to the state to adoptive parents. Even in cases of child maltreatment, however, birth parents' rights are still an important consideration for the courts. The courts prefer to keep families together and to return children to birth parents when safely possible.

To wit, in contested adoption situations, the rights of birth parents often prevail. For example, when a father has not consented to his child's adoption, the courts will remove a child from adoptive parents to whom the child has become emotionally attached and return the child to the father. Arguably, in terms of ongoing attachment relations, the child's best interests would dictate staying with the adoptive parents. Yet, in such cases birth parents' rights to their children are considered fundamental. As can be seen from these examples, the courts generally retain a fluid balance between child, state, and family interests that is sensitive to the specific situations in which children and families come into contact with the legal system.

Paradigms in Conflict

Psychology as a science operates under a different set of assumptions than does the law. The legal system is more concerned with justice than with truth, and thus with fairness. Psychology as a science is concerned with the truth. Differences in methods, language, and approaches add further to the gap between psychology and law.

Nevertheless, the legal system looks to developmental psychology for guidance on many issues concerning children. Scientists can contribute to a jurisprudence that is informed about children's abilities and needs, and thus one that is based more on fact than on intuition and tradition. Facts contribute importantly to fairness. However, even given relevant scientific findings, the courts struggle with what is fair when it comes to children. It is not in the public interest for courts to adopt research findings prematurely before the replicability, generalizability, and complexities of studies can be adequately explored. Moreover, developmental research has not always dealt with the full range of considerations relevant to children's best interests (e.g., economic factors or the effectiveness of intervention in improving children's lives). The courts play an important role in moderating premature application of science.

With these paradigm differences, how can psychology and law relate? Haney (1980) described three ways: psychology in the law, psychology and law, and psychology of law. Of the three, "psychology in the law" is the most frequent. In this situation, the legal system uses psychological knowledge for specific cases (e.g., by having a psychologist testify as an expert witness). The legal system decides when psychological knowledge will be used and maintains the power to ignore developmental research, reinterpret it, or accept it. Thus, within the "psychology in law" relationship, although the scientific method dictates how science is conducted, the legal system's methods dictate how science is used. Still, psychological research can have considerable influence in specific cases and even in determining the law of the land regarding children (e.g., *Brown v. Board of Education,* 1954; *Maryland v. Craig,* 1990).

"Psychology and law" refers to use of psychological science to examine the legal system from a psychological perspective, with the hope that valid principles will be adopted. Developmental psychologists working within this perspective might ask such questions as: Are legal assumptions about children empirically supported (e.g., that children should not decide with whom to live)? Are legal procedures valid when it comes to children (e.g., that cross-examination of a child is the best way for jurors to reach the truth)? Research intended to answer "psychology and law" questions has the potential to shape more profound legal change.

The third form of relationship, "psychology of law," is concerned with law as a determinant of behavior. How successful is the law in controlling behavior (e.g., in preventing child abuse)? Why are some laws tolerated (e.g., laws that permit religious exemptions for child abuse) and other laws not tolerated (e.g., there are no laws against parents' corporal punishment of children)? This third perspective addresses the heart of the legal system, questioning its justification, usefulness, and societal biases. Issues concerning children can be profitably addressed at each of the psychology/law interfaces. So far, however, relatively little developmental research has explored the "psychology of law" interface.

Developmental Research and Social Policy Decisions

Developmentalists need to apply their research to societal problems with care and caution. Although psychological research can inform policymakers and courts of children's abilities and needs, many important ethical issues are raised in the process.

One ethical issue concerns the applicability of research findings to actual cases. Methodological problems (e.g., lack of random assignment to divorced vs. nondivorced, adopted vs. nonadopted, or abused vs. nonabused groups) limit causal inferences. Constraints on the generalizability of many research findings limit application. Such issues must be considered and acknowledged in attempts to influence social policy regarding children.

Moreover, researchers should distinguish between normative ranges of adjustment and factors that place children at risk. One can obtain a statistically significant difference between two groups (e.g., abused vs. nonabused, adopted vs. nonadopted) and still have both groups score within normative ranges. As pointed out in connection with studies of adoption, although some studies show that adopted children exhibit more problems than nonadopted children, the differences are small and the adopted children are typically well within the range of normal behavior. A similar pattern is often found with respect to effects of divorce. The social policy implications of a small change in the normal range may be different from the implications of a large change or one that places children in a risk category.

Furthermore, because social policies that benefit some children may hurt others, it is important for developmentalists to determine how the outcomes of interventions affect different groups of children and then consider the risk-benefit ratio of the intervention. To do this, researchers should consider the full range of children in the full range of situations that actually confront the legal system. In the area of divorce, laws that state a preference for joint custody might do a disservice to children whose parents are in continual conflict. In the area of child maltreatment, policies relevant to eliminating false reports (e.g., abolishing mandatory reporting laws) might leave many abused children unprotected. In the area of foster care and adoption, some children might be better off returning to their birth parents even after several years in temporary foster care whereas others might benefit most from being adopted quickly.

These examples raise the issue of values. Social policy for children is not a purely scientific matter. Societal values necessarily come into play. Regarding the preceding examples, is it better to ensure that both parents have equal access to their children in custody cases or to protect children from conflict that may jeopardize their mental health? Is it better to eliminate false reports of abuse and thereby protect innocent adults, even at the risk of many children continuing to suffer maltreatment? Is it better to honor birth parents' rights to their children and children's rights to their birth parents or to move quickly to find permanent placements for children? To say whether a policy is "good" or "bad," "better" or "worse," one quickly has to venture beyond the limits of science.

Ideally, all children would be born into stable, happy families that treat children with kindness and respect. Ideally, we could prevent family disruption, child maltreatment, and foster-care placements for children. Complete prevention may never be possible, however, and in some cases (such as divorce or adoption situations) prevention may be undesirable. Therefore, scientists need to continue to investigate the best ways to intervene on behalf of children. Research presented in this chapter provides a partial basis on which sound interventions can be made, despite the need for more and better developmental research.

Unlike psychology, law is basically conservative. The courts do not seek out cases. Their decisions are based largely on disputes that come to their attention, and on precedence and tradition. In contrast, developmental psychologists are basically forward looking. As scientists, we can experiment with what could be rather than simply accepting what is. Developmentalists thus possess exciting opportunities to advance science and social policy on behalf of children.

ACKNOWLEDGMENTS

The authors thank David Brodzinsky for his substantial help with the development of this chapter. The authors also thank two anonymous reviewers. Jodi Quas, Daya Hutchins, and Elizabeth Encisco provided valuable assistance. Although the present chapter represents the collaborative effort of the three authors, major responsibility for each section should be attributed as follows: Robert Emery, divorce; Gail S. Goodman, child maltreatment; Jeffrey Haugaard, foster care and adoption.

REFERENCES

Aber, J., & Allen, J. P. (1987). The effects of maltreatment on children's socioemotional development: An attachment theory perspective. *Developmental Psychology, 23,* 406–414.

Ackerman, M. J. (1995). *Clinician's guide to child custody evaluations.* New York: Wiley.

Allen, M. E., Jones, P. D., & Nash, M. R. (1989, August). *Detection of sexual abuse among emotionally disturbed preschoolers.* Paper presented at the annual convention of the American Psychological Association, New Orleans, LA.

Allison, P., & Furstenberg, F. (1989). How marital dissolution affects children: Variations by age and sex. *Developmental Psychology, 25,* 540–549.

ALMA Society v. Mellon, 601 F. 2d 1225 (1979).

Alpert, J. L. (1995). Trauma, dissociation, and clinical study as a responsible beginning. *Consciousness and Cognition, 4,* 125–129.

Alpert, J. L., Brown, L., Ceci, S. J., Courtois, C., Loftus, E. F., & Ornstein, P. (1996). *Working group on investigation of memories of childhood abuse: Final report.* Washington, DC: American Psychological Association.

Amato, P. R. (1993). Children's adjustment to divorce: Theories, hypotheses, and empirical support. *Journal of Marriage and the Family, 55,* 23–38.

Amato, P. R., & Keith, B. (1991). Parental divorce and the well-being of children: A meta-analysis. *Psychological Bulletin, 110,* 26–46.

Amato, P. R., Loomis, L. S., & Booth, A. (1995). Parental divorce, marital conflict, and offspring well-being during early adulthood. *Social Forces, 73,* 895–915.

Amato, P. R., & Rezac, S. J. (1994). Contact with nonresident parents, interparental conflict, and children's behavior. *Journal of Family Issues, 15,* 191–207.

American Association for Protecting Children. (1988). *Highlights of official child neglect and abuse reporting, 1986.* Denver: American Humane Association.

American Professional Society on the Abuse of Children (APSAC). (1988). *Guidelines for psychosocial evaluation of suspected sexual abuse in young children.* Unpublished manuscript, Chicago.

American Professional Society on the Abuse of Children (APSAC). (1995). *Practice guidelines: Use of anatomical dolls in child sexual abuse assessments.* Unpublished document, Chicago.

American Psychological Association. (1994). Guidelines for child custody evaluations in divorce proceedings. *American Psychologist, 49,* 677–680.

Amersterdam, B., Brill, M., Bell, N. W., & Edwards, D. (1979). Coping with abuse: Adolescents' views. *Victimology, 4,* 278–284.

Ames, L. (1992). Open adoptions: Truth and consequences. *Law and Psychology Review, 16,* 137–152.

Andujo, E. (1988). Ethnic identity of transethnically adopted Hispanic adolescents. *Social Work, 33,* 531–535.

Anson, D. A., Golding, S. L., & Gully, K. J. (1993). Child sexual abuse allegations: Reliability of criteria-based content analyses. *Law and Human Behavior, 17,* 331–343.

Appell A. R., & Boyer, B. (1995). Parental rights vs. best interests of the child. *Duke Journal of Gender Law and Policy, 2,* 63–96.

Atkeson, B. M., Forehand, R. L., & Richard, K. M. (1982). The effects of divorce on children. In B. B. Lahey & A. E. Kazdin (Eds.), *Advances in clinical child psychology* (Vol. 5, pp. 255–281). New York: Plenum Press.

August, R. I., & Forman, B. D. (1989, Fall). A comparison of sexually abused and nonsexually abused children's behavioral responses to anatomically correct dolls. *Child Psychiatry and Human Development,* 39–47.

Axelrod, R. (1984). *The evolution of cooperation.* New York: Basic Books.

Bagley, C. (1993). Transracial adoption in Britain: A follow-up study, with policy considerations. *Child Welfare, 73,* 285–299.

Baker-Ward, L., Burgwyn, E., Ornstein, P. A., & Gordon, B. (1995, April). Children's reports of a minor medical emergency procedure. In G. Goodman & L. Baker-Ward (Chairs), *Children's memory for emotional and traumatic events.* Symposium conducted at the Society for Research in Child Development, Indianapolis, IN.

Baker-Ward, L., Hess, T. M., & Flannagan, D. A. (1990). The effects of involvement on children's memory for events. *Cognitive Development, 5,* 55–69.

Barber, B., & Eccles, J. (1992). Long-term influences of divorce and single parenting on adolescent family- and work-related values, behaviors, and aspirations. *Psychological Bulletin, 111,* 108–126.

Barnett, D., Manly, J. T., & Cicchetti, D. (1993). Defining child maltreatment: The interface between policy and research. In D. Cicchetti & S. Toth (Eds.), *Child abuse, child development, and social policy* (pp. 7–74). Norwood, NJ: ABLEX.

Barnhizel v. Ferrell, 47 Ind. 335 (1874).

Barth, R. P., & Beery, M. (1988). *Adoption and disruption.* New York: Aldine de Gruyter.

Barth, R. P., Courtney, M., Berrick J. D., & Albert, V. (1994). *From child abuse to permanency planning.* New York: Aldine de Gruyter.

Bartholet, E. (1993). *Family bonds: Adoption and politics of parenting.* Boston: Houghton Mifflin.

Bass, C. (1975). Matchmaker-matchmaker: Older-child adoption failures. *Child Welfare, 54,* 505–512.

Batterman-Faunce, J. M., & Goodman, G. S. (1993). Effects of context on the accuracy and suggestibility of child witnesses. In G. S. Goodman & B. L. Bottoms (Eds.), *Child victims, child witnesses: Understanding and improving children's testimony* (pp. 301–330). New York: Guilford Press.

Batterman-Faunce, J. M., & Goodman, G. S. (1996). *Assessing children's eyewitness reports after a four year delay.* Unpublished paper.

Baydar, N., & Brooks-Gunn, J. (1991). Effects of maternal employment and child-care arrangements on preschoolers' cognitive and behavioral outcomes: Evidence from the Children of the National Longitudinal Survey of Youth. *Developmental Psychology, 27,* 932–945.

Beal, C. R., Schmitt, K. L., & Dekle, D. J. (1995). Eyewitness identification of children: Effects of absolute judgments, nonverbal response options, and event encoding. *Law and Human Behavior, 19,* 197–216.

Beitchman, J., Zucker, K., Hood, J., DaCosta, G., Akman, D., & Cassavia, E. (1992). A review of the long-term effects of child sexual abuse. *Child Abuse and Neglect, 16,* 101–118.

Belbas, N. (1987). Staying in touch: Empathy in open adoptions. *Smith College Studies in Social Work, 57,* 184–198.

Benedek, E., & Schetky, D. (1985). Allegations of sexual abuse in child custody and visitation disputes. In D. Schetky & E. Benedek (Eds.), *Emerging issues in child psychiatry and law* (pp. 145–158). New York: Brunner/Mazel.

Benedict, M. I., & White, R. B. (1991). Factors associated with foster care length of stay. *Child Welfare, 70,* 45–58.

Benedict, M. I., Zuravin, S., Brandt, D., & Abbey, H. (1994). Types of frequency of child maltreatment by family foster care providers in an urban population. *Child Abuse and Neglect, 18,* 577–585.

Benson, B. A., & Gross, A. M. (1989). The effect of a congenitally handicapped child upon the marital dyad: A review of the literature. *Clinical Psychology Review, 9,* 747–758.

Berliner, L. (in press). The use of expert testimony in child sexual abuse cases. In S. J. Ceci & H. Hembrooke (Eds.), *What can (and should) an expert tell the court?* Washington, DC: American Psychological Association.

Berliner, L., & Conte, J. (1993). Sexual abuse evaluations: Conceptual and empirical obstacles. *Child Abuse and Neglect, 17,* 111–125.

Berliner, L., & Conte, J. (1995). The effects of disclosure and intervention on sexually abused children. *Child Abuse and Neglect, 19,* 371–384.

Berliner, L., & Elliott, D. (1996). Child sexual abuse. In J. Briere, L. Berliner, J. Bulkley, C. Jenny, & T. Reid (Eds.), *The APSAC handbook on child maltreatment* (pp. 51–71). Newbury Park, CA: Sage.

Berrick J. D., & Barth, R. P. (1994). Research on kinship foster care: What do we know? Where do we go from here? *Children and Youth Services Review, 16,* 1–5.

Berrick, J. D., Barth, R. P., & Needell, B. (1994). A comparison of kinship foster homes and foster family homes. *Children and Youth Services Review, 16,* 35–63.

Berry, M. (1993). Adoptive parents' perceptions of, and comfort with, open adoption. *Child Welfare, 72,* 231–253.

Bjorklund, B., Douglas, R., Park, C., Nelson, L., Sanders, L., Gache, J., Cassel, W., & Bjorklund, D. (1997). *When does misleading questioning cause children to change their minds as well as their answers?* Paper presented at the meeting of the Society for Research in Child Development, Washington, DC.

Block, J. H., Block, J., & Gjerde, P. F. (1986). The personality of children prior to divorce: A prospective study. *Child Development, 57,* 827–840.

Boat, B., & Everson, M. (1986). *Using anatomical dolls: Guidelines for interviewing young children in sexual abuse investigations.* Chapel Hill: University of North Carolina, Department of Psychiatry.

Boat, B., & Everson, M. (1993). The use of anatomical dolls in sexual abuse evaluations: Current research and practice. In G. Goodman & B. Bottoms (Eds.), *Child victims, child witnesses* (pp. 47–70). New York: Guilford Press.

Boat, B., & Everson, M. (1996). Concerning practices of interviewers when using anatomical dolls in child protective services investigations. *Child Maltreatment, 1,* 96–104.

Bohannon, J. N., & Symons, V. L. (1993). Flashbulb memories: Confidence, consistency, and quantity. In E. Winograd & U. Neisser (Eds.), *Affect and accuracy in recall: Studies of "flashbulb" memories* (pp. 65–91). New York: Cambridge University Press.

Bohman, M. (1971). A comparative study of adopted children, foster children, and children in their biological environment born after undesired pregnancies. *Acta Paediatrica Scandinavia, 221*(Suppl.), 5–38.

Bohman, M., & Sigvardsson, S. (1980). A prospective, longitudinal study of children registered for adoption. *Acta Psychiatrica Scandinavia, 61,* 339–355.

Bohman, M., & Sigvardsson S. (1990). Outcome in adoption: Lessons from longitudinal studies. In D. Brodzinsky & M. Schechter (Eds.), *The psychology of adoption* (pp. 93–106). New York: Oxford University Press.

Bolton, F. G., Laner, R., & Gai, D. (1981). For better or worse?: Foster parents and children in an officially reported child maltreatment population. *Children and Youth Services Review, 3,* 37–53.

Boneh, C. (1979). *Disruptions in adoptive placements.* Boston: Department of Public Welfare.

Borgatta, E. F., & Fanshel, D. (1965). *Behavioral characteristics of children known to psychiatric outpatient clinics.* New York: Child Welfare League of America.

Bottoms, B. L. (1993). Individual differences in perceptions of child sexual assault victims. In G. S. Goodman & B. L. Bottoms (Eds.), *Child victims, child witnesses.* New York: Guilford Press.

Bottoms, B. L., & Goodman, G. S. (1994). Evaluation of children's testimony: Factors influencing the jury. *Journal of Applied Social Psychology, 24,* 702–732.

Bottoms, B. L., & Goodman, G. S. (1996). *International perspectives on child abuse and children's testimony.* Newbury Park, CA: Sage.

Bottoms, B. L., Goodman, G. S., Schwartz-Kenney, B., Sachsenmaier, T., & Thomas, S. (1990, March). *Keeping secrets: Implications for children's testimony.* Presented at the meetings of the American Psychology and Law, Williamsburg, VA.

Bottoms, B. L., Shaver, P. R., & Goodman, G. S. (1996). An analysis of ritualistic and religion-related child abuse allegations. *Law and Human Behavior, 20,* 1–34.

Bottoms, B. L., Shaver, P. R., Goodman, G. S., & Qin, J. (1995). In the name of God: Religion and child abuse. *Journal of Social Issues, 51,* 85–111.

Bowlby, J. (1980). *Attachment and loss: Vol. 3. Loss, sadness, and depression.* New York: Basic Books.

Bradley, A., & Wood, J. (1996). How do children disclose? *Child Abuse and Neglect, 20,* 881–891.

Brainerd, C., & Ornstein, P. (1991). Children's memory for witnessed events: The developmental back drop. In J. Doris (Ed.), *The suggestibility of children's recollections* (pp. 10–20). Washington, DC: American Psychological Association.

Brainerd, C., Renya, V., Howe, M., & Kingma, J. (1990). The development of forgetting and reminiscence. *Monographs of Society for Research in Child Development, 55*(Serial No. 222).

Brassard, M., German, R., & Hart, S. (1987). *Psychological maltreatment of children and youth.* New York: Pergamon Press.

Brekke, N. J., Enko, P. J., Clavet, G., & Seelau, E. (1991). Of juries and court-appointed experts: The impact of nonadversarial versus adversarial expert testimony. *Law and Human Behavior, 15,* 451–475.

Bremner, R. (1970). *Children and youth in America* (Vol. 1). Cambridge, MA: Harvard University Press.

Brennan, M., & Brennan, R. (1988). *Strange language: Child victims under cross examination.* Riverina, Australia: Charles Stuart University.

Brewin, C. R., Andrews, B., & Gotlib, I. H. (1993). Psychopathology and early experience: A reappraisal of retrospective reports. *Psychological Bulletin, 113,* 82–98.

Briere, J. (1992). *Child abuse trauma.* Newbury Park, CA: Sage.

Briere, J., & Conte, J. (1993). Self reported amnesia for abuse in adults molested as children. *Journal of Traumatic Stress, 6,* 21–31.

Brodzinsky, D. M. (1987). Adjustment to adoption: A psychosocial perspective. *Clinical Psychology Review, 7,* 25–47.

Brodzinsky, D. M., Radice, C., Huffman, L., & Merkler, K. (1987). Prevalence of clinically significant symptomatology in a nonclinical sample of adopted and nonadopted children. *Journal of Clinical Child Psychology, 16,* 350–356.

Brodzinsky, D. M., Schechter, D. E., Graff, A. M., & Singer, L. M. (1984). Psychological and academic adjustment in adopted children. *Journal of Consulting and Clinical Psychology, 52,* 582–590.

Bross, D. (1984). Protecting child witnesses. In *Multidisciplinary advocacy for mistreated children* (pp. 195–203). Denver, CO: National Association of Counsel for Children.

Brown v. Board of Education of Topeka et al., 347 U.S. 483 (1954).

Browne, A., & Finkelhor, D. (1986). Impact of child sexual abuse: A review of the research. *Psychological Bulletin, 99,* 66–77.

Bruck, M., Ceci, S. J., Francoeur, E., & Barr, R. (1995). "I hardly cried when I got my shot!": Influencing children's reports about a visit to their pediatrician. *Child Development, 66,* 193–208.

Bruck, M., Ceci, S. J., Francoeur, E., & Renick, A. (1995). Anatomically detailed dolls do not facilitate preschoolers' reports of a pediatric examination involving genital touching. *Journal of Experimental Psychology: Applied, 1,* 95–109.

Bruck, M., Ceci, S. J., & Hembrooke, H. (in press). Children's reports of pleasant and unpleasant events. In D. Read & S. Lindsay (Eds.), *Recollections of trauma: Scientific research and clinical practice.* New York: Plenum Press.

Buchanan, C. M., Maccoby, E. E., & Dornbusch, S. M. (1991). Caught between parents: Adolescents' experience in divorced homes. *Child Development, 62,* 1008–1029.

Bugental, D. B., Blue, J., Cortez, V., Fleck, K., & Rodriguez, A. (1992). The influence of witnessed affect on information processing in children. *Child Development, 63,* 774–786.

Bull, R. (1995). Good practice for video recorded interviews with child witnesses for use in criminal proceedings. In G. Davies, S. Lloyd-Bostock, M. McMurran, & C. Wilson (Eds.), *Psychology, law, and criminal justice: International developments in research and practice* (pp. 100–117). Berlin, Germany: Walter de Gruyter.

Bumpass, L. L., & Raley, R. K. (1993). *Trends in the duration of single-parent families* (National Survey of Families and Households Working Paper No. 58). Center for Demography, University of Wisconsin, Madison.

Burton, R. V., & Strichartz, A. F. (1992). Liar, liar, pants afire. In S. J. Ceci, M. D. Leichtman, & M. Putnick (Eds.), *Cognitive and social factors in early deception* (pp. 11–28). Hillsdale, NJ: Erlbaum.

Bussey, K. (1992). Lying and truthfulness: Children's definitions, standards, and evaluative reactions. *Child Development, 63,* 129–137.

Bussey, K., Lee, K., & Grimbeek, E. J. (1993). Lies and secrets: Implications for children's reporting of sexual abuse. In G. S. Goodman & B. L. Bottoms (Eds.), *Child victims, child witnesses: Understanding and improving testimony* (pp. 147–168). New York: Guilford Press.

Butler, S., Gross, J., & Hayne, H. (1995). The effect of drawing on memory performance in young children. *Developmental Psychology, 31,* 597–608.

Bybee, D., & Mowbray, C. T. (1993). An analysis of allegations of sexual abuse in a multi-victim day-care center case. *Child Abuse and Neglect, 17,* 767–784.

Cahn, K., & Johnson, P. (1993). Critical issues in permanency planning. In K. Cahn & P. Johnson (Eds.), *Children can't wait.* Washington, DC: Child Welfare League.

Camara, K. A., & Resnick, G. (1987). Marital and parental subsystems in mother-custody, father-custody and two-parent households: Effects on children's social development. In J. Vincent (Ed.), *Advances in family assessment, intervention and research* (Vol. 4, pp. 165–196). Greenwich, CT: JAI Press.

Camara, K. A., & Resnick, G. (1989). Styles of conflict resolution and cooperation between divorced parents: Effects on child behavior and adjustment. *American Journal of Orthopsychiatry, 59,* 560–575.

Campbell, L., Silverman, P. R., & Patti, P. (1991). Reunions between adoptees and birth parents: The adoptees' experience. *Social Work, 36,* 329–335.

Camras, L., Ribordy, S., Hill, J., & Martino, S. (1988). Recognition and posing of emotional expressions by abused children and their mothers. *Developmental Psychology, 24,* 776–781.

Capaldi, D. M., & Patterson, G. R. (1991). Relation of parental transitions to boys' adjustment problems: I. A linear hypothesis. II. Mothers at risk for transitions and unskilled parenting. *Developmental Psychology, 3,* 489–504.

Carey, W. B., Lipton, W. L., & Myers, R. A. (1974). Temperament in adopted and foster babies. *Child Welfare, 53,* 352–359.

Carlson, V., Cicchetti, D., Barnett, D., & Braunwalk, K. (1989). Disorganized and disoriented attachment relationships in maltreated infants. *Developmental Psychology, 25,* 525–531.

Carrieri, J. R. (1991). *Child custody, foster care, and adoptions.* New York: Lexington Books.

Carter, C., Bottoms, B. L., & Levine, M. (1996). Linguistic and socioemotional influences on the accuracy of children's reports. *Law and Human Behavior, 20,* 335–358.

Case, R. (1991). *The mind's staircase: Exploring the conceptual underpinnings of children's thought and knowledge.* Hillsdale, NJ: Erlbaum.

Cashmore, J. (1992). *The use of closed-circuit television for child witnesses in the ACT.* Sydney, Australia: Australian Law Reform Commission.

Cassel, W., Roebers, C., & Bjorklund, D. (1996). Developmental patterns of eyewitness responses to repeated and increasingly suggestive questions. *Journal of Experimental Child Psychology, 61,* 116–133.

Catania, F. J. (1992). Accounting to ourselves for ourselves: An analysis of adjudication in the resolution of child custody disputes. *Nebraska Law Review, 71,* 1228–1271.

Ceci, S. J., & Bruck, M. (1993). Suggestibility of the child witness: A historical review and synthesis. *Psychological Bulletin, 113,* 403–439.

Ceci, S. J., & Bruck. M. (1995). *Jeopardy in the courtroom.* Washington, DC: American Psychological Association.

Ceci, S. J., Bruck, M., & Rosenthal, R. (1995). Children's allegations of sexual abuse: Forensic and scientific issues. The social science amicus brief in State of New Jersey v. Margaret Kelly Michaels. Psychology. *Public Policy and Law, 1,* 494–520.

Ceci, S. J., Huffman, M. L., Smith, E., & Loftus, E. F. (1994). Repeatedly thinking about a non-event: Source misattribution among preschoolers. *Consciousness and Cognition, 3,* 388–407.

Ceci, S. J., Leichtman, M., & Bruck, M. (1995). The suggestibility of children's eyewitness reports: Methodological issues. In F. Weinert & W. Schneider (Eds.), *Memory performance and competence* (pp. 323–374). Mahwah, NJ: Erlbaum.

Ceci, S. J., Leichtman, M., Putnick, M., & Nightingale, N. (1993). Age differences in suggestibility. In D. Cicchetti & S. Toth (Eds.), *Child abuse, child development, and social policy* (pp. 117–137). Norwood, NJ: ABLEX.

Ceci, S. J., Loftus, E., Leichtman, M., & Bruck, M. (1994). The role of source misattribution in the creation of false beliefs among preschoolers. *International Journal of Clinical and Experimental Hypnosis, 62,* 304–320.

Chase-Lansdale, P., & Hetherington, E. M. (1990). The impact of divorce on life-span development: Short and longterm effects. In P. B. Baltes, D. L. Featherman, & R. M. Learner (Eds.), *Life-span development and behavior* (Vol. 10, pp. 107–151). Hillsdale, NJ: Erlbaum.

Cherlin, A. J. (1992). *Marriage, divorce, remarriage* (2nd ed.). Cambridge, MA: Harvard University Press.

Cherlin, A. J., Furstenberg, F. F., Chase-Lansdale, P. L., Kiernan, K. E., Robins, P. K., Morrison, D. R., & Teitler, J. O. (1991). Longitudinal studies of effects of divorce on children in Great Britain and the United States. *Science, 252,* 1386–1389.

Child Abuse Prevention and Treatment Act. (1974). P.L. 93-247, 93d Cong., S1191.

Children's Defense Fund. (1987). *A children's defense budget.* Washington, DC: Author.

Chou, C. (1993). Renewing the good intentions of foster care. *Vanderbilt Law Review, 46,* 683–713.

Christianson, S. A. (1992). Emotional stress and eyewitness memory: A critical review. *Psychological Bulletin, 112,* 284–309.

Christianson, S. A., & Nilsson, L. (1989). Hysterical amnesia: A case of aversively motivated isolation of memory. In T. Archer & L. Nilsson (Eds.), *Aversion, avoidance, and anxiety: Perspectives on aversively motivated behavior* (pp. 289–310). Hillsdale, NJ: Erlbaum.

Cicchetti, D. (1990). The organization and coherence of socioemotional, cognitive, and representational development. In R. Thompson (Ed.), *Nebraska Symposium on Motivation* (Vol. 36, pp. 259–366). Lincoln: University of Nebraska Press.

Cicchetti, D., & Barnett, D. (1991). Attachment organization in maltreated preschoolers. *Development and Psychopathology, 3,* 397–412.

Cicchetti, D., & Carlson, V. (Eds.). (1989). *Child maltreatment.* New York: Cambridge University Press.

Clarke-Stewart, A., Thompson, R., & Lepore, S. (1989). Manipulating children's interpretations through interrogation. In G. Goodman (Chair), *Current topics in research on children's testimony.* Kansas City, MO: Society for Research in Child Development.

Cohen, N. (1995). Discussant comments. In P. Ornstein (Chair), *Remembering the distant past: Implications for research on children's memory for the recovered memory debate.* Symposium presented at the Society for Research in Child Development meetings, Indianapolis, IN.

Cohn, A., & Birch, T. (1988). Building resources for prevention programs. In D. Bross, R. Krugman, M. Lenherr, D. Rosenberg, & B. Schmitt (Eds.), *The new child protection team handbook* (pp. 598–615). New York: Garland.

Colorado Ex rel M.M., 726 P. 2d 1108 (1986).

Commonwealth of Pennsylvania v. Nancrede, 32 Pa. 389 (1859).

Compos v. McKeithen, 341 F. Supp. 264 (1972).

Conte, J., Sorenson, E., Fogarty, L., & Rosa, J. (1991). Evaluating children's reports of sexual abuse: A survey of professionals. *American Journal of Orthopsychiatry, 61,* 428–437.

Cook, L. W. (1991–1992). Open adoption: Can visitation with natural family members be in the child's best interest? *Journal of Family Law, 30,* 471–492.

Corwin, D., Berliner, L., Goodman, G. S., Goodwin, J., & White, S. (1987). Child sexual abuse and custody disputes—No easy answers. *Journal of Interpersonal Violence, 2,* 91–105.

Corwin, D., & Olafson, E. (1997). Videotaped discovery of a memory of abuse compared with earlier childhood interview. *Child Maltreatment, 2,* 91–112.

Coster, W., Gersten, M., Beeghly, M., & Cicchetti, D. (1989). Communicative functioning in maltreated toddlers. *Developmental Psychology, 25,* 1020–1029.

Costin, L. (1991). *Child welfare.* New York: Freeman.

Cowan, N. (1997). *The development of memory in childhood.* Hove, East Sussex, England: Psychology Press.

Cowen, E. L., Pedro-Carroll, J. L., & Alpert-Gillis, L. J. (1990). Relationship between support and adjustment among children of divorce. *Journal of Child Psychology and Psychiatry, 31,* 727–735.

Cox, M. J., & Cox, R. D. (1985). A brief history of policy for dependent and neglected children. In M. J. Cox & R. D. Cox (Eds.), *Foster care: Current issues, policies, and practices* (pp. 1–25). Norwood, NJ: ABLEX.

Coy v. Iowa, 108 S. Ct. 2798 (1988).

Cressler, D. E. (1993–1994). Requiring proof beyond a reasonable doubt in parental rights termination cases. *Journal of Family Law, 32,* 785–815.

Crittenden, P. (1988). Family and dyadic patterns of functioning in maltreating families. In K. Browne, C. Davies, & P. Stratton (Eds.), *Early prediction and prevention of child abuse* (pp. 161–189). Chichester, England: Wiley.

Crittenden, P., & Ainsworth, M. (1989). Child maltreatment and attachment theory. In D. Cicchetti & V. Carlson (Eds.), *Child maltreatment* (pp. 432–463). Cambridge, England: Cambridge University Press.

Cross, T. P., DeVos, E., & Whitcomb, D. (1994). Prosecution of child sexual abuse: Which cases are accepted? *Child Abuse and Neglect, 18,* 663–678.

Crowley, M. J., O'Callaghan, M. G., & Ball, P. J. (1994). The juridical impact of psychological expert testimony in a simulated child sexual abuse trial. *Law and Human Behavior, 18,* 89–105.

Cummings, E. M., & Davies, P. (1994). *Children and marital conflict.* New York: Guilford Press.

Dalenberg, C. (1995). *The accuracy of continuous and recovered memories of childhood sexual trauma.* Paper presented at the meeting of the Society for Applied Research in Memory and Cognition, Vancouver, Canada.

Daubert v. Merrell Dow Pharmaceuticals, 951 F.2d 1128 (9th Cir. 1991), vacated, 113 S.Ct. 2786 (1993).

Davies, G. (1993). Children's memory for other people: An integrative review. In C. A. Nelson (Ed.), *Memory and affect in development: Minnesota Symposium on Child Psychology* (Vol. 26, pp. 123–157). Hillsdale, NJ: Erlbaum.

Davies, G., & Noon, E. (1991). *An evaluation of live link for child witnesses.* London: Home Office.

Davies, G., Wilson, C., Mitchell, R., & Milsom, J. (1995). *Videotaping children's evidence: An evaluation.* London: Home Office.

Dawes, R. M. (1994). *House of cards: Psychology and psychotherapy built on myth.* New York: Free Press.

Deitrich-MacLean, G., & Walden, T. (1988). Distinguishing teaching interactions of physically abusive from nonabusive parent-child dyads. *Child Abuse and Neglect, 12,* 469–479.

Deloache, J. S. (1995). The use of dolls in interviewing young children. In M. S. Zaragoza, J. R. Graham, G. C. N. Hall, R. Hirschman, & Y. S. Ben-Porath (Eds.), *Memory and testimony in the child witness* (pp. 160–178). Newbury Park, CA: Sage.

Deloache, J. S., & Marzolf, D. (1995). The use of dolls to interview young children: Issues of symbolic representation. *Journal of Experimental Child Psychology, 60,* 155–173.

DeMause, L. (1975). *The history of childhood.* New York: Psychohistory Press.

Demick, J., & Wapner, S. (1988). Open and closed adoption: A developmental conceptualization. *Family Process, 27,* 229–249.

Dent, H. (1982). The effects of interviewing strategies on the results of interviews with child witnesses. In A. Trankell (Ed.), *Reconstructing the past: The role of psychologists in criminal trials* (pp. 279–298). Deventer, The Netherlands: Kluwer.

Dent, H., & Flin, R. (Eds.). (1992). *Children as witnesses.* Chichester, England: Wiley.

Derdeyn, A. P. (1976). Child custody contests in historical perspective. *American Journal of Psychiatry, 133,* 1369–1376.

Devlin, A. S., Brown, E. H., Beebe, J., & Parulis, E. (1992). Parent education for divorced fathers. *Family Relations, 41,* 290–296.

Diamond, R., & Carey, S. (1977). Developmental changes in the representation of faces. *Journal of Experimental Child Psychology, 23,* 1–22.

Dickson, L. R., Heffron, W. M., & Parker, C. (1990). Children from disrupted and adoptive homes on an inpatient unit. *American Journal of Orthopsychiatry, 60,* 594–602.

Dietze, P. M., & Thomson, D. M. (1993). Mental reinstatement of context: A technique for interviewing child witnesses. *Applied Cognitive Psychology, 7,* 97–108.

DiLalla, L., & Gottesman, I. (1991). Biological and genetic contributions to violence—Widom's untold tale. *Psychological Bulletin, 109,* 125–129.

Dillon, P., & Emery, R. E. (1996). Long term effects of divorce mediation in a field study of child custody dispute resolution. *American Journal of Orthopsychiatry, 66,* 131–140.

DiTomasso, M., & Routh, D. (1993). Recall of abuse in childhood and three measures of dissociation. *Child Abuse and Neglect, 17,* 477–486.

Dodge, K., Bates, J., & Pettit, G. S. (1990). Mechanisms in the cycle of violence. *Science, 250,* 1678–1683.

Doelling, J. L., & Johnson, J. H. (1990). Predicting success in foster placement. *American Journal of Orthopsychiatry, 60,* 585–593.

Doherty, W. J., & Needle, R. H. (1991). Psychological adjustment and substance use among adolescents before and after a parental divorce. *Child Development, 62,* 328–337.

Donnelly, D., & Finkelhor, D. (1993). Who has joint custody? Class differences in the determination of custody arrangements. *Family Relations, 42,* 57–60.

Dougherty, S. A. (1978). Single adoptive mothers and their children. *Social Work, 32,* 311–314.

Douglas, R. N. (1997, April). *Considering the witness in interviews.* Paper presented at the meeting of the Society for Research in Child Development, Washington, DC.

Downey, D. B., & Powell, B. (1993). Do children in single-parent households fare better living with same-sex parents? *Journal of Marriage and the Family, 55,* 55–71.

Drucker, P., Greco-Vigorito, C., Moore-Russell, M., & Avaltroni, J. (1997). *Drawing facilitates recall of traumatic past events in young children of substance abusers.* Paper presented at the meeting of the Society of Research in Child Development, Washington, DC.

Drummond v. Fulton County Department of Family and Children's Services, 563 F. 2d 1200 (1977).

Dubowitz, H., Feigelman, S., & Zuravin, S. (1993). A profile of kinship care. *Child Welfare, 72,* 153–169.

Duncan, G. J., & Hoffman, S. D. (1985). Economic consequences of marital instability. In M. David & T. Smeeding (Eds.), *Horizontal equity, uncertainty and well-being* (pp. 427–469). Chicago: University of Chicago Press.

Eagle, R. S. (1994). The separation experience of children in long-term care. *American Journal of Orthopsychiatry, 64,* 421–434.

Eckenrode, J., Laird, M., & Doris, J. (1993). School performance and disciplinary problems among abused and neglected children. *Developmental Psychology, 29,* 53–63.

Eckenrode, J., Rowe, E., Laird, M., & Brathwaite, J. (1995). Mobility as a mediator of the effects of child maltreatment on academic performance. *Child Development, 66,* 1130–1142.

Eekelaar, J. (1991). *Regulating divorce.* New York: Oxford University Press.

Egeland, B. (1988). Breaking the cycle of abuse: Implications for prediction and intervention. In K. Browne, C. Davies, & P. Stratton (Eds.), *Early prediction and prevention of child abuse.* New York: Wiley.

Egeland, B., Jacobvitz, D., & Sroufe, L. (1988). Breaking the cycle of abuse. *Child Development, 59,* 1080–1088.

Egeland, B., Sroufe, L., & Erikson, M. (1983). Developmental consequence of different patterns of attachment. *Child Abuse and Neglect, 7,* 459–469.

Eisen, M., Goodman, G. S., & Qin, J. (1995). *Eyewitness testimony in victims of child maltreatment: Stress, memory, and suggestibility.* Paper presented at the meeting of the Society for Applied Research on Memory and Cognition, Canada.

Eisen, M., Goodman, G. S., Qin, J. J., & Davis, S. L. (in press). Memory and suggestibility in maltreated children: New research relevant to evaluating allegations of abuse. In S. Lynn & K. McConkey (Eds.), *Truth in memory.* New York: Guilford Press.

Ellement, J. (1997, March 25). SJC finds trial flaws, but rejects Amirault appeals. *The Boston Globe,* pp. A1–A14.

Elliott, B. J., & Richards, M. P. M. (1991). Children and divorce: Educational performance and behavior before and after parental separation. *International Journal of Law and the Family, 5,* 258–276.

Ellis, H. (1995, August). *Emotion and memory: Thought processes and cognitive interference.* Paper presented at the American Psychological Association Convention, New York.

Ellis, J. W. (1990). Plans, protections, and professional intervention: Innovations in divorce custody reform and the role of legal professionals. *University of Michigan Journal of Law Reform, 24,* 65–188.

Emery, R. E. (1982). Interparental conflict and the children of discord and divorce. *Psychological Bulletin, 92,* 310–330.

Emery, R. E. (1988). *Marriage, divorce, and children's adjustment.* Beverly Hills, CA: Sage.

Emery, R. E. (1994). *Renegotiating family relationships: Divorce, child custody, and mediation.* New York: Guilford Press.

Emery, R. E., & Coiro, M. J. (in press). Some costs of coping: Stress and distress among children from divorced families. In D. Cicchetti & S. O. Toth (Eds.), *Rochester Symposium on Developmental Psychopathology: Vol. 8. The effects of trauma on developmental process.* Rochester, NY: University of Rochester Press.

Emery, R. E., Fincham, F. F., & Cummings, M. (1992). Parenting in context: Systemic thinking about parental conflict and its influence on children. *Journal of Consulting and Clinical Psychology, 60,* 909–912.

Emery, R. E., & Forehand, R. (1994). Parental divorce and children's well-being: A focus on resilience. In R. J. Haggerty, L. Sherrod, N. Garmezy, & M. Rutter (Eds.), *Risk and resilience in children* (pp. 64–99). London: Cambridge University Press.

Emery, R. E., Kitzmann, K., & Aaron, J. (1995). *Mothers' aggression before marriage and children's aggression after divorce.* Unpublished paper, University of Virginia.

Emery, R. E., Matthews, S., & Wyer (1991). Child custody mediation and litigation: Further evidence on the differing views of mothers and fathers. *Journal of Consulting and Clinical Psychology, 59,* 410–418.

Emery, R. E., & Rogers, K. C. (1990). The role of behavior therapists in child custody cases. In M. Hersen & R. M. Eisler (Eds.), *Progress in behavior modification* (pp. 60–89). Beverly Hills, CA: Sage.

Emery, R. E., & Wyer, M. M. (1987). Divorce mediation. *American Psychologist, 42,* 472–480.

Erdelyi, M. H. (1985). *Psychoanalysis: Freud's cognitive psychology.* New York: Freeman.

Erdelyi, M. H., & Becker, J. (1974). Hypermnesia for pictures: Incremental memory for pictures but not words in multiple recall trials. *Cognitive Psychology, 6,* 159–171.

Erel, O., & Burman, B. (1995). Interrelatedness of marital relations and parent-child relations: A meta-analytic review. *Psychological Bulletin, 118,* 108–132.

Erickson, M., & Egeland, B. (1996). Child neglect. In J. Breire, L. Berliner, J. Bulkley, C. Jenny, & T. Reid (Eds.), *The APSAC handbook on child maltreatment* (pp. 4–20). Newbury Park, CA: Sage.

Espenshade, T. J. (1979). The economic consequences of divorce. *Journal of Marriage and the Family, 41,* 615–625.

Everson, M. D., & Boat, B. W. (1990). Sexualized doll play among young children: Implications for the use of anatomical dolls in sexual abuse evaluations. *Journal of the American Academy of Child and Adolescent Psychiatry, 29*(5), 736–742.

Everson, M. D., & Boat, B. W. (1994). Putting the anatomical doll controversy in perspective: An examination of the major uses and criticisms of the dolls in child sexual abuse evaluations. *Child Abuse and Neglect, 18,* 113–129.

Everson, M. D., Hunter, W. M., Runyan, D. K., Edelsohn, G. A., & Coulter, M. L. (1989). Maternal support following disclosure of incest. *American Journal of Orthopsychiatry, 59,* 197–207.

Ewing, C. P. (1990). *When children kill.* Lexington, MA: Lexington Books.

Falk, P. J. (1989). Lesbian mothers: Psychosocial assumptions in family law. *American Psychologist, 44,* 941–947.

Faller, K. (1991). Possible explanations for child sexual abuse allegations in divorce. *American Journal of Orthopsychiatry, 61,* 552–557.

Fanshel, D., & Shinn, E. B. (1978). *Children in foster care: A longitudinal investigation.* New York: Columbia University Press.

Farrar, M. J., & Goodman, G. S. (1990). Developmental differences in the relation between episodic and semantic memory: Do they exist?. In R. Fivush & J. Hudson (Eds.), *Knowing and remembering in young children* (pp. 30–64). New York: Cambridge University Press.

Fauber, R., Forehand, R., Thomas, A. M., & Wierson, M. (1990). A mediational model of the impact of marital conflict on adolescent adjustment in intact and divorced families: The role of disruptive parenting. *Child Development, 61,* 1112–1123.

Feigelman, W., & Silverman, A. (1977). Single parent adoptions. *Social Casework, 58,* 418–425.

Feigelman, W., & Silverman, A. (1983). *Chosen children: New patterns of adoptive relationships.* New York: Praeger.

Fergusson, D., Lynskey, J., & Horwood, L. (1995). The adolescent outcomes of adoption: A 16-year longitudinal study. *Journal of Child Psychology and Psychiatry, 36,* 597–615.

Fergusson, D., & Lynskey, M. T. (1997). Physical punishment/maltreatment during childhood and adjustment in young adulthood. *Child Abuse and Neglect, 21,* 617–630.

Ferleger, N., Glenwick, D., Gaines, R. R., & Green, A. H. (1988). Identifying correlates of reabuse in maltreating parents. *Child Abuse and Neglect, 12,* 41–49.

Festinger, T. (1986). *Necessary risk: A study of adoptions and disrupted adoptive placements.* Washington, DC: Child Welfare League of America.

Festinger, T. (1990). Adoption disruption: Rates and correlates. In D. Brodzinsky & M. Schechter (Eds.), *The psychology of adoption.* New York: Oxford University Press.

Fineman, M. (1988). Dominant, discourse, professional language, and legal change in child custody decision making. *Harvard Law Review, 101,* 727–774.

Finkelhor, D. (1979). *Sexually victimized children.* New York: Free Press.

Finkelhor, D. (1984). *Child sexual abuse: New theory and research.* New York: Free Press.

Finkelhor, D., & Browne, A. (1985). The traumatic impact of child sexual abuse: A conceptualization. *American Journal of Orthopsychiatry, 55,* 530–541.

Finkelhor, D., & Dziuba-Leatherman, J. (1994). Children as victims of violence: A national survey. *Pediatrics, 94,* 413–420.

Finkelhor, D., Williams, L. M., & Burns, N. (1988). *Nursery crimes: Sexual abuse in day care.* Newbury Park, CA: Sage.

Fischer, K. W. (1980). A theory of cognitive development: The control and construction of hierarchies of skills. *Psychological Review, 87,* 477–531.

Fisher, C. (1995). American Psychological Association's 1992 ethics code and the validation of sexual abuse in day-care settings. *Psychology, Public Policy, and Law, 1,* 461–478.

Fivush, R. (1993). Developmental perspectives on autobiographical recall. In G. S. Goodman & B. L. Bottoms (Eds.), *Child victims, child witnesses* (pp. 1–24). New York: Guilford Press.

Fivush, R., & Hammond, N. (1989). Time and again: Effects of repetition and retention interval on 2 year olds' event recall. *Journal of Experimental Child Psychology, 47,* 259–273.

Fivush, R., & Schwarzmueller, A. (1995). Say it once again: Effects of repeated questions on children's event recall. *Journal of Traumatic Stress, 8,* 555–580.

Flin, R. (1991). Commentary: A grand memory for forgetting. In J. Doris (Ed.), *The suggestibility of children's recollections* (pp. 21–23). Washington, DC: American Psychological Association.

Flin, R., Boon, J., Knox, A., & Bull, R. (1992). The effects of a five-month delay on children's and adults' eyewitness memory. *British Journal of Psychology, 83,* 323–336.

Flin, R., Stevenson, Y., & Davies, G. M. (1989). Children's knowledge of court proceedings. *British Journal of Psychology, 80,* 285–297.

Folberg, J. (1991). *Joint custody and shared parenting.* New York: Guilford Press.

Foley, M. A., Harris, J. F., & Hermann, S. (1994). Developmental comparisons of the ability to discriminate between memories for symbolic play enactments. *Developmental Psychology, 30,* 206–217.

Forehand, R. (1992). Parental divorce and adolescent maladjustment: Scientific inquiry versus public information. *Behavioral Research and Therapy, 30,* 319–327.

Forehand, R., McCombs, A., Long, N., Brody, G., & Fauber, R. (1988). Early adolescent adjustment to recent parental divorce: The role of interparental conflict and adolescent sex as mediating variables. *Journal of Consulting and Clinical Psychology, 56,* 624–627.

Forehand, R., Thomas, A. M., Wierson, M., Brody, G., & Fauber, R. (1990). Role of maternal functioning and parenting skills in adolescent functioning following parental divorce. *Journal of Abnormal Psychology, 99,* 278–283.

Freed, D. J., & Walker, T. B. (1986). Family law in the fifty states: An overview. *Family Law Quarterly, 19,* 331–411.

Freed, D. J., & Walker, T. B. (1991). Family law in the fifty states: An overview. *Family Law Quarterly, 24,* 309–405.

Freud, S. (1957). Repression. In J. Strachey (Ed.), *The standard edition of the complete works of Sigmund Freud* (Vol. 14, pp. 146–158). London: Hogarth Press. (Original work published 1915)

Freyd, J., & Gleaves, D. (1996). "Remembering" words not presented in lists: Relevance to the current recovered/false memory controversy. *Journal of Experimental Psychology, 22,* 811–813.

Friedrich, W. N. (1988). Behavior problems in sexually abused children: An adaptional perspective. In G. Wyatt & G. J. Powell (Eds.), *Lasting effects of child sexual abuse* (pp. 171–192). Newbury Park, CA: Sage.

Friedrich, W. N. (1990). *Psychotherapy of sexually abused children and their families.* New York: Norton.

Friedrich, W. N. (1993). Sexual victimization and sexual behavior in children: A review of recent literature. *Child Abuse and Neglect, 17,* 59–66.

Friedrich, W. N., Einbender, A., & Luecke, W. (1983). Cognitive and behavioral characteristics of physically abused children. *Journal of Consulting and Clinical Psychology, 51,* 313–314.

Friedrich, W. N., Grambsch, P., Damon, L., Hewitt, S. K., Koverola, C., Lang, R. A., Wolfe, V., & Broughton, D. (1992). Child Sexual Abuse Inventory: Normative and clinical comparisons. *Psychological Assessments, 4,* 303–311.

Furstenberg, F., & Cherlin, A. (1991). *Divided families: What happens to children when parents part?* Cambridge, MA: Harvard University Press.

Furstenberg, F., Morgan, S., & Allison, P. (1987). Paternal participation and children's well-being after marital dissolution. *American Sociological Review, 52,* 695–701.

Gabora, N. J., Spanos, N. P., & Joab, A. (1993). The effects of complainant age and expert psychological testimony in a simulated child sexual abuse trial. *Law and Human Behavior, 17,* 103–119.

Ganaway, G. K. (1989). Historical versus narrative truth: Clarifying the role of exogenous trauma in the etiology of MPD and its variants. *Dissociation: Progress in the Dissociative Disorders, 2,* 205–220.

Garbarino, J. (1982). *Children and families in the social environment.* New York: Aldine.

Garbarino, J., & Gilliam, G. (1980). *Understanding abusive families.* Lexington, MA: Lexington Books.

Garbarino, J., Guttman, E., & Seeley,J. W. (1986). *The psychologically battered child.* San Francisco: Jossey-Bass.

Gardner, R. A. (1987). *The Parental Alienation Syndrome and the differentiation between fabricated and genuine child sex abuse.* Cresskill, NJ: Creative Therapeutics.

Gardner, R. A. (1991). *Sex abuse hysteria: Salem witch trials revisited.* Cresskill, NJ: Creative Therapeutics.

Garmezy, N. (1983). Stressors of childhood. In N. Garmezy & M. Rutter (Eds.), *Stress, coping, and development in children* (pp. 43–84). New York: McGraw-Hill.

Garmezy, N. (1994). Reflections and commentary on risk, resilience, and development. In R. J. Haggerty, L. Sherrod, N. Garmezy, & M. Rutter (Eds.), *Risk and resilience in children* (pp. 1–18). London: Cambridge University Press.

Garrison, E. G. (1991). Children's competence to participate in divorce custody decision making. *Journal of Clinical Child Psychology, 20,* 78–87.

Gaudin, J. (1993). *Child neglect: A guide for intervention.* Washington, DC: Department of Health and Human Services.

Gee, S., & Pipe, M.-E. (1995). Helping children remember: The influence of object cues on children's accounts of a real event. *Developmental Psychology, 31,* 746–758.

Geiselman, R. E., Fisher, R., MacKinnon, D. P., & Holland, H. L. (1985). Eyewitness memory enhancement in the police interview: Cognitive retrieval mnemonics versus hypnosis. *Journal of Applied Psychology, 70,* 401–412.

Geiselman, R. E., Saywitz, K. J., & Bornstein, G. K. (1993). Effects of cognitive questioning techniques on children's recall performance. In G. S. Goodman & B. L. Bottoms (Eds.), *Child victims, child witnesses: Understanding and improving testimony* (pp. 71–93). New York: Guilford Press.

Geiser, R. L. (1973). *The illusion of caring.* Boston: Beacon Press.

Gelles, R., & Straus, M. (1979). Violence in the American family. *Journal of Social Issues, 35,* 15–39.

Gelles, R., & Straus, M. (1987). Is violence toward children increasing? A comparison of 1975 and 1985 national survey rates. *Journal of Interpersonal Violence, 2,* 212–222.

George, C., & Main, M. (1979). Social interactions of young abused children: Approach, avoidance, and aggression. *Child Development, 50,* 306–318.

Giovannoni, J., & Becerra, R. M. (1979). *Defining child abuse.* New York: Free Press.

Glaser, D., & Collins, C. (1989). The response of young, nonsexually abused children to anatomically correct dolls. *Journal of Child Psychology and Psychiatry, 30,* 547–560.

Gleeson, J. P., & Craig, L. C. (1994). Kinship care in child welfare: An analysis of states' policies. *Children and Youth Services Review, 16,* 7–31.

Glueck, S., & Glueck, E. (1968). *Delinquents and nondelinquents in perspective.* Cambridge, MA: Harvard University Press.

Glynn, T. P. (1993). The role of race in adoptions proceedings: A constitutional critique of the Minnesota preference statute. *Minnesota Law Review, 77,* 925–952.

Golan v. Louise Wise Services, 514 N.Y. S. 2d 682 (1987).

Goldberg, D., & Wolkind, S. (1992). Patterns of psychiatric disorder in adopted girls: A research note. *Journal of Child Psychology and Psychiatry, 33,* 935–940.

Golding, J. M., Sanchez, R. P., & Sego, A. S. (1997). The believability of hearsay testimony in a child sexual assault trial. *Law and Human Behavior, 21,* 299–326.

Golding, S. (1991). Specialty guidelines for forensic psychologists. *Law and Human Behavior, 15,* 655–666.

Goldman, J., Graves, L. M., Ward, M., Albanese, I., Sorensen, E., & Chamberlain, C. (1993). Self-report of guardian ad litem: Provision of information to judges in child abuse and neglect cases. *Child Abuse and Neglect, 17,* 227–232.

Goldstein J., Freud, A., & Solnit, A. (1973). *Beyond the best interests of the child.* New York: Free Press.

Golombok, S., Spencer, A., & Rutter, M. (1983). Children in lesbian and single-parent households: Psychosexual and psychiatric appraisal. *Journal of Child Psychology and Psychiatry and Allied Disciplines, 24,* 551–572.

Goodman, G. S. (Ed.). (1984). The child witness. *Journal of Social Issues, 40*(2).

Goodman, G. S. (1990, August). Media effects and children's testimony. In D. Singer (Chair), *The impact of the media on the judicial system.* Invited symposium presented at the meeting of the American Psychological Association, Boston, MA.

Goodman, G. S., & Aman, C. J. (1991). Children's use of anatomically detailed dolls to recount an event. *Child Development, 61,* 1859–1871.

Goodman, G. S., Aman, C. J., & Hirschman, J. (1987). Child sexual and physical abuse: Children's testimony. In S. Ceci, M. Toglia, & D. Ross (Eds.), *Children's eyewitness memory* (pp. 1–23). New York: Springer-Verlag.

Goodman, G. S., Batterman, J., & Kenney, R. (1993). Optimizing children's testimony: Research and social policy issues concerning allegations of child sexual abuse. In D. Cicchetti & S. Toth (Eds.), *Child abuse, child development, and social policy* (pp. 139–166). Norwood, NJ: ABLEX.

Goodman, G. S., Bottoms, B. L., Herscovici, B. B., & Shaver, P. (1989). Determinants of the child victim's perceived credibility. In S. Ceci, D. Ross, & M. Toglia (Eds.), *Perspectives on children's testimony* (pp. 1–22). New York: Springer-Verlag.

Goodman, G. S., Bottoms, B. L., Schwartz-Kenney, B., & Rudy, L. (1991). Children's memory for a stressful event: Improving children's reports. *Journal of Narrative and Life History, 1,* 69–99.

Goodman, G. S., Golding, J., & Haith, M. M. (1984). Jurors' reactions to child witnesses. *Journal of Social Issues, 40*(2), 139–156.

Goodman, G. S., Golding, J., Helgeson, V., Haith, M., & Michelli, J. (1987). When a child takes the stand: Jurors' perceptions of children's eyewitness testimony. *Law and Human Behavior, 11,* 27–40.

Goodman, G. S., Hepps, D., & Reed, R. (1986). The child victim's testimony. In A. Haralambie (Ed.), *New issues for child advocates.* Phoenix: Arizona Council of Attorneys for Children.

Goodman, G. S., Hirschman, J., Hepps, D., & Rudy, L. (1991). Children's memory for stressful events. *Merrill-Palmer Quarterly, 37,* 109–158.

Goodman, G. S., Levine, M., Melton, G. B., & Ogden, D. (1991). Craig vs. Maryland. Amicus brief to the U.S. Supreme Court on behalf of the American Psychological Association. *Law and Human Behavior, 15,* 13–30.

Goodman, G. S., Pyle-Taub, E., Jones, D. P. H., England, P., Port, L., Rudy, L., & Prado, L. (1992). Testifying in criminal court: Emotional effects on child sexual assault victims. *Monographs of the Society for Research in Child Development, 57*(5, Serial No. 229).

Goodman, G. S., Quas, J. A., Batterman-Faunce, J. M., Riddlesberger, M., & Kuhn, J. (1994). Predictors of accurate and inaccurate memories of traumatic events experienced in childhood. *Consciousness and Cognition, 3,* 269–294.

Goodman, G. S., Quas, J. A., Batterman-Faunce, J. M., Riddlesberger, M., & Kuhn, J. (in press). Children's reactions to and memory for a stressful experience: Effects of age, knowledge, anatomical dolls, and parental attachment. *Applied Developmental Science.*

Goodman, G. S., & Reed, R. S. (1986). Age differences in eyewitness testimony. *Law and Human Behavior, 10,* 317–332.

Goodman, G. S., Rudy, L., Bottoms, B., & Aman, C. (1990). Children's concerns and memory: Issues of ecological validity in the study of children's eyewitness testimony. In R. Fivush & J. Hudson (Eds.), *Knowing and remembering in young children* (pp. 249–284). New York: Cambridge University Press.

Goodman, G. S., Rudy, L., Port, L. K., England, P., Bottoms, B. L., & Renouf, A. (1989, August). Do past abuse experiences intrude into children's reports? In G. S. Goodman, (Chair). *Child sexual abuse: Understanding and improving children's testimony.* Paper presented at the meetings of the American Psychological Association, New Orleans, LA.

Goodman, G. S., Sharma, A., Thomas, S., & Considine, M. (1995). Mother knows best: Effects of relationship status and interviewer bias on children's memory. *Journal of Experimental Child Psychology, 60,* 195–228.

Goodman, G. S., Wilson, M. E., Hazan, C., & Reed, R. S. (1989, April). *Children's testimony nearly four years after an event.* Boston, MA: Eastern Psychological Association.

Goodman, J., Silberstein, J., & Mandell W. (1963). Adopted children brought to a child psychiatric clinic. *Archives of General Psychiatry, 9,* 451–456.

Goodman-Delahunty, J. (1997). Forensic psychological expertise in the wake of Daubert. *Law and Human Behavior, 21,* 121–140.

Gordon, B. N., Ornstein, P. A., Nida, R. E., Follmer, A., Crenshaw, M. C., & Albert, G. (1993). Does the use of dolls facilitate children's memory of visits to the doctor? *Applied Cognitive Psychology, 7,* 459–474.

Gottman, J. S. (1990). Children of gay and lesbian parents. In F. Bozett & M. Sussman (Eds.), *Homosexuality and family relations* (pp. 177–196). New York: Harrington Park.

Gray, E. (1993). *Unequal justice.* New York: Free Press.

Graziano, A., & Namaste, K. (1990). Parental use of force in child discipline: A survey of 679 college students. *Journal of Interpersonal Violence, 5,* 449–463.

Green R. (1986). Lesbian mothers and their children: A comparison with solo parent heterosexual mothers and their children. *Archives of Sexual Behavior, 15,* 167–184.

Gregory, I. (1965). Anterospective data following childhood loss of a parent: Delinquency and high school dropout. *Archives of General Psychiatry, 13,* 99–109.

Grisso, T. (1981). *Juveniles' waiver of rights: Legal and psychological competence.* New York: Plenum Press.

Grossberg, M. (1985). *Governing the hearth.* Chapel Hill: University of North Carolina Press.

Grotevant, H. D., McRoy, R. G., Elde, C. L., & Fravel, D. L. (1994). Adoptive family system dynamics: Variations by level of openness in the adoption. *Family Process, 33,* 125–146.

Grow, L. J., & Shapiro, D. (1974). *Black children, White parents: A study of transracial adoption.* New York: Child Welfare League of America.

Groze, V., & Rosenthal, J. (1991). Single parents and their adopted children: A psychosocial analysis. *Families in Society, 9,* 67–77.

Grych, J. H., & Fincham, F. D. (1990). Marital conflict and children's adjustment: A cognitive-contextual framework. *Psychological Bulletin, 108,* 267–290.

Halem, L. C. (1981). *Divorce reform.* New York: Free Press.

Hammond, R., & Fivush, R. (1991). Memories of Mickey Mouse: Young children recount their trip to Disneyworld. *Cognitive Development, 6,* 433–448.

Haney, C. (1980). Psychology and legal change: On the limits of a factual jurisprudence. *Law and Human Behavior, 4,* 147–200.

Haralambie, A. M. (1993). *Handling child custody, abuse and adoption cases.* Colorado Springs, CO: Shepard's/McGraw-Hill.

Haugaard, J. J. (1993). Young children's classification of the corroboration of a false statement as the truth or lie. *Law and Human Behavior, 17,* 645–660.

Haugaard, J. J., & Emery, R. (1989). Methodological issues in child sexual abuse research. *Child Abuse and Neglect, 13,* 89–100.

Haugaard, J. J., & Feerick, M. (1996). The influences of child abuse and family violence on violence in the schools. In A. Hoffman (Ed.), *Schools: Violence and society* (pp. 79–100). Westport, CT: Praeger.

Haugaard, J. J., & Repucci, N. D. (1988). *Child sexual abuse.* San Francisco: Jossey-Bass.

Haugaard, J. J., Repucci, N. D., Laird, J., & Nauful, T. (1991). Children's definitions of the truth and their competency as witnesses in legal proceedings. *Law and Human Behavior, 15,* 253–271.

Healy, J. M., Malley, J. E., & Stewart, A. J. (1990). Children and their fathers after parental separation. *American Journal of Orthopsychiatry, 60,* 531–543.

Hembrooke, H., & Ceci, S. J. (1995). Traumatic memories: Do we need to invoke special mechanisms? *Consciousness and Cognition, 4,* 75–82.

Hendricks, C. L. (1993–1994). The trend toward mandatory mediation in custody and visitation disputes of minor children: An overview. *Journal of Family Law, 32,* 491–510.

Herman, J. L. (1981). *Father-daughter incest.* London: Harvard University Press.

Hernandez, D. J. (1993). *America's children: Resources from family, government, and the economy.* New York: Russell-Sage Foundation.

Herrenkohl, R., & Herrenkohl, E. (1981). Some antecedents and developmental consequences of child maltreatment. *New Directions for Child Development: Developmental Perspectives on Child Maltreatment, 11,* 57–76.

Herzberger, S. D., & Tennen, H. (1986). Coping with abuse: Children's perspectives on their abusive treatment. In R. Ashmore & D. Brodzinsky (Eds.), *Thinking about the family: Views of parents and children* (pp. 277–294). Hillsdale, NJ: Erlbaum.

Herzog, E., & Sudia, C. E. (1973). Children in fatherless families. In B. Caldwell & H. Ricciuti (Eds.), *Review of child development research* (Vol. 3, pp. 141–232). Chicago: University of Chicago Press.

Hetherington, E. M. (1989). Coping with family transitions: Winners, losers, and survivors. *Child Development, 60,* 1–14.

Hetherington, E. M. (1991). Presidential address: Families, lies, and videotapes. *Journal of Research on Adolescence, 1,* 323–348.

Hetherington, E. M. (1993). An overview of the Virginia Longitudinal Study of Divorce and Remarriage with a focus on early adolescence. *Journal of Family Psychology, 7,* 39–56.

Hetherington, E. M., & Clingempeel, W. G. (1992). Coping with marital transitions. *Monographs of the Society for Research in Child Development, 57,* 1–229.

Hetherington, E. M., Cox, M., & Cox, R., (1982). Effects of divorce on parents and children. In M. Lamb (Ed.), *Nontraditional families* (pp. 233–288). Hillsdale, NJ: Erlbaum.

Heuer, F., & Reisberg, D. (1992). Emotion, arousal, and memory for detail. In S. Christianson (Ed.), *The handbook of emotion and memory: Research and theory* (pp. 151–180). Hillsdale, NJ: Erlbaum.

Hill, P. E., & Hill, S. M. (1987). Videotaping children's testimony: An empirical view. *Michigan Law Review, 85,* 809–833.

Hill v. Moorman, 525 So. 2d 681 (1988).

Hoeffer, B. (1981). Children's acquisition of sex-role behavior in lesbian-mother families. *American Journal of Orthopsychiatry, 51,* 536–544.

Hoffman-Plotkin, D., & Twentyman, C. (1984). A multimodal assessment of behavioral and cognitive deficits in abused and neglected preschoolers. *Child Development, 55,* 794–802.

Hollinger, J. H. (Ed.). (1991). *Adoption law and practice.* New York: West.

Holmes, S. J., & Robins, L. (1987). The influence of childhood disciplinary experience on the development of alcoholism and depression. *Journal of Child Psychology and Psychiatry, 28,* 399–415.

Honts, C., Devitt, M., Tye, M., Peters, D., & Vondergeest, L. (1995). *Credibility assessment with children.* Paper presented at the meeting of the Socicty for Research in Child Development, Indianapolis, IN.

Hoopes, J. E., Lauder, E., Lower, K., Andrews, B., Sherman, E., & Hill, J. (1969). *Post-placement functioning of adopted children.* New York: Child Welfare League of America.

Horner, T. M., Guyer, M. J., & Kalter, N. M. (1993). Clinical expertise and the assessment of child sexual abuse. *Journal of the American Academy of Child and Adolescent Psychiatry, 32,* 925–931.

Howe, A., Herzberger, S., & Tennen, H. (1988). The influence of personal history of abuse and gender on clinicians' judgments of child abuse. *Journal of Family Violence, 3,* 105–119.

Howe, M. L., Courage, M. L., & Bryant-Brown, L. (1993). Reinstating preschoolers' memories. *Developmental Psychology, 5,* 854–869.

Howe, M. L., Courage, M. L., & Peterson, C. (1994). How can I remember when "I" wasn't there: Long-term retention of traumatic experiences of the cognitive self. *Consciousness and Cognition, 3,* 327–355.

Howes, C., & Eldridge, R. (1985). Responses of abused, neglected, and non-maltreated children to the behavior of peers. *Journal of Applied Developmental Psychology, 6,* 261–270.

Hudson, J. (1986). Memories are made of this: General event knowledge and development of autobiographical memory. In K. Nelson (Ed), *Event knowledge* (pp. 97–118). Hillsdale, NJ: Erlbaum.

Hudson, J., & Fivush, R. (1987). *As time goes by: Sixth graders remember a kindergarten experience* (Emery Cognition Project Report 13). Atlanta, GA: Emory University.

Huffman, M. L., Crossman, A., & Ceci, S. J. (1996, March). *An investigation of the long-term effects of source misattribution error: "Are false memories permanent?"* Paper presented at the biennial conference of the American Psychology-Law Society, Hilton Head, SC.

Huggins, S. L. (1989). A comparative study of self-esteem of adolescent children of divorced lesbian mothers and divorced heterosexual mothers. In F. Bozett (Ed.), *Homosexuality and the family* (pp. 123–136). New York: Haworth Press.

Hunter, R. S., & Kilstrom, N. (1979). Breaking the cycle of abusive families. *American Journal of Psychiatry, 136,* 1320–1322.

Huston, A. C. (1991). *Children in poverty: Child development and public policy.* New York: Cambridge University Press.

Hyman, I., & Billings, F. (1995). *Individual differences and the creation of false childhood memories.* Unpublished manuscript, Western Washington University, Bellvue.

Hyman, I. E., Husband, T. H., & Billings, F. J. (1995). False memories of childhood experiences. *Applied Cognitive Psychology, 9,* 181–197.

Idaho v. Wright, 110 S. Ct. 3139 (1990).

Iglehart, A. P. (1994). Kinship foster care: Placement, service, and outcome issues. *Children and Youth Services Review, 16,* 107–122.

In re Adoption of B.G.S., 614 A. 2d 1161 (1992).

In re Adoption of Charles B., 552 N.E. 2d 884 (1990).

In re Alison VV., 621 N.Y.S. 2d 739 (1995).

In re Amber B. (1987). 9 Cal.App. 3d 682.

In re Angel Lace M., 516 N.W. 2d 678 (1994).

In re Anonymous, 285 N.Y.S. 827 (1936).

In re Appeal in Pima County Juvenile Action, 876 P. 2d 1121 (1994).

In re Assalone, 512 A. 2d 1383 (1986).

In re Department of Public Welfare, 419 N.E. 2d 285 (1981).

In re Doe, 638 N.E. 2d 181, (1994).

In re Evan, 583 N.Y.S. 2d 997 (1992).

In re Gault, 387 US 1, 87 S Ct. 1428, 18 L. Ed. 2nd 527 (1967).

In re Gomez, 424 S.W. 2d 656 (1967).

In re J.R., 367 A. 2d 1168 (1980).

In re L.B.T., 318 N.W. 2d 200 (1982).

In re Moorehead, 600 N.E. 2d 778 (1991).

In re Raquel Marie X., 559 N.E. 2d 418 (1990).

In re R.M.G., 454 A. 2d 776 (1982).

In re Tammy, 619 N.E. 2d 315 (1993).

Isquith, P. K., Levine, M., & Scheiner, J. (1993). Blaming the child: Attribution of responsibility to victims of child sexual abuse. In G. S. Goodman & B. L. Bottoms (Eds.), *Child victims, child witnesses: Understanding and improving testimony* (pp. 203–228). New York: Guilford Press.

Jampole, L., & Weber, M. K. (1987). An assessment of the behavior of sexually abused and nonabused children with anatomically correct dolls. *Child Abuse and Neglect, 11,* 187–192.

Janet, P. (1925). *Psychological healing* (Vols. 1–2). New York: Macmillan. (Original work published 1919)

Jellinek, M. S., Little, M., Benedict, K., Murphy, J. M., & Pagano, M. (1995). Placement outcomes of 206 severely maltreated children in the Boston juvenile court system: A 7.5-year follow-up study. *Child Abuse and Neglect, 19,* 1051–1064.

Jellinek, M. S., Murphey, J. M., Poitrast, F., Quinn, D., Bishop, S., & Goshko, M. (1992). Serious child mistreatment in Massachusetts: The course of 206 children through the courts. *Child Abuse and Neglect, 16,* 179–186.

Jenkins, J. M., & Smith, M. A. (1990). Factors protecting children living in disharmonious homes. *Journal of the American Academy of Child and Adolescent Psychiatry, 29,* 60–69.

Johnson, J. R., Kline, M., & Tschann, J. M. (1989). Ongoing post-divorce conflict in families contesting custody: Effects on children of joint custody and frequent access. *American Journal of Orthopsychiatry, 59,* 576–592.

Johnson, M., & Foley, M. (1984). Differentiating fact from fantasy. *Journal of Social Issues, 40,* 33–50.

Johnson, M. K., & Raye, C. L. (1981). Reality monitoring. *Psychological Review, 114,* 3–28.

Johnston, J. R., Kline, M., & Tschann, J. M. (1989). Ongoing post-divorce conflict in families contesting custody: Effects on children of joint custody and frequent access. *American Journal of Orthopsychiatry, 59,* 576–592.

Jones, D., & McGraw, E. (1987). Reliable and fictitious accounts of sexual abuse of children. *Journal of Interpersonal Violence, 2,* 27–45.

Kadushin, A. (1980). *Child welfare services.* New York: Macmillan.

Kalichman, S. (1993). *Mandated reporting of suspected child abuse.* Washington, DC: American Psychological Association.

Kassin, S. M., Ellsworth, P. C., & Smith, V. (1989). The "general acceptance" of psychological research on eyewitness testimony: A survey of the experts. *American Psychologist, 44,* 1089–1098.

Katz, S., Schonfeld, D., Carter, A., Leventhal, J. M., & Cicchetti, D. V. (1995). The accuracy of children's reports with anatomically correct dolls. *Developmental and Behavioral Pediatrics, 16,* 71–76.

Kaufman, J., & Zigler, E. (1987). Do abused children become abusive parents? *American Journal of Orthopsychiatry, 57,* 186–192.

Kaye, K. (1990). Acknowledgment or rejection of differences. In D. Brodzinsky & M. Schechter (Eds.), *The psychology of adoption* (pp. 121–143). New York: Oxford University Press.

Keary, K., & Fitzpatrick, C. (1994). Children's disclosure of sexual abuse during formal investigation. *Child Abuse and Neglect, 18,* 543–548.

Keilin, W. G., & Bloom, L. J. (1986). Child custody evaluation practices: A survey of experienced professionals. *Professional Psychology, 17,* 338–348.

Kelly, J. B. (1990). *Mediated and adversarial divorce resolution processes: An analysis of post-divorce outcomes.* (Final report. Available from the author, Northern California Mediation Center, Corte Madera, CA)

Kelly, J. B., Gigy, L., & Hausman, S. (1988). Mediated and adversarial divorce: Initial findings from a longitudinal study. In J. Folberg & A. Milne (Eds.), *Divorce mediation: Theory and practices* (pp. 453–474). New York: Guilford Press.

Kempe, C. H., Silverman, F., Steele, B., Droegemueller, W., & Silver, H. (1962). The battered child syndrome. *Journal of the American Medical Association, 181,* 17–24.

Kempe, R., & Kempe, C. H. (1978). *Child abuse.* Cambridge, MA: Harvard University Press.

Kempton, T., Armistead, L., Wierson, M., & Forehand, R. (1991). Presence of a sibling as a potential buffer following parent divorce: An examination of young adolescents. *Journal of Clinical Child Psychology, 20,* 434–438.

Kendall-Tackett, K. A., Williams, L. M., & Finkelhor, D. (1993). Impact of sexual abuse on children: A review and synthesis of recent empirical studies. *Psychological Bulletin, 113,* 164–180.

Kinard, E. (1980). Emotional development in physically abused children. *American Journal of Orthopsychiatry, 50,* 686–696.

Kinard, E. (1982). Experiencing child abuse: Effects on emotional adjustment. *American Journal of Orthopsychiatry, 52,* 82–91.

King, M. A., & Yuille, J. (1987). Suggestibility and the child witness. In S. J. Ceci, M. P. Toglia, & D. F. Ross (Eds.), *Children's eyewitness memory* (pp. 24–35). New York: Springer-Verlag.

Kingsley v. Kingsley, 623 So. 2d 780 (1993).

Kirk, D. (1988). *Exploring adoptive family life.* Port Angeles, WA: Ben-Simon.

Kirkpatrick, M., Smith, C., & Roy, R. (1981). Lesbian mothers and their children: A comparative survey. *American Journal of Orthopsychiatry, 51,* 201–211.

Kitzmann, K. M., & Emery, R. E. (1994). Child and family coping one year after mediated and litigated child custody disputes. *Journal of Family Psychology, 8,* 150–157.

Kolko, D. (1992). Characteristics of child victims of physical violence. *Journal of Interpersonal Violence, 7,* 244–276.

Kolko, D. (1996). Child physical abuse. In J. Briere, L. Berliner, J. Bulkley, C. Jenny, & T. Reid (Eds.), *The APSAC handbook on child maltreatment* (pp. 21–50). Newbury Park, CA: Sage.

Koocher, G., Goodman, G. S., White, S., Friedrich, W., Sivan, A., & Reynolds, C. (1995). Psychological science and the use of anatomically detailed dolls in child sexual abuse assessments. *Psychological Bulletin, 118,* 199–222.

Korn, K. (1994). The struggle for the child: Preserving the family in adoption disputes between biological parents and third parties. *North Carolina Law Review, 72,* 1279–1331.

Kotsoupoulos, S., Cote, A., Joseph, L., Pentland, N., Stavrakaki, C., Sheahan, P., & Oke, L. (1988). Psychiatric disorders in adopted children: A controlled study. *American Journal of Orthopsychiatry, 58,* 608–612.

Kovera, M. B., & Borgida, E. (1996). The use of expert testimony and other procedural innovations in U.S. child sexual abuse trials. In B. Bottoms & G. Goodman (Eds.), *International perspectives on child abuse and children's testimony* (pp. 201–220). Newbury Park, CA: Sage.

Kramer, L., & Waho, C. A. (1993). Evaluation of a court-mandated prevention program for divorcing parents: The children's first program. *Family Relations, 42,* 179–186.

Kuhns, J. (1994). The sealed adoption records controversy: Breaking down the walls of secrecy. *Golden Gate University Law Review, 24,* 259–297.

Lamb, M. (1993). The investigation of child sexual abuse: An interdisciplinary consensus paper. *Child Abuse and Neglect, 18,* 1021–1028.

Lamb, M., Hershkowitz, I., Sternberg, K. J., Esplin, P. W., Hovav, M., Manor, T., & Yudilevitch, L. (1996). Effects of investigative style on Israeli children's responses. *International Journal of Behavioral Development, 19,* 627–637.

Lambert, L., & Streather, J. (1980). *Children in changing families: A study of adoption and illegitimacy.* London: Macmillan.

Landsman, K. J., & Minow, M. L. (1978). Lawyering for the child: Principles of representation in custody and visitation disputes arising from divorce. *Yale Law Journal, 87,* 1126–1190.

Lanktree, C., Briere, J., & Zaidi, L. (1991). Incidence and impact of sexual abuse in a child outpatient sample: The role of direct inquiry. *Child Abuse and Neglect, 15,* 447–453.

Lawson, L., & Chaffin, M. (1992). False negatives in sexual abuse disclosure interviews. *Journal of Interpersonal Violence, 7,* 532–542.

Lazoritz, S. (1990). What happened to Mary Ellen? *Child Abuse and Neglect, 14,* 143–149.

Leavitt, F. (1997). False attribution of suggestibility to explain recovered memory of childhood sexual abuse following extended amnesia. *Child Abuse and Neglect, 21,* 265–272.

Lehr v. Robertson, 463 U.S. 248 (1983).

Leichtman, M., & Ceci, S. J. (1995). Effects of stereotypes and suggestions on preschoolers' reports. *Developmental Psychology, 31,* 568–578.

Leippe, M. R., Manion, A., & Romanczyk, A. (1993). Discernability or discrimination?: Understanding jurors' reactions to accurate and inaccurate child and adult eyewitnesses. In G. Goodman & B. Bottoms (Eds.), *Child victims, child witnesses* (pp. 169–202). New York: Guilford Press.

Leitenberg, H., Burchard, J. D., Healy, D., & Fuller, E. J. (1981). Nondelinquent children in state custody: Does type of placement matter? *American Journal of Community Psychology, 9,* 347–360.

Lepore, S., & Sesco, B. (1994). Distorting children's reports and interpretations of events through suggestion. *Journal of Applied Psychology, 79,* 108–120.

Levine, M., & Levine, A. (1992). *Helping children.* New York: Oxford University Press.

Levy, H. B., Markovic, J., Kalinowski, M. N., Ahart, S., & Torres, R. (1995). Child sexual abuse interviews: The use of anatomic dolls and the reliability of information. *Journal of Interpersonal Violence, 10,* 334–353.

Lewis, C., Wilkins, R., Baker, L., & Woobey, A. (1995). "Is this man your daddy?" Suggestibility in children's eyewitness identification of a family member. *Child Abuse and Neglect, 19,* 739–744.

Limber, S. P., & Etheredge, S. (1989, August). *Prosecutors' perceptions of sexually abused children as witnesses.* Paper presented at the 97th American Psychological Association Convention, New Orleans, LA.

Lindholm, B. W., & Touliatos, J. (1980). Psychological adjustment of adopted and nonadopted children. *Psychological Reports, 46,* 307–310.

Lindsay, D. S. (1995). *Recovery of childhood memories.* Paper presented at the American Psychological Association Convention, New York.

Lindsay, D. S., Gonzales, V., & Eso, K. (1995). Aware and unaware uses of memories of postevent suggestions. In M. Zaragoza, J. Graham, G. Hall, R. Hirschman, & Y. S. Ben-Porath (Eds.), *Memory and testimony in the child witness* (pp. 86–108). Newbury Park, CA: Sage.

Lindsay, D. S., & Read, J. D. (1994). Psychotherapy and memories of childhood sexual abuse: A cognitive perspective. *Applied Cognitive Psychology, 8,* 281–338.

Lipman, E. L., Offord, D. R., Racine, Y. A., & Boyle, M. H. (1992). Psychiatric disorders in adopted children: A profile from the Ontario Child Health Study. *Canadian Journal of Psychiatry, 37,* 627–633.

Lipovsky, J. A., Tidwell, R., Crisp, J., Kilpatrick, D., Saunders, B., & Dawson, V. I. (1992). Child witnesses in criminal court: Descriptive information from three southern states. *Law and Human Behavior, 16,* 635–650.

Loftus, E. F. (1979). *Eyewitness testimony.* Cambridge, MA: Harvard University Press.

Loftus. E. F. (1993). The reality of repressed memories. *American Psychologist, 48,* 518–537.

Loftus, E. F., Garry, M., & Feldman, J. (1994). Forgetting sexual trauma: What does it mean when 38% forget? *Journal of Consulting and Clinical Psychology, 62,* 1177–1181.

Loftus, E. F., & Pickrell, J. (1995). The formation of false memories. *Psychiatric Annals, 25,* 720–725.

Loftus, E. F., Polonsky, S., & Fullilove, M. T. (1994). Memories of childhood sexual abuse: Remembering and repressing. *Psychology of Women Quarterly, 18,* 67–84.

Long, N., & Forehand, R. (1987). The effects of parental divorce and parental conflict on children: An overview. *Developmental and Behavioral Pediatrics, 8,* 292–296.

Lum, B. W. Y. (1993). Privacy v. secrecy: The open adoption records movement and its impact on Hawaii. *University of Hawaii Law Review, 15,* 483–522.

Lynch, M., & Cicchetti, D. (1991). Patterns of relatedness in maltreated and nonmaltreated children: Connections among multiple representational models. *Development and Psychopathology, 3,* 206–277.

Lyon, T. D. (1995). False allegations and false denials in child sexual abuse. *Psychology, Public Policy, and Law, 1,* 429–437.

Maccoby, E. E., Buchanan, C. M., Mnookin, R. H., & Dornbusch, S. M. (1993). Postdivorce roles of mothers and fathers in the lives of their children. *Journal of Family Psychology, 7,* 24–38.

Maccoby, E. E., & Mnookin, R. H. (1992). *Dividing the child: Social and legal dilemmas of custody.* Cambridge, MA: Harvard University Press.

Main, M., & George, C. (1985). Responses of abused and disadvantaged toddlers to distress in agemates: A study in the day care setting. *Developmental Psychology, 21,* 407–412.

Malinoski, P., Lynn, S. J., Martin, D., Aronoff, A., Neufeld, J., & Gedeon, S. (1995). *Individual differences in early memory reports: An empirical investigation.* Paper presented at the American Psychological Association Convention, New York.

Malinosky-Rummell, R., & Hansen, D. (1993). Long-term consequences of physical abuse. *Psychological Bulletin, 114,* 68–79.

Maluccio, A. N., & Fein, E. (1985). Growing up in foster care. *Children and Youth Services Review, 7,* 123–134.

Martin, H., & Beezley, P. (1977). Behavioral observations of abused children. *Developmental Medicine and Child Neurology, 19,* 373–387.

Maryland v. Craig, 110 S. Ct. 3157; 47 Cr.L. 2258 U.S. Sup. Ct. (1990).

Mason, M. A. (1991). A judicial dilemma: Expert witness testimony in child sexual abuse cases. *Journal of Psychiatry and the Law, 19,* 185–219.

Masson, J. (1984). *The assault on truth.* New York: Farrar, Straus and Giroux.

Maughan, B., & Pickles, A. (1990). Adopted and illegitimate children growing up. In L. Robins & M. Rutter (Eds.), *Straight and devious pathways from childhood to adulthood* (pp. 36–61). Cambridge, England: Cambridge University Press.

Maxfield, M., & Widom, C. (1996). The cycle of violence: Revisited 6 years later. *Archives of Pediatric Adolescent Medicine, 150,* 390–395.

McCord, J., McCord, W., & Thurber, E. (1962). Some effects of paternal absence on male children. *Journal of Abnormal and Social Psychology, 64,* 361–369.

McCurdy, K., & Daro, D. (1994). *Current trends in child abuse reporting and fatalities: The results of the 1993 annual 50 state survey.* Chicago: National Committee to Prevent Child Abuse.

McGee, R. A., & Wolfe, D. (1991). Psychological maltreatment: Toward an operational definition. *Development and Psychopathology, 3,* 3–18.

McGough, L. (1994). *Fragile voices: The child witness in American courts.* New Haven, CT: Yale University Press.

McGue, M., & Lykken, D. T. (1992). Genetic influence on risk of divorce. *Psychological Science, 3,* 368–373.

McIntosh, J. A., & Prinz, R. J. (1993). The incidence of alleged sexual abuse in 603 family court cases. *Law and Human Behavior, 17,* 95–102.

McLanahan, S., & Sandefur, G. (1994). *Growing up with a single parent: What hurts, what helps.* Cambridge, MA: Harvard University Press.

McRoy, R. G., Grotevant, H. D., & White, K. (1988). *Openness in adoption* . New York: Praeger.

McRoy, R. G., Zurcher, L. A., Lauderdale, M. L., & Anderson, R. N. (1982). Self-esteem and racial identity in transracial and inracial adoptees. *Social Work, 27,* 522–526.

Melton, G. B. (1992). Children as legal actors. In D. K. Kagehiro & W. S. Laufer (Eds.), *Handbook of psychology and law* (pp. 273–291). New York: Springer-Verlag.

Melton, G. B. (1994). Expert opinions: Not for cosmic understanding. In B. Sales & G. VanderBos (Eds.), *Psychology in litigation and law* (pp. 55–99). Washington, DC: American Psychological Association.

Melton, G. B., & Berliner, L. (1992, April). *Preparing sexually abused children for testimony: Children's perceptions of the legal process* (Final report). Washington, DC: National Center on Child Abuse and Neglect.

Melton, G. B., & Limber, S. (1989). Psychologists' involvement in cases of child maltreatment. *American Psychologist, 44,* 1225–1233.

Melton, G. B., & Lind, E. A. (1982). Procedural justice in family court: Does the adversary model make sense? *Child and Youth Services, 5,* 63–81.

Melton, G. B., Petrila, J., Poythress, N. G., & Slobogin, C. (1987). *Psychological evaluations for the courts.* New York: Guilford Press.

Memon, A., Cronin, O., Eaves, R., & Bull, R. (1995). An empirical test of the mnemonic components of the Cognitive Interview. In G. Davies, S. Lloyd-Bostock, M. McMurran, & C. Wilson (Eds.), *Psychology, law, and criminal justice: International developments in research and practice* (pp. 135–145). Berlin, Germany: Walter de Gruyter.

Merritt, K. A., Ornstein, P. A., & Spicker, B. (1994). Children's memory for a salient medical procedure: Implications for testimony. *Pediatrics, 94,* 17–23.

Meyer v. Nebraska, 262 U.S. 390 (1923).

Meyer, B. S., & Link M. K. (1990). *Kinship foster care: The doubled edged dilemma.* New York: Task Force on Permanency Planning for Foster Children.

Mikawa, J., & Boston, J. (1968). Psychological characteristics of adopted children. *Psychiatric Quarterly Supplement, 42,* 274–281.

Miller v. Youakim, 440 U.S. 125 (1979).

Mills v. Atlantic City Dept. of Vital Statistics, 372 A. 2d 646 (1977).

Mini, M. M. (1994). Breaking down the barriers to transracial adoption. *Hofstra Law Review, 22,* 897–968.

Mnookin, R. H., (1975). Child-custody adjudication: Judicial functions in the face of indeterminacy. *Law and Contemporary Problems, 39,* 226–292.

Mnookin, R. H. (1978). *Child, family, and state.* Boston: Little, Brown.

Mnookin, R. H. (1985). *In the interest of children: Advocacy law reform and public policy.* New York: Freeman.

Monahan, J. (Ed.). (1980). *Who is the client? The ethics of psychological intervention in the criminal justice system.* Washington: American Psychological Association.

Morgan, M. (1995). *How to interview sexual abuse victims.* Newbury Park, CA: Sage.

Moston, S. (1987). The suggestibility of children in interview studies. *Child Language, 7,* 67–78.

Moston, S., & Engelberg, T. (1992). The effects of social support on children's eyewitness testimony. *Applied Cognitive Psychology, 6,* 61–75.

Murachver, T., Pipe, M.-E., Gordon, R., Owens, J. L., & Fivush, R. (1997). Do, show, and tell: Children's event memories acquired through direct experience, observation, and stories. *Child Development, 67,* 3029–3044.

Murray, K. (1995). *Live television link.* Edinburgh, Scotland: The Scottish Office.

Myers, J. E. B. (1987). *Child witness law and practice.* New York: Wiley.

Myers, J. E. B. (1992). *Legal issues in child abuse and neglect.* Newbury Park, CA: Sage.

Myers, J. E. B. (1993). A call for forensically relevant research. *Child Abuse and Neglect, 17,* 573–579.

Myers, J. E. B. (1994). *The backlash.* Newbury Park, CA: Sage.

Myers, J. E. B. (1995a). Taint hearings for child witnesses?: A step in the wrong direction. *Baylor Law Review, 46,* 873–951.

Myers, J. E. B. (1995b). New era of skepticism regarding children's credibility. The social science amicus brief in State of New Jersey v. Margaret Kelly Michaels. *Psychology, Public Policy, and Law, 1,* 387–398.

Myers, J. E. B. (1996). A decade of international reform to accommodate child witnesses. *Criminal Justice and Behavior, 23,* 402–422.

Myers, J. E. B., Bays, J., Becker, J., Berliner, L., Corwin, D., & Saywitz, K. J. (1989). Expert testimony in child sexual abuse litigation. *Nebraska Law Review, 68,* 1–145.

Myers, J. E. B., Goodman, G. S., Qin, J. J., Quas, J. A., Schuder, M., Rogers, L., & Redlich, A. (1995). *Children's out-of-court statements: Effects of hearsay on jurors' decisions.* Paper presented at the National Institute of Justice Conference, Washington, DC.

Myers, J. E. B., Gordon, S. M., Pizzini, S., Saywitz, K. J., Stewart, D. C., & Walton, T. (1994). *Child victim witness investigative pilot projects.* Sacramento: California Attorney General's Office.

Myers, J. E. B., Saywitz, K., & Goodman, G. S. (1996). Psychological research on children as witnesses: Practical implications for children's interviews and courtroom testimony. *Pacific Law Journal, 28,* 1–91.

National Center on Child Abuse and Neglect. (1978). *Interdisciplinary glossary on child abuse and neglect.* Washington, DC: Department of Health, Education, and Welfare. (OHDS 78-30137)

National Center on Child Abuse and Neglect. (1997). *Child maltreatment 1995: Reports from the states to the National Center on Child Abuse and Neglect.* Washington, DC: Department of Health and Human Services.

National Commission on Child Welfare and Family Preservation. (1990). *A commitment to change: Interim report.* Washington, DC: American Public Welfare Association.

National Commission on Family Foster Care. (1991). *A blueprint for fostering infants, children, and youth in the 1990s.* Washington, DC: Child Welfare League.

National Committee for Adoption. (1989). *Adoption factbook.* Washington, DC: Author.

National Committee to Prevent Child Abuse. (1995). *Current trends in child abuse reporting and fatalities: Results of the 1994 annual 50 state survey.* Chicago: Author.

National Committee to Prevent Child Abuse. (1997). *Current trends in child abuse reporting and fatalities: Results of the 1996 annual 50 state survey.* Chicago: Author.

Nelson, B. J. (1984). *Making an issue of child abuse.* Chicago: University of Chicago Press.

Nelson, K. A. (1985). *On the frontier of adoption: A study of special needs adoptive families.* Washington, DC: Child Welfare League of America.

Nelson, K. A. (1993). Explaining the emergence of autobiographical memory in early childhood. In A. Collins, S. Gathercole, M. Conway, & P. Morris (Eds.), *Theories of memory* (pp. 355–385). Hillsdale, NJ: Erlbaum.

Nemiah, J. C. (1995). Early concepts of trauma, dissociation, and the unconscious: Their history and current implications. In D. Bremner & C. Marmar (Eds.), *Trauma, memory, and dissociation.* Washington, DC: American Psychiatric Press.

New Jersey Division of Youth & Family Services v. A.W., 512 A. 2d 438 (1986).

Ney, P. G. (1988). Transgenerational child abuse. *Child Psychiatry and Human Development, 18,* 151–168.

Nichols-Casebolt, A., (1986). The economic impact of child support reform on the poverty status of custodial and noncustodial families. *Journal of Marriage and the Family, 48,* 875–880.

Nitti, T. A. (1994). Stepping back from the psychological parenting theory: A comment on *In re J.C. Rutgers Law Review, 46,* 1003–1039.

Oates, R. K., & Shrimpton, S. (1991). Children's memories for stressful and non-stressful events. *Medicine, Science, and the Law, 31,* 4–10.

Ofshe, R., & Waters, E. (1994). *Making monsters.* New York: Wiley.

Orcutt, H. (1995). *Detecting deception: Jurors' abilities to assess the truth.* Unpublished dissertation, State University of New York at Buffalo.

Ornstein, P., Baker-Ward, L., Gordon, B., & Merritt, K. (1993). *Children's memory for medical procedures.* Paper presented at the Society for Research in Child Development Convention, New Orleans, LA.

Ornstein, P., Gordon, B., & Larus, D. (1992). Children's memory for a personally experienced event: Implications for testimony. *Applied Cognitive Psychology, 6,* 49–60.

Otto, R., & Melton, G. B. (1990). Trends in legislation and case law on child abuse and neglect. In R. T. Ammerman & M. Hersen (Eds.), *Children at risk: An evaluation of factors contributing to child abuse and neglect* (pp. 55–83). New York: Plenum Press.

Otto, R. K., & Butcher, J. N. (1995). Computer-assisted psychological assessment in child custody evaluations. *Family Law Quarterly, 29,* 79–96.

Palmer, S. E. (1979). Predicting outcome in long-term foster care. *Journal of Social Service Research, 3,* 201–214.

Parke, R. D. (1996). *Fatherhood.* Cambridge, MA: Harvard University Press.

Parker, J., Bahrick, L., Lundy, B., Fivush, R., & Levitt, M. (1995). *Children's memory for a natural disaster: Effects of stress.* Paper presented at the meeting of the Society for Applied Research in Memory and Cognition, Vancouver, Canada.

Parker, J., & Carranza, L. (1989). Eyewitness testimony of children in target-present and target-absent lineups. *Law and Human Behavior, 13,* 133–149.

Parker, J., Haverfield, E., & Baker-Thomas, S. (1986). Eyewitness testimony of children. *Journal of Applied Social Psychology, 16,* 287–302.

Parker, J. F., & Ryan, V. (1993). An attempt to reduce guessing behavior in children's and adults' eyewitness identifications. *Law and Human Behavior, 17,* 11–26.

Partridge, S., Hornby, H., & McDonald, T. (1986). *Legacies of loss—visions of gain.* Portland: University of Southern Maine.

Pasztor, E. M., & Wynne, S. F. (1995). *Foster parent retention and recruitment.* Washington, DC: Child Welfare League of America.

Patterson, C. J. (1992). Children of lesbian and gay parents. *Child Development, 63,* 1025–1042.

Pearson, J., & Thoennes, N. (1984). *Final report of the divorce mediation research project,* (Available from authors, 1720 Emerson St., Denver, CO)

Pearson, J., & Thoennes, N. (1988). Supporting children after divorce: The influence of custody and support levels and payments. *Family Law Quarterly, 22,* 319–339.

Pearson, J., & Thoennes, N. (1989). Divorce mediation: Reflections on a decade of research. In K. Kressel & D. Pruitt (Eds.), *Mediation research* (pp. 9–30). San Francisco: Jossey-Bass.

People ex rel. Sibley v. Sheppard, 445 N.Y. S. 2d 420 (1981).

Peters, D. (1990, March). *Confrontational stress and lying.* Paper presented at the biennial meeting of the American Psychology-Law Society, Williamsburg, VA.

Peters, D. P. (1991). The influence of stress and arousal on the child witness. In J. L. Doris (Ed.), *The suggestibility of children's recollections* (pp. 60–76). Washington DC: American Psychological Association.

Peterson, C., & Seligman, M. E. P. (1983). Causal explanations as a risk factor for depression: Theory and evidence. *Psychological Review, 91,* 347–374.

Peterson, J. L., & Zill, N. (1986). Marital disruption, parent-child relationships, and behavior problems in children. *Journal of Marriage and the Family, 48,* 295–307.

Pezdek, K. (1995, July). *Childhood memories: What types of false memories can be suggestively planted?* Paper presented at the meeting of the Society for Applied Research in Memory and Cognition, Vancouver, Canada.

Pezdek, K., & Banks, W. (1996). *The recovered memory/false memory debate.* New York: Academic Press.

Pezdek, K., & Roe, C. (1994). Memory for childhood events: How suggestible is it? *Consciousness and Cognition, 3,* 374–387.

Pezdek, K., & Roe, C. (1997). The suggestibility of children's memory for being touched: Planting, erasing, and changing memories. *Law and Human Behavior, 21,* 95–106.

Phares, V., & Compass, B. (1993). Where's poppa? The relative lack of attention to the role of fathers in child and adolescent psychopathology. *American Psychologist, 47,* 656–664.

Piaget, J. (1932). *The moral judgment of the child.* New York: Harcourt Brace.

Pianta, R., Egeland, B., & Erickson, M. (1989). The antecedents of maltreatment: Results of the Mother-Child Interaction Research Project. In D. Cicchetti & V. Carlson (Eds.), *Child maltreatment* (pp. 203–253). New York: Cambridge University Press.

Piersma, H. L. (1987). Adopted children and inpatient psychiatric treatment: A retrospective study. *Psychiatric Hospital, 18,* 153–158.

Pillemer, D. B., Picariello, M. L., & Pruett, J. C. (1994). Very long-term memories of a salient preschool event. *Applied Cognitive Psychology, 8,* 95–106.

Pipe, M.-E., Gee, S., & Wilson, C. (1993). Cues, props, and context: Do they facilitate children's reports? In G. S. Goodman & B. L. Bottoms (Eds.), *Child victims, child witnesses* (pp. 25–46). New York: Guilford Press.

Pipe, M.-E., & Goodman, G. S. (1991). Elements of secrecy: Implications for children's testimony. *Behavioral Sciences and the Law, 9,* 33–41.

Pipe, M.-E., Goodman, G. S., Quas, J. A., Bidrose, S., Ablin, D., & Craw, S. (in press). Remembering early experiences during childhood: Are stressful events special? In D. Read & S. Lindsay (Eds.), *Recollections of trauma: Scientific research and clinical practice.* New York: Plenum Press.

Pipe, M.-E., & Wilson, J. C. (1994). Cues and secrets: Influences on children's event reports. *Developmental Psychology, 30,* 515–525.

Plateris, A. (1974). *100 years of marriage and divorce statistics, 1867–1967. Vital and Health Statistics* (Series 21, No. 24. DHEW Pub. No. HRA 74-1902). Washington, DC: U.S. Government Printing Office, Health Resources Administration.

Plomin, R., & DeFries, J. (1985). *Origins of individual differences in infancy.* New York: Academic Press.

Poole, D. A., & Lindsay, D. S. (1995). Interviewing preschoolers: Effects of nonsuggestive techniques, parental coaching, and leading questions on reports of nonexperienced events. *Journal of Experimental Child Psychology, 60,* 129–154.

Poole, D. A., Lindsay, D. S., Memon, A., & Bull, R. (1995). Psychotherapy and the recovery of memories of childhood sexual abuse: U.S. & British practitioners' opinions, practices, and experiences. *Journal of Consulting and Clinical Psychology, 63,* 426–437.

Poole, D. A., & White, L. (1991). Effects of question repetition on the eyewitness testimony of children and adults. *Developmental Psychology, 27,* 975–986.

Popenoe, D. (1993). American family decline, 1960–1990: A review and appraisal. *Journal of Marriage and the Family, 55,* 527–555.

Presser, S. B. (1971). The historical background of the American law of adoption. *Journal of Family Law, 11,* 443–516.

Putnam, F. W. (1985). Dissociation as a response to extreme trauma. In R. P. Kluft (Ed.), *Childhood antecedents of multiple personality disorder* (pp. 65–97). Washington, DC: American Psychiatric Press.

Putnam, F. W. (1991). Dissociative disorders in children and adolescents: A developmental perspective. *Psychiatric Clinics of North America, 14,* 519–531.

Pynoos, R. S., & Eth, S. (1984). The child as witness to homicide. *Journal of Social Issues, 40,* 87–108.

Pynoos, R. S., & Nader, K. (1988). Children who witness the sexual assaults of their mothers. *Journal of the American Academy of Child and Adolescent Psychiatry, 27,* 567–572.

Qin, J., Eisen, M., Goodman, G. S., Davis, S., Hutchins, D., & Tyda, K. (1997, April). *Maltreated children's memory and suggestibility: Individual difference predictors.* Paper presented in J. Quas & G. S. Goodman (Chairs), Individual differences in children's memory and suggestibility, Society for Research in Child Development meetings, Washington, DC.

Quas, J. A., DeCicco, V., Bulkley, J., & Goodman, G. S. (1996). District attorneys' views of child witnesses. *American Psychology and Law Newsletter, 16,* 5–8.

Quas, J. A., Denton, M., Goodman, G. S., & Myers, J. (1996). *Consistency in children's true and false reports.* Paper presented at the meetings of the American Psychology and Law Society, Hilton Head, SC.

Quas, J. A., Goodman, G. S., Bidrose, S., Pipe, M.-E., Craw, S., & Ablin, D. (in press). Emotion and memory: Children's long-term remembering, forgetting, and suggestibility. *Journal of Experimental Child Psychology.*

Quilloin v. Walcott, 434 U.S. 246 (1978).

Quinn, K. M., White, S., & Santilli, G. (1989). Influences of an interviewer's behaviors in child sex abuse investigations. *Bulletin of the American Academy of Psychiatry and Law, 17,* 45–52.

Racusin, R. J., Albertini, R., Wishik, H. R., Schnurr, P., & Mayberry, J. (1989). Factors associated with joint custody awards. *Journal of the American Academy of Child and Adolescent Psychiatry, 28,* 164–170.

Raskin, D., & Esplin, P. (1991). Statement validity assessments: Interview procedures and context analysis of children's statements of sexual abuse. *Behavioural Assessment, 13,* 265–291.

Rawls, J. (in press). How question form and body-parts diagrams can affect the content of young children's disclosures. In D. Read & S. Lindsay (Eds.), *Recollections of trauma: Scientific research and clinical practice.* New York: Plenum Press.

Realmuto, G., & Wescoe, S. (1992). Agreement among professionals about child's sexual abuse status. *Child Abuse and Neglect, 16,* 719–725.

Regents of the University of California v. Bakke, 438 U.S. 265 (1978).

Reid, W. J., Kagan, R. M., Kaminsky, A., & Helmer, K. (1987). Adoptions of older institutionalized youth. *Social Casework, 68,* 140–149.

Renninger, K. A. (1990). Children's play interests, representation, and activity. In R. Fivush & J. Hudson (Eds.), *Knowing and remembering in young children* (pp. 127–165). New York: Cambridge University Press.

Ricci, C., Beal, C., & Dekle, D. (1995). *The effect of parent versus unfamiliar interviewers on young witnesses' memory and identification accuracy.* Unpublished paper.

Roediger, H. L., & McDermott, K. (1995). Creating false memories: Remembering words not presented in lists. *Journal of Experimental Psychology: Learning, Memory, and Cognition, 21,* 803–814.

Rogers, C. M. (1982). Child sexual abuse and the courts: Preliminary findings. *Journal of Social Work and Human Sexuality, 1,* 145–153.

Rohner, R., & Rohner, E. (1990). Antecedents and consequences of parental rejection: A theory of emotional abuse. *Child Abuse and Neglect, 4,* 189–198.

Rosenthal, J. A., Motz, J., Edmonson, D. A., & Groze, V. (1991). A descriptive study of abuse and neglect in out-of-home placement. *Child Abuse and Neglect, 15,* 249–260.

Rosenthal, J. A., Schmidt, D., & Conner, J. (1988). Predictors of special needs adoption disruption: An exploratory study. *Child and Youth Services Review, 10,* 101–107.

Ross, F., Hopkins, S., Hanson, E., Lindsay, R. C. L., Hazen, K., & Eslinger, T. (1994). The impact of protective shields and videotape testimony on conviction rates in a simulated trial of child sexual abuse. *Law and Human Behavior, 18,* 553–566.

Rothman, D. J. (1971). *The discovery of the asylum.* Boston: Little, Brown.

Rudy, L., & Goodman, G. S. (1991). Effects of participation on children's reports: Implications for children's testimony. *Developmental Psychology, 27,* 1–26.

Runyan, D. K., Everson, M. D., Edelsohn, G. A., Hunter, W. M., & Coulter, M. L. (1988). Impact of legal intervention on sexually abused children. *Journal of Pediatrics, 113,* 647–653.

Runyan, D. K., & Gould, C. L. (1985). Foster care for child maltreatment: Impact on delinquent behavior. *Pediatrics, 75,* 562–568.

Rush, F. (1980). *The best kept secret.* New York: McGraw-Hill.

Russ, G. H. (1993). Through the eyes of a child, "Gregory K.": A child's right to be heard. *Family Law Quarterly, 27,* 365–933.

Russell, D. (1983). The incidence and prevalence of intrafamilial and extra familial sexual abuse of female children. *Child Abuse and Neglect, 7,* 133–146.

Rutter, M. (1972). *Maternal deprivation reassessed.* Harmondsworth, England: Penguin.

St. Claire, L., & Osborn, A. F. (1987). The ability and behavior of children who have been "in-care" or separated from their parents. *Early Childhood Development and Care, 28,* 187–353.

Santosky v. Kramer, 455 U.S. 745 (1982).

Santrock, J. W., & Warshak, R. A. (1979). Father custody and social development in boys and girls. *Journal of Social Issues, 35,* 112–135.

Sas, L. D. (1991). *Reducing the system-induced trauma for child sexual abuse victims through court preparation.* Ontario, Canada: London Family Court.

Sas, L. D. (1993). *Three years after the verdict.* Ontario, Canada: London Family Court.

Sas, L. D., & Cunningham, A. H. (1995). *Tipping the balance to tell the secret.* Ontario, Canada: London Family Court.

Sauzier, M. (1989). Disclosure of child sexual abuse: For better or for worse. *Psychiatric Clinics of North America, 12,* 455–469.

Saywitz, K., Jaenicke, C., & Camparo, L. (1990). Children's knowledge of legal terminology. *Law and Human Behavior, 14*(6), 523–535.

Saywitz, K. J., Goodman, G. S., Nicholas, E., & Moan, S. F. (1991). Children's memories of a physical examination involving genital touch: Implications for reports of child sexual abuse. *Journal of Consulting and Clinical Psychology, 59,* 682–691.

Saywitz, K. J., & Lyon, T. D. (1995). *Sensitively assessing young children's testimonial competence.* Interim report to the National Center on Child Abuse and Neglect, Washington, DC.

Saywitz, K. J., & Snyder, L. (1993). Improving children's testimony with preparation. In G. S. Goodman & B. L. Bottoms (Eds.), *Child victims, child witnesses: Understanding and improving testimony* (pp. 117–146). New York: Guilford Press.

Schmitt, B., & Krugman, R. (1992). Abuse and neglect of children: In R. Behrman & R. Kliegman (Eds.), *Nelson textbook of pediatrics* (14th ed., pp. 78–83). Philadelphia: Saunders.

Scott, E. S. (1992). Pluralism, parental preference, and child custody. *California Law Review, 80,* 615–172.

Scott, E. S., & Derdeyn, A. P. (1984). Rethinking joint custody. *Ohio State Law Journal, 45,* 455–474.

Seglow, J., Pringle, M. K., & Wedge, P. (1972). *Growing up adopted.* Windsor, England: National Foundation for Educational Research in England and Wales.

Selman, M. E. (1994). For the sake of the child: Moving toward uniformity in adoption law. *Washington Law Review, 69,* 841–867.

Seltzer, J. A. (1991). Relationships between fathers and children who live apart: The father's role after separation. *Journal of Marriage and the Family, 53,* 79–101.

Seltzer, J. A. (1994a). Consequences of marital dissolution for children. *Annual Review of Sociology, 20,* 235–266.

Seltzer, J. A. (1994b). *Effects of joint legal custody on child support and time with children after divorce.* Paper presented at the annual meeting of the Population Association of America, Miami.

Senior, N., & Himadi, E. (1985). Emotionally disturbed, adopted, inpatient adolescents. *Child Psychiatry and Human Development, 15,* 189–197.

Shanley, M. L. (1995). Unwed fathers' rights, adoption, and sex equality: Gender-neutrality and the perpetuation of patriarchy. *Columbia Law Review, 95,* 60–97.

Shaw, D. S., Emery, R. E., & Tuer, M. (1993). Parental functioning and children's adjustment in families of divorce: A prospective look. *Journal of Abnormal Child Psychology, 29,* 119–134.

Shireman, J. (1988). *Growing up adopted: An examination of some major issues.* Chicago: Chicago Child Care Society.

Shireman, J. (1995). Adoptions by single parents. *Marriage and Family Review, 20,* 367–388.

Shireman, J., & Johnson, P. (1985). Single parent adoptions: A longitudinal study. *Children and Youth Services Review, 7,* 321–334.

Shyamalan, B., Lamb, S., & Sheldrick, R. (1995, August). *The effects of repeated questioning on preschoolers' reports.* Paper presented at the American Psychological Association annual convention, New York.

Simon, R. J., Altstein, H., & Melli, M. S. (1994). *The case for transracial adoption.* Washington, DC: American University Press.

Skinner, L., & Berry, K. (1993). Anatomically detailed dolls and the evaluation of child sexual abuse allegations. *Law and Human Behavior, 17,* 399–422.

Smith, B. E., Goretsky-Elstein, S., Trost, T., & Bulkley, J. (1994). *The prosecution of child sexual and physical abuse cases* (Final report to the National Center on Child Abuse and Neglect). Washington, DC: American Bar Association.

Sommer, C. D. (1994). Empowering children: Granting foster children the right to initiate parental rights termination proceedings. *Cornell Law Review, 79,* 1200–1262.

Soppe, H. (1986). Children's recognition of unfamiliar faces: Development and determinants. *International Journal of Behavioural Development, 9,* 219–233.

Sorenson, E., Goldman, J., Ward, M., Albanese, I., Graves, L., & Chamberlain, C. (1995). Judicial decision making in contested custody cases: The influence of reported child abuse, spouse abuse, and parental substance abuse. *Child Abuse and Neglect, 19,* 251–260.

Sorenson, T., & Snow, B. (1991). How children tell: The process of disclosure in child sexual abuse. *Child Welfare, 70,* 3–15.

Sorosky, A., Baran, A., & Pannor, R. (1978). *The adoption triangle.* Garden City, NY: Anchor Press.

Spanos, N. P. (1994). Multiple identity enactments and multiple personality disorder: A sociocognitive perspective. *Psychological Bulletin, 116,* 143–165.

Spencer, J., & Flin, R. (1993). *The evidence of children: The law and the psychology* (2nd ed.). London: Blackstone.

Stack, C. B. (1984). Cultural perspectives on child welfare. *New York University Review of Law and Social Change, 12,* 539–547.

Stahl, P. M. (1994). *Conducting child custody evaluations.* Newbury Park, CA: Sage.

State of Florida v. Cox, 627 So. 2d 1210 (1993).

State v. Michaels, 136 N.J. 299, 642 A.2d 1372 (N.J., 1994).

State v. Milbradt, 756 P.2d 620 (Or. 1988).

Stein, N., & Boyce, T. (1995, April). *The role of physiological reactivity in attending to, remembering, and responding to an emotional event.* In G. Goodman & L. Baker-Ward (Chairs), Children's memory for emotional and traumatic events. Symposium presented at the Society for Research in Child Development meetings, Indianapolis, IN.

Steverson, J. W. (1994). Stopping fetal abuse with no-pregnancy and drug treatment probation conditions. *Santa Clara Law Review, 34,* 295–372.

Steward, M., & Steward, D. (1989). *The development of a model interview for young child victims of sexual abuse: Comparing the effectiveness of anatomical dolls, drawings, and videographics* (Final Report to the National Center on Child Abuse and Neglect). Washington, DC: American Bar Association.

Steward, M., & Steward, D. (1996). Interviewing young children about body touch and handling. *Monographs of the Society for Research in Child Development, 61*(4/5, Serial No. 248).

Straus, M. A. (1995). *Beating the devil out of children.* New York: Lexington Books.

Straus, M. A., & Gelles, R. J. (1990). *Physical violence in American families.* New Brunswick, NJ: Transaction.

Straus, M., & Kantor, G. K. (1995, November). *Trends in physical abuse by parents from 1975 to 1992: A comparison of three national surveys.* Paper presented at the Amerian Society of Criminology, Boston, MA.

Sugarman, A. (Ed.). (1994). *Victims of abuse.* Madison, CT: International Universities Press.

Summit, R. C. (1983). The child sexual abuse accommodation syndrome. *Child Abuse and Neglect, 7,* 177–193.

Swim, J., Borgida, E., & McCoy, K. (1993). Videotaped versus in-court witness testimony: Does protecting the child witness jeopardize due process? *Journal of Applied Social Psychology, 23,* 603–631.

Taylor-Brown, S. (1991). The impact of AIDS on foster care. *Child Welfare, 70,* 193–209.

Tedesco, J., & Schnell, S. (1987). Children's reactions to sex abuse investigation and litigation. *Child Abuse and Neglect, 11,* 267–272.

Terr, L. (1988). What happens to early memories of trauma? A study of 20 children under age 5 at the time of the documented traumatic events. *Journal of the American Academy of Child and Adolescent Psychiatry, 27,* 96–104.

Terr, L. (1991). Child traumas: An outline and overview. *American Journal of Psychiatry, 148,* 10–20.

Terr, L. (1994). *Unchained memories: True stories of traumatic memories, lost and found.* New York: Basic Books.

Thibaut, J., & Walker, L. (1975). *Procedural justice: A psychological analysis.* Hillsdale, NJ: Erlbaum.

Thornton, J. L. (1991). Permanency planning for children in kinship foster homes. *Child Welfare, 70,* 593–601.

Tidwell, R. P., Lipovsky, J. A., Crisp, J., Plum, H., Kirkpatrick, D., Saunders, B., & Dawson, V. L. (1990). *Child victims and witnesses* (Final report. Grant No. 88-11J-D-064). State Justice Institute, Alexandria, VA.

Tizzard, B. (1991). Intercountry adoption—a review of the evidence. *Journal of Child Psychology and Psychiatry, 32,* 23–43.

Tjaden, P., & Thoennes, N. (1992). Predictors of legal intervention in child maltreatment cases. *Child Abuse and Neglect, 16,* 807–821.

Tobey, A., & Goodman, G. S. (1992). Children's eyewitness memory: Effects of participation and forensic context. *Child Abuse and Neglect, 16,* 779–796.

Tobey, A., Goodman, G. S., Batterman-Faunce, J. M., Orcutt, H., Thomas, S., & Sachsenmaier, T. (1995). Balancing the rights of children and defendants: Effects of closed-circuit television on children's accuracy and jurors' perceptions. In M. Zaragoza, J. Graham, G. Hall, R. Hirschman, & Y. S. Ben-Porath (Eds.), *Memory and testimony in the child witness* (pp. 214–239). Newbury Park, CA: Sage.

Tomaka, J., & Blascovich, J. (1994). Effects of justice beliefs on cognitive appraisal of and subjective, physiological, and behavioral responses to potential stress. *Journal of Personality and Social Psychology, 67,* 732–740.

Trattner, W. I. (1979). *From poor law to welfare state.* New York: Free Press.

Trisiliotis, J. (1973). *In search of origins: Experiences of adopted people.* New York: Routledge & Kegan Paul.

Undeutsch, U. (1982). Statement reality analysis. In A. Trankell (Ed.), *Reconstructing the past.* Stockholm: Norsted.

U.S. Advisory Board on Child Abuse and Neglect. (1995). *A nation's shame: Fatal child abuse and neglect in the United States.* Washington, DC: U.S. Department of Health and Human Services.

Usher, J., & Neisser, U. (1993). Childhood amnesia and the beginnings of memory for four early life events. *Journal of Experimental Psychology: General, 122,* 155–165.

van der Kolk, B. A., & Fisler, R. E. (1995). Dissociation and the fragmentary nature of traumatic memories: Overview and exploratory study. *Journal of Traumatic Stress, 8,* 505–525.

van der Kolk, B. A., & van der Hart, O. (1989). Pierre Janet and the breakdown of adaptation in psychological trauma. *American Journal of Psychiatry, 146,* 1530–1540.

Vandermaas, M. O., Hess, T. M., & Baker-Ward, L. (1992). Does anxiety affect children's reports of memory for a stressful event? *Journal of Applied Psychology, 7,* 109–128.

Vandermis v. Gilbert, 10 Pa. Super. 570 (1899).

Van Dyne v. Vreeland, 12 N. J. Eq. 142 (1857).

Wald, M. S. (1982). State intervention on behalf of endangered children: A proposed legal response. *Child Abuse and Neglect, 6,* 3–45.

Wald, M. S., Carlsmith, J., & Leiderman, P. (1988). *Protecting abused and neglected children.* Stanford, CA: Stanford University Press.

Walker, A. G. (1993). Questioning young children in court: A linguistic case study. *Law and Human Behavior, 17,* 59–81.

Waller, G., & Ruddock, A. (1993). Experiences of disclosure of child sexual abuse and psychopathology. *Child Abuse and Neglect, 2,* 185–195.

Wallerstein, J. S., & Blakeslee, S. (1989). *Second chances: Men, women, and children a decade after divorce.* New York: Ticknor & Fields.

Wallerstein, J. S., & Kelly, J. (1980). *Surviving the breakup: How children actually cope with divorce.* New York: Basic Books.

Warren, A., & Lane. P. (1995). The effects of timing and type of questioning on eyewitness accuracy and suggestibility. In M. Zaragoza, J. Graham, G. Hall, R. Hirschman, & Y. S. Ben-Porath (Eds.), *Memory and testimony in the child witness* (pp. 44–60). Newbury Park, CA: Sage.

Warren, A., Perry, N., Nelson, D., Porter, C., Elliott, K., Komori, L., Hunt, J., Gleason, T., Galas, J., & Kellen, L. (1995). *Interviewing children: Questions of structure and style.* Paper presented at the American Professional Society on the Abuse of Children Conference, Tempe, AZ.

Warren, A., Tulse-Trotter, & Tubbs, E. (1991). Inducing resistance to suggestibility in children. *Child Abuse and Neglect, 15,* 273–286.

Warren, A., Woodall, C., Ross, D., Bhagat, C., Thornberry, I., & Cowger, C. (1997, April). *How accurately do interviewers recall children's statements? The reliability of hearsay testimony.* Paper presented at the meetings of the Society for Research in Child Development, Washington, DC.

Warren-Leubecker, A., & Swartwood, J. (1992). Developmental issues in flashbulb memory research: Children recall the Challenger event. In E. Winograd & U. Neisser (Eds.), *Affect and accuracy in recall* (pp. 95–120). Cambridge, England: Cambridge University Press.

Warren-Leubecker, A., Tate, C. S., Hinton, I. D., & Ozbek, I. N. (1989). What do children know about the legal system and when do they know it? In S. J. Ceci, D. F. Ross, & M. P. Toglia (Eds.), *Perspectives on children's testimony* (pp. 131–157). New York: Springer-Verlag.

Warshak, R. A. (1986). Father-custody and child development: A review and analysis of psychological research. *Behavioral Sciences and the Law, 4,* 2–17.

Waters, E., & Noyes, D. (1984). Psychological parents vs. attachment theory. *New York University Review of Law and Social Change, 12,* 505–515.

Weidell, R. C. (1980). Unsealing sealed birth certificates in Minnesota. *Child Welfare, 59,* 113–119.

Weiss, R. S. (1979). Issues in the adjudication of custody when parents separate. In G. Levinger & O. C. Moles (Eds.), *Divorce and separation* (pp. 324–336). New York: Basic Books.

Weithorn, L. A., & Campbell, S. B. (1982). The competency of children and adolescents to make informed treatment decisions. *Child Development, 53,* 1589–1598.

Weitzman, L. J. (1985). *The divorce revolution.* New York: Free Press.

Weitzman, L. J., & Dixon, R. B. (1979). Child custody awards: Legal standards and empirical patterns for child custody, support, and visitation after divorce. *University of California, Davis Law Review, 12,* 471–521.

Welch-Ross, M., Diecidue, K., & Miller, S. (1997). Children's understanding of conflicting mental representation in relation to suggestibility. *Developmental Psychology, 33,* 43–53.

Wells, G., & Loftus, E. F. (1991). Is this child fabricating? Reactions to a new assessment technique. In J. Doris (Ed.), *The suggestibility of children's recollections* (pp. 168–171). Washington, DC: American Psychological Association.

Wells, G., Turtle, J., & Luus, C. A. E. (1989). The perceived credibility of child eyewitnesses. In S. J. Ceci, M. P. Toglia, & D. F. Ross (Eds.), *Perspectives on children's testimony* (pp. 23–46). New York: Springer-Verlag.

Whitcomb, D., Runyan, D. K., DeVos, E., Hunter, W., Cross, T., Everson, M. D., Peeler, N., Porter, C., Toth, P. A., & Cropper, C. (1991). *Child victims as witnesses: Research and development program* (Final report to the Office of Juvenile Justice and Delinquency Prevention). Washington, DC: American Bar Association.

White, S., Halprin, B. M., Strom, G. A., & Santilli, G. (1988). Behavioral comparisons of young sexually abused, neglected, and non-referred children. *Journal of Clinical Child Psychiatry, 17,* 53–61.

White, S., & Quinn, K. M. (1988). Investigatory independence in child sexual abuse evaluations: Conceptual considerations. *Bulletin of the American Academy of Psychiatry and the Law, 16,* 269–278.

White, S., Strom, G. A., Santilli, G., & Halpin, B. M. (1986). Interviewing young sexual abuse victims with anatomically correct dolls. *Child Abuse and Neglect, 10,* 519–529.

Whitfield, C. L. (1995). The forgotten difference: Ordinary memory versus traumatic memory. *Consciousness and Cognition, 4,* 88–94.

Widom, C. (1989). Does violence beget violence? A critical examination of the literature. *Psychological Bulletin, 106,* 3–28.

Widom, C. (1991). The role of placement experiences in mediating the criminal consequences of early childhood victimization. *American Journal of Orthopsychiatry, 6,* 195–209.

Widom, C., & Morris, S. (1993). *Accuracy of adult memories of earlier childhood sexual victimization: Preliminary findings.* Paper presented at the meeting of the American Society of Criminology, Phoenix, AZ.

Williams, L. M. (1994a). Recall of childhood trauma: A prospective study of women's memories of child sexual abuse. *Journal of Consulting and Clinical Psychology, 62,* 1167–1176.

Williams, L. M. (1994b). What does it mean to forget child sexual abuse?: A reply to Loftus, Garry, and Feldman. *Journal of Consulting and Clinical Psychology, 62,* 1182–1186.

Wolchik, S. A., Braver, S. L., & Sandler, I. N. (1985). Maternal versus joint custody: Children's post-separation experiences and adjustment. *Journal of Clinical Child Psychology, 14,* 118–141.

Wolfe, D. A., & Mosk, M. D. (1983). Behavioral comparisons of children from abusive and distressed families. *Journal of Consulting and Clinical Psychology, 51,* 702–708.

Wolfner, G. D., & Gelles, R. J. (1993). A profile of violence toward children: A national study. *Child Abuse and Neglect, 17,* 197–212.

Wyatt, G. (1985). The sexual abuse of Afro-American and White American women in childhood. *Child Abuse and Neglect, 10,* 231–240.

Youngblade, L. M., & Belsky, J. (1990). Social and emotional consequences of child maltreatment. In R. T. Ammerman & M. Hersen (Eds.), *Children at risk: An evaluation of factors contributing to child abuse and neglect* (pp. 109–149). New York: Plenum Press.

Yuille, J. C., & Cutshall, J. L. (1986). A case study of eyewitness memory of a crime. *Journal of Applied Psychology, 71,* 291–301.

Yuille, J. C., Hunter, R., Joffe, R., & Zaparniuk, J. (1993). Interviewing children in sexual abuse cases. In G. S. Goodman & B. L. Bottoms (Eds.), *Child victims, child witnesses: Understanding and improving children's testimony* (pp. 95–115). New York: Guilford Press.

Zaragoza, M., Graham, J., Hall, G., Hirschman, R., & Ben-Porath, Y. S. (Eds.). (1995). *Memory and testimony in the child witness.* Newbury Park, CA: Sage.

Zaslow, M. J. (1988). Sex differences in children's response to parental divorce: 1. Research methodology and postdivorce family forms. *American Journal of Orthopsychiatry, 58,* 355–378.

Zaslow, M. J. (1989). Sex differences in children's responses to parental divorce: 2. Samples, variables, ages, and sources. *American Journal of Orthopsychiatry, 59,* 118–141.

Zill, N. (1988). Behavior, achievement, and health problems among children in stepfamilies. In E. M. Hetherington & J. D. Arasteh (Eds.), *Impact of divorce, single parenting, and stepparenting on children* (pp. 324–368). Hillsdale, NJ: Erlbaum.

Zill, N., Morrison, D. R., & Coiro, M. J. (1993). Long-term effects of parental divorce on parent-child relationships, adjustment, and achievement in young adulthood. *Journal of Family Psychology, 7,* 91–103.

Zimrin, H. (1986). A profile of survival. *Child Abuse and Neglect, 10,* 339–349.

Zuravin, S. J., Benedict, M., & Somerfield, M. (1993). Child maltreatment in family foster care. *American Journal of Orthopsychiatry, 63,* 589–596.

Zwimpfer, D. M. (1983). Indicators of adoption breakdown. *Social Casework, 64,* 169–177.

Community and Culture

CHAPTER 13

School and Community Competence-Enhancement and Prevention Programs

ROGER P. WEISSBERG and MARK T. GREENBERG

Roger Weissberg acknowledges the NIMH's Prevention Research Branch and Office on AIDS for their support and funding of the University of Illinois at Chicago (UIC) Prevention Research Training Program in Urban Children's Mental Health and AIDS Prevention (1-T32-MH19933), directed by Roger Weissberg. He also appreciates the support of his research by the Irving B. Harris Foundation, the Ounce of Prevention Fund, the Surdna Foundation, the UIC Great Cities Program, and the Office of Educational Research and Improvement of the U.S. Department of Education through a grant to the Mid-Atlantic Laboratory for Student Success at the Temple University Center for Research in Human Development and Education.

The work of Mark Greenberg was supported by NIMH Grant R18 MH50951. The Center for Substance Abuse Prevention has also provided support through a memorandum of agreement with the NIMH.

> First we must seek out the causes of mental illness and mental retardation and eradicate them. Here, more than in any other area, "an ounce of prevention is worth more than a pound of cure." For prevention is far more desirable for all concerned. It is far more economical and it is far more likely to be successful. Prevention will require both selected specific programs directed especially at known causes, and the general strengthening of our fundamental community, social welfare, and educational programs which can do much to eliminate or correct the harsh environmental conditions which are often associated with mental retardation and mental illness. (Kennedy, 1963, p. 127)

In 1963, President Kennedy made "prevention" a national priority. He challenged the nation and scientific community to establish and disseminate effective prevention programs. Several recent reviews have described the progress made during the past 35 years (e.g., Carnegie Council on Adolescent Development, 1995; Consortium on the School-based Promotion of Social Competence, 1994; Dryfoos, 1990; Durlak, 1995; Durlak & Wells, 1997; Institute of Medicine, 1994; Millstein, Petersen, & Nightingale, 1993a; Moore, Sugland, Blumenthal, Glei, & Snyder, 1995; National Commission on Children, 1991; Price, Cowen, Lorion, & Ramos-McKay, 1989; Simeonsson, 1994; Tolan & Guerra, 1994; Trickett, Dahiyal, & Selby, 1994; Weissberg, Gullotta, Hampton, Ryan, & Adams, 1997a, 1997b). This chapter provides our assessment of the theoretical advances and empirical achievements of prevention researchers from the time of President Kennedy's challenge with respect to children and youth. We will describe diverse ways to conceptualize and evaluate school and community interventions, and highlight promising research findings and practices for competence enhancement and prevention.

The chapter will begin with a review of environmental circumstances and behavioral trends that prompt calls for school and community prevention and competence-enhancement programs for young people. Data about divorce, births to unmarried women, children who grow up in single-parent homes, two-career couples, and poverty suggest that too many children are growing up without adequate family support and guidance (Hernandez, 1995; Zill & Nord, 1994). Indicators of children's substance use, high-risk sexual behavior, delinquency, suicide, and school performance indicate that unacceptably large numbers of young people experience problems and engage in multiple high-risk behaviors that may limit their potential to develop into constructive, contributing members of society (Dryfoos, 1990, 1997).

Next, we will describe how developmental theory, with an emphasis on the development-ecological model, supports the promise of family, school, and community interventions both to prevent problem behaviors and to promote social competence (Bronfenbrenner, 1979, 1995; Perry, Kelder, & Komro, 1993). Research during the past 35 years has emphasized the prevention of educational, social, psychological, and physical problems, including school failure, violence, adolescent pregnancy, sexually transmitted diseases, substance abuse, and suicide (Institute of Medicine, 1994; Simeonsson, 1994). But preventing these problems is not an end unto itself. Young people who are not drug abusers, who are not teen parents, who are not in jail, and who are not dropouts may be considered "problem-free." However, they may still lack the skills, attitudes, and knowledge to be good family members, productive workers, and contributing citizens to their community. The commitment to prevention of specific problems must be matched with strong commitment to the promotion of competence in health, social relationships, school, and work (Carnegie Council on Adolescent Development, 1995; Pittman & Cahill, 1992; Weissberg, Caplan, & Harwood, 1991).

Another important research finding regarding adolescent problem behaviors is that they tend to cluster within the same person and to reinforce one another (Dryfoos, 1990; Jessor, Donovan, & Costa, 1991). Although drug abuse, unwanted pregnancy, crime, and school dropout are often considered independently by researchers and practitioners, the reality is that they often occur together. Dryfoos (1990) compellingly argued that the main emphasis of prevention should be in the schools because low achievement is a major risk factor for many problem behaviors. When young people develop low commitment to education, and when parents and teachers have low expectations for a child's performance, trouble often follows. Those who have a history of difficulties in school are more likely to smoke and drink in early adolescence, to initiate sex earlier than their peers, and to engage in antisocial behavior. Therefore, many of the prevention programs we will review involve an emphasis on promoting school success as both a protective factor for diverse problem behaviors as well as an important outcome in itself.

As a final step in clarifying the content and scope of this chapter's literature review, we will also discuss conceptual issues and definitions regarding prevention. Our perspective has been influenced by Cowen (1983), who wrote that primary prevention involves the dual goals of enhancing people's psychological health and reducing the development of psychological problems. Primary prevention programs are mass- or group-oriented, not targeted to individuals. They are directed to essentially well people rather than to those with behavioral problems, although targets may also include those who, by life circumstances or recent experiences, are considered to be epidemiologically at risk for adverse psychological outcomes. Finally, primary prevention programs should be based on theory and knowledge that suggest their operations hold promise for strengthening competence or reducing psychological maladjustment. Our definition of primary prevention encompasses programs that more recently have been labeled universal and selective preventive interventions (Gordon, 1983; Institute of Medicine, 1994), as well as programs to enhance social competence, wellness, health, and positive youth development (Cowen, 1995; Millstein et al., 1993a; Weissberg et al., 1991).

In our literature review, we will discuss primary prevention research involving family, school, and community programs for young people. We will first describe evaluations of programs for infants and young children, with emphases on home-based and center-school-based interventions. We will then describe school, family, and community programs to enhance the academic performance, social competence, and health behaviors of elementary-age children and adolescents. We will contend that multiyear, multicomponent interventions that target multiple outcomes represent a theoretically defensible and realistic approach to address adequately the needs of today's children and families.

Following our literature review, we will discuss issues involved in training the next generation of competence-enhancement and prevention researchers. We will focus on the conceptualization, design, implementation, and institutionalization of preventive interventions and highlight standards for program evaluation. We will also consider two alternative paradigms (i.e., Prevention Science and Collaborative Community Action Research) for approaching these tasks. The Prevention Science (PS) perspective was advanced by the 1994 Institute of Medicine (IOM) Report, which proposed that preventive intervention research involves the following cycle of tasks: (a) identify a problem or disorder, review epidemiological data to determine its extent, and work with communities to assess their level of concern about it; (b) consider relevant basic and applied information from the core behavioral and biological sciences to identify risk and protective factors associated with the onset of the disorder; (c) design and conduct pilot efficacy studies and confirmatory replication trials of preventive intervention programs; (d) design and conduct large-scale effectiveness trials; and (e) facilitate the dissemination, adoption, and ongoing evaluation of programs into community service settings. This framework follows a research, development, and diffusion (RD&D) model of change suggesting that prevention programs be designed largely by "experts" who are familiar with the latest theoretical perspectives, research findings, and intervention practices. The programs are then systematically field-tested and validated before wide-scale dissemination to local settings.

In contrast, the Collaborative Community Action Research (CCAR) model asserts that it is preferable to involve local community members as participants throughout the entire process of establishing an interrelated set of prevention programs (Berman & McLaughlin, 1978; Heller, 1996; Kelly, 1988; Rappaport, Seidman, & Davidson, 1979; Tolan, Keys, Chertok, & Jason, 1990). Assessing community needs, generating problem-resolution strategies, and selecting and shaping ecologically valid innovations that coordinate with ongoing efforts to address perceived problems all represent integral parts of the change process. Involving community members from the outset may foster better understanding of intervention goals, greater commitment to high-quality implementation, and more appropriate adaptation of programs. We will highlight the contributions and limitations of the PS and CCAR models for establishing and evaluating competence-enhancement and prevention programs and suggest ways to combine the best of both approaches to improve future research, theory, and practice.

SOCIAL-ENVIRONMENTAL TRENDS EXPERIENCED BY YOUNG PEOPLE

This section reviews changes in young people's living conditions between the 1960s and the present. We focus on four areas that influence the development and behavior of young people: total population, children living with single parents, labor participation by parents, and poverty. These circumstances support the need to establish effective school and community competence-enhancement and prevention programs.

Total Child Population

There has been considerable fluctuation in the total size of the child population since 1960. As a result of the post–World War II baby boom (1946–1964) and the subsequent "birth dearth" of the 1970s, the total number of young people increased from approximately 64 million in 1960 to almost 70 million in 1970 and back below 64 million in 1980 (Zill & Rogers, 1988). After relative stability during the early 1980s, the numbers again began to rise. As of 1995, there were approximately 69 million young people under the age of 18 living in the United States. That number is projected to increase by the year 2010 to 74 million, the largest absolute size in the nation's history (U.S. Bureau of the Census, 1993). According to Snyder and Sickmund (1995), this population growth alone will lead to increased numbers of children who experience abuse and neglect and engage in problem behavior and crime.

The U.S. population is also becoming more racially and ethnically diverse, due largely to immigration and differential birthrates. In 1980, 74% of young people under 18 were White (and not of Hispanic origin), 15% were Black, 9% were Hispanic, 2% were Asian American, and 1% were from other racial or ethnic groups. By 2010, the proportion of White young people will decline to 58%, whereas there will be a slight increase to 17% for Blacks and larger increases to 18% for Hispanics and 7% for Asian Americans (U.S. Department of Health and Human Services, 1996). Language barriers, poverty, and cultural isolation affect the educational and social needs of minority children, which, unless addressed, will contribute to more youth who engage in problem behaviors (Snyder & Sickmund, 1995). These demographic changes also make it clear that an important developmental task for young people of the twenty-first century will be to learn to respect diversity in our increasingly pluralistic society.

Children Living with Single Parents

Between 1960 and 1979, the annual U.S. divorce rate more than doubled from 9.2 divorces to an all-time high of 22.8 per 1,000 married women (Snyder & Fromboluti, 1993). Since then the rate has declined slightly. Currently, more than 40% of all first marriages end in divorce. Furthermore, the number of children born to unmarried women has also grown tremendously, rising from 21.6 per 1,000 unmarried women to 43.8 between 1960 and 1990 (Snyder & Fromboluti, 1993; Zill & Nord, 1994). Unmarried women gave birth to approximately 1.2 million babies in 1992, that is, 30.1% of all births. Between 1970 and 1991, the percentage of births to unmarried White women rose from 5.7% to 22.6%, and from 37.6% to 68.1% for unmarried Black women (U.S. Department of Health and Human Services, 1996). In addition, the percentage of children under 18 years old living in single-parent families increased from 13% in 1960 to 30% in 1994 (U.S. Department of Health and Human Services, 1996). In 1994, 23% of White children, 36% of Hispanic children, and 64% of Black children lived in single-parent homes. Estimates are that approximately half of all children will spend some time in a single-parent family.

The Myth of the "Ozzie and Harriet Family"

During the 1950s, the *Ozzie and Harriet* television show portrayed the ideal family as one in which the father worked full time, the mother was a full-time homemaker, and children were born after the parents' only marriage (Hernandez, 1995). In 1940, 87% of children under the age of 6 had a nonemployed parent who could provide full-time care; however, by 1989, this percentage decreased to 48% (Hernandez, 1995). This decline is due to the growing prevalence of dual-earner families and single-parent families with an employed head. Between 1940 and 1989, dual-earner, two-parent families increased from 5% to 38% (Hernandez, 1995). Maternal labor force participation rates rose substantially between 1960 and 1991; the percentage of married working mothers with children under 6 increased from 18.6% to 59.9%, and with children between 6 and 17 rose from 39% to 73.6% (Snyder & Fromboluti, 1993). Labor force participation by divorced women was even higher than for married women in 1991; 68.5% of divorced women with children under 6 and 84.6% of women with children between 6 and 17 were employed.

Poverty Rates

In 1960, 26.9% of children younger than 18 lived in poverty. This percentage dropped to 14.1% by 1969, but steadily increased to 22% by 1993. The number of children under 6 living in poverty has reached a record high of 6 million or 26% (Knitzer & Aber, 1995). Poverty can damage children's development in many ways. It can lead to housing problems and homelessness, residence in dangerous and deteriorating neighborhoods, poor nutrition, and can also contribute to parental stress and less effective parenting (Sherman, 1994). Poverty also can reduce children's access to good-quality child care, health care, schools, extracurricular and community activities, and college. In sum, children living in poverty experience double jeopardy: they are more vulnerable to elevated risks of every kind, resulting in the development of more social, behavioral, and physical problems; and there are fewer high-quality resources and supports to help them and their families cope with these problems. The costs of child poverty to the nation are enormous. Sherman (1994) estimated that every year of child poverty at current levels will cost the economy between $36 billion and $177 billion in lower future productivity and employment among those who grow up poor. Furthermore, these costs do not include the additional tens of billions of dollars that will be spent on teenage childbearing, special education, crime, and medical costs that result from child poverty.

Summary Regarding Social-Environmental Trends

The family situations in which children are reared have changed significantly since President Kennedy was our nation's leader in 1960. Divorce is more prevalent. It is more common for unmarried women to bear and rear children. Dual-career couples and employment of mothers outside the home have become the norm. These factors contribute to increased parental absence. The traditional family type with two biological parents, one working in the home and the other working in the formal labor market, now accounts for less than one-third of all U.S. families. Changes in socialization forces that historically have nurtured the development of children—especially in the family—necessitate reconceptualization of school and community program practices to support the family in its mission to raise successful children (Hernandez, 1995).

BEHAVIORAL TRENDS AMONG YOUNG PEOPLE

This section briefly reviews behavioral changes in young people between 1960 and the present, and discusses their implications for competence-enhancement and prevention programs. We describe findings in the areas of substance use, high-risk sexual behavior, delinquency and violence, suicide, and academic performance to provide a broad perspective regarding the overall functioning of young people. These problem areas are the ones most commonly addressed by prevention and competence-enhancement programs.

Tobacco, Alcohol, and Illicit Drugs

In the 1950s, fewer than 5% of young people experimented with an illicit drug before entering the tenth grade; during 1987, more than 30% of young people did so (National Commission on the Role of the School and the Community in Improving Adolescent Health, 1990). Although this increase is dramatic, it is not linear. Examination of changes between the late 1970s and early 1990s indicates considerable fluctuation in substance use. Since 1975, the Monitoring the Future Study has surveyed a nationally representative sample of high school seniors to describe their drug use patterns (Johnston, O'Malley, & Bachman, 1995). In 1993, drug use among high school seniors was lower than when the study began. Drug use increased during the late 1970s and early 1980s and then decreased into the 1990s (Johnston et al., 1995). Although there have been declines since the early 1980s, the percentages of drug and alcohol users remain high in an absolute sense. For example, among the 9th- to 12th-graders who completed the 1993 United States Youth Risk Behavior Survey, 30.5% reported current cigarette use during the past 30 days; 30.0% engaged in episodic heavy drinking (i.e., drank five or more drinks of alcohol on at least one occasion during the past 30 days); 32.8% had smoked marijuana during their lifetime and 17.7% had used marijuana during the past 30 days; and 4.9% admitted having used cocaine (Centers for Disease Control and Prevention, 1995). Furthermore, recent data suggests that drug use among young people is on the rise again and that more children initiate drug use at younger ages. Illustratively, recent data for eighth-graders indicated 30-day prevalence rates rose between 1991 and 1994 from 14.3% to 18.6% for cigarette smoking and from 6.2% to 13.0% for marijuana use (Johnston et al., 1995).

High-Risk Sexual Behavior

In 1993, 53% of U.S. ninth- to twelfth-graders reported ever having had intercourse, ranging from 37.7% of the ninth-graders to 68.3% of the twelfth-graders; in addition, 18.8% of this sample reported having four or more sex partners during their lifetime (Centers for Disease Control and Prevention, 1995). These rates have risen substantially during the past few decades (Alan Guttmacher Institute, 1994). Further, approximately 50% of adolescents did not use contraceptives the first time they had intercourse (Gans, Blyth, Elster, & Gaveras, 1990). In fact, only 52.8% of the sexually active respondents to the 1993 Youth Risk Behavior Survey reported condom use during last sexual intercourse (Centers for Disease Control and Prevention, 1995).

Negative consequences of early unprotected intercourse have also increased over time. The rate of births to unmarried teens tripled between 1960 and 1993 from 15.3 to 45.3 per 1,000 teenage girls (U.S. Department of Health and Human Services, 1996). Unmarried adolescents who have children are less likely to complete high school or fare well in the job market, and their children are more likely to live in poverty. Between 1965 and 1985, the number of U.S. adolescents with gonorrhea and syphilis rose from 4 to 12 reported cases per 1,000. The Centers for Disease Control and Prevention estimate that each year approximately 3 million adolescents contract a sexually transmitted disease (STD). About 25% of sexually active adolescents will become infected with a STD before graduating from high school. The growth of HIV infection and AIDS among adolescents is especially alarming (Centers for Disease Control and Prevention, 1994b).

Delinquent Behavior and Violence

Almost all children act out at one time or another by committing minor acts of vandalism or defying parents or teachers. This may represent normal development, reflecting neither current nor potential delinquency. In contrast, combinations of excessive fighting, stealing, cheating, truancy, or running away reflect more serious conduct problems. The most serious end of this continuum includes robbery, aggravated assault, rape, and murder. Based on self-report surveys, Dryfoos (1990) reported that about 1 in 5 young people commit acts that could result in their arrest. Only a small proportion of those who carry out these behaviors actually become court cases.

National crime rates have leveled off or declined during the past two decades. Following a peak of 41.4 million crime victimizations in 1981, that number declined to approximately 33.6 million by 1992 (U.S. Bureau of Justice Statistics, 1994). In contrast to the overall national trends, rates of juvenile crime have increased dramatically, especially since 1985 (Blumstein, 1995; Snyder & Sickmund, 1995). Bennett (1994) contended that the fastest growing segment of the criminal population is our nation's young people. Juvenile arrest rates for violent crime tripled from 137 to 431 per 100,000 between 1965 and 1990 (Federal Bureau of Investigation, 1994). Between 1982 and 1991, the following arrest rate increases occurred: 93% for murder, 72% for aggravated assault, 24% for forcible rape, and 97% for motor vehicle theft.

Our nation has become increasingly concerned about the large numbers of adolescents who engage in fights and carry weapons. According to 1993 Youth Risk Behavior Survey results, 51.2% of the ninth- to twelfth-grade males and 31.7% of the females reported being in a physical fight (Centers for Disease Control and Prevention, 1995). Approximately 22% of the students had carried some kind of weapon within 30 days of the survey and 7.9% indicated they had carried a gun. The Children's Defense Fund (1995) reported that more than 5,000 young people were killed by firearms in 1992—about 15 children every day. Approximately 63% of these children were victims of gun homicides, 26% used a gun for suicide, and 9% died from gun accidents. Forty percent of students from 10 inner-city high schools indicated that they have a male relative who carries a gun. Between 1985 and 1991, the murder rate for 15- to 19-year-olds increased from 13 to 33 per 100,000. Among Black males in this age group, the rate rose from 46 to 124 homicides.

Emotional Well-Being and Suicide

Zill and Rogers (1988) suggested that American children's emotional well-being has deteriorated during the past three decades. They reported that twice as many young people use mental health services now than in the 1960s and concluded that this increase is due to the facts that more young people need help and that helping services are more accessible and acceptable to children and families. Approximately 15% to 22% of young people in the United States have behavioral and emotional difficulties severe enough to warrant mental health intervention (Costello, 1990; Tuma, 1989). Unfortunately, 70% to 80% of children who need treatment still do not receive appropriate services (U.S. Congress, Office of Technology Assessment, 1986).

Between 1960 and 1990, the rate at which adolescents committed suicide more than tripled from 3.6 to 11.3 per 100,000 15- to 19-year-olds (Bennett, 1994). On the Youth Risk Behavior Survey, 24.1% of high school students indicated that they seriously thought about committing suicide during the past year, 19% made a suicide plan, and 8.6% actually attempted suicide (Centers for Disease Control and Prevention, 1995). These feelings and behaviors are more common among females than males, although males are more successful in actually committing suicide.

Academic Performance

Low achievement and grade retention are important predictors and consequences of adolescent risk behaviors, including substance use, early sexual intercourse, and delinquency (Dryfoos, 1990). Based on performance standards established by the National Educational Goals Panel (1995), only 32% of fourth-, eighth-, and twelfth-graders met reading achievement objectives and about 20% met math achievement standards. Approximately 18% of eighth-graders have already been held back a year. Rumberger (1995) found that students who were retained by eighth grade were 11 times more likely to drop out by tenth grade than those who were not. In spite of low achievement levels, the dropout rate among persons 16 to 24 improved from 17% in 1967 to 12.5% in 1991 (Snyder & Fromboluti, 1993). The dropout rate for Blacks declined rapidly from 28.6% in 1967 to 13.6% in 1991, while Hispanic rates have remained high and stable at 35.3%.

The quality of school climate also affects students' academic performance. Bennett (1994) reported that discipline problems in American schools have worsened. In 1994, 17% of tenth-graders reported that other students interfered with their own learning at least six times per week; 46% of all secondary teachers indicated that student misbehavior interfered with their teaching (National Educational Goals Panel, 1995). Almost one-third of the students had property stolen or damaged at school. Skipping school is a fairly common practice, with 11%, 18%, and 31% of eighth-, tenth-, and twelfth-graders acknowledging that they had done so during the past four weeks (National Educational Goals Panel, 1995).

Summary of Behavioral Trends

Several reports provide compelling evidence that there is an adolescent health crisis (Gans et al., 1990; Haveman & Wolfe, 1994; National Commission on the Role of the School and the Community in Improving Adolescent Health, 1990; Snyder & Sickmund, 1995). In certain domains, today's young people engage in substantially more health-risk behavior than their counterparts from the 1960s. On the other hand, there are areas where adolescent behavior has fluctuated or improved depending upon the years and the groups that are contrasted (Bennett, 1994; Males, 1992; Snyder & Fromboluti, 1993). Unfortunately, an unacceptably high number of children engage in high-risk behavior across several domains. Dryfoos (1990) estimated that 25% of young people are highly vulnerable to suffering the negative consequences of engaging in multiple high-risk behaviors, and that another 25% place themselves at risk by engaging in some problem behaviors. Although the remaining 50% are at low risk for involvement with damaging behaviors, they need strong and consistent support to avoid becoming involved. Based on an updated analysis, Dryfoos (1997) recently estimated that 30% of 14- to 17-year-olds regularly engage in multiple high-risk behaviors and an additional 35% experiment with various high-risk behaviors.

IMPLICATIONS OF SOCIAL-ENVIRONMENTAL AND BEHAVIORAL TRENDS FOR SCHOOL AND COMMUNITY COMPETENCE-ENHANCEMENT AND PREVENTION PROGRAMS

As we approach the 21st century, many young people face greater risks to their health and social development than ever before (Hamburg, 1992; Takanishi, 1993). Damaging adolescent problems such as drug abuse, teenage pregnancy, delinquency, suicide attempts, and school failure are strongly related to lack of parental monitoring, inconsistent discipline, poor communication, and family discord (Dryfoos, 1990). Zill and Nord (1994) pointed out that structural changes in families are not as critical for successful child development as how a family carries out three core responsibilities that society expects from it. First, families are expected to provide for the basic physical needs of young people, including food, clothing, and shelter. Second, families have the primary responsibility to educate children to respect the rights of others, to differentiate right from wrong, and to value other societal institutions. Third, it is important for families to monitor and supervise children's daily activities to protect them from harm and to make sure that they conform to society's rules.

Changes in the U.S. economy have made it increasingly difficult for many parents to provide for the basic needs of their children (Zill & Nord, 1994). It is also difficult for families to combat negative peer influences that may be contrary to the priorities of parents. Such influences are often extended and reinforced by the media. At the same time, adult authority has become weaker and more fragmented in recent years. It is a challenge for parents to maintain control as their children grow older. Parents face the task of helping their children become more independent as they mature, while concurrently monitoring the influences of peers and other forces in their children's lives.

In her assessment regarding the functioning of children and families, Dryfoos (1994) pointed out the following: (a) a significant proportion of children will fail to grow into contributing adults unless there are major changes in the way they are taught and nurtured; (b) although families and schools traditionally carried out the responsibilities for raising and educating children, they require transformation to fulfill these obligations more effectively; and (c) new kinds of community resources and arrangements are needed to support the development of children into responsible, productive, fully contributing members of society.

CONTRIBUTIONS OF DEVELOPMENTAL THEORY

Developmental Considerations

There is a growing emphasis on the integration of developmental theory with models from public health, epidemiology, sociology, and developmental psychopathology in conceptualizing, designing, and implementing preventive interventions (Cicchetti, 1984; Cicchetti & Cohen, 1995; Kellam & Rebok, 1992; Lorion, 1990a, 1990b; Sameroff, 1991; Sroufe & Rutter, 1984). As concepts in development have broadened to include ecological analysis (Belsky, 1993; Bronfenbrenner, 1979, 1995; Garbarino, 1992) and multivariate examination of causation and risk (Institute of Medicine, 1994; Rutter, 1987), developmental theory is more able to provide a powerful framework for organizing and building the field. Although developmental theory is based on the fundamental notion that growth and maturation of the individual is the result of interaction between the genotype and environment, there are a number of *other* fundamental characteristics of a developmental analysis that are central to the conceptualization, design, and evaluation of preventive interventions (Sroufe & Rutter, 1984).

Contextualism

The central notion here is that phenomena (e.g., a child's status) can only be understood within the context in which they exist (Schneirla, 1966). A careful analysis of an event or behavior cannot be conducted independently of the social-ecological-cultural context (Bronfenbrenner, 1979; Lerner, 1994). Thus, the meaning of an altruistic or aggressive act may differ for a toddler versus a teen, or in a rural, nontechnological ecology versus a modern, technological, urban setting.

Direction

Events occur in a purposeful direction across time. Individual differences are present from conception. How experiences affect the individual depends on the current developmental level of the individual at a variety of levels (e.g., neurological, biochemical/hormonal, cognitive, social, experiential). The growing child does not react passively. From the beginning, built-in response biases exist. Across time, children become increasing active shapers of their environment (Bell, 1968; Lerner, 1994). As Sroufe and Rutter (1984) stated, "later experience is not a random influence on individuals because persons selectively perceive, respond to and create experience based on all that has gone before" (p. 20).

Increasing Flexibility of Response

With increasing maturation and experience, the child develops a more varied and flexible repertoire of ways to respond to and cope with both internal and external events. The advent of representational processes (e.g., language and symbolic play) in the preschool years, the beginnings of logic, reason, and problem solving in middle childhood, and the development of hypothetical thought and progressively more complex communication and relational strategies in adolescence allow the developing person to draw on a wider array of approaches to internal challenges, demands of the social environment, and their interaction.

Sensitive Periods and Malleability

Given that many aspects of development are hierarchically organized, it appears that experience may have its greatest impact at earlier stages in development. This is believed to be true because early experiences are more likely to affect biological systems and to alter both the child's cognitions and expectancies as well as those of the caregiving environment. Further, there is a bidirectional relation between neuronal growth and the social environment such that both maturation and experience influence the growing brain;

contextual forces operate even at the cellular level (Cicchetti, 1990). Nevertheless, as neuronal pruning and sculpting occur primarily in infancy and the preschool years, interventions are less likely to impact neurological development after early childhood (Brown, 1994; Courchesne, Chisum, & Townsend, 1994; Greenough, Black, & Wallace, 1987).

This perspective might lead to the mistaken assumption that all interventions are best done at the earlier points in development. However, the dictum that earlier is better may be taken to the extreme and lead to misdirected interventions. Children may have different "sensitive" periods in which they are more responsive to the environment and to particular interventions. For example, educationally based interventions are more likely to benefit preschool children than infants or toddlers. Furthermore, in the domain of substance abuse prevention, interventions affecting normative attitudes about substance use may be more successful in the preadolescent and adolescent phase, whereas social skill interventions that emphasize substance-use refusal may be best taught in childhood.

Continuity and Change

The course of development is considered to be lawful. This implies both that there is a common developmental course experienced by all children and that an individual's course of development is coherent and understandable. This notion of coherence is distinct from stability; coherence means that both intra-individual continuity and discontinuity can be lawfully explained by understanding the person, the environment, and their transactions (Sackett, Sameroff, Cairns, & Suomi, 1981). Individual factors supporting continuity include the child's developing cognitive-affective understandings, sense of identity, and working models of relations (Main, Cassidy, & Kaplan, 1985) and actions (Caspi & Moffitt, 1993; Dodge, 1986). Events may have different effects depending upon the circumstances under which they occur, what precedes and follows them, and the child's developmental ability to appraise the events. A critical role in development is played by these self-regulatory and self-reflective processes (Bandura, 1986). The development of personal standards, one's sense of efficacy, and judgments about the capabilities of both the self and other have major influences on motivations, thoughts, and actions. Further, the human ability for self-directedness in coordination with cognitive-affective schemas provides some control of and influence on one's environment. Yet, prediction from intra-individual factors is modest, and continuities in the social network play a significant role in predicting continuity in behavior.

Developmental-Ecological Models

Given the principle that the developing organism is strongly influenced by context, Bronfenbrenner's (1979, 1995; Bronfenbrenner & Crouter, 1983) model of the nature and levels of context has catalyzed the field. The ecological model posits four levels for classifying context, beginning with those ecologies in which the child directly interacts and proceeding to increasingly distant levels of the social world that affect child development. The first level, the *microsystem,* is composed of those ecologies with which the child directly interacts, such as the family, school, peer group, and neighborhood. Although all of these settings influence development, until recently research with young children primarily involved the study of the child's direct interactions with parents, siblings, and other family members. As alternative care arrangements have become more common, the study of child care and school settings has become important (Minuchin & Shapiro, 1983). Similarly, the study of peer relations has increased (Hartup, 1983). Further, although direct interactions with the neighborhood as a context are limited in infancy, by the preschool years such interactions may begin to directly impact the child (Garbarino, 1992; Richters & Martinez, 1993). In summary, the study of the child's microsystem interactions has broadened gradually from the sole study of parent-child relations to the examination of peer, school/teacher, extended family, and neighborhood interactions.

Another significant contribution of the ecological model lies in the systemic characterization of the reciprocal systems of influence beyond the microsystem itself, and how these levels affect microsystem interactions and the developing child. The *mesosystem* encompasses the relationships among the various microsystems. As the developing child becomes directly involved and influenced by a greater variety of microsystem interactions, the nature and importance of the mesosystem is necessarily altered. Interactions between the parents and school, for example, the family-school connection (Epstein, 1990; Ryan, Adams, Gullotta, Weissberg, & Hampton, 1995; Stevenson & Baker, 1987), or between the parents and the child's peer group and peers' families, for example, parental monitoring (Patterson, Reid, & Dishion, 1992), assume increasing importance as the complexity of the child's network expands. It has been suggested that stronger and more reciprocal links among settings increase the likelihood that the mesosystem will influence a child's development (Garbarino & Abramowitz, 1992). The absence of mesosytem links may also be an important risk factor in development.

Interactions within both the microsystem and mesosystem are often affected by circumstances that do not directly involve the child. Bronfenbrenner (1979) defines the *exosystem* as those situations that indirectly impact the child's development. These situations are wide-ranging and may include both formal and informal social structures that affect microsystem interactions. Informal situations include circumstances such as the quality of the marriage within the nuclear family and the ways this affects parenting (Belsky, 1984); economic or social stresses within the extended family that affect parenting or the child's direct access to extended family members; and social interactions within the school, neighborhood, and parents' worksite that lead to widened or restricted opportunities for the child. Many of these interactions have been studied in the burgeoning literature on the direct and indirect effects of stress and social supports on parenting and parent-child relations (Yoshikawa, 1994). Other exosystem effects arise from more remote and formal aspects of the social and economic structure. For example, children and youth may be significantly affected by changes in the legal system (e.g., changing definitions of neglect or abuse; legal sanctions leading to the collection of child support payments from "deadbeat" parents; regulation of firearms, tobacco, and illegal drugs), the social welfare system (e.g., welfare reforms, boundary changes for categorical services), the mass media (e.g., controls on children's exposure to television violence, the widened horizons via the Internet), and the local school board, community associations, or other social structures that set policies and practices that alter microsystem and mesosystem interactions. Many preventive interventions may thus be viewed as changes at the exosystem level that alter interactions among lower system levels.

The *macrosystem* represents the widest level of systems influence, consisting of the broad ideological and institutional patterns and events that define a culture or subculture. Thus, macrosystem influences include the effects of historical events (e.g., wars, natural disasters), as well as more gradual changes in social structure (e.g., extension in life span, urbanization, development of a global economy) that influence both values and resources and thereby affect many exosystem-level changes. For instance, the decreased value of the U.S. dollar in the global market may lead to reductions in the federal budget that may yield fewer dollars for early childhood education.

Since many ideological assumptions within a culture are "accepted as the way life is," the macrosystem frame provides a sociocultural perspective to identify how values and beliefs alter interactions at other levels of the ecological system. For example, differing assumptions regarding whether there should be universal provision of early child care may lead to vastly different social policies (Cochran, 1993). At a deeper level, fundamental values regarding the role and rights of children or the role of government in regulating aspects of citizen life affect interactions at all levels. For example, differences in regulatory control of firearms in the United States versus Canada results in 4.8 times as many firearms deaths in the United States (Sloan et al., 1988), but entrenched values regarding firearm possession in the United States accounts for much resistance to regulatory change (O'Donnell, 1995).

In synchronicity with Bronfenbrenner's ecological model, Sameroff (1991) proposed the concept of the *environtype,* composed of subsystems that interact with the child as well as with each other. The environtype represents the structure of social organization and is analogous to a genotype. The environment is viewed as operating via cultural and family variables that provide or limit developmental opportunities for growing children. The environtype includes the levels of culture, family, and individual parent, with codes at each level that regulate both cognitive and social development. These codes are determined by such factors as the beliefs and values of families and culture. The cultural code is especially determinative in understanding features that organize child rearing, socialization, and education. Furthermore, important processes by which these codes are enacted include cultural and social controls and social supports. Sameroff speculated that the ineffectiveness of some intervention efforts may result from failures to understand these regulatory systems.

The value of developmental-ecological models is that they both present a framework for discussing different types of processes that affect the developing child, and encourage developmentalists to engage in cross-disciplinary interaction with community psychology, education, public health, public policy, medicine, social welfare, and other related fields. This fosters a broader analysis of how children grow and how they are affected by increasingly distant but nevertheless powerfully influential forces in their lives. Furthermore, they provide a conceptual framework for making explicit the assumptions of prevention theories and interventions and foster the capacity for clearer examination of the ways that natural or planned prevention efforts are intended to have their effects.

Developmental-ecological models can be used both to frame basic research attempts to understand layers of influence on behavior and to identify potential targets and mediators of intervention. It is important for researchers to specify, for example, whether their interventions focus primarily on the microsystem, or a particular portion of it;

multiple microsystems (e.g., interventions for both the home and school); the mesosystem (e.g., the family-school connection); informal networks that in turn affect the microsystem (e.g., the development of extended family or peer support to parents); or on developing new models of service delivery or regulatory reform (e.g., formal services in the exosystem). Further, one might ask if these different levels of intervention emphasize changing the behavior and attitudes of individuals at these levels (i.e., person-centered) or changing the nature of the system's operation itself (i.e., environment-focused; Cowen, 1977; Weissberg et al., 1991).

Contributions from Developmental Psychopathology

> Developmental psychopathology may indeed be the core integrative discipline for the knowledge base for preventive intervention research. (Institute of Medicine, 1994, p. 62)

Developmental psychopathology has been defined as "the study of the origins and course of individual patterns of behavioral maladaptation" (Sroufe & Rutter, 1984, p. 18). Given an adequate theory, prospective longitudinal studies can be powerful tools in identifying factors in young people and their ecology that contribute to the development of competence and various forms of psychopathology. Such research may assist in the identification of risk and protective factors that predict varying rates of maladaptation. However, risk or protective factors are not synonymous with cause; many factors may correlate with negative outcomes but are not causal in their development (Coie et al., 1993). When an intervention alters levels of risk or protection but not outcomes those factors are unlikely to be causal in the process, yet they may be valuable as markers of adaptive development or dysfunction.

Risk Factors and Their Operation

Theory and research support a number of observations about the development of behavioral maladaptation. First, development is complex and it is unlikely that there is a single cause of any disorder. As Rutter (1982) concluded, it is doubtful that most childhood social and behavioral disorders can be eliminated by treating only causes that are purported to reside in the child alone. Furthermore, a basic tenet of developmental psychopathology is the notion of multiple pathways for disorders. That is, different combinations of risk factors may lead to the same disorder, and no single cause may be sufficient to produce a specific negative outcome (Greenberg, Speltz, & DeKlyen, 1993). In addition, risk factors occur not only at individual or family levels, but at all levels within the ecological model (Kellam, 1990).

There appears to be a nonlinear relationship between risk factors and outcomes. Although one or two risk factors may show little prediction to poor outcomes, there are rapidly increasing rates of disorders with additional risk factors (Rutter 1979; Sameroff, Seifer, Barocas, Zax, & Greenspan, 1987). However, not all children who experience such contexts develop adjustment problems (e.g., Cowen et al., 1992), and no one factor alone accounts for children's adjustment problems (e.g., Sameroff & Seifer, 1990). Although research indicates that an increase in the number of risk factors experienced by a child results in a greater likelihood of developing adjustment problems, it remains unclear whether certain risk factors or combinations of risk factors matter more than others. In the domain of juvenile delinquency, Loeber and Dishion (1983) have demonstrated how the use of odds-ratios for different risk factors may assist in making these determinations.

Given the above findings, it is apparent that many developmental risk factors are not disorder-specific, but may relate instead to a variety of maladaptive outcomes. The notion of generic and interrelated risk factors has led to a strategy of targeting multiple factors simultaneously with the hope that the potential payoff will be greater than a focused attack on controlling a single risk factor. Coie et al. (1993, p. 1022) grouped empirically derived, generic risk factors into the following seven individual and environmental domains:

1. *Constitutional handicaps:* perinatal complications, neurochemical imbalance, organic handicaps, and sensory disabilities
2. *Skill development delays:* low intelligence, social incompetence, attentional deficits, reading disabilities, and poor work skills and habits
3. *Emotional difficulties:* apathy or emotional blunting, emotional immaturity, low self-esteem, and emotional disregulation
4. *Family circumstances:* low social class, mental illness in the family, large family size, child abuse, stressful life events, family disorganization, communication deviance, family conflict, and poor bonding to parents
5. *Interpersonal problems:* peer rejection, alienation, and isolation
6. *School problems:* scholastic demoralization and school failure
7. *Ecological context:* neighborhood disorganization, extreme poverty, racial injustice, and unemployment

Recent findings in behavioral epidemiology indicate that mental health problems, social problems, and health-risk behaviors often co-occur as an organized pattern of adolescent risk behaviors (Donovan, Jessor, & Costa, 1988; Dryfoos, 1990; Elliott, Huizinga, & Menard, 1989; Jessor et al., 1991; Jessor & Jessor, 1977). Thus, because risk factors may predict multiple outcomes and there is great overlap among problem behaviors, prevention efforts that focus on risk reduction of interacting risk factors may have direct effects on diverse outcomes (Coie et al., 1993; Dryfoos, 1990).

Certain risk factors may have differential action or influence at different ages. For example, parental education may be more important in children's early development, whereas cognitive ability and motivation may be more important in middle childhood, and parental norms regarding behavior may be more critical during adolescence. There is a need for basic research to elucidate the differential timing of risk factors. Risk factors may vary in influence with host factors such as gender and ethnicity, and with environmental factors such as population density and neighborhood organization.

Public health models have long based their interventions on reducing the risk factors for disease or disorder as well as promoting processes that buffer or protect against risk. Communitywide programs have focused on reducing environmental and individual behavioral risks for both heart and lung disease and have demonstrated positive effects on health behaviors as well as reductions in smoking (Farquhar et al., 1990; Jacobs et al., 1986; Pushka, Tuomilehto, Nissinen, & Korhonen, 1989). Similarly, substance abuse and delinquency are predicted by risk factors in the environment and within the individual (Hawkins, Catalano, & Miller, 1992; Newcomb, Maddahian, & Bentler, 1986; Yoshikawa, 1994). Risk factors for teenage substance use and delinquency include family history of psychopathology and criminality, high levels of family conflict and low levels of social support, family management problems, parental drug use and favorable attitudes toward use, early conduct problems, academic failure, little commitment to school, alienation or rebelliousness, antisocial behavior in childhood and early adolescence, peer influence to use drugs, community disorganization, economic deprivation, transitions and mobility, community laws and norms favorable to drug use, and easy availability of alcohol and other drugs (Hawkins, Catalano, & Miller, 1992). Although causal status is not conclusively established, these factors are consistent predictors. Thus, to the extent that they are malleable and can be changed, they serve as promising intervention targets (Catalano, Haggerty, Gainey, Hoppe, & Brewer, in press).

In addition, interactions among risk factors have been demonstrated and have implications for intervention. For example, difficult infant temperament, under conditions of poor social support for mothers, leads to insecure attachments (Crockenberg, 1981). Likewise, the relation between prematurity and poor educational and behavioral outcomes is affected by family adversity and parental social class (Werner & Smith, 1992). However, a factor that presumably confers risk may not do so in certain settings; in fact it may even be advantageous. For instance, Maziade and colleagues (Maziade, Cote, Bernier, Boutin, & Thivierge, 1989) found that difficult temperament in preschoolers in families with high adversity raised the risk of behavior problems. However, a further set of analyses on the same sample revealed that difficult infant temperament, combined with high family SES and good family communication, was associated with higher IQ (Maziade, Caron, Cote, Boutin, & Thivierge, 1990). Thus, since high IQ is a potential protective factor for conduct disorder (Schonfeld, Shaffer, O'Connor, & Portnoy, 1988; White, Moffitt, & Silva, 1989), difficult temperament may lead to widely divergent outcomes depending upon familial and neighborhood circumstances.

Protective Factors and Their Operation. Protective factors are variables that reduce the likelihood of maladaptive outcomes under conditions of risk. Although less is known about protective factors and their operation (Kazdin, 1991a; Luthar, 1993; Rutter, 1985), at least three broad domains of protective factors have been identified. The first domain includes characteristics of the individual such as cognitive skills, social-cognitive skills, temperamental characteristics, and social skills (Luthar & Zigler, 1992). The quality of the child's interactions with the environment comprise the second domain. These interactions include secure attachments to parents (Morisset, Barnard, Greenberg, Booth, & Spieker, 1990) and attachments to peers or other adults who engage in positive health behaviors and have prosocial values. A third protective domain involves aspects of the mesosystem and exosystem, such as school-home relations, quality of schools, and regulatory activities. Similar to risk factors, some protective factors may be more malleable and thus more effective targets for prevention.

There is considerable controversy regarding the designation of variables as risk versus protective factors (Luthar, 1993; Seifer, Sameroff, Baldwin, & Baldwin, 1993; Stouthamer-Loeber et al., 1993; Zimmerman & Arunkumar, 1994). In some studies, a factor (e.g., social class, attachment security, peer group) is conceptualized as a risk factor and in others as a protective factor, depending on which end of the spectrum is being studied, the nature of the sample population, and the theoretical bent of the investigator. Further, some factors that appear protective for one set of positive outcomes (e.g., academic or behavioral competence) may also relate to dysfunctional outcomes (e.g., depressive symptoms; Luthar, 1991).

Prospective longitudinal designs are critical to understanding how protective factors operate and how they interact with risk. Well-planned basic studies and clinical trials can identify which risk factors are predictive of different developmental stages of problems, the dynamic relationship between risk and protective factors at different developmental stages, and what factors are most likely to "protect" or buffer persons with multiple risk factors from negative outcomes. Coie et al. (1993) suggested that protective factors may work in one or more of the following four ways: (a) directly decrease dysfunction; (b) interact with risk factors to buffer their effects; (c) disrupt the mediational chain by which risk leads to disorder; or (d) prevent the initial occurrence of risk factors. By specifying links among protective factors, positive outcomes, and reduced problem behaviors, prevention researchers may more successfully identify relevant targets for intervention (Coie et al., 1993; Dryfoos, 1990).

Finally, just as problem behaviors co-occur, research indicates that health-enhancing behaviors also tend to cluster in young people (Elliott, 1993). Families, schools, and communities may promote healthy lifestyles and address common roots of both negative and positive behavioral clusters. The Carnegie Council on Adolescent Development (1995) labeled this a *generic* approach as opposed to a *categorical* or *targeted* approach that focuses on a single problem. Generic approaches provide education and opportunities to foster healthy lifestyles and responsible decision making regarding constructive alternatives to high-risk behaviors (Hamburg, 1990; Millstein et al., 1993a).

Keeping Our Eyes on the Prize: Competence as a Developmental Outcome

The specification of intervention goals is an important component of preventive-intervention research and practice. This requires both an understanding of risk and protective factors that contribute to outcomes and the identification of competencies that are presumed mediators or goals of the intervention. Although these goals may include the prevention of difficulties (e.g., absence of arrests, abstention from substance use, avoiding pregnancy), they also involve the promotion of healthy developmental outcomes (Pittman & Cahill, 1992). Further, the prevention of deleterious outcomes involves the enhancement of competency mediators (e.g., effective social problem solving as a mediator of reductions in delinquency).

There have been many conceptualizations of competence in childhood. Although some primarily enumerate skills (Anderson & Messick, 1974), there is considerable agreement that competence has broad features that cross developmental stages as well as competencies that arise or recede in importance during different developmental periods. For example, maintaining trusting relations is critical across developmental periods, although managing impulses is not a particularly salient construct during infancy. Within developmental models of competence, some focus primarily on resolving relevant developmental issues or challenges (Erikson, 1950; Loevinger, 1976; Sroufe, 1979; Waters & Sroufe, 1983), and others specify domains of competence that cross developmental periods but that are manifested differently at each stage, for example "to love and to work" (Kegan, 1982). Some themes will cross development, and others will ascend or attenuate, given the biological-cognitive-social growth of the child as well as the social demands during different developmental periods. From an Eriksonian perspective, researchers can posit certain competencies for children and also identify the different adults or groups within the mesosystem and exosystem structures who are most important in supporting their development. As most developmentalists have not considered these large systemic support issues, they are rarely considered in existing models.

Cowen (1994, 1995) called for a greater emphasis in prevention research on strategies that promote wellness. According to Cowen, these strategies should be communitywide, proactive, multidimensional, and ongoing. Specifying different emphases for different groups, circumstances, and ages, Cowen articulated general competencies and pathways of childhood, including wholesome early attachments; acquiring age-appropriate cognitive-behavioral skills; exposure to environments and settings that facilitate adaptation, autonomy, support, and empowerment; and effectively coping with stress. Further, the optimal development of wellness pathways requires integrated operations involving individuals, families, settings, community contexts, and macro-level social structures and policies.

Following Waters and Sroufe (1983), we define competence as "an integrative concept that refers to the ability to generate and coordinate flexible, adaptive responses to demands and to generate and capitalize on opportunities in the environment" (p. 80). This definition emphasizes (a) the individual's ability to coordinate affect, cognition, communication, and behavior (Greenberg, Kusche, & Speltz, 1991; Waters & Sroufe, 1983), and (b) the importance of environmental factors that nurture adaptive developmental outcomes (Weissberg, Caplan, & Sivo, 1989). Below, we present exemplars of competency models for each developmental period. These are illustrative rather than comprehensive and prescriptive.

The Early Years. Waters and Sroufe (1983) provided a rich, detailed model of developing competencies in the first five years and the role of the caregiver in supporting their emergence. However, they did not consider which factors outside the parent-child microsystem affect these developing attributes. In contrast, recent policy reports have provided new integrations that synthesize developmental and ecological theories and lead to clear recommendations regarding policy and practice concerns. For example, the Carnegie Task Force on Meeting the Needs of Young Children (1994) provided a model of developmental competence outcomes for 3-year-olds and also specified exosystem provisions necessary to foster them. The competence goals for 3-year-olds include being self-confident and trusting, intellectually inquisitive, able to use language to communicate, physically and mentally healthy, able to relate well to others, and empathic toward others. These competencies result from loving, caring parent-child interactions that lead to healthy attachments, as well as early experiences with adult caregivers that provide the building blocks for intellectual and communicative competence.

As parents model healthy ways to relate to children and others, teach acceptable behavior, guide healthy habits and routines, and help children to manage impulses, age-appropriate developmental competencies will unfold. For many parents to provide this rich milieu for healthy outcomes, the Carnegie Task Force (1994) recommended the following exosystem supports.

1. *Promote responsible parenthood* through encouraging planned child rearing and pre-conception care; ensuring comprehensive prenatal care and support; and providing parent education and support.
2. *Guarantee quality child care choices* through improving parental leave benefits; ensuring quality child care; providing parents with affordable child care options; and developing family-centered child care programs.
3. *Ensure good health and protection* through the provision of health care services for all infants and toddlers; protecting young children from injury and promoting their health; and creating safe environments for young children.
4. *Mobilize communities to support young children and families* through strengthening community networks; promoting a culture of responsibility; moving toward family-centered communities; and establishing governmental structures that serve children and families more effectively.

Elementary School Years. During the elementary school years, there are vast changes in children's cognitive and social-cognitive growth as well as in the powerful microsystem influences of the peer group and the school. A major goal of competence-enhancement programs during this period is to teach children to make use of personal and environmental resources to achieve prosocial goals (Waters & Sroufe, 1983). Modifiable personal resources, often targeted in prevention programs, include cognitive, affective, and behavioral skills; personal beliefs and social attitudes; tacit knowledge and acquired knowledge about developmentally and culturally relevant social issues and situations; self-perceptions of performance efficacy in specific social domains; and the ability to elicit the support of parents, teachers, and peers when needed. To enhance children's personal resources for coping adaptively with developmental challenges, social interactions, and life stresses, some programs emphasize the enhancement of social-information processing skills (e.g., Dodge, Pettit, McClaskey, & Brown, 1986; Weissberg et al., 1989), such as the capacities to control impulses and manage affect to engage in responsible problem solving; perceive the nature of social tasks and the feelings and perspectives of the people involved; be motivated to establish adaptive goals to resolve situations; feel confident in the ability to achieve a goal successfully; access or generate goal-directed alternatives and link them with realistic consequences; decide on an optimal strategy and, when necessary, develop elaborated implementation plans that anticipate potential obstacles; carry out solutions with behavioral skill; self-monitor behavioral performance and, when needed, abandon ineffective strategies, try alternative plans, or reformulate goals; and provide self-reinforcement for successful goal attainment or engage in emotion-focused coping when a desired goal cannot be reached.

The William T. Grant Consortium on the School-Based Promotion of Social Competence (1992) offered a developmental framework for social competencies during the middle childhood years. It proposed that programs educate students to coordinate emotions, cognitions, and behaviors to address developmental tasks in the following six domains of functioning.

1. *Personal development* emphasizes issues such as learning about self-management, social norms about appearance, healthy behaviors; recognizing and accepting early pubertal changes; understanding safety for latchkey children; and managing time effectively to balance study and play time.
2. *Family life* focuses on understanding roles of family members; making contributions at home through chores; relating with siblings; recognizing different family structures; and developing appropriate intimacy and boundaries with family members.
3. *Peer relations* involve making friends; sharing; taking turns; learning to cope with peer pressure; assertiveness; and handling teasing and aggression.
4. *School-related skills* include following school rules; accepting responsibility in the classroom; respecting authority; setting academic goals and responsibly completing them; working in teams; and accepting similarity and differences in ability levels and appearance.
5. *Community/citizenship* focuses on recognizing that we live in a diverse, pluralistic society; recognizing, accepting, and appreciating cultural differences; assuming responsibility for the environment; helping people in need; and joining prosocial groups or teams outside of school.
6. *Event-triggered stressors* involve coping with events such as family moves, divorce, death, or becoming a big brother or sister.

Hawkins, Catalano, and Associates (1992) suggested a transdevelopmental strategy for promoting health, social, and academic development. Their social development model suggests that children who are bonded to peers, adults, and institutions that promote healthy beliefs and clear prosocial standards are more likely to adopt similar views. Thus, healthy bonding fosters a motivational component that can protect children from exposure to risk. Three conditions are essential to this bonding process (Hawkins & Weis, 1985). First, children must experience challenging and meaningful opportunities to contribute to their family, school, peers, and other institutional and informal settings in ways that are developmentally appropriate and lead to feelings of responsibility and satisfaction. Second, they must be taught skills (e.g., academic, social) that allow them to utilize the opportunities they experience. Third, they need to receive recognition and acknowledgment for their efforts; appropriate recognition nurtures children's motivation to continue and refine their skilled performances. This tripartite notion of opportunities, skills, and recognition provides a model for the provision of supportive processes in the child's environment and places the motivational component of significant relationships at the center of interventions that provide protection from risk (Yoshikawa, 1994).

Middle School Years. Young people between the ages of 10 and 14 experience many predictable stressors and dramatic life changes. Rapid body changes, cognitive maturation, and increased social pressures profoundly influence the functioning of young adolescents. The transition from self-contained, elementary school classrooms to a less protective middle school culture is often difficult and introduces new stresses and challenges to compound those connected with growing up (Carnegie Council on Adolescent Development. Report of the Task Force on Education of Young Adolescents, 1989). All adolescents face decisions about choosing appropriate friends, resolving conflicts with peers, negotiating increased independence from parents, experimenting with alcohol or drugs, and having sex. While these are common experiences, the negative consequences of poor decision making may lead to serious physical, social, and emotional problems that negatively affect the current and future quality of one's life.

Young adolescents typically explore new options and possibilities with an experimental attitude common for this age group. Much of this exploratory behavior is adaptive. However, when carried to extremes, such behavior can become habitual and produce lifelong negative consequences. Early adolescence represents a critical period for the prevention of health-compromising and the promotion of health-enhancing lifestyles before damaging behaviors become entrenched (Elliott, 1993). To become healthy, constructive, productive adults, adolescents on an effective developmental pathway must accomplish the following (Carnegie Council on Adolescent Development, 1995): "Find a valued place in a constructive group; learn how to form close, durable human relationships; feel a sense of worth as a person; achieve a reliable basis for making informed choices; know how to use the support systems available to them; express constructive curiosity and exploratory behavior; find ways of being useful to others; believe in a promising future with real opportunities; . . . master social skills, including the ability to manage conflict peacefully; cultivate the inquiring and problem-solving habits of mind for life-long learning; become ethical persons; learn the requirements of responsible citizenship; and respect diversity in our pluralistic society" (pp. 10–11).

The Carnegie Council on Adolescent Development (1989, 1992, 1995) has disseminated three exemplary reports with suggested micro-, meso-, and exosystem changes to help adolescents achieve their developmental competencies. Core recommendations include reengaging families with their adolescent children through collaborative efforts with schools and community agencies; establishing safe, developmentally appropriate schools that offer challenging, nurturing, and health-promoting learning environments; providing life skills training to foster adaptive behavior; ensuring access to health services; providing growth-promoting, community settings for young people during the nonschool hours; and enhancing the constructive potential of the media.

High School Years. Pittman and Cahill (1992) identified five basic competency areas that define the range of skills and behaviors required for adult success.

1. *Health/physical competence* involves good current health status as well as evidence of knowledge, attitudes, and behaviors that will foster future health.
2. *Personal/social competence* emphasizes intrapersonal skills such as self-discipline and the capacity to understand personal emotions; interpersonal skills such as the ability to work and develop positive relationships with others through empathy, cooperation, communication, and negotiating; and judgment skills such as the capacity to plan, evaluate, solve problems, and make responsible decisions.
3. *Cognitive/creative competence* focuses on the ability to learn; motivation to learn and achieve; good oral and written language skills; appreciation and participation in different forms of creative expression; analytical and problem-solving skills; and development of a broad base of knowledge.
4. *Vocational competence* involves awareness of vocational and avocational options and the steps needed to accomplish goals; understanding the value and function of work and leisure; and adequate preparation for a chosen career.
5. *Citizenship (or ethics and participation) competence* emphasizes knowledge of and appreciation for the history and values of one's community and nation, as well as active participation in efforts that contribute to the community and nation.

Although some of the competencies (i.e., health/physical, personal/social, and cognitive/creative competence) show clear continuities with those in early and middle childhood, others emerge during adolescence (i.e., vocational, citizenship). In general, however, these competencies clearly establish a firm foundation for making positive contributions as a member of one's family, peer group, workplace, and community at large.

Connell, Aber, and Walker (1995) provided a comprehensive research-based framework that moves backwards from desired outcomes (i.e., competencies) to the developmental processes leading to these outcomes, to the social mediators (e.g., actors) most important to those outcomes, to community dimensions (e.g., primarily exosystem- and mesosystem-level functions) that facilitate these processes. Although economic capacity and opportunity, community demography, and the existence of social institutions (e.g., youth organizations) are viewed as important factors, Connell et al. placed crucial emphasis on the density of bonds and networks among community participants (e.g., parents, neighbors, teachers) who assume primary responsibility for healthy youth development. Microsystem interactions between social mediators and youth are core building blocks for the desired outcomes, while exosystem supports of parent-teen interactions facilitate these processes. The desired outcomes are grouped into three gross domains: economic self-sufficiency, healthy family and social relationships, and good citizenship practices. These outcomes are considered in relative terms with relative levels of success measured in relation to the degree of adversity experienced by the individual and the community.

CONCEPTUAL ISSUES REGARDING PREVENTION

Before presenting our review of programs, it is important to define prevention, competence enhancement, and health promotion to clarify the focus and scope of our program selection. Reaching consensus on definitions of these terms has proven difficult—especially because perceptions of these concepts may vary based on an investigator's disciplinary perspective and theoretical framework. However, clarifying conceptual perspectives and terminology is especially important because the field of prevention has long suffered from definitional confusion (Cowen, 1983). Currently, there is considerable debate about the most appropriate terminology for prevention scientists to employ and the kinds of interventions that should be considered preventive.

Investigators have developed several classification models for prevention (Caplan, 1964; Cowen, 1983; Gordon, 1983; Institute of Medicine, 1994). The most common terminology historically used for public health and preventive mental health includes the terms *primary, secondary,* and *tertiary* prevention. Recently, the influential IOM report (1994) contended that the terms *universal, selective,* and *indicated* may be more appropriate. Therefore, we will define both sets of terms, look for overlap between them, and identify areas where clarification is needed.

Historically, preventive interventions were classified as primary (i.e., actions to decrease the number of new cases or incidence of a disorder), secondary (i.e., early identification and efficient treatment to lower the prevalence of established cases), or tertiary (i.e., rehabilitation to reduce the severity of disability associated with an existing disorder) based on the behavioral or health status of the target group (Caplan, 1964; Cowen, 1983). However, characterizing behavioral status, which some view categorically in terms of *DSM-IV* diagnoses and others view dimensionally, is not necessarily straightforward. Should we consider school-based play therapy for an aggressive first-grader as secondary prevention (i.e., early symptom detection and treatment), or should it be classified as primary prevention for conduct disorder? Is a districtwide alcohol education program for ninth-graders primary prevention for nondrinkers and secondary prevention for their classmates who drank a six-pack of beer at a party during the past weekend?

Similarly, disagreements can occur when classifying services from different disciplines (e.g., education, juvenile justice, medicine, psychology) concerned with different outcomes. For example, counseling gang members who flunked out of school could be labeled as treatment for school failure, but primary prevention for drug abuse and pregnancy. However, we would classify this as secondary prevention because the program participants were singled out based on their problematic behavioral performance. When classifying prevention efforts, it seems necessary to consider several factors, including the target group's current behavioral status, their level of risk, the way they are selected, as well as the setting and mechanism through which an intervention is delivered. Thus, we would call a teacher-taught, classroom-based problem-solving program for all third-graders primary prevention even if some children with behavioral disorders were enrolled in the classes. On the other hand, a series of small-group problem-solving sessions run by the school social worker for impulsive first-graders represents secondary prevention. To discriminate reliably among various categories of prevention, further elaboration on terminology is warranted.

Primary, Secondary, and Tertiary Prevention

Primary Prevention

Kessler and Albee (1975) humorously noted that nearly everything has implications for primary prevention, for reducing emotional disturbance and strengthening mental health, including "children's group homes, titanium paint, parent-effectiveness-training, consciousness raising, Zoom, Sesame Street, the guaranteed annual wage, legalized abortion, school integration, limits on international cartels, unpolished rice, free prenatal clinics, antipollution laws, a yoghurt and vegetable free diet, free VD clinics, and a host of other topics" (p. 560). In addition, there is a widespread misperception that prevention is present in all aspects of mental health service and research (Institute of Medicine, 1994). As evidence to support the need for a reliable and valid classification system for prevention, the IOM report noted that some people consider it prevention to provide lithium medication to a patient with bipolar mood disorder to prevent a comorbid disorder of alcohol dependence. Although one technically could argue that this intervention is preventive in certain respects, it is more appropriately classified as treatment.

As stated at the chapter's outset, *primary prevention* is dually focused on forestalling the development of psychological problems and enhancing people's psychosocial competence and health (Cowen, 1977, 1983, 1994, 1995). Primary prevention programs reduce the incidence of problems through group- or population-oriented interventions, rather than targeting individuals who exhibit behavioral and emotional symptoms. They focus on well-functioning groups of people or those who, because of environmental circumstances or life events, are epidemiologically at risk for adverse psychological outcomes. Such programs are provided within the context of mainstream institutions, settings, and social policies rather than through specialized services for those manifesting psychological, social, or physical problems. In addition, primary prevention programs should be theoretically and empirically based, using information about risk and protective processes to increase the intervention's promise of promoting positive behavioral outcomes.

Other investigators have introduced additional concepts to clarify various forms of primary prevention. For example, Catalano and Dooley (1980) proposed dividing primary prevention into "proactive" programs that have the goal of avoiding risk factors altogether, and "reactive" programs that prepare people to cope effectively with unavoidable risk factors. Bloom (1983) distinguished among "total population," "milestone," and "high-risk" approaches. Total population approaches are communitywide efforts such as water purification or media-based mental health education. Milestone strategies focus on community members at times of predictable transitions or stressful life events, such as kindergarten entry, marriage, beginning a job, or retiring. Risk approaches target groups of people who are epidemiologically more vulnerable for developing certain types of dysfunction (e.g., children of parents with mental illness, drug problems, or a history of criminality).

Secondary Prevention

Secondary prevention programs seek to reduce the prevalence or to lower the rates of established cases of disorder or illness in the population. They reduce the duration of a disorder through early case finding combined with prompt and effective intervention. One pathway to secondary prevention involves identifying behavioral or emotional symptoms of dysfunction early in someone's development and providing treatment to reduce the potential for later, more severe psychopathology. The Primary Mental Health Project, a school-based program for the early detection and prevention of school maladaptation, is a well-known exemplar of secondary prevention (Cowen et al., 1996). A second pathway involves identifying prodromal signs of serious disorder early so that prompt, efficacious intervention (e.g., providing appropriate medication to someone during the initial stages of schizophrenia or depression) can avert more dire psychiatric consequences.

Tertiary Prevention

Tertiary prevention efforts focus on individuals with established disorders and seek to reduce the disorder's residual effects and to rehabilitate such individuals to a level where they may readjust to community life. For people who experience major mental illness, appropriate tertiary prevention goals are to reestablish some interpersonal and job effectiveness. Although these programs are needed and worthwhile, this form of intervention is more appropriately classified as rehabilitation rather than prevention (Cowen, 1983; Institute of Medicine, 1994).

Universal, Selective, and Indicated Preventive Intervention

The IOM report (1994) attempted to clarify the placement of preventive intervention within the broader mental health intervention framework by differentiating it from treatment (i.e., case identification; standard treatment for known disorders) and maintenance (i.e., compliance with long-term treatment to reduce relapse; aftercare, including rehabilitation). Based in part on Gordon's (1983, 1987) proposal to replace the terms primary, secondary, and tertiary prevention, the IOM report defined three forms of preventive intervention: universal, selective, and indicated.

Universal Preventive Interventions

These interventions target "the general public or a whole population group that has not been identified on the basis of individual risk. The intervention is desirable for everyone in that group" (Institute of Medicine, 1994, pp. 24–25). The IOM report exemplars include prenatal care, childhood immunization, and interventions designed to prevent distress and divorce in couples who are married or planning marriage and not currently experiencing relationship difficulties. Universal programs are desirable because they can contribute to adaptive coping across an array of experiences and settings. Because these programs are positive, proactive, and provide independent of risk status, their potential for stigmatizing participants is minimized and thus they may be more readily accepted and adopted.

Selective Preventive Interventions

Selective strategies target "individuals or a subgroup of the population whose risk of developing mental disorders is significantly higher than average. . . . Risk groups may be identified on the basis of biological, psychological, or social risk factors that are known to be associated with the onset of a mental disorder" (Institute of Medicine, 1994, p. 25). The IOM report offered the following examples of selective intervention programs: home visitation and infant day care for low-birthweight children, preschool programs for all children from poor neighborhoods, and support groups for elderly widows.

Indicated Preventive Interventions

These programs target "high-risk individuals who are identified as having minimal but detectable signs or symptoms foreshadowing mental disorder, or biological markers indicating a predisposition for mental disorder, but who do not meet DSM-III-R diagnostic levels at the current time" (Institute of Medicine, 1994, p. 25). The IOM committee's definition differs from Gordon's (1983), who intended that such interventions should be applied only to asymptomatic individuals. The IOM report characterized providing parent-child interaction training for families whose parents report a child to have behavioral problems as an example of an indicated intervention.

Commentary on the IOM Classification System

The objectives underlying the IOM classification scheme are worthy ones. Most valuable, it highlights the importance of considering risk and protective factors in designing preventive interventions. Unfortunately, this classification scheme has created confusion among prevention researchers for several reasons. First, it is unclear how much "higher than average" the risk of a target group should be before a program is considered selective rather than universal. For example, should the same violence prevention program be considered universal intervention in a middle-class suburban school but selective in a low-income, inner-city school? Given gender differences in risk for depression and suicide, would a depression prevention program be universal if offered to Boy Scouts and selective if offered to Girl Scouts? Given age differences in risk for substance abuse, are drug-prevention programs universal if targeted to elementary school students and selective if targeted to middle school students? Second, the meanings of *psychological* and *social* risk factors are ambiguous, making it difficult to discriminate reliably between selective and indicated interventions. Should we classify as selective or indicated a social skills training program for children who are disruptive and have poor peer relations? Since these programs involve early identification and efficient intervention, we would call such programs indicated. Yet the IOM report classified some of these programs as selective (e.g., Bierman & Furman, 1984; Coie & Krehbiel, 1984; Lochman, Coie, Underwood, & Terry, 1993) and others as indicated (e.g., Bry, 1982). Third, we return to the dilemma of how to classify universal programs that are delivered to groups of primarily well-functioning children in which there are subgroups who have behavioral problems. When researchers conducted subgroup analyses on problem-behavior children who participated in universal interventions, the IOM report classified these program recipients as having received an indicated preventive intervention (e.g., Hawkins, Doueck, & Lishner, 1988; Rotheram, 1982). To us, it seems counterintuitive to change the classification of the same program based on strategies of data analysis to determine if different adjustment subgroups responded in different ways to the intervention. Finally, although indicated preventive interventions represent an important form of service delivery, they are qualitatively different from universal interventions in their focus on symptomatic individuals rather than essentially well groups. In contrast to Gordon's (1983) approach, the IOM definition substantially overlaps with secondary prevention service delivery models that involve early detection or case finding, a rapid service delivery response, and efficient intervention or treatment. In summary, although the universal-selective-indicated classification scheme highlights important conceptual issues for consideration, definitions of these terms require clarification to promote interrater reliability in classifying the various prevention programs.

Prevention, Health Promotion, and Competence Enhancement

The IOM report (1994) recommended distinguishing prevention programs from health and competence-promotion efforts. It contended "The reason for not including it within the above spectrum is that health promotion is not driven by an emphasis on illness, but rather by a focus on the enhancement of well-being. It is provided to individuals, groups, or large populations to enhance competence, self-esteem, and a sense of well-being rather than to intervene to prevent psychological or social problems or mental disorders. This focus on health, rather than illness, is what distinguishes health promotion activities from the enhancement of protective factors within a risk reduction model for preventive interventions" (p. 27).

This distinction has been criticized for its narrow view by a number of prevention theorists who argue for a synthesis of these approaches (e.g., Cowen, 1995; Durlak & Wells, 1997). Perry et al. (1993) proposed a broader conceptualization of health promotion that incorporates models for reducing risk and enhancing protective factors. By applying social-psychological theory that emphasizes a focus on both young people and their social environments (Bandura, 1986; Bronfenbrenner, 1979), Perry et al. posited that the broad goal of health promotion involves the enhancement of competence across social, psychological, physical, and spiritual domains. They identified intervention components such as family involvement programs, peer leadership training, school-based life skills and social competency curricula, communitywide activities, health-enhancing mass media, and public policy initiatives to enhance health. This broad conceptualization of health promotion is similar to the competence-enhancement perspectives provided by others (e.g., Carnegie Council on Adolescent Development, 1995; Consortium on the School-Based Promotion of Social Competence, 1994; Pittman & Cahill, 1992).

Perry et al. (1993) highlighted programs that target psychosocial factors at individual, behavioral, and environmental levels. Programs that target *individual* factors include efforts such as identifying the social, legal, and health consequences of engaging in various forms of high-risk behavior; increasing critical understanding of media images and marketing methods; enhancing the value of prosocial norms and health concerns; and fostering self-efficacy to manage negative peer influences. Interventions that address *behavioral* factors include teaching social competencies to cope with stress and develop positive interpersonal relationships, and supporting and rewarding participation in prosocial activities. *Social environmental* factors include modeling of health-enhancing behaviors by family, peers, role models, and the media; establishing barriers to excessive mass media involvement and unsupervised time; and creating opportunities to foster intimacy and communication among young people and adults. Programs that positively influence these psychosocial factors are hypothesized to increase health-enhancing behaviors and reduce health-compromising behaviors. Perry et al.'s conceptualization of health promotion meshes with the risk-reduction model advanced by the IOM report, while it also actively embraces the competence-enhancement and protective-factors perspective. In addition, the broader focus on multiple domains of health, rather than just mental health, encourages a more holistic, developmental-ecological approach.

Millstein, Petersen, and Nightingale (1993b) suggested that attempts to draw clear distinctions among the paradigms of disease prevention, health protection, and health promotion are not likely to be useful, and that it is preferable to view them as overlapping with fluid definitional boundaries. Health promotion is "most broadly a philosophy of health or a set of activities that takes as its aim the promotion of health, not just the prevention of disease" (U.S. Congress, Office of Technology Assessment, 1991, p. 168). The IOM report correctly noted that there are many atheoretical programs that focus on improving one's quality of life but fail to conceptualize their efforts in the context of strengthening protective factors and building resistance against the development of dysfunction. However, there are also many well-researched health-promotion and competence-enhancement programs that have fostered protective factors and reduced behavioral dysfunction (see reviews by the Consortium on the School-Based Promotion of Social Competence, 1994; Cowen, 1995; DeFriese, Crossland, Pearson, & Sullivan, 1990; Durlak & Wells, 1997; Elias, 1995; Millstein et al., 1993a; Weissberg et al., 1991). Following the long-standing tradition of earlier reports (e.g., Commission on Chronic Illness 1957; Report of the Task Panel on Prevention, 1978), we contend that competence-enhancement and health-promotion programs comfortably fit within the context of primary or universal preventive intervention.

A Historical View on Definitions and Conceptual Issues Regarding Prevention and Health Promotion

One of the earliest, clearest statements on prevention and health promotion was offered by the Commission on Chronic Illness (1957). The Commission was established as an independent national agency to study the problems of chronic disease, illness, and disability by the American Hospital Association, American Medical Association, American Public Health Association, and American Public Welfare Association. The Commission indicated that the prevention of chronic illness and disability can be achieved only through united efforts toward health promotion, averting the occurrence of illness, and early detection of disease through mass screening and health examinations to assure treatment in early stages to reduce the chances of increased disability or premature death.

Following the World Health Organization's basic charter, the Commission (1957) defined health "as a state of complete physical, mental, and social well-being and not merely the absence of disease or infirmity" (p. 8). It also pointed out the difficulties inherent in trying to distinguish between the concept of "promotion of health" and that of "primary prevention" of chronic illness. It suggested that health promotion be viewed as "general primary prevention" because it helps to reduce the occurrences of illness through fostering optimum levels of health throughout life. In contrast, "specific primary prevention" relates more narrowly to the prevention of particular diseases. The Commission identified a sample of components for healthful living that play a critical role in preventing disabilities, including adequate nutrition; adequate housing, including safeguards against accidents; general education and education specifically for health; access to recreational activities; moderate and well-balanced personal habits, including appropriate amounts of exercise, careful attention to personal hygiene, and restraint in use of alcohol and tobacco; mental hygiene to support the development of equanimity in the face of the natural and inevitable frustrations of living; a productive role in society; and a sense of personal security related to job security, access to health care, and income maintenance during times of illness or following retirement.

The Commission (1957) also distinguished between primary and secondary prevention. It cautioned against defining primary prevention too narrowly (i.e., thinking only in terms of methods employed to prevent communicable diseases after the discovery of infectious agents), and pointed out that preventive measures have been successful before precise causes were identified. A classic example of general primary prevention was John Snow's 1854 effort to halt the epidemic of cholera by removing the handle from the Broad Street water pump in London. In spite of little understanding of the causal mechanisms involved, his action greatly reduced the incidence of cholera. More specific primary prevention efforts through environmental sanitation were mounted after the identification of the cholera vibrio and tracing its source to sewage-contaminated water supplies. A further step in specific primary prevention occurred with the development of an immunization against cholera that protected immunized people from serving as a favorable host for the cholera vibrio.

The Commission (1957) noted that definitional confusion regarding the prevention of disability is based on the fact that one person's negative outcome may also serve as a risk factor for another disability. The goals of primary prevention extend toward health promotion or increasing human resistance to the various factors that contribute to disease. Primary prevention objectives also extend toward secondary prevention. Illustratively, early detection and treatment of a malignant neoplasm (secondary) before it metastasizes to other organs prevents disseminated cancer. Thus, the Commission argued that the strict traditional definition of specific primary prevention must be broadened when applied to chronic illnesses because it is impossible to identify a clear starting point for these diseases.

The Focus and Scope of the Current Review

Primary prevention is a term that comfortably subsumes health promotion (i.e., general primary prevention), competence enhancement, universal preventive interventions, and selective interventions for epidemiologically at-risk groups. The next two sections review primary prevention programs first for infants and preschoolers and then for elementary-age children and adolescents. On the other hand, our review does not include secondary-prevention or indicated-preventive-intervention research studies in which individuals have been identified based on behavioral deficits and symptoms (e.g., Bierman & Furman, 1984; Bry, 1982; Coie & Krehbiel, 1984; Lochman et al., 1993; Tremblay, Pagani-Kurtz, Masse, Vitaro, & Pihl, 1995). These fit more appropriately in the domain of early detection and intervention.

We will provide a general summary regarding the nature and effects of primary prevention efforts across several key program areas and then discuss one or a few illustrative studies in some detail. Summary statements about intervention strategies are derived from our own examination of each domain as well as recent summary reviews or meta-analyses by others. We do not attempt to review comprehensively the literature as several excellent reviews already exist for young children (e.g., Barnett, 1995; Gomby, Larson, Lewit, & Behrman, 1993; Hawkins, Catalano, & Brewer, 1995; Institute of Medicine, 1994; Olds & Kitzman, 1993; St. Pierre, Layzar, & Barnes, 1995; Yoshikawa, 1994, 1995), and for elementary-age children and adolescents (e.g., Brewer, Hawkins, Catalano, & Neckerman, 1995; Consortium on the School-Based Promotion of Social Competence, 1994; DeFriese et al., 1990; Dryfoos, 1990; Durlak, 1995; Durlak & Wells, 1997; Hansen, 1992; Hawkins, Arthur, & Catalano, 1995; Institute of Medicine, 1994; Kirby, 1992; Moore et al., 1995; Tolan & Guerra, 1994). Illustrative studies are chosen for in-depth discussion because of the quality of research design, innovative nature of the intervention, and importance of their results.

Many studies reviewed in these sections have been designed as randomized clinical trials. Results from such studies have potential to offer more systematic and controlled information about intervention effects (Olds & Kitzman, 1993; Robins, 1992). When available, the following features of illustrative programs will be examined: (a) program description and procedures; (b) program effects at posttest as well as available follow-ups; (c) assessment of the quality of program implementation; (d) analyses of moderator variables (e.g., subject or setting characteristics associated with different outcomes); and (e) tests of mediational models that specify the manner in which outcomes were obtained or the relation between hypothesized mediators and outcomes.

PROGRAMS FOR INFANTS AND PRESCHOOLERS

> The development and expansion of family support programs have far outpaced the availability of research information on program implementation and effectiveness. This is not a field where science has played a major role in informing practice. (Powell, 1994, p. 441)

There have been significant developments during the past 35 years in the area of preventive intervention services for families with infants and young children. Two main types of interventions have been provided: home/family-based interventions and center/clinic/school-based interventions. Some programs have combined both types of intervention models. These interventions have been provided as primary prevention for all families, and for selected populations based on either family risk characteristics or physical risk characteristics of the child (e.g., preterm birth). The review is organized both by type of intervention and nature of the population. First, we describe the goals of home-based interventions. Then we review home-based interventions provided during the prenatal and infancy periods. Finally, we review home-based and center-based interventions in the preschool period.

The Goals of Home Visiting

During infancy, home visiting is a key component of most prevention models. However, there are a variety of potential goals of differing models and the field is often marked by the absence of theory regarding both program goals and which risk or protective factors are the focus of the program (Yoshikawa, 1994). Ramey and Ramey (1993) provided an overarching conceptual framework operationalizing eight domains that early childhood health and development programs may address. These eight domains, which focus on both enhancing the health and well-being of child and parents as well as on preventing negative outcomes that might arise through inadequate parental care, include survival (e.g., housing, food, income, safety, and transportation); values and goals (e.g., setting goals for family, school, and work success; valuing community resources); a sense of physical, social-emotional, and financial security for both parent and child; physical and mental health; social interaction with family members, peers, the neighborhood, and community; self-esteem, academic achievement motivation, and social competence; communication skills; and basic intellectual skills. They posited that home visiting programs need to consider the full range of child and family functioning in developing program goals.

These multiple goals are addressed by home-visiting programs that promote maternal sensitivity and responsiveness to the child, which promote healthy attachments; concrete parenting activities that enhance cognitive and communicative development; health education that assists parents in reducing risk behaviors (e.g., substance abuse) that impede positive parenting and child development; linkages between the parent and community services that provide instrumental support, including nutrition supplements; access to transportation for clinic visits, educational and vocational training, and employment assistance; and social support through the home visitor–parent relationships to build a parent's self-efficacy and sense of control and to support a parent's attempts at behavior change and effective parenting (Olds & Kitzman, 1993). Few programs to date provide such comprehensive models, and it is unlikely that paraprofessionals would have sufficient training to meet all of these wide-ranging goals. There has been a noticeable change in the emphasis of family-support programs from a deficit-based prevention model to an empowerment-based promotion model over the past decade (Cochran & Woolever, 1983; Dunst, Trivette, & Thompson, 1990; Weissbourd, 1994).

Home Visiting Programs for the Prevention of Low Birthweight and Premature Birth

Few evaluated programs have identified families prior to birth and provided ongoing preventive activities in the prenatal period. Olds and Kitzman (1993) reviewed such programs and found that most have the primary goal of preventing low birthweight (LBW) or preterm birth. In general, there is little empirical documentation that home visiting has successfully prevented prematurity. Most clinic-based programs have failed to prevent LBW (Collaborative Group on Preterm Prevention, 1993), although Hobel et al. (1994) reported a clinic-based program in West Los Angeles with a primarily Hispanic population that both significantly reduced preterm birth and proved cost-effective (M. Ross et al., 1994). Olds, Henderson, Chamberlin, and Tatelbaum (1986) found effects of home visiting on preterm birth, but only among a subset of their intervention sample who were smoking prior to the home visiting intervention (see below for further description). Similarly, they reported a significant increase in birthweights among another subsample—14- to 16-year-olds who were nurse home-visited. Thus far, the limited nature of these effects and lack of replication indicate that most home visiting models have not effectively prevented LBW.

In contrast to the minimal effects of home visiting on birthweight, there are several promising findings from studies of school-based models for teen girls (Levy, Perhats, Nash-Johnson, & Welter, 1992; Seitz & Apfel, 1994). Seitz and Apfel (1994) utilized a novel design to examine the role of a specialized public school program for pregnant teens that contained a strong health component with prenatal care and daily supervision by nurses. They reported a significant reduction in preterm birth (6% vs. 16%). As no specific health-related behaviors changed between the intervention and comparison groups, they ascribed program effects to the development of a nurturing, secure environment that provided psychological support and continuous monitoring of nutrition and health.

Paneth (1995) suggested that these interventions require a theoretical basis regarding which risk factors may be malleable to intervention to be effective. Known risk factors for LBW and preterm birth include smoking during pregnancy, low maternal weight gain, and low prepregnancy weight. However, these risk factors account for only a small percentage of high-risk births. Two recent reviews suggested that interventions that focus on health risk behaviors, especially quality of diet, smoking, and possible substance abuse, may have the greatest impact (Olds & Kitzman, 1993; Shiono & Behrman, 1995). Such interventions focus on successful ways to create behavior change during pregnancy. For example, it has been estimated that a smoking cessation program that is effective in 18% of the cases will be cost-effective if the program costs $80 or less per patient (Hueston, Mainous, & Farrell, 1994). However, these estimates are based only on the direct effect smoking has on the costs of premature birth and do not include cost savings that follow from the effect of prematurity (e.g., lowered health and educational costs) or other effects of maternal smoking on child development or maternal health (Olds, Henderson, & Tatelbaum, 1994a, 1994b).

In the area of preventing LBW, it has been difficult to develop focused interventions that reduce the probability of deleterious outcomes because few risk or protective factors have been identified. Given the lack of success, there has been little examination of moderator variables (e.g., subgroups that differentially affect intervention outcome). However, various investigations indicate that maternal smoking during pregnancy is a viable and possibly malleable risk factor. Olds et al. (1994a) also showed that compared to controls, nurse-visited mothers who smoked had a lower rate of preterm birth. However, analyses were not presented to show that reduction in smoking was the mediator of this outcome. Finally, no studies found that differences in quality of implementation or dosage of the intervention affected outcomes.

Home Visiting Programs with Families of Preterm Infants

Preterm infants provide an identifiable selective population for preventive intervention. They are at significant risk for negative outcomes in the domains of cognitive, communication, social, and emotional development, especially if they weigh less than 1,500 grams (Friedman & Sigman, 1992). Further, the birth of a preterm infant is a significant stressor for families, and the quality of family support systems as well as social-economic factors influence their outcomes (Beckwith & Cohen, 1984; Greenberg & Crnic, 1988; Werner & Smith, 1982). In general, family interventions for preterm infants have shown consistent, positive effects on both parent-child relations as well as cognitive outcomes (Olds & Kitzman, 1993; Seitz & Provence, 1990). Home visiting programs that focused primarily on the quality of the parent-child relationship and those that focused on cognitive stimulation have produced significant increases in infant and toddler mental development (Barrera, Rosenbaum, & Cunningham, 1986; Beckwith & Rodning, 1992; Field, Widmayer, Stringer, & Ignatoff, 1980; Rauh, Achenbach, Nurcombe, Howell, & Teti, 1988; Resnick, Armstrong, & Carter, 1988; Scarr-Salapatek & Williams, 1973). However, few studies have followed participants later in development to examine maintenance of effects.

The Infant Health and Development Program (IHDP)

The IHDP provides an excellent example for examining the effects of intervention on LBW infants. IHDP is the first multisite, randomized clinical trial to evaluate the efficacy of home- and center-based interventions among LBW preterm infants. The goals of IHDP were to reduce the developmental-cognitive, social-behavioral, and health problems of LBW infants. The intervention began after discharge from the neonatal nursery and continued until 36 months of age (corrected for prematurity). Infants were assigned randomly to the intervention or a comparison condition that also received pediatric follow-up and referral services. Randomization was conducted using an "adaptive randomization model" in which one infant was assigned to intervention for every two comparisons (balanced for infant and family characteristics), resulting in 377 intervention and 608 comparison subjects (Kraemer & Fendt, 1990). Twenty-one percent of families approached refused to participate and it is not known how they differed from the study population. Analyses contrasted the effects of intervention on children of heavier birthweight (HBW = 2,000–2,500 grams) versus LBW (< 2,000 grams). Assessments of cognitive development and behavior problems occurred on a regular basis. Retention was very high, with 93% participation in analyses at age 3 and 82% participation at age 5.

The intervention consisted of three interrelated components adapted from previous interventions for families with disadvantaged children (Ramey et al., 1992; Ramey & Campbell, 1987). Home visits were provided on a weekly basis in the first year and biweekly during the following two years. Home visiting was conducted by college-educated specialists who were trained in home visiting and received weekly individual and group supervision. Home visiting emphasized cognitive, linguistic, and social development through the use of over 300 developmentally graded activities, and focused on empowering parents to identify problems and goals and develop plans to solve them. Home visitors also provided developmental and health information as well as social support to families. Families received an average of 67 home visits during the three years.

For the second intervention component, children attended a free, specially designed child development center. This intervention began when children were 12 months old and continued through 36 months of age. The teaching staff consisted of early childhood educators who implemented learning activities drawn from the same curriculum as was used in the home visiting component. Children attended an average of 267 days of center-based programming; 14% of children never attended the center-based component. The final component involved bimonthly parent groups that began at 12 months. However, this component was low in intensity and only attended by parents on average 3.7 times (Ramey et al., 1992).

At the end of intervention (age 3), results indicated significant effects on both intelligence and behavior problems (The Infant Health and Development Program, 1990). However, significant differences within the intervention sample indicated the importance of birthweight to outcomes. The effect sizes (ES) of the intervention for IQ were .83 for HBW children and .41 for LBW children. Further, intervention had little effect for children with birthweights under 1,500 grams or children with IQs under 70. Further analyses of the IQ effects indicated that they were moderated by maternal education. The intervention provided significant benefits to children of women with a high school education or less. Children whose mothers attended college did not show differential IQ change (Brooks-Gunn, Gross, Kraemer, Spiker, & Shapiro, 1992). Additional analyses of IQ subcomponents indicated intervention effects both on verbal and nonverbal aspects of cognitive development (Brooks-Gunn, Liaw, & Klebanov, 1992). The intervention did not differentially affect aspects of the mother's life (e.g., returning to school, fertility), with the exceptions that the provision of free center-based education led mothers to return to work a few months earlier and home visiting referrals probably explain the fact that intervention mothers took greater advantage of public assistance and health insurance (Brooks-Gunn, McCormick, Shapiro, Benaisch, & Black, 1994). At 30 months, the dyads participated in a problem-solving task to assess the quality of maternal interactive behavior and child competence. Small, significant intervention effects (ES = .25) were found for the mother's quality of assistance as well as the child's persistence, enthusiasm, and on-task behavior. For the last two findings, it appeared that the intervention affected only Black children. As no effects were found for maternal supportiveness, the authors suggested that IHDP may have had less effect on the social as compared to the teaching aspect of parenting (Spiker, Ferguson, & Brooks-Gunn, 1993). Modest, significant intervention effects at age 3 were also found for parent report of behavior problems (ES = .18) and for observations of some aspects of home environment quality.

Ramey and colleagues (Blair, Ramey, & Hardin, 1995; Ramey et al., 1992) also examined how participation rates in the three intervention components related to outcomes at age 3 by dividing participants into three levels of involvement. They found significant and clinically meaningful differences: whereas 17% of the comparison sample scored in the mentally retarded range (IQ <70), only 13% of low-level, 4% of medium-level, and 2% of high-level participants did so. Thus, the most active participants had more than an eightfold reduction in relative incidence of mental retardation compared to the control group and a sixfold difference from low-level participants. Furthermore, no preexisting demographic characteristics of parents, child biological status, or site were related to level of participation. Thus, independent of family (i.e., social class, education, ethnicity) and child characteristics (i.e., birthweight, neonatal health), early, high-quality intensive interventions were associated with improved developmental outcomes, especially for families with low education levels. Finally, analyses of risk and protective factors indicated that only 11% of comparison LBW children born into poverty were functioning at normal levels across four domains at age 3, whereas 39% of the intervention group did so (Bradley et al., 1994); and, although the cumulative number of social risk factors affects cognitive outcomes, the intervention was successful at all levels of risk (Liaw & Brooks-Gunn, 1994).

A two-year follow-up of IHDP when the children were 5 years old showed significant attenuation of effects. In the HBW group, full-scale IQ differences were 3.7 points higher; there was no longer a significant difference in the percentage of children who were mentally delayed. Minor intervention differences in rates of behavioral problems at age 3 had attenuated for both weight groups at age 5. As IQ has been shown to be less affected by intervention than is school performance, the findings for the HBW children are inconclusive and further follow-up in the school years is warranted. Results also indicated that the LBW infants, who are of most concern, were not affected by the intervention. It is not clear if this is due to the fact that their biological or neurological status requires more intensive or longer interventions. The IHDP is marked by the quality of its intervention, its sample retention, complete analyses, and also for its analyses of how both level of participation and preexisting family and child status variables were related to intervention effectiveness. No estimates of cost or of cost benefit have been published to date.

The Vermont Intervention Program (VIP)

In contrast to the diminution of effects of the IHDP program, findings from the VIP indicated maintenance of effects through age 7 (Nurcombe et al., 1984; Rauh et al., 1988). This small clinical trial (60 LBW infants were randomized to intervention or comparison) included nurse visiting with the mother daily for seven days prior to discharge and then four times in the home over the first 90 days. The intervention focused on enhancing the mother's ability to appreciate her child's specific characteristics, become effective at reading the baby's cues, and respond to those cues to facilitate mutually satisfying interactions. Similarly to IHDP, no significant effects on infant development were found, but by age 3 meaningful differences between intervention and control groups were obtained. At ages 4 and 7, differences on intellectual performance were approximately 1 standard deviation, with intervention children performing similarly to normal birthweight comparison, and performing better than controls at each level of SES (Achenbach, Phares, Howell, Rauh, & Nurcombe, 1990). At ages 3 and 4, partial mediation of effects was found from nurse's ratings of mother's receptivity to the program. Three differences from IHDP are apparent: (a) the Vermont sample was more economically advantaged than the IHDP sample; (b) the VIP began earlier and was more intensive in the first months of life, but much shorter and less intensive overall; and (c) the VIP was provided by neonatal intensive care nurses who had more experience and knowledge regarding both LBW infants and their families than the IHDP home visitors.

Home Visiting Programs for Families with Infants and Preschoolers at Social and Economic Risk

In general, family-based support programs for families with significant social and economic disadvantages are based on the same premises and targeted to the same goals as discussed above. Olds and Kitzman (1993) reviewed programs that are primarily home-based and concluded that such programs have mildly beneficial effects on both parental caregiving and child cognitive outcomes in the preschool years. In addition, they show most benefit with low-SES unwed mothers. Further, they concluded that the professional training of the visitor impacts outcome, with programs using professional staff showing greater effects.

The Prenatal/Early Infancy Project (PEIP)

The PEIP is a nurse home visitation program designed for poor, unmarried, young women who are pregnant with their first child (Olds, 1988). The project was initially conducted in a semirural area of Upstate New York and had the following four goals: (a) improve the health outcomes of pregnancy; (b) improve the quality of care and stimulation that parents provide during infancy; (c) improve the women's own life course by motivating them to return to school and plan ahead for future pregnancies; and (d) reduce child neglect, maltreatment, and childhood injuries. The study design involved a randomized trial with four groups: Group 1 received only screening and referral, Group 2 received Group 1 services plus free transportation to well-child care clinics, Group 3 received the above services plus nurse home visiting every two weeks for an average of nine visits during pregnancy, and Group 4 received the above services plus continued nurse home visiting until the infants were 2 years old. Approximately 400 families were randomly assigned to the four groups and follow-up has been reported through age 4. Attrition ranged from 15% to 20%, and all analyses focused on Caucasians (89% of the sample).

During pregnancy, the nurse-visited groups, compared to Groups 1 and 2, improved the quality of their diets and decreased their amount of smoking. Nurse-visited women also reported greater informal social support and took better advantage of community-based services. At birth, among the women who smoked, there were 75% fewer preterm births as a result of home visiting. In addition, among young teens (ages 14 to 16), home visiting led to infants with higher birthweights. During the first two years after birth, within the subgroup of poor, unmarried teens in Group 4, there was an 80% reduction in state-verified cases of child maltreatment as compared to the comparison groups (19% vs. 4%). These findings were corroborated from other sources (Olds et al., 1986). This reduction in maltreatment did not extend for the two years after intervention ended (Olds, Henderson, & Kitzman, 1994), but nurse-visited homes were judged to be safer and the children made fewer emergency room visits (Olds, Henderson, Kitzman, & Cole, 1995). Similarly, only within the poor, unmarried teen subgroup who received the pre- and postnatal visiting, the following differences were found compared to Groups 1 and 2: (a) the rate of pregnancy was reduced by 42%; (b) the number of months women participated in the workforce increased by 83%; and (c) HOME scores on stimulation of language skills were significantly higher at 34 and 46 months. Among those who had not graduated from high school, a higher percentage of Group 4 women were enrolled in an educational program by the time their infant was 6 months old. At the end of the two-year intervention, Group 4 women had been on public assistance 157 fewer days; however, these effects did not maintain in the two years postintervention. Although there were no overall effects of child intelligence (Olds et al., 1994a), among mothers who were moderate to heavy smokers, those who received Group 3 or 4 interventions had children with higher IQs at age 4; after controlling for confounding factors, the mean difference was 4 IQ points. However, since there were no differences between Groups 3 and 4, these outcomes may have been mediated by prebirth changes in maternal smoking and diet (Olds et al., 1994a).

A cost-benefit analysis indicated that the net effect of the Group 4 intervention was $180 in 1992 dollars for low-income families, and $1,582 for the sample as a whole. Thus, the cost of the intervention was redeemed in the low-income portion of the sample. This is because reductions in Aid to Families with Dependent Children (AFDC) and food stamps accounted for 82% of the savings; 32% of the savings among low-income families was due to reduction in subsequent pregnancy and, thus, reductions in Medicaid, AFDC, and costs of Child Protective Services associated with the current child and with possible future children. Group 3, although less costly than the full treatment, did not show comparative cost savings. These analyses are conservative as they do not assess potential additional cost savings that might accrue from higher incomes or lower educational and social service costs past age 4 (S. Barnett, 1993b; Olds, Henderson, Phelps, Kitzman, & Hanks, 1993). Olds (1994b) posited that interventions will be most effective for low-income women when they foster a mother's sense of control over her life.

Olds (1995) attempted to replicate the PEIP with a low-income, inner-city African American sample in Memphis. Preliminary findings indicated that the intervention was more difficult to deliver in the urban environment, with a 50% turnover in nurse visitors during the intervention. The findings on reductions in smoking and increases in use of community services, as well as significant reductions in alcohol consumption, were replicated. Among mothers with low personal resources (e.g., low IQ, more mental health symptoms, passive coping style), the intervention increased maternal responsiveness and reduced child injuries and ingestions over the first two years.

Programs that are solely based on a home visiting model of service delivery for pregnant women and families in the first year or two of life have shown substantial impact on the behavior of both parents and young children. However, impact is likely to be highly dependent upon the intensity of service delivery as well as the professional training, supervision, and ongoing support of the home visiting staff. There is a clear need for research to examine both the dose-response relationship in this field as well as to study further how training and support of staff affect outcomes (Halpern, 1992; Olds & Kitzman, 1993).

Home- and Center-Based Programs for Families of Young Children at Social and Economic Risk

The great majority of evaluated programs for families at high social risk beginning before the child is 2 years old have been comprehensive in scope, although varying in time of initiation and duration of intervention. Programs that focus on both the family and parenting needs through home visiting and recruitment of community services and that attend to the child's direct educational needs through center-based programming have recently been termed "two-generation" programs (R. G. St. Pierre et al., 1995). The combination of home visiting and center-based educational stimulation is believed to maximize potential effects on both cognitive and behavioral outcomes (Hawkins, Catalano, & Brewer, 1995; Seitz, 1991; Yoshikawa, 1994). These programs have typically intervened with predominantly ethnic-minority, poorly educated parents living in poverty. As these programs have shown great promise, we describe a number of exemplary programs.

The Houston Parent-Child Development Center (H-PCDC)

The H-PCDC consisted of a comprehensive two-stage program for Hispanic families that required 550 hours of family involvement beginning when the child was 1 and ending at age 3 (Johnson, 1988). During the first year, mothers were visited at home 25 times by a paraprofessional who focused on child development, parenting skills, and educational stimulation. During the second year, mothers and children came to the Center four mornings per week. Mothers attended classes in child management and communication skills while the children were in nursery school. Families actually received an average of 400 hours of intervention from a combination of professionals and paraprofessionals. The evaluation design included random assignment of families in five yearly cohorts. However, approximately 50% of the intervention sample dropped out during the two years and were not followed, introducing a significant bias in interpretation of outcome. Most attrition was attributed to family mobility.

Results at posttest indicated (a) higher HOME scores; (b) on observation, program mothers showed greater praise and less criticism (average ES = .59); and (c) a trend toward higher IQ on the Stanford-Binet. At ages 4 to 9, no differences were found on IQ (Walker & Johnson, 1988), and there were no differences on school grades between 8 and 10 years (Johnson & Walker, 1991a). However, significant differences were found on composite achievement scores from the Iowa Test of Basic Abilities, as well as in vocabulary, reading, and language subdomains. Further, teachers reported significantly lower rates of externalizing behavior problems. This difference was clinically meaningful as comparison children showed an 8 times higher rate of "referral-level" difficulties (Johnson & Walker, 1987). There were no differences in retention or special education referral, but fewer program children attended bilingual classes. Thus, the project demonstrated continuing effects on both behavior and achievement five to eight years postintervention. However, these findings are limited in generalization to those families that remained both in the neighborhood and in the intervention. There were no analyses of mediational models, dosage levels, or implementation quality that might explain these effects.

The Brookline Early Education Project (BEEP)

The BEEP examined the effects of three levels of intervention in a birth to age 4 universal intervention model (Pierson, 1988). Families were randomly assigned to one of three levels of intensity. The most intensive level received home visits every three to four weeks, center-based parent meetings, and child care. The second level received the above services, but less frequent home visits. The least intensive level received only parent meetings and center-based services. No formal educational component began with children until age 3, when a morning kindergarten and extended day care were offered on a sliding fee scale. The sample was primarily suburban and advantaged; 50% were college graduates and 39% were ethnic minorities. A quasi-experimental design with comparison groups indicated improved reading and better academic standing in second grade. Across the entire sample, a dose-response relationship was found, with greater intensity leading to better outcomes. Also, for parents with limited education, children benefited only if they received the high-intensity program, suggesting that concerted outreach to the home environment was necessary to create involvement and change.

Avance

In most cases, programs that have been evaluated are considered to be model demonstration programs, often without continuance in the community. A major exception is the recent evaluation of Avance, a community-based, nonprofit organization that provides family support and education services to low-income Hispanic families with young children in San Antonio, Texas (Johnson & Walker, 1991b; Walker, Rodriguez, Johnson, & Cortez, 1995). Avance has the following goals: to foster parenting knowledge and skills relevant to child development; to encourage parents to improve their own educational and employment status; and to address broader family needs through linkages to community services. Avance intervention has two stages. In year 1, parents attend weekly three-hour parenting classes; monthly home visits, child care, and transportation are provided. In year 2, graduates of the parent education component are encouraged to take basic education, ESL, and community college classes provided at the Avance center. Most program staff are paraprofessionals who are often graduates of Avance. Professional staff are responsible for the parent education and staff supervision. Avance had been in operation for approximately a decade prior to evaluation. The evaluation was done separately at two locations: at one, random assignment was conducted; at the second, a matched comparison sample from a separate neighborhood was recruited. Evaluations were conducted at pretest and the end of years 1 and 2 on children who had a mean age of 2.

Results indicated that compared to controls, Avance parents showed higher total HOME scores at both times (ESs = approximately 1.0 at year 1 and .5 at year 2). Results regarding the provision of a more stimulating environment were bolstered by significant differences obtained through observations of mother-child interaction, indicating higher maternal positive communication and affect at both times, and the dyads having greater mutual enjoyment. At year 1, but not year 2, intervention mothers also reported more self-efficacy in their role as an educator. In addition, Avance mothers were more likely to access community resources and return for further education. There were no differences in child behavior during parent-child observations, tests of cognitive development, or reports of behavior problems. Thus, Avance showed significant impacts on the mothers' affect, cognitions, and behaviors, but no direct impact on the child's behavior or development.

Cluster analyses of families indicated three different types of families served by Avance: recent immigrants (traditionalists), families with high support and low depression (copers), and those with low support and high depression (strugglers). Analyses indicated equal effectiveness with all three types. The above results are qualified by substantial difficulties in attrition: 51% of parents dropped out of intervention (presumably mostly due to mobility), and only 21% of parents recruited into the intervention were assessed at the end of year 2. In comparison, 70% of the control group were pretested and 62% retained at posttest. This great difference in maintenance of the intervention sample is likely to have led to systematic biases. Those who were most interested and likely to be successful maintained interest through the entire intervention. The maxim

"Once randomized, always analyzed" is critical if one is to generalize the efficacy of interventions to the entire population, not only to those who are likely to complete it.

The Carolina Abecedarian Project (CAP)

The CAP has provided one of the most intensive demonstration programs that has been evaluated (Ramey, Bryant, Campbell, Sparling, & Wasik, 1988). Beginning at 6 to 12 weeks of age and continuing until age 5 (i.e., kindergarten entrance), the CAP program provided full-day developmental day care, occasional home visiting, a toy-lending library, parent-group meetings, and on-site medical care. Randomly assigned control parents received iron-fortified formula and free diapers through 15 months of age. This project is marked by its strong design and its high participation rates (98%) and low attrition rates through its 12-year follow-up (86%). At entrance to kindergarten, a second randomization within each group occurred, giving half of each preschool group a school-age intervention. The school-age intervention lasted three years (through grade 2) and consisted of a home-school resource teacher who provided an average of 15 home visits per year to assist parents in supplementing school instruction and who regularly consulted with teachers and served as a liaison to the family. Thus, the full project contrasted four groups: early and later intervention (E/E), early intervention only (E/C), later intervention only (C/E), and no intervention (C/C).

Results showed that by 18 months and thereafter through age 8, children with early intervention outperformed controls in IQ and school achievement and were retained in grade less often (50% for C/C vs. 16% for E/E; Horacek, Ramey, Campbell, Hoffman, & Fletcher, 1987; Martin, Ramey, & Ramey, 1990). The E/C group showed better outcomes than the C/E group, showing the impact of early intervention. A recent follow-up at age 12 (summer following sixth grade) showed strong intervention maintenance effects for both verbal IQ and school achievement, four years after the E/E intervention had ended (Campbell & Ramey, 1994). A dose-response relationship indicated that the E/E performed best (ESs of .9 on IQ and approximately .6 on achievement compared to C/C), somewhat less effect for E/C, and small or no effects of C/E. In contrast to other studies, mostly beginning in the preschool period (Lazar, Darlington, Murray, Royce, & Snipper, 1982), the CAP demonstrated that an intensive, multiple-setting intervention lasting into the school years can have a long-term impact on both IQ and achievement. Although remarkable for its care in design and follow-up, CAP has reported no data on issues in implementation or processes related to mediation or moderation, and it is unclear how often home visiting occurred in the early years. Thus far, no effects have been reported on social-emotional development, psychopathology, or parent outcomes.

Project CARE

Wasik, Ramey, Bryant, and Sparling (1990) reported on the evaluation of Project CARE, which is in part a replication of the Abecedarian model. Project CARE compared the enriched CAP day care model (with a regular home visiting component) to home visiting alone and a no-intervention control using a randomized design. Home visiting alone (averaging 2.5 times per month across the first three years) did not measurably affect family, parent, or child development, whereas the combination of intensive early education and home visiting resulted in higher IQ scores at age 3, but no effect on home environment quality. By 52 months, these differences had attenuated. Thus, at least at 52 months, this project did not replicate the long-term effects of CAP. The investigators speculated that the attenuation may be due to many comparison children's attending community day care and preschools.

As compared to other home visiting programs, negative findings regarding Project CARE's home-visiting-only intervention might be due to a number of factors: less intensive training and supervision of home visitors, the fact that home visitors were not nurses, and the fact that visits did not begin prenatally or in the neonatal period. Apparently, the strongest results occur in home visiting programs that begin early, use nurse visitors, and are intensive (Gutelius, Kirsch, MacDonald, Brooks, & McErlean, 1977; Gutelius et al., 1972; Olds, 1988; Powell & Grantham-McGregor, 1989). Powell and Grantham-McGregor compared weekly to bimonthly home visiting for poor urban children in Jamaica and concluded that "at least weekly visiting is necessary to make a substantial impact on the children's development" (p. 163).

Other Home and Home-Center Programs

Other influential, landmark home and home-center combination programs include the Yale Child Welfare Research Program (Provence & Naylor, 1983; Seitz, Rosenbaum, & Apfel, 1985), the Syracuse University Family Development Research Program (Lally, Mangione, & Honig, 1988), and the Mother-Child Home Project (Levenstein, 1992). They are notable for the breadth of intervention and the long-term follow-up of subjects (albeit with varying levels of attrition). Further, in all three cases, long-term effects were found on a combination of school achievement, behavioral problems, and parent behavior and education. However, in all three cases, random assignment to conditions was not accomplished (matched control samples were employed). As it is not possible to distinguish the motivation of those who enrolled in and completed a rigorous long-term intervention from those who were willing just to undergo assessment at posttest, definitive conclusions about outcome effects cannot be drawn. It should be noted that recent research has determined that nonrandomized matched control groups, even under the best of circumstances, are likely to lead to systematic biases (Grossman & Tierney, 1993).

The significant short-term and sometimes long-term results of intervention programs begun during infancy has led to their increasing use as a model for reducing risk factors for school failure across the United States. Noncontrolled evaluations of the Parents as Teachers (PAT) program in two primarily middle-class samples in Missouri has led to positive evaluations of both its acceptability to families and outcomes for children (Pfannenstiel, Lambson, & Yarnell, 1991). During the 1992–1993 school year, this state-mandated program served over 119,000 families in Missouri alone and is now in operation in over 1,500 locations in 44 states. Another widely discussed model is Healthy Start (Hawaii State Department of Health, 1992). Begun in Hawaii as a statewide early intervention program, screening is conducted at childbirth to determine family risk status. Home visiting is then conducted on a variable basis from infancy through age 5 for families determined to be at risk. Although it is now undergoing a rigorous evaluation in numerous demonstration sites in the United States, an uncontrolled study in Hawaii showed a significant reduction in child abuse and neglect (Breakey & Pratt, 1991).

Early Childhood Education

Early childhood education may be broadly defined as any group program for children under age 5 that provides them with cognitive skills and social competencies required for normal development or success in school (Haskins, 1989). This broad description includes a range of programs in terms of location (e.g., home day care, community center, or school) and educational approach (e.g., child-initiated learning, teacher-directed instruction). Research findings from the High/Scope Perry Preschool Study (Schweinhart, Barnes, & Weikart, 1993; Schweinhart & Weikart, 1988) and the Consortium for Longitudinal Studies (Lazar et al., 1982) demonstrate that *high-quality* preschool programs can produce positive, enduring changes in children's social and behavioral functioning. Based in part on these positive research findings, there is growing national support for the widespread dissemination of early childhood education programs (e.g., Committee for Economic Development, 1987). In particular, the U.S. Department of Health and Human Services, Public Health Service (1990) recommended that by the year 2000 the country "achieve for all disadvantaged children and children with disabilities access to high quality and developmentally appropriate preschool programs that help prepare children for school, thereby improving their prospects with regard to school performance, problem behaviors, and physical health" (p. 254).

However, the lasting benefits of early childhood education have been achieved *only* by high-quality programs characterized by a developmentally appropriate curriculum based on child-initiated activities; teaching teams that are knowledgeable in early childhood development and receive ongoing training and supervision; class size limited to fewer than 20 3- to 5-year-olds with at least two teachers; administrative leadership that includes support of the program; systematic efforts to involve parents as partners in their child's education, as well as sensitivity to the noneducational needs of the child and family; and evaluation procedures that are developmentally appropriate (Schweinhart & Weikart, 1988). These characteristics of program design and implementation appear to be central ingredients of most successful prevention efforts (Weissberg et al., 1989). In contrast, ample evidence suggests that early childhood education programs of lesser quality do not result in such positive effects (Haskins, 1989).

The High/Scope Perry Preschool Project

Between 1962 and 1967, the High/Scope Perry Preschool Project served low-income Black 3- and 4-year-olds with IQ scores between 70 and 90 (Schweinhart & Weikart, 1988, 1989). Evaluators randomly assigned 58 children to a preschool group and 65 children to a control group. The classroom program involved five 90-minute classes a week for seven months a year over a two-year period. Classroom groups had 25 children and four well-trained teachers who implemented the High/Scope Early Childhood Curriculum, an educational approach that promotes intellectual, social, and physical development through child-initiated learning activities. In addition, teachers made weekly 90-minute home visits to involve parents as partners in their child's education. Thus, the program attended to cognitive and social goals as well as parent involvement and empowerment. There was extremely low, nonbiased attrition through age 27.

Longitudinal follow-up data on children up to age 19 indicated that program children, relative to control subjects, showed stronger commitment to schooling, higher academic achievement, lower rates of grade retention, fewer placements in special education (16 % vs. 28%), and lower rates of classification of mental impairment (15% vs. 35%). Findings at age 27 showed better high school graduation rates (67% vs. 49%), fewer lifetime arrests (31% vs. 51%), a five-times lower rate of being arrested five or more times (5% vs. 35%), significantly higher monthly earnings, a higher rate of home ownership, and lower use of welfare assistance (15% vs. 32%). Gender analyses indicated that differences in high school graduation and the need for special education placements were found only for females. In addition, at age 27, program females were significantly more likely to be married. These findings withstood the fact that earlier differences found on intelligence tests faded to nonsignificance by age 6 or 7.

Cost estimates and cost-benefit analyses have been performed on several occasions (W. S. Barnett, 1993a; Schweinhart et al., 1993). The average cost of intervention for two years was $14,415 (in 1992 dollars). Cost-benefit analyses indicate between a 7:1 and 8:1 ratio of return to costs for taxpayers; a great majority of these costs are those incurred to taxpayers and crime victims as a result of reduction in criminality. As budgetary pressures have led to reductions in costs and services (average cost of $3,720/year in 1993 dollars), corresponding reductions in benefit and cost-benefit might be expected. Poorer teacher preparation, salary, and training, larger class sizes, and less home visiting are likely to reduce positive outcomes.

The Consortium for Longitudinal Studies

Other high-quality programs have also promoted multiple competencies and prevented problem behaviors in children. Most notably, the Consortium for Longitudinal Studies evaluated the long-term effects of 11 preschool programs (including the Perry Preschool Project) on 2,008 experimental and control children between ages 9 and 19. Program children were less likely to be retained or to require special education. Although for some programs the results were stronger than for others, findings also suggested that these programs have potential to affect rates of delinquency and crime, teen pregnancy, welfare use, and employment (Royce, Darlington, & Murray, 1983).

Head Start

Although the most widely experienced preschool program for disadvantaged children is Head Start, it is among the most inadequately evaluated. Research, evaluation, and demonstration efforts consumed less than 11% of costs by 1989. While the Head Start Synthesis Project, a meta-analysis of over 200 projects, indicated that graduates had better health and immunization rates as well as enhanced socioemotional development (McKey et al., 1985), technical problems of this study as well as others make these conclusions tentative (Zigler & Styfco, 1994). As Zigler and Styfco (1994) reiterated: "The empirical literature thus delivers good news and bad news. The bad news is that neither Head Start nor any preschool program can inoculate children against the ravages of poverty. Early intervention simply cannot overpower the effects of poor living conditions, inadequate nutrition and health care, negative role models, and substandard schools. But good programs can prepare children for school and possibly help them deliver better coping and adaptation skills that will enable better life outcomes, albeit not perfect ones" (p. 129).

The Chicago Child-Parent Center and Expansion Program (C-CPCEP)

Findings by Reynolds (1994, 1995a, 1995b) on the effects of the C-CPCEP have shown the importance of follow-up into the early school years. Reynolds contrasted the effects of quality preschool and kindergarten experience (combined with active parent involvement) alone, to a continuation of the program through grades 2 or 3, and to a nonintervention comparison group. Effects at both grades 5 and 8 indicated that having more than four years of program experience (regardless of whether it began in preschool or kindergarten) had significantly greater effects on school achievement, special education referral, and grade retention. By eighth grade, six-year participants had half the grade-retention rate of four-year participants and one-third the rate of comparison children. Thus, one or two years of participation (in preschool, kindergarten, or both) was not likely to promote lasting effects. Analyses also indicated that there was a significant relation between degree of parent involvement and educational outcomes for the full-intervention groups (five or six years). The results of both the Carolina Abecedarian Project and the Chicago program support the contention that follow-through programs and high-quality early elementary programs are critical to lasting success of initial preschool gains (Zigler & Styfco, 1994).

Concluding Comments

The great need to reduce the multiple risk factors experienced by many children and families and the success of family- and center-based programs for disadvantaged children have influenced social and legislative policies throughout the United States. Three important changes should be noted that have in part resulted from both the recognized need and the successes of the above efforts. First, the passage of Public Law 99–457 now places the family at the center of early intervention efforts to children diagnosed with developmental disabilities. Second, in 1988

Congress enacted the Comprehensive Child Development Act to establish two-generation family support programs designed to offer comprehensive and integrated services to children from low-income families from birth to entrance to elementary school and also to provide support services to parents to enhance their economic and social self-sufficiency. As a result, 34 model programs were funded by 1992. The first interim report of the Comprehensive Child Development Program (CCDP; U.S. Department of Health and Human Services, 1994) indicated that services are reaching a high percentage of families who were targeted (over 75% receiving home visiting and developmental and health screenings). Unique features of this project include having parents rather than program staff set goals and control program services received, an equal focus on child and family services, and significant efforts at communitywide coordination of services. Preliminary findings compared to a randomized control group across sites indicated initial successes in improved quality of mother-child interaction, more appropriate and positive expectations for child behavior, higher rates of child prosocial behavior, and more CCDP mothers who are enrolled in academic/vocational job training. The 1994 reauthorization of Head Start initiated 68 sites for model demonstrations of Early Head Start to provide comprehensive child development and family support services to low-income families with children under 3 and pregnant women.

Both the family support movement and Head Start have shown dramatic expansion in the past decade. State and local initiatives have led to broad expansion of programs such as PAT, Healthy Start, and others. It appears that the field is moving beyond the past debates regarding the relative value of home- versus center-based and infant versus preschool models. It is now recognized that family-based models that incorporate outreach to the home, offer center-based enriched preschool experiences, and facilitate optimal transitions to elementary school are part of a warranted developmental package of services (H. Weiss, 1993; Zigler, 1994). The major research task now facing the field is to assess how variation in program features, such as the age of the children at program initiation, intensity of delivery of services in both the home and center, and the quality of staff training and support, impact both behavioral and economic outcomes. There is also much to be learned from further in-depth study of the process of community adoption of such programs and how program effectiveness is affected by the coherence and coordination among agency services to children, early childhood education, mental health, schools, and other important stakeholders within communities (Gomby, Larner, Stevenson, Lewit, & Behrman, 1995; R. G. St. Pierre et al., 1995).

Although early intervention projects were initially conceptualized to help children at risk for school failure, these results also have implications for primary prevention in mental health. Many school-related variables (e.g., poor achievement motivation, low aspirations and expectations for educational accomplishment, poor school performance, and school dropout) are risk factors for a variety of later problem behaviors, including substance abuse, unwanted teen pregnancy, and conduct problems (Dryfoos, 1990; Elliott et al., 1989). Early school failure and placement in special education are two critical markers that constitute major turning points in the lives of many children, with long-term implications for future adjustment (Hawkins et al., 1988; Maughan, 1988). Thus, early childhood education, especially when combined with regular home visiting, should be viewed as an innovative mental health strategy that affects many risk and protective factors for diverse problem behaviors (W. Barnett, 1995; Hawkins, Catalano, & Brewer, 1995; Yoshikawa, 1994; Zigler, Taussig, & Black, 1992).

There is considerable debate about why some of these early interventions produce long-term effects. One causal model suggests that family support and preschool education promote cognitive and social skills that result in greater school readiness and a smoother transition to kindergarten. Subsequently, this preparation leads to positive responses by kindergarten teachers, which foster improved student attitudes and motivation about schooling and better school performance in later grades; school success, in turn, serves as a protective factor to prevent behavioral maladjustment and delinquency (Schweinhart et al., 1993). An alternative set of explanations emphasizes the importance of changing parents' behaviors, attitudes, and expectations (in terms of both the child and the school) as primary mechanisms to enhance children's adjustment (Sameroff, 1991). For example, extensive home visitations in high-quality preschool programs may enhance parental competence and involvement, leading parents to become more adept socializers and more involved in their child's education. These changes, in turn, provide firmer foundations for improved family functioning and child behavior. Overall, programs that focus on both children and their socializing environments appear to produce the most long-lasting gains (Hawkins, Catalano, & Brewer, 1995; Seitz, 1991; Yoshikawa, 1994, 1995).

Although some high-quality, comprehensive early interventions have promoted long-term competencies, researchers note that relying too heavily on any one time period or any one context for preventive interventions is a mistake (Zigler & Berman, 1983). Furthermore, although certain early interventions produce significant gains in the program relative to control students, the number of children experiencing school and social difficulties remains considerably higher than acceptable. For these reasons, as children and adolescents face the complex challenges inherent in growing up, it is necessary to create ongoing educational experiences and supports to promote their continued positive social and behavioral development.

PROGRAMS FOR ELEMENTARY-AGE CHILDREN AND ADOLESCENTS

> Whenever change in current educational practice is recommended to ameliorate a contemporary problem, the first question asked is, "will such a change make a positive difference?" An honest answer to this basic question of the impact and outcomes of school health education is a simple yes. . . . Yes, school health education makes a positive difference in the lives of children and adolescents. . . . A less simple, but more complete answer to the question is, yes school health education makes a positive difference, but its ultimate impact on behavior is heavily dependent upon a number of factors, such as teacher training, extent and degree of program implementation, time allotted for instruction, involvement of parents and family, community support, and the overall comprehensiveness of the curriculum. (Seffrin, 1990, p. 153)

Most reviews of competence-enhancement and prevention programs for elementary-age children and adolescents have focused categorically on a discrete area, such as substance abuse (e.g., Dusenbury & Falco, 1997; Hansen, 1992; Hawkins, Arthur, & Catalano, 1995; Tobler, 1986, 1992); delinquency and violence (e.g., Brewer et al., 1995; Murray, Guerra, & Williams, 1997; Tolan & Guerra, 1994); teen pregnancy and AIDS (e.g., Kirby, 1992; Kirby et al., 1994; Miller, Card, Paikoff, & Peterson, 1992; Moore et al., 1995; Sagrestano & Paikoff, 1997); mental disorders (e.g., Durlak & Wells, 1997; Institute of Medicine, 1994); or health (e.g., DeFriese et al., 1990). Occasionally, more comprehensive efforts have examined prevention programs across several psychosocial and health areas, noting that high-risk behaviors often co-occur, have many common risk factors, and may be addressed by similar intervention strategies (e.g., Botvin, Schinke, & Orlandi, 1995; Dryfoos, 1990; Durlak, 1995). Generally, most scientific reviews emphasize the theories, experimental designs, and outcomes of independent programs. They typically do not address a central challenge for school- and community-based practitioners who are the frontline decision makers and implementers of such programs: "how to integrate the many but different successful interventions that have been developed, that is how to 'put all of the pieces together' in one place" (Haggerty, 1988, p. 4). Rather than provide an exhaustive review, this section will describe selected prevention efforts and highlight their implications for a coordinated set of school and community competence-enhancement strategies.

Based on an analysis of approximately 100 programs and interviews with experts, Dryfoos (1990) contended that the main thrust of preventive interventions should be in the schools. Low achievement is a major risk factor for many problem behaviors. Thus, high-quality instruction and learning environments that foster the acquisition of basic fundamental skills are important foci for intervention. Furthermore, as compulsory institutions that have sustained contact with most young people during formative years of development (Rutter, Maughan, Mortimore, & Ouston, 1979), schools may serve as sites for widespread social competence and health-promotion efforts (Bond & Compas, 1989; Dryfoos, 1994, 1995; Durlak, 1995; Zigler & Finn-Stevenson, 1997; Zins & Forman, 1988). Sherman (1994) identified the following factors that help to prevent high-risk behaviors in young people. First, young people need strong basic academic skills and high-quality education; poor attendance, falling behind a grade level, and low achievement are predictive of school failure and other social and health problems. Second, young people can benefit from links to caring adults who provide positive role models, support, and values; parents are the most important sources of nurturing and guidance for young people, and our society must support parents in this role. Third, young people need social competence and health education focusing on problem-solving, decision-making, communication, and life-planning skills as well as information about health and social concerns. Finally, young people require a range of preventive, comprehensive, accessible health services.

The Task Force on Social Competence Instruction for Kindergarten through Fourth-Grade Students (1990), a group comprised of school administrators, teachers, curriculum and instruction supervisors, staff developers, and parents, provided recommendations about promising competence-enhancement programs based on the perspective of educators. They established the following prerequisite characteristics of high-quality programs: (a) sequenced, developmentally appropriate, multiyear, schoolwide instruction; (b) emphases on interrelated cognitive, affective, and behavioral skills as well as prosocial values and attitudes; (c) detailed lesson plans that incorporate sound instructional theory about skill acquisition and application; (d) emphases on improving classroom, school, and community climate; (e) parent-involvement and training activities; (f) training and on-site coaching for school staff and administrators; and (g) program evaluation data indicating positive impact on children's skills and behaviors. These priorities indicate that schools are best served by adopting multiyear programs that coordinate classroom, school, parent, and community interventions and provide sufficient training and support for coordinated, high-quality implementation.

There is growing national support for comprehensive, kindergarten through grade 12 health education that emphasizes personal and social skills training; promotes positive social values and health attitudes; and provides honest, relevant information about health issues such as substance abuse, sex, AIDS, violence, family life, and mental health (Carnegie Council on Adolescent Development, 1995; DeFriese et al., 1990; Mueller & Higgins, 1988; National Commission on the Role of the School and the Community in Improving Adolescent Health, 1990; Report of the National Mental Health Association Commission on the Prevention of Mental-Emotional Disabilities, 1986). The U.S. Department of Health and Human Services, Public Health Service (1990) proposed that by the year 2000 at least 75% of the nation's schools provide high-quality comprehensive health education. This advocacy offers a supportive context for researchers to introduce programming of sufficient scope and length to produce long-term positive behavioral outcomes.

Unfortunately, there is a gap between these multiyear, comprehensive programs and the limited scope and duration of most theory-driven, empirically based programs that scientists design and evaluate (Weissberg & Elias, 1993). Consequently, many schools adopt well-marketed programs that lack documented effectiveness. For example, Dusenbury and Falco (1995) estimated that schools spend more than $100 million annually on drug education curricula. The most aggressively marketed programs are DARE, QUEST, Here's Looking at You 2000, BABES, Project Charlie, Ombudsman, and Project Adventure. Dusenbury and Falco contended that DARE is the only project among these successfully disseminated programs to be adequately evaluated, and the DARE evaluation indicated it was less effective at reducing or preventing drug use behavior than programs that emphasize social skills, general social competencies, and interactive (especially peer-to-peer) teaching strategies (Ennett, Tobler, Ringwalt, & Flewelling, 1994). To date, there have been no controlled, longitudinal field experiments to evaluate the *long-term* effects of K to 12 social competence and health-promotion programs. Weissberg and Elias (1993) proposed that policymakers and funders support long-term collaborations among educators and researchers to design and assess such efforts.

In conclusion, a major challenge for schools across the United States involves addressing Haggerty's challenge of "putting all the pieces together" as they adopt, implement, and institutionalize theory-guided, empirically based practices to educate the whole child. Next, we will describe a selection of diverse multiyear school and community interventions that represent building blocks for comprehensive prevention programming. These programs contain the following research-based approaches: coordinated school-level organizational development and planning; classroom management and instructional practices; social competence promotion; comprehensive health education; and multicomponent strategies involving broader systemic school, family, and community influences on the child (Bronfenbrenner, 1979; Dryfoos, 1994).

Coordinated School-Level Organizational Development and Planning Strategies

In the absence of systematic decision making about how best to identify, adopt, and implement innovative practices, well-intentioned efforts to restructure and improve school functioning may unfortunately create chaos at the organization level, consternation among staff, and confusion among children and their parents. Before schools implement new interventions, they should critically examine how such efforts may duplicate, supplement, or conflict with current programming and priorities. Schools will be more successful at introducing new programs when they have structures and procedures in place to assess multiple informants (e.g., teachers, parents, students) about school resources and needs; make coordinated decisions about appropriate strategies to accomplish identified goals; support high-quality program implementation; and monitor the effects of innovations on the students, staff, and system. We will present two models that illustrate coordinated school-level management and planning.

The School Development Program (SDP)

The SDP introduces processes by which stakeholders collaboratively plan to help schools become learning and caring communities where children feel valued and motivated to achieve (Cauce, Comer, & Schwartz, 1987; Comer, 1988; Comer, Haynes, Joyner, & Ben-Avie, 1996; Haynes & Comer, 1993). Three mechanisms are central to SDP. First, a school planning and management team, composed of school administrators, teachers, support staff, and parents, serves as a representative policymaking and decision-making body. This group creates a comprehensive school plan that identifies social and academic goals, organizes staff development activities designed to address the goals outlined in the plan, and monitors and assesses program processes and outcomes to inform program modifications or establishment of new goals. Second, a multidisciplinary mental health team emphasizes global school climate issues, prevention and enhancement initiatives, and individual teacher and student concerns and problems. Third, a parent program involves parents in all facets of school life, including supporting children in academic and extracurricular activities, general school support, and policy and management issues.

The SDP was initiated in two elementary schools in 1968 as a collaborative effort between the Yale Child Study Center and the New Haven Public School System. As of 1995, the SDP has been implemented in more than 550 schools and 80 school districts across the nation. Haynes, Emmons, Gebreyesus, and Ben-Avie (1996) summarized SDP process and outcome findings and plans for future research. Several cross-sectional, quasi-experimental, and qualitative studies suggest that the SDP process has potential to affect positively school climate and the self-concept, attendance, and achievement of students. Furthermore, a three-year, post-only, follow-up study with 48 subjects indicated that seventh-graders who attended an SDP elementary school had higher achievement test scores, grades, and perceived school and self-competence than a comparison group who attended non-SDP schools. The SDP has developed a sensible, organized set of decision-making and management processes that enhance school-based collaborative planning and program coordination. For this reason, many educators have embraced the model enthusiastically. The SDP group plans to include more rigorous evaluation designs and implementation assessments in future evaluations (Haynes et al., 1996). These steps will help to clarify whether the positive outcomes reported to date occur only in certain types of schools. Furthermore, it is important to examine the extent to which SDP planning processes per se or other aspects of the program (e.g., charismatic principals and SDP facilitators, staff development efforts, parent involvement activities, or choices about specific curricula and programs) influence student academic and behavioral gains.

The Positive Action Through Holistic Education (PATHE) Project

Denise Gottfredson and colleagues (Gottfredson, 1986, 1987; Gottfredson, Fink, Skroban, & Gottfredson, in press; Gottfredson, Gottfredson, & Hybl, 1993) have conducted a series of organizational interventions to improve school functioning and reduce disruptive, antisocial behaviors in middle and high school students. This innovative, organizational intervention approach is exemplified in Gottfredson's (1986) evaluation of Project PATHE, which combined an environmental change approach with direct services to high-risk students to increase educational achievement and reduce antisocial behavior. PATHE established an organizational structure to foster shared decision making among school administrators, teachers, students, parents, and community agencies to review and revise school policies and to implement school change. Team members were trained to assess needs and resources, research problems, define objectives, develop and implement plans, assess progress, and redesign strategies. Other PATHE components included: (a) curriculum and discipline policy review and revision that resulted in staff training in classroom management and the development of classroom and school rules with student participation; (b) schoolwide academic innovations including study skills courses, a free reading period, and cooperative learning instruction; (c) schoolwide climate innovations to promote student and teacher morale, including a school pride campaign and peer counseling; (d) career exploration and job-seeking skills programs; and (e) affective and academic services for low-achieving and disruptive students.

Gottfredson (1986) employed a nonequivalent comparison group design to assess program effects in five middle schools (four program and one comparison) and four high schools (three program and one comparison) located in inner-city Charleston, South Carolina, and a neighboring impoverished rural area. Students in PATHE schools reported significantly less delinquency and drug use and fewer school suspensions and punishments over time, whereas control students reported modest increases in these areas. PATHE students self-reported decreases in alienation and increases in attachment to school (at the middle school level) as well as perceived fairness and clarity of rules, suggesting that PATHE created a sense of belonging in the school. Teachers' assessments of staff morale and teacher-administrator cooperation increased in PATHE schools and declined in comparison schools. Finally, although direct services for high-risk students did not reduce their delinquent behavior, they did enhance educational commitment, relative to controls, as evidenced by rates of graduation, dropout, retention, and achievement test scores. Although these overall positive program findings are qualified by the nonequivalent comparison design, the Gottfredsons' emphasis on the high-quality implementation of coordinated, theory-guided organizational and individual interventions represents a promising model for research and practice.

Classroom Organization, Management, and Instructional Strategies

Brewer et al. (1995) proposed that classroom organization, management, and instructional practices may foster protective factors, including "opportunities to participate actively in learning, skills to establish positive social relationships, and bonding to school and prosocial peers" (p. 70). At the same time, these strategies reduce risk factors such as low commitment to school, early and persistent antisocial behavior, and school failure. An attraction of these approaches is their capacity to improve students' academic achievement in traditional subject areas (e.g., reading, math) in addition to diminishing co-occurring social and health risk behaviors. Reviewing empirical studies, Brewer et al. identified a variety of efficacious practices, such as substantial reductions in class size in the primary grades, ability grouping, proactive classroom management, cooperative learning, computer-assisted instruction, tutoring, and interactive teaching. In this section, we will describe four multicomponent programs involving classroom organization, management, or instructional models that seek to enhance students' school performance and social behavior: Success for All (Slavin et al., 1995), the Child Development Project (Battistich, Schaps, Watson, & Solomon, in press), the Seattle Social Development Project (Hawkins, Catalano, Morrison, et al., 1992), and the School Transitional Environment Project (Felner et al., 1993)

Success for All (SFA)

SFA began in one Baltimore elementary school in 1987; as of the fall of 1995, it was in about 300 schools and 70 districts throughout the United States (Madden, Slavin, Karweit, Dolan, & Wasik, 1993; Slavin et al., 1995; Slavin, Madden, Karweit, Livermon, & Dolan, 1990). SFA is based on the view that success can be achieved with most children in the context of regular education classrooms by providing excellent preschool and primary grade programs; offering high-quality curriculum, instruction, and classroom management; assessing children frequently to assure that they are progressing adequately; and working cooperatively with parents so they can foster students' learning at home. SFA employs a reading curriculum with empirically based practices in beginning reading and cooperative learning. Teachers systematically assess student progress every eight weeks to reevaluate students' reading groups, to decide who is to receive tutoring, and to determine other types of assistance that students may require. Certified tutors work one-to-one in 20-minute sessions with students, mainly supporting students' achievement in the regular reading curriculum rather than working on different objectives. A family support team offers parenting education and involves parents in supporting students' home-based learning. A program facilitator coordinates the program and provides on-site coaching to teachers, tutors, and the family support team. Finally, a representative school advisory committee periodically monitors program progress and collaboratively problem-solves difficulties that arise.

Slavin et al. (1995) summarized data from several SFA evaluations conducted in nine districts across eight states. Overall, these studies indicated that the program increases student reading performance and reduces special education referrals and placements. In a major longitudinal study, Madden et al. (1993) assessed SFA effects in five Baltimore schools over a three- to four-year period. Program students, relative to matched controls in comparable schools, manifested significant gains on several individually administered reading tests. Retentions in grade were reduced considerably. Whereas 31% of fourth-grade-age children in control schools had been retained, only 4% of students at Abbottston Elementary (the initial SFA school) had been retained. Furthermore, attendance improved modestly over time, especially at SFA schools with strong family support programs. Another important finding is that SFA effects appear to get stronger the longer the program has been implemented in a particular setting (Slavin et al., 1995). Madden et al. contended that their data imply that *early and continued intervention* is required to ensure the cognitive progress of at-risk students throughout their schooling. It is important to determine how students in SFA elementary schools will fare in middle and high school. Furthermore, it is desirable to broaden future evaluations to assess children's social and health behaviors. Finally, given the expense of SFA, it is important to determine which program components are essential and how less costly versions of the program might affect students' school performance and behavior.

The Child Development Project (CDP)

The CDP is a comprehensive, elementary school program in which teachers and administrators build supportive relationships with students and encourage students to establish similarly warm, inclusive relationships with each other (Battistich et al., in press; Battistich & Solomon, 1995; Battistich, Solomon, Watson, Solomon, & Schaps, 1989; Solomon, Watson, Delucchi, Schaps, & Battistich, 1988). Five instructional practices encompass CDP's core: (a) cooperative learning activities that encourage student teamwork; (b) a literature-based, values-rich, multicultural language arts program that emphasizes students' critical thinking about relevant social and ethical issues; (c) "developmental discipline" techniques that emphasize proactive, democratic teaching approaches that foster responsibility, establish prosocial norms, and build conflict-resolution skills; (d) classroom and schoolwide community-building activities that introduce projects for students, teachers, parents, and extended family members; and (e) "homeside" activities that enhance communication between students and parents, build bridges between school and home, and encourage students' understanding about their family's heritage and culture.

One longitudinal evaluation focused on children from three CDP and three comparison suburban elementary schools as they moved from kindergarten through fourth grade between 1982 and 1987 (Battistich et al., 1989; Solomon et al., 1988). Observational, teacher-questionnaire, and student-interview data indicated significantly higher scores in CDP classrooms on five measures of the utilization of program-related practices: cooperative activities, developmental discipline, social understanding, prosocial values, and helping activities. CDP also positively changed children's cognitive problem-solving skills in the areas of interpersonal sensitivity, consideration of others' needs, means-ends thinking, and prosocial conflict resolution (Battistich et al., 1989). Observational data revealed positive changes in program children's supportive and friendly behavior as well as spontaneous prosocial behavior.

In 1991, the CDP initiated a longitudinal, multisite, quasi-experimental demonstration trial at 24 geographically diverse elementary schools (12 program and 12 comparison) from six school districts around the United States (Battistich et al., in press; Battistich & Solomon, 1995). Preliminary analyses after two years indicated positive effects on classroom teaching practices, student classroom behavior, and students' self-reported sense of community, school-related attitudes, concern for others, conflict-resolution skills, sense of efficacy, and altruistic behavior. Battistich et al. examined the CDP's impact on the substance use and delinquent behavior of fifth- and sixth-graders, and reported positive effects on alcohol use for the overall sample. Next, based on changes in observational measures of program practices, they divided the 12 demonstration schools into three groups of high, moderate, and low implementation. Students in high-implementation schools, relative to those in matched comparison schools, used less marijuana and engaged in fewer delinquent acts over time. Based on the research of CDP's developers, it appears that the CDP's combined emphases on the school environment, school-family partnerships, classroom instructional approaches, and curriculum content have promise for enhancing students' sense of school community and social competence. Independent evaluations, involving random assignment of this well-conceptualized and well-designed program to schools, will provide a more definitive picture of CDP's efficacy.

The Seattle Social Development Project (SSDP)

The theory that guides the SSDP, the social development model, proposes that positive social bonds to family and school develop when (a) family and school experiences foster skills for successful participation; (b) children have opportunities for active involvement; and (c) responsible adults and peers consistently reward children for constructive, prosocial involvement (Hawkins & Weis, 1985). The SSDP evaluated a six-year, multicomponent intervention for multiethnic urban students who entered first grade in eight Seattle Public Schools in 1981 (Hawkins, Catalano, Morrison, et al., 1992; O'Donnell, Hawkins, Catalano, Abbott, & Day, 1995). The SSDP trained classroom teachers in instructional methods with three major components: proactive classroom management, interactive teaching, and cooperative learning. These teaching approaches were used in combination with (a) classroom-based cognitive and social skills training in first and sixth grade; and (b) parent training that emphasized child behavior management in first or second grade, academic support in second or third grade, and preventing drug use and antisocial behavior in fifth or sixth grade.

Employing a true experimental design, Hawkins, Catalano, Morrison, et al. (1992) found that program students (by fifth grade), relative to controls, reported significantly better family management and communication practices as well as greater bonding to family and school. Program students were also significantly less likely than controls to have initiated alcohol use and delinquent behavior, although the groups did not differ in their attitudes and beliefs about these behaviors. O'Donnell et al. (1995) examined the SSDP's impact on low-income subgroups of males and females at the end of sixth grade and reported mixed effects. Relative to controls, intervention girls and boys evidenced positive impact on 7 and 6 of 35 outcome variables, respectively. Suggestive findings indicated that intervention girls perceived more opportunities for classroom involvement, more reinforcement for participation, and were less likely to have smoked cigarettes; intervention boys had higher achievement test scores and grades and were rated by teachers as more socially competent and persistent in school work. Although this ambitious program-evaluation effort indicates some potential for comprehensive, school-based risk-reduction strategies, it also suggests how factors such as student mobility, poor program-implementation quality, and lack of parent involvement can diminish program benefits.

The School Transitional Environment Project (STEP)

Normative transitions to large middle and high schools are often associated with declines in students' academic, socioemotional, and behavioral adjustment. Felner and colleagues (Felner & Adan, 1988; Felner et al., 1993; Felner, Ginter, & Primavera, 1982) have developed STEP to change the ecological features of the school setting in ways that reduce the adaptational demands of coping with the complexity of new school environments; increase access to support and guidance from school staff and other students; and enhance students' feelings of connectedness within the school. STEP reorganizes the school social system so that incoming students are assigned to units of 60 or 100 students or "smaller schools within the school." Homerooms and classes in primary academic subjects are composed of only peers in the same unit, and these classrooms are located in close physical proximity to each other. STEP also restructures the homeroom teachers' role so that they act as the main administrative and counseling link among the students, their parents, and the rest of the school. Teachers receive consultation from school guidance staff as well as training in team-building and student advisory skills to implement this redefined role.

Felner et al. (1982) reported that ninth-grade urban STEP students had significantly more positive perceptions of their school and teachers than did comparison students at the end of the intervention year. They also showed significantly smaller declines in academic performance and attendance during the transition between junior and senior high school. Long-term results indicated a significantly lower dropout rate for STEP students (24.3%) than for comparison students (42.7%) and better attendance throughout high school (Felner et al., 1993). Felner et al. (1993) also reported results from a two-year longitudinal study with a diverse sample of middle school students in which they found positive STEP effects on students' perceptions of school experiences, self-reported socioemotional adjustments, and teacher ratings of behavior. In conclusion, ecologically based restructuring of schools into smaller, more cohesive and supportive units is eminently sensible and developmentally appropriate for middle and high school students. Although the findings of Felner and colleagues are positive, their interpretation is qualified by the fact that pretest measures are not available for most outcome variables. Furthermore, replication attempts by other researchers have not been as positive (Reyes & Jason, 1991). Future research should examine the specific nature and content of homeroom teachers' interaction with students. Perhaps a combination of ecological restructuring and specific competence-enhancement activities will produce stronger, more consistent findings—especially with high-risk students.

Social Competence–Enhancement Programs

Given changing societal conditions, some researchers and practitioners contend that coordinated school-based planning and decision making, high-quality curriculum and instructional practices, and supportive school environments may be necessary but not sufficient to prevent high-risk behavior in young people (e.g., Consortium on the School-Based Promotion of Social Competence, 1994; The National Commission on the Role of the School and the Community in Improving Adolescent Health, 1990). They argue that educationally based life-skills, health education, and social and emotional learning programs are needed to develop productive, healthy, competent members of society (Carnegie Council on Adolescent Development, 1995).

Ever since the President's Commission on Mental Health (Report of the Task Panel on Prevention, 1978) highlighted the promise of competency training, much research has assessed the efficacy of this approach (Consortium on the School-Based Promotion of Social Competence, 1994). Research indicates that information- or knowledge-only programs have minimal effects on children's behaviors (Kirby, 1992; Tobler, 1986). In contrast, programs that teach broadly applicable personal and social competencies—such as self-control, stress management, problem solving, decision making, communication, peer resistance, and assertiveness—have yielded significant benefits regarding children's social adjustment, assertive and aggressive behavior, peer sociability, and coping with stressors (Elias et al., 1986; Gesten et al., 1982; Greenberg, 1996; Rotheram-Borus, 1988; Shure & Spivack, 1982, 1988; Weissberg, Gesten, Carnrike, et al., 1981; Weissberg, Gesten, Rapkin, et al., 1981).

Competence-enhancement programs that focus independently on the child are not as effective as those that simultaneously educate the child and instill positive changes in the environment. Consequently, it is important to distinguish between person-centered and ecologically oriented competence-enhancement training programs. Training programs are considered person-centered when skills are taught in the absence of creating environmental supports for continued skill application in daily interactions. For example, programs offered by "outside experts" who fail to coordinate efforts with a child's teacher or parents exemplify this approach. In contrast, ecologically oriented programs emphasize the teaching of skills, fostering meaningful opportunities to use skills, and establishing structures to reinforce effective skill application (Hawkins & Weis, 1985). From this perspective, the success of skills-training programs may depend largely on their attention to changing socialization patterns and supports in the intervention setting (Elias & Weissberg, 1990). For example, ecologically oriented problem-solving programs try to introduce a common social-information processing framework that children and teachers can use to communicate more effectively about problem situations (Shure & Spivack, 1988; Weissberg, Barton, & Shriver, 1997). In other words, they try to change not only the child's behavior, but also the teacher's behavior, the relationship between teacher and child, and classroom and school-level resources and procedures to support adaptive problem-solving efforts (Weissberg et al., 1989).

Person-centered skills training programs that teach students competencies without focusing on changing the environmental settings in which they function will produce limited benefits for a select group of children at best. Combining classroom instruction with efforts to create environmental support and reinforcement from peers, family members, school personnel, health professionals, other concerned community members, and the media increases the likelihood that students will adopt positive social and health practices (Perry & Jessor, 1985; Price, Cioci, Penner, & Trautlein, 1993). This section will summarize three school-based programs that emphasize ecologically oriented, social competence–enhancement programs (Elias & Clabby, 1992; Greenberg, 1996; Weissberg, Barton, & Shriver, 1997), and then will describe a fourth multiyear, multicomponent competence-enhancement effort that combines school, family, peer, and community programs (Conduct Problems Prevention Research Group, 1992).

The Improving Social Awareness–Social Problem Solving (ISA-SPS) Project

Elias and colleagues (Elias & Clabby, 1989, 1992; Elias, Gara, Schuyler, Branden-Muller, & Sayette, 1991; Elias et al., 1986) have designed a widely disseminated social competence–promotion program for elementary school children. During the instructional phase of the curriculum, teachers use scripted lessons to introduce classroom activities with the following general format: (a) group sharing of interpersonal successes, problem situations, and feelings that children wish to share with their teacher and classmates; (b) a brief overview of the cognitive, affective, or behavioral skills to be taught during the lesson; (c) written and video presentations of situations that call for and model skill application; (d) discussion of the situations and ways to use the new skills; (e) role plays encouraging behavioral rehearsal of skills in diverse, developmentally relevant situations; and (f) summary and review. This format emphasizes a number of features to foster the maintenance, generalization, and transfer of learning (Ladd & Mize, 1983). Then, during the application phase, teachers use problem-solving dialoguing methods to encourage student use of adaptive coping strategies to handle real-life problems effectively. Also, teachers integrate problem-solving and social-awareness activities into the regular classroom routine and their daily instruction.

Students receiving a two-year program emphasizing self-control, group participation and social awareness, problem solving, and social decision making evidenced skill acquisition and gains on teacher-rated behavior, sociometric ratings, and self-reported ability to cope with everyday problem situations. When cohorts of elementary-trained students were evaluated in the middle school to assess program effects on their transition, results from a quasi-experimental design suggested that they were better able than controls to handle a range of middle school stressors (Elias et al., 1986). Finally, cohorts of elementary-trained students were followed up in high school up to six years after exposure to the intervention. Condition by gender interactions indicated that control boys had higher rates of involvement with alcohol, violent behavior to others, and self-destructive/identity problems, whereas control girls had higher rates of cigarette smoking, chewing tobacco, and vandalism against parental property (Elias et al., 1991).

The Social-Competence Promotion Program for Young Adolescents (SCPP-YA)

Weissberg and his colleagues (Caplan & Weissberg, 1990; Kavanagh, Jackson, Gaffney, Caplan, & Weissberg, 1990; Weissberg, Caplan, Bennetto, & Jackson, 1990; Weissberg, Barton, & Shriver, 1997) designed a 45-session program for middle school students that provides classroom-based instruction and establishes environmental supports aimed at (a) promoting social competencies (conveyed via a "stop light" model) such as self-control, stress-management, responsible decision-making, social problem-solving, and communication skills; (b) enhancing the quality of communication between school personnel and students; and (c) preventing antisocial and aggressive behavior, substance use, and high-risk sexual behaviors.

The SCPP-YA problem-solving module improved program students, relative to controls, in terms of the number, effectiveness (e.g., fewer aggressive and passive alternatives and more nonconfrontational and compromise solutions), and planfulness of alternative solutions they generated to problem situations (Weissberg & Caplan, 1994). Program students also employed more adaptive stress-management strategies when faced with situations that made them upset or anxious (Caplan et al., 1992). Teacher ratings indicated that program students improved more than controls in constructive conflict resolution with peers, impulse control, and popularity (Weissberg & Caplan, 1994). These positive changes were reflected in ratings by both program teachers and teachers who observed students in other class settings such as music and gym. Furthermore, while the frequency of self-reported antisocial and delinquent behavior increased 36.8% in pre- to postassessments for control students, such behavior was stable for program students (Weissberg & Caplan, 1994). Arthur, Weissberg, and Caplan (1991) assessed the long-term effects of problem-solving training in a one-year follow-up study in which sixth- and seventh-graders who received two years of training were compared with those who received one year or no training. Only students with two years of training maintained improvements in problem-solving skills, prosocial values, and teacher-rated peer relations and behavioral conduct. These findings suggest that although one year of intervention may produce short-term benefits for students, multiple years of instruction may be needed to promote more enduring improvements.

Finally, program teachers have reacted positively on multiple levels. On anonymous surveys to maximize candor in responding, most teachers (96%) indicated that the curriculum addressed issues that are important for their students. They reported that SCPP-YA classes most positively affected students in the following areas: feeling good about themselves; recognizing the negative effects of drugs and avoiding drugs; recognizing behaviors that may lead to pregnancy and AIDS; and identifying behaviors that reduce the risk of pregnancy and AIDS (Kasprow et al., 1991). More than 90% of the teachers enjoyed teaching the lessons and felt confident about their ability to teach the program. Importantly, Caplan, Weissberg, and Shriver (1990) found that 89% of the teachers said the program helped them to communicate better with students; 85% indicated that the program helped them to deal with stress better in their own lives; and 96% believed the program had positive effects on them in applications of problem solving to their own problems.

Promoting Alternative THinking Strategies (PATHS) Curriculum

In a series of trials, Greenberg and his colleagues (Kusche & Greenberg, 1995) have examined the effectiveness of the PATHS Curriculum. This multiyear model for the elementary years is an extensive hybrid curriculum that combines models of self-control, emotional awareness, and social problem solving. Two unique features of PATHS are its central focus on emotion recognition and emotion regulation as necessary processes for effective coping and its focus on ongoing generalization techniques used in the classroom throughout the day. First used with deaf children (in the medium of both sign language and speech), a waiting-list control design indicated that the use of the PATHS Curriculum led to significant improvements in social-cognitive skills, teacher-reported social competence, and reading achievement (Greenberg & Kusche, 1993).

Using different versions of PATHS in regular education and special-needs classes, a randomized clinical trial with 300 second- and third-graders indicated the effectiveness of PATHS for both groups of children (Greenberg, 1996; Greenberg, Kusche, Cook, & Quamma, 1995). Compared to controls, regular education children showed posttest improvements in emotional understanding and social problem solving. At one-year follow-up, differences emerged on both teacher and self-report of conduct problems, teacher ratings of adaptive behavior, and cognitive abilities related to social planning and impulsivity. For special-needs children, results indicated posttest improvement on teacher-rated social competence, child report of depressive symptoms, and emotional understanding and social-cognitive skills. At one-year and two-year follow-up, both teachers and children separately reported significant improvements in both internalizing (e.g., depression and somatic complaints) and externalizing behavior problems, as well as improved social planning and decreased cognitive impulsivity.

Finally, a multiyear version of PATHS is being tested as the universal component of the Fast Track Program, which includes a randomized clinical trial of 50 elementary schools. Results using the classroom as the unit of analysis indicated that the use of PATHS in first grade improved teacher ratings of classroom conduct problems, students' sociometric report of the average level of peer aggression, and observers' ratings of the classroom atmosphere. In addition, quality of teacher implementation was significantly related to individual differences in classroom outcomes in the intervention sample (Conduct Problems Prevention Research Group, 1996a, 1996b).

The Fast Track Program

As children in any community population vary widely in both their risk factors and rate of disorders, it is surprising that comprehensive interventions have not been developed and evaluated that combine universal together with selective or targeted interventions in an integrated model. Recently, a consortium of prevention researchers has developed such a model, Fast Track, which is intended to provide a comprehensive longitudinal model for the prevention of conduct disorders and associated adolescent problem behaviors (Conduct Problems Prevention Research Group, 1992). This randomized clinical trial involves 50 elementary schools in four U.S. urban and rural locations. The universal intervention includes teacher consultation in the use of a series of grade-level versions of the PATHS Curriculum throughout the elementary years. The targeted intervention package includes a series of interventions that involve the family (e.g., home visiting, parenting skills, case management), the child (e.g., academic tutoring, social skills training), the school, the peer group, and the community. Targeted children and families are identified by a multistage screening for externalizing behavior problems during kindergarten and the 10% of children with the most extreme behavior problems in schools in neighborhoods with high crime and poverty rates. Results of the first year of intervention (post-first grade) include significant improvements in social-cognitive skills, reading skills, parent social cognitions regarding parenting, observations of appropriate discipline by parents and warmth by children in the home, lower rates of disruptive behavior during school observations, and greater peer liking by sociometric assessment. Fast Track is predicated on a long-term model (i.e., the intervention will continue through middle school) that assumes that prevention of antisocial behavior will be achieved by building competencies and protective factors in the child, family, school, and community. The results of the first year indicate strong evidence for improved social and academic development, although only partial indication of fewer conduct problems.

Targeted Prevention Programs

Although general competence-enhancement programs may enhance children's critical thinking skills and social behaviors, their positive impact does not consistently generalize to more problem-specific domains such as substance use, high-risk sexual behavior, or violence (Durlak, 1983). Combining general personal and social skills training—for example, in problem solving and decision making—with attempts to affect student knowledge, attitudes, and behavioral competence in specific domains appears to be a more promising approach for preventing specific problem behaviors (Caplan & Weissberg, 1989). Recent literature reviews and meta-analyses have suggested that certain targeted school and community prevention programs have achieved at least modest reductions in adolescent drug use, high-risk sexual behavior, and delinquency (e.g., Botvin, Schinke, et al., 1995; Brewer et al., 1995; Dryfoos, 1990; Durlak, 1995; Kirby et al., 1994; Moore et al., 1995; Tobler, 1986, 1992; Tolan & Guerra, 1994). Evaluations of these programs have increased in rigor during the past few decades, with more sophisticated research designs; larger, more racially and ethnically diverse samples; more valid and reliable assessment measures; greater concern for implementation fidelity; longer follow-ups; and more thorough data analyses.

Given space limitations, we will first cite the research of several investigators who have evaluated promising prevention programs in the areas of alcohol and drug use (e.g., Caplan et al., 1992; Ellickson & Bell, 1990; Ellickson, Bell, & McGuigan, 1993; Hansen & Graham, 1991; Pentz et al., 1989; Shope, Kloska, Dielman, & Maharg, 1994); high-risk sexual behavior (e.g., Allen, Kuperminc, Philliber, & Herre, 1994; Eisen, Zellman, & McAlister, 1990; Green & Sollie, 1989; Howard & McCabe, 1990; Jemmott, Jemmott, & Fong, 1992; Kirby, Barth, Leland, & Fetro, 1991; Koo, Dunteman, George, Green, & Vincent, 1994; Miller et al., 1993; St. Pierre, Mark, Kaltreider, & Aikin, 1995; Zabin, Hirsch, Smith, Streett, & Hardy, 1986; Zabin et al., 1988); and delinquency and aggression (The Committee for Children, 1988, 1989, 1990; Gainer, Webster, & Champion, 1993; Jones & Offord, 1989; Olweus, 1991; RCCP Research Team, 1996).

Next, we will highlight two exemplary prevention research trials that illustrate practices that could be incorporated into a comprehensive competence-enhancement effort. The first characterizes a theory-driven, classroom-based program that combines general and targeted skills training to prevent drug abuse (Botvin, Baker, Dusenbury, Botvin, & Diaz, 1995; Botvin, Baker, Dusenbury, Tortu, & Botvin, 1990; Botvin & Tortu, 1988). The second project involves a six-year, multicomponent, drug abuse prevention program including a school-based educational effort, parental involvement in homework, mass media programming, community organization, and health policy components (Pentz et al., 1989).

The Life Skills Training (LST) Program

Since 1977, Botvin and colleagues (Botvin, Baker, et al., 1995; Botvin et al., 1990; Botvin & Tortu, 1988) have developed and evaluated the LST program to prevent drug use in young adolescents. The three-year LST intervention consists of 15 class periods in seventh grade, 10 sessions in eighth grade, and 5 sessions in ninth grade. Classroom teachers teach students cognitive-behavioral skills for building self-esteem, making responsible decisions, problem solving, communicating effectively, developing interpersonal relationships, and asserting personal rights. The LST program also emphasizes skills and knowledge specifically related to resisting social and media influences to use tobacco, alcohol, and other drugs. These skills are taught through a variety of methods, including demonstration, role play, and behavioral homework assignments for out-of-class practice, feedback, and reinforcement for adaptive skill application.

Results from 10 separate evaluations of the LST program have demonstrated program effects on tobacco, alcohol, and other drug use, as well as on hypothesized attitudinal, informational, and skill mediational variables (Botvin, Schinke, & Orlandi, 1995). Evaluation results have indicated 40% to 80% reductions in initial drug use behavior and impact on more serious indicators of substance abuse. A major six-year longitudinal randomized evaluation of the LST program involved 3,597 predominantly White, middle-class twelfth-graders from 56 schools who participated in the three-year program (Botvin, Baker, et al., 1995). Analyses with the full sample indicated that the prevalence rates of weekly and monthly cigarette smoking, problem drinking, and weekly polydrug use (i.e., weekly cigarette smoking, alcohol use, and marijuana use) were significantly lower in the LST groups. Supplementary analyses on a "high-fidelity" subgroup of 2,752 students who received at least 60% of the LST program yielded even stronger effects; there were up to 44% fewer drug users and 66% fewer polydrug users. Botvin, Baker, et al. (1995) concluded that drug abuse prevention programs conducted in junior high school can produce meaningful reductions in tobacco, alcohol, and marijuana use at least three years postintervention when they teach a combination of social resistance and general life skills for three years, and when they are properly implemented.

The Midwestern Prevention Project (MPP)

In line with the ecological perspective, Pentz et al. (1989) contended that many school-based prevention programs may not produce significant and sustained behavioral changes because of a lack of integration between school-based training and community-based interventions, the mass media, and other environmental influences outside of school that conflict with the concepts taught in school. They proposed that multilevel, multicomponent prevention efforts that coordinate the efforts of multiple socializing influences—including parents, peers, community leaders, local school and government administrators, and mass media programmers—may be needed to produce long-term social, psychological, and health benefits. Specifically, Pentz et al. developed a substance abuse prevention program that combined 10 sessions of classroom-based peer-resistance skills training, 10 homework sessions interviewing parents and family members about issues related to drug abuse prevention, mass media programming, and community organization. Outcome analyses with 22,500 sixth- and seventh-graders indicated significantly lower prevalence rates for alcohol, cigarette, and marijuana use for the program participants compared with control subjects. Positive effects were sustained three years following the classroom intervention, with low-risk and high-risk subjects showing significant reductions in tobacco and marijuana use (Johnson et al., 1990).

Conclusions

Reviews of targeted prevention programs have identified several common, effective components (e.g., Botvin, Schinke, & Orlandi, 1995; Dryfoos, 1990; Dusenbury & Falco, 1995; Moore et al., 1995). First, effective interventions are based on a sound research foundation and are theory driven. Programs most successful at reducing high-risk behaviors place greater emphasis on both generic and problem-specific skills and focus less on general health information. They convey developmentally and culturally appropriate messages about the social influences promoting health-compromising behaviors, accurate information about the short-term consequences of these behaviors, prosocial norm-setting messages intended to modify normative expectations, and cognitive-affective-behavioral skills for resisting negative social influences. Effective programs employ interactive teaching techniques to promote the active participation of children, such as role plays, small-group discussions and activities, and opportunities for positive peer leadership as opposed to didactic lectures by adults. Multiyear programs have more enduring impact than briefer programs. Although much research remains to be done, there is growing agreement that the impact of school-based interventions are strengthened by peer, family, community, and media components. Finally, high-quality training and follow-up support to program deliverers to ensure implementation fidelity appears essential. Because research findings suggest that children have limited capacities to transfer and generalize skills, attitudes, and information for handling stressors in one domain to address problems in another (Dodge et al., 1986), a major task for future research involves developing skills-attitudes-information training models that target multiple social and health outcomes in the context of the same intervention. The next section focuses on comprehensive health education programs that lay the foundation for much broader impact.

Comprehensive Health Education Programs

The National Commission on the Role of the School and the Community in Improving Adolescent Health (1990), a joint task force established by the National Association of State Boards of Education and the American Medical Association, recommended that "young people receive a new kind of health education, a sophisticated, multi-faceted program that goes light years beyond present lectures about 'personal hygiene' or the four food groups" (p. 36). Similar to social competence–enhancement and targeted prevention programs, a major component of beneficial health instruction utilizes innovative behavioral teaching techniques—such as modeling, role play, performance feedback, and positive reinforcement—to encourage students to apply newly acquired concepts, skills, and attitudes to real-life social situations and health decisions. In addition, positive program effects have been enhanced by small-group participatory activities and peer leadership opportunities that teach students to work cooperatively and model prosocial values and behaviors for their schoolmates (Benard, Fafoglia, & Perone, 1987; Tobler, 1986). Finally, effective instruction in health education requires teaching methods that change the ways children and adults communicate about high-risk behaviors and problem situations.

This section will describe four landmark health education research efforts that document the efficacy of this approach. The first two involve large-scale, classroom-based training for fourth- to seventh-graders (Connell, Turner, & Mason, 1985) and junior high/middle school and high school students (Errecart et al., 1991). The third describes a five-year health education program for sixth- to tenth-graders in the context of a community intervention to enhance students' healthy food selection, physical activity, and nonuse of tobacco and alcohol (Perry, Klepp, & Sillers, 1989). We will also describe a school-linked health center that emphasizes the prevention of high-risk sexual behavior (Zabin, 1992).

The School Health Education Evaluation (SHEE)

The SHEE was a comprehensive research study involving more than 30,000 fourth- through seventh-graders in 1,071 classrooms (688 program and 383 comparison classes) from 20 states (Connell & Turner, 1985; Connell et al., 1986; Connell, Turner, Mason, & Olsen, 1986). The SHEE was commissioned to evaluate the School Health Curriculum Project (SHCP), a widely used health education program sponsored by the U.S. Public Health Service since 1967. The SHCP incorporates a "hands-on" learning approach that encourages critical thinking and peer discussion about health issues and involves family members and community agencies as resources. The program, which was taught five days a week for 10 to 12 weeks, involved students in diverse educational experiences, including learning center activities, experiments, role plays, film viewing, readings, and peer-group discussions to affect their health information, attitudes, and behaviors.

The SHCP was compared along with four other promising curricula: the Health Education Curriculum Guide; Project Prevention; and Reading, 'Riting, 'Rithmetic; and High Blood Pressure. Although random assignment did not take place, analyses with considerable statistical power indicated no group pretest differences in health-related knowledge, attitudes, or self-reported practices. All programs positively affected students; however, results expressed in terms of mean effect sizes indicated the largest overall effects for SHCP on students' program-specific knowledge (ES = .86), general health knowledge (ES = .83), attitudes (ES = .29), and practices (ES = .68). The quality and extent of program implementation related to student outcomes. Positive effects on students' knowledge, attitudes, and practices stabilized at about 50 hours of class instruction (Connell et al., 1985). In addition, two years of SHCP instruction produced stronger effects than one year of training (Connell & Turner, 1985).

The Teenage Health Teaching Modules (THTM) Evaluation

The THTM project was a large-scale, quasi-experimental evaluation with 4,806 junior high/middle school and high school students from 149 schools (Errecart et al., 1991; Gold et al., 1991; Ross, Luepker, Nelson, Saavedra, & Hubbard, 1991). The 16 THTM modules are organized by developmentally based health tasks of concern to adolescents instead of by content areas. Modules help students to develop five skills: self-assessment, communication, decision making, health advocacy, and healthy self-management. Nine of the 16 modules were selected for implementation in the current study. The four modules for junior high/middle school students were "Being Fit," "Having Friends," "Living with Feelings," and "Preventing Injuries." The five modules for senior high school students were "Eating Well," "Handling Stress," "Protecting Oneself and Others," "Promoting Health in Families," and "Planning a Healthy Future." The intervention required 36 to 38 45-minute classes taught during a 16- to 18-week semester.

Results, analyzed separately for junior and senior high students, revealed significant gains in health knowledge (ESs = .99 and .75), attitudes (ESs = .36 and .75), and practices (ESs = .36 and .42). Significant changes on self-reported priority health behaviors (i.e., cigarette smoking, use of smokeless tobacco, drinking alcohol, illegal drug use, seat belt use, and consumption of fried foods) occurred for senior high but not for junior high students (Errecart et al., 1991). Furthermore, teachers trained prior to teaching THTM implemented the program with greater fidelity and had more positive effects on students' knowledge and attitudes than did untrained teachers (Ross, Luepker, et al., 1991). Future THTM research must clarify the program's limited impact on the health behavior of junior high/middle school students. Gold et al. (1991) suggested that the content of the specific modules tested with this age group may not have focused sufficiently on the targeted outcomes. In addition, follow-up studies on multiple years of training are needed to assess the enduring effects of more intensive training.

The Minnesota Heart Health Program (MHHP) and the Class of 1989 Study

The MHHP provided the opportunity to implement and assess a five-year school health education program, for students moving from sixth through tenth grade, conducted in the context of a communitywide intervention to change eating, physical activity, and smoking habits (Kelder, Perry, & Klepp, 1993; Kelder, Perry, Klepp, & Lytle, 1994; Perry, Kelder, Murray, & Klepp, 1992; Perry et al., 1989). The MHHP's goal was to reduce morbidity and mortality from cardiovascular disease between 1980 and 1990 in three north central U.S. communities compared with three matched reference communities. The primary MHHP intervention components included cardiovascular risk screening for 70% of the adults; direct education regarding smoking, exercise, and healthy eating; citizen task forces to design annual risk factor educational campaigns; community quit-smoking contests; environmental changes in grocery stores and restaurants; mass media education via television, radio, and newsprint; adult education in work sites and churches; and youth education.

The Class of 1989 Study focused on cohorts of young adolescents in one of the two MHHP communities (Fargo, North Dakota, and Moorhead, Minnesota) and a matched reference community (Sioux Falls, South Dakota). Students were originally surveyed in 1983 when they were sixth-graders and prior to the initiation of any larger MHHP efforts. Subsequently, they were surveyed annually for seven years until they graduated from high school in 1989. The Fargo-Moorhead students also participated between 1983 and 1987 in school-based behavioral health programs emphasizing healthy eating habits, regular physical activity, and nonuse of tobacco and alcohol (Perry et al., 1989). These programs enhanced students' social skills, strengthened their ability to resist pressures to engage in health-compromising behaviors, generated health-enhancing alternatives, changed peer group norms, and provided alternative healthy role models. All programs used peer leaders, who were elected by their classmates and trained by community staff, as key trainers of new skills and information within the classroom setting. Reported findings regarding the intervention's long-term impact on smoking indicated that 14.6% of the twelfth-graders in the intervention community smoked weekly, compared with 24.1% of their counterparts in the reference community. Long-term assessments of healthy food choices, physical activities, and exercise showed positive effects for females but not males (Kelder et al., 1993; Kelder et al., 1994). These longitudinal findings offer some optimism regarding the long-term health benefits of multiyear school-based and complementary communitywide programs. A crucial next step is to determine whether similar strategies can be used to prevent a broader range of high-risk behaviors (e.g., Wagenaar & Perry, 1994). In addition, future research should replicate these findings beginning with a younger sample of students.

The Self Center

Although school and community education programs affect the health attitudes and behaviors of large numbers of young people, personal one-to-one communication between adolescents and primary health care providers represents an additional critical component of comprehensive health-promotion programming—especially with high-risk students (The National Commission on the Role of the School and the Community in Improving Adolescent Health, 1990). Many adolescents respect medical personnel and believe they can offer accurate answers to medical questions, including questions about sex, sexually transmitted diseases, and reproductive health. When adolescents and clinic staff have positive relationships, the adolescent may be especially receptive to information and counseling. As adolescents approach puberty, it is an ideal time for health care personnel to discuss sexual risk-taking behavior and ways to avoid risk.

The Self Center was a comprehensive school-linked reproductive health service program for inner-city junior and senior high school students, conducted collaboratively by the Johns Hopkins School of Medicine and the Baltimore City Department of Education (Zabin, 1992; Zabin et al., 1986; Zabin et al., 1988). The clinic provided services to a high school located across the street and a junior high school that was four blocks away. A social worker and a nurse offered sex education presentations in homeroom classes once each semester and were available for two and a half hours each day in a school health suite for group discussions, individual counseling, and to schedule clinic appointments. Clinic services included group education, individual counseling, and reproductive health care. The Self Center staff trained and supervised student peer leaders as resources to help with informal group discussions, serve as peer counselors, and publicize Center activities.

Using a quasi-experimental comparison group design, Zabin et al. (1986) found that students exposed to the Center's services increased in contraceptive knowledge and use compared to their counterparts at nonparticipating schools. Fewer than 20% of females in schools with the program for two years had unprotected sex, whereas 44% to 49% of students from comparison schools used no birth control. Also, postponement of sexual initiation by seven months (from 15 years and 7 months to 16 years and 2 months) was observed for high school students exposed to the program for three years. Finally, although the program and comparison schools had similar pregnancy rates at the start of the evaluation, pregnancy rates in Self Center schools declined by 30.1% after 28 months, whereas they increased by 57.6% in comparison schools. Although access to high-quality, free medical services, professional counseling, and open communication probably contributed to positive student outcomes, more research is needed to clarify which combination of program components produce positive effects.

School-, School District–, and Community-Based Efforts to "Put All the Pieces Together"

This section describes a school-level (Dryfoos, 1994), a school district–based (Shriver & Weissberg, 1996), and a community-based (Hawkins, Catalano, & Associates, 1992) model for establishing coordinated, multicomponent programming to enhance students' academic, social, and health behaviors. Our major goal is to articulate some of the processes involved in planning and implementing these comprehensive intervention efforts.

Full-Service Schools

Dryfoos (1994, 1995) presented a challenging vision for a full-service school in which she described how schools and communities can provide comprehensive programs to foster positive development in children and their families. According to Dryfoos (1995, p. 152), full-service schools could offer the following core components:

1. *Quality education provided by schools:* effective basic skills, individualized instruction, team teaching, cooperative learning, school-based management, healthy school climate, alternatives to tracking, parent involvement, effective discipline.
2. *Services provided by schools or community agencies:* comprehensive health education, health promotion, social skills training, preparation for the world of work (life planning).
3. *Support services provided by community agencies:* health screening and services, dental services, family planning, individual counseling, substance abuse treatment, mental health services, nutrition/weight management, referral with follow-up, basic services (housing, food, and clothes), recreation, sports, culture, mentoring, family welfare services, parent education and literacy, child care, employment training/jobs, case management, crisis intervention, community policing.

Dryfoos (1994, 1995) pointed out the importance and complexity of involving school personnel, parents, students, and community agencies in planning these efforts. She and others (Knapp, 1995; Stallings, 1995; Wang, Haertel, & Walberg, 1997) have elaborated on the challenging, innovative evaluation strategies required to assess the implementation and outcomes of full-service schools.

The New Haven Social Development Project

In 1987, the New Haven superintendent of schools (Weissberg, Shriver, Bose, & DeFalco, 1997) convened a school-community task force (composed of teachers, parents, administrators, students, pupil-personnel staff, community leaders, university researchers, and human service providers) to examine high-risk behaviors of students in the areas of drug use, teen pregnancy and AIDS, delinquency and aggressive behavior, truancy, and school failure. The task force found that significant percentages of students engaged in high-risk behaviors that jeopardized their academic performance, health, and futures. They also acknowledged that many of these problems had common roots, such as poor problem-solving and communication skills, limited constructive afterschool opportunities, and a lack of monitoring and guidance by positive adult role models.

To address these concerns, the task force recommended the creation of a comprehensive K to 12 social development curriculum. The superintendent and the board of education established a Social Development District Steering Committee and broadly representative elementary, middle, and high school curriculum committees with the following assignments: (a) articulate the broad mission and goals for the Project; (b) identify a scope and sequence of social development curriculum with student learning objectives at each grade level; (c) design or select social development and health-promotion programs to address these learning objectives; (d) coordinate school, parent, and community activities to support classroom instruction; and (e) design professional development programs to train and support school teachers, administrators, and pupil-personnel staff in program implementation.

Within a year, the superintendent and board established a Department of Social Development with a district-level supervisor and a staff of facilitators to strengthen the organizational infrastructure to support the successful systemwide implementation of social development initiatives. This structure ensured broad involvement by school, parents, and community members. Furthermore, the Department of Social Development collaborated with the Yale University Psychology Department to provide high-quality training, support, and on-site coaching to teachers who implemented the curriculum and to school-based planning and management teams who coordinated classroom instruction with complementary school and community programming (Shriver & Weissberg, 1996; Weissberg et al., in press).

The Social Development Project's mission emphasized educating students so that they (a) develop a sense of self-worth and feel effective as they deal with daily responsibilities and challenges; (b) engage in positive, safe, health-protective behavior practices; (c) become socially skilled and have positive relationships with peers and adults; (d) feel motivated to contribute responsibly to their peer group, family, school, and community; and (e) acquire a set of basic skills, work habits, and values as a foundation for a lifetime of meaningful work.

Since 1989, the Department of Social Development accomplished three main goals. First, it phased in a K to 12 curriculum with 25 to 50 hours of classroom-based instruction at each grade. The curriculum emphasized self-monitoring, problem solving, conflict resolution, and communication skills; values such as personal responsibility and respect for self and others; and content about health, culture, interpersonal relationships, and careers. Second, it created educational, recreational, and health-promotion opportunities at the school and community levels to reinforce classroom-based instruction. These included programs such as mentoring, peer-mediation and leadership groups, an Extended Day Academy with after-school clubs, health center services, and an outdoor adventure class. Third, each school's mental health planning team focused attention on the climate of the school and the coordinated implementation of school-based social development initiatives supported by all segments of the school community.

The New Haven Social Development Project has conducted several process and pre- to postoutcome evaluations (e.g., Caplan et al., 1990; Kasprow et al., 1991, 1992, 1993; Schwab-Stone et al., 1995). Anonymous consumer satisfaction surveys revealed that the program is perceived very positively by students, parents, teachers, and administrators. Teacher ratings of children's behavior suggested that programming benefited the social skills of 83% of a randomly selected sample of 1,400 kindergarten through third-grade students; further, these students showed improvements in frustration tolerance and acting-out behavior (Kasprow et al., 1992). Assessments of sixth-, eighth-, and tenth-graders' self-reported social and health attitudes and behaviors revealed positive changes from 1992 to 1994 in the percentages of students who participated in fights, felt safe at school or in the neighborhood, worried about getting AIDS, or felt positive about their future prospects; in contrast, students also reported increased tobacco, alcohol, and marijuana use during this time (Schwab-Stone et al., 1995). Without a comparison group, the causes of these changes cannot be identified. Perhaps the New Haven Social Development Project's major contribution has been its pioneering efforts to design, implement, and institutionalize a comprehensive, coordinated, districtwide, kindergarten through twelfth-grade model to enhance students' academic, social, and health behavior.

Communities That Care (CTC)

CTC is a comprehensive, communitywide, risk- and protective-factor prevention strategy that mobilizes community members to plan, implement, and evaluate coordinated positive youth development programs (Hawkins, Catalano, & Associates, 1992; Hirachi, Ayers, Hawkins, Catalano, & Cushing, 1996). The CTC process has three phases. First, key community leaders (e.g., the mayor, chief law enforcement officer, superintendent of schools, business and religious leaders) are oriented to the project. If they commit to the project, they agree to serve as an oversight board and appoint a prevention board of diverse community members. Second, the community board is trained to conduct a risk-and-resource assessment that provides an empirical foundation to identify priorities for preventive action. Third, during a planning and implementation phase, the board selects programs from a menu of interventions that have been evaluated for efficacy in addressing their priority risk areas and develops detailed action plans for program implementation. Baseline assessment data serve as the benchmark against which to measure community progress in targeted areas. Process evaluations and case examples demonstrate that the CTC strategy provides a promising framework for coordinating school and community prevention efforts in a range of communities. An important next step will be to evaluate the CTC approach in a controlled field trial.

Concluding Comments

In an ideal world, the combined efforts of responsible parents, quality child care, health care services, and family-centered communities would provide healthy and nurturing foundations so that as many young children as possible could come to school ready to learn (Carnegie Task Force on Meeting the Needs of Young Children, 1994). In addition, these young children would enter schools that manage, plan, and implement the highest quality academic programming and instruction and establish comprehensive, developmentally appropriate programming and organizational structures that foster children's social competence, emotional development, health, and citizenship. Multicomponent interventions in which peers, parents, and community members reinforce school-based academic, social, and health promotion efforts represent a central approach to address adequately the widespread behavioral problems of young people (Carnegie Council on Adolescent Development, 1995; Dryfoos, 1990, 1994; Zigler & Berman, 1983). Another key challenge involves coordinating school-based programming with effective programs offered during the nonschool hours (e.g., Carnegie Council on Adolescent Development, 1992; Jones & Offord, 1989; Price et al., 1993; Quinn, 1995; Tierney, Grossman, & Resch, 1995; Wagenaar & Perry, 1994).

Elias (1995) argued that comprehensive prevention programs should convey the value that positive academic, health, and social development are necessary to succeed in college and the work world. He contended that the carryover of health-related skills into everyday classroom routines and developmentally salient life issues is essential for maximal retention and flexible application. Thus, multifaceted programs should incorporate a common cognitive-affective-behavioral skills framework that students and teachers may apply to self-care; positive relationships with parents, siblings, peers, and adults; using alternatives to violence; preventing substance use, unwanted pregnancies, and sexually transmitted diseases; nutrition; cardiovascular fitness; and performing responsibly and effectively at school, at work, and in the community.

Ultimately, comprehensive programs that address academic, social, and health behaviors have greater potential to endure in school settings than discrete, short-term interventions that target a single, categorical problem behavior (DeFriese et al., 1990; Weissberg & Elias, 1993). Reviews of targeted prevention efforts indicate that some incorporate similar strategies to affect students' skills, attitudes, perceptions of norms, and practices (Botvin, Schinke, & Orlandi, 1995; Consortium on the School-Based Promotion of Social Competence, 1994; Dryfoos, 1990). From a long-term planning perspective, it is preferable to establish integrated models that provide age-appropriate information integrated across the domains of mental-emotional, social, and physical health. Competence and health-promotion programming should start before students are pressured to experiment with risky behaviors and continue through adolescence. Establishing K to 12 programming serves two important longitudinal functions. First, it provides continuous instruction, encouragement, and reinforcement to support students' ongoing, developmentally appropriate positive behavior. Second, K to 12 programming helps to build system recognition and support, thus increasing the likelihood of enduring program maintenance.

Prevention programs must be designed and delivered in ways that are acceptable to and reach populations at risk. The topics covered at each grade level should be shaped both by students' developmental needs and social experiences and by the values and the norms that parents and school staff hope to inculcate. Recently, innovative models showing greater cultural sensitivity to sociodemographically diverse students have been developed (Botvin, Schinke, & Orlandi, 1995; Hudley & Graham, 1995; U.S. General Accounting Office, 1992). For example, the GAO report indicated that many promising programs for poor rural or inner-city minority youth hire racially, ethnically, and culturally compatible staff drawn from the community served by the program. These programs also use culturally appropriate program activities, including ethnically relevant theater, music, and dance productions. Future research must clarify the extent to which culturally sensitive prevention approaches will improve the efficacy of program efforts—especially with economically and educationally disadvantaged youth (Botvin, Schinke, & Orlandi, 1995; Hudley & Graham, 1995). Also, programs must better address the needs and concerns of large numbers of students who have begun to engage in high-risk behaviors. It is critical to integrate classroom-based instruction with school-based health clinics, pupil-personnel service delivery systems, and community-based youth agencies to improve the continuity of services for students already experiencing serious social, psychological, and health problems (National Commission on the Role of the School and the Community in Improving Adolescent Health, 1990).

ESTABLISHING AND EVALUATING COMPETENCE-ENHANCEMENT AND PREVENTION PROGRAMS: TRAINING PRIORITIES, DEBATES, AND FUTURE DIRECTIONS

> There could be no wiser investment in our country than a commitment to foster the prevention of mental disorders and the promotion of mental health through rigorous research with the highest of methodological standards. Such a commitment would yield the potential for healthier lives for countless individuals and the general advancement of the nation's well-being. (Institute of Medicine, 1994, p. 550)

The preceding review offers evidence that important and meaningful progress has been made in competence-enhancement and prevention research with families, schools, and communities since President Kennedy's challenge in 1963. There have been advances in the theory, design, and evaluation of programs, and there is a growing number of demonstration projects with documented efficacy of beneficial impact. In turn, research findings have influenced public policy regarding how schools and communities can provide effective models of intervention for children and families.

Over time, the researchers, practitioners, and policymakers have developed a more realistic perspective on the necessary intensity and comprehensiveness of programming to prevent high-risk behavior and promote positive youth development, especially with children and adolescents growing up in high-risk environments (Panel on High-Risk Youth, National Research Council, 1993). Dryfoos (1990) summarized the following common findings regarding successful prevention programs for young people:

1. There is no single program component that can prevent multiple high-risk behaviors. A package of coordinated, collaborative strategies and programs is required in each community.
2. Short term preventive interventions produce time-limited benefits, at best, with at-risk groups, whereas multiyear programs are more likely to foster enduring benefits.
3. Preventive interventions should be directed at risk and protective factors rather than at categorical problem behaviors. With this perspective, it is both feasible and cost-effective to target multiple negative outcomes in the context of a coordinated set of programs.
4. Interventions should be aimed at changing institutions, environments, and individuals.

In spite of substantial gains in prevention research during the past 35 years, it is important to acknowledge that considerable progress is needed to affect more tangibly the lives of American children and families. Only a small group of researchers has designed and evaluated multiyear, multicomponent programs that target multiple social and health outcomes. Few successful efficacy trials have been replicated by independent investigators, and there have been even fewer attempts to evaluate the implementation process and impact of widely disseminated program models. In summary, although a solid scientific base is being created, the most important knowledge regarding preventive interventions will come from the next generation of prevention researchers!

Thus far in this chapter, we have argued that social environmental and behavioral trends among young people call strongly for the establishment of effective, enduring school and community competence-enhancement and prevention programs. We also reviewed developmental-ecological theory and intervention research supporting the promise of these programs. Given the urgent national need and the potential of prevention approaches, it is striking that the country's commitment to training prevention researchers, who could improve the quality of these efforts, has been so limited. The IOM report (1994) commented: "The current preventive intervention research training effort is organized in such a fashion and funded at such a low level that an outside observer could reasonably conclude that policy makers wish to phase out investment in this field" (p. 456).

Recently, the National Institutes of Health (1996) proposed a national plan for prevention research in which they called for increases in federal funding to increase training capacity in prevention research. In this section, we will highlight core training needs required by graduate students and postdoctoral trainees who aspire to become prevention researchers. We will focus on issues related to the conceptualization, design, implementation, institutionalization, and evaluation of preventive interventions. Finally, we will describe two contrasting models of prevention research—Prevention Science versus Collaborative Community Action Research—and contend that a combination of these approaches will advance prevention practice substantially.

Training Competence-Enhancement and Prevention Researchers

> Here we see the need for a new breed of investigator: one who can synthesize research from many disciplines, distill the essentials from a variety of programs, and develop new theories and methods to implement and then evaluate, the essential elements of an integrated intervention. We need researchers who can put the pieces together based upon a comprehensive theory of theories, and put the essential components of comprehensive programs in place in one school system. This is one of the many areas where it would appear that we need a broader approach by investigators who would link disciplines, develop new theories, apply old ones to new settings, and then evaluate these comprehensive programs. (Haggerty, 1988, p. 5)

Price (1983) described four roles for prevention researchers: the problem analyst, innovation designer, field researcher, and diffusion researcher. To carry out these roles effectively, prevention researchers who specialize in programming for young people require training in the following areas: developmental epidemiology and knowledge of social-environmental and behavioral trends; a life span developmental and ecological theoretical orientation with sensitivity to human diversity; knowledge of social, cognitive, and biological risk and protective factors for social, health, and mental/emotional problems; culturally appropriate assessment approaches with diverse populations; design and implementation of multicomponent prevention programs in natural settings—particularly with families, schools, and communities; multidisciplinary approaches to the prevention of problem behaviors such as substance use, unsafe sex, and delinquency; clinical field trial research designs and data-analytic techniques for longitudinal prospective interventions; methods to design, conduct, and evaluate collaborative, community action research; strategies to disseminate effective prevention practices; and principles of scientific integrity and ethics in conducting prevention research. Greater efforts during the twenty-first century must be made to establish freestanding multidisciplinary prevention research training programs as well as to strengthen prevention training for students within human service and behavioral science disciplines such as education, epidemiology, nursing, pediatrics, psychiatry (clinical, community, developmental, health, and social), psychology, public health, public policy, social work, and sociology.

Competence-enhancement and prevention research must be carried out systematically to establish and disseminate beneficial practices (Durlak, 1995; Institute of Medicine, 1994; Weissberg et al., 1989). As a part of problem analysis, epidemiological information about the extent of problem behaviors or stressful environmental circumstances informs scientists and practitioners about important priorities for preventive intervention. Some researchers then focus on problem behaviors or disorders in individuals and determine risk and protective factors that affect their incidence. Specifying markers and causal processes that enhance or mitigate the likelihood of negative biopsychosocial outcomes provides direction about the structure and content of preventive interventions (Hawkins, 1995; Institute of Medicine, 1994; Rutter, 1987). Alternatively, researchers may identify stressful life events or experiences that produce negative consequences in a significant proportion of the population, and mount interventions to prevent the occurrence of these circumstances or people's capacities to cope effectively with them (Report of the Task Panel on Prevention, 1978).

Well-trained problem analysts are not tied to a single methodological tradition. They utilize combinations of epidemiological information, survey data, ethnographic information, participant observation, and interviews with different people (e.g., children, parents, teachers, community leaders) holding diverse perspectives about the nature and causes of problems as well as ways to address them. Core objectives of problem analysis involve perceiving the problem from the cultural perspective of the population thought to be at risk as well as setting-related risks and resources that influence the development of positive and negative outcomes. The problem analyst's capacity to communicate what has been learned about modifiable risk and protective process provides a foundation for the conceptualization and design of preventive interventions (Price, 1983).

Although basic research can provide a generative foundation for creating preventive interventions, there is a separate group of executive steps that must be taken to establish enduring, beneficial prevention programming (Cowen, 1980). Five interrelated phases of program development include conceptualization, design, implementation, institutionalization, and evaluation (Weissberg et al., 1989). Innovation designers, who have broad knowledge about individual and organizational change methods, emphasize program conceptualization and design. Field researchers and diffusion researchers focus on evaluating the process and outcomes of interventions as they are implemented, disseminated, and institutionalized. Price (1983, p. 292) highlighted the need for "political sensitivity and scientific hardheadedness" to conduct prevention research effectively. We will describe considerations related to conceptualizing, designing, implementing, and institutionalizing prevention programs, and then highlight important design and methodological issues in evaluating them.

Conceptualization

Program conceptualization involves explicitly articulating the outcomes an intervention intends to achieve, the methods that will be used to accomplish these objectives, and theoretical models of human and organizational change that guide program strategies and practices. Theory, basic and applied research findings, and field experiences inform the identification of promising target variables on both individual and environmental levels that will mediate positive behavioral outcomes. Influential theoretical models of behavior change that have provided a foundation for program design to prevent diverse health problems include social-cognitive learning theory (Bandura, 1986, 1994), the health belief model (Becker, 1974; Janz & Becker, 1984; Rosenstock, Strecher, & Becker, 1994), the theory of reasoned action (Fishbein & Ajzen, 1975; Fishbein, Middlestadt, & Hitchcock, 1994), the theory of self-regulation and self-control (Karoly & Kanfer, 1982), adolescent problem behavior theory (Jessor, 1993; Jessor & Jessor, 1977; Perry & Jessor, 1985), the social development model (Hawkins & Weis, 1985), the theory of triadic influence (Flay & Petraitis, 1994), and the developmental-ecological model (Bronfenbrenner, 1979). When conducting school- and community-based preventive interventions, programs based on these models must be integrated with theoretical frameworks of community and organizational change (e.g., Fullan & Stiegelbauer, 1991; Hall & Hord, 1987; Kanter, Stein, & Jick, 1992; Kelly, 1987, 1988; Keys, 1986; Sarason, 1982).

Design

Innovation design involves translating conceptual models of behavioral and organizational change into replicable programs that explicitly describe methods to teach individuals the coordination of cognition, affect, and behavior to address socially relevant tasks adaptively, and to create environmental settings, opportunities, and resources that support using adaptive social and health behavior (Weissberg et al., 1989). Well-designed programs specify the scope of program content and the planned sequence by which behavioral skills and positive self-perceptions are enhanced; are based on effective educational and social learning principles; ensure that training is developmentally and culturally appropriate; coordinate different levels of programming, when appropriate, at the family, school, peer, and community levels; and identify organizational structures and policies that support program objectives. A central responsibility of innovation designers involves the development of detailed training manuals and materials that increase the likelihood that an intervention will be implemented with fidelity.

Implementation

Concern for high-quality program implementation stems from the recognition that well-conceptualized and -designed programs are necessary, but not sufficient, to produce behavior changes in target groups (Botvin et al., 1990; Connell et al., 1985). Potential for positive impact is diminished when program implementers are poorly trained; have inadequate support, time, or resources for effective program delivery; or lack the skills or motivation to provide competent training. Well-conceptualized and -designed programs that are implemented with low integrity may appear ineffective when in fact they are beneficial. Schools and community settings must allocate sufficient time and resources for proficient staff training, program planning, ongoing supervision, on-site coaching, and program monitoring to ensure high-quality implementation. A key shortcoming in many preventive intervention studies is that investigators assess program outcomes but fail to examine systematically the quality of program implementation. Research has identified clear links between the quality of implementation and program outcomes (Blakely et al., 1987; Botvin et al., 1990; Connell et al., 1985; Gottfredson et al., 1993; Ross, Luepker, et al., 1991). Overall, the results indicate that preimplementation training and on-site coaching enable service providers to implement programs with greater integrity and to have more positive effects on the children they serve. These findings highlight the importance of providing high-quality training, supervision, and monitoring for those who implement prevention programs. Thus, field researchers must possess more than research design and evaluation skills. They also must have the interpersonal skills to collaborate with the administrators, program implementers, and community groups who create the context for program implementation.

Institutionalization

Berman and McLaughlin (1978) reported that successful interventions are not easily disseminated; their replications in new sites usually produce less positive effects than their performance in the original site; and these projects have difficulty sustaining their success over a number of years. Given these realities, researchers must clarify which systems-level structures, practices, and policies enable effective programs to endure (McLaughlin, 1990). For example, program designers of school-based social-competence and health education efforts must ensure that program content and training approaches comply with evolving state and federal guidelines for drug, AIDS, and violence prevention. In addition, the successful institutionalization of prevention programs requires that program designers, deliverers, and recipients continuously monitor, assess, adapt, and improve programs to mesh with the evolving priorities, norms, and ecologies of the setting in which they are implemented (Price & Lorion, 1989; Price & Smith, 1985; Tolan et al., 1990).

Concluding Comments

Weissberg et al. (1989) argued that researchers should document that they have effectively conceptualized, designed, and implemented a preventive intervention before evaluating its effects. Without such documentation, it is difficult to explain which program characteristics contributed to positive outcomes or what shortcomings must be addressed when interventions fail to have impact. In contrast to some of the state-of-the-art research efforts reviewed in the previous sections, Durlak and Well's (1997) recent meta-analysis of 177 evaluations of primary prevention programs for children and adolescents provided disquieting data regarding the state-of-the-practice of most preventive intervention research.

Durlak and Wells (1997) classified only 36% of the studies as articulating specific intervention goals, whereas the remaining 64% were characterized as providing very broad or vague goals. Only 29.3% of the studies indicated that an intervention program manual was available, and 53.2% of the studies provided only general program descriptions. The race and ethnicity of participants were not reported in 48% of the studies—a problematic finding in a field where the sociocultural appropriateness of interventions is critical. Finally, because few investigations provided information about implementation, Durlak and Wells could not examine relations between the extent or quality of implementation efforts and outcomes. Given these shortcomings, it seems necessary to reiterate priorities for conducting sound evaluations of school and community interventions (Lorion, 1983; Moore et al., 1995; Price & Smith, 1985).

Standards for High-Quality Preventive Intervention Research

Flay and Cook (1996) identified seven major purposes for program evaluation.

1. *Impact assessment:* Does the intervention affect hypothesized mediators and targeted outcomes?
2. *Implementation assessment:* How well is the intervention delivered?
3. *Accountability:* Are the funds being spent in cost-effective and cost-beneficial ways?
4. *Formative:* Does information regarding implementation process or consumer reactions suggest needs for mid-course modifications or future program development?
5. *Community building:* Can an ongoing self-monitoring and self-assessment system be established so that communities can identify continuing program effectiveness, new needs, and areas for improvement?
6. *Theory development and testing:* Can we improve our conceptual models for intervention to enhance the design of future efforts?
7. *Social learning:* What lessons about intervention can be applied to the next generation?

Given limited resources and funding for programs, it is critical to evaluate the effectiveness of preventive interventions to ensure that such efforts have their intended effects without producing unintended negative consequences. Rigorous evaluations are necessary to provide credible data about what works and how it works. Such information is important to policymakers, funders, and service providers, who want to know about the impact of the programs being implemented. It is also critical for researchers and program developers so they have a solid foundation from which to improve their conceptual models, intervention practices, and evaluation strategies for establishing enduring, beneficial programs. There is no shortage of opinions about the types of programs that might enhance social competence and prevent high-risk behaviors. However, there remains a pressing need for more compelling empirical evidence about which programs work, under which circumstances and with whom, and why they work. We will now elaborate on critical research and methodological issues involved in conducting high-quality prevention research.

Specify Program Goals, Intended Outcomes, and Theoretical Models of Change

Every program evaluation should be designed based on the intervention's goals and intended outcomes; a realistic time frame in which outcomes will be achieved and maintained; and the theoretical models of change that guide intervention strategies (C. Weiss, 1995). The overall goals should be expressed in terms of concrete, feasible intervention objectives that can be measured reliably and validly. Program developers, implementers, and evaluators should be clear about specific positive outcomes they intend to enhance and specific negative outcomes they plan to reduce. Furthermore, they should indicate whether changes will be apparent after a short period of time or only after some time has passed. They should specify, for example, how long changes have to be maintained to consider the program a success. Finally, it is important to present a clear model explicating how changing selected personal and environmental risk and protective factors will help achieve desired outcomes.

Identify the Target Sample and Relevant Subsamples

Program evaluators must precisely identify the target population for the intervention, being clear about behavioral goals for different subgroups. For example, is a classroom-based AIDS prevention program expected to encourage virgins to delay having sex and nonvirgins to stop having sex? Or is the goal with nonvirgins to promote condom use or to refrain from sex with multiple partners? Similarly, should the goal of a high school alcohol abuse prevention program be nonuse for all students, drinking in moderation for some, or not driving or riding in a car when the driver is intoxicated? If one's conceptual framework posits different goals for different subgroups, it is critical to assess, prior to or early in the intervention, the proportion of the target population that meets the criteria for each subgroup. For example, the content of a ninth-grade sex education program might differ considerably if 90% of the participants were virgins or if 90% had already had sex with more than one partner.

In addition, sufficient demographic data should be provided about participants so that readers may determine the limits of generalizability from outcome results. Child participants should be described minimally in terms of their age, gender, grade level, race, ethnicity, family structure (e.g., one- or two-parent homes), and parents' educational, occupational, and socioeconomic background. It is also important to provide information regarding the settings or systems through which interventions are provided, the schools young people attend, and the neighborhoods in which they live.

Describe the Intervention and Measure the Quantity, Quality, and Process of Implementation

Program evaluations must describe the content and structure of the intervention; the number, duration, and frequency of intervention contacts; the demographic and educational background of program deliverers; and how the program implementers are trained, supervised, and supported. Then processes must be put into place to confirm that the services were delivered as intended. Dobson and Cook (1980) cautioned evaluators about the dangers of Type III errors, that is, measuring the effects of an intervention that one assumes has been implemented properly, when in reality it may have been delivered inappropriately or not at all. For example, without measuring implementation quality, one may incorrectly judge a program ineffective when, in fact, negative outcome findings are due to shortcomings in service delivery. Another important outcome of intervention research may be the finding that sufficient quality of implementation for a desired intervention cannot be achieved. This may be the case for some efficacy trials that are difficult to replicate in the context of an effectiveness trial or a wider-scale dissemination effort.

Scheirer (1987) suggested that it is preferable to begin program evaluations with the tentative stance that an unclear innovation is being provided in an uncertain fashion. Accordingly, prior to measuring outcomes, a comprehensive evaluation should specify the program components that are supposed to be implemented, identify which ones are actually delivered, and measure how effectively they are delivered. There is a critical need to assess the processes involved in each stage of the implementation process. For example, there has been little discussion of the processes that have been found most effective in building university-community coalitions for conducting and evaluating programs. Further, to conduct collaborative community initiatives that involve numerous agencies, schools, and government leaders, there is a need to develop guidelines that are likely to lead to effective working relationships (see Annie E. Casey Foundation, 1995, for an excellent example studying such processes). Another critical task involves identifying social system components (e.g., organizational structures and policies, characteristics of program deliverers) that foster high-quality implementation and increase potential for institutionalization. Finally, there are numerous issues to be studied in how to effectively disseminate (going to scale) and institutionalize empirically validated prevention models.

Some researchers have developed systematic methods to operationalize the core program components of social and educational innovations (Blakely et al., 1987; Fullan & Stiegelbauer, 1991; Hall & Hord, 1987). Through structured interviews and observations, they reliably measure the degree to which such components are implemented with fidelity to a validated program model or adapted by program implementers to meet perceived ecological needs of the context in which the program is being delivered. Using these approaches, they examine how program implementation processes relate to behavioral outcomes and to program institutionalization.

For example, Blakely et al. (1987) operationalized seven nationally disseminated education and criminal justice projects in terms of 60 to 100 specific program components that were judged to be implemented in an ideal, acceptable, or unacceptable manner. They also examined the extent to which local program adopters adapted these projects by changing or adding to essential program components. They reported: (a) program adopters generally implemented their programs at acceptable levels; (b) high-fidelity adopters produced more positive outcomes than low-fidelity adopters; and (c) program implementers who introduced new strategies to augment the impact of faithfully implemented components produced the most positive outcomes. These findings indicated that combining implementation fidelity with appropriate adaptation led to the best results. Weissberg (1990) noted that a combination of factors—including the content and structure of an intervention, the manner in which it is implemented, relationships between program implementers and participants, and a variety of system-level variables—all interact to influence the outcomes that a program produces as well as the program's future viability.

Conduct Cost-Benefit and Cost-Effectiveness Analyses

It is important to evaluate the costs of prevention programs relative to both their expected benefits as well as their cost compared to other interventions (Plotnick, 1994; Yates, 1994). Price et al. (1989) identified as critical the need for economic analysis of program effectiveness, including assessing the cost of program services, analyzing benefits relative to costs, and examining the relative cost of different programs to solve the same problem (i.e., cost-effectiveness). Given a more cost-driven and outcome-driven environment that has been generated by budgetary issues, market forces, and the advent of managed care models to contain health care costs, demonstrations of cost-benefits and cost-effectiveness will play a larger role in policy decisions to support the dissemination of competence-enhancement and prevention programs.

An initial step in assessing the economic impact of prevention programs involves a careful economic analysis of the costs of targeted problem outcomes, including associated benefits related to desisting or resisting risk behaviors. For example, what are the true costs of school dropout? Whereas one benefit of remaining in school is the differential income fostered by high school completion and associated earnings, there are also other, less quantifiable benefits (Barnett, 1993a, 1993b; Cohen, 1996). Recent examples of informative economic analyses include assessing the health and educational costs of birth defects (Waitzman, Romano, & Scheffler, 1994), hospital costs of firearms-related injuries (Kizer, Vassar, Hary, & Layton, 1995; Max & Rice, 1993), and charting the costs of a criminal career pathway, school dropout, and a career of hard substance use (Cohen, 1996; Haveman & Wolfe, 1984; T. Miller, Cohen, & Weirsma, 1996).

Although a program's efficacy should not *necessarily* be based solely on cost-effectiveness (some programs are expensive, e.g., foster care, but exist for the greater good), this will be one criterion of increasing salience to both consumers and policymakers. Future research must prospectively plan effective cost-benefits models that involve cost data collection from the outset, both on direct and possible indirect effects of the intervention. For example, the greatest cost savings identified in the Elmira Nursing Study were not benefits accrued directly to the target child of the intervention, but instead the cost savings of a substantially greater interval to the next pregnancy, which led to significant reductions in welfare, WIC, and other associated health and welfare costs (Olds et al., 1993). Cost-benefit analyses have also demonstrated the substantial savings accrued by diverse programs including the prevention of preterm birth (Ross et al., 1994) and the treatment of substance abuse (Harwood, Hubbard, Collins, & Rachal, 1988). Such evaluation models will require close collaboration between economists and social scientists.

If the costs of problem outcomes can be estimated, cost-benefit analyses can be conducted through clinical trials as well as less experimental models (Levin, 1983; Plotnick, 1994; Zerbe & Dively, 1993). An excellent example of a benefit-costs analysis using the clinical trials model is that of the Perry Preschool Project, which compared the benefits-to-costs ratio for both the intervention and comparison samples (Barnett, 1985, 1993a). These estimates examined the costs of the intervention compared to the benefits accrued from reduced special education costs, reduced criminal justice system and incarceration costs, increased wages, and lower use of welfare dollars. These studies found that the net benefits (minus costs) were estimated at approximately $90,000 per child. Even when the effects of crime and delinquency were omitted, economic benefits of the program were estimated to be approximately $30,000 per participant.

Once general estimates of cost savings accrued for each person who is protected by an intervention from initiating the target behaviors are known, these figures can be utilized in nonexperimental studies to indicate the potential economic effect of an intervention. For example, assume a high school runs a $300,000 dropout prevention program that includes a homework center and tutoring support. Given that the lifetime benefit of dropping out of school is estimated at between $200,000 and $400,000 (Cohen, 1996), to be cost-beneficial to society the program would need to reduce dropout for a certain number of children relative to previous recent estimates for that ecology. However, if cheaper programs could lead to the same outcome, then they would be shown to be more cost-effective.

There is also a growing literature on cost-effectiveness analyses that compare relative cost-to-effectiveness ratios of different programs. For example, analyses have suggested that legislative and communitywide programs to increase the use of bicycle helmets are more cost-effective than school-based interventions (Hatziandreu et al., 1995), and that high school incentive programs for graduation and parent training may be more cost-effective in prevention of delinquency than home-based infant and preschool programs (Greenwood, Model, Rydell, & Chiesa, 1996). However, in a context in which legislative changes have already been made (i.e., helmets are mandated), other interventions may show differing outcomes.

Benefit-cost analyses can provide important data in which the interests of the researcher, practitioner, and policymaker converge. Given the current interest in accountability models in prevention practice and the recent estimation of the costs of maladaptive outcomes, benefit-cost and cost-effectiveness analyses should be a central focus of future efforts in prevention research.

Use Some Form of Comparison Sample

Comparison groups should be employed whenever possible. It is not sufficient to report proportions of the intervention group that engaged in positive or antisocial behaviors without providing any indications as to whether these outcomes represent improvements over what might have occurred without the intervention. There are a variety of evaluation strategies that may be employed to provide some perspectives on program effects, including randomized controlled trials, field experiments comparing alternative treatments, nonequivalent control group designs, comparison-created groups from existing survey databases, comparison individuals matched with treatment individuals, and time series designs with data collection at multiple time points (Campbell & Stanley, 1963; Cook & Campbell, 1979; Grossman & Tierney, 1993; Hollister & Hill, 1995; Kaftarian & Hansen, 1994; Moore et al., 1995; Price & Smith, 1985). Although all of these research designs have potential to yield useful data, some scholars have argued that prevention research should be built primarily on findings from randomized controlled trials because "such a high standard lends credence to the results of these studies" (Institute of Medicine, 1994, p. 216). The next section highlights the virtues of this approach, some of its limitations, and alternative methodologies that are needed to advance prevention theory, research, and practice.

Prevention Science and Collaborative Community Action Research

> The choice of research methodologies is a major issue in examining preventive interventions and research trials designed to determine their outcomes. It heavily determines whether evidence is compelling that a preventive intervention could have produced its intended effect. The ideal research design in a preventive trial is a randomized controlled trial of adequate size embedded in a longitudinal study. (Institute of Medicine, 1994, p. 221)

> We should encourage the researcher to collaborate with research participants unless there is some good reason not to do so. From the empowerment perspective, it is wrong to assume that distancing oneself from research participants is always the best way to know anything useful. If the research method is itself disempowering (e.g., by disregarding the constructed reality of a participant), the process of doing research may be more likely to contribute to a degrading rather than to an empowering outcome, particularly if the person studied has a stake in the research findings. In short, for the empowerment researcher collaboration must be part of the research design—it begins "before the beginning" (Sarason, 1972). (Rappaport, 1990, pp. 55–56)

PS and CCAR represent two divergent approaches for developing and evaluating preventive interventions (Coie et al., 1993; Connell, Kubisch, Schorr, & Weiss, 1995; Cook, Anson, & Walchli, 1993; Flay & Cook, 1996; Heller, 1996; Institute of Medicine, 1994; Knapp, 1995; Robins, 1992; Tolan et al., 1990). These differing models profoundly influence the entire research enterprise and affect the manner in which research is defined, conceived, conducted, and interpreted. They arise from different historical and scientific traditions and, as with many schisms in the social sciences, indicate two valid and widely differing viewpoints on the nature of theory, research, and evidence (Cronbach, 1975; Gage, 1996; Gergen, 1985; Knapp, 1995). Next, we will identify features that are common to PS and CCAR, highlight ways in which the PS and CCAR frameworks differ, and offer thoughts about how integrating the productive and appropriate application of these research approaches is needed to advance significantly future competence-enhancement and prevention research and practice.

Prevention Science

The PS model has emerged from an interface of public health methodology, life course developmental psychology, and developmental psychopathology (Coie et al., 1993; Institute of Medicine, 1994). The PS approach is exemplified in the "preventive intervention research cycle" advanced in the IOM report (1994). In this model, after first identifying the problem, a review of risk and protective factors is a necessary precondition for intervention development. This model is based on constructing an epidemiology of the risk factors related to the development of a disorder, the protective factors that may buffer the disorder in the face of risk, and a causal model of their processes. Prevention designs are then informed by this model in establishing methods, contexts, and targets for intervention such that when risks are reduced and/or protective factors are increased, the risk of disorder declines. To do so requires examining the epidemiology of risk for particular disorders, conducting prospective longitudinal studies to examine the attributable risk (e.g., the expected contribution of exposure to a risk to the development of new cases of a disorder), and thus the causal nature of risk to outcome (Boyle & Offord, 1990; Rothman, 1986; Verhulst & Koot, 1992). Gordon (1983), however, noted that it is often very difficult to determine causal links between antecedents and outcomes in development and that understanding of the mechanism should not be a precondition to the implementation of intervention. Nevertheless, according to this approach, there should be at least a strong statistical association between the risk-focused nature of the intervention and the outcome.

Robins (1992, p. 3) contended that "randomized controlled experiments are recognized as the best method for evaluating treatments." A defining methodology for PS is the randomized controlled trial, which is employed to evaluate three phases of program development: (a) pilot efficacy studies and confirmatory replication trials; (b) large-scale effectiveness trials; and (c) the dissemination, adoption, and ongoing evaluation of programs into community service settings (Institute of Medicine, 1994). The power of randomized clinical trials stems from the view that only by carefully sampling the population and then randomly assigning children, families, schools, or communities to intervention or control samples, can one unequivocally know if the intervention is effective (Kazdin, 1991b; Kirk, 1968).

Without random assignment, it is not possible to know if pretest differences or sensitization are responsible for intervention outcomes. Without a control sample, one cannot ascertain if pre- to postintervention changes that occurred were due to the intervention, or if similar changes might have occurred due to development or chance occurrence in a comparison sample, or if changes in the level of risk or protective factors are related to the outcome. Further, it is only through replication of randomized field trials that sufficient evidence accumulates to ascertain efficacy with confidence (Lipsey, 1990). However, it should be recognized that the term *control* group is often a misnomer in real-world settings because, although researchers may be able to prevent the control group from receiving the specific intervention under study, it is not possible to control other multiple influences (e.g., media, changing principals or curricula in control schools, shifts to new models of health care) that may powerfully affect the behavior of young people. Therefore, in addition to examining program implementation in an experimental condition, randomized clinical trials must also assess the nature and quality of relevant programming efforts that are introduced in control settings.

Albee (1983) argued compellingly that scientists are likely to select theories and findings that are consistent with their personal beliefs, attitudes, and prejudices, and to seek facts that validate these beliefs—neglecting or denying observations that contradict their personal preferences. This provides a compelling rationale for the necessity of randomized clinical trials: to reduce potential biases in producing program outcomes. This has been pointed out by the pitfalls presented in the delinquency prevention literature, where several well-intentioned ideas that have been part of social policy and welfare worldviews have been shown through careful clinical trials to be ineffective (McCord & Tremblay, 1992). Further, numerous studies using quasi-experimental designs with nonrandomized control conditions show biases that are likely to invalidate findings (Lorion, 1983).

Although there are discrepancies in views within PS regarding its focus on experimental field trials, the IOM report only reviewed field experiments that involved experimental and control conditions because of their desire to support the scientific foundation for prevention. There are a number of assumptions that underlie the PS approach in its most straightforward form. First, this approach takes as the central unit of analysis the individual and its development. However, it is conceivable that the unit of analysis could be a school or community in which one had carefully studied the risk-protection-maladaptive outcome sequence. Second, this approach usually involves the researcher as either the "objective evaluator" or the participant-observer who develops, introduces, and/or directs the assessment of new programs. Thus, these programs are primarily drawn from theory and past empirical linkages regarding risk and outcomes, and the programs are usually university-developed rather than emergent from the community.

Limits of Randomized Control Trial Methodology

In spite of their central importance for the field of prevention research, there are limits to the practical use of randomized field trials as well as to the generalizability of their results. First, comprehensive interventions, such as large-scale efforts to alter and coordinate large service delivery systems, are difficult or impossible to assign randomly to intervention and control conditions. For example, if one sought to change the ways schools, children's services, and mental and public health centers operated in a community (e.g., to develop full-service schools; Dryfoos, 1994), it would be difficult to find communities that would agree to random assignment, could be carefully matched at pretest, or, if randomized to control, could be constrained to not initiate similar new ideas over the number of years necessary for assessment of the systems change (Connell, Aber, & Walker, 1995). In fact, it is often the unique, rather than randomly assigned, school or community that has the motivation, competence, and history of program development to provide an adequate foundation for the effective implementation of coordinated, comprehensive, multiyear interventions.

Further, even if all of these obstacles could be overcome, one would have to randomize many communities to have the statistical power necessary for effective evaluation (Lipsey, 1990). Thus, interventions that are relatively large scale and require substantial change among the relations of subsystems within a larger social context present considerable challenges to field trial methods. Recent examples concerning the use of schools or communities in randomized trials of universal interventions for substance abuse highlight both the value and difficulty in utilizing randomized trials (Pentz, 1994; Wagenaar, Murray, Wolfson, Forster, & Finnegan, 1994). Further, if the model is that intervention is emergent from the community, then it is unlikely that communities would willingly and effectively adopt the model developed from another community. Although it is possible to provide partial solutions to these issues, such as using more small communities, isolating treatment and control communities, or comparing alternative treatments (Flay & Cook, 1996), these options are only viable in certain circumstances.

A related but separable concern regarding field trials is their external validity or generalizability. As contextual influences are critical to the conceptualization, implementation, and evaluation of prevention services, Elias and Branden (1988, p. 589) stated, "context is the limiting factor in the replication of programs." Although experimental research may provide useful intervention materials and strategies, contextual influences in all levels of the ecological model will affect a community's motivation to employ them. Dumas (1989) similarly pointed out that it is necessary to understand how culture, context, and setting interact transactionally with the intervention and how interventions must be altered to fit different ecologies.

Additional limitations of this approach arise when investigators wish to explore questions about the feasibility of making such systemic changes and attempt to assess the issues involved in such restructuring efforts (e.g., What are the obstacles encountered in altering the culture of work when agencies are merged? What factors create obstacles to promoting social competence interventions within a school or school system? What are the meanings of the intervention to families involved?). Then experimental methodology, with its emphasis on standardization of implementation, may actually promote iatrogenic effects that complicate research attempts to examine these questions.

PS reflects the "investigator-driven" research, development, and diffusion (RD&D) model for program development that has predominated the field of social intervention research. The RD&D model and the IOM's prevention research cycle both assume that there is a rational sequence—research, development, packaging, and dissemination—for evolving and applying a new intervention. They also assume that there is a rational consumer who accepts and adopts the intervention. It is assumed that programs are effective because they incorporate the most recent findings from theory and research and that they have been through systematic development and field testing. The fact that most of these programs are never used on a widespread basis illustrates the danger in not understanding more about the user end of the RD&D continuum (Berman & McLaughlin, 1978; Hall & Hord, 1987; Heller, 1996). Next, we discuss the CCAR model, an alternative intervention research strategy, that places great emphasis on collaboration between researchers and research participants throughout all phases of program development and evaluation.

Collaborative Community Action Research

CCAR has its historical roots in the social reform movements of the late nineteenth and early twentieth centuries (Addams, 1910/1990); the action-research traditions of Lewin (1946, 1951); the action-science approaches of Argyris (Argyris, Putnam, & Smith, 1985); and intervention efforts in community organizing (Rothman & Tropman, 1987), community coalitions and partnerships (Butterfoss, Goodman, & Wandersman, 1993; Kaftarian & Hansen, 1994), comprehensive collaborative community initiatives

(Connell, Kubisch, Schorr, & Weiss, 1995; Knapp, 1995), and community psychology (Heller, Price, Reinharz, Riger, & Wandersman, 1984; Kelly, 1988; Levine & Perkins, 1987; Sarason, Levine, Goldenberg, Cherlin, & Bennett, 1966; Tolan et al., 1990).

CCAR is based on an ecological perspective that encourages close collaboration among researchers, practitioners, and citizens to foster constructive community development (Kelly, 1986, 1988). The ecological perspective (a) emphasizes how people, settings, and events can serve as resources for the positive development of communities; (b) considers how these resources can be managed, coordinated, conserved, and created; and (c) approaches prevention research with the priority of fostering the preservation and enhancement of community resources (Trickett, Barone, & Buchanan, 1996; Trickett, Kelly, & Vincent, 1985). This *resource* emphasis orients researchers toward a setting's strengths, competencies, and potential promise rather than its weaknesses, deficits, and problems. CCAR involves long-term reciprocal relationships and commitments between researchers and the host community that extend beyond and build upon the initial gathering of data. Philosophically, CCAR derives from the notion of active, empowering, participatory democracy in which citizens are encouraged to control their own lives and ecologies (Rappaport, 1990).

A central component of CCAR is that action and understanding must be grounded in the understanding of specific ecologies and contexts. A number of implications derive from this perspective. First, there is a focus on understanding the community or setting as the unit of analysis. Doing so requires an assessment of the setting that includes (a) an epidemiology of risks and strengths, (b) a model of the differing organizational structures in the setting, and (c) an ethnography of the community issues, needs, and resources that represent the views of the multiple stakeholders. Second, as a result of this assessment process, researchers and stakeholders are informed of the "problem" in the context of a developing collaboration. As a result, models for change are emergent from the collaboration. Also, it is often inappropriate to maintain standardization in delivery of an intervention across different settings comprised of different resources and participants. Third, evaluating the *processes* involved throughout the cycle of problem analysis and definition, intervention design, implementation, and institutionalization is itself a legitimate and important source of research findings. Fourth, the researcher is viewed as a participant-conceptualizer who does not control, but instead facilitates program development and evaluation. As a result, the researcher achieves the goal of richly studying the processes involved, but sometimes at the expenses of loss of evaluative control from which to draw causal inferences regarding program efficacy.

In proposing standards for collaborative research relationships, Fawcett (1990) posed the following questions to help assess the quality of collaboration.

> Does the research approach require researchers to become informed about community life and practices by participating in nonresearch activities of local origin before, during, and after the intervention?
>
> To what degree is the intervention designed, adapted, and implemented in collaboration with community members?
>
> Are the community's interests and priorities evident in the selection of new research goals that are not evident in the researcher's discipline or past topic choices?
>
> Does the intervention rely sufficiently on local resources (e.g., funding, practitioners, setting features), and is the intervention maintained by the local community?
>
> To what extent do the program and its impact remain if and when the researchers depart?

Given the need for alternative models to evaluate community programs, a number of recent reports have suggested strategy models (Connell, Kubisch, Schorr, & Weiss, 1995; Fetterman, Kaftarian, & Wandersman, 1995; Kaftarian & Hansen, 1994). Kim, Crutchfield, Williams, and Hepler (1994) pointed out that replicability of community-based projects are unlikely due to local conditions and given real-world constraints in field evaluations. They proposed a rigorous but uncontrolled threshold-gating model approach based on using already established markers, theorems, and generalizations and applying them to local projects at each stage of the project (e.g., design, training, implementation). Thus, what is already known is used as criterion measures for local projects. A second alternative described by Weiss and colleagues (Hollister & Hill, 1995; C. Weiss, 1995) focuses on theory-based evaluations as elaborated in the recent Aspen Institute model on nonexperimental program evaluation. Goodman and Wandersman (1994) highlighted the ways that structured, theory-guided formative evaluations can benefit project planning, design, and implementation.

Knapp (1995) suggested that research and evaluations of collaborative, comprehensive services should be strongly conceptualized, descriptive, comparative, and constructively skeptical. He proposed a variety of innovative approaches to study multicomponent interventions, including profiles of individual participation and change among program consumers; detailed, multiple-case descriptions of program impact on the attitudes and practices of service providers; single-subject and single-system time series research to measure effects on individuals or service systems; examinations of exemplary and typical practice; and quantitative and qualitative analyses regarding the costs of comprehensive programming. Given the current state of program development, he contended that these research approaches will provide more useful information to improve future program design, implementation, and outcomes than will group-comparative experimental studies that contrast recipients and nonrecipients.

Tolan et al. (1990) noted that community research often examines "ill-structured" problems. An example of such problems involves asking questions such as, Why is there so much youth violence in our community? What can be done to prevent or reduce it? and How will we know if our programs have been effective? Answers to these questions will vary according to the perspective of the stakeholder; that is, youth, business leaders, educators, and law enforcement officials are likely to define the problem, its potential solutions, and criteria for success differently. Thus, these variables must be considered from a relativistic, contextualized viewpoint that values the subjective notions of the stakeholders. As such, "the relation of knowledge to action is not reliable across encounters with the problem" (Tolan et al., 1990, p. 6). Thus, such problems may require substantially different interventions and evaluation strategies depending upon the context and its actors. Given this grounded model, there is significant resistance to the notion of determining context-free causes, solutions, and evaluation approaches. In closing, one of the contributions of the CCAR approach to inquiry is well captured by Tolan et al., who wrote: "The value of research knowledge, then, is in its descriptive richness, explanatory utility, and conceptual robustness, rather than in its situational independence, ability to prove a general fact, and generalizability of results. This view of research as the conversing of like-interested (but not necessarily like-minded) scientists looks for coherence and explanation in patterns rather than consistency of results and conclusions" (p. 7).

PS and CCAR Approaches, Levels of Collaboration, and the Establishment of Effective, Enduring, Competence-Enhancement and Prevention Programs

Weissberg (1995) examined differences between investigator-driven, randomized controlled PS and CCAR approaches using Selman's developmental model for intervention (Brion-Meisels & Selman, 1984; Selman, 1980; Selman et al., 1992; Yeates & Selman, 1989). According to Selman and his colleagues (Yeates & Selman, 1989), "Interpersonal Negotiation Strategies are the means by which an individual tries to meet personal needs via interaction with another individual when both participants' needs are in conflict" (pp. 75–76). Weissberg (1995) applied this model to explore relationships between university researchers and school-based practitioners who interact around the development, implementation, and evaluation of prevention programs. Although these groups have some overlapping goals—such as a desire to establish programming to enhance positive youth development—their primary concerns, motivations, and priorities are often quite different.

For example, academic researchers may be concerned primarily about contributing to the research literature through conducting a controlled, theory-guided intervention study with the highest possible experimental rigor. District administrators, building principals, or classroom teachers have other concerns, such as being asked to teach too much in too little time, handling daily student and personnel crises with limited resources, parent complaints, and the pressures of implementing new programs. These different underlying motivations profoundly affect the scope of programs that are designed and the quality of their implementation.

There are four levels of interpersonal negotiation strategies (Yeates & Selman, 1989). *Level 0 (impulsive) strategies* involve primarily impulsive and physical behavior to get what one wants or to avoid harm. Although principals and principal investigators are unlikely to have physical altercations, there is an array of nonphysical Level 0 strategies such as intentional decisions not to return phone calls or to attend meetings to hear the ideas and proposals of the other party. *Level 1 (unilateral) strategies* consist of attempts to either control or appease the other person through willful one-way orders to assert power and satisfy oneself. For example, this could involve a top-down, system-entry approach in which a superintendent or principal allow researchers and their staff of health educators to implement prevention programs in their school without the involvement of teachers. The researchers' goal is to implement an intervention in standardized fashion with fidelity to the program design. Sometimes researchers even keep the details of the intervention secret from teachers to obtain blind teacher ratings. In addition, researchers typically know little about what goes on in the school during times that they are not implementing the program. With Level 1 relationships, teachers typically remain uninvolved in program implementation; nor do they consider or share their views of how the program fits into the context of other related school-based efforts. In some instances, teachers leave the room when the health educators enter, reducing the likelihood that there will be any follow-up to reinforce the knowledge, attitudes, skills, and practices encouraged by the program.

Level 2 (reciprocal) strategies involve attempts to satisfy the needs of both participants in reciprocal fashion through trades, exchanges, and deals. The researchers' primary goal may be to implement and evaluate an intervention in accordance with the design of a funded grant application. In exchange, schools receive free innovative services, researchers train school staff to implement the program, and teachers may be paid or given college credits for participating in the staff development experience. There is an important trade-off between a Level 1 and Level 2 intervention strategy. The former may result in person-centered interventions that are implemented with greater fidelity (especially since the job of the health educator may depend on this!). The latter may be implemented with less integrity, but may offer a more powerful, ecologically oriented intervention that changes the child, the teacher, their interaction, and, to some extent, the organizational system in which the program is implemented.

Level 3 (collaborative) strategies involve collaborative attempts to change both one's own and the other person's wishes to develop mutual goals. At this level, strategies use self-reflection and shared reflection to facilitate the process of dialogue that leads to compromise and the construction of mutually satisfactory resolutions. They demonstrate concerns for a relationship's continuity and the understanding that solutions to immediate problems have a bearing in that regard. In Level 3 approaches, the researchers and school staff work collaboratively to develop ecologically valid interventions with an understanding of the goals and priorities of the school system. This involves, for example, knowledge of historical and ongoing prevention efforts and how proposed initiatives mesh with these; familiarity with the organizational structures and key decision makers in the system; and concern about how federal, state, and local policies, politics, and funding affect program selection, implementation, and maintenance. It also keeps in mind that the major priority of school involves teaching basic academic skills to children. Level 3 relationships are time consuming. Researchers often relinquish considerable experimental control in these collaborative undertakings. At the same time, school personnel feel more ownership and commitment to programs that they help to develop and implement.

Cognitive-developmental theories, such as Selman's, have been criticized for terming more sophisticated levels of development "better." Part of the difficulty has been the failure to answer the question: Better in what? In Selman's model, there is an underlying assumption that higher-level strategies involve a more thorough consideration and balancing of the participants' perspectives and, therefore, are more likely to lead to better outcomes for all involved. On the other hand, Selman readily acknowledges that higher-level strategies may not always be necessary or even adaptive in all contexts. So should we aspire to have *all* prevention research reflect collaborative Level 3 approaches? The answer is no. Whether investigators aspire to Level 1, 2, or 3 relationships with program implementers depends on their priorities. Clearly, Level 1 and Level 2 approaches permit more scientific control and rigor, such as random assignment of schools, teachers, and children to experimental and control conditions. Level 3 approaches yield greater interpersonal and organizational understanding; therefore, such strategies are likely to lead to more ecologically valid, contextually sensitive approaches. However, Level 3 approaches also reduce experimental control as well as the likelihood of standardized program implementation across settings. Thus, they offer less definitive and interpretable data regarding program efficacy. The bottom line is that those who design and evaluate prevention programs must have greater insight about the implications of operating at lower or higher levels of collaboration and recognize the benefits and limitations of operating at different levels. Giesbrecht and Ferris (1993) elaborated the many issues involved in community- or school-based initiatives and the tensions that surround the power and control arrangements that must be negotiated to create a balance among research interests, practitioner goals, and stakeholder needs.

It is important to examine the extent to which research from these differing approaches has the potential to provide an adequate foundation for comprehensive competence-enhancement and prevention programming. An examination of most randomized controlled clinical trials indicates a clear gap between the scope of most state-of-the-art prevention research program models and the multiyear, multicomponent intervention models called for by practitioners and policymakers (Weissberg & Elias, 1993). For example, Weissberg (1995) examined 19 exemplary school-based programs for school-age children and adolescents identified by Price et al. (1989) or the IOM report (1994). Of the 19 programs, 11 lasted less than one year and 6 lasted less than two years. Twelve of the 19 programs (or 63%) had a single component (such as a teacher-led, classroom-based skills training component), and 7 had two or more components. The dearth of well-evaluated comprehensive programs is problematic. If a superintendent and mayor asked prevention researchers to recommend a coordinated, multicomponent kindergarten through twelfth grade prevention strategy, intervention research from only a small proportion of prevention scientists could readily translate to informative, concrete recommendations.

Building an Integrative Model of Prevention Research

Although the development of the PS model has been an important step in the evolution of prevention research, its applicability may be limited for a variety of reasons that include both the nature of experimental control and the value of alternative models of program development that are more aligned with the CCAR approach. Although they can be seen as opposing, there is little question that there is substantial value in both approaches. However, we conceptualize their roles as representing somewhat overpolarized components of a dialectical process moving toward greater integration.

Prevention scientists often argue that programs should not be disseminated widely without documented support for their efficacy through a series of replicating clinical trials. On the other hand, collaborative community action researchers question the extent to which intervention models developed through clinical trials will benefit diverse communities. Prevention and competence-enhancement research must meet the challenge of combining the strengths of PS and CCAR approaches. On the one hand, clinical trial methodologies, including random assignment, are needed to provide a clearer foundation for identifying the effects of programs on risk and protective factors and outcomes. Clinical trials may inform collaborative researchers about which variables to address as they work with school and community settings to design ecologically valid, contextually responsive programs.

There are four parameters of these contrasting models that require recognition to build integration. First, both the investigator-driven, experimental field trial model and the contextually grounded, participant-conceptualizer models contribute critical insights into the conduct and evaluation of preventive interventions. Their utility will depend on the nature and goals of the questions being asked. Second, each approach should make an important contribution to the steps in any model of the prevention cycle. Third, depending on the problem and current knowledge of its course, when to rely more on one of these approaches may vary considerably. Fourth, a comprehensive approach to prevention research should be accepting and encouraging of what Shadish (1986) termed "planned critical multiplism." The concept of critical multiplism suggests that all theoretical and methodological approaches have advantages and strengths as well as disadvantages and weaknesses, such that the use of only one approach introduces both theoretical and systematic biases that affect both internal and external validity. Thus, understanding a set of phenomena more fully requires using multiple approaches in ways that best balance such biases as well as encourage researchers to develop self-reflective critiques of their methods. The utilization of multiple methodologies is an exciting prospect for prevention research and reflects significant recent changes in evaluation theory and practice (Shadish, Cook, & Leviton, 1991). Although the combining of a quantitative, experimental, summative model with a more qualitative, process, formative model is not without its difficulties, such integration is necessary for effective evaluation that meets the needs of multiple stakeholders and policymakers.

The future of large-scale prevention lies in part in the development of multilevel, multicomponent prevention efforts that coordinate the efforts of multiple socializing influences, including parents, peers, community leaders, local school and government administrators, and mass media programmers. Bronfenbrenner's (1979) developmental-ecological model points out the value of incorporating these higher systems and their relations versus focusing on just the individual and interactions with the "target individual." A major contribution of much investigator-driven research is that it plays a central role in creating controlled, short-term foundational studies that provide directions regarding intervention strategies for changes with specific groups in particular settings. However, short-term, one-shot programs promote sustainable changes neither in young people nor in settings. Comprehensive, coordinated programs have the potential to reduce duplication of services, identify gaps in prevention services, and create coordination among the numerous educational, legal, and social agencies that serve children, youth, and families. Such coordinated services are believed to offer the best chance for producing long-term social, psychological, and health benefits. That is, providing comprehensive, multifaceted programming and promoting lasting environmental and systems changes seem necessary to promote long-term positive effects on the psychosocial behavior of large groups of children and youth (Dryfoos, 1990, 1994; Hamburg, 1992; Rutter, 1987; Schorr, 1988; Zigler & Berman, 1983).

However, conducting such coordinated prevention programs does not mean that only large-scale projects will inform the field. Smaller, more time-limited studies that consist of more controlled designs are crucial for informing policymakers, researchers, and practitioners regarding the types of interventions that are more likely to produce effective outcomes when combined with other types of interventions in a larger model. Further, as preventive interventions will have differential effectiveness by participant and setting, understanding both the mediators and moderators of change at individual and systems levels is a necessary part of the productive dialogue that will lead to further improvement in prevention programs as well as refinement of the research enterprise. In other words, basic, controlled, preventive intervention research will help to create a stronger foundation for establishing more comprehensive, beneficial school and community competence-enhancement and prevention programs.

> Progress, far from consisting in change, depends on retentiveness. When change is absolute there remains no being to improve and no direction is set for possible improvement: and when experience is not retained, as among savages, infancy is perpetual. Those who can not remember the past are condemned to repeat it. (Santayana, 1948, p. 284)

ACKNOWLEDGMENTS

The authors express their appreciation to Ana Mari Cauce, Maurice Elias, Mary Hancock, Eva Patrikakou, Ann Renninger, Theresa Schultz, and Irving Sigel, who provided feedback on earlier versions of this manuscript.

REFERENCES

Achenbach, R. M., Phares, V., Howell, C. T., Rauh, V. A., & Nurcombe, B. (1990). Seven-year outcome of the Vermont Intervention Program for Low-Birthweight Infants. *Child Development, 61,* 1672–1681.

Addams, J. (1990). *Twenty years at Hull House.* Chicago: University of Illinois Press. (Original work published 1910)

Alan Guttmacher Institute. (1994). *Sex and America's teenagers.* New York: Author.

Albee, G. W. (1983). Psychopathology, prevention, and the just society. *Journal of Primary Prevention, 4,* 5–40.

Allen, J. P., Kuperminc, G., Philliber, S., & Herre, K. (1994). Programmatic prevention of adolescent problem behaviors: The role of autonomy, relatedness, and volunteer service in the Teen Outreach Program. *American Journal of Community Psychology, 22,* 617–638.

Anderson, S., & Messick, S. (1974). Social competence in young children. *Developmental Psychology, 10,* 282–293.

Annie E. Casey Foundation. (1995). *The path of most resistance: Reflections on lessons learned from new futures.* Baltimore: Author.

Argyris, C., Putnam, R., & Smith, D. M. (1985). *Action science.* San Francisco: Jossey-Bass.

Arthur, M. W., Weissberg, R. P., & Caplan, M. Z. (1991, August). *Promoting social competence in young urban adolescents: A follow-up study.* Paper presented at the annual meeting of the American Psychological Association, San Francisco.

Bandura, A. (1986). *Social foundations of thought and action.* Englewood Cliffs, NJ: Prentice-Hall.

Bandura, A. (1994). Social cognitive theory and exercise of control over HIV infection. In R. J. DiClemente & J. L. Petersen (Eds.), *Preventing AIDS: Theories and methods of behavioral interventions* (pp. 25–59). New York: Plenum Press.

Barnett, W. S. (1985). *The Perry Preschool Program and its long-term effects: A benefit-cost analysis* (High/Scope Early Childhood Policy Papers, No. 21). Ypsilanti, MI: High/Scope Educational Research Foundation.

Barnett, W. S. (1993a). Benefit-cost analysis of preschool education: Findings from a 25-year follow-up. *American Journal of Orthopsychiatry, 63,* 500–508.

Barnett, W. S. (1993b). Economic evaluation of home visiting programs. *Future of Children, 3,* 93–112.

Barnett, W. S. (1995). Long-term effects of early childhood programs on cognitive and school outcomes. *Future of Children, 5,* 25–50.

Barrera, M. E., Rosenbaum, P. L., & Cunnigham, C. E. (1986). Early home intervention with low-birth-weight infants and their parents. *Child Development, 57,* 20–23.

Battistich, V., Elias, M. J., & Branden-Muller, L. (1992). Two school-based approaches to promoting children's social competence. In G. W. Albee, L. A. Bond, & T. Monsey (Eds.), *Improving children's lives: Global approaches to prevention* (pp. 212–234). Newbury Park, CA: Sage.

Battistich, V., Schaps, E., Watson, M., & Solomon, D. (in press). Prevention effects of the Child Development Project: Early findings from an ongoing multi-site demonstration trial. *Journal of Adolescent Research.*

Battistich, V., & Solomon, D. (1995, April). Linking teacher change to student change. In E. Schaps (Chair), *Why restructuring must focus on thinking and caring: A model for deep, long-term change through staff development.* Symposium conducted at the meeting of the American Educational Research Association, San Francisco.

Battistich, V., Solomon, D., Watson, M., Solomon, J., & Schaps, E. (1989). Effects of an elementary school program to enhance prosocial behavior on children's cognitive social problem-solving skills and strategies. *Journal of Applied Developmental Psychology, 10,* 147–169.

Becker, M. H. (1974). The health belief model and personal health behavior. *Health Education Monographs, 2,* 324–508.

Beckwith, L., & Cohen, S. E. (1984). Home environment and cognitive competence in preterm children during the first five years of life. In A. W. Gottfried (Ed.), *Home environment and early cognitive development* (pp. 235–271). New York: Academic Press.

Beckwith, L., & Rodning, C. (1992). Evaluating effects of intervention with parents of preterm infants. In S. L. Friedman & M. D. Sigman (Eds.), *The psychological development of low birthweight children* (pp. 389–410). Norwood, NJ: ABLEX.

Bell, R. Q. (1968). A reinterpretation of the direction of effects in studies of child socialization. *Psychological Review, 75,* 81–95.

Belsky, J. (1984). The determinants of parenting: A process model. *Child Development, 55,* 83–96.

Belsky, J. (1993). Etiology of child maltreatment: A developmental-ecological analysis. *Psychological Bulletin, 114,* 413–434.

Benard, B., Fafoglia, B., & Perone, J. (1987). Knowing what to do—and not to do—reinvigorates drug education. *ASCD Curriculum Update,* 1–12.

Bennett, W. J. (1994). *The index of leading cultural indicators: Facts and figures on the state of American society.* New York: Simon & Schuster.

Berman, P., & McLaughlin, M. W. (1978). *Federal programs supporting educational change: Vol. 8. Implementing and sustaining innovations.* Santa Monica, CA: Rand.

Bierman, K. L., & Furman, W. (1984). The effects of social skills training and peer involvement on the social adjustments of preadolescents. *Child Development, 55,* 151–162.

Blair, C., Ramey, C. T., & Hardin, J. M. (1995). Early intervention for low birthweight, premature infants: Participation and intellectual development. *American Journal of Mental Retardation, 99,* 542–554.

Blakely, C. H., Mayer, J. P., Gottschalk, R. G., Schmitt, N., Davidson, W. S., Roitman, D. B., & Emshoff, J. G. (1987). The fidelity-adaptation debate: Implications for the implementation of public sector social programs. *American Journal of Community Psychology, 15,* 253–268.

Bloom, B. L. (1983). *Community mental health: A general introduction* (2nd ed.). Monterey, CA: Brooks/Cole.

Blumstein, A. (1995). Violence by young people: Why the deadly nexus? *National Institute of Justice Journal, 229*(9), 2–9.

Bond, L. A., & Compas, B. E. (Eds.). (1989). *Primary prevention and promotion in the schools.* Newbury Park, CA: Sage.

Botvin, G. J., Baker, E., Dusenbury, L., Botvin, E. M., & Diaz, T. (1995). Long-term follow-up results of a randomized drug abuse prevention trial in a white middle-class population. *Journal of the American Medical Association, 273,* 1106–1111.

Botvin, G. J., Baker, E., Dusenbury, L., Tortu, S., & Botvin, E. M. (1990). Preventing adolescent drug abuse through a multimodal cognitive-behavioral approach: Results of a 3-year study. *Journal of Consulting and Clinical Psychology, 58,* 437–446.

Botvin, G. J., Schinke, S., & Orlandi, M. A. (1995). School-based health promotion: Substance abuse and sexual behavior. *Applied and Preventive Psychology, 4,* 167–184.

Botvin, G. J., & Tortu, S. (1988). Preventing adolescent substance abuse through life skills training. In R. H. Price, E. L. Cowen, R. P. Lorion, & J. Ramos-McKay (Eds.), *14 ounces of prevention: A casebook for practitioners* (pp. 98–110). Washington, DC: American Psychological Association.

Boyle, M. H., & Offord, D. R. (1990). Primary prevention of conduct disorder: Issues and prospects. *Journal of the American Academy of Child and Adolescent Psychiatry, 29,* 227–233.

Bradley, R. H., Whiteside, L., Mundfrom, D. J., Casey, P. H., Caldwell, B. M., & Barnett, K. (1994). Impact of the Infant Health and Development Program (IHDP) on the home environments of infants born prematurely and with low birthweight. *Journal of Educational Psychology, 86,* 531–541.

Breakey, G., & Pratt, B. (1991). Healthy growth for Hawaii's "Healthy Start": Toward a systematic statewide approach to the prevention of child abuse and neglect. *Zero to Three,* 16–22.

Brewer, D. D., Hawkins, J. D., Catalano, R. F., & Neckerman, H. J. (1995). Preventing serious, violent, and chronic juvenile offending: A review of evaluations of selected strategies in childhood, adolescence, and the community. In J. C. Howell, B. Krisberg, J. J. Wilson, & J. D. Hawkins (Eds.), *A sourcebook on serious, violent, and chronic juvenile offenders* (pp. 61–141). Newbury Park, CA: Sage.

Brion-Meisels, S., & Selman, R. L. (1984). Early adolescent development of new interpersonal strategies: Understanding and intervention. *School Psychology Review, 13,* 278–291.

Bronfenbrenner, U. (1979). *The ecology of human development: Experiments by nature and design.* Cambridge, MA: Harvard University Press.

Bronfenbrenner, U. (1995). Developmental ecology through space and time: A future perspective. In P. Moen, G. H. Elder, Jr., & K. Luscher (Eds.), *Examining lives in context* (pp. 619–647). Washington, DC: American Psychological Association.

Bronfenbrenner, U., & Crouter, A. C. (1983). The evolution of environmental models in developmental research. In P. H. Mussen (Series Ed.) & W. Kessen (Vol. Ed.), *Handbook of child psychology: Vol. 1. History, theory, and methods* (4th ed., pp. 357–413). New York: Wiley.

Brooks-Gunn, J., Gross, R. T., Kraemer, H. C., Spiker, D., & Shapiro, S. (1992). Enhancing the cognitive outcomes of low birth weight, premature infants: For whom is the intervention most effective. *Pediatrics, 89,* 1209–1215.

Brooks-Gunn, J., Liaw, F., & Klebanov, P. K. (1992). Effects of early intervention on cognitive function of low birth weight preterm infants. *Journal of Pediatrics, 120,* 350–359.

Brooks-Gunn, J., McCormick, M. C., Shapiro, S., Benaisch, A., & Black, G. W. (1994). The effects of early education intervention on maternal employment, public assistance, and health insurance: The Infant Health and Development Program. *American Journal of Public Health, 84,* 924–931.

Brown, J. W. (1994). Morphogenesis and mental process. *Development and Psychopathology, 6,* 551–563.

Bry, B. H. (1982). Reducing the incidence of adolescent problems through preventive intervention: One- and five-year follow-up. *American Journal of Community Psychology, 10,* 265–276.

Butterfoss, F. D., Goodman, R. M., & Wandersman, A. (1993). Community coalitions for prevention and health promotion. *Health Education Research: Theory and Practice, 8,* 315–330.

Campbell, D. T., & Stanley, J. C. (1963). *Experimental and quasi-experimental designs for research.* Chicago: Rand McNally.

Campbell, F. A., & Ramey, C. T. (1994). Effects of early intervention on intellectual and academic achievement: A follow-up study of children from low-income families. *Child Development, 65,* 684–698.

Caplan, G. (1964). *Principles of preventive psychiatry.* New York: Basic Books.

Caplan, M., & Weissberg, R. P. (1989). Promoting social competence in early adolescence: Developmental considerations. In B. H. Schneider, G. Attili, J. Nadel, & R. P. Weissberg (Eds.), *Social competence in developmental perspective* (pp. 371–385). Boston: Kluwer.

Caplan, M., & Weissberg, R. P. (1990). *The substance use prevention module of the Yale-New Haven Social Development Program.* Chicago: University of Illinois.

Caplan, M., Weissberg, R. P., Grober, J. H., Sivo, P. J., Grady, K., & Jacoby, C. (1992). Social competence promotion with inner-city and suburban young adolescents: Effects on social adjustment and alcohol use. *Journal of Consulting and Clinical Psychology, 60,* 56–63.

Caplan, M., Weissberg, R. P., & Shriver, T. (1990). *Evaluation summary for the 1989–1990 Social Development Project.* New Haven, CT: New Haven Public Schools.

Carnegie Council on Adolescent Development. (1995). *Great transitions: Preparing adolescents for a new century* (Concluding report of the Carnegie Council on Adolescent Development). New York: Carnegie Corporation of New York.

Carnegie Council on Adolescent Development. Report of the Task Force on Education of Young Adolescents. (1989). *Turning points: Preparing American youth for the 21st century.* New York: Carnegie Corporation of New York.

Carnegie Council on Adolescent Development. Report of the Task Force on Youth Development and Community Programs. (1992). *A matter of time: Risk and opportunity in the non-school hours.* New York: Carnegie Corporation of New York.

Carnegie Task Force on Meeting the Needs of Young Children. (1994). *Starting points: Meeting the needs of our youngest children.* New York: Carnegie Corporation of New York.

Caspi, A., & Moffitt, T. E. (1993). When do individual differences matter? A paradoxical theory of personality coherence. *Psychological Inquiry, 4,* 247–271.

Catalano, R., & Dooley, D. (1980). Economic change in primary prevention. In R. H. Price, R. F. Ketterer, B. C. Bader, & J. Monahan (Eds.), *Prevention in mental health: Research, policy, and practice* (pp. 21–40). Beverly Hills, CA: Sage.

Catalano, R. F., Haggerty, K. P., Gainey, R. R., Hoppe, M. J., & Brewer, D. (in press). Effectiveness of primary prevention interventions with high-risk youth. In W. J. Bukoski & R. I. Evans (Eds.), *Cost benefit/cost effectiveness research of drug abuse prevention: Implications for programming and policy.* NIDA Research Monograph.

Cauce, A. M., Comer, J. P., & Schwartz, B. A. (1987). Long-term effects of a system-oriented school prevention program. *American Journal of Orthopsychiatry, 57,* 127–131.

Centers for Disease Control and Prevention. (1994a). *Pregnancy, sexually transmitted diseases, and related risk behaviors among U.S. adolescents.* Atlanta: Author.

Centers for Disease Control and Prevention. (1994b). *HIV/AIDS Surveillance Report, 6*(1), 12.

Centers for Disease Control and Prevention. (1995, March 24). *CDC Surveillance Summaries, MMWR, 44*(No. SS-1).

Children's Defense Fund. (1995). *The state of America's children yearbook: 1995.* Washington, DC: Author.

Cicchetti, D. (1984). The emergence of developmental psychopathology. *Child Development, 55,* 1–7.

Cicchetti, D. (1990). A historical perspective on the discipline of developmental psychopathology. In J. Rolf, A. S. Masten, D. Cicchetti, K. H. Nuechterlein, & S. Weintraub (Eds.), *Risk and protective factors in the development of psychopathology* (pp. 2–28). New York: Cambridge University Press.

Cicchetti, D., & Cohen, D. J. (1995). *Developmental psychopathology: Vol. 2. Risk, disorder, and adaptation.* New York: Wiley.

Cochran, M. (Ed.). (1993). *International handbook of child care policies and programs.* Westport, CT: Greenwood Press.

Cochran, M., & Woolever, F. (1983). Beyond the deficit model: The empowerment of parents with information and informal supports. In I. E. Siegel & L. M. Laosa (Eds.), *Changing families* (pp. 225–245). New York: Plenum Press.

Cohen, D. A., & Rice, J. C. (1995). A parent-targeted intervention for adolescent substance use prevention. *Evaluation Review, 19,* 159–180.

Cohen, M. A. (1996). *The monetary value of saving a high risk youth.* Unpublished manuscript, Owen Graduate School of Management, Vanderbilt University, Nashville, TN.

Coie, J. D., & Krehbiel, G. (1984). Effects of academic tutoring on the social status of low-achieving, socially rejected children. *Child Development, 55,* 1465–1478.

Coie, J. D., Watt, N. F., West, S. G., Hawkins, J. D., Asarnow, J. R., Markman, H. J., Ramey, S. L., Shure, M. B., & Long, B. (1993). The science of prevention: A conceptual framework and some directions for a national research program. *American Psychologist, 48,* 1013–1022.

Collaborative Group on Preterm Birth Prevention. (1993). Multicenter randomized, controlled trial of a preterm birth prevention program. *American Journal of Obstetrics and Gynecology, 169,* 362–366.

Comer, J. P. (1988). Educating poor minority children. *Scientific American, 259,* 42–48.

Comer, J. P., Haynes, N. M., Joyner, E. T., & Ben-Avie, M. (1996). *Rallying the whole village: The Comer process for reforming education.* New York: Teachers College Press.

Commission on Chronic Illness. (1957). *Chronic illness in the United States* (Vol. 1). Cambridge, MA: Harvard University Press.

Committee for Children, The. (1988). *Second step, grades 1–3, pilot project 1987–1988, summary report.* Seattle, WA: Author.

Committee for Children, The. (1989). *Second step, grades 4–5, pilot project 1988–1989, summary report.* Seattle, WA: Author.

Committee for Children, The. (1990). *Second step, grades 6–8, pilot project 1989–1990, summary report.* Seattle, WA: Author.

Committee for Economic Development. (1987). *Children in need: Investment strategies for the educationally disadvantaged.* New York: Author.

Conduct Problems Prevention Research Group. (1992). A developmental and clinical model for the prevention of conduct disorders: The FAST Track Program. *Development and Psychopathology, 4,* 509–527.

Conduct Problems Prevention Research Group. (1996a). *An initial evaluation of the FAST Track Program.* Paper presented at the fifth annual conference on Prevention Research, National Institute of Mental Health, Washington, DC.

Conduct Problems Prevention Research Group. (1996b). *The effectiveness of the universal component of FAST Track: The PATHS Curriculum.* Unpublished manuscript, Department of Psychology, University of Washington.

Connell, D. B., & Turner, R. R. (1985). The impact of instructional experience and the effects of cumulative instruction. *Journal of School Health, 55,* 324–331.

Connell, D. B., Turner, R. R., & Mason, E. F. (1985). Summary of the findings of the School Health Education Evaluation: Health promotion effectiveness, implementation, and costs. *Journal of School Health, 55,* 316–323.

Connell, D. B., Turner, R. R., Mason, E. F., & Olsen, L. K. (1986). School health education evaluation. *International Journal of Educational Research, 10,* 245–345.

Connell, J. P., Aber, J. L., & Walker, G. (1995). How do urban communities affect youth? Using social science research to inform the design and evaluation of comprehensive community initiatives. In J. P. Connell, A. C. Kubisch, L. B. Schorr, & C. H. Weiss (Eds.), *New approaches to evaluating community initiatives: Concepts, methods, and contexts* (pp. 93–125). Washington, DC: Aspen Institute.

Connell, J. P., Kubisch, A. C., Schorr, L. B., & Weiss, C. H. (Eds.). (1995). *New approaches to evaluating community initiatives: Concepts, methods, and contexts.* Washington, DC: Aspen Institute.

Consortium on the School-Based Promotion of Social Competence. (1994). The school-based promotion of social competence: Theory, research, practice, and policy. In R. J. Haggerty, L. R. Sherrod, N. Garmezy, & M. Rutter (Eds.), *Stress, risk, and resilience in children and adolescents: Processes, mechanisms, and interventions* (pp. 268–316). New York: Cambridge University Press.

Cook, R., Roehl, J., Oros, C., & Trudeau, J. (1994). Conceptual and methodological issues in the evaluation of community-based substance abuse prevention coalitions: Lessons learned from the national evaluation of the Community Partnership Program [Monograph] [Special issue]. *Journal of Community Psychology,* 155–169.

Cook, T. D., Anson, A. R., & Walchli, S. B. (1993). From causal description to causal explanation: Three already good evaluations of adolescent health program. In S. G. Millstein, A. C. Petersen, & E. O. Nightengale (Eds.), *Promoting the health of adolescents: New directions for the twenty-first century* (pp. 339–374). New York: Oxford University Press.

Cook, T. D., & Campbell, D. T. (1979). *Quasi-experimentation: Design and analysis issues for field settings.* Chicago: Rand McNally.

Costello, E. J. (1990). Child psychiatric epidemiology: Implications for clinical research and practice. In B. B. Lahey & A. E. Kazdin (Eds.), *Advances in clinical child psychology* (Vol. 13, pp. 53–90). New York: Plenum Press.

Courchesne, E., Chisum, H., & Townsend, J. (1994). Neural activity-dependent brain changes in development: Implications for psychopathology. *Development and Psychopathology, 6,* 697–722.

Cowen, E. L. (1977). Baby-steps toward primary prevention. *American Journal of Community Psychology, 5,* 1–22.

Cowen, E. L. (1980). The wooing of primary prevention. *American Journal of Community Psychology, 8,* 258–284.

Cowen, E. L. (1983). Primary prevention in mental health: Past, present, and future. In R. D. Felner, L. A. Jason, J. N. Moritsugu, & S. S. Farber (Eds.), *Preventive psychology: Theory, research, and practice* (pp. 11–25). New York: Pergamon Press.

Cowen, E. L. (1994). The enhancement of psychological wellness: Challenges and opportunities. *American Journal of Community Psychology, 22,* 149–178.

Cowen, E. L. (1995, August). *The ontogenesis of primary prevention: Lengthy strides and stubbed toes.* Paper presented at the meeting of the American Psychological Association, New York.

Cowen, E. L., Hightower, A. D., Pedro-Caroll, J. L., Work, W. C., Wyman, P. A., & Haffey, W. G. (1996). *School-based prevention of children at risk: The Primary Mental Health Project.* Washington, DC: American Psychological Association.

Cowen, E. L., Work, W. C., Wyman, P. A., Parker, G. R., Wannon, M., & Gribble, P. (1992). Test comparisons among stress-affected, stress-resilient, and nonclassified fourth- through sixth-grade urban children. *Journal of Community Psychology, 20,* 200–214.

Crockenberg, S. (1981). Infant irritability, mother responsiveness, and social influences on the security of infant-mother attachment. *Child Development, 52,* 857–865.

Cronbach, L. J. (1975). Beyond the two disciplines of scientific psychology. *American Psychologist, 30,* 116–127.

DeFriese, G. H., Crossland, C. L., Pearson, C. E., & Sullivan, C. J. (Eds.). (1990). Comprehensive school health programs: Current status and future prospects. *Journal of School Health, 60,* 127–190.

Dobson, D., & Cook, T. J. (1980). Avoiding Type III error in program evaluation: Results from a field experiment. *Evaluation and Program Planning, 3,* 269–276.

Dodge, K. A. (1986). A social information processing model of social competence in children. In M. Perlmutter (Ed.), *Cognitive perspectives on children's social behavior and behavioral development. Minnesota Symposium on Child Psychology* (Vol. 18, pp. 77–122). Hillsdale, NJ: Erlbaum.

Dodge, K. A., Pettit, G. S., McClaskey, C. L., & Brown, M. M. (1986). Social competence in children. *Monographs of the Society for Research in Child Development, 51*(2, Serial No. 213).

Donovan, J. E., Jessor, R., & Costa, F. M. (1988). Syndrome of problem behavior in adolescence: A replication. *Journal of Consulting and Clinical Psychology, 56,* 762–765.

Dryfoos, J. G. (1990). *Adolescents at risk: Prevalence and prevention.* New York: Oxford University Press.

Dryfoos, J. G. (1994). *Full-service schools: A revolution in health and social services for children, youth, and families.* San Francisco: Jossey-Bass.

Dryfoos, J. G. (1995). Full-service schools: Revolution or fad? *Journal of Research on Adolescence, 5,* 147–172.

Dryfoos, J. G. (1997). The prevalence of problem behaviors: Implications for programs. In R. P. Weissberg, T. P. Gullotta, R. L. Hampton, B. A. Ryan, & G. R. Adams (Eds.), *Healthy children 2010: Enhancing children's wellness* (pp. 17–46). Thousand Oaks, CA: Sage.

Dumas, J. E. (1989). Primary prevention: Toward an experimental paradigm sensitive to contextual variables. *Journal of Primary Prevention, 10,* 27–40.

Dunst, C. J., Trivette, C. M., & Thompson, R. B. (1990). New directions for family resource and support programs. In D. G. Unger & D. R. Powell (Eds.), *Families as nurturing systems: Support across the life-span* (pp. 19–44). New York: Haworth Press.

Durlak, J. A. (1983). Social problem solving as a primary prevention strategy. In R. D. Felner, L. A. Jason, J. N. Moritsugu, & S. S. Farber (Eds.), *Preventive psychology: Theory, research, and practice* (pp. 31–48). New York: Pergamon Press.

Durlak, J. A. (1995). *School-based prevention programs for children and adolescents.* Thousand Oaks, CA: Sage.

Durlak, J. A., & Wells, A. M. (1997). Primary prevention mental health programs for children and adolescents: A meta-analytic review. *American Journal of Community Psychology, 25,* 115–152.

Dusenbury, L., & Falco, M. (1995). Eleven components of effective drug abuse prevention curricula. *Journal of School Health, 65,* 420–425.

Dusenbury, L., & Falco, M. (1997). School-based drug abuse prevention strategies: From research to policy and practice. In R. P. Weissberg, T. P. Gullotta, R. L. Hampton, B. A. Ryan, & G. R. Adams (Eds.), *Healthy children 2010: Enhancing children's wellness* (pp. 47–75). Thousand Oaks, CA: Sage.

Eisen, M., Zellman, G. L., & McAlister, A. L. (1990). Evaluating the impact of a theory-based sexuality and contraceptive education program. *Family Planning Perspectives, 22,* 261–271.

Elias, M. J. (1995). Primary prevention as health and social competence promotion. *Journal of Primary Prevention, 16,* 5–14.

Elias, M. J., & Branden, L. R. (1988). Primary prevention of behavioral and emotional problems in school-aged populations. *School Psychology Review, 17,* 581–592.

Elias, M. J., & Clabby, J. (1989). *Social decision-making skills: A curriculum guide for the elementary grades.* Rockville, MD: Aspen.

Elias, M. J., & Clabby, J. (1992). *Building social problem-solving skills: Guidelines from a school-based program.* San Francisco: Jossey-Bass.

Elias, M. J., Gara, M. A., Schuyler, T. F., Branden-Muller, L. R., & Sayette, M. A. (1991). The promotion of social competence: Longitudinal study of a preventive school-based program. *American Journal of Orthopsychiatry, 61,* 409–417.

Elias, M. J., Gara, M., Ubriaco, M., Rothbaum, P. A., Clabby, J. F., & Schuyler, T. (1986). The impact of a preventive social problem-solving intervention on children's coping with middle-school stressors. *American Journal of Community Psychology, 14,* 259–275.

Elias, M. J., & Weissberg, R. P. (1990). School-based social competence promotion as a primary prevention strategy: A tale of two projects. In R. P. Lorion (Ed.), *Protecting the children: Strategies for optimizing emotional and behavioral development* (pp. 177–200). New York: Haworth Press.

Ellickson, P. L., & Bell, R. M. (1990). Drug prevention in junior high: A multi-site longitudinal test. *Science, 247,* 1299–1305.

Ellickson, P. L., Bell, R. M., & McGuigan, K. (1993). Preventing adolescent drug use: Long-term results of a junior high program. *American Journal of Public Health, 83,* 856–861.

Elliott, D. S. (1993). Health-enhancing and health-compromising lifestyles. In S. G. Millstein, A. C. Petersen, & E. O. Nightengale (Eds.), *Promoting the health of adolescents: New directions for the twenty-first century* (pp. 119–145). New York: Oxford University Press.

Elliott, D. S., Huizinga, D., & Menard, S. (1989). *Multiple-problem youth: Delinquency, substance use, and mental health problems.* New York: Springer-Verlag.

Ennett, S. T., Tobler, N. S., Ringwalt, C. L., & Flewelling, R. L. (1994). How effective is drug abuse resistance education? A meta-analysis of project DARE outcome evaluations. *American Journal of Public Health, 84,* 1394–1401.

Epstein, J. L. (1990). School and family connections: Theory, research, and implications for integrating sociologies of education and family. *Marriage and Family Review, 15,* 99–126.

Erikson, E. H. (1950). *Childhood and society.* New York: Norton.

Errecart, M. T., Walberg, H. J., Ross, J. G., Gold, R. S., Fiedler, J. L., & Kolbe, L. J. (1991). Effectiveness of teenage health teaching modules. *Journal of School Health, 61,* 26–30.

Farquhar, J. W., Fortmann, S. P., Flora, J. A., Taylor, C. B., Haskell, W. B., Williams, P. T., Maccoby, N., & Wood, P. D. (1990). Effects of community-wide education on cardiovascular disease risk factors: The Stanford Five-City Project. *Journal of the American Medical Association, 264,* 359–365.

Fawcett, S. B. (1990). Some emerging standards for community research and action: Aid from a behavioral perspective. In P. Tolan, C. Keys, F. Chertok, & L. Jason (Eds.), *Researching community psychology: Issues of theories and methods* (pp. 64–75). Washington, DC: American Psychological Association.

Federal Bureau of Investigation. (1994). *Age-specific arrest rates and race-specific arrest rates for selected offenses 1965–1992.* Washington, DC: U.S. Government Printing Office.

Felner, R. D., & Adan, A. M. (1988). The School Transitional Environment Project: An ecological intervention and evaluation. In R. H. Price, E. L. Cowen, R. P. Lorion, & J. Ramos-McKay (Eds.), *14 ounces of prevention: A casebook for practitioners* (pp. 111–122). Washington, DC: American Psychological Association.

Felner, R. D., Brand, S., Adan, A. M., Mulhall, P. F., Flowers, N., Sartain, B., & DuBois, D. L. (1993). Restructuring the ecology of the school as an approach to prevention during school transitions: Longitudinal follow-ups of the School Transitional Environment Project (STEP). *Prevention in Human Services, 10,* 103–136.

Felner, R. D., Ginter, M., & Primavera, J. (1982). Primary prevention during school transitions: Social support and environmental structure. *American Journal of Community Psychology, 10,* 277–290.

Fetterman, D. M., Kaftarian, S. J., & Wandersman, A. (Eds.). (1995). *Empowerment evaluation: Knowledge and tools for self-assessment and accountability.* Newbury Park, CA: Sage.

Field, T. M., Widmayer, S. M., Stringer, S., & Ignatoff, E. (1980). Teenage, lower-class, black mothers and their preterm infants: An intervention and developmental follow-up. *Child Development, 51,* 426–436.

Fishbein, M., & Ajzen, I. (1975). *Belief, attitude, intention, and behavior: An introduction to theory and research.* Boston: Addison-Wesley.

Fishbein, M., Middlestadt, S. E., & Hitchcock, P. J. (1994). Using information to change sexually transmitted disease-related behaviors: An analysis based on the theory of reasoned action. In R. J. DiClemente & J. L. Petersen (Eds.), *Preventing AIDS: Theories and methods of behavioral interventions* (pp. 61–78). New York: Plenum Press.

Flay, B. R., & Cook, T. D. (1996, May). *Relation of old and new methods for evaluating community interventions.* Presented at the fifth national conference on Prevention Research, Tysons Corner, VA.

Flay, B. R., & Petraitis, J. (1994). The theory of triadic influence: A new theory of health behavior with implications for preventive interventions. In G. S. Albrecht (Ed.), *Advances in medical sociology: Vol. 4. A reconsideration of models of health behavior change* (pp. 19–44). Greenwich, CT: JAI Press.

Friedman, S. L., & Sigman, M. D. (Eds.). (1992). *The psychological development of low birthweight children.* Norwood, NJ: ABLEX.

Fullan, M. G., & Stiegelbauer, S. (1991). *The new meaning of educational change* (2nd ed.). New York: Teachers College Press.

Gage, N. L. (1996). Confronting counsels of despair for the behavioral sciences. *Educational Researcher, 25,* 5–15.

Gainer, P. S., Webster, D. W., & Champion, H. R. (1993). A youth violence prevention program: Description and preliminary evaluation. *Archives of Surgery, 128,* 303–308.

Gans, J. E., Blyth, D. A., Elster, A. B., & Gaveras, L. L. (1990). *America's adolescents: How healthy are they?* Chicago: American Medical Association.

Garbarino, J. (1992). *Children and families in the social environment* (2nd ed.). New York: Aldine de Gruyter.

Garbarino, J., & Abramowitz, R. (1992). Sociocultural risk and opportunity. In J. Garbarino (Ed.), *Children and families in the social environment* (2nd ed., pp. 35–70). New York: Aldine de Gruyter.

Gergen, K. (1985). The social constructivist movement in modern psychology. *American Psychologist, 40,* 266–275.

Gesten, E. L., Rains, M., Rapkin, B. D., Weissberg, R. P., Flores de Apodaca, R., Cowen, E. L., & Bowen, R. (1982). Training children in social problem-solving skills: A competence building approach, first and second look. *American Journal of Community Psychology, 10,* 95–115.

Giesbrecht, N., & Ferris, J. (1993). Community-based research initiatives in prevention. *Addiction, 88*(Suppl.), (83S–93S).

Gold, R. S., Parcel, G. S., Walberg, H. J., Luepker, R. V., Portnoy, B., & Stone, E. J. (1991). Summary and conclusions of the THTM evaluation: The expert work group perspective. *Journal of School Health, 61,* 39–42.

Gomby, D. S., Larner, M. B., Stevenson, C. S., Lewit, E. M., & Behrman, R. E. (1995). Long-term outcomes of early childhood programs: Analysis and recommendation. *Future of Children, 5,* 6–24.

Gomby, D. S., Larson, C. S., Lewit, E. M., & Behrman, R. E. (1993). Home visiting: Analysis and recommendations. *Future of Children, 3,* 6–22.

Goodman, R. M., & Wandersman, A. (1994). FORECAST: A formative approach to evaluating community coalitions and community-based initiatives. In S. J. Kaftarian & W. B. Hansen (Eds.), Community partnership program center for substance abuse prevention [Monograph] [Special issue]. *Journal of Community Psychology,* 6–25.

Gordon, R. S. (1983). An operational classification of disease prevention. *Public Health Reports, 98,* 107–109.

Gordon, R. S. (1987). An operational classification of disease prevention. In J. A. Sternberg & M. M. Silverman (Eds.), *Preventing mental disorders: A research perspective* (pp. 20–26) (DHHS Publication No. ADM 87-1492). Washington, DC: U.S. Government Printing Office.

Gottfredson, D. C. (1986). An empirical test of school-based environmental and individual interventions to reduce the risk of delinquent behavior. *Criminology, 24,* 705–731.

Gottfredson, D. C. (1987). An evaluation of an organizational development approach to reducing school disorder. *Evaluation Review, 11,* 739–763.

Gottfredson, D. C., Fink, C. M., Skroban, S., & Gottfredson, G. D. (in press). Making prevention work. In R. P. Weissberg, T. P. Gullotta, R. L. Hampton, & G. R. Adams (Eds.), *Healthy children 2010: Strategies to enhance social, emotional, and physical wellness.* Newbury Park, CA: Sage.

Gottfredson, D. C., Gottfredson, G. D., & Hybl, L. G. (1993). Managing adolescent behavior: A multiyear, multischool study. *American Educational Research Journal, 30,* 179–216.

Green, S. K., & Sollie, D. L. (1989). Long-term effects of a church-based sex education program on adolescent communication. *Family Relations, 38,* 152–156.

Greenberg, M. T. (1996). *The PATHS project: Preventive intervention for children* (A final report to NIMH, Grant number: R01MH42131). University of Washington: Author.

Greenberg, M. T., & Crnic, K. A. (1988). Longitudinal predictors of developmental status and social interaction in premature and full-term infants at age two. *Child Development, 59,* 554–570.

Greenberg, M. T., & Kusche, C. A. (1993). *Promoting social and emotional development in deaf children: The PATHS Project.* Seattle: University of Washington Press.

Greenberg, M. T., Kusche, C. A., Cook, E. T., & Quamma, J. P. (1995). Promoting emotional competence in school-aged deaf children: The effects of the PATHS Curriculum. *Development and Psychopathology, 7,* 117–136.

Greenberg, M. T., Kusche, C. A., & Speltz, M. (1991). Emotional regulation, self-control, and psychopathology: The role of relationships in early childhood. In D. Cicchetti & S. L. Toth (Eds.), *Rochester Symposium on Developmental Psychopathology: Vol. 2. Internalizing and externalizing expressions of dysfunction* (pp. 21–56). Hillsdale, NJ: Erlbaum.

Greenberg, M. T., Speltz, M. L., & DeKlyen, M. (1993). The role of attachment in the early development of disruptive behavior problems. *Development and Psychopathology, 5,* 191–213.

Greenough, W. T., Black, J. E., & Wallace, C. S. (1987). Experience and brain development. *Child Development, 58,* 439–459.

Greenwood, P. W., Model, K. E., Rydell, C. P., & Chiesa, J. (1996). *Diverting children from a life of crime: Measuring costs and benefits* (MR-699-UCB/RC/IF). Santa Monica, CA: Rand.

Grossman, J., & Tierney, J. P. (1993). The fallibility of comparison groups. *Evaluation Review, 17,* 556–571.

Gutelius, M. F., Kirsch, A. D., MacDonald, S., Brooks, M. R., & McErlean, T. (1977). Controlled study of child health supervision: Behavioral results. *Pediatrics, 60,* 294–304.

Gutelius, M. F., Kirsch, A. D., MacDonald, S., Brooks, M. R., McErlean, T., & Newcomb, C. (1972). Promising results from a cognitive stimulation program in infancy. *Clinical Pediatrics, 11,* 585–593.

Haggerty, R. J. (1988). President's report. *William T. Grant Foundation Annual Report: 1988.* New York: William T. Grant Foundation.

Hall, G. E., & Hord, S. M. (1987). *Change in school: Facilitating the process.* Albany: State University of New York Press.

Halpern, R. (1992). Issues of program design and implementation. In M. Larner, R. Halpern, & O. Harkavy (Eds.), *Fair Start for children: Lessons learned from seven demonstration projects* (pp. 179–197). New Haven, CT: Yale University Press.

Hamburg, B. A. (1990). *Life skills training: Preventive interventions for young adolescents.* Washington, DC: Carnegie Council on Adolescent Development.

Hamburg, D. A. (1992). *Today's children: Creating a future for a generation in crisis.* New York: Times Books.

Hansen, W. B. (1992). School-based substance abuse prevention: A review of the state of the art in curriculum, 1980–1990. *Health Education Research, 7,* 403–430.

Hansen, W. B., & Graham, J. W. (1991). Preventing alcohol, marijuana, and cigarette use among adolescents: Peer pressure resistance training versus establishing conservative norms. *Preventive Medicine, 20,* 414–430.

Hartup, W. (1983). Peer relations. In P. H. Mussen (Series Ed.) & E. M. Hetherington (Vol. Ed.), *Handbook of child psychology: Vol. 4. Socialization, personality, and social development* (4th ed., pp. 103–195). New York: Wiley.

Harwood, H., Hubbard, R., Collins, J., & Rachal, J. V. (1988). The costs of crime and the benefits of drug abuse treatment: A cost-benefit analysis using TOPS data. In C. Leukefeld & F. Tims (Eds.), *Compulsory treatment of drug abuse: Research and clinical practice* (NIDA Research Monograph 96) (pp. 209–235). Washington DC: U.S. Government Printing Office.

Haskins, R. (1989). Beyond metaphor: The efficacy of early childhood education. *American Psychologist, 44,* 274–283.

Hatziandreu, E. J., Sacks, J. J., Brown, R., Taylor, W. R., Rosenberg, M. L., & Graham, J. D. (1995). The cost effectiveness of three programs to increase use of bicycle helmets among children. *Public Health Reports, 110,* 251–259.

Haveman, R., & Wolfe, B. L. (1984). Schooling and economic well-being: The role of nonmarket effects. *Journal of Human Resources, 19,* 377–407.

Haveman, R., & Wolfe, B. L. (1994). *Succeeding generations: On the effects of investments in children.* New York: Russell-Sage Foundation.

Hawaii State Department of Health. (1992). *Healthy Start: Hawaii's system of family support services.* Report to the 16th Legislature, State of Hawaii.

Hawkins, J. D. (1995). Controlling crime before it happens: Risk-focused prevention. *National Institute of Justice Journal, 229*(9), 10–18.

Hawkins, J. D., Arthur, M. W., & Catalano, R. F. (1995). Preventing substance abuse. In M. Tonry & D. Farringon (Eds.), *Crime and justice: A review of research: Vol. 19. Building a safer society: Strategic approaches to crime prevention* (pp. 343–427). Chicago: University of Chicago Press.

Hawkins, J. D., Catalano, R. F., & Associates. (1992). *Communities that care: Action for drug abuse prevention.* San Francisco: Jossey-Bass.

Hawkins, J. D., Catalano, R. F., & Brewer, D. D. (1995). Preventing serious, violent and chronic juvenile offending: Effective strategies from conception to age 6. In J. C. Howell, B. Krisberg, J. J. Wilson, & J. D. Hawkins (Eds.), *A sourcebook on serious, violent, and chronic juvenile offenders* (pp. 47–60). Newbury Park, CA: Sage.

Hawkins, J. D., Catalano, R. F., & Miller, J. Y. (1992). Risk and protective factors for alcohol and other drug problems in adolescence and early adulthood: Implications for substance abuse prevention. *Psychological Bulletin, 112,* 64–105.

Hawkins, J. D., Catalano, R. F., Morrison, D. M., O'Donnell, J., Abbott, R. D., & Day, L. E. (1992). The Seattle Social Development Project: Effects of the first four years on protective factors and problem behaviors. In J. McCord & R. E. Tremblay (Eds.), *Preventing antisocial behavior: Interventions from birth through adolescence* (pp. 139–161). New York: Guilford Press.

Hawkins, J. D., Doueck, H. J., & Lishner, D. M. (1988). Changing teaching practices in mainstream classrooms to improve bonding and behavior of low achievers. *American Educational Research Journal, 25,* 31–50.

Hawkins, J. D., & Weis, J. G. (1985). The social development model: An integrated approach to delinquency prevention. *Journal of Primary Prevention, 6,* 73–97.

Haynes, N., & Comer, J. P. (1993). The Yale School Development Program: Process, outcomes, and policy implications. *Urban Education, 28,* 166–199.

Haynes, N., Emmons, C. L., Gebreyesus, S., & Ben-Avie, M. (1996). The School Development Program evaluation process. In J. P. Comer, N. M. Haynes, E. T. Joyner, & M. Ben-Avie (Eds.), *Rallying the whole village: The Comer process for reforming education* (pp. 123–146). New York: Teachers College Press.

Heller, K. (1996, May). *Models of community adoption in prevention research.* Paper presented at the fifth national conference on Prevention Research, Tysons Corner, VA.

Heller, K., Price, R. H., Reinharz, S., Riger, S., & Wandersman, A. (1984). *Psychology and community change: Challenges of the future* (2nd ed.). Pacific Grove, CA: Brooks/Cole.

Hernandez, D. J. (1995). Changing demographics: Past and future demands for early childhood programs. *Future of Children, 5*(3), 145–160.

Hirachi, T. W., Ayers, C. D., Hawkins, J. D., Catalano, R. F., & Cushing, J. (1996). Empowering communities to prevent adolescent substance abuse: Process evaluation results from a risk- and protection-focused community mobilization effort. *Journal of Primary Prevention, 16,* 233–254.

Hobel, C. J., Ross, M. G., Bemis, R. L., Bragonier, J. R., Nessim, S., Sandhu, N., Bear, M. B., & Mori, B. (1994). The West Los Angeles Preterm Birth Prevention Project: I. Program impact on high-risk women. *American Journal of Obstetrics and Gynecology, 170,* 54–62.

Hollister, R. G., & Hill, J. (1995). Problems in evaluation of community-wide initiatives. In J. P. Connell, A. C. Kubish, L. B. Schorr, & C. H. Weiss (Eds.), *New approaches to evaluating community initiatives: Concept, methods, and context* (pp. 127–172). Washington, DC: Aspen Institute.

Horacek, H. J., Ramey, C. T., Campbell, F. A., Hoffman, K. P., & Fletcher, R. H. (1987). Predicting school failure and assessing early intervention with high-risk children. *Journal of the American Academy of Child and Adolescent Psychiatry, 36,* 758–763.

Howard, M., & McCabe, J. B. (1990). Helping teenagers postpone sexual involvement. *Family Planning Perspectives, 22,* 21–26.

Hudley, C., & Graham, S. (1995). School-based interventions for aggressive African-American boys. *Applied and Preventive Psychology, 4,* 185–195.

Hueston, W. J., Mainous, A. G., & Farrell, J. B. (1994). A cost-benefit analysis of smoking cessation programs during the first trimester of pregnancy for the prevention of low birthweight. *Journal of Family Practice, 39,* 353–357.

Infant Health and Development Program, The. (1990). Enhancing the outcomes of low-birth-weight, premature infants: A multisite, randomized trial. *Journal of the American Medical Association, 263,* 3035–3042.

Institute of Medicine. (1994). *Reducing risks for mental disorders: Frontiers for preventive intervention research.* Washington, DC: National Academy Press.

Jacobs, D. R., Luepker, R. V., Mittlemark, M. B., Folsom, A. R., Pirie, P. L., Mascioli, S. R., Hannan, P. J., Pechacek, T. F., Bracht, N. F., Carlaw, R. W., Kline, F. G., & Blackburn, H. (1986). Community-wide prevention strategies: Evaluation design of the Minnesota Heart Health Program. *Journal of Chronic Disease, 39,* 775–787.

Janz, N. K., & Becker, M. H. (1984). The health belief model: A decade later. *Health Education Quarterly, 11,* 1–47.

Jemmott, J. B., III, Jemmott, L. S., & Fong, G. T. (1992). Reductions in HIV risk-associated sexual behaviors among black male adolescents: Effects of an AIDS prevention intervention. *American Journal of Public Health, 82,* 372–377.

Jessor, R. (1993). Successful adolescent development among youth in high-risk settings. *American Psychologist, 48,* 117–126.

Jessor, R., Donovan, J. E., & Costa, F. M. (1991). *Beyond adolescence: Problem behavior and young adult development.* New York: Cambridge University Press.

Jessor, R., & Jessor, S. L. (1977). *Problem behavior and psychosocial development: A longitudinal study of youth.* New York: Academic Press.

Johnson, C. A., Pentz, M. A., Weber, M. D., Dwyer, J. H., Baer, N., MacKinnon, D. P., Hansen, W. B., & Flay, B. R. (1990). Relative effectiveness of comprehensive community programming for drug abuse prevention with high-risk and low-risk adolescents. *Journal of Consulting and Clinical Psychology, 58,* 447–456.

Johnson, D. L. (1988). Primary prevention of behavior problems in young children: The Houston Parent-Child Development Center. In R. H. Price, E. L. Cowen, R. P. Lorion, & J. Ramos-McKay (Eds.), *14 ounces of prevention: A casebook for practitioners* (pp. 44–52). Washington, DC: American Psychological Association.

Johnson, D. L., & Walker, T. B. (1987). Primary prevention of behavior problems in Mexican-American children. *American Journal of Community Psychology, 15,* 375–386.

Johnson, D. L., & Walker, T. B. (1991a). A follow-up evaluation of the Houston Parent-Child Development Center: School performance. *Journal of Early Intervention, 15,* 226–236.

Johnson, D. L., & Walker, T. B. (1991b). *Final report of an evaluation of the Avance parent education and family support program.* Unpublished manuscript, Carnegie Corporation of New York.

Johnston, L. D., O'Malley, P. M., & Bachman, J. G. (1995). *National survey results on drug use from the Monitoring the Future Study, 1975–1994.* Rockville, MD: National Institute on Drug Abuse.

Jones, M. B., & Offord, D. R. (1989). Reduction of antisocial behavior in poor children by nonschool skill-development. *Journal of Child Psychology and Psychiatry, 30,* 737–750.

Kaftarian, S. J., & Hansen, W. B. (Eds.). (1994). Community Partnership Program, Center for Substance Abuse Prevention [Monograph] [Special issue]. *Journal of Community Psychology,* 1–205.

Kanter, R. M., Stein, B. A., & Jick, T. D. (1992). *The challenge of organizational change: How companies experience it and leaders guide it.* New York: Free Press.

Karoly, P., & Kanfer, F. H. (Eds.). (1982). *Self-management and behavior change: From theory to practice.* New York: Pergamon Press.

Kasprow, W. J., Marmorstein, N., Voyce, C. K., Schwab-Stone, M., Shriver, T., DeFalco, K., Elder, W., Kavanagh, M., Speese-Linehan, D., & Camacho, M. (1993). *New Haven Public Schools Social Development Project: 1992–1993*

Evaluation report. Part 1: Consumer satisfaction surveys. New Haven, CT: New Haven Public Schools.

Kasprow, W. J., Weissberg, R. P., Voyce, C. K., Jackson, A. S., Fontana, T., Arthur, M. W., Borman, E., Marmorstein, N., Zeisz, J., Shriver, T., DeFalco, K., Elder, W., & Kavanagh, M. (1991). *New Haven Public Schools Social Development Project: 1990–1991 Evaluation report.* New Haven, CT: New Haven Public Schools.

Kasprow, W. J., Weissberg, R. P., Voyce, C. K., Jackson, A. S., Fontana, T., Ayers, T., Barone, C., Primavera, J., Marmorstein, N., Beauvais, J., Driscoll, L., Schwab-Stone, M., Shriver, T., DeFalco, K., Elder, W., Kavanagh, M., Speese-Linehan, D., & Camacho, M. (1992). *New Haven Public Schools Social Development Project: 1991–1992 Evaluation report.* New Haven, CT: New Haven Public Schools.

Kavanagh, M., Jackson, A. S., Gaffney, J., Caplan, M., & Weissberg, R. P. (1990). *The human growth and development, AIDS prevention, and teen pregnancy prevention module of the Yale-New Haven Social Development Program.* Chicago: University of Illinois.

Kazdin, A. E. (1991a). Prevention of conduct disorder. In *The prevention of mental disorders: Progress, problems, and prospects.* Washington, DC: National Institute of Mental Health.

Kazdin, A. E. (1991b). *Research design in clinical psychology* (2nd ed.). New York: HarperCollins.

Kegan, R. (1982). *The evolving self.* Cambridge, MA: Harvard University Press.

Kelder, S. H., Perry, C. L., & Klepp, K. (1993). Community-wide youth exercise promotion: Long-term outcomes of the Minnesota Heart Health Program and the Class of 1989 Study. *Journal of School Health, 63,* 218–223.

Kelder, S. H., Perry, C. L., Klepp, K., & Lytle, L. L. (1994). Longitudinal tracking of adolescent smoking, physical activity, and food choice behaviors. *American Journal of Public Health, 84,* 1121–1126.

Kellam, S. G. (1990). Developmental epidemiological framework for family research on depression and aggression. In G. R. Patterson (Ed.), *Depression and aggression in family interaction* (pp. 11–48). Hillsdale, NJ: Erlbaum.

Kellam, S. G., & Rebok, G. W. (1992). Building developmental and etiological theory through epidemiologically based preventive intervention trials. In J. McCord & R. E. Tremblay (Eds.), *Preventing antisocial behavior: Interventions from birth through adolescence* (pp. 162–194). New York: Guilford Press.

Kellam, S. G., Werthamer, L. L., Dolan, L. J., Brown, C. H., Mayer, L. S., Rebok, G. W., Anthony, J. C., Laudolff, J., Edelsohn, G., & Wheeler, L. (1991). Developmental epidemiologically based preventive trials: Baseline modeling of early target behaviors and depressive symptoms. *American Journal of Community Psychology, 19,* 563–584.

Kelly, J. G. (1987). An ecological paradigm: Defining mental health consultation as a preventive service. *Prevention in Human Services, 4,* 1–36.

Kelly, J. G. (1988). *A guide to conducting prevention research in the community: First steps.* Binghamton, NY: Haworth Press.

Kennedy, J. F. (1963, February 5). Special message to the Congress on mental illness and mental retardation. *Public Papers of the Presidents,* 126–137.

Kessler, M., & Albee, G. W. (1975). Primary prevention. In M. R. Rosenzweig & L. W. Porter (Eds.), *Annual Review of Psychology, 26,* 557–591.

Keys, C. B. (1986). Organization development: An approach to mental health consultation. In F. V. Mannino, E. J. Trickett, M. F. Shore, M. G. Kidder, & G. Levin (Eds.), *Handbook of mental health consultation* (pp. 81–112). Washington, DC: U.S. Government Printing Office.

Kim, S., Crutchfield, C., Williams, C., & Hepler, N. (1994). An innovative and unconventional approach to program evaluation in the field of substance abuse prevention: A threshold gating approach using single system evaluation designs [Monograph] [Special issue]. *Journal of Community Psychology: Community Partnership Program, Center for Substance Abuse Prevention,* 61–78.

Kirby, D. (1992). School-based programs to reduce sexual risk-taking behaviors. *Journal of School Health, 62,* 280–287.

Kirby, D., Barth, R. P., Leland, N., & Fetro, J. V. (1991). Reducing the risk: Impact of a new curriculum on sexual risk taking. *Family Planning Perspectives, 23,* 253–263.

Kirby, D., Short, L., Collins, J., Rugg, D., Kolby, L., Howard, L., Miller, B., Sonnenstein, F., & Zabin, L. S. (1994). School-based programs to reduce sexual risk behaviors: A review of effectiveness. *Public Health Reports, 109,* 339–360.

Kirk, R. E. (1968). *Experimental design: Procedures for the behavioral sciences.* Monterey, CA: Brooks/Cole.

Kizer, K. W., Vassar, M. J., Hary, R. L., & Layton, K. D. (1995). Hospitalization charges, costs, and income for firearm-related injuries in a university trauma center. *Journal of the American Medical Association, 273,* 1768–1773.

Knapp, M. S. (1995). How shall we study comprehensive, collaborative services for children and families? *Educational Researcher, 22*(4), 5–16.

Knitzer, J., & Aber, J. L. (1995). Young children and poverty: Facing the facts. *American Journal of Orthopsychiatry, 65,* 174–176.

Koo, H. P., Dunteman, G. H., George, C., Green, Y., & Vincent, M. (1994). Reducing adolescent pregnancy through a school- and community-based intervention: Denmark, South Carolina, revisited. *Family Planning Perspectives, 26*(5), 206–211, 217.

Kraemer, H., & Fendt, K. (1990). Random assignment in clinical trials: Issues in planning. *Journal of Clinical Epidemiology, 11,* 1157–1167.

Kusche, C. A., & Greenberg, M. T. (1995). *The PATHS curriculum.* Seattle, WA: Developmental Research and Programs.

Ladd, G. W., & Mize, J. (1983). A cognitive-social learning model of social-skill training. *Psychological Review, 90,* 127–157.

Lally, R. J., Mangione, P. L., & Honig, A. S. (1988). The Syracuse University Family Development Research Program: Long-range impact on an early intervention with low-income children and their families. In D. Powell (Ed.), *Parent education as early childhood intervention: Emerging directions in theory, research, and practice* (pp. 79–104). Norwood, NJ: ABLEX.

Lazar, I., Darlington, R. B., Murray, H., Royce, J., & Snipper, A. (1982). Lasting effects of early education: A report from the Consortium for Longitudinal Studies. *Monographs of the Society for Research in Child Development, 47*(2/3, Serial No. 195).

Lerner, R. M. (1994). *America's children and youth in crisis.* Thousand Oaks, CA: Sage.

Levenstein, P. (1992). The Mother-Child Home Project: Research methodology and the real world. In J. McCord & R. E. Tremblay (Eds.), *Preventing antisocial behavior* (pp. 43–66). New York: Guilford Press.

Levin, H. M. (1983). *Cost-effectiveness analysis: A primer.* Newbury Park, CA: Sage.

Levine, M., & Perkins, D. V. (1987). *Principles of community psychology: Perspectives and applications.* New York: Oxford University Press.

Levy, S. R., Perhats, C., Nash-Johnson, M., & Welter, J. F. (1992). Reducing the risks in pregnant teens who are very young and those with mild mental retardation. *Mental Retardation, 30,* 195–203.

Lewin, K. (1946). Action research and minority problems. *Journal of Social Issues, 2,* 34–46.

Lewin, K. (1951). *Field theory in social science.* New York: Harper & Row.

Liaw, F., & Brooks-Gunn, J. (1994). Cumulative familial risks and low-birthweight children's cognitive and behavioral development. *Journal of Clinical Child Psychology, 23,* 360–372.

Lipsey, M. W. (1990). *Design sensitivity: Statistical power for experimental research.* Newbury Park, CA: Sage.

Lochman, J. E., Coie, J. D., Underwood, M. K., & Terry, R. (1993). Effectiveness of a social relations intervention program for aggressive and nonaggressive rejected children. *Journal of Consulting and Clinical Psychology, 61,* 1053–1058.

Loeber, R., & Dishion, T. (1983). Early predictors of male delinquency: A review. *Psychological Bulletin, 93,* 68–99.

Loevinger, J. (1976). *Ego development.* San Francisco: Jossey-Bass.

Lorion, R. P. (1983). Evaluating preventive interventions: Guidelines for the serious social change agent. In R. D. Felner, L. A. Jason, J. N. Moritsugu, & S. S. Farber (Eds.), *Preventive psychology: Theory, research, and practice* (pp. 251–268). New York: Pergamon Press.

Lorion, R. P. (1990a). Developmental analyses of community phenomena. In P. Tolan, C. Keys, F. Chertok, & L. Jason (Eds.), *Researching community psychology: Issues of theories and methods* (pp. 32–41). Washington, DC: American Psychological Association.

Lorion, R. P. (Ed.). (1990b). Protecting the children: Strategies for optimizing emotional and behavioral development. *Prevention in Human Services, 7,* 1–275.

Lorion, R. P., Myers, T. G., Bartels, C., & Dennis, A. (1994). Preventive intervention research: Pathways for extending knowledge of child/adolescent health and pathology. In T. H. Ollendick & R. J. Prinz (Eds.), *Advances in clinical child psychology* (Vol. 16, pp. 109–139). New York: Plenum Press.

Luthar, S. S. (1991). Vulnerability and resiliency: A study of high-risk adolescents. *Child Development, 62,* 600–616.

Luthar, S. S. (1993). Annotation: Methodological and conceptual issues in research on childhood resilience. *Journal of Child Psychology and Psychiatry and Allied Disciplines, 34,* 441–453.

Luthar, S. S., & Zigler, E. (1992). Intelligence and social competence among high-risk adolescents. *Development and Psychopathology, 4,* 287–299.

Madden, N. A., Slavin, R. F., Karweit, N. I., Dolan, L. J., & Wasik, B. A. (1993). Success for all: Longitudinal effects of a restructuring program for inner-city elementary schools. *American Educational Research Journal, 30,* 123–148.

Main, M., Cassidy, J., & Kaplan, N. (1985). Security in infancy, childhood and adulthood: A move to the level of representation. In I. Bretherton & E. Waters (Eds.), Growing points in attachment theory and research. *Monographs of the Society for Research in Child Development, 50*(1/2, Serial No. 209).

Males, M. (1992). The Code Blue report: Call to action, or unwarranted "Dirism"? *Adolescence, 27,* 272–282.

Martin, S. L., Ramey, C. T., & Ramey, S. (1990). The prevention of intellectual impairment in children of impoverished families: Findings from a randomized trial of educational day care. *American Journal of Public Health, 80,* 844–847.

Maughan, B. (1988). School experiences as risk/protective factors. In M. Rutter (Ed.), *Studies of psychosocial risk: The power of longitudinal data* (pp. 200–220). New York: Cambridge University Press.

Max, W., & Rice, D. P. (1993). Shooting in the dark: Estimating the cost of firearm injuries. *Health Affairs, 12,* 171–185.

Maziade, M., Caron, C., Cote, R., Boutin, P., & Thivierge, J. (1990). Extreme temperament and diagnosis. *Archives of General Psychiatry, 47,* 477–484.

Maziade, M., Cote, R., Bernier, H., Boutin, P., & Thivierge, J. (1989). Significance of extreme temperament in infancy for clinical status in pre-school years: I. *British Journal of Psychiatry, 14,* 535–543.

McCord, J., & Tremblay, R. E. (Eds.). (1992). *Preventing antisocial behavior: Interventions from birth through adolescence.* New York: Guilford Press.

McKey, R. H., Condelli, L., Ganson, H., Barrett, B. J., McConkey, C., & Planz, M. C. (1985). *The impact of Head Start on children, families and communities* (DHHS Publication No. OHDS 85-31193). Washington, DC: U.S. Government Printing Office.

McLaughlin, M. W. (1990). The Rand Change Agent Study revisited: Macro perspectives and micro realities. *Educational Researcher, 19*(9), 11–16.

Miller, B. C., Card, J. J., Paikoff, R. L., & Peterson, J. L. (1992). *Preventing adolescent pregnancy: Model programs and evaluations.* Newbury Park, CA: Sage.

Miller, B. C., Norton, M. C., Jenson, G. O., Lee, T. R., Christopherson, C., & King, P. K. (1993). Pregnancy prevention programs: Impact evaluation of facts and feelings: A home-based video sex education curriculum. *Family Relations, 42,* 392–400.

Miller, T. R., Cohen, M. A., & Weirsma, B. (1996). *Victim costs and consequences: A new look* (National Institute of Justice Research Report, NCJ-155282). Washington, DC: National Institute of Justice.

Millstein, S. G., Petersen, A. C., & Nightingale, E. O. (Eds.). (1993a). *Promoting the health of adolescents: New directions for the twenty-first century.* New York: Oxford University Press.

Millstein, S. G., Petersen, A. C., & Nightingale, E. O. (1993b). Adolescent health promotion: Rationale, goals, and objectives. In S. G. Millstein, A. C. Petersen, & E. O. Nightingale (Eds.), *Promoting the health of adolescents: New directions for the twenty-first century* (pp. 3–10). New York: Oxford University Press.

Minuchin, P. P., & Shapiro, E. K. (1983). The school as a context for social development. In P. H. Mussen (Series Ed.) & E. M. Hetherington (Vol. Ed.), *Handbook of child psychology: Vol. 4. Socialization, personality, and social development* (4th ed., pp. 197–274). New York: Wiley.

Moore, K. A., Sugland, B. W., Blumenthal, C., Glei, D., & Snyder, N. (1995). *Adolescent pregnancy prevention programs: Interventions and evaluations.* Washington, DC: Child Trends.

Morissett, C. E., Barnard, K. E., Greenberg, M. T., Booth, C. L., & Spieker, S. J. (1990). Environmental influences on early language development: The context of social risk. *Development and Psychopathology, 2,* 127–149.

Mueller, D. P., & Higgins, P. S. (1988). *Funders' guide manual: A guide to prevention programs in human services: Focus on children and adolescents.* Saint Paul, MN: Amherst H. Wilder Foundation.

Murray, M. E., Guerra, N., & Williams, K. R. (1997). Violence prevention for the 21st century. In R. P. Weissberg, T. P. Gullotta, R. L. Hampton, B. A. Ryan, & G. R. Adams (Eds.), *Healthy children 2010: Enhancing children's wellness* (pp. 105–128). Thousand Oaks, CA: Sage.

National Commission on Children. (1991). *Beyond rhetoric: A new American agenda for children and families.* Washington, DC: U.S. Government Printing Office.

National Commission on the Role of the School and the Community in Improving Adolescent Health. (1990). *Code Blue: Uniting for healthier youth.* Alexandria, VA: National Association of State Boards of Education.

National Education Goals Panel. (1995). *Data for the National Education Goals Report: Vol. 1. National data.* Washington, DC: U.S. Government Printing Office.

National Institutes of Health, National Institute of Mental Health. (1996). *A plan for prevention research for the National Institute of Mental Health: A report to the National Advisory Mental Health Council* (NIH Publication No. 96-4093). Washington, DC: Author.

Newcomb, M. D., Maddahian, E., & Bentler, P. M. (1986). Risk factors for drug use among adolescents: Concurrent and longitudinal analyses. *American Journal of Public Health, 76,* 525–530.

Nurcombe, B., Howell, D. C., Rauh, V. A., Teti, D. M., Ruoff, P., & Brennan, J. (1984). An intervention program for mothers of low birthweight infants. *Journal of the American Academy of Child Psychiatry, 23,* 319–325.

O'Donnell, C. R. (1995). Firearm deaths among children and youth. *American Psychologist, 50,* 771–776.

O'Donnell, J., Hawkins, J. D., Catalano, R. F., Abbott, R. D., & Day, L. E. (1995). Preventing school failure, drug use, and delinquency among low-income children: Long-term intervention in elementary schools. *American Journal of Orthopsychiatry, 65,* 87–100.

Offord, D. R., & Jones, M. B. (1983). Skill development: A community intervention program for the prevention of antisocial behavior. In S. B. Guze, F. J. Earls, & J. E. Barrett (Eds.), *Childhood psychopathology and development* (pp. 165–188). New York: Raven Press.

Olds, D. L. (1988). The prenatal/early infancy project. In R. H. Price, E. L. Cowen, R. P. Lorion, & J. Ramos-McKay (Eds.), *14 ounces of prevention: A casebook for practitioners* (pp. 9–23). Washington, DC: American Psychological Association.

Olds, D. L. (1995, April). *Studies of prenatal and infancy nurse home visitation.* Paper presented at the meeting of the Society for Research in Child Development, Indianapolis, IN.

Olds, D. L., Henderson, C. R., Chamberlin, R., & Tatelbaum, R. (1986). Preventing child abuse and neglect: A randomized clinical trial of nurse home visitation. *Pediatrics, 78,* 65–78.

Olds, D. L., Henderson, C. R., & Kitzman, H. (1994). Does neonatal and infancy nurse home visitation have enduring effects on qualities of parental caregiving and child health at 25 to 50 months of life? *Pediatrics, 93,* 89–98.

Olds, D. L., Henderson, C. R., Kitzman, H., & Cole R. (1995). Effects of prenatal and infancy nurse home visitation on surveillance of child maltreatment. *Pediatrics, 95,* 365–372.

Olds, D. L., Henderson, C. R., Phelps, C., Kitzman, H., & Hanks, C. (1993). Effects of prenatal and infancy nurse home visiting on government spending. *Medical Care, 31,* 155–174.

Olds, D. L., Henderson, C. R., & Tatelbaum, R. (1994a). Intellectual impairment in children of women who smoke cigarettes during pregnancy. *Pediatrics, 93,* 221–227.

Olds, D. L., Henderson, C. R., & Tatelbaum, R. (1994b). Prevention of intellectual impairment in children of women who smoke cigarettes during pregnancy. *Pediatrics, 93,* 228–233.

Olds, D. L., & Kitzman, H. (1993). Review of research on home visiting for pregnant women and parents of young children. *Future of Children, 3,* 53–92.

Olweus, D. (1991). Bully/victim problems among schoolchildren: Basic facts and effects of an intervention program. In D. J. Pepler & K. H. Rubin (Eds.), *The development and treatment of childhood aggression* (pp. 411–448). Hillsdale, NJ: Erlbaum.

Panel on High-Risk Youth, National Research Council. (1993). *Losing generations: Adolescents in high-risk settings.* Washington, DC: National Academy Press.

Paneth, N. S. (1995). The problem of low birth weight. *Future of Children, 5,* 19–34.

Patterson, G. R., Reid, J. B., & Dishion, T. J. (1992). *Antisocial boys.* Eugene, OR: Castalia Press.

Pentz, M. A. (1994). Adaptive evaluation strategies for estimating effects of community-based drug abuse prevention programs [Monograph] [Special issue]. *Journal of Community Psychology: Community Partnership Program, Center for Substance Abuse Prevention,* 26–51.

Pentz, M. A., Dwyer, J. H., MacKinnon, D. P., Flay, B., Hansen, W. B., Wang, E. Y. I., & Johnson, C. A. (1989). A multicommunity trial for primary prevention of adolescent drug abuse. *Journal of the American Medical Association, 261,* 3259–3266.

Perry, C. L., & Jessor, R. (1985). The concept of health promotion and the prevention of adolescent drug abuse. *Health Education Quarterly, 12,* 169–184.

Perry, C. L., Kelder, S. H., & Komro, K. A. (1993). The social world of adolescents: Families, peers, schools, and the community. In S. G. Millstein, A. C. Petersen, & E. O. Nightingale (Eds.), *Promoting the health of adolescents: New directions for the twenty-first century* (pp. 73–96). New York: Oxford University Press.

Perry, C. L., Kelder, S., Murray, D. M., & Klepp, K. (1992). Community-wide smoking prevention: Long-term outcomes of the Minnesota Heart Health Program and the Class of 1989 Study. *American Journal of Public Health, 82,* 1210–1216.

Perry, C. L., Klepp, K., & Sillers, C. (1989). Community-wide strategies for cardiovascular health: The Minnesota Heart Health Youth Program. *Health Education Research, 4,* 87–101.

Pfannenstiel, J., Lambson, T., & Yarnell, V. (1991). *Second wave study of the Parents as Teachers Program* (Report for the Missouri Department of Elementary and Secondary Education). St. Louis, MO: Parents as Teachers National Center.

Pierson, D. E. (1988). The Brookline Early Education Project. In R. H. Price, E. L. Cowen, R. P. Lorion, & J. Ramos-McKay (Eds.), *14 ounces of prevention: A casebook for practitioners* (pp. 24–31). Washington, DC: American Psychological Association.

Pittman, K. J., & Cahill, M. (1992). *Pushing the boundaries of education: The implications of a youth development approach to education policies, structures, and collaborations.* Washington, DC: Council of Chief State School Officers.

Plotnick, R. (1994). Applying benefit-cost analysis to the substance abuse prevention programs. *International Journal of Addiction, 29,* 339–359.

Powell, C., & Grantham-McGregor, S. (1989). Home visiting of varying frequency and child development. *Pediatrics, 84,* 157–164.

Powell, D. R. (1994). Evaluating family support programs. In S. L. Kagan & B. Weissbourd (Eds.), *Putting families first: America's family support movement and the challenge of change* (pp. 441–470). San Francisco: Jossey-Bass.

Price, R. H. (1983). The education of a prevention psychologist. In R. D. Felner, L. A. Jason, J. N. Moritsugu, & S. S. Farber (Eds.), *Preventive psychology: Theory, research, and practice* (pp. 290–296). New York: Pergamon Press.

Price, R. H., Cioci, M., Penner, W., & Trautlein, B. (1993). Webs of influence: School and community programs that enhance adolescent health and education. *Teachers College Record, 94,* 487–521.

Price, R. H., Cowen, E. L., Lorion, R. P., & Ramos-McKay, J. (Eds.). (1988). *14 ounces of prevention: A casebook for practitioners.* Washington, DC: American Psychological Association.

Price, R. H., Cowen, E. L., Lorion, R. P., & Ramos-McKay, J. (1989). The search for effective prevention programs: What we have learned along the way. *American Journal of Orthopsychiatry, 59,* 49–58.

Price, R. H., & Lorion, R. P. (1989). Prevention programming as organizational reinvention: From research to implementation. In D. Shaffer, I. Philips, & N. B. Enzer (Eds.), *Prevention of mental disorders, alcohol, and other drug use in children and adolescents* (pp. 97–124). Washington, DC: Alcohol, Drug Abuse, and Mental Health Administration, U.S. Government Printing Office.

Price, R. H., & Smith, S. S. (1985). *A guide to evaluating prevention programs in mental health* (DHHS Publication No. ADM 85-1365). Washington, DC: National Institute of Mental Health.

Provence, S., & Naylor, A. (1983). *Working with disadvantaged parents and children: Scientific issues and practice.* New Haven, CT: Yale University Press.

Pushka, P., Tuomilehto, J., Nissinen, K., & Korhonen, H. J. (1989). The North Karelia project: 15 years of community-based prevention of coronary heart disease. *Annals of Medicine, 21,* 169–173.

Quinn, J. (1995). Positive effects of participation in youth organizations. In M. Rutter (Ed.), *Psychosocial disturbances in young people: Challenges for prevention* (pp. 274–304). New York: Cambridge University Press.

Ramey, C. T., Bryant, D. M., Campbell, F. A., Sparling, J. J., & Wasik, B. H. (1988). Early intervention for high-risk children: The Carolina Early Intervention Program. In R. H. Price, E. L. Cowen, R. P. Lorion, & J. Ramos-McKay (Eds.), *14 ounces of prevention: A casebook for practitioners* (pp. 32–43). Washington, DC: American Psychological Association.

Ramey, C. T., Bryant, D. M., Wasik, B. H., Sparling, J. J., Fendt, K. H., & LaVange, L. M. (1992). Infant Health and Development Program for low birth weight, premature infants: Program elements, family participation, and child intelligence. *Pediatrics, 89,* 454–465.

Ramey, C. T., & Campbell, F. A. (1987). The Carolina Abecedarian Project: An educational experiment concerning human malleability. In J. J. Gallagher & C. T. Ramey (Eds.), *The malleability of children* (pp. 127–140). Baltimore: Brookes.

Ramey, C. T., & Ramey, S. L. (1993). Home visiting programs and the health and development of young children. *Future of Children, 3,* 129–139.

Rappaport, J. (1990). Research methods and empowerment social agenda. In P. Tolan, C. Keys, F. Chertok, & L. Jason (Eds.), *Researching community psychology: Issues of theories and methods* (pp. 51–63). Washington, DC: American Psychological Association.

Rappaport, J., Seidman, E., & Davidson, W. S. (1979). Demonstration research and manifest versus true adoption: The natural history of a research project to divert adolescents from the legal system. In R. F. Munoz, L. R. Snowden, & J. G. Kelly (Eds.), *Social and psychological research in community settings* (pp. 101–144). San Francisco: Jossey-Bass.

Rauh, V. A., Achenbach, T. M., Nurcombe, B., Howell, C. T., & Teti, D. M. (1988). Minimizing adverse effects of low birthweight: Four-year results of an early intervention program. *Child Development, 59,* 544–553.

RCCP Research Team. (1996). *The evaluation of the Resolving Conflict Creatively Program: An overview.* Unpublished manuscript, National Center for Children in Poverty, Columbia University, New York.

Report of the National Mental Health Association Commission on the Prevention of Mental-Emotional Disabilities. (1986). *The prevention of mental-emotional disabilities.* Alexandria, VA: National Mental Health Association.

Report of the Task Panel on Prevention. (1978). *Task panel reports submitted to the President's Commission on Mental Health* (Vol. 4, pp. 1822–1863). Washington, DC: U.S. Government Printing Office.

Resnick, M. B., Armstrong, S., & Carter, R. L. (1988). Developmental intervention program for high risk premature infants: Effects on development and parent-infant interactions. *Developmental and Behavior Pediatrics, 9,* 73–78.

Reyes, O., & Jason, L. A. (1991). An evaluation of a high school dropout prevention program. *Journal of Community Psychology, 19,* 221–230.

Reynolds, A. J. (1994). Effects of a preschool plus follow-up intervention for children at risk. *Developmental Psychology, 30,* 787–804.

Reynolds, A. J. (1995a). One year of preschool intervention or two: Does it matter? *Early Childhood Research Quarterly, 10,* 1–31.

Reynolds, A. J. (1995b, October 20). *The Child-Parent Center and Expansion Program: Grade 8 findings from the Chicago Longitudinal Study.* Paper presented at the symposium Social Programs That Really Work, Institute of Government and Public Affairs, University of Illinois, Chicago.

Richters, J. E., & Martinez, P. E. (1993). Violent communities, family choices, and children's chances: An algorithm for improving the odds. *Development and Psychopathology, 5,* 609–627.

Robins, L. N. (1992). The role of prevention experiments in discovering causes of children's antisocial behavior. In J. McCord & R. E. Tremblay (Eds.), *Preventing antisocial behavior: Interventions from birth through adolescence* (pp. 3–18). New York: Guilford Press.

Rosenstock, I. M., Strecher, V. J., & Becker, M. H. (1994). The health belief model and HIV risk behavior change. In R. J. DiClemente & J. L. Petersen (Eds.), *Preventing AIDS: Theories and methods of behavioral interventions* (pp. 5–24). New York: Plenum Press.

Ross, J. G., Luepker, R. V., Nelson, G. D., Saavedra, P., & Hubbard, B. M. (1991). Teenage Health Teaching Modules: Impact of teacher training on implementation and student outcomes. *Journal of School Health, 61,* 31–34.

Ross, J. G., Nelson, G. D., & Kolbe, L. J. (1991). Teenage Health Teaching Modules evaluation. *Journal of School Health, 61,* 19–42.

Ross, M. G., Sandhu, M., Bemis, R., Nessim, S., Bragonier, J. R., & Hobel, C. (1994). The West Los Angeles Preterm Birth Prevention Project: II. Cost-effectiveness analysis of high-risk pregnancy interventions. *Obstetrics and Gynecology, 83,* 506–511.

Rotheram, M. J. (1982). Social skills training with underachievers, disruptive, and exceptional children. *Psychology in the Schools, 19,* 532–539.

Rothman, J., & Tropman, J. E. (1987). Models of community organization and macro practice perspectives: Their mixing and phasing. In F. M. Cox, J. L. Erlich, J. Rothman, & J. E. Tropman (Eds.), *Strategies of community organization: Macro practice* (4th ed., pp. 3–26). Itasca, IL: Peacock.

Rothman, K. J. (1986). *Modern epidemiology.* Boston: Little, Brown.

Rotheram-Borus, M. J. (1988). Assertiveness training with children. In R. H. Price, E. L. Cowen, R. P. Lorion, & J. Ramos-McKay (Eds.), *14 ounces of prevention: A casebook for practitioners* (pp. 83–97). Washington, DC: American Psychological Association.

Royce, J. M., Darlington, R. B., & Murray, H. W. (1983). Pooled analyses: Findings across studies. In Consortium for Longitudinal Studies (Ed.), *As the twig is bent: Lasting effects of preschool programs* (pp. 411–459). Hillsdale, NJ: Erlbaum.

Rumberger, R. W. (1995). Dropping out of middle school: A multilevel analysis of students and schools. *American Educational Research Journal, 32,* 583–625.

Rutter, M. (1979). Protective factors in children's responses to stress and disadvantage. In M. W. Kent & J. Rolf (Eds.), *Primary prevention of psychopathology: Vol. 3. Social competence in children* (pp. 49–74). Hanover, NH: University Press of New England.

Rutter, M. (1982). Prevention of children's psychosocial disorders: Myth and substance. *Pediatrics, 70,* 883–894.

Rutter, M. (1985). Resilience in the face of adversity: Protective factors and resistance to psychiatric disorder. *British Journal of Psychiatry, 147,* 598–611.

Rutter, M. (1987). Psychosocial resilience and protective mechanisms. *American Journal of Orthopsychiatry, 57,* 316–331.

Rutter, M., Maughan, B., Mortimore, P., & Ouston, J. (1979). *Fifteen thousand hours: Secondary schools and their effects on children.* Cambridge, MA: Harvard University Press.

Ryan, B. A., Adams, G. R., Gullotta, T. P., Weissberg, R. P., & Hampton, R. L. (Eds.). (1995). *The family-school connection: Theory, research, and practice.* Thousand Oaks, CA: Sage.

Sackett, G. P., Sameroff, A. J., Cairns, R. B., & Suomi, S. (1981). Continuities in behavioral development: Theoretical and empirical studies. In K. Imelmann (Ed.), *Behavioral development: The Bielefeld interdisciplinary project* (pp. 23–57). New York: Cambridge University Press.

Sagrestano, L. M., & Paikoff, R. L. (1997). Preventing high-risk sexual behavior, sexually transmitted diseases, and pregnancy among adolescents. In R. P. Weissberg, T. P. Gullotta, R. L. Hampton, B. A. Ryan, & G. R. Adams (Eds.), *Healthy children 2010: Enhancing children's wellness* (pp. 76–104). Thousand Oaks, CA: Sage.

St. Pierre, R. G., Layzer, J. I., & Barnes, H. V. (1995). Two-generation programs: Design, cost, and short-term effectiveness. *Future of Children, 5,* 76–93.

St. Pierre, T. L., Mark, M. M., Kaltreider, D. L., & Aikin, K. J. (1995). A 27-month evaluation of a sexual activity prevention program in Boys and Girls Clubs across the nation. *Family Relations, 44,* 69–77.

Sameroff, A. J. (1991). Prevention of developmental psychopathology using the transactional model: Perspectives on host, risk agent and environmental interactions. In *The prevention of mental disorders: Progress, problems, and prospects.* Washington, DC: National Institute of Mental Health.

Sameroff, A. J., & Seifer, R. (1990). Early contributors to developmental risk. In J. Rolf, A. S. Masten, D. Cicchetti, K. H. Neuchterlein, & S. Weintraub (Eds.), *Risk and protective factors in the development of psychopathology.* New York: Cambridge University Press.

Sameroff, A. J., Seifer, R., Barocas, R., Zax, M., & Greenspan, S. (1987). Intelligence quotient scores of 4-year-old children: Social-environmental risk factors. *Pediatrics, 79,* 343–350.

Santayana, G. (1948). *The life of reason.* New York: Charles Scribner's Sons.

Sarason, S. B. (1972). *The creation of settings and the future societies.* San Francisco: Jossey-Bass.

Sarason, S. B. (1982). *The culture of the school and the problem of change* (2nd ed.). Boston: Allyn & Bacon.

Sarason, S. B., Levine, M., Goldenberg, I. I., Cherlin, D. L., & Bennett, E. M. (1966). *Psychology in community settings: Clinical, educational, vocational, social aspects.* New York: Wiley.

Scarr-Salapatek, S., & Williams, M. L. (1973). The effects of early stimulation on low-birth-weight infants. *Child Development, 44,* 91–101.

Scheirer, M. A. (1987). Program theory and implementation theory: Implications for evaluators. In L. Bickman (Ed.), *Using program theory in evaluation* (pp. 59–76). San Francisco: Jossey-Bass.

Schinke, S. P., Blythe, B. J., & Gilchrist, L. D. (1981). Cognitive-behavioral prevention of adolescent pregnancy. *Journal of Counseling Psychology, 28,* 451–454.

Schneirla, T. C. (1966). Behavioral development and comparative psychology. *Quarterly Review of Biology, 41,* 283–302.

Schonfeld, I. S., Shaffer, D., O'Connor, P., & Portnoy, S. (1988). Conduct disorder and cognitive functioning: Testing three causal hypotheses. *Child Development, 59,* 993–1007.

Schorr, L. B. (1988). *Within our reach: Breaking the cycle of disadvantage.* New York: Anchor Press.

Schwab-Stone, M., Kasprow, W. J., Voyce, C. K., Crowther, B., Silver, D., Del Gobbo, P., DeFalco, K., Kavanagh, M., Speese-Linehan, D., Charest, N., Johnson, S. D., Jackson, C., & Verderame, A. (1995). *New Haven Public Schools Social Development Project: Report on the 1994 social and health assessment.* New Haven, CT: New Haven Public Schools.

Schweinhart, L. J., Barnes, H. V., & Weikart, D. P. (1993). *Significant benefits: The High/Scope Perry Preschool Study through age 27.* Ypsilanti, MI: High/Scope Press.

Schweinhart, L. J., & Weikart, D. P. (1988). The High/Scope Perry Preschool Program. In R. H. Price, E. L. Cowen, R. P. Lorion, & J. Ramos-McKay (Eds.), *14 ounces of prevention: A casebook for practitioners* (pp. 53–65). Washington, DC: American Psychological Association.

Schweinhart, L. J., & Weikart, D. P. (1989). The High/Scope Perry Preschool Study: Implications for early childhood care and education. *Prevention in Human Services, 7,* 109–132.

Seffrin, J. R. (1990). The comprehensive school health curriculum: Closing the gap between state-of-the-art and state-of-the-practice. *Journal of School Health, 60,* 151–156.

Seifer, R., Sameroff, A. J., Baldwin, C. P., & Baldwin, A. L. (1993). Child and family factors that ameliorate risk between 4 and 13 years of age. *Journal of the American Academy of Child and Adolescent Psychiatry, 31,* 893–903.

Seitz, V. (1991). Intervention programs for impoverished children: A comparison of educational and family support models. *Annals of Child Development, 7,* 73–103.

Seitz, V., & Apfel, N. H. (1994). Effects of a school for pregnant students on the incidence of low-birthweight deliveries. *Child Development, 65,* 666–676.

Seitz, V., & Provence, S. (1990). Protective factors in individual resilience. In S. J. Meisels & J. P. Shonkoff (Eds.), *Handbook of early childhood intervention* (pp. 400–427). New York: Cambridge University Press.

Seitz, V., Rosenbaum, L. K., & Apfel, N. H. (1985). Effects of family support intervention: A ten-year follow-up. *Child Development, 56,* 376–391.

Selman, R. L. (1980). *The growth of interpersonal understanding: Clinical and developmental analyses.* New York: Academic Press.

Selman, R. L., Schultz, L. H., Nakkula, M., Barr, D., Watts, C., & Richmond, J. B. (1992). Friendship and fighting: A developmental approach to the study of risk and prevention of violence. *Development and Psychopathology, 4,* 529–558.

Shadish, W. R. (1986). Planned critical multiplism: Some elaboration. *Behavioral Assessment, 8,* 75–103.

Shadish, W. R., Jr. (1990). Defining excellence criteria in community research. In P. H. Tolan, C. Keys, F. Chertok, & L. Jason (Eds.), *Researching community psychology: Issues of theories and methods* (pp. 9–20). Washington, DC: American Psychological Association.

Shadish, W. R., Jr., Cook, T. D., & Leviton, L. C. (1986). *Foundations of program evaluation: Theories of practice.* Newbury Park, CA: Sage.

Shadish, W. R., Jr., Cook, T. D., & Leviton, L. C. (1991). *Foundations of program evaluation: Theories of practice.* Newbury Park, CA: Sage.

Sherman, A. (1994). *Wasting America's future: The Children's Defense Fund Report on the Cost of Poverty.* Boston: Beacon Press.

Shiono, P. H., & Behrman, R. E. (1995). Low birth weight: Analysis and recommendations. *Future of Children, 5,* 4–18.

Shope, J. T., Kloska, D. D., Dielman, T. E., & Maharg, R. (1994). Longitudinal evaluation of an enhanced alcohol misuse prevention study (AMPS) curriculum for grades six–eight. *Journal of School Health, 64,* 160–166.

Shriver, T. P., & Weissberg, R. P. (1996, May 15). No new wars! *Education Week, 15*(34), 33–37.

Shure, M. B., & Spivack, G. (1982). Interpersonal problem-solving in young children: A cognitive approach to prevention. *American Journal of Community Psychology, 10,* 341–356.

Shure, M. B., & Spivack, G. (1988). Interpersonal cognitive problem solving. In R. H. Price, E. L. Cowen, R. P. Lorion, & J. Ramos-McKay (Eds.), *14 ounces of prevention: A casebook for practitioners* (pp. 69–82). Washington, DC: American Psychological Association.

Shweder, R. A. (1986). Divergent rationalities. In D. W. Fiske & R. A. Shweder (Eds.), *Metatheory in social sciences: Pluralism and subjectives* (pp. 163–196). Chicago: University of Chicago Press.

Simeonsson, R. J. (Ed.). (1994). *Risk, resilience, and prevention: Promoting the well-being of all children.* Baltimore: Brookes.

Slavin, R. E., Madden, N. A., Dolan, L. J., Wasik, B. A., Ross, S., Smith, L., & Dianda, M. (1995, April). *Success for All: A summary of research.* Paper presented at the meeting of the American Educational Research Association, San Francisco.

Slavin, R. E., Madden, N. A., Karweit, N. L., Livermon, B. J., & Dolan, L. (1990). Success for All: First-year outcomes of a comprehensive plan for reforming urban education. *American Educational Research Journal, 27,* 255–278.

Sloan, J. H., Kellerman, A. L., Reay, D. T., Ferris, J. A., Koepsell, T., Rivara, F. P., Rice, C., Gray, L., & LoGerfo, J. (1988). Handgun regulations, crime assaults, and homicide: A tale of two cities. *New England Journal of Medicine, 319,* 1256–1262.

Snyder, H. N., & Sickmund, M. (1995). *Juvenile offenders and victims: A national report.* Washington, DC: Office of Juvenile Justice and Delinquency Prevention.

Snyder, T. D., & Fromboluti, C. S. (1993). *Youth indicators 1993: Trends in the well-being of American youth.* Washington, DC: U.S. Department of Education, Office of Educational Research and Improvement.

Solomon, D., Watson, M. S., Delucchi, K. L., Schaps, E., & Battistich, V. (1988). Enhancing children's prosocial behavior in the classroom. *American Educational Research Journal, 25,* 527–554.

Spiker, D., Ferguson, J., & Brooks-Gunn, J. (1993). Enhancing maternal interactive behavior and child social competence in low birth weight premature infants. *Child Development, 64,* 754–768.

Springer, F. J., & Phillips, J. L. (1994). Policy learning and evaluation design: Lessons from the Community Partnership Demonstration Program [Monograph] [Special issue]. *Journal of Community Psychology: Community Partnership Program, Center for Substance Abuse Prevention,* 117–139.

Sroufe, L. A. (1979). The coherence of individual development: Early care, attachment, and subsequent developmental issues. *American Psychologist, 34,* 834–841.

Sroufe, L. A., & Rutter, M. (1984). The domain of developmental psychopathology. *Child Development, 83,* 173–189.

Stallings, J. A. (1995). Ensuring teaching and learning in the 21st century. *Educational Researcher, 24,* 4–8.

Stevenson, D. L., & Baker, D. P. (1987). The family-school relation and the child's school performance. *Child Development, 58,* 1348–1357.

Stouthamer-Loeber, M., Loeber, R., Farrington, D. P., Zhang, Q., Van Kammen, W., & Maguin, E. (1993). The double edge of protective and risk factors for delinquency: Interrelations and developmental patterns. *Development and Psychopathology, 5,* 683–701.

Takanishi, R. (1993). The opportunities of adolescence: Research, interventions, and policy. *American Psychologist, 48,* 85–87.

Task Force on Social Competence Instruction for Kindergarten through Fourth-Grade Students. (1990). *Promoting social development in elementary school children.* Westchester County: Westchester County Department of Community Mental Health, New York.

Tierney, J. P., Grossman, J. B., & Resch, N. L. (1995). *Making a difference: An impact study of Big Brothers/Big Sisters.* Philadelphia: Public/Private Ventures.

Tobler, N. S. (1986). Meta-analysis of 143 adolescent drug prevention programs: Quantitative outcome results of program participants compared to a control or comparison group. *Journal of Drug Issues, 16,* 537–567.

Tobler, N. S. (1992). Drug prevention programs can work: Research findings. *Journal of Addictive Diseases, 11,* 1–28.

Tolan, P., Keys, C., Chertok, F., & Jason, L. (Eds.). (1990). *Researching community psychology: Issues of theories and methods.* Washington, DC: American Psychological Association.

Tolan, P. H., & Guerra, N. G. (1994). Prevention of delinquency: Current status and issues. *Applied and Preventive Psychology, 3,* 251–273.

Tolan, P. H., Guerra, N. G., & Kendall, P. C. (1995). A developmental-ecological perspective on antisocial behavior in children and adolescents: Toward a unified risk and intervention framework. *Journal of Consulting and Clinical Psychology, 63,* 579–584.

Tremblay, R. E., Pagani-Kurtz, L., Masse, L. C., Vitaro, F., & Pihl, R. O. (1995). A bimodal preventive intervention for disruptive kindergarten boys: Its impact through mid-adolescence. *Journal of Consulting and Clinical Psychology, 63,* 560–568.

Trickett, E. J., Barone, C., & Buchanan, R. M. (1996). Elaborating developmental contextualism in adolescent research and intervention: Paradigm contributions from community psychology. *Journal of Research on Adolescence, 6,* 245–269.

Trickett, E. J., Dahiyal, C., & Selby, P. M. (1994). *Primary prevention in mental health: An annotated bibliography 1983–1991* (NIH Publication No. 94-3767). Rockville, MD: National Institutes of Health.

Trickett, E. J., Kelly, J. G., & Vincent, T. A. (1985). The spirit of ecological inquiry in community research. In E. Susskind & D. C. Klein (Eds.), *Community research: Methods, paradigms, and applications* (pp. 283–333). New York: Praeger.

Tuma, J. M. (1989). Mental health services for children: The state of the art. *American Psychologist, 44,* 188–199.

U.S. Bureau of the Census. (1993). *Current population reports, population projections of the United States by age, sex, race, and Hispanic origin: 1993 to 2050* (Series P25-1104). Washington, DC: Author.

U.S. Bureau of Justice Statistics. (1994). *Criminal victimization in the United States: 1973–1992 trends.* Washington, DC: U.S. Department of Justice.

U.S. Congress, Office of Technology Assessment. (1986). *Children's mental health: Problems and services. A background paper.* Washington, DC: U.S. Government Printing Office.

U.S. Congress, Office of Technology Assessment. (1991). *Adolescent health: Vol. 1. Summary and policy options* (OTA-H-468). Washington, DC: U.S. Government Printing Office.

U.S. Department of Education, National Center for Education Statistics. (1993). *The condition of education, 1993.* Washington, DC: U.S. Government Printing Office.

U.S. Department of Health and Human Services, Public Health Service. (1990). *Healthy people 2000: National health promotion and disease prevention objectives.* Washington, DC: Superintendent of Documents, U.S. Government Printing Office.

U.S. Department of Health and Human Services. (1994). *Comprehensive Child Development Project: Interim report to Congress.* Washington, DC: U.S. Government Printing Office.

U.S. Department of Health and Human Services. (1996). *Trends in the well-being of America's children and youth: 1996.* Washington, DC: Author.

U.S. General Accounting Office, Program Evaluation and Methodology Division. (1992, January). *Adolescent drug use prevention: Common features of promising community programs* (Report No. GAO/PEMD-92-2). Washington, DC: Author.

Verhulst, F. C., & Koot, H. M. (1992). *Child psychiatric epidemiology.* Newbury Park, CA: Sage.

Vincent, M. L., Clearie, A. F., & Schluchter, M. D. (1987). Reducing adolescent pregnancy through school and community-based education. *Journal of the American Medical Association, 257,* 3382–3386.

Wagenaar, A. C., Murray, D. M., Wolfson, M., Forster, J. L., & Finnegan, J. R. (1994). Community mobilizing for change on alcohol: Design of a randomized community trial [Monograph] [Special issue]. *Journal of Community Psychology: Community Partnership Program, Center for Substance Abuse Prevention,* 79–101.

Wagenaar, A. C., & Perry, C. L. (1994). Community strategies for the reduction of youth drinking: Theory and application. *Journal of Research on Adolescence, 4,* 319–345.

Waitzman, H. J., Romano, P. S., & Scheffler, R. M. (1994). Estimates of the economic costs of birth defects. *Inquiry, 33,* 188–205.

Walker, T., & Johnson, D. L. (1988). A follow-up of the Houston Parent-Child Development Center: Intelligence test results. *Journal of Genetic Psychology, 149,* 377–381.

Walker, T. B., Rodriguez, G. G., Johnson, D. L., & Cortez, C. P. (1995). Avance parent-child education program. In S. Smith & I. E. Siegel (Eds.), *Advances in applied developmental psychology: Vol. 9. Two-generation programs for families in poverty: A new intervention strategy* (pp. 67–90). Norwood, NJ: ABLEX.

Wang, M. C., Haertel, G. D., & Walberg, H. (1997). The effectiveness of collaborative school-linked services. In G. D. Haertel & M. C. Wang (Eds.), *Coordination, cooperation, collaboration: What we know about school-linked services* (pp. 3–23). Philadelphia: Temple University Center for Research in Human Development and Education.

Wasik, B. H., Ramey, C. T., Bryant, D. M., & Sparling, J. J. (1990). A longitudinal study of two early intervention strategies: Project CARE. *Child Development, 61,* 1682–1692.

Waters, E., & Sroufe, L. A. (1983). Social competence as a developmental construct. *Developmental Review, 3,* 79–97.

Weiss, C. H. (1995). The stakeholder approach to evaluation: Origins and promise. In J. P. Connell, A. C. Kubish, L. B. Schorr, & C. H. Weiss (Eds.), *New approaches to evaluating community initiatives: Concept, methods, and context* (pp. 3–14). Washington, DC: Aspen Institute.

Weiss, H. B. (1993). Home visits: Necessary but not sufficient. *Future of Children, 3,* 113–128.

Weissberg, R. P. (1989). Challenges inherent in translating theory and basic research into effective social competence promotion programs. In B. H. Schneider, G. Attili, J. Nadel, & R. P. Weissberg (Eds.), *Social competence in developmental perspective* (pp. 335–338). Boston: Kluwer.

Weissberg, R. P. (1990). Fidelity and adaptation: Combining the best of two perspectives. In P. Tolan, C. Keys, F. Chertok, & L. Jason (Eds.), *Researching community psychology: Issues of theories and methods* (pp. 186–190). Washington, DC: American Psychological Association.

Weissberg, R. P. (1995, August). *What I have learned about prevention research (so far!).* Paper presented at the meeting of the American Psychological Association, New York.

Weissberg, R. P., Barton, H. A., & Shriver, T. P. (1997). The Social-Competence Promotion Program for young adolescents. In G. W. Albee & T. P. Gullotta (Eds.), *Primary prevention exemplars: The Lela Rowland awards* (pp. 268–290). Thousand Oaks, CA: Sage.

Weissberg, R. P., & Caplan, M. (1994). *Promoting social competence and preventing antisocial behavior in young urban adolescents.* Unpublished manuscript, University of Illinois, Chicago.

Weissberg, R. P., Caplan, M., Bennetto, L., & Jackson, A. S. (1990). *The New Haven Social Development Program: Sixth-grade social problem-solving module.* Chicago: University of Illinois.

Weissberg, R. P., Caplan, M., & Harwood, R. L. (1991). Promoting competent young people in competence-enhancing environments: A systems-based perspective on primary prevention. *Journal of Consulting and Clinical Psychology, 59,* 830–841.

Weissberg, R. P., Caplan, M. Z., & Sivo, P. J. (1989). A new conceptual framework for establishing school-based social competence promotion programs. In L. A. Bond & B. E. Compas (Eds.), *Primary prevention and promotion in the schools* (pp. 255–296). Newbury Park, CA: Sage.

Weissberg, R. P., & Elias, M. J. (1993). Enhancing young people's social competence and health behavior: An important challenge for educators, scientists, policy makers, and funders.

Applied and Preventive Psychology: Current Scientific Perspectives, 3, 179–190.

Weissberg, R. P., Gesten, E. L., Carnrike, C. L., Toro, P. A., Rapkin, B. D., Davidson, E., & Cowen, E. L. (1981). Social problem-solving skills training: A competence building intervention with second- to fourth-grade children. *American Journal of Community Psychology, 9,* 411–423.

Weissberg, R. P., Gesten, E. L., Rapkin, B. D., Cowen, E. L., Davidson, E., Flores de Apodaca, R., & McKim, B. J. (1981). The evaluation of a social problem-solving training program for suburban and inner-city third-grade children. *Journal of Consulting and Clinical Psychology, 49,* 251–261.

Weissberg, R. P., Gullotta, T. P., Hampton, R. L., Ryan, B. A., & Adams, G. R. (Eds.). (1997a). *Healthy children 2010: Enhancing children's wellness.* Thousand Oaks, CA: Sage.

Weissberg, R. P., Gullotta, T. P., Hampton, R. L., Ryan, B. A., & Adams, G. R. (Eds.). (1997b). *Healthy children 2010: Establishing preventive services.* Thousand Oaks, CA: Sage.

Weissberg, R. P., Shriver, T. P., Bose, S., & DeFalco, K. (1997). Creating a districtwide social development project. *Educational Leadership, 54*(8), 37–39.

Weissbourd, B. (1994). The evolution of the family resource movement. In S. L. Kagan & B. Weissbourd (Eds.), *Putting families first: America's family support movement and the challenge of change* (pp. 28–47). San Francisco: Jossey-Bass.

Werner, E. E., & Smith, R. S. (1982). *Vulnerable but invincible: A study of resilient children and youth.* New York: McGraw-Hill.

Werner, E. E., & Smith, R. S. (1992). *Overcoming the odds: High-risk children from birth to adulthood.* New York: Cornell University Press.

White, J., Moffitt, T. E., & Silva, P. A. (1989). A prospective replication of the protective effects of IQ in subjects at high risk for juvenile delinquency. *Journal of Consulting and Clinical Psychology, 57,* 719–724.

William T. Grant Consortium on the School-Based Promotion of Social Competence. (1992). Drug and alcohol prevention curricula. In J. D. Hawkins, R. F. Catalano, & Associates (Eds.), *Communities that care: Action for drug abuse prevention* (pp. 129–148). San Francisco: Jossey-Bass.

Yates, B. (1994). Towards the incorporation of costs, cost-effectiveness analysis, and cost-benefit analysis into clinical research. *Journal of Consulting and Clinical Psychology, 62,* 729–736.

Yeates K. O., & Selman, R. L. (1989). Social competence in the schools: Toward an integrative developmental model for intervention. *Developmental Review, 9,* 64–100.

Yoshikawa, H. (1994). Prevention of cumulative protection: Effects of early family support and education on chronic delinquency and its risks. *Psychological Bulletin, 115,* 1–27.

Yoshikawa, H. (1995). Long-term effects of early childhood programs on social outcomes and delinquency. *Future of Children, 5*(3), 51–75.

Zabin, L. S. (1992). School-linked reproductive health services: The Johns Hopkins Program. In B. C. Miller, J. J. Card, R. L. Paikoff, & J. L. Peterson (Eds.), *Preventing adolescent pregnancy.* Newbury Park, CA: Sage.

Zabin, L. S., Hirsch, M. B., Smith, E. A., Street, R., & Hardy, J. B. (1986). Evaluation of a pregnancy prevention program for urban teenagers. *Family Planning Perspectives, 18*(3), 119–126.

Zabin, L. S., Hirsch, M. B., Street, R., Emmerson, M. R., Smith, M., Hardy, J. B., & King, T. M. (1988). The Baltimore pregnancy prevention program for urban teenagers: I. How did it work? *Family Planning Perspectives, 20*(4), 182–187.

Zerbe, R., & Dively, D. (1993). *Benefit-cost analysis in theory and practice.* New York: HarperCollins.

Zigler, E. (1994). Reshaping early childhood intervention to be a more effective weapon against poverty. *American Journal of Community Psychology, 22,* 37–48.

Zigler, E., & Berman, W. (1983). Discerning the future of early childhood intervention. *American Psychologist, 38,* 894–906.

Zigler, E., & Finn-Stevenson, M. (1997). Policy efforts to enhance child and family life: Goals for 2010. In R. P. Weissberg, T. P. Gullotta, R. L. Hampton, B. A. Ryan, & G. R. Adams (Eds.), *Healthy children 2010: Establishing preventive services* (pp. 47–75). Thousand Oaks, CA: Sage.

Zigler, E., & Styfco, S. J. (1994). Head Start: Criticisms in a constructive context. *American Psychologist, 49,* 127–132.

Zigler, E., Taussig, C., & Black, K. (1992). Early childhood intervention. *American Psychologist, 47,* 997–1006.

Zill, N., & Nord, C. W. (1994). *Running in place: How American families are faring in a changing economy and an individualistic society.* Washington, DC: Child Trends.

Zill, N., & Rogers, C. C. (1988). Recent trends in the well-being of children in the United States and their implications for public policy. In A. J. Cherlin (Ed.), *The changing American family and public policy* (pp. 31–115). Washington, DC: Urban Institute Press.

Zimmerman, M. A., & Arunkumar, R. (1994). Resiliency research: Implications for schools and social policy. *Social Policy Report, 8*(4), 1–20.

Zins, J., & Forman, S. G. (1988). Mini-series on primary prevention: From theory to practice. *School Psychology Review, 17*(4), 539–634.

CHAPTER 14

Issues in Community-Based Research and Program Evaluation

ROBERT B. McCALL, BETH L. GREEN, MARK S. STRAUSS, and CHRISTINA J. GROARK

Scientific research, it can be argued, invokes empirical rules of evidence to describe and understand nature for the purpose of improving life. In developmental psychology, the pursuit is focused on describing and understanding developmental change, particularly (but not exclusively) in human infants, children, adolescents, and families, for the purpose of improving their welfare.

Scientific Ideals and Basic versus Applied Research

Underlying this endeavor in psychology are two scientific ideals. First, the *ideal scientific methodology* consists of a large number of subjects who are randomly selected from a population of interest and are then randomly assigned to different treatment conditions that are tightly manipulated and controlled by the experimenter. Subject characteristics, treatments, and outcomes are precisely measured so that differences among the groups can be ascribed only to the variation in treatments. The closer we approach this methodological ideal, the more certain will be our inferences of cause and effect. Second, the *ideal scientific goal* is to amass empirical evidence, preferably by studies using the above methodological ideal, to discover general laws—cause-and-effect principles that apply to a great variety of particular circumstances.

The pursuit of these two ideals is central to *basic research*—the scientific description and understanding of natural phenomena. Much of the history of psychology in general and developmental psychology in particular through the 1970s might be characterized as an attempt by a behavioral science to attain these scientific ideals—in a phrase, "to be a science like physics." Many scholars, at least beginning with Skinner (1956), would argue that although these are worthy ideals, much actual behavioral research only vaguely approximates them. Instead, an increasing number of researchers (e.g., McCall, 1996; McCall & Green, 1997) are emphasizing the *purpose of research*—to improve life in general and the welfare of children and families in particular. They attempt to use empirical evidence to produce the best obtainable information, not necessarily the scientific ideal, that will help understand the practical issues of real-life development and will improve the welfare of children and families directly, not simply by inference from general theoretical principles or empirical laws.

This chapter was supported in part by Urban Communities Services Program grant P252A20082 from the U.S. Department of Education. We thank Hidenori Yamatani for his helpful comments on an early draft of this chapter.

Such *applied* research, which includes *action research* aimed at solving particular problems (Campbell, 1978; Cialdini, 1980; Lewin, 1946), accepts that society needs (but may not appreciate) basic research and that universities should produce it because basic research permits more certain understanding of cause and effect and has the potential for the greatest generality of application. But the use of basic research information to fulfill science's purpose as defined above is uncertain, inefficient, and sometimes incomplete. We hope, or have faith, that someone will make use of the information someday for the betterment of someone. Scholars also insist that at least some researchers (more than do so now) should attempt to apply theory, basic research information, and scientific methodology to create new knowledge and provide information that *directly* improves the human condition (McCall & Green, 1997). Returning to the analogy of the physical sciences, we need both basic research *and* engineering (and points between them).

The movement toward applied research may constitute one of the more substantial developments in our discipline in the past few decades. Society's problems, including those pertaining to children and families, are much more numerous and severe, and Congress is demanding that more money be spent on solving them. For example, Congress mandated that 60% of the National Science Foundation (NSF) budget, long the pillar of support for basic research, be spent on achieving the national science and technology goals, many of which are quite applied (Gladue, 1994). Further, Congress directed that 15% of the National Institute of Mental Health (NIMH) budget, which has supported basic research in psychology for decades, be spent on improving services, prominently including services for children and families (Gladue, 1994). As a result, an increasing amount of funding is directed more at solving social and behavioral problems than at acquiring basic knowledge, and solving social problems requires at least some scholars to conduct applied research.

Applied research shares many general principles of conduct with basic research, but it is also very different. For one thing, it is less precise. Sampling and the assignment of subjects to groups are unlikely to be random or even representative; manipulations are multifaceted and perhaps not uniformly administered; the researcher may not control the interventions; confounds are potentially numerous, measurement is less precise, data analyses may be more complicated, and conclusions are more tenuous (McCall & Green, 1997). In addition, applied research is more likely to be collaborative and interdisciplinary, and some of the collaborators may be service professionals who have no training in research and whose responsibilities are centered on helping the client, not generating research data. Finally, because of the collaborative nature of much applied research, it may require more complicated "research administration," including multiple funding arrangements, detailed contracts, and limitations on data ownership and the dissemination of results.

Although the applied research movement has been swift and strong in society, in legislatures, and at funding agencies, the academy has moved less rapidly (McCall, 1996). Our educational programs are very traditional. We train undergraduates and graduates to be clones of our traditional academic selves. We do not teach students about the value of other disciplines and how to collaborate with them, and our methodological and statistical training, which is largely the same as it was several decades ago, is most appropriate for basic laboratory research (Aiken, West, Sechrest, & Reno, 1990; McCall & Green, 1997). The academic system—embodied, for example, in the criteria used by journals, grant reviewers, and tenure review committees—still largely values theory-driven basic research conducted, according to the methodological ideal, within a single discipline by a single researcher and published in a traditional basic-research refereed journal. In short, the system clings to its methodological and scientific ideals.

The Focus of This Chapter

The disparity between how we train students and conduct traditional, basic laboratory research, and how we *might* train students and conduct applied research, especially within the community, is the focus of this chapter. We recognize that, in many respects, we have painted the basic–applied distinction to be an extreme dichotomy when it is actually a continuum and a difference in degree or emphasis. For example, applied research with community agencies is not new. NIMH has supported applied as well as basic research for decades, and many psychologists have devoted their careers to applied and action research. Also, applied researchers sometimes lament the lack of basic research and theory that might guide the creation and interpretation of interventions. Nevertheless, we focus here on the extremes for illustrative and pedagogical purposes, because, when compared to traditional laboratory basic scholarship, contemporary applied developmental psychology can be exceedingly different in every respect—from conception and funding to publishing.

This chapter is intended as an introduction and guide for students and faculty who have been trained in traditional methods for conducting applied research, especially research performed within the community in collaboration with human service agencies. We focus on the process of training for and performing such research—participating in interdisciplinary applied training programs, working in collaborative partnerships, administering such projects, and exploring scientific and methodological issues—rather than on the content of applied research, which is reviewed elsewhere in this volume. We have assumed, with some empirical justification (Aiken et al., 1990), that most faculty and contemporary students are trained in traditional methods and approaches. Finally, we have emphasized one type of applied research—the evaluation of community-based human service programs.

We selected program evaluation for two reasons. First, community-based program evaluation is one of the most applied research endeavors that developmental psychologists are likely to encounter, and it illustrates the most frequent and severe departures in approach from traditional laboratory basic research. Second, after a boom period through the 1970s and then a decline, the demand for program evaluation has recently increased. Many legislators, including Vice President Al Gore, as part of redefining government, have asserted that we can no longer be content with simply determining how many people are served by our educational and human service programs; we need to know whether the programs work. Furthermore, the United Way has demanded nationwide that agencies seeking its funds provide objective information on the effectiveness of their services. Finally, funders at all levels have increasingly allocated funds for evaluation in concert with funds for service demonstration programs, and some funders have required service programs specifically to engage universities to conduct the evaluations. Because more psychologists are trained to conduct research than members of most other behavioral disciplines, and because many human service programs are aimed at children and families, the evaluation of community-based service programs seems a particularly promising domain for applied developmental psychologists who can bring both their methodological skills and content knowledge to the enterprise.

Much of what is presented in this chapter is based on the collective experiences of the authors, and the generality of this information should be interpreted accordingly. However, the backgrounds of the authors represent the perspectives of traditional child development research, interdisciplinary training, academic administration, research in the public interest, science communication, program evaluation, and human services. While literatures exist within professional service disciplines (e.g., education, social work) on university–community collaborations (e.g., Friend & Cook, 1992; Mattessich & Monsey, 1992; Vandercook, York, & Sullivan, 1993), we have tried to present information that is especially relevant to developmental psychologists and that derives from our experience in living jointly, for more than a decade, the collaborations that we describe and encourage here (McCall, Groark, Strauss, & Johnson, 1995).

Some Definitions

A few definitions have guided the presentation in this chapter. "Applied research," including "action research," refers to research that has *direct* implications for action; its results point directly to a certain course of action or a modification of an existing course of action (e.g., implementing or modifying a particular intervention program). In contrast, "relevant research" has *less direct* or *inferred* implications for action (e.g., high-risk parents lack the perception of personal effectance, so intervention programs should aim to build a sense of effectance in clients).

"Community-based" projects are those in which the intervention is implemented in community settings (e.g., the home, a center), typically by "human service agencies" (e.g., a county department of human services or a county health department; public or private agencies that deliver drug and alcohol rehabilitation services, specialized foster care, family support programs, or family preservation services; Head Start; public or private preschools, early childhood centers, or primary/secondary schools). Usually, such agencies are directed and staffed by human service professionals (e.g., social workers, educators, public health specialists, child care professionals, community or clinical psychologists) whose training, values, roles, and responsibilities are aimed primarily at improving the well-being of their clients, not at producing scientifically credible research.

"Program evaluation" refers to the systematic application of research procedures to the study of the process and effectiveness of community-based human service intervention programs, which are typically designed to prevent or treat one or more problems or circumstances (e.g., child abuse and neglect, drug and alcohol abuse, school failure, unemployment, antisocial behavior) and/or to improve certain skills or conditions (e.g., school readiness, parenting skills, psychological and financial self-sufficiency). The focus may be on describing and monitoring the implementation of the intervention, called "process evaluation" or "formative evaluation," and/or on describing the change in clients, or in their circumstances, produced by the intervention, called "outcome evaluation" or "summative evaluation." Further, evaluations may range in purpose from (a) those that are most focused on the dynamics and cause–effect relations that occur within the program, as a basis for understanding how or why the intervention program works and generalizing such findings to other programs and situations, called "program evaluation research," to (b) those that are primarily directed at describing the process and/or effectiveness of a particular program per se, with relatively less concern about generalizing to other programs and situations (Prosavac & Carey, 1992; Rossi & Freeman, 1993).

Why Perform Evaluations of Community-Based Programs?

Developmental psychologists have long performed interventions and evaluated their effects, most notably early childhood enrichment/intervention programs. Typically, however, the researcher created and operated the intervention program, perhaps in a special center devoted solely to that program, and then evaluated its implementation and effectiveness. Such projects were controlled from start to finish by the researcher, and they were conducted independently of the massive educational and human service systems that are in place in communities. Moreover, the growth of program evaluation during the 1950s and on through the 1980s, while more tied to the community-based programs of the Great Society, was an attempt to bring traditional research methods, including the randomized experiment or clinical trial, to social programs (Rossi & Freeman, 1993). These two thrusts represented a research discipline reaching out toward applied issues (but on its own terms of control) and the pursuit of methodological and scientific ideals.

Today, legislators and funders are increasingly requesting systematic evaluation, not only of major new service demonstration programs especially designed for evaluation, but also of human services that have been performed in the community for years. Researchers, for their part, perhaps are feeling more confident about their methods for dealing with the lack of control and rigor that comes with studying such services. The result is that more researchers are not just dipping their toes in the waters of applied research but are actually taking the plunge into the sea of community-based services.

This is a worthy pursuit. Massive numbers of children and families are served by the educational and human service systems, and billions of tax dollars, which are increasingly in short supply, are spent predominantly by counties on a spectrum of programs. In the greater Pittsburgh area alone, for example, more than 550 agencies serve children and families. It is reasonable public policy to ask whether these agencies' services work. Understanding how their programs operate and the factors that contribute to their effectiveness will help to improve the programs, and this type of information may also help developmental scientists understand the factors that contribute to human development. The human service systems and developmental science share the same purpose of improving the lives of children and families, and the study and evaluation of human services is a way for both groups to work together toward this common purpose.

To accomplish this unity of effort, however, traditional psychological scientists must adjust their scientific ideals and practices to the realities of working in the community, and they should join with research colleagues in applied disciplines and with the human service professionals who already operate such programs, and work collaboratively in partnerships toward this goal. For most traditionally trained developmental psychologists, the collaboration will be a new experience from beginning to end. This chapter is directed at introducing psychologists to the differences they will encounter during this process.

FORGING SUCCESSFUL INTERDISCIPLINARY AND ACADEMIC/SERVICE PROFESSIONAL COLLABORATIONS

The entire process of conducting applied research, especially community-based studies and program evaluation, is very different from and much more complicated than traditional laboratory basic research, and few traditionally trained students or their faculty mentors are prepared for or trained in how to conduct this type of project, especially when intense collaboration with professionals from other disciplines is required. Therefore, we first examine the nature and issues of interdisciplinary training in applied human development.

Interdisciplinary Applied Educational Programming in Human Development

"Somebody once claimed the only thing connecting classes in many schools is the plumbing" (Klein, 1990). This humorous quote applies to most courses within a university, but it is an especially apt and regrettable description of courses pertaining to children, youth, and families. In both undergraduate and graduate classes, academics typically teach about children and families only from the perspective of their own discipline. Psychology, education, nursing, social work, public health, child care, sociology, pediatrics, and law all have different and important perspectives on children and families, yet scholars typically isolate themselves and their courses within the confines of a single academic discipline. Undergraduate students, who are required to take courses outside of their major to give them a "broad education," often are not required to obtain any breadth in the content areas related to their major. For example, developmental psychology majors typically are not required to take related courses in social work, education, or public health. Graduate programs are even more disciplinarily restrictive, and faculty from different disciplines rarely coordinate or collaborate to provide students with the breadth that comes from an interdisciplinary approach.

This is particularly unfortunate for students interested in applied issues of children and families. How does one become adequately educated about child abuse and neglect, for example, without some understanding of the medical, legal, ethical, sociological, educational, child welfare, and psychological issues that are involved in this complicated problem? In this section, we explore the value of interdisciplinary education for students interested in applied issues of children and families. We are not suggesting that traditional educational programs be abandoned in favor of programs that are amalgamations of existing fields. The strength of interdisciplinary education comes from an appreciation of the different perspectives, issues, and methodologies that each discipline brings to the topic. Rather, we will be discussing why we need a more interdisciplinary approach to education, the barriers that exist in developing such programs, and how these barriers may be overcome.

The Need for Interdisciplinary Educational Approaches

At least for undergraduates, perhaps the most important reason we should be developing interdisciplinary educational programs pertains to their practical career needs. Undergraduate programs are often reflections of the graduate programs that exist within a department or elsewhere, and there is a tacit guiding principle that all undergraduate students should be taught as if they will enter graduate programs in that discipline. In reality, most students interested in children and families do not eventually enroll in graduate programs; they seek employment in applied fields. With the continually increasing numbers of social welfare agencies and programs required to deal with the problems of contemporary society, a substantial demand for well-educated students is likely to continue. But applicants for employment will need a broad multidisciplinary understanding of the issues that confront children and parents. As Lawson and Hooper-Briar (1994) recently stated:

> [P]rofessional preparation programs cannot be relevant or effective unless colleges and universities are, at a minimum, responsive to the changing conditions of both service systems and children, youth and families. Beyond such responses, as part of a "catch-up game," are needs for proactive planning in professional preparation. After all, professional preparation is not merely a technical response to preexisting job requirements; it is also the chief means for creating new work roles, service designs and technologies. Neither will result if leaders in colleges and universities remain either ignorant, or passive observers on the sidelines, while interprofessional collaborations and service integration efforts develop. The costs of doing so are becoming apparent, especially in higher education institutions claiming to prepare helping professionals for the most vulnerable child, youth and families. (p. 13)

If universities are to respond to this challenge of preparing professionals to work with children and families, it will be critical to train students who understand both the limitations and the advantages of other professions and who view children in a holistic perspective (O'Neil & Wilson-Coker, 1986).

This issue may be particularly problematic for undergraduate students in developmental psychology. Specifically, most courses in this discipline are taught as if all the students will become psychological researchers, yet only a small percentage of students intend to study psychology in graduate school, and only a fraction of those who do will become active researchers. Should we not offer courses for the student who is not oriented toward a research career, and how will faculty members, who themselves have limited experience with applied interdisciplinary issues, teach such courses?

A holistic perspective may be difficult to achieve. Faculty tend to value and emphasize depth in a particular field rather than the breadth that would come from a more interdisciplinary approach. Upon receiving his degree in developmental psychology, one of the present authors remembers believing that too much truth was embodied in the joke line: "It's claimed that developmental psychologists can recognize two out of three children." He was an expert in research design and could intelligently debate many important theoretical issues concerning the nature of development, but he knew very little about the practical issues of how children develop. Indeed, while doing research as a new faculty member, his biggest concern was that the parents of his subjects might actually ask him a practical question concerning child development! It is certainly important for students to receive an in-depth education in their chosen area, but are we doing them a disservice by denying them the breadth and balance that would be contributed by a broader interdisciplinary perspective?

Besides being more useful to students, an interdisciplinary program can provide faculty with an exciting academic synergism. In our experience, collaborative efforts often begin with a degree of distrust or apprehension, but then the faculty in interdisciplinary educational programs typically become energized by the opportunity to discuss and think about issues of concern from the perspectives of other disciplines and professions. Indeed, faculty often benefit more from such educational collaborations than do students.

Barriers to the Development of Interdisciplinary Programs

Unfortunately, many barriers impede the development of interdisciplinary educational programs and discourage faculty from attempting to create them. These barriers pertain to the basic structure of universities as institutions, the way faculty function and develop their careers, and the manner in which we socialize students.

Institutional Barriers. One primary impediment is the lack of any tradition in American universities for developing interdisciplinary programs (Klein, 1990). For more than 100 years, our universities have been built around the model of strong, independent, disciplinary departments with little cross-communication. This is particularly true of departments that report to different deans, such as departments in the arts and sciences (e.g., psychology or sociology) and departments in professional schools (e.g., social work, education, public health). Indeed, at many universities, different departments compete with each other for economic resources and student enrollments. As university resources become increasingly scarce, departmental competition for faculty, student credit hours, and majors can become intense, potentially chilling the climate needed for cooperative or shared educational planning across disciplines rather than stimulating the need for collaboration.

Some scholars (e.g., Sewell, 1989) have argued that social science departments are even less supportive of interdisciplinary efforts than the physical and biological sciences, because they are in a relatively weaker position with respect to university resources. Because social science departments typically receive fewer funds for research, space, equipment, and salaries, they "tend to be much less supportive of interdisciplinary programs, unless additional funds for them can be brought in from the outside" (Sewell, 1989, p. 7). This may be even more applicable to faculty in the area of children and families. At least within large research universities, educational and research programs related to children typically have low status relative to highly technical "cutting edge" areas such as genetics, computers, or medical science. Programs concerned with the welfare of children and families are simply not a high priority within most universities, despite the large number of diverse faculty interested in children and families and the importance of these programs in dealing with significant societal problems, such as child abuse, youth violence, or teenage pregnancy.

Apart from university resources and values, another barrier to interdisciplinary education concerns how curricula and their requirements are typically developed. The number of courses required in the home department for both undergraduate and graduate degrees significantly limits the ability of students to take courses outside of their discipline. Students often are unable to take more than a course or two per term that are not a part of their core requirements. This is especially true for professional departments (e.g., clinical psychology, education, social work), which typically require a curriculum that satisfies external accreditation agencies. Nonclinical psychology students (e.g., developmental students) have fewer requirements and more flexibility in coursework, but psychology faculty tend to prefer depth in psychology, especially in research and methods, rather than breadth, and they tend to view their faculty colleagues in other disciplines, especially applied disciplines, as less scientifically astute (to put it diplomatically) and perhaps a bad influence on their students (to put it more frankly).

This problem of institutional barriers is well summarized by Damrosch (1995) in a book concerning the changing culture of the university:

> Academic work is institutionally arranged in a patterned isolation of disciplines, and then of specialized fields within disciplines. This patterning is not something inherent in the material; it stems from decisions made a century ago when the American university assumed its modern form. Those decisions reflected political and economic assumptions then current, and although conditions have changed in society at large, our academic structures have remained relatively constant, and the old assumptions built into our institutions continue to have largely unseen but pervasive effects. (p. 6)

Faculty Barriers. The traditional nature of faculty careers also tends to work against the development of interdisciplinary programs. As Damrosch (1995) has argued, academia tends to foster an ethos of "hyperindividualism." It is common for academicians to work alone. We often publish coauthored papers, but usually with individuals in our own fields; typically, each author separately contributes a part of the total study, based on his or her specialized knowledge. Much less common are true collaborative efforts that cross disciplinary lines to merge and extend the contributions of individuals.

Indeed, academic success largely depends on both individualism and limited interdisciplinary interactions. Consider what is required to receive tenure at most research universities. The first hurdle is the departmental promotion committee, which is composed solely of senior colleagues from a single academic department who have likely attained this status by conducting basic, unidisciplinary research. In judging the candidate, they will apply a set of standards (or biases) specific to that discipline. The degree to which that discipline values basic versus applied research, quantitative versus qualitative approaches, laboratory versus field studies, and primary or secondary analyses of data will all be part of the tenure decision process. The faculty member must be able to clearly demonstrate his or her individual contribution in a rather narrow area of specialization. This is done by publishing single- or first-authored papers in a limited number of refereed journals judged to be important (i.e., typically with a basic research focus) within that discipline. Thus, there are substantial pressures on new faculty members to follow a traditional academic course and limit their cross-disciplinary contacts.

For those who venture beyond their disciplinary boundaries, it is often difficult to establish, with faculty from other disciplines, meaningful relationships that will lead to interdisciplinary educational endeavors. For the past ten years, for example, we have been involved in interdisciplinary programs in the areas of child abuse and child welfare. Students and faculty have come from seven disciplines: psychology, nursing, law, social work, pediatrics, public health, and child care/development. Participating faculty members were frequently surprised at how much their disciplinary backgrounds and biases limited their ability to appreciate the values and contributions of colleagues from other disciplines. Indeed, even communicating across disciplinary boundaries can be difficult, because different disciplines have different vocabularies for the same referent (even the same statistical technique may be called by a different name) and the same word (e.g., "research") can refer to very different activities. But beyond vocabulary, different disciplinary values and practices created problems regarding which courses were important, how much research and/or internship experience should be required, and what common themes needed to be emphasized.

We, and others (e.g., Lawson & Hooper-Briar, 1994), have found that colleagues initially approach interdisciplinary collaborations with a high degree of wariness. This wariness can eventually lead to curiosity about the other disciplines and ultimately to true enjoyment in discussing new perspectives or common areas of interest. But this disciplinary ecumenism may be restricted to faculty who are directly involved in the planning of such a program. Initially, in our program, we had many complaints from faculty from one discipline, who wondered why students from a different discipline were in their classes. Indeed, some faculty were even hostile to this invasion of students. As core faculty, we had to do much public relations work prior to our students' enrolling in the classes of faculty who were not involved in the planning of the interdisciplinary program. It may be best to involve all relevant faculty in the planning of an interdisciplinary program as soon as it is practical.

Student Barriers. One might expect to encounter problems with faculty and administrators, who have long been indoctrinated in a particular discipline. More surprising are the barriers to interdisciplinary training that reside with students. By their junior year, undergraduate students have already adopted many of the biases and expectations of their newly declared disciplinary major, and this mindset grows stronger as exposure to a discipline increases. Undergraduate psychology students, for example, may be quite surprised at the reliance that social work students (among others from the helping professions) place on their personal experiences rather than on research data. Coming from a more research-oriented discipline, psychology students are quickly socialized to believe that opinions should be based on empirical research and not simply on personal experience. Conversely, social work students often object that empirical findings are sterile, unrealistic, and not descriptive of real-world experiences. Similarly, social work students may complain that law students have no appreciation of the practical and moral issues involved in child abuse and child welfare cases. Unfortunately, rather than appreciating the information one can get from different perspectives, students often have a bias about the approaches of one discipline versus those of another.

Biases must be confronted openly from the first day students enter an interdisciplinary program. It also helps to bring all students and faculty together on a regular basis to discuss areas of mutual interest. In our experience, students go through a process similar to that of the core faculty. Initially, they are skeptical of views outside of their own discipline, but eventually they appreciate and enjoy engaging the different perspectives that come from interdisciplinary collaborations. Indeed, observing this developmental process among students may be one of the strongest motivators for faculty to deal with the barriers discussed above and to push for more interdisciplinary educational programs on children and families.

Promoting Interdisciplinary Educational Initiatives

Among the many ways to structure interdisciplinary education are: truly blended degree programs, integrated subprograms or minors, certificate programs, nondegree training programs, coordinated courses, and individual courses that promote multidisciplinary viewpoints.

Formal Blended Degree Programs. The most difficult programs to establish and maintain, but the ones that make the most concerted effort to be thoroughly interdisciplinary, are formal degree programs that require students from different disciplines to take a common set of courses taught and promoted by faculty representing different disciplines. One of the oldest interdisciplinary programs pertaining to children and families is at Ohio State University and is sponsored by the Interprofessional Education Commission of Ohio. Based on many years of experience, its Director, Michael Casto (Casto & Julia, 1994), suggested that several important conditions are needed to sustain such a program: (a) a neutral base of operation that is outside the "turf" of the participating disciplines; (b) administrative support that includes such things as faculty release from disciplinary courses and special organizational structures; (c) strong commitments and shared interests among the participating faculty; (d) specific training in collaborative skills; (e) faculty rewards, including fair tenure and promotion reviews, and salary increases based on participation in the interdisciplinary program; and (f) administrative promises of continued institutional funding.

Unfortunately, few universities are willing to provide the resources needed to support such programs. This is a time of retrenchment at most universities, which means the goal is fewer courses and perhaps fewer degree programs, not more. And, as in all times of austerity, support for the traditional often triumphs over support for creative programs that may deal more effectively with the cause of the retrenchment (Kennedy, 1994). Instead, administration and faculty need to perceive interdisciplinary programs, not as a threat but as a means of solving some of their problems (e.g., not enough students, not enough student credit hours, insufficient faculty in an area to have a program, etc.). External training grants may provide an alternative source of funding, at least initially, but successful interdisciplinary programs still require some type of neutral organization and significant support from deans and provosts willing to deal with faculty rewards and the attribution of faculty time and student credit hours—among other issues.

Certificate Programs. Rather than creating an actual interdisciplinary major or degree program, it is much easier to develop certificate programs. Students in these programs continue to be enrolled in a traditional discipline and fulfill the degree requirements of that discipline. However, they also take a set of specialized courses, perhaps as electives, from a stipulated set of courses, plus a research or internship experience. Although not as integrative as an actual degree granting program, certificate programs require much less administrative support, do not require an involved university approval process, and are much less "threatening" to traditional departments. However, some professional schools have substantial degree requirements, and students must spend extra time fulfilling the demands of both the degree program and the certificate program, at a time when many students cannot afford more education.

Cross-Listed Courses. Full interdisciplinary degree or certificate programs are not the only ways to promote interdisciplinary education within universities. Perhaps the easiest approach is to cross-list courses in different disciplines. These courses will still be taught from a single disciplinary viewpoint, but their advertising at least may attract students from other disciplines. Many universities may have countless courses related to children and families that are known only to the students within the department offering the course. Some universities (Michigan State and the University of Pittsburgh, among others) publish booklets describing the different degree programs pertaining to children and families, as well as individual courses within each program that students from any program may take.

Team-Taught Courses. Another alternative is to offer team-taught courses open to students from different disciplines. The lecturers might be academics who represent a variety of disciplines, or even some people from the community (e.g., the school superintendent, a physician specializing in high-risk pregnancies). Each week, in our proseminar on applied issues of children and families, students from many different fields hear lectures from experts who represent a variety of disciplines and approaches. Response to this course has always been very positive. It provides an experience very different from the typical in-depth but narrow approach taken in most other courses.

Team-taught or proseminar courses have several advantages. Well-known professors who ordinarily do not teach full-time or who do not teach undergraduate or low-level graduate courses can be induced to give one or two lectures on their specialty. Also, some topics should be covered in a curriculum but do not need to constitute a whole course—a week or two of study would be sufficient. Finally, professional school students do not have time to take whole courses in other disciplines, but they can get substantial interdisciplinary exposure in one or two team-taught courses. The disadvantages of such courses are that teacher and student credit-hour assignments are more difficult to make, and students sometimes complain that the material is not integrated across topics. Also, unless faculty and professionals from different disciplines are brought together in the same class period, students and faculty may not experience the benefits of bringing different perspectives to bear on the same topic.

Mixing Classes. Mixing students from different classes is another approach. Students registered in different but related courses may be brought together occasionally for interdisciplinary discussions. For example, courses on adolescence taught by the psychology department and the school of social work may hold joint sessions to discuss common questions.

Sequencing Classes. Coordinating the sequencing of courses across disciplinary boundaries is another way to promote interdisciplinary education. Students might take an initial course from one discipline but then be required or encouraged to take additional or specialized courses from other disciplines.

Multidisciplinary Dissertations. With respect to graduate students, Damrosch (1995) has suggested that an alternative model should be allowed for dissertations from students interested in a multidisciplinary approach. The students should be permitted to conduct dissertations that consist of several different but related activities, each guided by different faculty representing different disciplines. Rather than a single mentor, the student would benefit from working with several different sponsors who give the attention usually provided by a single person. At the same time, the student would be able to explore the different disciplinary perspectives that are important to an issue. This type of project could provide the student with the opportunity to blend disciplinary perspectives around a single theme; however, the approach risks the student's getting caught in the disciplinary cross fire of his or her committee unless its faculty members are committed to and experienced in an interdisciplinary approach.

Whatever form the educational program takes, we believe it is critical for faculty concerned with applied issues of children, youth, and families to begin training students to function in an interdisciplinary field. The demands of this domain, whether in the realm of research or professional application, will require a new type of student, one who respects, appreciates, and integrates the perspectives of more than a single discipline in the pursuit of understanding and solving the problems that children and families face in a changing society.

It is not sufficient to just know about other disciplines; applied research frequently requires the research psychologist to work collaboratively with academics and service professionals trained in other disciplines. We now turn to issues pertaining to the actual conduct of interdisciplinary research collaboratives.

General Issues in Collaborating with Community Agencies

The traditional laboratory basic researcher typically works alone. He or she personally writes the grant applications, designs the studies, recruits the subjects, collects the data, conducts the data analyses, and writes the article, perhaps directing a few apprentices—graduate students—who assist. In contrast, research on and evaluation of community-based programs are typically done as a partnership or collaboration among researchers, service professionals, funders, perhaps policy makers, and, increasingly, participants in the services, who usually have complementary skills and values and who, ideally, work together with mutual trust and respect toward a common goal (Vandercook et al., 1993).

In many respects, the values, purposes, procedures, style, and atmosphere of the agency are very different and often conflict with those of traditional academics. If the researcher is to function smoothly in an agency context, these differences must be understood and accommodated. Groark and McCall (1993, 1996) and McCall (1990) have discussed a variety of barriers to successful academic/service provider collaborations, and they and others (e.g., Mattessich & Monsey, 1992) have provided some guidelines on how to overcome them. The summary presented below pertains specifically to research and evaluation collaborations with community agencies. Such researchers and all community service providers have been lumped into single contrasting groups for illustration purposes; the actual circumstance of any particular case is likely to fall between these end points.

Attitudes and Roles

In the extreme, academics and service professionals are wary or even distrustful of each other, because they seem to have conflicting goals. Researchers, for example, may believe they know much more about the problems the service provider is attempting to prevent or treat than does the service provider. This attitude may be viewed as arrogance by service professionals, especially those who regard a researcher's knowledge as "academic"—that is, irrelevant—to their service needs. For example, one scholar was invited to report to a meeting of service professionals to plan an integrated service program to combat teenage pregnancy, school dropout, and youth unemployment. The academic's report contained one-page summaries of the research and services outcome literature (i.e., "what works") for each of the three problem domains, plus a one-page summary of the implications of that literature for the proposed integrated service program system. The committee chairperson, a service professional, glanced at the report, ripped off the first three pages of literature reviews, threw them away, and announced that the fourth page was "what we need." Research knowledge, even about the rationale for the effectiveness of a particular service, may not be a valued and traditional part of service program development (although some service professionals have a broad and astute grasp of the research literature pertinent to their services).

In addition to not valuing research information, some service professionals and schools may have had previous experience with researchers who wanted access to subjects but contributed nothing to the agency in the process of conducting their research (Ellickson, 1994; Mordock, 1993). Instead of a need for or benefit from cooperating with researchers, service providers may see only substantial costs in terms of time and possibly a risk of disaffecting clients in the process (see below). As a result, service providers may view academics as irrelevant at best and mercantile and intrusive at worst (Mordock, 1993). Such attitudes may have been created on the basis of actual experience, or they may be generalizations of stereotypical images of researchers, or they may exist because the agency director wishes to maintain total control over the activities of the agency, its staff, and its clients, and not be "observed" or "reviewed" by anyone, especially someone he or she does not know and may not respect.

Special tensions may arise if the researcher's role is to evaluate the effectiveness of the service program (see below), and the potential friction may be greater if the agency's funder, rather than the agency itself, has insisted on the evaluation and has even designated the particular researcher to conduct it. Few professionals of any type enjoy being evaluated, especially if they distrust the evaluator or are uncertain that the evaluation methods will be appropriate and sensitive to the agency's procedures and outcomes. Such a situation tends to produce an antagonistic "we–they relationship," rather than a more comfortable and desirable attitude and relationship that might be characterized as "us."

Usually, such divergent attitudes reflect contrasting values, purposes, and reward structures for these two professional groups. Such negative attitudes between service professionals and researchers need not, and often do not, exist when the parties understand these differences. For example, researchers may have gathered more research-based information about problems and services *in general,* and service professionals may know more about the *particular* problems of the clients served by their agency, the types of services and approaches that are locally feasible, and how to cope with the legal, policy, and political constraints of the local system (Groark & McCall, 1993). Both types of knowledge are necessary for a successful community-based project, and good collaborations require that both parties view themselves as bringing complementary and necessary knowledge and skills to a partnership of mutual respect in which the members share responsibilities and benefits in working toward a common goal.

Purposes and Goals

Most researchers want to discover new knowledge about a phenomenon, publish their discovery, and gain tenure and/or the respect of their academic colleagues. The purpose of most agencies is to improve the welfare of a particular client group. They do this by delivering services to the group, and they must acquire and maintain funding to do so.

Superficially at least, these two purposes do not appear to intersect, and they may actually conflict. For example, research procedures may require agency staff to spend extra time with clients in spite of their already high caseloads. The assessment procedures (e.g., questions about depression and suicide) may upset clients and have the potential to injure the relationship of comfort and trust that agencies work to establish and maintain to keep clients in service and help them effectively. Service professionals may not understand the need for or may be unwilling to cooperate in obtaining a comparison group (especially a no-treatment control group) or conducting what the researcher may consider other methodological necessities.

Essentially, then, the service professional is likely to feel that the welfare of clients takes precedence over everything else, and that the research, or even an evaluation of the effectiveness of the service program, is a luxury that can be tolerated only if time, resources, professional ethics, and client welfare permit. After all, they may reason, nothing much happens if the researcher does not get an article published; but clients may die or not receive the services they need, and the agency may fold and its director and staff lose their jobs, if clients and then funders become disaffected.

Successful community-based collaborative projects must satisfy both sets of values and purposes. Agencies, including schools, are reluctant to grant access to children or clients unless the research activity provides some knowledge that is directly useful to the purposes of the agency. The research is more likely to be useful if the agency is treated as a partner in selecting, not just reviewing, the questions to be addressed and the procedures to be used. Conversely, the researcher may need to explain to the agency that the information to be gained from the research will be more useful to the agency if certain methodological procedures (e.g., comparison groups or other procedures) are permitted.

For example, most agencies resist random assignment of clients to a treatment group and a no-treatment or less-treatment comparison group. They do not want to deny services to a needy person just to satisfy the research design, and they feel that a policy of "best practices" dictates that they evaluate potential clients and, on that basis (not by random assignment), refer clients to the services that best match their needs. However, if the services program can serve only a small number relative to the total number of potential and equally needy clients, agencies may be persuaded that random assignment is a fairer way *for them* to decide who will receive the special treatment, rather than employing other approaches to this decision.

In this case, random assignment serves both scientific and service purposes. But this is not always possible, and the purposes of the researcher and agency may conflict. An agency, for example, may resist asking young people questions about whether they have ever contemplated suicide (an item on most depression scales), because they fear the question itself will increase the likelihood that depressed teenagers will actually attempt suicide. There may be no evidence, research or clinical, that asking such a question indeed contributes to the likelihood of suicide attempts or even of more severe depression, but the fear of the possible effect on a teenager, and the consequences to the agency if a suicide attempt is made, may be enough for the agency to resist such questions. To accommodate the agency's concern, the researcher may have to delete questions about suicide from an otherwise standardized assessment of depression.

Stakeholders

Stakeholders are individuals or institutions to whom the director and staff of the agency are responsible or who are directly affected by the program. They may include a board of directors, potential funders, policy makers, parents of program participants, and the media. Such stakeholders can wield enormous influence over the agency and may determine whether it is refunded and survives. Academics, on the other hand, have relatively few stakeholders, and those that do exist (e.g., funders, editors, tenure review committees) tend to be much more distant from the project than are the stakeholders of the agency.

In addition to power and proximity, the biggest difference between the two groups of stakeholders is that, compared to the stakeholders of researchers, agency stakeholders tend to make their judgments and decisions in a much more personal and subjective manner. For example, whereas a reviewer of a research grant who is too personally knowledgeable about or associated with an applicant may be recused from the review process, an individual with the same personal knowledge of an agency and its director and staff may be used as the primary basis for a local funding decision about a service program.

Similarly, interpersonal relationships are crucial with respect to an agency's board of directors, which in many cases is not merely advisory but holds legal authority over the agency and its staff. Some board members are selected because they are staunch advocates for the agency, but others may be placed on the board in recognition of their power in the community and in the hope that they will become advocates for the agency. Much of what a board member knows about an agency comes from the agency's briefings at board meetings and from what that board member hears about the agency from others in the community. The latter especially can be based on hearsay, rumor, competitive prejudice, and personal beliefs and attitudes of the board member as well as his or her friends and associates.

Policy makers frequently decide how much money will be available to agencies, and the kinds of services and programs on which the money can be spent. In addition to personal knowledge of agencies, policy making is influenced by a variety of considerations other than the effectiveness of programs that fill the needs of the community. For example, Mordock (1993) suggested that some programs for handicapped children are funded because they save costs, appeal to democratic ideals, or are considered to be the legal rights of such children.

These several stakeholders can wield substantial public and private, dependable and capricious, valid and invalid, knowledgeable and naïve power over the agency, and the agency must accommodate and contend with it (Groark & McCall, 1996). Academics, accustomed to more distant and impersonal stakeholders who presumably base their decisions on the objective merits of a proposal, article, or tenure application, are likely to find this an alien world. The academic may perceive the agency's deference to the attitudes and views of stakeholders as pandering at best and dishonest or irresponsible at worst, especially if the academic perceives that research-based "truth" is subordinated to idiosyncratic beliefs and attitudes of stakeholders who seem to not want to be "confused with the facts." Academics may also be shocked to find local funders influenced by individual academics, journalists, and others who are adept at pushing their approach to services but who may have little evidence to support their program and even less credibility within the academic community. But that "expert" may be a friend or acquaintance of the funder; or the funder may have given money to that expert; or the expert may be the most well-known person in the field whom the funder has met personally. Consequently, when a funder, who may be on the agency's board, suggests that the agency and researcher use the expert's approach, the scholar who offers the observation that "no evidence exists that such an approach works" and especially that its proponent is "not respected in the academic community" will not only fail to have any influence on the funder but may be perceived as an arrogant critic of someone who appears (to the funder) to be more prominent than the scholar.

Another crucial aspect of this emphasis on personal relations is that style may matter more than substance. Academics are accustomed to speaking their minds and openly criticizing others, sometimes in offensive ad hominem terms and in public forums. Not only is there little regard for the interpersonal consequences of such criticism and disagreement, but academics respect and value a crisp, incisive, definitive critique regardless of context or consequences. Service professionals—indeed, most other groups—do not, at least not in public.

Researchers who collaborate with agencies are likely to attend and eventually may become members of a board of advisers or directors for an agency or program, and they need to be sensitive to these differences in style. At an advisory board meeting of a federally funded service program, for example, an agency staff member described her approach to hiring indigenous case managers. She indicated that she asked applicants whether they intended to have children in the near future, their religion, and a variety of other personal questions. An academic member of the advisory board responded at the meeting that, although the agency could do what it wished, he felt it was his responsibility as a board member to indicate that many of these questions were not allowed under contemporary policies and law, and an applicant might choose to sue. Nothing further was said during the meeting, but afterward, community members were aghast at the academic's behavior. It was considered insulting to have publicly criticized the staff member in this way. Some community board meetings can become quite frank and heated (and community politicians can be more unrestrained than anonymous journal reviewers), but generally there is greater concern for diplomatic language and personal relations at community agency board meetings than at academic advisory meetings. In part, the reason may be that community advisory boards often include funders, and agencies do not like to be criticized in front of them. It would have been more appropriate, for example, for the academic to have offered his advice in private—perhaps to the agency director rather than to the staff member.

Regulations

Agencies operate under a variety of legal and policy standards, regulations, licensing requirements, guidelines, directives, and "best practices." The effect of these principles is to limit the agency's ability to accommodate some of the requests that researchers may deem reasonable and necessary for the scientific integrity of the project, such as being unable to alter the nature of services, staff–client ratios, staff qualifications, labor practices (e.g., breaks, lunch hours), certain features of the physical environment, space allocations, safety provisions, client rights, and other procedures (Groark & McCall, 1993). For example, the number of square feet per child in a room designated for certain functions (e.g., reading) may be prescribed by state government for preschools, but the requirement may be different if a facility is designated as a day-care center and if 3-year-olds rather than 4-year-olds will use the area. Therefore, because the agency does not have a room that conforms to state standards, the agency may not be able to conduct an experimental reading or literacy program, or may be able to have groups of four but not of five children, or may be able to offer the program for 3-year-olds but not 4-year-olds because of different state space regulations.

Some of these restrictions may be formally adopted (e.g., state regulations); others may be quite subjective (e.g., certain "best practices"). Researchers accustomed to having a free hand in controlling every aspect of a laboratory research project will find these regulations annoying and frustrating. This reaction is especially common toward "best practices," which may be grounded in the beliefs or convictions of the agency administrator or what happens to be popular in the service community at the time, with no research evidence that the practice is either "effective" or "best." The agency may be unwilling to try an experimental intervention instead of the service it currently offers, or to randomly assign subjects to two contrasting treatment approaches, both of which are unresearched but one of which the agency director or staff suspect will be more effective.

Resistance to a suggestion because it conflicts with such a belief will be hard to swallow for a researcher, who values empirical evidence above all else. For the agency, however, the consequences of violating "best practices" are both ethical and practical. Service providers frequently operate beyond the reach of research; every day, they make decisions, without benefit of research information, that profoundly affect people's lives (e.g., removing a child from a home, judging the likelihood of future abuse, determining who would be the best parent in custody decisions). Consequently, they are accustomed to relying not only on their personal professional judgment but on the prevailing opinions of their field, and to do otherwise might be considered below professional standards or unethical. Further, to violate even the unwritten and unsubstantiated (empirically, at least) beliefs of their field may jeopardize their reputation and their financial future. Agencies are often visited by regulators and may be required to submit reports documenting services, clients, and procedures. It may be difficult for them to justify to such regulators certain experimental practices.

Agency directors also make judgments about the best interests of their clients that researchers may regard as intensely subjective and idiosyncratic. For example, in attempting to plan a program evaluation for an agency serving severely financially and emotionally stressed parents of medically fragile infants, a researcher wanted the case workers to make a global rating of each parent's emotional status, ability to cope, and level of functioning as a parent. These ratings were to be used to chart the progress of the parent and assess the effectiveness of the service, at least in the eyes of the case workers. The agency director refused, fearing that such records could be subpoenaed by courts and used as a basis for removing children from the custody of their parents. Given her experience, which included several visits to the court, she did not have confidence that the court would use such information fairly and, in her professional judgment, in the best interests of every child or family (Groark & McCall, 1996).

Resources

Agencies have two major resources, money and personnel, and both are fragile and in short supply. Financially, most agencies are entirely "soft-money" operations. Core or general support funding may be unknown, and in some locales every agency that is publicly supported is funded year by year, occasionally by an administrator who is basically a political appointee and not a human service professional. The researcher may live under a "publish or perish" system, but perishing may occur more swiftly and severely for agencies than for academics, because most agencies constantly live on the financial edge. For example, if an agency loses one grant in a single year, the agency and its staff may go out of business immediately. In contrast, an untenured academic who loses a grant usually does not lose his or her job and has approximately seven years to establish a case for tenure. A tenured academic may have no repercussions at all, save loss of pride, to having a grant rejected.

Money buys personnel who are the heart and soul of every human service program. Except for unionized public school teachers and a few agency directors, most human service professionals are paid a pittance. It was not unknown in 1995 for a new social worker who had earned an MSW degree to be assigned 30 to 50 cases involving child abuse, family violence, and drug and alcohol abuse and be paid less than $20,000 a year, including two weeks' paid vacation. Routinely, this MSW hiree would visit families in violent neighborhoods, and would be substantially unappreciated by many clients and by society in general. From this perspective, the academic's job looks luxurious, stressless, respected, and safe.

Under these circumstances, if a policy maker, funder, or agency director is given a choice between investing $20,000 in research—even a program evaluation ostensibly to improve the effectiveness of the service—or in another case worker, the added case worker wins hands down. And time is money. It may appear reasonable, even trivial, for a researcher to ask case workers to spend 5 extra minutes asking each client a half-dozen questions, but the case worker calculates that 5 minutes times 30 clients equals 2.5 extra hours each week with no reduction in caseload (Groark & McCall, 1996). Also, some types of human service professionals must spend hours each week preparing documents to be used in court proceedings pertaining to termination of parental rights, prosecution of abusers, and the like. In contrast, filling out a child behavior problem checklist or conducting a short-form developmental assessment looks insignificant and trivial as well as burdensome.

But these same line staff members may function as the academic's research assistants when conducting community-based projects. These individuals may differ substantially from the typical graduate student employed in laboratory research, who has chosen research as a career path, is trained to conduct it, is paid to do so, and is partly beholden to the faculty member for his or her future career. In contrast, agency personnel are typically not trained in research, may not value it, come from a variety of disciplines other than that of the researcher, may have no more formal training than a bachelor's degree or less, and owe the academic nothing. Even well-trained and experienced service personnel rely on a different knowledge base than researchers; they trust their accumulated experience more than a collection of research literature. Teachers, for example, may believe that prenatal exposure to cocaine produces the hyperactivity of children whom they see in their special education classes, whereas researchers will argue that the evidence for the effects of prenatal exposure to cocaine is inconclusive at best (Groark & McCall, 1996). The disparity represents the long-standing contrast between the service professional's assertion, "I see it in the clinic every day," and the researcher's challenge, "What is the evidence that X causes Y?"

The Imperfect Laboratory

Compared to the ideal research context, community agencies represent an imperfect laboratory at best. Treatments may not be rigidly applied in the same way to each client; whole treatment programs and practices may change in midstudy; personnel may turn over; regulations may be revised; discipline-wide innovations may be implemented in the middle of a project; comparison groups may not be available; clients may fail to cooperate; agency personnel may not be diligent in recording information; and a funding crisis may precipitously terminate the entire service program or the agency itself (Campbell & Stanley, 1966; Rossi, 1978; Scheirer & Rezmovic; 1983; Sechrest & Rednor, 1979). Such circumstances do not represent a lack of professionalism, irresponsibility among administrators and staff, or disregard for research and program evaluation; instead, they are the facts of life in a world designed for purposes other than research. Researchers will not be in control; they will be guests in other people's houses, and they will likely be forced to accommodate to the purposes and practices of the agency if they wish to stay and function there. Those researchers unwilling to accept these premises and their implications may be better suited to the laboratory.

Conversely, from the standpoint of human services and helping children and families, the laboratory, not the community, is the imperfect context. It is unrealistic, artificial, and unique (Bronfenbrenner, 1977). How can results generated in such a context be applied to the world, environment, and circumstances in which low-income families, for example, actually live?

Historically, traditional laboratory psychological researchers scoffed at and denigrated colleagues, especially those from other disciplines, who attempted to do research in applied contexts because of its deviation from the aforementioned methodological ideal. Regardless of whether particular criticisms were justified, conducting research in community-based agencies implies that the cookbook methodologies and designs taught in graduate school cannot be applied without substantial modification. It takes more creativity and care to conduct such research, and it is easier to do poor research and more difficult to do good-quality research in this context. A distinction should be made between obtaining the scientific ideal, which is likely impossible in community settings, and producing the best obtainable research-based information. At the same time, although circumstances may dictate that applied research will be crude, there is never an excuse for sloppiness. Walking this fine line takes great skill and maturity, and it requires academics who are unusually innovative and sophisticated methodologically. Therefore, disciplines "that care enough should send their very best."

Administrative Issues in Conducting Evaluations of Community-Based Programs

The previous discussion could apply in varying degrees to nearly any kind of applied research conducted in community settings. Program evaluation is a particular type of applied research in which the primary goal is to describe the clients, procedures, and services of a particular intervention program as well as the outcomes for clients.

Our focus shifts now to program evaluation, because it involves most of the issues that pertain to conducting applied scholarship in community settings, and it provokes numerous other concerns more peculiar to program evaluation. Historically, program evaluation was popular a decade or more ago but then lost some of its emphasis. Its decline may have resulted from the style and approach toward program evaluation that were popular at that time. Interventions were seen as "social experiments," and methodology approximated, as closely as possible, the approach used in the laboratory. Evaluators were independent from the intervention, and their main purpose was to provide a funder or policy maker with a "report card" on the effectiveness of the service program. This approach made program evaluation expensive, tended to establish an adversarial relationship between program and evaluator, and sometimes produced little information other than pass/fail that the agency could use to improve its program.

Today, program evaluation has a new look and, perhaps partly as a consequence, a resurgence of interest. Independent outside evaluations are still conducted, but an evaluation is more likely to represent a partnership between an evaluator and the service agency. The agency is empowered to play a vital role in conducting the evaluation, which is aimed more at providing information that will help the agency improve the program than at simply reporting to a funding agency that the program works or does not work. Faced with increasing needs for services and decreasing funds relative to that need, policy makers are forced to make choices in funding different service options, and they need to ensure that services are delivered as effectively and efficiently as possible. As a result, state and federal governments are calling for more objective information on the effectiveness of programs, and private funders—including, most notably, the United Way—are requiring agencies to present objective evidence of the effectiveness of their programs to obtain continued funding.

In some communities, the demand for program evaluation far outstrips the available personnel who are trained, experienced, and willing to conduct evaluations of community-based human service programs. Psychologists, being more routinely and extensively trained in research than personnel in most other behavioral disciplines, represent a major potential personnel resource for conducting program evaluations. However, psychologists are typically trained to conduct laboratory research, whereas program evaluation is a much different enterprise administratively and scientifically. What follows here is a guide for traditionally trained developmental researchers on the difference between program evaluation and laboratory research procedures. In this section, we will discuss administrative issues. The next two sections will deal, respectively, with scientific concerns and with a hypothetical case example based on an amalgamation of the authors' experience.

Evaluator–Agency–Funder Relationships

Contemporary evaluation is likely to be a partnership between the evaluator and the agency (and perhaps also the funder, who may be a policy maker). These relationships are very different from those that are typical of traditional laboratory projects. The traditional academic research project begins solely with the researcher, who conceives of a set of questions and the procedures to address them, and then applies to a funder to support the proposed research. The funder is often a federal agency or national foundation. The researcher, who may not know anyone personally at the funding agency, presents in the application, in excruciating detail, the procedures of the intended work. The application is reviewed by several specialists in that field, and feedback from reviewers may be provided with a request for a revision. Once funding is granted, the funder is unlikely to have any influence on the conduct of the project, and the researcher is not obligated to follow the details of the proposal as long as the research is confined to the original intent expressed in the application. In conducting the research, the scientist typically exercises complete control over every aspect of the project, including the selection of participants, the design and implementation of the manipulations or interventions, the measurement of variables, the analyses of the data, and the writing and publication of the report. Typically, a single researcher controls every aspect of the project, working with a staff of graduate students but usually not with an equal collaborator. If collaborators are involved, they are typically other faculty at the same university (usually from the same discipline or department) or employees of the researcher. Except for proposing a budget that conforms to university fiscal policies, clearing the research with the Internal Review Board (IRB), writing position descriptions, abiding by university employment practices and pay scales, and submitting a final report to the granting agency, little administration is required.

As described below, essentially every aspect of this traditional procedure is likely to be different when performing a project in collaboration with a community-based service agency, especially if the project consists of an evaluation of the agency's service program.

Funding. Occasionally, program evaluations are funded by federal agencies and national foundations, but they are unlikely to be the product of an investigator-initiated application. Instead, the funder is primarily interested in supporting a particular kind of intervention and issues a Request for Proposals (RFP), primarily directed at human service agencies, that outlines in general terms or in great detail the type of intervention it seeks to fund. In conjunction with the service program, there will be an evaluation, which may take one of several forms. Most commonly, the RFP will stipulate that the service provider will at least cooperate with a national evaluator, who will require the agency to collect data with its personnel or who will send its own data collectors to the site. Alternatively, the applicant may be required to choose a university or research institute partner capable of performing the evaluation at that site. In this case, a specific percentage or amount of money may be required to be spent on the local evaluation, and an evaluation plan will be submitted as part of the service program application. Typically, if local evaluators will be involved, they will be required to work with a national evaluator who may dictate the entire evaluation protocol or coordinate the local evaluators in developing a common core protocol. But in other cases, the evaluation is established and planned completely after the service programs have been selected, funded, and perhaps even implemented.

Notice the important differences between this funding procedure and the traditional laboratory research grant application. First, the research is subordinate to the intervention and sometimes to the intervention agency. The funder will judge the service program first, and only if the program is acceptable will the evaluation be considered. Second, in some cases, the researcher may not propose the sample, create the research design, identify the assessments, or even conduct the data analysis. Instead, the evaluator may submit only credentials and relevant experience. The actual research procedure may be dictated by another party or created by a consortium of local evaluators representing all or a subset of the intervention sites ultimately funded. Alternatively, the evaluator may propose a detailed plan only to have it revised by the national consortium for evaluation. Also, the amount of funds available may be stipulated in the RFP, and the amount may or may not be reasonable for the task. Or, neither the task nor the amount may be specified, so the evaluator cannot judge whether the amount of funding will be reasonable for what will be required.

But most funding for services—and evaluations of them—comes from state and county agencies and local foundations, not from federal agencies or national foundations. Generally, local funders have less experience with researchers and program evaluation, and the funding process is more informal. As with national funding, money for evaluation is almost always linked to the service program, but a local funder, as a suggestion or a contingency for funding the service program, may instruct the agency to fund out of its service grant, with an amount specified, an evaluation after the service award has been made. In this case, the evaluator and the evaluation plan may never be reviewed by anyone other than the agency prior to conducting the project, and the amount of money will be determined solely by the funder—probably arbitrarily, rather than on the basis of much knowledge about what could, should, or will be done.

Who will conduct the evaluation? The local communication network where agencies or funders can advertise the need for evaluation, or the availability of funds to conduct an evaluation, is typically not well organized. Sometimes, RFPs are distributed only to 10 to 20 individuals or institutions known to the funder. The writer of the RFP may have almost no experience with research in general or even program evaluation in particular. As a result, the RFP may request a very extensive evaluation and offer $5,000 to do the job. Alternatively, it may not offer enough information about the goals of the program, the nature of the desired evaluation, or the amount of money available, for the potential applicant to determine what kind of evaluation is possible (i.e., number of clients, opportunity for comparison groups). Compared to the detail of many federal RFPs and the detail that researchers put into traditional laboratory research grant applications, this looks hopelessly ridiculous and not worth pursuing.

Instead, however, researchers are advised to call the funder and perhaps the service agency to inquire about the amount and type of information desired from the evaluation, the details on the service program (its specific goals, the number of individuals being served, the length of service, comparison group possibilities, the data the agency already collects, the availability of staff at the agency to make new assessments), the timetable for the evaluation, and the amount of money available (many funders do not want to stipulate an amount and do not know what is reasonable; see below). Do not be surprised if (a) neither the funder nor the agency can answer some of these questions and (b) the questions they want the evaluation to address cannot be answered as stated—or at all. Also, some funders or agencies may feel uncomfortable giving more information to one potential bidder than to others, but some do not. In any case, local funders typically do not want the level of detail that researchers are accustomed to providing in applications, and they may allow only two or three weeks for the preparation of the application, give themselves one week to decide, and expect the evaluation to begin forthwith upon notification of the award.

Often, when a service agency has been charged by a funder to obtain an evaluation, no formal announcement or RFP will be distributed. The agency simply contacts someone known to be a potential evaluator; or, the funder suggests a possible evaluator with whom it has some experience, or simply calls the university (i.e., calls the general switchboard or the school of social work or education). Psychologists who desire to conduct such evaluations may want to meet briefly with local funders (remember the personal element) to indicate their interest and their availability to perform evaluations, and to leave a one-page statement of identification, training, and experience (no traditional academic vitae). Potential funders might include the county department of human services, children and youth services, and foundations that are known to fund services. Psychologists might also communicate their interest to colleagues in schools or departments that are typically associated with services and service evaluations (e.g., schools of social work, education, public health). Collaborating with them on an evaluation will provide contacts and direct evaluation experience, if it has not yet been gained. Newcomers may be perceived as rivals if the demand for evaluation is less than the supply of evaluators.

Once contact between the agency and the evaluator has been made, a meeting is typically held to outline the service program and goals, the purpose of the evaluation, potential measurements, the extent of the agency's current record keeping, the ability of the agency to make the assessments, the potential for comparison groups or comparison strategies if needed, and the amount of money involved. Typically, such amounts are minuscule by federal standards (e.g., $2,000–$10,000, although some locally funded evaluations may be $200,000 to $1 million), but often an agency can collect the data with its own personnel, leaving the researcher to design the assessments, analyze the data, and write a report. The money may be sufficient to pay the researcher a consulting fee plus the hourly rate of a graduate student. The task is to strike a balance among the extent of the program, the certainty and comprehensiveness of the results that the evaluation will produce, and the available budget.

Agencies are likely to have a fixed (small) amount of money available for an evaluation. Funders, such as the county and local foundations, may be more flexible but also somewhat inexperienced. Helping a funder craft an RFP for an evaluation (for which the helper will not be an applicant) might make a substantial and lasting contribution to all concerned. As implied above, many local funders do not anticipate the kind of information a potential evaluator needs for a decision on whether and what to propose, and the result may be that the RFP needlessly generates no applicants or only substandard applicants. A specific issue is the amount of money that should be set aside for an evaluation and whether that figure should be communicated in the RFP. A very rough rule of thumb is that 10% of the cost of the service program should be invested in program evaluation. But sometimes the cost of the program used in this estimate should be summed over all the future years in which the program is likely to operate. Using such an approach, however, the estimate for the cost of the evaluation could exceed the cost of the program in the first year or two. It may be justified, but it will never fly with a funder.

Cost is also a function of the purpose of the evaluation. Policy makers, for example, often want to know simply whether the program "works" and maybe how much it will save in future services. Such a summative evaluation should be conducted only after the program is up, running, and refined ("Evaluate no program before its time"). The policy maker may be interested in only a few policy-related outcomes (i.e., dropout reduction, teenage pregnancies), and may estimate that the evaluation should not take long. But the agency, although concerned about funding, is more likely to want the evaluation to improve and refine the program, in which case it might start simultaneously with program creation, help the agency build monitoring and evaluation into its system, emphasize process initially and outcome somewhat later, and last several years.

Even if an amount for evaluation is established, funders often resist communicating that amount in the RFP, following a typical negotiating strategy of giving the "bidder" the "opportunity" to do the job more cheaply than the funder expected. But potential evaluators need to know the scope of what is desired, so the RFP must give either a dollar figure or sufficient methodological detail to guide an applicant and to make applications roughly comparable. We suggest that funders compromise: Provide as much detail in the RFP as possible, and state a maximum dollar figure plus the advice that "cost-efficiency will be a criterion for selecting the evaluator."

The researcher's continuing relationship to the funder will depend on both the type of funding and the personal disposition of the funder. In traditional research, once a grant is made, the funder plays almost no role in the design and conduct of the research itself. Many local foundations operate in the same manner, but others do not. In the latter case, because an evaluator may be picked on the basis of credentials alone, it is not unreasonable for such a funder to want to approve the evaluation plan once the evaluator and the agency have agreed on a design and a set of procedures. The funder may also want to make a personal judgment about the evaluator. After all, as noted above, personal knowledge of the potential grant recipient is a common requirement in deciding the allocation of funds for services, so it is reasonable for the funder to employ the same procedure and criterion when selecting an evaluator. This is especially true if the funder has had minimum experience with academics and harbors all or part of the stereotype of the irrelevant, obfuscatory, independent-to-the-point-of-uncooperative, arrogant academic. Once the funds are allocated, the funder may want periodic written and/or oral progress reports and may request changes (see below).

If the service agency itself is funding the evaluation out of its grant to deliver services, then the evaluator essentially works for the agency. This means that the agency determines who the evaluator is and can terminate the arrangement at any time. Potentially, this represents a great loss of independence and appears to threaten the integrity of the evaluation. In reality, however, the same cooperation with the agency is required for a meaningful, smoothly operating, insightful "outside, independent" evaluation.

Regardless of the application mechanism or the nature of the institution funding the evaluation, evaluators must communicate in a far different manner than is expected when applying for traditional federal research grants. Of paramount concern is the likelihood that none or almost none of the reviewers (if there are reviewers) and decision makers, as well as the agency with which the evaluation will be conducted, is experienced in research and evaluation. Therefore, all written and oral communication must be stripped of jargon, must get to the point immediately, and must provide only as much detail as the audience desires, needs, and can handle (see below). It helps to ask how the application will be judged and by whom.

Relations with the Agency. Regardless of the funding source and the nature and structure of the evaluation, a program evaluation is likely to be conducted as a collaborative partnership with the agency and perhaps with the funder, and the application for funding and all procedures thereafter must reflect an attitude and style that accept this reality. Research design, assessments, data collection procedures, and the interpretation of the results (but probably not the data analyses) will be conducted cooperatively, even though the evaluator is likely to take the lead and the responsibility for these activities. The agency must agree with all procedures. To do so, agency personnel must understand why they are necessary and why they will contribute information that is useful to the agency, not just to science.

We have found, especially in the early stages of discussing an evaluation with an agency, that it helps to spend most of the time listening—to a thorough description of the service program, to the goals of the program, to directors' and line staff's concerns about what they think the program actually can accomplish, the goals for the evaluation, and their uneasiness and even fear regarding the evaluation and the evaluators. Knowledge of child and family development may be very useful in program development, and it should be offered; but remember that the agency is designing the service program. To do so, it helps for the evaluator to sincerely take the attitude that the purpose of the evaluation is to help the agency improve its service program and perhaps secure subsequent funding (which, after all, may be the only initial motive of the agency for conducting an evaluation). Also, accept and emphasize to the agency that the project is a cooperative partnership in which the agency has ultimate control (a right of refusal) and also a substantial portion of the responsibility (e.g., they may use their own staff to collect the data), and that the utility of the results to the agency will depend on the sincerity and the cooperation of both parties.

In most cases, the ideal situation is for the program evaluator to be at the table with the program developers at the beginning of the program development process. This is important for three reasons. First, it allows time for a relationship to develop between the agency and the evaluator. This occurs best if the evaluator is seen as respecting the agency professionals for their knowledge of service program development and is perceived as a team player in a cooperative partnership. Rather than offering suggestions or advice, it is better for the evaluator to listen and ask questions at this stage.

Second, if the evaluator is involved in program development, adequate pretesting can likely be implemented, both to establish a pretreatment baseline and to obtain measures of factors that are likely to moderate treatment effects. Such assessments may be the only strategy available to determine whether the clients made progress in the program (i.e., an independent comparison group may not be available). Further, they may permit much greater precision and power in assessing program effects, and they may contribute immensely to determining who benefits most and least from the treatment, which information may contribute more precisely to program development than general group differences.

Third, the design of a program evaluation follows the same logical steps that the design of a good service program must follow, and the evaluator and service professionals can help each other think through the common issues they face, for example: Who are the clients and what problems do they present? What are the specific (and ultimately measurable) goals the agency hopes to attain? What services will the agency provide to attain those goals, and what is the rationale (and perhaps evidence supporting the rationale) that suggests those services are likely to accomplish those goals? How will we know when the services have been delivered, how many and what kinds of services were provided, and who received them? How will we know when the services are matched to client needs? How can we measure and know when client goals are attained so that the client can be moved to the next level of service or graduated from the program? How will we know that the program has achieved its goals? What types of clients are most likely to attain program goals, and what types are less likely to attain them, and why?

Often, the program evaluator has been trained to follow the above outline of questions more systematically and overtly than are many service providers, because, in some locales, the service system historically has supported *services,* not *outcomes* (i.e., it was sufficient for the agency to report to the funder how many clients from what geographical areas and of which races received how many services). If the evaluator can be viewed by the agency as supportively and gently organizing the discussion around these questions, the scholar can be seen as contributing to program development yet being deferential to the agency's greater experience in creating and managing service programs. This approach, however, can entail endless meetings, many of which will seem to have contributed only to relationship building, with little discernible progress on developing the evaluation plan. But these meetings will be worthwhile if mutual trust and confidence are established, which can be translated into cooperation and support for the evaluator and agency during the project.

Too often, however, the evaluator is identified and invited after the program has been created and perhaps after it has been in operation for several years. This approach may be appropriate for a policy maker's report-card summative evaluation, in which the agency has been given some years to refine its program before its effectiveness is assessed. But the approach sometimes imposes limits on the evaluation. For example, the evaluator must accept what is already done and cannot be changed, and the evaluator, agency, and funder must come to accept the more limited information that may be produced by such an evaluation. In some instances, for example, the only option for an outcome evaluation is to conduct a consumer satisfaction survey, because no pretest or other assessments were conducted to track progress during treatment, and no untreated comparison group may be available against which to compare treated clients at this point in time. Also, the evaluator may be dependent on the records the agency has routinely kept, which may be minimal and inconsistently maintained. In other cases, however, much creative design work and analyses are possible, even when the evaluator is called in after the program has been operating for years.

Relation with Other Evaluators. In some multisited demonstration programs, often funded by the federal government, the evaluator of a specific site may be required to cooperate with other site-specific evaluators as well as with a general evaluator overseeing all sites. Such arrangements vary in how much influence and control the local evaluators have. A packaged management information system (MIS) may be handed to each site to implement and maintain as specified, and the site also may be expected to send information periodically to a central contractor. Similarly, a central contractor (not necessarily the same contractor as for the MIS) may specify the measurements and even conduct the outcome assessments, with local evaluators being little more than research assistants for the central contractor. The local evaluators may have access to local data for analysis, but might be subordinate to the central contractor with respect to releasing results. The Comprehensive Child Development Program of the Administration for Children, Youth, and Families was operated in this way.

In other cases, local evaluators have a great deal of control and responsibility for their own evaluations, but they are asked to cooperate with other sites and with a central contractor to establish at least a common core of assessments that can be used to evaluate the success of the multisited consortium. Such arrangements require swift cooperation at the beginning, to be able to establish a common core of assessments across all sites by the time clients are enrolled in the demonstration programs. Throughout the process, each site must be subordinate to cross-site procedures and training of data collectors, to ensure quality control and uniformity.

Another possibility is that a local program is funded by several sources, each of which requires its own management and outcome evaluation data and perhaps even a different computer system to maintain the data.

Outside/Independent versus Self-Evaluation. The relationship among evaluator, agency, and funder will be influenced in part by the broad structural character of the evaluation. Historically, the typical and ideal arrangement was to have an evaluator come in from the outside to assess a service program. The advantages of such an *outside/independent evaluation* are that the evaluator is a specialist in such research, and the evaluation has substantial credibility because it is conducted independently of the agency's personnel. The disadvantages are the substantial cost of such an evaluation, the possible difficulties of outside data collectors' gaining access to and developing rapport with clients, and a tendency to have an adversarial "we–they" relationship between the evaluator and the agency. Also, because of their distance from the program, such evaluators may lack information about the program that could contribute to accurate measurement and interpretation, and agencies may fear that a "number might be done on them" by an evaluator who has great credibility but little knowledge of the program. Complete outside evaluations are less common today, but their independence and credibility are still favored by funders—most of whom, however, are reluctant to pay the steeper price.

At the other extreme is *self-evaluation,* in which the agency designs its own assessments, collects its own data, analyzes and interprets them, and reports on them to funders and others. The advantages of this approach are: the agency is in total control; the agency is most knowledgeable about its own program goals, appropriate measurements, and proper interpretations of results; the agency has a maximum relationship with its own clients and can obtain sensitive information that otherwise might not be forthcoming to an outside evaluator who has no established relationship with the client; and the evaluation potentially costs less. The disadvantages are that many agencies are not sufficiently trained or experienced to conduct such an evaluation; they are often not given the money to maintain the records and employ the personnel capable of analyzing the data and interpreting it properly; and they lack the credibility of an independent and presumably unbiased evaluation. Agencies tend to favor self-evaluations because of their greater control, but they typically lack the financial and personnel resources to conduct them, and funders are skeptical of their objectivity.

A compromise to these extremes is a partnership between trained evaluators and the agency, in an attempt to emphasize the advantages of both outside and self-evaluations and to minimize their respective disadvantages. The evaluator brings to the project skills in design, assessment, data analysis, and data interpretation. The agency maintains maximum control over the implementation of the evaluation, retains a right of refusal over its procedures and measurements, may use its own personnel to conduct the assessments, and is a cooperative partner in the design of the project and the interpretation of results. Presumably, however, this approach combines the expertise of the evaluator with the relationship the agency has established with clients in a cooperative partnership that represents the best blend of credibility, access to clients, and cost.

But partnerships require special skills and attitudes. The partners must mutually respect as well as depend on one another. Compromises on both sides must be made. The partners must perceive that they are working toward a common goal of improving the program, and mechanisms must be established to ensure quality control of data collection when case workers who are initially untrained in data collection (and may not value it) are the primary data collectors. The evaluator must balance the need to be cooperative with, even deferential to, the agency on some matters, with maintaining scholarly independence and credibility on other matters. If the results of the evaluation are not supportive, great care and diplomacy may be needed to maintain this balance.

Public Oversight Committees. A local or a state funder may establish a broadly representative public committee to select an evaluator and/or to monitor the evaluation of a large and usually innovative service demonstration program. For example, the United Way of Western Pennsylvania established three community collaboratives to deliver case-managed, comprehensive services to drug- and alcohol-abusing mothers. A committee of community leaders and a few academics was appointed to select an evaluator and to oversee the evaluation enterprise. In such arrangements, the evaluator may report directly to the committee, perhaps on a quarterly basis, or the evaluator may work on a day-to-day basis with a representative of the committee or funder (e.g., a staff member of the funding agency).

In either case, the committee is likely to be dominated by individuals who are not familiar with evaluation, although such committees may contain a few members who are knowledgeable about research methodology and evaluation. These few committee specialists may be the evaluator's harshest critics, but they are also likely to be his or her staunchest supporters. Evaluators would do well to establish and maintain a special relationship with these members, who can help the evaluator through well-meaning but impractical or burdensome suggestions made by nonresearchers on the committee. If the committee has broader responsibilities than this single project, the evaluator may request a subcommittee composed of a majority of individuals who are knowledgeable about evaluation. Nevertheless, the evaluator ultimately will be governed by a group composed predominantly of nonspecialists who meet only occasionally and have the right to approve, disapprove, and enforce new procedures on the evaluation. This means that the evaluator must (a) accept the fact that the committee is ultimately in control of the project; (b) be able to communicate clearly, concisely, and with only an appropriate amount of detail with this nonspecialist committee; and (c) be prepared, throughout the evaluation process, for suggestions from the committee that constitute "midcourse corrections" to the evaluation procedures.

The latter are anathema to researchers, who usually want to have procedures agreed on before data collection begins and then remain constant through the evaluation process. The evaluator should attempt to lay out proposed procedures in as much detail as possible, and with maximum consultation with the committee early in the process. Ask the committee what information they think they will need and how they will use such information in making decisions regarding the program, but accept the possibility that they will not know except in very general terms. As early in the process as possible, propose procedures that will deliver to them what they say they want. Explain the costs of changing procedures later, not in a threatening manner but as encouragement for the committee to work hard at the beginning and to understand the potential consequences should they wish to change their minds later. Even when this is done, the evaluator should expect requests for changes during midcourse, especially if the service program is itself still developing. Between meetings, committees do not think much about the projects they oversee, and they are likely to think of questions, measures, and procedures after several meetings that did not occur to them at the beginning. Also, if the goal of the evaluation is to improve the service program, then a change in the program that is stimulated by the evaluation is testimony to the evaluation's utility and *raison d'être,* even if it also gives evaluators gray hair.

Investigator-Initiated Interventions. Program evaluation is difficult because it pertains to and potentially threatens the essence of the agency (i.e., its service program and funding), and investigator-initiated interventions and observations pose a similar and no less formidable set of problems. Years ago, scholars had relatively little difficulty gaining access to children in schools, for example, to study topics that often bore no relation to the educational enterprise as practiced in that school.

Today, investigator-initiated research is much more difficult and perhaps nearly impossible in some places. Schools are overburdened with demands for projects and with their own program requirements; students and teachers have less time for such matters; informed consent and privacy issues are more onerous; and parents and school boards are more vocal and resistive for personal, social, religious, and political reasons. Projects that are not pertinent to the purpose of the agency may be rejected for reasons of time and irrelevancy. Projects that are related to the purpose and activities of the agency (e.g., a schoolwide behavior management system, a drug and alcohol education program, a pregnancy prevention intervention) may come under such intense scrutiny by diverse groups complaining about the program on any grounds—correct or incorrect, relevant or irrelevant—that school authorities may block even a project they value and want to implement, just to minimize the hassle and negative publicity (e.g., Ellickson, 1994; W. Pelham, personal communication, 1995).

Projects conducted in the community but without the need for agency cooperation also are now more difficult, because citizens are more skeptical and wary of researchers and of any "outside" project. Well-educated parents, out of curiosity or "to help science," may still volunteer for innocuous studies of their infants and children, but too many urban, low-income citizens have experienced demonstration or research projects that have studied them "like guinea pigs" while returning nothing of lasting benefit. They will no longer participate in any activity labeled "research" or "study" (we never use these terms with the community) or any "outside" project, especially one associated with a university. Participating in an intervention group may be perceived as beneficial to them, but assignment to—or the possibility of being randomly assigned to—the no-treatment, less-treatment, or even "different treatment" group may not be considered beneficial. Obtaining a control or comparison group in such communities may be impossible.

Community and personal "empowerment" is the guiding principle for contemporary services and community-based projects, and researchers should anticipate that citizens and agencies will expect to decide whether a project will be conducted in their communities as well as whether they personally will participate (i.e., "What will this project do for *us?*") and how it will be conducted. In the extreme, it will be *their* project or none at all. So, all of the suggestions for working cooperatively and in partnership with agencies, presented here and elsewhere (e.g., Ellickson, 1994), apply when the researcher wants to design and initiate the intervention or observation as well as when the researcher evaluates the agency's own service program.

Contractual Arrangements

A traditional grant for lab-based research, although it is a legal document, is hardly a binding contract for a specific piece of work. The grantor promises to deliver funds, but has the right to reduce them or stop them entirely. The researcher is not bound by the details of the procedures described in the application, although he or she is expected to pursue the same line of work with the same intent. In most cases, relatively little is irrevocably obligated in either direction, and, frankly, relatively little is at stake in the way of potential benefits or losses for either party.

In contrast, much may be at stake, especially for the agency, when a program evaluation is conducted. If the results are negative, the agency might lose service program funding. Moreover, when the evaluation is conducted jointly with the agency, unique issues arise (e.g., Who owns the data? Who can release the report?) that could be the source of misunderstanding and conflict. If the evaluator receives a grant or contract directly from a funder for an outside/independent evaluation in which the evaluator is solely responsible for all data collection, analyses, and report writing, a special contract may not be necessary, although the agency should be made aware of the evaluator's rights and privileges in the conduct of this evaluation. However, if the evaluation is funded by the agency or by a third party, but will be conducted in collaboration with the agency, having a contract with the agency (and possibly with the funder) is highly advisable, not as the basis of a future lawsuit but as a means of anticipating and coming to mutual understanding about the events that are likely to transpire during the course of the evaluation. These events could be sensitive at best or contentious at worst.

Most major universities, for example, have a standard contract for arrangements with profit-making entities. The contract can be modified to be specifically suitable for program evaluation with a nonprofit agency. A generic form with options in several sections can be created and preapproved by the university and easily adapted for each particular use.[1] Although useful and necessary, it is, like most legal documents, foreboding in length and language. We have found it useful to have a brief, common-language statement of the major issues available for agencies prior to receiving such a contract, although most of the time we simply discuss these points verbally and prepare the agency for the legalese to follow. Actually, it is conventional practice for the contractor (i.e., the agency or funder) to issue the contract rather than the contractee (the university), and a few agencies, such as the county children and youth services, may have their own contracts. However, these may be established to fund service provision and may therefore contain many provisions that are irrelevant (e.g., monthly billing, insurance provisions, legal clearances). The university's standard contract may be more appropriate, but such agencies, especially government agencies, may insist on their own contracts anyway.

Regardless of who writes the contract, the following issues usually need to be discussed and agreed on in such a document. For convenience, it will be assumed that the evaluator is at a university.

Workscope. The heart of any contract is the stipulation of who will do what, how, and when. This "workscope" is specific to each arrangement, and is included as an attachment to the generic contract. For example, for a full-scale, collaborative evaluation, the workscope might stipulate that the evaluator will be responsible—in cooperation with, and with the consent of the agency—for the design of the evaluation, the selection of measurements, the training of data collectors, the design of a management information system, and the management of the database. The evaluator might also be responsible for the analyses of the data, the interpretation of the results, and the writing of the final report. The agency might agree to provide access, cooperation, and, in some cases, its own personnel (e.g., case workers or case managers, child development specialists, or a separate staff) to collect the data.

Independence. The contract should indicate that the evaluator is operating as an independent contractor. Specifically, it will conduct its affairs cooperatively with the agency, but the independence provision guarantees that the evaluator has the ultimate authority and responsibility for drawing conclusions from the data. The agency should be provided some reasonable period of time to review a draft of all reports, although it is collegial to meet with them to discuss a draft after their review. Such provisions are crucial for establishing the independence and credibility of the evaluator and the report; the more positive the report, the more valuable this independence provision will be to the agency, not just to the evaluator.

Data Ownership. Typically, if the evaluator and his or her employees collect the data, they "own" the data and have all rights and privileges to it. However, if agency staff collect the data, then the agency would typically "own" the data. Ownership implies control over who has access to the data, under what conditions, for what purposes, and over what period of time. Therefore, the contract should stipulate the nature of the rights that the owner of the data will grant to the other party. If the agency owns the data (e.g., because its staff collected it), the contract may stipulate that the agency permits the evaluator: to have complete access to specified data, to use it for the purposes described in the workscope or for scholarly purposes (see below), to have a first right of refusal for future uses of the data or subsequent evaluations, to be able to use the data for educational purposes, and to use the data as illustrations in scholarly methodological papers. Also, some provision should be made to cover the sharing of data with third parties (e.g., it cannot be done without written permission

[1] An example of such a contract can be obtained from R. B. McCall, University of Pittsburgh, UCSUR, 121 University Place, Pittsburgh, PA 15260. Please send a 3¼-inch disk if you want a WordPerfect 6.1 version.

from both contracting parties, or it can be done only under circumstance X or Y).

Confidentiality. The contract should stipulate the confidentiality procedures to be used by all parties having access to identifiable information. If the agency retains all identifying information and only transmits to the evaluator data having an ID code, then only ordinary procedures of data security need be followed by the evaluator. However, if the evaluator receives identifying information, then extraordinary procedures, consistent with university policy, must be taken by the evaluator to safeguard confidentiality. Evaluators must recognize that such data are likely to be more sensitive than those typically collected in laboratory research, and the injudicious release of identifying information could do irreparable harm to the agency, which may be held responsible for such a breach by the client, community members, and the funder.

Although typically not in the contract, these issues raise a question about the role of the Internal Review Board in conducting program evaluations. The Board's role will depend partly on the procedures established at each university. However, program evaluations may straddle or stretch the definitions of major concepts in determining whether procedures must be reviewed at all by an IRB or the kinds of IRB procedures that are required of the evaluator. For example, does a program evaluation constitute research? Is the primary purpose the acquisition of knowledge or the monitoring and improvement of services? Is the main beneficiary the researcher, the client, or the agency? In the latter case, a program evaluation might not be considered research.

Is the university really responsible for safeguarding subject rights and protections? If the data are collected by employees of the agency and if identifying information is maintained by the agency and not provided to the university, the agency rather than the university may be responsible for protecting client rights. From the university's standpoint, such a project may be considered an analysis of nonidentifying, previously collected data or the provision of consulting and technical assistance. In this case, the project may not need university IRB review (but it may need to follow agency procedures).

Even if university IRB review is not ordinarily needed under the above circumstances, such a decision may be qualified by local university regulations if children are involved in assessments, even via questionnaires or surveys, or if sensitive information is being collected from adults or children (which is often the case when evaluating human service programs). University policies differ on these matters, so it will be useful for the researcher intending to conduct program evaluations, especially on a continuing basis, to have a thorough discussion with appropriate IRB representatives to determine the circumstances that govern the nature of the required IRB review or exemption from it.

Payments. Most contracts contain a payment schedule. Typically, some amount is to be paid within 30 to 60 days of signing the contract, intermediate amounts are to be paid with deliverables or on a time schedule, and a final amount is due within 30 to 60 days of the completion of the project and the delivery of the final report. Some agencies accustomed to funding services pay on a cost-reimbursement basis. They ask the university to fund the project up front and to request periodic (sometimes even monthly) reimbursement from the agency for costs that have been incurred. Typically, billing is done by the university, but the university may or may not know when certain products (e.g., reports) have been delivered (if payment is based on deliverables). Some cooperation must be forged between the evaluator and the university with respect to billing. If this is a single project, the university will typically handle all the billing, and the evaluator will inform the university of the delivery of products. However, if numerous evaluation projects are contemplated, it may be better if the unit that houses the several projects does the billing and gives copies to the university. In any event, these procedures need to be established between the unit and the university before a contract is written and signed.

Most research grants have a line-by-line budget and must account for the expenditure of money within those lines and within the budget period established in the grant. Local agencies, however, may be willing or may even prefer to have "fixed-fee contracts" in which a dollar amount is agreed on as payment for the evaluation services, and no accounting of the expenditure of funds is required to be given to the funder/agency. This option is especially common if the agency is funding the evaluation, but it may be used by county agencies as well. The advantages of a fixed-fee contract are: the evaluator may spend the money in any way that he or she deems appropriate; the money may be spent across the total budget period in any way; many typical provisions in contracts (especially from agencies that usually fund services) may be eliminated; and any excess funds over actual costs (i.e., "profit") need not be returned to the funder. The disadvantage is that if the project ultimately costs more out of pocket than the fixed fee, the evaluator is responsible for finding the money. Prior to signing a fixed-fee contract, the evaluator must make arrangements with the university for what will happen with a shortfall or an excess of funds. While not unknown, both circumstances are unusual events in universities, and such arrangements may be complicated and resisted by a university.

Indirect Costs. Federal funders typically pay an additional indirect cost stipulated by the university's federally audited indirect cost rate. Many local funders of evaluations (e.g., smaller human service agencies, some local foundations, and some municipal agencies) pay little or no indirect costs and may never have encountered such a request (e.g., having the university conduct an evaluation may be the first such subcontract between a university and a small agency). Larger units more experienced with contracting may have an indirect cost policy or may negotiate such a rate individually for each contract. Further, because agencies are likely to have a fixed amount of money available for evaluation, any contribution to indirect costs will be taken out of that fixed amount, which reduces the amount available for direct costs.

The evaluator should discuss such matters with appropriate university officials to determine university policies and procedures in this regard. Faculty must recognize that indirect costs do not represent "gravy" to the university; they are payment for real costs incurred in executing such a project (e.g., research administration, research accounting, space and utilities, and so on). Universities, however, need to understand that not all external funders are able or willing to pay the audited federal indirect cost rate or any such costs, and that a rigid university policy that does not accept contracts without full indirect costs is tantamount to disallowing certain types of scholarly activity. They may not pay indirect costs, but local funders of services are more accustomed to paying, as direct costs, many of the items typically paid out of the federal indirect cost, including rent for space, utilities, accounting services, janitorial services, and routine office supplies and services. Some arrangement should be worked out in which such items can be listed under a special heading and do not need to be accounted for by the university in the usual way.

The Distribution of the Report. Despite occasional frustrations with a reviewer, traditional academics are accustomed to publishing what they like, drawing whatever conclusions they can justify scholastically, and disseminating the results of their research in any way and as widely as they choose. In contrast, depending on the circumstances, a variety of restrictions may affect the dissemination of findings from a program evaluation. After all, whereas little typically happens (other than a citation or another study) as the result of an academic publication, the outcome of a program evaluation may literally be the life or death of a service agency, the jobs of its staff, and the welfare of its clients. Consequently, who shall control the distribution of an evaluation report must be agreed on in the contract.

Control over the distribution of the report may depend on how the evaluation project is funded. If a third party (e.g., a foundation, a county agency) independently contracts with the researcher to evaluate the program of a service agency, the funder may want the report delivered to it and may place no restriction on the evaluator's right to distribute it. On the other hand, such an independent funder may feel the report is a "work-for-hire"—the funder owns the rights to the report, and only the funder should distribute it as it sees fit. In such a case, the evaluator may need the funder's permission to send out a copy of the report to anyone. If the funder is a state or federal agency and the evaluation is of a local site in a state or national consortium, the funder may stipulate that no local report shall be issued before the state or national evaluation report is made public. This restriction may be imposed because of the significance of the findings for future funding from state or federal legislatures.

If the agency funds the evaluation, it is likely to desire control over the distribution of the report. At least, it will want to exercise damage control if the evaluation is not as complimentary as the agency would like. Evaluators must understand the reasonableness of the agency's self-preservation motivation, especially if the agency has never been evaluated before or has not worked with this evaluator before. Researchers, however, coming from a value system that emphasizes academic freedom and the open exchange of information, may be unaccustomed to and may therefore resist such a request. A possible compromise is to give the agency rights over all distribution for a limited period of time (e.g., a year).

Scholarly Distribution Rights. Giving the agency control over the distribution of the report is not very limiting to the evaluator as long as the evaluator maintains all rights to the scholarly distribution of the results. Scholarly distribution includes publication in academic and professional journals (in a form different from the report to the agency or funder), presentations at conferences and workshops, and use of data and other material for educational purposes (e.g., in brown bag presentations and in class). Academic publication lags are typically a year (although classroom use and conference presentations may be arranged in less time), so granting the agency sole distribution rights to the report for a year is not very restrictive.

The evaluator should retain all rights and responsibilities for scholarly communications, but certain courtesies should be included in the contract. First, the agency might be allowed a specific period of time to review and comment on all written manuscripts before they are submitted for scholarly publication, although such review may not be possible for some types of conference presentations and workshops. Second, the evaluator may promise reasonable attempts to write scholarly reports without information that clearly identifies the agency and program, although the agency should be informed that local funders and professionals who know services in the area may be able to identify the agency anyway.

Third, the evaluator may offer authorship status to particular agency personnel who are responsible for the creation and direction of the service program being evaluated and/or who contribute materially to the evaluation. This issue may or may not be included in the contract, because it may be difficult to specify in advance who should and can be a coauthor. For example, the policies and even the ethical guidelines regarding authorship vary from one discipline and journal to another. A case can be made that the individuals responsible for creating and managing the service program have made a necessary and crucial contribution to a scholarly report evaluating its process and effectiveness, and both program and evaluation directors probably would be coauthors if they were colleagues at the same university. However, certain public health and medical journals stipulate that no one can be listed as a coauthor unless he or she has contributed to the report per se (not just to the program that is being evaluated). As a practical matter, most agency personnel, including directors, do not have the opportunity to publish papers. Having their names on a scholarly report is as valuable to them as the first publication or two is to an academic, and such a publication conveys credibility and prestige that may be useful to the agency when securing funding. Consequently, much may be gained for the agency—and for a relationship of cooperation and trust between the agency and the evaluator—by granting coauthorship to program professionals under appropriate circumstances and when the accepting journal permits.

Other Provisions. Most contracts contain, as standard practice, a variety of other provisions that are not unique to evaluation projects. These include: procedures governing finances and the ownership of materials collected if the arrangement is prematurely terminated; several indemnifications of the university and agency in the event of various unanticipated circumstances (e.g., injury of employees, damages as a result of the nature of the report); an assurance of best efforts on the part of the university but no guarantee of specific results, and so on. Such provisions appear to be legal boilerplate, especially for behavioral contracts that do not involve potentially lucrative products, patents, or copyrights, but infrequent real instances do arise in which such provisions are necessary. Besides, the university legal department is likely to insist on them.

Reports to Agencies and Funders

The reports an evaluator issues to agencies or funders are different from scholarly articles. First, they must be written for nonacademics—specifically, service professionals, funders, and perhaps nonspecialist board members. Second, although the evaluator assumes ultimate independence and responsibility, reports should be interpreted collaboratively with the agency to ensure balance and to permit the agency to contribute insightful interpretations of both positive and less positive results. Third, they should be written in a manner that expresses the purpose and attitude of the evaluation: to help the agency improve the quality and effectiveness of its program, rather than to constitute a simplistic report card.

Writing for nonacademic audiences requires more than simply "translating technical jargon into plain English." In many ways, it is similar to communicating with the press and legislators (e.g., see McCall, 1987, 1993; McCartney, 1993). Reports of evaluations to agencies, funders, and policy makers should follow these guidelines:

1. Start with an executive summary of one or two pages that captures the most important findings and conclusions.
2. Write in "outline form"; use frequent headings, bullets, and paragraphs that begin with the conclusion (perhaps in boldface) followed by some illustrative detail and evidence that can be skipped by those who want to skim the report (e.g., policy makers).
3. Minimize methodological and statistical detail in the body of the report (place the details in tables, footnotes, or appendixes, if including them at all). Instead, emphasize simple charts and graphs.
4. Do not shy away from interpreting the data and drawing actionable conclusions. If done responsibly and in consultation with the agency, this is one of the skills that scholars bring to this enterprise. The conclusions, not the data, will be remembered and used by the agency in subsequent reports and funding applications.

5. Phrase results in a constructive, positive, forward-looking manner that is consistent with the evaluation's purpose of improving the program.

To illustrate this last suggestion, it helps to communicate negative findings, not as "failures," but as "areas in which current services might consider revisions to improve their effectiveness." For example, one service program was designed to help substance-abusing, single-parent mothers, especially teenagers, and their children. But the process evaluation showed, after the first 2 years, that the average age of the client mothers was 28 years and that only a small percentage of the mothers were teenagers. Instead of declaring that the program "has failed to reach its target population of teenage substance-abusing mothers," the report stated that "current recruitment practices were more successful at enrolling older than younger substance-abusing mothers. In the future the agency could decide that older mothers are more amenable to treatment and that services might be more successful with them, or they could consider new recruitment practices that would encourage younger mothers to use the service." If negative results are found, it is helpful for the evaluator to discuss them with agency directors and line staff to determine possible explanations for the result (e.g., "The teenage mothers I saw just didn't think they had a problem, because so many of their friends, who were not mothers, were doing drugs. But the older mothers, especially those who had a long history of substance abuse, knew they had a problem and knew they needed help with it").

Even when well crafted, the report may not be greeted with praise or thanks. If the report is negative, the agency will not be enthused and neither will its funder. To defuse these reactions, the evaluator must do a great deal of preparation with the agency and funder before issuing the report. Also, the messenger (i.e., the evaluator) may be shot for delivering an unpopular message (i.e., negative results for a powerful agency or a popular program). For example, the evaluator may be called on to explain or even to justify a negative result (e.g., "Why are they not enrolling teenage mothers?"), when the responsibility for the result is really the agency's.

Researchers are accustomed to explaining away findings on the basis of methodological details, so it should be no surprise to them when agencies complain that negative results were obtained because the measurement procedures were not appropriate to the program goals, or the "right" clients were not interviewed. Agencies may say, "We know this program works—we have been doing it for 20 years—why can't your procedures see it as well as we see it?" The reaction may be a version of "Don't confuse me with the facts," or it may reflect actual inappropriate or inadequate measurement. At the same time, the researcher cannot present a long list of qualifications and limitations in the name of scientific responsibility, because agencies, funders, and policy makers will decide that the evaluator could not draw any firm conclusions so they learned nothing from the evaluation.

Even if the results are positive, there may be critics. For example, "We did not need to spend $10,000 to find this out. We knew from our extensive experience that this program works; we did not need these costly procedures to tell us 'what we already knew.'"

In a very real sense, agencies, funders, and especially policy makers literally need "sound bites" in evaluation reports that may be quoted in applications for funding, told to the media, and presented in briefs to boards of directors. Nonacademics often rely on scholars to interpret data and provide them with something useful, preferably in a quotable phrase. Evaluators should also be prepared to meet with boards of directors, policy groups, funders, and even the press, depending on the circumstances, to release the report or to discuss its findings.

Finally, the evaluator may encounter unfilled and perhaps unrealistic expectations by agency professionals and policy makers about what an evaluation is likely to produce. Agencies, of course, want the good news of a scientific or university validation that they are doing a good job and contributing to the welfare of their clients. They may appreciate far less a list of suggestions of ways they can improve their service, even though such a list may ultimately be more useful than a global "Congratulations." Policy makers, especially those supporting a given program, want the most dramatic sound bite they can get. An evaluator of a family support program may be ecstatic if the initial report reveals that, compared to nontreatment controls, parents in the family support program feel a much greater sense of effectiveness and of being in control of their lives, because such a personal perception is thought to be a necessary mediator for psychological and financial self-sufficiency, the major goal of the program. But a policy maker, who must justify to a funding board or to legislators the substantial expense of a family support service, may be unhappy that the report did not declare that "40% of treated families were now economically self-sufficient" or that "the program prevented 9 cases of child abuse and 11 unwanted pregnancies," despite the fact that the program was only in existence for 15 months. Funders are increasingly demanding program evaluation, but it is still a new kid on the block, and evaluators must learn the values, needs, and procedures of policy makers and agencies just as the policy makers and agencies must learn how evaluation is conducted and what it can and cannot do for human services.

THE DESIGN AND ANALYSIS OF PROGRAM EVALUATIONS

Like funding, administration, contracting, and report writing activities, the design and analysis of evaluations of community-based service programs depart from those of traditional laboratory research (e.g., Appelbaum & McCall, 1983). Research designs and statistical analyses are, or should be, viewed as tools for answering research questions, not as strategies with independent lives of their own that shape the nature of the questions (Appelbaum & McCall, 1983; McCall, 1977, 1995; McCall & Green, 1997). In the laboratory, it is easy to confuse these purposes and the direction of influence, because the researcher has a relatively free hand to control the questions, the manipulations or interventions, and the design and analyses—one element (including the questions and interventions) can be made to fit the other (including the design and analyses). As discussed above, in community-based projects, the researcher will likely exert much less control over the questions, the intervention, the nature of a comparison sample or condition, the measures, and even the budget, which in the extreme may be established even before the researcher joins the project. As a result, the design and analysis more obviously must be created to answer the established questions about the existing intervention under the current circumstances rather than the reverse.

Because these circumstances vary much more than their laboratory counterparts from one community-based project to another, the design and analysis strategies of program evaluation are as many and varied as the programs and services being evaluated. Different evaluation strategies have emerged, largely through the application of various research paradigms to different service programs that operate under varying feasibility and political climates. Although some would argue that certain paradigms and approaches are unquestionably superior to others (e.g., the randomized experiment as the quintessential research strategy), Cronbach (1982) is probably correct in his assertion that "there is no single best plan for an evaluation, not even for an inquiry into a particular program, at a particular time, with a particular budget" (p. 231). Therefore, some have described program evaluation design and analysis as more a creative "art" than a "science" (Cronbach, 1982; Patton, 1990). Keeping this in mind, several of the most widely used approaches to program evaluation are reviewed below, as well as several strategies for developing collaborations among service programs, evaluators, and other stakeholders that can help ensure a "fit" between evaluation design and analysis on one hand and program interventions, questions, and approaches on the other.

The intent of this section is not to provide a complete tutorial on program evaluation research methods. Several texts and chapters represent suitable introductions (Berk & Rossi, 1990; Prosavac & Carey, 1992; Rossi & Freeman, 1993; Shadish, Cook, & Leviton, 1991) and advanced discussions of major topics and issues (Bickman, 1987; Cook & Campbell, 1979; Cook & Reichardt, 1979; Guba & Lincoln, 1981; Patton, 1986, 1990). Instead, as part of the intent of this chapter as a whole, this section is addressed to readers who are familiar with the design and analysis of laboratory experimental and observational research, and it represents a guide to the practical and contemporary scientific issues that pertain to extending that knowledge to conducting evaluations of community-based interventions.

Evaluation Approaches: A Brief Overview

Evaluation approaches can be loosely categorized into three major groupings: (a) summative approaches, (b) formative approaches, and (c) comprehensive approaches. In evaluation terminology, summative approaches are also known as "effectiveness," "outcome," and/or "impact studies." Formative approaches include "process," "accountability," and/or "implementation" evaluations.

Summative approaches tend to assume a relatively static program model, use quantitative design and data collection methods (especially experimental and quasi-experimental designs), and have as their primary purpose the evaluation of program effectiveness (e.g., Campbell & Stanley, 1966; Cook & Campbell, 1979; Rossi & Freeman, 1993; Stufflebeam, 1994; Stufflebeam et al., 1971). *Formative approaches* emphasize the description of ongoing program processes, use qualitative or a combination of qualitative and quantitative approaches to data collection and analysis methods, and have as their primary purpose program development and improvement (e.g., Lincoln & Guba, 1994; Patton, 1986, 1990). These are loose categories, however; most evaluators now recognize the importance of including components of both approaches in any one evaluation plan. Therefore, a third category of evaluation has emerged: *comprehensive approaches* (Rossi & Freeman, 1993; Rossi & Wright, 1984), which relies on a combination of quantitative and qualitative methods of data collection and analysis, and which typically serves both program development and program effectiveness purposes (e.g., Herman, Morris,

& Fitz-Gibbon, 1987; Rossi & Freeman, 1990; Rossi & Wright, 1984; Smith, 1994).

Summative Approaches to Evaluation

In the early days of the field of evaluation, much of the research was dominated by social scientists trained in a laboratory-based experimental approach. As was so eloquently put forth in Campbell's classic 1969 article, these researchers envisioned the application of experimental design to social programs that would result in conclusive evidence about program effectiveness. Campbell called for:

> an experimental approach to social reform, an approach in which we try out new programs designed to cure specific social problems, in which we learn whether or not these programs are effective, and in which we retain, imitate, modify, or discard them on the basis of apparent effectiveness on the multiple imperfect criteria available. (p. 409)

In this optimistic vein, a number of large-scale federal evaluations of demonstration service projects were carried out during the "Great Society" legislation of the 1960s and 1970s. Many of these were true field experiments, employing random assignment to treatment and control groups. The negative income tax experiments were one of the best known examples (Kershaw & Fair, 1975; Robins, Spiegelman, Weiner, & Bell, 1980; Rossi & Lyall, 1974; Watts & Rees, 1976). This approach was concerned largely with providing information about program effectiveness to funders and policy makers to help provide justification for the allocation of limited funding for social programs. In one sense, these studies provided a "report card" to policy makers. In another sense, many of these studies are best characterized as *evaluation research,* which is evaluation that is chiefly concerned with contributing to generalizable knowledge and theory (in contrast to *program evaluation,* which in its focused meaning is typically more program-specific). However, the results of many of these field experiments were disappointing; "a reasonable summary of the findings is that the expected value of the effect of any program hovers around zero" (Rossi & Wright, 1984, p. 58).

A legacy of Campbell's "experimenting society" approach remains, however, in the continuing preference for the randomized experiment in large-scale demonstration program evaluations (Boruch, 1994; Dennis & Boruch, 1994). In terms of determining the net effects of a given program, there is little question that the randomized experiment has the potential to bring the strongest data to bear on the question: "Did the program work?" However, methodological, ethical, and epistemological concerns surrounding the randomized experiment have raised questions about its usefulness and feasibility as the method of choice for program evaluation (Fetterman, 1982; Johnston & Swift, 1994; Lincoln & Guba, 1994; McCall & Green, 1997).

Methodologically, it is now acknowledged that conducting robust true experiments in the field—the scientific ideal described at the beginning of this chapter—is extremely difficult and often impossible. For example, there are numerous examples of failures to properly implement random assignment. Some researchers have even tried to devise decision rules about when randomization should be attempted (Dennis & Boruch, 1989). Such issues as diffusion of treatment into control groups (e.g., persons in the control group get some or all of the "treatment"), reactivity of control groups (e.g., control subjects knowledgeable about the treatment may "work" harder even though not treated), and administrative problems maintaining control over the randomization process plague randomized designs in field settings. Randomized experiments also raise ethical dilemmas; potentially useful treatments may be denied those who might benefit. Moreover, it has become evident that true experiments involving wide-reaching policy changes are difficult to carry out except under conditions in which policies have not yet been implemented; however, getting policy makers to wait until "the data are in" before implementing popular and potentially beneficial programs is extremely difficult.

Another issue in conducting randomized designs or any approach that requires a nontreated comparison group is locating and recruiting "nontreated subjects." Families living in low-income, high-risk neighborhoods of major cities that are frequently the geographic targets for major service programs may have access to several different service programs simultaneously. Families that do not participate in such programs may be qualitatively different from those who seek treatment (e.g., they may have fewer problems and be less in need of help, or they may be exceptionally isolated and high-risk).

Finally, it has been our experience, in working with community-based programs, that randomized experiments may violate the very goals and objectives of the program itself. For example, family support programs (e.g., Weissbourd, 1987), which are meant to serve as community centers for strengthening families, are not conducive to randomized designs. Family support programs are *supposed* to create a diffusion of treatment effects into the community by promoting community activism and empowering families, including families not enrolled in the focal treatment. The imposition of a random experiment on such a program would have the effect of artificially limiting the program to a select group of persons within that community and forcing staff to work only with those families, in order to create a comparable nontreated comparison group. Therefore, the net potential impact of the program on community-wide problems, which are thought to exacerbate personal and family problems, would be reduced simply as an artifact of the evaluation design.

In response to these difficulties, alternatives to the true randomized experiment, especially utilization of the "quasi-experiment" (that is, investigations not involving random assignment of participants), have become extremely widespread. Although in some ways methodologically inferior to true experiments (at least in terms of deriving strong causal relationships between programs and outcomes), quasi-experiments have been popular and widely used designs in evaluation research. Because quasi-experiments do not involve random assignment to experimental groups, the predominant concern of those using these designs has been with internal validity—that is, addressing the question of whether it was the program that caused change or "something else." Campbell and Stanley (1966) were among the first to put forward logical frameworks for guiding interpretations of such "threats to validity" in quasi-experimental designs.

Although the exploration of the strengths and weakness of various quasi-experimental designs is beyond the scope of this chapter (the interested reader is referred to Cook & Campbell, 1979, for more information), two categories of designs—(a) nonequivalent control group designs and (b) interrupted time-series designs—have become so popular that a brief description of each is in order.

Nonequivalent Control Group Designs. Perhaps the most widely used quasi-experimental design is the nonequivalent control group design, usually involving both pretest and posttest observations, in which the outcomes for a group exposed to the program or treatment are compared with another (nontreated) group that is similar to the program group at the pretest. A variation of the nonequivalent control group design includes programs in which different persons get similar service programs that differ in their qualitative nature (e.g., one emphasizes parenting and child development, and the other emphasizes parental job training and personal skills and supports) or their intensity (e.g., home visits by case managers/child development specialists once per week versus once per month). Because participants are not randomly assigned to treatment and comparison groups, a host of threats to the validity of such designs must be considered.

A particular problem with nonequivalent control group designs are the threats to validity that derive from the selection of subjects into the program or comparison group. Given that assignment to the groups is nonrandom, the researcher must address the question of what factors might contribute to how a person got into either group. In social service programs, for example, services are often delivered to those who are the first to "sign up." A common comparison group under these circumstances might be those persons who did not sign up for the program. This comparison, however, poses several threats to interpreting the program outcomes. For example, in the event that positive program effects are found, one plausible alternative hypothesis might be that those enrolling in the program were more highly motivated at the outset, and therefore would have achieved positive outcomes even without the program. A second plausible hypothesis might be that the program would not be as effective with less motivated participants. This type of validity threat has been labeled a "selection–maturation" interaction, and is especially problematic for evaluations of programs in which people not only volunteer or self-select into programs but also might be expected to change over time to some degree, even without the program (see Campbell & Stanley, 1966, and Cook & Campbell, 1979, for a complete discussion of threats to validity).

Like other threats to validity, those due to selection–maturation can be minimized if the researcher is able to anticipate these alternative hypotheses and measure related variables at the pretest. The plausibility of such alternative hypotheses can then be reduced by ensuring that the groups were similar on the variable representing the potential threat. For example, motivation or perception of efficacy could be measured in both groups at the pretest, and subjects could be selected to equate the groups on this variable. Another approach would be to use this variable as a covariate in data analyses, to minimize the likelihood that outcome differences were due to motivation rather than to the program itself.

The methods of analyzing data for nonequivalent control group designs involving change over time are controversial (Cook & Campbell, 1979; McCall & Appelbaum, 1973; Rogosa, 1988). In particular, techniques for measuring change over time (repeated measures, gain score analysis, and so on) and for controlling for possible selection effects (e.g., through matching, analysis of covariance, hierarchical multiple regression, and so on) pose many statistical and interpretive challenges.

One increasingly popular method of analysis is growth curve analysis, either regression-based (e.g., Bryk &

Raudenbush, 1987) or with latent variables (e.g., McArdle, 1991; McArdle & Epstein, 1987). This type of analysis is particularly useful because it allows the researcher to model both individual growth curves and between-subject variation (Bryk & Raudenbush, 1987; Burchinal & Appelbaum, 1991; McArdle & Epstein, 1987; Rogosa, Brandt, & Zimowski, 1982; Tate & Hokanson, 1992; Willet & Sayer, 1994). Growth curve analysis allows the researcher to examine several variables that are of particular interest in evaluating interventions for young children, including (a) the analysis of developmental changes over time at the individual level, (b) rates of change in addition to mean levels of change, and (c) correlates of rates of change (such as assignment to various treatment groups or demographic variables; Willet & Sayer, 1994). For example, growth curve analysis might be used to analyze the effectiveness of an early childhood intervention on children's developmental trajectories by comparing the developmental curves of the treatment group to the patterns found in an untreated group (Bailey, Burchinal, & McWilliam, 1993).

Growth curve analysis that uses hierarchical linear modeling can account for nonindependence of observations, a common situation in evaluations of interventions for young children (Burchinal & Appelbaum, 1991). For example, interventions often are delivered to groups of participants (e.g., schools, classes, or families). Hierarchical linear modeling basically conducts nested regressions in which individual correlates of outcome are modeled and nested within family or classroom correlates of outcome (Cook, 1994; Kenny & Judd, 1986). For example, a sample of Head Start centers might be obtained, as well as non-Head Start day-care centers serving a similar population. Hierarchical linear modeling would determine a regression between individual measures (e.g., SES, maternal knowledge of child development, maternal involvement, and so on) and child outcome (e.g., school readiness, social development). It would then nest that regression within a separate regression of classroom characteristics (e.g., teacher skills and enthusiasm, class size) on the same outcomes, and nest both of those regressions within a separate regression of center characteristics (e.g., expenditure per child, poverty of neighborhood, degree of racial segregation of neighborhood) on outcome when comparing Head Start and non-Head Start groups. Notice that none of the independent variables is necessarily "independent" of the others.

Increasing the usefulness of growth curve analysis for evaluators is the fact that these techniques are remarkably "forgiving" in terms of data requirements. In contrast to standard repeated-measures analysis of variance, for example, growth curve models do not require the same number of observations for each participant (randomly missing data, therefore, are not a problem). Although data should be assessed at the same intervals for participants (e.g., every 12 months), they do not have to be the same points in time (e.g., participants may start the program at different times; e.g., Bailey et al., 1993; Burchinal & Appelbaum, 1991). Finally, and importantly, these models should increase the power of the analysis by allowing individual growth patterns to be specified and by reducing error variance. However, it should be noted that no amount of statistical adjustment can completely or certainly eliminate sampling inequities, but they can contribute to the best obtainable results (Campbell & Boruch, 1975).

Interrupted Time-Series Designs. Another frequently used and relatively robust quasi-experimental design is the interrupted time-series design, in which numerous observations of the same variables are collected over time, both before and after the "interruption" represented by the introduction of the treatment program. This design is especially useful in evaluating wide-reaching policy changes that are implemented at a particular point in time for which data collection is routine and continuous (e.g., public health indicators). For example, interrupted time-series designs have been used to evaluate the effectiveness of changes in drunk-driving legislation (Ross, Campbell, & Glass, 1970; West, Hepworth, McCall, & Reich, 1989). Time-series analysis requires a large number of data points (e.g., "no fewer than 50" is sometimes used as a rule of thumb; West, Hepworth, McCall, & Reich, 1989), the same data must be collected consistently over time, and the data are often highly aggregated [i.e., rates of arrest for drunk driving, or the total number of driving-under-the-influence (DUI) tickets given in a geographic area]. Such designs are appropriate for developmental research in principle, but, in practice, few developmental studies are likely to meet these requirements. However, the data routinely collected by public agencies describe the health, education, economic, criminal, and welfare status of cities, counties, and sometimes municipalities and census tracks. Data such as rates of infant mortality, low-birth-weight newborns, use of prenatal care, births to teenage mothers, public assistance, free and reduced lunch usage, WIC participation, juvenile crime, substance abuse rates, drug abuse treatment referrals, and so on, are all potentially rich sources of information to the evaluator. These data represent frequent goals of service programs, may be collected frequently and consistently, and could be used to evaluate large-scale policy interventions or changes.

Data analysis of time series involves fairly complex modeling procedures that can indicate whether the intervention has caused changes in the pattern of data that differ from the naturally occurring trend patterns and account for the nonindependence of observations (i.e., a given observation is more highly correlated with adjacent observations than with nonadjacent observations). Autoregressive integrated moving average (ARIMA) modeling techniques have been the most widely used approaches for analysis of time-series data (Box & Jenkins, 1976; Cook & Campbell, 1979; West et al., 1989). The time-series design can be further strengthened by utilizing a nonequivalent control group for which parallel data are available. For example, in a time-series evaluation of drunk-driving legislation in Phoenix, Arizona, data from similar cities that were unaffected by the new law were used as comparisons (West et al., 1989).

No Comparison Group. As with methodologies in psychology in general (Wohlwill, 1973), program evaluation techniques have not typically been created with developmental interests in mind, and the curve-fitting and time-series approaches described above are two popular approaches suited to the case in which change over time is expected even without treatment. Because these developmental curves are expected, determining treatment effects is extremely difficult without comparison subjects. However, many community programs, even very large ones, are initially implemented without much thought to evaluation, and comparison groups are often difficult to find. Depending on when in the service implementation the evaluator is brought in, several options are possible.

One approach is to evaluate a dose-response function of individual differences within the treatment group. Presumably, those participants receiving the most frequent and intense treatment should have better outcomes. However, if participants who had more severe problems were given more frequent and intense services, there may be no dose-response effect or a negative dose-response effect may be found (i.e., the participants who had the most severe problems initially received the most services but made less progress on outcome measures). One approach to dealing with this problem may be to regress measures of services on measures of risk or problem severity, the residuals of which represent services relative to need and can be correlated with outcome.

A variant on the individual differences approach within the treatment group is to predict or retrospectively characterize those participants who showed the most improvement in the treatment. The correlates of improvement can often indicate what type of participant does well or less well in the program, suggesting that the program should concentrate on those participants most likely to succeed and/or devise a different treatment program for those who made less progress.

Sometimes the circumstances that make traditional approaches to design and analysis difficult can be used to forge a solution. For example, many service programs for young children enroll those children at different ages, the children remain in the program different lengths of time, no traditional comparison group exists, and the outcome variable can be expected to change over time in the target group even without an intervention (e.g., a measure of general mental performance for low-income children 2 to 6 years of age). Consequently, simple pre-post differences will be confounded with such non-intervention age changes, and a result of no pre-post differences that would ordinarily be interpreted as evidence that the program provided no benefit might actually have been successful in preventing the decline in general mental performance typical of low-income children of this age range. In such a situation, the pretest scores of program children (or their siblings) could be regressed on their ages (they entered the program at different ages) to obtain an estimate of the rate of change over age (e.g., per month) that would be expected in such children who have not (yet) experienced the program. The actual pre-post rate of change in these same children after experiencing the service program can be compared to this expected no-treatment estimate of rate of change to evaluate the effects of the intervention (McCall, Ryan, & Green, 1997).

The Problem of No-Difference Findings. Unfortunately, the heavy focus on threats to internal validity shown by early evaluation researchers was based on the assumption that social programs would produce positive effects, the challenge then would be to draw a causal inference about that change. The actual result was not anticipated: the majority of programs had effects "hovering near zero." One of the most widely known examples of negative research findings was the Westinghouse Learning Corporation evaluation of Head Start (1969). Many of those working with the Head Start program were disturbed not only by the lack of positive effects (which remain controversial; e.g., Bentler & Woodward, 1978; Magidson, 1977) but with "how far afield the evaluation seemed to have been from the real concerns, goals, and dreams of program personnel and participants" (Jacobs, 1988, p. 37).

Rethinking Summative Evaluation Approaches. Concerns such as these led to a reexamination of the purpose and methods of evaluation research. First, the fact that many programs were not being implemented as planned (or at all) became more widely recognized. Several programs that had shown a disappointing lack of positive effects appeared, after closer investigation, never to have really been implemented (e.g., the "Push-Excel" program, as reported by the American Institutes for Research, 1980). Thus, the importance of documenting program implementation (or "measuring the treatment") became more widespread, and evaluations began to take on the task of program monitoring (i.e., formative or process evaluation) as an essential component. Indeed, some researchers focused exclusively on the problem of implementation and studied the conditions under which complete implementation is more or less likely to occur (Williams & Elmore, 1976).

Second, evaluators began to "unpack the black-box model" of evaluation that was typical of the early experimental/quasi-experimental approaches. These researchers questioned the notion that a program, such as Head Start, was a single undifferentiated treatment implemented in the same way across different programs and sites. Treating programs as a single experimental manipulation was useful when the purpose of the evaluation was simply to measure net program effects (i.e., "Did the program in general work?"). But such an approach contributed much less information that might be used to improve the program, especially when the results of the evaluation were negative (i.e., "We know the program didn't work as expected, but we have no clues as to why").

One approach to unpacking the black box has been labeled "theory-driven evaluation" (Bickman, 1987, 1990; Chen, 1990; Chen & Rossi, 1983, 1989), which emphasizes the importance of understanding the procedures and activities of a program and how these link logically to expected program outcomes. The evaluation design and measurement, then, is guided by the understanding of the program theory and should yield information about why program effects did or did not occur. Although still primarily summative in approach, theory-driven evaluation emphasizes the elaboration and measurement of program processes, and perhaps theoretically important intervening variables, as a key to understanding outcomes. For example, family support programs are thought to produce positive long-term benefits by increasing personal perceptions of "effectance" in low-income, high-risk families that lead to greater psychological and financial self-sufficiency. In such a case, effectance might be measured to determine whether the program increased it and whether those parents who increased in effectance had better outcomes. Although Chen and Rossi (1989) have argued that theory-driven evaluation is suitable for a variety of methodologies, these approaches typically have been quantitative and analytic in nature. Recently, for example, many have applied more sophisticated statistical techniques, including path analyses and structural equation modeling, to more fully elaborate the theoretical causal paths underlying program effects (Chen & Rossi, 1989; Smith, 1990).

Finally, some evaluators rejected, to varying degrees, the positivistic, experimental approaches to knowledge as a way of understanding social programs (e.g., Lincoln & Guba, 1986; Patton, 1980). Instead, these researchers took the perspective that many, if not all, social programs were not ready for stringent experimental evaluations. The goals, methods, and procedures of these programs were evolving and constantly changing, and therefore they could not be identified and measured accurately as required by pretest–posttest models of experimental design. Thus, these researchers turned to more qualitative, formative evaluations as a method of choice for program evaluation.

Formative Approaches to Evaluation

Formative approaches to evaluation emphasize observation and documentation of program implementation processes and operations, and they have as their primary purpose program development and improvement. Often, although not always, formative evaluations utilize qualitative methods (e.g., content analysis of key program documents, open-ended interviews, and observations of program process). A striking contrast to this qualitative approach, however, is the growth of program monitoring, which relies primarily on quantitative data to ensure service delivery compliance (e.g., counts of number served, time spent delivering services, and staff caseload).

Formative evaluations are better suited for many of the rather loosely knit, multifaceted social programs that serve children and families, because they do not assume that the program is a stable unchanging unit with explicit goals and strategies for their achievement. Instead, formative approaches can reflect the more developmentally dynamic aspects of innovative programs, and are often viewed more favorably by program administrators and staff because they more closely mirror the program as it "really exists." Formative research is also less threatening to programs, because its role is to verify program implementation and development rather than to measure effectiveness. One common purpose of formative evaluation is to help to develop a clear picture of the program's goals and objectives, which is necessary for rigorous summative evaluations that might be conducted later. In this way, although typically not aimed directly at assessing program effectiveness (at least not at measuring the net effects of the program on its recipients), formative evaluations are often seen as "setting the stage" for summative evaluations.

Not all formative evaluation, however, is qualitative or is even aimed at program improvement. For example, many formative studies that primarily monitor program compliance and implementation collect only service delivery data (e.g., how many people with which characteristics received which services), and this may be considered sufficient reporting—no outcome evaluation is planned or considered. The use of such "head counting" as "evaluation" in social services has provoked a recent call (e.g., by the United Way) for "outcomes-oriented" evaluation approaches that focus on program effectiveness rather than just the nature of services delivered to x number of clients. We would suggest that data collection aimed solely at compliance monitoring of services delivery, although it can yield important information (e.g., "Is the program serving the target population? Does the service population need the services? Do they stay a sufficient time in the program? Why do they leave?"), often contributes too little to serve program improvement or development functions. As is true for summative evaluations, formative evaluations that combine quantitative and qualitative methods are more likely to yield a more complete picture of program functioning.

Quantitative and Qualitative Data in Evaluations. Happily for most evaluators, the quantitative–qualitative "debate" is, for the most part, a nonissue. A good illustration can be found in a recent issue of *Evaluation Practice,* in which numerous well-known evaluators commented on the "past and future" of evaluation. *Half* of the commentators discussed the qualitative–quantitative "debate"; for almost all, however, there was recognition that both quantitative and qualitative approaches served critical, although different and often complementary, functions in evaluation (Smith, 1994). In response to advocates of both sides of the debate who called each other "dinosaurs," Chen (1994) likened both to "cockroaches" instead: "Since program evaluation requires multiple functions . . . qualitative and quantitative methods are all bound to survive . . ." (p. 232). Again, the question for the evaluator becomes one of matching approach and methods to suit the nature of the program and the specific need for information (McCall, 1995; McCall & Green, 1997).

Often, even if both qualitative and quantitative methods are used, there is little conceptual or methodological understanding of how the two methods should be integrated. Quantitative and qualitative methods can have such diametrically opposed epistemological and methodological assumptions that combining the two has been compared to a "shotgun marriage" (Chen, 1994; Lincoln & Guba, 1985). Others have noted that, although mixed methods are undeniably the "wave of the future" for evaluations, there is little guidance for those employing such combined approaches as to when and under what circumstances different techniques might be more or less useful (Bickman, 1994; Boruch, 1994; Cook & Reichardt, 1979; Maxwell, Bashook, & Sandlow, 1986).

McCall (1995; McCall & Green, 1997) suggested using each approach to accomplish what its proponents argue it does best. Many qualitative methods (e.g., ethnography) are very good at describing "the lay of the land"—the major issues, independent and dependent variables, suspected cause-and-effect relations—something Wohlwill (1973) urged his colleagues to study before launching major quantitative studies. Thus, ethnography, for example, could provide valuable pilot data if conducted before a quantitative study, and/or insightful interpretations if conducted simultaneously or after the quantitative study. Quantitative approaches often have the advantage of better sampling, assessment of the pervasiveness of effects, the range and correlates of individual differences, more objective and systematic measurement, and a basis for generalizing the results. But those benefits may not be needed if the object of study is unique (e.g., a single culture).

The potential benefits of ethnographic approaches are not restricted to piloting for subsequent quantitative research. For example, quantitative program evaluation frequently requires that the goals of a service program and appropriate measures of them are established before the program is implemented and that these goals and measures do not change over the course of the evaluation. These assumptions are often not met. A new program designed to teach parenting skills may find participants need help with food, housing, or drug and alcohol problems, for example, which dominate the service program agenda for two or three years before staff can concentrate on teaching parenting skills. And if the purpose of an evaluation of an established program is continuous project improvement, the goals, outcome measures, and services may change over time as a result of the evaluation. Qualitative assessments can accommodate these changes more easily than quantitative approaches. Further, some types of situations and questions are more easily and directly addressed with qualitative methods. If one was interested in the social dynamics of adolescent gangs and the potential of a participant "big brother" social worker to guide the gang toward more constructive activities, an ethnographic evaluation might yield much more useful information than traditional quantitative approaches.

The use of both qualitative and quantitative approaches often produces conflicting rather than complementary results, and reconciliation sometimes can be difficult. For example, what interpretation should be made if numerous case studies of program participants show positive examples of program effects and glowing endorsement of the program, yet standardized measures of outcomes show little or no effects (hardly an unlikely scenario)? How can and should these data be reconciled, and how can and should evaluations be structured so that such gaps between quantitative and qualitative data are reduced? Although there is no clear answer to this question, the continued application of multiple methods in evaluation is likely to move the field toward a more fully integrated methodological approach (Bickman, 1994).

Comprehensive Evaluation Approaches

Just as many evaluators use both quantitative and qualitative methodologies, many evaluators also reconcile formative and summative approaches in designing more "comprehensive" evaluations. Contributing to the evolution of the comprehensive approach has been a growing recognition that evaluations can be rendered more useful by being responsive to the diverse needs of different stakeholder groups, including program administrators, staff, participants, and funders (e.g., Patton, 1986). Rossi (Rossi & Freeman, 1993; Rossi & Wright, 1984) conceptualized comprehensive evaluations as involving five different components:

1. Basic research to contribute to the development and rationale of social programs.
2. Needs assessment to identify the scope and magnitude of the social issue to be addressed (e.g., "How many people need service? What are their problems?").
3. Implementation research to explore methods of establishing a service program that will be most effective and cost-efficient.
4. Program monitoring to ensure that programs are implemented as planned.
5. Outcome evaluation to assess effectiveness.

As Rossi and Wright (1984) aptly point out, however, there have been few (if any) truly comprehensive evaluations of social programs. Issues of time, cost, and political climate usually do not allow for such a thorough approach. Further, this strategy is more suited to large-scale demonstration programs and is less feasible for smaller, community-based, grass-roots social programs that now struggle to exist in an outcomes-oriented world with little or no resources for evaluation. Not all programs need such an elaborate and comprehensive approach. The question in designing evaluations, then, becomes: Under what circumstances are certain approaches more or less appropriate, and what should be the primary focus of the evaluation? The issue becomes one of relative emphasis in the evaluation plan (e.g., Herman et al., 1987): What is the most appropriate information needed for the program, relative to its size and cost?

Jacobs (1988) suggests a more pragmatic approach to comprehensive evaluation, which she calls a "Five-Tiered Approach." This conceptualization is more directly aimed at program evaluation and program improvement, rather than program design and evaluation research. The Five-Tiered Approach was based on Jacobs's experience with early child development programs, evaluations, and, in particular, the burgeoning family support movement of the 1980s. The five "tiers" are:

1. The *preimplementation tier,* including needs and resources assessment, to provide the groundwork for developing a potentially successful program.
2. The *accountability tier,* in which data are collected to monitor service penetration, utilization, and delivery.
3. The *program clarifications tier,* which provides information that clarifies program goals and objectives, identifies barriers to program success and strategies for overcoming these barriers, and gives general information about the strengths and weaknesses of the program.
4. The *progress toward objectives tier,* which begins to document program effectiveness.
5. The *program impact tier,* in which evaluation "research" is conducted with the purpose of contributing to broader knowledge and theory.

Although it may come as a surprise to academic researchers unfamiliar with applied social services, many agencies have not progressed much beyond the first tier (presumably, if the program is funded and exists, it has successfully negotiated the preimplementation stage by such a definition). For example, in a survey of 387 family support programs, 20% reported not collecting any basic background information about participants or simple service data regarding the number of persons served (Weiss & Hite, 1986). If this sounds disheartening, consider that of the remaining 80% of programs that did collect some data, 66% had no evaluation requirements from funders and nearly 80% had no funds earmarked for evaluation purposes (Weiss & Hite, 1986).

The Five-Tiered Approach recognizes that not all programs need or have the capacity to perform rigorous evaluations using experimental or quasi-experimental designs, emphasizing that programs can benefit by undertaking more modest data collection efforts. This approach represents one of the newer, more program-friendly evaluation strategies that have been developed in an attempt to address some of the barriers to evaluations encountered by "real world" social programs.

Another popular approach has been labeled "developmental" evaluation (Patton, 1994). Developmental evaluation involves many of the tasks enumerated in the Five-Tiered Approach, but takes an even more explicit program improvement approach. Patton (1994) suggests that evaluators need to build true partnerships with evaluation stakeholders, and in particular with program staff and administrators, and they must function as "part of a team whose members collaborate to conceptualize, design, and test new approaches in a long-term, ongoing process of continuous improvement" (Patton, 1994, p. 317). This strategy also fits nicely within the "empowerment evaluation" framework, which suggests that evaluations should help to empower service agencies and participants to conduct their own evaluations (Fetterman, 1993; Fetterman, Kaftarian, & Wandersman, 1996). This approach requires a strong collaboration with evaluators who can teach and adapt evaluation techniques for use by persons with little formal research training.

Few now would argue that program evaluation and research are best served by a combination of methods and strategies, but the true "collaborative" and the somewhat controversial "empowerment" approaches have drawn their share of criticisms. Some have suggested, for example, that although empowerment evaluation, with its goal of fostering self-evaluation among programs and participants, has a valuable role, it is not evaluation (Scriven, 1980; Stufflebeam, 1994). This criticism centers around the definition of evaluation. For some, evaluation exclusively is "the systematic investigation of the worth or merit of an object" (Joint Committee on Standards for Educational Evaluation, 1994). Although acknowledging that evaluation may serve other purposes, its "essential nonvariant goal [is] determining something's value" (Stufflebeam, 1994, p. 324), and therefore evaluation should be a process of "valuing" whatever is the focus of the evaluation (e.g., Scriven, 1967, 1980; Shadish et al., 1991). Evaluation requires and relies on definitions of the relative merit of a given program, and *not simply the stated goals or beliefs of the stakeholders.* That is, evaluation is seen as a process that evaluates not only the program and whether it reaches its goals, but the worthiness of those goals themselves (Stufflebeam, 1994). One highly controversial approach to evaluation suggests that the only way an evaluator can truly remain objective (and thus retain his or her proper evaluative role) is to have *no knowledge of the program* or its goals prior to conducting the evaluation. This "goal-free" approach to evaluation makes explicit that the goals of a program should become obvious to the evaluator during the course of the evaluation; if they do not, then those goals and objectives are irrelevant (Scriven, 1967, 1980, 1983). This approach argues against not only collaborative, developmental evaluations, but also against those who would take a more traditional approach by attempting to outline and measure progress toward the goals and objectives set forth by the program.

However, this view is not terribly pragmatic in the rapidly changing world of human services. For example, what is considered a "good" method of dealing with participants (or "customers," or "clients," or "patients") changes frequently; we are still negotiating "best practices" and will likely continue to do so for some time. The goals of retaining scientific objectivity and making sound evaluative recommendations are worthy, but to do so without regard to the sociopolitical context of programs will not serve to advance the utility of evaluations for either the field of social services or evaluation methods. Just as programs that serve families and children have moved away from didactic approaches and methods to more creative and empowering service delivery, evaluation must keep abreast of these changes if it is to continue to be useful to these programs.

A Case Study in Evaluating a Community-Based Program

Few researchers are trained to develop partnerships or collaborations, even with other researchers. However, working with human service programs to develop and implement high-quality evaluations requires that mutual respect and a trusting relationship be developed among the evaluator and those who have a vested interest in the program and its evaluation. Developing such a partnership requires considerable effort because program staff, administrators, and program participants frequently have strong antievaluation and antiresearch sentiments.

The overriding threat is that negative evaluation findings will result in cutbacks or elimination of programs. For example, one of our evaluation colleagues reported, after an initial meeting with service program staff, "When I walked in, the very first thing I heard whispered was 'Better be quiet, the snitch is here.'" Such sentiments are not uncommon—and frankly, not completely unwarranted—but they stand in the way of building fruitful collaborations with stakeholders. Our best advice is to confront such feelings head-on. Get to know your stakeholders; some may be more or less receptive to the idea of an evaluation. Tell them upfront that you do not intend to be a "snitch" to the funders. More importantly, do not become one! If the evaluation will be developed in collaboration with the agency and its stakeholders, the evaluator must be willing to compromise and defer control over a great many decisions to the stakeholders—something that those trained in academic settings are not typically accustomed to doing. The issue of control is central, and a willingness to relinquish it to facilitate productive collaboration is paramount. The case study given here involves a currently active evaluation project. Several of the complex issues described above, related to (a) developing and implementing collaborative evaluations of community-based programs and (b) how taking a collaborative approach can help to overcome these difficulties, are illustrated in the study.

Building the Collaboration

The evaluation process described here is entering its second year. We received funding for conducting an evaluation as part of the service program funding at the beginning of the creation of the service program. Thus, in this project, we were in the happy position of being able to begin developing collaborations with several stakeholder groups prior to program implementation.

Stakeholders. Our original partnership was with a central coordinating agency, the Partnerships for Family Support (PFFS), which administered and provided technical assistance to the development of a family support program in two communities. Site 1 is an urban, low-income, predominantly African American neighborhood; Site 2 is a mixed-ethnic, mixed-SES transitional neighborhood. Although coordinated by the central office, each of the individual family support programs was directly administered by a different host agency, specifically a local YMCA and a health care provider. The funders for this program—the county department of human services, and private foundations—were interested in having a single evaluation, across both program sites, that would include process and outcome information. Both sites were to provide a core group of services, including case management, child development education, and parental support and training. The method in which the services were to be delivered was left to the individual communities, with the restriction that these core services be provided to a targeted number of families and that service delivery be based on a "family support" philosophy (e.g., Kagan, Powell, Weissbourd, & Zigler, 1987). To further complicate matters, one of the program sites was also being funded in part by state funds, and was required, as part of this funding, to participate in a separate statewide data collection effort.

Our formal agreement was with the county and private funders and the central coordinating agency, PFFS. However, because the programs were being developed through the work of local "community councils" comprised of community members, parents, and local service providers, we felt it imperative that the community councils be involved in helping to develop the evaluation plan. Thus, we began what has become a two-year, continuous, collaborative evaluation process with these several groups, which represent the diversity of the possible collaborators involved in a single project.

Initial Meetings. The stakeholders, in addition to the evaluators, included the funders, the coordinating agency director, the community council members, program staff (when they were hired), and each of the host agency directors. We held a series of meetings with these stakeholder groups to determine their perceptions of program goals, their information needs, and the principal questions they wanted the evaluation to address.

We met first with the funders, a policy maker, and foundation program officers, to determine their interests and needs for the evaluation. Not surprisingly, they wanted "hard data" on program effectiveness. Thus, our primary goal in working with the funders was to reach a common understanding of the goals of the programs and what would constitute realistic outcomes for the first, second, and third program years. At this juncture, we encountered a disparity between the funders' goals and realistic outcomes. Some adjustments in their conceptualization of the program were required. For example, school readiness was a highly desired goal for funders; however, the program was targeted at infants and children under age 3 years. We suggested that looking at age-appropriate cognitive and social developmental progress might be more realistic than trying to capture school readiness in 3-year olds. These meetings resulted in a set of goals that was acceptable to the funders and would apply to both program sites.

The sites were implemented sequentially, allowing us to work intensively with the first site to "pilot" the evaluation. Our initial meeting regarding Site 1 was with the community council. Significant resistance to the idea of university researchers doing *anything* in this community was encountered. Council members had extremely negative perceptions of research in general, based on experience with other researchers who had used this community for various research projects but gave nothing of benefit to the community in return. Our first step was to try to break down these negative attitudes and explain that our purpose was different than our predecessors. Our primary goal was to work with the program in developing ways to ensure that the community's needs were being met, and to help provide evidence that could be used to improve the program and help gain long-term funding. We tried to convey that the reason we were meeting with the community council was to allow them to have a real and meaningful voice in developing their own program and planning for its evaluation, albeit with our help.

Focusing the Evaluation

The approach that we took was to present a plan that we had developed based on the goals and objectives as stated in the service program proposals and in our meeting with funders. Discussion then centered around (a) whether those goals actually matched what community council members believed the purpose of the program should be, (b) what information could be collected to address these goals and objectives (there were some nonnegotiable requirements from the state), (c) from whom such information should be collected (there was strong pressure from funders to have, minimally, a quasi-experimental/control group design), and (d) how the information would be collected and aggregated. Because direct program staff were not yet hired, we worked with the community council to develop a general evaluation design, with the understanding that specifics would be negotiated after program staff had been hired.

Design Accommodations. Not surprisingly, one particularly inflammatory issue was the control group. As often happens, discussion of the possible nature of the evaluation design raised issues about the services program. Specifically, it was unclear whether the program was to serve all families in the community (less intensively) or relatively few families but with higher intensity. Most community council members were strongly opposed to the idea of excluding community members from the program. They argued, logically, that family support programs were intended to be open and supportive of the entire community and not limited to a select subset. However, funders were adamant that a certain level of intensity was required; that is, they did not want to simply fund a community drop-in center. Somewhat unexpectedly, the evaluation provided grounds for a compromise. We suggested an evaluation plan that would focus on a subset of families who would be served intensively and use as comparisons those families who used the center for drop-in purposes. Intensive services were subsequently defined by the program to include at least monthly contacts with case managers and child development staff, to do goal planning and child development activities; and weekly visits from a "family advocate" (paraprofessional workers hired from the community) for ongoing family support. Classes, workshops, recreational activities, and information and referral services were made available to the entire community. Here was an example of obtaining a needed methodological feature by having it serve program needs.

The next step was to make the critical decision about how families would be assigned to the intensive services group. Originally, we advocated a random assignment approach, based on the community council's belief that far more families needed the intensive services that the program could provide. Again, strong resistance to this idea was encountered in the community council, based largely, again, on past experience with researchers and strong antiresearch sentiments. Random assignment, it was felt, would detract from the family-friendly approach that the center was trying to take. In essence, random assignment was felt to violate the very philosophy that family support programs represent (Green, Mulvey, Fisher, & Woratschek, 1996). We agreed with this argument, and it was decided that the intensive services would be open on a "first come, first served" basis. The necessity to compromise, in terms of methodological rigor to accommodate stakeholders' values and philosophies, even when such values have little or no empirical evidence to support them, is perhaps one of the most difficult pills for applied researchers to swallow. In retrospect, however, we strongly believe that compromising some methodological rigor for continued community support was well worth it, and perhaps necessary to have an evaluation at all.

Protocol Development. After the general evaluation plan (which included developing a comprehensive management information system and conducting face-to-face pre/post interviews with a subset of intensive and comparison families) was approved by the community council and the funders, our next step was to present it to the site staff, program directors, and coordinating agency (PFFS). Because our approach was to attempt to couple service delivery with data collection (i.e., use service professionals to collect data), three priorities were arrived at, in terms of developing data collection protocols: (a) they must be easy for staff to complete; (b) they must be useful to staff in their day-to-day activities with families; and (c) they must be well-matched to the service delivery approach and process. To attain these goals, data collection protocols had to be developed with, not for, staff.

Program staff at the first site were presented with the evaluation plan, and issues around evaluation were discussed. Again, we tried to ensure that our goals as evaluators were perceived as congruent with program goals, and we sought to overcome negative attitudes and preconceptions about evaluation. Although staff were originally reticent about commenting on the evaluation, discussion livened up when they were presented with our first draft of the data collection instruments. These forms were designed (a) to collect demographic and family constellation information, service delivery data, and goal-setting and progress information, and (b) to provide tracking of prenatal care visits, immunizations, and child development assessments. One of the most fruitful things we did was to fulfill our promise that we would collaborate with the staff as well as the council and PFFS. After the first day of discussion of several of the forms, we negotiated clarifications and changes to the instruments to make them easier to complete, to collect additional information that staff wanted to have, to omit some information that was seen as unneeded, and to develop a more family-friendly approach to actually filling out the forms.

At the next session, less than a week later, we brought revised forms, updated procedures, and expanded service codes, in direct response to staff feedback. This immediate incorporation of staff comments made a substantial contribution to the development of a trusting relationship between staff and evaluators. We continued to make extensive adjustments to procedures and forms during the first 12 weeks of the program. Continuing adjustments to the data collection protocol is scientifically tricky, and evaluators must learn to judge when to allow changes and when to "stick to your scientific guns" around data collection issues. For example, a few staff felt very uncomfortable approaching families with questions related to income. Other staff felt that this was "not a big deal" and something that they would learn about anyway. We felt it was necessary to collect this information, because socioeconomic status is often a critical correlate of outcomes. Thus, we had an open debate about the worth of the data versus the perceived intrusiveness of collecting it. In this instance, it was ultimately decided that income data were important enough that efforts should be made to collect it. Relatively broad income categories were constructed, to reduce intrusiveness to families yet supply adequate information for the evaluation.

We wanted to ensure that the evaluation approach did not violate the principles and philosophies of the family support service program. Developing techniques and methods for collecting information that would not be perceived by families as unfriendly or typical of traditional social service programs (family support programs differ in important ways from traditional service approaches) was critical to implementing the evaluation. Staff suggested that rather than having the families answer a barrage of questions on their initial visit, the forms should be filled out during an initial "enrollment phase" lasting 6 to 8 weeks. Further, to minimize the intrusiveness of the forms, staff suggested that families sit down with staff and complete the forms in partnership, and have families initial all forms to give their "seal of approval" to the information contained in their files. This got around the traditional social-service approach in which a secret case file is kept on each family, and families rarely know what the service provider is writing down and filing away. Families were informed that they were welcome to look at their case file at any time.

To maintain the collaboration once the data began to be collected, the evaluator continued to attend a weekly meeting between the coordinating agency and the site program directors. Additionally, the evaluator attended at least one staff meeting at the sites per month. These meetings have allowed continuous refinement of the data collection process, and have provided a mechanism for periodic monitoring of program goals and objectives while keeping the evaluation in line with program activities.

Ongoing Review and Feedback. Because we were focusing on using the evaluation for continuous program improvement, we wanted to ensure a high-quality system for updating records and providing regular feedback to program staff and families. We did this through MIS reports and through regular meetings with staff, administrators, and others, to discuss and interpret the data.

One good example of using information to focus the program emerged through analysis of service delivery data. In Site 1, much of the original discussion regarding services focused on service penetration and delivery: "Are we serving families?" and "Are the services being delivered?" We wanted to describe family needs, the services that were being delivered, and the intensity of services. Initial analysis of the staff's contact logs (as reflected in the management information system) indicated that a good deal of staff time was devoted to outreach, informal discussions to engage families in the program, and getting families involved in recreational activities. Although they recognized that these activities were instrumental in getting people engaged in the program, funders were concerned that the services were too "soft." Therefore, several decisions were made—in collaboration with the funders, site staff and administrators, and PFFS—to focus on delivering services that were more explicitly linked to the program goals: child development services, education and training services, and health services. Here was an example of how a modification in the nature of the service program was stimulated by the process evaluation.

The next phase of the program was directed at long-term goal setting and problem solving with families. Child development workers, who had previously been working primarily with children in the drop-in center and conducting informal home visits, began to research curricula and were subsequently trained in the Parents as Teachers model. Case managers and the evaluation team fine-tuned the goal-planning instrument to allow families and staff to set goals in partnership, regularly reassess these goals, and keep a continuous record of progress toward them. Subsequent analysis of contact logs indicated that, after this refinement, substantially more work was done in child development, goal planning, and education and training. In this case, the process evaluation confirmed that a midcourse correction was indeed implemented.

The next phase involved working with the health services component of the program, especially tracking immunizations and prenatal visits, and ensuring that families were linked to a primary health care provider and had health insurance. County health department nurses trained the staff and evaluators to develop a method for obtaining immunization records for tracking purposes. The MIS was then programmed to allow "tickler" reports for staff to let them know when childrens' immunizations were due. Of all the functions that the evaluation can serve, being able to provide simple, easy-to-understand reports such as these perhaps is the most highly valued. These reports also provide incentive for continued attention to data collection, because program staff who collect the data can see that the data actually have application in their program.

Implementing the Evaluation at Site 2

As mentioned above, the sites were implemented sequentially, about 8 months apart. Presumably, this allowed us to "pilot" our methods and approach in the first program site (Site 1). However, Site 2 proved to be a new and formidable challenge. When the second site began to be implemented, attempts were made to conduct the same collaborative process that we had developed at Site 1. However, political problems and interagency disagreements rendered the atmosphere less than conducive to open discussion of evaluation within the community council. Although council members understood that there would be an evaluation component, their energies were directed at solving a myriad of other problems regarding service issues; thus, the program evaluation was not an immediate priority. After a few initial (unfruitful) attempts at bringing the issue of evaluation to the table, the decision was made to let the program get started and then to approach the program director and staff about implementing the evaluation. Although this was somewhat frustrating to us, again, in retrospect, it was likely the correct decision. Evaluators need to be acutely aware of the often sensitive political and interpersonal dynamics in which programs are implemented. In this case, the atmosphere initially did not allow productive discussion of evaluation issues.

We presented staff and administrators with the evaluation plan as it had evolved at Site 1 and encountered no resistance at first, other than some minimal suggestions for changes. However, as the program began to develop, it became clear that it was quite different from Site 1 in method and approach. For example, Site 1 served a subset of families intensively and had developed clear definitions for what constituted intensive service. Site 2, although never formally rejecting this program model, in practice took a much more inclusive approach, enrolling large numbers of families but serving them less intensively. Site 1 utilized a team approach in which each family was assigned a team of staff including a case manager, a child development specialist, and a family advocate. This team worked collaboratively with a small number of families. Site 2 utilized a less formal approach; families could work with whichever staff member they felt best suited their needs or personalities. So, if a family had issues mostly around obtaining basic services and planning adult goals, they might decide to work mainly with a case manager, having minimal contact with the child development specialist. The result was that some staff worked with large numbers of families, and not all families received the different types of services with the same intensity.

There was a diffusion of responsibility regarding completion of paperwork, because there was no formal assignment of families to particular staff members. Site 2 continued to be plagued by internal and external political conflict, reducing the conduciveness to a collaborative approach, which relies on staff and administrators to be open about issues and difficulties. Often, we found out about problems only in offhand remarks and informal conversations; rarely were such issues brought up in formal staff meetings. This underlined the importance of the collaborative atmosphere within the service program as a determinant of the collaborative atmosphere between program and evaluators.

The differences we unearthed required a major retooling not so much of the instruments (although some was needed) but of the procedures for collecting the data and ensuring timely and accurate data collection. To address this problem, we held a series of meetings with staff, focused around the issue of "What are you actually *doing* with the families?" The program was not being implemented in the same manner as in Site 1; therefore, the evaluators and coordinating agency staff needed to more thoroughly understand the program model. Decisions had to be made about whether the evaluation still made sense for this program, and how it could be adapted to better match the program activities. But a different evaluation might threaten the funders' goal of having one evaluation for both sites. Fortunately, the one constant was that the program *goals* remained the same. Thus, we felt that the outcome interviews could remain consistent with Site 1 and still reflect the intended outcomes of the program.

It became clear, however, that an understanding of the evaluation outcomes, especially possible differences between sites, would be strongly linked to differences between the programs at each site, and the analysis strategy would need to analyze sites separately and in comparison to each other, rather than collapsing data across the sites. In essence, instead of evaluating one program delivered in two sites, we were analyzing two programs with similar goals but markedly different service delivery models. Although we had not yet reached the data analysis stage, we had to make decisions about altering the data analysis strategy to increase power and the ability to detect differences. Budgetary constraints kept us from doing what we might do in the laboratory—that is, run more subjects. We are currently considering analysis strategies that involve statistical procedures, such as hierarchical linear modeling, which have a greater potential to detect differences, can allow modeling of individual growth curves, and permit testing for differences between the two program models. Both sites continue to use their data for ongoing monitoring and program development. Site 2 has continued to be a challenge from an evaluation standpoint because of its internal and external sociopolitical struggles. Information continues to be collected, but putting the data to *use* has been much more difficult because of these conflicts.

Conclusion

We have attempted to present some of the challenges we have faced and the lessons we have learned in 10 years of working collaboratively with agencies on a variety of university–community research and training projects. Our collaborative projects rarely follow the scientific ideal, as illustrated in the case study. Instead, this work stretches the traditional skills and resources of the laboratory researcher and requires considerably more compromise and negotiation than does working within more traditional academic venues. In the most applied research, program evaluation, the researcher often must compromise even the basic scientific questions to be asked. The questions ultimately addressed may reflect the information needs of the program and its funders more than the academic interests of the researcher. Lack of autonomy; loss of control over research questions, measures, design, and analysis; and the need for constant attention to the sociopolitical context are part of conducting community-based studies. However, we have found that the payoff, both personally and in terms of producing useful, important, and contextually valid information, far outweighs these costs.

The direct application of research to social problems and to all of the attendant difficulties will continue to challenge psychologists in the future. As funding mechanisms increasingly demand research that provides direct information about social programs and how they work, psychologists must learn to bring their considerable skills to bear on real-world issues. Meeting this challenge, however, may require fundamental changes in the way that we train students, work with other disciplines, and develop and test research questions. In the long run, however, our discipline is more likely to attain its goal—contributing to human welfare, especially the welfare of children, youth, and families—if some psychologists venture along the path we have described above.

REFERENCES

Aiken, L. S., West, S. G., Sechrest, L., & Reno, R. R. (1990). Graduate training in statistics, methodology, and measurement in psychology: A survey of PhD programs in North America. *American Psychologist, 45,* 721–734.

American Institutes for Research. (1980). *The national evaluation of the PUSH for excellence project.* Washington, DC: Author.

Appelbaum, M. I., & McCall, R. B. (1983). Design and analysis in developmental psychology. In W. Kessen (Ed.), *Handbook of child psychology* (3rd ed.) (Vol. 1, pp. 415–476). New York: Wiley.

Bailey, D. B., Burchinal, M. R., & McWilliam, R. A. (1993). Relationship between age of peers and early child development: A longitudinal study. *Child Development, 64,* 848–862.

Bentler, P. M., & Woodward, J. A. (1978). A Head Start reevaluation: Positive effects are not yet demonstrable. *Evaluation Quarterly, 2,* 493–510.

Berk, R. A., & Rossi, P. H. (1990). *Thinking about program evaluation.* Newbury Park, CA: Sage.

Bickman, L. (1987). The functions of program theory. In L. Bickman (Ed.), *Using program theory in evaluation.* San Francisco: Jossey-Bass.

Bickman, L. (1990). *Advances in program theory.* San Francisco: Jossey-Bass.

Bickman, L. (1994). An optimistic view of evaluation. *Evaluation Practice, 15*(3), 255–259.

Boruch, R. F. (1994). The future of controlled randomized experiments: A briefing. *Evaluation Practice, 15*(3), 265–274.

Box, G. E., & Jenkins, G. W. (1976). *Time series analysis: Forecasting and control.* San Francisco: Holden-Day.

Bronfenbrenner, U. (1977). Toward an experimental ecology of human development. *American Psychologist, 32,* 513–531.

Bryk, A. S., & Raudenbush, S. W. (1987). Application of hierarchical linear models to assessing change. *Psychological Bulletin, 101,* 147–158.

Burchinal, M., & Appelbaum, M. I. (1991). Estimating individual developmental functions: Methods and their assumptions. *Child Development, 62,* 23–43.

Campbell, D. T. (1969). Reforms as experiments. *American Psychologist, 24,* 409–429.

Campbell, D. T. (1978). Qualitative knowing in action research. In M. Brenner, P. Marsh, & M. Brenner (Eds.), *The social contexts of method* (pp. 184–209). London: Croom Helm.

Campbell, D. T., & Boruch, R. F. (1975). Making the case for randomized assignment to treatments by considering the alternatives. In C. A. Bennett & A. A. Lumsdaine (Eds.), *Evaluation and experiment* (pp. 347–367). New York: Academic Press.

Campbell, D. T., & Stanley, J. C. (1966). *Experimental and quasi-experimental designs for research.* Skokie, IL: Rand McNally.

Casto, R., & Julia, M. (1994). *Interprofessional care and collaborative practice.* Pacific Grove, CA: Brooks/Cole.

Chen, H. T. (1990). *Theory-driven evaluations.* Newbury, CA: Sage.

Chen, H. T. (1994). Theory-driven evaluations: Needs, difficulties, and options. *Evaluation Practice, 15*(1), 79–82.

Chen, H. T., & Rossi, P. H. (1983). Evaluating with sense: The theory-driven approach. *Evaluation Review, 7,* 283–302.

Chen, H. T., & Rossi, P. H. (1989). Issues in the theory-driven perspective. *Evaluation and Program Planning, 12,* 299–306.

Cialdini, R. B. (1980). Full cycle social psychology. In L. Bickman (Ed.), *Applied social psychology annual.* Newbury Park, CA: Sage.

Cook, T. D., & Campbell, D. T. (1979). *Quasi-experimentation: Design and analysis issues for field settings.* Boston: Houghton Mifflin.

Cook, T. D., & Reichardt, C. S. (1979). *Qualitative and quantitative methods in evaluation research.* Newbury, CA: Sage.

Cook, W. L. (1994). A structural equation model of dyadic relationships within the family system. *Journal of Consulting and Clinical Psychology, 62*(3), 500–509.

Cronbach, L. J. (1982). *Designing evaluations of educational and social programs.* San Francisco: Jossey-Bass.

Damrosch, D. (1995). *We scholars. Changing the culture of the university.* Cambridge, MA: Harvard University Press.

Dennis, M. L., & Boruch, R. F. (1989). Randomized experiments for planning and testing projects in developing countries: Threshold conditions. *Evaluation Review, 13,* 292–309.

Denniš, M. L., & Boruch, R. F. (1994, Fall). Improving the quality of randomized field experiments: Tricks of the trade. *New Directions for Program Evaluation,* 67–71.

Ellickson, P. L. (1994). Getting and keeping schools and kids for evaluation studies [Special issue]. *Journal of Community Psychology,* 102–116.

Fetterman, D. M. (1982). Ibsen's baths: Reactivity and insensitivity (a misapplication of the treatment-control design in a national evaluation). *Educational Evaluation and Policy Analysis, 4*(3), 261–279.

Fetterman, D. M. (1993, Spring). Empowerment evaluation. *Evaluation Practice, 15*(1), 1–15.

Fetterman, D. M., Kaftarian, S. J., & Wandersman, A. (1996). *Empowerment evaluation: Knowledge and tools for self-assessment and accountability.* Thousand Oaks, CA: Sage.

Friend, M., & Cook, L. (1992). *Interactions: Collaboration skills for school professionals.* White Plains, NY: Longman.

Gladue, B. A. (1994, March/April). Making the case for basic research. *Psychological Science Agenda,* 8.

Green, B., Mulvey, L., Fisher, H., & Woratschek, F. (1996). Integrating program and evaluation values: A family support approach to program evaluation. *Evaluation Practice, 17*(3), 261–272.

Groark, C. J., & McCall, R. B. (1993, Spring). Building mutually beneficial collaborations between researchers and community service professionals. *Newsletter of the Society for Research in Child Development,* 6–14.

Groark, C. J., & McCall, R. B. (1996). Building successful university-community human service agency collaborations. In C. D. Fisher, J. P. Murray, & I. E. Sigel (Eds.), *Applied developmental science: Graduate training for diverse disciplines and educational settings* (pp. 000–000). Norwood, NJ: ABLEX.

Guba, E. G., & Lincoln, Y. S. (1981). *Effective evaluation: Improving the usefulness of evaluation results through responsive and naturalistic approaches.* San Francisco: Jossey-Bass.

Herman, J. L., Morris, L. L., & Fitz-Gibbon, C. T. (1987). *Evaluator's handbook.* Newbury Park, CA: Sage.

Jacobs, F. H. (1988). The five-tiered approach to evaluation: Context and implementation. In H. B. Weiss & F. H. Jacobs (Eds.), *Evaluating family programs* (pp. 37–68). New York: Aldine de Gruyter.

Johnston, P., & Swift, P. (1994, Fall). Effects of randomization on a homeless services initiative: A comment. *New Directions for Program Evaluation,* 67–71.

Joint Committee on Standards for Educational Evaluation. (1994). *The program evaluation standards.* Thousand Oaks, CA: Sage.

Kagan, S. L., Powell, D. R., Weissbourd, B., & Zigler, E. F. (1987). Past accomplishments: Future challenges. In S. L. Kagan, D. R. Powell, B. Weissbourd, & E. W. Zigler (Eds.),

America's family support programs. New Haven, CT: Yale University Press.

Kennedy, D. (1994). Making choices in the research university. In J. R. Cole, E. G. Barber, & S. R. Graubard (Eds.), *The research university in a time of discontent.* Baltimore: Johns Hopkins University Press.

Kenny, D. A., & Judd, C. M. (1986). Consequences of violating the independence assumption in analysis of variance. *Psychological Bulletin, 99,* 422–431.

Kershaw, D., & Fair, J. (1975). *The New Jersey–Pennsylvania income maintenance experiment.* New York: Academic Press.

Klein, J. T. (1990). IDS: Interdisciplinary education. In J. T. Klein (Ed.), *Interdisciplinarity: History, theory, and practice.* Detroit, MI: Wayne State University Press.

Lawson, H. A., & Hooper-Briar, K. (1994). *Expanding partnerships: Involving colleges and universities in interprofessional collaboration and service integration.* A report presented to The Danforth Foundation and The Institute for Educational Renewal, Miami University, Oxford, OH.

Lewin, K. (1946). Action research and minority problems. *Journal of Social Issues, 2,* 34–35.

Lincoln, Y. S., & Guba, E. G. (1985). *Naturalistic inquiry.* Newbury Park, CA: Sage.

Lincoln, Y. S., & Guba, E. G. (1986). But is it rigorous? Trustworthiness and authenticity in naturalistic evaluation. In D. D. Williams (Ed.), *Naturalistic evaluation. New directions for program evaluation* (pp. 73–84). San Francisco: Jossey-Bass.

Lincoln, Y. S., & Guba, E. G. (1994). RSVP: We are pleased to accept your invitation. *Evaluation Practice, 15*(1), 179–192.

Magidson, J. (1977). Toward a causal model approach for adjusting for pre-existing differences in the nonequivalent control group situation: A general alternative to ANCOVA. *Evaluation Quarterly, 1,* 399–420.

Mattessich, P. W., & Monsey, B. R. (1992). *Collaboration: What makes it work? A review of research literature on factors influencing successful collaborations.* St. Paul, MN: Amherst H. Wilder Foundation.

Maxwell, J. A., Bashook, P. G., & Sandlow, L. J. (1986). Combining ethnographic and experimental methods in educational evaluation: A case study. In D. M. Fetterman & M. A. Pitman (Eds.), *Educational evaluation: Ethnography in theory, practice, and politics* (pp. 121–143). Beverly Hills, CA: Sage.

McArdle, J. J. (1991). Structural models of development theory in psychology. *Annals of Theoretical Psychology, 7,* 139–159.

McArdle, J. J., & Epstein, D. (1987). Latent growth curves within developmental structural equation models. *Child Development, 58,* 110–133.

McCall, R. B. (1977). Challenges to a science of developmental psychology. *Child Development, 48,* 333–344.

McCall, R. B. (1987). The media, society, and child development research. In J. D. Osofsky (Ed.), *Handbook of infant development* (2nd ed., pp. 1199–1255). New York: Wiley.

McCall, R. B. (1990). Promoting interdisciplinary and faculty-service professional relations. *American Psychologist, 45,* 1319–1324.

McCall, R. B. (1993). A guide to communicating through the media. In K. McCartney (Ed.), *An insider's guide to providing expert testimony before Congress* (pp. 16–24). Ann Arbor, MI: Society for Research in Child Development.

McCall, R. B. (1995). Quantitative methods, qualitative methods, and value-based critical inquiry. In B. Crabtree, R. Addison, V. Gilchrist, A. Kuzel, & W. Miller (Eds.), *Developing collaborative research in primary care* (pp. 255–259). Newbury Park, CA: Sage.

McCall, R. B. (1996). The concept and practice of education, research, and public service in university psychology departments. *American Psychologist, 51*(4), 379–388.

McCall, R. B., & Appelbaum, M. I. (1973). Bias in the analysis of repeated measures designs: Some alternative approaches. *Child Development, 44,* 401–415.

McCall, R. B., & Green, B. L. (1997). *Beyond the methodological gold standards of behavioral research.* Pittsburgh: University of Pittsburgh Office of Child Development.

McCall, R. B., Groark, C. J., Strauss, M. S., & Johnson, C. N. (1995). The University of Pittsburgh office of child development—An experiment in promoting interdisciplinary applied human development. *Journal of Applied Developmental Psychology, 16,* 593–612.

McCall, R. B., Ryan, C. S., & Green, B. L. (1997). *Some nonrandomized constructed comparison groups for evaluating age-related outcomes of intervention programs.* Pittsburgh: University of Pittsburgh Office of Child Development.

McCartney, K. (Ed.). (1993). *An insider's guide to providing expert testimony before Congress.* Ann Arbor, MI: Society for Research in Child Development.

Mordock, J. B. (1993, Fall). Diversity: More on collaboration. *Society for Research in Child Development Newsletter, 1,* 12.

O'Neil, M. J., & Wilson-Coker, P. (1986, March–April). The child welfare specialist: An interdisciplinary graduate curriculum. *Child Welfare,* 99–117.

Patton, M. Q. (1980). *Qualitative evaluation methods.* Beverly Hills, CA: Sage.

Patton, M. Q. (1986). *Utilization-focused evaluation* (2nd ed.). Newbury Park, CA: Sage.

Patton, M. Q. (1990). *Qualitative evaluation and research methods* (2nd ed.). Newbury Park, CA: Sage.

Patton, M. Q. (1994). Developmental evaluation. *Evaluation Practice, 15*(3), 311–319.

Prosavac, E., & Carey, R. (1992). *Program evaluation: Methods and case studies* (4th ed.). Englewood Cliffs, NJ: Prentice-Hall.

Reichardt, C. S., & Cook, T. D. (1979). Beyond qualitative versus quantitative methods. In T. D. Cook & C. S. Reichardt (Eds.), *Qualitative and quantitative methods in evaluation* (pp. 7–32). Beverly Hills, CA: Sage.

Robins, P. K., Spiegelman, R. G., Weiner, S., & Bell, J. G. (1980). *A guaranteed annual income: Evidence from a social experiment.* New York: Academic Press.

Rogosa, D. R. (1988). Myths about longitudinal research. In K. W. Schaie, R. T. Campbell, W. Meredith, & S. C. Rawlings (Eds.), *Methodological issues in aging research* (pp. 171-210). New York: Springer.

Rogosa, D. R., Brandt, D., & Zimowski, M. (1982). A growth curve approach to the measurement of change. *Psychological Bulletin, 90,* 726–748.

Ross, H. L., Campbell, D. T., & Glass, G. V. (1970). Determining the effects of a legal reform: The British "breathalyser" crackdown of 1967. *American Behavioral Scientist, 13,* 493–509.

Rossi, P. H. (1978). Issues in the evaluation of human services delivery. *Evaluation Quarterly, 2*(4), 573–599.

Rossi, P. H., & Freeman, H. E. (1993). *Evaluation: A systematic approach* (5th ed.). Newbury Park, CA: Sage.

Rossi, P. H., & Lyall, K. (1974). *Reforming public welfare.* New York: Russell-Sage Foundation.

Rossi, P. H., & Wright, J. D. (1984). Evaluation research: An assessment. *Annual Review of Sociology, 10,* 48–69.

Scheirer, M. A., & Rezmovic, E. L. (1983). Measuring the degree of program implementation: A methodological review. *Evaluation Review, 7*(5), 599–633.

Scriven, M. (1967). The methodology of evaluation. In R. E. Stake (Ed.), *Perspectives on curriculum evaluation: American Educational Research Association Monograph Series* (No. 1). Chicago, IL: Rand McNally.

Scriven, M. (1980). *The logic of evaluation.* Pt. Reyes, CA: Edge-press.

Scriven, M. (1983). *Word magic: Evaluating and selecting word processing.* Belmont, CA: Wadsworth Van Nostrand.

Sechrest, L., & Rednor, R. (1979). Strength and integrity of treatments in evaluation studies. In *How well does it work? Review of Criminal Justice Evaluation, 1978.* Washington, DC: US Department of Justice, National Criminal Justice Reference Service.

Sewell, W. H. (1989). Some reflections on the golden age of interdisciplinary social psychology. *Annual Review of Sociology, 15,* 1–16.

Shadish, W. R., Cook, T. D., & Leviton, L. C. (1991). *Foundations of program evaluation.* Newbury Park, CA: Sage.

Skinner, B. F. (1956). A case history in scientific method. *American Psychologist, 11,* 221–233.

Smith, N. L. (1990). Using path analysis to develop and evaluate program theory and impact. In L. Bickman (Ed.), *Advances in program theory: New directions for program evaluation* (Special ed.) (Vol. 47, pp. 53–57). San Francisco: Jossey-Bass.

Smith, N. L. (1994). Clarifying and expanding the application of program theory-driven evaluations. *Evaluation Practice, 15*(1), 83–87.

Stufflebeam, D. L. (1994). Empowerment evaluation, objectivist evaluation, and evaluation standards: Where the future of evaluation should not go and where it needs to go. *Evaluation Practice, 15*(3), 321–338.

Stufflebeam, D. L., Foley, W. J., Gephart, W. J., Guba, E. G., Hammond, R. L., Merriman, H. O., & Provus, M. M. (1971). *Educational evaluation and decision-making.* Itasca, IL: Peacock.

Tate, R. L., & Hokanson, J. E. (1992). Analyzing individual status and change with hierarchical linear models: Illustration with depression in college students. *Journal of Personality, 61*(2), 181–206.

Vandercook, T., York, J., & Sullivan, B. (1993, Winter). TRUE OR FALSE? Truly collaborative relationships can exist between university and public school personnel. *OSERS News in Print,* 31–37.

Watts, H. W., & Rees, A. (1976). *The New Jersey income-maintenance experiment.* New York: Academic Press.

Weiss, H., & Hite, S. (1986). Evaluation: Who's doing it and how? A report from a national program survey conducted by the Harvard Family Research Project. *Family Resource Coalition,* 4–11.

Weissbourd, B. (1987). A brief history of family support programs. In S. L. Kagan, D. R. Powell, B. Weissbourd, & E. F. Zigler (Eds.), *America's family support programs* (pp. 38–56). New Haven, CT: Yale University Press.

West, S. G., Hepworth, J. T., McCall, M. A., & Reich, J. W. (1989). An evaluation of Arizona's July 1982 drunk driving law: Effects on the city of Phoenix. *Journal of Applied Social Psychology, 19,* 1212–1237.

Westinghouse Learning Corporation. (1969). *The impact of Head Start on children's cognitive and affective development.* Athens: Ohio University.

Willett, J. B., & Sayer, A. G. (1994). Using covariance structure analysis to detect correlates and predictors of individual change over time. *Psychological Bulletin, 116*(2), 363–381.

Williams, W., & Elmore, R. F. (1976). *Social program implementation.* New York: Academic Press.

Wohlwill, J. F. (1973). *The study of behavioral development.* New York: Academic Press.

CHAPTER 15

Mass Media and Children's Development

ALETHA C. HUSTON and JOHN C. WRIGHT

The 20th century has witnessed a radical transformation of the media environment. In less than 100 years, radio, movies, comic books, television, video games, CD-ROM, and audiotapes and videotapes have become a routine part of most children's environments. Digital television, the Internet, and virtual reality are spreading rapidly. In the United States, mass media have typically been commercial enterprises for which the primary purpose was entertainment.

With the introduction of each new medium, public opinion ranged from great optimism about its potential for informing and expanding horizons to concern about potentially damaging effects on children. Research was heavily influenced by these popular concerns, particularly about negative effects. In each case, people initially expressed fears about the medium itself—that it would displace other presumably more valued activities (e.g., reading and homework) and that it was so seductive that children might become addicted or suffer harmful effects from overexposure. Within a short time, the content of the medium was criticized with special attention to violence, sex, and immorality.

In this chapter, we concentrate primarily on television because it is the subject of most of the recent research. Moreover, it can be argued that television has stronger effects on development than other media. It occupies many hours of children's time each day; it is readily available in almost all homes; it has an auditory and visual immediacy that attracts the interest of even very young children.

The literature reviewed is limited to children and adolescents except in a few cases when studies of college students or adults provide seminal information on an issue. Empirical studies conducted from 1980 through 1995 are given most extensive presentation. The interested reader can find detailed reviews of earlier work in several sources (Comstock, 1991; Condry, 1989; Huston et al., 1992; Stein & Friedrich, 1975; Van Evra, 1990).

ORGANIZATION OF THE CHAPTER

We begin with a description of the ecology of television, providing information on viewing patterns and the influences of family, parent work, and social contexts on television use. Then we turn to an examination of the effects of the medium itself. Television spread rapidly from about 10% of the U.S. households in 1950 to about 90% in 1960 (Condry, 1989), raising questions about its effects on school achievement, reading, and time in other leisure activities, as well as questions about whether the medium of television leads to modes of processing information that are fundamentally different from those inspired by print. The conclusion from much of this research was that the content of television is more important than the properties of the medium itself in determining its effects on intellectual development. Hence, the last part of this section is devoted to research on television that is designed to teach both intellectual skills and social behavior.

After comparing television with other media, we turn to a large literature investigating how children process information presented on television. In the past 20 years, most scholars have abandoned the stereotyped notion that television induces passive, mindless states. Children are active users of television. Their patterns of attention and comprehension of content show that they are selective in what they attend to, and that they can learn a wide range of information from television. Moreover, we now know a great deal about how variations in the forms and content of programs help or hinder attention and comprehension. One topic of particular interest is the child's perception of television as real or unreal.

The discussion of how television as a medium affects learning and how children process information from television leads to an examination of newer audiovisual technologies associated with, and derived from, television. In this section, we consider interactive television, CD-ROM disks, video games, computer games and instructional tools, and the Internet.

Some of the most persistent questions about television revolve around the social effects of its content. Violence is by far the most frequently studied content, but sexuality, social stereotypes, emotionally arousing content, and moral values arise repeatedly in both research and public discourse about television. Although the importance of these topics has not diminished with time, most of the research was conducted in the 1960s and 1970s. We refer briefly to these earlier studies, but concentrate on more recent investigations, most of which go well beyond the simple question of effects to more complex issues of how those effects come about and how they are moderated.

In the final section, we consider how research on television is used in the formation of policy, by schools, and by parents. Unlike many other socializing institutions in our society, most television is not designed for the benefit of children. We consider issues of commercial exploitation of children as well as positive uses of television to teach, or to enhance children's well-being.

THE ECOLOGY OF TELEVISION VIEWING

When television was introduced as a consumer product shortly after World War II, it spread rapidly into homes throughout much of the economically developed world. In the United States and elsewhere, people reported spending 10 to 20 hours a week viewing shortly after they acquired television sets (Robinson & Bachman, 1972), and the amount of viewing has gradually increased over the years since then (Comstock, 1991).

The popular press is filled with statements about how much time children spend watching television. It is true that many children watch a lot of television, but one of the most striking facts about viewing is large individual differences. In one of our early studies, a sample of 320 preschool children's viewing ranged from 0 to 80 hours of television in one week.

We have used an ecological model derived from Bryant and Anderson (1983) for understanding why, when, where, and with whom children use television (Huston & Wright, 1996; Piñon, Huston, & Wright, 1989). The model includes four levels of influence: individual characteristics of children (levels of cognitive development, interests); family characteristics (parent viewing patterns, parent education, parent regulation, and mediation of television); larger institutions affecting the family (school, parent work, the television industry); and macrosocial influences (culture, income, social groups, socioeconomic status). Although much of the research is descriptive, it can be organized within this general framework.

Measuring Viewing

Before examining what affects children's viewing, however, we raise a cautionary note. Determining how much and what kind of television children watch in their natural environments can be difficult.

Methods of Measurement

A common method of measuring viewing is time estimates—questions asking the respondent how much time he or she (or her child) usually watches television during a given interval. Viewing diaries are another; respondents record their own viewing (and often that of other family members) for one or more days. Commercial ratings services (e.g., A. C. Nielsen) use diaries, but they also use direct electronic recording in the form of "people meters" installed in respondents' homes. The family members are instructed to press buttons for each individual who enters or leaves the viewing area. In a few intensive studies, video cameras have been installed in homes to record viewing directly (e.g., Anderson, Field, Collins, Lorch, & Nathan, 1985).

Validity of Measures

Most of these measurement methods are potentially subject to problems of biased reporting, subjects' inability to provide accurate estimates of their time use, incomplete or inadequate recall, and incomplete or inaccurate recording (see Anderson & Field, 1991, for review). More important, they may rely on different definitions of "viewing"—a subjective judgment, presence in the room while the television set is on, or checklists for particular programs. We know from videotaped records that people often engage in other activities while watching television (e.g., eating, playing, homework), and they come and go from the room (Anderson & Field, 1991; Bechtel, Achelpohl, & Akers, 1972).

The absolute amount of viewing tends to be overestimated when parents are asked for time estimates and, to a lesser extent, when diaries are kept (Anderson & Field, 1991), but both types of measures reflect individual differences in the *relative* amount of viewing fairly accurately. In the most extensive validation study available, cameras recorded all viewing in approximately 100 families for a 10-day period while the families also completed a viewing diary. The total amount of viewing recorded in the diaries was slightly higher than that observed on videotape, probably because diaries included some brief periods when individuals left the room during viewing. The correlation between the two methods was quite high for preschoolers (.84), however, indicating that individual differences among families were measured consistently. Time estimates by parents were also correlated with diaries ($r = .60$) (Anderson et al., 1985).

Parental reports about children's viewing appear to be more subject to distortions of social desirability than are time-use diaries. In our "Early Window Study," parents of young children reported more educational programs and fewer cartoons on checklists than on the diaries (Huston & Wright, 1993). Children's own estimates of time spent viewing are correlated with diaries they keep after about age 12 (van der Voort & Vooijs, 1990), but it is doubtful that younger children have the time concepts necessary to provide accurate reports.

Videotapes of home viewing showed that there was no correlation between the amount of exposure (time in the room) and the *percentage* of attention (Anderson & Field, 1983). That is, children who had many hours of exposure were no more or less likely to be looking at the set when they were in the room than children with few hours of exposure. Therefore, one can assume that individual differences in exposure time are reasonable indicators of individual differences in actual viewing.

Although estimates of absolute amounts of viewing are subject to problems, diaries and carefully defined time estimates by parents or older children appear to be reasonably valid indicators of the relative amounts of viewing by different children.

Individual Characteristics of Children

Age Changes

Total viewing time increases with age from infancy to early adolescence, then declines (see Figure 15.1). At the high point, children average 3 to 4 hours a day (Comstock, 1991; Medrich, Roizen, Rubin, & Buckley, 1982; Timmer, Eccles, & O'Brien, 1985), but that average obscures large individual

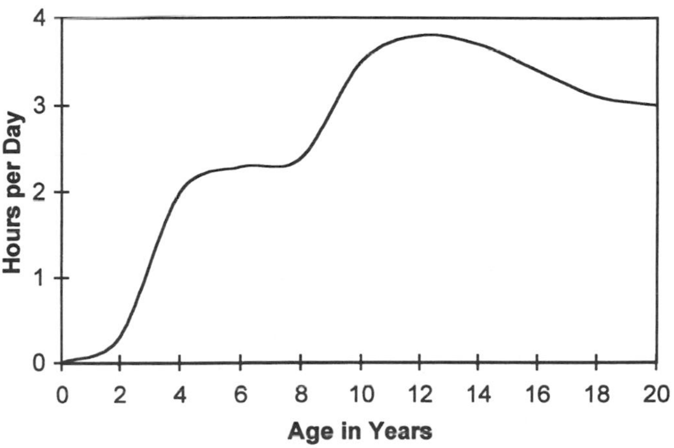

Figure 15.1 Average hours of television viewing per day by age. From "Children's use of television and other media," by J. Lyle and H. R. Hoffman, 1972, in Television and social behavior. Vol. 4. Television in day-to-day life: Patterns of use (p. 178), by E. A. Rubinstein, G. A. Comstock, and J. P. Murray (Eds.), Washington, D.C.: Government Printing Office.

differences. As viewing declines in adolescence, listening to radio (primarily music) increases (Brown, Childers, Bauman, & Koch, 1990; Larson, Kubey, & Colletti, 1989). Attention or the percentage of time children look at the set increases rapidly during the first few years of life, and peaks by early adolescence (Anderson & Field, 1983). The types of programs viewed change with age. Viewing educational programs peaks around age 4; viewing cartoons increases to about age 5, then levels off (Huston, Wright, Rice, Kerkman, & St. Peters, 1990; Wright & Huston, 1995). By the early years of middle childhood, situation comedies are typically the most popular shows (Condry, 1989).

Although viewing patterns change with age, longitudinal studies show that individual differences in viewing are quite stable over time (Huesmann & Eron, 1986; Huston et al., 1990; J. Singer & Singer, 1981; Tangney & Feshbach, 1988; Wright & Huston, 1995). Children who are heavy viewers of a particular genre at one age are likely to be heavy viewers of that genre at a later age.

Gender

During the preschool years, boys become more frequent viewers than girls, particularly of cartoons and action adventure programs (Huston et al., 1990; J. Singer & Singer, 1981; Wright & Huston, 1995). That difference continues at least until late childhood (McKenzie, Sallis, Nader, & Broyles, 1992; Ridley-Johnson, Chance, & Cooper, 1984; Timmer et al., 1985). For adolescents, however, patterns of gender differences are less consistent (Brown et al., 1990; Timmer et al., 1985). For both children and adults, there is some tendency for males to be more attentive when they are viewing than females (Alvarez, Huston, Wright, & Kerkman, 1988; Anderson, Lorch, Field, Collins, & Nathan, 1986).

Family Influences

Family members play a central role in inculcating patterns of media use. Parents' own viewing patterns, their encouragement and regulation of children's viewing, and media use by siblings and other family members have a direct influence on what and how much children watch.

Coviewing with Parents and Siblings

Preschool children often watch television with their parents, but such coviewing occurs more often during general audience programs than during programs designed for children (see Figure 15.2). Coviewing tends to increase with age, probably because children come to enjoy the general

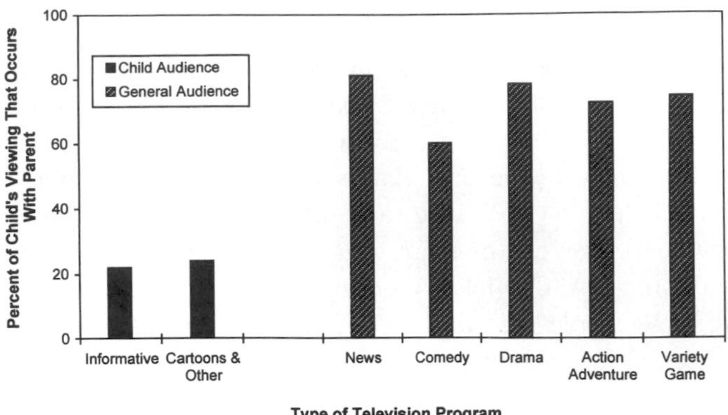

Figure 15.2 Coviewing with parent as a function of program type. From "Television and families: What do young children watch with their parents?" by M. St. Peters, M. Fitch, A. C. Huston, J. C. Wright, and D. Eakins, 1991, *Child Development, 62,* p. 1414. Copyright 1991 by Society for Research in Child Development, Inc. Adapted with permission.

audience programs that their parents like to watch (Dorr, Kovaric, & Doubleday, 1989; St. Peters, Fitch, Huston, Wright, & Eakins, 1991). In one investigation, young adolescents who watched a lot of television tended to do so with their parents. The authors interpreted television as an activity that reinforces adult values, contrasting it with pop music as an activity that reinforces peer values (Larson et al., 1989).

Children also watch television with their siblings, and the preferences of siblings affect what is viewed. For example, children with older siblings move away from viewing preschool educational programs at an earlier age than firstborn children do; conversely, those with younger siblings continue to view preschool programs longer than do those with no younger siblings (Piñon et al., 1989). Siblings use television as a source of play and interaction; older siblings sometimes explain and interpret content to younger ones (Alexander, Ryan, & Munoz, 1984; Haefner & Wartella, 1987).

Parental Mediation, Regulation, and Encouragement

Despite the widespread public concern about children's use of television, many parents do relatively little to guide or regulate their children's viewing (Comstock, 1991). Parents who do restrict either viewing time or program content have children who watch less television than unrestricted children (D. Atkin, Greenberg, & Baldwin, 1991; St. Peters et al., 1991; Wright, St. Peters, & Huston, 1990).

Perhaps more interesting is that parental encouragement to watch particular programs is not just the obverse of regulation. Preschoolers who were encouraged to watch programming their parents considered beneficial watched more educational programs and were more likely to coview with parents than other children (St. Peters et al., 1991).

Children's uses of television are also influenced by the overall climate of communication and discipline in the family. When parents are warm and communicative, children watch less television, particularly less violent television (Desmond, Singer, & Singer, 1990; Tangney, 1988). It is difficult, however, to determine why. Parents who provide a positive family climate may regulate television differently or may have different viewing habits than less positive parents. It is also possible that children in a negative family climate use television as a refuge. In one investigation, parents reporting high levels of life stress were more likely to watch "escapist" programs like situation comedies, game shows (mothers), or action-adventure shows (fathers) (Anderson, Collins, Schmitt, Jacobvitz, & Dondis, 1996).

Parent Work and Child Care

It is widely assumed that children of employed mothers watch television to excess, presumably because they are unsupervised. In fact, among preschool and early elementary school children, those whose mothers are employed watch less television than children of full-time homemakers because they are in child-care settings where viewing may be less likely than at home (Huston, Wright, Murphy, Derley, & Soh, 1995; Piñon et al., 1989; Timmer et al., 1985). The reduction in viewing, however, occurs primarily for daytime programs designed for children, including educational television, rather than for general audience entertainment.

Among children old enough to be unsupervised when parents are at work, the results are mixed. In one review, the authors found little evidence of differences in viewing as a function of maternal employment (Messaris & Hornik, 1983), but two studies did show higher viewing when mothers were employed than when they were not (Brown et al., 1990; Medrich et al., 1982).

Whether or how maternal employment affects viewing appears to depend on the viewing patterns of mothers when they are home, the child's location when mothers are not home, and the functions that television serves in the family. In one investigation, children who attended organized after-school child care watched less television than those who went to a home setting with an adult present, whether the home was their own or that of another caregiver. Children who were unsupervised after school, however, watched more television than those in any form of adult care (Posner & Vandell, 1994). Among sixth graders in Oakland, California, children of well-educated mothers watched less television when their mothers did not work than when they did. African American children, however, watched more afternoon television when their mothers were not employed than when they were, possibly because their mothers were viewing. In addition, when employed mothers perceived their neighborhoods as unsafe, children watched television in the afternoon, probably because they were required to stay indoors (Medrich et al., 1982).

Socioeconomic Status and Ethnic Group

In general, parent education, occupational status, and income are inversely related to the amount of television that children and adults watch (Comstock, 1991; Condry, 1989). African American children and adults watch more television than European Americans, even with socioeconomic status controlled (Brown et al., 1990; Comstock, 1991; Medrich et al., 1982; Tangney & Feshbach, 1988). In fact, among African Americans, well-educated, middle-class families and their children watch about as much television as those in other educational or occupational groups (Condry, 1989; Medrich et al., 1982). We have less information about other ethnic groups, but it appears that Hispanic adults and children watch more than European Americans (Comstock & Cobbey, 1982; Greenberg, Burgoon, Burgoon, & Korzenny, 1983).

There is some evidence that children prefer watching programs with characters of their own ethnic group (Greenberg & Brand, 1994). With the proliferation of cable stations aimed at many nationalities, there may be an increasing pattern of ethnic differences in programs viewed, but little systematic evidence on children appears to be available.

These descriptive patterns provide little insight into why different groups use television differently. One explanation seems to lie in sheer opportunity. The more waking time that individuals spend at home, the more time they spend on television. Many ethnic minority families and many families with low socioeconomic status have few alternatives to home entertainment; they lack the income to do other things, and they may live in neighborhoods that provide little access to alternative activities.

Individuals from different cultural groups sometimes use television to serve different functions. In our Early Window Study, Hispanic children watched more children's educational programs than European American or African American children (Wright & Huston, 1995). Anecdotes suggested that Latino parents sometimes used *Sesame*

Street and other children's programs to increase their own and their children's English proficiency. In another investigation, foreign children living in the United States not only watched more television than American-born children, but used television to learn and considered it more realistic (Zohoori, 1988). African Americans consider television a reliable source of information about world events and social customs and conventions (Comstock, 1991; Greenberg & Brand, 1994). When one of us (JW) took his adolescent children to England on sabbatical, they spent the first few weeks watching British television avidly as a means of getting acquainted with the culture.

TELEVISION EFFECTS: IS THE MEDIUM THE MESSAGE?

The pervasiveness of television has led many theorists and social critics to speculate about the effects of the medium itself, independent of its content, on the lives of children. Some blame television for reductions in reading, school achievement, and SAT scores; others cite it as a deterrent to active family life, physical fitness, and social relationships with peers. McLuhan (1964) proposed that film (and presumably television) cultivated new nonlinear modes of thought. The hypotheses about television effects are, in most instances, vaguely formulated and poorly developed, but we have attempted to summarize them here:

- *Time Displacement.* Television viewing is thought to take time from more valuable intellectual activities (e.g., reading and homework), from other valuable leisure activities (e.g., sports, organized groups), and to reduce the opportunity and need for active social engagement among family members and friends.
- *Cultivating Passivity.* Because television is ubiquitous and demands relatively little intellectual effort, it teaches a habit of choosing easy, passive ways of spending time; by providing ready-made entertainment and fantasy images, it relieves the child of having to find and create play activities.
- *Shallow Information Processing.* Rapid pace, short segments, superficial presentation, and nonlinguistic visual images are typical of the medium. The result is short attention spans and difficulty in sustaining interest when exposed to the pace of a classroom (Healy, 1990; J. Singer, 1980).
- *Modes of Representation.* Television uses visual, iconic representation; audio and print media rely more heavily on verbal forms. Therefore, children learn visually presented information, including spatial skills, from television, but acquire language-related information more efficiently from other media (Greenfield, 1984; Hornik, 1981; Salomon, 1979). Moreover, television provides concrete detail, both visual and verbal, so it provides little impetus for the consumer to imagine or infer what is not explicitly given in the presentation.
- *Amount of Invested Mental Effort.* Children perceive television as easy and print as more difficult, partly because of the inherent ease of learning the representational codes, but also because of the predominant use of television for light entertainment and print for education (Salomon, 1979, 1983).
- *Source of Information.* Television can be a source of language and vocabulary as well as stimulating interest in topics the child does not encounter in everyday life (Hornik, 1981). As a result of seeing a program about whales, for example, a child may search out books, toys, or other sources of information about whales.

Time Use and Displacement Models

If children spend an average of 2 to 4 hours a day watching television, it seems obvious that other activities must decline as a result. Time, however, is more elastic than one might expect. Moreover, television viewing can be combined with many activities; rather than displacing some activities, television may bring about a change in the nature of time spent in those activities.

Radio and Movies

Attending movies and listening to the radio are the activities most often displaced by television. Both declined when television was introduced in the United States and Canada in the 1950s (Robinson & Bachman, 1972; Schramm, Lyle, & Parker, 1961; Williams & Boyes, 1986). More systematic information was collected when television was introduced in South Africa in 1975. A large sample of children in Grades 5 to 12 responded to time-use questionnaires in 1975, before television was available, and samples of children in these grades were questioned during the years from 1976 through 1981 to provide cross-sectional comparisons. A second group was followed from sixth grade in 1975 to 12th grade in 1981 to examine intraindividual change over time (Mutz, Roberts, & van Vuuren, 1993). Both the cross-sectional and longitudinal comparisons showed a marked decline in time spent with radio and movies. The most common interpretation of these patterns is that new media displace activities that are "functionally equivalent." Radio and movies were the principal media used for leisure entertainment and, to a lesser extent for news, and television fulfilled those functions.

Active Leisure and Social Activities

Popular stereotypes envisage the child viewer as a couch potato sitting absorbed and inactive in front of the set. More serious hypotheses about time use suggest that viewing is incompatible with physical activity and social interaction. The evidence supports a modest effect of television viewing on both physical and social activity; but the effect may be most pronounced when television is new.

Williams (1986) and her associates observed a natural experiment in a remote part of British Columbia in the 1970s. One town (Notel), which did not receive television, was compared with a town that received only the Canadian public channel (Unitel) and a town that received several U.S. channels (Multitel). Assessments were repeated two years later after the Canadian public channel was introduced in Notel. In that investigation, and in the South African study already mentioned, there was a decline in participation in organized sports and social activities outside the home (Mutz et al., 1993; Williams & Handford, 1986).

Early studies in the United States indicated that families spent slightly more time together after television was introduced than before, but that levels of interaction were reduced (Maccoby, 1964). At a more microscopic level, observations of children show considerably lower levels of social interaction with mothers or peers when a television set is turned on than when it is not (Gadberry, 1974; St. Peters, 1993).

Reduced physical activity may account for the finding that frequent television viewing contributes to obesity. In a large sample of children examined twice (once between ages 6 and 11 and once in adolescence), early television viewing predicted increased obesity in adolescence, even with initial levels of obesity controlled (Dietz & Gortmaker, 1985). This finding could be due to low activity level; to increased calorie intake as a result of advertising that promotes foods with high amounts of sugar and fat; or to the tendency to graze on such foods while viewing. Lowered activity was implicated in a later longitudinal study: Viewing predicted increased body fat, but showed no relation to calorie intake (Shannon, Peacock, & Brown, 1991). A survey of mothers of young children (3–8), however, showed that the amount of television viewing was positively related to requests for foods advertised on television and to caloric intake (Taras, Sallis, Patterson, Nader, et al., 1989).

Time displacement models tend to be static, but the ways in which television is integrated into lives changes continually over time. Recent investigations in the United States show little relation between viewing and leisure activities. In one extensive time-use study, television viewing was unrelated to most leisure activities (Timmer et al., 1985). Among sixth graders, Medrich et al. (1982) found few relations of television to organized sports or social activities. A survey of 6th to 8th graders showed that heavy television viewers participated less in organized groups (musical, school, church), and were more likely to play videogames in arcades than light viewers (Selnow & Reynolds, 1984).

Reading and Being Read To

It is widely believed that television has displaced leisure reading, but the evidence for that belief is shaky at best. Numerous correlational studies show that heavy television viewers spend less time reading than light viewers (Allen, Cipielewski, & Stanovich, 1992; Beentjes & van der Voort, 1988; Medrich et al., 1982; Ritchie, Price, & Roberts, 1987; Van Lil, Vooijs, & van der Voort, 1988), but this association could be due to socioeconomic factors, family characteristics, or individual attributes that contribute to both. The correlations are small or nonexistent when even minimal controls for age, gender, and parent education are included (Neuman, 1986; Timmer et al., 1985).

Longitudinal Findings. In a longitudinal study of children ranging from second to eighth grades, there was slight support for the hypothesis that television displaced reading as children moved from Grade 3 to Grade 5, but for older children, the data suggested that increased reading led to decreased television viewing (Ritchie et al., 1987). In another sample followed from Grade 6 to Grade 9, time spent with television was initially associated with low time on reading, but predicted later leisure reading positively (Morgan & Gross, 1982).

Media Introduction Results. Perhaps the most stringent tests are provided by changes occurring when television is introduced in a society. In the United States, the amount of time spent on leisure reading has remained steady since 1945—about 15 minutes a day (Neuman, 1991). In the cross-sectional samples studied in South Africa, children spent significantly less time reading after television became available than had children of comparable ages before television. The difference was more pronounced among adolescents than among younger children; the adolescents were questioned several years after television became available. The analysis following the same children over time, however, did not show that changes in reading were associated with changes in television viewing (Mutz et al., 1993).

Reducing Viewing. The effects of reducing television viewing time were also studied in two small experiments in which a randomly assigned group of parents agreed to curtail their children's television use (Beentjes & van der Voort, 1988). Parents reported increases in reading by their children, but it seems likely that parents participating in such experiments would be primed to notice and encourage positive behavior. There was no evidence in the South African study that reductions in television viewing led to increases in reading (Mutz et al., 1993).

Effects of Program Content. Whether television viewing complements or interferes with reading depends on the content of the programs viewed. In two studies of children from ages 2 to 7, heavy viewers of educational television spent more time using print (reading and being read to) than light viewers. Children who watched a lot of cartoons or adult entertainment programs were infrequent print users (Truglio, Huston, & Wright, 1986; Wright & Huston, 1995). Moreover, heavy cartoon viewing at age 5 predicted a decline in children's frequency of using books and magazines by age 7 (Truglio et al., 1986).

Although children who read more watch television less (and vice versa), there is slight basis for concluding that television viewing displaces time that would otherwise have been spent reading. The relations of television viewing to reading depend on the content of programs viewed. As Neuman (1991) notes, children did very little reading before television, and they continued that pattern after television.

Homework

Contrary to popular belief, there is little or no reason to believe that television displaces homework. In an analysis of eight statewide assessments and the data from the National Assessment of Educational Progress including thousands of cases (Neuman, 1986), the correlations between homework and television viewing were slightly negative for 13- and 17-year-olds, but not for 9-year-olds. In another survey of 12th graders, however, homework time was not related to television viewing (Keith, Reimers, Fehrman, Pottebaum, & Aubey, 1986). Moreover, there was no evidence of changes in time spent on homework after television was introduced in South Africa (Mutz et al., 1993).

Although television may not displace homework, some have argued that young people do homework while watching television; hence, television may result in less concentration and learning from the time spent studying. In a survey of 7- to 15-year-olds in Great Britain, about half of those who had homework reported doing it with the television on. Most who combined television with homework thought it helped them to study by screening out distractions in the home environment or reducing the likelihood that other people would interrupt them. Respondents who preferred not to do homework with television cited interference with concentration as a problem (Wober, 1992).

Evaluation of Displacement Hypothesis

Overall, the displacement hypothesis in its simple form is not well supported by the evidence. The most pronounced effects of television are reduction in use of other media that satisfy some of the same functions that television serves. There is slight evidence that television may reduce leisure reading, but it is inconsistent.

The major problem in making sense of this research is that the displacement conceptualization is too simple. Even when there are time trade-offs between television and other activities, the causal relations involved are far from clear. Television may be the default, filling in time when there are few opportunities for other activities, rather than a force luring children away from alternatives. Moreover the ways in which people incorporate television into their lives are complex, and the patterns probably change over time. Television is used for many purposes—information, entertainment, social contact, accompanying boring tasks, and relaxation. Whether it replaces, overlaps, or is combined with other activities depends partly on the function it is serving at the moment. Neuman (1991) proposed that television and print, as well as other media, can have a synergistic relationship, often complementing and reinforcing one another. Children go frequently from one medium to another; they watch stories on television and read books containing similar or identical stories. Media forms are often integrated, using print and visual representations in complex ways.

Finally, the relations of television to other activities depend on the content of the television viewed. There is some suggestion in this literature (it becomes more apparent as we discuss television and achievement) that the time spent viewing educational and informational television has quite different relations to other activities than does time devoted to entertainment programs.

Television and School Achievement

Most educators are persuaded that television inhibits school achievement. The empirical case, however, is weak

(Anderson & Collins, 1988). Extensive television viewing (e.g., more than 30 hours a week) may inhibit the development and maintenance of reading skills, but even that relationship is not consistently supported.

Correlational and Longitudinal Studies

School Readiness. Well-designed studies show little or no relation between home television viewing and performance in reading or other school subjects in the early years of school. In one extensive investigation of second graders, for example, early television viewing habits (measured at age 5) did not predict reading acquisition (Scarborough, 1989). In two longitudinal studies at CRITC (Center for Research on the Influences of Television on Children), children's television viewing was measured intensively over two or three years. The relations of viewing to school-related skills depended on the content of the programs viewed. With controls for home environment, viewing educational programs during the preschool years positively predicted prereading skills in the first study (Truglio et al., 1986) and school readiness, math, and reading skills at age 5 in the second (Wright & Huston, 1995). Viewing general entertainment programs, on the other hand, was generally not related to academic skills when family characteristics and home environments were controlled.

Achievement in the School Years. Among children in late elementary school and adolescence, there are reliable, but low negative relationships of total television viewing to performance on achievement tests and school grades (e.g., Allen et al., 1992; Comstock, 1991; Keith et al., 1986; Neuman, 1991). In 1982, P. Williams, Haertel, Walberg, and Haertel reported a meta-analysis of 23 large-scale studies. The average correlation of time viewing television with achievement was –.05. In fact, the relation was curvilinear. Children who watched 10 hours a week performed slightly better than those who watched less, but as viewing increased beyond 10 hours a week achievement declined dramatically. Comstock (1991) disputed the curvilinear relation, using an analysis of the California Assessment Study to demonstrate that the relationship of viewing to achievement is linear and negative.

Two other studies suggest that there may be a threshold around 30 hours a week beyond which additional viewing interferes with achievement. In Neuman's (1988) analysis of several large-scale surveys, there was little relation between television viewing and reading skill for students who watched 2 to 4 hours a day, but performance dropped considerably when viewing exceeded 4 hours a day. In a sample of 8th to 12th graders, television viewing was negatively related to achievement for children who exceeded 30 hours a week (Potter, 1987). Students who watched news performed better in school than nonviewers; viewing sports and cartoons predicted low school performance.

A correlation between television viewing and achievement does not, of course, demonstrate a causal relationship. Both are undoubtedly influenced by family and socioeconomic variables and by individual differences among children. Among high school seniors in the High-School-and-Beyond Survey, television viewing had a minimal negative relation to achievement when family characteristics, IQ, and time spent on homework were included in the prediction model (Keith et al., 1986).

In two longitudinal investigations, no relations between early viewing and later achievement were found once appropriate third variables were controlled. Children in the National Health Examination were seen twice (at 6–11 years and again at 12–16 years). Although time watching television at both ages was negatively associated with performance on achievement tests in adolescence, the relation dropped to zero when controls for grade-school test performance, region, and family characteristics were included (Gortmaker, Salter, Walker, & Dietz, 1990). Similarly, in another investigation, changes in achievement between Grades 10 and 12 were not predicted by television viewing at Grade 10. In fact, cross-lag analyses suggested a marginal tendency for poor achievement at Grade 10 to predict higher television viewing by Grade 12 (Gaddy, 1986).

Reading. Investigations focused on reading proficiency rather than school achievement in general do suggest a small negative influence of extensive television viewing. Interview questions and viewing diaries were included in one longitudinal study following three panels of children over three years (Grades 1–3, Grades 3–5, and Grades 6–8). The temporal patterns supported the hypothesis that television viewing contributed to lowered reading skill over time, at least among the oldest cohort of children studied (Ritchie et al., 1987).

Some negative effects of television on reading acquisition in the early years were also suggested in the British Columbia study of the introduction of television. Children in Grades 2, 3, and 8 were studied. The design of the study allowed a cross-sectional comparison of Notel with the towns receiving television at Time 1 as well as an examination of changes after television was introduced. For both analyses, there was some evidence of a negative effect of television viewing on early reading skills, but the effect was weak. No effects were observed for older children (Corteen & Williams, 1986).

Are Some Groups Affected More than Others?

When negative effects of television viewing on achievement occur, they are most likely for children with the highest probability of educational attainment—children with high IQs and those from White, highly educated and affluent families. In many studies, the negative correlation of television viewing with achievement is strongest for children with high IQs (Morgan & Gross, 1982; Williams et al., 1982), students from families with high socioeconomic status (Comstock, 1991), and students with access to many educational resources (Gaddy, 1986). The negative correlation is higher for White than for Black or other minority group students (Comstock, 1991; Gaddy, 1986) and for females than for males (Gaddy, 1986; Williams et al., 1982). In some studies, children with low IQs actually perform better at reading the more television they watch (Morgan & Gross, 1982). Two large surveys did not find these group differences (Gortmaker et al., 1990; Neuman, 1988), but where they occur, the direction is consistent.

Privileged and intellectually able children may use their time away from television for more educationally valuable activities than most entertainment television has to offer; hence, their performance is enhanced by eschewing television. Children with low ability or children from environments that offer few educational options may glean more from watching television than from many of the alternative pursuits available to them.

There is little basis for believing that television viewing has a generally negative effect on children's school performance, but some support for the hypothesis that general entertainment television viewing in large amounts may inhibit the development of reading skills (Beentjes & van der Voort, 1988). Inhibiting effects appear to be most likely for girls, children with high IQs, and those from advantaged families. Television viewing alone, however, accounts for very little variation in reading skill. Family background, ability, exposure to print, and time spent doing homework account for much more of the variation in reading and school achievement than does television viewing.

Television versus Other Media

Hypotheses that television stimulates different modes of representing and acting on information than print or exclusively auditory media (e.g., radio) have been tested in numerous cross-media experimental studies in which similar content was presented to children in different modalities (see Meringoff et al., 1983 for early work).

Television versus Auditory Presentations

In several investigations, televised stories were presented to one group, and a "radio" version of the same story, usually with an identical sound track, was presented to another. Television viewers typically perform better than children receiving auditory versions on recall of actions, recall of information that is central to the story, accuracy, reproducing the sequence of events in the story, and inferences about visually presented information and actions. Children exposed to audio presentations typically perform better than television viewers on recall of dialogue and sound effects, inferences using verbal information and outside-story information, and recall of expressive or figurative language (Beentjes & van der Voort, 1991; Greenfield & Beagles-Roos, 1988; Greenfield, Farrar, & Beagles-Roos, 1986; Hayes, Kelly, & Mandel, 1986; Pezdek & Hartman, 1983). Hayes et al. (1986) found that the children who received an audio presentation recalled more dialogue and sound effects than the television group, but the content of the material recalled was trivial and peripheral to the story.

A consistent methodological problem in these studies is that, because the radio versions relied almost entirely on verbal representation, they may have been more complex than the televised versions. In one study of preschool children, the amount and complexity of information was controlled by matching the audio and video versions for actions and dialogue. All actions shown on the video version were described in the audio version; the dialogue was identical on both. Both verbal and nonverbal methods of recall were used. Children who saw the video version had higher recall of both the actions and the utterances of the characters than those in the audio group (Gibbons, Anderson, Smith, Field, & Fischer, 1986).

Children learn most types of content more effectively from television than from audio-only presentations, but children who listen to auditory presentations sometimes recall dialogue and figurative language well. Those exposed to television use language to describe actions and to paraphrase story themes.

Television versus Print

Salomon's proposal that children exert less mental effort during a television presentation than when they read was supported in a series of early studies of children in the United States. In one experiment, children exposed to print or television were given instructions designed to vary mental effort; they were told to attend "just for fun" or "see how much you can learn." The instructions had little effect on recall and inference from print, but led to considerably better recall for those exposed to television (Salomon, 1983).

In two more recent studies of Dutch children, however, children who saw a televised story performed better than those who read the story. In the first (Beentjes & van der Voort, 1991), television viewers generated more complete reproductions and more indirect speech while making fewer errors; the print group gave more descriptive information, more specifics about characters, and more direct speech. In the second (Beentjes & van der Voort, 1993), children's mental effort during the televised or printed presentation was measured by their reaction times to a secondary task (more rapid response indicates low involvement in the primary task) and reports of mental effort at the end of the presentation. When children were reading, they showed more rapid reaction times (less mental effort) than when they viewed television, but their reports of mental effort after the presentations were higher for reading than for television. Children who viewed television had better recall and inference about the content, especially when tested two or three weeks later. Other investigations in the United States have found no differences in recall of printed text and television (Pezdek, Lehrer, & Simon, 1984) and no differences in children's self-reported thinking processes as they read text or viewed television matched for content (Neuman, 1992).

One reason for the discrepant findings may be children's prior experience with the media. Much of the programming on Dutch television is imported and has printed subtitles. Publicly supported television with informative and relatively nonviolent content is also more widely viewed in the Netherlands than in the United States. Hence, Dutch children may perceive television as demanding more effort than U.S. children do.

There may also be both developmental and individual differences among children in the effectiveness of televised and printed presentations. During the first few years of school, much of a child's effort while reading is devoted to decoding the text. Reading for comprehension (as well as for pleasure) becomes more likely in the later elementary years once the technical skills have been mastered (Chall, 1983). Individual differences were suggested in an investigation in which the same children received a televised version of one story and a printed version of the other. Memory and comprehension on the televised version were not correlated with performance on the printed version; some children did well with one medium and some did well with the other (Pezdek et al., 1984).

The evidence contradicts the hypothesis that television as a medium leads to poorer or lower level processing of information than print or auditory presentations. Children generally recall information well from a televised presentation, and they succeed in identifying central themes and drawing inferences. They sometimes recall specific language better from print or audio media, perhaps because those media are almost exclusively verbal. To the extent that children process information differently as a function of the medium of presentation, those differences may be due partly to their expectations and experience in using those media.

Imagination

Because television supplies concrete images, some theorists have proposed that viewers have little need to go beyond what is given; radio and print media, by contrast, stimulate consumers to generate visual images. At the same time, television supplies a vast array of stories and characters that may stimulate fantasy and imagination, though some would argue that much of what is generated is stereotyped and constrained by the formulaic content of entertainment television.

In evaluating these hypotheses, it is important to distinguish among related constructs: creativity (fluency or originality of ideas); imagination (adding elements or combining elements not given in the stimulus); fantasy play (acting out themes in play), and daydreaming (mental musing, wandering, fantasy).

Creativity

In a recent review, the authors concluded that there is very modest support for the hypothesis that television viewing reduces creativity and imagination. Some correlational studies show no relation of viewing to creativity; others show negative correlations, but fail to control for demographic variables and intelligence (Valkenburg & van der Voort, 1994). In the British Columbia study of the introduction of television, children were given two measures of creative fluency (the ability to generate many alternatives). Children without television scored higher than those receiving TV, and their scores were reduced 2 years later, on a verbal measure, but not on a test of visual pattern fluency (Harrison & Williams, 1986).

Experimental studies comparing audiovisual with exclusively auditory presentations of stories have also produced mixed results. When asked to complete a story that was stopped just before it ended, children produced more actions and words that did not appear in the story after hearing an audio version than after a televised version (Greenfield & Beagles-Roos, 1988; Greenfield et al., 1986).

Using the same stimuli, Runco and Pezdek (1984) found that radio and television presentations did not lead to any differences in the fluency, flexibility, or originality of the events children imagined at the end of the story. Television may offer more specific and concrete elements for use in story completions, but the medium appears to have little effect on children's ability to generate novel and original ideas (Anderson & Collins, 1988).

Fantasy and Daydreaming

Television can stimulate fantasy play and daydreaming, but the content of the programs viewed is related to the content of the fantasies generated. Both experimental and naturalistic studies of young children suggest that viewing violent television leads to lowered imaginative play or to fantasies with aggressive themes (van der Voort & Valkenberg, 1994). In a longitudinal study of preschool children, those who were heavy viewers of violence showed less imaginative play than other children (J. Singer & Singer, 1981). Similar patterns appeared in an experimental study in which children who saw television with low violence or who saw no television showed an increase in imaginative play; those who saw programs with high action and violence declined in imaginative play (Huston-Stein, Fox, Greer, Watkins, & Whitaker, 1981).

There is weak evidence that prosocial television content can stimulate fantasy (van der Voort & Valkenberg, 1994). In one field experiment, preschool children were exposed to several episodes of *Mr. Rogers' Neighborhood.* A control group saw neutral films. Those who viewed *Mr. Rogers* showed an increase in imaginative fantasy in their classrooms, but only when play materials related to those themes were available (Friedrich-Cofer, Huston-Stein, Kipnis, Susman, & Clewett, 1979).

Both correlational and longitudinal studies indicate that television content affects the nature of children's daydreams (see review by Valkenberg & van der Voort, 1994). In two longitudinal analyses conducted in the Netherlands, the investigators identified three types of daydreaming styles: positive-intense (realistic, absorbing daydreams with generally positive affect), aggressive-heroic (competitive, aggressive themes), and dysphoric (frightening or sad themes). Children who watched educational programs designed for children more often had positive-intense daydreams, and those who watched violent dramatic programs more often had aggressive-heroic daydreams. The temporal patterns suggested that television influenced daydreams, not that daydream style affected television viewing choices. There was no relation between viewing and dysphoric daydreams (Valkenberg & van der Voort, 1995; Valkenberg, Vooijs, van der Voort, & Wiegman, 1992).

Distractibility and Attention Span

The hypothesis that television reduces children's attention spans is popular among teachers and the public, but repeated attempts to test it have produced almost universally negative results (see Anderson & Collins, 1988; Comstock, 1991; Neuman, 1991). Recent investigations have continued the trend. In one study, 5-year-olds' total viewing and viewing of 17 different program categories were examined as predictors of impulsivity, task persistence, and activity level. Total viewing predicted mothers' ratings of activity level, but the vast majority of the correlations were nonsignificant (P. Collins, 1991).

Students in 8th through 12th grades were studied on two occasions separated by 1 to 4 years. They rated themselves on a 100-item questionnaire in which 15 items formed a distractibility index. Cross-sectional analyses of the initial wave of data indicated a slight positive relation between the amount of television viewed and distractibility for one group of 8th graders, but not a second group. In longitudinal analyses controlling for initial level of distractibility, there were no effects of television viewing on later distractibility (Roberts, Henriksen, Voelker, & van Vuuren, 1993).

If television has any effects on attention span or willingness to persist on tasks, those effects are more likely to be a function of the content and form of the programs viewed than of the medium per se. In one early study, for example, children who were shown *Mr. Rogers' Neighborhood* each day in preschool were more persistent (i.e., stayed with activities longer) during classroom free play than children who saw neutral films. Some of the episodes of the *Mr. Rogers* program stressed trying again when failure occurs. By contrast, children who saw violent cartoons were less willing to wait for toys or activities than the other groups (Friedrich & Stein, 1972). Similar effects of violent programs have appeared in some other investigations (Comstock, 1991).

Sesame Street has been a particular target of critics expressing concern about the effects of rapidly paced presentations on children's attention spans (Healy, 1990; J. Singer & Singer, 1981). The magazine format of *Sesame Street* was chosen to fit the natural attention patterns of young children, but its formal features are not identical to animated commercial programs for children. Episodes of *Sesame Street* broadcast in 1977 and 1978 were coded for action, pace, visual and auditory special effects, dialogue and narration, and singing. *Sesame Street* was similar to other public educational programs and different from Saturday morning programs on most of these features (Huston & Wright, 1994).

There is no evidence that children who view *Sesame Street* are more distractible or impatient with the pace and quality of teaching when they reach school. On the contrary, in the first large-scale evaluation of the program conducted by Educational Testing Service, first-grade teachers rated heavy viewers of *Sesame Street* as being better prepared for school and as having a more positive attitude to school than infrequent viewers (Bogatz & Ball, 1971). In a recent longitudinal study, there was a slight positive relationship between *Sesame Street* viewing and teacher ratings of school adjustment once family characteristics were taken into account (Wright & Huston, 1995).

TELEVISION AS TEACHER

Most discussions of television emphasize negative effects, eclipsing our understanding of television's great potential for teaching. One theme emerging consistently from tests of general media effects is that content is important. It is not television per se, but particular types of television that have positive or negative effects on achievement, reading, persistence, and the like. Children can learn language and information from programs intended primarily for entertainment, but the real power of the medium is probably better realized in programming designed intentionally to teach.

Language

General Television Viewing

Under some circumstances, children acquire vocabulary from viewing entertainment television. In one of the earliest studies comparing children in a United States city that received television and one that did not, it was reported that 6-year-olds exposed to television had more advanced vocabularies than those without television (Schramm et al., 1961). Immigrants often use television to become proficient in the language of a new country. Among students with limited English proficiency, the amount of television viewed was positively associated with school achievement in a large study of California pupils (Comstock, 1991). More recent investigations of communities receiving television for the first time have not shown effects on vocabulary (Harrison & Williams, 1986; Lonner, Thorndike, Forbes, & Ashworth, 1985), but the samples were small and the patterns of findings were quite complex.

Planned Programming

Children also learn vocabulary from planned educational programming in which language appropriate to the child's comprehension level is used, visual referents are often shown as words are said, and words are repeated in different contexts (Rice, Huston, Truglio, & Wright, 1990). Children exposed to *Sesame Street* in its early years showed improvement in vocabulary (Bogatz & Ball, 1971). In both of our longitudinal studies, children who watched *Sesame Street* and other educational programs during the period from age 2 to 5 showed more rapid increases in receptive vocabulary than nonviewers even when demographic and family characteristics were controlled (Rice et al., 1990; Wright & Huston, 1995). In an experimental study preschool children learned new vocabulary words after just two exposures to televised stories containing those words (Rice & Woodsmall, 1988).

Spatial Skills

Because it shows moving visual images, television may be especially well suited to teach skills involving visual-spatial relationships (Greenfield, 1984), but the evidence is sparse. In British Columbia and Alaska, children were given the Block Design test before and after television was introduced; there were no differences in performance as a function of exposure to television (Harrison & Williams, 1986; Lonner et al., 1985). When television was introduced in Israel, however, both naturalistic and experimental studies showed that exposure to *Sesame Street* predicted children's skill in visual analysis, embedded figures, and perspective-taking (Salomon, 1979).

Educational Programming

History of Planned Programming in the United States

In the early days of television in the United States, educational programs for children were part of standard commercial offerings. The number peaked in 1953, dropped precipitously by 1959, increased some in the 1960s, and steadily declined after that time (See Figure 15.3). In 1967, the Public Broadcasting Act established federal support for a nonprofit, public broadcasting system in the United States, largely because commercial broadcasting was not serving the public need for information and education (Watkins, 1987). Programs for children, including *Mr. Rogers' Neighborhood* were shown on public stations, but they typically garnered relatively small audiences.

At the same time, the national consciousness of poverty and its effects on school readiness led to the inception of Head Start and other early interventions designed for children in low-income families. The next logical step was to use television to teach young children, and *Sesame Street* was born. The creators of *Sesame Street* broke new ground

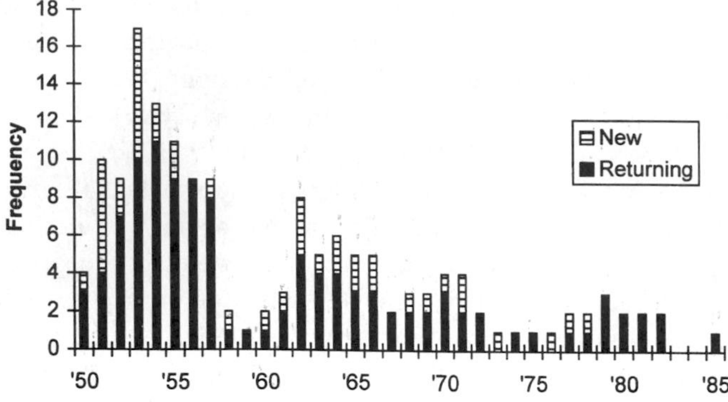

Figure 15.3 Number of educational children's programs from 1950–1985. From The Psychology of Television (p. 56), by J. Condry, 1989, Hillsdale, NJ: Lawrence Erlbaum Associates, Inc. Copyright 1989 by Lawrence Erlbaum Associates, Inc. Reprinted with permission.

by (a) reaching audiences that were much larger than even the most optimistic forecasts had envisioned, (b) basing the design and production of the program on current knowledge about child development and preschool curriculum, and (c) establishing a model for production based on an intensive and continuing program of formative and summative research.

The success of the program shattered the stereotype that public television would reach only a minuscule audience of children from highly educated, elite families. As a result, the 1970s were something of a heyday for programs funded by the Corporation for Public Broadcasting, the Department of Education, the National Science Foundation, and private foundations. Commercial broadcasters also responded with educational efforts (e.g., *Fat Albert and the Cosby Kids, Schoolhouse Rock*).

The 1980s produced a hiatus as funding for publicly supported production and distribution was reduced, and deregulation removed pressures on commercial broadcasters. By the end of the 1980s, in response to the "Goals 2000" panel, Congress instructed the Public Broadcasting System to undertake a new "Ready to Learn" initiative using educational television. Both existing and new programs for children were packaged in a unified format with interspersed short bits emphasizing educational messages. Local stations designed community outreach efforts to involve child-care providers and parents in using the *Ready-to-Learn* television broadcasts in conjunction with adult participation and other activities in their homes and centers.

At the same time, the obligation of commercial broadcasters to serve children's needs for education and information were codified in the 1990 Children's Television Act (see Public Policy section). As a result, some new programs appeared on commercial stations.

Defining Educational Content

In the policy debates surrounding enforcement of the Children's Television Act, one of the thorniest issues concerns the definitions of *educational* and *informative*. One hallmark of educational programming is that it is planned around developmental or educational goals. Children's Television Workshop, which created *Sesame Street* and many other programs for children, follows a model in which content goals are written at a global and specific level. Other producers may use less formal or detailed goal statements, but they have a curriculum or an agenda for the educational messages to be conveyed.

Informative programming is targeted to a relatively narrow age range (e.g., 3 to 5 or 8 to 11) rather than the 2 to 12 used by most commercial broadcasters. Good educational programming is based on expert knowledge about child development and on research and evaluation to develop and improve programs. At Children's Television Workshop, programs are planned and designed by a team of researchers, experts on content, formative research, and creative artists. Formative studies provide information about children's level of understanding and interest. When *Sesame Street* undertook a race relations curriculum, it was based on extensive formative research investigating children's understanding of and attitudes about race and ethnicity as well as careful examination of children's interpretations and misinterpretations of messages presented (Sesame Street Research, 1992).

Educational programming can include a broad range of topics. In one analysis (Neapolitan & Huston, 1994a), educational content was defined by six content areas listed as school-readiness skills by the Technical Planning Subgroup on School Readiness for the National Educational Goals Panel:

1. Physical well-being and motor development (motor skills and health-related knowledge).
2. Social and emotional development (intrapersonal and interpersonal skills).
3. Approaches to learning (developing a positive attitude to learning, developing creativity and curiosity, classroom and study skills).
4. Language skills, vocabulary flexibility and fluency (language arts, literacy).
5. Cognitive skills (classification, discrimination, problem-solving, reasoning, number-related skills).
6. Social and natural science.

In public television programs, social/emotional themes and approaches to learning, especially creativity, were the most frequent types of content. In commercial programs, natural and social science represented the most frequent educational content, but a considerable amount of time was spent on noneducational content (including commercials) (see Figures 15.4 and 15.5). In both types of program, themes stressing narrowly defined academic content—language and cognitive skills—were less prominent (Neapolitan & Huston, 1994a).

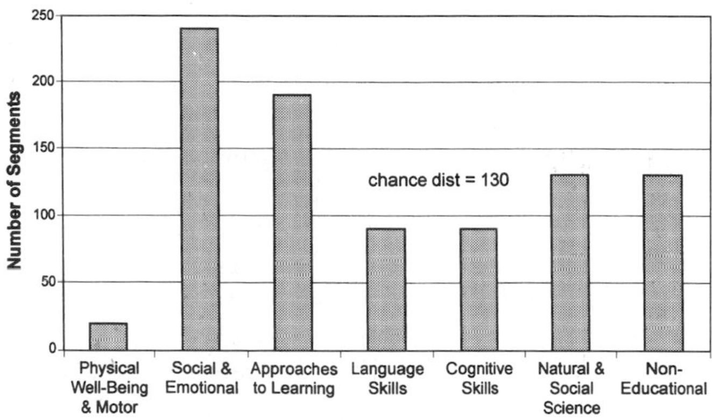

Figure 15.5 Content of educational programming—PBS programs. Neapolitan, D. M. & Huston, A. C. (1994). *Educational content of children's programs on public & commercial television.* Report to the Public Broadcasting System, Center for Research on the Influences of Television on Children, University of Kansas, Lawrence, KS. Reprinted with permission of authors.

Effects of Viewing

Evaluation of effects was an integral part of the planning for *Sesame Street* because it represented a large investment of federal and foundation funds, and evaluation became an expected component of publicly supported programs thereafter. Evaluations can follow one of two basic models: *tests of efficacy*—what an intervention achieves under optimal conditions—and *tests of effectiveness*—what the intervention produces in typical or usual conditions (Cook & Curtin, 1986). An evaluation of efficacy is designed to determine what the program *can* teach when children are regularly exposed and reasonably attentive. The method of choice is a random-assignment experiment. Studies of effectiveness, on the other hand, determine what effects the program *has* under normal real-world conditions. The usual methods are surveys or longitudinal studies that do not involve intervention.

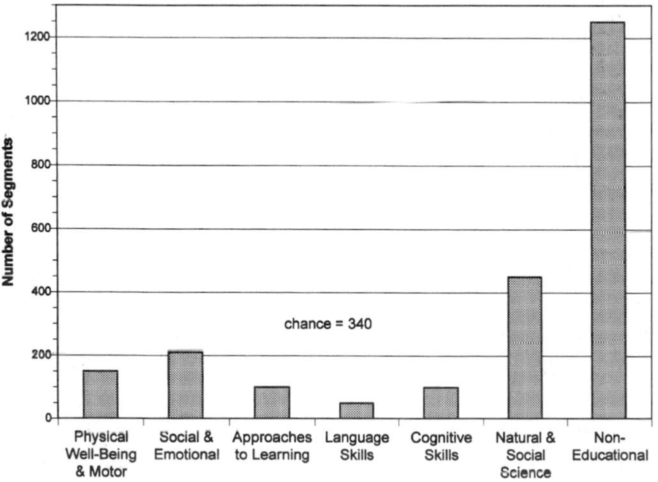

Figure 15.4 Content of educational programming—commercial programs. Neapolitan, D. M. & Huston, A. C. (1994). *Educational content of children's programs on public & commercial television.* Report to the Public Broadcasting System, Center for Research on the Influences of Television on Children, University of Kansas, Lawrence, KS. Reprinted with permission of authors.

Measurement of appropriate outcomes is a thorny issue in either type of evaluation. The outcomes studied may be closely tied to program objectives (e.g., letter recognition) or they may be broad domains expected to be affected indirectly (e.g., general knowledge, vocabulary). Cognitive and intellectual outcomes are generally easier to measure than social/emotional characteristics. Children's knowledge about an area is more readily measured than changes in behavior (e.g., being helpful and cooperative).

Sesame Street. In the first two seasons of *Sesame Street,* large multisite evaluations were conducted by the Educational Testing Service (Ball & Bogatz, 1970; Bogatz & Ball, 1971). The sample consisted primarily of economically disadvantaged children. In both years, a random assignment experiment was undertaken; parents of children in the experimental group ("encouraged to view") were told about the program and asked to encourage their children to watch it. In Year 1, the experimental design became correlational because of the unexpected success of the program—the control group watched, too. In Year 2, the experimental design was successful because sites were chosen in which the public station was on cable or UHF; experimental families were given reception devices. All children were given pre- and posttests measuring seven skill areas taught on the program and a vocabulary test to measure generalized effects. When naturally occurring viewing differences were examined, children who watched frequently gained more on these skills than those who did not; the experimental group in Year 2 gained more than the control.

Moreover, in Year 2, viewers improved on a measure of vocabulary more than controls, indicating that effects generalized beyond the specific skills taught (Bogatz & Ball, 1971; Stein & Friedrich, 1975).

A Mexican adaptation, *Plaza Sesamo,* was tested in two experimental studies in day-care centers over several months. In the first, conducted when the program was introduced on Mexican television, viewers performed better than nonviewers on most cognitive skills tested (Diaz-Guererro & Holtzman, 1974), but few effects were demonstrated in a similar study two years later (Diaz-Guererro, Reyes-Lagunes, Witzke, & Holtzman, 1976).

The ETS studies were interpreted by many as solid support for the efficacy of *Sesame Street* for teaching school-readiness skills to young children. A less sanguine view appeared in a reanalysis of the data raising two major criticisms (Cook et al., 1975). First, the experimental treatment, "encouragement to view," included more than viewing the program because parents were asked to be involved. In fact, encouragement had effects on children's performance even when the actual amount of reported viewing was controlled (Ball & Bogatz, 1970). Cook et al. argued that only the nonencouraged control group provided a pure test of the relation between viewing and outcome and that viewing predicted only one or two subtests within the nonencouraged samples. These samples were relatively small, however, leaving the analyses with lower power to detect differences than that for the overall study.

The second criticism was that *Sesame Street* was not closing the gap between affluent and poor children, but might actually be widening it. The authors did not deny that economically disadvantaged children learned as much as advantaged children when they watched frequently. Moreover, among children who did *not* view often, advantaged children gained more than disadvantaged children, probably because the latter group had other sources for learning basic intellectual skills. But, disadvantaged children were less likely than advantaged preschoolers to watch in real-world circumstances. That is, *Sesame Street* might be *efficacious* for children living in poverty, but less *effective* than for children in middle-income families.

This argument does not apply in the 1990s. In 1993, a nationally representative sample of parents was interviewed in the National Household Education Survey. More than 75% of preschool children and 60% of kindergartners were reported to watch *Sesame Street* at least once a week. Moreover, viewing was as common or slightly more common among children in low-income families as for those in higher-income families and was slightly more frequent for ethnic minority children than for White children (Zill, Davies, & Daly, 1994).

Our Early Window Study of children in low- and moderate-income families provided evidence that viewing *Sesame Street* and other educational programs for children in the preschool years was effective in contributing to children's school readiness (Wright & Huston, 1995). For a group of children followed from age 2 to 5, preschool viewing predicted improvement in performance on tests of vocabulary, prereading, math, and school readiness skills. The effects of viewing were independent of parents' education, income, primary language spoken at home (English or Spanish), and the overall quality of the home environment as measured by the H.O.M.E. (Caldwell & Bradley, 1984). For a second cohort, followed from age 4 through 7, no effects of viewing appeared.

In the National Household Educational Survey, *Sesame Street* viewing was positively related to parent reports that their children had literacy skills (e.g., knowing colors, letter recognition, reading), even with controls for a number of relevant demographic variables. Viewing-related differences were larger for 4-year-olds in low-income families than those in higher-income families (Zill et al., 1994). The strengths and weaknesses of surveys and intensive longitudinal studies are complementary. Surveys offer large, representative samples and superficial measurement; longitudinal studies are based on small samples of convenience and high-quality, extensive measures. Together, they support the conclusion that educational television viewing can be both an efficacious and effective contributor to acquisition of school-related skills for young children from a wide range of social and demographic circumstances.

Barney and Friends. In the 1990s, *Barney and Friends* became a hit program for young children; it attracted larger audiences than any educational program except *Sesame Street.* The goals of the program included intellectual skills, social knowledge (e.g., identifying emotions, occupations, manners), knowledge about nature and health, and multicultural awareness. Its efficacy was tested in two experiments conducted in preschool settings—one with middle-class White children and one with an ethnically diverse group of children located in five different cities (J. L. Singer & Singer, 1994; D. G. Singer & Singer, 1994a). The treatments included viewing 10 episodes of *Barney* with associated activities provided by teachers; viewing without associated activities; or control conditions with no special treatment. (A small group received associated play activities without viewing but was not appreciably different from the other controls.)

In a pre- and posttest design, viewers in Study 1 (with or without associated activities) performed significantly better than nonviewers on 5 or 6 of 13 subtests, including counting and vocabulary, but the control group was higher on 2 (J. L. Singer & Singer, 1994). In the multisite study, children who viewed *Barney* with associated activities showed greater gains in knowledge of the goal areas than the control group, but viewing alone did not produce significant improvement (D. G. Singer & Singer, 1994a). These studies support the efficacy of the program for teaching preacademic skills as part of a preschool curriculum, but do not provide strong support for its effects without supporting activities. Moreover, it would be useful to have information about the effectiveness of home viewing, particularly for children in the age range from 1 to 3, among whom the program is extremely popular.

Reading Programs. If television can prepare children to enter school, perhaps it can be used to teach basic academic skills during the school years as well. Shortly after *Sesame Street* began, *Electric Company* was launched. Its goal was to teach basic reading skills at a second-grade level; the emphasis was on phonics. Although the program was popular, a large-scale evaluation showed no effects of home viewing on reading skills. Viewing in school led to improved performance on the Electric Battery, a test designed to measure specific skills taught on the program, but did not lead to generalized improvement on a standard reading test (Ball & Bogatz, 1973).

Home television may not be well suited to teach basic decoding skills that children are simultaneously being taught in school, but it could serve to increase children's motivation, interest, and perceived value for those skills. That assumption guided the development of subsequent programs emphasizing literacy, including *Reading Rainbow, Storytime,* and *Ghostwriter.* All of them present books and literacy skills as fun and useful, and all have attracted reasonably large numbers of their target audiences. In 1994, Nielsen ratings showed that *Ghostwriter* was among the top 15 out of 81 programs in the number of 6- to 11-year-old viewers (Children's Television Workshop, 1994).

Little evaluation information has been collected for these series. A nationally representative sample of children's librarians reported that *Reading Rainbow* influenced children's requests for books and reading habits. Half of them said they routinely order duplicate copies of books featured on the program, and approximately 80% thought the program increased circulation of some or all titles. No direct indicators of children's behavior or book circulation were collected (RMC Research Corporation, 1989).

Math and Science. Programs featuring math and science content have also emphasized motivation and interest at least as much as specific skills or content. The goals for *Square One* were "to promote positive attitudes toward, and enthusiasm for, mathematics; . . . to encourage the use and application of problem-solving processes; and . . . to present sound mathematical content in an interesting, accessible, and meaningful manner" (Hall, Esty, & Fisch, 1990, p. 162).

The efficacy of *Square One* was evaluated in an experimental design with fifth graders in which the treatment group watched 30 half-hour programs in school over a 6-week period. Both experimental and control groups continued normal math instruction, and teachers did not incorporate the television programs into classroom activity. Before and after viewing, children were tested on solving nonroutine mathematical problems and on their views about math. Although the number of subjects was small (a total of 48), viewers improved significantly more than nonviewers on problem-solving skills—the number and variety of actions and heuristics used as well as the completeness and sophistication of the solutions obtained. That is, they were not learning arithmetic; they were learning complex strategies and approaches to mathematics (Hall et al., 1990). Children in the experimental group also expressed more enjoyment of math and problem solving than those in the control group (Bennett, Debold, & Solan, 1991).

Other experimental evaluations have also provided some evidence that children's knowledge and attitudes about science was influenced by such programs as *3–2–1 Contact,* and *CRO* (Chen, 1984; Goodman, Rylander, & Ross, 1993; Johnston, 1980).

There has been a trend away from large summative evaluations since the 1970s. They are expensive, and producers have little incentive to initiate them. Evaluation data are most likely to be collected if demanded by outside funding sources; as funding for production by government and foundations was reduced, so was the pressure for evaluation.

Children's Television Workshop has been the leader in using research as an integral part of the design and production process. It has also conducted or funded many formative and summative studies of its programs. One's interpretations of these findings must be tempered with the knowledge that the sponsor has a vested interest in positive outcomes, and methodological rigor should be scrutinized very carefully. In the major studies reported here, high standards of experimental design, appropriate measures to reduce observer bias, and peer review of findings are typical. We judge the conclusions to be reliable.

History. *School House Rock* was shown on Saturday morning by ABC from 1976 through 1979. History, math, science, and English grammar lessons were presented in 2- to 3-minute animated stories and songs. One such segment contained a singing version of the Preamble to the United States Constitution. Many years after the series ended, college students who had been frequent viewers recalled the Preamble better than nonviewers did, and they remembered it in musical form. In an experimental study exposing students to single or repeated presentations of either the musical version or a verbal version without music, those who saw repetitions of the musical version demonstrated better short-term and long-term (5 weeks later) recall than students in the other conditions (Calvert & Tart, 1993). In our experience, mentioning *School House Rock* to young adults in the cohort of likely viewers elicits a barrage of smiles, recollections of specific bits, and singing.

A subsequent set of investigations suggested limits on the usefulness of songs. For both children and adults, songs improved verbatim recall and knowledge of the sequential order of events, but did not improve recall of discretely presented factual material (Calvert, 1995). Songs may work well for sequenced information, but less well for other types of content.

Prosocial Content

As noted earlier, much of the content of public television programs for children is social, focusing on intrapersonal themes (e.g., self-worth and understanding one's feelings) and interpersonal behavior (e.g., cooperation, sharing). In the 1970s, a number of investigations demonstrated that viewing programs designed to promote prosocial behavior (or even entertainment programs with prosocial themes) led to changes in children's social behavior. A meta-analysis of research on prosocial television concluded that there was a significant and fairly large effect size (.63) associated with viewing prosocial content (Hearold, 1986).

Mr. Rogers' Neighborhood

Mr. Rogers was one of the first planned programs addressing social and emotional development of young children. Much of the research on prosocial television used *Mr. Rogers* programs; there were fairly consistent findings that viewing led to increases in such prosocial behaviors as helping, sharing, cooperation, and verbalizing feelings as well as to increases in task persistence and imagination (see Stein & Friedrich, 1975, for review).

In one field experiment with children attending Head Start programs, some children saw the program in classrooms containing activities and materials reinforcing the prosocial themes in the television programs; other groups saw *Mr. Rogers,* but their classrooms received new activities and materials unrelated to prosocial themes. A control group saw "neutral" television shows and unrelated activities. Children who viewed *Mr. Rogers* with supplementary activities showed increases in observed positive social interactions with peers and adults and in imaginative play, but those who viewed without associated activities did not differ from the control group (Friedrich-Cofer et al., 1979).

Programs for Older Children

Measuring prosocial outcomes is particularly problematic because behavioral indices are difficult and expensive to assess. Most evaluations of programs for older children have relied largely on verbal reports of message comprehension, attitudes, and hypothetical actions. Such evaluations have found positive effects of several programs designed to convey nonstereotyped attitudes (*Freestyle*—Johnston & Ettema, 1982), adolescent coping skills (*Degrassi Junior High*—D. Singer & Singer, 1994b), and social problem-solving skills (*Talking with TJ*—Johnston, Bauman, Milne, & Urdan, 1993).

Adult Mediation

As is true with any media experience, educational television is likely to produce larger effects when adults are involved in the child's viewing activity, particularly if they provide relevant lessons or activities following viewing. When mothers were asked to watch *Sesame Street* with their children, the children learned more than a control group not instructed to coview (Salomon, 1977), and the effects of encouragement to view, independent of actual viewing, in the ETS evaluations of *Sesame Street* probably reflect maternal involvement as well (Ball & Bogatz, 1970). Several of the studies already discussed show that learning and behavior change in a preschool setting is more likely when the curriculum reinforces the content of the television programs than when the programs must stand alone.

In the real world, however, it appears that true adult mediation is the exception rather than the rule. When children watch educational television at home, an adult is in the room only about 25% of the time (St. Peters et al., 1991). Even in preschools and schools, anecdotal evidence suggests that teachers often treat television viewing for children as an opportunity to disengage. When teachers are given specific lesson plans or instructions, they generally use them, but we have little information about their mediation efforts under uninstructed conditions (Friedrich-Cofer et al., 1979; D. G. Singer & Singer, 1994a).

The overall conclusion from these evaluations is that well-designed educational programs can and often do teach a wide range of academic and social skills. Children can learn literacy and numeracy skills, information about science and history, and prosocial attitudes and behavior from television. Planned programs can also stimulate children's interest in books, science, and history. Although the educational benefits of television are enhanced by a supportive home environment, adult involvement, and relevant materials in the child's environment, children can learn from viewing without these supports. Educational television can be valuable for children of all income groups, but it has particular importance as a resource for children living in circumstances that place them at risk for school failure.

Knowing that children can learn from television is a first step. The more interesting questions have to do with "how." What program features are most powerful? What excites children's interest and attention? What formats are most effective in communicating information? Do these differ by age or demographic group? In the next section, we turn to these questions by examining a large literature on children's attention to and comprehension of what they see on television.

CHILDREN'S PROCESSING AND COMPREHENSION OF TELEVISION

Visual Attention

Phenomena of Attention

We begin with some facts about attention. Although researchers in the area of memory often assume that attention and encoding are inseparable, and thus that implicit attention may be inferred from amount and accuracy of recall, research on children's attention has converged on visual fixation of the television screen as the preferred measure (Anderson, Alwitt, Lorch, & Levin, 1979). Little effort has been expended on determining exactly where the child is visually fixating *within* the screen (but see Flagg, 1978; Krull, 1983).

Attentional Inertia. Attentional inertia appears to counteract the more familiar habituation of attention that occurs with repeated or unchanging visual stimulation (Anderson et al., 1979). Inertia is seen in the fact that the longer one has been looking (or not looking), the higher the probability that the look (or nonlook) will continue for *n* seconds more. Thus there is a resistance to change between looking and nonlooking, in either direction, that grows with the length of time one has been doing one or the other. It has been suggested that this inertial phenomenon serves to maintain attention to an otherwise informative stimulus across break boundaries and the less interesting moments that are inevitably encountered during longer bouts of viewing (Anderson, Choi, & Lorch, 1987; Calvert, Brune, Eguia, & Marcato, 1991; Meadowcroft, 1994).

Auditory Attention. Visual orientation does not inform us about listening. A few attempts have been made to measure auditory attention by the method of periodic degradation and distortion of the sound track, which can be restored to clear audio by the viewer's manual response. The latency of such restore responses after the beginning of a progressive degrade is defined as the inverse of auditory attention. A quick restoration of the sound track indicates that the child is attending closely to it (Rolandelli, Wright, Huston, & Eakins, 1991).

Determinants of Attention. Attention is recruited and maintained by auditory features (changes in sounds, peculiar noises or voices, vocalizations, and loud music) and such visual features as movement, character action, animation, and visual special effects. Children are likely to attend to women's and children's voices, but to turn away when adult males speak (Anderson et al., 1979; Anderson & Levin, 1976; Calvert, Huston, Watkins, & Wright, 1982). At a more global level, children over about age 5 attend more to stories than to disconnected magazine formats (Wright et al., 1984). Overall pace (i.e., rate of change of scenes, characters, and content) does not, however, affect children's attention (Anderson, Levin, & Lorch, 1977; Wright et al., 1984).

Active versus Passive Viewer Models

Perhaps the most persistent debate about children's processing of mass media concerns whether the child's role in viewing television is active or passive (Huston & Wright, 1989). Those most critical of television (e.g., Healy, 1990; Postman, 1979; Winn, 1987) have asserted that the child is a victim, almost forced to attend to the screen as a passive and potentially addicted respondent to the demanding perceptual features of the medium. Its bells and whistles, its special effects and violations of natural cause and effect make the child an involuntary and uncritical consumer of its powerful images and messages, both explicit and implied. According to other critics, the rapid pace used in many children's programs allows only superficial rather than optimal processing (J. Singer, 1980).

Aligned against this view have been those who see the child as an active processor, determined to master the images and implicit messages of the medium and to decode its structure as well as its content (Bryant & Anderson, 1983; W. Collins, 1983a, 1983b; Huston & Wright, 1989). Anderson championed the position that children are cognitively active in attempts to comprehend media content, and that attention is guided by these attempts (e.g., Anderson & Burns, 1991; Anderson & Lorch, 1983). For example, when comprehensibility of *Sesame Street* segments was varied by showing some with Greek language or backward speech and others with English, children's attention to the incomprehensible language segments declined (Anderson, Lorch, Field, & Sanders, 1981; Hawkins, Kim, & Pingree, 1991).

Integrated Models

A better statement than active versus passive would be strategic versus automatic according to Anderson & Lorch (1983). Active attention is usually schema-dependent and schema-driven. Prior knowledge, a story schema, or some other age-appropriate advanced organizer seems to make thoughtful processing of some sort possible at almost any age (Meadowcroft & Reeves, 1989). Social schemas relevant to individual children can affect the deployment of attention. For example, once children understand that gender is a constant and lasting attribute, boys attend to male characters more than to female characters (Luecke-Alesca, Anderson, Collins, & Schmitt, 1995; Slaby & Frey, 1975).

In our early work, we proposed that television viewing could be active or passive, depending on the attributes of the medium and on the cognitive structures and experiences the child brings to the viewing context (Huston & Wright, 1983; Wright & Huston, 1983). At very young ages, or with material that is shallow, superficially humorous, or stereotyped, the perceptual salience of the production techniques used, or "formal features" were expected to determine both selective attention and level of processing. With increasing age or experience with the medium, children were expected to shift to more internally governed, goal-directed patterns of attention based on their interest in the content presented.

Stimulus features identified by Berlyne (1960) as defining attributes of salience included intensity, contrast, change, movement, novelty, and incongruity. Such features, correlated with a statistical definition of information content can be seen in the entropy or complexity of the patterning on a television screen as it changes over time and arouses visual fixation, pretty much independently of content (Krull & Husson, 1979).

Although most of the effects so noted reveal visual attention as a rising function of complexity, the finding of nonattention to very complex and incomprehensible stimuli makes it clear that the function must be curvilinear, where maximum attention and interest are associated with intermediate degrees of information input rate. Indices of mental effort expended and level of processing attempted also show the inverted U-shaped function when plotted against amount, rate, or complexity of meaningful stimulus input in a video presentation (Oppenheimer, 1993; Salomon, 1983).

The accumulated evidence shows that even very young children often make periodic, informed decisions about attention-worthiness of television programs based on their understanding of its content and expectations about its likely comprehensibility and interest value (Anderson et al., 1981; Huston & Wright, 1983, 1994).

Feature-Signal Hypothesis. Formal program attributes may produce orienting responses on the basis of their perceptual salience, but, more importantly, they can serve as signals of content that guide children's selective attention. Although the content of televised material will always play an important role in determining children's interest, the forms and formats are stable cues to its probable comprehensibility and interest level. According to a model by Huston and Wright (1983), the formal production features are the recognizable constants, and they, like the superordinate story scripts underlying the content, are the markers of what kind of television is being seen. Children can, after a moment's glance at a new channel, determine from form, rather than content, the genre of the program—whether it is for adults or children, whether it is funny or serious, whether it is informative or entertaining in intent, and whether it is worthy of their further investment of attention.

This hypothesis was tested by comparing two versions of brief educational films with identical content. One contained such features as animation, children's voices, and sound effects that signal child-appropriate content; the other was produced with adult male voices and live photography signaling adult content. Children attended to the version with child-oriented features more than to that with adult-oriented features (Campbell, Wright, & Huston, 1987).

Stimulus Sampling. With increasing maturation and viewing experience, children learn to sample the program by periodic visual fixation of the screen, and to use the formal visual and auditory features as markers of the kinds of content being presented. They make decisions about further attention based on these signals of forthcoming program comprehensibility, type of program, intended audience, and entertaining versus informative intent (Hawkins, Pingree, Bruce, & Tapper, 1995; Hawkins, Tapper, Bruce, & Pingree, 1995; Huston & Wright, 1983, 1989; Wright & Huston, 1981, 1983). All else being equal, they are more interested in characters and events that have intermediate complexity, novelty, incongruity, and the like than in those that do not (Anderson & Levin, 1976; Hawkins et al., 1991).

The Traveling Lens Model

Most models of children's attention are somewhat static, accounting for processes at one point in time. Our model for the dynamic changes over time in children's attention to, and interest in televised stimuli is illustrated in Figure 15.6 (from Rice, Huston, & Wright, 1982). On the abscissa may be placed any variable stimulus attribute that indexes amount of information to be processed or its complexity. At the high (right) end are all the attributes that should contribute to incomprehensibility, including not only features that make comprehension difficult, but also those that violate expectations, require accommodation, and do not readily permit assimilation.

Over time, two processes modify the lens of the model. One is habituation of attention to the most familiar attributes and readily comprehensible scripts and schemas of the simplest kinds. The other is familiarization and gradual understanding of forms and organization found at the limits of comprehension, where repetition extends the nonzero

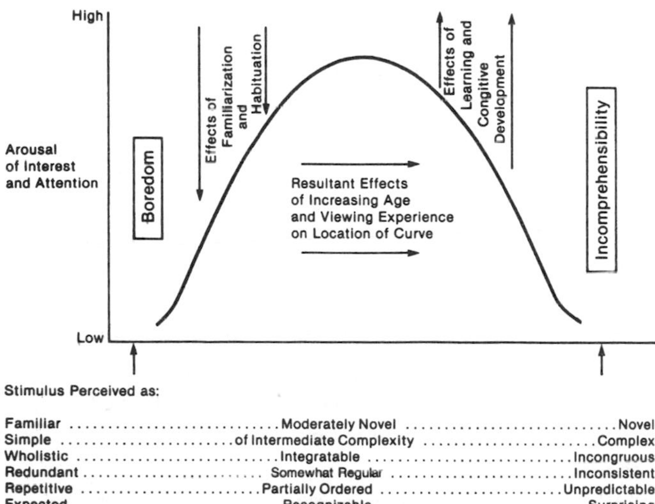

Figure 15.6 The traveling lens model. Rice, M. L., Huston, A. C., & Wright, J. C. (1982). The forms and codes of television: Effects on children's attention, comprehension, and social behavior. In D. Pearl (Ed.), *Television and behavior: Ten years of scientific progress and implications for the 80s* (pp. 24–38). Washington, DC: Government Printing Office.

portion of the curve into the domain of the previously incomprehensible. Thus, for any one child, the entire attentional lens moves steadily to the right, with interest focusing more and more on material that was previously judged to be incomprehensible.

The application of this model sometimes clarifies ambiguities in the empirical literature by requiring for any given intermediate level of attention and interest, that the investigator determine whether the corresponding stimulus is to the left or the right of the point of maximum attention. If attention has already peaked and is starting down (e.g., to thoroughly familiar stimuli), then it is to the left of the peak. If understanding is just being acquired for the first time, then interest should be rising over repeated exposures, and the stimulus is determined to lie to the right of the point of maximum attention. The model serves the practical function of providing a means (direction of change over repeated exposures) for determining optimal levels of complexity for teaching and learning that is analogous to the zone of proximal development proposed by Vygotsky (1978).

Comprehension of Television Content

Relation of Attention and Comprehension

Attention is of interest to both basic and applied researchers at least in part because they assume that it leads to cognitive processing and, hence, to comprehension and recall of the information presented. Anderson and his associates challenged that assumption, arguing that the observed correlation between attention and comprehension was primarily due to the effects of comprehension on subsequent attention (e.g., Anderson & Lorch, 1983). The evidence for this assertion comes from studies in which attention was experimentally manipulated by providing toys during viewing to one group and no distractors to another. Although children with toys available had much lower percentages of visual attention, their comprehension scores were not different from those without toys (Landau, Lorch, & Milich, 1992; Lorch, Anderson, & Levin, 1979). In other studies, however, in which attention was experimentally manipulated by child-oriented versus adult-oriented formal features (Campbell et al., 1987) or by adding narration (Rolandelli et al., 1991), comprehension was affected. The latter manipulations appear more likely to engage the child's mental effort as contrasted with extrinsic conditions that affect visual orientation to the set.

Parallel discussions have occurred during the brief history of producing public television for children. The naive view that getting children to look at the screen assures transmission of a message has given way to understanding that children's cognitive processing efforts must be engaged. Evaluations of programs, therefore, need to go beyond visual attention to measuring learning.

What the Child Brings to the Viewing Situation

Both developmental psychologists and communication scholars in the 1970s rejected the model of television viewer as passive recipient. The natural consequence was to investigate individual differences—what viewers bring to the television viewing experience—as important determinants of what viewers take away from the experience. In communication studies, the "uses and gratifications" perspective emphasizes the functions of television or viewers' motivations (Rosengren, Wenner, & Palmgreen, 1985). In developmental psychology, the role of cognitive developmental changes was extensively investigated, particularly in the work of W. Collins (1983a, 1983b).

Developmental Level. Using general audience programs (e.g., action adventures or situation comedies), Collins and his associates demonstrated that it was not until middle childhood (fourth or fifth grade) that children were able to make inferences from televised presentations or to connect logically and causally related plot elements that were separated by incidental material, subplot events, or even commercial breaks (W. A. Collins, 1983a, 1983b).

Available Schemas. Children's understanding of television narrative is enhanced by their social schemas or prior knowledge about the general content being presented. Children from two social class groups (middle and working classes), each subdivided into European American and African American ethnic groups, saw one of two situation comedies. One featured a middle-class European American family, the other a working-class African American family. Children recalled more information from the program that matched their family's social class; ethnic group did not influence recall (Newcomb & Collins, 1979). Apparently, children's social class experiences provided schemas and/or levels of interest in television families that matched their own background leading to more recall of the content viewed.

Cultural Expectations. Salomon's (1983) model, discussed in an earlier section, defines amount of invested mental effort (AIME) as a mediator between interest and attention on the one hand, and effective comprehension on the other. An important determinant of mental effort is the role played by television in the society. Children in Israel follow the cultural and familial pattern of taking television seriously because it informs citizens of political and military crises, and they process informative programming with greater effort and recall more of its instructional content than do North American youngsters. By contrast, Japanese children in one investigation, were more visually attentive to a television program presented in a laboratory than U.S. children, but had lower scores on a comprehension task (Rolandelli, Siguhara, & Wright, 1992). The Japanese children may be more conforming to the task demands of an experiment, but not necessarily likely to process an entertainment program more thoroughly.

Form and Content as Influences on Comprehension

Comprehension obviously depends on the complexity and familiarity of content, but the forms and formats used to present the content can also be important influences on the messages children extract from what they see.

Syntax of Television. Formal features (e.g., cuts, fades, laugh tracks, music) are the syntax of television; they mark beginnings and endings, time shifts, place changes, and mood, to name only a few. Format cues (e.g., adults sitting at a desk in front of a weather map) mark program genres, providing almost instantaneous information about the type of program and its level of reality. Understanding the content of television depends partly on comprehending its syntax and formats (Salomon, 1979).

Preschool children can make sense of such media conventions as cutting from one time to another so long as the content is simple. Children made correct inferences about event sequences (e.g., a child getting up in pajamas, then eating breakfast fully dressed) shown with such complex film codes as ellipsis and simultaneous action sequences (Smith, Anderson, & Fischer, 1985). Until about age 6 or 7, however, children appear to have difficulty understanding television conventions that violate real-world possibility. Young children interpreted instant replays as actual repetitions of events rather than a television convention (Rice, Huston, & Wright, 1986).

Young children have difficulty determining boundaries between program units and separations between programs and advertisements. The code adopted by the Children's Advertising Review Board includes a requirement that "separators" mark shifts from program to commercial. Children's comprehension is not, however, improved by the separators typically used on Saturday morning television (Palmer & McDowell, 1979). Separators that included a stop sign and an explicit statement that a commercial was coming did improve comprehension, but these conventions were not readily adopted by the television industry (Ballard-Campbell, cited in Dorr, 1986).

Connotative Meaning. Television forms and formats can carry connotative meaning because of their associations with content in television production or because they mimic symbolic meanings in the larger culture. For example, advertisements for masculine sex-typed toys (action figures and vehicles) have rapid pace, high action, loud sound effects, and rapid cuts; commercials for feminine toys (dolls and toy makeup) use fades and dissolves, singing narration, and soft colors (Welch, Huston-Stein, Wright, & Plehal, 1979). Children as young as kindergarten age understand the sex-typed meanings of such features, even when they are shown without obvious content cues (Huston, Greer, Wright, Welch, & Ross, 1984; Leary, Huston, & Wright, 1983).

Formal features also provide cues about whether the content is fictional or real, a topic to be discussed in detail in a subsequent section.

Visual and Verbal Presentation. Television content can be encoded as auditory and visual imagery directly, called *iconic representation,* and as verbal symbols, called *symbolic encoding* (Bruner, Olver, & Greenfield, 1966). The distinction is referred to by Van Evra (1990) as holistic versus linguistic. In general, iconic encoding appears at a younger age, and is more stimulus driven, whereas with increasing age more and more encoding is verbal, though imagery remains a strong option. The early literature showed that children seem to prefer visual to auditory and iconic to symbolic/linguistic representation (Ackerman, 1981; Hayes & Birnbaum, 1980; Watkins, Calvert, Huston-Stein, & Wright, 1980). This "visual superiority hypothesis" is well reviewed in Rolandelli (1989). More recently, researchers have emphasized the increasing independence of visual and verbal representation with age (Calvert, Huston, & Wright, 1987; Field & Anderson, 1985; Gibbons et al., 1986).

When verbal information and concrete visual images occur simultaneously, younger children's processing is enhanced (Anderson & Levin, 1976). Children in middle childhood, by contrast, appear to try harder to understand when the verbal content is abstract. But even they begin to lose interest and reduce their cognitive investment when different messages are simultaneously presented on-screen in print and by verbal narration. Like the younger children, they appear to be turned off by cognitive overload, but at a higher threshold (Oppenheimer, 1993).

Advance Organizers. Educators have known for some time that students learn more from an instructional TV program when they have some preparation about what information to look for—when they have advance organizers. Both visual and verbal advance organizers can be incorporated in a television program to improve children's comprehension of televised information. Calvert et al. (1987) used an insert of a fortune-teller who presented and narrated "preplays" of central content from her crystal ball; children's comprehension of program content improved as a result. Intraprogram synopses, consisting of narrated bits from scenes in the program, facilitated recognition of central content (Kelly & Spear, 1991), as did brief previews without explanatory narration (Neuman, Burden, & Holden, 1990).

Selection of Central Content. Within a program, formal features can provide emphasis and direction that either enhance the central content message just as a spotlight directs attention on a stage, or detracts from it with such techniques as slapstick jokes that are incidental to the message. Young children are more likely to understand and recall content that is marked with such salient formal features as a distinctive sound effect, character action, or visual special effect than content presented primarily with low action dialogue (Calvert & Gersh, 1987; Calvert et al., 1982). Narration can, however, be used effectively to recruit children's attention to important content elements as well as to enhance verbal encoding (Rolandelli et al., 1991).

Children's cognitive processing of television is typically active, involving choices about when to attend and when not to attend and judgments about the comprehensibility and interest value of the material being broadcast. Children use both content and form in processing what they see and hear. Knowledge about the effects of developmental and individual differences in ability and motivation on children's intellectual processing can benefit our understanding of development and inform production of television that is maximally beneficial to children.

Perceived Reality of Television

Children's investment of mental effort and the level of processing achieved depend in part on the perceived level of reality and credibility of the message (Dorr, 1983). The cultivation hypothesis suggests that heavy television viewing may alter people's perceptions of social reality by making the world seem a more violent and dangerous place than it actually is, or than low TV-viewers perceive it to be (Gerbner, Gross, Morgan, & Signorielli, 1994). The notion that real-world schemas are influenced by television-based schemas in the same domains is logically dependent on some sort of cognitive acceptance of TV as an accurate portrayal of the real social world.

Hawkins (1977) proposed a two-dimensional model of TV reality that distinguishes between "magic window" (the belief that people and events on television exist outside the world of television) and "social expectations" (the belief that television fiction shows life in a realistic way). Our model of perceived reality distinguishes between factuality ("Did it happen in the unrehearsed real world?") and social realism ("How like real life is it, even if it is fictional?") (Wright, Huston, Reitz, & Piemyat, 1994).

Potter (1988) proposed a three-dimensional model of TV reality involving (a) a magic-window belief (accepting television content as factual and blurring the lines between actors' roles on television and their real-life activities), (b) an instructional dimension, corresponding to Hawkins's utility or social expectations, as indexed by applicability of content to real-life situations, and (c) an identity dimension (identification of self with leading characters), which corresponds also to social realism, except that it is focused on persons rather than on events and situations.

Factuality

The magic-window dimension that we call factuality refers sometimes to the naivete of very young children about whether television images are present as people and things in the set, and at other times to uncritical acceptance of what is shown even after the viewer's understanding of iconic representation and mediated imagery has developed. Between ages 2 and 4, children acquire the understanding that the objects seen on television are not literally in the set (Flavell, Flavell, Green, & Korfmacher, 1990). Among preschoolers, Nikken and Peeters (1988) found evidence for magic-window thinking of three distinct kinds: (a) Sesame Street really exists as a place where people live; (b) television characters can see and hear us when they are on our TV; and (c) everything you see actually exists as you see it inside the TV set.

Age and Cognitive Level. The accurate discrimination of factuality is a function of level of cognitive functioning and real-world experience as indexed by age. Belief that programs other than news or documentaries are factual declines with age (Hawkins, 1977), accompanied by a corresponding increase in correct discrimination between factual and nonfactual programs. In one investigation, 7-year-olds understood better than 5-year-olds that fictional characters do not retain their TV roles in their off-TV lives. The older children also understood that fictional shows are scripted, rehearsed, made up, and synthetic. This understanding of factuality was predicted by cognitive level, as indexed by a vocabulary test, as well as by age. Neither accurate discrimination of factuality nor a bias toward judging nonfactual programs as factual was influenced by amount or type of the child's television viewing experience (Wright et al., 1994).

Cues Used by Children. Our research (Fitch, Huston, & Wright, 1993) indicates that factuality is discriminated mostly as a consequence of genre (e.g., news is factual; drama is not), which in turn depends primarily on formal production features (e.g., talking heads and on-screen graphics indicate news or documentaries). Condry and Freund (1989) found a steady improvement with age when comparing second, fourth, and sixth graders on a task requiring them to identify 5-second samples of programs as "real" or "make-believe." Another study, conducted just after the *Challenger* shuttle disaster, showed that 9- to 12-year-old children knew the televised events were factual and not just space fiction primarily by noting the formal features characteristic of live news and not simply by judging the plausibility of the content (Wright, Kunkel, Piñon, & Huston, 1989).

When children perceive that a program is factual, they process the information presented more extensively and deeply. Third- and fourth-grade children who perceived the content of a TV story as factual recalled more complex, inferential content, and more psychological and emotional states of characters than did those who perceived the story as fictional (Huston, Wright, Alvarez, et al., 1995). In another study, 8- and 11-year-old children, after seeing televised natural disasters in fiction versus in news stories, rated those in the news format as more factual and those in the dramatic format as more fictional. Those who saw the factual (news) format recalled more of the content details than did those who saw the fictional format (Moghaddam & Wright, 1991). A particularly strong indicator of differential schematic processing of fiction and fact in both studies was the finding that when the children were asked to extrapolate from what they had seen to what else occurred in the original programs, those who saw the news or documentary versions extrapolated to more factual unseen content than those who had viewed fiction.

Social Realism

The second dimension—perceived social realism—has to do with the perceived similarity between the televised presentation and the child's life experience or, sometimes, the child's perception that television portrayals of unfamiliar people and places are plausible and true to life. Unlike the perception of factuality, the judgment of social realism appears to be influenced by viewing experience rather than age or cognitive level. The direction of the effect (a bias, rather than an accuracy predictor) is that the more television one has habitually watched, the more socially realistic one believes TV in general to be, and the more one finds information in entertainment programming to be applicable to and useful in the real world (Elliott & Slater, 1980; Greenberg, Neuendorf, Buerkel-Rothfuss, & Henderson, 1982; Slater & Elliott, 1982). Analogous results have been obtained regarding perceptions of the reality of televised violence (Huesmann, Lagerspetz, & Eron, 1984; McLeod, Atkin, & Chaffee, 1972).

At a more microlevel, in a study assessing children's occupational schemas about jobs shown on television or jobs in real life, children who judged television as both factual and socially realistic were the ones whose real-world occupational schemas were most like television portrayals of those occupations (Wright, Huston, Truglio, et al., 1995).

Motives for viewing affect judgments that television is realistic and applicable to real life. Those who report watching for information or to learn more about people and life perceive it as providing more useful information (Ostman & Jeffers, 1990; Rubin, 1983). That may be one reason young people of color or from low-income families perceive television as more realistic than do individuals lacking those characteristics (Greenberg & Dominick, 1969; Greenberg & Gordon, 1972; Lyle & Hoffman, 1972).

TV as a whole is rated as less realistic than a particular familiar character in a particular familiar show, while intermediate degrees of specificity, such as "TV families" or "TV cops" are rated as intermediate in social realism (Dorr, 1983). Dorr, Kovaric, and Doubleday (1990) studied perceptions of social realism of TV families in relation to children's experience in their own family by asking them to estimate the percentage of American families who are really like the TV family shown on 13 characteristics. They found little evidence of developmental change in judgments of social realism. The level of factuality ascribed to TV declined with age of child, a trend that is compatible with the hypothesis that discrimination of factuality increases with age. Despite the decline in proportion of American families with traditional family structure, children in this study saw traditional families on TV as more realistic than nontraditional ones.

The Reality of "Reality-Based" Programs

In the past several years, a new genre of "reality-based" television show has become popular with the North American viewing public, young and old. It presents factual content in production formats that resemble those of entertainment television. Production involves narration of a factual story, blended with actual footage taken at the time, interviews with the real people involved in the story, and dramatizations of what happened employing actors and scripted reenactments (Neapolitan, 1993). A characteristic of such programs (e.g., *Rescue 911*) is the repeated verbal assurances that everything shown is "true" and "really happened." Instructional statements that a program's content is real give that program a relatively strong effect on the viewer's cognitions about reality (Potter, 1986).

In two studies, reality-based programs were judged by school-age children to be both slightly more factual than news, and more socially realistic than fictional drama. One presented the same fictional story about a fistfight in three formats: news-documentary, dramatic fiction, or reality-based (Soh, Neapolitan, Wright, & Todd, 1993). In a second, children saw one of four versions of the World Trade Center bombing: news, reality-based documentary, docudrama, or pure fiction (Soh, 1995). Children's judgments of factuality and credibility put the reality version not only higher than the fictional and docudrama versions, but more like news than news itself. This phenomenon appears to be a result of the interaction of source credibility and the arousing effect of dramatic production style.

In the first study (Soh et al., 1993), the reality formats were each shown in two content versions: the aggressive model succeeded or was punished. The outcome variables were approval of aggression as a means of resolving conflicts; judged effectiveness of aggression; and willingness to aggress if provoked. As predicted, the magnitude of the difference associated with consequences to the model was significantly higher in the news and reality-based formats than it was in the fictional dramatic one. Such interactive findings in the absence of main effects argue for a moderating, rather than a mediating role of perceived reality.

A Proposed Structure of Reality of Television

It is perhaps not too presumptuous to suggest a structure and a convention to standardize the discussion of perceived reality of television. It seems that there is fairly good agreement that perceived reality is multidimensional, each dimension having different antecedents and perhaps discriminably different consequences among child viewers.

1. *Factuality.* This dimension corresponds to magic window, and perhaps to possibility. It refers to whether one believes that the events shown actually happened in the unstaged, unscripted, unrehearsed world outside of television. Like all the other dimensions, it can be subdivided: "Did the portrayed events actually happen in that real world pretty much as shown on TV?" "Did the TV show those events or part of them when they actually happened?" (as opposed to a reenactment of the factual event). A "yes" answer to the main question establishes the content as factual. A yes answer to the second enhances the factuality, while a "no" answer diminishes it,

2. *Social Realism.* This second major dimension corresponds approximately to plausibility and incorporates the notions of similarity to real life as experienced as well as utility and applicability to real-world situations, and therefore appropriateness for instruction and appeal to those whose motivation for watching is informational. Its subdivisions include whether its social realism is characteristic of events and situations, and separately, whether its similarity to one's own life is based on identification of self with an individual character in the program ("identity"). The former is an actuarial sort of judgment, while the latter is entirely personal and subjective in its reference. Although factuality has a to-be-agreed-on true value, social realism, by definition, will differ depending on the life circumstances and cultural identity of the respondent.

3. *Videotypy.* This third possible dimension is offered rather tentatively. It deals with form and style rather than substantive content and refers to the degree to which the formal features of the program, the manner and style in which production and editing techniques are used, are heavy-handed, intrusive, and otherwise dominate the consciousness of viewers so as continually to remind them that "this is a television program." Sports shows, quiz shows, stand-up comedy, live-audience talk shows, and animated cartoons have in common a high score in this dimension of unreality. Relatively low scores, by contrast, would characterize soap operas, most family dramas, and dramatic presentations of classic and other serious fictional literature. Among children's programs, *Sesame Street, Barney,* and *Ghostwriter* are high in videotypy; *Mr.Rogers, Storytime,* and *Reading Rainbow* are relatively low.

NEW TECHNOLOGIES

The past two decades have witnessed an explosion of new modalities of electronic communication and entertainment, each of which has portions of its spectrum designed for and used especially by children. The Telecommunications Act signed into law in 1996 eases the way for even more changes in the media environment. In discussing the entire landscape of children's electronic media, Wartella (1994) provides a history lesson showing that, as each new medium gains mass popularity, social commentators see both a wonderful enhancement of children's development and learning and a sociocultural disaster for children's taste and values. The likely future for both educational and entertainment functions of new children's media probably lies in a mixed bag of effects between the extremes of our hopes and fears.

We begin this section with a consideration of "interactive television," as seen in children's use of remote controls and videocassettes. We then discuss video games created and marketed for children contrasted with computer programs for children, including stories and virtual environments on CD-ROM, especially those, like LOGO and Sim City, in which children learn to construct systems on the computer by doing their own programming. Finally we present what little is known about children's use of the Internet and World Wide Web as their entre to cyberspace.

Interactive Television

Remote Controls

Adult viewers use VCRs and remote controls to manipulate the duration, sequence, deletion, and repetition of bits of television, but little is known about children's patterns. About 88% of American families had a remote control device in their homes in 1992 (Krendl, Troiano, Dawson, & Clark, 1992), and about 80% of homes had a VCR. About three quarters of the 3- to 6-year-olds asked by Krendl, Clark, Dawson, and Troiano (1993) if they could insert and play a videotape claimed that they could. About half actually succeeded in doing so. Some children as young as 3 could manipulate the VCR with the remote control, though they could not yet explain what they were doing. Most of the children understood that tapes had to be rewound before replaying and could do so.

CD-ROM Disks

The recent integration of CD-ROM discs containing video images and digital sound with personal computers presents the opportunity for children to interact with televisionlike stories using professionally constructed computer graphics, a sound card with amplifier and speakers, and a mouse. The initial offerings for children in this medium have been mostly based on well-known children's books. Children see a page of the original children's book (e.g., *The Tortoise and the Hare*) with the full-page color illustration and the text. They hear the text read by a narrator/character in the story, with synchronous highlighting of each word of the text. Animation and various character voices are interlaced with the reading. Then a cursor appears and the mouse is activated. The child can "click" on almost any object on the screen and see and hear a preprogrammed few seconds of activity, song, sound effects, or a "sight gag." If the child clicks on main characters, they paraphrase what has been going on in the story from their perspective. Clicking on any word of text produces that word from the sound track. Thus children can review, select, or even rearrange the auditory verbal presentation at will. The child can page forward or backward, but with the restriction that on arrival at any page, the mouse is temporarily deactivated until the story text has been read and highlighted.

Derley and Wright (1996) compared first graders' recall of a story after being exposed to an interactive CD-ROM disc program, a passive version of the same CD-ROM program in which the mouse was deactivated, or a video version made from the original book and the CD-ROM sound track. Those assigned to the passive CD-ROM version recalled more about the story than those in the interactive version; the difference was attributed in part to the eagerness with which the children moved on to the next page and the next opportunity to click on objects with entertaining consequences. In effect, the interactivity became an end in itself, especially to the boys, who focused so much on the bells and whistles that they actually turned pages faster and retained less of the central plot than those with access only to the story.

Strommen (1991, 1994) compared a presentation containing verbal commands from *Sesame Street* characters that could be executed by preschoolers using a mouse with a condition in which they could use a mouse to explore a CD-ROM-based virtual forest. Speech was much less effective alone than when presented with supporting visual display changes.

Video Games

Beginning with Atari in the 1970s, games that can be played on Nintendo® and Sega® equipment have become popular with young children, especially boys between the ages of about 5 and 12. The games are widely available for purchase or rental at video outlets. It was estimated in 1994 that 34% of American homes had video game equipment (Greenfield, 1994).

"Action" Games

Where elaborate manipulanda and vertically oriented screens are used in arcade games for a general audience, Nintendo and Sega, using home TV sets as monitors, typically use a mouse, a track ball, or most commonly a joystick as input devices. The speed and action games usually involve moving, evading, shooting, ducking, and other simple chase and targeting behaviors in scenarios with simple, often violent plots. Hand-to-hand combat and aerial dogfights are more common than are reflective, verbal, keyboard-operated exploratory or adventure games, such as *Dungeons and Dragons.*

Visual-Spatial Skill Development

A clearly documented outcome of action video game play among children is the development of rapid and efficient sensorimotor skills within the genre of the program (Greenfield, 1994). Among college students, long-term expertise in action video games, but not concentrated short-term practice, predicted spatial skills in a mental paperfolding test requiring mental construction and rotation of three-dimensional objects (Greenfield, Brannon, & Lohr, 1994). Skill at dividing visual attention in a vigilance task is enhanced by practice on action video games (Greenfield, deWinstanley, Kilpatrick, & Kaye, 1994).

The action/speed games appear to exercise and develop spatial skills that can be carried out much more quickly than the verbal-analytic strategy skills required for adventure games (Lowery & Knirk, 1982–1983). The work of Goffinet, DeVolder, Bol, and Michel (1990 cited in Greenfield, 1994), indicates that "action video games hyperactivate the visual cortex, while depressing activity in the prefrontal cortex, the part of the brain responsible for complex linguistic grammar and sequential motor planning" (p. 8).

Sociocultural and Gender Effects

To the extent that social content of video games has been analyzed, frequent themes of violence, exploitation, implicit sexuality, and stereotyping, both by gender and by ethnic group have been noted (Kinder, 1996). Silvern and Williamson (1987) found that playing an aggressive video game augmented children's aggression and hostility to exactly the same degree as watching a violent television cartoon. Cardiovascular arousal indicators and subsequent hostile behavior tracked three levels of violence in video game play (Ballard & Wiest, 1995). In a virtual-reality adventure game, interactive players reported more aggressive thoughts and had greater increases in heart rate than those who "observed" the virtual reality action, but did not actively participate (Calvert & Tan, 1994). Some of the same effects, such as aggressive social play and desensitization to violence, as have been observed from watching violent television have also been attributed to playing video games (Cocking & Greenfield, 1996; Gailey, 1993).

Very large sex differences favoring males are consistently observed in the liking for and use of video games, and the vast majority of game plots are male oriented. A small number designed for girls are not enjoying wide sales (Kafai, 1996). Skill differences between boys and girls in complex mental rotation tasks were sharply reduced following practice with an action video game, but not after practice on a verbal game (Subrahmanyam & Greenfield, 1994).

Time use analyses among young children have shown that video game use and viewing commercial entertainment cartoons are positively correlated, whereas time spent on video games is negatively related to time spent with print media and time spent watching educational television programs (Wright & Huston, 1995).

Using Computers

An imperfect, but functional distinction can be drawn between action video games on the one hand and computer activities, including verbal-strategic adventure games, on the other. Although the line of demarcation is somewhat fuzzy, computer programs for children seem to have more constructive content, more challenging cognitive demands, less focus on sensorimotor skills, and more conceptual and strategic emphases (Greenfield, 1994).

A generally positive and confident orientation toward computers can result from early exposure to programs designed to familiarize children with computer use and simple firststeps of programming. Graphic and pictorial forms often predominate over linguistic forms, whether written or voiced, providing a special opportunity for disciplined thought among children with especially strong iconic and visual processing orientations or with some weakness or reluctance where reading, writing, and keyboard skills are involved (Greenfield, Camaioni, et al., 1994). Moreover there is vast potential for engaging children in animation, simulation, and kinetic imagery, when movement over time is added to graphic representation (Klein, 1985). Imagery fluency is associated with high involvement in visual media of several kinds (Wober & Fazal, 1988).

Educational computer software for children too young to read has made use of speech to communicate to them, and simple speech recognition systems to enable their spoken control of the program (Strommen, 1991; Strommen & Frome, 1993). Authoring languages for children like LOGO can help them to create animation, stories, and even games designed for other children, as well as to construct systems for others to explore and games for others to play (Kafai, 1995).

Tutorials accompanying operating system software and word and number-processing programs can be made into computer-literacy training packages for young people. Educational software and computer-assisted instruction are especially effective when the subject matter has a graphic, parallel logic, rather than a verbal, serial structure (Okagaki & Frensch, 1994).

Divergent thinking skills may result from programs that encourage children to explore complex domains and discover or construct recurrent regularities in the computerized world. By contrast computer-assisted instruction is often designed to be convergent in its effects—to provide basic classroomlike instruction in simulation of a Socratic educational setting. Cooperative discovery has been shown superior to competitive game formats for acquisition of content knowledge (Strommen, 1993). For example, first graders can learn from team use of a computer environment for studying science without teacher assistance (Strommen, 1994).

Although it is beyond the scope of this chapter to discuss the research literature on formal computer-assisted instruction (CAI), suffice it to say that collectively the literature shows that, beyond providing drill in basic facts, the best CAI software does as well or better than traditional instructional methods at teaching basic knowledge and skills, even to children at very young ages.

Other Media

Although the medium is older than any previously discussed, children's theater has just begun to receive significant cognitive developmental research on such variables as attention and comprehension, interest in plot levels, identification with characters, and the perennial "willing suspension of disbelief." The work of Klein (1991, 1995) has adopted the theoretical models and some of the research techniques developed for the study of children's television, and adapted them to create a new approach to the study of live, in-person dramatic performances as perceived by children.

Another old/new medium is popular music and music videos. Christenson and Roberts (1990) surveyed the literature and concluded that effects of rock music on young people are not large or general and depend on listener characteristics as well as the context of listening. Children's comprehension of rock music increases with age, but lyrics are often misunderstood, and taken at a more literal, less metaphoric level than intended (Greenfield et al., 1987). The same authors found that music videos provide less stimulation of imagination and are enjoyed less than the songs alone. Correspondingly, rock songs alone elicit more emotion and affect than when they are presented as a music video.

The Internet

Although there is virtually no published research on children's use of on-line networks to communicate by e-mail; to visit sites on the World Wide Web; or to post their own work, play games, or "chat" in real time, there is no doubt that they are becoming active in all these formats. Child-oriented pages on the World Wide Web reveal not only the activities of those who develop communications and activities to sell to kids, but a wealth of storytelling, and pen-pal sources. There are, in addition, several children's media bulletin boards and lists as well as groups concerned with policy matters, media literacy, and general child advocacy.

The new technologies, like television itself, have been exploited to deliver entertainment of questionable taste and value at considerable cost to children and profit to the industry. The vast educational and prosocial potentials of the media have been touched, sampled, proved valuable, but not yet developed to even a fraction of that potential.

The power of stories to hold the attention of children is reaffirmed, and it is ironic that the straight stories, unembellished by interactive glitz, seem to do the best job of conveying the plot, characters, and themes in a comprehensible and memorable fashion. Interactivity per se motivates children, especially boys in middle childhood, but it does not accomplish enhanced communication unless it is properly designed to emphasize rather than distract from the intended content. Good intentions are not enough to produce good interactive programs; careful formative research and knowledge about children's learning processes are needed. Action video games designed to entertain appear to occupy a slot in children's lives that is more akin to cartoon watching than it is to book reading. By contrast, the use of generative computer programs designed to stimulate constructive thinking and problem solving may cultivate some educationally relevant skills.

EFFECTS OF SOCIAL CONTENT

Much of the public concern about television, popular music, and video games arises from their social content—messages about violence, sex, social stereotypes, family life, and social roles. At the same time, many of the clearest successes of planned programming for children and young people have fallen in the realms of prosocial behavior (e.g., helping others, empathy), reduced stereotypes, and understanding complex human relationships and feelings.

Social messages in the mass media can have both immediate and long-term effects. Viewing a television program may change a person's state by inducing emotional arousal (increased or reduced), inhibition or disinhibition of impulses, and activation of thoughts or associations, and it may contribute to enduring learned patterns of behavior, cognitive structures (e.g., scripts and schemas), attitudes, and beliefs about the real world.

Media effects are bidirectional. Children are not just recipients of media messages; they choose the content to which they are exposed, and they interpret the content within their own frames of reference. They receive media messages in contexts of family, peers, and social institutions, all of which may modify or determine how children integrate messages into their existing store of information and beliefs.

Acknowledging the multidirectional processes involved in children's interactions with media does not obviate the possibility of drawing conclusions about content effects. If the causal directions go from individual to media exposure as well as from exposure to individual, each direction can still be important: It is likely that the observed correlation between viewing violence and aggressive behavior is due not only to the effects of viewing on aggression, but also to greater preference for violence by aggressive individuals. One can still consider the "effects" of social content messages as one part of the process.

Theories of Media and Social Behavior

Social Cognitive Theory of Observational Learning

Much of the early research on television content and children's behavior was guided by observational learning theory (Bandura & Walters, 1963). Bandura (1994) expanded his original formulation by elaborating the cognitive and motivational processes that intervene between observing a modeled event and behaving in a way that matches that event. These processes, summarized in Figure 15.7, fall in four "subfunctions," each of which is influenced by characteristics of the modeled event and by characteristics of the observer. *Attention* determines what is taken in and how it is interpreted. *Retention* then depends on how the observed actions are encoded and rehearsed; for children, both the level of cognitive development and the cognitive structures available are important influences on what is retained.

Much observational learning stops with retention; some residue of the modeled events remains stored in memory, but the person does not act immediately on this knowledge. *Production processes* are used to generate actions that match or are similar to those observed. *Motivational processes* include the child's judgment about the likely

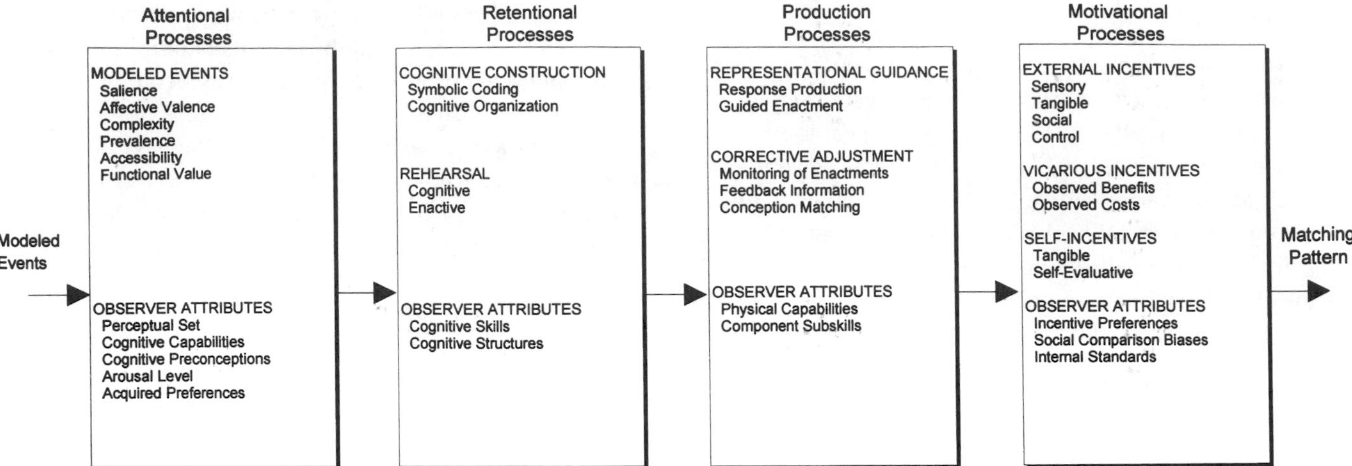

Figure 15.7 Bandura's observational learning model. From "Social cognitive theory of mass communication," by A. Bandura, 1994, from *Media effects: Advances in theory and research* (p. 67), in J. Bryant and D. Zillmann (Eds.), 1994, Hillsdale, NJ: Lawrence Erlbaum Associates, Inc. Copyright 1994 by Lawrence Erlbaum Associates, Inc. Adapted with permission.

consequences of imitation as well as internalized goals, standards, and self-evaluative processes (Bandura, 1994).

Cognitive Neoassociationist Theory

According to this theory (Berkowitz, 1990; Jo & Berkowitz, 1994), thoughts, emotions, and action tendencies are organized in networks of associations; activation of one component in a network elicits related components. Viewing television violence can have a *priming* effect by activating aggressive thoughts that lead to emotion (anger) and aggressive action tendencies. This activation may last for some time after viewing with the result that there is increased probability that viewers will "(a) have hostile thoughts that can color their interpretation of other people, (b) believe other forms of aggressive conduct are justified and/or will bring them benefits, and (c) be aggressively inclined" (Jo & Berkowitz, 1994, p. 46).

Durable effects of media exposure are proposed through two processes: People may continue to think about what was shown, so that related networks of associations are repeatedly activated, or they may encounter reminders of the television show in a later situation. Evidence for the first proposition comes from studies cited earlier showing a relation between watching violent television and aggressive daydreams (Valkenburg & van der Voort, 1994). Support for the second was found in an experiment with second- and third-grade boys. Children were shown a violent program in which characters used walkie-talkies or a nonviolent television program. Half of each group were subsequently interviewed by a person using a walkie-talkie. All boys then played a game of floor hockey. Boys who had seen the violent movie and who had been exposed to the walkie-talkie were more aggressive than the other groups (Josephson, 1987). It appears that the walkie-talkie activated the aggression-related ideas and actions portrayed in the violent television show.

Arousal Theory

Exposure to many types of content (e.g., violence, erotic scenes, suspense, humor) produces a state of nonspecific emotional and physiological arousal, according to Zillmann and Bryant (1994). While viewing, the arousal is linked to the content of the program; that is, the person feels sad, angry, or sexually aroused depending on what is being shown, but after viewing ends, the arousal remains independent of the content with which it was associated. The person's subsequent emotion depends on his or her interpretation of the current situation. If the person perceives someone as being insulting, the resultant emotional state will be anger; if a happy ending follows fearful suspense, the person will feel happy. The *intensity* of that emotion, however, is affected by a process of "excitation transfer." The lingering sympathetic arousal from the viewing experience combines with the arousal produced by the current situation to make one feel and react more intensely than one would solely on the basis of the current context.

One prediction from this theory is that the effects of media may have little relation to the particular content of the program because the important mediator is nonspecific arousal. Viewing highly arousing violence could increase a person's inclination to help in an emergency; viewing nonviolent eroticism could increase violence if a person were threatened or instigated by peers to engage in violence.

Information Processing Theory

Huesmann (1986, Huesmann & Miller, 1994) proposed that television violence contributes to children's cognitive scripts—learned patterns of action that serve as guides concerning expectations about others, one's own behavior, and acceptable forms of social problem solving. Using information processing theory, three steps are proposed: (a) encoding of a representation of an external stimulus in memory; (b) rehearsal and elaboration through fantasy or repeated exposure to similar stimuli; and (c) retrieval for action when a child encounters a social problem situation.

Media produce long-term cumulative effects by repeatedly providing material for certain scripts (e.g., violent resolution of conflict). Immediate effects occur when media provide cues for retrieval of existing scripts. Because repeated retrieval solidifies and expands existing scripts, it can produce some long-term effects as well. Young children are especially susceptible to learning new scripts from television; longitudinal data show lasting effects of viewing during middle childhood (Huesmann & Eron, 1986).

Cultivation Theory

In the theories discussed so far, the level of analysis is the individual. Cultivation theorists discuss mass media at the level of society and culture, arguing that television presents a narrow and consistent set of social messages that reflect the political and economic forces in society. Viewers who are immersed in those messages for many hours a week gradually absorb them as part of their worldviews (Gerbner et al., 1994; Signorielli & Morgan, 1990).

In tests of the theory, two complementary methods are used: message system analysis to examine the content of television, and cultivation analysis to test individuals' conceptions of social reality. People's beliefs about the real world are compared with the aggregate picture presented by television. Heavy viewers are expected to have distorted beliefs about events that are misrepresented on television (e.g., the percentage of the population who are police or the probability of being a victim of violent crime).

Although some of the research on social content effects has been designed to test one or more of these theories, much of it has not been theoretically guided. In what follows, we will discuss the evidence about television content and its relations to children's beliefs and behavior in the domains of violence, emotion, sex, and social roles, referring to these theories when possible.

Violence

Questions about media violence have plagued modern societies, especially the United States, at least since the introduction of movies and radio early in the century. Television raised this debate to a new level of concern because it has the visual immediacy of movies and virtually constant availability in homes and many public places. The United States as a nation has an overwhelming ambivalence about violence that is reflected in public dialogues bemoaning the high rates of criminal and domestic violence juxtaposed with refusal to regulate the availability of weapons.

Violent Content on Television

Violence pervades much of the programming available on television and associated media (videotapes and movies) in the United States. Moreover, U.S. television is exported throughout the world, often constituting a majority of the programming in both industrialized and developing countries. Annual content analyses of network television since 1967 report violence, portrayals of different social groups, portrayals of occupations, and many other forms of social content (Gerbner et al., 1994; Gerbner, Morgan, & Signorielli, 1993; Signorielli & Morgan, 1990). The method is a strictly quantitative count of instances of using or threatening physical harm to another, but portrayals of violence are interpreted as symbols for power, conveying messages about social structure and broadly shared cultural values.

In the 20 years from 1973 to 1993, 71.2% of prime time network programs and 92.% of Saturday morning dramatic programs (aimed at children) contained some violence (see Figure 15.8). In prime time, the average number of violent scenes per hour was 5.3; on Saturday morning, it was 23.0. Whether the decline in the early 1990s represents a trend is not certain. In the early 1990s, "reality" and variety

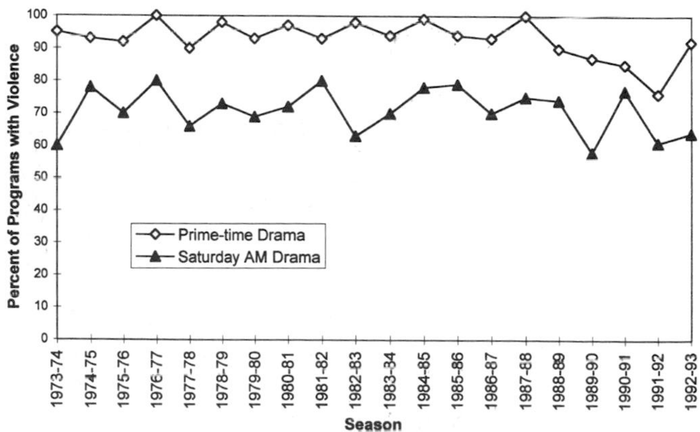

Figure 15.8 Proportion of programs containing violence, by year. Gerbner, G., Morgan, M., & Signorielli, N. (1993, December). *Television violence profile No. 16: The turning point from research to action.* Unpublished manuscript, Annenberg School of Communication, University of Pennsylvania, Philadelphia, PA. Reprinted with permission of authors.

programs became popular with children and adults. In 1993, the rates of violent incidents per hour were 13.0 for variety programs and 7.5 for reality programs, higher than any other prime time genres. Cable programming for children was less violent (17.3 acts per hour) than network fare, but cable offerings for general audiences were more violent (9.2 acts per hour) (Gerbner et al., 1993).

Effects on Beliefs

A review of the few studies with children concluded that there is some evidence that television viewing contributes to children's beliefs that violence is frequent in the real world, but the content chosen for viewing appears to be important. Viewers of action adventure were most likely to have such beliefs (Hawkins & Pingree, 1982).

Effects on Behavior

Congress and various government commissions have considered issues of television violence for four decades (Liebert & Sprafkin, 1988). In the 1960s and 1970s, federal funds supported programs of research designed to determine whether television violence "caused" aggressive behavior. The National Institute of Mental Health organized a major research effort for the Surgeon General's Scientific Advisory Committee on Television and Social Behavior around 1970. On the basis of numerous studies, the Committee concluded that there was "a preliminary and tentative indication of a causal relation between viewing violence on television and aggressive behavior; . . . any such causal relation operates only on some children (who are predisposed to be aggressive); . . . only in some environmental contexts" (Surgeon General's Scientific Advisory Committee on Television and Social Behavior, 1972, p. 11).

Ten years later, a review of the literature by the National Institute of Mental Health (Pearl, Bouthilet, & Lazar, 1982) was much less tentative, concluding, "The consensus among most of the research community is that violence on television does lead to aggressive behavior by children and teenagers who watch the programs" (p. 6). In 1985, the American Psychological Association adopted a resolution stating that the research evidence supported the conclusion that "viewing television violence can lead to increases in aggressive attitudes, values, and behavior, particularly in children" (p. 3).

Scholars reviewing the literature have, with few exceptions, reached similar conclusions (Comstock, 1991; Friedrich-Cofer & Huston, 1986; Huesmann, 1982; Huesmann & Malamuth, 1986; Liebert & Sprafkin, 1988; Stein & Friedrich, 1975). Industry representatives have consistently demurred, with support from a few scholars (Freedman, 1984, 1986; Milavsky, Stipp, Kessler, & Rubens, 1982). No serious scholars advocate the opposite view—that viewing violence reduces aggression through catharsis or some similar process.

The empirical literature on the effects of television violence on aggression is much too vast to consider in detail here. Our strategy, therefore, will be to use reviews, including meta-analyses to present the summary picture; then to discuss in more detail some exemplary studies that illustrate the methods used; and finally to consider a series of questions about interpretation of the research.

Meta-Analyses. The research on television violence constitutes a good methodological case study illustrating the strengths and weaknesses of different approaches. Two major strategies have been used: experiments using random assignment and correlational studies intended to capture the naturally occurring relations between viewing and behavior. Within each type, both short-term and longer-term patterns of relations have been investigated. Most experiments have been short-term—one session in which individuals were exposed to television programs varying in violence and then tested or observed immediately after viewing either in a contrived task (e.g., interfering with another child's activity) or in free play. Field experiments lasting from one to several weeks have also been conducted; individuals were repeatedly exposed to different types of television, and subsequent behavior in a natural setting was observed.

Naturalistic studies include correlational investigations relating the amount of violence viewed to behavior on one occasion and longitudinal studies examining repeated measures over time. Most were conducted before 1985, and they are well summarized in several review sources (Comstock, 1991; Condry, 1989; Liebert & Sprafkin, 1988; Stein & Friedrich, 1975).

Four meta-analyses of this literature were published between 1977 and 1994; all concluded that viewing violence was related to aggression (Andison, 1977; Hearold, 1986; Paik & Comstock, 1994; Wood, Wong, & Chachere, 1991). The analysis by Hearold (1986) included experimental studies in the laboratory and in field settings, cross-sectional correlational investigations, longitudinal studies, and time series analyses. Antisocial behavior was broadly defined to include not only aggression, but materialism and stereotyping. Effect sizes ranged from 0.25 to 0.41, depending on how they were calculated; the estimated summary effect size was 0.30.

In 47 of those studies, prosocial behavior was also coded (e.g., altruism, nonstereotyping, social interaction). There were no effects of antisocial television on prosocial behavior. Hence, viewing violence appears to contribute to antisocial behavior, but to have no impact on prosocial tendencies.

The meta-analysis by Paik and Comstock (1994) limited the outcome measures to behaviors that were clearly aggressive (i.e., self-reports of aggressive intention, observed aggressive behavior in laboratory simulations or real-world situations, and illegal behavior). About half of the 217 studies analyzed were part of Hearold's sample. The overall effect size was 0.65 when multiple contrasts within studies were included; with each study entered only once, it was 0.73.

Many studies in these analyses relied on indirect measures—self-report or laboratory simulations of aggression. Wood et al. (1991) restricted their meta-analysis to experiments with random assignment in which the dependent measure was observed aggression toward another person who was physically present to evaluate causal effects on "real" aggressive behavior. For the total sample of 28 experiments, there was a significant effect of viewing violence on aggression. Effect sizes could be calculated for 12 studies; they were 0.27 weighted for sample size, and 0.40 unweighted.

These meta-analyses are consistent in supporting a positive relation of viewing violence to aggressive and antisocial behavior, but Paik and Comstock (1994) found larger effect sizes than the other two. For experimental studies alone, their effect size was 0.80 in contrast to 0.40 in Wood et al.'s (1991) analysis. Paik and Comstock (1994) included many more studies, lending stability to their estimates, but some of those studies may be the less ecologically valid laboratory experiments excluded by Wood et al. (1991). Hearold (1986) found that effect sizes decreased as the external validity of the studies increased. Investigations using natural settings and naturally occurring measures of aggression are probably subject to more influences from variables extraneous to the experimental manipulation than are highly controlled measures and settings. What is impressive about these results is the consistency of pattern.

Longitudinal Studies. In three different studies, viewing was measured by having children mark programs they watched often on a list of popular television programs; aggression was measured by peer nominations. Milavsky et al. (1982), measured these variables for boys on six occasions over 3 years. Regressions were used to determine whether viewing at one occasion predicted aggression at the next occasion with prior aggression statistically controlled. Most of the coefficients were positive, but did not reach statistical significance. The authors, who were employed by NBC, concluded that no effects of viewing were found. Other methodological experts (Cook, Kendziersky, & Thomas, 1983), however, concluded that the pattern of coefficients did indicate positive effects.

Among boys assessed at ages 8 and 18 in another investigation, preference for television violence at age 8 predicted aggression at age 18 (Eron, Lefkowitz, Huesmann, & Walder, 1972). More recently, the sample was studied again at age 30. Viewing violence at age 8 predicted violent crime at age 30 (though this finding is tenuous because of reduced sample size) (Huesmann & Miller, 1994). There were no significant relations for females.

In the 1980s, parallel studies were conducted in the United States, Poland, Israel (both kibbutz and city), Australia, Finland, and the Netherlands (Huesmann & Eron, 1986; Huesmann & Miller, 1994; Wiegerman, Kuttschreuter, & Baarda; 1992). First- and third-grade children were followed for 2 years (until they reached third and fifth grades). Violence viewing was measured by children's reports, and aggression was assessed by peer nominations. Children living in a kibbutz in Israel showed no relations between viewing and aggressive behavior, but there were positive relations for boys in all the other groups. Viewing violence in earlier grades predicted later aggression; coefficients were statistically significant in four of six comparisons. Similar patterns occurred for girls in all except one sample (Australia), but the coefficients were statistically significant in only two of the six comparisons. There were no instances in which viewing was negatively related to aggression. These studies also provided evidence for a bidirectional effect of violence viewing and behavior; in most samples, early measures of aggression also predicted later viewing of violence.

Overall, the longitudinal studies support theories predicting that violence contributes to children's learned patterns of behavior or scripts in ways that can be manifested in behavior well beyond childhood.

Perceived Reality and Responses to Violence

Adults (including college students) react to violence perceived as "real" with more aggression than to violence they believe is fictional (Jo & Berkowitz, 1994). The evidence is less consistent for children. In the 1950s, Himmelweit, Oppenheim, and Vince (1958) found that children reported more discomfort about realistic violence than about ritualized violence (cartoons). Feshbach (1972) showed 9- to 11-year-olds film footage of a campus riot experimentally attributed as real versus staged. In a help-hurt game after viewing, there was more game aggression from those assigned to the "real" attribution. Nevertheless, almost all of the research testing violence effects concerns fictional programs, including cartoons. It may be the case that real or realistic violence has greater effects, but behavior *is* influenced by fictional television.

Issues of Interpretation

Few if any would dispute that a relation of viewing violence to aggressive behavior has been demonstrated. There is disagreement, however, on why that relation exists and how important it is.

Some argue that viewing and aggression do not cause one another, but are both a result of other antecedents. This argument does not apply to experiments, but possible "third variables" are always a concern in naturalistic studies. Wiegerman et al. (1992) concluded that the small association of viewing with aggression in their Dutch sample was due to the effects of low intelligence on preference for violent television and on aggression (even though they measured intelligence at the end of the study). In several major studies, however, many of the likely candidates for common antecedents have been controlled, and the associations of viewing with aggression remained (cf., Friedrich-Cofer & Huston, 1986).

A second issue is the magnitude of effects. Are effect sizes of .27 to .40 socially important? The bulk of the correlations between viewing and aggression are in the range from .16 to .30 (i.e., viewing accounts for 2.6% to 9% of the variance in aggression). Some (e.g., McGuire, 1986) argue that such small effects are unimpressive or unimportant. Others see the cup as half full rather than half empty, emphasizing the consistency of the findings. Rosenthal (1986) demonstrated that even small correlations represent associations with practical significance. For example, when the correlation is .16, 42% of the children whose viewing is below the median are highly aggressive, and 58% of those with viewing above the median are highly aggressive. When the correlation is .30, the difference is 35% versus 65%. We believe that such differences do have practical significance.

Sex

Sexual Content on Television

The sexual content in television programs, movies, and popular music is a continuing source of public debate and concern. Over the past 20+ years, direct and indirect references to erotic sexual acts have become more prevalent and explicit in broadcast television. Sexual acts (e.g., kissing, hugging, erotic touching) are shown often, and, although sexual intercourse is shown relatively infrequently on broadcast television, it is often implied by context and verbal references (Harris, 1994; Sapolsky & Tabarlet, 1991; Truglio, 1993). Moreover, movies on pay cable and videotape offer explicit depictions of nudity and sexual intercourse.

What has not changed over time are the contextual messages. Sex is shown as recreational; themes of competition, emphasis on physical attractiveness, and portraying sexuality as a defining attribute of masculinity or femininity are frequent (Ward, 1995). The partners involved are usually not married, at least to each other, nor are they in a committed relationship (Fernandez-Collado, Greenberg, Korzenny, & Atkin, 1978; Greenberg et al., 1993; Trugio, 1993; Ward, 1995). For example, in one content analysis, two-thirds of the verbal and contextual references to intercourse involved uncommitted couples; only 14% involved couples who were married to each other (see Figure 15.9) (Truglio, 1993).

Television sexual messages rarely refer to contraception, abortion, or "safer sex" practices; yet, people do not often get pregnant or contract sexually transmitted diseases (Lowry & Towles, 1987; Sapolsky & Tabarlet, 1991; Truglio, 1993). There are relatively few references to socially discouraged sexual behaviors (e.g., prostitution, rape, voyeurism).

Children's Knowledge, Attitudes, and Behavior

Television may play a more important role in sexual socialization than in other domains because of: "(1) the adult nature of most programming children watch; (2) children's

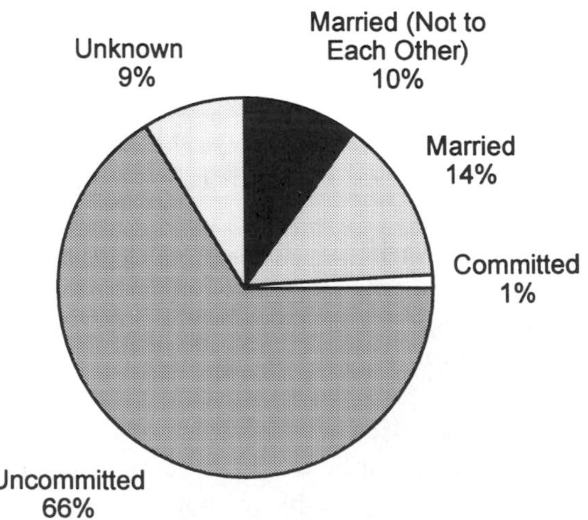

Figure 15.9 Frequency of verbal references to sexual intercourse in conversations of couples on prime-time television by marital status of couples involved (Truglio, 1993). *Sex in the 90s: What are the lessons from prime-time TV?* Paper presented at the Meeting of the Society for Research in Child Development, New Orleans. Reprinted with permission of author.

limited access to countervailing information and/or ideas; (3) the 'realism' with which roles, relationships, and lifestyles are portrayed; and (4) the overwhelming consistency of the messages about sexuality which are communicated" (Roberts, 1982, p. 209).

The small number of studies conducted with adolescents (there are none with children) provide few answers about whether, how, or under what circumstances such socializing effects occur. Two studies show positive correlations of television viewing with sexually permissive attitudes (D. Greenberg, cited in Godbold & Cantor, 1994) and reported intercourse (Brown & Newcomer, 1991). One longitudinal study, however, demonstrated no relation between viewing television in general or sexual content in particular and adolescents' initiation of sexual activity (Peterson, Moore, & Furstenberg, 1991).

As children enter adolescence, they understand many of the sexual innuendoes and messages on television (Silverman-Watkins & Sprafkin, 1983), and many of them are aware of how the sexuality portrayed on television differs from real life. When adolescents from 8th to 12th grade were asked to describe sexual scenarios on television and in real life, they showed awareness that television overrepresents the probability of having sex with someone you meet for the first time and underrepresents the negative consequences of sexual intercourse. They rated the likelihood of getting a sexually transmitted disease, getting pregnant, and using contraception as higher in real life than on television. Nevertheless, heavy television viewers reported using television as a guide to interpersonal behavior (Truglio, 1990).

Because this review does not extend to research on college students and adults, we have not included a large literature investigating the effects of erotic content and violent sexuality on attitudes and behavior of young adults. In those populations, portrayals of sexual violence lead to negative attitudes about women, desensitization about violence against women, and acceptance of the myth that women enjoy rape. Some investigators argue that nonviolent sexual content produces similar effects, but there is considerable disagreement about that conclusion (cf., Harris, 1994, for review). As children and adolescents are exposed to erotic content, it is likely that some of the same effects occur for them as for older individuals.

Television presents a consistent set of messages portraying erotic sexuality as a casual, recreational activity with little emotional or personal commitment and few negative consequences. Theory and common sense suggests that such messages are incorporated by children, but little evidence exists. Public discussion of sex in the United States is dominated by strong ideologically based disagreements, making research with children and adolescents difficult, if not impossible, to conduct.

Emotion

Emotional arousal is at the core of some of the theories of media effects, but the research on children's emotional responses to media portrayals has had little formal guidance by these overarching theories. Instead a problem-oriented, general developmental model, focused to some extent on cognitive and empathic changes in the determinants of children's emotional reactions has prevailed (Cantor, 1994, 1996). On the whole, young children (below 7 or 8) respond emotionally primarily to concrete observable stimuli on television; older children increasingly respond with empathy to the plight of people they observe and to abstract or psychological instigators of emotion.

Emotional Expression

Television can teach children about forms of expressing emotion and about recognizing emotions in others (Huston et al., 1992). Following a content analysis of emotional themes in family-based situation comedies, two studies of children's cognitive and emotional responses to such programs were conducted (Weiss & Wilson 1993, 1994, 1995). Older children (8–10) and frequent viewers had a deeper understanding of the typical emotional storyline and differentiated between positive and negative emotions of characters, although they, like the younger (5–7) and less frequent viewers had a generally positive and prosocial schema for emotions in such programs. Introduction of a humorous subplot confused the younger children's understanding of the main plot and weakened the discrimination between the main character's fear and anger at both age levels.

Fear

Attraction to Horror. Why are children and adults attracted to horror films? Many parents have had the experience reported by a friend whose teenage son insisted on watching *Friday Fright Night* week after week, even though he often awakened later feeling terrified. Viewers' attraction to films that arouse fear is a paradox (Cantor & Reilly, 1982). The happy ending and just resolution of the plot is one major reason that adults report liking scary films (Tamborini & Stiff, 1987; Zillman, Weaver, Mundorf, & Aust, 1986), and 3- to 11-year-olds mentioned relief from threat or danger as a reason for liking movies and TV shows (Cantor & Hoffner, 1991).

Zillman (1980) proposed that the more suspense is provided by foreshadowing of danger, and the longer that suspense is maintained with some degree of uncertainty, the greater should be the emotional response to the scary events when they do occur, and the more liked the show should be if it is happily and justly resolved. This hypothesis was tested by showing stories with resolved or unresolved endings. Viewers who experienced the most worry or fear reported the greatest enjoyment, regardless of the ending. People with high negative affect showed a weak tendency to enjoy the resolved ending and not to enjoy the unresolved ending (Hoffner & Cantor, 1991).

Developmental Changes. In general, younger children are more afraid of concrete creatures and things; children in middle childhood fear less visible threats to life and family; and adolescents fear threats to community, society, and civilization (Cantor, Wilson, & Hoffner, 1986). This change is accompanied, and perhaps caused by a shift in focus from frightening objects and actions to empathy with the emotional and verbal reactions of others.

Wilson and Cantor (1985) showed that whereas 3- to 5-year-olds were frightened by a scary stimulus, 9- to 11-year-olds were more frightened by shots of a character's facial, vocal, or verbal reactions to that stimulus. In a subsequent study, Wilson, Cantor, Gordon, and Zillman (1986) compared 7- and 8-year-olds with low and average IQs on empathy for a character who initially behaved either badly or well, and who subsequently either felt happy or sad. The low-IQ children felt similar emotions to those of the protagonist, regardless of his behavior; the average-IQ children reported affect similar to the protagonist who behaved well and opposite to the protagonist who behaved badly.

Reducing Fear through Desensitization. Presenting successively increasing approximations of a frightening stimulus in a supportive and nonthreatening context is a common technique for reducing fear. In several studies, children's fearful reactions to programs portraying such animals as snakes, tarantulas, lizards, and earthworms were reduced by prior exposure to videos showing them in nonthreatening contexts or by actual interaction with the animals (Weiss, Imrich, & Wilson, 1993; Wilson, 1987, 1989a; Wilson & Cantor, 1987). In a TV adventure series called *The Incredible Hulk,* children were frightened by the scenes in which a mild-mannered scientist was transformed into a large, ugly, green creature who expressed anger and terrified the "bad guys" before triumphing over them. The desensitization video showed the familiar, gentle "Mr. Rogers" visiting the set of *The Incredible Hulk* and observing the makeup artists transform the actor into the frightening superhero. Children from 3 to 10 who viewed this video showed less affect while watching the Hulk in his monster role than did those who had not seen the *Mr. Rogers* documentary first (Cantor, Sparks, & Hoffner, 1988).

Fact versus Fiction

Television often exposes children to real events or fictional simulations that are potentially frightening. During the Persian Gulf War, the *Challenger* disaster, and the much-anticipated movie about a nuclear disaster, *The Day After,* our center received many calls asking whether children ought to be shielded from exposure. Several investigations indicate that children are affected by naturally occurring exposure to news or fiction about wars and technological disasters, but few children seem to experience long-term, serious emotional consequences (Cantor, 1992). During the Persian Gulf War, few parents reported chronic worry and sleep disturbance associated with viewing televised coverage of war news (Cantor, Mares, & Oliver, 1993). On the other hand, viewing fictional disasters increases children's estimates of their probability in the real world (Cantor & Omdahl, 1991).

There are developmental and gender differences in the ways that children respond to disaster news. Young children (K-3) mentioned disaster stories when asked whether any news frightened them, whereas older children (Grades 4–6) cited crime stories as scary and personalized the emotions of people in the news, often applying the stories to themselves (Wilson & Smith, 1995). During the Persian Gulf War, elementary school students were more often frightened by concrete things shown (e.g., weapons, victims getting hurt, dying), whereas adolescents mentioned the larger issues of oil, Saddam Hussein, U. S. involvement, terrorism in the United States, and nuclear war. Young children's questions were concrete ("How far away is it?" "Can it get to here?"); older children asked "why" questions about the geopolitical and economic causes of the war (Cantor et al., 1993).

Shortly after the *Challenger* disaster, which was seen on television at school almost immediately after it occurred, boys and girls in Grades 4 to 6 reported anxiety, grief, sleep disturbance, obsessive thoughts about the event, and fears that it might occur again. Boys more often expressed concern about the loss of equipment, training time, data, and valuable astronauts; the girls more often focused their reported negative affect on the families of the victims, and the personal tragedies resulting from loss of life (Wright et al., 1989).

It is reasonable that children old enough to understand the difference between televised fiction and reality would react more strongly to real events than to fictional ones, but the evidence from experimental studies is mixed. In one study (Piemyat, 1992), children saw a short film about an earthquake or a tornado; half of each group saw news footage, and the other half saw a fictional story. The level of reality had no effect on children's reported fear, but children who saw news expressed more sadness about the suffering of the people in the video than those who saw fiction. Reality cues may affect empathy with the people viewed more than the raw emotion of fear.

Social Roles

Television programs are rarely designed to convey information about gender, cultural diversity, work, family life, or social roles, but such messages are implicit in the selection of people and activities presented. In the 1960s and early 1970s, advocates seeking equality for African Americans and women pinpointed media portrayals as a target for change. Theories emphasizing social learning, schema formation, or cultivation all imply that television messages can be conveyed by the number of people in different groups who appear as well as by their actions and status when they are shown. All predict that television portrayals of social roles can influence children's beliefs, attitudes, and adoption of roles.

In this section, we discuss media influences on children's understanding of gender, ethnic group, occupations, and family life. There are many other social groups (e.g., children, the elderly, people with disabilities) to which the principles identified here probably apply (Huston et al., 1992).

Content of the Medium—What's On

Gender. On television, women are underrepresented in relation to their numbers in the population (Huston et al., 1992). Over the 17 years from 1967 through 1985, the proportion of women increased from one-fourth in the late 1960s to about one-third of all characters in the 1980s. In entertainment programs designed for children, however, the ratio of male to female characters is very unbalanced (4 or 5 to 1) (Signorielli, 1993b). Educational and informative programs on both public and commercial stations had much more balanced ratios (less than 2 to 1) in one analysis (Neapolitan & Huston, 1994b). In another, the ratios in educational programs did not differ from noneducational shows (Williams & Cox, 1995).

Portrayals of men and women conform to social stereotypes, and many of them did not change from 1967 to 1985. Women are more likely than men to be young, to be attractive and nurturing, to be in a context of romance, home, or family, and to be victimized. Men are powerful and dominant; women are nurturant and complementary. In advertisements, voice-overs are overwhelmingly male. Both men and women are unlikely to be married, but when women are married, only 25% are employed (compared with 75% of married men). Gender roles are particularly stereotyped in children's programs (Comstock, 1991; Durkin, 1985a; Signorielli, 1989, 1993b).

Women are shown more often than men as sex objects, in skimpy attire, with cameras focused on their bodies (Williams, Baron, Phillips, Travis, & Jackson, 1986). Rock videos and advertisements accompanying them show White men as predominant characters. Women are submissive, passive, attractive, sensual, decorative, and sexual (Signorielli, 1993b; Signorielli, McLeod, & Healy, 1994).

Women's work lives on television did change by the 1980s. More women had an occupation, and more were in typically male occupations than in earlier years (Huston et al., 1992; Signorielli, 1993b).

Ethnic Group. Most of the major characters on television are White men. African Americans are the only ethnic minority with numbers on television even close to their percentage of the population. In the early 1990s, African Americans constituted 11% of prime-time characters, 9% on daytime serials, but only 3% on Saturday morning children's programs (Greenberg & Brand, 1994). Because of a gender imbalance for minority characters, African American females are seen infrequently. People of Hispanic, Asian, or Native American origins are virtually absent from the television world (Greenberg & Brand, 1994).

In programming for children, educational shows (both public and commercial) present a rich array of ethnic diversity, but commercial entertainment programs have very little. In a content analysis of PBS and commercial *educational* programs broadcast in the early 1990s, 38% and 27%, respectively, of all characters were minorities (Neapolitan & Huston, 1994b). Another analysis of United States and Canadian channels found that 70% of the informative programs and 33% of the noninformative programs showed at least one major character from a minority ethnic group. Ethnic characters were shown in a position of power or authority in 59% of the informative programs and 11%

of the noninformative programs (Williams & Cox, 1995). Programs on public television show people from many ethnic groups interacting with other, and they often feature content about cultural patterns (e.g., food, holidays) (Greenberg & Brand, 1993).

Work and Occupational Roles. In the world of television, a great many people have professional occupations (e.g., doctors, artists, writers, athletes) or law enforcement jobs. In the real world, a much larger proportion of the population comprises blue-collar workers, secretaries, and managers than one would guess from watching television (Signorielli, 1993a).

Television portrayals of many occupations reinforce sex stereotypes and show the glamorous, dramatic aspects of jobs, while the hard work, boredom, and routine elements are deemphasized. Medical professionals are shown in hospital settings; doctors are male and powerful; nurses are female and submissive; they treat pathology more than they engage in prevention; acute illnesses prevail over chronic illnesses; and they use drugs and biomedical treatments more than psychological-behavioral treatments (DeFleur, 1964; Signorielli, 1993a; Turow & Coe, 1985). Police officers on entertainment television are hardened, tough characters who spend time solving violent crimes, and they usually succeed in tracking down and arresting criminals (Dominick, 1973; Lichter & Lichter, 1983).

Negative stereotypes of some occupations abound. In one analysis of popular children's programs, scientists were compared with characters who used technology or supernatural forces. Scientists were more often mentally ill (the "mad scientist" image); more often had harmful or selfish motives; were more often unsuccessful and were punished in the plot resolution. No female scientists appeared (Potts, Martinez, & Dedmon, 1993).

Family. Although most adults in the United States are married, the majority of television adults are not. Women are more likely than men to be married, and non-White women are married more often than White women (Signorielli, 1991). Home, family, and marriage constitute an important part of some genres (e.g., situation comedies), but are rarely shown in others (e.g., adventure programs). Both two-parent and single-parent families populate television; in fact, some have argued that single-parent families, particularly single-father families, are overrepresented (cf., Huston et al., 1992). Family life on television is often, but not always idealized. On the whole, television families communicate effectively with each other and engage in conflict resolution more often than in conflict escalation (Skill, Wallace, & Cassata, 1990). Nevertheless, family programs popular with children showed somewhat more conflict in 1989–1990 than in the late 1970s (Heintz, 1992), and informal observation suggests that patterns of sarcasm and hostility among family members have become more prevalent in the 1990s.

Relations of Viewing to Beliefs, Attitudes, and Behavior

Gender. Detecting the contribution of television to children's conceptions of gender roles is particularly difficult because many of the stereotypic images on television reflect widespread beliefs and attitudes to which children are exposed in many contexts. Viewing entertainment television is weakly correlated with stereotypic beliefs, but less with attitudes and sex-typed behavior (Durkin, 1985b). In a meta-analysis of studies investigating children's sex stereotypes, heavy viewing of entertainment programs was associated with sex stereotype knowledge (Signorella, Bigler, & Liben, 1993).

Cultivation analyses have included both longitudinal assessments and statistical controls for parent education, child's academic achievement, and other potential confounds. Morgan (1982) tested the same children in sixth, seventh, and eighth grades. For girls, reports of television viewing in early waves predicted increased scores on a measure of sexist attitudes by eighth grade, but early sexism scores predicted later viewing for boys. In a later study, adolescents were asked about sex-typed chores (e.g., doing dishes, yard work) on two occasions. Television viewing predicted later sex-stereotyped beliefs about chores, but not how likely individuals were to perform the chores (Morgan, 1987). This finding was replicated for fourth and fifth graders tested on a single occasion (Signorielli & Lears, 1992).

Boys may be especially likely to learn stereotypes for their own gender because they choose to watch same-sex characters and programs featuring behaviors stereotyped for their gender. Boys attend to same-sex characters within a program and select programs with predominantly male characters (cartoons, sports, and adventure), especially after they have achieved cognitive gender constancy (Huston et al., 1990; Luecke-Aleksa et al., 1995).

The influence of television is more evident when counterstereotypes are shown, though their impact depends on children's initial attitudes and receptivity (Durkin, 1985c). The changes in women's occupational roles on television in the 1980s provided a natural context for testing children's reactions. In one study, it appeared that girls had incorporated the new messages. Girls' television viewing predicted positive attitudes and aspirations for nontraditional occupations shown often on television (e.g., lawyer), but not their attitudes and aspirations for nontraditional occupations that were not shown on television. No relations appeared for boys (Wroblewski & Huston, 1988).

Several small-scale experiments have shown some effects of counterstereotyped portrayals (Durkin, 1985c; Jeffery & Durkin, 1989), but the most ambitious experiment was the program, *Freestyle,* produced around 1980. Thirteen half-hour episodes were broadcast on public television; both in-school and home viewing were evaluated for children in fourth to sixth grade. When school viewing was accompanied by class discussion, changes in stereotypes and attitudes occurred and endured in a 9-month follow-up. Girls expressed intentions to participate in some "masculine" activities as a consequence of viewing (Comstock, 1991; Johnston & Ettema, 1982, 1984).

Race and Ethnic Group. Images of minorities on television may affect others' beliefs about them, though the data for children are remarkably scarce (Greenberg & Brand, 1994). Slightly more attention has been devoted to the impact of images (or lack thereof) on children's views of themselves and their own ethnic group (see Berry & Asaman, 1993 for reviews). Almost all of the empirical work has been conducted with African Americans.

Media might influence images of minorities through two mechanisms: whether the group appears at all (representation) and the content of portrayals when they do appear. The mere presence of African Americans on television appears to be important to African American children. As noted earlier, African American children and adolescents use television more extensively and rely on it as a source of knowledge more heavily than European Americans. They choose programs with African American characters as favorites, and they identify with African American characters (Greenberg & Brand, 1994).

Children's attitudes and beliefs about their own ethnic group must be distinguished from self-esteem. One's feeling of self-worth does not derive solely (or perhaps even primarily) from one's beliefs about a reference group to which one belongs (Cross, 1985). Nevertheless, if television presents positive role models, both racial attitudes and self-perceptions may be influenced.

Some evidence suggests that viewing television with African American characters can contribute to children's self-esteem even when the attributes portrayed are not all positive, perhaps because representation itself is affirming. Stroman (1986) found a positive correlation of television viewing with self-esteem for 7- to 13-year-old African American girls, but no correlation for boys. In another study of African American fourth and fifth graders, the regularity with which children watched "Black" TV shows was positively related to self-esteem; the association was especially strong when children had positive perceptions of Black characters (McDermott & Greenberg, 1984).

Experiments have produced mixed results. In one experimental study, children were shown cartoons with Black characters; children's positive attitudes to their race increased regardless of whether the portrayals were positive or negative. This finding was reversed in a subsequent study using a situation comedy (Graves, 1993). Freeman (1993) found that boys' racial attitudes were more positive after viewing cartoons showing prosocial male African American characters; there were no effects for girls.

Occupations. Television serves as one source of information about the world of work (DeFleur & DeFleur, 1967). A cultivation analysis of a national survey of high school seniors demonstrated that heavy viewers subscribed to two views of work promoted by TV: value on high status and money, and value on relaxed pace and freedom (Signorielli, 1993a). Potts and Martinez (1994) found that children's evaluations of scientists were negatively related to cartoon viewing (in which negative images of scientists predominate), not to viewing other genres. Experimental studies also show that children acquire beliefs about the activities and attributes of particular occupations from fictional dramas on television as well as from factual programs (Huston, Wright, Fitch, Wroblewski, & Piemyat, 1993).

By middle childhood, children are somewhat aware of the distortions in televised occupational portrayals, at least for jobs with which they have some real-world contact. When asked what police officers or nurses do on television or in real life, children who described television police and nurses rated them as more sex-stereotyped, more affluent, more involved in dramatic activities such as catching criminals, and having to expend less effort than did the children describing real-life police and nurses (Wright et al., 1995).

Families. Television families serve as models for children, often embodying the cohesion, communication, and caring they wish for in their own families (Schiff & Truglio, 1995). Critics' concerns about television cultivating antifamily attitudes do not appear well-founded for children, but receive slight support among adolescents. Children consider conventional family structures (two parents) more normative than other family structures (Dorr et al., 1990). In a survey of high school seniors controlling for gender, political views, parent education, and grades, White high school seniors who were heavy television viewers more often said they intended to marry and have children than did light viewers. For non-White respondents, however, heavy viewing predicted low intention to marry and have children. At the same time, frequent TV viewers were more apt to endorse the idea that marriages don't last, people should live together before marrying, and monogamy is too restrictive (Signorielli, 1991).

HOW RESEARCH IS USED

Television, video games, and other electronic media generate wide public concern and, as a result, interest in research findings. Research on television and its effects is used in discussions of public policy that involve decisions about government funding for public television or about regulation of content. Organizations of advocates, professionals, and industry representatives often use research to buttress their positions in policy discussions.

Both formative and summative research play important roles in creating and evaluating educational programs designed for children. Research on children's comprehension and social responses to television can also help to guide media literacy education. And, research can inform parents about the positive and negative effects of television as well as about ways of helping their children to use the medium intelligently.

Public Policy

The two major avenues through which government can influence media are regulation and funding; both are severely limited in the United States. The federal government can regulate broadcasters through the Communications Act of 1934, which established that the airwaves belong to the public. A broadcaster (i.e., a station) is granted a license for a fixed period of time and is required to serve in the "public interest, convenience, and necessity" (Communications Act of 1934, p. 51). The Federal Communications Commission (FCC) is responsible for determining whether stations meet this requirement. The FCC has no jurisdiction over such nonbroadcast outlets as videotapes, video games, or films, and it has very limited authority to regulate cable distribution.

The second policy avenue is funding, usually for noncommercial television. In many industrialized countries (e.g., Great Britain, Japan, Germany), publicly funded television was available before commercial television and continues to occupy a major role. In the United States, commercial television was well established in the 1950s; public television began in the late 1960s and has remained relatively weak.

Despite these limitations, research has been used to inform policy in three areas: (a) reducing socially harmful content, particularly violence and sex; (b) promoting programs with educational and informational value to children; and (c) protecting children from commercial exploitation. Research is cited frequently in these debates, but it seems to be used more often to buttress already-formed positions than to drive the debate or define the political agenda in any meaningful way (Huston, Watkins, & Kunkel, 1989).

Socially Harmful Content

Congressional committees began investigating the possible effects of violence in 1955; hearings and legislative proposals have occurred every 5 to 10 years since then. Social science research on the effects of television violence has formed part of the case for action. For example, in a hearing of the Senate Committee on the Judiciary, attended by one of the authors in 1987, three large tables were conspicuously piled high with books, journals, and papers containing reports of research on television violence.

In 1969, the Senate Subcommittee on Communications initiated research by requesting that the Surgeon General appoint a Scientific Advisory Committee on Television and Social Behavior to evaluate the scientific evidence. The National Institute of Mental Health was instructed to allocate $1,000,000 for a program of research to inform the deliberations of that committee (Rowland, 1983). The result was a strong core of research on the topic.

Research has been used to document the need for regulation by showing the pervasiveness of violence or its effects on viewers, but the methods used to regulate have typically not been based on empirical data. In 1990, a law was enacted allowing (not requiring) television broadcasters and cable companies to develop industry-wide codes to regulate content and advertising. This legislation was needed because earlier codes had been interpreted as violations of federal antitrust laws, but there is little evidence that it has had any effect.

Another approach is a rating system like that used for films. The 1996 Telecommunications Act requires television manufacturers to incorporate a "V chip" that allows a consumer to block programs designated with particular ratings. There are major difficulties in producing consensus about the definitions to be used in a rating system. Moreover, some people argue that labeling a program as sexual or violent would be counterproductive because it would increase its attraction to young audiences, a hypothesis supported for boys, but not girls, in a recent survey (Cantor & Harrison, 1996).

Audience research showing that children are heavy viewers in prime time formed one basis in the mid-1970s for the "family viewing hour," an agreement among broadcasters not to show programs that were inappropriate for general family viewing during the hour before prime time and the first hour of prime time (i.e., 7–9 P.M. on the East and West coasts; 6–8 P.M. in the middle of the country). This practice was ultimately ruled illegal (Rowland, 1983). Even if such a restriction were imposed, it would not protect most children from most of the violence available on television. Programs designed for children (e.g., Saturday morning cartoons) would be unaffected, and many children watch television well after 8 or 9 P.M.

Barriers to Government Action

Despite the long-term and repeated interest in television violence in the Congress, and despite a general consensus that the research evidence supports some causal effects of violent television on aggression, almost no legislation has been enacted that would regulate television content. Two important factors impede attempts to regulate media content through legislation or regulatory action in the United States. First, any limitation on content risks violating First Amendment rights to freedom of expression, and, as a result, encounters opposition from journalists, broadcasters, and civil libertarians who express understandable opposition to establishing a principle of government control over media content. Moreover, even those who support such regulation do not agree on which content is objectionable and which is not.

The second major barrier is economic. In the United States, most broadcasting is commercially supported; its first goal is to make a profit. The industry has a powerful lobby that opposes most forms of regulation (Huston et al., 1989). The television industry also uses research to support its position. In the 1970s, both NBC and CBS supported large-scale studies of violence effects on boys (Milavsky et al., 1982; Wells, 1973). Industry representatives regularly participate in hearings and research discussions, presenting the case that the available research does not merit the conclusion that viewing violence is causally related to aggression.

Promoting Educational and Informational Programs

Governments and publicly controlled agencies throughout the world play a major role in funding the production, distribution, and broadcasting of educational and informational programs for children. Many countries collect a monthly fee from every television owner; the proceeds are used to pay for noncommercial, public television. In the United States, the federal government pays a smaller and smaller portion of the costs of public broadcasting; government agencies can and sometimes do make grants to producers.

Evaluative research is often cited in arguments promoting public support of educational programs, and funding agencies sometimes require evaluation as a condition for grants. In the first two seasons of *Sesame Street,* an extensive evaluation of impact by the Educational Testing Service was a part of the overall plan. Private producers occasionally commission research as well, either to help them improve their product or to justify it. For example, the producers of the controversial *Channel One* news program for schools funded evaluation studies to determine what students learned from it, and they used the information to improve the program over a 3-year period (Johnston, Brzezinski, & Anderman, 1994). They specifically excluded, however, any test of the effects of the commercials that schools are required to include with the news show.

In the United States, regulation is also designed to promote educational and informational programs for children on commercial outlets. The Children's Television Act of 1990 required broadcasters to provide programming that serves the educational and informational needs of children, but did not specify any minimum time that stations should devote to such programs.

Research played a role in passage of the law and has been useful in subsequent discussions of enforcement. The legislation begins by stating that "it has been demonstrated that television can assist children to learn important information, skills, values and behavior," (Children's Television Act, 1990). The law itself, however, had little initial impact because enforcement was minimal. Kunkel and Canepa (1994) examined the program titles listed by stations as "educational" in license renewal applications filed in 1992. Although many of the titles appeared to be legitimately educational (e.g., *Beakman's World, Real News for Kids*), many others were entertainment programs that few would regard as informative (e.g., *Teenage Mutant Ninja Turtles, Bugs and Tweety Show*).

Partly as a result of good data produced by researchers, in April 1995 the Federal Communications Commission issued a Notice of Proposed Rule Making to institute additional procedures to enforce the law and to make it more effective. In 1996, they issued a decision interpreting the law as requiring broadcasters to provide at least 3 hours per week of educational and informative programs for children. Research was cited in their deliberations, but the decision was reached only after intensive negotiation with the broadcasters by Vice President Gore, with the clear support of President Clinton.

Although research on the positive effects of educational television is useful in this debate, many of the questions about what regulations would be effective have received little research attention. For example, the Commission debated whether or not to allow short segments (e.g., less than 5 minutes) to satisfy the requirement. Research on the relative impacts and utility of educational programming of different lengths would have been quite useful. Similarly, they debated requiring stations to label and advertise programming as educational, but wondered whether such labels might reduce young viewers' attraction to the program.

Protecting Children from Advertising

Children became a "market" for advertisers early in the history of television. The first goal of commercial programs is to increase the sales of their advertisers' products. In the 1970s, there was a great deal of research on children's responses to advertising establishing that very young children often fail to distinguish advertising from program material and do not understand the intent of commercials (C. Atkin, 1982; Federal Trade Commission, 1978). Research was central to regulatory efforts by both the Federal Communication Commission and the Federal Trade Commission; nonetheless, those efforts failed (Kunkel & Roberts, 1991). The same evidence may have been important in 1990, however, when Congress placed limits on the amount of time devoted to advertising in programs for children (Children's Television Act, 1990).

In the 1980s, a new method of merchandising appeared in the form of product-related programs (or program-length commercials) in which the central character(s) was based on a toy that was promoted simultaneously in the marketplace. By the end of the 1980s, the majority of syndicated weekday and network shows were toy-related, and the majority of toy advertisements were for products featured in children's programs (Wartella, 1995).

Both theory and common sense suggest that the combination of product-related programs and advertisements could make it more difficult for children to distinguish programs from commercials; such confusion might be especially likely if commercials and programs containing the same "characters" were adjacent. In two experiments, this prediction was confirmed for young children; when they saw both a program and an ad with the same toy or cartoon character, they were less likely to distinguish the two than when they saw a program and ad containing different toys or cartoon characters (Kunkel, 1988; Wilson & Weiss, 1992). Although neither of these studies demonstrated clear effects on children's attitudes about or desire for the product shown, these findings support the value of a prohibition on "host selling" by the Federal Communications Commission.

Product-related programming is of concern for reasons other than its commercial intent. Its content is formulaic, violent, and stereotypic (showing few minority or female characters), even compared with other cartoon television, according to a content analysis of 16 hours of children's programs (Eaton & Dominick, 1991). Moreover, when programs featured toys, children's play with those toys was more imitative and less imaginative than when the toys available did not match the program (Greenfield et al., 1990). Because product-related programs are offered under terms that make them very inexpensive for stations to broadcast, they essentially squeeze more creative works out of the market.

Another controversial development of the 1990s was *Channel One,* a daily television broadcast consisting of 10 minutes of news and 2 minutes of advertisements. Schools are offered video equipment in return for showing the program daily to their students. By 1995, it was being used by 12,000 schools and reaching 40% of children in Grades 6 through 12 (Wartella, 1995). Teachers and principals generally liked the service, and students showed modest gains in knowledge of current events, particularly after the program was revised to include more serious news (Johnston et al., 1994). Nonetheless, critics have expressed concern that the school environment may lend authority and credence to advertisements shown there. In fact, one study demonstrated that students in *Channel One* schools, compared with those in schools without *Channel One,* expressed more positive affect toward products advertised and more frequent intention to purchase them, as well as greater consumer orientation generally (Brand & Greenberg, 1994).

Program Production

Both formative and summative research play an important role in the design and evaluation of educational programming. Children's Television Workshop, the producers of *Sesame Street* and several other educational programs has developed a model of production that includes continuous collaboration of formative researchers with writers and producers. The Sesame Street Research Department is responsible for writing the curriculum goals and objectives. When new content areas are introduced, research on children's knowledge about them is regularly conducted to determine what aspects of the content should be emphasized (e.g., Mielke, 1983; Sesame Street Research, 1992).

What Parents Can Do

Parents' greatest influence on children's television use occurs through modeling and the television environment they provide at home. What, how, and how much television parents view has a direct impact on children not only because it provides a model, but because children are directly exposed to programs that parents are viewing.

Coviewing

Many psychologists recommend that parents and children watch television together. Coviewing can provide an opportunity to discuss or reinforce content messages, making the viewing experience richer for the child. For example, in observations of toddlers watching *Sesame Street,* parents often used it as a "talking picture book," labeling and pointing to characters and events on the program (Lemish & Rice, 1986). Similarly, mothers used *Sesame Street* as a source of informal teaching interactions with young children in laboratory observations (St. Peters, 1993). For older children, when adults provide explanatory comments, children understand social content messages better than they do without such comments (W. Collins, Sobol, & Westby, 1981; Watkins, Calvert, Huston-Stein, & Wright, 1980).

Coviewing with someone the child knows, parents or siblings, can also help a child cope with fear produced by television programming. When children were asked by Wilson, Hoffner, and Cantor (1987) to check which of eight popular coping strategies they thought would help them feel better if they were frightened by something on TV, the item, "sit by mom or dad" was chosen most. In an experiment, preschool children were shown a scary story while viewing with an older sibling or alone. The coviewing preschoolers were less emotionally aroused and liked the program better than did those who watched alone, but were less likely to understand instructions that the scary part was all a dream (Wilson & Weiss, 1993).

Much of the evidence suggests, however, that coviewing does not involve such active parent-child interaction, but occurs because the parent is viewing and the child is nearby. In one investigation, the amount of coviewing could be predicted simply from the total amount of individual viewing that parents and children did (Field, 1989). In another (St. Peters et al., 1991), the amount of time spent coviewing general audience programs was predicted by the amount of time parents viewed similar programs without children present, but not by the child's individual viewing patterns. Parent preferences and viewing habits appeared to determine coviewing; parents did not seem to be making efforts to join children in watching programs of particular interest to the child. They were present only 25% of the time that children were watching child audience programs.

There is little evidence that naturally occurring coviewing has strong beneficial effects. Frequent coviewing did not reduce children's perceptions that situation comedies were socially realistic; in fact, coviewers said they could use the program content as a means of learning about the world (Dorr et al., 1989). Both interviews and home observations indicate that parents and children talk about television, but that occasions when parents explain content, discuss values, and interpret programs are relatively rare (Comstock, 1991; Desmond, Singer, & Singer, 1990; Messaris & Sarett, 1981).

Regulation and Encouragement

Parental regulation of children's viewing is relatively effective for young children, but as children advance into middle childhood and adolescence, it becomes increasingly difficult to control their exposure to television. The evidence amassed by Cantor and Wilson (1984, 1988) suggests that efforts to prevent exposure to frightening programs are doomed to fail as children gain gradual independence from parental control.

Another strategy is to instruct children in techniques for avoiding emotionally arousing content. In one study (Wilson, 1989b), children in Grades K–1 or Grades 3–5 were told to turn off the TV whenever they started to feel afraid or to "cover your eyes" or "cover your ears" when the scary material begins. The "turn off the TV" strategy had no effect, and the "cover your eyes" strategy was partially effective for the younger children, but it actually enhanced emotional reactions and threatening interpretations of the content among the older children.

Explanations about Reality and Fiction

Parents can help children understand television by explanations designed to present factual information and to get the child to process and remember it. One popular technique among parents is simply telling the child that the events on TV are not real. Experimental studies show that this technique is effective with older children (roughly 8 and above), who understand the difference between factual and fictional television content, but not with younger children (Cantor & Wilson, 1984). In the ratings of effective and ineffective techniques for coping with frightening television, older children chose "tell yourself it's not real" more than younger ones (Wilson et al., 1987). Two reality explanations were compared as ameliorating treatments for fear reactions to the horror film, *Squirm.* One emphasized the special tricks used to create the frightening scene. The other explanation stressed the difference between TV magic and real life. Young children were not influenced by either treatment. The special-tricks explanation reduced older children's emotional reactions, but did not affect their cognitive interpretations. The real-life explanation had only weak effects on the children's interpretations (Wilson & Weiss, 1991).

When the threat in the frightening stimulus is a real or realistic one, as it is in news and documentaries and some fiction, an explanation that the risk, though real, is very, very small in the real world has opposite effects for older and for younger children. It makes younger children *more* afraid and older ones less so (Wilson & Cantor, 1987).

What Teachers and Child-Care Providers Can Do

Television in Child Care

Television is a pariah for many teachers and early childhood educators. They reject it as a source of beneficial learning, even when the content is educational. Child-care providers in family or home settings use television more than child-care centers or preschools, but both groups tend to show general child entertainment rather than using educational programming. They may be wasting an important opportunity, not only to use television to teach children, but in teaching children about how to use television. If the message about television is that one uses it for "down time" only to relax with undemanding entertainment, then children will build that habit. If the message is that television, like books and computers, can be an exciting source of learning, then children may use it for learning as well as entertainment in other contexts.

In the past several years, the distributors of both *Sesame Street* and *Mr. Rogers' Neighborhood* have produced and distributed supplementary curriculum materials and activities to be used in child care settings in conjunction with the television programs. Such materials are useful in helping children to rehearse prosocial and educational television messages and generalize them to their own environments (Friedrich & Stein, 1975; Friedrich-Cofer et al., 1979; D. Singer & Singer, 1994; J. Singer & Singer, 1994; Stein & Friedrich, 1975). Teachers can use a combination of television, books, play activities, and songs in teacher-led group activities or with individual children.

Media Literacy Education

For good or ill, television in all its forms is a central part of life in most industrialized societies. Many educators and others have argued that children should be taught media literacy or critical viewing skills, and a number of experimental tests of media literacy programs were carried out in the early 1980s. In most, elementary school-age children were exposed to a set of lessons covering a wide range of topics: the commercial and economic basis of television, the unreality of television content (especially violence), the production techniques used to create illusions on television, techniques for evaluating and understanding television programming (particularly its lack of realism), evaluating advertising critically, and making intelligent decisions about one's own viewing (J. Anderson, 1983; Corder-Bolz, 1982). Some concentrated specifically on advertising (e.g., Feshbach, Feshbach, & Cohen, 1982) and others included a range of content (e.g., Dorr, Graves, & Phelps, 1980; D. Singer, Zuckerman, & Singer, 1980; Sprafkin, Gadow, & Kant, 1988; Sprafkin, Watkins, & Gadow, 1990; Vooijs & van der Voort, 1993; Watkins, Sprafkin, Gadow, & Sadetsky, 1988).

The results are fairly consistent in showing that children learn the content of the curriculum, becoming more skeptical about advertising and more aware of the ways in which television distorts reality, but the curricula were less successful in producing attitudinal or behavioral changes. In two studies of children with emotional disturbance, learning disabilities, or no identified problem, children exposed to critical viewing skills curricula showed greater ability to distinguish real and fictional television, recognize television special effects, and evaluate commercials than control groups, but there were no differences in attitudes about television or reported viewing habits (Sprafkin et al., 1990; Watkins et al., 1988).

In one experiment, children who watched a lot of television violence were randomly assigned to a treatment group that received lessons about television violence or a control group. Children in the treatment group were significantly less aggressive than controls 3 months later even though the lessons did not lead to significant changes in attitudes, judged realism, or the amount of television violence viewed. Perhaps more interesting, the correlation between viewing and aggression was diminished in the experimental group (Huesmann, Eron, Klein, Brice, & Fischer, 1983).

Media literacy lessons can also be used successfully to teach children to recognize prosocial content on television, perhaps enabling them to extract positive messages from what they view (Abelman, 1987, 1991).

CONCLUSION

Why should psychologists study children's interactions with mass media? Television and other media occupy more time than any other activity except sleeping. Communications media can serve as socializing influences on children and youth, but whether those influences are large and powerful or peripheral and trivial is unclear. Television provides an ecologically valid, naturally controlled laboratory for studying many problems of development because its content and form are standard for large numbers of children who share its culture.

Although children watch an average of 3 to 4 hours a day by late childhood, there are vast individual variations in the amount and types of programming viewed. Family patterns of television use and regulation, as well as interpersonal communication are important influences on children's viewing, but the amount of viewing is also a function of opportunity provided by time at home when other activities are not readily available.

Some social critics have argued that television as a medium is inherently superficial, concrete, and potentially harmful to intellectual development. The evidence shows that watching television in and of itself, independently of content, has few demonstrable effects on school achievement, reading, creativity, or attention span. The notion that television displaces more valuable activities is too simplistic and receives little support in the literature. For children who watch a great deal of television (e.g., more than 30 hours a week), viewing may interfere with school achievement and reading skill, but popular attempts to blame the educational ills of the United States on television appear to be misguided. The influences of viewing on creativity, imagination, and task persistence appear to be a function of different types of content rather than of something about the medium of television itself. For example, children learn language and verbal information from television, especially when the language is well coordinated with the visual messages.

Perhaps the most important message from all this research is that the medium is not the message; the content of the medium is much more important than its audiovisual form. Nowhere is this fact more apparent than in the evidence that television can be an effective teacher when programs are well designed. Children can learn literacy and numeracy skills, information about science and history, and prosocial attitudes and behavior from television. Educational television can be valuable for children of all income groups, but it has particular importance as a resource for children living in circumstances that place them at risk for school failure.

When children "watch" television, they are generally not passive zombies. They actively invest mental effort to evaluate and understand what is being presented. They select relevant, informative, entertaining, and comprehensible content to attend to, and within the limits of their level of cognitive development, they work to process the material they have selected in ways that match their sense of the real world. They develop schematic knowledge, often different for the world of television and the world of reality, but the two inevitably influence one another.

The use of television to understand the real world is in part contingent on its perceived reality. The ability to discriminate between genres of programming that are factual and those that are fictional improves gradually with age and level of cognitive development. Making use of format production features to discriminate factual from fictional content, the child manifests a skill in so doing that is not particularly dependent on that child's history of viewing television. The appreciation of television content as applicable to one's own life, even if fictional, by contrast, depends very much on viewing history, and hardly at all on age or cognitive abilities.

Many critics of television greeted new technologies (computers, the Internet, interactive television) with enthusiasm, but many of these, like television itself, have been exploited to deliver entertainment of questionable taste and value at considerable cost to children and profit to the industry. Interactivity per se motivates children, especially boys in middle childhood, but it does not enhance communication unless it is properly designed. Good intentions are not enough to produce good interactive programs; careful formative research and knowledge about children's learning processes are needed.

Television presents a social world emphasizing violence, frightening events, and somewhat impersonal and casual sex. It is disproportionately peopled by Whites, males, people with power, and single people who lead glamorous, adventurous lives. Violence and one-sided, stereotyped images are particularly prevalent in commercial noneducational programs designed for children.

Both attitudes and behavior are affected by the social messages viewed. There is little doubt that viewing television violence has a causal effect on aggressive behavior, though there is disagreement about the magnitude and social importance of the effect. Television readily arouses emotion; it also provides a version of social reality that goes far beyond the child's own direct experience of life and is readily consensually validated by peers, who watch many of the same programs on the same day.

Research on television can be used to inform public policy. It appears to be a necessary, but not sufficient condition to influence either regulation or funding decisions by public agencies. Research is also used to guide production;

to provide information to parents and others responsible for children about how to use television; and to help educators in teaching children about television. We have relatively little information, however, on how parents, child-care providers, and teachers can help children to use television effectively and selectively. With the majority of preschool children in child care, efforts by public television stations to do outreach and provide supplementary print and curriculum materials for child-care providers are welcome, but overdue. At the elementary level, a flurry of "media literacy" or "critical viewing skills" curricula were investigated in the early 1980s, then largely disappeared, perhaps because of their limited effectiveness. Moreover, their focus on the negative aspects of television left us with little research investigating techniques for teaching children how to learn constructive and useful information from television or how to use television production techniques creatively. After almost 50 years, we have allowed the medium to treat children as a market for sales and have not begun to capitalize on its potential for education or quality entertainment.

REFERENCES

Abelman, R. (1987). TV literacy: II. Amplifying the affective level effects of television's prosocial fare through curriculum intervention. *Journal of Research and Development in Education, 20*(2), 40–49.

Abelman, R. (1991). TV literacy: III. Gifted and learning disabled children: Amplifying prosocial learning through curriculum intervention. *Journal of Research and Development in Education, 24*(4), 51–60.

Ackerman, B. P. (1981). Encoding specificity in the recall of pictures and words in children and adults. *Journal of Experimental Child Psychology, 31,* 193–211.

Alexander, A., Ryan, M. S., & Munoz, P. (1984). Creating a learning context: Investigations on the interaction of siblings during television viewing. *Critical Studies in Mass Communication, 1,* 345–364.

Allen, L., Cipielewski, J., & Stanovich, K. E. (1992). Multiple indicators of children's reading habits and attitudes: Construct validity and cognitive correlates *Journal of Educational Psychology, 84*(4), 489–503.

Alvarez, M., Huston, A. C., Wright, J. C., & Kerkman, D. (1988). Gender differences in visual attention to television form and content. *Journal of Applied Developmental Psychology, 9,* 459–476.

American Psychological Association. (1985). *Violence on television.* Washington, DC: APA Board of Ethical and Social Responsibility for Psychology.

Anderson, D. R., Alwitt, L. F., Lorch, E. P., & Levin, S. R. (1979). Watching children watch television. In G. A. Hale & M. Lewis (Eds.), *Attention and cognitive development.* New York: Plenum Press.

Anderson, D. R., & Burns, J. (1991). Paying attention to television. In J. Bryant & D. Zillmann (Eds.), *Responding to the screen: Reception and reaction processes* (pp. 3–25). Hillsdale, NJ: Erlbaum.

Anderson, D. R., Choi, H. P., & Lorch, E. P. (1987). Attentional inertia reduces distractibility during young children's television viewing. *Child Development, 58,* 798–806.

Anderson, D. R., & Collins, P. A. (1988). *The impact on children's education: Television's influence on cognitive development.* Washington, DC: U.S. Department of Education.

Anderson, D. R., Collins, P. A., Schmitt, K. L., & Jacobvitz, R. S. (1996). Stressful life events and television viewing. *Communication Research, 23,* 243–260.

Anderson, D. R., & Field, D. E. (1983). Children's attention to television: Implications for production. In M. Meyer (Ed.), *Children and the formal features of television.* Munchen: Saur.

Anderson, D. R., & Field, D. E. (1991). Online and offline assessment of the television audience. In J. Bryant & D. Zillmann (Eds.), *Responding to the screen: Reception and reaction processes* (pp. 199–216). Hillsdale, NJ: Erlbaum.

Anderson, D. R., Field, D. E., Collins, P. A., Lorch, E. P., & Nathan, J. G. (1985). Estimates of young children's time with television: A methodological comparison of parent reports with time-lapse video home observation. *Child Development, 56,* 1345–1357.

Anderson, D. R., & Levin, S. R. (1976). Young children's attention to "Sesame Street." *Child Development, 47,* 806–811.

Anderson, D. R., Levin, S. R., & Lorch, E. P. (1977). The effects of TV program pacing on the behavior of preschool children. *AV Communication Review, 25,* 154–166.

Anderson, D. R., & Lorch, E. P. (1983). Looking at television: Action or reaction? In J. Bryant & D. R. Anderson (Eds.), *Children's understanding of television: Research on attention and comprehension* (pp. 1–33). New York: Academic Press.

Anderson, D. R., Lorch, E. P., Field, D. E., Collins, P. A., & Nathan, J. G. (1986). Television viewing at home: Age trends in visual attention and time with TV. *Child Development, 57,* 1024–1033.

Anderson, D. R., Lorch, E. P., Field, D. E., & Sanders, J. (1981). The effects of TV program comprehensibility on preschool children's visual attention to television. *Child Development, 52,* 151–157.

Anderson, J. A. (1983). Television literacy and the critical viewer. In J. Bryant & D. R. Anderson (Eds.), *Children's understanding of television: Research on attention and comprehension* (pp. 297–330). San Diego, CA: Academic Press.

Andison, F. S. (1977). TV violence and viewer aggression: Accumulation of study results 1956–1976. *Public Opinion Quarterly, 41,* 314–331.

Atkin, C. K. (1982). Television advertising and socialization to consumer roles. In D. Pearl, L. Bouthilet, & J. Lazar (Eds.), *Television and behavior: Ten years of scientific progress and implications for the eighties* (pp. 191–200). Washington, DC: U.S. Government Printing Office.

Atkin, D. J., Greenberg, B. S., & Baldwin, T. F. (1991). The home ecology of children's television viewing: Parental mediation and the new video environment. *Journal of Communication, 41*(3), 40–52.

Ball, S., & Bogatz, G. A. (1970). *The first year of Sesame Street: An evaluation.* Princeton, NJ: Educational Testing Service.

Ball, S., & Bogatz, G. A. (1973). *Reading with television: An evaluation of the Electric Company* (2 vols.). Princeton, NJ: Educational Testing Service.

Ballard, M. E., & Wiest, J. R. (1995, March). *Mortal Kombat: The effects of violent video technology on males' hostility and cardiovascular responding.* Paper presented at the meeting of the Society for Research in Child Development, Indianapolis.

Bandura, A. (1994). Social cognitive theory of mass communication. In J. Bryant & D. Zillmann (Eds.), *Media effects: Advances in theory and research* (pp. 61–90). Hillsdale, NJ: Erlbaum.

Bandura, A., & Walters, R. H. (1963). *Social learning and personality development.* New York: Holt, Rinehart and Winston.

Bechtel, R. B., Achelpohl, C., & Akers, R. (1972). Correlates between observed behavior and questionnaire responses on television viewing. In E. A. Rubinstein, G. A. Comstock, & J. P. Murray (Eds.), *Television and social behavior: Vol. 4. Television in day-to-day life: Patterns of use* (pp. 274–344). Washington, DC: U.S. Government Printing Office.

Beentjes, J. W. J., & van der Voort, T. H. A. (1988). Television's impact on children's reading skills: A review of research. *Reading Research Quarterly, 23*(4), 389–413.

Beentjes, J. W. J., & van der Voort, T. H. A. (1991). Children's written accounts of televised and printed stories. *Educational Technology Research and Development, 39*(3), 15–26.

Beentjes, J. W. J., & van der Voort, T. H. A. (1993). Television viewing versus reading: Mental effort, retention, and inferential learning. *Communication Education, 42*(3), 191–205.

Beentjes, J. W. J., Vooijs, M. W., & van der Voort, T. H. (1993). Children's recall of televised and printed news as a function of test expectations. *Journal of Educational Television, 19*(1), 5–14.

Bennett, D. T., Debold, E., & Solan, S. V. (1991). *Children and mathematics: Enjoyment, motivation, and Square One TV.* Paper presented at the biennial meeting of the Society for Research in Child Development, Seattle, WA.

Berkowitz, L. (1990). On the formation and regulation of anger and aggression: A cognitive-neoassociationistic analysis *American Psychologist, 45,* 494–503.

Berlyne, D. E. (1960). *Conflict, arousal, and curiosity.* New York: McGraw-Hill.

Berry, G. L., & Asamen, J. K. (Eds.). (1993). *Children and television: Images in a changing sociocultural world.* Newbury Park, CA: Sage.

Bogatz, G. A., & Ball, S. (1971). *The second year of "Sesame Street": A continuing evaluation* (2 vols.). Princeton, NJ: Educational Testing Service.

Brand, J. E., & Greenberg, B. S. (1994). Commercials in the classroom: The impact of Channel One advertising. *Journal of Advertising Research, 34,* 18–27.

Brown, J., & Newcomer, S. (1991). Television viewing and adolescents' sexual behavior. *Journal of Homosexuality, 21,* 77–91.

Brown, J. D., Childers, K. W., Bauman, K. E., & Koch, G. G. (1990). The influences of new media and family structure on young adolescents' television and radio use. *Communication Research, 17,* 65–82.

Bruner, J., Olver, R., & Greenfield, O. M. (1966). *Studies in cognitive growth.* New York: Wiley.

Bryant, J., & Anderson, D. R. (Eds.). (1983). *Children's understanding of TV: Research on attention and comprehension.* New York: Academic Press.

Caldwell, B. M., & Bradley, R. (1984). *Home observation for measurement of the environment.* Little Rock: University of Arkansas.

Calvert, S. L. (1988). Television production feature effects on children's comprehension of time. *Journal of Applied Developmental Psychology, 9,* 263–273.

Calvert, S. L. (1995). *Impact of televised songs on children's and young adults' memory of verbally-presented content.* Unpublished manuscript, Department of Psychology, Georgetown University, Washington, DC.

Calvert, S. L., Brune, C., Eguia, M., & Marcato, J. (1991, April). *Attentional inertia and distractibility during children's educational computer interactions.* Poster presented at the meeting of the Society for Research in Child Development, Seattle, WA.

Calvert, S. L., & Gersh, T. L. (1987). The selective use of sound effects and visual inserts for children's television story comprehension. *Journal of Applied Developmental Psychology, 8,* 363–376.

Calvert, S. L., Huston, A. C., Watkins, B. A., & Wright, J. C. (1982). The relation between selective attention to television forms and children's comprehension of content. *Child Development, 53,* 601–610.

Calvert, S. L., Huston, A. C., & Wright, J. C. (1987). Effects of television preplay formats on children's attention and story comprehension. *Journal of Applied Developmental Psychology, 8,* 329–342.

Calvert, S. L., & Tan, S.-L. (1994). Impact of virtual reality on young adults' physiological arousal and aggressive thoughts: Interaction vs. observation. *Journal of Applied Developmental Psychology, 15,* 125–139.

Calvert, S. L., & Tart, M. (1993). Song versus verbal forms for very-long-term, long-term, and short-term verbatim recall. *Journal of Applied Developmental Psychology, 14,* 245–260.

Campbell, T. A., Wright, J. C., & Huston, A. C. (1987). Form cues and content difficulty as determinants of children's cognitive processing of televised educational messages. *Journal of Experimental Child Psychology, 43,* 311–327.

Cantor, J. (1991). Fright responses to mass media productions. In J. Bryant & D. Zillmann (Eds.), *Responding to the screen: Reception and reaction processes* (pp. 169–197). Hillsdale, NJ: Erlbaum.

Cantor, J. (1992). Children's emotional reactions to technological disasters conveyed by the mass media. In J. M. Wober (Ed.), *Television and nuclear power: Making the public mind.* Norwood, NJ: ABLEX.

Cantor, J. (1994). Fright reactions to mass media. In J. Bryant & D. Zillmann (Eds.), *Media effects: Advances in theory and research* (pp. 213–245). Hillsdale, NJ: Erlbaum.

Cantor, J. (1996). Television and children's fear. In T. M. MacBeth (Ed.), *Tuning in to young viewers: Social science perspectives on television* (pp. 87–116). Newbury Park, CA: Sage.

Cantor, J., & Harrison, K. (1996). Ratings and advisories for television programming: University of Wisconsin, Madison study. In *National Television Violence Study: Scientific Papers 1994–1995.* Los Angeles: Mediascope.

Cantor, J., & Hoffner C. (1991, April). *Children's reports of media events that produce happiness and sadness.* Presented at the meeting of the Society for Research in Child Development, Seattle, WA.

Cantor, J., Mares, M. L., & Oliver, M. B. (1993). Parents' and children's emotional reactions to TV coverage of the Gulf War. In B. S. Greenberg & W. Gantz (Eds.), *Desert Storm and the mass media* (pp. 325–340). Cresskill, NJ: Hampton Press.

Cantor, J., & Omdahl, B. L. (1991). Effect of fictional media depictions of realistic threats on children's emotional responses, expectations, worries, and linking for related activities. *Communication Monographs, 58,* 384–401.

Cantor, J., & Reilly, S. (1982). Adolescents' fright reactions to television and films. *Journal of Communication, 32*(4), 87–99.

Cantor, J., Sparks, G. G., & Hoffner, C. (1988). Calming children's television fears: Mr. Rogers vs. The Incredible Hulk. *Journal of Broadcasting and Electronic Media, 32*(3), 271–288.

Cantor, J., & Wilson, B. J. (1984). Modifying fear responses to mass media in preschool and elementary school children. *Journal of Broadcasting, 28,* 431–443.

Cantor, J., & Wilson, B. J. (1988). Helping children cope with frightening media presentations. *Current Psychology: Research and Reviews, 7*(1), 58–75.

Cantor, J., Wilson, B. J., & Hoffner, C. (1986). Emotional responses to a televised nuclear holocaust film. *Communication Research, 13*(2), 257–277.

Caron, A., & Meunier, D. (1994). The appropriation of play in interactive technologies. *Society and Leisure, 17*(1), 51–80.

Chall, J. S. (1983). *Stages of reading development.* New York: McGraw-Hill.

Chen, M. (1984). *A review of research on the educational potential of 3-2-1 Contact: A children's TV series on science and technology.* New York: Children's Television Workshop.

Children's Television Act of 1990. (1990). Public Law No. 101-437.

Children's Television Workshop. (1994). *Learning from ghostwriter: Strategies and outcomes.* New York: Children's Television Workshop.

Christenson, P. G., & Roberts, D. F. (1990). *Popular music in early adolescence.* New York: Carnegie Council on Adolescent Development.

Cocking, R. R., & Greenfield, P. M. (1996). Introduction. In P. M. Greenfield & R. Cocking (Eds.), *Interacting with video* (pp. 3–7). Norwood, NJ: ABLEX.

Collins, P. A. (1991, April). *The impact of television on preschoolers' perseverance, impulsivity, and restlessness.* Paper presented at the meeting of the Society for Research in Child Development, Seattle, WA.

Collins, W. A. (1983a). Social antecedents, cognitive processing, and comprehension of social portrayals on television. In E. T. Higgins, D. N. Ruble, & W. W. Hartup (Eds.), *Social cognition and social development* (pp. 110–133). Cambridge, England: Cambridge University Press.

Collins, W. A. (1983b). Interpretation and inference in children's television viewing. In J. Bryant & D. R. Anderson (Eds.), *Children's understanding of television: Research on attention and comprehension.* New York: Academic Press.

Collins, W. A., Sobol, B. L., & Westby, S. (1981). Effects of adult commentary on children's comprehension and inferences about a televised aggressive portrayal. *Child Development, 52,* 158–163.

Comstock, G. (1991). *Television and the American child.* Orlando, FL: Academic Press.

Comstock, G., & Cobbey, R. E. (1982). Television and the children of ethnic minorities: Perspectives from research. In G. L. Berry & C. Mitchell-Kernan (Eds.), *Television and the socialization of the minority child* (pp. 245–260). New York: Academic Press.

Communications Act. (1934). 47 U.S.C. 151-610 (1982).

Condry, J. (1989). *The psychology of television.* Hillsdale, NJ: Erlbaum.

Condry, J. C., & Freund, S. (1989, April). *Discriminating real from make-believe: A developmental study.* Paper presented at the meeting of the Society for Research in Child Development, Kansas City.

Cook, T. D., Appleton, H., Conner, R. F., Shaffer, A., Tamkin, G., & Weber, S. J. (1975). *"Sesame Street" revisited.* New York: Russell-Sage Foundation.

Cook, T. D., & Curtin, T. R. (1986). An evaluation of the models used to evaluate television series. In G. Comstock (Ed.), *Public communication and behavior* (Vol. 1, pp. 1–64). Orlando, FL: Academic Press.

Cook, T. D., Kendziersky, D. A., & Thomas, S. V. (1983). The implicit assumptions of television: An analysis of the 1982 NIMH Report on Television and Behavior. *Public Opinion Quarterly, 47,* 161–201.

Corder-Bolz, C. R. (1982). Television literacy and critical television viewing skills. In D. Pearl, L. Bouthilet, & J. Lazar (Eds.), *Television and human behavior: Ten years of scientific progress and implications for the eighties: Vol. 2. Technical reports* (pp. 91–102). Washington, DC: U.S. Department of Health and Human Services.

Corteen, R. S., & Williams, T. M. (1986). Television and reading skills. In T. M. Williams (Ed.), *The impact of television: A natural experiment in three communities* (pp. 39–85). Orlando, FL: Academic Press.

Cross, W. E., Jr. (1985). Black identity: Rediscovering the distinction between personal identity and reference group orientation. In M. B. Spencer, G. K. Brookins, & W. R. Allen (Eds.), *Beginnings: The social and affective development of Black children.* Hillsdale, NJ: Erlbaum.

DeFleur, M. L. (1964). Occupational roles as portrayed on television. *Public Opinion Quarterly, 28,* 57–74.

DeFleur, M. L., & DeFleur, L. B. (1967). The relative contribution of television as a learning source for children's occupational knowledge. *American Sociological Review, 32,* 777–789.

Derley, R., & Wright, J. C. (1996, April). *Interactive vs. passive media presentation of a story: Processing and gender differences.* Paper presented at the biennial meeting of the Society for Research in Child Development, Washington, DC.

Desmond, R. J., Singer, J. L., & Singer, D. G. (1990). Family mediation: Parental communication patterns and the influences of television on children. In J. Bryant (Ed.), *Television and the American family* (pp. 253–274). Hillsdale, NJ: Erlbaum.

Desmond, R. J., Singer, J. L., Singer, D. G., Calam, R., & Colimore, K. (1985). Family mediation patterns and television viewing: Young children's use and grasp of the medium. *Human Communication Research, 11,* 461–480.

Diaz-Guerrero, R., & Holtzman, W. H. (1974). Learning by televised "Plaza Sesamo" in Mexico. *Journal of Educational Psychology, 66,* 632–643.

Diaz-Guerrero, R., Reyes-Lagunes, I., Witzke, D. B., & Holtzman, W. H. (1976). Plaza Sesamo in Mexico: An evaluation. *Journal of Communication, 26,* 145–155.

Dietz, W. H., Jr., & Gortmaker, S. L. (1985). Do we fatten our children at the television set? Obesity and television viewing in children and adolescents. *Pediatrics, 75,* 807–812.

Dominick, J. R. (1973). Crime and law enforcement on prime-time television. *Public Opinion Quarterly, 37,* 241–250.

Dorr, A. (1983). No shortcuts to judging reality. In J. Bryant & D. R. Anderson (Eds.), *Children's understanding of television: Research on attention and comprehension* (pp. 199–220). New York: Academic Press.

Dorr, A. (1986). *Television and children: A special medium for a special audience.* Beverly Hills, CA: Sage.

Dorr, A., Graves, S. B., & Phelps, E. (1980). Television literacy for young children. *Journal of Communication, 30,* 71–83.

Dorr, A., Kovaric, P., & Doubleday, C. (1989). Parent-child coviewing of television. *Journal of Broadcasting and Electronic Media, 33,* 35–51.

Dorr, A., Kovaric, P., & Doubleday, C. (1990). Age and content influences on children's perceptions of the realism of television families. *Journal of Broadcasting and Electronic Media, 34*(4), 377–397.

Durkin, K. (1985a). Television and sex-role acquisition: 1. Content. *British Journal of Social Psychology, 24,* 101–113.

Durkin, K. (1985b). Television and sex-role acquisition: 2. Effects. *British Journal of Social Psychology, 24,* 191–210.

Durkin, K. (1985c). Television and sex-role acquisition: 3. Counter-stereotyping. *British Journal of Social Psychology, 24,* 211–222.

Eaton, B. C., & Dominick, J. R. (1991). Product-related programming and children's TV: A content analysis. *Journalism Quarterly, 68,* 67–75.

Elliott, W. R., & Slater, D. (1980). Exposure, experience, and perceived TV reality for adolescents. *Journalism Quarterly, 57,* 409–414.

Eron, L. D., Lefkowitz, M. M., Huesmann, L. R., & Walder, L. O. (1972). Does television violence cause aggression? *American Psychologist, 27,* 253–263.

Federal Trade Commission. (1978). *FTC staff report on television advertising to children.* Washington, DC: U.S. Government Printing Office.

Fernandez-Collado, C., Greenberg, B., Korzenny, F., & Atkin, C. (1978). Sexual intimacy and drug use in TV series. *Journal of Communication, 28*(3), 30–37.

Feshbach, S. (1972). Reality and fantasy in filmed violence. In J. P. Murray, E. A. Rubenstein, & G. A. Comstock (Eds.), *Television and social behavior: Vol. 2. Television and social learning* (pp. 318–345). Washington, DC: Government Printing Office.

Feshbach, S., Feshbach, N. D., & Cohen, S. E. (1982). Enhancing children's discrimination in response to television advertising: The effects of psychoeducational training in two elementary schools-age groups. *Developmental Review, 2,* 385–403.

Field, D. E. (1989). *Television coviewing related to family characteristics and cognitive performance.* Unpublished doctoral dissertation, University of Massachusetts, Amherst.

Field, D. E., & Anderson, D. R. (1985). Instruction and modality effects on children's television attention and comprehension. *Journal of Educational Psychology, 77,* 91–100.

Fitch, M., Huston, A. C., & Wright, J. C. (1993). From television forms to genre schemata: Children's perceptions of television reality. In G. L. Berry & J. K. Asamen (Eds.), *Children and television: Images in a changing sociocultural world* (pp. 38–52). Newbury Park, CA: Sage.

Flagg, B. N. (1978). Children and television: Effects of stimulus repetition on eye activity. In J. W. Senders, D. F. Fisher, & R. A. Monty (Eds.), *Eye movements and higher psychological functioning.* Hillsdale, NJ: Erlbaum.

Flavell, J. H., Flavell, E. R., Green, F. L., & Korfmacher, J. E. (1990). Do young children think of television images as pictures or real objects? *Journal of Broadcasting and Electronic Media, 34,* 399–419.

Freedman, J. L. (1984). Effect of television violence on aggressiveness. *Psychological Bulletin, 96,* 227–246.

Freedman, J. L. (1986). Television violence and aggression: A rejoinder. *Psychological Bulletin, 100,* 372–278.

Freeman, J. (1995, April). *Effects of prosocial television on racial attitudes of African American children.* Paper presented at the meeting of the Society for Research in Child Development, Indianapolis.

Friedrich, L. K., & Stein, A. H. (1973). Aggressive and prosocial television programs and the natural behavior of preschool children. *Monographs of the Society for Research in Child Development, 38*(No. 4, Whole No. 151).

Friedrich, L. K., & Stein, A. H. (1975). Prosocial television and young children's behavior: The effect of verbal labeling and role playing training. *Child Development, 46,* 27–38.

Friedrich-Cofer, L., & Huston, A. C. (1986). Television violence and aggression: The debate continues. *Psychological Bulletin, 100,* 364–371.

Friedrich-Cofer, L., Huston-Stein, A., Kipnis, D. M., Susman, E. J., & Clewett, A. S. (1979). Environmental enhancement of prosocial television content: Effects on interpersonal behavior, imaginative play, and self-regulation in a natural setting. *Developmental Psychology, 15,* 637–646.

Gadberry, S. (1974). Television as baby-sitter: A field comparison of preschoolers' behavior during playtime and during television viewing time. *Child Development, 45,* 1132–1136.

Gadberry, S. (1980). Effects of restricting first graders' TV-viewing on leisure time use, IQ change, and cognitive style. *Journal of Applied Developmental Psychology, 1,* 45–58.

Gaddy, G. D. (1986). Television's impact on high school achievement. *Public Opinion Quarterly, 50,* 340–359.

Gailey, C. W. (1993). Mediated messages: Gender, class, and cosmos in home video games. *Journal of Popular Culture, 27*(1), 81–97.

Gerbner, G., Gross, L., Morgan, M., & Signorielli, N. (1994). Growing up with television: The cultivation perspective. In J. Bryant & D. Zillmann (Eds.), *Media effects: Advances in theory and research* (pp. 17–42). Hillsdale, NJ: Erlbaum.

Gerbner, G., Morgan, M., & Signorielli, N. (1993, December). *Television violence profile No. 16: The turning point from research to action.* Unpublished manuscript, Annenberg School of Communication, University of Pennsylvania, Philadelphia.

Gibbons, J., Anderson, D. R., Smith, R., Field, D. E., & Fischer, C. (1986). Young children's recall and reconstruction of audio and audio visual narratives. *Child Development, 57,* 1014–1023.

Godbold, L. C., & Cantor, J. (1995). *The relationship between television viewing and adolescents' perceptions, attitudes and behaviors regarding sexuality.* Unpublished manuscript, Department of Communication Arts, University of Wisconsin, Madison.

Goldberg, M. E. (1990). A quasi-experiment assessing the effectiveness of TV advertising directed to children. *Journal of Marketing Research, 27*(4), 445–454.

Goodman, I. F., Rylander, K., & Ross, S. (1993). *CRO: Season I summative evaluation.* Cambridge, MA: Sierra Research Associates.

Gortmaker, S. L., Salter, C. A., Walker, D. K., Dietz, W. H. (1990). The impact of television viewing on mental aptitude and achievement: A longitudinal study. *Public Opinion Quarterly, 54,* 594–604.

Graves, S. B. (1993). Television, the portrayal of African Americans, and the development of children's attitudes. In G. L. Berry & J. K. Asamen (Eds.), *Children and television: Images in a changing sociocultural world* (pp. 179–190). Newbury Park, CA: Sage.

Greenberg, B. S., & Brand, J. E. (1993). Cultural diversity on Saturday morning television. In G. L. Berry & J. K. Asamen (Eds.), *Children and television: Images in a changing sociocultural world* (pp. 132–142). Newbury Park, CA: Sage.

Greenberg, B. S., & Brand, J. E. (1994). Minorities and the mass media: 1970s to 1990s. In J. Bryant & D. Zillmann (Eds.), *Media effects: Advances in theory and research* (pp. 273–314). Hillsdale, NJ: Erlbaum.

Greenberg, B. S., Burgoon, M., Burgoon, J., & Korzenny (Eds.). (1983). *Mexican Americans and the mass media.* Norwood, NJ: ABLEX.

Greenberg, B. S., & Dominick, J. R. (1969). Racial and social class differences in teenagers' use of television. *Journal of Broadcasting, 13,* 331–334.

Greenberg, B. S., & Gordon, T. F. (1972). Children's perceptions of television violence: A replication. In G. A. Comstock, E. A. Rubinstein, & J. P. Murray (Eds.), *Television and social behavior: Vol. 5. Television's effects: Further explorations* (pp. 211–230). Washington, DC: U.S. Government Printing Office.

Greenberg, B. S., Neuendorf, K., Buerkel-Rothfuss, N., & Henderson, L. (1982). The soaps: What's on, and who cares? *Journal of Broadcasting, 26,* 519–535.

Greenberg, B. S., & Reeves, B. (1976). Children and the perceived reality of television. *Journal of Social Issues, 32,* 86–97.

Greenberg, B. S., Stanley, C., Siemicki, M., Heeter, C., Soderman, A., & Linsangan, R. (1993). Sex content on soaps and prime-time television series most viewed by adolescents. In B. S. Greenberg, J. D. Brown, & N. Buerkel-Rothfuss (Eds.), *Media, sex and the adolescent* (pp. 29–44). Cresskill, NJ: Hampton Press.

Greenfield, P. M. (1984). *Mind and media: The effects of television, video games, and computers.* Cambridge, MA: Harvard University Press.

Greenfield, P. M. (1994). Video games as cultural artifacts. *Journal of Applied Developmental Psychology, 15,* 3–11.

Greenfield, P. M., & Beagles-Roos, J. (1988). Radio vs. television: Their cognitive impact on children of different socioeconomic and ethnic groups. *Journal of Communication, 38*(2), 71–92.

Greenfield, P. M., Brannon, C., & Lohr, D. (1994). Two-dimensional representation of movement through three-dimensional space: The role of video game expertise. *Journal of Applied Developmental Psychology, 15,* 87–103.

Greenfield, P. M., Bruzzone, L., Koyamatsu, K., Satuloff, W., Nixon, K., Brodie, M., & Kingsdale, D. (1987). What is rock music doing to the minds of our youth? A first experimental look at the effects of rock music lyrics and music videos. *Journal of Early Adolescence, 7,* 315–330.

Greenfield, P. M., Camaioni, L., Ercolani, P., Weiss, L., Lauber, B. A., & Perrucchini, P. (1994). Cognitive socialization by computer games in two cultures: Inductive discovery or mastery of an iconic code? *Journal of Applied Developmental Psychology, 15,* 59–85.

Greenfield, P. M., deWinstanley, P., Kilpatrick, H., & Kaye, D. (1994). Action video games and informal education: Effects on strategies for dividing visual attention. *Journal of Applied Developmental Psychology, 15,* 105–123.

Greenfield, P. M., Farrar, D., & Beagles-Ross, J. (1986). Is the medium the message? An experimental comparison of the effects of radio and television on imagination. *Journal of Applied Developmental Psychology, 7*(3), 201–218.

Greenfield, P. M., Yut, E., Chung, M., Land, D., Kreider, H., Pantoja, M., & Horsley, K. (1990). The program-length commercial: A study of the effects of television/toy tie-ins on imaginative play. *Psychology and Marketing, 7*(4), 237–255.

Gunter, B., McAleer, J., & Clifford, B. R. (1991). Television police dramas and children's beliefs about the police. *Journal of Educational Television, 17*(2), 81–100.

Haefner, M. J., & Wartella, E. A. (1987). Effects of sibling coviewing on children's interpretations of television programs. *Journal of Broadcasting and Electronic Media, 31,* 153–168.

Hall, E. R., Esty, E. T., & Fisch, S. M. (1990). Television and children's problem-solving behavior: A synopsis of an evaluation of the effects of Square One TV. *Journal of Mathematical Behavior, 9,* 161–174.

Harris, R. J. (1994). The impact of sexually explicit media. In J. Bryant & D. Zillmann (Eds.), *Media effects: Advances in theory and research* (pp. 247–272). Hillsdale, NJ: Erlbaum.

Harrison, L. F., & Williams, T. M. (1986). Television and cognitive development. In T. M. Williams (Ed.), *The impact of television: A natural experiment in three communities* (pp. 87–142). Orlando, FL: Academic Press.

Hawkins, R. P. (1977). The dimensional structure of children's perceptions of television reality. *Communications Research, 4,* 299–320.

Hawkins, R. P., Kim, Y. H., & Pingree, S. (1991). The ups and downs of attention to television. *Communication Research, 18*(1), 53–76.

Hawkins, R. P., & Pingree, S. (1982). Television's influence on social reality. In D. Pearl, L. Bouthilet, & J. Lazar (Eds.), *Television and behavior: Ten years of scientific progress implications for the eighties* (pp. 224–247). Washington, DC: U.S. Government Printing Office.

Hawkins, R. P., Pingree, S., Bruce, L., & Tapper, J. (1995). *Strategy and style in attention to television.* Unpublished manuscript, Mass Communication Research Center, University of Wisconsin, Madison.

Hawkins, R. P., Tapper J., Bruce, L., & Pingree, S. (1995). Strategic and nonstrategic explanations for attentional inertia. *Communication Research, 22*(2), 188–206.

Hayes, D. S., & Birnbaum, D. W. (1980). Preschoolers' retention of televised events: Is a picture worth a thousand words? *Developmental Psychology, 16,* 410–416.

Hayes, D. S., Kelly, S. B., & Mandel, M. (1986). Media differences in children's story synopses: Radio and television contrasted. *Journal of Educational Psychology, 78,* 341–346.

Healy, J. M. (1990). *Endangered minds: Why our children don't think.* New York: Simon & Schuster.

Hearold, S. (1986). A synthesis of 1043 effects of television on social behavior. In G. Comstock (Ed.), *Public communication and behavior* (Vol. 1, pp. 65–130). Orlando, FL: Academic Press.

Heintz, K. E. (1992). Children's favorite television families: A descriptive analysis of role interactions. *Journal of Broadcasting and Electronic Media, 36,* 309–320.

Himmelweit, H. T., Oppenheim, A. N., & Vince, P. (1958). *Television and the child.* London: Oxford University Press.

Hoffner, C., & Cantor, J. (1991). Factors affecting children's enjoyment of a frightening film sequence. *Communication Monographs, 58,* 41–62.

Hornik, R. (1981). Out-of-school television and schooling: Hypotheses and methods. *Review of Educational Research, 51,* 193–214.

Huesmann, L. R. (1982). Television violence and aggressive behavior. In D. Pearl, L. Bouthilet, & J. Lazar (Eds.), *Television and behavior: Ten years of scientific progress and implications for the eighties: Vol. 2. Technical reviews* (pp. 220–256). Washington, DC: National Institute of Mental Health.

Huesmann, L. R. (1986). Psychological processes promoting the relation between exposure to media violence and aggressive behavior by the viewer. *Journal of Social Issues, 42,* 125–140.

Huesmann, L. R., & Eron, L. D. (Eds.). (1986). *Television and the aggressive child: A cross-national comparison.* Hillsdale, NJ: Erlbaum.

Huesmann, L. R., Eron, L. D., Klein, R., Brice, P., & Fischer, P. (1983). Mitigating the imitation of aggressive behaviors by changing children's attitudes about media violence. *Journal of Personality and Social Psychology, 44,* 899–910.

Huesmann, L. R., Lagerspetz, K., & Eron, L. D. (1984). Intervening variables in the TV violence-aggression relation: Evidence from two countries. *Developmental Psychology, 20,* 746–775.

Huesmann, L. R., & Malamuth, N. M. (1986). Media violence and antisocial behavior: An overview. *Journal of Social Issues, 42*(3), 1–6.

Huesmann, L. R., & Miller, L. S. (1994). Long-term effects of repeated exposure to media violence in childhood. In L. R. Huesmann (Ed.), *Aggressive behavior: Current perspectives* (pp. 153–186). New York: Plenum Press.

Huston, A. C., Donnerstein, E., Fairchild, H., Feshbach, N., Katz, P., Murray, J., Rubinstein, E., Wilcox, B., & Zuckerman, D. (1992). *Big world, small screen: The role of television in American society.* Lincoln: University of Nebraska Press.

Huston, A. C., Greer, D., Wright, J. C., Welch, R., & Ross, R. (1984). Children's comprehension of televised formal features with masculine and feminine connotations. *Developmental Psychology, 20,* 707–716.

Huston, A. C., Watkins, B. A., & Kunkel, D. (1989). Public policy and children's television. *American Psychologist, 44,* 424–433.

Huston, A. C., & Wright, J. C. (1983). Children's processing of television: The informative functions of formal features. In J. Bryant & D. R. Anderson (Eds.), *Children's understanding of television: Research on attention and comprehension.* New York: Academic Press.

Huston, A. C., & Wright, J. C. (1989). The forms of television and the child viewer. In G. Comstock (Ed.), *Public communication and behavior* (Vol. 2, pp. 103–159). Orlando, FL: Academic Press.

Huston, A. C., & Wright, J. C. (1993). Center for Research on the Influences of Television on Children, University of Kansas, Lawrence.

Huston, A. C., & Wright, J. C. (1994). Educating children with television: The forms of the medium. In D. Zillmann, J. Bryant, & A. C. Huston (Eds.), *Media, children and the family: Social scientific, psychodynamic, and clinical perspectives* (pp. 73–84). Hillsdale, NJ: Erlbaum.

Huston, A. C., & Wright, J. C. (1996). Television and socialization of young children. In T. M. MacBeth (Ed.), *Tuning in to young viewers: Social science perspectives on television* (pp. 37–60). Thousand Oaks, CA: Sage.

Huston, A. C., Wright, J. C., Alvarez, M., Truglio, R., Fitch, M., & Piemyat, S. (1995). Perceived television reality and children's emotional and cognitive responses to its social content. *Journal of Applied Developmental Psychology, 16,* 231–251.

Huston, A. C., Wright, J. C., Fitch, M., Wroblewski, R., & Piemyat, S. (1993). *Effects of documentary and fictional television formats on children's acquisition of schemata for unfamiliar occupations.* Paper presented at the meeting of the Society for Research in Child Development, New Orleans, LA.

Huston, A. C., Wright, J. C., Murphy, K., Derley, R., & Soh, R. (1995, December). *Use of new media among young children from low and moderate income families* (Early Window Project Report No. 5). Center for Research on the Influences of Television on Children, University of Kansas, Lawrence.

Huston, A. C., Wright, J. C., Rice, M. L., Kerkman, D., & St. Peters, M. (1990). The development of television viewing patterns in early childhood: A longitudinal investigation. *Developmental Psychology, 26,* 409–420.

Huston, A. C., Wright, J. C., Wartella, E., Rice, M. L., Watkins, B. A., Campbell, T., & Potts, R. (1981). Communicating more than content: Formal features of children's television programs. *Journal of Communication, 31,* 32–48.

Huston-Stein, A., Fox, S., Greer, D., Watkins, B. A., & Whitaker, J., (1981). The effects of action and violence in television programs on the social behavior and imaginative play of preschool children. *Journal of Genetic Psychology, 138,* 183–191.

Jeffery, L., & Durkin, K. (1989). Children's reactions to televised counterstereotyped male sex role behavior as a function of age, sex, and perceived power.

Jo, E., & Berkowitz, L. (1994). A priming effect analysis of media influences: An update. In J. Bryant & D. Zillmann (Eds.), *Media effects: Advances in theory and research* (pp. 43–60). Hillsdale, NJ: Erlbaum.

Johnston, J. (1980, May). *An exploratory study of the effects of viewing the first season of 3-2-1 Contact.* Ann Arbor, MI: Institute for Social Research, University of Michigan.

Johnston, J., Bauman, J, Milne, L., & Urdan, T. (1993). *Taking the measure of Talking with TJ: An evaluation of the first implementation of Talking with TJ, Series 1.* Ann Arbor: Institute for Social Research, University of Michigan.

Johnston, J., Brzezinski, E. J., & Anderman, E. M. (1994). *Taking the measure of Channel One: A three year perspective.* Institute for Social Research, Ann Arbor: University of Michigan, University of Michigan.

Johnston, J., & Ettema, J. S. (1982). *Positive images: Breaking stereotypes with children's television.* Beverly Hills, CA: Sage.

Johnston, J., & Ettema, J. S. (1984). Using television to best advantage: Research for prosocial television. In J. Bryant & D. Zillmann (Eds.), *Perspectives on media effects* (pp. 143–164). Hillsdale, NJ: Erlbaum.

Josephson, W. L. (1987). Television violence and children's aggression: Testing the priming, social script, and disinhibition predictions. *Journal of Personality and Social Psychology, 53,* 882–890.

Kafai, Y. B. (1995). *Minds in play: Computer game design as a context for children's learning.* Hillsdale, NJ: Erlbaum.

Kafai, Y. B. (1996). Gender differences in children's constructions of video games. In P. M. Greenfield & R. R. Cocking (Eds.), *Interacting with video* (pp. 39–66). Norwood, NJ: ABLEX.

Keith, T. Z., Reimers, T. M., Fehrmann, P. G., Pottebaum, S. M., & Aubey, L. W. (1986). Parental involvement, homework, and TV time: Direct and indirect effects on high school achievement. *Journal of Educational Psychology, 78,* 373–380.

Kelly, A. E., & Spear, P. S. (1991). Intraprogram synopses for children's comprehension of television content. *Journal of Experimental Child Psychology, 52,* 87–98.

Kinder, M. (1996). Contextualizing video game violence: From Teenage Mutant Ninja Turtles to Mortal Kombat 2. In P. M. Greenfield & R. R. Cocking (Eds.), *Interacting with video* (pp. 25–37). Norwood, NJ: ABLEX.

Klein, E. L. (Ed.). (1985). *Children and computers. New directions in child development* (Vol. 85). San Francisco: Jossey-Bass.

Klein, J. (1991). Applying research to artistic practices: This is not a pipe dream. *Youth Theatre Journal, 7*(3), 13–17.

Klein, J. (1995). Reading empathy in a Quebecois play: Crying to laugh. *Theatre Research in Canada, 15,* 20–41.

Krendl, K. A., Clark, G., Dawson, R., & Troiano, C. (1993). Preschoolers and VCRs in the home: A multiple methods approach. *Journal of Broadcasting and Electronic Media, 37,* 293–312.

Krendl, K. A., Troiano, C. A., Dawson, R., & Clark, G. (1992). "OK, Where's the remote?" Children, families, and remote control devices. In J. R. Walker & R. V. Bellamy, Jr. (Eds.), *The remote control in the new age of television.* Westport, CT: Greenwood Press/Praeger.

Krull, R. (1983). Children learning to watch television. In J. Bryant & D. R. Anderson (Eds.), *Children's understanding of television* (pp. 103–123.) New York: Academic Press.

Krull, R., & Husson, W. (1979). Children's attention: The case of TV viewing. In E. Wartella (Ed.), *Children communicating: Media and development of thought, speech, and understanding.* Beverly Hills, CA: Sage.

Kunkel, D. (1988). Children and host selling television commercials. *Communication Research, 15,* 71–92.

Kunkel, D., & Canepa, J. (1994). Broadcasters' license renewal claims regarding children's educational programming. *Journal of Broadcasting and Electronic Media, 38,* 397–416.

Kunkel, D., & Roberts, D. (1991). Young minds and marketplace values: Issues in children's television advertising *Journal of Social Issues, 47*(1), 57–72.

Kunkel, D., & Watkins, B. (1987). Evolution of children's television regulatory policy. *Journal of Broadcasting and Electronic Media, 31,* 367–389.

Landau, S., Lorch, E. P., & Milich, R. (1992). Visual attention to and comprehension of television in attention deficit hyperactivity disordered and normal boys. *Child Development, 63,* 928–937.

Larson, R., Kubey, R. W., & Colletti, J. (1989). Changing channels: Early adolescent media choices and shifting investments in family and friends. *Journal of Youth and Adolescence, 18,* 583–599.

Leary, A., Huston, A. C., & Wright, J. C. (1983, April). *The influence of television production features with masculine and feminine connotations on children's comprehension and play behavior.* Paper presented at the biennial meeting of the Society for Research in Child Development, Detroit.

Lemish, D., & Rice, M. L. (1986). Television as a talking picture book: A prop for language acquisition. *Journal of Child Language, 13,* 251–274.

Lichter, L. S., & Lichter, R. (1983). *Prime time crime.* Washington, DC: Media Institute.

Liebert, R. M., & Sprafkin, J. (1988). *The early window: Effects of television on children and youth* (3rd ed.). New York: Pergamon Press.

List, J. A., Collins, W. A., & Westby, S. (1983). Comprehension and inferences from traditional and nontraditional sex-role portrayals on television. *Child Development, 54,* 1580–1587.

Lonner, W. J., Thorndike, R. M., Forbes, N. E., & Ashworth, C. (1985). The influence of television on measured cognitive abilities: A study with native Alaskan children. *Journal of Cross-Cultural Psychology, 16,* 355–380.

Lorch, E. P., Anderson, D. R., & Levin, S. R. (1979). The relationship of visual attention to children's comprehension of television. *Child Development, 50,* 722–727.

Lowery, B. R., & Knirk, F. G. (1982–1983). Microcomputer video games and spatial visualization acquisition. *Journal of Educational Technology Systems, 11,* 155–166.

Lowry, D. T., & Towles, D. E. (1987). Prime time TV portrayals of sex, contraception and venereal diseases. *Journalism Quarterly, 64,* 347–352.

Luecke-Aleksa, D., Anderson, D. R., Collins, P. A., & Schmitt, K. L. (1995). Gender constancy and television viewing. *Developmental Psychology, 31,* 773–780.

Lyle, J., & Hoffman, H. R. (1972). Children's use of television and other media. In E. A. Rubinstein, G. A. Comstock, & J. P. Murray (Eds.), *Television and social behavior:Television in day-to-day life: Vol. 4. Patterns of use* (pp. 129–256). Washington, DC: U.S. Government Printing Office.

Maccoby, E. E. (1964). Effects of the mass media. In M. Hoffman & L. W. Hoffman (Eds.), *Review of child development research* (Vol. 1, pp. 323–348). New York: Russell-Sage Foundation.

McDermott, S., & Greenberg, B. (1984). Parents, peers and television as determinants of Black children's esteem. In R. Bostrom (Ed.), *Communication yearbook* (Vol. 8, pp. 164–177). Beverly Hills, CA: Sage.

McGuire, W. J. (1986). The myth of massive media impact: Savagings and salvagings. In G. Comstock (Ed.), *Public communication and behavior* (Vol. 1, pp. 173–258). Orlando, FL: Academic Press.

McKenzie, T. L., Sallis, J. F., Nader, P. R., & Broyles, S. L. (1992). Anglo- and Mexican-American preschoolers at home and at recess: Activity patterns and environmental influences. *Journal of Developmental and Behavioral Pediatrics, 13,* 173–180.

McLeod, J. M., Atkin, C. K., & Chaffee, S. H. (1972). Adolescents, parents, and television use: Adolescent self-report measures from Maryland and Wisconsin samples. In G. A. Comstock & E. A. Rubinstein (Eds.), *Television and social behavior: Vol. 3. Television and adolescent aggressiveness* (pp. 173–238). Washington, DC: U.S. Government Printing Office.

McLuhan, H. M. (1964). *Understanding media: The extensions of man.* New York: McGraw-Hill.

Meadowcroft, J. M. (1994). Attention span cycles. In J. H. Watt & A. Van Lear, Jr. (Eds.), *Cycles and dynamic patterns in communication processes.* Newbury Park, CA: Sage.

Meadowcroft, J. M., & Reeves, B. (1989). Influence of story schema development on children's attention to television. *Communication Research,16,* 352–374.

Medrich, E. A., Roizen, J. A., Rubin, V., & Buckley, S. (1982). *The serious business of growing up: A study of children's lives outside school.* Berkeley: University of California Press.

Meringoff, L. K., Vibbert, M. M., Char, C. A., Fernie, D. E., Banker, G. S., & Gardner, H. (1983). How is children's learning from television distinctive? Exploiting the medium methodologically. In J. Bryant & D. R. Anderson (Eds.), *Children's understanding of television: Research on attention and comprehension* (pp. 151–180). New York: Academic Press.

Messaris, P., & Hornik, R. C. (1983). Work status, television exposure, and educational outcomes. In C. Hayes & S. B. Kamerman (Eds.), *Children of working parents: Experiences and outcomes* (pp. 44–72). Washington, DC: National Academy Press.

Messaris, P., & Sarett, C. (1981). On the consequences of television-related parent-child interaction. *Human Communication Research, 7,* 226–244.

Mielke, K. (1983). Formative research on appeal and comprehension in 3-2-1 CONTACT. In J. Bryant & D. R. Anderson (Eds.), *Children's understanding of television: Research on attention and comprehension* (pp. 241–264). San Diego, CA: Academic Press.

Milavsky, J. R., Stipp, H. H., Kessler, R. C., & Rubens, W. S. (1982). *Television and aggression: A panel study.* New York: Academic Press.

Moghaddam, M., & Wright, J. C. (1991). *Understanding television: The effect of fictional and factual portrayals on children's cognitive processing.* Unpublished manuscript, Center for Research on the Influences of Television on Children, University of Kansas, Lawrence.

Morgan, M. (1982). Television and adolescents' sex role stereotypes: A longitudinal study. *Journal of Personality and Social Psychology, 43,* 947–955.

Morgan, M. (1987). Television, sex-role attitudes, and sex-role behavior. *Journal of Early Adolescence, 7,* 269–282.

Morgan, M., & Gross, L. (1982). Television and educational achievement and aspiration. In D. Pearl, L. Bouthilet, & J. Lazar (Eds.), *Television and behavior: Ten years of scientific progress and implications for the eighties: Vol. 2.*

Technical reports (pp. 78–90). Washington, DC: U.S. Government Printing Office.

Mutz, D. C., Roberts, D. F., & van Vuuren, D. P. (1993). Reconsidering the displacement hypothesis: Television's influence on children's time use. *Communication Research, 20,* 51–75.

Neapolitan, D. M. (1993). *An analysis of the formal features of "reality-based" television programs.* Lawrence: Center for Research on the Influences of Television on Children, University of Kansas.

Neapolitan, D. M., & Huston, A. C. (1994a). *Educational content of children's programs on public and commercial television.* Lawrence: Center for Research on the Influences of Television on Children, University of Kansas.

Neapolitan, D. M., & Huston, A. C. (1994b). *Female and minority characters on educational and informative television programs for children Report to the Public Broadcasting Service.* Lawrence: Center for Research on the Influences of Television on Children, University of Kansas.

Neuman, S. B. (1986). Television, reading and the home environment. *Reading Research and Instruction, 25,* 173–183.

Neuman, S. B. (1988). The displacement effect: Assessing the relation between television viewing and reading performance. *Reading Research Quarterly, 23,* 415–439.

Neuman, S. B. (1991). *Literacy in the television age: The myth of the TV effect.* Norwood, NJ: ABLEX.

Neuman, S. B. (1992). Is learning from media distinctive? Examining children's inferencing strategies. *American Educational Research Journal, 29*(1), 119–140.

Neuman, S. B., Burden, D., & Holden, E. (1990). Enhancing children's comprehension of a televised story through previewing. *Journal of Educational Research, 83,* 258–265.

Newcomb, A. F., & Collins, W. A. (1979). Children's comprehension of family role portrayals in televised dramas: Effects of socioeconomic status, ethnicity, and age. *Developmental Psychology, 15,* 417–423.

Nikken, P., & Peeters, A. L. (1988). Children's perceptions of television reality. *Journal of Broadcasting and Electronic Media, 32*(4), 441–452.

Okagaki, L., & Frensch, P. A. (1994). Effects of video game playing on measures of spatial performance: Gender effects in late adolescence. *Journal of Applied Developmental Psychology, 15,* 33–58.

Oppenheimer, S. (1993). *Subjective time estimation and information processing in children: Effects of motion, narration, and subtitles.* Unpublished Ph.D. dissertation, University of Kansas, Lawrence.

Ostman, R. E., & Jeffers, D. W. (1990). *The relationship of life stage to motives for using television and the perceived reality of TV.* Paper presented at the meeting of the International Communication Association, Acapulco, Mexico.

Paik, H., & Comstock, G. (1994). The effects of television violence on antisocial behavior: A meta-analysis. *Communication Research, 21,* 516–546.

Palmer, E. L., & McDowell, C. N. (1979). Program/commercial separators in children's television programming. *Journal of Communication, 29,* 197–201.

Pearl, D., Bouthilet, L., & Lazar, J. (Eds.). (1982). *Television and behavior: Ten years of scientific progress and implications for the eighties: Vol. 1. Summary report.* Washington, DC: U.S. Government Printing Office.

Peterson, J. L., Moore, K. A., & Furstenberg, F. F. (1991). Television viewing and early initiation of sexual intercourse: Is there a link? *Journal of Homosexuality, 21,* 93–118.

Pezdek, K., & Hartman, E. F. (1983). Children's television viewing: Attention and comprehension of auditory versus visual information. *Child Development, 54,* 1015–1023.

Pezdek, K., Lehrer, A., & Simon, S. (1984). The relationship between reading and cognitive processing of television and radio. *Child Development, 55,* 2072–2082.

Piemyat, S. (1992). *Children's emotional responses to real and fictional, and effects on their recall and prosocial behaviors.* Unpublished Ph.D. dissertation, University of Kansas, Lawrence.

Piñon, M. F., Huston, A. C., & Wright, J. C. (1989). Family ecology and child characteristics that predict young children's educational television viewing. *Child Development, 60,* 846–856.

Posner, J. K., & Vandell, D. L. (1994). Low-income children's after-school care: Are there beneficial effects of after-school programs? *Child Development, 65,* 440–456.

Postman, N. (1979). *Teaching as a conserving activity.* New York: Delacourt Press.

Potter, W. J. (1986). Perceived reality and the cultivation hypothesis. *Journal of Broadcasting and Electronic Media, 30,* 159–174.

Potter, W. J. (1987). Does television viewing hinder academic achievement among adolescents? *Human Communication Research, 14,* 27–46.

Potter, W. J. (1988). Perceived reality in television effects research. *Journal of Broadcasting and Electronic Media, 32,* 23–41.

Potts, R., & Martinez, I. (1994). Television viewing and children's beliefs about scientists. *Journal of Applied Developmental Psychology, 15,* 287–300.

Potts, R., Martinez, I., & Dedmon, A. (1993, May). *An analysis of scientific and supernatural content in children's television programs.* Paper presented at the meeting of the Southwestern Psychological Association, Corpus Christi, TX.

Rice, M. L., Huston, A. C., Truglio, R., & Wright, J. C. (1990). Words from Sesame Street: Learning vocabulary while viewing. *Developmental Psychology, 26,* 421–428.

Rice, M. L., Huston, A. C., & Wright, J. C. (1982). The forms and codes of television: Effects on children's attention, comprehension, and social behavior. In D. Pearl (Ed.), *Television and behavior: Ten years of scientific progress and implications for the 80s* (pp. 24–38). Washington, DC: Government Printing Office.

Rice, M. L., Huston, A. C., & Wright, J. C. (1986). Replays as repetitions: Young children's interpretation of television forms. *Journal of Applied Developmental Psychology, 7,* 61–76.

Rice, M. L., & Woodsmall, L. (1988). Lessons from television: Children's word learning when viewing. *Child Development, 59,* 420–429.

Ridley-Johnson, R., Chance, J. E., & Cooper, H. (1984). Correlates of children's television viewing: Expectancies, age, and sex. *Journal of Applied Developmental Psychology, 5,* 225–235.

Ritchie, D., Price, V., & Roberts, D. F. (1987). Television, reading, and reading achievement: A reappraisal. *Communication Research, 14,* 292–315.

RMC Research Corporation. (1989). *The impact of Reading Rainbow on libraries.* Hampton, NH: RMC Corporation.

Roberts, D. F., Henriksen, L., Voelker, D. H., & van Vuuren, D. P. (1993). Television and schooling: Displacement and distraction hypotheses. *Australian Journal of Education, 37,* 198–211.

Roberts, E. J. (1982). Television and sexual learning in childhood. In D. Pearl (Ed.), *Television and behavior: Ten years of scientific progress and implications for the 80s* (pp. 209–223). Washington, DC: Government Printing Office.

Robinson, J. P., & Bachman, J. G. (1972). Television viewing habits and aggression. In G. A. Comstock & E. A. Rubinstein (Eds.), *Television and social behavior: Vol. 3. Television and adolescent aggressiveness* (pp. 372–382). Washington, DC: U.S. Government Printing Office.

Rolandelli, D. R. (1989). Children and television: The visual superiority effect reconsidered. *Journal of Broadcasting and Electronic Media, 33*(1), 69–81.

Rolandelli, D. R., Sugihara, K., & Wright, J. C. (1992). Visual processing of televised information by Japanese and American children. *Journal of Cross-Cultural Psychology, 23*(1), 5–24.

Rolandelli, D. R., Wright, J. C., Huston, A. C., & Eakins, D. (1991). Children's auditory and visual processing of narrated and non-narrated television programming. *Journal of Experimental Child Psychology, 51,* 90–122.

Rosengren, K. E., Wenner, L. A., & Palmgreen, P. (Eds.). (1985). *Media gratification research: Current perspectives.* Beverly Hills, CA: Sage.

Rosenthal, R. (1986). Media violence, antisocial behavior, and the social consequences of small effects. *Journal of Social Issues, 42*(3), 141–154.

Rowland, W. D., Jr. (1983). *The politics of TV violence: Policy uses of communication research.* Beverly Hills, CA: Sage.

Rubin, A. M. (1983). Television uses and gratifications: The interactions of viewing patterns and motivations. *Journal of Broadcasting, 27,* 37–51.

Runco, M. A., & Pezdek, K. (1984). The effect of television and radio on children's creativity. *Human Communication Research, 11,* 109–120.

St. Peters, M. (1993). *The ecology of mother child interaction.* Unpublished doctoral dissertation, University of Kansas, Lawrence.

St. Peters, M., Fitch, M., Huston, A. C., Wright, J. C., & Eakins, D. (1991). Television and families: What do young children watch with their parents? *Child Development, 62,* 1409–1423.

Salomon, G. (1977). Effects of encouraging Israeli mothers to co-observe "Sesame Street" with their five-year-olds. *Child Development, 48,* 1146–1151.

Salomon, G. (1979). *Interaction of media, cognition, and learning.* San Francisco: Jossey-Bass.

Salomon, G. (1983). Television watching and mental effort: A social psychological view. In J. Bryant & D. R. Anderson (Eds.), *Children's understanding of television: Research on attention and comprehension* (pp. 181–198). New York: Academic Press.

Sapolsky, B. S., & Tabarlet, J. O. (1991). Sex in primetime television: 1979 versus 1989. *Journal of Broadcasting and Electronic Media, 35,* 505–516.

Scarborough, H. S. (1989). Prediction of reading disability from familial and individual differences. *Journal of Educational Psychology, 81,* 101–108,

Schiff, J. L., & Truglio, R. T. (1995, April). *In search of the ideal family: The use of television family portrayals during early adolescence.* Paper presented at the biennial meeting of the Society for Research in Child Development, Indianapolis, IN.

Schramm, W., Lyle, J., & Parker, E. B. (1961). *Television in the lives of our children.* Stanford, CA: Stanford University Press.

Selnow, G. W., & Reynolds, H. (1984). Some opportunity costs of television viewing. *Journal of Broadcasting, 28,* 315–322.

Sesame Street Research. (1992). *Puerto Rican, African American, White, and Crow Indian self awareness and race relations.* New York: Children's Television Workshop.

Shannon, B., Peacock, J., & Brown, M. J. (1991). Body fatness, television viewing and caloric intake of a sample of Pennsylvania sixth grade children. *Journal of Nutrition Education, 23,* 262–268.

Signorella, M. L., Bigler, R. S., & Liben, L. S. (1993). Developmental differences in children's gender schemata about others: A meta-analytic review. *Developmental Review, 13,* 147–183.

Signorielli, N. (1989). Television and conceptions about sex-roles: Maintaining conventionality and the status quo. *Sex Roles, 21,* 341–360.

Signorielli, N. (1991). Adolescents and ambivalence toward marriage: A cultivation analysis. *Youth and Society, 23,* 121–149.

Signorielli, N. (1993a). Television and adolescents' perceptions about work. *Youth and Society, 24,* 314–341.

Signorielli, N. (1993b). Television, the portrayal of women, and children's attitudes. In G. Berry & J. K. Asamen (Eds.), *Children and television: Images in a changing sociocultural world* (pp. 229–242). Newbury Park, CA: Sage.

Signorielli, N., & Lears, M. (1992). Children, television, and conceptions about chores: Attitudes and behaviors. *Sex Roles, 27,* 157–170.

Signorielli, N., McLeod, D., & Healy, E. (1994). Gender stereotypes in MTV commercials: The beat goes on. *Journal of Broadcasting and Electronic Media, 38,* 91–101.

Signorielli, N., & Morgan, M. (Eds.). (1990). *Cultivation analysis: New directions in media effects research.* Newbury Park, CA: Sage.

Silverman-Watkins, T., & Sprafkin, J. N. (1983). Adolescents' comprehension of televised sexual innuendos. *Journal of Applied Developmental Psychology, 4,* 359–369.

Silvern, S. B., & Williamson, P. A. (1987). The effects of video game play on young children's aggression, fantasy, and prosocial behavior. *Journal of Applied Developmental Psychology, 8,* 453–462.

Singer, D. G., & Singer, J. L. (1994a). *Barney & Friends as education and entertainment: Phase 3. A national study: Can preschoolers learn through exposure to Barney & Friends?* New Haven, CT: Yale University Family Television Research and Consultation Center.

Singer, D. G., & Singer, J. L. (1994b). Evaluating the classroom viewing of a television series: "Degrassi Junior High." In D. Zillmann, J. Bryant, & A. C. Huston (Eds.), *Media, children, and the family: Social scientific, psychodynamic, and clinical perspectives* (pp. 97–116). Hillsdale, NJ: Erlbaum.

Singer, D. G., Zuckerman, D. M., & Singer, J. L. (1980). Helping elementary school children learn about TV. *Journal of Communication, 30,* 84–93.

Singer, J. L. (1980). The power and limits of television: A cognitive-affective analysis. In P. Tannenbaum (Ed.), *The entertainment function of television.* Hillsdale, NJ: Erlbaum.

Singer, J. L., & Singer, D. G. (1981). *Television, imagination and aggression: A study of preschoolers.* Hillsdale, NJ: Erlbaum.

Singer, J. L., & Singer, D. G. (1994). *Barney & Friends as education and entertainment: Phase 2. Can children learn through preschool exposure to Barney & Friends?* New Haven, CT: Yale University Family Television Research and Consultation Center.

Skill, T., Wallace, S., & Cassata, M. (1990). Families on prime-time television: Patterns of conflict escalation and resolution across intact, nonintact, and mixed-family settings. In J. Bryant (Ed.), *Television and the American family* (pp. 129–164). Hillsdale, NJ: Erlbaum.

Slaby, R. G., & Frey, K. S. (1975). Development of gender constancy and selective attention to same-sex models. *Child Development, 46,* 849–856.

Slater, D., & Elliott, W. R. (1982). Television's influence on social reality. *Quarterly Journal of Speech, 68,* 69–70.

Smith, R., Anderson, D. R., & Fischer, C. R. (1985). Young children's comprehension of montage. *Child Development, 56,* 962–971.

Soh, R. S. (1995). *Effects of TV hybred genres on children's cognitive, emotional, and prosocial behaviors.* Unpublished Ph.D. dissertation, University of Kansas, Lawrence.

Soh, R. S., Neapolitan, D., Wright, J. C., & Todd, M. (1993, March). *Television factuality and consequences to models: Effects of violent content on children's self reports about aggression.* Paper presented at the meeting of the Society for Research in Child Development, New Orleans.

Sprafkin, J., Gadow, K. D., & Kant, G. (1988). Teaching emotionally disturbed children to discriminate reality from fantasy on television. *Journal of Special Education, 21*(4), 99–107.

Sprafkin, J., Watkins, L. T., & Gadow, K. D. (1990). Efficacy of a television literacy curriculum for emotionally disturbed and learning disabled children. *Journal of Applied Developmental Psychology, 11*(2), 225–244.

Stein, A. H., & Friedrich, L. K. (1975). The impact of television on children and youth. In E. M. Hetherington (Ed.), *Review of child development research* (Vol. 5, pp. 183–256). Chicago: University of Chicago Press.

Stroman, C. A. (1986). Television viewing and self-concept among Black children. *Journal of Broadcasting and Electronic Media, 30,* 87–93.

Strommen, E. F. (1991). "What did he say?": Speech output in preschool software. *Proceedings of the National Educational Computing Conference,* 149–151.

Strommen, E. F. (1993). "Does yours eat leaves?": Cooperative learning in an educational software task. *Journal of Computing in Childhood Education, 4,* 45–56.

Strommen, E. F. (1994, April). Children's use of mouse-based interfaces to control virtual travel. *Proceedings of the National Educational Computing Conference,* 405–410.

Strommen, E. F., & Frome, F. S. (1993). Talking back to Big Bird: Preschool users and a simple speech recognition system. *Educational Technology Research and Development, 41,* 5–16.

Strommen, E. F., Revelle, G. L., Medoff, L. M., & Razavi, S. (in press). Slow and steady wins the race?: Three-year-olds and pointing device use. *Behavior and Information Technology.*

Subrahmanyam, K., & Greenfield, P. M. (1994). Effect of video game practice on spatial skills in girls and boys. *Journal of Applied Developmental Psychology, 15,* 13–32.

Surgeon General's Scientific Advisory Committee on Television and Social Behavior. (1972). *Television and growing up: The impact of televised violence.* Washington, DC: U.S. Government Printing Office.

Tamborini, R., & Stiff, J. (1987). Predictors of horror-film attendance and appeal: An analysis of the audience for frightening films. *Communication Research, 14,* 415–436.

Tangney, J. P. (1988). Aspects of the family and children's television viewing content preferences. *Child Development, 59,* 1070–1079.

Tangney, J. P., & Feshbach, S. (1988). Children's television viewing frequency: Individual differences and demographic correlates. *Personality and Social Psychology Bulletin, 14,* 145–158.

Taras, H. L., Sallis, J. F., Patterson, T. L., & Nader, P. R. (1989). Television's influence on children's diet and physical activity. *Journal of Developmental and Behavioral Pediatrics, 10*(4), 176–180.

Timmer, S. G., Eccles, J., & O'Brien, K. (1985). How children use time. In F. T. Juster & F. P. Stafford (Eds.), *Time, goods, and well-being* (pp. 353–382). Ann Arbor, MI: Survey Research Center, Institute for Social Research.

Truglio, R. T. (1990). *The socializing effects of prime-time television on adolescents' learning about sexuality.* Report to Center for Population Options, University of Kansas, Lawrence.

Truglio, R. T. (1993). *Sex in the 90s: What are the lessons from prime-time TV?* Paper presented at the meeting of the Society for Research in Child Development, New Orleans.

Truglio, R., Huston, A. C., & Wright, J. C. (1986, August). *The relation between types of television viewing and young children's reading abilities.* Paper presented at the meeting of the American Psychological Association, Washington, DC.

Turow, J., & Coe, L. (1985). Curing television's ills: The portrayal of health care. *Journal of Communication, 35*(4), 36–51.

Valkenburg, P. M., & van der Voort, T. H. A. (1994). Influence of TV on daydreaming and creative imagination: A review of research. *Psychological Bulletin, 116,* 316–339.

Valkenburg, P. M., & van der Voort, T. H. A. (1995). The influence of television on children's daydreaming styles: A 1-year panel study. *Communication Research, 22,* 267–287.

Valkenburg, P. M., Vooijs, M. W., van der Voort, T. H., & Weigman, O. (1992). The influence of television on children's fantasy styles: A secondary analysis. *Imagination, Cognition, and Personality, 12*(1), 55–67.

van der Voort, T. H., & Valkenburg, P. M. (1994). Television's impact on fantasy play: A review of research. *Developmental Review, 14,* 227–251.

van der Voort, T. H., & Vooijs, M. W. (1990). Validity of children's direct estimates of time spent television viewing. *Journal of Broadcasting and Electronic Media, 34,* 93–99.

Van Evra, J. (1990). *Television and child development.* Hillsdale, NJ: Erlbaum.

Van Lil, J. E., Vooijs, M. W., & van der Voort, T. H. (1988). The relationship between television viewing and leisure reading: A cross-sectional study. *Pedagogische Studien, 64*(10), 377–389.

Vooijs, M. W., & van der Voort, T. H. (1993). Learning about television violence: The impact of a critical viewing curriculum on children's attitudinal judgments of crime series. *Journal of Research and Development in Education, 26,* 133–142.

Vygotsky, L. S. (1978). The zone of proximal development. In M. Cole, V. John-Steiner, S. Scribner, & E. Souberman (Eds.), *Mind in society.* Cambridge, MA: Harvard University Press.

Ward, L. M. (1995). Talking about sex: Common themes about sexuality in the prime-time television programs children and adolescents view most. *Journal of Youth and Adolescence, 24,* 595–616.

Wartella, E. (1994). *Living an electronic childhood.* The Cologne Conference, Cologne, Germany.

Wartella, E. (1995). The commercialization of youth: Channel One in context. *Phi Delta Kappan,* 448–451.

Watkins, B. A. (1987). Improving educational and informational television for children: When the marketplace fails. *Yale Law and Policy Review, 5,* 345–381.

Watkins, B. A., Calvert, S. L., Huston-Stein, A., & Wright, J. C. (1980). Children's recall of television material: Effects of presentation mode and adult labeling. *Developmental Psychology, 16,* 672–674.

Watkins, L. T., Sprafkin, J., Gadow, K. D., & Sadetsky, I. (1988). Effects of a critical viewing skills curriculum on elementary school children's knowledge and attitudes about television. *Journal of Educational Research, 81*(3), 165–170.

Weiss, A. J., Imrich, D. J., & Wilson, B. J. (1993). Prior exposure to creatures from a horror film: Live vs. photographic representations. *Human Communication Research, 20*(1), 41–66.

Weiss, A. J., & Wilson, B. J. (1993). *Developmental differences in children's understanding of emotions and emotional storylines in family-formatted situation comedies.* Paper presented at the biennial meeting of the Society for Research in Child Development, New Orleans.

Weiss, A. J., & Wilson, B. J. (1994). *Children's cognitive and emotional responses to the portrayal of negative emotions in family-formatted situation comedies.* Paper presented at the meeting of the International Communication Association, Sydney, Australia.

Weiss, A. J., & Wilson, B. J. (1995). *Emotional portrayals in family television series that are popular among children.* Unpublished manuscript, University of California, Santa Barbara.

Welch, R. L., Huston-Stein, A., Wright, J. C., & Plehal, R. (1979). Subtle sex-role cues in children's commercials. *Journal of Communication, 29*(3), 202–209.

Wells, W. D. (1973). *Television and aggression: Replication of an experimental field study.* Unpublished manuscript, University of Chicago, Graduate School of Business.

Wiegerman, O., Kuttschreuter, M., & Baarda, B. (1992). A longitudinal study of the effects of television viewing on aggressive and prosocial behaviors. *British Journal of Social Psychology, 31,* 147–164.

Williams, P. A., Haertel, E. H., Walberg, H. J., & Haertel, G. D. (1982). The impact of leisure-time television on school learning: A research synthesis. *American Educational Research Journal, 19,* 19–50.

Williams, T. M. (Ed.). (1986). *The impact of television: A natural experiment in three communities.* Orlando, FL: Academic Press.

Williams, T. M., Baron, D., Phillips, S., Travis, L., & Jackson, D. (1986). *The portrayal of sex roles on Canadian and U.S. television.* Paper presented at the conference of the International Association for Mass Communication Research, New Delhi, India.

Williams, T. M., & Boyes, M. C. (1986). Television-viewing patterns and use of other media. In T. M. Williams (Ed.), *The impact of television: A natural experiment in three communities* (pp. 215–264). Orlando, FL: Academic Press.

Williams, T. M., & Cox, R. (1995). *Informative versus other children's TV programs: Portrayals of ethnic diversity, gender, and aggression.* Paper presented at the meeting of the Society for Research in Child Development, Indianapolis, IN.

Williams, T. M., & Handford, A. G. (1986). Television and other leisure activities. In T. M. Williams (Ed.), *The impact of television: A natural experiment in three communities* (pp. 143–214). Orlando, FL: Academic Press.

Wilson, B. J. (1987). Reducing children's emotional reactions to mass media through rehearsed explanation and exposure to a replica of a fear object. *Human Communication Research, 14*(1), 3–26.

Wilson, B. J. (1989a). Desensitizing children's emotional reactions to the mass media. *Communication Research, 16,* 723–745.

Wilson, B. J. (1989b). The effects of two control strategies on children's emotional reactions to a frightening movie scene. *Journal of Broadcasting and Electronic Media, 33,* 397–418.

Wilson, B. J., & Cantor, J. (1985). Developmental differences in empathy with a television protagonist's fear. *Journal of Experimental Child Psychology, 39,* 284–299.

Wilson, B. J., & Cantor, J. (1987). Reducing fear reactions to mass media: Effects of visual exposure and verbal explanation. In M. McLoughlin (Ed.), *Communication yearbook* (Vol. 10, pp. 553–573). Newbury Park, CA: Sage.

Wilson, B. J., Cantor, J., Gordon, L., & Zillmann, D. (1986). Affective response of nonretarded and retarded children to the emotions of a protagonist. *Child Study Journal, 16*(2), 77–93.

Wilson, B. J., Hoffner, C., & Cantor, J. (1987). Children's perceptions of the effectiveness of techniques to reduce fear from mass media. *Journal of Applied Developmental Psychology, 8,* 39–52.

Wilson, B. J., & Smith, S. L. (1995). *Children's comprehension of, and emotional reactions to, television news.* Paper presented at the meeting of the International Communication Association, Albuquerque.

Wilson, B. J., & Weiss, A. J. (1991). The effects of two reality explanations on children's reactions to a frightening movie scene. *Communication Monographs, 58,* 307–326.

Wilson, B. J., & Weiss, A. J. (1992). Developmental differences in children's reactions to a toy advertisement linked to a toy-based cartoon. *Journal of Broadcasting and Electronic Media, 36,* 371–394.

Wilson, B. J., & Weiss, A. J. (1993). The effects of sibling coviewing on preschooler's reactions to a suspenseful movie scene. *Communication Research, 20,* 214–248.

Winker, J. B. (1949). Age trends and sex differences in the wishes, identifications, activities, and fears of children. *Child Development, 20,* 191–200.

Winn, M. (1987). *Unplugging the plug-in drug.* New York: Penguin Books.

Wober, J. M. (1992). Text in a texture of television: Children's homework experience. *Journal of Educational Television, 18*(1), 23–34.

Wober, J. M., & Fazal, S. (1988). *Children's imagery and uses of television, computers, and other communication equipment* (Research Paper). London: Independent Broadcasting Authority.

Wood, W., Wong, F. Y., & Chachere, J. G. (1991). Effects of media violence on viewers' aggression in unconstrained social interaction. *Psychological Bulletin, 109,* 371–383.

Wright, J. C., & Huston, A. C. (1981). The forms of television: Nature and development of television literacy in children. In H. Gardner & H. Kelly (Eds.), *New directions in child development: Vol. 13. Viewing children through television* (pp. 73–88). San Francisco: Jossey-Bass.

Wright, J. C., & Huston, A. C. (1983). A matter of form: Potentials of television for young viewers. *American Psychologist, 38,* 835–843.

Wright, J. C., & Huston, A. C. (1995, June). *Effects of educational TV viewing of lower income preschoolers on academic skills, school readiness, and school adjustment one to three years later.* Report to Children's Television Workshop, Center for Research on the Influences of Television on Children, University of Kansas, Lawrence.

Wright, J. C., Huston, A. C., Alvarez, M., Truglio, R., Fitch, M., & Piemyat, S. (1995). Perceived television reality and children's emotional and cognitive responses to its social content. *Journal of Applied Developmental Psychology, 16,* 231–251.

Wright, J. C., Huston, A. C., Reitz, A. L., & Piemyat, S. (1994). Young children's perception of television reality: Determinants and developmental differences. *Developmental Psychology, 30,* 229–239.

Wright, J. C., Huston, A. C., Ross, R. P., Calvert, S. L., Rolandelli, D., Weeks, L. A., Raeissi, P., & Potts, R. (1984). Pace and continuity of television programs: Effects on children's attention and comprehension. *Developmental Psychology, 20,* 653–666.

Wright, J. C., Huston, A. C., Truglio, R., Fitch, M., Smith, E., & Piemyat, S. (1995). Occupational portrayals on television: Children's role schemata, career aspirations, and perceptions of reality. *Child Development, 66,* 1706–1718.

Wright, J. C., Kunkel, D., Piñon, M., & Huston, A. C. (1989). Children's affective and cognitive reactions to televised coverage of the space shuttle disaster. *Journal of Communication, 39* (2), 27–45.

Wright, J. C., St. Peters, M., & Huston, A. C. (1990). Family television use and its relation to children's cognitive skills and social behavior. In J. Bryant (Ed.), *Television and the American family* (pp. 227–252). Hillsdale, NJ: Erlbaum.

Wright, J. C., & Vlietstra, A. C. (1975). The development of selective attention: From perceptual exploration to logical search. In H. Reese (Ed.), *Advances in child development and behavior* (Vol. 10). New York: Academic Press.

Wroblewski, R., & Huston, A. C. (1987). Televised occupational stereotypes and their effects on early adolescents: Are they changing? *Journal of Early Adolescence, 7,* 283–298.

Zill, N., Davies, E., & Daly, M. (1994). *Viewing of Sesame Street by preschool children in the United States and its relationship to school readiness.* Rockville, MD: Westat.

Zillmann, D. (1980). Anatomy of suspense. In P. H. Tannenbaum (Ed.), *The entertainment functions of television* (pp. 133–163). Hillsdale, NJ: Erlbaum.

Zillmann, D. (1982). Television viewing and arousal. In D. Pearl, L. Bouthilet, & J. Lazar (Eds.), *Television and behavior:Ten years of scientific progress and implications for the eighties* (pp. 53–67). Washington, DC: U.S. Government Printing Office.

Zillmann, D., & Bryant, J. (1994). Entertainment as media effect. In J. Bryant & D. Zillmann (Eds.), *Media effects: Advances in theory and research* (pp. 437–462). Hillsdale, NJ: Erlbaum.

Zillmann, D., Weaver, J. B. V., Mundorf, N., & Aust, C. F. (1986). Effects of opposite-gender companion's affect to horror on distress, delight, and distraction. *Journal of Personality and Social Psychology, 51,* 586–594.

Zohoori, A. R. (1988). Children, television, and the acculturation process. In S. Thomas (Ed.), *Communication and culture: Language, performance, technology, and media. Studies in communication* (Vol. 4, pp. 255–264). Norwood, NJ: ABLEX.

CHAPTER 16

Culture and Human Development: Implications for Parenting, Education, Pediatrics, and Mental Health

PATRICIA M. GREENFIELD and LALITA K. SUZUKI

Culture and child development are inextricably intertwined. From the child's perspective, an important aspect of development is the acquisition of cultural knowledge, Bruner (1990). From the societal perspective, children from birth are exposed to the culture surrounding them. This cultural surround spans everything from sleeping arrangements and feeding practices to the child's eventual value systems, school experiences, and interpersonal interactions. The child's active acquisition of cultural knowledge from the cultural surround constitutes the relationship between culture and child development that is the focus of this chapter.

In multicultural societies, the cultural surround in which a child develops comprises myriad influences; these can be broadly categorized as *home culture* and *societal culture*. Home culture refers to the values, practices, and cultural background of the child's immediate family. The child interacts in this home culture on a daily basis, absorbing and learning from the implicit values transmitted through interactions with family members. The child is also exposed to societal culture, or the culture of the society at large. Through interactions with outside sources (schools, peers, media, etc.), the child can also learn the more general cultural values communicated by the dominant society. Children are thus raised in a dual climate of the culture within the home and the culture of the external world.

In some cases, the cultural climate within the home is derivative of the general cultural climate, mirroring the value systems of the surround. In other situations, the cultural climate of the home may differ significantly from the cultural climate of society at large, as is often the case for recently immigrated families from many foreign countries. When home culture and societal culture differ for any particular family, interesting, and at times vexing, situations arise. Children may be faced with conflicting messages from home and from the outside world (particularly from school) as to the proper values, attitudes, and behaviors they should follow. Parents also must reassess their cultural framework in a new setting where many of their own values may be in direct conflict with those of society at large. These parents need to choose which values in what contexts they should use in raising their children.

The difficulty of such choices is all the greater because cultures are "invisible" (Philips, 1972). That is, they are interpretive lenses that are taken for granted by the wearers. Like the air one breathes, under ordinary conditions, these value frameworks do not rise to conscious awareness. This lack of awareness exacerbates the potential for both personal conflict and interpersonal misunderstanding in multicultural environments.

Because they have the task of assessing the behaviors of parents and children who come from diverse cultural backgrounds, counselors, social workers, educators, and health care professionals who work with families must be aware of these intercultural dynamics. Behaviors that may appear strange and perhaps dysfunctional in one cultural context could in fact be seen as normal in others. The professional community that comes into contact with families of differing backgrounds has the challenge of understanding the values and child developmental goals behind cultural differences. Otherwise, they cannot hope to correctly diagnose the source of any problems that arise.

Perhaps even more important, an understanding of diverse cultural values and associated rearing practices reveals the strengths of socialization and child-care practices used in diverse cultural groups. Equally important is the awareness of the losses that come from giving up one's ancestral culture in the process of assimilating to the dominant cultural surround.

In this chapter, behavioral and value differences that exist in different cultures will be discussed from this dual-culture (home and society) perspective. Each home culture and the dominant societal culture has ancestral roots in other countries (Greenfield & Cocking, 1994). For example, the dominant American culture and the home culture of many European Americans stems primarily from northern Europe, whereas the home culture of Chinese Americans stems from China. These cross-cultural roots allow us to relate ethnic diversity within the multicultural societies of North America (and elsewhere) to cross-cultural variability on a global level. Conversely, the understanding of ancestral cultures helps us to understand the cultural frameworks that constitute an ethnically diverse society.

Two alternative cultural frameworks are particularly basic. In one framework or model, the preferred endpoint of development is independence (Greenfield, 1994; Markus & Kitayama, 1991). The primary goal of socialization in this model is an autonomous, self-fulfilled individual who enters into social relationships and responsibilities by personal choice (Miller, 1994; Miller, Bersoff, & Harwood, 1990). In the other model, the preferred endpoint of development is interdependence (Greenfield, 1994; Markus & Kitayama, 1991). The primary goal of socialization in this model is for the mature person to be embedded in a network of relationships and responsibilities to others; personal achievements are ideally in the service of a collectivity, most often the family.

These models not only generate preferred developmental endpoints and socialization goals, they also function as interpretive frameworks, generating evaluations of others' thinking, feeling, and acting. As interpretive frameworks, the models elucidate the reasons for cultural differences, the values behind cross-cultural variability in behaviors, thoughts, and feelings.

The independence framework is part of a broader philosophical and social model called individualism (Triandis, 1988). The interdependence framework is part of a broader philosophical and social model called collectivism (Triandis, 1988). These cultural models are often taken for granted; yet they generate socialization preferences and developmental goals across a wide variety of behavioral domains. To use Shore's (1996) terminology, they are foundational schemata.

Traditional research in developmental psychology has implicitly assumed the independence model or script. By also acknowledging an alternative course of development—the interdependence script—we have a more universal theory of development.

Because of this generative quality, the cultural models of individualism and collectivism integrate group differences across different domains and different periods of development. They provide theoretical, cultural, and developmental coherence to what otherwise would be an array of unconnected group differences. Because of this coherence, we have used these alternative cultural models as an organizing framework for four periods and domains of development: infant care, socialization, and development; parent-child relations; peer relations; and home-school relations. These constitute the four major sections of this chapter.

The contrasting cultural models of individualism and collectivism also provide a framework that can account for cultural diversity in a multicultural society such as the United States (Greenfield & Cocking, 1994). Many immigrant and other minority groups have entered the United States, a society built on individualistic principles (Raeff, in press), bringing with them a collectivistic value system and frame of reference from their ancestral cultures (Greenfield & Cocking, 1994). This historical situation leads to a dynamic in which the socialization goals of a child's home culture are more collectivistic, while those of the broader society are more individualistic. This state of affairs produces a dialectical process that has important social ramifications. This dialectic will be a focus of our concern as we draw out implications of culture and human development for parents and practitioners.

ORGANIZATION OF THE CHAPTER

Infant Care, Socialization, and Development; Parent-Child Relations; Peer Relations; and Home-School relations were selected as organizing domains because interaction with parents, peers, and schools constitutes the process by which children are socialized to become human beings and to become members of a particular culture. These social relationships are, moreover, important determinants of children's adjustment and mental health.

The first two major sections of the chapter will focus on variations in existing home cultures during infancy (first section) and later development (second section). The second two major sections focus on extrafamilial sources of cultural knowledge: peers and school. All four sections explore what can occur when home culture differs from societal culture. An introduction to each section follows.

Infant Care, Socialization, and Development

Infancy is commonly described as the period of life between birth and the emergence of language, when a child is approximately 1½ to 2 years of age (Bornstein & Lamb, 1992). During this time, children are first fully exposed to the cultural place that surrounds them. This "cultural place," or the cultural beliefs, practices, and meanings characteristic of members of the child's community, is perhaps the single most important factor in influencing the future life of the child (Weisner, 1996).

The first section, on infant care and development, will analyze the dominant North American cultural model of development, while presenting important alternatives to it. This is critical for professionals who work directly with infants and their families; they need to know the strengths and weaknesses of each cultural model before prescribing infant care practices and developmental diagnoses based on one rather than another. Although our examples often come from the United States, the contrasting cultural models apply to many other societies, including multicultural societies in which European-based culture is dominant.

Our chapter will profile different cultural models of development, their expressions during infancy, and their diverse patterns of strength and weakness. How cultural models influence infant sleeping arrangements, feeding, attachment, and communication will be our substantive focus.

From a theoretical perspective, infancy is critical because it is when a culture sets the gyroscope of development along a particular pathway. From an applied perspective, this period of development is of immediate importance to pediatricians and other health care workers, because they are the primary professionals who interface with infants and their families.

Although infant care advice is generally put forth by pediatricians in books and in person as scientific and therefore culturally "neutral," cross-national differences and changes over historical time in infant care advice (e.g., Métraux, 1955; Young, 1990) make it clear that these professionals are, in fact, providing culture-specific models of children's care and development (Harkness, Super, Keefer, Raghavan, & Campbell, 1996). Because they are unfamiliar with alternative models, pediatricians and their allied workers may promulgate an implicit individualistic cultural model to their patients without being aware of its cultural specificity.

This lack of awareness of one's own cultural assumptions, combined with a lack of understanding of the other's cultural foundations, can cause problems in communicating with and advising patients who enter the medical encounter with a contrasting set of assumptions regarding child development and socialization. Furthermore, when advice concerning infant care and development based on the dominant North American cultural model is put forth as *the* right way, it can make parents who have been brought up with other cultural models feel confused, guilty, or inadequate.

Cultural knowledge of infancy is also important for professionals such as educators, who meet families when their children are older. An understanding of the diverse developmental courses that have been set in infancy provides insight into the different behavioral patterns that are seen when children arrive in preschool or elementary school. The bottom line is that implicit learning at home significantly impacts what educators have to begin working with at school.

Parent-Child Relations

Taking a developmental approach, the second section will focus on older children and how interactions and relations between parents and children may differ in various cultural contexts. Issues such as parent-child communication, parenting styles, and discipline will be addressed. By organizing the first two sections chronologically, the reader will be able to see how the same set of cultural models—specifically models stressing independence or interdependence as developmental goals—show up at earlier and later stages of development. This cultural consistency reinforces and provides continuity for particular paths of development (Greenfield & Childs, 1991).

This section also has practical implications beyond the family. For example, teachers must know the developmental goals that parents are working toward at home, to prevent children from being caught in the middle of home-school value conflict (e.g., Raeff, Greenfield, & Quiroz, in press), the topic of the fourth section.

Similarly, counselors and clinical psychologists must know the developmental goals that parents are working toward at home. Here is an example of the usefulness of such knowledge in a culturally diverse counseling practice:

When a Korean adolescent of immigrant parents complains that his or her parents are dictating a field of study for the child, a counselor in the United States or Canada may not realize that, in the Korean culture, the goal of education is not to bring out the unique potential of a maximally autonomous individual; rather, education is for the benefit of the whole family, including parents. Within this cultural framework, parents are justifiably concerned that their child find a field that can ensure future economic security for the whole family.

With an understanding of this kind of alternative developmental model, counselors and clinical psychologists are less likely to accuse the parents of depriving their child of autonomy or producing an unhealthy guilt trip. They are more likely to correctly diagnose the adolescent as caught between two opposing value frameworks. Equally important, they will be able to explain this value conflict to immigrant parents who are often more strongly identified with the ancestral culture than are their more assimilated children.

Peer Relations

The third section focuses on implications of contrasting value assumptions for peer relations. When peers from differing cultural backgrounds interact, certain assumptions about communication, allocation of rewards, conflict resolution, and other interpersonal issues may be violated, leading to potential hurt and confusion. The implications of these potential cross-cultural misunderstandings will be discussed for parents, educators, and clinicians.

The direct relevance of cultural variability in peer relations for educational practice is illustrated in the following example (Quiroz & Greenfield, in press):

A kindergarten teacher and her class are of similar ethnic background; all the families have immigrated from Mexico or Central America. The teacher sets out crayons in cups for the class. Each cup holds multiple crayons of a given color. On a mentoring visit, a supervisor tells the teacher that she should abandon the communal crayons and, instead, give each child his or her individual cup of multicolor crayons. By doing this, the supervisor says, children will not have to use the broken crayons created by other children; they will enjoy the activity more.

After following this advice, the teacher discovers that the children, who had been interested in taking care of the "group" crayons, have no interest whatsoever in taking care of their "individual" crayons; if anything, their interest and enjoyment of the coloring activity diminishes.

In essence, the supervisor is enforcing a cultural model of development that emphasizes the independence of each member of a peer group; the concept of personal property (in this case, applied to crayons) is part of that independence. The teacher and class, in contrast, are actualizing a contrasting model of development that emphasizes interdependence and sharing among peers. This is the model of peer relations that these children have brought with them from home.

Through understanding the two cultural models for peer relations, the supervisor could have discussed the strengths and weaknesses of the alternative practices with the teacher, so that an informed choice could be made. Instead, the supervisor rather unconsciously created a value conflict between peer relations valued at home and school, a dichotomy that could potentially alienate children (and teachers) from home, school, or from both, while interfering with the joy and process of learning.

On the theoretical level, such conflicts give us a clue concerning contrasting models of human development. On the applied level, it is to the avoidance of such unconscious, yet destructive cross-cultural value conflicts that this chapter is dedicated.

Home-School Relations

As the preceeding section implies, relations between families and school personnel are crucially important for parents, children, and teachers. The final major section of this chapter will emphasize schools as institutional contexts with a distinct culture and with the potential for inducing value conflicts between school and home.

As an example of such conflict, teachers often complain that Asian American and Mexican American children do not speak up enough or ask questions in class (e.g., Greenfield, Quiroz, & Raeff, in press; Muto, Kubo, & Oshima-Takane, 1980). But do these teachers realize that, in many Mexican families, it is considered disrespectful to express opinions to adults (Delgado-Gaitan, 1994)? Do teachers realize that, for Japanese families, questions to the teacher are considered a challenge to the pedagogical competence of the teacher or an admission of failure to understand on the part of the student (Muto et al., 1980)?

Armed with such knowledge, teachers will at least understand that the quiet child of Mexican or Japanese immigrant parents is not detached or stupid, but merely expressing a different style. This section of the chapter will present home-school value differences. Such differences will be analyzed as part of contrasting cultural models of human development and socialization—models of independence and interdependence as developmental priorities.

GUIDING PRINCIPLES

With particular attention to ethnic diversity, our goal in this chapter is to give coherence and meaning to cultural differences. Hence, we concentrate not on the level of discrete behaviors, but on the level of cultural models: deep conceptual frameworks that generate myriad specific cultural practices and provide automatic interpretations of the cultural practices of others. It is important to note that these "cultural models" are not limited to national or ethnic differences, but can include the influences of socioeconomic class, rural/urban locality, level of education, and many other dimensions as well. Thus, these models are not group labels, but they reveal themselves in the socialization practices and developmental goals that parents and the broader society have for children.

LeVine et al. (1994), based on the work of Geertz (1983), Holland and Quinn (1987), and D'Andrade and Strauss (1992), term the cultural software of parental behavior a "'commonsense' folk model" (p. 248). This model is implicit, rather than explicit. The folk model generates specific behaviors and activities that are conscious, but the underlying model is not. As applied to child rearing, this cultural model is often called a parental ethnotheory (cf., Harkness & Super, 1995) or parental belief system (Sigel, 1985; Sigel, McGillicuddy-DeLisi, & Goodnow, 1992). Although there are individual differences in parental ethnotheories within any cultural group, many of these variations occur around a particular cultural theme.

At the same time, cultural models and developmental goals operate in a context of economic, social, psychological, and physical factors that both influence the goals and provide constraints or facilitating conditions for translating goals into socialization practices. These factors include biology, physical environment, family structure, parental work, intergroup relations, and societal economy. Our chapter considers the role of such factors in the cultural enactment of developmental goals.

In selecting topics for inclusion in this chapter, two criteria were paramount: Would the topic reveal the operation of important, yet culturally variable developmental goals? Would the topic be useful for professionals who deal with children and their families? Because of this intended audience, we have evaluated research and selected what seemed useful both theoretically and practically for parents, educators, and health-care professionals. It is our hope that these criteria have been successfully implemented.

INFANT CARE, SOCIALIZATION, AND DEVELOPMENT

A recent article in *Mothering,* a magazine for mothers of young infants in the United States, contained an article on infant sleeping arrangements called "Tossing and Turning over 'Crying It Out,'" by Carol Smaldino (1995). Smaldino's article begins with a description from *Can't You Sleep, Little Bear?* by Martin Waddell and Barbara Firth

(1995) and a discussion of her own confusion and concern about infants' sleeping arrangements, an issue of great concern among many new parents:

> Little Bear can't sleep because he is afraid of the dark. Big Bear, while busy reading a book, checks on him intermittently, bringing bigger and better lanterns each time. Finally, Big Bear takes Little Bear in his arms and goes outside to show him the moon and stars. By the time they step into the night air, Little Bear is already asleep, safely cradled in the warmth of Big Bear's arms. Big Bear has fallen on success shamelessly. Obviously, he has read few bear-rearing books warning him about the hazards of too much comforting.
>
> In my first days of mothering, putting Paul to sleep was about the only thing that came easily. The evening events would exhaust him, then nursing would rescue him from the stresses of the day. During our peaceful ritual of bedtime nursing, he drifted into a sleep that told me first that he was all right, and second that by nursing him to sleep I had contributed to his well-being. I felt like a good mother.
>
> Then the bad news broke. Parenting advice from well-respected professionals came pouring in. *Beware of putting your child to sleep, for you risk encouraging a lifetime of dependency and impairing the development of your child's* own *resources.* The prediction of future sorrows and regrets struck an immediate chord. How could I possibly ignore advice that promised to avert years of suffering? Pangs of guilt rose up in the night. (Smaldino, 1995, p. 33)

As explicit in this example, culture inundates us with information on what constitutes "appropriate" infant rearing, which can lead to feelings of confusion and guilt. Although considerable diversity exists even within middle-class American methods of infant rearing, when we look cross-culturally, we see an even greater variance in child-rearing practices. What may seem risky to child care experts in the United States may be normative in other cultures. Within the United States, mothers from divergent cultural, economic, or educational backgrounds can have very different behavioral practices and goals for their young infants.

What Are Parental Goals for Infants and Children?

In general, parental goals for their children include some combination of the following: infant survival and health, the acquisition of economic capabilities, and the attainment of culturally appropriate values (LeVine, 1988). These values will vary from culture to culture and yield culturally variable child development goals. Culturally defined parental goals are crucial in parental behavior toward the child and in the child's eventual socialization process. Normative parental goals both reflect and affect the structure and functioning of society as a whole.

In the United States, parents have many goals for their children, but one of the most basic and general is the desire to have children grow up to be independent and individuated adults. Guiding children to learn to make their own decisions and establish their separate individual existences was found to be one of the most important parental goals mentioned by mothers in Boston, Massachusetts (Richman, Miller, & Johnson Solomon, 1988). This is the developmental goal underlying the "professional" advice reported by Carol Smaldino concerning putting a baby to sleep alone. Similarly, Hess, Kashiwagi, Azuma, Price, and Dickson (1980) found that U.S. mothers tended to value skills in their children's behaviors that related to matters of individual action, such as self-assertion and standing up for one's rights (Hess et al., 1980). These goals are associated with the cultural model of individualism.

Such goals socialize children to operate effectively in an individualistic society such as the United States. "So basic is the concept of individualism to American society," it has been said, "that every major issue which faces us as a nation invariably poses itself in these terms" (Gross & Osterman, 1971, p. xi).

In contrast, parents in Japan show a different trend in parental goals. Rather than focusing on independence, in Japan, parents "want their children to develop a sense of what can be loosely translated as dependence from the very beginning" (Nugent, 1994, p. 6). In the study of maternal values conducted by Hess et al. (1980), Japanese mothers contrasted with U.S. mothers in their greater concern about issues of self-control, compliance to adult authority, and social interaction in child development.

Japanese mothers are more likely to perceive themselves as being "one" with their infants. In a paper presented in Tokyo in 1987, Kawakami claimed, "An American mother-infant relationship consists of two individuals . . . on the other hand a Japanese mother-infant relationship consists of only one individual; i.e., mother and infant are not divided" (p. 5) (in Morelli, Rogoff, Oppenheim, & Goldsmith, 1992). This value of extreme closeness between mother and infant is another indication of the interdependent goals of Japanese parenting and is manifested in patterns of interaction, such as in *amae* behavior (variously translated as dependence or interdependence) that children express toward their mothers (Lebra, 1994, Shwalb & Shwalb, 1996).

Just as the United States is a society that both values and institutionalizes individualism, Japan is a society in which collectivism—an emphasis on strong, cohesive in-groups

(Hofstede, 1991)—is both valued and institutionalized. Considering these issues, how might Japanese mothers react to Big Bear's method for getting Little Bear to sleep in the opening example?

Perhaps Japanese parents, who put their babies to sleep by nursing and holding them would agree with the U.S. experts that this practice encourages dependence. However, the Japanese interpretation of dependence would be quite different. Certainly, the Japanese would be in profound disagreement with the experts' negative evaluation of dependence as a risk factor that could impair a child's development. This notion of developmental risk is clearly culture-bound (Nugent, 1994).

How Are Sleeping and Feeding Arrangements Affected by Parental Goals?

Smaldino (1995) continues her article in *Mothering:*

> When Paul turned 10 months old, my husband Lino and I became so concerned about wakeful episodes a few times each night that we scheduled an appointment with our pediatrician. He informed us, almost jovially, that the definitive cure would be to let Paul "cry it out." My insides rebelled. I felt an anticipatory wave of depression at the thought of abandoning him. (pp. 33–34)

Although behaviors toward infants vary by culture, one readily observable behavior in all cultures is the organization of infant sleeping arrangements. Infant sleep is a particularly important issue to many U.S. mothers. In the United States, the leading complaint heard by pediatricians is from parents struggling to get infants to sleep alone through the night at as early an age as possible (Lozoff, Wolf, & Davis, 1984). There are also widespread cross-cultural differences in infant sleeping arrangements, and it can be argued that cultural views of infancy, manifest in parental goals, can play a part in determining infant sleeping arrangements.

Where Do Infants Sleep Worldwide?

In the United States, most infants sleep alone in a separate crib, most often in a separate room from their parents (Morelli et al., 1992). In many cultures around the world (particularly non-Western cultures), however, cosleeping is the predominant sleeping arrangement (Konner & Worthman, 1980). In fact, in a survey taken of sleeping practices around the world, it was found that mothers in approximately two thirds of the cultures slept with their infants in their beds, and this portion was much higher if mothers sleeping with their babies in the same room were included (Barry & Paxson, 1971; Burton & Whiting, 1961). Examples of cosleeping cultures include Japan, where children typically sleep with their parents until five or six years of age (Caudill & Plath, 1966). This cosleeping is often referred to as *kawa,* or "river," in which the parents form the symbolic riverbanks for the children sleeping in their own futons between them (Brazelton, 1990). People from many other cultures have similar cosleeping arrangements with their children.

Although the dominant culture in the United States adheres to separate sleeping practices, many minority and immigrant groups still hold on to cosleeping practices from their ancestral cultures. Many people in the United States have immigrated from countries in which infant-mother cosleeping is customary. For example, Schachter, Fuchs, Bijur, and Stone (1989) found that 20% of Hispanic American families in Harlem slept with their children at least three times a week. This was in contrast to the 6% of European American families that did so. Lozoff et al. (1984) found a similar pattern, with more African American than European American infants and toddlers regularly cosleeping with their parent or parents.

What Preferences and Constraints Do Sleeping Arrangements Reflect in the Dominant U.S. Culture?

In the dominant culture of the United States, there is a distinct pressure on parents to push their infants to sleep alone (Brazelton, 1990). In fact, middle-class families who practice cosleeping realize they are going against cultural norms (Hanks & Rebelsky, 1977). According to Morelli et al. (1992), since the early 1900s, American folk wisdom has considered early nighttime separation to be crucial for healthy infant development.

A stress on independence training is an important factor connected to separate sleeping among middle-class parents in the United States (Munroe, Munroe, & Whiting, 1981). Parents have goals of training infants to be independent and self-reliant from the first few months of life, before an undesirable habit of cosleeping may be established that can be difficult to break (Morelli et al., 1992).

Another side of the coin may be parents' need for independence. Adults from the dominant U.S. culture constitute the developmental endpoint of independence training. A dependent infant threatens their own autonomy; therefore, an important motive for separate sleeping arrangements in infancy must be the parents' need to maintain their own independence. Research on the interrelations between parents' goals for themselves and for their children is very much needed.

Loss of privacy associated with parental intimacy is another reason for the disapproval of cosleeping (Shweder, Jensen, & Goldstein, 1995). The privileging of marital ties is typical of cultures that stress autonomy or independence as a developmental goal. In contrast, the privileging of intergenerational ties, such as that between mother and child, is typical of cultures that stress interdependence as a developmental goal (Lebra, 1994; Shweder et al., 1995).

Survival as a reason for separate sleeping arrangements has also been cited by U.S. parents. This includes reducing risks such as smothering or catching a contagious illness (Bundesen, 1944; Holt, 1957; Morelli et al., 1992). Other reasons include psychoanalytic oedipal issues and fear of incestual sexual abuse (Brazelton, 1990; Shweder et al., 1995). These rationales have led many middle-class European American women (and others who are part of the dominant culture) to adhere to sleeping separately from their infants.

Pediatricians, and even the federal government, reinforce this practice. Lozoff et al. (1984) cite sources, from pediatric advice books to government publications, that advise parents not to take their children into their bed for any reason (e.g., Spock, 1976). When parents read such advice, however, the authors are viewed as "well-respected professionals" (Smaldino, 1995), rather than bearers of folk wisdom or carriers of culture-specific ethnotheories of development.

What Preferences and Constraints Does Cosleeping Reflect?

In many cultures, however, cosleeping is considered a desirable practice. In fact, separate infant sleeping arrangements are often met with shock. For example, Brahmans in India believe that it is wrong to let young children sleep alone in a separate room in case the child awakens in the middle of the night. They believe that it is the parents' obligation to protect their children from fear and distress at night (Shweder, Mahapatra, & Miller, 1990). Mayan Indians and Japanese also express shock and pity when first learning of the American practice of having infants sleep apart from parents (Brazelton, 1990; Morelli et al., 1992). On learning that American infants sleep in a separate room from their parents, one shocked Mayan mother remarked, "But there's someone else with them there, isn't there?" (Morelli et al., 1992, p. 608).

Case studies of infant sleeping arrangements done by UCLA undergraduates of diverse cultural origin indicate that deviations from the U.S. norm of separate beds and separate rooms for mother and baby are often motivated by this value of interpersonal closeness. The infant sleeping arrangements of many immigrants to the United States reflect a compromise between the infant-parent separation that is normative here and the infant-parent closeness that is normative in their ancestral cultures of Asia, Mexico, Central America, and the Middle East.

It has been suggested that resource constraints such as lack of space may also be a factor in cosleeping (Brazelton, 1990; Shweder et al., 1995). In many cultures homes have fewer beds or fewer rooms allotted for sleeping purposes. Resource constraints, however, may play a relatively small role. For example, the shock and sadness that Mayan mothers express when learning of the North American practice of separate sleeping arrangements is an indication that cosleeping is not merely a practical concern. Rather, it constitutes a commitment to a particular kind of relationship with the infant (Morelli et al., 1992).

Indeed, in their study of cultural variability within the United States, Lozoff et al. (1984) found that there was no significant relationship between space constraints (number of sleeping rooms available, household size, or the ratio of household size to sleeping rooms) and sleeping arrangements during infancy and toddlerhood. Instead of resource constraints (Shweder et al., 1995), there seem to be reasons related to cultural values and goals that affect even the seemingly simplest of practices, such as infant sleeping arrangements.

Other kinds of ecological factors, however, can play a role in moderating the enactment of a culturally specified developmental goal such as independence. In Lozoff et al.'s (1984) study, there was evidence that European American babies were accepted in their parents' bed under constraining conditions, such as when there was familial stress (such as a move or marital tension) or infant illness, or when the baby was old enough to get out of bed by him- or herself and walk into the parents' bedroom or bed.

The changing ecology of parenting in the United States also provides a moderating influence on the early push toward independence. Brazelton (1990) notes several groups of parents who often sleep with their infants and small children; these include: "(1) single parents, whose needs for company at night may dominate the decision: (2) working parents, who feel torn away during the day and want to reconstitute closeness with their babies at night" (p. 1). In these cases, an ecological factor pushes against the dominant norm in the United States, moving practices in the direction of the norms in most of the rest of the world.

Perhaps working outside the home has rendered nighttime closeness desirable for working mothers, single or married. Another constraining factor might be that working mothers cannot afford the lost sleep engendered by having to get up and feed their waking infants sleeping in another room, or even in another bed.

The Relationship of Sleep to Feeding, Holding, Carrying, and Nursing

Like Big Bear, parents in Asia, Africa, and indigenous America do put their babies to sleep by nursing and holding (e.g., LeVine et al., 1994; Miyake, Chen, & Campos, 1985; Morelli et al., 1992; Super & Harkness, 1982). This practice is part of a pattern of almost continual holding, carrying, and nursing (e.g., Brazelton, Robey, & Collier, 1969; Konner, 1977; Miyake et al., 1985; Super & Harkness, 1982). This pattern may work because of a better fit with the physiology of the young infant. Klein (1995), drawing on Konner (1982), summarizes the research of Blurton-Jones (1972) on this matter:

> There are two types of mammals; those that "nest" their young and those that remain in continuous proximity to their young. Mammals that raise their young in nests produce milk with a high protein and fat content, and feed their offspring at widely spaced intervals. Mammals that carry their young produce milk with a low protein and fat content, and feed their young more or less continuously. Humans, like all higher primates, have the milk composition and suckling characteristics of "carrier" species. !Kung mothers, in keeping with this biological reality, nurse their infants about four times an hour. (p. 308)

The Zinacantecans, a Mayan group in Chiapas, Mexico, also nurse, carry, and hold their infants very frequently (Brazelton et al., 1969).

From a neurological perspective, Restak's (1979) research shows that "physical holding and carrying of the infant turns out to be the most important factor responsible for the infant's normal mental and social development" (p. 122). Hence, we must strongly consider the possibility, suggested by Konner (1982), that sleep problems are a major cultural problem in infant care in the United States precisely because professional advice and the culturally dominant practice are fighting the biology of the human infant that has evolved over hundreds of thousands of years.

What would drive a culture to ignore the physiological imperatives of the infancy period? The words of the professionals hold a clue: *"Beware of putting your child to sleep, for you risk encouraging a lifetime of dependency and impairing the development of your child's* own *resources"* (Smaldino, 1995, p. 33). Could this fear of dependency hinder parents from utilizing broader resources and ideas for child-rearing practices used in other cultures?

What Can We Learn from a Cross-Cultural Perspective on Infant Care Practices? Implications for Parents, Pediatricians, and Other Practitioners

Cultural views and goals may often make it difficult for people to realize and incorporate different modes of behavior, but much can be gained by observing and understanding the practices of other cultures.

Sleep

Many have claimed that in North America, sleep disturbance is one of the most common concerns among parents of young infants today (Brazelton, 1990; Dawes, 1989; Nugent, 1994), as it was for Carol Smaldino. Yet sleep problems are less common or even nonexistent in a number of other cultures. For example, Nugent (1994) reports that "sleep problems or night waking are less commonly reported as clinical concerns in Japanese settings" (p. 6). Similarly, Super and Harkness (1982) noted that sleep problems were nonexistent among the Kipsigis in Kenya.

Why is infant sleep a large problem in the United States, but not in Japan or Kenya? Why are the United States and Western Europe unique in having to call on pediatricians (Spock & Rothenberg, 1985), psychotherapists (Dawes, 1990), and neurologists (Ferber, 1985, 1990) to solve infant sleep problems? Can cross-cultural research be used to address infant sleep problems in North America? Can it help us to evaluate the method used by Big Bear versus that advocated by Smaldino's "well-respected professionals?"

Cross-Cultural Exchange. Much can be learned from infant-rearing techniques practiced in different cultures. Being open to various modes of behavior can often be helpful in introducing new ideas and modes of thought. Parents and pediatricians in North America may benefit from being more accepting of cosleeping practices, since cosleeping has been found to have a number of advantages, such as easier nighttime feeding. For example, Mayan mothers "reported that they generally did not notice having to feed their babies in the night. Mothers said that they did not have to waken, just to turn and make the breast accessible" (Morelli et al., 1992, pp. 606–607). In contrast to these Mayan mothers, night-feeding for middle-class European American mothers is often a laborious task (Morelli et al., 1992), requiring mothers to lose many precious hours of sleep because of having to get up to feed.

It is not that Mayan or Kipsigis babies sleep longer than U.S. babies; rather, the ecology and values are such that the same behavior (night waking) is not viewed as problematic because of the convenience associated with cosleeping arrangements. Indeed, because of the absence of cultural pressure on babies to sleep through the night or to have regular bedtimes, babies in fact wake more often and sleep for shorter periods than in the United States. Super and Harkness (1982) found that Kipsigis babies in Kenya had an average sleep period of only 3 hours from 1 to 8 months of age.

In terms of the superordinate goal of infant survival, cosleeping may play a part in fostering the development of optimal sleeping patterns in infants (McKenna et al., 1993). This may be because cosleeping permits the sleeping infant to take tactile and rhythmic cues from his or her parent, and these cues help regulate an immature breathing system. This interactive process, in turn, may decrease the risk of sudden infant death syndrome (SIDS) (McKenna, 1986). In many countries worldwide, cosleeping is associated with low rates of SIDS (McKenna & Mosko, 1994).

McKenna and Mosko's (1994) recent research indicates that infants arouse more frequently and their sleep stages are altered when they cosleep. This finding is important because past studies have found that near-miss SIDS infants have less frequent spontaneous awakenings (e.g., Coons & Guilleminault, 1985; Kahn, Picard, & Blum, 1986) and that siblings of SIDS victims have relatively longer periods of uninterrupted sleep. These findings suggest a difficulty in switching from sleep to wakefulness as a factor in SIDS (Harper et al., 1981; Hoppenbrouwers, Hodgman, Arakawa, & Sterman, 1989).

Conclusion. Many issues surround infant care practices such as sleeping arrangements. Of import for the consideration of parents and pediatricians alike are the child's physical well-being (e.g., reducing the risk of SIDS), emotional well-being (e.g., night-time comforting), parental sleep patterns (e.g., parental privacy, night-time feeding issues), practical constraints (e.g., housing situation), family ecology (e.g., single parenthood vs. married parents), adult needs (e.g., for autonomy) and cultural goals (e.g., independence vs. interdependence).

Sleeping arrangements are an integral part of whole systems of cultural meaning and ecological constraints. On the one hand, a cross-cultural look at these practices opens up new options for potential cross-cultural exchange. However, to borrow one part of a cultural system and insert it into a totally different system often brings on problems in itself. For example, Brazelton (1990) warns of parents from the dominant U.S. culture who "sleep with a small infant and a toddler but then become desperate to assign the child to a separate room and bed—and may desert the child by letting him or her "scream it out" (p. 7). Perhaps this outcome stems from a mismatch between the child's socialized dependence on cosleeping and the parents' own culturally shaped needs for independence. But, whatever the reason, Brazelton notes, "This anger and desertion are not deserved, and leaving the child to cry it out only blames the victim (p. 5). Hence, the long-term and systemic implications of cross-cultural borrowing must always be taken into account.

Nonetheless, Brazelton (1990, p. 7) asks an important question of practitioners: "Should we reevaluate our stance toward children's sleep?" Pediatricians have traditionally concluded that infant-parent cosleeping was a risk factor for healthy development. However, have they considered infant sleeping arrangements from all of the relevant angles: physiological, psychological, and cultural? As Nugent (1994) points out, cross-cultural studies demonstrate that the notion of risk is a cultural construction. Pediatricians must be cautious before imposing their own cultural construction on members of ethnic or social groups with whom they do not share a common culture or common ecocultural niche for infant development.

Carrying

Given the cross-cultural variability of infant carrying, it is interesting to explore the developmental implications of this practice. Anisfeld, Casper, Nozyce, and Cunningham (1990) experimentally tested whether increased carrying of infants, using a device adapted from African baby carriers, affected security of attachment, as measured by the Ainsworth Strange Situation (Ainsworth, Blehar, Waters, & Wall, 1978). In their research design, mothers of newborns were randomly assigned to receive either a Snugli® baby carrier (which permits the mother to carry a baby against the front of her body) or an infant seat (which permits the baby to sit in physical independence of the mother); the overall sample was selected so that attitudes toward the two devices were the same in all subjects. The mothers were recruited from a low-income clinic population. After using the infant carrier an average of 8.5 months, the experimental group showed a much higher rate of secure infant attachment in the Ainsworth Strange Situation at 13 months: 83% of the infants whose mothers had received the baby carriers were rated as securely attached; only 38% of the babies whose mothers had used infant seats were securely attached.

This study is a model of research that experimentally tests the value of cross-cultural exchange in child-rearing practices. More experimental research such as this is greatly needed.

At the same time, we need to keep in mind that we have new immigrants who are bringing practices such as infant carrying into the United States and other industrial countries on a constant basis. Many immigrants from Mexico and Central America come from cultures in which carrying infants is standard practice. What the research of Anisfeld et al. (1990) shows is that we can learn from these mothers. On a substantive level, the research of Anisfeld and colleagues indicates that our ultimate developmental goal of independence may often be applied too early, at the cost of secure attachment.

Differences, Not Deficits

For many ethnic and immigrant groups in the United States (and other industrial nations), cosleeping, holding, and carrying are part of their ancestral heritage of infant care practices. Being aware and accepting of these cultural differences is, in itself, important and beneficial. Because multicultural societies such as the United States contain many ethnic groups and family contexts with varied sleeping practices, parents deviating from the dominant norm should not be made to feel they are doing something harmful to their child.

Understanding that sleeping alone and cosleeping are two different cultural modes, each with its own set of risks and benefits, will lead to pride in rather than shame for diverse cultural heritages. For members of the dominant majority, such understanding leads to respect for rather than denigration of nonstandard practices such as cosleeping. Similarly, understanding the reasons behind alternative practices can also help immigrants understand the cultural norms in their new cultural surround. The dissemination of information on such practices among pediatricians and parents can help in developing this kind of mutual respect.

The Issues of Security and Independence

Ferber recommends that if the child climbs out of bed and tries to enter the parents' bedroom, they are to hold the door closed (Smaldino, 1995): "Remember your goal is to help your child learn to sleep alone. You are using the door as a controlled way of enforcing this, not to scare him. So reassure him by talking through the door" (Ferber, 1985, p. 75). Given the strength of infants' evolved mechanisms for keeping the caregiver close, research is needed to assess the extent to which such a regime leads to independence, as well as the extent to which it leads to sleep, separation, or attachment problems later on in life.

As Carol Smaldino found out, dominant U.S. culture also has specific advice for nighttime infant crying: Let the child "cry it out." Ferber reassures parents, "Allowing some crying while you help your child to improve his sleep will never lead to psychological harm" (p. 75). Yet this assurance goes against the classical finding of Ainsworth (1985) that rapid response to crying is associated with more secure attachments. If this is so, then the failure to respond to crying could lead to insecure attachment, which could, in turn, be manifested as a separation issue.

Bowlby (1969) pointed out that crying is one of the evolutionarily important mechanisms whose function is to keep the caregiver close. In the words of Lee Salk, crying *is* the baby's resource (Smaldino, 1995). In letting the baby cry it out, parents are using a behavioristic method to extinguish the baby's first and only means of communicating with his social world. This method seems to go against the nature of adults as well; Bowlby noted that the caregiver's response to crying—acting to stop the crying by reestablishing proximity and satisfying other needs—is also part of the human evolutionary heritage. This is why letting the baby cry is so painful for parents like Carol Smaldino.

The cross-cultural evidence indicates that, even if independence is the ultimate goal for raising children, the complex of constant contact, continuous feeding, and cosleeping may be most effective. As Klein (1995) points out, !Kung babies grow up to be even more independent than children living in the United States despite initial cosleeping and nurturant behaviors (Konner, 1982, p. 313). The implication is that children can still be raised to be independent adults, despite behaving in ways that may be categorized as "dependent" when they are young.

How Are Attachment Behaviors Affected by Parental Goals?

Although the role of cultural goals is readily observed in infant sleeping practices, cross-cultural differences in parental goals are also manifest in attachment behaviors. Harwood, Miller, and Lucca Irizarry (1995) begin their book, *Culture and Attachment,* with Bowlby's (1969) classic definition of "attachment as 'the bond that ties' the child to his or her primary caretaker" (p. 4) and attachment behaviors as "those behaviors that allow the infant to seek and maintain proximity to his primary attachment figure" (p. 4). These views of attachment have been ingrained in developmental psychological literature, leading to major research paradigms, including the classic Strange Situation presented by Ainsworth and Wittig in 1969.

Infant Responses to the Strange Situation

In the Strange Situation paradigm, "securely" attached children are differentiated from "insecurely" attached children through the usage of a laboratory test involving leaving an infant alone with various combinations of mother, stranger, both, or neither. From observations of infant behavior in these situations, infants can be assigned into the categories of avoidant attachment (Group A), secure attachment (Group B), and resistant attachment (Group C). The Group B behavior pattern in the Strange Situation has long been seen as an indicator of such things as healthy mother-infant interaction and emotional growth (Ainsworth, Blehar, Waters, & Wall, 1978).

The role of the mother, particularly maternal sensitivity, is also seen as important in infant attachment. For example, it has been proposed that mothers of future "A" babies express anger and rejection of their babies and mothers of "C" babies are insensitive and inept, whereas mothers of "B" babies are more affectionate and effective in soothing their babies (Ainsworth, 1979; Campos, Barrett, Lamb, Goldsmith, & Stenberg, 1983; Main & Weston, 1982).

These generalizations, however, do not take into consideration the cultural reasons for an infant's behavior and for a mother's interpretation of that behavior. Because mothers are the carriers of culture to the next generation, especially during their child's infancy, it is important to consider cultural reasons for the mother's behavior as well.

In Japan, compared with the United States, there are more "C" or "resistant" babies. In contrast, "A" or avoidant babies are common in the United States, but rare or absent in Japan (Miyake et al., 1985; Takahashi, 1990; van IJzendoorn & Kroonenberg, 1988). Why this difference in the way cultures deviate from the "norm"? Cultural differences in parental goals may be the reason. Japanese mothers, with parental goals such as having the parent and child "become one" (Kawakami, 1987), rarely leave their babies in the care of strangers such as babysitters. Thus, the separations that take place in the Strange Situation paradigm cause extreme and unusual stress to the infants (Miyake et al., 1985; Takahashi, 1990). Confirming this point, studies in the United States by Lamb and colleagues (Lamb & Sternberg, 1990; Roopnarine & Lamb, 1978, 1980) show that unaccustomed separations from the mother, as when a baby begins day care, can raise anxiety about separation that is revealed in Strange Situation behavior, but that habituation to temporary separations removes the behavioral manifestations of this anxiety.

Supporting this hypothesis, a study of working Japanese mothers found the same distribution of attachment patterns as in the United States (Durrett, Otaki, & Richards, 1984); there were avoidant, as well as resistant and secure attachments. Such babies would have had experience with temporary separations from their mothers.

As Takahashi (1990) had proposed, the separation history of the child affects responses to the Strange Situation; this separation history is conditioned both by cross-cultural variability in value orientations and by ecological factors within a culture, such as day care. The higher proportion of resistant babies found in Japan could therefore be due to different modal patterns of separation that take place in the daily interactions of Japanese and U.S. mother-child dyads.

In another study, German babies were found to be more likely to be categorized as "A" group, or avoidant, and less likely to be labeled as "C" group, or resistant, when compared with children in both Japan and the United States (Grossmann, Grossmann, Spangler, Suess, & Unzner, 1985; van IJzendoorn & Kroonenberg, 1988). Like the Japanese and U.S. patterns, this pattern can also be attributed to culture-specific parental goals for children. In Germany, parents desire their children to be nonclingy and independent (Grossmann et al., 1985). Therefore, the greater proportion of "A" infants in Germany may be a culturally desired outcome of German parental goals and strategies (Campos et al., 1983).

In Japan, on the other hand, parental goals include, as mentioned earlier, intense mother-child closeness, in which the mother is said to view her child as "an extension of herself" (Caudill, 1972, p. 195). In this context, the interdependence of mother and child is highly valued. This mother-child closeness could in turn lead to more shock and more resistance when infants are separated from their mothers.

The United States is between Japan and Germany in the frequency of both avoidant, independent (Type A) and dependent, resistant (Type C) babies (van IJzendoorn & Kroonenberg, 1988). If we think of the independence value as having originated in Germany and other parts of northern Europe, then this pattern makes sense. The value would have attenuated in its travels to the United States, where it came into contact with people from all over the world, including indigenous Americans, most of whom valued interdependence in their ancestral cultures (Greenfield & Cocking, 1994). In line with this explanation, Grossman et al. (1985) observe that in Germany:

> As soon as infants become mobile, most mothers feel that they should now be weaned from close bodily contact. To carry a baby who can move on its own or to respond to its every cry by picking it up would be considered as spoiling. (p. 253)

LeVine (1994) notes that German infants not only sleep alone; they are also left alone in the morning for an hour after waking up. In addition, mothers leave babies alone to shop, and German babies are left alone in the evening after one year of age. These methods of fostering independence seem more extreme than those used by mothers in the United States. Hence, it is logical for the United States to be between Germany and Japan in both avoidant, independent "A" type babies and resistant, dependent "C" type ones.

Within the United States, however, it has been suggested that day care is also associated with more avoidant attachments (Belsky, 1989). This is an ecological factor that could push the value of independence farther than would otherwise be the case. Clarke-Stewart (1989) has suggested, "although children who are accustomed to brief separations by virtue of repeated day care experiences may behave 'avoidantly,' their behavior might actually reflect a developmentally precocious pattern of independence and confidence rather than insecurity" (Lamb & Sternberg, 1990, p. 360).

Note that "B," or securely attached babies are predominant in all three cultures (Takahashi, 1986; van IJzendoorn & Kroonenberg, 1988). A possible conclusion is that the "B" pattern represents the human species norm for a mother-infant system, whereas variations around this norm reflect cultural variations in developmental goals and socialization practices.

Adult Interpretations of the Strange Situation

Parental interpretations of children going through the Strange Situation paradigm are also quite indicative of the cultural structuring of parental goals (Harwood et al., 1995). In an anecdotal account of a Strange Situation observation, Weisner (1996) spoke with a woman whose child had acted in a way that would, in the standard system, be classified as avoidant attachment. The woman, on seeing her child act in an avoidant manner, demonstrated strong approval of her child's behavior. She mentioned that she was proud of how independent her child was in playing by himself. The woman, in fact, was a single mother by choice, and one of her parental goals was to have the child be independent enough to be alone at day care while she was out working. Having the child behave in a nonchalant manner on separation and reunion, therefore, was desirable to this mother, given her goals for her child. This mother shows how a particular family factor—being a single, working parent—might strengthen the independence/autonomy goal even within a culture that already values these qualities.

Cultural variation in parents' perceptions of attachment behavior was also studied by Harwood (1992). She compared European American and Puerto Rican parental reactions to separation situations and their relationship to parental goals for their children. Once again, European American mothers focused on issues of individual autonomy for their children in the context of their attachment behaviors; they wanted a balance between autonomy and relatedness (Harwood et al., 1995). Puerto Rican mothers, on the other hand, placed a greater emphasis on their child's ability to maintain a "proper demeanor" in a social context, even when the child is separated from the parent; they wanted a balance between respect and caring. Both groups of mothers found the desired qualities in "B" type behavior, but the culturally normative interpretations of the same behavior were different.

Implications for Practice of Cross-Cultural Differences in Attachment

What, in a multicultural society, is the adaptive significance of minority interpretations of attachment that differ from those of the majority? This is an important question for practice that has not been explored in research. Are minority infants at risk for later maladaptation to the majority culture because their mothers have a different interpretation of the attachment relationship? For example, what happens to Puerto Ricans who bring their interpretations of secure attachment behavior with them to the mainland United States? Psychologists and practitioners concerned with attachment should keep this issue in mind; for clinical purposes, it may be necessary to go beyond attachment behaviors to understand the culture-specific meaning of those behaviors for the mother-child dyad.

Mother-infant behaviors are deeply rooted in a cultural value system. Therefore, one must not be too quick to judge attachment behaviors that may seem insecure to us:

> In Japan a greater valuing of emotional interdependence is associated with limited separation experiences, therefore heightening the distress experienced by many Japanese infants in the Strange Situation. However, because the family environment of those infants is in accord with the values and expectations of the larger sociocultural setting, the mental health implications of their heightened distress is not the same as it would be in the dominant U.S. culture, which values the cultivation of independence. (Harwood et al., 1995, pp. 14–15)

When attempting to interpret attachment behaviors in mother-child dyads from diverse cultural backgrounds, clinicians must understand the system of cultural meanings and practices of which they are a part. Although there may be cross-cultural agreement on normative attachment behavior, deviations from this norm may have diametrically opposed implications for social pathology, depending on the cultural value context in which they occur.

Finally, the stress level engendered by the Strange Situation in Japan raises the question as to whether the measuring instrument itself is too culture-specific for cross-cultural research. Because it is based on reactions to separation from mother and reactions to strangers, is it a valid measure of attachment in cultures characterized by almost continuous mother-infant contact and the absence of contact with strangers?

How Are Communication Behaviors Affected by Parental Goals of Cognitive and Social Development?

Parental goals for child development are also realized through communication strategies used by parents toward their infants. Mundy-Castle (1974) conceptualizes the European-based (Western) way of socializing children as geared to the goal of technological intelligence, and the African way as geared to the goal of social intelligence. The early socialization of technological intelligence involves a focus on objects and their manipulation. In addition, technological intelligence involves an emphasis on cognitive development in isolation from social development. In contrast, the early socialization of social intelligence involves a focus on interpersonal relationships. These emphases are expressed in the communication patterns used in parent-infant interaction.

The African emphasis on social intelligence is seen in Bakeman, Adamson, Konner, and Barr's (1990) research among the !Kung, African hunter-gatherers in Botswana. In !Kung society, no toys are made for infants. Instead, natural objects, such as twigs, grass, stones, and nutshells, are always available, along with cooking implements. However, adults do not encourage babies to play with these objects. In fact, adults are unlikely to interact with infants while they are exploring objects independently. Thus, technological intelligence for its own sake is not actively encouraged.

It is only when a baby offers an object to another person that adults become highly responsive, encouraging and vocalizing much more than at other times. For example, when babies are between 6 and 12 months, !Kung grandmothers start to train babies in the importance of giving to others by guiding them to hand beads to relatives. Thus, the !Kung cultural emphasis on the interpersonal rather than physical aspects of existence is reflected in how adults communicate the importance of objects as social mediators in their interactions with the very youngest members of their community (Bakeman et al., 1990).

In line with the !Kung's emphasis on social rather than technological intelligence, the communication of West Africans in Africa and West African immigrants in Paris focuses on integrating the infant into a social group (Rabain, 1979; Rabain-Jamain, 1994; Zempleni-Rabain, 1973). African mothers manifest this emphasis by using verbalizations that relate their infant to a third party, either real (e.g., telling the baby to share some food with brothers or sisters) or imaginary (e.g., "Grandma told you," said by the mother of a family that has immigrated to France, leaving the grandmother in Africa). They also respond more frequently to child-initiated social activity than French mothers do.

French mothers, in contrast, focus on the child-centered mother-child dyad and on their infants' technological competence, i.e., object manipulation (Rabain, 1979; Rabain-Jamain, 1994; Zempleni-Rabain, 1973). Compared with the African mothers, they manifest this focus by more frequent reference to the child's speech (e.g., "What are you saying to your mommy?"; "Is that all you've got to say?"), by less frequently relating the child to a third party, and by responding more frequently to child-initiated object manipulation. In this way, the French mothers display a heavier emphasis on technological than on social intelligence.

This emphasis on technological intelligence can also be seen in the actual utterances used by parents toward their infants. For example, in a study of mother-infant dyads playing with toys, American mothers tended to focus on calling attention to the object names of the toys (Fernald & Morikawa, 1993). An example of a typical American interaction was, "That's a car. See the car? You like it? It's got wheels" (p. 653). Many U.S. mothers explained that their goals in the interaction were to attract their child's attention and to teach them new words. Here, a distinct value is placed on cognitive development.

In contrast, Japanese mothers explained that their goals were to talk gently and to use sounds that the infant could easily imitate. The Japanese concern for explicit teaching of cultural norms for politeness in speech was also expressed (Clancy, 1986; Fernald & Morikawa, 1993). Thus, Japanese mothers were less interested in object labeling, but, instead, focused more attention on acting out polite verbal exchanges. An example of such an interaction is translated as, "Here! It's a vroom vroom. I give it to you. Now give it to me. Give me. Yes! Thank you" (p. 653). Japanese mothers were also more likely to engage in routines that arouse empathy with the object, encouraging positive feelings toward the toy by saying things like, "Here! It's a doggy. Give it love. Love love love." (p. 653), while patting the toy. As in Africa, social intelligence seems to have priority as a developmental goal in the Japanese mothers' communication pattern. In this way, parental values are reflected in the communication patterns of parents toward their infants.

One conclusion is that there may be a connection between an independent orientation and technological intelligence. An absence of emphasis on social relations in individualistic societies seems correlated with the presence of an emphasis on the physical world. Although our earlier discussion of sleeping arrangements focused on whether an infant was alone or with a parent, there is another aspect of this difference: When European American infants are left alone in a crib or playpen, they are usually given toys (e.g., mobiles, rattles) to amuse themselves with. Because toys provide early cognitive socialization for technological intelligence, there is a connection between the socialization of independence and the socialization of technological intelligence. The child left alone with toys is both learning to be alone and learning to interact with the physical world of objects. In contrast, interpersonal relations are more important than the object world in the development of an interdependent orientation or social intelligence for the African mothers; this expresses a collectivistic orientation.

Implications for Parents, Teachers, and Child Care Workers

In communication, as in other areas, we see that different culturally based developmental goals lead to different child-rearing practices. In the United States, where the learning of object names is culturally important, mothers spend a good deal of time labeling objects in their communicative interactions with their children. Although this tendency seems perfectly reasonable in this cultural context, it would be important to understand that other parents may have other cultural goals for their children. Teachers and child care workers who interact with infants on a daily basis should be sensitive to the alternative of using communication to actualize children's social intelligence, not merely their knowledge of the physical world, and to actualize social skills in dealing with groups rather than only dyads. Again, through cross-cultural exchange, both styles of communication could be used to socialize children for both technological and social intelligence.

Cultural Models

Cultural Coherence and Individual Differences

The different customs and practices of infant care that we have described are not random. They are motivated by underlying cultural models with overarching socialization goals that provide continuity from one developmental domain to another. Cross-domain continuity emerges when we take a comparative look at Japan, the United States, and Germany, in the areas of infant care practices, parental ethnotheories, and experimentally assessed attachment behaviors. In Germany, infants are left alone as much as possible, in line with a developmental ethnotheory that stresses independence (LeVine, 1994). German infants also develop the most independent behavior in the Strange Situation (van IJzendoorn & Kroonenberg, 1988).

In contrast, Japanese babies sleep with and are given virtually continual access to their mothers. This fits with the Japanese developmental goal of empathy and interdependence. It also fits with the fact that, in the Strange Situation, Japanese babies become extremely upset after a separation from their mother, something that rarely happens in their everyday life.

European American babies fall in between German and Japanese ones on these dimensions. Although the majority of parents sleep apart from their infants, some cosleeping does take place under certain circumstances (Lozoff et al., 1984; Morelli et al., 1992). This pattern is consistent with their ethnotheory of secure attachment, where parents want a balance between independence and relatedness in their infants (Harwood et al., 1995). Also consistent with this pattern, the proportion of independent (Type C) and dependent (Type A) attached infants is midway between Japan and Germany.

This in-between position of the United States could stem from the multicultural influences on the dominant model in a country composed of people with ancestral roots in Europe, Asia, Africa, and indigenous America. The balance between independence and relatedness favored by mothers for their infants then becomes a balance that is favored by psychologists for mature adults (Guisinger & Blatt, 1994).

Cultural continuity provides developmental continuity as well. For example, Gusii and Zinacantecan babies who are spoken to with imperatives as toddlers become obedient, nonquestioning children (Greenfield, Brazelton, & Childs, 1989; LeVine et al., 1994). In contrast, U.S. babies who are spoken to with interrogatives as toddlers often become questioning, self-assertive children (LeVine et al., 1994).

Each culture also has its own view of the socialization process. Often cultures oriented toward interdependence see the infant as an asocial being who must be socialized. In contrast, cultures with an independence-oriented developmental script often see the baby as starting out as a dependent being who must learn independence. Thus, the developmental progression is seen as from independent to interdependent in one group of cultures, while a reverse progression is the model in the other.

But, although, they differ, each cultural model has its own form of developmental change and continuity built in. The way that infants are viewed, the developmental goals of the parents for the child, and parental behavior toward the child are all inextricably intertwined with the cultural background of the parents and the child. The coherence, on a cultural level, of developmental goals, socialization practices, child outcomes, and adult interpretations is illustrated in Table 16.1, which summarizes this section.

Philosophical Differences in Child Rearing between Individualistic and Collectivistic Cultures

The two models presented in Table 16.1 must be taken as two idealized systems of cultural norms. Within each ideal type, different societies and cultures will exemplify varieties of both individualism and collectivism (Kim & Choi, 1994).

Because individual differences are central to our culture and to psychology as a discipline, it is important to point out that, within every culture, there will always be important individual variation around each cultural norm. Cultural typologies do not eradicate or minimize individual differences; they simply point to the norms around which those differences range.

In addition, situations of culture contact or culture change will cause conflict and compromise between the two idealized models presented in Table 16.1. Culture contact is particularly important in multicultural societies. Culture change is particularly important in societies undergoing technological development.

Cultural Frameworks and Ethnocentrism

Through the lens of one cultural model, it is an all-too-natural response to criticize the attitudes and practices generated by a different cultural model, with no understanding of the model behind the overt behaviors. LeVine et al. (1994) provide a wonderful example of ethnocentric criticism in their comparative look at the Gussii in Kenya and the middle class in the United States. According to LeVine et al. (1994):

> The Gusii would be shocked at the slow or casual responsiveness of American mothers to the crying of young infants. . . . This signals incompetent caregiving from their perspective. They would be similarly appalled by the practice of putting babies to sleep in separate beds or rooms, where they cannot be closely monitored at night, rather than with the mother. (pp. 255–256)

According to LeVine et al. (1994), the Gusii would think American toddlers unruly and disobedient as well, largely due to excessive praise and maternal solicitations of their preferences as toddlers.

Likewise, LeVine et al. (1994) believe that Americans would also find problems with the way that the Gusii choose to raise their infants. For example, leaving an infant under the supervision of a 5- or 6-year-old child, a common practice among the Gusii, would be viewed as neglect in the United States. LeVine et al. (1994) also believe:

> They [Americans] would be appalled that Gusii mothers often do not look at their babies when breastfeeding them . . . and that praise is more or less prohibited in the Gusii script of maternal response. . . . They would see the Gusii mothers as unacceptably authoritarian and punitive with children. (pp. 255–256)

In this way, infant care practices that are viewed as moral and pragmatic in one cultural context can be viewed as "misguided, ineffective, and even immoral" (LeVine et al., 1994, p. 256) in others.

In a multicultural society, ethnocentric criticism has disastrous practical and social consequences, as seen in the United States and other multicultural societies with varied cultural models. It is necessary to understand how each model has made sense in its historical context. This means that assessments of pathology or deviance by parents, pediatricians, teachers, and clinicians must always be based on an understanding of the cultural meaning that particular behaviors have for the participants in a social system.

For example, Schroen (1995) explores how a lack of cultural understanding can lead to misinterpretations by social workers. She documents how negative judgments by social workers of cultural practices they do not understand, using criteria from their own culture, can lead to

Table 16.1 Contrasting Cultural Models of Infant Development and Socialization

	Developmental Goals	
	Independence	Interdependence
Valued intelligence	Technological	Social
Socialization practices	Infant sleeps alone; more use of devices (baby seats, strollers, cribs, playpens) that allow separation of awake infant; objects to explore and amuse	Parent-child cosleeping; more holding and carrying; objects to mediate social relationships
Parental interpretation of secure attachment	Balance of autonomy and relatedness	Balance of respect and caring
Attachment behaviors	More avoidant attachments	More resistant attachments

tragedy. For instance, social workers can misinterpret sibling care (a practice utilized in many cultures worldwide) as child neglect, leading to children being taken away from loving parents who may have been following a different cultural model of competent parenting and child development. One can imagine other situations in which cultural practices may be misinterpreted as abuse. Cosleeping or cobathing practices (acceptable in many cultures, such as in Japan) may be misinterpreted as sexual in nature. Social workers, like other clinicians, must therefore be trained to recognize differences between cultural variations in practice and truly abusive situations.

Teachers and day-care workers must also be made aware of these differences in infant-rearing practices. For example, the crying (or lack thereof) of children when they are dropped off at school in the morning may be partially attributable to cultural differences in the "strangeness" of separation. Through a better understanding of these differences, infant care professionals can become more understanding and helpful to the child's transition between home and day care.

Each cultural model has its own set of benefits and costs (LeVine et al., 1994). These can still be seen in adulthood, the endpoint of development. For example, the mother-child bond remains strong throughout life in Japan, but the husband-wife tie is of a less romantic and close nature than in the United States (Lebra, 1994).

The costs and benefits of each cultural model are perceived by the participants and can also be perceived by a culturally sensitive outside observer. Although European American mothers generally subscribe to the benefits of autonomy as a developmental goal, its cost to them could be seen as the "empty nest" syndrome. In this culture, adult children are often "gone" physically, as well as emotionally.

Differing patterns of costs and benefits provide opportunities for useful cross-cultural exchange. From the perspective of both insider and outsider, each cultural model has its strengths and weaknesses, its costs and benefits, and its pathological extremes. For this reason, cross-cultural exchange of values and practices can sometimes serve as a corrective force to counteract the weaknesses, costs, and pathologies of any given cultural system. For example, McKenna and Mosko's (1994) current experimental research documents the potential physiological benefits of cosleeping for infants in a society (the United States) with a relatively high rate of sudden infant death syndrome. Cosleeping is a practice which many of their subjects have brought with them from Mexico and Central America. The findings have direct relevance to pediatric advice on sleeping arrangements.

As a related example, falling asleep with an infant, the practice criticized by Dr. Spock but practiced in many cultures, also reduces thumbsucking (Wolf & Lozoff, 1989), often considered a problem in the United States. Again, pediatricians could utilize this information in advising parents on how to avoid or stop thumbsucking in their children.

However, recommendations for cross-cultural exchange of infant care practices must be tempered by the finding of Weisner, Bausano, and Kornfein's (1983) that there are strong ecological and cultural constraints on cross-cultural exchange in this domain. An example of such a constraint is that parent-infant cosleeping, while decreasing the risk of SIDS, also decreases husband-wife intimacy, so valued in the United States. Consequently, ecologically valid research on the benefits and costs of adapting infant care practices from other cultures is needed.

Parents, pediatricians, clinicians, and day-care workers are often not fully aware of the options available for infant caregiving practices. Many infant-care practices (as well as behavior in general) utilized in other cultures may seem impractical and even strange from a different cultural perspective. To truly understand why these differences exist, it is necessary to carefully examine the core cultural values behind the behaviors. By being open to learning about different cultural values and behavioral options, a new appreciation, and perhaps even successful implementation, of a broader range of practices may be attained.

PARENT-CHILD RELATIONS

Parent-child relations are an important aspect of both child development and child socialization; parents embody and represent the broader cultural context as children learn to become members of their culture. Parents and children become a sort of family microculture with specific norms, customs, and values that reflect cultural and ethnic norms. From the parents' perspective, we examine cross-cultural variation in parents' behavior and attitudes toward their progeny beyond infancy, the topic of the preceding section. From the child's perspective, children's treatment of their parents is explored as an important (although understudied) aspect of their social development. Drawing on the material available, we discuss both facets of parent-child relations in this section.

To begin, consider the following scenario:

A week ago, you had gone shopping with your mother, and at the register, she had realized that she was short $10. You *lent her the money, and after a week, she gives no indication of remembering the loan. What would you do? Why?*

How would children and adolescents choose to behave in such a situation? Would there be any cross-cultural or ethnic variation in children's tendency to self-sacrifice for their parents?

This scenario was used in a study by Suzuki and Greenfield (1997) to determine whether there are ethnic differences in older adolescents' tendency to choose to sacrifice self for their parents or to preserve their personal goals. The following is a reply given by an undergraduate student:

> I would tell my mom nicely she owes me $10 and ask her when I might receive it. Because I'm sure she'd have forgotten and not try to "screw me over."

In contrast, the following is a reply given by a different undergraduate student:

> I would not ask her about the money at all. Because she's my mother. She has been sacrificing all her life to raise me, giving me everything I need, providing me education, love, shelter, food, etc. She's giving me more than I could ever ask for. I'd be happy to lend her the money without asking it back—that's the least I could do to thank her for everything.

The first reply was given by a European American student, and the second was given by an Asian American student. Are these solutions indicative simply of individual differences, or are there broader cultural differences between European Americans and Asians or Asian Americans in general in attitudes and behavior toward parents? Does each response also signify a cultural difference in parents' attitudes and behaviors toward their children? These are some of the issues that we address in this section of the chapter.

Children's Behavior toward Parents

In response to scenarios like the one described here, Suzuki and Greenfield (1997) found an interesting effect. Asian American students, particularly those closer to Asian culture in their acculturative levels and activity preferences, were significantly more likely than European American students to sacrifice certain personal goals for their parents. This finding seems to reflect the collectivistic emphasis on filial piety and respect for parents found in the Confucian worldview of East Asia.

The Confucian value of filial piety deeply influences the desired behavior of children toward their parents. According to Tseng (1973), "[Confucius] viewed the parent-child relationship as the foundation from which interpersonal love and trust would grow, and thus interpreted filial piety as the virtue for every person to follow" (p. 199). Some of the tenets of filial piety are "obeying and honoring one's parents, providing for the material and mental well-being of one's aged parents, performing the ceremonial duties of ancestral worship, taking care to avoid harm to one's body, ensuring the continuity of the family line, and in general conducting oneself so as to bring honor and not disgrace to the family name" (Ho, 1994, p. 287). This multidimensional concept of filial piety is believed to be a virtue that everyone must practice, since "the love and affection of a child for his parents, particularly the mother, is the prototype of goodness in interpersonal relationships" (Tseng, 1973, p. 195). From a very young age, children are introduced to these concepts and ideals, and by the time that they are teenagers, the extent of filial piety felt among Asians is such that it is not uncommon for Chinese teenagers to hand over entire paychecks to their parents for family use (Sung, 1985).

On the other hand, the European American response seemed to reflect the importance of individual goals and personal property prominent in the dominant North American worldview. Implicit in the response is a certain personal distance between parent and child; this is consonant with a view of human development that emphasizes the achievement of autonomy by late adolescence. It is also consonant with the Judeo-Christian religious background of the West. This background contrasts with Confucianism in that a person's relationship with God is individual and direct, rather than mediated by interpersonal relations. Contrasting responses to the scenario manifest and highlight differing models of children's relationships with their parents that have deep cultural roots. Given that assimilation to U.S. culture reduced self-sacrifice in Asian Americans in Suzuki and Greenfield's study, we would expect an even stronger pattern of difference when comparing Asians in Asia with European Americans in the United States.

Other Asian countries have similar emphases on children's lifelong duties toward their parents. Some parallel differences emerged when Miller and Bersoff (1995) gave subjects in India and the United States the following scenario:

Because of his job, a married son had to live in a city that was a 4-hour drive from his parents' home. The son made a point of keeping in touch with his parents by either visiting, calling, or writing them on a regular basis. (p. 274)

The authors note that a typical subject in the United States evaluated "the son's behavior as satisfying in that it enabled him to enhance his relationship with his parents, while still retaining a sense of individual autonomy" (p. 30). A typical Indian subject, in contrast, "focused on the satisfaction associated with fulfilling the obligations of care towards one's parents and of knowing that their welfare needs are being met" (p. 275).

In both scenarios, the contrast is between a response that values children's obligations to their parents versus one that emphasizes children's autonomy and personal choices concerning their relationship to their parents. In both cases, the dominant cultural response in the United States is toward autonomy and choice. In contrast to that response, less acculturated Asian Americans emphasized self-sacrifice for parents, whereas Indians in India emphasized children's obligations to their parents as a positive value.

Parents' Behavior toward Children

Styles of Parenting

Baumrind's (1967, 1971) classical formulation of three parenting styles—authoritarian, authoritative, and permissive—defines core relationships between parents and children. The children that have been studied range from preschool (Baumrind, 1967) to high school age (Dornbusch, Ritter, Leiderman, Roberts, & Fraleigh (1987). The *authoritative* parent is controlling, demanding, warm, rational, and receptive to the child's communication. The *authoritarian* parent is detached and controlling without exhibiting warmth. The *permissive* parent is noncontrolling, nondemanding, and relatively warm (Baumrind, 1983).

How Does Parenting Style Relate to European American Parents' Goals for Their Children? Although not generally acknowledged in the developmental literature, Baumrind's typology is closely tied to the normative goals for child development in North America. Authoritative parenting is considered to be the most adaptive style because it is associated with children who are "self-reliant, self-controlled, explorative, and content" (Baumrind, 1983, p. 121). These are the qualities of the independent individual so valued in the cultural model of individualism in countries such as the United States.

Cross-Cultural Variability in Styles of Parenting. Authoritative parenting, however, is not the norm in every group. Different ethnic groups within the United States and many Eastern and developing countries have been found to utilize an authoritarian parenting style to a greater degree than do middle-class European American parents in the United States. Authoritarian parenting is common in East Asia (Ho, 1994; Kim & Choi, 1994), Africa (LeVine et al., 1994; Nsamenang & Lamb, 1994), and Mexico (Delgado-Gaitan, 1994), as well as in ethnic groups derived from these ancestral cultures: Asian Americans (Chao, 1994), African Americans (Baumrind, 1972), and Mexican Americans (Delgado-Gaitan, 1994; Reese, Balzano, Gallimore, & Goldenberg, 1995). (Baumrind's third style, permissive parenting, has not been found to be normative in any identifiable cultural group.)

How Does Cross-Cultural Variability in Parenting Style Relate to Child Behavior and Parental Goals? Most important in considering cross-cultural variation in parenting styles is that different parental goals can give different meanings and a different emotional context to the same behaviors. Notably, the social and emotional accompaniments of classical "authoritarian" parenting behavior such as the usage of imperatives may be quite different where the culture has an interdependence-oriented developmental script (Greenfield, 1994). Chao (1994) points out the inadequacy of the notion of authoritarian parenting to describe the Chinese ethnotheory of child socialization. She invokes indigenous Chinese child-rearing ideologies reflected in the concepts of *chiao shun* (training children in the appropriate or expected behaviors) and *guan* (to govern).

For the European American mothers in this study, the word *training* often evoked associations such as "militaristic," "regimented," or "strict" that were interpreted as being very negative aspects of authoritarian parenting. However, whereas authoritarian parenting was associated with negative effects and images in the United States, the Chinese versions of authoritarianism, *chaio shun* (training) and *guan* (governing), were perceived in a more positive light from within the culture, emphasizing harmonious relations and parental concern (Chao, 1994). Chinese *chiao shun* and *guan* were seen not as punitive or emotionally unsupportive, but as associated with rigorous and responsible teaching, high involvement, and physical closeness (Chao, 1994).

Although *chiao shun* and *guan* may be interpreted as authoritarian parenting, the roots behind this type of parenting are very different from that in the United States. According to Chao (1994), Baumrind's (1971) original conceptions of authoritarian parenting emphasized "a set standard of conduct, usually an absolute standard without explaining, listening, or providing emotional support" (p. 1113). In the United States, this style of parenting has been linked to an evangelical "religious fervor" that stresses the "domination" and "breaking of the child's will" and is associated with hostility, rejection, and uninvolved parental behaviors (Chao, 1994; Smuts & Hagan, 1985). Chao (1994) points out that although the negative connotations of authoritarian were derived from a specific historical and sociocultural context, they "have been applied to describe the parenting styles of individuals who in no way share this same historical and sociocultural context" (p. 1117). Authoritarian parenting received its negative connotations from, *The Authoritarian Personality,* by Adorno, Frenkel-Brunswik, Levinson, and Sanford (1950). Written after World War II, it attempted to use a culturally reinforced personality syndrome to explain the racist slaughter that occurred in Nazi Germany.

The roots behind *chiao shun* and *guan,* on the other hand, evolved from the Confucian emphasis on hierarchical relationships and social order (Chao, 1994). In Confucianism, the standards that may be viewed as authoritarian are used, not to dominate the child, but rather to preserve the integrity of the family unit and to assure harmonious relationships with others (Chao, 1994; Lau & Cheung, 1987). The Chinese version also emphasizes high concern and care for the children (Chao, 1994). The goals and behaviors behind this form of authoritarian parenting are thus quite different from those originally posed by Baumrind (1971).

Authoritarian parenting from China (Ho, 1994) persists in the practices of Chinese immigrants to the United States (Chao, 1994). Chao demonstrates that middle-class immigrant Chinese parents in Los Angeles subscribe to child-rearing ideologies related to *chiao shun* and *guan* more than do their European American counterparts, even after statistically equating scores on measures of authoritarian parenting, parental control, and authoritative parenting. That is, the Chinese child-rearing concepts could not be reduced to the U.S. concepts originated by Baumrind.

Another interesting finding indicative of qualitatively different cultural patterning was that, while Chinese American parents were higher on authoritarian parenting than European American parents, they did not differ on the measure of authoritative parenting. In other words, Chinese parents more often subscribed to authoritarian items (sample authoritarian item: "I do not allow my child to question my decisions"). However, there was no difference between the groups in subscribing to authoritative items (sample authoritative item: "I talk it over and reason with my child when he misbehaves"). In this group, authoritarianism and aspects of authoritativeness such as affection and rational guidance (illustrated in the example) were complementary, not contradictory.

Besides Chinese Americans, there are other groups in the United States for whom authoritarian parenting is not always associated with the negative child development outcomes (e.g., discontent, withdrawal, distrust, lack of instrumental competence) it has for European American children. Baumrind (1972) found that, in lower-middle-class African American families, authoritarian parenting was more frequent and seemed to produce different effects on child development than in European American families. Rather than resulting in negative outcomes, authoritarian parenting by African Americans was associated with self-assertive, independent behavior in preschool girls. (Baumrind did not have enough information to carry out the same kind of analysis with African American preschool boys.)

One possibility is that this difference in the frequency and effects of authoritarian parenting may be related to different ecological demands of the African American environment. African Americans have traditionally been on the bottom of society's power, and economic hierarchy may have led them to develop obedience in their children through authoritarian directives.

Another possibility is that African Americans have some different goals for child development. According to Sudarkasa (1988), "research has documented the persistence of some African cultural patterns among contemporary African American families" (Harrison, Wilson, Pine, Chan, & Buriel, 1990, p. 354). One relevant pattern would be the emphasis on obedience and respect as the most important goal in African child development (LeVine et al., 1994; Nsamenang & Lamb, 1994). On the side of socialization, this pattern is achieved by strictness (Nsamenang & Lamb, 1994) and the use of parental commands as a communication strategy (LeVine et al., 1994). Such a socialization pattern would fit into the rubric of Baumrind's authoritarian parenting.

An important hypothesis is that, like African parents, African American parents use so-called authoritarian means because, through the retention of some African values at an implicit level, they are more interested in instilling respect and obedience than are parents in the dominant North American culture. Similarly, poor immigrant Latino families bring from Mexico and Central America the developmental goal of respect and the socialization mode of authoritarian parenting to achieve parental respect (Reese et al., 1995).

Parent-Child Communication

Another important aspect of parent-child relations includes the styles and modes that parents employ in communicating with their children. Although parents everywhere utilize an array of styles and modes, the emphasis is quite different from culture to culture. In this section, we take up several dimensions of this variability, relating each style to parental goals and cultural models of human development.

Nonverbal Communication or Verbalization? The Cultural Role of Empathy, Observation, and Participation. Azuma (1994) notes that Japanese mothers (and nursery school teachers) rely more on empathy and nonverbal communication, whereas mothers in the United States rely more on verbal communication with their children. He sees a connection between the physical closeness of the Japanese mother-child pair (discussed in the infancy section of this chapter) and the development of empathy as a mode of communication.

He points out that verbalization is necessary when there is greater physical and psychological distance between parent and child. The development of empathy paves the way for learning by osmosis, in which the mother does not need to teach directly; she simply prepares a learning environment and makes suggestions. In turn, the child's empathy for the mother motivates learning; this tradition survives in the families of third-generation Japanese American immigrants (Schneider, Hieshima, Lee, & Plank, 1994).

Closely related to empathy and learning by osmosis are the use of observation and participation as forms of parent-child communication and socialization. Whereas verbal instruction is particularly important in school-based learning, observation and coparticipation of learner and teacher are central to the apprentice-style learning common in many cultures (Rogoff, 1990). Often master and apprentice are parent and child, as in Childs and Greenfield's (1980) study of informal learning of weaving in a Mayan community of highland Chiapas, Mexico.

Both learning by observation and coparticipation with a parent imply a kind of closeness and empathy between parent and child. For example, in Zinacantecan weaving apprenticeship, the teacher would sometimes sit behind the learner, positioned so that two bodies, the learner's and the teacher's, were functioning as one at the loom (Maynard, Greenfield, & Childs, in press). Verbal communication and instruction, in contrast, imply using words to bridge the distance through explicitness, thus reducing the need for empathetic communication.

A discourse study by Choi (1992) reveals a similar pattern of differences between Korean and Canadian mothers interacting with their young children. Comparing middle-class mothers in Korea and Canada, Choi found that Korean mothers and their children manifest a communicative pattern that is relationally attuned to one another in a "fused" state (Choi, 1992), "where the mothers freely enter their children's reality and speak for them, 'merging themselves with the children'" (Kagitçibasi, 1996, p. 69). Canadian mothers, in contrast, "withdraw themselves from the children's reality, so that the child's reality can remain autonomous" (Choi, 1992, pp. 119–120).

Development of Comprehension versus Self-Expression. Authoritarian parenting brings with it an associated style of parent-to-child communication: frequent use of directives and imperatives, with encouragement of obedience and respect (Greenfield et al., 1989; Harkness, 1988; Kagitçibasi, 1996). This style is used where the primary goal of child communication development is comprehension rather than speaking (e.g., Harkness & Super, 1982). A basic aspect of the imperative style is that it elicits action, rather than verbalization from the child. This style is found in cultures such as that in Africa (Harkness & Super, 1982) and Mexico (Tapia Uribe, LeVine, & LeVine, 1994), and in Latino populations in the United States (Delgado-Gaitan, 1994).

The comprehension skill developed in children by an imperative style on the part of parents is particularly functional in agrarian societies in which the obedient learning of chores and household skills is an important socializing experience (e.g., Childs & Greenfield, 1980), with the ultimate goal of developing obedient, respectful, and socially responsible children (Harkness & Super, 1982; Kagitçibasi, 1996; LeVine et al., 1994). This style of interaction is also useful for apprenticeship learning of manual skills, but it is not so functional for school, where verbal expression is much more important than nonverbal action.

On the other hand, more democratic parenting brings with it a communication style that encourages self-expression and autonomy in the child. This parenting style often features a high rate of questions from the parent, particularly "test questions," in which the answer is already known to the parent (Duranti & Ochs, 1986), as well as parent-child negotiation (cf., Delgado-Gaitan, 1994). Child-initiated questions are also encouraged and accepted. This style is intrinsic to the process of formal education in which the teacher, paradigmatically, asks questions to which he or she already knows the answer and tests children on their verbal expression. An important aspect of the interrogative style is that it elicits verbalization from the child. Such verbal expresssion is an important part of becoming a formally educated person and is particularly functional and common in commercial and technological societies where academic achievement, autonomy, and creativity are important child development goals. This style is the cultural norm in North America and northern Europe.

Teaching and Learning: The Role of Reinforcement. In societies that put an emphasis on commands in parental communication, there also tends to be little praise used in parent-child communication (e.g., Childs & Greenfield, 1980). Where schooling comes into play, praise and positive reinforcement take on importance. Duranti and Ochs

(1986) make the following observation of Samoan children who go to school:

> In their primary socialization [home], they learn not to expect praises and compliments for carrying out directed tasks. Children are expected to carry out these tasks for their elders and family. In their secondary socialization [school], they learn to expect recognition and positive assessments, given successful accomplishment of a task. In their primary socialization, Samoan children learn to consider tasks as cooperatively accomplished, as social products. In their secondary socialization, they learn to consider tasks as an individual's work and accomplishment. (p. 229)

Thus, there is a connection between more individualistic child development goals and the use of praise and other positive reinforcers.

Correlatively, there is a connection between a tighter primary in-group and the absence of praise and compliments. Where role-appropriate behavior is expected rather than chosen, positive reinforcement does not make sense. J. G. Miller (1995) has described how people do not say "thank you" in India; once you are part of the group, you are completely accepted and expected to fulfill your social roles and obligations. B. Whiting and J. Whiting (1975) noted the lesser need for positive reinforcement where the intrinsic worth of the work is evident, as it is in household tasks and chores.

Parents Helping Children

Miller, Bersoff, and Harwood (1990) have explored cross-cultural variability in helping behaviors, another aspect of parent-child relations. Using two samples coming from New Haven, Connecticut, and Mysore, India, Miller et al. used scenarios to elicit responses that would reflect how subjects felt about a wide range of helping situations involving different potential help recipients.

What they found was the following: When children are in life-threatening need, college students in both India and the United States are in agreement that parents should help their children. Subjects in both countries see this as a moral matter; that is, the response to a child's life-threatening need is understood similarly by everyone. In India, however, a lesser degree of need did not affect the responses; Indian subjects thought it was a moral matter of social obligation for parents to help their children, even if their need for assistance was less acute.

In the United States, the findings were very different: Responses showed a gradient from situations of extreme need (e.g., the need for mouth-to-mouth resuscitation) to moderate need (e.g., the need for psychological support before surgery) to minor need (e.g., the need for directions to a store). At each level of need, fewer U.S. subjects saw the help from parent to child as a moral matter and more saw it as a matter of personal choice. Under conditions of a child's minor need, most U.S. subjects saw the helping behavior as a matter of personal choice for the parents. In contrast, the Indian sample still interpreted the situation as a moral matter, a context in which society had the right to regulate behavior.

From a developmental perspective, the basic patterns in both India and the United States are established as early as in the second grade. However, there is a developmental shift in the United States from a less to a more restricted view of the social obligation to help a child. For example, for children ranging from the second grade to sixth grade to college, there was a linear drop in the proportion of U. S. subjects who thought parents had a moral obligation to help a child in minor need. In contrast, Indian subjects believed that parents should always help children in minor need.

Cultural Models of Parent-Child Relations: Developmental Goals over the Life Span

There are basically two cultural models describing parent-child relations over the life span. These models are the underlying frameworks that generate many of the specific cross-cultural differences discussed up to now in this chapter. Each model has its cross-cultural variants. Furthermore, sometimes the models come into contact and influence each other. Without considering both models, however, we cannot adequately encompass cross-cultural variability in child development, parental behavior, and parent-child relations.

In the individualistic model, children are viewed as starting life as dependent on their parents and as achieving increasing independence from their parents as they grow older (Greenfield, 1994). In the collectivistic model, children are viewed as starting life as asocial creatures and as achieving an increasing concept and practice of social responsibility and interdependence as they grow older (e.g., Ochs & Schieffelin, 1984). Under this model, infants are often indulged, whereas older children are socialized to comprehend, follow, and internalize directives from elders, particularly parents. The developmental outcome of the first model is the independent, individuated self; the developmental outcome of the second model is the interdependent self (Markus & Kitayama, 1991).

Kagitçibasi (1996) refers to these two models as the family models of interdependence and independence. She describes these two models on the basis of extensive cross-cultural research in many societies all over the world. In the interdependent family model, socialization stresses family loyalties, control, dependence, and obedience of children.

> When socialized this way, children grow up to be "loyal" adult offspring who uphold family needs and invest in their (elderly) parents, whereas "independent" children are more likely to look after their own individual interests. . . .
>
> The intergenerational dependencies shift direction during the family life cycle in the model of interdependence. First, the child is dependent on the parent. This dependence is later reversed when the elderly parent becomes dependent on the grown-up offspring. The resultant familial and interpersonal relations in the family model of interdependence are characterized by interdependence along both emotional and material dimensions. (Kagitçibasi, 1996, p. 82)

Given this framework, the results found in the example of self-sacrifice toward parents (Suzuki & Greenfield, 1997) at the beginning of this section are not surprising. Asians as well as Asian Americans often abide by values of the interdependent model of family relations, in which family and group needs are placed before individual needs. Therefore, sacrificing money for one's mother is seen as a matter of course. In the interdependent model found in Japan, the mother-child relationship lasts a lifetime and is seen as the model for all human relationships throughout life (Lebra, 1994). The importance of continued respect up the generational ladder is seen in other cultures that subscribe to this model, such as Mexican, Mexican American (Delgado-Gaitan, 1994), and Korean (Kim, seminar given in Psychology Department at UCLA, April, 1996).

In contrast, the independent model of family relations is distinguished by the "separateness of the generations and both emotional and material investments channeled toward the child, rather than to the older generation" (Kagitçibasi, 1996, p. 84). As Lebra (1994) points out, in this model, characteristic of the United States, the paradigmatic model of parent-child relations is the rebellious adolescent son, who is breaking away from his family of origin. Under this model, it would be more appropriate for a child to exert his rights and ask for a loan to be returned from one's parents.

Currently, there are many immigrants who have brought a family model of interdependence into a society in which intrafamily independence is the norm. The following is an excerpt from a family analysis done by a student from a Persian Jewish family in Los Angeles:

> Being a first generation immigrant I have had to deal with . . . adjusting a collectivistic upbringing to an environment of individualism. In my home my parents and family coming from a country and culture . . . [with] beliefs of family as the central and dominant unit in life, endeavored to instill in us a sense of family in the collectivistic sense.
>
> We were brought up in a home where the "we" consciousness was stressed, rather than the "I" consciousness. We were taught that our behavior not only had implications for . . . ourselves but also for the rest of the family, for example, if I stayed out late at night, not only would I be taking the chance of getting robbed, raped, and/or murdered (implications of that experience for me), but also my younger brother and sister who looked up to me would also learn to go out late at night and their lives would also be jeopardized (implications of my actions for others) . . . .
>
> We were also taught to be responsible not only for ourselves, but also responsible for every other family member; thereby sharing the responsibility for both good and bad outcomes and playing a major part in each other's lives. For example, if my brother did bad in school, I was also responsible because as his older sister I was responsible to help him and take care of him and teach him right from wrong. I was, to an extent, as responsible for his actions as he, and my parents were. (Yafai, 1992, p. 3)

To be socialized with this moral sense of family interdependence within a society that stresses the independence of each person often presents itself as a conflict for the immigrant or minority child. What happens when the values that a child learns at home conflict with the values learned at school and in the larger society? We shall return to this example and issue in the last section, on home-school relations.

Ecological Factors

The interdependence model is particularly adaptive in poor rural/agrarian societies, where it utilizes a "functionally extended family" to carry out subsistence tasks, including child care (Kagitçibasi, 1996). Due to the high poverty levels and agricultural lifestyles, such shared work is highly adaptive for survival (Kagitçibasi, 1996). The interdependence between generations, with the younger ultimately responsible for the old-age security of the older, is particularly adaptive in societies lacking old-age pensions and Social Security systems (Kagitçibasi, 1996).

Conversely, the independence model of family relations is particularly adaptive in industrial, technological societies, where the unit of economic employment is the individual, not the family. Furthermore, independence and self-reliance are valued in a sociocultural-economic context where intergenerational material dependencies are minimal, and children's loyalty to their elderly parents is not required to support parents in their old age (Kagitçibasi, 1996). With increasing affluence and education, the interdependence model tends to wane, as the independence model waxes (Kagitçibasi, 1996).

Implications for Practice

What Can We Learn from a Cross-Cultural Perspective on Parenting Styles?

In this section, we will draw out implications of the previous section for the practice of developmental researchers, parents, educators, social workers, and clinicians. We emphasize the implications for practice in a multicultural society, and note particularly the opportunities for interethnic exchange concerning parenting and parent-child relations.

For Researchers: You Can't Take It with You. There is an important methodological lesson here: It is not always valid to take the same measuring instrument from one culture to another, with the goal of making a direct cross-cultural comparison. The same behavior may have a different meaning and therefore a different outcome in other cultures (Greenfield, in press). This is true when looking at the styles of parental interaction and discipline used by diverse cultural groups. For example, taking a measure of authoritarian parenting developed in the United States and using it to study parenting styles in China would provide an inaccurate and incomplete perspective on parenting practices there (Chao, 1994). It would therefore be important to explore different methods of research that utilize the ideas and opinions of people native to the society under study.

One way to do this would be to encourage the usage of the indigenous psychologies approach when studying culture. Kim and Berry (1993) define this approach as "the scientific study of human behavior (or the mind) that is native, that is not transported from other regions, and that is designed for its people" (p. 2). Instead of taking concepts, methods, and measures from one culture and forcing them into the framework of another, it may be more appropriate and more fruitful to work from within the culture to form concepts, methods, and measures designed for that environment. If this is done, indigenous concepts (e.g., *chiao shun* and *guan*) can be discovered and investigated from a more culturally-salient perspective.

For Parents, Educators, Social Workers, and Other Clinicians: Differences, Not Deficits. Each style of parenting will be perceived to have its own strengths and weaknesses *within its own cultural sphere.* Note that each culture has different goals, so that weaknesses from the perspective of one culture may be strengths from the perspective of another. For example, a strength of authoritative parenting is the encouragement of independence in the child (Baumrind, 1983); but this quality is seen as a weakness in some cultures, such as in Mexico (Raeff, Greenfield, & Quiroz, in press) and Japan (Nugent, 1994), where independent children are not the cultural ideal.

Each pattern of child development that results from each cultural style of parenting is different; one is not inferior to another. Each is adaptive in different contexts; each has its own pattern of strengths and weaknesses. What is important is to understand the meanings and the cultural child development goals behind each pattern.

Multicultural understanding has direct implications for clinical work with families. Consider the following case (Carolyn McCarty, personal communication, June 1996): A child in an African American family is punished when a younger sibling, under her care, falls off the bed. The older child feels as though the punishment is unfair and complains of holding too much responsibility in the family. The family seeks family therapy for these issues. In this case, armed with unconscious cultural assumptions about the developmental goal and value of independence, the first reaction of the therapist is to blame the parents for "parentifying" the older child; in this framework parentification is considered pathological. Parentification of a child compromises the autonomy and opportunities for self-actualization that are implicit developmental goals in psychotherapy, itself an outgrowth of an individualistic framework.

However, after some training concerning the two cultural models described earlier, the clinician understood another possibility: that the parents could be developing familial responsibility in the older child by having her take care of the younger child. In accordance with this value system, the older child's punishment makes sense; it helps socialize the child to carry out the familial responsibility associated with child care. Having understood this perspective, the clinician is in a position to explore the issue of culture conflict. Is this situation, in fact, simply a conflict between an older child who has internalized the individualistic notion of fairness and responsibility for self and parents who hold dear the value of familial responsibility? If so, the clinician can now mediate between the two cultures represented by the two generations within the family.

In such cases, therapists and counselors may help minority and immigrant parents reach a better understanding of the behavior of their children. They can do this by guiding parents to view their children as behaving in ways that are in accord with the majority culture, rather than in ways that are in direct conflict with the parent's own values. Children, particularly those with immigrant parents, could also be counseled on how their clashes with their parents could be due to differences in cultural perspective, rather than to parental stubbornness or insensitivity, and children can be encouraged to better understand their parents' perspective.

Parent-Child Relations: Differential Acculturation of Parents and Children

Because parents often acculturate more slowly to a host culture (Kim & Choi, 1994), there is a great potential for parent-child conflict when parents immigrate from a collectivistic to an individualistic society. Parents may expect respect; but their children have been taught to argue and negotiate (Delgado-Gaitan, 1994). Parents may see strictness as a sign of caring; adolescents may see it as robbing them of autonomy and self-direction (Rohner & Pettengill, 1985).

An example of the plight of the immigrant parent is provided by a parent who had immigrated from Peru. She told her American-born college-age daughter that when she was young in Peru, she had to defer to the older generation. She expected that someday she would be older and her children would defer to her. But as an adult she immigrated to the United States where the older generation defers to the younger. She felt cheated: Because the cultural rules changed, she had ended up on the bottom all her life (Elsie Beach, personal communication, 1994, Winter).

Sometimes immigrant parents bring their children, particularly teenagers, to mental health clinics for problem behaviors, such as rebelliousness, that are considered normal for adolescents in the dominant U.S. society (V. Chavira, personal communication, June 1996). When this happens, a clinician may easily assume the perspective of the dominant culture and simply take the side of the child. However, this approach denigrates the parents without understanding the value perspective that has generated their attitudes and behavior. It should be much more helpful if the clinician could accurately diagnose the parent-child problem as a problem of cross-cultural value conflict and differential acculturation. In this way, the perspectives of both parent and child would be validated and understood, and a way opened for compromise and mutual understanding.

Parental Goals and Practices: Implications for Educational and Clinical Practice. An implication of the preceding is that professionals (e.g., social workers, counselors, clinical psychologists, pediatricians, and educators) who advise parents on discipline and other parenting practices need to bear in mind that any advice must be relative to a particular set of child development goals. Often they may not realize that particular goals are implicit in a piece of advice on an issue such as discipline. Insofar as members of many ethnic groups in a multicultural society will not share the socially dominant developmental model with the clinician or teacher, practitioners may need to think twice about whether it is appropriate either to ignore or to change parents' developmental goals for their children.

An example would be an adolescent who feels her immigrant parents are being too restrictive. Should the therapist take the side of the American-born child and urge the parents to provide more autonomy to the adolescent? In so doing, she will make the child happy, but the parents' cultural expectations of respect and interdependence will be thwarted. In addition, because of the reliance on social controls in an interdependence-oriented culture, parents may not have instilled the internal controls in the child that are so necessary for constructive autonomy. Consequently, it would seem more fruitful for the therapist to begin with an understanding that normal behavior for the American-born child is not normal child behavior for the foreign-born parents. Similarly, normal parental behavior for the American-born child is not normal for the foreign-born parents. With these understandings in place, the therapist, rather than pathologizing the parents' behavior from the therapist's implicit cultural perspective, will recognize the "normality" of both sides' behavior within two different cultural frameworks.

Implications of Cross-Cultural Differences in Parenting Style: Cross-Ethnic Exchange

Within the United States, cultural diversity is such that parent-child relations are not limited to one culturally dominant model. Because the weaknesses of one model are the strengths of another, there is a possibility that cross-ethnic exchange can solve some common child-rearing problems in our multicultural society.

For example, impulsiveness is a common behavior problem in the dominant U.S. milieu (Maccoby, 1980). Maccoby notes that adolescent impulsiveness is associated with a parenting style in which parents have not assigned tasks or chores. However, systematic task assignment is a component of a more authoritarian parent-child relationship featuring parental directives and child obedience. The possibility therefore arises that one causal factor in developing impulsiveness may be an excess of family democracy in which all chores and tasks are either a matter of discussion and negotiation between parent and child or are simply left up to the child.

Thus, task and chore assignment, underplayed in the dominant U.S. style of parenting (Whiting & Whiting, 1994/1973), could perhaps be a helpful clinical tool in combating impulse control problems. There are already groups in the United States, such as Latino immigrants from Mexico and Central America, that expect children to help with chores (Raeff et al., in press). Clinicians could make parents aware of household chores as a potential strategy to prevent child and adolescent problems in this area. Clinicians from ethnic groups in which this strategy is already used can lead the way.

On the other hand, the inability to ask questions and assert opinions verbally is a detriment for the school achievement of certain ethnic groups in the United States, such as Latino immigrant children (Greenfield et al., 1995). The soliciting of children's views, a component of the authoritative parenting style favored in the dominant U.S. culture, can encourage such behavior, thus enhancing school adaptation (Delgado-Gaitan, 1994). By confining such routines to school-related activities such as reading, Delgado-Gaitan shows how immigrant Latino families can strike a bicultural pose that enhances children's school achievement, while maintaining the value of respect in other family situations.

Another opportunity for cross-cultural exchange lies in the relative importance assigned to verbal and nonverbal communication in the socialization process. It is well documented in the socialization literature that when there is a conflict between parental word and deed, "actions speak louder than words." Actions can socialize in two ways: by providing models, and through coparticipation in an activity. Where a particular skill is pretty much universal within a culture, we may speak of no-failure learning. For example, weaving is a no-failure learning activity for Zinacantecan girls; driving is a no-failure learning activity for adolescents in the United States. If we look at the characteristics of no-failure learning around the world, such learning always seems rich in the availability of models and/or coparticipants. No-failure learning privileges action rather than verbal modes of teaching. This is a characteristic of the apprenticeship model of learning that is so important in many other cultures.

The apprenticeship model may also be useful in solving problems of noncompliance, a frequent issue in child behavior in the United States. High rates of noncompliance are not surprising, because, as our analysis has shown, authoritarian parenting, which would foster compliance or obedience, is a culturally disfavored style of parenting in the United States. The dominant culture, both professional and lay, both denigrates obedient children and abhors noncompliant ones. That would seem a paradox, if not an out-and-out contradiction.

Nonetheless, noncompliance problems could perhaps be ameliorated if parents were to rely more on modeling and participating in the desired child behaviors. This conclusion is suggested by our interpretation of the findings of Vaughn, Kopp, and Krakow (1984). These researchers tested compliance in young children between the ages of 18 and 30 months in the following situation: A female experimenter comes in with a basket of toys and dumps them on the floor next to the child. Then the mother tells the child to pick up the toys. Very few young children complied with this request, or, to put it another way, followed the mother's directive.

In this situation, however, the mother neither models nor helps (participates with) the child with the desired task. Quite the contrary, an adult functions as an antisocial model in this situation by dumping the toys out and making a mess. Our hypothesis is that, holding child age constant, if the mother picked up the toys with the child, thus serving as both a model and a participant, compliance rates would have been much higher.

If so, then cultures in which the scaffolding techniques of modeling and coparticipation are a stronger tradition than they are in European American culture can teach us something about parenting; they may provide a technique that could be used to avoid the excesses of our own preferred cultural mode—verbalization—of parent-child socialization and communication. Influenced by models of apprenticeship around the world (Lave & Wenger, 1991), formal education is now trying to incorporate apprenticeship models into more effective formal education (Collins, Brown, & Newman, 1989). They may be equally effective as clinical interventions into parental teaching style (cf., Rogoff, 1990).

Summary

Again, we find evidence of cultural coherence. This coherence has developmental continuity as well. The two cultural models of infant development and socialization, independence and interdependence (Table 16.1) continue

Table 16.2 Contrasting Cultural Models of Parent-Child Relations

	Developmental Goals	
	Independence	Interdependence
Developmental trajectory	From dependent to independent self	From asocial to socially responsible self
Children's relations to parents	Personal choice concerning relationship to parents	Obligations to parents
Communication	Verbal emphasis	Nonverbal emphasis (empathy, observation, participation)
	Autonomous self-expression by child	Child comprehension, mother speaks for child
	Frequent parental questions to child	Frequent parental directives to child
	Frequent praise	Infrequent praise
	Child negotiation	Harmony, respect, obedience
Parenting style	Authoritative: controlling, demanding, warm, rational	Rigorous and responsible teaching, high involvement, physical closeness
Parents helping children	A matter of personal choice except under extreme need	A moral obligation under all circumstances

to be expressed in the parent-child relations of children (Table 16.2).

There is a paucity of information in the developmental research literature on parent-child relations. Totally absent is information about children's attitudes and behavior toward their parents. Instead, there is a tremendous amount of work on the effects of parent behavior on their children. Our hypothesis is that this paucity is the unwitting result of an individualistic cultural lens that is centered on the child as separate being, rather than on a two-way relationship between parent and child, a focus of the interdependence model of family functioning.

PEER RELATIONS

Although the home environment is crucial in the socialization of a child, childhood peer relations are also important and cannot be ignored in the study of development. Children often approach peer relations by acting in terms of the invisible cultures of their homes. Where that culture differs from the invisible culture of peers, cross-cultural conflict in peer relations may arise. Peer relations are the child's first opportunity to take the cultural values and practices learned at home and go forth into a wider world of people who may or may not share these values and practices.

Clashes in cultural understanding can occur even in the most seemingly mundane of actions between peers and friends. Peer interactions that are taken for granted as being "normal" in one cultural context can, in fact, seem strange and even unacceptable in others. Such reactions can then be experienced as prejudice and discrimination, although that may not be the motive.

Take the following situation described by Markus and Kitayama (1991):

> Imagine that one has a friend over for lunch and has decided to make a sandwich for him. The conversation might be: "Hey, Tom, what do you want in your sandwich? I have turkey, salami, and cheese." Tom responds, "Oh, I like turkey." (p. 229)

According to Markus and Kitayama (1991), this scene would be completely natural between friends who share an independent view of the self, in which people are perceived to have a right to express their preferences and desires. With such a perspective, offering guests a choice of food would be seen as the courteous thing to do. The friend is given a choice and is in the position of actively voicing a preference in creating the meal. Similar situations occur frequently in the daily interaction of peers in cultures such as in the United States.

Between people with an interdependent view of the self, however, such a situation would be met with bewilderment and confusion, for it would ordinarily be assumed that the host has the responsibility of understanding the desires of his or her friends without their asking. In Japan, people often feel uncomfortable in expressing their desires through choices, and hosts must interpret their guests' wants without directly questioning them (Wierzbicka, 1991). Instead, the following scenario would be more likely to take place between people with an interdependent view of the self:

> "Hey, Tomio, I made you a turkey sandwich because I remember that last week you said you like turkey more than beef." And Tomio would respond, "Oh, thank you, I really like turkey." (Markus & Kitayama, 1991, p. 229)

This is an example of how cultural differences can make an impact on interactions among one's peers and friends.

On the surface, the interaction that takes place in this second scenario may appear to be only subtly different from the first scenario, but is in fact indicative of a different set of assumptions between the peers involved.

Each scenario indicates a different developmental endpoint concerning the guiding assumptions in peer relations. In the first scenario, friendship is based partly on respect for each other's autonomy; as a consequence, one friend offers another free choice. In the second scenario, friendship is based partly on empathy for the other person; as a consequence, one friend offers the other understanding of the other's wishes. In the latter case, it is appropriate to inhibit the "I" perspective in an attempt to read the guest's viewpoint by taking the "thou" perspective (Hsu, 1981; Markus & Kitayama, 1991).

As Markus and Kitayama (1991) point out, the former scenario would be part of the development of an independent self, while the latter would be part of the development of an interdependent self. The themes of the preceding two sections apply to cross-cultural variability in peer relations: In cultures where parents foster interdependence and empathy with others, we would expect Tomio's style of peer interaction. In cultures where parents foster independence and autonomy, we would expect Tom's style.

Tom is a European American and Tomio is Japanese. Imagine what would happen if Tom and Tomio were friends in a multicultural society such as the United States. As the two scenarios show, "proper" peer interaction differs greatly, depending on one's values and beliefs. In the same situation, two people with different cultural perspectives can interpret a situation and act in ways that are completely foreign to each other. Tom might feel upset if Tomio did not give him a choice of menu; or Tomio might feel uncomfortable if Tom did not anticipate his desires. When this type of subtle misunderstanding occurs, it is hard enough for adults to realize that a cross-cultural value conflict may be taking place; among children, this realization would be rarer still.

This section will start with an overview of different cultural elements that can come into play during peer interaction. As with the sandwich example, our general strategy will be to make inferences from cross-cultural variability in peer behavior when peers belong to the same cultural group to potential intergroup conflict when interacting peers belong to different cultural groups. We will analyze cultural differences and intergroup peer conflict in a number of different behavioral areas: communication, self-presentation, helping behaviors, competition/cooperation, reward allocation, and conflict resolution.

In several cases, we will use adult social-psychological literature to establish developmental endpoints for peer behavior in different cultures and developmental literature (where available) to see how peer relations develop across cultures. A cross-cultural perspective on adult behavior is important because adults provide the goals for child socialization. As a consequence, child behavior grows toward the developmental endpoints expressed in adult behavior.

Communication

Communication requires shared knowledge (Krauss & Fussell, 1991) or common ground in the areas of information, beliefs, attitudes (Clark, 1985), and practices. Culturally distinctive beliefs and the practices they generate are important sources of common ground. Communication in each of the sandwich scenarios presupposes this sort of cultural common ground.

In Japan, the common ground would be an understanding of the importance of anticipating others' needs and wants in order to spare them the necessity of voicing their own needs. This common ground leads to communication that is implicit rather than explicit: The guest has communicated what he wants without saying anything on this occasion, and the host has communicated that he has understood the guest's desires. Recall that the use of empathy, rather than explicit communication, begins in infancy in Japanese mother-child communication, contrasting from the beginning with the emphasis on verbalization in European American mother-child communication (Azuma, 1994). Schneider et al. (1994) demonstrate how the implicit verbal style continues into maternal communications to school-age children, even among Japanese Americans who have lived in the United States for several generations.

Among European Americans in North America, the common ground would be an understanding of the importance of recognizing others as autonomous individuals by allowing them to make conscious choices. This common ground leads to communication that is explicit rather than implicit. Even if the host remembers the turkey sandwich from last week, it is considerate to give the guest an opportunity to express a new choice today. Thus, the host explicitly asks what the guest wants; he does not utilize the implicit information from the previous week.

When a Japanese and a European American come together, this example suggests that the common ground on which good communication is based may be lacking. Each party may make assumptions about desirable behavior and communication styles not shared by the other. This situation can lead to unrecognized misunderstandings in cross-cultural communication.

When communicating with others, emotions that are indigenous to one culture but not another may come into play, adding subtlety and complexity to the communicative interaction. For example, the Japanese feeling of restraint, or *enryo,* may lead guests to refrain from expressing their true desires (e.g., "I would like turkey in my sandwich"), in an attempt to be polite. Japanese communicative style, therefore utilizes indirectness in speech and continual awareness of others as a form of culturally valued courtesy (Miyamoto, 1986–1987). Although *enryo,* or restraint, may be seen as a form of politeness in Japan, it is ironic to think that this culturally bound form of courtesy in Japan may not be perceived as courteous at all in other cultures. Behaving in a way that shows *enryo* may be confusing and frustrating to people who are accustomed to more direct and inquisitive modes of communication.

Value conflicts such as these can lead to conflicts in peer interactions. One can imagine the misunderstandings that can take place between a Japanese child and an American child. The Japanese child might constantly refrain from voicing her true opinions in an effort to be polite, whereas the American child, taking this at face value, would be frustrated in her wishy-washy and ambivalent style of communication. In turn, the Japanese child would be constantly taken aback by the American child's forthrightness in expressing his desires and frustrated at his lack of intuition in realizing her unspoken desires.

Similar misunderstandings might occur between Japanese American and European American children because of their contrasting ancestral value systems. This is just one example of countless ways in which discrepant developmental goals produce conflicting communicative styles that lead to misunderstandings and frustrations in peer interactions.

Self-Presentation

In many individualistic societies, people like to perceive themselves as the origin of good effects but not of bad effects (Greenwald, 1980), and the confident attribution of successes to personal ability is commonly practiced (e.g., Miller & Ross, 1975; Mullen & Riordan, 1988). Consequently, self-esteem is a highly desirable quality in these societies. For example, in the United States, people who scored highest on self-esteem tests (by saying nice things about themselves) also tended to say nice things about themselves when explaining their successes and failures (LeVine & Uleman, 1979). It appears that self-esteem is somehow correlated to a positive representation of the self.

In collectivistic societies, this tendency to present oneself in a positive light is not as highly valued. Markus and Kitayama (1991) note a striking example of this difference with anecdotes from an article in the *New York Times.* In this article, company policies to boost productivity were described. Employees of a small Texas corporation were instructed to look into a mirror and say, "I am beautiful" 100 times before coming to work. In contrast, employees of a Japanese supermarket opening in New Jersey were encouraged to hold hands and tell each other that "he" or "she is beautiful" before work each day ("A Japanese Supermarket," 1989, in Markus & Kitayama, 1991). Further research has shown that Americans tend to self-enhancement, whereas Japanese tend to self-deprecation (Kitayama, Markus, Matsumoto, & Norasakkunkit, 1997). The effect of culture in molding self-presentation, and therefore peer relations, is indeed far-reaching.

This cultural difference in peer relations begins in childhood. In a study conducted on the opinions of second, third, and fifth graders in Japan, students were asked to evaluate a hypothetical peer who was either modest and self-restrained or self-enhancing in commenting on his or her athletic performance (Markus & Kitayama, 1991; Yoshida, Kojo, & Kaku, 1982). Yoshida et al. (1982) found that the personality of the person giving the modest comment was perceived much more positively than that of the person giving the self-enhancing comment at all ages. A developmental trend was also found: second graders believed the self-enhancing comment of the hypothetical peer to be true, whereas fifth graders did not. In other words, whereas second graders believed that the self-enhancing peer was truly superb in athletics, fifth graders believed that the modest peer was more competent. Therefore, although the cultural value of restraint and modesty was understood as early as second grade, this value expanded with age to incorporate positive attributes of ability and competence (Markus & Kitayama, 1991).

This tendency to value modesty of self-presentation is also reflected in Hong Kong, where people giving humble or self-effacing attributions following successes were more positively perceived than people giving a self-enhancing attribution (Bond, Leung, & Wan, 1982; Markus & Kitayama, 1991). Indeed, behaviors such as the verbal devaluation of oneself and even of one's family members is a norm in many East Asian cultures (Toupin, 1980).

In collectivistic cultures such as Japan, group harmony is highly valued, whereas in individualistic cultures such as the United States, individuality is crucial. This dichotomy in desired interactive styles is underscored in Lebra's (1976) observation that the Japanese nightmare is exclusion and failure to connect with others whereas the American nightmare is the failure to separate from others, ending up in being unnoticed and undifferentiated from others. The modest, self-restrained, interactive style of the Japanese people is just one way of preserving group harmony, while the more self-confident style of the dominant American culture complements its cultural goals of individuality and assertiveness.

Implications for Intergroup Peer Relations

Both modes of self-presentation conform perfectly with their respective cultural goals, but one can see how people from one culture can misinterpret and even decry the preferred self-presentation styles of other cultures. For example, in college interview situations, Asian American students can be viewed as uninteresting applicants because of their modesty and desire to fit in rather than stand out.

Two more examples come from a multiethnic high school sports team (B. Quiroz, unpublished data, January 1996):

After a winning game, the European American coach picks out the scorers for recognition and praise but he never mentions the supporting players. One of the two immigrant Latinas on the team later bursts into tears because no credit is given for supporting positions, which she and the other Latina member play.

The European American coach gives selective recognition to the stars, individuals who are perceived to stand out from the team. This individualistic interpretation of who has contributed to the team's success then offends the Latina players, who play supporting positions, but are not given credit for their considerate and skillful effort to support the scorers. Standing out versus contributing to the unit is the issue but these modes are not of equal power; the coach as authority figure represents and promotes the individualistic value of standing out.

In the next example, a parallel value conflict between self-promotion and modesty is at play (B. Quiroz, unpublished data, January 1996):

A team vote for most improved player takes place. Each European American girl nominates herself. Although they recognize that they are most improved, the two Latina girls do not feel comfortable nominating themselves, so they do not vote. According to the coaches, one of the Latina girls was actually most improved. However, since she received no votes, the prize was not awarded. The "most improved" player is then upset when she does not receive recognition as such.

Whereas self-aggrandizement is considered a positive aspect of self-esteem in the individualistic framework, it is negatively considered in the collectivistic model of human behavior (Kitayama, Markus, & Lieberman, in press; Markus & Kitayama, 1991). Whereas individual achievement is applauded and idealized from the European American perspective, acknowledgment of others, conversely, is more valued in the more collectivistic view held by the immigrant Latinas. Not only must the Latina players accommodate to a conflicting value system, but also no social structures are in place to allow expression of their own value system.

These two examples show how differences in the valued mode of self-presentation can lead to problems in peer relations in a multicultural situation. Each of these occurrences is a manifestation of negative interpersonal processes that occur when youth from differing home cultures come together in a joint activity. The misunderstandings are subtle, but very real and painful. Note that none is manifest as an overt conflict; yet each involves a negative interpersonal experience with members of a different ethnic group.

Note also that the protagonists were not aware of the reasons behind the problems. They were not aware that they have two contrasting sets of presuppositions about what is desirable in human development and behavior. The two contrasting cultural value systems were invisible to all concerned. Each party in each conflict took her own perspective for granted and was therefore unaware of how the other group might be interpreting her actions. Each party was completely ignorant of cultural models that differed from her own.

Helping Behavior

The desirability of helping behaviors is almost universal, valued in most cultures around the world. People's perceptions of helping behaviors and when they are appropriate, however, can vary drastically from culture to culture. Although some societies view helping as a personal choice, others view this as a moral obligation. It has been shown that American children believe that only justice obligations, and not helping behavior, should be governed by others (Miller & Bersoff, 1992; Smetana, Killen, & Turiel, 1991). More specifically, they feel that it is a matter of personal choice, not moral responsibility, to help a friend in moderate or minor need (Miller et al., 1990), but it is a matter of moral responsibility to help a friend in extreme need or to uphold justice. An example of fulfilling a justice obligation is refusing a request to destroy someone else's garden—(Miller et al., 1990). Caring and interpersonal responsiveness are seen as a matter of personal choice (Higgins, Power, & Kohlberg, 1984; Miller &

Bersoff, 1992; Nunner-Winkler, 1984). This value of personal choice is highlighted in individualistic societies, such as the United States, where Miller et al. (1990) found virtually the same pattern of results from second grade to college age.

In collectivistic societies that value group harmony and cooperation, however, helping behaviors can be perceived at a different level of urgency and obligation. This is particularly true in India, where helping is seen not as a personal choice, but rather as a moral necessity (Miller, 1994; Miller & Bersoff, 1992, Miller et al., 1990). Virtually all Indians from second grade to college age felt it was legitimate to punish a person who failed to help a friend, even in minor need.

In another study (Miller, 1995), it was found that most U.S. college students would not inconvenience themselves to help their best friend if she had not helped them or others in the past. Although Indian college students agreed with U.S. college students that not helping in the past was undesirable behavior, this history would not deter them from helping their best friend.

Choosing not to help others may be met with harsh disapproval in cultures that value the preservation of group interests. In Cameroon, asserting individual rights and interests over those of the community would cause the Cameroonian to be acting "at the expense of his or her peace of mind and at great risk of losing the psychological comfort of a feeling of belonging" (Nsamenang, 1987, p. 279). Such a person would be considered deviant under traditional African thinking (Nsamenang, 1987). Given this difference, one can imagine how an Indian or Nigerian child might be confused and even shocked when a child from another culture chooses not to help a group member in a time of need.

Ecological Factors

Whiting and Whiting (1994/1973) put forth the hypothesis that complex societies must suppress altruistic or helping behavior to friends (as well as to family) to maintain the economic order, "a system of open and achievable occupational statuses" (p. 279). A complex technological society requires the egoistic behaviors of self-development; the essence of obtaining a position in the economic system is individual merit, not social or family connections. Based partly on their cross-cultural child observation data, Whiting and Whiting view the United States, a complex technological society, as occupying an extreme position on the egoistic side of the egoism/altruism dimension.

They further hypothesize that, when a society takes an extreme view on any value, as our society has done with respect to egoism/altruism, there is a psychic cost to its members; this cost must be mitigated by some sort of social defense mechanism. Whiting and Whiting (1994/1973) continue:

> The traditional defense of complex societies against too great an emphasis on egoistic behavior is what might be called *displaced altruism.* Taught as children that they should outdo their parents and compete with their siblings, friends, and neighbors, men and women feel guilty and isolated, and find solace in helping the poor, the ignorant, and the "culturally deprived." Missionary work has long characterized the more complex societies. . . . The concern of the middle class with the poor and the culturally deprived in our own culture, as expressed by the civil rights movement and Vista, as well as the concern of the psychically normal with the mentally retarded and psychotic, are further examples of displacing altruism from friends and relatives to strangers. The culturally approved defense of displaced altruism apparently permits some members of our society to live at relative peace with strong competitive egoistic demands and permits them to continue to teach their children that to do well in school and to get the best jobs are the most important of values. (p. 280)

In essence, the Whitings are saying that self-development and achievement are required in complex, technological societies such as the United States, whereas helping behaviors or altruism are optional, a matter of choice. The importance of helping strangers through "displaced altruism" fits with this analysis, for in the United States, helping strangers is perceived as more a matter of choice than is helping a child or a friend by subjects at all age levels: second grade, sixth grade, and college (Miller et al., 1990).

Play: Cooperation, Competition, and Reward Allocation

Peer games can bring up important cross-cultural differences in the tendency to emphasize cooperation versus competition and in the ways rewards are allocated. These differences can then create difficulties in peer relations in a culturally diverse society. Interestingly, the classic research in this area was done in the 1960s and 1970s. The topic has received little research attention since.

Competition versus Cooperation

In Western societies, both cooperation and competition are valued, and children often learn to interact with one another utilizing both concepts. However, children in the United States are often placed in situations where competition is more likely to be utilized and even encouraged.

School is an environment where this tendency takes place. According to Aronson and Bridgeman (1979):

> In the typical American classroom, children are almost never engaged in the pursuit of common goals. During the past several years, we and our colleagues have systematically observed scores of elementary school classrooms and found that, in the vast majority of these cases, the process of education is highly competitive. Children vie with one another for good grades, the respect of the teacher, etc. (p. 340)

In a society where children are constantly evaluated and rewarded based on individual achievement, a tendency toward competitiveness is to be expected.

In the United States, this tendency to be competitive with one another increases with age (Kagan & Madsen, 1972). This developmental trend was depicted in a study by Madsen (1971) that utilized an interpersonal game in which children could either cooperate with one another (and be more likely to receive a prize) or compete with one another (and be less likely to receive a prize). The result showed a striking effect. In the United States, it was found that younger children (4–5) were more successful than older children (7–8, 10–11) in cooperating in order to receive a prize. In older children, the motivation to compete was so strong that it overcame the tendency to act for mutual self-interest (Madsen, 1971). In contrast, Mexican children from a small agricultural community behaved cooperatively at the older ages. Small community size may be important because of its role in leading to within-group cohesion.

However, in-group cooperation is often associated with out-group competition. This was the case for highly cooperative kibbutz children from Israel (Shapira & Madsen, 1969). Israeli kibbutzim are small, collectivistic, agricultural communities with strong in-group ties. Using a game to examine cooperation and competition in peer relations, Shapira and Madsen (1969) found that kibbutz children's tendency to cooperate in a game overshadowed their competitive tendencies under various reward conditions. In contrast, city children would cooperate when there was a group reward, but as soon as rewards were distributed on an individual basis, competition took over.

In kibbutzim, children are prepared from an early age to cooperate and work as a group, and competition is not seen as a socially desirable norm (Shapira & Madsen, 1969). At the time this study was done, kibbutz teachers reported that anticompetitive attitudes were so strong that children sometimes felt ashamed for being consistently at the top of their class (Shapira & Madsen, 1969). Under such cultural norms, it is not surprising that children in kibbutz communities were much more likely to cooperate rather than compete with one another in gaming situations. A high-level of within-group cooperation was associated with a desire to do better than other groups who had played the game before.

Insofar as an emphasis on cooperation is part of a collectivistic value orientation, it may be that greater differentiation of relations between in-group and out-group members may characterize collectivistic cultures, in comparison with individualistic ones. (An in-group is one to which you belong; an out-group is one to which you do not.) Triandis, Bontempo, Villareal, Asai, and Lucca (1988) have data confirming this idea. In a study comparing Japanese and American students in conflict situations against differing opponents, they found that the Japanese subjects showed a greater behavioral difference between their interactions with in-group members and their interactions with out-group members.

It is too simplistic to say that children from collectivistic cultures are, on the average, more cooperative than children from individualistic cultures. Instead, children from more collectivistic cultures are more cooperative with in-groups and more competitive with out-groups. Second, the cross-cultural mean differences are far from absolute. For example, children from more individualistic environments will cooperate when competition is dysfunctional and there are strong cues for cooperating, such as group reward (Shapira & Madsen, 1969). In addition, differences in cultural values concerning cooperation and competition often reflect ecological conditions.

Ecological factors. As with helping behavior, cooperative behavior appears to be more functional and encouraged in small, simple, nontechnological groups with low levels of formal education and to be less functional in large, complex, technological groups with high levels of formal education (Graves & Graves, 1978). Therefore, when members of a small, simple, nontechnological group come into contact with members of a large, complex, technological group, competitiveness in peer relations increases, as Madsen and Lancy (1981) found in New Guinea.

The role of urbanization in stimulating competition is confirmed by studies comparing two ecologies in one country. In one such study, Madsen (1967) found that urban Mexican children were much more competitive and less cooperative than rural Mexican children from a small, agricultural community. This pattern of findings points to the conclusion that the greater cooperation of Mexican immigrants to the United States may be, to a great extent, a function of their rural, agricultural background.

Urbanization may play its role in reducing cooperation and increasing competition by loosening the strength of in-group ties in an ethnically diverse milieu. This was the conclusion of Madsen and Lancy (1981), who, in a study of 10 sites in New Guinea, found that, when primary group identification could be separated from rural residence, it was by far the most important factor in children's choice between a cooperative and competitive strategy in a peer game situation. Children who came from ethnic groups that had retained their tribal coherence were more cooperative, even when exposed to urban centers, than were rural children whose groups had less stability and whose traditional way of life had largely disappeared.

Reward Allocation

Leung and Iwawaki (1988) claim that people from individualistic backgrounds are more likely to want to allocate rewards in proportion to each individual's contribution, whereas people from collectivistic backgrounds tended to allocate rewards equally to everyone in the group. This has been found to be true in numerous studies of adults, such as those comparing Hong Kong and the United States (Leung & Iwawaki, 1988), Korea and the United States (Leung & Park, 1986), as well as Japan and Australia (Kashima, Siegel, Tanaka, & Isaka, 1988).

Kibbutz children, coming from a collectivistic background, fit this pattern and show that the principle starts in middle childhood. In fact, when faced with a game situation in which reward allocation could differ, the kibbutz children showed a concern that "everyone should get the same" and "when, in some isolated cases, one of the children tried to compete against the others, the group usually restrained him" (Shapira & Madsen, 1969, p. 617). Because the city children did not show this same concern, there was some indication that equity of rewards goes with a cooperative approach to playing games and, perhaps, other activities.

Implications for Intergroup Peer Relations

With this in mind, it is apparent that children (as well as adults) with different cultural backgrounds can easily have divergent ideas concerning cooperation, competition, and the allocation of rewards. Without proper awareness of such differentiation in viewpoints, one can imagine the possible confusion and misunderstanding that might occur when one child's assumptions about cooperation, competition, and reward allocation fundamentally differs from that of her playmate. This difference can indeed be yet another source of cross-cultural conflict that can occur among children, particularly following immigration from a collectivistic milieu to an individualistic one.

Kagan and Madsen (1972) found Mexican American children to be midway between Mexican and U.S. children in cooperativeness. This pattern of findings confirms the hypothesis that Mexican immigrants from rural areas bring a collectivistic orientation with them to the United States. There, collectivistic values come into conflict with an individualistic value system and subsequently diminish (Delgado-Gaitan, 1994; Raeff et al., in press). Nonetheless, differential cooperativeness can potentially affect peer relations between Latino and European American children, with the most severe conflicts likely to occur for immigrant Latino children playing with European American peers. This kind of situation occurs in multiethnic sports teams. Here is an example of the difficulty in peer relations that can occur when immigrant Latina players are on the same team with European American players. The example comes from a girls' high school varsity volleyball team (B. Quiroz, January 1996, unpublished data):

Two immigrant Latina players talk about wanting the team to work as a unit. They complain that the European American girls just want themselves to look good, sometimes even at the expense of the team's performance.

In this example, the European American players try to act like "stars," sometimes even at a perceived cost to team performance. The Latina players are upset at the European American girls' tendency to value individual attention instead of the overall group goal of cooperating as a team to play the game. What is viewed as natural and even desirable from the European American perspective, is seen as an act of bad faith from the immigrant Latina perspective.

Sometimes, in contrast to the situation for most immigrant Latinos, immigrants may arrive in North America with an approach to play that is more similar to the competitive framework of the dominant society. For example, Madsen and Yi (1975) found urban children to be more competitive than rural children in Korea. Unlike Mexican immigrants, most Korean immigrants to North America are urban professionals, and according to Madsen and Yi's (1975) findings, this means that they arrive in North America with some degree of competitive emphasis already present in their socialization and development. This could make adjustment to the dominant mode of peer relations in North America easier than it is for most Latino immigrants coming to the United States from rural backgrounds.

Conflict Resolution

Conflicts among children are inevitable within any culture. The preceding descriptions underscore that the potential for conflict (especially culturally based conflict) is even greater between children of differing backgrounds. However, it is ironic that acceptable and preferred measures of conflict resolution also differ from culture to culture.

Cultural Bases of Conflict Resolution

In the United States, success, freedom, and justice are "central strands" of culture (Bellah, Madsen, Sullivan, Swindler, & Tipton, 1985). These values are considered "individual" rights and are treasured concepts, written into the Constitution and worthy of fighting wars for. Under the precepts of these rights and the resulting economic system of capitalism, competition among people is seen as healthy, necessary, and even desirable. Thus, resolution of conflict may be competitive and confrontational, based on the concept that the individual, rather than the collective, has rights that may, and should be, actively pursued.

In other societies, however, behavioral ideals lead to different types of desired behavior. Chinese people were found to prefer nonconfrontational approaches to conflict resolution more than Westerners did (Leung, 1988). In fact, there appears to be a strong inverse relationship between the presence of Chinese values and the degree of competitiveness used in handling conflicts (Chiu & Kosinski, 1994), suggesting a strong tie between cultural values and conflict behavior. In general, Toupin (1980) suggests that East Asian cultures share certain norms, including that of deference to others, absence of verbal aggression, and avoidance of confrontation.

Conflict resolution in West Africa also emphasizes the importance of group harmony. According to Nsamenang (1987), West Africans emphasize reconciliation as a means of handling disputes and domestic conflicts to "reinforce the spirit of communal life" (p. 279). The preservation of group harmony during conflict resolution is once again crucial in this cultural context.

Both the means and the goals of conflict resolution vary according to the values and ideals to which each culture aspires. We would expect these cultural modes of adult conflict resolution to furnish the developmental goals for the socialization of conflict resolution in children.

Children's Methods of Conflict Resolution Reflect Their Cultural Foundations

In every society, cultural ideals are manifested in the conflict resolution tactics encouraged by the adults. According to Whiting and Edwards (1988), "The manner in which socializers handle children's disputes is one of the ways in which the former transmit their values concerning the legitimate power ascribed to gender and age" (p. 189). Through adult intervention, cultural and societal ideals and values are transmitted to the children.

For example, in American preschools, one is generally encouraged to use his or her words to "defend oneself from accusations and to seek redress when one feels wronged" (Tobin, Wu, & Davidson, 1989, p. 167). American parents also encourage children to use their words to "negotiate disputes or label their emotions" (Whiting & Edwards, 1988) when having conflicts with their peers. In a culture that highly values equality, individual rights, and justice, expressing one's personal point of view is very important. By doing so, the hope is that justice can emerge out of learning about each child's individual perspective. Note that the emphasis on verbal dispute resolution reflects the emphasis of European American parents on verbalization.

Another tactic used by American adults to reduce conflict among children is "time out." A clear example of this technique is seen in *Preschool in Three Cultures,* a chronicle of preschool observations in Japan, China, and the United States by Tobin et al. (1989). In an observation of a U.S. classroom, the authors describe an encounter in which a teacher isolates Kerry, a boy who refuses to put away toys, until he admits to playing with the toys and becomes willing to help clean up the Legos that he had played with. Repeatedly, the teacher approaches Kerry and attempts to reason with him before finally resorting to a time-out measure.

This individualized attention given to misbehaving children, while heralded as an appropriate and effective means of child management in this particular cultural context, would appear strange in others. In the United States, it is quite common and even desirable for teachers, parents, and children to use negotiation, lobbying, voting, pleading, litigation, encouraging, arbitration, and isolation to resolve conflicts in a just or fair manner (Tobin et al., 1989). However, giving such individualized attention to disobedient children may not be approved of in more collectivistic cultures.

In the same observational field study, Tobin et al. (1989) also observed classroom activities in Komatsudani, a preschool in Japan. Here, teachers were described as being "careful not to isolate a disruptive child from the group by singling him out for punishment or censure or excluding him from a group activity" (Tobin et al., 1989, p. 43). In a society that highly values group interactions and collectivism, such a punishment would be seen as extreme. In this cultural framework, the teachers at Komatsudani would instead take a more unintrusive and collective approach to conflict resolution. When Hiroki, a misbehaving child, causes a stir among his classmates, the Japanese teacher's response is not to single him out but rather to instruct other children to take care of the problem themselves. This technique is in stark contrast to the American tactic of immediate adult intervention and arbitration, followed by later isolation.

The philosophy behind this mode of conflict resolution at Komatsudani is also closely linked to cultural beliefs. In Japan, group interactions are highly salient, and teachers therefore believe that "children learn best to control their behavior when the impetus to change comes spontaneously through interactions with their peers rather than from above" (Lewis, 1984; quoted in Tobin et al., 1989, p. 28). On being interviewed, Fukui-sensei, the teacher at Komatsudani, said that she believed that other classmates' disapproval would have a greater effect on misbehaving children, perhaps more so than would any form of adult intervention. Here we see peer pressure as an effective means of conflict control.

In the United States, in contrast, peer pressure is usually seen not as a means of controlling behavior in a positive way, but rather, as a negative form of conformity and lack of personal freedom. In this context, having children "work things out on their own" without intervention and assessment by others would be unusual indeed.

Implications for Intergroup Peer Relations

Conflict is unavoidable in any cultural context. However, modes of dealing with conflict can differ greatly. Conflict resolution is difficult enough in a homogenous society where children subscribe to the same cultural scripts and norms. When children from differing backgrounds attempt to reconcile their differences, their task is even further exacerbated by an incongruence between the children's conflict resolution styles. Thus, events such as minor playground altercations can lead to schisms in children's perceptions of people from other backgrounds and beliefs.

Implications for Practice

Education

Teachers may interact with large groups of children of differing backgrounds where cultural differences in interactive style would be constantly exposed. Many situations might arise in which a teacher could negatively interpret a child's culturally bound peer interactions. Teachers should therefore be trained to become aware of the differing cultural belief systems and modes of behavior that may lead children to peer conflict or make peer conflicts difficult to resolve.

When interethnic misunderstandings occur, Quiroz (personal communication, January 1996) observed that the injured party often attributes the behavior of the other group to prejudice and discrimination. This might be especially true when the injured party belongs to a minority ethnicity. An understanding of the cultural reasons for peer behavior has the power to decrease attributions of prejudice and discrimination, thus contributing to improved intergroup peer relations.

Making each group aware of the cultural model behind the behavior of their own and other ethnic groups may be a powerful means for improving intergroup understanding and intergroup relations. This may be achieved through the training of teachers, counselors, and coaches to be more aware of cultural issues (Rothstein-Fisch, Trumbull, Quiroz, & Greenfield, 1997). Workshops may also be started for children and adolescents to increase dialogue on these issues.

Teachers may also choose to change their curriculum to accommodate different modes of participation and interaction among students. Because class activities are generally competitive, the addition of class projects focusing more on cooperative participation may encourage and inspire children to work together in new ways while putting children who are used to cooperative modes of interaction more at ease. This issue will be discussed in more detail in the final section of the chapter on home-school relations.

Parents

When parents have their children in a multicultural environment in which different cultural goals for human development are idealized, it would be important to recognize these differences and prepare their children for this possibility.

In the United States, conflict resolution between peers depends on a clear presentation of one's personal needs and a recognition of self-responsibility to accomplish change and solve the conflict. This is wholly unlike collectivistic views of conflict resolution, in which the self is responsible for the other and for the acknowledgment of the other's needs. In many home cultures, strongly voicing and defending one's point of view is not encouraged. Yet this skill is often required of children faced with peers in multicultural or bicultural social environments. Parents should therefore be aware of this difference and help their children cope with it.

Summary

Despite some degree of intracultural variation and multicultural influences, overall cultural patterns of interpersonal interaction exist. Differences in peer relations in the areas of communication, self-presentation, helping behavior, play, and conflict resolution organize themselves around what has become a familiar dimension: an idealized cultural model of independent or interdependent functioning. When interacting peers come from home cultures that have contrasting models concerning this dimension, the potential for problematic peer relations arises.

An important source of perceived prejudice and discrimination is failure to understand the cultural values that generate the behavior of others. Behavior that is valued at home in one ethnic group may be devalued, and even made fun of, by members of another ethnic group. Students can end up criticizing each other for acting in ways that actualize different sets of cultural ideals, learned at home, about behavior and human relations.

Differences in cultural value systems have the potential to cause deep misunderstanding and conflict between children from diverse cultural backgrounds. Interaction between children is never completely conflict free, but when children play among other children who share their cultural values, peer interaction can often be smoother, based on similar assumptions of what consists of fair play, proper methods of conflict resolution, ideal interactive behaviors, and so forth.

In a multicultural society such as the United States, children from various cultural backgrounds have the opportunity to interact with one another. However, interaction alone does not breed awareness of other value systems. There is a tendency for each interactant to see the other's behavior through the implicit lens of his or her own value system. Therefore parents and teachers need to be aware of the potential differences between children to help each child to better understand that children may have different perspectives on proper peer interaction, and that these differences can be acknowledged, respected, and even appreciated.

It is necessary first to educate parents and teachers concerning cultural differences and then have them, in turn, educate children. Teaching children about cultural differences in values and behavior can be an important first step to help children become more aware, accepting, and fulfilled in their interaction with one another as children, as well as to prepare them for their interactions with one another as functioning, socially conscious adults.

HOME-SCHOOL RELATIONS

Cultural models of human development and socialization are embodied in infant care practices and parent-child relations. These practices and relations then influence the cultural models and behaviors that children bring into their peer relations. The school is an important institution in the forging of peer relations. Schooling involves more than just peer relations, however. It also involves relations between children and teachers and between parents and teachers. These relationships will be the focus of the present section.

By the age of 4 or 5, most children venture from their homes to enter a brand-new environment: school. In a culturally homogenous society, this shift between home culture and the culture of the schools is a relatively smooth transition, based on shared goals and assumptions (Raeff et al., in press). In a multicultural society such as the United States, however, families come from many cultural backgrounds. Although colorful and joyous, this diversity can also lead to potential misunderstandings and value conflict between school personnel and parents. Some of these misunderstandings occur in the context of peer relations at school, an area where the analysis of the preceding section is relevant. Still others occur between parents and teachers or between children and teachers. Such culture-based misunderstandings will be the central issue of this section.

In the cross-cultural peer conflicts analyzed in the preceding section, contrasting cultural values were, to an extent, on an equal footing. In school, however, this is not the case. The power belongs to the dominant culture that is part and parcel of formal education in the United States or any other country. This inequality of power between the dominant value system exemplified in school and contrasting value systems present in the homes of various ethnic groups is exemplified in the following incident from an elementary school in West Los Angeles serving low-income Latino families (Greenfield, 1995; Quiroz & Greenfield, in press):

> There had just been a major conflagration involving the federally funded school breakfast program. The problem, as seen by the school, was that immigrant Latino mothers were accompanying their children to school, bringing younger siblings, eating the school breakfast together with their children, and, as a consequence, eating food that "belonged" to the school-aged children. When the school tried to stop families from having breakfast with their children, there was a major blow-up. Latino immigrant parents who had previously not been involved in school affairs suddenly became very activist. The school personnel, who felt strongly about their position, were astounded at the reaction. (Greenfield, 1995, p. 3)

How Does This Narrative of Social Conflict Reflect Contrasting Developmental Goals?

This is a situation in which parents and school administrators differed in their opinions about what is best for the child. From the school's point of view, the sharing of school breakfasts that took place between students and their family members was unacceptable. First of all, this situation violated federal regulations guiding the school breakfast program, an antipoverty nutritional program designed as an individual rather than family-based entitlement. Therefore, the child's individual rights to *all* his or her food were being violated.

A second problem, as seen by the school personnel, was that these mothers were literally spoon-feeding their school-age kids instead of letting them eat by themselves. Such behavior was seen as leading to dependency, rather than to the self-sufficiency advocated by the schools. From a Eurocentric point of view, the indignation and perplexity felt on the part of school administrators toward the Latino parents is readily understandable.

When viewing the school breakfast situation through the lenses of the cultural goals shared by the Latino parents, however, their desire to take part in their children's meals is equally understandable. For the Latino parents, sharing the school breakfasts with their school-age children reflected a desire to emphasize the family unit. In their view, the child's breakfast was not the sole, personal property of the child, but something that could be shared with the entire family. Nutrition was something needed by the whole family, not merely the school-age child or children. Helping the children eat their food also reflected Latino cultural values: Being helpful toward one another is a highly desirable trait. In this situation, differences between the goals of the Latino families and the assumptions and expectations of school personnel came into direct conflict, causing misunderstandings and conflict between Latino immigrant parents and the school.

Because both the individualistic framework that generated the school's interpretation and response and the collectivistic framework that generated the parents' were invisible to all, there was no possibility of each side understanding the perspective of the other. Instead, each side used their own model of human development and behavior to negatively evaluate the behavior of the other side.

Developmental Goals of "School Culture"

How general was this conflict over school breakfasts? Would it be correct to say that it reflected two contrasting cultural models of development? Raeff et al. (in press) conducted experimental research to investigate this. They administered a set of scenarios concerning social dilemmas at home and at school in two different schools. Each dilemma could be solved in a number of different ways, some consonant with an individualistic model of development and socialization, some consonant with a collectivistic model. Parents, teachers, and children were tested in each school. In one school, the families were primarily European American; in the other, they were Latino immigrants.

Here is an example of a dilemma that relates to the school breakfast example. In this dilemma, which takes place at school, the issue is whether to help or not:

> It is the end of the school day, and the class is cleaning up. Denise isn't feeling well, and she asks Jasmine to help her with her job for the day which is cleaning the blackboard. Jasmine isn't sure that she will have time to do both jobs. What do you think the teacher should do? (Raeff et al., in press)

Just as the school was unified in the opinion that mothers should not help their school-age children to eat, teachers (at both schools) were in broad agreement that Jasmine should not be required to help Denise. Most often they thought a third person should be found to do the job, on a volunteer basis.

Although the situation is quite different in many respects from the school breakfast problem, the issue of helpfulness seems to evoke the same underlying model and reveal its generality among school personnel. Teacher ethnicity did not affect the response; teachers as a professional group had been socialized into the culture of the school.

Not only did Raeff et al. (in press) find generality of the cultural model from a real-world incident to an experimental scenario; there was also generality across scenarios and across settings, from school to home. Across a number of different scenarios, the overwhelming number of teacher responses reflected an individualistic model of child socialization and development. Because the scenarios were diverse, we can conclude that a single underlying individualistic model generates coordinated responses in a range of social situations.

Home-School Harmony and Conflict

Raeff et al. (in press) had expected that European American parents would be generally in tune with the school's individualistic model of development. That is exactly what was found: European American parents shared the teachers' view that Jasmine should not be required to help Denise.

Based on information concerning Latino immigrant models of development (discussed in the sections on infancy and parent-child relations) and based on reactions to the school breakfast program, Raeff et al. (in press) expected that Latino immigrant parents would be in sharp conflict with the school's approach to the school jobs dilemma.

Just as the Latino parents thought mothers should help their children eat their school breakfasts, Raeff et al. (in press) expected Latino parents to think that Jasmine should help Denise. And that is exactly what they found: Latino parents were in broad agreement that Jasmine should help Denise. This response was shown to be part of a more general model of development: Across a number of diverse scenarios, they overwhelmingly constructed responses that reflected an underlying collectivistic model of development.

From the point of view of home-school relations, the Latino parents are completely out of tune with the school's value system, whereas correlatively, the teachers are completely out of tune with the Latino parents' value system. This is in sharp contrast to the picture of home-school value harmony that exists for European American families.

Children Caught between Home Culture and School Culture

As a consequence of value harmony between their parents and their teachers, European American children are receiving consistent socialization messages at home and at school. The children of Latino immigrants are not. The results reflect these dynamics: Whereas there are no significant differences between the responses of European American children and their parents, there are significant differences between Latino children and their immigrant parents (Raeff et al., in press).

The Latino children are, overall, significantly more individualistic than their parents and significantly more collectivistic than their teachers. That is, they are different from both their major socializing agents. Little is known about whether such children have successfully integrated two cultures or they are caught in the middle. It has been noted (R. Paredes, personal communication, 1996) that they express Chicano culture, the culture of Mexican Americans in the United States. Although this research was done with a particular population, it is potentially applicable to the children of other collectivistic groups who come to the United States.

The most common problem derives from immigrant parents' collectivistic expectations of children suffused with individualism from the surrounding society, particularly the school. (Recall that problems of differential acculturation rate between parents and children were also discussed in the section on parent-child relations.) The following is an articulately expressed experience of a first-generation college student of Persian Jewish immigrant parents:

> Although the collectivistic ideology dominated my home life, at school and within the greater community, a different, and sometimes contradictory, ideology of individualism was taught and had been established as the norm. The "I" consciousness was the norm here; you had to watch out for yourself, you were responsible for your actions, your successes and your failures. I was no longer responsible for whether my brother did well on his tests or not, that was now his problem, not mine. In school my non-Persian friends could not relate nor understand why I had to drive my brother around or why my mother was upset at me because my sister had made a mess in the living room and it had been my responsibility to help her and make sure she cleaned it. In their families, if you had a responsibility and you didn't fulfill it, only you suffered the consequences, not your brother or sister or anyone else.
>
> In school and in the community life seemed to be so much simpler, you had only to do things for yourself, you weren't bound to any other entity. If your sister was sick, you could go out, you didn't have to stay home and take care of her. You could go away to college and "experience life," you weren't bound to the home and family as in the Persian society and in my family. Their parents weren't strict about curfews, when you could go out, and where you could go; it was your choice and your responsibility. (Yafai, 1992, pp. 3–4)

Bringing a Collectivistic Model of Development to School: The Potential for Home-School Conflict

In the United States, many schooling options are available to children and their families: public schools, private schools, parochial schools, language immersion schools, college preparatory boarding schools . . . the list goes on. Despite this diversity, research indicates that schools often reflect aspects of individualism that highlight independence as a goal of development. Classroom interactions and activities emphasize individual achievement, the encouragement of children's autonomous choice and initiative, and the development of logico-rational, rather than social skills (Delgado-Gaitan, 1993, 1994; Reese et al., 1995).

Academic activities are also intrinsically individualistic insofar as evaluations are generally made on the basis of independent work accomplished by individual students (Whiting & Whiting, 1994/1973) rather than on group endeavors. This focus on individual achievement and evaluation is a predominant theme in academic settings; individual achievement and evaluation are the foundation on which many schools are built.

These aspects of school culture often come into direct conflict with the collectivistic orientation toward education favored not only by Latinos, but by many minority and immigrant cultures (e.g., Asian American, Native American, and African American), whose cultures emphasize values such as cherishing interpersonal relationships, respecting elders and native traditions, feeling a responsibility for others, and cooperation (Blake, 1993, 1994; Delgado-Gaitan, 1993, 1994; Ho, 1994; Kim & Choi, 1994; Suina & Smolkin, 1994). This perspective is antithetical to the school's emphasis on individual achievement.

Individual Achievement from a Collectivistic Perspective

Encouraging children's individual achievements can be seen in some cultures (e.g., Nigeria) as devaluing cooperation (Oloko, 1993, 1994) or group harmony. Research on conferences between immigrant Latino parents and their children's elementary school teachers revealed incidents when the teacher's praise of an individual child's outstanding achievement made a parent feel distinctly uncomfortable (Greenfield, Quiroz, & Raeff, in press).

Parents seemed to feel most comfortable with a child's school achievement if the academic skill in question could be applied to helping other family members. For example, in one parent-teacher conference, a Latino mother (with a first-grade education) created common ground with the teacher when she responded to a question about her daughter's home reading by telling the teacher that her daughter had been reading to a younger family member (Greenfield et al., in press).

In this example, mother and teacher have cooperatively constructed a symbolic child who both practices a skill (reading) and shares this skill within the family (reading to a younger child). Individual achievement is made more consonant with a collectivistic model of development by using the achievement to enrich the experience of another family member.

Written Knowledge from a Collectivistic Perspective

The reliance on textbooks used in many school settings may also be cause for conflict. In some cultures, the acquisition of knowledge is seen as something that is gleaned not from impersonal texts, but rather from the wisdom and knowledge of relevant others. In the Pueblo Indian worldview, parents and grandparents are seen as the repositories of knowledge, and this fact provides a social connection between the older and younger generations. In cultures such as these, when objects rather than people become the authorities of knowledge, the introduction of resources such as encyclopedias, reference books, and the like is seen to undermine "the very fiber of the connectedness" (Suina, 1991, p. 153) between people. From this perspective, the school's emphasis on learning through written material may appear to be an impersonal and even undesirable way of acquiring knowledge.

Object Knowledge from a Collectivistic Perspective

Children whose cultural background has emphasized social relations and social knowledge may not understand the privileged position of decontextualized object knowledge in the culture of the school. The following is an example of culture conflict that can occur between teachers and children:

> In a Los Angeles prekindergarten class mostly comprising Hispanic children, the teacher was showing the class a real chicken egg that would be hatching soon. She was explaining the physical properties of the egg, and she asked the children to describe eggs by thinking about the times they had cooked and eaten eggs. One of the children tried three times to talk about how she cooked eggs with her grandmother, but the teacher disregarded these comments in favor of a child who explained how eggs are white and yellow when they are cracked. (Greenfield et al., 1995)

From the Latino point of view, the first child's answer was typical of the associations encouraged in her invisible home culture of interdependence: Objects are most meaningful when they mediate social interactions. The child therefore acted on this value of interpersonal relations in answering the teacher's question. The teacher, however, did not recognize this effort on the part of the child and considered the social descriptions of the time they had eaten eggs as irrelevant; only physical descriptions of these occasions were valued (Greenfield et al., 1995).

The teacher did not even see the invisible culture that generated a description of cooking eggs with one's grandmother; the teacher devalued the child's contribution, and implicitly, the value orientation it reflected. Because she did not understand the collectivistic value orientation, she was also unaware that her question was ambiguous in the following way: Children who shared her value orientation would assume that she was interested in the physical properties of the eggs, even though she did not make this point explicit. Those children who did not share the teacher's value orientation would make different assumptions.

Assertiveness from a Collectivistic Perspective

To give another example, in many collectivistic cultures, the value placed on respecting authority may go as far as to undermine the more individualistic styles of learning that require children to articulate and even argue their views with teachers and other elders on a relatively egalitarian basis (Delgado-Gaitan, 1993, 1994). The following extract describes the cultural ideal for child communicative behavior for many people of Mexican background. According to Delgado-Gaitan (1994):

> Children are expected to politely greet their elders; they are not supposed to argue with them. In the company of adults, children are to be good listeners and participate in a conversation only when solicited. To raise questions is to be rebellious. (p. 64)

A similar view of questioning is found in Japan (Muto et al., 1980). Given this cultural ideal in child communication, one can imagine the scenario in a U.S. school in which a teacher might falsely interpret a Mexican American child's compliance or a Japanese child's absence of questioning as a lack of motivation or intellectual curiosity.

As noted in the section on parent-child relations, many children from different ethnic groups are raised with the notion of respecting and accepting the opinions of elders without question, and this value may be carried with the children to the school setting. The school's emphasis on rational argumentation can be seen to undermine respect for elders. Thus, when children are not vocal and adept at logico-rational modes of argumentation, they can be subjected to criticism by teachers, who focus on fostering individual assertiveness and opinions.

In a study of conferences between immigrant Latino parents and their children's elementary school teachers, Greenfield et al. (in press) showed that the teacher criticized every single child for not sufficiently expressing his or her views in class. The teacher was unaware that such behavior would be contrary to the Latino parents' goals for their own children's development.

Implications for Educational Practice

In this section, we detail methods for overcoming home-school conflict that occurs when children with a collectivistic background come to school. We also stress the relevance of cross-cultural exchange in educational practice.

Teaching to the Whole Class

In many collectivistic societies, schools have found ways of integrating indigenous cultural values into the school system. In Japanese and Chinese classrooms, classroom practices that focus the attention of teaching on the class as a whole rather than promoting attention to individual students are common and widely accepted (Stigler & Perry, 1988). This technique might be useful in U.S. classrooms that are homogenous in the sense of containing only children who come from collectivistic backgrounds. Classrooms for immigrants would be one such example.

Cooperative Learning in the Classroom

In the United States, there has been considerable experimentation with cooperative learning, particular in classrooms featuring cultural diversity (Aronson & Bridgeman, 1979). Cooperative learning methods represent a compromise with the school's bias toward individual achievement and evaluation (Whiting & Whiting, 1994/1973) and a more collectivistic or interdependent approach. Effective cooperative learning methods have two necessary characteristics (Slavin, 1986, p. 8):

1. Rewards must be given to the group as a whole, rather than to individuals within it.
2. The group's success must depend on the individual learning of each group member.

Thus, individual learning is placed in a context of interdependence.

One method for accomplishing this is the Jigsaw Classroom of Aronson and colleagues (Aronson, Stephan, Sikes, Blaney, & Snapp, 1978). In this method, each student in a small group has access to a part of the information required for a total lesson. Students have to master their own parts and then teach them to the other members of the group. Team members are ultimately tested individually, but they are totaled into team scores and recognition is given to the team as a whole, rather than to individuals within it.

Consonant with the idea that African American and Latino students generally have their cross-cultural ancestral roots in collectivistic cultures, the academic achievement of these minorities was better in the cooperative than in the normal, individualistic learning conditions (Lucker, Rosenfield, Sikes, & Aronson, 1977). Consonant with the idea that European American children more often have their cultural roots in the individualism of the United States and Northern Europe, their academic achievement was not improved by the cooperative conditions. But neither was the academic achievement of European American children hampered by the Jigsaw Classroom. At the same time for all ethnic groups, the liking of students for others within their cooperating group increased, both within and across ethnic boundaries.

This pattern of results indicates that cooperative learning can be of use in the culturally diverse classroom. Cooperative techniques such as jigsaw teaching seem to make children who come to school with cooperative backgrounds feel more at ease with learning (Widaman & Kagan, 1987) while teaching cooperative behavior to children from more individualistic backgrounds. Most important, cooperating groups become in-groups with positive bonds; these bonds can extend across ethnic lines.

Cooperative learning might be particularly effective with children from cultures in which respectful deference to authority, rather than speaking up to adults, is expected (e.g., Greenfield et al., 1995). In such cultures, free communication among peers is expected. It therefore might be much more consonant with cultural conventions of communication to speak out in teaching a peer in a Jigsaw Classroom than to speak out to an adult authority figure such as a teacher.

Barriers to Introducing the Collectivistic Model of Development into Classroom Management

Blanca Quiroz, then a bilingual kindergarten teacher, incorporated cooperative classroom management practices into her classroom, composed of children of Latino immigrants. However, she consistently encountered resistance from the supervisory administration. Here is an example:

> Three groups were alternating activities; one activity consisted of playing with toys on the carpet. Instead of having each child in each group pick up and put away the toys before each activity switch, the whole class was cleaning up the toys at the end of the complete rotation. Furthermore, they expressed enjoyment at helping out. Yet the single comment that the assistant principal stated on her review was "You have an excellent rapport with the students, but I would like you to work on having every student pick up after themselves, you know, to be more independent. . . . " It is particularly notable that the assistant principal considered the fostering of independence more important than the teacher's rapport with the children. The teacher, in contrast, considered her rapport to be more important than independence. In addition, the children were cooperating to pick up after themselves as a group (Quiroz & Greenfield, in press).

In this example, as in the sharing example presented early in this chapter, the teacher incorporates a collectivistic framework into classroom practice and management. She succeeds in playing to the strengths Latino children typically bring with them from home to school.

In both cases, however, this strategy goes unappreciated (and is even criticized) by her mentor-trainers, who evaluate her methods through the interpretive lens of individualism. The implication is that strong individualistic constraints are acculturated into educational personnel and the educational system. At an automatic level, these limit and constrain the transformation of classroom practice in a collectivistic direction.

Cross-Cultural Exchange in Classroom Practice

It is possible to introduce collectivistic values and practices into the classroom, while still making explicit the individualistic values that guide education for children who may not have met these values in their home cultures. This process yields the integration of multicultural values in classroom practice.

For example, in response to the egg incident described earlier, the teacher could both validate family experiences as legitimate responses in the discussion and also be explicit about expectations for a focus on physical knowledge when that is the topic of study. This kind of approach would create a bidirectional culture exchange at school: Some collectivistic values and practices would become part of the normally individualistic classroom; at the same time, children whose invisible cultures are collectivistic would receive practice in the individualistic cognitive operations necessary for school success. In a similar vein, Suina and Smolkin (1994) discuss the necessity for Native American children to be explicitly taught the cultural demands of the school, insofar as these differ from what they have learned at home.

Sometimes cross-cultural exchange involves a compromise between a collectivistic practice and an individualistic one. In dealing with Latino immigrants who have experienced poverty and little opportunity for education, teachers could, in their parent-teacher conferences, emphasize the child's academic needs and abilities, without downplaying the importance that the parents place on the child's correct social behavior.

On the other hand, teachers could also use this dual emphasis in parent-teacher conferences for European American children. The point here would be to add discussion of correct social behavior to those conferences.

Another example of potential cross-cultural exchange is to establish day-care centers for preschool children in elementary schools, where school-age children could help as caregivers. Through these interactions, the egoistic or individualistic children described by Whiting and Whiting (1994/1973) in the United States could develop the sense of social responsibility that child-care activities engender. This model has been used by the City and Country School in New York, where every 12-year-old is paired to take care of a 4-year-old (H. Davis, personal communication, June 1996).

At the same time, children who came from home backgrounds in which child care was an important socializing experience would have a chance to enact their cultural values at school. This educational practice would also test the idea that all children, not just immigrant or minority children, could benefit from a heightened balance between social responsibility and individual achievement in their socialization and education.

Teacher as Ethnographer

Current approaches to education and teacher training that treat immigrant children as *tabulae rasae* (blank slates) need to be replaced by an understanding of the values and practices that children from diverse cultures bring to the classroom. To do this, the teacher must become an ethnographer, a participant-observer in the child's home culture. Observation of parent behavior is one method for gaining ethnographic data. Talking to parents about their hopes, aspirations, and lives is another. The parent-teacher conference could become a two-way street in which both parent and teacher would provide information to the other. Teachers would devote part of the conference to learning about the parents' lives, backgrounds, and goals for their children.

Cross-Cultural Exchange: Parents and Teachers

Parents, as well as teachers, may not understand that their children's success in school is partly based on mastering modes of activity and interaction that are different from those emphasized at home, and that these modes of acting may stem from a conflicting value orientation. The school's emphasis on developing each individual child's potential may be perceived by collectivistically oriented Latino immigrant parents as encouraging undesirable selfishness. Yet, they might have to accept that this is a necessary means to the school achievement that they desire for their children. At the same time, the teacher could encourage sharing and helping behavior in the classroom and come to understand and appreciate the sacrifice of cultural values that immigrant parents must make in the socialization of their children.

We have carried out an intervention program for teachers to help them become aware of the individualistic and collectivistic belief systems that exist among different groups of students and their families (Rothstein-Fisch et al., 1997). We have implemented a teacher-training program beginning with analysis and discussion of hypothetical scenarios such as the school jobs scenario presented earlier; each scenario presents an interpersonal dilemma that can be resolved along an individualistic or collectivistic pathway. Our goal was to make teachers who served immigrant Latino families aware of these fundamentally contrasting cultural perspectives. Teachers were encouraged to apply the cultural models of individualism and collectivism to understanding and modifying educational practice in their own schools and classrooms. By the end of a series of three workshops, teachers had increased their understanding of the collectivistic value system typical of Latino immigrant homes (Delgado-Gaitan, 1994), and they had developed ways of working with this value system in their educational practice (Rothstein-Fisch et al., 1997).

Historical Relations between Majority and Minority Groups: Implications for Home-School Conflict and for Educational Practice

Both the ancestral culture, discussed up to now, and the historical context of the arrival of a minority group affect the relations between majority and minority groups. Because schools are an institution of the majority, this context is important in affecting home-school relations.

Ogbu (e.g., 1993, 1994) emphasizes the importance of the history and of the power relations between minority and majority groups within a given society. Ogbu believes that two major classifications of minority groups can be identified: involuntary minority groups (those who become incorporated into a nation through conquest, slavery, or colonization), and voluntary minority groups (those who become incorporated into a nation through voluntary immigration).

Voluntary minorities try to maintain their preexisting cultural values but are interested in using institutions such as the school to help improve their opportunities for success in their new country. Because the ancestral cultures of voluntary minorities are often more tolerated by the countries to which they immigrate, "they do not perceive or interpret learning the selected aspects of North American culture as threatening to their cultural identity" (Ogbu, 1994, p. 375). Asian Americans are viewed as a voluntary minority; and schooling is seen and used by them as an effective pathway to achievement in the broader society. Because of the framework of the voluntary immigrant, Asian parents will tend to support educational institutions, even when they challenge their ancestral values of interdependence.

Involuntary minorities, in contrast, tend to define themselves and their culture in opposition to the cultural values of the majority (Ogbu, 1993, 1994), in response to their history of conquerors, enslavers, and colonizers who have tried to wipe out or repress their indigenous cultures. Therefore, unlike voluntary minorities, involuntary minorities feel they cannot adopt any of the majority's ways without losing their own. African Americans (through slavery),

Native Americans (through conquest) and, to some extent, Mexican Americans and Puerto Ricans (through conquest of the American Southwest from Mexico) fall under the definition of involuntary minorities (Ogbu, 1994). Because schools are identified as a majority institution, academic achievement can challenge the group loyalties and ethnic identities of involuntary minorities.

Involuntary minorities find historical justification for the belief that their ancestral or ethnic culture and European American culture, including its schools, are mutually exclusive. For example, Native American children were forcibly put into government boarding schools, a major goal of which was to eradicate Native American culture and languages. For this reason, the most successful schooling for Native Americans has been their own community-run institutions, such as tribal colleges. Among involuntary immigrants, there will tend to be suspicion of educational institutions; there will be a low degree of tolerance for value conflicts with the home culture.

It is therefore possible that a general implication for educational practice might be the importance of community-controlled educational institutions for involuntary minorities. Otherwise, there is no chance of home-school harmony.

Summary

By and large, the educational implications of cross-cultural research revolve around a single major theme: the need to recognize that patterns and norms of development and education previously thought to be universal are often specific to European American culture and the culture of the schools. Immigrant families often come from collectivistic cultures, but they must put their children into the highly individualistic institution of the school. On the other hand, members of the dominant culture find relative harmony between their individualistic value framework and that of the school. Finally, particular histories of contact between dominant majority and minority groups can develop particular frames of reference with which to approach the school experience. For example, the oppositional framework that involuntary minorities learn at home (Ogbu, 1994) produces another source of home-school conflict.

The major educational implication of involuntary minority status for educational practice is community-controlled schools with emphasis on retaining and restoring ancestral culture and language. The major educational implication of cross-cultural value conflict is for teachers to acquire an understanding of the collectivistic framework and to then encourage mutual understanding and accommodation between the two value frameworks in both children and their parents.

CONCLUSION

Every generalization obscures some things while illuminating others. Cultural variability is no exception. It calls attention to normative cultural patterns at the expense of individual differences. However, individual differences always occur around a culturally defined norm, which also serves as the starting point for historical change. Without knowledge of the norm, individual differences become uninterpretable. This chapter has contributed to a deeper understanding of culturally variable norms around which individual differences can range. It has also contributed to an understanding of the dynamics of intercultural conflict, as these affect development and socialization.

The analysis of cultural variability calls attention to cultures at one point in time, thereby obscuring historical change. It is therefore important to bear in mind that culture is not static; rather, it is constantly reinventing itself through the addition of new ethnic groups to multicultural societies, through changes in educational practices, through widening effects of the mass media, and through transformations in economy and technology. These sociohistorical changes produce constantly evolving cultural modes of socialization and human development.

In a diverse society such as the United States, cross-cultural conflict is unavoidable, manifesting itself in interpersonal misunderstandings and altercations. Every culture must find its own compromise between functioning as individuals and as members of a group, between independence and interdependence. Some cultures stress one, some the other. Although individual differences in this tendency are present in every culture, each of them also has an ideal model of whether independence or interdependence is more important. Differences in these models and emphases generate cross-cultural differences in many domains of child development.

Throughout this chapter, we have seen that cultural models of individualism and collectivism have connected what would otherwise appear to be unrelated cross-cultural differences and, more important, provided an explanation for these differences. The diverse ethnicities that comprise the United States and other multicultural societies have their ancestral roots in cultures that have different positions in the cultural complexes of individualism and collectivism. Prior research (Greenfield & Cocking, 1994) has shown that these constructs therefore also generate a historical understanding of cultural diversity in child development and socialization in diverse societies like the United States. In this chapter, many cross-cultural differences and intergroup conflicts reflected patterned manifestations of individualism and collectivism.

Although it is clear that such cross-cultural conflicts exist, it is not enough to simply acknowledge their existence. By educating parents, teachers, clinicians, and health care professionals to recognize and deal with cross-cultural difference and conflict, children's social, psychological, and educational needs can be better served. It is hoped that in this increasingly multicultural society, children will learn to prepare for and to appreciate the cultural differences that they will inevitably encounter between themselves and others.

One of our main messages for the application of a cultural perspective on human development is the opportunity for cross-cultural exchange in socialization strategies. Cultural differences are a resource for pediatricians, educators, and mental health professionals who work with parents and children. At the same time, there is an important secondary effect of such cross-cultural exchange: no ethnic group feels that they are parenting the wrong way; parents from all ethnocultural backgrounds can receive the message that they have something to contribute to the raising of children in a multicultural society. At the same time, the message can go out to members of the dominant culture that, in a changing world, they have much to learn from other cultural modes of socialization and human development.

ACKNOWLEDGMENTS

The authors express special appreciation to Helen Davis for insightful comments on earlier drafts, for editing, and for help with manuscript preparation. We also thank Ashley Maynard and Rodney Cocking for reading and commenting on earlier drafts. A grant from the Carnegie Corporation to Patricia Greenfield provided support for the preparation of this chapter.

REFERENCES

Adorno, T. W., Frenkel-Brunswik, E., Levinson, D. J., & Sanford, R. N. (1950). *The authoritarian personality.* New York: Harper.

Ainsworth, M. D. S., Blehar, M. C., Waters, E., & Wall, S. (1978). *Patterns of attachment.* Hillsdale, NJ: Erlbaum.

Ainsworth, M. D. S., & Wittig, B. A. (1969). Attachment and the exploratory behavior of one-year-olds in a Strange Situation. In B. M. Foss (Ed.), *Determinants of infant behavior* (Vol. 4). London: Methuen.

Ainsworth, M. S. (1979). Infant-mother attachment. *American Psychologist, 34*(10), 932–937.

Ainsworth, M. S. (1985). Patterns of attachment. *Clinical Psychologist, 38*(2), 27–29.

Anisfeld, E., Casper, V., Nozyce, M., & Cunningham, N. (1990). Does infant carrying promote attachment? An experimental study of the effects of increased physical contact on the development of attachment. *Child Development, 61*(5), 1617–1627.

Aronson, E., & Bridgeman, D. (1979). Jigsaw groups and the desegregated classroom: In pursuit of common goals. *Personality and Social Psychology Bulletin, 5*(4), 438–446.

Aronson, E., Stephan, C., Sikes, J., Blaney, N., & Snapp, M. (1978). *The jigsaw classroom.* Beverly Hills, CA: Sage.

Azuma, H. (1994). Two modes of cognitive socialization in Japan and the United States. In P. M. Greenfield & R. R. Cocking (Eds.), *Cross-cultural roots of minority child development* (pp. 275–284). Hillsdale, NJ: Erlbaum.

Bakeman, R., Adamson, L. B., Konner, M., & Barr, R. G. (1990). !Kung infancy: The social context of object exploration. *Child Development, 61,* 794–809.

Baldwin, A. L.(1983). Socialization and the parent-child relationship. In W. Damon (Ed.), *Social and personality development: Essays on the growth of the child* (pp. 110–120). New York: Norton.

Barry, H., III, & Paxson, L. M. (1971). Infancy and early childhood: Cross-cultural codes: 2. *Ethology, 10,* 466–508.

Baumrind, D. (1967). Child care practices antedating three patterns of preschool behavior. *Genetic Psychology Monographs, 75,* 43–88.

Baumrind, D. (1971). Current patterns of parental authority. *Developmental Psychology Monographs, 4*(1, Part 2).

Baumrind, D. (1972). An exploratory study of socialization effects on black children: Some black-white comparisons. *Child Development, 43,* 261–267.

Baumrind, D. (1983). Socialization and instrumental competence in young children. In W. Damon (Ed.), *Social and personality development: Essays on the growth of the child* (pp. 121–138). New York: Norton.

Bellah, R. N., Madsen, R., Sullivan, W. M., Swindler, A., & Tipton, S. M. (1985). *Habits of the heart.* Berkeley: University of California Press.

Belsky, J. (1989). Infant-parent attachment and daycare: In defense of the Strange Situation. In J. Lande, S. Scarr, & N. Gunzenhauser (Eds.), *Caring for children: Challenge to America* (pp. 23–48). Hillsdale, NJ: Erlbaum.

Blake, I. K. (1993). Learning language in context: The social-emotional orientation of African-American mother-child communication. *International Journal of Behavioral Development, 16,* 443–464.

Blake, I. K. (1994). Language development and socialization in young African-American children. In P. M. G. Greenfield & R. R. Cocking (Eds.), *Cross-cultural roots of minority child development.* Hillsdale, NJ: Erlbaum.

Blurton-Jones, N. (1972). *Comparative aspects of mother-child contact: Ethological studies of child behavior* (pp. 305–328). Cambridge, England: Cambridge University Press.

Bond, M. H., Leung, K., & Wan, K. C. (1982). How does cultural collectivism operate? The impact of task and maintenance contributions on reward distribution. *Journal of Cross-Cultural Psychology, 13,* 186–200.

Bornstein, M. H., & Lamb, M. E. (1992). *Development in infancy: An introduction.* New York: McGraw-Hill.

Bowlby, J. (1969). *Attachment and loss: Vol. 1. Attachment.* New York: Basic Books.

Brazelton, T. B. (1990). Commentary: Parent-infant co-sleeping revisited. *Ab Initio, 2*(1), 1–7.

Brazelton, T. B., Robey, J. S., & Collier, G. A. (1969). Infant development in the Zinacanteco Indians of southern Mexico. *Pediatrics, 44,* 274–290.

Bundesen, H. (1944). *The baby manual.* New York: Simon & Schuster.

Bruner, J. S. (1990). Culture and human development: A new look. *Human Development, 33,* 344–355.

Burton, R. V., & Whiting, J. W. M. (1961). The absent father and cross-sex identity. *Merrill-Palmer Quarterly, 7,* 85–95.

Campos, J. J., Barrett, K. C., Lamb, M. E., Goldsmith, H. H., & Stenberg, C. (1983). Socioemotional development. In P. H. Mussen (Series Ed.) & M. M. Haith & J. J. Campos (Vol. Eds.), *Handbook of child psychology: Vol. 2. Infancy and developmental psychobiology* (pp. 783–915). New York: Wiley.

Caudill, W. (1972). Tiny dramas: Vocal communication between mother and infant in Japanese and American families. In W. P. Lebra (Ed.), *Mental health research in Asia and the Pacific* (Vol. 2, pp. 25–48). Honolulu: East-West Center Press.

Caudill, W., & Plath, D. (1966). Who sleeps by whom? Parent-child involvement in urban Japanese families. *Psychiatry, 29,* 344–366.

Chao, R. (1994). Beyond parental control and authoritarian parenting style: Understanding Chinese parenting through the cultural notion of training. *Child Development, 65,* 1111–1119.

Childs, C. P., & Greenfield, P. M. (1980). Informal modes of learning and teaching: The case of Zinacanteco weaving. In N. Warren (Ed.), *Studies in cross-cultural psychology* (Vol. 2, pp. 269–316). London: Academic Press.

Chiu, R. K., & Kosinski, F. A. (1994). Is Chinese conflict-handling behavior influenced by Chinese values? *Social Behavior and Personality, 22*(1), 81–90.

Choi, S. H. (1992). Communicative socialization processes: Korea and Canada. In S. Iwawaki, Y. Kashima, & K. Leung (Eds.), *Innovations in cross-cultural psychology* (pp. 103–121). Lisse, The Netherlands: Swets & Zeitlinger.

Clancy, P. M. (1986). The acquisition of communicative style in Japanese. In B. B. Schieffelin & E. Ochs (Eds.), *Language socialization across cultures.* Cambridge, England: Cambridge University Press.

Clark, H. H. (1985). Language use and language users. In G. Lindzey & E. Aronson (Eds.), *Handbook of social psychology* (pp. 179–231). New York: Random House.

Clarke-Stewart, A. (1989). Infant day care: Maligned or malignant? *American Psychologist, 44,* 266–273.

Cole, M., & Bruner, J. S. (1971). Cultural differences and inferences about psychological processes. *American Psychologist, 26,* 876–896.

Collins, A., Brown, J. S., & Newman, S. E. (1989). Cognitive apprenticeship: Teaching the crafts of reading, writing, and mathematics. In L. B. Resnick (Ed.), *Knowing, learning, and instruction: Essays in honor of Robert Glaser.* Hillsdale, NJ: Erlbaum.

Coons, S., & Guilleminault, C. (1985). Motility and arousal in near-miss Sudden Infant Death Syndrome. *Journal of Pediatrics, 107,* 728–732.

D'Andrade, R. G., & Strauss, C. (Eds.). (1992). *Human motives and cultural models.* Cambridge, England: Cambridge University Press.

Dawes, D. (1989). *Through the night: Helping parents and sleepless infants.* London: Free Association Books.

Dawes, D. (1990). Brief psychoanalytic infant-parent therapy for sleep problems. *Ab Initio, 2*(1), 4–7.

Delgado-Gaitan, C. (1993). Socializing young children in Mexican American families: An intergenerational perspective. *International Journal of Behavioral Development, 16,* 409–427.

Delgado-Gaitan, C. (1994). Socializing young children in Mexican-American families: An intergenerational perspective. In P. M. Greenfield & R. R. Cocking (Eds.), *Cross-cultural roots of minority child development.* Hillsdale, NJ: Erlbaum.

Dornbusch, S. M., Ritter, P. L., Leiderman, P. H., Roberts, D. F., & Fraleigh, M. J. (1987). The relation of parenting style to adolescent school performance. *Child Development, 58,* 1244–1257.

Duranti, A., & Ochs, E. (1986). Literacy instruction in a Samoan village. In B. B. Schieffelin & P. Gilmore (Eds.), *Acquisition of literacy: Ethnographic perspectives* (pp. 213–232). Norwood, NJ: ABLEX.

Durrett, M. E., Otaki, M., & Richards, P. (1984). Attachment and mothers' perception of support from the father. *International Journal of Behavioral Development, 7*(2), 167–176.

Eagley, A. H., & Crowley, M. (1986). Gender and helping behavior: A metal-analysis of social influence studies. *Psychological Bulletin, 90,* 1–20.

Ferber, R. (1985). *Solve your child's sleep problems.* New York: Simon & Schuster.

Ferber, R. (1990). An approach to sleep management. *Ab Initio, 2*(1), 2.

Fernald, A., & Morikawa, H. (1993). Common themes and cultural variation in Japanese and American mothers' speech to infants. *Child Development, 64,* 637–656.

Geertz, C. (1983). *Local knowledge.* New York: Basic Books.

Graves, N. B., & Graves, T. D. (1978, August 31). *Learning cooperation in a cooperative society: Implications for the classroom. Cooperate, cooperating to learn.* Symposium conducted at the annual meeting of the American Psychological Association, Toronto, Canada.

Greenfield, P. M. (1994). Independence and interdependence as developmental scripts: Implications for theory, research, and practice. In P. M. Greenfield & R. R. Cocking (Eds.), *Cross-cultural roots of minority child development* (pp. 1–40). Hillsdale, NJ: Erlbaum.

Greenfield, P. M. (1995). *Conflicting values in Hispanic immigrant families and the schools.* Invited address, American Psychological Association Division 7, cosponsored by the Developmental and Ethnic Psychology Divisions, New York.

Greenfield, P. M. (in press). You can't take it with you. *American Psychologist.*

Greenfield, P. M., Brazelton, T. B., & Childs, C. (1989). From birth to maturity in Zinacantan: Ontogenesis in cultural context. In V. Bricker & G. Gossen (Eds.), *Ethnographic encounters in southern Mesoamerica: Celebratory essays in honor of Evon Z. Vogt.* Albany: Institute of Mesoamerica, State University of New York.

Greenfield, P. M., & Childs, C. P. (1991). Developmental continuity in biocultural context. In R. Cohen & A. W. Siegel (Eds.), *Context and development* (pp. 135–159). Hillsdale, NJ: Erlbaum.

Greenfield, P. M., & Cocking, R. R. (1994). *Cross-cultural roots of minority child development.* Hillsdale, NJ: Erlbaum.

Greenfield, P. M., & Lave, J. (1982). Cognitive aspects of informal education. In D. Wagner & H. Stevenson (Eds.), *Cultural perspectives on child development* (pp. 181–207). San Francisco: Freeman.

Greenfield, P. M., Quiroz, B., & Raeff, C. (in press). Cross-cultural conflict and harmony in the social construction of the child. In S. Harkness, C. Raeff, & C. M. Super (Eds.), *The social construction of the child: The nature of variability. New directions in child development.* San Francisco: Jossey-Bass.

Greenfield, P. M., Raeff, C., & Quiroz, B. (1995). Cultural values in learning and education. In B. Williams (Ed.), *Closing the achievement gap.* Alexandria, VA: Association for Curriculum Supervision.

Greenwald, A. G. (1980). The totalitarian ego: Fabrication and revision of personal history. *American Psychologist, 35*(7), 603–618.

Gross, R., & Osterman, P. (1971). Introduction. In R. Gross & P. Osterman (Eds.), *Individualism: Man in modern society.* New York: Dell.

Grossmann, K., Grossmann, K. E., Spangler, G., Suess, G., & Unzner, L. (1985). Maternal sensitivity and newborns' orientation responses as related to quality of attachment in northern Germany. In I. Bretherton & E. Waters (Eds.), Growing points of attachment theory and research. *Monographs of the Society for Research in Child Development, 50*(1/2, Serial No. 209).

Guisinger, S., & Blatt, S. (1994). Individuality and relatedness: Evolution of a fundamental dialectic. *American Psychologist, 49,* 104–111.

Hanks, C., & Rebelsky, F. (1977). Mommy and the midnight visitor: A study of occasional co-sleeping. *Psychiatry, 40,* 277–280.

Harkness, S. (1988). The cultural construction of semantic contingency in mother-child speech. *Language Sciences, 10*(1), 53–67.

Harkness, S., & Super, C. (1982). Why African children are so hard to test. In L. L. Adler (Ed.), *Cross-cultural research at issue* (pp. 145–152). New York: Academic Press.

Harkness, S., & Super, C. (1995). Culture and parenting. In M. H. Bornstein (Ed.), *Handbook of parenting.* Hillsdale, NJ: Erlbaum.

Harkness, S., Super, C., Keefer, C. H., Raghavan, C. S., & Campbell, E. K. (1996). Ask the doctor: The negotiation of cultural models in American parent-pediatrician discourse. In S. Harkness & C. M. Super (Eds.), *Parents' cultural belief systems: Their origins, expressions, and consequences* (pp. 289–310). New York: Guilford Press.

Harper, R. M., Leake, B., Hoffman, H., Walter, D. O., Hoppenbrouwers, T., Hodgman, J., & Sterman, M. B. (1981). Periodicity of sleep states is altered in infants at risk of Sudden Infant Death Syndrome. *Science, 213,* 1030–1032.

Harrison, A. O., Wilson, M. N., Pine, C. J., Chan, S. Q., & Buriel, R. (1990). Family ecologies of ethnic minority children. *Child Development, 61*(2), 347–362.

Harwood, R. (1992). The influence of culturally derived values on Anglo and Puerto Rican mothers' perceptions of attachment behavior. *Child Development, 63,* 822–839.

Harwood, R., Miller, J., & Lucca Irizarry, N. (1995). *Culture and attachment: Perceptions of the child in context.* New York: Guilford Press.

Hess, R. D., Kashiwagi, K., Azuma, H., Price, G. G., & Dickson, W. P. (1980). Maternal expectation for mastery of developmental tasks in Japan and the United States. *International Journal of Psychology, 15,* 259–271.

Higgins, A., Power, C., & Kohlberg, L. (1984). The relationship of moral atmosphere to judgments of responsibility. In W. M. Kurtiness & J. L. Gewirtz (Eds.), *Morality, moral behavior, and moral development* (pp. 74–106). New York: Wiley.

Ho, D. Y. F. (1994). Cognitive socialization in Confucian heritage cultures. In P. M. Greenfield & R. R. Cocking (Eds.), *Cross-cultural roots of minority child development* (pp. 285–313). Hillsdale, NJ: Erlbaum.

Hofstede, G. (1991). *Software of the mind.* New York: McGraw-Hill.

Holland, D., & Quinn, N. (1987). *Cultural models in language and thought.* New York: Cambridge University Press.

Holt, E. (1957). *How children fail.* New York: Dell.

Hoppenbrouwers, T., Hodgman, J. E., Arakawa, K., & Sterman, M. B. (1989). Polysomnographic sleep and waking states are similar in subsequent siblings of SIDS and control infants during the first six months of life. *Sleep, 12,* 265–276.

Hsu, F. L. K. (1981). *American and Chinese: Passage to differences.* Honolulu: University of Hawaii Press.

A Japanese supermarket in New Jersey. (1989, April 6). *New York Times,* p. 4.

Kagan, S., & Madsen, M. C. (1971). Cooperation and competition of Mexican, Mexican-American, and Anglo-American children of two ages under four instructional sets. *Developmental Psychology, 5,* 32–39.

Kagan, S., & Madsen, M. C. (1972). Rivalry in Anglo-American and Mexican children of two ages. *Journal of Personality and Social Psychology, 24*(2), 214–220.

Kagitçibasi, Ç. (1996). *Family and human development across cultures: A view from the other side.* Mahwah, NJ: Erlbaum.

Kahn, A., Picard, E., & Blum, D. (1986). Auditory arousal threshold and normal and near-miss SIDS infants. *Developmental Medical Child Neurology, 28,* 299–302.

Kashima, Y., Siegal, M., Tanaka, K., & Isaka, H. (1988). Universalism in lay conceptions of distributive justice: A cross-cultural examination. *International Journal of Psychology, 23,* 51–63.

Kawakami, K. (1987, July). *Comparison of mother-infant relationships in Japanese and American families.* Paper presented at the meeting of the International Society for the Study of Behavioral Development, Tokyo, Japan.

Kim, U. (1984). *Psychological acculturation of Korean immigrants in Toronto: A study of modes of acculturation, identity, language, and acculturative stress.* Unpublished master's thesis, Queen's University, Kingston, Ontario, Canada.

Kim, U. (1992). *The parent-child relationship: The core of Korean collectivism.* Unpublished manuscript, University of Hawaii, Department of Psychology, Honolulu.

Kim, U. (1994). Significance of paternalism and communalism in the occupational welfare system of Korean firms: A national survey. In U. Kim, H. C. Triandis, Ç. Kâgitçibasi, S. Choi, & G. Yoon (Eds.), *Individualism and collectivism: Theory, method, and applications* (pp. 251–266). Thousand Oaks, CA: Sage.

Kim, U., & Berry, J. W. (1993). *Indigenous psychologies-research and experience in cultural context. Cross-cultural research and methodologies series* (Vol. 17). Newbury Park, CA: Sage.

Kim, U., & Choi, S. H. (1994). Individualism, collectivism, and child development. In P. M. Greenfield & R. R. Cocking (Eds.), *Cross-cultural roots of minority child development* (pp. 227–258). Hillsdale, NJ: Erlbaum.

Kitayama, S., Markus, H. R., & Lieberman, C. (in press). The collective construction of self esteem: Implications for culture, self, and emotion. In J. Russell, J. Wellenkamp, T. Manstead, & J. M. F. Dols (Eds.), *Everyday conceptions of emotions.* Dordrecht, The Netherlands: Kluwer Academic.

Kitayama, S., Markus, H. R., Matsumoto, H., & Norasakkunkit, V. (1997). Individual and collective processes in the construction of the self: Self-enhancement in the United States and self-depreciation in Japan. *Journal of Personality and Social Psychology, 72,* 1245–1267.

Klein, P. F. (1995, Spring). The needs of children. *Mothering,* 39–45.

Konner, M. (1977). Infancy among the Kalahari Desert San. In P. H. Leiderman, S. R. Tulkin, & A. Rosenfeld (Eds.), *Culture and infancy: Variations in the human experience* (pp. 287–328). New York: Academic Press.

Konner, M. (1982). *The tangled wing: Biological constraints on the human spirit.* New York: Holt, Rinehart and Winston.

Konner, M. J., & Worthman, C. (1980). Nursing frequency, gonadal function and birth-spacing among !Kung hunters and gatherers. *Science, 207,* 788–791.

Krauss, R. M., & Fussell, S. R. (1991). Constructing shared communicative environments. In L. B. Resnick, J. M. Levine, & S. D. Teasley (Eds.), *Perspectives on socially shared cognition* (pp. 172–200). Washington, DC: American Psychological Association.

Lamb, M., & Sternberg, K. J. (1990). Do we really know how daycare affects children? *Journal of Applied Developmental Psychology, 11*(3), 351–379.

Lau, S., & Cheung, P. C. (1987). Relations between Chinese adolescents' perception of parental control and organization and their perception of parental warmth. *Developmental Psychology, 23*(5), 726–729.

Lave, J., & Wenger, E. (1991). *Situated learning: Legitimate peripheral participation.* Cambridge, England: Cambridge University Press.

Lebra, T. S. (1976). *Japanese patterns of behavior.* Honolulu: University of Hawaii Press.

Lebra, T. S. (1994). Mother and child in Japanese socialization: A Japan-US comparison. In P. M. Greenfield & R. R. Cocking (Eds.), *Cross-cultural roots of minority child development* (pp. 259–274). Hillsdale, NJ: Erlbaum.

Leung, K. (1988). Some determinants of conflict avoidance. *Journal of Cross-Cultural Psychology, 19,* 125–136.

Leung, K., & Bond, M. H. (1984). The impact of cultural collectivism on reward allocation. *Journal of Personality and Social Psychology, 47,* 793–804.

Leung, K., & Iwawaki, S. (1988). Cultural collectivism and distributive behavior. *Journal of Cross-Cultural Psychology, 19,* 35–49.

Leung, K., & Park, H. J. (1986). Effects of interactional goal on choice allocation rule: A cross-national study. *Organizational Behavior and Human Decision Processes, 37,* 111–120.

LeVine, R. A. (1988). Human and parental care: Universal goals, cultural strategies, individual behavior. In R. A. Levine, P. M. Miller, & M. M. West (Eds.), *Parental behavior in diverse societies. New directions for child development* (Vol. 40, pp. 3–12). San Francisco: Jossey-Bass.

LeVine, R. A. (1994, July). *Culture and infant-mother attachment.* Paper presented at the meeting of the International Society for the Study of Behavioral Development, Amsterdam, The Netherlands.

LeVine, R. A. (1995). Foreword. In R. Harwood, J. Miller, & N. Lucca Irizarry, *Culture and attachment: Perceptions of the child in context* (pp. ix–xi). New York: Guilford Press.

LeVine, R. A., Dixon, S., LeVine, S., Richman, A., Leiderman, P., Keefer, C., & Brazelton, T. (1994). *Child care and culture: Lessons from Africa.* Cambridge, England: Cambridge University Press.

LeVine, R. A., & Uleman, J. S. (1979). Perceived locus of control, chronic self-esteem, and attributions to success and failure. *Journal of Personality and Social Psychology, 5,* 69–72.

Lewis, C. (1984). Cooperation and control in Japanese nursery schools. *Comparative Education Review, 28,* 69–84.

Lozoff, B., Wolf, A., & Davis, N. (1984). Cosleeping in urban families with young children in the United States. *Pediatrics, 74*(2), 171–182.

Lucker, G. W., Rosenfield, D., Sikes, J., & Aronson, E. (1976). Performance in the interdependent classroom: A field study. *American Educational Research Journal, 13*(2), 115–123.

Maccoby, E. E. (1980). *Social development: Psychological growth and the parent-child relationship.* New York: Harcourt Brace Jovanovich.

Madsen, M. C. (1967), Cooperative and competitive motivation of children in three Mexican subcultures. *Psychological Reports, 20,* 1307–1320.

Madsen, M. C. (1971). Developmental and cross-cultural differences in the cooperative and competitive behavior of young children. *Journal of Cross-Cultural Psychology, 2*(4), 365–371.

Madsen, M. C., & Lancy, D. F. (1981). Cooperative and competitive behavior: Experiments related to ethnic identity and urbanization in Papua, New Guinea. *Journal of Cross-Cultural Psychology, 12*(4), 389–408.

Madsen, M. C., & Yi, S. (1975). Cooperation and competition of urban and rural children in the Republic of South Korea. *International Journal of Psychology, 10*(4), 269–274.

Main, M., & Weston, D. (1982). Avoidance of the attachment figure in infancy: Descriptions and interpretations. In J. Stevenson-Hinde & C. Murray Parkes (Eds.), *The place of attachment in human infancy.* New York: Basics Books.

Markus, H., & Kitayama, S. (1991). Culture and the self: Implications for cognition, emotion, and motivation. *Psychological Review, 98*(2), 224–253.

Maynard, A., Greenfield, P. M., & Childs, C. P. (in press). *Culture, history, biology, and body: Native and non-native acquisition of technological skill.* Revision of paper presented at a symposium on Culture and the Uses of the Body, Fondation Fyssen, Paris.

McKenna, J. J. (1986). An anthropological perspective on the Sudden Infant Death Syndrome (SIDS): The role of parental breathing cues and speech breathing adaptations. *Medical Anthropology, 10*(1), 9–92.

McKenna, J. J., & Mosko, S. S. (1994). Sleep and arousal, synchrony and independence, among mothers and infants sleeping apart and together (same bed): An experiment in evolutionary medicine. *Acta Paediatric Supplement, 397,* 94–102.

McKenna, J. J., Thoman, E. B., Anders, T. F., Sadeh, A., Schectman, V. L., & Glotzbach, S. F. (1993). Infant-parent co-sleeping in an evolutionary perspective: Implication for understanding infant sleep development in the Sudden Infant Death Syndrome. *Sleep, 16*(3), 23–282.

Métraux, R. (1955). Parents and children: An analysis of contemporary German child-care and youth-guidance literature. In M. Mead & M. Wolfenstein (Eds.), *Childhood in contemporary cultures* (pp. 204–228). Chicago: University of Chicago Press.

Miller, D. T., & Ross, M. (1975). Self-serving biases in the attribution of causality: Fact or fiction? *Psychological Bulletin, 82,* 213–225.

Miller, J. G. (1994). Cultural diversity in the morality of caring: Individually oriented versus duty-based interpersonal moral codes. *Cross-Cultural Research, 28*(1), 3–39.

Miller, J. G. (1995). In C. Raeff (Chair), *Individualism and collectivism as cultural contexts for developing different modes of independence and interdependence.* Symposium presented at the Society for Research in Child Development, Indianapolis.

Miller, J. G., & Bersoff, D. M. (1992). Culture and moral judgment: How are conflicts between justice and interpersonal responsibilities resolved? *Journal of Personality and Social Psychology, 62*(4), 541–554.

Miller, J. G., & Bersoff, D. M. (1995). Development in the context of everyday family relationships: Culture, interpersonal morality and adaptation. In M. Killen & D. Hart (Eds.), *Morality in everyday life: A developmental perspective* (pp. 259–282). New York: Cambridge University Press.

Miller, J. G., Bersoff, D. M., & Harwood, R. L. (1990). Perceptions of social responsibilities in India and in the United States: Moral imperatives or personal decisions? *Journal of Personality and Social Psychology, 58*(1), 33–47.

Miyake, K., Chen, S., & Campos, J. J. (1985). Infant temperament, mother's mode of interaction, and attachment in Japan: An interim report. In I. Bretherton & E. Waters (Eds.), Growing points in attachment theory and research. *Monographs of Cross-Cultural Human Development, 50*(1/2, Serial No. 209).

Miyamoto, S. F. (1986–1987). Problems of interpersonal style among the Nisei. *Amerasia, 13*(2), 29–45.

Morelli, G. A., Rogoff, B., Oppenheim, D., & Goldsmith, D. (1992). Cultural variation in infants' sleeping arrangements: Questions of independence. *Developmental Psychology, 28*(4), 604–613.

Mullen, B., & Riordan, C. A. (1988). Self-serving attribution in naturalistic settings: A meta-analytic review. *Journal of Applied Social Psychology, 18,* 3–22.

Mundy-Castle, A. C. (1974). Social and technological intelligence in Western and non-Western cultures. *Universitas, 4,* 46–52.

Munroe, R. L., Munroe, R. H., & Whiting, J. W. M. (1981). Male sex-role resolutions. In R. H. Munroe, R. L. Munroe, & B. B. Whiting (Eds.), *Handbook of cross-cultural human development* (pp. 611–632). New York: Garland.

Muto, T., Kubo, Y., & Oshima-Takane, Y. (1980). Why don't Japanese ask questions? *Japanese Psychological Review (Shinrigaku Hyouron), 23,* 71–88.

Nsamenang, A. B. (1987). A West African perspective. In M. E. Lamb (Ed.), *Cross-cultural perspectives* (pp. 273–293). Hillsdale, NJ: Erlbaum.

Nsamenang, A. B., & Lamb, M. E. (1994). Socialization of Nso children in the Bamenda grassfields of Northwest Cameroon. In P. M. Greenfield & R. R. Cocking (Eds.), *Cross-cultural roots of minority child development* (pp. 133–146). Hillsdale, NJ: Erlbaum.

Nugent, J. K. (1994). Cross-cultural studies of child development: Implications for clinicians. *Zero to Three, 15*(2), 1, 3–8.

Nunner-Winkler, G. (1984). Two moralities? A critical discussion of an ethic of care and responsibility versus an ethic of rights and justice. In W. M. Kurtiness & J. L. Gewirtz (Eds.), *Morality, moral behavior, and moral development* (pp. 348–361). New York: Wiley.

Ochs, E., & Schieffelin, B. B. (1984). Language acquisition and socialization: Three developmental stories and their implications. In R. Shweder & R. LeVine (Eds.), *Culture theory: Essays on mind, self, and emotion* (pp. 276–320). Cambridge, England: Cambridge University Press.

Ogbu, J. U. (1993). Differences in cultural frame of reference. *International Journal of Behavioral Development, 16,* 483–506.

Ogbu, J. U. (1994). From cultural differences to differences in cultural frame of reference. In P. M. Greenfield & R. R. Cocking (Eds.), *Cross-cultural roots of minority child development* (pp. 365–391). Hillsdale, NJ: Erlbaum.

Oloko, B. A. (1993). Children's street work in urban Nigeria: Dilemma of modernizing tradition. *Journal of Behavioral Development, 16,* 465–482.

Oloko, B. A. (1994). Children's street work in urban Nigeria: Dilemma of modernizing tradition. In P. M. Greenfield & R. R. Cocking (Eds.), *Cross-cultural roots of minority and child development.* Hillsdale, NJ: Erlbaum.

Oshima-Takane, Y., & Muto, T. (1993, May). *Analysis of question-asking behaviors: A comparison between Japanese and Canadian students.* Paper presented at the meeting of the Canadian Psychological Association, Montreal.

Pettengill, S. M., & Rohner, R. P. (1985). Korean-American adolescent's perceptions of parental control, parental acceptance-rejection and parent-adolescent conflict. In I. R. Lagunes & Y. H. Poortinga (Eds.), *From different perspective: Studies of behavior across cultures* (pp. 241–249). Lisse, The Netherlands: Swets & Zeitlinger.

Philips, S. U. (1972). Participant structures and communicative competence: Warm Springs children in community and classroom. In C. B. Cazden, V. P. John, & D. Hymes (Eds.), *Functions of language in the classroom.* New York: Teachers College Press.

Phinney, J. S., & Rotheram, M. J. (Eds.). (1987). *Children's ethnic socialization: Pluralism and development.* Newbury Park, CA: Sage.

Quiroz, B., & Greenfield, P. (in press). Cross-cultural value conflict: Removing a barrier to Latino school achievement. In R. Paredes & K. Gutierrez (Eds.), *Latino academic achievement.* Berkeley: Latino Eligibility Task Force, University of California.

Rabain, J. (1979). *L'enfant du lignage.* Paris: Payot.

Rabain-Jamain, J. (1994). Language and socialization of the child in African families living in France. In P. M. Greenfield & R. R. Cocking (Eds.), *Cross-cultural roots of minority child development.* Hillsdale, NJ: Erlbaum.

Raeff, C. (in press). Individuals in relationships: Cultural values, children's social interactions, and the development of an American individualistic self. *Developmental Review.*

Raeff, C., Greenfield, P. M., & Quiroz, B. (in press). Conceptualizing interpersonal relationships in the cultural contexts of individualism and collectivism. In S. Harkness, C. Raeff, &

C. M. Super (Eds.), *The social construction of the child: The nature of the variability. New directions in child development.* San Francisco: Jossey-Bass.

Reese, L., Balzano, S., Gallimore, R., & Goldenberg C. (1995). The concept of *educación:* Latino family values and American schooling. *International Journal of Educational Research, 23*(1), 57–81.

Restak, R. (1979). *The brain.* New York: Doubleday.

Richman, A. L., Miller, P. M., & Johnson Solomon, M. (1988). The socialization of infants in suburban Boston. In R. A. LeVine, P. M. Miller, & M. West (Eds.), *Parental behavior in diverse societies* (pp. 65–74). San Francisco: Jossey-Bass.

Rogoff, B. (1990). *Apprenticeship in thinking: Cognitive development in social context.* Oxford, England: Oxford University Press.

Rogoff, B., & Morelli, G. (1989). Perspectives on children's development from cultural psychology. *American Psychologist, 44,* 343–348.

Rohner, R. P., & Pettengill, S. M. (1985). Perceived parental acceptance-rejection and parental control among Korean adolescents [Special Issue]. *Child Development, 56,* 524–528.

Roopnarine, J. L., & Lamb, M. E. (1978). The effects of daycare on attachment and exploratory behavior in a Strange Situation. *Merrill-Palmer Quarterly, 24,* 85–95.

Roopnarine, J. L., & Lamb, M. E. (1980). Peer and parent-child interaction before and after enrollment in nursery school. *Journal of Applied Developmental Psychology, 1,* 77–81.

Rothstein-Fisch, C., Trumbull, E., Quiroz, B., & Greenfield, P. M. (1997). *Bridging cultures in the classroom.* Poster session presented at the annual meeting of the Jean Piaget Society, Santa Monica, CA.

Schachter, F. F., Fuchs, M. L., Bijur, P. E., & Stone, R. (1989). Co-sleeping and sleep problems in Hispanic-American urban young children. *Pediatrics, 84,* 522–530.

Schneider, B., Hieshima, J. A., Lee, S., & Plank, S. (1994). Continuities and discontinuities in the cognitive socialization of Asian-oriented children: The case of Japanese Americans. In P. M. Greenfield & R. R. Cocking (Eds.), *Cross-cultural roots of minority child development* (pp. 323–350). Hillsdale, NJ: Erlbaum.

Schroen, C. (1995, May). *Is it child abuse?: Toward a multicultural field guide for social workers.* Paper presented at the University of California, Undergraduate Psychology Conference, Los Angeles.

Shapira, A., & Madsen, M. C. (1969). Cooperative and competitive behavior of kibbutz and urban children in Israel. *Child Development, 40*(2), 609–617.

Shore, B. (1996). *Culture in mind: Cognition, culture, and the problem of meaning.* New York: Oxford University Press.

Shwalb, D. W., & Shwalb, B. J. (Eds.). (1996). *Japanese childrearing: Two generations of scholarship.* New York: Guilford Press.

Shweder, R. A., Jensen, L., & Goldstein, W. (1995, Spring). Who sleeps by whom revisited: A method for extracting the moral goods implicit in practice. In J. Goodnow, P. Miller, & F. Kessel (Eds.), *Cultural practices as contexts for development. New directions for child development* (Vol. 67, pp. 21–39). San Francisco: Jossey-Bass.

Shweder, R. A., Mahapatra, M., & Miller, J. G. (1990). Culture and moral development. In J. W. Stigler, R. A. Shweder, & G. Herdt (Eds.), *Cultural psychology: Essays of comparative human development* (pp. 130–203). Cambridge, England: Cambridge University Press.

Sigel, I. E. (Ed.). (1985). *Parental belief systems: The psychological consequences for children.* Hillsdale, NJ: Erlbaum.

Sigel, I. E., McGillicuddy-DeLisi, A. V., & Goodnow, J. J. (Eds.). (1992). *Parental belief systems: The psychological consequences for children* (2nd ed.). Hillsdale, NJ: Erlbaum.

Slavin, R. E. (1986). Learning together. *American Educator, 10*(2), 6–13.

Smaldino, C. (1995, Spring). Tossing and turning over "crying it out." *Mothering, 74,* 32–37.

Smetana, J. G., Killen, M., & Turiel, E. (1991). Children's reasoning about interpersonal and moral conflicts. *Child Development, 62*(3), 629–644.

Smuts, A. B., & Hagen, J. W. (1985). History of the family and of child development: Introduction to Part 1. *Monographs of the Society for Research in Child Development, 50*(4/5, Serial No. 211).

Spock, B. (1976). *Baby and child care.* New York: Pocket Books.

Spock, B., & Rothenberg, M. (1985). *Dr. Spock's baby and child care* (p. 222). New York: Dutton.

Steinberg, L., Elman, J. D., & Mounts, S. (1989). Authoritative parenting, psychosocial maturity, and academic success among adolescents. *Child Development, 60,* 1424–1436.

Stigler, J. W., & Perry, M. (1988). Mathematics learning in Japanese, Chinese, and American classrooms. In G. B. Saxe & M. Gearhart (Eds.), *Children's mathematics. New directions of child development* (Vol. 41). San Francisco: Jossey-Bass.

Sudarkasa, N. (1988). Interpreting the African heritage in Afro-American family organization. In H. P. McAdoo (Ed.), *Black families* (2nd ed.). Newbury Park, CA: Sage.

Suina, J. H. (1991, June/July). Discussion. In P. M. Greenfield & R. R. Cocking (Eds.), *Continuities and discontinuities in the cognitive socialization of minority children.* Proceedings of a workshop, Department of Health and Human Services, Public Health Service, Alcohol, Drug Abuse, and Mental Health Administration, Washington, DC.

Suina, J. H., & Smolkin, L. B. (1994). From natal culture to school culture to dominant society culture: Supporting transitions for Pueblo Indian students. In P. M. Greenfield & R. R. Cocking (Eds.), *Cross-cultural roots of minority child development.* Hillsdale, NJ: Erlbaum.

Sung, B. L. (1985). Bicultural conflicts in Chinese immigrant children. *Journal of Comparative Family Studies, 16,* 255–269.

Super, C., & Harkness, S. (1982). The infant's niche in rural Kenya and metropolitan America. In L. L. Adler (Ed.), *Cross-cultural research at issue* (pp. 47–55). New York: Academic Press.

Suzuki, L. K., & Greenfield, P. M. (1997). *Self-sacrifice in Asian-American and Euro-American older adolescents: The effects of ethnicity and acculturation.* Manuscript submitted for publication.

Takahashi, K. (1986). Examining the Strange Situation procedure with Japanese mothers and 12-month-old infants. *Developmental Psychology, 22,* 265–270.

Takahashi, K. (1990). Are the key assumptions of the "Strange Situation" procedure universal? A view from Japanese research. *Human Development, 33,* 23–30.

Tapia Uribe, F., LeVine, R. A., & LeVine, S. E. (1994). Maternal behavior in a Mexican community: The changing environments of children. In P. M. Greenfield & R. R. Cocking (Eds.), *Cross-cultural roots of minority child development.* Hillsdale, NJ: Erlbaum.

Tharp, R. G., & Gallimore, R. (1988). *Rousing minds to life: Teaching, learning, and schooling in social context.* Cambridge, England: Cambridge University Press.

Tobin, J., Wu, D., & Davidson, D. (1989). *Preschool in three cultures: Japan, China, and the United States.* New Haven, CT: Yale University Press.

Toupin, E. A. (1980). Counseling Asians: Psychotherapy in context of racism and Asian American history. *American Journal of Orthopsychiatry, 50,* 76–86.

Triandis, H. C. (1988). Collectivism vs. individualism: A reconceptualization of a basic concept in cross-cultural social psychology. In C. Bargley & G. K. Verma (Eds.), *Personality, cognition, and values: Cross-cultural perspectives of childhood and adolescence.* London: Macmillan.

Triandis, H. C., Bontempo, R., Villareal, M., Asai, M., & Lucca, M. (1988). Individualism and collectivism: Cross-cultural perspectives on self-ingroup relationships. *Journal of Personality and Social Psychology, 54,* 323–338.

Tseng, W.-S. (1973). The concept of personality in Confucian thought. *Psychiatry, 36,* 191–202.

van IJzendoorn, M., & Kroonenberg, P. (1988). Cross-cultural patterns of attachment: A meta-analysis of the Strange Situation. *Child Development, 59,* 147–156.

Vaughn, B. E., Kopp, C. B., & Krakow, J. B. (1984). The emergence and consolidation of self-control from eighteen to thirty months of age: Normative trends and individual differences. *Child Development, 55*(3), 990–1004.

Waddel, M., & Firth, B. (1995). *Can't you sleep little bear?* London: Candlewick Press.

Watson-Gegeo, K. A., & Gegeo, D. W. (1989). In P. G. Zukow (Ed.), *Sibling interaction across cultures* (pp. 54–76). New York: Springer-Verlag.

Weisner, T. S. (1996). Why ethnography should be the most important method in the study of human development. In A. Colby, R. Jessor, & R. Shweder (Eds.), *Ethnography and human development* (pp. 305–324). Chicago: University of Chicago Press.

Weisner, T. S., Bausano, M., & Kornfein, M. (1983, Winter). Putting family ideals into practice: Pronaturalism in conventional and nonconventional California families. *Ethos, 11*(4), 278–304.

Whiting, B. B., & Edwards, C. (1988). *Children of different worlds: The formation of social behavior.* Cambridge, MA: Harvard University Press.

Whiting, B. B., & Whiting, J. W. M. (1975). *Children of six cultures.* Cambridge, MA: Harvard University Press.

Whiting, J. W. M., & Whiting, B. B. (1994). Altruistic and egoistic behavior in six cultures. In E. H. Chasdi (Ed.), *Culture and human development* (pp. 267–281). New York: Cambridge University Press. (Reprinted from *Cultural illness and health: Essays in human adaption,* pp. 56–66, by L. Nader & T. W. Maretzki (Eds.), 1973, Washington, DC: American Anthropological Association)

Widaman, K. F., & Kagan, S. (1987). Cooperativeness and achievement: Interaction of student cooperativeness with cooperative vs. competitive classroom organization. *Journal of Social Psychology, 25,* 355–365.

Wierzbicka, A. (1991). Japanese key words and core cultural values. *Language and Society, 20,* 333–385.

Wolf, A., & Lozoff, B. (1989). Object attachment, thumb sucking, and the passage to sleep. *Journal of the American Academy of Child and Adolescent Psychiatry, 28,* 287–292.

Yafai, S. (1992). *Individualism vs. collectivism: What to do?* Unpublished paper, Department of Psychology, University of California, Los Angeles.

Yoshida, T., Kojo, K., & Kaku, H. (1982). A study on the development of self-presentation in children. *Japanese Journal of Educational Psychology, 30,* 30–37.

Young, K. T. (1990). American conceptions of infant development from 1955 to 1984: What the experts are telling parents. *Child Development, 61,* 17–28.

Zempleni-Rabain, J. (1973). Food and the strategy involved in learning fraternal exchange among Wolof children. In P. Alexandre (Ed.), *French perspectives in African studies.* London: Oxford University Press.

Epilogue

CHAPTER 17

Practice and Research: A Problem in Developing Communication and Cooperation

IRVING E. SIGEL

The focus of this chapter will be on the use and application of child development research to practitioners, service providers, and policymakers in real-life settings who are dedicated to the health and welfare of children. There is a continuing interest in turning to the research generated by behavioral scientists for valid information which can be applied to everyday, real-life issues in real-life situations such as schools, clinics, hospitals, and, in fact, any setting where the welfare of children is at issue.

There is a commonly held view that the community of behavioral scientists is the preeminent source of knowledge that can be of service to children in every walk of life and in any setting. The belief is that behavioral sciences have the know-how and the wherewithal to make meaningful contributions to the understanding of human development and that this information is necessary for working toward alleviating many of the social and behavioral problems facing our society. Whenever social questions are posed that are crying for solutions, social and behavioral scientists claim that their science can be useful.

Efforts by the U.S. Congress to make major reductions in budgets for behavioral science research were rescinded when professional behavioral science groups claimed that they could address these basic social problems and come up with useful information to help alleviate the problems. They argue that empirical science functions as a master problem solver, a belief held by most members of the behavioral science professions and probably the educated elements of the general society. So, society places a demand on the professionals and provides financial support to find solutions to origins and treatment of diseases, illnesses, and social problems such as juvenile crime, and educational failure. The history of scientific advances in virtually every aspect of our daily lives provides the rationale for belief that if there is a problem to be fixed, the scientist can fix it. Psychologists have joined the ranks of the empirical scientists making the same claims for their scientific enterprise as have the natural and physical sciences. Psychology is defined as behavioral science employing all the rituals and procedures that meet the criteria of a scientific discipline which will provide the needed information to accomplish these goals.

These aspirations for behavioral science contributions to the social good have been voiced most eloquently as far back as 1964 by Hoffman and Hoffman, who advocated greater communication between researchers and service providers. They wrote:

> A more basic problem for the practitioner is that most research topics are determined largely by the concerns of a particular scientific discipline. Rather than being addressed to a solution of practical problems, they follow the logic of guiding theories and the dictates of the research designs. From the standpoint of long-range progress this is as it should be. The researcher should be free to pursue the data wherever they may lead, unhampered by premature pressures toward practical application. But the theoretical and conceptual focus of such research can obscure the relevance for practice even when it exists, because of difference between the concept and terminology of the researcher and the practitioner. (p. 1)

Ironically, in 1997, the need for such interprofessional communication is still needed. Did the previous efforts fail and if so, why? If they succeeded, is the preparation of this volume just another update or does it take a different approach? Is it time to evaluate the state of affairs? These issues are still timely (McCall, 1996).

I think it is appropriate to reassess practice-research relationships. Adding this new volume to the *Handbook* series indicates that the Advisory Board believes that the time has come to have an archival volume dedicated to a dialogue between research and practice by inviting authors to review research in child psychology, to set up a dialogue between researchers and practitioners.

WHAT IS CHILD PSYCHOLOGY?

Diversity in the Conceptual System

What is difficult is getting a handle on what child psychology is and where it is in the firmament of science. The common theme that seems to define the field is the interest in children and how they develop. So far so good.

Beyond this shared interest and a general commitment to scientific research, there is considerable diversity among researchers in their theoretical orientation, the problems studied, and their mode of working. Scientific approaches range from studies of normal child to the development of psychopathology. Interestingly enough, there is similar diversity of interests among practitioners. There is often overlap in the theoretical persuasions of practitioners and researchers. The difference is in the practice of the profession. One is the scientific model; the other is the practitioner, service provider model.

Shared conceptual orientations do not necessarily lead to sharing information. The researchers or the practitioners may see no reason to communicate or read each other's publications, even though they are in the same intellectual community. One reason for this is that there is no mutual understanding of the discourse or the issues confronting the particular field. Practitioners are unwilling to read experimental literature since it is too distant from their field of interest. The researchers are uninterested in the mechanics of program development as well as the ways of carrying them out.

Another condition that contributes to the diversity and subsequent fragmentation of the field is the firm belief in scientific freedom, freedom of inquiry and publication. This cardinal value is significant because it enables scientists to explore any problems they wish within ethical and legal constraints. In effect, there is contradiction since freedom of inquiry and practice harbors the germs of fragmentation, not coherence, yet a coherent science is a goal. This state of affairs is inherent in any organic living system, and the scientific study of children is no exception. The range of activity and rate of change among the science and practice professionals in child psychology will be limited by social and political forces that support or prevent change. In the long run, the ingenuity and creativity of the researcher and the practitioner will effect change. Meanwhile, the field is diversified and fragmented.

The diversity is evidenced by an array of conceptual systems flourishing among all members of the profession. There are the Piagetians, neo-Piagetians, Vygotskyans, Wernerians, Freudians, and Skinnerians. Even within each of these conceptual perspectives, there are differences of interpretation. There are other writers who have developed their own "school" and have no defined leader. Among them are those who have defined themselves as specialists in particular areas of development, such as cognitive science, neural development, behavior modification, and social cognition with a social psychological twist. If that is not enough, there are problem-centered investigators who select a theoretical problem, such as children's concept of mind, language development, or development of self, and devise their own minitheories incorporating many of the available perspectives that meet their fancy. Each of these theoretical and problem themes often forms the basis of a group or an organization creating a community of interests each with a language common to the members and not to the out-group.

Diversity in Communication

Piagetian-oriented practitioners generally are able to communicate with Piagetian researchers, and the same pattern exists for other communities where research and practice groups share the same ideology and vocabulary. The problem inherent in this state of affairs is that no one theory or ideology covers all of the bases. Chances are a Piagetian based curriculum does not provide the teaching strategies that are extensions of the theoretical perspective. Nor is there much attention paid in that approach to affective and emotional development. These omissions force practitioners to improvise and interpret their own actions. Such efforts add to the diversity within "schools" because they create divisions for adherents to the basic school of thought, as well as generate disputes, precluding purists, practitioner or researcher from accepting or integrating alternative views as authentic, thereby legitimate, deviations from the basic system. When I proposed my distancing theory of the development of representation as derived from a Piagetian perspective (Sigel, 1970), I was duly reprimanded by an orthodox Piagetian because Piaget never used the word *distance.* Anticipating criticism from this authentic Piagetian, I had found the word in the "sacred" text, reported same, and therefore was temporarily absolved of heresy. This example, which is by no means rare among researchers and scholars, precludes authentic sharing and conceptual change. Regretfully, openmindedness and willingness to change are not universal characteristics of many investigators (Sigel, 1996).

Diversity in Professional Functions

Not only is there diversity in areas and methods of study, but diversity in how developmental psychologists define their professional functions. Child psychology researchers have tended to perceive themselves as engaged in basic theory-driven research in contrast to the atheoretical concrete applied researchers who are, by implication, second rate. The orientation of the basic researcher is to search for scientific generalization through the use of experimental research, with little or no interest in developing technologies or practical suggestions (Polanyi, 1958). These are *the* scientists. I suspect that there is still a strong bent among child psychologists to perceive themselves as theoretically oriented scientists (McCall, 1996). In this *Handbook* series a full volume is dedicated just to developmental theory. Does that not reflect the scientific face of child psychology?

On the other hand, there is a growing interest in blending science with application. *Science practitioner* is a recently coined label applied to those professionals who are engaged in research and practice. In this volume, Cicchetti and Toth; Cowan, Cowan, and Powell; and Renninger represent that approach. They are science-practitioners. Other authors tend to be engaged in scientific research dealing with real-life problems; they are not service providers in the sense of being clinicians, but the topics they pursue, and how they pursue them, place them in this venue (e.g., Adams, Treiman, & Pressley; Ceci & Bruck; and Lamb, this volume).

Psychologists as Practitioners

A third group of child development psychologists are indeed practitioners working within a practical psychological perspective. Those so identified use psychological principles with children in child guidance clinics, hospitals, schools, juvenile courts, and social institutions sharing the responsibility for helping children (and often their families) cope with the worlds in which they live. They are the clinicians who may be, or should be, consumers who could use the products of research if and when they become accessible and are appropriate for the program.

A Move toward Problem-Centered Research

The field in all its diversity of interests and theoretical orientations has seemed to have created a mixed and blurry image of the science of child psychology. Despite the substantial growth of scientific laboratory research, there seems to be an increased interest in investigating developmental problems. Scientists have begun to recognize that as a field, child psychology has much to offer for mitigating social and individual dysfunctions and for improving the health and well-being of the society. Thus what has been in the past an intense debate defining child psychology as a basic or applied science, has shifted to how researchers in the field can work on real-life problems. Now the argument is, Can the application of scientific methods to real-life problems realistically follow the rules of the scientific game without compromising the science or minimizing how to study the questions? Does the scientific study of complex social problems preclude careful science, or does the use of rigid scientific procedures narrow the problems for study and lead to the study of trivial questions? This is the issue, not the nature of the problem. There seems to be unanimity that the framing of the problem to be studied defines its place in the category of basic or applied. I shall address this issue later in the chapter in the context of proximal-distal relationship to application. There are differences of opinion as how best to undertake studies that have practical value, but this is a disagreement of method, not of substance. To come to terms with this vexing and long-standing problem, it might be helpful to delineate some sources of the problem and to consider the reasonable expectations of scientific research findings that will contribute effectively to social change and even social transformations.

Child psychology as a scientific discipline can be characterized as diversified in focus and interests. It reflects diverse problems of study. It contains many voices and languages. It contains different methods, yet each claims an allegiance to the science, and there are equally diverse voices among practitioners who work with children. And each of these groups reveals varying degrees of interface with other self-defined child psychology interest groups.

THE CONCEPTUAL BASES OF CHILD PSYCHOLOGY

The Concept of Science That Seems Prevalent among Child Psychologists

Although the researchers in this volume developed their material on the basis of the research literature, there is no reason to believe that all studies work within the same view of child psychology as science. Debates on this issue abound, not only as to the definition, but also as to the appropriateness of the model of science in use. This is reflected in articles by Bevan and Kessel (1994) and by Kimble (1994), in the *American Psychologist:*

> Psychology's methods and methodology must be far less rigid and our discipline's view of what is scientifically acceptable must be far more pragmatic than has been the case for many decades. (Bevan & Kessel, 1994, p. 507)

They agree with Sigmund Koch, who argues that psychology needs an "indigenous" methodology with the sensitivity to human experience that characterizes humanistic scholarship. This is a far cry from the position taken by Kimble (1994), who writes:

> If psychology is to be a science, it must play by the scientific rules, of which the most important is that it must be about observables. It must be a science of stimuli and responses, because the only public facts available are the things that organisms do (responses) and the situations in which they do them (stimuli). (p. 510)

The profound difference between these two views of science leads to confusion among users of scientific research information. The fundamental question is the confidence practitioners can have in research reports if they are reflections of the fractured field. I will discuss this in a later section of the chapter.

A comprehensive exegesis of the research to practice interface that reflects some of the objectives described by Hoffman and Hoffman (1964) is too complex a topic to deal with in a single chapter of moderate size. My goal, however, is to diagnose the problems seemingly intrinsic to the research-practitioner relationship and propose constructive solutions of mutual benefit to practitioners and researchers. By implication, the belief is that scientific efforts will provide a database from which practitioners will be able to draw information to deal with general or particular problems. Ideally, all clinicians will have to learn more about a problem they are facing in their practice and to search the appropriate database to find the information available on that topic.

Where Is the Information for Practitioners?

However, finding the necessary information is not as simple as checking into a database and retrieving abstract articles, journal references, or even journal articles. What the practitioner needs to know is how to frame the question to set out on the search, and also, and equally important, how the answers to the search fit into the service program in question, and by doing so make the knowledge functional.

So the knowledge retrieval process is not as simple as it may appear. Data sources are not necessarily user-friendly; answers may be there, but they may be in a language too technical or obtuse to be readily accessible.

A more complicated issue is that at times the information is not limited to one field. For example, to find literature on teenage pregnancy, the practitioner might have to search psychological, sociological, and even medical journals. Rarely is a complex social issue studied within only a single discipline. In fact, understanding of research for application is an interdisciplinary search. This complicates the matter further because the languages of the behavioral and social sciences are not the same (e.g., the languages of research in sociology and in psychology are divergent). Within psychology itself, there are considerable divergences. The learning theory of Skinner, the developmental theory of Piaget, and the sociocultural theory of Vygotsky differ in concept and in style of communicating. Literature searches have their complications, but another more serious dilemma here is due to the diversity in the field alluded to earlier.

Some Current Views of Psychology among Psychologists—Is There Disunity of the Field as a Whole?

My thesis is that despite the claims made by psychologists as to their actual and potential contributions to the social welfare, (Wiggins, 1994), there are those who are dismayed by psychology's failure to address important human questions. Bevan and Kessel (1994) write, "In their eagerness to be seen as 'scientists,' psychologists have tended to cling to a metaphysics that fails to address in a meaningful way many of the essential, and essentially, human questions" (p. 507).

A similar trend seems to be developing with advocates calling for a special field of applied developmental psychology or applied developmental science (Fisher & Lerner, 1994). There are child developmental psychologists who argue that setting up a separate field will lead to eschewing basic scientific research as intrinsic to the field (Morrison, Lord, & Keating, 1984). Developmental psychology emerged as a branch of the science of psychology. Parallel to this development there has been a continued interest in the use of psychological principles to working on real-life problems. Over the years, the scientific tradition evolved, divorced from service and application. Basic science became so divorced from the practical world that it seemed as though there were two separate fields. This separation is expressed in the various organizations and publications, e.g., The American Psychological Society is an organization of science practitioners in contrast to the American Psychological Association, which is an umbrella organization dedicated to the field of psychology with multiple foci, including the practice of psychology. The difference between these two organizations may be more political than substantive. Even more divisive are the attitudes each type of psychologist holds toward the other. Some scientists tend to hold practitioners in mild, or even venomous, contempt, whereas the practitioners claim that scientists are arrogant and demeaning and have little of practical value to offer (Fox, 1996).

These polemics among psychologists do little to help the service providers who want guidance in using the research in their work. Chances are, they disregard the scientific research as irrelevant and have little confidence in the applied research psychologist because most of their work is not within the genre of conventional scientific methodology. The upshot of all this internecine conflict is a lack of partnering between researchers and service providers. From a social and economic perspective, the waste of resources for the social good is considerable. The fallout from all this is wasted energy, time, and money in the field.

We might reassess our ways of working to help mitigate some of the failures in the past and the present by finding ways to influence appropriate segments of our professional communities to enter into partnerships to use our collective knowledge in the service of the social good. My argument is that because we know more, we can educate the appropriate segments of our society to attend to what we have learned over the years. In that way, the research can be of use to practitioners. To achieve this confidence, we must learn how to become effective change agents.

Actions Become Change Agents

The criticism of researchers by practitioners is based in part on promises made and promises unfulfilled. A promise that research will be of social value has to be tempered by the consumer's awareness that there is an inevitable time lag between the time a project has begun to its acceptance and use in the field. The medical research on poliomyelitis and diphtheria are good examples from the past. Research on AIDS, cancer, and many other diseases shows that the time lag between the onset of the research and completion is highly unpredictable. A further complication is the trajectory of the implementation of child psychological research. It is slower than we would like because of the complexity of child development. There are so many factors in the life of a child that are reasonable sources of influence that it is difficult to evaluate each one's role and influence.

The service provider interested in using the research information to inform practice has a difficult task in comprehending and integrating it because the information is complex and it is difficult to translate the material into practice. On the other hand, communicating the current knowledge base has been slow and difficult because of inherent problems with practitioners accepting research and generating dialogues where differences exist in theory and practice. Service providers and policymakers have their own agendas, which must be reconciled within meaningful differences for anything useful to come out of this effort. Scientific research can be a helpmate to achieve a comprehensible dialogue between the worlds of science and practice.

ARE RESEARCHERS REALLY INTERESTED IN REAL-LIFE PROBLEMS?

Using this context, in the following sections I address some of the unstated and implied issues that create difficulties and disappointments for researchers and practitioners in communicating and establishing a relationship of mutual influence. The practical question is how this task is to be done: My goal in this chapter is to provide some answers. Since the time is *now* for making extended efforts to encourage a reciprocal interaction because our society is in crisis on many fronts and could use behavioral science knowledge to address the social problems.

A Misconception Clarified?

Before considering specific topics, it is important to clarify some of the confusion in the field and refute the often repeated generalization that child psychology researchers are not interested in understanding the roots of real-life problems. At the level of uncovering knowledge about real-life problems, there is considerable overlap between researchers, whatever their persuasion, and service providers. A careful analysis of some samples of ongoing research publications dispels the belief that interest in real-life problems is lacking or is limited to the clinically oriented psychologist or practitioner. Examination of the abstracts in the April 1995 volume of *PsycSCAN: Developmental Psychology,* provides evidence that developmental research psychologists do formulate research projects directed at meaningful human development questions. Of the 37 journals reviewed, 14 contain abstracts of articles specifically devoted to the study of practical problems (e.g., development of self-concept, intellectual development, and parent-child relations). These studies generally seek to discover normative developmental trends, but the topic of the research deals with questions at the human functioning level. For example, the *Journal of Applied Developmental Psychology* is devoted to theory-based research dealing with human development.

All these journals are refereed and must meet strict scientific publication standards. These can be considered to be applied if the definition of *applied* refers to the problems addressed and their role in the lives of humans. Attention to a wide array of variables is necessary to identify and to understand how and why developing children evolve the way they do. This is basic to the search for developmental patterns. These investigations, however, abjure an interest in the practical problems of society. The scientific methods used to gather facts help researchers arrive at a theoretical understanding of development, but do not explain how to implement their findings. The practical significance of these studies is by implication, not application (Shuell, 1993). There is little guidance for the practitioner in using or implementing the findings in practice. Chances are the investigator does not know how to apply the research findings obtained under controlled conditions to the appropriate practical setting. For evidence of this assertion, the reader can examine any scientific research journal in developmental psychology in detail, looking for the technology of application.

An example of the application problem is reflected in the report, "Basic Behavioral Science Research for Mental Health: A National Investment," (National Advisory Mental Health Council, 1995). This report poses a basic science question for study: "What are the patterns of emergence of children's coping strategies for controlling their emotions and thereby their social relationships?" (p. 129).

I interpret this as a defined basic research question that is integral to applied psychology. Why else would they do it? Scientists can generate knowledge that sets the practice agenda because it supplies the basic information needed to work on real-life problems. What is not provided are the technologies that flow from their work. The lack of targeted prescriptions to alleviate, to correct, or to prevent the occurrence of the conditions described may not be due to disinterest as much as to the inherent difficulty in the way research findings are obtained and the basic epistemology of scientific thinking and reasoning that seeks generalizations, not particulars. The distinction is between the traditional notion of basic research with little or no attention to application to the real world. Rather, it is a contribution to scientific understanding of the problem in question; it deals with the world of scientific study. Where the practitioner seeks a practical way to use scientific knowledge for real-life problems, the scientist seeks explanations at a theoretical level. The issue is framed in another section of the NAMHC report where it is written:

> Understanding in detail how biological, psychological, and social-environmental factors interact to produce behavior is a fundamental task for basic behavioral science research. This knowledge is essential to understand the roots of normal behavior and to reduce the enormous emotional, social, and economic burden of mental illness in America. (NAMHC, 1995, p. 8)

Although the report focuses on the basic behavioral science in mental health, the argument of the significance of behavioral science knowledge for alleviating social problems in our society is equally relevant for child psychology, where they write in the same report:

> Because pathology is often the result of faulty development, greater understanding of normal developmental processes is key to planning effective interventions for preventing and ameliorating psychopathology. (p. 7)

Wherein lies the belief that basic research does not deal with real-life problems? In reality, research and practice should be interdependent. The scientist works from the belief that valid generalizable knowledge can only be derived from scientific study. The process is cumulative with increased understanding of the phenomena as more research is done. Science is a feedback system. As more knowledge is gained, it feeds and expands the theory. We come to know more and more. At least that is the ideal.

In ideal terms, the scientific discovery of the "facts" by the researcher should serve practitioners, provided they have the same or similar conceptual perspective. It is the responsibility of the practitioner to access and use the research relevant to his or her field. This is probably the only way each community, researchers and practitioners, can share the fruits of the research. To do so, practitioners and researchers must be intimately familiar with the way the other works and how to interpret that in the context of one's own activities. Can access to the information be made more user-friendly?

The irony is that it is not the way the system, if there is a system, operates. The commonality of interest does not bring researchers and practitioners together. It is not the commonality of interest that separates practitioners from researchers, but rather, factors such as mutual interest, the attitudes many researchers have toward practitioners, and questions about the feasibility of application. Researchers feel that their time is better spent doing the research and letting the practitioners fend for themselves. After all, the information is available in publications. If the investigators believe their time is better spent in the laboratory than in the field, then can there ever be a shared connection between them?

What Are the Views of Researchers and Practitioners and What Are Their Expectations for Each Other?

In the world of research and the world of practice, tight boundaries often seem to exist between the professionals engaged in the scientific enterprise and those in practice. There has been (and probably still is) a case of mutual disrespect between the typical researcher and the service provider. Researchers view practitioners as being concrete, theoretical, and ultimate pragmatists. Practitioners view researchers as engaged in elegant approaches to trivial questions, driven by sometimes esoteric and unworldly theory tested by rigid, meaningless, scientific methods. Practitioners often find the research reports are couched in probability terms that are utterly useless for their day-to-day work and accuse scientists of engaging with a fanatic and uncritical devotion to science. Why should a busy practitioner waste time reading such meaningless material? Not to be outdone by this criticism, researchers are often disdainful of practitioners' lack of understanding of science and the significance of data derived from careful methodology. Practitioners are perceived as unable to extrapolate from the theoretical to the practical because they have limited knowledge of how to use the research data.

Can Mutual Disrespect Be Ameliorated?

For some, a reconciliation is possible if research and practice were to be wedded into the same field of inquiry. Fisher and Lerner (1994) and Morrison et al. (1984) offer different strategies to cope with this issue.

Fisher and Lerner (1994) describe a collaborative model in their publication. This approach involves a separate field of applied psychology discipline, collaborating with the relevant service and practitioner groups in the university and the community. In contrast, Morrison et al. (1984) offer an alternative, a unified science of psychology with basic and applied fields evolving interdependently. Those who want to identify themselves as applied psychologists may eschew the traditional labels of applied psychologists such as child clinical psychologists, school psychologists, and educational therapists. Child psychologists on the other hand, have identified themselves as part of the behavioral science community of research scientists working within the tradition of science. Individuals so engaged are usually oriented toward research within any one of a number of theoretical persuasions.

Ironically, Bevan and Kessel's (1994) position, referred to earlier, is even more radical than these. They suggested a model of psychology that is not separated overtly into the basic and applied but loosens up approaches to science that extend psychology to other fields of endeavor.

What Is the Image of Child Development among Researchers and Service Providers?

The image of how to study children is not of one cloth. The reasons can be summarized in a single sentence. There is no definitive center that gives the field a coherent view of the phenomena of childhood:

> Images [of childhood] are basic assumptions or conceptions about children and the factors that influence their ontogeny. Images thus include beliefs regarding the existence of innate tendencies or dispositions, the susceptibility to external influences, the limits of human modifiability, the special importance of early experience, and the role of the individual. (Hwang, Lamb, & Sigel, 1996, p. 3)

Using this definition to assess whether developmental psychology manifests a common image of childhood, my colleague Myung-In Kim and I reviewed two major journals in the field as exemplars of change and diversity. Our argument was that the different images stem from different perceptions of childhood, and the differences suggest the important child variables to study to get at some important developmental questions. We compared the topics studied, the methods used, and the sample description during a 5-year interval in the two leading refereed journals, *Developmental Psychology* and *Child Development.* We found significant changes in problems chosen to study, age levels addressed, and research methods used. There are occasional allusions to implications for practice or application. There are rarely even references suggesting how to use the information.

Miller (1989) succinctly describes the reason for these diverse images and selection of study topics:

> The diverse answers to this question (of finding a singular image of childhood) illustrate why an integration of theories is so difficult. The theorists attend to very different levels of behavior and select different context areas. The stage theorists look at stage-defining characteristics and therefore operate at a general level. In their view, the most important developments are cognitive structures (Piaget) or personality structures (Freud and Erikson). The other theorists focus on more specific acquisitions, often limited to certain situations or types of stimulation. . . . With respect to content, the theories range from stressing social behaviors and personality (Freud, Erikson, social learning theory, ethology) to thinking. . . . No one theory has unraveled this complex process. (p. 423)

This quotation can apply to practices and services for children as well as for research. Researchers hold no monopoly on diversity of theory or image of children and childhood. In fact, it appears that variations in concepts of childhood are an endemic to the field old problem. So what is there to do?

In the following section, I address four derived issues which emerge for these analyses: knowledge generation and problem finding, practitioner-initiated research, knowledge dissemination, and knowledge interpretation.

KNOWLEDGE AND ITS GENERATING, DISSEMINATING, AND APPLICATIONS

Knowledge Generation and Problem Finding

In a field as diverse as child psychology, investigators have a wide universe from which to select problems of interest. The sources are virtually limitless, constrained only by ethical, technical, and financial limitations.

There are three least major ways to generate problems for study. One is the traditional way of an investigator who selects a problem that meets his or her theoretical interests and perceptions of what is publishable in quality refereed journals. This approach satisfies academic requirements for tenure, promotions, and salary adjustments.

Such studies may be in any genre, proximal or distal to applied research, but are focused and limited in scope. The articles published in *Developmental Psychology* usually fit this model. In the typical academic context, research designated as applied may not be done because it has lower status; yet the research may well be appropriately designated as applied. If we are consistent with the definition, the problem under study is an applied one (e.g., children's developing self-concept, or the relationship between mothers' depression and children's school adjustment). Academically based investigations, however, will usually be couched in the register of theory-driven research with careful adherence to the scientific canons. Still, such research may have practical implications when read by practitioners who share a similar theory.

In another approach, a researcher decides to study an applied problem because he or she is either interested in it or has a needed source of funding. Many government contracts fall into this category (e.g., evaluation studies of Headstart or other government programs). Another type may be those initiated by policymakers or program evaluators who hire researchers to do a specific job.

Any of these types of research may contribute to both the theoretical and practical service literature although each has a different contribution to make toward practice.

Practitioner-Initiated Research

A practitioner may wish to study a particular question and to do so must have a working relationship with a researcher. It may be an evaluation of a curriculum, or a mode of psychotherapy, or whatever. This kind of partnership requires a mutually reciprocal, coequal status so that the study meets the interests of both parties. Whether or not the partnership is authentic will depend on how the relationship is structured, the personalities of the principals, clarification of theoretical views, and shared goals. Most of these so-called partnerships are not truly coequal where the researchers take charge because of their expertise. This asymmetry usually is accepted and justified, but researchers often treat the practitioners insensitively and arrogantly. Such interactions occur in educational circles where teachers are at times coerced by the administration to participate in an experimental research project. Often they have no real choice or interest in participating. If the teacher is a reluctant participant, can the data be trusted?

Many models are used in generating research ideas. Each has its limitations and complexities. To create effective teams and partnerships for an effective project requires an awareness of the political situation and the interpersonal relationships. Although these factors are peripheral to the substance of the project, they may well determine its success or failure.

Knowledge Dissemination

How and when research information is disseminated depends on the target audience and the person disseminating the information. The audiences targeted to receive reports of research are the scientific community (including students in training to become researchers and practitioners), practitioners, and the lay public. Usually this task involves different discourses. More to the point are the traditional, and hence conventional, methods of reporting research.

Typically, research findings are written and published in formal formats in books and journals accessible to the science communities. Researchers look to publish their work in scholarly journals, meeting many of the standard criteria required for acceptance by the journal editors and consequently made available to colleagues. Because these journals are archival, the work is available in perpetuity and available in the public domain. Its accessibility is only limited by its comprehensibility and that depends on the reader's familiarization with the particular discourse of the author. For scientists, the discourse may be familiar. For the practitioners, especially those unfamiliar with the scientific jargon and style of writing, the research findings and their interpretation are meaningless and hence neither accessible nor useful. Research findings are also reported during professional meetings which are usually a community of scientists. These contributions help to further the development of their science.

Another audience is the practitioner who looks to the research as a resource for programmatic use. The language of such reports is often inappropriate. An alternative language register that is comprehensible within the discourse for practice is not even considered. Ironically, most researchers are not willing, or even able, to write for such audiences. This creates a dilemma because if there is no translation of the technical report into comprehensible language, the findings are not accessible to practical-minded readers.

The language, the conclusions, the recommendations, and the actual findings need to be written in a way the practitioner can understand and use. If researchers should be intimately acquainted with the setting to which they claim their research applies, so too practitioners should assume some responsibility for becoming informed about how to read and interpret this material in order to rationally evaluate the quality and the appropriateness of what he or she finds.

Research reviews, if carefully structured to clarify concepts and alter the style as in this volume, can serve as a dissemination medium. These reviews are unlikely to be accessible to the lay public who would still need other nontechnical expositions of research linked to practical use.

On the informal level, disseminating research findings can be done by researchers while consulting with service providers. Depending on the relationship of the researcher to the service partners, consultations can provide the opportunity for face-to-face meetings; discussions can follow the flow of the practitioner's needs. Usually consultants are used where common interests and common conceptual frameworks are in place and thus the discourse should involve shared meanings. In this context, verbal and interpersonal skills are the necessary coin. Also in this setting, the application of the research to practice can be dealt with in a concrete, and, if necessary, elaborated fashion.

Mass media provide still another way to report research findings to the practitioners and the lay public. The writers of these news releases are not trained in developmental psychology, but rather, are sophisticated journalists. They often report on research findings by interviewing the researchers and then translating the work into lay people's language. Inherent problems in this venue range from oversimplification and overgeneralization to downright distortion. This type of reporting involves ethical issues such as accuracy, misinterpretation, or misquoting (Sigel, 1990). The scientist or the science practitioner has little control over the material used because all research publications in standard professional journals are in the public domain and accessible to the reading public. The only place the researcher has some control is in the granting of interviews and public appearances. Here the individual is the responsible agent. Can one apply information from one setting to another without entering into the conceptual framework of the researcher? Are application assertions by researchers often assertions of practicality without suggestions for specific practice? Or, have findings been validated so they can be transported with confidence?

Knowledge Interpretation

Research results are usually presented in quantitative terms. The assumption is that numbers tell an objective story whose meaning is shared by every reader. The numbers, however, are derived from the investigator's perspective. He or she chooses the methods by which to collect the data and the means of quantification. Since every quantitative method has its limits and biases, the reported numbers are subject to interpretation. The decision how to evaluate the input goes back to the initial organization and classification of the data. The reader of this research now has numerous interpretative entrance points for evaluating the merits of the study for application. Irrespective of where the reader enters the evaluation, all the subsequent information can become suspect or accepted. The study's flaws, wherever found, cast doubt on all subsequent sections and therefore negate the validity of the results.

Suggestions for six key aspects of research validity have been proposed by Morgan and Gliner (1996). They are instruments of reliability and statistics, equivalence of subject characteristics, control of experience/environment variables, instrument reliability and statistics, external validity of operations and instrument validity, population external validity, and ecological external validity. They demonstrate how these criteria can be employed by most readers of research to evaluate a study's appropriateness and trustworthiness.

These evaluations are easy to deal with since the standards of assessment are generally accepted. Now the challenge. The spin one places on the implications of these so-called objective findings is equally contentious. A correlation is reported as significant statistically, say of the magnitude of .45, $p > .05$. The researcher's hypothesis is supported. The skeptic says the researcher is confusing statistical significance with psychological significance. Is accounting for 16% of the variance any big deal? It gives a hint of the possible, but some error sources here make the results of questionable value for real-life use. Statistical tools, we need to remind ourselves, are tools, not truths. They have no meaning beyond that we give them. The demystification of quantitative analysis is difficult for the devoted quantifiers. If a study deals with a trivial problem, it matters little whether it is well conceived and executed and the results are statistically significant. Service providers do not usually have the background to interpret statistical information, thus results should become verbal descriptions in lieu of numbers.

LIMITATIONS OF RESEARCH FOR PRACTITIONERS

Narrowness in Problem

Another limitation of the studies as sources of practical value is their narrow scope. Research reports in research-oriented journals usually are for small-scale studies with limited sample sizes and types. In part, this is why the bibliographies in the previous chapters are so extensive. They contain relatively large numbers of studies on the same topic. However, the differences among them need interpretation. What reviewers do when they try to create order out of disorder or chaos is to select the common features as they see them and ignore the warts and foibles. I suggest the reader take any topic in the preceding volumes and look at the number of references for any given topic. The number of studies referred to reflects not only the number of direct converging replications, but also many studies that may or may not confirm the intended results. Often the decision is based on the frequency of studies supporting a particular finding, rather than on any objective criterion. It is literally confirmation or disconfirmation by inference made by the reviewer and not by any scientific replication.

One reason for some of the difficulty is that all these studies are small and narrow. In keeping the design so carefully controlled, it is questionable whether the variables involved are truly equivalent. If they are, well and good, but if they are named the same but investigators have defined them differently, these variables must be separated accordingly. For example, if the need is to review the literature on high-risk children, and all the studies have been gathered, the first issue is the comparability of the concept *high risk.* If different definitions of "high risk" are found, how does a reviewer use this information to create a generalization from the research with such groups? The choice is going to be a function of the reviewer's orientation and preference for one or the other definition.

Limited Number of Variables

The number of variables used in small-scale studies is usually limited by the size of the sample. Thus, the probability is great that they will create a constricted experimental environment that, in effect, decontextualizes the child. The child's humanness is sacrificed so that he or she becomes a partitioned object of study as defined by the variables of interest to the investigator. Most of the studies investigating children's conservation of quantity or number rarely ask whether or not these children were studying these subjects in school. Is it not possible that the child's academic experience confounds the findings? The child in the experiment is treated as a subject unrelated to any other source of influence.

The approach to controlled studies works on the assumption that randomization of children to experimental conditions is sufficient to deal with these other confounding sources of error. If that is the case, how can the practitioner use any information obtained under such precious conditions? It is not difficult to figure this problem out. No research study or collection of studies, however brought together can prescribe a specific technology because they may have approached the problem differently or dealt with different aspects of the whole. Basically, phenomena are studied by partitioning not only the child, but also the problem. It is as though studies of cognition or motivation are insulated from other psychological systems. Yet, the whole child is the person responding to whatever is being asked of him or her. Maybe yes or maybe no?

Research Results Can Be Contradictory

Even if the research is accessible and expertly executed in one theoretical frame, the studies may not necessarily be accepted by some from another persuasion, although the problem is similar. There is often a critical and cynical attitude toward replications when not "pure" and exact. Similar rejection of disconfirmation studies is frequent when they conflict with the convictions of the initial investigator, especially if the mental functions are labeled in identical terms. This can be illustrated by a study by Noelting and his colleagues who confirm Inhelder and Piaget's description of the stages in formal operation, in contrast to Ennis who disconfirmed the same developmental pattern (Ennis, 1976; Noelting, Rousseau, & Coudé, 1996). Much research has been conducted by others to test the same theory; some have found it wanting, others confirmatory. The differences in findings create confusion for the practitioner who might be interested in using such information in planning educational programs. The antagonist will claim that Inhelder and Piaget's results are artifacts of poorly controlled experiments without the proper checks and balances for reliability and validity of scoring responses. Well, the argument can be reversed because the critics' experimental design can only approximate a replication—true replications are impossible in psychology.

The conditions of previous studies can never be reproduced except by inference, in contrast to a physics experiment where reproducibility is in every respect possible except for the time frame. All psychological experiments, no matter how well controlled, include unaccounted for variables from the time of day the experiment is run, to the reproducibility of the sample. Samples are merely randomized selections of subjects, not clones of the original sample, and despite experiment controls, there are unaccounted differences in subject characteristics. So, for example, how can educators deal with these contradictions when making curriculum decisions? With such contradictions in the literature, why bother with the research? They might use their own experience to better advantage. In this case, certainty is elusive. Although each study addresses a similar problem, each uses different measures, tasks, and statistical analyses, so which is right? Which one can an educator rely on for planning a curriculum?

Data from these studies are aggregated to report group variability, but not how individuals vary. Yet, the practitioner needs to know how a specific child might function based on those particular findings, or how a particular strategy will affect a specific child. If this is the case, what are the limits for how the teacher, therapist, or clinician can work with this child in *that* particular setting? The researcher who is testing hypotheses to support his or her theory hence can generalize how a phenomenon functions. The practitioner, on the other hand, is interested in individual differences in that particular classroom, with that child or those children, at that particular point in time.

CONCEPTUALIZATION OF RESEARCH: DESIGN AND ANALYSIS OF DATA

In their research design and analysis, investigators work from a nomothetic model eschewing idiographics or ipsative analyses, probably because of their interest in generalizing on the basis of aggregating analyses. Generalizations are more problematic from an idiographic analysis. Yet, from a practitioner's perspective, idiographic reports are more meaningful because they present an integrated view of the person, more akin to profile analyses or case histories in contrast to the partitioned approach of the nomothetic stance. The former approaches are more typical of clinical methodologies, often rejected by the scientist committed to a traditional experimental paradigm as a research strategy. It seems to me that child development research actually eschews, and at times ridicules, the value of idiographic research opting for nomothetic studies. I believe that using nomothetic approaches limits the practical contributions our field can make to practice, but it does provide useful information for scientific theory building. Is it not possible to use both approaches, accepting them as equally significant contributions? The argument of holistic research versus partitioned studies needs to be reconstituted with each having its own place. The decision whether to use a nomothetic or idiographic approach will depend on the problem studied. It is time to begin to revisit the issues involved in broadening the scope of our research efforts and communicating them (Fisher, Murray, & Sigel, 1996).

Definitions Are Often Constructions Emerging from a Worldview of the Definition Maker

Scientific constructs, be they operational or hypothetical, are all inventions of the scientist. Why some researchers opt for one type of approach compared with another is a vexing, unresolved question that must wait for another time. The fact of the matter is that this is the case. In this context, the core concept of development can serve as an illustration. It is central enough to the field to make the point. The context in which development is usually described can vary from an evolutionary perspective to an accretion of incremental growth to a transformational model of structural change (Wozniak, 1996). Take your pick. After all, rational selection is tempered by the root metaphor that the investigator works with in his or her conceptualization of human nature and how to study it (Pepper, 1942/1970).

Not only is there extensive diversity in the use of the same word with a different meaning, but there are also different meanings for the same phenomenon. A dramatic, illustrative example of differences in theory and practice is found in a fascinating small volume commenting on the similarities and differences between Piaget and Vygotsky. This book, reflects the divergences among a dedicated group of thoughtful scientists, some committed to Piaget, others to Vygotsky (Tryphon & Vonèche, 1996).

A researcher who reads this book might be enthralled by the level of discussion and erudition among the writers. If an educator interested in developing a conceptual position regarding child development reads it, he or she would find that whereas two different conceptions of development share some overlapping interests, they have basic epistemological differences that, in my mind, are irreconcilable. For example, Vygotsky's position of development is anchored in the sociocultural historical context, a traditional Marxist position, using a comparative method for studying animals, humans, preliterate peoples, and children. He held that the development of intelligence involves the invention of tools. Piaget's position as a structuralist can be characterized in this way by Wozniak (1996): "Development was simply defined as change (in cognitive structure) leading from lower forms to higher forms of equilibrium" (p. 18), where equilibrium is the "joint co-ordination of parts and whole" (Wozniak, 1996).

The practitioner might be tempted to leave the book soon after struggling with the first chapter because he or she would not find a clear path for practice. Here is where the practitioner would need to read further because toward the end of the book there is an eminently practical discussion of Piaget and Vygotsky in an educational science program authored by Brown, Metz, and Campione (1996), who describe how these two great thinkers have much to offer if the reader approaches the texts eclectically and pragmatically paying little or no attention to the epistemological differences. This example demonstrates that practitioners need to decide the level of theory they can work with. Adapting and taking whatever seems relevant from each one may be most useful and beneficial. The theoretical bases of the theories may have little significance to the world of praxis affairs. Purism can be dysfunctional at any level of action.

Another area that contributes to the difficulty in assessing the overall field is the use of the same methods for problems other than the one originally intended because they seem to be "cute" or manageable. Under these circumstances, it is often the method that dictates the problem. Many studies that use the "stranger situation" developed by Mary Ainsworth are excellent examples. That the procedure is a useful measure for studying attachment seems clear-cut. But someone thought it might be a good idea to use it to evaluate day care. Does the measure fit? What is the connection between attending day care and attachment? Lamb and Sternberg (1990) have argued persuasively that the "stranger situation" measure was not created for evaluating daycare attendance. Attachment theory research has yet to clarify the day-care separation issues on the basis of the stranger separation method of assessment. Although the conventional wisdom is that methods should be intrinsic to the testing of the research question, the convenience of the measures is rationalized as justification for their use. As some of these movements occur in the field, concomitant research strategies often become prevalent because of their presumed value.

The use of IQ measures to evaluate the effectiveness of preschool programs including Headstart is another instance of inappropriate use of measures because the programs under study were not intended to raise IQ, but rather to prepare children for school. However rationalized by evaluators, the claims are not justified. In fact IQ tests were devised to measure intellectual functioning. No agreement is extant defining the basis of the IQ scores. The heritability issues are still prevalent (Plomin, DeFries, & Fulker, 1988). So, a conceptual rationale is necessary for using IQ level as an assessment measure, rather than assuming the IQ to be depressed because of socioeconomic deprivation—the usual justification (Sigel, 1990).

Distinctions between Proximal and Distal Relevance of Research for Practitioners

Discourse or communication questions have already been dealt with; the next step is to devise a systematic way to evaluate the usability, and hence applicability, of the research information. Application is not only on the basis of the class of problems deemed in need of solution, but also on any research findings from whatever source in the service of practice or policy. It may come from research findings offering new ways to teach mathematics or planning recreation for children.

Effective linkage between research and its application can be effective if, and only if, the problem is addressed in the genre of communication. The communication efforts need to be directed toward shared meaning and mutual understanding of the task of research and the demands for transforming research findings to real-life problems. To deal with this crucial question, it is necessary to identify the functions research serves and the products of such efforts, and then how and when these products can be used by appropriate service providers.

The following thought experiment represents the applicability of research findings to any setting.

I will call this the *proximity index,* defined as a metric assessing the distance between the readiness for findings to be used interacting with the understanding of the meaning and the comprehensibility of the text. These are interdependent factors. The findings from research can only be applied if the practitioner understands how to use them in the course of the practice. Understanding in this context is limited to a minimal level of operation. A crude analogy is that of an individual who buys a new television set and needs to follow instructions on how to set it up at home. There is no need to understand the hardware of the TV set, only the mechanistic application of the instructions.

In the interpersonal application setting, however, the practitioner needs to ask: Are these results compatible with the goals of my program or do they conflict with my objectives? Thus, if a teacher reads about the virtues of an inquiry discovery approach but has taught with a directive authoritative approach, he or she needs to assess the implications for shifting approaches without mastery of the procedures. In this case, the research results are compatible with the objectives of education, but incompatible with the goals of the instructor. If on the other hand, there is compatibility between the research and the atmosphere in the class, the new findings may aid the teacher in elaborating the approaches in the classroom. This is a Level 1 application.

Each subsequent score on our hypothetical index has to make additional judgments. At Level 2 the practitioners judge the findings of the study as being closer in terms of specific techniques used, but somewhat uncertain about the level of comparability. Now the practitioner moves into a more active role of evaluator or interpreter of the research to a particular setting. It is these criteria that become working ideas as one moves from 2 to 3 and 3 to 4. As one approaches 5, the research is not deemed applicable. Weighting the degrees of comparability will involve comparability of the sample, how similar the children in the study were to those in one's practice, the validity of the study, and the reliability of the measures. In effect, the practitioner needs to reflect on the number of extrapolations that have to be made before there is some comfort in applying the research to any one's personal setting (see Morgan & Gliner, 1996).

Applicability does not need to be action based. Practitioners can use the research to rethink the way they do their work, and to reflect about other areas to explore, all in the service of the practice or program. For example, if one becomes involved in the effects of culture on schooling (see Greenfield & Suzuki, this volume), then there is reason to expect that the instructor will change his or her understanding of some of the events in his her classroom or clinic. This index is then a way to informally structure one's thinking to generate plans for application and research results.

The practitioner should always be concerned about the generality of the findings. To make these judgments requires some understanding of the research process. Mastering elementary information about reliability, validity, and replicability of the research are all important for undergirding its applicability. To paraphrase a commercial slogan, "The better informed practitioners are about fundamental research practices, the better the practice."

The Collaborative-Consultant Model as a Way to Ensure Shared Meaning of the Research and Practice

The researcher and the service provider sometimes do establish a coequal working relationship dealing with problems of mutual interest. The researcher may be seeking to test a hypothesis of interest to him or her and the service provider is interested in the outcome of the study because it will be applicable to his or her particular program. In this scenario, each participant has sufficient information to determine the degree to which the findings will be applicable and under what conditions (see Fisher & Lerner, 1994, for a detailed description of a collaborative model).

This process of close collaboration will lead to a good sense of the possibilities for the research to be relevant to the program. The closer the major players in the program perceive themselves as coequals, each with something to gain, the better the outcomes will be for all of the parties. This is in contrast to the top-down approach taken by Headstart evaluators, which in my view is a prime negative example. The questions posed for the evaluation were determined by a research committee to rate a multitude of variable and inconsistent programs, all under the aegis of Headstart. The service providers were not part of the evaluation except as targets of study. The children were evaluated on the basis of criteria deemed consistent with the Headstart mandate to help children get ready for school. Investigators defined the research in terms of what they held were the important questions. Too often, the issues addressed were intellectual development, school readiness on an intellectual basis with little attention to the details of family interactions and ways of child care, communication patterns at home, and the like. The studies, although complex in their overall design, still lacked input from the practitioners. In essence, such research is from the outside looking in and not from the inside looking out.

Suggestions for Broadening the Scope of Research to Establish a Collaborative Climate between Basic Science and Practice

If we accept the premise that there is still much more work to be done to increase the contributions of behavioral science research to the world of practice, what are some of the possible directions for such efforts to take?

In an introduction to a volume published by the Foundation on Meta analysis, Eric Wanner (1992) President of the Russell Sage Foundation, writes:

> The practical value of social science depends upon its ability to deliver usable knowledge about causes of social problems and the effectiveness of policies and programs designed to alleviate them. The immense diversity of social life, however, and the great welter of factors underlying social phenomenon make it difficult, if not impossible, to derive conclusive knowledge from any single study, no matter how well designed or intelligently analyzed. The causal process that appears so essential at one time or place may prove less important in another. The program that works well with one group under certain conditions may be less effective with another group when the circumstances are a bit different.
>
> These basic facts of social life render the success of social science crucially dependent upon its ability to accumulate results across the many studies of a given social process or program. The accumulation of results and the gradual convergence on information of higher quality is one hallmark of progress in any science, but it is particularly key in social science, where there may be no single, uniform answer to a given question, but rather a family of answers, related by principles that emerge only over the course of much research.
>
> Traditionally, this process of distilling reliable generalizations from the history of research on a given problem has been considered something of an art. Experience, good judgement, and a sound understanding of methodological principles should enable a seasoned scientist to make useful sense of a related set of studies, but with no guarantee that a similarly experienced analyst would reach a similar conclusion. This potential for disagreement among the experts—often realized in spades for certain socially important issues—has undoubtedly weakened social science as a source of social policy. If social scientists cannot agree, how can policymakers be guided by their results? (pp. vii–viii)

This state of affairs is not just limited to concerns of policymakers. It also characterizes the problems with utilization of behavioral research in every aspect of children's lives. Eric Wanner uses these arguments as a basis for justification of the growing interest in meta-analysis as a way of creating research syntheses that can be replicable because the same methods can be used by other social and behavioral science researchers.

Undoubtedly, Wanner is justified in his advocacy. Further, his suggestion is intended to reduce fragmentation and diversity. His is one solution that poses some of the same problems alluded to in the forgoing discussion. The studies used in such meta-analytic studies will be narrow in scope, limited in number of variables attended to, and diverse in terms of concept and maybe even method. Whether they will contain the critical information on how to transform research findings into practice remains to be seen. But this approach, despite limitations, still has the potential to reduce fragmentation. The Wanner argument is an ideal whose time has yet to come, and whose logic provides guidance for linking research to practice because it is geared to generate knowledge for answering some questions or solving some problems. It reduces the need to integrate the studies by practitioners themselves.

The offering of meta-analysis to bring together the many studies addressing a common problem is but one operational approach to reduce the fragmented reporting of research results. Other statistical procedures have been, or are still in place that enable behavioral scientists to create complex and multivariable models to address any research problems of interest. What the Eric Wanner statement does is address the fundamental question of how to incorporate and demonstrate the interdependence of the factors inherent in any problem in everyday life.

What all these changes provide is an increased confidence in research findings. It does not matter how the problem of study is classified, organized, or reported, there is still the underlying question of how to use the knowledge that is reported. This is the nub of the issue: Why is there a gap between research and its implementation in the field of action, be it in the home, the schools, the clinics, or the courts? Is the paradigm of the research a problem? Is the structure or the struggle between epistemologies, or is another institutional arrangement needed as an interface between the science of discovery and the assimilation of such knowledge into the world of practice? That question is no longer one of basic or applied science. The question becomes one of the practical level of use of any scientifically acquired knowledge. And we all agree that getting to know ourselves in our various worlds is a tough job. Nevertheless, we continue the struggle for understanding and control of our lives. In this final major section, I examine some reasons for the discrepancy between what we know and what we are continuing to learn about human functioning and its use in helping to reduce social ills and the number of dysfunctional individuals and families.

BASES FOR DIFFICULTY ASSIMILATING RESEARCH FINDINGS INTO PRACTICE

The primary difficulties are framed as follows: (a) The question of who poses the research question; (b) recognition that there is an inevitable time gap between the onset of the research and the final report; and (c) the conflict between general findings and specifications for application and the practical problems integrating the research into the practice.

Who Poses the Question?

The posing of the research question can be an intellectual challenge because it is often difficult to get consensus between researchers and practitioners. Where practitioners usually frame questions in atheoretical and practical terms, researchers prefer theoretically based inquiries.

The structuring of the research question is part and parcel of the scientist's way of working. Each participant in any collaborative effort will frame the question of interest from his or her own frame of reference. The scientist will put it into the genre of science with the precision necessary for subsequently setting up a study. The practitioner may phrase the question within an action-based practical way consistent with his or her setting. This is difficult and will require considerable discussion. This may be one reason why this is not a popular approach. There are studies where the practitioner and the researcher share the same approach, and the practitioner and researcher may even be the same person. For example, some of the evaluation work of Elaine Blechman in therapy with children in her clinic reflects this congruence. The therapist's perspective is the same point of view as the researcher's. There is no conflict and the results of the study can be readily used in the subsequent practice (Blechman, 1990).

In the more usual situation, the researcher and the practitioner come from two different settings, such as in educational settings. These situations require the kind of dialoguing I described earlier. However, the topic of choice may vary as already described, whether applied or basic. Whoever does the definition, the approach meets the rules of science, which may be limited in scope for practical reasons.

Research Takes Time

To carry out any research project takes time. This is a trite observation, yet, there are efforts to shortcut the process. There are advocates of formative assessments that alter the control and rigor usually expected in carrying out these experiments. Such procedures are often employed in intervention studies in the form of quality control. This is not the place to discuss the intricacies and implications for such approaches. It is the case that the luxury of reflective and thoughtful research strategies may have to be compromised in the service of the urgency of the problems under study.

The gap between discovery and implementation is due not only to the length of time required to do the research, but also to the resistance of practitioners to acknowledge the findings. The commitment of scientists and practitioners to their own construction of knowledge of where truth resides and how to move the discussion from a pseudoconviction of scientific objectivity to the reality of scientists' and practitioners' biases poses problems integrating new knowledge (McCall, 1996). This state of affairs is a constant factor in the scientist-practitioner gap.

Researchers Are Not Experienced as Practitioners and Vice Versa

The research findings cannot usually be applied because of the limited background of the researcher for implementation. Intervention studies offer an excellent example. Many studies in education are carried out by academic educational psychologists who have had little if any experience in classrooms and are not intimately acquainted with how practices are to be effectively used. It is obvious that advising and consulting as an observer have limited value for the actual doing. Because most research studies done in the traditional way can only be suggestive, it is unlikely that the researcher can create prescriptions for what to do or how to use the findings in a real situation. One way to handle this state of affairs may be through the creation of a mutually acceptable true collaboration of research and practice in the development of the project to begin with. In this way, the experience gap and mutual understanding is enhanced and the reality of the research approximates the real-life events in classroom management.

To be sure, a new professional group, referred to as "science practitioners," is emerging. In such cases, because the practitioner and the researcher are one, implementation may arise directly out of practice (Blechman, 1990; Cicchetti & Toth, this volume). For the most part, however, researchers are not necessarily practitioners. Thus, modes of implementation are not part of their professional repertoire. Therefore it is the practitioner who has to interpret what would be appropriate procedures for implementation. For example, in studies on day care, most of the research is done by developmental psychologists who have probably not been directly involved in working with the children. Their expertise resides in the research acumen; thus there is little reason to expect them to provide the technology or the explicit means to implement their research.

Researchers and their spokespersons usually report findings in cautious terms because findings are always in need of validation. Most laboratory studies are not followed up with studies in real-life settings. So in reporting the results from the laboratory as suggestive of application, the researcher is often tentative, at times equivocal, and usually couched with qualifications as to how the results should be interpreted. A good example is the dilemma facing the practitioner who wants to use research data reporting some of the difficulties young children from deprived environments have in relating to other children. How does a practitioner implement any findings derived from such limited research (see McLoyd, this volume). Usually the researchers have little experience in recommending types of intervention, and the results from their studies cannot be directly applied to classroom or to a clinic. An example of this situation is found in the Piagetian conservation studies done under laboratory conditions. Training studies revealed that conservation can be "taught," but it required the creation of teaching strategies appropriate for the classroom (Sigel, Roeper, & Hooper, 1966). Findings from this and similar studies were difficult to implement in school settings because of insufficient details about the methods to use in following through on the research. Practitioners may be unconvinced that the studies reported anything different from what had actually already been reported, and most important, the aggregated findings were not helpful where individualized programming is the order of the day.

Now the practitioner is faced with an interesting dilemma—reject the research as problematic, offer new questions for the investigators to address, or reinterpret their findings. This level of collaboration or interaction is probably more influenced by the interpersonal relationships and mutual trust than by the science.

A Case of Professional Cooperation and Threat

Several years ago, I participated in an intervention program in a middle-class elementary school system. The program was derived from Piagetian theory. One of the stipulations in their curriculum required the teachers to ask questions, to engage in dialogue, and to get the children to interact with each other, and with the teacher. The study was undertaken to observe teachers' question-asking techniques and follow-through, how they engaged the group, and whether or not they allowed the children to discover and share ideas. Observers went into the classroom with permission of the teacher and set up a rigorous observation schedule and observed teachers' verbalizations every 6 seconds during a 30-minute extended play period. The results showed that the teachers asked many questions, but the questions were didactic and directive, such as: "What is the name of this?" "What is the color of that?" There was very little, if any, follow-through. Considerable attention was paid to the precise way in which the children spoke their answers. After the program was evaluated, it was found that these children were no different in responsiveness and verbalization from children enrolled in traditional programs in that same school system, and that teachers' questions never created a dialogue or a discussion. When these results were reported to the school committee, immediate objections were raised that the observers were new, unknown to the teachers, segmented in their approach, and so on. Rather than discussing the implications of these findings, the committee rejected them out of hand because they were not what was expected.

Resolution of this conflict took intense discussion and explanations why their criticism of the research was not valid by having the committee listen to audiotapes of the classroom using the observation schedule. They eventually accepted the researchers' observations. The point was that it was not the quality of science that resolved the issue but the developing of interpersonal trust and willingness for everyone to examine the work differently. Ironically, these procedures confirmed the earlier findings and the committee was assuaged. They decided to alter their intervention efforts consistent with the research findings.

The Need for Mutual and Honest Involvement

Another set of issues inherent in the assimilation of research to practice settings involves the level of mutual involvement and decision making between researchers and practitioners in the project. Many researchers enter into field settings to gather data for research and then do not report the findings to the agency or institution that gave them the hospitality of their facilities. This is particularly true in education. It would be an interesting task to review the number of studies that have been done within public, and even private, schools by graduate students and faculty members in education and to find out the consequences of these investigations. They are always presented to boards of education, principals, and superintendents as being significant for the enhancement or understanding of educational process. For whom? For the teacher? For the parents? For the clinicians? For the investigator and his or her faculty colleagues? Chances are that the gainers in this enterprise are not the children, not the teachers, not the parents, but rather the academic investigators who have carried out these projects. If this is the case, there is little reason for educational systems to trust investigators who wish to come and work in their schools.

Reporting results is almost a minimal follow-through in responsibility. Of course, it is often said, "Yes, we did send them a report of what our findings were. They were instructed in how to use the findings. We fulfilled our commitments." This approach is no different from having a physician say, "Here are some pills. Take them and you will be all right." You don't know why to take them, how to take them, and so on. The physician doesn't tell you that. Optimally, the physician provides specific details on when and how often the particular drug should be used and informs the patient what side effects might occur and which ones should be reported immediately. We do not have this kind of interactive responsibility with educators, yet we frequently blame teachers or practitioners for not being properly trained, properly advised, and properly motivated to engage in this whole research effort.

CONCLUSION

The child psychologist's interest is in every context in which children are functioning. Despite all the work and publication of research, and despite the increase in practitioners working with children, there is a malaise in the field. It is as though the challenge and the promise of behavioral sciences to be socially useful leaves much to be desired. The time is the ever-present *now* that behavioral science research should become more accessible to the practicing fields. But how? What mechanisms can be devised that bring empirical research to the fore in answering questions about *how* and *why* children develop as they do? What mechanisms aid in keeping the trajectory of development optimal? What contributions can be made to prevent dysfunctional development? What are the requirements to optimal development? Should not developmental research offer useful and meaningful explanations for the course of development and where needed provide approaches to prevent and ameliorate conditions that may interfere with the developmental trajectory?

Does this description of the world of child psychology and its place in the world of science and service connote a state of chaos and of unending complexity, never to be resolved? Do these efforts have an indigenous self-regulating force or is there a developing reconstituting of itself as it broadens its base and reinvents itself? These are the basic questions we are facing. But these long-range or ultimate questions may be approached with some analysis of where we are and what we can do.

SOME AFTERTHOUGHTS

My aim in this chapter was to lay out some of the issues about practitioner-researcher relations. As I reread this chapter, I was struck with the range of my observation; there is some disillusion about the lack of communication between research and practice or discouragement about progress in the behavioral sciences to discover more about human development that would or could become part of current practice at home, in school, in the clinic, and the community and despair that all we are finding is a confirmation of common sense and everyday folk psychology. One might ask, are we kidding ourselves that progress in the behavioral sciences is being made because as Fiske and Shweder (1986) write:

> . . . each scientist [is] holding that "progress is being made on the problem on which I am working." At the same time, and perhaps paradoxically, there has been in the social sciences, at least in recent years, a vague sense of unease about the overall rate of progress of the disciplines. (p. 1)

On the other hand, the behavioral scientists are bemoaning the current states of their collective fields and are being criticized for not contributing to the social good at a significant rate and the "science" qua science contribution is fragile (Lindblom, 1990). Others see new horizons if they are willing to take some risks. For some it is too narrow and for others it is too grandiose. For some, behavioral science employs the incorrect model, and for others there is no other way to acquire sound and unequivocal results (Campbell, 1986).

The field is in a ferment. In the past, we accepted this because we believed ourselves to be members of a young science and we just needed to grow and mature. Scientific knowledge was, we believed, cumulative and linear in its development. However, now, 100 years later, we can no longer use that argument. Now we are mature, and our experience should replace youthful idealism and naivete.

The ferment some may bemoan, others relish. Fermentation reflects an effervescence, a bubbling change that alters the character of substance. To carry on the analogy, the process is not linear, and in addition, it is in the current vernacular "chaotic," becoming transformed into a new whole. In a sense, those of us in child psychology are sharing the same crisis that our idealized physics colleagues are facing—the new scientific revolution, *the science of chaos* (Gleick, 1987). Does that not sound like an oxymoron? We have been encouraged to think in terms of stability, equilibrium, and homeostasis. But, I believe that chaos, as a natural state of existence, is not only relevant for all science, but is inherent in the universe, bar none. We struggle with this perspective with an awareness that the process of discovery, of seeking order out of chaos is our goal.

Acceptance of this is counterintuitive to the psychological assumption that humans prefer order and stability. Psychologists are no exceptions. Our science is grounded in the precepts of prediction, another seemingly fundamental universal desire. To predict means to be able to control, to define, to be precise, and to identify the ingredients of the whole.

Yet we have moved away from a dogmatic set of expectancies because we accept the simple fact that we live in a probabilistic world. There is not, and cannot be, absolute prediction—absolute control. The reason underlying all our efforts, and even our belief in the accumulation of knowledge, is that in a metaphoric sense it is ephemeral—all these efforts at science are attempts to take hold and to be in control. If, however, the natural state of affairs is a chaotic world, with pervasive perturbations, then it seems to be the case that we move in tandem with this reality and seek to evolve new systems that will expand understanding of the process of growth.

Working within such an awareness and recognizing that all our controls are tentative and approximate requires surrendering some of our precious beliefs in the religion of scientism of today with the evolving science of tomorrow. This is not rhetoric, but requires a different orientation from what is current among child psychologists.

The necessary changes require a move away from a linear model of development to a dynamic, transforming growth whose pattern may become apparent if we change from a narrow focal lens to wider and wider lenses, integrating and reintegrating as we expand our viewing lens view and incorporate more of what we see as functional. The seeds of these ideas were discussed long ago by Heinz Werner in his principle of orthogenesis where development is an ongoing integration and reintegration in hierarchical fashion (Werner, 1978/1957). Piaget (1947/1950) also describes perturbations as an inherent attribute development.

Now for the most difficult task. Are we willing to engage in this process of change and recognize that our implicit scientific mentors (who by the way we are usually encouraged to adjure, the physicist and the mathematicians) are moving into the acceptance of a nonlinear world?

We can only move into new ways of looking at the world if we come to realize part of the problem for recognizing the nonlinear universe resides in ourselves. Most of us are committed to a model of the world and the basic belief that there is truth out there that we can discover. There are protests to the contrary that we use models which presume a discoverable and certain validity. As we move into the phase model of dynamic systems emerging from our broadening lenses we will find some sense for understanding how we move through our existence.

We have many unfulfilled trends in the history of our field. If we can come to believe in mutual and reciprocal trust and recognize that our own rigidities and biases are at the crux of restricting change in our science, then we can enjoy sharing and cooperating in the process of development. To quote a political metaphor, let us gather into the big tent and cooperate with all disciplines that touch on our own. Finally, a realization that understanding can come from many sources—research in the laboratory, research in the field, practice in the consulting room, watching children in the classroom, and taking a step back and reflecting on all we see. The process of trying to understand and share, although it may sound Pollyannaish and sentimental, is the route we ought to try. We may all like it. Psychology has traditionally been a science that both in principle and in practice has opted for the same model of science as the physicist. Now researchers will have to find their way in concert with the consumers of their work—the practitioners—the folks in the real world.

ACKNOWLEDGMENTS

I wish to acknowledge the valuable comments of K. Ann Renninger for a careful reading of this chapter and her wise substantive and organizational advice; to Brian Vandenburg my gratitude for his constructive comments substantive questions on research aspractice; and to Linda Kozelski for her patience and skill in preparing this document for publication.

REFERENCES

Bevan, W., & Kessel, F. (1994). Plain truths and home cooking: Thoughts on the making and remaking of psychology. *American Psychologist, 49,* 505–509.

Blechman, E. (1990). A new look at emotions and the family: A model of effective family communication. In E. A. Blechman (Ed.), *Emotions and the family: For better or for worse.* Hillsdale, NJ: Erlbaum.

Brown, A. L., Metz, K. E., & Campione, J. C. (1996). *Social interaction and individual understanding in a community of learners: The influence of Piaget and Vygotsky.* In A. Tryphon & J. Vonèche (Eds.), *Piaget—Vygotsky: The social genesis of thought* (pp. 145–170). East Sussex, England: Psychology Press.

Campbell, D. T. (1986). Science's social system of validity-enhancing collective belief change and the problems of the social sciences. In D. W. Fiske & R. A. Shweder (Eds.), *Metatheory in social science: Pluralisms and subjectives* (pp. 108–136). Chicago: University of Chicago Press.

Ennis, R. H. (1976). An alternative to Piaget's conceptualization of logical competence. *Child Development, 47,* 903–919.

Fisher, C. B., & Lerner, R. M. (Eds.). (1994). Applied developmental psychology. *New York: McGraw-Hill.*

Fisher, C. B., Murray, J. P., & Sigel, I. E. (Eds.). (1996). *Applied developmental science: Graduate training for diverse disciplines and educational settings.* Norwood, NJ: ABLEX.

Fiske, D. W., & Shweder, R. A. (Eds.). (1986). *Metatheory in social science: Pluralisms and subjectives.* Chicago: University of Chicago Press.

Fox, R. E. (1996). Charlatanism, scientism, and psychology's social contract. *American Psychologist, 51,* 777–784.

Gleick, J. (1987). *Chaos: Making a new science.* New York: Penguin Books.

Hoffman, M. L., & Hoffman, L. W. (Eds.). (1964). *Review of child development research* (Vol. 1). New York: Russell-Sage Foundation.

Kimble, G. A. (1994). A frame of reference for psychology. *American Psychologist, 49,* 510–519.

Hwang, C. P., Lamb, M. E., & Sigel, I. E. (Eds.). (1996). *Images of childhood.* Mahway, NJ; Erlbaum.

Lamb, M. E., & Sternberg, K. J. (1990). Do we really know how day care affects children? *Journal of Applied Developmental Psychology, 11,* 351–379.

Lindblom, C. E. (1990). *Inquiry and change: The troubled attempt to understand and shape society.* New Haven, CT: Yale University Press.

McCall, R. B. (1996). The concept and practice of education, research, and public service in university psychology departments. *American Psychologist, 51,* 379–388.

Miller, P. H. (1989). *Theories of developmental psychology* (2nd ed.). New York: Freeman.

Morgan, G. A., & Gliner, J. A. (1996). *Evaluating the validity of research.* Manuscript submitted for publication.

Morrison, F. J., Lord, C., & Keating, D. P. (Eds.). (1984). *Applied developmental psychology* (Vol. 1). Orlando, FL: Academic Press.

National Advisory Mental Health Council. (1995). *Basic behavioral science research for mental health: A national investment* (NIH Publication No. 96-3682). Washington, DC: U.S. Government Printing Office.

Noelting, G., Rousseau, J. P., & Coudé, G, (1996, June) *Operating stages as a composition of relations and the onset of formal operations.* Paper presented at the annual Symposium of the Jean Piaget Society, Philadelphia, PA.

Pepper, S. C. (1970). *World hypotheses: A study in evidence.* Berkeley: University of California Press. (Original work published 1942)

Piaget, J. (1950). *The psychology of intelligence* (M. Piercy & D. E. Berlyne, Trans.). London: Routledge & Kegan Paul. (Original work published 1947)

Polanyi, M. (1958). *Personal knowledge: Toward a post-critical philosophy.* Chicago: University of Chicago Press.

Shuell, T. J. (1993). Toward an integrated theory of teaching and learning. *Educational Psychologist, 28,* 291–311.

Sigel, I. E. (1970). The distancing hypothesis: A causal hypothesis for the acquisition of representational thought. In M. R. Jones (Ed.), *Miami Symposium on the Prediction of Behavior, 1968: Effects of early experience* (pp. 99–118). Coral Gables, FL: University of Miami Press.

Sigel, I. E. (1990). Ethical concerns for the use of research findings in applied settings. In C. B. Fisher & W. W. Tryon (Eds.), *Advances in applied developmental psychology: Vol. 4. Ethics in applied developmental psychology: Emerging issues in an emerging field* (pp. 133–142). Norwood, NJ: ABLEX.

Sigel, I. E. (1996). Applied developmental psychology graduate training should be grounded in a social-cultural framework. In C. B. Fisher, J. P. Murray, & I. E. Sigel (Eds.), *Applied developmental science: Graduate training for diverse disciplines and educational settings* (pp. 190–219). Norwood, NJ: ABLEX.

Sigel, I. E., & Kim, M.-I. (1996). The images of children in developmental psychology. In C. P. Hwang, M. E. Lamb, & I. E. Sigel (Eds.), *Images of childhood* (pp. 47–62). Mahway, NJ: Erlbaum.

Sigel, I. E., Roeper, A., & Hooper, F. H. (1966). A training procedure for acquisition of Piaget's conservation of quantity: A pilot study and its replication. *The British Journal of Educational Psychology, 36,* 301–311.

Tryphon, A., & Vonèche, J. (Eds.). (1996). *Piaget—Vygotsky: The social genesis of thought.* East Sussex, England: Psychology Press.

Wanner, E. (1992). Foreward. In T. D. Cook, H. D. Cooper, D. S. Cordray, H. Hartmann, L. V. Hedges, R. J. Light, T. A. Louis, & F. Mosteller (Eds.), *Meta-analysis for explanation: A casebook* (pp. vii-x). New York: Russell-Sage Foundation.

Werner, H. (1978). The concept of development from a comparative and organismic point of view. In S. S. Barten & M. B. Franklin (Eds.), *Developmental processes: Heinz Werner's selected writings: Vol. 1. General theory and perceptual experiences* (pp. 107–130). New York: International Universities Press. (Original work published 1957)

Wiggins, J. G., Jr. (1994). Would you want your child to be a psychologist? *American Psychologist, 49,* 485–492.

Wozniak, R. H. (1996). Qu'est-ce que l'intelligence? Piaget, Vygotsky, and the 1920s crisis in psychology. In A. Tryphon & J. Vonèche (Eds.), *Piaget—Vygotsky: The social genesis of thought* (pp. 12–24). East Sussex, England: Psychology Press.

Author Index

Subject Index